Collins

Collins German Dictionary

William Collins' dream of knowledge for all began with the publication of his first book in 1819. A self-educated mill worker, he not only enriched millions of lives, but also founded a flourishing publishing house. Today, staying true to this spirit, Collins books are packed with inspiration, innovation, and practical expertise. They place you at the centre of a world of possibility and give you exactly what you need to explore it.

Language is the key to this exploration, and at the heart of Collins Dictionaries is language as it is really used. New words, phrases, and meanings spring up every day, and all of them are captured and analysed by the Collins Word Web. Constantly updated, and with over 2.5 billion entries, this living language resource is unique to our dictionaries.

Words are tools for life. And a Collins Dictionary makes them work for you.

Collins. Do more.

Collins

Collins German Dictionary

HarperCollins Publishers
Westerhill Road
Bishopbriggs
Glasgow
G64 2QT
Great Britain

Fifth Edition 2007

Reprint 10 9 8 7 6 5 4 3

ISBN-13 978-0-00-725342-5
ISBN-10 0-00-725342-7

www.collins.co.uk

A catalogue record for this book is available from the British Library

HarperCollins Publishers, 10 East 53rd Street, New York, NY 10022

COLLINS GERMAN CONCISE DICTIONARY.
Fourth US Edition 2007

ISBN-13 978-0-06-114183-6
ISBN-10 0-06-114183-6

Library of Congress Cataloging-in-Publication Data has been applied for

www.harpercollins.com

HarperCollins books may be purchased for educational, business, or sales promotional use. For information, please write to: Special Markets Department, HarperCollins Publishers, 10 East 53rd Street, New York, NY 10022

Typeset by Wordcraft, Glasgow

Printed in Italy by Legoprint S.p.A.

Acknowledgements
We would like to thank those authors and publishers who kindly gave permission for copyright material to be used in the Collins Word Web. We would also like to thank Times Newspapers Ltd for providing valuable data.

Inhalt

Contents

GESAMTLEITUNG/PUBLISHING DIRECTOR
Lorna Sinclair Knight

PROJEKTLEITUNG/PROJECT MANAGEMENT
Maree Airlie

LEITENDE REDAKTEURE/SENIOR EDITORS
Horst Kopleck, Joyce Littlejohn

MITARBEITER/CONTRIBUTIONS FROM
Dagmar Förtsch, Hildegard Pesch, Veronika Schnorr, Gisela Moohan, Ulrike Seeberger, Elspeth Anderson, Val McNulty, Eva Vennebusch, Robin Sawers, Ilse MacLean, Beate Wengel

DATENVERARBEITUNG/COMPUTING STAFF
Thomas Callan

Einleitung

Sie möchten Englisch lernen oder vielleicht bereits vorhandene Kenntnisse vertiefen. Sie möchten sich auf Englisch ausdrücken, englische Texte lesen oder übersetzen, oder Sie möchten sich ganz einfach mit Englisch sprechenden Menschen unterhalten können. Ganz gleich ob Sie Englisch an der Schule oder an der Universität lernen, in einem Büro oder in einem Unternehmen tätig sind: Sie haben sich den richtigen Begleiter für Ihre Arbeit ausgesucht! Dieses Buch ist der ideale Helfer, wenn Sie sich in englischer Sprache ausdrücken und verständlich machen wollen, ob Sie nun sprechen oder schreiben. Unser Wörterbuch ist ganz bewusst praktisch und modern, es räumt vor allem der Alltagssprache und der Sprache, wie sie Ihnen in Zeitungen und Nachrichten, im Geschäftsleben, im Büro und im Urlaub begegnet, großen Raum ein. Wie in allen unseren Wörterbüchern haben wir das Hauptgewicht auf zeitgenössische Sprache und idiomatische Redewendungen gelegt.

Wie man dieses Buch benutzt

Im Folgenden geben wir einige Erklärungen darüber, wie die Einträge Ihres Wörterbuchs aufgebaut sind. Unser Ziel: Wir wollen Ihnen so viel Information wie möglich bieten, ohne dabei an Klarheit und Verständlichkeit einzubüßen.

Die Wörterbucheinträge

Ein typischer Eintrag in Ihres Wörterbuchs besteht aus folgenden Elementen:

Lautschrift

Wie die meisten modernen Wörterbücher geben wir die Aussprache mit Zeichen an, die zum „internationalen phonetischen Alphabet“ gehören. Weiter unten (auf den Seiten xiv) finden Sie eine vollständige Liste der Zeichen, die in diesem System benutzt werden. Die Aussprache englischer Wörter geben wir auf der englisch-deutschen Seite unmittelbar hinter dem jeweiligen Wort in eckigen Klammern an. Die deutsche Aussprache erscheint im deutsch-englischen Teil ebenfalls auf diese Weise unmittelbar hinter den Worteinträgen. Allerdings wird sie nicht immer angegeben, zum Beispiel bei zusammengesetzten Wörtern wie Liebesbrief, deren Bestandteile schon an anderer Stelle im Wörterbuch zu finden sind.

Grammatik-Information

Alle Wörter gehören zu einer der folgenden grammatischen Klassen: Substantiv, Verb, Adjektiv, Pronomen, Artikel, Konjunktion, Präposition, Interjektion, Abkürzung. Substantive können im Deutschen männlich, weiblich oder sächlich sein. Verben können transitiv, intransitiv, reflexiv oder auch unpersönlich sein. Die Wortart folgt auf die Lautschrift und ist in *Kursivschrift* angegeben. Wo bei Übersetzungen eine Geschlechtsangabe erforderlich ist, wird diese ebenfalls in *Kursivschrift* gegeben.

Oft gehören Wörter zu zwei oder mehr grammatischen Klassen. So kann das deutsche Wort **gut** ein Adjektiv („good“) oder auch ein Adverb („well“) sein, und das englische Wort **spell** ist sowohl ein Substantiv („Zauber“) als auch ein Verb („schreiben, buchstabieren“). Das Verb **reden** ist manchmal transitiv, d. h. es hat ein Objekt („sie redet Unsinn“), manchmal intransitiv, d.h. es wird ohne Objekt gebraucht („er redet ständig vom Wetter“). Zur besseren Übersichtlichkeit sind verschiedene Wortarten durch das Symbol ▹ abgegrenzt; alle Beispielsätze werden dann unter den entsprechenden grammatischen Kategorien gegeben.

Bedeutungsunterschiede

Die meisten Wörter haben mehr als eine Bedeutung. So kann z.B. **Rad** einen Teil eines Autos oder Fahrrads bezeichnen, aber auch ein Wort für das Fahrrad selbst sein. Andere Wörter haben je nach Kontext verschiedene Übersetzungen; so bedeutet das Verb **to recede** abhängig vom Subjekt des Satzes entweder „zurückgehen“ oder „verschwinden“. Damit Sie in jedem Zusammenhang immer die richtige Übersetzung finden, haben wir die Einträge nach Bedeutungen eingeteilt: jede Kategorie wird durch einen „Verwendungshinweis“ bestimmt, der *kursiv* gedruckt ist und in

Klammern steht. Die beiden Beispiele von oben sehen dann so aus:

Rad *nt* wheel; (*Fahrrad*) bike
recede *vi* (*tide*) zurückgehen; (*lights etc*) verschwinden

Andere Wörter haben in verschiedenen Sachzusammenhängen unterschiedliche Bedeutungen. Das Wort **Rezept** z. B. bezeichnet eine Koch- oder Backanleitung, bezieht sich in medizinischen Zusammenhängen jedoch auf ein ärztlich verordnetes Medikament. Wir zeigen Ihnen, welche Übersetzung Sie auswählen sollten, indem wir wieder in Klammern solche Fachgebiete in *kursiven* Buchstaben angeben, mit dem Anfangsbuchstaben großgeschrieben, im vorigen Fall *Koch* als Abkürzung für *Kochen* und *Med* als Abkürzung für *Medizin*:

Rezept *nt* (*Koch*) recipe; (*Med*) prescription

Sie finden eine Liste aller in diesem Wörterbuch benutzten Abkürzungen für solche Sachgebiete auf den Seiten x–xii.

Übersetzungen

Die meisten deutschen Wörter können mit einem einzigen englischen Wort übersetzt werden und umgekehrt. Aber manchmal gibt es eine solche genaue Entsprechung nicht. In diesen Fällen haben wir eine ungefähre Entsprechung angegeben, gekennzeichnet durch ≈. Dies ist z. B. der Fall bei **Gymnasium** mit den englischen bzw. amerikanischen Äquivalenten „grammar school" und „high school", die aufgrund der unterschiedlichen Ausbildungssysteme lediglich ungefähre Entsprechungen sein können.

Gymnasium *nt* ≈ grammar school (*Brit*), high school (*US*)

Manchmal kann man nicht einmal ein ungefähres Äquivalent finden. Besonders oft ist das der Fall beim Essen, insbesondere bei lokalen Spezialitäten wie dieser schottischen Speise:

haggis (*Scot*) *n Gericht aus gehackten Schafsinnereien und Haferschrot, im Schafsmagen gekocht*

Hier wird statt einer Übersetzung (die es einfach gar nicht gibt) eine Erklärung gegeben, die durch *Kursivschrift* als solche kenntlich gemacht ist.

Im Deutschen wissen Sie , in welcher Situation Sie den Ausdruck **ich bin pleite** verwenden würden, wann Sie **ich bin knapp bei Kasse** sagen und wann **ich bin in Geldschwierigkeiten.** Wenn Sie jedoch Englisch verstehen oder selbst sprechen wollen, ist es wichtig zu wissen, welcher Ausdruck etwa höflich ist und welcher nicht. Um Ihnen hierbei zu helfen, haben wir für umgangssprachliche Ausdrücke die Kennzeichnung (*umg*) bzw. (*inf*) verwendet. Besonders anstößige Ausdrücke sind zusätzlich mit einem Ausrufezeichen versehen, also (*umg!*) bzw. (*inf!*), um den Benutzer zu warnen, diese nur mit großer Vorsicht zu verwenden. Angaben wie (*umg*) oder (*inf*) werden bei Übersetzungen in der Regel nicht wiederholt, wenn das Sprachniveau der Zielsprache dem der Ausgangssprache entspricht.

Schlüsselwörter

Im Text als **SCHLÜSSELWÖRTER** hervorgehobene Einträge, wie etwa **to be** und **to do** und ihre deutschen Entsprechungen **sein** und **machen**, werden als Grundelemente der Sprache besonders ausführlich behandelt.

Landeskundliche Informationen

In vom restlichen Text durch eine senkrechte Reihe schattierter Punkte abgesetzten Artikeln werden landeskundliche Aspekte in deutsch- und englischsprachigen Ländern behandelt. Die Themen umfassen Politik, Ausbildung, Medien und Feiertage, z. B. **Bundestag**, **Abitur**, **BBC** und **Hallowe'en**.

Introduction

You may be starting to learn German, or you may wish to extend your knowledge of the language. Perhaps you want to read and study German books, newspapers and magazines, or perhaps simply have a conversation with German speakers. Whatever the reason, whether you're a student, a tourist or want to use German for business, this is the ideal book to help you understand and communicate. This modern, user-friendly dictionary gives priority to everyday vocabulary and the language of current affairs, business and tourism. As in all Collins dictionaries, the emphasis is firmly placed on contemporary language and expressions.

How To Use This Dictionary

You will find below an outline of the way in which information is presented in your dictionary. Our aim is to give you the maximum amount of information whilst still providing a text which is clear and user-friendly.

Entries

A typical entry in your dictionary will be made up of the following elements:

Phonetic transcription

Phonetics appear in square brackets immediately after the headword. They are shown using the International Phonetic Alphabet (IPA), and a complete list of the symbols used in this system can be found on pages xiv and xv.

Grammatical information

All words belong to one of the following parts of speech: noun, verb, adjective, adverb, pronoun, article, conjunction, preposition, exclamation, abbreviation. Nouns can be singular or plural and, in German, masculine, feminine or neuter. Verbs can be transitive, intransitive, reflexive or impersonal. Parts of speech appear in *italics* immediately after the phonetic spelling of the headword. The gender of the translation appears in *italics* immediately following the key element of the translation.

Often a word can have more than one part of speech. Just as the English word **next** can be an adjective or an adverb, the German word **gut** can be an adjective ("good") or an adverb ("well"). In the same way the verb **to walk** is sometimes transitive, i.e. it takes an object ("to walk the dog") and sometimes intransitive, i.e. it doesn't take an object ("to walk to school"). To help you find the meaning you are looking for quickly and for clarity of presentation, the different part of speech categories are separated by an open white triangle ▷.

Meaning divisions

Most words have more than one meaning. Take, for example, **punch** which can be, amongst other things, a blow with the fist or an object used for making holes. Other words are translated differently depending on the context in which they are used. The intransitive verb **to recede**, for example, can be translated by "zurückgehen" or "verschwinden" depending on *what* is receding. To help you select the most appropriate translation in every context, entries are divided according to meaning. Each different meaning is introduced by an "indicator" in *italics* and in brackets. Thus, the examples given above will be shown as follows:

> **punch** *n* (*blow*) Schlag *m*; (*tool*) Locher *m*
> **recede** *vi* (*tide*) zurückgehen; (*lights etc*) verschwinden

Likewise, some words can have a different meaning when used to talk about a specific subject area or field. For example, **bishop**, which in a religious context means a high-ranking clergyman, is also the name of a chess piece. To show English speakers which translation to use, we have added "subject field labels" in italics with initial capitals and in brackets, in this case (*Rel*) and (*Chess*):

bishop *n* (*Rel*) Bischof *m*; (*Chess*) Läufer *m*

Field labels are often shortened to save space. You will find a complete list of abbreviations used in the dictionary on pages x to xii

Translations

Most English words have a direct translation in German and vice versa, as shown in the examples given above. Sometimes, however, no exact equivalent exists in the target language. In such cases we have given an approximate equivalent, indicated by the sign ≈. Such is the case of **high school**, the German equivalent of which is "Oberschule *f*". This is not an exact translation since the systems of the two countries in question are quite different:

high school *n* ≈ Oberschule *f*

On occasion it is impossible to find even an approximate equivalent. This may be the case, for example, with the names of culinary specialities like this German cake:

Streuselkuchen *m cake with crumble topping*

Here the translation (which doesn't exist) is replaced by an explanation. For increased clarity the explanation, or "gloss", is shown in *italics*.

Register

In English you instinctively know when to say **I'm broke** *or* **I'm a bit short of cash** and when to say **I don't have any money**. When you are trying to understand someone who is speaking German, however, or when you yourself try to speak German, it is especially important to know what is polite and what is less so. To help you with this, we have added the register labels (*umg*) and (*inf*) to colloquial or offensive expressions. Those expressions which are particularly vulgar are also given an exclamation mark (*umg!*) or (*inf!*), warning you to use them with extreme care. Please note that the register labels (*umg*) and (*inf*) are not repeated in the target language when the register of the translation matches that of the word or phrase being translated.

Keywords

Words labelled in the text as **KEYWORDS**, such as **be** and **do** or their German equivalents **sein** and **machen**, have been given special treatment because they form the basic elements of the language. This extra help will ensure that you know how to use these complex words with confidence.

Cultural information

Entries which appear separated by a column of dots explain aspects of culture in German- and English-speaking countries. Subject areas covered include politics, education, media and national festivals, for example **Bundestag**, **Abitur**, **BBC** and **Hallowe'en**.

Abkürzungen		Abbreviations
Abkürzung	*abk, abbr*	abbreviation
Adjektiv	*adj*	adjective
Verwaltung	*Admin*	administration
Adverb	*adv*	adverb
Landwirtschaft	*Agr*	agriculture
Akkusativ	*akk, acc*	accusative
Anatomie	*Anat*	anatomy
Architektur	*Archit*	architecture
Artikel	*art*	article
Kunst	*Art*	art
Astrologie	*Astrol*	astrology
Astronomie	*Astron*	astronomy
attributiv	*attrib*	attributive
Kraftfahrzeuge	*Aut*	automobiles
Hilfsverb	*aux*	auxiliary
Luftfahrt	*Aviat*	aviation
Bergbau	*Bergb*	mining
besonders	*bes*	especially
Biologie	*Biol*	biology
Botanik	*Bot*	botany
britisch	*Brit*	British
Kartenspiel	*Cards*	cards
Chemie	*Chem*	chemistry
Film	*Cine*	cinema
Handel	*Comm*	commerce
Komparativ	*comp*	comparative
Computer	*Comput*	computers
Konjunktion	*conj*	conjunction
Bauwesen	*Constr*	building
zusammengesetztes Wort	*cpd*	compound
Kochen und Backen	*Culin*	cooking
Dativ	*dat*	dative
bestimmt	*def*	definite
diminutiv	*dimin*	diminutive
dekliniert	*dekl*	declined
kirchlich	*Eccl*	ecclesiastical
Volkswirtschaft	*Econ*	economics
Eisenbahn	*Eisenb*	railways
Elektrizität	*Elek, Elec*	electricity
besonders	*esp*	especially
und so weiter	*etc*	et cetera
etwas	*etw*	something
Euphemismus	*euph*	euphemism
Ausruf	*excl*	exclamation
Femininum	*f*	feminine
übertragen	*fig*	figurative
Film	*Film*	cinema
Finanzen	*Fin*	finance
formell	*form*	formal
'phrasal verb', bei dem Partikel und Verb nicht getrennt werden können	*fus*	fused: phrasal verb where the particle cannot be separated from the verb
gehoben	*geh*	elevated

Genitiv	*gen*	genitive
Geografie	*Geog*	geography
Geologie	*Geol*	geology
Geometrie	*Geom*	geometry
Grammatik	*Gram*	grammar
Geschichte	*Hist*	history
scherzhaft	*hum*	humorous
Imperfekt	*imperf*	imperfect
unpersönlich	*impers*	impersonal
unbestimmt	*indef*	indefinite
umgangssprachlich	*inf*	informal
untrennbares Verb	*insep*	inseparable
Interjektion	*interj*	interjection
Interrogativ	*interrog*	interrogative
unveränderlich	*inv*	invariable
unregelmäßig	*irreg*	irregular
jemand	*jd*	somebody
jemandem	*jdm*	(to) somebody
jemanden	*jdn*	somebody
jemandes	*jds*	somebody's
Rechtswesen	*Jur*	law
Kartenspiel	*Karten*	cards
Kochen und Backen	*Koch*	cooking
Komparativ	*komp*	comparative
Konjunktion	*konj*	conjunction
Rechtswesen	*Law*	law
Sprachwissenschaft	*Ling*	linguistics
wörtlich	*lit*	literal
literarisch	*liter*	literary
Literatur	*Liter*	literature
Maskulinum	*m*	masculine
Mathematik	*Math*	mathematics
Medizin	*Med*	medicine
Meteorologie	*Met*	meteorology
Militärwesen	*Mil*	military
Bergbau	*Min*	mining
Musik	*Mus*	music
Substantiv	*n*	noun
nautisch	*Naut*	nautical
Nominativ	*nom*	nominative
norddeutsch	*Nordd*	North Germany
Neutrum	*nt*	neuter
Zahlwort	*num*	numeral
Objekt	*obj*	object
oder	*od*	or
veraltet	*old*	
sich	*o.s.*	oneself
österreichisch	*Österr*	Austria
Parlament	*Parl*	parliament
pejorativ	*pej*	pejorative
Person/persönlich	*pers*	person/personal
Pharmazie	*Pharm*	pharmacy
Fotografie	*Phot*	photography
Physik	*Phys*	physics
Physiologie	*Physiol*	physiology

Plural	*pl*	plural
Politik	*Pol*	politics
possessiv	*poss*	possessive
Partizip Perfekt	*pp*	past participle
Präfix	*präf, pref*	prefix
Präposition	*präp, prep*	preposition
Präsens	*präs, pres*	present
Pronomen	*pron*	pronoun
Psychologie	*Psych*	psychology
Imperfekt	*pt*	past tense
Radio	*Radio*	radio
Eisenbahn	*Rail*	railways
Religion	*Rel*	religion
Relativ-	*rel*	relative
Rundfunk	*Rundf*	broadcasting
jemand (-en, -en)	*sb*	somebody
Schulwesen	*Sch*	school
Naturwissenschaft	*Sci*	science
Schulwesen	*Scol*	school
schottisch	*Scot*	Scottish
Singular	*sing*	singular
Skisport	*Ski*	skiing
etwas	*sth*	something
Süddeutschland	*Südd*	South German
Suffix	*suff*	suffix
Superlativ	*superl*	superlative
Technik	*Tech*	technology
Telekommunikation	*Tel*	telecommunications
Theater	*Theat*	theatre
Fernsehen	*TV*	television
Typografie	*Typ*	typography
umgangssprachlich	*umg*	colloquial
Universität	*Univ*	university
unpersönlich	*unpers*	impersonal
unregelmäßig	*unreg*	irregular
untrennbar	*untr*	inseparable
unveränderlich	*unver*	invariable
(nord)amerikanisch	US	(North)American
gewöhnlich	*usu*	usually
und so weiter	*usw*	et cetera
Verb	*vb*	verb
intransitives Verb	*vi*	intransitive verb
reflexives Verb	*vr*	reflexive verb
transitives Verb	*vt*	transitive verb
Wirtschaft	*Wirts*	economy
Zoologie	*Zool*	zoology
zusammengesetztes Wort	*zW*	compound
ungefähre Entsprechung	≈	cultural equivalent
eingetragene Marke	®	registered trademark

German Noun Endings

After many noun entries on the German-English side of the dictionary, you will find two pieces of grammatical information, separated by commas, to help you with the declension of the noun, e.g. **-**, **-n** or **-(e)s**, **-e**. The first item shows you the genitive singular form, and the second gives the plural form. The hyphen stands for the word itself and the other letters are endings. Sometimes an umlaut is shown over the hyphen, which means an umlaut must be placed on the vowel of the word, e.g.:

DICTIONARY ENTRY	GENITIVE SINGULAR	PLURAL
Mann *m* **-(e)s, ¨-er**	**Mannes** *or* **Manns**	**Männer**
Jacht *f* **-, -en**	**Jacht**	**Jachten**

This information is not given when the noun has one of the regular German noun endings below, and you should refer to this table in such cases. Similarly, genitive and plural endings are not shown when the German entry is a compound consisting of two or more words which are to be found elsewhere in the dictionary, since the compound form takes the endings of the LAST word of which it is formed, e.g.:

for **Nebenstraße** *see* **Straße**
for **Schneeball** *see* **Ball**

Regular German Noun Endings

NOM	GEN	PL
-ant *m*	-anten	-anten
-anz *f*	-anz	-anzen
-ar *m*	-ar(e)s	-are
-chen *nt*	-chens	-chen
-ei *f*	-ei	-eien
-elle *f*	-elle	-ellen
-ent *m*	-enten	-enten
-enz *f*	-enz	-enzen
-ette *f*	-ette	-etten
-eur *m*	-eurs	-eure
-euse *f*	-euse	-eusen
-heit *f*	-heit	-heiten
-ie *f*	-ie	-ien
-ik *f*	-ik	-iken
-in *f*	-in	-innen
-ine *f*	-ine	-inen
-ion *f*	-ion	-ionen
-ist *m*	-isten	-isten
-ium *nt*	-iums	-ien
-ius *m*	-ius	-iusse
-ive *f*	-ive	-iven
-keit *f*	-keit	-keiten
-lein *nt*	-leins	-lein
-ling *m*	-lings	-linge
-ment *nt*	-ments	-mente
-mus *m*	-mus	-men
-schaft *f*	-schaft	-schaften
-tät *f*	-tät	-täten
-tor *m*	-tors	-toren
-ung *f*	-ung	-ungen
-ur *f*	-ur	-uren

Phonetic Symbols

NB: All vowels sounds are approximate only.

Lautschrift

NB: Alle Vokallaute sind nur ungefähre Entsprechungen.

Vowels		Vokale
matt	[a]	
Fahne	[aː]	
Vater	[ər]	
	[ɑː]	calm, part
	[æ]	sat
Rendezvous	[ã]	
Chance	[aː]	
	[ãː]	clientele
Etage	[e]	
Seele, Mehl	[eː]	
Wäsche, Bett	[ɛ]	egg
zählen	[ɛː]	
Teint	[ɛ̃ː]	
mache	[ə]	above
	[əː]	burn, earn
Kiste	[ɪ]	pit, awfully
Vitamin	[i]	
Ziel	[iː]	peat
Oase	[o]	
oben	[oː]	
Champignon	[õ]	
Salon	[õː]	
Most	[ɔ]	cot
	[ɔː]	born, jaw
ökonomisch	[ø]	
blöd	[øː]	
Göttin	[œ]	
	[ʌ]	hut
zuletzt	[u]	put
Mut	[uː]	pool
Mutter	[ʊ]	
Physik	[y]	
Kübel	[yː]	
Sünde	[ʏ]	

Diphthongs		**Diphthonge**
Styling	[ai]	
w*ei*t	[aɪ]	b*uy*, d*ie*, m*y*
umb*au*en	[au]	h*ou*se, n*ow*
H*au*s	[aʊ]	
	[eɪ]	p*ay*, m*a*te
	[ɛə]	p*air*, m*are*
	[əu]	n*o*, b*oa*t
	[ɪə]	m*ere*, sh*ear*
H*eu*, H*äu*ser	[ɔʏ]	
	[ɔɪ]	b*oy*, c*oi*n
	[uə]	t*our*, p*oor*

Consonants		**Konsonanten**
Ball	[b]	*b*all
mi*ch*	[ç]	
	[tʃ]	*ch*ild
*f*ern	[f]	*f*ield
*g*ern	[g]	*g*ood
Hand	[h]	*h*and
*j*a	[j]	*y*et, mill*i*on
	[dʒ]	*j*ust
Kind	[k]	*k*ind, *c*atch
*l*inks, Pult	[l]	*l*eft, *l*itt*l*e
*m*att	[m]	*m*at
Nest	[n]	*n*est
la*ng*	[ŋ]	lo*ng*
Paar	[p]	*p*ut
*r*ennen	[r]	*r*un
fast, fassen	[s]	*s*it
*Ch*ef, *S*tein, *Sch*lag	[ʃ]	*sh*all
Tafel	[t]	tab
	[θ]	*th*ing
	[ð]	*th*is
*w*er	[v]	*v*ery
	[w]	*w*et
Lo*ch*	[x]	lo*ch*
fi*x*	[ks]	box
*s*ingen	[z]	pods, zip
Zahn	[ts]	
*g*enieren	[ʒ]	measure

Other signs		**Andere Zeichen**
glottal stop	|	Knacklaut
main stress	[ˈ]	Hauptton
long vowel	[ː]	Längezeichen

German Irregular Verbs

* with "sein"

INFINITIV	PRÄSENS 2., 3. SINGULAR	PRÄTERITUM	PARTIZIP PERFEKT
abwägen	wägst ab, wägt ab	wog ab	abgewogen
ausbedingen	bedingst aus, bedingt aus	bedang *od* bedingte aus	ausbedungen
backen	bäckst, bäckt	backte *od* buk	gebacken
befehlen	befiehlst, befiehlt	befahl	befohlen
beginnen	beginnst, beginnt	begann	begonnen
beißen	beißt, beißt	biss	gebissen
bergen	birgst, birgt	barg	geborgen
bersten*	birst, birst	barst	geborsten
betrügen	betrügst, betrügt	betrog	betrogen
bewegen	bewegst, bewegt	bewog	bewogen
biegen	biegst, biegt	bog	gebogen
bieten	bietest, bietet	bot	geboten
binden	bindest, bindet	band	gebunden
bitten	bittest, bittet	bat	gebeten
blasen	bläst, bläst	blies	geblasen
bleiben*	bleibst, bleibt	blieb	geblieben
braten	brätst, brät	briet	gebraten
brechen*	brichst, bricht	brach	gebrochen
brennen	brennst, brennt	brannte	gebrannt
bringen	bringst, bringt	brachte	gebracht
denken	denkst, denkt	dachte	gedacht
dreschen	drischst, drischt	drosch	gedroschen
dringen*	dringst, dringt	drang	gedrungen
dürfen	darfst, darf	durfte	gedurft
empfangen	empfängst, empfängt	empfing	empfangen
empfehlen	empfiehlst, empfiehlt	empfahl	empfohlen
empfinden	empfindest, empfindet	empfand	empfunden
erbleichen*	erbleichst, erbleicht	erbleichte	erblichen
erloschen*	erlischst, erlischt	erlosch	erloschen
erschrecken*	erschrickst, erschrickt	erschrak	erschrocken
erwägen	erwägst, erwägt	erwog	erwogen
essen	isst, isst	aß	gegessen
fahren*	fährst, fährt	fuhr	gefahren
fallen*	fällst, fällt	fiel	gefallen
fangen	fängst, fängt	fing	gefangen
fechten	fichst, ficht	focht	gefochten
finden	findest, findet	fand	gefunden
flechten	flichtst, flicht	flocht	geflochten
fliegen*	fliegst, fliegt	flog	geflogen
fliehen*	fliehst, flieht	floh	geflohen
fließen*	fließt, fließt	floss	geflossen
fressen	frisst, frisst	fraß	gefressen
frieren	frierst, friert	fror	gefroren
gären*	gärst, gärt	gor	gegoren
gebären	gebierst, gebiert	gebar	geboren
geben	gibst, gibt	gab	gegeben
gedeihen*	gedeihst, gedeiht	gedieh	gediehen
gehen*	gehst, geht	ging	gegangen

* with "sein"

INFINITIV	PRÄSENS 2., 3. SINGULAR	PRÄTERITUM	PARTIZIP PERFEKT
gelingen*	–, gelingt	gelang	gelungen
gelten	giltst, gilt	galt	gegolten
genesen*	genest, genest	genas	genesen
genießen	genießt, genießt	genoss	genossen
geraten*	gerätst, gerät	geriet	geraten
geschehen*	–, geschieht	geschah	geschehen
gewinnen	gewinnst, gewinnt	gewann	gewonnen
gießen	gießt, gießt	goss	gegossen
gleichen	gleichst, gleicht	glich	geglichen
gleiten*	gleitest, gleitet	glitt	geglitten
glimmen	glimmst, glimmt	glomm	geglommen
graben	gräbst, gräbt	grub	gegraben
greifen	greifst, greift	griff	gegriffen
haben	hast, hat	hatte	gehabt
halten	hältst, hält	hielt	gehalten
hängen	hängst, hängt	hing	gehangen
hauen	haust, haut	haute	gehauen
heben	hebst, hebt	hob	gehoben
heißen	heißt, heißt	hieß	geheißen
helfen	hilfst, hilft	half	geholfen
kennen	kennst, kennt	kannte	gekannt
klimmen*	klimmst, klimmt	klomm	geklommen
klingen	klingst, klingt	klang	geklungen
kneifen	kneifst, kneift	kniff	gekniffen
kommen*	kommst, kommt	kam	gekommen
können	kannst, kann	konnte	gekonnt
kriechen*	kriechst, kriecht	kroch	gekrochen
laden	lädst, lädt	lud	geladen
lassen	lässt, lässt	ließ	gelassen
laufen*	läufst, läuft	lief	gelaufen
leiden	leidest, leidet	litt	gelitten
leihen	leihst, leiht	lieh	geliehen
lesen	liest, liest	las	gelesen
liegen	liegst, liegt	lag	gelegen
lügen	lügst, lügt	log	gelogen
mahlen	mahlst, mahlt	mahlte	gemahlen
meiden	meidest, meidet	mied	gemieden
melken	melkst, melkt	melkte *od* molk	gemolken
messen	misst, misst	maß	gemessen
misslingen*	–, misslingt	misslang	misslungen
mögen	magst, mag	mochte	gemocht
müssen	musst, muss	musste	gemusst
nehmen	nimmst, nimmt	nahm	genommen
nennen	nennst, nennt	nannte	genannt
pfeifen	pfeifst, pfeift	pfiff	gepfiffen
preisen	preist, preist	pries	gepriesen
quellen*	quillst, quillt	quoll	gequollen
raten	rätst, rät	riet	geraten
reiben	reibst, reibt	rieb	gerieben

* with "sein"

INFINITIV	PRÄSENS 2., 3. SINGULAR	PRÄTERITUM	PARTIZIP PERFEKT
reißen*	reißt, reißt	riss	gerissen
reiten*	reitest, reitet	ritt	geritten
rennen*	rennst, rennt	rannte	gerannt
riechen	riechst, riecht	roch	gerochen
ringen	ringst, ringt	rang	gerungen
rinnen*	rinnst, rinnt	rann	geronnen
rufen	rufst, ruft	rief	gerufen
salzen	salzt, salzt	salzte	gesalzen
saufen	säufst, säuft	soff	gesoffen
saugen	saugst, saugt	sog *od* saugte	-gesogen *od* gesaugt
schaffen	schaffst, schafft	schuf	geschaffen
schallen	schallst, schallt	scholl	geschollen
scheiden*	scheidest, scheidet	schied	geschieden
scheinen	scheinst, scheint	schien	geschienen
scheißen	scheißt, scheißt	schiss	geschissen
schelten	schiltst, schilt	schalt	gescholten
scheren	scherst, schert	schor	geschoren
schieben	schiebst, schiebt	schob	geschoben
schießen	schießt, schießt	schoss	geschossen
schinden	schindest, schindet	schindete	geschunden
schlafen	schläfst, schläft	schlief	geschlafen
schlagen	schlägst, schlägt	schlug	geschlagen
schleichen*	schleichst, schleicht	schlich	geschlichen
schleifen	schleifst, schleift	schliff	geschliffen
schließen	schließt, schließt	schloss	geschlossen
schlingen	schlingst, schlingt	schlang	geschlungen
schmeißen	schmeißt, schmeißt	schmiss	geschmissen
schmelzen*	schmilzt, schmilzt	schmolz	geschmolzen
schneiden	schneidest, schneidet	schnitt	geschnitten
schreiben	schreibst, schreibt	schrieb	geschrieben
schreien	schreist, schreit	schrie	geschrie(e)n
schreiten	schreitest, schreitet	schritt	geschritten
schweigen	schweigst, schweigt	schwieg	geschwiegen
schwellen*	schwillst, schwillt	schwoll	geschwollen
schwimmen*	schwimmst, schwimmt	schwamm	geschwommen
schwinden*	schwindest, schwindet	schwand	geschwunden
schwingen	schwingst, schwingt	schwang	geschwungen
schwören	schwörst, schwört	schwor	geschworen
sehen	siehst, sieht	sah	gesehen
sein*	bist, ist	war	gewesen
senden	sendest, sendet	sandte	gesandt
singen	singst, singt	sang	gesungen
sinken*	sinkst, sinkt	sank	gesunken
sinnen	sinnst, sinnt	sann	gesonnen
sitzen	sitzt, sitzt	saß	gesessen
sollen	sollst, soll	sollte	gesollt
speien	speist, speit	spie	gespie(e)n
spinnen	spinnst, spinnt	spann	gesponnen
sprechen	sprichst, spricht	sprach	gesprochen
sprießen*	sprießt, sprießt	spross	gesprossen
springen*	springst, springt	sprang	gesprungen

* with "sein"

INFINITIV	PRÄSENS 2., 3. SINGULAR	PRÄTERITUM	PARTIZIP PERFEKT
stechen	stichst, sticht	stach	gestochen
stecken	steckst, steckt	steckte *od* stack	gesteckt
stehen	stehst, steht	stand	gestanden
stehlen	stiehlst, stiehlt	stahl	gestohlen
steigen*	steigst, steigt	stieg	gestiegen
sterben*	stirbst, stirbt	starb	gestorben
stinken	stinkst, stinkt	stank	gestunken
stoßen	stößt, stößt	stieß	gestoßen
streichen	streichst, streicht	strich	gestrichen
streiten	streitest, streitet	stritt	gestritten
tragen	trägst, trägt	trug	getragen
treffen	triffst, trifft	traf	getroffen
treiben*	treibst, treibt	trieb	getrieben
treten*	trittst, tritt	trat	getreten
trinken	trinkst, trinkt	trank	getrunken
trügen	trügst, trügt	trog	getrogen
tun	tust, tut	tat	getan
verderben	verdirbst, verdirbt	verdarb	verdorben
verdrießen	verdrießt, verdrießt	verdross	verdrossen
vergessen	vergisst, vergisst	vergaß	vergessen
verlieren	verlierst, verliert	verlor	verloren
verschleißen	verschleißt, verschleißt	verschliss	verschlissen
verschwinden	verschwindest, verschwindet	verschwand	verschwunden
verzeihen	verzeihst, verzeiht	verzieh	verziehen
wachsen*	wächst, wächst	wuchs	gewachsen
wägen	wägst, wägt	wog	gewogen
waschen	wäschst, wäscht	wusch	gewaschen
weben	webst, webt	webte *od* wob	gewoben
weichen*	weichst, weicht	wich	gewichen
weisen	weist, weist	wies	gewiesen
wenden	wendest, wendet	wandte	gewandt
werben	wirbst, wirbt	warb	geworben
werden*	wirst, wird	wurde	geworden
werfen	wirfst, wirft	warf	geworfen
wiegen	wiegst, wiegt	wog	gewogen
winden	windest, windet	wand	gewunden
wissen	weißt, weiß	wusste	gewusst
wollen	willst, will	wollte	gewollt
wringen	wringst, wringt	wrang	gewrungen
zeihen	zeihst, zeiht	zieh	geziehen
ziehen*	ziehst, zieht	zog	gezogen
zwingen	zwingst, zwingt	zwang	gezwungen

Deutsch–Englisch

German–English

Aa

A¹, a [aː] *nt* A, a; **A wie Anton** ≈ A for Andrew, ≈ A for Able (*US*); **das A und O** the be-all and end-all; (*eines Wissensgebietes*) the basics *pl*; **wer A sagt, muss auch B sagen** (*Sprichwort*) in for a penny, in for a pound (*Sprichwort*)
A² *f abk* (= *Autobahn*) ≈ M (*Brit*)
a. *abk* = **am**
à [aː] *präp* (*bes Comm*) at
AA *nt abk* (= *Auswärtiges Amt*) F.O. (*Brit*)
Aachen [ˈaːxən] (**-s**) *nt* Aachen
Aal [aːl] (**-(e)s, -e**) *m* eel
aalen [ˈaːlən] (*umg*) *vr*: **sich in der Sonne ~** to bask in the sun
a. a. O. *abk* (= *am angegebenen od angeführten Ort*) loc. cit.
Aas [aːs] (**-es, -e** *od* **Äser**) *nt* carrion; **Aasgeier** *m* vulture

SCHLÜSSELWORT

ab [ap] *präp +dat* from; **ab Werk** (*Comm*) ex works; **Kinder ab 12 Jahren** children from the age of 12; **ab morgen** from tomorrow; **ab sofort** as of now
▷ *adv* **1** off; **links ab** to the left; **der Knopf ist ab** the button has come off; **ab nach Hause!** off home with you!; **ab durch die Mitte!** (*umg*) beat it!
2 (*zeitlich*): **von da ab** from then on; **von heute ab** from today, as of today
3 (*auf Fahrplänen*): **München ab 12.20** leaving Munich 12.20
4: ab und zu *od* **an** now and then *od* again

abändern [ˈap|ɛndərn] *vt*: **~ (in** *+akk***)** to alter (to); (*Gesetzentwurf*) to amend (to); (*Strafe, Urteil*) to revise (to)
Abänderung *f* alteration; amendment; revision
Abänderungsantrag *m* (*Parl*) proposed amendment
abarbeiten [ˈap|arbaɪtən] *vr* to slave away
Abart [ˈap|aːrt] *f* (*Biol*) variety
abartig *adj* abnormal
Abb. *abk* (= *Abbildung*) illus.
Abbau [ˈapbaʊ] (**-(e)s**) *m* (*+gen*) dismantling; (*Verminderung*) reduction (in); (*Verfall*) decline (in); (*Min*) mining; (*über Tage*) quarrying; (*Chem*) decomposition
abbaubar *adj*: **biologisch ~** biodegradable
abbauen *vt* to dismantle; (*verringern*) to reduce; (*Min*) to mine; to quarry; (*Chem*) to break down; **Arbeitsplätze ~** to make job cuts
Abbaurechte *pl* mineral rights *pl*
abbeißen [ˈapbaɪsən] *unreg vt* to bite off
abbekommen [ˈapbəkɔmən] *unreg vt*: **etwas ~** to get some (of it); (*beschädigt werden*) to get damaged; (*verletzt werden*) to get hurt
abberufen [ˈapbəruːfən] *unreg vt* to recall
Abberufung *f* recall
abbestellen [ˈapbəʃtɛlən] *vt* to cancel
abbezahlen [ˈapbətsaːlən] *vt* to pay off
abbiegen [ˈapbiːgən] *unreg vi* to turn off; (*Straße*) to bend ▷ *vt* to bend; (*verhindern*) to ward off
Abbiegespur *f* turning lane
Abbild [ˈapbɪlt] *nt* portrayal; (*einer Person*) image, likeness; **abbilden** [ˈapbɪldən] *vt* to portray; **Abbildung** *f* illustration; (*Schaubild*) diagram
abbinden [ˈapbɪndən] *unreg vt* (*Med: Arm, Bein etc*) to ligature
Abbitte [ˈapbɪtə] *f*: **~ leisten** *od* **tun (bei)** to make one's apologies (to)
abblasen [ˈapblaːzən] *unreg vt* to blow off; (*fig: umg*) to call off
abblättern [ˈapblɛtərn] *vi* (*Putz, Farbe*) to flake (off)
abblenden [ˈapblɛndən] *vt* (*Aut*) to dip (*Brit*), dim (*US*) ▷ *vi* to dip (*Brit*) *od* dim (*US*) one's headlights
Abblendlicht [ˈapblɛntlɪçt] *nt* dipped (*Brit*) *od* dimmed (*US*) headlights *pl*
abblitzen [ˈapblɪtsən] (*umg*) *vi*: **jdn ~ lassen** to send sb packing
abbrechen [ˈapbrɛçən] *unreg vt* to break off; (*Gebäude*) to pull down; (*Zelt*) to take down; (*aufhören*) to stop; (*Comput*) to abort ▷ *vi* to break off; to stop; **sich** *dat* **einen ~** (*umg: sich sehr anstrengen*) to bust a gut
abbrennen [ˈapbrɛnən] *unreg vt* to burn off; (*Feuerwerk*) to let off ▷ *vi* (*Hilfsverb sein*) to burn down; **abgebrannt sein** (*umg*) to be broke
abbringen [ˈapbrɪŋən] *unreg vt*: **jdn von etw ~** to dissuade sb from sth; **jdn vom Weg ~** to divert sb; **ich bringe den Verschluss nicht ab** (*umg*) I can't get the top off

abbröckeln ['apbrœkəln] *vi* to crumble off *od* away; (*Börse: Preise*) to ease
Abbruch ['apbrʊx] *m* (*von Verhandlungen etc*) breaking off; (*von Haus*) demolition; (*Comput*) abort; **jdm/etw ~ tun** to harm sb/sth; **Abbrucharbeiten** *pl* demolition work *sing*; **abbruchreif** *adj* only fit for demolition
abbrühen ['apbry:ən] *vt* to scald
abbuchen ['apbu:xən] *vt* to debit; (*durch Dauerauftrag*): **~ (von)** to pay by standing order (from)
abbürsten ['apbʏrstən] *vt* to brush off
abbüßen ['apby:sən] *vt* (*Strafe*) to serve
ABC-Waffen *pl abk* (= *atomare, biologische und chemische Waffen*) ABC weapons (= atomic, biological and chemical weapons)
abdampfen ['apdampfən] *vi* (*fig: umg: losgehen/-fahren*) to hit the road
abdanken ['apdaŋkən] *vi* to resign; (*König*) to abdicate
Abdankung *f* resignation; abdication
abdecken ['apdɛkən] *vt* to uncover; (*Tisch*) to clear; (*Loch*) to cover
abdichten ['apdɪçtən] *vt* to seal; (*Naut*) to caulk
abdrängen ['apdrɛŋən] *vt* to push off
abdrehen ['apdre:ən] *vt* (*Gas*) to turn off; (*Licht*) to switch off; (*Film*) to shoot ▷ *vi* (*Schiff*) to change course; **jdm den Hals ~** to wring sb's neck
abdriften ['apdrɪftən] *vi* to drift (away)
abdrosseln ['apdrɔsəln] *vt* to throttle; (*Aut*) to stall; (*Produktion*) to cut back
Abdruck ['apdrʊk] *m* (*Nachdrucken*) reprinting; (*Gedrucktes*) reprint; (*Gipsabdruck, Wachsabdruck*) impression; (*Fingerabdruck*) print; **abdrucken** *vt* to print
abdrücken ['apdrʏkən] *vt* to make an impression of; (*Waffe*) to fire; (*umg: Person*) to hug, squeeze ▷ *vr* to leave imprints; (*abstoßen*) to push o.s. away; **jdm die Luft ~** to squeeze all the breath out of sb
abdüsen ['apdy:sən] (*umg*) *vi* to dash *od* whizz off
abebben ['ap|ɛbən] *vi* to ebb away
Abend ['a:bənt] (**-s, -e**) *m* evening; **gegen ~** towards (the) evening; **den ganzen ~ (über)** the whole evening; **zu ~ essen** to have dinner *od* supper; **heute ~** this evening; **Abendanzug** *m* dinner jacket (*Brit*), tuxedo (*US*); **Abendbrot** *nt* supper; **Abendessen** *nt* supper; **abendfüllend** *adj* taking up the whole evening; **Abendgymnasium** *nt* night school; **Abendkasse** *f* (*Theat*) box office; **Abendkleid** *nt* evening gown; **Abendkurs** *m* evening classes *pl*; **Abendland** *nt* West; **abendlich** *adj* evening; **Abendmahl** *nt* Holy Communion; **Abendrot** *nt* sunset
abends *adv* in the evening
Abend- *zW*: **Abendvorstellung** *f* evening performance; **Abendzeitung** *f* evening paper
Abenteuer ['a:bəntɔʏər] (**-s, -**) *nt* adventure; (*Liebesabenteuer*) affair; **abenteuerlich** *adj* adventurous; **Abenteuerspielplatz** *m* adventure playground
Abenteurer (**-s, -**) *m* adventurer; **Abenteurerin** *f* adventuress
aber ['a:bər] *konj* but; (*jedoch*) however ▷ *adv*: **oder ~** or else; **bist du ~ braun!** aren't you brown!; **das ist ~ schön** that's really nice; **nun ist ~ Schluss!** now that's enough!; **Aber** *nt* but
Aberglaube ['a:bərglaʊbə] *m* superstition
abergläubisch ['a:bərglɔʏbɪʃ] *adj* superstitious
aberkennen ['ap|ɛrkɛnən] *unreg vt*: **jdm etw ~** to deprive sb of sth, take sth (away) from sb
Aberkennung *f* taking away
abermalig *adj* repeated
abermals *adv* once again
Abertausend, abertausend ['a:bərtaʊznt] *num*: **Tausend und ~** thousands upon thousands
Abf. *abk* (= *Abfahrt*) dep.
abfahren ['apfa:rən] *unreg vi* to leave, depart ▷ *vt* to take *od* cart away; (*Film*) to start; (*Film, TV: Kamera*) to roll; (*Strecke*) to drive; (*Reifen*) to wear; (*Fahrkarte*) to use; **der Zug ist abgefahren** (*lit*) the train has left; (*fig*) we've/you've *etc* missed the boat; **der Zug fährt um 8.00 von Bremen ab** the train leaves Bremen at 8 o'clock; **jdn ~ lassen** (*umg: abweisen*) to tell sb to get lost; **auf jdn ~** (*umg*) to really go for sb
Abfahrt ['apfa:rt] *f* departure; (*Autobahnabfahrt*) exit; (*Ski*) descent; (*Piste*) run; **Vorsicht bei der ~ des Zuges!** stand clear, the train is about to leave!
Abfahrts- *zW*: **Abfahrtslauf** *m* (*Ski*) downhill; **Abfahrtstag** *m* day of departure; **Abfahrtszeit** *f* departure time
Abfall ['apfal] *m* waste; (*von Speisen etc*) rubbish (*Brit*), garbage (*US*); (*Neigung*) slope; (*Verschlechterung*) decline; **Abfalleimer** *m* rubbish bin (*Brit*), garbage can (*US*)
abfallen *unreg vi* (*lit, fig*) to fall *od* drop off; (*Pol, vom Glauben*) to break away; (*sich neigen*) to fall *od* drop away; **wie viel fällt bei dem Geschäft für mich ab?** (*umg*) how much do I get out of the deal?
abfällig ['apfɛlɪç] *adj* disparaging, deprecatory
Abfallprodukt *nt* (*lit, fig*) waste product
abfangen ['apfaŋən] *unreg vt* to intercept; (*Person*) to catch; (*unter Kontrolle bringen*) to check; (*Aufprall*) to absorb; (*Kunden*) to lure away
Abfangjäger *m* (*Mil*) interceptor
abfärben ['apfɛrbən] *vi* (*lit*) to lose its colour; (*Wäsche*) to run; (*fig*) to rub off
abfassen ['apfasən] *vt* to write, draft
abfeiern ['apfaɪərn] (*umg*) *vt*: **Überstunden ~** to take time off in lieu of overtime pay
abfertigen ['apfɛrtɪgən] *vt* to prepare for dispatch, process; (*an der Grenze*) to clear; (*Kundschaft*) to attend to; **jdn kurz ~** to give sb short shrift
Abfertigung *f* preparing for dispatch, processing; clearance; (*Bedienung: von Kunden*) service; (*: von Antragstellern*): **~ von** dealing with

abfeuern ['apfɔʏərn] *vt* to fire
abfinden ['apfındən] *unreg vt* to pay off ▷ *vr* to come to terms; **sich mit jdm ~/nicht ~** to put up with/not to get on with sb; **er konnte sich nie damit ~, dass ...** he could never accept the fact that ...
Abfindung *f* (*von Gläubigern*) payment; (*Geld*) sum in settlement
abflachen ['apflaxən] *vt* to level (off), flatten (out) ▷ *vi* (*fig: sinken*) to decline
abflauen ['apflaʊən] *vi* (*Wind, Erregung*) to die away, subside; (*Nachfrage, Geschäft*) to fall *od* drop off
abfliegen ['apfli:gən] *unreg vi* to take off ▷ *vt* (*Gebiet*) to fly over
abfließen ['apfli:sən] *unreg vi* to drain away; **ins Ausland ~** (*Geld*) to flow out of the country
Abflug ['apflu:k] *m* departure; (*Start*) take-off
Abflugterminal ['apflu:ktœrmınəl] **(-s, -s)** *m* departure terminal; **Abflugzeit** *f* departure time
Abfluss ['apflʊs] *m* draining away; (*Öffnung*) outlet; **Abflussrohr** *nt* drainpipe; (*von sanitären Anlagen*) wastepipe
abfragen ['apfra:gən] *vt* to test; (*Comput*) to call up; **jdn etw ~** to question sb on sth
abfrieren ['apfri:rən] *unreg vi*: **ihm sind die Füße abgefroren** his feet got frostbitten, he got frostbite in his feet
abfrühstücken ['apfry:ʃtykən] (*umg*) *vt* (*jdn*) to fob off, snub; (*Sache*) to get through with
Abfuhr ['apfu:r] **(-, -en)** *f* removal; (*fig*) snub, rebuff; **sich** *dat* **eine ~ holen** to meet with a rebuff
abführen ['apfy:rən] *vt* to lead away; (*Gelder, Steuern*) to pay ▷ *vi* (*Med*) to have a laxative effect
Abführmittel *nt* laxative, purgative
Abfüllanlage *f* bottling plant
abfüllen ['apfʏlən] *vt* to draw off; (*in Flaschen*) to bottle
Abgabe ['apga:bə] *f* handing in; (*von Ball*) pass; (*Steuer*) tax; (*einer Erklärung*) giving
abgabenfrei *adj* tax-free
abgabenpflichtig *adj* liable to tax
Abgabetermin *m* closing date; (*für Dissertation etc*) submission date
Abgang ['apgaŋ] *m* (*von Schule*) leaving; (*Theat*) exit; (*Med: Ausscheiden*) passing; (*: Fehlgeburt*) miscarriage; (*Abfahrt*) departure; (*der Post, von Waren*) dispatch
Abgangszeugnis *nt* leaving certificate
Abgas ['apga:s] *nt* waste gas; (*Aut*) exhaust
Abgasgrenzwert *m* exhaust emission standard
ABGB *nt abk* (*Österr: = Allgemeines Bürgerliches Gesetzbuch*) *Civil Code in Austria*
abgeben ['apge:bən] *unreg vt* (*Gegenstand*) to hand *od* give in; (*Ball*) to pass; (*Wärme*) to give off; (*Amt*) to hand over; (*Schuss*) to fire; (*Erklärung, Urteil*) to give; (*darstellen*) to make ▷ *vr*: **sich mit jdm/etw ~** to associate with sb/ bother with sth; **„Kinderwagen abzugeben"** "pram for sale"; **jdm etw ~** (*überlassen*) to let sb have sth
abgebrannt ['apgəbrant] (*umg*) *adj* broke
abgebrüht ['apgəbry:t] (*umg*) *adj* (*skrupellos*) hard-boiled, hardened
abgedroschen ['apgədrɔʃən] *adj* trite; (*Witz*) corny
abgefahren ['apgəfa:rən] *pp von* **abfahren**
abgefeimt ['apgəfaımt] *adj* cunning
abgegeben ['apgəge:bən] *pp von* **abgeben**
abgegriffen ['apgəgrıfən] *adj* (*Buch*) well-thumbed; (*Redensart*) trite
abgehackt ['apgəhakt] *adj* clipped
abgehalftert ['apgəhalftərt] *adj* (*fig: umg*) run-down, dead beat
abgehangen ['apgəhaŋən] *pp von* **abhängen** ▷ *adj*: **(gut) ~** (*Fleisch*) well-hung
abgehärtet ['apgəhɛrtət] *adj* tough, hardy; (*fig*) hardened
abgehen ['apge:ən] *unreg vi* to go away, leave; (*Theat*) to exit; (*Post*) to go; (*Med*) to be passed; (*sterben*) to die; (*Knopf etc*) to come off; (*abgezogen werden*) to be taken off; (*Straße*) to branch off; (*abweichen*): **von einer Forderung ~** to give up a demand ▷ *vt* (*Strecke*) to go *od* walk along; (*Mil: Gelände*) to patrol; **von seiner Meinung ~** to change one's opinion; **davon gehen 5% ab** 5% is taken off that; **etw geht jdm ab** (*fehlt*) sb lacks sth
abgekämpft ['apgəkɛmpft] *adj* exhausted
abgekartet ['apgəkartət] *adj*: **ein ~es Spiel** a rigged job
abgeklärt ['apgəklɛ:rt] *adj* serene, tranquil
abgelegen ['apgəle:gən] *adj* remote
abgelten ['apgɛltən] *unreg vt* (*Ansprüche*) to satisfy
abgemacht ['apgəmaxt] *adj* fixed; **~!** done!
abgemagert ['apgəma:gərt] *adj* (*sehr dünn*) thin; (*ausgemergelt*) emaciated
abgeneigt ['apgənaıkt] *adj* averse
abgenutzt ['apgənʊtst] *adj* worn, shabby; (*Reifen*) worn; (*fig: Klischees*) well-worn
Abgeordnete, r ['apgə|ɔrdnətə(r)] *f(m)* elected representative; (*von Parlament*) member of parliament
Abgesandte, r ['apgəzantə(r)] *f(m)* delegate; (*Pol*) envoy
abgeschieden ['apgəʃi:dən] *adv* (*einsam*): **~ leben/wohnen** to live in seclusion
abgeschlagen ['apgəʃla:gən] *adj* (*besiegt*) defeated; (*erschöpft*) exhausted, worn-out
abgeschlossen ['apgəʃlɔsən] *pp von* **abschließen** ▷ *adj attrib* (*Wohnung*) self-contained
abgeschmackt ['apgəʃmakt] *adj* tasteless; **Abgeschmacktheit** *f* lack of taste; (*Bemerkung*) tasteless remark
abgesehen ['apgəze:ən] *adj*: **es auf jdn/etw ~ haben** to be after sb/sth; **~ von ...** apart from ...
abgespannt ['apgəʃpant] *adj* tired out
abgestanden ['apgəʃtandən] *adj* stale; (*Bier*) flat

abgestorben ['apgəʃtɔrbən] *adj* numb; (*Biol, Med*) dead
abgestumpft ['apgəʃtʊmpft] *adj* (*gefühllos: Person*) insensitive; (*Gefühle, Gewissen*) dulled
abgetakelt ['apgəta:kəlt] *adj* (*fig*) decrepit, past it
abgetan ['apgəta:n] *adj*: **damit ist die Sache ~** that settles the matter
abgetragen ['apgətra:gən] *adj* worn
abgewinnen ['apgəvɪnən] *unreg vt*: **jdm Geld ~** to win money from sb; **einer Sache etw/Geschmack ~** to get sth/pleasure from sth
abgewogen ['apgəvo:gən] *adj* (*Urteil, Worte*) balanced
abgewöhnen ['apgəvø:nən] *vt*: **jdm/sich etw ~** to cure sb of sth/give sth up
abgießen ['apgi:sən] *unreg vt* (*Flüssigkeit*) to pour off
Abglanz ['apglants] *m* (*auch fig*) reflection
abgleiten ['apglaɪtən] *unreg vi* to slip, slide
Abgott ['apgɔt] *m* idol
abgöttisch ['apgœtɪʃ] *adj*: **~ lieben** to idolize
abgrasen ['apgra:zən] *vt* (*Feld*) to graze; (*umg: Thema*) to do to death
abgrenzen ['apgrɛntsən] *vt* (*lit, fig*) to mark off; (*Gelände*) to fence off ▷ *vr*: **sich ~ (gegen)** to dis(as)sociate o.s. (from)
Abgrund ['apgrʊnt] *m* (*lit, fig*) abyss
abgründig ['apgrʏndɪç] *adj* unfathomable; (*Lächeln*) cryptic
abgrundtief *adj* (*Hass, Verachtung*) profound
abgucken ['apgʊkən] *vt, vi* to copy
Abguss ['apgʊs] *m* (*Kunst, Metallurgie: Vorgang*) casting; (*: Form*) cast
abhaben ['apha:bən] *unreg* (*umg*) *vt* (*abbekommen*): **willst du ein Stück ~?** do you want a bit?
abhacken ['aphakən] *vt* to chop off
abhaken ['apha:kən] *vt* to tick off (*Brit*), check off (*US*)
abhalten ['aphaltən] *unreg vt* (*Versammlung*) to hold; **jdn von etw ~** (*fernhalten*) to keep sb away from sth; (*hindern*) to keep sb from sth
abhandeln ['aphandəln] *vt* (*Thema*) to deal with; **jdm die Waren/10 Euro ~** to do a deal with sb for the goods/beat sb down 10 euros
abhandenkommen [ap'handən-] *vi* to get lost
Abhandlung ['aphandlʊŋ] *f* treatise, discourse
Abhang ['aphaŋ] *m* slope
abhängen ['aphɛŋən] *unreg vt* (*Bild*) to take down; (*Anhänger*) to uncouple; (*Verfolger*) to shake off ▷ *vi* (*Fleisch*) to hang; **von jdm/etw ~** to depend on sb/sth; **das hängt ganz davon ab** it all depends; **er hat abgehängt** (*Tel: umg*) he hung up (on me *etc*)
abhängig ['aphɛŋɪç] *adj*: **~ (von)** dependent (on); **Abhängigkeit** *f*: **Abhängigkeit (von)** dependence (on)
abhärten ['aphɛrtən] *vt* to toughen up ▷ *vr* to toughen (o.s.) up; **sich gegen etw ~** to harden o.s. to sth
abhauen ['aphaʊən] *unreg vt* to cut off; (*Baum*) to cut down ▷ *vi* (*umg*) to clear off *od* out; **hau ab!** beat it!
abheben ['aphe:bən] *unreg vt* to lift (up); (*Karten*) to cut; (*Masche*) to slip; (*Geld*) to withdraw, take out ▷ *vi* (*Flugzeug*) to take off; (*Rakete*) to lift off; (*Karten*) to cut ▷ *vr*: **sich ~ von** to stand out from, contrast with
abheften ['aphɛftən] *vt* (*Rechnungen etc*) to file away; (*Nähen*) to tack, baste
abhelfen ['aphɛlfən] *unreg vi +dat* to remedy
abhetzen ['aphɛtsən] *vr* to wear *od* tire o.s. out
Abhilfe ['aphɪlfə] *f* remedy; **~ schaffen** to put things right
abholen ['apho:lən] *vt* (*Gegenstand*) to fetch, collect; (*Person*) to call for; (*am Bahnhof etc*) to pick up, meet
Abholmarkt *m* cash and carry
abholzen ['aphɔltsən] *vt* (*Wald*) to clear, deforest
abhorchen ['aphɔrçən] *vt* (*Med*) to listen to, sound
abhören ['aphø:rən] *vt* (*Vokabeln*) to test; (*Telefongespräch*) to tap; (*Tonband etc*) to listen to; **abgehört werden** (*umg*) to be bugged
Abhörgerät *nt* bug
abhungern ['aphʊŋərn] *vr*: **sich** *dat* **10 Kilo ~** to lose 10 kilos by going on a starvation diet
Abi ['abi] **(-s, -s)** *nt* (*Sch: umg*) = **Abitur**
Abitur [abi'tu:r] **(-s, -e)** *nt German school-leaving examination*, ≈ A-levels *pl* (*Brit*); **(das) ~ machen** to take one's school-leaving exam *od* A-levels; *see culture note*

ABITUR

The *Abitur* is the German school-leaving examination which is taken at the age of 18 or 19 by pupils at a *Gymnasium*. It is taken in four subjects and is necessary for entry to a university education.

Abiturient, in [abitʊri'ɛnt(ɪn)] *m(f)* candidate for school-leaving certificate
abkämmen ['apkɛmən] *vt* (*Gegend*) to comb, scour
abkanzeln ['apkantsəln] (*umg*) *vt*: **jdn ~** to give sb a dressing-down
abkapseln ['apkapsəln] *vr* to shut *od* cut o.s. off
abkarten ['apkartən] (*umg*) *vt*: **die Sache war von vornherein abgekartet** the whole thing was a put-up job
abkaufen ['apkaʊfən] *vt*: **jdm etw ~** to buy sth from sb
abkehren ['apke:rən] *vt* (*Blick*) to avert, turn away ▷ *vr* to turn away
abklappern ['apklapərn] (*umg*) *vt* (*Kunden*) to call on; (*: Läden, Straße*): **~ (nach)** to scour (for), comb (for)
abklären ['apklɛ:rən] *vt* (*klarstellen*) to clear up, clarify ▷ *vr* (*sich setzen*) to clarify
Abklatsch ['apklatʃ] **(-es, -e)** *m* (*fig*) (poor) copy
abklemmen ['apklɛmən] *vt* (*Leitung*) to clamp
abklingen ['apklɪŋən] *unreg vi* to die away;

(*Rundf*) to fade out
abknallen ['apknalən] (*umg*) *vt* to shoot down
abknöpfen ['apknœpfən] *vt* to unbutton; **jdm etw ~** (*umg*) to get sth off sb
abkochen ['apkɔxən] *vt* to boil; (*keimfrei machen*) to sterilize (by boiling)
abkommandieren ['apkɔmandi:rən] *vt* (*Mil: zu Einheit*) to post; (*zu bestimmtem Dienst*): **~ zu** to detail for
abkommen ['apkɔmən] *unreg vi* to get away; **(vom Thema) ~** to get off the subject, digress; **von der Straße/einem Plan ~** to leave the road/give up a plan
Abkommen (**-s, -**) *nt* agreement
abkömmlich ['apkœmlıç] *adj* available, free
Abkömmling *m* (*Nachkomme*) descendant; (*fig*) adherent
abkönnen ['apkœnən] *unreg* (*umg*) *vt* (*mögen*): **das kann ich nicht ab** I can't stand it
abkratzen ['apkratsən] *vt* to scrape off ▷ *vi* (*umg*) to kick the bucket
abkriegen ['apkri:gən] (*umg*) *vt* = **abbekommen**
abkühlen ['apky:lən] *vt* to cool down ▷ *vr* (*Mensch*) to cool down *od* off; (*Wetter*) to get cool; (*Zuneigung*) to cool
Abkunft ['apkʊnft] (-) *f* origin, birth
abkürzen ['apkʏrtsən] *vt* to shorten; (*Wort*) to abbreviate; **den Weg ~** to take a short cut
Abkürzung *f* abbreviation; short cut
abladen ['apla:dən] *unreg vi* to unload ▷ *vt* to unload; (*fig: umg*): **seinen Ärger (bei jdm) ~** to vent one's anger (on sb)
Ablage ['apla:gə] *f* place to keep/put sth; (*Aktenordnung*) filing; (*für Akten*) tray
ablagern ['apla:gərn] *vt* to deposit ▷ *vr* to be deposited ▷ *vi* to mature
Ablagerung *f* (*abgelagerter Stoff*) deposit
ablassen ['aplasən] *unreg vt* (*Wasser, Dampf*) to let out *od* off; (*vom Preis*) to knock off ▷ *vi*: **von etw ~** to give sth up, abandon sth
Ablauf *m* (*Abfluss*) drain; (*von Ereignissen*) course; (*einer Frist, Zeit*) expiry (*Brit*), expiration (*US*); **nach ~ des Jahres/dieser Zeit** at the end of the year/this time
Ablaufdatum *nt* (*Österr*) expiry date; (*von Lebensmitteln*) use-by *od* best-before date
ablaufen ['aplaʊfən] *unreg vi* (*abfließen*) to drain away; (*Ereignisse*) to happen; (*Frist, Zeit, Pass*) to expire ▷ *vt* (*Sohlen*) to wear (down *od* out); **~ lassen** (*abspulen, abspielen: Platte, Tonband*) to play; (*Film*) to run; **sich** *dat* **die Beine** *od* **Hacken nach etw ~** (*umg*) to walk one's legs off looking for sth; **jdm den Rang ~** to steal a march on sb
Ableben ['aple:bən] *nt* (*form*) demise (*form*)
ablegen ['aple:gən] *vt* to put *od* lay down; (*Kleider*) to take off; (*Gewohnheit*) to get rid of; (*Prüfung*) to take, sit (*Brit*); (*Zeugnis*) to give; (*Schriftwechsel*) to file (away); (*nicht mehr tragen: Kleidung*) to discard, cast off; (*Schwur, Eid*) to swear ▷ *vi* (*Schiff*) to cast off
Ableger (**-s, -**) *m* layer; (*fig*) branch, offshoot
ablehnen ['aple:nən] *vt* to reject; (*missbilligen*) to disapprove of; (*Einladung*) to decline, refuse ▷ *vi* to decline, refuse
Ablehnung *f* rejection; refusal; **auf ~ stoßen** to meet with disapproval
ableisten ['aplaıstən] *vt* (*form: Zeit*) to serve
ableiten ['aplaıtən] *vt* (*Wasser*) to divert; (*deduzieren*) to deduce; (*Wort*) to derive
Ableitung *f* diversion; deduction; derivation; (*Wort*) derivative
ablenken ['aplɛŋkən] *vt* to turn away, deflect; (*zerstreuen*) to distract ▷ *vi* to change the subject; **das lenkt ab** (*zerstreut*) it takes your mind off things; (*stört*) it's distracting
Ablenkung *f* deflection; distraction
Ablenkungsmanöver *nt* diversionary tactic; (*um vom Thema abzulenken*) red herring
ablesen ['aple:zən] *unreg vt* to read; **jdm jeden Wunsch von den Augen ~** to anticipate sb's every wish
ableugnen ['aplɔygnən] *vt* to deny
ablichten ['aplıçtən] *vt* to photocopy; (*fotografieren*) to photograph
abliefern ['apli:fərn] *vt* to deliver; **etw bei jdm/einer Dienststelle ~** to hand sth over to sb/in at an office
Ablieferung *f* delivery
abliegen ['apli:gən] *unreg vi* to be some distance away; (*fig*) to be far removed
ablisten ['aplıstən] *vt*: **jdm etw ~** to trick *od* con sb out of sth
ablösen ['aplø:zən] *vt* (*abtrennen*) to take off, remove; (*in Amt*) to take over from; (*Fin: Schuld, Hypothek*) to pay off, redeem; (*Methode, System*) to supersede ▷ *vr* (*auch*: **einander ablösen**) to take turns; (*Fahrer, Kollegen, Wachen*) to relieve each other
Ablösung *f* removal; relieving
abluchsen ['aplʊksən] (*umg*) *vt*: **jdm etw ~** to get *od* wangle sth out of sb
Abluft *f* (*Tech*) used air
ABM *pl abk* (= *Arbeitsbeschaffungsmaßnahmen*) *job-creation scheme*
abmachen ['apmaxən] *vt* to take off; (*vereinbaren*) to agree; **etw mit sich allein ~** to sort sth out for o.s.
Abmachung *f* agreement
abmagern ['apma:gərn] *vi* to get thinner, become emaciated
Abmagerungskur *f* diet; **eine ~ machen** to go on a diet
Abmarsch ['apmarʃ] *m* departure;
abmarschbereit *adj* ready to start
abmarschieren ['apmarʃi:rən] *vi* to march off
abmelden ['apmɛldən] *vt* (*Auto*) to take off the road; (*Telefon*) to have disconnected; (*Comput*) to log off ▷ *vr* to give notice of one's departure; (*im Hotel*) to check out; **ein Kind von einer Schule ~** to take a child away from a school; **er/sie ist bei mir abgemeldet** (*umg*) I don't want anything to do with him/her; **jdn bei der Polizei ~** to register sb's departure with the police
abmessen ['apmɛsən] *unreg vt* to measure

Abmessung *f* measurement; (*Ausmaß*) dimension
abmontieren ['apmɔnti:rən] *vt* to take off; (*Maschine*) to dismantle
ABM-Stelle *f temporary post created as part of a job creation scheme*
abmühen ['apmy:ən] *vr* to wear o.s. out
abnabeln ['apna:bəln] *vt*: **jdn ~** (*auch fig*) to cut sb's umbilical cord
abnagen ['apna:gən] *vt* to gnaw off; (*Knochen*) to gnaw
Abnäher ['apnɛ:ər] (**-s, -**) *m* dart
Abnahme ['apna:mə] *f (+gen)* removal; (*Comm*) buying; (*Verringerung*) decrease (in)
abnehmen ['apne:mən] *unreg vt* to take off, remove; (*Führerschein*) to take away; (*Prüfung*) to hold; (*Maschen*) to decrease; (*Hörer*) to lift, pick up; (*begutachten: Gebäude, Auto*) to inspect ▷ *vi* to decrease; (*schlanker werden*) to lose weight; **jdm etw ~** (*Geld*) to get sth out of sb; (*kaufen: auch umg: glauben*) to buy sth from sb; **kann ich dir etwas ~?** (*tragen*) can I take something for you?; **jdm Arbeit ~** to take work off sb's shoulders; **jdm ein Versprechen ~** to make sb promise sth
Abnehmer (**-s, -**) *m* purchaser, customer; **viele/wenige ~ finden** (*Comm*) to sell well/ badly
Abneigung ['apnaɪgʊŋ] *f* aversion, dislike
abnicken ['apnɪkən] (*umg*) *vt*: **etw ~** to nod sth through
abnorm [ap'nɔrm] *adj* abnormal
abnötigen ['apnø:tɪgən] *vt*: **jdm etw/Respekt ~** to force sth from sb/gain sb's respect
abnutzen ['apnʊtsən] *vt* to wear out
Abnutzung *f* wear (and tear)
Abo ['abo] (**-s, -s**) (*umg*) *nt* = **Abonnement**
Abonnement [abɔn(ə)'mã:] (**-s, -s** *od* **-e**) *nt* subscription; (*Theaterabonnement*) season ticket
Abonnent, in [abɔ'nɛnt(ɪn)] *m(f)* subscriber
abonnieren [abɔ'ni:rən] *vt* to subscribe to
abordnen ['ap|ordnən] *vt* to delegate
Abordnung *f* delegation
Abort [a'bɔrt] (**-(e)s, -e**) *m* (*veraltet*) lavatory
abpacken ['appakən] *vt* to pack
abpassen ['appasən] *vt* (*Person, Gelegenheit*) to wait for; (*warten auf*) to catch; (*jdm auflauern*) to waylay; **etw gut ~** to time sth well
abpausen ['appaʊzən] *vt* to make a tracing of
abpfeifen ['appfaɪfən] *unreg vt, vi* (*Sport*): **(das Spiel) ~** to blow the whistle (for the end of the game)
Abpfiff ['appfɪf] *m* final whistle
abplagen ['appla:gən] *vr* to struggle (away)
Abprall ['appral] *m* rebound; (*von Kugel*) ricochet
abprallen ['appralən] *vi* to bounce off; to ricochet; **an jdm ~** (*fig*) to make no impression on sb
abputzen ['appʊtsən] *vt* to clean; (*Nase etc*) to wipe
abquälen ['apkvɛ:lən] *vr* to struggle (away)
abrackern ['aprakərn] (*umg*) *vr* to slave away
abraten ['apra:tən] *unreg vi*: **jdm von etw ~** to advise sb against sth, warn sb against sth
abräumen ['aprɔʏmən] *vt* to clear up *od* away; (*Tisch*) to clear ▷ *vi* to clear up *od* away
abreagieren ['apreagi:rən] *vt*: **seinen Zorn (an jdm/etw) ~** to work one's anger off (on sb/sth) ▷ *vr* to calm down; **seinen Ärger an anderen ~** to take it out on others
abrechnen ['aprɛçnən] *vt* to deduct, take off ▷ *vi* (*lit*) to settle up; (*fig*) to get even; **darf ich ~?** would you like your bill (*Brit*) *od* check (*US*) now?
Abrechnung *f* settlement; (*Rechnung*) bill; (*Aufstellung*) statement; (*Bilanz*) balancing; (*fig: Rache*) revenge; **in ~ stellen** (*form: Abzug*) to deduct; **~ über** *+akk* bill/statement for
Abrechnungszeitraum *m* accounting period
Abrede ['apre:də] *f*: **etw in ~ stellen** to deny *od* dispute sth
abregen ['apre:gən] (*umg*) *vr* to calm *od* cool down
abreiben ['apraɪbən] *unreg vt* to rub off; (*säubern*) to wipe; **jdn mit einem Handtuch ~** to towel sb down
Abreibung (*umg*) *f* (*Prügel*) hiding, thrashing
Abreise ['apraɪzə] *f* departure
abreisen *vi* to leave, set off
abreißen ['apraɪsən] *unreg vt* (*Haus*) to tear down; (*Blatt*) to tear off ▷ *vi*: **den Kontakt nicht ~ lassen** to stay in touch
abrichten ['aprɪçtən] *vt* to train
abriegeln ['apri:gəln] *vt* (*Tür*) to bolt; (*Straße, Gebiet*) to seal off
abringen ['aprɪŋən] *unreg vt*: **sich** *dat* **ein Lächeln ~** to force a smile
Abriss ['aprɪs] (**-es, -e**) *m* (*Übersicht*) outline; (*Abbruch*) demolition
abrollen ['aprɔlən] *vt* (*abwickeln*) to unwind ▷ *vi* (*vonstattengehen: Programm*) to run; (*: Veranstaltung*) to go off; (*: Ereignisse*) to unfold
Abruf ['apru:f] *m*: **auf ~** on call
abrufen *unreg vt* (*Mensch*) to call away; (*Comm: Ware*) to request delivery of; (*Comput*) to recall, retrieve
abrunden ['aprʊndən] *vt* to round off
abrüsten ['aprʏstən] *vi* to disarm
Abrüstung *f* disarmament
abrutschen ['aprʊtʃən] *vi* to slip; (*Aviat*) to sideslip
Abs. *abk* = **Absender**; (= *Absatz*) par., para
absacken ['apzakən] *vi* (*sinken*) to sink; (*Boden, Gebäude*) to subside
Absage ['apza:gə] (**-, -n**) *f* refusal; (*auf Einladung*) negative reply
absagen *vt* to cancel, call off; (*Einladung*) to turn down ▷ *vi* to cry off; (*ablehnen*) to decline; **jdm ~** to tell sb that one can't come
absägen ['apzɛ:gən] *vt* to saw off
absahnen ['apza:nən] *vt* (*lit*) to skim; **das Beste für sich ~** (*fig*) to take the cream
Absatz ['apzats] *m* (*Comm*) sales *pl*; (*Jur*) section; (*Bodensatz*) deposit; (*neuer Abschnitt*) paragraph; (*Treppenabsatz*) landing;

(*Schuhabsatz*) heel; **Absatzflaute** *f* slump in the market; **Absatzförderung** *f* sales promotion; **Absatzgebiet** *nt* (*Comm*) market; sales territory; **Absatzplus** *nt* increase in sales; **Absatzprognose** *f* sales forecast; **Absatzschwierigkeiten** *pl* sales problems *pl*; **Absatzziffern** *pl* sales figures *pl*

absaufen ['apzaʊfən] *unreg* (*umg*) *vi* (*ertrinken*) to drown; (: *Motor*) to flood; (: *Schiff etc*) to go down

absaugen ['apzaʊgən] *vt* (*Flüssigkeit*) to suck out *od* off; (*Teppich, Sofa*) to hoover®, vacuum

abschaben ['apʃa:bən] *vt* to scrape off; (*Möhren*) to scrape

abschaffen ['apʃafən] *vt* to abolish, do away with

Abschaffung *f* abolition

abschalten ['apʃaltən] *vt, vi* (*lit: umg*) to switch off

abschattieren ['apʃati:rən] *vt* to shade

abschätzen ['apʃɛtsən] *vt* to estimate; (*Lage*) to assess; (*Person*) to size up

abschätzig ['apʃɛtsɪç] *adj* disparaging, derogatory

Abschaum ['apʃaʊm] (**-(e)s**) *m* scum

Abscheu ['apʃɔʏ] (**-(e)s**) *m* loathing, repugnance; **abscheuerregend** *adj* repulsive, loathsome; **abscheulich** *adj* abominable

abschicken ['apʃɪkən] *vt* to send off

abschieben ['apʃi:bən] *unreg vt* to push away; (*Person*) to pack off; (*ausweisen: Ausländer*) to deport; (*fig: Verantwortung, Schuld*): **~ (auf** *+akk*) to shift (onto)

Abschied ['apʃi:t] (**-(e)s, -e**) *m* parting; (*von Armee*) discharge; **(von jdm) ~ nehmen** to say goodbye (to sb), take one's leave (of sb); **seinen ~ nehmen** (*Mil*) to apply for discharge; **zum ~** on parting

Abschiedsbrief *m* farewell letter

Abschiedsfeier *f* farewell party

abschießen ['apʃi:sən] *unreg vt* (*Flugzeug*) to shoot down; (*Geschoss*) to fire; (*umg: Minister*) to get rid of

abschirmen ['apʃɪrmən] *vt* to screen; (*schützen*) to protect ▷ *vr* (*sich isolieren*): **sich ~ (gegen)** to cut o.s. off (from)

abschlaffen ['apʃlafən] (*umg*) *vi* to flag

abschlagen ['apʃla:gən] *unreg vt* (*abhacken, Comm*) to knock off; (*ablehnen*) to refuse; (*Mil*) to repel

abschlägig ['apʃlɛ:gɪç] *adj* negative; **jdn/etw ~ bescheiden** (*form*) to turn sb/sth down

Abschlagszahlung *f* interim payment

abschleifen ['apʃlaɪfən] *unreg vt* to grind down; (*Holzboden*) to sand (down) ▷ *vr* to wear off

Abschleppdienst *m* (*Aut*) breakdown service (*Brit*), towing company (*US*)

abschleppen ['apʃlɛpən] *vt* to (take in) tow

Abschleppseil *nt* towrope

abschließen ['apʃli:sən] *unreg vt* (*Tür*) to lock; (*beenden*) to conclude, finish; (*Vertrag, Handel*) to conclude; (*Versicherung*) to take out; (*Wette*) to place ▷ *vr* (*sich isolieren*) to cut o.s. off; **mit abgeschlossenem Studium** with a degree; **mit der Vergangenheit ~** to break with the past

abschließend *adj* concluding ▷ *adv* in conclusion, finally

Abschluss ['apʃlʊs] *m* (*Beendigung*) close, conclusion; (*Comm: Bilanz*) balancing; (*von Vertrag, Handel*) conclusion; **zum ~** in conclusion; **Abschlussfeier** *f* (*Sch*) school-leavers' ceremony; **Abschlussprüfer** *m* accountant; **Abschlussprüfung** *f* (*Sch*) final examination; (*Univ*) finals *pl*; **Abschlussrechnung** *f* final account; **Abschlusszeugnis** *nt* (*Sch*) leaving certificate, diploma (*US*)

abschmecken ['apʃmɛkən] *vt* (*kosten*) to taste; (*würzen*) to season

abschmieren ['apʃmi:rən] *vt* (*Aut*) to grease, lubricate

abschminken ['apʃmɪŋkən] *vt*: **sich ~** to remove one's make-up

abschmirgeln ['apʃmɪrgəln] *vt* to sand down

abschnallen ['apʃnalən] *vr* to unfasten one's seat belt ▷ *vi* (*umg: nicht mehr folgen können*) to give up; (: *fassungslos sein*) to be staggered

abschneiden ['apʃnaɪdən] *unreg vt* to cut off ▷ *vi* to do, come off; **bei etw gut/schlecht ~** (*umg*) to come off well/badly in sth

Abschnitt ['apʃnɪt] *m* section; (*Mil*) sector; (*Kontrollabschnitt*) counterfoil (*Brit*), stub (*US*); (*Math*) segment; (*Zeitabschnitt*) period

abschnüren ['apʃny:rən] *vt* to constrict

abschöpfen ['apʃœpfən] *vt* to skim off

abschrauben ['apʃraʊbən] *vt* to unscrew

abschrecken ['apʃrɛkən] *vt* to deter, put off; (*mit kaltem Wasser*) to plunge into cold water

abschreckend *adj* deterrent; **~es Beispiel** warning; **eine abschreckende Wirkung haben, ~ wirken** to act as a deterrent

abschreiben ['apʃraɪbən] *unreg vt* to copy; (*verloren geben*) to write off; (*Comm*) to deduct; **er ist bei mir abgeschrieben** I'm finished with him

Abschreibung *f* (*Comm*) deduction; (*Wertverminderung*) depreciation

Abschrift ['apʃrɪft] *f* copy

abschuften ['apʃʊftən] (*umg*) *vr* to slog one's guts out (*umg*)

abschürfen ['apʃʏrfən] *vt* to graze

Abschuss ['apʃʊs] *m* (*eines Geschützes*) firing; (*Herunterschießen*) shooting down; (*Tötung*) shooting

abschüssig ['apʃʏsɪç] *adj* steep

Abschussliste *f*: **er steht auf der ~** (*umg*) his days are numbered

Abschussrampe *f* launch(ing) pad

abschütteln ['apʃʏtəln] *vt* to shake off

abschütten ['apʃʏtən] *vt* (*Flüssigkeit etc*) to pour off

abschwächen ['apʃvɛçən] *vt* to lessen; (*Behauptung, Kritik*) to tone down ▷ *vr* to lessen

abschweifen ['apʃvaɪfən] *vi* to wander; (*Redner*) to digress

Abschweifung *f* digression

abschwellen ['apʃvɛlən] *unreg vi* (*Geschwulst*) to go down; (*Lärm*) to die down
abschwenken ['apʃvɛŋkən] *vi* to turn away
abschwören ['apʃvø:rən] *unreg vi +dat* to renounce
absehbar ['apze:ba:r] *adj* foreseeable; **in ~er Zeit** in the foreseeable future; **das Ende ist ~** the end is in sight
absehen *unreg vt* (*Ende, Folgen*) to foresee ▷ *vi*: **von etw ~** to refrain from sth; (*nicht berücksichtigen*) to leave sth out of consideration; **jdm etw ~** (*erlernen*) to copy sth from sb
abseilen ['apzaɪlən] *vt* to lower down on a rope ▷ *vr* (*Bergsteiger*) to abseil (down)
Abseits ['apzaɪts] *nt* (*Sport*) offside; **im ~ stehen** to be offside; **im ~ leben** (*fig*) to live in the shadows
abseits *adv* out of the way ▷ *präp +gen* away from
absenden ['apzɛndən] *unreg vt* to send off, dispatch
Absender *m* sender
Absendung *f* dispatch
absetzbar ['apzɛtsba:r] *adj* (*Beamter*) dismissible; (*Waren*) saleable; (*von Steuer*) deductible
absetzen ['apzɛtsən] *vt* (*niederstellen, aussteigen lassen*) to put down; (*abnehmen; auch Theaterstück*) to take off; (*Comm: verkaufen*) to sell; (*Fin: abziehen*) to deduct; (*entlassen*) to dismiss; (*König*) to depose; (*streichen*) to drop; (*Fußballspiel, Termin*) to cancel; (*hervorheben*) to pick out ▷ *vi*: **er trank das Glas aus, ohne abzusetzen** he emptied his glass in one ▷ *vr* (*sich entfernen*) to clear off; (*sich ablagern*) to be deposited; **das kann man ~** that is tax-deductible
Absetzung *f* (*Fin: Abzug*) deduction; (*Entlassung*) dismissal; (*von König*) deposing; (*Streichung*) dropping
absichern ['apzɪçərn] *vt* to make safe; (*schützen*) to safeguard ▷ *vr* to protect o.s.
Absicht ['apzɪçt] *f* intention; **mit ~** on purpose;
absichtlich *adj* intentional, deliberate
absichtslos *adj* unintentional
absinken ['apzɪŋkən] *unreg vi* to sink; (*Temperatur, Geschwindigkeit*) to decrease
absitzen ['apzɪtsən] *unreg vi* to dismount ▷ *vt* (*Strafe*) to serve
absolut [apzo'lu:t] *adj* absolute
Absolutheitsanspruch *m* claim to absolute right
Absolutismus [apzolu:'tɪsmʊs] *m* absolutism
Absolvent, in *m(f)*: **die ~en eines Lehrgangs** the students who have completed a course
absolvieren [apzɔl'vi:rən] *vt* (*Sch*) to complete
absonderlich [ap'zɔndərlɪç] *adj* odd, strange
absondern *vt* to separate; (*ausscheiden*) to give off, secrete ▷ *vr* to cut o.s. off
Absonderung *f* separation; (*Med*) secretion
absorbieren [apzɔr'bi:rən] *vt* (*lit, fig*) to absorb
abspalten ['apʃpaltən] *vt* to split off
Abspannung ['apʃpanʊŋ] *f* (*Ermüdung*) exhaustion
absparen ['apʃpa:rən] *vt*: **sich** *dat* **etw ~** to scrimp and save for sth
abspecken ['apʃpɛkən] (*umg*) *vt* to shed ▷ *vi* to lose weight
abspeisen ['apʃpaɪzən] *vt* (*fig*) to fob off
abspenstig ['apʃpɛnstɪç] *adj*: **(jdm) ~ machen** to lure away (from sb)
absperren ['apʃpɛrən] *vt* to block *od* close off; (*Tür*) to lock
Absperrung *f* (*Vorgang*) blocking *od* closing off; (*Sperre*) barricade
abspielen ['apʃpi:lən] *vt* (*Platte, Tonband*) to play; (*Sport: Ball*) to pass ▷ *vr* to happen; **vom Blatt ~** (*Mus*) to sight-read
absplittern ['apʃplɪtərn] *vt, vi* to chip off
Absprache ['apʃpra:xə] *f* arrangement; **ohne vorherige ~** without prior consultation
absprechen ['apʃprɛçən] *unreg vt* (*vereinbaren*) to arrange ▷ *vr*: **die beiden hatten sich vorher abgesprochen** they had agreed on what to do/say *etc* in advance; **jdm etw ~** to deny sb sth; (*in Abrede stellen: Begabung*) to dispute sb's sth
abspringen ['apʃprɪŋən] *unreg vi* to jump down/off; (*Farbe, Lack*) to flake off; (*Aviat*) to bale out; (*sich distanzieren*) to back out
Absprung ['apʃprʊŋ] *m* jump; **den ~ schaffen** (*fig*) to make the break (*umg*)
abspulen ['apʃpu:lən] *vt* (*Kabel, Garn*) to unwind
abspülen ['apʃpy:lən] *vt* to rinse; **Geschirr ~** to wash up (*Brit*), do the dishes
abstammen ['apʃtamən] *vi* to be descended; (*Wort*) to be derived
Abstammung *f* descent; derivation; **französischer ~** of French extraction *od* descent
Abstand ['apʃtant] *m* distance; (*zeitlich*) interval; **davon ~ nehmen, etw zu tun** to refrain from doing sth; **~ halten** (*Aut*) to keep one's distance; **~ von etw gewinnen** (*fig*) to distance o.s. from sth; **mit großem ~ führen** to lead by a wide margin; **mit ~ der Beste** by far the best
Abstandssumme *f* compensation
abstatten ['apʃtatən] *vt* (*form: Dank*) to give; (*: Besuch*) to pay
abstauben ['apʃtaʊbən] *vt, vi* to dust; (*umg: mitgehen lassen*) to help oneself to, pinch; **(den Ball) ~** (*Sport*) to tuck the ball away
Abstauber, in ['apʃtaʊbər(ɪn)] **(-s, -)** (*umg*) *m(f)* (*Person*) somebody on the make
abstechen ['apʃtɛçən] *unreg vt* to cut; (*Tier*) to cut the throat of ▷ *vi*: **~ gegen** *od* **von** to contrast with
Abstecher **(-s, -)** *m* detour
abstecken ['apʃtɛkən] *vt* (*Fläche*) to mark out; (*Saum*) to pin
abstehen ['apʃte:ən] *unreg vi* (*Ohren, Haare*) to stick out; (*entfernt sein*) to stand away
Absteige *f* cheap hotel
absteigen ['apʃtaɪgən] *unreg vi* (*vom Rad etc*) to

get off, dismount; **in einem Gasthof** ~ to put up at an inn; **(in die Zweite Liga)** ~ to be relegated (to the second division); **auf dem ~den Ast sein** *(umg)* to be going downhill, be on the decline

abstellen ['apʃtɛlən] *vt (niederstellen)* to put down; *(entfernt stellen)* to pull out; *(hinstellen: Auto)* to park; *(ausschalten)* to turn *od* switch off; *(Missstand, Unsitte)* to stop; *(abkommandieren)* to order off; *(ausrichten)*: ~ **auf** *+akk* to gear to; **das lässt sich nicht/lässt sich** ~ nothing/something can be done about that

Abstellgleis *nt* siding; **jdn aufs ~ schieben** *(fig)* to cast sb aside

Abstellraum *m* storeroom

abstempeln ['apʃtɛmpəln] *vt* to stamp; *(fig)*: ~ **zu** *od* **als** to brand as

absterben ['apʃtɛrbən] *unreg vi* to die; *(Körperteil)* to go numb

Abstieg ['apʃti:k] **(-(e)s, -e)** *m* descent; *(Sport)* relegation; *(fig)* decline

Abstiegskampf *m (Sport)* relegation battle

abstimmen ['apʃtɪmən] *vi* to vote ▷*vt*: ~ **(auf** *+akk***)** *(Instrument)* to tune (to); *(Interessen)* to match (with); *(Termine, Ziele)* to fit in (with) ▷*vr* to agree

Abstimmung *f* vote; *(geheime Abstimmung)* ballot

abstinent [apsti'nɛnt] *adj (von Alkohol)* teetotal

Abstinenz [apsti'nɛnts] *f* teetotalism

Abstinenzler, in (-s, -) *m(f)* teetotaller

abstoßen ['apʃto:sən] *unreg vt* to push off *od* away; *(anekeln)* to repel; *(Comm: Ware, Aktien)* to sell off

abstoßend *adj* repulsive

abstottern ['apʃtɔtərn] *(umg) vt* to pay off in instalments

abstrahieren [apstra'hi:rən] *vt, vi* to abstract

abstrakt [ap'strakt] *adj* abstract ▷*adv* abstractly, in the abstract

Abstraktion [apstraktsi'o:n] *f* abstraction

Abstraktum [ap'straktʊm] **(-s, Abstrakta)** *nt* abstract concept; *(Gram)* abstract noun

abstrampeln ['apʃtrampəln] *vr (fig: umg)* to sweat (away)

abstreifen ['apʃtraɪfən] *vt (abtreten: Schuhe, Füße)* to wipe; *(abziehen: Schmuck)* to take off, slip off

abstreiten ['apʃtraɪtən] *unreg vt* to deny

Abstrich ['apʃtrɪç] *m (Abzug)* cut; *(Med)* smear; **~e machen** to lower one's sights

abstufen ['apʃtu:fən] *vt (Hang)* to terrace; *(Farben)* to shade; *(Gehälter)* to grade

abstumpfen ['apʃtʊmpfən] *vt (lit, fig)* to dull, blunt ▷*vi* to become dulled

Absturz ['apʃtʊrts] *m* fall; *(Aviat)* crash

abstürzen ['apʃtʏrtsən] *vi* to fall; *(Aviat)* to crash

absuchen ['apzu:xən] *vt* to scour, search

absurd [ap'zʊrt] *adj* absurd

Abszess [aps'tsɛs] **(-es, -sse)** *m* abscess

Abt [apt] **(-(e)s, ¨-e)** *m* abbot

Abt. *abk (= Abteilung)* dept.

abtasten ['aptastən] *vt* to feel, probe; *(Elek)* to scan; *(bei Durchsuchung)*: ~ **(auf** *+akk***)** to frisk (for)

abtauen ['aptaʊən] *vt, vi* to thaw; *(Kühlschrank)* to defrost

Abtei [ap'taɪ] **(-, -en)** *f* abbey

Abteil [ap'taɪl] **(-(e)s, -e)** *nt* compartment

abteilen ['aptaɪlən] *vt* to divide up; *(abtrennen)* to divide off

Abteilung *f (in Firma, Kaufhaus)* department; *(Mil)* unit; *(in Krankenhaus, Jur)* section

Abteilungsleiter, in *m(f)* head of department; *(in Kaufhaus)* department manager(ess)

abtelefonieren ['aptelefoni:rən] *(umg) vi* to telephone to say one can't make it

Äbtissin [ɛp'tɪsɪn] *f* abbess

abtönen ['aptø:nən] *vt (Phot)* to tone down

abtöten ['aptøtən] *vt (lit, fig)* to destroy, kill (off); *(Nerv)* to deaden

abtragen ['aptra:gən] *unreg vt (Hügel, Erde)* to level down; *(Essen)* to clear away; *(Kleider)* to wear out; *(Schulden)* to pay off

abträglich ['aptrɛ:klɪç] *adj (+dat)* harmful (to)

Abtragung *f (Geol)* erosion

Abtransport (-(e)s, -e) *m* transportation; *(aus Katastrophengebiet)* evacuation

abtransportieren ['aptranspɔrti:rən] *vt* to transport; to evacuate

abtreiben ['aptraɪbən] *unreg vt (Boot, Flugzeug)* to drive off course; *(Kind)* to abort ▷*vi* to be driven off course; *(Frau)* to have an abortion

Abtreibung *f* abortion

Abtreibungsparagraf *m* abortion law

Abtreibungsversuch *m* attempted abortion

abtrennen ['aptrɛnən] *vt (lostrennen)* to detach; *(entfernen)* to take off; *(abteilen)* to separate off

abtreten ['aptre:tən] *unreg vt* to wear out; *(überlassen)* to hand over, cede; *(Rechte, Ansprüche)* to transfer ▷*vi* to go off; *(zurücktreten)* to step down; **sich** *dat* **die Füße** ~ to wipe one's feet; **~!** *(Mil)* dismiss!

Abtritt ['aptrɪt] *m (Rücktritt)* resignation

abtrocknen ['aptrɔknən] *vt* to dry ▷*vi* to do the drying-up

abtropfen ['aptrɔpfən] *vi*: **etw ~ lassen** to let sth drain

abtrünnig ['aptrʏnɪç] *adj* renegade

abtun ['aptu:n] *unreg vt* to take off; *(fig)* to dismiss; **etw kurz** ~ to brush sth aside

aburteilen ['ap|ʊrtaɪlən] *vt* to condemn

abverlangen ['apfɛrlaŋən] *vt*: **jdm etw** ~ to demand sth from sb

abwägen ['apvɛ:gən] *unreg vt* to weigh up

abwählen ['apvɛ:lən] *vt* to vote out (of office); *(Sch: Fach)* to give up

abwälzen ['apvɛltsən] *vt*: ~ **(auf** *+akk***)** *(Schuld, Verantwortung)* to shift (onto); *(Arbeit)* to unload (onto); *(Kosten)* to pass on (to)

abwandeln ['apvandəln] *vt* to adapt

abwandern ['apvandərn] *vi* to move away

Abwärme ['apvɛrmə] *f* waste heat

abwarten ['apvartən] *vt* to wait for ▷*vi* to wait; **das Gewitter** ~ to wait till the storm is over; **~ und Tee trinken** *(umg)* to wait and see; **eine ~de Haltung einnehmen** to play a waiting game

abwärts ['apvɛrts] *adv* down; **mit ihm/dem Land geht es ~** he/the country is going downhill

Abwasch ['apvaʃ] **(-(e)s)** *m* washing-up; **du kannst das auch machen, das ist (dann) ein ~** *(umg)* you could do that as well and kill two birds with one stone

abwaschen *unreg vt (Schmutz)* to wash off; *(Geschirr)* to wash (up)

Abwasser ['apvasər] **(-s, -wässer)** *nt* sewage; **Abwasseraufbereitung** *f* sewage treatment; **Abwasserkanal** *m* sewer

abwechseln ['apvɛksəln] *vi, vr* to alternate; *(Personen)* to take turns

abwechselnd *adj* alternate

Abwechslung *f* change; *(Zerstreuung)* diversion; **für ~ sorgen** to provide entertainment

abwechslungsreich *adj* varied

Abweg ['apve:k] *m*: **auf ~e geraten/führen** to go/lead astray

abwegig ['apve:gıç] *adj* wrong; *(Verdacht)* groundless

Abwehr ['apve:r] (-) *f* defence; *(Schutz)* protection; *(Abwehrdienst)* counter-intelligence (service); **auf ~ stoßen** to be repulsed; **abwehren** *vt* to ward off; *(Ball)* to stop; **abwehrende Geste** dismissive gesture; **Abwehrreaktion** *f (Psych)* defence *(Brit) od* defense *(US)* reaction; **Abwehrstoff** *m* antibody

abweichen ['apvaıçən] *unreg vi* to deviate; *(Meinung)* to differ; **vom rechten Weg ~** *(fig)* to wander off the straight and narrow

abweichend *adj* deviant; differing

Abweichler **(-s, -)** *m (Pol)* maverick

Abweichung *f (zeitlich, zahlenmäßig)* allowance; **zulässige ~** *(Tech)* tolerance

abweisen ['apvaızən] *unreg vt* to turn away; *(Antrag)* to turn down; **er lässt sich nicht ~** he won't take no for an answer

abweisend *adj (Haltung)* cold

abwenden ['apvɛndən] *unreg vt* to avert ▷ *vr* to turn away

abwerben ['apvɛrbən] *unreg vt*: **(jdm) ~** to woo away (from sb)

abwerfen ['apvɛrfən] *unreg vt* to throw off; *(Profit)* to yield; *(aus Flugzeug)* to drop; *(Spielkarte)* to discard

abwerten ['apvɛrtən] *vt (Fin)* to devalue

abwertend *adj* pejorative

Abwertung *f* devaluation

abwesend ['apve:zənt] *adj* absent; *(zerstreut)* far away

Abwesenheit ['apve:zənhaıt] *f* absence; **durch ~ glänzen** *(ironisch)* to be conspicuous by one's absence

abwickeln ['apvıkəln] *vt* to unwind; *(Geschäft)* to transact, conclude; *(fig: erledigen)* to deal with

Abwicklungskosten ['apvıkluŋskɔstən] *pl* transaction costs *pl*

abwiegen ['apvi:gən] *unreg vt* to weigh out

abwimmeln ['apvıməln] *(umg) vt (Person)* to get rid of; *(: Auftrag)* to get out of

abwinken ['apvıŋkən] *vi* to wave it/him *etc* aside; *(fig: ablehnen)* to say no

abwirtschaften ['apvırtʃaftən] *vi* to go downhill

abwischen ['apvıʃən] *vt* to wipe off *od* away; *(putzen)* to wipe

abwracken ['apvrakən] *vt (Schiff)* to break (up); **ein abgewrackter Mensch** a wreck (of a person)

Abwurf ['apvʊrf] *m* throwing off; *(von Bomben etc)* dropping; *(von Reiter, Sport)* throw

abwürgen ['apvʏrgən] *(umg) vt* to scotch; *(Motor)* to stall; **etw von vornherein ~** to nip sth in the bud

abzahlen ['aptsa:lən] *vt* to pay off

abzählen ['aptsɛ:lən] *vt* to count (up); **abgezähltes Fahrgeld** exact fare

Abzählreim ['aptsɛ:lraım] *m* counting rhyme *(e.g. eeny meeny miney mo)*

Abzahlung *f* repayment; **auf ~ kaufen** to buy on hire purchase *(Brit) od* the installment plan *(US)*

abzapfen ['aptsapfən] *vt* to draw off; **jdm Blut ~** to take blood from sb

abzäunen ['aptsɔynən] *vt* to fence off

Abzeichen ['aptsaıçən] *nt* badge; *(Orden)* decoration

abzeichnen ['aptsaıçnən] *vt* to draw, copy; *(unterschreiben)* to initial ▷ *vr* to stand out; *(fig: bevorstehen)* to loom

Abziehbild *nt* transfer

abziehen ['aptsi:ən] *unreg vt* to take off; *(Tier)* to skin; *(Bett)* to strip; *(Truppen)* to withdraw; *(subtrahieren)* to take away, subtract; *(kopieren)* to run off; *(Schlüssel)* to take out, remove ▷ *vi* to go away; *(Truppen)* to withdraw; *(abdrücken)* to pull the trigger, fire

abzielen ['aptsi:lən] *vi*: **~ auf** *+akk* to be aimed at

Abzocke ['aptsɔkə] *(umg) f* rip-off

Abzug ['aptsu:k] *m* departure; *(von Truppen)* withdrawal; *(Kopie)* copy; *(Subtraktion)* subtraction; *(Betrag)* deduction; *(Rauchabzug)* flue; *(von Waffen)* trigger; *(Rabatt)* discount; *(Korrekturfahne)* proof; *(Phot)* print; **jdm freien ~ gewähren** to grant sb safe passage

abzüglich ['aptsy:klıç] *präp +gen* less

abzweigen ['aptsvaıgən] *vi* to branch off ▷ *vt* to set aside

Abzweigung *f* junction

Accessoires [aksɛso'a:rs] *pl* accessories *pl*

ach [ax] *interj* oh; **~ so!** I see!; **mit A~ und Krach** by the skin of one's teeth; **~ was** *od* **wo, das ist doch nicht so schlimm!** come on now, it's not that bad!

Achillesferse [a'xılɛsfɛrzə] *f* Achilles heel

Achse ['aksə] **(-, -n)** *f* axis; *(Aut)* axle; **auf ~ sein** *(umg)* to be on the move

Achsel ['aksəl] **(-, -n)** *f* shoulder; **Achselhöhle**

f armpit; **Achselzucken** *nt* shrug (of one's shoulders)
Achsenbruch *m* (*Aut*) broken axle
Achsenkreuz *nt* coordinate system
Acht[1] [axt] (**-, -en**) *f* eight; (*beim Eislaufen etc*) figure (of) eight
Acht[2] (**-**) *f* attention; **hab ~** (*Mil*) attention!; **~ geben** = **achtgeben**; **sich in ~ nehmen (vor** *+dat*) to be careful (of), watch out (for); **etw außer ~ lassen** to disregard sth
acht *num* eight; **~ Tage** a week
achtbar *adj* worthy
achte, r, s *adj* eighth
Achteck *nt* octagon
Achtel *nt* eighth; **Achtelnote** *f* quaver, eighth note (*US*)
achten *vt* to respect ▷ *vi*: **~ (auf** *+akk*) to pay attention (to); **darauf ~, dass ...** to be careful that ...
ächten ['ɛçtən] *vt* to outlaw, ban
Achterbahn *f* roller coaster
Achterdeck *nt* (*Naut*) afterdeck
achtfach *adj* eightfold
achtgeben *unreg vi*: **~ (auf** *+akk*) to take care (of); (*aufmerksam sein*) to pay attention (to)
achtlos *adj* careless; **viele gehen ~ daran vorbei** many people just pass by without noticing
achtmal *adv* eight times
achtsam *adj* attentive
Achtstundentag *m* eight-hour day
Achtung ['axtʊŋ] *f* attention; (*Ehrfurcht*) respect ▷ *interj* look out!; (*Mil*) attention!; **alle ~!** good for you/him *etc*!; **~, fertig, los!** ready, steady, go!; **„~ Hochspannung!"** "danger, high voltage"; **„~ Lebensgefahr/Stufe!"** "danger/mind the step!"
Achtungserfolg *m* reasonable success
achtzehn *num* eighteen
achtzig *num* eighty; **Achtziger, in (-s, -)** *m(f)* octogenarian
ächzen ['ɛçtsən] *vi*: **~ (vor** *+dat*) to groan (with)
Acker ['akər] (**-s, ¨-**) *m* field; **Ackerbau** *m* agriculture; **Ackerbau und Viehzucht** farming
ackern *vi* to plough; (*umg*) to slog away
a conto [a 'kɔnto] *adv* (*Comm*) on account
A. D. *abk* (= *Anno Domini*) A.D.
a. D. *abk* = **außer Dienst**
a. d. *abk* = **an der** (*bei Ortsnamen*)
ad absurdum [at ap'zʊrdʊm] *adv*: **~ führen** (*Argument etc*) to reduce to absurdity
ADAC (**-**) *m abk* (= *Allgemeiner Deutscher Automobil-Club*) *German motoring organization*, ≈ AA (*Brit*), AAA (*US*)
ad acta [at 'akta] *adv*: **etw ~ legen** (*fig*) to consider sth finished; (*Frage, Problem*) to consider sth closed
Adam ['a:dam] *m*: **bei ~ und Eva anfangen** (*umg*) to start right from scratch *od* from square one
adaptieren [adap'ti:rən] *vt* to adapt
adäquat [adɛ'kva:t] *adj* (*Belohnung, Übersetzung*) adequate; (*Stellung, Verhalten*) suitable
addieren [a'di:rən] *vt* to add (up)
Addis Abeba ['adıs'a:beba] (**-, -s**) *nt* Addis Ababa
Addition [aditsi'o:n] *f* addition
ade *interj* bye!
Adel ['a:dəl] (**-s**) *m* nobility; **~ verpflichtet** noblesse oblige
adelig *adj* noble
Adelsstand *m* nobility
Ader ['a:dər] (**-, -n**) *f* vein; (*fig: Veranlagung*) bent
Adhäsionsverschluss [athɛzi'o:nsfɛrʃlʊs] *m* adhesive seal
Adjektiv ['atjɛkti:f] (**-s, -e**) *nt* adjective
Adler ['a:dlər] (**-s, -**) *m* eagle
adlig *adj* = **adelig**
Admiral [atmi'ra:l] (**-s, -e**) *m* admiral
Admiralität *f* admiralty
adoptieren [adɔp'ti:rən] *vt* to adopt
Adoption [adɔptsi'o:n] *f* adoption
Adoptiveltern *pl* adoptive parents *pl*
Adoptivkind *nt* adopted child
Adr. *abk* (= *Adresse*) add.
Adressant [adrɛ'sant] *m* sender
Adressat [adrɛ'sa:t] (**-en, -en**) *m* addressee
Adressbuch *nt* directory; (*privat*) address book
Adresse [a'drɛsə] (**-, -n**) *f* (*auch Comput*) address; **an der falschen ~ sein** (*umg*) to have gone/come to the wrong person; **absolute ~** absolute address; **relative ~** relative address
adressieren [adrɛ'si:rən] *vt*: **~ (an** *+akk*) to address (to)
Adria ['a:dria] (**-**) *f* Adriatic Sea
Adriatisches Meer [adri'a:tıʃəs me:r] *nt* (*form*) Adriatic Sea
Advent [at'vɛnt] (**-(e)s, -e**) *m* Advent; **der erste/zweite ~** the first/second Sunday in Advent
Advents- *zW*: **Adventskalender** *m* Advent calendar; **Adventskranz** *m* Advent wreath
Adverb [at'vɛrp] *nt* adverb
adverbial [atverbi'a:l] *adj* adverbial
aero- [aero] *präf* aero-
Aerobic [ae'ro:bik] (**-s**) *nt* aerobics *sing*
Affäre [a'fɛ:rə] (**-, -n**) *f* affair; **sich aus der ~ ziehen** (*umg*) to get (o.s.) out of it
Affe ['afə] (**-n, -n**) *m* monkey; (*umg: Kerl*) berk (*Brit*)
Affekt (**-(e)s, -e**) *m*: **im ~ handeln** to act in the heat of the moment
affektiert [afɛk'ti:rt] *adj* affected
Affen- *zW*: **affenartig** *adj* like a monkey; **mit affenartiger Geschwindigkeit** (*umg*) like a flash; **affengeil** (*umg*) *adj* magic, fantastic; **Affenhitze** (*umg*) *f* incredible heat; **Affenliebe** *f*: **Affenliebe (zu)** blind adoration (of); **Affenschande** (*umg*) *f* crying shame; **Affentempo** (*umg*) *nt*: **in** *od* **mit einem Affentempo** at breakneck speed; **Affentheater** (*umg*) *nt*: **ein Affentheater aufführen** to make a fuss
affig ['afıç] *adj* affected
Afghane [af'ga:nə] (**-n, -n**) *m* Afghan

Afghanin [af'ga:nɪn] *f* Afghan
afghanisch *adj* Afghan
Afghanistan [af'ga:nɪsta:n] (**-s**) *nt* Afghanistan
Afrika ['a:frika] (**-s**) *nt* Africa
Afrikaans [afri'ka:ns] (-) *nt* Afrikaans
Afrikaner, in [afri'ka:nər(ɪn)] (**-s, -**) *m(f)* African
afrikanisch *adj* African
afroamerikanisch ['a:fro|ameri'ka:nɪʃ] *adj* Afro-American
After ['aftər] (**-s, -**) *m* anus
AG (-) *f abk* (*= Aktiengesellschaft*) ≈ plc (*Brit*), corp., inc. (*US*)
Ägäis [ɛ'gɛ:ɪs] (-) *f* Aegean (Sea)
Ägäisches Meer *nt* Aegean Sea
Agent, in [a'gɛnt(ɪn)] *m(f)* agent
Agententätigkeit *f* espionage
Agentur [agɛn'tu:r] *f* agency; **Agenturbericht** *m*, **Agenturmeldung** *f* (news) agency report
Aggregat [agre'ga:t] (**-(e)s, -e**) *nt* aggregate; (*Tech*) unit; **Aggregatzustand** *m* (*Phys*) state
Aggression [agrɛsi'o:n] *f* aggression
aggressiv [agrɛ'si:f] *adj* aggressive
Aggressivität [agrɛsivi'tɛ:t] *f* aggressiveness
Aggressor [a'grɛso:r] (**-s, -en**) *m* aggressor
Agitation [agitatsi'o:n] *f* agitation
Agrarpolitik *f* agricultural policy
Agrarstaat *m* agrarian state
AGV *f abk* (*= Arbeitsgemeinschaft der Verbraucherverbände) consumer groups' association*
Ägypten [ɛ'gʏptən] (**-s**) *nt* Egypt
Ägypter, in (**-s, -**) *m(f)* Egyptian
ägyptisch *adj* Egyptian
aha [a'ha:] *interj* aha!
Aha-Erlebnis *nt* sudden insight
ahd. *abk* (*= althochdeutsch*) OHG
Ahn [a:n] (**-en, -en**) *m* forebear
ahnden ['a:ndən] *vt* (*geh: Freveltat, Verbrechen*) to avenge; (*Übertretung, Verstoß*) to punish
ähneln ['ɛ:nəln] *vi +dat* to be like, resemble ▷ *vr* to be alike *od* similar
ahnen ['a:nən] *vt* to suspect; (*Tod, Gefahr*) to have a presentiment of; **nichts Böses ~** to be unsuspecting; **du ahnst es nicht!** you have no idea!; **davon habe ich nichts geahnt** I didn't have the slightest inkling of it
Ahnenforschung *f* genealogy
ähnlich ['ɛ:nlɪç] *adj (+dat)* similar (to); **das sieht ihm (ganz) ~!** (*umg*) that's just like him!, that's him all over!; **Ähnlichkeit** *f* similarity
Ahnung ['a:nʊŋ] *f* idea, suspicion; (*Vorgefühl*) presentiment
ahnungslos *adj* unsuspecting
Ahorn ['a:hɔrn] (**-s, -e**) *m* maple
Ähre ['ɛ:rə] (**-, -n**) *f* ear
AHS *f abk* (*Österr: = allgemeinbildende höhere Schule*) ≈ secondary school
Aids [e:dz] (-) *nt* Aids
Airbag ['ɛ:bɛ:g] (**-s, -s**) *m* (*Aut*) airbag
Akademie [akade'mi:] *f* academy
Akademiker, in [aka'de:mikər(ɪn)] (**-s, -**) *m(f)* university graduate
akademisch *adj* academic
Akazie [a'ka:tsiə] (**-, -n**) *f* acacia
Akk. *abk* = **Akkusativ**
akklimatisieren [aklimati'zi:rən] *vr* to become acclimatized
Akkord [a'kɔrt] (**-(e)s, -e**) *m* (*Mus*) chord; **im ~ arbeiten** to do piecework; **Akkordarbeit** *f* piecework
Akkordeon [a'kɔrdeɔn] (**-s, -s**) *nt* accordion
Akkordlohn *m* piece wages *pl*, piece rate
Akkreditiv [akredi'ti:f] (**-s, -e**) *nt* (*Comm*) letter of credit
Akku ['aku] (**-s, -s**) (*umg*) *m* (*Akkumulator*) battery
akkurat [aku'ra:t] *adj* precise; (*sorgfältig*) meticulous
Akkusativ ['akuzati:f] (**-s, -e**) *m* accusative (case); **Akkusativobjekt** *nt* accusative *od* direct object
Akne ['aknə] (**-, -n**) *f* acne
Akribie [akri'bi:] *f* (*geh*) meticulousness
Akrobat, in [akro'ba:t(ɪn)] (**-en, -en**) *m(f)* acrobat
Akt [akt] (**-(e)s, -e**) *m* act; (*Kunst*) nude
Akte ['aktə] (**-, -n**) *f* file; **etw zu den ~n legen** (*lit, fig*) to file sth away
Akten- *zW*: **Aktendeckel** *m* folder; **Aktenkoffer** *m* attaché case; **aktenkundig** *adj* on record; **Aktennotiz** *f* memo(randum); **Aktenordner** *m* file; **Aktenschrank** *m* filing cabinet; **Aktentasche** *f* briefcase; **Aktenzeichen** *nt* reference
Aktie ['aktsiə] (**-, -n**) *f* share; **wie stehen die ~n?** (*hum: umg*) how are things?
Aktien- *zW*: **Aktienbank** *f* joint-stock bank; **Aktienemission** *f* share issue; **Aktiengesellschaft** *f* joint-stock company; **Aktienindex** *m* share index; **Aktienkapital** *nt* share capital; **Aktienkurs** *m* share price
Aktion [aktsi'o:n] *f* campaign; (*Polizeiaktion, Suchaktion*) action
Aktionär, in [aktsio'nɛ:r(ɪn)] (**-s, -e**) *m(f)* shareholder
Aktionismus [aktsio'nɪsmʊs] *m* (*Pol*) actionism
Aktionsradius [aktsi'o:nzra:diʊs] (**-, -ien**) *m* (*Aviat, Naut*) range; (*fig: Wirkungsbereich*) scope
aktiv [ak'ti:f] *adj* active; (*Mil*) regular; **Aktiv** (**-s**) *nt* (*Gram*) active (voice)
Aktiva [ak'ti:va] *pl* assets *pl*
aktivieren [akti'vi:rən] *vt* to activate; (*fig: Arbeit, Kampagne*) to step up; (*Mitarbeiter*) to get moving
Aktivität [aktivi'tɛ:t] *f* activity
Aktivposten *m* (*lit, fig*) asset
Aktivsaldo *m* (*Comm*) credit balance
Aktivurlaub *m* activity holiday
aktualisieren [aktuali'zi:rən] *vt* (*Comput*) to update
Aktualität [aktuali'tɛ:t] *f* topicality; (*einer Mode*) up-to-dateness
aktuell [aktu'ɛl] *adj* topical; up-to-date; **eine ~e Sendung** (*Rundf, TV*) a current affairs

programme
Akupunktur [akupuŋk'tu:ər] *f* acupuncture
Akustik [a'kʊstɪk] *f* acoustics *pl*
akustisch [a'kʊstɪʃ] *adj* acoustic; **ich habe dich rein ~ nicht verstanden** I simply didn't catch what you said (properly)
akut [a'ku:t] *adj* acute; (*Frage*) pressing, urgent
AKW *nt abk* = **Atomkraftwerk**
Akzent [ak'tsɛnt] (**-(e)s, -e**) *m* accent; (*Betonung*) stress; **~e setzen** (*fig*) to bring out *od* emphasize the main points; **Akzentverschiebung** *f* (*fig*) shift of emphasis
Akzept (**-(e)s, -e**) *nt* (*Comm: Wechsel*) acceptance
akzeptabel [aktsɛp'ta:bl] *adj* acceptable
akzeptieren [aktsɛp'ti:rən] *vt* to accept
AL *f abk* (= *Alternative Liste*) *siehe* **alternativ**
Alarm [a'larm] (**-(e)s, -e**) *m* alarm; (*Zustand*) alert; **~ schlagen** to give *od* raise the alarm; **Alarmanlage** *f* alarm system; **alarmbereit** *adj* standing by; **Alarmbereitschaft** *f* stand-by
alarmieren [alar'mi:rən] *vt* to alarm
Alaska [a'laska] (**-s**) *nt* Alaska
Albaner, in [al'ba:nər(ɪn)] (**-s, -**) *m(f)* Albanian
Albanien [al'ba:niən] (**-s**) *nt* Albania
albanisch *adj* Albanian
albern ['albərn] *adj* silly
Albtraum ['alptraʊm] *m* nightmare
Album ['albʊm] (**-s, Alben**) *nt* album
Alcopops ['alkopɔps] *pl* alcopops *pl*
Aleuten [ale'u:tən] *pl* Aleutian Islands *pl*
Alge ['algə] (**-, -n**) *f* alga
Algebra ['algebra] (**-**) *f* algebra
Algerien [al'ge:riən] (**-s**) *nt* Algeria
Algerier, in (**-s, -**) *m(f)* Algerian
algerisch [al'ge:rɪʃ] *adj* Algerian
Algier ['alʒi:ər] (**-s**) *nt* Algiers
ALGOL ['algɔl] (**-(s)**) *nt* (*Comput*) ALGOL
alias ['a:lias] *adv* alias
Alibi ['a:libi] (**-s, -s**) *nt* alibi
Alimente [ali'mɛntə] *pl* alimony *sing*
Alkohol ['alkohɔl] (**-s, -e**) *m* alcohol; **unter ~ stehen** to be under the influence (of alcohol); **alkoholarm** *adj* low alcohol; **Alkoholexzess** *m* binge drinking; **alkoholfrei** *adj* non-alcoholic; **Alkoholgehalt** *m* proof
Alkoholika [alko'ho:lika] *pl* alcoholic drinks *pl*, liquor (*US*)
Alkoholiker, in [alko'ho:likər(ɪn)] (**-s, -**) *m(f)* alcoholic
alkoholisch *adj* alcoholic
Alkoholverbot *nt* ban on alcohol
All [al] (**-s**) *nt* universe; (*Raumfahrt*) space; (*außerhalb unseres Sternsystems*) outer space
allabendlich *adj* every evening
allbekannt *adj* universally known
alle *adj siehe* **alle(r, s)**
alledem ['alədeːm] *pron*: **bei/trotz** *etc* **~** with/in spite of *etc* all that; **zu ~** moreover
Allee [a'le:] (**-, -n**) *f* avenue
allein [a'laɪn] *adj, adv* alone; (*ohne Hilfe*) on one's own, by oneself ▷ *konj* (*geh*) but, only; **von ~** by oneself/itself; **nicht ~** (*nicht nur*) not only; **~ schon der Gedanke** the very *od* mere thought ..., the thought alone ...; **alleinerziehend** *adj* single-parent; **Alleinerziehende, r** *f(m)*, **Alleinerzieher, in** *m(f)* single parent; **Alleingang** *m*: **im Alleingang** on one's own; **Alleinherrscher, in** *m(f)* autocrat; **Alleinhersteller, in** *m(f)* sole manufacturer
alleinig [a'laɪnɪç] *adj* sole
allein- *zW*: **Alleinsein** *nt* being on one's own; (*Einsamkeit*) loneliness; **alleinstehend** *adj* single; **Alleinunterhalter, in** *m(f)* solo entertainer; **Alleinvertretung** *f* (*Comm*) sole agency; **Alleinvertretungsvertrag** *m* (*Comm*) exclusive agency agreement
allemal ['alə'ma:l] *adv* (*jedes Mal*) always; (*ohne Weiteres*) with no bother; *siehe auch* **Mal**
allenfalls ['alən'fals] *adv* at all events; (*höchstens*) at most

SCHLÜSSELWORT

alle, r, s *adj* **1** (*sämtliche*) all; **wir alle** all of us; **alle Kinder waren da** all the children were there; **alle Kinder mögen ...** all children like ...; **alle beide** both of us/them; **sie kamen alle** they all came; **alles Gute** all the best; **alles in allem** all in all; **vor allem** above all; **das ist alles andere als ...** that's anything but ...; **es hat alles keinen Sinn mehr** nothing makes sense any more; **was habt ihr alles gemacht?** what did you get up to?

2 (*mit Zeit- oder Maßangaben*) every; **alle vier Jahre** every four years; **alle fünf Meter** every five metres

▷ *pron* everything; **alles was er sagt** everything he says, all that he says; **trotz allem** in spite of everything

▷ *adv* (*zu Ende, aufgebraucht*) finished; **die Milch ist alle** the milk's all gone, there's no milk left; **etw alle machen** to finish sth up

allerbeste, r, s ['alər'bɛstə(r, s)] *adj* very best
allerdings ['alər'dɪŋs] *adv* (*zwar*) admittedly; (*gewiss*) certainly
Allergie [alɛr'gi:] *f* allergy
allergisch [a'lɛrgɪʃ] *adj* allergic; **auf etw** *akk* **~ reagieren** to be allergic to sth
allerhand (*umg*) *adj inv* all sorts of; **das ist doch ~!** that's a bit much!; **~!** (*lobend*) good show!
Allerheiligen *nt* All Saints' Day; *see culture note*

ALLERHEILIGEN

Allerheiligen (All Saints' Day) is a public holiday in Germany and in Austria. It is a day in honour of all the saints. *Allerseelen* (All Souls' Day) is celebrated on November 2nd in the Roman Catholic Church. It is customary to visit cemeteries and place lighted candles on the graves of deceased relatives and friends.

aller- *zW*: **allerhöchste, r, s** *adj* very highest; **es wird allerhöchste Zeit, dass ...** it's really high time that ...; **allerhöchstens** *adv* at the very most; **allerlei** *adj inv* all sorts of; **allerletzte, r, s** *adj* very last; **der/das ist das Allerletzte** (*umg*) he's/it's the absolute end!; **allerneueste, allerneuste, r, s** *adj* very latest

Allerseelen (**-s**) *nt* All Soul's Day; *siehe auch* **Allerheiligen**; **allerseits** *adv* on all sides; **prost allerseits!** cheers everyone!

Allerwelts- *in zW* (*Durchschnitts-*) common; (*nichtssagend*) commonplace

allerwenigste, r, s *adj* very least; **die ~n Menschen wissen das** very few people know that

Allerwerteste, r *m* (*hum*) posterior (*hum*)

alles *pron* everything; *siehe auch* **alle(r, s)**

allesamt *adv* all (of them/us *etc*)

Alleskleber (**-s, -**) *m* all-purpose adhesive

Allgäu ['algɔʏ] *nt part of the alpine region of Bavaria*

allgegenwärtig *adj* omnipresent, ubiquitous

allgemein ['algəmaɪn] *adj* general ▷ *adv*: **es ist ~ üblich** it's the general rule; **~ verständlich** generally intelligible; **im A~** in general; **im ~en Interesse** in the common interest; **auf ~en Wunsch** by popular request; **Allgemeinbildung** *f* general *od* all-round education; **allgemeingültig** *adj* generally accepted; **Allgemeinheit** *f* (*Menschen*) general public; **Allgemeinheiten** *pl* (*Redensarten*) general remarks *pl*; **Allgemeinwissen** *nt* general knowledge

Allheilmittel [al'haɪlmɪtəl] *nt* cure-all, panacea (*bes fig*)

Alliierte, r [ali'i:rtə(r)] *f(m)* ally

all- *zW*: **alljährlich** *adj* annual; **allmächtig** *adj* all-powerful, omnipotent; **allmählich** *adv* gradually; **es wird allmählich Zeit** (*umg*) it's about time; **Allradantrieb** *m* all-wheel drive; **allseitig** *adj* (*allgemein*) general; (*ausnahmslos*) universal; **Alltag** *m* everyday life; **alltäglich** *adj* daily; (*gewöhnlich*) commonplace; **alltags** *adv* on weekdays; **Alltagskultur** *f* everyday culture

Allüren [a'ly:rən] *pl* odd behaviour (*Brit*) *od* behavior (*US*) *sing*; (*eines Stars etc*) airs and graces *pl*

all- *zW*: **allwissend** *adj* omniscient; **Allzeithoch** *nt* all-time high; **Allzeittief** *nt* all-time low; **allzu** *adv* all too; **allzu gern** (*mögen*) only too much; (*bereitwillig*) only too willingly; **allzu oft** all too often; **allzu viel** too much

Allzweck- ['altsvɛk-] *in zW* all-purpose

Alm [alm] (**-, -en**) *f* alpine pasture

Almosen ['almo:zən] (**-s, -**) *nt* alms *pl*

Alpen ['alpən] *pl* Alps *pl*; **Alpenblume** *f* alpine flower; **Alpenveilchen** *nt* cyclamen; **Alpenvorland** *nt* foothills *pl* of the Alps

Alphabet [alfa'be:t] (**-(e)s, -e**) *nt* alphabet

alphabetisch *adj* alphabetical

alphanumerisch [alfanu'me:rɪʃ] *adj* (*Comput*) alphanumeric

Alptraum ['alptraʊm] *m* = **Albtraum**

SCHLÜSSELWORT

als [als] *konj* **1** (*zeitlich*) when; (*gleichzeitig*) as; **damals als ...** (in the days) when ...; **gerade als ...** just as ...

2 (*in der Eigenschaft*) than; **als Antwort** as an answer; **als Kind** as a child

3 (*bei Vergleichen*) than; **ich kam später als er** I came later than he (did) *od* later than him; **lieber ... als ...** rather ... than ...; **alles andere als** anything but; **nichts als Ärger** nothing but trouble; **so viel/so weit als möglich** (*bei Vergleichen*) as much/far as possible

4: als ob/wenn as if

alsbaldig [als'baldɪç] *konj*: **„zum ~en Verbrauch bestimmt"** "for immediate use only"

also ['alzo:] *konj* so; (*folglich*) therefore; **~ wie ich schon sagte** well (then), as I said before; **ich komme ~ morgen** so I'll come tomorrow; **~ gut** *od* **schön!** okay then; **~, so was!** well really!; **na ~!** there you are then!

Alt [alt] (**-s, -e**) *m* (*Mus*) alto

alt *adj* old; **ich bin nicht mehr der A~e** I am not the man I was; **alles beim A~en lassen** to leave everything as it was; **ich werde heute nicht ~ (werden)** (*umg*) I won't last long today/tonight *etc*; **~ aussehen** (*fig: umg*) to be in a pickle

Altar [al'ta:r] (**-(e)s, -äre**) *m* altar

alt- *zW*: **Altbau** *m* old building; **Altbauwohnung** *f* flat (*Brit*) *od* apartment (*US*) in an old building; **altbekannt** *adj* well-known; **altbewährt** *adj* (*Methode etc*) well-tried; (*Tradition etc*) long-standing; **Altbier** *nt top-fermented German dark beer*; **alteingesessen** *adj* old-established; **Alteisen** *nt* scrap iron

Altenheim *nt* old people's home

Altenteil ['altəntaɪl] *nt*: **sich aufs ~ setzen** *od* **zurückziehen** (*fig*) to retire from public life

Alter ['altər] (**-s, -**) *nt* age; (*hohes*) old age; **er ist in deinem ~** he's your age; **im ~ von** at the age of

älter ['ɛltər] *adj* (*comp*) older; (*Bruder, Schwester*) elder; (*nicht mehr jung*) elderly

altern ['altərn] *vi* to grow old, age

Alternativ- [altɛrna'ti:f] *in zW* alternative

alternativ *adj*: **A~e Liste** *electoral pact between the Greens and alternative parties*; **~ leben** to live an alternative way of life

Alternative [altɛrna'ti:və] *f* alternative

Alternativ- *zW*: **Alternativmedizin** *f* alternative medicine; **Alternativszene** *f* alternative scene; **Alternativtechnologie** *f* alternative technology

alters ['altərs] *adv* (*geh*): **von** *od* **seit ~ (her)** from time immemorial

Alters- *zW*: **Altersarmut** *f* old-age poverty; **altersbedingt** *adj* related to a particular age;

caused by old age; **Altersgrenze** *f* age limit; **flexible Altersgrenze** flexible retirement age; **Altersheim** *nt* old people's home; **Altersrente** *f* old age pension; **Altersruhegeld** *nt* retirement benefit; **altersschwach** *adj* (*Mensch*) old and infirm; (*Auto, Möbel*) decrepit; **Altersversorgung** *f* provision for old age

Altertum ['altərtu:m] *nt* antiquity

altertümlich *adj* (*aus dem Altertum*) ancient; (*veraltet*) antiquated

alt- *zW*: **altgedient** *adj* long-serving; **Altglas** *nt* used glass (*for recycling*), scrap glass; **Altglascontainer** *m* bottle bank; **althergebracht** *adj* traditional; **Altherrenmannschaft** *f* (*Sport*) *team of players over thirty*; **altklug** *adj* precocious; **Altlasten** *pl* legacy *sing* of dangerous waste; **Altmaterial** *nt* scrap; **Altmetall** *nt* scrap metal; **altmodisch** *adj* old-fashioned; **Altpapier** *nt* waste paper; **Altstadt** *f* old town

Altstimme *f* alto

Altwarenhändler *m* second-hand dealer

Altweibersommer *m* Indian summer

Alu ['a:lu] (*umg*) *abk* = **Arbeitslosenunterstützung; Aluminium**

Alufolie ['a:lufo:liə] *f* tinfoil

Aluminium [alu'mi:niʊm] (**-s**) *nt* aluminium, aluminum (*US*); **Aluminiumfolie** *f* tinfoil

Alzheimerkrankheit ['altshaɪmər'kraŋkhaɪt] *f* Alzheimer's disease

am [am] = **an dem**; **am Sterben** on the point of dying; **am 15. März** on March 15th; **am letzten Sonntag** last Sunday; **am Morgen/Abend** in the morning/evening; **am besten/schönsten** best/most beautiful

Amalgam [amal'ga:m] (**-s, -e**) *nt* amalgam

Amateur [ama'tø:r] *m* amateur

Amazonas [ama'tso:nas] (**-**) *m* Amazon (river)

Ambiente [ambi'ɛntə] (**-**) *nt* ambience

Ambition [ambitsi'o:n] *f*: **~en auf etw** *akk* **haben** to have ambitions of getting sth

Amboss ['ambɔs] (**-es, -e**) *m* anvil

ambulant [ambu'lant] *adj* outpatient

Ameise ['a:maɪzə] (**-, -n**) *f* ant

Ameisenhaufen *m* anthill

Amerika [a'me:rika] (**-s**) *nt* America

Amerikaner [ameri'ka:nər] (**-s, -**) *m* American; (*Gebäck*) *flat iced cake*; **Amerikanerin** *f* American

amerikanisch *adj* American

Ami ['ami] (**-s, -s**) (*umg*) *m* Yank; (*Soldat*) GI

Amme ['amə] (**-, -n**) *f* (*veraltet*) foster mother; (*Nährmutter*) wet nurse

Ammenmärchen ['amənmɛ:rçən] *nt* fairy tale *od* story

Amok ['a:mɔk] *m*: **~ laufen** to run amok *od* amuck

Amortisation [amɔrtizatsi'o:n] *f* amortization

amortisieren [amɔrti'zi:rən] *vr* to pay for itself

Ampel ['ampəl] (**-, -n**) *f* traffic lights *pl*

amphibisch [am'fi:bɪʃ] *adj* amphibious

Ampulle [am'pʊlə] (**-, -n**) *f* (*Behälter*) ampoule

amputieren [ampu'ti:rən] *vt* to amputate

Amsel ['amzəl] (**-, -n**) *f* blackbird

Amsterdam [amstər'dam] *nt* (**-s**) Amsterdam

Amt [amt] (**-(e)s, ⸚er**) *nt* office; (*Pflicht*) duty; (*Tel*) exchange; **zum zuständigen ~ gehen** to go to the relevant authority; **von ~s wegen** (*auf behördliche Anordnung hin*) officially

amtieren [am'ti:rən] *vi* to hold office; (*fungieren*): **als ...** ~ to act as ...

amtierend *adj* incumbent

amtlich *adj* official; **~es Kennzeichen** registration (number), license number (*US*)

Amtmann (**-(e)s**, *pl* **-männer** *od* **-leute**) *m* (*Verwaltung*) senior civil servant

Amtmännin *f* (*Verwaltung*) senior civil servant

Amts- *zW*: **Amtsarzt** *m* medical officer; **amtsärztlich** *adj*: **amtsärztlich untersucht werden** to have an official medical examination; **Amtsdeutsch**, **Amtsdeutsche** *nt* officialese; **Amtseid** *m*: **den Amtseid ablegen** to be sworn in, take the oath of office; **Amtsgeheimnis** *nt* (*geheime Sache*) official secret; (*Schweigepflicht*) official secrecy; **Amtsgericht** *nt* county (*Brit*) *od* district (*US*) court; **Amtsmissbrauch** *m* abuse of one's position; **Amtsperiode** *f* term of office; **Amtsperson** *f* official; **Amtsrichter** *m* district judge; **Amtsschimmel** *m* (*hum*) officialdom; **Amtssprache** *f* official language; **Amtsstunden** *pl* office hours *pl*; **Amtsträger** *m* office bearer; **Amtswechsel** *m* change of office; (*in Behörde*) rotation (in office); **Amtsweg** *m*: **auf dem Amtsweg** through official channels; **Amtszeit** *f* period of office

amüsant [amy'zant] *adj* amusing

Amüsement [amyzə'mã:] *nt* amusement

amüsieren [amy'zi:rən] *vt* to amuse ▷ *vr* to enjoy o.s.; **sich über etw** *akk* ~ to find sth funny; (*unfreundlich*) to make fun of sth

SCHLÜSSELWORT

an [an] *präp +dat* **1** (*räumlich: wo?*) at; (*auf, bei*) on; (*nahe bei*) near; **an diesem Ort** at this place; **an der Wand** on the wall; **zu nahe an etw** too near to sth; **unten am Fluss** down by the river; **Köln liegt am Rhein** Cologne is on the Rhine; **an der gleichen Stelle** at *od* on the same spot; **jdn an der Hand nehmen** to take sb by the hand; **sie wohnen Tür an Tür** they live next door to one another; **es an der Leber** *etc* **haben** (*umg*) to have liver *etc* trouble

2 (*zeitlich: wann?*) on; **an diesem Tag** on this day; **an Ostern** at Easter

3: arm an Fett low in fat; **jung an Jahren sein** to be young in years; **an der ganzen Sache ist nichts** there is nothing in it; **an etw sterben** to die of sth; **an (und für) sich** actually

▷ *präp +akk* **1** (*räumlich: wohin?*) to; **er ging ans Fenster** he went (over) to the window; **etw an die Wand hängen/schreiben** to hang/write sth on the wall; **an die Arbeit gehen** to get down to work

2 (*zeitlich: woran?*): **an etw denken** to think of

sth
3 (*gerichtet an*) to; **ein Gruß/eine Frage an dich** greetings/a question to you
▷ *adv* **1** (*ungefähr*) about; **an die Hundert** about a hundred; **an die 10 Euro** around 10 euros
2 (*auf Fahrplänen*): **Frankfurt an 18.30** arriving Frankfurt 18.30
3 (*ab*): **von dort/heute an** from there/today onwards
4 (*angeschaltet, angezogen*) on; **an sein** (*umg*) to be on; **das Licht ist an** the light is on; **ohne etwas an** with nothing on; *siehe auch* **am**

analog [ana'lo:k] *adj* analogous
Analogie [analo'gi:] *f* analogy
Analogrechner [ana'lo:krɛçnər] *m* analog computer
Analphabet, in [an|alfa'be:t(ɪn)] (**-en, -en**) *m(f)* illiterate (person)
Analyse [ana'ly:zə] (**-, -n**) *f* analysis
analysieren [analy'zi:rən] *vt* to analyse (*Brit*), analyze (*US*)
Anämie [anɛ'mi:] (**-, -n**) *f* anaemia (*Brit*), anemia (*US*)
Ananas ['ananas] (**-,** *-od* **-se**) *f* pineapple
Anarchie [anar'çi:] *f* anarchy
anarchisch [a'narçɪʃ] *adj* anarchic
Anarchist, in [anar'çɪst(ɪn)] *m(f)* (**-en, -en**) anarchist
Anästhesist, in [an|ɛste'zɪst(ɪn)] (**-en, -en**) *m(f)* anaesthetist (*Brit*), anesthesiologist (*US*)
Anatomie [anato'mi:] *f* anatomy
anbahnen ['anba:nən] *vr* to open up; (*sich andeuten*) to be in the offing; (*Unangenehmes*) to be looming ▷ *vt* to initiate
Anbahnung *f* initiation
anbändeln ['anbɛndəln] (*umg*) *vi* to flirt
Anbau ['anbaʊ] *m* (*Agr*) cultivation; (*Gebäude*) extension
anbauen *vt* (*Agr*) to cultivate; (*Gebäudeteil*) to build on
Anbaugebiet *nt*: **ein gutes ~ für etw** a good area for growing sth
Anbaumöbel *pl* unit furniture *sing*
anbehalten ['anbəhaltən] *unreg vt* to keep on
anbei [an'baɪ] *adv* enclosed (*form*); **~ schicken wir Ihnen ...** please find enclosed ...
anbeißen ['anbaɪsən] *unreg vt* to bite into ▷ *vi* (*lit*) to bite; (*fig*) to swallow the bait; **zum A~ aussehen** (*umg*) to look good enough to eat
anbelangen ['anbəlaŋən] *vt* to concern; **was mich anbelangt** as far as I am concerned
anberaumen ['anbəraʊmən] *vt* (*form*) to fix, arrange
anbeten ['anbe:tən] *vt* to worship
Anbetracht ['anbətraxt] *m*: **in ~** *+gen* in view of
Anbetung *f* worship
anbiedern ['anbi:dərn] (*pej*) *vr*: **sich ~ (bei)** to curry favour (with)
anbieten ['anbi:tən] *unreg vt* to offer ▷ *vr* to volunteer; **das bietet sich als Lösung an** that would provide a solution
anbinden ['anbɪndən] *unreg vt* to tie up; (*verbinden*) to connect
Anblick ['anblɪk] *m* sight
anblicken *vt* to look at
anbraten ['anbra:tən] *unreg vt* (*Fleisch*) to brown
anbrechen ['anbrɛçən] *unreg vt* to start; (*Vorräte*) to break into ▷ *vi* to start; (*Tag*) to break; (*Nacht*) to fall
anbrennen ['anbrɛnən] *unreg vi* to catch fire; (*Koch*) to burn
anbringen ['anbrɪŋən] *unreg vt* to bring; (*Ware*) to sell; (*festmachen*) to fasten; (*Telefon etc*) to install
Anbruch ['anbrʊx] *m* beginning; **~ des Tages** dawn; **~ der Nacht** nightfall
anbrüllen ['anbrʏlən] *vt* to roar at
Andacht ['andaxt] (**-, -en**) *f* devotion; (*Versenkung*) rapt interest; (*Gottesdienst*) prayers *pl*; (*Ehrfurcht*) reverence
andächtig ['andɛçtɪç] *adj* devout
andauern ['andaʊərn] *vi* to last, go on
andauernd *adj* continual
Anden ['andən] *pl*: **die ~** the Andes *pl*
Andenken ['andɛŋkən] (**-s, -**) *nt* memory; (*Reiseandenken*) souvenir; (*Erinnerungsstück*): **ein ~ (an** *+akk*) a memento (of), a keepsake (from)
andere, r, s *adj* other; (*verschieden*) different; **am ~n Tage** the next day; **ein ~s Mal** another time; **kein ~r** nobody else; **alles ~ als zufrieden** anything but pleased, far from pleased; **von etwas ~m sprechen** to talk about something else; **es blieb mir nichts ~s übrig als selbst hinzugehen** I had no alternative but to go myself; **unter ~m** among other things; **von einem Tag zum ~n** overnight; **sie hat einen ~n** she has someone else
andererseits *adv* on the other hand
andermal *adv*: **ein ~** some other time
ändern ['ɛndərn] *vt* to alter, change ▷ *vr* to change
andernfalls *adv* otherwise
andernorts ['andərn'ɔrts] *adv* elsewhere
anders *adv*: **~ (als)** differently (from); **wer ~?** who else?; **niemand ~** no-one else; **wie nicht ~ zu erwarten** as was to be expected; **wie könnte es ~ sein?** how could it be otherwise?; **ich kann nicht ~** (*kann es nicht lassen*) I can't help it; (*muss leider*) I have no choice; **~ ausgedrückt** to put it another way; **jemand/irgendwo ~** somebody/somewhere else; **~ aussehen/klingen** to look/sound different; **~ lautend = anderslautend**
andersartig *adj* different
Andersdenkende, r *f(m)* dissident, dissenter
anderseits ['andər'zaɪts] *adv* = **andererseits**
anders- *zW*: **andersfarbig** *adj* of a different colour; **andersgläubig** *adj* of a different faith; **andersherum** *adv* the other way round; **anderslautend** *adj*: **anderslautende Berichte** reports to the contrary; **anderswo** *adv* elsewhere; **anderswoher** *adv* from elsewhere; **anderswohin** *adv* elsewhere
anderthalb ['andərt'halp] *adj* one and a half

Änderung ['ɛndərʊŋ] *f* alteration, change
Änderungsantrag ['ɛndərʊŋs|antra:k] *m* (*Parl*) amendment
anderweitig ['andər'vaɪtɪç] *adj* other ▷ *adv* otherwise; (*anderswo*) elsewhere
andeuten ['andɔʏtən] *vt* to indicate; (*Wink geben*) to hint at
Andeutung *f* indication; hint
andeutungsweise *adv* (*als Anspielung, Anzeichen*) by way of a hint; (*als flüchtiger Hinweis*) in passing
andichten ['andɪçtən] *vt*: **jdm etw ~** (*umg: Fähigkeiten*) to credit sb with sth
Andorra [an'dɔra] **(-s)** *nt* Andorra
Andorraner, in [andɔ'ra:nər(ɪn)] *m(f)* Andorran
Andrang ['andraŋ] *m* crush
andrehen ['andre:ən] *vt* to turn *od* switch on; **jdm etw ~** (*umg*) to unload sth onto sb
androhen ['andro:ən] *vt*: **jdm etw ~** to threaten sb with sth
Androhung *f*: **unter ~ von Gewalt** with the threat of violence
anecken ['an|ɛkən] (*umg*) *vi*: **(bei jdm/allen) ~** to rub (sb/everyone) up the wrong way
aneignen ['an|aɪgnən] *vt*: **sich** *dat* **etw ~** to acquire sth; (*widerrechtlich*) to appropriate sth; (*sich mit etw vertraut machen*) to learn sth
aneinander [an|aɪ'nandər] *adv* at/on/to *etc* one another *od* each other; **aneinanderfügen** *vt* to put together; **aneinandergeraten** *vi* to clash; **aneinanderlegen** *vt* to put together
anekeln ['an|e:kəln] *vt* to disgust
Anemone [ane'mo:nə] **(-, -n)** *f* anemone
anerkannt ['an|ɛrkant] *adj* recognized, acknowledged
anerkennen ['an|ɛrkɛnən] *unreg vt* to recognize, acknowledge; (*würdigen*) to appreciate; **das muss man ~** (*zugeben*) you can't argue with that; (*würdigen*) one has to appreciate that
anerkennend *adj* appreciative
anerkennenswert *adj* praiseworthy
Anerkennung *f* recognition, acknowledgement; appreciation
anerzogen ['an|ɛrtso:gən] *adj* acquired
anfachen ['anfaxən] *vt* (*lit*) to fan into flame; (*fig*) to kindle
anfahren ['anfa:rən] *unreg vt* to deliver; (*fahren gegen*) to hit; (*Hafen*) to put into; (*umg*) to bawl at ▷ *vi* to drive up; (*losfahren*) to drive off
Anfahrt ['anfa:rt] *f* (*Anfahrtsweg, Anfahrtszeit*) journey; (*Zufahrt*) approach
Anfall ['anfal] *m* (*Med*) attack; **in einem ~ von** (*fig*) in a fit of
anfallen *unreg vt* to attack ▷ *vi* (*Arbeit*) to come up; (*Produkt, Nebenprodukte*) to be obtained; (*Zinsen*) to accrue; (*sich anhäufen*) to accumulate; **die ~den Kosten/Reparaturen** the costs/repairs incurred
anfällig ['anfɛlɪç] *adj* delicate; **~ für etw** prone to sth
Anfang ['anfaŋ] **(-(e)s, -fänge)** *m* beginning, start; **von ~ an** right from the beginning; **zu ~** at the beginning; **~ fünfzig** in one's early fifties; **~ Mai/1994** at the beginning of May/1994
anfangen ['anfaŋən] *unreg vt* to begin, start; (*machen*) to do ▷ *vi* to begin, start; **damit kann ich nichts ~** (*nützt mir nichts*) that's no good to me; (*verstehe ich nicht*) it doesn't mean a thing to me; **mit dir ist heute (aber) gar nichts anzufangen!** you're no fun at all today!; **bei einer Firma ~** to start working for a firm
Anfänger, in ['anfɛŋər(ɪn)] **(-s, -)** *m(f)* beginner
anfänglich ['anfɛŋlɪç] *adj* initial
anfangs *adv* at first; **wie ich schon ~ erwähnte** as I mentioned at the beginning; **Anfangsbuchstabe** *m* initial *od* first letter; **Anfangsgehalt** *nt* starting salary; **Anfangsstadium** *nt* initial stages *pl*
anfassen ['anfasən] *vt* to handle; (*berühren*) to touch ▷ *vi* to lend a hand ▷ *vr* to feel
anfechtbar ['anfɛçtba:r] *adj* contestable
anfechten ['anfɛçtən] *unreg vt* to dispute; (*Meinung, Aussage*) to challenge; (*Urteil*) to appeal against; (*beunruhigen*) to trouble
anfeinden ['anfaɪndən] *vt* to treat with hostility
anfertigen ['anfɛrtɪgən] *vt* to make
anfeuchten ['anfɔʏçtən] *vt* to moisten
anfeuern ['anfɔʏərn] *vt* (*fig*) to spur on
anflehen ['anfle:ən] *vt* to implore
anfliegen ['anfli:gən] *unreg vt* to fly to ▷ *vi* to fly up
Anflug ['anflu:k] *m* (*Aviat*) approach; (*Spur*) trace
anfordern ['anfɔrdərn] *vt* to demand; (*Comm*) to requisition
Anforderung *f* (*+gen*) demand (for); (*Comm*) requisition
Anfrage ['anfra:gə] *f* inquiry; (*Parl*) question
anfragen ['anfra:gən] *vi* to inquire
anfreunden ['anfrɔʏndən] *vr* to make friends; **sich mit etw ~** (*fig*) to get to like sth
anfügen ['anfy:gən] *vt* to add; (*beifügen*) to enclose
anfühlen ['anfy:lən] *vt, vr* to feel
anführen ['anfy:rən] *vt* to lead; (*zitieren*) to quote; (*umg: betrügen*) to lead up the garden path
Anführer, in **(-s, -)** *m(f)* leader
Anführung *f* leadership; (*Zitat*) quotation
Anführungszeichen *pl* quotation marks *pl*, inverted commas *pl* (*Brit*)
Angabe ['anga:bə] *f* statement; (*Tech*) specification; (*umg: Prahlerei*) boasting; (*Sport*) service; **Angaben** *pl* (*Auskunft*) particulars *pl*; **ohne ~ von Gründen** without giving any reasons; **~n zur Person** (*form*) personal details *od* particulars
angeben ['ange:bən] *unreg vt* to give; (*anzeigen*) to inform on; (*bestimmen*) to set ▷ *vi* (*umg*) to boast; (*Sport*) to serve
Angeber, in **(-s, -)** (*umg*) *m(f)* show-off
Angeberei [ange:bə'raɪ] (*umg*) *f* showing off

angeblich ['ange:plıç] *adj* alleged
angeboren ['angəbo:rən] *adj (+dat)* inborn, innate (in); *(Med, fig)*: **~ (bei)** congenital (to)
Angebot ['angəbo:t] *nt* offer; *(Comm)*: **~ (an** *+dat***)** supply (of); **im ~** *(umg)* on special offer
angeboten ['angəbo:tən] *pp von* **anbieten**
Angebotspreis *m* offer price
angebracht ['angəbraxt] *adj* appropriate
angebrannt ['angəbrant] *adv*: **es riecht hier so ~** there's a smell of burning here
angebrochen ['angəbrɔxən] *adj (Packung, Flasche)* open(ed); **was machen wir mit dem ~en Abend?** *(umg)* what shall we do with the rest of the evening?
angebunden ['angəbʊndən] *adj*: **kurz ~ sein** *(umg)* to be abrupt *od* curt
angefangen *pp von* **anfangen**
angegeben *pp von* **angeben**
angegossen ['angəgɔsən] *adj*: **wie ~ sitzen** to fit like a glove
angegriffen ['angəgrıfən] *adj*: **er wirkt ~** he looks as if he's under a lot of strain
angehalten ['angəhaltən] *pp von* **anhalten** ▷ *adj*: **~ sein, etw zu tun** to be required *od* obliged to do sth
angehaucht ['angəhaʊxt] *adj*: **links/rechts ~ sein** to have left-/right-wing tendencies *od* leanings
angeheiratet ['angəhaıratət] *adj* related by marriage
angeheitert ['angəhaıtərt] *adj* tipsy
angehen ['ange:ən] *unreg vt* to concern; *(angreifen)* to attack; *(bitten)*: **jdn ~ (um)** to approach sb (for) ▷ *vi (Feuer)* to light; *(umg: beginnen)* to begin; **das geht ihn gar nichts an** that's none of his business; **gegen jdn ~** *(entgegentreten)* to fight sb; **gegen etw ~** *(entgegentreten)* to fight sth; *(Missstände, Zustände)* to take measures against sth
angehend *adj* prospective; *(Musiker, Künstler)* budding
angehören ['angəhø:rən] *vi +dat* to belong to
Angehörige, r *f(m)* relative
Angeklagte, r ['angəkla:ktə(r)] *f(m)* accused, defendant
angeknackst ['angəknakst] *(umg) adj (Mensch)* uptight; (: *Selbstbewusstsein*) weakened
angekommen ['angəkɔmən] *pp von* **ankommen**
Angel ['aŋəl] **(-, -n)** *f* fishing rod; *(Türangel)* hinge; **die Welt aus den ~n heben** *(fig)* to turn the world upside down
Angelegenheit ['angəle:gənhaıt] *f* affair, matter
angelernt ['angəlɛrnt] *adj (Arbeiter)* semi-skilled
Angelhaken *m* fish hook
angeln ['aŋəln] *vt* to catch ▷ *vi* to fish; **Angeln (-s)** *nt* angling, fishing
Angelpunkt *m* crucial *od* central point; *(Frage)* key *od* central issue
Angelrute *f* fishing rod
Angelsachse ['aŋəlzaksə] **(-n, -n)** *m* Anglo-Saxon
Angelsächsin ['aŋəlzɛksın] *f* Anglo-Saxon
angelsächsisch ['aŋəlzɛksıʃ] *adj* Anglo-Saxon
Angelschein *m* fishing permit
angemessen ['angəmɛsən] *adj* appropriate, suitable; **eine der Leistung ~e Bezahlung** payment commensurate with the input
angenehm ['angəne:m] *adj* pleasant; **~!** *(bei Vorstellung)* pleased to meet you; **das A~e mit dem Nützlichen verbinden** to combine business with pleasure
angenommen ['angənɔmən] *pp von* **annehmen** ▷ *adj* assumed; *(Kind)* adopted; **~, wir ...** assuming we ...
angepasst ['angəpast] *adj* conformist
angerufen ['angəru:fən] *pp von* **anrufen**
angesäuselt ['angəzɔʏzəlt] *adj* tipsy, merry
angeschlagen ['angəʃla:gən] *(umg) adj (Mensch, Aussehen, Nerven)* shattered; *(Gesundheit)* poor
angeschlossen ['angəʃlɔsən] *adj (+dat)* affiliated (to *od* with), associated (with)
angeschmiert ['angəʃmi:rt] *(umg) adj* in trouble; **der/die A~e sein** to have been had
angeschrieben ['angəʃri:bən] *(umg) adj*: **bei jdm gut/schlecht ~ sein** to be in sb's good/bad books
angesehen ['angəze:ən] *pp von* **ansehen** ▷ *adj* respected
Angesicht ['angəzıçt] *nt (geh)* face
angesichts ['angəzıçts] *präp +gen* in view of, considering
angespannt ['angəʃpant] *adj (Aufmerksamkeit)* close; *(Nerven, Lage)* tense, strained; *(Comm: Markt)* tight, overstretched; *(Arbeit)* hard
Angest. *abk* = **Angestellte(r)**
angestammt ['angəʃtamt] *adj (überkommen)* traditional; *(ererbt: Rechte)* hereditary; (: *Besitz*) inherited
Angestellte, r ['angəʃtɛltə(r)] *f(m)* employee; *(Büroangestellte)* white-collar worker
angestrengt ['angəʃtrɛŋt] *adv* as hard as one can
angetan ['angəta:n] *adj*: **von jdm/etw ~ sein** to be taken with sb/sth; **es jdm ~ haben** to appeal to sb
angetrunken ['angətrʊŋkən] *adj* inebriated
angewiesen ['angəvi:zən] *adj*: **auf jdn/etw ~ sein** to be dependent on sb/sth; **auf sich selbst ~ sein** to be left to one's own devices
angewöhnen ['angəvø:nən] *vt*: **jdm/sich etw ~** to accustom sb/become accustomed to sth
Angewohnheit ['angəvo:nhaıt] *f* habit
angewurzelt ['angəvʊrtsəlt] *adj*: **wie ~ dastehen** to be rooted to the spot
angiften ['angıftən] *(pej: umg) vt* to snap at
angleichen ['anglaıçən] *unreg vt, vr* to adjust
Angler ['aŋlər] **(-s, -)** *m* angler
angliedern ['angli:dərn] *vt*: **~ (an** *+akk***)** *(Verein, Partei)* to affiliate (to *od* with); *(Land)* to annex (to)
Anglist, in [aŋ'glıst(ın)] **(-en, -en)** *m(f)* English specialist; *(Student)* English student; *(Professor*

etc) English lecturer/professor
Angola [aŋ'go:la] (**-s**) *nt* Angola
angolanisch [aŋgo'la:nɪʃ] *adj* Angolan
angreifen ['angraɪfən] *unreg vt* to attack; (*anfassen*) to touch; (*Arbeit*) to tackle; (*beschädigen*) to damage
Angreifer, in (**-s, -**) *m(f)* attacker
angrenzen ['angrɛntsən] *vi*: **an etw** *akk* **~** to border on sth, adjoin sth
Angriff ['angrɪf] *m* attack; **etw in ~ nehmen** to make a start on sth
Angriffsfläche *f*: **jdm/etw eine ~ bieten** (*lit, fig*) to provide sb/sth with a target
angriffslustig *adj* aggressive
Angst [aŋst] (**-, ¨e**) *f* fear; **~ haben (vor** *+dat***)** to be afraid *od* scared (of); **~ um jdn/etw haben** to be worried about sb/sth; **jdm ~ einflößen** *od* **einjagen** to frighten sb; **jdm ~ machen** to scare sb; **nur keine ~!** don't be scared; **angst** *adj*: **jdm ist angst** sb is afraid *od* scared; **angstfrei** *adj* free of fear; **Angsthase** (*umg*) *m* chicken, scaredy-cat
ängstigen ['ɛŋstɪgən] *vt* to frighten ▷ *vr*: **sich ~ (vor** *+dat od* **um)** to worry (o.s.) (about)
ängstlich *adj* nervous; (*besorgt*) worried; (*schüchtern*) timid; **Ängstlichkeit** *f* nervousness
Angstschweiß *m*: **mir brach der ~ aus** I broke out in a cold sweat
angurten ['angʊrtən] *vt, vr* = **anschnallen**
Anh. *abk* (= *Anhang*) app.
anhaben ['anha:bən] *unreg vt* to have on; **er kann mir nichts ~** he can't hurt me
anhaften ['anhaftən] *vi* (*lit*): **~ (an** *+dat***)** to stick (to); (*fig*): **~** *+dat* to stick to, stay with
anhalten ['anhaltən] *unreg vt* to stop ▷ *vi* to stop; (*andauern*) to persist; (*werben*): **um die Hand eines Mädchens ~** to ask for a girl's hand in marriage; **(jdm) etw ~** to hold sth up (against sb); **jdn zur Arbeit/Höflichkeit ~** to get sb to work/teach sb to be polite
anhaltend *adj* persistent
Anhalter, in (**-s, -**) *m(f)* hitch-hiker; **per ~ fahren** to hitch-hike
Anhaltspunkt *m* clue
anhand [an'hant] *präp +gen* with; **~ eines Beispiels** by means of an example
Anhang ['anhaŋ] *m* appendix; (*Leute*) family; (*Anhängerschaft*) supporters *pl*
anhängen ['anhɛŋən] *unreg vt* to hang up; (*Wagen*) to couple up; (*Zusatz*) to add (on); (*Comput*) to append; **sich an jdn ~** to attach o.s. to sb; **jdm etw ~** (*umg: nachsagen, anlasten*) to blame sb for sth, blame sth on sb; (*: Verdacht, Schuld*) to pin sth on sb
Anhänger (**-s, -**) *m* supporter; (*Aut*) trailer; (*am Koffer*) tag; (*Schmuck*) pendant; **Anhängerschaft** *f* supporters *pl*
Anhängeschloss *nt* padlock
anhängig *adj* (*Jur*) sub judice; **etw ~ machen** to start legal proceedings over sth
anhänglich *adj* devoted; **Anhänglichkeit** *f* devotion
Anhängsel (**-s, -**) *nt* appendage
anhauen ['anhaʊən] (*umg*) *vt* (*ansprechen*): **jdn ~ (um)** to accost sb (for)
anhäufen ['anhɔʏfən] *vt* to accumulate, amass ▷ *vr* to accrue
Anhäufung ['anhɔʏfʊŋ] *f* accumulation
anheben ['anhe:bən] *unreg vt* to lift up; (*Preise*) to raise
anheimelnd ['anhaɪməlnt] *adj* comfortable, cosy
anheimstellen [an'haɪmʃtɛlən] *vt*: **jdm etw ~** to leave sth up to sb
anheizen ['anhaɪtsən] *vt* (*Ofen*) to light; (*fig: umg: Wirtschaft*) to stimulate; (*verschlimmern: Krise*) to aggravate
anheuern ['anhɔʏərn] *vt, vi* (*Naut, fig*) to sign on *od* up
Anhieb ['anhi:b] *m*: **auf ~** straight off, first go; **es klappte auf ~** it was an immediate success
anhimmeln ['anhɪməln] (*umg*) *vt* to idolize, worship
Anhöhe ['anhø:ə] *f* hill
anhören ['anhø:rən] *vt* to listen to; (*anmerken*) to hear ▷ *vr* to sound
Anhörung *f* hearing
Animierdame [ani'mi:rda:mə] *f* nightclub/bar hostess
animieren [ani'mi:rən] *vt* to encourage, urge on
Anis [a'ni:s] (**-es, -e**) *m* aniseed
Ank. *abk* (= *Ankunft*) arr.
ankämpfen ['ankɛmpfən] *vi*: **gegen etw ~** to fight (against) sth; (*gegen Wind, Strömung*) to battle against sth
Ankara ['aŋkara] (**-s**) *nt* Ankara
Ankauf ['ankaʊf] *m*: **~ und Verkauf von ...** we buy and sell ...; **ankaufen** *vt* to purchase, buy
Anker ['aŋkər] (**-s, -**) *m* anchor; **vor ~ gehen** to drop anchor
ankern *vt, vi* to anchor
Ankerplatz *m* anchorage
Anklage ['ankla:gə] *f* accusation; (*Jur*) charge; **gegen jdn ~ erheben** (*Jur*) to bring *od* prefer charges against sb; **Anklagebank** *f* dock
anklagen ['ankla:gən] *vt* to accuse; **jdn (eines Verbrechens) ~** (*Jur*) to charge sb (with a crime)
Anklagepunkt *m* charge
Ankläger, in ['anklɛ:gər(ɪn)] (**-s, -**) *m(f)* accuser
Anklageschrift *f* indictment
anklammern ['anklamərn] *vt* to clip, staple ▷ *vr*: **sich an etw** *akk od dat* **~** to cling to sth
Anklang ['anklaŋ] *m*: **bei jdm ~ finden** to meet with sb's approval
ankleben ['ankle:bən] *vt*: **„Plakate ~ verboten!"** "stick no bills"
Ankleidekabine *f* changing cubicle
ankleiden ['anklaɪdən] *vt, vr* to dress
anklingen ['anklɪŋən] *vi* (*angeschnitten werden*) to be touched (up)on; (*erinnern*): **~ an** *+akk* to be reminiscent of
anklopfen ['anklɔpfən] *vi* to knock
anknipsen ['anknɪpsən] *vt* to switch on; (*Schalter*) to flick

anknüpfen ['anknʏpfən] *vt* to fasten *od* tie on; (*Beziehungen*) to establish; (*Gespräch*) to start up ▷ *vi* (*anschließen*): **~ an** *+akk* to refer to
Anknüpfungspunkt *m* link
ankommen ['ankɔmən] *unreg vi* to arrive; (*näher kommen*) to approach; (*Anklang finden*): **bei jdm (gut) ~** to go down well with sb ▷ *vi unpers*: **er ließ es auf einen Streit/einen Versuch ~** he was prepared to argue about it/to give it a try; **es kommt darauf an** it depends; (*wichtig sein*) that is what matters; **es kommt auf ihn an** it depends on him; **es darauf ~ lassen** to let things take their course; **gegen jdn/etw ~** to cope with sb/sth; **damit kommst du bei ihm nicht an!** you won't get anywhere with him like that
ankreiden ['ankraɪdən] *vt* (*fig*): **jdm etw (dick** *od* **übel) ~** to hold sth against sb
ankreuzen ['ankrɔʏtsən] *vt* to mark with a cross
ankündigen ['ankʏndɪgən] *vt* to announce
Ankündigung *f* announcement
Ankunft ['ankʊnft] (**-, -künfte**) *f* arrival
Ankunftszeit *f* time of arrival
ankurbeln ['ankʊrbəln] *vt* (*Aut*) to crank; (*fig*) to boost
Anl. *abk* (= *Anlage*) enc(l).
anlachen ['anlaxən] *vt* to smile at; **sich** *dat* **jdn ~** (*umg*) to pick sb up
Anlage ['anla:gə] *f* disposition; (*Begabung*) talent; (*Park*) gardens *pl*; (*Beilage*) enclosure; (*Tech*) plant; (*Einrichtung*: *Mil, Elek*) installation(s *pl*); (*Sportanlage etc*) facilities *pl*; (*umg*: *Stereoanlage*) (stereo) system; (*Fin*) investment; (*Entwurf*) layout; **als ~** *od* **in der ~ erhalten Sie ...** please find enclosed ...; **Anlageberater, in** *m(f)* investment consultant; **Anlagekapital** *nt* fixed capital
Anlagenabschreibung *f* capital allowance
Anlagengeschäft *nt* investment deal; (*Branche*) investment banking
Anlagevermögen *nt* capital assets *pl*, fixed assets *pl*
anlangen ['anlaŋən] *vi* (*ankommen*) to arrive
Anlass ['anlas] (**-es, -lässe**) *m*: **~ (zu)** cause (for); (*Ereignis*) occasion; **aus ~** *+gen* on the occasion of; **~ zu etw geben** to give rise to sth; **beim geringsten/bei jedem ~** for the slightest reason/at every opportunity; **etw zum ~ nehmen** to take the opportunity of sth
anlassen *unreg vt* to leave on; (*Motor*) to start ▷ *vr* (*umg*) to start off
Anlasser (**-s, -**) *m* (*Aut*) starter
anlässlich ['anlɛslɪç] *präp +gen* on the occasion of
anlasten ['anlastən] *vt*: **jdm etw ~** to blame sb for sth
Anlauf ['anlaʊf] *m* run-up; (*fig*: *Versuch*) attempt, try
anlaufen *unreg vi* to begin; (*Film*) to be showing; (*Sport*) to run up; (*Fenster*) to mist up; (*Metall*) to tarnish ▷ *vt* to call at; **rot ~** to turn *od* go red; **gegen etw ~** to run into *od* up against sth; **angelaufen kommen** to come running up
Anlauf- *zW*: **Anlaufstelle** *f* place to go (with one's problems); **Anlaufzeit** *f* (*fig*) time to get going *od* started
anläuten ['anlɔʏtən] *vi* to ring
anlegen ['anle:gən] *vt* to put; (*anziehen*) to put on; (*gestalten*) to lay out; (*Kartei, Akte*) to start; (*Comput*: *Datei*) to create; (*Geld*) to invest ▷ *vi* to dock; (*Naut*) to berth; **etw an etw** *akk* **~** to put sth against *od* on sth; **ein Gewehr ~ (auf** *+akk***)** to aim a weapon (at); **es auf etw** *akk* **~** to be out for sth/to do sth; **strengere Maßstäbe ~ (bei)** to lay down *od* impose stricter standards (in); **sich mit jdm ~** (*umg*) to quarrel with sb
Anlegeplatz *m* landing place
Anleger, in (**-s, -**) *m(f)* (*Fin*) investor
Anlegestelle *f* landing place
anlehnen ['anle:nən] *vt* to lean; (*Tür*) to leave ajar; **(sich) an etw** *akk* **~** to lean on *od* against sth
Anlehnung *f* (*Imitation*): **in ~ an jdn/etw** following sb/sth
Anlehnungsbedürfnis *nt* need of loving care
anleiern ['anlaɪərn] (*umg*) *vt* to get going
Anleihe ['anlaɪə] (**-, -n**) *f* (*Fin*) loan; (*Wertpapier*) bond
anleiten ['anlaɪtən] *vt* to instruct
Anleitung *f* instructions *pl*
anlernen ['anlɛrnən] *vt* to teach, instruct
anlesen ['anle:zən] *unreg vt* (*aneignen*): **sich** *dat* **etw ~** to learn sth by reading
Anliegen ['anli:gən] (**-s, -**) *nt* matter; (*Wunsch*) wish
anliegen *unreg vi* (*Kleidung*) to cling
anliegend *adj* adjacent; (*beigefügt*) enclosed
Anlieger (**-s, -**) *m* resident; **~ frei** no thoroughfare – residents only
anlocken ['anlɔkən] *vt* to attract; (*Tiere*) to lure
anlügen ['anly:gən] *unreg vt* to lie to
Anm. *abk* (= *Anmerkung*) n.
anmachen ['anmaxən] *vt* to attach; (*Elektrisches*) to put on; (*Salat*) to dress; **jdn ~** (*umg*) to try and pick sb up
anmalen ['anma:lən] *vt* to paint ▷ *vr* (*pej*: *schminken*) to paint one's face *od* o.s.
Anmarsch ['anmarʃ] *m*: **im ~ sein** to be advancing; (*hum*) to be on the way; **im ~ sein auf** *+akk* to be advancing on
anmaßen ['anma:sən] *vt*: **sich** *dat* **etw ~** to lay claim to sth
anmaßend *adj* arrogant
Anmaßung *f* presumption
Anmeldeformular ['anmɛldəfɔrmʊla:r] *nt* registration form
anmelden *vt* to announce; (*geltend machen*: *Recht, Ansprüche, zu Steuerzwecken*) to declare; (*Comput*) to log on ▷ *vr* (*sich ankündigen*) to make an appointment; (*polizeilich, für Kurs etc*) to register; **ein Gespräch nach Deutschland ~** (*Tel*) to book a call to Germany
Anmeldung *f* announcement; appointment; registration; **nur nach vorheriger ~** by appointment only

anmerken ['anmɛrkən] *vt* to observe; (*anstreichen*) to mark; **jdm seine Verlegenheit** *etc* ~ to notice sb's embarrassment *etc*; **sich** *dat* **nichts ~ lassen** not to give anything away
Anmerkung *f* note
Anmut ['anmu:t] (**-**) *f* grace
anmuten *vt* (*geh*): **jdn** ~ to appear *od* seem to sb
anmutig *adj* charming
annähen ['annɛ:ən] *vt* to sew on
annähern ['annɛ:ərn] *vr* to get closer
annähernd *adj* approximate; **nicht ~ so viel** not nearly as much
Annäherung *f* approach
Annäherungsversuch *m* advances *pl*
Annahme ['anna:mə] (**-, -n**) *f* acceptance; (*Vermutung*) assumption; **Annahmestelle** *f* counter; (*für Reparaturen*) reception; **Annahmeverweigerung** *f* refusal
annehmbar ['anne:mba:r] *adj* acceptable
annehmen *unreg vt* to accept; (*Namen*) to take; (*Kind*) to adopt; (*vermuten*) to suppose, assume ▷ *vr* (*+gen*) to take care (of); **jdn an Kindes statt** ~ to adopt sb; **angenommen, das ist so** assuming that is so
Annehmlichkeit *f* comfort
annektieren [anɛk'ti:rən] *vt* to annex
anno ['ano] *adj*: **von ~ dazumal** (*umg*) from the year dot
Annonce [a'nõ:sə] (**-, -n**) *f* advertisement
annoncieren [anõ'si:rən] *vt, vi* to advertise
annullieren [anʊ'li:rən] *vt* to annul
Anode [a'no:də] (**-, -n**) *f* anode
anöden ['an|ø:dən] (*umg*) *vt* to bore stiff
anomal [ano'ma:l] *adj* (*regelwidrig*) unusual, abnormal; (*nicht normal*) strange, odd
anonym [ano'ny:m] *adj* anonymous
Anorak ['anorak] (**-s, -s**) *m* anorak
anordnen ['an|ɔrdnən] *vt* to arrange; (*befehlen*) to order
Anordnung *f* arrangement; order; **~en treffen** to give orders
anorganisch ['an|ɔrga:nɪʃ] *adj* (*Chem*) inorganic
anpacken ['anpakən] *vt* to grasp; (*fig*) to tackle; **mit** ~ to lend a hand
anpassen ['anpasən] *vt* (*Kleidung*) to fit; (*fig*) to adapt ▷ *vr* to adapt
Anpassung *f* fitting; adaptation
Anpassungsdruck *m* pressure to conform (*to society*)
anpassungsfähig *adj* adaptable
anpeilen ['anpaɪlən] *vt* (*mit Radar, Funk etc*) to take a bearing on; **etw** ~ (*fig: umg*) to have one's sights on sth
Anpfiff ['anpfɪf] *m* (*Sport*) (starting) whistle; (*Spielbeginn: Fußball etc*) kick-off; **einen ~ bekommen** (*umg*) to get a rocket (*Brit*)
anpöbeln ['anpø:bəln] *vt* to abuse; (*umg*) to pester
Anprall ['anpral] *m*: **~ gegen** *od* **an** *+akk* impact on *od* against
anprangern ['anpraŋərn] *vt* to denounce
anpreisen ['anpraɪzən] *unreg vt* to extol; **sich ~ (als)** to sell o.s. (as); **etw** ~ to extol (the virtues of) sth; **seine Waren ~** to cry one's wares
Anprobe ['anpro:bə] *f* trying on
anprobieren ['anprobi:rən] *vt* to try on
anpumpen ['anpʊmpən] (*umg*) *vt* to borrow from
anquatschen ['ankvatʃən] (*umg*) *vt* to speak to; (*: Mädchen*) to try to pick up
Anrainer ['anraɪnər] (**-s, -**) *m* neighbour (*Brit*), neighbor (*US*)
anranzen ['anrantsən] (*umg*) *vt*: **jdn ~** to tick sb off
anraten ['anra:tən] *unreg vt* to recommend; **auf A~ des Arztes** *etc* on the doctor's *etc* advice *od* recommendation
anrechnen ['anrɛçnən] *vt* to charge; (*fig*) to count; **jdm etw hoch ~** to think highly of sb for sth
Anrecht ['anrɛçt] *nt*: **~ auf** *+akk* right (to); **ein ~ auf etw haben** to be entitled to sth, have a right to sth
Anrede ['anre:də] *f* form of address
anreden *vt* to address
anregen ['anre:gən] *vt* to stimulate; **angeregte Unterhaltung** lively discussion
anregend *adj* stimulating
Anregung *f* stimulation; (*Vorschlag*) suggestion
anreichern ['anraɪçərn] *vt* to enrich
Anreise ['anraɪzə] *f* journey there/here
anreisen *vi* to arrive
anreißen ['anraɪsən] *unreg vt* (*kurz zur Sprache bringen*) to touch on
Anreiz ['anraɪts] *m* incentive
anrempeln ['anrɛmpəln] *vt* (*anstoßen*) to bump into; (*absichtlich*) to jostle
anrennen ['anrɛnən] *unreg vi*: **gegen etw ~** (*gegen Wind etc*) to run against sth; (*Mil*) to storm sth
Anrichte ['anrɪçtə] (**-, -n**) *f* sideboard
anrichten *vt* to serve up; **Unheil ~** to make mischief; **da hast du aber etwas angerichtet!** (*umg: verursacht*) you've started something there all right!; (*: angestellt*) you've really made a mess there!
anrüchig ['anrʏçɪç] *adj* dubious
anrücken ['anrʏkən] *vi* to approach; (*Mil*) to advance
Anruf ['anru:f] *m* call; **Anrufbeantworter** *m* (telephone) answering machine, answerphone
anrufen *unreg vt* to call out to; (*bitten*) to call on; (*Tel*) to ring up, phone, call
anrühren ['anry:rən] *vt* to touch; (*mischen*) to mix
ans [ans] = **an das**
Ansage ['anza:gə] *f* announcement
ansagen *vt* to announce ▷ *vr* to say one will come
Ansager, in (**-s, -**) *m(f)* announcer
ansammeln ['anzaməln] *vt* to collect ▷ *vr* to accumulate; (*fig: Wut, Druck*) to build up
Ansammlung *f* collection; (*Leute*) crowd
ansässig ['anzɛsɪç] *adj* resident

Ansatz ['anzats] *m* start; (*Haaransatz*) hairline; (*Halsansatz*) base; (*Verlängerungsstück*) extension; (*Veranschlagung*) estimate; **die ersten Ansätze zu etw** the beginnings of sth; **Ansatzpunkt** *m* starting point; **Ansatzstück** *nt* (*Tech*) attachment
anschaffen ['anʃafən] *vt* to buy, purchase ▷ *vi*: **~ gehen** (*umg*: *durch Prostitution*) to be on the game; **sich** *dat* **Kinder ~** (*umg*) to have children
Anschaffung *f* purchase
anschalten ['anʃaltən] *vt* to switch on
anschauen ['anʃaʊən] *vt* to look at
anschaulich *adj* illustrative
Anschauung *f* (*Meinung*) view; **aus eigener ~** from one's own experience
Anschauungsmaterial *nt* illustrative material
Anschein ['anʃaɪn] *m* appearance; **allem ~ nach** to all appearances; **den ~ haben** to seem, appear
anscheinend *adj* apparent
anschieben ['anʃi:bən] *unreg vt* (*Fahrzeug*) to push
Anschiss ['anʃɪs] (*umg*) *m*: **einen ~ bekommen** to get a telling-off *od* ticking-off (*bes Brit*)
Anschlag ['anʃla:k] *m* notice; (*Attentat*) attack; (*Comm*) estimate; (*auf Klavier*) touch; (*auf Schreibmaschine*) keystroke; **einem ~ zum Opfer fallen** to be assassinated; **ein Gewehr im ~ haben** (*Mil*) to have a rifle at the ready; **Anschlagbrett** *nt* notice board (*Brit*), bulletin board (*US*)
anschlagen ['anʃla:gən] *unreg vt* to put up; (*beschädigen*) to chip; (*Akkord*) to strike; (*Kosten*) to estimate ▷ *vi* to hit; (*wirken*) to have an effect; (*Glocke*) to ring; (*Hund*) to bark; **einen anderen Ton ~** (*fig*) to change one's tune; **an etw** *akk* **~** to hit against sth
anschlagfrei *adj*: **~er Drucker** non-impact printer
Anschlagzettel *m* notice
anschleppen ['anʃlɛpən] (*umg*) *vt* (*unerwünscht mitbringen*) to bring along
anschließen ['anʃli:sən] *unreg vt* to connect up; (*Sender*) to link up; (*in Steckdose*) to plug in; (*fig*: *hinzufügen*) to add ▷ *vi*: **an etw** *akk* **~** (*zeitlich*) to follow sth ▷ *vr*: **sich jdm/etw ~** to join sb/sth; (*beipflichten*) to agree with sb/sth; **sich an etw** *akk* **~** (*angrenzen*) to adjoin sth
anschließend *adj* adjacent; (*zeitlich*) subsequent ▷ *adv* afterwards; **~ an** *+akk* following
Anschluss ['anʃlʊs] *m* (*Elek, Eisenb, Tel*) connection; (*weiterer Apparat*) extension; (*von Wasser etc*) supply; (*Comput*) port; **im ~ an** *+akk* following; **~ finden** to make friends; **~ bekommen** to get through; **kein ~ unter dieser Nummer** number unobtainable; **den ~ verpassen** (*Eisenb etc*) to miss one's connection; (*fig*) to miss the boat
anschmiegen ['anʃmi:gən] *vr*: **sich an jdn/etw ~** (*Kind, Hund*) to snuggle *od* nestle up to *od* against sb/sth
anschmiegsam ['anʃmi:kza:m] *adj* affectionate
anschmieren ['anʃmi:rən] *vt* to smear; (*umg*) to take in
anschnallen ['anʃnalən] *vt* to buckle on ▷ *vr* to fasten one's seat belt
Anschnallpflicht *f*: **für Kinder besteht ~** children must wear seat belts
anschnauzen ['anʃnaʊtsən] (*umg*) *vt* to yell at
anschneiden ['anʃnaɪdən] *unreg vt* to cut into; (*Thema*) to introduce
Anschnitt ['anʃnɪt] *m* first slice
anschreiben ['anʃraɪbən] *unreg vt* to write (up); (*Comm*) to charge up; (*benachrichtigen*) to write to; **bei jdm gut/schlecht angeschrieben sein** to be well/badly thought of by sb, be in sb's good/bad books
anschreien ['anʃraɪən] *unreg vt* to shout at
Anschrift ['anʃrɪft] *f* address
Anschriftenliste *f* mailing list
Anschub *m* (*bei Firmengründung*) start-up (funds *pl*)
Anschuldigung ['anʃʊldɪgʊŋ] *f* accusation
anschwärzen ['anʃvɛrtsən] *vt* (*fig*: *umg*): **jdn ~ (bei)** to blacken sb's name (with)
anschwellen ['anʃvɛlən] *unreg vi* to swell (up)
anschwemmen ['anʃvɛmən] *vt* to wash ashore
anschwindeln ['anʃvɪndəln] (*umg*) *vt* to lie to
ansehen ['anze:ən] *unreg vt* to look at; **jdm etw ~** to see sth (from sb's face); **jdn/etw als etw ~** to look on sb/sth as sth; **~ für** to consider; **(sich** *dat***) etw ~** to (have a) look at sth; (*Fernsehsendung*) to watch sth; (*Film, Stück, Sportveranstaltung*) to see sth; **etw (mit) ~** to watch sth, see sth happening
Ansehen (-s) *nt* respect; (*Ruf*) reputation; **ohne ~ der Person** (*Jur*) without respect of person
ansehnlich ['anze:nlɪç] *adj* fine-looking; (*beträchtlich*) considerable
anseilen ['anzaɪlən] *vt*: **jdn/sich ~** to rope sb/o.s. up
an sein ['anzaɪn] *siehe* **an**
ansetzen ['anzɛtsən] *vt* (*festlegen*) to fix; (*entwickeln*) to develop; (*Fett*) to put on; (*Blätter*) to grow; (*zubereiten*) to prepare ▷ *vi* (*anfangen*) to start, begin; (*Entwicklung*) to set in; (*dick werden*) to put on weight ▷ *vr* (*Rost etc*) to start to develop; **~ an** *+akk* (*anfügen*) to fit on to; (*anlegen, an Mund etc*) to put to; **zu etw ~** to prepare to do sth; **jdn/etw auf jdn/etw ~** to set sb/sth on sb/sth
Ansicht ['anzɪçt] *f* (*Anblick*) sight; (*Meinung*) view, opinion; **zur ~** on approval; **meiner ~ nach** in my opinion
Ansichtskarte *f* picture postcard
Ansichtssache *f* matter of opinion
ansiedeln ['anzi:dəln] *vt* to settle; (*Tierart*) to introduce ▷ *vr* to settle; (*Industrie etc*) to get established
ansonsten [an'zɔnstən] *adv* otherwise
anspannen ['anʃpanən] *vt* to harness; (*Muskel*) to strain

Anspannung *f* strain
Anspiel ['anʃpi:l] *nt* (*Sport*) start of play
anspielen *vt* (*Sport*) to play the ball *etc* to ▷ *vi*: **auf etw** *akk* **~** to refer *od* allude to sth
Anspielung *f*: **~ (auf** *+akk***)** reference (to), allusion (to)
Ansporn ['anʃpɔrn] (**-(e)s**) *m* incentive
Ansprache ['anʃpra:xə] *f* (*Rede*) address
ansprechen ['anʃprɛçən] *unreg vt* to speak to; (*bitten, gefallen*) to appeal to; (*Eindruck machen auf*) to make an impression on ▷ *vi*: **~ auf** *+akk* (*Patient*) to respond (to); (*Messgerät*) to react (to); **jdn auf etw** *akk* **(hin) ~** to ask sb about sth
ansprechend *adj* attractive
Ansprechpartner *m* contact
anspringen ['anʃprɪŋən] *unreg vi* (*Aut*) to start ▷ *vt* (*anfallen*) to jump; (*Raubtier*) to pounce (up)on; (*Hund: hochspringen*) to jump up at
Anspruch ['anʃprʊx] (**-s, -sprüche**) *m* (*Recht*): **~ (auf** *+akk***)** claim (to); **den Ansprüchen gerecht werden** to meet the requirements; **hohe Ansprüche stellen/haben** to demand/ expect a lot; **jdn/etw in ~ nehmen** to occupy sb/take up sth
anspruchslos *adj* undemanding
anspruchsvoll *adj* demanding; (*Comm*) upmarket
anspucken ['anʃpʊkən] *vt* to spit at
anstacheln ['anʃtaxəln] *vt* to spur on
Anstalt ['anʃtalt] (**-, -en**) *f* institution; **~en machen, etw zu tun** to prepare to do sth
Anstand ['anʃtant] *m* decency; (*Manieren*) (good) manners *pl*
anständig ['anʃtɛndɪç] *adj* decent; (*umg*) proper; (*groß*) considerable; **Anständigkeit** *f* propriety, decency
anstandshalber ['anʃtantshalbər] *adv* out of politeness
anstandslos *adv* without any ado
anstarren ['anʃtarən] *vt* to stare at
anstatt [an'ʃtat] *präp +gen* instead of ▷ *konj*: **~ etw zu tun** instead of doing sth
anstauen ['anʃtaʊən] *vr* to accumulate; (*Blut in Adern etc*) to congest; (*fig: Gefühle*) to build up
anstechen ['anʃtɛçən] *unreg vt* to prick; (*Fass*) to tap
anstecken ['anʃtɛkən] *vt* to pin on; (*Ring*) to put *od* slip on; (*Med*) to infect; (*Pfeife*) to light; (*Haus*) to set fire to ▷ *vr*: **ich habe mich bei ihm angesteckt** I caught it from him ▷ *vi* (*fig*) to be infectious
ansteckend *adj* infectious
Ansteckung *f* infection
anstehen ['anʃte:ən] *unreg vi* to queue (up) (*Brit*), line up (*US*); (*Verhandlungspunkt*) to be on the agenda
ansteigen ['anʃtaɪgən] *unreg vi* to rise; (*Straße*) to climb
anstelle, an Stelle [an'ʃtɛlə] *präp +gen* in place of
anstellen ['anʃtɛlən] *vt* (*einschalten*) to turn on; (*Arbeit geben*) to employ; (*umg: Unfug treiben*) to get up to; (*: machen*) to do ▷ *vr* to queue (up) (*Brit*), line up (*US*); (*umg*) to act; (*: sich zieren*) to make a fuss, act up
Anstellung *f* employment; (*Posten*) post, position; **~ auf Lebenszeit** tenure
ansteuern ['anʃtɔyərn] *vt* to make *od* steer *od* head for
Anstich ['anʃtɪç] *m* (*von Fass*) tapping, broaching
Anstieg ['anʃti:k] (**-(e)s, -e**) *m* climb; (*fig: von Preisen etc*) increase
anstiften ['anʃtɪftən] *vt* (*Unglück*) to cause; **jdn zu etw ~** to put sb up to sth
Anstifter (**-s, -**) *m* instigator
Anstiftung *f* (*von Tat*) instigation; (*von Mensch*): **~ (zu)** incitement (to)
anstimmen ['anʃtɪmən] *vt* (*Lied*) to strike up (with); (*Geschrei*) to set up ▷ *vi* to strike up
Anstoß ['anʃto:s] *m* impetus; (*Ärgernis*) offence (*Brit*), offense (*US*); (*Sport*) kick-off; **der erste ~** the initiative; **ein Stein des ~es** (*umstrittene Sache*) a bone of contention; **~ nehmen an** *+dat* to take offence at
anstoßen *unreg vt* to push; (*mit Fuß*) to kick ▷ *vi* to knock, bump; (*mit der Zunge*) to lisp; (*mit Gläsern*) to drink a toast; **an etw** *akk* **~** (*angrenzen*) to adjoin sth; **~ auf** *+akk* to drink (a toast) to
anstößig ['anʃtø:sɪç] *adj* offensive, indecent; **Anstößigkeit** *f* indecency, offensiveness
anstrahlen ['anʃtra:lən] *vt* to floodlight; (*strahlend ansehen*) to beam at
anstreben ['anʃtre:bən] *vt* to strive for
anstreichen ['anʃtraɪçən] *unreg vt* to paint; **(jdm) etw als Fehler ~** to mark sth wrong
Anstreicher, in (**-s, -**) *m(f)* painter
anstrengen ['anʃtrɛŋən] *vt* to strain; (*strapazieren: jdn*) to tire out; (*: Patienten*) to fatigue; (*Jur*) to bring ▷ *vr* to make an effort; **eine Klage ~ (gegen)** (*Jur*) to initiate *od* institute proceedings (against)
anstrengend *adj* tiring
Anstrengung *f* effort
Anstrich ['anʃtrɪç] *m* coat of paint
Ansturm ['anʃtʊrm] *m* rush; (*Mil*) attack
Ansuchen ['anzu:xən] (**-s, -**) *nt* request
ansuchen ['anzu:xən] *vi*: **um etw ~** to apply for sth
Antagonismus [antago'nɪsmʊs] *m* antagonism
antanzen ['antantsən] (*umg*) *vi* to turn *od* show up
Antarktis [ant'|arktɪs] (**-**) *f* Antarctic
antarktisch *adj* Antarctic
antasten ['antastən] *vt* to touch; (*Recht*) to infringe upon; (*Ehre*) to question
Anteil ['antaɪl] (**-s, -e**) *m* share; (*Mitgefühl*) sympathy; **~ nehmen an** *+dat* to share in; (*sich interessieren*) to take an interest in; **~ an etw** *dat* **haben** (*beitragen*) to contribute to sth; (*teilnehmen*) to take part in sth
anteilig *adj* proportionate, proportional
anteilmäßig *adj* pro rata
Anteilnahme (**-**) *f* sympathy

Antenne [an'tɛnə] (**-, -n**) *f* aerial; (*Zool*) antenna; **eine/keine ~ für etw haben** (*fig: umg*) to have a/no feeling for sth
Anthrazit [antra'tsi:t] (**-s, -e**) *m* anthracite
Anthropologie [antropolo'gi:] (**-**) *f* anthropology
Anti- ['anti] *in zW* anti; **Antialkoholiker** *m* teetotaller; **antiautoritär** *adj* anti-authoritarian; **Antibabypille** *f* (contraceptive) pill; **Antibiotikum** (**-s, -ka**) *nt* antibiotic; **Antiheld** *m* antihero
antik [an'ti:k] *adj* antique
Antike (**-, -n**) *f* (*Zeitalter*) ancient world; (*Kunstgegenstand*) antique
Antikörper *m* antibody
Antillen [an'tɪlən] *pl* Antilles *pl*
Antilope [anti'lo:pə] (**-, -n**) *f* antelope
Antipathie [antipa'ti:] *f* antipathy
antippen ['antɪpən] *vt* to tap; (*Pedal, Bremse*) to touch; (*fig: Thema*) to touch on
Antiquariat [antikvari'a:t] (**-(e)s, -e**) *nt* secondhand bookshop; **modernes ~** remainder bookshop/department
antiquiert [anti'kvi:rt] (*pej*) *adj* antiquated
Antiquitäten [antikvi'tɛ:tən] *pl* antiques *pl*; **Antiquitätenhandel** *m* antique business; **Antiquitätenhändler, in** *m(f)* antique dealer
Antisemitismus [antizemi'tɪsmʊs] *m* anti-semitism
antiseptisch [anti'zɛptɪʃ] *adj* antiseptic
Antlitz ['antlɪts] (**-es, -e**) *nt* (*liter*) countenance (*liter*), face
antörnen ['antœrnən] (*umg*) *vt* (*Drogen, Musik*) to turn on ▷ *vi*: **... törnt an** ... turns you on
Antrag ['antra:k] (**-(e)s, -träge**) *m* proposal; (*Parl*) motion; (*Gesuch*) application; **einen ~ auf etw** *akk* **stellen** to make an application for sth; (*Jur etc*) to file a petition/claim for sth
Antragsformular *nt* application form
Antragsgegner, in *m(f)* (*Jur*) respondent
Antragsteller, in (**-s, -**) *m(f)* claimant; (*für Kredit etc*) applicant
antreffen ['antrɛfən] *unreg vt* to meet
antreiben ['antraɪbən] *unreg vt* to drive on; (*Motor*) to drive; (*anschwemmen*) to wash up ▷ *vi* to be washed up; **jdn zur Eile/Arbeit ~** to urge sb to hurry up/to work
Antreiber (**-s, -**) (*pej*) *m* slave-driver (*pej*)
antreten ['antre:tən] *unreg vt* (*Amt*) to take up; (*Erbschaft*) to come into; (*Beweis*) to offer; (*Reise*) to start, begin ▷ *vi* (*Mil*) to fall in; (*Sport*) to line up; (*zum Dienst*) to report; **gegen jdn ~** to play/fight against sb
Antrieb ['antri:p] *m* (*lit, fig*) drive; **aus eigenem ~** of one's own accord
Antriebskraft *f* (*Tech*) power
antrinken ['antrɪŋkən] *unreg vt* (*Flasche, Glas*) to start to drink from; **sich** *dat* **Mut/einen Rausch ~** to give o.s. Dutch courage/get drunk; **angetrunken sein** to be tipsy
Antritt ['antrɪt] *m* beginning, commencement; (*eines Amts*) taking up
antun ['antu:n] *unreg vt*: **jdm etw ~** to do sth to sb; **sich** *dat* **Zwang ~** to force o.s.
anturnen ['antœrnən] (*umg*) *vt* = **antörnen**
Antwerpen [ant'vɛrpən] (**-s**) *nt* Antwerp
Antwort ['antvɔrt] (**-, -en**) *f* answer, reply; **um ~ wird gebeten** RSVP
antworten *vi* to answer, reply
anvertrauen ['anfɛrtraʊən] *vt*: **jdm etw ~** to entrust sb with sth; **sich jdm ~** to confide in sb
anvisieren ['anvizi:rən] *vt* (*fig*) to set one's sights on
anwachsen ['anvaksən] *unreg vi* to grow; (*Pflanze*) to take root
Anwalt ['anvalt] (**-(e)s, -wälte**) *m* solicitor; lawyer; (*fig: Fürsprecher*) advocate; (*: der Armen etc*) champion
Anwältin ['anvɛltɪn] *f siehe* **Anwalt**
Anwalts- *zW*: **Anwaltshonorar** *nt* retainer, retaining fee; **Anwaltskammer** *f professional association of lawyers*, ≈ Law Society (*Brit*); **Anwaltskosten** *pl* legal expenses *pl*
Anwandlung ['anvandlʊŋ] *f* caprice; **eine ~ von etw** a fit of sth
anwärmen ['anvɛrmən] *vt* to warm up
Anwärter, in ['anvɛrtər(ɪn)] *m(f)* candidate
anweisen ['anvaɪzən] *unreg vt* to instruct; (*zuteilen*) to assign
Anweisung *f* instruction; (*Comm*) remittance; (*Postanweisung, Zahlungsanweisung*) money order
anwendbar ['anvɛntba:r] *adj* practicable, applicable
anwenden ['anvɛndən] *unreg vt* to use, employ; (*Gesetz, Regel*) to apply
Anwenderprogramm *nt* (*Comput*) application program
Anwendersoftware *f* application package
Anwendung *f* use; application
anwerfen ['anvɛrfən] *unreg vt* (*Tech*) to start up
anwesend ['anve:zənt] *adj* present; **die A~en** those present
Anwesenheit *f* presence
Anwesenheitsliste *f* attendance register
anwidern ['anvi:dərn] *vt* to disgust
Anwohner, in ['anvo:nər(ɪn)] (**-s, -**) *m(f)* resident
Anwuchs ['anvu:ks] *m* growth
Anzahl ['antsa:l] *f*: **~ (an** *+dat***)** number (of)
anzahlen *vt* to pay on account
Anzahlung *f* deposit, payment on account
anzapfen ['antsapfən] *vt* to tap
Anzeichen ['antsaɪçən] *nt* sign, indication; **alle ~ deuten darauf hin, dass ...** all the signs are that ...
Anzeige ['antsaɪgə] (**-, -n**) *f* (*Zeitungsanzeige*) announcement; (*Werbung*) advertisement; (*Comput*) display; (*bei Polizei*) report; **gegen jdn ~ erstatten** to report sb (to the police)
anzeigen *vt* (*zu erkennen geben*) to show; (*bekannt geben*) to announce; (*bei Polizei*) to report
Anzeigenteil *m* advertisements *pl*
anzeigepflichtig *adj* notifiable
Anzeiger *m* indicator

anzetteln ['antsɛtəln] *(umg) vt* to instigate
anziehen ['antsi:ən] *unreg vt* to attract; *(Kleidung)* to put on; *(Mensch)* to dress; *(Schraube, Seil)* to pull tight; *(Knie)* to draw up; *(Feuchtigkeit)* to absorb ▷ *vr* to get dressed
anziehend *adj* attractive
Anziehung *f (Reiz)* attraction
Anziehungskraft *f* power of attraction; *(Phys)* force of gravitation
Anzug ['antsu:k] *m* suit; **im ~ sein** to be approaching
anzüglich ['antsy:klɪç] *adj* personal; *(anstößig)* offensive; **Anzüglichkeit** *f* offensiveness; *(Bemerkung)* personal remark
anzünden ['antsʏndən] *vt* to light
Anzünder *m* lighter
anzweifeln ['antsvaɪfəln] *vt* to doubt
AOK (-) *f abk (= Allgemeine Ortskrankenkasse) siehe* **Ortskrankenkasse**; *see culture note*

AOK

The *AOK* (Allgemeine Ortskrankenkasse) forms part of a compulsory medical insurance scheme for people who are not members of a private scheme. In every large town there is an independently run AOK office. Foreign nationals may also receive help from these offices if they fall ill while in Germany.

APA *f abk (= Austria Presse-Agentur) Austrian news agency*
apart [a'part] *adj* distinctive
Apartheid [a'pa:rthaɪt] *f* apartheid
Apartment [a'partmənt] (**-s, -s**) *nt* flat *(Brit)*, apartment *(bes US)*
Apathie [apa'ti:] *f* apathy
apathisch [a'pa:tɪʃ] *adj* apathetic
Apenninen [apɛ'ni:nən] *pl* Apennines *pl*
Apfel ['apfəl] (**-s, ¨**) *m* apple; **in den sauren ~ beißen** *(fig: umg)* to swallow the bitter pill; **etw für einen ~ und ein Ei kaufen** *(umg)* to buy sth dirt cheap *od* for a song; **Apfelmus** *nt* apple purée; *(als Beilage)* apple sauce; **Apfelsaft** *m* apple juice
Apfelsine [apfəl'zi:nə] (**-, -n**) *f* orange
Apfeltasche *f* apple turnover
Apfelwein *m* strong cider
apl. *abk* = **außerplanmäßig**
APO, Apo ['a:po] (-) *f abk (= außerparlamentarische Opposition) extraparliamentary opposition; see culture note*

APO

The *APO* was an extraparliamentary opposition group formed in West Germany in the late 1960's by those who felt that their interests were not being sufficiently represented in parliament. It was disbanded in the 1970's. Some of its members then formed the RAF, a terrorist organisation. Some formed the Green Party *(die Grünen)*.

apolitisch ['apoli:tɪʃ] *adj* non-political, apolitical
Apostel [a'pɔstəl] (**-s, -**) *m* apostle
Apostroph [apo'stro:f] (**-s, -e**) *m* apostrophe
Apotheke [apo'te:kə] (**-, -n**) *f* chemist's (shop) *(Brit)*, drugstore *(US)*; *see culture note*

APOTHEKE

The *Apotheke* is a pharmacy where prescribed drugs and other medicines only available on prescription are sold. It also sells toiletries. The pharmacist is qualified to give advice on medicines and treatment.

Apotheker, in (**-s, -**) *m(f)* pharmacist, (dispensing) chemist *(Brit)*, druggist *(US)*
Appalachen [apa'laxən] *pl* Appalachian Mountains *pl*
Apparat [apa'ra:t] (**-(e)s, -e**) *m* piece of apparatus; *(Fotoapparat)* camera; *(Telefon)* telephone; *(Rundf, TV)* set; *(Verwaltungsapparat, Parteiapparat)* machinery, apparatus; **am ~** on the phone; *(als Antwort)* speaking; **am ~ bleiben** to hold the line
Apparatur [apara'tu:r] *f* apparatus
Appartement [apart(ə)'mã:] (**-s, -s**) *nt* flat *(Brit)*, apartment *(bes US)*
Appell [a'pɛl] (**-s, -e**) *m (Mil)* muster, parade; *(fig)* appeal
appellieren [apɛ'li:rən] *vi*: **~ (an** *+akk***)** to appeal (to)
Appetit [ape'ti:t] (**-(e)s, -e**) *m* appetite; **guten ~!** enjoy your meal; **appetitlich** *adj* appetizing; **Appetitlosigkeit** *f* lack of appetite
Applaus [ap'laʊs] (**-es, -e**) *m* applause
Appretur [apre'tu:r] *f* finish; *(Wasserundurchlässigkeit)* waterproofing
approbiert [apro'bi:rt] *adj (Arzt)* registered, certified
Apr. *abk (= April)* Apr.
Aprikose [apri'ko:zə] (**-, -n**) *f* apricot
April [a'prɪl] (**-(s), -e**) *(pl selten) m* April; **jdn in den ~ schicken** to make an April fool of sb; *siehe auch* **September**; **Aprilwetter** *nt* April showers *pl*
apropos [apro'po:] *adv* by the way, that reminds me
Aquaplaning [akva'pla:nɪŋ] (**-(s)**) *nt* aquaplaning
Aquarell [akva'rɛl] (**-s, -e**) *nt* watercolour *(Brit)*, watercolor *(US)*
Aquarium [a'kva:riʊm] *nt* aquarium
Äquator [ɛ'kva:tɔr] (**-s**) *m* equator
Äquivalent [ɛkviva'lɛnt] (**-(e)s, -e**) *nt* equivalent
Ar [a:r] (**-s, -e**) *nt od m (Maß)* are ($100\ m^2$)
Ära ['ɛ:ra] (**-, Ären**) *f* era
Araber, in ['a:rabər(ɪn)] (**-s, -**) *m(f)* Arab
Arabien [a'ra:biən] (**-s**) *nt* Arabia

arabisch *adj* Arab; (*Arabien betreffend*) Arabian; (*Sprache*) Arabic; **A~er Golf** Arabian Gulf; **A~es Meer** Arabian Sea; **A~e Wüste** Arabian Desert

Arbeit ['arbaɪt] (**-, -en**) *f* work; (*Stelle*) job; (*Erzeugnis*) piece of work; (*wissenschaftliche*) dissertation; (*Klassenarbeit*) test; **Tag der ~** Labour (*Brit*) *od* Labor (*US*) Day; **sich an die ~ machen, an die ~ gehen** to get down to work, start working; **jdm ~ machen** (*Mühe*) to put sb to trouble; **das war eine ~** that was a hard job

arbeiten *vi* to work ▷ *vt* to make ▷ *vr*: **sich nach oben/an die Spitze ~** (*fig*) to work one's way up/to the top

Arbeiter, in (**-s, -**) *m(f)* worker; (*ungelernt*) labourer (*Brit*), laborer (*US*)

Arbeiter- *zW*: **Arbeiterfamilie** *f* working-class family; **Arbeiterkammer** *f* (*Österr*) Chambers of Labour; **Arbeiterkind** *nt* child from a working-class family; **Arbeitermitbestimmung** *f* employee participation; **Arbeiterschaft** *f* workers *pl*, labour (*Brit*) *od* labor (*US*) force; **Arbeiterselbstkontrolle** *f* workers' control; **Arbeiter-und-Bauern-Staat** *m* (*DDR*) workers' and peasants' state; **Arbeiterwohlfahrt** *f* workers' welfare association

Arbeit- *zW*: **Arbeitgeber** (**-s, -**) *m* employer; **Arbeitnehmer** (**-s, -**) *m* employee

Arbeitsagentur *f* job agency

Arbeits- *in zW* labour (*Brit*), labor (*US*); **arbeitsam** *adj* industrious

Arbeits- *zW***: **Arbeitsamt** *nt* employment exchange, Job Centre (*Brit*); **Arbeitsaufwand** *m* expenditure of energy; (*Industrie*) use of labour (*Brit*) *od* labor (*US*); **Arbeitsbedingungen** *pl* working conditions *pl*; **Arbeitsbeschaffung** *f* (*Arbeitsplatzbeschaffung*) job creation; **Arbeitserlaubnis** *f* work permit; **arbeitsfähig** *adj* fit for work, able-bodied; **Arbeitsgang** *m* operation; **Arbeitsgemeinschaft** *f* study group; **Arbeitsgericht** *nt* industrial tribunal; **arbeitsintensiv** *adj* labour-intensive (*Brit*), labor-intensive (*US*); **Arbeitskonflikt** *m* industrial dispute; **Arbeitskraft** *f* worker; **Arbeitskräfte** *pl* workers *pl*, labour (*Brit*), labor (*US*); **arbeitslos** *adj* unemployed, out-of-work; **Arbeitslosengeld** *nt* unemployment benefit; **Arbeitslosenhilfe** *f* supplementary benefit; **Arbeitslosenunterstützung** *f* unemployment benefit; **Arbeitslosenversicherung** *f* *compulsory insurance against unemployment*; **Arbeitslosigkeit** *f* unemployment; **Arbeitsmarkt** *m* job market; **Arbeitsmoral** *f* attitude to work; (*in Betrieb*) work climate; **Arbeitsniederlegung** *f* walkout; **Arbeitsplatte** *f* (*Küche*) work-top, work surface; **Arbeitsplatz** *m* place of work; (*Stelle*) job; **Arbeitsplatzrechner** *m* (*Comput*) work station; **Arbeitsplatzverlust** *m* job loss; **Arbeitsrecht** *nt* industrial law; **arbeitsscheu** *adj* workshy; **Arbeitsschutz** *m* *maintenance of health and safety standards at work*; **Arbeitstag** *m* work(ing) day; **Arbeitsteilung** *f* division of labour (*Brit*) *od* labor (*US*); **Arbeitstier** *nt* (*fig: umg*) glutton for work, workaholic; **arbeitsunfähig** *adj* unfit for work; **Arbeitsunfall** *m* industrial accident; **Arbeitsverhältnis** *nt* employee-employer relationship; **Arbeitsvermittler, in** *m(f)*: **(privater) Arbeitsvermittler** employment officer, job placement officer; **Arbeitsvermittlung** *f* (*Amt*) employment exchange; (*privat*) employment agency; **Arbeitsvertrag** *m* contract of employment; **Arbeitszeit** *f* working hours *pl*; **Arbeitszeitkonto** *nt* record of hours worked; **Arbeitszeitmodell** *nt* model of working hours; **Arbeitszeitregelung** *f* regulation of working hours; **Arbeitszeitverkürzung** *f* reduction in working hours; **Arbeitszimmer** *nt* study

Archäologe [arçɛo'lo:gə] (**-n, -n**) *m* arch(a)eologist

Archäologin [arçɛo'lo:gɪn] *f* arch(a)eologist

Arche ['arçə] (**-, -n**) *f*: **die ~ Noah** Noah's Ark

Architekt, in [arçi'tɛkt(ɪn)] (**-en, -en**) *m(f)* architect

architektonisch [arçitɛk'to:nɪʃ] *adj* architectural

Architektur [arçitɛk'tu:r] *f* architecture

Archiv [ar'çi:f] (**-s, -e**) *nt* archive

ARD *f* archive; *see culture note*

ARD

The *ARD* (Arbeitsgemeinschaft der öffentlich-rechtlichen Rundfunkanstalten der Bundesrepublik Deutschland) is the name of the German broadcasting corporation founded as a result of several mergers after 1945. It is financed by licence fees and advertising and transmits the First Programme nationwide as well as the Third and other regional programmes. News and educational programmes make up about a third of its transmissions.

Arena [a're:na] (**-, Arenen**) *f* (*lit, fig*) arena; (*Zirkusarena, Stierkampfarena*) ring

arg [ark] *adj* bad, awful ▷ *adv* awfully, very; **es zu ~ treiben** to go too far

Argentinien [argɛn'ti:niən] (**-s**) *nt* Argentina, the Argentine

Argentinier, in (**-s, -**) *m(f)* Argentine, Argentinian (*Brit*), Argentinean (*US*)

argentinisch [argɛn'ti:nɪʃ] *adj* Argentine, Argentinian (*Brit*), Argentinean (*US*)

Ärger ['ɛrgər] (**-s**) *m* (*Wut*) anger; (*Unannehmlichkeit*) trouble; **jdm ~ machen** *od* **bereiten** to cause sb a lot of trouble *od* bother; **ärgerlich** *adj* (*zornig*) angry; (*lästig*) annoying, aggravating

ärgern *vt* to annoy ▷ *vr* to get annoyed

Ärgernis (**-ses, -se**) *nt* annoyance; (*Anstoß*) offence (*Brit*), offense (*US*), outrage; **öffentliches ~ erregen** to be a public nuisance

arg- *zW*: **arglistig** *adj* cunning, insidious;

arglistige Täuschung fraud; **arglos** *adj* guileless, innocent; **Arglosigkeit** *f* guilelessness, innocence
Argument [argu'mɛnt] *nt* argument
argumentieren [argumɛn'ti:rən] *vi* to argue
Argusauge ['argʊs|aʊgə] *nt* (*geh*): **mit ~n** eagle-eyed
Argwohn *m* suspicion
argwöhnisch *adj* suspicious
Arie ['a:riə] *f* aria
Aristokrat, in [arɪsto'kra:t(ɪn)] (**-en, -en**) *m(f)* aristocrat
Aristokratie [arɪstokra:'ti:] *f* aristocracy
aristokratisch *adj* aristocratic
arithmetisch [arɪt'me:tɪʃ] *adj* arithmetical; **~es Mittel** arithmetic mean
Arkaden [ar'ka:dən] *pl* (*Bogengang*) arcade *sing*
Arktis ['arktɪs] (-) *f* Arctic
arktisch *adj* Arctic
arm [arm] *adj* poor; **~ dran sein** (*umg*) to have a hard time of it
Arm (**-(e)s, -e**) *m* arm; (*Flussarm*) branch; **jdn auf den ~ nehmen** (*fig: umg*) to pull sb's leg; **jdm unter die ~e greifen** (*fig*) to help sb out; **einen langen/den längeren ~ haben** (*fig*) to have a lot of/more pull (*umg*) *od* influence
Armatur [arma'tu:r] *f* (*Elek*) armature
Armaturenbrett *nt* instrument panel; (*Aut*) dashboard
Armband *nt* bracelet; **Armbanduhr** *f* (wrist) watch
Arme, r *f(m)* poor man/woman; **die ~n** the poor
Armee [ar'me:] (**-, -n**) *f* army; **Armeekorps** *nt* army corps
Ärmel ['ɛrməl] (**-s, -**) *m* sleeve; **etw aus dem ~ schütteln** (*fig*) to produce sth just like that
Ärmelkanal *m* (English) Channel
Armenien [ar'me:niən] (**-s**) *nt* Armenia
Armenier, in [ar'me:niər(ɪn)] (**-s, -**) *m(f)* Armenian
armenisch [ar'me:nɪʃ] *adj* Armenian
Armenrecht *nt* (*Jur*) legal aid
Armer *m siehe* **Arme(r)**
Armlehne *f* armrest
Armleuchter (*pej: umg*) *m* (*Dummkopf*) twit (*Brit*), fool
ärmlich ['ɛrmlɪç] *adj* poor; **aus ~en Verhältnissen** from a poor family
armselig *adj* wretched, miserable; (*mitleiderregend*) pathetic, pitiful
Armut ['armu:t] (-) *f* poverty
Armutsgrenze *f* poverty line
Armutsrisiko *nt* poverty risk
Armutszeugnis *nt* (*fig*): **jdm/sich ein ~ ausstellen** to show sb's/one's shortcomings
Aroma [a'ro:ma] (**-s, Aromen**) *nt* aroma; **Aromatherapie** *f* aromatherapy
aromatisch [aro'ma:tɪʃ] *adj* aromatic
arrangieren [arã:'ʒi:rən] *vt* to arrange ▷ *vr* to come to an arrangement
Arrest [a'rɛst] (**-(e)s, -e**) *m* detention
arretieren [are'ti:rən] *vt* (*Tech*) to lock (in place)
arrogant [aro'gant] *adj* arrogant
Arroganz *f* arrogance
Arsch [arʃ] (**-es, ¨-e**) (*umg!*) *m* arse (*!*); **leck mich am ~!** (*lass mich in Ruhe*) get stuffed! (*!*), fuck off! (*!*); **am ~ der Welt** (*umg*) in the back of beyond; **Arschkriecher** (*umg!*) *m* arse licker (*!*), crawler; **Arschloch** (*umg!*) *nt* (*Mensch*) bastard (*!*)
Arsen [ar'ze:n] (**-s**) *nt* arsenic
Art [a:rt] (**-, -en**) *f* (*Weise*) way; (*Sorte*) kind, sort; (*Biol*) species; **eine ~ (von) Frucht** a kind of fruit; **Häuser aller ~** houses of all kinds; **einzig in seiner ~ sein** to be the only one of its kind, be unique; **auf diese ~ und Weise** in this way; **das ist doch keine ~!** that's no way to behave!; **es ist nicht seine ~, das zu tun** it's not like him to do that; **ich mache das auf meine ~** I do that my (own) way; **Schnitzel nach ~ des Hauses** chef's special escalope
arten *vi*: **nach jdm ~** to take after sb; **der Mensch ist so geartet, dass ...** human nature is such that ...
Artenschutz *m* protection of endangered species
Arterie [ar'te:riə] *f* artery
Arterienverkalkung *f* arteriosclerosis
Artgenosse ['a:rtgənɔsə] *m* animal/plant of the same species; (*Mensch*) person of the same type
Arthritis [ar'tri:tɪs] (**-, -ritiden**) *f* arthritis
artig ['a:rtɪç] *adj* good, well-behaved
Artikel [ar'ti:kəl] (**-s, -**) *m* article
Artillerie [artɪlə'ri:] *f* artillery
Artischocke [arti'ʃɔkə] (**-, -n**) *f* artichoke
Artistik [ar'tɪstɪk] (-) *f* artistry; (*Zirkus-/Varietékunst*) circus/variety performing
Arznei [a:rts'naɪ] *f* medicine; **Arzneimittel** *nt* medicine, medicament
Arzt [a:rtst] (**-es, ¨-e**) *m* doctor; **praktischer ~** general practitioner, GP
Ärztekammer *f* ≈ General Medical Council (*Brit*), State Medical Board of Registration (*US*)
Arzthelferin *f* doctor's assistant
Ärztin ['ɛ:rtstɪn] *f* woman doctor; *siehe auch* **Arzt**
ärztlich ['ɛ:rtstlɪç] *adj* medical
Arztpraxis *f* doctor's practice; (*Räume*) doctor's surgery (*Brit*) *od* office (*US*)
As [as] (**-ses, -se**) *nt* (*Mus*) A flat; *siehe auch* **Ass**
Asbest [as'bɛst] (**-(e)s, -e**) *m* asbestos
Asche ['aʃə] (**-, -n**) *f* ash
Aschen- *zW*: **Aschenbahn** *f* cinder track; **Aschenbecher** *m* ashtray; **Aschenbrödel** *nt* (*Liter, fig*) Cinderella; **Aschenputtel** *nt* (*Liter, fig*) Cinderella
Aschermittwoch *m* Ash Wednesday
Aserbaidschan [azɛrbaɪ'dʒa:n] (**-s**) *nt* Azerbaijan
aserbaidschanisch *adj* Azerbaijani
Asiat, in [azi'a:t(ɪn)] (**-en, -en**) *m(f)* Asian
asiatisch *adj* Asian, Asiatic
Asien ['a:ziən] (**-s**) *nt* Asia

asozial ['azotsia:l] *adj* antisocial; (*Familie*) asocial
Asoziale, r *(pej) f(m) dekl wie adj* antisocial person; **Asoziale** *pl* antisocial elements
Aspekt [as'pɛkt] (**-(e)s, -e**) *m* aspect
Asphalt [as'falt] (**-(e)s, -e**) *m* asphalt
asphaltieren [asfal'ti:rən] *vt* to asphalt
Asphaltstraße *f* asphalt road
aß *etc* [a:s] *vb siehe* **essen**
Ass [as] (**-es, -e**) *nt* ace
Ass. *abk* = **Assessor**
Assekurant, in [aseku'rant(ɪn)] (**-en, -en**) *m(f)* underwriter
Assemblersprache [ə'sɛmblərʃpra:xə] *f* (*Comput*) assembly language
Assessor, in [a'sɛsɔr, -'so:rɪn] (**-s, -en**) *m(f)* *graduate civil servant who has completed his/her traineeship*
Assistent, in [asɪs'tɛnt(ɪn)] *m(f)* assistant
Assistenzarzt [asɪs'tɛntsa:rtst] *m* houseman (*Brit*), intern (*US*)
Assoziation [asotsiatsi'o:n] *f* association
assoziieren [asotsi'i:rən] *vt* (*geh*) to associate
Ast [ast] (**-(e)s, ¨e**) *m* branch; **sich** *dat* **einen ~ lachen** (*umg*) to double up (with laughter)
AStA ['asta] (**-(s), -(s)**) *m abk* (*= Allgemeiner Studentenausschuss*) *students' association*
ästhetisch [ɛs'te:tɪʃ] *adj* aesthetic (*Brit*), esthetic (*US*)
Asthma ['astma] (**-s**) *nt* asthma
Asthmatiker, in [ast'ma:tikər(ɪn)] (**-s, -**) *m(f)* asthmatic
astrein ['astraɪn] *adj* (*fig: umg: moralisch einwandfrei*) straight, on the level; (*: echt*) genuine; (*prima*) fantastic
Astrologe [astro'lo:gə] (**-n, -n**) *m* astrologer
Astrologie [astrolo'gi:] *f* astrology
Astrologin *f* astrologer
Astronaut, in [astro'naʊt(ɪn)] (**-en, -en**) *m(f)* astronaut
Astronautik *f* astronautics
Astronom, in [astro'no:m(ɪn)] (**-en, -en**) *m(f)* astronomer
Astronomie [astrono'mi:] *f* astronomy
ASU *f abk* (*= Arbeitsgemeinschaft selbstständiger Unternehmer*) *association of private traders*; (*= Abgassonderuntersuchung*) exhaust emission test
ASW *f abk* (*= außersinnliche Wahrnehmung*) ESP
Asyl [a'zy:l] (**-s, -e**) *nt* asylum; (*Heim*) home; (*Obdachlosenasyl*) shelter
Asylant, in [azy'lant(ɪn)] (**-en, -en**) *m(f)* person seeking (political) asylum
Asylrecht *nt* (*Pol*) right of (political) asylum
A.T. *abk* (*= Altes Testament*) O.T.
Atelier [atəli'e:] (**-s, -s**) *nt* studio
Atem ['a:təm] (**-s**) *m* breath; **den ~ anhalten** to hold one's breath; **außer ~** out of breath; **jdn in ~ halten** to keep sb in suspense *od* on tenterhooks; **das verschlug mir den ~** it took my breath away; **einen langen/den längeren ~ haben** to have a lot of staying power; **atemberaubend** *adj* breathtaking; **atemlos** *adj* breathless; **Atempause** *f* breather; **Atemwege** *pl* (*Anat*) respiratory tract; **Atemzug** *m* breath
Atheismus [ate'ɪsmʊs] *m* atheism
Atheist, in *m(f)* atheist; **atheistisch** *adj* atheistic
Athen [a'te:n] (**-s**) *nt* Athens
Athener, in (**-s, -**) *m(f)* Athenian
Äther ['ɛ:tər] (**-s, -**) *m* ether
Äthiopien [ɛti'o:piən] (**-s**) *nt* Ethiopia
Äthiopier, in (**-s, -**) *m(f)* Ethiopian
äthiopisch *adj* Ethiopian
Athlet, in [at'le:t(ɪn)] (**-en, -en**) *m(f)* athlete
Athletik *f* athletics *sing*
Atlanten *pl von* **Atlas**
Atlantik [at'lantɪk] (**-s**) *m* Atlantic
atlantisch *adj* Atlantic; **der A~e Ozean** the Atlantic Ocean
Atlas ['atlas] (**-** *od* **-ses, -se** *od* **Atlanten**) *m* atlas; **Atlasgebirge** *nt* Atlas Mountains *pl*
atmen ['a:tmən] *vt, vi* to breathe
Atmosphäre [atmo'sfɛ:rə] (**-, -n**) *f* atmosphere
atmosphärisch *adj* atmospheric
Atmung ['a:tmʊŋ] *f* respiration
Ätna ['ɛ:tna] (**-(s)**) *m* Etna
Atom [a'to:m] (**-s, -e**) *nt* atom
atomar [ato'ma:r] *adj* atomic, nuclear; (*Drohung*) nuclear
Atom- *zW*: **Atombombe** *f* atom bomb; **Atomenergie** *f* nuclear *od* atomic energy; **Atomgegner** *m*: **Atomgegner sein** to be antinuclear; **Atomkern** *m* atomic nucleus; **Atomkraft** *f* nuclear power; **Atomkraftwerk** *nt* nuclear power station; **Atomkrieg** *m* nuclear *od* atomic war; **Atomlobby** *f* nuclear lobby; **Atommacht** *f* nuclear *od* atomic power; **Atommeiler** *m* nuclear reactor; **Atommüll** *m* nuclear waste; **Atomphysik** *f* nuclear physics *sing*; **Atompilz** *m* mushroom cloud; **Atomsperrvertrag** *m* (*Pol*) nuclear non-proliferation treaty; **Atomsprengkopf** *m* nuclear *od* atomic warhead; **Atomstrom** *m* *electricity generated by nuclear power*; **Atomtest** *m* nuclear test; **Atomtestgelände** *nt* nuclear testing range; **Atomwaffen** *pl* nuclear *od* atomic weapons *pl*; **atomwaffenfrei** *adj* (*Zone*) nuclear-free; **Atomwirtschaft** *f* nuclear industry; **Atomzeitalter** *nt* atomic age
Attacke [a'takə] (**-, -n**) *f* (*Angriff*) attack
Attentat [atɛn'ta:t] (**-(e)s, -e**) *nt*: **~ (auf** *+akk*) (attempted) assassination (of)
Attentäter, in [atɛn'tɛ:tər(ɪn)] (**-s, -**) *m(f)* (would-be) assassin
Attest [a'tɛst] (**-(e)s, -e**) *nt* certificate
Attraktion [atraktsi'o:n] *f* attraction
attraktiv [atrak'ti:f] *adj* attractive
Attrappe [a'trapə] (**-, -n**) *f* dummy; **bei ihr ist alles ~** everything about her is false
Attribut [atri'bu:t] (**-(e)s, -e**) *nt* (*Gram*) attribute
ätzen ['ɛtsən] *vi* to be caustic
ätzend *adj* (*lit: Säure*) corrosive; (*Geruch*) pungent; (*fig: umg: furchtbar*) dreadful, horrible; (*: toll*) magic

SCHLÜSSELWORT

auch [aʊx] *adv* **1** (*ebenfalls*) also, too, as well; **das ist auch schön** that's nice too *od* as well; **er kommt — ich auch** he's coming — so am I *od* me too; **auch nicht** not ... either; **ich auch nicht** nor I, me neither; **oder auch** or; **auch das noch!** not that as well!; **nicht nur ..., sondern auch ...** not only ... but also ...
2 (*selbst, sogar*) even; **auch wenn das Wetter schlecht ist** even if the weather is bad; **ohne auch nur zu fragen** without even asking
3 (*wirklich*) really; **du siehst müde aus — bin ich auch** you look tired — (so) I am; **so sieht es auch aus** (and) that's what it looks like
4 (*auch immer*): **wer auch** whoever; **was auch** whatever; **wozu auch?** (*emphatisch*) whatever for?; **wie dem auch sei** be that as it may; **wie sehr er sich auch bemühte** however much he tried

Audienz [aʊdi'ɛnts] (**-, -en**) *f* (*bei Papst, König etc*) audience
Audimax [aʊdi'maks] *nt* (*Univ: umg*) main lecture hall
audiovisuell [aʊdiovizu'ɛl] *adj* audiovisual
Auditorium [aʊdi'to:riʊm] *nt* (*Hörsaal*) lecture hall; (*geh: Zuhörerschaft*) audience

SCHLÜSSELWORT

auf [aʊf] *präp +dat* (*wo?*) on; **auf dem Tisch** on the table; **auf der Reise** on the way; **auf der Post/dem Fest** at the post office/party; **auf der Straße** on the road; **auf dem Land/der ganzen Welt** in the country/the whole world; **was hat es damit auf sich?** what does it mean?
▷ *präp +akk* **1** (*wohin?*) on(to); **auf den Tisch** on(to) the table; **auf die Post gehen** to go to the post office; **auf das Land** into the country; **etw auf einen Zettel schreiben** to write sth on a piece of paper; **auf eine Tasse Kaffee/eine Zigarette(nlänge)** for a cup of coffee/a smoke; **die Nacht (von Montag) auf Dienstag** Monday night; **auf einen Polizisten kommen 1.000 Bürger** there is one policeman to every 1,000 citizens
2: **auf Deutsch** in German; **auf Lebenszeit** for my/his lifetime; **bis auf ihn** except for him; **auf einmal** at once; **auf seinen Vorschlag (hin)** at his suggestion
▷ *adv* **1** (*offen*) open; **auf sein** to be open; **das Fenster ist auf** the window is open
2 (*hinauf*) up; **auf und ab** up and down; **auf und davon** up and away; **auf!** (*los!*) come on!; **von klein auf** from childhood onwards
3 (*aufgestanden*) up; **auf sein** (*Person*) to be up; **ist er schon auf?** is he up yet?
▷ *konj*: **auf dass** (so) that

aufarbeiten ['aʊf|arbaɪtən] *vt* (*erledigen: Korrespondenz etc*) to catch up with
aufatmen ['aʊf|a:tmən] *vi* to heave a sigh of relief
aufbahren ['aʊfba:rən] *vt* to lay out
Aufbau ['aʊfbaʊ] *m* (*Bauen*) building, construction; (*Struktur*) structure; (*aufgebautes Teil*) superstructure
aufbauen ['aʊfbaʊən] *vt* to erect, build (up); (*Existenz*) to make; (*gestalten*) to construct; (*gründen*): **~ (auf +dat)** to found (on), base (on) ▷ *vr*: **sich vor jdm ~** to draw o.s. up to one's full height in front of sb
aufbäumen ['aʊfbɔʏmən] *vr* to rear; (*fig*) to revolt, rebel
aufbauschen ['aʊfbaʊʃən] *vt* to puff out; (*fig*) to exaggerate
aufbegehren ['aʊfbəge:rən] *vi* (*geh*) to rebel
aufbehalten ['aʊfbəhaltən] *unreg vt* to keep on
aufbekommen ['aʊfbəkɔmən] *unreg* (*umg*) *vt* (*öffnen*) to get open; (*: Hausaufgaben*) to be given
aufbereiten ['aʊfbəraɪtən] *vt* to process; (*Trinkwasser*) to purify; (*Text etc*) to work up
Aufbereitungsanlage *f* processing plant
aufbessern ['aʊfbɛsərn] *vt* (*Gehalt*) to increase
aufbewahren ['aʊfbəva:rən] *vt* to keep; (*Gepäck*) to put in the left-luggage office
Aufbewahrung *f* (safe)keeping; (*Gepäckaufbewahrung*) left-luggage office (*Brit*), baggage check (*US*); **jdm etw zur ~ geben** to give sb sth for safekeeping
Aufbewahrungsort *m* storage place
aufbieten ['aʊfbi:tən] *unreg vt* (*Kraft*) to summon (up); (*Armee, Polizei*) to mobilize
Aufbietung *f*: **unter ~ aller Kräfte ...** summoning (up) all his/her *etc* strength ...
aufbinden ['aʊfbɪndən] *unreg vt*: **lass dir doch so etwas nicht ~** (*fig*) don't fall for that
aufblähen ['aʊfblɛ:ən] *vr* to blow out; (*Segel*) to billow out; (*Med*) to become swollen; (*fig: pej*) to puff o.s. up
aufblasen ['aʊfbla:zən] *unreg vt* to blow up, inflate ▷ *vr* (*umg*) to become big-headed
aufbleiben ['aʊfblaɪbən] *unreg vi* (*Laden*) to remain open; (*Person*) to stay up
aufblenden ['aʊfblɛndən] *vt* (*Scheinwerfer*) to turn on full beam
aufblicken ['aʊfblɪkən] *vi* to look up; **~ zu** (*lit*) to look up at; (*fig*) to look up to
aufblühen ['aʊfbly:ən] *vi* to blossom; (*fig*) to blossom, flourish
aufblühend *adj* (*Comm*) booming
aufbocken ['aʊfbɔkən] *vt* (*Auto*) to jack up
aufbrauchen ['aʊfbraʊxən] *vt* to use up
aufbrausen ['aʊfbraʊzən] *vi* (*fig*) to flare up
aufbrausend *adj* hot-tempered
aufbrechen ['aʊfbrɛçən] *unreg vt* to break open, to prise (*Brit*) *od* pry (*US*) open ▷ *vi* to burst open; (*gehen*) to start, set off
aufbringen ['aʊfbrɪŋən] *unreg vt* (*öffnen*) to open; (*in Mode*) to bring into fashion; (*beschaffen*) to procure; (*Fin*) to raise; (*ärgern*) to irritate; **Verständnis für etw ~** to be able to

understand sth
Aufbruch ['aʊfbrʊx] *m* departure
aufbrühen ['aʊfbry:ən] *vt* (*Tee*) to make
aufbrummen ['aʊfbrʊmən] (*umg*) *vt*: **jdm die Kosten ~** to land sb with the costs
aufbürden ['aʊfbʏrdən] *vt*: **jdm etw ~** to burden sb with sth
aufdecken ['aʊfdɛkən] *vt* to uncover; (*Spielkarten*) to show
aufdrängen ['aʊfdrɛŋən] *vt*: **jdm etw ~** to force sth on sb ▷ *vr*: **sich jdm ~** to intrude on sb
aufdrehen ['aʊfdre:ən] *vt* (*Wasserhahn etc*) to turn on; (*Ventil*) to open; (*Schraubverschluss*) to unscrew; (*Radio etc*) to turn up; (*Haar*) to put in rollers
aufdringlich ['aʊfdrɪŋlɪç] *adj* pushy; (*Benehmen*) obtrusive; (*Parfüm*) powerful
aufeinander [aʊf|aɪ'nandər] *adv* on top of one another; (*schießen*) at each other; (*warten*) for one another; (*vertrauen*) each other; **Aufeinanderfolge** *f* succession, series; **aufeinanderfolgen** *vi* to follow one another; **aufeinanderfolgend** *adj* consecutive; **aufeinanderlegen** *vt* to lay on top of one another; **aufeinanderprallen** *vi* (*Autos etc*) to collide; (*Truppen, Meinungen*) to clash
Aufenthalt ['aʊf|ɛnthalt] *m* stay; (*Verzögerung*) delay; (*Eisenb: Halten*) stop; (*Ort*) haunt
Aufenthalts- *zW*: **Aufenthaltserlaubnis** *f*, **Aufenthaltsgenehmigung** *f* residence permit; **Aufenthaltsraum** *m* day room; (*in Betrieb*) recreation room
auferlegen ['aʊf|ɛrle:gən] *vt*: **(jdm) ~** to impose (upon sb)
auferstehen ['aʊf|ɛrʃte:ən] *unreg vi untr* to rise from the dead
Auferstehung *f* resurrection
aufessen ['aʊf|ɛsən] *unreg vt* to eat up
auffahren ['aʊffa:rən] *unreg vi* (*herankommen*) to draw up; (*hochfahren*) to jump up; (*wütend werden*) to flare up; (*in den Himmel*) to ascend ▷ *vt* (*Kanonen, Geschütz*) to bring up; **~ auf** *+akk* (*Auto*) to run *od* crash into
auffahrend *adj* hot-tempered
Auffahrt *f* (*Hausauffahrt*) drive; (*Autobahnauffahrt*) slip road (*Brit*), entrance ramp (*US*)
Auffahrunfall *m* pile-up
auffallen ['aʊffalən] *unreg vi* to be noticeable; **angenehm/unangenehm ~** to make a good/bad impression; **jdm ~** (*bemerkt werden*) to strike sb
auffallend *adj* striking
auffällig ['aʊffɛlɪç] *adj* conspicuous, striking
auffangen ['aʊffaŋən] *unreg vt* to catch; (*Funkspruch*) to intercept; (*Preise*) to peg; (*abfangen: Aufprall etc*) to cushion, absorb
Auffanglager *nt* reception camp
auffassen ['aʊffasən] *vt* to understand, comprehend; (*auslegen*) to see, view
Auffassung *f* (*Meinung*) opinion; (*Auslegung*) view, conception; (*auch*: **Auffassungsgabe**) grasp
auffindbar ['aʊffɪntba:r] *adj* to be found
aufflammen ['aʊfflamən] *vi* (*lit, fig: Feuer, Unruhen etc*) to flare up
auffliegen ['aʊffli:gən] *unreg vi* to fly up; (*umg: Rauschgiftring etc*) to be busted
auffordern ['aʊffɔrdərn] *vt* to challenge; (*befehlen*) to call upon, order; (*bitten*) to ask
Aufforderung *f* (*Befehl*) order; (*Einladung*) invitation
aufforsten ['aʊffɔrstən] *vt* (*Gebiet*) to reafforest; (*Wald*) to restock
auffrischen ['aʊffrɪʃən] *vt* to freshen up; (*Kenntnisse*) to brush up; (*Erinnerungen*) to reawaken ▷ *vi* (*Wind*) to freshen
aufführen ['aʊffy:rən] *vt* (*Theat*) to perform; (*in einem Verzeichnis*) to list, specify ▷ *vr* (*sich benehmen*) to behave; **einzeln ~** to itemize
Aufführung *f* (*Theat*) performance; (*Liste*) specification
auffüllen ['aʊffʏlən] *vt* to fill up; (*Vorräte*) to replenish; (*Öl*) to top up
Aufgabe ['aʊfga:bə] **(-, -n)** *f* task; (*Sch*) exercise; (*Hausaufgabe*) homework; (*Verzicht*) giving up; (*von Gepäck*) registration; (*von Post*) posting; (*von Inserat*) insertion; **sich** *dat* **etw zur ~ machen** to make sth one's job *od* business
aufgabeln ['aʊfga:bəln] *vt* (*fig: umg: jdn*) to pick up; (*: Sache*) to get hold of
Aufgabenbereich *m* area of responsibility
Aufgang ['aʊfgaŋ] *m* ascent; (*Sonnenaufgang*) rise; (*Treppe*) staircase
aufgeben ['aʊfge:bən] *unreg vt* (*verzichten auf*) to give up; (*Paket*) to send, post; (*Gepäck*) to register; (*Bestellung*) to give; (*Inserat*) to insert; (*Rätsel, Problem*) to set ▷ *vi* to give up
aufgeblasen ['aʊfgəbla:zən] *adj* (*fig*) puffed up, self-important
Aufgebot ['aʊfgəbo:t] *nt* supply; (*von Kräften*) utilization; (*Eheaufgebot*) banns *pl*
aufgedonnert ['aʊfgədɔnərt] (*pej: umg*) *adj* tarted up
aufgedreht ['aʊfgədre:t] (*umg*) *adj* excited
aufgedunsen ['aʊfgedʊnzən] *adj* swollen, puffed up
aufgegeben ['aʊfgəge:bən] *pp von* **aufgeben**
aufgehen ['aʊfge:ən] *unreg vi* (*Sonne, Teig*) to rise; (*sich öffnen*) to open; (*Theat: Vorhang*) to go up; (*Knopf, Knoten etc*) to come undone; (*klar werden*) to become clear; (*Math*) to come out exactly; **~ (in** *+dat***)** (*sich widmen*) to be absorbed (in); **in Rauch/Flammen ~** to go up in smoke/flames
aufgeilen ['aʊfgaɪlən] (*umg*) *vt* to turn on ▷ *vr* to be turned on
aufgeklärt ['aʊfgəklɛ:rt] *adj* enlightened; (*sexuell*) knowing the facts of life
aufgekratzt ['aʊfgəkratst] (*umg*) *adj* in high spirits, full of beans
aufgelaufen ['aʊfgəlaʊfən] *adj*: **~e Zinsen** *pl* accrued interest *sing*
Aufgeld *nt* premium
aufgelegt ['aʊfgəle:kt] *adj*: **gut/schlecht ~**

sein to be in a good/bad mood; **zu etw ~ sein** to be in the mood for sth
aufgenommen ['aʊfgənɔmən] *pp von* **aufnehmen**
aufgeregt ['aʊfgəre:kt] *adj* excited
aufgeschlossen ['aʊfgəʃlɔsən] *adj* open, open-minded
aufgeschmissen ['aʊfgəʃmɪsən] (*umg*) *adj* in a fix, stuck
aufgeschrieben ['aʊfgəʃri:bən] *pp von* **aufschreiben**
aufgestanden ['aʊfgəʃtandən] *pp von* **aufstehen**
aufgetakelt ['aʊfgəta:kəlt] *adj* (*fig: umg*) dressed up to the nines
aufgeweckt ['aʊfgəvɛkt] *adj* bright, intelligent
aufgießen ['aʊfgi:sən] *unreg vt* (*Wasser*) to pour over; (*Tee*) to infuse
aufgliedern ['aʊfgli:dərn] *vr*: **sich ~ (in** *+akk***)** to (sub)divide (into), break down (into)
aufgreifen ['aʊfgraɪfən] *unreg vt* (*Thema*) to take up; (*Verdächtige*) to pick up, seize
aufgrund, auf Grund [aʊf'grʊnt] *präp +gen*: **~ von** on the basis of; (*wegen*) because of
Aufgussbeutel ['aʊfgʊsbɔʏtəl] *m* sachet (containing coffee/herbs *etc*) for brewing; (*Teebeutel*) tea bag
aufhaben ['aʊfha:bən] *unreg vt* (*Hut etc*) to have on; (*Arbeit*) to have to do
aufhalsen ['aʊfhalzən] (*umg*) *vt*: **jdm etw ~** to saddle *od* lumber sb with sth
aufhalten ['aʊfhaltən] *unreg vt* (*Person*) to detain; (*Entwicklung*) to check; (*Tür, Hand*) to hold open; (*Augen*) to keep open ▷ *vr* (*wohnen*) to live; (*bleiben*) to stay; **jdn (bei etw) ~** (*abhalten, stören*) to hold *od* keep sb back (from sth); **sich über etw/jdn ~** to go on about sth/sb; **sich mit etw ~** to waste time over sth; **sich bei etw ~** (*sich befassen*) to dwell on sth
aufhängen ['aʊfhɛŋən] *unreg vt* (*Wäsche*) to hang up; (*Menschen*) to hang ▷ *vr* to hang o.s.
Aufhänger (-s, -) *m* (*am Mantel*) hook; (*fig*) peg
Aufhängung *f* (*Tech*) suspension
aufheben ['aʊfhe:bən] *unreg vt* (*hochheben*) to raise, lift; (*Sitzung*) to wind up; (*Urteil*) to annul; (*Gesetz*) to repeal, abolish; (*aufbewahren*) to keep; (*ausgleichen*) to offset, make up for ▷ *vr* to cancel itself out; **viel A~(s) machen (von)** to make a fuss (about); **bei jdm gut aufgehoben sein** to be well looked after at sb's
aufheitern ['aʊfhaɪtərn] *vt, vr* (*Himmel, Miene*) to brighten; (*Mensch*) to cheer up
Aufheiterungen *pl* (*Met*) bright periods *pl*
aufheizen ['aʊfhaɪtsən] *vt*: **die Stimmung ~** to stir up feelings
aufhelfen ['aʊfhɛlfən] *unreg vi* (*lit: beim Aufstehen*): **jdm ~** to help sb up
aufhellen ['aʊfhɛlən] *vt, vr* to clear up; (*Farbe, Haare*) to lighten
aufhetzen ['aʊfhɛtsən] *vt* to stir up
aufheulen ['aʊfhɔʏlən] *vi* to howl; (*Sirene*) to (start to) wail; (*Motor*) to (give a) roar
aufholen ['aʊfho:lən] *vt* to make up ▷ *vi* to catch up
aufhorchen ['aʊfhɔrçən] *vi* to prick up one's ears
aufhören ['aʊfhø:rən] *vi* to stop; **~, etw zu tun** to stop doing sth
aufkaufen ['aʊfkaʊfən] *vt* to buy up
aufklappen ['aʊfklapən] *vt* to open; (*Verdeck*) to fold back
aufklären ['aʊfklɛ:rən] *vt* (*Geheimnis etc*) to clear up; (*Person*) to enlighten; (*sexuell*) to tell the facts of life to; (*Mil*) to reconnoitre ▷ *vr* to clear up
Aufklärung *f* (*von Geheimnis*) clearing up; (*Unterrichtung, Zeitalter*) enlightenment; (*sexuell*) sex education; (*Mil, Aviat*) reconnaissance
Aufklärungsarbeit *f* educational work
aufkleben ['aʊfkle:bən] *vt* to stick on
Aufkleber (-s, -) *m* sticker
aufknöpfen ['aʊfknœpfən] *vt* to unbutton
aufkochen ['aʊfkɔxən] *vt* to bring to the boil
aufkommen ['aʊfkɔmən] *unreg vi* (*Wind*) to come up; (*Zweifel, Gefühl*) to arise; (*Mode*) to start; **für jdn/etw ~** to be liable *od* responsible for sb/sth; **für den Schaden ~** to pay for the damage; **endlich kam Stimmung auf** at last things livened up
aufkreuzen ['aʊfkrɔʏtsən] (*umg*) *vi* (*erscheinen*) to turn *od* show up
aufkündigen ['aʊfkʏndɪgən] *vt* (*Vertrag etc*) to terminate
aufladen ['aʊfla:dən] *unreg vt* to load ▷ *vr* (*Batterie etc*) to be charged; (*neu aufladen*) to be recharged; **jdm/sich etw ~** (*fig*) to saddle sb/o.s. with sth
Auflage ['aʊfla:gə] *f* edition; (*Zeitung*) circulation; (*Bedingung*) condition; **jdm etw zur ~ machen** to make sth a condition for sb
Auflagehöhe, Auflagenhöhe *f* (*von Buch*) number of copies published; (*von Zeitung*) circulation
auflassen ['aʊflasən] *unreg* (*umg*) *vt* (*offen*) to leave open; (*: aufgesetzt*) to leave on; **die Kinder länger ~** to let the children stay up (longer)
auflauern ['aʊflaʊərn] *vi*: **jdm ~** to lie in wait for sb
Auflauf ['aʊflaʊf] *m* (*Koch*) pudding; (*Menschenauflauf*) crowd
auflaufen *unreg vi* (*auf Grund laufen: Schiff*) to run aground; **jdn ~ lassen** (*umg*) to drop sb in it
Auflaufform *f* (*Koch*) ovenproof dish
aufleben ['aʊfle:bən] *vi* to revive
auflegen ['aʊfle:gən] *vt* to put on; (*Hörer*) to put down; (*Typ*) to print ▷ *vi* (*Tel*) to hang up
auflehnen ['aʊfle:nən] *vt* to lean on ▷ *vr* to rebel
Auflehnung *f* rebellion
auflesen ['aʊfle:zən] *unreg vt* to pick up
aufleuchten ['aʊflɔʏçtən] *vi* to light up
aufliegen ['aʊfli:gən] *unreg vi* to lie on; (*Comm*) to be available
auflisten ['aʊflɪstən] *vt* (*auch Comput*) to list

auflockern ['aʊflɔkərn] *vt* to loosen; (*fig: Eintönigkeit etc*) to liven up; (*entspannen, zwangloser machen*) to make relaxed; (*Atmosphäre*) to make more relaxed, ease
auflösen ['aʊflø:zən] *vt* to dissolve; (*Missverständnis*) to sort out; (*Konto*) to close; (*Firma*) to wind up; (*Haushalt*) to break up; **in Tränen aufgelöst sein** to be in tears
Auflösung *f* dissolving; (*fig*) solution; (*Bildschirm*) resolution
aufmachen ['aʊfmaxən] *vt* to open; (*Kleidung*) to undo; (*zurechtmachen*) to do up ▷ *vr* to set out
Aufmacher *m* (*Presse*) lead
Aufmachung *f* (*Kleidung*) outfit, get-up; (*Gestaltung*) format
aufmerksam ['aʊfmɛrkza:m] *adj* attentive; **auf etw** *akk* **~ werden** to become aware of sth; **jdn auf etw** *akk* **~ machen** to point sth out to sb; **(das ist) sehr ~ von Ihnen** (*zuvorkommend*) (that's) most kind of you; **Aufmerksamkeit** *f* attention, attentiveness; (*Geschenk*) token (gift)
aufmöbeln ['aʊfmø:bəln] (*umg*) *vt* (*Gegenstand*) to do up; (*: beleben*) to buck up, pep up
aufmucken ['aʊfmʊkən] (*umg*) *vi*: **~ gegen** to protest at *od* against
aufmuntern ['aʊfmʊntərn] *vt* (*ermutigen*) to encourage; (*erheitern*) to cheer up
aufmüpfig ['aʊfmʏpfɪç] (*umg*) *adj* rebellious
Aufnahme ['aʊfna:mə] **(-, -n)** *f* reception; (*Beginn*) beginning; (*in Verein etc*) admission; (*in Liste etc*) inclusion; (*Notieren*) taking down; (*Phot*) shot; (*auf Tonband etc*) recording; **Aufnahmeantrag** *m* application for membership *od* admission; **aufnahmefähig** *adj* receptive; **Aufnahmeleiter** *m* (*Film*) production manager; (*Rundf, TV*) producer; **Aufnahmeprüfung** *f* entrance test; **Aufnahmestopp** *m* (*für Flüchtlinge etc*) freeze on immigration
aufnehmen ['aʊfne:mən] *unreg vt* to receive; (*hochheben*) to pick up; (*beginnen*) to take up; (*in Verein etc*) to admit; (*in Liste etc*) to include; (*fassen*) to hold; (*begreifen*) to take in, grasp; (*beim Stricken: Maschen*) to increase, make; (*notieren*) to take down; (*fotografieren*) to photograph; (*auf Tonband, Platte*) to record; (*Fin: leihen*) to take out; **es mit jdm ~ können** to be able to compete with sb
aufnötigen ['aʊfnø:tɪgən] *vt*: **jdm etw** ~ to force sth on sb
aufoktroyieren ['aʊf|ɔktroaji:rən] *vt*: **jdm etw** ~ (*geh*) to impose *od* force sth on sb
aufopfern ['aʊf|ɔpfərn] *vt* to sacrifice ▷ *vr* to sacrifice o.s.
aufopfernd *adj* selfless
aufpassen ['aʊfpasən] *vi* (*aufmerksam sein*) to pay attention; **auf jdn/etw** ~ to look after *od* watch sb/sth; **aufgepasst!** look out!
Aufpasser, in (-s, -) (*pej*) *m(f)* (*Aufseher, Spitzel*) spy, watchdog; (*Beobachter*) supervisor; (*Wächter*) guard
aufpflanzen ['aʊfpflantsən] *vr*: **sich vor jdm ~** to plant o.s. in front of sb
aufplatzen ['aʊfplatsən] *vi* to burst open
aufplustern ['aʊfplu:stərn] *vr* (*Vogel*) to ruffle (up) its feathers; (*Mensch*) to puff o.s. up
aufprägen ['aʊfprɛ:gən] *vt*: **jdm/etw seinen Stempel ~** (*fig*) to leave one's mark on sb/sth
Aufprall ['aʊfpral] **(-(e)s, -e)** *m* impact
aufprallen *vi* to hit, strike
Aufpreis ['aʊfpraɪs] *m* extra charge
aufpumpen ['aʊfpʊmpən] *vt* to pump up
aufputschen ['aʊfpʊtʃən] *vt* (*aufhetzen*) to inflame; (*erregen*) to stimulate
Aufputschmittel *nt* stimulant
aufraffen ['aʊfrafən] *vr* to rouse o.s.
aufräumen ['aʊfrɔymən] *vt, vi* (*Dinge*) to clear away; (*Zimmer*) to tidy up
Aufräumungsarbeiten *pl* clearing-up operations *pl*
aufrecht ['aʊfrɛçt] *adj* (*lit, fig*) upright
aufrechterhalten *unreg vt* to maintain
aufregen ['aʊfre:gən] *vt* to excite; (*ärgerlich machen*) to irritate, annoy; (*nervös machen*) to make nervous; (*beunruhigen*) to disturb ▷ *vr* to get excited
aufregend *adj* exciting
Aufregung *f* excitement
aufreiben ['aʊfraɪbən] *unreg vt* (*Haut*) to rub raw; (*erschöpfen*) to exhaust; (*Mil: völlig vernichten*) to wipe out, annihilate
aufreibend *adj* strenuous
aufreihen ['aʊfraɪən] *vt* (*in Linie*) to line up; (*Perlen*) to string
aufreißen ['aʊfraɪsən] *unreg vt* (*Umschlag*) to tear open; (*Augen*) to open wide; (*Tür*) to throw open; (*Straße*) to take up; (*umg: Mädchen*) to pick up
Aufreißer (-s, -) *m* (*Person*) smooth operator
aufreizen ['aʊfraɪtsən] *vt* to incite, stir up
aufreizend *adj* exciting, stimulating
aufrichten ['aʊfrɪçtən] *vt* to put up, erect; (*moralisch*) to console ▷ *vr* to rise; (*moralisch*): **sich ~ (an** *+dat***)** to take heart (from); **sich im Bett ~** to sit up in bed
aufrichtig ['aʊfrɪçtɪç] *adj* sincere; honest; **Aufrichtigkeit** *f* sincerity
aufrollen ['aʊfrɔlən] *vt* (*zusammenrollen*) to roll up; (*Kabel*) to coil *od* wind up; *siehe auch* **wiederaufrollen**
aufrücken ['aʊfrʏkən] *vi* to move up; (*beruflich*) to be promoted
Aufruf ['aʊfru:f] *m* summons; (*zur Hilfe*) call; (*des Namens*) calling out
aufrufen *unreg vt* (*Namen*) to call out; (*auffordern*): **jdn ~ (zu)** to call upon sb (for); **einen Schüler ~** to ask a pupil (to answer) a question
Aufruhr ['aʊfru:r] **(-(e)s, -e)** *m* uprising, revolt; **in ~ sein** to be in uproar
Aufrührer, in (-s, -) *m(f)* rabble-rouser
aufrührerisch ['aʊfry:rərɪʃ] *adj* rebellious
aufrunden ['aʊfrʊndən] *vt* (*Summe*) to round up
aufrüsten ['aʊfrʏstən] *vt, vi* to arm
Aufrüstung *f* rearmament

aufrütteln ['aʊfrʏtəln] *vt* (*lit, fig*) to shake up
aufs [aʊfs] = **auf das**
aufsagen ['aʊfza:gən] *vt* (*Gedicht*) to recite; (*geh: Freundschaft*) to put an end to
aufsammeln ['aʊfzaməln] *vt* to gather up
aufsässig ['aʊfzɛsɪç] *adj* rebellious
Aufsatz ['aʊfzats] *m* (*Geschriebenes*) essay, composition; (*auf Schrank etc*) top
aufsaugen ['aʊfzaʊgən] *unreg vt* to soak up
aufschauen ['aʊfʃaʊən] *vi* to look up
aufscheuchen ['aʊfʃɔʏçən] *vt* to scare, startle
aufschichten ['aʊfʃɪçtən] *vt* to stack, pile up
aufschieben ['aʊfʃi:bən] *unreg vt* to push open; (*verzögern*) to put off, postpone
Aufschlag ['aʊfʃla:k] *m* (*Ärmelaufschlag*) cuff; (*Jackenaufschlag*) lapel; (*Hosenaufschlag*) turn-up (*Brit*), cuff (*US*); (*Aufprall*) impact; (*Preisaufschlag*) surcharge; (*Tennis*) service
aufschlagen ['aʊfʃla:gən] *unreg vt* (*öffnen*) to open; (*verwunden*) to cut; (*hochschlagen*) to turn up; (*aufbauen: Zelt, Lager*) to pitch, erect; (*Wohnsitz*) to take up ▷ *vi* (*aufprallen*) to hit; (*teurer werden*) to go up; (*Tennis*) to serve; **schlagt Seite 111 auf** open your books at page 111
aufschließen ['aʊfʃli:sən] *unreg vt* to open up, unlock ▷ *vi* (*aufrücken*) to close up
Aufschluss ['aʊfʃlʊs] *m* information
aufschlüsseln ['aʊfʃlʏsəln] *vt*: **~ (nach)** to break down (into); (*klassifizieren*) to classify (according to)
aufschlussreich *adj* informative, illuminating
aufschnappen ['aʊfʃnapən] *vt* (*umg*) to pick up ▷ *vi* to fly open
aufschneiden ['aʊfʃnaɪdən] *unreg vt* to cut open; (*Brot*) to cut up; (*Med: Geschwür*) to lance ▷ *vi* (*umg*) to brag
Aufschneider (**-s, -**) *m* boaster, braggart
Aufschnitt ['aʊfʃnɪt] *m* (slices of) cold meat
aufschnüren ['aʊfʃny:rən] *vt* to unlace; (*Paket*) to untie
aufschrauben ['aʊfʃraʊbən] *vt* (*festschrauben*) to screw on; (*lösen*) to unscrew
aufschrecken ['aʊfʃrɛkən] *vt* to startle ▷ *vi* (*unreg*) to start up
Aufschrei ['aʊfʃraɪ] *m* cry
aufschreiben ['aʊfʃraɪbən] *unreg vt* to write down
aufschreien *unreg vi* to cry out
Aufschrift ['aʊfʃrɪft] *f* (*Inschrift*) inscription; (*Etikett*) label
Aufschub ['aʊfʃu:p] (**-(e)s, -schübe**) *m* delay, postponement; **jdm ~ gewähren** to grant sb an extension
aufschürfen ['aʊfʃʏrfən] *vt*: **sich** *dat* **die Haut/das Knie ~** to graze *od* scrape o.s./one's knee
aufschütten ['aʊfʃʏtən] *vt* (*Flüssigkeit*) to pour on; (*Kohle*) to put on (the fire); (*Damm, Deich*) to throw up; **Kaffee ~** to make coffee
aufschwatzen ['aʊfʃvatsən] (*umg*) *vt*: **jdm etw ~** to talk sb into (getting/having *etc*) sth
Aufschwung ['aʊfʃvʊŋ] *m* (*Elan*) boost; (*wirtschaftlich*) upturn, boom; (*Sport: an Gerät*) mount
aufsehen ['aʊfze:ən] *unreg vi* to look up; **~ zu** (*lit*) to look up at; (*fig*) to look up to; **Aufsehen** (**-s**) *nt* sensation, stir; **aufsehenerregend** *adj* sensational
Aufseher, in (**-s, -**) *m(f)* guard; (*im Betrieb*) supervisor; (*Museumsaufseher*) attendant; (*Parkaufseher*) keeper
auf sein ['aʊfzaɪn] *siehe* **auf**
aufseiten, **auf Seiten** [aʊf'zaɪtn] *präp +gen*: **~ von** on the part of
aufsetzen ['aʊfzɛtsən] *vt* to put on; (*Flugzeug*) to put down; (*Dokument*) to draw up ▷ *vr* to sit upright ▷ *vi* (*Flugzeug*) to touch down
Aufsicht ['aʊfzɪçt] *f* supervision; **die ~ haben** to be in charge; **bei einer Prüfung ~ führen** to invigilate (*Brit*) *od* supervise an exam
Aufsichtsrat *m* board (of directors)
aufsitzen ['aʊfzɪtsən] *unreg vi* (*aufgerichtet sitzen*) to sit up; (*aufs Pferd, Motorrad*) to mount, get on; (*Schiff*) to run aground; **jdn ~ lassen** (*umg*) to stand sb up; **jdm ~** (*umg*) to be taken in by sb
aufspalten ['aʊfʃpaltən] *vt* to split
aufspannen ['aʊfʃpanən] *vt* (*Netz, Sprungtuch*) to stretch *od* spread out; (*Schirm*) to put up, open
aufsparen ['aʊfʃpa:rən] *vt* to save (up)
aufsperren ['aʊfʃpɛrən] *vt* to unlock; (*Mund*) to open wide; **die Ohren ~** (*umg*) to prick up one's ears
aufspielen ['aʊfʃpi:lən] *vr* to show off; **sich als etw ~** to try to come on as sth
aufspießen ['aʊfʃpi:sən] *vt* to spear
aufspringen ['aʊfʃprɪŋən] *unreg vi* (*hochspringen*) to jump up; (*sich öffnen*) to spring open; (*Hände, Lippen*) to become chapped; **~ auf** *+akk* to jump onto
aufspüren ['aʊfʃpy:rən] *vt* to track down, trace
aufstacheln ['aʊfʃtaxəln] *vt* to incite
aufstampfen ['aʊfʃtampfən] *vi*: **mit dem Fuß ~** to stamp one's foot
Aufstand ['aʊfʃtant] *m* insurrection, rebellion
aufständisch ['aʊfʃtɛndɪʃ] *adj* rebellious, mutinous
aufstauen ['aʊfʃtaʊən] *vr* to collect; (*fig: Ärger*) to be bottled up
aufstechen ['aʊfʃtɛçən] *unreg vt* to prick open, puncture
aufstecken ['aʊfʃtɛkən] *vt* to stick on; (*mit Nadeln*) to pin up; (*umg*) to give up
aufstehen ['aʊfʃte:ən] *unreg vi* to get up; (*Tür*) to be open; **da musst du früher** *od* **eher ~!** (*fig: umg*) you'll have to do better than that!
aufsteigen ['aʊfʃtaɪgən] *unreg vi* (*hochsteigen*) to climb; (*Rauch*) to rise; **~ auf** *+akk* to get onto; **in jdm ~** (*Hass, Verdacht, Erinnerung etc*) to well up in sb
Aufsteiger (**-s, -**) *m* (*Sport*) promoted team; **(sozialer) ~** social climber
aufstellen ['aʊfʃtɛlən] *vt* (*aufrecht stellen*) to put up; (*Maschine*) to install; (*aufreihen*) to line up; (*Kandidaten*) to nominate; (*Forderung, Behauptung*) to put forward; (*formulieren: Programm etc*) to draw up;

(*leisten*: *Rekord*) to set up
Aufstellung *f* (*Sport*) line-up; (*Liste*) list
Aufstieg ['aʊfʃti:k] (**-(e)s, -e**) *m* (*auf Berg*) ascent; (*Fortschritt*) rise; (*beruflich, Sport*) promotion
Aufstiegschance *f* prospect of promotion
aufstöbern ['aʊfʃtø:bərn] *vt* (*Wild*) to start, flush; (*umg*: *entdecken*) to run to earth
aufstocken ['aʊfʃtɔkən] *vt* (*Vorräte*) to build up
aufstoßen ['aʊfʃto:sən] *unreg vt* to push open ▷ *vi* to belch
aufstrebend ['aʊfʃtre:bənd] *adj* ambitious; (*Land*) striving for progress
Aufstrich ['aʊfʃtrɪç] *m* spread
aufstülpen ['aʊfʃtʏlpən] *vt* (*Ärmel*) to turn up; (*Hut*) to put on
aufstützen ['aʊfʃtʏtsən] *vt* (*Körperteil*) to prop, lean; (*Person*) to prop up ▷ *vr*: **sich ~ auf** *+akk* to lean on
aufsuchen ['aʊfzu:xən] *vt* (*besuchen*) to visit; (*konsultieren*) to consult
auftakeln ['aʊfta:kəln] *vt* (*Naut*) to rig (out) ▷ *vr* (*pej*: *umg*) to deck o.s. out
Auftakt ['aʊftakt] *m* (*Mus*) upbeat; (*fig*) prelude
auftanken ['aʊftaŋkən] *vi* to get petrol (*Brit*) *od* gas (*US*) ▷ *vt* to refuel
auftauchen ['aʊftaʊxən] *vi* to appear; (*gefunden werden, kommen*) to turn up; (*aus Wasser etc*) to emerge; (*U-Boot*) to surface; (*Zweifel*) to arise
auftauen ['aʊftaʊən] *vt* to thaw ▷ *vi* to thaw; (*fig*) to relax
aufteilen ['aʊftaɪlən] *vt* to divide up; (*Raum*) to partition
Aufteilung *f* division; partition
auftischen ['aʊftɪʃən] *vt* to serve (up); (*fig*) to tell
Auftr. *abk* = **Auftrag**
Auftrag ['aʊftra:k] (**-(e)s, -träge**) *m* order; (*Anweisung*) commission; (*Aufgabe*) mission; **etw in ~ geben (bei)** to order/commission sth (from); **im ~ von** on behalf of; **im ~** *od* **i. A. J. Burnett** pp J. Burnett
auftragen ['aʊftra:gən] *unreg vt* (*Essen*) to serve; (*Farbe*) to put on; (*Kleidung*) to wear out ▷ *vi* (*dick machen*): **die Jacke trägt auf** the jacket makes one look fat; **jdm etw ~** to tell sb sth; **dick ~** (*umg*) to exaggerate
Auftraggeber, in (**-s, -**) *m(f)* client; (*Comm*) customer
Auftragsbestätigung *f* confirmation of order
auftreiben ['aʊftraɪbən] *unreg* (*umg*) *vt* (*beschaffen*) to raise
auftrennen ['aʊftrɛnən] *vt* to undo
auftreten ['aʊftre:tən] *unreg vt* to kick open ▷ *vi* to appear; (*mit Füßen*) to tread; (*sich verhalten*) to behave; (*fig*: *eintreten*) to occur; (*Schwierigkeiten etc*) to arise; **als Vermittler** *etc* **~** to act as intermediary *etc*; **geschlossen ~** to put up a united front
Auftreten (**-s**) *nt* (*Vorkommen*) appearance; (*Benehmen*) behaviour (*Brit*), behavior (*US*)
Auftrieb ['aʊftri:p] *m* (*Phys*) buoyancy, lift; (*fig*) impetus
Auftritt ['aʊftrɪt] *m* (*des Schauspielers*) entrance; (*lit, fig*: *Szene*) scene
auftrumpfen ['aʊftrʊmpfən] *vi* to show how good one is; (*mit Bemerkung*) to crow
auftun ['aʊftu:n] *unreg vt* to open ▷ *vr* to open up
auftürmen ['aʊftʏrmən] *vr* (*Gebirge etc*) to tower up; (*Schwierigkeiten*) to pile *od* mount up
aufwachen ['aʊfvaxən] *vi* to wake up
aufwachsen ['aʊfvaksən] *unreg vi* to grow up
Aufwand ['aʊfvant] (**-(e)s**) *m* expenditure; (*Kosten*) expense; (*Luxus*) show; **bitte, keinen ~!** please don't go out of your way
aufwändig ['aʊfvɛndɪç] *adj, adv* costly
Aufwandsentschädigung *f* expense allowance
aufwärmen ['aʊfvɛrmən] *vt* to warm up; (*alte Geschichten*) to rake up
aufwarten ['aʊfvartən] *vi* (*zu bieten haben*): **mit etw ~** to offer sth
aufwärts ['aʊfvɛrts] *adv* upwards; **es geht ~** things are looking up; **Aufwärtsentwicklung** *f* upward trend
aufwecken ['aʊfvɛkən] *vt* to wake(n) up
aufweichen ['aʊfvaɪçən] *vt* to soften; (*Brot*) to soak
aufweisen ['aʊfvaɪzən] *unreg vt* to show
aufwenden ['aʊfvɛndən] *unreg vt* to expend; (*Geld*) to spend; (*Sorgfalt*) to devote
aufwendig ['aʊfvɛndɪç] *adj, adv* costly
aufwerfen ['aʊfvɛrfən] *unreg vt* (*Fenster etc*) to throw open; (*Probleme*) to throw up, raise ▷ *vr*: **sich zu etw ~** to make o.s. out to be sth
aufwerten ['aʊfvɛrtən] *vt* (*Fin*) to revalue; (*fig*) to raise in value
Aufwertung *f* revaluation
aufwickeln ['aʊfvɪkəln] *vt* (*aufrollen*) to roll up; (*umg*: *Haar*) to put in curlers; (*lösen*) to untie
aufwiegeln ['aʊfvi:gəln] *vt* to stir up, incite
aufwiegen ['aʊfvi:gən] *unreg vt* to make up for
Aufwind ['aʊfvɪnt] *m* up-current; **neuen ~ bekommen** (*fig*) to get new impetus
aufwirbeln ['aʊfvɪrbəln] *vt* to whirl up; **Staub ~** (*fig*) to create a stir
aufwischen ['aʊfvɪʃən] *vt* to wipe up
aufwühlen ['aʊfvy:lən] *vt* (*lit*: *Erde, Meer*) to churn (up); (*Gefühle*) to stir
aufzählen ['aʊftsɛ:lən] *vt* to count out
aufzeichnen ['aʊftsaɪçnən] *vt* to sketch; (*schriftlich*) to jot down; (*auf Band*) to record
Aufzeichnung *f* (*schriftlich*) note; (*Tonbandaufzeichnung, Filmaufzeichnung*) recording
aufzeigen ['aʊftsaɪgən] *vt* to show, demonstrate
aufziehen ['aʊftsi:ən] *unreg vt* (*hochziehen*) to raise, draw up; (*öffnen*) to pull open; (: *Reißverschluss*) to undo; (*Gardinen*) to draw (back); (*Uhr*) to wind; (*großziehen*: *Kinder*) to raise, bring up; (*Tiere*) to rear; (*umg*: *necken*) to tease; (: *veranstalten*) to set up; (: *Fest*) to arrange ▷ *vi* (*Gewitter, Wolken*) to gather
Aufzucht ['aʊftsʊxt] *f* (*das Großziehen*) rearing, raising

Aufzug ['aʊftsu:k] *m* (*Fahrstuhl*) lift (*Brit*), elevator (*US*); (*Aufmarsch*) procession, parade; (*Kleidung*) get-up; (*Theat*) act
aufzwingen ['aʊftsvɪŋən] *unreg vt*: **jdm etw ~** to force sth upon sb
Aug. *abk* (*= August*) Aug.
Augapfel ['aʊk|apfəl] *m* eyeball; (*fig*) apple of one's eye
Auge ['aʊgə] (**-s, -n**) *nt* eye; (*Fettauge*) globule of fat; **unter vier ~n** in private; **vor aller ~n** in front of everybody, for all to see; **jdn/etw mit anderen ~n (an)sehen** to see sb/sth in a different light; **ich habe kein ~ zugetan** I didn't sleep a wink; **ein ~/beide ~n zudrücken** (*umg*) to turn a blind eye; **jdn/etw aus den ~n verlieren** to lose sight of sb/sth; (*fig*) to lose touch with sb/sth; **etw ins ~ fassen** to contemplate sth; **das kann leicht ins ~ gehen** (*fig*: *umg*) it might easily go wrong
Augenarzt *m* eye specialist, ophthalmologist
Augenblick *m* moment; **im ~** at the moment; **im ersten ~** for a moment; **augenblicklich** *adj* (*sofort*) instantaneous; (*gegenwärtig*) present
Augen- *zW*: **Augenbraue** *f* eyebrow; **Augenhöhe** *f*: **in Augenhöhe** at eye level; **Augenmerk** *nt* (*Aufmerksamkeit*) attention; **Augenschein** *m*: **jdn/etw in Augenschein nehmen** to have a close look at sb/sth; **augenscheinlich** *adj* obvious; **Augenweide** *f* sight for sore eyes; **Augenwischerei** *f* (*fig*) eye-wash; **Augenzeuge** *m* eye witness; **Augenzeugin** *f* eye witness
August [aʊ'gʊst] (**-(e)s** *od* **-, -e**) (*pl selten*) *m* August; *siehe auch* **September**
Auktion [aʊktsi'o:n] *f* auction
Auktionator [aʊktsio'na:tɔr] *m* auctioneer
Aula ['aʊla] (**-, Aulen** *od* **-s**) *f* assembly hall
Aus [aʊs] (**-**) *nt* (*Sport*) outfield; **ins ~ gehen** to go out

SCHLÜSSELWORT

aus [aʊs] *präp+dat* **1** (*räumlich*) out of; (*von ... her*) from; **er ist aus Berlin** he's from Berlin; **aus dem Fenster** out of the window
2 (*gemacht/hergestellt aus*) made of; **ein Herz aus Stein** a heart of stone
3 (*auf Ursache deutend*) out of; **aus Mitleid** out of sympathy; **aus Erfahrung** from experience; **aus Spaß** for fun
4: **aus ihr wird nie etwas** she'll never get anywhere
▷ *adv* **1** (*zu Ende*) finished, over; **aus sein** to be over; **es ist aus mit ihm** he is finished, he has had it; **aus und vorbei** over and done with
2 (*ausgeschaltet, ausgezogen*) off; **aus sein** to be out; **Licht aus!** lights out!
3 (*in Verbindung mit von*): **von Rom aus** from Rome; **vom Fenster aus** out of the window; **von sich aus** (*selbstständig*) of one's own accord; **von mir aus** as far as I'm concerned
4: **aus und ein gehen** to come and go; (*bei jdm*) to visit frequently; **weder aus noch ein wissen** to be at one's wits' end; **auf etw** *akk* **aus sein** to be after sth

ausarbeiten ['aʊs|arbaɪtən] *vt* to work out
ausarten ['aʊs|artən] *vi* to degenerate; (*Kind*) to become overexcited
ausatmen ['aʊs|a:tmən] *vi* to breathe out
ausbaden ['aʊsba:dən] (*umg*) *vt*: **etw ~ müssen** to carry the can for sth
Ausbau ['aʊsbaʊ] *m* extension, expansion; removal
ausbauen *vt* to extend, expand; (*herausnehmen*) to take out, remove
ausbaufähig *adj* (*fig*) worth developing
ausbedingen ['aʊsbədɪŋən] *unreg vt*: **sich** *dat* **etw ~** to insist on sth
ausbeißen ['aʊsbaɪsən] *unreg vr*: **sich** *dat* **an etw** *dat* **die Zähne ~** (*fig*) to have a tough time of it with sth
ausbessern ['aʊsbɛsərn] *vt* to mend, repair
Ausbesserungsarbeiten *pl* repair work *sing*
ausbeulen ['aʊsbɔʏlən] *vt* to beat out
Ausbeute ['aʊsbɔʏtə] *f* yield; (*Gewinn*) profit, gain; (*Fische*) catch
ausbeuten *vt* to exploit; (*Min*) to work
ausbezahlen ['aʊsbətsa:lən] *vt* (*Geld*) to pay out
ausbilden ['aʊsbɪldən] *vt* to educate; (*Lehrling, Soldat*) to instruct, train; (*Fähigkeiten*) to develop; (*Geschmack*) to cultivate
Ausbilder, in (**-s, -**) *m(f)* instructor, instructress
Ausbildung *f* education; training, instruction; development; cultivation; **er ist noch in der ~** he's still a trainee; he hasn't finished his education
Ausbildungs- *zW*: **Ausbildungsförderung** *f* (provision of) grants for students and trainees; (*Stipendium*) grant; **Ausbildungsplatz** *m* (*Stelle*) training vacancy
ausbitten ['aʊsbɪtən] *unreg vt*: **sich** *dat* **etw ~** (*geh*: *erbitten*) to ask for sth; (*verlangen*) to insist on sth
ausblasen ['aʊsbla:zən] *unreg vt* to blow out; (*Ei*) to blow
ausbleiben ['aʊsblaɪbən] *unreg vi* (*Personen*) to stay away, not come; (*Ereignisse*) to fail to happen, not happen; **es konnte nicht ~, dass ...** it was inevitable that ...
ausblenden ['aʊsblɛndən] *vt, vi* (*TV etc*) to fade out
Ausblick ['aʊsblɪk] *m* (*lit, fig*) prospect, outlook, view
ausbomben ['aʊsbɔmbən] *vt* to bomb out
ausbooten ['aʊsbo:tən] (*umg*) *vt* (*jdn*) to kick *od* boot out
ausbrechen ['aʊsbrɛçən] *unreg vi* to break out ▷ *vt* to break off; **in Tränen/Gelächter ~** to burst into tears/out laughing
Ausbrecher, in (**-s, -**) (*umg*) *m(f)* (*Gefangener*) escaped prisoner, escapee
ausbreiten ['aʊsbraɪtən] *vt* to spread (out); (*Arme*) to stretch out ▷ *vr* to spread; **sich über**

ein Thema ~ to expand *od* enlarge on a topic
ausbrennen ['aʊsbrɛnən] *unreg vt* to scorch; (*Wunde*) to cauterize ▷ *vi* to burn out
ausbringen ['aʊsbrɪŋən] *unreg vt* (*ein Hoch*) to propose
Ausbruch ['aʊsbrʊx] *m* outbreak; (*von Vulkan*) eruption; (*Gefühlsausbruch*) outburst; (*von Gefangenen*) escape
ausbrüten ['aʊsbry:tən] *vt* (*lit, fig*) to hatch
Ausbuchtung ['aʊsbʊxtʊŋ] *f* bulge; (*Küste*) cove
ausbügeln ['aʊsby:gəln] *vt* to iron out; (*umg: Fehler, Verlust*) to make good
ausbuhen ['aʊsbu:ən] *vt* to boo
Ausbund ['aʊsbʊnt] *m*: **ein ~ an** *od* **von Tugend/Sparsamkeit** a paragon of virtue/a model of thrift
ausbürgern ['aʊsbʏrgərn] *vt* to expatriate
ausbürsten ['aʊsbʏrstən] *vt* to brush out
Ausdauer ['aʊsdaʊər] *f* stamina; (*Beharrlichkeit*) perseverance
ausdauernd *adj* persevering
ausdehnen ['aʊsde:nən] *vt, vr* (*räumlich*) to expand; (*zeitlich, auch Gummi*) to stretch; (*Nebel, fig: Macht*) to extend
ausdenken ['aʊsdɛŋkən] *unreg vt* (*zu Ende denken*) to think through; **sich** *dat* **etw ~** to think sth up; **das ist nicht auszudenken** (*unvorstellbar*) it's inconceivable
ausdiskutieren ['aʊsdɪskuti:rən] *vt* to talk out
ausdrehen ['aʊsdre:ən] *vt* to turn *od* switch off
Ausdruck ['aʊsdrʊk] (**-s, -drücke**) *m* expression, phrase; (*Kundgabe, Gesichtsausdruck*) expression; (*Fachausdruck*) term; (*Comput*) hard copy; **mit dem ~ des Bedauerns** (*form*) expressing regret
ausdrucken *vt* (*Text*) to print out
ausdrücken ['aʊsdrʏkən] *vt* (*auch vr: formulieren, zeigen*) to express; (*Zigarette*) to put out; (*Zitrone*) to squeeze
ausdrücklich *adj* express, explicit
Ausdrucks- *zW*: **Ausdrucksfähigkeit** *f* expressiveness; (*Gewandtheit*) articulateness; **ausdruckslos** *adj* expressionless, blank; **ausdrucksvoll** *adj* expressive; **Ausdrucksweise** *f* mode of expression
Ausdünstung ['aʊsdʏnstʊŋ] *f* (*Dampf*) vapour (*Brit*), vapor (*US*); (*Geruch*) smell
auseinander [aʊs|aɪ'nandər] *adv* (*getrennt*) apart; **weit ~** far apart
auseinander- *zW*: **auseinanderbringen** *unreg vt* to separate; **auseinanderfallen** *unreg vi* to fall apart; **auseinandergehen** *unreg vi* (*Menschen*) to separate; (*Meinungen*) to differ; (*Gegenstand*) to fall apart; (*umg: dick werden*) to put on weight; **auseinanderhalten** *unreg vt* to tell apart; **auseinanderklaffen** *vi* to gape open; (*fig: Meinungen*) to be far apart, diverge (wildly); **auseinanderlaufen** *unreg vi* (*Menge*) to disperse; (*umg: sich trennen*) to break up; **auseinanderleben** *vr* to drift apart; **auseinandernehmen** *unreg vt* to take to pieces, dismantle; **auseinanderschreiben** *unreg vt* to write as separate words; **auseinandersetzen** *unreg vt* to set forth, explain ▷ *vr* (*sich verständigen*) to come to terms, settle; (*sich befassen*) to concern o.s.; **sich mit jdm auseinandersetzen** to talk with sb; (*sich streiten*) to argue with sb; **Auseinandersetzung** *f* argument
auserkoren ['aʊs|ɛrko:rən] *adj* (*liter*) chosen, selected
auserlesen ['aʊs|ɛrle:zən] *adj* select, choice
ausersehen ['aʊs|ɛrze:ən] *unreg vt* (*geh*): **dazu ~ sein, etw zu tun** to be chosen to do sth
ausfahrbar *adj* extendable; (*Antenne, Fahrgestell*) retractable
ausfahren ['aʊsfa:rən] *unreg vi* to drive out; (*Naut*) to put out (to sea) ▷ *vt* to take out; (*Aut*) to drive flat out; (*ausliefern: Waren*) to deliver; **ausgefahrene Wege** rutted roads
Ausfahrt *f* (*des Zuges etc*) leaving, departure; (*Autobahnausfahrt, Garagenausfahrt*) exit, way out; (*Spazierfahrt*) drive, excursion
Ausfall ['aʊsfal] *m* loss; (*Nichtstattfinden*) cancellation; (*das Versagen: Tech, Med*) failure; (*von Motor*) breakdown; (*Produktionsstörung*) stoppage; (*Mil*) sortie; (*Fechten*) lunge; (*radioaktiv*) fallout
ausfallen ['aʊsfalən] *unreg vi* (*Zähne, Haare*) to fall *od* come out; (*nicht stattfinden*) to be cancelled; (*wegbleiben*) to be omitted; (*Person*) to drop out; (*Lohn*) to be stopped; (*nicht funktionieren*) to break down; (*Resultat haben*) to turn out; **wie ist das Spiel ausgefallen?** what was the result of the game?; **die Schule fällt morgen aus** there's no school tomorrow
ausfallend *adj* impertinent
Ausfallstraße *f* arterial road
Ausfallzeit *f* (*Maschine*) downtime
ausfegen ['aʊsfe:gən] *vt* to sweep out
ausfeilen ['aʊsfaɪlən] *vt* to file out; (*Stil*) to polish up
ausfertigen ['aʊsfɛrtɪgən] *vt* (*form*) to draw up; (*Rechnung*) to make out; **doppelt ~** to duplicate
Ausfertigung *f* (*form*) drawing up; making out; (*Exemplar*) copy; **in doppelter/dreifacher ~** in duplicate/triplicate
ausfindig ['aʊsfɪndɪç] *adj*: **~ machen** to discover
ausfliegen ['aʊsfli:gən] *unreg vi* to fly away ▷ *vt* to fly out; **sie sind ausgeflogen** (*umg*) they're out
ausfließen ['aʊsfli:sən] *unreg vi*: **~ (aus)** (*herausfließen*) to flow out (of); (*auslaufen: Öl etc*) to leak (out of); (*Eiter etc*) to be discharged (from)
ausflippen ['aʊsflɪpən] (*umg*) *vi* to freak out
Ausflucht ['aʊsflʊxt] (**-, -flüchte**) *f* excuse
Ausflug ['aʊsflu:k] *m* excursion, outing
Ausflügler, in ['aʊsfly:klər(ɪn)] (**-s, -**) *m(f)* tripper (*Brit*), excursionist (*US*)
Ausfluss ['aʊsflʊs] *m* outlet; (*Med*) discharge
ausfragen ['aʊsfra:gən] *vt* to interrogate, question
ausfransen ['aʊsfranzən] *vi* to fray

ausfressen ['aʊsfrɛsən] *unreg* (*umg*) *vt* (*anstellen*) to be up to

Ausfuhr ['aʊsfu:r] (**-, -en**) *f* export, exportation; (*Ware*) export ▷ *in zW* export

ausführbar ['aʊsfy:rba:r] *adj* feasible; (*Comm*) exportable

ausführen ['aʊsfy:rən] *vt* (*verwirklichen*) to carry out; (*Person*) to take out; (*Hund*) to take for a walk; (*Comm*) to export; (*erklären*) to give details of; **die ~de Gewalt** (*Pol*) the executive

Ausfuhrgenehmigung *f* export licence

ausführlich *adj* detailed ▷ *adv* in detail; **Ausführlichkeit** *f* detail

Ausführung *f* execution, performance; (*von Waren*) design; (*von Thema*) exposition; (*Durchführung*) completion; (*Herstellungsart*) version; (*Erklärung*) explanation

Ausfuhrzoll *m* export duty

ausfüllen ['aʊsfʏlən] *vt* to fill up; (*Fragebogen etc*) to fill in; (*Beruf*) to be fulfilling for; **jdn (ganz) ~** (*Zeit in Anspruch nehmen*) to take (all) sb's time

Ausg. *abk* (= *Ausgabe*) ed.

Ausgabe ['aʊsga:bə] *f* (*Geld*) expenditure, outlay; (*Aushändigung*) giving out; (*Schalter*) counter; (*Ausführung*) version; (*Buch*) edition; (*Nummer*) issue

Ausgang ['aʊsgaŋ] *m* way out, exit; (*Ende*) end; (*Ausgangpunkt*) starting point; (*Ergebnis*) result; (*Ausgehtag*) free time, time off; **ein Unfall mit tödlichem ~** a fatal accident; **kein ~** no exit

Ausgangs- *zW*: **Ausgangsbasis** *f* starting point; **Ausgangspunkt** *m* starting point; **Ausgangssperre** *f* curfew

ausgeben ['aʊsge:bən] *unreg vt* (*Geld*) to spend; (*austeilen*) to issue, distribute; (*Comput*) to output ▷ *vr*: **sich für etw/jdn ~** to pass o.s. off as sth/sb; **ich gebe heute Abend einen aus** (*umg*) it's my treat this evening

ausgebeult ['aʊsgəbɔʏlt] *adj* (*Kleidung*) baggy; (*Hut*) battered

ausgebucht ['aʊsgəbu:xt] *adj* fully booked

Ausgeburt ['aʊsgəbu:rt] (*pej*) *f* (*der Fantasie etc*) monstrous product *od* invention

ausgedehnt ['aʊsgəde:nt] *adj* (*breit, groß, fig: weitreichend*) extensive; (*Spaziergang*) long; (*zeitlich*) lengthy

ausgedient ['aʊsgədi:nt] *adj* (*Soldat*) discharged; (*verbraucht*) no longer in use; **~ haben** to have come to the end of its useful life

ausgefallen ['aʊsgəfalən] *adj* (*ungewöhnlich*) exceptional

ausgefuchst ['aʊsgəfʊkst] (*umg*) *adj* clever; (*listig*) crafty

ausgegangen ['aʊsgəgaŋən] *pp von* **ausgehen**

ausgeglichen ['aʊsgəglɪçən] *adj* (well-)balanced; **Ausgeglichenheit** *f* balance; (*von Mensch*) even-temperedness

Ausgehanzug *m* good suit

ausgehen ['aʊsge:ən] *unreg vi* (*auch Feuer, Ofen, Licht*) to go out; (*zu Ende gehen*) to come to an end; (*Benzin*) to run out; (*Haare, Zähne*) to fall *od* come out; (*Strom*) to go off; (*Resultat haben*) to turn out; (*spazieren gehen*) to go (out) for a walk; (*abgeschickt werden: Post*) to be sent off; **mir ging das Benzin aus** I ran out of petrol (*Brit*) *od* gas (*US*); **auf etw** *akk* **~** to aim at sth; **von etw ~** (*wegführen*) to lead away from sth; (*herrühren*) to come from sth; (*zugrunde legen*) to proceed from sth; **wir können davon ~, dass ...** we can proceed from the assumption that ..., we can take as our starting point that ...; **leer ~** to get nothing; **schlecht ~** to turn out badly

ausgehungert ['aʊsgəhʊŋərt] *adj* starved; (*abgezehrt: Mensch etc*) emaciated

Ausgehverbot *nt* curfew

ausgeklügelt ['aʊsgəkly:gəlt] *adj* ingenious

ausgekocht ['aʊsgəkɔxt] (*pej: umg*) *adj* (*durchtrieben*) cunning; (*fig*) out-and-out

ausgelassen ['aʊsgəlasən] *adj* boisterous, high-spirited, exuberant; **Ausgelassenheit** *f* boisterousness, high spirits *pl*, exuberance

ausgelastet ['aʊsgəlastət] *adj* fully occupied

ausgeleiert ['aʊsgəlaɪərt] *adj* worn; (*Gummiband*) stretched

ausgelernt ['aʊsgəlɛrnt] *adj* trained, qualified

ausgemacht ['aʊsgəmaxt] *adj* settled; (*umg: Dummkopf etc*) out-and-out, downright; **es gilt als ~, dass ...** it is settled that ...; **es war eine ~e Sache, dass ...** it was a foregone conclusion that ...

ausgemergelt ['aʊsgəmɛrgəlt] *adj* (*Gesicht*) emaciated, gaunt

ausgenommen ['aʊsgənɔmən] *konj* except; **Anwesende sind ~** present company excepted

ausgepowert ['aʊsgəpo:vərt] *adj*: **~ sein** (*umg*) to be tired, be exhausted

ausgeprägt ['aʊsgəprɛ:kt] *adj* prominent; (*Eigenschaft*) distinct

ausgerechnet ['aʊsgərɛçnət] *adv* just, precisely; **~ du** you of all people; **~ heute** today of all days

ausgeschlossen ['aʊsgəʃlɔsən] *pp von* **ausschließen** ▷ *adj* (*unmöglich*) impossible, out of the question; **es ist nicht ~, dass ...** it cannot be ruled out that ...

ausgeschnitten ['aʊsgəʃnɪtən] *adj* (*Kleid*) low-necked

ausgesehen ['aʊsgəze:ən] *pp von* **aussehen**

ausgesprochen ['aʊsgəʃprɔxən] *adj* (*Faulheit, Lüge etc*) out-and-out; (*unverkennbar*) marked ▷ *adv* decidedly

ausgestorben ['aʊsgəʃtɔrbən] *adj* (*Tierart*) extinct; (*fig*) deserted

ausgewogen ['aʊsgəvo:gən] *adj* balanced; (*Maß*) equal

ausgezeichnet ['aʊsgətsaɪçnət] *adj* excellent

ausgiebig ['aʊsgi:bɪç] *adj* (*Gebrauch*) full, good; (*Essen*) generous, lavish; **~ schlafen** to have a good sleep

ausgießen ['aʊsgi:sən] *unreg vt* (*aus einem Behälter*) to pour out; (*Behälter*) to empty; (*weggießen*) to pour away

Ausgleich ['aʊsglaɪç] (**-(e)s, -e**) *m* balance; (*von Fehler, Mangel*) compensation; (*Sport*): **den ~ erzielen** to equalize; **zum ~** *+gen* in order to offset sth; **das ist ein guter ~** (*entspannend*) that's very relaxing

ausgleichen ['aʊsglaɪçən] *unreg vt* to balance (out); (*Konflikte*) to reconcile; (*Höhe*) to even up ▷ *vi* (*Sport*) to equalize; **~de Gerechtigkeit** poetic justice

Ausgleichssport *m* keep-fit activity

Ausgleichstor *nt* equalizer

ausgraben ['aʊsgra:bən] *unreg vt* to dig up; (*Leichen*) to exhume; (*fig*) to unearth

Ausgrabung *f* excavation

ausgrenzen ['aʊsgrɛntsən] *vt* to shut out, separate

Ausgrenzung *f* shut-out, separation

Ausguck ['aʊsgʊk] *m* look-out

Ausguss ['aʊsgʊs] *m* (*Spüle*) sink; (*Abfluss*) outlet; (*Tülle*) spout

aushaben ['aʊsha:bən] *unreg* (*umg*) *vt* (*Kleidung*) to have taken off; (*Buch*) to have finished

aushalten ['aʊshaltən] *unreg vt* to bear, stand; (*umg*: *Geliebte*) to keep ▷ *vi* to hold out; **das ist nicht zum A~** that is unbearable; **sich von jdm ~ lassen** to be kept by sb

aushandeln ['aʊshandəln] *vt* to negotiate

aushändigen ['aʊshɛndɪgən] *vt*: **jdm etw ~** to hand sth over to sb

Aushang ['aʊshaŋ] *m* notice

aushängen ['aʊshɛŋən] *unreg vt* (*Meldung*) to put up; (*Fenster*) to take off its hinges ▷ *vi* to be displayed ▷ *vr* to hang out

Aushängeschild *nt* (shop) sign; (*fig*): **als ~ für etw dienen** to promote sth

ausharren ['aʊsharən] *vi* to hold out

aushäusig ['aʊshɔʏzɪç] *adj* gallivanting around, on the tiles

ausheben ['aʊshe:bən] *unreg vt* (*Erde*) to lift out; (*Grube*) to hollow out; (*Tür*) to take off its hinges; (*Diebesnest*) to clear out; (*Mil*) to enlist

aushecken ['aʊshɛkən] (*umg*) *vt* to concoct, think up

aushelfen ['aʊshɛlfən] *unreg vi*: **jdm ~** to help sb out

Aushilfe ['aʊshɪlfə] *f* help, assistance; (*Person*) (temporary) worker

Aushilfs- *zW*: **Aushilfskraft** *f* temporary worker; **Aushilfslehrer, in** *m(f)* supply teacher; **aushilfsweise** *adv* temporarily, as a stopgap

aushöhlen ['aʊshø:lən] *vt* to hollow out; (*fig*: *untergraben*) to undermine

ausholen ['aʊsho:lən] *vi* to swing one's arm back; (*zur Ohrfeige*) to raise one's hand; (*beim Gehen*) to take long strides; **zum Gegenschlag ~** (*lit, fig*) to prepare for a counter-attack

aushorchen ['aʊshɔrçən] *vt* to sound out, pump

aushungern ['aʊshʊŋərn] *vt* to starve out

auskennen ['aʊskɛnən] *unreg vr* to know a lot; (*an einem Ort*) to know one's way about; (*in Fragen etc*) to be knowledgeable; **man kennt sich bei ihm nie aus** you never know where you are with him

auskippen ['aʊskɪpən] *vt* to empty

ausklammern ['aʊsklamərn] *vt* (*Thema*) to exclude, leave out

Ausklang ['aʊsklaŋ] *m* (*geh*) end

ausklappbar ['aʊsklapba:r] *adj*: **dieser Tisch ist ~** this table can be opened out

auskleiden ['aʊsklaɪdən] *vr* (*geh*) to undress ▷ *vt* (*Wand*) to line

ausklingen ['aʊsklɪŋən] *unreg vi* to end; (*Ton, Lied*) to die away; (*Fest*) to come to an end

ausklinken ['aʊsklɪŋkən] *vt* (*Bomben*) to release ▷ *vi* (*umg*) to flip one's lid

ausklopfen ['aʊsklɔpfən] *vt* (*Teppich*) to beat; (*Pfeife*) to knock out

auskochen ['aʊskɔxən] *vt* to boil; (*Med*) to sterilize

auskommen ['aʊskɔmən] *unreg vi*: **mit jdm ~** to get on with sb; **mit etw ~** to get by with sth; **Auskommen (-s)** *nt*: **sein Auskommen haben** to get by; **mit ihr ist kein Auskommen** she's impossible to get on with

auskosten ['aʊskɔstən] *vt* to enjoy to the full

auskramen ['aʊskra:mən] (*umg*) *vt* to dig out, unearth; (*fig*: *alte Geschichten etc*) to bring up

auskratzen ['aʊskratsən] *vt* (*auch Med*) to scrape out

auskugeln ['aʊsku:gəln] *vr*: **sich** *dat* **den Arm ~** to dislocate one's arm

auskundschaften ['aʊskʊntʃaftən] *vt* to spy out; (*Gebiet*) to reconnoitre (*Brit*), reconnoiter (*US*)

Auskunft ['aʊskʊnft] **(-, -künfte)** *f* information; (*nähere*) details *pl*, particulars *pl*; (*Stelle*) information office; (*Tel*) inquiries; **jdm ~ erteilen** to give sb information

auskuppeln ['aʊskʊpəln] *vi* to disengage the clutch

auskurieren ['aʊskuri:rən] (*umg*) *vt* to cure

auslachen ['aʊslaxən] *vt* to laugh at, mock

ausladen ['aʊsla:dən] *unreg vt* to unload; (*umg*: *Gäste*) to cancel an invitation to ▷ *vi* (*Äste*) to spread

ausladend *adj* (*Gebärden, Bewegung*) sweeping

Auslage ['aʊsla:gə] *f* shop window (display)

Auslagen *pl* outlay *sing*, expenditure *sing*

Ausland ['aʊslant] *nt* foreign countries *pl*; **im ~** abroad; **ins ~** abroad

Ausländer, in ['aʊslɛndər(ɪn)] **(-s, -)** *m(f)* foreigner

Ausländerfeindlichkeit *f* hostility to foreigners, xenophobia

ausländisch *adj* foreign

Auslands- *zW*: **Auslandsaufenthalt** *m* stay abroad; **Auslandsgespräch** *nt* international call; **Auslandskorrespondent, in** *m(f)* foreign correspondent; **Auslandsreise** *f* trip abroad; **Auslandsschutzbrief** *m* international travel cover; **Auslandsvertretung** *f* agency abroad; (*von Firma*) foreign branch

auslassen ['aʊslasən] *unreg vt* to leave out; (*Wort etc*) to omit; (*Fett*) to melt; (*Kleidungsstück*) to let out ▷ *vr*: **sich über etw** *akk* **~** to speak one's mind about sth; **seine Wut** *etc* **an jdm ~** to vent one's rage *etc* on sb

Auslassung *f* omission
Auslassungszeichen *nt* apostrophe
auslasten ['aʊslastən] *vt* (*Fahrzeug*) to make full use of; (*Maschine*) to use to capacity; (*jdn*) to occupy fully
Auslauf ['aʊslaʊf] *m* (*für Tiere*) run; (*Ausfluss*) outflow, outlet
auslaufen *unreg vi* to run out; (*Behälter*) to leak; (*Naut*) to put out (to sea); (*langsam aufhören*) to run down
Ausläufer ['aʊslɔʏfər] *m* (*von Gebirge*) spur; (*Pflanze*) runner; (*Met*: *von Hoch*) ridge; (: *von Tief*) trough
ausleeren ['aʊsle:rən] *vt* to empty
auslegen ['aʊsle:gən] *vt* (*Waren*) to lay out; (*Köder*) to put down; (*Geld*) to lend; (*bedecken*) to cover; (*Text etc*) to interpret
Ausleger (**-s, -**) *m* (*von Kran etc*) jib, boom
Auslegung *f* interpretation
Ausleihe ['aʊslaɪə] (**-, -n**) *f* issuing; (*Stelle*) issue desk
ausleihen ['aʊslaɪən] *unreg vt* (*verleihen*) to lend; **sich** *dat* **etw ~** to borrow sth
auslernen ['aʊslɛrnən] *vi* (*Lehrling*) to finish one's apprenticeship; **man lernt nie aus** (*Sprichwort*) you live and learn
Auslese ['aʊsle:zə] (**-, -n**) *f* selection; (*Elite*) elite; (*Wein*) choice wine
auslesen ['aʊsle:zən] *unreg vt* to select; (*umg*: *zu Ende lesen*) to finish
ausliefern ['aʊsli:fərn] *vt* to hand over; (*Comm*) to deliver ▷ *vr*: **sich jdm ~** to give o.s. up to sb; **~ (an** *+akk***)** to deliver (up) (to), hand over (to); (*an anderen Staat*) to extradite (to); **jdm/etw ausgeliefert sein** to be at the mercy of sb/sth
Auslieferungsabkommen *nt* extradition treaty
ausliegen ['aʊsli:gən] *unreg vi* (*zur Ansicht*) to be displayed; (*Zeitschriften etc*) to be available (to the public); (*Liste*) to be up
auslöschen ['aʊslœʃən] *vt* to extinguish; (*fig*) to wipe out, obliterate
auslosen ['aʊslo:zən] *vt* to draw lots for
auslösen ['aʊslø:zən] *vt* (*Explosion, Schuss*) to set off; (*hervorrufen*) to cause, produce; (*Gefangene*) to ransom; (*Pfand*) to redeem
Auslöser (**-s, -**) *m* trigger; (*Phot*) release; (*Anlass*) cause
ausloten ['aʊslo:tən] *vt* (*Naut*: *Tiefe*) to sound; (*fig geh*) to plumb
ausmachen ['aʊsmaxən] *vt* (*Licht, Radio*) to turn off; (*Feuer*) to put out; (*entdecken*) to make out; (*vereinbaren*) to agree; (*beilegen*) to settle; (*Anteil darstellen, betragen*) to represent; (*bedeuten*) to matter; **das macht ihm nichts aus** it doesn't matter to him; **macht es Ihnen etwas aus, wenn ...?** would you mind if ...?
ausmalen ['aʊsma:lən] *vt* to paint; (*fig*) to describe; **sich** *dat* **etw ~** to imagine sth
Ausmaß ['aʊsma:s] *nt* dimension; (*fig*) scale
ausmerzen ['aʊsmɛrtsən] *vt* to eliminate
ausmessen ['aʊsmɛsən] *unreg vt* to measure
ausmisten ['aʊsmɪstən] *vt* (*Stall*) to muck out; (*fig*: *umg*: *Schrank etc*) to tidy out; (: *Zimmer*) to clean out
ausmustern ['aʊsmʊstərn] *vt* (*Maschine, Fahrzeug etc*) to take out of service; (*Mil*: *entlassen*) to invalid out
Ausnahme ['aʊsna:mə] (**-, -n**) *f* exception; **eine ~ machen** to make an exception; **Ausnahmeerscheinung** *f* exception, one-off example; **Ausnahmefall** *m* exceptional case; **Ausnahmezustand** *m* state of emergency
ausnahmslos *adv* without exception
ausnahmsweise *adv* by way of exception, for once
ausnehmen ['aʊsne:mən] *unreg vt* to take out, remove; (*Tier*) to gut; (*Nest*) to rob; (*umg*: *Geld abnehmen*) to clean out; (*ausschließen*) to make an exception of ▷ *vr* to look, appear
ausnehmend *adj* exceptional
ausnüchtern ['aʊsnʏçtərn] *vt, vi* to sober up
Ausnüchterungszelle *f* drying-out cell
ausnutzen ['aʊsnʊtsən] *vt* (*Zeit, Gelegenheit*) to use, turn to good account; (*Einfluss*) to use; (*Mensch, Gutmütigkeit*) to exploit
auspacken ['aʊspakən] *vt* to unpack ▷ *vi* (*umg*: *alles sagen*) to talk
auspfeifen ['aʊspfaɪfən] *unreg vt* to hiss/boo at
ausplaudern ['aʊsplaʊdərn] *vt* (*Geheimnis*) to blab
ausposaunen ['aʊspozaʊnən] (*umg*) *vt* to tell the world about
ausprägen ['aʊsprɛ:gən] *vr* (*Begabung, Charaktereigenschaft*) to reveal *od* show itself
auspressen ['aʊsprɛsən] *vt* (*Saft, Schwamm etc*) to squeeze out; (*Zitrone etc*) to squeeze
ausprobieren ['aʊsprobi:rən] *vt* to try (out)
Auspuff ['aʊspʊf] (**-(e)s, -e**) *m* (*Tech*) exhaust; **Auspuffrohr** *nt* exhaust (pipe); **Auspufftopf** *m* (*Aut*) silencer (*Brit*), muffler (*US*)
ausquartieren ['aʊskvarti:rən] *vt* to move out
ausquetschen ['aʊskvɛtʃən] *vt* (*Zitrone etc*) to squeeze; (*umg*: *ausfragen*) to grill; (: *aus Neugier*) to pump
ausradieren ['aʊsradi:rən] *vt* to erase, rub out
ausrangieren ['aʊsrãʒi:rən] (*umg*) *vt* to chuck out; (*Maschine, Auto*) to scrap
ausrauben ['aʊsraʊbən] *vt* to rob
ausräumen ['aʊsrɔʏmən] *vt* (*Dinge*) to clear away; (*Schrank, Zimmer*) to empty; (*Bedenken*) to put aside
ausrechnen ['aʊsrɛçnən] *vt* to calculate, reckon
Ausrechnung *f* calculation, reckoning
Ausrede ['aʊsre:də] *f* excuse
ausreden ['aʊsre:dən] *vi* to have one's say ▷ *vt*: **jdm etw ~** to talk sb out of sth; **er hat mich nicht mal ~ lassen** he didn't even let me finish (speaking)
ausreichen ['aʊsraɪçən] *vi* to suffice, be enough
ausreichend *adj* sufficient, adequate; (*Sch*) adequate
Ausreise ['aʊsraɪzə] *f* departure; **bei der ~** when leaving the country; **Ausreiseerlaubnis**

f exit visa
ausreisen ['aʊsraɪzən] *vi* to leave the country
ausreißen ['aʊsraɪsən] *unreg vt* to tear *od* pull out ▷*vi* (*Riss bekommen*) to tear; (*umg*) to make off, scram; **er hat sich** *dat* **kein Bein ausgerissen** (*umg*) he didn't exactly overstrain himself
ausrenken ['aʊsrɛŋkən] *vt* to dislocate
ausrichten ['aʊsrɪçtən] *vt* (*Botschaft*) to deliver; (*Gruß*) to pass on; (*Hochzeit etc*) to arrange; (*in gerade Linie bringen*) to get in a straight line; (*angleichen*) to bring into line; (*Typ etc*) to justify; **etwas/nichts bei jdm ~** to get somewhere/nowhere with sb; **jdm etw ~** to take a message for sb; **ich werde es ihm ~** I'll tell him
ausrotten ['aʊsrɔtən] *vt* to stamp out, exterminate
ausrücken ['aʊsrʏkən] *vi* (*Mil*) to move off; (*Feuerwehr, Polizei*) to be called out; (*umg: weglaufen*) to run away
Ausruf ['aʊsru:f] *m* (*Schrei*) cry, exclamation; (*Verkünden*) proclamation
ausrufen *unreg vt* to cry out, exclaim; to call out; **jdn ~ (lassen)** (*über Lautsprecher etc*) to page sb
Ausrufezeichen *nt* exclamation mark
ausruhen ['aʊsru:ən] *vt, vi, vr* to rest
ausrüsten ['aʊsrʏstən] *vt* to equip, fit out
Ausrüstung *f* equipment
ausrutschen ['aʊsrʊtʃən] *vi* to slip
Ausrutscher (-s, -) (*umg*) *m* (*lit, fig*) slip
Aussage ['aʊsza:gə] **(-, -n)** *f* (*Jur*) statement; **der Angeklagte/Zeuge verweigerte die ~** the accused/witness refused to give evidence
aussagekräftig *adj* expressive, full of expression
aussagen ['aʊsza:gən] *vt* to say, state ▷*vi* (*Jur*) to give evidence
Aussatz ['aʊszats] **(-es)** *m* (*Med*) leprosy
aussaugen ['aʊszaʊgən] *vt* (*Saft etc*) to suck out; (*Wunde*) to suck the poison out of; (*fig: ausbeuten*) to drain dry
ausschalten ['aʊsʃaltən] *vt* to switch off; (*fig*) to eliminate
Ausschank ['aʊsʃaŋk] **(-(e)s, -schänke)** *m* dispensing, giving out; (*Comm*) selling; (*Theke*) bar
Ausschankerlaubnis *f* licence (*Brit*), license (*US*)
Ausschau ['aʊsʃaʊ] *f*: **~ halten (nach)** to look out (for), watch (for)
ausschauen *vi*: **~ (nach)** to look out (for), be on the look-out (for)
ausscheiden ['aʊsʃaɪdən] *unreg vt* (*aussondern*) to take out; (*Med*) to excrete ▷*vi*: **~ (aus)** to leave; (*aus einem Amt*) to retire (from); (*Sport*) to be eliminated (from), be knocked out (of); **er scheidet für den Posten aus** he can't be considered for the job
Ausscheidung *f* (*Aussondern*) removal; (*Med*) excretion; (*Sport*) elimination
ausschenken ['aʊsʃɛŋkən] *vt* to pour out; (*am Ausschank*) to serve
ausscheren ['aʊsʃe:rən] *vi* (*Fahrzeug*) to leave the line *od* convoy; (*zum Überholen*) to pull out
ausschildern ['aʊsʃɪldərn] *vt* to signpost
ausschimpfen ['aʊsʃɪmpfən] *vt* to scold, tell off
ausschlachten ['aʊsʃlaxtən] *vt* (*Auto*) to cannibalize; (*fig*) to make a meal of
ausschlafen ['aʊsʃla:fən] *unreg vi, vr* to sleep late ▷*vt* to sleep off; **ich bin nicht ausgeschlafen** I didn't have *od* get enough sleep
Ausschlag ['aʊsʃla:k] *m* (*Med*) rash; (*Pendelausschlag*) swing; (*von Nadel*) deflection; **den ~ geben** (*fig*) to tip the balance
ausschlagen ['aʊsʃla:gən] *unreg vt* to knock out; (*auskleiden*) to deck out; (*verweigern*) to decline ▷*vi* (*Pferd*) to kick out; (*Bot*) to sprout; (*Zeiger*) to be deflected
ausschlaggebend *adj* decisive
ausschließen ['aʊsʃli:sən] *unreg vt* to shut *od* lock out; (*Sport*) to disqualify; (*Fehler, Möglichkeit etc*) to rule out; (*fig*) to exclude; **ich will mich nicht ~** myself not excepted
ausschließlich *adj* exclusive ▷*adv* exclusively ▷*präp +gen* excluding, exclusive of
ausschlüpfen ['aʊsʃlʏpfən] *vi* to slip out; (*aus Ei, Puppe*) to hatch out
Ausschluss ['aʊsʃlʊs] *m* exclusion; **unter ~ der Öffentlichkeit stattfinden** to be closed to the public; (*Jur*) to be held in camera
ausschmücken ['aʊsʃmʏkən] *vt* to decorate; (*fig*) to embellish
ausschneiden ['aʊsʃnaɪdən] *unreg vt* to cut out; (*Büsche*) to trim
Ausschnitt ['aʊsʃnɪt] *m* (*Teil*) section; (*von Kleid*) neckline; (*Zeitungsausschnitt*) cutting (*Brit*), clipping (*US*); (*aus Film etc*) excerpt
ausschöpfen ['aʊsʃœpfən] *vt* to ladle out; (*fig*) to exhaust; **Wasser** *etc* **aus etw ~** to ladle water *etc* out of sth
ausschreiben ['aʊsʃraɪbən] *unreg vt* (*ganz schreiben*) to write out (in full); (*Scheck, Rechnung etc*) to write (out); (*Stelle, Wettbewerb etc*) to announce, advertise
Ausschreibung *f* (*Bekanntmachung: von Wahlen*) calling; (*: von Stelle*) advertising
Ausschreitung ['aʊsʃraɪtʊŋ] *f* excess
Ausschuss ['aʊsʃʊs] *m* committee, board; (*Abfall*) waste, scraps *pl*; (*Comm: auch:* **Ausschussware**) reject
ausschütten ['aʊsʃʏtən] *vt* to pour out; (*Eimer*) to empty; (*Geld*) to pay ▷*vr* to shake (with laughter)
Ausschüttung *f* (*Fin*) distribution
ausschwärmen ['aʊsʃvɛrmən] *vi* (*Bienen, Menschen*) to swarm out; (*Mil*) to fan out
ausschweifend ['aʊsʃvaɪfənt] *adj* (*Leben*) dissipated, debauched; (*Fantasie*) extravagant
Ausschweifung *f* excess
ausschweigen ['aʊsʃvaɪgən] *unreg vr* to keep silent
ausschwitzen ['aʊsʃvɪtsən] *vt* to sweat out
aussehen ['aʊsze:ən] *unreg vi* to look; **gut ~** to look good/well; **wie siehts aus?** (*umg: wie*

stehts?) how's things?; **das sieht nach nichts aus** that doesn't look anything special; **es sieht nach Regen aus** it looks like rain; **es sieht schlecht aus** things look bad;
Aussehen (**-s**) *nt* appearance
aus sein ['aussaın] *siehe* **aus**
außen ['aʊsən] *adv* outside; (*nach außen*) outwards; **~ ist es rot** it's red (on the) outside
Außen- *zW*: **Außenantenne** *f* outside aerial; **Außenarbeiten** *pl* work *sing* on the exterior; **Außenaufnahme** *f* outdoor shot; **Außenbezirk** *m* outlying district; **Außenbordmotor** *m* outboard motor
aussenden ['aʊszɛndən] *unreg vt* to send out, emit
Außen- *zW*: **Außendienst** *m* outside *od* field service; (*von Diplomat*) foreign service; **Außenhandel** *m* foreign trade; **Außenminister** *m* foreign minister; **Außenministerium** *nt* foreign office; **Außenpolitik** *f* foreign policy; **Außenseite** *f* outside; **Außenseiter, in** (**-s, -**) *m(f)* outsider; **Außenspiegel** *m* (*Aut*) outside mirror; **Außenstände** *pl* (*bes Comm*) outstanding debts *pl*, arrears *pl*; **Außenstehende, r** *f(m)* outsider; **Außenstelle** *f* branch; **Außenwelt** *f* outside world
außer ['aʊsər] *präp +dat* (*räumlich*) out of; (*abgesehen von*) except ▷ *konj* (*ausgenommen*) except; **~ Gefahr sein** to be out of danger; **~ Zweifel** beyond any doubt; **~ Betrieb** out of order; **~ sich** *dat* **sein/geraten** to be beside o.s.; **~ Dienst** retired; **~ Landes** abroad; **~ wenn** unless; **~ dass** except; **außeramtlich** *adj* unofficial, private
außerdem *konj* besides, in addition ▷ *adv* anyway
außerdienstlich *adj* private
äußere, r, s ['ɔʏsərə(r,s)] *adj* outer, external; **Äußere, s** *nt* exterior; (*fig: Aussehen*) outward appearance
außer- *zW*: **außerehelich** *adj* extramarital; **außergewöhnlich** *adj* unusual; **außerhalb** *präp +gen* outside ▷ *adv* outside; **außerirdisch** *adj* extraterrestrial; **Außerkraftsetzung** *f* repeal
äußerlich *adj* external; **rein ~ betrachtet** on the face of it; **Äußerlichkeit** *f* (*fig*) triviality; (*Oberflächlichkeit*) superficiality; (*Formalität*) formality
äußern *vt* to utter, express; (*zeigen*) to show ▷ *vr* to give one's opinion; (*sich zeigen*) to show itself
außer- *zW*: **außerordentlich** *adj* extraordinary; **außerplanmäßig** *adj* unscheduled; **außersinnlich** *adj*: **außersinnliche Wahrnehmung** extrasensory perception
äußerst ['ɔʏsərst] *adv* extremely, most
außerstande, außer Stande [aʊsər'ʃtandə] *adv* (*nicht in der Lage*) not in a position; (*nicht fähig*) unable
Äußerste, s *nt*: **bis zum ~n gehen** to go to extremes
äußerste, r, s *adj* utmost; (*räumlich*) farthest; (*Termin*) last possible; (*Preis*) highest; **mein ~s Angebot** my final offer
äußerstenfalls *adv* if the worst comes to the worst
Äußerung *f* (*Bemerkung*) remark, comment; (*Behauptung*) statement; (*Zeichen*) expression
aussetzen ['aʊszɛtsən] *vt* (*Kind, Tier*) to abandon; (*Boote*) to lower; (*Belohnung*) to offer; (*Urteil, Verfahren*) to postpone ▷ *vi* (*aufhören*) to stop; (*Pause machen*) to have a break; **jdn/sich einer Sache** *dat* **~** to lay sb/o.s. open to sth; **jdm/etw ausgesetzt sein** to be exposed to sb/sth; **was haben Sie daran auszusetzen?** what's your objection to it?; **an jdm/etw etwas ~** to find fault with sb/sth
Aussicht ['aʊszıçt] *f* view; (*in Zukunft*) prospect; **in ~ sein** to be in view; **etw in ~ haben** to have sth in view; **jdm etw in ~ stellen** to promise sb sth
Aussichts- *zW*: **aussichtslos** *adj* hopeless; **Aussichtspunkt** *m* viewpoint; **aussichtsreich** *adj* promising; **Aussichtsturm** *m* observation tower
Aussiedler, in ['aʊszi:dlər(ın)] (**-s, -**) *m(f)* (*Auswanderer*) emigrant; *see culture note*

AUSSIEDLER

Aussiedler are people of German origin from East and South-East Europe who have resettled in Germany. Many come from the former Soviet Union. They are given free German language tuition and receive financial help. The number of *Aussiedler* increased dramatically in the early 1990s.

aussöhnen ['aʊszø:nən] *vt* to reconcile ▷ *vr* (*einander*) to become reconciled; **sich mit jdm/etw ~** to reconcile o.s. with sb/to sth
Aussöhnung *f* reconciliation
aussondern ['aʊszɔndərn] *vt* to separate off, select
aussorgen ['aʊszɔrgən] *vi*: **ausgesorgt haben** to have no more money worries
aussortieren ['aʊszɔrti:rən] *vt* to sort out
ausspannen ['aʊsʃpanən] *vt* to spread *od* stretch out; (*Pferd*) to unharness; (*umg: Mädchen*): **jdm jdn ~** to steal sb from sb ▷ *vi* to relax
aussparen ['aʊsʃpa:rən] *vt* to leave open
aussperren ['aʊsʃpɛrən] *vt* to lock out
Aussperrung *f* (*Industrie*) lock-out
ausspielen ['aʊsʃpi:lən] *vt* (*Karte*) to lead; (*Geldprämie*) to offer as a prize ▷ *vi* (*Karten*) to lead; **ausgespielt haben** to be finished; **jdn gegen jdn ~** to play sb off against sb
Ausspielung *f* (*im Lotto*) draw
ausspionieren ['aʊsʃpioni:rən] *vt* (*Pläne etc*) to spy out; (*Person*) to spy on
Aussprache ['aʊsʃpra:xə] *f* pronunciation; (*Unterredung*) (frank) discussion
aussprechen ['aʊsʃprɛçən] *unreg vt* to pronounce; (*zu Ende sprechen*) to speak; (*äußern*)

to say, express ▷ *vr* (*sich äußern*): **sich ~ (über** *+akk*) to speak (about); (*sich anvertrauen*) to unburden o.s. (about *od* on); (*diskutieren*) to discuss ▷ *vi* (*zu Ende sprechen*) to finish speaking; **der Regierung das Vertrauen ~** to pass a vote of confidence in the government

Ausspruch ['aʊsʃprʊx] *m* remark; (*geflügeltes Wort*) saying

ausspucken ['aʊsʃpʊkən] *vt* to spit out ▷ *vi* to spit

ausspülen ['aʊsʃpy:lən] *vt* to wash out; (*Mund*) to rinse

ausstaffieren ['aʊsʃtafi:rən] *vt* to equip, kit out; (*Zimmer*) to furnish

Ausstand ['aʊsʃtant] *m* strike; **in den ~ treten** to go on strike; **seinen ~ geben** to hold a leaving party

ausstatten ['aʊsʃtatən] *vt* (*Zimmer etc*) to furnish; **jdn mit etw ~** to equip sb *od* kit sb out with sth

Ausstattung *f* (*Ausstatten*) provision; (*Kleidung*) outfit; (*Aussteuer*) dowry; (*Aufmachung*) make-up; (*Einrichtung*) furnishing

ausstechen ['aʊsʃtɛçən] *unreg vt* (*Torf, Kekse*) to cut out; (*Augen*) to gouge out; (*übertreffen*) to outshine

ausstehen ['aʊsʃte:ən] *unreg vt* to stand, endure ▷ *vi* (*noch nicht da sein*) to be outstanding

aussteigen ['aʊsʃtaɪgən] *unreg vi* to get out, alight; **alles ~!** (*von Schaffner*) all change!; **aus der Gesellschaft ~** to drop out (of society)

Aussteiger, in (*umg*) *m(f)* dropout

ausstellen ['aʊsʃtɛlən] *vt* to exhibit, display; (*umg: ausschalten*) to switch off; (*Rechnung etc*) to make out; (*Pass, Zeugnis*) to issue

Aussteller, in *m(f)* (*auf Messe*) exhibitor; (*von Scheck*) drawer

Ausstellung *f* exhibition; (*Fin*) drawing up; (*einer Rechnung*) making out; (*eines Passes etc*) issuing

Ausstellungsdatum *nt* date of issue

Ausstellungsstück *nt* (*in Ausstellung*) exhibit; (*in Schaufenster etc*) display item

aussterben ['aʊsʃtɛrbən] *unreg vi* to die out; **Aussterben** *nt* extinction

Aussteuer ['aʊsʃtɔʏər] *f* dowry

aussteuern ['aʊsʃtɔʏərn] *vt* (*Verstärker*) to adjust

Ausstieg ['aʊsʃti:k] (**-(e)s, -e**) *m* (*Ausgang*) exit; **~ aus der Atomenergie** abandonment of nuclear energy

ausstopfen ['aʊsʃtɔpfən] *vt* to stuff

ausstoßen ['aʊsʃto:sən] *unreg vt* (*Luft, Rauch*) to give off, emit; (*aus Verein etc*) to expel, exclude; (*herstellen: Teile, Stückzahl*) to turn out, produce

ausstrahlen ['aʊsʃtra:lən] *vt, vi* to radiate; (*Rundf*) to broadcast

Ausstrahlung *f* radiation; (*fig*) charisma

ausstrecken ['aʊsʃtrɛkən] *vt, vr* to stretch out

ausstreichen ['aʊsʃtraɪçən] *unreg vt* to cross out; (*glätten*) to smooth out

ausstreuen ['aʊsʃtrɔʏən] *vt* to scatter; (*fig: Gerücht*) to spread

ausströmen ['aʊsʃtrø:mən] *vi* (*Gas*) to pour out, escape ▷ *vt* to give off; (*fig*) to radiate

aussuchen ['aʊszu:xən] *vt* to select, pick out

Austausch ['aʊstaʊʃ] *m* exchange; **austauschbar** *adj* exchangeable

austauschen *vt* to exchange, swop

Austauschmotor *m* replacement engine; (*gebraucht*) factory-reconditioned engine

Austauschstudent, in *m(f)* exchange student

austeilen ['aʊstaɪlən] *vt* to distribute, give out

Auster ['aʊstər] (**-, -n**) *f* oyster

austoben ['aʊsto:bən] *vr* (*Kind*) to run wild; (*Erwachsene*) to let off steam; (*sich müde machen*) to tire o.s. out

austragen ['aʊstra:gən] *unreg vt* (*Post*) to deliver; (*Streit etc*) to decide; (*Wettkämpfe*) to hold; **ein Kind ~** (*nicht abtreiben*) to have a child

Austräger ['aʊstrɛ:gər] *m* delivery boy; (*Zeitungsausträger*) newspaper boy

Austragungsort *m* (*Sport*) venue

Australien [aʊs'tra:liən] (**-s**) *nt* Australia

Australier, in (**-s, -**) *m(f)* Australian

australisch *adj* Australian

austreiben ['aʊstraɪbən] *unreg vt* to drive out, expel; (*Teufel etc*) to exorcize; **jdm etw ~** to cure sb of sth; (*bes durch Schläge*) to knock sth out of sb

austreten ['aʊstre:tən] *unreg vi* (*zur Toilette*) to be excused ▷ *vt* (*Feuer*) to tread out, trample; (*Schuhe*) to wear out; (*Treppe*) to wear down; **aus etw ~** to leave sth

austricksen ['aʊstrɪksən] (*umg*) *vt* (*Sport, fig*) to trick

austrinken ['aʊstrɪŋkən] *unreg vt* (*Glas*) to drain; (*Getränk*) to drink up ▷ *vi* to finish one's drink, drink up

Austritt ['aʊstrɪt] *m* emission; (*aus Verein, Partei etc*) retirement, withdrawal

austrocknen ['aʊstrɔknən] *vt, vi* to dry up

austüfteln ['aʊstʏftəln] (*umg*) *vt* to work out; (*ersinnen*) to think up

ausüben ['aʊs|y:bən] *vt* (*Beruf*) to practise (*Brit*), practice (*US*), carry out; (*innehaben: Amt*) to hold; (*Funktion*) to perform; (*Einfluss*) to exert; **einen Reiz auf jdn ~** to hold an attraction for sb; **eine Wirkung auf jdn ~** to have an effect on sb

Ausübung *f* practice, exercise; **in ~ seines Dienstes/seiner Pflicht** (*form*) in the execution of his duty

ausufern ['aʊs|u:fərn] *vi* (*fig*) to get out of hand; (*Konflikt etc*): **~ (zu)** to escalate (into)

Ausverkauf ['aʊsfɛrkaʊf] *m* sale; (*fig: Verrat*) sell-out

ausverkaufen *vt* to sell out; (*Geschäft*) to sell up

ausverkauft *adj* (*Karten, Artikel*) sold out; (*Theat: Haus*) full

auswachsen ['aʊsvaksən] *unreg vi*: **das ist (ja) zum A~** (*umg*) it's enough to drive you mad

Auswahl ['aʊsva:l] *f*: **eine ~ (an** *+dat*) a selection (of), a choice (of)

auswählen ['aʊsvɛ:lən] *vt* to select, choose

Auswahlmöglichkeit *f* choice

Auswanderer ['aʊsvandərər] (**-s, -**) *m* emigrant
Auswanderin ['aʊsvandərɪn] *f* emigrant
auswandern *vi* to emigrate
Auswanderung *f* emigration
auswärtig ['aʊsvɛrtɪç] *adj* (*nicht am/vom Ort*) out-of-town; (*ausländisch*) foreign; **das A~e Amt** the Foreign Office (*Brit*), the State Department (*US*)
auswärts ['aʊsvɛrts] *adv* outside; (*nach außen*) outwards; **~ essen** to eat out; **Auswärtsspiel** *nt* away game
auswaschen ['aʊsvaʃən] *unreg vt* to wash out; (*spülen*) to rinse (out)
auswechseln ['aʊsvɛksəln] *vt* to change, substitute
Ausweg ['aʊsve:k] *m* way out; **der letzte ~** the last resort; **ausweglos** *adj* hopeless
ausweichen ['aʊsvaɪçən] *unreg vi*: **jdm/etw ~** (*lit*) to move aside *od* make way for sb/sth; (*fig*) to sidestep sb/sth; **jdm/einer Begegnung ~** to avoid sb/a meeting
ausweichend *adj* evasive
Ausweichmanöver *nt* evasive action
ausweinen ['aʊsvaɪnən] *vr* to have a (good) cry
Ausweis ['aʊsvaɪs] (**-es, -e**) *m* identity card; passport; (*Mitgliedsausweis, Bibliotheksausweis etc*) card; **~, bitte** your papers, please
ausweisen ['ausvaɪzən] *unreg vt* to expel, banish ▷ *vr* to prove one's identity
Ausweis- *zW*: **Ausweiskarte** *f* identity papers *pl*; **Ausweiskontrolle** *f* identity check; **Ausweispapiere** *pl* identity papers *pl*
Ausweisung *f* expulsion
ausweiten ['aʊsvaɪtən] *vt* to stretch
auswendig ['aʊsvɛndɪç] *adv* by heart; **~ lernen** to learn by heart
auswerfen ['aʊsvɛrfən] *unreg vt* (*Anker, Netz*) to cast
auswerten ['aʊsvɛrtən] *vt* to evaluate
Auswertung *f* evaluation, analysis; (*Nutzung*) utilization
auswickeln ['aʊsvɪkəln] *vt* (*Paket, Bonbon etc*) to unwrap
auswirken ['aʊsvɪrkən] *vr* to have an effect
Auswirkung *f* effect
auswischen ['aʊsvɪʃən] *vt* to wipe out; **jdm eins ~** (*umg*) to put one over on sb
Auswuchs ['aʊsvu:ks] *m* (out)growth; (*fig*) product; (*Missstand, Übersteigerung*) excess
auswuchten ['aʊsvʊxtən] *vt* (*Aut*) to balance
auszacken ['aʊstsakən] *vt* (*Stoff etc*) to pink
auszahlen ['aʊstsa:lən] *vt* (*Lohn, Summe*) to pay out; (*Arbeiter*) to pay off; (*Miterben*) to buy out ▷ *vr* (*sich lohnen*) to pay
auszählen ['aʊstsɛ:lən] *vt* (*Stimmen*) to count; (*Boxen*) to count out
auszeichnen ['aʊstsaɪçnən] *vt* to honour (*Brit*), honor (*US*); (*Mil*) to decorate; (*Comm*) to price ▷ *vr* to distinguish o.s.; **der Wagen zeichnet sich durch ... aus** one of the car's main features is ...
Auszeichnung *f* distinction; (*Comm*) pricing; (*Ehrung*) awarding of decoration; (*Ehre*) honour (*Brit*), honor (*US*); (*Orden*) decoration; **mit ~** with distinction
ausziehen ['aʊstsi:ən] *unreg vt* (*Kleidung*) to take off; (*Haare, Zähne, Tisch etc*) to pull out ▷ *vr* to undress ▷ *vi* (*aufbrechen*) to leave; (*aus Wohnung*) to move out
Auszubildende, r ['aʊstsʊbɪldəndə(r)] *f(m)* trainee; (*als Handwerker*) apprentice
Auszug ['aʊstsu:k] *m* (*aus Wohnung*) removal; (*aus Buch etc*) extract; (*Kontoauszug*) statement; (*Ausmarsch*) departure
autark [aʊ'tark] *adj* self-sufficient (*auch fig*); (*Comm*) autarkical
Auto ['aʊto] (**-s, -s**) *nt* (motor-)car, automobile (*US*); **mit dem ~ fahren** to go by car; **~ fahren** to drive
Autoatlas *m* road atlas
Autobahn *f* motorway (*Brit*), expressway (*US*); *see culture note*

AUTOBAHN

Autobahn is the German for a motorway. In the former West Germany there is an widespread network but in the former DDR the motorways are somewhat less extensive. There is no overall speed limit but a limit of 130 km per hour is recommended and there are lower mandatory limits on certain stretches of road. As yet there are no tolls payable on German Autobahns.

Autobahndreieck *nt* motorway (*Brit*) *od* expressway (*US*) junction
Autobahnkreuz *nt* motorway (*Brit*) *od* expressway (*US*) intersection
Autobahnzubringer *m* motorway feeder *od* access road
Autobiografie [aʊtobiogra'fi:] *f* autobiography
Auto- *zW*: **Autobombe** *f* car bomb; **Autobus** *m* bus; (*Reisebus*) coach (*Brit*), bus (*US*); **Autofähre** *f* car ferry; **Autofahrer, in** *m(f)* motorist, driver; **Autofahrt** *f* drive; **Autofriedhof** (*umg*) *m* car dump
autogen [aʊto'ge:n] *adj* autogenous; **~es Training** (*Psych*) relaxation through self-hypnosis
Autogramm [aʊto'gram] *nt* autograph
Automat (**-en, -en**) *m* machine
Automatik [aʊto'ma:tɪk] *f* automatic mechanism (*auch fig*); (*Gesamtanlage*) automatic system; (*Aut*) automatic transmission
automatisch *adj* automatic
Automatisierung [aʊtomati'zi:rʊŋ] *f* automation
Automobilausstellung [aʊtomo'bi:laʊsʃtɛlʊŋ] *f* motor show
autonom [aʊto'no:m] *adj* autonomous
Autopsie [aʊtɔ'psi:] *f* post-mortem, autopsy
Autor ['aʊtɔr] (**-s, -en**) *m* author

Auto- *zW*: **Autoradio** *nt* car radio; **Autoreifen** *m* car tyre (*Brit*) *od* tire (*US*); **Autoreisezug** *m* motorail train; **Autorennen** *nt* motor race; (*Sportart*) motor racing
Autorin [aʊ'toːrɪn] *f* authoress
autoritär [aʊtori'tɛːr] *adj* authoritarian
Autorität *f* authority
Auto- *zW*: **Autoschalter** *m* drive-in bank (counter); **Autotelefon** *nt* car phone; **Autounfall** *m* car *od* motor accident; **Autoverleih** *m*, **Autovermietung** *f* car hire (*Brit*) *od* rental (*US*)
AvD (-) *m abk* (= *Automobilclub von Deutschland*) *German motoring organization*, ≈ AA (*Brit*), AAA (*US*)
Axt [akst] (-, ¨-e) *f* axe (*Brit*), ax (*US*)
AZ, **Az.** *abk* (= *Aktenzeichen*) ref.
Azoren [a'tsoːrən] *pl* (*Geog*) Azores *pl*
Azteke [ats'teːkə] (-n, -n) *m* Aztec
Azubi [a'tsuːbi] (-s, -s) (*umg*) *f(m) abk* = **Auszubildende(r)**

Bb

B¹, b [beː] *nt* (*letter*) B, b; **B wie Bertha** ≈ B for Benjamin, B for Baker (*US*); **B-Dur/b-Moll** (the key of) B flat major/minor
B² [beː] *f abk* = **Bundesstraße**
Baby ['beːbi] (**-s, -s**) *nt* baby; **Babyausstattung** *f* layette; **Babyklappe** *f anonymous drop-off point for unwanted babies*; **Babyraum** *m* (*Flughafen etc*) nursing room; **babysitten** *vi* to babysit; **Babysitter** ['beːbisɪtər] (**-s, -**) *m* baby-sitter; **Babyspeck** (*umg*) *m* puppy fat
Bach [bax] (**-(e)s, ¨-e**) *m* stream, brook
Backblech *nt* baking tray
Backbord (**-(e)s, -e**) *nt* (*Naut*) port
Backe (**-, -n**) *f* cheek
backen ['bakən] *unreg vt, vi* to bake; **frisch/knusprig gebackenes Brot** fresh/crusty bread
Backenbart *m* sideboards *pl*
Backenzahn *m* molar
Bäcker, in ['bɛkər(ɪn)] (**-s, -**) *m(f)* baker
Bäckerei [bɛkə'raɪ] *f* bakery; (*Bäckerladen*) baker's (shop)
Bäckerjunge *m* (*Lehrling*) baker's apprentice
Back- *zW*: **Backfisch** *m* fried fish; (*veraltet*) teenager; **Backform** *f* baking tin (*Brit*) *od* pan (*US*); **Backhähnchen** *nt* fried chicken in breadcrumbs; **Backobst** *nt* dried fruit; **Backofen** *m* oven; **Backpflaume** *f* prune; **Backpulver** *nt* baking powder; **Backstein** *m* brick
bäckt [bɛkt] *vb siehe* **backen**
Bad [baːt] (**-(e)s, ¨-er**) *nt* bath; (*Schwimmen*) bathing; (*Ort*) spa
Bade- *zW*: **Badeanstalt** *f* swimming pool; **Badeanzug** *m* bathing suit; **Badehose** *f* bathing *od* swimming trunks *pl*; **Badekappe** *f* bathing cap; **Bademantel** *m* bath(ing) robe; **Bademeister** *m* swimming pool attendant
baden ['baːdən] *vi* to bathe, have a bath ▷ *vt* to bath; **~ gehen** (*fig: umg*) to come a cropper
Bade- *zW*: **Badeort** *m* spa; **Badesachen** *pl* swimming things *pl*; **Badetuch** *nt* bath towel; **Badewanne** *f* bath(tub); **Badezimmer** *nt* bathroom
baff [baf] *adj*: **~ sein** (*umg*) to be flabbergasted
BAföG, Bafög [baːføk] *nt abk* = **Bundesausbildungsförderungsgesetz**; *see culture note*

BAFÖG

Bafög is the system which awards grants for living expenses to students at universities and certain training colleges. The amount is based on parental income. Part of the grant must be paid back a few years after graduating.

BAG (**-**) *nt abk* (= *Bundesarbeitsgericht*) *German industrial tribunal*
Bagatelle [baga'tɛlə] (**-, -n**) *f* trifle
Bagdad ['bakdat] (**-s**) *nt* Baghdad
Bagger ['bagər] (**-s, -**) *m* excavator; (*Naut*) dredger
baggern *vt, vi* to excavate; (*Naut*) to dredge
Baggersee *m* (flooded) gravel pit
Bahamas [ba'haːmas] *pl*: **die ~** the Bahamas *pl*
Bahn [baːn] (**-, -en**) *f* railway (*Brit*), railroad (*US*); (*Weg*) road, way; (*Spur*) lane; (*Rennbahn*) track; (*Astron*) orbit; (*Stoffbahn*) length; **mit der ~** by train *od* rail/tram; **frei ~** (*Comm*) carriage free to station of destination; **jdm/etw die ~ ebnen** (*fig*) to clear the way for sb/sth; **von der rechten ~ abkommen** to stray from the straight and narrow; **jdn aus der ~ werfen** (*fig*) to shatter sb; **Bahnbeamte, r** *m* railway (*Brit*) *od* railroad (*US*) official; **bahnbrechend** *adj* pioneering; **Bahnbrecher, in** (**-s, -**) *m(f)* pioneer; **Bahndamm** *m* railway embankment
bahnen *vt*: **sich einen Weg ~** to clear a way
Bahnfahrt *f* railway (*Brit*) *od* railroad (*US*) journey
Bahnhof *m* station; **auf dem ~** at the station; **ich verstehe nur ~** (*hum: umg*) it's all Greek to me
Bahnhofshalle *f* station concourse
Bahnhofsmission *f charitable organization for helping rail travellers*; *see culture note*

BAHNHOFSMISSION

The *Bahnhofsmission* is a charitable organization set up by and run jointly by various churches. They have an office at railway stations in most big cities to which people in need of advice and help can go.

Bahnhofswirtschaft *f* station restaurant
Bahn- *zW*: **bahnlagernd** *adj* (*Comm*) to be collected from the station; **Bahnlinie** *f* (railway (*Brit*) *od* railroad (*US*)) line; **Bahnschranke** *f* level (*Brit*) *od* grade (*US*) crossing barrier; **Bahnsteig** *m* platform; **Bahnsteigkarte** *f* platform ticket; **Bahnstrecke** *f* railway (*Brit*) *od* railroad (*US*) line; **Bahnübergang** *m* level (*Brit*) *od* grade (*US*) crossing; **beschrankter Bahnübergang** crossing with gates; **unbeschrankter Bahnübergang** unguarded crossing; **Bahnwärter** *m* signalman
Bahrain [ba'raın] (**-s**) *nt* Bahrain
Bahre ['ba:rə] (**-, -n**) *f* stretcher
Baiser [bɛ'ze:] (**-s, -s**) *nt* meringue
Baisse ['bɛ:sə] (**-, -n**) *f* (*Börse*) fall; (*plötzlich*) slump
Bajonett [bajo'nɛt] (**-(e)s, -e**) *nt* bayonet
Bakelit® [bake'li:t] (**-s**) *nt* Bakelite®
Bakterien [bak'te:riən] *pl* bacteria *pl*
Balance [ba'lã:sə] (**-, -n**) *f* balance, equilibrium
balancieren *vt, vi* to balance
bald [balt] *adv* (*zeitlich*) soon; (*beinahe*) almost; **~ ... ~ ...** now ... now ...; **~ darauf** soon afterwards; **bis ~!** see you soon
baldig ['baldıç] *adj* early, speedy
baldmöglichst *adv* as soon as possible
Baldrian ['baldria:n] (**-s, -e**) *m* valerian
Balearen [bale'a:rən] *pl*: **die ~** the Balearics *pl*
Balg [balk] (**-(e)s, ¨-er**) (*pej: umg*) *m od nt* (*Kind*) brat
balgen ['balgən] *vr*: **sich ~ (um)** to scrap (over)
Balkan ['balka:n] *m*: **der ~** the Balkans *pl*
Balken ['balkən] (**-s, -**) *m* beam; (*Tragbalken*) girder; (*Stützbalken*) prop
Balkon [bal'kõ:] (**-s, -s** *od* **-e**) *m* balcony; (*Theat*) (dress) circle
Ball [bal] (**-(e)s, ¨-e**) *m* ball; (*Tanz*) dance, ball
Ballade [ba'la:də] (**-, -n**) *f* ballad
Ballast ['balast] (**-(e)s, -e**) *m* ballast; (*fig*) weight, burden; **Ballaststoffe** *pl* (*Med*) roughage *sing*
Ballen ['balən] (**-s, -**) *m* bale; (*Anat*) ball
ballen *vt* (*formen*) to make into a ball; (*Faust*) to clench ▷ *vr* to build up; (*Menschen*) to gather
ballern ['balərn] (*umg*) *vi* to shoot, fire
Ballett [ba'lɛt] (**-(e)s, -e**) *nt* ballet; **Balletttänzer, in** *m(f)* ballet dancer
Ballistik [ba'lıstık] *f* ballistics *sing*
Balljunge *m* ball boy
Ballkleid *nt* evening dress
Ballon [ba'lõ:] (**-s, -s** *od* **-e**) *m* balloon
Ballspiel *nt* ball game
Ballung ['balʊŋ] *f* concentration; (*von Energie*) build-up
Ballungs- *zW*: **Ballungsgebiet** *nt*, **Ballungsraum** *m* conurbation; **Ballungszentrum** *nt* centre (*Brit*) *od* center (*US*) (*of population, industry etc*)
Balsam ['balza:m] (**-s, -e**) *m* balsam; (*fig*) balm
Balte ['baltə] (**-n, -n**) *m* Balt; **er ist ~** he comes from the Baltic
Baltikum ['baltikʊm] (**-s**) *nt*: **das ~** the Baltic States *pl*
baltisch *adj* Baltic *attrib*
Balz [balts] (**-, -en**) *f* (*Paarungsspiel*) courtship display; (*Paarungszeit*) mating season
Bambus ['bambʊs] (**-ses, -se**) *m* bamboo; **Bambusrohr** *nt* bamboo cane
Bammel ['baməl] (**-s**) (*umg*) *m*: **(einen) ~ vor jdm/etw haben** to be scared of sb/sth
banal [ba'na:l] *adj* banal
Banalität [banali'tɛ:t] *f* banality
Banane [ba'na:nə] (**-, -n**) *f* banana
Bananenschale *f* banana skin
Bananenstecker *m* jack plug
Banause [ba'naʊzə] (**-n, -n**) *m* philistine
Band[1] [bant] (**-(e)s, ¨-e**) *m* (*Buchband*) volume; **das spricht Bände** that speaks volumes
Band[2] (**-(e)s, ¨-er**) *nt* (*Stoffband*) ribbon, tape; (*Fließband*) production line; (*Fassband*) hoop; (*Zielband, Tonband*) tape; (*Anat*) ligament; **etw auf ~ aufnehmen** to tape sth; **am laufenden ~** (*umg*) non-stop
Band[3] (**-(e)s, -e**) *nt* (*Freundschaftsband etc*) bond
Band[4] [bɛnt] (**-, -s**) *f* band, group
band *etc* [bant] *vb siehe* **binden**
Bandage [ban'da:ʒə] (**-, -n**) *f* bandage
bandagieren *vt* to bandage
Bandbreite *f* (*von Meinungen etc*) range
Bande ['bandə] (**-, -n**) *f* band; (*Straßenbande*) gang
bändigen ['bɛndıgən] *vt* (*Tier*) to tame; (*Trieb, Leidenschaft*) to control, restrain
Bandit [ban'di:t] (**-en, -en**) *m* bandit
Band- *zW*: **Bandmaß** *nt* tape measure; **Bandnudeln** *pl* tagliatelle *pl*; **Bandsäge** *f* band saw; **Bandscheibe** *f* (*Anat*) disc; **Bandscheibenschaden** *m* slipped disc; **Bandwurm** *m* tapeworm
bange ['baŋə] *adj* scared; (*besorgt*) anxious; **jdm wird es ~** sb is becoming scared; **jdm B~ machen** to scare sb; **Bangemacher** (**-s, -**) *m* scaremonger
bangen *vi*: **um jdn/etw ~** to be anxious *od* worried about sb/sth
Bangkok ['baŋkɔk] (**-s**) *nt* Bangkok
Bangladesch [baŋgla'dɛʃ] (**-s**) *nt* Bangladesh
Banjo ['banjo, 'bɛndʒo] (**-s, -s**) *nt* banjo
Bank[1] [baŋk] (**-, ¨-e**) *f* (*Sitzbank*) bench; (*Sandbank etc*) (sand)bank, (sand)bar; **etw auf die lange ~ schieben** (*umg*) to put sth off
Bank[2] (**-, -en**) *f* (*Geldbank*) bank; **bei der ~** at the bank; **Geld auf der ~ haben** to have money in the bank; **Bankanweisung** *f* banker's order; **Bankautomat** *m* cash dispenser; **Bankbeamte, r** *m* bank clerk; **Bankeinlage** *f* (bank) deposit
Bankett [baŋ'kɛt] (**-(e)s, -e**) *nt* (*Essen*) banquet; (*Straßenrand*) verge (*Brit*), shoulder (*US*)
Bank- *zW*: **Bankfach** *nt* (*Schließfach*) safe-deposit box; **Bankgebühr** *f* bank charge;

Bankgeheimnis *nt* confidentiality in banking
Bankier [baŋki'eː] **(-s, -s)** *m* banker
Bank- *zW*: **Bankkonto** *nt* bank account; **Bankleitzahl** *f* bank code number; **Banknote** *f* banknote; **Bankraub** *m* bank robbery
bankrott [baŋ'krɔt] *adj* bankrupt; **Bankrott** **(-(e)s, -e)** *m* bankruptcy; **Bankrott machen** to go bankrupt; **den Bankrott anmelden** *od* **erklären** to declare o.s. bankrupt; **Bankrotterklärung** *f* (*lit*) declaration of bankruptcy; (*fig: umg*) declaration of failure
Banküberfall *m* bank raid
Bann [ban] **(-(e)s, -e)** *m* (*Hist*) ban; (*Kirchenbann*) excommunication; (*fig: Zauber*) spell; **bannen** *vt* (*Geister*) to exorcize; (*Gefahr*) to avert; (*bezaubern*) to enchant; (*Hist*) to banish
Banner **(-s, -)** *nt* banner, flag
Bar [baːr] **(-, -s)** *f* bar
bar *adj* (*+gen*) (*unbedeckt*) bare; (*frei von*) lacking (in); (*offenkundig*) utter, sheer; **~e(s) Geld** cash; **etw (in) ~ bezahlen** to pay sth (in) cash; **etw für ~e Münze nehmen** (*fig*) to take sth at face value; **~ aller Hoffnung** (*liter*) devoid of hope, completely without hope
Bär [bɛːr] **(-en, -en)** *m* bear; **jdm einen ~en aufbinden** (*umg*) to have sb on
Baracke [ba'rakə] **(-, -n)** *f* hut
barbarisch [bar'baːrɪʃ] *adj* barbaric, barbarous
Barbestand *m* money in hand
Bardame *f* barmaid
Bärenhunger (*umg*) *m*: **einen ~ haben** to be famished
bärenstark (*umg*) *adj* strapping, strong as an ox; (*fig*) terrific
barfuß *adj* barefoot
barg *etc* [bark] *vb siehe* **bergen**
Bargeld *nt* cash, ready money
bargeldlos *adj* non-cash; **~er Zahlungsverkehr** non-cash *od* credit transactions *pl*
barhäuptig *adj* bareheaded
Barhocker *m* bar stool
Bariton ['baːritɔn] *m* baritone
Barkauf *m* cash purchase
Barkeeper ['baːrkiːpər] **(-s, -)** *m* barman, bartender
Barkredit *m* cash loan
Barmann **(-(e)s**, *pl* **-männer)** *m* barman
barmherzig [barm'hɛrtsɪç] *adj* merciful, compassionate; **Barmherzigkeit** *f* mercy, compassion
Barock [ba'rɔk] **(-s** *od* **-)** *nt od m* baroque
Barometer [baro'meːtər] **(-s, -)** *nt* barometer; **das ~ steht auf Sturm** (*fig*) there's a storm brewing
Baron [ba'roːn] **(-s, -e)** *m* baron
Baronesse [baro'nɛsə] **(-, -n)** *f* baroness
Baronin *f* baroness
Barren ['barən] **(-s, -)** *m* parallel bars *pl*; (*Goldbarren*) ingot
Barriere [bari'ɛːrə] **(-, -n)** *f* barrier
Barrikade [bari'kaːdə] **(-, -n)** *f* barricade
Barsch [barʃ] **(-(e)s, -e)** *m* perch
barsch [barʃ] *adj* brusque, gruff; **jdn ~ anfahren** to snap at sb
Barschaft *f* ready money
Barscheck *m* open *od* uncrossed cheque (*Brit*), open check (*US*)
barst *etc* [barst] *vb siehe* **bersten**
Bart [baːrt] **(-(e)s, ¨-e)** *m* beard; (*Schlüsselbart*) bit
bärtig ['bɛːrtɪç] *adj* bearded
Barvermögen *nt* liquid assets *pl*
Barzahlung *f* cash payment
Basar [ba'zaːr] **(-s, -e)** *m* bazaar
Base ['baːzə] **(-, -n)** *f* (*Chem*) base; (*Cousine*) cousin
Basel ['baːzəl] **(-s)** *nt* Basle
Basen *pl von* **Base; Basis**
basieren [ba'ziːrən] *vt* to base ▷ *vi* to be based
Basilikum [ba'ziːlikʊm] **(-s)** *nt* basil
Basis ['baːzɪs] **(-**, *pl* **Basen)** *f* basis; (*Archit, Mil, Math*) base; **~ und Überbau** (*Pol, Soziologie*) foundation and superstructure; **die ~** (*umg*) the grass roots
basisch ['baːzɪʃ] *adj* (*Chem*) alkaline
Basisgruppe *f* action group
Baske ['baskə] **(-n, -n)** *m* Basque
Baskenland *nt* Basque region
Baskenmütze *f* beret
Baskin *f* Basque
Bass [bas] **(-es, ¨-e)** *m* bass
Bassin [ba'sɛ̃ː] **(-s, -s)** *nt* pool
Bassist [ba'sɪst] *m* bass
Bassschlüssel *m* bass clef
Bassstimme *f* bass voice
Bast [bast] **(-(e)s, -e)** *m* raffia
basta ['basta] *interj*: **(und damit) ~!** (and) that's that!
basteln ['bastəln] *vt* to make ▷ *vi* to do handicrafts; **an etw** *dat* **~** (*an etw herumbasteln*) to tinker with sth
Bastler ['bastlər] **(-s, -)** *m* do-it-yourselfer; (*handwerklich*) handicrafts enthusiast
BAT *m abk* (*= Bundesangestelltentarif*) *German salary scale for employees*
bat *etc* [baːt] *vb siehe* **bitten**
Bataillon [batal'joːn] **(-s, -e)** *nt* battalion
Batist [ba'tɪst] **(-(e)s, -e)** *m* batiste
Batterie [batə'riː] *f* battery
Bau [baʊ] **(-(e)s)** *m* (*Bauen*) building, construction; (*Aufbau*) structure; (*Körperbau*) frame; (*Baustelle*) building site; (*pl Baue: Tierbau*) hole, burrow; (*: Min*) working(s); (*pl Bauten: Gebäude*) building; **sich im ~ befinden** to be under construction; **Bauarbeiten** *pl* (*Straßenbau*) roadworks *pl* (*Brit*), roadwork *sing* (*US*); building *od* construction work *sing*; **Bauarbeiter** *m* building worker
Bauch [baʊx] **(-(e)s, Bäuche)** *m* belly; (*Anat*) stomach, abdomen; **sich** *dat* **(vor Lachen) den ~ halten** (*umg*) to split one's sides (laughing); **mit etw auf den ~ fallen** (*umg*) to come a cropper with sth; **Bauchansatz** *m* beginning of a paunch; **Bauchfell** *nt* peritoneum
bauchig *adj* bulging

Bauch- *zW*: **Bauchlandung** *f*: **eine Bauchlandung machen** (*fig*) to experience a failure, to flop; **Bauchmuskel** *m* abdominal muscle; **Bauchnabel** *m* navel, belly-button (*umg*); **Bauchredner** *m* ventriloquist; **Bauchschmerzen** *pl* stomachache *sing*; **Bauchspeicheldrüse** *f* pancreas; **Bauchtanz** *m* belly dance; belly dancing; **Bauchweh** *nt* stomachache

Baudrate [baʊt'ra:tə] *f* (*Comput*) baud rate

bauen ['baʊən] *vt* to build; (*Tech*) to construct; (*umg*: *verursachen*: *Unfall*) to cause ▷ *vi* to build; **auf jdn/etw ~** to depend *od* count upon sb/sth; **da hast du Mist gebaut** (*umg*) you really messed that up

Bauer[1] ['baʊər] (**-n** *od* **-s, -n**) *m* farmer; (*Schach*) pawn

Bauer[2] (**-s, -**) *nt od m* (*Vogelbauer*) cage

Bäuerchen ['bɔʏərçən] *nt* (*Kindersprache*) burp

Bäuerin ['bɔʏərɪn] *f* farmer; (*Frau des Bauern*) farmer's wife

bäuerlich *adj* rustic

Bauern- *zW*: **Bauernbrot** *nt* black bread; **Bauernfängerei** *f* deception, confidence trick(s); **Bauernfrühstück** *nt* bacon and potato omelette (*Brit*) *od* omelet (*US*); **Bauernhaus** *nt* farmhouse; **Bauernhof** *m* farm; **Bauernschaft** *f* farming community; **Bauernschläue** *f* native cunning, craftiness, shrewdness

Bau- *zW*: **baufällig** *adj* dilapidated; **Baufälligkeit** *f* dilapidation; **Baufirma** *f* construction firm; **Bauführer** *m* site foreman; **Baugelände** *nt* building site; **Baugenehmigung** *f* building permit; **Baugerüst** *nt* scaffolding; **Bauherr** *m* client (*of construction firm*); **Bauingenieur** *m* civil engineer

Bauj. *abk* = **Baujahr**

Bau- *zW*: **Baujahr** *nt* year of construction; (*von Auto*) year of manufacture; **Baukasten** *m* box of bricks; **Bauklötzchen** *nt* (building) block; **Baukosten** *pl* construction costs *pl*; **Bauland** *nt* building land; **Bauleute** *pl* building workers *pl*; **baulich** *adj* structural; **Baulöwe** *m* building speculator; **Baulücke** *f* undeveloped building plot

Baum [baʊm] (**-(e)s**, *pl* **Bäume**) *m* tree; **heute könnte ich Bäume ausreißen** I feel full of energy today

Baumarkt *m* DIY superstore

baumeln ['baʊməln] *vi* to dangle

bäumen ['bɔʏmən] *vr* to rear (up)

Baum- *zW*: **Baumgrenze** *f* tree line; **Baumschule** *f* nursery; **Baumstamm** *m* tree trunk; **Baumstumpf** *m* tree stump; **Baumwolle** *f* cotton

Bau- *zW*: **Bauplan** *m* architect's plan; **Bauplatz** *m* building site; **Bausachverständige, r** *f(m)* quantity surveyor; **Bausatz** *m* construction kit

Bausch [baʊʃ] (**-(e)s**, *pl* **Bäusche**) *m* (*Wattebausch*) ball, wad; **in ~ und Bogen** (*fig*) lock, stock, and barrel

bauschen *vt, vi, vr* to puff out

bauschig *adj* baggy, wide

Bau- *zW*: **bausparen** *vi untr* to save with a building society (*Brit*) *od* a building and loan association (*US*); **Bausparkasse** *f* building society (*Brit*), building and loan association (*US*); **Bausparvertrag** *m* savings contract with a building society (*Brit*) *od* building and loan association (*US*); **Baustein** *m* building stone, freestone; **Baustelle** *f* building site; **Baustil** *m* architectural style; **bautechnisch** *adj* in accordance with building *od* construction methods; **Bauteil** *nt* prefabricated part (of building); **Bauten** *pl von* **Bau**; **Bauunternehmer** *m* contractor, builder; **Bauweise** *f* (method of) construction; **Bauwerk** *nt* building; **Bauzaun** *m* hoarding

b. a. W. *abk* (= *bis auf Weiteres*) until further notice

Bayer, in ['baɪər(ɪn)] (**-n, -n**) *m(f)* Bavarian

bayerisch, bayrisch *adj* Bavarian

Bayern *nt* Bavaria

Bazillus [ba'tsɪlʊs] (**-**, *pl* **Bazillen**) *m* bacillus

Bd. *abk* (= *Band*) vol.

Bde. *abk* (= *Bände*) vols.

beabsichtigen [bə'|apzɪçtɪgən] *vt* to intend

beachten [bə'|axtən] *vt* to take note of; (*Vorschrift*) to obey; (*Vorfahrt*) to observe

beachtenswert *adj* noteworthy

beachtlich *adj* considerable

Beachtung *f* notice, attention, observation; **jdm keine ~ schenken** to take no notice of sb

Beamte, r [bə'|amtə(r)] (**-n, -n**) *m* official; (*Staatsbeamte*) civil servant; (*Bankbeamte etc*) employee

Beamtenlaufbahn *f*: **die ~ einschlagen** to enter the civil service

Beamtenverhältnis *nt*: **im ~ stehen** to be a civil servant

beamtet *adj* (*form*) appointed on a permanent basis (*by the state*)

Beamtin *f siehe* **Beamte(r)**

beängstigend [bə'|ɛŋstɪgənt] *adj* alarming

beanspruchen [bə'|anʃprʊxən] *vt* to claim; (*Zeit, Platz*) to take up, occupy; **jdn ~** to take up sb's time; **etw stark ~** to put sth under a lot of stress

beanstanden [bə'|anʃtandən] *vt* to complain about, object to; (*Rechnung*) to query

Beanstandung *f* complaint

beantragen [bə'|antra:gən] *vt* to apply for, ask for

beantworten [bə'|antvɔrtən] *vt* to answer

Beantwortung *f* reply

bearbeiten [bə'|arbaɪtən] *vt* to work; (*Material*) to process; (*Thema*) to deal with; (*Land*) to cultivate; (*Chem*) to treat; (*Buch*) to revise; (*umg*: *beeinflussen wollen*) to work on

Bearbeitung *f* processing; cultivation; treatment; revision; **die ~ meines Antrags hat lange gedauert** it took a long time to deal with my claim

Bearbeitungsgebühr *f* handling charge

beatmen [bəˈ|aːtmən] *vt*: **jdn künstlich ~** to give sb artificial respiration
Beatmung [bəˈ|aːtmʊŋ] *f* respiration
beaufsichtigen [bəˈ|aʊfzɪçtɪgən] *vt* to supervise
Beaufsichtigung *f* supervision
beauftragen [bəˈ|aʊftraːgən] *vt* to instruct; **jdn mit etw ~** to entrust sb with sth
Beauftragte, r *f(m)* representative
bebauen [bəˈbaʊən] *vt* to build on; (*Agr*) to cultivate
beben [ˈbeːbən] *vi* to tremble, shake; **Beben (-s, -)** *nt* earthquake
bebildern [bəˈbɪldərn] *vt* to illustrate
Becher [ˈbɛçər] (**-s, -**) *m* mug; (*ohne Henkel*) tumbler
bechern [ˈbɛçərn] (*umg*) *vi* (*trinken*) to have a few (drinks)
Becken [ˈbɛkən] (**-s, -**) *nt* basin; (*Mus*) cymbal; (*Anat*) pelvis
Bedacht [bəˈdaxt] *m*: **mit ~** (*vorsichtig*) prudently, carefully; (*absichtlich*) deliberately
bedacht *adj* thoughtful, careful; **auf etw** *akk* **~ sein** to be concerned about sth
bedächtig [bəˈdɛçtɪç] *adj* (*umsichtig*) thoughtful, reflective; (*langsam*) slow, deliberate
bedanken [bəˈdaŋkən] *vr*: **sich (bei jdm) ~** to say thank you (to sb); **ich bedanke mich herzlich** thank you very much
Bedarf [bəˈdarf] (**-(e)s**) *m* need; (*Bedarfsmenge*) requirements *pl*; (*Comm*) demand; supply; **alles für den häuslichen ~** all household requirements; **je nach ~** according to demand; **bei ~** if necessary; **~ an etw** *dat* **haben** to be in need of sth
Bedarfs- *zW*: **Bedarfsartikel** *m* requisite; **Bedarfsdeckung** *f* satisfaction of sb's needs; **Bedarfsfall** *m* case of need; **Bedarfshaltestelle** *f* request stop
bedauerlich [bəˈdaʊərlɪç] *adj* regrettable
bedauern [bəˈdaʊərn] *vt* to be sorry for; (*bemitleiden*) to pity; **wir ~, Ihnen mitteilen zu müssen, ...** we regret to have to inform you ...; **Bedauern** (**-s**) *nt* regret
bedauernswert *adj* (*Zustände*) regrettable; (*Mensch*) pitiable, unfortunate
bedecken [bəˈdɛkən] *vt* to cover
bedeckt *adj* covered; (*Himmel*) overcast
bedenken [bəˈdɛŋkən] *unreg vt* to think over, consider; **ich gebe zu ~, dass ...** (*geh*) I would ask you to consider that ...; **Bedenken** (**-s, -**) *nt* (*Überlegen*) consideration; (*Zweifel*) doubt; (*Skrupel*) scruple; **mir kommen Bedenken** I am having second thoughts
bedenklich *adj* doubtful; (*bedrohlich*) dangerous, risky
Bedenkzeit *f* time to consider; **zwei Tage ~** two days to think about it
bedeuten [bəˈdɔʏtən] *vt* to mean; to signify; (*wichtig sein*) to be of importance; **das bedeutet nichts Gutes** that means trouble
bedeutend *adj* important; (*beträchtlich*) considerable
bedeutsam *adj* significant; (*vielsagend*) meaningful
Bedeutung *f* meaning; significance; (*Wichtigkeit*) importance
bedeutungslos *adj* insignificant, unimportant
bedeutungsvoll *adj* momentous, significant
bedienen [bəˈdiːnən] *vt* to serve; (*Maschine*) to work, operate ▷ *vr* (*beim Essen*) to help o.s.; (*gebrauchen*): **sich jds/einer Sache ~** to make use of sb/sth; **werden Sie schon bedient?** are you being served?; **damit sind Sie sehr gut bedient** that should serve you very well; **ich bin bedient!** (*umg*) I've had enough
Bedienung *f* service; (*Kellner etc*) waiter/waitress; (*Zuschlag*) service (charge); (*von Maschinen*) operation
Bedienungsanleitung *f* operating instructions *pl*
bedingen [bəˈdɪŋən] *vt* (*voraussetzen*) to demand, involve; (*verursachen*) to cause, occasion
bedingt *adj* limited; (*Straferlass*) conditional; (*Reflex*) conditioned; **(nur) ~ gelten** to be (only) partially valid; **~ geeignet** suitable up to a point
Bedingung *f* condition; (*Voraussetzung*) stipulation; **mit** *od* **unter der ~, dass ...** on condition that ...; **zu günstigen ~en** (*Comm*) on favourable (*Brit*) *od* favorable (*US*) terms
Bedingungsform *f* (*Gram*) conditional
bedingungslos *adj* unconditional
bedrängen [bəˈdrɛŋən] *vt* to pester, harass
Bedrängnis [bəˈdrɛŋnɪs] *f* (*seelisch*) distress, torment
Bedrängung *f* trouble
bedrohen [bəˈdroːən] *vt* to threaten
bedrohlich *adj* ominous, threatening
Bedrohung *f* threat, menace
bedrucken [bəˈdrʊkən] *vt* to print on
bedrücken [bədrʏkən] *vt* to oppress, trouble
bedürfen [bəˈdʏrfən] *unreg vi +gen* (*geh*) to need, require; **ohne dass es eines Hinweises bedurft hätte, ...** without having to be asked ...
Bedürfnis [bəˈdʏrfnɪs] (**-ses, -se**) *nt* need; **das ~ nach etw haben** to need sth; **Bedürfnisanstalt** *f* (*form*) public convenience (*Brit*), comfort station (*US*); **bedürfnislos** *adj* frugal, modest
bedürftig *adj* in need, poor, needy
Beefsteak [ˈbiːfsteːk] (**-s, -s**) *nt* steak; **deutsches ~** hamburger
beehren [bəˈ|eːrən] *vt* (*geh*) to honour (*Brit*), honor (*US*); **wir ~ uns ...** we have pleasure in ...
beeilen [bəˈ|aɪlən] *vr* to hurry
beeindrucken [bəˈ|aɪndrʊkən] *vt* to impress, make an impression on
beeinflussen [bəˈ|aɪnflʊsən] *vt* to influence
Beeinflussung *f* influence
beeinträchtigen [bəˈ|aɪntrɛçtɪgən] *vt* to affect adversely; (*Sehvermögen*) to impair; (*Freiheit*) to

infringe upon
beenden [bəˈ|ɛndən], **beendigen** [bəˈ|ɛndɪgən] *vt* to end, finish, terminate
Beendung, Beendigung *f* end(ing), finish(ing)
beengen [bəˈ|ɛŋən] *vt* to cramp; (*fig*) to hamper, inhibit; **~de Kleidung** restricting clothing
beengt *adj* cramped; (*fig*) stifled
beerben [bəˈ|ɛrbən] *vt* to inherit from
beerdigen [bəˈ|eːrdɪgən] *vt* to bury
Beerdigung *f* funeral, burial
Beerdigungsunternehmer *m* undertaker
Beere [ˈbeːrə] (**-, -n**) *f* berry; (*Traubenbeere*) grape
Beerenauslese *f wine made from specially selected grapes*
Beet [beːt] (**-(e)s, -e**) *nt* (*Blumenbeet*) bed
befähigen [bəˈfɛːɪgən] *vt* to enable
befähigt *adj* (*begabt*) talented; (*fähig*): **~ (für)** capable (of)
Befähigung *f* capability; (*Begabung*) talent, aptitude; **die ~ zum Richteramt** the qualifications to become a judge
befahl *etc* [bəˈfaːl] *vb siehe* **befehlen**
befahrbar [bəˈfaːrbaːr] *adj* passable; (*Naut*) navigable; **nicht ~ sein** (*Straße, Weg*) to be closed (to traffic); (*wegen Schnee etc*) to be impassable
befahren [bəˈfaːrən] *unreg vt* to use, drive over; (*Naut*) to navigate ▷ *adj* used
befallen [bəˈfalən] *unreg vt* to come over
befangen [bəˈfaŋən] *adj* (*schüchtern*) shy, self-conscious; (*voreingenommen*) bias(s)ed; **Befangenheit** *f* shyness; bias
befassen [bəˈfasən] *vr* to concern o.s.
Befehl [bəˈfeːl] (**-(e)s, -e**) *m* command, order; (*Comput*) command; **auf ~ handeln** to act under orders; **zu ~, Herr Hauptmann!** (*Mil*) yes, sir; **den ~ haben** *od* **führen (über** *+akk***)** to be in command (of)
befehlen *unreg vt* to order ▷ *vi* to give orders; **jdm etw ~** to order sb to do sth; **du hast mir gar nichts zu ~** I won't take orders from you
befehligen *vt* to be in command of
Befehls- *zW*: **Befehlsempfänger** *m* subordinate; **Befehlsform** *f* (*Gram*) imperative; **Befehlshaber** (**-s, -**) *m* commanding officer; **Befehlsnotstand** *m* (*Jur*) obligation to obey orders; **Befehlsverweigerung** *f* insubordination
befestigen [bəˈfɛstɪgən] *vt* to fasten; (*stärken*) to strengthen; (*Mil*) to fortify; **~ an** *+dat* to fasten to
Befestigung *f* fastening; strengthening; (*Mil*) fortification
Befestigungsanlage *f* fortification
befeuchten [bəˈfɔʏçtən] *vt* to damp(en), moisten
befinden [bəˈfɪndən] *unreg vr* to be; (*sich fühlen*) to feel ▷ *vt*: **jdn/etw für** *od* **als etw ~** to deem sb/sth to be sth ▷ *vi*: **~ (über** *+akk***)** to decide (on), adjudicate (on)
Befinden (**-s**) *nt* health, condition; (*Meinung*) view, opinion
beflecken [bəˈflɛkən] *vt* (*lit*) to stain; (*fig geh: Ruf, Ehre*) to besmirch
befliegen [bəˈfliːgən] *unreg vt* (*Strecke*) to fly
beflügeln [bəˈflyːgəln] *vt* (*geh*) to inspire
befohlen [bəˈfoːlən] *pp von* **befehlen**
befolgen [bəˈfɔlgən] *vt* to comply with, follow
befördern [bəˈfœrdərn] *vt* (*senden*) to transport, send; (*beruflich*) to promote; **etw mit der Post/per Bahn ~** to send sth by post/by rail
Beförderung *f* transport; promotion
Beförderungskosten *pl* transport costs *pl*
befragen [bəˈfraːgən] *vt* to question; (*um Stellungnahme bitten*): **~ (über** *+akk***)** to consult (about)
Befragung *f* poll
befreien [bəˈfraɪən] *vt* to set free; (*erlassen*) to exempt
Befreier, in (**-s, -**) *m(f)* liberator
befreit *adj* (*erleichtert*) relieved
Befreiung *f* liberation, release; (*Erlassen*) exemption
Befreiungs- *zW*: **Befreiungsbewegung** *f* liberation movement; **Befreiungskampf** *m* struggle for liberation; **Befreiungsversuch** *m* escape attempt
befremden [bəˈfrɛmdən] *vt* to surprise; (*unangenehm*) to disturb; **Befremden** (**-s**) *nt* surprise, astonishment
befreunden [bəˈfrɔʏndən] *vr* to make friends; (*mit Idee etc*) to acquaint o.s.
befreundet *adj* friendly; **wir sind schon lange (miteinander) ~** we have been friends for a long time
befriedigen [bəˈfriːdɪgən] *vt* to satisfy
befriedigend *adj* satisfactory
Befriedigung *f* satisfaction, gratification
befristet [bəˈfrɪstət] *adj* limited; (*Arbeitsverhältnis, Anstellung*) temporary
befruchten [bəˈfrʊxtən] *vt* to fertilize; (*fig*) to stimulate
Befruchtung *f*: **künstliche ~** artificial insemination
Befugnis [bəˈfuːknɪs] (**-, -se**) *f* authorization, powers *pl*
befugt *adj* authorized, entitled
befühlen [bəˈfyːlən] *vt* to feel, touch
Befund [bəˈfʊnt] (**-(e)s, -e**) *m* findings *pl*; (*Med*) diagnosis; **ohne ~** (*Med*) (results) negative
befürchten [bəˈfʏrçtən] *vt* to fear
Befürchtung *f* fear, apprehension
befürworten [bəˈfyːrvɔrtən] *vt* to support, speak in favour (*Brit*) *od* favor (*US*) of
Befürworter, in (**-s, -**) *m(f)* supporter, advocate
Befürwortung *f* support(ing), favouring (*Brit*), favoring (*US*)
begabt [bəˈgaːpt] *adj* gifted
Begabung [bəˈgaːbʊŋ] *f* talent, gift
begann *etc* [bəˈgan] *vb siehe* **beginnen**
begatten [bəˈgatən] *vr* to mate ▷ *vt* to mate *od* pair (with)
begeben [bəˈgeːbən] *unreg vr* (*gehen*) to proceed; (*geschehen*) to occur; **sich ~ nach** *od*

zu to proceed to(wards); **sich in ärztliche Behandlung ~** to undergo medical treatment; **sich in Gefahr ~** to expose o.s. to danger; **Begebenheit** *f* occurrence

begegnen [bə'ge:gnən] *vi*: **jdm ~** to meet sb; (*behandeln*) to treat; **Blicke ~ sich** eyes meet

Begegnung *f* meeting; (*Sport*) match

begehen [bə'ge:ən] *unreg vt* (*Straftat*) to commit; (*Weg etc*) to use, negotiate; (*geh: feiern*) to celebrate

begehren [bə'ge:rən] *vt* to desire

begehrenswert *adj* desirable

begehrt *adj* in demand; (*Junggeselle*) eligible

begeistern [bə'gaɪstərn] *vt* to fill with enthusiasm; (*inspirieren*) to inspire ▷ *vr*: **sich für etw ~** to get enthusiastic about sth; **er ist für nichts zu ~** he's not interested in doing anything

begeistert *adj* enthusiastic

Begeisterung *f* enthusiasm

Begierde [bə'gi:rdə] (**-, -n**) *f* desire, passion

begierig [bə'gi:rɪç] *adj* eager, keen; (*voll Verlangen*) hungry, greedy

begießen [bə'gi:sən] *unreg vt* to water; (*mit Fett: Braten etc*) to baste; (*mit Alkohol*) to drink to

Beginn [bə'gɪn] (**-(e)s**) *m* beginning; **zu ~** at the beginning

beginnen *unreg vt, vi* to start, begin

beglaubigen [bə'glaʊbɪgən] *vt* to countersign; (*Abschrift*) to authenticate; (*Echtheit, Übersetzung*) to certify

Beglaubigung *f* countersignature

Beglaubigungsschreiben *nt* credentials *pl*

begleichen [bə'glaɪçən] *unreg vt* to settle, pay; **mit Ihnen habe ich noch eine Rechnung zu ~** (*fig*) I've a score to settle with you

begleiten [bə'glaɪtən] *vt* to accompany; (*Mil*) to escort

Begleiter, in (**-s, -**) *m(f)* companion; (*zum Schutz*) escort; (*Mus*) accompanist

Begleit- *zW*: **Begleiterscheinung** *f* side effect; **Begleitmusik** *f* accompaniment; **Begleitpapiere** *pl* (*Comm*) accompanying documents *pl*; **Begleitschiff** *nt* escort vessel; **Begleitschreiben** *nt* covering letter; **Begleitumstände** *pl* attendant circumstances

Begleitung *f* company; (*Mil*) escort; (*Mus*) accompaniment

beglücken [bə'glʏkən] *vt* to make happy, delight

beglückwünschen [bə'glʏkvʏnʃən] *vt*: **~ (zu)** to congratulate (on)

begnadet [bə'gna:dət] *adj* gifted

begnadigen [bə'gna:dɪgən] *vt* to pardon

Begnadigung *f* pardon

begnügen [bə'gny:gən] *vr*: **sich ~ mit** to be satisfied with, content o.s. with

Begonie [bə'go:niə] *f* begonia

begonnen [bə'gɔnən] *pp von* **beginnen**

begossen [bə'gɔsən] *pp von* **begießen** ▷ *adj*: **er stand da wie ein ~er Pudel** (*umg*) he looked so sheepish

begraben [bə'gra:bən] *unreg vt* to bury; (*aufgeben: Hoffnung*) to abandon; (*beenden: Streit etc*) to end; **dort möchte ich nicht ~ sein** (*umg*) I wouldn't like to be stuck in that hole

Begräbnis [bə'grɛ:pnɪs] (**-ses, -se**) *nt* burial, funeral

begradigen [bə'gra:dɪgən] *vt* to straighten (out)

begreifen [bə'graɪfən] *unreg vt* to understand, comprehend

begreiflich [bə'graɪflɪç] *adj* understandable; **ich kann mich ihm nicht ~ machen** I can't make myself clear to him

begrenzen [bə'grɛntsən] *vt* (*beschränken*): **~ (auf +akk)** to restrict (to), limit (to)

Begrenztheit [bə'grɛntsthaɪt] *f* limitation, restriction; (*fig*) narrowness

Begriff [bə'grɪf] (**-(e)s, -e**) *m* concept, idea; **im ~ sein, etw zu tun** to be about to do sth; **sein Name ist mir ein/kein ~** his name means something/doesn't mean anything to me; **du machst dir keinen ~ (davon)** you've no idea; **für meine ~e** in my opinion; **schwer von ~** (*umg*) slow on the uptake

Begriffsbestimmung *f* definition

begriffsstutzig *adj* slow-witted, dense

begrub *etc* [bə'gru:p] *vb siehe* **begraben**

begründen [bə'grʏndən] *vt* (*Gründe geben*) to justify; **etw näher ~** to give specific reasons for sth

Begründer, in (**-s, -**) *m(f)* founder

begründet *adj* well-founded, justified; **sachlich ~** founded on fact

Begründung *f* justification, reason

begrünen [bə'gry:nən] *vt* to plant with greenery

begrüßen [bə'gry:sən] *vt* to greet, welcome

begrüßenswert *adj* welcome

Begrüßung *f* greeting, welcome

begünstigen [bə'gʏnstɪgən] *vt* (*Person*) to favour (*Brit*), favor (*US*); (*Sache*) to further, promote

Begünstigte, r *f(m)* beneficiary

begutachten [bə'gu:t|axtən] *vt* to assess; (*umg: ansehen*) to have a look at

begütert [bə'gy:tərt] *adj* wealthy, well-to-do

begütigend *adj* (*Worte etc*) soothing; **~ auf jdn einreden** to calm sb down

behaart [bə'ha:rt] *adj* hairy

behäbig [bə'hɛ:bɪç] *adj* (*dick*) portly, stout; (*geruhsam*) comfortable

behaftet [bə'haftət] *adj*: **mit etw ~ sein** to be afflicted by sth

behagen [bə'ha:gən] *vi*: **das behagt ihm nicht** he does not like it; **Behagen** (**-s**) *nt* comfort, ease; **mit Behagen essen** to eat with relish

behaglich [bə'ha:klɪç] *adj* comfortable, cosy; **Behaglichkeit** *f* comfort, cosiness

behält [bə'hɛlt] *vb siehe* **behalten**

behalten [bə'haltən] *unreg vt* to keep, retain; (*im Gedächtnis*) to remember; **~ Sie (doch) Platz!** please don't get up!

Behälter [bə'hɛltər] (**-s, -**) *m* container,

receptacle

behämmert [bə'hɛmərt] *(umg) adj* screwy, crazy

behandeln [bə'handəln] *vt* to treat; *(Thema)* to deal with; *(Maschine)* to handle; **der ~de Arzt** the doctor in attendance

Behändigkeit [bə'hɛndıçkaıt] *f* agility, quickness

Behandlung *f* treatment; *(von Maschine)* handling

behängen [bə'hɛŋən] *vt* to decorate

beharren [bə'harən] *vi*: **auf etw** *dat* **~** to stick *od* keep to sth

beharrlich [bə'harlıç] *adj (ausdauernd)* steadfast, unwavering; *(hartnäckig)* tenacious, dogged; **Beharrlichkeit** *f* steadfastness; tenacity

behaupten [bə'haʊptən] *vt* to claim, assert, maintain; *(sein Recht)* to defend ▷ *vr* to assert o.s.; **von jdm ~, dass ...** to say (of sb) that ...; **sich auf dem Markt ~** to establish itself on the market

Behauptung *f* claim, assertion

Behausung [bə'haʊzʊŋ] *f* dwelling, abode; *(armselig)* hovel

beheben [bə'he:bən] *unreg vt (beseitigen)* to remove; *(Missstände)* to remedy; *(Schaden)* to repair; *(Störung)* to clear

beheimatet [bə'haıma:tət] *adj*: **~ (in +dat)** domiciled (at/in); *(Tier, Pflanze)* native (to)

beheizen [bə'haıtsən] *vt* to heat

Behelf [bə'hɛlf] **(-(e)s, -e)** *m* expedient, makeshift; **behelfen** *unreg vr*: **sich mit etw behelfen** to make do with sth

behelfsmäßig *adj* improvised, makeshift; *(vorübergehend)* temporary

behelligen [bə'hɛlıgən] *vt* to trouble, bother

Behendigkeit [bə'hɛndıçkaıt] *f siehe* **Behändigkeit**

beherbergen [bə'hɛrbɛrgən] *vt (lit, fig)* to house

beherrschen [bə'hɛrʃən] *vt (Volk)* to rule, govern; *(Situation)* to control; *(Sprache, Gefühle)* to master ▷ *vr* to control o.s.

beherrscht *adj* controlled; **Beherrschtheit** *f* self-control

Beherrschung *f* rule; control; mastery; **die ~ verlieren** to lose one's temper

beherzigen [bə'hɛrtsıgən] *vt* to take to heart

beherzt *adj* spirited, brave

behielt *etc* [bə'hi:lt] *vb siehe* **behalten**

behilflich [bə'hılflıç] *adj* helpful; **jdm ~ sein (bei)** to help sb (with)

behindern [bə'hındərn] *vt* to hinder, impede

Behinderte, r *f(m)* disabled person

Behinderung *f* hindrance; *(Körperbehinderung)* handicap

Behörde [bə'hø:rdə] **(-, -n)** *f* authorities *pl*; *(Amtsgebäude)* office(s *pl*)

behördlich [bə'hø:rtlıç] *adj* official

behüten [bə'hy:tən] *vt* to guard; **jdn vor etw** *dat* **~** to preserve sb from sth

behütet *adj (Jugend etc)* sheltered

behutsam [bə'hu:tza:m] *adj* cautious, careful; **man muss es ihr ~ beibringen** it will have to be broken to her gently; **Behutsamkeit** *f* caution, carefulness

SCHLÜSSELWORT

bei [baı] *präp +dat* **1** *(nahe bei)* near; *(zum Aufenthalt)* at, with; *(unter, zwischen)* among; **bei München** near Munich; **bei uns** at our place; **beim Friseur** at the hairdresser's; **bei seinen Eltern wohnen** to live with one's parents; **bei einer Firma arbeiten** to work for a firm; **etw bei sich haben** to have sth on one; **jdn bei sich haben** to have sb with one; **bei Goethe** in Goethe; **beim Militär** in the army

2 *(zeitlich)* at, on; *(während)* during; *(Zustand, Umstand)* in; **bei Nacht** at night; **bei Nebel** in fog; **bei Regen** if it rains; **bei solcher Hitze** in such heat; **bei meiner Ankunft** on my arrival; **bei der Arbeit** when I'm *etc* working; **beim Fahren** while driving; **bei offenem Fenster schlafen** to sleep with the window open; **bei Feuer Scheibe einschlagen** in case of fire break glass; **bei seinem Talent** with his talent

beibehalten ['baıbəhaltən] *unreg vt* to keep, retain

Beibehaltung *f* keeping, retaining

Beiblatt ['baıblat] *nt* supplement

beibringen ['baıbrıŋən] *unreg vt (Beweis, Zeugen)* to bring forward; *(Gründe)* to adduce; **jdm etw ~** *(zufügen)* to inflict sth on sb; *(zu verstehen geben)* to make sb understand sth; *(lehren)* to teach sb sth

Beichte ['baıçtə] *f* confession

beichten *vt* to confess ▷ *vi* to go to confession

Beichtgeheimnis *nt* secret of the confessional

Beichtstuhl *m* confessional

beide ['baıdə] *pron, adj* both; **meine ~n Brüder** my two brothers, both my brothers; **die ersten ~n** the first two; **wir ~** we two; **einer von ~n** one of the two; **alles ~s** both (of them); **~ Mal** both times

beider- *zW*: **beiderlei** *adj inv* of both; **beiderseitig** *adj* mutual, reciprocal; **beiderseits** *adv* mutually ▷ *präp +gen* on both sides of

beidhändig ['baıthɛndıç] *adj* ambidextrous

beidrehen ['baıdre:ən] *vi* to heave to

beidseitig ['baıtzaıtıç] *adj (auf beiden Seiten)* on both sides

beieinander [baı|aı'nandər] *adv* together; **gut ~ sein** *(umg: gesundheitlich)* to be in good shape; *(: geistig)* to be all there

Beifahrer, in ['baıfa:rər(ın)] **(-s, -)** *m(f)* passenger; **Beifahrerairbag** *m (Aut)* passenger airbag; **Beifahrersitz** *m* passenger seat

Beifall ['baıfal] **(-(e)s)** *m* applause; *(Zustimmung)* approval; **~ heischend** fishing for applause/approval

beifällig ['baıfɛlıç] *adj* approving; *(Kommentar)* favourable (Brit), favorable (US)

Beifilm ['baıfılm] *m* supporting film

beifügen ['baɪfy:gən] *vt* to enclose
Beigabe ['baɪga:bə] *f* addition
beige ['be:ʒ] *adj* beige
beigeben ['baɪge:bən] *unreg vt* (*zufügen*) to add; (*mitgeben*) to give ▷ *vi*: **klein ~** (*nachgeben*) to climb down
Beigeschmack ['baɪgeʃmak] *m* aftertaste
Beihilfe ['baɪhɪlfə] *f* aid, assistance; (*Studienbeihilfe*) grant; (*Jur*) aiding and abetting; **wegen ~ zum Mord** (*Jur*) because of being an accessory to the murder
beikommen ['baɪkɔmən] *unreg vi +dat* to get at; (*einem Problem*) to deal with
Beil [baɪl] (**-(e)s, -e**) *nt* axe (*Brit*), ax (*US*), hatchet
Beilage ['baɪla:gə] *f* (*Buchbeilage etc*) supplement; (*Koch*) accompanying vegetables; (*getrennt serviert*) side dish
beiläufig ['baɪlɔʏfɪç] *adj* casual, incidental ▷ *adv* casually, by the way
beilegen ['baɪle:gən] *vt* (*hinzufügen*) to enclose, add; (*beimessen*) to attribute, ascribe; (*Streit*) to settle
beileibe [baɪ'laɪbə] *adv*: **~ nicht** by no means
Beileid ['baɪlaɪt] *nt* condolence, sympathy; **herzliches** ~ deepest sympathy
beiliegend ['baɪli:gənt] *adj* (*Comm*) enclosed
beim [baɪm] = **bei dem**
beimessen ['baɪmɛsən] *unreg vt* to attribute, ascribe
Bein [baɪn] (**-(e)s, -e**) *nt* leg; **jdm ein ~ stellen** (*lit, fig*) to trip sb up; **wir sollten uns auf die ~e machen** (*umg*) we ought to be making tracks; **jdm ~e machen** (*umg: antreiben*) to make sb get a move on; **die ~e in die Hand nehmen** (*umg*) to take to one's heels; **sich** *dat* **die ~e in den Bauch stehen** (*umg*) to stand about until one is fit to drop; **etw auf die ~e stellen** (*fig*) to get sth off the ground
beinah [baɪ'na:], **beinahe** [baɪ'na:ə] *adv* almost, nearly
Beinbruch *m* fracture of the leg; **das ist kein ~** (*fig: umg*) it could be worse
beinhalten [bə'|ɪnhaltən] *vt* to contain
beipflichten ['baɪpflɪçtən] *vi*: **jdm/etw** ~ to agree with sb/sth
Beiprogramm ['baɪprogram] *nt* supporting programme (*Brit*) *od* program (*US*)
Beirat ['baɪra:t] *m* advisory council; (*Elternbeirat*) parents' council
beirren [bə'|ɪrən] *vt* to confuse, muddle; **sich nicht ~ lassen** not to let o.s. be confused
Beirut [baɪ'ru:t] (**-s**) *nt* Beirut
beisammen [baɪ'zamən] *adv* together; **beisammenhaben** *unreg vt*: **er hat (sie) nicht alle beisammen** (*umg*) he's not all there; **Beisammensein** (**-s**) *nt* get-together
Beischlaf ['baɪʃla:f] *m* (*Jur*) sexual intercourse
Beisein ['baɪzaɪn] (**-s**) *nt* presence
beiseite [baɪ'zaɪtə] *adv* to one side, aside; (*stehen*) on one side, aside; **Spaß ~!** joking apart!; **beiseitelegen** *vt* (*sparen*) to put by; **beiseiteschaffen** *vt* to get rid of
beisetzen ['baɪzɛtsən] *vt* to bury
Beisetzung *f* funeral
Beisitzer, in ['baɪzɪtsər(ɪn)] (**-s, -**) *m(f)* (*Jur*) assessor; (*bei Prüfung*) observer
Beispiel ['baɪʃpi:l] (**-(e)s, -e**) *nt* example; **mit gutem ~ vorangehen** to set a good example; **sich** *dat* **an jdm ein ~ nehmen** to take sb as an example; **zum** ~ for example; **beispielhaft** *adj* exemplary; **beispiellos** *adj* unprecedented
beispielsweise *adv* for instance, for example
beispringen ['baɪʃprɪŋən] *unreg vi +dat* to come to the aid of
beißen ['baɪsən] *unreg vt, vi* to bite; (*stechen: Rauch, Säure*) to burn ▷ *vr* (*Farben*) to clash
beißend *adj* biting, caustic; (*Geruch*) pungent, sharp; (*fig*) sarcastic
Beißzange ['baɪstsaŋə] *f* pliers *pl*
Beistand ['baɪʃtant] (**-(e)s, ¨-e**) *m* support, help; (*Jur*) adviser; **jdm ~ leisten** to give sb assistance/one's support
beistehen ['baɪʃte:ən] *unreg vi*: **jdm** ~ to stand by sb
Beistelltisch ['baɪʃtɛltɪʃ] *m* occasional table
beisteuern ['baɪʃtɔʏərn] *vt* to contribute
beistimmen ['baɪʃtɪmən] *vi +dat* to agree with
Beistrich ['baɪʃtrɪç] *m* comma
Beitrag ['baɪtra:k] (**-(e)s, ¨-e**) *m* contribution; (*Zahlung*) fee, subscription; (*Versicherungsbeitrag*) premium; **einen ~ zu etw leisten** to make a contribution to sth
beitragen ['baɪtra:gən] *unreg vt, vi*: **~ (zu)** to contribute (to); (*mithelfen*) to help (with)
Beitrags- *zW*: **beitragsfinanziert** *adj* financed by fees/contributions; **beitragsfrei** *adj* non-contributory; **beitragspflichtig** *adj* contributory; **beitragspflichtig sein** (*Mensch*) to have to pay contributions; **Beitragszahler, in** *m(f)* contributor
beitreten ['baɪtre:tən] *unreg vi +dat* to join
Beitritt ['baɪtrɪt] *m* joining; membership
Beitrittserklärung *f* declaration of membership
Beitrittsland *nt* (*zu EU etc*) acceding country
Beiwagen ['baɪva:gən] *m* (*Motorradbeiwagen*) sidecar; (*Straßenbahnbeiwagen*) extra carriage
beiwohnen ['baɪvo:nən] *vi* (*geh*): **einer Sache** *dat* ~ to attend *od* be present at sth
Beiwort ['baɪvɔrt] *nt* adjective
Beize ['baɪtsə] (**-, -n**) *f* (*Holzbeize*) stain; (*Koch*) marinade
beizeiten [baɪ'tsaɪtən] *adv* in time
bejahen [bə'ja:ən] *vt* (*Frage*) to say yes to, answer in the affirmative; (*gutheißen*) to agree with
bejahrt [bə'ja:rt] *adj* elderly, advanced in years
bejammern [bə'jamərn] *vt* to lament, bewail
bejammernswert *adj* lamentable
bekakeln [bə'ka:kəln] (*umg*) *vt* to discuss
bekam *etc* [bə'kam] *vb siehe* **bekommen**
bekämpfen [bə'kɛmpfən] *vt* (*Gegner*) to fight; (*Seuche*) to combat ▷ *vr* to fight
Bekämpfung *f*: ~ (*+gen*) fight (against),

struggle (against)

bekannt [bə'kant] *adj* (well-)known; (*nicht fremd*) familiar; **~ geben** to announce publicly; **mit jdm ~ sein** to know sb; **~ machen** to announce; **jdn mit jdm ~ machen** to introduce sb to sb; **sich mit etw ~ machen** to familiarize o.s. with sth; **das ist mir ~** I know that; **es/sie kommt mir ~ vor** it/she seems familiar; **durch etw ~ werden** to become famous because of sth

Bekannte, r *f(m)* friend, acquaintance

Bekanntenkreis *m* circle of friends

bekanntermaßen *adv* as is known

bekannt- *zW*: **Bekanntgabe** *f* announcement; **Bekanntheitsgrad** *m* degree of fame; **bekanntlich** *adv* as is well known, as you know; **Bekanntmachung** *f* publication; (*Anschlag etc*) announcement; **Bekanntschaft** *f* acquaintance

bekehren [bə'ke:rən] *vt* to convert ▷ *vr* to be *od* become converted

Bekehrung *f* conversion

bekennen [bə'kɛnən] *unreg vt* to confess; (*Glauben*) to profess ▷ *vr*: **sich zu jdm/etw ~** to declare one's support for sb/sth; **Farbe ~** (*umg*) to show where one stands

Bekenntnis [bə'kɛntnɪs] (**-ses, -se**) *nt* admission, confession; (*Religion*) confession, denomination; **ein ~ zur Demokratie ablegen** to declare one's belief in democracy; **Bekenntnisschule** *f* denominational school

beklagen [bə'kla:gən] *vt* to deplore, lament ▷ *vr* to complain

beklagenswert *adj* lamentable, pathetic; (*Mensch*) pitiful; (*Zustand*) deplorable; (*Unfall*) terrible

beklatschen [bə'klatʃən] *vt* to applaud, clap

bekleben [bə'kle:bən] *vt*: **etw mit Bildern ~** to stick pictures onto sth

bekleckern [bə'klɛkərn] (*umg*) *vt* to stain

bekleiden [bə'klaɪdən] *vt* to clothe; (*Amt*) to occupy, fill

Bekleidung *f* clothing; (*form: eines Amtes*) tenure

Bekleidungsindustrie *f* clothing industry, rag trade (*umg*)

beklemmen [bə'klɛmən] *vt* to oppress

Beklemmung *f* oppressiveness; (*Gefühl der Angst*) feeling of apprehension

beklommen [bə'klɔmən] *adj* anxious, uneasy; **Beklommenheit** *f* anxiety, uneasiness

bekloppt [bə'klɔpt] (*umg*) *adj* (*Mensch*) crazy; (*: Sache*) lousy

beknackt [bə'knakt] (*umg*) *adj* = **bekloppt**

beknien [bə'kni:ən] (*umg*) *vt* (*jdn*) to beg

bekommen [bə'kɔmən] *unreg vt* to get, receive; (*Kind*) to have; (*Zug*) to catch, get ▷ *vi*: **jdm ~** to agree with sb; **es mit jdm zu tun ~** to get into trouble with sb; **wohl bekomms!** your health!

bekömmlich [bə'kœmlɪç] *adj* easily digestible

beköstigen [bə'kœstɪgən] *vt* to cater for

bekräftigen [bə'krɛftɪgən] *vt* to confirm, corroborate

Bekräftigung *f* corroboration

bekreuzigen [bə'krɔʏtsɪgən] *vr* to cross o.s.

bekritteln [bə'krɪtəln] *vt* to criticize, pick holes in

bekümmern [bə'kʏmərn] *vt* to worry, trouble

bekunden [bə'kʊndən] *vt* (*sagen*) to state; (*zeigen*) to show

belächeln [bə'lɛçəln] *vt* to laugh at

beladen [bə'la:dən] *unreg vt* to load

Belag [bə'la:k] (**-(e)s, ¨-e**) *m* covering, coating; (*Brotbelag*) spread; (*auf Pizza, Brot*) topping; (*auf Tortenboden, zwischen Brotscheiben*) filling; (*Zahnbelag*) tartar; (*auf Zunge*) fur; (*Bremsbelag*) lining

belagern [bə'la:gərn] *vt* to besiege

Belagerung *f* siege

Belagerungszustand *m* state of siege

belämmert [bəlɛmərt] (*umg*) *adj* sheepish

Belang [bə'laŋ] (**-(e)s**) *m* importance

Belange *pl* interests *pl*, concerns *pl*

belangen *vt* (*Jur*) to take to court

belanglos *adj* trivial, unimportant

Belanglosigkeit *f* triviality

belassen [bə'lasən] *unreg vt* (*in Zustand, Glauben*) to leave; (*in Stellung*) to retain; **es dabei ~** to leave it at that

Belastbarkeit *f* (*von Brücke, Aufzug*) load-bearing capacity; (*von Menschen, Nerven*) ability to take stress

belasten [bə'lastən] *vt* (*lit*) to burden; (*fig: bedrücken*) to trouble, worry; (*Comm: Konto*) to debit; (*Jur*) to incriminate ▷ *vr* to weigh o.s. down; (*Jur*) to incriminate o.s.; **etw (mit einer Hypothek) ~** to mortgage sth

belastend *adj* (*Jur*) incriminating

belästigen [bə'lɛstɪgən] *vt* to annoy, pester

Belästigung *f* annoyance, pestering; (*körperlich*) molesting

Belastung [bə'lastʊŋ] *f* (*lit*) load; (*fig: Sorge etc*) weight; (*Comm*) charge, debit(ing); (*mit Hypothek*): **~** (*+gen*) mortgage (on); (*Jur*) incriminating evidence

Belastungs- *zW*: **Belastungsmaterial** *nt* (*Jur*) incriminating evidence; **Belastungsprobe** *f* capacity test; (*fig*) test; **Belastungszeuge** *m* witness for the prosecution

belaubt [bə'laʊpt] *adj*: **dicht ~ sein** to have thick foliage

belaufen [bə'laʊfən] *unreg vr*: **sich ~ auf** *+akk* to amount to

belauschen [bə'laʊʃən] *vt* to eavesdrop on

beleben [bə'le:bən] *vt* (*anregen*) to liven up; (*Konjunktur, jds Hoffnungen*) to stimulate

belebt [bə'le:pt] *adj* (*Straße*) crowded

Beleg [bə'le:k] (**-(e)s, -e**) *m* (*Comm*) receipt; (*Beweis*) documentary evidence, proof; (*Beispiel*) example

belegen [bə'le:gən] *vt* to cover; (*Kuchen, Brot*) to spread; (*Platz*) to reserve, book; (*Kurs, Vorlesung*) to register for; (*beweisen*) to verify, prove

Belegschaft *f* personnel, staff

belegt *adj* (*Zunge*) furred; (*Stimme*) hoarse; (*Zimmer*) occupied; **~e Brote** open sandwiches

belehren [bə'le:rən] *vt* to instruct, teach; **jdn**

eines Besseren ~ to teach sb better; **er ist nicht zu ~** he won't be told
Belehrung *f* instruction
beleibt [bə'laɪpt] *adj* stout, corpulent
beleidigen [bə'laɪdɪgən] *vt* to insult; to offend
beleidigt *adj* insulted; (*gekränkt*) offended; **die ~e Leberwurst spielen** (*umg*) to be in a huff
Beleidigung *f* insult; (*Jur*) slander; (*: schriftlich*) libel
beleihen [bə'laɪən] *unreg vt* (*Comm*) to lend money on
belemmert [bə'lɛmərt] (*umg*) *adj siehe* **belämmert**
belesen [bə'le:zən] *adj* well-read
beleuchten [bə'lɔʏçtən] *vt* to light, illuminate; (*fig*) to throw light on
Beleuchter, in (**-s, -**) *m(f)* lighting technician
Beleuchtung *f* lighting, illumination
beleumdet [bə'lɔʏmdət] *adj*: **gut/schlecht ~ sein** to have a good/bad reputation
beleumundet [bə'lɔʏmʊndət] *adj* = **beleumdet**
Belgien ['bɛlgiən] (**-s**) *nt* Belgium
Belgier, in (**-s, -**) *m(f)* Belgian
belgisch *adj* Belgian
Belgrad ['bɛlgra:t] (**-s**) *nt* Belgrade
belichten [bə'lɪçtən] *vt* to expose
Belichtung *f* exposure
Belichtungsmesser *m* exposure meter
Belieben [bə'li:bən] *nt*: **(ganz) nach ~** (just) as you wish
belieben *vi unpers* (*geh*): **wie es Ihnen beliebt** as you wish
beliebig [bə'li:bɪç] *adj* any you like, as you like; **~ viel** as much as you like; **in ~er Reihenfolge** in any order whatever; **ein ~es Thema** any subject you like *od* want
beliebt [bə'li:pt] *adj* popular; **sich bei jdm ~ machen** to make o.s. popular with sb;
Beliebtheit *f* popularity
beliefern [bə'li:fərn] *vt* to supply
Belize [bɛ'li:z] (**-s**) *nt* Belize
bellen ['bɛlən] *vi* to bark
Belletristik [bɛle'trɪstɪk] *f* fiction and poetry
belohnen [bə'lo:nən] *vt* to reward
Belohnung *f* reward
Belüftung [bə'lʏftʊŋ] *f* ventilation
belügen [bə'ly:gən] *unreg vt* to lie to, deceive
belustigen [bə'lʊstɪgən] *vt* to amuse
Belustigung *f* amusement
bemächtigen [bə'mɛçtɪgən] *vr*: **sich einer Sache** *gen* **~** to take possession of sth, seize sth
bemalen [bə'ma:lən] *vt* to paint ▷ *vr* (*pej: schminken*) to put on one's war paint (*umg*)
bemängeln [bə'mɛŋəln] *vt* to criticize
bemannen [bə'manən] *vt* to man
Bemannung *f* manning; (*Naut, Aviat etc*) crew
bemänteln [bə'mɛntəln] *vt* to cloak, hide
bemerkbar *adj* perceptible, noticeable; **sich ~ machen** (*Person*) to make *od* get o.s. noticed; (*Unruhe*) to become noticeable
bemerken [bə'mɛrkən] *vt* (*wahrnehmen*) to notice, observe; (*sagen*) to say, mention; **nebenbei bemerkt** by the way
bemerkenswert *adj* remarkable, noteworthy
Bemerkung *f* remark, comment; (*schriftlich*) comment, note
bemitleiden [bə'mɪtlaɪdən] *vt* to pity
bemittelt [bə'mɪtəlt] *adj* well-to-do, well-off
bemühen [bə'my:ən] *vr* to take trouble; **sich um eine Stelle ~** to try to get a job
bemüht *adj*: **(darum) ~ sein, etw zu tun** to endeavour (*Brit*) *od* endeavor (*US*) *od* be at pains to do sth
Bemühung *f* trouble, pains *pl*, effort
bemüßigt [bə'my:sɪçt] *adj*: **sich ~ fühlen/sehen** (*geh*) to feel called upon
bemuttern [bə'mʊtərn] *vt* to mother
benachbart [bə'naxba:rt] *adj* neighbouring (*Brit*), neighboring (*US*)
benachrichtigen [bə'na:xrɪçtɪgən] *vt* to inform
Benachrichtigung *f* notification
benachteiligen [bə'na:xtaɪlɪgən] *vt* to (put at a) disadvantage, victimize
benehmen [bə'ne:mən] *unreg vr* to behave;
Benehmen (**-s**) *nt* behaviour (*Brit*), behavior (*US*); **kein Benehmen haben** not to know how to behave
beneiden [bə'naɪdən] *vt* to envy
beneidenswert *adj* enviable
Beneluxländer ['be:nelʊkslɛndər] *pl* Benelux (countries *pl*)
Beneluxstaaten *pl* Benelux (countries *pl*)
benennen [bə'nɛnən] *unreg vt* to name
Bengel ['bɛŋəl] (**-s, -**) *m* (little) rascal *od* rogue
Benimm [bə'nɪm] (**-s**) (*umg*) *m* manners *pl*
Benin [be'ni:n] (**-s**) *nt* Benin
benommen [bə'nɔmən] *adj* dazed
benoten [bə'no:tən] *vt* to mark
benötigen [bə'nø:tɪgən] *vt* to need
benutzen [bə'nʊtsən] *vt* to use
benützen [bə'nʏtsən] *vt* to use
Benutzer, in (**-s, -**) *m(f)* user; **benutzerdefiniert** *adj* (*Comput*) user-defined; **benutzerfreundlich** *adj* user-friendly; **Benutzername** *m* username
Benutzung *f* utilization, use; **jdm etw zur ~ überlassen** to put sth at sb's disposal
Benzin [bɛnt'si:n] (**-s, -e**) *nt* (*Aut*) petrol (*Brit*), gas(oline) (*US*); **Benzineinspritzanlage** *f* (*Aut*) fuel injection system; **Benzinkanister** *m* petrol (*Brit*) *od* gas (*US*) can; **Benzintank** *m* petrol (*Brit*) *od* gas (*US*) tank; **Benzinuhr** *f* petrol (*Brit*) *od* gas (*US*) gauge
beobachten [bə'|o:baxtən] *vt* to observe
Beobachter, in (**-s, -**) *m(f)* observer; (*eines Unfalls*) witness; (*Presse, TV*) correspondent
Beobachtung *f* observation
beordern [bə'|ɔrdərn] *vt*: **jdn zu sich ~** to send for sb
bepacken [bə'pakən] *vt* to load, pack
bepflanzen [bə'pflantsən] *vt* to plant
bequatschen [bə'kvatʃən] (*umg*) *vt* (*überreden*) to persuade; **etw ~** to talk sth over
bequem [bə'kve:m] *adj* comfortable; (*Ausrede*) convenient; (*Person*) lazy, indolent
bequemen [bə'kve:mən] *vr*: **sich ~, etw zu**

tun to condescend to do sth
Bequemlichkeit *f* convenience, comfort; (*Faulheit*) laziness, indolence
Ber. *abk* = **Bericht; Beruf**
berät [bə'rɛ:t] *vb siehe* **beraten**
beraten [bə'ra:tən] *unreg vt* to advise; (*besprechen*) to discuss, debate ▷ *vr* to consult; **gut/schlecht ~ sein** to be well/ill advised; **sich ~ lassen** to get advice
beratend *adj* consultative; **jdm ~ zur Seite stehen** to act in an advisory capacity to sb
Berater, in (**-s, -**) *m(f)* adviser; **Beratervertrag** *m* consultancy contract
beratschlagen [bə'ra:tʃla:gən] *vi* to deliberate, confer ▷ *vt* to deliberate on, confer about
Beratung *f* advice; (*Besprechung*) consultation
Beratungsstelle *f* advice centre (*Brit*) *od* center (*US*)
berauben [bə'raʊbən] *vt* to rob
berauschen [bə'raʊʃən] *vt* (*lit, fig*) to intoxicate
berauschend *adj*: **das war nicht sehr ~** (*ironisch*) that wasn't very exciting
berechenbar [bə'rɛçənba:r] *adj* calculable; (*Verhalten*) predictable
berechnen [bə'rɛçnən] *vt* to calculate; (*Comm: anrechnen*) to charge
berechnend *adj* (*Mensch*) calculating, scheming
Berechnung *f* calculation; (*Comm*) charge
berechtigen [bə'rɛçtɪgən] *vt* to entitle; (*bevollmächtigen*) to authorize; (*fig*) to justify
berechtigt [bə'rɛçtɪçt] *adj* justifiable, justified
Berechtigung *f* authorization; (*fig*) justification
bereden [bə're:dən] *vt* (*besprechen*) to discuss; (*überreden*) to persuade ▷ *vr* to discuss
beredt [bə're:t] *adj* eloquent
Bereich [bə'raɪç] (**-(e)s, -e**) *m* (*Bezirk*) area; (*Ressort, Gebiet*) sphere; **im ~ des Möglichen liegen** to be within the bounds of possibility
bereichern [bə'raɪçərn] *vt* to enrich ▷ *vr* to get rich; **sich auf Kosten anderer ~** to feather one's nest at the expense of other people
Bereifung [bə'raɪfʊŋ] *f* (set of) tyres (*Brit*) *od* tires (*US*) *pl*; (*Vorgang*) fitting with tyres (*Brit*) *od* tires (*US*)
bereinigen [bə'raɪnɪgən] *vt* to settle
bereisen [bə'raɪzən] *vt* to travel through; (*Comm: Gebiet*) to travel, cover
bereit [bə'raɪt] *adj* ready, prepared; **zu etw ~ sein** to be ready for sth; **sich ~ erklären** to declare o.s. willing; **(sich) ~ machen** to prepare, to get ready
bereiten *vt* to prepare, make ready; (*Kummer, Freude*) to cause; **einer Sache** *dat* **ein Ende ~** to put an end to sth
bereit- *zW*: **bereithalten** *unreg vt* to keep in readiness; **bereitlegen** *vt* to lay out; **bereitmachen** *vt, vr siehe* **bereit**
bereits *adv* already
bereit- *zW*: **Bereitschaft** *f* readiness; (*Polizei*) alert; **in Bereitschaft sein** to be on the alert *od* on stand-by; **Bereitschaftsarzt** *m* doctor on call; (*im Krankenhaus*) duty doctor; **Bereitschaftsdienst** *m* emergency service; **bereitstehen** *unreg vi* (*Person*) to be prepared; (*Ding*) to be ready; **bereitstellen** *vt* (*Kisten, Pakete etc*) to put ready; (*Geld etc*) to make available; (*Truppen, Maschinen*) to put at the ready
Bereitung *f* preparation
bereitwillig *adj* willing, ready; **Bereitwilligkeit** *f* willingness, readiness
bereuen [bə'rɔʏən] *vt* to regret
Berg [bɛrk] (**-(e)s, -e**) *m* mountain; (*kleiner*) hill; **mit etw hinterm ~ halten** (*fig*) to keep quiet about sth; **über alle ~e sein** to be miles away; **da stehen einem ja die Haare zu ~e** it's enough to make your hair stand on end; **bergab** *adv* downhill; **bergan** *adv* uphill; **Bergarbeiter** *m* miner; **bergauf** *adv* uphill; **Bergbahn** *f* mountain railway (*Brit*) *od* railroad (*US*); **Bergbau** *m* mining
bergen ['bɛrgən] *unreg vt* (*retten*) to rescue; (*Ladung*) to salvage; (*enthalten*) to contain
Bergführer *m* mountain guide
Berggipfel *m* mountain top, peak, summit
bergig ['bɛrgɪç] *adj* mountainous, hilly
Berg- *zW*: **Bergkamm** *m* crest, ridge; **Bergkette** *f* mountain range; **Bergkristall** *m* rock crystal; **Bergmann** (**-(e)s**, *pl* **~leute**) *m* miner; **Bergnot** *f*: **in Bergnot sein/geraten** to be in/get into difficulties while climbing; **Bergpredigt** *f* (*Rel*) Sermon on the Mount; **Bergrettungsdienst** *m* mountain rescue service; **Bergrutsch** *m* landslide; **Bergschuh** *m* walking boot; **Bergsteigen** *nt* mountaineering; **Bergsteiger, in** *m(f)* mountaineer, climber; **Berg-und-Tal-Bahn** *f* big dipper, roller-coaster
Bergung ['bɛrgʊŋ] *f* (*von Menschen*) rescue; (*von Material*) recovery; (*Naut*) salvage
Bergwacht *f* mountain rescue service
Bergwerk *nt* mine
Bericht [bə'rɪçt] (**-(e)s, -e**) *m* report, account; **berichten** *vt, vi* to report; **Berichterstatter** (**-s, -**) *m* reporter, (newspaper) correspondent; **Berichterstattung** *f* reporting
berichtigen [bə'rɪçtɪgən] *vt* to correct
Berichtigung *f* correction
berieseln [bə'ri:zəln] *vt* to spray with water
Berieselung *f* watering; **die dauernde ~ mit Musik ...** (*fig*) the constant stream of music ...
Berieselungsanlage *f* sprinkler (system)
Beringmeer ['be:rɪŋme:r] *nt* Bering Sea
beritten [bə'rɪtən] *adj* mounted
Berlin [bɛr'li:n] (**-s**) *nt* Berlin
Berliner[1] *adj attrib* Berlin
Berliner[2] (**-s, -**) *m* (*Person*) Berliner; (*Koch*) jam doughnut
Berlinerin *f* Berliner
berlinerisch (*umg*) *adj* (*Dialekt*) Berlin *attr*
Bermudas [bɛr'mu:das] *pl*: **auf den ~** in Bermuda
Bern [bɛrn] (**-s**) *nt* Berne
Bernhardiner [bɛrnhar'di:nər] (**-s, -**) *m* Saint

Bernard (dog)
Bernstein ['bɛrnʃtaɪn] *m* amber
bersten ['bɛrstən] *unreg vi* to burst, split
berüchtigt [bə'rʏçtɪçt] *adj* notorious, infamous
berücksichtigen [bə'rʏkzɪçtɪgən] *vt* to consider, bear in mind
Berücksichtigung *f* consideration; **in** *od* **unter ~ der Tatsache, dass ...** in view of the fact that ...
Beruf [bə'ru:f] (**-(e)s, -e**) *m* occupation, profession; (*Gewerbe*) trade; **was sind Sie von ~?** what is your occupation *etc*?, what do you do for a living?; **seinen ~ verfehlt haben** to have missed one's vocation
berufen *unreg vt* (*in Amt*): **jdn in etw** *akk* **~** to appoint sb to sth ▷ *vr*: **sich auf jdn/etw ~** to refer *od* appeal to sb/sth ▷ *adj* competent, qualified; (*ausersehen*): **zu etw ~ sein** to have a vocation for sth
beruflich *adj* professional; **er ist ~ viel unterwegs** he is away a lot on business
Berufs- *zW*: **Berufsakademie** *f* college of advanced vocational studies; **Berufsausbildung** *f* vocational *od* professional training; **berufsbedingt** *adj* occupational; **Berufsberater** *m* careers adviser; **Berufsberatung** *f* vocational guidance; **Berufsbezeichnung** *f* job description; **Berufseinsteiger, in** *m(f)* first-time employee; **Berufserfahrung** *f* (professional) experience; **Berufsfeuerwehr** *f* fire service; **Berufsgeheimnis** *nt* professional secret; **Berufskrankheit** *f* occupational disease; **Berufskriminalität** *f* professional crime; **Berufsleben** *nt* professional life; **im Berufsleben stehen** to be working *od* in employment; **berufsmäßig** *adj* professional; **Berufsperspektive** *f* job *od* career prospects *pl*; **Berufsrisiko** *nt* occupational hazard; **Berufsschule** *f* vocational *od* trade school; **Berufssoldat** *m* professional soldier, regular; **Berufssportler** *m* professional (sportsman); **berufstätig** *adj* employed; **berufsunfähig** *adj* unable to work (at one's profession); **Berufsunfall** *m* occupational accident; **Berufsverbot** *nt*: **jdm Berufsverbot erteilen** to ban sb from his/her profession; (*einem Arzt, Anwalt*) to strike sb off; **Berufsverkehr** *m* commuter traffic; **Berufswahl** *f* choice of a job
Berufung *f* vocation, calling; (*Ernennung*) appointment; (*Jur*) appeal; **~ einlegen** to appeal; **unter ~ auf etw** *akk* (*form*) with reference to sth
Berufungsgericht *nt* appeal court, court of appeal
beruhen [bə'ru:ən] *vi*: **auf etw** *dat* **~** to be based on sth; **etw auf sich ~ lassen** to leave sth at that; **das beruht auf Gegenseitigkeit** the feeling is mutual
beruhigen [bə'ru:ɪgən] *vt* to calm, pacify, soothe ▷ *vr* (*Mensch*) to calm (o.s.) down; (*Situation*) to calm down
beruhigend *adj* (*Gefühl, Wissen*) reassuring; (*Worte*) comforting; (*Mittel*) tranquillizing
Beruhigung *f* reassurance; (*der Nerven*) calming; **zu jds ~** to reassure sb
Beruhigungsmittel *nt* sedative
Beruhigungspille *f* tranquillizer
berühmt [bə'ry:mt] *adj* famous; **das war nicht ~** (*umg*) it was nothing to write home about; **berühmt-berüchtigt** *adj* infamous, notorious; **Berühmtheit** *f* (*Ruf*) fame; (*Mensch*) celebrity
berühren [bə'ry:rən] *vt* to touch; (*gefühlsmäßig bewegen*) to affect; (*flüchtig erwähnen*) to mention, touch on ▷ *vr* to meet, touch; **von etw peinlich berührt sein** to be embarrassed by sth
Berührung *f* contact
berührungsempfindlich *adj* touch-sensitive
Berührungspunkt *m* point of contact
bes. *abk* (= *besonders*) esp
besagen [bə'za:gən] *vt* to mean
besagt *adj* (*form: Tag etc*) in question
besaiten [bə'zaɪtən] *vt*: **neu ~** (*Instrument*) to restring
besänftigen [bə'zɛnftɪgən] *vt* to soothe, calm
besänftigend *adj* soothing
Besänftigung *f* soothing, calming
besaß *etc* [bə'za:s] *vb siehe* **besitzen**
besät [bə'zɛ:t] *adj* covered; (*mit Blättern etc*) strewn
Besatz [bə'zats] (**-es, ¨-e**) *m* trimming, edging
Besatzung *f* garrison; (*Naut, Aviat*) crew
Besatzungsmacht *f* occupying power
Besatzungszone *f* occupied zone
besaufen [bə'zaufən] *unreg* (*umg*) *vr* to get drunk *od* stoned
beschädigen [bə'ʃɛ:dɪgən] *vt* to damage
Beschädigung *f* damage; (*Stelle*) damaged spot
beschaffen [bə'ʃafən] *vt* to get, acquire ▷ *adj* constituted; **so ~ sein wie ...** to be the same as ...; **Beschaffenheit** *f* constitution, nature; **je nach Beschaffenheit der Lage** according to the situation
Beschaffung *f* acquisition
beschäftigen [bə'ʃɛftɪgən] *vt* to occupy; (*beruflich*) to employ; (*innerlich*): **jdn ~** to be on sb's mind ▷ *vr* to occupy *od* concern o.s.
beschäftigt *adj* busy, occupied; (*angestellt*): **(bei einer Firma) ~** employed (by a firm)
Beschäftigung *f* (*Beruf*) employment; (*Tätigkeit*) occupation; (*geistige Beschäftigung*) preoccupation; **einer ~ nachgehen** (*form*) to be employed
Beschäftigungsgesellschaft *f regional job creation scheme in areas with high unemployment*
Beschäftigungsprogramm *nt* employment scheme
Beschäftigungstherapie *f* occupational therapy
beschämen [bə'ʃɛ:mən] *vt* to put to shame
beschämend *adj* shameful; (*Hilfsbereitschaft*) shaming
beschämt *adj* ashamed
beschatten [bə'ʃatən] *vt* to shade; (*Verdächtige*) to shadow

beschaulich [bəˈʃaulɪç] *adj* contemplative; (*Leben, Abend*) quiet, tranquil
Bescheid [bəˈʃaɪt] (**-(e)s, -e**) *m* information; (*Weisung*) directions *pl*; **~ wissen (über** *+akk***)** to be well-informed (about); **ich weiß ~** I know; **jdm ~ geben** *od* **sagen** to let sb know; **jdm ordentlich ~ sagen** (*umg*) to tell sb where to go
bescheiden [bəˈʃaɪdən] *unreg vr* to content o.s. ▷ *vt*: **etw abschlägig ~** (*form*) to turn sth down ▷ *adj* modest; **Bescheidenheit** *f* modesty
bescheinen [bəˈʃaɪnən] *unreg vt* to shine on
bescheinigen [bəˈʃaɪnɪgən] *vt* to certify; (*bestätigen*) to acknowledge; **hiermit wird bescheinigt, dass ...** this is to certify that ...
Bescheinigung *f* certificate; (*Quittung*) receipt
bescheißen [bəˈʃaɪsən] *unreg* (*umg!*) *vt* to cheat
beschenken [bəˈʃɛŋkən] *vt* to give presents to
bescheren [bəˈʃeːrən] *vt*: **jdm etw ~** to give sb sth as a present; **jdn ~** to give presents to sb
Bescherung *f* giving of presents; (*umg*) mess; **da haben wir die ~!** (*umg*) what did I tell you!
bescheuert [bəˈʃɔʏərt] (*umg*) *adj* stupid
beschichten [bəˈʃɪçtən] *vt* (*Tech*) to coat, cover
beschießen [bəˈʃiːsən] *unreg vt* to shoot *od* fire at
beschildern [bəˈʃɪldərn] *vt* to signpost
beschimpfen [bəˈʃɪmpfən] *vt* to abuse
Beschimpfung *f* abuse, insult
beschirmen [bəˈʃɪrmən] *vt* (*geh: beschützen*) to shield
Beschiss [bəˈʃɪs] (**-es**) (*umg*) *m*: **das ist ~** that is a cheat
beschiss *etc vb siehe* **bescheißen**
beschissen *pp von* **bescheißen** ▷ *adj* (*umg!*) bloody awful, lousy
Beschlag [bəˈʃlaːk] (**-(e)s, ¨-e**) *m* (*Metallband*) fitting; (*auf Fenster*) condensation; (*auf Metall*) tarnish; finish; (*Hufeisen*) horseshoe; **jdn/etw in ~ nehmen** *od* **mit ~ belegen** to monopolize sb/sth
beschlagen [bəˈʃlaːgən] *unreg vt* to cover; (*Pferd*) to shoe; (*Fenster, Metall*) to cover ▷ *vi, vr* (*Fenster etc*) to mist over; **~ sein (in** *od* **auf** *+dat***)** to be well versed (in)
beschlagnahmen *vt* to seize, confiscate
Beschlagnahmung *f* confiscation
beschleunigen [bəˈʃlɔʏnɪgən] *vt* to accelerate, speed up ▷ *vi* (*Aut*) to accelerate
Beschleunigung *f* acceleration
beschließen [bəˈʃliːsən] *unreg vt* to decide on; (*beenden*) to end, close
beschlossen [bəˈʃlɔsən] *pp von* **beschließen** ▷ *adj* (*entschieden*) decided, agreed; **das ist ~e Sache** that's been settled
Beschluss [bəˈʃlʊs] (**-es, ¨-e**) *m* decision, conclusion; (*Ende*) close, end; **einen ~ fassen** to pass a resolution
beschlussfähig *adj*: **~ sein** to have a quorum
Beschlusslage *f* policy position
beschmieren [bəˈʃmiːrən] *vt* (*Wand*) to bedaub
beschmutzen [bəˈʃmʊtsən] *vt* to dirty, soil
beschneiden [bəˈʃnaɪdən] *unreg vt* to cut; (*stutzen*) to trim; (*: Strauch*) to prune; (*Rel*) to circumcise
beschnuppern [bəˈʃnʊpərn] *vr* (*Hunde*) to sniff each other; (*fig: umg*) to size each other up
beschönigen [bəˈʃøːnɪgən] *vt* to gloss over; **~der Ausdruck** euphemism
beschränken [bəˈʃrɛŋkən] *vt, vr*: **(sich) ~ (auf** *+akk***)** to limit *od* restrict (o.s.) (to)
beschrankt [bəˈʃraŋkt] *adj* (*Bahnübergang*) with barrier
beschränkt [bəˈʃrɛŋkt] *adj* confined, narrow; (*Mensch*) limited, narrow-minded; (*pej: geistig*) dim; **Gesellschaft mit ~er Haftung** limited company (*Brit*), corporation (*US*); **Beschränktheit** *f* narrowness
Beschränkung *f* limitation
beschreiben [bəˈʃraɪbən] *unreg vt* to describe; (*Papier*) to write on
Beschreibung *f* description
beschrieb *etc* [bəˈʃriːp] *vb siehe* **beschreiben**
beschrieben [bəˈʃriːbən] *pp von* **beschreiben**
beschriften [bəˈʃrɪftən] *vt* to mark, label
Beschriftung *f* lettering
beschuldigen [bəˈʃʊldɪgən] *vt* to accuse
Beschuldigung *f* accusation
beschummeln [bəˈʃʊməln] (*umg*) *vt, vi* to cheat
Beschuss [bəˈʃʊs] *m*: **jdn/etw unter ~ nehmen** (*Mil*) to (start to) bombard *od* shell sb/sth; (*fig*) to attack sb/sth; **unter ~ geraten** (*lit, fig*) to come into the firing line
beschützen [bəˈʃʏtsən] *vt*: **~ (vor** *+dat***)** to protect (from)
Beschützer, in (**-s, -**) *m(f)* protector
Beschützung *f* protection
beschwatzen [bəˈʃvatsən] (*umg*) *vt* (*überreden*) to talk over
Beschwerde [bəˈʃveːrdə] (**-, -n**) *f* complaint; (*Mühe*) hardship; (*Industrie*) grievance; **Beschwerden** *pl* (*Leiden*) trouble; **~ einlegen** (*form*) to lodge a complaint; **beschwerdefrei** *adj* fit and healthy; **Beschwerdefrist** *f* (*Jur*) *period of time during which an appeal may be lodged*
beschweren [bəˈʃveːrən] *vt* to weight down; (*fig*) to burden ▷ *vr* to complain
beschwerlich *adj* tiring, exhausting
beschwichtigen [bəˈʃvɪçtɪgən] *vt* to soothe, pacify
Beschwichtigung *f* soothing, calming
beschwindeln [bəˈʃvɪndəln] *vt* (*betrügen*) to cheat; (*belügen*) to fib to
beschwingt [bəˈʃvɪŋt] *adj* cheery, in high spirits
beschwipst [bəˈʃvɪpst] *adj* tipsy
beschwören [bəˈʃvøːrən] *unreg vt* (*Aussage*) to swear to; (*anflehen*) to implore; (*Geister*) to conjure up
beseelen [bəˈzeːlən] *vt* to inspire
besehen [bəˈzeːən] *unreg vt* to look at; **genau ~** to examine closely
beseitigen [bəˈzaɪtɪgən] *vt* to remove
Beseitigung *f* removal
Besen [ˈbeːzən] (**-s, -**) *m* broom; (*pej: umg: Frau*) old bag; **ich fresse einen ~, wenn das stimmt** (*umg*) if that's right, I'll eat my hat;

Besenstiel *m* broomstick
besessen [bə'zɛsən] *adj* possessed; (*von einer Idee etc*): **~ (von)** obsessed (with)
besetzen [bə'zɛtsən] *vt* (*Haus, Land*) to occupy; (*Platz*) to take, fill; (*Posten*) to fill; (*Rolle*) to cast; (*mit Edelsteinen*) to set
besetzt *adj* full; (*Tel*) engaged, busy; (*Platz*) taken; (*WC*) engaged; **Besetztzeichen** *nt* engaged tone (*Brit*), busy signal (*US*)
Besetzung *f* occupation; (*von Stelle*) filling; (*von Rolle*) casting; (*die Schauspieler*) cast; **zweite ~** (*Theat*) understudy
besichtigen [bə'zıçtıgən] *vt* to visit, look at
Besichtigung *f* visit
besiedeln *vt*: **dicht/dünn besiedelt** densely/thinly populated
Besiedelung [bə'zi:dəlʊŋ], **Besiedlung** [bə'zi:dlʊŋ] *f* population
besiegeln [bə'zi:gəln] *vt* to seal
besiegen [bə'zi:gən] *vt* to defeat, overcome
Besiegte, r [bə'zi:ktə(r)] *f(m)* loser
besinnen [bə'zınən] *unreg vr* (*nachdenken*) to think, reflect; (*erinnern*) to remember; **sich anders ~** to change one's mind
besinnlich *adj* contemplative
Besinnung *f* consciousness; **bei/ohne ~ sein** to be conscious/unconscious; **zur ~ kommen** to recover consciousness; (*fig*) to come to one's senses
besinnungslos *adj* unconscious; (*fig*) blind
Besitz [bə'zıts] (**-es**) *m* possession; (*Eigentum*) property; **Besitzanspruch** *m* claim of ownership; (*Jur*) title; **besitzanzeigend** *adj* (*Gram*) possessive
besitzen *unreg vt* to possess, own; (*Eigenschaft*) to have
Besitzer, in (**-s, -**) *m(f)* owner, proprietor
Besitz- *zW*: **Besitzergreifung** *f* seizure; **Besitznahme** *f* seizure; **Besitztum** *nt* (*Grundbesitz*) estate(*s pl*), property; **Besitzurkunde** *f* title deeds *pl*
besoffen [bə'zɔfən] (*umg*) *adj* sozzled
besohlen [bə'zo:lən] *vt* to sole
Besoldung [bə'zɔldʊŋ] *f* salary, pay
besondere, r, s [bə'zɔndərə(r, s)] *adj* special; (*eigen*) particular; (*gesondert*) separate; (*eigentümlich*) peculiar
Besonderheit *f* peculiarity
besonders *adv* especially, particularly; (*getrennt*) separately; **das Essen/der Film war nicht ~** the food/film was nothing special *od* out of the ordinary; **wie gehts dir? — nicht ~** how are you? — not too hot
besonnen [bə'zɔnən] *adj* sensible, level-headed; **Besonnenheit** *f* level-headedness
besorgen [bə'zɔrgən] *vt* (*beschaffen*) to acquire; (*kaufen*) to purchase; (*erledigen: Geschäfte*) to deal with; (*sich kümmern um*) to take care of; **es jdm ~** (*umg*) to sort sb out
Besorgnis (**-, -se**) *f* anxiety, concern; **besorgniserregend** *adj* alarming, worrying
besorgt [bə'zɔrkt] *adj* anxious, worried; **Besorgtheit** *f* anxiety, worry
Besorgung *f* acquisition; (*Kauf*) purchase; (*Einkauf*): **~en machen** to do some shopping
bespannen [bə'ʃpanən] *vt* (*mit Saiten, Fäden*) to string
bespielbar *adj* (*Rasen etc*) playable
bespielen [bə'ʃpi:lən] *vt* (*Tonband, Kassette*) to make a recording on
bespitzeln [bə'ʃpıtsəln] *vt* to spy on
besprechen [bə'ʃprɛçən] *unreg vt* to discuss; (*Tonband etc*) to record, speak onto; (*Buch*) to review ▷ *vr* to discuss, consult
Besprechung *f* meeting, discussion; (*von Buch*) review
bespringen [bə'ʃprıŋən] *unreg vt* (*Tier*) to mount, cover
bespritzen [bə'ʃprıtsən] *vt* to spray; (*beschmutzen*) to spatter
besser ['bɛsər] *adj* better; **nur ein ~er ...** just a glorified ...; **~e Leute** a better class of people; **es geht ihm ~** he feels better; *siehe auch* **besserstehen**
bessern *vt* to make better, improve ▷ *vr* to improve; (*Mensch*) to reform
besserstehen *unreg vr* (*umg*) to be better off
Besserung *f* improvement; **auf dem Weg(e) der ~ sein** to be getting better, be improving; **gute ~!** get well soon!
Besserwisser, in (**-s, -**) *m(f)* know-all (*Brit*), know-it-all (*US*)
Bestand [bə'ʃtant] (**-(e)s, ¨-e**) *m* (*Fortbestehen*) duration, continuance; (*Kassenbestand*) amount, balance; (*Vorrat*) stock; **eiserner ~** iron rations *pl*; **~ haben, von ~ sein** to last long, endure
bestand *etc vb siehe* **bestehen**
bestanden *pp von* **bestehen** ▷ *adj*: **nach ~er Prüfung** after passing the exam
beständig [bə'ʃtɛndıç] *adj* (*ausdauernd*) constant (*auch fig*); (*Wetter*) settled; (*Stoffe*) resistant; (*Klagen etc*) continual
Bestandsaufnahme *f* stocktaking
Bestandsüberwachung *f* stock control, inventory control
Bestandteil *m* part, component; (*Zutat*) ingredient; **sich in seine ~e auflösen** to fall to pieces
bestärken [bə'ʃtɛrkən] *vt*: **jdn in etw** *dat* **~** to strengthen *od* confirm sb in sth
bestätigen [bə'ʃtɛ:tıgən] *vt* to confirm; (*anerkennen, Comm*) to acknowledge; **jdn (im Amt) ~** to confirm sb's appointment
Bestätigung *f* confirmation; acknowledgement
bestatten [bə'ʃtatən] *vt* to bury
Bestatter (**-s, -**) *m* undertaker
Bestattung *f* funeral
Bestattungsinstitut *nt* undertaker's (*Brit*), mortician's (*US*)
bestäuben [bə'ʃtɔʏbən] *vt* to powder, dust; (*Pflanze*) to pollinate
beste, r, s ['bɛstə(r, s)] *adj* best; **sie singt am ~n** she sings best; **so ist es am ~n** it's best that way; **am ~n gehst du gleich** you'd better

go at once; **jdn zum B~n haben** to pull sb's leg; **einen Witz** *etc* **zum B~n geben** to tell a joke *etc*; **aufs B~** in the best possible way; **zu jds B~n** for the benefit of sb; **es steht nicht zum B~n** it does not look too promising

bestechen [bəˈʃtɛçən] *unreg vt* to bribe ▷ *vi* (*Eindruck machen*): **(durch etw) ~** to be impressive (because of sth)

bestechend *adj* (*Schönheit, Eindruck*) captivating; (*Angebot*) tempting

bestechlich *adj* corruptible; **Bestechlichkeit** *f* corruptibility

Bestechung *f* bribery, corruption

Bestechungsgelder *pl* bribe *sing*

Bestechungsversuch *m* attempted bribery

Besteck [bəˈʃtɛk] **(-(e)s, -e)** *nt* knife, fork and spoon, cutlery; (*Med*) set of instruments; **Besteckkasten** *m* cutlery canteen

bestehen [bəˈʃteːən] *unreg vi* to exist; (*andauern*) to last ▷ *vt* (*Probe, Prüfung*) to pass; (*Kampf*) to win; **~ bleiben** to last, endure; (*Frage, Hoffnung*) to remain; **die Schwierigkeit/das Problem besteht darin, dass ...** the difficulty/problem lies in the fact that ..., the difficulty/problem is that ...; **~ auf** *+dat* to insist on; **~ aus** to consist of; **Bestehen** *nt*: **seit Bestehen der Firma** ever since the firm came into existence *od* has existed

bestehlen [bəˈʃteːlən] *unreg vt* to rob

besteigen [bəˈʃtaɪgən] *unreg vt* to climb, ascend; (*Pferd*) to mount; (*Thron*) to ascend

Bestellbuch *nt* order book

bestellen [bəˈʃtɛlən] *vt* to order; (*kommen lassen*) to arrange to see; (*nominieren*) to name; (*Acker*) to cultivate; (*Grüße, Auftrag*) to pass on; **wie bestellt und nicht abgeholt** (*hum: umg*) like orphan Annie; **er hat nicht viel/nichts zu ~** he doesn't have much/any say here; **ich bin für 10 Uhr bestellt** I have an appointment for *od* at 10 o'clock; **es ist schlecht um ihn bestellt** (*fig*) he is in a bad way

Bestell- *zW*: **Bestellformular** *nt* purchase order; **Bestellnummer** *f* order number; **Bestellschein** *m* order coupon

Bestellung *f* (*Comm*) order; (*Bestellen*) ordering; (*Ernennung*) nomination, appointment

bestenfalls [ˈbɛstənˈfals] *adv* at best

bestens [ˈbɛstəns] *adv* very well

besteuern [bəˈʃtɔʏərn] *vt* to tax

bestialisch [bɛstiˈaːlɪʃ] (*umg*) *adj* awful, beastly

besticken [bəˈʃtɪkən] *vt* to embroider

Bestie [ˈbɛstiə] *f* (*lit, fig*) beast

bestimmen [bəˈʃtɪmən] *vt* (*Regeln*) to lay down; (*Tag, Ort*) to fix; (*prägen*) to characterize; (*ausersehen*) to mean; (*ernennen*) to appoint; (*definieren*) to define; (*veranlassen*) to induce ▷ *vi*: **du hast hier nicht zu ~** you don't make the decisions here; **er kann über sein Geld allein ~** it is up to him what he does with his money

bestimmend *adj* (*Faktor, Einfluss*) determining, decisive

bestimmt *adj* (*entschlossen*) firm; (*gewiss*) certain, definite; (*Artikel*) definite ▷ *adv* (*gewiss*) definitely, for sure; **suchen Sie etwas B~es?** are you looking for anything in particular?; **Bestimmtheit** *f* certainty; **in** *od* **mit aller Bestimmtheit** quite categorically

Bestimmung *f* (*Verordnung*) regulation; (*Festsetzen*) determining; (*Verwendungszweck*) purpose; (*Schicksal*) fate; (*Definition*) definition

Bestimmungs- *zW*: **Bestimmungsbahnhof** *m* (*Eisenb*) destination; **bestimmungsgemäß** *adj* as agreed; **Bestimmungshafen** *m* (port of) destination; **Bestimmungsort** *m* destination

Bestleistung *f* best performance

bestmöglich *adj* best possible

Best.-Nr. *abk* = **Bestellnummer**

bestrafen [bəˈʃtraːfən] *vt* to punish

Bestrafung *f* punishment

bestrahlen [bəˈʃtraːlən] *vt* to shine on; (*Med*) to treat with X-rays

Bestrahlung *f* (*Med*) X-ray treatment, radiotherapy

Bestreben [bəˈʃtreːbən] **(-s)** *nt* endeavour (*Brit*), endeavor (*US*), effort

bestrebt [bəˈʃtreːpt] *adj*: **~ sein, etw zu tun** to endeavour (*Brit*) *od* endeavor (*US*) to do sth

Bestrebung [bəˈʃtreːbʊŋ] *f* = **Bestreben**

bestreichen [bəˈʃtraɪçən] *unreg vt* (*Brot*) to spread

bestreiken [bəˈʃtraɪkən] *vt* (*Industrie*) to black; **die Fabrik wird zur Zeit bestreikt** there's a strike on in the factory at the moment

bestreiten [bəˈʃtraɪtən] *unreg vt* (*abstreiten*) to dispute; (*finanzieren*) to pay for, finance; **er hat das ganze Gespräch allein bestritten** he did all the talking

bestreuen [bəˈʃtrɔʏən] *vt* to sprinkle, dust; (*Straße*) to (spread with) grit

Bestseller [ˈbɛstsɛlər] **(-s, -)** *m* best-seller

bestürmen [bəˈʃtʏrmən] *vt* (*mit Fragen, Bitten etc*) to overwhelm, swamp

bestürzen [bəˈʃtʏrtsən] *vt* to dismay

bestürzt *adj* dismayed

Bestürzung *f* consternation

Bestzeit *f* (*bes Sport*) best time

Besuch [bəˈzuːx] **(-(e)s, -e)** *m* visit; (*Person*) visitor; **einen ~ bei jdm machen** to pay sb a visit *od* call; **~ haben** to have visitors; **bei jdm auf** *od* **zu ~ sein** to be visiting sb

besuchen *vt* to visit; (*Sch etc*) to attend; **gut besucht** well-attended

Besucher, in (-s, -) *m(f)* visitor, guest

Besuchserlaubnis *f* permission to visit

Besuchszeit *f* visiting hours *pl*

besudeln [bəˈzuːdəln] *vt* (*Wände*) to smear; (*fig: Namen, Ehre*) to sully

betagt [bəˈtaːkt] *adj* aged

betasten [bəˈtastən] *vt* to touch, feel

betätigen [bəˈtɛːtɪgən] *vt* (*bedienen*) to work, operate ▷ *vr* to involve o.s.; **sich politisch ~** to be involved in politics; **sich als etw ~** to work as sth

Betätigung *f* activity; (*beruflich*) occupation; (*Tech*) operation

betäuben [bə'tɔʏbən] *vt* to stun; (*fig: Gewissen*) to still; (*Med*) to anaesthetize (*Brit*), anesthetize (*US*); **ein ~der Duft** an overpowering smell
Betäubung *f* (*Narkose*): **örtliche ~** local anaesthetic (*Brit*) *od* anesthetic (*US*)
Betäubungsmittel *nt* anaesthetic (*Brit*), anesthetic (*US*)
Bete ['be:tə] (**-, -n**) *f*: **Rote ~** beetroot (*Brit*), beet (*US*)
beteiligen [bə'taılıgən] *vr*: **sich (an etw** *dat***) ~** to take part (in sth), participate (in sth); (*an Geschäft: finanziell*) to have a share (in sth) ▷ *vt*: **jdn (an etw** *dat***) ~** to give sb a share *od* interest (in sth); **sich an den Unkosten ~** to contribute to the expenses
Beteiligung *f* participation; (*Anteil*) share, interest; (*Besucherzahl*) attendance
Beteiligungsgesellschaft *f* associated company
beten ['be:tən] *vi* to pray ▷ *vt* (*Rosenkranz*) to say
beteuern [bə'tɔʏərn] *vt* to assert; (*Unschuld*) to protest; **jdm etw ~** to assure sb of sth
Beteuerung *f* assertion; protestation; assurance
Beton [be'tõ:] (**-s, -s**) *m* concrete
betonen [bə'to:nən] *vt* to stress
betonieren [beto'ni:rən] *vt* to concrete
Betonmischmaschine *f* concrete mixer
betont [bə'to:nt] *adj* (*Höflichkeit*) emphatic, deliberate; (*Kühle, Sachlichkeit*) pointed
Betonung *f* stress, emphasis
betören [bə'tø:rən] *vt* to beguile
Betr. *abk* = **Betreff**
betr. *abk* (= *betreffend, betreffs*) re
Betracht [bə'traxt] *m*: **in ~ kommen** to be concerned *od* relevant; **nicht in ~ kommen** to be out of the question; **etw in ~ ziehen** to consider sth; **außer ~ bleiben** not to be considered
betrachten *vt* to look at; (*fig*) to consider, look at
Betrachter, in (**-s, -**) *m(f)* onlooker
beträchtlich [bə'trɛçtlıç] *adj* considerable
Betrachtung *f* (*Ansehen*) examination; (*Erwägung*) consideration; **über etw** *akk* **~en anstellen** to reflect on *od* contemplate sth
betraf *etc* [bə'tra:f] *vb siehe* **betreffen**
Betrag [bə'tra:k] (**-(e)s, ¨-e**) *m* amount, sum; **~ erhalten** (*Comm*) sum received
betragen [bə'tra:gən] *unreg vt* to amount to ▷ *vr* to behave
Betragen (**-s**) *nt* behaviour (*Brit*), behavior (*US*); (*bes in Zeugnis*) conduct
beträgt [bə'trɛ:kt] *vb siehe* **betragen**
betrat *etc* [bə'tra:t] *vb siehe* **betreten**
betrauen [bə'traʊən] *vt*: **jdn mit etw ~** to entrust sb with sth
betrauern [bə'traʊərn] *vt* to mourn
beträufeln [bə'trɔʏfəln] *vt*: **den Fisch mit Zitrone ~** to sprinkle lemon juice on the fish
Betreff *m*: **~: Ihr Schreiben vom ...** re *od* reference your letter of ...
betreffen [bə'trɛfən] *unreg vt* to concern, affect; **was mich betrifft** as for me
betreffend *adj* relevant, in question
betreffs [bə'trɛfs] *präp +gen* concerning, regarding
betreiben [bə'traıbən] *unreg vt* (*ausüben*) to practise (*Brit*), practice (*US*); (*Politik*) to follow; (*Studien*) to pursue; (*vorantreiben*) to push ahead; (*Tech: antreiben*) to drive; **auf jds B~** *akk* **hin** (*form*) at sb's instigation
Betreiberfirma [bə'traıbərfırma] *f* operating company
betreten [bə'tre:tən] *unreg vt* to enter; (*Bühne etc*) to step onto ▷ *adj* embarrassed; **„B~ verboten"** "keep off/out"
betreuen [bə'trɔʏən] *vt* to look after
Betreuer, in (**-s, -**) *m(f)* carer; (*Kinderbetreuer*) child-minder
Betreuung *f*: **er wurde mit der ~ der Gruppe beauftragt** he was put in charge of the group
Betrieb (**-(e)s, -e**) *m* (*Firma*) firm, concern; (*Anlage*) plant; (*Tätigkeit*) operation; (*Treiben*) bustle; (*Verkehr*) traffic; **außer ~ sein** to be out of order; **in ~ sein** to be in operation; **eine Maschine in/außer ~ setzen** to start a machine up/stop a machine; **eine Maschine/Fabrik in ~ nehmen** to put a machine/factory into operation; **in den Geschäften herrscht großer ~** the shops are very busy; **er hält den ganzen ~ auf** (*umg*) he's holding everything up
betrieb *etc* [bə'tri:p] *vb siehe* **betreiben**
betrieben [bə'tri:bən] *pp von* **betreiben**
betrieblich *adj* company *attr* ▷ *adv* (*regeln*) within the company
Betriebs- *zW*: **Betriebsanleitung** *f* operating instructions *pl*; **Betriebsausflug** *m* firm's outing; **Betriebsausgaben** *pl* revenue expenditure *sing*; **betriebseigen** *adj* company *attr*; **Betriebsergebnis** *nt* trading *od* operating result; **Betriebserlaubnis** *f* operating permission/licence (*Brit*) *od* license (*US*); **betriebsfähig** *adj* in working order; **Betriebsferien** *pl* company holidays *pl* (*Brit*) *od* vacation *sing* (*US*); **Betriebsführung** *f* management; **Betriebsgeheimnis** *nt* trade secret; **Betriebskapital** *nt* capital employed; **Betriebsklima** *nt* (working) atmosphere; **Betriebskosten** *pl* running costs; **Betriebsleitung** *f* management; **Betriebsrat** *m* workers' council; **Betriebsrente** *f* company pension; **betriebssicher** *adj* safe, reliable; **Betriebsstoff** *m* fuel; **Betriebsstörung** *f* breakdown; **Betriebssystem** *nt* (*Comput*) operating system; **Betriebsunfall** *m* industrial accident; **Betriebswirt** *m* management expert; **Betriebswirtschaft** *f* business management
betrifft [bə'trıft] *vb siehe* **betreffen**
betrinken [bə'trıŋkən] *unreg vr* to get drunk
betritt [bə'trıt] *vb siehe* **betreten**
betroffen [bə'trɔfən] *pp von* **betreffen** ▷ *adj* (*bestürzt*) amazed, perplexed; **von etw ~**

werden *od* **sein** to be affected by sth
betrüben [bə'try:bən] *vt* to grieve
betrübt [bə'try:pt] *adj* sorrowful, grieved
Betrug (-(e)s) *m* deception; (*Jur*) fraud
betrug *etc* [bə'tru:k] *vb siehe* **betragen**
betrügen [bə'try:gən] *unreg vt* to cheat; (*Jur*) to defraud; (*Ehepartner*) to be unfaithful to ▷ *vr* to deceive o.s.
Betrüger, in (-s, -) *m(f)* cheat, deceiver
betrügerisch *adj* deceitful; (*Jur*) fraudulent; **in ~er Absicht** with intent to defraud
betrunken [bə'trʊŋkən] *adj* drunk
Betrunkene, r *f(m)* drunk
Bett [bɛt] **(-(e)s, -en)** *nt* bed; **im ~** in bed; **ins** *od* **zu ~ gehen** to go to bed; **Bettbezug** *m* duvet cover; **Bettdecke** *f* blanket; (*Daunenbettdecke*) quilt; (*Überwurf*) bedspread
bettelarm ['bɛtəl|arm] *adj* very poor, destitute
Bettelei [bɛtə'laɪ] *f* begging
Bettelmönch *m* mendicant *od* begging monk
betteln *vi* to beg
betten *vt* to make a bed for
Bett- *zW*: **Betthupferl** (*Südd*) *nt* bedtime sweet; **bettlägerig** *adj* bedridden; **Bettlaken** *nt* sheet; **Bettlektüre** *f* bedtime reading
Bettler, in ['bɛtlər(ɪn)] **(-s, -)** *m(f)* beggar
Bett- *zW*: **Bettnässer (-s, -)** *m* bedwetter; **Bettschwere** (*umg*) *f*: **die nötige Bettschwere haben/bekommen** to be/get tired enough to sleep; **Betttuch** *nt* sheet; **Bettvorleger** *m* bedside rug; **Bettwäsche** *f* bedclothes *pl*, bedding; **Bettzeug** *nt* = **Bettwäsche**
betucht [bə'tu:xt] (*umg*) *adj* well-to-do
betulich [bə'tu:lɪç] *adj* (*übertrieben besorgt*) fussing *attr*; (*Redeweise*) twee
betupfen [bə'tʊpfən] *vt* to dab; (*Med*) to swab
Beugehaft ['bɔʏgəhaft] *f* (*Jur*) coercive detention
beugen ['bɔʏgən] *vt* to bend; (*Gram*) to inflect ▷ *vr* (*+dat*) (*sich fügen*) to bow (to)
Beule ['bɔʏlə] **(-, -n)** *f* bump
beunruhigen [bə'|ʊnru:ɪgən] *vt* to disturb, alarm ▷ *vr* to become worried
Beunruhigung *f* worry, alarm
beurkunden [bə'|u:rkʊndən] *vt* to attest, verify
beurlauben [bə'|u:rlaʊbən] *vt* to give leave *od* holiday to (*Brit*), grant vacation to (*US*); **beurlaubt sein** to have leave of absence; (*suspendiert sein*) to have been relieved of one's duties
beurteilen [bə'|ʊrtaɪlən] *vt* to judge; (*Buch etc*) to review
Beurteilung *f* judgement; (*von Buch etc*) review; (*Note*) mark
Beute ['bɔʏtə] **(-)** *f* booty, loot; (*von Raubtieren etc*) prey
Beutel (-s, -) *m* bag; (*Geldbeutel*) purse; (*Tabaksbeutel*) pouch
bevölkern [bə'fœlkərn] *vt* to populate
Bevölkerung *f* population
Bevölkerungs- *zW*: **Bevölkerungsexplosion** *f* population explosion; **Bevölkerungsschicht** *f* social stratum; **Bevölkerungsstatistik** *f* vital statistics *pl*
bevollmächtigen [bə'fɔlmɛçtɪgən] *vt* to authorize
Bevollmächtigte, r *f(m)* authorized agent
Bevollmächtigung *f* authorization
bevor [bə'fo:r] *konj* before; **bevormunden** *vt untr* to dominate; **bevorstehen** *unreg vi*: **(jdm) bevorstehen** to be in store (for sb); **bevorstehend** *adj* imminent, approaching; **bevorzugen** *vt untr* to prefer; **bevorzugt** [bə'fo:rtsu:kt] *adv*: **etw bevorzugt abfertigen** *etc* to give sth priority; **Bevorzugung** *f* preference
bewachen [bə'vaxən] *vt* to watch, guard
bewachsen [bə'vaksən] *adj* overgrown
Bewachung *f* (*Bewachen*) guarding; (*Leute*) guard, watch
bewaffnen [bə'vafnən] *vt* to arm
Bewaffnung *f* (*Vorgang*) arming; (*Ausrüstung*) armament, arms *pl*
bewahren [bə'va:rən] *vt* to keep; **jdn vor jdm/etw ~** to save sb from sb/sth; **(Gott) bewahre!** (*umg*) heaven *od* God forbid!
bewähren [bə'vɛ:rən] *vr* to prove o.s.; (*Maschine*) to prove its worth
bewahrheiten [bə'va:rhaɪtən] *vr* to come true
bewährt *adj* reliable
Bewährung *f* (*Jur*) probation; **ein Jahr Gefängnis mit ~** a suspended sentence of one year with probation
Bewährungs- *zW*: **Bewährungsfrist** *f* (period of) probation; **Bewährungshelfer** *m* probation officer; **Bewährungsprobe** *f*: **etw einer Bewährungsprobe** *dat* **unterziehen** to put sth to the test
bewaldet [bə'valdət] *adj* wooded
bewältigen [bə'vɛltɪgən] *vt* to overcome; (*Arbeit*) to finish; (*Portion*) to manage; (*Schwierigkeiten*) to cope with
bewandert [bə'vandərt] *adj* expert, knowledgeable
Bewandtnis [bə'vantnɪs] *f*: **damit hat es folgende ~** the fact of the matter is this
bewarb *etc* [bə'varp] *vb siehe* **bewerben**
bewässern [bə'vɛsərn] *vt* to irrigate
Bewässerung *f* irrigation
bewegen [bə've:gən] *vt, vr* to move; **der Preis bewegt sich um die 50 Euro** the price is about 50 euros; **jdn zu etw ~** to induce sb to do sth
Beweggrund *m* motive
beweglich *adj* movable, mobile; (*flink*) quick
bewegt [bə've:kt] *adj* (*Leben*) eventful; (*Meer*) rough; (*ergriffen*) touched
Bewegung *f* movement, motion; (*innere*) emotion; (*körperlich*) exercise; **sich** *dat* **~ machen** to take exercise
Bewegungsfreiheit *f* freedom of movement; (*fig*) freedom of action
bewegungslos *adj* motionless
Beweis [bə'vaɪs] **(-es, -e)** *m* proof; (*Zeichen*) sign; **Beweisaufnahme** *f* (*Jur*) taking *od* hearing of

evidence; **beweisbar** *adj* provable
beweisen *unreg vt* to prove; (*zeigen*) to show; **was zu ~ war** QED
Beweis- *zW*: **Beweisführung** *f* reasoning; (*Jur*) presentation of one's case; **Beweiskraft** *f* weight, conclusiveness; **beweiskräftig** *adj* convincing, conclusive; **Beweislast** *f* (*Jur*) onus, burden of proof; **Beweismittel** *nt* evidence; **Beweisnot** *f* (*Jur*) lack of evidence; **Beweisstück** *nt* exhibit
bewenden [bə'vɛndən] *vi*: **etw dabei ~ lassen** to leave sth at that
bewerben [bə'vɛrbən] *unreg vr*: **sich ~ (um)** to apply (for)
Bewerber, in (-s, -) *m(f)* applicant
Bewerbung *f* application
Bewerbungsfrist *f* application deadline
Bewerbungsmappe *f*, **Bewerbungsunterlagen** *pl* application documents *pl*
bewerkstelligen [bə'vɛrkʃtɛlɪgən] *vt* to manage, accomplish
bewerten [bə'veːrtən] *vt* to assess
bewies *etc* [bə'viːs] *vb siehe* **beweisen**
bewiesen [bə'viːzən] *pp von* **beweisen**
bewilligen [bə'vɪlɪgən] *vt* to grant, allow
Bewilligung *f* granting
bewirbt [bə'vɪrpt] *vb siehe* **bewerben**
bewirken [bə'vɪrkən] *vt* to cause, bring about
bewirten [bə'vɪrtən] *vt* to entertain
bewirtschaften [bə'vɪrtʃaftən] *vt* to manage
Bewirtung *f* hospitality; **die ~ so vieler Gäste** catering for so many guests
bewog *etc* [bə'voːk] *vb siehe* **bewegen**
bewogen [bə'voːgən] *pp von* **bewegen**
bewohnbar *adj* inhabitable
bewohnen [bə'voːnən] *vt* to inhabit, live in
Bewohner, in (-s, -) *m(f)* inhabitant; (*von Haus*) resident
bewölkt [bə'vœlkt] *adj* cloudy, overcast
Bewölkung *f* clouds *pl*
Bewölkungsauflockerung *f* break-up of the cloud
beworben [bə'vɔrbən] *pp von* **bewerben**
Bewunderer, in (-s, -) *m(f)* admirer
bewundern [bə'vʊndərn] *vt* to admire
bewundernswert *adj* admirable, wonderful
Bewunderung *f* admiration
bewusst [bə'vʊst] *adj* conscious; (*absichtlich*) deliberate; **jdm etw ~ machen** to make sb conscious of sth; **sich** *dat* **etw ~ machen** to realize sth; **sich** *dat* **einer Sache** *gen* **~ sein** to be aware of sth; **bewusstlos** *adj* unconscious; **Bewusstlosigkeit** *f* unconsciousness; **bis zur Bewusstlosigkeit** (*umg*) ad nauseam; **Bewusstsein** *nt* consciousness; **bei Bewusstsein** conscious; **im Bewusstsein, dass ...** in the knowledge that ...
Bewusstseins- *zW*: **Bewusstseinsbildung** *f* (*Pol*) shaping of political ideas; **bewusstseinserweiternd** *adj*: **bewusstseinserweiternde Drogen** mind-expanding drugs; **Bewusstseinserweiterung** *f* consciousness raising
Bez. *abk* = **Bezirk**
bez. *abk* (= *bezüglich*) re.
bezahlen [bə'tsaːlən] *vt* to pay (for); **es macht sich bezahlt** it will pay
Bezahlfernsehen *nt* pay TV
Bezahlung *f* payment; **ohne/gegen** *od* **für ~** without/for payment
bezaubern [bə'tsaʊbərn] *vt* to enchant, charm
bezeichnen [bə'tsaɪçnən] *vt* (*kennzeichnen*) to mark; (*nennen*) to call; (*beschreiben*) to describe; (*zeigen*) to show, indicate
bezeichnend *adj*: **~ (für)** characteristic (of), typical (of)
Bezeichnung *f* (*Zeichen*) mark, sign; (*Beschreibung*) description; (*Ausdruck*) expression, term
bezeugen [bə'tsɔʏgən] *vt* to testify to
bezichtigen [bə'tsɪçtɪgən] *vt* (*+gen*) to accuse (of)
Bezichtigung *f* accusation
beziehen [bə'tsiːən] *unreg vt* (*mit Überzug*) to cover; (*Haus, Position*) to move into; (*Standpunkt*) to take up; (*erhalten*) to receive; (*Zeitung*) to subscribe to, take ▷ *vr* (*Himmel*) to cloud over; **die Betten frisch ~** to change the beds; **etw auf jdn/etw ~** to relate sth to sb/sth; **sich ~ auf** *+akk* to refer to
Beziehung *f* (*Verbindung*) connection; (*Zusammenhang*) relation; (*Verhältnis*) relationship; (*Hinsicht*) respect; **diplomatische ~en** diplomatic relations; **seine ~en spielen lassen** to pull strings; **in jeder ~** in every respect; **~en haben** (*vorteilhaft*) to have connections *od* contacts
Beziehungskiste (*umg*) *f* relationship
beziehungsweise *adv* or; (*genauer gesagt*) that is, or rather; (*im anderen Fall*) and ... respectively
beziffern [bə'tsɪfərn] *vt* (*angeben*): **~ auf** *+akk od* **mit** to estimate at
Bezirk [bə'tsɪrk] **(-(e)s, -e)** *m* district
bezirzen [bə'tsɪrtsən] (*umg*) *vt* to bewitch
bezogen [bə'tsoːgən] *pp von* **beziehen**
Bezogene, r [bə'tsoːgənə(r)] *f(m)* (*von Scheck etc*) drawee
Bezug [bə'tsuːk] **(-(e)s, ¨-e)** *m* (*Hülle*) covering; (*Comm*) ordering; (*Gehalt*) income, salary; (*Beziehung*): **~ (zu)** relationship (to); **in ~ auf** *+akk* with reference to; **mit** *od* **unter ~ auf** *+akk* regarding; (*form*) with reference to; **~ nehmen auf** *+akk* to refer to
bezüglich [bə'tsyːklɪç] *präp +gen* concerning, referring to ▷ *adj* concerning; (*Gram*) relative
Bezugnahme *f*: **~ (auf** *+akk***)** reference (to)
Bezugs- *zW*: **Bezugsperson** *f*: **die wichtigste Bezugsperson des Kleinkindes** the person to whom the small child relates most closely; **Bezugspreis** *m* retail price; **Bezugsquelle** *f* source of supply
bezuschussen [bə'tsuːʃʊsən] *vt* to subsidize
bezwecken [bə'tsvɛkən] *vt* to aim at
bezweifeln [bə'tsvaɪfəln] *vt* to doubt
bezwingen [bə'tsvɪŋən] *unreg vt* to conquer;

(*Feind*) to defeat, overcome
bezwungen [bə'tsvʊŋən] *pp von* **bezwingen**
Bf. *abk* = **Bahnhof; Brief**
BfA (-) *f abk* (= *Bundesversicherungsanstalt für Angestellte*) *Federal insurance company for employees*
BfV (-) *nt abk* (= *Bundesamt für Verfassungsschutz*) *Federal Office for Protection of the Constitution*
BG (-) *f abk* (= *Berufsgenossenschaft*) *professional association*
BGB (-) *nt abk* (= *Bürgerliches Gesetzbuch*) *siehe* **bürgerlich**
BGH (-) *m abk* (= *Bundesgerichtshof*) *Federal Supreme Court*
BGS (-) *m abk* = **Bundesgrenzschutz**
BH (**-s, -(s)**) *m abk* (= *Büstenhalter*) bra
Bhf. *abk* = **Bahnhof**
BI *f abk* = **Bürgerinitiative**
Biathlon ['bi:atlɔn] (**-s, -s**) *nt* biathlon
bibbern ['bɪbərn] (*umg*) *vi* (*vor Kälte*) to shiver
Bibel ['bi:bəl] (**-, -n**) *f* Bible
bibelfest *adj* well versed in the Bible
Biber ['bi:bər] (**-s, -**) *m* beaver
Biberbettuch *nt* flannelette sheet
Bibliografie [bibliogra'fi:] *f* bibliography
Bibliothek [biblio'te:k] (**-, -en**) *f* (*auch Comput*) library
Bibliothekar, in [bibliote'ka:r(ɪn)] (**-s, -e**) *m(f)* librarian
biblisch ['bi:blɪʃ] *adj* biblical
bieder ['bi:dər] *adj* upright, worthy; (*pej*) conventional; (*Kleid etc*) plain
Biedermann (**-(e)s,** *pl* **-männer**) (*pej*) *m* (*geh*) petty bourgeois
biegbar ['bi:kba:r] *adj* flexible
Biege *f*: **die ~ machen** (*umg*) to buzz off, split
biegen ['bi:gən] *unreg vt, vr* to bend ▷ *vi* to turn; **sich vor Lachen ~** (*fig*) to double up with laughter; **auf B~ oder Brechen** (*umg*) by hook or by crook
biegsam ['bi:kza:m] *adj* supple
Biegung *f* bend, curve
Biene ['bi:nə] (**-, -n**) *f* bee; (*veraltet: umg: Mädchen*) bird (*Brit*), chick (*bes US*)
Bienen- *zW*: **Bienenhonig** *m* honey; **Bienenkorb** *m* beehive; **Bienenstich** *m* (*Koch*) *sugar-and-almond coated cake filled with custard or cream*; **Bienenstock** *m* beehive; **Bienenwachs** *nt* beeswax
Bier [bi:r] (**-(e)s, -e**) *nt* beer; **zwei ~, bitte!** two beers, please; **Bierbauch** (*umg*) *m* beer belly; **Bierbrauer** *m* brewer; **Bierdeckel** *m* beer mat; **Bierfilz** *m* beer mat; **Bierkrug** *m* beer mug; **Bierschinken** *m* ham sausage; **Bierseidel** *nt* beer mug; **Bierwurst** *f* ham sausage
Biest [bi:st] (**-(e)s, -er**) (*pej: umg*) *nt* (*Mensch*) (little) wretch; (*Frau*) bitch (*!*)
biestig *adj* beastly
bieten ['bi:tən] *unreg vt* to offer; (*bei Versteigerung*) to bid ▷ *vr* (*Gelegenheit*): **sich jdm ~** to present itself to sb; **sich** *dat* **etw ~ lassen** to put up with sth
Bigamie [biga'mi:] *f* bigamy
Bikini [bi'ki:ni] (**-s, -s**) *m* bikini
Bilanz [bi'lants] *f* balance; (*fig*) outcome; **eine ~ aufstellen** to draw up a balance sheet; **~ ziehen (aus)** to take stock (of); **Bilanzprüfer** *m* auditor
bilateral ['bi:latera:l] *adj* bilateral; **~er Handel** bilateral trade; **~es Abkommen** bilateral agreement
Bild [bɪlt] (**-(e)s, -er**) *nt* (*lit, fig*) picture; photo; (*Spiegelbild*) reflection; (*fig: Vorstellung*) image, picture; **ein ~ machen** to take a photo *od* picture; **im ~e sein (über** *+akk***)** to be in the picture (about); **Bildauflösung** *f* (*TV, Comput*) resolution; **Bildband** *m* illustrated book; **Bildbericht** *m* pictorial report; **Bildbeschreibung** *f* (*Sch*) description of a picture; **Bilddatei** *f* picture file
bilden ['bɪldən] *vt* to form; (*erziehen*) to educate; (*ausmachen*) to constitute ▷ *vr* to arise; (*durch Lesen etc*) to improve one's mind; (*erziehen*) to educate o.s.
bildend *adj*: **die ~e Kunst** art
Bilderbuch *nt* picture book
Bilderrahmen *m* picture frame
Bild- *zW*: **Bildfläche** *f* screen; (*fig*) scene; **von der Bildfläche verschwinden** (*fig: umg*) to disappear (from the scene); **bildhaft** *adj* (*Sprache*) vivid; **Bildhauer** *m* sculptor; **bildhübsch** *adj* lovely, pretty as a picture; **bildlich** *adj* figurative; pictorial; **sich** *dat* **etw bildlich vorstellen** to picture sth in one's mind's eye
Bildnis ['bɪltnɪs] *nt* (*liter*) portrait
Bild- *zW*: **Bildplatte** *f* videodisc; **Bildröhre** *f* (*TV*) cathode ray tube; **Bildschirm** *m* (*TV, Comput*) screen; **Bildschirmgerät** *nt* (*Comput*) visual display unit, VDU; **Bildschirmschoner** (**-s, -**) *m* (*Comput*) screen saver; **Bildschirmtext** *m* teletext; ≈ Ceefax®, Oracle®; **bildschön** *adj* lovely
Bildtelefon *nt* videophone
Bildung ['bɪldʊŋ] *f* formation; (*Wissen, Benehmen*) education
Bildungs- *zW*: **Bildungsgang** *m* school (and university/college) career; **Bildungsgut** *nt* cultural heritage; **Bildungslücke** *f* gap in one's education; **Bildungspolitik** *f* educational policy; **Bildungsroman** *m* (*Liter*) Bildungsroman, *novel relating hero's intellectual/spiritual development*; **Bildungsurlaub** *m* educational holiday; **Bildungsweg** *m*: **auf dem zweiten Bildungsweg** through night school/the Open University *etc*; **Bildungswesen** *nt* education system
Bildweite *f* (*Phot*) distance
Bildzuschrift *f* reply enclosing photograph
Billard ['bɪljart] (**-s, -e**) *nt* billiards; **Billardball** *m* billiard ball; **Billardkugel** *f* billiard ball
billig ['bɪlɪç] *adj* cheap; (*gerecht*) fair, reasonable; **~e Handelsflagge** flag of convenience; **~es Geld** cheap/easy money
billigen ['bɪlɪgən] *vt* to approve of; **etw stillschweigend ~** to condone sth
billigerweise *adv* (*veraltet*) in all fairness,

reasonably
Billig- *zW:* **Billigflieger** *m*, **Billigfluglinie** *f* cheap *od* low-cost airline; **Billigladen** *m* discount store; **Billigpreis** *m* low price; **Billigprodukt** *nt* low-price product
Billigung *f* approval
Billion [bɪli'o:n] *f* billion (*Brit*), trillion (*US*)
bimmeln ['bɪməln] *vi* to tinkle
Bimsstein ['bɪmsʃtaɪn] *m* pumice stone
bin [bɪn] *vb siehe* **sein**
binär [bi'nɛ:r] *adj* binary; **Binärzahl** *f* binary number
Binde ['bɪndə] **(-, -n)** *f* bandage; (*Armbinde*) band; (*Med*) sanitary towel (*Brit*) *od* napkin (*US*); **sich** *dat* **einen hinter die ~ gießen** *od* **kippen** (*umg*) to put a few drinks away
Binde- *zW:* **Bindeglied** *nt* connecting link; **Bindehautentzündung** *f* conjunctivitis; **Bindemittel** *nt* binder
binden *unreg vt* to bind, tie ▷ *vr* (*sich verpflichten*): **sich ~ (an** *+akk***)** to commit o.s. (to)
bindend *adj* binding; (*Zusage*) definite; **~ für** binding on
Bindestrich *m* hyphen
Bindewort *nt* conjunction
Bindfaden *m* string; **es regnet Bindfäden** (*umg*) it's sheeting down
Bindung *f* bond, tie; (*Ski*) binding
binnen ['bɪnən] *präp* (*+dat od gen*) within; **Binnenhafen** *m* inland harbour (*Brit*) *od* harbor (*US*); **Binnenhandel** *m* internal trade; **Binnenmarkt** *m* home market; **Europäischer Binnenmarkt** single European market; **Binnennachfrage** *f* domestic demand
Binse ['bɪnzə] **(-, -n)** *f* rush, reed; **in die ~n gehen** (*fig: umg*) to be a wash-out
Binsenwahrheit *f* truism
Biografie [biogra'fi:] *f* biography
Bioladen ['biola:dən] *m* health food shop (*Brit*) *od* store (*US*); *see culture note*

BIOLADEN

A *Bioladen* is a shop which specializes in selling environmentally-friendly products such as phosphate-free washing powders, recycled paper and organically-grown vegetables.

Biologe [bio'lo:gə] **(-n, -n)** *m* biologist
Biologie [biolo'gi:] *f* biology
Biologin *f* biologist
biologisch [bio'lo:gɪʃ] *adj* biological; **~e Vielfalt** biodiversity; **~e Uhr** biological clock
Bio- [bio-] *zW:* **Biosphäre** *f* biosphere; **Biotechnik** [bio'tɛçnɪk] *f* biotechnology; **Bioterrorismus** *m* bioterrorism; **Biotreibstoff** ['bi:otraipʃtɔf] *m* biofuel
birgt [bɪrkt] *vb siehe* **bergen**
Birke ['bɪrkə] **(-, -n)** *f* birch
Birma ['bɪrma] **(-s)** *nt* Burma
Birnbaum *m* pear tree
Birne ['bɪrnə] **(-, -n)** *f* pear; (*Elek*) (light) bulb
birst [bɪrst] *vb siehe* **bersten**

SCHLÜSSELWORT

bis [bɪs] *adv, präp +akk* **1** (*zeitlich*) till, until; (*bis spätestens*) by; **Sie haben bis Dienstag Zeit** you have until *od* till Tuesday; **bis zum Wochenende** up to *od* until the weekend; (*spätestens*) by the weekend; **bis Dienstag muss es fertig sein** it must be ready by Tuesday; **bis wann ist das fertig?** when will that be finished?; **bis auf Weiteres** until further notice; **bis in die Nacht** into the night; **bis bald!/gleich!** see you later/soon
2 (*räumlich*) (up) to; **ich fahre bis Köln** I'm going as far as Cologne; **bis an unser Grundstück** (right *od* up) to our plot; **bis hierher** this far; **bis zur Straße kommen** to get as far as the road
3 (*bei Zahlen, Angaben*) up to; **bis zu** up to; **Gefängnis bis zu 8 Jahren** a maximum of 8 years' imprisonment
4: bis auf etw *akk* (*außer*) except sth; (*einschließlich*) including sth
▷ *konj* **1** (*mit Zahlen*) to; **10 bis 20** 10 to 20
2 (*zeitlich*) till, until; **bis es dunkel wird** till *od* until it gets dark; **von ... bis ...** from ... to ...

Bisamratte ['bi:zamratə] *f* muskrat (beaver)
Bischof ['bɪʃɔf] **(-s, ¨-e)** *m* bishop
bischöflich ['bɪʃø:flɪç] *adj* episcopal
bisexuell [bizɛksu'ɛl] *adj* bisexual
bisher [bɪs'he:r] *adv* till now, hitherto
bisherig [bɪs'he:rɪç] *adj* till now
Biskaya [bɪs'ka:ya] *f*: **Golf von ~** Bay of Biscay
Biskuit [bɪs'kvi:t] **(-(e)s, -s** *od* **-e)** *m od nt* biscuit; **Biskuitgebäck** *nt* sponge cake(s); **Biskuitteig** *m* sponge mixture
bislang [bɪs'laŋ] *adv* hitherto
Biss (-es, -e) *m* bite
biss *etc* [bɪs] *vb siehe* **beißen**
bisschen ['bɪsçən] *adj, adv* bit
Bissen ['bɪsən] **(-s, -)** *m* bite, morsel; **sich** *dat* **jeden ~ vom** *od* **am Munde absparen** to watch every penny one spends
bissig ['bɪsɪç] *adj* (*Hund*) snappy; vicious; (*Bemerkung*) cutting, biting; **„Vorsicht, ~er Hund"** "beware of the dog"
bist [bɪst] *vb siehe* **sein**
Bistum ['bɪstu:m] *nt* bishopric
bisweilen [bɪs'vaɪlən] *adv* at times, occasionally
Bit [bɪt] **(-(s), -(s))** *nt* (*Comput*) bit
Bittbrief *m* petition
Bitte ['bɪtə] **(-, -n)** *f* request; **auf seine ~ hin** at his request; **bitte** *interj* please; (*als Antwort auf Dank*) you're welcome; **wie bitte?** (I beg your) pardon?; **bitte schön!** it was a pleasure; **bitte schön?** (*in Geschäft*) can I help you?; **na bitte!** there you are!
bitten *unreg vt* to ask ▷ *vi* (*einladen*): **ich lasse ~** would you ask him/her *etc* to come in now?; **~ um** to ask for; **aber ich bitte dich!** not at all;

ich bitte darum *(form)* if you wouldn't mind; **ich muss doch (sehr) ~!** well I must say!
bittend *adj* pleading, imploring
bitter ['bɪtər] *adj* bitter; *(Schokolade)* plain; **etw ~ nötig haben** to be in dire need of sth; **bitterböse** *adj* very angry; **bitterernst** *adj*: **damit ist es mir bitterernst** I am deadly serious *od* in deadly earnest; **Bitterkeit** *f* bitterness; **bitterlich** *adj* bitter ▷ *adv* bitterly
Bittsteller, in (**-s, -**) *m(f)* petitioner
Biwak ['bi:vak] (**-s, -s** *od* **-e**) *nt* bivouac
Bj. *abk* = **Baujahr**
Blabla [bla:'bla:] (**-s**) *(umg) nt* waffle
blähen ['blɛ:ən] *vt, vr* to swell, blow out ▷ *vi* *(Speisen)* to cause flatulence *od* wind
Blähungen *pl* *(Med)* wind *sing*
blamabel [bla'ma:bəl] *adj* disgraceful
Blamage [bla'ma:ʒə] (**-, -n**) *f* disgrace
blamieren [bla'mi:rən] *vr* to make a fool of o.s., disgrace o.s. ▷ *vt* to let down, disgrace
blank [blaŋk] *adj* bright; *(unbedeckt)* bare; *(sauber)* clean, polished; *(umg: ohne Geld)* broke; *(offensichtlich)* blatant
blanko ['blaŋko] *adv* blank; **Blankoscheck** *m* blank cheque *(Brit)* *od* check *(US)*; **Blankovollmacht** *f* carte blanche
Bläschen ['blɛ:sçən] *nt* bubble; *(Med)* small blister
Blase ['bla:zə] (**-, -n**) *f* bubble; *(Med)* blister; *(Anat)* bladder
Blasebalg *m* bellows *pl*
blasen *unreg vt, vi* to blow; **zum Aufbruch ~** *(fig)* to say it's time to go
Blasenentzündung *f* cystitis
Bläser, in ['blɛ:zər(ɪn)] (**-s, -**) *m(f)* *(Mus)* wind player; **die ~** the wind (section)
blasiert [bla'zi:rt] *(pej) adj* *(geh)* blasé
Blas- *zW*: **Blasinstrument** *nt* wind instrument; **Blaskapelle** *f* brass band; **Blasmusik** *f* brass band music
blass [blas] *adj* pale; *(Ausdruck)* weak, insipid; *(fig: Ahnung, Vorstellung)* faint, vague; **~ vor Neid werden** to go green with envy
Blässe ['blɛsə] (**-**) *f* paleness, pallor
Blatt [blat] (**-(e)s, ¨er**) *nt* leaf; *(von Papier)* sheet; *(Zeitung)* newspaper; *(Karten)* hand; **vom ~ singen/spielen** to sight-read; **kein ~ vor den Mund nehmen** not to mince one's words
blättern ['blɛtərn] *vi*: **in etw** *dat* **~** to leaf through sth
Blätterteig *m* flaky *od* puff pastry
Blattlaus *f* greenfly, aphid
blau [blaʊ] *adj* blue; *(umg)* drunk, stoned; *(Koch)* boiled; *(Auge)* black; **~er Fleck** bruise; **mit einem ~en Auge davonkommen** *(fig)* to get off lightly; **~er Brief** *(Sch) letter telling parents a child may have to repeat a year*; **er wird sein ~es Wunder erleben** *(umg)* he won't know what's hit him; **blauäugig** *adj* blue-eyed; **Blaubeere** *f* bilberry
Blaue *nt*: **Fahrt ins ~** mystery tour; **das ~ vom Himmel (herunter) lügen** *(umg)* to tell a pack of lies
blau- *zW*: **Blauhelm** *(umg) m* UN Soldier; **Blaukraut** *nt* red cabbage; **Blaulicht** *nt* flashing blue light; **blaumachen** *(umg) vi* to skive off work; **Blaupause** *f* blueprint; **Blausäure** *f* prussic acid; **Blaustrumpf** *m (fig)* bluestocking
Blech [blɛç] (**-(e)s, -e**) *nt* tin, sheet metal; *(Backblech)* baking tray; **~ reden** *(umg)* to talk rubbish *od* nonsense; **Blechbläser** *pl* the brass (section); **Blechbüchse** *f* tin, can; **Blechdose** *f* tin, can
blechen *(umg) vt, vi* to pay
Blechschaden *m (Aut)* damage to bodywork
Blechtrommel *f* tin drum
blecken ['blɛkən] *vt*: **die Zähne ~** to bare *od* show one's teeth
Blei [blaɪ] (**-(e)s, -e**) *nt* lead
Bleibe (**-, -n**) *f* roof over one's head
bleiben *unreg vi* to stay, remain; **bitte, ~ Sie doch sitzen** please don't get up; **wo bleibst du so lange?** *(umg)* what's keeping you?; **das bleibt unter uns** *(fig)* that's (just) between ourselves; **~ lassen** *(aufgeben)* to give up; **etw ~ lassen** *(unterlassen)* to give sth a miss
bleich [blaɪç] *adj* faded, pale; **bleichen** *vt* to bleach; **Bleichgesicht** *(umg) nt* *(blasser Mensch)* pasty-face
bleiern *adj* leaden
Blei- *zW*: **bleifrei** *adj* lead-free; **Bleigießen** *nt* *New Year's Eve fortune-telling using lead shapes*; **bleihaltig** *adj*: **bleihaltig sein** to contain lead; **Bleistift** *m* pencil; **Bleistiftabsatz** *m* stiletto heel *(Brit)*, spike heel *(US)*; **Bleistiftspitzer** *m* pencil sharpener; **Bleivergiftung** *f* lead poisoning
Blende ['blɛndə] (**-, -n**) *f* *(Phot)* aperture; *(: Einstellungsposition)* f-stop
blenden *vt* to blind, dazzle; *(fig)* to hoodwink
blendend *(umg) adj* grand; **~ aussehen** to look smashing
Blender (**-s, -**) *m* con-man
blendfrei ['blɛntfraɪ] *adj* *(Glas)* non-reflective
Blick [blɪk] (**-(e)s, -e**) *m* *(kurz)* glance, glimpse; *(Anschauen)* look, gaze; *(Aussicht)* view; **Liebe auf den ersten ~** love at first sight; **den ~ senken** to look down; **den bösen ~ haben** to have the evil eye; **einen (guten) ~ für etw haben** to have an eye for sth; **mit einem ~** at a glance
blicken *vi* to look; **das lässt tief ~** that's very revealing; **sich ~ lassen** to put in an appearance
Blick- *zW*: **Blickfang** *m* eye-catcher; **Blickfeld** *nt* range of vision *(auch fig)*; **Blickkontakt** *m* visual contact; **Blickpunkt** *m*: **im Blickpunkt der Öffentlichkeit stehen** to be in the public eye
blieb *etc* [bli:p] *vb siehe* **bleiben**
blies *etc* [bli:s] *vb siehe* **blasen**
blind [blɪnt] *adj* blind; *(Glas etc)* dull; *(Alarm)* false; **~er Passagier** stowaway
Blinddarm *m* appendix; **Blinddarmentzündung** *f* appendicitis

Blindekuh ['blındəku:] *f*: **~ spielen** to play blind man's buff
Blindenhund *m* guide dog
Blindenschrift *f* braille
Blind- *zW*: **Blindgänger** *m* (*Mil, fig*) dud; **Blindheit** *f* blindness; **mit Blindheit geschlagen sein** (*fig*) to be blind; **blindlings** *adv* blindly; **Blindschleiche** *f* slow worm; **blindschreiben** *unreg vi* to touch-type
blinken ['blıŋkən] *vi* to twinkle, sparkle; (*Licht*) to flash, signal; (*Aut*) to indicate ▷ *vt* to flash, signal
Blinker (**-s, -**) *m* (*Aut*) indicator
Blinklicht *nt* (*Aut*) indicator
blinzeln ['blıntsəln] *vi* to blink, wink
Blitz [blıts] (**-es, -e**) *m* (flash of) lightning; **wie ein ~ aus heiterem Himmel** (*fig*) like a bolt from the blue; **Blitzableiter** *m* lightning conductor; (*fig*) vent *od* safety valve for feelings; **blitzen** *vi* (*aufleuchten*) to glint, shine; **es blitzt** (*Met*) there's a flash of lightning; **Blitzgerät** *nt* (*Phot*) flash(gun); **Blitzlicht** *nt* flashlight; **blitzsauber** *adj* spick and span; **blitzschnell** *adj, adv* as quick as a flash; **Blitzwürfel** *m* (*Phot*) flashcube
Block [blɔk] (**-(e)s, ¨-e**) *m* (*lit, fig*) block; (*von Papier*) pad; (*Pol: Staatenblock*) bloc; (*Fraktion*) faction
Blockade [blɔ'ka:də] (**-, -n**) *f* blockade
Block- *zW*: **Blockbuchstabe** *m* block letter *od* capital; **Blockflöte** *f* recorder; **blockfrei** *adj* (*Pol*) non-aligned; **Blockhaus** *nt* log cabin; **Blockhütte** *f* log cabin
blockieren [blɔ'ki:rən] *vt* to block ▷ *vi* (*Räder*) to jam
Block- *zW*: **Blockschokolade** *f* cooking chocolate; **Blockschrift** *f* block letters *pl*; **Blockstunde** *f* double period
blöd [blø:t] *adj* silly, stupid
blödeln ['blø:dəln] (*umg*) *vi* to fool around
Blödheit *f* stupidity
Blödian ['blø:dian] (**-(e)s, -e**) (*umg*) *m* idiot
blöd- *zW*: **Blödmann** (**-(e)s**, *pl* **-männer**) (*umg*) *m* idiot; **Blödsinn** *m* nonsense; **blödsinnig** *adj* silly, idiotic
blöken ['blø:kən] *vi* (*Schaf*) to bleat
blond [blɔnt] *adj* blond(e), fair-haired
Blondine [blɔn'di:nə] *f* blonde

SCHLÜSSELWORT

bloß [blo:s] *adj* **1** (*unbedeckt*) bare; (*nackt*) naked; **mit der bloßen Hand** with one's bare hand; **mit bloßem Auge** with the naked eye
2 (*alleinig: nur*) mere; **der bloße Gedanke** the very thought; **bloßer Neid** sheer envy
▷ *adv* only, merely; **lass das bloß!** just don't do that!; **wie ist das bloß passiert?** how on earth did that happen?

Blöße ['blø:sə] (**-, -n**) *f* bareness; nakedness; (*fig*) weakness; **sich** *dat* **eine ~ geben** (*fig*) to lay o.s. open to attack
bloßlegen *vt* to expose
bloßstellen *vt* to show up
blühen ['bly:ən] *vi* (*lit*) to bloom, be in bloom; (*fig*) to flourish; (*umg: bevorstehen*): **(jdm) ~** to be in store (for sb)
blühend *adj*: **wie das ~e Leben aussehen** to look the very picture of health
Blume ['blu:mə] (**-, -n**) *f* flower; (*von Wein*) bouquet; **jdm etw durch die ~ sagen** to say sth in a roundabout way to sb
Blumen- *zW*: **Blumengeschäft** *nt* flower shop, florist's; **Blumenkasten** *m* window box; **Blumenkohl** *m* cauliflower; **Blumenstrauß** *m* bouquet, bunch of flowers; **Blumentopf** *m* flowerpot; **Blumenzwiebel** *f* bulb
Bluse ['blu:zə] (**-, -n**) *f* blouse
Blut [blu:t] (**-(e)s**) *nt* (*lit, fig*) blood; **(nur) ruhig ~** keep your shirt on (*umg*); **jdn/sich bis aufs ~ bekämpfen** to fight sb/fight bitterly; **~ stillend** styptic; **blutarm** *adj* anaemic (*Brit*), anemic (*US*); (*fig*) penniless; **Blutbahn** *f* bloodstream; **Blutbank** *f* blood bank; **blutbefleckt** *adj* bloodstained; **Blutbild** *nt* blood count; **Blutbuche** *f* copper beech; **Blutdruck** *m* blood pressure
Blüte ['bly:tə] (**-, -n**) *f* blossom; (*fig*) prime
Blutegel ['blu:t|e:gəl] *m* leech
bluten *vi* to bleed
Blütenstaub *m* pollen
Bluter (**-s, -**) *m* (*Med*) haemophiliac (*Brit*), hemophiliac (*US*)
Bluterguss *m* haemorrhage (*Brit*), hemorrhage (*US*); (*auf Haut*) bruise
Blütezeit *f* flowering period; (*fig*) prime
Blutgerinnsel *nt* blood clot
Blutgruppe *f* blood group
blutig *adj* bloody; (*umg: Anfänger*) absolute; (*: Ernst*) deadly
Blut- *zW*: **blutjung** *adj* very young; **Blutkonserve** *f* unit *od* pint of stored blood; **Blutkörperchen** *nt* blood corpuscle; **Blutprobe** *f* blood test; **blutrünstig** *adj* bloodthirsty; **Blutschande** *f* incest; **Blutsenkung** *f* (*Med*): **eine Blutsenkung machen** to test the sedimentation rate of the blood; **Blutspender** *m* blood donor; **blutstillend** *adj* styptic; **Blutsturz** *m* haemorrhage (*Brit*), hemorrhage (*US*)
blutsverwandt *adj* related by blood
Blutübertragung *f* blood transfusion
Blutung *f* bleeding, haemorrhage (*Brit*), hemorrhage (*US*)
Blut- *zW*: **blutunterlaufen** *adj* suffused with blood; (*Augen*) bloodshot; **Blutvergießen** *nt* bloodshed; **Blutvergiftung** *f* blood poisoning; **Blutwurst** *f* black pudding; **Blutzuckerspiegel** *m* blood sugar level
BLZ *abk* = **Bankleitzahl**
BMX-Rad *nt* BMX
BND (**-s, -**) *m abk* = **Bundesnachrichtendienst**
Bö (**-, -en**) *f* squall
Boccia ['bɔtʃa] *nt od f* bowls *sing*
Bock [bɔk] (**-(e)s, ¨-e**) *m* buck, ram; (*Gestell*)

trestle, support; (*Sport*) buck; **alter ~** (*umg*) old goat; **den ~ zum Gärtner machen** (*fig*) to choose the worst possible person for the job; **einen ~ schießen** (*fig: umg*) to (make a) boob; **~ haben, etw zu tun** (*umg: Lust*) to fancy doing sth

Bockbier *nt* bock (beer) (*type of strong beer*)

bocken ['bɔkən] (*umg*) *vi* (*Auto, Mensch*) to play up

Bocksbeutel *m wide, rounded (dumpy) bottle containing Franconian wine*

Bockshorn *nt*: **sich von jdm ins ~ jagen lassen** to let sb upset one

Bocksprung *m* leapfrog; (*Sport*) vault

Bockwurst *f* bockwurst (*large frankfurter*)

Boden ['bo:dən] (**-s, ¨**) *m* ground; (*Fußboden*) floor; (*Meeresboden, Fassboden*) bottom; (*Speicher*) attic; **den ~ unter den Füßen verlieren** (*lit*) to lose one's footing; (*fig: in Diskussion*) to get out of one's depth; **ich hätte (vor Scham) im ~ versinken können** (*fig*) I was so ashamed, I wished the ground would swallow me up; **am ~ zerstört sein** (*umg*) to be shattered; **etw aus dem ~ stampfen** (*fig*) to conjure sth up out of nothing; (*Häuser*) to build overnight; **auf dem ~ der Tatsachen bleiben** (*fig: Grundlage*) to stick to the facts; **zu ~ fallen** to fall to the ground; **festen ~ unter den Füßen haben** to be on firm ground, be on terra firma; **Bodenkontrolle** *f* (*Raumfahrt*) ground control; **bodenlos** *adj* bottomless; (*umg*) incredible; **Bodenpersonal** *nt* (*Aviat*) ground personnel *pl*, ground staff; **Bodensatz** *m* dregs *pl*, sediment; **Bodenschätze** *pl* mineral wealth *sing*

Bodensee ['bo:dənze:] *m*: **der ~** Lake Constance

Bodenturnen *nt* floor exercises *pl*

Böe (**-, -n**) *f* squall

bog *etc* [bo:k] *vb siehe* **biegen**

Bogen ['bo:gən] (**-s, -**) *m* (*Biegung*) curve; (*Archit*) arch; (*Waffe, Mus*) bow; (*Papier*) sheet; **den ~ heraushaben** (*umg*) to have got the hang of it; **einen großen ~ um jdn/etw machen** (*meiden*) to give sb/sth a wide berth; **jdn in hohem ~ hinauswerfen** (*umg*) to fling sb out; **Bogengang** *m* arcade; **Bogenschütze** *m* archer

Bohle ['bo:lə] (**-, -n**) *f* plank

Böhme ['bø:mə] (**-n, -n**) *m* Bohemian

Böhmen (**-s**) *nt* Bohemia

Böhmin *f* Bohemian woman

böhmisch ['bø:mɪʃ] *adj* Bohemian; **das sind für mich ~e Dörfer** (*umg*) that's all Greek to me

Bohne ['bo:nə] (**-, -n**) *f* bean; **blaue ~** (*umg*) bullet; **nicht die ~** not one little bit

Bohnen- *zW*: **Bohnenkaffee** *m* real coffee; **Bohnenstange** *f* (*fig: umg*) beanpole; **Bohnenstroh** *nt*: **dumm wie Bohnenstroh** (*umg*) (as) thick as two (short) planks

bohnern *vt* to wax, polish

Bohnerwachs *nt* floor polish

bohren ['bo:rən] *vt* to bore; (*Loch*) to drill ▷ *vi* to drill; (*fig: drängen*) to keep on; (*peinigen: Schmerz, Zweifel etc*) to gnaw; **nach Öl/Wasser ~** drill for oil/water; **in der Nase ~** to pick one's nose

Bohrer (**-s, -**) *m* drill

Bohr- *zW*: **Bohrinsel** *f* oil rig; **Bohrmaschine** *f* drill; **Bohrturm** *m* derrick

Boiler ['bɔʏlər] (**-s, -**) *m* water heater

Boje ['bo:jə] (**-, -n**) *f* buoy

Bolivianer, in [bolivi'a:nər(ɪn)] (**-s, -**) *m(f)* Bolivian

Bolivien [bo'li:viən] *nt* Bolivia

bolivisch [bo'li:vɪʃ] *adj* Bolivian

Bollwerk ['bɔlvɛrk] *nt* (*lit, fig*) bulwark

Bolschewismus [bɔlʃe'vɪsmʊs] (**-**) *m* Bolshevism

Bolzen ['bɔltsən] (**-s, -**) *m* bolt

bombardieren [bɔmbar'di:rən] *vt* to bombard; (*aus der Luft*) to bomb

Bombe ['bɔmbə] (**-, -n**) *f* bomb; **wie eine ~ einschlagen** to come as a (real) bombshell

Bomben- *zW*: **Bombenalarm** *m* bomb scare; **Bombenangriff** *m* bombing raid; **Bombenanschlag** *m* bomb attack; **Bombenerfolg** (*umg*) *m* huge success; **Bombengeschäft** (*umg*) *nt*: **ein Bombengeschäft machen** to do a roaring trade; **bombensicher** (*umg*) *adj* dead certain

bombig (*umg*) *adj* great, super

Bon [bɔŋ] (**-s, -s**) *m* voucher; (*Kassenzettel*) receipt

Bonbon [bõ'bõ:] (**-s, -s**) *nt od m* sweet

Bonn [bɔn] (**-s**) *nt* Bonn

Bonus ['bo:nʊs] (**-, -se**) *m* bonus

Bonusmeile *f* bonus mile

Bonze ['bɔntsə] (**-n, -n**) *m* big shot (*umg*)

Bonzenviertel (*umg*) *nt* posh quarter (*of town*)

Boot [bo:t] (**-(e)s, -e**) *nt* boat

Bord [bɔrt] (**-(e)s, -e**) *m* (*Aviat, Naut*) board ▷ *nt* (*Brett*) shelf; **über ~ gehen** to go overboard; (*fig*) to go by the board; **an ~** on board

Bordell [bɔr'dɛl] (**-s, -e**) *nt* brothel

Bordfunkanlage *f* radio

Bordstein *m* kerb(stone) (*Brit*), curb(stone) (*US*)

borgen ['bɔrgən] *vt* to borrow; **jdm etw ~** to lend sb sth

Borneo ['bɔrneo] (**-s**) *nt* Borneo

borniert [bɔr'ni:rt] *adj* narrow-minded

Börse ['bœ:rzə] (**-, -n**) *f* stock exchange; (*Geldbörse*) purse

Börsen- *zW*: **Börsenmakler** *m* stockbroker; **börsennotiert** *adj*: **börsennotierte Firma** listed company; **Börsennotierung** *f* quotation (on the stock exchange)

Borste ['bɔrstə] (**-, -n**) *f* bristle

Borte ['bɔrtə] (**-, -n**) *f* edging; (*Band*) trimming

bös [bø:s] *adj* = **böse**; **bösartig** *adj* malicious; (*Med*) malignant

Böschung ['bœʃʊŋ] *f* slope; (*Uferböschung etc*) embankment

böse ['bø:zə] *adj* bad, evil; (*zornig*) angry; **das war nicht ~ gemeint** I/he *etc* didn't mean it nastily

Bösewicht (*umg*) *m* baddy

boshaft ['bo:shaft] *adj* malicious, spiteful

Bosheit *f* malice, spite
Bosnien ['bɔsniən] (**-s**) *nt* Bosnia
Bosnien-Herzegowina ['bɔsniənhɛrtsə-'go:vi:na] (**-s**) *nt* Bosnia-Herzegovina
Bosnier, in (**-s, -**) *m(f)* Bosnian
bosnisch *adj* Bosnian
Boss [bɔs] (**-es, -e**) (*umg*) *m* boss
böswillig ['bø:svɪlɪç] *adj* malicious
bot *etc* [bo:t] *vb siehe* **bieten**
Botanik [bo'ta:nɪk] *f* botany
botanisch [bo'ta:nɪʃ] *adj* botanical
Bote ['bo:tə] (**-n, -n**) *m* messenger
Botengang *m* errand
Botenjunge *m* errand boy
Botin ['bo:tɪn] *f* messenger
Botschaft *f* message, news; (*Pol*) embassy; **die Frohe ~** the Gospel; **Botschafter** (**-s, -**) *m* ambassador
Botswana [bɔ'tsva:na] (**-s**) *nt* Botswana
Bottich ['bɔtɪç] (**-(e)s, -e**) *m* vat, tub
Bouillon [bʊ'ljõ:] (**-, -s**) *f* consommé
Boulevard- [bulə'va:r] *zW*: **Boulevardblatt** (*umg*) *nt* tabloid; **Boulevardpresse** *f* tabloid press; **Boulevardstück** *nt* light play/comedy
Boutique [bu'ti:k] (**-, -n**) *f* boutique
Bowle ['bo:lə] (**-, -n**) *f* punch
Bowlingbahn ['bo:lɪŋba:n] *f* bowling alley
Box [bɔks] *f* (*Lautsprecherbox*) speaker
boxen *vi* to box
Boxer (**-s, -**) *m* boxer
Boxhandschuh *m* boxing glove
Boxkampf *m* boxing match
Boykott [bɔʏ'kɔt] (**-(e)s, -s**) *m* boycott
boykottieren [bɔʏkɔ'ti:rən] *vt* to boycott
BR *abk* (*= Bayerischer Rundfunk*) *German radio station*
brach *etc* [bra:x] *vb siehe* **brechen**
brachial [braxi'a:l] *adj*: **mit ~er Gewalt** by brute force
brachliegen ['bra:xli:gən] *unreg vi* (*lit, fig*) to lie fallow
brachte *etc* ['braxtə] *vb siehe* **bringen**
Branche ['brã:ʃə] (**-, -n**) *f* line of business
Branchenführer, in *m(f)* market leader
Branchenverzeichnis *nt* trade directory
Brand [brant] (**-(e)s, ¨-e**) *m* fire; (*Med*) gangrene
Brandanschlag *m* arson attack
branden ['brandən] *vi* to surge; (*Meer*) to break
Brandenburg ['brandənbʊrk] (**-s**) *nt* Brandenburg
Brandherd *m* source of the fire
brandmarken *vt* to brand; (*fig*) to stigmatize
brandneu (*umg*) *adj* brand-new
Brand- *zW*: **Brandsalbe** *f* ointment for burns; **Brandsatz** *m* incendiary device; **Brandstifter** *m* arsonist, fire-raiser; **Brandstiftung** *f* arson
Brandung *f* surf
Brandwunde *f* burn
brannte *etc* ['brantə] *vb siehe* **brennen**
Branntwein ['brantvaɪn] *m* brandy; **Branntweinsteuer** *f* tax on spirits
Brasilianer, in [brazili'a:nər(ɪn)] (**-s, -**) *m(f)* Brazilian
brasilianisch *adj* Brazilian
Brasilien [bra'zi:liən] *nt* Brazil
brät [brɛt] *vb siehe* **braten**
Bratapfel *m* baked apple
braten ['bra:tən] *unreg vt* to roast; (*in Pfanne*) to fry; **Braten** (**-s, -**) *m* roast, joint; **den Braten riechen** (*umg*) to smell a rat, suss something
Brat- *zW*: **Brathähnchen** *nt* (*Südd, Österr*) roast chicken; **Brathendl** *nt* roast chicken; **Brathuhn** *nt* roast chicken; **Bratkartoffeln** *pl* fried/roast potatoes *pl*; **Bratpfanne** *f* frying pan; **Bratrost** *m* grill
Bratsche ['bra:tʃə] (**-, -n**) *f* viola
Bratspieß *m* spit
Bratwurst *f* grilled sausage
Brauch [braʊx] (**-(e)s**, *pl* **Bräuche**) *m* custom
brauchbar *adj* usable, serviceable; (*Person*) capable
brauchen *vt* (*bedürfen*) to need; (*müssen*) to have to; (*verwenden*) to use; **wie lange braucht man, um ...?** how long does it take to ...?
Brauchtum *nt* customs *pl*, traditions *pl*
Braue ['braʊə] (**-, -n**) *f* brow
brauen ['braʊən] *vt* to brew
Brauerei [braʊə'raɪ] *f* brewery
braun [braʊn] *adj* brown; (*von Sonne*) tanned; **~ gebrannt** tanned; (*pej*) Nazi
Bräune ['brɔʏnə] (**-, -n**) *f* brownness; (*Sonnenbräune*) tan
bräunen *vt* to make brown; (*Sonne*) to tan
Braunkohle *f* brown coal
Braunschweig ['braʊnʃvaɪk] (**-s**) *nt* Brunswick
Brause ['braʊzə] (**-, -n**) *f* shower; (*von Gießkanne*) rose; (*Getränk*) lemonade
brausen *vi* to roar; (*auch vr: duschen*) to take a shower
Brausepulver *nt* lemonade powder
Brausetablette *f* lemonade tablet
Braut [braʊt] (**-**, *pl* **Bräute**) *f* bride; (*Verlobte*) fiancée
Bräutigam ['brɔʏtɪgam] (**-s, -e**) *m* bridegroom; (*Verlobter*) fiancé
Braut- *zW*: **Brautjungfer** *f* bridesmaid; **Brautkleid** *nt* wedding dress; **Brautpaar** *nt* bride and bridegroom, bridal pair
brav [bra:f] *adj* (*artig*) good; (*ehrenhaft*) worthy, honest; (*bieder: Frisur, Kleid*) plain; **sei schön ~!** be a good boy/girl
BRD (**-**) *f abk* (*= Bundesrepublik Deutschland*) FRG; **die alte ~** former West Germany; *see culture note*

BRD

The *BRD* (Bundesrepublik Deutschland) is the official name for the Federal Republic of Germany. It comprises 16 *Länder* (see *Land*). It was the name given to the former West Germany as opposed to East Germany (the *DDR*). The two Germanies were reunited on 3rd October 1990.

Brechbohne *f* French bean
Brecheisen *nt* crowbar

brechen *unreg vt, vi* to break; (*Licht*) to refract; (*speien*) to vomit; **die Ehe ~** to commit adultery; **mir bricht das Herz** it breaks my heart; **~d voll sein** to be full to bursting
Brechmittel *nt*: **er/das ist das reinste ~** (*umg*) he/it makes me feel ill
Brechreiz *m* nausea
Brechung *f* (*des Lichts*) refraction
Brei [braɪ] (**-(e)s, -e**) *m* (*Masse*) pulp; (*Koch*) gruel; (*Haferbrei*) porridge (*Brit*), oatmeal (*US*); (*für Kinder, Kranke*) mash; **um den heißen ~ herumreden** (*umg*) to beat about the bush
breit [braɪt] *adj* broad; (*bei Maßangabe*) wide; **die ~e Masse** the masses *pl* ▷ *adv*: **ein ~ gefächertes Angebot** a wide range; **Breitband** *nt* (*Comput*) broadband; **Breitbandanschluss** *m* (*Comput*) broadband connection; **breitbeinig** *adj* with one's legs apart
Breite (**-, -n**) *f* breadth; (*bei Maßangabe*) width; (*Geog*) latitude
breiten *vt*: **etw über etw** *akk* **~** to spread sth over sth
Breitengrad *m* degree of latitude
Breitensport *m* popular sport
breit- *zW*: **breitmachen** *unreg* (*umg*) *vr* to spread o.s. out; **breitschlagen** *unreg* (*umg*) *vt*: **sich breitschlagen lassen** to let o.s. be talked round; **breitschulterig, breitschultrig** *adj* broad-shouldered; **breittreten** *unreg* (*umg*) *vt* to go on about; **Breitwandfilm** *m* wide-screen film
Bremen ['bre:mən] (**-s**) *nt* Bremen
Bremsbelag *m* brake lining
Bremse ['brɛmzə] (**-, -n**) *f* brake; (*Zool*) horsefly
bremsen *vi* to brake, apply the brakes ▷ *vt* (*Auto*) to brake; (*fig*) to slow down ▷ *vr*: **ich kann mich ~** (*umg*) not likely!
Brems- *zW*: **Bremsflüssigkeit** *f* brake fluid; **Bremslicht** *nt* brake light; **Bremspedal** *nt* brake pedal; **Bremsschuh** *m* brake shoe; **Bremsspur** *f* tyre (*Brit*) *od* tire (*US*) marks *pl*; **Bremsweg** *m* braking distance
brennbar *adj* inflammable; **leicht ~** highly inflammable
Brennelement *nt* fuel element
brennen ['brɛnən] *unreg vi* to burn, be on fire; (*Licht, Kerze etc*) to burn ▷ *vt* (*Holz etc*) to burn; (*Ziegel, Ton*) to fire; (*Kaffee*) to roast; (*Branntwein*) to distil; **wo brennts denn?** (*fig: umg*) what's the panic?; **darauf ~, etw zu tun** to be dying to do sth
Brenn- *zW*: **Brennmaterial** *nt* fuel; **Brennnessel** *f* nettle; **Brennofen** *m* kiln; **Brennpunkt** *m* (*Math, Optik*) focus; **Brennspiritus** *m* methylated spirits *pl*; **Brennstoff** *m* liquid fuel
brenzlig ['brɛntslɪç] *adj* smelling of burning, burnt; (*fig*) precarious
Bresche ['brɛʃə] (**-, -n**) *f*: **in die ~ springen** (*fig*) to step into the breach
Bretagne [bre'tanjə] *f*: **die ~** Brittany
Bretone [bre'to:nə] (**-n, -n**) *m* Breton
Bretonin [bre'to:nɪn] *f* Breton
Brett [brɛt] (**-(e)s, -er**) *nt* board, plank; (*Bord*) shelf; (*Spielbrett*) board; **Bretter** *pl* (*Ski*) skis *pl*; (*Theat*) boards *pl*; **Schwarzes ~** notice board; **er hat ein ~ vor dem Kopf** (*umg*) he's really thick
brettern (*umg*) *vi* to speed
Bretterzaun *m* wooden fence
Brezel ['bre:tsəl] (**-, -n**) *f* pretzel
bricht [brɪçt] *vb siehe* **brechen**
Brief [bri:f] (**-(e)s, -e**) *m* letter; **Briefbeschwerer** (**-s, -**) *m* paperweight; **Briefdrucksache** *f* circular; **Brieffreund, in** *m(f)* pen friend, pen-pal; **Briefkasten** *m* letter box; (*Comput*) mailbox; **Briefkopf** *m* letterhead; **brieflich** *adj, adv* by letter; **Briefmarke** *f* postage stamp; **Brieföffner** *m* letter opener; **Briefpapier** *nt* notepaper; **Briefqualität** *f* (*Comput*) letter quality; **Brieftasche** *f* wallet; **Brieftaube** *f* carrier pigeon; **Briefträger** *m* postman; **Briefumschlag** *m* envelope; **Briefwahl** *f* postal vote; **Briefwechsel** *m* correspondence
briet *etc* [bri:t] *vb siehe* **braten**
Brigade [bri'ga:də] (**-, -n**) *f* (*Mil*) brigade; (*DDR*) (work) team *od* group
Brikett [bri'kɛt] (**-s, -s**) *nt* briquette
brillant [brɪl'jant] *adj* (*fig*) sparkling, brilliant; **Brillant** (**-en, -en**) *m* brilliant, diamond
Brille ['brɪlə] (**-, -n**) *f* spectacles *pl*; (*Schutzbrille*) goggles *pl*; (*Toilettenbrille*) (toilet) seat
Brillenschlange *f* (*hum*) four-eyes
Brillenträger, in *m(f)*: **er ist ~** he wears glasses
bringen ['brɪŋən] *unreg vt* to bring; (*mitnehmen, begleiten*) to take; (*einbringen: Profit*) to bring in; (*veröffentlichen*) to publish; (*Theat, Film*) to show; (*Rundf, TV*) to broadcast; (*in einen Zustand versetzen*) to get; (*umg: tun können*) to manage; **jdn dazu ~, etw zu tun** to make sb do sth; **jdn zum Lachen/Weinen ~** to make sb laugh/cry; **es weit ~** to do very well, get far; **jdn nach Hause ~** to take sb home; **jdn um etw ~** to make sb lose sth; **jdn auf eine Idee ~** to give sb an idea
brisant [bri'zant] *adj* (*fig*) controversial
Brisanz [bri'zants] *f* (*fig*) controversial nature
Brise ['bri:zə] (**-, -n**) *f* breeze
Brite ['bri:tə] (**-n, -n**) *m* Briton, Britisher (*US*); **die ~n** the British
Britin *f* Briton, Britisher (*US*)
britisch ['bri:tɪʃ] *adj* British; **die B~en Inseln** the British Isles
bröckelig ['brœkəlɪç] *adj* crumbly
Brocken ['brɔkən] (**-s, -**) *m* piece, bit; (*Felsbrocken*) lump of rock; **ein paar ~ Spanisch** a smattering of Spanish; **ein harter ~** (*umg*) a tough nut to crack
brodeln ['bro:dəln] *vi* to bubble
Brokat [bro'ka:t] (**-(e)s, -e**) *m* brocade
Brokkoli ['brɔkoli] *pl* broccoli
Brombeere ['brɔmbe:rə] *f* blackberry, bramble (*Brit*)
bronchial [brɔnçi'a:l] *adj* bronchial
Bronchien ['brɔnçiən] *pl* bronchial tubes *pl*

Bronchitis [brɔn'çi:tɪs] (**-, -tiden**) *f* bronchitis
Bronze ['brõ:sə] (**-, -n**) *f* bronze
Brosame ['bro:za:mə] (**-, -n**) *f* crumb
Brosche ['brɔʃə] (**-, -n**) *f* brooch
Broschüre [brɔ'ʃy:rə] (**-, -n**) *f* pamphlet
Brot [bro:t] (**-(e)s, -e**) *nt* bread; (*Brotlaib*) loaf; **das ist ein hartes ~** (*fig*) that's a hard way to earn one's living
Brötchen ['brø:tçən] *nt* roll; **kleine ~ backen** (*fig*) to set one's sights lower; **Brötchengeber** *m* (*hum*) employer, provider (*hum*)
brotlos ['bro:tlo:s] *adj* (*Person*) unemployed; (*Arbeit etc*) unprofitable
Brotzeit (*Südd*) *f* (*Pause*) ≈ tea break
browsen ['brauzən] *vi* (*Comput*) to browse
BRT *abk* (= *Bruttoregistertonne*) GRT
Bruch [brʊx] (**-(e)s, ¨-e**) *m* breakage; (*zerbrochene Stelle*) break; (*fig*) split, breach; (*Med: Eingeweidebruch*) rupture, hernia; (*Beinbruch etc*) fracture; (*Math*) fraction; **zu ~ gehen** to get broken; **sich einen ~ heben** to rupture o.s.; **Bruchbude** (*umg*) *f* shack
brüchig ['brʏçɪç] *adj* brittle, fragile
Bruch- *zW*: **Bruchlandung** *f* crash landing; **Bruchschaden** *m* breakage; **Bruchstelle** *f* break; (*von Knochen*) fracture; **Bruchstrich** *m* (*Math*) line; **Bruchstück** *nt* fragment; **Bruchteil** *m* fraction
Brücke ['brʏkə] (**-, -n**) *f* bridge; (*Teppich*) rug; (*Turnen*) crab
Bruder ['bru:dər] (**-s, ¨-**) *m* brother; **unter Brüdern** (*umg*) between friends
brüderlich *adj* brotherly; **Brüderlichkeit** *f* fraternity
Brudermord *m* fratricide
Brüderschaft *f* brotherhood, fellowship; **~ trinken** to agree to use the familiar "du" (*over a drink*)
Brühe ['bry:ə] (**-, -n**) *f* broth, stock; (*pej*) muck
brühwarm ['bry:'varm] (*umg*) *adj*: **er hat das sofort ~ weitererzählt** he promptly spread it around
Brühwürfel *m* stock cube (*Brit*), bouillon cube (*US*)
brüllen ['brʏlən] *vi* to bellow, roar
Brummbär *m* grumbler
brummeln ['brʊməln] *vt, vi* to mumble
brummen *vi* (*Bär, Mensch etc*) to growl; (*Insekt, Radio*) to buzz; (*Motor*) to roar; (*murren*) to grumble ▷ *vt* to growl; **jdm brummt der Kopf** sb's head is buzzing
Brummer ['brʊmər] (**-s, -**) (*umg*) *m* (*Lastwagen*) juggernaut
brummig (*umg*) *adj* grumpy
Brummschädel (*umg*) *m* thick head
brünett [brʏ'nɛt] *adj* brunette, brown-haired
Brunnen ['brʊnən] (**-s, -**) *m* fountain; (*tief*) well; (*natürlich*) spring; **Brunnenkresse** *f* watercress
Brunst [brʊnst] *f* (*von männlichen Tieren*) rut; (*von weiblichen Tieren*) heat; **Brunstzeit** *f* rutting season
brüsk [brʏsk] *adj* abrupt, brusque
brüskieren [brʏs'ki:rən] *vt* to snub
Brüssel ['brʏsəl] (**-s**) *nt* Brussels
Brust [brʊst] (**-, ¨-e**) *f* breast; (*Männerbrust*) chest; **einem Kind die ~ geben** to breast-feed (*Brit*) *od* nurse (*US*) a baby
brüsten ['brʏstən] *vr* to boast
Brust- *zW*: **Brustfellentzündung** *f* pleurisy; **Brustkasten** *m* chest; **Brustkorb** *m* (*Anat*) thorax; **Brustschwimmen** *nt* breast-stroke; **Brustton** *m*: **im Brustton der Überzeugung** in a tone of utter conviction
Brüstung ['brʏstʊŋ] *f* parapet
Brustwarze *f* nipple
Brut [bru:t] (**-, -en**) *f* brood; (*Brüten*) hatching
brutal [bru'ta:l] *adj* brutal; **Brutalität** *f* brutality
Brutapparat *m* incubator
brüten ['bry:tən] *vi* (*auch fig*) to brood; **~de Hitze** oppressive *od* stifling heat
Brüter (**-s, -**) *m* (*Tech*): **Schneller ~** fast-breeder (reactor)
Brutkasten *m* incubator
Brutstätte *f* (*+gen*) (*lit, fig*) breeding ground (for)
brutto ['brʊto] *adv* gross; **Bruttoeinkommen** *nt* gross salary; **Bruttogehalt** *nt* gross salary; **Bruttogewicht** *nt* gross weight; **Bruttogewinn** *m* gross profit; **Bruttoinlandsprodukt** *nt* gross domestic product; **Bruttolohn** *m* gross wages *pl*; **Bruttosozialprodukt** *nt* gross national product
brutzeln ['brʊtsəln] (*umg*) *vi* to sizzle away ▷ *vt* to fry (up)
Btx *abk* = **Bildschirmtext**
Bub [bu:p] (**-en, -en**) *m* boy, lad
Bube ['bu:bə] (**-n, -n**) *m* (*Schurke*) rogue; (*Karten*) jack
Bubikopf *m* bobbed hair
Buch [bu:x] (**-(e)s, ¨-er**) *nt* book; (*Comm*) account book; **er redet wie ein ~** (*umg*) he never stops talking; **ein ~ mit sieben Siegeln** (*fig*) a closed book; **über etw** *akk* **~ führen** to keep a record of sth; **zu ~(e) schlagen** to make a significant difference, tip the balance; **Buchbinder** *m* bookbinder; **Buchdrucker** *m* printer
Buche (**-, -n**) *f* beech tree
buchen *vt* to book; (*Betrag*) to enter; **etw als Erfolg ~** to put sth down as a success
Bücherbord ['by:çər-] *nt* bookshelf
Bücherbrett *nt* bookshelf
Bücherei [by:çə'raɪ] *f* library
Bücherregal *nt* bookshelves *pl*, bookcase
Bücherschrank *m* bookcase
Bücherwurm (*umg*) *m* bookworm
Buchfink ['bu:xfɪŋk] *m* chaffinch
Buch- *zW*: **Buchführung** *f* book-keeping, accounting; **Buchhalter, in** (**-s, -**) *m(f)* book-keeper; **Buchhandel** *m* book trade; **im Buchhandel erhältlich** available in bookshops; **Buchhändler, in** *m(f)* bookseller; **Buchhandlung** *f* bookshop; **Buchprüfung** *f* audit; **Buchrücken** *m* spine

Büchse ['bʏksə] (**-, -n**) *f* tin, can; (*Holzbüchse*) box; (*Gewehr*) rifle
Büchsenfleisch *nt* tinned meat
Büchsenöffner *m* tin *od* can opener
Buchstabe (**-ns, -n**) *m* letter (of the alphabet)
buchstabieren [bu:xʃta'bi:rən] *vt* to spell
buchstäblich ['bu:xʃtɛ:plɪç] *adj* literal
Buchstütze *f* book end
Bucht ['bʊxt] (**-, -en**) *f* bay
Buchung ['bu:xʊŋ] *f* booking; (*Comm*) entry
Buchweizen *m* buckwheat
Buchwert *m* book value
Buckel ['bʊkəl] (**-s, -**) *m* hump; **er kann mir den ~ runterrutschen** (*umg*) he can (go and) take a running jump
buckeln (*pej*) *vi* to bow and scrape
bücken ['bʏkən] *vr* to bend; **sich nach etw ~** to bend down *od* stoop to pick sth up
Bückling ['bʏklɪŋ] *m* (*Fisch*) kipper; (*Verbeugung*) bow
Budapest ['bu:dapɛst] (**-s**) *nt* Budapest
buddeln ['bʊdəln] (*umg*) *vi* to dig
Bude ['bu:də] (**-, -n**) *f* booth, stall; (*umg*) digs *pl* (*Brit*) *od* place (*US*); **jdm die ~ einrennen** (*umg*) to pester sb; **Leben in die ~ bringen** to liven up the place
Budget [bʏ'dʒe:] (**-s, -s**) *nt* budget
Büfett [bʏ'fɛt] (**-s, -s**) *nt* (*Anrichte*) sideboard; (*Geschirrschrank*) dresser; **kaltes ~** cold buffet
Büffel ['bʏfəl] (**-s, -**) *m* buffalo
büffeln ['bʏfəln] (*umg*) *vi* to swot, cram ▷ *vt* (*Lernstoff*) to swot up
Bug [bu:k] (**-(e)s, -e**) *m* (*Naut*) bow; (*Aviat*) nose
Bügel ['by:gəl] (**-s, -**) *m* (*Kleiderbügel*) hanger; (*Steigbügel*) stirrup; (*Brillenbügel*) arm; **Bügelbrett** *nt* ironing board; **Bügeleisen** *nt* iron; **Bügelfalte** *f* crease; **bügelfrei** *adj* non-iron; (*Hemd*) drip-dry
bügeln *vt, vi* to iron
Buhmann ['bu:man] (*umg*) *m* bogeyman
Bühne ['by:nə] (**-, -n**) *f* stage
Bühnenbild *nt* set, scenery
Buhruf ['bu:ru:f] *m* boo
buk *etc* [bu:k] *vb* (*veraltet*) *siehe* **backen**
Bukarest ['bu:karɛst] (**-s**) *nt* Bucharest
Bulette [bu'lɛtə] *f* meatball
Bulgare [bʊl'ga:rə] (**-n, -n**) *m* Bulgarian
Bulgarien (**-s**) *nt* Bulgaria
Bulgarin *f* Bulgarian
bulgarisch *adj* Bulgarian
Bulimie [bʊli'mi:] *f* (*Med*) bulimia
Bull- *zW*: **Bullauge** *nt* (*Naut*) porthole; **Bulldogge** *f* bulldog; **Bulldozer** ['bʊldo:zər] (**-s, -**) *m* bulldozer
Bulle (**-n, -n**) *m* bull; **die ~n** (*pej: umg*) the fuzz *sing*, the cops
Bullenhitze (*umg*) *f* sweltering heat
Bummel ['bʊməl] (**-s, -**) *m* stroll; (*Schaufensterbummel*) window-shopping (expedition)
Bummelant [bʊmə'lant] *m* slowcoach
Bummelei [bʊmə'laɪ] *f* wandering; dawdling; skiving
bummeln *vi* to wander, stroll; (*trödeln*) to dawdle; (*faulenzen*) to skive (*Brit*), loaf around
Bummelstreik *m* go-slow (*Brit*), slowdown (*US*)
Bummelzug *m* slow train
Bummler, in ['bʊmlər(ɪn)] (**-s, -**) *m(f)* (*langsamer Mensch*) dawdler (*Brit*), slowpoke (*US*); (*Faulenzer*) idler, loafer
bumsen ['bʊmzən] *vi* (*schlagen*) to thump; (*prallen, stoßen*) to bump, bang; (*umg: koitieren*) to bonk, have it off (*Brit*)
Bund[1] [bʊnt] (**-(e)s, ¨-e**) *m* (*Freundschaftsbund etc*) bond; (*Organisation*) union; (*Pol*) confederacy; (*Hosenbund, Rockbund*) waistband; **den ~ fürs Leben schließen** to take the marriage vows
Bund[2] [bʊnt] (**-(e)s, -e**) *nt* bunch; (*Strohbund*) bundle
Bündchen ['bʏntçən] *nt* ribbing; (*Ärmelbündchen*) cuff
Bündel (**-s, -**) *nt* bundle, bale
bündeln *vt* to bundle
Bundes- ['bʊndəs] *in zW* Federal; **Bundesagentur** *f*: **Bundesagentur für Arbeit** ≈ Department of Employment; **Bundesbahn** *f*: **die Deutsche Bundesbahn** German Federal Railways *pl*; **Bundesbank** *f* Federal Bank, Bundesbank; **Bundesbürger** *m* German citizen; (*vor 1990*) West German citizen; **Bundesgebiet** *nt* Federal territory; **Bundesgerichtshof** *m* Federal Supreme Court; **Bundesgrenzschutz** *m* Federal Border Guard; **Bundeshauptstadt** *f* Federal capital; **Bundeshaushalt** *m* (*Pol*) National Budget; **Bundeskanzler** *m* Federal Chancellor; *see culture note*

BUNDESKANZLER

The *Bundeskanzler*, head of the German government, is elected for 4 years and determines government guidelines. He is formally proposed by the *Bundespräsident* but needs a majority in parliament to be elected to office.

Bundes- *zW*: **Bundesland** *nt* state, Land; **Bundesliga** *f* (*Sport*) national league; **Bundesministerium** *nt* Federal Ministry; **Bundesnachrichtendienst** *m* Federal Intelligence Service; **Bundespost** *f* (*früher*): **die (Deutsche) Bundespost** the (German) Federal Post (Office); **Bundespräsident** *m see culture note*

BUNDESPRÄSIDENT

The *Bundespräsident* is the head of state of the Federal Republic of Germany who is elected every 5 years by the members of the *Bundestag* and by delegates of the *Landtage* (regional parliaments). His role is that of a figurehead who represents Germany at home and abroad. He can only be elected twice.

Bundesrat *m see culture note*

BUNDESRAT

The *Bundesrat* is the Upper House of the German Parliament whose 68 members are not elected but determined by the parliaments of the individual *Länder*. Its most important function is the approval of federal laws which concern jurisdiction of the Länder. It can raise objections to all other laws but can be outvoted by the *Bundestag*.

Bundes- *zW*: **Bundesrechnungshof** *m* Federal Audit Office; **Bundesregierung** *f* Federal Government; **Bundesrepublik** *f* Federal Republic (of Germany); **Bundesstaat** *m* Federal state; **Bundesstraße** *f* Federal Highway, main road; **Bundestag** *m see culture note*

BUNDESTAG

The *Bundestag* is the Lower House of the German Parliament, elected by the people. There are 646 MPs, half of them elected directly from the first vote (*Erststimme*), and half from the regional list of parliamentary candidates resulting from the second vote (*Zweitstimme*), and giving proportional representation to the parties. The Bundestag exercises parliamentary control over the government.

Bundes- *zW*: **Bundestagsabgeordnete, r** *f(m)* member of the German Parliament; **Bundestagswahl** *f* (Federal) parliamentary elections *pl*; **Bundesverfassungsgericht** *nt* Federal Constitutional Court; **Bundeswehr** *f* German *od* (*vor 1990*) West German Armed Forces *pl*; *see culture note*

BUNDESWEHR

The *Bundeswehr* is the name for the German armed forces. It was established in 1955, first of all for volunteers, but since 1956 there has been compulsory military service for all able-bodied young men of 18 (see *Wehrdienst*). In peacetime the Defence Minister is the head of the Bundeswehr, but in wartime, the *Bundeskanzler* takes over. The Bundeswehr comes under the jurisdiction of NATO.

Bundfaltenhose *f* pleated trousers *pl*
Bundhose *f* knee breeches *pl*
bündig ['bʏndɪç] *adj* (*kurz*) concise
Bündnis ['bʏntnɪs] (**-ses, -se**) *nt* alliance
Bunker ['bʊŋkər] (**-s, -**) *m* bunker; (*Luftschutzbunker*) air-raid shelter
bunt [bʊnt] *adj* coloured (*Brit*), colored (*US*); (*gemischt*) mixed; **jdm wird es zu ~** it's getting too much for sb; **Buntstift** *m* coloured (*Brit*) *od* colored (*US*) pencil, crayon
Bürde ['bʏrdə] (**-, -n**) *f* (*lit, fig*) burden
Burg [bʊrk] (**-, -en**) *f* castle, fort
Bürge ['bʏrgə] (**-n, -n**) *m* guarantor
bürgen *vi* to vouch; **für jdn ~** (*fig*) to vouch for sb; (*Fin*) to stand surety for sb
Bürger, in (**-s, -**) *m(f)* citizen; member of the middle class; **bürgerfreundlich** *adj* citizen-friendly; **Bürgerinitiative** *f* citizen's initiative; **Bürgerkrieg** *m* civil war; **bürgerlich** *adj* (*Rechte*) civil; (*Klasse*) middle-class; (*pej*) bourgeois; **bürgerliches Gesetzbuch** Civil Code; **Bürgermeister** *m* mayor; **Bürgerrecht** *nt* civil rights *pl*; **Bürgerrechtler, in** *m(f)* civil rights campaigner; **Bürgerschaft** *f* population, citizens *pl*; **Bürgerschaftswahl** *f* metropolitan council election; **Bürgerschreck** *m* bogey of the middle classes; **Bürgersteig** *m* pavement (*Brit*), sidewalk (*US*); **Bürgertum** *nt* citizens *pl*; **Bürgerversicherung** *f* citizens' insurance; **Bürgerwehr** *f* vigilantes *pl*
Burgfriede, Burgfrieden *m* (*fig*) truce
Bürgin *f* guarantor
Bürgschaft *f* surety; **~ leisten** to give security
Burgund [bʊr'gʊnt] (**-(s)**) *nt* Burgundy
Burgunder (**-s, -**) *m* (*Wein*) burgundy
Büro [by'ro:] (**-s, -s**) *nt* office; **Büroangestellte, r** *f(m)* office worker; **Büroklammer** *f* paper clip; **Bürokraft** *f* (office) clerk
Bürokrat [byro'kra:t] (**-en, -en**) *m* bureaucrat
Bürokratie [byrokra'ti:] *f* bureaucracy
bürokratisch *adj* bureaucratic
Bürokratismus *m* red tape
Büroschluss *m* office closing time
Büroturm *m* office tower
Bursch ['bʊrʃ(ə)] (**-en, -en**) *m* = **Bursche**
Bursche (**-n, -n**) *m* lad, fellow; (*Diener*) servant
Burschenschaft *f* student fraternity
burschikos [bʊrʃi'ko:s] *adj* (*jungenhaft*) (tom)boyish; (*unbekümmert*) casual
Bürste ['bʏrstə] (**-, -n**) *f* brush
bürsten *vt* to brush
Bus [bʊs] (**-ses, -se**) *m* bus
Busch [bʊʃ] (**-(e)s, ¨-e**) *m* bush, shrub; **bei jdm auf den ~ klopfen** (*umg*) to sound sb out
Büschel ['bʏʃəl] (**-s, -**) *nt* tuft
buschig *adj* bushy
Busen ['bu:zən] (**-s, -**) *m* bosom; (*Meerbusen*) inlet, bay; **Busenfreund, in** *m(f)* bosom friend
Bushaltestelle *f* bus stop
Bussard ['bʊsart] (**-s, -e**) *m* buzzard
Buße ['bu:sə] (**-, -n**) *f* atonement, penance; (*Geld*) fine
büßen ['by:sən] *vi* to do penance, atone ▷ *vt* to atone for
Bußgeld *nt* fine
Buß- und Bettag *m* day of prayer and repentance
Büste ['bʏstə] (**-, -n**) *f* bust
Büstenhalter *m* bra
Butan [bu'ta:n] (**-s**) *nt* butane

Büttenrede ['bʏtənre:də] *f* carnival speech
Butter ['bʊtər] (-) *f* butter; **alles (ist) in ~** (*umg*) everything is fine *od* hunky-dory; **Butterberg** (*umg*) *m* butter mountain; **Butterblume** *f* buttercup; **Butterbrot** *nt* (piece of) bread and butter; **Butterbrotpapier** *nt* greaseproof paper; **Buttercremetorte** *f* gateau with buttercream filling; **Butterdose** *f* butter dish; **Butterkeks** *m* ≈ Rich Tea® biscuit; **Buttermilch** *f* buttermilk; **butterweich** *adj* soft as butter; (*fig: umg*) soft
Butzen ['bʊtsən] (**-s, -**) *m* core
BVG *nt abk* (= *Betriebsverfassungsgesetz*) ≈ Industrial Relations Act; = **Bundesverfassungsgericht**
b. w. *abk* (= *bitte wenden*) p.t.o
Byte [baɪt] (**-s, -s**) *nt* (*Comput*) byte
Bz. *abk* = **Bezirk**
bzgl. *abk* (= *bezüglich*) re.
bzw. *abk* = **beziehungsweise**

Cc

C¹, c [tse:] *nt* C, c; **C wie Cäsar** ≈ C for Charlie
C² [tse:] *abk* (= *Celsius*) C
ca. [ka] *abk* (= *circa*) approx.
Cabriolet [kabrio'le:] (**-s, -s**) *nt* (*Aut*) convertible
Café [ka'fe:] (**-s, -s**) *nt* café
Cafeteria [kafete'ri:a] (**-, -s**) *f* cafeteria
cal *abk* (= *Kalorie*) cal
Calais [ka'lɛ:] (**-'**) *nt*: **die Straße von ~** the Straits of Dover
Callcenter ['kɔ:lsɛntər] *nt* call centre (*Brit*), call center (*US*)
Camcorder (**-s, -**) *m* camcorder
campen ['kɛmpən] *vi* to camp
Camper, in (**-s, -**) *m(f)* camper
Camping ['kɛmpɪŋ] (**-s**) *nt* camping; **Campingbus** *m* camper; **Campingplatz** *m* camp(ing) site
Caravan ['karavan] (**-s, -s**) *m* caravan
Cargo ['kargo] (**-s, -s**) *m* (*Comm*) cargo
Cäsium ['tsɛ:ziʊm] *nt* caesium (*Brit*), cesium (*US*)
ccm *abk* (= *Kubikzentimeter*) cm³
CD *f abk* (= *Compact Disc*) CD; **CD-Brenner** *m* CD burner; **CD-ROM** (**-, -s**) *f* CD-ROM; **CD-Spieler** *m* CD player
CDU [tse:de:'|u:] (**-**) *f abk* (= *Christlich-Demokratische Union (Deutschlands)*) Christian Democratic Union; *see culture note*

CDU

The CDU (Christlich-Demokratische Union) is a Christian and conservative political party founded in 1945. It operates in all the *Länder* apart from Bavaria where its sister party the *CSU* is active. In the *Bundestag* the two parties form a coalition. It is the second largest party in Germany after the *SPD*, the Social Democratic Party.

Celli *pl von* **Cello**
Cellist, in [tʃɛ'lɪst(ɪn)] *m(f)* cellist
Cello ['tʃɛlo] (**-s, -s** *od* **Celli**) *nt* cello
Celsius ['tsɛlziʊs] *m* Celsius
Cent [(t)sɛnt] (**-(s), -(s)**) *m* cent
Ces [tsɛs] (**-, -**) *nt* (*Mus*) C flat
ces [tsɛs] (**-, -**) *nt* (*Mus*) C flat
Ceylon ['tsaɪlɔn] (**-s**) *nt* Ceylon
Chamäleon [ka'mɛ:leɔn] (**-s, -s**) *nt* chameleon
Champagner [ʃam'panjər] (**-s, -**) *m* champagne
Champignon ['ʃampɪnjõ] (**-s, -s**) *m* button mushroom
Chance ['ʃã:s(ə)] (**-, -n**) *f* chance, opportunity
chancengleich *adj* with equal opportunities
Chancengleichheit *f* equality of opportunity
Chaos ['ka:ɔs] (**-**) *nt* chaos
Chaot, in [ka'o:t(ɪn)] (**-en, -en**) *m(f)* (*Pol: pej*) anarchist (*pej*)
chaotisch [ka'o:tɪʃ] *adj* chaotic
Charakter [ka'raktər] (**-s, -e**) *m* character; **charakterfest** *adj* of firm character
charakterisieren [karakteri'zi:rən] *vt* to characterize
Charakteristik [karakte'rɪstɪk] *f* characterization
charakteristisch [karakte'rɪstɪʃ] *adj*: **~ (für)** characteristic (of), typical (of)
Charakter- *zW*: **charakterlos** *adj* unprincipled; **Charakterlosigkeit** *f* lack of principle; **Charakterschwäche** *f* weakness of character; **Charakterstärke** *f* strength of character; **Charakterzug** *m* characteristic, trait
charmant [ʃar'mant] *adj* charming
Charme [ʃarm] (**-s**) *m* charm
Charta ['karta] (**-, -s**) *f* charter
Charterflug ['tʃartərflu:k] *m* charter flight
Chartermaschine ['tʃartərmaʃi:nə] *f* charter plane
chartern ['tʃartərn] *vt* to charter
Chassis [ʃa'si:] (**-, -**) *nt* chassis
Chatroom ['tʃɛtru:m] *m* (*Comput*) chatroom
Chauffeur [ʃɔ'fø:r] *m* chauffeur
Chaussee [ʃo'se:] (**-, -n**) *f* (*veraltet*) high road
Chauvi ['ʃovi] (**-s, -s**) (*umg*) *m* male chauvinist
Chauvinismus [ʃovi'nɪsmʊs] *m* chauvinism
Chauvinist [ʃovi'nɪst] *m* chauvinist
checken ['tʃɛkən] *vt* (*überprüfen*) to check; (*umg: verstehen*) to get
Chef, in [ʃɛf(ɪn)] (**-s, -s**) *m(f)* head; (*umg*) boss; **Chefarzt** *m* senior consultant; **Chefetage** *f* executive floor; **Chefredakteur** *m* editor-in-chief; **Chefsekretärin** *f* personal assistant/secretary; **Chefvisite** *f* (*Med*) consultant's round
Chemie [çe'mi:] (**-**) *f* chemistry; **Chemiefaser** *f*

man-made fibre (*Brit*) *od* fiber (*US*)
Chemikalie [çemi'ka:liə] *f* chemical
Chemiker, in ['çe:mikər(ın)] (**-s, -**) *m(f)* (industrial) chemist
chemisch ['çe:mıʃ] *adj* chemical; **~e Reinigung** dry cleaning
Chemotherapie [çemotera'pi:] *f* chemotherapy
chic [ʃık] *adj inv* stylish, chic
Chicorée [ʃiko're:] (**-s**) *f od m* chicory
Chiffre ['ʃıfrə] (**-, -n**) *f* (*Geheimzeichen*) cipher; (*in Zeitung*) box number
Chiffriermaschine [ʃı'fri:rmaʃi:nə] *f* cipher machine
Chile ['tʃi:le] (**-s**) *nt* Chile
Chilene [tʃi'le:nə] (**-n, -n**) *m* Chilean
Chilenin [tʃi'le:nın] *f* Chilean
chilenisch *adj* Chilean
China ['çi:na] (**-s**) *nt* China
Chinakohl *m* Chinese leaves *pl*
Chinese [çi'ne:zə] (**-n, -n**) *m* Chinaman, Chinese
Chinesin *f* Chinese woman
chinesisch *adj* Chinese
Chinin [çi'ni:n] (**-s**) *nt* quinine
Chipkarte ['tʃıpkartə] *f* smart card
Chips [tʃıps] *pl* crisps *pl* (*Brit*), chips *pl* (*US*)
Chirurg, in [çi'rʊrg(ın)] (**-en, -en**) *m(f)* surgeon
Chirurgie [çirʊr'gi:] *f* surgery
chirurgisch *adj* surgical; **ein ~er Eingriff** surgery
Chlor [klo:r] (**-s**) *nt* chlorine
Chloroform [kloro'fɔrm] (**-s**) *nt* chloroform
chloroformieren [klorofor'mi:rən] *vt* to chloroform
Chlorophyll [kloro'fʏl] (**-s**) *nt* chlorophyll
Cholera ['ko:lera] (**-**) *f* cholera
Choleriker, in [ko'le:rikər(ın)] (**-s, -**) *m(f)* hot-tempered person
cholerisch [ko'le:rıʃ] *adj* choleric
Cholesterin [kolɛste'ri:n] (**-s**) *nt* cholesterol; **Cholesterinspiegel** [kolɛste'ri:nʃpigəl] *m* cholesterol level
Chor [ko:r] (**-(e)s, ⸚e**) *m* choir; (*Musikstück, Theat*) chorus
Choral [ko'ra:l] (**-s, -äle**) *m* chorale
Choreograf, in [koreo'gra:f(ın)] (**-en, -en**) *m(f)* choreographer
Choreografie [koreogra'fi:] *f* choreography
Chorgestühl *nt* choir stalls *pl*
Chorknabe *m* choirboy
Chose ['ʃo:zə] (**-, -n**) (*umg*) *f* (*Angelegenheit*) thing
Chr. *abk* = **Christus; Chronik**
Christ [krıst] (**-en, -en**) *m* Christian; **Christbaum** *m* Christmas tree
Christenheit *f* Christendom
Christentum (**-s**) *nt* Christianity
Christin *f* Christian
Christkind *nt* ≈ Father Christmas; (*Jesus*) baby Jesus
christlich *adj* Christian; **C~er Verein Junger Männer** Young Men's Christian Association
Christus (**Christi**) *m* Christ; **Christi Himmelfahrt** Ascension Day
Chrom [kro:m] (**-s**) *nt* (*Chem*) chromium; chrome
Chromosom [kromo'zo:m] (**-s, -en**) *nt* (*Biol*) chromosome
Chronik ['kro:nık] *f* chronicle
chronisch *adj* chronic
Chronologie [kronolo'gi:] *f* chronology
chronologisch *adj* chronological
Chrysantheme [kryzan'te:mə] (**-, -n**) *f* chrysanthemum
CIA ['si:aı'eı] (**-**) *f od m abk* (= *Central Intelligence Agency*) CIA
circa ['tsırka] *adv* (round) about
Cis [tsıs] (**-, -**) *nt* (*Mus*) C sharp
cis [tsıs] (**-, -**) *nt* (*Mus*) C sharp
City ['sıti] (**-, -s**) *f* city centre (*Brit*); **in der ~** in the city centre (*Brit*), downtown (*US*); **die ~ von Berlin** the (city) centre of Berlin (*Brit*), downtown Berlin (*US*)
clean [kli:n] *adj* (*Drogen: umg*) off drugs
clever ['klɛvər] *adj* clever; (*gerissen*) crafty
Clique ['klıkə] (**-, -n**) *f* set, crowd
Clou [klu:] (**-s, -s**) *m* (*von Geschichte*) (whole) point; (*von Show*) highlight, high spot
Clown [klaʊn] (**-s, -s**) *m* clown
cm *abk* (= *Zentimeter*) cm.
COBOL ['ko:bɔl] *nt* COBOL
Cockpit ['kɔkpıt] (**-s, -s**) *nt* cockpit
Cocktail ['kɔkte:l] (**-s, -s**) *m* cocktail
Code [ko:t] (**-s, -s**) *m* code
Cola ['ko:la] (**-(s), -s**) *nt od f* Coke®
Collier [kɔli'e:] (**-s, -s**) *nt* necklet, necklace
Comicheft ['kɔmıkhɛft] *nt* comic
Computer [kɔm'pju:tər] (**-s, -**) *m* computer; **computergesteuert** *adj* computer-controlled; **computergestützt** *adj* computer-based; **computergestütztes Design** computer-aided design; **Computerkriminalität** *f* computer crime; **Computerspiel** *nt* computer game; **Computertechnik** *f* computer technology
Conférencier [kõferãsi'e:] (**-s, -s**) *m* compère
Container [kɔn'te:nər] (**-s, -**) *m* container; **Containerschiff** *nt* container ship
Contergankind [kɔntɛr'gankınt] (*umg*) *nt* thalidomide child
cool [ku:l] (*umg*) *adj* (*gefasst*) cool
Cord [kɔrt] (**-(e)s, -e** *od* **-s**) *m* corduroy
Cornichon [kɔrni'ʃõ:] (**-s, -s**) *nt* gherkin
Couch [kaʊtʃ] (**-, -es** *od* **-en**) *f* couch; **Couchgarnitur** ['kaʊtʃgarni'tu:r] *f* three-piece suite
Couleur [ku'lø:r] (**-s, -s**) *f* (*geh*) kind, sort
Coupé [ku'pe:] (**-s, -s**) *nt* (*Aut*) coupé, sports version
Coupon [ku'põ:, ku'pɔŋ] (**-s, -s**) *m* coupon, voucher; (*Stoffcoupon*) length of cloth
Courage [ku'ra:ʒə] (**-**) *f* courage
Cousin [ku'zɛ̃:] (**-s, -s**) *m* cousin
Cousine [ku'zi:nə] (**-, -n**) *f* cousin
Crack [krɛk] (**-**) *nt* (*Droge*) crack

Creme [krɛːm] (**-, -s**) *f* (*lit, fig*) cream; (*Schuhcreme*) polish; (*Koch*) mousse; **cremefarben** *adj* cream(-coloured (*Brit*) *od* -colored (*US*))

cremig ['kreːmɪç] *adj* creamy

Crux [krʊks] (-) *f* = **Krux**

CSU [tseː|ɛs'|uː] (-) *f abk* (= *Christlich-Soziale Union*) Christian Social Union; *see culture note*

CSU

The *CSU* (Christlich-Soziale Union) is a party founded in 1945 in Bavaria. Like its sister party the *CDU* it is a Christian, right-wing party.

CT-Scanner [tseː'teːskenər] *m* CT scanner

Curriculum [kʊ'riːkulʊm] (**-s, -cula**) *nt* (*geh*) curriculum

Curry ['kari] (**-s**) *m od nt* curry powder; **Currypulver** ['karipʊlfər] *nt* curry powder; **Currywurst** *f* curried sausage

Cursor ['kørːsər] (**-s**) *m* (*Comput*) cursor; **Cursortaste** *f* cursor key

Cutter, in ['katər(ɪn)] (**-s, -**) *m(f)* (*Film*) editor

CVJM [tseːfaʊjɔt'|ɛm] (-) *m abk* (= *Christlicher*

Dd

D, d [de:] *nt* D, d; **D wie Dora** ≈ D for David, D for Dog (*US*)
D. *abk* = **Doktor** (*der evangelischen Theologie*)

SCHLÜSSELWORT

da [da:] *adv* **1** (*örtlich*) there; (*hier*) here; **da draußen** out there; **da sein** to be there; **ein Arzt, der immer für seine Patienten da ist** a doctor who always has time for his patients; **da bin ich** here I am; **da hast du dein Geld** (there you are,) there's your money; **da, wo** where; **ist noch Milch da?** is there any milk left?
2 (*zeitlich*) then; (*folglich*) so; **es war niemand im Zimmer, da habe ich ...** there was nobody in the room, so I ...
3: da haben wir Glück gehabt we were lucky there; **was gibts denn da zu lachen?** what's so funny about that?; **da kann man nichts machen** there's nothing one can do (in a case like that)
▷ *konj* (*weil*) as, since

d. Ä. *abk* (= *der Ältere*) Sen., sen.
DAAD (-) *m abk* (= *Deutscher Akademischer Austauschdienst*) *German Academic Exchange Service*
dabehalten *unreg vt* to keep
dabei [da'baɪ] *adv* (*räumlich*) close to it; (*noch dazu*) besides; (*zusammen mit*) with them/it *etc*; (*zeitlich*) during this; (*obwohl doch*) but, however; **~ sein** (*anwesend*) to be present; (*beteiligt*) to be involved; **ich bin ~!** count me in!; **was ist schon ~?** what of it?; **es ist doch nichts ~, wenn ...** it doesn't matter if ...; **bleiben wir ~** let's leave it at that; **es soll nicht ~ bleiben** this isn't the end of it; **es bleibt ~** that's settled; **das Dumme/Schwierige ~** the stupid/difficult part of it; **er war gerade ~ zu gehen** he was just leaving; **hast du ~ etwas gelernt?** did you learn anything from it?; **~ darf man nicht vergessen, dass ...** it shouldn't be forgotten that ...; **die ~ entstehenden Kosten** the expenses arising from this; **es kommt doch nichts ~ heraus** nothing will come of it; **ich finde gar nichts ~** I don't see any harm in it; **dabeistehen** *unreg vi* to stand around

Dach [dax] (**-(e)s, ⸚er**) *nt* roof; **unter ~ und Fach sein** (*abgeschlossen*) to be in the bag (*umg*); (*Vertrag, Geschäft*) to be signed and sealed; (*in Sicherheit*) to be safe; **jdm eins aufs ~ geben** (*umg: ausschimpfen*) to give sb a (good) talking to; **Dachboden** *m* attic, loft; **Dachdecker** (**-s, -**) *m* slater, tiler; **Dachfenster** *nt* skylight; (*ausgestellt*) dormer window; **Dachfirst** *m* ridge of the roof; **Dachgepäckträger** *m* (*Aut*) roof rack; **Dachgeschoss** *nt* attic storey (*Brit*) *od* story (*US*); (*oberster Stock*) top floor *od* storey (*Brit*) *od* story (*US*); **Dachluke** *f* skylight; **Dachpappe** *f* roofing felt; **Dachrinne** *f* gutter
Dachs [daks] (**-es, -e**) *m* badger
Dachschaden (*umg*) *m*: **einen ~ haben** to have a screw loose
dachte *etc* ['daxtə] *vb siehe* **denken**
Dach- *zW*: **Dachterrasse** *f* roof terrace; **Dachverband** *m* umbrella organization; **Dachziegel** *m* roof tile
Dackel ['dakəl] (**-s, -**) *m* dachshund
dadurch [da'dʊrç] *adv* (*räumlich*) through it; (*durch diesen Umstand*) thereby, in that way; (*deshalb*) because of that, for that reason
▷ *konj*: **~, dass** because
dafür [da'fy:r] *adv* for it; (*anstatt*) instead; (*zum Ausgleich*): **in Latein ist er schlecht, ~ kann er gut Fußball spielen** he's bad at Latin but he makes up for it at football; **er ist bekannt ~** he is well-known for that; **was bekomme ich ~?** what will I get for it?; **~ ist er immer zu haben** he never says no to that; **~ bin ich ja hier** that's what I'm here for; **er kann nichts ~ (, dass ...)** he can't help it (that ...); **Dafürhalten** (**-s**) *nt* (*geh*): **nach meinem Dafürhalten** in my opinion
DAG *f abk* (= *Deutsche Angestellten-Gewerkschaft*) *Clerical and Administrative Workers' Union*
dagegen [da'ge:gən] *adv* against it; (*im Vergleich damit*) in comparison with it; (*bei Tausch*) for it
▷ *konj* however; **haben Sie etwas ~, wenn ich rauche?** do you mind if I smoke?; **ich habe nichts ~** I don't mind; **ich war ~** I was against it; **ich hätte nichts ~ (einzuwenden)** that's okay by me; **~ kann man nichts tun** one can't do anything about it; **dagegenhalten** *unreg vt* (*vergleichen*) to compare with it; (*entgegnen*) to put forward as an objection

daheim [da'haɪm] *adv* at home; **bei uns ~** back home; **Daheim** (**-s**) *nt* home
daher [da'he:r] *adv* (*räumlich*) from there; (*Ursache*) from that ▷ *konj* (*deshalb*) that's why; **das kommt ~, dass ...** that is because ...; **~ kommt er auch** that's where he comes from too; **~ die Schwierigkeiten** that's what is causing the difficulties; **dahergelaufen** *adj*: **jeder dahergelaufene Kerl** any Tom, Dick or Harry; **daherreden** *vi* to talk away ▷ *vt* to say without thinking
dahin [da'hɪn] *adv* (*räumlich*) there; (*zeitlich*) then; (*vergangen*) gone; **ist es noch weit bis ~?** is there still far to go?; **~ gehend** on this matter; **das tendiert ~** it is tending towards that; **er bringt es noch ~, dass ich ...** he'll make me ...; **dahingegen** *konj* on the other hand; **dahingehen** *unreg vi* (*Zeit*) to pass; **dahingestellt** *adv*: **dahingestellt bleiben** to remain to be seen; **etw dahingestellt sein lassen** to leave sth open *od* undecided; **dahinschleppen** *vr* (*lit: sich fortbewegen*) to drag o.s. along; (*fig: Verhandlungen, Zeit*) to drag on; **dahinschmelzen** *vi* to be enthralled
dahinten [da'hɪntən] *adv* over there
dahinter [da'hɪntər] *adv* behind it; **sich ~ klemmen** *od* **knien** (*umg*) to put one's back into it; **~ kommen** (*umg*) to find out
dahinvegetieren [da'hɪnvege'ti:rən] *vi* to vegetate
Dahlie ['da:liə] (**-, -n**) *f* dahlia
DAK (**-**) *f abk* (= *Deutsche Angestellten-Krankenkasse*) *health insurance company for employees*
Dakar ['dakar] (**-s**) *nt* Dakar
dalassen ['da:lasən] *unreg vt* to leave (behind)
dalli ['dali] (*umg*) *adv*: **dalli, ~!** on (*Brit*) *od* at (*US*) the double!
damalig ['da:ma:lɪç] *adj* of that time, then
damals ['da:ma:ls] *adv* at that time, then
Damaskus [da'maskʊs] *nt* Damascus
Damast [da'mast] (**-(e)s, -e**) *m* damask
Dame ['da:mə] (**-, -n**) *f* lady; (*Schach, Karten*) queen; (*Spiel*) draughts (*Brit*), checkers (*US*)
Damen- *zW*: **Damenbesuch** *m* lady visitor *od* visitors; **Damenbinde** *f* sanitary towel (*Brit*) *od* napkin (*US*); **damenhaft** *adj* ladylike; **Damensattel** *m*: **im Damensattel reiten** to ride side-saddle; **Damenwahl** *f* ladies' excuse-me
Damespiel *nt* draughts (*Brit*), checkers (*US*)
damit [da'mɪt] *adv* with it; (*begründend*) by that ▷ *konj* in order that *od* to; **was meint er ~?** what does he mean by that?; **was soll ich ~?** what am I meant to do with that?; **muss er denn immer wieder ~ ankommen?** must he keep on about it?; **was ist ~?** what about it?; **genug ~!** that's enough!; **~ basta!** and that's that!; **~ eilt es nicht** there's no hurry
dämlich ['dɛ:mlɪç] (*umg*) *adj* silly, stupid
Damm [dam] (**-(e)s, ⸚e**) *m* dyke (*Brit*), dike (*US*); (*Staudamm*) dam; (*Hafendamm*) mole; (*Bahndamm, Straßendamm*) embankment
dämmen ['dɛmən] *vt* (*Wasser*) to dam up; (*Schmerzen*) to keep back
dämmerig *adj* dim, faint
Dämmerlicht *nt* twilight; (*abends*) dusk; (*Halbdunkel*) half-light
dämmern ['dɛmərn] *vi* (*Tag*) to dawn; (*Abend*) to fall; **es dämmerte ihm, dass ...** (*umg*) it dawned on him that ...
Dämmerung *f* twilight; (*Morgendämmerung*) dawn; (*Abenddämmerung*) dusk
Dämmerzustand *m* (*Halbschlaf*) dozy state; (*Bewusstseinstrübung*) semi-conscious state
Dämmung *f* insulation
Dämon ['dɛ:mɔn] (**-s, -en**) *m* demon
dämonisch [dɛ'mo:nɪʃ] *adj* demonic
Dampf [dampf] (**-(e)s, ⸚e**) *m* steam; (*Dunst*) vapour (*Brit*), vapor (*US*); **jdm ~ machen** (*umg*) to make sb get a move on; **~ ablassen** (*lit, fig*) to let off steam; **dampfen** *vi* to steam
dämpfen ['dɛmpfən] *vt* (*Koch*) to steam; (*bügeln*) to iron with a damp cloth; (*mit Dampfbügeleisen*) to steam iron; (*fig*) to dampen, subdue
Dampfer ['dampfər] (**-s, -**) *m* steamer; **auf dem falschen ~ sein** (*fig*) to have got the wrong idea
Dämpfer (**-s, -**) *m* (*Mus: bei Klavier*) damper; (*bei Geige, Trompete*) mute; **er hat einen ~ bekommen** (*fig*) it dampened his spirits
Dampf- *zW*: **Dampfkochtopf** *m* pressure cooker; **Dampfmaschine** *f* steam engine; **Dampfschiff** *nt* steamship; **Dampfwalze** *f* steamroller
Damwild ['damvɪlt] *nt* fallow deer
danach [da'na:x] *adv* after that; (*zeitlich*) afterwards; (*gemäß*) accordingly; (*laut diesem*) according to which *od* that; **mir war nicht ~ (zumute)** I didn't feel like it; **er griff schnell ~** he grabbed at it; **~ kann man nicht gehen** you can't go by that; **er sieht ~ aus** he looks it
Däne ['dɛ:nə] (**-n, -n**) *m* Dane, Danish man/boy
daneben [da'ne:bən] *adv* beside it; (*im Vergleich*) in comparison; **~ sein** (*umg: verwirrt sein*) to be completely confused; **danebenbenehmen** *unreg vr* to misbehave; **danebengehen** *unreg vi* to miss; (*Plan*) to fail; **danebengreifen** *unreg vi* to miss; (*fig: mit Schätzung etc*) to be wide of the mark
Dänemark ['dɛ:nəmark] (**-s**) *nt* Denmark
Dänin ['dɛ:nɪn] *f* Dane, Danish woman *od* girl
dänisch *adj* Danish
Dank [daŋk] (**-(e)s**) *m* thanks *pl*; **vielen** *od* **schönen ~** many thanks; **jdm ~ sagen** to thank sb; **mit (bestem) ~ zurück!** many thanks for the loan; **dank** *präp* (*+dat od gen*) thanks to; **dankbar** *adj* grateful; (*Aufgabe*) rewarding; (*haltbar*) hard-wearing; **Dankbarkeit** *f* gratitude
danke *interj* thank you, thanks
danken *vi +dat* to thank; **nichts zu ~!** don't mention it; **~d erhalten/ablehnen** to receive/decline with thanks
dankenswert *adj* (*Arbeit*) worthwhile; rewarding; (*Bemühung*) kind
Dank- *zW*: **Dankgottesdienst** *m* service of

thanksgiving; **danksagen** *vi* to express one's thanks; **Dankschreiben** *nt* letter of thanks
dann [dan] *adv* then; **~ und wann** now and then; **~ eben nicht** well, in that case (there's no more to be said); **erst ~, wenn ...** only when ...; **~ erst recht nicht!** in that case no way (*umg*)
dannen ['danən] *adv*: **von ~** (*liter*: *weg*) away
daran [da'ran] *adv* on it; (*stoßen*) against it; **es liegt ~, dass ...** the cause of it is that ...; **gut/schlecht ~ sein** to be well/badly off; **das Beste/Dümmste ~** the best/stupidest thing about it; **ich war nahe ~, zu ...** I was on the point of ...; **im Anschluss ~** (*zeitlich*: *danach anschließend*) following that *od* this; **wir können nichts ~ machen** we can't do anything about it; **es ist nichts ~** (*ist nicht fundiert*) there's nothing in it; (*ist nichts Besonderes*) it's nothing special; **er ist ~ gestorben** he died from *od* of it; **darangehen** *unreg vi* to start; **daranmachen** (*umg*) *vr*: **sich daranmachen, etw zu tun** to set about doing sth; **daransetzen** *vt* to stake; **er hat alles darangesetzt, von Glasgow wegzukommen** he has done his utmost to get away from Glasgow
darauf [da'raʊf] *adv* (*räumlich*) on it; (*zielgerichtet*) towards it; (*danach*) afterwards; **~ folgend** following; **es kommt ganz ~ an, ob ...** it depends whether ...; **seine Behauptungen stützen sich ~, dass ...** his claims are based on the supposition that ...; **wie kommst du ~?** what makes you think that?; **die Tage ~** the days following *od* thereafter; **am Tag ~** the next day; **darauffolgend** *adj* (*Tag, Jahr*) next, following; **daraufhin** *adv* (*im Hinblick darauf*) in this respect; (*aus diesem Grund*) as a result; **wir müssen es daraufhin prüfen, ob ...** we must test it to see whether ...; **drauflegen** *vt* to lay *od* put on top
daraus [da'raʊs] *adv* from it; **was ist ~ geworden?** what became of it?; **~ geht hervor, dass ...** this means that ...
darbieten ['da:rbi:tən] *vt* (*vortragen*: *Lehrstoff*) to present ▷ *vr* to present itself
Darbietung *f* performance
Dardanellen [darda'nɛlən] *pl* Dardanelles *pl*
darein- *präf* = **drein-**
Daressalam [darɛsa'la:m] *nt* Dar-es-Salaam
darf [darf] *vb siehe* **dürfen**
darin [da'rɪn] *adv* in (there), in it; **der Unterschied liegt ~, dass ...** the difference is that ...
darlegen ['da:rle:gən] *vt* to explain, expound, set forth
Darlegung *f* explanation
Darlehen, Darlehn (**-s, -**) *nt* loan
Darm [darm] (**-(e)s, ¨-e**) *m* intestine; (*Wurstdarm*) skin; **Darmausgang** *m* anus; **Darmgrippe** *f* gastric influenza; **Darmsaite** *f* gut string
darstellen ['da:rʃtɛlən] *vt* (*abbilden, bedeuten*) to represent; (*Theat*) to act; (*beschreiben*) to describe ▷ *vr* to appear to be
Darsteller, in (**-s, -**) *m(f)* actor, actress
darstellerisch *adj*: **eine ~e Höchstleistung** a magnificent piece of acting
Darstellung *f* portrayal, depiction
darüber [da'ry:bər] *adv* (*räumlich*) over/above it; (*fahren*) over it; (*mehr*) more; (*währenddessen*) meanwhile; (*sprechen, streiten*) about it; **~ hinweg sein** (*fig*) to have got over it; **~ hinaus** over and above that; **~ geht nichts** there's nothing like it; **seine Gedanken ~** his thoughts about *od* on it; **~ liegen** (*fig*) to be higher
darum [da'rʊm] *adv* (*räumlich*) round it ▷ *konj* that's why; **~ herum** round about (it); **er bittet ~** he is pleading for it; **es geht ~, dass ...** the thing is that ...; **~ geht es mir/ geht es mir nicht** that's my point/that's not the point for me; **er würde viel ~ geben, wenn ...** he would give a lot to ...; *siehe auch* **drum**
darunter [da'rʊntər] *adv* (*räumlich*) under it; (*dazwischen*) among them; (*weniger*) less; **ein Stockwerk ~** one floor below (it); **was verstehen Sie ~?** what do you understand by that?; **~ kann ich mir nichts vorstellen** that doesn't mean anything to me; **~ fallen** to be included; **~ mischen** (*Mehl*) to mix in; **sich ~ mischen** to mingle; **~ setzen** (*Unterschrift*) to put to it
das [das] *pron* that ▷ *def art* the; *siehe auch* **der**; **~ heißt** that is; **~ und ~** such and such
Dasein ['da:zaɪn] (**-s**) *nt* (*Leben*) life; (*Anwesenheit*) presence; (*Bestehen*) existence
da sein *unreg vi siehe* **da**
Daseinsberechtigung *f* right to exist
Daseinskampf *m* struggle for survival
dass [das] *konj* that
dasselbe [das'zɛlbə] *nt pron* the same
dastehen ['da:ʃte:ən] *unreg vi* to stand there; (*fig*): **gut/schlecht ~** to be in a good/bad position; **allein ~** to be on one's own
Dat. *abk* = **Dativ**
Datei [da'taɪ] *f* (*Comput*) file; **Dateimanager** *m* file manager; **Dateiname** *m* file name; **Dateiverwaltung** *f* file management
Daten ['da:tən] *pl* (*Comput*) data; (*Angaben*) data *pl*, particulars; *siehe auch* **Datum**; **Datenabgleich** *m* data comparison; **Datenautobahn** *f* information (super)highway; **Datenbank** *f* database; **Datenerfassung** *f* data capture; **Datenleitung** *f* data line; **Datenmüll** *m* (*aus dem Internet*) Internet buildup; (*auf Festplatte*) hard disk clutter; **Datennetz** *nt* data network; **Datensatz** *m* record; **Datenschutz** *m* data protection; **Datensichtgerät** *nt* visual display unit, VDU; **Datenträger** *m* data carrier; **Datenübertragung** *f* data transmission; **Datenverarbeitung** *f* data processing; **Datenverarbeitungsanlage** *f* data processing equipment, DP equipment
datieren [da'ti:rən] *vt* to date

Dativ ['da:ti:f] (**-s, -e**) *m* dative; **Dativobjekt** *nt* (*Gram*) indirect object
dato ['da:to] *adv*: **bis ~** (*Comm: umg*) to date
Dattel ['datəl] (**-, -n**) *f* date
Datum ['da:tʊm] (**-s, Daten**) *nt* date; **das heutige ~** today's date
Datumsgrenze *f* (*Geog*) (international) date line
Dauer ['daʊər] (**-, -n**) *f* duration; (*gewisse Zeitspanne*) length; (*Bestand, Fortbestehen*) permanence; **es war nur von kurzer ~** it didn't last long; **auf die ~** in the long run; (*auf längere Zeit*) indefinitely; **Dauerauftrag** *m* standing order; **dauerhaft** *adj* lasting, durable; **Dauerhaftigkeit** *f* durability; **Dauerkarte** *f* season ticket; **Dauerlauf** *m* long-distance run
dauern *vi* to last; **es hat sehr lang gedauert, bis er ...** it took him a long time to ...
dauernd *adj* constant
Dauer- *zW*: **Dauerobst** *nt* fruit suitable for storing; **Dauerredner** (*pej*) *m* long-winded speaker; **Dauerregen** *m* continuous rain; **Dauerschlaf** *m* prolonged sleep; **Dauerstellung** *f* permanent position; **Dauerwelle** *f* perm, permanent wave; **Dauerwurst** *f* German salami; **Dauerzustand** *m* permanent condition
Daumen ['daʊmən] (**-s, -**) *m* thumb; **jdm die ~ drücken** *od* **halten** to keep one's fingers crossed for sb; **über den ~ peilen** to guess roughly; **Daumenlutscher** *m* thumb-sucker
Daune ['daʊnə] (**-, -n**) *f* down
Daunendecke *f* down duvet
davon [da'fɔn] *adv* of it; (*räumlich*) away; (*weg von*) away from it; (*Grund*) because of it; (*mit Passiv*) by it; **das kommt ~!** that's what you get; **~ abgesehen** apart from that; **wenn wir einmal ~ absehen, dass ...** if for once we overlook the fact that ...; **~ sprechen/wissen** to talk/know of *od* about it; **was habe ich ~?** what's the point?; **~ betroffen werden** to be affected by it; **davongehen** *unreg vi* to leave, go away; **davonkommen** *unreg vi* to escape; **davonlassen** *unreg vt*: **die Finger davonlassen** (*umg*) to keep one's hands *od* fingers off (it); **davonlaufen** *unreg vi* to run away; **davonmachen** *vr* to make off; **davontragen** *unreg vt* to carry off; (*Verletzung*) to receive
davor [da'fo:r] *adv* (*räumlich*) in front of it; (*zeitlich*) before (that); **~ warnen** to warn about it
dazu [da'tsu:] *adv* (*legen, stellen*) by it; (*essen*) with it; **und ~ noch** and in addition; **ein Beispiel/seine Gedanken ~** one example for/his thoughts on this; **wie komme ich denn ~?** why should I?; **... aber ich bin nicht ~ gekommen** ... but I didn't get around to it; **das Recht ~** the right to do it; **~ bereit sein, etw zu tun** to be prepared to do sth; **~ fähig sein** to be capable of it; **sich ~ äußern** to say something on it; **dazugehören** *vi* to belong to it; **das gehört dazu** (*versteht sich von selbst*) it's all part of it; **es gehört schon einiges dazu, das zu tun** it takes a lot to do that; **dazugehörig** *adj* appropriate; **dazukommen** *unreg vi* (*Ereignisse*) to happen too; (*an einen Ort*) to come along; **kommt noch etwas dazu?** will there be anything else?; **dazulernen** *vt*: **schon wieder was dazugelernt!** you learn something (new) every day!; **dazumal** ['da:tsuma:l] *adv* in those days; **dazutun** *unreg vt* to add; **er hat es ohne dein Dazutun geschafft** he managed it without your doing *etc* anything
dazwischen [da'tsvɪʃən] *adv* in between; (*zusammen mit*) among them; **der Unterschied ~** the difference between them; **dazwischenfahren** *unreg vi* (*eingreifen*) to intervene; **dazwischenfunken** (*umg*) *vi* (*eingreifen*) to put one's oar in; **dazwischenkommen** *unreg vi* (*hineingeraten*) to get caught in it; **es ist etwas dazwischengekommen** something (has) cropped up; **dazwischenreden** *vi* (*unterbrechen*) to interrupt; (*sich einmischen*) to interfere; **dazwischentreten** *unreg vi* to intervene
DB *f abk* (*= Deutsche Bahn*) *German railways*
DBP *f abk* (*früher*) = **Deutsche Bundespost**
DDR (**-**) *f abk* (*früher: = Deutsche Demokratische Republik*) GDR; *see culture note*

DDR

The *DDR* (Deutsche Demokratische Republik) was the name by which the former Communist German Democratic Republic was known. It was founded in 1949 from the Soviet-occupied zone. After the building of the Berlin Wall in 1961 it was virtually sealed off from the West until mass demonstrations and demands for reform forced the opening of the borders in 1989. It then merged in 1990 with the BRD.

DDT® *nt abk* DDT
Dealer, in ['di:lər(ɪn)] (**-s, -**) (*umg*) *m(f)* pusher
Debatte [de'batə] (**-, -n**) *f* debate; **das steht hier nicht zur ~** that's not the issue
debattieren [deba'ti:rən] *vt* to debate
Debet ['de:bɛt] (**-s, -s**) *nt* (*Fin*) debits *pl*
Debüt [de'by:] (**-s, -s**) *nt* debut
dechiffrieren [deʃɪ'fri:rən] *vt* to decode; (*Text*) to decipher
Deck [dɛk] (**-(e)s, -s** *od* **-e**) *nt* deck; **an ~ gehen** to go on deck
Deckbett *nt* feather quilt
Deckblatt *nt* (*Schutzblatt*) cover
Decke (**-, -n**) *f* cover; (*Bettdecke*) blanket; (*Tischdecke*) tablecloth; (*Zimmerdecke*) ceiling; **unter einer ~ stecken** to be hand in glove; **an die ~ gehen** to hit the roof; **mir fällt die ~ auf den Kopf** (*fig*) I feel really claustrophobic
Deckel (**-s, -**) *m* lid; **du kriegst gleich eins auf**

den ~ (*umg*) you're going to catch it
Deckelung *f* capping
decken *vt* to cover ▷ *vr* to coincide ▷ *vi* to lay the table; **mein Bedarf ist gedeckt** I have all I need; (*fig*) I've had enough; **sich an einen gedeckten Tisch setzen** (*fig*) to be handed everything on a plate
Deckmantel *m*: **unter dem ~ von** under the guise of
Deckname *m* assumed name
Deckung *f* (*das Schützen*) covering; (*Schutz*) cover; (*Sport*) defence (*Brit*), defense (*US*); (*Übereinstimmen*) agreement; **zur ~ seiner Schulden** to meet his debts
deckungsgleich *adj* congruent
Decoder *m* (*TV*) decoder
de facto [de: 'fakto] *adv* de facto
Defekt [de'fɛkt] (**-(e)s, -e**) *m* fault, defect; **defekt** *adj* faulty
defensiv [defɛn'si:f] *adj* defensive
Defensive *f*: **jdn in die ~ drängen** to force sb onto the defensive
definieren [defi'ni:rən] *vt* to define
Definition [definitsi'o:n] *f* definition
definitiv [defini'ti:f] *adj* definite
Defizit ['de:fitsɪt] (**-s, -e**) *nt* deficit
defizitär [defitsi'tɛ:r] *adj*: **eine ~e Haushaltspolitik führen** to follow an economic policy which can only lead to deficit
Deflation [deflatsi'o:n] *f* (*Econ*) deflation
deflationär [deflatsio'nɛ:r] *adj* deflationary
deftig ['dɛftɪç] *adj* (*Essen*) large; (*Witz*) coarse
Degen ['de:gən] (**-s, -**) *m* sword
degenerieren [degene'ri:rən] *vi* to degenerate
degradieren [degra'di:rən] *vt* to degrade
dehnbar ['de:nba:r] *adj* elastic; (*fig*: *Begriff*) loose; **Dehnbarkeit** *f* elasticity; looseness
dehnen *vt, vr* to stretch
Dehnung *f* stretching
Deich [daɪç] (**-(e)s, -e**) *m* dyke (*Brit*), dike (*US*)
Deichsel ['daɪksəl] (**-, -n**) *f* shaft
deichseln *vt* (*fig*: *umg*) to wangle
dein [daɪn] *pron* your; (*adjektivisch*): **herzliche Grüße, D~e Elke** with best wishes, yours *od* (*herzlicher*) love, Elke
deine, r, s *poss pron* yours
deiner *gen von* **du** *pron* of you
deinerseits *adv* on your part
deinesgleichen *pron* people like you
deinetwegen ['daɪnət've:gən] *adv* (*für dich*) for your sake; (*wegen dir*) on your account
deinetwillen ['daɪnət'vɪlən] *adv*: **um ~ = deinetwegen**
deinige *pron*: **der/die/das D~** yours
dekadent [deka'dɛnt] *adj* decadent
Dekadenz *f* decadence
Dekan [de'ka:n] (**-s, -e**) *m* dean
deklassieren [dekla'si:rən] *vt* (*Soziologie*: *herabsetzen*) to downgrade; (*Sport*: *übertreffen*) to outclass
Deklination [deklinatsi'o:n] *f* declension
deklinieren [dekli'ni:rən] *vt* to decline
Dekolleté, Dekolletee [dekɔl'te:] (**-s, -s**) *nt* low neckline
dekomprimieren *vt* (*Comput*) to decompress
Dekor [de'ko:r] (**-s, -s** *od* **-e**) *m od nt* decoration
Dekorateur, in [dekora'tø:r(ɪn)] *m(f)* window dresser
Dekoration [dekoratsi'o:n] *f* decoration; (*in Laden*) window dressing
dekorativ [dekora'ti:f] *adj* decorative
dekorieren [deko'ri:rən] *vt* to decorate; (*Schaufenster*) to dress
Dekostoff ['de:koʃtɔf] *m* (*Textil*) furnishing fabric
Dekret [de'kre:t] (**-(e)s, -e**) *nt* decree
Delegation [delegatsi'o:n] *f* delegation
delegieren [dele'gi:rən] *vt*: **~ (an** *+akk*) to delegate (to)
Delegierte, r *f(m)* delegate
Delfin [dɛl'fi:n] (**-s, -e**) *m* dolphin
Delfinschwimmen *nt* butterfly (stroke)
Delhi ['de:lɪ] (**-s**) *nt* Delhi
delikat [deli'ka:t] *adj* (*zart, heikel*) delicate; (*köstlich*) delicious
Delikatesse [delika'tɛsə] (**-, -n**) *f* delicacy
Delikatessengeschäft *nt* delicatessen (shop)
Delikt [de'lɪkt] (**-(e)s, -e**) *nt* (*Jur*) offence (*Brit*), offense (*US*)
Delinquent [delɪŋ'kvɛnt] *m* (*geh*) offender
Delirium [de'li:riʊm] *nt*: **im ~ sein** to be delirious; (*umg*: *betrunken*) to be paralytic
Delle ['dɛlə] (**-, -n**) (*umg*) *f* dent
Delphin *etc* [dɛl'fi:n] (**-s, -e**) *m* = **Delfin** *etc*
Delta ['dɛlta] (**-s, -s**) *nt* delta
dem [de(:)m] *art dat von* **der; das**; **wie ~ auch sei** be that as it may
Demagoge [dema'go:gə] (**-n, -n**) *m* demagogue
Demarkationslinie [demarkatsi'o:nzli:niə] *f* demarcation line
Dementi [de'mɛnti] (**-s, -s**) *nt* denial
dementieren [demɛn'ti:rən] *vt* to deny
dem- *zW*: **dementsprechend** *adj* appropriate ▷ *adv* correspondingly; (*demnach*) accordingly; **demgemäß** *adv* accordingly; **demnach** *adv* accordingly; **demnächst** *adv* shortly
Demo ['de:mo] (**-s, -s**) (*umg*) *f* demo
Demografie [demogra'fi:] *f* demography
Demokrat, in [demo'kra:t(ɪn)] (**-en, -en**) *m(f)* democrat
Demokratie [demokra'ti:] *f* democracy; **Demokratieverständnis** *nt* understanding of (the meaning of) democracy
demokratisch *adj* democratic
demokratisieren [demokrati'zi:rən] *vt* to democratize
demolieren [demo'li:rən] *vt* to demolish
Demonstrant, in [demɔn'strant(ɪn)] *m(f)* demonstrator
Demonstration [demɔnstratsi'o:n] *f* demonstration
demonstrativ [demɔnstra'ti:f] *adj* demonstrative; (*Protest*) pointed
demonstrieren [demɔn'stri:rən] *vt, vi* to demonstrate
Demontage [demɔn'ta:ʒə] (**-, -n**) *f* (*lit, fig*)

dismantling
demontieren [demɔn'ti:rən] *vt (lit, fig)* to dismantle; *(Räder)* to take off
demoralisieren [demorali'zi:rən] *vt* to demoralize
Demoskopie [demosko'pi:] *f* public opinion research
demselben *dat von* **derselbe; dasselbe**
Demut ['de:mu:t] (-) *f* humility
demütig ['de:my:tıç] *adj* humble
demütigen ['de:my:tıgən] *vt* to humiliate
Demütigung *f* humiliation
demzufolge ['de:mtsu'fɔlgə] *adv* accordingly
den [de(:)n] *art akk von* **der**
denen ['de:nən] *pron dat pl von* **der; die; das**
Denk- *zW:* **Denkanstoß** *m:* **jdm Denkanstöße geben** to give sb food for thought; **Denkart** *f* mentality; **denkbar** *adj* conceivable
denken ['dɛŋkən] *unreg vi* to think ▷ *vt:* **für jdn/etw gedacht sein** to be intended *od* meant for sb/sth ▷ *vr (vorstellen):* **das kann ich mir ~** I can imagine; *(beabsichtigen):* **sich** *dat* **etw bei etw ~** to mean sth by sth; **wo ~ Sie hin!** what an idea!; **ich denke schon** I think so; **an jdn/etw ~** to think of sb/sth; **daran ist gar nicht zu ~** that's (quite) out of the question; **ich denke nicht daran, das zu tun** there's no way I'm going to do that *(umg)*
Denken (-s) *nt* thinking
Denker, in (-s, -) *m(f)* thinker; **das Volk der Dichter und ~** the nation of poets and philosophers
Denk- *zW:* **Denkfähigkeit** *f* intelligence; **denkfaul** *adj* mentally lazy; **Denkfehler** *m* logical error; **Denkhorizont** *m* mental horizon
Denkmal (-s, ¨-er) *nt* monument; **Denkmalschutz** *m:* **etw unter Denkmalschutz stellen** to classify sth as a historical monument
Denk- *zW:* **Denkpause** *f:* **eine Denkpause einlegen** to have a break to think things over; **Denkschrift** *f* memorandum; **Denkvermögen** *nt* intellectual capacity; **denkwürdig** *adj* memorable; **Denkzettel** *m:* **jdm einen Denkzettel verpassen** to teach sb a lesson
denn [dɛn] *konj* for; *(konzessiv):* **es sei ~, (dass)** unless ▷ *adv* then; *(nach Komparativ)* than
dennoch ['dɛnnɔx] *konj* nevertheless ▷ *adv:* **und ~, ...** and yet ...
denselben *akk von* **derselbe** ▷ *dat von* **dieselben**
Denunziant, in [denʊntsi'ant(ın)] *m(f)* informer
denunzieren [denʊn'tsi:rən] *vt* to inform against
Deospray ['de:ɔʃpreı] *nt od m* deodorant spray
Depesche [de'pɛʃə] (-, -n) *f* dispatch
deplatziert [depla'tsi:rt] *adj* out of place
Deponent, in [depo'nɛnt(ın)] *m(f)* depositor
Deponie *f* dump, disposal site
deponieren [depo'ni:rən] *vt (Comm)* to deposit
deportieren [depɔr'ti:rən] *vt* to deport
Depot [de'po:] (-s, -s) *nt* warehouse; *(Busdepot, Eisenb)* depot; *(Bankdepot)* strongroom *(Brit)*, safe *(US)*
Depp [dɛp] (-en, -en) *m (Dialekt: pej)* twit
Depression [deprɛsi'o:n] *f* depression
depressiv *adj* depressive; *(Fin)* depressed
deprimieren [depri'mi:rən] *vt* to depress

SCHLÜSSELWORT

der [de(:)r] *(f* **die**, *nt* **das**, *gen* **des, der, des**, *dat* **dem, der, dem**, *akk* **den**) *def art* the; **der Rhein** the Rhine; **der Klaus** *(umg)* Klaus; **die Frau** *(im Allgemeinen)* women; **der Tod/das Leben** death/life; **der Fuß des Berges** the foot of the hill; **gib es der Frau** give it to the woman; **er hat sich** *dat* **die Hand verletzt** he has hurt his hand
▷ *rel pron (bei Menschen)* who, that; *(bei Tieren, Sachen)* which, that; **der Mann, den ich gesehen habe** the man who *od* whom *od* that I saw
▷ *demon pron* he/she/it; *(jener, dieser)* that; *(pl)* those; **der/die war es** it was him/her; **der mit der Brille** the one with the glasses; **ich will den (da)** I want that one

derart ['de:r'a:rt] *adv (Art und Weise)* in such a way; *(Ausmaß: vor adj)* so; *(: vor vb)* so much
derartig *adj* such, this sort of
derb [dɛrp] *adj* sturdy; *(Kost)* solid; *(grob)* coarse; **Derbheit** *f* sturdiness; solidity; coarseness
deren ['de:rən] *rel pron (gen sing von die)* whose; *(von Sachen)* of which; *(gen pl von der, die, das)* their; whose; of whom
derentwillen ['de:rənt'vılən] *adv:* **um ~** *(rel)* for whose sake; *(von Sachen)* for the sake of which
dergestalt *adv (geh):* **~, dass ...** in such a way that ...
der- *zW:* **dergleichen** *pron* such; *(substantivisch):* **er tat nichts dergleichen** he did nothing of the kind; **und dergleichen (mehr)** and suchlike; **derjenige** *pron* he; she; it; *(rel)* the one (who); that (which); **dermaßen** *adv* to such an extent, so; **derselbe** *m pron* the same; **derweil, derweilen** *adv* in the meantime; **derzeit** *adv (jetzt)* at present, at the moment; **derzeitig** *adj* present, current; *(damalig)* then
des [dɛs] *art gen von* **der**
Des [dɛs] (-) *nt (Mus: auch:* **des**) D flat
Deserteur [dezɛr'tø:r] *m* deserter
desertieren [dezɛr'ti:rən] *vi* to desert
desgl. *abk* = **desgleichen**
desgleichen ['dɛs'glaıçən] *pron* the same
deshalb ['dɛs'halp] *adv, konj* therefore, that's why
Design [di'zaın] (-s, -s) *nt* design
designiert [dezi'gni:rt] *adj attrib:* **der ~e Vorsitzende/Nachfolger** the chairman designate/prospective successor
Desinfektion [dezınfɛktsi'o:n] *f* disinfection
Desinfektionsmittel *nt* disinfectant
desinfizieren [dezınfi'tsi:rən] *vt* to disinfect
Desinteresse [dɛs|ıntə'rɛsə] (-s) *nt:* **~ (an** +*dat)**

lack of interest (in)

desinteressiert [dɛs|ɪntərɛ'siːrt] *adj* uninterested

desselben *gen von* **derselbe; dasselbe**

dessen ['dɛsən] *pron gen von* **der; das**; **~ ungeachtet** nevertheless, regardless

Dessert [dɛ'sɛːr] **(-s, -s)** *nt* dessert

Dessin [dɛ'sɛ̃ː] **(-s, -s)** *nt* (*Textil*) pattern, design

Destillation [dɛstɪlatsi'oːn] *f* distillation

destillieren [dɛstɪ'liːrən] *vt* to distil

desto ['dɛsto] *adv* all *od* so much the; **~ besser** all the better

destruktiv [destrʊk'tiːf] *adj* destructive

deswegen ['dɛs'veːgən] *konj* therefore, hence

Detail [de'taɪ] **(-s, -s)** *nt* detail

detaillieren [deta'jiːrən] *vt* to specify, give details of

Detektiv [detɛk'tiːf] **(-s, -e)** *m* detective; **Detektivroman** *m* detective novel

Detektor [de'tɛktɔr] *m* (*Tech*) detector

Detonation [detonatsi'oːn] *f* explosion, blast

Deut *m*: **(um) keinen ~** not one iota *od* jot

deuten ['dɔʏtən] *vt* to interpret; (*Zukunft*) to read ▷ *vi*: **~ (auf +akk)** to point (to *od* at)

deutlich *adj* clear; (*Unterschied*) distinct; **jdm etw ~ zu verstehen geben** to make sth perfectly clear *od* plain to sb; **Deutlichkeit** *f* clarity; distinctness

deutsch [dɔʏtʃ] *adj* German; **~e Schrift** Gothic script; **auf D~** in German; **auf gut D~ (gesagt)** (*fig: umg*) ≈ in plain English; **D~e Demokratische Republik** (*Hist*) German Democratic Republic

Deutsche, r *f(m)*: **er ist ~r** he is (a) German

Deutschland *nt* Germany; **Deutschlandlied** *nt German national anthem*; **Deutschlandpolitik** *f* home *od* domestic policy; (*von fremdem Staat*) policy towards Germany

deutschsprachig *adj* (*Bevölkerung, Gebiete*) German-speaking; (*Zeitung, Ausgabe*) German-language; (*Literatur*) German

deutschstämmig *adj* of German origin

Deutung *f* interpretation

Devise [de'viːzə] **(-, -n)** *f* motto, device; **Devisen** *pl* (*Fin*) foreign currency *od* exchange

Devisenausgleich *m* foreign exchange offset

Devisenkontrolle *f* exchange control

Dez. *abk* (= *Dezember*) Dec.

Dezember [de'tsɛmbər] **(-(s), -)** *m* December; *siehe auch* **September**

dezent [de'tsɛnt] *adj* discreet

Dezentralisation [detsɛntralizatsi'oːn] *f* decentralization

Dezernat [detsɛr'naːt] **(-(e)s, -e)** *nt* (*Verwaltung*) department

Dezibel [detsi'bɛl] **(-s, -)** *nt* decibel

dezidiert [detsi'diːrt] *adj* firm, determined

dezimal [detsi'maːl] *adj* decimal; **Dezimalbruch** *m* decimal (fraction); **Dezimalsystem** *nt* decimal system

dezimieren [detsi'miːrən] *vt* (*fig*) to decimate ▷ *vr* to be decimated

DFB *m abk* (= *Deutscher Fußball-Bund*) *German Football Association*

DFG *f abk* (= *Deutsche Forschungsgemeinschaft*) *German Research Council*

DGB *m abk* (= *Deutscher Gewerkschaftsbund*) ≈ TUC

dgl. *abk* = **dergleichen**

d. h. *abk* (= *das heißt*) i.e.

Di. *abk* = **Dienstag**

Dia ['diːa] **(-s, -s)** *nt* = **Diapositiv**

Diabetes [dia'beːtɛs] **(-, -)** *m* (*Med*) diabetes

Diabetiker, in [dia'beːtikər(ɪn)] **(-s, -)** *m(f)* diabetic

Diagnose [dia'gnoːzə] **(-, -n)** *f* diagnosis

diagnostizieren [diagnɔsti'tsiːrən] *vt, vi* (*Med, fig*) to diagnose

diagonal [diago'naːl] *adj* diagonal

Diagonale (-, -n) *f* diagonal

Diagramm [dia'gram] *nt* diagram

Diakonie [diako'niː] *f* (*Rel*) social welfare work

Dialekt [dia'lɛkt] **(-(e)s, -e)** *m* dialect; **Dialektausdruck** *m* dialect expression *od* word; **dialektfrei** *adj* without an accent

dialektisch *adj* dialectal; (*Logik*) dialectical

Dialog [dia'loːk] **(-(e)s, -e)** *m* dialogue

Diamant [dia'mant] *m* diamond

Diapositiv [diapozi'tiːf] **(-s, -e)** *nt* (*Phot*) slide, transparency

Diaprojektor *m* slide projector

Diät [di'ɛːt] (-) *f* diet; **Diäten** *pl* (*Pol*) allowance *sing*; **~ essen** to eat according to a diet; **(nach einer) ~ leben** to be on a special diet

dich [dɪç] *akk von* **du** ▷ *pron* you ▷ *refl pron* yourself

dicht [dɪçt] *adj* dense; (*Nebel*) thick; (*Gewebe*) close; (*undurchlässig*) (water)tight; (*fig*) concise; (*umg: zu*) shut, closed ▷ *adv*: **~ an/bei** close to; **er ist nicht ganz ~** (*umg*) he's crackers; **~ machen** to make watertight/airtight; **~ hintereinander** right behind one another; **~ bevölkert** densely *od* heavily populated; *siehe auch* **dichtmachen**

Dichte (-, -n) *f* density; thickness; closeness; (water)tightness; (*fig*) conciseness

dichten *vt* (*dicht machen*) to make watertight; to seal; (*Naut*) to caulk; (*Liter*) to compose, write ▷ *vi* (*Liter*) to compose, write

Dichter, in (-s, -) *m(f)* poet; (*Autor*) writer; **dichterisch** *adj* poetical; **dichterische Freiheit** poetic licence (*Brit*) *od* license (*US*)

dichthalten *unreg* (*umg*) *vi* to keep one's mouth shut

dichtmachen (*umg*) *vt* (*Geschäft*) to wind up ▷ *vi* (*Person*) to close one's mind; *siehe auch* **dicht**

Dichtung *f* (*Tech*) washer; (*Aut*) gasket; (*Gedichte*) poetry; (*Prosa*) (piece of) writing; **~ und Wahrheit** (*fig*) fact and fantasy

dick [dɪk] *adj* thick; (*fett*) fat; **durch ~ und dünn** through thick and thin; **Dickdarm** *m* (*Anat*) colon

Dicke (-, -n) *f* thickness; fatness

dickfellig *adj* thick-skinned

dickflüssig *adj* viscous

Dickicht (-s, -e) *nt* thicket

dick- *zW*: **Dickkopf** *m* mule; **Dickmilch** *f* soured

milk; **Dickschädel** *m* = **Dickkopf**
die [di:] *def art* the; *siehe auch* **der**
Dieb, in [di:p, 'di:bɪn] (**-(e)s, -e**) *m(f)* thief; **haltet den ~!** stop thief!; **diebisch** *adj* thieving; (*umg*) immense; **Diebstahl** *m* theft; **diebstahlsicher** *adj* theft-proof
diejenige ['di:je:nɪgə] *pron siehe* **derjenige**
Diele ['di:lə] (**-, -n**) *f* (*Brett*) board; (*Flur*) hall, lobby; (*Eisdiele*) ice-cream parlour (*Brit*) *od* parlor (*US*)
dienen ['di:nən] *vi*: **(jdm)** ~ to serve (sb); **womit kann ich Ihnen ~?** what can I do for you?; (*in Geschäft*) can I help you?
Diener (**-s, -**) *m* servant; (*umg: Verbeugung*) bow; **Dienerin** *f* (maid)servant
dienern *vi* (*fig*): ~ **(vor** *+dat***)** to bow and scrape (to)
Dienerschaft *f* servants *pl*
dienlich *adj* useful, helpful
Dienst [di:nst] (**-(e)s, -e**) *m* service; (*Arbeit, Arbeitszeit*) work; **~ am Kunden** customer service; **jdm zu ~en stehen** to be at sb's disposal; **außer** ~ retired; **~ haben** to be on duty; **~ habend** = **diensthabend**; **~ tuend** = **diensttuend**; **der öffentliche ~** the civil service
Dienstag *m* Tuesday; **am** ~ on Tuesday; **~ in acht Tagen** *od* **in einer Woche** a week on Tuesday, Tuesday week; **~ vor einer Woche** *od* **acht Tagen** a week (ago) last Tuesday
dienstags *adv* on Tuesdays
Dienst- *zW*: **Dienstalter** *nt* length of service; **dienstbeflissen** *adj* zealous; **Dienstbote** *m* servant; **Dienstboteneingang** *m* tradesmen's *od* service entrance; **diensteifrig** *adj* zealous; **dienstfrei** *adj* off duty; **Dienstgebrauch** *m* (*Mil, Verwaltung*): **nur für den Dienstgebrauch** for official use only; **Dienstgeheimnis** *nt* professional secret; **Dienstgespräch** *nt* business call; **Dienstgrad** *m* rank; **diensthabend** *adj* (*Arzt, Offizier*) on duty; **Dienstleistung** *f* service; **Dienstleistungsbereich** *m* service sector *od* industry; **Dienstleistungsbetrieb** *m* service industry business; **Dienstleistungsgewerbe** *nt* service industries *pl*; **Dienstleistungssektor** *m* service sector *od* industry; **dienstlich** *adj* official; (*Angelegenheiten*) business *attrib*; **Dienstmädchen** *nt* domestic servant; **Dienstplan** *m* duty rota; **Dienstreise** *f* business trip; **Dienststelle** *f* office; **diensttuend** *adj* on duty; **Dienstvorschrift** *f* service regulations *pl*; **Dienstwagen** *m* (*von Beamten*) official car; **Dienstweg** *m* official channels *pl*; **Dienstzeit** *f* office hours *pl*; (*Mil*) period of service
diesbezüglich *adj* (*Frage*) on this matter
diese, r, s *pron* this (one) ▷ *adj* this; **~ Nacht** tonight
Diesel ['di:zəl] (**-s**) *m* (*Kraftstoff*) diesel fuel
dieselbe [di:'zɛlbə] *f pron* the same
dieselben [di:'zɛlbən] *pl pron* the same
Dieselöl ['di:zəlø:l] *nt* diesel oil
diesig *adj* drizzly
dies- *zW*: **diesjährig** *adj* this year's; **diesmal** *adv* this time; **Diesseits** (**-**) *nt* this life; **diesseits** *präp +gen* on this side
Dietrich ['di:trɪç] (**-s, -e**) *m* picklock
Diffamierungskampagne [dɪfa'mi:rʊŋskampanjə] *f* smear campaign
differential *etc* [dɪfɛrɛntsi'a:l] *adj* = **differenzial** *etc*
Differenz [dɪfe'rɛnts] *f* difference; **Differenzbetrag** *m* difference, balance
differenzial [dɪferɛntsi'a:l] *adj* differential; **Differenzialgetriebe** *nt* differential gear; **Differenzialrechnung** *f* differential calculus
differenzieren [dɪferɛn'tsi:rən] *vt* to make distinctions in ▷ *vi*: **~ (bei)** to make distinctions (in)
differenziert *adj* complex
diffus [dɪ'fu:s] *adj* (*Gedanken etc*) confused
Digital- [digi'ta:l-] *zW*: **Digitalanzeige** *f* digital display; **Digitalfernsehen** *nt* digital TV; **Digitalrechner** *m* digital computer; **Digitaluhr** *f* digital watch
Diktafon, Diktaphon [dɪkta'fo:n] *nt* dictaphone®
Diktat [dɪk'ta:t] (**-(e)s, -e**) *nt* dictation; (*fig: Gebot*) dictate; (*Pol*) diktat, dictate
Diktator [dɪk'ta:tɔr] *m* dictator; **diktatorisch** [-a'to:rɪʃ] *adj* dictatorial
Diktatur [dɪkta'tu:r] *f* dictatorship
diktieren [dɪk'ti:rən] *vt* to dictate
Diktion [dɪktsi'o:n] *f* style
Dilemma [di'lɛma] (**-s, -s** *od* **-ta**) *nt* dilemma
Dilettant [dilɛ'tant] *m* dilettante, amateur; **dilettantisch** *adj* dilettante
Dimension [dimɛnzi'o:n] *f* dimension
DIN *f abk* (= *Deutsche Industrie-Norm*) *German Industrial Standard*; **~ A4** A4
Ding [dɪŋ] (**-(e)s, -e**) *nt* thing; object; **das ist ein ~ der Unmöglichkeit** that is totally impossible; **guter ~e sein** to be in good spirits; **so wie die ~e liegen, nach Lage der ~e** as things are; **es müsste nicht mit rechten ~en zugehen, wenn ...** it would be more than a little strange if ...; **ein krummes ~ drehen** to commit a crime; to do something wrong; **dingfest** *adj*: **jdn dingfest machen** to arrest sb; **dinglich** *adj* real, concrete
Dings (**-**) (*umg*) *nt* thingummyjig (*Brit*)
Dingsbums ['dɪŋsbʊms] (**-**) (*umg*) *nt* thingummybob (*Brit*)
Dingsda (**-**) (*umg*) *nt* thingummyjig (*Brit*)
Dinosaurier [dino'zaʊriər] *m* dinosaur
Diözese [diø'tse:zə] (**-, -n**) *f* diocese
Diphtherie [dɪfte'ri:] *f* diphtheria
Dipl.-Ing. *abk* = **Diplom-Ingenieur**
Diplom [di'plo:m] (**-(e)s, -e**) *nt* diploma; (*Hochschulabschluss*) degree; **Diplomarbeit** *f* dissertation
Diplomat [diplo'ma:t] (**-en, -en**) *m* diplomat
Diplomatie [diploma'ti:] *f* diplomacy
diplomatisch [diplo'ma:tɪʃ] *adj* diplomatic
Diplom-Ingenieur *m* academically qualified

engineer

dir [diːr] *dat von* **du** ▷ *pron* (to) you

direkt [di'rɛkt] *adj* direct; ~ **fragen** to ask outright *od* straight out

Direktion [dirɛktsi'oːn] *f* management; (*Büro*) manager's office

Direktmandat *nt* (*Pol*) direct mandate

Direktor, in *m(f)* director; (*von Hochschule*) principal; (*von Schule*) principal, head (teacher) (*Brit*)

Direktorium [direk'toːriʊm] *nt* board of directors

Direktübertragung *f* live broadcast

Direktverkauf *m* direct selling

Dirigent, in [diri'gɛnt(ɪn)] *m(f)* conductor

dirigieren [diri'giːrən] *vt* to direct; (*Mus*) to conduct

Dirne ['dɪrnə] (**-, -n**) *f* prostitute

Dis [dɪs] (**-, -**) *nt* (*Mus*) D sharp

dis [dɪs] (**-, -**) *nt* (*Mus*) D sharp

Disco ['dɪsko] (**-, -s**) *f* disco

Disharmonie [dɪsharmo'niː] *f* (*lit, fig*) discord

Diskette [dɪs'kɛtə] *f* disk, diskette

Diskettenlaufwerk *nt* disk drive

Disko ['dɪsko] (**-, -s**) *f* disco

Diskont [dɪs'kɔnt] (**-s, -e**) *m* discount; **Diskontsatz** *m* rate of discount

Diskothek [dɪsko'teːk] (**-, -en**) *f* disco(theque)

diskreditieren [dɪskredi'tiːrən] *vt* (*geh*) to discredit

Diskrepanz [dɪskre'pants] *f* discrepancy

diskret [dɪs'kreːt] *adj* discreet

Diskretion [dɪskretsi'oːn] *f* discretion; **strengste ~ wahren** to preserve the strictest confidence

diskriminieren [dɪskrimi'niːrən] *vt* to discriminate against

Diskriminierung *f*: ~ **(von)** discrimination (against)

Diskussion [dɪskʊsi'oːn] *f* discussion; **zur ~ stehen** to be under discussion

Diskussionsbeitrag *m* contribution to the discussion

Diskuswerfen ['dɪskʊsvɛrfən] *nt* throwing the discus

diskutabel [dɪsku'taːbəl] *adj* debatable

diskutieren [dɪsku'tiːrən] *vt, vi* to discuss; **darüber lässt sich** ~ that sounds like something we could talk about

disponieren [dɪspo'niːrən] *vi* (*geh: planen*) to make arrangements

Disposition [dɪspozitsi'oːn] *f* (*geh: Verfügung*): **jdm zur** *od* **zu jds ~ stehen** to be at sb's disposal

disqualifizieren [dɪskvalifi'tsiːrən] *vt* to disqualify

dissen ['dɪsən] (*umg*) *vt* to slag off (*Brit*), to diss (*esp US*)

Dissertation [dɪsɛrtatsi'oːn] *f* dissertation; doctoral thesis

Dissident, in [dɪsi'dɛnt(ɪn)] *m(f)* dissident

Distanz [dɪs'tants] *f* distance; (*fig: Abstand, Entfernung*) detachment; (*Zurückhaltung*) reserve

distanzieren [dɪstan'tsiːrən] *vr*: **sich von jdm/etw** ~ to dissociate o.s. from sb/sth

distanziert *adj* (*Verhalten*) distant

Distel ['dɪstəl] (**-, -n**) *f* thistle

Disziplin [dɪstsi'pliːn] (**-, -en**) *f* discipline

Disziplinarverfahren [dɪstsipli'narfɛrfaːrən] *nt* disciplinary proceedings *pl*

dito ['diːto] *adv* (*hum, Comm*) ditto

Diva ['diːva] (**-, -s**) *f* star; (*Film*) screen goddess

divers [di'vɛrs] *adj* various

Diverses *pl* sundries *pl*; **„~"** "miscellaneous"

Dividende [divi'dɛndə] (**-, -n**) *f* dividend

dividieren [divi'diːrən] *vt*: ~ **(durch)** to divide (by)

d. J. *abk* (= *der Jüngere*) jun.

Djakarta [dʒa'karta] *nt* Jakarta

DJH *nt abk* (= *Deutsches Jugendherbergswerk*) *German Youth Hostel Association*

DKP *f abk* (= *Deutsche Kommunistische Partei*) *German Communist Party*

DLV *m abk* (= *Deutscher Leichtathletik-Verband*) *German track and field association*

DM *f abk* (*Hist*: = *Deutsche Mark*) DM

d. M. *abk* (= *dieses Monats*) inst.

D-Mark ['deːmark] (**-, -**) *f* (*Hist*) deutschmark

DNS *f abk* (= *Desoxyribo(se)nukleinsäure*) DNA

Do. *abk* = **Donnerstag**

SCHLÜSSELWORT

doch [dɔx] *adv* **1** (*dennoch*) after all; (*sowieso*) anyway; **er kam doch noch** he came after all; **du weißt es ja doch besser** you know more about it (than I do) anyway; **es war doch ganz interessant** it was actually quite interesting; **und doch, ...** and yet ...

2 (*als bejahende Antwort*) yes I do/it does *etc*; **das ist nicht wahr — doch!** that's not true — yes it is!

3 (*auffordernd*): **komm doch** do come; **lass ihn doch** just leave him; **nicht doch!** oh no!

4: **sie ist doch noch so jung** but she's still so young; **Sie wissen doch, wie das ist** you know how it is(, don't you?); **wenn doch** if only

▷ *konj* (*aber*) but; (*trotzdem*) all the same; **und doch hat er es getan** but still he did it

Docht [dɔxt] (**-(e)s, -e**) *m* wick

Dock [dɔk] (**-s, -s** *od* **-e**) *nt* dock; **Dockgebühren** *pl* dock dues *pl*

Dogge ['dɔgə] (**-, -n**) *f* bulldog; **Deutsche ~** Great Dane

Dogma ['dɔgma] (**-s, -men**) *nt* dogma

dogmatisch [dɔ'gmaːtɪʃ] *adj* dogmatic

Dohle ['doːlə] (**-, -n**) *f* jackdaw

Doktor ['dɔktɔr] (**-s, -en**) *m* doctor; **den ~ machen** (*umg*) to do a doctorate *od* Ph.D.

Doktorand, in [dɔkto'rant (-dɪn)] (**-en, -en**) *m(f)* Ph.D. student

Doktor- *zW*: **Doktorarbeit** *f* doctoral thesis; **Doktortitel** *m* doctorate; **Doktorvater** *m* supervisor

doktrinär [dɔktri'nɛ:r] *adj* doctrinal; (*stur*) doctrinaire
Dokument [doku'mɛnt] *nt* document
Dokumentar- *zW*: **Dokumentarbericht** *m* documentary; **Dokumentarfilm** *m* documentary (film); **dokumentarisch** *adj* documentary; **Dokumentarspiel** *nt* docudrama
Dokumentationszentrum *nt* documentation centre (*Brit*) *od* center (*US*)
dokumentieren [dokumɛn'ti:rən] *vt* to document; (*fig: zu erkennen geben*) to reveal, show
Dolch [dɔlç] **(-(e)s, -e)** *m* dagger; **Dolchstoß** *m* (*bes fig*) stab
dolmetschen ['dɔlmɛtʃən] *vt, vi* to interpret
Dolmetscher, in **(-s, -)** *m(f)* interpreter
Dolomiten [dolo'mi:tən] *pl* (*Geog*): **die ~** the Dolomites *pl*
Dom [do:m] **(-(e)s, -e)** *m* cathedral
Domäne [do'mɛ:nə] **(-, -n)** *f* (*fig*) domain, province
dominieren [domi'ni:rən] *vt* to dominate ▷ *vi* to predominate
Dominikanische Republik [domini'ka:nɪʃə-repu'bli:k] *f* Dominican Republic
Dompfaff ['do:mpfaf] **(-en, -en)** *m* bullfinch
Dompteur [dɔmp'tø:r] *m* (*Zirkus*) trainer
Dompteuse [dɔmp'tø:zə] *f* (*Zirkus*) trainer
Donau ['do:naʊ] *f*: **die ~** the Danube
Donner ['dɔnər] **(-s, -)** *m* thunder; **wie vom ~ gerührt** (*fig*) thunderstruck
donnern *vi unpers* to thunder ▷ *vt* (*umg*) to slam, crash
Donnerschlag *m* thunderclap
Donnerstag *m* Thursday; *siehe auch* **Dienstag**
Donnerwetter *nt* thunderstorm; (*fig*) dressing-down ▷ *interj* good heavens!; (*anerkennend*) my word!
doof [do:f] (*umg*) *adj* daft, stupid
Dopingkontrolle ['dɔpɪŋkɔntrɔlə] *f* (*Sport*) dope check
Doppel ['dɔpəl] **(-s, -)** *nt* duplicate; (*Sport*) doubles; **Doppelband** *m* (*von doppeltem Umfang*) double-sized volume; (*zwei Bände*) two volumes *pl*; **Doppelbett** *nt* double bed; **doppelbödig** *adj* (*fig*) ambiguous; **doppeldeutig** *adj* ambiguous; **Doppelfenster** *nt* double glazing; **Doppelgänger, in** **(-s, -)** *m(f)* double; **Doppelkorn** *m type of schnapps*; **Doppelpunkt** *m* colon; **doppelseitig** *adj* (*auch Comput: Diskette*) double-sided; (*Lungenentzündung*) double; **doppelseitige Anzeige** double-page advertisement; **doppelsinnig** *adj* ambiguous; **Doppelstecker** *m* two-way adaptor; **Doppelstunde** *f* (*Sch*) double period
doppelt *adj* double; (*Comm: Buchführung*) double-entry; (*Staatsbürgerschaft*) dual ▷ *adv*: **die Karte habe ich ~** I have two of these cards; **~ gemoppelt** (*umg*) saying the same thing twice over; **in ~er Ausführung** in duplicate
Doppel- *zW*: **Doppelverdiener** *pl* two-income family; **Doppelzentner** *m* 100 kilograms; **Doppelzimmer** *nt* double room
Dorf [dɔrf] **(-(e)s, ¨-er)** *nt* village; **Dorfbewohner** *m* villager
dörflich ['dœrflɪç] *adj* village *attrib*
Dorn[1] [dɔrn] **(-(e)s, -en)** *m* (*Bot*) thorn; **das ist mir ein ~ im Auge** (*fig*) it's a thorn in my flesh
Dorn[2] [dɔrn] **(-(e)s, -e)** *m* (*Schnallendorn*) tongue, pin
dornig *adj* thorny
Dornröschen *nt* Sleeping Beauty
dörren ['dœrən] *vt* to dry
Dörrobst ['dœro:pst] *nt* dried fruit
dort [dɔrt] *adv* there; **~ drüben** over there; **dorther** *adv* from there; **dorthin** *adv* (to) there
dortig *adj* of that place; in that town
Dose ['do:zə] **(-, -n)** *f* box; (*Blechdose*) tin, can; **in ~n** (*Konserven*) canned, tinned (*Brit*)
Dosen *pl von* **Dose; Dosis**
dösen ['dø:zən] (*umg*) *vi* to doze
Dosenmilch *f* evaporated milk
Dosenöffner *m* tin (*Brit*) *od* can opener
Dosenpfand *nt* deposit on drink cans; (*allgemein: Einwegpfand*) deposit on drink cans and disposable bottles
dosieren [do'zi:rən] *vt* (*lit, fig*) to measure out
Dosis ['do:zɪs] **(-, Dosen)** *f* dose
Dotierung [do'ti:rʊŋ] *f* endowment; (*von Posten*) remuneration
Dotter ['dɔtər] **(-s, -)** *m* egg yolk
Double ['du:bəl] **(-s, -s)** *nt* (*Film etc*) stand-in
Download ['daunlo:d] *m* (*Comput*) download
downloaden ['daunlo:dən] *vti* (*Comput*) to download
Downsyndrom *nt no pl* (*Med*) Down's Syndrome
Doz. *abk* = **Dozent(in)**
Dozent, in [do'tsɛnt(ɪn)] **(-en, -en)** *m(f)*: **~ (für)** lecturer (in), professor (of) (*US*)
dpa (-) *f abk* (= *Deutsche Presse-Agentur*) *German Press Agency*
Dr. *abk* = **Doktor**
Drache ['draxə] **(-n, -n)** *m* (*Tier*) dragon
Drachen **(-s, -)** *m* kite; **einen ~ steigen lassen** to fly a kite; **drachenfliegen** *vi* to hang-glide; **Drachenfliegen** *nt* (*Sport*) hang-gliding
Dragee, Dragée [dra'ʒe:] **(-s, -s)** *nt* (*Pharm*) dragee, sugar-coated pill
Draht [dra:t] **(-(e)s, ¨-e)** *m* wire; **auf ~ sein** to be on the ball; **Drahtesel** *m* (*hum*) trusty bicycle; **Drahtgitter** *nt* wire grating; **drahtlos** *adj* cordless; (*Telefon*) mobile; **Drahtseil** *nt* cable; **Nerven wie Drahtseile** (*umg*) nerves of steel; **Drahtseilbahn** *f* cable railway; **Drahtzange** *f* pliers *pl*; **Drahtzieher, in** *m(f)* (*fig*) wire-puller
Drall *m* (*fig: Hang*) tendency; **einen ~ nach links haben** (*Aut*) to pull to the left
drall [dral] *adj* strapping; (*Frau*) buxom
Drama ['dra:ma] **(-s, Dramen)** *nt* drama
Dramatiker, in [dra'ma:tikər(ɪn)] **(-s, -)** *m(f)* dramatist
dramatisch [dra'ma:tɪʃ] *adj* dramatic
Dramaturg, in [drama'tʊrk (-gɪn)] **(-en, -en)**

m(f) artistic director; (TV) drama producer

dran [dran] (*umg*) *adv* (*an der Reihe*): **jetzt bist du ~** it's your turn now; **früh/spät ~ sein** to be early/late; **ich weiß nicht, wie ich (bei ihm) ~ bin** I don't know where I stand (with him); *siehe auch* **daran**; **dranbleiben** *unreg* (*umg*) *vi* to stay close; (*am Apparat*) to hang on

Drang (**-(e)s, ⸚**) *m* (*Trieb*) urge, yearning; (*Druck*) pressure; **~ nach** urge *od* yearning for

drang *etc* [draŋ] *vb siehe* **dringen**

drängeln ['drɛŋəln] *vt, vi* to push, jostle

drängen ['drɛŋən] *vt* (*schieben*) to push, press; (*antreiben*) to urge ▷ *vi* (*eilig sein*) to be urgent; (*Zeit*) to press; **auf etw** *akk* **~** to press for sth

drangsalieren [draŋza'li:rən] *vt* to pester, plague

dranhalten (*umg*) *vr* to get a move on

drankommen (*umg*: *unreg*: *vi* (*an die Reihe kommen*) to have one's turn; (*Sch: beim Melden*) to be called; (*Frage, Aufgabe etc*) to come up

drannehmen (*umg*: *unreg*: *vt* (*Schüler*) to ask

drastisch ['drastɪʃ] *adj* drastic

drauf [draʊf] (*umg*) *adv*: **~ und dran sein, etw zu tun** to be on the point of doing sth; *siehe auch* **darauf**; **Draufgänger** (**-s, -**) *m* daredevil; **draufgehen** *unreg vi* (*verbraucht werden*) to be used up; (*kaputtgehen*) to be smashed up; **draufhaben** (*umg*) *unreg vt*: **etw draufhaben** (*können*) to be able to do sth just like that; (*Kenntnisse*) to be well up on sth; **draufzahlen** *vi* (*fig: Einbußen erleiden*) to pay the price

draußen ['draʊsən] *adv* outside, out-of-doors

Drechsler, in ['drɛkslər(ɪn)] (**-s, -**) *m(f)* (wood) turner

Dreck [drɛk] (**-(e)s**) *m* mud, dirt; **~ am Stecken haben** (*fig*) to have a skeleton in the cupboard; **das geht ihn einen ~ an** (*umg*) that's none of his business

dreckig *adj* dirty, filthy; **es geht mir ~** (*umg*) I'm in a bad way

Dreckskerl (*umg!*) *m* dirty swine (*!*)

Dreh [dre:] *m*: **den ~ raushaben** *od* **weghaben** (*umg*) to have got the hang of it

Dreh- *zW*: **Drehachse** *f* axis of rotation; **Dreharbeiten** *pl* (*Film*) shooting *sing*; **Drehbank** *f* lathe; **drehbar** *adj* revolving; **Drehbuch** *nt* (*Film*) script

drehen *vt* to turn, rotate; (*Zigaretten*) to roll; (*Film*) to shoot ▷ *vi* to turn, rotate ▷ *vr* to turn; (*handeln von*): **sich um etw ~** to be about sth; **ein Ding ~** (*umg*) to play a prank

Dreher, in (**-s, -**) *m(f)* lathe operator

Dreh- *zW*: **Drehorgel** *f* barrel organ; **Drehort** *m* (*Film*) location; **Drehscheibe** *f* (*Eisenb*) turntable; **Drehtür** *f* revolving door

Drehung *f* (*Rotation*) rotation; (*Umdrehung, Wendung*) turn

Dreh- *zW*: **Drehwurm** (*umg*) *m*: **einen Drehwurm haben/bekommen** to be/become dizzy; **Drehzahl** *f* rate of revolution; **Drehzahlmesser** *m* rev(olution) counter

drei [draɪ] *num* three; **~ viertel** three quarters; **aller guten Dinge sind ~!** (*Sprichwort*) all good things come in threes!; (*nach zwei missglückten Versuchen*) third time lucky!; **Dreieck** *nt* triangle; **dreieckig** *adj* triangular; **Dreiecksverhältnis** *nt* eternal triangle; **dreieinhalb** *num* three and a half; **Dreieinigkeit** [-'|aɪnɪçkaɪt] *f* Trinity

dreierlei *adj inv* of three kinds

drei- *zW*: **dreifach** *adj* triple, treble ▷ *adv* three times; **die dreifache Menge** three times the amount; **Dreifaltigkeit** *f* trinity; **Dreifuß** *m* tripod; (*Schemel*) three-legged stool; **Dreigangschaltung** *f* three-speed gear; **dreihundert** *num* three hundred; **Dreikäsehoch** (*umg*) *m* tiny tot; **Dreikönigsfest** *nt* Epiphany; **dreimal** *adv* three times, thrice; **dreimalig** *adj* three times

dreinblicken ['draɪnblɪkən] *vi*: **traurig** *etc* **~** to look sad *etc*

dreinreden ['draɪnre:dən] *vi*: **jdm ~** (*dazwischenreden*) to interrupt sb; (*sich einmischen*) to interfere with sb

Dreirad *nt* tricycle

Dreisprung *m* triple jump

dreißig ['draɪsɪç] *num* thirty

dreist [draɪst] *adj* bold, audacious

Dreistigkeit *f* boldness, audacity

drei- *zW*: **Dreiviertelstunde** *f* three-quarters of an hour; **Dreivierteltakt** *m*: **im Dreivierteltakt** in three-four time; **dreizehn** *num* thirteen; **jetzt schlägts dreizehn!** (*umg*) that's a bit much

dreschen ['drɛʃən] *unreg vt* to thresh; **Skat ~** (*umg*) to play skat

Dresden ['dre:sdən] (**-s**) *nt* Dresden

dressieren [drɛ'si:rən] *vt* to train

Dressur [drɛ'su:r] *f* training; (*für Dressurreiten*) dressage

Dr. h. c. *abk* (*= Doktor honoris causa*) honorary doctor

driften ['drɪftən] *vi* (*Naut, fig*) to drift

Drillbohrer *m* light drill

drillen ['drɪlən] *vt* (*bohren*) to drill, bore; (*Mil*) to drill; (*fig*) to train; **auf etw** *akk* **gedrillt sein** (*fig: umg*) to be practised (*Brit*) *od* practiced (*US*) at doing sth

Drilling *m* triplet

drin [drɪn] (*umg*) *adv*: **bis jetzt ist noch alles ~** everything is still quite open; *siehe auch* **darin**

dringen ['drɪŋən] *unreg vi* (*Wasser, Licht, Kälte*): **~ (durch/in** *+akk***)** to penetrate (through/into); **auf etw** *akk* **~** to insist on sth; **in jdn ~** (*geh*) to entreat sb

dringend ['drɪŋənt] *adj* urgent; **~ empfehlen** to recommend strongly

dringlich ['drɪŋlɪç] *adj* = **dringend**

Dringlichkeit *f* urgency

Dringlichkeitsstufe *f* priority; **~ 1** top priority

drinnen ['drɪnən] *adv* inside, indoors

drinstecken ['drɪnʃtɛkən] (*umg*) *vi*: **da steckt eine Menge Arbeit drin** a lot of work has gone into it

drischt [drɪʃt] *vb siehe* **dreschen**

dritt *adv*: **wir kommen zu ~** three of us are

coming together
dritte, r, s *adj* third; **D~ Welt** Third World; **im Beisein D~r** in the presence of a third party
Drittel (**-s, -**) *nt* third
drittens *adv* thirdly
drittklassig *adj* third-rate, third-class
Dr. jur. *abk* (= *Doktor der Rechtswissenschaften*) ≈ L.L.D.
DRK (-) *nt abk* (= *Deutsches Rotes Kreuz*) ≈ R.C.
Dr. med. *abk* (= *Doktor der Medizin*) ≈ M.D.
droben ['dro:bən] *adv* above, up there
Droge ['dro:gə] (**-, -n**) *f* drug
dröge ['drøgə] (*Nordd*) *adj* boring
Drogen- *zW*: **drogenabhängig** *adj* addicted to drugs; **Drogenhändler, in** *m(f)* peddler, pusher; **drogensüchtig** *adj* addicted to drugs
Drogerie [drogə'ri:] *f* chemist's shop (*Brit*), drugstore (*US*); *see culture note*

DROGERIE

The *Drogerie* as opposed to the *Apotheke* sells medicines not requiring a prescription. It tends to be cheaper and also sells cosmetics, perfume and toiletries.

Drogist, in [dro'gɪst(ɪn)] *m(f)* pharmacist, chemist (*Brit*)
Drohbrief *m* threatening letter
drohen ['dro:ən] *vi*: **(jdm)** ~ to threaten (sb)
Drohgebärde *f* (*lit, fig*) threatening gesture
Drohne ['dro:nə] (**-, -n**) *f* drone
dröhnen ['drø:nən] *vi* (*Motor*) to roar; (*Stimme, Musik*) to ring, resound
Drohung ['dro:ʊŋ] *f* threat
drollig ['drɔlɪç] *adj* droll
Drops [drɔps] (**-, -**) *m od nt* fruit drop
drosch *etc* [drɔʃ] *vb siehe* **dreschen**
Droschke ['drɔʃkə] (**-, -n**) *f* cab
Droschkenkutscher *m* cabman
Drossel ['drɔsəl] (**-, -n**) *f* thrush
drosseln ['drɔsəln] *vt* (*Motor etc*) to throttle; (*Heizung*) to turn down; (*Strom, Tempo, Produktion etc*) to cut down
Dr. phil. *abk* (= *Doktor der Geisteswissenschaften*) ≈ Ph.D.
Dr. theol. *abk* (= *Doktor der Theologie*) ≈ D.D.
drüben ['dry:bən] *adv* over there, on the other side
drüber ['dry:bər] (*umg*) *adv* = **darüber**
Druck [drʊk] (**-(e)s, -e**) *m* (*Zwang, Phys*) pressure; (*Typ: Vorgang*) printing; (*: Produkt*) print; (*fig: Belastung*) burden, weight; **~ hinter etw** *akk* **machen** to put some pressure on sth; **Druckbuchstabe** *m* block letter; **in Druckbuchstaben schreiben** to print
Drückeberger ['drʏkəbɛrgər] (**-s, -**) *m* shirker, dodger
drucken ['drʊkən] *vt, vi* (*Typ, Comput*) to print
drücken ['drʏkən] *vt* (*Knopf, Hand*) to press; (*zu eng sein*) to pinch; (*fig: Preise*) to keep down; (*: belasten*) to oppress, weigh down ▷ *vi* to press; to pinch ▷ *vr*: **sich vor etw** *dat* **~** to get out of (doing) sth; **jdm etw in die Hand ~** to press sth into sb's hand
drückend *adj* oppressive; (*Last, Steuern*) heavy; (*Armut*) grinding; (*Wetter, Hitze*) oppressive, close
Drucker (**-s, -**) *m* printer
Drücker (**-s, -**) *m* button; (*Türdrücker*) handle; (*Gewehrdrücker*) trigger; **am ~ sein** *od* **sitzen** (*fig: umg*) to be the key person; **auf den letzten ~** (*fig: umg*) at the last minute
Druckerei [drʊkə'raɪ] *f* printing works, press
Druckerschwärze *f* printer's ink
Druck- *zW*: **Druckfahne** *f* galley(-proof); **Druckfehler** *m* misprint; **Druckknopf** *m* press stud (*Brit*), snap fastener; **Druckkopf** *m* printhead; **Druckluft** *f* compressed air; **Druckmittel** *nt* leverage; **druckreif** *adj* ready for printing, passed for press; (*fig*) polished; **Drucksache** *f* printed matter; **Druckschrift** *f* printing; (*gedrucktes Werk*) pamphlet; **Drucktaste** *f* push button; **Druckwelle** *f* shock wave
drum [drʊm] (*umg*) *adv* around; **mit allem D~ und Dran** with all the bits and pieces *pl*; (*Mahlzeit*) with all the trimmings *pl*
Drumherum *nt* trappings *pl*
drunten ['drʊntən] *adv* below, down there
Drüse ['dry:zə] (**-, -n**) *f* gland
DSB (-) *m abk* (= *Deutscher Sportbund*) *German Sports Association*
Dschungel ['dʒʊŋəl] (**-s, -**) *m* jungle
DSD *nt abk* (= *Duales System Deutschland*) *German waste collection and recycling service*; *see culture note*

DSD

The *DSD* (Duales System Deutschland) is a scheme introduced in Germany for separating domestic refuse into two types so as to reduce environmental damage. Normal refuse is disposed of in the usual way by burning or dumping at land-fill sites; packets and containers with a green spot (*Grüner Punkt*) imprinted on them are kept separate and are then collected for recycling.

dt. *abk* = **deutsch**
DTC (-) *m abk* (= *Deutscher Touring Automobil Club*) *German motoring organization*
DTP (-) *nt abk* (= *Desktop publishing*) DTP
Dtzd. *abk* (= *Dutzend*) doz.
du [du:] *pron* you; **mit jdm per du sein** to be on familiar terms with sb; **Du** *nt*: **jdm das Du anbieten** to suggest that sb uses "du", suggest that sb uses the familiar form of address
Dübel ['dy:bəl] (**-s, -**) *m* plug; (*Holzdübel*) dowel
dübeln ['dy:bəln] *vt, vi* to plug
Dublin ['dablɪn] *nt* Dublin
ducken ['dʊkən] *vt* (*Kopf*) to duck; (*fig*) to take down a peg or two ▷ *vr* to duck
Duckmäuser ['dʊkmɔʏzər] (**-s, -**) *m* yes-man
Dudelsack ['du:dəlzak] *m* bagpipes *pl*

Duell [du'ɛl] (**-s, -e**) *nt* duel
Duett [du'ɛt] (**-(e)s, -e**) *nt* duet
Duft [dʊft] (**-(e)s, ⸚e**) *m* scent, odour (*Brit*), odor (*US*); **duften** *vi* to smell, be fragrant
duftig *adj* (*Stoff, Kleid*) delicate, diaphanous; (*Muster*) fine
Duftnote *f* (*von Parfüm*) scent
dulden ['dʊldən] *vt* to suffer; (*zulassen*) to tolerate ▷ *vi* to suffer
duldsam *adj* tolerant
dumm [dʊm] *adj* stupid; **das wird mir zu ~** that's just too much; **der D~e sein** to be the loser; **der ~e August** (*umg*) the clown; **du willst mich wohl für ~ verkaufen** you must think I'm stupid; **sich ~ und dämlich reden** (*umg*) to talk till one is blue in the face; **so etwas D~es** how stupid; what a nuisance; **dummdreist** *adj* impudent
dummerweise *adv* stupidly
Dummheit *f* stupidity; (*Tat*) blunder, stupid mistake
Dummkopf *m* blockhead
dumpf [dʊmpf] *adj* (*Ton*) hollow, dull; (*Luft*) close; (*Erinnerung, Schmerz*) vague; **Dumpfheit** *f* hollowness, dullness; closeness; vagueness
dumpfig *adj* musty
Dumpingpreis ['dampɪŋpraɪs] *m* give-away price
Düne ['dy:nə] (**-, -n**) *f* dune
Dung [dʊŋ] (**-(e)s**) *m* manure
düngen ['dyŋən] *vt* to fertilize
Dünger (**-s, -**) *m* fertilizer; (*Dung*) manure
dunkel ['dʊŋkəl] *adj* dark; (*Stimme*) deep; (*Ahnung*) vague; (*rätselhaft*) obscure; (*verdächtig*) dubious, shady; **im D~n tappen** (*fig*) to grope in the dark
Dünkel ['dʏŋkəl] (**-s**) *m* self-conceit; **dünkelhaft** *adj* conceited
Dunkelheit *f* darkness; (*fig*) obscurity; **bei Einbruch der ~** at nightfall
Dunkelkammer *f* (*Phot*) dark room
dunkeln *vi unpers* to grow dark
Dunkelziffer *f* estimated number of unnotified cases
dünn [dʏn] *adj* thin ▷ *adv*: **~ gesät** scarce; **Dünndarm** *m* small intestine; **dünnflüssig** *adj* watery, thin; **Dünnheit** *f* thinness; **Dünnschiss** (*umg*) *m* the runs
Dunst [dʊnst] (**-es, ⸚e**) *m* vapour (*Brit*), vapor (*US*); (*Wetter*) haze; **Dunstabzugshaube** *f* extractor hood
dünsten ['dʏnstən] *vt* to steam
Dunstglocke *f* haze; (*Smog*) pall of smog
dunstig ['dʊnstɪç] *adj* vaporous; (*Wetter*) hazy, misty
düpieren [dy'pi:rən] *vt* to dupe
Duplikat [dupli'ka:t] (**-(e)s, -e**) *nt* duplicate
Dur [du:r] (**-, -**) *nt* (*Mus*) major

SCHLÜSSELWORT

durch [dʊrç] *präp+akk* **1** (*hindurch*) through; **durch den Urwald** through the jungle; **durch die ganze Welt reisen** to travel all over the world
2 (*mittels*) through, by (means of); (*aufgrund*) due to, owing to; **Tod durch Herzschlag/den Strang** death from a heart attack/by hanging; **durch die Post** by post; **durch seine Bemühungen** through his efforts
▷ *adj* **1** (*hindurch*) through; **die ganze Nacht durch** all through the night; **den Sommer durch** during the summer; **8 Uhr durch** past 8 o'clock; **durch und durch** completely; **das geht mir durch und durch** that goes right through me
2 (*Koch: umg: durchgebraten*) done; **(gut) durch** well-done

durcharbeiten *vt, vi* to work through ▷ *vr*: **sich durch etw ~** to work one's way through sth
durchatmen *vi* to breathe deeply
durchaus [dʊrç'aʊs] *adv* completely; (*unbedingt*) definitely; **~ nicht** (*in verneinten Sätzen: als Verstärkung*) by no means; (*: als Antwort*) not at all; **das lässt sich ~ machen** that sounds feasible; **ich bin ~ Ihrer Meinung** I quite *od* absolutely agree with you
durchbeißen *unreg vt* to bite through ▷ *vr* (*fig*) to battle on
durchblättern *vt* to leaf through
Durchblick ['dʊrçblɪk] *m* view; (*fig*) comprehension; **den ~ haben** (*fig: umg*) to know what's what
durchblicken *vi* to look through; (*umg: verstehen*): **(bei etw) ~** to understand (sth); **etw ~ lassen** (*fig*) to hint at sth
Durchblutung [dʊrç'blu:tʊŋ] *f* circulation (of blood)
durchbohren *vt untr* to bore through, pierce
durchboxen ['dʊrçbɔksən] *vr* (*fig: umg*): **sich (durch etw) ~** to fight one's way through (sth)
durchbrechen[1] ['dʊrçbrɛçən] *unreg vt, vi* to break
durchbrechen[2] [dʊrç'brɛçən] *unreg vt untr* (*Schranken*) to break through
durchbrennen *unreg vi* (*Draht, Sicherung*) to burn through; (*umg*) to run away
durchbringen *unreg vt* to get through; (*Geld*) to squander ▷ *vr* to make a living
Durchbruch ['dʊrçbrʊx] *m* (*Öffnung*) opening; (*Mil*) breach; (*von Gefühlen etc*) eruption; (*der Zähne*) cutting; (*fig*) breakthrough; **zum ~ kommen** to break through
durchdacht [dʊrç'daxt] *adj* well thought-out
durchdenken *unreg vt untr* to think out
durch- *zW*: **durchdiskutieren** *vt* to talk over, discuss; **durchdrängen** *vr* to force one's way through; **durchdrehen** *vt* (*Fleisch*) to mince ▷ *vi* (*umg*) to crack up
durchdringen[1] ['dʊrçdrɪŋən] *unreg vi* to penetrate, get through
durchdringen[2] [dʊrç'drɪŋən] *unreg vt untr* to penetrate
durchdringend *adj* piercing; (*Kälte, Wind*) biting; (*Geruch*) pungent

durchdrücken ['dʊrçdrʏkən] *vt* (*durch Presse*) to press through; (*Creme, Teig*) to pipe; (*fig: Gesetz, Reformen etc*) to push through; (*seinen Willen*) to get; (*Knie, Kreuz etc*) to straighten

durcheinander [dʊrç|aɪ'nandər] *adv* in a mess, in confusion; (*verwirrt*) confused; **Durcheinander** (**-s**) *nt* (*Verwirrung*) confusion; (*Unordnung*) mess; **durcheinanderbringen** *vt* to mess up; (*verwirren*) to confuse; **durcheinanderreden** *vi* to talk at the same time; **durcheinandertrinken** *vi* to mix one's drinks; **durcheinanderwerfen** *vt* to muddle up

durch- *zW*: **durchfahren** *unreg vi*: **er ist bei Rot durchgefahren** he jumped the lights ▷ *vt*: **die Nacht durchfahren** to travel through the night; **Durchfahrt** *f* transit; (*Verkehr*) thoroughfare; **Durchfahrt bitte freihalten!** please keep access free; **Durchfahrt verboten!** no through road; **Durchfall** *m* (*Med*) diarrhoea (*Brit*), diarrhea (*US*); **durchfallen** *unreg vi* to fall through; (*in Prüfung*) to fail; **durchfinden** *unreg vr* to find one's way through; **durchfliegen** *unreg* (*umg*) *vi* (*in Prüfung*): **(durch etw** *od* **in etw** *dat***) durchfliegen** to fail (sth); **Durchflug** *m*: **Passagiere auf dem Durchflug** transit passengers

durchforschen *vt untr* to explore

durchforsten [dʊrç'fɔrstən] *vt untr* (*fig: Akten etc*) to go through

durchfragen *vr* to find one's way by asking

durchfressen *unreg vr* to eat one's way through

durchführbar *adj* feasible, practicable

durchführen ['dʊrçfy:rən] *vt* to carry out; (*Gesetz*) to implement; (*Kursus*) to run

Durchführung *f* execution, performance

Durchgang ['dʊrçgaŋ] *m* passage(way); (*bei Produktion, Versuch*) run; (*Sport*) round; (*bei Wahl*) ballot; **~ verboten** no thoroughfare

durchgängig ['dʊrçgɛŋɪç] *adj* universal, general

Durchgangs- *zW*: **Durchgangshandel** *m* transit trade; **Durchgangslager** *nt* transit camp; **Durchgangsstadium** *nt* transitory stage; **Durchgangsverkehr** *m* through traffic

durchgeben ['dʊrçge:bən] *unreg vt* (*Rundf, TV: Hinweis, Wetter*) to give; (*Lottozahlen*) to announce

durchgefroren ['dʊrçgəfro:rən] *adj* (*See*) completely frozen; (*Mensch*) frozen stiff

durchgehen ['dʊrçge:ən] *unreg vt* (*behandeln*) to go over *od* through ▷ *vi* to go through; (*ausreißen: Pferd*) to break loose; (*Mensch*) to run away; **mein Temperament ging mit mir durch** my temper got the better of me; **jdm etw ~ lassen** to let sb get away with sth

durchgehend *adj* (*Zug*) through; (*Öffnungszeiten*) continuous

durchgeschwitzt ['dʊrçgəʃvɪtst] *adj* soaked in sweat

durch- *zW*: **durchgreifen** *unreg vi* to take strong action; **durchhalten** *unreg vi* to last out ▷ *vt* to keep up; **Durchhaltevermögen** *nt* staying power; **durchhängen** *unreg vi* (*lit, fig*) to sag; **durchhecheln** (*umg*) *vt* to gossip about; **durchkommen** *unreg vi* to get through; (*überleben*) to pull through

durchkreuzen *vt untr* to thwart, frustrate

durchlassen *unreg vt* (*Person*) to let through; (*Wasser*) to let in

durchlässig *adj* leaky

Durchlaucht ['dʊrçlaʊxt] (**-, -en**) *f*: **(Euer) ~** Your Highness

Durchlauf ['dʊrçlaʊf] *m* (*Comput*) run

durchlaufen *unreg vt untr* (*Schule, Phase*) to go through

Durchlauferhitzer (**-s, -**) *m* continuous-flow water heater

Durchlaufzeit *f* (*Comput*) length of the run

durch- *zW*: **durchleben** *vt untr* (*Zeit*) to live *od* go through; (*Jugend, Gefühl*) to experience; **durchlesen** *unreg vt* to read through; **durchleuchten** *vt untr* to X-ray; **durchlöchern** *vt untr* to perforate; (*mit Löchern*) to punch holes in; (*mit Kugeln*) to riddle; **durchmachen** *vt* to go through; **die Nacht durchmachen** to make a night of it

Durchmarsch *m* march through

Durchmesser (**-s, -**) *m* diameter

durchnässen *vt untr* to soak (through)

durch- *zW*: **durchnehmen** *unreg vt* to go over; **durchnummerieren** *vt* to number consecutively; **durchorganisieren** *vt* to organize down to the last detail; **durchpausen** *vt* to trace; **durchpeitschen** *vt* (*lit*) to whip soundly; (*fig: Gesetzentwurf, Reform*) to force through

durchqueren [dʊrç'kve:rən] *vt untr* to cross

durch- *zW*: **durchrechnen** *vt* to calculate; **durchregnen** *vi unpers*: **es regnet durchs Dach durch** the rain is coming through the roof; **Durchreiche** (**-, -n**) *f* (serving) hatch, pass-through (*US*); **Durchreise** *f* transit; **auf der Durchreise** passing through; (*Güter*) in transit; **Durchreisevisum** *nt* transit visa; **durchringen** *unreg vr* to make up one's mind finally; **durchrosten** *vi* to rust through; **durchrutschen** *vi*: **(durch etw) durchrutschen** (*lit*) to slip through (sth); (*bei Prüfung*) to scrape through (sth)

durchs [dʊrçs] = **durch das**

Durchsage ['dʊrçza:gə] *f* intercom *od* radio announcement

Durchsatz ['dʊrçzats] *m* (*Produktion, Comput*) throughput

durchschauen[1] ['dʊrçʃaʊən] *vt, vi* (*lit*) to look *od* see through

durchschauen[2] [dʊrç'ʃaʊən] *vt untr* (*Person, Lüge*) to see through

durchscheinen ['dʊrçʃaɪnən] *unreg vi* to shine through

durchscheinend *adj* translucent

durchschlafen ['dʊrçʃla:fən] *unreg vi* to sleep through

Durchschlag ['dʊrçʃla:k] *m* (*Doppel*) carbon copy; (*Sieb*) strainer

durchschlagen *unreg vt* (*entzweischlagen*) to split (in two); (*sieben*) to sieve ▷ *vi* (*zum Vorschein kommen*) to emerge, come out ▷ *vr* to get by
durchschlagend *adj* resounding; **(eine) ~e Wirkung haben** to be totally effective
Durchschlagpapier *nt* flimsy; (*Kohlepapier*) carbon paper
Durchschlagskraft *f* (*von Geschoss*) penetration; (*fig: von Argument*) decisiveness
durch- *zW*: **durchschlängeln** *vr* (*durch etw: Mensch*) to thread one's way through; **durchschlüpfen** *vi* to slip through; **durchschneiden** *unreg vt* to cut through
Durchschnitt ['dʊrçʃnɪt] *m* (*Mittelwert*) average; **über/unter dem ~** above/below average; **im ~** on average; **durchschnittlich** *adj* average ▷ *adv* on average; **durchschnittlich begabt/groß** *etc* of average ability/height *etc*
Durchschnitts- *zW*: **Durchschnittsgeschwindigkeit** *f* average speed; **Durchschnittsmensch** *m* average man, man in the street; **Durchschnittswert** *m* average
durch- *zW*: **Durchschrift** *f* copy; **Durchschuss** *m* (*Loch*) bullet hole; **durchschwimmen** *unreg vt untr* to swim across; **durchsegeln** (*umg*) *vi* (*nicht bestehen*): **durch** *od* **bei etw durchsegeln** to fail *od* flunk (*umg*) (sth); **durchsehen** *unreg vt* to look through
durchsetzen¹ ['dʊrçzɛtsən] *vt* to enforce ▷ *vr* (*Erfolg haben*) to succeed; (*sich behaupten*) to get one's way; **seinen Kopf ~** to get one's own way
durchsetzen² [dʊrç'zɛtsən] *vt untr* to mix
Durchsicht ['dʊrçzɪçt] *f* looking through, checking
durchsichtig *adj* transparent; **Durchsichtigkeit** *f* transparency
durch- *zW*: **durchsickern** *vi* to seep through; (*fig*) to leak out; **durchsieben** *vt* to sieve; **durchsitzen** *unreg vt* (*Sessel etc*) to wear out (the seat of); **durchspielen** *vt* to go *od* run through; **durchsprechen** *unreg vt* to talk over; **durchstehen** *unreg vt* to live through; **Durchstehvermögen** *nt* endurance, staying power; **durchstellen** *vt* (*Tel*) to put through; **durchstöbern** [-'ʃtø:bərn] *vt untr* to ransack, search through; **durchstoßen** *unreg vt, vi* to break through (*auch Mil*); **durchstreichen** *unreg vt* to cross out; **durchstylen** *vt* to ponce up (*umg*); **durchsuchen** *vt untr* to search; **Durchsuchung** *f* search; **Durchsuchungsbefehl** *m* search warrant; **durchtrainieren** *vt* (*Sportler, Körper*): **gut durchtrainiert** in superb condition; **durchtränken** *vt untr* to soak; **durchtreten** *unreg vt* (*Pedal*) to step on; (*Starter*) to kick; **durchtrieben** *adj* cunning, wily; **durchwachsen** *adj* (*lit: Speck*) streaky; (*fig: mittelmäßig*) so-so
Durchwahl ['dʊrçva:l] *f* (*Tel*) direct dialling; (*bei Firma*) extension
durch- *zW*: **durchweg** *adv* throughout, completely; **durchwursteln** (*umg*) *vr* to muddle through; **durchzählen** *vt* to count ▷ *vi* to count *od* number off; **durchzechen** *vt untr*: **eine durchzechte Nacht** a night of drinking; **durchziehen** *unreg vt* (*Faden*) to draw through ▷ *vi* to pass through; **eine Sache durchziehen** to finish off sth; **durchzucken** *vt untr* to shoot *od* flash through; **Durchzug** *m* (*Luft*) draught (*Brit*), draft (*US*); (*von Truppen, Vögeln*) passage; **durchzwängen** *vt, vr* to squeeze *od* force through

SCHLÜSSELWORT

dürfen ['dʏrfən] *unreg vi* **1** (*Erlaubnis haben*) to be allowed to; **ich darf das** I'm allowed to (do that); **darf ich?** may I?; **darf ich ins Kino?** can *od* may I go to the cinema?; **es darf geraucht werden** you may smoke
2 (*in Verneinungen*): **er darf das nicht** he's not allowed to (do that); **das darf nicht geschehen** that must not happen; **da darf sie sich nicht wundern** that shouldn't surprise her; **das darf doch nicht wahr sein!** that can't be true!
3 (*in Höflichkeitsformeln*): **darf ich Sie bitten, das zu tun?** may *od* could I ask you to do that?; **wir freuen uns, Ihnen mitteilen zu dürfen** we are pleased to be able to tell you; **was darf es sein?** what can I get for you?
4 (*können*): **das dürfen Sie mir glauben** you can believe me
5 (*Möglichkeit*): **das dürfte genug sein** that should be enough; **es dürfte Ihnen bekannte sein, dass ...** as you will probably know ...

durfte *etc* ['dʊrftə] *vb siehe* **dürfen**
dürftig ['dʏrftɪç] *adj* (*ärmlich*) needy, poor; (*unzulänglich*) inadequate
dürr [dʏr] *adj* dried-up; (*Land*) arid; (*mager*) skinny
Dürre **(-, -n)** *f* aridity; (*Zeit*) drought
Durst [dʊrst] **(-(e)s)** *m* thirst; **~ haben** to be thirsty; **einen über den ~ getrunken haben** (*umg*) to have had one too many
durstig *adj* thirsty
Durststrecke *f* hard times *pl*
Dusche ['dʊʃə] **(-, -n)** *f* shower; **das war eine kalte ~** (*fig*) that really brought him/her *etc* down with a bump
duschen *vi, vr* to have a shower
Duschgelegenheit *f* shower facilities *pl*
Düse ['dy:zə] **(-, -n)** *f* nozzle; (*Flugzeugdüse*) jet
Dusel ['du:zəl] (*umg*) *m*: **da hat er (einen) ~ gehabt** he was lucky
Düsen- *zW*: **Düsenantrieb** *m* jet propulsion; **Düsenflugzeug** *nt* jet (plane); **Düsenjäger** *m* jet fighter
Dussel ['dʊsəl] **(-s, -)** (*umg*) *m* twit, berk
Düsseldorf ['dʏsəldɔrf] *nt* Dusseldorf
dusselig ['dʊsəlɪç], **dusslig** ['dʊslɪç] (*umg*) *adj* stupid

düster ['dy:stər] *adj* dark; (*Gedanken, Zukunft*) gloomy; **Düsterkeit** *f* darkness, gloom; gloominess

Dutzend ['dʊtsənt] (**-s, -e**) *nt* dozen; **~(e) Mal** a dozen times; **Dutzendware** (*pej*) *f* (cheap) mass-produced item; **dutzendweise** *adv* by the dozen

duzen ['du:tsən] *vt* to address with the familiar "du" form ▷ *vr* to address each other with the familiar "du" form; *siehe auch* **siezen**; *see culture note*

DUZEN/SIEZEN

There are two different forms of address in German: du and Sie. *Duzen* means addressing someone as "du" and *siezen* means addressing someone as "Sie". "Du" is used to address children, family and close friends. Students almost always use "du" to each other. "Sie" is used for all grown-ups and older teenagers.

Duzfreund *m* good friend

DVD (**-, -s**) *f abk* (= *Digital Versatile Disc*) DVD

Dynamik [dy'na:mɪk] *f* (*Phys*) dynamics; (*fig: Schwung*) momentum; (*von Mensch*) dynamism

dynamisch [dy'na:mɪʃ] *adj* (*lit, fig*) dynamic; (*rentendynamisch*) index-linked

Dynamit [dyna'mi:t] (**-s**) *nt* dynamite

Dynamo [dy'na:mo] (**-s, -s**) *m* dynamo

dz *abk* = **Doppelzentner**

D-Zug ['de:tsu:k] *m* through train; **ein alter Mann ist doch kein ~** (*umg*) I am going as fast as I can

Ee

E[1], **e** [eː] *nt* E, e; **E wie Emil** ≈ E for Edward, E for Easy (*US*)

E[2] [eː] *abk* = **Eilzug; Europastraße**

Ebbe ['ɛbə] (**-, -n**) *f* low tide; **~ und Flut** ebb and flow

eben ['eːbən] *adj* level; (*glatt*) smooth ▷ *adv* just; (*bestätigend*) exactly; **das ist ~ so** that's just the way it is; **mein Bleistift war doch ~ noch da** my pencil was there (just) a minute ago; **~ deswegen** just because of that

Ebenbild *nt*: **das genaue ~ seines Vaters** the spitting image of his father

ebenbürtig *adj*: **jdm ~ sein** to be sb's peer

Ebene (**-, -n**) *f* plain; (*Math, Phys*) plane; (*fig*) level

eben- *zW*: **ebenerdig** *adj* at ground level; **ebenfalls** *adv* likewise; **Ebenheit** *f* levelness; (*Glätte*) smoothness; **Ebenholz** *nt* ebony; **ebenso** *adv* just as; **ebenso gut** just as well; **ebenso oft** just as often; **ebenso viel** just as much; **ebenso weit** just as far; **ebenso wenig** just as little

Eber ['eːbər] (**-s, -**) *m* boar

Eberesche *f* mountain ash, rowan

ebnen ['eːbnən] *vt* to level; **jdm den Weg ~** (*fig*) to smooth the way for sb

Echo ['ɛço] (**-s, -s**) *nt* echo; **(bei jdm) ein lebhaftes ~ finden** (*fig*) to meet with a lively response (from sb)

Echolot ['ɛçoloːt] *nt* (*Naut*) echo-sounder, sonar

Echse ['ɛksə] (**-, -n**) *f* (*Zool*) lizard

echt [ɛçt] *adj* genuine; (*typisch*) typical; **ich hab ~ keine Zeit** (*umg*) I really don't have any time; **Echtheit** *f* genuineness

Eckball ['ɛkbal] *m* corner (kick)

Ecke ['ɛkə] (**-, -n**) *f* corner; (*Math*) angle; **gleich um die ~** just around the corner; **an allen ~n und Enden sparen** (*umg*) to pinch and scrape; **jdn um die ~ bringen** (*umg*) to bump sb off; **mit jdm um ein paar ~n herum verwandt sein** (*umg*) to be distantly related to sb, be sb's second cousin twice removed (*hum*)

eckig *adj* angular

Eckzahn *m* eye tooth

Eckzins *m* (*Fin*) minimum lending rate

Ecstasy ['ɛkstəsɪ] *nt* (*Droge*) ecstasy

Ecuador [ekua'doːr] (**-s**) *nt* Ecuador

edel ['eːdəl] *adj* noble; **Edelganove** *m* gentleman criminal; **Edelgas** *nt* rare gas; **Edelmetall** *nt* rare metal; **Edelstein** *m* precious stone

Edinburg, Edinburgh ['eːdɪnbʊrk] *nt* Edinburgh

EDV (**-**) *f abk* (= *elektronische Datenverarbeitung*) EDP

EEG (**-**) *nt abk* (= *Elektroenzephalogramm*) EEG

Efeu ['eːfɔʏ] (**-s**) *m* ivy

Effeff [ɛf'|ɛf] (**-**) (*umg*) *nt*: **etw aus dem ~ können** to be able to do sth standing on one's head

Effekt [ɛ'fɛkt] (**-(e)s, -e**) *m* effect

Effekten [ɛ'fɛktən] *pl* stocks *pl*; **Effektenbörse** *f* Stock Exchange

Effekthascherei [ɛfɛkthaʃə'raɪ] *f* sensationalism

effektiv [ɛfɛk'tiːf] *adj* effective, actual

Effet [ɛ'feː] (**-s**) *m* spin

EG (**-**) *f abk* (= *Europäische Gemeinschaft*) EC

egal [e'gaːl] *adj* all the same; **das ist mir ganz ~** it's all the same to me

egalitär [egali'tɛːr] *adj* (*geh*) egalitarian

Egge ['ɛgə] (**-, -n**) *f* (*Agr*) harrow

Egoismus [ego'ɪsmʊs] *m* selfishness, egoism

Egoist, in *m(f)* egoist; **egoistisch** *adj* selfish, egoistic

egozentrisch [ego'tsɛntrɪʃ] *adj* egocentric, self-centred (*Brit*), self-centered (*US*)

eh [eː] *adv*: **seit eh und je** for ages, since the year dot (*umg*); **ich komme eh nicht dazu** I won't get around to it anyway

e. h. *abk* = **ehrenhalber**

Ehe ['eːə] (**-, -n**) *f* marriage; **die ~ eingehen** (*form*) to enter into matrimony; **sie leben in wilder ~** (*veraltet*) they are living in sin

ehe *konj* before

Ehe- *zW*: **Ehebrecher** (**-s, -**) *m* adulterer; **Ehebrecherin** *f* adulteress; **Ehebruch** *m* adultery; **Ehefrau** *f* wife; **Eheleute** *pl* married couple *pl*; **ehelich** *adj* matrimonial; (*Kind*) legitimate

ehemalig *adj* former

ehemals *adv* formerly

Ehe- *zW*: **Ehemann** *m* married man; (*Partner*) husband; **Ehepaar** *nt* married couple; **Ehepartner** *m* husband; **Ehepartnerin** *f* wife

eher ['eːər] *adv* (*früher*) sooner; (*lieber*) rather, sooner; (*mehr*) more; **nicht ~ als** not before;

umso ~, als the more so because

Ehe- *zW*: **Ehering** *m* wedding ring; **Ehescheidung** *f* divorce; **Eheschließung** *f* marriage; **Ehestand** *m*: **in den Ehestand treten** *(form)* to enter into matrimony

eheste, r, s ['e:əstə(r, s)] *adj (früheste)* first, earliest; **am ~n** *(am liebsten)* soonest; *(meist)* most; *(am wahrscheinlichsten)* most probably

Ehevermittlung *f (Büro)* marriage bureau

Eheversprechen *nt (Jur)* promise to marry

ehrbar ['e:rba:r] *adj* honourable *(Brit)*, honorable *(US)*, respectable

Ehre **(-, -n)** *f* honour *(Brit)*, honor *(US)*; **etw in ~n halten** to treasure *od* cherish sth

ehren *vt* to honour *(Brit)*, honor *(US)*

Ehren- *zW*: **ehrenamtlich** *adj* honorary; **Ehrenbürgerrecht** *nt*: **die Stadt verlieh ihr das Ehrenbürgerrecht** she was given the freedom of the city; **Ehrengast** *m* guest of honour *(Brit) od* honor *(US)*; **ehrenhaft** *adj* honourable *(Brit)*, honorable *(US)*; **ehrenhalber** *adv*: **er wurde ehrenhalber zum Vorsitzenden auf Lebenszeit ernannt** he was made honorary president for life; **Ehrenmann** *m* man of honour *(Brit) od* honor *(US)*; **Ehrenmitglied** *nt* honorary member; **Ehrenplatz** *m* place of honour *(Brit) od* honor *(US)*; **Ehrenrechte** *pl* civic rights *pl*; **ehrenrührig** *adj* defamatory; **Ehrenrunde** *f* lap of honour *(Brit) od* honor *(US)*; **Ehrensache** *f* point of honour *(Brit) od* honor *(US)*; **Ehrensache!** *(umg)* you can count on me; **Ehrentag** *m (Geburtstag)* birthday; *(großer Tag)* big day; **ehrenvoll** *adj* honourable *(Brit)*, honorable *(US)*; **Ehrenwort** *nt* word of honour *(Brit) od* honor *(US)*; **Urlaub auf Ehrenwort** parole

Ehr- *zW*: **ehrerbietig** *adj* respectful; **Ehrfurcht** *f* awe, deep respect; **Ehrfurcht gebietend** awesome; *(Stimme)* authoritative; **Ehrgefühl** *nt* sense of honour *(Brit) od* honor *(US)*; **Ehrgeiz** *m* ambition; **ehrgeizig** *adj* ambitious; **ehrlich** *adj* honest; **ehrlich verdientes Geld** hard-earned money; **ehrlich gesagt ...** quite frankly *od* honestly ...; **Ehrlichkeit** *f* honesty; **ehrlos** *adj* dishonourable *(Brit)*, dishonorable *(US)*

Ehrung *f* honour(ing) *(Brit)*, honor(ing) *(US)*

ehrwürdig *adj* venerable

Ei [aɪ] **(-(e)s, -er)** *nt* egg; **Eier** *pl (umg!: Hoden)* balls *pl (!)*; **jdn wie ein rohes Ei behandeln** *(fig)* to handle sb with kid gloves; **wie aus dem Ei gepellt aussehen** *(umg)* to look spruce

ei *interj* well, well; *(beschwichtigend)* now, now

Eibe ['aɪbə] **(-, -n)** *f (Bot)* yew

Eichamt ['aɪç|amt] *nt* Office of Weights and Measures

Eiche **(-, -n)** *f* oak (tree)

Eichel **(-, -n)** *f* acorn; *(Karten)* club; *(Anat)* glans

eichen *vt* to calibrate

Eichhörnchen *nt* squirrel

Eichmaß *nt* standard

Eichung *f* standardization

Eid ['aɪt] **(-(e)s, -e)** *m* oath; **eine Erklärung an ~es statt abgeben** *(Jur)* to make a solemn declaration

Eidechse ['aɪdɛksə] **(-, -n)** *f* lizard

eidesstattlich *adj*: **~e Erklärung** affidavit

Eid- *zW*: **Eidgenosse** *m* Swiss; **Eidgenossenschaft** *f*: **Schweizerische Eidgenossenschaft** Swiss Confederation; **eidlich** *adj* (sworn) upon oath

Eidotter *nt* egg yolk

Eier- *zW*: **Eierbecher** *m* egg cup; **Eierkuchen** *m* pancake; *(Omelett)* omelette *(Brit)*, omelet *(US)*; **Eierlikör** *m* advocaat

eiern ['aɪərn] *(umg) vi* to wobble

Eier- *zW*: **Eierschale** *f* eggshell; **Eierstock** *m* ovary; **Eieruhr** *f* egg timer

Eifel ['aɪfəl] **(-)** *f* Eifel (Mountains)

Eifer ['aɪfər] **(-s)** *m* zeal, enthusiasm; **mit großem ~ bei der Sache sein** to put one's heart into it; **im ~ des Gefechts** *(fig)* in the heat of the moment; **Eifersucht** *f* jealousy; **eifersüchtig** *adj*: **eifersüchtig (auf** *+akk***)** jealous (of)

eifrig ['aɪfrɪç] *adj* zealous, enthusiastic

Eigelb ['aɪgɛlp] **(-(e)s, -e** *od* **-)** *nt* egg yolk

eigen ['aɪgən] *adj* own; *(eigenartig)* peculiar; *(ordentlich)* particular; *(übergenau)* fussy; **ich möchte kurz in ~er Sache sprechen** I would like to say something on my own account; **mit dem ihm ~en Lächeln** with that smile peculiar to him; **sich** *dat* **etw zu ~ machen** to make sth one's own; **Eigenart** *f (Besonderheit)* peculiarity; *(Eigenschaft)* characteristic; **eigenartig** *adj* peculiar; **Eigenbau** *m*: **er fährt ein Fahrrad Marke Eigenbau** *(hum: umg)* he rides a home-made bike; **Eigenbedarf** *m* one's own requirements *pl*; **Eigenbrötler, in** **(-s, -)** *m(f)* loner, lone wolf; *(komischer Kauz)* oddball *(umg)*; **Eigengewicht** *nt* dead weight; **eigenhändig** *adj* with one's own hand; **Eigenheim** *nt* owner-occupied house; **Eigenheit** *f* peculiarity; **Eigeninitiative** *f* initiative of one's own; **Eigenkapital** *nt* personal capital; *(von Firma)* company capital; **Eigenlob** *nt* self-praise; **eigenmächtig** *adj* high-handed; *(eigenverantwortlich)* taken/done *etc* on one's own authority; *(unbefugt)* unauthorized; **Eigenname** *m* proper name; **Eigennutz** *m* self-interest

eigens *adv* expressly, on purpose

eigen- *zW*: **Eigenschaft** *f* quality, property, attribute; **Eigenschaftswort** *nt* adjective; **Eigensinn** *m* obstinacy; **eigensinnig** *adj* obstinate; **eigenständig** *adj* independent; **Eigenständigkeit** *f* independence

eigentlich *adj* actual, real ▷ *adv* actually, really; **was willst du ~ hier?** what do you want here anyway?

eigen- *zW*: **Eigentor** *nt* own goal; **Eigentum** *nt* property; **Eigentümer, in** **(-s, -)** *m(f)* owner, proprietor; **eigentümlich** *adj* peculiar; **Eigentümlichkeit** *f* peculiarity

Eigentumsdelikt *nt (Jur: Diebstahl)* theft

Eigentumswohnung *f* freehold flat
Eigenvorsorge *f* private provision (*for retirement etc*)
eigenwillig *adj* with a mind of one's own
eignen ['aɪgnən] *vr* to be suited
Eignung *f* suitability
Eignungsprüfung *f* aptitude test
Eignungstest (**-(e)s, -s** *od* **-e**) *m* aptitude test
Eilbote *m* courier; **per** *od* **durch ~n** express
Eilbrief *m* express letter
Eile (-) *f* haste; **es hat keine ~** there's no hurry
Eileiter ['aɪlaɪtər] *m* (*Anat*) Fallopian tube
eilen *vi* (*Mensch*) to hurry; (*dringend sein*) to be urgent
eilends *adv* hastily
Eilgut *nt* express goods *pl*, fast freight (US)
eilig *adj* hasty, hurried; (*dringlich*) urgent; **es ~ haben** to be in a hurry
Eil- *zW*: **Eiltempo** *nt*: **etw im Eiltempo machen** to do sth in a rush; **Eilzug** *m* fast stopping train; **Eilzustellung** *f* special delivery
Eimer ['aɪmər] (**-s, -**) *m* bucket, pail; **im ~ sein** (*umg*) to be up the spout
ein, e ['aɪn(ə)] *num* one ▷ *indef art* a, an ▷ *adv*: **nicht ~ noch aus wissen** not to know what to do; **E~/Aus** (*an Geräten*) on/off; **er ist ihr E~ und Alles** he means everything to her; **er geht bei uns ~ und aus** he is always round at our place
einander [aɪ'nandər] *pron* one another, each other
einarbeiten ['aɪn|arbaɪtən] *vr*: **sich (in etw** *akk***) ~** to familiarize o.s. (with sth)
Einarbeitungszeit *f* training period
einarmig ['aɪn|armɪç] *adj* one-armed
einäschern ['aɪn|ɛʃərn] *vt* (*Leichnam*) to cremate; (*Stadt etc*) to reduce to ashes
einatmen ['aɪn|a:tmən] *vt, vi* to inhale, breathe in
einäugig ['aɪn|ɔʏgɪç] *adj* one-eyed
Einbahnstraße ['aɪnba:nʃtrasə] *f* one-way street
Einband ['aɪnbant] *m* binding, cover
einbändig ['aɪnbɛndɪç] *adj* one-volume
einbauen ['aɪnbaʊən] *vt* to build in; (*Motor*) to install, fit
Einbau- *zW*: **Einbauküche** *f* (fully-)fitted kitchen; **Einbaumöbel** *pl* built-in furniture *sing*; **Einbauschrank** *m* fitted cupboard
einbegriffen ['aɪnbəgrɪfən] *adj* included, inclusive
einbehalten ['aɪnbəhaltən] *unreg vt* to keep back
einberufen *unreg vt* to convene; (*Mil*) to call up (*Brit*), draft (US)
Einberufung *f* convocation; call-up (*Brit*), draft (US)
Einberufungsbefehl *m*, **Einberufungsbescheid** *m* (*Mil*) call-up (*Brit*) *od* draft (US) papers *pl*
einbetten ['aɪnbɛtən] *vt* to embed
Einbettzimmer *nt* single room
einbeziehen ['aɪnbətsi:ən] *unreg vt* to include
einbiegen ['aɪnbi:gən] *unreg vi* to turn
einbilden ['aɪnbɪldən] *vr*: **sich** *dat* **etw ~** to imagine sth; **sich** *dat* **viel auf etw** *akk* **~**: *stolz sein*) to be conceited about sth
Einbildung *f* imagination; (*Dünkel*) conceit
Einbildungskraft *f* imagination
einbinden ['aɪnbɪndən] *unreg vt* to bind (up)
einbläuen ['aɪnblɔʏən] (*umg*) *vt*: **jdm etw ~** to hammer sth into sb
einblenden ['aɪnblɛndən] *vt* to fade in
Einblick ['aɪnblɪk] *m* insight; **~ in die Akten nehmen** to examine the files; **jdm ~ in etw** *akk* **gewähren** to allow sb to look at sth
einbrechen ['aɪnbrɛçən] *unreg vi* (*einstürzen*) to fall in; (*Einbruch verüben*) to break in; **bei ~der Dunkelheit** at nightfall
Einbrecher (**-s, -**) *m* burglar
einbringen ['aɪnbrɪŋən] *unreg vt* to bring in; (*Geld, Vorteil*) to yield; (*mitbringen*) to contribute; **das bringt nichts ein** (*fig*) it's not worth it
einbrocken ['aɪnbrɔkən] (*umg*) *vt*: **jdm/sich etwas ~** to land sb/o.s. in it
Einbruch ['aɪnbrʊx] *m* (*Hauseinbruch*) break-in, burglary; (*des Winters*) onset; (*Einsturz, Fin*) collapse; (*Mil*: *in Front*) breakthrough; **bei ~ der Nacht** at nightfall
einbruchssicher *adj* burglar-proof
Einbuchtung ['aɪnbʊxtʊŋ] *f* indentation; (*Bucht*) inlet, bay
einbürgern ['aɪnbʏrgərn] *vt* to naturalize ▷ *vr* to become adopted; **das hat sich so eingebürgert** that's become a custom
Einbürgerung *f* naturalization
Einbuße ['aɪnbu:sə] *f* loss, forfeiture
einbüßen ['aɪnby:sən] *vt* to lose, forfeit
einchecken ['aɪntʃɛkən] *vt, vi* to check in
eincremen ['aɪnkre:mən] *vt* to put cream on
eindämmen ['aɪndɛmən] *vt* (*Fluss*) to dam; (*fig*) to check, contain
eindecken ['aɪndɛkən] *vr*: **sich ~ (mit)** to lay in stocks (of) ▷ *vt* (*umg*: *überhäufen*): **mit Arbeit eingedeckt sein** to be inundated with work
eindeutig ['aɪndɔʏtɪç] *adj* unequivocal
eindeutschen ['aɪndɔʏtʃən] *vt* (*Fremdwort*) to Germanize
eindösen ['aɪndø:zən] (*umg*) *vi* to doze off
eindringen ['aɪndrɪŋən] *unreg vi*: **~ (in** *+akk***)** to force one's way in(to); (*in Haus*) to break in(to); (*in Land*) to invade; (*Gas, Wasser*) to penetrate; **auf jdn ~** (*mit Bitten*) to pester sb
eindringlich *adj* forcible, urgent; **ich habe ihn ~ gebeten ...** I urged him ...
Eindringling *m* intruder
Eindruck ['aɪndrʊk] *m* impression
eindrücken ['aɪndrʏkən] *vt* to press in
eindrucksfähig *adj* impressionable
eindrucksvoll *adj* impressive
eine, r, s *pron* one; (*jemand*) someone; **wie kann ~r nur so dumm sein!** how could anybody be so stupid!; **es kam ~s zum anderen** it was (just) one thing after another; **sich** *dat* **~n genehmigen** (*umg*) to have a quick one
einebnen ['aɪn|e:bnən] *vt* (*lit*) to level (off); (*fig*)

to level out
Einehe ['aɪn|eːə] *f* monogamy
eineiig ['aɪn|aɪɪç] *adj* (*Zwillinge*) identical
eineinhalb ['aɪn|aɪn'halp] *num* one and a half
einengen ['aɪn|ɛŋən] *vt* to confine, restrict
Einer ['aɪnər] (-) *m* (*Math*) unit; (*Ruderboot*) single scull
Einerlei ['aɪnər'laɪ] (**-s**) *nt* monotony; **einerlei** *adj* (*gleichartig*) the same kind of; **es ist mir einerlei** it is all the same to me
einerseits *adv* on the one hand
einfach ['aɪnfax] *adj* simple; (*nicht mehrfach*) single ▷ *adv* simply; **Einfachheit** *f* simplicity
einfädeln ['aɪnfɛːdəln] *vt* (*Nadel*) to thread; (*fig*) to contrive
einfahren ['aɪnfaːrən] *unreg vt* to bring in; (*Barriere*) to knock down; (*Auto*) to run in ▷ *vi* to drive in; (*Zug*) to pull in; (*Min*) to go down
Einfahrt *f* (*Vorgang*) driving in; pulling in; (*Min*) descent; (*Ort*) entrance; (*von Autobahn*) slip road (*Brit*), entrance ramp (*US*)
Einfall ['aɪnfal] *m* (*Idee*) idea, notion; (*Lichteinfall*) incidence; (*Mil*) raid
einfallen *unreg vi* (*einstürzen*) to fall in, collapse; (*Licht*) to fall; (*Mil*) to raid; (*einstimmen*): ~ **(in** *+akk***)** to join in (with); **etw fällt jdm ein** sth occurs to sb; **das fällt mir gar nicht ein!** I wouldn't dream of it; **sich** *dat* **etwas ~ lassen** to have a good idea; **dabei fällt mir mein Onkel ein, der ...** that reminds me of my uncle who ...; **es fällt mir jetzt nicht ein** I can't think of it *od* it won't come to me at the moment
einfallslos *adj* unimaginative
einfallsreich *adj* imaginative
einfältig ['aɪnfɛltɪç] *adj* simple(-minded)
Einfaltspinsel ['aɪnfaltspɪnzəl] (*umg*) *m* simpleton
Einfamilienhaus [aɪnfa'miːliənhaʊs] *nt* detached house
einfangen ['aɪnfaŋən] *unreg vt* to catch
einfarbig ['aɪnfarbɪç] *adj* all one colour (*Brit*) *od* color (*US*); (*Stoff etc*) self-coloured (*Brit*), self-colored (*US*)
einfassen ['aɪnfasən] *vt* (*Edelstein*) to set; (*Beet, Stoff*) to edge
Einfassung *f* setting; border
einfetten ['aɪnfɛtən] *vt* to grease
einfinden ['aɪnfɪndən] *unreg vr* to come, turn up
einfliegen ['aɪnfliːgən] *unreg vt* to fly in
einfließen ['aɪnfliːsən] *unreg vi* to flow in
einflößen ['aɪnfløːsən] *vt*: **jdm etw ~** (*lit*) to give sb sth; (*fig*) to instil sth into sb
Einfluss ['aɪnflʊs] *m* influence; **~ nehmen** to bring an influence to bear; **Einflussbereich** *m* sphere of influence; **einflussreich** *adj* influential
einflüstern ['aɪnflʏstərn] *vt*: **jdm etw ~** to whisper sth to sb; (*fig*) to insinuate sth to sb
einförmig ['aɪnfœrmɪç] *adj* uniform; (*eintönig*) monotonous; **Einförmigkeit** *f* uniformity; monotony
einfrieren ['aɪnfriːrən] *unreg vi* to freeze (in) ▷ *vt* to freeze; (*Pol: Beziehungen*) to suspend
einfügen ['aɪnfyːgən] *vt* to fit in; (*zusätzlich*) to add; (*Comput*) to insert
einfühlen ['aɪnfyːlən] *vr*: **sich in jdn ~** to empathize with sb
einfühlsam ['aɪnfyːlzaːm] *adj* sensitive
Einfühlungsvermögen *nt* empathy; **mit großem ~** with a great deal of sensitivity
Einfuhr ['aɪnfuːr] (-) *f* import; **Einfuhrartikel** *m* imported article
einführen ['aɪnfyːrən] *vt* to bring in; (*Mensch, Sitten*) to introduce; (*Ware*) to import; **jdn in sein Amt ~** to install sb (in office)
Einfuhr- *zW*: **Einfuhrgenehmigung** *f* import permit; **Einfuhrkontingent** *nt* import quota; **Einfuhrsperre** *f* ban on imports; **Einfuhrstopp** *m* ban on imports
Einführung *f* introduction
Einführungspreis *m* introductory price
Einfuhrzoll *m* import duty
einfüllen ['aɪnfʏlən] *vt* to pour in
Eingabe ['aɪngaːbə] *f* petition; (*Dateneingabe*) input; **~/Ausgabe** (*Comput*) input/output
Eingang ['aɪngaŋ] *m* entrance; (*Comm: Ankunft*) arrival; (*Sendung*) post; **wir bestätigen den ~ Ihres Schreibens vom ...** we acknowledge receipt of your letter of the ...
eingängig ['aɪngɛŋɪç] *adj* catchy
eingangs *adv* at the outset ▷ *präp +gen* at the outset of
Eingangs- *zW*: **Eingangsbestätigung** *f* acknowledgement of receipt; **Eingangshalle** *f* entrance hall; **Eingangsstempel** *m* (*Comm*) receipt stamp
eingeben ['aɪngeːbən] *unreg vt* (*Arznei*) to give; (*Daten etc*) to enter; (*Gedanken*) to inspire
eingebettet ['aɪngəbɛtət] *adj*: **in** *od* **zwischen Hügeln ~** nestling among the hills
eingebildet ['aɪngəbɪldət] *adj* imaginary; (*eitel*) conceited; **~er Kranker** hypochondriac
Eingeborene, r ['aɪngəboːrənə(r)] *f(m)* native
Eingebung *f* inspiration
eingedenk ['aɪngədɛŋk] *präp +gen* bearing in mind
eingefahren ['aɪngəfaːrən] *adj* (*Verhaltensweise*) well-worn
eingefallen ['aɪngəfalən] *adj* (*Gesicht*) gaunt
eingefleischt ['aɪngəflaɪʃt] *adj* inveterate; **~er Junggeselle** confirmed bachelor
eingefroren ['aɪngəfroːrən] *adj* frozen
eingehen ['aɪngeːən] *unreg vi* (*Aufnahme finden*) to come in; (*Sendung, Geld*) to be received; (*Tier, Pflanze*) to die; (*Firma*) to fold; (*schrumpfen*) to shrink ▷ *vt* (*abmachen*) to enter into; (*Wette*) to make; **auf etw** *akk* **~** to go into sth; **auf jdn ~** to respond to sb; **jdm ~** (*verständlich sein*) to be comprehensible to sb; **auf einen Vorschlag/Plan ~** (*zustimmen*) to go along with a suggestion/plan; **bei dieser Hitze/Kälte geht man ja ein!** (*umg*) this heat/cold is just too much!
eingehend *adj* in-depth, thorough
eingekeilt ['aɪngəkaɪlt] *adj* hemmed in; (*fig*)

trapped
eingekesselt ['aɪngəkɛsəlt] *adj*: **~ sein** to be encircled *od* surrounded
Eingemachte, s ['aɪngəma:xtə(s)] *nt* preserves *pl*
eingemeinden ['aɪngəmaɪndən] *vt* to incorporate
eingenommen ['aɪngənɔmən] *adj*: **~ (von)** fond (of), partial (to); **~ (gegen)** prejudiced (against)
eingeschnappt ['aɪngəʃnapt] (*umg*) *adj* cross; **~ sein** to be in a huff
eingeschrieben ['aɪngəʃri:bən] *adj* registered
eingeschworen ['aɪngəʃvo:rən] *adj* confirmed; (*Gemeinschaft*) close
eingesessen ['aɪngəzɛsən] *adj* old-established
eingespannt ['aɪngəʃpant] *adj* busy
eingespielt ['aɪngəʃpi:lt] *adj*: **aufeinander ~ sein** to be in tune with each other
Eingeständnis ['aɪngəʃtɛntnɪs] *nt* admission, confession
eingestehen ['aɪngəʃte:ən] *unreg vt* to confess
eingestellt ['aɪngəʃtɛlt] *adj*: **ich bin im Moment nicht auf Besuch ~** I'm not prepared for visitors
eingetragen ['aɪngətra:gən] *adj* (*Comm*) registered; **~er Gesellschaftssitz** registered office; **~es Warenzeichen** registered trademark
Eingeweide ['aɪngəvaɪdə] **(-s, -)** *nt* innards *pl*, intestines *pl*
Eingeweihte, r ['aɪngəvaɪtə(r)] *f(m)* initiate
eingewöhnen ['aɪngəvø:nən] *vr*: **sich ~ (in** *+dat***)** to settle down (in)
eingezahlt ['aɪngətsa:lt] *adj*: **~es Kapital** paid-up capital
eingießen ['aɪngi:sən] *unreg vt* to pour (out)
eingleisig ['aɪnglaɪzɪç] *adj* single-track; **er denkt sehr ~** (*fig*) he's completely single-minded
eingliedern ['aɪngli:dərn] *vt*: **~ (in** *+akk***)** to integrate (into) ▷ *vr*: **sich ~ (in** *+akk***)** to integrate o.s. (into)
eingraben ['aɪngra:bən] *unreg vt* to dig in ▷ *vr* to dig o.s. in; **dieses Erlebnis hat sich seinem Gedächtnis eingegraben** this experience has engraved itself on his memory
eingreifen ['aɪngraɪfən] *unreg vi* to intervene, interfere; (*Zahnrad*) to mesh
Eingreiftruppe *f* (*Mil*) strike force
eingrenzen ['aɪngrɛntsən] *vt* to enclose; (*fig: Problem*) to delimit
Eingriff ['aɪngrɪf] *m* intervention, interference; (*Operation*) operation
einhaken ['aɪnha:kən] *vt* to hook in ▷ *vr*: **sich bei jdm ~** to link arms with sb ▷ *vi* (*sich einmischen*) to intervene
Einhalt ['aɪnhalt] *m*: **~ gebieten** *+dat* to put a stop to
einhalten *unreg vt* (*Regel*) to keep ▷ *vi* to stop
einhämmern ['aɪnhɛmərn] *vt*: **jdm etw ~** (*fig*) to hammer sth into sb
einhandeln ['aɪnhandəln] *vt*: **etw gegen** *od* **für etw ~** to trade sth for sth
einhändig ['aɪnhɛndɪç] *adj* one-handed
einhändigen ['aɪnhɛndɪgən] *vt* to hand in
einhängen ['aɪnhɛŋən] *vt* to hang; (*Telefon: auch vi*) to hang up; **sich bei jdm ~** to link arms with sb
einheimisch ['aɪnhaɪmɪʃ] *adj* native
Einheimische, r *f(m)* local
einheimsen (*umg*) *vt* to bring home
einheiraten ['aɪnhaɪra:tən] *vi*: **in einen Betrieb ~** to marry into a business
Einheit ['aɪnhaɪt] *f* unity; (*Maß, Mil*) unit; **eine geschlossene ~ bilden** to form an integrated whole; **einheitlich** *adj* uniform
Einheits- *zW*: **Einheitsfront** *f* (*Pol*) united front; **Einheitsliste** *f* (*Pol*) single *od* unified list of candidates; **Einheitspreis** *m* uniform price
einheizen ['aɪnhaɪtsən] *vi*: **jdm (tüchtig) ~** (*umg: die Meinung sagen*) to make things hot for sb
einhellig ['aɪnhɛlɪç] *adj* unanimous ▷ *adv* unanimously
einholen ['aɪnho:lən] *vt* (*Tau*) to haul in; (*Fahne, Segel*) to lower; (*Vorsprung aufholen*) to catch up with; (*Verspätung*) to make up; (*Rat, Erlaubnis*) to ask ▷ *vi* (*einkaufen*) to buy, shop
Einhorn ['aɪnhɔrn] *nt* unicorn
einhüllen ['aɪnhʏlən] *vt* to wrap up
einhundert ['aɪn'hʊndərt] *num* one hundred
einig ['aɪnɪç] *adj* (*vereint*) united; **sich** *dat* **~ sein** to be in agreement; **~ werden** to agree
einige, r, s *adj, pron* some ▷ *pl* some; (*mehrere*) several; **mit Ausnahme ~r weniger** with a few exceptions; **vor ~n Tagen** the other day, a few days ago; **dazu ist noch ~s zu sagen** there are still one or two things to say about that; **~ Mal** a few times
einigen *vt* to unite ▷ *vr*: **sich (auf etw** *akk***) ~** to agree (on sth)
einigermaßen *adv* somewhat; (*leidlich*) reasonably
einiges *pron siehe* **einige(r, s)**
einiggehen *unreg vi* to agree
Einigkeit *f* unity; (*Übereinstimmung*) agreement
Einigung *f* agreement; (*Vereinigung*) unification
einimpfen ['aɪn|ɪmpfən] *vt*: **jdm etw ~** to inoculate sb with sth; (*fig*) to impress sth upon sb
einjagen ['aɪnja:gən] *vt*: **jdm Furcht/einen Schrecken ~** to give sb a fright
einjährig ['aɪnjɛ:rɪç] *adj* of *od* for one year; (*Alter*) one-year-old; (*Pflanze*) annual
einkalkulieren ['aɪnkalkuli:rən] *vt* to take into account, allow for
einkassieren ['aɪnkasi:rən] *vt* (*Geld, Schulden*) to collect
Einkauf ['aɪnkaʊf] *m* purchase; (*Comm: Abteilung*) purchasing (department)
einkaufen *vt* to buy ▷ *vi* to shop; **~ gehen** to go shopping
Einkäufer, in ['aɪnkɔʏfər(ɪn)] *m(f)* (*Comm*) buyer
Einkaufs- *zW*: **Einkaufsbummel** *m*: **einen**

Einkaufsbummel machen to go on a shopping spree; **Einkaufskorb** *m* shopping basket; **Einkaufsleiter, in** *m(f)* (*Comm*) chief buyer; **Einkaufsnetz** *nt* string bag; **Einkaufspreis** *m* cost price, wholesale price; **Einkaufswagen** *m* trolley (*Brit*), cart (*US*); **Einkaufszentrum** *nt* shopping centre

einkehren ['aɪnke:rən] *vi* (*geh: Ruhe, Frühling*) to come; **in einem Gasthof ~** to (make a) stop at an inn

einkerben ['aɪnkɛrbən] *vt* to notch

einklagen ['aɪnkla:gən] *vt* (*Schulden*) to sue for (the recovery of)

einklammern ['aɪnklamərn] *vt* to put in brackets, bracket

Einklang ['aɪnklaŋ] *m* harmony

einkleiden ['aɪnklaɪdən] *vt* to clothe; (*fig*) to express

einklemmen ['aɪnklɛmən] *vt* to jam

einknicken ['aɪnknɪkən] *vt* to bend in; (*Papier*) to fold ▷ *vi* (*Knie*) to give way

einkochen ['aɪnkɔxən] *vt* to boil down; (*Obst*) to preserve, bottle

Einkommen ['aɪnkɔmən] **(-s, -)** *nt* income

einkommensschwach *adj* low-income *attrib*

einkommensstark *adj* high-income *attrib*

Einkommenssteuer, **Einkommensteuer** *f* income tax; **Einkommenssteuererklärung, Einkommensteuererklärung** *f* income tax return

Einkommensverhältnisse *pl* (level of) income *sing*

einkreisen ['aɪnkraɪzən] *vt* to encircle

einkriegen ['aɪnkri:gən] (*umg*) *vr*: **sie konnte sich gar nicht mehr darüber ~, dass ...** she couldn't get over the fact that ...

Einkünfte ['aɪnkʏnftə] *pl* income *sing*, revenue *sing*

einladen ['aɪnla:dən] *unreg vt* (*Person*) to invite; (*Gegenstände*) to load; **jdn ins Kino ~** to take sb to the cinema

Einladung *f* invitation

Einlage ['aɪnla:gə] *f* (*Programmeinlage*) interlude; (*Spareinlage*) deposit; (*Fin: Kapitaleinlage*) investment; (*Schuheinlage*) insole; (*Fußstütze*) support; (*Zahneinlage*) temporary filling; (*Koch*) *noodles, vegetables etc (in clear soup)*

einlagern ['aɪnla:gərn] *vt* to store

Einlass ['aɪnlas] **(-es, ¨-e)** *m* admission; **jdm ~ gewähren** to admit sb

einlassen *unreg vt* to let in; (*einsetzen*) to set in ▷ *vr*: **sich mit jdm/auf etw** *akk* **~** to get involved with sb/sth; **sich auf einen Kompromiss ~** to agree to a compromise; **ich lasse mich auf keine Diskussion ein** I'm not having any discussion about it

Einlauf ['aɪnlaʊf] *m* arrival; (*von Pferden*) finish; (*Med*) enema

einlaufen *unreg vi* to arrive, come in; (*Sport*) to finish; (*Wasser*) to run in; (*Stoff*) to shrink ▷ *vt* (*Schuhe*) to break in ▷ *vr* (*Sport*) to warm up; (*Motor, Maschine*) to run in; **jdm das Haus ~** to invade sb's house; **in den Hafen ~** to enter the harbour

einläuten ['aɪnlɔʏtən] *vt* (*neues Jahr*) to ring in; (*Sport: Runde*) to sound the bell for

einleben ['aɪnle:bən] *vr* to settle down

Einlegearbeit *f* inlay

einlegen ['aɪnle:gən] *vt* (*einfügen: Blatt, Sohle*) to insert; (*Koch*) to pickle; (*in Holz etc*) to inlay; (*Geld*) to deposit; (*Pause*) to have; (*Protest*) to make; (*Veto*) to use; (*Berufung*) to lodge; **ein gutes Wort bei jdm ~** to put in a good word with sb

Einlegesohle *f* insole

einleiten ['aɪnlaɪtən] *vt* to introduce, start; (*Geburt*) to induce

Einleitung *f* introduction; induction

einlenken ['aɪnlɛŋkən] *vi* (*fig*) to yield, give way

einlesen ['aɪnle:zən] *unreg vr*: **sich in ein Gebiet ~** to get into a subject ▷ *vt*: **etw in etw** *+akk* **~** (*Daten*) to feed sth into sth

einleuchten ['aɪnlɔʏçtən] *vi*: **(jdm) ~** to be clear *od* evident (to sb)

einleuchtend *adj* clear

einliefern ['aɪnli:fərn] *vt*: **~ (in** *+akk***)** to take (into); **jdn ins Krankenhaus ~** to admit sb to hospital

Einlieferungsschein *m* certificate of posting

einlochen ['aɪnlɔxən] (*umg*) *vt* (*einsperren*) to lock up

einlösen ['aɪnlø:zən] *vt* (*Scheck*) to cash; (*Schuldschein, Pfand*) to redeem; (*Versprechen*) to keep

einmachen ['aɪnmaxən] *vt* to preserve

Einmachglas *nt* bottling jar

einmal ['aɪnma:l] *adv* once; (*erstens*) first of all, firstly; (*später*) one day; **nehmen wir ~ an** just let's suppose; **noch ~** once more; **nicht ~** not even; **auf ~** all at once; **es war ~** once upon a time there was/were; **~ ist keinmal** (*Sprichwort*) once doesn't count; **waren Sie schon ~ in Rom?** have you ever been to Rome?

Einmaleins *nt* multiplication tables *pl*; (*fig*) ABC, basics *pl*

einmalig *adj* unique; (*einmal geschehend*) single; (*prima*) fantastic

Einmalzahlung *f* one-off payment

Einmannbetrieb *m* one-man business

Einmannbus *m* one-man-operated bus

Einmarsch ['aɪnmarʃ] *m* entry; (*Mil*) invasion

einmarschieren *vi* to march in

einmengen ['aɪnmɛŋən] *vr*: **sich (in etw** *+akk***) ~** to interfere (with sth)

einmieten ['aɪnmi:tən] *vr*: **sich bei jdm ~** to take lodgings with sb

einmischen ['aɪnmɪʃən] *vr*: **sich (in etw** *+akk***) ~** to interfere (with sth)

einmotten ['aɪnmɔtən] *vt* (*Kleider etc*) to put in mothballs

einmünden ['aɪnmʏndən] *vi*: **~ in** *+akk* (*subj: Fluss*) to flow *od* run into, join; (*: Straße: in Platz*) to run into; (*: in andere Straße*) to run into, join

einmütig ['aɪnmy:tɪç] *adj* unanimous

einnähen ['aɪnnɛ:ən] *vt* (*enger machen*) to take in

Einnahme ['aɪnna:mə] (**-, -n**) *f* (*Geld*) takings *pl*, revenue; (*von Medizin*) taking; (*Mil*) capture, taking; **~n und Ausgaben** income and expenditure; **Einnahmeausfall** *f* (*Wirts*) drop in takings *od* revenue; (*von Staat*) revenue shortfall; **Einnahmequelle** *f* source of income
einnehmen ['aɪnne:mən] *unreg vt* to take; (*Stellung, Raum*) to take up; **~ für/gegen** to persuade in favour of/against
einnehmend *adj* charming
einnicken ['aɪnnɪkən] *vi* to nod off
einnisten ['aɪnnɪstən] *vr* to nest; (*fig*) to settle o.s.
Einöde ['aɪn|ø:də] (**-, -n**) *f* desert, wilderness
einordnen ['aɪn|ɔrdnən] *vt* to arrange, fit in ▷ *vr* to adapt; (*Aut*) to get in(to) lane
einpacken ['aɪnpakən] *vt* to pack (up)
einparken ['aɪnparkən] *vt, vi* to park
einpauken ['aɪnpaʊkən] (*umg*) *vt*: **jdm etw ~** to drum sth into sb
einpendeln ['aɪnpɛndəln] *vr* to even out
einpennen ['aɪnpɛnən] (*umg*) *vi* to drop off
einpferchen ['aɪnpfɛrçən] *vt* to pen in; (*fig*) to coop up
einpflanzen ['aɪnpflantsən] *vt* to plant; (*Med*) to implant
einplanen ['aɪnpla:nən] *vt* to plan for
einprägen ['aɪnprɛ:gən] *vt* to impress, imprint; (*beibringen*): **jdm etw ~** to impress sth on sb; **sich** *dat* **etw ~** to memorize sth
einprägsam ['aɪnprɛ:kza:m] *adj* easy to remember; (*Melodie*) catchy
einprogrammieren ['aɪnprogrami:rən] *vt* (*Comput*) to feed in
einprügeln ['aɪnpry:gəln] (*umg*) *vt*: **jdm etw ~** to din sth into sb
einquartieren ['aɪnkvarti:rən] *vt* (*Mil*) to billet; **Gäste bei Freunden ~** to put visitors up with friends
einrahmen ['aɪnra:mən] *vt* to frame
einrasten ['aɪnrastən] *vi* to engage
einräumen ['aɪnrɔʏmən] *vt* (*ordnend*) to put away; (*überlassen: Platz*) to give up; (*zugestehen*) to admit, concede
einrechnen ['aɪnrɛçnən] *vt* to include; (*berücksichtigen*) to take into account
einreden ['aɪnre:dən] *vt*: **jdm/sich etw ~** to talk sb/o.s. into believing sth ▷ *vi*: **auf jdn ~** to keep on and on at sb
Einreibemittel *nt* liniment
einreiben ['aɪnraɪbən] *unreg vt* to rub in
einreichen ['aɪnraɪçən] *vt* to hand in; (*Antrag*) to submit
einreihen ['aɪnraɪən] *vt* (*einordnen, einfügen*) to put in; (*klassifizieren*) to classify ▷ *vr* (*Auto*) to get in lane; **etw in etw** *akk* **~** to put sth into sth
Einreise ['aɪnraɪzə] *f* entry; **Einreisebestimmungen** *pl* entry regulations *pl*; **Einreiseerlaubnis** *f* entry permit; **Einreisegenehmigung** *f* entry permit
einreisen ['aɪnraɪzən] *vi*: **in ein Land ~** to enter a country
Einreiseverbot *nt* refusal of entry
Einreisevisum *nt* entry visa
einreißen ['aɪnraɪsən] *unreg vt* (*Papier*) to tear; (*Gebäude*) to pull down ▷ *vi* to tear; (*Gewohnheit werden*) to catch on
einrenken ['aɪnrɛŋkən] *vt* (*Gelenk, Knie*) to put back in place; (*fig: umg*) to sort out ▷ *vr* (*fig: umg*) to sort itself out
einrichten ['aɪnrɪçtən] *vt* (*Haus*) to furnish; (*schaffen*) to establish, set up; (*arrangieren*) to arrange; (*möglich machen*) to manage ▷ *vr* (*in Haus*) to furnish one's house; **sich ~ (auf** *+akk***)** (*sich vorbereiten*) to prepare o.s. (for); (*sich anpassen*) to adapt (to)
Einrichtung *f* (*Wohnungseinrichtung*) furnishings *pl*; (*öffentliche Anstalt*) organization; (*Dienste*) service; (*Laboreinrichtung etc*) equipment; (*Gewohnheit*): **zur ständigen ~ werden** to become an institution
Einrichtungsgegenstand *m* item of furniture
einrosten ['aɪnrɔstən] *vi* to get rusty
einrücken ['aɪnrʏkən] *vi* (*Mil: Soldat*) to join up; (*: in Land*) to move in ▷ *vt* (*Anzeige*) to insert; (*Zeile, Text*) to indent
Eins [aɪns] (**-, -en**) *f* one; **eins** *num* one; **es ist mir alles eins** it's all one to me; **eins zu eins** (*Sport*) one all; **eins a** (*umg*) first-rate
einsalzen ['aɪnzaltsən] *vt* to salt
einsam ['aɪnza:m] *adj* lonely, solitary; **~e Klasse/Spitze** (*umg: hervorragend*) absolutely fantastic; **Einsamkeit** *f* loneliness, solitude
einsammeln ['aɪnzaməln] *vt* to collect
Einsatz ['aɪnzats] *m* (*Teil*) insert; (*an Kleid*) insertion; (*Tischeinsatz*) leaf; (*Verwendung*) use, employment; (*Spieleinsatz*) stake; (*Risiko*) risk; (*Mil*) operation; (*Mus*) entry; **im ~** in action; **etw unter ~ seines Lebens tun** to risk one's life to do sth; **Einsatzbefehl** *m* order to go into action; **einsatzbereit** *adj* ready for action; **Einsatzkommando** *nt* (*Mil*) task force
einschalten ['aɪnʃaltən] *vt* (*Elek*) to switch on; (*einfügen*) to insert; (*Pause*) to make; (*Aut: Gang*) to engage; (*Anwalt*) to bring in ▷ *vr* (*dazwischentreten*) to intervene
Einschaltquote *f* (*TV*) viewing figures *pl*
einschärfen ['aɪnʃɛrfən] *vt*: **jdm etw ~** to impress sth on sb
einschätzen ['aɪnʃɛtsən] *vt* to estimate, assess ▷ *vr* to rate o.s.
einschenken ['aɪnʃɛŋkən] *vt* to pour out
einscheren ['aɪnʃe:rən] *vi* to get back (into lane)
einschicken ['aɪnʃɪkən] *vt* to send in
einschieben ['aɪnʃi:bən] *unreg vt* to push in; (*zusätzlich*) to insert; **eine Pause ~** to have a break
einschiffen ['aɪnʃɪfən] *vt* to ship ▷ *vr* to embark, go on board
einschl. *abk* (= *einschließlich*) inc.
einschlafen ['aɪnʃla:fən] *unreg vi* to fall asleep, go to sleep; (*fig: Freundschaft*) to peter out
einschläfern ['aɪnʃlɛ:fərn] *vt* (*schläfrig machen*) to make sleepy; (*Gewissen*) to soothe; (*narkotisieren*) to give a soporific to; (*töten: Tier*)

to put to sleep
einschläfernd *adj* (*Med*) soporific; (*langweilig*) boring; (*Stimme*) lulling
Einschlag ['aɪnʃla:k] *m* impact; (*Aut*) lock; (*fig: Beimischung*) touch, hint
einschlagen ['aɪnʃla:gən] *unreg vt* to knock in; (*Fenster*) to smash, break; (*Zähne, Schädel*) to smash in; (*Steuer*) to turn; (*kürzer machen*) to take up; (*Ware*) to pack, wrap up; (*Weg, Richtung*) to take ▷ *vi* to hit; (*sich einigen*) to agree; (*Anklang finden*) to work, succeed; **es muss irgendwo eingeschlagen haben** something must have been struck by lightning; **gut ~** (*umg*) to go down well, be a big hit; **auf jdn ~** to hit sb
einschlägig ['aɪnʃlɛ:gɪç] *adj* relevant; **er ist ~ vorbestraft** (*Jur*) he has a previous conviction for a similar offence
einschleichen ['aɪnʃlaɪçən] *unreg vr* (*in Haus, fig: Fehler*) to creep in, steal in; (*in Vertrauen*) to worm one's way in
einschleppen ['aɪnʃlɛpən] *vt* (*fig: Krankheit etc*) to bring in
einschleusen ['aɪnʃlɔʏzən] *vt*: **~ (in +*akk*)** to smuggle in(to)
einschließen ['aɪnʃli:sən] *unreg vt* (*Kind*) to lock in; (*Häftling*) to lock up; (*Gegenstand*) to lock away; (*Bergleute*) to cut off; (*umgeben*) to surround; (*Mil*) to encircle; (*fig*) to include, comprise ▷ *vr* to lock o.s. in
einschließlich *adv* inclusive ▷ *präp +gen* inclusive of, including
einschmeicheln ['aɪnʃmaɪçəln] *vr*: **sich (bei jdm) ~** to ingratiate o.s. (with sb)
einschmuggeln ['aɪnʃmʊgəln] *vt*: **~ (in +*akk*)** to smuggle in(to)
einschnappen ['aɪnʃnapən] *vi* (*Tür*) to click to; (*fig*) to be touchy; **eingeschnappt sein** to be in a huff
einschneidend ['aɪnʃnaɪdənt] *adj* incisive
einschneien ['aɪnʃnaɪən] *vi*: **eingeschneit sein** to be snowed in
Einschnitt ['aɪnʃnɪt] *m* (*Med*) incision; (*im Tal, Gebirge*) cleft; (*im Leben*) decisive point
einschnüren ['aɪnʃny:rən] *vt* (*einengen*) to cut into; **dieser Kragen schnürt mir den Hals ein** this collar is strangling me
einschränken ['aɪnʃrɛŋkən] *vt* to limit, restrict; (*Kosten*) to cut down, reduce ▷ *vr* to cut down (on expenditure); **~d möchte ich sagen, dass ...** I'd like to qualify that by saying ...
einschränkend *adj* restrictive
Einschränkung *f* restriction, limitation; reduction; (*von Behauptung*) qualification
Einschreibbrief, **Einschreibebrief** *m* registered (*Brit*) *od* certified (*US*) letter
einschreiben ['aɪnʃraɪbən] *unreg vt* to write in; (*Post*) to send by registered (*Brit*) *od* certified (*US*) mail ▷ *vr* to register; (*Univ*) to enrol; **Einschreiben** *nt* registered (*Brit*) *od* certified (*US*) letter
einschreiten ['aɪnʃraɪtən] *unreg vi* to step in, intervene; **~ gegen** to take action against
Einschub ['aɪnʃu:p] **(-(e)s, ¨-e)** *m* insertion
einschüchtern ['aɪnʃʏçtərn] *vt* to intimidate
Einschüchterung ['aɪnʃʏçtərʊŋ] *f* intimidation
einschulen ['aɪnʃu:lən] *vt*: **eingeschult werden** (*Kind*) to start school
einschweißen ['aɪnʃvaɪsən] *vt* (*in Plastik*) to shrink-wrap; (*Tech*): **etw in etw** *akk* **~** to weld sth into sth
einschwenken ['aɪnʃvɛŋkən] *vi*: **~ (in +*akk*)** to turn *od* swing in(to)
einsehen ['aɪnze:ən] *unreg vt* (*prüfen*) to inspect; (*Fehler etc*) to recognize; (*verstehen*) to see; **das sehe ich nicht ein** I don't see why; **Einsehen** **(-s)** *nt* understanding; **ein Einsehen haben** to show understanding
einseifen ['aɪnzaɪfən] *vt* to soap, lather; (*fig: umg*) to take in, con
einseitig ['aɪnzaɪtɪç] *adj* one-sided; (*Pol*) unilateral; (*Ernährung*) unbalanced; (*Diskette*) single-sided; **Einseitigkeit** *f* one-sidedness
einsenden ['aɪnzɛndən] *unreg vt* to send in
Einsender, in **(-s, -)** *m(f)* sender, contributor
Einsendeschluss *m* closing date (for entries)
Einsendung *f* sending in
einsetzen ['aɪnzɛtsən] *vt* to put (in); (*in Amt*) to appoint, install; (*Geld*) to stake; (*verwenden*) to use; (*Mil*) to employ ▷ *vi* (*beginnen*) to set in; (*Mus*) to enter, come in ▷ *vr* to work hard; **sich für jdn/etw ~** to support sb/sth; **ich werde mich dafür ~, dass ...** I will do what I can to see that ...
Einsicht ['aɪnzɪçt] *f* insight; (*in Akten*) look, inspection; **zu der ~ kommen, dass ...** to come to the conclusion that ...
einsichtig *adj* (*Mensch*) judicious; **jdm etw ~ machen** to make sb understand *od* see sth
Einsichtnahme **(-, -n)** *f* (*form*) perusal; **„zur ~"** "for attention"
einsichtslos *adj* unreasonable
einsichtsvoll *adj* understanding
Einsiedler ['aɪnzi:dlər] **(-s, -)** *m* hermit
einsilbig ['aɪnzɪlbɪç] *adj* (*lit, fig*) monosyllabic; **Einsilbigkeit** *f* (*fig*) taciturnity
einsinken ['aɪnzɪŋkən] *unreg vi* to sink in
Einsitzer ['aɪnzɪtsər] **(-s, -)** *m* single-seater
einspannen ['aɪnʃpanən] *vt* (*Werkstück, Papier*) to put (in), insert; (*Pferde*) to harness; (*umg: Person*) to rope in; **jdn für seine Zwecke ~** to use sb for one's own ends
einsparen ['aɪnʃpa:rən] *vt* to save, economize on; (*Kosten*) to cut down on; (*Posten*) to eliminate
Einsparung *f* saving
einspeichern ['aɪnʃpaɪçərn] *vt*: **etw (in etw *akk*) ~** (*Comput*) to feed sth in(to sth)
einsperren ['aɪnʃpɛrən] *vt* to lock up
einspielen ['aɪnʃpi:lən] *vr* (*Sport*) to warm up ▷ *vt* (*Film: Geld*) to bring in; (*Instrument*) to play in; **sich aufeinander ~** to become attuned to each other; **gut eingespielt** running smoothly

einsprachig ['aɪnʃpra:xɪç] *adj* monolingual
einspringen ['aɪnʃprɪŋən] *unreg vi* (*aushelfen*) to stand in; (*mit Geld*) to help out
einspritzen ['aɪnʃprɪtsən] *vt* to inject
Einspritzmotor *m* (*Aut*) injection engine
Einspruch ['aɪnʃprʊx] *m* protest, objection; **~ einlegen** (*Jur*) to file an objection
Einspruchsfrist *f* (*Jur*) period for filing an objection
Einspruchsrecht *nt* veto
einspurig ['aɪnʃpu:rɪç] *adj* single-lane; (*Eisenb*) single-track
einst [aɪnst] *adv* once; (*zukünftig*) one *od* some day
Einstand ['aɪnʃtant] *m* (*Tennis*) deuce; (*Antritt*) entrance (to office); **er hat gestern seinen ~ gegeben** yesterday he celebrated starting his new job
einstechen ['aɪnʃtɛçən] *unreg vt* to pierce
einstecken ['aɪnʃtɛkən] *vt* to stick in, insert; (*Brief*) to post, mail (*US*); (*Elek: Stecker*) to plug in; (*Geld*) to pocket; (*mitnehmen*) to take; (*überlegen sein*) to put in the shade; (*hinnehmen*) to swallow
einstehen ['aɪnʃte:ən] *unreg vi*: **für jdn ~** to vouch for sb; **für etw ~** to guarantee sth, vouch for sth; (*Ersatz leisten*) to make good sth
einsteigen ['aɪnʃtaɪgən] *unreg vi* to get in *od* on; (*in Schiff*) to go on board; (*sich beteiligen*) to come in; (*hineinklettern*) to climb in; **~!** (*Eisenb etc*) all aboard!
Einsteiger **(-s, -)** (*umg*) *m* beginner
einstellbar *adj* adjustable
einstellen ['aɪnʃtɛlən] *vt* (*in Firma*) to employ, take on; (*aufhören*) to stop; (*Geräte*) to adjust; (*Kamera etc*) to focus; (*Sender, Radio*) to tune in to; (*unterstellen*) to put ▷ *vi* to take on staff/workers ▷ *vr* (*anfangen*) to set in; (*kommen*) to arrive; **Zahlungen ~** to suspend payment; **etw auf etw** *akk* **~** to adjust sth to sth; to focus sth on sth; **sich auf jdn/etw ~** to adapt to sb/prepare o.s. for sth
einstellig *adj* (*Zahl*) single-digit
Einstellplatz *m* (*auf Hof*) carport; (*in Großgarage*) (covered) parking space
Einstellung *f* (*Aufhören*) suspension, cessation; (*von Gerät*) adjustment; (*von Kamera etc*) focusing; (*von Arbeiter etc*) appointment; (*Haltung*) attitude
Einstellungsgespräch *nt* interview
Einstellungsstopp *m* halt in recruitment
Einstieg ['aɪnʃti:k] **(-(e)s, -e)** *m* entry; (*fig*) approach; (*von Bus, Bahn*) door; **kein ~** exit only
einstig ['aɪnstɪç] *adj* former
einstimmen ['aɪnʃtɪmən] *vi* to join in ▷ *vt* (*Mus*) to tune; (*in Stimmung bringen*) to put in the mood
einstimmig *adj* unanimous; (*Mus*) for one voice; **Einstimmigkeit** *f* unanimity
einstmalig *adj* former
einstmals *adv* once, formerly
einstöckig ['aɪnʃtœkɪç] *adj* two-storeyed (*Brit*), two-storied (*US*)
einstöpseln ['aɪnʃtœpsəln] *vt*: **etw (in etw** *+akk*) **~**: *Elek*) to plug sth in(to sth)
einstudieren ['aɪnʃtudi:rən] *vt* to study, rehearse
einstufen ['aɪnʃtu:fən] *vt* to classify
Einstufung *f*: **nach seiner ~ in eine höhere Gehaltsklasse** after he was put on a higher salary grade
einstündig ['aɪnʃtʏndɪç] *adj* one-hour *attrib*
einstürmen ['aɪnʃtʏrmən] *vi*: **auf jdn ~** to rush at sb; (*Eindrücke*) to overwhelm sb
Einsturz ['aɪnʃtʊrts] *m* collapse
einstürzen ['aɪnʃtʏrtsən] *vi* to fall in, collapse; **auf jdn ~** (*fig*) to overwhelm sb
Einsturzgefahr *f* danger of collapse
einstweilen *adv* meanwhile; (*vorläufig*) temporarily, for the time being
einstweilig *adj* temporary; **~e Verfügung** (*Jur*) temporary *od* interim injunction
eintägig ['aɪntɛ:gɪç] *adj* one-day
Eintagsfliege ['aɪnta:ksfli:gə] *f* (*Zool*) mayfly; (*fig*) nine-day wonder
eintauchen ['aɪntaʊxən] *vt* to immerse, dip in ▷ *vi* to dive
eintauschen ['aɪntaʊʃən] *vt* to exchange
eintausend ['aɪn'taʊzənt] *num* one thousand
einteilen ['aɪntaɪlən] *vt* (*in Teile*) to divide (up); (*Menschen*) to assign
einteilig *adj* one-piece
eintönig ['aɪntø:nɪç] *adj* monotonous; **Eintönigkeit** *f* monotony
Eintopf ['aɪntɔpf] *m* stew
Eintopfgericht ['aɪntɔpfgərɪçt] *nt* stew
Eintracht ['aɪntraxt] **(-)** *f* concord, harmony
einträchtig ['aɪntrɛçtɪç] *adj* harmonious
Eintrag ['aɪntra:k] **(-(e)s, ¨-e)** *m* entry; **amtlicher ~** entry in the register
eintragen ['aɪntra:gən] *unreg vt* (*in Buch*) to enter; (*Profit*) to yield ▷ *vr* to put one's name down; **jdm etw ~** to bring sb sth
einträglich ['aɪntrɛ:klɪç] *adj* profitable
Eintragung *f*: **~ (in** *+akk*) entry (in)
eintreffen ['aɪntrɛfən] *unreg vi* to happen; (*ankommen*) to arrive; (*fig: wahr werden*) to come true
eintreiben ['aɪntraɪbən] *unreg vt* (*Geldbeträge*) to collect
eintreten ['aɪntre:tən] *unreg vi* (*hineingehen*) to enter; (*sich ereignen*) to occur ▷ *vt* (*Tür*) to kick open; **in etw** *akk* **~** to enter sth; (*in Klub, Partei*) to join sth; **für jdn/etw ~** to stand up for sb/sth
eintrichtern ['aɪntrɪçtərn] (*umg*) *vt*: **jdm etw ~** to drum sth into sb
Eintritt ['aɪntrɪt] *m* (*Betreten*) entrance; (*in Klub etc*) joining; **~ frei** admission free; **„~ verboten"** "no admittance"; **bei ~ der Dunkelheit** at nightfall
Eintritts- *zW*: **Eintrittsgeld** *nt* admission charge; **Eintrittskarte** *f* (admission) ticket; **Eintrittspreis** *m* admission charge
eintrocknen ['aɪntrɔknən] *vi* to dry up
eintrudeln ['aɪntru:dəln] (*umg*) *vi* to drift in
eintunken ['aɪntʊŋkən] *vt* (*Brot*): **etw in etw**

akk ~ to dunk sth in sth
einüben ['aɪn|y:bən] *vt* to practise (*Brit*), practice (*US*), drill
einverleiben ['aɪnfɛrlaɪbən] *vt* to incorporate; (*Gebiet*) to annex; **sich** *dat* **etw** ~ (*fig: geistig*) to assimilate sth
Einvernehmen ['aɪnfɛrne:mən] (**-s, -**) *nt* agreement, understanding
einverstanden ['aɪnfɛrʃtandən] *interj* agreed ▷ *adj*: ~ **sein** to agree, be agreed; **sich mit etw ~ erklären** to give one's agreement to sth
Einverständnis ['aɪnfɛrʃtɛntnɪs] (**-ses**) *nt* understanding; (*gleiche Meinung*) agreement; **im ~ mit jdm handeln** to act with sb's consent
Einwand ['aɪnvant] (**-(e)s, ¨e**) *m* objection; **einen ~ erheben** to raise an objection
Einwanderer ['aɪnvandərər] *m* immigrant
Einwanderin *f* immigrant
einwandern *vi* to immigrate
Einwanderung *f* immigration
einwandfrei *adj* perfect; **etw ~ beweisen** to prove sth beyond doubt
einwärts ['aɪnvɛrts] *adv* inwards
Einwegflasche ['aɪnve:gflaʃə] *f* non-returnable bottle
Einwegpfand *nt* deposit on non-returnables
Einwegspritze *f* disposable (hypodermic) syringe
einweichen ['aɪnvaɪçən] *vt* to soak
einweihen ['aɪnvaɪən] *vt* (*Kirche*) to consecrate; (*Brücke*) to open; (*Gebäude*) to inaugurate; (*Person*): **in etw** *akk* ~ to initiate in sth; **er ist eingeweiht** (*fig*) he knows all about it
Einweihung *f* consecration; opening; inauguration; initiation
einweisen ['aɪnvaɪzən] *unreg vt* (*in Amt*) to install; (*in Arbeit*) to introduce; (*in Anstalt*) to send; (*in Krankenhaus*): ~ **(in** *+akk***)** to admit (to)
Einweisung *f* installation; introduction; sending
einwenden ['aɪnvɛndən] *unreg vt*: **etwas ~ gegen** to object to, oppose
einwerfen ['aɪnvɛrfən] *unreg vt* to throw in; (*Brief*) to post; (*Geld*) to put in, insert; (*Fenster*) to smash; (*äußern*) to interpose
einwickeln ['aɪnvɪkəln] *vt* to wrap up; (*fig: umg*) to outsmart
einwilligen ['aɪnvɪlɪgən] *vi*: **(in etw** *akk***)** ~ to consent (to sth), agree (to sth)
Einwilligung *f* consent
einwirken ['aɪnvɪrkən] *vi*: **auf jdn/etw** ~ to influence sb/sth
Einwirkung *f* influence
Einwohner, in ['aɪnvo:nər(ɪn)] (**-s, -**) *m(f)* inhabitant; **Einwohnermeldeamt** *nt* registration office; **sich beim Einwohnermeldeamt (an)melden** ≈ to register with the police; **Einwohnerschaft** *f* population, inhabitants *pl*
Einwurf ['aɪnvʊrf] *m* (*Öffnung*) slot; (*Einwand*) objection; (*Sport*) throw-in
Einzahl ['aɪntsa:l] *f* singular
einzahlen *vt* to pay in
Einzahlung *f* payment; (*auf Sparkonto*) deposit
einzäunen ['aɪntsɔʏnən] *vt* to fence in
einzeichnen ['aɪntsaɪçnən] *vt* to draw in
Einzel ['aɪntsəl] (**-s, -**) *nt* (*Tennis*) singles *pl*
Einzel- *zW*: **Einzelaufstellung** *f* (*Comm*) itemized list; **Einzelbett** *nt* single bed; **Einzelblattzuführung** *f* sheet feed; **Einzelfall** *m* single instance, individual case; **Einzelgänger, in** *m(f)* loner; **Einzelhaft** *f* solitary confinement; **Einzelhandel** *m* retail trade; **im Einzelhandel erhältlich** available retail; **Einzelhandelsgeschäft** *nt* retail outlet; **Einzelhandelspreis** *m* retail price; **Einzelhändler** *m* retailer; **Einzelheit** *f* particular, detail; **Einzelkind** *nt* only child
Einzeller ['aɪntsɛlər] (**-s, -**) *m* (*Biol*) single-celled organism
einzeln *adj* single; (*von Paar*) odd ▷ *adv* singly; ~ **angeben** to specify; **E~e** some (people), a few (people); **der/die E~e** the individual; **das E~e** the particular; **ins E~e gehen** to go into detail(s); **etw im E~en besprechen** to discuss sth in detail; ~ **aufführen** to list separately *od* individually; **bitte ~ eintreten** please come in one (person) at a time
Einzelteil *nt* individual part; (*Ersatzteil*) spare part; **etw in seine ~e zerlegen** to take sth to pieces, dismantle sth
Einzelzimmer *nt* single room
einziehen ['aɪntsi:ən] *unreg vt* to draw in, take in; (*Kopf*) to duck; (*Fühler, Antenne, Fahrgestell*) to retract; (*Steuern, Erkundigungen*) to collect; (*Mil*) to call up, draft (*US*); (*aus dem Verkehr ziehen*) to withdraw; (*konfiszieren*) to confiscate ▷ *vi* to move in; (*Friede, Ruhe*) to come; (*Flüssigkeit*): ~ **(in** *+akk***)** to soak in(to)
einzig ['aɪntsɪç] *adj* only; (*ohnegleichen*) unique ▷ *adv*: ~ **und allein** solely; **das E~e** the only thing; **der/die E~e** the only one; **kein ~es Mal** not once, not one single time; **kein E~er** nobody, not a single person; **einzigartig** *adj* unique
Einzug ['aɪntsu:k] *m* entry, moving in
Einzugsauftrag *m* (*Fin*) direct debit
Einzugsbereich *m* catchment area
Einzugsverfahren *nt* (*Fin*) direct debit
Eis [aɪs] (**-es, -**) *nt* ice; (*Speiseeis*) ice cream; **~ am Stiel** ice lolly (*Brit*), popsicle® (*US*); **Eisbahn** *f* ice *od* skating rink; **Eisbär** *m* polar bear; **Eisbecher** *m* sundae; **Eisbein** *nt* pig's trotters *pl*; **Eisberg** *m* iceberg; **Eisbeutel** *m* ice pack; **Eiscafé** *nt* = **Eisdiele**
Eischnee ['aɪʃne:] *m* (*Koch*) beaten white of egg
Eisdecke *f* sheet of ice
Eisdiele *f* ice-cream parlour (*Brit*) *od* parlor (*US*)
Eisen ['aɪzən] (**-s, -**) *nt* iron; **zum alten ~ gehören** (*fig*) to be on the scrap heap
Eisenbahn *f* railway, railroad (*US*); **es ist (aller)höchste ~** (*umg*) it's high time; **Eisenbahner** (**-s, -**) *m* railwayman, railway employee, railroader (*US*); **Eisenbahnnetz** *nt* rail network; **Eisenbahnschaffner** *m*

railway guard, (railroad) conductor (*US*); **Eisenbahnüberführung** *f* footbridge; **Eisenbahnübergang** *m* level crossing, grade crossing (*US*); **Eisenbahnwagen** *m* railway *od* railroad (*US*) carriage; **Eisenbahnwaggon**, **Eisenbahnwagon** *m* (*Güterwagen*) goods wagon

Eisen- *zW*: **Eisenerz** *nt* iron ore; **eisenhaltig** *adj* containing iron; **Eisenmangel** *m* iron deficiency; **Eisenwarenhandlung** *f* ironmonger's (*Brit*), hardware store (*US*)

eisern ['aɪzərn] *adj* iron; (*Gesundheit*) robust; (*Energie*) unrelenting; (*Reserve*) emergency; **der E~e Vorhang** the Iron Curtain; **in etw** *dat* **~ sein** to be adamant about sth; **er ist ~ bei seinem Entschluss geblieben** he stuck firmly to his decision

Eis- *zW*: **Eisfach** *nt* freezer compartment, icebox; **eisfrei** *adj* clear of ice; **eisgekühlt** *adj* chilled; **Eishockey** *nt* ice hockey

eisig ['aɪzɪç] *adj* icy

Eis- *zW*: **Eiskaffee** *m* iced coffee; **eiskalt** *adj* icy cold; **Eiskunstlauf** *m* figure skating; **Eislaufen** *nt* ice-skating; **Eisläufer** *m* ice-skater; **Eismeer** *nt*: **Nördliches/Südliches Eismeer** Arctic/ Antarctic Ocean; **Eispickel** *m* ice-axe (*Brit*), ice-ax (*US*)

Eisprung ['aɪʃprʊŋ] *m* ovulation

Eis- *zW*: **Eisschießen** *nt* ≈ curling; **Eisscholle** *f* ice floe; **Eisschrank** *m* fridge, icebox (*US*); **Eisstadion** *nt* ice *od* skating rink; **Eiswürfel** *m* ice cube; **Eiszapfen** *m* icicle; **Eiszeit** *f* Ice Age

eitel ['aɪtəl] *adj* vain; **Eitelkeit** *f* vanity

Eiter ['aɪtər] (**-s**) *m* pus

eiterig *adj* suppurating

eitern *vi* to suppurate

Ei- *zW*: **Eiweiß** (**-es, -e**) *nt* white of an egg; (*Chem*) protein; **Eiweißgehalt** *m* protein content; **Eizelle** *f* ovum

EKD *f abk* (*= Evangelische Kirche in Deutschland*) *German Protestant Church*

Ekel[1] ['e:kəl] (**-s**) *m* nausea, disgust; **vor jdm/ etw einen ~ haben** to loathe sb/sth

Ekel[2] ['e:kəl] (**-s, -**) (*umg*) *nt* (*Mensch*) nauseating person

ekelerregend *adj* nauseating, disgusting

ekelhaft *adj*, **ekelig** *adj* nauseating, disgusting

ekeln *vt* to disgust ▷ *vr*: **sich vor etw** *dat* **~** to be disgusted at sth; **es ekelt ihn** he is disgusted

EKG (-) *nt abk* (*= Elektrokardiogramm*) ECG

Eklat [e'kla:] (**-s**) *m* (*geh: Aufsehen*) sensation

eklig *adj* nauseating, disgusting

Ekstase [ɛk'sta:zə] (**-, -n**) *f* ecstasy; **jdn in ~ versetzen** to send sb into ecstasies

Ekzem [ɛk'tse:m] (**-s, -e**) *nt* (*Med*) eczema

Elan [e'lã:] (**-s**) *m* élan

elastisch [e'lastɪʃ] *adj* elastic

Elastizität [elastitsi'tɛ:t] *f* elasticity

Elbe ['ɛlbə] *f* (*Fluss*) Elbe

Elch [ɛlç] (**-(e)s, -e**) *m* elk

Elefant [ele'fant] *m* elephant; **wie ein ~ im Porzellanladen** (*umg*) like a bull in a china shop

elegant [ele'gant] *adj* elegant

Eleganz [ele'gants] *f* elegance

Elektrifizierung [elɛktrifi'tsi:rʊŋ] *f* electrification

Elektriker [e'lɛktrikər] (**-s, -**) *m* electrician

elektrisch [e'lɛktrɪʃ] *adj* electric

elektrisieren [elɛktri'zi:rən] *vt* (*lit, fig*) to electrify; (*Mensch*) to give an electric shock to ▷ *vr* to get an electric shock

Elektrizität [elɛktritsi'tɛ:t] *f* electricity

Elektrizitätswerk *nt* electric power station

Elektroartikel [e'lɛktro|artɪkəl] *m* electrical appliance

Elektrode [elɛk'tro:də] (**-, -n**) *f* electrode

Elektro- *zW*: **Elektrogerät** *nt* electrical appliance; **Elektroherd** *m* electric cooker; **Elektrokardiogramm** *nt* (*Med*) electrocardiogram

Elektrolyse [elektro'ly:zə] (**-, -n**) *f* electrolysis

Elektromotor *m* electric motor

Elektron [e'lɛktrɔn] (**-s, -en**) *nt* electron

Elektronengehirn, **Elektronenhirn** *nt* electronic brain

Elektronenrechner *m* computer

Elektronik [elɛk'tro:nɪk] *f* electronics *sing*; (*Teile*) electronics *pl*

elektronisch *adj* electronic; **~e Post** electronic mail

Elektro- *zW*: **Elektrorasierer** (**-s, -**) *m* electric razor; **Elektroschock** *m* (*Med*) electric shock, electroshock; **Elektrotechniker** *m* electrician; (*Ingenieur*) electrical engineer

Element [ele'mɛnt] (**-s, -e**) *nt* element; (*Elek*) cell, battery

elementar [elemɛn'ta:r] *adj* elementary; (*naturhaft*) elemental; **Elementarteilchen** *nt* (*Phys*) elementary particle

Elend ['e:lɛnt] (**-(e)s**) *nt* misery; **da kann man das heulende ~ kriegen** (*umg*) it's enough to make you scream; **elend** *adj* miserable; **mir ist ganz elend** I feel really awful

elendiglich ['e:lɛndɪklɪç] *adv* miserably; **~ zugrunde gehen** to come to a wretched end

Elendsviertel *nt* slum

elf [ɛlf] *num* eleven; **Elf** (**-, en**) *f* (*Sport*) eleven

Elfe (**-, -n**) *f* elf

Elfenbein *nt* ivory; **Elfenbeinküste** *f* Ivory Coast

Elfmeter *m* (*Sport*) penalty (kick)

Elfmeterschießen *nt* (*Sport*) penalty shoot-out

eliminieren [elimi'ni:rən] *vt* to eliminate

elitär [eli'tɛ:r] *adj* elitist ▷ *adv* in an elitist fashion

Elite [e'li:tə] (**-, -n**) *f* elite

Elixier [elɪ'ksi:r] (**-s, -e**) *nt* elixir

Ellbogen *m* = **Ellenbogen**

Elle ['ɛlə] (**-, -n**) *f* ell; (*Maß*) ≈ yard

Ellenbogen *m* elbow; **die ~ gebrauchen** (*umg*) to be pushy; **Ellenbogenfreiheit** *f* (*fig*) elbow room; **Ellenbogengesellschaft** *f* dog-eat-dog society

Ellipse [ɛ'lɪpsə] (**-, -n**) *f* ellipse

E-Lok ['e:lɔk] (-) *f abk* (*= elektrische Lokomotive*)

electric locomotive *od* engine
Elsass ['ɛlzas] *nt*: **das ~** Alsace
Elsässer ['ɛlzɛsər] *adj* Alsatian
Elsässer, in (**-s, -**) *m(f)* Alsatian, inhabitant of Alsace
elsässisch *adj* Alsatian
Elster ['ɛlstər] (**-, -n**) *f* magpie
elterlich *adj* parental
Eltern ['ɛltərn] *pl* parents *pl*; **nicht von schlechten ~ sein** (*umg*) to be quite something; **Elternabend** *m* (*Sch*) parents' evening; **Elternhaus** *nt* home; **elternlos** *adj* orphaned; **Elternsprechtag** *m* open day (for parents); **Elternteil** *m* parent
Email [e'ma:j] (**-s, -s**) *nt* enamel
E-Mail ['i:me:l] (**-, -s**) *f* E-mail, e-mail; **E-Mail-Adresse** *f* E-mail address
e-mailen ['i:me:lən] *vt* to e-mail
emaillieren [ema'ji:rən] *vt* to enamel
Emanze (**-, -n**) (*pej*) *f* women's libber (*umg*)
Emanzipation [emantsipatsi'o:n] *f* emancipation
emanzipieren [emantsi'pi:rən] *vt* to emancipate
Embargo [ɛm'bargo] (**-s, -s**) *nt* embargo
Embryo ['ɛmbryo] (**-s, -s** *od* **-nen**) *m* embryo
Embryonenforschung *f* embryo research
Emigrant, in [emi'grant(ɪn)] *m(f)* emigrant
Emigration [emigratsi'o:n] *f* emigration
emigrieren [emi'gri:rən] *vi* to emigrate
Emissionen *pl* emissions *pl*
emissionsarm [emɪsi'o:nsarm] *adj* low in emissions
Emissionshandel *m* emissions trading
Emissionskurs *m* (*Aktien*) issued price
EMNID *m abk* (*= Erforschung, Meinung, Nachrichten, Informationsdienst*) *opinion poll organization*
emotional [emotsio'na:l] *adj* emotional; (*Ausdrucksweise*) emotive
emotionsgeladen [emotsi'o:nsgəla:dən] *adj* emotionally-charged
Empf. *abk* = **Empfänger**
empfahl *etc* [ɛm'pfa:l] *vb siehe* **empfehlen**
empfand *etc* [ɛm'pfant] *vb siehe* **empfinden**
Empfang [ɛm'pfaŋ] (**-(e)s, ⸚e**) *m* reception; (*Erhalten*) receipt; **in ~ nehmen** to receive; **(zahlbar) nach** *od* **bei ~** *+gen* (payable) on receipt (of)
empfangen *unreg vt* to receive ▹ *vi* (*schwanger werden*) to conceive
Empfänger, in [ɛm'pfɛŋər(ɪn)] (**-s, -**) *m(f)* receiver; (*Comm*) addressee, consignee; **~ unbekannt** (*auf Briefen*) not known at this address
empfänglich *adj* receptive, susceptible
Empfängnis (**-, -se**) *f* conception; **empfängnisverhütend** *adj*: **empfängnisverhütende Mittel** contraceptives *pl*; **Empfängnisverhütung** *f* contraception
Empfangs- *zW*: **Empfangsbestätigung** *f* (acknowledgement of) receipt; **Empfangschef** *m* (*von Hotel*) head porter; **Empfangsdame** *f* receptionist; **Empfangsschein** *m* receipt; **Empfangsstörung** *f* (*Rundf, TV*) interference; **Empfangszimmer** *nt* reception room
empfehlen [ɛm'pfe:lən] *unreg vt* to recommend ▹ *vr* to take one's leave
empfehlenswert *adj* recommendable
Empfehlung *f* recommendation; **auf ~ von** on the recommendation of
Empfehlungsschreiben *nt* letter of recommendation
empfiehlt [ɛm'pfi:lt] *vb siehe* **empfehlen**
empfinden [ɛm'pfɪndən] *unreg vt* to feel; **etw als Beleidigung ~** to find sth insulting; **Empfinden** (**-s**) *nt*: **meinem Empfinden nach** to my mind
empfindlich *adj* sensitive; (*Stelle*) sore; (*reizbar*) touchy; **deine Kritik hat ihn ~ getroffen** your criticism cut him to the quick; **Empfindlichkeit** *f* sensitiveness; (*Reizbarkeit*) touchiness
empfindsam *adj* sentimental; (*Mensch*) sensitive
Empfindung *f* feeling, sentiment
empfindungslos *adj* unfeeling, insensitive
empfing *etc* [ɛm'pfɪŋ] *vb siehe* **empfangen**
empfohlen [ɛm'pfo:lən] *pp von* **empfehlen** ▹ *adj*: **~er Einzelhandelspreis** recommended retail price
empfunden [ɛm'pfʊndən] *pp von* **empfinden**
empor [ɛm'po:r] *adv* up, upwards
emporarbeiten *vr* (*geh*) to work one's way up
Empore [ɛm'po:rə] (**-, -n**) *f* (*Archit*) gallery
empören [ɛm'pø:rən] *vt* to make indignant; to shock ▹ *vr* to become indignant
empörend *adj* outrageous
emporkommen *unreg vi* to rise; (*vorankommen*) to succeed
Emporkömmling *m* upstart, parvenu
empört *adj*: **~ (über** *+akk*) indignant (at), outraged (at)
Empörung *f* indignation
emsig ['ɛmzɪç] *adj* diligent, busy
End- ['ɛnt] *in zW* final; **Endauswertung** *f* final analysis; **Endbahnhof** *m* terminus; **Endbetrag** *m* final amount
Ende ['ɛndə] (**-s, -n**) *nt* end; **am ~** at the end; (*schließlich*) in the end; **am ~ sein** to be at the end of one's tether; **~ Dezember** at the end of December; **zu ~ sein** to be finished; **zu ~ gehen** to come to an end; **zu ~ führen** to finish (off); **letzten ~s** in the end, at the end of the day; **ein böses ~ nehmen** to come to a bad end; **ich bin mit meiner Weisheit am ~** I'm at my wits' end; **er wohnt am ~ der Welt** (*umg*) he lives at the back of beyond
Endeffekt *m*: **im ~** (*umg*) when it comes down to it
enden *vi* to end
Endergebnis *nt* final result
endgültig *adj* final, definite
Endivie [ɛn'di:viə] *f* endive
End- *zW*: **Endkunde** *m* end customer *od* consumer; **Endlager** *nt* permanent waste disposal site; **Endlagerung** *f* permanent

disposal; **endlich** *adj* final; (*Math*) finite ▷ *adv* finally; **endlich!** at last!; **hör endlich damit auf!** will you stop that!; **endlos** *adj* endless; **Endlospapier** *nt* continuous paper; **Endprodukt** *nt* end *od* final product; **Endspiel** *nt* final(s); **Endspurt** *m* (*Sport*) final spurt; **Endstation** *f* terminus

Endung *f* ending

Endverbraucher *m* consumer, end-user

Energie [enɛr'gi:] *f* energy; **Energieaufwand** *m* energy expenditure; **Energiebedarf** *m* energy requirement; **Energieeinsparung** *f* energy saving; **Energiegewinnung** *f* generation of energy; **energielos** *adj* lacking in energy, weak; **Energiequelle** *f* source of energy; **Energieversorgung** *f* supply of energy; **Energiewirtschaft** *f* energy industry

energisch [e'nɛrgɪʃ] *adj* energetic; **~ durchgreifen** to take vigorous *od* firm action

eng [ɛŋ] *adj* narrow; (*Kleidung*) tight; (*fig: Horizont*) narrow, limited; (*Freundschaft, Verhältnis*) close; **~ an etw** *dat* close to sth; **in die ~ere Wahl kommen** to be short-listed (*Brit*)

Engadin ['ɛŋgadi:n] (**-s**) *nt*: **das ~** the Engadine

Engagement [ãgaʒə'mã:] (**-s, -s**) *nt* engagement; (*Verpflichtung*) commitment

engagieren [ãga'ʒi:rən] *vt* to engage ▷ *vr* to commit o.s.; **ein engagierter Schriftsteller** a committed writer

Enge ['ɛŋə] (**-, -n**) *f* (*lit, fig*) narrowness; (*Landenge*) defile; (*Meerenge*) straits *pl*; **jdn in die ~ treiben** to drive sb into a corner

Engel ['ɛŋəl] (**-s, -**) *m* angel; **engelhaft** *adj* angelic; **Engelmacher, in** (**-s, -**) (*umg*) *m(f)* backstreet abortionist

Engelsgeduld *f*: **sie hat eine ~** she has the patience of a saint

Engelszungen *pl*: **(wie) mit ~ reden** to use all one's own powers of persuasion

engherzig *adj* petty

engl. *abk* = **englisch**

England ['ɛŋlant] *nt* England

Engländer ['ɛŋlɛndər] (**-s, -**) *m* Englishman; English boy; **die Engländer** *pl* the English, the Britishers (*US*); **Engländerin** *f* Englishwoman; English girl

englisch ['ɛŋlɪʃ] *adj* English

engmaschig ['ɛŋmaʃɪç] *adj* close-meshed

Engpass *m* defile, pass; (*fig: Verkehr*) bottleneck

en gros [ã'gro] *adv* wholesale

engstirnig ['ɛŋʃtɪrnɪç] *adj* narrow-minded

Enkel ['ɛŋkəl] (**-s, -**) *m* grandson; **Enkelin** *f* granddaughter; **Enkelkind** *nt* grandchild

en masse [ã'mas] *adv* en masse

enorm [e'nɔrm] *adj* enormous; (*umg: herrlich, kolossal*) tremendous

en passant [ãpa'sã] *adv* en passant, in passing

Ensemble [ã'sãbəl] (**-s, -s**) *nt* ensemble

entarten [ɛnt'|a:rten] *vi* to degenerate

entbehren [ɛnt'be:rən] *vt* to do without, dispense with

entbehrlich *adj* superfluous

Entbehrung *f* privation; **~en auf sich** *akk* **nehmen** to make sacrifices

entbinden [ɛnt'bɪndən] *unreg vt (+gen)* to release (from); (*Med*) to deliver ▷ *vi* (*Med*) to give birth

Entbindung *f* release; (*Med*) delivery, birth

Entbindungsheim *nt* maternity hospital

Entbindungsstation *f* maternity ward

entblößen [ɛnt'blø:sən] *vt* to denude, uncover; (*berauben*): **einer Sache** *gen* **entblößt** deprived of sth

entbrennen [ɛnt'brɛnən] *unreg vi* (*liter: Kampf, Streit*) to flare up; (*: Liebe*) to be aroused

entdecken [ɛnt'dɛkən] *vt* to discover; **jdm etw ~** to disclose sth to sb

Entdecker, in (**-s, -**) *m(f)* discoverer

Entdeckung *f* discovery

Ente ['ɛntə] (**-, -n**) *f* duck; (*fig*) canard, false report; (*Aut*) Citroën 2CV, deux-chevaux

entehren [ɛnt'|e:rən] *vt* to dishonour (*Brit*), dishonor (*US*), disgrace

enteignen [ɛnt'|aɪgnən] *vt* to expropriate; (*Besitzer*) to dispossess

enteisen [ɛnt'|aɪzən] *vt* to de-ice; (*Kühlschrank*) to defrost

enterben [ɛnt'|ɛrbən] *vt* to disinherit

Enterhaken ['ɛntərha:kən] *m* grappling iron *od* hook

entfachen [ɛnt'faxən] *vt* to kindle

entfallen [ɛnt'falən] *unreg vi* to drop, fall; (*wegfallen*) to be dropped; **jdm ~** (*vergessen*) to slip sb's memory; **auf jdn ~** to be allotted to sb

entfalten [ɛnt'faltən] *vt* to unfold; (*Talente*) to develop ▷ *vr* to open; (*Mensch*) to develop one's potential

Entfaltung *f* unfolding; (*von Talenten*) development

entfernen [ɛnt'fɛrnən] *vt* to remove; (*hinauswerfen*) to expel ▷ *vr* to go away, retire, withdraw

entfernt *adj* distant ▷ *adv*: **nicht im E~esten!** not in the slightest!; **weit davon ~ sein, etw zu tun** to be far from doing sth

Entfernung *f* distance; (*Wegschaffen*) removal; **unerlaubte ~ von der Truppe** absence without leave

Entfernungsmesser *m* (*Phot*) rangefinder

entfesseln [ɛnt'fɛsəln] *vt* (*fig*) to arouse

entfetten [ɛnt'fɛtən] *vt* to take the fat from

entflammen [ɛnt'flamən] *vt* (*fig*) to (a)rouse ▷ *vi* to burst into flames; (*fig: Streit*) to flare up; (*: Leidenschaft*) to be (a)roused *od* inflamed

entfremden [ɛnt'frɛmdən] *vt* to estrange, alienate

Entfremdung *f* estrangement, alienation

entfrosten [ɛnt'frɔstən] *vt* to defrost

Entfroster (**-s, -**) *m* (*Aut*) defroster

entführen [ɛnt'fy:rən] *vt* to abduct, kidnap; (*Flugzeug*) to hijack

Entführer (**-s, -**) *m* kidnapper (*Brit*), kidnaper (*US*); hijacker

Entführung *f* abduction, kidnapping (*Brit*), kidnaping (*US*); hijacking

entgegen [ɛnt'ge:gən] *präp +dat* contrary to,

against ▷ *adv* towards; **entgegenbringen** *unreg vt* to bring; (*fig*): **jdm etw entgegenbringen** to show sb sth; **entgegengehen** *unreg vi +dat* to go to meet, go towards; **Schwierigkeiten entgegengehen** to be heading for difficulties; **entgegengesetzt** *adj* opposite; (*widersprechend*) opposed; **entgegenhalten** *unreg vt* (*fig*): **einer Sache** *dat* **entgegenhalten, dass ...** to object to sth that ...; **Entgegenkommen** *nt* obligingness; **entgegenkommen** *unreg vi +dat* to come towards, approach; (*fig*): **jdm entgegenkommen** to accommodate sb; **das kommt unseren Plänen sehr entgegen** that fits in very well with our plans; **entgegenkommend** *adj* obliging; **entgegenlaufen** *unreg vi +dat* to run towards *od* to meet; (*fig*) to run counter to; **Entgegennahme** *f* (*form: Empfang*) receipt; (*Annahme*) acceptance; **entgegennehmen** *unreg vt* to receive, accept; **entgegensehen** *unreg vi +dat* to await; **entgegensetzen** *vt* to oppose; **dem habe ich entgegenzusetzen, dass ...** against that I'd like to say that ...; **jdm/etw Widerstand entgegensetzen** to put up resistance to sb/sth; **entgegenstehen** *unreg vi*: **dem steht nichts entgegen** there's no objection to that; **entgegentreten** *unreg vi +dat* (*lit*) to step up to; (*fig*) to oppose, counter; **entgegenwirken** *vi +dat* to counteract

entgegnen [ɛnt'ge:gnən] *vt* to reply, retort

Entgegnung *f* reply, retort

entgehen [ɛnt'ge:ən] *unreg vi* (*fig*): **jdm ~** to escape sb's notice; **sich** *dat* **etw ~ lassen** to miss sth

entgeistert [ɛnt'gaɪstərt] *adj* thunderstruck

Entgelt [ɛnt'gɛlt] **(-(e)s, -e)** *nt* remuneration

entgelten *unreg vt*: **jdm etw ~** to repay sb for sth

entgleisen [ɛnt'glaɪzən] *vi* (*Eisenb*) to be derailed; (*fig: Person*) to misbehave; **~ lassen** to derail

Entgleisung *f* derailment; (*fig*) faux pas, gaffe

entgleiten [ɛnt'glaɪtən] *unreg vi*: **jdm ~** to slip from sb's hand

entgräten [ɛnt'grɛ:tən] *vt* to fillet, bone

Enthaarungsmittel [ɛnt'ha:rʊŋsmɪtəl] *nt* depilatory

enthält [ɛnt'hɛlt] *vb siehe* **enthalten**

enthalten [ɛnt'haltən] *unreg vt* to contain ▷ *vr +gen* to abstain from, refrain from; **sich (der Stimme) ~** to abstain

enthaltsam [ɛnt'haltza:m] *adj* abstinent, abstemious; **Enthaltsamkeit** *f* abstinence

enthärten [ɛnt'hɛrtən] *vt* (*Wasser*) to soften; (*Metall*) to anneal

enthaupten [ɛnt'haʊptən] *vt* to decapitate; (*als Hinrichtung*) to behead

enthäuten [ɛnt'hɔʏtən] *vt* to skin

entheben [ɛnt'he:bən] *unreg vt*: **jdn einer Sache** *gen* **~** to relieve sb of sth

enthemmen [ɛnt'hɛmən] *vt*: **jdn ~** to free sb from his/her inhibitions

enthielt *etc* [ɛnt'hi:lt] *vb siehe* **enthalten**

enthüllen [ɛnt'hʏlən] *vt* to reveal, unveil

Enthüllung *f* revelation; (*von Skandal*) exposure

Enthusiasmus [ɛntuzi'asmʊs] *m* enthusiasm

entjungfern [ɛnt'jʊŋfərn] *vt* to deflower

entkalken [ɛnt'kalkən] *vt* to decalcify

entkernen [ɛnt'kɛrnən] *vt* (*Kernobst*) to core; (*Steinobst*) to stone

entkleiden [ɛnt'klaɪdən] *vt, vr* (*geh*) to undress

entkommen [ɛnt'kɔmən] *unreg vi* to get away, escape; **jdm/etw** *od* **aus etw ~** to get away *od* escape from sb/sth

entkorken [ɛnt'kɔrkən] *vt* to uncork

entkräften [ɛnt'krɛftən] *vt* to weaken, exhaust; (*Argument*) to refute

entkrampfen [ɛnt'krampfən] *vt* (*fig*) to relax, ease

entladen [ɛnt'la:dən] *unreg vt* to unload; (*Elek*) to discharge ▷ *vr* (*Gewehr, Elek*) to discharge; (*Ärger etc*) to vent itself

entlang [ɛnt'laŋ] *präp* (*+akk od dat*) along ▷ *adv* along; **~ dem Fluss, den Fluss entlang** along the river; **hier ~** this way; **entlanggehen** *unreg vi* to walk along

entlarven [ɛnt'larfən] *vt* to unmask, expose

entlassen [ɛnt'lasən] *unreg vt* to discharge; (*Arbeiter*) to dismiss; (*nach Stellenabbau*) to make redundant

entlässt [ɛnt'lɛst] *vb siehe* **entlassen**

Entlassung *f* discharge; dismissal; **es gab 20 ~en** there were 20 redundancies

Entlassungswelle *f* wave of redundancies *od* job losses

Entlassungszeugnis *nt* (*Sch*) school-leaving certificate

entlasten [ɛnt'lastən] *vt* to relieve; (*Arbeit abnehmen*) to take some of the load off; (*Angeklagte*) to exonerate; (*Konto*) to clear

Entlastung *f* relief; (*Comm*) crediting

Entlastungszeuge *m* defence (*Brit*) *od* defense (*US*) witness

Entlastungszug *m* relief train

entledigen [ɛnt'le:dɪgən] *vr*: **sich jds/einer Sache ~** to rid o.s. of sb/sth

entleeren [ɛnt'le:rən] *vt* to empty; (*Darm*) to evacuate

entlegen [ɛnt'le:gən] *adj* remote

entließ *etc* [ɛnt'li:s] *vb siehe* **entlassen**

entlocken [ɛnt'lɔkən] *vt*: **jdm etw ~** to elicit sth from sb

entlohnen *vt* to pay; (*fig*) to reward

entlüften [ɛnt'lʏftən] *vt* to ventilate

entmachten [ɛnt'maxtən] *vt* to deprive of power

entmenscht [ɛnt'mɛnʃt] *adj* inhuman, bestial

entmilitarisiert [ɛntmilitari'zi:rt] *adj* demilitarized

entmündigen [ɛnt'mʏndɪgən] *vt* to certify; (*Jur*) to (legally) incapacitate, declare incapable of managing one's own affairs

entmutigen [ɛnt'mu:tɪgən] *vt* to discourage

Entnahme [ɛnt'na:mə] **(-, -n)** *f* removal, withdrawal

Entnazifizierung [ɛntnatsifi'tsi:rʊŋ] *f*

denazification

entnehmen [ɛnt'ne:mən] *unreg vt +dat* to take out of, take from; (*folgern*) to infer from; **wie ich Ihren Worten entnehme, ...** I gather from what you say that ...

entpuppen [ɛnt'pʊpən] *vr* (*fig*) to reveal o.s., turn out; **sich als etw ~** to turn out to be sth

entrahmen [ɛnt'ra:mən] *vt* to skim

entreißen [ɛnt'raɪsən] *unreg vt*: **jdm etw ~** to snatch sth (away) from sb

entrichten [ɛnt'rɪçtən] *vt* (*form*) to pay

entrosten [ɛnt'rɔstən] *vt* to derust

entrüsten [ɛnt'rʏstən] *vt* to incense, outrage ▷ *vr* to be filled with indignation

entrüstet *adj* indignant, outraged

Entrüstung *f* indignation

Entsafter [ɛnt'zaftər] **(-s, -)** *m* juice extractor

entsagen [ɛnt'za:gən] *vi +dat* to renounce

entschädigen [ɛnt'ʃɛ:dɪgən] *vt* to compensate

Entschädigung *f* compensation

entschärfen [ɛnt'ʃɛrfən] *vt* to defuse; (*Kritik*) to tone down

Entscheid [ɛnt'ʃaɪt] **(-(e)s, -e)** *m* (*form*) decision

entscheiden *unreg vt, vi, vr* to decide; **darüber habe ich nicht zu ~** that is not for me to decide; **sich für jdn/etw ~** to decide in favour of sb/sth; to decide on sb/sth

entscheidend *adj* decisive; (*Stimme*) casting; **das E~e** the decisive *od* deciding factor

Entscheidung *f* decision; **wie ist die ~ ausgefallen?** which way did the decision go?

Entscheidungs- *zW*: **Entscheidungsbefugnis** *f* decision-making powers *pl*; **entscheidungsfähig** *adj* capable of deciding; **Entscheidungsspiel** *nt* play-off; **Entscheidungsträger** *m* decision-maker

entschied *etc* [ɛnt'ʃi:t] *vb siehe* **entscheiden**

entschieden [ɛnt'ʃi:dən] *pp von* **entscheiden** ▷ *adj* decided; (*entschlossen*) resolute; **das geht ~ zu weit** that's definitely going too far; **Entschiedenheit** *f* firmness, determination

entschlacken [ɛnt'ʃlakən] *vt* (*Med: Körper*) to purify

entschließen [ɛnt'ʃli:sən] *unreg vr* to decide; **sich zu nichts ~ können** to be unable to make up one's mind; **kurz entschlossen** straight away

Entschließungsantrag *m* (*Pol*) resolution proposal

entschloss *etc* [ɛnt'ʃlɔs] *vb siehe* **entschließen**

entschlossen [ɛnt'ʃlɔsən] *pp von* **entschließen** ▷ *adj* determined, resolute; **Entschlossenheit** *f* determination

entschlüpfen [ɛnt'ʃlʏpfən] *vi* to escape, slip away; (*fig: Wort etc*) to slip out

Entschluss [ɛnt'ʃlʊs] *m* decision; **aus eigenem ~ handeln** to act on one's own initiative; **es ist mein fester ~** it is my firm intention

entschlüsseln [ɛnt'ʃlʏsəln] *vt* to decipher; (*Funkspruch*) to decode

entschlussfreudig *adj* decisive

Entschlusskraft *f* determination, decisiveness

entschuldbar [ɛnt'ʃʊltba:r] *adj* excusable

entschuldigen [ɛnt'ʃʊldɪgən] *vt* to excuse ▷ *vr* to apologize ▷ *vi*: **~ Sie (bitte)!** excuse me; (*Verzeihung*) sorry; **jdn bei jdm ~** to make sb's excuses *od* apologies to sb; **sich ~ lassen** to send one's apologies

entschuldigend *adj* apologetic

Entschuldigung *f* apology; (*Grund*) excuse; **jdn um ~ bitten** to apologize to sb; **~!** excuse me; (*Verzeihung*) sorry

entschwefeln [ɛnt'ʃvɛ:fəln] *vt* to desulphurize

Entschwefelungsanlage *f* desulphurization plant

entschwinden [ɛnt'ʃvɪndən] *unreg vi* to disappear

entsetzen [ɛnt'zɛtsən] *vt* to horrify ▷ *vr* to be horrified *od* appalled; **Entsetzen (-s)** *nt* horror, dismay

entsetzlich *adj* dreadful, appalling

entsetzt *adj* horrified

entsichern [ɛnt'zɪçərn] *vt* to release the safety catch of

entsinnen [ɛnt'zɪnən] *unreg vr +gen* to remember

entsorgen [ɛnt'zɔrgən] *vt*: **eine Stadt ~** to dispose of a town's refuse and sewage

Entsorgung *f* waste disposal; (*von Chemikalien*) disposal

entspannen [ɛnt'ʃpanən] *vt, vr* (*Körper*) to relax; (*Pol: Lage*) to ease

Entspannung *f* relaxation, rest; (*Pol*) détente

Entspannungspolitik *f* policy of détente

Entspannungsübungen *pl* relaxation exercises *pl*

entspr. *abk* = **entsprechend**

entsprach *etc* [ɛnt'ʃprax] *vb siehe* **entsprechen**

entsprechen [ɛnt'ʃprɛçən] *unreg vi +dat* to correspond to; (*Anforderungen, Wünschen*) to meet, comply with

entsprechend *adj* appropriate ▷ *adv* accordingly ▷ *präp +dat*: **er wird seiner Leistung ~ bezahlt** he is paid according to output

entspricht [ɛnt'ʃprɪçt] *vb siehe* **entsprechen**

entspringen [ɛnt'ʃprɪŋən] *unreg vi (+dat)* to spring (from)

entsprochen [ɛnt'ʃprɔxən] *pp von* **entsprechen**

entstaatlichen [ɛnt'ʃta:tlɪçən] *vt* to denationalize

entstammen [ɛnt'ʃtamən] *vi +dat* to stem *od* come from

entstand *etc* [ɛnt'ʃtant] *vb siehe* **entstehen**

entstanden [ɛnt'ʃtandən] *pp von* **entstehen**

entstehen [ɛnt'ʃte:ən] *unreg vi*: **~ (aus** *od* **durch)** to arise (from), result (from); **wir wollen nicht den Eindruck ~ lassen, ...** we don't want to give rise to the impression that ...; **für ~den** *od* **entstandenen Schaden** for damages incurred

Entstehung *f* genesis, origin

entstellen [ɛnt'ʃtɛlən] *vt* to disfigure; (*Wahrheit*) to distort

Entstellung *f* distortion; disfigurement

entstören [ɛnt'ʃtø:rən] *vt* (*Rundf*) to eliminate

interference from; (*Aut*) to suppress
enttäuschen [ɛnt'tɔyʃən] *vt* to disappoint
Enttäuschung *f* disappointment
entwachsen [ɛnt'vaksən] *unreg vi +dat* to outgrow, grow out of; (*geh: herauswachsen aus*) to spring from
entwaffnen [ɛnt'vafnən] *vt* (*lit, fig*) to disarm
entwaffnend *adj* disarming
Entwarnung [ɛnt'varnʊŋ] *f* all clear (signal)
entwässern [ɛnt'vɛsərn] *vt* to drain
Entwässerung *f* drainage
entweder [ɛnt've:dər] *konj* either; **~ ... oder ...** either ... or ...
entweichen [ɛnt'vaɪçən] *unreg vi* to escape
entweihen [ɛnt'vaɪən] *unreg vt* to desecrate
entwenden [ɛnt'vɛndən] *unreg vt* to purloin, steal
entwerfen [ɛnt'vɛrfən] *unreg vt* (*Zeichnung*) to sketch; (*Modell*) to design; (*Vortrag, Gesetz etc*) to draft
entwerten [ɛnt've:rtən] *vt* to devalue; (*stempeln*) to cancel
Entwerter (**-s, -**) *m* (ticket-)cancelling (*Brit*) *od* canceling (*US*) machine
entwickeln [ɛnt'vɪkəln] *vt* to develop (*auch Phot*); (*Mut, Energie*) to show, display ▷ *vr* to develop
Entwickler (**-s, -**) *m* developer
Entwicklung [ɛnt'vɪklʊŋ] *f* development; (*Phot*) developing; **in der ~** at the development stage; (*Jugendliche etc*) still developing
Entwicklungs- *zW*: **Entwicklungsabschnitt** *m* stage of development; **Entwicklungshelfer, in** *m(f)* VSO worker (*Brit*), Peace Corps worker (*US*); **Entwicklungshilfe** *f* aid for developing countries; **Entwicklungsjahre** *pl* adolescence *sing*; **Entwicklungsland** *nt* developing country; **Entwicklungszeit** *f* period of development; (*Phot*) developing time
entwirren [ɛnt'vɪrən] *vt* to disentangle
entwischen [ɛnt'vɪʃən] *vi* to escape
entwöhnen [ɛnt'vø:nən] *vt* to wean; (*Süchtige*): **(einer Sache** *dat od* **von etw) ~** to cure (of sth)
Entwöhnung *f* weaning; cure, curing
entwürdigend [ɛnt'vʏrdɪgənt] *adj* degrading
Entwurf [ɛnt'vʊrf] *m* outline, design; (*Vertragsentwurf, Konzept*) draft
entwurzeln [ɛnt'vʊrtsəln] *vt* to uproot
entziehen [ɛnt'tsi:ən] *unreg vt (+dat)* to withdraw (from), take away (from); (*Flüssigkeit*) to draw (from), extract (from) ▷ *vr (+dat)* to escape (from); (*jds Kenntnis*) to be outside *od* beyond; (*der Pflicht*) to shirk (from); **sich jds Blicken ~** to be hidden from sight
Entziehung *f* withdrawal
Entziehungsanstalt *f* drug addiction/alcoholism treatment centre (*Brit*) *od* center (*US*)
Entziehungskur *f* treatment for drug addiction/alcoholism
entziffern [ɛnt'tsɪfərn] *vt* to decipher; (*Funkspruch*) to decode
entzücken [ɛnt'tsʏkən] *vt* to delight; **Entzücken** (**-s**) *nt* delight
entzückend *adj* delightful, charming
Entzug [ɛnt'tsu:k] (**-(e)s**) *m* (*einer Lizenz etc, Med*) withdrawal
Entzugserscheinung *f* withdrawal symptom
entzündbar *adj*: **leicht ~** highly inflammable; (*fig*) easily roused
entzünden [ɛnt'tsʏndən] *vt* to light, set light to; (*fig, Med*) to inflame; (*Streit*) to spark off ▷ *vr* (*lit, fig*) to catch fire; (*Streit*) to start; (*Med*) to become inflamed
Entzündung *f* (*Med*) inflammation
entzwei [ɛnt'tsvaɪ] *adv* in two; broken; **entzweibrechen** *unreg vt, vi* to break in two
entzweien *vt* to set at odds ▷ *vr* to fall out
entzweigehen *unreg vi* to break (in two)
Enzian ['ɛntsia:n] (**-s, -e**) *m* gentian
Enzyklika [ɛn'tsy:klika] (**-, -liken**) *f* (*Rel*) encyclical
Enzyklopädie [ɛntsyklopɛ'di:] *f* encyclop(a)edia
Enzym [ɛn'tsy:m] (**-s, -e**) *nt* enzyme
Epen *pl von* **Epos**
Epidemie [epide'mi:] *f* epidemic
Epilepsie [epile'psi:] *f* epilepsy
episch ['e:pɪʃ] *adj* epic
Episode [epi'zo:də] (**-, -n**) *f* episode
Epoche [e'pɔxə] (**-, -n**) *f* epoch; **epochemachend** *adj* epoch-making
Epos ['e:pɔs] (**-, Epen**) *nt* epic (poem)
Equipe [e'kɪp] (**-, -n**) *f* team
er [e:r] *pron* he; it
erachten [ɛr'|axtən] *vt* (*geh*): **~ für** *od* **als** to consider (to be); **meines E~s** in my opinion
erarbeiten [ɛr'|arbaɪtən] *vt* to work for, acquire; (*Theorie*) to work out
Erbanlage ['ɛrp|anla:gə] *f* hereditary factor(s *pl*)
erbarmen [ɛr'barmən] *vr (+gen)* to have pity *od* mercy (on) ▷ *vt*: **er sieht zum E~ aus** he's a pitiful sight; **Herr, erbarme dich (unser)!** Lord, have mercy (upon us)!; **Erbarmen** (**-s**) *nt* pity
erbärmlich [ɛr'bɛrmlɪç] *adj* wretched, pitiful; **Erbärmlichkeit** *f* wretchedness
Erbarmungs- *zW*: **erbarmungslos** *adj* pitiless, merciless; **erbarmungsvoll** *adj* compassionate; **erbarmungswürdig** *adj* pitiable, wretched
erbauen [ɛr'baʊən] *vt* to build, erect; (*fig*) to edify; **er ist von meinem Plan nicht besonders erbaut** (*umg*) he isn't particularly enthusiastic about my plan
Erbauer (**-s, -**) *m* builder
erbaulich *adj* edifying
Erbauung *f* construction; (*fig*) edification
erbberechtigt *adj* entitled to inherit
erbbiologisch *adj*: **~es Gutachten** (*Jur*) blood test (*to establish paternity*)
Erbe[1] ['ɛrbə] (**-n, -n**) *m* heir; **jdn zum** *od* **als ~n einsetzen** to make sb one's/sb's heir
Erbe[2] ['ɛrbə] (**-s**) *nt* inheritance; (*fig*) heritage

erben *vt* to inherit; (*umg: geschenkt bekommen*) to get, be given
erbeuten [ɛr'bɔʏtən] *vt* to carry off; (*Mil*) to capture
Erb- *zW*: **Erbfaktor** *m* gene; **Erbfehler** *m* hereditary defect; **Erbfeind** *m* traditional *od* arch enemy; **Erbfolge** *f* (line of) succession
Erbin *f* heiress
erbitten [ɛr'bɪtən] *unreg vt* to ask for, request
erbittern [ɛr'bɪtərn] *vt* to embitter; (*erzürnen*) to incense
erbittert [ɛr'bɪtərt] *adj* (*Kampf*) fierce, bitter
erblassen [ɛr'blasən] *vi* to (turn) pale
Erblasser, in ['ɛrblasər(ɪn)] (**-s, -**) *m(f)* (*Jur*) *person who leaves an inheritance*
erbleichen [ɛr'blaɪçən] *unreg vi* to (turn) pale
erblich ['ɛrplɪç] *adj* hereditary; **er/sie ist ~ (vor)belastet** it runs in the family
erblichen *pp von* **erbleichen**
erblicken [ɛr'blɪkən] *vt* to see; (*erspähen*) to catch sight of
erblinden [ɛr'blɪndən] *vi* to go blind
Erbmasse ['ɛrpmasə] *f* estate; (*Biol*) genotype
erbosen [ɛr'bo:zən] *vt* (*geh*) to anger ▷ *vr* to grow angry
erbrechen [ɛr'brɛçən] *unreg vt, vr* to vomit
Erbrecht *nt* hereditary right; (*Gesetze*) law of inheritance
Erbschaft *f* inheritance, legacy
Erbschaftssteuer *f* estate *od* death duties *pl*
Erbschleicher, in ['ɛrpʃlaɪçər(ɪn)] (**-s, -**) *m(f)* legacy-hunter
Erbse ['ɛrpsə] (**-, -n**) *f* pea
Erb- *zW*: **Erbstück** *nt* heirloom; **Erbsünde** *f* (*Rel*) original sin; **Erbteil** *nt* inherited trait; (*Jur*) (portion of) inheritance
Erd- *zW*: **Erdachse** *f* earth's axis; **Erdapfel** (*Österr*) *m* potato; **Erdatmosphäre** *f* earth's atmosphere; **Erdbahn** *f* orbit of the earth; **Erdbeben** *nt* earthquake; **Erdbeere** *f* strawberry; **Erdboden** *m* ground; **etw dem Erdboden gleichmachen** to level sth, raze sth to the ground
Erde (**-, -n**) *f* earth; **zu ebener ~** at ground level; **auf der ganzen ~** all over the world; **du wirst mich noch unter die ~ bringen** (*umg*) you'll be the death of me yet
erden *vt* (*Elek*) to earth
erdenkbar [ɛr'dɛŋkba:r] *adj* conceivable; **sich** *dat* **alle ~e Mühe geben** to take the greatest (possible) pains
erdenklich [ɛr'dɛŋklɪç] *adj* = **erdenkbar**
Erdg. *abk* = **Erdgeschoss**
Erd- *zW*: **Erdgas** *nt* natural gas; **Erdgeschoss** *nt* ground floor (*Brit*), first floor (*US*); **Erdkunde** *f* geography; **Erdnuss** *f* peanut; **Erdoberfläche** *f* surface of the earth; **Erdöl** *nt* (mineral) oil; **Erdölfeld** *nt* oilfield; **Erdölindustrie** *f* oil industry; **Erdreich** *nt* soil, earth
erdreisten [ɛr'draɪstən] *vr* to dare, have the audacity (*to do sth*)
erdrosseln [ɛr'drɔsəln] *vt* to strangle, throttle
erdrücken [ɛr'drʏkən] *vt* to crush; **~de Übermacht/~des Beweismaterial** overwhelming superiority/evidence
Erd- *zW*: **Erdrutsch** *m* landslide; **Erdstoß** *m* (seismic) shock; **Erdteil** *m* continent
erdulden [ɛr'dʊldən] *vt* to endure, suffer
ereifern [ɛr'|aɪfərn] *vr* to get excited
ereignen [ɛr'|aɪgnən] *vr* to happen
Ereignis [ɛr'|aɪgnɪs] (**-ses, -se**) *nt* event; **ereignislos** *adj* uneventful; **ereignisreich** *adj* eventful
Eremit [ere'mi:t] (**-en, -en**) *m* hermit
erfahren [ɛr'fa:rən] *unreg vt* to learn, find out; (*erleben*) to experience ▷ *adj* experienced
Erfahrung *f* experience; **~en sammeln** to gain experience; **etw in ~ bringen** to learn *od* find out sth
Erfahrungsaustausch *m* exchange of experiences
erfahrungsgemäß *adv* according to experience
erfand *etc* [ɛr'fant] *vb siehe* **erfinden**
erfassen [ɛr'fasən] *vt* to seize; (*fig: einbeziehen*) to include, register; (*verstehen*) to grasp
erfinden [ɛr'fɪndən] *unreg vt* to invent; **frei erfunden** completely fictitious
Erfinder, in (**-s, -**) *m(f)* inventor; **erfinderisch** *adj* inventive
Erfindung *f* invention
Erfindungsgabe *f* inventiveness
Erfolg [ɛr'fɔlk] (**-(e)s, -e**) *m* success; (*Folge*) result; **~ versprechend** promising; **viel ~!** good luck!
erfolgen [ɛr'fɔlgən] *vi* to follow; (*sich ergeben*) to result; (*stattfinden*) to take place; (*Zahlung*) to be effected; **nach erfolgter Zahlung** when payment has been made
Erfolg- *zW*: **erfolglos** *adj* unsuccessful; **Erfolglosigkeit** *f* lack of success; **erfolgreich** *adj* successful
Erfolgserlebnis *nt* feeling of success, sense of achievement
erfolgversprechend *adj siehe* **Erfolg**
erforderlich *adj* requisite, necessary
erfordern [ɛr'fɔrdərn] *vt* to require, demand
Erfordernis (**-ses, -se**) *nt* requirement, prerequisite
erforschen [ɛr'fɔrʃən] *vt* (*Land*) to explore; (*Problem*) to investigate; (*Gewissen*) to search
Erforscher, in (**-s, -**) *m(f)* explorer; investigator
Erforschung *f* exploration; investigation; searching
erfragen [ɛr'fra:gən] *vt* to inquire, ascertain
erfreuen [ɛr'frɔʏən] *vr*: **sich ~ an** *+dat* to enjoy ▷ *vt* to delight; **sich einer Sache** *gen* **~** (*geh*) to enjoy sth; **sehr erfreut!** (*form: bei Vorstellung*) pleased to meet you!
erfreulich [ɛr'frɔʏlɪç] *adj* pleasing, gratifying
erfreulicherweise *adv* happily, luckily
erfrieren [ɛr'fri:rən] *unreg vi* to freeze (to death); (*Glieder*) to get frostbitten; (*Pflanzen*) to be killed by frost
erfrischen [ɛr'frɪʃən] *vt* to refresh
Erfrischung *f* refreshment

Erfrischungsraum *m* snack bar, cafeteria
erfüllen [ɛrˈfʏlən] *vt* (*Raum etc*) to fill; (*fig: Bitte etc*) to fulfil (*Brit*), fulfill (*US*) ▷ *vr* to come true; **ein erfülltes Leben** a full life
Erfüllung *f*: **in ~ gehen** to be fulfilled
erfunden [ɛrˈfʊndən] *pp von* **erfinden**
ergab *etc* [ɛrˈgaːp] *vb siehe* **ergeben**
ergänzen [ɛrˈgɛntsən] *vt* to supplement, complete ▷ *vr* to complement one another
Ergänzung *f* completion; (*Zusatz*) supplement
ergattern [ɛrˈgatərn] (*umg*) *vt* to get hold of, hunt up
ergaunern [ɛrˈgaʊnərn] (*umg*) *vt*: **sich** *dat* **etw ~** to get hold of sth by underhand methods
ergeben [ɛrˈgeːbən] *unreg vt* to yield, produce ▷ *vr* to surrender; (*folgen*) to result ▷ *adj* devoted; (*demütig*) humble; **sich einer Sache** *dat* **~** (*sich hingeben*) to give o.s. up to sth, yield to sth; **es ergab sich, dass unsere Befürchtungen ...** it turned out that our fears ...; **dem Trunk ~** addicted to drink; **Ergebenheit** *f* devotion; humility
Ergebnis [ɛrˈgeːpnɪs] (**-ses, -se**) *nt* result; **zu einem ~ kommen** to come to *od* reach a conclusion; **ergebnislos** *adj* without result, fruitless; **ergebnislos bleiben** *od* **verlaufen** to come to nothing
ergehen [ɛrˈgeːən] *unreg vi* (*form*) to be issued, go out ▷ *vi unpers*: **es ergeht ihm gut/schlecht** he's faring *od* getting on well/badly ▷ *vr*: **sich in etw** *dat* **~** to indulge in sth; **etw über sich** *akk* **~ lassen** to put up with sth; **sich (in langen Reden) über ein Thema ~** (*fig*) to hold forth at length on sth
ergiebig [ɛrˈgiːbɪç] *adj* productive
ergo [ˈɛrgo] *konj* therefore, ergo (*liter, hum*)
Ergonomie [ɛrgonoˈmiː] *f* ergonomics *pl*
ergötzen [ɛrˈgœtsən] *vt* to amuse, delight
ergrauen [ɛrˈgraʊən] *vi* to turn *od* go grey (*Brit*) *od* gray (*US*)
ergreifen [ɛrˈgraɪfən] *unreg vt* (*lit, fig*) to seize; (*Beruf*) to take up; (*Maßnahmen*) to resort to; (*rühren*) to move; **er ergriff das Wort** he began to speak
ergreifend *adj* moving, affecting
ergriff *etc* [ɛrˈgrɪf] *vb siehe* **ergreifen**
ergriffen *pp von* **ergreifen** ▷ *adj* deeply moved
Ergriffenheit *f* emotion
ergründen [ɛrˈgrʏndən] *vt* (*Sinn etc*) to fathom; (*Ursache, Motive*) to discover
Erguss [ɛrˈgʊs] (**-es, ¨-e**) *m* discharge; (*fig*) outpouring, effusion
erhaben [ɛrˈhaːbən] *adj* (*lit*) raised, embossed; (*fig*) exalted, lofty; **über etw** *akk* **~ sein** to be above sth
Erhalt *m*: **bei** *od* **nach ~** on receipt
erhält [ɛrˈhɛlt] *vb siehe* **erhalten**
erhalten [ɛrˈhaltən] *unreg vt* to receive; (*bewahren*) to preserve, maintain; **das Wort ~** to receive permission to speak; **jdn am Leben ~** to keep sb alive; **gut ~** in good condition
erhältlich [ɛrˈhɛltlɪç] *adj* obtainable, available
Erhaltung *f* maintenance, preservation
erhängen [ɛrˈhɛŋən] *vt, vr* to hang
erhärten [ɛrˈhɛrtən] *vt* to harden; (*These*) to substantiate, corroborate
erhaschen [ɛrˈhaʃən] *vt* to catch
erheben [ɛrˈheːbən] *unreg vt* to raise; (*Protest, Forderungen*) to make; (*Fakten*) to ascertain ▷ *vr* to rise (up); **sich über etw** *akk* **~** to rise above sth
erheblich [ɛrˈheːplɪç] *adj* considerable
erheitern [ɛrˈhaɪtərn] *vt* to amuse, cheer (up)
Erheiterung *f* exhilaration; **zur allgemeinen ~** to everybody's amusement
erhellen [ɛrˈhɛlən] *vt* (*lit, fig*) to illuminate; (*Geheimnis*) to shed light on ▷ *vr* (*Fenster*) to light up; (*Himmel, Miene*) to brighten (up); (*Gesicht*) to brighten up
erhielt *etc* [ɛrˈhiːlt] *vb siehe* **erhalten**
erhitzen [ɛrˈhɪtsən] *vt* to heat ▷ *vr* to heat up; (*fig*) to become heated *od* aroused
erhoffen [ɛrˈhɔfən] *vt* to hope for; **was erhoffst du dir davon?** what do you hope to gain from it?
erhöhen [ɛrˈhøːən] *vt* to raise; (*verstärken*) to increase; **erhöhte Temperatur haben** to have a temperature
Erhöhung *f* (*Gehalt*) increment
erholen [ɛrˈhoːlən] *vr* to recover; (*entspannen*) to have a rest; (*fig: Preise, Aktien*) to rally, pick up
erholsam *adj* restful
Erholung *f* recovery; relaxation, rest
erholungsbedürftig *adj* in need of a rest, run-down
Erholungsgebiet *nt* holiday (*Brit*) *od* vacation (*US*) area
Erholungsheim *nt* convalescent home
erhören [ɛrˈhøːrən] *vt* (*Gebet etc*) to hear; (*Bitte etc*) to yield to
Erika [ˈeːrika] (**-, Eriken**) *f* heather
erinnern [ɛrˈ|ɪnərn] *vt*: **~ (an** *+akk***)** to remind (of) ▷ *vr*: **sich (an etw** *akk***) ~** to remember (sth)
Erinnerung *f* memory; (*Andenken*) reminder; **Erinnerungen** *pl* (*Lebenserinnerung*) reminiscences *pl*; (*Liter*) memoirs *pl*; **jdn/etw in guter ~ behalten** to have pleasant memories of sb/sth
Erinnerungsschreiben *nt* (*Comm*) reminder
Erinnerungstafel *f* commemorative plaque
Eritrea [eriˈtreːa] (**-s**) *nt* Eritrea
erkalten [ɛrˈkaltən] *vi* to go cold, cool (down)
erkälten [ɛrˈkɛltən] *vr* to catch cold; **sich** *dat* **die Blase ~** to catch a chill in one's bladder
erkältet *adj* with a cold; **~ sein** to have a cold
Erkältung *f* cold
erkämpfen [ɛrˈkɛmpfən] *vt* to win, secure
erkannt [ɛrˈkant] *pp von* **erkennen**
erkannte *etc vb siehe* **erkennen**
erkennbar *adj* recognizable
erkennen [ɛrˈkɛnən] *unreg vt* to recognize; (*sehen, verstehen*) to see; **jdm zu ~ geben, dass ...** to give sb to understand that ...
erkenntlich *adj*: **sich ~ zeigen** to show one's appreciation; **Erkenntlichkeit** *f* gratitude; (*Geschenk*) token of one's gratitude

Erkenntnis (**-, -se**) *f* knowledge; (*das Erkennen*) recognition; (*Einsicht*) insight; **zur ~ kommen** to realize
Erkennung *f* recognition
Erkennungsdienst *m* police records department
Erkennungsmarke *f* identity disc
Erker ['ɛrkər] (**-s, -**) *m* bay; **Erkerfenster** *nt* bay window
erklärbar *adj* explicable
erklären [ɛr'klɛ:rən] *vt* to explain; (*Rücktritt*) to announce; (*Politiker, Pressesprecher etc*) to say; **ich kann mir nicht ~, warum ...** I can't understand why ...
erklärlich *adj* explicable; (*verständlich*) understandable
erklärt *adj attrib* (*Gegner etc*) professed, avowed; (*Favorit, Liebling*) acknowledged
Erklärung *f* explanation; (*Aussage*) declaration
erklecklich [ɛr'klɛklɪç] *adj* considerable
erklimmen [ɛr'klɪmən] *unreg vt* to climb to
erklingen [ɛr'klɪŋən] *unreg vi* to resound, ring out
erklomm *etc* [ɛr'klɔm] *vb siehe* **erklimmen**
erklommen *pp von* **erklimmen**
erkranken [ɛr'kraŋkən] *vi*: **~ (an** *+dat***)** to be taken ill (with); (*Organ, Pflanze, Tier*) to become diseased (with)
Erkrankung *f* illness
erkunden [ɛr'kʊndən] *vt* to find out, ascertain; (*bes Mil*) to reconnoitre (*Brit*), reconnoiter (*US*)
erkundigen *vr*: **sich ~ (nach)** to inquire (about); **ich werde mich ~** I'll find out
Erkundigung *f* inquiry; **~en einholen** to make inquiries
Erkundung *f* (*Mil*) reconnaissance, scouting
erlahmen [ɛr'la:mən] *vi* to tire; (*nachlassen*) to flag, wane
erlangen [ɛr'laŋən] *vt* to attain, achieve
Erlass [ɛr'las] (**-es, -e**) *m* decree; (*Aufhebung*) remission
erlassen *unreg vt* (*Verfügung*) to issue; (*Gesetz*) to enact; (*Strafe*) to remit; **jdm etw ~** to release sb from sth
erlauben [ɛr'laʊbən] *vt* to allow, permit ▷ *vr*: **sich** *dat* **etw ~** (*Zigarette, Pause*) to permit o.s. sth; (*Bemerkung, Verschlag*) to venture sth; (*sich leisten*) to afford sth; **jdm etw ~** to allow *od* permit sb (to do) sth; **~ Sie?** may I?; **~ Sie mal!** do you mind!; **was ~ Sie sich (eigentlich)!** how dare you!
Erlaubnis [ɛr'laʊpnɪs] (**-, -se**) *f* permission
erläutern [ɛr'lɔʏtərn] *vt* to explain
Erläuterung *f* explanation; **zur ~** in explanation
Erle ['ɛrlə] (**-, -n**) *f* alder
erleben [ɛr'le:bən] *vt* to experience; (*Zeit*) to live through; (*miterleben*) to witness; (*noch miterleben*) to live to see; **so wütend habe ich ihn noch nie erlebt** I've never seen *od* known him so furious
Erlebnis [ɛr'le:pnɪs] (**-ses, -se**) *nt* experience
erledigen [ɛr'le:dɪgən] *vt* to take care of, deal with; (*Antrag etc*) to process; (*umg: erschöpfen*) to wear out; (*ruinieren*) to finish; (*umbringen*) to do in ▷ *vr*: **das hat sich erledigt** that's all settled; **das ist erledigt** that's taken care of, that's been done; **ich habe noch einiges in der Stadt zu ~** I've still got a few things to do in town
erledigt (*umg*) *adj* (*erschöpft*) shattered, done in; (*: ruiniert*) finished, ruined
erlegen [ɛr'le:gən] *vt* to kill
erleichtern [ɛr'laɪçtərn] *vt* to make easier; (*fig: Last*) to lighten; (*lindern, beruhigen*) to relieve
erleichtert *adj* relieved; **~ aufatmen** to breathe a sigh of relief
Erleichterung *f* facilitation; lightening; relief
erleiden [ɛr'laɪdən] *unreg vt* to suffer, endure
erlernbar *adj* learnable
erlernen [ɛr'lɛrnən] *vt* to learn, acquire
erlesen [ɛr'le:zən] *adj* select, choice
erleuchten [ɛr'lɔʏçtən] *vt* to illuminate; (*fig*) to inspire
Erleuchtung *f* (*Einfall*) inspiration
erliegen [ɛr'li:gən] *unreg vi +dat* (*lit, fig*) to succumb to; (*einem Irrtum*) to be the victim of; **zum E~ kommen** to come to a standstill
erlischt [ɛr'lɪʃt] *vb siehe* **erlöschen**
erlogen [ɛr'lo:gən] *adj* untrue, made-up
Erlös [ɛr'lø:s] (**-es, -e**) *m* proceeds *pl*
erlosch *etc* [ɛr'lɔʃ] *vb siehe* **erlöschen**
erlöschen [ɛr'lœʃən] *unreg vi* (*Feuer*) to go out; (*Interesse*) to cease, die; (*Vertrag, Recht*) to expire; **ein erloschener Vulkan** an extinct volcano
erlösen [ɛr'lø:zən] *vt* to redeem, save
Erlöser (**-s, -**) *m* (*Rel*) Redeemer; (*Befreier*) saviour (*Brit*), savior (*US*)
Erlösung *f* release; (*Rel*) redemption
ermächtigen [ɛr'mɛçtɪgən] *vt* to authorize, empower
Ermächtigung *f* authorization
ermahnen [ɛr'ma:nən] *vt* to admonish, exhort
Ermahnung *f* admonition, exhortation
Ermangelung [ɛr'maŋəlʊŋ], **Ermanglung** [ɛr'maŋlʊŋ] *f*: **in Ermang(e)lung** *+gen* because of the lack of
ermäßigen [ɛr'mɛsɪgən] *vt* to reduce
Ermäßigung *f* reduction
ermessen [ɛr'mɛsən] *unreg vt* to estimate, gauge; **Ermessen** (**-s**) *nt* estimation; discretion; **in jds Ermessen** *dat* **liegen** to lie within sb's discretion; **nach meinem Ermessen** in my judgement
Ermessensfrage *f* matter of discretion
ermitteln [ɛr'mɪtəln] *vt* to determine; (*Täter*) to trace ▷ *vi*: **gegen jdn ~** to investigate sb
Ermittlung [ɛr'mɪtlʊŋ] *f* determination; (*Polizeiermittlung*) investigation; **~en anstellen (über** *+akk***)** to make inquiries (about)
Ermittlungsverfahren *nt* (*Jur*) preliminary proceedings *pl*
ermöglichen [ɛr'mø:klɪçən] *vt* (*+dat*) to make possible (for)
ermorden [ɛr'mɔrdən] *vt* to murder
Ermordung *f* murder

ermüden [ɛr'myːdən] *vt* to tire; (*Tech*) to fatigue ▷ *vi* to tire
ermüdend *adj* tiring; (*fig*) wearisome
Ermüdung *f* fatigue
Ermüdungserscheinung *f* sign of fatigue
ermuntern [ɛr'mʊntərn] *vt* to rouse; (*ermutigen*) to encourage; (*beleben*) to liven up; (*aufmuntern*) to cheer up
ermutigen [ɛr'muːtɪgən] *vt* to encourage
ernähren [ɛr'nɛːrən] *vt* to feed, nourish; (*Familie*) to support ▷ *vr* to support o.s., earn a living; **sich ~ von** to live on
Ernährer, in (**-s, -**) *m(f)* breadwinner
Ernährung *f* nourishment; (*Med*) nutrition; (*Unterhalt*) maintenance
ernennen [ɛr'nɛnən] *unreg vt* to appoint
Ernennung *f* appointment
erneuern [ɛr'nɔʏərn] *vt* to renew; (*restaurieren*) to restore; (*renovieren*) to renovate
Erneuerung *f* renewal; restoration; renovation
erneut *adj* renewed, fresh ▷ *adv* once more
erniedrigen [ɛr'niːdrɪgən] *vt* to humiliate, degrade
Ernst [ɛrnst] (**-es**) *m* seriousness; **das ist mein ~** I'm quite serious; **im ~** in earnest; **~ machen mit etw** to put sth into practice; **ernst** *adj* serious ▷ *adv*: **es steht ernst um ihn** things don't look too good for him; **ernst gemeint** meant in earnest, serious; **Ernstfall** *m* emergency; **ernsthaft** *adj* serious; **Ernsthaftigkeit** *f* seriousness; **ernstlich** *adj* serious
Ernte ['ɛrntə] (**-, -n**) *f* harvest; **Erntedankfest** *nt* harvest festival
ernten *vt* to harvest; (*Lob etc*) to earn
ernüchtern [ɛr'nʏçtərn] *vt* to sober up; (*fig*) to bring down to earth
Ernüchterung *f* sobering up; (*fig*) disillusionment
Eroberer [ɛr'|obərər] (**-s, -**) *m* conqueror
erobern *vt* to conquer
Eroberung *f* conquest
eröffnen [ɛr'|œfnən] *vt* to open ▷ *vr* to present itself; **jdm etw ~** (*geh*) to disclose sth to sb
Eröffnung *f* opening
Eröffnungsansprache *f* inaugural *od* opening address
Eröffnungsfeier *f* opening ceremony
erogen [ero'geːn] *adj* erogenous
erörtern [ɛr'|œrtərn] *vt* to discuss (in detail)
Erörterung *f* discussion
Erotik [e'roːtɪk] *f* eroticism
erotisch *adj* erotic
Erpel ['ɛrpəl] (**-, -**) *m* drake
erpicht [ɛr'pɪçt] *adj*: **~ (auf** *+akk***)** keen (on)
erpressen [ɛr'prɛsən] *vt* (*Geld etc*) to extort; (*jdn*) to blackmail
Erpresser (**-s, -**) *m* blackmailer
Erpressung *f* blackmail; extortion
erproben [ɛr'proːbən] *vt* to test; **erprobt** tried and tested
erraten [ɛr'raːtən] *unreg vt* to guess
errechnen [ɛr'rɛçnən] *vt* to calculate, work out
erregbar [ɛr'reːkbaːr] *adj* excitable; (*reizbar*) irritable; **Erregbarkeit** *f* excitability; irritability
erregen [ɛr'reːgən] *vt* to excite; (*sexuell*) to arouse; (*ärgern*) to infuriate; (*hervorrufen*) to arouse, provoke ▷ *vr* to get excited *od* worked up
Erreger (**-s, -**) *m* causative agent
Erregtheit *f* excitement; (*Beunruhigung*) agitation
Erregung *f* excitement; (*sexuell*) arousal
erreichbar *adj* accessible, within reach
erreichen [ɛr'raɪçən] *vt* to reach; (*Zweck*) to achieve; (*Zug*) to catch; **wann kann ich Sie morgen ~?** when can I get in touch with you tomorrow?; **vom Bahnhof leicht zu ~** within easy reach of the station
errichten [ɛr'rɪçtən] *vt* to erect, put up; (*gründen*) to establish, set up
erringen [ɛr'rɪŋən] *unreg vt* to gain, win
erröten [ɛr'røːtən] *vi* to blush, flush
Errungenschaft [ɛr'rʊŋənʃaft] *f* achievement; (*umg: Anschaffung*) acquisition
Ersatz [ɛr'zats] (**-es**) *m* substitute; replacement; (*Schadenersatz*) compensation; (*Mil*) reinforcements *pl*; **als ~ für jdn einspringen** to stand in for sb; **Ersatzbefriedigung** *f* vicarious satisfaction; **Ersatzdienst** *m* (*Mil*) alternative service; **Ersatzkasse** *f* private health insurance; **Ersatzmann** *m* replacement; (*Sport*) substitute; **Ersatzmutter** *f* substitute mother; **ersatzpflichtig** *adj* liable to pay compensation; **Ersatzreifen** *m* (*Aut*) spare tyre (*Brit*) *od* tire (*US*); **Ersatzteil** *nt* spare (part); **ersatzweise** *adv* as an alternative
ersaufen [ɛr'zaʊfən] *unreg* (*umg*) *vi* to drown
ersäufen [ɛr'zɔʏfən] *vt* to drown
erschaffen [ɛr'ʃafən] *unreg vt* to create
erscheinen [ɛr'ʃaɪnən] *unreg vi* to appear
Erscheinung *f* appearance; (*Geist*) apparition; (*Gegebenheit*) phenomenon; (*Gestalt*) figure; **in ~ treten** (*Merkmale*) to appear; (*Gefühle*) to show themselves
Erscheinungsform *f* manifestation
Erscheinungsjahr *nt* (*von Buch*) year of publication
erschien *etc* [ɛr'ʃiːn] *vb siehe* **erscheinen**
erschienen *pp von* **erscheinen**
erschießen [ɛr'ʃiːsən] *unreg vt* to shoot (dead)
erschlaffen [ɛr'ʃlafən] *vi* to go limp; (*Mensch*) to become exhausted
erschlagen [ɛr'ʃlaːgən] *unreg vt* to strike dead ▷ *adj* (*umg: todmüde*) worn out, dead beat (*umg*)
erschleichen [ɛr'ʃlaɪçən] *unreg vt* to obtain by stealth *od* dubious methods
erschließen [ɛr'ʃliːsən] *unreg vt* (*Gebiet, Absatzmarkt*) to develop, open up; (*Bodenschätze*) to tap
erschlossen [ɛr'ʃlɔsən] *adj* (*Gebiet*) developed
erschöpfen [ɛr'ʃœpfən] *vt* to exhaust
erschöpfend *adj* exhaustive, thorough
erschöpft *adj* exhausted

Erschöpfung *f* exhaustion
erschossen [ɛrˈʃɔsən] *(umg) adj*: **(völlig) ~ sein** to be whacked, be dead (beat)
erschrak *etc* [ɛrˈʃraːk] *vb siehe* **erschrecken²**
erschrecken¹ [ɛrˈʃrɛkən] *vt* to startle, frighten
erschrecken² [ɛrˈʃrɛkən] *unreg vi* to be frightened *od* startled
erschreckend *adj* alarming, frightening
erschrickt [ɛrˈʃrɪkt] *vb siehe* **erschrecken²**
erschrocken [ɛrˈʃrɔkən] *pp von* **erschrecken²** ▷ *adj* frightened, startled
erschüttern [ɛrˈʃʏtərn] *vt* to shake; *(ergreifen)* to move deeply; **ihn kann nichts ~** he always keeps his cool *(umg)*
erschütternd *adj* shattering
Erschütterung *f (des Bodens)* tremor; *(tiefe Ergriffenheit)* shock
erschweren [ɛrˈʃveːrən] *vt* to complicate; **~de Umstände** *(Jur)* aggravating circumstances; **es kommt noch ~d hinzu, dass …** to compound matters …
erschwindeln [ɛrˈʃvɪndəln] *vt* to obtain by fraud
erschwinglich *adj* affordable
ersehen [ɛrˈzeːən] *unreg vt*: **aus etw ~, dass …** to gather from sth that …
ersehnt [ɛrˈzeːnt] *adj* longed-for
ersetzbar *adj* replaceable
ersetzen [ɛrˈzɛtsən] *vt* to replace; **jdm Unkosten** *etc* **~** to pay sb's expenses *etc*
ersichtlich [ɛrˈzɪçtlɪç] *adj* evident, obvious
ersparen [ɛrˈʃpaːrən] *vt (Ärger etc)* to spare; *(Geld)* to save; **ihr blieb auch nichts erspart** she was spared nothing
Ersparnis (-, -se) *f* saving
ersprießlich [ɛrˈʃpriːslɪç] *adj* profitable, useful; *(angenehm)* pleasant

SCHLÜSSELWORT

erst [eːrst] *adv* **1** first; **mach erst (ein)mal die Arbeit fertig** finish your work first; **wenn du das erst (ein)mal hinter dir hast** once you've got that behind you
2 *(nicht früher als, nur)* only; *(nicht bis)* not till; **erst gestern** only yesterday; **erst morgen** not until tomorrow; **erst als** only when, not until; **wir fahren erst später** we're not going until later; **er ist (gerade) erst angekommen** he's only just arrived
3: wäre er doch erst zurück! if only he were back!; **da fange ich erst gar nicht an** I simply won't bother to begin; **jetzt erst recht!** that just makes me all the more determined; **da gings erst richtig los** then things really got going

erstarren [ɛrˈʃtarən] *vi* to stiffen; *(vor Furcht)* to grow rigid; *(Materie)* to solidify
erstatten [ɛrˈʃtatən] *vt (Unkosten)* to refund; **Anzeige gegen jdn ~** to report sb; **Bericht ~** to make a report
Erstattung *f (von Unkosten)* reimbursement
Erstaufführung [ˈeːrst|aʊffyːrʊŋ] *f* first performance
erstaunen [ɛrˈʃtaʊnən] *vt* to astonish ▷ *vi* to be astonished; **Erstaunen (-s)** *nt* astonishment
erstaunlich *adj* astonishing
Erstausgabe *f* first edition
erstbeste, r, s *adj* first that comes along
erste, r, s *adj* first; **als E~s** first of all; **in ~r Linie** first and foremost; **fürs E~** for the time being; **E~ Hilfe** first aid; **das ~ Mal** the first time
erstechen [ɛrˈʃtɛçən] *unreg vt* to stab (to death)
erstehen [ɛrˈʃteːən] *unreg vt* to buy ▷ *vi* to (a)rise
ersteigen [ɛrˈʃtaɪgən] *unreg vt* to climb, ascend
ersteigern [ɛrˈʃtaɪgərn] *vt* to buy at an auction
erstellen [ɛrˈʃtɛlən] *vt* to erect, build
erstens *adv* firstly, in the first place
erstere, r, s *pron* (the) former; **der/die/das E~** the former
ersticken [ɛrˈʃtɪkən] *vt (lit, fig)* to stifle; *(Mensch)* to suffocate; *(Flammen)* to smother ▷ *vi (Mensch)* to suffocate; *(Feuer)* to be smothered; **mit erstickter Stimme** in a choked voice; **in Arbeit ~** to be snowed under with work
Erstickung *f* suffocation
erst- *zW*: **erstklassig** *adj* first-class; **Erstkommunion** *f* first communion; **erstmalig** *adj* first; **erstmals** *adv* for the first time; **erstrangig** *adj* first-rate
erstrebenswert [ɛrˈʃtreːbənsveːrt] *adj* desirable, worthwhile
erstrecken [ɛrˈʃtrɛkən] *vr* to extend, stretch
Erststimme *f* first vote; *see culture note*

ERSTSTIMME/ZWEITSTIMME

The *Erststimme* and *Zweitstimme* (first and second vote) system is used to elect MPs to the *Bundestag*. Each elector is given two votes. The first is to choose a candidate in his constituency; the candidate with the most votes is elected MP. The second is to choose a party. All the second votes in each *Land* are counted and a proportionate number of MP's from each party is sent to the *Bundestag*.

Ersttagsbrief *m* first-day cover
Ersttagsstempel *m* first-day (date) stamp
erstunken [ɛrˈʃtʊŋkən] *adj*: **das ist ~ und erlogen** *(umg)* that's a pack of lies
Erstwähler (-s, -) *m* first-time voter
ersuchen [ɛrˈzuːxən] *vt* to request
ertappen [ɛrˈtapən] *vt* to catch, detect
erteilen [ɛrˈtaɪlən] *vt* to give
ertönen [ɛrˈtøːnən] *vi* to sound, ring out
Ertrag [ɛrˈtraːk] **(-(e)s, ¨-e)** *m* yield; *(Gewinn)* proceeds *pl*
ertragen *unreg vt* to bear, stand
erträglich [ɛrˈtrɛːklɪç] *adj* tolerable, bearable
ertragreich *adj (Geschäft)* profitable, lucrative
ertrank *etc* [ɛrˈtraŋk] *vb siehe* **ertrinken**
ertränken [ɛrˈtrɛŋkən] *vt* to drown

erträumen [ɛr'trɔʏmən] *vt*: **sich** *dat* **etw** ~ to dream of sth, imagine sth
ertrinken [ɛr'trɪŋkən] *unreg vi* to drown; **Ertrinken** (**-s**) *nt* drowning
ertrunken [ɛr'trʊŋkən] *pp von* **ertrinken**
erübrigen [ɛr'|y:brɪgən] *vt* to spare ▷ *vr* to be unnecessary
erwachen [ɛr'vaxən] *vi* to awake; **ein böses E~** (*fig*) a rude awakening
erwachsen [ɛr'vaksən] *adj* grown-up ▷ *vi unreg*: **daraus erwuchsen ihm Unannehmlichkeiten** that caused him some trouble
Erwachsene, r *f(m)* adult
Erwachsenenbildung *f* adult education
erwägen [ɛr'vɛ:gən] *unreg vt* to consider
Erwägung *f* consideration; **etw in ~ ziehen** to take sth into consideration
erwähnen [ɛr'vɛ:nən] *vt* to mention
erwähnenswert *adj* worth mentioning
Erwähnung *f* mention
erwarb *etc* [ɛr'varp] *vb siehe* **erwerben**
erwärmen [ɛr'vɛrmən] *vt* to warm, heat ▷ *vr* to get warm, warm up; **sich ~ für** to warm to
erwarten [ɛr'vartən] *vt* to expect; (*warten auf*) to wait for; **etw kaum ~ können** to hardly be able to wait for sth
Erwartung *f* expectation; **in ~ Ihrer baldigen Antwort** (*form*) in anticipation of your early reply
erwartungsgemäß *adv* as expected
erwartungsvoll *adj* expectant
erwecken [ɛr'vɛkən] *vt* to rouse, awake; **den Anschein ~** to give the impression; **etw zu neuem Leben ~** to resurrect sth
erwehren [ɛr've:rən] *vr +gen* (*geh*) to fend off, ward off; (*des Lachens etc*) to refrain from
erweichen [ɛr'vaɪçən] *vt* to soften; **sich nicht ~ lassen** to be unmoved
erweisen [ɛr'vaɪzən] *unreg vt* to prove ▷ *vr*: **sich ~ als** to prove to be; **jdm einen Gefallen/ Dienst ~** to do sb a favour/service; **sich jdm gegenüber dankbar ~** to show one's gratitude to sb
erweitern [ɛr'vaɪtərn] *vt, vr* to widen, enlarge; (*Geschäft*) to expand; (*Med*) to dilate; (*fig: Kenntnisse*) to broaden; (*Macht*) to extend
Erweiterung *f* expansion
Erwerb [ɛr'vɛrp] (**-(e)s, -e**) *m* acquisition; (*Beruf*) trade
erwerben [ɛr'vɛrbən] *unreg vt* to acquire; **er hat sich** *dat* **große Verdienste um die Firma erworben** he has done great service for the firm
Erwerbs- *zW*: **erwerbsfähig** *adj* (*form*) capable of gainful employment; **Erwerbsgesellschaft** *f* acquisitive society; **erwerbslos** *adj* unemployed; **Erwerbsquelle** *f* source of income; **erwerbstätig** *adj* (gainfully) employed; **erwerbsunfähig** *adj* unable to work
erwidern [ɛr'vi:dərn] *vt* to reply; (*vergelten*) to return
Erwiderung *f*: **in ~ Ihres Schreibens vom ...** (*form*) in reply to your letter of the ...
erwiesen [ɛr'vi:zən] *adj* proven
erwirbt [ɛr'vɪrpt] *vb siehe* **erwerben**
erwirtschaften [ɛr'vɪrtʃaftən] *vt* (*Gewinn etc*) to make by good management
erwischen [ɛr'vɪʃən] (*umg*) *vt* to catch, get; **ihn hats erwischt!** (*umg: verliebt*) he's got it bad; (*: krank*) he's got it; **kalt ~** (*umg*) to catch off-balance
erworben [ɛr'vɔrbən] *pp von* **erwerben**
erwünscht [ɛr'vʏnʃt] *adj* desired
erwürgen [ɛr'vʏrgən] *vt* to strangle
Erz [e:rts] (**-es, -e**) *nt* ore
erzählen [ɛr'tsɛ:lən] *vt, vi* to tell; **dem werd ich was ~!** (*umg*) I'll have something to say to him; **~de Dichtung** narrative fiction
Erzähler, in (**-s, -**) *m(f)* narrator
Erzählung *f* story, tale
Erzbischof *m* archbishop
Erzengel *m* archangel
erzeugen [er'tsɔʏgən] *vt* to produce; (*Strom*) to generate
Erzeuger (**-s, -**) *m* producer; **Erzeugerpreis** *m* manufacturer's price
Erzeugnis (**-ses, -se**) *nt* product, produce
Erzeugung *f* production; generation
Erzfeind *m* arch enemy
erziehbar *adj*: **ein Heim für schwer ~e Kinder** a home for difficult children
erziehen [ɛr'tsi:ən] *unreg vt* to bring up; (*bilden*) to educate, train
Erzieher, in (**-s, -**) *m(f)* educator; (*in Kindergarten*) nursery school teacher
Erziehung *f* bringing up; (*Bildung*) education
Erziehungs- *zW*: **Erziehungsberechtigte, r** *f(m)* parent, legal guardian; **Erziehungsgeld** *nt* payment for new parents; **Erziehungsheim** *nt* community home; **Erziehungsurlaub** *m* leave for a new parent
erzielen [ɛr'tsi:lən] *vt* to achieve, obtain; (*Tor*) to score
erzkonservativ ['ɛrtskɔnzɛrva'ti:f] *adj* ultraconservative
erzog *etc* [ɛr'tso:k] *vb siehe* **erziehen**
erzogen [ɛr'tso:gən] *pp von* **erziehen**
erzürnen [ɛr'tsʏrnən] *vt* (*geh*) to anger, incense
erzwingen [ɛr'tsvɪŋən] *unreg vt* to force, obtain by force
Es [ɛs] (**-**) *nt* (*Mus: Dur*) E flat
es [ɛs] *nom, akk pron* it
Esche ['ɛʃə] (**-, -n**) *f* ash
Esel ['e:zəl] (**-s, -**) *m* donkey, ass; **ich ~!** (*umg*) silly me!
Eselsbrücke *f* (*Gedächtnishilfe*) mnemonic, aide-mémoire
Eselsohr *nt* dog-ear
Eskalation [ɛskalatsi'o:n] *f* escalation
eskalieren [ɛska'li:rən] *vt, vi* to escalate
Eskimo ['ɛskimo] (**-s, -s**) *m* eskimo
Eskorte [ɛs'kɔrtə] (**-, -n**) *f* (*Mil*) escort
eskortieren [ɛskɔr'ti:rən] *vt* (*geh*) to escort
Espenlaub ['ɛspənlaʊp] *nt*: **zittern wie ~** to shake like a leaf

essbar ['ɛsba:r] *adj* eatable, edible
Essecke *f* dining area
essen ['ɛsən] *unreg vt, vi* to eat; **~ gehen** (*auswärts*) to eat out; **~ Sie gern Äpfel?** do you like apples?; **Essen** (**-s, -**) *nt* (*Mahlzeit*) meal; (*Nahrung*) food; **Essen auf Rädern** meals on wheels
Essens- *zW*: **Essensausgabe** *f* serving of meals; (*Stelle*) serving counter; **Essensmarke** *f* meal voucher; **Essenszeit** *f* mealtime
Essgeschirr *nt* dinner service
Essig ['ɛsɪç] (**-s, -e**) *m* vinegar; **damit ist es ~** (*umg*) it's all off; **Essiggurke** *f* gherkin
Esskastanie *f* sweet chestnut
Essl. *abk* (= *Esslöffel*) tbsp.
Ess- *zW*: **Esslöffel** *m* tablespoon; **Esstisch** *m* dining table; **Esswaren** *pl* foodstuffs *pl*; **Esszimmer** *nt* dining room
Establishment [ɪs'tæblɪʃmənt] (**-s, -s**) *nt* establishment
Este ['e:stə] (**-n, -n**) *m*, **Estin** *f* Estonian
Estland ['e:stlant] *nt* Estonia
estnisch ['e:stnɪʃ] *adj* Estonian
Estragon ['ɛstragɔn] (**-s**) *m* tarragon
Estrich ['ɛstrɪç] (**-s, -e**) *m* stone/clay *etc* floor
etablieren [eta'bli:rən] *vr* to establish o.s.; (*Comm*) to set up
Etage [e'ta:ʒə] (**-, -n**) *f* floor, storey (*Brit*), story (*US*)
Etagenbetten *pl* bunk beds *pl*
Etagenwohnung *f* flat (*Brit*), apartment (*US*)
Etappe [e'tapə] (**-, -n**) *f* stage
etappenweise *adv* step by step, stage by stage
Etat [e'ta:] (**-s, -s**) *m* budget; **Etatjahr** *nt* financial year; **Etatposten** *m* budget item
etc *abk* (= *et cetera*) etc.
etepetete [e:təpe'te:tə] (*umg*) *adj* fussy
Ethik ['e:tɪk] *f* ethics *sing*
ethisch ['e:tɪʃ] *adj* ethical
ethnisch ['ɛtnɪʃ] *adj* ethnic; **~e Säuberung** ethnic cleansing
Etikett [eti'kɛt] (**-(e)s, -e**) *nt* (*lit, fig*) label
Etikette *f* etiquette, manners *pl*
Etikettenschwindel *m* (*Pol*): **es ist reinster ~, wenn ...** it is just playing *od* juggling with names if ...
etikettieren [etikɛ'ti:rən] *vt* to label
etliche, r, s ['ɛtlɪçə(r, s)] *adj* quite a lot of ▷ *pron pl* some, quite a few; **~s** quite a lot
Etüde [e'ty:də] (**-, -n**) *f* (*Mus*) étude
Etui [ɛt'vi:] (**-s, -s**) *nt* case
etwa ['ɛtva] *adv* (*ungefähr*) about; (*vielleicht*) perhaps; (*beispielsweise*) for instance; (*entrüstet, erstaunt*): **hast du ~ schon wieder kein Geld dabei?** don't tell me you haven't got any money again! ▷ *adv* (*zur Bestätigung*): **Sie kommen doch, oder ~ nicht?** you are coming, aren't you?; **nicht ~** by no means; **willst du ~ schon gehen?** (surely) you don't want to go already?
etwaig ['ɛtvaɪç] *adj* possible
etwas *pron* something; (*fragend, verneinend*) anything; (*ein wenig*) a little ▷ *adv* a little; **er kann ~** he's good; **Etwas** *nt*: **das gewisse Etwas** that certain something
Etymologie [etymolo'gi:] *f* etymology
EU [e:'|u:] (**-**) *f abk* (= *Europäische Union*) EU
euch [ɔʏç] *pron* (*akk von ihr*) you; yourselves; (*dat von ihr*) (to/for) you ▷ *refl pron* yourselves
euer ['ɔʏər] *pron gen von* **ihr** of you ▷ *adj* your
EU-Erweiterung *f* enlargement of the EU
EU-Kommissar, in *m(f)* EU commissioner
EU-Kommission *f* EU commission
Eule ['ɔʏlə] (**-, -n**) *f* owl
EU-Osterweiterung *f* eastward expansion of the EU
Euphemismus [ɔʏfe'mɪsmʊs] *m* euphemism
Eurasien [ɔʏ'ra:ziən] *nt* Eurasia
Euratom [ɔʏra'to:m] *f abk* (= *Europäische Atomgemeinschaft*) Euratom
eure, r, s ['ɔʏrə(r, s)] *pron* yours
eurerseits *adv* on your part
euresgleichen *pron* people like you
euretwegen ['ɔʏrət'vegən] *adv* (*für euch*) for your sakes; (*wegen euch*) on your account
euretwillen ['ɔʏrət'vɪlən] *adv*: **um ~** = **euretwegen**
eurige *pron*: **der/die/das E~** (*geh*) yours
Euro ['ɔʏro] (**-, -s**) *m* (*Fin*) euro
Eurocheque [ɔʏro'ʃɛk] (**-s, -s**) *m* Eurocheque
Eurokrat [ɔʏro'kra:t] (**-en, -en**) *m* eurocrat
Europa [ɔʏ'ro:pa] (**-s**) *nt* Europe
Europäer, in [ɔʏro'pɛ:ər(ɪn)] (**-s, -**) *m(f)* European
europäisch *adj* European; **das E~e Parlament** the European Parliament; **E~e Union** European Union; **E~e (Wirtschafts)gemeinschaft** European (Economic) Community, Common Market
Europa- *zW*: **Europameister** *m* European champion; **Europarat** *m* Council of Europe; **Europastraße** *f* Euroroute
Euter ['ɔʏtər] (**-s, -**) *nt* udder
Euthanasie [ɔʏtana'zi:] *f* euthanasia
EU-Verfassung *f* EU constitution
E. V., e. V. *abk* (= *eingetragener Verein*) registered association
ev. *abk* = **evangelisch**
evakuieren [evaku'i:rən] *vt* to evacuate
evangelisch [evaŋ'ge:lɪʃ] *adj* Protestant
Evangelium [evaŋ'ge:liʊm] *nt* Gospel
Evaskostüm *nt*: **im ~** in her birthday suit
eventuell [evɛntu'ɛl] *adj* possible ▷ *adv* possibly, perhaps
Evolution [evolutsi'o:n] *f* evolution
Evolutionstheorie *f* theory of evolution
evtl. *abk* = **eventuell**
EWG [e:ve:'ge:] (**-**) *f abk* (*früher*: = *Europäische Wirtschaftsgemeinschaft*) EEC
ewig ['e:vɪç] *adj* eternal ▷ *adv*: **auf ~** forever; **ich habe Sie ~ lange nicht gesehen** (*umg*) I haven't seen you for ages; **Ewigkeit** *f* eternity; **bis in alle Ewigkeit** forever
EWS (**-**) *nt abk* (= *Europäisches Währungssystem*) EMS
EWU (**-**) *f abk* (= *Europäische Währungsunion*) EMU

ex [ɛks] (*umg*) *adv*: **etw ex trinken** to drink sth down in one
exakt [ɛ'ksakt] *adj* exact
exaltiert [ɛksal'ti:rt] *adj* exaggerated, effusive
Examen [ɛ'ksa:mən] (**-s, -** *od* **Examina**) *nt* examination
Examensarbeit *f* dissertation
Exekutionskommando [ɛksekutsi'o:nskɔmando] *nt* firing squad
Exekutive [ɛkseku'ti:və] *f* executive
Exempel [ɛ'ksɛmpəl] (**-s, -**) *nt* example; **die Probe aufs ~ machen** to put it to the test
Exemplar [ɛksɛm'pla:r] (**-s, -e**) *nt* specimen; (*Buchexemplar*) copy; **exemplarisch** *adj* exemplary
exerzieren [ɛksɛr'tsi:rən] *vi* to drill
Exhibitionist [ɛkshibitsio'nɪst] *m* exhibitionist
Exil [ɛ'ksi:l] (**-s, -e**) *nt* exile
existentiell [ɛksɪstɛntsi'ɛl] *adj* = **existenziell**
Existenz [ɛksɪs'tɛnts] *f* existence; (*Unterhalt*) livelihood, living; (*pej: Mensch*) character; **Existenzberechtigung** *f* right to exist; **Existenzgrundlage** *f* basis of one's livelihood
existenziell [ɛksɪstɛntsi'ɛl] *adj*: **von ~er Bedeutung** of vital significance
Existenzkampf *m* struggle for existence
Existenzminimum (**-s, -ma**) *nt* subsistence level
existieren [ɛksɪs'ti:rən] *vi* to exist
exkl. *abk* = **exklusive**
exklusiv [ɛksklu'zi:f] *adj* exclusive; **Exklusivbericht** *m* (*Presse*) exclusive report
exklusive [ɛksklu'zi:və] *präp +gen* exclusive of, not including ▷ *adv* exclusive of, excluding
Exkursion [ɛkskʊrzi'o:n] *f* (study) trip
Exmatrikulation [ɛksmatrikulatsi'o:n] *f* (*Univ*): **bei seiner ~** when he left university
exorzieren [ɛksɔr'tsi:rən] *vt* to exorcize
exotisch [ɛ'kso:tɪʃ] *adj* exotic
expandieren [ɛkspan'di:rən] *vi* (*Econ*) to expand
Expansion [ɛkspanzi'o:n] *f* expansion
expansiv [ɛkspan'zi:f] *adj* expansionist; (*Wirtschaftszweige*) expanding
Expedition [ɛkspeditsi'o:n] *f* expedition; (*Comm*) forwarding department
Experiment [ɛksperi'mɛnt] *nt* experiment
experimentell [ɛksperimɛn'tɛl] *adj* experimental
experimentieren [ɛksperimɛn'ti:rən] *vi* to experiment
Experte [ɛks'pɛrtə] (**-n, -n**) *m* expert, specialist; **Expertenkommission** *f* think tank; **Expertenmeinung** *f* expert opinion
Expertin [ɛks'pɛrtɪn] *f* expert, specialist
explodieren [ɛksplo'di:rən] *vi* to explode
Explosion [ɛksplozi'o:n] *f* explosion
explosiv [ɛksplo'zi:f] *adj* explosive
Exponent [ɛkspo'nɛnt] *m* exponent
exponieren [ɛkspo'ni:rən] *vt*: **an exponierter Stelle stehen** to be in an exposed position
Export [ɛks'pɔrt] (**-(e)s, -e**) *m* export
Exportartikel *m* export
Exporteur [ɛkspɔr'tø:r] *m* exporter
Exporthandel *m* export trade
Exporthaus *nt* export house
exportieren [ɛkspɔr'ti:rən] *vt* to export
Exportkaufmann *m* exporter
Exportland *nt* exporting country
Exportvertreter *m* export agent
Exportwirtschaft *f* export business *od* sector
Expressgut [ɛks'prɛsgut] *nt* express goods *pl od* freight
Expressionismus [ɛksprɛsio'nɪsmʊs] *m* expressionism
Expresszug *m* express (train)
extra ['ɛkstra] *adj inv* (*umg: gesondert*) separate; (*besondere*) extra ▷ *adv* (*gesondert*) separately; (*speziell*) specially; (*absichtlich*) on purpose; (*vor Adjektiven, zusätzlich*) extra; **Extra** (**-s, -s**) *nt* extra; **Extraausgabe** *f* special edition; **Extrablatt** *nt* special edition
Extrakt [ɛks'trakt] (**-(e)s, -e**) *m* extract
Extratour *f* (*fig: umg*): **sich** *dat* **~en leisten** to do one's own thing
extravagant [ɛkstrava'gant] *adj* extravagant; (*Kleidung*) flamboyant
Extrawurst (*umg*) *f* (*Sonderwunsch*): **er will immer eine ~ (gebraten haben)** he always wants something different
Extrem [ɛks'tre:m] (**-s, -e**) *nt* extreme; **extrem** *adj* extreme; **Extremfall** *m* extreme (case)
Extremist, in *m(f)* extremist
Extremistenerlass [ɛkstre'mɪstən|ɛrlas] *m* *law(s) governing extremism*
extremistisch [ɛkstre'mɪstɪʃ] *adj* (*Pol*) extremist
Extremitäten [ɛkstremi'tɛ:tən] *pl* extremities *pl*
extrovertiert [ɛkstrovɛr'ti:rt] *adj* extrovert
Exzellenz [ɛkstsɛ'lɛnts] *f* excellency
exzentrisch [ɛks'tsɛntrɪʃ] *adj* eccentric
Exzess [ɛks'tsɛs] (**-es, -e**) *m* excess

Ff

F, f[1] [ef] (**-, -**) *nt* F, f; **F wie Friedrich** ≈ F for Frederick, F for Fox (*US*); **nach Schema F** (*umg*) in the usual old way

f[2] *abk* (= *feminin*) fem.

Fa. *abk* (= *Firma*) co.

Fabel ['fa:bəl] (**-, -n**) *f* fable; **fabelhaft** *adj* fabulous, marvellous (*Brit*), marvelous (*US*)

Fabrik [fa'bri:k] *f* factory; **Fabrikanlage** *f* plant; (*Gelände*) factory premises *pl*

Fabrikant [fabri:'kant] *m* (*Hersteller*) manufacturer; (*Besitzer*) industrialist

Fabrikarbeiter, in *m(f)* factory worker

Fabrikat [fabri:'ka:t] (**-(e)s, -e**) *nt* product; (*Marke*) make

Fabrikation [fabri:katsi'o:n] *f* manufacture, production

Fabrikbesitzer *m* factory owner

Fabrikgelände *nt* factory site

fabrizieren [fabri'tsi:rən] *vt* (*geistiges Produkt*) to produce; (*Geschichte*) to concoct, fabricate

Fach [fax] (**-(e)s, ¨-er**) *nt* compartment; (*in Schrank, Regal etc*) shelf; (*Sachgebiet*) subject; **ein Mann/eine Frau vom ~** an expert; **Facharbeiter** *m* skilled worker; **Facharzt** *m* (medical) specialist; **Fachausdruck** *m* technical term; **Fachbereich** *m* (special) field; (*Univ*) school, faculty; **Fachbuch** *nt* reference book

Fächer ['fɛçər] (**-s, -**) *m* fan

Fach- *zW*: **Fachfrau** *f* expert; **Fachgebiet** *nt* (special) field; **Fachgeschäft** *nt* specialist shop (*Brit*) *od* store (*US*); **Fachhändler** *m* stockist; **Fachhochschule** *f* college; **Fachidiot** (*umg*) *m* narrow-minded specialist; **Fachkraft** *f* qualified employee; **Fachkräftemangel** *m* lack of skilled *od* qualified personnel; **Fachkreise** *pl*: **in Fachkreisen** among experts; **fachkundig** *adj* expert, specialist; **Fachlehrer** *m* specialist subject teacher; **fachlich** *adj* technical; (*beruflich*) professional; **Fachmann** (**-(e)s**, *pl* **~leute**) *m* expert; **fachmännisch** *adj* professional; **Fachrichtung** *f* subject area; **Fachschule** *f* technical college; **fachsimpeln** *vi* to talk shop; **fachspezifisch** *adj* technical; **Fachverband** *m* trade association; **Fachwelt** *f* profession; **Fachwerk** *nt* timber frame; **Fachwerkhaus** *nt* half-timbered house

Fackel ['fakəl] (**-, -n**) *f* torch

fackeln (*umg*) *vi* to dither

Fackelzug *m* torchlight procession

fad, fade *adj* insipid; (*langweilig*) dull; (*Essen*) tasteless

Faden ['fa:dən] (**-s, ¨-**) *m* thread; **der rote ~** (*fig*) the central theme; **alle Fäden laufen hier zusammen** this is the nerve centre (*Brit*) *od* center (*US*) of the whole thing; **Fadennudeln** *pl* vermicelli *sing*; **fadenscheinig** *adj* (*lit, fig*) threadbare

Fagott [fa'gɔt] (**-(e)s, -e**) *nt* bassoon

fähig ['fɛ:ıç] *adj*: **~ (zu** *od* **+***gen***)** capable (of); able (to); **zu allem ~ sein** to be capable of anything; **Fähigkeit** *f* ability

Fähnchen ['fɛ:nçən] *nt* pennon, streamer

fahnden ['fa:ndən] *vi*: **~ nach** to search for

Fahndung *f* search

Fahndungsliste *f* list of wanted criminals, wanted list

Fahne ['fa:nə] (**-, -n**) *f* flag; standard; **mit fliegenden ~n zu jdm/etw überlaufen** to go over to sb/sth; **eine ~ haben** (*umg*) to smell of drink

Fahnenflucht *f* desertion

Fahrausweis *m* (*form*) ticket

Fahrbahn *f* carriageway (*Brit*), roadway

fahrbar *adj*: **~er Untersatz** (*hum*) wheels *pl*

Fähre ['fɛ:rə] (**-, -n**) *f* ferry

fahren ['fa:rən] *unreg vt* to drive; (*Rad*) to ride; (*befördern*) to drive, take; (*Rennen*) to drive in ▷ *vi* (*sich bewegen*) to go; (*Schiff*) to sail; (*abfahren*) to leave; **mit dem Auto/Zug ~** to go *od* travel by car/train; **mit dem Aufzug ~** to take the lift, ride the elevator (*US*); **links/rechts ~** to drive on the left/right; **gegen einen Baum ~** to drive *od* go into a tree; **die U-Bahn fährt alle fünf Minuten** the underground goes *od* runs every five minutes; **mit der Hand ~ über** *+akk* to pass one's hand over; **(bei etw) gut/schlecht ~** (*zurechtkommen*) to do well/badly (with sth); **was ist (denn) in dich ge~?** what's got (*Brit*) *od* gotten (*US*) into you?; **einen ~ lassen** (*umg*) to fart (*!*)

fahrend *adj*: **~es Volk** travelling people

Fahrer, in ['fa:rər(ın)] (**-s, -**) *m(f)* driver; **Fahrerflucht** *f* hit-and-run driving

Fahr- *zW*: **Fahrgast** *m* passenger; **Fahrgeld** *nt* fare; **Fahrgelegenheit** *f* transport; **Fahrgestell**

nt chassis; (*Aviat*) undercarriage
fahrig ['fa:rɪç] *adj* nervous; (*unkonzentriert*) distracted
Fahr- *zW*: **Fahrkarte** *f* ticket; **Fahrkartenausgabe** *f* ticket office; **Fahrkartenautomat** *m* ticket machine; **Fahrkartenschalter** *m* ticket office
fahrlässig *adj* negligent; **~e Tötung** manslaughter; **Fahrlässigkeit** *f* negligence
Fahr- *zW*: **Fahrlehrer** *m* driving instructor; **Fahrplan** *m* timetable; **fahrplanmäßig** *adj* (*Eisenb*) scheduled; **Fahrpraxis** *f* driving experience; **Fahrpreis** *m* fare; **Fahrprüfung** *f* driving test; **Fahrrad** *nt* bicycle; **Fahrradweg** *m* cycle path; **Fahrrinne** *f* (*Naut*) shipping channel, fairway; **Fahrschein** *m* ticket; **Fahrschule** *f* driving school; **Fahrschüler** *m* learner (driver); **Fahrspur** *f* lane; **Fahrstuhl** *m* lift (*Brit*), elevator (*US*); **Fahrstunde** *f* driving lesson
Fahrt [fa:rt] **(-, -en)** *f* journey; (*kurz*) trip; (*Aut*) drive; (*Geschwindigkeit*) speed; **gute ~!** safe journey!; **volle ~ voraus!** (*Naut*) full speed ahead!
fährt [fɛ:rt] *vb siehe* **fahren**
fahrtauglich ['fa:rtaʊklɪç] *adj* fit to drive
Fährte ['fɛ:rtə] **(-, -n)** *f* track, trail; **jdn auf eine falsche ~ locken** (*fig*) to put sb off the scent
Fahrtenschreiber *m* tachograph
Fahrtkosten *pl* travelling expenses *pl*
Fahrtrichtung *f* course, direction
Fahr- *zW*: **fahrtüchtig** ['fa:rtʏçtɪç] *adj* fit to drive; **Fahrverhalten** *nt* (*von Fahrer*) behaviour (*Brit*) *od* behavior (*US*) behind the wheel; (*von Wagen*) road performance; **Fahrzeug** *nt* vehicle; **Fahrzeughalter (-s, -)** *m* owner of a vehicle; **Fahrzeugpapiere** *pl* vehicle documents *pl*
Faible ['fɛ:bl] **(-s, -s)** *nt* (*geh*) liking; (*Schwäche*) weakness; (*Vorliebe*) penchant
fair [fɛ:r] *adj* fair
Fäkalien [fɛ'ka:liən] *pl* faeces *pl*
Faksimile [fak'zi:mile] **(-s, -s)** *nt* facsimile
faktisch ['faktɪʃ] *adj* actual
Faktor *m* factor
Faktum (-s, -ten) *nt* fact
fakturieren [faktu'ri:rən] *vt* (*Comm*) to invoice
Fakultät [fakʊl'tɛ:t] *f* faculty
Falke ['falkə] **(-n, -n)** *m* falcon
Falklandinseln ['falklant'ɪnzəln] *pl* Falkland Islands, Falklands
Fall [fal] **(-(e)s, ¨-e)** *m* (*Sturz*) fall; (*Sachverhalt, Jur, Gram*) case; **auf jeden ~, auf alle Fälle** in any case; (*bestimmt*) definitely; **gesetzt den ~** assuming (that); **jds ~ sein** (*umg*) to be sb's cup of tea; **klarer ~!** (*umg*) sure thing!, you bet!; **das mache ich auf keinen ~** there's no way I'm going to do that
Falle (-, -n) *f* trap; (*umg*: *Bett*) bed; **jdm eine ~ stellen** to set a trap for sb
fallen *unreg vi* to fall; (*im Krieg*) to fall, be killed; **etw ~ lassen** to drop sth; (*Bemerkung*) to make sth; (*Plan*) to abandon sth, to drop sth
fällen ['fɛlən] *vt* (*Baum*) to fell; (*Urteil*) to pass
fällig ['fɛlɪç] *adj* due; (*Wechsel*) mature(d); **längst ~** long overdue; **Fälligkeit** *f* (*Comm*) maturity
Fallobst *nt* fallen fruit, windfall
falls *adv* in case, if
Fall- *zW*: **Fallschirm** *m* parachute; **Fallschirmjäger** *m* paratrooper; **Fallschirmspringer, in** *m(f)* parachutist; **Fallschirmtruppe** *f* paratroops *pl*; **Fallstrick** *m* (*fig*) trap, snare; **Fallstudie** *f* case study
fällt [fɛlt] *vb siehe* **fallen**
Falltür *f* trap door
fallweise *adj* from case to case
falsch [falʃ] *adj* false; (*unrichtig*) wrong; **ein ~es Spiel (mit jdm) treiben** to play (sb) false; **etw ~ verstehen** to misunderstand sth, get sth wrong; *siehe auch* **falschliegen**
fälschen ['fɛlʃən] *vt* to forge
Fälscher, in (-s, -) *m(f)* forger
Falschgeld *nt* counterfeit money
Falschheit *f* falsity, falseness; (*Unrichtigkeit*) wrongness
fälschlich *adj* false
fälschlicherweise *adv* mistakenly
falschliegen *unreg vi* to be wrong; **~ bei/mit** to be wrong about/in
Falschmeldung *f* (*Presse*) false report
Fälschung *f* forgery
fälschungssicher *adj* forgery-proof
Faltblatt *nt* leaflet; (*in Zeitschrift etc*) insert
Fältchen ['fɛltçən] *nt* crease, wrinkle
Falte ['faltə] **(-, -n)** *f* (*Knick*) fold, crease; (*Hautfalte*) wrinkle; (*Rockfalte*) pleat
falten *vt* to fold; (*Stirn*) to wrinkle
faltenlos *adj* without folds; without wrinkles
Faltenrock *m* pleated skirt
Falter ['faltər] **(-s, -)** *m* (*Tagfalter*) butterfly; (*Nachtfalter*) moth
faltig ['faltɪç] *adj* (*Haut*) wrinkled; (*Rock usw*) creased
falzen ['faltsən] *vt* (*Papierbogen*) to fold
Fam. *abk* = **Familie**
familiär [famili'ɛ:r] *adj* familiar
Familie [fa'mi:liə] *f* family; **~ Otto Francke** (*als Anschrift*) Mr & Mrs Otto Francke and family; **zur ~ gehören** to be one of the family
Familien- *zW*: **Familienanschluss** *m*: **Unterkunft mit Familienanschluss** *accommodation where one is treated as one of the family*; **Familienkreis** *m* family circle; **Familienmitglied** *nt* member of the family; **Familienname** *m* surname; **Familienpackung** *f* family(-size) pack; **Familienplanung** *f* family planning; **Familienstand** *m* marital status; **Familienunternehmen** *nt* family business; **Familienvater** *m* head of the family; **Familienverhältnisse** *pl* family circumstances *pl*
Fanatiker, in [fa'na:tikər(ɪn)] **(-s, -)** *m(f)* fanatic
fanatisch *adj* fanatical

Fanatismus [fana'tɪsmʊs] *m* fanaticism
fand *etc* [fant] *vb siehe* **finden**
Fang [faŋ] **(-(e)s, ¨-e)** *m* catch; (*Jagen*) hunting; (*Kralle*) talon, claw
fangen *unreg vt* to catch ▷ *vr* to get caught; (*Flugzeug*) to level out; (*Mensch: nicht fallen*) to steady o.s.; (*fig*) to compose o.s.; (*in Leistung*) to get back on form
Fangfrage *f* catch *od* trick question
Fanggründe *pl* fishing grounds *pl*
fängt [fɛŋkt] *vb siehe* **fangen**
Fantasie [fanta'zi:] *f* imagination; **in seiner ~** in his mind; **Fantasiegebilde** *nt* (*Einbildung*) figment of the imagination; **fantasielos** *adj* unimaginative
fantasieren [fanta'zi:ren] *vi* to fantasize; (*Med*) to be delirious
fantasievoll *adj* imaginative
Fantast [fan'tast] **(-en, -en)** *m* dreamer
fantastisch *adj* fantastic
Farb- *zW*: **Farbabzug** *m* coloured (*Brit*) *od* colored (*US*) print; **Farbaufnahme** *f* colour (*Brit*) *od* color (*US*) photograph; **Farbband** *nt* typewriter ribbon
Farbe ['fa:rbə] **(-, -n)** *f* colour (*Brit*), color (*US*); (*zum Malen etc*) paint; (*Stofffarbe*) dye; (*Karten*) suit
farbecht ['farp|ɛçt] *adj* colourfast (*Brit*), colorfast (*US*)
färben ['fɛrbən] *vt* to colour (*Brit*), color (*US*); (*Stoff, Haar*) to dye
farben- *zW*: **farbenblind** *adj* colour-blind (*Brit*), color-blind (*US*); **farbenfroh** *adj* colourful (*Brit*), colorful (*US*); **farbenprächtig** *adj* colourful (*Brit*), colorful (*US*)
Farbfernsehen *nt* colour (*Brit*) *od* color (*US*) television
Farbfilm *m* colour (*Brit*) *od* color (*US*) film
Farbfoto *nt* colour (*Brit*) *od* color (*US*) photo
farbig *adj* coloured (*Brit*), colored (*US*)
Farbige, r *f(m)* coloured (*Brit*) *od* colored (*US*) person
Farb- *zW*: **Farbkasten** *m* paintbox; **farblos** *adj* colourless (*Brit*), colorless (*US*); **Farbstift** *m* coloured (*Brit*) *od* colored (*US*) pencil; **Farbstoff** *m* dye; (*Lebensmittelfarb*) (artificial) colouring (*Brit*) *od* coloring (*US*); **Farbton** *m* hue, tone
Färbung ['fɛrbʊŋ] *f* colouring (*Brit*), coloring (*US*); (*Tendenz*) bias
Farn [farn] **(-(e)s, -e)** *m* fern; (*Adlerfarn*) bracken
Farnkraut [farn] *nt* = **Farn**
Färöer [fɛ'rø:ər] *pl* Faeroe Islands *pl*
Fasan [fa'za:n] **(-(e)s, -e(n))** *m* pheasant
Fasching ['faʃɪŋ] **(-s, -e** *od* **-s)** *m* carnival
Faschismus [fa'ʃɪsmʊs] *m* fascism
Faschist, in *m(f)* fascist
faschistisch [fa'ʃɪstɪʃ] *adj* fascist
faseln ['fa:zəln] *vi* to talk nonsense, drivel
Faser ['fa:zər] **(-, -n)** *f* fibre
Fass [fas] **(-es, ¨-er)** *nt* vat, barrel; (*für Öl*) drum; **Bier vom ~** draught beer; **ein ~ ohne Boden** (*fig*) a bottomless pit
Fassade [fa'sa:də] *f* (*lit, fig*) façade
fassbar *adj* comprehensible
Fassbier *nt* draught beer
fassen ['fasən] *vt* (*ergreifen*) to grasp, take; (*inhaltlich*) to hold; (*Entschluss etc*) to take; (*verstehen*) to understand; (*Ring etc*) to set; (*formulieren*) to formulate, phrase ▷ *vr* to calm down; **nicht zu ~** unbelievable; *siehe auch* **kurzfassen**
fasslich ['faslɪç] *adj* comprehensible
Fasson [fa'sõ:] **(-, -s)** *f* style; (*Art und Weise*) way; **aus der ~ geraten** (*lit*) to lose its shape
Fassung ['fasʊŋ] *f* (*Umrahmung*) mounting; (*Lampenfassung*) socket; (*Wortlaut*) version; (*Beherrschung*) composure; **jdn aus der ~ bringen** to upset sb; **völlig außer ~ geraten** to lose all self-control
fassungslos *adj* speechless
Fassungsvermögen *nt* capacity; (*Verständnis*) comprehension
fast [fast] *adv* almost, nearly; **~ nie** hardly ever
fasten ['fastən] *vi* to fast; **Fasten (-s)** *nt* fasting; **Fastenzeit** *f* Lent
Fastnacht *f* Shrovetide carnival
faszinieren [fastsi'ni:rən] *vt* to fascinate
fatal [fa'ta:l] *adj* fatal; (*peinlich*) embarrassing
fauchen ['faʊxən] *vt, vi* to hiss
faul [faʊl] *adj* rotten; (*Person*) lazy; (*Ausreden*) lame; **daran ist etwas ~** there's something fishy about it
faulen *vi* to rot
faulenzen ['faulɛntsən] *vi* to idle
Faulenzer, in (-s, -) *m(f)* idler, loafer
Faulheit *f* laziness
faulig *adj* putrid
Fäulnis ['fɔʏlnɪs] **(-)** *f* decay, putrefaction
Faulpelz (*umg*) *m* lazybones *sing*
Faust ['faʊst] **(-, Fäuste)** *f* fist; **das passt wie die ~ aufs Auge** (*passt nicht*) it's all wrong; **auf eigene ~** (*fig*) on one's own initiative
Fäustchen ['fɔʏstçən] *nt*: **sich** *dat* **ins ~ lachen** to laugh up one's sleeve
faustdick (*umg*) *adj*: **er hat es ~ hinter den Ohren** he's a crafty one
Fausthandschuh *m* mitten
Faustregel *f* rule of thumb
Favorit, in [favo'ri:t(ɪn)] **(-en, -en)** *m(f)* favourite (*Brit*), favorite (*US*)
Fax [faks] **(-, -e)** *nt* fax; **faxen** *vt* to fax
Faxen ['faksən] *pl*: **~ machen** to fool around
Fazit ['fa:tsɪt] **(-s, -s** *od* **-e)** *nt*: **wenn wir aus diesen vier Jahren das ~ ziehen** if we take stock of these four years
FCKW (-s, -s) *m abk* (= *Fluorchlorkohlenwasserstoff*) CFC
FdH (*umg*) *abk* (= *Friss die Hälfte*) eat less
FDP, F.D.P. *f abk* (= *Freie Demokratische Partei*) Free Democratic Party; *see culture note*

FDP

The FDP (Freie Demokratische Partei) was founded in 1948 and is Germany's centre party. It is a liberal party which has formed governing coalitions with both the *SPD* and the *CDU/CSU* at times, both in the regions and in the *Bundestag*.

Feb. *abk* (= *Februar*) Feb.
Februar ['fe:brua:r] **(-(s), -e)** *(pl selten) m* February; *siehe auch* **September**
fechten ['fɛçtən] *unreg vi* to fence
Feder ['fe:dər] **(-, -n)** *f* feather; (*Schreibfeder*) pen nib; (*Tech*) spring; **in den ~n liegen** (*umg*) to be/stay in bed; **Federball** *m* shuttlecock; **Federballspiel** *nt* badminton; **Federbett** *nt* continental quilt; **federführend** *adj* (*Behörde*): **federführend (für)** in overall charge (of); **Federhalter** *m* pen; **federleicht** *adj* light as a feather; **Federlesen** *nt*: **nicht viel Federlesens mit jdm/etw machen** to make short work of sb/sth
federn *vi* (*nachgeben*) to be springy; (*sich bewegen*) to bounce ▷ *vt* to spring
Federung *f* suspension
Federvieh *nt* poultry
Federweiße, r *m* new wine
Federzeichnung *f* pen-and-ink drawing
Fee [fe:] **(-, -n)** *f* fairy
feenhaft ['fe:ənhaft] *adj* (*liter*) fairylike
Fegefeuer ['fe:gəfɔʏər] *nt* purgatory
fegen ['fe:gən] *vt* to sweep
fehl [fe:l] *adj*: **~ am Platz** *od* **Ort** out of place; **Fehlanzeige** (*umg*) *f* dead loss
fehlen *vi* to be wanting *od* missing; (*abwesend sein*) to be absent ▷ *vi unpers*: **es fehlte nicht viel und ich hätte ihn verprügelt** I almost hit him; **etw fehlt jdm** sb lacks sth; **du fehlst mir** I miss you; **was fehlt ihm?** what's wrong with him?; **der/das hat mir gerade noch gefehlt!** (*ironisch*) he/that was all I needed; **weit gefehlt!** (*fig*) you're way out! (*umg*); (*ganz im Gegenteil*) far from it!; **mir ~ die Worte** words fail me; **wo fehlt es?** what's the trouble?, what's up? (*umg*)
Fehlentscheidung *f* wrong decision
Fehlentwicklung *f* mistake
Fehler (-s, -) *m* mistake, error; (*Mangel, Schwäche*) fault; **ihr ist ein ~ unterlaufen** she's made a mistake; **Fehlerbeseitigung** *f* (*Comput*) debugging; **fehlerfrei** *adj* faultless; without any mistakes; **fehlerhaft** *adj* incorrect; faulty; **fehlerlos** *adj* = **fehlerfrei**; **Fehlermeldung** *f* (*Comput*) error message; **Fehlersuchprogramm** *nt* (*Comput*) debugger
fehl- *zW*: **Fehlgeburt** *f* miscarriage; **fehlgehen** *unreg vi* to go astray; **Fehlgriff** *m* blunder; **Fehlkonstruktion** *f*: **eine Fehlkonstruktion sein** to be badly designed; **Fehlleistung** *f*: **freudsche Fehlleistung** Freudian slip; **Fehlschlag** *m* failure; **fehlschlagen** *unreg vi* to fail; **Fehlschluss** *m* wrong conclusion; **Fehlstart** *m* (*Sport*) false start; **Fehltritt** *m* false move; (*fig*) blunder, slip; (*: Affäre*) indiscretion; **Fehlurteil** *nt* miscarriage of justice; **Fehlzündung** *f* (*Aut*) misfire, backfire
Feier ['faɪər] **(-, -n)** *f* celebration; **Feierabend** *m* time to stop work; **Feierabend machen** to stop, knock off; **was machst du am Feierabend?** what are you doing after work?; **jetzt ist Feierabend!** that's enough!
feierlich *adj* solemn; **das ist ja nicht mehr ~** (*umg*) that's beyond a joke; **Feierlichkeit** *f* solemnity; **Feierlichkeiten** *pl* festivities *pl*
feiern *vt, vi* to celebrate
Feiertag *m* holiday
feig *adj* cowardly
Feige ['faɪgə] **(-, -n)** *f* fig
feige *adj* cowardly
Feigheit *f* cowardice
Feigling *m* coward
Feile ['faɪlə] **(-, -n)** *f* file
feilen *vt, vi* to file
feilschen ['faɪlʃən] *vi* to haggle
fein [faɪn] *adj* fine; (*vornehm*) refined; (*Gehör etc*) keen; **~!** great!; **er ist ~ raus** (*umg*) he's sitting pretty; **sich ~ machen** to get all dressed up
Feind, in [faɪnt, 'faɪndɪn] **(-(e)s, -e)** *m(f)* enemy; **Feindbild** *nt* concept of an/the enemy; **feindlich** *adj* hostile; **Feindschaft** *f* enmity; **feindselig** *adj* hostile; **Feindseligkeit** *f* hostility
Fein- *zW*: **feinfühlend** *adj* sensitive; **feinfühlig** *adj* sensitive; **Feingefühl** *nt* delicacy, tact; **Feinheit** *f* fineness; refinement; keenness; **Feinkostgeschäft** *nt* delicatessen (shop), deli; **Feinschmecker (-s, -)** *m* gourmet; **Feinwaschmittel** *nt* mild(-action) detergent
feist [faɪst] *adj* fat
feixen ['faɪksən] (*umg*) *vi* to smirk
Feld [fɛlt] **(-(e)s, -er)** *nt* field; (*Schach*) square; (*Sport*) pitch; **Argumente ins ~ führen** to bring arguments to bear; **das ~ räumen** (*fig*) to bow out; **Feldarbeit** *f* (*Agr*) work in the fields; (*Geog etc*) fieldwork; **Feldblume** *f* wild flower; **Feldherr** *m* commander; **Feldjäger** *pl* (*Mil*) the military police; **Feldlazarett** *nt* (*Mil*) field hospital; **Feldsalat** *m* lamb's lettuce; **Feldstecher** *m* (pair of) binoculars *pl od* field glasses *pl*
Feld-Wald-und-Wiesen- (*umg*) *in zW* common-or-garden
Feld- *zW*: **Feldwebel (-s, -)** *m* sergeant; **Feldweg** *m* path; **Feldzug** *m* (*lit, fig*) campaign
Felge ['fɛlgə] **(-, -n)** *f* (wheel) rim
Felgenbremse *f* caliper brake
Fell [fɛl] **(-(e)s, -e)** *nt* fur; coat; (*von Schaf*) fleece; (*von toten Tieren*) skin; **ein dickes ~ haben** to be thick-skinned, have a thick skin; **ihm sind die ~e weggeschwommen** (*fig*) all his hopes were dashed
Fels [fɛls] **(-en, -en)** *m* = **Felsen**
Felsen ['fɛlzən] **(-s, -)** *m* rock; (*Klippe*) cliff; **felsenfest** *adj* firm
felsig *adj* rocky
Felsspalte *f* crevice
Felsvorsprung *m* ledge
feminin [femi'ni:n] *adj* feminine; (*pej*) effeminate
Feministin [femi'nɪstɪn] *f* feminist

Fenchel ['fɛnçəl] (**-s**) *m* fennel
Fenster ['fɛnstər] (**-s, -**) *nt* window; **weg vom ~** (*umg*) out of the game, finished; **Fensterbrett** *nt* windowsill; **Fensterladen** *m* shutter; **Fensterleder** *nt* chamois, shammy (leather); **Fensterplatz** *m* window seat; **Fensterputzer** (**-s, -**) *m* window cleaner; **Fensterscheibe** *f* windowpane; **Fenstersims** *m* windowsill
Ferien ['fe:riən] *pl* holidays *pl*, vacation (*US*); **die großen ~** the summer holidays (*Brit*), the long vacation (*US Univ*); **~ haben** to be on holiday; **Ferienkurs** *m* holiday course; **Ferienreise** *f* holiday; **Ferienwohnung** *f* holiday flat (*Brit*), vacation apartment (*US*); **Ferienzeit** *f* holiday period
Ferkel ['fɛrkəl] (**-s, -**) *nt* piglet
fern [fɛrn] *adj, adv* far-off, distant; **~ von hier** a long way (away) from here; *siehe auch* **fernhalten, fernliegen**; **Fernamt** *nt* (*Tel*) exchange; **Fernbedienung** *f* remote control; **fernbleiben** *unreg vi*: **fernbleiben (von** *od +dat*) to stay away (from)
Ferne (**-, -n**) *f* distance
ferner *adj, adv* further; (*weiterhin*) in future; **unter „~ liefen" rangieren** (*umg*) to be an also-ran
fern- *zW*: **Fernfahrer** *m* long-distance lorry (*Brit*) *od* truck driver; **Fernflug** *m* long-distance flight; **Ferngespräch** *nt* long-distance call (*Brit*), toll call (*US*); **ferngesteuert** *adj* remote-controlled; (*Rakete*) guided; **Fernglas** *nt* binoculars *pl*; **fernhalten** *unreg vt* to keep away; **Fernkopie** *f* fax; **Fernkopierer** *m* fax machine; **Fernkurs**, **Fernkursus** *m* correspondence course; **Fernlenkung** *f* remote control; **Fernlicht** *nt* (*Aut*): **mit Fernlicht fahren** to drive on full beam; **fernliegen** *unreg vi*: **jdm fernliegen** to be far from sb's mind
Fernmelde- *in zW* telecommunications; (*Mil*) signals
fern- *zW*: **Fernost aus/in Fernost** from/in the Far East; **fernöstlich** *adj* Far Eastern *attrib*; **Fernrohr** *nt* telescope; **Fernschreiben** *nt* telex; **Fernschreiber** *m* teleprinter; **fernschriftlich** *adj* by telex
Fernsehapparat *m* television (set)
Fernsehduell *nt* TV duel *od* debate
fernsehen ['fɛrnze:ən] *unreg vi* to watch television; **Fernsehen** (**-s**) *nt* television; **im Fernsehen** on television
Fernseher (**-s, -**) *m* television (set)
Fernseh- *zW*: **Fernsehgebühr** *f* television licence (*Brit*) *od* license (*US*) fee; **Fernsehgerät** *nt* television set; **Fernsehprogramm** *nt* (*Kanal*) channel, station (*US*); (*Sendung*) programme (*Brit*), program (*US*); (*Fernsehzeitschrift*) (television) programme (*Brit*) *od* program (*US*) guide; **Fernsehsendung** *f* television programme (*Brit*) *od* program (*US*); **Fernsehüberwachungsanlage** *f* closed-circuit television; **Fernsehzuschauer** *m* (television) viewer
Fern- *zW*: **Fernsprecher** *m* telephone; **Fernsprechzelle** *f* telephone box (*Brit*) *od* booth (*US*); **Fernsteuerung** *f* remote control
Fernstudium *nt* multimedia course, ≈ Open University course (*Brit*); *see culture note*

FERNSTUDIUM

Fernstudium is a distance-learning degree course where students do not go to university but receive their tuition by letter, television or radio programmes. There is no personal contact between student and lecturer. The first *Fernstudium* was founded in 1974. Students are free to practise their career or to bring up a family at the same time as studying.

Fernverkehr *m* long-distance traffic
Fernweh *nt* wanderlust
Ferse ['fɛrzə] (**-, -n**) *f* heel
Fersengeld *nt*: **~ geben** to take to one's heels
fertig ['fɛrtɪç] *adj* (*bereit*) ready; (*beendet*) finished; (*gebrauchsfertig*) ready-made; **~ ausgebildet** fully qualified; **mit jdm/etw ~ werden** to cope with sb/sth; **mit den Nerven ~ sein** to be at the end of one's tether; **~ bringen** *od* **machen** (*beenden*) to finish; **sich ~ machen** to get ready; **~ essen/lesen** to finish eating/reading; **~ stellen** to complete; **Fertigbau** *m* prefab(ricated house)
fertigbringen *unreg vt* (*fähig sein*) to manage, be capable of; (*beenden*) to finish
fertigen ['fɛrtɪgən] *vt* to manufacture
Fertig- *zW*: **Fertiggericht** *nt* ready-to-serve meal; **Fertighaus** *nt* prefab(ricated house); **Fertigkeit** *f* skill; **fertigmachen** (*umg*) *vt* (*Person*) to finish; (*körperlich*) to exhaust; (*moralisch*) to get down; *siehe auch* **fertig**; **fertigstellen** *vt* to complete
Fertigung *f* production
Fertigungs- *in zW* production; **Fertigungsstraße** *f* production line
Fertigware *f* finished product
fertigwerden *unreg vi siehe* **fertig**
fesch [fɛʃ] (*umg*) *adj* (*modisch*) smart; (*: hübsch*) attractive
Fessel ['fɛsəl] (**-, -n**) *f* fetter
fesseln *vt* to bind; (*mit Fesseln*) to fetter; (*fig*) to grip; **ans Bett gefesselt** (*fig*) confined to bed
fesselnd *adj* gripping
Fest [fɛst] (**-(e)s, -e**) *nt* (*Feier*) celebration; (*Party*) party; **man soll die ~e feiern wie sie fallen** (*Sprichwort*) make hay while the sun shines
fest *adj* firm; (*Nahrung*) solid; (*Gehalt*) regular; (*Gewebe, Schuhe*) strong, sturdy; (*Freund(in)*) steady ▷ *adv* (*schlafen*) soundly; **~ angestellt** employed on a permanent basis; **~ entschlossen sein** to be absolutely determined; **~ umrissen** clearcut; **~e Kosten** (*Comm*) fixed costs *pl*
Festbeleuchtung *f* illumination
festbinden *unreg vt* to tie, fasten

festbleiben *unreg vi* to stand firm
Festessen *nt* banquet
festfahren *unreg vr* to get stuck
Festgeldkonto *nt* time-deposit account
festhalten *unreg vt* to seize, hold fast; (*Ereignis*) to record ▷ *vr*: **sich ~ (an** *+dat***)** to hold on (to)
festigen *vt* to strengthen
Festigkeit *f* strength
fest- *zW*: **festklammern** *vr*: **sich festklammern (an** *+dat***)** to cling on (to); **festklemmen** *vt* to wedge fast; **Festkomma** *nt* (*Comput*) fixed point; **Festland** *nt* mainland; **festlegen** *vt* to fix ▷ *vr* to commit o.s.; **jdn auf etw** *akk* **festlegen** (*festnageln*) to tie sb (down) to sth; (*verpflichten*) to commit sb to sth
festlich *adj* festive
fest- *zW*: **festliegen** *unreg vi* (*Fin: Geld*) to be tied up; **festmachen** *vt* to fasten; (*Termin etc*) to fix; **festnageln** *vt*: **jdn festnageln (auf** *+akk***)** (*fig: umg*) to pin sb down (to); **Festnahme (-, -n)** *f* capture; **festnehmen** *unreg vt* to capture, arrest; **Festnetztelefon** *nt* fixed-line phone; **Festplatte** *f* (*Comput*) hard disk; **Festpreis** *m* (*Comm*) fixed price
Festrede *f* speech, address
festschnallen *vt* to strap down ▷ *vr* to fasten one's seat belt
festsetzen *vt* to fix, settle
Festspiel *nt* festival
fest- *zW*: **feststehen** *unreg vi* to be certain; **feststellbar** *adj* (*herauszufinden*) ascertainable; **feststellen** *vt* to establish; (*sagen*) to remark; (*Tech*) to lock (fast); **Feststellung** *f*: **die Feststellung machen, dass ...** to realize that ...; (*bemerken*) to remark *od* observe that ...; **Festtag** *m* holiday
Festung *f* fortress
festverzinslich *adj* fixed-interest *attrib*
Festwertspeicher *m* (*Comput*) read-only memory
Festzelt *nt* marquee
Fête ['fe:tə] **(-, -n)** *f* party
Fett [fɛt] **(-(e)s, -e)** *nt* fat, grease; **fett** *adj* fat; (*Essen etc*) greasy; **fett gedruckt** bold-type; **fettarm** *adj* low fat; **fetten** *vt* to grease; **Fettfleck** *m* grease spot *od* stain; **fettfrei** *adj* fat-free; **Fettgehalt** *m* fat content; **fettig** *adj* greasy, fatty; **Fettnäpfchen** *nt*: **ins Fettnäpfchen treten** to put one's foot in it; **Fettpolster** *nt* (*hum: umg*): **Fettpolster haben** to be well-padded
Fetzen ['fɛtsən] **(-s, -)** *m* scrap; **..., dass die ~ fliegen** (*umg*) ... like mad
feucht [fɔʏçt] *adj* damp; (*Luft*) humid; **feuchtfröhlich** *adj* (*hum*) boozy
Feuchtigkeit *f* dampness; humidity
Feuchtigkeitscreme *f* moisturizer
feudal [fɔy'da:l] *adj* (*Pol, Hist*) feudal; (*umg*) plush
Feuer ['fɔʏər] **(-s, -)** *nt* fire; (*zum Rauchen*) a light; (*fig: Schwung*) spirit; **für jdn durchs ~ gehen** to go through fire and water for sb; **~ und Flamme (für etw) sein** (*umg*) to be dead keen (on sth); **~ für etw/jdn fangen** (*fig*) to develop a great interest in sth/sb; **Feueralarm** *m* fire alarm; **Feuereifer** *m* zeal; **feuerfest** *adj* fireproof; **Feuergefahr** *f* danger of fire; **bei Feuergefahr** in the event of fire; **feuergefährlich** *adj* inflammable; **Feuerleiter** *f* fire escape ladder; **Feuerlöscher (-s, -)** *m* fire extinguisher; **Feuermelder (-s, -)** *m* fire alarm
feuern *vt, vi* (*lit, fig*) to fire
Feuer- *zW*: **feuerpolizeilich** *adj* (*Bestimmungen*) laid down by the fire authorities; **Feuerprobe** *f* acid test; **feuerrot** *adj* fiery red
Feuersbrunst *f* (*geh*) conflagration
Feuer- *zW*: **Feuerschlucker** *m* fire-eater; **Feuerschutz** *m* (*Vorbeugung*) fire prevention; (*Mil: Deckung*) covering fire; **feuersicher** *adj* fireproof; **Feuerstein** *m* flint; **Feuerstelle** *f* fireplace; **Feuertreppe** *f* fire escape; **Feuerversicherung** *f* fire insurance; **Feuerwaffe** *f* firearm; **Feuerwehr** *f* fire brigade; **Feuerwehrauto** *nt* fire engine; **Feuerwerk** *nt* fireworks *pl*; **Feuerwerkskörper** *m* firework; **Feuerzangenbowle** *f red wine punch containing rum which has been flamed off*; **Feuerzeug** *nt* (cigarette) lighter
Feuilleton [fœjə'tõ:] **(-s, -s)** *nt* (*Presse*) feature section; (*Artikel*) feature (article)
feurig ['fɔʏrɪç] *adj* fiery
Fiche [fi:ʃ] **(-s, -s)** *m od nt* (micro)fiche
ficht [fɪçt] *vb siehe* **fechten**
Fichte ['fɪçtə] **(-, -n)** *f* spruce
ficken ['fɪkən] (*umg!*) *vt, vi* to fuck (*!*)
fickerig ['fɪkərɪç], **fickrig** ['fɪkrɪç] (*umg*) *adj* fidgety
fidel [fi'de:l] (*umg*) *adj* jolly
Fidschi-Inseln, **Fidschiinseln** ['fɪdʒi|ɪnzəln] *pl* Fiji Islands
Fieber ['fi:bər] **(-s, -)** *nt* fever, temperature; (*Krankheit*) fever; **~ haben** to have a temperature; **fieberhaft** *adj* feverish; **Fiebermesser** *m* thermometer; **Fieberthermometer** *nt* thermometer
fiel *etc* [fi:l] *vb siehe* **fallen**
fies [fi:s] (*umg*) *adj* nasty
Figur [fi'gu:r] **(-, -en)** *f* figure; (*Schachfigur*) chessman, chess piece; **eine gute/schlechte/traurige ~ abgeben** to cut a good/poor/sorry figure
fiktiv [fɪk'ti:f] *adj* fictitious
Filet [fi'le:] **(-s, -s)** *nt* (*Koch*) fillet; (*Rinderfilet*) fillet steak; (*zum Braten*) piece of sirloin *od* tenderloin (*US*)
Filiale [fili'a:lə] **(-, -n)** *f* (*Comm*) branch
Filipino [fili'pi:no] **(-s, -s)** *m* Filipino
Film [fɪlm] **(-(e)s, -e)** *m* film, movie (*bes US*); **da ist bei mir der ~ gerissen** (*umg*) I had a mental blackout; **Filmaufnahme** *f* shooting
Filmemacher, in *m(f)* film-maker
filmen *vt, vi* to film
Film- *zW*: **Filmfestspiele** *pl* film festival *sing*; **Filmkamera** *f* cine-camera; **Filmriss** (*umg*) *m* mental blackout; **Filmschauspieler, in** *m(f)* film *od* movie (*bes US*) actor, film *od* movie

actress; **Filmverleih** *m* film distributors *pl*; **Filmvorführgerät** *nt* cine-projector
Filter ['fɪltər] (**-s, -**) *m* filter; **Filterkaffee** *m* filter *od* drip (*US*) coffee; **Filtermundstück** *nt* filter tip
filtern *vt* to filter
Filterpapier *nt* filter paper
Filterzigarette *f* tipped cigarette
Filz [fɪlts] (**-es, -e**) *m* felt
filzen *vt* (*umg*) to frisk ▷ *vi* (*Wolle*) to mat
Filzstift *m* felt-tip (pen)
Fimmel ['fɪməl] (**-s, -**) (*umg*) *m*: **du hast wohl einen ~!** you're crazy!
Finale [fi'na:lə] (**-s, -(s)**) *nt* finale; (*Sport*) final(s *pl*)
Finanz [fi'nants] *f* finance; **Finanzen** *pl* finances *pl*; **das übersteigt meine ~en** that's beyond my means; **Finanzamt** *nt* ≈ Inland Revenue Office (*Brit*), Internal Revenue Office (*US*); **Finanzbeamte, r** *f(m)* revenue officer; **Finanzdienstleister, in** *m(f)* (*Bank etc*) financial services provider
finanziell [finantsi'ɛl] *adj* financial
finanzieren [finan'tsi:rən] *vt* to finance, to fund
Finanzierung *f* financing, funding
Finanz- *zW*: **Finanzminister** *m* ≈ Chancellor of the Exchequer (*Brit*), Minister of Finance; **finanzschwach** *adj* financially weak; **Finanzwesen** *nt* financial system; **Finanzwirtschaft** *f* public finances *pl*
finden ['fɪndən] *unreg vt* to find; (*meinen*) to think ▷ *vr* to be (found); (*sich fassen*) to compose o.s. ▷ *vi*: **ich finde schon allein hinaus** I can see myself out; **ich finde nichts dabei, wenn ...** I don't see what's wrong if ...; **das wird sich ~** things will work out
Finder, in (**-s, -**) *m(f)* finder; **Finderlohn** *m* reward (for the finder)
findig *adj* resourceful
fing *etc* [fɪŋ] *vb siehe* **fangen**
Finger ['fɪŋər] (**-s, -**) *m* finger; **mit ~n auf jdn zeigen** (*fig*) to look askance at sb; **das kann sich jeder an den (fünf) ~n abzählen** (*umg*) it sticks out a mile; **sich** *dat* **etw aus den ~n saugen** to conjure sth up; **lange ~ machen** (*umg*) to be light-fingered; **Fingerabdruck** *m* fingerprint; **Fingerhandschuh** *m* glove; **Fingerhut** *m* thimble; (*Bot*) foxglove; **Fingernagel** *m* fingernail; **Fingerring** *m* ring; **Fingerspitze** *f* fingertip; **Fingerspitzengefühl** *nt* sensitivity; **Fingerzeig** (**-(e)s, -e**) *m* hint, pointer
fingieren [fɪŋ'gi:rən] *vt* to feign
fingiert *adj* made-up, fictitious
Fink ['fɪŋk] (**-en, -en**) *m* finch
Finne ['fɪnə] (**-n, -n**) *m* Finn
Finnin ['fɪnɪn] *f* Finn
finnisch *adj* Finnish
Finnland *nt* Finland
finster ['fɪnstər] *adj* dark, gloomy; (*verdächtig*) dubious; (*verdrossen*) grim; (*Gedanke*) dark; **jdn ~ ansehen** to give sb a black look; **Finsternis** (**-**) *f* darkness, gloom
Finte ['fɪntə] (**-, -n**) *f* feint, trick
Firlefanz ['fɪrləfants] (*umg*) *m* (*Kram*) frippery; (*Albernheit*): **mach keinen ~** don't clown around
firm [fɪrm] *adj* well-up
Firma (**-, -men**) *f* firm; **die ~ dankt** (*hum*) much obliged (to you)
Firmen- *zW*: **Firmeninhaber** *m* proprietor (*of firm*); **Firmenregister** *nt* register of companies; **Firmenschild** *nt* (shop) sign; **Firmenübernahme** *f* takeover; **Firmenwagen** *m* company car; **Firmenzeichen** *nt* trademark
Firmung *f* (*Rel*) confirmation
Firnis ['fɪrnɪs] (**-ses, -se**) *m* varnish
Fis [fɪs] (**-, -**) *nt* (*Mus*) F sharp
Fisch [fɪʃ] (**-(e)s, -e**) *m* fish; **Fische** *pl* (*Astrol*) Pisces *sing*; **das sind kleine ~e** (*fig: umg*) that's child's play; **Fischbestand** *m* fish population
fischen *vt, vi* to fish
Fischer (**-s, -**) *m* fisherman
Fischerei [fɪʃə'raɪ] *f* fishing, fishery
Fisch- *zW*: **Fischfang** *m* fishing; **Fischgeschäft** *nt* fishmonger's (shop); **Fischgräte** *f* fishbone; **Fischgründe** *pl* fishing grounds *pl*, fisheries *pl*; **Fischstäbchen** *nt* fish finger (*Brit*), fish stick (*US*); **Fischzucht** *f* fish-farming; **Fischzug** *m* catch of fish
Fisimatenten [fizima'tɛntən] (*umg*) *pl* (*Ausflüchte*) excuses *pl*; (*Umstände*) fuss *sing*
Fiskus ['fɪskʊs] *m* (*fig: Staatskasse*) Treasury
fit [fɪt] *adj* fit
Fitness ['fɪtnəs] *nt* fitness
Fittich ['fɪtɪç] (**-(e)s, -e**) *m* (*liter*): **jdn unter seine ~e nehmen** (*hum*) to take sb under one's wing
fix [fɪks] *adj* (*flink*) quick; (*Person*) alert, smart; **~e Idee** obsession, idée fixe; **~ und fertig** finished; (*erschöpft*) done in; **jdn ~ und fertig machen** (*nervös machen*) to drive sb mad
fixen (*umg*) *vi* (*Drogen spritzen*) to fix
Fixer, in ['fɪksər(ɪn)] (*umg*) *m(f)* junkie (*inf*); **Fixerstube** (*umg*) *f* junkies' centre (*inf*)
fixieren [fɪ'ksi:rən] *vt* to fix; (*anstarren*) to stare at; **er ist zu stark auf seine Mutter fixiert** (*Psych*) he has a mother fixation
Fixkosten *pl* (*Comm*) fixed costs *pl*
FKK *abk* = **Freikörperkultur**
flach [flax] *adj* flat; (*Gefäß*) shallow; **auf dem ~en Land** in the middle of the country
Fläche ['flɛçə] (**-, -n**) *f* area; (*Oberfläche*) surface
Flächeninhalt *m* surface area
Flach- *zW*: **flachfallen** *unreg* (*umg*) *vi* to fall through; **Flachheit** *f* flatness; shallowness; **Flachland** *nt* lowland; **flachliegen** *unreg* (*umg*) *vi* to be laid up; **Flachmann** (**-(e)s**, *pl* **-männer**) (*umg*) *m* hip flask
flachsen ['flaksən] (*umg*) *vi* to kid around
flackern ['flakərn] *vi* to flare, flicker
Fladen ['fla:dən] (**-s, -**) *m* (*Koch*) round flat dough-cake; (*umg: Kuhfladen*) cowpat
Flagge ['flagə] (**-, -n**) *f* flag; **~ zeigen** (*fig*) to nail one's colours to the mast

flaggen *vi* to fly flags *od* a flag
flagrant [fla'grant] *adj* flagrant; **in ~i** red-handed
Flak [flak] **(-s, -)** *f* (= *Flug(zeug)abwehrkanone*) anti-aircraft gun; (*Einheit*) anti-aircraft unit
flambieren [flam'bi:rən] *vt* (*Koch*) to flambé
Flame ['fla:mə] **(-n, -n)** *m* Fleming
Flämin ['flɛ:mɪn] *f* Fleming
flämisch ['flɛ:mɪʃ] *adj* Flemish
Flamme ['flamə] **(-, -n)** *f* flame; **in ~n stehen/aufgehen** to be in/go up in flames
Flandern ['flandərn] *nt* Flanders *sing*
Flanell [fla'nɛl] **(-s, -e)** *m* flannel
Flanke ['flaŋkə] **(-, -n)** *f* flank; (*Sport: Seite*) wing
Flasche ['flaʃə] **(-, -n)** *f* bottle; (*umg: Versager*) wash-out; **zur ~ greifen** (*fig*) to hit the bottle
Flaschen- *zW*: **Flaschenbier** *nt* bottled beer; **Flaschenöffner** *m* bottle opener; **Flaschenwein** *m* bottled wine; **Flaschenzug** *m* pulley
flatterhaft *adj* flighty, fickle
flattern ['flatərn] *vi* to flutter
flau [flaʊ] *adj* (*Brise, Comm*) slack; **jdm ist ~ (im Magen)** sb feels queasy
Flaum [flaʊm] **(-(e)s)** *m* (*Feder*) down
flauschig ['flaʊʃɪç] *adj* fluffy
Flausen ['flaʊzən] *pl* silly ideas *pl*; (*Ausflüchte*) weak excuses *pl*
Flaute ['flaʊtə] **(-, -n)** *f* calm; (*Comm*) recession
Flechte ['flɛçtə] **(-, -n)** *f* (*Med*) dry scab; (*Bot*) lichen
flechten *unreg vt* to plait; (*Kranz*) to twine
Fleck [flɛk] **(-(e)s, -e)** *m* (*Schmutzfleck*) stain; (*Farbfleck*) patch; (*Stelle*) spot; **nicht vom ~ kommen** (*lit, fig*) not to get any further; **sich nicht vom ~ rühren** not to budge; **vom ~ weg** straight away
Fleckchen *nt*: **ein schönes ~ (Erde)** a lovely little spot
Flecken **(-s, -)** *m* = **Fleck**; **fleckenlos** *adj* spotless; **Fleckenmittel** *nt* stain remover; **Fleckenwasser** *nt* stain remover
fleckig *adj* marked; (*schmutzig*) stained
Fledermaus ['fle:dərmaʊs] *f* bat
Flegel ['fle:gəl] **(-s, -)** *m* flail; (*Person*) lout; **flegelhaft** *adj* loutish, unmannerly; **Flegeljahre** *pl* adolescence *sing*
flegeln *vr* to loll, sprawl
flehen ['fle:ən] *vi* (*geh*) to implore
flehentlich *adj* imploring
Fleisch [flaɪʃ] **(-(e)s)** *nt* flesh; (*Essen*) meat; **sich** *dat od akk* **ins eigene ~ schneiden** to cut off one's nose to spite one's face (*Sprichwort*); **es ist mir in ~ und Blut übergegangen** it has become second nature to me; **Fleischbrühe** *f* meat stock
Fleischer **(-s, -)** *m* butcher
Fleischerei [flaɪʃə'raɪ] *f* butcher's (shop)
fleischig *adj* fleshy
Fleisch- *zW*: **Fleischkäse** *m* meat loaf; **fleischlich** *adj* carnal; **Fleischpastete** *f* meat pie; **Fleischsalat** *m* diced meat salad with mayonnaise; **Fleischvergiftung** *f* food poisoning (*from meat*); **Fleischwolf** *m* mincer; **Fleischwunde** *f* flesh wound; **Fleischwurst** *f* pork sausage
Fleiß ['flaɪs] **(-es)** *m* diligence, industry; **ohne ~ kein Preis** (*Sprichwort*) success never comes easily
fleißig *adj* diligent, industrious; **~ studieren/arbeiten** to study/work hard
flektieren [flɛk'ti:rən] *vt* to inflect
flennen ['flɛnən] (*umg*) *vi* to cry, blubber
fletschen ['flɛtʃən] *vt* (*Zähne*) to show
Fleurop® ['flɔyrɔp] *f* ≈ Interflora®
flexibel [flɛ'ksi:bəl] *adj* flexible
Flexibilität [flɛksibili'tɛ:t] *f* flexibility
flicht [flɪçt] *vb siehe* **flechten**
Flicken ['flɪkən] **(-s, -)** *m* patch
flicken *vt* to mend
Flickschusterei ['flɪkʃu:stəraɪ] *f*: **das ist ~** that's a patch-up job
Flieder ['fli:dər] **(-s, -)** *m* lilac
Fliege ['fli:gə] **(-, -n)** *f* fly; (*Schlips*) bow tie; **zwei ~n mit einer Klappe schlagen** (*Sprichwort*) to kill two birds with one stone; **ihn stört die ~ an der Wand** every little thing irritates him
fliegen *unreg vt, vi* to fly; **auf jdn/etw ~** (*umg*) to be mad about sb/sth; **aus der Kurve ~** to skid off the bend; **aus der Firma ~** (*umg*) to get the sack
fliegend *adj attrib* flying; **~e Hitze** hot flushes *pl*
Fliegengewicht *nt* (*Sport, fig*) flyweight
Fliegenklatsche ['fli:gənklatʃə] *f* fly-swat
Fliegenpilz *m* fly agaric
Flieger **(-s, -)** *m* flier, airman; **Fliegeralarm** *m* air-raid warning
fliehen ['fli:ən] *unreg vi* to flee
Fliehkraft ['fli:kraft] *f* centrifugal force
Fliese ['fli:zə] **(-, -n)** *f* tile
Fließband ['fli:sbant] *nt* assembly *od* production line; **am ~ arbeiten** to work on the assembly *od* production line; **Fließbandarbeit** *f* production-line work; **Fließbandproduktion** *f* assembly-line production
fließen *unreg vi* to flow
fließend *adj* flowing; (*Rede, Deutsch*) fluent; (*Übergang*) smooth
Fließ- *zW*: **Fließheck** *nt* fastback; **Fließkomma** *nt* (*Comput*) ≈ floating point; **Fließpapier** *nt* blotting paper (*Brit*), fleece paper (*US*)
Flimmerkasten (*umg*) *m* (*Fernsehen*) box
Flimmerkiste (*umg*) *f* (*Fernsehen*) box
flimmern ['flɪmərn] *vi* to glimmer; **es flimmert mir vor den Augen** my head's swimming
flink [flɪŋk] *adj* nimble, lively; **mit etw ~ bei der Hand sein** to be quick (off the mark) with sth; **Flinkheit** *f* nimbleness, liveliness
Flinte ['flɪntə] **(-, -n)** *f* shotgun; **die ~ ins Korn werfen** to throw in the sponge
Flirt [flœrt] **(-s, -s)** *m* flirtation; **einen ~ (mit jdm) haben** flirt (with sb)
flirten ['flɪrtən] *vi* to flirt

Flittchen (*pej: umg*) *nt* floozy
Flitter (**-s, -**) *m* (*Flitterschmuck*) sequins *pl*
Flitterwochen *pl* honeymoon *sing*
flitzen ['flɪtsən] *vi* to flit
Flitzer (**-s, -**) (*umg*) *m* (*Auto*) sporty car
floaten ['flo:tən] *vt, vi* (*Fin*) to float
flocht *etc* [flɔxt] *vb siehe* **flechten**
Flocke ['flɔkə] (**-, -n**) *f* flake
flockig *adj* flaky
flog *etc* [flo:k] *vb siehe* **fliegen**
Floh [flo:] (**-(e)s, ¨-e**) *m* flea; **jdm einen ~ ins Ohr setzen** (*umg*) to put an idea into sb's head
floh *etc vb siehe* **fliehen**
Flohmarkt *m* flea market
Flora ['flo:ra] (**-, -ren**) *f* flora
Florenz [flo'rɛnts] *nt* Florence
florieren [flo'ri:rən] *vi* to flourish
Florist, in *m(f)* florist
Floskel ['flɔskəl] (**-, -n**) *f* set phrase; **floskelhaft** *adj* cliché-ridden, stereotyped
Floß [flo:s] (**-es, ¨-e**) *nt* raft
floss *etc* [flɔs] *vb siehe* **fließen**
Flosse ['flɔsə] (**-, -n**) *f* fin; (*Taucherflosse*) flipper; (*umg: Hand*) paw
Flöte ['flø:tə] (**-, -n**) *f* flute; (*Blockflöte*) recorder
flöten gehen ['flø:tənge:ən] (*umg*) *unreg vi* to go for a burton
Flötist, in [flø'tɪst(ɪn)] *m(f)* flautist, flutist (*bes US*)
flott [flɔt] *adj* lively; (*elegant*) smart; (*Naut*) afloat
Flotte (**-, -n**) *f* fleet
Flottenstützpunkt *m* naval base
flottmachen *vt* (*Schiff*) to float off; (*Auto, Fahrrad etc*) to put back on the road
Flöz [flø:ts] (**-es, -e**) *nt* layer, seam
Fluch [flu:x] (**-(e)s, ¨-e**) *m* curse; **fluchen** *vi* to curse, swear
Flucht [flʊxt] (**-, -en**) *f* flight; (*Fensterflucht*) row; (*Reihe*) range; (*Zimmerflucht*) suite; (*geglückt*) flight, escape; **jdn/etw in die ~ schlagen** to put sb/sth to flight
fluchtartig *adj* hasty
flüchten ['flʏçtən] *vi* to flee ▷ *vr* to take refuge
Fluchthilfe *f*: **~ leisten** to aid an escape
flüchtig *adj* fugitive; (*Chem*) volatile; (*oberflächlich*) cursory; (*eilig*) fleeting; **~er Speicher** (*Comput*) volatile memory; **jdn ~ kennen** to have met sb briefly; **Flüchtigkeit** *f* transitoriness; volatility; cursoriness; **Flüchtigkeitsfehler** *m* careless slip
Flüchtling *m* refugee
Flüchtlingslager *nt* refugee camp
Flucht- *zW*: **Fluchtversuch** *m* escape attempt; **Fluchtweg** *m* escape route
Flug [flu:k] (**-(e)s, ¨-e**) *m* flight; **im** ~ airborne, in flight; **wie im ~(e)** (*fig*) in a flash; **Flugabwehr** *f* anti-aircraft defence; **Flugbahn** *f* flight path; (*Kreisbahn*) orbit; **Flugbegleiter, in** *m(f)* (*Aviat*) flight attendant; **Flugblatt** *nt* pamphlet
Flügel ['fly:gəl] (**-s, -**) *m* wing; (*Mus*) grand piano; **Flügeltür** *f* double door
flugfähig *adj* able to fly; (*Flugzeug: in Ordnung*) airworthy
Fluggast *m* airline passenger
flügge ['flʏgə] *adj* (fully-)fledged; **~ werden** (*lit*) to be able to fly; (*fig*) to leave the nest
Flug- *zW*: **Fluggeschwindigkeit** *f* flying *od* air speed; **Fluggesellschaft** *f* airline (company); **Flughafen** *m* airport; **Flughöhe** *f* altitude (of flight); **Fluglotse** *m* air traffic *od* flight controller; **Flugplan** *m* flight schedule; **Flugplatz** *m* airport; (*klein*) airfield; **Flugreise** *f* flight
flugs [flʊks] *adv* speedily
Flug- *zW*: **Flugsand** *m* drifting sand; **Flugschein** *m* pilot's licence (*Brit*) *od* license (*US*); **Flugschreiber** *m* flight recorder; **Flugschrift** *f* pamphlet; **Flugsteig** *m* gate; **Flugstrecke** *f* air route; **Flugverkehr** *m* air traffic; **Flugwesen** *nt* aviation
Flugzeug (**-(e)s, -e**) *nt* plane, aeroplane (*Brit*), airplane (*US*); **Flugzeugentführung** *f* hijacking of a plane; **Flugzeughalle** *f* hangar; **Flugzeugträger** *m* aircraft carrier
fluktuieren [flʊktu'i:rən] *vi* to fluctuate
Flunder ['flʊndər] (**-, -n**) *f* flounder
flunkern ['flʊŋkərn] *vi* to fib, tell stories
Fluor ['flu:ɔr] (**-s**) *nt* fluorine
Flur[1] [flu:r] (**-(e)s, -e**) *m* hall; (*Treppenflur*) staircase
Flur[2] [flu:r] (**-, -en**) *f* (*geh*) open fields *pl*; **allein auf weiter ~ stehen** (*fig*) to be out on a limb
Fluss [flʊs] (**-es, ¨-e**) *m* river; (*Fließen*) flow; **im ~ sein** (*fig*) to be in a state of flux; **etw in** ~ *akk* **bringen** to get sth moving; **flussab, flussabwärts** *adv* downstream; **flussauf, flussaufwärts** *adv* upstream; **Flussdiagramm** *nt* flow chart
flüssig ['flʏsɪç] *adj* liquid; (*Stil*) flowing; **~es Vermögen** (*Comm*) liquid assets *pl*; **Flüssigkeit** *f* liquid; (*Zustand*) liquidity; **flüssigmachen** *vt* (*Geld*) to make available
Flussmündung *f* estuary
Flusspferd *nt* hippopotamus
flüstern ['flʏstərn] *vt, vi* to whisper
Flüsterpropaganda *f* whispering campaign
Flut [flu:t] (**-, -en**) *f* (*lit, fig*) flood; (*Gezeiten*) high tide; **fluten** *vi* to flood; **Flutlicht** *nt* floodlight
flutschen ['flʊtʃən] (*umg*) *vi* (*rutschen*) to slide; (*funktionieren*) to go well
Flutwelle *f* tidal wave
fl. W. *abk* (= *fließendes Wasser*) running water
focht *etc* [fɔxt] *vb siehe* **fechten**
föderativ [fødera'ti:f] *adj* federal
Fohlen ['fo:lən] (**-s, -**) *nt* foal
Föhn [fø:n] (**-(e)s, -e**) *m* foehn, *warm dry alpine wind*; (*Haartrockner*) hairdryer
föhnen *vt* to blow-dry
Föhre ['fø:rə] (**-, -n**) *f* Scots pine
Folge ['fɔlgə] (**-, -n**) *f* series, sequence; (*Fortsetzung*) instalment (*Brit*), installment (*US*); (*TV, Rundf*) episode; (*Auswirkung*) result; **in rascher ~** in quick succession; **etw zur ~ haben** to result in sth; **~n haben** to have

consequences; **einer Sache** *dat* **~ leisten** to comply with sth; **Folgeerscheinung** *f* result, consequence
folgen *vi +dat* to follow ▷ *vi* (*gehorchen*) to obey; **jdm ~ können** (*fig*) to follow *od* understand sb; **daraus folgt, dass ...** it follows from this that ...
folgend *adj* following; **im F~en** in the following; (*schriftlich*) below
folgendermaßen ['fɔlgəndər'ma:sən] *adv* as follows, in the following way
folgenreich *adj* momentous
folgenschwer *adj* momentous
folgerichtig *adj* logical
folgern *vt*: **~ (aus)** to conclude (from)
Folgerung *f* conclusion
folgewidrig *adj* illogical
folglich ['fɔlklɪç] *adv* consequently
folgsam ['fɔlkza:m] *adj* obedient
Folie ['fo:liə] **(-, -n)** *f* foil
Folienschweißgerät *nt* shrink-wrap machine
Folklore ['fɔlklo:ər] **(-)** *f* folklore
Folter ['fɔltər] **(-, -n)** *f* torture; (*Gerät*) rack; **jdn auf die ~ spannen** (*fig*) to keep sb on tenterhooks
foltern *vt* to torture
Fön® [fø:n] **(-(e)s, -e)** *m* hairdryer
Fonds [fõ:] **(-, -)** *m* (*lit, fig*) fund; (*Fin: Schuldverschreibung*) government bond; **Fondsmanager, in** *m(f)* fund manager
fönen *vt siehe* **föhnen**
Fono-, fono- *in zW* = **Phono-, phono-**
Fontäne [fɔn'tɛ:nə] **(-, -n)** *f* fountain
foppen ['fɔpən] *vt* to tease
forcieren [fɔr'si:rən] *vt* to push; (*Tempo*) to force; (*Konsum, Produktion*) to push *od* force up
Förderband ['fœrdərbant] *nt* conveyor belt
Förderer (-s, -) *m* patron
Fördergebiet *nt* development area
Förderin *f* patroness
Förderkorb *m* pit cage
Förderleistung *f* (*Min*) output
förderlich *adj* beneficial
fordern ['fɔrdərn] *vt* to demand; (*fig: kosten: Opfer*) to claim; (*: herausfordern*) to challenge
fördern ['fœrdərn] *vt* to promote; (*unterstützen*) to help; (*Kohle*) to extract; (*finanziell: Projekt*) to sponsor; (*jds Talent, Neigung*) to encourage, foster
Förderplattform *f* production platform
Förderstufe *f* (*Sch*) *first stage of secondary school where abilities are judged*
Förderturm *m* (*Min*) winding tower; (*auf Bohrstelle*) derrick
Forderung ['fɔrdərʊŋ] *f* demand
Förderung ['fœrdərʊŋ] *f* promotion; help; extraction
Forelle [fo'rɛlə] *f* trout
Form [fɔrm] **(-, -en)** *f* shape; (*Gestaltung*) form; (*Gussform*) mould; (*Backform*) baking tin; **in ~ von** in the shape of; **in ~ sein** to be in good form *od* shape; **die ~ wahren** to observe the proprieties; **in aller ~** formally
formal [fɔr'ma:l] *adj* formal; (*Besitzer, Grund*) technical
formalisieren [fɔrmali'zi:rən] *vt* to formalize
Formalität [fɔrmalɪ'tɛ:t] *f* formality; **alle ~en erledigen** to go through all the formalities
Format [fɔr'ma:t] **(-(e)s, -e)** *nt* format; (*fig*) quality
formatieren [fɔrma'ti:rən] *vt* (*Text, Diskette*) to format
Formation [fɔrmatsi'o:n] *f* formation
formbar *adj* malleable
Formblatt *nt* form
Formel (-, -n) *f* formula; (*von Eid etc*) wording; (*Floskel*) set phrase; **formelhaft** *adj* (*Sprache, Stil*) stereotyped
formell [fɔr'mɛl] *adj* formal
formen *vt* to form, shape
Formfehler *m* faux pas, gaffe; (*Jur*) irregularity
Formfleisch *nt* pressed meat
formieren [fɔr'mi:rən] *vt* to form ▷ *vr* to form up
förmlich ['fœrmlɪç] *adj* formal; (*umg*) real; **Förmlichkeit** *f* formality
formlos *adj* shapeless; (*Benehmen etc*) informal; (*Antrag*) unaccompanied by a form *od* any forms
Formsache *f* formality
Formular [fɔrmu'la:r] **(-s, -e)** *nt* form
formulieren [fɔrmu'li:rən] *vt* to formulate
Formulierung *f* wording
formvollendet *adj* perfect; (*Vase etc*) perfectly formed
forsch [fɔrʃ] *adj* energetic, vigorous
forschen [fɔrʃən] *vi* to search; (*wissenschaftlich*) to (do) research; **~ nach** to search for
forschend *adj* searching
Forscher (-s, -) *m* research scientist; (*Naturforscher*) explorer
Forschung ['fɔrʃʊŋ] *f* research; **~ und Lehre** research and teaching; **~ und Entwicklung** research and development
Forschungsreise *f* scientific expedition
Forst [fɔrst] **(-(e)s, -e)** *m* forest; **Forstarbeiter** *m* forestry worker
Förster ['fœrstər] **(-s, -)** *m* forester; (*für Wild*) gamekeeper
Forstwesen *nt* forestry
Forstwirtschaft *f* forestry
fort [fɔrt] *adv* away; (*verschwunden*) gone; (*vorwärts*) on; **und so ~** and so on; **in einem ~** incessantly; **fortbestehen** *unreg vi* to continue to exist; **fortbewegen** *vt, vr* to move away; **fortbilden** *vr* to continue one's education; **Fortbildung** *f* further education; **fortbleiben** *unreg vi* to stay away; **fortbringen** *unreg vt* to take away; **Fortdauer** *f* continuance; **fortdauernd** *adj* continuing; (*in der Vergangenheit*) continued ▷ *adv* constantly, continuously; **fortfahren** *unreg vi* to depart; (*fortsetzen*) to go on, continue; **fortführen** *vt* to continue, carry on; **Fortgang** *m* (*Verlauf*) progress; (*Weggang*): **Fortgang (aus)** departure (from); **fortgehen** *unreg vi* to go away;

fortgeschritten *adj* advanced; **fortkommen** *unreg vi* to get on; (*wegkommen*) to get away; **fortkönnen** *unreg vi* to be able to get away; **fortlassen** *vt* (*auslassen*) to leave out, omit; (*weggehen lassen*): **jdn fortlassen** to let sb go; **fortlaufend** *adj*: **fortlaufend nummeriert** consecutively numbered; **fortmüssen** *unreg vi* to have to go; **fortpflanzen** *vr* to reproduce; **Fortpflanzung** *f* reproduction

FORTRAN ['fɔrtran] *nt* FORTRAN

Forts. *abk* = **Fortsetzung**

fortschaffen *vt* to remove

fortschreiten *unreg vi* to advance

Fortschritt ['fɔrtʃrɪt] *m* advance; **~e machen** to make progress; **dem ~ dienen** to further progress; **fortschrittlich** *adj* progressive

fortschrittsgläubig *adj* believing in progress

fort- *zW*: **fortsetzen** *vt* to continue; **Fortsetzung** *f* continuation; (*folgender Teil*) instalment (*Brit*), installment (*US*); **Fortsetzung folgt** to be continued; **Fortsetzungsroman** *m* serialized novel; **fortwährend** *adj* incessant, continual; **fortwirken** *vi* to continue to have an effect; **fortziehen** *unreg vt* to pull away ▷ *vi* to move on; (*umziehen*) to move away

Foto ['fo:to] (**-s, -s**) *nt* photo(graph); **ein ~ machen** to take a photo(graph); **Fotoalbum** *nt* photograph album; **Fotoapparat** *m* camera; **Fotograf, in** (**-en, -en**) *m(f)* photographer; **Fotografie** *f* photography; (*Bild*) photograph; **fotografieren** *vt* to photograph ▷ *vi* to take photographs; **Fotohandy** *nt* camera phone; **Fotokopie** *f* photocopy; **fotokopieren** *vt* to photocopy; **Fotokopierer** *m* photocopier; **Fotokopiergerät** *nt* photocopier

Foul [faʊl] (**-s, -s**) *nt* foul

Foyer [foa'je:] (**-s, -s**) *nt* foyer; (*in Hotel*) lobby, foyer

FPÖ (**-**) *f abk* (= *Freiheitliche Partei Österreichs*) Austrian Freedom Party

Fr. *abk* (= *Frau*) Mrs, Ms

Fracht [fraxt] (**-, -en**) *f* freight; (*Naut*) cargo; (*Preis*) carriage; **~ zahlt Empfänger** (*Comm*) carriage forward; **Frachtbrief** *m* consignment note, waybill

Frachter (**-s, -**) *m* freighter

Fracht- *zW*: **frachtfrei** *adj* (*Comm*) carriage paid *od* free; **Frachtgut** *nt* freight; **Frachtkosten** *pl* (*Comm*) freight charges *pl*

Frack [frak] (**-(e)s, ⸚e**) *m* tails *pl*, tail coat

Frage ['fra:gə] (**-, -n**) *f* question; **jdm eine ~ stellen** to ask sb a question, put a question to sb; **das ist gar keine ~, das steht außer ~** there's no question about it; *siehe auch* **infrage**; **Fragebogen** *m* questionnaire

fragen *vt, vi* to ask ▷ *vr* to wonder; **nach Arbeit/Post ~** to ask whether there is/was any work/mail; **da fragst du mich zu viel** (*umg*) I really couldn't say; **nach** *od* **wegen** (*umg*) **jdm ~** to ask for sb; (*nach jds Befinden*) to ask after sb; **ohne lange zu ~** without asking a lot of questions

Fragerei [fra:gə'raɪ] *f* questions *pl*

Fragestunde *f* (*Parl*) question time

Fragezeichen *nt* question mark

fraglich *adj* questionable, doubtful; (*betreffend*) in question

fraglos *adv* unquestionably

Fragment [fra'gmɛnt] *nt* fragment

fragmentarisch [fragmɛn'ta:rɪʃ] *adj* fragmentary

fragwürdig ['fra:kvʏrdɪç] *adj* questionable, dubious

Fraktion [fraktsi'o:n] *f* parliamentary party

Fraktionsvorsitzende, r *f(m)* (*Pol*) party whip

Fraktionszwang *m* requirement to obey the party whip

Franchisekette ['frɛnʃaɪskɛtə] *f* franchise chain

frank [fraŋk] *adj* frank, candid

Franken[1] ['fraŋkən] *nt* Franconia

Franken[2] ['fraŋkən] (**-, -**) *m*: **(Schweizer) ~** (Swiss) Franc

Frankfurt ['fraŋkfʊrt] (**-s**) *nt* Frankfurt

Frankfurter, in *m(f)* native of Frankfurt ▷ *adj* Frankfurt; **Frankfurter Würstchen** *pl* frankfurters

frankieren [fraŋ'ki:rən] *vt* to stamp, frank

Frankiermaschine *f* franking machine

fränkisch ['fraŋkɪʃ] *adj* Franconian

franko *adv* carriage paid; (*Post*) post-paid

Frankreich ['fraŋkraɪç] (**-s**) *nt* France

Franse ['franzə] (**-, -n**) *f* fringe

fransen *vi* to fray

franz. *abk* = **französisch**

Franzbranntwein *m* alcoholic liniment

Franzose [fran'tso:zə] (**-n, -n**) *m* Frenchman; French boy

Französin [fran'tsø:zɪn] *f* Frenchwoman; French girl

französisch *adj* French; **~es Bett** double bed

Fräse ['frɛ:zə] (**-, -n**) *f* (*Werkzeug*) milling cutter; (*für Holz*) moulding cutter

Fraß (**-es, -e**) (*pej: umg*) *m* (*Essen*) muck

fraß *etc* [fra:s] *vb siehe* **fressen**

Fratze ['fratsə] (**-, -n**) *f* grimace; **eine ~ schneiden** to pull *od* make a face

Frau [fraʊ] (**-, -en**) *f* woman; (*Ehefrau*) wife; (*Anrede*) Mrs, Ms; **~ Doktor** Doctor

Frauen- *zW*: **Frauenarzt** *m* gynaecologist (*Brit*), gynecologist (*US*); **Frauenbewegung** *f* feminist movement; **frauenfeindlich** *adj* anti-women, misogynous; **Frauenhaus** *nt* women's refuge; **Frauenquote** *f* recommended proportion of women (employed); **Frauenrechtlerin** *f* feminist; **Frauenzentrum** *nt* women's advice centre; **Frauenzimmer** (*pej*) *nt* female, broad (*US*)

Fräulein ['frɔʏlaɪn] *nt* young lady; (*Anrede*) Miss; (*Verkäuferin*) assistant (*Brit*), sales clerk (*US*); (*Kellnerin*) waitress

fraulich ['fraʊlɪç] *adj* womanly

frech [frɛç] *adj* cheeky, impudent; **~ wie Oskar sein** (*umg*) to be a little monkey; **Frechdachs** *m* cheeky monkey; **Frechheit** *f* cheek, impudence; **sich** *dat* **(einige) Frechheiten erlauben** to be a bit cheeky (*bes Brit*) *od* fresh (*bes US*)

Fregatte [fre'gatə] (**-, -n**) *f* frigate

frei [fraɪ] *adj* free; (*Stelle*) vacant; (*Mitarbeiter*) freelance; (*Geld*) available; (*unbekleidet*) bare; **aus ~en Stücken** *od* **~em Willen** of one's own free will; **~ nach ...** based on ...; **für etw ~e Fahrt geben** (*fig*) to give sth the go-ahead; **der Film ist ~ ab 16 (Jahren)** the film may be seen by people of 16 years (of age) and over; **unter ~em Himmel** in the open (air); **morgen/Mittwoch ist ~** tomorrow/Wednesday is a holiday; **„Zimmer ~"** "vacancies"; **auf ~er Strecke** (*Eisenb*) between stations; (*Aut*) on the road; **~er Wettbewerb** fair/open competition; **~ Haus** (*Comm*) carriage paid; **~ Schiff** (*Comm*) free on board; **~e Marktwirtschaft** free market economy; **von etw ~ sein** to be free of sth; **im F~en** in the open air; **~ halten** (*Ausfahrt etc*) to keep free; **~ sprechen** to talk without notes; **Freibad** *nt* open-air swimming pool; **freibekommen** *unreg vt*: **jdn/einen Tag freibekommen** to get sb freed/get a day off; **freiberuflich** *adj* self-employed; **Freibetrag** *m* tax allowance

Freier (**-s, -**) *m* suitor

Frei- *zW*: **Freiexemplar** *nt* free copy; **freigeben** *unreg vt*: **etw zum Verkauf freigeben** to allow sth to be sold on the open market; **freigebig** *adj* generous; **Freigebigkeit** *f* generosity; **Freihafen** *m* free port; **freihalten** *unreg vt* (*bezahlen*) to pay for; *siehe auch* **frei**; **Freihandel** *m* free trade; **Freihandelszone** *f* free trade area; **freihändig** *adv* (*fahren*) with no hands

Freiheit *f* freedom; **sich** *dat* **die ~ nehmen, etw zu tun** to take the liberty of doing sth; **freiheitlich** *adj* liberal; (*Verfassung*) based on the principle of liberty; (*Demokratie*) free

Freiheits- *zW*: **Freiheitsberaubung** *f* (*Jur*) wrongful deprivation of personal liberty; **Freiheitsdrang** *m* urge/desire for freedom; **Freiheitskampf** *m* fight for freedom; **Freiheitskämpfer, in** *m(f)* freedom fighter; **Freiheitsrechte** *pl* civil liberties *pl*; **Freiheitsstrafe** *f* prison sentence

frei- *zW*: **freiheraus** *adv* frankly; **Freikarte** *f* free ticket; **freikaufen** *vt*: **jdn/sich freikaufen** to buy sb's/one's freedom; **freikommen** *unreg vi* to get free; **Freikörperkultur** *f* nudism; **freilassen** *unreg vt* to (set) free; **Freilauf** *m* freewheeling; **freilaufend** *adj* (*Hühner*) free-range; **freilegen** *vt* to expose; **freilich** *adv* certainly, admittedly; **ja freilich!** yes of course; **Freilichtbühne** *f* open-air theatre; **freimachen** *vt* (*Post*) to frank ▷ *vr* to arrange to be free; **Tage freimachen** to take days off; **sich freimachen** (*beim Arzt*) to take one's clothes off, strip; **Freimaurer** *m* Mason, Freemason

freimütig ['fraɪmy:tɪç] *adj* frank, honest

Frei- *zW*: **freinehmen** *vt*: **sich** *dat* **einen Tag freinehmen** to take a day off; **Freiraum** *m*: **Freiraum (zu)** (*fig*) freedom (for); **freischaffend** *adj attrib* freelance; **Freischaltcode** *m* (*Tel*) connecting *od* enabling code; **Freischärler** (**-s, -**) *m* guerrilla; **freischwimmen** *vr* (*fig*) to learn to stand on one's own two feet; **freisetzen** *vt* (*Energien*) to release; **freisinnig** *adj* liberal; **Freisprechanlage** *f* hands-free (headset); (*im Auto*) hands-free (car kit); **freisprechen** *unreg vt*: **freisprechen (von)** to acquit (of); **Freispruch** *m* acquittal; **freistehen** *unreg vi*: **es steht dir frei, das zu tun** you are free to do so; **das steht Ihnen völlig frei** that is completely up to you; **freistellen** *vt*: **jdm etw freistellen** to leave sth (up) to sb; **Freistoß** *m* free kick; **Freistunde** *f* free hour; (*Sch*) free period

Freitag *m* Friday; *siehe auch* **Dienstag**

freitags *adv* on Fridays

Frei- *zW*: **Freitod** *m* suicide; **Freiübungen** *pl* (physical) exercises *pl*; **Freiumschlag** *m* reply-paid envelope; **Freiwild** *nt* (*fig*) fair game; **freiwillig** *adj* voluntary; **Freiwillige, r** *f(m)* volunteer; **Freizeichen** *nt* (*Tel*) ringing tone; **Freizeit** *f* spare *od* free time; **Freizeitgestaltung** *f* organization of one's leisure time; **freizügig** *adj* liberal, broad-minded; (*mit Geld*) generous

fremd [frɛmt] *adj* (*unvertraut*) strange; (*ausländisch*) foreign; (*nicht eigen*) someone else's; **etw ist jdm ~** sth is foreign to sb; **ich bin hier ~** I'm a stranger here; **sich ~ fühlen** to feel like a stranger; **fremdartig** *adj* strange

Fremde (**-**) *f* (*liter*): **die ~** foreign parts *pl*

Fremde, r *f(m)* stranger; (*Ausländer*) foreigner

Fremden- *zW*: **Fremdenführer** *m* (tourist) guide; (*Buch*) guide (book); **Fremdenlegion** *f* foreign legion; **Fremdenverkehr** *m* tourism; **Fremdenzimmer** *nt* guest room

fremd- *zW*: **fremdgehen** *unreg* (*umg*) *vi* to be unfaithful; **Fremdkapital** *nt* loan capital; **Fremdkörper** *m* foreign body; **fremdländisch** *adj* foreign; **Fremdling** *m* stranger; **Fremdsprache** *f* foreign language; **Fremdsprachenkorrespondentin** *f* bilingual secretary; **fremdsprachig** *adj attrib* foreign-language; **Fremdwort** *nt* foreign word

frenetisch [fre'ne:tɪʃ] *adj* frenetic

Frequenz [fre'kvɛnts] *f* (*Rundf*) frequency

Fresse (**-, -n**) (*umg!*) *f* (*Mund*) gob; (*Gesicht*) mug

fressen ['frɛsən] *unreg vt, vi* to eat ▷ *vr*: **sich satt ~** to gorge o.s.; **einen Narren an jdm/etw gefressen haben** to dote on sb/sth

Freude ['frɔʏdə] (**-, -n**) *f* joy, delight; **~ an etw** *dat* **haben** to get *od* derive pleasure from sth; **jdm eine ~ machen** *od* **bereiten** to make sb happy

Freudenhaus *nt* (*veraltet*) house of ill repute

Freudentanz *m*: **einen ~ aufführen** to dance with joy

freudestrahlend *adj* beaming with delight

freudig *adj* joyful, happy

freudlos *adj* joyless
freuen ['frɔʏən] *vt unpers* to make happy *od* pleased ▷ *vr* to be glad *od* happy; **sich auf etw** *akk* ~ to look forward to sth; **sich über etw** *akk* ~ to be pleased about sth; **sich zu früh** ~ to get one's hopes up too soon
Freund ['frɔʏnt] (**-(e)s, -e**) *m* friend; (*Liebhaber*) boyfriend; **ich bin kein ~ von so etwas** I'm not one for that sort of thing; **Freundin** *f* friend; (*Liebhaberin*) girlfriend; **freundlich** *adj* kind, friendly; **bitte recht freundlich!** smile please!; **würden Sie bitte so freundlich sein und das tun?** would you be so kind as to do that?; **freundlicherweise** *adv* kindly; **Freundlichkeit** *f* friendliness, kindness; **Freundschaft** *f* friendship; **freundschaftlich** *adj* friendly
Frevel ['fre:fəl] (**-s, -**) *m*: **~ (an** *+dat***)** crime *od* offence (against); **frevelhaft** *adj* wicked
Frieden ['fri:dən] (**-s, -**) *m* peace; **im ~** in peacetime; **~ schließen** to make one's peace; (*Pol*) to make peace; **um des lieben ~s willen** (*umg*) for the sake of peace and quiet; **ich traue dem ~ nicht** (*umg*) something (fishy) is going on
Friedens- *zW*: **Friedensbewegung** *f* peace movement; **Friedensrichter** *m* justice of the peace; **Friedensschluss** *m* peace agreement; **Friedenstruppe** *f* peace-keeping force; **Friedensverhandlungen** *pl* peace negotiations *pl*; **Friedensvertrag** *m* peace treaty; **Friedenszeit** *f* peacetime
fried- *zW*: **friedfertig** *adj* peaceable; **Friedhof** *m* cemetery; **friedlich** *adj* peaceful; **etw auf friedlichem Wege lösen** to solve sth by peaceful means
frieren ['fri:rən] *unreg vi* to freeze ▷ *vt unpers* to freeze ▷ *vi unpers*: **heute Nacht hat es gefroren** it was below freezing last night; **ich friere, es friert mich** I am freezing, I'm cold; **wie ein Schneider ~** (*umg*) to be *od* get frozen to the marrow
Fries [fri:s] (**-es, -e**) *m* (*Archit*) frieze
Friese ['fri:zə] (**-n, -n**) *m* Fri(e)sian
Friesin ['fri:zɪn] *f* Fri(e)sian
frigid, frigide *adj* frigid
Frikadelle [frika'dɛlə] *f* meatball
frisch [frɪʃ] *adj* fresh; (*lebhaft*) lively; **~ gestrichen!** wet paint!; **sich ~ machen** to freshen (o.s.) up; **jdn auf ~er Tat ertappen** to catch sb red-handed *od* in the act
Frische (**-**) *f* freshness; liveliness; **in alter ~** (*umg*) as always
Frischhaltebeutel *m* airtight bag
Frischhaltefolie *f* clingfilm
frischweg *adv* (*munter*) straight out
Friseur [fri'zø:r] *m* hairdresser
Friseuse [fri'zø:zə] *f* hairdresser
frisieren [fri'zi:rən] *vt* (*Haar*) to do; (*fig: Abrechnung*) to fiddle, doctor ▷ *vr* to do one's hair; **jdn ~, jdm das Haar ~** to do sb's hair
Frisiersalon *m* hairdressing salon
Frisiertisch *m* dressing table
Frisör [fri'zø:r] (**-s, -e**) *m* = **Friseur**
frisst [frɪst] *vb siehe* **fressen**
Frist [frɪst] (**-, -en**) *f* period; (*Termin*) deadline; **eine ~ einhalten/verstreichen lassen** to meet a deadline/let a deadline pass; (*bei Rechnung*) to pay/not to pay within the period stipulated; **jdm eine ~ von vier Tagen geben** to give sb four days' grace
fristen *vt* (*Dasein*) to lead; (*kümmerlich*) to eke out
Fristenlösung *f* abortion law (*permitting abortion in the first three months*)
fristgerecht *adj* within the period stipulated
fristlos *adj* (*Entlassung*) instant
Frisur [fri'zu:r] *f* hairdo, hairstyle
Fritteuse [fri'tø:zə] (**-, -n**) *f* chip pan (*Brit*), deep fat fryer
frittieren [fri'ti:rən] *vt* to deep fry
frivol [fri'vo:l] *adj* frivolous
Frl. *abk* (= *Fräulein*) Miss
froh [fro:] *adj* happy, cheerful; **ich bin ~, dass ...** I'm glad that ...
fröhlich ['frø:lɪç] *adj* merry, happy; **Fröhlichkeit** *f* merriment, gaiety
frohlocken *vi* (*geh*) to rejoice; (*pej*) to gloat
Frohsinn *m* cheerfulness
fromm [frɔm] *adj* pious, good; (*Wunsch*) idle
Frömmelei [frœmə'laɪ] *f* false piety
Frömmigkeit *f* piety
frönen ['frø:nən] *vi +dat* to indulge in
Fronleichnam [fro:n'laɪçna:m] (**-(e)s**) *m* Corpus Christi
Front [frɔnt] (**-, -en**) *f* front; **klare ~en schaffen** (*fig*) to clarify the position
frontal [frɔn'ta:l] *adj* frontal; **Frontalangriff** *m* frontal attack
fror *etc* [fro:r] *vb siehe* **frieren**
Frosch [frɔʃ] (**-(e)s, ¨-e**) *m* frog; (*Feuerwerk*) squib; **sei kein ~!** (*umg*) be a sport!; **Froschmann** *m* frogman; **Froschperspektive** *f*: **etw aus der Froschperspektive sehen** to get a worm's-eye view of sth; **Froschschenkel** *m* frog's leg
Frost [frɔst] (**-(e)s, ¨-e**) *m* frost; **frostbeständig** *adj* frost-resistant; **Frostbeule** *f* chilblain
frösteln ['frœstəln] *vi* to shiver
frostig *adj* frosty
Frostschutzmittel *nt* anti-freeze
Frottee, Frotté [frɔ'te:] (**-(s), -s**) *nt od m* towelling
frottieren [frɔ'ti:rən] *vt* to rub, towel
Frottierhandtuch *nt* towel
Frottiertuch *nt* towel
frotzeln ['frɔtsəln] (*umg*) *vt, vi* to tease
Frucht [frʊxt] (**-, ¨-e**) *f* (*lit, fig*) fruit; (*Getreide*) corn; (*Embryo*) foetus; **fruchtbar** *adj* fruitful, fertile; **Fruchtbarkeit** *f* fertility; **Fruchtbecher** *m* fruit sundae
Früchtchen ['frʏçtçən] (*umg*) *nt* (*Tunichtgut*) good-for-nothing
fruchten *vi* to be of use
fruchtlos *adj* fruitless
Fruchtsaft *m* fruit juice
früh [fry:] *adj, adv* early; **heute ~** this morning;

von ~ auf from an early age; **Frühaufsteher** (**-s, -**) *m* early riser; **Frühdienst** *m*: **Frühdienst haben** to be on early shift
Frühe (**-**) *f* early morning; **in aller ~** at the crack of dawn
früher *adj* earlier; (*ehemalig*) former ▷ *adv* formerly; **~ war das anders** that used to be different; **~ oder später** sooner or later
frühestens *adv* at the earliest
Frühgeburt *f* premature birth; (*Kind*) premature baby
Frühjahr *nt* spring
Frühjahrsmüdigkeit *f* springtime lethargy
Frühjahrsputz *m* spring-cleaning
Frühling *m* spring; **im ~** in spring
früh- *zW*: **frühreif** *adj* precocious; **Frührentner** *m person who has retired early*; **Frühschicht** *f* early shift; **Frühschoppen** *m* morning/lunchtime drink; **Frühsport** *m* early morning exercise; **Frühstück** *nt* breakfast; **frühstücken** *vi* to (have) breakfast; **Frühwarnsystem** *nt* early warning system; **frühzeitig** *adj* early; (*vorzeitig*) premature
Frust (**-(e)s**) (*umg*) *m* frustration
frustrieren [frʊsˈtriːrən] *vt* to frustrate
frz. *abk* = **französisch**
FSV *abk* (= *Fußball-Sportverein*) F.C.
FU (**-**) *f abk* (= *Freie Universität Berlin*) *Berlin University*
Fuchs [fʊks] (**-es, ¨-e**) *m* fox
fuchsen (*umg*) *vt* to rile, annoy ▷ *vr* to be annoyed
Füchsin [ˈfʏksɪn] *f* vixen
fuchsteufelswild *adj* hopping mad
Fuchtel [ˈfʊxtl] (**-, -n**) *f* (*fig: umg*): **unter jds ~** under sb's control *od* thumb
fuchteln [ˈfʊxtəln] *vi* to gesticulate wildly
Fuge [ˈfuːgə] (**-, -n**) *f* joint; (*Mus*) fugue
fügen [ˈfyːgən] *vt* to place, join ▷ *vr unpers* to happen ▷ *vr*: **sich ~ (in** *+akk*) to be obedient (to); (*anpassen*) to adapt o.s. (to)
fügsam [ˈfyːkzaːm] *adj* obedient
fühlbar *adj* perceptible, noticeable
fühlen [ˈfyːlən] *vt, vi, vr* to feel
Fühler (**-s, -**) *m* feeler
Fühlung *f*: **mit jdm in ~ bleiben/stehen** to stay/be in contact *od* touch with sb
fuhr *etc* [fuːr] *vb siehe* **fahren**
Fuhre (**-, -n**) *f* (*Ladung*) load
führen [ˈfyːrən] *vt* to lead; (*Geschäft*) to run; (*Name*) to bear; (*Buch*) to keep; (*im Angebot haben*) to stock ▷ *vi* to lead ▷ *vr* to behave; **was führt Sie zu mir?** (*form*) what brings you to me?; **Geld/seine Papiere bei sich ~** (*form*) to carry money/one's papers on one's person; **das führt zu nichts** that will come to nothing
Führer, in [ˈfyːrər(ɪn)] (**-s, -**) *m(f)* leader; (*Fremdenführer*) guide; **Führerhaus** *nt* cab; **Führerschein** *m* driving licence (*Brit*), driver's license (*US*); **den Führerschein machen** (*Aut*) to learn to drive; (*die Prüfung ablegen*) to take one's (driving) test; **Führerscheinentzug** *m* disqualification from driving
Fuhrmann [ˈfuːrman] (**-(e)s**, *pl* **-leute**) *m* carter
Führung [ˈfyːrʊŋ] *f* leadership; (*eines Unternehmens*) management; (*Mil*) command; (*Benehmen*) conduct; (*Museumsführung*) conducted tour
Führungs- *zW*: **Führungskraft** *f* executive; **Führungsstab** *m* (*Mil*) command; (*Comm*) top management; **Führungsstil** *m* management style; **Führungszeugnis** *nt* certificate of good conduct
Fuhrunternehmen *nt* haulage business
Fuhrwerk *nt* cart
Fülle [ˈfʏlə] (**-**) *f* wealth, abundance
Füllen (**-s, -**) *nt* foal
füllen *vt* to fill; (*Koch*) to stuff ▷ *vr* to fill (up)
Füller (**-s, -**) *m* fountain pen
Füllfederhalter *m* fountain pen
Füllgewicht *nt* (*Comm*) weight at time of packing; (*auf Dosen*) net weight
füllig [ˈfʏlɪç] *adj* (*Mensch*) corpulent, portly; (*Figur*) ample
Füllung *f* filling; (*Holzfüllung*) panel
fummeln [ˈfʊməln] (*umg*) *vi* to fumble
Fund [fʊnt] (**-(e)s, -e**) *m* find
Fundament [fʊndaˈmɛnt] *nt* foundation
fundamental *adj* fundamental
Fundamentalismus *m* fundamentalism
Fundbüro *nt* lost property office, lost and found (*US*)
Fundgrube *f* (*fig*) treasure trove
fundieren [fʊnˈdiːrən] *vt* to back up
fundiert *adj* sound
fündig [ˈfʏndɪç] *adj* (*Min*) rich; **~ werden** to make a strike; (*fig*) to strike it lucky
Fundsachen *pl* lost property *sing*
fünf [fʏnf] *num* five; **seine ~ Sinne beisammen haben** to have all one's wits about one; **~(e) gerade sein lassen** (*umg*) to turn a blind eye; **fünfhundert** *num* five hundred; **fünfjährig** *adj* (*Frist, Plan*) five-year; (*Kind*) five-year-old; **Fünfkampf** *m* pentathlon
Fünfprozentklausel *f* (*Parl*) *clause debarring parties with less than 5% of the vote from Parliament*; *see culture note*

FÜNFPROZENTKLAUSEL

The *Fünfprozentklausel* is a rule in German Federal elections whereby only those parties who collect at least 5% of the second vote (*Zweitstimme*) receive a parliamentary seat. This is to avoid the parliament being made up of a large number of very small parties which, in the Weimar Republic, led to political instability.

Fünftagewoche *f* five-day week
fünfte, r, s *adj* fifth
Fünftel (**-s, -**) *nt* fifth
fünfzehn *num* fifteen
fünfzig *num* fifty
fungieren [fʊŋˈgiːrən] *vi* to function; (*Person*) to act
Funk [fʊŋk] (**-s**) *m* radio, wireless (*Brit old*);

Funkausstellung *f* radio and television exhibition
Funke (**-ns, -n**) *m* (*lit, fig*) spark
funkeln *vi* to sparkle
funkelnagelneu (*umg*) *adj* brand-new
Funken (**-s, -**) *m* = **Funke**
funken *vt* to radio
Funker (**-s, -**) *m* radio operator
Funk- *zW*: **Funkgerät** *nt* radio set; **Funkhaus** *nt* broadcasting centre; **Funkkolleg** *nt* educational radio broadcasts *pl*; **Funkrufempfänger** *m* (*Telec*) pager, paging device; **Funkspot** *m* advertisement on the radio; **Funksprechgerät** *nt* radio telephone; **Funkspruch** *m* radio signal; **Funkstation** *f* radio station; **Funkstille** *f* (*fig*) ominous silence; **Funkstreife** *f* police radio patrol; **Funktaxi** *nt* radio taxi; **Funktelefon** *nt* cell phone; **Funktelefonnetz** *nt* radio telephone network
Funktion [fʊŋktsi'o:n] *f* function; **in ~ treten/sein** to come into/be in operation
Funktionär, in [fʊŋktsio'nɛ:r(ɪn)] (**-s, -e**) *m(f)* functionary, official
funktionieren [fʊŋktsio'ni:rən] *vi* to work, function
Funktions- *zW*: **Funktionsbekleidung** *f* functional wear; **funktionsfähig** *adj* working; **Funktionstaste** *f* (*Comput*) function key; **funktionstüchtig** *adj* in working order
Funzel [funtsəl] (**-, -n**) (*umg*) *f* dim lamp
für [fy:r] *präp +akk* for; **was ~** what kind *od* sort of; **~s Erste** for the moment; **was Sie da sagen, hat etwas ~ sich** there's something in what you're saying; **Tag ~ Tag** day after day; **Schritt ~ Schritt** step by step; **das F~ und Wider** the pros and cons *pl*; **Fürbitte** *f* intercession
Furche ['fʊrçə] (**-, -n**) *f* furrow
furchen *vt* to furrow
Furcht [fʊrçt] (**-**) *f* fear; **furchtbar** *adj* terrible, awful
fürchten ['fʏrçtən] *vt* to be afraid of, fear ▹*vr*: **sich ~ (vor** *+dat***)** to be afraid (of)
fürchterlich *adj* awful
furchtlos *adj* fearless
furchtsam *adj* timorous
füreinander [fy:r|aɪ'nandər] *adv* for each other
Furie ['fu:riə] (**-, -n**) *f* (*Mythologie*) fury; (*fig*) hellcat
Furnier [fʊr'ni:r] (**-s, -e**) *nt* veneer
Furore [fu'ro:rə] *f od nt*: **~ machen** (*umg*) to cause a sensation
fürs [fy:rs] = **für das**
Fürsorge ['fy:rzɔrgə] *f* care; (*Sozialfürsorge*) welfare; **von der ~ leben** to live on social security (*Brit*) *od* welfare (*US*); **Fürsorgeamt** *nt* welfare office
Fürsorger, in (**-s, -**) *m(f)* welfare worker
Fürsorgeunterstützung *f* social security (*Brit*), welfare benefit (*US*)
fürsorglich *adj* caring
Fürsprache *f* recommendation; (*um Gnade*) intercession
Fürsprecher *m* advocate
Fürst [fʏrst] (**-en, -en**) *m* prince
Fürstentum *nt* principality
Fürstin *f* princess
fürstlich *adj* princely
Furt [fʊrt] (**-, -en**) *f* ford
Furunkel [fu'rʊŋkəl] (**-s, -**) *nt od m* boil
Fürwort ['fy:rvɔrt] *nt* pronoun
furzen ['fʊrtsən] (*umg!*) *vi* to fart (*!*)
Fusion [fuzi'o:n] *f* amalgamation; (*von Unternehmen*) merger; (*von Atomkernen, Zellen*) fusion
fusionieren [fuzio'ni:rən] *vt* to amalgamate
Fuß [fu:s] (**-es, ¨-e**) *m* foot; (*von Glas, Säule etc*) base; (*von Möbel*) leg; **zu ~** on foot; **bei ~!** heel!; **jdm etw vor die Füße werfen** (*lit*) to throw sth at sb; (*fig*) to tell sb to keep sth; **(festen) ~ fassen** (*lit, fig*) to gain a foothold; (*sich niederlassen*) to settle down; **mit jdm auf gutem ~ stehen** to be on good terms with sb; **auf großem ~ leben** to live the high life
Fußball *m* football; **Fußballplatz** *m* football pitch; **Fußballspiel** *nt* football match; **Fußballspieler** *m* footballer (*Brit*), football player (*US*); **Fußballtoto** *m od nt* football pools *pl*
Fußboden *m* floor; **Fußbodenheizung** *f* underfloor heating
Fußbremse *f* (*Aut*) foot brake
fusselig ['fʊsəlɪç] *adj*: **sich** *dat* **den Mund ~ reden** (*umg*) to talk till one is blue in the face
fusseln ['fʊsəln] *vi* (*Stoff, Kleid etc*) to go bobbly (*umg*)
fußen *vi*: **~ auf** *+dat* to rest on, be based on
Fuß- *zW*: **Fußende** *nt* foot; **Fußgänger, in** (**-s, -**) *m(f)* pedestrian; **Fußgängerüberführung** *f* pedestrian bridge; **Fußgängerzone** *f* pedestrian precinct; **Fußleiste** *f* skirting board (*Brit*), baseboard (*US*); **Fußnagel** *m* toenail; **Fußnote** *f* footnote; **Fußpfleger** *m* chiropodist; **Fußpilz** *m* (*Med*) athlete's foot; **Fußspur** *f* footprint; **Fußstapfen** (**-s, -**) *m*: **in jds Fußstapfen treten** (*fig*) to follow in sb's footsteps; **Fußtritt** *m* kick; (*Spur*) footstep; **Fußvolk** *nt* (*fig*): **das Fußvolk** the rank and file; **Fußweg** *m* footpath
futsch [fʊtʃ] (*umg*) *adj* (*weg*) gone, vanished
Futter ['fʊtər] (**-s, -**) *nt* fodder, feed; (*Stoff*) lining
Futteral [fʊtə'ra:l] (**-s, -e**) *nt* case
futtern ['fʊtərn] *vi* (*hum: umg*) to stuff o.s. ▹*vt* to scoff
füttern ['fʏtərn] *vt* to feed; (*Kleidung*) to line; **„F~ verboten"** "do not feed the animals"
Futur [fu'tu:r] (**-s, -e**) *nt* future

Gg

G, g[1] [geː] *nt* G, g; **G wie Gustav** ≈ G for George
g[2] *abk* (*Österr*) = **Groschen**; (= *Gramm*) g
gab *etc* [gaːp] *vb siehe* **geben**
Gabe ['gaːbə] (**-, -n**) *f* gift
Gabel ['gaːbəl] (**-, -n**) *f* fork; (*Tel*) rest, cradle; **Gabelfrühstück** *nt* mid-morning light lunch; **gabeln** *vr* to fork; **Gabelstapler** (**-s, -**) *m* fork-lift truck; **Gabelung** *f* fork
Gabentisch ['gaːbəntɪʃ] *m table for Christmas or birthday presents*
Gabun [ga'buːn] *nt* Gabon
gackern ['gakərn] *vi* to cackle
gaffen ['gafən] *vi* to gape
Gag [gɛk] (**-s, -s**) *m* (*Filmgag*) gag; (*Werbegag*) gimmick
Gage ['gaːʒə] (**-, -n**) *f* fee
gähnen ['gɛːnən] *vi* to yawn; **~de Leere** total emptiness
GAL (**-**) *f abk* (= *Grün-Alternative Liste*) *electoral pact of Greens and alternative parties*
Gala ['gala] (**-**) *f* formal dress
galant [ga'lant] *adj* gallant, courteous
Galavorstellung *f* (*Theat*) gala performance
Galerie [galə'riː] *f* gallery
Galgen ['galgən] (**-s, -**) *m* gallows *pl*; **Galgenfrist** *f* respite; **Galgenhumor** *m* macabre humour (*Brit*) *od* humor (*US*); **Galgenstrick** (*umg*) *m*, **Galgenvogel** (*umg*) *m* gallows bird
Galionsfigur [gali'oːnsfiguːr] *f* figurehead
gälisch ['gɛːlɪʃ] *adj* Gaelic
Galle ['galə] (**-, -n**) *f* gall; (*Organ*) gall bladder; **jdm kommt die ~ hoch** sb's blood begins to boil
Galopp [ga'lɔp] (**-s, -s** *od* **-e**) *m* gallop; **im ~** (*lit*) at a gallop; (*fig*) at top speed
galoppieren [galɔ'piːrən] *vi* to gallop
galt *etc* [galt] *vb siehe* **gelten**
galvanisieren [galvani'ziːrən] *vt* to galvanize
Gamasche [ga'maʃə] (**-, -n**) *f* gaiter; (*kurz*) spat
Gameboy® ['geːmbɔʏ] *m* (*Comput*) games console
Gammastrahlen ['gamaʃtraːlən] *pl* gamma rays *pl*
gammelig ['gaməlɪç], **gammlig** ['gamlɪç] (*umg*) *adj* (*Kleidung*) tatty
gammeln ['gaməln] (*umg*) *vi* to loaf about
Gammler, in ['gamlər(ɪn)] (**-s, -**) *m(f)* dropout
Gämse ['gɛmzə] (**-, -n**) *f* chamois
Gang[1] [gaŋ] (**-(e)s, ¨-e**) *m* walk; (*Botengang*) errand; (*Gangart*) gait; (*Abschnitt eines Vorgangs*) operation; (*Essensgang, Ablauf*) course; (*Flur etc*) corridor; (*Durchgang*) passage; (*Aut, Tech*) gear; (*in Kirche, Theat, Aviat*) aisle; **den ersten ~ einlegen** to engage first (gear); **einen ~ machen/tun** to go on an errand/for a walk; **den ~ nach Canossa antreten** (*fig*) to eat humble pie; **seinen gewohnten ~ gehen** (*fig*) to run its usual course; **in ~ bringen** to start up; (*fig*) to get off the ground; **in ~ sein** to be in operation; (*fig*) to be under way
Gang[2] [gɛŋ] (**-, -s**) *f* gang
gang *adj*: **~ und gäbe** usual, normal
Gangart *f* way of walking, walk, gait; (*von Pferd*) gait; **eine härtere ~ einschlagen** (*fig*) to apply harder tactics
gangbar *adj* passable; (*Methode*) practicable
Gängelband ['gɛŋəlbant] *nt*: **jdn am ~ halten** (*fig*) to spoon-feed sb
gängeln *vt* to spoonfeed; **jdn ~** to treat sb like a child
gängig ['gɛŋɪç] *adj* common, current; (*Ware*) in demand, selling well
Gangschaltung *f* gears *pl*
Gangway ['gæŋweɪ] *f* (*Naut*) gangway; (*Aviat*) steps *pl*
Ganove [ga'noːvə] (**-n, -n**) (*umg*) *m* crook
Gans [gans] (**-, ¨-e**) *f* goose
Gänse- *zW*: **Gänseblümchen** *nt* daisy; **Gänsebraten** *m* roast goose; **Gänsefüßchen** (*umg*) *pl* inverted commas *pl* (*Brit*), quotes *pl*; **Gänsehaut** *f* goose pimples *pl*; **Gänsemarsch** *m*: **im Gänsemarsch** in single file
Gänserich (**-s, -e**) *m* gander
ganz [gants] *adj* whole; (*vollständig*) complete ▷ *adv* quite; (*völlig*) completely; (*sehr*) really; (*genau*) exactly; **~ Europa** all Europe; **im (Großen und) G~en genommen** on the whole, all in all; **etw wieder ~ machen** to mend sth; **sein ~es Geld** all his money; **~ gewiss!** absolutely!; **ein ~ klein wenig** just a tiny bit; **das mag ich ~ besonders gern(e)** I'm particularly fond of that; **sie ist ~ die Mutter** she's just *od* exactly like her mother; **~ und gar nicht** not at all
Ganze, s *nt*: **es geht ums ~** everything's at stake; **aufs ~ gehen** to go for the lot

Ganzheitsmethode ['gantshaɪtsmeto:də] *f* (*Sch*) look-and-say method
gänzlich ['gɛntslɪç] *adj* complete, entire ▷ *adv* completely, entirely
ganztägig ['gantstɛ:gɪç] *adj* all-day *attrib*
ganztags *adv* (*arbeiten*) full time
gar [ga:r] *adj* cooked, done ▷ *adv* quite; **~ nicht/nichts/keiner** not/nothing/nobody at all; **~ nicht schlecht** not bad at all; **~ kein Grund** no reason whatsoever *od* at all; **er wäre ~ zu gern noch länger geblieben** he would really have liked to stay longer
Garage [ga'ra:ʒə] (**-, -n**) *f* garage
Garantie [garan'ti:] *f* guarantee; **das fällt noch unter die ~** that's covered by the guarantee
garantieren *vt* to guarantee
garantiert *adv* guaranteed; (*umg*) I bet
Garantieschein *m* guarantee
Garaus ['ga:raus] (*umg*) *m*: **jdm den ~ machen** to do sb in
Garbe ['garbə] (**-, -n**) *f* sheaf; (*Mil*) burst of fire
Garde ['gardə] (**-, -n**) *f* guard(s); **die alte ~** the old guard
Garderobe [gardə'ro:bə] (**-, -n**) *f* wardrobe; (*Abgabe*) cloakroom (*Brit*), checkroom (*US*); (*Kleiderablage*) hall stand; (*Theat: Umkleideraum*) dressing room
Garderobenfrau *f* cloakroom attendant
Garderobenständer *m* hall stand
Gardine [gar'di:nə] (**-, -n**) *f* curtain
Gardinenpredigt (*umg*) *f*: **jdm eine ~ halten** to give sb a talking-to
Gardinenstange *f* curtain rail; (*zum Ziehen*) curtain rod
garen ['ga:rən] *vt, vi* (*Koch*) to cook
gären ['gɛ:rən] *unreg vi* to ferment
Garn [garn] (**-(e)s, -e**) *nt* thread; (*Häkelgarn, fig*) yarn
Garnele [gar'ne:lə] (**-, -n**) *f* shrimp, prawn
garnieren [gar'ni:rən] *vt* to decorate; (*Speisen*) to garnish
Garnison [garni'zo:n] (**-, -en**) *f* garrison
Garnitur [garni'tu:r] *f* (*Satz*) set; (*Unterwäsche*) set of (matching) underwear; **erste ~** (*fig*) top rank; **zweite ~** second rate
garstig ['garstɪç] *adj* nasty, horrid
Garten ['gartən] (**-s, ¨**) *m* garden; **Gartenarbeit** *f* gardening; **Gartenbau** *m* horticulture; **Gartenfest** *nt* garden party; **Gartengerät** *nt* gardening tool; **Gartenhaus** *nt* summerhouse; **Gartenkresse** *f* cress; **Gartenlaube** *f* (*Gartenhäuschen*) summerhouse; **Gartenlokal** *nt* beer garden; **Gartenschere** *f* pruning shears *pl*; **Gartentür** *f* garden gate; **Gartenzaun** *m* garden fence; **Gartenzwerg** *m* garden gnome; (*pej: umg*) squirt
Gärtner, in ['gɛrtnər(ɪn)] (**-s, -**) *m(f)* gardener
Gärtnerei [gɛrtnə'raɪ] *f* nursery; (*Gemüsegärtnerei*) market garden (*Brit*), truck farm (*US*)
gärtnern *vi* to garden
Gärung ['gɛ:rʊŋ] *f* fermentation
Gas [ga:s] (**-es, -e**) *nt* gas; **~ geben** (*Aut*) to accelerate, step on the gas
Gascogne [gas'kɔnjə] *f* Gascony
Gas- *zW*: **Gasflasche** *f* bottle of gas, gas canister; **gasförmig** *adj* gaseous; **Gashahn** *m* gas tap; **Gasherd** *m* gas cooker; **Gaskocher** *m* gas cooker; **Gasleitung** *f* gas pipeline; **Gasmaske** *f* gas mask; **Gaspedal** *nt* accelerator, gas pedal (*US*); **Gaspistole** *f* gas pistol
Gasse ['gasə] (**-, -n**) *f* lane, alley
Gassenhauer (**-s, -**) (*veraltet: umg*) *m* popular melody
Gassenjunge *m* street urchin
Gast [gast] (**-es, ¨e**) *m* guest; **bei jdm zu ~ sein** to be sb's guest(s); **Gastarbeiter** *m* foreign worker
Gäste- *zW*: **Gästebett** *nt* spare bed; **Gästebuch** *nt* visitors' book; **Gästezimmer** *nt* guest room
Gast- *zW*: **gastfreundlich** *adj* hospitable; **Gastfreundlichkeit** *f* hospitality; **Gastfreundschaft** *f* hospitality; **Gastgeber, in** (**-s, -**) *m(f)* host(ess); **Gasthaus** *nt* hotel, inn; **Gasthof** *m* hotel, inn; **Gasthörer, in** *m(f)* (*Univ*) observer, auditor (*US*)
gastieren [gas'ti:rən] *vi* (*Theat*) to (appear as a) guest
Gast- *zW*: **Gastland** *nt* host country; **gastlich** *adj* hospitable; **Gastlichkeit** *f* hospitality; **Gastrolle** *f* (*Theat*) guest role; **eine Gastrolle spielen** to make a guest appearance
Gastronomie [gastrono'mi:] *f* (*form: Gaststättengewerbe*) catering trade
gastronomisch [gastro'no:mɪʃ] *adj* gastronomic(al)
Gast- *zW*: **Gastspiel** *nt* (*Sport*) away game; **ein Gastspiel geben** (*Theat*) to give a guest performance; (*fig*) to put in a brief appearance; **Gaststätte** *f* restaurant; (*Trinklokal*) pub; **Gastwirt** *m* innkeeper; **Gastwirtschaft** *f* hotel, inn; **Gastzimmer** *nt* guest room
Gas- *zW*: **Gasvergiftung** *f* gas poisoning; **Gasversorgung** *f* (*System*) gas supply; **Gaswerk** *nt* gasworks *sing od pl*; **Gaszähler** *m* gas meter
Gatte ['gatə] (**-n, -n**) *m* (*form*) husband, spouse; **die ~n** husband and wife
Gatter ['gatər] (**-s, -**) *nt* grating; (*Tür*) gate
Gattin *f* (*form*) wife, spouse
Gattung ['gatʊŋ] *f* (*Biol*) genus; (*Sorte*) kind
GAU [gaʊ] *m abk* (*= größter anzunehmender Unfall*) MCA, maximum credible accident
Gaudi ['gaʊdi] (*Südd, Österr: umg*) *nt od f* fun
Gaukler ['gaʊklər] (**-s, -**) *m* (*liter*) travelling entertainer; (*Zauberkünstler*) conjurer, magician
Gaul [gaʊl] (**-(e)s, Gäule**) (*pej*) *m* nag
Gaumen ['gaʊmən] (**-s, -**) *m* palate
Gauner ['gaʊnər] (**-s, -**) *m* rogue
Gaunerei [gaʊnə'raɪ] *f* swindle
Gaunersprache *f* underworld jargon
Gaze ['ga:zə] (**-, -n**) *f* gauze
Geäst [gə|'ɛst] *nt* branches *pl*
geb. *abk* = **geboren**

Gebäck [gəˈbɛk] (**-(e)s, -e**) *nt* (*Kekse*) biscuits *pl* (*Brit*), cookies *pl* (*US*); (*Teilchen*) pastries *pl*
gebacken [gəˈbakən] *pp von* **backen**
Gebälk [gəˈbɛlk] (**-(e)s**) *nt* timberwork
gebannt [gəˈbant] *adj* spellbound
gebar *etc* [gəˈbaːr] *vb siehe* **gebären**
Gebärde [gəˈbɛːrdə] (**-, -n**) *f* gesture
gebärden *vr* to behave
Gebaren [gəˈbaːrən] (**-s**) *nt* behaviour (*Brit*), behavior (*US*); (*Geschäftsgebaren*) conduct
gebären [gəˈbɛːrən] *unreg vt* to give birth to
Gebärmutter *f* uterus, womb
Gebäude [gəˈbɔydə] (**-s, -**) *nt* building; **Gebäudekomplex** *m* (building) complex; **Gebäudereinigung** *f* (*das Reinigen*) commercial cleaning; (*Firma*) cleaning contractors *pl*
Gebein [gəˈbaɪn] (**-(e)s, -e**) *nt* bones *pl*
Gebell [gəˈbɛl] (**-(e)s**) *nt* barking
geben [ˈgeːbən] *unreg vt, vi* to give; (*Karten*) to deal ▷ *vt unpers*: **es gibt** there is/are; there will be ▷ *vr* (*sich verhalten*) to behave, act; (*aufhören*) to abate; **jdm etw ~** to give sb sth *od* sth to sb; **in die Post ~** to post; **das gibt keinen Sinn** that doesn't make sense; **er gibt Englisch** he teaches English; **viel/nicht viel auf etw** *akk* **~** to set great store/not much store by sth; **etw von sich ~** (*Laute etc*) to utter; **ein Wort gab das andere** one angry word led to another; **ein gutes Beispiel ~** to set a good example; **~ Sie mir bitte Herrn Braun** (*Tel*) can I speak to Mr Braun please?; **ein Auto in Reparatur ~** to have a car repaired; **was gibts?** what's the matter?, what's up?; **was gibts zum Mittagessen?** what's for lunch?; **das gibts doch nicht!** that's impossible!; **sich geschlagen ~** to admit defeat; **das wird sich schon ~** that'll soon sort itself out
Geberkonferenz [ˈgeːbər-] *f* (*Pol*) donor conference
Gebet [gəˈbeːt] (**-(e)s, -e**) *nt* prayer; **jdn ins ~ nehmen** (*fig*) to take sb to task
gebeten [gəˈbeːtən] *pp von* **bitten**
gebeugt [gəˈbɔykt] *adj* (*Haltung*) stooped; (*Kopf*) bowed; (*Schultern*) sloping
gebiert [gəˈbiːrt] *vb siehe* **gebären**
Gebiet [gəˈbiːt] (**-(e)s, -e**) *nt* area; (*Hoheitsgebiet*) territory; (*fig*) field
gebieten *unreg vt* to command, demand
Gebieter (**-s, -**) *m* master; (*Herrscher*) ruler; **Gebieterin** *f* mistress; **gebieterisch** *adj* imperious
Gebietshoheit *f* territorial sovereignty
Gebilde [gəˈbɪldə] (**-s, -**) *nt* object, structure
gebildet *adj* cultured, educated
Gebimmel [gəˈbɪməl] (**-s**) *nt* (continual) ringing
Gebirge [gəˈbɪrgə] (**-s, -**) *nt* mountains *pl*
gebirgig *adj* mountainous
Gebirgs- *zW*: **Gebirgsbahn** *f railway crossing a mountain range*; **Gebirgskette** *f*, **Gebirgszug** *m* mountain range
Gebiss [gəˈbɪs] (**-es, -e**) *nt* teeth *pl*; (*künstlich*) dentures *pl*
gebissen *pp von* **beißen**
Gebläse [gəˈblɛːzə] (**-s, -**) *nt* fan, blower
geblasen [gəˈblaːzən] *pp von* **blasen**
geblichen [gəˈblɪçən] *pp von* **bleichen**
geblieben [gəˈbliːbən] *pp von* **bleiben**
geblümt [gəˈblyːmt] *adj* flowered; (*Stil*) flowery
Geblüt [gəˈblyːt] (**-(e)s**) *nt* blood, race
gebogen [gəˈboːgən] *pp von* **biegen**
geboren [gəˈboːrən] *pp von* **gebären** ▷ *adj* born; (*Frau*) née; **wo sind Sie ~?** where were you born?
geborgen [gəˈbɔrgən] *pp von* **bergen** ▷ *adj* secure, safe
geborsten [gəˈbɔrstən] *pp von* **bersten**
Gebot (**-(e)s, -e**) *nt* (*Gesetz*) law; (*Rel*) commandment; (*bei Auktion*) bid; **das ~ der Stunde** the needs of the moment
gebot *etc* [gəˈboːt] *vb siehe* **gebieten**
geboten [gəˈboːtən] *pp von* **bieten; gebieten** ▷ *adj* (*geh: ratsam*) advisable; (*: notwendig*) necessary; (*: dringend geboten*) imperative
Gebr. *abk* (= *Gebrüder*) Bros., bros.
gebracht [gəˈbraxt] *pp von* **bringen**
gebrannt [gəˈbrant] *pp von* **brennen** ▷ *adj*: **ein ~es Kind scheut das Feuer** (*Sprichwort*) once bitten twice shy (*Sprichwort*)
gebraten [gəˈbraːtən] *pp von* **braten**
Gebräu [gəˈbrɔy] (**-(e)s, -e**) *nt* brew, concoction
Gebrauch [gəˈbraʊx] (**-(e)s, Gebräuche**) *m* use; (*Sitte*) custom; **zum äußerlichen/innerlichen ~** for external use/to be taken internally
gebrauchen *vt* to use; **er/das ist zu nichts zu ~** he's/that's (of) no use to anybody
gebräuchlich [gəˈbrɔyçlɪç] *adj* usual, customary
Gebrauchs- *zW*: **Gebrauchsanweisung** *f* directions *pl* for use; **Gebrauchsartikel** *m* article of everyday use; **gebrauchsfertig** *adj* ready for use; **Gebrauchsgegenstand** *m* commodity
gebraucht [gəˈbraʊxt] *adj* used; **Gebrauchtwagen** *m* second-hand *od* used car
gebrechlich [gəˈbrɛçlɪç] *adj* frail; **Gebrechlichkeit** *f* frailty
gebrochen [gəˈbrɔxən] *pp von* **brechen**
Gebrüder [gəˈbryːdər] *pl* brothers *pl*
Gebrüll [gəˈbrʏl] (**-(e)s**) *nt* (*von Mensch*) yelling; (*von Löwe*) roar
gebückt [gəˈbʏkt] *adj*: **eine ~e Haltung** a stoop
Gebühr [gəˈbyːr] (**-, -en**) *f* charge; (*Postgebühr*) postage *no pl*; (*Honorar*) fee; **zu ermäßigter ~** at a reduced rate; **~ (be)zahlt Empfänger** postage to be paid by addressee; **nach ~** suitably; **über ~** excessively
gebühren *vi* (*geh*): **jdm ~** to be sb's due *od* due to sb ▷ *vr* to be fitting
gebührend *adj* (*verdient*) due; (*angemessen*) suitable
Gebühren- *zW*: **Gebühreneinheit** *f* (*Tel*) tariff unit; **Gebührenerlass** *m* remission of fees; **Gebührenermäßigung** *f* reduction of fees; **gebührenfrei** *adj* free of charge;

Gebührenmanager *m* tariff meter; **gebührenpflichtig** *adj* subject to charges; **gebührenpflichtige Verwarnung** (*Jur*) fine

gebunden [gə'bʊndən] *pp von* **binden** ▷ *adj*: **vertraglich ~ sein** to be bound by contract

Geburt [gə'bu:rt] (**-, -en**) *f* birth; **das war eine schwere ~!** (*fig: umg*) that took some doing

Geburten- *zW*: **Geburtenkontrolle** *f* birth control; **Geburtenregelung** *f* birth control; **Geburtenrückgang** *m* drop in the birth rate; **geburtenschwach** *adj* (*Jahrgang*) with a low birth rate; **Geburtenziffer** *f* birth rate

gebürtig [gə'bʏrtɪç] *adj* born in, native of; **~e Schweizerin** native of Switzerland, Swiss-born woman

Geburts- *zW*: **Geburtsanzeige** *f* birth notice; **Geburtsdatum** *nt* date of birth; **Geburtsfehler** *m* congenital defect; **Geburtshelfer** *m* (*Arzt*) obstetrician; **Geburtshelferin** *f* (*Ärztin*) obstetrician; (*Hebamme*) midwife; **Geburtshilfe** *f* (*als Fach*) obstetrics *sing*; (*von Hebamme*) midwifery; **Geburtsjahr** *nt* year of birth; **Geburtsort** *m* birthplace; **Geburtstag** *m* birthday; **herzlichen Glückwunsch zum Geburtstag!** happy birthday!, many happy returns (of the day)!; **Geburtsurkunde** *f* birth certificate

Gebüsch [gə'bʏʃ] (**-(e)s, -e**) *nt* bushes *pl*

gedacht [gə'daxt] *pp von* **denken; gedenken**

gedachte *etc vb siehe* **gedenken**

Gedächtnis [gə'dɛçtnɪs] (**-ses, -se**) *nt* memory; **wenn mich mein ~ nicht trügt** if my memory serves me right; **Gedächtnisfeier** *f* commemoration; **Gedächtnishilfe** *f* memory aid, mnemonic; **Gedächtnisschwund** *m* loss of memory; **Gedächtnisverlust** *m* amnesia

gedämpft [gə'dɛmpft] *adj* (*Geräusch*) muffled; (*Farben, Instrument, Stimmung*) muted; (*Licht, Freude*) subdued

Gedanke [gə'daŋkə] (**-ns, -n**) *m* thought; (*Idee, Plan, Einfall*) idea; (*Konzept*) concept; **sich über etw** *akk* **~n machen** to think about sth; **jdn auf andere ~n bringen** to make sb think about other things; **etw ganz in ~n** *dat* **tun** to do sth without thinking; **auf einen ~n kommen** to have *od* get an idea

Gedanken- *zW*: **Gedankenaustausch** *m* exchange of ideas; **Gedankenfreiheit** *f* freedom of thought; **gedankenlos** *adj* thoughtless; **Gedankenlosigkeit** *f* thoughtlessness; **Gedankensprung** *m* mental leap; **Gedankenstrich** *m* dash; **Gedankenübertragung** *f* thought transference, telepathy; **gedankenverloren** *adj* lost in thought; **gedankenvoll** *adj* thoughtful

Gedärme [gə'dɛrmə] *pl* intestines *pl*

Gedeck [gə'dɛk] (**-(e)s, -e**) *nt* cover(ing); (*Menü*) set meal; **ein ~ auflegen** to lay a place

gedeckt *adj* (*Farbe*) muted

Gedeih *m*: **auf ~ und Verderb** for better or for worse

gedeihen [gə'daɪən] *unreg vi* to thrive, prosper; **die Sache ist so weit gediehen, dass ...** the matter has reached the point *od* stage where ...

gedenken [gə'dɛŋkən] *unreg vi +gen* (*geh: denken an*) to remember; (*beabsichtigen*) to intend; **Gedenken** *nt*: **zum Gedenken an jdn** in memory *od* remembrance of sb

Gedenk- *zW*: **Gedenkfeier** *f* commemoration; **Gedenkminute** *f* minute's silence; **Gedenkstätte** *f* memorial; **Gedenktag** *m* remembrance day

Gedicht [gə'dɪçt] (**-(e)s, -e**) *nt* poem

gediegen [gə'di:gən] *adj* (good) quality; (*Mensch*) reliable; (*rechtschaffen*) honest; **Gediegenheit** *f* quality; reliability; honesty

gedieh *etc* [gə'di:] *vb siehe* **gedeihen**

gediehen *pp von* **gedeihen**

gedr. *abk* = **gedruckt**

Gedränge [gə'drɛŋə] (**-s**) *nt* crush, crowd; **ins ~ kommen** (*fig*) to get into difficulties

gedrängt *adj* compressed; **~ voll** packed

gedroschen [gə'drɔʃən] *pp von* **dreschen**

gedruckt [gə'drʊkt] *adj* printed; **lügen wie ~** (*umg*) to lie left, right and centre

gedrungen [gə'drʊŋən] *pp von* **dringen** ▷ *adj* thickset, stocky

Geduld [gə'dʊlt] (-) *f* patience; **mir reißt die ~, ich verliere die ~** my patience is wearing thin, I'm losing my patience

gedulden [gə'dʊldən] *vr* to be patient

geduldig *adj* patient

Geduldsprobe *f* trial of (one's) patience

gedungen [gə'dʊŋən] (*pej*) *adj* (*geh: Mörder*) hired

gedunsen [gə'dʊnzən] *adj* bloated

gedurft [gə'dʊrft] *pp von* **dürfen**

geehrt [gə'|e:rt] *adj*: **Sehr ~e Damen und Herren!** Ladies and Gentlemen!; (*in Briefen*) Dear Sir or Madam

geeignet [gə'|aɪgnət] *adj* suitable; **im ~en Augenblick** at the right moment

Gefahr [gə'fa:r] (**-, -en**) *f* danger; **~ laufen, etw zu tun** to run the risk of doing sth; **auf eigene ~** at one's own risk; **außer ~** (*nicht gefährdet*) not in danger; (*nicht mehr gefährdet*) out of danger; (*Patienten*) off the danger list

gefährden [gə'fɛ:rdən] *vt* to endanger

gefahren [gə'fa:rən] *pp von* **fahren**

Gefahren- *zW*: **Gefahrenquelle** *f* source of danger; **Gefahrenschwelle** *f* threshold of danger; **Gefahrenstelle** *f* danger spot; **Gefahrenzulage** *f* danger money

gefährlich [gə'fɛ:rlɪç] *adj* dangerous

Gefährte [gə'fɛ:rtə] (**-n, -n**) *m* companion

Gefährtin [gə'fɛ:rtɪn] *f* companion

Gefälle [gə'fɛlə] (**-s, -**) *nt* (*von Land, Straße*) slope; (*Neigungsgrad*) gradient; **starkes ~!** steep hill

Gefallen[1] [gə'falən] (**-s, -**) *m* favour; **jdm etw zu ~ tun** to do sth to please sb

Gefallen[2] [gə'falən] (**-s**) *nt* pleasure; **an etw** *dat* **~ finden** to derive pleasure from sth; **an jdm ~ finden** to take to sb

gefallen *pp von* **fallen; gefallen** ▷ *vi* (*unreg*): **jdm**

~ to please sb; **er/es gefällt mir** I like him/it; **das gefällt mir an ihm** that's one thing I like about him; **sich** *dat* **etw ~ lassen** to put up with sth

Gefallene, r *m* soldier killed in action

gefällig [gə'fɛlɪç] *adj* (*hilfsbereit*) obliging; (*erfreulich*) pleasant; **sonst noch etwas ~?** (*veraltet, ironisch*) will there be anything else?; **Gefälligkeit** *f* favour (*Brit*), favor (*US*); helpfulness; **etw aus Gefälligkeit tun** to do sth as a favour (*Brit*) *od* favor (*US*)

gefälligst (*umg*) *adv* kindly; **sei ~ still!** will you kindly keep your mouth shut!

gefällt [gə'fɛlt] *vb siehe* **gefallen**

gefangen [gə'faŋən] *pp von* **fangen** ▷ *adj* captured; (*fig*) captivated; **~ halten** to keep prisoner; **~ nehmen** to capture

Gefangene, r *f(m)* prisoner, captive

Gefangenenlager *nt* prisoner-of-war camp

Gefangen- *zW*: **Gefangennahme** (**-, -n**) *f* capture; **Gefangenschaft** *f* captivity

Gefängnis [gə'fɛŋnɪs] (**-ses, -se**) *nt* prison; **zwei Jahre ~ bekommen** to get two years' imprisonment; **Gefängnisstrafe** *f* prison sentence; **Gefängniswärter** *m* prison warder (*Brit*) *od* guard

gefärbt [gə'fɛrpt] *adj* (*fig: Bericht*) biased; (*Lebensmittel*) coloured (*Brit*), colored (*US*)

Gefasel [gə'fa:zəl] (**-s**) *nt* twaddle, drivel

Gefäß [gə'fɛ:s] (**-es, -e**) *nt* vessel (*auch Anat*), container

gefasst [gə'fast] *adj* composed, calm; **auf etw** *akk* **~ sein** to be prepared *od* ready for sth; **er kann sich auf etwas ~ machen** (*umg*) I'll give him something to think about

Gefecht [gə'fɛçt] (**-(e)s, -e**) *nt* fight; (*Mil*) engagement; **jdn/etw außer ~ setzen** (*lit, fig*) to put sb/sth out of action

gefedert [gə'fe:dərt] *adj* (*Matratze*) sprung

gefeiert [gə'faɪərt] *adj* celebrated

gefeit [gə'faɪt] *adj*: **gegen etw ~ sein** to be immune to sth

gefestigt [gə'fɛstɪçt] *adj* (*Charakter*) steadfast

Gefieder [gə'fi:dər] (**-s, -**) *nt* plumage, feathers *pl*

gefiedert *adj* feathered

gefiel *etc* [gə'fi:l] *vb siehe* **gefallen**

Geflecht [gə'flɛçt] (**-(e)s, -e**) *nt* (*lit, fig*) network

gefleckt [gə'flɛkt] *adj* spotted; (*Blume, Vogel*) speckled

Geflimmer [gə'flɪmər] (**-s**) *nt* shimmering; (*Film, TV*) flicker(ing)

geflissentlich [gə'flɪsəntlɪç] *adj* intentional ▷ *adv* intentionally

geflochten [gə'flɔxtən] *pp von* **flechten**

geflogen [gə'flo:gən] *pp von* **fliegen**

geflohen [gə'flo:ən] *pp von* **fliehen**

geflossen [gə'flɔsən] *pp von* **fließen**

Geflügel [gə'fly:gəl] (**-s**) *nt* poultry

Geflügelpest *f* poultry plague

geflügelt *adj*: **~e Worte** familiar quotations

Geflüster [gə'flʏstər] (**-s**) *nt* whispering

gefochten [gə'fɔxtən] *pp von* **fechten**

Gefolge [gə'fɔlgə] (**-s, -**) *nt* retinue

Gefolgschaft [gə'fɔlkʃaft] *f* following

Gefolgsmann (**-(e)s**, *pl* **-leute**) *m* follower

gefragt [ge'fra:kt] *adj* in demand

gefräßig [gə'frɛ:sɪç] *adj* voracious

Gefreite, r [gə'fraɪtə(r)] *m* (*Mil*) lance corporal (*Brit*), private first class (*US*); (*Naut*) able seaman (*Brit*), seaman apprentice (*US*); (*Aviat*) aircraftman (*Brit*), airman first class (*US*)

gefressen [gə'frɛsən] *pp von* **fressen** ▷ *adj*: **den hab(e) ich ~** (*umg*) I'm sick of him

gefrieren [gə'fri:rən] *unreg vi* to freeze

Gefrier- *zW*: **Gefrierfach** *nt* freezer compartment; **Gefrierfleisch** *nt* frozen meat; **gefriergetrocknet** *adj* freeze-dried; **Gefrierpunkt** *m* freezing point; **Gefrierschutzmittel** *nt* antifreeze; **Gefriertruhe** *f* deep-freeze

gefror *etc* [gə'fro:r] *vb siehe* **gefrieren**

gefroren *pp von* **frieren, gefrieren**

Gefüge [gə'fy:gə] (**-s, -**) *nt* structure

gefügig *adj* submissive; (*gehorsam*) obedient

Gefühl [gə'fy:l] (**-(e)s, -e**) *nt* feeling; **etw im ~ haben** to have a feel for sth; **gefühllos** *adj* unfeeling; (*Glieder*) numb

Gefühls- *zW*: **gefühlsbetont** *adj* emotional; **Gefühlsduselei** [-du:zə'laɪ] (*pej*) *f* mawkishness; **Gefühlsleben** *nt* emotional life; **gefühlsmäßig** *adj* instinctive; **Gefühlsmensch** *m* emotional person

gefühlvoll *adj* (*empfindsam*) sensitive; (*ausdrucksvoll*) expressive; (*liebevoll*) loving

gefüllt [gə'fʏlt] *adj* (*Koch*) stuffed; (*Pralinen*) with soft centres

gefunden [gə'fʊndən] *pp von* **finden** ▷ *adj*: **das war ein ~es Fressen für ihn** that was handing it to him on a plate

gegangen [gə'gaŋən] *pp von* **gehen**

gegeben [gə'ge:bən] *pp von* **geben** ▷ *adj* given; **zu ~er Zeit** in due course

gegebenenfalls [gə'ge:bənənfals] *adv* if need be

SCHLÜSSELWORT

gegen ['ge:gən] *präp+akk* **1** against; **nichts gegen jdn haben** to have nothing against sb; **X gegen Y** (*Sport, Jur*) X versus Y; **ein Mittel gegen Schnupfen** something for colds

2 (*in Richtung auf*) towards; **gegen Osten** to(wards) the east; **gegen Abend** towards evening; **gegen einen Baum fahren** to drive into a tree

3 (*ungefähr*) round about; **gegen 3 Uhr** around 3 o'clock

4 (*gegenüber*) towards; (*ungefähr*) around; **gerecht gegen alle** fair to all

5 (*im Austausch für*) for; **gegen bar** for cash; **gegen Quittung** against a receipt

6 (*verglichen mit*) compared with

Gegen- *zW*: **Gegenangriff** *m* counter-attack; **Gegenbesuch** *m* return visit; **Gegenbeweis** *m*

counter-evidence

Gegend ['ge:gənt] (**-, -en**) *f* area, district

Gegen- *zW*: **Gegendarstellung** *f* (*Presse*) reply; **gegeneinander** *adv* against one another; **Gegenfahrbahn** *f* opposite carriageway; **gegenfinanzieren** *vt* to counterfinance; **Gegenfinanzierung** *f financing of state expenditure by means of cuts, tax increases etc*; **Gegenfrage** *f* counterquestion; **Gegengewicht** *nt* counterbalance; **Gegengift** *nt* antidote; **Gegenkandidat** *m* rival candidate; **gegenläufig** *adj* contrary; **Gegenleistung** *f* service in return; **Gegenlichtaufnahme** *f* back lit photograph; **Gegenliebe** *f* requited love; (*fig: Zustimmung*) approval; **Gegenmaßnahme** *f* countermeasure; **Gegenmittel** *nt*: **Gegenmittel (gegen)** (*Med*) antidote (to); **Gegenprobe** *f* cross-check

Gegensatz (**-es, ⸚e**) *m* contrast; **Gegensätze überbrücken** to overcome differences

gegensätzlich *adj* contrary, opposite; (*widersprüchlich*) contradictory

Gegen- *zW*: **Gegenschlag** *m* counter-attack; **Gegenseite** *f* opposite side; (*Rückseite*) reverse; **gegenseitig** *adj* mutual, reciprocal; **sich gegenseitig helfen** to help each other; **in gegenseitigem Einverständnis** by mutual agreement; **Gegenseitigkeit** *f* reciprocity; **Gegenspieler** *m* opponent; **Gegensprechanlage** *f* (two-way) intercom; **Gegenstand** *m* object; **gegenständlich** *adj* objective, concrete; (*Kunst*) representational; **gegenstandslos** *adj* (*überflüssig*) irrelevant; (*grundlos*) groundless; **Gegenstimme** *f* vote against; **Gegenstoß** *m* counterblow; **Gegenstück** *nt* counterpart; **Gegenteil** *nt* opposite; **im Gegenteil** on the contrary; **das Gegenteil bewirken** to have the opposite effect; (*Mensch*) to achieve the exact opposite; **ganz im Gegenteil** quite the reverse; **ins Gegenteil umschlagen** to swing to the other extreme; **gegenteilig** *adj* opposite, contrary; **ich habe nichts Gegenteiliges gehört** I've heard nothing to the contrary

gegenüber [ge:gən'|y:bər] *präp +dat* opposite; (*zu*) to(wards); (*in Bezug auf*) with regard to; (*im Vergleich zu*) in comparison with; (*angesichts*) in the face of ▷ *adv* opposite; **mir ~ hat er das nicht geäußert** he didn't say that to me; **Gegenüber** (**-s, -**) *nt* person opposite; (*bei Kampf*) opponent; (*bei Diskussion*) opposite number; **gegenüberliegen** *unreg vr* to face each other; **gegenüberstehen** *unreg vr* to be opposed (to each other); **gegenüberstellen** *vt* to confront; (*fig*) to contrast; **Gegenüberstellung** *f* confrontation; (*fig*) contrast; (*: Vergleich*) comparison; **gegenübertreten** *unreg vi +dat* to face

Gegen- *zW*: **Gegenveranstaltung** *f* counter-meeting; **Gegenverkehr** *m* oncoming traffic; **Gegenvorschlag** *m* counterproposal

Gegenwart ['ge:gənvart] *f* present; **in ~ von** in the presence of

gegenwärtig *adj* present ▷ *adv* at present; **das ist mir nicht mehr ~** that has slipped my mind

gegenwartsbezogen *adj* (*Roman etc*) relevant to present times

Gegen- *zW*: **Gegenwert** *m* equivalent; **Gegenwind** *m* headwind; **Gegenwirkung** *f* reaction; **gegenzeichnen** *vt* to countersign; **Gegenzug** *m* countermove; (*Eisenb*) corresponding train in the other direction

gegessen [gə'gɛsən] *pp von* **essen**

geglichen [gə'glıçən] *pp von* **gleichen**

gegliedert [gə'gli:dərt] *adj* jointed; (*fig*) structured

geglitten [gə'glıtən] *pp von* **gleiten**

geglommen [gə'glɔmən] *pp von* **glimmen**

geglückt [gə'glʏkt] *adj* (*Feier*) successful; (*Überraschung*) real

Gegner, in ['ge:gnər(ın)] (**-s, -**) *m(f)* opponent; **gegnerisch** *adj* opposing; **Gegnerschaft** *f* opposition

gegolten [gə'gɔltən] *pp von* **gelten**

gegoren [gə'go:rən] *pp von* **gären**

gegossen [gə'gɔsən] *pp von* **gießen**

gegr. *abk* (*= gegründet*) estab.

gegraben [gə'gra:bən] *pp von* **graben**

gegriffen [gə'grıfən] *pp von* **greifen**

Gehabe [gə'ha:bə] (**-s**) (*umg*) *nt* affected behaviour (*Brit*) *od* behavior (*US*)

gehabt [gə'ha:pt] *pp von* **haben**

Gehackte, s [ge'haktə(s)] *nt* mince(d meat) (*Brit*), ground meat (*US*)

Gehalt[1] [gə'halt] (**-(e)s, -e**) *m* content

Gehalt[2] [gə'halt] (**-(e)s, ⸚er**) *nt* salary

gehalten [gə'haltən] *pp von* **halten** ▷ *adj*: **~ sein, etw zu tun** (*form*) to be required to do sth

Gehalts- *zW*: **Gehaltsabrechnung** *f* salary statement; **Gehaltsempfänger** *m* salary earner; **Gehaltserhöhung** *f* salary increase; **Gehaltsklasse** *f* salary bracket; **Gehaltskonto** *nt* current account (*Brit*), checking account (*US*); **Gehaltszulage** *f* salary increment

gehaltvoll [gə'haltfɔl] *adj* (*Speise, Buch*) substantial

gehandicapt, gehandikapt [gə'hɛndikɛpt] *adj* handicapped

gehangen [gə'haŋən] *pp von* **hängen**

geharnischt [gə'harnıʃt] *adj* (*fig*) forceful, sharp

gehässig [gə'hɛsıç] *adj* spiteful, nasty; **Gehässigkeit** *f* spite(fulness)

gehäuft [gə'hɔʏft] *adj* (*Löffel*) heaped

Gehäuse [gə'hɔʏzə] (**-s, -**) *nt* case; (*Radiogehäuse, Uhrgehäuse*) casing; (*von Apfel etc*) core

gehbehindert ['ge:behındərt] *adj* disabled

Gehege [gə'he:gə] (**-s, -**) *nt* enclosure, preserve; **jdm ins ~ kommen** (*fig*) to poach on sb's preserve

geheim [gə'haım] *adj* secret; (*Dokumente*) classified; **streng ~** top secret; **~ halten** to keep secret; **Geheimdienst** *m* secret service, intelligence service; **Geheimfach** *nt* secret

compartment
Geheimnis (**-ses, -se**) *nt* secret; (*rätselhaftes Geheimnis*) mystery; **Geheimniskrämer** *m* mystery-monger; **geheimnisvoll** *adj* mysterious
Geheim- *zW*: **Geheimnummer** *f* (*Tel*) secret number; **Geheimpolizei** *f* secret police; **Geheimrat** *m* privy councillor; **Geheimratsecken** *pl*: **er hat Geheimratsecken** he is going bald at the temples; **Geheimschrift** *f* code, secret writing; **Geheimtipp** *m* (personal) tip
Geheiß [gəˈhaɪs] (**-es**) *nt* (*geh*) command; **auf jds ~** *akk* at sb's bidding
geheißen [gəˈhaɪsən] *pp von* **heißen**
gehemmt [gəˈhɛmt] *adj* inhibited
gehen [ˈgeːən] *unreg vi* (*auch Auto, Uhr*) to go; (*zu Fuß gehen*) to walk; (*funktionieren*) to work; (*Teig*) to rise ▷ *vt* to go; to walk ▷ *vi unpers*: **wie geht es dir?** how are you *od* things?; **~ nach** (*Fenster*) to face; **in sich** *akk* **~** to think things over; **nach etw ~** (*urteilen*) to go by sth; **sich ~ lassen** to lose one's self-control; (*nachlässig sein*) to let o.s. go; **wie viele Leute ~ in deinen Wagen?** how many people can you get in your car?; **nichts geht über** *+akk* **...** there's nothing to beat ..., there's nothing better than ...; **schwimmen/schlafen ~** to go swimming/to bed; **in die Tausende ~** to run into (the) thousands; **mir/ihm geht es gut** I'm/he's (doing) fine; **geht das?** is that possible?; **gehts noch?** can you manage?; **es geht** not too bad, O.K.; **das geht nicht** that's not on; **es geht um etw** it concerns sth, it's about sth; **lass es dir gut ~** look after yourself, take care of yourself; **so geht das, das geht so** that/this is how it's done; **darum geht es (mir) nicht** that's not the point; (*spielt keine Rolle*) that's not important to me; **morgen geht es nicht** tomorrow's no good; **wenn es nach mir ginge ...** if it were *od* was up to me ...
gehetzt [gəˈhɛtst] *adj* harassed
geheuer [gəˈhɔʏər] *adj*: **nicht ~** eerie; (*fragwürdig*) dubious
Geheul [gəˈhɔʏl] (**-(e)s**) *nt* howling
Gehilfe [gəˈhɪlfə] (**-n, -n**) *m* assistant
Gehilfin [gəˈhɪlfɪn] *f* assistant
Gehirn [gəˈhɪrn] (**-(e)s, -e**) *nt* brain; **Gehirnerschütterung** *f* concussion; **Gehirnschlag** *m* stroke; **Gehirnwäsche** *f* brainwashing
gehoben [gəˈhoːbən] *pp von* **heben** ▷ *adj*: **~er Dienst** *professional and executive levels of the civil service*
geholfen [gəˈhɔlfən] *pp von* **helfen**
Gehör [gəˈhøːr] (**-(e)s**) *nt* hearing; **musikalisches ~** ear; **absolutes ~** perfect pitch; **~ finden** to gain a hearing; **jdm ~ schenken** to give sb a hearing
gehorchen [gəˈhɔrçən] *vi +dat* to obey
gehören [gəˈhøːrən] *vi* to belong ▷ *vr unpers* to be right *od* proper; **das gehört nicht zur Sache** that's irrelevant; **dazu gehört (schon) einiges** *od* **etwas** that takes some doing (*umg*); **er gehört ins Bett** he should be in bed
gehörig *adj* proper; **~ zu** *od +dat* (*geh*) belonging to
gehörlos *adj* (*form*) deaf
gehorsam [gəˈhoːrzaːm] *adj* obedient; **Gehorsam** (**-s**) *m* obedience
Gehörsinn *m* sense of hearing
Gehsteig [ˈgeːʃtaɪk] *m*, **Gehweg** [ˈgeːvɛk] *m* pavement (*Brit*), sidewalk (*US*)
Geier [ˈgaɪər] (**-s, -**) *m* vulture; **weiß der ~!** (*umg*) God knows
geifern [ˈgaɪfərn] *vi* to slaver; (*fig*) to be bursting with venom
Geige [ˈgaɪgə] (**-, -n**) *f* violin; **die erste/zweite ~ spielen** (*lit*) to play first/second violin; (*fig*) to call the tune/play second fiddle
Geiger, in (**-s, -**) *m(f)* violinist
Geigerzähler *m* geiger counter
geil [gaɪl] *adj* randy (*Brit*), horny (*US*); (*pej*: *lüstern*) lecherous; (*umg*: *gut*) fantastic
Geisel [ˈgaɪzəl] (**-, -n**) *f* hostage; **Geiselnahme** (-) *f* taking of hostages
Geißel [ˈgaɪsəl] (**-, -n**) *f* scourge, whip
geißeln *vt* to scourge
Geist [gaɪst] (**-(e)s, -er**) *m* spirit; (*Gespenst*) ghost; (*Verstand*) mind; **von allen guten ~ern verlassen sein** (*umg*) to have taken leave of one's senses; **hier scheiden sich die ~er** this is the parting of the ways; **den** *od* **seinen ~ aufgeben** to give up the ghost
Geister- *zW*: **Geisterfahrer** (*umg*) *m* ghost-driver (*US*), *person driving in the wrong direction*; **geisterhaft** *adj* ghostly; **Geisterhand** *f*: **wie von Geisterhand** as if by magic
Geistes- *zW*: **geistesabwesend** *adj* absent-minded; **Geistesakrobat** *m* mental acrobat; **Geistesblitz** *m* brain wave; **Geistesgegenwart** *f* presence of mind; **geistesgegenwärtig** *adj* quick-witted; **geistesgestört** *adj* mentally disturbed; (*stärker*) (mentally) deranged; **Geisteshaltung** *f* mental attitude; **geisteskrank** *adj* mentally ill; **Geisteskranke, r** *f(m)* mentally ill person; **Geisteskrankheit** *f* mental illness; **Geistesstörung** *f* mental disturbance; **Geistesverfassung** *f* frame of mind; **Geisteswissenschaften** *pl* arts (subjects) *pl*; **Geisteszustand** *m* state of mind; **jdn auf seinen Geisteszustand untersuchen** to give sb a psychiatric examination
geistig *adj* intellectual; (*Psych*) mental; (*Getränke*) alcoholic; **~ behindert** mentally handicapped; **~-seelisch** mental and spiritual
geistlich *adj* spiritual; (*religiös*) religious; **Geistliche, r** *m* clergyman; **Geistlichkeit** *f* clergy
geist- *zW*: **geistlos** *adj* uninspired, dull; **geistreich** *adj* intelligent; (*witzig*) witty; **geisttötend** *adj* soul-destroying; **geistvoll** *adj* intellectual; (*weise*) wise
Geiz [gaɪts] (**-es**) *m* miserliness, meanness; **geizen** *vi* to be miserly; **Geizhals** *m* miser

geizig *adj* miserly, mean
Geizkragen *m* miser
gekannt [gə'kant] *pp von* **kennen**
Gekicher [gə'kɪçər] (**-s**) *nt* giggling
Geklapper [gə'klapər] (**-s**) *nt* rattling
Geklimper [gə'klɪmpər] (**-s**) (*umg*) *nt* (*Klaviergeklimper*) tinkling; (*: stümperhaft*) plonking; (*von Geld*) jingling
geklungen [gə'klʊŋən] *pp von* **klingen**
geknickt [gə'knɪkt] *adj* (*fig*) dejected
gekniffen [gə'knɪfən] *pp von* **kneifen**
gekommen [gə'kɔmən] *pp von* **kommen**
gekonnt [gə'kɔnt] *pp von* **können** ▷ *adj* skilful (*Brit*), skillful (*US*)
Gekritzel [gə'krɪtsəl] (**-s**) *nt* scrawl, scribble
gekrochen [gə'krɔxən] *pp von* **kriechen**
gekünstelt [ge'kʏnstəlt] *adj* artificial; (*Sprache, Benehmen*) affected
Gel [ge:l] (**-s, -e**) *nt* gel
Gelaber [gə'la:bər], **Gelabere** [gə'la:bərə] (**-s**) (*umg*) *nt* prattle
Gelächter [gə'lɛçtər] (**-s, -**) *nt* laughter; **in ~ ausbrechen** to burst out laughing
gelackmeiert [gə'lakmaɪərt] (*umg*) *adj* conned
geladen [ge'la:dən] *pp von* **laden** ▷ *adj* loaded; (*Elek*) live; (*fig*) furious
Gelage [gə'la:gə] (**-s, -**) *nt* feast, banquet
gelagert [gə'la:gərt] *adj*: **in anders/ähnlich ~en Fällen** in different/similar cases
gelähmt [gə'lɛ:mt] *adj* paralysed
Gelände [gə'lɛndə] (**-s, -**) *nt* land, terrain; (*von Fabrik, Sportgelände*) grounds *pl*; (*Baugelände*) site; **Geländefahrzeug** *nt* cross-country vehicle; **geländegängig** *adj* able to go cross-country; **Geländelauf** *m* cross-country race
Geländer [gə'lɛndər] (**-s, -**) *nt* railing; (*Treppengeländer*) banister(s)
gelang *etc vb siehe* **gelingen**
gelangen [gə'laŋən] *vi*: **~ an** *+akk od* **zu** to reach; (*erwerben*) to attain; **in jds Besitz** *akk* ~ to come into sb's possession; **in die richtigen/falschen Hände ~** to fall into the right/wrong hands
gelangweilt *adj* bored
gelassen [gə'lasən] *pp von* **lassen** ▷ *adj* calm; (*gefasst*) composed; **Gelassenheit** *f* calmness; composure
Gelatine [ʒela'ti:nə] *f* gelatine
gelaufen [gə'laʊfən] *pp von* **laufen**
geläufig [gə'lɔʏfɪç] *adj* (*üblich*) common; **das ist mir nicht ~** I'm not familiar with that; **Geläufigkeit** *f* commonness; familiarity
gelaunt [gə'laʊnt] *adj*: **schlecht/gut ~** in a bad/good mood; **wie ist er ~?** what sort of mood is he in?
Geläut [gə'lɔʏt] (**-(e)s**) *nt* ringing; (*Läutwerk*) chime
Geläute (**-s**) *nt* ringing
gelb [gɛlp] *adj* yellow; (*Ampellicht*) amber (*Brit*), yellow (*US*); **~e Seiten** Yellow Pages; **gelblich** *adj* yellowish
Gelbsucht *f* jaundice
Geld [gɛlt] (**-(e)s, -er**) *nt* money; **etw zu ~ machen** to sell sth off; **er hat ~ wie Heu** (*umg*) he's stinking rich; **am ~ hängen** *od* **kleben** to be tight with money; **staatliche/öffentliche ~er** state/public funds *pl od* money; **Geldadel** *m*: **der Geldadel** the moneyed aristocracy; (*hum: die Reichen*) the rich; **Geldanlage** *f* investment; **Geldautomat** *m* cash dispenser; **Geldautomatenkarte** *f* cash card; **Geldbeutel** *m* purse; **Geldbörse** *f* purse; **Geldeinwurf** *m* slot; **Geldgeber** (**-s, -**) *m* financial backer; **geldgierig** *adj* avaricious; **Geldinstitut** *nt* financial institution; **Geldmittel** *pl* capital *sing*, means *pl*; **Geldquelle** *f* source of income; **Geldschein** *m* banknote; **Geldschrank** *m* safe, strongbox; **Geldstrafe** *f* fine; **Geldstück** *nt* coin; **Geldverlegenheit** *f*: **in Geldverlegenheit sein/kommen** to be/run short of money; **Geldverleiher** *m* moneylender; **Geldwäsche** *f* money-laundering; **Geldwechsel** *m* exchange (of money); **„Geldwechsel"** "bureau de change"; **Geldwert** *m* cash value; (*Fin: Kaufkraft*) currency value
geleckt [gə'lɛkt] *adj*: **wie ~ aussehen** to be neat and tidy
Gelee [ʒe'le:] (**-s, -s**) *nt od m* jelly
gelegen [gə'le:gən] *pp von* **liegen** ▷ *adj* situated; (*passend*) convenient, opportune; **etw kommt jdm ~** sth is convenient for sb; **mir ist viel/nichts daran ~** (*wichtig*) it matters a great deal/doesn't matter to me
Gelegenheit [gə'le:gənhaɪt] *f* opportunity; (*Anlass*) occasion; **bei ~** some time (or other); **bei jeder ~** at every opportunity
Gelegenheits- *zW*: **Gelegenheitsarbeit** *f* casual work; **Gelegenheitsarbeiter** *m* casual worker; **Gelegenheitskauf** *m* bargain
gelegentlich [gə'le:gəntlɪç] *adj* occasional ▷ *adv* occasionally; (*bei Gelegenheit*) some time (or other) ▷ *präp +gen* on the occasion of
gelehrig [gə'le:rɪç] *adj* quick to learn
gelehrt *adj* learned; **Gelehrte, r** *f(m)* scholar; **Gelehrtheit** *f* scholarliness
Geleise [gə'laɪzə] (**-s, -**) *nt* = **Gleis**
Geleit [gə'laɪt] (**-(e)s, -e**) *nt* escort; **freies** *od* **sicheres ~** safe conduct; **geleiten** *vt* to escort; **Geleitschutz** *m* escort
Gelenk [gə'lɛŋk] (**-(e)s, -e**) *nt* joint
gelenkig *adj* supple
gelernt [gə'lɛrnt] *adj* skilled
gelesen [gə'le:zən] *pp von* **lesen**
Geliebte *f* sweetheart; (*Liebhaberin*) mistress
Geliebte, r *m* sweetheart; (*Liebhaber*) lover
geliefert [gə'li:fərt] *adj*: **ich bin ~** (*umg*) I've had it
geliehen [gə'li:ən] *pp von* **leihen**
gelind [gə'lɪnt] *adj* = **gelinde**
gelinde [gə'lɪndə] *adj* (*geh*) mild; **~ gesagt** to put it mildly
gelingen [gə'lɪŋən] *unreg vi* to succeed; **die Arbeit gelingt mir nicht** I'm not doing very well with this work; **es ist mir gelungen, etw zu tun** I succeeded in doing sth; **Gelingen**

nt (*geh*: *Glück*) success; (: *erfolgreiches Ergebnis*) successful outcome
gelitten [gə'lɪtən] *pp von* **leiden**
gellen ['gɛlən] *vi* to shrill
gellend *adj* shrill, piercing
geloben [gə'lo:bən] *vt, vi* to vow, swear; **das Gelobte Land** (*Rel*) the Promised Land
gelogen [gə'lo:gən] *pp von* **lügen**
gelten ['gɛltən] *unreg vt* (*wert sein*) to be worth ▹ *vi* (*gültig sein*) to be valid; (*erlaubt sein*) to be allowed ▹ *vb unpers* (*geh*): **es gilt, etw zu tun** it is necessary to do sth; **was gilt die Wette?** do you want a bet?; **das gilt nicht!** that doesn't count!; (*nicht erlaubt*) that's not allowed; **etw gilt bei jdm viel/wenig** sb values sth highly/doesn't value sth very highly; **jdm viel/wenig ~** to mean a lot/not mean much to sb; **jdm ~** (*gemünzt sein auf*) to be meant for *od* aimed at sb; **etw ~ lassen** to accept sth; **für diesmal lasse ichs ~** I'll let it go this time; **als** *od* **für etw ~** to be considered to be sth; **jdm** *od* **für jdn ~** (*betreffen*) to apply to sb
geltend *adj* (*Preise*) current; (*Gesetz*) in force; (*Meinung*) prevailing; **etw ~ machen** to assert sth; **sich ~ machen** to make itself/o.s. felt; **einen Einwand ~ machen** to raise an objection
Geltung ['gɛltʊŋ] *f*: **~ haben** to have validity; **sich/etw** *dat* **~ verschaffen** to establish o.s./ sth; **etw zur ~ bringen** to show sth to its best advantage; **zur ~ kommen** to be seen/heard *etc* to its best advantage
Geltungsbedürfnis *nt* desire for admiration
geltungssüchtig *adj* craving admiration
Gelübde [gə'lʏpdə] (**-s, -**) *nt* vow
gelungen [gə'lʊŋən] *pp von* **gelingen** ▹ *adj* successful
Gem. *abk* = **Gemeinde**
gemächlich [gə'mɛ:çlɪç] *adj* leisurely
gemacht [gə'ma:xt] *adj* (*gewollt, gekünstelt*) false, contrived; **ein ~er Mann sein** to be made
Gemahl [gə'ma:l] (**-(e)s, -e**) *m* (*geh, form*) spouse, husband
gemahlen [gə'ma:lən] *pp von* **mahlen**
Gemahlin *f* (*geh, form*) spouse, wife
Gemälde [gə'mɛ:ldə] (**-s, -**) *nt* picture, painting
gemasert [gə'ma:zərt] *adj* (*Holz*) grained
gemäß [gə'mɛ:s] *präp +dat* in accordance with ▹ *adj +dat* appropriate to
gemäßigt *adj* moderate; (*Klima*) temperate
Gemauschel [gə'maʊʃəl] (**-s**) (*umg*) *nt* scheming
Gemecker [gə'mɛkər] (**-s**) *nt* (*von Ziegen*) bleating; (*umg*: *Nörgelei*) moaning
gemein [gə'maɪn] *adj* common; (*niederträchtig*) mean; **etw ~ haben (mit)** to have sth in common (with)
Gemeinde [gə'maɪndə] (**-, -n**) *f* district; (*Bewohner*) community; (*Pfarrgemeinde*) parish; (*Kirchengemeinde*) congregation; **Gemeindeabgaben** *pl* rates and local taxes *pl*; **Gemeindebau** *m* (*Österr*) subsidized housing; (*Gebäude*) subsidized house; **Gemeindeordnung** *f* by(e) laws *pl*, ordinances *pl* (*US*); **Gemeinderat** *m* district council; (*Mitglied*) district councillor; **Gemeindeschwester** *f* district nurse (*Brit*); **Gemeindesteuer** *f* local rates *pl*; **Gemeindeverwaltung** *f* local administration; **Gemeindevorstand** *m* local council; **Gemeindewahl** *f* local election
Gemein- *zW*: **Gemeineigentum** *nt* common property; **gemeingefährlich** *adj* dangerous to the public; **Gemeingut** *nt* public property; **Gemeinheit** *f* (*Niedertracht*) meanness; **das war eine Gemeinheit** that was a mean thing to do/to say; **gemeinhin** *adv* generally; **Gemeinkosten** *pl* overheads *pl*; **Gemeinnutz** *m* public good; **gemeinnützig** *adj* of benefit to the public; (*wohltätig*) charitable; **Gemeinplatz** *m* commonplace, platitude; **gemeinsam** *adj* joint, common (*auch Math*) ▹ *adv* together; **gemeinsame Sache mit jdm machen** to be in cahoots with sb; **der Gemeinsame Markt** the Common Market; **gemeinsames Konto** joint account; **etw gemeinsam haben** to have sth in common; **Gemeinsamkeit** *f* common ground; **Gemeinschaft** *f* community; **in Gemeinschaft mit** jointly *od* together with; **eheliche Gemeinschaft** (*Jur*) matrimony; **Gemeinschaft Unabhängiger Staaten** Commonwealth of Independent States; **gemeinschaftlich** *adj* = **gemeinsam**; **Gemeinschaftsantenne** *f* party aerial (*Brit*) *od* antenna (*US*); **Gemeinschaftsarbeit** *f* teamwork; **Gemeinschaftsbesitz** *m* collective ownership; **Gemeinschaftserziehung** *f* coeducation; **Gemeinschaftskunde** *f* social studies *pl*; **Gemeinschaftsraum** *m* common room; **Gemeinschaftswährung** *f* common *od* single currency; (*innerhalb der EU*) single European currency; **Gemeinsinn** *m* public spirit; **gemeinverständlich** *adj* generally comprehensible; **Gemeinwesen** *nt* community; **Gemeinwohl** *nt* common good
Gemenge [gə'mɛŋə] (**-s, -**) *nt* mixture; (*Handgemenge*) scuffle
gemessen [gə'mɛsən] *pp von* **messen** ▹ *adj* measured
Gemetzel [gə'mɛtsəl] (**-s, -**) *nt* slaughter, carnage
gemieden [gə'mi:dən] *pp von* **meiden**
Gemisch [gə'mɪʃ] (**-es, -e**) *nt* mixture
gemischt *adj* mixed
gemocht [gə'mɔxt] *pp von* **mögen**
gemolken [gə'mɔlkən] *pp von* **melken**
Gemse ['gɛmzə] (**-, -n**) *f siehe* **Gämse**
Gemunkel [gə'mʊŋkəl] (**-s**) *nt* gossip
Gemurmel [gə'mʊrməl] (**-s**) *nt* murmur(ing)
Gemüse [gə'my:zə] (**-s, -**) *nt* vegetables *pl*; **Gemüsegarten** *m* vegetable garden; **Gemüsehändler** *m* greengrocer (*Brit*), vegetable dealer (*US*); **Gemüseplatte** *f* (*Koch*): **eine Gemüseplatte** assorted vegetables
gemusst [gə'mʊst] *pp von* **müssen**

gemustert [gə'mʊstərt] *adj* patterned
Gemüt [gə'my:t] **(-(e)s, -er)** *nt* disposition, nature; (*fig: Mensch*) person; **sich** *dat* **etw zu ~e führen** (*umg*) to indulge in sth; **die ~er erregen** to arouse strong feelings; **wir müssen warten, bis sich die ~er beruhigt haben** we must wait until feelings have cooled down
gemütlich *adj* comfortable, cosy; (*Person*) good-natured; **wir verbrachten einen ~en Abend** we spent a very pleasant evening; **Gemütlichkeit** *f* comfortableness, cosiness; amiability
Gemüts- *zW*: **Gemütsbewegung** *f* emotion; **gemütskrank** *adj* emotionally disturbed; **Gemütsmensch** *m* sentimental person; **Gemütsruhe** *f* composure; **in aller Gemütsruhe** (*umg*) (as) cool as a cucumber; (*gemächlich*) at a leisurely pace; **Gemütszustand** *m* state of mind
gemütvoll *adj* warm, tender
Gen [ge:n] **(-s, -e)** *nt* gene
Gen. *abk* = **Genossenschaft**; (= *Genitiv*) gen.
gen. *abk* (= *genannt*) named, called
genannt [gə'nant] *pp von* **nennen**
genas *etc* [gə'na:s] *vb siehe* **genesen**
genau [gə'naʊ] *adj* exact, precise ▷ *adv* exactly, precisely; **etw ~ nehmen** to take sth seriously; **~ genommen** strictly speaking; **G~eres** further details *pl*; **etw ~ wissen** to know sth for certain; **~ auf die Minute, auf die Minute genau** exactly on time
Genauigkeit *f* exactness, accuracy
genauso [gə'naʊzo:] *adv* (*vor Adjektiv*) just as; (*allein stehend*) just *od* exactly the same
genehm [gə'ne:m] *adj* agreeable, acceptable
genehmigen *vt* to approve, authorize; **sich** *dat* **etw ~** to indulge in sth
Genehmigung *f* approval, authorization
geneigt [gə'naɪkt] *adj* (*geh*) well-disposed, willing; **~ sein, etw zu tun** to be inclined to do sth
Genera *pl von* **Genus**
General [gene'ra:l] **(-s, -e** *od* **¨-e)** *m* general; **Generaldirektor** *m* chairman (*Brit*), president (*US*); **Generalkonsulat** *nt* consulate general; **Generalprobe** *f* dress rehearsal; **Generalsekretär** *m* secretary-general; **Generalstabskarte** *f* ordnance survey map; **Generalstreik** *m* general strike; **generalüberholen** *vt* to overhaul thoroughly; **Generalvertretung** *f* sole agency
Generation [generatsi'o:n] *f* generation
Generationskonflikt *m* generation gap
Generator [gene'ra:tɔr] *m* generator, dynamo
generell [genə'rɛl] *adj* general
genesen [ge'ne:zən] *unreg vi* (*geh*) to convalesce, recover
Genesende, r *f(m)* convalescent
Genesung *f* recovery, convalescence
Genetik [ge'ne:tɪk] *f* genetics
genetisch [ge'ne:tɪʃ] *adj* genetic
Genf ['gɛnf] **(-s)** *nt* Geneva
Genfer *adj attrib*: **der ~ See** Lake Geneva; **die ~ Konvention** the Geneva Convention
genial [geni'a:l] *adj* brilliant
Genialität [geniali'tɛ:t] *f* brilliance, genius
Genick [gə'nɪk] **(-(e)s, -e)** *nt* (back of the) neck; **jdm/etw das ~ brechen** (*fig*) to finish sb/sth; **Genickstarre** *f* stiff neck
Genie [ʒe'ni:] **(-s, -s)** *nt* genius
genieren [ʒe'ni:rən] *vr* to be embarrassed ▷ *vt* to bother; **geniert es Sie, wenn ...?** do you mind if ...?
genießbar *adj* edible; (*trinkbar*) drinkable
genießen [gə'ni:sən] *unreg vt* to enjoy; (*essen*) to eat; (*trinken*) to drink; **er ist heute nicht zu ~** (*umg*) he is unbearable today
Genießer, in (-s, -) *m(f)* connoisseur; (*des Lebens*) pleasure-lover; **genießerisch** *adj* appreciative ▷ *adv* with relish
Genitalien [geni'ta:liən] *pl* genitals *pl*
Genitiv ['ge:niti:f] *m* genitive
Genmais *m* GM maize
genmanipuliert *adj* genetically modified
genommen [gə'nɔmən] *pp von* **nehmen**
genoss *etc* [gə'nɔs] *vb siehe* **genießen**
Genosse [gə'nɔsə] **(-n, -n)** *m* comrade (*bes Pol*), companion
genossen *pp von* **genießen**
Genossenschaft *f* cooperative (association)
Genossin [gə'nɔsɪn] *f* comrade (*bes Pol*), companion
genötigt [gə'nø:tɪçt] *adj*: **sich ~ sehen, etw zu tun** to feel obliged to do sth
Genre [ʒã:rə] **(-s, -s)** *nt* genre
Gent [gɛnt] **(-s)** *nt* Ghent
Gentechnik *f*, **Gentechnologie** *f* gene technology
Genua ['ge:nua] **(-s)** *nt* Genoa
genug [gə'nu:k] *adv* enough; **jetzt ist(s) aber ~!** that's enough!
Genüge [gə'ny:gə] *f*: **jdm/etw ~ tun** *od* **leisten** to satisfy sb/sth; **etw zur ~ kennen** to know sth well enough; (*abwertender*) to know sth only too well
genügen *vi* to be enough; (*den Anforderungen etc*) to satisfy; **jdm ~** to be enough for sb
genügend *adj* enough, sufficient; (*befriedigend*) satisfactory
genügsam [gə'ny:kza:m] *adj* modest, easily satisfied; **Genügsamkeit** *f* moderation
Genugtuung [gə'nu:ktu:ʊŋ] *f* satisfaction
Genus ['ge:nʊs] **(-, Genera)** *nt* (*Gram*) gender
Genuss [gə'nʊs] **(-es, ¨-e)** *m* pleasure; (*Zusichnehmen*) consumption; **etw mit ~ essen** to eat sth with relish; **in den ~ von etw kommen** to receive the benefit of sth
genüsslich [gə'nʏslɪç] *adv* with relish
Genussmittel *pl* (semi-)luxury items *pl*
geöffnet [gə'œfnət] *adj* open
Geograf [geo'gra:f] **(-en, -en)** *m* geographer
Geografie [geogra'fi:] *f* geography
Geografin *f* geographer
geografisch *adj* geographical
Geologe [geo'lo:gə] **(-n, -n)** *m* geologist

Geologie [geolo:'gi:] *f* geology
Geologin *f* geologist
Geometrie [geome'tri:] *f* geometry
geordnet [gə'ɔrdnət] *adj*: **in ~en Verhältnissen leben** to live a well-ordered life
Georgien [ge'ɔrgiən] (**-s**) *nt* Georgia
Gepäck [gə'pɛk] (**-(e)s**) *nt* luggage, baggage; **mit leichtem ~ reisen** to travel light; **Gepäckabfertigung** *f* luggage desk/office; **Gepäckannahme** *f* (*Bahnhof*) baggage office; (*Flughafen*) baggage check-in; **Gepäckaufbewahrung** *f* left-luggage office (*Brit*), baggage check (*US*); **Gepäckausgabe** *f* (*Bahnhof*) baggage office; (*Flughafen*) baggage reclaim; **Gepäcknetz** *nt* luggage rack; **Gepäckschein** *m* luggage *od* baggage ticket; **Gepäckstück** *nt* piece of baggage; **Gepäckträger** *m* porter; (*Fahrrad*) carrier; **Gepäckwagen** *m* luggage van (*Brit*), baggage car (*US*)
Gepard ['ge:part] (**-(e)s, -e**) *m* cheetah
gepfeffert [gə'pfɛfərt] (*umg*) *adj* (*Preise*) steep; (*Fragen, Prüfung*) tough; (*Kritik*) biting
gepfiffen [gə'pfɪfən] *pp von* **pfeifen**
gepflegt [gə'pfle:kt] *adj* well-groomed; (*Park etc*) well looked after; (*Atmosphäre*) sophisticated; (*Ausdrucksweise, Sprache*) cultured
Gepflogenheit [gə'pflo:gənhaɪt] *f* (*geh*) custom
Geplapper [gə'plapər] (**-s**) *nt* chatter
Geplauder [gə'plaʊdər] (**-s**) *nt* chat(ting)
Gepolter [gə'pɔltər] (**-s**) *nt* din
gepr. *abk* (= *geprüft*) tested
gepriesen [gə'pri:zən] *pp von* **preisen**
gequält [gə'kvɛ:lt] *adj* (*Lächeln*) forced; (*Miene, Ausdruck*) pained; (*Gesang, Stimme*) strained
Gequatsche [gə'kvatʃə] (**-s**) (*pej*: *umg*) *nt* gabbing; (*Blödsinn*) twaddle
gequollen [gə'kvɔlən] *pp von* **quellen**
Gerade [gə'ra:də] (**-n, -n**) *f* straight line

SCHLÜSSELWORT

gerade [gə'ra:də] *adj* straight; (*aufrecht*) upright; **eine gerade Zahl** an even number
▷ *adv* **1** (*genau*) just, exactly; (*speziell*) especially; **gerade deshalb** that's just *od* exactly why; **das ist es ja gerade!** that's just it; **gerade du** you especially; **warum gerade ich?** why me (of all people)?; **jetzt gerade nicht!** not now!; **gerade neben** right next to; **nicht gerade schön** not exactly beautiful; **gerade biegen** to straighten out; **gerade stehen** (*aufrecht*) to stand up straight
2 (*eben, soeben*) just; **er wollte gerade aufstehen** he was just about to get up; **da wir gerade von Geld sprechen ...** talking of money ...; **gerade erst** only just; **gerade noch** (only) just

gerade- *zW*: **geradeaus** *adv* straight ahead; **geradebiegen** *unreg vt* (*fig*) to straighten out; **geradeheraus** *adv* straight out, bluntly
gerädert [gə'rɛ:dərt] *adj*: **wie ~ sein, sich wie ~ fühlen** to be *od* feel (absolutely) whacked (*umg*)
geradeso *adv* just so; **~ dumm** *etc* just as stupid *etc*; **~ wie** just as
geradestehen *unreg vi*: **für jdn/etw ~** (*fig*) to answer *od* be answerable for sb/sth
geradezu *adv* (*beinahe*) virtually, almost
geradlinig *adj* straight
gerammelt [gə'raməlt] *adv*: **~ voll** (*umg*) (jam-)packed
Geranie [gɛ'ra:niə] *f* geranium
gerannt [gə'rant] *pp von* **rennen**
Gerät [gə'rɛ:t] (**-(e)s, -e**) *nt* device; (*Apparat*) gadget; (*elektrisches Gerät*) appliance; (*Werkzeug*) tool; (*Sport*) apparatus; (*Zubehör*) equipment *no pl*
gerät [gə'rɛ:t] *vb siehe* **geraten**
geraten [gə'ra:tən] *unreg pp von* **raten; geraten** ▷ *vi* (*gedeihen*) to thrive; (*gelingen*): **(jdm) ~** to turn out well (for sb); (*zufällig gelangen*): **~ in** *+akk* to get into; **gut/schlecht ~** to turn out well/badly; **an jdn ~** to come across sb; **an den Richtigen/Falschen ~** to come to the right/wrong person; **in Angst ~** to get frightened; **nach jdm ~** to take after sb
Geräteturnen *nt* apparatus gymnastics
Geratewohl [gəra:tə'vo:l] *nt*: **aufs ~** on the off chance; (*bei Wahl*) at random
geraum [gə'raʊm] *adj*: **seit ~er Zeit** for some considerable time
geräumig [gə'rɔʏmɪç] *adj* roomy
Geräusch [gə'rɔʏʃ] (**-(e)s, -e**) *nt* sound; (*unangenehm*) noise; **geräuscharm** *adj* quiet; **Geräuschkulisse** *f* background noise; (*Film, Rundf, TV*) sound effects *pl*; **geräuschlos** *adj* silent; **Geräuschpegel** *m* sound level; **geräuschvoll** *adj* noisy
gerben ['gɛrbən] *vt* to tan
Gerber (**-s, -**) *m* tanner
Gerberei [gɛrbə'raɪ] *f* tannery
gerecht [gə'rɛçt] *adj* just, fair; **jdm/etw ~ werden** to do justice to sb/sth; **gerechtfertigt** *adj* justified
Gerechtigkeit *f* justice, fairness
Gerechtigkeits- *zW*: **Gerechtigkeitsfanatiker** *m* justice fanatic; **Gerechtigkeitsgefühl** *nt* sense of justice; **Gerechtigkeitssinn** *m* sense of justice
Gerede [gə're:də] (**-s**) *nt* talk; (*Klatsch*) gossip
geregelt [gə're:gəlt] *adj* (*Arbeit, Mahlzeiten*) regular; (*Leben*) well-ordered
gereizt [gə'raɪtst] *adj* irritable; **Gereiztheit** *f* irritation
Gericht [gə'rɪçt] (**-(e)s, -e**) *nt* court; (*Essen*) dish; **jdn/einen Fall vor ~ bringen** to take sb/a case to court; **mit jdm ins ~ gehen** (*fig*) to judge sb harshly; **über jdn zu ~ sitzen** to sit in judgement on sb; **das Jüngste ~** the Last Judgement; **gerichtlich** *adj* judicial, legal ▷ *adv* judicially, legally; **ein gerichtliches Nachspiel haben** to finish up in court; **gerichtlich gegen jdn vorgehen** to take legal proceedings against sb

Gerichts- *zW*: **Gerichtsakten** *pl* court records *pl*; **Gerichtsbarkeit** *f* jurisdiction; **Gerichtshof** *m* court (of law); **Gerichtskosten** *pl* (legal) costs *pl*; **gerichtsmedizinisch** *adj* forensic medical *attrib*; **Gerichtssaal** *m* courtroom; **Gerichtsstand** *m* court of jurisdiction; **Gerichtsverfahren** *nt* legal proceedings *pl*; **Gerichtsverhandlung** *f* court proceedings *pl*; **Gerichtsvollzieher** *m* bailiff

gerieben [gəˈriːbən] *pp von* **reiben** ▷ *adj* grated; (*umg: schlau*) smart, wily

geriet *etc* [gəˈriːt] *vb siehe* **geraten**

gering [gəˈrɪŋ] *adj* slight, small; (*niedrig*) low; (*Zeit*) short ▷ *adv*: **~ achten** to think little of; **geringfügig** *adj* slight, trivial; **geringfügig Beschäftigte** ≈ part-time workers *pl*; **geringschätzig** *adj* disparaging; **Geringschätzung** *f* disdain

geringste, r, s *adj* slightest, least; **nicht im G~n** not in the least *od* slightest

Geringverdiener, in *m(f)* low-income earner

gerinnen [gəˈrɪnən] *unreg vi* to congeal; (*Blut*) to clot; (*Milch*) to curdle

Gerinnsel [gəˈrɪnzəl] **(-s, -)** *nt* clot

Gerippe [gəˈrɪpə] **(-s, -)** *nt* skeleton

gerissen [gəˈrɪsən] *pp von* **reißen** ▷ *adj* wily, smart

geritten [gəˈrɪtən] *pp von* **reiten**

geritzt [gəˈrɪtst] (*umg*) *adj*: **die Sache ist ~** everything's fixed up *od* settled

Germanist, in [gɛrmaˈnɪst(ɪn)] *m(f)* Germanist, German specialist; (*Student*) German student

Germanistik *f* German (studies *pl*)

gern [gɛrn] *adv* willingly, gladly; **(aber) ~!** of course!; **~ mögen** to like; **etw ~ tun** to like doing sth; **~ geschehen!** you're welcome!, not at all!; **ein ~ gesehener Gast** a welcome visitor; **ich hätte** *od* **möchte ~ ...** I would like ...; *siehe auch* **gernhaben**

gerne [ˈgɛrnə] *adv* = **gern**

Gernegroß **(-, -e)** *m* show-off; **gernhaben** *unreg vt* to like; **du kannst mich mal gernhaben!** (*umg*) (you can) go to hell!

gerochen [gəˈrɔxən] *pp von* **riechen**

Geröll [gəˈrœl] **(-(e)s, -e)** *nt* scree

geronnen [gəˈrɔnən] *pp von* **rinnen; gerinnen**

Gerste [ˈgɛrstə] **(-, -n)** *f* barley

Gerstenkorn *nt* (*im Auge*) stye

Gerte [ˈgɛrtə] **(-, -n)** *f* switch, rod

gertenschlank *adj* willowy

Geruch [gəˈrʊx] **(-(e)s, ¨-e)** *m* smell, odour (*Brit*), odor (*US*); **geruchlos** *adj* odourless (*Brit*), odorless (*US*)

Geruchssinn *m* sense of smell

Gerücht [gəˈrʏçt] **(-(e)s, -e)** *nt* rumour (*Brit*), rumor (*US*)

geruchtilgend *adj* deodorant

gerufen [gəˈruːfən] *pp von* **rufen**

geruhen [gəˈruːən] *vi* to deign

geruhsam [gəˈruːzaːm] *adj* peaceful; (*Spaziergang etc*) leisurely

Gerümpel [gəˈrʏmpəl] **(-s)** *nt* junk

gerungen [gəˈrʊŋən] *pp von* **ringen**

Gerüst [gəˈrʏst] **(-(e)s, -e)** *nt* (*Baugerüst*) scaffold(ing); (*fig*) framework

Ges. *abk* (= *Gesellschaft*) Co., co.

gesalzen [gəˈzaltsən] *pp von* **salzen** ▷ *adj* (*fig: umg: Preis, Rechnung*) steep, stiff

gesamt [gəˈzamt] *adj* whole, entire; (*Kosten*) total; (*Werke*) complete; **im G~en** all in all; **Gesamtauflage** *f* gross circulation; **Gesamtausgabe** *f* complete edition; **Gesamtbetrag** *m* total (amount); **gesamtdeutsch** *adj* all-German; **Gesamteindruck** *m* general impression; **Gesamtheit** *f* totality, whole

Gesamthochschule *f* polytechnic (*Brit*); *see culture note*

GESAMTHOCHSCHULE

A *Gesamthochschule* is an institution combining several different kinds of higher education organizations eg. a university, teacher training college and institute of applied science. Students can study for various degrees within the same subject area and it is easier to change course than it is in an individual institution.

Gesamt- *zW*: **Gesamtmasse** *f* (*Comm*) total assets *pl*; **Gesamtnachfrage** *f* (*Comm*) composite demand; **Gesamtschaden** *m* total damage

Gesamtschule *f* ≈ comprehensive school; *see culture note*

GESAMTSCHULE

The *Gesamtschule* is a comprehensive school teaching pupils who have different aims. Traditionally pupils would go to one of three different schools, the *Gymnasium*, *Realschule* or *Hauptschule*, depending on ability. The *Gesamtschule* seeks to avoid the elitist element prevalent in many *Gymnasium*, but in Germany these schools are still very controversial. Many parents still prefer the traditional system.

Gesamtwertung *f* (*Sport*) overall placings *pl*

gesandt *pp von* **senden**

Gesandte, r [gəˈzantə(r)] *f(m)* envoy

Gesandtschaft [gəˈzantʃaft] *f* legation

Gesang [gəˈzaŋ] **(-(e)s, ¨-e)** *m* song; (*Singen*) singing; **Gesangbuch** *nt* (*Rel*) hymn book

Gesäß [gəˈzɛːs] **(-es, -e)** *nt* seat, bottom

gesättigt [gəˈzɛtɪçt] *adj* (*Chem*) saturated

gesch. *abk* (= *geschieden*) div.

Geschädigte, r [gəˈʃɛːdɪçtə(r)] *f(m)* victim

geschaffen [gəˈʃafən] *pp von* **schaffen**

Geschäft [gəˈʃɛft] **(-(e)s, -e)** *nt* business; (*Laden*) shop; (*Geschäftsabschluss*) deal; **mit jdm ins ~ kommen** to do business with sb; **dabei**

hat er ein ~ gemacht he made a profit by it; **im** ~ at work; (*im Laden*) in the shop; **sein ~ verrichten** to do one's business (*euph*)

Geschäftemacher *m* wheeler-dealer

geschäftig *adj* active, busy; (*pej*) officious

geschäftlich *adj* commercial ▷ *adv* on business; ~ **unterwegs** away on business

Geschäfts- *zW*: **Geschäftsabschluss** *m* business deal *od* transaction; **Geschäftsaufgabe** *f* closure of a/the business; **Geschäftsauflösung** *f* closure of a/the business; **Geschäftsbedingungen** *pl* terms of business; **Geschäftsbereich** *m* (*Parl*) responsibilities *pl*; **Minister ohne Geschäftsbereich** minister without portfolio; **Geschäftsbericht** *m* financial report; **Geschäftsbeziehungen** *pl* business relations; **Geschäftscomputer** *m* business computer; **Geschäftsessen** *nt* business lunch; **Geschäftsführer** *m* manager; (*Klub*) secretary; **Geschäftsgeheimnis** *nt* trade secret; **Geschäftsinhaber** *m* owner; **Geschäftsjahr** *nt* financial year; **Geschäftslage** *f* business conditions *pl*; **Geschäftsleitung** *f* management; **Geschäftsmann** (**-(e)s**, *pl* **-leute**) *m* businessman; **geschäftsmäßig** *adj* businesslike; **Geschäftsordnung** *f* standing orders *pl*; **eine Frage zur Geschäftsordnung** a question on a point of order; **Geschäftspartner** *m* partner; **Geschäftsreise** *f* business trip; **Geschäftsschluss** *m* closing time; **Geschäftssinn** *m* business sense; **Geschäftsstelle** *f* office(s *pl*), place of business; **geschäftstüchtig** *adj* business-minded; **Geschäftsviertel** *nt* shopping centre (*Brit*) *od* center (*US*); (*Banken etc*) business quarter, commercial district; **Geschäftswagen** *m* company car; **Geschäftswesen** *nt* business; **Geschäftszeit** *f* business hours *pl*; **Geschäftszweig** *m* branch (of a business)

geschah *etc* [gəˈʃaː] *vb siehe* **geschehen**

geschehen [gəˈʃeːən] *unreg vi* to happen; **das geschieht ihm (ganz) recht** it serves him (jolly well (*umg*)) right; **was soll mit ihm/damit ~?** what is to be done with him/it?; **es war um ihn ~** that was the end of him

gescheit [gəˈʃaɪt] *adj* clever; (*vernünftig*) sensible

Geschenk [gəˈʃɛŋk] (**-(e)s, -e**) *nt* present, gift; **Geschenkartikel** *m* gift; **Geschenkgutschein** *m* gift voucher; **Geschenkpackung** *f* gift pack; **Geschenksendung** *f* gift parcel

Geschichte [gəˈʃɪçtə] (**-, -n**) *f* story; (*Sache*) affair; (*Historie*) history

Geschichtenerzähler *m* storyteller

geschichtlich *adj* historical; (*bedeutungsvoll*) historic

Geschichtsfälschung *f* falsification of history

Geschichtsschreiber *m* historian

Geschick [gəˈʃɪk] (**-(e)s, -e**) *nt* skill; (*geh: Schicksal*) fate

Geschicklichkeit *f* skill, dexterity

Geschicklichkeitsspiel *nt* game of skill

geschickt *adj* skilful (*Brit*), skillful (*US*); (*taktisch*) clever; (*beweglich*) agile

geschieden [gəˈʃiːdən] *pp von* **scheiden** ▷ *adj* divorced

geschieht [gəˈʃiːt] *vb siehe* **geschehen**

geschienen [gəˈʃiːnən] *pp von* **scheinen**

Geschirr [gəˈʃɪr] (**-(e)s, -e**) *nt* crockery; (*Küchengeschirr*) pots and pans *pl*; (*Pferdegeschirr*) harness; **Geschirrspülmaschine** *f* dishwasher; **Geschirrtuch** *nt* tea towel (*Brit*), dishtowel (*US*)

geschissen [gəˈʃɪsən] *pp von* **scheißen**

geschlafen [gəˈʃlaːfən] *pp von* **schlafen**

geschlagen [gəˈʃlaːgən] *pp von* **schlagen**

geschlaucht [gəˈʃlaʊxt] *adv*: ~ **sein** (*umg*) to be exhausted *od* knackered

Geschlecht [gəˈʃlɛçt] (**-(e)s, -er**) *nt* sex; (*Gram*) gender; (*Gattung*) race; (*Abstammung*) lineage; **geschlechtlich** *adj* sexual

Geschlechts- *zW*: **Geschlechtskrankheit** *f* sexually-transmitted disease; **geschlechtsreif** *adj* sexually mature; **geschlechtsspezifisch** *adj* (*Soziologie*) sex-specific; **Geschlechtsteil** *nt od m* genitals *pl*; **Geschlechtsverkehr** *m* sexual intercourse; **Geschlechtswort** *nt* (*Gram*) article

geschlichen [gəˈʃlɪçən] *pp von* **schleichen**

geschliffen [gəˈʃlɪfən] *pp von* **schleifen**

geschlossen [gəˈʃlɔsən] *pp von* **schließen** ▷ *adj*: **~e Gesellschaft** (*Fest*) private party ▷ *adv*: **~ hinter jdm stehen** to stand solidly behind sb; **~e Ortschaft** built-up area

geschlungen [gəˈʃlʊŋən] *pp von* **schlingen**

Geschmack [gəˈʃmak] (**-(e)s, ¨-e**) *m* taste; **nach jds ~** to sb's taste; **~ an etw** *dat* **finden** to (come to) like sth; **je nach ~** to one's own taste; **er hat einen guten ~** (*fig*) he has good taste; **geschmacklos** *adj* tasteless; (*fig*) in bad taste

Geschmacks- *zW*: **Geschmackssache** *f* matter of taste; **Geschmackssinn** *m* sense of taste; **Geschmacksverirrung** *f*: **unter Geschmacksverirrung leiden** (*ironisch*) to have no taste

geschmackvoll *adj* tasteful

Geschmeide [gəˈʃmaɪdə] (**-s, -**) *nt* jewellery (*Brit*), jewelry (*US*)

geschmeidig *adj* supple; (*formbar*) malleable

Geschmeiß *nt* vermin *pl*

Geschmiere [gəˈʃmiːrə] (**-s**) *nt* scrawl; (*Bild*) daub

geschmissen [gəˈʃmɪsən] *pp von* **schmeißen**

geschmolzen [gəˈʃmɔltsən] *pp von* **schmelzen**

Geschnetzelte, s [gəˈʃnɛtsəltə(s)] *nt* (*Koch*) *meat cut into strips and stewed to produce a thick sauce*

geschnitten [gəˈʃnɪtən] *pp von* **schneiden**

geschoben [gəˈʃoːbən] *pp von* **schieben**

geschollen [gəˈʃɔlən] *pp von* **schallen**

gescholten [gəˈʃɔltən] *pp von* **schelten**

Geschöpf [gəˈʃœpf] (**-(e)s, -e**) *nt* creature

geschoren [gəˈʃoːrən] *pp von* **scheren**

Geschoss [gəˈʃɔs] (**-es, -e**) *nt*, **Geschoß** [gəˈʃoːs] (**-sses, -sse**) (*Österr*) *nt* (*Mil*) projectile; (*Rakete*) missile; (*Stockwerk*) floor

geschossen [gəˈʃɔsən] *pp von* **schießen**

geschraubt [gəˈʃraʊpt] *adj* stilted, artificial
Geschrei [gəˈʃraɪ] **(-s)** *nt* cries *pl*, shouting; (*fig: Aufheben*) noise, fuss
geschrieben [gəˈʃriːbən] *pp von* **schreiben**
geschrieen [gəˈʃriːən], **geschrien** [gəˈʃriːn] *pp von* **schreien**
geschritten [gəˈʃrɪtən] *pp von* **schreiten**
geschunden [gəˈʃʊndən] *pp von* **schinden**
Geschütz [gəˈʃʏts] **(-es, -e)** *nt* gun, piece of artillery; **ein schweres ~ auffahren** (*fig*) to bring out the big guns; **Geschützfeuer** *nt* artillery fire, gunfire
geschützt *adj* protected; (*Winkel, Ecke*) sheltered
Geschw. *abk* = **Geschwister**
Geschwader [gəˈʃvaːdər] **(-s, -)** *nt* (*Naut*) squadron; (*Aviat*) group
Geschwafel [gəˈʃvaːfəl] **(-s)** *nt* silly talk
Geschwätz [gəˈʃvɛts] **(-es)** *nt* chatter; (*Klatsch*) gossip
geschwätzig *adj* talkative; **Geschwätzigkeit** *f* talkativeness
geschweige [gəˈʃvaɪgə] *adv*: **~ (denn)** let alone, not to mention
geschwiegen [gəˈʃviːgən] *pp von* **schweigen**
geschwind [gəˈʃvɪnt] *adj* quick, swift
Geschwindigkeit [gəˈʃvɪndɪçkaɪt] *f* speed, velocity
Geschwindigkeits- *zW*: **Geschwindigkeitsbegrenzung** *f*, **Geschwindigkeitsbeschränkung** *f* speed limit; **Geschwindigkeitsmesser** *m* (*Aut*) speedometer; **Geschwindigkeitsüberschreitung** *f* speeding
Geschwister [gəˈʃvɪstər] *pl* brothers and sisters *pl*
geschwollen [gəˈʃvɔlən] *pp von* **schwellen** ▷ *adj* pompous
geschwommen [gəˈʃvɔmən] *pp von* **schwimmen**
geschworen [gəˈʃvoːrən] *pp von* **schwören**
Geschworene, r *f(m)* juror; **die Geschworenen** *pl* the jury
Geschwulst [gəˈʃvʊlst] **(-, ¨-e)** *f* growth, tumour
geschwunden [gəˈʃvʊndən] *pp von* **schwinden**
geschwungen [gəˈʃvʊŋən] *pp von* **schwingen** ▷ *adj* curved
Geschwür [gəˈʃvyːr] **(-(e)s, -e)** *nt* ulcer; (*Furunkel*) boil
gesehen [gəˈzeːən] *pp von* **sehen**
Geselle [gəˈzɛlə] **(-n, -n)** *m* fellow; (*Handwerksgeselle*) journeyman
gesellen *vr*: **sich zu jdm ~** to join sb
Gesellenbrief *m* articles *pl*
Gesellenprüfung *f* examination to become a journeyman
gesellig *adj* sociable; **~es Beisammensein** get-together; **Geselligkeit** *f* sociability
Gesellschaft *f* society; (*Begleitung, Comm*) company; (*Abendgesellschaft etc*) party; (*pej*) crowd (*umg*); (*Kreis von Menschen*) group of people; **in schlechte ~ geraten** to get into bad company; **geschlossene ~** private party; **jdm ~ leisten** to keep sb company
Gesellschafter, in (-s, -) *m(f)* shareholder; (*Partner*) partner
gesellschaftlich *adj* social
Gesellschafts- *zW*: **Gesellschaftsanzug** *m* evening dress; **gesellschaftsfähig** *adj* socially acceptable; **Gesellschaftsordnung** *f* social structure; **Gesellschaftsreise** *f* group tour; **Gesellschaftsschicht** *f* social stratum; **Gesellschaftssystem** *nt* social system
gesessen [gəˈzɛsən] *pp von* **sitzen**
Gesetz [gəˈzɛts] **(-es, -e)** *nt* law; (*Parl*) act; (*Satzung, Regel*) rule; **vor dem ~** in (the eyes of the) law; **nach dem ~** under the law; **das oberste ~ (der Wirtschaft** *etc***)** the golden rule (of industry *etc*); **Gesetzblatt** *nt* law gazette; **Gesetzbuch** *nt* statute book; **Gesetzentwurf** *m* bill
Gesetzeshüter *m* (*ironisch*) guardian of the law
Gesetzesvorlage *f* bill
Gesetz- *zW*: **gesetzgebend** *adj* legislative; **Gesetzgeber (-s, -)** *m* legislator; **Gesetzgebung** *f* legislation; **gesetzlich** *adj* legal, lawful; **Gesetzlichkeit** *f* legality, lawfulness; **gesetzlos** *adj* lawless; **gesetzmäßig** *adj* lawful
gesetzt *adj* (*Mensch*) sedate ▷ *konj*: **~ den Fall ...** assuming (that) ...
gesetzwidrig *adj* illegal; (*unrechtmäßig*) unlawful
ges. gesch. *abk* (= *gesetzlich geschützt*) reg.
Gesicht [gəˈzɪçt] **(-(e)s, -er)** *nt* face; **das Zweite ~** second sight; **das ist mir nie zu ~ gekommen** I've never laid eyes on that; **jdn zu ~ bekommen** to clap eyes on sb; **jdm etw ins ~ sagen** to tell sb sth to his face; **sein wahres ~ zeigen** to show (o.s. in) one's true colours; **jdm wie aus dem ~ geschnitten sein** to be the spitting image of sb
Gesichts- *zW*: **Gesichtsausdruck** *m* (facial) expression; **Gesichtsfarbe** *f* complexion; **Gesichtspackung** *f* face pack; **Gesichtspunkt** *m* point of view; **Gesichtswasser** *nt* face lotion; **Gesichtszüge** *pl* features *pl*
Gesindel [gəˈzɪndəl] **(-s)** *nt* rabble
gesinnt [gəˈzɪnt] *adj* disposed, minded
Gesinnung [gəˈzɪnʊŋ] *f* disposition; (*Ansicht*) views *pl*
Gesinnungs- *zW*: **Gesinnungsgenosse** *m* like-minded person; **Gesinnungslosigkeit** *f* lack of conviction; **Gesinnungsschnüffelei** (*pej*) *f*: **Gesinnungsschnüffelei betreiben** to pry into people's political convictions; **Gesinnungswandel** *m* change of opinion
gesittet [gəˈzɪtət] *adj* well-mannered
gesoffen [gəˈzɔfən] *pp von* **saufen**
gesogen [gəˈzoːgən] *pp von* **saugen**
gesollt [gəˈzɔlt] *pp von* **sollen**
gesondert [gəˈzɔndərt] *adj* separate
gesonnen [gəˈzɔnən] *pp von* **sinnen**
gespalten [gəˈʃpaltən] *adj* (*Bewusstsein*) split; (*Lippe*) cleft
Gespann [gəˈʃpan] **(-(e)s, -e)** *nt* team; (*umg*) couple

gespannt *adj* tense, strained; (*neugierig*) curious; (*begierig*) eager; **ich bin ~, ob** I wonder if *od* whether; **auf etw/jdn ~ sein** to look forward to sth/to meeting sb; **ich bin ~ wie ein Flitzebogen** (*hum: umg*) I'm on tenterhooks

Gespenst [gəˈʃpɛnst] (**-(e)s, -er**) *nt* ghost; (*fig: Gefahr*) spectre (*Brit*), specter (*US*); **~er sehen** (*fig: umg*) to imagine things

gespensterhaft, gespenstisch *adj* ghostly

gespieen [gəʃpi:ən], **gespien** [gəʃpi:n] *pp von* **speien**

gespielt [gəˈʃpi:lt] *adj* feigned

gesponnen [gəʃpɔnən] *pp von* **spinnen**

Gespött [gəˈʃpœt] (**-(e)s**) *nt* mockery; **zum ~ werden** to become a laughing stock

Gespräch [gəˈʃprɛ:ç] (**-(e)s, -e**) *nt* conversation; (*Diskussion*) discussion; (*Anruf*) call; **zum ~ werden** to become a topic of conversation; **ein ~ unter vier Augen** a confidential *od* private talk; **mit jdm ins ~ kommen** to get into conversation with sb; (*fig*) to establish a dialogue with sb

gesprächig *adj* talkative; **Gesprächigkeit** *f* talkativeness

Gesprächs- *zW*: **Gesprächseinheit** *f* (*Tel*) unit; **Gesprächsgegenstand** *m* topic; **Gesprächspartner** *m*: **mein Gesprächspartner bei den Verhandlungen** my opposite number at the talks; **Gesprächsstoff** *m* topics *pl*; **Gesprächsthema** *nt* subject *od* topic (of conversation)

gesprochen [gəˈʃprɔxən] *pp von* **sprechen**

gesprossen [gəˈʃprɔsən] *pp von* **sprießen**

gesprungen [gəˈʃprʊŋən] *pp von* **springen**

Gespür [gəˈʃpy:r] (**-s**) *nt* feeling

gest. *abk* (= *gestorben*) dec.

Gestalt [gəˈʃtalt] (**-, -en**) *f* form, shape; (*Person*) figure; (*Liter: pej: Mensch*) character; **in ~ von** in the form of; **~ annehmen** to take shape

gestalten *vt* (*formen*) to shape, form; (*organisieren*) to arrange, organize ▷ *vr*: **sich ~ (zu)** to turn out (to be); **etw interessanter** *etc* **~** to make sth more interesting *etc*

Gestaltung *f* formation; organization

gestanden [gəʃtandən] *pp von* **stehen; gestehen**

geständig [gəˈʃtɛndɪç] *adj*: **~ sein** to have confessed

Geständnis [gəˈʃtɛntnɪs] (**-ses, -se**) *nt* confession

Gestank [gəˈʃtaŋk] (**-(e)s**) *m* stench

gestatten [gəˈʃtatən] *vt* to permit, allow; **~ Sie?** may I?; **sich** *dat* **~, etw zu tun** to take the liberty of doing sth

Geste [ˈgɛstə] (**-, -n**) *f* gesture

Gesteck [gəˈʃtɛk] (**-(e)s, -e**) *nt* flower arrangement

gestehen [gəˈʃte:ən] *unreg vt* to confess; **offen gestanden** quite frankly

Gestein [gəˈʃtaɪn] (**-(e)s, -e**) *nt* rock

Gestell [gəˈʃtɛl] (**-(e)s, -e**) *nt* stand; (*Regal*) shelf; (*Bettgestell, Brillengestell*) frame

gestellt *adj* (*unecht*) posed

gestern [ˈgɛstərn] *adv* yesterday; **~ Abend/Morgen** yesterday evening/morning; **er ist nicht von ~** (*umg*) he wasn't born yesterday

gestiefelt [gəˈʃti:fəlt] *adj*: **der G~e Kater** Puss-in-Boots

gestiegen [gəˈʃti:gən] *pp von* **steigen**

Gestik (-) *f* gestures *pl*

gestikulieren [gɛstikuˈli:rən] *vi* to gesticulate

Gestirn [gəˈʃtɪrn] (**-(e)s, -e**) *nt* star

gestoben [gəˈʃto:bən] *pp von* **stieben**

Gestöber [gəˈʃtø:bər] (**-s, -**) *nt* flurry; (*länger*) blizzard

gestochen [gəˈʃtɔxən] *pp von* **stechen** ▷ *adj* (*Handschrift*) clear, neat

gestohlen [gəˈʃto:lən] *pp von* **stehlen** ▷ *adj*: **der/das kann mir ~ bleiben** (*umg*) he/it can go hang

gestorben [gəˈʃtɔrbən] *pp von* **sterben**

gestört [gəˈʃtø:rt] *adj* disturbed; (*Rundfunkempfang*) poor, with a lot of interference

gestoßen [gəˈʃto:sən] *pp von* **stoßen**

Gestotter [gəˈʃtɔtər] (**-s**) *nt* stuttering, stammering

Gesträuch [gəˈʃtrɔʏç] (**-(e)s, -e**) *nt* shrubbery, bushes *pl*

gestreift [gəˈʃtraɪft] *adj* striped

gestrichen [gəˈʃtrɪçən] *pp von* **streichen** ▷ *adj*: **~ voll** (*genau voll*) level; (*sehr voll*) full to the brim; **ein ~er Teelöffel voll** a level teaspoon(ful)

gestrig [ˈgɛstrɪç] *adj* yesterday's

gestritten [gəˈʃtrɪtən] *pp von* **streiten**

Gestrüpp [gəˈʃtrʏp] (**-(e)s, -e**) *nt* undergrowth

gestunken [gəˈʃtʊŋkən] *pp von* **stinken**

Gestüt [gəˈʃty:t] (**-(e)s, -e**) *nt* stud farm

Gesuch [gəˈzu:x] (**-(e)s, -e**) *nt* petition; (*Antrag*) application

gesucht *adj* (*begehrt*) sought after

gesund [gəˈzʊnt] *adj* healthy; **wieder ~ werden** to get better; **~ und munter** hale and hearty; **Gesundheit** *f* health; (*Sportlichkeit, fig*) healthiness; **Gesundheit!** bless you!; **bei guter Gesundheit** in good health; **gesundheitlich** *adj* health *attrib*, physical ▷ *adv* physically; **wie geht es Ihnen gesundheitlich?** how's your health?

Gesundheits- *zW*: **Gesundheitsamt** *nt* public health department; **Gesundheitsapostel** *m* (*ironisch*) health freak (*umg*); **Gesundheitsfarm** *f* health farm; **Gesundheitsfürsorge** *f* health care; **Gesundheitsreform** *f* health service reforms *pl*; **Gesundheitsrisiko** *nt* health hazard; **gesundheitsschädlich** *adj* unhealthy; **Gesundheitssystem** *nt* health (care) system; **Gesundheitswesen** *nt* health service; **Gesundheitszeugnis** *nt* health certificate; **Gesundheitszustand** *m* state of health

gesundschreiben *unreg vt*: **jdn ~** to certify sb (as) fit

gesungen [gəˈzʊŋən] *pp von* **singen**

gesunken [gəˈzʊŋkən] *pp von* **sinken**

getan [gəˈta:n] *pp von* **tun** ▷ *adj*: **nach ~er**

Arbeit when the day's work is done
Getier [gə'ti:ər] (**-(e)s, -e**) *nt* (*Tiere, bes Insekten*) creatures *pl*; (*einzelnes*) creature
Getöse [gə'tø:zə] (**-s**) *nt* din, racket
getragen [gə'tra:gən] *pp von* **tragen**
Getränk [gə'trɛŋk] (**-(e)s, -e**) *nt* drink
Getränkeautomat *m* drinks machine *od* dispenser
Getränkekarte *f* (*in Café*) list of beverages; (*in Restaurant*) wine list
getrauen [gə'traʊən] *vr* to dare
Getreide [gə'traɪdə] (**-s, -**) *nt* cereal, grain; **Getreidespeicher** *m* granary
getrennt [gə'trɛnt] *adj* separate; **~ leben** to be separated, live apart
getreten [gə'tre:tən] *pp von* **treten**
getreu [gə'trɔʏ] *adj* faithful
Getriebe [gə'tri:bə] (**-s, -**) *nt* (*Leute*) bustle; (*Aut*) gearbox
getrieben *pp von* **treiben**
Getriebeöl *nt* transmission oil
getroffen [gə'trɔfən] *pp von* **treffen**
getrogen [gə'tro:gən] *pp von* **trügen**
getrost [gə'tro:st] *adv* confidently; **~ sterben** to die in peace; **du kannst dich ~ auf ihn verlassen** you need have no fears about relying on him
getrunken [gə'trʊŋkən] *pp von* **trinken**
Getto ['gɛto] (**-s, -s**) *nt* ghetto
Gettoblaster ['gɛtobla:stər] (**-s, -s**) *m* ghettoblaster
Getue [gə'tu:ə] (**-s**) *nt* fuss
Getümmel [gə'tʏməl] (**-s**) *nt* turmoil
geübt [gə'y:pt] *adj* experienced
GEW (**-**) *f abk* (*= Gewerkschaft Erziehung und Wissenschaft*) *union of employees in education and science*
Gew. *abk* = **Gewerkschaft**
Gewächs [gə'vɛks] (**-es, -e**) *nt* growth; (*Pflanze*) plant
gewachsen [gə'vaksən] *pp von* **wachsen** ▷ *adj*: **jdm/etw ~ sein** to be sb's equal/equal to sth
Gewächshaus *nt* greenhouse
gewagt [gə'va:kt] *adj* daring, risky
gewählt [gə'vɛ:lt] *adj* (*Sprache*) refined, elegant
gewahr [gə'va:r] *adj*: **eine** *od* **einer Sache** *gen* **~ werden** to become aware of sth
Gewähr [gə'vɛ:r] (**-**) *f* guarantee; **keine ~ übernehmen für** to accept no responsibility for; **die Angabe erfolgt ohne ~** this information is supplied without liability
gewähren *vt* to grant; (*geben*) to provide; **jdn ~ lassen** not to stop sb
gewährleisten *vt* to guarantee
Gewährleistungspflicht *f* warranty obligation
Gewahrsam [gə'va:rza:m] (**-s, -e**) *m* safekeeping; (*Polizeigewahrsam*) custody
Gewährsmann *m* informant, source
Gewährung *f* granting
Gewalt [gə'valt] (**-, -en**) *f* power; (*große Kraft*) force; (*Gewalttaten*) violence; **mit aller ~** with all one's might; **die ausübende/gesetzgebende/richterliche ~** the executive/legislature/judiciary; **elterliche ~** parental authority; **höhere ~** acts/an act of God; **Gewaltanwendung** *f* use of force
Gewaltenteilung *f* separation of powers
Gewaltherrschaft *f* tyranny
gewaltig *adj* tremendous; (*Irrtum*) huge; **sich ~ irren** to be very much mistaken
Gewalt- *zW*: **gewaltlos** *adj* non-violent ▷ *adv* without force/violence; **Gewaltmarsch** *m* forced march; **Gewaltmonopol** *nt* monopoly on the use of force; **gewaltsam** *adj* forcible; **gewalttätig** *adj* violent; **Gewaltverbrechen** *nt* crime of violence; **Gewaltverzicht** *m* non-aggression
Gewand [gə'vant] (**-(e)s, ¨er**) *nt* garment
gewandt [gə'vant] *pp von* **wenden** ▷ *adj* deft, skilful (*Brit*), skillful (*US*); (*erfahren*) experienced; **Gewandtheit** *f* dexterity, skill
gewann *etc* [gə'van] *vb siehe* **gewinnen**
gewaschen [gə'vaʃən] *pp von* **waschen**
Gewässer [gə'vɛsər] (**-s, -**) *nt* waters *pl*
Gewebe [gə've:bə] (**-s, -**) *nt* (*Stoff*) fabric; (*Biol*) tissue
Gewehr [gə've:r] (**-(e)s, -e**) *nt* (*Flinte*) rifle; (*Schrotbüchse*) shotgun; **Gewehrlauf** *m* rifle barrel; barrel of a shotgun
Geweih [gə'vaɪ] (**-(e)s, -e**) *nt* antlers *pl*
Gewerbe [gə'vɛrbə] (**-s, -**) *nt* trade, occupation; **Handel und ~** trade and industry; **fahrendes ~** mobile trade; *siehe auch* **gewerbetreibend**; **Gewerbeaufsichtsamt** *nt* ≈ factory inspectorate; **Gewerbepark** *m* trading estate, business park; **Gewerbeschein** *m* trading licence; **Gewerbeschule** *f* technical school
gewerbetreibend *adj* carrying on a trade
gewerblich *adj* industrial
gewerbsmäßig *adj* professional
Gewerbszweig *m* line of trade
Gewerkschaft [gə'vɛrkʃaft] *f* trade *od* labor (*US*) union
Gewerkschafter, **Gewerkschaftler, in** *m(f)* trade *od* labor (*US*) unionist
gewerkschaftlich *adj*: **wir haben uns ~ organisiert** we organized ourselves into a union
Gewerkschaftsbund *m* federation of trade *od* labor (*US*) unions, ≈ Trades Union Congress (*Brit*), Federation of Labor (*US*)
gewesen [gə've:zən] *pp von* **sein**
gewichen [gə'vɪçən] *pp von* **weichen**
Gewicht [gə'vɪçt] (**-(e)s, -e**) *nt* weight; (*fig*) importance
gewichten *vt* to evaluate
Gewichtheben (**-s**) *nt* (*Sport*) weight-lifting
gewichtig *adj* weighty
Gewichtsklasse *f* (*Sport*) weight (category)
gewieft [gə'vi:ft] (*umg*) *adj* shrewd, cunning
gewiesen [gə'vi:zən] *pp von* **weisen**
gewillt [gə'vɪlt] *adj* willing, prepared
Gewimmel [gə'vɪməl] (**-s**) *nt* swarm; (*Menge*) crush

Gewinde [gə'vɪndə] (**-s, -**) *nt* (*Kranz*) wreath; (*von Schraube*) thread

Gewinn [gə'vɪn] (**-(e)s, -e**) *m* profit; (*bei Spiel*) winnings *pl*; **~ bringend** profitable; **etw mit ~ verkaufen** to sell sth at a profit; **aus etw ~ schlagen** (*umg*) to make a profit out of sth; **Gewinnanteil** *m* (*Comm*) dividend; **Gewinnausschüttung** *f* prize draw; **Gewinnbeteiligung** *f* profit-sharing; **gewinnbringend** *adj* profitable; **Gewinnchancen** *pl* (*beim Wetten*) odds *pl*; **Gewinneinbruch** *m* slump in profits

gewinnen *unreg vt* to win; (*erwerben*) to gain; (*Kohle, Öl*) to extract ▷ *vi* to win; (*profitieren*) to gain; **jdn (für etw) ~** to win sb over (to sth); **an etw** *dat* **~** to gain in sth

gewinnend *adj* winning, attractive

Gewinner, in (**-s, -**) *m(f)* winner

Gewinn- *zW*: **Gewinnmitnahme** *f* profit-taking; **Gewinnnummer** *f* winning number; **Gewinnspanne** *f* profit margin; **Gewinnsucht** *f* love of gain; **Gewinn- und Verlustrechnung** *f* profit and loss account

Gewinnung *f* (*von Kohle etc*) mining; (*von Zucker etc*) extraction

Gewinnwarnung *f* (*Comm*) profit warning

Gewirr [gə'vɪr] (**-(e)s, -e**) *nt* tangle; (*von Straßen*) maze

gewiss [gə'vɪs] *adj* certain ▷ *adv* certainly; **in ~em Maße** to a certain extent

Gewissen [gə'vɪsən] (**-s, -**) *nt* conscience; **jdm ins ~ reden** to have a serious talk with sb; **gewissenhaft** *adj* conscientious; **Gewissenhaftigkeit** *f* conscientiousness; **gewissenlos** *adj* unscrupulous

Gewissens- *zW*: **Gewissensbisse** *pl* pangs of conscience *pl*, qualms *pl*; **Gewissensfrage** *f* matter of conscience; **Gewissensfreiheit** *f* freedom of conscience; **Gewissenskonflikt** *m* moral conflict

gewissermaßen [gəvɪsər'ma:sən] *adv* more or less, in a way

Gewissheit *f* certainty; **sich** *dat* **~ verschaffen** to find out for certain

gewisslich *adv* surely

Gewitter [gə'vɪtər] (**-s, -**) *nt* thunderstorm

gewittern *vi unpers*: **es gewittert** there's a thunderstorm

gewitterschwül *adj* sultry and thundery

Gewitterwolke *f* thundercloud; (*fig: umg*) storm cloud

gewitzt [gə'vɪtst] *adj* shrewd, cunning

gewoben [gə'vo:bən] *pp von* **weben**

gewogen [gə'vo:gən] *pp von* **wiegen** ▷ *adj (+dat)* well-disposed (towards)

gewöhnen [gə'vø:nən] *vt*: **jdn an etw** *akk* **~** to accustom sb to sth; (*erziehen zu*) to teach sb sth ▷ *vr*: **sich an etw** *akk* **~** to get used *od* accustomed to sth

Gewohnheit [gə'vo:nhaɪt] *f* habit; (*Brauch*) custom; **aus ~** from habit; **zur ~ werden** to become a habit; **sich** *dat* **etw zur ~ machen** to make a habit of sth

Gewohnheits- *in zW* habitual; **Gewohnheitsmensch** *m* creature of habit; **Gewohnheitsrecht** *nt* common law; **Gewohnheitstier** (*umg*) *nt* creature of habit

gewöhnlich [gə'vø:nlɪç] *adj* usual; (*durchschnittlich*) ordinary; (*pej*) common; **wie ~** as usual

gewohnt [gə'vo:nt] *adj* usual; **etw ~ sein** to be used to sth

Gewöhnung *f*: **~ (an** *+akk***)** getting accustomed (to); (*das Angewöhnen*) training (in)

Gewölbe [gə'vœlbə] (**-s, -**) *nt* vault

gewollt [gə'vɔlt] *pp von* **wollen** ▷ *adj* forced, artificial

gewonnen [gə'vɔnən] *pp von* **gewinnen**

geworben [gə'vɔrbən] *pp von* **werben**

geworden [gə'vɔrdən] *pp von* **werden**

geworfen [gə'vɔrfən] *pp von* **werfen**

gewrungen [gə'vrʊŋən] *pp von* **wringen**

Gewühl [gə'vy:l] (**-(e)s**) *nt* throng

gewunden [gə'vʊndən] *pp von* **winden**

gewunken [gə'vʊŋkən] *pp von* **winken**

Gewürz [gə'vʏrts] (**-es, -e**) *nt* spice; (*Pfeffer, Salz*) seasoning; **Gewürzgurke** *f* pickled gherkin; **Gewürznelke** *f* clove

gewusst [gə'vʊst] *pp von* **wissen**

gez. *abk* (*= gezeichnet*) signed

gezackt [gə'tsakt] *adj* (*Fels*) jagged; (*Blatt*) serrated

gezähnt [gə'tsɛ:nt] *adj* serrated, toothed

gezeichnet [gə'tsaɪçnət] *adj* marked

Gezeiten [gə'tsaɪtən] *pl* tides *pl*

Gezeter [gə'tse:tər] (**-s**) *nt* nagging

gezielt [gə'tsi:lt] *adj* (*Frage, Maßnahme*) specific; (*Hilfe*) well-directed; (*Kritik*) pointed

geziemen [gə'tsi:mən] *vr unpers* to be fitting

geziemend *adj* proper

geziert [gə'tsi:rt] *adj* affected; **Geziertheit** *f* affectation

gezogen [gə'tso:gən] *pp von* **ziehen**

Gezwitscher [gə'tsvɪtʃər] (**-s**) *nt* twitter(ing), chirping

gezwungen [gə'tsvʊŋən] *pp von* **zwingen** ▷ *adj* forced; (*Atmosphäre*) strained

gezwungenermaßen *adv* of necessity; **etw ~ tun** to be forced to do sth, do sth of necessity

GG *abk* = **Grundgesetz**

ggf. *abk* = **gegebenenfalls**

Ghetto ['gɛto] (**-s, -s**) *nt* = **Getto**

Gibraltar [gi'braltar] (**-s**) *nt* Gibraltar

gibst [gi:pst] *vb siehe* **geben**

gibt *vb siehe* **geben**

Gicht [gɪçt] (**-**) *f* gout; **gichtisch** *adj* gouty

Giebel ['gi:bəl] (**-s, -**) *m* gable; **Giebeldach** *nt* gable(d) roof; **Giebelfenster** *nt* gable window

Gier [gi:r] (**-**) *f* greed

gierig *adj* greedy

Gießbach *m* torrent

gießen ['gi:sən] *unreg vt* to pour; (*Blumen*) to water; (*Metall*) to cast; (*Wachs*) to mould ▷ *vi unpers*: **es gießt in Strömen** it's pouring down

Gießerei [gi:sə'raɪ] *f* foundry

Gießkanne *f* watering can

Gift [gɪft] **(-(e)s, -e)** *nt* poison; **das ist ~ für ihn** (*umg*) that is very bad for him; **darauf kannst du ~ nehmen** (*umg*) you can bet your life on it; **giftgrün** *adj* bilious green

giftig *adj* poisonous; (*fig: boshaft*) venomous

Giftler, in ['gɪftlər] *m(f)* (*Österr: umg*) junkie

Gift- *zW*: **Giftmüll** *m* toxic waste; **Giftpilz** *m* poisonous toadstool; **Giftstoff** *m* toxic substance; **Giftwolke** *f* poisonous cloud; **Giftzahn** *m* fang; **Giftzwerg** (*umg*) *m* spiteful little devil

Gigabyte ['gɪgabaɪt] *nt* (*Comput*) gigabyte

Gilde ['gɪldə] **(-, -n)** *f* guild

gilt [gɪlt] *vb siehe* **gelten**

ging *etc* [gɪŋ] *vb siehe* **gehen**

Ginseng ['gɪnzɛŋ] **(-s, -s)** *m* ginseng

Ginster ['gɪnstər] **(-s, -)** *m* broom

Gipfel ['gɪpfəl] **(-s, -)** *m* summit, peak; (*fig*) height; **das ist der ~!** (*umg*) that's the limit!; **Gipfelkonferenz** *f* (*Pol*) summit conference

gipfeln *vi* to culminate

Gipfeltreffen *nt* summit (meeting)

Gips [gɪps] **(-es, -e)** *m* plaster; (*Med*) plaster (of Paris); **Gipsabdruck** *m* plaster cast; **Gipsbein** (*umg*) *nt* leg in plaster; **gipsen** *vt* to plaster; **Gipsfigur** *f* plaster figure; **Gipsverband** *m* plaster (cast)

Giraffe [gi'rafə] **(-, -n)** *f* giraffe

Girlande [gɪr'landə] **(-, -n)** *f* garland

Giro ['ʒi:ro] **(-s, -s)** *nt* giro; **Girokonto** *nt* current account (*Brit*), checking account (*US*)

girren ['gɪrən] *vi* to coo

Gis [gɪs] **(-, -)** *nt* (*Mus*) G sharp

Gischt [gɪʃt] **(-(e)s, -e)** *m od f* spray, foam

Gitarre [gi'tarə] **(-, -n)** *f* guitar

Gitter ['gɪtər] **(-s, -)** *nt* grating, bars *pl*; (*für Pflanzen*) trellis; (*Zaun*) railing(s); **Gitterbett** *nt* cot (*Brit*), crib (*US*); **Gitterfenster** *nt* barred window; **Gitterzaun** *m* railing(s)

Glacéhandschuh, **Glaceehandschuh** [gla'se:hantʃu:] *m* kid glove

Gladiole [gladi'o:lə] **(-, -n)** *f* gladiolus

Glanz [glants] **(-es)** *m* shine, lustre (*Brit*), luster (*US*); (*fig*) splendour (*Brit*), splendor (*US*); **Glanzabzug** *m* (*Phot*) glossy *od* gloss print

glänzen ['glɛntsən] *vi* to shine (*also fig*), gleam

glänzend *adj* shining; (*fig*) brilliant; **wir haben uns ~ amüsiert** we had a marvellous *od* great time

Glanz- *zW*: **Glanzlack** *m* gloss (paint); **Glanzleistung** *f* brilliant achievement; **glanzlos** *adj* dull; **Glanzstück** *nt* pièce de résistance; **Glanzzeit** *f* heyday

Glas [gla:s] **(-es, ¨er)** *nt* glass; (*Brillenglas*) lens *sing*; **zwei ~ Wein** two glasses of wine; **Glasbläser** *m* glass blower; **Glaser (-s, -)** *m* glazier; **Glasfaser** *f* fibreglass (*Brit*), fiberglass (*US*); **Glasfaserkabel** *nt* optical fibre (*Brit*) *od* fiber (*US*) cable

Glasgow ['gla:sgoʊ] *nt* Glasgow

glasieren [gla'zi:rən] *vt* to glaze

glasig *adj* glassy; (*Zwiebeln*) transparent

glasklar *adj* crystal clear

Glasscheibe *f* pane

Glasur [gla'zu:r] *f* glaze; (*Koch*) icing, frosting (*bes US*)

glatt [glat] *adj* smooth; (*rutschig*) slippery; (*Absage*) flat; (*Lüge*) downright; (*Haar*) straight; (*Med: Bruch*) clean; (*pej: allzu gewandt*) smooth, slick ▷ *adv*: **~ rasiert** (*Mann, Kinn*) clean-shaven; **~ streichen** to smooth out; *siehe auch* **glattgehen**

Glätte ['glɛtə] **(-, -n)** *f* smoothness; slipperiness

Glatteis *nt* (black) ice; **„Vorsicht ~!"** "danger, black ice!"; **jdn aufs ~ führen** (*fig*) to take sb for a ride

glätten *vt* to smooth out

glattgehen *unreg vi* to go smoothly

Glatze ['glatsə] **(-, -n)** *f* bald head; **eine ~ bekommen** to go bald

glatzköpfig *adj* bald

Glaube ['glaʊbə] **(-ns, -n)** *m*: **~ (an** *+akk***)** faith (in); (*Überzeugung*) belief (in); **den ~n an jdn/etw verlieren** to lose faith in sb/sth

glauben *vt, vi* to believe; (*meinen*) to think; **jdm ~** to believe sb; **~ an** *+akk* to believe in; **jdm (etw) aufs Wort ~** to take sb's word (for sth); **wers glaubt, wird selig** (*ironisch*) a likely story

Glaubens- *zW*: **Glaubensbekenntnis** *nt* creed; **Glaubensfreiheit** *f* religious freedom; **Glaubensgemeinschaft** *f* religious sect; (*christliche*) denomination

glaubhaft ['glaʊbhaft] *adj* credible; **jdm etw ~ machen** to satisfy sb of sth

Glaubhaftigkeit *f* credibility

gläubig ['glɔʏbɪç] *adj* (*Rel*) devout; (*vertrauensvoll*) trustful; **Gläubige, r** *f(m)* believer; **die Gläubigen** *pl* the faithful

Gläubiger, in (-s, -) *m(f)* creditor

glaubwürdig ['glaʊbvʏrdɪç] *adj* credible; (*Mensch*) trustworthy; **Glaubwürdigkeit** *f* credibility; trustworthiness

gleich [glaɪç] *adj* equal; (*identisch*) (the) same, identical ▷ *adv* equally; (*sofort*) straight away; (*bald*) in a minute; (*räumlich*): **~ hinter dem Haus** just behind the house; (*zeitlich*): **~ am Anfang** at the very beginning; **es ist mir ~** it's all the same to me; **zu ~en Teilen** in equal parts; **das ~e, aber nicht dasselbe Auto** a similar car, but not the same one; **ganz ~ wer/was** *etc* no matter who/what *etc*; **2 mal 2 ~ 4** 2 times 2 is *od* equals 4; **bis ~!** see you soon!; **wie war doch ~ Ihr Name?** what was your name again?; **es ist ~ drei Uhr** it's very nearly three o'clock; **~ gesinnt** like-minded; **~ lautend** identical; **sie sind ~ groß** they are the same size; **~ nach/an** right after/at; **gleichaltrig** *adj* of the same age; **gleichartig** *adj* similar; **gleichbedeutend** *adj* synonymous; **gleichberechtigt** *adj* with equal rights; **Gleichberechtigung** *f* equal rights *pl*; **gleichbleibend** *adj* constant; **bei gleichbleibendem Gehalt** when one's salary stays the same

gleichen *unreg vi*: **jdm/etw ~** to be like sb/sth

▷*vr* to be alike
gleichermaßen *adv* equally
gleich- *zW*: **gleichfalls** *adv* likewise; **danke gleichfalls!** the same to you; **Gleichförmigkeit** *f* uniformity; **gleichgestellt** *adj*: **rechtlich gleichgestellt** equal in law; **Gleichgewicht** *nt* equilibrium, balance; **jdm aus dem Gleichgewicht bringen** to throw sb off balance; **gleichgültig** *adj* indifferent; (*unbedeutend*) unimportant; **Gleichgültigkeit** *f* indifference; **Gleichheit** *f* equality; (*Identität*) identity; (*Industrie*) parity; **Gleichheitsprinzip** *nt* principle of equality; **Gleichheitszeichen** *nt* (*Math*) equals sign; **gleichkommen** *unreg vi +dat* to be equal to; **gleichlautend** *adj* identical; **Gleichmacherei** *f* egalitarianism, levelling down (*pej*); **gleichmäßig** *adj* even, equal; **Gleichmut** *m* equanimity
Gleichnis (**-ses, -se**) *nt* parable
gleich- *zW*: **gleichrangig** *adj* (*Probleme etc*) equally important; **gleichrangig (mit)** (*Beamte etc*) equal in rank (to), at the same level (as); **gleichsam** *adv* as it were; **gleichschalten** (*pej*) *vt* to bring into line; **Gleichschritt** *m*: **im Gleichschritt, marsch!** forward march!; **gleichsehen** *unreg vi*: **jdm gleichsehen** to be *od* look like sb; **gleichstellen** *vt* (*rechtlich etc*) to treat as equal; **Gleichstrom** *m* (*Elek*) direct current; **gleichtun** *unreg vi*: **es jdm gleichtun** to match sb
Gleichung *f* equation
gleich- *zW*: **gleichviel** *adv* no matter; **gleichwertig** *adj* of the same value; (*Leistung, Qualität*) equal; (*Gegner*) evenly matched; **gleichwohl** *adv* (*geh*) nevertheless; **gleichzeitig** *adj* simultaneous
Gleis [glaɪs] (**-es, -e**) *nt* track, rails *pl*; (*am Bahnhof*) platform (*Brit*), track (*US*)
gleißend ['glaɪsənt] *adj* glistening, gleaming
gleiten *unreg vi* to glide; (*rutschen*) to slide
gleitend ['glaɪtənt] *adj*: **~e Arbeitszeit** flexible working hours *pl*, flex(i)time
Gleit- *zW*: **Gleitflug** *m* glide; **Gleitklausel** *f* (*Comm*) escalator clause; **Gleitkomma** *nt* floating point; **Gleitzeit** *f* flex(i)time
Gletscher ['glɛtʃər] (**-s, -**) *m* glacier; **Gletscherspalte** *f* crevasse
glich *etc* [glɪç] *vb siehe* **gleichen**
Glied [gli:t] (**-(e)s, -er**) *nt* member; (*Arm, Bein*) limb; (*Penis*) penis; (*von Kette*) link; (*Mil*) rank(s); **der Schreck steckt ihr noch in den ~ern** she is still shaking with the shock
gliedern *vt* to organize, structure
Gliederreißen *nt* rheumatic pains *pl*
Gliederschmerz *m* rheumatic pains *pl*
Gliederung *f* structure, organization
Gliedmaßen *pl* limbs *pl*
glimmen ['glɪmən] *unreg vi* to glow
Glimmer (**-s, -**) *m* (*Mineral*) mica
Glimmstängel (*umg*) *m* fag (*Brit*), butt (*US*)
glimpflich ['glɪmpflɪç] *adj* mild, lenient; **~ davonkommen** to get off lightly
glitschig ['glɪtʃɪç] (*umg*) *adj* slippery, slippy
glitt *etc* [glɪt] *vb siehe* **gleiten**
glitzern ['glɪtsərn] *vi* to glitter; (*Stern*) to twinkle
global [glo'ba:l] *adj* (*weltweit*) global, worldwide; (*ungefähr, pauschal*) general
Globalisierung [globalɪ'zi:rʊŋ] *f* globalization; **Globalisierungsfalle** *f* globalization trap
Globus ['glo:bʊs] (**-** *od* **-ses, Globen** *od* **-se**) *m* globe
Glöckchen ['glœkçən] *nt* (little) bell
Glocke ['glɔkə] (**-, -n**) *f* bell; **etw an die große ~ hängen** (*fig*) to shout sth from the rooftops
Glocken- *zW*: **Glockengeläut** *nt* peal of bells; **Glockenschlag** *m* stroke (of the bell); (*von Uhr*) chime; **Glockenspiel** *nt* chime(s); (*Mus*) glockenspiel; **Glockenturm** *m* belfry, bell-tower
glomm *etc* [glɔm] *vb siehe* **glimmen**
Glorie ['glo:riə] *f* glory; (*von Heiligen*) halo
glorreich ['glo:rraɪç] *adj* glorious
Glossar [glɔ'sa:r] (**-s, -e**) *nt* glossary
Glosse ['glɔsə] (**-, -n**) *f* comment
Glotze (**-, -n**) (*umg*) *f* gogglebox (*Brit*), TV set
glotzen ['glɔtsən] (*umg*) *vi* to stare
Glück [glʏk] (**-(e)s**) *nt* luck, fortune; (*Freude*) happiness; **~ haben** to be lucky; **viel ~** good luck; **zum ~** fortunately; **ein ~!** how lucky!, what a stroke of luck!; **auf gut ~** (*aufs Geratewohl*) on the off-chance; (*unvorbereitet*) trusting to luck; (*wahllos*) at random; **sie weiß noch nichts von ihrem ~** (*ironisch*) she doesn't know anything about it yet; **er kann von ~ sagen, dass ...** he can count himself lucky that ...; **Glückauf** *nt*: **„Glückauf"** (*Bergleute*) (cry of) "good luck"
Glucke (**-, -n**) *f* (*Bruthenne*) broody hen; (*mit Jungen*) mother hen
glücken *vi* to succeed; **es glückte ihm, es zu bekommen** he succeeded in getting it
gluckern ['glʊkərn] *vi* to glug
glücklich *adj* fortunate; (*froh*) happy ▷*adv* happily; (*umg: endlich, zu guter Letzt*) finally, eventually
glücklicherweise *adv* fortunately
glücklos *adj* luckless
Glücksbringer (**-s, -**) *m* lucky charm
glückselig [glʏk'ze:lɪç] *adj* blissful
Glücks- *zW*: **Glücksfall** *m* stroke of luck; **Glückskind** *nt* lucky person; **Glückspilz** *m* lucky beggar (*umg*); **Glückssache** *f* matter of luck; **Glücksspiel** *nt* game of chance; **Glücksstern** *m* lucky star; **Glückssträhne** *f* lucky streak
glückstrahlend *adj* radiant (with happiness)
Glückszahl *f* lucky number
Glückwunsch *m*: **~ (zu)** congratulations *pl* (on), best wishes *pl* (on)
Glühbirne *f* light bulb
glühen ['gly:ən] *vi* to glow
glühend *adj* glowing; (*heiß glühend: Metall*) red-hot; (*Hitze*) blazing; (*fig: leidenschaftlich*) ardent; (*: Hass*) burning; (*Wangen*) flushed, burning
Glüh- *zW*: **Glühfaden** *m* (*Elek*) filament;

Glühwein *m* mulled wine; **Glühwürmchen** *nt* glow-worm

Glut [glu:t] (**-, -en**) *f* (*Röte*) glow; (*Feuersglut*) fire; (*Hitze*) heat; (*fig*) ardour (*Brit*), ardor (*US*)

GmbH (**-, -s**) *f abk* (= *Gesellschaft mit beschränkter Haftung*) ≈ Ltd. (*Brit*), plc (*Brit*), Inc. (*US*)

Gnade ['gna:də] (**-, -n**) *f* (*Gunst*) favour (*Brit*), favor (*US*); (*Erbarmen*) mercy; (*Milde*) clemency; **~ vor Recht ergehen lassen** to temper justice with mercy

gnaden *vi*: **(dann) gnade dir Gott!** (then) God help you *od* heaven have mercy on you!

Gnaden- *zW*: **Gnadenbrot** *nt*: **jdm/einem Tier das Gnadenbrot geben** to keep sb/an animal in his/her/its old age; **Gnadenfrist** *f* reprieve; **Gnadengesuch** *nt* petition for clemency; **gnadenlos** *adj* merciless; **Gnadenstoß** *m* coup de grâce

gnädig ['gnɛ:dıç] *adj* gracious; (*voll Erbarmen*) merciful; **~e Frau** (*form*) madam, ma'am

Gockel ['gɔkəl] (**-s, -**) *m* (*bes Südd*) cock

Gold [gɔlt] (**-(e)s**) *nt* gold; **nicht mit ~ zu bezahlen** *od* **aufzuwiegen sein** to be worth one's weight in gold; **golden** *adj* golden; **goldene Worte** words of wisdom; **der Tanz ums Goldene Kalb** (*fig*) the worship of Mammon; **Goldfisch** *m* goldfish; **Goldgrube** *f* gold mine; **Goldhamster** *m* (golden) hamster

goldig ['gɔldıç] *adj* (*fig: umg*) sweet, cute

Gold- *zW*: **Goldregen** *m* laburnum; (*fig*) riches *pl*; **goldrichtig** (*umg*) *adj* dead right; **Goldschmied** *m* goldsmith; **Goldschnitt** *m* gilt edging; **Goldstandard** *m* gold standard; **Goldstück** *nt* piece of gold; (*fig: umg*) treasure; **Goldwaage** *f*: **jedes Wort auf die Goldwaage legen** (*fig*) to weigh one's words; **Goldwährung** *f* gold standard

Golf[1] [gɔlf] (**-(e)s, -e**) *m* gulf; **der (Persische) ~** the Gulf

Golf[2] [gɔlf] (**-s**) *nt* golf; **Golfplatz** *m* golf course; **Golfschläger** *m* golf club; **Golfspieler** *m* golfer

Golfstaaten *pl*: **die ~** the Gulf States *pl*

Golfstrom *m* (*Geog*) Gulf Stream

Gondel ['gɔndəl] (**-, -n**) *f* gondola; (*von Seilbahn*) cable car

gondeln (*umg*) *vi*: **durch die Welt ~** to go globetrotting

Gong [gɔŋ] (**-s, -s**) *m* gong; (*bei Boxkampf etc*) bell

gönnen ['gœnən] *vt*: **jdm etw ~** not to begrudge sb sth; **sich** *dat* **etw ~** to allow o.s. sth

Gönner (**-s, -**) *m* patron; **gönnerhaft** *adj* patronizing; **Gönnerin** *f* patroness; **Gönnermiene** *f* patronizing air

googeln ['gu:gəln] *vi* (*Comput: umg*) to google®

gor *etc* [go:r] *vb siehe* **gären**

Gorilla [go'rıla] (**-s, -s**) *m* gorilla; (*umg: Leibwächter*) heavy

goss *etc* [gɔs] *vb siehe* **gießen**

Gosse ['gɔsə] (**-, -n**) *f* gutter

Gote ['go:tə] (**-n, -n**) *m* Goth

Gotik ['go:tık] *f* (*Kunst*) Gothic (style); (*Epoche*) Gothic period

Gotin ['go:tın] *f* Goth

Gott [gɔt] (**-es, ¨-er**) *m* god; (*als Name*) God; **um ~es Willen!** for heaven's sake!; **~ sei Dank!** thank God!; **grüß ~!** (*bes Südd, Österr*) hello, good morning/afternoon/evening; **den lieben ~ einen guten Mann sein lassen** (*umg*) to take things as they come; **ein Bild für die Götter** (*hum: umg*) a sight for sore eyes; **das wissen die Götter** (*umg*) God (only) knows; **über ~ und die Welt reden** (*fig*) to talk about everything under the sun; **wie ~ in Frankreich leben** (*umg*) to be in clover

Götterspeise *f* (*Koch*) jelly (*Brit*), jello (*US*)

Gottes- *zW*: **Gottesdienst** *m* service; **gottesfürchtig** *adj* god-fearing; **Gotteshaus** *nt* place of worship; **Gotteskrieger, in** *m(f)* religious terrorist; **Gotteslästerung** *f* blasphemy

Gottheit *f* deity

Göttin ['gœtın] *f* goddess

göttlich *adj* divine

Gott- *zW*: **gottlob** *interj* thank heavens!; **gottlos** *adj* godless; **gottverdammt** *adj* goddamn(ed); **gottverlassen** *adj* godforsaken; **Gottvertrauen** *nt* trust in God

Götze ['gœtsə] (**-n, -n**) *m* idol

Grab [gra:p] (**-(e)s, ¨-er**) *nt* grave

grabbeln ['grabəln] (*Nordd: umg*) *vt* to rummage

Graben ['gra:bən] (**-s, ¨-**) *m* ditch; (*Mil*) trench

graben *unreg vt* to dig

Grabesstille *f* (*liter*) deathly hush

Grab- *zW*: **Grabmal** *nt* monument; (*Grabstein*) gravestone; **Grabrede** *f* funeral oration; **Grabstein** *m* gravestone

gräbt *vb siehe* **graben**

Gracht [graxt] (**-, -en**) *f* canal

Grad [gra:t] (**-(e)s, -e**) *m* degree; **im höchsten ~(e)** extremely; **Verbrennungen ersten ~es** (*Med*) first-degree burns; **Gradeinteilung** *f* graduation; **gradlinig** *adj* straight; **gradweise** *adv* gradually

Graf [gra:f] (**-en, -en**) *m* count, earl (*Brit*)

Grafik ['gra:fık] (**-, -en**) *f* (*Comput, Tech*) graphics; (*Art*) graphic arts *pl*

Grafiker, in ['gra:fıkər(ın)] (**-s, -**) *m(f)* graphic artist; (*Illustrator*) illustrator

Gräfin ['grɛ:fın] *f* countess

grafisch *adj* ['gra:fıʃ] ▷*adj* graphic; **~e Darstellung** graph

Grafschaft *f* county

Grahambrot ['gra:hambro:t] *nt* type of wholemeal (*Brit*) *od* whole-wheat (*US*) bread

Gralshüter ['gra:lzhy:tər] (**-s, -**) *m* (*fig*) guardian

Gram [gra:m] (**-(e)s**) *m* (*geh*) grief, sorrow

grämen ['grɛ:mən] *vr* to grieve; **sich zu Tode ~** to die of grief *od* sorrow

Gramm [gram] (**-s, -e**) *nt* gram(me)

Grammatik [gra'matık] *f* grammar

grammatisch *adj* grammatical

Grammofon, Grammophon [gramo'fo:n] (**-s, -e**) *nt* gramophone

Granat [gra'na:t] (**-(e)s, -e**) *m* (*Stein*) garnet; **Granatapfel** *m* pomegranate

Granate (**-, -n**) *f* (*Mil*) shell; (*Handgranate*) grenade
grandios [gran'dio:s] *adj* magnificent, superb
Granit [gra'ni:t] (**-s, -e**) *m* granite; **auf ~ beißen (bei ...)** to bang one's head against a brick wall (with ...)
grantig ['grantıç] (*umg*) *adj* grumpy
Graphik *etc* ['gra:fık] = **Grafik** *etc*
grapschen ['grapʃən] (*umg*) *vt, vi* to grab; **(sich** *dat***) etw ~** to grab sth
Gras [gra:s] (**-es, ¨-er**) *nt* grass; (*auch umg: Marihuana*) grass; **über etw** *akk* **~ wachsen lassen** (*fig*) to let the dust settle on sth; **grasen** *vi* to graze; **Grashalm** *m* blade of grass
grasig *adj* grassy
Grasnarbe *f* turf
grassieren [gra'si:rən] *vi* to be rampant, rage
grässlich ['grɛslıç] *adj* horrible
Grat [gra:t] (**-(e)s, -e**) *m* ridge
Gräte ['grɛ:tə] (**-, -n**) *f* fish-bone
Gratifikation [gratifikatsi'o:n] *f* bonus
gratis ['gra:tıs] *adj, adv* free (of charge); **Gratisprobe** *f* free sample
Grätsche ['grɛ:tʃə] (**-, -n**) *f* (*Sport*) straddle
Gratulant, in [gratu'lant(ın)] *m(f)* well-wisher
Gratulation [gratulatsi'o:n] *f* congratulation(s)
gratulieren [gratu'li:rən] *vi*: **jdm (zu etw) ~** to congratulate sb (on sth); **(ich) gratuliere!** congratulations!
Gratwanderung *f* (*fig*) tightrope walk
grau [graʊ] *adj* grey (*Brit*), gray (*US*); **der ~e Alltag** drab reality; **~ meliert** grey-flecked (*Brit*), gray-flecked (*US*); **Graubrot** *nt* = **Mischbrot**
Gräuel ['grɔyəl] (**-s, -**) *m* horror; (*Gräueltat*) atrocity; **etw ist jdm ein ~** sb loathes sth; **Gräuelpropaganda** *f* atrocity propaganda; **Gräueltat** *f* atrocity
Grauen (**-s**) *nt* horror
grauen *vi* (*Tag*) to dawn ▷ *vi unpers*: **es graut jdm vor etw** sb dreads sth, sb is afraid of sth ▷ *vr*: **sich ~ vor** to dread
grauenhaft, grauenvoll *adj* horrible
grauhaarig *adj* grey-haired (*Brit*), gray-haired (*US*)
gräulich ['grɔylıç] *adj* horrible
Graupelregen ['graupəlre:gən] *m* sleet
Graupelschauer *m* sleet
Graupen ['graʊpən] *pl* pearl barley *sing*
grausam ['graʊza:m] *adj* cruel; **Grausamkeit** *f* cruelty
Grausen ['graʊzən] (**-s**) *nt* horror; **da kann man das kalte ~ kriegen** (*umg*) it's enough to give you the creeps
grausen *vb* = **grauen**
Grauzone *f* (*fig*) grey (*Brit*) *od* gray (*US*) area
gravieren [gra'vi:rən] *vt* to engrave
gravierend *adj* grave
Grazie ['gra:tsiə] *f* grace
graziös [gratsi'ø:s] *adj* graceful
Greencard, Green Card ['gri:nka:əd] (**-, -s**) *f* green card
greifbar *adj* tangible, concrete; **in ~er Nähe** within reach
greifen ['graıfən] *unreg vt* (*nehmen*) to grasp; (*grapschen*) to seize, grab ▷ *vi* (*nicht rutschen, einrasten*) to grip; **nach etw ~** to reach for sth; **um sich ~** (*fig*) to spread; **zu etw ~** (*fig*) to turn to sth; **diese Zahl ist zu niedrig gegriffen** (*fig*) this figure is too low; **aus dem Leben gegriffen** taken from life
Greifer (**-s, -**) *m* (*Tech*) grab
Greifvogel *m* bird of prey
Greis [graıs] (**-es, -e**) *m* old man
Greisenalter *nt* old age
greisenhaft *adj* very old
Greisin ['graızın] *f* old woman
grell [grɛl] *adj* harsh
Gremium ['gre:miʊm] *nt* body; (*Ausschuss*) committee
Grenadier [grena'di:ər] (**-s, -e**) *m* (*Mil: Infanterist*) infantryman
Grenzbeamte, r *m* frontier official
Grenze (**-, -n**) *f* border; (*zwischen Grundstücken, fig*) boundary; (*Staatsgrenze*) frontier; (*Schranke*) limit; **über die ~ gehen/fahren** to cross the border; **hart an der ~ des Erlaubten** bordering on the limits of what is permitted
grenzen *vi*: **~ an** *+akk* to border on
grenzenlos *adj* boundless
Grenz- *zW*: **Grenzfall** *m* borderline case; **Grenzgänger** *m* (*Arbeiter*) international commuter (*across a local border*); **Grenzgebiet** *nt* (*lit, fig*) border area; **Grenzkosten** *pl* marginal cost *sing*; **Grenzlinie** *f* boundary; **Grenzübergang** *m* frontier crossing; **Grenzwert** *m* limit; **Grenzzwischenfall** *m* border incident
Gretchenfrage ['gre:tçənfra:gə] *f* (*fig*) crunch question, sixty-four-thousand-dollar question (*umg*)
Greuel *etc* ['grɔyəl] *siehe* **Gräuel**
greulich ['grɔylıç] *siehe* **gräulich**
Grieche ['gri:çə] (**-n, -n**) *m* Greek
Griechenland *nt* Greece
Griechin ['gri:çın] *f* Greek
griechisch *adj* Greek
griesgrämig ['gri:sgrɛ:mıç] *adj* grumpy
Grieß [gri:s] (**-es, -e**) *m* (*Koch*) semolina; **Grießbrei** *m* cooked semolina
Griff [grıf] (**-(e)s, -e**) *m* grip; (*Vorrichtung*) handle; (*das Greifen*): **der ~ nach etw** reaching for sth; **jdn/etw in den ~ bekommen** (*fig*) to gain control of sb/sth; **etw in den ~ bekommen** (*geistig*) to get a grasp of sth
griff *etc vb siehe* **greifen**
griffbereit *adj* handy
Griffel ['grıfəl] (**-s, -**) *m* slate pencil; (*Bot*) style
griffig ['grıfıç] *adj* (*Fahrbahn etc*) that has a good grip; (*fig: Ausdruck*) useful, handy
Grill [grıl] (**-s, -s**) *m* grill; (*Aut*) grille
Grille ['grılə] (**-, -n**) *f* cricket; (*fig*) whim
grillen *vt* to grill
Grimasse [gri'masə] (**-, -n**) *f* grimace; **~n schneiden** to make faces

grimmig *adj* furious; (*heftig*) fierce, severe
grinsen ['grɪnzən] *vi* to grin; (*höhnisch*) to smirk
Grippe ['grɪpə] (**-, -n**) *f* influenza, flu
Grips [grɪps] (**-es, -e**) (*umg*) *m* sense
grob [gro:p] *adj* coarse, gross; (*Fehler, Verstoß*) gross; (*brutal, derb*) rough; (*unhöflich*) ill-mannered; **~ geschätzt** at a rough estimate; **Grobheit** *f* coarseness; (*Beschimpfung*) coarse expression
Grobian ['gro:bia:n] (**-s, -e**) *m* ruffian
grobknochig *adj* large-boned
groggy ['grɔgɪ] *adj* (*Boxen*) groggy; (*umg: erschöpft*) bushed
grölen ['grø:lən] (*pej*) *vt, vi* to bawl
Groll [grɔl] (**-(e)s**) *m* resentment; **grollen** *vi* (*Donner*) to rumble; **grollen (mit** *od* *+dat*) to bear ill will (towards)
Grönland ['grø:nlant] (**-s**) *nt* Greenland
Grönländer, in (**-s, -**) *m(f)* Greenlander
Groschen ['grɔʃən] (**-s, -**) (*umg*) *m* 10-pfennig piece; (*Österr*) groschen; (*fig*) penny, cent (*US*); **Groschenroman** (*pej*) *m* cheap *od* dime (*US*) novel
groß [gro:s] *adj* big, large; (*hoch*) tall; (*Freude, Werk*) great ▷ *adv* greatly; **im G~en und Ganzen** on the whole; **wie ~ bist du?** how tall are you?; **die G~en** (*Erwachsene*) the grown-ups; **mit etw ~ geworden sein** to have grown up with sth; **die G~en Seen** the Great Lakes *pl*; **~en Hunger haben** to be very hungry; **~e Mode sein** to be all the fashion; **~ angelegt** large-scale, on a large scale; **~ und breit** (*fig: umg*) at great *od* enormous length; *siehe auch* **großschreiben**; **Großabnehmer** *m* (*Comm*) bulk buyer; **Großalarm** *m* red alert; **großartig** *adj* great, splendid; **Großaufnahme** *f* (*Film*) close-up; **Großbritannien** (**-s**) *nt* (Great) Britain; **Großbuchstabe** *m* capital (letter)
Größe ['grø:sə] (**-, -n**) *f* size; (*Länge*) height; (*fig*) greatness; **eine unbekannte ~** (*lit, fig*) an unknown quantity
Groß- *zW*: **Großeinkauf** *m* bulk purchase; **Großeinsatz** *m*: **Großeinsatz der Polizei** *etc* large-scale operation by the police *etc*; **Großeltern** *pl* grandparents *pl*
Größenordnung *f* scale; (*Größe*) magnitude; (*Math*) order (of magnitude)
großenteils *adv* for the most part
Größen- *zW*: **Größenunterschied** *m* difference in size; **Größenwahn** *m*, **Größenwahnsinn** *m* megalomania, delusions *pl* of grandeur
Groß- *zW*: **Großformat** *nt* large size; **Großhandel** *m* wholesale trade; **Großhandelspreisindex** *m* wholesale-price index; **Großhändler** *m* wholesaler; **großherzig** *adj* generous; **Großhirn** *nt* cerebrum; **Großindustrielle, r** *f(m)* major industrialist; **großkotzig** (*umg*) *adj* show-offish, bragging; **Großkundgebung** *f* mass rally; **Großmacht** *f* great power; **Großmaul** *m* braggart; **Großmut** (-) *f* magnanimity; **großmütig** *adj* magnanimous; **Großmutter** *f* grandmother; **Großraum** *m*: **der Großraum München** the Munich area *od* conurbation, Greater Munich; **Großraumbüro** *nt* open-plan office; **Großrechner** *m* mainframe; **Großreinemachen** *nt* thorough cleaning, ≈ spring cleaning; **großschreiben** *unreg vt*: **ein Wort großschreiben** to write a word with a capital; **großgeschrieben werden** (*umg*) to be stressed; **Großschreibung** *f* capitalization; **großspurig** *adj* pompous; **Großstadt** *f* city
größte, r, s [grø:stə(r, s)] *adj superl von* **groß**
größtenteils *adv* for the most part
Groß- *zW*: **Großtuer** (**-s, -**) *m* boaster; **großtun** *unreg vi* to boast; **Großvater** *m* grandfather; **Großverbraucher** *m* (*Comm*) heavy user; **Großverdiener** *m* big earner; **Großwild** *nt* big game; **großziehen** *unreg vt* to raise; **großzügig** *adj* generous; (*Planung*) on a large scale
grotesk [gro'tɛsk] *adj* grotesque
Grotte ['grɔtə] (**-, -n**) *f* grotto
grub *etc* [gru:p] *vb siehe* **graben**
Grübchen ['gry:pçən] *nt* dimple
Grube ['gru:bə] (**-, -n**) *f* pit; (*Bergwerk*) mine
grübeln ['gry:bəln] *vi* to brood
Grubenarbeiter *m* miner
Grubengas *nt* firedamp
Grübler ['gry:blər] (**-s, -**) *m* brooder; **grüblerisch** *adj* brooding, pensive
Gruft [gruft] (**-, ¨-e**) *f* tomb, vault
grün [gry:n] *adj* green; (*ökologisch*) green; (*Pol*): **die G~en** the Greens; **~e Minna** (*umg*) Black Maria (*Brit*), paddy wagon (*US*); **~e Welle** phased traffic lights; **~e Versicherungskarte** (*Aut*) green card; **sich ~ und blau** *od* **gelb ärgern** (*umg*) to be furious; **auf keinen ~en Zweig kommen** (*fig: umg*) to get nowhere; **jdm ~es Licht geben** to give sb the green light; **Grünanlage** *f* park
Grund [grʊnt] (**-(e)s, ¨-e**) *m* ground; (*von See, Gefäß*) bottom; (*fig*) reason; **von ~ auf** entirely, completely; **aus gesundheitlichen** *etc* **Gründen** for health *etc* reasons; **im ~e genommen** basically; **ich habe ~ zu der Annahme, dass ...** I have reason to believe that ...; **einer Sache** *dat* **auf den ~ gehen** (*fig*) to get to the bottom of sth; **in ~ und Boden** (*fig*) utterly, thoroughly; *siehe auch* **aufgrund; zugrunde**; **Grundausbildung** *f* basic training; **Grundbedeutung** *f* basic meaning; **Grundbedingung** *f* fundamental condition; **Grundbegriff** *m* basic concept; **Grundbesitz** *m* land(ed property), real estate; **Grundbuch** *nt* land register; **grundehrlich** *adj* thoroughly honest
gründen [grʏndən] *vt* to found ▷ *vr*: **sich ~ auf** *+akk* to be based on; **~ auf** *+akk* to base on
Gründer, in (**-s, -**) *m(f)* founder
Grund- *zW*: **grundfalsch** *adj* utterly wrong; **Grundgebühr** *f* basic charge; **Grundgedanke** *m* basic idea; **Grundgesetz** *nt* constitution
Grundierung [grʊn'di:rʊŋ] *f* (*Farbe*) primer
Grund- *zW*: **Grundkapital** *nt* nominal capital; **Grundkurs** *m* basic course; **Grundlage** *f* foundation; **jeder Grundlage** *gen* **entbehren**

to be completely unfounded; **grundlegend** *adj* fundamental
gründlich *adj* thorough; **jdm ~ die Meinung sagen** to give sb a piece of one's mind
Grund- *zW*: **grundlos** *adj* (*fig*) groundless; **Grundmauer** *f* foundation wall; **Grundnahrungsmittel** *nt* basic food(stuff)
Gründonnerstag *m* Maundy Thursday
Grund- *zW*: **Grundordnung** *f*: **die freiheitlich-demokratische Grundordnung** (*Brd Pol*) *the German constitution based on democratic liberty*; **Grundrechenart** *f* basic arithmetical operation; **Grundrecht** *nt* basic *od* constitutional right; **Grundregel** *f* basic *od* ground rule; **Grundriss** *m* plan; (*fig*) outline; **Grundsatz** *m* principle; **grundsätzlich** *adj* fundamental; (*Frage*) of principle ▷ *adv* fundamentally; (*prinzipiell*) on principle; **das ist grundsätzlich verboten** it is absolutely forbidden; **Grundsatzurteil** *nt judgement that establishes a principle*
Grundschule *f* primary (*Brit*) *od* elementary school; *see culture note*

GRUNDSCHULE

The *Grundschule* is a primary school which children attend for 4 years from the age of 6 to 10. There are no formal examinations in the *Grundschule* but parents receive a report on their child's progress twice a year. Many children attend a *Kindergarten* from 3-6 years before going to the *Grundschule*, but no formal instruction takes place in the *Kindergarten*.

Grund- *zW*: **Grundsicherung** *f* (*Wirts*) guaranteed minimum income; **Grundstein** *m* foundation stone; **Grundsteuer** *f* rates *pl*; **Grundstück** *nt* plot (of land); (*Anwesen*) estate; **Grundstücksmakler** *m* estate agent (*Brit*), realtor® (*US*); **Grundstufe** *f* first stage; (*Sch*) ≈ junior (*Brit*) *od* grade (*US*) school
Gründung *f* foundation
Gründungsurkunde *f* (*Comm*) certificate of incorporation
Gründungsversammlung *f* (*Aktiengesellschaft*) statutory meeting
Grund- *zW*: **grundverschieden** *adj* utterly different; **Grundwasser** *nt* ground water; **Grundwasserspiegel** *m* water table, ground-water level; **Grundzug** *m* characteristic; **etw in seinen Grundzügen darstellen** to outline (the essentials of) sth
Grüne (**-n**) *nt*: **im ~n** in the open air; **ins ~ fahren** to go to the country
Grüne, r *f(m)* (*Pol*) Ecologist, Green; **die Grünen** *pl* (*als Partei*) the Greens; *see culture note*

DIE GRÜNEN

Die Grünen is the name given to the Green or ecological party in Germany which was founded in 1980. Since 1993 they have been allied with the originally East German party, *Bündnis 90*.

GRÜNER PUNKT

The *Grüner Punkt* is the green spot symbol which appears on packaging, indicating that the packaging should not be thrown into the normal household refuse but kept separate to be recycled through the *DSD* system. The recycling is financed by licences bought by the manufacturer from the *DSD* and the cost of this is often passed on to the consumer.

Grün- *zW*: **Grünkohl** *m* kale; **Grünschnabel** *m* greenhorn; **Grünspan** *m* verdigris; **Grünstreifen** *m* central reservation
grunzen ['grʊntsən] *vi* to grunt
Gruppe ['grʊpə] (**-, -n**) *f* group
Gruppen- *zW*: **Gruppenarbeit** *f* teamwork; **Gruppendynamik** *f* group dynamics *pl*; **Gruppentherapie** *f* group therapy; **gruppenweise** *adv* in groups
gruppieren [grʊ'pi:rən] *vt, vr* to group
gruselig *adj* creepy
gruseln ['gru:zəln] *vi unpers*: **es gruselt jdm vor etw** sth gives sb the creeps ▷ *vr* to have the creeps
Gruß [gru:s] (**-es, ⸚e**) *m* greeting; (*Mil*) salute; **viele Grüße** best wishes; **Grüße an** *+akk* regards to; **einen (schönen) ~ an Ihre Frau!** (*geh*) my regards to your wife; **mit freundlichen Grüßen** (*als Briefformel*) Yours sincerely
grüßen ['gry:sən] *vt* to greet; (*Mil*) to salute; **jdn von jdm ~** to give sb sb's regards; **jdn ~ lassen** to send sb one's regards
Grütze ['grʏtsə] (**-, -n**) *f* (*Brei*) gruel; **rote ~** (type of) red fruit jelly
Guatemala [guate'ma:la] (**-s**) *nt* Guatemala
Guayana [gua'ja:na] (**-s**) *nt* Guyana
gucken ['gʊkən] *vi* to look
Guckloch *nt* peephole
Guinea [gi'ne:a] (**-s**) *nt* Guinea
Gulasch ['gu:laʃ] (**-(e)s, -e**) *nt* goulash; **Gulaschkanone** *f* (*Mil: umg*) field kitchen
gültig ['gʏltıç] *adj* valid; **~ werden** to become valid; (*Gesetz, Vertrag*) to come into effect; (*Münze*) to become legal tender; **Gültigkeit** *f* validity; **Gültigkeitsdauer** *f* period of validity
Gummi ['gʊmi] (**-s, -s**) *nt od m* rubber; (*Gummiharze*) gum; (*umg: Kondom*) rubber, Durex®; (*Gummiband*) rubber *od* elastic band; (*Hosengummi*) elastic; **Gummiband** *nt* rubber *od* elastic band; **Gummibärchen** *nt* jelly baby; **Gummigeschoss** *nt* rubber bullet; **Gummiknüppel** *m* rubber truncheon; **Gummiparagraf** *m* ambiguous *od* meaningless law *od* statute; **Gummistiefel** *m* rubber boot, wellington (boot) (*Brit*); **Gummistrumpf** *m* elastic stocking;

Gummizelle *f* padded cell
Gunst [gʊnst] (-) *f* favour (*Brit*), favor (*US*); *siehe auch* **zugunsten**
günstig ['gʏnstɪç] *adj* favourable (*Brit*), favorable (*US*); (*Angebot, Preis etc*) reasonable, good; **bei ~er Witterung** weather permitting; **im ~sten Fall(e)** with luck
Gurgel ['gʊrgəl] (**-, -n**) *f* throat
gurgeln *vi* to gurgle; (*im Rachen*) to gargle
Gurke ['gʊrkə] (**-, -n**) *f* cucumber; **saure ~** pickled cucumber, gherkin
Gurt [gʊrt] (**-(e)s, -e**) *m* belt
Gurtanlegepflicht *f* (*form*) *obligation to wear a safety belt in vehicles*
Gürtel ['gʏrtəl] (**-s, -**) *m* belt; (*Geog*) zone; **Gürtelreifen** *m* radial tyre; **Gürtelrose** *f* shingles *sing od pl*
GUS [ge:|u:'|ɛs] *f abk* (= *Gemeinschaft Unabhängiger Staaten*) CIS
Guss [gʊs] (**-es, ¨-e**) *m* casting; (*Regenguss*) downpour; (*Koch*) glazing; **Gusseisen** *nt* cast iron
Gut [gu:t] (**-(e)s, ¨-er**) *nt* (*Besitz*) possession; (*Landgut*) estate; **Güter** *pl* (*Waren*) goods *pl*

SCHLÜSSELWORT

gut *adj* good; **das ist gut gegen** *od* **für** (*umg*) **Husten** it's good for coughs; **sei so gut (und) gib mir das** would you mind giving me that; **dafür ist er sich zu gut** he wouldn't stoop to that sort of thing; **das ist ja alles gut und schön, aber ...** that's all very well but ...; **du bist gut!** (*umg*) you're a fine one!; **alles Gute** all the best; **also gut** all right then
▷ *adv* well; **gut gehen** to work, come off; **es geht jdm gut** sb's doing fine; **das ist noch einmal gut gegangen** it turned out all right; **gut gehend** thriving; **gut gelaunt** cheerful, in a good mood; **gut gemeint** well meant; **du hast es gut!** you've got it made!; **gut situiert** well-off; **gut unterrichtet** well-informed; **gut, aber ...** OK, but ...; **(na) gut, ich komme** all right, I'll come; **gut drei Stunden** a good three hours; **das kann gut sein** that may well be; **gut und gern** easily; **lass es gut sein** that'll do; *siehe auch* **guttun**

Gut- *zW*: **Gutachten** (**-s, -**) *nt* report; **Gutachter** (**-s, -**) *m* expert; **Gutachterkommission** *f* quango; **gutartig** *adj* good-natured; (*Med*) benign; **gutbürgerlich** *adj* (*Küche*) (good) plain; **Gutdünken** *nt*: **nach Gutdünken** at one's discretion
Güte ['gy:tə] (-) *f* goodness, kindness; (*Qualität*) quality; **ach du liebe** *od* **meine ~!** (*umg*) goodness me!; **Güteklasse** *f* (*Comm*) grade; **Güteklasseneinteilung** *f* (*Comm*) grading
Güter- *zW*: **Güterabfertigung** *f* (*Eisenb*) goods office; **Güterbahnhof** *m* goods station; **Gütertrennung** *f* (*Jur*) separation of property; **Güterverkehr** *m* freight traffic; **Güterwagen** *m* goods waggon (*Brit*), freight car (*US*); **Güterzug** *m* goods train (*Brit*), freight train (*US*)
Gütesiegel *nt* (*Comm*) stamp of quality
gut- *zW*: **gutgläubig** *adj* trusting; **Guthaben** (**-s**) *nt* credit; **guthaben** *unreg vt*: **30 Euro (bei jdm) guthaben** to be in credit (with sb) to the tune of 30 euros; **gutheißen** *unreg vt* to approve (of); **gutherzig** *adj* kind(-hearted)
gütig ['gy:tɪç] *adj* kind
gütlich ['gy:tlɪç] *adj* amicable
gut- *zW*: **gutmachen** *vt* (*in Ordnung bringen: Fehler*) to put right, correct; (*Schaden*) to make good; **gutmütig** *adj* good-natured; **Gutmütigkeit** *f* good nature
Gutsbesitzer, in *m(f)* landowner
Gut- *zW*: **Gutschein** *m* voucher; **gutschreiben** *unreg vt* to credit; **Gutschrift** *f* credit
Gutsherr *m* squire
Gutshof *m* estate
guttun *unreg vi*: **jdm ~** to do sb good
Gutverdienende, r *f(m)* high-income earner
gutwillig *adj* willing
Gymnasiallehrer, in [gʏmnazi'a:lle:rər(ɪn)] *m(f)* ≈ grammar school teacher (*Brit*), high school teacher (*US*)
Gymnasium [gʏm'na:ziʊm] *nt* ≈ grammar school (*Brit*), high school (*US*); *see culture note*

GYMNASIUM

The *Gymnasium* is a selective secondary school. There are nine years of study at a *Gymnasium* leading to the *Abitur* which gives access to higher education. Pupils who successfully complete six years automatically gain the *mittlere Reife*.

Gymnastik [gʏm'nastɪk] *f* exercises *pl*, keep-fit; **~ machen** to do keep-fit (exercises)/ gymnastics
Gynäkologe [gynɛko'lo:gə] (**-n, -n**) *m* gynaecologist (*Brit*), gynecologist (*US*)
Gynäkologin [gynɛko'lo:gɪn] *f* gynaecologist (*Brit*), gynecologist (*US*)

Hh

H, h [haː] *nt* H, h; (*Mus*) B; **H wie Heinrich** ≈ H for Harry, H for How (*US*)
ha *abk* = **Hektar**
Haag [haːk] **(-s)** *m*: **Den ~** The Hague
Haar [haːr] **(-(e)s, -e)** *nt* hair; **um ein ~** nearly; **~e auf den Zähnen haben** to be a tough customer; **sich die ~e raufen** (*umg*) to tear one's hair; **sich** *dat* **in die ~e kriegen** (*umg*) to quarrel; **das ist an den ~en herbeigezogen** that's rather far-fetched; **Haaransatz** *m* hairline; **Haarbürste** *f* hairbrush
haaren *vi, vr* to lose hair
Haaresbreite *f*: **um ~** by a hair's-breadth
Haarfestiger (-s, -) *m* setting lotion
haargenau *adv* precisely
haarig *adj* hairy; (*fig*) nasty
Haar- *zW*: **Haarklammer** *f*, **Haarklemme** *f* hair grip (*Brit*), barrette (*US*); **haarklein** *adv* in minute detail; **haarlos** *adj* hairless; **Haarnadel** *f* hairpin; **haarscharf** *adv* (*beobachten*) very sharply; (*verfehlen*) by a hair's breadth; **Haarschnitt** *m* haircut; **Haarschopf** *m* head of hair; **Haarsieb** *nt* fine sieve; **Haarspalterei** *f* hair-splitting; **Haarspange** *f* hair slide; **haarsträubend** *adj* hair-raising; **Haarteil** *nt* hairpiece; **Haarwaschmittel** *nt* shampoo; **Haarwasser** *nt* hair lotion
Hab [haːp] *nt*: **~ und Gut** possessions *pl*, belongings *pl*, worldly goods *pl*
Habe ['haːbə] **(-)** *f* property
haben ['haːbən] *unreg vt, hilfsverb* to have ▷ *vr unpers*: **und damit hat es sich** (*umg*) and that's that; **Hunger/Angst ~** to be hungry/afraid; **da hast du 10 Mark** there's 10 Marks; **die ~s (ja)** (*umg*) they can afford it; **Ferien ~** to be on holiday; **es am Herzen ~** (*umg*) to have heart trouble; **sie ist noch zu ~** (*umg: nicht verheiratet*) she's still single; **für etw zu ~ sein** to be keen on sth; **sie werden schon merken, was sie an ihm ~** they'll see how valuable he is; **haste was, biste was** (*Sprichwort*) money brings status; **wie gehabt!** some things don't change; **das hast du jetzt davon** now see what's happened; **woher hast du das?** where did you get that from?; **was hast du denn?** what's the matter (with you)?; **ich habe zu tun** I'm busy
Haben (-s, -) *nt* (*Comm*) credit
Habenseite *f* (*Comm*) credit side
Habgier *f* avarice
habgierig *adj* avaricious
habhaft *adj*: **jds/einer Sache ~ werden** (*geh*) to get hold of sb/sth
Habicht ['haːbɪçt] **(-(e)s, -e)** *m* hawk
Habilitation [habilitatsi'oːn] *f* (*Lehrberechtigung*) postdoctoral lecturing qualification
Habseligkeiten ['haːpzeːlɪçkaɪtən] *pl* belongings *pl*
Habsucht ['haːpzʊxt] *f* greed
Hachse ['haksə] **(-, -n)** *f* (*Koch*) knuckle
Hackbraten *m* meat loaf
Hackbrett *nt* chopping board; (*Mus*) dulcimer
Hacke ['hakə] **(-, -n)** *f* hoe; (*Ferse*) heel
hacken *vt* to hack, chop; (*Erde*) to hoe
Hacker ['hakər] **(-s, -)** *m* (*Comput*) hacker
Hackfleisch *nt* mince, minced meat, ground meat (*US*)
Hackordnung *f* (*lit, fig*) pecking order
Häcksel ['hɛksəl] **(-s)** *m od nt* chopped straw, chaff
hadern ['haːdərn] *vi* (*geh*): **~ mit** to quarrel with; (*unzufrieden sein*) to be at odds with
Hafen ['haːfən] **(-s, ¨)** *m* harbour, harbor (*US*), port; (*fig*) haven; **Hafenanlagen** *pl* docks *pl*; **Hafenarbeiter** *m* docker; **Hafendamm** *m* jetty, mole; **Hafengebühren** *pl* harbo(u)r dues *pl*; **Hafenstadt** *f* port
Hafer ['haːfər] **(-s, -)** *m* oats *pl*; **ihn sticht der ~** (*umg*) he is feeling his oats; **Haferbrei** *m* porridge (*Brit*), oatmeal (*US*); **Haferflocken** *pl* rolled oats *pl* (*Brit*), oatmeal (*US*); **Haferschleim** *m* gruel
Haff [haf] **(-s, -s** *od* **-e)** *nt* lagoon
Haft [haft] **(-)** *f* custody; **Haftanstalt** *f* detention centre (*Brit*) *od* center (*US*); **haftbar** *adj* liable, responsible; **Haftbefehl** *m* warrant (for arrest); **einen Haftbefehl gegen jdn ausstellen** to issue a warrant for sb's arrest
haften *vi* to stick, cling; **~ für** to be liable *od* responsible for; **für Garderobe kann nicht gehaftet werden** all articles are left at owner's risk; **~ bleiben (an** *+dat***)** to stick (to)
Häftling ['hɛftlɪŋ] *m* prisoner
Haft- *zW*: **Haftpflicht** *f* liability; **Haftpflichtversicherung** *f* third party insurance; **Haftrichter** *m* magistrate

Haftschalen *pl* contact lenses *pl*
Haftung *f* liability
Hagebutte ['ha:gəbʊtə] (**-, -n**) *f* rose hip
Hagedorn *m* hawthorn
Hagel ['ha:gəl] (**-s**) *m* hail; **Hagelkorn** *nt* hailstone; (*Med*) eye cyst
hageln *vi unpers* to hail
Hagelschauer *m* (short) hailstorm
hager ['ha:gər] *adj* gaunt
Häher ['hɛ:ər] (**-s, -**) *m* jay
Hahn [ha:n] (**-(e)s, ¨-e**) *m* cock; (*Wasserhahn*) tap, faucet (*US*); (*Abzug*) trigger; **~ im Korb sein** (*umg*) to be cock of the walk; **danach kräht kein ~ mehr** (*umg*) no one cares two hoots about that any more
Hähnchen ['hɛ:nçən] *nt* cockerel; (*Koch*) chicken
Hai ['haɪ], **Haifisch** ['haɪfɪʃ] (**-(e)s, -e**) *m* shark
Haiti [ha'i:ti] (**-s**) *nt* Haiti
Häkchen ['hɛ:kçən] *nt* small hook
Häkelarbeit *f* crochet work
häkeln ['hɛ:kəln] *vt* to crochet
Häkelnadel *f* crochet hook
Haken ['ha:kən] (**-s, -**) *m* hook; (*fig*) catch; **einen ~ schlagen** to dart sideways; **Hakenkreuz** *nt* swastika; **Hakennase** *f* hooked nose
halb [halp] *adj* half ▷ *adv* (*beinahe*) almost; **~ eins** half past twelve; **~ offen** half-open; **ein ~es Dutzend** half a dozen; **nichts H~es und nichts Ganzes** neither one thing nor the other; **(noch) ein ~es Kind sein** to be scarcely more than a child; **das ist ~ so schlimm** it's not as bad as all that; **mit jdm ~e-halbe machen** (*umg*) to go halves with sb
halb- *zW*: **Halbblut** *nt* (*Tier*) crossbreed; **Halbbruder** *m* half-brother; **Halbdunkel** *nt* semi-darkness
halber ['halbər] *präp +gen* (*wegen*) on account of; (*für*) for the sake of
Halb- *zW*: **halbfett** *adj* medium fat; **Halbfinale** *nt* semi-final; **Halbheit** *f* half-measure; **halbherzig** *adj* half-hearted
halbieren [hal'bi:rən] *vt* to halve
Halb- *zW*: **Halbinsel** *f* peninsula; **halbjährlich** *adj* half-yearly; **Halbkreis** *m* semicircle; **Halbkugel** *f* hemisphere; **halblang** *adj*: **nun mach mal halblang!** (*umg*) now wait a minute!; **halblaut** *adv* in an undertone; **Halbleiter** *m* (*Phys*) semiconductor; **halbmast** *adv* at half-mast; **Halbmond** *m* half-moon; (*fig*) crescent; **Halbpension** *f* half-board (*Brit*), European plan (*US*); **Halbschuh** *m* shoe; **Halbschwester** *f* half-sister; **halbseiden** *adj* (*lit*) fifty per cent silk; (*fig: Dame*) fast; (*: homosexuell*) gay; **halbseitig** *adj* (*Anzeige*) half-page; **Halbstarke, r** *f(m)* hooligan, rowdy; **halbtags** *adv*: **halbtags arbeiten** to work part-time; **Halbtagsarbeit** *f* part-time work; **Halbtagskraft** *f* part-time worker; **Halbton** *m* half-tone; (*Mus*) semitone; **halbtrocken** *adj* medium-dry; **Halbwaise** *f child/person who has lost one parent*; **halbwegs** *adv* half-way; **halbwegs besser** more or less better; **Halbwelt** *f* demimonde; **Halbwertzeit** *f* half-life; **Halbwüchsige, r** *f(m)* adolescent; **Halbzeit** *f* (*Sport*) half; (*Pause*) half-time
Halde ['haldə] *f* tip; (*Schlackenhalde*) slag heap
half *etc* [half] *vb siehe* **helfen**
Hälfte ['hɛlftə] (**-, -n**) *f* half; **um die ~ steigen** to increase by half
Halfter[1] ['halftər] (**-s, -**) *m od nt* (*für Tiere*) halter
Halfter[2] ['halftər] (**-, -n** *od* **-s, -**) *f od nt* (*Pistolenhalfter*) holster
Hall [hal] (**-(e)s, -e**) *m* sound
Halle ['halə] (**-, -n**) *f* hall; (*Aviat*) hangar
hallen *vi* to echo, resound
Hallen- *in zW* indoor; **Hallenbad** *nt* indoor swimming pool
hallo [ha'lo:] *interj* hallo
Halluzination [halutsinatsi'o:n] *f* hallucination
Halm ['halm] (**-(e)s, -e**) *m* blade, stalk
Hals [hals] (**-es, ¨-e**) *m* neck; (*Kehle*) throat; **sich** *dat* **nach jdm/etw den ~ verrenken** (*umg*) to crane one's neck to see sb/sth; **jdm um den ~ fallen** to fling one's arms around sb's neck; **aus vollem ~(e)** at the top of one's voice; **~ über Kopf** in a rush; **jdn auf dem** *od* **am ~ haben** (*umg*) to be lumbered *od* saddled with sb; **das hängt mir zum ~ raus** (*umg*) I'm sick and tired of it; **sie hat es in den falschen ~ bekommen** (*falsch verstehen*) she took it wrongly; **Halsabschneider** (*pej: umg*) *m* shark; **Halsband** *nt* (*Hundehalsband*) collar; **halsbrecherisch** *adj* (*Tempo*) breakneck; (*Fahrt*) hair-raising; **Halskette** *f* necklace; **Halskrause** *f* ruff; **Hals-Nasen-Ohren-Arzt** *m* ear, nose and throat specialist; **Halsschlagader** *f* carotid artery; **Halsschmerzen** *pl* sore throat *sing*; **halsstarrig** *adj* stubborn, obstinate; **Halstuch** *nt* scarf; **Hals- und Beinbruch** *interj* good luck; **Halsweh** *nt* sore throat; **Halswirbel** *m* cervical vertebra
Halt [halt] (**-(e)s, -e**) *m* stop; (*fester Halt*) hold; (*innerer Halt*) stability; **~!, halt!** stop!, halt!; **~ machen** to stop
hält [hɛlt] *vb siehe* **halten**
Halt- *zW*: **haltbar** *adj* durable; (*Lebensmittel*) non-perishable; (*Mil, fig*) tenable; **haltbar bis 6.11.** use by 6 Nov.; **Haltbarkeit** *f* durability; (non-)perishability; tenability; (*von Lebensmitteln*) shelf life; **Haltbarkeitsdatum** *nt* best-before date
halten ['haltən] *unreg vt* to keep; (*festhalten*) to hold ▷ *vi* to hold; (*frisch bleiben*) to keep; (*stoppen*) to stop ▷ *vr* (*frisch bleiben*) to keep; (*sich behaupten*) to hold out; **den Mund ~** (*umg*) to keep one's mouth shut; **~ für** to regard as; **~ von** to think of; **das kannst du ~ wie du willst** that's completely up to you; **der Film hält nicht, was er verspricht** the film doesn't live up to expectations; **davon halt(e) ich nichts** I don't think much of it; **zu jdm ~** to stand *od* stick by sb; **an sich** *akk* **~** to restrain o.s.; **auf sich** *akk* **~** (*auf Äußeres*

achten) to take a pride in o.s.; **er hat sich gut gehalten** (*umg*) he's well-preserved; **sich an ein Versprechen ~** to keep a promise; **sich rechts/links ~** to keep to the right/left
Halter ['haltər] (**-s, -**) *m* (*Halterung*) holder
Haltestelle *f* stop
Halteverbot *nt*: **absolutes ~** no stopping; **eingeschränktes ~** no waiting; **hier ist ~** you cannot stop here
haltlos *adj* unstable
Haltlosigkeit *f* instability
haltmachen *vi* to stop
Haltung *f* posture; (*fig*) attitude; (*Selbstbeherrschung*) composure; **~ bewahren** to keep one's composure
Halunke [ha'lʊŋkə] (**-n, -n**) *m* rascal
Hamburg ['hambʊrk] (**-s**) *nt* Hamburg
Hamburger (**-s, -**) *m* (*Koch*) burger, hamburger
Hamburger, in (**-s, -**) *m(f)* native of Hamburg
Hameln ['ha:məln] *nt* Hamelin
hämisch ['hɛ:mɪʃ] *adj* malicious
Hammel ['haməl] (**-s, ⸚** *od* **-**) *m* wether; **Hammelfleisch** *nt* mutton; **Hammelkeule** *f* leg of mutton
Hammelsprung *m* (*Parl*) division
Hammer ['hamər] (**-s, ⸚**) *m* hammer; **das ist ein ~!** (*umg: unerhört*) that's absurd!
hämmern ['hɛmərn] *vt, vi* to hammer
Hammondorgel ['hæmənd|ɔrgəl] *f* electric organ
Hämorrhoiden [hɛmɔro'i:dən], **Hämorriden** [hɛmɔ'ri:dən] *pl* piles *pl*, haemorrhoids *pl* (*Brit*), hemorrhoids *pl* (*US*)
Hampelmann ['hampəlman] *m* (*lit, fig*) puppet
Hamster ['hamstər] (**-s, -**) *m* hamster
Hamsterei [hamstə'raɪ] *f* hoarding
Hamsterer (**-s, -**) *m* hoarder
hamstern *vi* to hoard
Hand [hant] (**-, ⸚e**) *f* hand; **etw zur ~ haben** to have sth to hand; (*Ausrede, Erklärung*) to have sth ready; **jdm zur ~ gehen** to lend sb a helping hand; **zu Händen von jdm** for the attention of sb; **in festen Händen sein** to be spoken for; **die ~ für jdn ins Feuer legen** to vouch for sb; **hinter vorgehaltener ~** on the quiet; **~ aufs Herz** cross your heart; **jdn auf Händen tragen** to cherish sb; **bei etw die** *od* **seine ~ im Spiel haben** to have a hand in sth; **eine ~ wäscht die andere** (*Sprichwort*) if you scratch my back I'll scratch yours; **das hat weder ~ noch Fuß** that doesn't make sense; **das liegt auf der ~** (*umg*) that's obvious; **unter der ~** secretly; (*verkaufen*) privately; *siehe auch* **anhand**; **Handarbeit** *f* manual work; (*Nadelarbeit*) needlework; **Handarbeiter** *m* manual worker; **Handball** *m* handball; **Handbesen** *m* brush; **Handbetrieb** *m*: **mit Handbetrieb** hand-operated; **Handbewegung** *f* gesture; **Handbibliothek** *f* (*in Bibliothek*) reference section; (*auf Schreibtisch*) reference books *pl*; **Handbremse** *f* handbrake; **Handbuch** *nt* handbook, manual
Händedruck *m* handshake
Händeklatschen *nt* clapping, applause
Handel[1] ['handəl] (**-s**) *m* trade; (*Geschäft*) transaction; **im ~ sein** to be on the market; **(mit jdm) ~ treiben** to trade (with sb); **etw in den ~ bringen/aus dem ~ ziehen** to put sth on/take sth off the market
Handel[2] (**-s, ⸚**) *m* quarrel
handeln ['handəln] *vi* to trade; (*tätig werden*) to act ▷ *vr unpers*: **sich ~ um** to be a question of, be about; **~ von** to be about; **ich lasse mit mir ~** I'm open to persuasion; (*in Bezug auf Preis*) I'm open to offers
Handeln (**-s**) *nt* action
handelnd *adj*: **die ~en Personen in einem Drama** the characters in a drama
Handels- *zW*: **Handelsbank** *f* merchant bank (*Brit*), commercial bank; **Handelsbilanz** *f* balance of trade; **aktive/passive Handelsbilanz** balance of trade surplus/deficit; **Handelsdelegation** *f* trade mission; **handelseinig** *adj*: **mit jdm handelseinig werden** to conclude a deal with sb; **Handelsgesellschaft** *f* commercial company; **Handelskammer** *f* chamber of commerce; **Handelsklasse** *f* grade; **Handelsmarine** *f* merchant navy; **Handelsmarke** *f* trade name; **Handelsname** *m* trade name; **Handelsrecht** *nt* commercial law; **Handelsregister** *nt* register of companies; **Handelsreisende, r** *f(m)* = **Handlungsreisende(r)** commercial traveller; **Handelssanktionen** *pl* trade sanctions *pl*; **Handelsschule** *f* business school; **Handelsspanne** *f* gross margin, mark-up; **Handelssperre** *f* trade embargo; **handelsüblich** *adj* customary; **Handelsvertreter** *m* sales representative; **Handelsvertretung** *f* trade mission; **Handelsware** *f* commodity
händeringend ['hɛndərɪŋənd] *adv* wringing one's hands; (*fig*) imploringly
Hand- *zW*: **Handfeger** (**-s, -**) *m* brush; **Handfertigkeit** *f* dexterity; **handfest** *adj* hefty; **Handfläche** *f* palm *od* flat (of one's hand); **handgearbeitet** *adj* handmade; **Handgelenk** *nt* wrist; **aus dem Handgelenk** (*umg: ohne Mühe*) effortlessly; (*: improvisiert*) off the cuff; **Handgemenge** *nt* scuffle; **Handgepäck** *nt* hand baggage *od* luggage; **handgeschrieben** *adj* handwritten; **Handgranate** *f* hand grenade; **handgreiflich** *adj* palpable; **handgreiflich werden** to become violent; **Handgriff** *m* flick of the wrist; **Handhabe** *f*: **ich habe gegen ihn keine Handhabe** (*fig*) I have no hold on him; **handhaben** *unreg vt untr* to handle; **Handkarren** *m* handcart; **Handkäse** *m* *strong-smelling, round German cheese*; **Handkuss** *m* kiss on the hand; **Handlanger** (**-s, -**) *m* odd-job man, handyman; (*fig: Untergeordneter*) dogsbody
Händler ['hɛndlər] (**-s, -**) *m* trader, dealer
handlich ['hantlɪç] *adj* handy
Handlung ['handlʊŋ] *f* action; (*Tat*) act; (*in*

Buch) plot; (*Geschäft*) shop
Handlungs- *zW*: **Handlungsablauf** *m* plot; **Handlungsbevollmächtigte, r** *f(m)* authorized agent; **handlungsfähig** *adj* (*Regierung*) able to act; (*Jur*) empowered to act; **Handlungsfreiheit** *f* freedom of action; **handlungsorientiert** *adj* action-orientated; **Handlungsreisende, r** *f(m)* commercial traveller (*Brit*), traveling salesman (*US*); **Handlungsvollmacht** *f* proxy; **Handlungsweise** *f* manner of dealing
Hand- *zW*: **Handpflege** *f* manicure; **Handschelle** *f* handcuff; **Handschlag** *m* handshake; **keinen Handschlag tun** not to do a stroke (of work); **Handschrift** *f* handwriting; (*Text*) manuscript; **handschriftlich** *adj* handwritten ▷ *adv* (*korrigieren, einfügen*) by hand; **Handschuh** *m* glove; **Handschuhfach** *nt* (*Aut*) glove compartment; **Handtasche** *f* handbag (*Brit*), pocket book (*US*), purse (*US*); **Handtuch** *nt* towel; **Handumdrehen** *nt*: **im Handumdrehen** (*fig*) in the twinkling of an eye
Handwerk *nt* trade, craft; **jdm das ~ legen** (*fig*) to put a stop to sb's game
Handwerker (**-s, -**) *m* craftsman, artisan; **wir haben seit Wochen die ~ im Haus** we've had workmen in the house for weeks
Handwerkskammer *f* trade corporation
Handwerkszeug *nt* tools *pl*
Handwörterbuch *nt* concise dictionary
Handy ['hɛndi] (**-s, -s**) *nt* (*Tel*) mobile (phone)
Handzeichen *nt* signal; (*Geste*) sign; (*bei Abstimmung*) show of hands
Handzettel *m* leaflet, handbill
Hanf [hanf] (**-(e)s**) *m* hemp
Hang [haŋ] (**-(e)s, ¨-e**) *m* inclination; (*Abhang*) slope
Hänge- ['hɛŋə] *in zW* hanging; **Hängebrücke** *f* suspension bridge; **Hängematte** *f* hammock
Hängen ['hɛŋən] *nt*: **mit ~ und Würgen** (*umg*) by the skin of one's teeth
hängen *unreg vi* to hang ▷ *vt*: **~ (an** *+akk***)** to hang (on(to)); **an jdm ~** (*fig*) to be attached to sb; **~ bleiben** to be caught; (*fig*) to remain, stick; **~ bleiben an** *+dat* to catch *od* get caught on; **es bleibt ja doch alles an mir ~** (*fig: umg*) in the end it's all down to me anyhow; **~ lassen** (*vergessen*) to leave behind; **sich ~ lassen** to let o.s. go; **den Kopf ~ lassen** (*fig*) to be downcast; **die ganze Sache hängt an ihm** it all depends on him; **sich ~ an** *+akk* to hang on to, cling to
hängend *adj*: **mit ~er Zunge kam er angelaufen** (*fig*) he came running up panting
Hängeschloss *nt* padlock
Hanglage *f*: **in ~** situated on a slope
Hannover [ha'no:fər] (**-s**) *nt* Hanover
Hannoveraner, in [hanovə'ra:nər(ɪn)] (**-s, -**) *m(f)* Hanoverian
hänseln ['hɛnzəln] *vt* to tease
Hansestadt ['hanzəʃtat] *f* Hanseatic *od* Hanse town
Hanswurst [hans'vʊrst] (**-(e)s, -e** *od* **-würste**) *m* clown
Hantel ['hantəl] (**-, -n**) *f* (*Sport*) dumb-bell
hantieren [han'ti:rən] *vi* to work, be busy; **mit etw ~** to handle sth
hapern ['ha:pərn] *vi unpers*: **es hapert an etw** *dat* there is a lack of sth
Happen ['hapən] (**-s, -**) *m* mouthful
happig ['hapɪç] (*umg*) *adj* steep
Hardware ['ha:dwɛə] (**-, -s**) *f* hardware
Harfe ['harfə] (**-, -n**) *f* harp
Harke ['harkə] (**-, -n**) *f* rake
harken *vt, vi* to rake
harmlos ['harmlo:s] *adj* harmless
Harmlosigkeit *f* harmlessness
Harmonie [harmo'ni:] *f* harmony
harmonieren *vi* to harmonize
Harmonika [har'mo:nika] (**-, -s**) *f* (*Ziehharmonika*) concertina
harmonisch [har'mo:nɪʃ] *adj* harmonious
Harmonium [har'mo:niʊm] (**-s, -nien** *od* **-s**) *nt* harmonium
Harn ['harn] (**-(e)s, -e**) *m* urine; **Harnblase** *f* bladder
Harnisch ['harnɪʃ] (**-(e)s, -e**) *m* armour, armor (*US*); **jdn in ~ bringen** to infuriate sb; **in ~ geraten** to become angry
Harpune [har'pu:nə] (**-, -n**) *f* harpoon
harren ['harən] *vi*: **~ auf** *+akk* to wait for
Harsch [harʃ] (**-(e)s**) *m* frozen snow
harschig *adj* (*Schnee*) frozen
hart [hart] *adj* hard; (*fig*) harsh ▷ *adv*: **das ist ~ an der Grenze** that's almost going too far; **~e Währung** hard currency; **~ bleiben** to stand firm; **~ gekocht** hard-boiled; **~ gesotten** (*Ei*) hard-boiled; **es geht ~ auf ~** it's a tough fight
Härte ['hɛrtə] (**-, -n**) *f* hardness; (*fig*) harshness; **soziale ~n** social hardships; **Härtefall** *m* case of hardship; (*umg: Mensch*) hardship case; **Härteklausel** *f* hardship clause
härten *vt, vr* to harden
hart- *zW*: **Hartfaserplatte** *f* hardboard, fiberboard (*US*); **hartgesotten** *adj* (*Kerl*) tough, hard-boiled; **hartherzig** *adj* hard-hearted; **hartnäckig** *adj* stubborn; **Hartnäckigkeit** *f* stubbornness
Harz[1] [ha:rts] (**-es, -e**) *nt* resin
Harz[2] (**-es**) *m* (*Geog*) Harz Mountains *pl*
Haschee [ha'ʃe:] (**-s, -s**) *nt* hash
haschen ['haʃən] *vt* to catch, snatch ▷ *vi* (*umg*) to smoke hash
Haschisch ['haʃɪʃ] (**-**) *nt* hashish
Hase ['ha:zə] (**-n, -n**) *m* hare; **falscher ~** (*Koch*) meat loaf; **wissen, wie der ~ läuft** (*fig: umg*) to know which way the wind blows; **mein Name ist ~(, ich weiß von nichts)** I don't know anything about anything
Haselnuss ['ha:zəlnʊs] *f* hazelnut
Hasenfuß *m* coward
Hasenscharte *f* harelip
Haspel (**-, -n**) *f* reel, bobbin; (*Winde*) winch
Hass [has] (**-es**) *m* hate, hatred; **einen ~ (auf**

jdn) haben (*umg*: *Wut*) to be really mad (with sb)
hassen ['hasən] *vt* to hate; **etw ~ wie die Pest** (*umg*) to detest sth
hassenswert *adj* hateful
hässlich ['hɛslɪç] *adj* ugly; (*gemein*) nasty; **Hässlichkeit** *f* ugliness; nastiness
Hassliebe *f* love-hate relationship
Hast [hast] (-) *f* haste
hast *vb siehe* **haben**
hasten *vi, vr* to rush
hastig *adj* hasty
hat [hat] *vb siehe* **haben**
hätscheln ['hɛtʃəln] *vt* to pamper; (*zärtlich*) to cuddle
hatte *etc* ['hatə] *vb siehe* **haben**
hätte *etc* ['hɛtə] *vb siehe* **haben**
Haube ['haʊbə] (**-, -n**) *f* hood; (*Mütze*) cap; (*Aut*) bonnet (*Brit*), hood (*US*); **unter der ~ sein/ unter die ~ kommen** (*hum*) to be/get married
Hauch [haʊx] (**-(e)s, -e**) *m* breath; (*Lufthauch*) breeze; (*fig*) trace; **hauchdünn** *adj* extremely thin; (*Scheiben*) wafer-thin; (*fig*: *Mehrheit*) extremely narrow; **hauchen** *vi* to breathe; **hauchfein** *adj* very fine
Haue ['haʊə] (**-, -n**) *f* hoe; (*Pickel*) pick; (*umg*) hiding
hauen *unreg vt* to hew, cut; (*umg*) to thrash
Hauer ['haʊər] (**-s, -**) *m* (*Min*) face-worker
Häufchen ['hɔʏfçən] *nt*: **ein ~ Unglück** *od* **Elend** a picture of misery
Haufen ['haʊfən] (**-s, -**) *m* heap; (*Leute*) crowd; **ein ~ (Bücher)** (*umg*) loads *od* a lot (of books); **auf einem ~** in one heap; **etw über den ~ werfen** (*umg*: *verwerfen*) to chuck sth out; **jdn über den ~ rennen** *od* **fahren** *etc* (*umg*) to knock sb down
häufen ['hɔʏfən] *vt* to pile up ▷ *vr* to accumulate
haufenweise *adv* in heaps; in droves; **etw ~ haben** to have piles of sth
häufig ['hɔʏfɪç] *adj* frequent ▷ *adv* frequently; **Häufigkeit** *f* frequency
Haupt [haʊpt] (**-(e)s, Häupter**) *nt* head; (*Oberhaupt*) chief ▷ *in zW* main; **Hauptakteur** *m* (*lit, fig*) leading light; (*pej*) main figure; **Hauptaktionär** *m* major shareholder; **Hauptbahnhof** *m* central station; **hauptberuflich** *adv* as one's main occupation; **Hauptbuch** *nt* (*Comm*) ledger; **Hauptdarsteller, in** *m(f)* leading actor, leading actress; **Haupteingang** *m* main entrance; **Hauptfach** *nt* (*Sch, Univ*) main subject, major (*US*); **etw im Hauptfach studieren** to study sth as one's main subject, major in sth (*US*); **Hauptfilm** *m* main film; **Hauptgericht** *nt* main course; **Hauptgeschäftsstelle** *f* head office; **Hauptgeschäftszeit** *f* peak (shopping) period; **Hauptgewinn** *m* first prize; **einer der Hauptgewinne** one of the main prizes; **Hauptleitung** *f* mains *pl*
Häuptling ['hɔʏptlɪŋ] *m* chief(tain)

Haupt- *zW*: **Hauptmahlzeit** *f* main meal; **Hauptmann** (**-(e)s**, *pl* **-leute**) *m* (*Mil*) captain; **Hauptnahrungsmittel** *nt* staple food; **Hauptperson** *f* (*im Roman usw*) main character; (*fig*) central figure; **Hauptpostamt** *nt* main post office; **Hauptquartier** *nt* headquarters *pl*; **Hauptrolle** *f* leading part; **Hauptsache** *f* main thing; **in der Hauptsache** in the main, mainly; **hauptsächlich** *adj* chief ▷ *adv* chiefly; **Hauptsaison** *f* peak *od* high season; **Hauptsatz** *m* main clause; **Hauptschlagader** *f* aorta; **Hauptschlüssel** *m* master key
Hauptschule *f* ≈ secondary modern (school) (*Brit*), junior high (school) (*US*); *see culture note*

HAUPTSCHULE

The *Hauptschule* is a non-selective school which pupils attend after the *Grundschule*. They complete five years of study and most go on to do some training in a practical subject or trade.

Haupt- *zW*: **Hauptsendezeit** *f* (*TV*) prime time; **Hauptstadt** *f* capital; **Hauptstraße** *f* main street; **Hauptverkehrsstraße** *f* (*in Stadt*) main street; (*Durchgangsstraße*) main thoroughfare; (*zwischen Städten*) main highway, trunk road (*Brit*); **Hauptverkehrszeit** *f* rush hour; **Hauptversammlung** *f* general meeting; **Hauptwohnsitz** *m* main place of residence; **Hauptwort** *nt* noun
hau ruck ['hau 'rʊk] *interj* heave-ho
Haus [haʊs] (**-es, Häuser**) *nt* house; **nach ~e** home; **zu ~e** at home; **fühl dich wie zu ~e!** make yourself at home!; **ein Freund des ~es** a friend of the family; **~ halten** (*sparen*) to economize; **wir liefern frei ~** (*Comm*) we offer free delivery; **das erste ~ am Platze** (*Hotel*) the best hotel in town; **Hausangestellte** *f* domestic servant; **Hausarbeit** *f* housework; (*Sch*) homework; **Hausarrest** *m* (*im Internat*) detention; (*Jur*) house arrest; **Hausarzt** *m* family doctor; **Hausaufgabe** *f* (*Sch*) homework; **Hausbesetzung** *f* squat; **Hausbesitzer** *m* house-owner; **Hausbesuch** *m* home visit; (*von Arzt*) house call
Häuschen ['hɔʏsçən] *nt*: **ganz aus dem ~ sein** (*fig*: *umg*) to be out of one's mind (with excitement/fear *etc*)
Haus *zW*: **Hausdurchsuchung** *f* police raid; **Hausdurchsuchungsbefehl** *m* search warrant
Hauseigentümer *m* house-owner
hausen ['haʊzən] *vi* to live (in poverty); (*pej*) to wreak havoc
Häuser- *zW*: **Häuserblock** *m* block (of houses); **Häusermakler** *m* estate agent (*Brit*), real estate agent (*US*); **Häuserreihe** *f*, **Häuserzeile** *f* row of houses; (*aneinandergebaut*) terrace (*Brit*)
Haus- *zW*: **Hausfrau** *f* housewife; **Hausfreund** *m* family friend; (*umg*) lover; **Hausfriedensbruch** *m* (*Jur*) trespass (*in sb's house*); **Hausgebrauch** *m*: **für den**

Hausgebrauch (*Gerät*) for domestic *od* household use; **hausgemacht** *adj* home-made; **Hausgemeinschaft** *f* household (community); **Haushalt** *m* household; (*Pol*) budget; **haushalten** *unreg vi* (*old*) to keep house; (*sparen*) to economize; **Haushälterin** *f* housekeeper

Haushalts- *zW*: **Haushaltsauflösung** *f* dissolution of the household; **Haushaltsbuch** *nt* housekeeping book; **Haushaltsdebatte** *f* (*Parl*) budget debate; **Haushaltsgeld** *nt* housekeeping (money); **Haushaltsgerät** *nt* domestic appliance; **Haushaltshilfe** *f* domestic *od* home help; **Haushaltsjahr** *nt* (*Pol, Wirts*) financial *od* fiscal year; **Haushaltsperiode** *f* budget period; **Haushaltsplan** *m* budget

Haus- *zW*: **Haushaltung** *f* housekeeping; **Hausherr** *m* host; (*Vermieter*) landlord; **haushoch** *adv*: **haushoch verlieren** to lose by a mile

hausieren [haʊ'zi:rən] *vi* to peddle

Hausierer (**-s, -**) *m* pedlar (*Brit*), peddler (*US*)

hausintern ['haus|ɪntɛrn] *adj* internal company *attrib*

häuslich ['hɔʏslɪç] *adj* domestic; **sich irgendwo ~ einrichten** *od* **niederlassen** to settle in somewhere; **Häuslichkeit** *f* domesticity

Hausmacherart ['hausmaxər|a:rt] *f*: **Wurst** *etc* **nach ~** home-made-style sausage *etc*

Haus- *zW*: **Hausmann** (**-(e)s**, *pl* **-männer**) *m* (*den Haushalt versorgender Mann*) househusband; **Hausmarke** *f* (*eigene Marke*) own brand; (*bevorzugte Marke*) favourite (*Brit*) *od* favorite (*US*) brand; **Hausmeister** *m* caretaker, janitor; **Hausmittel** *nt* household remedy; **Hausnummer** *f* house number; **Hausordnung** *f* house rules *pl*; **Hausputz** *m* house cleaning; **Hausratversicherung** *f* (household) contents insurance; **Hausschlüssel** *m* front-door key; **Hausschuh** *m* slipper; **Hausschwamm** *m* dry rot

Hausse ['ho:sə] (**-, -n**) *f* (*Wirts*) boom; (*Börse*) bull market; **~ an** *+dat* boom in

Haus- *zW*: **Haussegen** *m*: **bei ihnen hängt der Haussegen schief** (*hum*) they're a bit short on domestic bliss; **Hausstand** *m*: **einen Hausstand gründen** to set up house *od* home; **Haussuchung** *f* = **Hausdurchsuchung**; **Haussuchungsbefehl** *m* = **Hausdurchsuchungsbefehl**; **Haustier** *nt* domestic animal; **Haustür** *f* front door; **Hausverbot** *nt*: **jdm Hausverbot erteilen** to ban sb from the house; **Hausverwalter** *m* property manager; **Hausverwaltung** *f* property management; **Hauswirt** *m* landlord; **Hauswirtschaft** *f* domestic science; **Haus-zu-haus-Verkauf** *m* door-to-door selling

Haut [haʊt] (**-, Häute**) *f* skin; (*Tierhaut*) hide; **mit ~ und Haar(en)** (*umg*) completely; **aus der ~ fahren** (*umg*) to go through the roof; **Hautarzt** *m* skin specialist, dermatologist

häuten ['hɔʏtən] *vt* to skin ▷ *vr* to shed one's skin

hauteng *adj* skintight

Hautfarbe *f* complexion

Hautkrebs *m* (*Med*) skin cancer

Havanna [ha'vana] (**-s**) *nt* Havana

Havel ['ha:fəl] (-) *f* (*Fluss*) Havel

Haxe ['haksə] (**-, -n**) *f* = **Hachse**

Hbf. *abk* = **Hauptbahnhof**

H-Bombe ['ha:bɔmbə] *f abk* H-bomb

Hebamme ['he:p|amə] *f* midwife

Hebel ['he:bəl] (**-s, -**) *m* lever; **alle ~ in Bewegung setzen** (*umg*) to move heaven and earth; **am längeren ~ sitzen** (*umg*) to have the whip hand

heben ['he:bən] *unreg vt* to raise, lift; (*steigern*) to increase; **einen ~ gehen** (*umg*) to go for a drink

Hebräer, in [he'brɛ:ər(ɪn)] (**-s, -**) *m(f)* Hebrew

hebräisch [he'brɛ:ɪʃ] *adj* Hebrew

Hebriden [he'bri:dən] *pl*: **die ~** the Hebrides *pl*

hecheln ['hɛçəln] *vi* (*Hund*) to pant

Hecht [hɛçt] (**-(e)s, -e**) *m* pike; **Hechtsprung** *m* (*beim Schwimmen*) racing dive; (*beim Turnen*) forward dive; (*Fussball: umg*) dive

Heck [hɛk] (**-(e)s, -e**) *nt* stern; (*von Auto*) rear

Hecke ['hɛkə] (**-, -n**) *f* hedge

Heckenrose *f* dog rose

Heckenschütze *m* sniper

Heck- *zW*: **Heckfenster** *nt* (*Aut*) rear window; **Heckklappe** *f* tailgate; **Heckmotor** *m* rear engine

heda ['he:da] *interj* hey there

Heer [he:r] (**-(e)s, -e**) *nt* army

Hefe ['he:fə] (**-, -n**) *f* yeast

Heft ['hɛft] (**-(e)s, -e**) *nt* exercise book; (*Zeitschrift*) number; (*von Messer*) haft; **jdm das ~ aus der Hand nehmen** (*fig*) to seize control *od* power from sb

Heftchen *nt* (*Fahrkartenheftchen*) book of tickets; (*Briefmarkenheftchen*) book of stamps

heften *vt*: **~ (an** *+akk***)** to fasten (to); (*nähen*) to tack (on (to)); (*mit Heftmaschine*) to staple *od* fasten (to) ▷ *vr*: **sich an jds Fersen** *od* **Sohlen ~** (*fig*) to dog sb's heels

Hefter (**-s, -**) *m* folder

heftig *adj* fierce, violent; **Heftigkeit** *f* fierceness, violence

Heft- *zW*: **Heftklammer** *f* staple; **Heftmaschine** *f* stapling machine; **Heftpflaster** *nt* sticking plaster; **Heftzwecke** *f* drawing pin (*Brit*), thumb tack (*US*)

hegen ['he:gən] *vt* to nurse; (*fig*) to harbour (*Brit*), harbor (*US*), foster

Hehl [he:l] *m od nt*: **kein(en) ~ aus etw machen** to make no secret of sth

Hehler (**-s, -**) *m* receiver (of stolen goods), fence

Heide[1] ['haɪdə] (**-, -n**) *f* heath, moor; (*Heidekraut*) heather

Heide[2] ['haɪdə] (**-n, -n**) *m* heathen, pagan

Heidekraut *nt* heather

Heidelbeere *f* bilberry

Heiden- *zW*: **Heidenangst** (*umg*) *f*: **eine**

Heidenangst vor etw/jdm haben to be scared stiff of sth/sb; **Heidenarbeit** (*umg*) *f* real slog; **heidenmäßig** (*umg*) *adj* terrific; **Heidentum** *nt* paganism

Heidin *f* heathen, pagan

heidnisch ['haɪdnɪʃ] *adj* heathen, pagan

heikel ['haɪkəl] *adj* awkward, thorny; (*wählerisch*) fussy

Heil [haɪl] **(-(e)s)** *nt* well-being; (*Seelenheil*) salvation ▷ *interj* hail; **Ski/Petri ~!** good skiing/fishing!

heil *adj* in one piece, intact; **mit ~er Haut davonkommen** to escape unscathed; **die ~e Welt** an ideal world (*without problems etc*)

Heiland **(-(e)s, -e)** *m* saviour (*Brit*), savior (*US*)

Heil- *zW*: **Heilanstalt** *f* nursing home; (*für Sucht- oder Geisteskranke*) home; **Heilbad** *nt* (*Bad*) medicinal bath; (*Ort*) spa; **heilbar** *adj* curable

Heilbutt ['haɪlbʊt] **(-s, -e)** *m* halibut

heilen *vt* to cure ▷ *vi* to heal; **als geheilt entlassen werden** to be discharged with a clean bill of health

heilfroh *adj* very relieved

Heilgymnastin *f* physiotherapist

heilig ['haɪlɪç] *adj* holy; **jdm ~ sein** (*lit, fig*) to be sacred to sb; **die H~e Schrift** the Holy Scriptures *pl*; **es ist mein ~er Ernst** I am deadly serious; *siehe auch* **heiligsprechen**; **Heiligabend** *m* Christmas Eve

Heilige, r *f(m)* saint

heiligen *vt* to sanctify, hallow; **der Zweck heiligt die Mittel** the end justifies the means

Heiligenschein *m* halo

Heiligkeit *f* holiness

heiligsprechen *unreg vt* to canonize

Heiligtum *nt* shrine; (*Gegenstand*) relic

Heilkunde *f* medicine

heillos *adj* unholy; (*Schreck*) terrible

Heil- *zW*: **Heilmittel** *nt* remedy; **Heilpraktiker, in** **(-s, -)** *m(f)* non-medical practitioner; **heilsam** *adj* (*fig*) salutary

Heilsarmee *f* Salvation Army

Heilung *f* cure

heim [haɪm] *adv* home

Heim **(-(e)s, -e)** *nt* home; (*Wohnheim*) hostel

Heimarbeit *f* (*Industrie*) homework, outwork

Heimat ['haɪma:t] **(-, -en)** *f* home (town/country *etc*); **Heimatfilm** *m sentimental film in idealized regional setting*; **Heimatkunde** *f* (*Sch*) local history; **Heimatland** *nt* homeland; **heimatlich** *adj* native, home *attrib*; (*Gefühle*) nostalgic; **heimatlos** *adj* homeless; **Heimatmuseum** *nt* local history museum; **Heimatort** *m* home town *od* area; **Heimatvertriebene, r** *f(m)* displaced person

heimbegleiten *vt* to accompany home

Heimchen *nt*: **~ (am Herd)** (*pej: Frau*) housewife

Heimcomputer *m* home computer

heimelig ['haɪməlɪç] *adj* homely

Heim- *zW*: **heimfahren** *unreg vi* to drive *od* go home; **Heimfahrt** *f* journey home; **Heimgang** *m* return home; (*Tod*) decease; **heimgehen** *unreg vi* to go home; (*sterben*) to pass away; **heimisch** *adj* (*gebürtig*) native; **sich heimisch fühlen** to feel at home; **Heimkehr** **(-, -en)** *f* homecoming; **heimkehren** *vi* to return home; **Heimkind** *nt child brought up in a home*; **heimkommen** *unreg vi* to come home; **Heimleiter** *m* warden of a home/hostel

heimlich *adj* secret ▷ *adv*: **~, still und leise** (*umg*) quietly, on the quiet; **Heimlichkeit** *f* secrecy; **Heimlichtuerei** *f* secrecy

Heim- *zW*: **Heimreise** *f* journey home; **Heimspiel** *nt* home game; **heimsuchen** *vt* to afflict; (*Geist*) to haunt; **heimtückisch** *adj* malicious; **heimwärts** *adv* homewards; **Heimweg** *m* way home; **Heimweh** *nt* homesickness; **Heimweh haben** to be homesick; **Heimwerker** *m* handyman; **heimzahlen** *vt*: **jdm etw heimzahlen** to pay back sb for sth

Heini ['haɪni] **(-s, -s)** *m*: **blöder ~** (*umg*) silly idiot

Heirat ['haɪra:t] **(-, -en)** *f* marriage; **heiraten** *vt, vi* to marry

Heirats- *zW*: **Heiratsantrag** *m* proposal (of marriage); **Heiratsanzeige** *f* (*Annonce*) advertisement for a marriage partner; **Heiratsschwindler** *m person who makes a marriage proposal under false pretences*; **Heiratsurkunde** *f* marriage certificate

heiser ['haɪzər] *adj* hoarse; **Heiserkeit** *f* hoarseness

heiß [haɪs] *adj* hot; (*Thema*) hotly disputed; (*Diskussion, Kampf*) heated, fierce; (*Begierde, Liebe, Wunsch*) burning; **es wird nichts so ~ gegessen, wie es gekocht wird** (*Sprichwort*) things are never as bad as they seem; **~er Draht** hot line; **~es Eisen** (*fig: umg*) hot potato; **~es Geld** hot money; **~ ersehnt** longed for; **~ umstritten** hotly debated; **jdn/etw ~ und innig lieben** to love sb/sth madly; **heißblütig** *adj* hot-blooded

heißen ['haɪsən] *unreg vi* to be called; (*bedeuten*) to mean ▷ *vt* to command; (*nennen*) to name ▷ *vi unpers*: **es heißt hier ...** it says here ...; **es heißt, dass ...** they say that ...; **wie ~ Sie?** what's your name?; **... und wie sie alle ~ ...** and the rest of them; **das will schon etwas ~** that's quite something; **jdn willkommen ~** to bid sb welcome; **das heißt** that is; (*mit anderen Worten*) that is to say

Heiß- *zW*: **Heißhunger** *m* ravenous hunger; **heißlaufen** *unreg vi, vr* to overheat; **Heißluft** *f* hot air; **Heißwasserbereiter** *m* water heater

heiter ['haɪtər] *adj* cheerful; (*Wetter*) bright; **aus ~em Himmel** (*fig*) out of the blue; **Heiterkeit** *f* cheerfulness; (*Belustigung*) amusement

heizbar *adj* heated; (*Raum*) with heating; **leicht ~** easily heated

Heizdecke *f* electric blanket

heizen *vt* to heat

Heizer **(-s, -)** *m* stoker

Heiz- *zW*: **Heizgerät** *nt* heater; **Heizkörper**

m radiator; **Heizöl** *nt* fuel oil; **Heizsonne** *f* electric fire
Heizung *f* heating
Heizungsanlage *f* heating system
Hektar [hɛk'ta:r] **(-s, -e)** *nt od m* hectare
Hektik [['hɛktɪk]] *f* hectic rush; (*von Leben etc*) hectic pace
hektisch ['hɛktɪʃ] *adj* hectic
Hektoliter [hɛkto'li:tər] *m od nt* hectolitre (*Brit*), hectoliter (*US*)
Held [hɛlt] **(-en, -en)** *m* hero; **heldenhaft** ['hɛldənhaft] *adj* heroic; **Heldin** *f* heroine
helfen ['hɛlfən] *unreg vi* to help; (*nützen*) to be of use ▷ *vb unpers*: **es hilft nichts, du musst ...** it's no use, you'll have to ...; **jdm (bei etw) ~** to help sb (with sth); **sich** *dat* **zu ~ wissen** to be resourceful; **er weiß sich** *dat* **nicht mehr zu ~** he's at his wits' end
Helfer, in **(-s, -)** *m(f)* helper, assistant
Helfershelfer *m* accomplice
Helgoland ['helgolant] **(-s)** *nt* Heligoland
hell [hɛl] *adj* clear; (*Licht, Himmel*) bright; (*Farbe*) light; **~es Bier** ≈ lager; **von etw ~ begeistert sein** to be very enthusiastic about sth; **es wird ~** it's getting light; **hellblau** *adj* light blue; **hellblond** *adj* ash-blond
Helle (-) *f* clearness; brightness
Heller **(-s, -)** *m* (*Hist*) farthing; **auf ~ und Pfennig** (down) to the last penny
hellhörig *adj* keen of hearing; (*Wand*) poorly soundproofed
hellicht ['hɛlɪçt] *adj siehe* **helllicht**
Helligkeit *f* clearness; brightness; lightness
helllicht ['hɛllɪçt] *adj*: **am ~en Tage** in broad daylight
hell- *zW*: **Hellraumprojektor** *m* (*Schweiz*) overhead projector; **hellsehen** *vi*: **hellsehen können** to be clairvoyant; **Hellseher, in** *m(f)* clairvoyant; **hellwach** *adj* wide-awake
Helm ['hɛlm] **(-(e)s, -e)** *m* helmet
Helsinki ['hɛlzɪŋki] **(-s)** *nt* Helsinki
Hemd [hɛmt] **(-(e)s, -en)** *nt* shirt; (*Unterhemd*) vest; **Hemdbluse** *f* blouse
Hemdenknopf *m* shirt button
hemdsärmelig *adj* shirt-sleeved; (*fig: umg: salopp*) pally; (*Ausdrucksweise*) casual
Hemisphäre [hemi'sfɛ:rə] *f* hemisphere
hemmen ['hɛmən] *vt* to check, hold up; **gehemmt sein** to be inhibited
Hemmschuh *m* (*fig*) impediment
Hemmung *f* check; (*Psych*) inhibition; (*Bedenken*) scruple
hemmungslos *adj* unrestrained, without restraint
Hengst [hɛŋst] **(-es, -e)** *m* stallion
Henkel ['hɛŋkəl] **(-s, -)** *m* handle; **Henkelkrug** *m* jug; **Henkelmann** (*umg*) *m* (*Gefäß*) canteen
henken ['hɛŋkən] *vt* to hang
Henker **(-s, -)** *m* hangman
Henne ['hɛnə] **(-, -n)** *f* hen
Hepatitis [hepa'ti:tɪs] *f* **(-, Hepatitiden)** hepatitis

SCHLÜSSELWORT

her [he:r] *adv* **1** (*Richtung*): **komm her zu mir** come here (to me); **von England her** from England; **von weit her** from a long way away; **her damit!** hand it over!; **wo bist du her?** where do you come from?; **wo hat er das her?** where did he get that from?; **hinter jdm/etw her sein** to be after sb/sth
2 (*Blickpunkt*): **von der Form her** as far as the form is concerned
3 (*zeitlich*): **das ist 5 Jahre her** that was 5 years ago; **ich kenne ihn von früher her** I know him from before

herab [hɛ'rap] *adv* down, downward(s); **herabhängen** *unreg vi* to hang down; **herablassen** *unreg vt* to let down ▷ *vr* to condescend; **herablassend** *adj* condescending; **Herablassung** *f* condescension; **herabsehen** *unreg vi*: **herabsehen (auf** *+akk***)** to look down (on); **herabsetzen** *vt* to lower, reduce; (*fig*) to belittle, disparage; **zu stark herabgesetzten Preisen** at greatly reduced prices; **Herabsetzung** *f* reduction; disparagement; **herabstufen** *vt* to downgrade; **herabstürzen** *vi* to fall off; (*Felsbrocken*) to fall down; **von etw herabstürzen** to fall off sth; to fall down from sth; **herabwürdigen** *vt* to belittle, disparage
heran [hɛ'ran] *adv*: **näher ~!** come closer!; **~ zu mir!** come up to me!; **heranbilden** *vt* to train; **heranbringen** *unreg vt*: **heranbringen (an** *+akk***)** to bring up (to); **heranfahren** *unreg vi*: **heranfahren (an** *+akk***)** to drive up (to); **herangehen** *unreg vi*: **an etw** *akk* **herangehen** (*an Problem, Aufgabe*) to tackle sth; **herankommen** *unreg vi*: **(an jdn/etw) herankommen** to approach (sb/sth), come near ((to) sb/sth); **er lässt alle Probleme an sich herankommen** he always adopts a wait-and-see attitude; **heranmachen** *vr*: **sich an jdn heranmachen** to make up to sb; (*umg*) to approach sb; **heranwachsen** *unreg vi* to grow up; **Heranwachsende, r** *f(m)* adolescent; **heranwinken** *vt* to beckon over; (*Taxi*) to hail; **heranziehen** *unreg vt* to pull nearer; (*aufziehen*) to raise; (*ausbilden*) to train; (*zu Hilfe holen*) to call in; (*Literatur*) to consult; **etw zum Vergleich heranziehen** to use sth by way of comparison; **jdn zu etw heranziehen** to call upon sb to help in sth
herauf [hɛ'raʊf] *adv* up, upward(s), up here; **heraufbeschwören** *unreg vt* to conjure up, evoke; **heraufbringen** *unreg vt* to bring up; **heraufsetzen** *vt* to increase; **heraufziehen** *unreg vt* to draw *od* pull up ▷ *vi* to approach; (*Sturm*) to gather
heraus [hɛ'raʊs] *adv* out; **nach vorn ~ wohnen** to live at the front (of the house); **aus dem Gröbsten ~ sein** to be over the worst; **~ mit der Sprache!** out with it!; **herausarbeiten** *vt* to work out; **herausbekommen** *unreg vt* to

get out; (*fig*) to find *od* figure out; (*Wechselgeld*) to get back; **herausbringen** *unreg vt* to bring out; (*Geheimnis*) to elicit; **jdn/etw ganz groß herausbringen** (*umg*) to give sb/sth a big build-up; **aus ihm war kein Wort herauszubringen** they couldn't get a single word out of him; **herausfinden** *unreg vt* to find out; **herausfordern** *vt* to challenge; (*provozieren*) to provoke; **Herausforderung** *f* challenge; provocation; **herausgeben** *unreg vt* to give up, surrender; (*Geld*) to give back; (*Buch*) to edit; (*veröffentlichen*) to publish ▷ *vi* (*Wechselgeld geben*): **können Sie (mir) herausgeben?** can you give me change?; **Herausgeber (-s, -)** *m* editor; (*Verleger*) publisher; **herausgehen** *unreg vi*: **aus sich herausgehen** to come out of one's shell; **heraushalten** *unreg vr*: **sich aus etw heraushalten** to keep out of sth; **heraushängen** *unreg vt, vi* to hang out; **herausholen** *vt*: **herausholen (aus)** to get out (of); **heraushören** *vt* (*wahrnehmen*) to hear; (*fühlen*): **heraushören (aus)** to detect (in); **herauskehren** *vt* (*fig*): **den Vorgesetzten herauskehren** to act the boss; **herauskommen** *unreg vi* to come out; **dabei kommt nichts heraus** nothing will come of it; **er kam aus dem Staunen nicht heraus** he couldn't get over his astonishment; **es kommt auf dasselbe heraus** it comes (down) to the same thing; **herausnehmen** *unreg vt* to take out; **sich** *dat* **Freiheiten herausnehmen** to take liberties; **Sie nehmen sich zu viel heraus** you're going too far; **herausputzen** *vt*: **sich herausputzen** to get dressed up; **herausreden** *vr* to talk one's way out of it (*umg*); **herausreißen** *unreg vt* to tear out; (*Zahn, Baum*) to pull out; **herausrücken** *vt* (*Geld*) to fork out, hand over; **mit etw herausrücken** (*fig*) to come out with sth; **herausrutschen** *vi* to slip out; **herausschlagen** *unreg vt* to knock out; (*fig*) to obtain; **herausstellen** *vr*: **sich herausstellen (als)** to turn out (to be); **das muss sich erst herausstellen** that remains to be seen; **herausstrecken** *vt* to stick out; **heraussuchen** *vt*: **sich** *dat* **jdn/etw heraussuchen** to pick out sb/sth; **heraustreten** *unreg vi*: **heraustreten (aus)** to come out (of); **herauswachsen** *unreg vi*: **herauswachsen aus** to grow out of; **herauswinden** *unreg vr* (*fig*): **sich aus etw herauswinden** to wriggle out of sth; **herauswollen** *vi*: **nicht mit etw herauswollen** (*umg: sagen wollen*) to not want to come out with sth; **herausziehen** *unreg vt* to pull out, extract

herb [hɛrp] *adj* (slightly) bitter, acid; (*Wein*) dry; (*fig: schmerzlich*) bitter; (*: streng*) stern, austere

herbei [hɛr'baɪ] *adv* (over) here; **herbeiführen** *vt* to bring about; **herbeischaffen** *vt* to procure; **herbeisehnen** *vt* to long for

herbemühen ['he:rbəmy:ən] *vr* to take the trouble to come

Herberge ['hɛrbɛrgə] (**-, -n**) *f* (*Jugendherberge etc*) hostel

Herbergsmutter *f* warden

Herbergsvater *m* warden

herbitten *unreg vt* to ask to come (here)

herbringen *unreg vt* to bring here

Herbst [hɛrpst] (**-(e)s, -e**) *m* autumn, fall (*US*); **im ~** in autumn, in the fall (*US*); **herbstlich** *adj* autumnal

Herd [he:rt] (**-(e)s, -e**) *m* cooker; (*fig, Med*) focus, centre (*Brit*), center (*US*)

Herde ['he:rdə] (**-, -n**) *f* herd; (*Schafherde*) flock

Herdentrieb *m* (*lit, fig: pej*) herd instinct

Herdplatte *f* (*von Elektroherd*) hotplate

herein [hɛ'raɪn] *adv* in (here), here; **~!** come in!; **hereinbitten** *unreg vt* to ask in; **hereinbrechen** *unreg vi* to set in; **hereinbringen** *unreg vt* to bring in; **hereindürfen** *unreg vi* to have permission to enter; **Hereinfall** *m* letdown; **hereinfallen** *unreg vi* to be caught, be taken in; **hereinfallen auf** *+akk* to fall for; **hereinkommen** *unreg vi* to come in; **hereinlassen** *unreg vt* to admit; **hereinlegen** *vt*: **jdn hereinlegen** to take sb in; **hereinplatzen** *vi* to burst in; **hereinschneien** (*umg*) *vi* to drop in; **hereinspazieren** *vi*: **hereinspaziert!** come right in!

her- *zW*: **Herfahrt** *f* journey here; **herfallen** *unreg vi*: **herfallen über** *+akk* to fall upon; **Hergang** *m* course of events, circumstances *pl*; **hergeben** *unreg vt* to give, hand (over); **sich zu etw hergeben** to lend one's name to sth; **das Thema gibt viel/nichts her** there's a lot/nothing to this topic; **hergebracht** *adj*: **in hergebrachter Weise** in the traditional way; **hergehen** *unreg vi*: **hinter jdm hergehen** to follow sb; **es geht hoch her** there are a lot of goings-on; **herhaben** *unreg* (*umg*) *vt*: **wo hat er das her?** where did he get that from?; **herhalten** *unreg vt* to hold out; **herhalten müssen** (*umg*) to have to suffer; **herhören** *vi* to listen; **hör mal her!** listen here!

Hering ['he:rɪŋ] (**-s, -e**) *m* herring; (*Zeltpflock*) (tent) peg

herkommen *unreg vi* to come; **komm mal her!** come here!

herkömmlich *adj* traditional

Herkunft (**-, -künfte**) *f* origin

Herkunftsland *nt* (*Comm*) country of origin

her- *zW*: **herlaufen** *unreg vi*: **herlaufen hinter** *+dat* to run after; **herleiten** *vr* to derive; **hermachen** *vr*: **sich hermachen über** *+akk* to set about *od* upon ▷ *vt* (*umg*): **viel hermachen** to look impressive

Hermelin [hɛrmə'li:n] (**-s, -e**) *m od nt* ermine

hermetisch [hɛr'me:tɪʃ] *adj* hermetic; **~ abgeriegelt** completely sealed off

her- *zW*: **hernach** *adv* afterwards; **hernehmen** *unreg vt*: **wo soll ich das hernehmen?** where am I supposed to get that from?; **hernieder** *adv* down

Heroin [hero'i:n] (**-s**) *nt* heroin; **heroinsüchtig**

adj addicted to heroin; **Heroinsüchtige, r** *f(m)* heroin addict

heroisch [he'ro:ɪʃ] *adj* heroic

Herold ['he:rɔlt] (**-(e)s, -e**) *m* herald

Herpes [['hɛrpɛs]] *m* (-) (*Med*) herpes

Herr [hɛr] (**-(e)n, -en**) *m* master; (*Mann*) gentleman; (*adliger, Rel*) Lord; (*vor Namen*) Mr; **mein ~!** sir!; **meine ~en!** gentlemen!; **Lieber ~ A, Sehr geehrter ~ A** (*in Brief*) Dear Mr A; **„~en"** (*Toilette*) "gentlemen" (*Brit*), "men's room" (*US*); **die ~en der Schöpfung** (*hum: Männer*) the gentlemen

Herrchen (*umg*) *nt* (*von Hund*) master

Herren- *zW*: **Herrenbekanntschaft** *f* gentleman friend; **Herrenbekleidung** *f* menswear; **Herrenbesuch** *m* gentleman visitor *od* visitors; **Herrendoppel** *nt* men's doubles; **Herreneinzel** *nt* men's singles; **Herrenhaus** *nt* mansion; **herrenlos** *adj* ownerless; **Herrenmagazin** *nt* men's magazine

Herrgott *m*: **~ noch mal!** (*umg*) damn it all!

Herrgottsfrühe *f*: **in aller ~** (*umg*) at the crack of dawn

herrichten ['he:rrɪçtən] *vt* to prepare

Herrin *f* mistress

herrisch *adj* domineering

herrje [hɛr'je:] *interj* goodness gracious!

herrjemine [hɛr'je:mine] *interj* goodness gracious!

herrlich *adj* marvellous (*Brit*), marvelous (*US*), splendid; **Herrlichkeit** *f* splendour (*Brit*), splendor (*US*), magnificence

Herrschaft *f* power, rule; (*Herr und Herrin*) master and mistress; **meine ~en!** ladies and gentlemen!

herrschen ['hɛrʃən] *vi* to rule; (*bestehen*) to prevail, be; **hier ~ ja Zustände!** things are in a pretty state round here!

Herrscher, in (**-s, -**) *m(f)* ruler

Herrschsucht *f* domineeringness

her- *zW*: **herrühren** *vi* to arise, originate; **hersagen** *vt* to recite; **hersehen** *unreg vi*: **hinter jdm/etw hersehen** to follow sb/sth with one's eyes

her sein *siehe* **her**

her- *zW*: **herstammen** *vi* to descend *od* come from; **herstellen** *vt* to make, manufacture; (*zustande bringen*) to establish; **Hersteller** (**-s, -**) *m* manufacturer; **Herstellung** *f* manufacture; **Herstellungskosten** *pl* manufacturing costs *pl*; **hertragen** *unreg vt*: **etw hinter jdm hertragen** to carry sth behind sb

herüber [hɛ'ry:bər] *adv* over (here), across

herum [hɛ'rʊm] *adv* about, (a)round; **um etw ~** around sth; **herumärgern** *vr*: **sich herumärgern (mit)** to get annoyed (with); **herumblättern** *vi*: **herumblättern in** *+dat* to browse *od* flick through; **herumdoktern** (*umg*) *vi* to fiddle *od* tinker about; **herumdrehen** *vt*: **jdm das Wort im Mund herumdrehen** to twist sb's words; **herumdrücken** *vr* (*vermeiden*): **sich um etw herumdrücken** to dodge sth; **herumfahren** *unreg vi* to travel around; (*mit Auto*) to drive around; (*sich rasch umdrehen*) to spin (a)round; **herumführen** *vt* to show around; **herumgammeln** (*umg*) *vi* to bum around; **herumgehen** *unreg vi* (*herumspazieren*) to walk about; **um etw herumgehen** to walk *od* go round sth; **etw herumgehen lassen** to circulate sth; **herumhacken** *vi* (*fig: umg*): **auf jdm herumhacken** to pick on sb; **herumirren** *vi* to wander about; **herumkommen** *unreg* (*umg*) *vi*: **um etw herumkommen** to get out of sth; **er ist viel herumgekommen** he has been around a lot; **herumkriegen** *vt* to bring *od* talk round; **herumlungern** *vi* to lounge about; (*umg*) to hang around; **herumquälen** *vr*: **sich mit Rheuma herumquälen** to be plagued by rheumatism; **herumreißen** *unreg vt* to swing around (hard); **herumschlagen** *unreg vr*: **sich mit etw herumschlagen** (*umg*) to tussle with sth; **herumschleppen** *vt*: **etw mit sich herumschleppen** (*Sorge, Problem*) to be troubled by sth; (*Krankheit*) to have sth; **herumsprechen** *unreg vr* to get around, be spread; **herumstochern** (*umg*) *vi*: **im Essen herumstochern** to pick at one's food; **herumtreiben** *unreg vi, vr* to drift about; **Herumtreiber, in** (**-s, -**) (*pej*) *m(f)* tramp; **herumziehen** *unreg vi, vr* to wander about

herunter [hɛ'rʊntər] *adv* downward(s), down (there); **mit den Nerven/der Gesundheit ~ sein** (*umg*) to be at the end of one's tether/be run-down; **herunterbrechen** *unreg vt* (*Zahlen, Kalkulation*) to break down; **herunterfahren** *unreg vti* (*Comput, Tech*) to shut down; **heruntergekommen** *adj* run-down; **herunterhandeln** (*umg*) *vt* (*Preis*) to beat down; **herunterhängen** *unreg vi* to hang down; **herunterholen** *vt* to bring down; **herunterkommen** *unreg vi* to come down; (*fig*) to come down in the world; **herunterleiern** (*umg*) *vt* to reel off; **heruntermachen** *vt* to take down; (*schlechtmachen*) to run down, knock; **herunterputzen** (*umg*) *vt*: **jdn herunterputzen** to tear sb off a strip; **herunterspielen** *vt* to play down; **herunterwirtschaften** (*umg*) *vt* to bring to the brink of ruin

hervor [hɛr'fo:r] *adv* out, forth; **hervorbrechen** *unreg vi* to burst forth, break out; **hervorbringen** *unreg vt* to produce; (*Wort*) to utter; **hervorgehen** *unreg vi* to emerge, result; **daraus geht hervor, dass ...** from this it follows that ...; **hervorheben** *unreg vt* to stress; (*als Kontrast*) to set off; **hervorragend** *adj* excellent; (*lit*) projecting; **hervorrufen** *unreg vt* to cause, give rise to; **hervorstechen** *unreg vi* (*lit, fig*) to stand out; **hervorstoßen** *unreg vt* (*Worte*) to gasp (out); **hervortreten** *unreg vi* to come out; **hervortun** *unreg vr* to distinguish o.s.; (*umg: sich wichtigtun*) to show off; **sich mit etw hervortun** to show off sth

Herz [hɛrts] (**-ens, -en**) *nt* heart; (*Karten: Farbe*)

hearts *pl*; **mit ganzem ~en** wholeheartedly; **etw auf dem ~en haben** to have sth on one's mind; **sich** *dat* **etw zu ~en nehmen** to take sth to heart; **du sprichst mir aus dem ~en** that's just what I feel; **es liegt mir am ~en** I am very concerned about it; **seinem ~en Luft machen** to give vent to one's feelings; **sein ~ an jdn/etw hängen** to commit o.s. heart and soul to sb/sth; **ein ~ und eine Seele sein** to be the best of friends; **jdn/etw auf ~ und Nieren prüfen** to examine sb/sth very thoroughly; **Herzanfall** *m* heart attack; **Herzbeschwerden** *pl* heart trouble *sing*

herzen *vt* to caress, embrace

Herzenslust *f*: **nach ~** to one's heart's content

Herz- *zW*: **herzergreifend** *adj* heart-rending; **herzerweichend** *adj* heartrending; **Herzfehler** *m* heart defect; **herzhaft** *adj* hearty

herziehen ['he:rtsi:ən] *vi*: **über jdn/etw ~** (*umg*) to pull sb/sth to pieces (*fig*)

Herz- *zW*: **Herzinfarkt** *m* heart attack; **Herzklappe** *f* (heart) valve; **Herzklopfen** *nt* palpitation; **herzkrank** *adj* suffering from a heart condition

herzlich *adj* cordial ▷ *adv* (*sehr*): **~ gern!** with the greatest of pleasure!; **~en Glückwunsch** congratulations *pl*; **~e Grüße** best wishes; **Herzlichkeit** *f* cordiality

herzlos *adj* heartless; **Herzlosigkeit** *f* heartlessness

Herzog ['hɛrtso:k] **(-(e)s, ¨-e)** *m* duke; **Herzogin** *f* duchess; **herzoglich** *adj* ducal; **Herzogtum** *nt* duchy

Herz- *zW*: **Herzschlag** *m* heartbeat; (*Med*) heart attack; **Herzschrittmacher** *m* pacemaker; **herzzerreißend** *adj* heartrending

Hesse ['hɛsə] **(-n, -n)** *m* Hessian

Hessen ['hɛsən] **(-s)** *nt* Hesse

Hessin *f* Hessian

hessisch *adj* Hessian

heterogen [hetero'ge:n] *adj* heterogeneous

heterosexuell [heterozɛksu'ɛl] *adj* heterosexual

Hetze ['hɛtsə] *f* (*Eile*) rush

hetzen *vt* to hunt; (*verfolgen*) to chase ▷ *vi* (*eilen*) to rush; **jdn/etw auf jdn/etw ~** to set sb/sth on sb/sth; **~ gegen** to stir up feeling against; **~ zu** to agitate for

Hetzerei [hɛtsə'raɪ] *f* agitation; (*Eile*) rush

Hetzkampagne ['hɛtskampanjə] *f* smear campaign

Heu [hɔʏ] **(-(e)s)** *nt* hay; **Heuboden** *m* hayloft

Heuchelei [hɔʏçə'laɪ] *f* hypocrisy

heucheln ['hɔʏçəln] *vt* to pretend, feign ▷ *vi* to be hypocritical

Heuchler, in [hɔʏçlər(ɪn)] **(-s, -)** *m(f)* hypocrite; **heuchlerisch** *adj* hypocritical

Heuer ['hɔʏər] **(-, -n)** *f* (*Naut*) pay

heuer *adv* this year

heuern ['hɔʏərn] *vt* to sign on, hire

Heugabel *f* pitchfork

Heuhaufen *m* haystack

heulen ['hɔʏlən] *vi* to howl; (*weinen*) to cry; **das ~de Elend bekommen** to get the blues

heurig ['hɔʏrɪç] *adj* this year's

Heuschnupfen *m* hay fever

Heuschrecke *f* grasshopper; (*in heißen Ländern*) locust

heute ['hɔʏtə] *adv* today; **~ Abend/früh** this evening/morning; **~ Morgen** this morning; **~ in einer Woche** a week today, today week; **von ~ auf morgen** (*fig: plötzlich*) overnight, from one day to the next; **das H~** today

heutig ['hɔʏtɪç] *adj* today's; **unser ~es Schreiben** (*Comm*) our letter of today('s date)

heutzutage ['hɔʏttsuta:gə] *adv* nowadays

Hexe ['hɛksə] **(-, -n)** *f* witch

hexen *vi* to practise witchcraft; **ich kann doch nicht ~** I can't work miracles

Hexen- *zW*: **Hexenhäuschen** *nt* gingerbread house; **Hexenkessel** *m* (*lit, fig*) cauldron; **Hexenmeister** *m* wizard; **Hexenschuss** *m* lumbago

Hexerei [hɛksə'raɪ] *f* witchcraft

HG *f abk* = **Handelsgesellschaft**

Hg. *abk* (= *Herausgeber*) ed.

hg. *abk* (= *herausgegeben*) ed.

HGB (-) *nt abk* (= *Handelsgesetzbuch*) *statutes of commercial law*

Hieb (-(e)s, -e) *m* blow; (*Wunde*) cut, gash; (*Stichelei*) cutting remark; **~e bekommen** to get a thrashing

hieb *etc* [hi:p] *vb* (*veraltet*) *siehe* **hauen**

hieb- und stichfest *adj* (*fig*) watertight

hielt *etc* [hi:lt] *vb siehe* **halten**

hier [hi:r] *adv* here; **~ spricht Dr. Müller** (*Tel*) this is Dr Müller (speaking); **er ist von ~** he's a local (man); *siehe auch* **hierbehalten; hierbleiben; hierlassen**

Hierarchie [hierar'çi:] *f* hierarchy

hier- *zW*: **hierauf** *adv* thereupon; (*danach*) after that; **hieraus** *adv*: **hieraus folgt, dass ...** from this it follows that ...; **hierbehalten** *unreg vt* to keep here; **hierbei** *adv* (*bei dieser Gelegenheit*) on this occasion; **hierbleiben** *unreg vi* to stay here; **hierdurch** *adv* by this means; (*örtlich*) through here; **hierher** *adv* this way, here; **hierher gehören** to belong here; (*fig: relevant sein*) to be relevant; **hierlassen** *unreg vt* to leave here; **hiermit** *adv* hereby; **hiermit erkläre ich ...** (*form*) I hereby declare ...; **hiernach** *adv* hereafter; **hiervon** *adv* about this, hereof; **hiervon abgesehen** apart from this; **hierzu** *adv* (*dafür*) for this; (*dazu*) with this; (*außerdem*) in addition to this, moreover; (*zu diesem Punkt*) about this; **hierzulande, hier zu Lande** *adv* in this country

hiesig ['hi:zɪç] *adj* of this place, local

hieß *etc* [hi:s] *vb siehe* **heißen**

Hi-Fi-Anlage ['haɪfianla:gə] *f* hi-fi set *od* system

Hightechindustrie ['haɪtɛkɪndʊs'tri:] *f* high tech *od* hi-tech industry

Hilfe ['hɪlfə] **(-, -n)** *f* help; (*für Notleidende*) aid; **Erste ~** first aid; **jdm ~ leisten** to help sb; **~!** help!; **Hilfeleistung** *f*: **unterlassene**

Hilfeleistung (*Jur*) denial of assistance;
Hilfestellung *f* (*Sport, fig*) support
Hilf- *zW*: **hilflos** *adj* helpless; **Hilflosigkeit** *f* helplessness; **hilfreich** *adj* helpful
Hilfs- *zW*: **Hilfsaktion** *f* relief action, relief measures *pl*; **Hilfsarbeiter** *m* labourer (*Brit*), laborer (*US*); **hilfsbedürftig** *adj* needy; **hilfsbereit** *adj* ready to help; **Hilfskraft** *f* assistant, helper; **Hilfsmittel** *nt* aid; **Hilfsschule** *f* school for backward children; **Hilfszeitwort** *nt* auxiliary verb
hilft [hɪlft] *vb siehe* **helfen**
Himalaja [hiˈmaːlaja] **(-s)** *m*: **der ~** the Himalayas *pl*
Himbeere [ˈhɪmbeːrə] **(-, -n)** *f* raspberry
Himmel [ˈhɪməl] **(-s, -)** *m* sky; (*Rel*) heaven; **um ~s willen** (*umg*) for Heaven's sake; **zwischen ~ und Erde** in midair; **himmelangst** *adj*: **es ist mir himmelangst** I'm scared to death; **Himmelbett** *nt* four-poster bed; **himmelblau** *adj* sky-blue
Himmelfahrt *f* Ascension
Himmelfahrtskommando *nt* (*Mil: umg*) suicide squad; (*Unternehmen*) suicide mission
Himmelreich *nt* (*Rel*) Kingdom of Heaven
himmelschreiend *adj* outrageous
Himmelsrichtung *f* direction; **die vier ~en** the four points of the compass
himmelweit *adj*: **ein ~er Unterschied** a world of difference
himmlisch [ˈhɪmlɪʃ] *adj* heavenly

SCHLÜSSELWORT

hin [hɪn] *adv* **1** (*Richtung*): **hin und zurück** there and back; **einmal London hin und zurück** a return to London (*Brit*), a roundtrip ticket to London (*US*); **hin und her** to and fro; **etw hin und her überlegen** to turn sth over and over in one's mind; **bis zur Mauer hin** up to the wall; **wo ist er hin?** where has he gone?; **nichts wie hin!** (*umg*) let's go then!; **nach außen hin** (*fig*) outwardly; **Geld hin, Geld her** money or no money
2 (*auf ... hin*): **auf meine Bitte hin** at my request; **auf seinen Rat hin** on the basis of his advice; **auf meinen Brief hin** on the strength of my letter
3: hin sein (*umg: kaputt sein*) to have had it; (*Ruhe*) to be gone; **mein Glück ist hin** my happiness has gone; **hin und wieder** (every) now and again

hinab [hɪˈnap] *adv* down; **hinabgehen** *unreg vi* to go down; **hinabsehen** *unreg vi* to look down
hinarbeiten [ˈhɪnarbaɪtən] *vi*: **auf etw** *akk* **~** (*auf Ziel*) to work towards sth
hinauf [hɪˈnaʊf] *adv* up; **hinaufarbeiten** *vr* to work one's way up; **hinaufsteigen** *unreg vi* to climb
hinaus [hɪˈnaʊs] *adv* out; **hinten/vorn ~** at the back/front; **darüber ~** over and above this; **auf Jahre ~** for years to come;
hinausbefördern *vt* to kick *od* throw out;
hinausfliegen *unreg* (*umg*) *vi* to be kicked out;
hinausführen *vi*: **über etw** *akk* **hinausführen** (*lit, fig*) to go beyond sth; **hinausgehen** *unreg vi* to go out; **hinausgehen über** *+akk* to exceed; **hinauslaufen** *unreg vi* to run out; **hinauslaufen auf** *+akk* to come to, amount to; **hinausschieben** *unreg vt* to put off, postpone; **hinausschießen** *unreg vi*: **über das Ziel hinausschießen** (*fig*) to overshoot the mark; **hinauswachsen** *unreg vi*: **er wuchs über sich selbst hinaus** he surpassed himself; **hinauswerfen** *unreg vt* to throw out; **hinauswollen** *vi* to want to go out; **hoch hinauswollen** to aim high; **hinauswollen auf** *+akk* to drive at, get at; **hinausziehen** *unreg vt* to draw out ▷ *vr* to be protracted; **hinauszögern** *vt* to delay, put off ▷ *vr* to be delayed, be put off
hinbekommen *unreg* (*umg*) *vt*: **das hast du gut ~** you've made a good job of it
hinblättern (*umg*) *vt* (*Geld*) to fork out
Hinblick [ˈhɪnblɪk] *m*: **in *od* im ~ auf** *+akk* in view of
hinderlich [ˈhɪndərlɪç] *adj* awkward; **jds Karriere** *dat* **~ sein** to be a hindrance to sb's career
hindern *vt* to hinder, hamper; **jdn an etw** *dat* **~** to prevent sb from doing sth
Hindernis **(-ses, -se)** *nt* obstacle; **Hindernislauf** *m*, **Hindernisrennen** *nt* steeplechase
Hinderungsgrund *m* obstacle
hindeuten [ˈhɪndɔʏtən] *vi*: **~ auf** *+akk* to point to
Hinduismus [hɪnduˈɪsmʊs] *m* Hinduism
hindurch [hɪnˈdʊrç] *adv* through; across; (*zeitlich*) over
hindürfen [hɪnˈdʏrfən] *unreg vi*: **~ (zu)** to be allowed to go (to)
hinein [hɪˈnaɪn] *adv* in; **bis tief in die Nacht ~** well into the night; **hineinfallen** *unreg vi* to fall in; **hineinfallen in** *+akk* to fall into; **hineinfinden** *unreg vr* (*fig: sich vertraut machen*) to find one's feet; (*sich abfinden*) to come to terms with it; **hineingehen** *unreg vi* to go in; **hineingehen in** *+akk* to go into, enter; **hineingeraten** *unreg vi*: **hineingeraten in** *+akk* to get into; **hineinknien** *vr* (*fig: umg*): **sich in etw** *akk* **hineinknien** to get into sth; **hineinlesen** *unreg vt*: **etw in etw** *akk* **hineinlesen** to read sth into sth; **hineinpassen** *vi* to fit in; **hineinpassen in** *+akk* to fit into; **hineinprügeln** *vt*: **etw in jdn hineinprügeln** to cudgel sth into sb; **hineinreden** *vi*: **jdm hineinreden** to interfere in sb's affairs; **hineinstecken** *vt*: **Geld/Arbeit in etw** *akk* **hineinstecken** to put money/some work into sth; **hineinsteigern** *vr* to get worked up; **hineinversetzen** *vr*: **sich in jdn hineinversetzen** to put o.s. in sb's position; **hineinziehen** *unreg vt*: **hineinziehen (in** *+akk***)** to pull in (to); **jdn in etw hineinziehen** (*in Konflikt, Gespräch*) to draw sb into sth

hin- *zW*: **hinfahren** *unreg vi* to go; to drive ▷ *vt* to take; to drive; **Hinfahrt** *f* journey there; **hinfallen** *unreg vi* to fall down; **hinfällig** *adj* frail, decrepit; (*Regel etc*) unnecessary; **hinfliegen** *unreg vi* to fly there; (*umg: hinfallen*) to fall over; **Hinflug** *m* outward flight

hing *etc* [hɪŋ] *vb siehe* **hängen**

hin- *zW*: **Hingabe** *f* devotion; **mit Hingabe tanzen/singen** *etc* (*fig*) to dance/sing *etc* with abandon; **hingeben** *unreg vr +dat* to give o.s. up to, devote o.s. to; **hingebungsvoll** ['hɪnge:bʊŋsfɔl] *adv* (*begeistert*) with abandon; (*lauschen*) raptly

hingegen [hɪn'ge:gən] *konj* however

hin- *zW*: **hingehen** *unreg vi* to go; (*Zeit*) to pass; **gehst du auch hin?** are you going too?; **hingerissen** *adj*: **hingerissen sein** to be enraptured; **hin- und hergerissen sein** (*fig*) to be torn; **ich bin ganz hin- und hergerissen** (*ironisch*) that's absolutely great; **hinhalten** *unreg vt* to hold out; (*warten lassen*) to put off, stall; **Hinhaltetaktik** *f* stalling *od* delaying tactics *pl*

hinhauen ['hɪnhaʊən] *unreg* (*umg*) *vi* (*klappen*) to work; (*ausreichen*) to do

hinhören ['hɪnhø:rən] *vi* to listen

hinken ['hɪŋkən] *vi* to limp; (*Vergleich*) to be unconvincing

hin- *zW*: **hinkommen** *unreg* (*umg*) *vi* (*auskommen*) to manage; (*: ausreichen, stimmen*) to be right; **hinlänglich** *adj* adequate ▷ *adv* adequately; **hinlegen** *vt* to put down ▷ *vr* to lie down; **sich der Länge nach hinlegen** (*umg*) to fall flat; **hinnehmen** *unreg vt* (*fig*) to put up with, take; **hinreichen** *vi* to be adequate ▷ *vt*: **jdm etw hinreichen** to hand sb sth; **hinreichend** *adj* adequate; (*genug*) sufficient; **Hinreise** *f* journey out; **hinreißen** *unreg vt* to carry away, enrapture; **sich hinreißen lassen, etw zu tun** to get carried away and do sth; **hinreißend** *adj* (*Landschaft, Anblick*) enchanting; (*Schönheit, Mensch*) captivating; **hinrichten** *vt* to execute; **Hinrichtung** *f* execution; **hinsehen** *unreg vi*: **bei genauerem Hinsehen** on closer inspection

hin sein ['hɪnzaɪn] *siehe* **hin**

hin- *zW*: **hinsetzen** *vr* to sit down; **Hinsicht** *f*: **in mancher** *od* **gewisser Hinsicht** in some respects *od* ways; **hinsichtlich** *präp +gen* with regard to; **hinsollen** (*umg*) *vi*: **wo soll ich/das Buch hin?** where do I/does the book go?; **Hinspiel** *nt* (*Sport*) first leg; **hinstellen** *vt* to put (down) ▷ *vr* to place o.s.

hintanstellen [hɪnt'|anʃtɛlən] *vt* (*fig*) to ignore

hinten ['hɪntən] *adv* behind; (*rückwärtig*) at the back; **~ und vorn** (*fig: betrügen*) left, right and centre; **das reicht ~ und vorn nicht** that's nowhere near enough; **hintendran** (*umg*) *adv* at the back; **hintenherum** *adv* round the back; (*fig*) secretly

hinter ['hɪntər] *präp* (*+dat od akk*) behind; (*: nach*) after; **~ jdm her sein** to be after sb; **~ die Wahrheit kommen** to get to the truth; **sich ~ jdn stellen** (*fig*) to support sb; **etw ~ sich** *dat* **haben** (*zurückgelegt haben*) to have got through sth; **sie hat viel ~ sich** she has been through a lot; **Hinterachse** *f* rear axle; **Hinterbänkler** (**-s, -**) *m* (*Pol: pej*) backbencher; **Hinterbein** *nt* hind leg; **sich auf die Hinterbeine stellen** to get tough; **Hinterbliebene, r** *f(m)* surviving relative; **hinterdrein** *adv* afterwards

hintere, r, s *adj* rear, back

hinter- *zW*: **hintereinander** *adv* one after the other; **zwei Tage hintereinander** two days running; **hinterfotzig** (*umg*) *adj* underhanded; **hinterfragen** *vt untr* to analyse; **Hintergedanke** *m* ulterior motive; **hintergehen** *unreg vt untr* to deceive; **Hintergrund** *m* background; **hintergründig** *adj* cryptic, enigmatic; **Hintergrundprogramm** *nt* (*Comput*) background program; **Hinterhalt** *m* ambush; **etw im Hinterhalt haben** to have sth in reserve; **hinterhältig** *adj* underhand, sneaky; **hinterher** *adv* afterwards, after; **er ist hinterher, dass ...** (*fig*) he sees to it that ...; **Hinterhof** *m* back yard; **Hinterkopf** *m* back of one's head; **Hinterland** *nt* hinterland; **hinterlassen** *unreg vt untr* to leave; **Hinterlassenschaft** *f* (testator's) estate; **hinterlegen** *vt untr* to deposit; **Hinterlegungsstelle** *f* depository; **Hinterlist** *f* cunning, trickery; (*Handlung*) trick, dodge; **hinterlistig** *adj* cunning, crafty; **Hintermann** (**-(e)s**, *pl* **-männer**) *m* person behind; **die Hintermänner des Skandals** the men behind the scandal

Hintern ['hɪntərn] (**-s, -**) (*umg*) *m* bottom, backside; **jdm den ~ versohlen** to smack sb's bottom

hinter- *zW*: **Hinterrad** *nt* back wheel; **Hinterradantrieb** *m* (*Aut*) rear-wheel drive; **hinterrücks** *adv* from behind; **Hinterteil** *nt* behind; **Hintertreffen** *nt*: **ins Hintertreffen kommen** to lose ground; **hintertreiben** *unreg vt untr* to prevent, frustrate; **Hintertreppe** *f* back stairs *pl*; **Hintertür** *f* back door; (*fig: Ausweg*) escape, loophole; **Hinterwäldler** (**-s, -**) (*umg*) *m* backwoodsman, hillbilly (*bes US*); **hinterziehen** *unreg vt untr* (*Steuern*) to evade (paying)

hintun ['hɪntu:n] *unreg* (*umg*) *vt*: **ich weiß nicht, wo ich ihn ~ soll** (*fig*) I can't (quite) place him

hinüber [hɪ'ny:bər] *adv* across, over; **hinübergehen** *unreg vi* to go over *od* across

hinunter [hɪ'nʊntər] *adv* down; **hinunterbringen** *unreg vt* to take down; **hinunterschlucken** *vt* (*lit, fig*) to swallow; **hinunterspülen** *vt* to flush away; (*Essen, Tablette*) to wash down; (*fig: Ärger*) to soothe; **hinuntersteigen** *unreg vi* to descend

Hinweg ['hɪnve:k] *m* journey out

hinweg- [hɪn'vɛk] *zW*: **hinweggehen** *unreg vi*: **über etw** *akk* **hinweggehen** (*fig*) to pass over sth; **hinweghelfen** *unreg vi*: **jdm**

über etw *akk* **hinweghelfen** to help sb to get over sth; **hinwegkommen** *unreg vi* (*fig*): **über etw** *akk* **hinwegkommen** to get over sth; **hinwegsehen** *unreg vi*: **darüber hinwegsehen, dass ...** to overlook the fact that ...; **hinwegsetzen** *vr*: **sich hinwegsetzen über** *+akk* to disregard

Hinweis ['hɪnvaɪs] (**-es, -e**) *m* (*Andeutung*) hint; (*Anweisung*) instruction; (*Verweis*) reference; **sachdienliche ~e** relevant information

hinweisen *unreg vi*: **~ auf** *+akk* to point to; (*verweisen*) to refer to; **darauf ~, dass ...** to point out that ...; (*anzeigen*) to indicate that ...

Hinweisschild *nt* sign

Hinweistafel *f* sign

hinwerfen *unreg vt* to throw down; **eine hingeworfene Bemerkung** a casual remark

hinwirken *vi*: **auf etw** *akk* **~** to work towards sth

Hinz [hɪnts] *m*: **~ und Kunz** (*umg*) every Tom, Dick and Harry

hinziehen *unreg vr* (*fig*) to drag on

hinzielen *vi*: **~ auf** *+akk* to aim at

hinzu [hɪn'tsu:] *adv* in addition; **hinzufügen** *vt* to add; **Hinzufügung** *f*: **unter Hinzufügung von etw** (*form*) by adding sth; **hinzukommen** *unreg vi*: **es kommt noch hinzu, dass ...** there is also the fact that ...; **hinzuziehen** *unreg vt* to consult

Hiobsbotschaft ['hi:ɔpsbo:tʃaft] *f* bad news

Hirn [hɪrn] (**-(e)s, -e**) *nt* brain(s); **Hirngespinst** (**-(e)s, -e**) *nt* fantasy; **Hirnhautentzündung** *f* (*Med*) meningitis; **hirntot** *adj* braindead; **hirnverbrannt** *adj* (*umg*) harebrained

Hirsch [hɪrʃ] (**-(e)s, -e**) *m* stag

Hirse ['hɪrzə] (**-, -n**) *f* millet

Hirt ['hɪrt] (**-en, -en**) *m*, **Hirte** (**-n, -n**) *m* herdsman; (*Schafhirt, fig*) shepherd

Hirtin *f* herdswoman; (*Schafhirtin*) shepherdess

hissen ['hɪsən] *vt* to hoist

Historiker [hɪs'to:rikər] (**-s, -**) *m* historian

historisch [hɪs'to:rɪʃ] *adj* historical

Hit [hɪt] (**-s, -s**) (*umg*) *m* (*Mus, fig*) hit; **Hitparade** *f* hit parade

Hitze ['hɪtsə] (**-**) *f* heat; **hitzebeständig** *adj* heat-resistant; **Hitzefrei** (**-**) *nt*: **Hitzefrei haben** *to have time off school/work because of excessive heat*; **Hitzewelle** *f* heat wave

hitzig *adj* hot-tempered; (*Debatte*) heated

Hitz- *zW*: **Hitzkopf** *m* hothead; **hitzköpfig** *adj* fiery, hot-headed; **Hitzschlag** *m* heatstroke

HIV-negativ *adj* HIV-negative

HIV-positiv *adj* HIV-positive

hl. *abk* = **heilig**

H-Milch ['ha:mɪlç] *f* long-life milk, UHT milk

HNO-Arzt *m* ENT specialist

hob *etc* [ho:p] *vb siehe* **heben**

Hobby ['hɔbi] (**-s, -s**) *nt* hobby

Hobel ['ho:bəl] (**-s, -**) *m* plane; **Hobelbank** *f* carpenter's bench

hobeln *vt, vi* to plane

Hobelspäne *pl* wood shavings *pl*

hoch [ho:x] (*attrib* **hohe(r, s)**) *adj* high ▷ *adv*: **~ achten** to respect; **~ begabt** = **hochbegabt**; **~ dotiert** highly paid; **~ entwickelt** (*Kultur, Land*) highly developed; (*Geräte, Methoden*) sophisticated; **wenn es ~ kommt** (*umg*) at (the) most, at the outside; **das ist mir zu ~** (*umg*) that's above my head; **ein hohes Tier** (*umg*) a big fish; **es ging ~ her** (*umg*) we/they *etc* had a whale of a time; **~ und heilig versprechen** to promise faithfully; *siehe auch* **hochempfindlich; hochgestellt**

Hoch (**-s, -s**) *nt* (*Ruf*) cheer; (*Met, fig*) high

hoch- *zW*: **Hochachtung** *f* respect, esteem; **mit vorzüglicher Hochachtung** (*form: Briefschluss*) yours faithfully; **hochachtungsvoll** *adv* yours faithfully; **hochaktuell** *adj* highly topical; **Hochamt** *nt* high mass; **hocharbeiten** *vr* to work one's way up; **hochbegabt** *adj* extremely gifted, aged; **hochbetagt** *adj* very old, aged; **Hochbetrieb** *m* intense activity; (*Comm*) peak time; **Hochbetrieb haben** to be at one's *od* its busiest; **hochbringen** *unreg vt* to bring up; **Hochburg** *f* stronghold; **Hochdeutsch** *nt* High German; **Hochdruck** *m* high pressure; **Hochebene** *f* plateau; **hochempfindlich** *adj* highly sensitive; (*Film*) high-speed; **hocherfreut** *adj* highly delighted; **hochfahren** *unreg vi* (*erschreckt*) to jump; (*Comput, Tech*) to start up; **hochfliegend** *adj* ambitious; (*fig*) high-flown; **Hochform** *f* top form; **Hochgebirge** *nt* high mountains *pl*; **Hochgefühl** *nt* elation; **hochgehen** *unreg* (*umg*) *vi* (*explodieren*) to blow up; (*Bombe*) to go off; **Hochgenuss** *m* great *od* special treat; (*großes Vergnügen*) great pleasure; **hochgeschlossen** *adj* (*Kleid etc*) high-necked; **hochgestellt** *adj* (*fig: Persönlichkeit*) high-ranking; **Hochglanz** *m* high polish; (*Phot*) gloss; **hochgradig** *adj* intense, extreme; **hochhalten** *unreg vt* to hold up; (*fig*) to uphold, cherish; **Hochhaus** *nt* multi-storey building; **hochheben** *unreg vt* to lift (up); **hochkant** *adv*: **jdn hochkant hinauswerfen** (*fig: umg*) to chuck sb out on his/her ear; **hochkommen** *unreg vi* (*nach oben*) to come up; (*fig: gesund werden*) to get back on one's feet; (*beruflich, gesellschaftlich*) to come up in the world; **Hochkonjunktur** *f* boom; **hochkrempeln** *vt* to roll up; **Hochland** *nt* highlands *pl*; **hochleben** *vi*: **jdn hochleben lassen** to give sb three cheers; **Hochleistungssport** *m* competitive sport; **hochmodern** *adj* very modern, ultra-modern; **Hochmut** *m* pride; **hochmütig** *adj* proud, haughty; **hochnäsig** *adj* stuck-up, snooty; **hochnehmen** *unreg vt* to pick up; **jdn hochnehmen** (*umg: verspotten*) to pull sb's leg; **Hochofen** *m* blast furnace; **hochprozentig** *adj* (*Alkohol*) strong; **Hochrechnung** *f* projected result; **Hochsaison** *f* high season; **Hochschätzung** *f* high esteem

Hochschulabschluss *m* degree

Hochschulbildung *f* higher education

Hochschule *f* college; (*Universität*) university

Hochschulreife *f*: **er hat (die) ~** ≈ he's got

his A-levels (*Brit*), he's graduated from high school (*US*)

hoch- *zW*: **hochschwanger** *adj* heavily pregnant, well advanced in pregnancy; **Hochseefischerei** *f* deep-sea fishing; **Hochsitz** *m* (*Jagd*) (raised) hide; **Hochsommer** *m* middle of summer; **Hochspannung** *f* high tension; **hochspielen** *vt* (*fig*) to blow up; **Hochsprache** *f* standard language; **hochspringen** *unreg vi* to jump up; **Hochsprung** *m* high jump

höchst [hø:çst] *adv* highly, extremely

Hochstapler ['ho:xsta:plər] (**-s, -**) *m* swindler

höchste, r, s *adj* highest; (*äußerste*) extreme; **die ~ Instanz** (*Jur*) the supreme court of appeal

höchstens *adv* at the most

Höchstgeschwindigkeit *f* maximum speed

Höchstgrenze *f* upper limit

Hochstimmung *f* high spirits *pl*

Höchst- *zW*: **Höchstleistung** *f* best performance; (*bei Produktion*) maximum output; **höchstpersönlich** *adv* personally, in person; **Höchstpreis** *m* maximum price; **Höchststand** *m* peak; **höchstwahrscheinlich** *adv* most probably

Hoch- *zW*: **Hochtechnologie** *f* high technology; **hochtechnologisch** *adj* high-tech; **Hochtemperaturreaktor** *m* high-temperature reactor; **Hochtour** *f*: **auf Hochtouren laufen** *od* **arbeiten** to be working flat out; **hochtrabend** *adj* pompous; **Hoch- und Tiefbau** *m* structural and civil engineering; **Hochverrat** *m* high treason; **Hochwasser** *nt* high water; (*Überschwemmung*) floods *pl*; **hochwertig** *adj* high-class, first-rate; **Hochwürden** *m* Reverend; **Hochzahl** *f* (*Math*) exponent

Hochzeit ['hɔxtsaɪt] (**-, -en**) *f* wedding; **man kann nicht auf zwei ~en tanzen** (*Sprichwort*) you can't have your cake and eat it

Hochzeitsreise *f* honeymoon

Hochzeitstag *m* wedding day; (*Jahrestag*) wedding anniversary

hochziehen *unreg vt* (*Rollladen, Hose*) to pull up; (*Brauen*) to raise

Hocke ['hɔkə] (**-, -n**) *f* squatting position; (*beim Turnen*) squat vault; (*beim Skilaufen*) crouch

hocken ['hɔkən] *vi, vr* to squat, crouch

Hocker (**-s, -**) *m* stool

Höcker ['hœkər] (**-s, -**) *m* hump

Hockey ['hɔki] (**-s**) *nt* hockey

Hoden [['ho:dən]] (**-s, -**) *m* testicle

Hodensack *m* scrotum

Hof [ho:f] (**-(e)s, ¨-e**) *m* (*Hinterhof*) yard; (*Bauernhof*) farm; (*Königshof*) court; **einem Mädchen den ~ machen** (*veraltet*) to court a girl

hoffen ['hɔfən] *vi*: **~ (auf** *+akk***)** to hope (for)

hoffentlich *adv* I hope, hopefully

Hoffnung ['hɔfnʊŋ] *f* hope; **jdm ~en machen** to raise sb's hopes; **sich** *dat* **~en machen** to have hopes; **sich** *dat* **keine ~en machen** not to hold out any hope(s)

Hoffnungs- *zW*: **hoffnungslos** *adj* hopeless; **Hoffnungslosigkeit** *f* hopelessness; **Hoffnungsschimmer** *m* glimmer of hope; **hoffnungsvoll** *adj* hopeful

höflich ['hø:flɪç] *adj* courteous, polite; **Höflichkeit** *f* courtesy, politeness

hohe, r, s ['ho:ə(r, s)] *adj siehe* **hoch**

Höhe ['hø:ə] (**-, -n**) *f* height; (*Anhöhe*) hill; **nicht auf der ~ sein** (*fig: umg*) to feel below par; **ein Scheck in ~ von ...** a cheque (*Brit*) *od* check (*US*) for the amount of ...; **das ist doch die ~** (*fig: umg*) that's the limit; **er geht immer gleich in die ~** (*umg*) he always flares up; **auf der ~ der Zeit sein** to be up-to-date

Hoheit ['ho:haɪt] *f* (*Pol*) sovereignty; (*Titel*) Highness

Hoheits- *zW*: **Hoheitsgebiet** *nt* sovereign territory; **Hoheitsgewalt** *f* (national) jurisdiction; **Hoheitsgewässer** *nt* territorial waters *pl*; **Hoheitszeichen** *nt* national emblem

Höhen- *zW*: **Höhenangabe** *f* altitude reading; (*auf Karte*) height marking; **Höhenflug** *m*: **geistiger Höhenflug** intellectual flight; **Höhenlage** *f* altitude; **Höhenluft** *f* mountain air; **Höhenmesser** *m* altimeter; **Höhensonne** *f* sun lamp; **Höhenunterschied** *m* difference in altitude; **Höhenzug** *m* mountain chain

Höhepunkt *m* climax; (*des Lebens*) high point

höher *adj, adv* higher

hohl [ho:l] *adj* hollow; (*umg: dumm*) hollow(-headed)

Höhle ['hø:lə] (**-, -n**) *f* cave; hole; (*Mundhöhle*) cavity; (*fig, Zool*) den

Hohl- *zW*: **Hohlheit** *f* hollowness; **Hohlkreuz** *nt* (*Med*) hollow back; **Hohlmaß** *nt* measure of volume; **Hohlraum** *m* hollow space; (*Gebäude*) cavity; **Hohlsaum** *m* hemstitch; **Hohlspiegel** *m* concave mirror

Hohn [ho:n] (**-(e)s**) *m* scorn; **das ist der reinste ~** it's sheer mockery

höhnen ['hø:nən] *vt* to taunt, scoff at

höhnisch *adj* scornful, taunting

Hokuspokus [ho:kʊs'po:kʊs] (**-**) *m* (*Zauberformel*) hey presto; (*fig: Täuschung*) hocus-pocus

hold [hɔlt] *adj* charming, sweet

holen ['ho:lən] *vt* to get, fetch; (*Atem*) to take; **jdn/etw ~ lassen** to send for sb/sth; **sich** *dat* **eine Erkältung ~** to catch a cold

Holland ['hɔlant] (**-s**) *nt* Holland

Holländer ['hɔlɛndər] (**-s, -**) *m* Dutchman

Holländerin *f* Dutchwoman, Dutch girl

holländisch *adj* Dutch

Hölle ['hœlə] (**-, -n**) *f* hell; **ich werde ihm die ~ heißmachen** (*umg*) I'll give him hell

Höllenangst *f*: **eine ~ haben** to be scared to death

Höllenlärm *m* infernal noise (*umg*)

höllisch ['hœlɪʃ] *adj* hellish, infernal

Hologramm [holo'gram] (**-s, -e**) *nt* hologram

holperig ['hɔlpərɪç] *adj* rough, bumpy

holpern ['hɔlpərn] *vi* to jolt

Holunder [ho'lʊndər] (**-s, -**) *m* elder

Holz [hɔlts] (**-es, ⸚er**) *nt* wood; **aus ~** made of wood, wooden; **aus einem anderen/demselben ~ geschnitzt sein** (*fig*) to be cast in a different/the same mould; **gut ~!** (*Kegeln*) have a good game!; **Holzbläser** *m* woodwind player

hölzern ['hœltsərn] *adj* (*lit, fig*) wooden

Holz- *zW*: **Holzfäller** (**-s, -**) *m* lumberjack, woodcutter; **Holzfaserplatte** *f* (wood) fibreboard (*Brit*) *od* fiberboard (*US*); **holzfrei** *adj* (*Papier*) wood-free

holzig *adj* woody

Holz- *zW*: **Holzklotz** *m* wooden block; **Holzkohle** *f* charcoal; **Holzkopf** *m* (*fig: umg*) blockhead, numbskull; **Holzscheit** *nt* log; **Holzschuh** *m* clog; **Holzweg** *m* (*fig*) wrong track; **Holzwolle** *f* fine wood shavings *pl*; **Holzwurm** *m* woodworm

Homecomputer ['hoʊmkɔm'pju:tər] (**-s, -**) *m* home computer

Homepage ['hoʊm'pa:gə] *nt* (*Comput*) home page

Homo-Ehe ['ho:mo|e:ə] (*umg*) *f* gay marriage

homogen [homo'ge:n] *adj* homogenous

Homöopath [homøo'pa:t] (**-en, -en**) *m* homeopath

Homöopathie [homøopa'ti:] *f* homeopathy, homeopathic medicine

homosexuell [homozɛksu'ɛl] *adj* homosexual

Honduras [hɔn'du:ras] (**-**) *nt* Honduras

Hongkong [hɔŋ'kɔŋ] (**-s**) *nt* Hong Kong

Honig ['ho:nɪç] (**-s, -e**) *m* honey; **Honiglecken** *nt* (*fig*): **das ist kein Honiglecken** it's no picnic; **Honigmelone** *f* honeydew melon; **Honigwabe** *f* honeycomb

Honorar [hono'ra:r] (**-s, -e**) *nt* fee

Honoratioren [honoratsi'o:rən] *pl* dignitaries

honorieren [hono'ri:rən] *vt* to remunerate; (*Scheck*) to honour (*Brit*), honor (*US*)

Hopfen ['hɔpfən] (**-s, -**) *m* hops *pl*; **bei ihm ist ~ und Malz verloren** (*umg*) he's a dead loss

hoppla ['hɔpla] *interj* whoops

hopsen ['hɔpsən] *vi* to hop

hörbar *adj* audible

horch [hɔrç] *interj* listen

horchen *vi* to listen; (*pej*) to eavesdrop

Horcher (**-s, -**) *m* listener; eavesdropper

Horde ['hɔrdə] (**-, -n**) *f* horde

hören ['hø:rən] *vt, vi* to hear; **auf jdn/etw ~** to listen to sb/sth; **ich lasse von mir ~** I'll be in touch; **etwas/nichts von sich ~ lassen** to get/not to get in touch; **Hören** *nt*: **es verging ihm Hören und Sehen** (*umg*) he didn't know whether he was coming or going

Hörensagen *nt*: **vom ~** from hearsay

Hörer (**-s, -**) *m* (*Rundf*) listener; (*Univ*) student; (*Telefonhörer*) receiver

Hörfunk *m* radio

Hörgerät *nt* hearing aid

hörig ['hø:rɪç] *adj*: **sie ist ihm (sexuell) ~** he has (sexual) power over her

Horizont [hori'tsɔnt] (**-(e)s, -e**) *m* horizon; **das geht über meinen ~** (*fig*) that is beyond me

horizontal [horitsɔ'ta:l] *adj* horizontal

Hormon [hɔr'mo:n] (**-s, -e**) *nt* hormone

Hörmuschel *f* (*Tel*) earpiece

Horn [hɔrn] (**-(e)s, ⸚er**) *nt* horn; **ins gleiche** *od* **in jds ~ blasen** to chime in; **sich** *dat* **die Hörner abstoßen** (*umg*) to sow one's wild oats; **Hornbrille** *f* horn-rimmed spectacles *pl*

Hörnchen ['hœrnçən] *nt* (*Gebäck*) croissant

Hornhaut *f* horny skin; (*des Auges*) cornea

Hornisse [hɔr'nɪsə] (**-, -n**) *f* hornet

Hornochs, Hornochse *m* (*fig: umg*) blockhead, idiot

Horoskop [horo'sko:p] (**-s, -e**) *nt* horoscope

Hör- *zW*: **Hörrohr** *nt* ear trumpet; (*Med*) stethoscope; **Hörsaal** *m* lecture room; **Hörspiel** *nt* radio play

Hort [hɔrt] (**-(e)s, -e**) *m* hoard; (*Sch*) nursery school; **horten** *vt* to hoard

Hörweite *f*: **in/außer ~** within/out of hearing *od* earshot

Hose ['ho:ze] (**-, -n**) *f* trousers *pl*, pants *pl* (*US*); **in die ~ gehen** (*umg*) to be a complete flop

Hosen- *zW*: **Hosenanzug** *m* trouser suit, pantsuit (*US*); **Hosenboden** *m*: **sich auf den Hosenboden setzen** (*umg*) to get stuck in; **Hosenrock** *m* culottes *pl*; **Hosentasche** *f* trouser pocket; **Hosenträger** *pl* braces *pl* (*Brit*), suspenders *pl* (*US*)

Hostie ['hɔstiə] *f* (*Rel*) host

Hotel [ho'tɛl] (**-s, -s**) *nt* hotel; **Hotelfach** *nt* hotel management; **Hotel garni** *nt* bed and breakfast hotel

Hotelier [hotɛli'e:] (**-s, -s**) *m* hotelier

Hr. *abk* (= *Herr*) Mr

Hrsg. *abk* (= *Herausgeber*) ed.

hrsg. *abk* (= *herausgegeben*) ed.

HTML *abk* (= *Hyper Text Markup Language*) HTML

Hub [hu:p] (**-(e)s, ⸚e**) *m* lift; (*Tech*) stroke

hüben ['hy:bən] *adv* on this side, over here; **~ und drüben** on both sides

Hubraum *m* (*Aut*) cubic capacity

hübsch [hypʃ] *adj* pretty, nice; **immer ~ langsam!** (*umg*) nice and easy

Hubschrauber (**-s, -**) *m* helicopter

Hucke ['hʊkə] (**-, -n**) *f*: **jdm die ~ vollhauen** (*umg*) to give sb a good hiding

huckepack ['hʊkəpak] *adv* piggy-back, pick-a-back

hudeln ['hu:dəln] *vi* to be sloppy

Huf ['hu:f] (**-(e)s, -e**) *m* hoof; **Hufeisen** *nt* horseshoe; **Hufnagel** *m* horseshoe nail

Hüfte ['hyftə] (**-, -n**) *f* hip

Hüftgürtel *m* girdle

Hüfthalter *m* girdle

Hüfthose *f* hip huggers *pl*

Huftier *nt* hoofed animal, ungulate

Hügel ['hy:gəl] (**-s, -**) *m* hill

hügelig, hüglig *adj* hilly

Huhn [hu:n] (**-(e)s, ⸚er**) *nt* hen; (*Koch*) chicken; **da lachen ja die Hühner** (*umg*) it's enough to make a cat laugh; **er sah aus wie ein gerupftes ~** (*umg*) he looked as if he'd been dragged through a hedge backwards

Hühnchen ['hy:nçən] *nt* young chicken; **mit jdm ein ~ zu rupfen haben** (*umg*) to have a bone to pick with sb
Hühner- *zW*: **Hühnerauge** *nt* corn; **Hühnerbrühe** *f* chicken broth; **Hühnerklein** *nt* (*Koch*) chicken trimmings *pl*
Huld [hʊlt] (-) *f* favour (*Brit*), favor (*US*)
huldigen ['hʊldɪgən] *vi*: **jdm ~** to pay homage to sb
Huldigung *f* homage
Hülle ['hʏlə] (**-, -n**) *f* cover(ing); (*Zellophanhülle*) wrapping; **in ~ und Fülle** galore; **die ~n fallen lassen** (*fig*) to strip off
hüllen *vt*: **~ (in** *+akk***)** to cover (with); to wrap (in)
Hülse ['hʏlzə] (**-, -n**) *f* husk, shell
Hülsenfrucht *f* pulse
human [hu'ma:n] *adj* humane
humanistisch [huma'nɪstɪʃ] *adj*: **~es Gymnasium** *secondary school with bias on Latin and Greek*
humanitär [humani'tɛ:r] *adj* humanitarian
Humanität *f* humanity
Humanmedizin *f* (human) medicine
Hummel ['hʊməl] (**-, -n**) *f* bumblebee
Hummer ['hʊmər] (**-s, -**) *m* lobster
Humor [hu'mo:r] (**-s, -e**) *m* humour (*Brit*), humor (*US*); **~ haben** to have a sense of humo(u)r; **Humorist, in** *m(f)* humorist; **humoristisch** *adj* humorous; **humorvoll** *adj* humorous
humpeln ['hʊmpəln] *vi* to hobble
Humpen ['hʊmpən] (**-s, -**) *m* tankard
Humus ['hu:mʊs] (-) *m* humus
Hund [hʊnt] (**-(e)s, -e**) *m* dog; **auf den ~ kommen, vor die Hunde gehen** (*fig: umg*) to go to the dogs; **~e, die bellen, beißen nicht** (*Sprichwort*) empty vessels make most noise (*Sprichwort*); **er ist bekannt wie ein bunter ~** (*umg*) everybody knows him
Hunde- *zW*: **hundeelend** (*umg*) *adj*: **mir ist hundeelend** I feel lousy; **Hundehütte** *f* (dog) kennel; **Hundekuchen** *m* dog biscuit; **Hundemarke** *f* dog licence disc, dog tag (*US*); **hundemüde** (*umg*) *adj* dog-tired
hundert ['hʊndərt] *num* hundred; **Hundert** (**-s, -e**) *nt* hundred; **Hunderte von Menschen** hundreds of people
Hunderter (**-s, -**) *m* hundred; (*umg: Geldschein*) hundred (euro/pound/dollar *etc* note)
hundert- *zW*: **Hundertjahrfeier** *f* centenary; **Hundertmeterlauf** *m* (*Sport*): **der/ein Hundertmeterlauf** the/a hundred metres (*Brit*) *od* meters (*US*) *sing*; **hundertprozentig** *adj, adv* one hundred per cent
hundertste, r, s *adj* hundredth; **von H~n ins Tausendste kommen** (*fig*) to get carried away
Hundesteuer *f* dog licence (*Brit*) *od* license (*US*) fee
Hundewetter (*umg*) *nt* filthy weather
Hündin ['hʏndɪn] *f* bitch
Hüne ['hy:nə] (**-n, -n**) *m*: **ein ~ von Mensch** a giant of a man
Hünengrab *nt* megalithic tomb
Hunger ['hʊŋər] (**-s**) *m* hunger; **~ haben** to be hungry; **ich sterbe vor ~** (*umg*) I'm starving; **Hungerlohn** *m* starvation wages *pl*
hungern *vi* to starve
Hungersnot *f* famine
Hungerstreik *m* hunger strike
Hungertuch *nt*: **am ~ nagen** (*fig*) to be starving
hungrig ['hʊŋrɪç] *adj* hungry
Hunsrück ['hʊnsrʏk] *m* Hunsruck (Mountains *pl*)
Hupe ['hu:pə] (**-, -n**) *f* horn
hupen *vi* to hoot, sound one's horn
hupfen ['hʊpfən] *vi* to hop, jump; **das ist gehupft wie gesprungen** (*umg*) it's six of one and half a dozen of the other
hüpfen ['hʏpfən] *vi* = **hupfen**
Hupkonzert (*umg*) *nt* hooting (of car horns)
Hürde ['hʏrdə] (**-, -n**) *f* hurdle; (*für Schafe*) pen
Hürdenlauf *m* hurdling
Hure ['hu:rə] (**-, -n**) *f* whore
Hurensohn (*pej: umg!*) *m* bastard (*!*), son of a bitch (*!*)
hurra [hʊ'ra:] *interj* hurray, hurrah
hurtig ['hʊrtɪç] *adj* brisk, quick ▷ *adv* briskly, quickly
huschen ['hʊʃən] *vi* to flit, scurry
Husten ['hu:stən] (**-s**) *m* cough; **husten** *vi* to cough; **auf etw** *akk* **husten** (*umg*) not to give a damn for sth; **Hustenanfall** *m* coughing fit; **Hustenbonbon** *m od nt* cough drop; **Hustensaft** *m* cough mixture
Hut[1] [hu:t] (**-(e)s, ¨-e**) *m* hat; **unter einen ~ bringen** (*umg*) to reconcile; (*Termine etc*) to fit in
Hut[2] [hu:t] (-) *f* care; **auf der ~ sein** to be on one's guard
hüten ['hy:tən] *vt* to guard ▷ *vr* to watch out; **das Bett/Haus ~** to stay in bed/indoors; **sich ~ zu** to take care not to; **sich ~ vor** *+dat* to beware of; **ich werde mich ~!** not likely!
Hutschnur *f*: **das geht mir über die ~** (*umg*) that's going too far
Hütte ['hʏtə] (**-, -n**) *f* hut; (*Holzhütte, Blockhütte*) cabin; (*Eisenhütte*) forge; (*umg: Wohnung*) pad; (*Tech: Hüttenwerk*) iron and steel works
Hüttenindustrie *f* iron and steel industry
Hüttenkäse *m* cottage cheese
Hüttenwerk *nt* iron and steel works
hutzelig ['hʊtsəlɪç] *adj* shrivelled
Hyäne [hy'ɛ:nə] (**-, -n**) *f* hyena
Hyazinthe [hya'tsɪntə] (**-, -n**) *f* hyacinth
Hydrant [hy'drant] *m* hydrant
hydraulisch [hy'draʊlɪʃ] *adj* hydraulic
Hydrierung [hy'dri:rʊŋ] *f* hydrogenation
Hygiene [hygi'e:nə] (-) *f* hygiene
hygienisch [hygi'e:nɪʃ] *adj* hygienic
Hymne ['hʏmnə] (**-, -n**) *f* hymn, anthem
hyper- ['hʏpɛr] *präf* hyper-
Hypnose [hʏp'no:zə] (**-, -n**) *f* hypnosis
hypnotisch *adj* hypnotic
Hypnotiseur [hʏpnoti'zø:r] *m* hypnotist
hypnotisieren [hʏpnoti|zi:rən] *vt* to

hypnotize

Hypotenuse [[hypote'nu:zə]] (**-, -n**) *f* hypotenuse

Hypothek [hypo'te:k] (**-, -en**) *f* mortgage; **eine ~ aufnehmen** to raise a mortgage; **etw mit einer ~ belasten** to mortgage sth

Hypothese [hypo'te:zə] (**-, -n**) *f* hypothesis

hypothetisch [hypo'te:tɪʃ] *adj* hypothetical

Hysterie [hyste'ri:] *f* hysteria

hysterisch [hʏs'te:rɪʃ] *adj* hysterical; **einen ~en Anfall bekommen** (*fig*) to have hysterics

I i

I, i [iː] *nt* I, i; **I wie Ida** ≈ I for Isaac, I for Item (*US*); **das Tüpfelchen auf dem i** (*fig*) the final touch
i. *abk* = **in; im**
i. A. *abk* (= *im Auftrag*) p.p.
iberisch [i'beːrɪʃ] *adj* Iberian; **die I~e Halbinsel** the Iberian Peninsula
IC (-) *m abk* = **Intercityzug**
ICE *m abk* (= *Intercity-Expresszug*) inter-city train
ich [ɪç] *pron* I; **~ bins!** it's me!; **Ich (-(s), -(s))** *nt* self; (*Psych*) ego; **Ichform** *f* first person; **Ichroman** *m* novel in the first person
Ideal [ide'aːl] (**-s, -e**) *nt* ideal; **ideal** *adj* ideal; **Idealfall** *m*: **im Idealfall** ideally
Idealismus [idea'lɪsmʊs] *m* idealism
Idealist, in *m(f)* idealist
idealistisch *adj* idealistic
Idealvorstellung *f* ideal
Idee [i'deː] (**-, -n**) *f* idea; (*ein wenig*) shade, trifle; **jdn auf die ~ bringen, etw zu tun** to give sb the idea of doing sth
ideell [ide'ɛl] *adj* ideal
identifizieren [idɛntifi'tsiːrən] *vt* to identify
identisch [i'dɛntɪʃ] *adj* identical
Identität [idɛnti'tɛːt] *f* identity
Ideologe [ideo'loːgə] (**-n, -n**) *m* ideologist
Ideologie [ideolo'giː] *f* ideology
Ideologin [ideo'loːgɪn] *f* ideologist
ideologisch [ideo'loːgɪʃ] *adj* ideological
idiomatisch [idio'maːtɪʃ] *adj* idiomatic
Idiot [idi'oːt] (**-en, -en**) *m* idiot
Idiotenhügel *m* (*hum: umg*) beginners' *od* nursery slope
idiotensicher (*umg*) *adj* foolproof
Idiotin *f* idiot
idiotisch *adj* idiotic
Idol [i'doːl] *nt* (**-s, -e**) idol
idyllisch [i'dʏlɪʃ] *adj* idyllic
IG *abk* (= *Industriegewerkschaft*) *industrial trade union*
IGB (-) *m abk* (= *Internationaler Gewerkschaftsbund*) International Trades Union Congress
Igel ['iːgəl] (**-s, -**) *m* hedgehog
igitt [i'gɪt], **igittigitt** [i'gɪti'gɪt] *interj* ugh!
Iglu ['iːglu] (**-s, -s**) *m od nt* igloo
Ignorant [ɪgno'rant] (**-en, -en**) *m* ignoramus
ignorieren [ɪgno'riːrən] *vt* to ignore
IHK *f abk* = **Industrie- und Handelskammer**
ihm [iːm] *pron dat von* **er, es** (to) him, (to) it; **es ist ~ nicht gut** he doesn't feel well
ihn [iːn] *pron akk von* **er** him; (*bei Tieren, Dingen*) it
ihnen ['iːnən] *pron dat pl von* **sie** (to) them; (*nach Präpositionen*) them
Ihnen *pron dat von* **Sie** (to) you; (*nach Präpositionen*) you

SCHLÜSSELWORT

ihr [iːr] *pron* **1** (*nom pl*) you; **ihr seid es** it's you
2 (*dat von sie*) (to) her; (*bei Tieren, Dingen*) (to) it; **gib es ihr** give it to her; **er steht neben ihr** he is standing beside her
▷ *poss pron* **1** (*sing*) her; (*: bei Tieren, Dingen*) its; **ihr Mann** her husband
2 (*pl*) their; **die Bäume und ihre Blätter** the trees and their leaves

Ihr *poss pron* your
Ihre, r, s *poss pron* yours; **tun Sie das ~** (*geh*) you do your bit
ihre, r, s *poss pron* hers; (*eines Tieres*) its; (*von mehreren*) theirs; **sie taten das I~** (*geh*) they did their bit
ihrer ['iːrər] *pron gen sing von* **sie** of her; (*pl*) of them
Ihrer *pron gen von* **Sie** of you
Ihrerseits *adv* for your part
ihrerseits *adv* for her/their part
ihresgleichen *pron* people like her/them; (*von Dingen*) others like it; **eine Frechheit, die ~ sucht!** an incredible cheek!
ihretwegen *adv* (*für sie*) for her/its/their sake; (*wegen ihr, ihnen*) on her/its/their account; **sie sagte, ~ könnten wir gehen** she said that, as far as she was concerned, we could go
ihretwillen *adv*: **um ~** for her/its/their sake
ihrige ['iːrɪgə] *pron*: **der/die/das ~** *od* **Ihrige** hers; its; theirs
i. J. *abk* (= *im Jahre*) in (the year)
Ikone [i'koːnə] (**-, -n**) *f* icon
IKRK *nt abk* (= *Internationales Komitee vom Roten Kreuz*) ICRC
illegal ['ɪlegaːl] *adj* illegal
illegitim ['ɪlegitiːm] *adj* illegitimate
Illusion [ɪluzi'oːn] *f* illusion; **sich** *dat* **~en machen** to delude o.s.
illusorisch [ɪlu'zoːrɪʃ] *adj* illusory

Illustration [ɪlʊstratsi'o:n] *f* illustration
illustrieren [ɪlʊs'tri:rən] *vt* to illustrate
Illustrierte (**-n, -n**) *f* picture magazine
Iltis ['ɪltɪs] (**-ses, -se**) *m* polecat
im [ɪm] = **in dem** *präp*: **etw im Liegen/Stehen tun** do sth lying down/standing up
Image ['ɪmɪtʃ] (**-(s), -s**) *nt* image; **Imagekampagne** ['ɪmɪtʃkampanjə] *f* image-building campaign; **Imagepflege** ['ɪmɪtʃpfle:gə] (*umg*) *f* image-building; **Imageschaden** *f* damage to one's image
imaginär [imagi'nɛ:r] *adj* imaginary
Imbiss ['ɪmbɪs] (**-es, -e**) *m* snack; **Imbisshalle** *f* snack bar; **Imbissstand** *m*, **Imbissstube** *f* snack bar
Imissionswert [imisi'o:nsve:rt] *m* pollution count
imitieren [imi'ti:rən] *vt* to imitate
Imker ['ɪmkər] (**-s, -**) *m* beekeeper
immanent [ɪma'nɛnt] *adj* inherent, intrinsic
Immatrikulation [ɪmatrikulatsi'o:n] *f* (*Univ*) registration
immatrikulieren [ɪmatriku'li:rən] *vi, vr* to register
immer ['ɪmər] *adv* always; ~ **wieder** again and again; **etw ~ wieder tun** to keep on doing sth; ~ **noch** still; ~ **noch nicht** still not; **für ~** forever; ~ **wenn ich ...** every time I ...; ~ **schöner** more and more beautiful; ~ **trauriger** sadder and sadder; **was/wer (auch)** ~ whatever/whoever; **immerhin** *adv* all the same; **immerzu** *adv* all the time
Immigrant, in [ɪmi'grant(ɪn)] *m(f)* immigrant
Immobilien [ɪmo'bi:liən] *pl* real property (*Brit*), real estate (*US*); (*in Zeitungsannoncen*) property *sing*; **Immobilienhändler**, **Immobilienmakler** *m* estate agent (*Brit*), realtor (*US*)
immun [ɪ'mu:n] *adj* immune
immunisieren [ɪmuni'zi:rən] *vt* to immunize
Immunität [ɪmu:ni'tɛ:t] *f* immunity
Immunschwäche *f* immunodeficiency
Immunsystem *nt* immune system
imperativ ['ɪmperati:f] *adj*: **~es Mandat** imperative mandate
Imperativ (**-s, -e**) *m* imperative
Imperfekt ['ɪmpɛrfɛkt] (**-s, -e**) *nt* imperfect (tense)
Imperialismus [ɪmperia'lɪsmʊs] *m* imperialism
Imperialist [ɪmperia'lɪst] *m* imperialist; **imperialistisch** *adj* imperialistic
impfen ['ɪmpfən] *vt* to vaccinate
Impf- *zW*: **Impfpass** *m* vaccination card; **Impfschutz** *m* protection given by vaccination; **Impfstoff** *m* vaccine; **Impfung** *f* vaccination; **Impfzwang** *m* compulsory vaccination
implizieren [ɪmpli'tsi:rən] *vt* to imply
imponieren [ɪmpo'ni:rən] *vi +dat* to impress
Import [ɪm'pɔrt] (**-(e)s, -e**) *m* import
Importeur [ɪmpɔr'tø:r] (**-s, -e**) *m* importer
importieren [ɪmpɔr'ti:rən] *vt* to import
imposant [ɪmpo'zant] *adj* imposing
impotent ['ɪmpotɛnt] *adj* impotent
Impotenz ['ɪmpotɛnts] *f* impotence
imprägnieren [ɪmprɛ'gni:rən] *vt* to (water)proof
Impressionismus [ɪmprɛsio'nɪsmʊs] *m* impressionism
Impressum [ɪm'prɛsʊm] (**-s, -ssen**) *nt* imprint
Improvisation [ɪmprovizatsi'o:n] *f* improvisation
improvisieren [ɪmprovi'zi:rən] *vt, vi* to improvise
Impuls [ɪm'pʊls] (**-es, -e**) *m* impulse; **etw aus einem ~ heraus tun** to do sth on impulse
impulsiv [ɪmpʊl'zi:f] *adj* impulsive
imstande, im Stande [ɪm'ʃtandə] *adj*: ~ **sein** to be in a position; (*fähig*) to be able; **er ist zu allem** ~ he's capable of anything

SCHLÜSSELWORT

in [ɪn] *präp +akk* **1** (*räumlich: wohin*) in, into; **in die Stadt** into town; **in die Schule gehen** to go to school; **in die Hunderte gehen** to run into (the) hundreds
2 (*zeitlich*): **bis ins 20. Jahrhundert** into *od* up to the 20th century
▷ *präp +dat* **1** (*räumlich: wo*) in; **in der Stadt** in town; **in der Schule sein** to be at school; **es in sich haben** (*umg: Text*) to be tough; (*: Drink*) to have quite a kick
2 (*zeitlich: wann*): **in diesem Jahr** this year; (*in jenem Jahr*) in that year; **heute in zwei Wochen** two weeks today

inaktiv ['ɪn|akti:f] *adj* inactive; (*Mitglied*) non-active
Inangriffnahme [ɪn'|angrɪfna:mə] (**-, -n**) *f* (*form*) commencement
Inanspruchnahme [ɪn'|anʃprʊxna:mə] (**-, -n**) *f*: ~ (*+gen*) demands *pl* (on); **im Falle einer ~ der Arbeitslosenunterstützung** (*form*) where unemployment benefit has been sought
inbegr. *abk* (= *inbegriffen*) enc.
Inbegriff ['ɪnbəgrɪf] *m* embodiment, personification
inbegriffen *adv* included
Inbetriebnahme [ɪnbə'tri:pna:mə] (**-, -n**) *f* (*form*) commissioning; (*von Gebäude, U-Bahn etc*) inauguration
inbrünstig ['ɪnbrʏnstɪç] *adj* ardent
indem [ɪn'de:m] *konj* while; ~ **man etw macht** (*dadurch*) by doing sth
Inder, in ['ɪndər(ɪn)] (**-s, -**) *m(f)* Indian
indes [ɪn'dɛs], **indessen** [ɪn'dɛsən] *adv* meanwhile ▷ *konj* while
Index ['ɪndɛks] (**-(es), -e** *od* **Indizes**) *m*: **auf dem ~ stehen** (*fig*) to be banned; **Indexzahl** *f* index number
Indianer, in [ɪndi'a:nər(ɪn)] (**-s, -**) *m(f)* (Red *od* American) Indian
indianisch *adj* (Red *od* American) Indian
Indien ['ɪndiən] (**-s**) *nt* India

indigniert [ɪndɪ'gniːrt] *adj* indignant
Indikation [ɪndikatsi'oːn] *f*: **medizinische/soziale ~** medical/social grounds *pl* for the termination of pregnancy
Indikativ ['ɪndikatiːf] (**-s, -e**) *m* indicative
indirekt ['ɪndirɛkt] *adj* indirect; **~e Steuer** indirect tax
indisch ['ɪndɪʃ] *adj* Indian; **I~er Ozean** Indian Ocean
indiskret ['ɪndɪskreːt] *adj* indiscreet
Indiskretion [ɪndɪskretsi'oːn] *f* indiscretion
indiskutabel ['ɪndɪskutaːbəl] *adj* out of the question
indisponiert ['ɪndɪsponiːrt] *adj* (*geh*) indisposed
Individualist [ɪndividua'lɪst] *m* individualist
Individualität [ɪndividuali'tɛt] *f* individuality
Individualtourismus *m* individual tourism
individuell [ɪndividu'ɛl] *adj* individual; **etw ~ gestalten** to give sth a personal note
Individuum [ɪndi'viːduʊm] (**-s, -duen**) *nt* individual
Indiz [ɪn'diːts] (**-es, -ien**) *nt* (*Jur*) clue; **~ (für)** sign (of)
Indizes ['ɪnditseːz] *pl von* **Index**
Indizienbeweis *m* circumstantial evidence
indizieren [ɪndi'tsiːrən] *vt, vi* (*Comput*) to index
Indochina ['ɪndo'çiːna] (**-s**) *nt* Indochina
indogermanisch ['ɪndogɛr'maːnɪʃ] *adj* Indo-Germanic, Indo-European
indoktrinieren [ɪndɔktri'niːrən] *vt* to indoctrinate
Indonesien [ɪndo'neːziən] (**-s**) *nt* Indonesia
Indonesier, in (**-s, -**) *m(f)* Indonesian
indonesisch [ɪndo'neːzɪʃ] *adj* Indonesian
Indossament [ɪndɔsa'mɛnt] *nt* (*Comm*) endorsement
Indossant [ɪndɔ'sant] *m* endorser
Indossat [ɪndɔ'saːt] (**-en, -en**) *m* endorsee
indossieren *vt* to endorse
industrialisieren [ɪndʊstriali'ziːrən] *vt* to industrialize
Industrialisierung *f* industrialization
Industrie [ɪndʊs'triː] *f* industry; **in der ~ arbeiten** to be in industry; **Industriegebiet** *nt* industrial area; **Industriegelände** *nt* industrial *od* trading estate; **Industriekaufmann** *m* industrial manager
industriell [ɪndʊstri'ɛl] *adj* industrial; **~e Revolution** industrial revolution
Industrielle, r *f(m)* industrialist
Industrie- *zW*: **Industriestaat** *m* industrial nation; **Industrie- und Handelskammer** *f* chamber of industry and commerce; **Industriezone** *f* (*bes Österr, Schweiz*) industrial zone; **Industriezweig** *m* branch of industry
ineinander [ɪn|aɪ'nandər] *adv* in(to) one another *od* each other; **~ übergehen** to merge (into each other)
ineinandergreifen *unreg vi* (*lit*) to interlock; (*Zahnräder*) to mesh; (*fig: Ereignisse etc*) to overlap
Infanterie [ɪnfantə'riː] *f* infantry
Infarkt [ɪn'farkt] (**-(e)s, -e**) *m* coronary (thrombosis)
Infektion [ɪnfɛktsi'oːn] *f* infection
Infektionsherd *m* focus of infection
Infektionskrankheit *f* infectious disease
Infinitiv ['ɪnfinitiːf] (**-s, -e**) *m* infinitive
infizieren [ɪnfi'tsiːrən] *vt* to infect ▷ *vr*: **sich (bei jdm) ~** to be infected (by sb)
in flagranti [ɪn fla'granti] *adv* in the act, red-handed
Inflation [ɪnflatsi'oːn] *f* inflation
inflationär [ɪnflatsio'nɛːr] *adj* inflationary
inflationsbereinigt *adj* inflation-adjusted
Inflationsrate *f* rate of inflation
inflatorisch [ɪnfla'toːrɪʃ] *adj* inflationary
Info ['ɪnfo] (**-s, -s**) (*umg*) *nt* (information) leaflet
Infobrief ['ɪnfo-] *m* info letter
infolge [ɪn'fɔlgə] *präp +gen* as a result of, owing to; **infolgedessen** *adv* consequently
Informatik [ɪnfɔr'maːtɪk] *f* information studies *pl*
Informatiker, in (**-s, -**) *m(f)* computer scientist
Information [ɪnfɔrmatsi'oːn] *f* information *no pl*; **Informationen** *pl* (*Comput*) data; **zu Ihrer ~** for your information
Informationsabruf *m* (*Comput*) information retrieval
Informationsgesellschaft *f* information society
Informationstechnik *f* information technology
informativ [ɪnfɔrma'tiːf] *adj* informative
informieren [ɪnfɔr'miːrən] *vt*: **~ (über** *+akk***)** to inform (about) ▷ *vr*: **sich ~ (über** *+akk***)** to find out (about)
Infotelefon *nt* information line
infrage, in Frage [ɪn'fraːgə] *adv*: **etw ~ stellen** to question sth; **~ kommend** possible; (*Bewerber*) worth considering; **nicht ~ kommen** to be out of the question
Infrastruktur ['ɪnfraʃtrʊktuːr] *f* infrastructure
Infusion [ɪnfuzi'oːn] *f* infusion
Ing. *abk* = **Ingenieur**
Ingenieur [ɪnʒeni'øːr] *m* engineer; **Ingenieurschule** *f* school of engineering
Ingwer ['ɪŋvər] (**-s**) *m* ginger
Inh. *abk* (= *Inhaber(in)*) prop.; (= *Inhalt*) cont.
Inhaber, in ['ɪnhaːbər(ɪn)] (**-s, -**) *m(f)* owner; (*Comm*) proprietor; (*Hausinhaber*) occupier; (*Lizenzinhaber*) licensee, holder; (*Fin*) bearer
inhaftieren [ɪnhaf'tiːrən] *vt* to take into custody
inhalieren [ɪnha'liːrən] *vt, vi* to inhale
Inhalt ['ɪnhalt] (**-(e)s, -e**) *m* contents *pl*; (*eines Buchs etc*) content; (*Math: Flächen*) area; (*: Rauminhalt*) volume; **inhaltlich** *adj* as regards content
Inhalts- *zW*: **Inhaltsangabe** *f* summary; **Inhaltslos** *adj* empty; **Inhaltsreich** *adj* full; **Inhaltsverzeichnis** *nt* table of contents; (*Comput*) directory
inhuman ['ɪnhumaːn] *adj* inhuman
initialisieren [initsiaːli'ziːrən] *vt* (*Comput*) to initialize
Initialisierung *f* (*Comput*) initialization

Initiative [initsia'ti:və] *f* initiative; **die ~ ergreifen** to take the initiative
Initiator, in [initsi'a:tɔr, -'to:rɪn] *m(f)* *(geh)* initiator
Injektion [ɪnjɛktsi'o:n] *f* injection
injizieren [ɪnji'tsi:rən] *vt* to inject; **jdm etw ~** to inject sb with sth
Inka ['ɪŋka] **(-(s), -s)** *f(m)* Inca
Inkaufnahme [ɪn'kaʊfna:mə] *f* *(form)*: **unter ~ finanzieller Verluste** accepting the inevitable financial losses
inkl. *abk (= inklusive)* inc.
inklusive [ɪnklu'zi:və] *präp +gen* inclusive of ▷ *adv* inclusive
Inklusivpreis *m* all-in rate
inkognito [ɪn'kɔgnito] *adv* incognito
inkonsequent ['ɪnkɔnzekvɛnt] *adj* inconsistent
inkorrekt ['ɪnkɔrɛkt] *adj* incorrect
Inkrafttreten [ɪn'krafttre:tən] **(-s)** *nt* coming into force
Inkubationszeit [ɪnkubatsi'o:nstsaɪt] *f* *(Med)* incubation period
Inland ['ɪnlant] **(-(e)s)** *nt* *(Geog)* inland; *(Pol, Comm)* home (country); **im ~ und Ausland** at home and abroad; **Inlandflug** *m* domestic flight
Inlandsporto *nt* inland postage
inmitten [ɪn'mɪtən] *präp +gen* in the middle of; **~ von** amongst
innehaben ['ɪnəha:bən] *unreg vt* to hold
innehalten ['ɪnəhaltən] *unreg vi* to pause, stop
innen ['ɪnən] *adv* inside; **nach ~** inwards; **von ~** from the inside; **Innenarchitekt** *m* interior designer; **Innenaufnahme** *f* indoor photograph; **Innenbahn** *f* *(Sport)* inside lane; **Innendienst** *m*: **im Innendienst sein** to work in the office; **Inneneinrichtung** *f* (interior) furnishings *pl*; **Innenleben** *nt* *(seelisch)* emotional life; *(umg: körperlich)* insides *pl*; **Innenminister** *m* minister of the interior, Home Secretary *(Brit)*; **Innenpolitik** *f* domestic policy; **innenpolitisch** *adj* relating to domestic policy, domestic; **Innenstadt** *f* town *od* city centre *(Brit)* *od* center *(US)*
innerbetrieblich *adj* in-house; **etw ~ regeln** to settle sth within the company
innerdeutsch *adj*: **~e(r) Handel** domestic trade in Germany
Innere, s *nt* inside; *(Mitte)* centre *(Brit)*, center *(US)*; *(fig)* heart
innere, r, s *adj* inner; *(im Körper, inländisch)* internal
Innereien [ɪnə'raɪən] *pl* innards *pl*
inner- *zW*: **innerhalb** *adv* within; *(räumlich)* inside ▷ *prep +dat* within; inside; **innerlich** *adj* internal; *(geistig)* inward; **Innerlichkeit** *f* *(Liter)* inwardness; **innerparteilich** *adj*: **innerparteiliche Demokratie** democracy (with)in the party structure
Innerste, s *nt* heart; **bis ins ~ getroffen** hurt to the quick
innerste, r, s *adj* innermost

innewohnen ['ɪnəvo:nən] *vi +dat* *(geh)* to be inherent in
innig ['ɪnɪç] *adj* profound; *(Freundschaft)* intimate; **mein ~ster Wunsch** my dearest wish
Innovation [ɪnovatsi'o:n] *f* innovation
Innovationsschub [ɪnovatsi'o:nsʃu:p] *f* surge of innovations
Innung ['ɪnʊŋ] *f* (trade) guild; **du blamierst die ganze ~** *(hum: umg)* you are letting the whole side down
inoffiziell ['ɪn|ofitsiɛl] *adj* unofficial
ins [ɪns] = **in das**
Insasse ['ɪnzasə] **(-n, -n)** *m*, **Insassin** *f* *(einer Anstalt)* inmate; *(Aut)* passenger
insbesondere [ɪnsbə'zɔndərə] *adv* (e)specially
Inschrift ['ɪnʃrɪft] *f* inscription
Insekt [ɪn'zɛkt] **(-(e)s, -en)** *nt* insect
Insektenvertilgungsmittel *nt* insecticide
Insel ['ɪnzəl] **(-, -n)** *f* island
Inserat [ɪnze'ra:t] **(-(e)s, -e)** *nt* advertisement
Inserent [ɪnze'rɛnt] *m* advertiser
inserieren [ɪnze'ri:rən] *vt, vi* to advertise
insgeheim [ɪnsgə'haɪm] *adv* secretly
insgesamt [ɪnsgə'zamt] *adv* altogether, all in all
Insiderhandel ['ɪnsaɪdər-] *m* insider dealing *od* trading
Insidertipp ['ɪnsaɪdər-] *m* insider tip
insofern [ɪnzo'fɛrn] *adv* in this respect ▷ *konj* if; *(deshalb)* (and) so; **~ als** in so far as
insolvent ['ɪnzɔlvɛnt] *adj* bankrupt, insolvent
Insolvenz ['ɪnzɔlvɛnts] *f* *(Comm)* insolvency; **Insolvenzantrag** *m* application for insolvency proceedings; **Insolvenzverfahren** *nt* insolvency proceedings *pl*; **Insolvenzverwalter, in** *m(f)* official receiver
insoweit *adv, konj* = **insofern**
in spe [ɪn'ʃpe:] *(umg)* *adj*: **unser Schwiegersohn ~** our son-in-law to be, our future son-in-law
Inspektion [ɪnspɛktsi'o:n] *f* inspection; *(Aut)* service
Inspektor, in [ɪn'spɛktɔr, -'to:rɪn] **(-s, -en)** *m(f)* inspector
Inspiration [ɪnspiratsi'o:n] *f* inspiration
inspirieren [ɪnspi'ri:rən] *vt* to inspire; **sich von etw ~ lassen** to get one's inspiration from sth
inspizieren [ɪnspi'tsi:rən] *vt* to inspect
Installateur [ɪnstala'tø:r] *m* plumber; *(Elektroinstallateur)* electrician
installieren [ɪnsta'li:rən] *vt* to install *(auch fig, Comput)*
Instandhaltung [ɪn'ʃtanthaltʊŋ] *f* maintenance
inständig [ɪn'ʃtɛndɪç] *adj* urgent; **~ bitten** to beg
Instandsetzung *f* overhaul; *(eines Gebäudes)* restoration
Instanz [ɪn'stants] *f* authority; *(Jur)* court; **Verhandlung in erster/zweiter ~** first/second court case

Instanzenweg *m* official channels *pl*
Instinkt [ɪn'stɪŋkt] (**-(e)s, -e**) *m* instinct
instinktiv [ɪnstɪŋk'ti:f] *adj* instinctive
Institut [ɪnsti'tu:t] (**-(e)s, -e**) *nt* institute
Institution [ɪnstitutsi'o:n] *f* institution
Instrument [ɪnstru'mɛnt] *nt* instrument
Insulin [ɪnzu'li:n] (**-s**) *nt* insulin
inszenieren [ɪnstse'ni:rən] *vt* to direct; (*fig*) to stage-manage
Inszenierung *f* production
intakt [ɪn'takt] *adj* intact
Integralrechnung [ɪnte'gra:lrɛçnʊŋ] *f* integral calculus
Integration [ɪntegratsi'o:n] *f* integration
integrieren [ɪnte'gri:rən] *vt* to integrate; **integrierte Gesamtschule** comprehensive school (*Brit*)
Integrität [ɪntegri'tɛ:t] *f* integrity
Intellekt [ɪntɛ'lɛkt] (**-(e)s**) *m* intellect
intellektuell [ɪntɛlɛktu'ɛl] *adj* intellectual
Intellektuelle, r *f(m)* intellectual
intelligent [ɪnteli'gɛnt] *adj* intelligent
Intelligenz [ɪnteli'gɛnts] *f* intelligence; (*Leute*) intelligentsia *pl*; **Intelligenzquotient** *m* IQ, intelligence quotient
Intendant [ɪntɛn'dant] *m* director
Intensität [ɪntɛnzi'tɛ:t] *f* intensity
intensiv [ɪntɛn'zi:f] *adj* intensive
intensivieren [ɪntɛnzi'vi:rən] *vt* to intensify
Intensivkurs *m* intensive course
Intensivstation *f* intensive care unit
interaktiv *adj* (*Comput*) interactive
Intercityzug [ɪntər'sɪtitsu:k] *m* inter-city train
interessant [ɪnterɛ'sant] *adj* interesting; **sich ~ machen** to attract attention
interessanterweise *adv* interestingly enough
Interesse [ɪnte'rɛsə] (**-s, -n**) *nt* interest; **~ haben an** *+dat* to be interested in
Interessengebiet *nt* field of interest
Interessengegensatz *m* clash of interests
Interessent, in [ɪnterɛ'sɛnt(ɪn)] *m(f)* interested party; **es haben sich mehrere ~en gemeldet** several people have shown interest
Interessenvertretung *f* representation of interests; (*Personen*) group representing (one's) interests
interessieren [ɪnterɛ'si:rən] *vt*: **jdn (für etw** *od* **an etw** *dat*) **~** to interest sb (in sth) ▷ *vr*: **sich ~ für** to be interested in
interessiert *adj*: **politisch ~** interested in politics
Interkontinentalrakete [ɪntərkɔntinɛn'ta:lrake:tə] *f* intercontinental missile
interkulturell *adj* intercultural
intern [ɪn'tɛrn] *adj* internal
Internat [ɪntɛr'na:t] (**-(e)s, -e**) *nt* boarding school
international [ɪntɛrnatsio'na:l] *adj* international
Internatsschüler, in *m(f)* boarder
Internet ['ɪntɛrnɛt] (**-s**) *nt*: **das ~** the internet; **Internetanbieter, in** *m(f)* internet provider; **internetbasiert** *adj* internet-based; **internetbasierte Anwendung** internet-based application; **Internetcafé** *nt* internet café; **Internethändler, in** *m(f)* online trader *od* dealer; **Internetportal** *nt* web *od* internet portal; **Internetseite** *f* web page
internieren [ɪntɛr'ni:rən] *vt* to intern
Internierungslager *nt* internment camp
Internist, in *m(f)* internist
Interpol ['ɪntərpo:l] (**-**) *f abk* (*= Internationale Polizei*) Interpol
Interpret [ɪntər'pre:t] (**-en, -en**) *m*: **Lieder verschiedener ~en** songs by various singers
Interpretation [ɪntərpretatsi'o:n] *f* interpretation
interpretieren [ɪntɛrpre'ti:rən] *vt* to interpret
Interpretin *f siehe* **Interpret**
Interpunktion [ɪntɛrpʊŋktsi'o:n] *f* punctuation
Intervall [ɪntɛr'val] (**-s, -e**) *nt* interval
intervenieren [ɪntɛrve'ni:rən] *vi* to intervene
Interview [ɪntər'vju:] (**-s, -s**) *nt* interview; **interviewen** [-'vju:ən] *vt* to interview
intim [ɪn'ti:m] *adj* intimate; **Intimbereich** *m* (*Anat*) genital area
Intimität [ɪntimi'tɛ:t] *f* intimacy
Intimsphäre *f*: **jds ~ verletzen** to invade sb's privacy
intolerant ['ɪntolerant] *adj* intolerant
intransitiv ['ɪntranziti:f] *adj* (*Gram*) intransitive
Intrige [ɪn'tri:gə] (**-, -n**) *f* intrigue, plot
intrinsisch [ɪn'trɪnzɪʃ] *adj*: **~er Wert** intrinsic value
introvertiert [ɪntrovɛr'ti:rt] *adj*: **~ sein** to be an introvert
intuitiv [ɪntui'ti:f] *adj* intuitive
intus ['ɪntʊs] *adj*: **etw ~ haben** (*umg: Wissen*) to have got sth into one's head; (*Essen, Trinken*) to have got sth down one (*umg*)
Invalide [ɪnva'li:də] (**-n, -n**) *m* disabled person, invalid
Invalidenrente *f* disability pension
Invasion [ɪnvazi'o:n] *f* invasion
Inventar [ɪnvɛn'ta:r] (**-s, -e**) *nt* inventory; (*Comm*) assets and liabilities *pl*
Inventur [ɪnvɛn'tu:r] *f* stocktaking; **~ machen** to stocktake
investieren [ɪnvɛs'ti:rən] *vt* to invest
investiert *adj*: **~es Kapital** capital employed
Investition [ɪnvɛstitsi'o:n] *f* investment
Investitionszulage *f* investment grant
Investmentgesellschaft [ɪn'vɛstməntgəzɛlʃaft] *f* unit trust
inwiefern [ɪnvi'fɛrn] *adv* how far, to what extent
inwieweit [ɪnvi'vaɪt] *adv* how far, to what extent
Inzest [ɪn'tsɛst] (**-(e)s, -e**) *m* incest *no pl*
inzwischen [ɪn'tsvɪʃən] *adv* meanwhile
IOK *nt abk* (*= Internationales Olympisches Komitee*) IOC
Ion [i'o:n] (**-s, -en**) *nt* ion
ionisch [i'o:nɪʃ] *adj* Ionian; **I~es Meer** Ionian

Sea

IP *abk* (*Comput:* = *Internet Protocol*) IP

IQ *m abk* (= *Intelligenzquotient*) IQ

i. R. *abk* (= *im Ruhestand*) retd

IRA *f abk* (= *Irisch-Republikanische Armee*) IRA

Irak [i'ra:k] (**-s**) *m*: **(der) ~** Iraq

Iraker, in (**-s, -**) *m(f)* Iraqi

irakisch *adj* Iraqi

Iran [i'ra:n] (**-s**) *m*: **(der) ~** Iran

Iraner, in (**-s, -**) *m(f)* Iranian

iranisch *adj* Iranian

irdisch ['ɪrdɪʃ] *adj* earthly; **den Weg alles I~en gehen** to go the way of all flesh

Ire ['i:rə] (**-n, -n**) *m* Irishman; **die ~n** the Irish

irgend ['ɪrgənt] *adv* at all; **wann/was/wer ~** whenever/whatever/whoever; **irgendein, e, s** *adj* some, any; **haben Sie (sonst) noch irgendeinen Wunsch?** is there anything else you would like?; **irgendeine, r, s** *pron* (*Person*) somebody; (*Ding*) something; (*fragend, verneinend*) anybody/anything; **ich will nicht bloß irgendein(e)s** I don't want any old one; **irgendeinmal** *adv* sometime or other; (*fragend*) ever; **irgendetwas** *pron* something; (*fragend, verneinend*) anything; **irgendjemand** *pron* somebody; (*fragend, verneinend*) anybody; **irgendwann** *adv* sometime; **irgendwer** (*umg*) *pron* somebody; (*fragend, verneinend*) anybody; **irgendwie** *adv* somehow; **irgendwo** *adv* somewhere (*Brit*), someplace (*US*); (*fragend, verneinend, bedingend*) anywhere (*Brit*), any place (*US*); **irgendwohin** *adv* somewhere (*Brit*), someplace (*US*); (*fragend, verneinend, bedingend*) anywhere (*Brit*), any place (*US*)

Irin ['i:rɪn] *f* Irishwoman; Irish girl

Iris ['i:rɪs] (**-, -**) *f* iris

irisch *adj* Irish; **I~e See** Irish Sea

IRK *nt abk* (= *Internationales Rotes Kreuz*) IRC

Irland ['ɪrlant] (**-s**) *nt* Ireland; (*Republik Irland*) Eire

Irländer ['ɪrlɛndər] (**-s, -**) *m* = **Ire**; **Irländerin** *f* = **Irin**

Ironie [iro'ni:] *f* irony

ironisch [i'ro:nɪʃ] *adj* ironic(al)

irre ['ɪrə] *adj* crazy, mad; **~ gut** (*umg*) way out (*umg*); **Irre, r** *f(m)* lunatic; **irreführen** *vt* to mislead; **Irreführung** *f* fraud

irrelevant ['ɪrelevant] *adj*: **~ (für)** irrelevant (for *od* to)

irremachen *vt* to confuse

irren *vi* to be mistaken; (*umherirren*) to wander, stray ▷ *vr* to be mistaken; **jeder kann sich mal ~** anyone can make a mistake; **Irrenanstalt** *f* (*veraltet*) lunatic asylum; **Irrenhaus** *nt*: **hier geht es zu wie im Irrenhaus** (*umg*) this place is an absolute madhouse

Irrfahrt ['ɪrfa:rt] *f* wandering

irrig ['ɪrɪç] *adj* incorrect, wrong

irritieren [ɪri'ti:rən] *vt* (*verwirren*) to confuse, muddle; (*ärgern*) to irritate

Irr- *zW*: **Irrlicht** *nt* will-o'-the-wisp; **Irrsinn** *m* madness; **so ein Irrsinn, das zu tun!** what a crazy thing to do!; **irrsinnig** *adj* mad, crazy; (*umg*) terrific; **irrsinnig komisch** incredibly funny; **Irrtum** (**-s, -tümer**) *m* mistake, error; **im Irrtum sein** to be wrong *od* mistaken; **Irrtum!** wrong!; **irrtümlich** *adj* mistaken

ISBN *f abk* (= *Internationale Standardbuchnummer*) ISBN

Ischias ['ɪʃias] (**-**) *m od nt* sciatica

ISDN-Anlage [i:|ɛsde:'|ɛn-] *m* (*Tel*) ISDN connection

Islam ['ɪslam] (**-s**) *m* Islam

islamisch [ɪs'la:mɪʃ] *adj* Islamic

Island ['i:slant] (**-s**) *nt* Iceland

Isländer, in ['i:slɛndər(ɪn)] (**-s, -**) *m(f)* Icelander

isländisch *adj* Icelandic

Isolation [izolatsi'o:n] *f* isolation; (*Elek*) insulation; (*von Häftlingen*) solitary confinement

Isolator [izo'la:tɔr] *m* insulator

Isolierband *nt* insulating tape

isolieren [ɪzo'li:rən] *vt* to isolate; (*Elek*) to insulate

Isolierstation *f* (*Med*) isolation ward

Isolierung *f* isolation; (*Elek*) insulation

Israel ['ɪsrae:l] (**-s**) *nt* Israel

Israeli[1] [ɪsra'e:li] (**-(s), -s**) *m* Israeli

Israeli[2] [ɪsra'e:li] (**-, -(s)**) *f* Israeli

israelisch *adj* Israeli

isst [ɪst] *vb siehe* **essen**

ist [ɪst] *vb siehe* **sein**

Istanbul ['ɪstambu:l] (**-s**) *nt* Istanbul

Istbestand *m* (*Geld*) cash in hand; (*Waren*) actual stock

Italien [i'ta:liən] (**-s**) *nt* Italy

Italiener, in [itali'e:nər(ɪn)] (**-s, -**) *m(f)* Italian

italienisch *adj* Italian; **die ~e Schweiz** Italian-speaking Switzerland

i. V., I. V. *abk* (= *in Vertretung*) on behalf of; (= *in Vollmacht*) by proxy

IWF *m abk* (= *Internationaler Währungsfonds*) IMF

Jj

J, j [jɔt] *nt* J, j; **J wie Julius** ≈ J for Jack, J for Jig (*US*)

SCHLÜSSELWORT

ja [jaː] *adv* **1** yes; **haben Sie das gesehen? — ja** did you see it? — yes(, I did); **ich glaube ja** (yes) I think so; **zu allem Ja und Amen sagen** (*umg*) to accept everything without question
2 (*fragend*) really; **ich habe gekündigt — ja?** I've quit — have you?; **du kommst, ja?** you're coming, aren't you?
3: sei ja vorsichtig do be careful; **Sie wissen ja, dass ...** as you know, ...; **tu das ja nicht!** don't do that!; **sie ist ja erst fünf** (after all) she's only five; **Sie wissen ja, wie das so ist** you know how it is; **ich habe es ja gewusst** I just knew it; **ja, also ...** well you see ...

Jacht [jaxt] **(-, -en)** *f* yacht
Jacke ['jakə] **(-, -n)** *f* jacket; (*Wolljacke*) cardigan
Jacketkrone ['dʒɛ'kɪtkroːnə] *f* (*Zahnkrone*) jacket crown
Jackett [ʒa'kɛt] **(-s, -s** *od* **-e)** *nt* jacket
Jagd [jaːkt] **(-, -en)** *f* hunt; (*Jagen*) hunting; **Jagdbeute** *f* kill; **Jagdflugzeug** *nt* fighter; **Jagdgewehr** *nt* sporting gun; **Jagdhund** *m* hunting dog; **Jagdschein** *m* hunting licence (*Brit*) *od* license (*US*); **Jagdwurst** *f* smoked sausage
jagen ['jaːgən] *vi* to hunt; (*eilen*) to race ▷ *vt* to hunt; (*wegjagen*) to drive (off); (*verfolgen*) to chase; **mit diesem Essen kannst du mich ~** (*umg*) I wouldn't touch that food with a barge pole (*Brit*) *od* ten-foot pole (*US*)
Jäger ['jɛːgər] **(-s, -)** *m* hunter; **Jägerin** *f* huntress, huntswoman; **Jägerlatein** (*umg*) *nt* hunters' tales *pl*; **Jägerschnitzel** *nt* (*Koch*) *cutlet served with mushroom sauce*
jäh [jɛː] *adj* abrupt, sudden; (*steil*) steep, precipitous; **jählings** *adv* abruptly
Jahr [jaːr] **(-(e)s, -e)** *nt* year; **im ~(e) 1066** in (the year) 1066; **die Sechzigerjahre** *od* **sechziger ~e** the sixties *pl*; **mit dreißig ~en** at the age of thirty; **in den besten ~en sein** to be in the prime of (one's) life; **nach ~ und Tag** after (many) years; **zwischen den ~en** (*umg*) between Christmas and New Year; **jahraus** *adv*: **jahraus, jahrein** year in, year out; **Jahrbuch** *nt* annual, year book
jahrelang *adv* for years
Jahres- *zW*: **Jahresabonnement** *nt* annual subscription; **Jahresabschluss** *m* end of the year; (*Comm*) annual statement of account; **Jahresbeitrag** *m* annual subscription; **Jahresbericht** *m* annual report; **Jahreshauptversammlung** *f* (*Comm*) annual general meeting, AGM; **Jahreskarte** *f* annual season ticket; **Jahrestag** *m* anniversary; **Jahresumsatz** *m* (*Comm*) yearly turnover; **Jahreswechsel** *m* turn of the year; **Jahreszahl** *f* date, year; **Jahreszeit** *f* season
Jahr- *zW*: **Jahrgang** *m* age group; (*von Wein*) vintage; **er ist Jahrgang 1950** he was born in 1950; **Jahrhundert** *nt* century; **Jahrhundertfeier** *f* centenary; **Jahrhundertwende** *f* turn of the century
jährlich ['jɛːrlɪç] *adj, adv* yearly; **zweimal ~** twice a year
Jahr- *zW*: **Jahrmarkt** *m* fair; **Jahrtausend** *nt* millennium; **Jahrzehnt** *nt* decade
Jähzorn ['jɛːtsɔrn] *m* hot temper
jähzornig *adj* hot-tempered
Jalousie [ʒalu'ziː] *f* venetian blind
Jamaika [ja'maɪka] **(-s)** *nt* Jamaica
Jammer ['jamər] **(-s)** *m* misery; **es ist ein ~, dass ...** it is a crying shame that ...
jämmerlich ['jɛmərlɪç] *adj* wretched, pathetic; **Jämmerlichkeit** *f* wretchedness
jammern *vi* to wail ▷ *vt unpers*: **es jammert mich** it makes me feel sorry
jammerschade *adj*: **es ist ~** it is a crying shame
Jan. *abk* (= *Januar*) Jan.
Januar ['januaːr] **(-s, -e)** (*pl selten*) *m* January; *siehe auch* **September**
Japan ['jaːpan] **(-s)** *nt* Japan
Japaner, in [ja'paːnər(ɪn)] **(-s, -)** *m(f)* Japanese
japanisch *adj* Japanese
Jargon [ʒar'gõː] **(-s, -s)** *m* jargon
Jasager ['jaːzaːgər] **(-s, -)** (*pej*) *m* yes man
Jastimme *f* vote in favour (*Brit*) *od* favor (*US*) (of)
jäten ['jɛːtən] *vt, vi* to weed
Jauche ['jaʊxə] *f* liquid manure; **Jauchegrube** *f* cesspool, cesspit
jauchzen ['jaʊxtsən] *vi* to rejoice, shout (with

joy)
Jauchzer (**-s, -**) *m* shout of joy
jaulen ['jaʊlən] *vi* to howl
Jause ['jaʊzə] (*Österr*) *f* snack
jawohl *adv* yes (of course)
Jawort *nt* consent; **jdm das ~ geben** to consent to marry sb; (*bei Trauung*) to say "I do"
Jazz [dʒæz] (**-**) *m* jazz; **Jazzkeller** *m* jazz club

SCHLÜSSELWORT

je [je:] *adv* **1** (*jemals*) ever; **hast du so was je gesehen?** did you ever see anything like it?
2 (*jeweils*) every, each; **sie zahlten je 15 Euro** they paid 15 euros each
▷ *konj* **1: je nach** depending on; **je nachdem** it depends; **je nachdem, ob ...** depending on whether ...
2: je eher, desto *od* **umso besser** the sooner the better; **je länger, je lieber** the longer the better

Jeans [dʒi:nz] *pl* jeans *pl*; **Jeansanzug** *m* denim suit
jede, r, s ['je:də(r, s)] *adj* (*einzeln*) each; (*von zweien*) either; (*jede von allen*) every ▷ *indef pron* (*einzeln*) each (one); (*jede von allen*) everyone, everybody; **ohne ~ Anstrengung** without any effort; **~r Zweite** every other (one); **~s Mal** every time, each time
jedenfalls *adv* in any case
jedermann *pron* everyone; **das ist nicht ~s Sache** it's not everyone's cup of tea
jederzeit *adv* at any time
jedoch [je'dɔx] *adv* however
jeher ['je:he:r] *adv*: **von ~** all along
jein [jaɪn] *adv* (*hum*) yes no
jemals ['je:ma:ls] *adv* ever
jemand ['je:mant] *indef pron* someone, somebody; (*bei Fragen, bedingenden Sätzen, Negation*) anyone, anybody
Jemen ['je:mən] (**-s**) *m* Yemen
Jemenit, in [jeme'ni:t(ɪn)] (**-en, -en**) *m(f)* Yemeni
jemenitisch *adj* Yemeni
Jenaer Glas® ['je:naərgla:s] *nt* heatproof glass, ≈ Pyrex®
jene, r, s ['je:nə(r, s)] *adj* that; (*pl*) those ▷ *pron* that one; (*pl*) those; (*der Vorherige, die Vorherigen*) the former
jenseits ['je:nzaɪts] *adv* on the other side ▷ *präp +gen* on the other side of, beyond; **Jenseits** *nt*: **das Jenseits** the hereafter, the beyond; **jdn ins Jenseits befördern** (*umg*) to send sb to kingdom come
Jesus ['je:zʊs] (**Jesu**) *m* Jesus; **~ Christus** Jesus Christ
jetten ['dʒɛtən] (*umg*) *vi* to jet (*inf*)
jetzig ['jɛtsɪç] *adj* present
jetzt [jɛtst] *adv* now; **~ gleich** right now
jeweilig *adj* respective; **die ~e Regierung** the government of the day
jeweils *adv*: **~ zwei zusammen** two at a time; **zu ~ 10 Euro** at 10 euros each; **~ das Erste** the first each time; **~ am Monatsletzten** on the last day of each month
Jg. *abk* = **Jahrgang**
Jh. *abk* (= *Jahrhundert*) cent.
jiddisch ['jɪdɪʃ] *adj* Yiddish
Job [dʒɔp] (**-s, -s**) (*umg*) *m* job
jobben ['dʒɔbən] (*umg*) *vi* to work, have a job
Jobcenter ['dʒɔpsɛntər] *nt* job centre (*Brit*) *od* center
Jobmaschine ['dʒɔp-] *f* (*umg*) job-creation machine
Joch [jɔx] (**-(e)s, -e**) *nt* yoke
Jochbein *nt* cheekbone
Jockey, Jockei ['dʒɔke] (**-s, -s**) *m* jockey
Jod [jo:t] (**-(e)s**) *nt* iodine
jodeln ['jo:dəln] *vi* to yodel
joggen ['dʒɔgən] *vi* to jog
Joghurt, Jogurt ['jo:gʊrt] (**-s, -s**) *m od nt* yog(h)urt
Johannisbeere [jo'hanɪsbe:rə] *f*: **Rote ~** redcurrant; **Schwarze ~** blackcurrant
johlen ['jo:lən] *vi* to yell
Joint [dʒɔɪnt] (**-s, -s**) (*umg*) *m* joint
Joint Venture ['dʒɔɪntventʃə^r] (**-, -s**) *nt* joint venture
Jolle ['jɔlə] (**-, -n**) *f* dinghy
Jongleur [ʒõ'glø:r] (**-s, -e**) *m* juggler
jonglieren [ʒõ'gli:rən] *vi* to juggle
Joppe ['jɔpə] (**-, -n**) *f* jacket
Jordanien [jɔr'da:niən] (**-s**) *nt* Jordan
Jordanier, in (**-s, -**) *m(f)* Jordanian
jordanisch *adj* Jordanian
Journalismus [ʒʊrna'lɪsmʊs] *m* journalism
Journalist, in [ʒʊrna'lɪst(ɪn)] *m(f)* journalist; **journalistisch** *adj* journalistic
Jubel ['ju:bəl] (**-s**) *m* rejoicing; **~, Trubel, Heiterkeit** laughter and merriment; **Jubeljahr** *nt*: **alle Jubeljahre (einmal)** (*umg*) once in a blue moon
jubeln *vi* to rejoice
Jubilar, in [jubi'la:r(ɪn)] (**-s, -e**) *m(f) person celebrating an anniversary*
Jubiläum [jubi'lɛ:ʊm] (**-s, Jubiläen**) *nt* jubilee; (*Jahrestag*) anniversary
jucken ['jʊkən] *vi* to itch ▷ *vt*: **es juckt mich am Arm** my arm is itching; **das juckt mich** that's itchy; **das juckt mich doch nicht** (*umg*) I don't care
Juckpulver *nt* itching powder
Juckreiz *m* itch
Judaslohn ['ju:daslo:n] *m* (*liter*) blood money
Jude ['ju:də] (**-n, -n**) *m* Jew
Juden- *zW*: **Judenstern** *m* star of David; **Judentum** (**-s**) *nt* (*die Juden*) Jewry; **Judenverfolgung** *f* persecution of the Jews
Jüdin ['jy:dɪn] *f* Jewess
jüdisch *adj* Jewish
Judo ['ju:do] (**-(s)**) *nt* judo
Jugend ['ju:gənt] (**-**) *f* youth; **Jugendamt** *nt* youth welfare department; **jugendfrei** *adj* suitable for young people; (*Film*) U(-certificate), G (*US*); **Jugendherberge** *f*

youth hostel; **Jugendhilfe** *f* youth welfare scheme; **Jugendkriminalität** *f* juvenile crime; **jugendlich** *adj* youthful; **Jugendliche, r** *f(m)* teenager, young person; **Jugendliebe** *f* (*Geliebte(r)*) love of one's youth; **Jugendrichter** *m* juvenile court judge; **Jugendschutz** *m* protection of children and young people; **Jugendstil** *m* (*Kunst*) Art Nouveau; **Jugendstrafanstalt** *f* youth custody centre (*Brit*); **Jugendsünde** *f* youthful misdeed; **Jugendzentrum** *nt* youth centre (*Brit*) *od* center (*US*)

Jugoslawe [jugo'sla:və] (**-n, -n**) *m* Yugoslav

Jugoslawien [jugo'sla:viən] (**-s**) *nt* Yugoslavia

Jugoslawin [jugo'sla:vɪn] *f* Yugoslav

jugoslawisch *adj* Yugoslav(ian)

Juli ['ju:li] (**-(s), -s**) (*pl selten*) *m* July; *siehe auch* **September**

jun. *abk* (*= junior*) jun.

jung [jʊŋ] *adj* young

Junge (**-n, -n**) *m* boy, lad ▷ *nt* young animal; (*pl*) young *pl*

Jünger ['jʏŋər] (**-s, -**) *m* disciple

jünger *adj* younger

Jungfer (**-, -n**) *f*: **alte ~** old maid

Jungfernfahrt *f* maiden voyage

Jung- *zW*: **Jungfrau** *f* virgin; (*Astrol*) Virgo; **Junggeselle** *m* bachelor; **Junggesellin** *f* bachelor girl; (*älter*) single woman

Jüngling ['jʏŋlɪŋ] *m* youth

Jungsozialist *m* (*Brd Pol*) Young Socialist

jüngst [jʏŋst] *adv* lately, recently

jüngste, r, s *adj* youngest; (*neueste*) latest; **das J~ Gericht** the Last Judgement; **der J~ Tag** Doomsday, the Day of Judgement

Jungwähler, in *m(f)* young voter

Juni ['ju:ni] (**-(s), -s**) (*pl selten*) *m* June; *siehe auch* **September**

Junior ['ju:niɔr] (**-s, -en**) *m* junior

Junta ['xʊnta] (**-, -ten**) *f* (*Pol*) junta

jur. *abk* = **juristisch**

Jura ['ju:ra] *no art* (*Univ*) law

Jurist, in [ju'rɪst(ɪn)] *m(f)* jurist, lawyer; (*Student*) law student; **juristisch** *adj* legal

Juso ['ju:zo] (**-s, -s**) *m abk* = **Jungsozialist**

just [jʊst] *adv* just

Justiz [jʊs'ti:ts] (-) *f* justice; **Justizbeamte, r** *m* judicial officer; **Justizirrtum** *m* miscarriage of justice; **Justizminister** *m* minister of justice; **Justizmord** *m* judicial murder

Juwel [ju've:l] (**-s, -en**) *m od nt* jewel

Juwelier [juve'li:r] (**-s, -e**) *m* jeweller (*Brit*), jeweler (*US*); **Juweliergeschäft** *nt* jeweller's (*Brit*) *od* jeweler's (*US*) (shop)

Jux [jʊks] (**-es, -e**) *m* joke, lark; **etw aus ~ tun/sagen** (*umg*) to do/say sth in fun

jwd [jɔtve:'de:] *adv* (*hum*) in the back of beyond

Kk

K, k [ka:] *nt* K, k; **K wie Kaufmann** ≈ K for King
Kabarett [kaba'rɛt] (**-s, -e** *od* **-s**) *nt* cabaret; **Kabarettist, in** [kabarɛ'tɪst(ɪn)] *m(f)* cabaret artiste
Kabel ['ka:bəl] (**-s, -**) *nt* (*Elek*) wire; (*stark*) cable; **Kabelanschluss** *m*: **~anschluss haben** to have cable television; **Kabelfernsehen** *nt* cable television
Kabeljau ['ka:bəljaʊ] (**-s, -e** *od* **-s**) *m* cod
kabeln *vt, vi* to cable
Kabelsalat (*umg*) *m* tangle of cable
Kabine [ka'bi:nə] *f* cabin; (*Zelle*) cubicle
Kabinett [kabi'nɛt] (**-s, -e**) *nt* (*Pol*) cabinet; (*kleines Zimmer*) small room ▷ *m high-quality German white wine*
Kabriolett [kabrio'lɛt] (**-s, -s**) *nt* (*Aut*) convertible
Kachel ['kaxəl] (**-, -n**) *f* tile
kacheln *vt* to tile
Kachelofen *m* tiled stove
Kacke ['kakə] (**-, -n**) (*umg!*) *f* crap (*!*)
Kadaver [ka'da:vər] (**-s, -**) *m* carcass
Kader ['ka:dər] (**-s, -**) *m* (*Mil, Pol*) cadre; (*Sport*) squad; (*DDR, Schweiz: Fachleute*) group of specialists; **Kaderschmiede** *f* (*Pol: umg*) *institution for the training of cadre personnel*
Kadett [ka'dɛt] (**-en, -en**) *m* cadet
Käfer ['kɛ:fər] (**-s, -**) *m* beetle
Kaff [kaf] (**-s, -s**) (*umg*) *nt* dump, hole
Kaffee ['kafe] (**-s, -s**) *m* coffee; **zwei ~, bitte!** two coffees, please; **das ist kalter ~** (*umg*) that's old hat; **Kaffeekanne** *f* coffeepot; **Kaffeeklatsch** *m*, **Kaffeekränzchen** *nt* coffee circle; **Kaffeelöffel** *m* coffee spoon; **Kaffeemaschine** *f* coffee maker; **Kaffeemühle** *f* coffee grinder; **Kaffeesatz** *m* coffee grounds *pl*; **Kaffeetante** *f* (*hum*) coffee addict; (*in Café*) old biddy; **Kaffeewärmer** *m* cosy (*for coffeepot*)
Käfig ['kɛ:fɪç] (**-s, -e**) *m* cage
kahl [ka:l] *adj* bald; **~ fressen** to strip bare; **~ geschoren** shaven, shorn; **Kahlheit** *f* baldness; **kahlköpfig** *adj* bald-headed; **Kahlschlag** *m* (*in Wald*) clearing
Kahn [ka:n] (**-(e)s, ¨-e**) *m* boat, barge
Kai [kaɪ] (**-s, -e** *od* **-s**) *m* quay
Kairo ['kaɪro] (**-s**) *nt* Cairo
Kaiser ['kaɪzər] (**-s, -**) *m* emperor; **Kaiserin** *f* empress; **kaiserlich** *adj* imperial; **Kaiserreich** *nt* empire; **Kaiserschmarren** ['kaizərʃmarən] *m* (*Koch*) *sugared, cut-up pancake with raisins*; **Kaiserschnitt** *m* (*Med*) Caesarean (*Brit*) *od* Cesarean (*US*) (section)
Kajak ['ka:jak] (**-s, -s**) *m or nt* kayak
Kajüte [ka'jy:tə] (**-, -n**) *f* cabin
Kakao [ka'ka:o] (**-s, -s**) *m* cocoa; **jdn durch den ~ ziehen** (*umg: veralbern*) to make fun of sb; (*: boshaft reden*) to run sb down
Kakerlak ['ka:kərlak] (**-en, -en**) *m* cockroach
Kaktee [kak'te:ə] (**-, -n**) *f* cactus
Kaktus ['kaktʊs] (**-, -se**) *m* cactus
Kalabrien [ka'la:briən] (**-s**) *nt* Calabria
Kalauer ['ka:laʊər] (**-s, -**) *m* corny joke; (*Wortspiel*) corny pun
Kalb [kalp] (**-(e)s, ¨-er**) *nt* calf; **kalben** ['kalbən] *vi* to calve; **Kalbfleisch** *nt* veal
Kalbsleder *nt* calf(skin)
Kalender [ka'lɛndər] (**-s, -**) *m* calendar; (*Taschenkalender*) diary
Kali ['ka:li] (**-s, -s**) *nt* potash
Kaliber [ka'li:bər] (**-s, -**) *nt* (*lit, fig*) calibre (*Brit*), caliber (*US*)
Kalifornien [kali'fɔrniən] (**-s**) *nt* California
Kalk [kalk] (**-(e)s, -e**) *m* lime; (*Biol*) calcium; **Kalkstein** *m* limestone
Kalkül [kal'ky:l] (**-s, -e**) *m od nt* (*geh*) calculation
Kalkulation [kalkulatsi'o:n] *f* calculation
Kalkulator [kalku'la:tɔr] *m* cost accountant
kalkulieren [kalku'li:rən] *vt* to calculate
kalkuliert *adj*: **~es Risiko** calculated risk
Kalkutta [kal'kʊta] (**-s**) *nt* Calcutta
Kalorie [kalo'ri:] (**-, -n**) *f* calorie
kalorienarm *adj* low-calorie
kalt [kalt] *adj* cold; **mir ist (es) ~** I am cold; **~e Platte** cold meat; **der K~e Krieg** the Cold War; **etw ~ stellen** to chill, to put sth to chill; **die Wohnung kostet ~ 500 Euro** the flat costs 500 euros without heating; **~ bleiben** to be unmoved; **~ lächelnd** (*ironisch*) cool as you please; **kaltblütig** *adj* cold-blooded; (*ruhig*) cool; **Kaltblütigkeit** *f* cold-bloodedness; coolness
Kälte ['kɛltə] (**-**) *f* coldness; (*Wetter*) cold; **Kälteeinbruch** *m* cold spell; **Kältegrad** *m* degree of frost *od* below zero; **Kältewelle** *f* cold spell
kalt- *zW*: **kaltherzig** *adj* cold-hearted;

kaltmachen (*umg*) *vt* to do in; **Kaltmiete** *f* rent exclusive of heating; **Kaltschale** *f* (*Koch*) *cold sweet soup*; **kaltschnäuzig** *adj* cold, unfeeling; **kaltstellen** *vt* (*fig*) to leave out in the cold
Kalzium ['kaltsiʊm] (**-s**) *nt* calcium
kam *etc* [ka:m] *vb siehe* **kommen**
Kambodscha [kam'bɔdʒa] *nt* Cambodia
Kamel [ka'me:l] (**-(e)s, -e**) *nt* camel
Kamera ['kamera] (**-, -s**) *f* camera
Kamerad, in [kamə'ra:t, -'ra:dɪn] (**-en, -en**) *m(f)* comrade, friend; **Kameradschaft** *f* comradeship; **kameradschaftlich** *adj* comradely
Kamera- *zW*: **Kameraführung** *f* camera work; **Kameramann** (**-(e)s**, *pl* **-männer**) *m* cameraman; **Kamerarekorder** *m* camcorder; **Kameratelefon** *nt* cameraphone
Kamerun ['kaməru:n] (**-s**) *nt* Cameroon
Kamille [ka'mɪlə] (**-, -n**) *f* camomile
Kamillentee *m* camomile tea
Kamin [ka'mi:n] (**-s, -e**) *m* (*außen*) chimney; (*innen*) fireside; (*Feuerstelle*) fireplace; **Kaminfeger** (**-s, -**) *m* chimney sweep; **Kaminkehrer** (**-s, -**) *m* chimney sweep
Kamm [kam] (**-(e)s, ¨-e**) *m* comb; (*Bergkamm*) ridge; (*Hahnenkamm*) crest; **alle/alles über einen ~ scheren** (*fig*) to lump everyone/ everything together
kämmen ['kɛmən] *vt* to comb
Kammer ['kamər] (**-, -n**) *f* chamber; (*Zimmer*) small bedroom; **Kammerdiener** *m* valet; **Kammerjäger** *m* (*Schädlingsbekämpfer*) pest controller; **Kammermusik** *f* chamber music; **Kammerzofe** *f* chambermaid
Kammstück *nt* (*Koch*) shoulder
Kampagne [kam'panjə] (**-, -n**) *f* campaign
Kampf [kampf] (**-(e)s, ¨-e**) *m* fight, battle; (*Wettbewerb*) contest; (*fig: Anstrengung*) struggle; **jdm/etw den ~ ansagen** (*fig*) to declare war on sb/sth; **kampfbereit** *adj* ready for action
kämpfen ['kɛmpfən] *vi* to fight; **ich habe lange mit mir ~ müssen, ehe ...** I had a long battle with myself before ...
Kampfer ['kampfər] (**-s**) *m* camphor
Kämpfer, in (**-s, -**) *m(f)* fighter, combatant
Kampf- *zW*: **Kampfflugzeug** *nt* fighter (aircraft); **Kampfgeist** *m* fighting spirit; **Kampfhandlung** *f* action; **Kampfkunst** *f* martial arts *pl*; **kampflos** *adj* without a fight; **kampflustig** *adj* pugnacious; **Kampfplatz** *m* battlefield; (*Sport*) arena, stadium; **Kampfrichter** *m* (*Sport*) referee; **Kampfsport** *m* martial art
Kampuchea [kampʊ'tʃe:a] (**-s**) *nt* Kampuchea
Kanada ['kanada] (**-s**) *nt* Canada
Kanadier, in [ka'na:diər(ɪn)] (**-s, -**) *m(f)* Canadian
kanadisch [ka'na:dɪʃ] *adj* Canadian
Kanal [ka'na:l] (**-s, Kanäle**) *m* (*Fluss*) canal; (*Rinne*) channel; (*für Abfluss*) drain; **der ~** (*auch*: **der Ärmelkanal**) the (English) Channel
Kanalinseln *pl* Channel Islands *pl*
Kanalisation [kanalizatsi'o:n] *f* sewage system
kanalisieren [kanali'zi:rən] *vt* to provide with a sewage system; (*fig: Energie etc*) to channel
Kanaltunnel *m* Channel Tunnel
Kanarienvogel [ka'na:riənfo:gəl] *m* canary
Kanarische Inseln [ka'na:rɪʃə'ɪnzəln] *pl* Canary Islands *pl*, Canaries *pl*
Kandare [kan'da:rə] (**-, -n**) *f*: **jdn an die ~ nehmen** (*fig*) to take sb in hand
Kandidat, in [kandi'da:t(ɪn)] (**-en, -en**) *m(f)* candidate; **jdn als ~en aufstellen** to nominate sb
Kandidatur [kandida'tu:r] *f* candidature, candidacy
kandidieren [kandi'di:rən] *vi* (*Pol*) to stand, run
kandiert [kan'di:rt] *adj* (*Frucht*) candied
Kandis ['kandɪs], **Kandiszucker** ['kandɪstsʊkər] (**-**) *m* rock candy
Känguru ['kɛŋguru] (**-s, -s**) *nt* kangaroo
Kaninchen [ka'ni:nçən] *nt* rabbit
Kanister [ka'nɪstər] (**-s, -**) *m* can, canister
kann [kan] *vb siehe* **können**
Kännchen ['kɛnçən] *nt* pot; (*für Milch*) jug
Kanne ['kanə] (**-, -n**) *f* (*Krug*) jug; (*Kaffeekanne*) pot; (*Milchkanne*) churn; (*Gießkanne*) watering can
Kannibale [kani'ba:lə] (**-n, -n**) *m* cannibal
kannte *etc* ['kantə] *vb siehe* **kennen**
Kanon ['ka:nɔn] (**-s, -s**) *m* canon
Kanone [ka'no:nə] (**-, -n**) *f* gun; (*Hist*) cannon; (*fig: Mensch*) ace; **das ist unter aller ~** (*umg*) that defies description
Kanonenfutter (*umg*) *nt* cannon fodder
Kant. *abk* = **Kanton**
Kantate [kan'ta:tə] (**-, -n**) *f* cantata
Kante ['kantə] (**-, -n**) *f* edge; **Geld auf die hohe ~ legen** (*umg*) to put money by
kantig ['kantɪç] *adj* (*Holz*) edged; (*Gesicht*) angular
Kantine [kan'ti:nə] *f* canteen
Kanton [kan'to:n] (**-s, -e**) *m* canton
Kantor ['kantɔr] *m* choirmaster
Kanu ['ka:nu] (**-s, -s**) *nt* canoe
Kanzel ['kantsəl] (**-, -n**) *f* pulpit; (*Aviat*) cockpit
Kanzlei [kants'laɪ] *f* chancery; (*Büro*) chambers *pl*
Kanzler, in ['kantslər] (**-s, -**) *m(f)* chancellor
Kanzlerkandidatur *f* candidacy for the chancellorship
Kap [kap] (**-s, -s**) *nt* cape; **das ~ der guten Hoffnung** the Cape of Good Hope
Kapazität [kapatsi'tɛ:t] *f* capacity; (*Fachmann*) authority
Kapelle [ka'pɛlə] *f* (*Gebäude*) chapel; (*Mus*) band
Kapellmeister, in *m(f)* director of music; (*Mil, von Tanzkapelle etc*) bandmaster, bandleader
Kaper ['ka:pər] (**-, -n**) *f* caper
kapern *vt* to capture
kapieren [ka'pi:rən] (*umg*) *vt, vi* to understand
Kapital [kapi'ta:l] (**-s, -e** *od* **-ien**) *nt* capital; **aus etw ~ schlagen** (*pej: lit, fig*) to make capital out of sth; **Kapitalanlage** *f*

investment; **Kapitalaufwand** *m* capital expenditure; **Kapitalertrag** *m* capital gains *pl*; **Kapitalertragssteuer** *f* capital gains tax; **Kapitalflucht** *f* flight of capital; **Kapitalgesellschaft** *f* (*Comm*) joint-stock company; **Kapitalgüter** *pl* capital goods *pl*; **kapitalintensiv** *adj* capital-intensive

Kapitalismus [kapita'lɪsmʊs] *m* capitalism

Kapitalist [kapita'lɪst] *m* capitalist

kapitalistisch *adj* capitalist

Kapital- *zW*: **kapitalkräftig** *adj* wealthy; **Kapitalmarkt** *m* money market; **kapitalschwach** *adj* financially weak; **kapitalstark** *adj* financially strong; **Kapitalverbrechen** *nt* serious crime; (*mit Todesstrafe*) capital crime

Kapitän [kapi'tɛːn] (**-s, -e**) *m* captain

Kapitel [ka'pɪtəl] (**-s, -**) *nt* chapter; **ein trauriges ~** (*Angelegenheit*) a sad story

Kapitulation [kapitulatsi'oːn] *f* capitulation

kapitulieren [kapitu'liːrən] *vi* to capitulate

Kaplan [ka'plaːn] (**-s, Kapläne**) *m* chaplain

Kappe ['kapə] (**-, -n**) *f* cap; (*Kapuze*) hood; **das nehme ich auf meine ~** (*fig: umg*) I'll take the responsibility for that

kappen *vt* to cut

Kapsel ['kapsəl] (**-, -n**) *f* capsule

Kapstadt ['kapʃtat] *nt* Cape Town

kaputt [ka'pʊt] (*umg*) *adj* smashed, broken; (*Person*) exhausted, knackered; **etw ~ machen/schlagen** to break/smash sth; **der Fernseher ist ~** the TV's not working; **ein ~er Typ** a bum; *siehe auch* **kaputtmachen**; **kaputtgehen** *unreg vi* to break; (*Schuhe*) to fall apart; (*Firma*) to go bust; (*Stoff*) to wear out; (*sterben*) to cop it (*umg*); **kaputtlachen** *vr* to laugh o.s. silly; **kaputtmachen** *vt* to break; (*Mensch*) to exhaust, wear out; **kaputtschlagen** *unreg vt* to smash

Kapuze [ka'puːtsə] (**-, -n**) *f* hood

Karabiner [kara'biːnər] (**-s, -**) *m* (*Gewehr*) carbine

Karacho [ka'raxo] (**-s**) *nt*: **mit ~** (*umg*) hell for leather

Karaffe [ka'rafə] (**-, -n**) *f* carafe; (*geschliffen*) decanter

Karambolage [karambo'laːʒə] (**-, -n**) *f* (*Zusammenstoß*) crash

Karamell [kara'mɛl] (**-s**) *m* caramel; **Karamellbonbon** *m od nt* toffee

Karat [ka'raːt] (**-(e)s, -e**) *nt* carat

Karate (**-s**) *nt* karate

Karawane [kara'vaːnə] (**-, -n**) *f* caravan

Kardinal [kardi'naːl] (**-s, Kardinäle**) *m* cardinal; **Kardinalfehler** *m* cardinal error; **Kardinalzahl** *f* cardinal number

Karenzzeit [ka'rɛntstsaɪt] *f* waiting period

Karfreitag [kaːr'fraɪtaːk] *m* Good Friday

karg [kark] *adj* scanty, poor; (*Mahlzeit*) meagre (*Brit*), meager (*US*); **etw ~ bemessen** to be mean with sth; **Kargheit** *f* poverty, scantiness; meagreness (*Brit*), meagerness (*US*)

kärglich ['kɛrklɪç] *adj* poor, scanty

Kargo ['kargo] (**-s, -s**) *m* (*Comm*) cargo

Karibik [ka'riːbɪk] (-) *f*: **die ~** the Caribbean

karibisch *adj* Caribbean; **das K~e Meer** the Caribbean Sea

kariert [ka'riːrt] *adj* (*Stoff*) checked (*Brit*), checkered (*US*); (*Papier*) squared; **~ reden** (*umg*) to talk rubbish *od* nonsense

Karies ['kaːriɛs] (-) *f* caries

Karikatur [karika'tuːr] *f* caricature; **Karikaturist, in** [karikatuː'rɪst(ɪn)] *m(f)* cartoonist

karikieren [kari'kiːrən] *vt* to caricature

karitativ [karita'tiːf] *adj* charitable

Karneval ['karnəval] (**-s, -e** *od* **-s**) *m* carnival; *see culture note*

KARNEVAL

Karneval is the name given to the days immediately before Lent when people gather to sing, dance, eat, drink and generally make merry before the fasting begins. *Rosenmontag*, the day before Shrove Tuesday, is the most important day of Karneval on the Rhine. Most firms take a day's holiday on that day to enjoy the parades and revelry. In South Germany Karneval is called "Fasching".

Karnickel [kar'nɪkəl] (**-s, -**) (*umg*) *nt* rabbit

Kärnten ['kɛrntən] (**-s**) *nt* Carinthia

Karo ['kaːro] (**-s, -s**) *nt* square; (*Karten*) diamonds; **Karoass** *nt* ace of diamonds

Karosse [ka'rɔsə] (**-, -n**) *f* coach, carriage

Karosserie [karɔsə'riː] *f* (*Aut*) body(work)

Karotte [ka'rɔtə] (**-, -n**) *f* carrot

Karpaten [kar'paːtən] *pl* Carpathians *pl*

Karpfen ['karpfən] (**-s, -**) *m* carp

Karre ['karə] (**-, -n**) *f* = **Karren**

Karree [kaː'reː] (**-s, -s**) *nt*: **einmal ums ~ gehen** (*umg*) to walk around the block

karren ['karən] *vt* to cart, transport; **Karren** (**-s, -**) *m* cart, barrow; **den Karren aus dem Dreck ziehen** (*umg*) to get things sorted out

Karriere [kari'ɛːrə] (**-, -n**) *f* career; **~ machen** to get on, get to the top; **Karrieremacher, in** *m(f)* careerist

Karsamstag [kaːr'zamstaːk] *m* Easter Saturday

Karst [karst] (**-s, -e**) *m* (*Geog, Geol*) karst, *barren landscape*

Karte ['kartə] (**-, -n**) *f* card; (*Landkarte*) map; (*Speisekarte*) menu; (*Eintrittskarte, Fahrkarte*) ticket; **mit offenen ~n spielen** (*fig*) to put one's cards on the table; **alles auf eine ~ setzen** to put all one's eggs in one basket

Kartei [kar'taɪ] *f* card index; **Karteikarte** *f* index card; **Karteileiche** (*umg*) *f* sleeping *od* non-active member; **Karteischrank** *m* filing cabinet

Kartell [kar'tɛl] (**-s, -e**) *nt* cartel; **Kartellamt** *nt* monopolies commission; **Kartellgesetzgebung** *f* anti-trust legislation

Karten- *zW*: **Kartenhaus** *nt* (*lit, fig*) house of cards; **Kartenlegen** *nt* fortune-telling (*using cards*); **Kartenspiel** *nt* card game; (*Karten*) pack (*Brit*) *od* deck (*US*) of cards; **Kartentelefon** *nt* cardphone; **Kartenvorverkauf** *m* advance sale of tickets
Kartoffel [kar'tɔfəl] (**-, -n**) *f* potato; **Kartoffelbrei** *m* mashed potatoes *pl*; **Kartoffelchips** *pl* potato crisps *pl* (*Brit*), potato chips *pl* (*US*); **Kartoffelpüree** *nt* mashed potatoes *pl*; **Kartoffelsalat** *m* potato salad
Karton [kar'tõ:] (**-s, -s**) *m* cardboard; (*Schachtel*) cardboard box
kartoniert [karto'ni:rt] *adj* hardback
Karussell [karʊ'sɛl] (**-s, -s**) *nt* roundabout (*Brit*), merry-go-round
Karwoche ['ka:rvɔxə] *f* Holy Week
Karzinom [kartsi'no:m] (**-s, -e**) *nt* (*Med*) carcinoma
Kasachstan [kazaxs'ta:n] (**-s**) *nt* (*Geog*) Kazakhstan
Kaschemme [ka'ʃɛmə] (**-, -n**) *f* dive
kaschieren [ka'ʃi:rən] *vt* to conceal, cover up
Kaschmir ['kaʃmi:r] (**-s**) *nt* (*Geog*) Kashmir
Käse ['kɛ:zə] (**-s, -**) *m* cheese; (*umg*: *Unsinn*) rubbish, twaddle; **Käseblatt** (*umg*) *nt* (local) rag; **Käseglocke** *f* cheese cover; **Käsekuchen** *m* cheesecake
Kaserne [ka'zɛrnə] (**-, -n**) *f* barracks *pl*
Kasernenhof *m* parade ground
käsig ['kɛ:zɪç] *adj* (*fig*: *umg*: *Gesicht, Haut*) pasty, pale; (*vor Schreck*) white; (*lit*) cheesy
Kasino [ka'zi:no] (**-s, -s**) *nt* club; (*Mil*) officers' mess; (*Spielkasino*) casino
Kaskoversicherung ['kaskofɛrzɪçərʊŋ] *f* (*Aut*: *Teilkaskoversicherung*) ≈ third party, fire and theft insurance; (: *Vollkaskoversicherung*) fully comprehensive insurance
Kasper ['kaspər] (**-s, -**) *m* Punch; (*fig*) clown
Kasperletheater ['kaspərləteа:tər], **Kasperltheater** ['kaspərltea:tər] *nt* Punch and Judy (show)
Kaspisches Meer ['kaspɪʃəs'me:r] *nt* Caspian Sea
Kasse ['kasə] (**-, -n**) *f* (*Geldkasten*) cashbox; (*in Geschäft*) till, cash register; (*Kinokasse, Theaterkasse etc*) box office; (*Krankenkasse*) health insurance; (*Sparkasse*) savings bank; **die ~ führen** to be in charge of the money; **jdn zur ~ bitten** to ask sb to pay up; **~ machen** to count the money; **getrennte ~ führen** to pay separately; **an der ~** (*in Geschäft*) at the (cash) desk; **gut bei ~ sein** to be in the money
Kasseler ['kasələr] (**-s, -**) *nt* *lightly smoked pork loin*
Kassen- *zW*: **Kassenarzt** *m* ≈ National Health doctor (*Brit*), ≈ panel doctor (*US*); **Kassenbestand** *m* cash balance; **Kassenführer** *m* (*Comm*) cashier; **Kassenpatient** *m* ≈ National Health patient (*Brit*); **Kassenprüfung** *f* audit; **Kassenschlager** (*umg*) *m* (*Theat etc*) box-office hit; (: *Ware*) big seller; **Kassensturz** *m*: **Kassensturz machen** to check one's money; **Kassenwart** *m* (*von Klub etc*) treasurer; **Kassenzettel** *m* sales slip
Kasserolle [kasə'rɔlə] (**-, -n**) *f* casserole
Kassette [ka'sɛtə] *f* small box; (*Tonband, Phot*) cassette; (*Comput*) cartridge, cassette; (*Bücherkassette*) case
Kassettenrekorder (**-s, -**) *m* cassette recorder
Kassiber [ka'si:bər] (**-s, -**) *m* (*in Gefängnis*) secret message
kassieren [ka'si:rən] *vt* (*Gelder etc*) to collect; (*umg*: *wegnehmen*) to take (away) ▷ *vi*: **darf ich ~?** would you like to pay now?
Kassierer, in [ka'si:rər(ɪn)] (**-s, -**) *m(f)* cashier; (*von Klub*) treasurer
Kastanie [kas'ta:niə] *f* chestnut
Kastanienbaum *m* chestnut tree
Kästchen ['kɛstçən] *nt* small box, casket
Kaste ['kastə] (**-, -n**) *f* caste
Kasten ['kastən] (**-s, ¨**) *m* box (*auch Sport*), case; (*Truhe*) chest; **er hat was auf dem ~** (*umg*) he's brainy; **Kastenform** *f* (*Koch*) (square) baking tin (*Brit*) *od* pan (*US*); **Kastenwagen** *m* van
kastrieren [kas'tri:rən] *vt* to castrate
Kat (**-, -s**) *m abk* (*Aut*) = **Katalysator**
katalanisch [kata'la:nɪʃ] *adj* Catalan
Katalog [kata'lo:k] (**-(e)s, -e**) *m* catalogue (*Brit*), catalog (*US*)
katalogisieren [katalogi'zi:rən] *vt* to catalogue (*Brit*), catalog (*US*)
Katalysator [kataly'za:tɔr] *m* (*lit, fig*) catalyst; (*Aut*) catalytic converter; **~-Auto** vehicle fitted with a catalytic converter
Katapult [kata'pʊlt] (**-(e)s, -e**) *nt or m* catapult
katapultieren [katapʊl'ti:rən] *vt* to catapult ▷ *vr* to catapult o.s.; (*Pilot*) to eject
Katar ['ka:tar] *nt* Qatar
Katarrh, Katarr [ka'tar] (**-s, -e**) *m* catarrh
Katasteramt [ka'tastəramt] *nt* land registry
katastrophal [katastro'fa:l] *adj* catastrophic
Katastrophe [kata'stro:fə] (**-, -n**) *f* catastrophe, disaster
Katastrophen- *zW*: **Katastrophenalarm** *m* emergency alert; **Katastrophengebiet** *nt* disaster area; **Katastrophenmedizin** *f* medical treatment in disasters; **Katastrophenmeldung** *f* news of a/the catastrophe; **Katastrophenschutz** *m* disaster control
Katechismus [katɛ'çɪsmʊs] *m* catechism
Kategorie [katego'ri:] *f* category
kategorisch [kate'go:rɪʃ] *adj* categorical
kategorisieren [kategori'zi:rən] *vt* to categorize
Kater ['ka:tər] (**-s, -**) *m* tomcat; (*umg*) hangover; **Katerfrühstück** *nt* *breakfast (of pickled herring etc) to cure a hangover*
kath. *abk* = **katholisch**
Katheder [ka'te:dər] (**-s, -**) *nt* (*Sch*) teacher's desk; (*Univ*) lectern
Kathedrale [kate'dra:lə] (**-, -n**) *f* cathedral
Katheter [ka'te:tər] (**-s, -**) *m* (*Med*) catheter
Kathode [ka'to:də] (**-, -n**) *f* cathode
Katholik, in [kato'li:k(ɪn)] (**-en, -en**) *m(f)* Catholic

katholisch [ka'to:lɪʃ] *adj* Catholic
Katholizismus [katoli'tsɪsmʊs] *m* Catholicism
Katode [ka'to:də] **(-, -n)** *f* = **Kathode**
katzbuckeln ['katsbʊkəln] *(pej: umg) vi* to bow and scrape
Kätzchen ['kɛtsçən] *nt* kitten
Katze ['katsə] **(-, -n)** *f* cat; **die ~ im Sack kaufen** to buy a pig in a poke; **für die Katz** *(umg)* in vain, for nothing
Katzen- *zW:* **Katzenauge** *nt* cat's-eye *(Brit)*; *(am Fahrrad)* rear light; **Katzenjammer** *(umg) m* hangover; **Katzenmusik** *f (fig)* caterwauling; **Katzensprung** *(umg) m* stone's throw, short distance; **Katzentür** *f* cat flap; **Katzenwäsche** *f* a lick and a promise
Kauderwelsch ['kaʊdərvɛlʃ] **(-(s))** *nt* jargon; *(umg)* double Dutch *(Brit)*
kauen ['kaʊən] *vt, vi* to chew
kauern ['kaʊərn] *vi* to crouch
Kauf [kaʊf] **(-(e)s, Käufe)** *m* purchase, buy; *(Kaufen)* buying; **ein guter ~** a bargain; **etw in ~ nehmen** to put up with sth
kaufen *vt* to buy; **dafür kann ich mir nichts ~** *(ironisch)* what use is that to me!
Käufer, in ['kɔʏfər(ɪn)] **(-s, -)** *m(f)* buyer
Käuferverhalten *nt* buying habits *pl*
Kauf- *zW:* **Kauffrau** *f* businesswoman; *(Einzelhandelskauffrau)* shopkeeper; **kauffreudig** *adj* consumerist; **Kaufhaus** *nt* department store; **Kaufkraft** *f* purchasing power; **Kaufladen** *m* shop, store
käuflich ['kɔʏflɪç] *adj* purchasable, for sale; *(pej)* venal ▷ *adv:* **~ erwerben** to purchase
Kauf- *zW:* **Kauflust** *f* desire to buy things; *(Börse)* buying; **kauflustig** *adj* interested in buying; **Kaufmann** **(-(e)s,** *pl* **-leute)** *m* businessman; *(Einzelhandelskaufmann)* shopkeeper; **kaufmännisch** *adj* commercial; **kaufmännischer Angestellter** clerk; **Kaufpreis** *m* purchase price; **kaufsüchtig** *adj:* **kaufsüchtig sein** to be a shopaholic *(umg)*; **Kaufvertrag** *m* bill of sale; **Kaufwillige, r** *f(m)* potential buyer; **Kaufzurückhaltung** *f* consumer reticence; **Kaufzwang** *m:* **kein/ohne Kaufzwang** no/without obligation
Kaugummi ['kaʊgʊmi] *m* chewing gum
Kaukasus ['kaʊkazʊs] *m:* **der ~** the Caucasus
Kaulquappe ['kaʊlkvapə] **(-, -n)** *f* tadpole
kaum [kaʊm] *adv* hardly, scarcely; **wohl ~, ich glaube ~** I hardly think so
Kausalzusammenhang [kaʊ'za:ltsuzamənhaŋ] *m* causal connection
Kaution [kaʊtsi'o:n] *f* deposit; *(Jur)* bail
Kautschuk ['kaʊtʃʊk] **(-s, -e)** *m* India rubber
Kauz [kaʊts] **(-es, Käuze)** *m* owl; *(fig)* queer fellow
Kavalier [kava'li:r] **(-s, -e)** *m* gentleman
Kavaliersdelikt *nt* peccadillo
Kavallerie [kavalə'ri:] *f* cavalry
Kavallerist [kavalə'rɪst] *m* cavalryman
Kaviar ['ka:viar] *m* caviar
KB *nt abk (= Kilobyte)* KB, kbyte
Kcal *abk (= Kilokalorie)* kcal
keck [kɛk] *adj* daring, bold; **Keckheit** *f* daring, boldness
Kegel ['ke:gəl] **(-s, -)** *m* skittle; *(Math)* cone; **Kegelbahn** *f* skittle alley, bowling alley; **kegelförmig** *adj* conical
kegeln *vi* to play skittles
Kehle ['ke:lə] **(-, -n)** *f* throat; **er hat das in die falsche ~ bekommen** *(lit)* it went down the wrong way; *(fig)* he took it the wrong way; **aus voller ~** at the top of one's voice
Kehl- *zW:* **Kehlkopf** *m* larynx; **Kehlkopfkrebs** *m* cancer of the throat; **Kehllaut** *m* guttural
Kehre ['ke:rə] **(-, -n)** *f* turn(ing), bend
kehren *vt, vi (wenden)* to turn; *(mit Besen)* to sweep; **sich an etw** *dat* **nicht ~** not to heed sth; **in sich** *akk* **gekehrt** *(versunken)* pensive; *(verschlossen)* introspective, introverted
Kehricht **(-s)** *m* sweepings *pl*
Kehr- *zW:* **Kehrmaschine** *f* sweeper; **Kehrreim** *m* refrain; **Kehrseite** *f* reverse, other side; *(ungünstig)* wrong *od* bad side; **die Kehrseite der Medaille** the other side of the coin
kehrtmachen *vi* to turn about, about-turn
Kehrtwendung *f* about-turn
keifen ['kaɪfən] *vi* to scold, nag
Keil [kaɪl] **(-(e)s, -e)** *m* wedge; *(Mil)* arrowhead; **keilen** *vt* to wedge ▷ *vr* to fight
Keilerei [kaɪlə'raɪ] *(umg) f* punch-up
Keilriemen *m (Aut)* fan belt
Keim [kaɪm] **(-(e)s, -e)** *m* bud; *(Med, fig)* germ; **etw im ~ ersticken** to nip sth in the bud
keimen *vi* to germinate
Keim- *zW:* **keimfrei** *adj* sterile; **keimtötend** *adj* antiseptic, germicidal; **Keimzelle** *f (fig)* nucleus
kein ['kaɪn], **keine** ['kaɪnə] *pron* none ▷ *adj* no, not any; **~e schlechte Idee** not a bad idea; **~e Stunde/drei Monate** *(nicht einmal)* less than an hour/three months
keine, r, s *indef pron* no one, nobody; *(von Gegenstand)* none
keinerlei ['kaɪnər'laɪ] *adj attrib* no ... whatever
keinesfalls *adv* on no account
keineswegs *adv* by no means
keinmal *adv* not once
Keks [ke:ks] **(-es, -e)** *m od nt* biscuit *(Brit)*, cookie *(US)*
Kelch [kɛlç] **(-(e)s, -e)** *m* cup, goblet, chalice
Kelle ['kɛlə] **(-, -n)** *f* ladle; *(Maurerkelle)* trowel
Keller ['kɛlər] **(-s, -)** *m* cellar; **Kellerassel** **(-, -n)** *f* woodlouse
Kellerei [kɛlə'raɪ] *f* wine cellars *pl*; *(Firma)* wine producer
Kellergeschoss *nt* basement
Kellerwohnung *f* basement flat *(Brit) od* apartment *(US)*
Kellner, in ['kɛlnər(ɪn)] **(-s, -)** *m(f)* waiter, waitress
kellnern *(umg) vi* to work as a waiter/waitress *(Brit)*, wait on tables *(US)*
Kelte ['kɛltə] **(-n, -n)** *m* Celt
Kelter **(-, -n)** *f* winepress; *(Obstkelter)* press
keltern ['kɛltərn] *vt* to press

Keltin ['kɛltɪn] *f* (female) Celt
keltisch *adj* Celtic
Kenia ['ke:nia] (**-s**) *nt* Kenya
kennen ['kɛnən] *unreg vt* to know; **~ Sie sich schon?** do you know each other (already)?; **kennst du mich noch?** do you remember me?
kennenlernen *vt* to get to know ▷ *vr* to get to know each other; (*zum ersten Mal*) to meet
Kenner, in (**-s, -**) *m(f)*: **~ (von** *od* **+gen)** connoisseur (of); expert (on)
Kennkarte *f* identity card
kenntlich *adj* distinguishable, discernible; **etw ~ machen** to mark sth
Kenntnis (**-, -se**) *f* knowledge *no pl*; **etw zur ~ nehmen** to note sth; **von etw ~ nehmen** to take notice of sth; **jdn in ~ setzen** to inform sb; **über ~se von etw verfügen** to be knowledgeable about sth
Kenn- *zW*: **Kennwort** *nt* (*Chiffre*) code name; (*Losungswort*) password, code word; **Kennzeichen** *nt* mark, characteristic; **(amtliches/polizeiliches) Kennzeichen** (*Aut*) number plate (*Brit*), license plate (*US*); **kennzeichnen** *vt untr* to characterize; **kennzeichnenderweise** *adv* characteristically; **Kennziffer** *f* (code) number; (*Comm*) reference number
kentern ['kɛntərn] *vi* to capsize
Keramik [ke'ra:mɪk] (**-, -en**) *f* ceramics *pl*, pottery; (*Gegenstand*) piece of ceramic work *od* pottery
Kerbe ['kɛrbə] (**-, -n**) *f* notch, groove
Kerbel (**-s, -**) *m* chervil
kerben *vt* to notch
Kerbholz *nt*: **etw auf dem ~ haben** to have done sth wrong
Kerker ['kɛrkər] (**-s, -**) *m* prison
Kerl [kɛrl] (**-s, -e**) (*umg*) *m* chap, bloke (*Brit*), guy; **du gemeiner ~!** you swine!
Kern [kɛrn] (**-(e)s, -e**) *m* (*Obstkern*) pip, stone; (*Nusskern*) kernel; (*Atomkern*) nucleus; (*fig*) heart, core; **Kernenergie** *f* nuclear energy; **Kernfach** *nt* (*Sch*) core subject; **Kernfamilie** *f* nuclear family; **Kernforschung** *f* nuclear research; **Kernfrage** *f* central issue; **Kernfusion** *f* nuclear fusion; **Kerngehäuse** *nt* core; **kerngesund** *adj* thoroughly healthy, fit as a fiddle
kernig *adj* robust; (*Ausspruch*) pithy
Kern- *zW*: **Kernkompetenz** *f* core competence; **Kernkraftwerk** *nt* nuclear power station; **Kernland** *f* heartland; **kernlos** *adj* seedless, pipless; **Kernphysik** *f* nuclear physics *sing*; **Kernreaktion** *f* nuclear reaction; **Kernreaktor** *m* nuclear reactor; **Kernschmelze** *f* meltdown; **Kernseife** *f* washing soap; **Kernspaltung** *f* nuclear fission; **Kernstück** *nt* (*fig*) main item; (*von Theorie etc*) central part, core; **Kernwaffen** *pl* nuclear weapons *pl*; **kernwaffenfrei** *adj* nuclear-free; **Kernzeit** *f* core time
Kerze ['kɛrtsə] (**-, -n**) *f* candle; (*Zündkerze*) plug
Kerzen- *zW*: **kerzengerade** *adj* straight as a die; **Kerzenhalter** *m* candlestick; **Kerzenständer** *m* candleholder
kess [kɛs] *adj* saucy
Kessel ['kɛsəl] (**-s, -**) *m* kettle; (*von Lokomotive etc*) boiler; (*Mulde*) basin; (*Geog*) depression; (*Mil*) encirclement; **Kesselstein** *m* scale, fur (*Brit*); **Kesseltreiben** *nt* (*fig*) witch-hunt
Kette ['kɛtə] (**-, -n**) *f* chain; **jdn an die ~ legen** (*fig*) to tie sb down
ketten *vt* to chain
Ketten- *zW*: **Kettenfahrzeug** *nt* tracked vehicle; **Kettenhund** *m* watchdog; **Kettenkarussell** *nt* merry-go-round (*with gondolas on chains*); **Kettenladen** *m* chain store; **Kettenrauchen** *nt* chain smoking; **Kettenreaktion** *f* chain reaction
Ketzer, in ['kɛtsər(ɪn)] (**-s, -**) *m(f)* heretic; **Ketzerei** [kɛtsə'raɪ] *f* heresy; **ketzerisch** *adj* heretical
keuchen ['kɔʏçən] *vi* to pant, gasp
Keuchhusten *m* whooping cough
Keule ['kɔʏlə] (**-, -n**) *f* club; (*Koch*) leg
Keulung ['kɔʏlʊŋ] *f* cull, culling
keusch [kɔʏʃ] *adj* chaste; **Keuschheit** *f* chastity
Kfm. *abk* = **Kaufmann**
kfm. *abk* = **kaufmännisch**
Kfz (**-(s), -(s)**) *f abk* = **Kraftfahrzeug**
KG (**-, -s**) *f abk* = **Kommanditgesellschaft**
kg *abk* (= *Kilogramm*) kg
kHz *abk* (= *Kilohertz*) kHz
Kibbuz [kɪ'bu:ts] (**-, Kibbuzim** *od* **-e**) *m* kibbutz
kichern ['kɪçərn] *vi* to giggle
kicken ['kɪkən] *vt, vi* (*Fußball*) to kick
kidnappen ['kɪtnɛpən] *vt* to kidnap
Kidnapper, in (**-s, -**) *m(f)* kidnapper
Kiebitz ['ki:bɪts] (**-es, -e**) *m* peewit
Kiefer[1] ['ki:fər] (**-s, -**) *m* jaw
Kiefer[2] ['ki:fər] (**-, -n**) *f* pine
Kiefernholz *nt* pine(wood)
Kiefernzapfen *m* pine cone
Kieferorthopäde *m* orthodontist
Kieker ['ki:kər] (**-s, -**) *m*: **jdn auf dem ~ haben** (*umg*) to have it in for sb
Kiel [ki:l] (**-(e)s, -e**) *m* (*Federkiel*) quill; (*Naut*) keel; **Kielwasser** *nt* wake
Kieme ['ki:mə] (**-, -n**) *f* gill
Kies [ki:s] (**-es, -e**) *m* gravel; (*umg: Geld*) money, dough
Kiesel ['ki:zəl] (**-s, -**) *m* pebble; **Kieselstein** *m* pebble
Kiesgrube *f* gravel pit
Kiesweg *m* gravel path
Kiew ['ki:ɛf] (**-s**) *nt* Kiev
kiffen ['kɪfən] (*umg*) *vt* to smoke pot *od* grass
Kilimandscharo [kiliman'dʒa:ro] (**-s**) *m* Kilimanjaro
Killer ['kɪlər] (**-s, -**) (*umg*) *m* killer, murderer; (*gedungener*) hit man; **Killerin** (*umg*) *f* killer, female murderer, murderess
Kilo ['ki:lo] (**-s, -(s)**) *nt* kilo; **Kilobyte** [kilo'baɪt] *nt* (*Comput*) kilobyte; **Kilogramm** [kilo'gram] *nt* kilogram
Kilometer [kilo'me:tər] *m* kilometre (*Brit*), kilometer (*US*); **Kilometerfresser** (*umg*)

m long-haul driver; **Kilometergeld** *nt* ≈ mileage (allowance); **Kilometerstand** *m* ≈ mileage; **Kilometerstein** *m* ≈ milestone; **Kilometerzähler** *m* ≈ mileometer

Kilowatt [kilo'vat] *nt* kilowatt

Kimme ['kɪmə] (**-, -n**) *f* notch; (*Gewehr*) back sight

Kind [kɪnt] (**-(e)s, -er**) *nt* child; **sich freuen wie ein ~** to be as pleased as Punch; **mit ~ und Kegel** (*hum: umg*) with the whole family; **von ~ auf** from childhood

Kinderarzt *m* paediatrician (*Brit*), pediatrician (*US*)

Kinderbett *nt* cot (*Brit*), crib (*US*)

Kinderei [kɪndə'raɪ] *f* childishness

Kindererziehung *f* bringing up of children; (*durch Schule*) education of children

kinderfeindlich *adj* anti-children; (*Architektur, Planung*) not catering for children

Kinderfreibetrag *m* child allowance

Kindergarten *m* nursery school; *see culture note*

KINDERGARTEN

A *Kindergarten* is a nursery school for children aged between 3 and 6 years. The children sing, play and do handicrafts. They are not taught the three Rs at this stage. Most Kindergartens are financed by the town or the church and not by the state. Parents pay a monthly contribution towards the cost.

Kinder- *zW*: **Kindergärtner, in** *m(f)* nursery-school teacher; **Kindergeld** *nt* child benefit (*Brit*); **Kinderheim** *nt* children's home; **Kinderkrankheit** *f* childhood illness; **Kinderladen** *m* (alternative) playgroup; **Kinderlähmung** *f* polio(myelitis); **kinderleicht** *adj* childishly easy; **kinderlieb** *adj* fond of children; **Kinderlied** *nt* nursery rhyme; **kinderlos** *adj* childless; **Kindermädchen** *nt* nursemaid; **Kinderpflegerin** *f* child minder; **kinderreich** *adj* with a lot of children; **Kinderschuh** *m*: **es steckt noch in den Kinderschuhen** (*fig*) it's still in its infancy; **Kinderspiel** *nt* child's play; **ein Kinderspiel sein** to be a doddle; **Kinderstube** *f*: **eine gute Kinderstube haben** to be well-mannered; **Kindertagesstätte** *f* day-nursery; **Kinderteller** *m* children's dish; **Kinderwagen** *m* pram (*Brit*), baby carriage (*US*); **Kinderzimmer** *nt* child's/children's room; (*für Kleinkinder*) nursery

Kindes- *zW*: **Kindesalter** *nt* infancy; **Kindesbeine** *pl*: **von Kindesbeinen an** from early childhood; **Kindesmisshandlung** *f* child abuse

Kind- *zW*: **kindgemäß** *adj* suitable for a child *od* children; **Kindheit** *f* childhood; **kindisch** *adj* childish; **kindlich** *adj* childlike

kindsköpfig *adj* childish

Kinkerlitzchen ['kɪŋkərlɪtsçən] (*umg*) *pl* knick-knacks *pl*

Kinn [kɪn] (**-(e)s, -e**) *nt* chin; **Kinnhaken** *m* (*Boxen*) uppercut; **Kinnlade** *f* jaw

Kino ['ki:no] (**-s, -s**) *nt* cinema (*Brit*), movies (*US*); **Kinobesucher** *m*, **Kinogänger** *m* cinema-goer (*Brit*), movie-goer (*US*); **Kinoprogramm** *nt* film programme (*Brit*), movie program (*US*)

Kiosk [ki'ɔsk] (**-(e)s, -e**) *m* kiosk

Kippe ['kɪpə] (**-, -n**) *f* (*umg*) cigarette end; **auf der ~ stehen** (*fig*) to be touch and go

kippen *vi* to topple over, overturn ▷*vt* to tilt

Kipper ['kɪpər] (**-s, -**) *m* (*Aut*) tipper, dump(er) truck

Kippschalter *m* rocker switch

Kirche ['kɪrçə] (**-, -n**) *f* church

Kirchen- *zW*: **Kirchenchor** *m* church choir; **Kirchendiener** *m* churchwarden; **Kirchenfest** *nt* church festival; **Kirchenlied** *nt* hymn; **Kirchenschiff** *nt* (*Längsschiff*) nave; (*Querschiff*) transept; **Kirchensteuer** *f* church tax; **Kirchentag** *m* church congress

Kirch- *zW*: **Kirchgänger, in** (**-s, -**) *m(f)* churchgoer; **Kirchhof** *m* churchyard; **kirchlich** *adj* ecclesiastical; **Kirchturm** *m* church tower, steeple; **Kirchweih** *f* fair, kermis (*US*)

Kirgistan ['kɪrgista:n] (**-s**) *nt* (*Geog*) Kirghizia

Kirmes ['kɪrmɛs] (**-, -sen**) *f* (*Dialekt*) fair, kermis (*US*)

Kirschbaum ['kɪrʃbaʊm] *m* cherry tree; (*Holz*) cherry (wood)

Kirsche ['kɪrʃə] (**-, -n**) *f* cherry; **mit ihm ist nicht gut ~n essen** (*fig*) it's best not to tangle with him

Kirschtorte *f*: **Schwarzwälder ~** Black Forest Gateau

Kirschwasser *nt* kirsch

Kissen ['kɪsən] (**-s, -**) *nt* cushion; (*Kopfkissen*) pillow; **Kissenbezug** *m* pillow case

Kiste ['kɪstə] (**-, -n**) *f* box; (*Truhe*) chest; (*umg: Bett*) sack; (*: Fernsehen*) box (*Brit*), tube (*US*)

Kita ['kɪta] *f abk* = **Kindertagesstätte**

Kitsch [kɪtʃ] (**-(e)s**) *m* trash

kitschig *adj* trashy

Kitt [kɪt] (**-(e)s, -e**) *m* putty

Kittchen (*umg*) *nt* clink

Kittel (**-s, -**) *m* overall; (*von Arzt, Laborant etc*) (white) coat

kitten *vt* to putty; (*fig*) to patch up

Kitz [kɪts] (**-es, -e**) *nt* kid; (*Rehkitz*) fawn

kitzelig ['kɪtsəlɪç] *adj* (*lit, fig*) ticklish

kitzeln *vt, vi* to tickle

Kiwi ['ki:vi] (**-, -s**) *f* kiwi fruit

KKW (**-, -s**) *nt abk* = **Kernkraftwerk**

Kl. *abk* (= *Klasse*) cl.

Klacks [klaks] (**-es, -e**) (*umg*) *m* (*von Kartoffelbrei, Sahne*) dollop; (*von Senf, Farbe etc*) blob

Kladde ['kladə] (**-, -n**) *f* rough book; (*Block*) scribbling pad

klaffen ['klafən] *vi* to gape

kläffen ['klɛfən] *vi* to yelp

Klage ['kla:gə] (**-, -n**) *f* complaint; (*Jur*) action; **eine ~ gegen jdn einreichen** *od* **erheben** to

institute proceedings against sb; **Klagelied** *nt*: **ein Klagelied über jdn/etw anstimmen** (*fig*) to complain about sb/sth; **Klagemauer** *f*: **die Klagemauer** the Wailing Wall
klagen *vi* (*wehklagen*) to lament, wail; (*sich beschweren*) to complain; (*Jur*) to take legal action; **jdm sein Leid/seine Not ~** to pour out one's sorrow/distress to sb
Kläger, in ['klɛːgər(ɪn)] (**-s, -**) *m(f)* (*Jur: im Zivilrecht*) plaintiff; (*: im Strafrecht*) prosecuting party; (*: in Scheidung*) petitioner
Klageschrift *f* (*Jur*) charge; (*bei Scheidung*) petition
kläglich ['klɛːklɪç] *adj* wretched
Klamauk [kla'maʊk] (**-s**) (*umg*) *m* (*Alberei*) tomfoolery; (*im Theater*) slapstick
Klamm [klam] (**-, -en**) *f* ravine
klamm *adj* (*Finger*) numb; (*feucht*) damp
Klammer ['klamər] (**-, -n**) *f* clamp; (*in Text*) bracket; (*Büroklammer*) clip; (*Wäscheklammer*) peg (*Brit*), pin (*US*); (*Zahnklammer*) brace; **~ auf/zu** open/close brackets
klammern *vr*: **sich ~ an** *+akk* to cling to
klammheimlich [klam'haɪmlɪç] (*umg*) *adj* secret ▷ *adv* on the quiet
Klamotte [kla'mɔtə] (**-, -n**) *f* (*pej: Film etc*) rubbishy old film *etc*; **Klamotten** *pl* (*umg: Kleider*) clothes *pl*; (*: Zeug*) stuff
Klampfe ['klampfə] (**-, -n**) (*umg*) *f* guitar
klang *etc* [klaŋ] *vb siehe* **klingen**
Klang (**-(e)s, ¨-e**) *m* sound
klangvoll *adj* sonorous
Klappbett *nt* folding bed
Klappe ['klapə] (**-, -n**) *f* valve; (*an Oboe etc*) key; (*Film*) clapperboard; (*Ofenklappe*) damper; (*umg: Mund*) trap; **die ~ halten** to shut one's trap
klappen *vi* (*Geräusch*) to click; (*Sitz etc*) to tip ▷ *vt* to tip ▷ *vi unpers* to work; **hat es mit den Karten/dem Job geklappt?** did you get the tickets/job O.K.?
Klappentext *m* blurb
Klapper ['klapər] (**-, -n**) *f* rattle
klapperig *adj* run-down, worn-out
klappern *vi* to clatter, rattle
Klapperschlange *f* rattlesnake
Klapperstorch *m* stork; **er glaubt noch an den ~** he still thinks babies are found under the gooseberry bush
Klapp- *zW*: **Klappmesser** *nt* jackknife; **Klapprad** *nt* collapsible *od* folding bicycle; **Klappstuhl** *m* folding chair; **Klapptisch** *m* folding table
Klaps [klaps] (**-es, -e**) *m* slap; **einen ~ haben** (*umg*) to have a screw loose; **klapsen** *vt* to slap
klar [klaːr] *adj* clear; (*Naut*) ready to sail; (*Mil*) ready for action; **bei ~em Verstand sein** to be in full possession of one's faculties; **sich** *dat* **im K~en sein über** *+akk* to be clear about; **ins K~e kommen** to get clear; **~ sehen** to see clearly; **sich** *dat* **über etw** *akk* **~ werden** to get sth clear in one's mind
Kläranlage *f* sewage plant; (*von Fabrik*) purification plant
Klare, r (*umg*) *m* schnapps
klären *vt* (*Flüssigkeit*) to purify; (*Probleme*) to clarify ▷ *vr* to clear (itself) up
Klarheit *f* clarity; **sich** *dat* **~ über etw** *akk* **verschaffen** to get sth straight
Klarinette [klari'nɛtə] *f* clarinet
klar- *zW*: **klarkommen** *unreg* (*umg*) *vi*: **mit jdm/etw klarkommen** to be able to cope with sb/sth; **klarlegen** *vt* to clear up, explain; **klarmachen** *vt* (*Schiff*) to get ready for sea; **jdm etw klarmachen** to make sth clear to sb; **Klarsichtfolie** *f* transparent film; **klarstellen** *vt* to clarify; **Klartext** *m*: **im Klartext** in clear; (*fig: umg*) ≈ in plain English
Klärung ['klɛːrʊŋ] *f* purification; clarification
Klärungsbedarf *m* need for clarification
Klasse ['klasə] (**-, -n**) *f* class; (*Sch*) class, form; (*auch:* **Steuerklasse**) bracket; (*Güterklasse*) grade
klasse (*umg*) *adj* smashing
Klassen- *zW*: **Klassenarbeit** *f* test; **Klassenbewusstsein** *nt* class-consciousness; **Klassenbuch** *nt* (*Sch*) (class) register; **Klassengesellschaft** *f* class society; **Klassenkamerad, in** *m(f)* classmate; **Klassenkampf** *m* class conflict; **Klassenlehrer, in** *m(f)* class teacher; **klassenlos** *adj* classless; **Klassensprecher, in** *m(f)* class spokesperson; **Klassenziel** *nt*: **das Klassenziel nicht erreichen** (*Sch*) not to reach the required standard (for the year); (*fig*) not to make the grade; **Klassenzimmer** *nt* classroom
klassifizieren [klasifi'tsiːrən] *vt* to classify
Klassifizierung *f* classification
Klassik ['klasɪk] *f* (*Zeit*) classical period; (*Stil*) classicism; **Klassiker** (**-s, -**) *m* classic
klassisch *adj* (*lit, fig*) classical
Klassizismus [klasi'tsɪsmʊs] *m* classicism
Klatsch [klatʃ] (**-(e)s, -e**) *m* smack, crack; (*Gerede*) gossip; **Klatschbase** *f* gossip(monger)
klatschen *vi* (*tratschen*) to gossip; (*Beifall spenden*) to applaud, to clap ▷ *vt*: **(jdm) Beifall ~** to applaud *od* clap (sb)
Klatsch- *zW*: **Klatschmohn** *m* (corn) poppy; **klatschnass** *adj* soaking wet; **Klatschspalte** *f* gossip column; **Klatschtante** (*pej: umg*) *f* gossip(monger)
klauben ['klaʊbən] *vt* to pick
Klaue ['klaʊə] (**-, -n**) *f* claw; (*umg: Schrift*) scrawl
klauen *vt* to claw; (*umg*) to pinch
Klause ['klaʊzə] (**-, -n**) *f* cell; (*von Mönch*) hermitage
Klausel ['klaʊzəl] (**-, -n**) *f* clause; (*Vorbehalt*) proviso
Klausur [klaʊ'zuːr] *f* seclusion; **Klausurarbeit** *f* examination paper
Klaviatur [klavia'tuːr] *f* keyboard
Klavier [kla'viːr] (**-s, -e**) *nt* piano; **Klavierauszug** *m* piano score
Klebeband *nt* adhesive tape
Klebemittel *nt* glue
kleben ['kleːbən] *vt, vi*: **~ (an** *+akk***)** to stick (to); **jdm eine ~** (*umg*) to belt sb one

Klebezettel *m* gummed label
klebrig *adj* sticky
Klebstoff *m* glue
Klebstreifen *m* adhesive tape
kleckern ['klɛkərn] *vi* to slobber
Klecks [klɛks] (**-es, -e**) *m* blot, stain; **klecksen** *vi* to blot; (*pej*) to daub
Klee [kle:] (**-s**) *m* clover; **jdn/etw über den grünen ~ loben** (*fig*) to praise sb/sth to the skies; **Kleeblatt** *nt* cloverleaf; (*fig*) trio
Kleid [klaɪt] (**-(e)s, -er**) *nt* garment; (*Frauenkleid*) dress; **Kleider** *pl* clothes *pl*
kleiden ['klaɪdən] *vt* to clothe, dress ▷ *vr* to dress; **jdn ~** to suit sb
Kleider- *zW*: **Kleiderbügel** *m* coat hanger; **Kleiderbürste** *f* clothes brush; **Kleiderschrank** *m* wardrobe; **Kleiderständer** *m* coat-stand
kleidsam *adj* becoming
Kleidung *f* clothing
Kleidungsstück *nt* garment
Kleie ['klaɪə] (**-, -n**) *f* bran
klein [klaɪn] *adj* little, small; **haben Sie es nicht ~er?** haven't you got anything smaller?; **ein ~es Bier, ein K~es** (*umg*) ≈ half a pint, ≈ a half; **von ~ an** *od* **auf** (*von Kindheit an*) from childhood; (*von Anfang an*) from the very beginning; **das ~ere Übel** the lesser evil; **sein Vater war (ein) ~er Beamter** his father was a minor civil servant; **~ anfangen** to start off in a small way; **~ geschrieben werden** (*umg*) to count for (very) little; **~ hacken** to chop up; **~ schneiden** to chop up; **Kleinanzeige** *f* small ad (*Brit*), want ad (*US*); **Kleinanzeigen** *pl* classified advertising *sing*; **Kleinarbeit** *f*: **in zäher/mühseliger Kleinarbeit** with rigorous/painstaking attention to detail; **Kleinasien** *nt* Asia Minor; **Kleinbürgertum** *nt* petite bourgeoisie; **Kleinbus** *m* minibus
Kleine, r *f(m)* little one
klein- *zW*: **Kleinfamilie** *f* small family, nuclear family (*Soziologie*); **Kleinformat** *nt* small size; **im Kleinformat** small-scale; **Kleingedruckte, s** *nt* small print; **Kleingeld** *nt* small change; **das nötige Kleingeld haben** (*fig*) to have the wherewithal (*umg*); **kleingläubig** *adj* of little faith; **kleinhacken** *vt* to chop up; **Kleinholz** *nt* firewood; **Kleinholz aus jdm machen** to make mincemeat of sb
Kleinigkeit *f* trifle; **wegen** *od* **bei jeder ~** for the slightest reason; **eine ~ essen** to have a bite to eat
klein- *zW*: **kleinkariert** *adj*: **kleinkariert denken** to think small; **Kleinkind** *nt* infant; **Kleinkram** *m* details *pl*; **Kleinkredit** *m* personal loan; **kleinkriegen** (*umg*) *vt* (*gefügig machen*) to bring into line; (*unterkriegen*) to get down; (*körperlich*) to tire out; **kleinlaut** *adj* dejected, quiet; **kleinlich** *adj* petty, paltry; **Kleinlichkeit** *f* pettiness, paltriness; **kleinmütig** *adj* fainthearted
Kleinod ['klaɪno:t] (**-s, -odien**) *nt* gem; (*fig*) treasure
klein- *zW*: **Kleinrechner** *m* minicomputer; **kleinschneiden** *unreg vt* to chop up; **kleinschreiben** *unreg vt*: **ein Wort kleinschreiben** to write a word with a small initial letter; **Kleinschreibung** *f* use of small initial letters; **Kleinstadt** *f* small town; **kleinstädtisch** *adj* provincial
kleinstmöglich *adj* smallest possible
Kleinwagen *m* small car
Kleister ['klaɪstər] (**-s, -**) *m* paste
kleistern *vt* to paste
Klemme ['klɛmə] (**-, -n**) *f* clip; (*Med*) clamp; (*fig*) jam; **in der ~ sitzen** *od* **sein** (*fig: umg*) to be in a fix
klemmen *vt* (*festhalten*) to jam; (*quetschen*) to pinch, nip ▷ *vr* to catch o.s.; (*sich hineinzwängen*) to squeeze o.s. ▷ *vi* (*Tür*) to stick, jam; **sich hinter jdn/etw ~** to get on to sb/get down to sth
Klempner ['klɛmpnər] (**-s, -**) *m* plumber
Kleptomanie [klɛptoma'ni:] *f* kleptomania
Kleriker ['kle:rikər] (**-s, -**) *m* cleric
Klerus ['kle:rʊs] (-) *m* clergy
Klette ['klɛtə] (**-, -n**) *f* burr; **sich wie eine ~ an jdn hängen** to cling to sb like a limpet
Kletterer ['klɛtərər] (**-s, -**) *m* climber
Klettergerüst *nt* climbing frame
klettern *vi* to climb
Kletterpflanze *f* creeper
Kletterseil *nt* climbing rope
Klettverschluss *m* Velcro® fastener
klicken ['klɪkən] *vi* to click
Klient, in [kli'ɛnt(ɪn)] *m(f)* client
Klima ['kli:ma] (**-s, -s** *od* **-te**) *nt* climate; **Klimaanlage** *f* air conditioning
Klimaschutz *m* climate protection; **Klimaschutzabkommen** *nt* agreement on climate change
klimatisieren [kli:mati'zi:rən] *vt* to air-condition
klimatisiert *adj* air-conditioned
Klimawechsel *m* change of air
Klimawandel *m* climate change#
Klimbim [klɪm'bɪm] (**-s**) (*umg*) *m* odds and ends *pl*
klimpern ['klɪmpərn] *vi* to tinkle; (*auf Gitarre*) to strum
Klinge ['klɪŋə] (**-, -n**) *f* blade, sword; **jdn über die ~ springen lassen** (*fig: umg*) to allow sb to run into trouble
Klingel ['klɪŋəl] (**-, -n**) *f* bell; **Klingelbeutel** *m* collection bag; **Klingelknopf** *m* bell push
klingeln *vi* to ring; **es hat geklingelt** (*an Tür*) somebody just rang the doorbell, the doorbell just rang
Klingelton *m* ringtone
klingen ['klɪŋən] *unreg vi* to sound; (*Gläser*) to clink
Klinik ['kli:nɪk] *f* clinic
klinisch ['kli:nɪʃ] *adj* clinical
Klinke ['klɪŋkə] (**-, -n**) *f* handle
Klinker ['klɪŋkər] (**-s, -**) *m* clinker
Klippe ['klɪpə] (**-, -n**) *f* cliff; (*im Meer*) reef; (*fig*) hurdle

klippenreich *adj* rocky
klipp und klar ['klɪp|ʊntkla:r] *adj* clear and concise
Klips [klɪps] **(-es, -e)** *m* clip; (*Ohrklips*) earring
klirren ['klɪrən] *vi* to clank, jangle; (*Gläser*) to clink; **~de Kälte** biting cold
Klischee [klɪ'ʃe:] **(-s, -s)** *nt* (*Druckplatte*) plate, block; (*fig*) cliché; **Klischeevorstellung** *f* stereotyped idea
Klitoris ['kli:torɪs] **(-, -)** *f* clitoris
Klo [klo:] **(-s, -s)** (*umg*) *nt* loo (*Brit*), john (*US*)
Kloake [klo'a:kə] **(-, -n)** *f* sewer
klobig ['klo:bɪç] *adj* clumsy
Klon [klo:n] **(-s, -e)** *m* clone
Klonschaf *nt* cloned sheep
Klopapier (*umg*) *nt* toilet paper
klopfen ['klɔpfən] *vi* to knock; (*Herz*) to thump ▷ *vt* to beat; **es klopft** somebody's knocking; **jdm auf die Finger ~** (*lit, fig*) to give sb a rap on the knuckles; **jdm auf die Schulter ~** to tap sb on the shoulder
Klopfer (-s, -) *m* (*Teppichklopfer*) beater; (*Türklopfer*) knocker
Klöppel ['klœpəl] **(-s, -)** *m* (*von Glocke*) clapper
klöppeln *vi* to make lace
Klops [klɔps] **(-es, -e)** *m* meatball
Klosett [klo'zɛt] **(-s, -e** *od* **-s)** *nt* lavatory, toilet; **Klosettbrille** *f* toilet seat; **Klosettpapier** *nt* toilet paper
Kloß [klo:s] **(-es, ¨-e)** *m* (*Erdkloß*) clod; (*im Hals*) lump; (*Koch*) dumpling
Kloster ['klo:stər] **(-s, ¨-)** *nt* (*Männerkloster*) monastery; (*Frauenkloster*) convent; **ins ~ gehen** to become a monk/nun
klösterlich ['klø:stərlɪç] *adj* monastic; convent
Klotz [klɔts] **(-es, ¨-e)** *m* log; (*Hackklotz*) block; **jdm ein ~ am Bein sein** (*fig*) to be a millstone round sb's neck
Klub [klʊp] **(-s, -s)** *m* club; **Klubjacke** *f* blazer; **Klubsessel** *m* easy chair
Kluft [klʊft] **(-, ¨-e)** *f* cleft, gap; (*Geog*) chasm; (*Uniform*) uniform; (*umg: Kleidung*) gear
klug [klu:k] *adj* clever, intelligent; **ich werde daraus nicht ~** I can't make head or tail of it; **Klugheit** *f* cleverness, intelligence; **Klugscheißer** (*umg*) *m* smart-ass
Klümpchen ['klʏmpçən] *nt* clot, blob
klumpen ['klʊmpən] *vi* to go lumpy, clot
Klumpen (-s, -) *m* (*Koch*) lump; (*Erdklumpen*) clod; (*Blutklumpen*) clot; (*Goldklumpen*) nugget
Klumpfuß ['klʊmpfu:s] *m* club foot
Klüngel ['klʏŋəl] **(-s, -)** (*umg*) *m* (*Clique*) clique
Klunker ['klʊŋkər] **(-s, -)** (*umg*) *m* (*Schmuck*) rock(s *pl*)
km *abk* (= *Kilometer*) km
km/h *abk* (= *Kilometer pro Stunde*) km/h
knabbern ['knabərn] *vt, vi* to nibble; **an etw** *dat* **~** (*fig: umg*) to puzzle over sth
Knabe ['kna:bə] **(-n, -n)** *m* boy
knabenhaft *adj* boyish
Knäckebrot ['knɛkəbro:t] *nt* crispbread
knacken ['knakən] *vi* (*lit, fig*) to crack ▷ *vt* (*umg: Auto*) to break into
knackfrisch (*umg*) *adj* oven-fresh, crispy-fresh
knackig *adj* crisp
Knacks [knaks] **(-es, -e)** *m*: **einen ~ weghaben** (*umg*) to be uptight about sth
Knackwurst *f type of frankfurter*
Knall [knal] **(-(e)s, -e)** *m* bang; (*Peitschenknall*) crack; **~ auf Fall** (*umg*) just like that; **einen ~ haben** (*umg*) to be crazy *od* crackers; **Knallbonbon** *nt* cracker; **Knalleffekt** *m* surprise effect, spectacular effect; **knallen** *vi* to bang; to crack ▷ *vt*: **jdm eine knallen** (*umg*) to clout sb; **Knallfrosch** *m* jumping jack; **knallhart** (*umg*) *adj* really hard; (*: Worte*) hard-hitting; (*: Film*) brutal; (*: Porno*) hard-core; **Knallkopf** (*umg*) *m* dickhead; **knallrot** *adj* bright red
knapp [knap] *adj* tight; (*Geld*) scarce; (*kurz*) short; (*Mehrheit, Sieg*) narrow; (*Sprache*) concise; **meine Zeit ist ~ bemessen** I am short of time; **mit ~er Not** only just; *siehe auch* **knapphalten**
Knappe (-n, -n) *m* (*Edelmann*) young knight
knapphalten *unreg vt*: **jdn (mit etw) ~** to keep sb short (of sth)
Knappheit *f* tightness; scarcity; conciseness
Knarre ['knarə] **(-, -n)** (*umg*) *f* (*Gewehr*) shooter
knarren *vi* to creak
Knast [knast] **(-(e)s)** (*umg*) *m* clink, can (*US*)
Knatsch [kna:tʃ] **(-es)** (*umg*) *m* trouble
knattern ['knatərn] *vi* to rattle; (*Maschinengewehr*) to chatter
Knäuel ['knɔʏəl] **(-s, -)** *m od nt* (*Wollknäuel*) ball; (*Menschenknäuel*) knot
Knauf [knaʊf] **(-(e)s, Knäufe)** *m* knob; (*Schwertknauf*) pommel
Knauser ['knaʊzər] **(-s, -)** *m* miser
knauserig *adj* miserly
knausern *vi* to be mean
knautschen ['knaʊtʃən] *vt, vi* to crumple
Knebel ['kne:bəl] **(-s, -)** *m* gag
knebeln *vt* to gag; (*Naut*) to fasten
Knecht [knɛçt] **(-(e)s, -e)** *m* servant; (*auf Bauernhof*) farm labourer (*Brit*) *od* laborer (*US*)
knechten *vt* to enslave
Knechtschaft *f* servitude
kneifen ['knaɪfən] *unreg vt* to pinch ▷ *vi* to pinch; (*sich drücken*) to back out; **vor etw** *dat* **~** to dodge sth
Kneifzange *f* pliers *pl*; (*kleine*) pincers *pl*
Kneipe ['knaɪpə] **(-, -n)** (*umg*) *f* pub (*Brit*), bar, saloon (*US*)
Kneippkur ['knaɪpku:r] *f* Kneipp cure, *type of hydropathic treatment combined with diet, rest etc*
Knete ['kne:tə] (*umg*) *f* (*Geld*) dough
kneten *vt* to knead; (*Wachs*) to mould (*Brit*), mold (*US*)
Knetgummi *m od nt* Plasticine®
Knetmasse *f* Plasticine®
Knick [knɪk] **(-(e)s, -e)** *m* (*Sprung*) crack; (*Kurve*) bend; (*Falte*) fold
knicken *vt, vi* (*springen*) to crack; (*brechen*) to break; (*Papier*) to fold; **„nicht ~!"** "do not bend"; **geknickt sein** to be downcast

Knicks [knɪks] (**-es, -e**) *m* curts(e)y; **knicksen** *vi* to curts(e)y
Knie [kniː] (**-s, -**) *nt* knee; **in die ~ gehen** to kneel; (*fig*) to be brought to one's knees; **Kniebeuge** (**-, -n**) *f* knee bend; **Kniefall** *m* genuflection; **Kniegelenk** *nt* knee joint; **Kniekehle** *f* back of the knee
knien *vi* to kneel ▷ *vr*: **sich in die Arbeit ~** (*fig*) to get down to (one's) work
Kniescheibe *f* kneecap
Kniestrumpf *m* knee-length sock
kniff *etc* [knɪf] *vb siehe* **kneifen**
Kniff (**-(e)s, -e**) *m* (*Zwicken*) pinch; (*Falte*) fold; (*fig*) trick, knack
kniffelig *adj* tricky
knipsen ['knɪpsən] *vt* (*Fahrkarte*) to punch; (*Phot*) to take a snap of, snap ▷ *vi* (*Phot*) to take snaps/a snap
Knirps [knɪrps] (**-es, -e**) *m* little chap; **er hat einen neuen ~® gekauft** he has bought a new Knirps® (*folding umbrella*)
knirschen ['knɪrʃən] *vi* to crunch; **mit den Zähnen ~** to grind one's teeth
knistern ['knɪstərn] *vi* to crackle; (*Papier, Seide*) to rustle
Knitterfalte *f* crease
knitterfrei *adj* non-crease
knittern *vi* to crease
knobeln ['knoːbəln] *vi* (*würfeln*) to play dice; (*um eine Entscheidung*) to toss for it
Knoblauch ['knoːplaʊx] (**-(e)s**) *m* garlic
Knöchel ['knœçəl] (**-s, -**) *m* knuckle; (*Fußknöchel*) ankle
Knochen ['knɔxən] (**-s, -**) *m* bone; **Knochenarbeit** (*umg*) *f* hard work; **Knochenbau** *m* bone structure; **Knochenbruch** *m* fracture; **Knochengerüst** *nt* skeleton; **Knochenmark** *nt* bone marrow
knöchern ['knœçərn] *adj* bone
knochig ['knɔxɪç] *adj* bony
Knödel ['knøːdəl] (**-s, -**) *m* dumpling
Knolle ['knɔlə] (**-, -n**) *f* bulb
Knopf [knɔpf] (**-(e)s, ¨-e**) *m* button; **Knopfdruck** *m* touch of a button
knöpfen ['knœpfən] *vt* to button
Knopfloch *nt* buttonhole
Knorpel ['knɔrpəl] (**-s, -**) *m* cartilage, gristle
knorpelig *adj* gristly
knorrig ['knɔrɪç] *adj* gnarled, knotted
Knospe ['knɔspə] (**-, -n**) *f* bud
knospen *vi* to bud
knoten ['knoːtən] *vt* to knot; **Knoten** (**-s, -**) *m* knot; (*Haar*) bun; (*Bot*) node; (*Med*) lump
Knotenpunkt *m* junction
knuffen ['knʊfən] (*umg*) *vt* to cuff
Knüller ['knʏlər] (**-s, -**) (*umg*) *m* hit; (*Reportage*) scoop
knüpfen ['knʏpfən] *vt* to tie; (*Teppich*) to knot; (*Freundschaft*) to form
Knüppel ['knʏpəl] (**-s, -**) *m* cudgel; (*Polizeiknüppel*) baton, truncheon; (*Aviat*) (joy)stick; **jdm ~ zwischen die Beine werfen** (*fig*) to put a spoke in sb's wheel; **knüppeldick** (*umg*) *adj* very thick; (*fig*) thick and fast; **Knüppelschaltung** *f* (*Aut*) floor-mounted gear change
knurren ['knʊrən] *vi* (*Hund*) to snarl, growl; (*Magen*) to rumble; (*Mensch*) to mutter
knusperig ['knʊspərɪç], **knusprig** ['knʊsprɪç] *adj* crisp; (*Keks*) crunchy
knutschen ['knuːtʃən] (*umg*) *vt* to snog with ▷ *vi, vr* to snog
k. o. *adj* (*Sport*) knocked out; (*fig: umg*) whacked
Koalition [koalitsi'oːn] *f* coalition
Koalitionsabsprache *f* coalition agreement
koalitionsfähig *f* in a position to form a coalition
Kobalt ['koːbalt] (**-s**) *nt* cobalt
Kobold ['koːbɔlt] (**-(e)s, -e**) *m* imp
Kobra ['koːbra] (**-, -s**) *f* cobra
Koch [kɔx] (**-(e)s, ¨-e**) *m* cook; **Kochbuch** *nt* cookery book, cookbook; **kochecht** *adj* (*Farbe*) fast
kochen *vi* to cook; (*Wasser*) to boil ▷ *vt* (*Essen*) to cook; **er kochte vor Wut** (*umg*) he was seething; **etw auf kleiner Flamme ~** to simmer sth over a low heat
Kocher (**-s, -**) *m* stove, cooker
Köcher ['kœçər] (**-s, -**) *m* quiver
Kochgelegenheit *f* cooking facilities *pl*
Köchin ['kœçɪn] *f* cook
Koch- *zW*: **Kochkunst** *f* cooking; **Kochlöffel** *m* kitchen spoon; **Kochnische** *f* kitchenette; **Kochplatte** *f* hotplate; **Kochsalz** *nt* cooking salt; **Kochtopf** *m* saucepan, pot; **Kochwäsche** *f* washing that can be boiled
Kode [koːt] (**-s, -s**) *m* code
Köder ['køːdər] (**-s, -**) *m* bait, lure
ködern *vt* to lure, entice
Koexistenz [koɛksɪs'tɛnts] *f* coexistence
Koffein [kɔfe'iːn] (**-s**) *nt* caffeine; **koffeinfrei** *adj* decaffeinated
Koffer ['kɔfər] (**-s, -**) *m* suitcase; (*Schrankkoffer*) trunk; **die ~ packen** (*lit, fig*) to pack one's bags; **Kofferkuli** *m* (luggage) trolley (*Brit*), cart (*US*); **Kofferradio** *nt* portable radio; **Kofferraum** *m* (*Aut*) boot (*Brit*), trunk (*US*)
Kognak ['kɔnjak] (**-s, -s**) *m* brandy, cognac
Kohl [koːl] (**-(e)s, -e**) *m* cabbage
Kohldampf (*umg*) *m*: **~ haben** to be famished
Kohle ['koːlə] (**-, -n**) *f* coal; (*Holzkohle*) charcoal; (*Chem*) carbon; (*umg: Geld*): **die ~n stimmen** the money's right; **Kohlehydrat** (**-(e)s, -e**) *nt* carbohydrate; **Kohlekraftwerk** *nt* coal-fired power station
kohlen ['koːlən] (*umg*) *vi* to tell white lies
Kohlen- *zW*: **Kohlenbergwerk** *nt* coal mine, pit, colliery (*Brit*); **Kohlendioxid** (**-(e)s, -e**) *nt* carbon dioxide; **Kohlengrube** *f* coal mine, pit; **Kohlenhändler** *m* coal merchant, coalman; **Kohlensäure** *f* carbon dioxide; **ein Getränk ohne Kohlensäure** a non-fizzy *od* still drink; **Kohlenstoff** *m* carbon
Kohlepapier *nt* carbon paper
Köhler ['køːlər] (**-s, -**) *m* charcoal burner
Kohlestift *m* charcoal pencil

Kohlezeichnung *f* charcoal drawing
Kohl- *zW*: **kohlpechrabenschwarz, kohlrabenschwarz** *adj* (*Haar*) jet-black; (*Nacht*) pitch-black; **Kohlrübe** *f* turnip; **kohlschwarz** *adj* coal-black
Koitus ['ko:itʊs] (**-,** - *od* **-se**) *m* coitus
Koje ['ko:jə] (**-, -n**) *f* cabin; (*Bett*) bunk
Kokain [koka'i:n] (**-s**) *nt* cocaine
kokett [ko'kɛt] *adj* coquettish, flirtatious
kokettieren [kokɛ'ti:rən] *vi* to flirt
Kokosnuss ['ko:kɔsnʊs] *f* coconut
Koks [ko:ks] (**-es, -e**) *m* coke
Kolben ['kɔlbən] (**-s, -**) *m* (*Gewehrkolben*) butt; (*Keule*) club; (*Chem*) flask; (*Tech*) piston; (*Maiskolben*) cob
Kolchose [kɔl'ço:zə] (**-, -n**) *f* collective farm
Kolik ['ko:lɪk] *f* colic, gripe
Kollaborateur, in [kɔlabora'tø:r(ɪn)] *m(f)* (*Pol*) collaborator
Kollaps [kɔ'laps] (**-es, -e**) *m* collapse
Kolleg [kɔl'e:k] (**-s, -s** *od* **-ien**) *nt* lecture course
Kollege [kɔ'le:gə] (**-n, -n**) *m* colleague
kollegial [kɔlegi'a:l] *adj* cooperative
Kollegin [kɔ'le:gɪn] *f* colleague
Kollegium *nt* board; (*Sch*) staff
Kollekte [kɔ'lɛktə] (**-, -n**) *f* (*Rel*) collection
Kollektion [kɔlɛktsi'o:n] *f* collection; (*Sortiment*) range
kollektiv [kɔlɛk'ti:f] *adj* collective
Koller ['kɔlər] (**-s, -**) (*umg*) *m* (*Anfall*) funny mood; (*Wutanfall*) rage; (*Tropenkoller, Gefängniskoller*) madness
kollidieren [kɔli'di:rən] *vi* to collide; (*zeitlich*) to clash
Kollier [kɔli'e:] (**-s, -s**) *nt* = **Collier**
Kollision [kɔlizi'o:n] *f* collision; (*zeitlich*) clash
Kollisionskurs *m*: **auf ~ gehen** (*fig*) to be heading for trouble
Köln [kœln] (**-s**) *nt* Cologne
Kölnischwasser *nt* eau de Cologne
kolonial [koloni'a:l] *adj* colonial; **Kolonialmacht** *f* colonial power; **Kolonialwarenhändler** *m* grocer
Kolonie [kolo'ni:] *f* colony
kolonisieren [koloni'zi:rən] *vt* to colonize
Kolonist, in [kolo'nɪst(ɪn)] *m(f)* colonist
Kolonne [ko'lɔnə] (**-, -n**) *f* column; (*von Fahrzeugen*) convoy
Koloss [ko'lɔs] (**-es, -e**) *m* colossus
kolossal [kolɔ'sa:l] *adj* colossal
Kolumbianer, in [kolʊmbi'a:nər(ɪn)] *m(f)* Columbian
kolumbianisch *adj* Columbian
Kolumbien [ko'lʊmbiən] (**-s**) *nt* Columbia
Koma ['ko:ma] (**-s, -s** *od* **-ta**) *nt* (*Med*) coma
Kombi ['kɔmbi] (**-s, -s**) *m* (*Aut*) estate (car) (*Brit*), station wagon (*US*)
Kombination [kɔmbinatsi'o:n] *f* combination; (*Vermutung*) conjecture; (*Hemdhose*) combinations *pl*; (*Aviat*) flying suit
Kombinationsschloss *nt* combination lock
kombinieren [kɔmbi'ni:rən] *vt* to combine ▷ *vi* to deduce, work out; (*vermuten*) to guess
Kombiwagen *m* (*Aut*) estate (car) (*Brit*), station wagon (*US*)
Kombizange *f* (pair of) pliers
Komet [ko'me:t] (**-en, -en**) *m* comet
kometenhaft *adj* (*fig*: *Aufstieg*) meteoric
Komfort [kɔm'fo:r] (**-s**) *m* luxury; (*von Möbel etc*) comfort; (*von Wohnung*) amenities *pl*; (*von Auto*) luxury features *pl*; (*von Gerät*) extras *pl*
komfortabel [kɔmfɔr'ta:bəl] *adj* comfortable
Komik ['ko:mɪk] *f* humour (*Brit*), humor (*US*), comedy; **Komiker** (**-s, -**) *m* comedian
komisch ['ko:mɪʃ] *adj* funny; **mir ist so ~** (*umg*) I feel funny *od* strange *od* odd; **komischerweise** ['ko:mɪʃər'vaɪzə] *adv* funnily enough
Komitee [komi'te:] (**-s, -s**) *nt* committee
Komm. *abk* (= *Kommission*) comm.
Komma ['kɔma] (**-s, -s** *od* **-ta**) *nt* comma; (*Math*) decimal point; **fünf ~ drei** five point three
Kommandant [kɔman'dant] *m* commander, commanding officer
Kommandeur [kɔman'dø:r] *m* commanding officer
kommandieren [kɔman'di:rən] *vt* to command ▷ *vi* to command; (*Befehle geben*) to give orders
Kommanditgesellschaft [kɔman'di:tgəzɛlʃaft] *f* limited partnership
Kommando [kɔ'mando] (**-s, -s**) *nt* command, order; (*Truppe*) detachment, squad; **auf ~** to order; **Kommandobrücke** *f* (*Naut*) bridge; **Kommandowirtschaft** *f* command economy
kommen ['kɔmən] *unreg vi* to come; (*näher kommen*) to approach; (*passieren*) to happen; (*gelangen, geraten*) to get; (*Blumen, Zähne, Tränen etc*) to appear; (*in die Schule, ins Gefängnis etc*) to go; **was kommt diese Woche im Kino?** what's on at the cinema this week? ▷ *vi unpers*: **es kam eins zum anderen** one thing led to another; **~ lassen** to send for; **in Bewegung ~** to start moving; **jdn besuchen ~** to come and visit sb; **das kommt davon!** see what happens?; **du kommst mir gerade recht** (*ironisch*) you're just what I need; **das kommt in den Schrank** that goes in the cupboard; **an etw** *akk* **~** (*berühren*) to touch sth; (*sich verschaffen*) to get hold of sth; **auf etw** *akk* **~** (*sich erinnern*) to think of sth; (*sprechen über*) to get onto sth; **das kommt auf die Rechnung** that goes onto the bill; **hinter etw** *akk* **~** (*herausfinden*) to find sth out; **zu sich ~** to come round *od* to; **zu etw ~** to acquire sth; **um etw ~** to lose sth; **nichts auf jdn/etw ~ lassen** to have nothing said against sb/sth; **jdm frech ~** to get cheeky with sb; **auf jeden vierten kommt ein Platz** there's one place to every fourth person; **mit einem Anliegen ~** to have a request (to make); **wer kommt zuerst?** who's first?; **wer zuerst kommt, mahlt zuerst** (*Sprichwort*) first come first served; **unter ein Auto ~** to be run over by a car; **das kommt zusammen auf 20 Euro** that comes to 20 euros altogether; **und so kam es, dass ...** and that is how it happened that ...;

daher kommt es, dass … that's why …
Kommen (**-s**) *nt* coming
kommend *adj* (*Jahr, Woche, Generation*) coming; (*Ereignisse, Mode*) future; (*Trend*) upcoming; **(am) ~en Montag** next Monday
Kommentar [kɔmɛn'taːr] *m* commentary; **kein ~** no comment; **kommentarlos** *adj* without comment
Kommentator [kɔmɛn'taːtɔr] *m* (*TV*) commentator
kommentieren [kɔmɛn'tiːrən] *vt* to comment on; **kommentierte Ausgabe** annotated edition
kommerziell [kɔmɛrtsi'ɛl] *adj* commercial
Kommilitone [kɔmili'toːnə] (**-n, -n**) *m*, **Kommilitonin** *f* fellow student
Kommiss [kɔ'mɪs] (**-es**) *m* (life in the) army
Kommissar [kɔmɪ'saːr] *m* police inspector
Kommissbrot *nt* army bread
Kommission [kɔmɪsi'oːn] *f* (*Comm*) commission; (*Ausschuss*) committee; **in ~ geben** to give (to a dealer) for sale on commission
Kommode [kɔ'moːdə] (**-, -n**) *f* (chest of) drawers
kommunal [kɔmu'naːl] *adj* local; (*von Stadt*) municipal; **Kommunalabgaben** *pl* local rates and taxes *pl*; **Kommunalpolitik** *f* local government politics; **Kommunalverwaltung** *f* local government; **Kommunalwahlen** *pl* local (government) elections *pl*
Kommune [kɔ'muːnə] (**-, -n**) *f* commune
Kommunikation [kɔmunɪkatsi'oːn] *f* communication
Kommunikator, in [kɔmuni'kaːtɔr, -'toːrɪn] *m(f)* communicator
Kommunikee [kɔmyni'keː] (**-s, -s**) *nt* = **Kommuniqué**
Kommunion [kɔmuni'oːn] *f* communion
Kommuniqué [kɔmyni'keː] (**-s, -s**) *nt* communiqué
Kommunismus [kɔmu'nɪsmʊs] *m* communism
Kommunist, in [kɔmu'nɪst(ɪn)] *m(f)* communist; **kommunistisch** *adj* communist
kommunizieren [kɔmuni'tsiːrən] *vi* to communicate; (*Eccl*) to receive communion
Komödiant [komødi'ant] *m* comedian; **Komödiantin** *f* comedienne
Komödie [ko'møːdiə] *f* comedy; **~ spielen** (*fig*) to put on an act
Kompagnon [kɔmpan'jõː] (**-s, -s**) *m* (*Comm*) partner
kompakt [kɔm'pakt] *adj* compact
Kompaktanlage *f* (*Rundf*) audio system
Kompanie [kɔmpa'niː] *f* company
Komparativ ['kɔmparatiːf] (**-s, -e**) *m* comparative
Kompass ['kɔmpas] (**-es, -e**) *m* compass
kompatibel [kɔmpa'tiːbəl] *adj* (*auch Comput*) compatible
Kompatibilität [kɔmpatibili'tɛːt] *f* (*auch Comput*) compatibility
kompensieren [kɔmpɛn'ziːrən] *vt* to compensate for, offset
kompetent [kɔmpe'tɛnt] *adj* competent
Kompetenz *f* competence, authority; **Kompetenzstreitigkeiten** *pl* dispute over respective areas of responsibility; **Kompetenzverteilung** *f* distribution of powers; **Kompetenzzentrum** *f* competence centre (*Brit*) *od* center (*US*)
komplett [kɔm'plɛt] *adj* complete
komplex [kɔm'plɛks] *adj* complex; **Komplex** (**-es, -e**) *m* complex
Komplikation [kɔmplikatsi'oːn] *f* complication
Kompliment [kɔmpli'mɛnt] *nt* compliment
Komplize [kɔm'pliːtsə] (**-n, -n**) *m* accomplice
komplizieren [kɔmpli'tsiːrən] *vt* to complicate
kompliziert *adj* complicated; (*Med: Bruch*) compound
Komplizin [kɔm'pliːtsɪn] *f* accomplice
Komplott [kɔm'plɔt] (**-(e)s, -e**) *nt* plot
komponieren [kɔmpo'niːrən] *vt* to compose
Komponist, in [kɔmpo'nɪst(ɪn)] *m(f)* composer
Komposition [kɔmpozitsi'oːn] *f* composition
Kompost [kɔm'pɔst] (**-(e)s, -e**) *m* compost; **Komposthaufen** *m* compost heap
Kompott [kɔm'pɔt] (**-(e)s, -e**) *nt* stewed fruit
Kompresse [kɔm'prɛsə] (**-, -n**) *f* compress
Kompressor [kɔm'prɛsɔr] *m* compressor
Kompromiss [kɔmpro'mɪs] (**-es, -e**) *m* compromise; **einen ~ schließen** to compromise; **kompromissbereit** *adj* willing to compromise; **Kompromisslösung** *f* compromise solution
kompromittieren [kɔmpromɪ'tiːrən] *vt* to compromise
Kondensation [kɔndɛnzatsi'oːn] *f* condensation
Kondensator [kɔndɛn'zaːtɔr] *m* condenser
kondensieren [kɔndɛn'ziːrən] *vt* to condense
Kondensmilch *f* condensed milk
Kondensstreifen *m* vapour (*Brit*) *od* vapor (*US*) trail
Kondition [kɔnditsi'oːn] *f* condition, shape; (*Durchhaltevermögen*) stamina
Konditionalsatz [kɔnditsio'naːlzats] *m* conditional clause
Konditionstraining *nt* fitness training
Konditor [kɔn'diːtɔr] *m* pastry-cook
Konditorei [kɔndito'raɪ] *f* cake shop; (*mit Café*) café
kondolieren [kɔndo'liːrən] *vi*: **jdm ~** to condole with sb, offer sb one's condolences
Kondom [kɔn'doːm] (**-s, -e**) *m or nt* condom
Konfektion [kɔnfɛktsi'oːn] *f* (production of) ready-to-wear *od* off-the-peg clothing
Konfektionsgröße *f* clothes size
Konfektionskleidung *f* ready-to-wear *od* off-the-peg clothing
Konferenz [kɔnfe'rɛnts] *f* conference; (*Besprechung*) meeting; **Konferenzschaltung** *f* (*Tel*) conference circuit; (*Rundf, TV*) television *od* radio link-up

konferieren [kɔnfe'ri:rən] *vi* to confer; to have a meeting
Konfession [kɔnfɛsi'o:n] *f* religion; (*christlich*) denomination; **konfessionell** [-'nɛl] *adj* denominational
Konfessions- *zW*: **konfessionsgebunden** *adj* denominational; **konfessionslos** *adj* non-denominational; **Konfessionsschule** *f* denominational school
Konfetti [kɔn'fɛti] (**-(s)**) *nt* confetti
Konfiguration [kɔnfiguratsi'o:n] *f* (*Comput*) configuration
Konfirmand, in [kɔnfɪr'mant, -'mandɪn] *m(f)* candidate for confirmation
Konfirmation [kɔnfɪrmatsi'o:n] *f* (*Eccl*) confirmation
konfirmieren [kɔnfɪr'mi:rən] *vt* to confirm
konfiszieren [kɔnfɪs'tsi:rən] *vt* to confiscate
Konfitüre [kɔnfi'ty:rə] (**-, -n**) *f* jam
Konflikt [kɔn'flɪkt] (**-(e)s, -e**) *m* conflict; **Konfliktherd** *m* (*Pol*) centre (*Brit*) *od* center (*US*) of conflict; **Konfliktstoff** *m* cause of conflict
konform [kɔn'fɔrm] *adj* concurring; **~ gehen** to be in agreement
Konfrontation [kɔnfrɔntatsi'o:n] *f* confrontation
konfrontieren [kɔnfrɔn'ti:rən] *vt* to confront
konfus [kɔn'fu:s] *adj* confused
Kongo ['kɔŋgo] (**-(s)**) *m* Congo
Kongress [kɔn'grɛs] (**-es, -e**) *m* congress
Kongruenz [kɔngru'ɛnts] *f* agreement, congruence
König ['kø:nɪç] (**-(e)s, -e**) *m* king
Königin ['kø:nɪgɪn] *f* queen
königlich *adj* royal ▷ *adv*: **sich ~ amüsieren** (*umg*) to have the time of one's life
Königreich *nt* kingdom
Königtum ['kø:nɪçtu:m] (**-(e)s, -tümer**) *nt* kingship; (*Reich*) kingdom
konisch ['ko:nɪʃ] *adj* conical
Konj. *abk* (= *Konjunktiv*) conj.
Konjugation [kɔnjugatsi'o:n] *f* conjugation
konjugieren [kɔnju'gi:rən] *vt* to conjugate
Konjunktion [kɔnjʊŋktsi'o:n] *f* conjunction
Konjunktiv ['kɔnjʊŋkti:f] (**-s, -e**) *m* subjunctive
Konjunktur [kɔnjʊŋk'tu:r] *f* economic situation; (*Hochkonjunktur*) boom; **steigende/fallende ~** upward/downward economic trend; **Konjunkturbarometer** *nt* economic indicators *pl*; **Konjunktureinbruch** *nt* economic slump; **Konjunkturklima** *nt* economic climate; **Konjunkturloch** *nt* temporary economic dip; **Konjunkturpolitik** *f* *policies aimed at preventing economic fluctuations*
konkav [kɔn'ka:f] *adj* concave
konkret [kɔn'kre:t] *adj* concrete
Konkurrent, in [kɔnkʊ'rɛnt(ɪn)] *m(f)* competitor
Konkurrenz [kɔnkʊ'rɛnts] *f* competition; **jdm ~ machen** (*Comm, fig*) to compete with sb; **konkurrenzfähig** *adj* competitive; **Konkurrenzkampf** *m* competition; (*umg*) rat race
konkurrieren [kɔnkʊ'ri:rən] *vi* to compete
Konkurs [kɔn'kʊrs] (**-es, -e**) *m* bankruptcy; **in ~ gehen** to go into receivership; **~ machen** (*umg*) to go bankrupt; **Konkursverfahren** *nt* bankruptcy proceedings *pl*; **Konkursverwalter** *m* receiver; (*von Gläubigern bevollmächtigt*) trustee

SCHLÜSSELWORT

können ['kœnən] (*pt* **konnte**, *pp* **gekonnt** *od* (*als Hilfsverb*) **können**) *vt, vi* **1** to be able to; **ich kann es machen** I can do it, I am able to do it; **ich kann es nicht machen** I can't do it, I'm not able to do it; **ich kann nicht ...** I can't ..., I cannot ...; **was können Sie?** what can you do?; **ich kann nicht mehr** I can't go on; **ich kann nichts dafür** I can't help it; **du kannst mich (mal)!** (*umg*) get lost!
2 (*wissen, beherrschen*) to know; **können Sie Deutsch?** can you speak German?; **er kann gut Englisch** he speaks English well; **sie kann keine Mathematik** she can't do mathematics
3 (*dürfen*) to be allowed to; **kann ich gehen?** can I go?; **könnte ich ...?** could I ...?; **kann ich mit?** (*umg*) can I come with you?
4 (*möglich sein*): **Sie könnten recht haben** you may be right; **das kann sein** that's possible; **kann sein** maybe

Können (**-s**) *nt* ability
Könner (**-s, -**) *m* expert
Konnossement [kɔnɔsə'mɛnt] *nt* (*Export*) bill of lading
konnte *etc* ['kɔntə] *vb siehe* **können**
konsequent [kɔnze'kvɛnt] *adj* consistent; **ein Ziel ~ verfolgen** to pursue an objective single-mindedly
Konsequenz [kɔnze'kvɛnts] *f* consistency; (*Folgerung*) conclusion; **die ~en tragen** to take the consequences; **(aus etw) die ~en ziehen** to take the appropriate steps
konservativ [kɔnzɛrva'ti:f] *adj* conservative
Konservatorium [kɔnzɛrva'to:riʊm] *nt* academy of music, conservatory
Konserve [kɔn'zɛrvə] (**-, -n**) *f* tinned (*Brit*) *od* canned food
Konservenbüchse *f*, **Konservendose** *f* tin (*Brit*), can
konservieren [kɔnzɛr'vi:rən] *vt* to preserve
Konservierung *f* preservation
Konservierungsstoff *m* preservative
Konsole [kɔnzo:lə] *f* games console
konsolidiert [kɔnzoli'di:rt] *adj* consolidated
Konsolidierung *f* consolidation
Konsonant [kɔnzo'nant] *m* consonant
Konsortium [kɔn'zɔrtsiʊm] *nt* consortium, syndicate
konspirativ [kɔnspira'ti:f] *adj*: **~e Wohnung** conspirators' hideaway
konstant [kɔn'stant] *adj* constant
Konstellation [kɔnstɛlatsi'o:n] *f* constellation;

(*fig*) line-up; (*von Faktoren etc*) combination
Konstitution [kɔnstitutsi'o:n] *f* constitution
konstitutionell [kɔnstitutsio'nɛl] *adj* constitutional
konstruieren [kɔnstru'i:rən] *vt* to construct
Konstrukteur, in [kɔnstrʊk'tø:r(ɪn)] *m(f)* designer
Konstruktion [kɔnstrʊktsi'on] *f* construction
Konstruktionsfehler *m* (*im Entwurf*) design fault; (*im Aufbau*) structural defect
konstruktiv [kɔnstrʊk'ti:f] *adj* constructive
Konsul ['kɔnzʊl] (**-s, -n**) *m* consul
Konsulat [kɔnzʊ'la:t] (**-(e)s, -e**) *nt* consulate
konsultieren [kɔnzʊl'ti:rən] *vt* to consult
Konsum[1] [kɔn'zu:m] (**-s**) *m* consumption
Konsum[2] ['kɔnzu:m] (**-s, -s**) *m* (*Genossenschaft*) cooperative society; (*Laden*) cooperative store, co-op (*umg*)
Konsumartikel *m* consumer article
Konsument [kɔnzu'mɛnt] *m* consumer
konsumfreudig *f* consumption-oriented, consumerist
Konsumgesellschaft *f* consumer society
konsumieren [kɔnzu'mi:rən] *vt* to consume
Konsumtempel *m* temple of consumerism
Konsumterror *m* pressures *pl* of a materialistic society
Konsumzwang *m* compulsion to buy
Kontakt [kɔn'takt] (**-(e)s, -e**) *m* contact; **mit jdm ~ aufnehmen** to get in touch with sb; **Kontaktanzeige** *f* lonely hearts ad; **kontaktarm** *adj* unsociable; **kontaktfreudig** *adj* sociable
kontaktieren [kɔntak'ti:rən] *vt* to contact
Kontakt- *zW*: **Kontaktlinsen** *pl* contact lenses *pl*; **Kontaktmann** (**-(e)s**, *pl* **-männer**) *m* (*Agent*) contact; **Kontaktsperre** *f* ban on visits and letters (*to a prisoner*)
Konterfei ['kɔntərfaɪ] (**-s, -s**) *nt* likeness, portrait
kontern ['kɔntərn] *vt, vi* to counter
Konterrevolution ['kɔntərrevolutsio:n] *f* counter-revolution
Kontinent [kɔnti'nɛnt] *m* continent
Kontingent [kɔntɪŋ'gɛnt] (**-(e)s, -e**) *nt* quota; (*Truppenkontingent*) contingent
kontinuierlich [kɔntinu'i:rlɪç] *adj* continuous
Kontinuität [kɔntinui'tɛ:t] *f* continuity
Konto ['kɔnto] (**-s, Konten**) *nt* account; **das geht auf mein ~** (*umg: ich bin schuldig*) I am to blame for this; (*ich zahle*) this is on me (*umg*); **Kontoauszug** *m* statement (of account); **Kontoinhaber, in** *m(f)* account holder
Kontor [kɔn'to:r] (**-s, -e**) *nt* office
Kontorist, in [kɔnto'rɪst(ɪn)] *m(f)* clerk, office worker
Kontostand *m* bank balance
kontra ['kɔntra] *präp +akk* against; (*Jur*) versus
Kontra (**-s, -s**) *nt* (*Karten*) double; **jdm ~ geben** (*fig*) to contradict sb
Kontrabass *m* double bass
Kontrahent [-'hɛnt] *m* contracting party; (*Gegner*) opponent
Kontrapunkt *m* counterpoint
Kontrast [kɔn'trast] (**-(e)s, -e**) *m* contrast
Kontrollabschnitt *m* (*Comm*) counterfoil, stub
Kontrollampe [kɔn'trɔllampə] *f siehe* **Kontrolllampe**
Kontrolle [kɔn'trɔlə] (**-, -n**) *f* control, supervision; (*Passkontrolle*) passport control
Kontrolleur [kɔntrɔ'lø:r] *m* inspector
kontrollieren [kɔntrɔ'li:rən] *vt* to control, supervise; (*nachprüfen*) to check
Kontrolllampe [kɔn'trɔllampə] *f* pilot lamp; (*Aut: für Ölstand etc*) warning light
Kontrollturm *m* control tower
Kontroverse [kɔntro'vɛrzə] (**-, -n**) *f* controversy
Kontur [kɔn'tu:r] *f* contour
Konvention [kɔnvɛntsi'o:n] *f* convention
Konventionalstrafe [kɔnvɛntsio'na:lʃtra:fə] *f* penalty *od* fine (*for breach of contract*)
konventionell [kɔnvɛntsio'nɛl] *adj* conventional
Konversation [kɔnvɛrzatsi'o:n] *f* conversation
Konversationslexikon *nt* encyclopaedia
konvex [kɔn'vɛks] *adj* convex
Konvoi ['kɔnvɔʏ] (**-s, -s**) *m* convoy
Konzentrat [kɔntsɛn'tra:t] (**-s, -e**) *nt* concentrate
Konzentration [kɔntsɛntratsi'o:n] *f* concentration
Konzentrationsfähigkeit *f* power of concentration
Konzentrationslager *nt* concentration camp
konzentrieren [kɔntsɛn'tri:rən] *vt, vr* to concentrate
konzentriert *adj* concentrated ▷ *adv* (*zuhören, arbeiten*) intently
Konzept [kɔn'tsɛpt] (**-(e)s, -e**) *nt* rough draft; (*Plan, Programm*) plan; (*Begriff, Vorstellung*) concept; **jdn aus dem ~ bringen** to confuse sb; **Konzeptpapier** *nt* rough paper
Konzern [kɔn'tsɛrn] (**-s, -e**) *m* combine
Konzert [kɔn'tsɛrt] (**-(e)s, -e**) *nt* concert; (*Stück*) concerto; **Konzertsaal** *m* concert hall
Konzession [kɔntsɛsi'o:n] *f* licence (*Brit*), license (*US*); (*Zugeständnis*) concession; **die ~ entziehen** *+dat: Comm*) to disenfranchise
Konzessionär [kɔntsɛsio'nɛ:r] (**-s, -e**) *m* concessionaire
konzessionieren [kɔntsɛsio'ni:rən] *vt* to license
Konzil [kɔn'tsi:l] (**-s, -e** *od* **-ien**) *nt* council
konzipieren [kɔntsi'pi:rən] *vt* to conceive; (*entwerfen*) to design
kooperativ [ko|opera'ti:f] *adj* cooperative
kooperieren [ko|ope'ri:rən] *vi* to cooperate
koordinieren [ko|ɔrdi'ni:rən] *vt* to coordinate
Kopenhagen [ko:pən'ha:gən] (**-s**) *nt* Copenhagen
Kopf [kɔpf] (**-(e)s, ¨-e**) *m* head; **~ hoch!** chin up!; **~ an Kopf** shoulder to shoulder; (*Sport*) neck and neck; **pro ~** per person *od* head; **~ oder Zahl?** heads or tails?; **jdm den ~ waschen** (*fig: umg*) to give sb a piece of one's mind; **jdm über den ~ wachsen** (*lit*) to outgrow

sb; (*fig: Sorgen etc*) to be more than sb can cope with; **jdn vor den ~ stoßen** to antagonize sb; **sich** *dat* **an den ~ fassen** (*fig*) to be speechless; **sich** *dat* **über etw** *akk* **den ~ zerbrechen** to rack one's brains over sth; **sich** *dat* **etw durch den ~ gehen lassen** to think about sth; **sich** *dat* **etw aus dem ~ schlagen** to put sth out of one's mind; **... und wenn du dich auf den ~ stellst!** (*umg*) ... no matter what you say/do!; **er ist nicht auf den ~ gefallen** he's no fool; **Kopfbahnhof** *m* terminus station; **Kopfbedeckung** *f* headgear

Köpfchen ['kœpfçən] *nt*: **~ haben** to be brainy

köpfen ['kœpfən] *vt* to behead; (*Baum*) to lop; (*Ei*) to take the top off; (*Ball*) to head

Kopf- *zW*: **Kopfende** *nt* head; **Kopfhaut** *f* scalp; **Kopfhörer** *m* headphone; **Kopfkissen** *nt* pillow; **kopflastig** *adj* (*fig*) completely rational; **kopflos** *adj* panic-stricken; **Kopflosigkeit** *f* panic; **kopfrechnen** *vi* to do mental arithmetic; **Kopfsalat** *m* lettuce; **kopfscheu** *adj*: **jdn kopfscheu machen** to intimidate sb; **Kopfschmerzen** *pl* headache *sing*; **Kopfsprung** *m* header, dive; **Kopfstand** *m* headstand; **Kopfsteinpflaster** *nt*: **eine Straße mit Kopfsteinpflaster** a cobbled street; **Kopfstütze** *f* headrest; (*im Auto*) head restraint; **Kopftuch** *nt* headscarf; **kopfüber** *adv* head-first; **Kopfweh** *nt* headache; **Kopfzerbrechen** *nt*: **jdm Kopfzerbrechen machen** to give sb a lot of headaches

Kopie [ko'pi:] *f* copy

kopieren [ko'pi:rən] *vt* to copy

Kopierer (**-s, -**) *m* (photo)copier

Kopilot, in ['ko:pilo:t(ɪn)] *m(f)* co-pilot

Koppel[1] ['kɔpəl] (**-, -n**) *f* (*Weide*) enclosure

Koppel[2] ['kɔpəl] (**-s, -**) *nt* (*Gürtel*) belt

koppeln *vt* to couple

Koppelung *f* coupling

Koppelungsmanöver *nt* docking manoeuvre (*Brit*) *od* maneuver (*US*)

Koralle [ko'ralə] (**-, -n**) *f* coral

Korallenkette *f* coral necklace

Korallenriff *nt* coral reef

Korb [kɔrp] (**-(e)s, ¨-e**) *m* basket; **jdm einen ~ geben** (*fig*) to turn sb down; **Korbball** *m* basketball

Körbchen ['kœrpçən] *nt* (*von Büstenhalter*) cup

Korbstuhl *m* wicker chair

Kord [kɔrt] (**-(e)s, -e** *od* **-s**) *m* = **Cord**

Kordel ['kɔrdəl] (**-, -n**) *f* cord, string

Korea [ko're:a] (**-s**) *nt* Korea

Koreaner, in (**-s, -**) *m(f)* Korean

Korfu ['kɔrfu] (**-s**) *nt* Corfu

Korinthe [ko'rɪntə] (**-, -n**) *f* currant

Korinthenkacker [ko'rɪntənkakər] (**-s, -**) (*umg*) *m* fusspot, hair-splitter

Kork [kɔrk] (**-(e)s, -e**) *m* cork

Korken (**-s, -**) *m* stopper, cork; **Korkenzieher** (**-s, -**) *m* corkscrew

Korn[1] [kɔrn] (**-(e)s, ¨-er**) *nt* corn, grain

Korn[2] [kɔrn] (**-(e)s, -e**) *nt* (*Gewehr*) sight; **etw aufs ~ nehmen** (*fig: umg*) to hit out at sth

Korn[3] [kɔrn] (**-, -s**) *m* (*Kornbranntwein*) corn schnapps

Kornblume *f* cornflower

Körnchen ['kœrnçən] *nt* grain, granule

körnig ['kœrnɪç] *adj* granular, grainy

Kornkammer *f* granary

Körnung ['kœrnʊŋ] *f* (*Tech*) grain size; (*Phot*) granularity

Körper ['kœrper] (**-s, -**) *m* body; **Körperbau** *m* build; **körperbehindert** *adj* disabled; **Körpergeruch** *m* body odour (*Brit*) *od* odor (*US*); **Körpergewicht** *nt* weight; **Körpergröße** *f* height; **Körperhaltung** *f* carriage, deportment; **körperlich** *adj* physical; **körperliche Arbeit** manual work; **Körperpflege** *f* personal hygiene; **Körperschaft** *f* corporation; **Körperschaft des öffentlichen Rechts** public corporation *od* body; **Körperschaftssteuer** *f* corporation tax; **Körpersprache** *f* body language; **Körperteil** *m* part of the body; **Körperverletzung** *f* (*Jur*): **schwere Körperverletzung** grievous bodily harm

Korps [ko:r] (**-, -**) *nt* (*Mil*) corps; (*Univ*) students' club

korpulent [kɔrpu'lɛnt] *adj* corpulent

korrekt [kɔ'rɛkt] *adj* correct; **Korrektheit** *f* correctness

Korrektor, in [kɔ'rɛktɔr, -'to:rɪn] (**-s, -**) *m(f)* proofreader

Korrektur [kɔrɛk'tu:r] *f* (*eines Textes*) proofreading; (*Text*) proof; (*Sch*) marking, correction; **(bei etw) ~ lesen** to proofread (sth); **Korrekturfahne** *f* (*Typ*) proof

Korrespondent, in [kɔrɛspɔn'dɛnt(ɪn)] *m(f)* correspondent

Korrespondenz [kɔrɛspɔn'dɛnts] *f* correspondence; **Korrespondenzqualität** *f* (*Drucker*) letter quality

korrespondieren [kɔrɛspɔn'di:rən] *vi* to correspond

Korridor ['kɔrido:r] (**-s, -e**) *m* corridor

korrigieren [kɔri'gi:rən] *vt* to correct; (*Meinung, Einstellung*) to change

Korrosion [kɔrozi'o:n] *f* corrosion

Korrosionsschutz *m* corrosion protection

korrumpieren [kɔrʊm'pi:rən] *vt* (*auch Comput*) to corrupt

korrupt [kɔ'rʊpt] *adj* corrupt

Korruption [kɔrʊptsi'o:n] *f* corruption

Korsett [kɔr'zɛt] (**-(e)s, -e**) *nt* corset

Korsika ['kɔrzika] (**-s**) *nt* Corsica

Koseform ['ko:zəfɔrm] *f* pet form

kosen *vt* to caress ▷ *vi* to bill and coo

Kosename *m* pet name

Kosewort *nt* term of endearment

Kosmetik [kɔs'me:tɪk] *f* cosmetics *pl*

Kosmetikerin *f* beautician

kosmetisch *adj* cosmetic; (*Chirurgie*) plastic

kosmisch ['kɔsmɪʃ] *adj* cosmic

Kosmonaut [kɔsmo'naʊt] (**-en, -en**) *m* cosmonaut

Kosmopolit [kɔsmopo'li:t] (**-en, -en**) *m*

cosmopolitan; **kosmopolitisch** [-po'li:tiʃ] *adj* cosmopolitan

Kosmos ['kɔsmɔs] **(-)** *m* cosmos

Kost [kɔst] **(-)** *f* (*Nahrung*) food; (*Verpflegung*) board; **~ und Logis** board and lodging

kostbar *adj* precious; (*teuer*) costly, expensive; **Kostbarkeit** *f* preciousness; costliness, expensiveness; (*Wertstück*) treasure

Kosten *pl* cost(s); (*Ausgaben*) expenses *pl*; **auf ~ von** at the expense of; **auf seine ~ kommen** (*fig*) to get one's money's worth

kosten *vt* to cost; (*versuchen*) to taste ▷ *vi* to taste; **koste es, was es wolle** whatever the cost

Kosten- *zW*: **Kostenanschlag** *m* estimate; **kostendeckend** *adj* cost-effective; **Kostenerstattung** *f* reimbursement of expenses; **Kostenkontrolle** *f* cost control; **kostenlos** *adj* free (of charge); **Kosten-Nutzen-Analyse** *f* cost-benefit analysis; **kostenpflichtig** *adj*: **ein Auto kostenpflichtig abschleppen** to tow away a car at the owner's expense; **Kostenstelle** *f* (*Comm*) cost centre (*Brit*) *od* center (*US*); **Kostenvoranschlag** *m* (costs) estimate

Kostgeld *nt* board

köstlich ['kœstlɪç] *adj* precious; (*Einfall*) delightful; (*Essen*) delicious; **sich ~ amüsieren** to have a marvellous time

Kostprobe *f* taste; (*fig*) sample

kostspielig *adj* expensive

Kostüm [kɔs'ty:m] **(-s, -e)** *nt* costume; (*Damenkostüm*) suit; **Kostümfest** *nt* fancy-dress party

kostümieren [kɔsty'mi:rən] *vt, vr* to dress up

Kostümprobe *f* (*Theat*) dress rehearsal

Kostümverleih *m* costume agency

Kot [ko:t] **(-(e)s)** *m* excrement

Kotelett [kotə'lɛt] **(-(e)s, -e** *od* **-s)** *nt* cutlet, chop

Koteletten *pl* sideboards *pl* (*Brit*), sideburns *pl* (*US*)

Köter ['kø:tər] **(-s, -)** *m* cur

Kotflügel *m* (*Aut*) wing

kotzen ['kɔtsən] (*umg!*) *vi* to puke (*!*), throw up; **das ist zum K~** it makes you sick

KP **(-, -s)** *f abk* (= *Kommunistische Partei*) C.P.

KPÖ **(-)** *f abk* (= *Kommunistische Partei Österreichs*) Austrian Communist Party

Kr. *abk* = **Kreis**

Krabbe ['krabə] **(-, -n)** *f* shrimp

krabbeln *vi* to crawl

Krach [krax] **(-(e)s, -s** *od* **-e)** *m* crash; (*andauernd*) noise; (*umg: Streit*) quarrel, argument; **~ schlagen** to make a fuss; **krachen** *vi* to crash; (*beim Brechen*) to crack ▷ *vr* (*umg*) to argue, quarrel

krächzen ['krɛçtsən] *vi* to croak

Kräcker ['krɛkər] **(-s, -)** *m* (*Koch*) cracker

kraft [kraft] *präp +gen* by virtue of

Kraft **(-, ⸚e)** *f* strength; (*von Stimme, fig*) power, force; (*Arbeitskraft*) worker; **mit vereinten Kräften werden wir ...** if we combine our efforts we will ...; **nach (besten) Kräften** to the best of one's abilities; **außer ~ sein** (*Jur: Geltung*) to be no longer in force; **in ~ treten** to come into effect

Kraft- *zW*: **Kraftaufwand** *m* effort; **Kraftausdruck** *m* swearword; **Kraftbrühe** *f* beef tea

Kräfteverhältnis ['krɛftəfɛrhɛltnɪs] *nt* (*Pol*) balance of power; (*von Mannschaften etc*) relative strength

Kraftfahrer *m* motor driver

Kraftfahrzeug *nt* motor vehicle; **Kraftfahrzeugbrief** *m* (*Aut*) logbook (*Brit*), motor-vehicle registration certificate (*US*); **Kraftfahrzeugschein** *m* (*Aut*) car licence (*Brit*) *od* license (*US*); **Kraftfahrzeugsteuer** *f* ≈ road tax

kräftig ['krɛftɪç] *adj* strong; (*Suppe, Essen*) nourishing; **kräftigen** ['krɛftɪgən] *vt* to strengthen

Kraft- *zW*: **kraftlos** *adj* weak; powerless; (*Jur*) invalid; **Kraftmeierei** (*umg*) *f showing off of physical strength*; **Kraftprobe** *f* trial of strength; **Kraftrad** *nt* motorcycle; **Kraftstoff** *m* fuel; **Krafttraining** *nt* weight training; **kraftvoll** *adj* vigorous; **Kraftwagen** *m* motor vehicle; **Kraftwerk** *nt* power station; **Kraftwerker** *m* power station worker

Kragen ['kra:gən] **(-s, -)** *m* collar; **da ist mir der ~ geplatzt** (*umg*) I blew my top; **es geht ihm an den ~** (*umg*) he's in for it; **Kragenweite** *f* collar size; **das ist nicht meine Kragenweite** (*fig: umg*) that's not my cup of tea

Krähe ['krɛ:ə] **(-, -n)** *f* crow

krähen *vi* to crow

krakeelen [kra'ke:lən] (*umg*) *vi* to make a din

krakelig ['kra:kəlɪç] (*umg*) *adj* (*Schrift*) scrawly, spidery

Kralle ['kralə] **(-, -n)** *f* claw; (*Vogelkralle*) talon

krallen *vt* to clutch; (*krampfhaft*) to claw

Kram [kra:m] **(-(e)s)** *m* stuff, rubbish; **den ~ hinschmeißen** (*umg*) to chuck the whole thing; **kramen** *vi* to rummage; **Kramladen** (*pej*) *m* small shop

Krampf [krampf] **(-(e)s, ⸚e)** *m* cramp; (*zuckend*) spasm; (*Unsinn*) rubbish; **Krampfader** *f* varicose vein; **krampfhaft** *adj* convulsive; (*fig: Versuche*) desperate

Kran [kra:n] **(-(e)s, ⸚e)** *m* crane; (*Wasserkran*) tap (*Brit*), faucet (*US*)

Kranich ['kra:nɪç] **(-s, -e)** *m* (*Zool*) crane

krank [kraŋk] *adj* ill, sick; **das macht mich ~!** (*umg*) it gets on my nerves!, it drives me round the bend!; **sich ~ stellen** to pretend to be ill, malinger

Kranke, r *f(m)* sick person, invalid; (*Patient*) patient

kränkeln ['krɛŋkəln] *vi* to be in bad health

kranken ['kraŋkən] *vi*: **an etw** *dat* **~** (*fig*) to suffer from sth

kränken ['krɛŋkən] *vt* to hurt

Kranken- *zW*: **Krankenbericht** *m* medical

report; **Krankenbesuch** *m* visit to a sick person; **Krankengeld** *nt* sick pay; **Krankengeschichte** *f* medical history; **Krankengymnastik** *f* physiotherapy; **Krankenhaus** *nt* hospital; **Krankenkasse** *f* health insurance; **Krankenpfleger** *m* orderly; (*mit Schwesternausbildung*) male nurse; **Krankenpflegerin** *f* nurse; **Krankenschein** *m* medical insurance certificate; **Krankenschwester** *f* nurse; **Krankenversicherung** *f* health insurance; **Krankenwagen** *m* ambulance

krankfeiern (*umg*) *vi* to be off sick; (*vortäuschend*) to skive (*Brit*)

krankhaft *adj* diseased; (*Angst etc*) morbid; **sein Geiz ist schon ~** his meanness is almost pathological

Krankheit *f* illness; disease; **nach langer schwerer ~** after a long serious illness

Krankheitserreger *m* disease-causing agent

kränklich ['krɛŋklɪç] *adj* sickly

krankmelden *vr* to let one's boss *etc* know that one is ill; (*telefonisch*) to phone in sick; (*bes Mil*) to report sick

krankschreiben *unreg vt* to give sb a medical certificate; (*bes Mil*) to put sb on the sick list

Kränkung *f* insult, offence (*Brit*), offense (*US*)

Kranz [krants] (**-es, ¨-e**) *m* wreath, garland

Kränzchen ['krɛntsçən] *nt* small wreath; (*fig: Kaffeekränzchen*) coffee circle

Krapfen ['krapfən] (**-s, -**) *m* fritter; (*Berliner*) doughnut (*Brit*), donut (*US*)

krass [kras] *adj* crass; (*Unterschied*) extreme

Krater ['kra:tər] (**-s, -**) *m* crater

Kratzbürste ['kratsbʏrstə] *f* (*fig*) crosspatch

Krätze ['krɛtsə] *f* (*Med*) scabies *sing*

kratzen ['kratsən] *vt, vi* to scratch; (*abkratzen*): **etw von etw ~** to scrape sth off sth

Kratzer (**-s, -**) *m* scratch; (*Werkzeug*) scraper

Kraul [kraʊl] (**-s**) *nt* (*auch*: **Kraulschwimmen**) crawl; **kraulen** *vi* (*schwimmen*) to do the crawl ▷ *vt* (*streicheln*) to tickle

kraus [kraʊs] *adj* crinkly; (*Haar*) frizzy; (*Stirn*) wrinkled

Krause ['kraʊzə] (**-, -n**) *f* frill, ruffle

kräuseln ['krɔʏzəln] *vt* (*Haar*) to make frizzy; (*Stoff*) to gather; (*Stirn*) to wrinkle ▷ *vr* (*Haar*) to go frizzy; (*Stirn*) to wrinkle; (*Wasser*) to ripple

Kraut [kraʊt] (**-(e)s, Kräuter**) *nt* plant; (*Gewürz*) herb; (*Gemüse*) cabbage; **dagegen ist kein ~ gewachsen** (*fig*) there's nothing anyone can do about that; **ins ~ schießen** (*lit*) to run to seed; (*fig*) to get out of control; **wie ~ und Rüben** (*umg*) extremely untidy

Kräutertee ['krɔʏtərte:] *m* herb tea

Krawall [kra'val] (**-s, -e**) *m* row, uproar

Krawatte [kra'vatə] (**-, -n**) *f* tie

kreativ [krea'ti:f] *adj* creative

Kreativität [kreativi'tɛ:t] *f* creativity

Kreatur [krea'tu:r] *f* creature

Krebs [kre:ps] (**-es, -e**) *m* crab; (*Med*) cancer; (*Astrol*) Cancer; **krebserregend** *adj* carcinogenic; **krebskrank** *adj* suffering from cancer; **krebskrank sein** to have cancer; **Krebskranke, r** *f(m)* cancer victim; (*Patient*) cancer patient; **krebsrot** *adj* red as a lobster

Kredit [kre'di:t] (**-(e)s, -e**) *m* credit; (*Darlehen*) loan; (*fig*) standing; **Kreditdrosselung** *f* credit squeeze; **kreditfähig** *adj* creditworthy; **Kreditgrenze** *f* credit limit; **Kredithai** (*umg*) *m* loan-shark; **Kreditkarte** *f* credit card; **Kreditkonto** *nt* credit account; **Kreditpolitik** *f* lending policy; **kreditwürdig** *adj* creditworthy; **Kreditwürdigkeit** *f* creditworthiness, credit status

Kreide ['kraɪdə] (**-, -n**) *f* chalk; **bei jdm (tief) in der ~ stehen** to be (deep) in debt to sb; **kreidebleich** *adj* as white as a sheet

Kreis [kraɪs] (**-es, -e**) *m* circle; (*Stadtkreis etc*) district; **im ~ gehen** (*lit, fig*) to go round in circles; **(weite) ~e ziehen** (*fig*) to have (wide) repercussions; **weite ~e der Bevölkerung** wide sections of the population; **eine Feier im kleinen ~e** a celebration for a few close friends and relatives

kreischen ['kraɪʃən] *vi* to shriek, screech

Kreisel ['kraɪzəl] (**-s, -**) *m* top; (*Verkehrskreisel*) roundabout (*Brit*), traffic circle (*US*)

kreisen ['kraɪzən] *vi* to spin; (*fig: Gedanken, Gespräch*): **~ um** to revolve around

Kreis- *zW*: **kreisförmig** *adj* circular; **Kreislauf** *m* (*Med*) circulation; (*fig: der Natur etc*) cycle; **Kreislaufkollaps** *m* circulatory collapse; **Kreislaufstörungen** *pl* circulation trouble *sing*; **Kreissäge** *f* circular saw

Kreißsaal ['kraɪsza:l] *m* delivery room

Kreisstadt *f* ≈ county town

Kreisverkehr *m* roundabout (*Brit*), traffic circle (*US*)

Krematorium [krema'to:riʊm] *nt* crematorium

Kreml ['kre:ml] (**-s**) *m*: **der ~** the Kremlin

Krempe ['krɛmpə] (**-, -n**) *f* brim

Krempel (**-s**) (*umg*) *m* rubbish

krepieren [kre'pi:rən] (*umg*) *vi* (*sterben*) to die, kick the bucket

Krepp [krɛp] (**-s, -s** *od* **-e**) *m* crêpe

Krepppapier *nt* crêpe paper

Kreppsohle *f* crêpe sole

Kresse ['krɛsə] (**-, -n**) *f* cress

Kreta ['kre:ta] (**-s**) *nt* Crete

Kreter, in [kre:tər(ɪn)] (**-s, -**) *m(f)* Cretan

kretisch *adj* Cretan

kreuz [krɔʏts] *adj*: **~ und quer** all over

Kreuz (**-es, -e**) *nt* cross; (*Anat*) small of the back; (*Karten*) clubs; (*Mus*) sharp; (*Autobahnkreuz*) intersection; **zu ~e kriechen** (*fig*) to eat humble pie, eat crow (*US*); **jdn aufs ~ legen** to throw sb on his back; (*fig: umg*) to take sb for a ride

kreuzen *vt* to cross ▷ *vr* to cross; (*Meinungen etc*) to clash ▷ *vi* (*Naut*) to cruise; **die Arme ~** to fold one's arms

Kreuzer (**-s, -**) *m* (*Schiff*) cruiser

Kreuz- *zW*: **Kreuzfahrt** *f* cruise; **Kreuzfeuer** *nt* (*fig*): **im Kreuzfeuer stehen** to be caught in

the crossfire; **Kreuzgang** *m* cloisters *pl*
kreuzigen *vt* to crucify
Kreuzigung *f* crucifixion
Kreuzotter *f* adder
Kreuzschmerzen *pl* backache *sing*
Kreuzung *f* (*Verkehrskreuzung*) crossing, junction; (*Züchtung*) cross
Kreuz- *zW*: **kreuzunglücklich** *adj* absolutely miserable; **Kreuzverhör** *nt* cross-examination; **ins Kreuzverhör nehmen** to cross-examine; **Kreuzweg** *m* crossroads; (*Rel*) Way of the Cross; **Kreuzworträtsel** *nt* crossword puzzle; **Kreuzzeichen** *nt* sign of the cross; **Kreuzzug** *m* crusade
kribbelig ['krıbəlıç], **kribblig** ['krıblıç] (*umg*) *adj* fidgety; (*kribbelnd*) tingly
kribbeln ['krıbəln] *vi* (*jucken*) to itch; (*prickeln*) to tingle
kriechen ['kri:çən] *unreg vi* to crawl, creep; (*pej*) to grovel, crawl
Kriecher (**-s, -**) *m* crawler
kriecherisch *adj* grovelling (*Brit*), groveling (*US*)
Kriechspur *f* crawler lane (*Brit*)
Kriechtier *nt* reptile
Krieg [kri:k] (**-(e)s, -e**) *m* war; ~ **führen (mit** *od* **gegen)** to wage war (on)
kriegen ['kri:gən] (*umg*) *vt* to get
Krieger (**-s, -**) *m* warrior; **Kriegerdenkmal** *nt* war memorial; **kriegerisch** *adj* warlike
Kriegführung *f* warfare
Kriegs- *zW*: **Kriegsbeil** *nt*: **das Kriegsbeil begraben** (*fig*) to bury the hatchet; **Kriegsbemalung** *f* war paint; **Kriegsdienstverweigerer** *m* conscientious objector; **Kriegserklärung** *f* declaration of war; **Kriegsfuß** *m*: **mit jdm/etw auf Kriegsfuß stehen** to be at loggerheads with sb/not to get on with sth; **Kriegsgefangene, r** *f(m)* prisoner of war; **Kriegsgefangenschaft** *f* captivity; **Kriegsgericht** *nt* court-martial; **Kriegsrat** *m* council of war; **Kriegsrecht** *nt* (*Mil*) martial law; **Kriegsschauplatz** *m* theatre (*Brit*) *od* theater (*US*) of war; **Kriegsschiff** *nt* warship; **Kriegsschuld** *f* war guilt; **Kriegsverbrecher** *m* war criminal; **Kriegsversehrte, r** *f(m)* person disabled in the war; **Kriegszustand** *m* state of war
Krim [krım] *f*: **die** ~ the Crimea
Krimi ['kri:mi] (**-s, -s**) (*umg*) *m* thriller
kriminal [krimi'na:l] *adj* criminal; **Kriminalbeamte, r** *m* detective; **Kriminalfilm** *m* crime thriller *od* movie (*esp US*)
Kriminalität [kriminali'tε:t] *f* criminality
Kriminalpolizei *f* ≈ Criminal Investigation Department (*Brit*), ≈ Federal Bureau of Investigation (*US*)
Kriminalroman *m* detective story
kriminell [kri:mi'nεl] *adj* criminal
Kriminelle, r *f(m)* criminal
Krimskrams ['krımskrams] (**-es**) (*umg*) *m* odds and ends *pl*
Kringel ['krıŋəl] (**-s, -**) *m* (*der Schrift*) squiggle; (*Koch*) ring
kringelig *adj*: **sich ~ lachen** (*umg*) to kill o.s. laughing
Kripo ['kri:po] (**-, -s**) *f abk* (= *Kriminalpolizei*) ≈ CID (*Brit*), ≈ FBI (*US*)
Krippe ['krıpə] (**-, -n**) *f* manger, crib; (*Kinderkrippe*) crèche
Krippenspiel *nt* nativity play
Krippentod *m* cot death
Krise ['kri:zə] (**-, -n**) *f* crisis
kriseln *vi*: **es kriselt** there's a crisis looming, there is trouble brewing
Krisen- *zW*: **krisenfest** *adj* stable; **Krisenherd** *m* flash point; trouble spot; **Krisenstab** *m* action *od* crisis committee
Kristall[1] [krıs'tal] (**-s, -e**) *m* crystal
Kristall[2] (**-s**) *nt* (*Glas*) crystal; **Kristallzucker** *m* refined sugar crystals *pl*
Kriterium [kri'te:riʊm] *nt* criterion
Kritik [kri'ti:k] *f* criticism; (*Zeitungskritik*) review, write-up; **an jdm/etw ~ üben** to criticize sb/sth; **unter aller ~ sein** (*umg*) to be beneath contempt
Kritiker, in ['kri:tikər(ın)] (**-s, -**) *m(f)* critic
kritiklos *adj* uncritical
kritisch ['kri:tıʃ] *adj* critical
kritisieren [kriti'zi:rən] *vt, vi* to criticize
kritteln ['krıtəln] *vi* to find fault, carp
kritzeln ['krıtsəln] *vt, vi* to scribble, scrawl
Kroate [kro'a:tə] (**-n, -n**) *m* Croat
Kroatien [kro'a:tsiən] (**-s**) *nt* Croatia
Kroatin *f* Croat
kroatisch *adj* Croatian
kroch *etc* [krɔx] *vb siehe* **kriechen**
Krokodil [kroko'di:l] (**-s, -e**) *nt* crocodile
Krokodilstränen *pl* crocodile tears *pl*
Krokus ['kro:kʊs] (**-, -** *od* **-se**) *m* crocus
Krone ['kro:nə] (**-, -n**) *f* crown; (*Baumkrone*) top; **einen in der ~ haben** (*umg*) to be tipsy
krönen ['krø:nən] *vt* to crown
Kron- *zW*: **Kronkorken** *m* bottle top; **Kronleuchter** *m* chandelier; **Kronprinz** *m* crown prince
Krönung ['krø:nʊŋ] *f* coronation
Kronzeuge *m* (*Jur*) person who turns Queen's/King's (*Brit*) *od* State's (*US*) evidence; (*Hauptzeuge*) principal witness
Kropf [krɔpf] (**-(e)s, ⸚e**) *m* (*Med*) goitre (*Brit*), goiter (*US*); (*von Vogel*) crop
Krösus ['krø:zʊs] (**-ses, -se**) *m*: **ich bin doch kein** ~ (*umg*) I'm not made of money
Kröte ['krø:tə] (**-, -n**) *f* toad; **Kröten** *pl* (*umg: Geld*) pennies *pl*
Krs. *abk* = **Kreis**
Krücke ['krʏkə] (**-, -n**) *f* crutch
Krug [kru:k] (**-(e)s, ⸚e**) *m* jug; (*Bierkrug*) mug
Krümel ['kry:məl] (**-s, -**) *m* crumb
krümeln *vt, vi* to crumble
krumm [krʊm] *adj* (*lit, fig*) crooked; (*kurvig*) curved; **keinen Finger ~ machen** (*umg*) not to lift a finger; **ein ~es Ding drehen** (*umg*) to do something crooked; *siehe auch* **krummnehmen**; **krummbeinig** *adj* bandy-legged

krümmen ['krʏm:ən] *vt* to bend ▷ *vr* to bend, curve
krummlachen (*umg*) *vr* to laugh o.s. silly; **sich krumm- und schieflachen** to fall about laughing
krummnehmen *unreg* (*umg*) *vt*: **jdm etw ~** (*umg*) to take sth amiss
Krümmung *f* bend, curve
Krüppel ['krʏpəl] (**-s, -**) *m* cripple
Kruste ['krʊstə] (**-, -n**) *f* crust
Krux [krʊks] (-) *f* (*Schwierigkeit*) trouble, problem
Kruzifix [krutsi'fɪks] (**-es, -e**) *nt* crucifix
Kt. *abk* = **Kanton**
Kto. *abk* (= *Konto*) a/c
Kuba ['ku:ba] (**-s**) *nt* Cuba
Kubaner, in [ku'ba:nər(ɪn)] (**-s, -**) *m(f)* Cuban
kubanisch [ku'ba:nɪʃ] *adj* Cuban
Kübel ['ky:bəl] (**-s, -**) *m* tub; (*Eimer*) pail
Kubik- [ku'bi:k] *in zW* cubic; **Kubikmeter** *m* cubic metre (*Brit*) *od* meter (*US*)
Küche ['kʏçə] (**-, -n**) *f* kitchen; (*Kochen*) cooking, cuisine
Kuchen ['ku:xən] (**-s, -**) *m* cake; **Kuchenblech** *nt* baking tray; **Kuchenform** *f* baking tin (*Brit*) *od* pan (*US*); **Kuchengabel** *f* pastry fork
Küchen- *zW*: **Küchengerät** *nt* kitchen utensil; (*elektrisch*) kitchen appliance; **Küchenherd** *m* cooker, stove; **Küchenmaschine** *f* food processor; **Küchenmesser** *nt* kitchen knife; **Küchenschabe** *f* cockroach; **Küchenschrank** *m* kitchen cabinet
Kuchenteig *m* cake mixture
Kuckuck ['kʊkʊk] (**-s, -e**) *m* cuckoo; (*umg: Siegel des Gerichtsvollziehers*) bailiff's seal (*for distraint of goods*); **das weiß der ~** heaven (only) knows
Kuckucksuhr *f* cuckoo clock
Kuddelmuddel ['kʊdəlmʊdəl] (**-s**) (*umg*) *m od nt* mess
Kufe ['ku:fə] (**-, -n**) *f* (*Fasskufe*) vat; (*Schlittenkufe*) runner; (*Aviat*) skid
Kugel ['ku:gəl] (**-, -n**) *f* ball; (*Math*) sphere; (*Mil*) bullet; (*Erdkugel*) globe; (*Sport*) shot; **eine ruhige ~ schieben** (*umg*) to have a cushy number; **kugelförmig** *adj* spherical; **Kugelkopf** *m* (*Schreibmaschine*) golf ball; **Kugelkopfschreibmaschine** *f* golf-ball typewriter; **Kugellager** *nt* ball bearing
kugeln *vt* to roll; (*Sport*) to bowl ▷ *vr* (*vor Lachen*) to double up
Kugel- *zW*: **kugelrund** *adj* (*Gegenstand*) round; (*umg: Person*) tubby; **Kugelschreiber** *m* ball-point (pen), Biro®; **kugelsicher** *adj* bulletproof; **Kugelstoßen** (**-s**) *nt* shot put
Kuh [ku:] (**-, ¨-e**) *f* cow; **Kuhdorf** (*pej: umg*) *nt* one-horse town; **Kuhhandel** (*pej: umg*) *m* horse-trading; **Kuhhaut** *f*: **das geht auf keine Kuhhaut** (*fig: umg*) that's absolutely incredible
kühl [ky:l] *adj* (*lit, fig*) cool; **Kühlanlage** *f* refrigeration plant
Kühle (-) *f* coolness
kühlen *vt* to cool
Kühler (**-s, -**) *m* (*Aut*) radiator; **Kühlerhaube** *f* (*Aut*) bonnet (*Brit*), hood (*US*)
Kühl- *zW*: **Kühlflüssigkeit** *f* coolant; **Kühlhaus** *nt* cold-storage depot; **Kühlraum** *m* cold-storage chamber; **Kühlschrank** *m* refrigerator; **Kühltasche** *f* cool bag; **Kühltruhe** *f* freezer
Kühlung *f* cooling
Kühlwagen *m* (*Lastwagen, Eisenb*) refrigerator van
Kühlwasser *nt* coolant
kühn [ky:n] *adj* bold, daring; **Kühnheit** *f* boldness
Kuhstall *m* cow-shed
k. u. k. *abk* (= *kaiserlich und königlich*) imperial and royal
Küken ['ky:kən] (**-s, -**) *nt* chicken; (*umg: Nesthäkchen*) baby of the family
kulant [ku'lant] *adj* obliging
Kulanz [ku'lants] *f* accommodating attitude, generousness
Kuli ['ku:li] (**-s, -s**) *m* coolie; (*umg: Kugelschreiber*) Biro®
kulinarisch [kuli'na:rɪʃ] *adj* culinary
Kulisse [ku'lɪsə] (**-, -n**) *f* scene
Kulissenschieber, in *m(f)* stagehand
Kulleraugen ['kʊləraʊgən] (*umg*) *pl* wide eyes *pl*
kullern ['kʊlərn] *vi* to roll
Kult [kʊlt] (**-(e)s, -e**) *m* worship, cult; **mit etw ~ treiben** to make a cult out of sth
kultivieren [kʊlti'vi:rən] *vt* to cultivate
kultiviert *adj* cultivated, refined
Kultstätte *f* place of worship
Kultstatus *m*: **~ haben/genießen** to have/enjoy cult status
Kultur [kʊl'tu:r] *f* culture; (*Lebensform*) civilization; (*des Bodens*) cultivation; **Kulturbanause** (*umg*) *m* philistine, low-brow; **Kulturbetrieb** *m* culture industry; **Kulturbeutel** *m* toilet bag (*Brit*), washbag
kulturell [kʊltu'rɛl] *adj* cultural
Kulturfilm *m* documentary film
Kulturhauptstadt *f*: **Europäische ~** European City of Culture
Kulturteil *m* (*von Zeitung*) arts section
Kultusminister ['kʊltʊsminɪstər] *m* minister of education and the arts
Kümmel ['kʏməl] (**-s, -**) *m* caraway seed; (*Branntwein*) kümmel
Kummer ['kʊmər] (**-s**) *m* grief, sorrow
kümmerlich ['kʏmərlɪç] *adj* miserable, wretched
kümmern *vr*: **sich um jdn ~** to look after sb ▷ *vt* to concern; **sich um etw ~** to see to sth; **das kümmert mich nicht** that doesn't worry me
Kumpan, in [kʊm'pa:n(ɪn)] (**-s, -e**) *m(f)* mate; (*pej*) accomplice
Kumpel ['kʊmpəl] (**-s, -**) (*umg*) *m* mate
kündbar ['kʏntba:r] *adj* redeemable, recallable; (*Vertrag*) terminable
Kunde[1] ['kʊndə] (**-n, -n**) *m* customer
Kunde[2] ['kʊndə] (**-, -n**) *f* (*Botschaft*) news
Kunden- *zW*: **Kundenberatung** *f* customer

advisory service; **Kundendienst** *m* after-sales service; **Kundenfang** *(pej) m*: **auf Kundenfang sein** to be touting for customers; **Kundenfänger** *m* tout *(umg)*; **Kundenkonto** *nt* charge account; **Kundenkreis** *m* customers *pl*, clientele; **kundenorientiert** *m* customer-oriented; **Kundenservice** *f* customer service; **Kundenwerbung** *f* publicity *(aimed at attracting custom or customers)*

Kund- *zW*: **Kundgabe** *f* announcement; **kundgeben** *unreg vt* to announce; **Kundgebung** *f* announcement; *(Versammlung)* rally

kundig *adj* expert, experienced

kündigen ['kʏndɪgən] *vi* to give in one's notice ▷ *vt* to cancel; **jdm** ~ to give sb his notice; **zum 1. April** ~ to give one's notice for April 1st; *(Mieter)* to give notice for April 1st; *(bei Mitgliedschaft)* to cancel one's membership as of April 1st; **(jdm) die Stellung** ~ to give (sb) notice; **sie hat ihm die Freundschaft gekündigt** she has broken off their friendship

Kündigung *f* notice

Kündigungsfrist *f* period of notice

Kündigungsschutz *m* protection against wrongful dismissal

Kundin *f* customer

Kundschaft *f* customers *pl*, clientele

Kundschafter (**-s, -**) *m* spy; *(Mil)* scout

künftig ['kʏnftɪç] *adj* future ▷ *adv* in future

Kunst [kʊnst] (**-, ¨-e**) *f (auch Sch)* art; *(Können)* skill; **das ist doch keine** ~ it's easy; **mit seiner** ~ **am Ende sein** to be at one's wits' end; **das ist eine brotlose** ~ there's no money in that; **Kunstakademie** *f* academy of art; **Kunstdruck** *m* art print; **Kunstdünger** *m* artificial manure; **Kunsterziehung** *f (Sch)* art; **Kunstfaser** *f* synthetic fibre *(Brit)* *od* fiber *(US)*; **Kunstfehler** *m* professional error; *(weniger ernst)* slip; **Kunstfertigkeit** *f* skilfulness *(Brit)*, skillfulness *(US)*; **Kunstflieger** *m* stunt flyer; **kunstgerecht** *adj* skilful *(Brit)*, skillful *(US)*; **Kunstgeschichte** *f* history of art; **Kunstgewerbe** *nt* arts and crafts *pl*; **Kunstgriff** *m* trick, knack; **Kunsthändler** *m* art dealer; **Kunstharz** *nt* artificial resin; **Kunstleder** *nt* artificial leather

Künstler, in ['kʏnstlər(ɪn)] (**-s, -**) *m(f)* artist; **künstlerisch** *adj* artistic; **Künstlername** *m* pseudonym; *(von Schauspieler)* stage name; **Künstlerpech** *(umg) nt* hard luck

künstlich ['kʏnstlɪç] *adj* artificial; **~e Intelligenz** *(Comput)* artificial intelligence; **sich ~ aufregen** *(umg)* to get all worked up about nothing

Kunst- *zW*: **Kunstsammler** *m* art collector; **Kunstseide** *f* artificial silk; **Kunststoff** *m* synthetic material; **Kunststopfen** (**-s**) *nt* invisible mending; **Kunststück** *nt* trick; **das ist kein Kunststück** *(fig)* there's nothing to it; **Kunstturnen** *nt* gymnastics *sing*; **kunstvoll** *adj* artistic; **Kunstwerk** *nt* work of art

kunterbunt ['kʊntərbʊnt] *adj* higgledy-piggledy

Kupee [ku'pe:] (**-s, -s**) *nt* = **Coupé**

Kupfer ['kʊpfər] (**-s, -**) *nt* copper; **Kupfergeld** *nt* coppers *pl*

kupfern *adj* copper ▷ *vt (fig: umg)* to plagiarize, copy, imitate

Kupferstich *m* copperplate engraving

Kupon [ku'põ:] (**-s, -s**) *m* = **Coupon**

Kuppe ['kʊpə] (**-, -n**) *f (Bergkuppe)* top; *(Fingerkuppe)* tip

Kuppel (**-, -n**) *f* cupola, dome

Kuppelei [kʊpə'laɪ] *f (Jur)* procuring

kuppeln *vi (Jur)* to procure; *(Aut)* to operate *od* use the clutch ▷ *vt* to join

Kuppler ['kʊplər] (**-s, -**) *m* procurer; **Kupplerin** *f* procuress

Kupplung *f (auch Tech)* coupling; *(Aut etc)* clutch; **die ~ (durch)treten** to disengage the clutch

Kur [ku:r] (**-, -en**) *f (im Kurort)* (health) cure, (course of) treatment; *(Schlankheitskur)* diet; **eine ~ machen** to take a cure (in a health resort)

Kür [ky:r] (**-, -en**) *f (Sport)* free exercises *pl*

Kuratorium [kura'to:riʊm] *nt (Vereinigung)* committee

Kurbel ['kʊrbəl] (**-, -n**) *f* crank, winder; *(Aut)* starting handle; **Kurbelwelle** *f* crankshaft

Kürbis ['kʏrbɪs] (**-ses, -se**) *m* pumpkin; *(exotisch)* gourd

Kurde ['kʊrdə] (**-n, -n**) *m*, **Kurdin** *f* Kurd

Kurfürst ['ku:rfʏrst] *m* Elector, electoral prince

Kurgast *m* visitor (to a health resort)

Kurier [ku'ri:r] (**-s, -e**) *m* courier, messenger

kurieren [ku'ri:rən] *vt* to cure

kurios [kuri'o:s] *adj* curious, odd

Kuriosität [kuriozi'tɛ:t] *f* curiosity

Kur- *zW*: **Kurkonzert** *nt* concert *(at a health resort)*; **Kurort** *m* health resort; **Kurpfuscher** *m* quack

Kurs [kʊrs] (**-es, -e**) *m* course; *(Fin)* rate; **hoch im ~ stehen** *(fig)* to be highly thought of; **einen ~ besuchen** *od* **mitmachen** to attend a class; **harter/weicher** ~ *(Pol)* hard/soft line; **Kursänderung** *f (lit, fig)* change of course; **Kursbuch** *nt* timetable

Kürschner, in ['kʏrʃnər(ɪn)] (**-s, -**) *m(f)* furrier

kursieren [kʊr'zi:rən] *vi* to circulate

kursiv *adv* in italics

Kursnotierung *f* quotation

Kursus ['kʊrzʊs] (**-, Kurse**) *m* course

Kurswagen *m (Eisenb)* through carriage

Kurswert *m (Fin)* market value

Kurtaxe *f* spa tax *(paid by visitors)*

Kurve ['kʊrvə] (**-, -n**) *f* curve; *(Straßenkurve)* bend; *(statistisch, Fieberkurve etc)* graph; **die ~ nicht kriegen** *(umg)* not to get around to it

kurvenreich *adj*: **„~e Strecke"** "bends"

kurvig *adj (Straße)* bendy

kurz [kʊrts] *adj* short ▷ *adv*: **~ und bündig** concisely; **zu ~ kommen** to come off badly; **den Kürzeren ziehen** to get the worst of it; **~ und gut** in short; **über ~ oder lang** sooner or

later; **eine Sache ~ abtun** to dismiss sth out of hand; **~ gefasst** concise; **darf ich mal ~ stören?** could I just interrupt for a moment?; *siehe auch* **kurzfassen; kurzhalten; kurztreten**
Kurzarbeit *f* short-time work; *see culture note*

KURZARBEIT

Kurzarbeit is the term used to describe a shorter working week made necessary by a lack of work. It has been introduced in recent years as a preferable alternative to redundancy. It has to be approved by the Arbeitsamt, the job centre, which pays some compensation to the worker for loss of pay.

kurzärmelig, kurzärmlig *adj* short-sleeved
kurzatmig *adj* (*fig*) feeble, lame; (*Med*) short-winded
Kürze ['kʏrtsə] (**-, -n**) *f* shortness, brevity
kürzen *vt* to cut short; (*in der Länge*) to shorten; (*Gehalt*) to reduce
kurzerhand ['kʊrtsər'hant] *adv* without further ado; (*entlassen*) on the spot
kurz- *zW*: **kurzfassen** *vr* to be brief; **Kurzfassung** *f* shortened version; **kurzfristig** *adj* short-term; **kurzfristige Verbindlichkeiten** current liabilities *pl*; **Kurzgeschichte** *f* short story; **kurzhalten** *unreg vt* to keep short; **kurzlebig** *adj* short-lived
kürzlich ['kʏrtslɪç] *adv* lately, recently
Kurz- *zW*: **Kurzmeldung** *f* news flash; **Kurzparker** *m* short-stay parker; **Kurzschluss** *m* (*Elek*) short circuit; **Kurzschlusshandlung** *f* (*fig*) rash action; **Kurzschrift** *f* shorthand; **kurzsichtig** *adj* short-sighted; **Kurzstrecken-** *in zW* short-range; **Kurzstreckenläufer, in** *m(f)* sprinter; **kurztreten** *unreg vi* (*fig: umg*) to go easy; **kurzum** *adv* in a word
Kürzung *f* cutback
Kurzwaren *pl* haberdashery (*Brit*), notions *pl* (*US*)
Kurzwelle *f* short wave
kuschelig *adj* cuddly
kuscheln ['kʊʃəln] *vr* to snuggle up
kuschen ['kʊʃən] *vi, vr* (*Hund etc*) to get down; (*fig*) to knuckle under
Kusine [ku'zi:nə] *f* cousin
Kuss [kʊs] (**-es, ¨-e**) *m* kiss
küssen ['kʏsən] *vt, vr* to kiss
Küste ['kʏstə] (**-, -n**) *f* coast, shore
Küsten- *zW*: **Küstengewässer** *pl* coastal waters *pl*; **Küstenschiff** *nt* coaster; **Küstenwache** *f* coastguard (station)
Küster ['kʏstər] (**-s, -**) *m* sexton, verger
Kutsche ['kʊtʃə] (**-, -n**) *f* coach, carriage
Kutscher (**-s, -**) *m* coachman
kutschieren [kʊ'tʃi:rən] *vi*: **durch die Gegend ~** (*umg*) to drive around
Kutte ['kʊtə] (**-, -n**) *f* cowl
Kuvert [ku'vɛrt] (**-s, -e** *od* **-s**) *nt* envelope; (*Gedeck*) cover
Kuwait [ku'vaɪt] (**-s**) *nt* Kuwait
KV *abk* (*Mus: = Köchelverzeichnis*): **KV 280** K. (number) 280
KW *abk* (*= Kurzwelle*) SW
kW *abk* (*= Kilowatt*) kW
Kybernetik [kybɛr'ne:tɪk] *f* cybernetics *sing*
kybernetisch [kybɛr'ne:tɪʃ] *adj* cybernetic
KZ (**-s, -s**) *nt abk* = **Konzentrationslager**

Ll

L, l¹ [ɛl] *nt* L, l; **L wie Ludwig** ≈ L for Lucy, ≈ L for Love (*US*)
l² [ɛl] *abk* (= *Liter*) l
laben ['la:bən] *vt* to refresh ▷ *vr* to refresh o.s.; (*fig*): **sich an etw** *dat* **~** to relish sth
labern ['la:bərn] (*umg*) *vi* to prattle (on) ▷ *vt* to talk
labil [la'bi:l] *adj* (*physisch: Gesundheit*) delicate; (*: Kreislauf*) poor; (*psychisch*) unstable
Labor [la'bo:r] (**-s, -e** *od* **-s**) *nt* lab(oratory)
Laborant, in [labo'rant(ɪn)] *m(f)* lab(oratory) assistant
Laboratorium [labora'to:riʊm] *nt* lab(oratory)
Labyrinth [laby'rɪnt] (**-s, -e**) *nt* labyrinth
Lache ['laxə] (**-, -n**) *f* (*Wasser*) pool, puddle; (*umg: Gelächter*) laugh
lächeln ['lɛçəln] *vi* to smile; **Lächeln** (**-s**) *nt* smile
lachen ['laxən] *vi* to laugh; **mir ist nicht zum L~ (zumute)** I'm in no laughing mood; **dass ich nicht lache!** (*umg*) don't make me laugh!; **das wäre doch gelacht** it would be ridiculous; **Lachen** *nt*: **dir wird das Lachen schon noch vergehen!** you'll soon be laughing on the other side of your face
Lacher (**-s, -**) *m*: **die ~ auf seiner Seite haben** to have the last laugh
lächerlich ['lɛçərlɪç] *adj* ridiculous; **Lächerlichkeit** *f* absurdity
Lach- *zW*: **Lachgas** *nt* laughing gas; **lachhaft** *adj* laughable; **Lachkrampf** *m*: **einen Lachkrampf bekommen** to go into fits of laughter
Lachs [laks] (**-es, -e**) *m* salmon
Lachsalve ['laxzalvə] *f* burst *od* roar of laughter
Lachsschinken *m* *smoked, rolled fillet of ham*
Lack [lak] (**-(e)s, -e**) *m* lacquer, varnish; (*von Auto*) paint
lackieren [la'ki:rən] *vt* to varnish; (*Auto*) to spray
Lackierer [la'ki:rər] (**-s, -**) *m* varnisher
Lackleder *nt* patent leather
Lackmus ['lakmʊs] (**-**) *m od nt* litmus
Lade ['la:də] (**-, -n**) *f* box, chest; **Ladebaum** *m* derrick; **Ladefähigkeit** *f* load capacity; **Ladefläche** *f* load area; **Ladegewicht** *nt* tonnage; **Ladehemmung** *f*: **das Gewehr hat Ladehemmung** the gun is jammed
Laden ['la:dən] (**-s, ¨**) *m* shop; (*Fensterladen*) shutter; (*umg: Betrieb*) outfit; **der ~ läuft** (*umg*) business is good
laden ['la:dən] *unreg vt* (*Lasten, Comput*) to load; (*Jur*) to summon; (*einladen*) to invite; **eine schwere Schuld auf sich** *akk* **~** to place o.s. under a heavy burden of guilt
Laden- *zW*: **Ladenaufsicht** *f* shopwalker (*Brit*), floorwalker (*US*); **Ladenbesitzer** *m* shopkeeper; **Ladendieb** *m* shoplifter; **Ladendiebstahl** *m* shoplifting; **Ladenhüter** (**-s, -**) *m* unsaleable item; **Ladenöffnungszeit** *f* shop opening hours *pl*; **Ladenpreis** *m* retail price; **Ladenschluss** *m*, **Ladenschlusszeit** *f* closing time; **Ladentisch** *m* counter
Laderampe *f* loading ramp
Laderaum *m* (*Naut*) hold
lädieren [lɛ'di:rən] *vt* to damage
lädt [lɛ:t] *vb siehe* **laden**
Ladung ['la:dʊŋ] *f* (*Last*) cargo, load; (*Beladen*) loading; (*Jur*) summons; (*Einladung*) invitation; (*Sprengladung*) charge
lag *etc* [la:k] *vb siehe* **liegen**
Lage ['la:gə] (**-, -n**) *f* position, situation; (*Schicht*) layer; **in der ~ sein** to be in a position; **eine gute/ruhige ~ haben** to be in a good/peaceful location; **Herr der ~ sein** to be in control of the situation; **Lagebericht** *m* report; (*Mil*) situation report; **Lagebeurteilung** *f* situation assessment
lagenweise *adv* in layers
Lager ['la:gər] (**-s, -**) *nt* camp; (*Comm*) warehouse; (*Schlaflager*) bed; (*von Tier*) lair; (*Tech*) bearing; **etw auf ~ haben** to have sth in stock; **Lagerarbeiter** *m* storehand; **Lagerbestand** *m* stocks *pl*; **Lagerfeuer** *nt* camp fire; **Lagergeld** *nt* storage (charges *pl*); **Lagerhaus** *nt* warehouse, store
Lagerist, in [la:gə'rɪst(ɪn)] *m(f)* storeman, storewoman
lagern ['la:gərn] *vi* (*Dinge*) to be stored; (*Menschen*) to camp; (*auch vr: rasten*) to lie down ▷ *vt* to store; (*betten*) to lay down; (*Maschine*) to bed
Lager- *zW*: **Lagerraum** *m* storeroom; (*in Geschäft*) stockroom; **Lagerschuppen** *m* store shed; **Lagerstätte** *f* resting place
Lagerung *f* storage

Lagune [la'gu:nə] (**-, -n**) *f* lagoon
lahm [la:m] *adj* lame; (*umg: langsam, langweilig*) dreary, dull; (*Geschäftsgang*) slow, sluggish; **eine ~e Ente sein** (*umg*) to have no zip; *siehe auch* **lahmlegen**; **lahmarschig** ['la:m|arʃıç] (*umg*) *adj* bloody *od* damn (*!*) slow
lahmen *vi* to be lame, limp
lähmen ['lɛ:mən], **lahmlegen** *vt* to paralyse (*Brit*), paralyze (*US*)
Lähmung *f* paralysis
Lahn [la:n] (-) *f* (*Fluss*) Lahn
Laib [laıp] (**-s, -e**) *m* loaf
Laich [laıç] (**-(e)s, -e**) *m* spawn; **laichen** *vi* to spawn
Laie ['laıə] (**-n, -n**) *m* layman; (*fig, Theat*) amateur
laienhaft *adj* amateurish
Lakai [la'kaı] (**-en, -en**) *m* lackey
Laken ['la:kən] (**-s, -**) *nt* sheet
Lakritze [la'krıtsə] (**-, -n**) *f* liquorice
lala ['la'la] (*umg*) *adv*: **so ~** so-so, not too bad
lallen ['lalən] *vt, vi* to slur; (*Baby*) to babble
Lama ['la:ma] (**-s, -s**) *nt* llama
Lamelle [la'mɛlə] *f* lamella; (*Elek*) lamina; (*Tech*) plate
lamentieren [lamɛn'ti:rən] *vi* to lament
Lametta [la'mɛta] (**-s**) *nt* tinsel
Lamm [lam] (**-(e)s, ¨er**) *nt* lamb; **Lammfell** *nt* lambskin; **lammfromm** *adj* like a lamb; **Lammwolle** *f* lambswool
Lampe ['lampə] (**-, -n**) *f* lamp
Lampenfieber *nt* stage fright
Lampenschirm *m* lampshade
Lampion [lampi'õ:] (**-s, -s**) *m* Chinese lantern
Land [lant] (**-(e)s, ¨er**) *nt* land; (*Nation, nicht Stadt*) country; (*Bundesland*) state; **auf dem ~(e)** in the country; **an ~ gehen** to go ashore; **endlich sehe ich ~** (*fig*) at last I can see the light at the end of the tunnel; **einen Auftrag an ~ ziehen** (*umg*) to land an order; **aus aller Herren Länder** from all over the world; *siehe auch* **hierzulande**; *see culture note*

LAND

A *Land* (plural *Länder*) is a member state of the BRD. There are 16 *Länder*, namely Baden-Württemberg, Bayern, Berlin, Brandenburg, Bremen, Hamburg, Hessen, Mecklenburg-Vorpommern, Niedersachsen, Nordrhein-Westfalen, Rheinland-Pfalz, Saarland, Sachsen, Sachsen-Anhalt, Schleswig-Holstein and Thüringen. Each *Land* has its own parliament and constitution.

Landarbeiter *m* farm *od* agricultural worker
Landbesitz *m* landed property
Landbesitzer *m* landowner
Landebahn *f* runway
Landeerlaubnis *f* permission to land
landeinwärts [lant'|aınvɛrts] *adv* inland
landen ['landən] *vt, vi* to land; **mit deinen Komplimenten kannst du bei mir nicht ~** your compliments won't get you anywhere with me
Ländereien [lɛndə'raıən] *pl* estates *pl*
Länderspiel *nt* international (match)
Landes- *zW*: **Landesfarben** *pl* national colours *pl* (*Brit*) *od* colors *pl* (*US*); **Landesgrenze** *f* (national) frontier; (*von Bundesland*) state boundary; **Landesinnere, s** *nt* inland region; **Landeskind** *nt native of a German state*; **Landeskunde** *f* regional studies *pl*; **Landestracht** *f* national costume; **landesüblich** *adj* customary; **Landesverrat** *m* high treason; **Landesverweisung** *f* banishment; **Landeswährung** *f* national currency; **landesweit** *adj* countrywide
Landeverbot *nt* refusal of permission to land
Land- *zW*: **Landflucht** *f* emigration to the cities; **Landgut** *nt* estate; **Landhaus** *nt* country house; **Landkarte** *f* map; **Landkreis** *m* administrative region; **landläufig** *adj* customary
ländlich ['lɛntlıç] *adj* rural
Land- *zW*: **Landrat** *m head of administration of a Landkreis*; **Landschaft** *f* countryside; (*Kunst*) landscape; **die politische Landschaft** the political scene; **landschaftlich** *adj* scenic; (*Besonderheiten*) regional
Landsmann (**-(e)s**, *pl* **-leute**) *m* compatriot, fellow countryman
Landsmännin *f* compatriot, fellow countrywoman
Land- *zW*: **Landstraße** *f* country road; **Landstreicher** (**-s, -**) *m* tramp; **Landstrich** *m* region; **Landtag** *m* (*Pol*) regional parliament
Landung ['landʊŋ] *f* landing
Landungs- *zW*: **Landungsboot** *nt* landing craft; **Landungsbrücke** *f* jetty, pier; **Landungsstelle** *f* landing place
Landurlaub *m* shore leave
Landvermesser *m* surveyor
landw. *abk* (= *landwirtschaftlich*) agricultural
Land- *zW*: **Landwirt** *m* farmer; **Landwirtschaft** *f* agriculture; **Landwirtschaft betreiben** to farm; **Landzunge** *f* spit
lang [laŋ] *adj* long; (*umg: Mensch*) tall ▷ *adv*: **~ anhaltender Beifall** prolonged applause; **~ ersehnt** longed-for; **hier wird mir die Zeit nicht ~** I won't get bored here; **er machte ein ~es Gesicht** his face fell; **~ und breit** at great length; **langatmig** *adj* long-winded
lange *adv* for a long time; (*dauern, brauchen*) a long time; **~ nicht so ...** not nearly as ...; **wenn der das schafft, kannst du das schon ~** if he can do it, you can do it easily
Länge ['lɛŋə] (**-, -n**) *f* length; (*Geog*) longitude; **etw der ~ nach falten** to fold sth lengthways; **etw in die ~ ziehen** to drag sth out (*umg*); **der ~ nach hinfallen** to fall flat (on one's face)
langen ['laŋən] *vi* (*ausreichen*) to do, suffice; (*fassen*): **~ nach** to reach for; **es langt mir** I've had enough; **jdm eine ~** (*umg*) to give sb a clip on the ear

Längengrad *m* longitude
Längenmaß *nt* linear measure
Langeweile *f* boredom
lang- *zW*: **langfristig** *adj* long-term ▷ *adv* in the long term; (*planen*) for the long term; **langfristige Verbindlichkeiten** long-term liabilities *pl*; **langjährig** *adj* (*Freundschaft, Gewohnheit*) long-standing; (*Erfahrung, Verhandlungen*) many years of; (*Mitarbeiter*) of many years' standing; **Langlauf** *m* (*Ski*) cross-country skiing; **langlebig** *adj* long-lived; **langlebige Gebrauchsgüter** consumer durables *pl*
länglich *adj* longish
Langmut *f* forbearance, patience
langmütig *adj* forbearing
längs [lɛŋs] *präp* (*+gen od dat*) along ▷ *adv* lengthways
langsam *adj* slow; **immer schön ~!** (*umg*) easy does it!; **ich muss jetzt ~ gehen** I must be getting on my way; **~ (aber sicher) reicht es mir** I've just about had enough; **Langsamkeit** *f* slowness
Langschläfer *m* late riser
Langspielplatte *f* long-playing record
längsseit, längsseits *adv* alongside ▷ *präp +gen* alongside
längst [lɛŋst] *adv*: **das ist ~ fertig** that was finished a long time ago, that has been finished for a long time
längste, r, s *adj* longest
Langstrecken- *in zW* long-distance; **Langstreckenflugzeug** *nt* long-range aircraft
Languste [laŋ'gʊstə] (**-, -n**) *f* crayfish, crawfish (*US*)
lang- *zW*: **langweilen** *vt untr* to bore ▷ *vr untr* to be *od* get bored; **Langweiler** (**-s, -**) *m* bore; **langweilig** *adj* boring, tedious; **Langwelle** *f* long wave; **langwierig** *adj* lengthy, long-drawn-out
Lanze ['lantsə] (**-, -n**) *f* lance
Lanzette [lan'tsɛtə] *f* lancet
Laos ['la:ɔs] (**-**) *nt* Laos
Laote [la'o:tə] (**-n, -n**) *m*, **Laotin** *f* Laotian
laotisch [la'o:tɪʃ] *adj* Laotian
lapidar [lapi'da:r] *adj* terse, pithy
Lappalie [la'pa:liə] *f* trifle
Lappe ['lapə] (**-n, -n**) *m* Lapp, Laplander
Lappen (**-s, -**) *m* cloth, rag; (*Anat*) lobe; **jdm durch die ~ gehen** (*umg*) to slip through sb's fingers
läppern ['lɛpərn] (*umg*) *vr unpers*: **es läppert sich zusammen** it (all) mounts up
Lappin ['lapɪn] *f* Lapp, Laplander
läppisch ['lɛpɪʃ] *adj* foolish
Lappland ['laplant] (**-s**) *nt* Lapland
Lappländer, in ['laplɛndər(ɪn)] (**-s, -**) *m(f)* Lapp, Laplander
lappländisch *adj* Lapp
Lapsus ['lapsʊs] (**-, -**) *m* slip
Laptop ['lɛptɔp] (**-s, -s**) *m* laptop
Lärche ['lɛrçə] (**-, -n**) *f* larch
Lärm [lɛrm] (**-(e)s**) *m* noise; **Lärmbelästigung** *f* noise nuisance; **Lärmemission** *f* noise emission; (*stärker*) noise pollution; **lärmen** *vi* to be noisy, make a noise
Larve ['larfə] (**-, -n**) *f* mask; (*Biol*) larva
las *etc* [la:s] *vb siehe* **lesen**
Lasagne [la'zanjə] *pl* lasagne *sing*
lasch [laʃ] *adj* slack; (*Geschmack*) tasteless
Lasche ['laʃə] (**-, -n**) *f* (*Schuhlasche*) tongue; (*Eisenb*) fishplate
Laser ['le:zər] (**-s, -**) *m* laser; **Laserdrucker** *m* laser printer

SCHLÜSSELWORT

lassen ['lasən] (*pt* **ließ**, *pp* **gelassen** *od (als Hilfsverb)* **lassen**) *vt* **1** (*unterlassen*) to stop; (*momentan*) to leave; **lass das (sein)!** don't (do it)!; (*hör auf*) stop it!; **lass mich!** leave me alone!; **lassen wir das!** let's leave it; **er kann das Trinken nicht lassen** he can't stop drinking; **tu, was du nicht lassen kannst!** if you must, you must!
2 (*zurücklassen*) to leave; **etw lassen, wie es ist** to leave sth (just) as it is
3 (*erlauben*) to let, allow; **lass ihn doch** let him; **jdn ins Haus lassen** to let sb into the house; **das muss man ihr lassen** (*zugestehen*) you've got to grant her that
▷ *vi*: **lass mal, ich mache das schon** leave it, I'll do it
▷ *hilfsverb* **1** (*veranlassen*): **etw machen lassen** to have *od* get sth done; **jdn etw machen lassen** to get sb to do sth; (*durch Befehl usw*) to make sb do sth; **er ließ mich warten** he kept me waiting; **mein Vater wollte mich studieren lassen** my father wanted me to study; **sich** *dat* **etw schicken lassen** to have sth sent (to one)
2 (*zulassen*): **jdn etw wissen lassen** to let sb know sth; **das Licht brennen lassen** to leave the light on; **einen Bart wachsen lassen** to grow a beard; **lass es dir gut gehen!** take care of yourself!
3: lass uns gehen let's go
▷ *vr*: **das lässt sich machen** that can be done; **es lässt sich schwer sagen** it's difficult to say

lässig ['lɛsɪç] *adj* casual; **Lässigkeit** *f* casualness
lässlich ['lɛslɪç] *adj* pardonable, venial
lässt [lɛst] *vb siehe* **lassen**
Last [last] (**-, -en**) *f* load; (*Traglast*) burden; (*Naut, Aviat*) cargo; (*meist pl: Gebühr*) charge; **jdm zur ~ fallen** to be a burden to sb; **Lastauto** *nt* lorry (*Brit*), truck
lasten *vi*: **~ auf** *+dat* to weigh on
Lastenaufzug *m* hoist, goods lift (*Brit*) *od* elevator (*US*)
Lastenausgleichsgesetz *nt law on financial compensation for losses suffered in WWII*
Laster ['lastər] (**-s, -**) *nt* vice ▷ *m* (*umg*) lorry (*Brit*), truck
Lästerer ['lɛstərər] (**-s, -**) *m* mocker;

(*Gotteslästerer*) blasphemer
lasterhaft *adj* immoral
lästerlich *adj* scandalous
lästern ['lɛstərn] *vt, vi* (*Gott*) to blaspheme; (*schlecht sprechen*) to mock
Lästerung *f* jibe; (*Gotteslästerung*) blasphemy
lästig ['lɛstɪç] *adj* troublesome, tiresome; **(jdm) ~ werden** to become a nuisance (to sb); (*zum Ärgernis werden*) to get annoying (to sb)
Last- *zW*: **Lastkahn** *m* barge; **Lastkraftwagen** *m* heavy goods vehicle; **Lastschrift** *f* debiting; (*Eintrag*) debit item; **Lasttier** *nt* beast of burden; **Lastträger** *m* porter; **Lastwagen** *m* lorry (*Brit*), truck; **Lastzug** *m* truck and trailer
Latein [la'taɪn] **(-s)** *nt* Latin; **mit seinem ~ am Ende sein** (*fig*) to be stumped (*umg*); **Lateinamerika** *nt* Latin America; **lateinamerikanisch** *adj* Latin-American; **lateinisch** *adj* Latin
latent [la'tɛnt] *adj* latent
Laterne [la'tɛrnə] **(-, -n)** *f* lantern; (*Straßenlaterne*) lamp, light
Laternenpfahl *m* lamppost
Latinum [la'ti:nʊm] **(-s)** *nt*: **kleines/großes ~** ≈ Latin O-/A-level exams (*Brit*)
Latrine [la'tri:nə] *f* latrine
Latsche ['latʃə] **(-, -n)** *f* dwarf pine
Latschen ['la:tʃən] (*umg*) *m* (*Hausschuh*) slipper; (*pej: Schuh*) worn-out shoe
latschen (*umg*) *vi* (*gehen*) to wander, go; (*lässig*) to slouch
Latte ['latə] **(-, -n)** *f* lath; (*Sport*) goalpost; (*quer*) crossbar
Lattenzaun *m* lattice fence
Latz [lats] **(-es, ¨-e)** *m* bib; (*Hosenlatz*) front flap
Lätzchen ['lɛtsçən] *nt* bib
Latzhose *f* dungarees *pl*
lau [laʊ] *adj* (*Nacht*) balmy; (*Wasser*) lukewarm; (*fig: Haltung*) half-hearted
Laub [laʊp] **(-(e)s)** *nt* foliage; **Laubbaum** *m* deciduous tree
Laube ['laʊbə] **(-, -n)** *f* arbour (*Brit*), arbor (*US*); (*Gartenhäuschen*) summerhouse
Laub- *zW*: **Laubfrosch** *m* tree frog; **Laubsäge** *f* fretsaw; **Laubwald** *m* deciduous forest
Lauch [laʊx] **(-(e)s, -e)** *m* leek
Lauer ['laʊər] *f*: **auf der ~ sein** *od* **liegen** to lie in wait
lauern *vi* to lie in wait; (*Gefahr*) to lurk
Lauf [laʊf] **(-(e)s, Läufe)** *m* run; (*Wettlauf*) race; (*Entwicklung, Astron*) course; (*Gewehrlauf*) barrel; **im ~e des Gesprächs** during the conversation; **sie ließ ihren Gefühlen freien ~** she gave way to her feelings; **einer Sache** *dat* **ihren ~ lassen** to let sth take its course; **Laufbahn** *f* career; **eine Laufbahn einschlagen** to embark on a career; **Laufbursche** *m* errand boy
laufen ['laʊfən] *unreg vi* to run; (*umg: gehen*) to walk; (*Uhr*) to go; (*funktionieren*) to work; (*Elektrogerät: eingeschaltet sein*) to be on; (*gezeigt werden: Film, Stück*) to be on; (*Bewerbung, Antrag*) to be under consideration ▷ *vt* to run; **es lief mir eiskalt über den Rücken** a chill ran up my spine; **ihm läuft die Nase** he's got a runny nose; **~ lassen** (*Person*) to let go; **die Dinge ~ lassen** to let things slide; **die Sache ist ge~** (*umg*) it's in the bag; **das Auto läuft auf meinen Namen** the car is in my name; **Ski/Schlittschuh/Rollschuh** *etc* **~** to ski/ skate/rollerskate *etc*
laufend *adj* running; (*Monat, Ausgaben*) current; **auf dem L~en sein/halten** to be/keep up to date; **am ~en Band** (*fig*) continuously; **~e Nummer** serial number; (*von Konto*) number; **~e Kosten** running costs *pl*
Läufer ['lɔʏfər] **(-s, -)** *m* (*Teppich, Sport*) runner; (*Fußball*) half-back; (*Schach*) bishop
Lauferei [laʊfə'raɪ] (*umg*) *f* running about
Läuferin *f* (*Sport*) runner
Lauf- *zW*: **lauffähig** *adj* (*Comput*): **das Programm is unter Windows lauffähig** the program can be run under Windows; **Lauffeuer** *nt*: **sich wie ein Lauffeuer verbreiten** to spread like wildfire; **Laufkundschaft** *f* passing trade; **Laufmasche** *f* run, ladder (*Brit*); **Laufpass** *m*: **jdm den Laufpass geben** (*umg*) to give sb his/her marching orders; **Laufschritt** *m*: **im Laufschritt** at a run; **Laufstall** *m* playpen; **Laufsteg** *m* catwalk
läuft [lɔʏft] *vb siehe* **laufen**
Lauf- *zW*: **Laufwerk** *nt* running gear; (*Comput*) drive; **Laufzeit** *f* (*von Wechsel, Vertrag*) period of validity; (*von Maschine*) life; **Laufzettel** *m* circular
Lauge ['laʊgə] **(-, -n)** *f* soapy water; (*Chem*) alkaline solution
Laune ['laʊnə] **(-, -n)** *f* mood, humour (*Brit*), humor (*US*); (*Einfall*) caprice; (*schlechte Laune*) temper
launenhaft *adj* capricious, changeable
launisch *adj* moody
Laus [laʊs] **(-, Läuse)** *f* louse; **ihm ist (wohl) eine ~ über die Leber gelaufen** (*umg*) something's biting him; **Lausbub** *m* rascal, imp
Lauschangriff *m*: **~ (gegen)** bugging operation (on)
lauschen ['laʊʃən] *vi* to eavesdrop, listen in
Lauscher, in (-s, -) *m(f)* eavesdropper
lauschig ['laʊʃɪç] *adj* snug
Lausejunge (*umg*) *m* little devil; (*wohlwollend*) rascal
lausen ['laʊzən] *vt* to delouse
lausig ['laʊzɪç] (*umg*) *adj* lousy; (*Kälte*) perishing ▷ *adv* awfully
laut [laʊt] *adj* loud ▷ *adv* loudly; (*lesen*) aloud ▷ *präp* (*+gen od dat*) according to
Laut (-(e)s, -e) *m* sound
Laute ['laʊtə] **(-, -n)** *f* lute
lauten ['laʊtən] *vi* to say; (*Urteil*) to be
läuten ['lɔʏtən] *vt, vi* to ring, sound; **er hat davon (etwas) ~ hören** (*umg*) he has heard something about it
lauter ['laʊtər] *adj* (*Wasser*) clear, pure;

(*Wahrheit, Charakter*) honest ▷ *adj inv* (*Freude, Dummheit etc*) sheer ▷ *adv* (*nur*) nothing but, only; **Lauterkeit** *f* purity; honesty, integrity
läutern ['lɔʏtərn] *vt* to purify
Läuterung *f* purification
laut- *zW*: **lauthals** *adv* at the top of one's voice; **lautlos** *adj* noiseless, silent; **lautmalend** *adj* onomatopoeic; **Lautschrift** *f* phonetics *pl*; **Lautsprecher** *m* loudspeaker; **Lautsprecheranlage** *f*: **öffentliche Lautsprecheranlage** public-address *od* PA system; **Lautsprecherwagen** *m* loudspeaker van; **lautstark** *adj* vociferous; **Lautstärke** *f* (*Rundf*) volume
lauwarm ['laʊvarm] *adj* (*lit, fig*) lukewarm
Lava ['la:va] (**-, Laven**) *f* lava
Lavendel [la'vɛndəl] (**-s, -**) *m* lavender
Lawine [la'vi:nə] *f* avalanche
Lawinengefahr *f* danger of avalanches
lax [laks] *adj* lax
Layout, Lay-out ['le:|aʊt] (**-s, -s**) *nt* layout
Lazarett [latsa'rɛt] (**-(e)s, -e**) *nt* (*Mil*) hospital, infirmary
Ldkrs. *abk* = **Landkreis**
leasen ['li:zən] *vt* to lease
Leasing ['li:zɪŋ] (**-s, -s**) *nt* (*Comm*) leasing
Lebehoch *nt* three cheers *pl*
Lebemann (**-(e)s**, *pl* **-männer**) *m* man about town
Leben ['le:bən] (**-s, -**) *nt* life; **am ~ sein/bleiben** to be/stay alive; **ums ~ kommen** to die; **etw ins ~ rufen** to bring sth into being; **seines ~s nicht mehr sicher sein** to fear for one's life; **etw für sein ~ gern tun** to love doing sth
leben *vt, vi* to live
lebend *adj* living; **~es Inventar** livestock
lebendig [le'bɛndɪç] *adj* living, alive; (*lebhaft*) lively; **Lebendigkeit** *f* liveliness
Lebens- *zW*: **Lebensabend** *m* old age; **Lebensalter** *nt* age; **Lebensanschauung** *f* philosophy of life; **Lebensart** *f* way of life; **lebensbejahend** *adj* positive; **Lebensdauer** *f* life (span); (*von Maschine*) life; **Lebenserfahrung** *f* experience of life; **Lebenserwartung** *f* life expectancy; **lebensfähig** *adj* able to live; **lebensfroh** *adj* full of the joys of life; **Lebensgefahr** *f*: **Lebensgefahr!** danger!; **in Lebensgefahr** critically *od* dangerously ill; **lebensgefährlich** *adj* dangerous; (*Krankheit, Verletzung*) critical; **Lebensgefährte** *m*: **ihr Lebensgefährte** the man she lives with; **Lebensgefährtin** *f*: **seine Lebensgefährtin** the woman he lives with; **Lebensgröße** *f*: **in Lebensgröße** life-size(d); **Lebenshaltungskosten** *pl* cost of living *sing*; **Lebensinhalt** *m* purpose in life; **Lebensjahr** *nt* year of life; **Lebenskünstler** *m* master in the art of living; **Lebenslage** *f* situation in life; **lebenslänglich** *adj* (*Strafe*) for life; **Lebenslauf** *m* curriculum vitae, CV; **lebenslustig** *adj* cheerful, lively; **Lebensmittel** *pl* food *sing*; **Lebensmittelgeschäft** *nt* grocer's; **Lebensmittelvergiftung** *f* food poisoning; **lebensmüde** *adj* tired of life; **Lebenspartnerschaft** *f* long-term relationship; **eingetragene Lebenspartnerschaft** registered *or* civil (*Brit*) partnership; **Lebensqualität** *f* quality of life; **Lebensraum** *m* (*Pol*) Lebensraum; (*Biol*) biosphere; **Lebensretter** *m* lifesaver; **Lebensstandard** *m* standard of living; **Lebensstellung** *f* permanent post; **Lebensstil** *m* life style; **Lebensunterhalt** *m* livelihood; **Lebensversicherung** *f* life insurance; **Lebenswandel** *m* way of life; **Lebensweise** *f* way of life, habits *pl*; **Lebensweisheit** *f* maxim; (*Lebenserfahrung*) wisdom; **Lebenswichtig** *adj* vital; **Lebenszeichen** *nt* sign of life; **Lebenszeit** *f* lifetime; **Beamter auf Lebenszeit** permanent civil servant
Leber ['le:bər] (**-, -n**) *f* liver; **frei** *od* **frisch von der ~ weg reden** (*umg*) to speak out frankly; **Leberfleck** *m* mole; **Leberkäse** *m* ≈ meat loaf; **Lebertran** *m* cod-liver oil; **Leberwurst** *f* liver sausage
Lebewesen *nt* creature
Lebewohl *nt* farewell, goodbye
leb- *zW*: **lebhaft** *adj* lively, vivacious; **Lebhaftigkeit** *f* liveliness, vivacity; **Lebkuchen** *m* gingerbread; **leblos** *adj* lifeless; **Lebtag** *m* (*fig*): **das werde ich mein Lebtag nicht vergessen** I'll never forget that as long as I live; **Lebzeiten** *pl*: **zu jds Lebzeiten** (*Leben*) in sb's lifetime
lechzen ['lɛçtsən] *vi*: **nach etw ~** to long for sth
leck [lɛk] *adj* leaky, leaking; **Leck** (**-(e)s, -e**) *nt* leak
lecken[1] *vi* (*Loch haben*) to leak
lecken[2] *vt, vi* (*schlecken*) to lick
lecker ['lɛkər] *adj* delicious, tasty; **Leckerbissen** *m* dainty morsel; **Leckermaul** *nt*: **ein Leckermaul sein** to enjoy one's food
led. *abk* = **ledig**
Leder ['le:dər] (**-s, -**) *nt* leather; (*umg*: *Fußball*) ball; **Lederhose** *f* leather trousers *pl*; (*von Tracht*) leather shorts *pl*
ledern *adj* leather
Lederwaren *pl* leather goods *pl*
ledig ['le:dɪç] *adj* single; **einer Sache** *gen* **~ sein** to be free of sth; **lediglich** *adv* merely, solely
leer [le:r] *adj* empty; (*Blick*) vacant; **~ gefegt** (*Straße*) deserted; **~ stehend** empty
Leere (-) *f* emptiness; **(eine) gähnende ~** a gaping void
leeren *vt* to empty ▷ *vr* to (become) empty
Leer- *zW*: **Leergewicht** *nt* unladen weight; **Leergut** *nt* empties *pl*; **Leerlauf** *m* (*Aut*) neutral; **Leertaste** *f* (*Schreibmaschine*) space-bar
Leerung *f* emptying; (*Post*) collection
legal [le'ga:l] *adj* legal, lawful
legalisieren [legali'zi:rən] *vt* to legalize
Legalität [legali'tɛ:t] *f* legality; **(etwas) außerhalb der ~** (*euph*) (slightly) outside the law
Legasthenie [legaste'ni:] *f* dyslexia

Legastheniker, in [legas'te:nikər(ın)] (**-s, -**) *m(f)* dyslexic
Legebatterie *f* laying battery
legen ['le:gən] *vt* to lay, put, place; (*Ei*) to lay ▷ *vr* to lie down; (*fig*) to subside; **sich ins Bett ~** to go to bed
Legende [le'gɛndə] (**-, -n**) *f* legend
leger [le'ʒɛ:r] *adj* casual
legieren [le'gi:rən] *vt* to alloy
Legierung *f* alloy
Legislative [legısla'ti:və] *f* legislature
Legislaturperiode [legısla'tu:rperio:də] *f* parliamentary (*Brit*) *od* congressional (*US*) term
legitim [legi'ti:m] *adj* legitimate
Legitimation [legiti:matsi'o:n] *f* legitimation
legitimieren [legiti:'mi:rən] *vt* to legitimate ▷ *vr* to prove one's identity
Legitimität [legitimi'tɛ:t] *f* legitimacy
Lehm [le:m] (**-(e)s, -e**) *m* loam
lehmig *adj* loamy
Lehne ['le:nə] (**-, -n**) *f* arm; (*Rückenlehne*) back
lehnen *vt, vr* to lean
Lehnstuhl *m* armchair
Lehr- *zW*: **Lehramt** *nt* teaching profession; **Lehrbefähigung** *f* teaching qualification; **Lehrbrief** *m* indentures *pl*; **Lehrbuch** *nt* textbook
Lehre ['le:rə] (**-, -n**) *f* teaching, doctrine; (*beruflich*) apprenticeship; (*moralisch*) lesson; (*Tech*) gauge; **bei jdm in die ~ gehen** to serve one's apprenticeship with sb
lehren *vt* to teach
Lehrer, in (**-s, -**) *m(f)* teacher; **Lehrerausbildung** *f* teacher training; **Lehrerkollegium** *nt* teaching staff; **Lehrerzimmer** *nt* staff room
Lehr- *zW*: **Lehrgang** *m* course; **Lehrgeld** *nt*: **Lehrgeld für etw zahlen müssen** (*fig*) to pay dearly for sth; **Lehrjahre** *pl* apprenticeship *sing*; **Lehrkraft** *f* (*form*) teacher; **Lehrling** *m* apprentice; trainee; **Lehrmittel** *nt* teaching aid; **Lehrplan** *m* syllabus; **Lehrprobe** *f* demonstration lesson, crit (*umg*); **lehrreich** *adj* instructive; **Lehrsatz** *m* proposition; **Lehrstelle** *f* apprenticeship; **Lehrstuhl** *m* chair; **Lehrzeit** *f* apprenticeship
Leib [laıp] (**-(e)s, -er**) *m* body; **halt ihn mir vom ~!** keep him away from me!; **etw am eigenen ~(e) spüren** to experience sth for o.s.
leiben ['laıbən] *vi*: **wie er leibt und lebt** to a T (*umg*)
Leibes- *zW*: **Leibeserziehung** *f* physical education; **Leibeskräfte** *pl*: **aus Leibeskräften schreien** *etc* to shout *etc* with all one's might; **Leibesübung** *f* physical exercise; **Leibesvisitation** *f* body search
Leibgericht *nt* favourite (*Brit*) *od* favorite (*US*) meal
Leib- *zW*: **leibhaftig** *adj* personified; (*Teufel*) incarnate; **leiblich** *adj* bodily; (*Vater etc*) natural; **Leibrente** *f* life annuity; **Leibwache** *f* bodyguard
Leiche ['laıçə] (**-, -n**) *f* corpse; **er geht über ~n** (*umg*) he'd stick at nothing
Leichen- *zW*: **Leichenbeschauer** (**-s, -**) *m* doctor conducting a post-mortem; **Leichenhalle** *f* mortuary; **Leichenhemd** *nt* shroud; **Leichenträger** *m* bearer; **Leichenwagen** *m* hearse
Leichnam ['laıçna:m] (**-(e)s, -e**) *m* corpse
leicht [laıct] *adj* light; (*einfach*) easy ▷ *adv*: **~ zerbrechlich** very fragile; **es sich** *dat* **~ machen** to make things easy for o.s.; (*nicht gewissenhaft sein*) to take the easy way out; **~ verletzt** slightly injured; **nichts ~er als das!** nothing (could be) simpler!; *siehe auch* **leichtfallen; leichtnehmen**; **Leichtathletik** *f* athletics *sing*; **leichtfallen** *unreg vi*: **jdm leichtfallen** to be easy for sb; **leichtfertig** *adj* thoughtless; **leichtgläubig** *adj* gullible, credulous; **Leichtgläubigkeit** *f* gullibility, credulity; **leichthin** *adv* lightly
Leichtigkeit *f* easiness; **mit ~** with ease
leicht- *zW*: **leichtlebig** *adj* easy-going; **Leichtmatrose** *m* ordinary seaman; **Leichtmetall** *nt* light alloy; **leichtnehmen** *unreg vt* to take lightly; **Leichtsinn** *m* carelessness; **sträflicher Leichtsinn** criminal negligence; **leichtsinnig** *adj* careless
Leid [laıt] (**-(e)s**) *nt* grief, sorrow; **jdm sein ~ klagen** to tell sb one's troubles
leid *adj*: **etw ~ haben** *od* **sein** to be tired of sth; *siehe auch* **leidtun**
leiden ['laıdən] *unreg vt* to suffer; (*erlauben*) to permit ▷ *vi* to suffer; **jdn/etw nicht ~ können** not to be able to stand sb/sth; **Leiden** (**-s, -**) *nt* suffering; (*Krankheit*) complaint
Leidenschaft *f* passion; **leidenschaftlich** *adj* passionate
Leidens- *zW*: **Leidensgenosse** *m*, **Leidensgenossin** *f* fellow sufferer; **Leidensgeschichte** *f*: **die Leidensgeschichte (Christi)** (*Rel*) Christ's Passion
leider ['laıdər] *adv* unfortunately; **ja, ~** yes, I'm afraid so; **~ nicht** I'm afraid not
leidig ['laıdıç] *adj* miserable, tiresome
leidlich [laıtlıç] *adj* tolerable ▷ *adv* tolerably
Leidtragende, r *f(m)* bereaved; (*Benachteiligter*) one who suffers
leidtun *unreg vi*: **es tut mir/ihm leid** I am/he is sorry; **er/das tut mir leid** I am sorry for him/about it; **sie kann einem ~** you can't help feeling sorry for her
Leidwesen *nt*: **zu jds ~** to sb's dismay
Leier ['laıər] (**-, -n**) *f* lyre; (*fig*) old story
Leierkasten *m* barrel organ
leiern *vt* (*Kurbel*) to turn; (*umg*: *Gedicht*) to rattle off ▷ *vi* (*drehen*): **~ an** *+dat* to crank
Leih- *zW*: **Leiharbeit** *f* subcontracted labour; **Leiharbeiter, in** *m(f)* subcontracted worker; **Leihbibliothek** *f*, **Leihbücherei** *f* lending library
leihen ['laıən] *unreg vt* to lend; **sich** *dat* **etw ~** to borrow sth
Leih- *zW*: **Leihgabe** *f* loan; **Leihgebühr** *f* hire charge; **Leihhaus** *nt* pawnshop;

Leihmutter *f* surrogate mother; **Leihschein** *m* pawn ticket; (*in der Bibliothek*) borrowing slip; **Leihunternehmen** *nt* hire service; (*Arbeitsmarkt*) temp service; **Leihwagen** *m* hired car (*Brit*), rental car (*US*); **leihweise** *adv* on loan

Leim [laɪm] (**-(e)s, -e**) *m* glue; **jdm auf den ~ gehen** to be taken in by sb; **leimen** *vt* to glue

Leine ['laɪnə] (**-, -n**) *f* line, cord; (*Hundeleine*) leash, lead; **~ ziehen** (*umg*) to clear out

Leinen (**-s, -**) *nt* linen; (*grob, segeltuchartig*) canvas; (*als Bucheinband*) cloth

leinen *adj* linen

Lein- *zW*: **Leinsamen** *m* linseed; **Leintuch** *nt* linen cloth; (*Bettuch*) sheet; **Leinwand** *f* (*Kunst*) canvas; (*Film*) screen

leise ['laɪzə] *adj* quiet; (*sanft*) soft, gentle; **mit ~r Stimme** in a low voice; **nicht die ~ste Ahnung haben** not to have the slightest (idea)

Leisetreter (*pej: umg*) *m* pussyfoot(er)

Leiste ['laɪstə] (**-, -n**) *f* ledge; (*Zierleiste*) strip; (*Anat*) groin

leisten ['laɪstən] *vt* (*Arbeit*) to do; (*Gesellschaft*) to keep; (*Ersatz*) to supply; (*vollbringen*) to achieve; **sich** *dat* **etw ~** to allow o.s. sth; (*sich gönnen*) to treat o.s. to sth; **sich** *dat* **etw ~ können** to be able to afford sth

Leistenbruch *m* (*Med*) hernia, rupture

Leistung *f* performance; (*gute*) achievement; (*eines Motors*) power; (*von Krankenkasse etc*) benefit; (*Zahlung*) payment

Leistungs- *zW*: **Leistungsabfall** *m* (*in Bezug auf Qualität*) drop in performance; (*in Bezug auf Quantität*) drop in productivity; **Leistungsbeurteilung** *f* performance appraisal; **Leistungsdruck** *m* pressure; **leistungsfähig** *adj* efficient; **Leistungsfähigkeit** *f* efficiency; **Leistungsgesellschaft** *f* meritocracy; **Leistungskurs** *m* (*Sch*) set; **Leistungskürzung** *f* reduction of benefit; **leistungsorientiert** *adj* performance-orientated; **Leistungsprinzip** *nt* achievement principle; **Leistungssport** *m* competitive sport; **Leistungszulage** *f* productivity bonus

Leitartikel *m* leader

Leitbild *nt* model

leiten ['laɪtən] *vt* to lead; (*Firma*) to manage; (*in eine Richtung*) to direct; (*Elek*) to conduct; **sich von jdm/etw ~ lassen** (*lit, fig*) to (let o.s.) be guided by sb/sth

leitend *adj* leading; (*Gedanke, Idee*) dominant; (*Stellung, Position*) managerial; (*Ingenieur, Beamter*) in charge; (*Phys*) conductive; **~er Angestellter** executive

Leiter[1] ['laɪtər] (**-s, -**) *m* leader, head; (*Elek*) conductor

Leiter[2] ['laɪtər] (**-, -n**) *f* ladder

Leiterin *f* leader, head

Leiterplatte *f* (*Comput*) circuit board

Leit- *zW*: **Leitfaden** *m* guide; **Leitfähigkeit** *f* conductivity; **Leitgedanke** *m* central idea; **Leitmotiv** *nt* leitmotiv; **Leitplanke** *f* crash barrier; **Leitspruch** *m* motto

Leitung *f* (*Führung*) direction; (*Film, Theat etc*) production; (*von Firma*) management; directors *pl*; (*Wasserleitung*) pipe; (*Kabel*) cable; **eine lange ~ haben** to be slow on the uptake; **da ist jemand in der ~** (*umg*) there's somebody else on the line

Leitungs- *zW*: **Leitungsdraht** *m* wire; **Leitungsmast** *m* telegraph pole; **Leitungsrohr** *nt* pipe; **Leitungswasser** *nt* tap water

Leitwerk *nt* (*Aviat*) tail unit

Leitzins *m* (*Fin*) base rate

Lektion [lɛktsi'o:n] *f* lesson; **jdm eine ~ erteilen** (*fig*) to teach sb a lesson

Lektor, in ['lɛktɔr, lɛk'to:rɪn] *m(f)* (*Univ*) lector; (*Verlag*) editor

Lektüre [lɛk'ty:rə] (**-, -n**) *f* (*Lesen*) reading; (*Lesestoff*) reading matter

Lende ['lɛndə] (**-, -n**) *f* loin

Lendenbraten *m* roast sirloin

Lendenstück *nt* fillet

lenkbar ['lɛŋkba:r] *adj* (*Fahrzeug*) steerable; (*Kind*) manageable

lenken *vt* to steer; (*Kind*) to guide; (*Gespräch*) to lead; **~ auf** *+akk* (*Blick, Aufmerksamkeit*) to direct at; (*Verdacht*) to throw on(to); (*: auf sich*) to draw onto

Lenkrad *nt* steering wheel

Lenkstange *f* handlebars *pl*

Lenkung *f* steering; (*Führung*) direction

Lenz [lɛnts] (**-es, -e**) *m* (*liter*) spring; **sich** *dat* **einen (faulen) ~ machen** (*umg*) to laze about, swing the lead

Leopard [leo'part] (**-en, -en**) *m* leopard

Lepra ['le:pra] (**-**) *f* leprosy; **Leprakranke, r** *f(m)* leper

Lerche ['lɛrçə] (**-, -n**) *f* lark

lernbegierig *adj* eager to learn

lernbehindert *adj* educationally handicapped (*Brit*) *od* handicaped (*US*)

lernen *vt* to learn ▷*vi*: **er lernt bei der Firma Braun** he's training at Braun's

Lernhilfe *f* educational aid

lesbar ['le:sba:r] *adj* legible

Lesbierin ['lɛsbiərɪn] *f* lesbian

lesbisch *adj* lesbian

Lese ['le:zə] (**-, -n**) *f* (*Weinlese*) harvest

Lesebuch *nt* reading book, reader

lesen *unreg vt* to read; (*ernten*) to gather, pick ▷*vi* to read; **~/schreiben** (*Comput*) to read/write

Leser, in (**-s, -**) *m(f)* reader

Leseratte ['le:zəratə] (*umg*) *f* bookworm

Leser- *zW*: **Leserbrief** *m* reader's letter; **„Leserbriefe"** "letters to the editor"; **Leserkreis** *m* readership; **leserlich** *adj* legible

Lese- *zW*: **Lesesaal** *m* reading room; **Lesestoff** *m* reading material; **Lesezeichen** *nt* bookmark; **Lesezirkel** *m* magazine club

Lesotho [le'zo:to] (**-s**) *nt* Lesotho

Lesung ['le:zʊŋ] *f* (*Parl*) reading; (*Eccl*) lesson

lethargisch [le'targɪʃ] *adj* (*Med, fig*) lethargic

Lette ['lɛtə] (**-n, -n**) *m*, **Lettin** *f* Latvian

lettisch *adj* Latvian
Lettland ['lɛtlant] (**-s**) *nt* Latvia
Letzt *f*: **zu guter ~** finally, in the end
letzte, r, s ['lɛtstə(r, s)] *adj* last; (*neueste*) latest; **der L~ Wille** the last will and testament; **bis zum L~n** to the utmost; **zum ~n Mal** for the last time; **in ~r Zeit** recently
Letzte, s *nt*: **das ist ja das ~!** (*umg*) that really is the limit!
letztens *adv* lately
letztere, r, s *adj* the latter
letztlich *adv* in the end
Leuchte ['lɔʏçtə] (**-, -n**) *f* lamp, light; (*umg: Mensch*) genius
leuchten *vi* to shine, gleam
Leuchter (**-s, -**) *m* candlestick
Leucht- *zW*: **Leuchtfarbe** *f* fluorescent colour (*Brit*) *od* color (*US*); **Leuchtfeuer** *nt* beacon; **Leuchtkäfer** *m* glow-worm; **Leuchtkugel** *f* flare; **Leuchtpistole** *f* flare pistol; **Leuchtrakete** *f* flare; **Leuchtreklame** *f* neon sign; **Leuchtröhre** *f* strip light; **Leuchtturm** *m* lighthouse; **Leuchtzifferblatt** *nt* luminous dial
leugnen ['lɔʏgnən] *vt, vi* to deny
Leugnung *f* denial
Leukämie [lɔʏkɛ'mi:] *f* leukaemia (*Brit*), leukemia (*US*)
Leukoplast® [lɔʏko'plast] (**-(e)s, -e**) *nt* Elastoplast®
Leumund ['lɔʏmʊnt] (**-(e)s, -e**) *m* reputation
Leumundszeugnis *nt* character reference
Leute ['lɔʏtə] *pl* people *pl*; **kleine ~** (*fig*) ordinary people; **etw unter die ~ bringen** (*umg: Gerücht etc*) to spread sth around
Leutnant ['lɔʏtnant] (**-s, -s** *od* **-e**) *m* lieutenant
leutselig ['lɔʏtze:lɪç] *adj* affable; **Leutseligkeit** *f* affability
Leviten [le'vi:tən] *pl*: **jdm die ~ lesen** (*umg*) to haul sb over the coals
lexikalisch [lɛksi'ka:lɪʃ] *adj* lexical
Lexikografie [lɛksikogra'fi:] *f* lexicography
Lexikon ['lɛksikɔn] (**-s, Lexiken** *od* **Lexika**) *nt* encyclopedia
lfd. *abk* = **laufend**
Libanese [liba'ne:zə] (**-n, -n**) *m*, **Libanesin** *f* Lebanese
libanesisch *adj* Lebanese
Libanon ['li:banɔn] (**-s**) *m*: **der ~** the Lebanon
Libelle [li'bɛlə] (**-, -n**) *f* dragonfly; (*Tech*) spirit level
liberal [libe'ra:l] *adj* liberal
Liberale, r *f(m)* (*Pol*) Liberal
Liberalisierung [liberali'zi:rʊŋ] *f* liberalization
Liberalismus [libera'lɪsmʊs] *m* liberalism
Liberia [li'be:ria] (**-s**) *nt* Liberia
Liberianer, in [liberi'a:nər(ɪn)] (**-s, -**) *m(f)* Liberian
liberianisch *adj* Liberian
Libero ['li:bero] (**-s, -s**) *m* (*Fussball*) sweeper
Libyen ['li:byən] (**-s**) *nt* Libya
Libyer, in (**-s, -**) *m(f)* Libyan
libysch *adj* Libyan
Licht [lɪçt] (**-(e)s, -er**) *nt* light; **~ machen** (*anschalten*) to turn on a light; (*anzünden*) to light a candle *etc*; **mir geht ein ~ auf** it's dawned on me; **jdn hinters ~ führen** (*fig*) to lead sb up the garden path
licht *adj* light, bright
Licht- *zW*: **Lichtbild** *nt* photograph; (*Dia*) slide; **Lichtblick** *m* cheering prospect; **lichtempfindlich** *adj* sensitive to light
lichten ['lɪçtən] *vt* to clear; (*Anker*) to weigh ▷ *vr* (*Nebel*) to clear; (*Haar*) to thin
lichterloh ['lɪçtər'lo:] *adv*: **~ brennen** to blaze
Licht- *zW*: **Lichtgeschwindigkeit** *f* speed of light; **Lichtgriffel** *m* (*Comput*) light pen; **Lichthupe** *f* flashing of headlights; **Lichtjahr** *nt* light year; **Lichtmaschine** *f* dynamo; **Lichtmess** (**-**) *f* Candlemas; **Lichtpause** *f* photocopy; (*bei Blaupausverfahren*) blueprint; **Lichtschalter** *m* light switch; **lichtscheu** *adj* averse to light; (*fig: Gesindel*) shady
Lichtung *f* clearing, glade
Lid [li:t] (**-(e)s, -er**) *nt* eyelid; **Lidschatten** *m* eyeshadow
lieb [li:p] *adj* dear; **(viele) ~e Grüße, Deine Silvia** love, Silvia; **Liebe Anna, ~er Klaus! ...** Dear Anna and Klaus, ...; **am ~sten lese ich Kriminalromane** best of all I like detective novels; **den ~en langen Tag** (*umg*) all the livelong day; **sich bei jdm ~ Kind machen** (*pej*) to suck up to sb (*umg*); **~ gewinnen** to get fond of; **~ haben** to love; (*weniger stark*) to be (very) fond of
liebäugeln ['li:p|ɔʏgəln] *vi untr*: **mit dem Gedanken ~, etw zu tun** to toy with the idea of doing sth
Liebe ['li:bə] (**-, -n**) *f* love; **liebebedürftig** *adj*: **liebebedürftig sein** to need love
Liebelei *f* flirtation
lieben ['li:bən] *vt* to love; (*weniger stark*) to like; **etw ~d gern tun** to love to do sth
liebens- *zW*: **liebenswert** *adj* loveable; **liebenswürdig** *adj* kind; **liebenswürdigerweise** *adv* kindly; **Liebenswürdigkeit** *f* kindness
lieber ['li:bər] *adv* rather, preferably; **ich gehe ~ nicht** I'd rather not go; **ich trinke ~ Wein als Bier** I prefer wine to beer; **bleib ~ im Bett** you'd better stay in bed
Liebes- *zW*: **Liebesbrief** *m* love letter; **Liebesdienst** *m* good turn; **Liebeskummer** *m*: **Liebeskummer haben** to be lovesick; **Liebespaar** *nt* courting couple, lovers *pl*; **Liebesroman** *m* romantic novel
liebevoll *adj* loving
lieb- *zW*: **Liebhaber, in** (**-s, -**) *m(f)* lover; (*Sammler*) collector; **Liebhaberei** *f* hobby; **liebkosen** *vt untr* to caress; **lieblich** *adj* lovely, charming; (*Duft, Wein*) sweet
Liebling *m* darling
Lieblings- *in zw* favourite (*Brit*), favorite (*US*)
lieblos *adj* unloving
Liebschaft *f* love affair

Liechtenstein ['lɪçtənʃtaɪn] (**-s**) *nt* Liechtenstein
Lied [li:t] (**-(e)s, -er**) *nt* song; (*Eccl*) hymn; **davon kann ich ein ~ singen** (*fig*) I could tell you a thing or two about that (*umg*)
Liederbuch *nt* songbook; (*Rel*) hymn book
liederlich ['li:dərlɪç] *adj* slovenly; (*Lebenswandel*) loose, immoral; **Liederlichkeit** *f* slovenliness; immorality
lief *etc* [li:f] *vb siehe* **laufen**
Lieferant [li:fə'rant] *m* supplier
Lieferanteneingang *m* tradesmen's entrance; (*von Warenhaus etc*) goods entrance
lieferbar *adj* (*vorrätig*) available
Lieferbedingungen *pl* terms of delivery
Lieferfrist *f* delivery period
liefern ['li:fərn] *vt* to deliver; (*versorgen mit*) to supply; (*Beweis*) to produce
Lieferschein *m* delivery note
Liefertermin *m* delivery date
Lieferung *f* delivery; (*Versorgung*) supply
Lieferwagen *m* (delivery) van, panel truck (*US*)
Lieferzeit *f* delivery period; **~ 6 Monate** delivery six months
Liege ['li:gə] (**-, -n**) *f* bed; (*Campingliege*) camp bed (*Brit*), cot (*US*); **Liegegeld** *nt* (*Hafen, Flughafen*) demurrage
liegen ['li:gən] *unreg vi* to lie; (*sich befinden*) to be (situated); **mir liegt nichts/viel daran** it doesn't matter to me/it matters a lot to me; **es liegt bei Ihnen, ob ...** it rests with you whether ...; **Sprachen ~ mir nicht** languages are not my line; **woran liegt es?** what's the cause?; **so, wie die Dinge jetzt ~** as things stand at the moment; **an mir soll es nicht ~, wenn die Sache schiefgeht** it won't be my fault if things go wrong; **~ bleiben** (*Person*) to stay in bed; (*nicht aufstehen*) to stay lying down; (*Ding*) to be left (behind); (*nicht ausgeführt werden*) to be left (undone); **~ lassen** (*vergessen*) to leave behind; **Liegenschaft** *f* real estate
Liege- *zW*: **Liegeplatz** *m* (*auf Schiff, in Zug etc*) berth; (*Ankerplatz*) moorings *pl*; **Liegesitz** *m* (*Aut*) reclining seat; **Liegestuhl** *m* deck chair; **Liegestütz** *m* (*Sport*) press-up (*Brit*), push-up (*US*); **Liegewagen** *m* (*Eisenb*) couchette car; **Liegewiese** *f* lawn (*for sunbathing*)
lieh *etc* [li:] *vb siehe* **leihen**
ließ *etc* [li:s] *vb siehe* **lassen**
liest [li:st] *vb siehe* **lesen**
Lift [lɪft] (**-(e)s, -e** *od* **-s**) *m* lift
Liga ['li:ga] (**-, Ligen**) *f* (*Sport*) league
liieren [li'i:rən] *vt*: **liiert sein** (*Firmen etc*) to be working together; (*ein Verhältnis haben*) to have a relationship
Likör [li'kø:r] (**-s, -e**) *m* liqueur
lila ['li:la] *adj inv* purple; **Lila** (**-s, -s**) *nt* (*Farbe*) purple
Lilie ['li:liə] *f* lily
Liliputaner, in [lilipu'ta:nər(ɪn)] (**-s, -**) *m(f)* midget
Limit ['lɪmɪt] (**-s, -s** *od* **-e**) *nt* limit; (*Fin*) ceiling
Limonade [limo'na:də] (**-, -n**) *f* lemonade
lind [lɪnt] *adj* gentle, mild
Linde ['lɪndə] (**-, -n**) *f* lime tree, linden
lindern ['lɪndərn] *vt* to alleviate, soothe
Linderung *f* alleviation
lindgrün *adj* lime green
Lineal [line'a:l] (**-s, -e**) *nt* ruler
linear [line'a:r] *adj* linear
Linguist, in [lɪŋgu'ɪst(ɪn)] *m(f)* linguist
Linguistik *f* linguistics *sing*
Linie ['li:niə] *f* line; **in erster ~** first and foremost; **auf die ~ achten** to watch one's figure; **fahren Sie mit der ~ 2** take the number 2 (bus *etc*)
Linien- *zW*: **Linienblatt** *nt* ruled sheet; **Linienbus** *m* service bus; **Linienflug** *m* scheduled flight; **Linienrichter** *m* (*Sport*) linesman; **linientreu** *adj* loyal to the (party) line
linieren [li'ni:rən], **liniieren** [lini'i:rən] *vt* to line
Link [lɪŋk] (**-s, -s**) *m* (*Comput*) link
Linke ['lɪŋkə] (**-, -n**) *f* left side; left hand; (*Pol*) left
Linke, r *f(m)* (*Pol*) left-winger, leftie (*pej*)
linke, r, s *adj* left; **~ Masche** purl
linkisch *adj* awkward, gauche
links *adv* left; to *od* on the left; **~ von mir** on *od* to my left; **~ von der Mitte** left of centre; **jdn ~ liegen lassen** (*fig: umg*) to ignore sb; **das mache ich mit ~** (*umg*) I can do that with my eyes shut; **Linksabbieger** *m* motorist/vehicle turning left; **Linksaußen** (**-s, -**) *m* (*Sport*) outside left; **Linkshänder, in** (**-s, -**) *m(f)* left-handed person; **Linkskurve** *f* left-hand bend; **linkslastig** *adj*: **linkslastig sein** to list *od* lean to the left; **linksradikal** *adj* (*Pol*) radically left-wing; **Linksrutsch** *m* (*Pol*) swing to the left; **Linkssteuerung** *f* (*Aut*) left-hand drive; **Linksverkehr** *m* driving on the left
Linse ['lɪnzə] (**-, -n**) *f* lentil; (*optisch*) lens
linsen (*umg*) *vi* to peek
Lippe ['lɪpə] (**-, -n**) *f* lip
Lippenbekenntnis *nt* lip service
Lippenstift *m* lipstick
Liquidation [likvidatsi'o:n] *f* liquidation
Liquidationswert *m* break-up value
liquid [lik'vi:t], **liquide** [lik'vi:də] *adj* (*Firma*) solvent
Liquidator [likvi'da:tɔr] *m* liquidator
liquidieren [likvi'di:rən] *vt* to liquidate
Liquidität [likvidi'tɛ:t] *f* liquidity
lispeln ['lɪspəln] *vi* to lisp
Lissabon ['lɪsabɔn] *nt* Lisbon
List [lɪst] (**-, -en**) *f* cunning; (*Plan*) trick, ruse; **mit ~ und Tücke** (*umg*) with a lot of coaxing
Liste ['lɪstə] (**-, -n**) *f* list
Listenplatz *m* (*Pol*) place on the party list
Listenpreis *m* list price
listig *adj* cunning, sly
Litanei [lita'naɪ] *f* litany
Litauen ['li:taʊən] (**-s**) *nt* Lithuania
Litauer, in (**-s, -**) *m(f)* Lithuanian
litauisch *adj* Lithuanian

Liter ['li:tər] (**-s, -**) *m od nt* litre (*Brit*), liter (*US*)
literarisch [lıte'ra:rıʃ] *adj* literary
Literatur [lıtera'tu:r] *f* literature; **Literaturpreis** *m* award *od* prize for literature; **Literaturwissenschaft** *f* literary studies *pl*
literweise ['li:tərvaızə] *adv* (*lit*) by the litre (*Brit*) *od* liter (*US*); (*fig*) by the gallon
Litfaßsäule ['lıtfaszɔʏlə] *f* advertising (*Brit*) *od* advertizing (*US*) pillar
Lithografie [litogra'fi:] *f* lithography
litt *etc* [lıt] *vb siehe* **leiden**
Liturgie [litʊr'gi:] *f* liturgy
liturgisch [li'tʊrgıʃ] *adj* liturgical
Litze ['lıtsə] (**-, -n**) *f* braid; (*Elek*) flex
live [laıf] *adj, adv* (*Rundf, TV*) live
Livree [li'vre:] (**-, -n**) *f* livery
Lizenz [li'tsɛnts] *f* licence (*Brit*), license (*US*); **Lizenzausgabe** *f* licensed edition; **Lizenzgebühr** *f* licence fee; (*im Verlagswesen*) royalty
Lkw, LKW (**-(s), -(s)**) *m abk* = **Lastkraftwagen**
Lkw-Maut, LKW-Maut *f* toll for trucks
l. M. *abk* (= *laufenden Monats*) inst.
Lob [lo:p] (**-(e)s**) *nt* praise
Lobby ['lɔbi] (**-, -s**) *f* lobby
loben ['lo:bən] *vt* to praise; **das lob ich mir** that's what I like (to see/hear *etc*)
lobenswert *adj* praiseworthy
löblich ['lø:plıç] *adj* praiseworthy, laudable
Loblied *nt*: **ein ~ auf jdn/etw singen** to sing sb's/sth's praises
Lobrede *f* eulogy
Loch [lɔx] (**-(e)s, ⸚er**) *nt* hole; **lochen** *vt* to punch holes in; **Locher** (**-s, -**) *m* punch
löcherig ['lœçərıç] *adj* full of holes
löchern (*umg*) *vt*: **jdn ~** to pester sb with questions
Loch- *zW*: **Lochkarte** *f* punch card; **Lochstreifen** *m* punch tape; **Lochzange** *f* punch
Locke ['lɔkə] (**-, -n**) *f* lock, curl
locken *vt* to entice; (*Haare*) to curl
lockend *adj* tempting
Lockenwickler (**-s, -**) *m* curler
locker ['lɔkər] *adj* loose; (*Kuchen, Schaum*) light; (*umg*) cool; **lockerlassen** *unreg vi*: **nicht lockerlassen** not to let up
lockern *vt* to loosen ▷ *vr* (*Atmosphäre*) to get more relaxed
Lockerungsübung *f* loosening-up exercise; (*zum Warmwerden*) limbering-up exercise
lockig ['lɔkıç] *adj* curly
Lockmittel *nt* lure
Lockruf *m* call
Lockung *f* enticement
Lockvogel *m* decoy, bait; **Lockvogelangebot** *nt* (*Comm*) loss leader
Lodenmantel ['lo:dənmantəl] *m* thick woollen coat
lodern ['lo:dərn] *vi* to blaze
Löffel ['lœfəl] (**-s, -**) *m* spoon
löffeln *vt* to spoon
löffelweise *adv* by the spoonful
log *etc* [lo:k] *vb siehe* **lügen**
Logarithmentafel [loga'rıtmənta:fəl] *f* log(arithm) tables *pl*
Logarithmus [loga'rıtmʊs] *m* logarithm
Loge ['lo:ʒə] (**-, -n**) *f* (*Theat*) box; (*Freimaurerloge*) (masonic) lodge; (*Pförtnerloge*) office
logieren [lo'ʒi:rən] *vi* to lodge, stay
Logik ['lo:gık] *f* logic
Logis [lo'ʒi:] (**-, -**) *nt*: **Kost und ~** board and lodging
logisch ['lo:gıʃ] *adj* logical; (*umg: selbstverständlich*): **gehst du auch hin? — ~** are you going too? — of course
logo ['logo] (*umg*) *interj* obvious!
Logopäde [logo'pɛ:də] (**-n, -n**) *m* speech therapist
Logopädin [logo'pɛ:dın] *f* speech therapist
Lohn [lo:n] (**-(e)s, ⸚e**) *m* reward; (*Arbeitslohn*) pay, wages *pl*; **Lohnabrechnung** *f* wages slip; **Lohnausfall** *m* loss of earnings; **Lohnbüro** *nt* wages office; **Lohndiktat** *nt* wage dictate; **Lohndumping** *nt* wage dumping; **Lohnempfänger** *m* wage earner
lohnen ['lo:nən] *vt* (*liter*): **jdm etw ~** to reward sb for sth ▷ *vr unpers* to be worth it
lohnend *adj* worthwhile
Lohn- *zW*: **Lohnerhöhung** *f* wage increase, pay rise; **Lohnforderung** *f* wage claim; **Lohnfortzahlung** *f* continued payment of wages; **Lohnfortzahlungsgesetz** *nt law on continued payment of wages*; **Lohngefälle** *nt* wage differential; **Lohnkosten** *pl* labour (*Brit*) *od* labor (*US*) costs; **Lohnpolitik** *f* wages policy; **Lohnrunde** *f* pay round; **Lohnsteuer** *f* income tax; **Lohnsteuerjahresausgleich** *m* income tax return; **Lohnsteuerkarte** *f* (income) tax card; **Lohnstopp** *m* pay freeze; **Lohnstreifen** *m* pay slip; **Lohntüte** *f* pay packet
Lok [lɔk] (**-, -s**) *f abk* (= *Lokomotive*) loco (*umg*)
lokal [lo'ka:l] *adj* local
Lokal (**-(e)s, -e**) *nt* pub(lic house) (*Brit*)
Lokalblatt (*umg*) *nt* local paper
lokalisieren [loka:li'zi:rən] *vt* to localize
Lokalisierung *f* localization
Lokalität [lokali'tɛ:t] *f* locality; (*Raum*) premises *pl*
Lokal- *zW*: **Lokalpresse** *f* local press; **Lokalteil** *m* (*Zeitung*) local section; **Lokaltermin** *m* (*Jur*) visit to the scene of the crime
Lokomotive [lokomo'ti:və] (**-, -n**) *f* locomotive
Lokomotivführer *m* engine driver (*Brit*), engineer (*US*)
Lombardei [lɔmbar'daı] *f* Lombardy
London ['lɔndɔn] (**-s**) *nt* London
Londoner *adj attrib* London
Londoner, in (**-s, -**) *m(f)* Londoner
Lorbeer ['lɔrbe:r] (**-s, -en**) *m* (*lit, fig*) laurel; **Lorbeerblatt** *nt* (*Koch*) bay leaf
Lore ['lo:rə] (**-, -n**) *f* (*Min*) truck
Los [lo:s] (**-es, -e**) *nt* (*Schicksal*) lot, fate; (*in der Lotterie*) lottery ticket; **das große ~ ziehen** (*lit, fig*) to hit the jackpot; **etw durch das ~ entscheiden** to decide sth by drawing lots

los *adj* loose ▷ *adv*: **~!** go on!; **etw ~ sein** to be rid of sth; **was ist ~?** what's the matter?; **dort ist nichts/viel ~** there's nothing/a lot going on there; **ich bin mein ganzes Geld ~** (*umg*) I'm cleaned out; **irgendwas ist mit ihm ~** there's something wrong with him; **wir wollen früh ~** we want to be off early; **nichts wie ~!** let's get going; **losbinden** *unreg vt* to untie; **losbrechen** *unreg vi* (*Sturm, Gewitter*) to break

losch *etc* [lɔʃ] *vb siehe* **löschen**

Löschblatt ['lœʃblat] *nt* sheet of blotting paper

löschen ['lœʃən] *vt* (*Feuer, Licht*) to put out, extinguish; (*Durst*) to quench; (*Comm*) to cancel; (*Tonband*) to erase; (*Fracht*) to unload; (*Comput*) to delete; (*Tinte*) to blot ▷ *vi* (*Feuerwehr*) to put out a fire; (*Papier*) to blot

Lösch- *zW*: **Löschfahrzeug** *nt* fire engine; **Löschgerät** *nt* fire extinguisher; **Löschpapier** *nt* blotting paper; **Löschtaste** *f* (*Comput*) delete key

Löschung *f* extinguishing; (*Comm*) cancellation; (*Fracht*) unloading

lose ['lo:zə] *adj* loose

Lösegeld *nt* ransom

losen ['lo:zən] *vi* to draw lots

lösen ['lø:zən] *vt* to loosen; (*Handbremse*) to release; (*Husten, Krampf*) to ease; (*Rätsel etc*) to solve; (*Verlobung*) to call off; (*Chem*) to dissolve; (*Partnerschaft*) to break up; (*Fahrkarte*) to buy ▷ *vr* (*aufgehen*) to come loose; (*Schuss*) to go off; (*Zucker etc*) to dissolve; (*Problem, Schwierigkeit*) to (re)solve itself

los- *zW*: **losfahren** *unreg vi* to leave; **losgehen** *unreg vi* to set out; (*anfangen*) to start; (*Bombe*) to go off; **jetzt gehts los!** here we go!; **nach hinten losgehen** (*umg*) to backfire; **auf jdn losgehen** to go for sb; **loskaufen** *vt* (*Gefangene, Geiseln*) to pay ransom for; **loskommen** *unreg vi* (*sich befreien*) to free o.s.; **von etw loskommen** to get away from sth; **loslassen** *unreg vt* (*Seil etc*) to let go of; **der Gedanke lässt mich nicht mehr los** the thought haunts me; **loslaufen** *unreg vi* to run off; **loslegen** (*umg*) *vi*: **nun leg mal los und erzähl(e) ...** now come on and tell me/us ...

löslich ['lø:slɪç] *adj* soluble; **Löslichkeit** *f* solubility

loslösen *vt* to free ▷ *vr*: **sich (von etw) ~** to detach o.s. (from sth)

losmachen *vt* to loosen; (*Boot*) to unmoor ▷ *vr* to get free

Losnummer *f* ticket number

los- *zW*: **lossagen** *vr*: **sich von jdm/etw lossagen** to renounce sb/sth; **losschießen** *unreg vi*: **schieß los!** (*fig: umg*) fire away!; **losschrauben** *vt* to unscrew; **lossprechen** *unreg vt* to absolve; **losstürzen** *vi*: **auf jdn/etw losstürzen** to pounce on sb/sth

Losung ['lo:zʊŋ] *f* watchword, slogan

Lösung ['lø:zʊŋ] *f* (*Lockermachen*) loosening; (*eines Rätsels, Chem*) solution

Lösungsmittel *nt* solvent

loswerden *unreg vt* to get rid of

losziehen *unreg vi* (*sich aufmachen*) to set out; **gegen jdn ~** (*fig*) to run sb down

Lot [lo:t] (**-(e)s, -e**) *nt* plumbline; (*Math*) perpendicular; **im ~** vertical; (*fig*) on an even keel; **die Sache ist wieder im ~** things have been straightened out; **loten** *vt* to plumb, sound

löten ['lø:tən] *vt* to solder

Lothringen ['lo:trɪŋən] (**-s**) *nt* Lorraine

Lötkolben *m* soldering iron

Lotse ['lo:tsə] (**-n, -n**) *m* pilot; (*Aviat*) air traffic controller

lotsen *vt* to pilot; (*umg*) to lure

Lotterie [lɔtə'ri:] *f* lottery

Lotterleben ['lɔtərle:bən] (*umg*) *nt* dissolute life

Lotto ['lɔto] (**-s, -s**) *nt* ≈ National Lottery

Lottozahlen *pl* winning Lotto numbers *pl*

Löwe ['lø:və] (**-n, -n**) *m* lion; (*Astrol*) Leo

Löwen- *zW*: **Löwenanteil** *m* lion's share; **Löwenmaul** *nt*, **Löwenmäulchen** *nt* antirrhinum, snapdragon; **Löwenzahn** *m* dandelion

Löwin ['lø:vɪn] *f* lioness

loyal [loa'ja:l] *adj* loyal

Loyalität [loajali'tɛ:t] *f* loyalty

LP (**-, -s**) *f abk* (= *Langspielplatte*) LP

LSD (**-(s)**) *nt abk* (= *Lysergsäurediäthylamid*) LSD

lt. *abk* = **laut**

Luchs [lʊks] (**-es, -e**) *m* lynx

Lücke ['lʏkə] (**-, -n**) *f* gap; (*Gesetzeslücke*) loophole; (*in Versorgung*) break

Lücken- *zW*: **Lückenbüßer** (**-s, -**) *m* stopgap; **lückenhaft** *adj* full of gaps; (*Versorgung*) deficient; **lückenlos** *adj* complete

lud *etc* [lu:t] *vb siehe* **laden**

Luder ['lu:dər] (**-s, -**) (*pej*) *nt* (*Frau*) hussy; (*bedauernswert*) poor wretch

Luft [lʊft] (**-, ¨e**) *f* air; (*Atem*) breath; **die ~ anhalten** (*lit*) to hold one's breath; **seinem Herzen ~ machen** to get everything off one's chest; **in der ~ liegen** to be in the air; **dicke ~** (*umg*) a bad atmosphere; **(frische) ~ schnappen** (*umg*) to get some fresh air; **in die ~ fliegen** (*umg*) to explode; **diese Behauptung ist aus der ~ gegriffen** this statement is (a) pure invention; **die ~ ist rein** (*umg*) the coast is clear; **jdn an die (frische) ~ setzen** (*umg*) to show sb the door; **er ist ~ für mich** I'm not speaking to him; **jdn wie ~ behandeln** to ignore sb; **Luftangriff** *m* air raid; **Luftaufnahme** *f* aerial photo; **Luftballon** *m* balloon; **Luftblase** *f* air bubble; **Luftbrücke** *f* airlift; **luftdicht** *adj* airtight; **Luftdruck** *m* atmospheric pressure; **luftdurchlässig** *adj* pervious to air

lüften ['lʏftən] *vt* to air; (*Hut*) to lift, raise ▷ *vi* to let some air in

Luft- *zW*: **Luftfahrt** *f* aviation; **Luftfeuchtigkeit** *f* humidity; **Luftfracht** *f* air cargo; **luftgekühlt** *adj* air-cooled; **Luftgewehr** *nt* air rifle

luftig *adj* (*Ort*) breezy; (*Raum*) airy; (*Kleider*)

summery
Luft- *zW*: **Luftkissenfahrzeug** *nt* hovercraft; **Luftkrieg** *m* war in the air, aerial warfare; **Luftkurort** *m* health resort; **luftleer** *adj*: **luftleerer Raum** vacuum; **Luftlinie** *f*: **in der Luftlinie** as the crow flies; **Luftloch** *nt* air hole; (*Aviat*) air pocket; **Luftmatratze** *f* Lilo® (*Brit*), air mattress; **Luftpirat** *m* hijacker; **Luftpost** *f* airmail; **Luftpumpe** *f* (*für Fahrrad*) (bicycle) pump; **Luftraum** *m* air space; **Luftröhre** *f* (*Anat*) windpipe; **Luftschlange** *f* streamer; **Luftschloss** *nt* (*fig*) castle in the air; **Luftschutz** *m* anti-aircraft defence (*Brit*) *od* defense (*US*); **Luftschutzbunker** *m*, **Luftschutzkeller** *m* air-raid shelter; **Luftsprung** *m* (*fig*): **einen Luftsprung machen** to jump for joy
Lüftung ['lʏftʊŋ] *f* ventilation
Luft- *zW*: **Luftveränderung** *f* change of air; **Luftverkehr** *m* air traffic; **Luftverschmutzung** *f* air pollution; **Luftwaffe** *f* air force; **Luftweg** *m*: **etw auf dem Luftweg befördern** to transport sth by air; **Luftzufuhr** *f* air supply; **Luftzug** *m* draught (*Brit*), draft (*US*)
Lüge ['ly:gə] (**-, -n**) *f* lie; **jdn/etw ~n strafen** to give the lie to sb/sth
lügen ['ly:gən] *unreg vi* to lie; **wie gedruckt ~** (*umg*) to lie like mad
Lügendetektor ['ly:gəndetɛktɔr] *m* lie detector
Lügner, in (**-s, -**) *m(f)* liar
Luke ['lu:kə] (**-, -n**) *f* hatch; (*Dachluke*) skylight
lukrativ [lukra'ti:f] *adj* lucrative
Lümmel ['lʏməl] (**-s, -**) *m* lout
lümmeln *vr* to lounge (about)
Lump [lʊmp] (**-en, -en**) *m* scamp, rascal
lumpen ['lʊmpən] *vt*: **sich nicht ~ lassen** not to be mean
Lumpen (**-s, -**) *m* rag
Lumpensammler *m* rag and bone man
lumpig ['lʊmpɪç] *adj* shabby; **~e 10 Euro** (*umg*) 10 measly euros
Lüneburger Heide ['ly:nəbʊrgər 'haɪdə] *f* Lüneburg Heath
Lunge ['lʊŋə] (**-, -n**) *f* lung
Lungen- *zW*: **Lungenentzündung** *f* pneumonia; **lungenkrank** *adj* suffering from a lung disease; **Lungenkrankheit** *f* lung disease
lungern ['lʊŋərn] *vi* to hang about
Lunte ['lʊntə] (**-, -n**) *f* fuse; **~ riechen** to smell a rat
Lupe ['lu:pə] (**-, -n**) *f* magnifying glass; **unter die ~ nehmen** (*fig*) to scrutinize
lupenrein *adj* (*lit*: *Edelstein*) flawless
Lupine [lu'pi:nə] *f* lupin
Lurch [lʊrç] (**-(e)s, -e**) *m* amphibian
Lust [lʊst] (**-, ¨-e**) *f* joy, delight; (*Neigung*) desire; (*sexuell*) lust (*pej*); **~ haben zu** *od* **auf etw** *akk*/ **etw zu tun** to feel like sth/doing sth; **hast du ~?** how about it?; **er hat die ~ daran verloren** he has lost all interest in it; **je nach ~ und Laune** just depending on how I *od* you *etc* feel; **lustbetont** *adj* pleasure-orientated
lüstern ['lʏstərn] *adj* lustful, lecherous
Lustgefühl *nt* pleasurable feeling
Lustgewinn *m* pleasure
lustig ['lʊstɪç] *adj* (*komisch*) amusing, funny; (*fröhlich*) cheerful; **sich über jdn/etw ~ machen** to make fun of sb/sth
Lüstling *m* lecher
Lust- *zW*: **lustlos** *adj* unenthusiastic; **Lustmord** *m* sex(ual) murder; **Lustprinzip** *nt* (*Psych*) pleasure principle; **Lustspiel** *nt* comedy; **lustwandeln** *vi* to stroll about
luth. *abk* = **lutherisch**
Lutheraner, in [lʊtə'ra:nər(ɪn)] *m(f)* Lutheran
lutherisch ['lʊtərɪʃ] *adj* Lutheran
lutschen ['lʊtʃən] *vt, vi* to suck; **am Daumen ~** to suck one's thumb
Lutscher (**-s, -**) *m* lollipop
Luxemburg ['lʊksəmbʊrk] (**-s**) *nt* Luxembourg
Luxemburger, in ['lʊksəmburgər(ɪn)] (**-s, -**) *m(f)* citizen of Luxembourg, Luxembourger
luxemburgisch *adj* Luxembourgian
luxuriös [lʊksuri'ø:s] *adj* luxurious
Luxus ['lʊksʊs] (**-**) *m* luxury; **Luxusartikel** *pl* luxury goods *pl*; **Luxusausführung** *f* de luxe model; **Luxusdampfer** *m* luxury cruise ship; **Luxushotel** *nt* luxury hotel; **Luxussteuer** *f* tax on luxuries
LVA (**-**) *f abk* (= *Landesversicherungsanstalt*) *county insurance company*
LW *abk* (= *Langwelle*) LW
Lycra ['ly:kra] (**-(s)**) *no pl nt* Lycra®
Lymphe ['lʏmfə] (**-, -n**) *f* lymph
Lymphknoten *m* lymph(atic) gland
lynchen ['lʏnçən] *vt* to lynch
Lynchjustiz *f* lynch law
Lyrik ['ly:rɪk] *f* lyric poetry; **Lyriker, in** (**-s, -**) *m(f)* lyric poet
lyrisch ['ly:rɪʃ] *adj* lyrical

Mm

M, m[1] [ɛm] *nt* M, m; **M wie Martha** ≈ M for Mary, ≈ M for Mike (US)
m[2] *abk* (= *Meter*) m; (= *männlich*) m.
M. *abk* = **Monat**
MA. *abk* = **Mittelalter**
Maat [maːt] **(-s, -e** *od* **-en)** *m* (*Naut*) (ship's) mate
Machart *f* make
machbar *adj* feasible
Machbarkeitsstudie *f* feasibility study
Mache (-) (*umg*) *f* show, sham; **jdn in der ~ haben** to be having a go at sb

SCHLÜSSELWORT

machen [ˈmaxən] *vt* **1** to do; **was machst du da?** what are you doing there?; **das ist nicht zu machen** that can't be done; **was machen Sie (beruflich)?** what do you do for a living?; **mach, dass du hier verschwindest!** (you just) get out of here!; **mit mir kann mans ja machen!** (*umg*) the things I put up with!; **das lässt er nicht mit sich machen** he won't stand for that; **eine Prüfung machen** to take an exam
2 (*herstellen*) to make; **das Radio leiser machen** to turn the radio down; **aus Holz gemacht** made of wood; **das Essen machen** to get the meal; **Schluss machen** to finish (off)
3 (*verursachen, bewirken*) to make; **jdm Angst machen** to make sb afraid; **das macht die Kälte** it's the cold that does that
4 (*ausmachen*) to matter; **das macht nichts** that doesn't matter; **die Kälte macht mir nichts** I don't mind the cold
5 (*kosten: ergeben*) to be; **3 und 5 macht 8** 3 and 5 is *od* are 8; **was** *od* **wie viel macht das?** how much does that come to?
6: was macht die Arbeit? how's the work going?; **was macht dein Bruder?** how is your brother doing?; **das Auto machen lassen** to have the car done; **machs gut!** take care!; (*viel Glück*) good luck!
▷ *vi*: **mach schnell!** hurry up!; **mach schon!** come on!; **jetzt macht sie auf große Dame** (*umg*) she's playing the lady now; **lass mich mal machen** (*umg*) let me do it; (*ich bringe das in Ordnung*) I'll deal with it; **groß/klein machen** (*umg: Notdurft*) to do a big/little job; **sich** *dat* **in die Hose machen** to wet o.s.; **ins Bett machen** to wet one's bed; **das macht müde** it makes you tired; **in etw** *dat* **machen** to be *od* deal in sth
▷ *vr* to come along (nicely); **sich an etw** *akk* **machen** to set about sth; **sich verständlich machen** to make o.s. understood; **sich** *dat* **viel aus jdm/etw machen** to like sb/sth; **mach dir nichts daraus** don't let it bother you; **sich auf den Weg machen** to get going; **sich an etw** *akk* **machen** to set about sth

Machenschaften *pl* wheelings and dealings *pl*
Macher (-s, -) (*umg*) *m* man of action
Macho [ˈmatʃo] (*umg*) *adj* macho
Macho (-s, -s) (*umg*) *m* macho type
Macht [maxt] **(-, ¨-e)** *f* power; **mit aller ~** with all one's might; **an der ~ sein** to be in power; **alles in unserer ~ Stehende** everything in our power; **Machtergreifung** *f* seizure of power; **Machthaber (-s, -)** *m* ruler
mächtig [ˈmɛçtɪç] *adj* powerful, mighty; (*umg: ungeheuer*) enormous
Macht- *zW*: **machtlos** *adj* powerless; **Machtprobe** *f* trial of strength; **Machtstellung** *f* position of power; **Machtwort** *nt*: **ein Machtwort sprechen** to lay down the law
Machwerk *nt* work; (*schlechte Arbeit*) botched job
Macke [ˈmakə] **(-, -n)** (*umg*) *f* (*Tick, Knall*) quirk; (*Fehler*) fault
Macker (-s, -) (*umg*) *m* fellow, guy
MAD (-) *m abk* (= *Militärischer Abschirmdienst*) ≈ MI5 (*Brit*), ≈ CIA (*US*)
Madagaskar [madaˈgaskar] **(-s)** *nt* Madagascar
Mädchen [ˈmɛːtçən] *nt* girl; **ein ~ für alles** (*umg*) a dogsbody; (*im Büro etc*) a girl Friday; **mädchenhaft** *adj* girlish; **Mädchenname** *m* maiden name
Made [ˈmaːdə] **(-, -n)** *f* maggot
Madeira[1] [maˈdeːra] **(-s)** *nt* (*Geog*) Madeira
Madeira[2] **(-s, -s)** *m* (*Wein*) Madeira
Mädel [ˈmɛːdl] **(-s, -(s))** *nt* (*Dialekt*) lass, girl
madig [ˈmaːdɪç] *adj* maggoty; **madigmachen** *vt*: **jdm etw madigmachen** to spoil sth for sb

Madrid [ma'drɪt] (**-s**) *nt* Madrid
mag [ma:k] *vb siehe* **mögen**
Mag. *abk* = **Magister**
Magazin [maga'tsi:n] (**-s, -e**) *nt* (*Zeitschrift, am Gewehr*) magazine; (*Lager*) storeroom; (*Bibliotheksmagazin*) stockroom
Magd [ma:kt] (**-, ⸗e**) *f* maid(servant)
Magen ['ma:gən] (**-s, -** *od* **⸗**) *m* stomach; **jdm auf den ~ schlagen** (*umg*) to upset sb's stomach; (*fig*) to upset sb; **sich** *dat* **den ~ verderben** to upset one's stomach; **Magenbitter** *m* bitters *pl*; **Magengeschwür** *nt* stomach ulcer; **Magenschmerzen** *pl* stomachache *sing*; **Magenverstimmung** *f* stomach upset
mager ['ma:gər] *adj* lean; (*dünn*) thin; **Magerkeit** *f* leanness; thinness; **Magermilch** *f* skimmed milk; **Magerquark** *m* low-fat soft cheese; **Magersucht** *f* (*Med*) anorexia; **magersüchtig** *adj* anorexic
Magie [ma'gi:] *f* magic
Magier ['ma:giər] (**-s, -**) *m* magician
magisch ['ma:gɪʃ] *adj* magical
Magister [ma'gɪstər] (**-s, -**) *m* (*Univ*) M.A., Master of Arts
Magistrat [magɪs'tra:t] (**-(e)s, -e**) *m* municipal authorities *pl*
Magnat [ma'gna:t] (**-en, -en**) *m* magnate
Magnet [ma'gne:t] (**-s** *od* **-en, -en**) *m* magnet; **Magnetbahn** *f* magnetic railway; **Magnetband** *nt* (*Comput*) magnetic tape; **magnetisch** *adj* magnetic
magnetisieren [magneti'zi:rən] *vt* to magnetize
Magnetnadel *f* magnetic needle
Magnettafel *f* magnetic board
Mahagoni [maha'go:ni] (**-s**) *nt* mahogany
Mähdrescher (**-s, -**) *m* combine (harvester)
mähen ['mɛ:ən] *vt, vi* to mow
Mahl [ma:l] (**-(e)s, -e**) *nt* meal
mahlen *unreg vt* to grind
Mahlstein *m* grindstone
Mahlzeit *f* meal ▷ *interj* enjoy your meal!
Mahnbrief *m* reminder
Mähne ['mɛ:nə] (**-, -n**) *f* mane
mahnen ['ma:nən] *vt* to remind; (*warnend*) to warn; (*wegen Schuld*) to demand payment from; **jdn zur Eile/Geduld** *etc* **~** (*auffordern*) to urge sb to hurry/be patient *etc*
Mahn- *zW*: **Mahngebühr** *f* reminder fee; **Mahnmal** *nt* memorial; **Mahnschreiben** *nt* reminder
Mahnung *f* admonition, warning; (*Mahnbrief*) reminder
Mähre ['mɛ:rə] (**-, -n**) *f* mare
Mähren ['mɛ:rən] (**-s**) *nt* Moravia
Mai [maɪ] (**-(e)s, -e**) (*pl selten*) *m* May; *siehe auch* **September**; **Maibaum** *m* maypole; **Maibowle** *f* white wine punch (*flavoured with woodruff*); **Maiglöckchen** *nt* lily of the valley; **Maikäfer** *m* cockchafer
Mail [me:l] (**-, -s**) *f* (*Comput*) e-mail
Mailand ['maɪlant] (**-s**) *nt* Milan
Main [maɪn] (**-(e)s**) *m* (*Fluss*) Main
Mais [maɪs] (**-es, -e**) *m* maize, corn (*US*); **Maiskolben** *m* corncob
Majestät [majɛs'tɛ:t] *f* majesty
majestätisch *adj* majestic
Majestätsbeleidigung *f* lese-majesty
Majonäse [majɔ'nɛ:zə] (**-, -n**) *f* mayonnaise
Major [ma'jo:r] (**-s, -e**) *m* (*Mil*) major; (*Aviat*) squadron leader
Majoran [majo'ra:n] (**-s, -e**) *m* marjoram
makaber [ma'ka:bər] *adj* macabre
Makedonien [make'do:niən] (**-s**) *nt* Macedonia
makedonisch *adj* Macedonian
Makel ['ma:kəl] (**-s, -**) *m* blemish; (*moralisch*) stain; **ohne ~** flawless; **makellos** *adj* immaculate, spotless
mäkeln ['mɛ:kəln] *vi* to find fault
Make-up [me:k'|ap] (**-s, -s**) *nt* make-up; (*flüssig*) foundation
Makkaroni [maka'ro:ni] *pl* macaroni *sing*
Makler ['ma:klər] (**-s, -**) *m* broker; (*Grundstücksmakler*) estate agent (*Brit*), realtor (*US*); **Maklergebühr** *f* broker's commission, brokerage
Makrele [ma'kre:lə] (**-, -n**) *f* mackerel
Makro- *in zW* macro-
Makrone [ma'kro:nə] (**-, -n**) *f* macaroon
Makroökonomie *f* macroeconomics *sing*
Mal [ma:l] (**-(e)s, -e**) *nt* mark, sign; (*Zeitpunkt*) time; **ein für alle ~** once and for all; **mit einem ~(e)** all of a sudden; **das erste ~** the first time; **jedes ~** every time, each time; **zum letzten ~** for the last time; **ein paar ~** a few times
mal *adv* times
-mal *suff* -times
Malaie [ma'laɪə] (**-n, -n**) *m*, **Malaiin** *f* Malay
malaiisch *adj* Malayan
Malawi [ma'la:vi] (**-s**) *nt* Malawi
Malaysia [ma'laɪzia] (**-s**) *nt* Malaysia
Malaysier, in (**-s, -**) *m(f)* Malaysian
malaysisch *adj* Malaysian
Malediven [male'di:vən] *pl*: **die ~** the Maldive Islands
malen *vt, vi* to paint
Maler (**-s, -**) *m* painter
Malerei [ma:lə'raɪ] *f* painting
malerisch *adj* picturesque
Malkasten *m* paintbox
Mallorca [ma'jɔrka, ma'lɔrka] (**-s**) *nt* Majorca
Mallorquiner, in [majɔr'ki:nər(ɪn), malɔr'ki:nər(ɪn)] (**-s, -**) *m(f)* Majorcan
mallorquinisch *adj* Majorcan
malnehmen *unreg vt, vi* to multiply
Malta ['malta] (**-s**) *nt* Malta
Malteser, in [mal'te:zər(ɪn)] (**-s, -**) *m(f)* Maltese
Malteser-Hilfsdienst *m* ≈ St. John's Ambulance Brigade (*Brit*)
maltesisch *adj* Maltese
malträtieren [maltrɛ'ti:rən] *vt* to ill-treat, maltreat
Malz [malts] (**-es**) *nt* malt; **Malzbonbon** *nt or m* cough drop; **Malzkaffee** *m coffee substitute made*

from malt barley
Mama ['mama:] (**-, -s**) (*umg*) *f* mum(my) (*Brit*), mom(my) (*US*)
Mami ['mami] (**-, -s**) *f* = **Mama**
Mammografie [mamɔgra'fi:] *f* (*Med*) mammography
Mammut ['mamʊt] (**-s, -e** *od* **-s**) *nt* mammoth ▷ *in zw* mammoth, giant; **Mammutanlagen** *pl* (*Industrie*) mammoth plants
mampfen ['mampfən] (*umg*) *vt, vi* to munch, chomp
man [man] *pron* one, you, people *pl*; **~ hat mir gesagt ...** I was told ...
managen ['mɛnɪdʒən] *vt* to manage; **ich manage das schon!** (*umg*) I'll fix it somehow!
Manager, in (**-s, -**) *m(f)* manager
manch [manç] *pron*: **~ ein(e) ...** many a ...; **~ eine(r)** many a person
manche, r, s *adj* many a; (*pl*) a number of ▷ *pron* some
mancherlei [mançər'laɪ] *adj inv* various ▷ *pron* a variety of things
manchmal *adv* sometimes
Mandant, in [man'dant(ɪn)] *m(f)* (*Jur*) client
Mandarine [manda'ri:nə] *f* mandarin, tangerine
Mandat [man'da:t] (**-(e)s, -e**) *nt* mandate; **sein ~ niederlegen** (*Parl*) to resign one's seat
Mandel ['mandəl] (**-, -n**) *f* almond; (*Anat*) tonsil; **Mandelentzündung** *f* tonsillitis
Mandschurei (**-**) [mandʒu'raɪ] *f*: **die ~** Manchuria
Manege [ma'ne:ʒə] (**-, -n**) *f* ring, arena
Mangel[1] ['maŋəl] (**-, -n**) *f* mangle; **durch die ~ drehen** (*fig: umg*) to put through it; (*Prüfling etc*) to put through the mill
Mangel[2] ['maŋəl] (**-s, ¨-**) *m* lack; (*Knappheit*) shortage; (*Fehler*) defect, fault; **~ an** *+dat* shortage of
Mängelbericht ['mɛŋəlbərɪçt] *m* list of faults
Mangelerscheinung *f* deficiency symptom
mangelhaft *adj* poor; (*fehlerhaft*) defective, faulty; (*Schulnote*) unsatisfactory
mangeln *vi unpers*: **es mangelt jdm an etw** *dat* sb lacks sth ▷ *vt* (*Wäsche*) to mangle
mangels *präp +gen* for lack of
Mangelware *f* scarce commodity
Manie [ma'ni:] *f* mania
Manier [ma'ni:r] (**-**) *f* manner; (*Stil*) style; (*pej*) mannerism
Manieren *pl* manners *pl*; (*pej*) mannerisms *pl*
manieriert [mani'ri:rt] *adj* mannered, affected
manierlich *adj* well-mannered
Manifest [mani'fɛst] (**-es, -e**) *nt* manifesto
Maniküre [mani'ky:rə] (**-, -n**) *f* manicure
maniküren *vt* to manicure
Manipulation [manipulatsi'o:n] *f* manipulation; (*Trick*) manoeuvre (*Brit*), maneuver (*US*)
manipulieren [manipu'li:rən] *vt* to manipulate
Manko ['maŋko] (**-s, -s**) *nt* deficiency; (*Comm*) deficit
Mann [man] (**-(e)s, ¨-er** *od* (*Naut*) **Leute**) *m* man; (*Ehemann*) husband; (*Naut*) hand; **pro ~** per head; **mit ~ und Maus untergehen** to go down with all hands; (*Passagierschiff*) to go down with no survivors; **seinen ~ stehen** to hold one's own; **etw an den ~ bringen** (*umg*) to get rid of sth; **einen kleinen ~ im Ohr haben** (*hum: umg*) to be crazy
Männchen ['mɛnçən] *nt* little man; (*Tier*) male; **~ machen** (*Hund*) to (sit up and) beg
Mannequin [manə'kɛ̃:] (**-s, -s**) *nt* fashion model
Männersache ['mɛnərzaxə] *f* (*Angelegenheit*) man's business; (*Arbeit*) man's job
mannigfaltig ['manɪçfaltɪç] *adj* various, varied; **Mannigfaltigkeit** *f* variety
männlich ['mɛnlɪç] *adj* (*Biol*) male; (*fig, Gram*) masculine
Mannsbild *nt* (*veraltet: pej*) fellow
Mannschaft *f* (*Sport, fig*) team; (*Naut, Aviat*) crew; (*Mil*) other ranks *pl*
Mannschaftsgeist *m* team spirit
Mannsleute (*umg*) *pl* menfolk *pl*
Mannweib (*pej*) *nt* mannish woman
Manometer [mano'me:tər] *nt* (*Tech*) pressure gauge; **~!** (*umg*) wow!
Manöver [ma'nø:vər] (**-s, -**) *nt* manoeuvre (*Brit*), maneuver (*US*)
manövrieren [manø'vri:rən] *vt, vi* to manoeuvre (*Brit*), maneuver (*US*)
Mansarde [man'zardə] (**-, -n**) *f* attic
Manschette [man'ʃɛtə] *f* cuff; (*Papiermanschette*) paper frill; (*Tech*) sleeve
Manschettenknopf *m* cufflink
Mantel ['mantəl] (**-s, ¨-**) *m* coat; (*Tech*) casing, jacket; **Manteltarif** *m* general terms of employment; **Manteltarifvertrag** *m* general agreement on conditions of employment
Manuskript [manu'skrɪpt] (**-(e)s, -e**) *nt* manuscript
Mappe ['mapə] (**-, -n**) *f* briefcase; (*Aktenmappe*) folder
Marathonlauf ['ma:ratɔnlaʊf] *m* marathon
Märchen ['mɛ:rçən] *nt* fairy tale; **märchenhaft** *adj* fabulous; **Märchenprinz** *m* prince charming
Marder ['mardər] (**-s, -**) *m* marten
Margarine [marga'ri:nə] *f* margarine
Marge ['marʒə] (**-, -n**) *f* (*Comm*) margin
Maria [ma'ri:a] (**-**) *f* Mary
Marienbild *nt* picture of the Virgin Mary
Marienkäfer *m* ladybird
Marihuana [marihu'a:na] (**-s**) *nt* marijuana
Marinade [mari'na:də] (**-, -n**) *f* (*Koch*) marinade; (*Soße*) mayonnaise-based sauce
Marine [ma'ri:nə] *f* navy; **marineblau** *adj* navy-blue
marinieren [mari'ni:rən] *vt* to marinate
Marionette [mario'nɛtə] *f* puppet
Mark[1] [mark] (**-, -**) *f* (*Hist: Geld*) mark
Mark[2] [mark] (**-(e)s**) *nt* (*Knochenmark*) marrow; **jdn bis ins ~ treffen** (*fig*) to cut sb to the quick; **jdm durch ~ und Bein gehen** to go

right through sb
markant [mar'kant] *adj* striking
Marke ['markə] (**-, -n**) *f* mark; (*Warensorte*) brand; (*Fabrikat*) make; (*Rabattmarke, Briefmarke*) stamp; (*Essen(s)marke*) luncheon voucher; (*aus Metall etc*) token, disc
Marken- *zW*: **Markenartikel** *m* proprietary article; **markenbewusst** *adj* brand conscious; **Markenbutter** *f* best quality butter; **Markenkleidung** *f* designer clothes; **Markenzeichen** *nt* trademark
Marketing ['markətɪŋ] (**-s**) *nt* marketing
markieren [mar'ki:rən] *vt* to mark; (*umg*) to act ▷ *vi* (*umg*) to act it
Markierung *f* marking
markig ['markɪç] *adj* (*fig*) pithy
Markise [mar'ki:zə] (**-, -n**) *f* awning
Markstück *nt* (*Hist*) one-mark piece
Markt [markt] (**-(e)s, ⁻e**) *m* market; **Marktanalyse** *f* market analysis; **Marktanteil** *m* market share; **marktfähig** *adj* marketable; **Marktforschung** *f* market research; **marktgängig** *adj* marketable; **marktgerecht** *adj* geared to market requirements; **Marktlücke** *f* gap in the market; **Marktmacht** *f* market power; **Marktplatz** *m* market place; **Marktpotenzial**, **Marktpotential** *nt* market potential; **Marktpreis** *m* market price; **Marktwert** *m* market value; **Marktwirtschaft** *f* market economy; **marktwirtschaftlich** *adj* free enterprise
Marmelade [marmə'la:də] (**-, -n**) *f* jam
Marmor ['marmɔr] (**-s, -e**) *m* marble
marmorieren [marmo'ri:rən] *vt* to marble
Marmorkuchen *m* marble cake
marmorn *adj* marble
Marokkaner, in [marɔ'ka:nər(ɪn)] (**-s, -**) *m(f)* Moroccan
marokkanisch *adj* Moroccan
Marokko [ma'rɔko] (**-s**) *nt* Morocco
Marone [ma'ro:nə] (**-, -n**) *f* chestnut
Marotte [ma'rɔtə] (**-, -n**) *f* fad, quirk
Marsch[1] [marʃ] (**-, -en**) *f* marsh
Marsch[2] (**-(e)s, ⁻e**) *m* march; **jdm den ~ blasen** (*umg*) to give sb a rocket; **marsch!** *interj* march!; **marsch ins Bett!** off to bed with you!
Marschbefehl *m* marching orders *pl*
marschbereit *adj* ready to move
marschieren [mar'ʃi:rən] *vi* to march
Marschverpflegung *f* rations *pl*; (*Mil*) field rations *pl*
Marseille [mar'sɛ:j] (**-s**) *nt* Marseilles
Marsmensch ['marsmɛnʃ] *m* Martian
Marter ['martər] (**-, -n**) *f* torment
martern *vt* to torture
Martinshorn ['marti:nshɔrn] *nt* siren (*of police etc*)
Märtyrer, in ['mɛrtyrər(ɪn)] (**-s, -**) *m(f)* martyr
Martyrium [mar'ty:riʊm] *nt* (*fig*) ordeal
Marxismus [mar'ksɪsmʊs] *m* Marxism
März [mɛrts] (**-(es), -e**) (*pl selten*) *m* March; *siehe auch* **September**
Marzipan [martsi'pa:n] (**-s, -e**) *nt* marzipan
Masche ['maʃə] (**-, -n**) *f* mesh; (*Strickmasche*) stitch; **das ist die neueste ~** that's the latest dodge; **durch die ~n schlüpfen** to slip through the net
Maschendraht *m* wire mesh
maschenfest *adj* runproof
Maschine [ma'ʃi:nə] *f* machine; (*Motor*) engine; **~ schreiben** to type
maschinell [maʃi'nɛl] *adj* machine(-), mechanical
Maschinen- *zW*: **Maschinenausfallzeit** *f* machine downtime; **Maschinenbauer** *m* mechanical engineer; **Maschinenführer** *m* machinist; **maschinengeschrieben** *adj* typewritten; **Maschinengewehr** *nt* machine gun; **maschinenlesbar** *adj* (*Comput*) machine-readable; **Maschinenpistole** *f* submachine gun; **Maschinenraum** *m* plant room; (*Naut*) engine room; **Maschinensaal** *m* machine shop; **Maschinenschaden** *m* mechanical fault; **Maschinenschlosser** *m* fitter; **Maschinenschrift** *f* typescript; **Maschinensprache** *f* (*Comput*) machine language
Maschinerie [maʃinə'ri:] *f* (*fig*) machinery
Maschinist, in [maʃi'nɪst(ɪn)] *m(f)* engineer
Maser ['ma:zər] (**-, -n**) *f* grain
Masern *pl* (*Med*) measles *sing*
Maserung *f* grain(ing)
Maske ['maskə] (**-, -n**) *f* mask
Maskenball *m* fancy-dress ball
Maskenbildner, in *m(f)* make-up artist
Maskerade [maskə'ra:də] *f* masquerade
maskieren [mas'ki:rən] *vt* to mask; (*verkleiden*) to dress up ▷ *vr* to disguise o.s., dress up
Maskottchen [mas'kɔtçən] *nt* (lucky) mascot
Maskulinum [masku'li:nʊm] (**-s, Maskulina**) *nt* (*Gram*) masculine noun
Masochist [mazɔ'xɪst] (**-en, -en**) *m* masochist
Maß[1] [ma:s] (**-es, -e**) *nt* measure; (*Mäßigung*) moderation; (*Grad*) degree, extent; **über alle ~en** (*liter*) extremely, beyond measure; **~ halten** = **maßhalten**; **mit zweierlei ~ messen** (*fig*) to operate a double standard; **sich** *dat* **etw nach ~ anfertigen lassen** to have sth made to measure *od* order (*US*); **in besonderem ~e** especially; **das ~ ist voll** (*fig*) that's enough (of that)
Maß[2] (**-, -(e)**) *f* litre (*Brit*) *od* liter (*US*) of beer
maß *etc vb siehe* **messen**
Massage [ma'sa:ʒə] (**-, -n**) *f* massage
Massaker [ma'sa:kər] (**-s, -**) *nt* massacre
Maßanzug *m* made-to-measure suit
Maßarbeit *f* (*fig*) neat piece of work
Masse ['masə] (**-, -n**) *f* mass; **eine ganze ~** (*umg*) a great deal
Maßeinheit *f* unit of measurement
Massen- *zW*: **Massenartikel** *m* mass-produced article; **Massenblatt** *nt* tabloid; **Massengrab** *nt* mass grave; **massenhaft** *adj* masses of; **Massenmedien** *pl* mass media *pl*; **Massenproduktion** *f* mass production; **Massenveranstaltung** *f* mass meeting;

Massenvernichtungswaffen *pl* weapons of mass destruction; **Massenware** *f* mass-produced article; **massenweise** *adv* in huge numbers
Masseur [ma'søːr] *m* masseur
Masseuse [ma'søːzə] *f* masseuse
Maß- *zW*: **maßgebend** *adj* authoritative; **maßgebende Kreise** influential circles; **maßgeblich** *adj* definitive; **maßgeschneidert** *adj* (*Anzug*) made-to-measure, made-to-order (*US*), custom *attrib* (*US*); **maßhalten** *unreg vi* to exercise moderation
massieren [ma'siːrən] *vt* to massage; (*Mil*) to mass
massig ['masɪç] *adj* massive; (*umg*) a massive amount of
mäßig ['mɛːsɪç] *adj* moderate; **mäßigen** ['mɛːsɪgən] *vt* to restrain, moderate; **sein Tempo mäßigen** to slacken one's pace; **Mäßigkeit** *f* moderation
massiv [ma'siːf] *adj* solid; (*fig*) heavy, rough; **~ werden** (*umg*) to turn nasty; **Massiv** (**-s, -e**) *nt* massif
Maß- *zW*: **Maßkrug** *m* tankard; **maßlos** *adj* (*Verschwendung, Essen, Trinken*) excessive, immoderate; (*Enttäuschung, Ärger etc*) extreme; **Maßnahme** (**-, -n**) *f* measure, step; **maßregeln** *vt untr* to reprimand
Maßstab *m* rule, measure; (*fig*) standard; (*Geog*) scale; **als ~ dienen** to serve as a model
maßstabgetreu, **maßstabsgetreu** *adj* (true) to scale
maßvoll *adj* moderate
Mast [mast] (**-(e)s, -e(n)**) *m* mast; (*Elek*) pylon
Mastdarm *m* rectum
mästen ['mɛstən] *vt* to fatten
masturbieren [mastʊr'biːrən] *vi* to masturbate
Material [materi'aːl] (**-s, -ien**) *nt* material(s); **Materialfehler** *m* material defect
Materialismus [materia'lismus] *m* materialism
Materialist, in *m(f)* materialist; **materialistisch** *adj* materialistic
Materialkosten *pl* cost *sing* of materials
Materialprüfung *f* material(s) control
Materie [ma'teːriə] *f* matter, substance
materiell [materi'ɛl] *adj* material
Mathe ['matə] (**-**) *f* (*Sch: umg*) maths (*Brit*), math (*US*)
Mathematik [matema'tiːk] *f* mathematics *sing*; **Mathematiker, in** [mate'maːtɪkər(ɪn)] (**-s, -**) *m(f)* mathematician
mathematisch [mate'maːtɪʃ] *adj* mathematical
Matjeshering ['matjəsheːrɪŋ] (*umg*) *m* salted young herring
Matratze [ma'tratsə] (**-, -n**) *f* mattress
Matrixdrucker *m* dot-matrix printer
Matrixzeichen *nt* matrix character
Matrize [ma'triːtsə] (**-, -n**) *f* matrix; (*zum Abziehen*) stencil
Matrose [ma'troːzə] (**-n, -n**) *m* sailor
Matsch [matʃ] (**-(e)s**) *m* mud; (*Schneematsch*) slush
matschig *adj* muddy; slushy
matt [mat] *adj* weak; (*glanzlos*) dull; (*Phot*) matt; (*Schach*) mate; **jdn ~ setzen** (*lit*) to checkmate sb; *siehe auch* **mattsetzen**; **Matt** (**-s, -s**) *nt* (*Schach*) checkmate
Matte ['matə] (**-, -n**) *f* mat; **auf der ~ stehen** (*am Arbeitsplatz etc*) to be in
Mattigkeit *f* weakness; dullness
Mattscheibe *f* (*TV*) screen; **~ haben** (*umg*) to be not quite with it
mattsetzen *vt* (*fig*) to checkmate
Matura [ma'tuːra] (**-**) (*Österr, Schweiz*) *f* = **Abitur**
Mätzchen ['mɛtsçən] (*umg*) *nt* antics *pl*; **~ machen** to fool around
mau [maʊ] (*umg*) *adj* poor, bad
Mauer ['maʊər] (**-, -n**) *f* wall; **Mauerblümchen** (*umg*) *nt* (*fig*) wallflower
mauern *vi* to build, lay bricks ▷ *vt* to build
Mauer- *zW*: **Mauerschwalbe** *f* swift; **Mauersegler** *m* swift; **Mauerwerk** *nt* brickwork; (*Stein*) masonry
Maul [maʊl] (**-(e)s, Mäuler**) *nt* mouth; **ein loses** *od* **lockeres ~ haben** (*umg: frech sein*) to be an impudent so-and-so; (*: indiskret sein*) to be a blabbermouth; **halts ~!** (*umg*) shut your face! (*!*); **darüber werden sich die Leute das ~ zerreißen** (*umg*) that will start people's tongues wagging; **dem Volk** *od* **den Leuten aufs ~ schauen** (*umg*) to listen to what ordinary people say; **maulen** (*umg*) *vi* to grumble; **Maulesel** *m* mule; **Maulkorb** *m* muzzle; **Maulsperre** *f* lockjaw; **Maultier** *nt* mule; **Maul- und Klauenseuche** *f* (*Tiere*) foot-and-mouth disease
Maulwurf *m* mole
Maulwurfshaufen *m* molehill
Maurer ['maʊrər] (**-s, -**) *m* bricklayer; **pünktlich wie die ~** (*hum*) super-punctual
Mauretanien [maʊrə'taːniən] (**-s**) *nt* Mauritania
Maus [maʊs] (**-, Mäuse**) *f* (*auch Comput*) mouse; **Mäuse** *pl* (*umg: Geld*) bread *sing*, dough *sing*
mauscheln ['maʊʃəln] (*umg*) *vt, vi* (*manipulieren*) to fiddle
mäuschenstill ['mɔʏsçən'ʃtɪl] *adj* very quiet
Mausefalle *f* mousetrap
mausen *vt* (*umg*) to pinch ▷ *vi* to catch mice
mausern *vr* to moult (*Brit*), molt (*US*)
mausetot *adj* stone dead
mausgesteuert *adj* (*Comput*) mouse-driven
Mausklick [maʊsklɪk] *nt* (*Comput*) (mouse) click
Maut [maʊt] (**-, -en**) *f* toll; **Mautsystem** *nt* toll system
max. *abk* (= *maximal*) max.
maximal [maksi'maːl] *adj* maximum
Maxime [ma'ksiːmə] (**-, -n**) *f* maxim
maximieren [maksi'miːrən] *vt* to maximize
Maximierung *f* (*Wirts*) maximization
Maximum ['maksimʊm] (**-s, Maxima**) *nt* maximum
Mayonnaise [majɔ'nɛːzə] (**-, -n**) *f* mayonnaise

Mazedonien [matse'do:niən] (**-s**) *nt* Macedonia
Mäzen [mɛ'tse:n] (**-s, -e**) *m* (*gen*) patron, sponsor
MdB *nt abk* (= *Mitglied des Bundestages*) *member of the Bundestag*, ≈ MP
MdL *nt abk* (= *Mitglied des Landtages*) *member of the Landtag*
m. E. *abk* (= *meines Erachtens*) in my opinion
Mechanik [me'ça:nɪk] *f* mechanics *sing*; (*Getriebe*) mechanics *pl*; **Mechaniker** (**-s, -**) *m* mechanic, engineer
mechanisch *adj* mechanical
Mechanisierung *f* mechanization
Mechanismus [meça'nɪsmʊs] *m* mechanism
meckern ['mɛkərn] *vi* to bleat; (*umg*) to moan
Mecklenburg ['me:klənbʊrk] (**-s**) *nt* Mecklenburg
Mecklenburg-Vorpommern (**-s**) *nt* (state of) Mecklenburg-Vorpommern
Medaille [me'daljə] (**-, -n**) *f* medal
Medaillon [medal'jõ:] (**-s, -s**) *nt* (*Schmuck*) locket
Medien ['me:diən] *pl* media *pl*; **Medienbericht** *m* (*meist pl*) media report; **Medienberichten zufolge** according to reports in the media; **Medienforschung** *f* media research; **Mediengesellschaft** *f* media society; **Medienmogul** *m* media mogul; **medienübergreifend** *adj* cross-media *attrib*; **Medienvielfalt** *f* mixture of media
Medikament [medika'mɛnt] *nt* medicine
Meditation [meditatsi'o:n] *f* meditation
meditieren [medi'ti:rən] *vi* to meditate
Medium ['me:diʊm] *nt* medium
Medizin [medi'tsi:n] (**-, -en**) *f* medicine
Mediziner, in (**-s, -**) *m(f)* doctor; (*Univ*) medic (*umg*)
medizinisch *adj* medical; **~-technische Assistentin** medical assistant
Meer [me:r] (**-(e)s, -e**) *nt* sea; **am ~(e)** by the sea; **ans ~ fahren** to go to the sea(side); **Meerbusen** *m* bay, gulf; **Meerenge** *f* straits *pl*
Meeres- *zW*: **Meeresfrüchte** *pl* seafood; **Meeresklima** *nt* maritime climate; **Meeresspiegel** *m* sea level
Meer- *zW*: **Meerjungfrau** *f* mermaid; **Meerrettich** *m* horseradish; **Meerschweinchen** *nt* guinea pig; **Meerwasser** *nt* sea water
Mega-, mega- [mɛga-] *in zw* mega-; **Megabyte** [mega'baɪt] *nt* megabyte; **Megafon, Megaphon** [mega'fo:n] (**-s, -e**) *nt* megaphone; **Megawatt** [mɛga'vat] *nt* megawatt
Mehl [m'e:l] (**-(e)s, -e**) *nt* flour
mehlig *adj* floury
Mehlschwitze *f* (*Koch*) roux
mehr [me:r] *adv* more; **nie ~** never again, nevermore (*liter*); **es war niemand ~ da** there was no one left; **nicht ~ lange** not much longer; **Mehraufwand** *m* additional expenditure; **Mehrbelastung** *f* excess load; (*fig*) additional burden; **mehrdeutig** *adj* ambiguous
mehrere *indef pron* several; (*verschiedene*) various; **~s** several things
mehrfach *adj* multiple; (*wiederholt*) repeated
Mehrheit *f* majority
Mehrheitsprinzip *nt* principle of majority rule
Mehrheitswahlrecht *nt* first-past-the-post voting system
mehr- *zW*: **mehrjährig** *adj attrib* of several years; **Mehrkosten** *pl* additional costs *pl*; **mehrmalig** *adj* repeated; **mehrmals** *adv* repeatedly; **Mehrparteiensystem** *nt* multi-party system; **Mehrplatzsystem** *nt* (*Comput*) multi-user system; **Mehrprogrammbetrieb** *m* (*Comput*) multiprogramming; **mehrsprachig** *adj* multilingual; **mehrstimmig** *adj* for several voices; **mehrstimmig singen** to harmonize; **Mehrwegflasche** *f* returnable bottle; **Mehrwertsteuer** *f* value added tax, VAT; **Mehrzahl** *f* majority; (*Gram*) plural
Mehrzweck- *in zw* multipurpose
meiden ['maɪdən] *unreg vt* to avoid
Meile ['maɪlə] (**-, -n**) *f* mile; **das riecht man drei ~n gegen den Wind** (*umg*) you can smell that a mile off
Meilenstein *m* milestone
meilenweit *adj* for miles
mein [maɪn] *pron* my
meine, r, s *poss pron* mine
Meineid ['maɪn|aɪt] *m* perjury
meinen ['maɪnən] *vt* to think; (*sagen*) to say; (*sagen wollen*) to mean ▷ *vi* to think; **wie Sie ~!** as you wish; **damit bin ich gemeint** that refers to me; **das will ich ~** I should think so
meiner *gen von* **ich** ▷ *pron* of me
meinerseits *adv* for my part
meinesgleichen ['maɪnəs'glaɪçən] *pron* people like me
meinetwegen ['maɪnət've:gən] *adv* (*für mich*) for my sake; (*wegen mir*) on my account; (*von mir aus*) as far as I'm concerned; (*ich habe nichts dagegen*) I don't care *od* mind
meinetwillen ['maɪnət'vɪlən] *adv*: **um ~ = meinetwegen**
meinige *pron*: **der/die/das ~** *od* **Meinige** mine
meins [maɪns] *pron* mine
Meinung ['maɪnʊŋ] *f* opinion; **meiner ~ nach** in my opinion; **einer ~ sein** to think the same; **jdm die ~ sagen** to give sb a piece of one's mind
Meinungs- *zW*: **Meinungsaustausch** *m* exchange of views; **Meinungsbildungsprozess** *f* opinion-forming process; **Meinungsforscher, in** *m(f)* pollster; **Meinungsforschungsinstitut** *nt* opinion research institute; **Meinungsfreiheit** *f* freedom of speech; **Meinungsumfrage** *f* opinion poll; **Meinungsverschiedenheit** *f* difference of opinion
Meise ['maɪzə] (**-, -n**) *f* tit(mouse); **eine ~ haben** (*umg*) to be crackers
Meißel ['maɪsəl] (**-s, -**) *m* chisel
meißeln *vt* to chisel
meist [maɪst] *adj* most ▷ *adv* mostly;

Meistbegünstigungsklausel *f* (*Comm*) most-favoured-nation clause; **meistbietend** *adj*: **meistbietend versteigern** to sell to the highest bidder

meiste, r, s *superl von* **viel**

meistens *adv* mostly

Meister ['maɪstər] (**-s, -**) *m* master; (*Sport*) champion; **seinen ~ machen** to take one's master craftsman's diploma; **es ist noch kein ~ vom Himmel gefallen** (*Sprichwort*) no one is born an expert; **Meisterbrief** *m* master craftsman's diploma; **meisterhaft** *adj* masterly

Meisterin *f* (*auf einem Gebiet*) master, expert; (*Sport*) (woman) champion

meistern *vt* to master; **sein Leben ~** to come to grips with one's life

Meister- *zW*: **Meisterschaft** *f* mastery; (*Sport*) championship; **Meisterstück** *nt* masterpiece; **Meisterwerk** *nt* masterpiece

meistgekauft *adj attrib* best-selling

Mekka ['mɛka] (**-s, -s**) *nt* (*Geog, fig*) Mecca

Melancholie [melaŋko'li:] *f* melancholy

melancholisch [melaŋ'ko:lɪʃ] *adj* melancholy

Meldebehörde *f* registration authorities *pl*

Meldefrist *f* registration period

melden *vt* to report; (*registrieren*) to register ▹ *vr* to report; to register; (*Sch*) to put one's hand up; (*freiwillig*) to volunteer; (*auf etw, am Telefon*) to answer; **nichts zu ~ haben** (*umg*) to have no say; **wen darf ich ~?** who shall I say (is here)?; **sich ~ bei** to report to; to register with; **sich auf eine Anzeige ~** to answer an advertisement; **es meldet sich niemand** there's no answer; **sich zu Wort ~** to ask to speak

Meldepflicht *f* obligation to register with the police

Meldestelle *f* registration office

Meldung ['mɛldʊŋ] *f* announcement; (*Bericht*) report

meliert [me'li:rt] *adj* mottled, speckled

melken ['mɛlkən] *unreg vt* to milk

Melodie [melo'di:] *f* melody, tune

melodisch [me'lo:dɪʃ] *adj* melodious, tuneful

melodramatisch [melodra'ma:tɪʃ] *adj* (*auch fig*) melodramatic

Melone [me'lo:nə] (**-, -n**) *f* melon; (*Hut*) bowler (hat)

Membran [mem'bra:n] (**-, -en**) *f* (*Tech*) diaphragm; (*Anat*) membrane

Memme ['mɛmə] (**-, -n**) (*umg*) *f* cissy, yellow-belly

Memoiren [memo'a:rən] *pl* memoirs *pl*

Menge ['mɛŋə] (**-, -n**) *f* quantity; (*Menschenmenge*) crowd; (*große Anzahl*) lot (of); **jede ~** (*umg*) masses *pl*, loads *pl*

mengen *vt* to mix ▹ *vr*: **sich ~ in** *+akk* to meddle with

Mengen- *zW*: **Mengeneinkauf** *m* bulk buying; **Mengenlehre** *f* (*Math*) set theory; **Mengenrabatt** *m* bulk discount

Menorca [me'nɔrka] (**-s**) *nt* Menorca

Mensa ['mɛnza] (**-, -s** *od* **Mensen**) *f* (*Univ*) refectory (*Brit*), commons (*US*)

Mensch [mɛnʃ] (**-en, -en**) *m* human being, man; (*Person*) person; **kein ~** nobody; **ich bin auch nur ein ~!** I'm only human; **~ ärgere dich nicht** *nt* (*Spiel*) ludo

Menschen- *zW*: **Menschenalter** *nt* generation; **Menschenfeind** *m* misanthrope; **menschenfreundlich** *adj* philanthropical; **Menschengedenken** *nt*: **der kälteste Winter seit Menschengedenken** the coldest winter in living memory; **Menschenhandel** *m* slave trade; (*Jur*) trafficking in human beings; **Menschenkenner** *m* judge of human nature; **Menschenkenntnis** *f* knowledge of human nature; **menschenleer** *adj* deserted; **Menschenliebe** *f* philanthropy; **Menschenmasse** *f* crowd (of people); **Menschenmenge** *f* crowd (of people); **menschenmöglich** *adj* humanly possible; **Menschenrechte** *pl* human rights *pl*; **menschenscheu** *adj* shy; **Menschenschlag** (*umg*) *m* kind of people; **Menschenseele** *f*: **keine Menschenseele** (*fig*) not a soul

Menschenskind *interj* good heavens!

Menschen- *zW*: **menschenunwürdig** *adj* degrading; **Menschenverachtung** *f* contempt for human beings *od* of mankind; **Menschenverstand** *m*: **gesunder Menschenverstand** common sense; **Menschenwürde** *f* human dignity; **menschenwürdig** *adj* (*Behandlung*) humane; (*Unterkunft*) fit for human habitation

Mensch- *zW*: **Menschheit** *f* humanity, mankind; **menschlich** *adj* human; (*human*) humane; **Menschlichkeit** *f* humanity

Menstruation [mɛnstruatsi'o:n] *f* menstruation

Mentalität [mɛntali'tɛ:t] *f* mentality

Menü [me'ny:] (**-s, -s**) *nt* (*auch Comput*) menu; **Menüführung** *f* (*Comput*) menu assistance; **menügesteuert** *adj* (*Comput*) menu-driven

Merkblatt *nt* instruction sheet *od* leaflet

merken ['mɛrkən] *vt* to notice; **sich** *dat* **etw ~** to remember sth; **sich** *dat* **eine Autonummer ~** to make a (mental) note of a licence (*Brit*) *od* license (*US*) number

merklich *adj* noticeable

Merkmal *nt* sign, characteristic

merkwürdig *adj* odd

meschugge [me'ʃʊgə] (*umg*) *adj* nuts, meshuga (*US*)

Mess- *zW*: **Messband** *nt* tape measure; **messbar** *adj* measurable; **Messbecher** *m* measuring cup

Messbuch *nt* missal

Messdiener *m* (*Rel*) server, acolyte (*form*)

Messe ['mɛsə] (**-, -n**) *f* fair; (*Eccl*) mass; (*Mil*) mess; **auf der ~** at the fair; **Messegelände** *nt* exhibition centre (*Brit*) *od* center (*US*)

messen *unreg vt* to measure ▹ *vr* to compete

Messer (**-s, -**) *nt* knife; **auf des ~s Schneide stehen** (*fig*) to hang in the balance; **jdm**

ins offene ~ laufen (*fig*) to walk into a trap; **messerscharf** *adj* (*fig*): **messerscharf schließen** to conclude with incredible logic (*ironisch*); **Messerspitze** *f* knife point; (*in Rezept*) pinch; **Messerstecherei** *f* knife fight
Messestadt *f* (town with an) exhibition centre (*Brit*) *od* center (*US*)
Messestand *m* exhibition stand
Messgerät *nt* measuring device, gauge
Messgewand *nt* chasuble
Messing ['mɛsɪŋ] (**-s**) *nt* brass
Messstab *m* (*Aut: Ölmessstab etc*) dipstick
Messung *f* (*das Messen*) measuring; (*von Blutdruck*) taking; (*Messergebnis*) measurement
Messwert *m* measurement; (*Ableseergebnis*) reading
Metall [me'tal] (**-s, -e**) *nt* metal; **die ~ verarbeitende Industrie** the metal-processing industry; **metallen** *adj* metallic; **metallisch** *adj* metallic
Metallurgie [metalʊr'giː] *f* metallurgy
Metapher [me'tafər] (**-, -n**) *f* metaphor
metaphorisch [meta'foːrɪʃ] *adj* metaphorical
Metaphysik [metafy'ziːk] *f* metaphysics *sing*
Metastase [meta'staːzə] (**-, -n**) *f* (*Med*) secondary growth
Meteor [mete'oːr] (**-s, -e**) *m* meteor
Meteorologe [meteoro'loːgə] (**-n, -n**) *m* meteorologist
Meter ['meːtər] (**-s, -**) *m od nt* metre (*Brit*), meter (*US*); **in 500 ~ Höhe** at a height of 500 metres; **Metermaß** *nt* tape measure; **Meterware** *f* (*Textil*) piece goods
Methode [me'toːdə] (**-, -n**) *f* method
Methodik [me'toːdɪk] *f* methodology
methodisch [me'toːdɪʃ] *adj* methodical
Metier [meti'eː] (**-s, -s**) *nt* (*hum*) job, profession
metrisch ['meːtrɪʃ] *adj* metric, metrical
Metropole [metro'poːlə] (**-, -n**) *f* metropolis
Mettwurst ['mɛtvʊrst] *f* (smoked) sausage
Metzger ['mɛtsgər] (**-s, -**) *m* butcher
Metzgerei [mɛtsgə'raɪ] *f* butcher's (shop)
Meuchelmord ['mɔʏçəlmɔrt] *m* assassination
Meute ['mɔʏtə] (**-, -n**) *f* pack
Meuterei [mɔʏtə'raɪ] *f* mutiny
meutern *vi* to mutiny
Mexikaner, in [mɛksi'kaːnər(ɪn)] (**-s, -**) *m(f)* Mexican
mexikanisch *adj* Mexican
Mexiko ['mɛksiko] (**-s**) *nt* Mexico
MEZ *abk* (= *mitteleuropäische Zeit*) C.E.T.
MFG *abk* = **Mitfahrgelegenheit**
MfG *abk* (= *mit freundlichen Grüßen*) (with) best wishes
MG (**-(s), -(s)**) *nt abk* = **Maschinengewehr**
mg *abk* (= *Milligramm*) mg
mhd. *abk* (= *mittelhochdeutsch*) MHG
MHz *abk* (= *Megahertz*) MHz
Mi. *abk* = **Mittwoch**
miauen [mi'aʊən] *vi* to miaow
mich [mɪç] *akk von* **ich** ▷ *pron* me; (*reflexiv*) myself
mickerig ['mɪkərɪç], **mickrig** ['mɪkrɪç] (*umg*) *adj* pathetic; (*altes Männchen*) puny
mied *etc* [miːt] *vb siehe* **meiden**
Miederwaren ['miːdərvaːrən] *pl* corsetry *sing*
Mief [miːf] (**-s**) (*umg*) *m* fug; (*muffig*) stale air; (*Gestank*) stink, pong (*Brit*)
miefig (*umg*) *adj* smelly, pongy (*Brit*)
Miene ['miːnə] (**-, -n**) *f* look, expression; **gute ~ zum bösen Spiel machen** to grin and bear it
Mienenspiel *nt* facial expressions *pl*
mies [miːs] (*umg*) *adj* lousy
Miese ['miːzə] (*umg*) *pl*: **in den ~n sein** to be in the red
Miesmacher, in (*umg*) *m(f)* killjoy
Mietauto *nt* hired car (*Brit*), rental car (*US*)
Miete ['miːtə] (**-, -n**) *f* rent; **zur ~ wohnen** to live in rented accommodation *od* accommodations (*US*)
mieten *vt* to rent; (*Auto*) to hire (*Brit*), rent
Mieter, in (**-s, -**) *m(f)* tenant; **Mieterschutz** *m* rent control
Mietshaus *nt* tenement, block of flats (*Brit*) *od* apartments (*US*)
Miet- *zW*: **Mietverhältnis** *nt* tenancy; **Mietvertrag** *m* tenancy agreement; **Mietwagen** *m* = **Mietauto**; **Mietwucher** *m* the charging of exorbitant rent(s)
Mieze ['miːtsə] (**-, -n**) (*umg*) *f* (*Katze*) pussy; (*Mädchen*) chick, bird (*Brit*)
Migräne [mi'grɛːnə] (**-, -n**) *f* migraine
migrieren [mi'griːrən] *vi* to migrate
Mikado [mi'kaːdo] (**-s**) *nt* (*Spiel*) pick-a-stick
Mikro- ['miːkro] *in zW* micro-
Mikrobe [mi'kroːbə] (**-, -n**) *f* microbe
Mikro- *zW*: **Mikrochip** *m* microchip; **Mikrocomputer** *m* microcomputer; **Mikrofiche** *m od nt* microfiche; **Mikrofilm** *m* microfilm
Mikrofon [mikro'foːn] (**-s, e**) *nt* microphone
Mikroökonomie *f* microeconomics *pl*
Mikrophon [mikro'foːn] (**-s, -e**) *nt* microphone
Mikroprozessor (**-s, -oren**) *m* microprocessor
Mikroskop [mikro'skoːp] (**-s, -e**) *nt* microscope; **mikroskopisch** *adj* microscopic
Mikrowelle ['miːkrovɛlə] *f* microwave
Mikrowellenherd *m* microwave (oven)
Milbe ['mɪlbə] (**-, -n**) *f* mite
Milch [mɪlç] (**-**) *f* milk; (*Fischmilch*) milt, roe; **Milchdrüse** *f* mammary gland; **Milchglas** *nt* frosted glass
milchig *adj* milky
Milch- *zW*: **Milchkaffee** *m* white coffee; **Milchmixgetränk** *nt* milk shake; **Milchpulver** *nt* powdered milk; **Milchstraße** *f* Milky Way; **Milchtüte** *f* milk carton; **Milchzahn** *m* milk tooth
mild [mɪlt] *adj* mild; (*Richter*) lenient; (*freundlich*) kind, charitable
Milde ['mɪldə] (**-, -n**) *f* mildness; leniency
mildern *vt* to mitigate, soften; (*Schmerz*) to alleviate; **~de Umstände** extenuating circumstances
Milieu [mili'øː] (**-s, -s**) *nt* background, environment; **milieugeschädigt** *adj*

maladjusted
militant [mili'tant] *adj* militant
Militär [mili'tɛːr] (**-s**) *nt* military, army; **Militärdienst** *m* military service; **Militäreinsatz** *m* use of troops; (*Kampfhandlung*) military action; **Militärgericht** *nt* military court; **militärisch** *adj* military
Militarismus [milita'rɪsmʊs] *m* militarism
militaristisch *adj* militaristic
Militärpflicht *f* (compulsory) military service
Mill. *abk* (= *Million(en)*) m
Milli- *in zw* milli-
Milliardär, in [mɪliar'dɛːr(ɪn)] (**-s, -e**) *m(f)* multimillionaire
Milliarde [mɪli'ardə] (**-, -n**) *f* milliard, billion (*bes US*); **Milliardengrab** *nt* (*fig*) money burner, white elephant
Millimeter *m* millimetre (*Brit*), millimeter (*US*); **Millimeterpapier** *nt* graph paper
Million [mɪli'oːn] (**-, -en**) *f* million
Millionär, in [mɪlio'nɛːr(ɪn)] (**-s, -e**) *m(f)* millionaire
millionenschwer (*umg*) *adj* worth a few million
Milz [mɪlts] (**-, -en**) *f* spleen
Mimik ['miːmɪk] *f* mime
Mimose [mi'moːzə] (**-, -n**) *f* mimosa; (*fig*) sensitive person
minder ['mɪndər] *adj* inferior ▷ *adv* less; **minderbegabt** *adj* less able; **minderbemittelt** *adj*: **geistig minderbemittelt** (*ironisch*) intellectually challenged
Minderheit *f* minority
Minderheitsbeteiligung *f* (*Aktien*) minority interest
Minderheitsregierung *f* minority government
minderjährig *adj* minor; **Minderjährige, r** *f(m)* minor; **Minderjährigkeit** *f* minority
mindern *vt, vr* to decrease, diminish
minderqualifiziert *adj* less qualified; **Minderqualifizierte, r** *f(m)* less qualified person
Minderung *f* decrease
minder- *zW*: **minderwertig** *adj* inferior; **Minderwertigkeitsgefühl** *nt* inferiority complex; **Minderwertigkeitskomplex** (**-es, -e**) *m* inferiority complex
Mindestalter *nt* minimum age
Mindestbetrag *m* minimum amount
mindeste, r, s *adj* least
mindestens *adv* at least
Mindest- *zW*: **Mindestlohn** *m* minimum wage; **Mindestmaß** *nt* minimum; **Mindeststand** *m* (*Comm*) minimum stock; **Mindeststudiendauer** *nt* (*Österr*) minimum length of study; **Mindestumtausch** *m* minimum obligatory exchange
Mine ['miːnə] (**-, -n**) *f* mine; (*Bleistiftmine*) lead; (*Kugelschreibermine*) refill
Minenfeld *nt* minefield
Minensuchboot *nt* minesweeper
Mineral [mine'raːl] (**-s, -e** *od* **-ien**) *nt* mineral; **mineralisch** *adj* mineral; **Mineralölsteuer** *f* tax on oil and petrol (*Brit*) *od* gasoline (*US*); **Mineralwasser** *nt* mineral water
Miniatur [minia'tuːr] *f* miniature
Minigolf ['mɪnigɔlf] *nt* miniature golf
minimal [mini'maːl] *adj* minimal
Minimum ['miːnimʊm] (**-s, Minima**) *nt* minimum
Minirock ['mɪnirɔk] *m* miniskirt
Minister, in [mi'nɪstər(ɪn)] (**-s, -**) *m(f)* (*Pol*) minister
ministeriell [minɪsteri'ɛl] *adj* ministerial
Ministerium [minɪs'teːriʊm] *nt* ministry
Ministerpräsident, in *m(f)* prime minister
Minna ['mɪna] *f*: **jdn zur ~ machen** (*umg*) to give sb a piece of one's mind
minus ['miːnʊs] *adv* minus; **Minus** (**-, -**) *nt* deficit; **Minuspol** *m* negative pole; **Minuszeichen** *nt* minus sign
Minute [mi'nuːtə] (**-, -n**) *f* minute; **auf die ~ (genau** *od* **pünktlich)** (right) on the dot
Minutenzeiger *m* minute hand
Mio. *abk* (= *Million(en)*) m
mir [miːr] *dat von* **ich** ▷ *pron* (to) me; **von ~ aus!** I don't mind; **wie du ~, so ich dir** (*Sprichwort*) tit for tat (*umg*); (*als Drohung*) I'll get my own back; **~ nichts, dir nichts** just like that
Mirabelle [mira'bɛlə] *f* mirabelle, *small yellow plum*
Misch- *zW*: **Mischbatterie** *f* mixer tap; **Mischbrot** *nt bread made from more than one kind of flour*; **Mischehe** *f* mixed marriage
mischen *vt* to mix; (*Comput: Datei, Text*) to merge; (*Karten*) to shuffle ▷ *vi* (*Karten*) to shuffle
Misch- *zW*: **Mischfinanzierung** *m* (*Wirts*) mixed financing; **Mischkonzern** *m* conglomerate; **Mischling** *m* half-caste; **Mischmasch** (*umg*) *m* hotchpotch; (*Essen*) concoction; **Mischpult** *nt* (*Rundf, TV*) mixing panel
Mischung *f* mixture
Mischwald *m* mixed (deciduous and coniferous) woodland
miserabel [mizə'raːbəl] (*umg*) *adj* lousy; (*Gesundheit*) wretched; (*Benehmen*) dreadful
Misere [mi'zeːrə] (**-, -n**) *f* (*von Leuten, Wirtschaft etc*) plight; (*von Hunger, Krieg etc*) misery, miseries *pl*
Miss- *zW*: **missachten** *vt untr* to disregard; **Missachtung** *f* disregard; **Missbehagen** *nt* uneasiness; (*Missfallen*) discontent; **Missbildung** *f* deformity; **missbilligen** *vt untr* to disapprove of; **Missbilligung** *f* disapproval; **Missbrauch** *m* abuse; (*falscher Gebrauch*) misuse; **missbrauchen** *vt untr* to abuse; to misuse; (*vergewaltigen*) to assault; **jdn zu** *od* **für etw missbrauchen** to use sb for *od* to do sth; **missdeuten** *vt untr* to misinterpret
missen *vt* to do without; (*Erfahrung*) to miss
Misserfolg *m* failure
Missernte *f* crop failure
Missetat ['mɪsətaːt] *f* misdeed
Missetäter *m* criminal; (*umg*) scoundrel

Miss- *zW*: **missfallen** *unreg vi untr*: **jdm missfallen** to displease sb; **Missfallen (-s)** *nt* displeasure; **Missgeburt** *f* freak; (*fig*) failure; **Missgeschick** *nt* misfortune; **missglücken** *vi untr* to fail; **jdm missglückt etw** sb does not succeed with sth; **missgönnen** *vt untr*: **jdm etw missgönnen** to (be)grudge sb sth; **Missgriff** *m* mistake; **Missgunst** *f* envy; **missgünstig** *adj* envious; **misshandeln** *vt untr* to ill-treat; **Misshandlung** *f* ill-treatment; **Misshelligkeit** *f*: **Misshelligkeiten haben** to be at variance

Mission [mɪsi'o:n] *f* mission

Missionar, in [mɪsio'na:r(ɪn)] *m(f)* missionary

Missklang *m* discord

Misskredit *m* discredit

misslang *etc* [mɪs'laŋ] *vb siehe* **misslingen**

missliebig *adj* unpopular

misslingen [mɪs'lɪŋən] *unreg vi untr* to fail; **Misslingen (-s)** *nt* failure

misslungen [mɪs'lʊŋən] *pp von* **misslingen**

Miss- *zW*: **Missmut** *m* bad temper; **missmutig** *adj* cross; **missraten** *unreg vi untr* to turn out badly ▷ *adj* ill-bred; **Missstand** *m* deplorable state of affairs; **Missstimmung** *f* discord; (*Missmut*) ill feeling

misst *vb siehe* **messen**

Miss- *zW*: **misstrauen** *vi untr* to mistrust; **Misstrauen (-s)** *nt*: **Misstrauen (gegenüber)** distrust (of), suspicion (of); **Misstrauensantrag** *m* (*Pol*) motion of no confidence; **Misstrauensvotum** *nt* (*Pol*) vote of no confidence; **misstrauisch** *adj* distrustful, suspicious; **Missverhältnis** *nt* disproportion; **missverständlich** *adj* unclear; **Missverständnis** *nt* misunderstanding; **missverstehen** *unreg vt untr* to misunderstand

Misswahl ['mɪsva:l] *f* beauty contest

Misswirtschaft *f* mismanagement

Mist [mɪst] **(-(e)s)** *m* dung; (*umg*) rubbish; **~!** (*umg*) blast!; **das ist nicht auf seinem ~ gewachsen** (*umg*) he didn't think that up himself

Mistel (-, -n) *f* mistletoe

Mist- *zW*: **Mistgabel** *f* pitchfork (*used for shifting manure*); **Misthaufen** *m* dungheap; **Miststück** (*umg!*) *nt*, **Mistvieh** (*umg!*) *nt* (*Mann*) bastard (*!*); (*Frau*) bitch (*!*)

mit [mɪt] *präp +dat* with; (*mittels*) by ▷ *adv* along, too; **~ der Bahn** by train; **~ dem nächsten Flugzeug/Bus kommen** to come on the next plane/bus; **~ Bleistift schreiben** to write in pencil; **~ Verlust** at a loss; **er ist ~ der Beste in der Gruppe** he is among the best in the group; **wie wärs ~ einem Bier?** (*umg*) how about a beer?; **~ 10 Jahren** at the age of 10; **wollen Sie ~?** do you want to come along?

Mitarbeit ['mit|arbaɪt] *f* cooperation; **mitarbeiten** *vi*: **mitarbeiten (an** *+dat***)** to cooperate (on), collaborate (on)

Mitarbeiter, in *m(f)* (*an Projekt*) collaborator; (*Kollege*) colleague; (*Angestellter*) member of staff ▷ *pl* staff; **Mitarbeiterstab** *m* staff

mit- *zW*: **mitbekommen** *unreg vt* to get *od* be given; (*umg: verstehen*) to get; **mitbestimmen** *vi*: **(bei etw) mitbestimmen** to have a say (in sth) ▷ *vt* to have an influence on; **Mitbestimmung** *f* participation in decision-making; (*Pol*) determination; **mitbringen** *unreg vt* to bring along; **Mitbringsel** ['mɪtbrɪŋzəl] **(-s, -)** *nt* (*Geschenk*) small present; (*Andenken*) souvenir; **Mitbürger, in** *m(f)* fellow citizen; **mitdenken** *unreg vi* to follow; **du hast ja mitgedacht!** good thinking!; **mitdürfen** *unreg vi*: **wir durften nicht mit** we weren't allowed to go along; **Miteigentümer** *m* joint owner

miteinander [mɪt|aɪ'nandər] *adv* together, with one another

miterleben *vt* to see, witness

Mitesser ['mɪt|ɛsər] **(-s, -)** *m* blackhead

mit- *zW*: **mitfahren** *unreg vi*: **(mit jdm) mitfahren** to go (with sb); (*auf Reise auch*) to go *od* travel (with sb); **Mitfahrerzentrale** *f* agency for arranging lifts; **Mitfahrgelegenheit** *f* lift; **mitfühlen** *vi*: **mit jdm/etw mitfühlen** to sympathize with sb/sth; **mitfühlend** *adj* sympathetic; **mitführen** *vt* (*Papiere, Ware etc*) to carry (with one); (*Fluss*) to carry along; **mitgeben** *unreg vt* to give; **Mitgefühl** *nt* sympathy; **mitgehen** *unreg vi* to go *od* come along; **etw mitgehen lassen** (*umg*) to pinch sth; **mitgenommen** *adj* done in, in a bad way; **Mitgift** *f* dowry

Mitglied ['mɪtgli:t] *nt* member

Mitgliedsbeitrag *m* membership fee, subscription

Mitgliedschaft *f* membership

mit- *zW*: **mithaben** *unreg vt*: **etw mithaben** to have sth (with one); **mithalten** *unreg vi* to keep up; **mithelfen** *vi unreg* to help, lend a hand; **bei etw mithelfen** to help with sth; **Mithilfe** *f* help, assistance; **mithören** *vt* to listen in to; **mitkommen** *unreg vi* to come along; (*verstehen*) to keep up, follow; **Mitläufer** *m* hanger-on; (*Pol*) fellow traveller

Mitleid *nt* sympathy; (*Erbarmen*) compassion

Mitleidenschaft *f*: **in ~ ziehen** to affect

mitleidig *adj* sympathetic

mitleidslos *adj* pitiless, merciless

mit- *zW*: **mitmachen** *vt* to join in, take part in; (*umg: einverstanden sein*): **da macht mein Chef nicht mit** my boss won't go along with that; **Mitmensch** *m* fellow man; **mitmischen** (*umg*) *vi* (*sich beteiligen*): **mitmischen (in** *+dat od* **bei)** to be involved (in); (*sich einmischen*) to interfere (in); **mitnehmen** *unreg vt* to take along *od* away; (*anstrengen*) to wear out, exhaust; **mitgenommen aussehen** to look the worse for wear; **mitreden** *vi* (*Meinung äußern*): **(bei etw) mitreden** to join in (sth); (*mitbestimmen*) to have a say (in sth) ▷ *vt*: **Sie haben hier nichts mitzureden** this is none of your concern; **mitreißen** *vt unreg* to sweep away; (*fig: begeistern*) to carry away; **mitreißend** *adj* (*Rhythmus*) infectious; (*Reden*) rousing; (*Film,*

Fußballspiel) thrilling, exciting
mitsamt [mɪt'zamt] *präp +dat* together with
mitschneiden *vt unreg* to record
Mitschnitt ['mɪtʃnɪt] (**-(e)s, -e**) *m* recording
mitschreiben *unreg vt* to write *od* take down ▷ *vi* to take notes
Mitschuld *f* complicity
mitschuldig *adj*: **~ (an** *+dat***)** implicated (in); (*an Unfall*) partly responsible (for)
Mitschuldige, r *f(m)* accomplice
mit- *zW*: **Mitschüler, in** *m(f)* schoolmate; **mitspielen** *vi* to join in, take part; **er hat ihr übel** *od* **hart mitgespielt** (*Schaden zufügen*) he has treated her badly; **Mitspieler, in** *m(f)* partner; **Mitspracherecht** *nt* voice, say
Mittag ['mɪta:k] (**-(e)s, -e**) *m* midday, noon, lunchtime; **morgen ~** tomorrow at lunchtime *od* noon; **~ machen** to take one's lunch hour; **(zu) ~ essen** to have lunch; **Mittagessen** *nt* lunch, dinner
mittags *adv* at lunchtime *od* noon
Mittags- *zW*: **Mittagspause** *f* lunch break; **Mittagsruhe** *f* period of quiet (after lunch); (*in Geschäft*) midday closing; **Mittagsschlaf** *m* early afternoon nap, siesta; **Mittagszeit** *f*: **während** *od* **in der Mittagszeit** at lunchtime
Mittäter, in ['mɪttɛ:tər(ɪn)] *m(f)* accomplice
Mitte ['mɪtə] (**-, -n**) *f* middle; **aus unserer ~** from our midst
mitteilen ['mɪttaɪlən] *vt*: **jdm etw ~** to inform sb of sth, communicate sth to sb ▷ *vr*: **sich (jdm) ~** to communicate (with sb)
mitteilsam *adj* communicative
Mitteilung *f* communication; **jdm (eine) ~ von etw machen** (*form*) to inform sb of sth; (*bekannt geben*) to announce sth to sb
Mitteilungsbedürfnis *nt* need to talk to other people
Mittel ['mɪtəl] (**-s, -**) *nt* means; (*Methode*) method; (*Math*) average; (*Med*) medicine; **kein ~ unversucht lassen** to try everything; **als letztes ~** as a last resort; **ein ~ zum Zweck** a means to an end; **Mittelalter** *nt* Middle Ages *pl*; **mittelalterlich** *adj* medieval; **Mittelamerika** *nt* Central America (and the Caribbean); **mittelamerikanisch** *adj* Central American; **mittelbar** *adj* indirect; **Mittelding** *nt* (*Mischung*) cross; **Mitteleuropa** *nt* Central Europe; **Mitteleuropäer, in** *m(f)* Central European; **mitteleuropäisch** *adj* Central European; **mittelfristig** *adj* (*Finanzplanung, Kredite*) medium-term; **Mittelgebirge** *nt* low mountain range; **mittelgroß** *adj* medium-sized; **mittellos** *adj* without means; **Mittelmaß** *nt*: **das (gesunde) Mittelmaß** the happy medium; **mittelmäßig** *adj* mediocre, middling; **Mittelmäßigkeit** *f* mediocrity; **Mittelmeer** *nt* Mediterranean (Sea); **mittelprächtig** *adj* not bad; **Mittelpunkt** *m* centre (*Brit*), center (*US*); **im Mittelpunkt stehen** to be centre-stage
mittels *präp +gen* by means of
Mittelschicht *f* middle class
Mittelsmann (**-(e)s**, *pl* **Mittelsmänner** *od* **Mittelsleute**) *m* intermediary
Mittel- *zW*: **Mittelstand** *m* middle class; **Mittelstreckenrakete** *f* medium-range missile; **Mittelstreifen** *m* central reservation (*Brit*), median strip (*US*); **Mittelstufe** *f* (*Sch*) middle school (*Brit*), junior high (*US*); **Mittelstürmer** *m* centre forward; **Mittelweg** *m* middle course; **Mittelwelle** *f* (*Rundf*) medium wave; **Mittelwert** *m* average value, mean
mitten ['mɪtən] *adv* in the middle; **~ auf der Straße/in der Nacht** in the middle of the street/night; **mittendrin** *adv* (right) in the middle of it; **mittendurch** *adv* (right) through the middle
Mitternacht ['mɪtərnaxt] *f* midnight
mittlere, r, s ['mɪtlərə(r, s)] *adj* middle; (*durchschnittlich*) medium, average; **der M~ Osten** the Middle East; **~s Management** middle management; **~ Reife**; *see culture note*

MITTLERE REIFE

The *mittlere Reife* is the standard certificate achieved at a *Realschule* on successful completion of 6 years' education there. If a pupil at a *Realschule* attains good results in several subjects he or she is allowed to enter the 11th class of a *Gymnasium* to study for the *Abitur*.

mittlerweile ['mɪtlər'vaɪlə] *adv* meanwhile
Mittwoch ['mɪtvɔx] (**-(e)s, -e**) *m* Wednesday; *siehe auch* **Dienstag**
mittwochs *adv* on Wednesdays
mitunter [mɪt'|ʊntər] *adv* occasionally, sometimes
mit- *zW*: **mitverantwortlich** *adj* also responsible; **mitverdienen** *vi* to (go out to) work as well; **Mitverfasser** *m* co-author; **Mitverschulden** *nt* contributory negligence; **mitwirken** *vi*: **(bei etw) mitwirken** to contribute (to sth); (*Theat*) to take part (in sth); **Mitwirkende, r** *f(m)*: **die Mitwirkenden** (*Theat*) the cast; **Mitwirkung** *f* contribution; participation; **unter Mitwirkung von** with the help of; **Mitwisser** (**-s, -**) *m*: **Mitwisser (einer Sache** *gen***) sein** to be in the know (about sth); **jdn zum Mitwisser machen** to tell sb (all) about it
Mixer ['mɪksər] (**-s, -**) *m* (*Barmixer*) cocktail waiter; (*Küchenmixer*) blender; (*Rührmaschine, Rundf, TV*) mixer
ml *abk* (= *Milliliter*) ml
mm *abk* (= *Millimeter*) mm
MMS® *m* (= *Multimedia Messaging Service*) MMS
Mnemonik [mne'mo:nɪk] *f* mnemonic
Mo. *abk* = **Montag**
mobben ['mɔbən] *vt* to bully (at work)
Mobbing ['mɔbɪŋ] (**-s**) *nt* workplace bullying
Möbel ['mø:bəl] (**-s, -**) *nt* (piece of) furniture;

Möbelpacker *m* removal man (*Brit*), (furniture) mover (*US*); **Möbelwagen** *m* furniture *od* removal van (*Brit*), moving van (*US*)
mobil [mo'bi:l] *adj* mobile; (*Mil*) mobilized
Mobilfunk *m* cellular telephone service
Mobiliar [mobili'a:r] (**-s, -e**) *nt* movable assets *pl*
mobilisieren [mobili'zi:rən] *vt* (*Mil*) to mobilize
Mobilmachung *f* mobilization
Mobiltelefon *nt* (*Telec*) mobile phone
möbl. *abk* = **möbliert**
möblieren [mø'bli:rən] *vt* to furnish; **möbliert wohnen** to live in furnished accommodation
mochte *etc* ['mɔxtə] *vb siehe* **mögen**
Möchtegern- ['mœçtəgɛrn] *in zw* (*ironisch*) would-be
Modalität [modali'tɛ:t] *f* (*von Plan, Vertrag etc*) arrangement
Mode ['mo:də] (**-, -n**) *f* fashion; **Modefarbe** *f* in colour (*Brit*) *od* color (*US*); **Modeheft** *nt* fashion magazine; **Modejournal** *nt* fashion magazine
Modell [mo'dɛl] (**-s, -e**) *nt* model; **Modelleisenbahn** *f* model railway; (*als Spielzeug*) train set; **Modellfall** *m* textbook case
modellieren [modɛ'li:rən] *vt* to model
Modellversuch *m* (*bes Sch*) pilot scheme
Modem ['mo:dɛm] (**-s, -s**) *nt* (*Comput*) modem
Modenschau *f* fashion show
Modepapst *m* high priest of fashion
Moder ['mo:dər] (**-s**) *m* mustiness; (*Schimmel*) mildew
moderat [mode'ra:t] *adj* moderate
Moderator, in [mode'ra:tɔr, -a'to:rɪn] *m(f)* presenter
moderieren [mode'ri:rən] *vt, vi* (*Rundf, TV*) to present
modern [mo'dɛrn] *adj* modern; (*modisch*) fashionable
modernisieren [modɛrni'zi:rən] *vt* to modernize
Mode- *zW*: **Modeschmuck** *m* fashion jewellery (*Brit*) *od* jewelry (*US*); **Modeschöpfer, in** *m(f)* fashion designer; **Modewort** *nt* fashionable word
modifizieren [modifi'tsi:rən] *vt* to modify
modisch ['mo:dɪʃ] *adj* fashionable
Modul ['mo:dʊl] (**-s, -n**) *nt* (*Comput*) module
Modus ['mo:dʊs] (**-, Modi**) *m* way; (*Gram*) mood; (*Comput*) mode
Mofa ['mo:fa] (**-s, -s**) *nt* (*= Motorfahrrad*) small moped
Mogadischu (**-s**) [moga'dɪʃu] *nt* Mogadishu
mogeln ['mo:gəln] (*umg*) *vi* to cheat

SCHLÜSSELWORT

mögen ['mø:gən] (*pt* **mochte**, *pp* **gemocht** *od (als Hilfsverb)* **mögen**) *vt, vi* to like; **magst du/mögen Sie ihn?** do you like him?; **ich möchte ...** I would like ..., I'd like ...; **er möchte in die Stadt** he'd like to go into town; **ich möchte nicht, dass du ...** I wouldn't like you to ...; **ich mag nicht mehr** I've had enough; (*bin am Ende*) I can't take any more; **man möchte meinen, dass ...** you would think that ...
▷ *hilfsverb* to like to; (*wollen*) to want; **möchtest du etwas essen?** would you like something to eat?; **sie mag nicht bleiben** she doesn't want to stay; **das mag wohl sein** that may very well be; **was mag das heißen?** what might that mean?; **Sie möchten zu Hause anrufen** could you please call home?

möglich ['mø:klɪç] *adj* possible; **er tat sein M~stes** he did his utmost
möglicherweise *adv* possibly
Möglichkeit *f* possibility; **nach ~** if possible
möglichst *adv* as ... as possible
Mohammedaner, in [mohame'da:nər(ɪn)] (**-s, -**) *m(f)* Mohammedan, Muslim
Mohikaner [mohi'ka:nər] (**-s, -**) *m*: **der letzte ~** (*hum: umg*) the very last one
Mohn [mo:n] (**-(e)s, -e**) *m* (*Mohnblume*) poppy; (*Mohnsamen*) poppy seed
Möhre ['mø:rə] (**-, -n**) *f* carrot
Mohrenkopf ['mo:rənkɔpf] *m chocolate-covered marshmallow*
Mohrrübe *f* carrot
mokieren [mo'ki:rən] *vr*: **sich über etw** *akk* **~** to make fun of sth
Mokka ['mɔka] (**-s**) *m* mocha, *strong coffee*
Moldau ['mɔldaʊ] *f*: **die ~** the Vltava
Moldawien [mɔl'da:viən] (**-s**) *nt* Moldavia
moldawisch *adj* Moldavian
Mole ['mo:lə] (**-, -n**) *f* (*Naut*) mole
Molekül [mole'ky:l] (**-s, -e**) *nt* molecule
molk *etc* [mɔlk] *vb siehe* **melken**
Molkerei [mɔlkə'raɪ] *f* dairy; **Molkereibutter** *f* blended butter
Moll [mɔl] (**-, -**) *nt* (*Mus*) minor (key)
mollig *adj* cosy; (*dicklich*) plump
Molotowcocktail ['mo:lotɔfkɔkte:l] *m* Molotov cocktail
Moment [mo'mɛnt] (**-(e)s, -e**) *m* moment ▷ *nt* factor, element; **im ~** at the moment; **~ mal!** just a minute!; **im ersten ~** for a moment
momentan [momɛn'ta:n] *adj* momentary ▷ *adv* at the moment
Monaco [mo'nako, 'mo:nako] (**-s**) *nt* Monaco
Monarch [mo'narç] (**-en, -en**) *m* monarch
Monarchie [monar'çi:] *f* monarchy
Monat ['mo:nat] (**-(e)s, -e**) *m* month; **sie ist im sechsten ~ (schwanger)** she's five months pregnant; **was verdient er im ~?** how much does he earn a month?
monatelang *adv* for months
monatlich *adj* monthly
Monats- *zW*: **Monatsblutung** *f* menstrual period; **Monatskarte** *f* monthly ticket; **Monatsrate** *f* monthly instalment (*Brit*) *od* installment (*US*)
Mönch [mœnç] (**-(e)s, -e**) *m* monk

Mond [mo:nt] (**-(e)s, -e**) *m* moon; **auf** *od* **hinter dem ~ leben** (*umg*) to be behind the times; **Mondfähre** *f* lunar (excursion) module; **Mondfinsternis** *f* eclipse of the moon; **mondhell** *adj* moonlit; **Mondlandung** *f* moon landing; **Mondschein** *m* moonlight; **Mondsonde** *f* moon probe

Monegasse [mone'gasə] (**-n, -n**) *m* Monegasque

Monegassin [mone'gasɪn] *f* Monegasque

monegassisch *adj* Monegasque

Monetarismus [moneta'rɪsmʊs] *m* (*Econ*) monetarism

Monetarist *m* monetarist

Moneten [mo'ne:tən] (*umg*) *pl* (*Geld*) bread *sing*, dough *sing*

Mongole [mɔŋ'go:lə] (**-n, -n**) *m* Mongolian, Mongol

Mongolei [mɔŋgo'laɪ] *f*: **die ~** Mongolia

Mongolin *f* Mongolian, Mongol

mongolisch [mɔŋ'go:lɪʃ] *adj* Mongolian

mongoloid [mɔŋgolo'i:t] *adj* (*Med*) mongoloid

monieren [mo'ni:rən] *vt* to complain about ▷ *vi* to complain

Monitor ['mo:nitɔr] *m* (*Bildschirm*) monitor

Mono- [mono] *in zW* mono

monogam [mono'ga:m] *adj* monogamous

Monogamie [monoga'mi:] *f* monogamy

Monolog [mono'lo:k] (**-s, -e**) *m* monologue

Monopol (**-s, -e**) *nt* monopoly

monopolisieren [monopoli'zi:rən] *vt* to monopolize

Monopolstellung *f* monopoly

monoton [mono'to:n] *adj* monotonous

Monotonie [monoto'ni:] *f* monotony

Monstrum ['mɔnstrʊm] (**-s, Monstren**) *nt* (*lit, fig*) monster; **ein ~ von einem/einer ...** a hulking great ...

Monsun [mɔn'zu:n] (**-s, -e**) *m* monsoon

Montag ['mo:nta:k] (**-(e)s, -e**) *m* Monday; *siehe auch* **Dienstag**

Montage [mɔn'ta:ʒə] (**-, -n**) *f* (*Phot etc*) montage; (*Tech*) assembly; (*Einbauen*) fitting

montags *adv* on Mondays

Montanindustrie [mɔn'ta:nɪndʊstri:] *f* coal and steel industry

Montblanc [mõ'blã:] *m* Mont Blanc

Monte Carlo ['mɔntə 'karlo] (**-s**) *nt* Monte Carlo

Montenegro [mɔnte'ne:gro] (**-s**) *nt* Montenegro

Monteur [mɔn'tø:r] *m* fitter, assembly man

montieren [mɔn'ti:rən] *vt* to assemble, set up

Montur [mɔn'tu:r] (*umg*) *f* (*Spezialkleidung*) gear, rig-out

Monument [monu'mɛnt] *nt* monument

monumental [monumɛn'ta:l] *adj* monumental

Moor [mo:r] (**-(e)s, -e**) *nt* moor; **Moorbad** *nt* mud bath

Moos [mo:s] (**-es, -e**) *nt* moss

Moped ['mo:pɛt] (**-s, -s**) *nt* moped

Mops [mɔps] (**-es, ¨-e**) *m* (*Hund*) pug

Moral [mo'ra:l] (**-, -en**) *f* morality; (*einer Geschichte*) moral; (*Disziplin: von Volk, Soldaten*) morale; **Moralapostel** *m* upholder of moral standards; **moralisch** *adj* moral; **einen** *od* **den moralischen haben** (*umg*) to have (a fit of) the blues

Moräne [mo'rɛ:nə] (**-, -n**) *f* moraine

Morast [mo'rast] (**-(e)s, -e**) *m* morass, mire

morastig *adj* boggy

Mord [mɔrt] (**-(e)s, -e**) *m* murder; **dann gibt es ~ und Totschlag** (*umg*) there'll be hell to pay; **Mordanschlag** *m* murder attempt

Mörder ['mœrdər] (**-s, -**) *m* murderer; **Mörderin** *f* murderess

mörderisch *adj* (*fig: schrecklich*) dreadful, terrible; (*Preise*) exorbitant; (*Konkurrenzkampf*) cut-throat ▷ *adv* (*umg: entsetzlich*) dreadfully, terribly

Mordkommission *f* murder squad

Mords- *zW*: **Mordsding** (*umg*) *nt* whopper; **Mordsglück** (*umg*) *nt* amazing luck; **Mordskerl** (*umg*) *m* (*verwegen*) hell of a guy; **mordsmäßig** (*umg*) *adj* terrific, enormous; **Mordsschreck** (*umg*) *m* terrible fright

Mord- *zW*: **Mordverdacht** *m* suspicion of murder; **Mordversuch** *m* murder attempt; **Mordwaffe** *f* murder weapon

morgen ['mɔrgən] *adv* tomorrow; **bis ~!** see you tomorrow!; **~ in acht Tagen** a week (from) tomorrow; **~ um diese Zeit** this time tomorrow; **~ früh** tomorrow morning; **Morgen** (**-s, -**) *m* morning; (*Maß*) ≈ acre; **am Morgen** in the morning; **guten Morgen!** good morning!

Morgen- *zW*: **Morgengrauen** *nt* dawn, daybreak; **Morgenmantel** *m* dressing gown; **Morgenrock** *m* dressing gown; **Morgenrot** *nt*, **Morgenröte** *f* dawn

morgens *adv* in the morning; **von ~ bis abends** from morning to night

Morgenstunde *f*: **Morgenstund(e) hat Gold im Mund(e)** (*Sprichwort*) the early bird catches the worm (*Sprichwort*)

morgig ['mɔrgɪç] *adj* tomorrow's; **der ~e Tag** tomorrow

Morphium ['mɔrfiʊm] *nt* morphine

morsch [mɔrʃ] *adj* rotten

Morsealphabet ['mɔrzə|alfabe:t] *nt* Morse code

morsen *vi* to send a message by Morse code

Mörser ['mœrzər] (**-s, -**) *m* mortar (*auch Mil*)

Mörtel ['mœrtəl] (**-s, -**) *m* mortar

Mosaik [moza'i:k] (**-s, -en** *od* **-e**) *nt* mosaic

Mosambik [mosam'bi:k] (**-s**) *nt* Mozambique

Moschee [mɔ'ʃe:] (**-, -n**) *f* mosque

Mosel[1] ['mo:zəl] *f* (*Geog*) Moselle

Mosel[2] (**-s, -**) *m* (*auch*: **Moselwein**) Moselle (wine)

mosern ['mo:zərn] (*umg*) *vi* to gripe, bellyache

Moskau ['mɔskaʊ] (**-s**) *nt* Moscow

Moskauer *adj* Moscow *attrib*

Moskauer, in (**-s, -**) *m(f)* Muscovite

Moskito [mɔs'ki:to] (**-s, -s**) *m* mosquito

Moslem ['mɔslɛm] **(-s, -s)** *m* Muslim
moslemisch [mɔs'le:mɪʃ] *adj* Muslim
Most [mɔst] **(-(e)s, -e)** *m* (unfermented) fruit juice; (*Apfelwein*) cider
Motel [mo'tɛl] **(-s, -s)** *nt* motel
Motiv [mo'ti:f] **(-s, -e)** *nt* motive; (*Mus*) theme
Motivation [motivatsi'o:n] *f* motivation
motivieren [moti'vi:rən] *vt* to motivate
Motivierung *f* motivation
Motor ['mo:tɔr] **(-s, -en)** *m* engine; (*bes Elek*) motor; **Motorboot** *nt* motorboat
Motorenöl *nt* engine oil
Motorhaube *f* (*Aut*) bonnet (*Brit*), hood (*US*)
motorisch *adj* (*Physiologie*) motor *attrib*
motorisieren [motori'zi:rən] *vt* to motorize
Motor- *zW*: **Motorrad** *nt* motorcycle; **Motorradfahrer** *m* motorcyclist; **Motorroller** *m* motor scooter; **Motorschaden** *m* engine trouble *od* failure; **Motorsport** *m* motor sport
Motte ['mɔtə] **(-, -n)** *f* moth
Motten- *zW*: **mottenfest** *adj* mothproof; **Mottenkiste** *f*: **etw aus der Mottenkiste hervorholen** (*fig*) to dig sth out; **Mottenkugel** *f* mothball
Motto ['mɔto] **(-s, -s)** *nt* motto
motzen ['mɔtsən] (*umg*) *vi* to grouse, beef
Mountainbike *nt* mountain bike
Möwe ['mø:və] **(-, -n)** *f* seagull
MP (-) *f abk* = **Maschinenpistole**
MP3 *abk* (*Comput*) MP3
MP3-Spieler *m* (*Comput*) MP3 player
Mrd. *abk* = **Milliarde(n)**
MS *abk* (= *Motorschiff*) motor vessel, MV; (= *multiple Sklerose*) MS
MTA (-, -s) *f abk* (= *medizinisch-technische Assistentin*) medical assistant
mtl. *abk* = **monatlich**
Mucke ['mʊkə] **(-, -n)** *f* (*meist pl*) caprice; (*von Ding*) snag, bug; **seine ~n haben** to be temperamental
Mücke ['mʏkə] **(-, -n)** *f* midge, gnat; **aus einer ~ einen Elefanten machen** (*umg*) to make a mountain out of a molehill
Muckefuck ['mʊkəfʊk] **(-s)** (*umg*) *m* coffee substitute
mucken *vi*: **ohne zu ~** without a murmur
Mückenstich *m* midge *od* gnat bite
Mucks [mʊks] **(-es, e)** *m*: **keinen ~ sagen** not to make a sound; (*nicht widersprechen*) not to say a word
mucksen (*umg*) *vr* to budge; (*Laut geben*) to open one's mouth
mucksmäuschenstill ['mʊks'mɔʏsçənʃtɪl] (*umg*) *adj* (as) quiet as a mouse
müde ['my:də] *adj* tired; **nicht ~ werden, etw zu tun** never to tire of doing something
Müdigkeit ['my:dɪçkaɪt] *f* tiredness; **nur keine ~ vorschützen!** (*umg*) don't (you) tell me you're tired!
Muff [mʊf] **(-(e)s, -e)** *m* (*Handwärmer*) muff
Muffel (-s, -) (*umg*) *m* killjoy, sourpuss
muffig *adj* (*Luft*) musty
Mühe ['my:ə] **(-, -n)** *f* trouble, pains *pl*; **mit Müh(e) und Not** with great difficulty; **sich** *dat* **~ geben** to go to a lot of trouble; **mühelos** *adj* effortless, easy
muhen ['mu:ən] *vi* to low, moo
mühevoll *adj* laborious, arduous
Mühle ['my:lə] **(-, -n)** *f* mill; (*Kaffeemühle*) grinder; (*Mühlespiel*) nine men's morris
Mühlrad *nt* millwheel
Mühlstein *m* millstone
Mühsal (-, -e) *f* tribulation
mühsam *adj* arduous, troublesome ▷ *adv* with difficulty
mühselig *adj* arduous, laborious
Mulatte [mu'latə] **(-, -n)** *m* mulatto
Mulattin *f* mulatto
Mulde ['mʊldə] **(-, -n)** *f* hollow, depression
Mull [mʊl] **(-(e)s, -e)** *m* thin muslin
Müll [mʏl] **(-(e)s)** *m* refuse, rubbish, garbage (*US*); **Müllabfuhr** *f* refuse *od* garbage (*US*) collection; (*Leute*) dustmen *pl* (*Brit*), garbage collectors *pl* (*US*); **Müllabladeplatz** *m* rubbish dump; **Müllbeutel** *m* bin liner (*Brit*), trashcan liner (*US*)
Mullbinde *f* gauze bandage
Mülldeponie *f* waste disposal site, rubbish tip
Mülleimer *m* rubbish bin (*Brit*), garbage can (*US*)
Müller (-s, -) *m* miller
Müll- *zW*: **Müllhalde** *f*, **Müllhaufen** *m* rubbish *od* garbage (*US*) heap; **Müllmann (-(e)s,** *pl* **Müllmänner)** (*umg*) *m* dustman (*Brit*), garbage collector (*US*); **Müllsack** *m* rubbish *od* garbage (*US*) bag; **Müllschlucker** *m* waste (*Brit*) *od* garbage (*US*) disposal unit; **Mülltonne** *f* dustbin (*Brit*), trashcan (*US*); **Müllverbrennung** *f* rubbish *od* garbage (*US*) incineration; **Müllverbrennungsanlage** *f* incinerator, incinerating plant; **Müllwagen** *m* dustcart (*Brit*), garbage truck (*US*)
mulmig ['mʊlmɪç] *adj* rotten; (*umg*) uncomfortable; **jdm ist ~** sb feels funny
Multi ['mʊlti] **(-s, -s)** (*umg*) *m* multinational (organization)
multi- *in zw* multi; **multilateral** *adj*: **multilateraler Handel** multilateral trade; **multinational** *adj* multinational; **multinationaler Konzern** multinational organization
multiple Sklerose [mʊl'ti:plə skle'ro:zə] *f* multiple sclerosis
multiplizieren [mʊltipli'tsi:rən] *vt* to multiply
Mumie ['mu:miə] *f* (*Leiche*) mummy
Mumm [mʊm] **(-s)** (*umg*) *m* gumption, nerve
Mumps [mʊmps] **(-)** *m od f* mumps *sing*
München ['mʏnçən] *nt* Munich
Münchener, **Münchner, in (-s, -)** *m(f)* person from Munich
Mund [mʊnt] **(-(e)s, ¨er)** *m* mouth; **den ~ aufmachen** (*fig: seine Meinung sagen*) to speak up; **sie ist nicht auf den ~ gefallen** (*umg*) she's never at a loss for words; **Mundart** *f* dialect
Mündel ['mʏndəl] **(-s, -)** *nt* (*Jur*) ward

münden ['mʏndən] *vi*: **in etw** *akk* ~ to flow into sth

Mund- *zW*: **mundfaul** *adj* uncommunicative; **mundgerecht** *adj* bite-sized; **Mundgeruch** *m* bad breath; **Mundharmonika** *f* mouth organ

mündig ['mʏndɪç] *adj* of age; **Mündigkeit** *f* majority

mündlich ['mʏntlɪç] *adj* oral; **~e Prüfung** oral (exam); **~e Verhandlung** (*Jur*) hearing; **alles Weitere ~!** let's talk about it more when I see you

Mund- *zW*: **Mundraub** *m* (*Jur*) theft of food for personal consumption; **Mundstück** *nt* mouthpiece; (*von Zigarette*) tip; **mundtot** *adj*: **jdn mundtot machen** to muzzle sb

Mündung ['mʏndʊŋ] *f* estuary; (*von Fluss, Rohr etc*) mouth; (*Gewehrmündung*) muzzle

Mund- *zW*: **Mundwasser** *nt* mouthwash; **Mundwerk** *nt*: **ein großes Mundwerk haben** to have a big mouth; **Mundwinkel** *m* corner of the mouth; **Mund-zu-mund-Beatmung** *f* mouth-to-mouth resuscitation

Munition [munitsi'o:n] *f* ammunition

Munitionslager *nt* ammunition dump

munkeln ['mʊŋkəln] *vi* to whisper, mutter; **man munkelt, dass ...** there's a rumour (*Brit*) *od* rumor (*US*) that ...

Münster ['mʏnstər] (**-s, -**) *nt* minster

munter ['mʊntər] *adj* lively; (*wach*) awake; (*aufgestanden*) up and about; **Munterkeit** *f* liveliness

Münzanstalt *f* mint

Münzautomat *m* slot machine

Münze ['mʏntsə] (**-, -n**) *f* coin

münzen *vt* to coin, mint; **auf jdn gemünzt sein** to be aimed at sb

Münzfernsprecher ['mʏntsfɛrnʃprɛçər] *m* callbox (*Brit*), pay phone (*US*)

Münzwechsler *m* change machine

mürb ['mʏrb], **mürbe** ['mʏrbə] *adj* (*Gestein*) crumbly; (*Holz*) rotten; (*Gebäck*) crisp; **jdn ~(e) machen** to wear sb down

Mürbeteig, Mürbteig *m* shortcrust pastry

Murmel ['mʊrməl] (**-, -n**) *f* marble

murmeln *vt, vi* to murmur, mutter

Murmeltier ['mʊrməlti:r] *nt* marmot; **schlafen wie ein** ~ to sleep like a log

murren ['mʊrən] *vi* to grumble, grouse

mürrisch ['mʏrɪʃ] *adj* sullen

Mus [mu:s] (**-es, -e**) *nt* purée

Muschel ['mʊʃəl] (**-, -n**) *f* mussel; (*Muschelschale*) shell; (*Telefonmuschel*) receiver

Muse ['mu:zə] (**-, -n**) *f* muse

Museum [mu'ze:ʊm] (**-s, Museen**) *nt* museum

museumsreif *adj*: **~ sein** to be almost a museum piece

Musik [mu'zi:k] *f* music; (*Kapelle*) band

musikalisch [muzi:'ka:lɪʃ] *adj* musical

Musikbox *f* jukebox

Musiker, in ['mu:zikər(ɪn)] (**-s, -**) *m(f)* musician

Musik- *zW*: **Musikhochschule** *f* music school; **Musikinstrument** *nt* musical instrument; **Musikkapelle** *f* band; **Musikstück** *nt* piece of music; **Musikstunde** *f* music lesson

musisch ['mu:zɪʃ] *adj* artistic

musizieren [muzi'tsi:rən] *vi* to make music

Muskat [mʊs'ka:t] (**-(e)s, -e**) *m* nutmeg

Muskel ['mʊskəl] (**-s, -n**) *m* muscle; **Muskeldystrophie** *f* muscular dystrophy; **Muskelkater** *m*: **einen Muskelkater haben** to be stiff; **Muskelpaket** (*umg*) *nt* muscleman; **Muskelzerrung** (*umg*) *f* pulled muscle

Muskulatur [mʊskula'tu:r] *f* muscular system

muskulös [mʊsku'lø:s] *adj* muscular

Müsli ['my:sli] (**-s, -**) *nt* muesli

Muss [mʊs] (**-**) *nt* necessity, must

muss *vb siehe* **müssen**

Muße ['mu:sə] (**-**) *f* leisure

SCHLÜSSELWORT

müssen ['mʏsən] (*pt* **musste**, *pp* **gemusst** *od* (*als Hilfsverb*) **müssen**) *vi* **1** (*Zwang*) must (*nur im Präsens*), to have to; **ich muss es tun** I must do it, I have to do it; **ich musste es tun** I had to do it; **er muss es nicht tun** he doesn't have to do it; **muss ich?** must I?, do I have to?; **wann müsst ihr zur Schule?** when do you have to go to school?; **der Brief muss heute noch zur Post** the letter must be posted (*Brit*) *od* mailed (*US*) today; **er hat gehen müssen** he (has) had to go; **muss das sein?** is that really necessary?; **wenn es (unbedingt) sein muss** if it's absolutely necessary; **ich muss mal** (*umg*) I need to go to the loo (*Brit*) *od* bathroom (*US*)

2 (*sollen*): **das musst du nicht tun!** you oughtn't to *od* shouldn't do that; **das müsstest du eigentlich wissen** you ought to *od* you should know that; **Sie hätten ihn fragen müssen** you should have asked him

3: **es muss geregnet haben** it must have rained; **es muss nicht wahr sein** it needn't be true

Mussheirat (*umg*) *f* shotgun wedding

müßig ['my:sɪç] *adj* idle; **Müßiggang** *m* idleness

musst [mʊst] *vb siehe* **müssen**

musste *etc* ['mʊstə] *vb siehe* **müssen**

Muster ['mʊstər] (**-s, -**) *nt* model; (*Dessin*) pattern; (*Probe*) sample; **~ ohne Wert** free sample; **Musterbeispiel** *nt* classic example; **mustergültig** *adj* exemplary; **musterhaft** *adj* exemplary

mustern *vt* (*betrachten, Mil*) to examine; (*Truppen*) to inspect

Musterprozess *m* test case

Musterschüler *m* model pupil

Musterung *f* (*von Stoff*) pattern; (*Mil*) inspection

Mut [mu:t] *m* courage; **nur ~!** cheer up!; **jdm ~ machen** to encourage sb; **~ fassen** to pluck up courage

mutig *adj* courageous

mutlos *adj* discouraged, despondent

mutmaßen *vt untr* to conjecture ▷ *vi untr* to conjecture
mutmaßlich ['mu:tma:slıç] *adj* presumed ▷ *adv* probably
Mutprobe *f* test of courage
Mutter[1] ['mʊtər] (**-, -n**) *f* (*Schraubenmutter*) nut
Mutter[2] ['mʊtər] (**-, ¨-**) *f* mother; **Mutterfreuden** *pl* the joys *pl* of motherhood; **Muttergesellschaft** *f* (*Comm*) parent company; **Mutterkuchen** *m* (*Anat*) placenta; **Mutterland** *nt* mother country; **Mutterleib** *m* womb
mütterlich ['mʏtərlıç] *adj* motherly
mütterlicherseits *adv* on the mother's side
Mutter- *zW*: **Mutterliebe** *f* motherly love; **Muttermal** *nt* birthmark; **Muttermilch** *f* mother's milk
Mutterschaft *f* motherhood
Mutterschaftsgeld *nt* maternity benefit
Mutterschaftsurlaub *m* maternity leave
Mutter- *zW*: **Mutterschutz** *m* maternity regulations *pl*; **mutterseelenallein** *adj* all alone; **Muttersprache** *f* native language; **Muttertag** *m* Mother's Day
Mutti (**-, -s**) (*umg*) *f* mum(my) (*Brit*), mom(my) (*US*)
mutwillig ['mu:tvılıç] *adj* deliberate
Mütze ['mʏtsə] (**-, -n**) *f* cap
MV *f abk* (= *Mitgliederversammlung*) general meeting
MW *abk* (= *Mittelwelle*) MW
MwSt, Mw.-St. *abk* (= *Mehrwertsteuer*) VAT
mysteriös [mʏsteri'ø:s] *adj* mysterious
Mystik ['mʏstık] *f* mysticism
Mystiker, in (**-s, -**) *m(f)* mystic
mystisch ['mʏstıʃ] *adj* mystical; (*rätselhaft*) mysterious
Mythologie [mytolo'gi:] *f* mythology
Mythos ['my:tɔs] (**-, Mythen**) *m* myth

Nn

N¹, n [ɛn] *nt* N, n; **N wie Nordpol** ≈ N for Nellie, N for Nan (*US*)
N² [ɛn] *abk* (= *Norden*) N
na [na] *interj* well; **na gut** (*umg*) all right, OK; **na also!** (well,) there you are (then)!; **na so was!** well, I never!; **na und?** so what?
Nabel ['na:bəl] (**-s, -**) *m* navel; **der ~ der Welt** (*fig*) the hub of the universe; **Nabelschnur** *f* umbilical cord

SCHLÜSSELWORT

nach [na:x] *präp +dat* **1** (*örtlich*) to; **nach Berlin** to Berlin; **nach links/rechts** (to the) left/right; **nach oben/hinten** up/back; **er ist schon nach London abgefahren** he has already left for London
2 (*zeitlich*) after; **einer nach dem anderen** one after the other; **nach Ihnen!** after you!; **zehn (Minuten) nach drei** ten (minutes) past *od* after (*US*) three
3 (*gemäß*) according to; **nach dem Gesetz** according to the law; **die Uhr nach dem Radio stellen** to put a clock right by the radio; **ihrer Sprache nach (zu urteilen)** judging by her language; **dem Namen nach** judging by his/her name; **nach allem, was ich weiß** as far as I know
▷ *adv*: **ihm nach!** after him!; **nach und nach** gradually, little by little; **nach wie vor** still

nachäffen ['na:x|ɛfən] *vt* to ape
nachahmen ['na:x|a:mən] *vt* to imitate
nachahmenswert *adj* exemplary
Nachahmung *f* imitation; **etw zur ~ empfehlen** to recommend sth as an example
Nachbar, in ['naxba:r(ɪn)] (**-s, -n**) *m(f)* neighbour (*Brit*), neighbor (*US*); **Nachbarhaus** *nt*: **im Nachbarhaus** next door; **nachbarlich** *adj* neighbourly (*Brit*), neighborly (*US*); **Nachbarschaft** *f* neighbourhood (*Brit*), neighborhood (*US*); **Nachbarstaat** *m* neighbouring (*Brit*) *od* neighboring (*US*) state
nach- *zW*: **Nachbehandlung** *f* (*Med*) follow-up treatment; **nachbestellen** *vt* to order again; **Nachbestellung** *f* (*Comm*) repeat order; **nachbeten** (*pej*: *umg*) *vt* to repeat parrot-fashion; **nachbezahlen** *vt* to pay; (*später*) to pay later; **nachbilden** *vt* to copy; **Nachbildung** *f* imitation, copy; **nachblicken** *vi* to look *od* gaze after; **nachdatieren** *vt* to postdate
nachdem [na:x'de:m] *konj* after; (*weil*) since; **je ~ (ob)** it depends (whether)
nach- *zW*: **nachdenken** *unreg vi*: **über etw** *akk* **nachdenken** to think about sth; **darüber darf man gar nicht nachdenken** it doesn't bear thinking about; **Nachdenken** *nt* reflection, meditation; **nachdenklich** *adj* thoughtful, pensive; **nachdenklich gestimmt sein** to be in a thoughtful mood
Nachdruck ['na:xdrʊk] *m* emphasis; (*Typ*) reprint, reproduction; **besonderen ~ darauf legen, dass ...** to stress *od* emphasize particularly that ...
nachdrücklich ['na:xdrʏklɪç] *adj* emphatic; **~ auf etw** *dat* **bestehen** to insist firmly (up)on sth
nacheifern ['na:x|aɪfərn] *vi*: **jdm ~** to emulate sb
nacheinander [na:x|aɪ'nandər] *adv* one after the other; **kurz ~** shortly after each other; **drei Tage ~** three days running, three days on the trot (*umg*)
nachempfinden ['na:x|ɛmpfɪndən] *unreg vt*: **jdm etw ~** to feel sth with sb
nacherzählen ['na:x|ɛrtsɛ:lən] *vt* to retell
Nacherzählung *f* reproduction (of a story)
Nachf. *abk* = **Nachfolger**
Nachfahr ['na:xfa:r] (**-en, -en**) *m* descendant
Nachfolge ['na:xfɔlgə] *f* succession; **die/jds ~ antreten** to succeed/succeed sb
nachfolgen *vi* (*lit*): **jdm/etw ~** to follow sb/sth
nachfolgend *adj* following
Nachfolger, in (**-s, -**) *m(f)* successor
nachforschen *vt, vi* to investigate
Nachforschung *f* investigation; **~en anstellen** to make enquiries
Nachfrage ['na:xfra:gə] *f* inquiry; (*Comm*) demand; **es besteht eine rege ~** (*Comm*) there is a great demand; **danke der ~** (*form*) thank you for your concern; (*umg*) nice of you to ask; **nachfragemäßig** *adj* according to demand
nachfragen *vi* to inquire
nach- *zW*: **nachfühlen** *vt* = **nachempfinden**; **nachfüllen** *vt* to refill; **nachgeben** *unreg vi* to give way, yield

Nachgebühr *f* surcharge; (*Post*) excess postage
Nachgeburt *f* afterbirth
nachgehen ['na:xge:ən] *unreg vi (+dat)* to follow; (*erforschen*) to inquire (into); (*Uhr*) to be slow; **einer geregelten Arbeit ~** to have a steady job
Nachgeschmack ['na:xgəʃmak] *m* aftertaste
nachgiebig ['na:xgi:bıç] *adj* soft, accommodating; **Nachgiebigkeit** *f* softness
nachgrübeln ['na:xgry:bəln] *vi*: **über etw** *akk* ~ to think about sth; (*sich Gedanken machen*) to ponder on sth
nachgucken ['na:xgʊkən] *vt, vi* = **nachsehen**
nachhaken ['na:xha:kən] (*umg*) *vi* to dig deeper
Nachhall ['na:xhal] *m* resonance
nachhallen *vi* to resound
nachhaltig ['na:xhaltıç] *adj* lasting; (*Widerstand*) persistent
nachhängen ['na:xhɛŋən] *unreg vi*: **seinen Erinnerungen ~** to lose o.s. in one's memories
nachhause *adv* home
Nachhauseweg [na:x'haʊzəve:k] *m* way home
nachhelfen ['na:xhɛlfən] *unreg vi*: **jdm ~** to help *od* assist sb; **er hat dem Glück ein bisschen nachgeholfen** he engineered himself a little luck
nachher [na:x'he:r] *adv* afterwards; **bis ~** see you later!
Nachhilfe ['na:xhılfə] *f* (*auch*: **Nachhilfeunterricht**) extra (private) tuition
Nachhinein ['na:xhınaın] *adv*: **im ~** afterwards; (*rückblickend*) in retrospect
Nachholbedarf *m*: **einen ~ an etw** *dat* **haben** to have a lot of sth to catch up on
nachholen ['na:xho:lən] *vt* to catch up with; (*Versäumtes*) to make up for
Nachkomme ['na:xkɔmə] **(-n, -n)** *m* descendant
nachkommen *unreg vi* to follow; (*einer Verpflichtung*) to fulfil; **Sie können Ihr Gepäck ~ lassen** you can have your luggage sent on (after)
Nachkommenschaft *f* descendants *pl*
Nachkriegs- ['na:xkri:ks] *in zw* postwar; **Nachkriegszeit** *f* postwar period
Nach- *zW*: **Nachlass** **(-es, -lässe)** *m* (*Comm*) discount, rebate; (*Erbe*) estate; **nachlassen** *unreg vt* (*Strafe*) to remit; (*Summe*) to take off; (*Schulden*) to cancel ▷ *vi* to decrease, ease off; (*Sturm*) to die down; (*schlechter werden*) to deteriorate; **er hat nachgelassen** he has got worse; **nachlässig** *adj* negligent, careless; **Nachlässigkeit** *f* negligence, carelessness; **Nachlasssteuer** *f* death duty; **Nachlassverwalter** *m* executor
nachlaufen ['na:xlaʊfən] *unreg vi*: **jdm ~** to run after *od* chase sb
nachliefern ['na:xli:fərn] *vt* (*später liefern*) to deliver at a later date; (*zuzüglich liefern*) to make a further delivery of
nachlösen ['na:xlø:zən] *vi* to pay on the train/when one gets off; (*zur Weiterfahrt*) to pay the extra
nachm. *abk* (= *nachmittags*) p.m.
nachmachen ['na:xmaxən] *vt* to imitate, copy; (*fälschen*) to counterfeit; **jdm etw ~** to copy sth from sb; **das soll erst mal einer ~!** I'd like to see anyone else do that!
Nachmieter, in ['na:xmi:tər(ın)] *m(f)*: **wir müssen einen ~ finden** we have to find someone to take over the flat *etc*
Nachmittag ['na:xmıta:k] *m* afternoon; **am ~** in the afternoon; **gestern/heute ~** yesterday/this afternoon
nachmittags *adv* in the afternoon
Nachmittagsvorstellung *f* matinée (performance)
Nachn. *abk* = **Nachnahme**
Nachnahme **(-, -n)** *f* cash on delivery (*Brit*), collect on delivery (*US*); **per ~** C.O.D.
Nachname *m* surname
Nachporto *nt* excess postage
nachprüfbar ['na:xpry:fba:r] *adj* verifiable
nachprüfen ['na:xpry:fən] *vt* to check, verify
nachrechnen ['na:xrɛçnən] *vt* to check
Nachrede ['na:xre:də] *f*: **üble ~** (*Jur*) defamation of character
nachreichen ['na:xraıçən] *vt* to hand in later
Nachricht ['na:xrıçt] **(-, -en)** *f* (piece of) news *sing*; (*Mitteilung*) message
Nachrichten *pl* news *sing*; **Nachrichtenagentur** *f* news agency; **Nachrichtendienst** *m* (*Mil*) intelligence service; **Nachrichtensatellit** *m* (tele)communications satellite; **Nachrichtensperre** *f* news blackout; **Nachrichtensprecher, in** *m(f)* newsreader; **Nachrichtentechnik** *f* telecommunications *sing*
nachrücken ['na:xrʏkən] *vi* to move up
Nachruf ['na:xru:f] *m* obituary (notice)
nachrüsten ['na:xrʏstən] *vt* (*Kraftwerk etc*) to modernize; (*Auto etc*) to refit; (*Waffen*) to keep up to date ▷ *vi* (*Mil*) to deploy new arms
nachsagen ['na:xza:gən] *vt* to repeat; **jdm etw ~** to say sth of sb; **das lasse ich mir nicht ~!** I'm not having that said of me!
Nachsaison ['na:xzɛzõ:] *f* off season
nachschenken ['na:xʃɛŋkən] *vt, vi*: **darf ich Ihnen noch (etwas) ~?** may I top up your glass?
nachschicken ['na:xʃıkən] *vt* to forward
nachschlagen ['na:xʃla:gən] *unreg vt* to look up ▷ *vi*: **jdm ~** to take after sb
Nachschlagewerk *nt* reference book
Nachschlüssel *m* master key
nachschmeißen ['na:xʃmaısən] *unreg* (*umg*) *vt*: **das ist ja nachgeschmissen!** it's a real bargain!
Nachschrift ['na:xʃrıft] *f* postscript
Nachschub ['na:xʃu:p] *m* supplies *pl*; (*Truppen*) reinforcements *pl*
nachsehen ['na:xze:ən] *unreg vt* (*prüfen*) to check ▷ *vi* (*erforschen*) to look and see; **jdm etw ~** to forgive sb sth; **jdm ~** to gaze after sb
Nachsehen *nt*: **das ~ haben** to be left empty-handed

nachsenden ['na:xzɛndən] *unreg vt* to send on, forward
Nachsicht ['na:xzɪçt] **(-)** *f* indulgence, leniency
nachsichtig *adj* indulgent, lenient
Nachsilbe ['na:xzɪlbə] *f* suffix
nachsitzen ['na:xzɪtsən] *unreg vi* (*Sch*) to be kept in
Nachsorge ['na:xzɔrgə] *f* (*Med*) aftercare
Nachspann ['na:xʃpan] *m* credits *pl*
Nachspeise ['na:xʃpaɪzə] *f* dessert, sweet (*Brit*)
Nachspiel ['na:xʃpi:l] *nt* epilogue; (*fig*) sequel
nachspionieren ['na:xʃpioni:rən] (*umg*) *vi*: **jdm ~** to spy on sb
nachsprechen ['na:xʃprɛçən] *unreg vt*: **(jdm) ~** to repeat (after sb)
nächst [nɛ:çst] *präp +dat* (*räumlich*) next to; (*außer*) apart from; **nächstbeste, r, s** *adj* first that comes along; (*zweitbeste*) next-best
Nächste, r, s *f(m)* neighbour (*Brit*), neighbor (*US*)
nächste, r, s *adj* next; (*nächstgelegen*) nearest; **aus ~r Nähe** from close by; (*betrachten*) at close quarters; **Ende ~n Monats** at the end of next month; **am ~n Tag** (the) next day; **bei ~r Gelegenheit** at the earliest opportunity; **in ~r Zeit** some time soon; **der ~ Angehörige** the next of kin
nachstehen ['na:xʃte:ən] *unreg vi*: **jdm in nichts ~** to be sb's equal in every way
nachstehend *adj attrib* following
nachstellen ['na:xʃtɛlən] *vi*: **jdm ~** to follow sb; (*aufdringlich umwerben*) to pester sb
Nächstenliebe *f* love for one's fellow men
nächstens *adv* shortly, soon
nächstliegend *adj* (*lit*) nearest; (*fig*) obvious
nächstmöglich *adj* next possible
nachsuchen ['na:xzu:xən] *vi*: **um etw ~** to ask *od* apply for sth
Nacht [naxt] **(-, ¨-e)** *f* night; **gute ~!** good night!; **heute ~** tonight; **in der ~** at night; **in der ~ auf Dienstag** during Monday night; **in der ~ vom 12. zum 13. April** during the night of April 12th to 13th; **über ~** (*auch fig*) overnight; **bei ~ und Nebel** (*umg*) at dead of night; **sich** *dat* **die ~ um die Ohren schlagen** (*umg*) to stay up all night; (*mit Feiern, arbeiten*) to make a night of it
Nachtdienst *m* night duty
Nachteil ['na:xtaɪl] *m* disadvantage; **im ~ sein** to be at a disadvantage
nachteilig *adj* disadvantageous
Nachtfalter *m* moth
Nachthemd *nt* (*Herrennachthemd*) nightshirt; nightdress (*Brit*), nightgown
Nachtigall ['naxtɪgal] **(-, -en)** *f* nightingale
Nachtisch ['na:xtɪʃ] *m* = **Nachspeise**
Nachtleben *nt* night life
nächtlich ['nɛçtlɪç] *adj* nightly
Nacht- *zW*: **Nachtlokal** *nt* night club; **Nachtmensch** ['naxtmɛnʃ] *m* night person; **Nachtportier** *m* night porter
nach- *zW*: **Nachtrag** ['na:xtra:k] **(-(e)s, -träge)** *m* supplement; **nachtragen** *unreg vt* (*zufügen*) to add; **jdm etw nachtragen** to carry sth after sb; (*fig*) to hold sth against sb; **nachtragend** *adj* resentful; **nachträglich** *adj* later, subsequent; (*zusätzlich*) additional ▷ *adv* later, subsequently; (*zusätzlich*) additionally; **nachtrauern** *vi*: **jdm/etw nachtrauern** to mourn the loss of sb/sth
Nachtruhe ['naxtru:ə] *f* sleep
nachts *adv* by night
Nachtschicht *f* night shift
Nachtschwester *f* night nurse
nachtsüber *adv* during the night
Nacht- *zW*: **Nachttarif** *m* off-peak tariff; **Nachttisch** *m* bedside table; **Nachttopf** *m* chamber pot; **Nachtwache** *f* night watch; (*im Krankenhaus*) night duty; **Nachtwächter** *m* night watchman
Nach- *zW*: **Nachuntersuchung** *f* checkup; **nachvollziehen** *unreg vt* to understand, comprehend; **nachwachsen** *unreg vi* to grow again; **Nachwahl** *f* ≈ by-election (*bes Brit*); **Nachwehen** *pl* afterpains *pl*; (*fig*) aftereffects *pl*; **nachweinen** *vi +dat* to mourn ▷ *vt*: **dieser Sache** *dat* **weine ich keine Träne nach** I won't shed any tears over that
Nachweis ['na:xvaɪs] **(-es, -e)** *m* proof; **den ~ für etw erbringen** *od* **liefern** to furnish proof of sth; **nachweisbar** *adj* provable, demonstrable; **nachweisen** ['na:xvaɪzən] *unreg vt* to prove; **jdm etw nachweisen** to point sth out to sb; **nachweislich** *adj* evident, demonstrable
nach- *zW*: **Nachwelt** *f*: **die Nachwelt** posterity; **nachwinken** *vi*: **jdm nachwinken** to wave after sb; **nachwirken** *vi* to have aftereffects; **Nachwirkung** *f* aftereffect; **Nachwort** *nt* appendix; **Nachwuchs** *m* offspring; (*beruflich etc*) new recruits *pl*; **nachzahlen** *vt, vi* to pay extra; **nachzählen** *vt* to count again; **Nachzahlung** *f* additional payment; (*zurückdatiert*) back pay
nachziehen ['na:xtsi:ən] *unreg vt* (*Linie*) to go over; (*Lippen*) to paint; (*Augenbrauen*) to pencil in; (*hinterherziehen*): **etw ~** to drag sth behind one
Nachzügler **(-s, -)** *m* straggler
Nackedei ['nakədaɪ] **(-(e)s, -e** *od* **-s)** *m* (*hum: umg: Kind*) little bare monkey
Nacken ['nakən] **(-s, -)** *m* nape of the neck; **jdm im ~ sitzen** (*umg*) to breathe down sb's neck
nackt [nakt] *adj* naked; (*Tatsachen*) plain, bare; **Nacktheit** *f* nakedness; **Nacktkultur** *f* nudism
Nadel ['na:dəl] **(-, -n)** *f* needle; (*Stecknadel*) pin; **Nadelbaum** *m* conifer; **Nadelkissen** *nt* pincushion; **Nadelöhr** *nt* eye of a needle; **Nadelwald** *m* coniferous forest
Nagel ['na:gəl] **(-s, ¨)** *m* nail; **sich** *dat* **etw unter den ~ reißen** (*umg*) to pinch sth; **etw an den ~ hängen** (*fig*) to chuck sth in (*umg*); **Nägel mit Köpfen machen** (*umg*) to do the job properly; **Nagelbürste** *f* nailbrush; **Nagelfeile** *f* nailfile; **Nagelhaut** *f* cuticle;

Nagellack *m* nail varnish (*Brit*) *od* polish; **Nagellackentferner** (**-s, -**) *m* nail polish remover
nageln *vt, vi* to nail
nagelneu *adj* brand-new
Nagelschere *f* nail scissors *pl*
nagen ['na:gən] *vt, vi* to gnaw
Nagetier ['na:gəti:r] *nt* rodent
nah *adj* = **nahe**
Nahaufnahme *f* close-up
Nahe *f* (*Fluss*) Nahe
nahe *adj* (*räumlich*) near(by); (*Verwandte*) near, close; (*Freunde*) close; (*zeitlich*) near, close ▷ *adv*: **von nah und fern** from near and far ▷ *präp +dat* near (to), close to; **von N~m** at close quarters; **der N~ Osten** the Middle East; **jdm ~ kommen** to get close to sb; **~ stehend** close; **jdm zu ~ treten** (*fig*) to offend sb; **mit jdm ~ verwandt sein** to be closely related to sb; *siehe auch* **naheliegen; nahestehen** *etc*
Nähe ['nɛ:ə] (-) *f* nearness, proximity; (*Umgebung*) vicinity; **in der ~** close by; at hand; **aus der ~** from close to
nahebei *adv* nearby
nahebringen *unreg vt* (*fig*): **jdm etw ~** to bring sth home to sb
nahegehen *unreg vi* (*fig*): **jdm ~** to grieve sb
nahelegen *vi* (*fig*): **jdm etw ~** to suggest sth to sb
naheliegen *unreg vi* (*fig*) to be obvious; **der Verdacht liegt nahe, dass ...** it seems reasonable to suspect that ...; **~d** obvious
nahen *vi, vr* to approach, draw near
nähen ['nɛ:ən] *vt, vi* to sew
näher *adj* nearer; (*Erklärung, Erkundigung*) more detailed ▷ *adv* nearer; in greater detail; **~ kommen** to get closer; **ich kenne ihn nicht ~** I don't know him well
Nähere, s *nt* details *pl*, particulars *pl*
Näherei [nɛ:ə'raɪ] *f* sewing, needlework
Naherholungsgebiet *nt* recreational area (*close to a centre of population*)
Näherin *f* seamstress
nähern *vr* to approach
Näherungswert *m* approximate value
nahestehen *unreg vi* (*fig*): **jdm ~** to be close to sb; **einer Sache ~** to sympathize with sth
nahezu *adv* nearly
Nähgarn *nt* thread
Nahkampf *m* hand-to-hand fighting
Nähkasten *m* workbox, sewing basket
nahm *etc* [na:m] *vb siehe* **nehmen**
Nähmaschine *f* sewing machine
Nähnadel *f* (sewing) needle
Nahost [na:'ɔst] *m*: **aus ~** from the Middle East
Nährboden *m* (*lit*) fertile soil; (*fig*) breeding ground
nähren ['nɛ:rən] *vt* to feed ▷ *vr* (*Person*) to feed o.s.; (*Tier*) to feed; **er sieht gut genährt aus** he looks well fed
Nährgehalt ['nɛ:rgəhalt] *m* nutritional value
nahrhaft ['na:rhaft] *adj* (*Essen*) nourishing
Nährstoffe *pl* nutrients *pl*
Nahrung ['na:rʊŋ] *f* food; (*fig*) sustenance
Nahrungs- *zW*: **Nahrungsaufnahme** *f*: **die Nahrungsaufnahme verweigern** to refuse food; **Nahrungskette** *f* food chain; **Nahrungsmittel** *nt* food(stuff); **Nahrungsmittelindustrie** *f* food industry; **Nahrungssuche** *f* search for food
Nährwert *m* nutritional value
Naht [na:t] (**-, ¨-e**) *f* seam; (*Med*) suture; (*Tech*) join; **aus allen Nähten platzen** (*umg*) to be bursting at the seams; **nahtlos** *adj* seamless; **nahtlos ineinander übergehen** to follow without a gap
Nahverkehr *m* local traffic
Nahverkehrszug *m* local train
Nähzeug *nt* sewing kit, sewing things *pl*
Nahziel *nt* immediate objective
naiv [na'i:f] *adj* naïve
Naivität [naivi'tɛ:t] *f* naïveté, naïvety
Name ['na:mə] (**-ns, -n**) *m* name; **im ~n von** on behalf of; **dem ~n nach müsste sie Deutsche sein** judging by her name she must be German; **die Dinge beim ~n nennen** (*fig*) to call a spade a spade; **ich kenne das Stück nur dem ~n nach** I've heard of the play but that's all
namens *adv* by the name of
Namensänderung *f* change of name
Namenstag *m* name day, saint's day; *see culture note*

NAMENSTAG

In Catholic areas of Germany the *Namenstag* is often a more important celebration than a birthday. It is the day dedicated to the saint after whom a person is called, and on that day the person receives presents and invites relatives and friends round to celebrate.

namentlich ['na:məntlɪç] *adj* by name ▷ *adv* particularly, especially
namhaft ['na:mhaft] *adj* (*berühmt*) famed, renowned; (*beträchtlich*) considerable; **~ machen** to name, identify
Namibia [na'mi:bia] (**-s**) *nt* Namibia
nämlich ['nɛ:mlɪç] *adv* that is to say, namely; (*denn*) since; **der/die/das N~e** the same
nannte *etc* ['nantə] *vb siehe* **nennen**
nanu [na'nu:] *interj* well I never!
Napalm ['na:palm] (**-s**) *nt* napalm
Napf [napf] (**-(e)s, ¨-e**) *m* bowl, dish; **Napfkuchen** *m* ≈ ring-shaped pound cake
Narbe ['narbə] (**-, -n**) *f* scar
narbig ['narbɪç] *adj* scarred
Narkose [nar'ko:ze] (**-, -n**) *f* anaesthetic (*Brit*), anesthetic (*US*)
Narr [nar] (**-en, -en**) *m* fool; **jdn zum ~en halten** to make a fool of sb; **narren** *vt* to fool
Narrenfreiheit *f*: **sie hat bei ihm ~** he gives her (a) free rein
narrensicher *adj* foolproof

Narrheit *f* foolishness
Närrin ['nɛrɪn] *f* fool
närrisch *adj* foolish, crazy; **die ~en Tage** *Fasching and the period leading up to it*
Narzisse [nar'tsɪsə] (**-, -n**) *f* narcissus
narzisstisch [nar'tsɪstɪʃ] *adj* narcissistic
NASA ['na:za] (**-**) *f abk* (= *National Aeronautics and Space Administration*) NASA
naschen ['naʃən] *vt* to nibble; (*heimlich*) to eat secretly ▷ *vi* to nibble sweet things; **~ von** *od* **an** *+dat* to nibble at
naschhaft *adj* sweet-toothed
Nase ['na:zə] (**-, -n**) *f* nose; **sich** *dat* **die ~ putzen** to wipe one's nose; (*sich schnäuzen*) to blow one's nose; **jdm auf der ~ herumtanzen** (*umg*) to play sb up; **jdm etw vor der ~ wegschnappen** (*umg*) to just beat sb to sth; **die ~ vollhaben** (*umg*) to have had enough; **jdm etw auf die ~ binden** (*umg*) to tell sb all about sth; **(immer) der ~ nachgehen** (*umg*) to follow one's nose; **jdn an der ~ herumführen** (*als Täuschung*) to lead sb by the nose; (*als Scherz*) to pull sb's leg
Nasen- *zW*: **Nasenbluten** (**-s**) *nt* nosebleed; **Nasenloch** *nt* nostril; **Nasenrücken** *m* bridge of the nose; **Nasentropfen** *pl* nose drops *pl*
naseweis *adj* pert, cheeky; (*neugierig*) nosey
Nashorn ['na:shɔrn] *nt* rhinoceros
nass [nas] *adj* wet
Nassauer ['nasaʊər] (**-s, -**) (*umg*) *m* scrounger
Nässe ['nɛsə] (**-**) *f* wetness
nässen *vt* to wet
nasskalt *adj* wet and cold
Nassrasur *f* wet shave
Nation [natsi'o:n] *f* nation
national [natsio'na:l] *adj* national; **Nationalelf** *f* international (football) team; **Nationalfeiertag** *m* national holiday; **Nationalhymne** *f* national anthem
nationalisieren [natsiona:li'zi:rən] *vt* to nationalize
Nationalisierung *f* nationalization
Nationalismus [natsiona:'lɪsmʊs] *m* nationalism
nationalistisch [natsiona:'lɪstɪʃ] *adj* nationalistic
Nationalität [natsionali'tɛ:t] *f* nationality
National- *zW*: **Nationalmannschaft** *f* international team; **Nationalsozialismus** *m* National Socialism; **Nationalsozialist** *m* National Socialist
NATO, Nato ['na:to] (-) *f abk*: **die ~** NATO
Natrium ['na:triʊm] (**-s**) *nt* sodium
Natron ['na:trɔn] (**-s**) *nt* soda
Natter ['natər] (**-, -n**) *f* adder
Natur [na'tu:r] *f* nature; (*körperlich*) constitution; (*freies Land*) countryside; **das geht gegen meine ~** it goes against the grain
Naturalien [natu'ra:liən] *pl* natural produce *sing*; **in ~** in kind
Naturalismus [natu:ra'lɪsmʊs] *m* naturalism
Naturell [natu'rɛl] (**-s, -e**) *nt* temperament, disposition
Natur- *zW*: **Naturerscheinung** *f* natural phenomenon *od* event; **naturfarben** *adj* natural-coloured (*Brit*) *od* -colored (*US*); **Naturforscher** *m* natural scientist; **Naturfreak** (**-s, -s**) (*umg*) *m* back-to-nature freak; **naturgemäß** *adj* natural; **Naturgeschichte** *f* natural history; **Naturgesetz** *nt* law of nature; **naturgetreu** *adj* true to life; **Naturheilverfahren** *nt* natural cure; **Naturkatastrophe** *f* natural disaster; **Naturkostladen** *m* health food shop; **Naturkunde** *f* natural history; **Naturlehrpfad** *m* nature trail
natürlich [na'ty:rlɪç] *adj* natural ▷ *adv* naturally; **eines ~en Todes sterben** to die of natural causes
natürlicherweise [na'ty:rlɪçər'vaɪzə] *adv* naturally, of course
Natürlichkeit *f* naturalness
Natur- *zW*: **Naturprodukt** *nt* natural product; **naturrein** *adj* natural, pure; **Naturschutz** *m*: **unter Naturschutz stehen** to be legally protected; **Naturschutzgebiet** *nt* nature reserve (*BRIT*), national park (*US*); **Naturtalent** *nt* natural prodigy; **naturverbunden** *adj* nature-loving; **Naturwissenschaft** *f* natural science; **Naturwissenschaftler** *m* scientist; **Naturzustand** *m* natural state
Nautik ['naʊtɪk] *f* nautical science, navigation
nautisch ['naʊtɪʃ] *adj* nautical
Navelorange ['na:vəlorã:ʒə] *f* navel orange
Navigation [navigatsi'o:n] *f* navigation
Navigationsfehler *m* navigational error
Navigationsinstrumente *pl* navigation instruments *pl*
Nazi ['na:tsi] (**-s, -s**) *m* Nazi
NB *abk* (= *nota bene*) NB
n. Br. *abk* (= *nördlicher Breite*) northern latitude
NC *m abk* (= *numerus clausus*) *siehe* **Numerus**
Nchf. *abk* = **Nachfolger**
n. Chr. *abk* (= *nach Christus*) A.D.
NDR (**-**) *m abk* (= *Norddeutscher Rundfunk*) North German Radio
Neapel [ne'a:pəl] (**-s**) *nt* Naples
Neapolitaner, in [neapoli'ta:nər(ɪn)] (**-s, -**) *m(f)* Neapolitan
neapolitanisch [neapoli'ta:nɪʃ] *adj* Neapolitan
Nebel ['ne:bəl] (**-s, -**) *m* fog, mist
nebelig *adj* foggy, misty
Nebel- *zW*: **Nebelleuchte** *f* (*Aut*) rear fog-light; **Nebelscheinwerfer** *m* fog-lamp; **Nebelschlussleuchte** *f* (*Aut*) rear fog-light
neben ['ne:bən] *präp +akk* next to ▷ *präp +dat* next to; (*außer*) apart from, besides; **nebenan** [ne:bən|'an] *adv* next door; **Nebenanschluss** *m* (*Tel*) extension; **Nebenausgaben** *pl* incidental expenses *pl*; **nebenbei** [ne:bən'baɪ] *adv* at the same time; (*außerdem*) additionally; (*beiläufig*) incidentally; **nebenbei bemerkt** *od* **gesagt** by the way, incidentally; **Nebenberuf** *m* second occupation; **er ist im Nebenberuf ...** he has a second job as a ...; **Nebenbeschäftigung** *f* sideline; (*Zweitberuf*)

extra job; **Nebenbuhler, in (-s, -)** *m(f)* rival; **nebeneinander** [ne:bənaɪ'nandər] *adv* side by side; **nebeneinanderlegen** *vt* to put next to each other; **Nebeneingang** *m* side entrance; **Nebeneinkünfte** *pl*, **Nebeneinnahmen** *pl* supplementary income *sing*; **Nebenerscheinung** *f* side effect; **Nebenfach** *nt* subsidiary subject; **Nebenfluss** *m* tributary; **Nebengeräusch** *nt* (*Rundf*) atmospherics *pl*, interference; **Nebenhandlung** *f* (*Liter*) subplot; **nebenher** [ne:bən'he:r] *adv* (*zusätzlich*) besides; (*gleichzeitig*) at the same time; (*daneben*) alongside; **nebenherfahren** *unreg vi* to drive alongside; **Nebenkläger** *m* (*Jur*) joint plaintiff; **Nebenkosten** *pl* extra charges *pl*, extras *pl*; **Nebenmann (-(e)s,** *pl* **-männer)** *m*: **Ihr Nebenmann** the person next to you; **Nebenprodukt** *nt* by-product; **Nebenrolle** *f* minor part; **Nebensache** *f* trifle, side issue; **nebensächlich** *adj* minor, peripheral; **Nebensaison** *f* low season; **Nebensatz** *m* (*Gram*) subordinate clause; **nebenstehend** *adj*: **nebenstehende Abbildung** illustration opposite; **Nebenstraße** *f* side street; **Nebenstrecke** *f* (*Eisenb*) branch *od* local line; **Nebenverdienst** *m* secondary income; **Nebenzimmer** *nt* adjoining room

neblig ['ne:blɪç] *adj* = **nebelig**

nebst [ne:pst] *präp +dat* together with

Necessaire [nesɛ'sɛ:r] **(-s, -s)** *nt* (*Nähnecessaire*) needlework box; (*Nagelnecessaire*) manicure case

Neckar ['nɛkar] **(-s)** *m* (*Fluss*) Neckar

necken ['nɛkən] *vt* to tease

Neckerei [nɛkə'raɪ] *f* teasing

neckisch *adj* coy; (*Einfall, Lied*) amusing

nee [ne:] (*umg*) *adv* no, nope

Neffe ['nɛfə] **(-n, -n)** *m* nephew

negativ ['ne:gati:f] *adj* negative; **Negativ (-s, -e)** *nt* (*Phot*) negative

Neger ['ne:gər] **(-s, -)** (*pej*) *m* negro (*pej*); **Negerin** (*pej*) *f* negress (*pej*); **Negerkuss** *m chocolate-covered marshmallow*

negieren [ne'gi:rən] *vt* (*bestreiten*) to deny; (*verneinen*) to negate

nehmen ['ne:mən] *unreg vt, vi* to take; **etw zu sich ~** to take sth, partake of sth (*liter*); **jdm etw ~** to take sth (away) from sb; **sich ernst ~** to take o.s. seriously; **~ Sie sich doch bitte** help yourself; **man nehme ...** (*Koch*) take ...; **wie mans nimmt** depending on your point of view; **die Mauer nimmt einem die ganze Sicht** the wall blocks the whole view; **er ließ es sich** *dat* **nicht ~, es persönlich zu tun** he insisted on doing it himself

Nehrung ['ne:rʊŋ] *f* (*Geog*) spit (of land)

Neid [naɪt] **(-(e)s)** *m* envy

Neider ['naɪdər] **(-s, -)** *m* envier

Neidhammel (*umg*) *m* envious person

neidisch *adj* envious, jealous

Neige (-, -n) *f* (*geh: Ende*): **die Vorräte gehen zur ~** the provisions are fast becoming exhausted

neigen ['naɪgən] *vt* to incline, lean; (*Kopf*) to bow ▷ *vi*: **zu etw ~** to tend to sth

Neigung *f* (*des Geländes*) slope; (*Tendenz*) tendency, inclination; (*Vorliebe*) liking; (*Zuneigung*) affection

Neigungswinkel *m* angle of inclination

nein [naɪn] *adv* no

Nelke ['nɛlkə] **(-, -n)** *f* carnation, pink; (*Gewürznelke*) clove

nennen ['nɛnən] *unreg vt* to name; (*mit Namen*) to call; **das nenne ich Mut!** that's what I call courage!

nennenswert *adj* worth mentioning

Nenner (-s, -) *m* denominator; **etw auf einen ~ bringen** (*lit, fig*) to reduce sth to a common denominator

Nennung *f* naming

Nennwert *m* nominal value; (*Comm*) par

neokonservativ *adj* neo-conservative, neo-con (*umg*)

neoliberal *adj* neo-liberal, neo-lib (*umg*)

Neon ['ne:ɔn] **(-s)** *nt* neon

Neonazi [neo'na:tsi] *m* Neonazi

Neon- *zW*: **Neonlicht** *nt* neon light; **Neonreklame** *f* neon sign; **Neonröhre** *f* neon tube

Nepal ['ne:pal] **(-s)** *nt* Nepal

Nepp [nɛp] **(-s)** (*umg*) *m*: **der reinste ~** daylight robbery, a rip-off

Nerv [nɛrf] **(-s, -en)** *m* nerve; **die ~en sind mit ihm durchgegangen** he lost control, he snapped (*umg*); **jdm auf die ~en gehen** to get on sb's nerves

nerven (*umg*) *vt*: **jdn ~** to get on sb's nerves

Nerven- *zW*: **Nervenaufreibend** *adj* nerve-racking; **Nervenbündel** *nt* bundle of nerves; **Nervengas** *nt* (*Mil*) nerve gas; **Nervenheilanstalt** *f* mental hospital; **Nervenklinik** *f* psychiatric clinic; **nervenkrank** *adj* mentally ill; **Nervensäge** (*umg*) *f* pain (in the neck); **Nervenschwäche** *f* neurasthenia; **Nervensystem** *nt* nervous system; **Nervenzusammenbruch** *m* nervous breakdown

nervig ['nɛrvɪç] (*umg*) *adj* exasperating, annoying

nervös [nɛr'vø:s] *adj* nervous

Nervosität [nɛrvozi'tɛ:t] *f* nervousness

nervtötend *adj* nerve-racking; (*Arbeit*) soul-destroying

Nerz [nɛrts] **(-es, -e)** *m* mink

Nessel ['nɛsəl] **(-, -n)** *f* nettle; **sich in die ~n setzen** (*fig: umg*) to put o.s. in a spot

Nessessär [nesɛ'sɛ:r] **(-s, -s)** *nt* = **Necessaire**

Nest [nɛst] **(-(e)s, -er)** *nt* nest; (*umg: Ort*) dump; (*fig: Bett*) bed; (*: Schlupfwinkel*) hide-out, lair; **da hat er sich ins warme ~ gesetzt** (*umg*) he's got it made; **Nestbeschmutzung** (*pej*) *f* running-down (*umg*) *od* denigration (of one's family/country)

nesteln *vi*: **an etw** *+dat* **~** to fumble *od* fiddle about with sth

Nesthäkchen ['nɛsthɛ:kçən] *nt* baby of the

family

nett [nɛt] *adj* nice; **sei so ~ und räum auf!** would you mind clearing up?

netterweise ['nɛtər'vaɪzə] *adv* kindly

netto *adv* net; **Nettoeinkommen** *nt* net income; **Nettogewicht** *nt* net weight; **Nettogewinn** *m* net profit; **Nettogewinnspanne** *f* net margin; **Nettolohn** *m* take-home pay; **Nettozahler** *m* (*Land etc*) net contributor

Netz [nɛts] (**-es, -e**) *nt* net; (*Gepäcknetz*) rack; (*Einkaufsnetz*) string bag; (*Spinnennetz*) web; (*System, Comput*) network; (*Stromnetz*) mains *sing od pl*; **das soziale ~** the social security network; **jdm ins ~ gehen** (*fig*) to fall into sb's trap; **Netzanbieter** *m* (*Comput*) Internet provider; **Netzanschluss** *m* mains connection; **Netzbetreiber** *m* (*Comput*) Internet provider; **Netzcomputer** *m* network computer; **Netzhaut** *f* retina; **Netzkarte** *f* (*Eisenb*) runabout ticket (*Brit*); **Netzplantechnik** *f* network analysis; **Netzspannung** *f* mains voltage; **Netzzugang** *m* (*Comput*) network access

neu [nɔʏ] *adj* new; (*Sprache, Geschichte*) modern; **der/die N~e** the new person, the newcomer; **seit N~estem** (since) recently; **~ schreiben** to rewrite, write again; **auf ein N~es!** (*Aufmunterung*) let's try again; **was gibts N~es?** (*umg*) what's the latest?; **von N~em** (*von vorn*) from the beginning; (*wieder*) again; **sich ~ einkleiden** to buy o.s. a new set of clothes; **~ eröffnet** newly-opened; (*wieder geöffnet*) reopened; **Neuankömmling** *m* newcomer; **Neuanschaffung** *f* new purchase *od* acquisition; **neuartig** *adj* new kind of; **Neuauflage** *f* new edition; **Neuausgabe** *f* new edition; **Neubau** (**-(e)s, -ten**) *m* new building; **Neubauwohnung** *f* newly-built flat; **Neubearbeitung** *f* revised edition; (*das Neubearbeiten*) revision, reworking; **Neudruck** *m* reprint; **Neuemission** *f* (*Aktien*) new issue

neuerdings *adv* (*kürzlich*) (since) recently; (*von Neuem*) again

Neuerscheinung *f* (*Buch*) new publication; (*Schallplatte*) new release

Neuerung *f* innovation, new departure

Neufassung *f* revised version

Neufundland [nɔʏ'fʊntlant] *nt* Newfoundland; **Neufundländer, in** (**-s, -**) *m(f)* Newfoundlander; **neufundländisch** *adj* Newfoundland *attrib*

neugeboren *adj* newborn; **sich wie ~ fühlen** to feel (like) a new man/woman

Neugier *f* curiosity

Neugierde (**-**) *f*: **aus ~** out of curiosity

neugierig *adj* curious

Neuguinea [nɔʏgi'ne:a] (**-s**) *nt* New Guinea

Neuheit *f* novelty; (*neuartige Ware*) new thing

Neuigkeit *f* news *sing*

neu- *zW*: **Neujahr** *nt* New Year; **Neuland** *nt* virgin land; (*fig*) new ground; **neulich** *adv* recently, the other day; **Neuling** *m* novice; **neumodisch** *adj* fashionable; (*pej*) newfangled; **Neumond** *m* new moon

neun [nɔʏn] *num* nine; **Neun** (**-, -en**) *f* nine; **ach du grüne Neune!** (*umg*) well I'm blowed!

neunmalklug *adj* (*ironisch*) smart-aleck *attrib*

neunzehn *num* nineteen

neunzig *num* ninety

Neuregelung, Neureglung *f* adjustment

neureich *adj* nouveau riche; **Neureiche, r** *f(m)* nouveau riche

Neurologie [nɔʏrolo'gi:] *f* neurology

neurologisch [nɔʏro'lo:gɪʃ] *adj* neurological

Neurose [nɔʏ'ro:zə] (**-, -n**) *f* neurosis

Neurotiker, in [nɔʏ'ro:tikər(ɪn)] (**-s, -**) *m(f)* neurotic

neurotisch *adj* neurotic

Neu- *zW*: **Neuschnee** *m* fresh snow; **Neuseeland** [nɔʏ'ze:lant] *nt* New Zealand; **Neuseeländer, in** (**-s, -**) *m(f)* New Zealander; **neuseeländisch** *adj* New Zealand *attrib*; **neusprachlich** *adj*: **neusprachliches Gymnasium** grammar school (*Brit*) *od* high school (*bes US*) stressing modern languages

neutral [nɔʏ'tra:l] *adj* neutral

neutralisieren [nɔʏtrali'zi:rən] *vt* to neutralize

Neutralität [nɔʏtrali'tɛ:t] *f* neutrality

Neutron ['nɔʏtrɔn] (**-s, -en**) *nt* neutron

Neutrum ['nɔʏtrʊm] (**-s, Neutra** *od* **Neutren**) *nt* neuter

Neu- *zW*: **Neuwert** *m* purchase price; **neuwertig** *adj* as new; **Neuzeit** *f* modern age; **neuzeitlich** *adj* modern, recent

N. H. *abk* (= *Normalhöhenpunkt*) normal peak (level)

nhd. *abk* (= *neuhochdeutsch*) NHG

Nicaragua [nika'ra:gua] (**-s**) *nt* Nicaragua; **Nicaraguaner, in** [nikaragu'a:nər(ɪn)] (**-s, -**) *m(f)* Nicaraguan; **nicaraguanisch** [nikaragu'a:nɪʃ] *adj* Nicaraguan

SCHLÜSSELWORT

nicht [nɪçt] *adv* **1** (*Verneinung*) not; **er ist es nicht** it's not him, it isn't him; **nicht rostend** stainless; **er raucht nicht** (*gerade*) he isn't smoking; (*gewöhnlich*) he doesn't smoke; **ich kann das nicht — ich auch nicht** I can't do it — neither *od* nor can I; **es regnet nicht mehr** it's not raining any more; **nicht mehr als** no more than

2 (*Bitte, Verbot*): **nicht!** don't!, no!; **nicht berühren!** do not touch!; **nicht doch!** don't!

3 (*rhetorisch*): **du bist müde, nicht (wahr)?** you're tired, aren't you?; **das ist schön, nicht (wahr)?** it's nice, isn't it?

4: was du nicht sagst! the things you say!

▷ *präf* non-

Nicht- *zW*: **Nichtachtung** *f* disregard; **Nichtanerkennung** *f* repudiation; **Nichtangriffspakt** *m* non-aggression pact

Nichte ['nɪçtə] (**-, -n**) *f* niece

Nicht- *zW*: **Nichteinhaltung** *f* (+*gen*) non-

compliance (with); **Nichteinmischung** *f* (*Pol*) nonintervention; **Nichtgefallen** *nt*: **bei Nichtgefallen (zurück)** if not satisfied (return)
nichtig ['nɪçtɪç] *adj* (*ungültig*) null, void; (*wertlos*) futile; **Nichtigkeit** *f* nullity, invalidity; (*Sinnlosigkeit*) futility
Nichtraucher *m* nonsmoker; **ich bin ~** I don't smoke
nichts [nɪçts] *pron* nothing; **~ ahnend** unsuspecting; **~ sagend** meaningless; **~ als** nothing but; **~ da!** (*ausgeschlossen*) nothing doing (*umg*); **~ wie raus/hin** *etc* (*umg*) let's get out/over there *etc* (on the double); **für ~ und wieder nichts** for nothing at all; **Nichts** (**-s**) *nt* nothingness; (*pej: Person*) nonentity
Nichtschwimmer (**-s, -**) *m* nonswimmer
nichts- *zW*: **nichtsdestotrotz** *adv* notwithstanding (*form*), nonetheless; **nichtsdestoweniger** *adv* nevertheless; **Nichtsnutz** (**-es, -e**) *m* good-for-nothing; **nichtsnutzig** *adj* worthless, useless; **nichtssagend** *adj* meaningless; **Nichtstun** (**-s**) *nt* idleness
Nichtzutreffende, s *nt*: **~s (bitte) streichen** (please) delete as applicable
Nickel ['nɪkəl] (**-s**) *nt* nickel; **Nickelbrille** *f* metal-rimmed glasses *pl*
nicken ['nɪkən] *vi* to nod
Nickerchen ['nɪkərçən] *nt* nap; **ein ~ machen** (*umg*) to have forty winks
Nicki ['nɪki] (**-s, -s**) *m* velours pullover
nie [ni:] *adv* never; **~ wieder** *od* **mehr** never again; **~ und nimmer** never ever; **fast ~** hardly ever
nieder ['ni:dər] *adj* low; (*gering*) inferior ▷ *adv* down; **niederdeutsch** *adj* (*Ling*) Low-German; **Niedergang** *m* decline; **niedergedrückt** *adj* depressed; **niedergehen** *unreg vi* to descend; (*Aviat*) to come down; (*Regen*) to fall; (*Boxer*) to go down; **niedergeschlagen** *adj* depressed, dejected; **Niedergeschlagenheit** *f* depression, dejection; **Niederkunft** *f* (*veraltet*) delivery, giving birth; **Niederlage** *f* defeat
Niederlande ['ni:dərlandə] *pl*: **die ~** the Netherlands *pl*
Niederländer, in ['ni:dərlɛndər(ɪn)] (**-s, -**) *m(f)* Dutchman, Dutchwoman
niederländisch *adj* Dutch, Netherlands *attrib*
nieder- *zW*: **niederlassen** *unreg vr* (*sich setzen*) to sit down; (*an Ort*) to settle (down); (*Arzt, Rechtsanwalt*) to set up in practice; **Niederlassung** *f* settlement; (*Comm*) branch; **niederlegen** *vt* to lay down; (*Arbeit*) to stop; (*Amt*) to resign; **niedermachen** *vt* to mow down; **Niederösterreich** *nt* Lower Austria; **Niederrhein** *m* Lower Rhine; **niederrheinisch** *adj* Lower Rhine *attrib*; **Niedersachsen** *nt* Lower Saxony; **Niederschlag** *m* (*Chem*) precipitate; (*Bodensatz*) sediment; (*Met*) precipitation (*form*), rainfall; (*Boxen*) knockdown; **radioaktiver Niederschlag** (radioactive) fallout; **niederschlagen** *unreg vt* (*Gegner*) to beat down; (*Gegenstand*) to knock down; (*Augen*) to lower; (*Jur: Prozess*) to dismiss; (*Aufstand*) to put down ▷ *vr* (*Chem*) to precipitate; **sich in etw** *dat* **niederschlagen** (*Erfahrungen etc*) to find expression in sth; **niederschlagsfrei** ['ni:dərʃla:ksfraɪ] *adj* dry, without precipitation (*form*); **niederschmetternd** *adj* (*Nachricht, Ergebnis*) shattering; **niederschreiben** *unreg vt* to write down; **Niederschrift** *f* transcription; **niedertourig** *adj* (*Motor*) low-revving; **niederträchtig** *adj* base, mean; **Niederträchtigkeit** *f* despicable *od* malicious behaviour
Niederung *f* (*Geog*) depression
niederwalzen ['ni:dərvaltsən] *vt*: **jdn/etw ~** (*umg*) to mow sb/sth down
niederwerfen ['ni:dərvɛrfən] *unreg vt* to throw down; (*fig*) to overcome; (*Aufstand*) to suppress
niedlich ['ni:tlɪç] *adj* sweet, nice, cute
niedrig ['ni:drɪç] *adj* low; (*Stand*) lowly, humble; (*Gesinnung*) mean
Niedriglohnsektor *m* low-wage sector
niemals ['ni:ma:ls] *adv* never
niemand ['ni:mant] *pron* nobody, no-one
Niemandsland ['ni:mantslant] *nt* no-man's-land
Niere ['ni:rə] (**-, -n**) *f* kidney; **künstliche ~** kidney machine
Nierenentzündung *f* kidney infection
nieseln ['ni:zəln] *vi* to drizzle
Nieselregen *m* drizzle
niesen ['ni:zən] *vi* to sneeze
Niespulver *nt* sneezing powder
Niet [ni:t] (**-(e)s, -e**) *m* (*Tech*) rivet
Niete ['ni:tə] (**-, -n**) *f* (*Tech*) rivet; (*Los*) blank; (*Reinfall*) flop; (*Mensch*) failure
nieten *vt* to rivet
Nietenhose *f* (pair of) studded jeans *pl*
niet- und nagelfest (*umg*) *adj* nailed down
Niger[1] ['ni:gər] (**-s**) *nt* (*Staat*) Niger
Niger[2] ['ni:gər] (**-s**) *m* (*Fluss*) Niger
Nigeria [ni'ge:ria] (**-s**) *nt* Nigeria; **Nigerianer, in** [nigeri'a:nər(ɪn)] *m(f)* Nigerian; **nigerianisch** [nige:ri'a:nɪʃ] *adj* Nigerian
Nihilismus [nihi'lɪsmʊs] *m* nihilism
Nihilist [nihi'lɪst] *m* nihilist; **nihilistisch** *adj* nihilistic
Nikolaus ['ni:kolaʊs] (**-, -e** *od (hum: umg)* **-läuse**) *m* ≈ Santa Claus, ≈ Father Christmas
Nikosia [niko'zi:a] (**-s**) *nt* Nicosia
Nikotin [niko'ti:n] (**-s**) *nt* nicotine; **nikotinarm** *adj* low-nicotine
Nil [ni:l] (**-s**) *m* Nile; **Nilpferd** *nt* hippopotamus
Nimbus ['nɪmbʊs] (**-, -se**) *m* (*Heiligenschein*) halo; (*fig*) aura
nimmersatt ['nɪmərzat] *adj* insatiable; **Nimmersatt** (**-(e)s, -e**) *m* glutton
Nimmerwiedersehen (*umg*) *nt*: **auf ~!** I never want to see you again
nimmt [nɪmt] *vb siehe* **nehmen**
nippen ['nɪpən] *vt, vi* to sip
Nippes ['nɪpəs] *pl* knick-knacks *pl*, bric-a-brac

sing
Nippsachen ['nɪpzaxən] *pl* knick-knacks *pl*
nirgends ['nɪrgənts] *adv* nowhere; **überall und ~** here, there and everywhere
nirgendwo ['nɪrgəntvo] *adv* = **nirgends**
nirgendwohin *adv* nowhere
Nische ['ni:ʃə] (**-, -n**) *f* niche
nisten ['nɪstən] *vi* to nest
Nitrat [ni'tra:t] (**-(e)s, -e**) *nt* nitrate
Niveau [ni'vo:] (**-s, -s**) *nt* level; **diese Schule hat ein hohes ~** this school has high standards; **unter meinem ~** beneath me
Nivellierung [nivɛ'li:rʊŋ] *f* (*Ausgleichung*) levelling out
nix [nɪks] (*umg*) *pron* = **nichts**
Nixe ['nɪksə] (**-, -n**) *f* water nymph
Nizza ['nɪtsa] (**-s**) *nt* Nice
n. J. *abk* (= *nächsten Jahres*) next year
n. M. *abk* (= *nächsten Monats*) next month
NN *abk* (= *Normalnull*) m.s.l.
N. N. *abk* = **NN**
NO *abk* (= *Nordost*) NE
no. *abk* (= *netto*) net
nobel ['no:bəl] *adj* (*großzügig*) generous; (*elegant*) posh (*umg*)
Nobelpreis [no'bɛlpraɪs] *m* Nobel prize; **Nobelpreisträger, in** *m(f)* Nobel prize winner

SCHLÜSSELWORT

noch [nɔx] *adv* **1** (*weiterhin*) still; **noch nicht** not yet; **noch nie** never (yet); **noch immer** *od* **immer noch** still; **bleiben Sie doch noch** stay a bit longer; **ich gehe kaum noch aus** I hardly go out any more
2 (*in Zukunft*) still, yet; (*irgendwann einmal*) one day; **das kann noch passieren** that might still happen; **er wird noch kommen** he'll come (yet); **das wirst du noch bereuen** you'll come to regret it (one day)
3 (*nicht später als*): **noch vor einer Woche** only a week ago; **noch am selben Tag** the very same day; **noch im 19. Jahrhundert** as late as the 19th century; **noch heute** today
4 (*zusätzlich*): **wer war noch da?** who else was there?; **noch (ein)mal** once more, again; **noch dreimal** three more times; **noch einer** another one; **und es regnete auch noch** and on top of that it was raining
5 (*bei Vergleichen*): **noch größer** even bigger; **das ist noch besser** that's better still; **und wenn es noch so schwer ist** however hard it is
6: Geld noch und noch heaps (and heaps) of money; **sie hat noch und noch versucht, ...** she tried again and again to ...
▷ *konj*: **weder A noch B** neither A nor B

nochmal, nochmals *adv siehe* **noch**
nochmalig *adj* repeated
Nockenwelle ['nɔkənvɛlə] *f* camshaft
NOK *nt abk* (= *Nationales Olympisches Komitee*) National Olympic Committee
Nom. *abk* = **Nominativ**
Nominalwert [nomi'na:lve:rt] *m* (*Fin*) nominal *od* par value
Nominativ ['no:minati:f] (**-s, -e**) *m* nominative
nominell [nomi'nɛl] *adj* nominal
nominieren [nomi'ni:rən] *vt* to nominate
Nonne ['nɔnə] (**-, -n**) *f* nun
Nonnenkloster *nt* convent
Nonplusultra [nɔnplʊs'|ʊltra] (**-s**) *nt* ultimate
Non-Profit-Unternehmen, Nonprofitunternehmen [nɔn'prɔfit-] *nt* non-profit company
Nord [nɔrt] (**-s**) *m* north; **Nordafrika** ['nɔrt'|a:frika] *nt* North Africa; **Nordamerika** *nt* North America; **nordamerikanisch** ['nɔrt|ameri'ka:nɪʃ] *adj* North American
nordd. *abk* = **norddeutsch**
norddeutsch *adj* North German
Norddeutschland *nt* North(ern) Germany
Norden ['nɔrdən] *m* north
Nord- *zW*: **Nordengland** *nt* the North of England; **Nordirland** *nt* Northern Ireland, Ulster; **nordisch** *adj* northern; **nordische Kombination** (*Ski*) nordic combination; **Nordkap** *nt* North Cape; **Nordkorea** ['nɔrtko're:a] *nt* North Korea
nördlich ['nœrtlɪç] *adj* northerly, northern ▷ *präp +gen* (to the) north of; **der ~e Polarkreis** the Arctic Circle; **N~es Eismeer** Arctic Ocean; **~ von** north of
Nord- *zW*: **Nordlicht** *nt* northern lights *pl*, aurora borealis; **Nord-Ostsee-Kanal** *m* Kiel Canal; **Nordpol** *m* North Pole; **Nordpolargebiet** *nt* Arctic (Zone)
Nordrhein-Westfalen ['nɔrtraɪnvɛst'fa:lən] (**-s**) *nt* North Rhine-Westphalia
Nordsee *f* North Sea
nordwärts *adv* northwards
Nörgelei [nœrgə'laɪ] *f* grumbling
nörgeln *vi* to grumble
Nörgler, in (**-s, -**) *m(f)* grumbler
Norm [nɔrm] (**-, -en**) *f* norm; (*Leistungssoll*) quota; (*Größenvorschrift*) standard (specification)
normal [nɔr'ma:l] *adj* normal; **bist du noch ~?** (*umg*) have you gone mad?; **Normalbenzin** *nt* two-star petrol (*Brit veraltet*), regular gas (*US*)
normalerweise *adv* normally
Normalfall *m*: **im ~** normally
Normalgewicht *nt* normal weight; (*genormt*) standard weight
normalisieren [nɔrmali'zi:rən] *vt* to normalize ▷ *vr* to return to normal
Normalzeit *f* (*Geog*) standard time
Normandie [nɔrman'di:] *f* Normandy
normen *vt* to standardize
Norwegen ['nɔrve:gən] (**-s**) *nt* Norway
Norweger, in (**-s, -**) *m(f)* Norwegian
norwegisch *adj* Norwegian
Nostalgie [nɔstal'gi:] *f* nostalgia
Not [no:t] (**-, ¨-e**) *f* need; (*Mangel*) want; (*Mühe*) trouble; (*Zwang*) necessity; **~ leidend** needy;

zur ~ if necessary; (*gerade noch*) just about; **wenn ~ am Mann ist** if you/they *etc* are short (*umg*); (*im Notfall*) in an emergency; **er hat seine liebe ~ mit ihr/damit** he really has problems with her/it; **in seiner ~** in his hour of need

Notar, in [no'ta:r(ɪn)] **(-s, -e)** *m(f)* notary; **notariell** *adj* notarial; **notariell beglaubigt** attested by a notary

Not- *zW*: **Notarzt** *m* doctor on emergency call; **Notausgang** *m* emergency exit; **Notbehelf** *m* stopgap; **Notbremse** *f* emergency brake; **Notdienst** *m*: **Notdienst haben** (*Apotheke*) to be open 24 hours; (*Arzt*) to be on call; **notdürftig** *adj* scanty; (*behelfsmäßig*) makeshift; **sich notdürftig verständigen können** to be able to communicate to some extent

Note ['no:tə] **(-, -n)** *f* note; (*Sch*) mark (*Brit*), grade (*US*); **Noten** *pl* (*Mus*) music *sing*; **eine persönliche ~** a personal touch

Noten- *zW*: **Notenbank** *f* issuing bank; **Notenblatt** *nt* sheet of music; **Notenschlüssel** *m* clef; **Notenständer** *m* music stand

Not- *zW*: **Notfall** *m* (case of) emergency; **notfalls** *adv* if need be; **notgedrungen** *adj* necessary, unavoidable; **etw notgedrungen machen** to be forced to do sth; **Notgroschen** ['no:tgrɔʃən] *m* nest egg

notieren [no'ti:rən] *vt* to note; (*Comm*) to quote

Notierung *f* (*Comm*) quotation

nötig ['nø:tɪç] *adj* necessary ▷ *adv* (*dringend*): **etw ~ brauchen** to need sth urgently; **etw ~ haben** to need sth; **das habe ich nicht ~!** I can do without that!

nötigen *vt* to compel, force; **nötigenfalls** *adv* if necessary

Nötigung *f* compulsion, coercion (*Jur*)

Notiz [no'ti:ts] **(-, -en)** *f* note; (*Zeitungsnotiz*) item; **~ nehmen** to take notice; **Notizblock** *m* notepad; **Notizbuch** *nt* notebook; **Notizzettel** *m* piece of paper

Not- *zW*: **Notlage** *f* crisis, emergency; **notlanden** *vi* to make a forced *od* emergency landing; **Notlandung** *f* forced *od* emergency landing; **Notlösung** *f* temporary solution; **Notlüge** *f* white lie

notorisch [no'to:rɪʃ] *adj* notorious

Not- *zW*: **Notruf** *m* emergency call; **Notrufsäule** *f* emergency telephone; **notschlachten** *vt* (*Tiere*) to destroy; **Notstand** *m* state of emergency; **Notstandsgebiet** *nt* (*wirtschaftlich*) depressed area; (*bei Katastrophen*) disaster area; **Notstandsgesetz** *nt* emergency law; **Notunterkunft** *f* emergency accommodation; **Notverband** *m* emergency dressing; **Notwehr** (-) *f* self-defence; **notwendig** *adj* necessary; **Notwendigkeit** *f* necessity; **Notzucht** *f* rape

Nov. *abk* (= *November*) Nov.

Novelle [no'vɛlə] **(-, -n)** *f* novella; (*Jur*) amendment

November [no'vɛmbər] **(-(s), -)** *m* November; *siehe auch* **September**

Novum ['no:vʊm] **(-s, Nova)** *nt* novelty

NPD (-) *f abk* (= *Nationaldemokratische Partei Deutschlands*) National Democratic Party

Nr. *abk* (= *Nummer*) no.

NRW *abk* = **Nordrhein-Westfalen**

NS *abk* = **Nachschrift; Nationalsozialismus**

NS- *in zW* Nazi

N. T. *abk* (= *Neues Testament*) N.T.

Nu [nu:] *m*: **im Nu** in an instant

Nuance [ny'ã:sə] **(-, -n)** *f* nuance; (*Kleinigkeit*) shade

nüchtern ['nʏçtərn] *adj* sober; (*Magen*) empty; (*Urteil*) prudent; **Nüchternheit** *f* sobriety

Nudel ['nu:dəl] **(-, -n)** *f* noodle; (*umg*: *Mensch*: *dick*) dumpling; ((: *komisch*) character; **Nudelholz** *nt* rolling pin

Nugat ['nu:gat] **(-s, -s)** *m od nt* nougat

nuklear [nukle'a:r] *adj attrib* nuclear

null [nʊl] *num* zero; (*Fehler*) no; **~ Uhr** midnight; **in ~ Komma nichts** (*umg*) in less than no time; **die Stunde ~** the new starting point; **gleich ~ sein** to be absolutely nil; **~ und nichtig** null and void; **Null (-, -en)** *f* nought, zero; (*pej*: *Mensch*) dead loss; **nullachtfünfzehn** (*umg*) *adj* run-of-the-mill; **Nulldiät** *f* starvation diet; **Nulllösung** *f* (*Pol*) zero option; **Nullpunkt** *m* zero; **auf dem Nullpunkt** at zero; **Nulltarif** *m* (*für Verkehrsmittel*) free travel; **zum Nulltarif** free of charge

numerieren [nume'ri:rən] *vt siehe* **nummerieren**

numerisch [nu'me:rɪʃ] *adj* numerical; **~es Tastenfeld** (*Comput*) numeric pad

Numerus ['nu:merʊs] **(-, Numeri)** *m* (*Gram*) number; **~ clausus** (*Univ*) restricted entry

Nummer ['nʊmər] **(-, -n)** *f* number; **auf ~ sicher gehen** (*umg*) to play (it) safe

nummerieren [nume'ri:rən] *vt* to number

Nummern- *zW*: **Nummernkonto** *nt* numbered bank account; **Nummernscheibe** *f* telephone dial; **Nummernschild** *nt* (*Aut*) number *od* license (*US*) plate

nun [nu:n] *adv* now ▷ *interj* well

nur [nu:r] *adv* just, only; **nicht ~ ..., sondern auch ...** not only ... but also ...; **alle, ~ ich nicht** everyone but me; **ich hab das ~ so gesagt** I was just talking

Nürnberg ['nʏrnbɛrk] **(-s)** *nt* Nuremberg

nuscheln ['nʊʃəln] (*umg*) *vt, vi* to mutter, mumble

Nuss [nʊs] **(-, ¨-e)** *f* nut; **eine doofe ~** (*umg*) a stupid twit; **eine harte ~** a hard nut (to crack); **Nussbaum** *m* walnut tree; **Nussknacker (-s, -)** *m* nutcracker

Nüster ['ny:stər] **(-, -n)** *f* nostril

Nutte ['nʊtə] **(-, -n)** *f* tart (*Brit*), hooker (*US*)

nutz [nʊts] *adj* = **nütze**; **nutzbar** *adj*: **nutzbar machen** to utilize; **Nutzbarmachung** *f* utilization; **nutzbringend** *adj* profitable; **etw nutzbringend anwenden** to use sth to good effect, put sth to good use

nütze ['nʏtsə] *adj*: **zu nichts ~ sein** to be useless
nutzen *vi* to be of use ▷ *vt*: **(zu etw) ~** to use (for sth); **was nutzt es?** what's the use?, what use is it?; **Nutzen** (**-s**) *m* usefulness; (*Gewinn*) profit; **von Nutzen** useful
nützen *vt, vi* = **nutzen**
Nutz- *zW*: **Nutzfahrzeug** *nt farm od military vehicle etc*; (*Comm*) commercial vehicle; **Nutzfläche** *f* us(e)able floor space; (*Agr*) productive land; **Nutzlast** *f* maximum load, payload
nützlich ['nʏtslıç] *adj* useful; **Nützlichkeit** *f* usefulness
Nutz- *zW*: **nutzlos** *adj* useless; (*unnötig*) needless; **Nutzlosigkeit** *f* uselessness; **Nutznießer** (**-s, -**) *m* beneficiary
Nutzung *f* (*Gebrauch*) use; (*das Ausnutzen*) exploitation
NW *abk* (= *Nordwest*) NW
Nylon ['naılɔn] (**-s**) *nt* nylon
Nymphe ['nʏmfə] (**-, -n**) *f* nymph

Oo

O¹, o [oː] *nt* O, o; **O wie Otto** ≈ O for Olive, ≈ O for Oboe (*US*)
O² [oː] *abk* (*= Osten*) E
o. Ä. *abk* (*= oder Ähnliche(s)*) or similar
Oase [o'aːzə] (**-, -n**) *f* oasis
OB (**-s, -s**) *m abk* = **Oberbürgermeister**
ob [ɔp] *konj* if, whether; **ob das wohl wahr ist?** can that be true?; **ob ich (nicht) lieber gehe?** maybe I'd better go; **(so) tun als ob** (*umg*) to pretend; **und ob!** you bet!
Obacht ['oːbaxt] *f*: **~ geben** to pay attention
Obdach ['ɔpdax] (**-(e)s**) *nt* shelter, lodging; **obdachlos** *adj* homeless; **Obdachlosenasyl** *nt* hostel *od* shelter for the homeless; **Obdachlosenheim** *nt* = **Obdachlosenasyl**; **Obdachlose, r** *f(m)* homeless person
Obduktion [ɔpdʊktsi'oːn] *f* postmortem
obduzieren [ɔpdu'tsiːrən] *vt* to do a postmortem on
O-Beine ['oːbaɪnə] *pl* bow *od* bandy legs *pl*
oben ['oːbən] *adv* above; (*in Haus*) upstairs; (*am oberen Ende*) at the top; **~ erwähnt, ~ genannt** above-mentioned; **nach ~** up; **von ~** down; **siehe ~** see above; **ganz ~** right at the top; **~ ohne** topless; **die Abbildung ~ links** *od* **links oben** the illustration in the top left-hand corner; **jdn von ~ herab behandeln** to treat sb condescendingly; **jdn von ~ bis unten ansehen** to look sb up and down; **Befehl von ~** orders from above; **die da ~** (*umg: die Vorgesetzten*) the powers that be; **oben'an** *adv* at the top; **oben'auf** *adv* up above, on the top ▷ *adj* (*munter*) in form; **oben'drein** *adv* into the bargain; **oben'hin** *adv* cursorily, superficially
Ober ['oːbər] (**-s, -**) *m* waiter
Ober- *zW*: **Oberarm** *m* upper arm; **Oberarzt** *m* senior physician; **Oberaufsicht** *f* supervision; **Oberbayern** *nt* Upper Bavaria; **Oberbefehl** *m* supreme command; **Oberbefehlshaber** *m* commander-in-chief; **Oberbegriff** *m* generic term; **Oberbekleidung** *f* outer clothing; **Oberbett** *nt* quilt; **Oberbürgermeister** *m* lord mayor; **Oberdeck** *nt* upper *od* top deck
obere, r, s *adj* upper; **die O~n** the bosses; (*Eccl*) the superiors; **die ~n Zehntausend** (*umg*) high society
Ober- *zW*: **Oberfläche** *f* surface; **oberflächlich** *adj* superficial; **bei oberflächlicher Betrachtung** at a quick glance; **jdn (nur) oberflächlich kennen** to know sb (only) slightly; **Obergeschoss** *nt* upper storey *od* story (*US*); **im zweiten Obergeschoss** on the second floor (*Brit*), on the third floor (*US*); **oberhalb** *adv* above ▷ *präp +gen* above; **Oberhand** *f* (*fig*): **die Oberhand gewinnen (über** *+akk*) to get the upper hand (over); **Oberhaupt** *nt* head, chief; **Oberhaus** *nt* (*in Großbritannien*) upper house, House of Lords; **Oberhemd** *nt* shirt; **Oberherrschaft** *f* supremacy, sovereignty
Oberin *f* matron; (*Eccl*) Mother Superior
Ober- *zW*: **oberirdisch** *adj* above ground; (*Leitung*) overhead; **Oberitalien** *nt* Northern Italy; **Oberkellner** *m* head waiter; **Oberkiefer** *m* upper jaw; **Oberkommando** *nt* supreme command; **Oberkörper** *m* upper part of body; **Oberlauf** *m*: **am Oberlauf des Rheins** in the upper reaches of the Rhine; **Oberleitung** *f* (*Elek*) overhead cable; **Oberlicht** *nt* skylight; **Oberlippe** *f* upper lip; **Oberösterreich** *nt* Upper Austria; **Oberprima** *f* (*früher*) *final year of German secondary school*; **Oberschenkel** *m* thigh; **Oberschicht** *f* upper classes *pl*; **Oberschule** *f* grammar school (*Brit*), high school (*US*); **Oberschwester** *f* (*Med*) matron; **Oberseite** *f* top (side); **Obersekunda** *f* (*früher*) *seventh year of German secondary school*
Oberst ['oːbərst] (**-en** *od* **-s, -en** *od* **-e**) *m* colonel
oberste, r, s *adj* very top, topmost
Ober- *zW*: **Oberstübchen** (*umg*) *nt*: **er ist nicht ganz richtig im Oberstübchen** he's not quite right up top; **Oberstufe** *f* upper school; **Oberteil** *nt* upper part; **Obertertia** *f* (*früher*) *fifth year of German secondary school*; **Oberwasser** *nt*: **Oberwasser haben/bekommen** to be/get on top (of things); **Oberweite** *f* bust *od* chest measurement
obgleich [ɔp'glaɪç] *konj* although
Obhut ['ɔphuːt] (**-**) *f* care, protection; **in jds ~** *dat* **sein** to be in sb's care
obig ['oːbɪç] *adj* above
Objekt [ɔp'jɛkt] (**-(e)s, -e**) *nt* object
objektiv [ɔpjɛk'tiːf] *adj* objective
Objektiv (**-s, -e**) *nt* lens *sing*
Objektivität [ɔpjɛktivi'tɛːt] *f* objectivity
Oblate [o'blaːtə] (**-, -n**) *f* (*Gebäck*) wafer; (*Eccl*)

host

obligatorisch [obliga'to:rɪʃ] *adj* compulsory, obligatory

Oboe [o'bo:ə] (**-, -n**) *f* oboe

Obrigkeit ['o:brɪçkaɪt] *f* (*Behörden*) authorities *pl*, administration; (*Regierung*) government

Obrigkeitsdenken *nt* acceptance of authority

obschon [ɔp'ʃo:n] *konj* although

Observatorium [ɔpzɛrva'to:riʊm] *nt* observatory

obskur [ɔps'ku:r] *adj* obscure; (*verdächtig*) dubious

Obst [o:pst] (**-(e)s**) *nt* fruit; **Obstbau** *m* fruit-growing; **Obstbaum** *m* fruit tree; **Obstgarten** *m* orchard; **Obsthändler** *m* fruiterer (*Brit*), fruit merchant; **Obstkuchen** *m* fruit tart; **Obstsaft** *m* fruit juice; **Obstsalat** *m* fruit salad

obszön [ɔps'tsø:n] *adj* obscene

Obszönität [ɔpstøni'tɛ:t] *f* obscenity

Obus ['o:bʊs] (**-ses, -se**) (*umg*) *m* trolleybus

obwohl [ɔp'vo:l] *konj* although

Ochse ['ɔksə] (**-n, -n**) *m* ox; (*umg: Dummkopf*) twit; **er stand da wie der ~ vorm Berg** (*umg*) he stood there utterly bewildered

ochsen (*umg*) *vt, vi* to cram, swot (*Brit*)

Ochsenschwanzsuppe *f* oxtail soup

Ochsenzunge *f* ox tongue

Ocker ['ɔkər] (**-s, -**) *m od nt* ochre (*Brit*), ocher (*US*)

öd [ø:t(ə)] *adj* = **öde**

öde *adj* (*Land*) waste, barren; (*fig*) dull; **~ und leer** dreary and desolate

Öde (**-, -n**) *f* desert, waste(land); (*fig*) tedium

oder ['o:dər] *konj* or; **entweder ...** ~ either ... or; **du kommst doch, ~?** you're coming, aren't you?

Ofen ['o:fən] (**-s, ¨**) *m* oven; (*Heizofen*) fire, heater; (*Kohleofen*) stove; (*Hochofen*) furnace; (*Herd*) cooker, stove; **jetzt ist der ~ aus** (*umg*) that does it!; **Ofenrohr** *nt* stovepipe

offen ['ɔfən] *adj* open; (*aufrichtig*) frank; (*Stelle*) vacant; (*Bein*) ulcerated; (*Haare*) loose; **~er Wein** wine by the carafe *od* glass; **auf ~er Strecke** (*Straße*) on the open road; (*Eisenb*) between stations; **Tag der ~en Tür** open day (*Brit*), open house (*US*); **~e Handelsgesellschaft** (*Comm*) general *od* ordinary (*US*) partnership; **~ bleiben** (*Fenster*) to stay open; **~ halten** to keep open; **~ lassen** to leave open; **~ stehen** to be open; **seine Meinung ~ sagen** to speak one's mind; **ein ~es Wort mit jdm reden** to have a frank talk with sb; ~ **gesagt** to be honest; *siehe auch* **offenbleiben; offenstehen**

offenbar *adj* obvious; (*vermutlich*) apparently

offenbaren [ɔfən'ba:rən] *vt* to reveal, manifest

Offenbarung *f* (*Rel*) revelation

Offenbarungseid *m* (*Jur*) oath of disclosure

Offen- *zW*: **offenbleiben** *unreg vi* (*fig: Frage, Entscheidung*) to remain open; *siehe auch* **offen**; **Offenheit** *f* candour (*Brit*), candor (*US*), frankness; **offenherzig** *adj* candid, frank; (*hum: Kleid*) revealing; **Offenherzigkeit** *f* frankness; **offenkundig** *adj* well-known; (*klar*) evident; **offensichtlich** *adj* evident, obvious

offensiv [ɔfɛn'zi:f] *adj* offensive

Offensive (**-, -n**) *f* offensive

offenstehen *unreg vi* (*fig: Rechnung*) to be unpaid; **es steht Ihnen offen, es zu tun** you are at liberty to do it; **die (ganze) Welt steht ihm offen** he has the (whole) world at his feet; *siehe auch* **offen**

öffentlich ['œfəntlɪç] *adj* public; **die ~e Hand** (central/local) government; **Anstalt des ~en Rechts** public institution; **Ausgaben der ~en Hand** public spending *sing*

Öffentlichkeit *f* (*Leute*) public; (*einer Versammlung etc*) public nature; **in aller ~** in public; **an die ~ dringen** to reach the public ear; **unter Ausschluss der ~** in secret; (*Jur*) in camera

Öffentlichkeitsarbeit *f* public relations work

öffentlich-rechtlich *adj attrib* (under) public law

offerieren [ɔfe'ri:rən] *vt* to offer

Offerte [ɔ'fɛrtə] (**-, -n**) *f* offer

offiziell [ɔfitsi'ɛl] *adj* official

Offizier [ɔfi'tsi:r] (**-s, -e**) *m* officer

Offizierskasino *nt* officers' mess

öffnen ['œfnən] *vt, vr* to open; **jdm die Tür ~** to open the door for sb

Öffner ['œfnər] (**-s, -**) *m* opener

Öffnung ['œfnʊŋ] *f* opening

Öffnungsklausel *f* (*Jur*) escape clause; (*fig: Schlupfloch*) loophole

Öffnungszeiten *pl* opening times *pl*

Offsetdruck ['ɔfsɛtdrʊk] *m* offset (printing)

oft [ɔft] *adv* often

öfter ['œftər] *adv* more often *od* frequently; **des Öfteren** quite frequently; **~ mal was Neues** (*umg*) variety is the spice of life (*Sprichwort*)

öfters *adv* often, frequently

oftmals *adv* often, frequently

o. G. *abk* (= *ohne Gewähr*) without liability

OHG *f abk* (= *offene Handelsgesellschaft*) *siehe* **offen**

ohne ['o:nə] *präp +akk, konj* without; **das Darlehen ist ~ Weiteres bewilligt worden** the loan was granted without any problem; **das kann man nicht ~ Weiteres voraussetzen** you can't just assume that automatically; **das ist nicht ~** (*umg*) it's not bad; **~ Weiteres** without a second thought; (*sofort*) immediately; **ohnedies** *adv* anyway; **ohneeinander** [o:nə|aɪ'nandər] *adv* without each other; **ohnegleichen** *adj* unsurpassed, without equal; **ohnehin** *adv* anyway, in any case; **es ist ohnehin schon spät** it's late enough already

Ohnmacht ['o:nmaxt] *f* faint; (*fig*) impotence; **in ~ fallen** to faint

ohnmächtig ['o:nmɛçtɪç] *adj* in a faint, unconscious; (*fig*) weak, impotent; **sie ist ~** she has fainted; **ohnmächtige Wut, ~er Zorn** helpless rage; **einer Sache** *dat* **~ gegenüberstehen** to be helpless in the face of sth

Ohr [o:r] (**-(e)s, -en**) *nt* ear; (*Gehör*) hearing; **sich aufs ~ legen** *od* **hauen** (*umg*) to kip down; **jdm die ~en lang ziehen** (*umg*) to tweak sb's ear(s); **jdm in den ~en liegen** to keep on at sb; **jdn übers ~ hauen** (*umg*) to pull a fast one on sb; **auf dem ~ bin ich taub** (*fig*) nothing doing (*umg*); **schreib es dir hinter die ~en** (*umg*) will you (finally) get that into your (thick) head!; **bis über die** *od* **beide ~en verliebt sein** to be head over heels in love; **viel um die ~en haben** (*umg*) to have a lot on (one's plate); **halt die ~en steif!** keep a stiff upper lip!

Öhr [ø:r] (**-(e)s, -e**) *nt* eye

Ohren- *zW*: **Ohrenarzt** *m* ear specialist; **ohrenbetäubend** *adj* deafening; **Ohrensausen** *nt* (*Med*) buzzing in one's ears; **Ohrenschmalz** *nt* earwax; **Ohrenschmerzen** *pl* earache *sing*; **Ohrenschützer** (**-s, -**) *m* earmuff

Ohr- *zW*: **Ohrfeige** *f* slap on the face; (*als Strafe*) box on the ears; **ohrfeigen** *vt untr*: **jdn ohrfeigen** to slap sb's face; to box sb's ears; **ich könnte mich selbst ohrfeigen, dass ich das gemacht habe** I could kick myself for doing that; **Ohrläppchen** *nt* ear lobe; **Ohrringe** *pl* earrings *pl*; **Ohrwurm** *m* earwig; (*Mus*) catchy tune

o. J. *abk* (= *ohne Jahr*) no year given

okkupieren [ɔku'pi:rən] *vt* to occupy

Öko- ['øko-] *in zw* eco-, ecological; **Ökofonds** ['ø:kofo˜:] *m* eco-fund, green fund; **Ökoladen** ['ø:kola:dən] *m* wholefood shop

Ökologie [økolo'gi:] *f* ecology

ökologisch [øko'lo:gɪʃ] *adj* ecological, environmental

Ökonometrie [økonome'tri:] *f* econometrics *pl*

Ökonomie [økono'mi:] *f* economy; (*als Wissenschaft*) economics *sing*

ökonomisch [øko'no:mɪʃ] *adj* economical

Ökopax [øko'paks] (**-en, -e**) (*umg*) *m* environmentalist

Ökosystem ['ø:kozʏste:m] *nt* ecosystem

Okt. *abk* (= *Oktober*) Oct.

Oktan [ɔk'ta:n] (**-s, -e**) *nt* octane; **Oktanzahl** *f* octane rating

Oktave [ɔk'ta:və] (**-, -n**) *f* octave

Oktober [ɔk'to:bər] (**-(s), -**) *m* October; *siehe auch* **September**

Oktoberfest *nt see culture note*

OKTOBERFEST

The annual October beer festival, the *Oktoberfest*, takes place in Munich on a huge field where beer tents, roller coasters and many other amusements are set up. People sit at long wooden tables, drink beer from enormous litre beer mugs, eat pretzels and listen to brass bands. It is a great attraction for tourists and locals alike.

ökumenisch [øku'me:nɪʃ] *adj* ecumenical

Öl [ø:l] (**-(e)s, -e**) *nt* oil; **auf Öl stoßen** to strike oil

Öl- *zW*: **Ölbaum** *m* olive tree; **ölen** *vt* to oil; (*Tech*) to lubricate; **wie ein geölter Blitz** (*umg*) like greased lightning; **Ölfarbe** *f* oil paint; **Ölfeld** *nt* oilfield; **Ölfilm** *m* film of oil; **Ölheizung** *f* oil-fired central heating

ölig *adj* oily

Oligopol [oligo'po:l] (**-s, -e**) *nt* oligopoly

oliv [o'li:f] *adj* olive-green

Olive [o'li:və] (**-, -n**) *f* olive

Olivenöl *nt* olive oil

Öljacke *f* oilskin jacket

oll [ɔl] (*umg*) *adj* old; **das sind ~e Kamellen** that's old hat

Öl- *zW*: **Ölmessstab** *m* dipstick; **Ölpest** *f* oil pollution; **Ölplattform** *f* oil rig; **Ölsardine** *f* sardine; **Ölscheich** *m* oil sheik; **Ölstand** *m* oil level; **Ölstandanzeiger** *m* (*Aut*) oil level indicator; **Öltanker** *m* oil tanker; **Ölteppich** *m* oil slick

Ölung *f* oiling; (*Eccl*) anointment; **die Letzte ~** Extreme Unction

Ölwanne *f* (*Aut*) sump (*Brit*), oil pan (*US*)

Ölwechsel *m* oil change

Olymp [o'lʏmp] (**-s**) *m* (*Berg*) Mount Olympus

Olympiade [olʏmpi'a:də] (**-, -n**) *f* Olympic Games *pl*

Olympiasieger, in [o'lʏmpiazi:gər(ɪn)] *m(f)* Olympic champion

olympisch [o'lʏmpɪʃ] *adj* Olympic

Ölzeug *nt* oilskins *pl*

Oma ['o:ma] (**-, -s**) (*umg*) *f* granny

Oman [o'ma:n] (**-s**) *nt* Oman

Omelett [ɔm(ə)'lɛt] (**-(e)s, -s**) *nt* omelette (*Brit*), omelet (*US*)

Omelette [ɔm(ə)'lɛt] *f* = **Omelett**

Omen ['o:mɛn] (**-s, -** *od* **Omina**) *nt* omen

Omnibus ['ɔmnibʊs] *m* (omni)bus

Onanie [ona'ni:] *f* masturbation

onanieren *vi* to masturbate

ondulieren [ɔndu'li:rən] *vt, vi* to crimp

Onkel ['ɔŋkəl] (**-s, -**) *m* uncle

online ['ɔnlaɪn] *adj* (*Comput*) on-line

Onlineauktion *f* on-line auction

Onlinedienst *m* (*Comput*) on-line service

OP *m abk* = **Operationssaal**

Opa ['o:pa] (**-s, -s**) (*umg*) *m* grandpa

Opal [o'pa:l] (**-s, -e**) *m* opal

Oper ['o:pər] (**-, -n**) *f* opera; (*Opernhaus*) opera house

Operation [operatsi'o:n] *f* operation

Operationssaal *m* operating theatre (*Brit*) *od* theater (*US*)

operativ [opəra'ti:f] *adv* (*Med*): **eine Geschwulst ~ entfernen** to remove a growth by surgery

Operette [ope'rɛtə] *f* operetta

operieren [ope'ri:rən] *vt, vi* to operate; **sich ~ lassen** to have an operation

Opern- *zW*: **Opernglas** *nt* opera glasses *pl*; **Opernhaus** *nt* opera house; **Opernsänger, in** *m(f)* opera singer

Opfer ['ɔpfər] (**-s, -**) *nt* sacrifice; (*Mensch*)

victim; **Opferbereitschaft** *f* readiness to make sacrifices
opfern *vt* to sacrifice
Opferstock *m* (*Eccl*) offertory box
Opferung *f* sacrifice; (*Eccl*) offertory
Opium ['o:piʊm] (**-s**) *nt* opium
opponieren [ɔpo'ni:rən] *vi*: **gegen jdn/etw ~** to oppose sb/sth
opportun [ɔpɔr'tu:n] *adj* opportune; **Opportunismus** [-'nɪsmʊs] *m* opportunism; **Opportunist, in** [-'nɪst(ɪn)] *m(f)* opportunist
Opposition [ɔpozitsi'o:n] *f* opposition
oppositionell [ɔpozitsio:'nɛl] *adj* opposing
Oppositionsführer *m* leader of the opposition
optieren [ɔp'ti:rən] *vi* (*Pol: form*): **~ für** to opt for
Optik ['ɔptɪk] *f* optics *sing*
Optiker, in (**-s, -**) *m(f)* optician
optimal [ɔpti'ma:l] *adj* optimal, optimum
Optimismus [ɔpti'mɪsmʊs] *m* optimism
Optimist, in [ɔpti'mɪst(ɪn)] *m(f)* optimist; **optimistisch** *adj* optimistic
optisch ['ɔptɪʃ] *adj* optical; **~e Täuschung** optical illusion
Orakel [o'ra:kəl] (**-s, -**) *nt* oracle
Orange [o'rã:ʒə] (**-, -n**) *f* orange; **orange** *adj* orange
Orangeade [orã'ʒa:də] (**-, -n**) *f* orangeade
Orangeat [orã'ʒa:t] (**-s, -e**) *nt* candied peel
Orangen- *zW*: **Orangenmarmelade** *f* marmalade; **Orangensaft** *m* orange juice; **Orangenschale** *f* orange peel
Oratorium [ora'to:riʊm] *nt* (*Mus*) oratorio
Orchester [ɔr'kɛstər] (**-s, -**) *nt* orchestra
Orchidee [ɔrçi'de:ə] (**-, -n**) *f* orchid
Orden ['ɔrdən] (**-s, -**) *m* (*Eccl*) order; (*Mil*) decoration
Ordensgemeinschaft *f* religious order
Ordensschwester *f* nun
ordentlich ['ɔrdəntlɪç] *adj* (*anständig*) decent, respectable; (*geordnet*) tidy, neat; (*umg: annehmbar*) not bad; (*: tüchtig*) real, proper; (*Leistung*) reasonable; **~es Mitglied** full member; **~er Professor** (full) professor; **eine ~e Tracht Prügel** a proper hiding; **~ arbeiten** to be a thorough and precise worker; **Ordentlichkeit** *f* respectability; tidiness
Order (**-, -s** *od* **-n**) *f* (*Comm: Auftrag*) order
ordern *vt* (*Comm*) to order
Ordinalzahl [ɔrdi'na:ltsa:l] *f* ordinal number
ordinär [ɔrdi'nɛ:r] *adj* common, vulgar
Ordinarius [ɔrdi'na:riʊs] (**-, Ordinarien**) *m* (*Univ*): **~ (für)** professor (of)
ordnen ['ɔrdnən] *vt* to order, put in order
Ordner (**-s, -**) *m* steward; (*Comm*) file
Ordnung *f* order; (*Ordnen*) ordering; (*Geordnetsein*) tidiness; **geht in ~** (*umg*) that's all right *od* OK (*umg*); **~ schaffen, für ~ sorgen** to put things in order, tidy things up; **jdn zur ~ rufen** to call sb to order; **bei ihm muss alles seine ~ haben** (*räumlich*) he has to have everything in its proper place; (*zeitlich*) he has to do everything according to a fixed schedule; **das Kind braucht seine ~** the child needs a routine
Ordnungs- *zW*: **Ordnungsamt** *nt* ≈ town clerk's office; **ordnungsgemäß** *adj* proper, according to the rules; **ordnungshalber** *adv* as a matter of form; **Ordnungsliebe** *f* tidiness, orderliness; **Ordnungsstrafe** *f* fine; **ordnungswidrig** *adj* contrary to the rules, irregular; **Ordnungswidrigkeit** *f* infringement (*of law or rule*); **Ordnungszahl** *f* ordinal number
ORF (**-**) *m abk* (= *Österreichischer Rundfunk*)
Organ [ɔr'ga:n] (**-s, -e**) *nt* organ; (*Stimme*) voice
Organisation [ɔrganizatsi'o:n] *f* organization
Organisationstalent *nt* organizing ability; (*Person*) good organizer
Organisator [ɔrgani'za:tɔr] *m* organizer
organisch [ɔr'ga:nɪʃ] *adj* organic; (*Erkrankung, Leiden*) physical
organisieren [ɔrgani'zi:rən] *vt* to organize, arrange; (*umg: beschaffen*) to acquire ▷ *vr* to organize
Organismus [ɔrga'nɪsmʊs] *m* organism
Organist [ɔrga'nɪst] *m* organist
Organspender *m* donor (of an organ)
Organspenderausweis *m* donor card
Organverpflanzung *f* transplantation (of an organ)
Orgasmus [ɔr'gasmʊs] *m* orgasm
Orgel ['ɔrgəl] (**-, -n**) *f* organ; **Orgelpfeife** *f* organ pipe; **wie die Orgelpfeifen stehen** to stand in order of height
Orgie ['ɔrgiə] *f* orgy
Orient ['o:riɛnt] (**-s**) *m* Orient, east; **der Vordere ~** the Near East
Orientale [o:riɛn'ta:lə] (**-n, -n**) *m* Oriental
Orientalin [o:riɛn'ta:lɪn] *f* Oriental
orientalisch *adj* oriental
orientieren [o:riɛn'ti:rən] *vt* (*örtlich*) to locate; (*fig*) to inform ▷ *vr* to find one's way *od* bearings; (*fig*) to inform o.s.
Orientierung [o:riɛn'ti:rʊŋ] *f* orientation; (*fig*) information; **die ~ verlieren** to lose one's bearings
Orientierungssinn *m* sense of direction
Orientierungsstufe *m* *see culture note*

ORIENTIERUNGSSTUFE

The *Orientierungsstufe* is the name given to the first two years spent in a *Realschule* or *Gymnasium*, during which a child is assessed as to his or her suitability for the school. At the end of the two years it may be decided to transfer the child to a school more suited to his or her ability.

original [origi'na:l] *adj* original; **~ Meißener Porzellan** genuine Meissen porcelain; **Original** (**-s, -e**) *nt* original; (*Mensch*) character; **Originalausgabe** *f* first edition; **Originalfassung** *f* original version
Originalität [originali'tɛ:t] *f* originality
Originalübertragung *f* live broadcast
originell [origi'nɛl] *adj* original

Orkan [ɔr'ka:n] (**-(e)s, -e**) *m* hurricane; **orkanartig** *adj* (*Wind*) gale-force; (*Beifall*) thunderous
Orkneyinseln ['ɔ:knɪ|ɪnzəln] *pl* Orkney Islands *pl*, Orkneys *pl*
Ornament [ɔrna'mɛnt] *nt* decoration, ornament
ornamental [ɔrnamɛn'ta:l] *adj* decorative, ornamental
Ornithologe [ɔrnito'lo:gə] (**-n, -n**) *m* ornithologist
Ornithologin [ɔrnito'lo:gɪn] *f* ornithologist
Ort[1] [ɔrt] (**-(e)s, -e**) *m* place; **an ~ und Stelle** on the spot; **am ~** in the place; **am angegebenen ~** in the place quoted, loc. cit.; **~ der Handlung** (*Theat*) scene of the action; **das ist höheren ~(e)s entschieden worden** (*hum: form*) the decision came from above
Ort[2] [ɔrt] (**-(e)s, ¨er**) *m*: **vor ~** at the (coal) face; (*auch fig*) on the spot
Örtchen ['œrtçən] (*umg*) *nt* loo (*Brit*), john (*US*)
orten *vt* to locate
orthodox [ɔrto'dɔks] *adj* orthodox
Orthografie [ɔrtogra'fi:] *f* spelling, orthography
orthografisch [ɔrto'gra:fɪʃ] *adj* orthographic
Orthopäde [ɔrto'pɛ:də] (**-n, -n**) *m* orthopaedic (*Brit*) *od* orthopedic (*US*) specialist, orthopaedist (*Brit*), orthopedist (*US*)
Orthopädie [ɔrtopɛ'di:] *f* orthopaedics *sing* (*Brit*), orthopedics *sing* (*US*)
orthopädisch *adj* orthopaedic (*Brit*), orthopedic (*US*)
örtlich ['œrtlɪç] *adj* local; **jdn ~ betäuben** to give sb a local anaesthetic (*Brit*) *od* anesthetic (*US*); **Örtlichkeit** *f* locality; **sich mit den Örtlichkeiten vertraut machen** to get to know the place
Ortsangabe *f* (name of the) town; **ohne ~** (*Buch*) no place of publication indicated
ortsansässig *adj* local
Ortschaft *f* village, small town; **geschlossene ~** built-up area
Orts- *zW*: **ortsfremd** *adj* nonlocal; **Ortsfremde, r** *f(m)* stranger; **Ortsgespräch** *nt* local (phone) call; **Ortsgruppe** *f* local branch *od* group; **Ortskenntnis** *f*: **(gute) Ortskenntnisse haben** to know one's way around (well); **Ortskrankenkasse** *f*: **Allgemeine Ortskrankenkasse** *compulsory medical insurance scheme*; **ortskundig** *adj* familiar with the place; **ortskundig sein** to know one's way around; **Ortsname** *m* place name; **Ortsnetz** *nt* (*Tel*) local telephone exchange area; **Ortsnetzkennzahl** *f* (*Tel*) dialling (*Brit*) *od* area (*US*) code; **Ortsschild** *nt* place name sign; **Ortssinn** *m* sense of direction; **Ortstarif** *m* (*Tel*) charge for local calls; **Ortsvorschriften** *pl* by(e)-laws *pl*; **Ortszeit** *f* local time; **Ortszuschlag** *m* (local) weighting allowance
Ortung *f* locating
öS. *abk* (*= österreichischer Schilling*)
Öse ['ø:zə] (**-, -n**) *f* loop; (*an Kleidung*) eye
Oslo ['ɔslo] (**-s**) *nt* Oslo
Ossi ['ɔsi] (**-s, -s**) (*umg*) *m* East German; *see culture note*

OSSI

Ossi is a colloquial and rather derogatory word used to describe a German from the former *DDR*.

öst. *abk* (*= österreichisch*) Aust.
Ost- *zW*: **Ostafrika** *nt* East Africa; **ostdeutsch** *adj* East German; **Ostdeutsche, Ostdeutscher** *f(m)* East German; **Ostdeutschland** *nt* (*Pol: früher*) East Germany; (*Geog*) Eastern Germany
Osten (**-s**) *m* east; **der Ferne ~** the Far East; **der Nahe ~** the Middle East, the Near East
ostentativ [ɔstɛnta'ti:f] *adj* pointed, ostentatious
Oster- *zW*: **Osterei** *nt* Easter egg; **Osterfest** *nt* Easter; **Osterglocke** *f* daffodil; **Osterhase** *m* Easter bunny; **Osterinsel** *f* Easter Island; **Ostermarsch** *m* Easter demonstration; **Ostermontag** *m* Easter Monday
Ostern (**-s, -**) *nt* Easter; **frohe** *od* **fröhliche ~!** Happy Easter!; **zu ~** at Easter
Österreich ['ø:stəraɪç] (**-s**) *nt* Austria
Österreicher, in (**-s, -**) *m(f)* Austrian
österreichisch *adj* Austrian
Ostersonntag *m* Easter Day *od* Sunday
Osteuropa *nt* East(ern) Europe
osteuropäisch *adj* East European
östlich ['œstlɪç] *adj* eastern, easterly
Östrogen [œstro'ge:n] (**-s, -e**) *nt* oestrogen (*Brit*), estrogen (*US*)
Ost- *zW*: **Ostsee** *f* Baltic Sea; **ostwärts** *adv* eastwards; **Ostwind** *m* east wind
oszillieren [ɔstsɪ'li:rən] *vi* to oscillate
Otter[1] ['ɔtər] (**-s, -**) *m* otter
Otter[2] ['ɔtər] (**-, -n**) *f* (*Schlange*) adder
ÖTV (**-**) *f abk* (*= Gewerkschaft öffentliche Dienste, Transport und Verkehr*) ≈ Transport and General Workers' Union
Ouvertüre [uvɛr'ty:rə] (**-, -n**) *f* overture
oval [o'va:l] *adj* oval
Ovation [ovatsi'o:n] *f* ovation
Overall ['oʊvərɔ:l] (**-s, -s**) *m* (*Schutzanzug*) overalls *pl*
ÖVP (**-**) *f abk* (*= Österreichische Volkspartei*) Austrian People's Party
Ovulation [ovulatsi'o:n] *f* ovulation
Oxid, Oxyd [ɔ'ksy:t] (**-(e)s, -e**) *nt* oxide
oxidieren, oxydieren [ɔksy'di:rən] *vt, vi* to oxidize
Oxidierung, Oxydierung *f* oxidization
Ozean ['o:tsea:n] (**-s, -e**) *m* ocean; **Ozeandampfer** *m* (ocean-going) liner
Ozeanien [otse'a:niən] (**-s**) *nt* Oceania
ozeanisch [otse'a:nɪʃ] *adj* oceanic; (*Sprachen*) Oceanic
Ozeanriese (*umg*) *m* ocean liner
Ozon [o'tso:n] (**-s**) *nt* ozone; **Ozonloch** *nt* hole in the ozone layer; **Ozonschicht** *f* ozone layer

Pp

P, p [pe:] *nt* P, p; **P wie Peter** ≈ P for Peter
P. *abk* = **Pastor; Pater**
Paar [pa:r] (**-(e)s, -e**) *nt* pair; (*Liebespaar*) couple
paar *adj inv*: **ein ~** a few; (*zwei oder drei*) a couple of; *siehe auch* **paarmal**
paaren *vt, vr* (*Tiere*) to mate, pair
Paar- *zW*: **Paarhufer** *pl* (*Zool*) cloven-hoofed animals *pl*; **Paarlauf** *m* pair skating; **paarmal** *adv*: **ein paarmal** a few times
Paarung *f* combination; (*von Tieren*) mating
paarweise *adv* in pairs; in couples
Pacht [paxt] (**-, -en**) *f* lease; (*Entgelt*) rent; **pachten** *vt* to lease; **du hast das Sofa doch nicht für dich gepachtet** (*umg*) don't hog the sofa
Pächter, in ['pɛçtər(ɪn)] (**-s, -**) *m(f)* leaseholder; tenant
Pachtvertrag *m* lease
Pack[1] [pak] (**-(e)s, -e** *od* **-̈e**) *m* bundle, pack
Pack[2] [pak] (**-(e)s**) (*pej*) *nt* mob, rabble
Päckchen ['pɛkçən] *nt* small package; (*Zigaretten*) packet; (*Postpäckchen*) small parcel
Packeis *nt* pack ice
Packen (**-s, -**) *m* bundle; (*fig: Menge*) heaps (of); **packen** *vt, vi* (*auch Comput*) to pack; (*fassen*) to grasp, seize; (*umg: schaffen*) to manage; (*fig: fesseln*) to grip; **packen wirs!** (*umg: gehen*) let's go
Packer, in (**-s, -**) *m(f)* packer
Packesel *m* pack mule; (*fig*) packhorse
Packpapier *nt* brown paper, wrapping paper
Packung *f* packet; (*Pralinenpackung*) box; (*Med*) compress
Packzettel *m* (*Comm*) packing slip
Pädagoge [pɛda'go:gə] (**-n, -n**) *m* educationalist
Pädagogik *f* education
Pädagogin [pɛda'go:gɪn] *f* educationalist
pädagogisch *adj* educational, pedagogical; **~e Hochschule** college of education
Paddel ['padəl] (**-s, -**) *nt* paddle; **Paddelboot** *nt* canoe
paddeln *vi* to paddle
pädophil [pɛdo'fi:l] *adj* paedophile (*Brit*), pedophile (*US*)
Pädophilie [pɛdofɪ'li:] *f* paedophilia (*Brit*), pedophilia (*US*)
paffen ['pafən] *vt, vi* to puff
Page ['pa:ʒə] (**-n, -n**) *m* page(boy)
Pagenkopf *m* pageboy cut
paginieren [pagi'ni:rən] *vt* to paginate
Paginierung *f* pagination
Paillette [paɪ'jɛtə] *f* sequin
Paket [pa'ke:t] (**-(e)s, -e**) *nt* packet; (*Postpaket*) parcel; **Paketannahme** *f* parcels office; **Paketausgabe** *f* parcels office; **Paketkarte** *f* dispatch note; **Paketpost** *f* parcel post; **Paketschalter** *m* parcels counter
Pakistan ['pa:kɪsta:n] (**-s**) *nt* Pakistan
Pakistaner, in [pakɪs'ta:nər(ɪn)] (**-s, -**) *m(f)* Pakistani
Pakistani [pakɪs'ta:ni] (**-(s), -(s)**) *m* Pakistani
pakistanisch *adj* Pakistani
Pakt [pakt] (**-(e)s, -e**) *m* pact
Paläontologie [palɛɔntolo'gi:] *f* palaeontology (*Brit*), paleontology (*US*)
Palast [pa'last] (**-es, Paläste**) *m* palace
Palästina [palɛ'sti:na] (**-s**) *nt* Palestine
Palästinenser, in [palɛsti'nɛnzər(ɪn)] (**-s, -**) *m(f)* Palestinian
palästinensisch *adj* Palestinian
Palaver [pa'la:vər] (**-s, -**) *nt* (*auch fig: umg*) palaver
Palette [pa'lɛtə] *f* palette; (*fig*) range; (*Ladepalette*) pallet
Palme ['palmə] (**-, -n**) *f* palm (tree); **jdn auf die ~ bringen** (*umg*) to make sb see red
Palmsonntag *m* Palm Sunday
Pampelmuse ['pampəlmu:zə] (**-, -n**) *f* grapefruit
pampig ['pampɪç] (*umg*) *adj* (*frech*) fresh
Panama ['panama] (**-s**) *nt* Panama; **Panamakanal** *m* Panama Canal
Panflöte ['pa:nflø:tə] *f* panpipes *pl*, Pan's pipes *pl*
panieren [pa'ni:rən] *vt* (*Koch*) to coat with egg and breadcrumbs
Paniermehl [pa'ni:rme:l] *nt* breadcrumbs *pl*
Panik ['pa:nɪk] *f* panic; **nur keine ~!** don't panic!; **in ~ ausbrechen** to panic; **Panikkäufe** *pl* panic buying *sing*; **Panikkäufemache** (*umg*) *f* panicmongering
panisch ['pa:nɪʃ] *adj* panic-stricken
Panne ['panə] (**-, -n**) *f* (*Aut etc*) breakdown; (*Missgeschick*) slip; **uns ist eine ~ passiert** we've boobed (*Brit*) (*umg*) *od* goofed (*US*) (*umg*)

Pannendienst *m* breakdown service
Pannenhilfe *f* breakdown service
Panorama [pano'ra:ma] (**-s, -men**) *nt* panorama
panschen ['panʃən] *vi* to splash about ▷ *vt* to water down
Panther, **Panter** ['pantər] (**-s, -**) *m* panther
Pantoffel [pan'tɔfəl] (**-s, -n**) *m* slipper; **Pantoffelheld** (*umg*) *m* henpecked husband
Pantomime [panto'mi:mə] (**-, -n**) *f* mime
Panzer ['pantsər] (**-s, -**) *m* armour (*Brit*), armor (*US*); (*fig*) shield; (*Platte*) armo(u)r plate; (*Fahrzeug*) tank; **Panzerfaust** *f* bazooka; **Panzerglas** *nt* bulletproof glass; **Panzergrenadier** *m* armoured (*Brit*) *od* armored (*US*) infantryman
panzern *vt* to armour (*Brit*) *od* armor (*US*) plate ▷ *vr* (*fig*) to arm o.s.
Panzerschrank *m* strongbox
Panzerwagen *m* armoured (*Brit*) *od* armored (*US*) car
Papa [pa'pa:] (**-s, -s**) (*umg*) *m* dad(dy), pa
Papagei [papa:'gaɪ] (**-s, -en**) *m* parrot
Papier [pa'pi:r] (**-s, -e**) *nt* paper; (*Wertpapier*) share; **Papiere** *pl* (identity) papers *pl*; (*Urkunden*) documents *pl*; **seine ~e bekommen** (*entlassen werden*) to get one's cards; **Papierfabrik** *f* paper mill; **Papiergeld** *nt* paper money; **Papierkorb** *m* wastepaper basket; **Papierkram** (*umg*) *m* bumf (*Brit*) (*umg*); **Papierkrieg** *m* red tape; **Papiertüte** *f* paper bag; **Papiervorschub** *m* (*Drucker*) paper advance
Pappbecher *m* paper cup
Pappdeckel (**-, -n**) *m* cardboard
Pappe ['papə] *f* cardboard; **das ist nicht von ~** (*umg*) that is really something
Pappeinband *m* pasteboard
Pappel (**-, -n**) *f* poplar
pappen (*umg*) *vt, vi* to stick
Pappenheimer *pl*: **ich kenne meine ~** (*umg*) I know you lot/that lot (inside out)
Pappenstiel (*umg*) *m*: **keinen ~ wert sein** not to be worth a thing; **für einen ~ bekommen** to get for a song
papperlapapp [papərla'pap] *interj* rubbish!
pappig *adj* sticky
Pappmaschee, **Pappmaché** [papma'ʃe:] (**-s, -s**) *nt* papier-mâché
Pappteller *m* paper plate
Paprika ['paprika] (**-s, -s**) *m* (*Gewürz*) paprika; (*Paprikaschote*) pepper; **Paprikaschote** *f* pepper; **gefüllte Paprikaschoten** stuffed peppers
Papst [pa:pst] (**-(e)s, ¨-e**) *m* pope
päpstlich ['pɛ:pstlɪç] *adj* papal; **~er als der Papst sein** to be more Catholic than the Pope
Parabel [pa'ra:bəl] (**-, -n**) *f* parable; (*Math*) parabola
Parabolantenne [para'bo:l|antɛnə] *f* (*TV*) satellite dish
Parade [pa'ra:də] (**-, -n**) *f* (*Mil*) parade, review; (*Sport*) parry; **Paradebeispiel** *nt* prime example; **Parademarsch** *m* march past; **Paradeschritt** *m* goose step
Paradies [para'di:s] (**-es, -e**) *nt* paradise; **paradiesisch** *adj* heavenly
Paradox [para'dɔks] (**-es, -e**) *nt* paradox; **paradox** *adj* paradoxical
Paraffin [para'fi:n] (**-s, -e**) *nt* (*Chem: Paraffinöl*) paraffin (*Brit*), kerosene (*US*); (*Paraffinwachs*) paraffin wax
Paragraf [para'gra:f] (**-en, -en**) *m* paragraph; (*Jur*) section
Paragrafenreiter (*umg*) *m* pedant
Paraguay [paragu'a:i] (**-s**) *nt* Paraguay
Paraguayer, in [para'gua:jər(ɪn)] (**-s, -**) *m(f)* Paraguayan
paraguayisch *adj* Paraguayan
parallel [para'le:l] *adj* parallel; **~ schalten** (*Elek*) to connect in parallel
Parallele (**-, -n**) *f* parallel
Parameter [pa'ra:metər] *m* parameter
paramilitärisch [paramili'tɛ:rɪʃ] *adj* paramilitary
Paranuss ['pa:ranʊs] *f* Brazil nut
paraphieren [para'fi:rən] *vt* (*Vertrag*) to initial
Parasit [para'zi:t] (**-en, -en**) *m* (*lit, fig*) parasite
parat [pa'ra:t] *adj* ready
Pärchen ['pɛ:rçən] *nt* couple
Parcours [par'ku:r] (**-, -**) *m* showjumping course; (*Sportart*) showjumping
Pardon [par'dõ:] (**-s**) (*umg*) *m od nt*: **~!** (*Verzeihung*) sorry!; **kein ~ kennen** to be ruthless
Parfüm [par'fy:m] (**-s, -s** *od* **-e**) *nt* perfume
Parfümerie [parfymə'ri:] *f* perfumery
Parfümflasche *f* scent bottle
parfümieren [parfy'mi:rən] *vt* to scent, perfume
parieren [pa'ri:rən] *vt* to parry ▷ *vi* (*umg*) to obey
Paris [pa'ri:s] (**-**) *nt* Paris
Pariser [pa'ri:zər] (**-s, -**) *m* Parisian; (*umg: Kondom*) rubber ▷ *adj attrib* Parisian, Paris *attrib*
Pariserin *f* Parisian
Parität [pari'tɛ:t] *f* parity; **paritätisch** *adj*: **paritätische Mitbestimmung** equal representation
Pariwert ['pa:rive:rt] *m* par value, parity
Park [park] (**-s, -s**) *m* park
Parka ['parka] (**-(s), -s**) *m* parka
Parkanlage *f* park; (*um Gebäude*) grounds *pl*
Parkbucht *f* parking bay
parken *vt, vi* to park; **„P~ verboten!"** "No Parking"
Parkett [par'kɛt] (**-(e)s, -e**) *nt* parquet (floor); (*Theat*) stalls *pl* (*Brit*), orchestra (*US*); **Parketthandel** *m* (*Fin*) floor trading
Park- *zW*: **Parkhaus** *nt* multistorey car park; **Parklücke** *f* parking space; **Parkplatz** *m* car park, parking lot (*US*); parking place; **Parkscheibe** *f* parking disc; **Parkuhr** *f* parking meter; **Parkverbot** *nt* parking ban
Parlament [parla'mɛnt] *nt* parliament
Parlamentarier [parlamɛn'ta:riər] (**-s, -**) *m* parliamentarian

parlamentarisch *adj* parliamentary
Parlaments- *zW*: **Parlamentsausschuss** *m* parliamentary committee; **Parlamentsbeschluss** *m* vote of parliament; **Parlamentsferien** *pl* recess *sing*; **Parlamentsmitglied** *nt* Member of Parliament (*Brit*), Congressman (*US*); **Parlamentssitzung** *f* sitting (of parliament)
Parodie [paro'di:] *f* parody
parodieren *vt* to parody
Parodontose [parodɔn'to:zə] **(-, -n)** *f* shrinking gums *pl*
Parole [pa'ro:lə] **(-, -n)** *f* password; (*Wahlspruch*) motto
Partei [par'taɪ] *f* party; (*im Mietshaus*) tenant, party (*form*); **für jdn ~ ergreifen** to take sb's side; **Parteibuch** *nt* party membership book; **Parteiführung** *f* party leadership; **Parteigenosse** *m* party member; **parteiisch** *adj* partial, bias(s)ed; **parteilich** *adj* party *attrib*; **Parteilinie** *f* party line; **parteilos** *adj* neutral; **Parteinahme (-, -n)** *f* partisanship; **parteipolitisch** *adj* party political; **Parteiprogramm** *nt* (party) manifesto; **Parteitag** *m* party conference; **Parteivorsitzende, r** *f(m)* party leader
Parterre [par'tɛr] **(-s, -s)** *nt* ground floor; (*Theat*) stalls *pl* (*Brit*), orchestra (*US*)
Partie [par'ti:] *f* part; (*Spiel*) game; (*Ausflug*) outing; (*Mann, Frau*) catch; (*Comm*) lot; **mit von der ~ sein** to join in
partiell [partsi'ɛl] *adj* partial
Partikel [par'ti:kəl] **(-, -n)** *f* particle
Partisan, in [parti'za:n(ɪn)] **(-s** *od* **-en, -en)** *m(f)* partisan
Partitur [parti'tu:r] *f* (*Mus*) score
Partizip [parti'tsi:p] **(-s, -ien)** *nt* participle; **~ Präsens/Perfekt** (*Gram*) present/past participle
Partner, in ['partnər(ɪn)] **(-s, -)** *m(f)* partner; **Partnerschaft** *f* partnership; (*Städtepartnerschaft*) twinning; **partnerschaftlich** *adj* as partners; **Partnerstadt** *f* twin town (*Brit*)
partout [par'tu:] *adv*: **er will ~ ins Kino gehen** he insists on going to the cinema
Party ['pa:rti] **(-, -s)** *f* party
Parzelle [par'tsɛlə] *f* plot, lot
Pascha ['paʃa] **(-s, -s)** *m*: **wie ein ~** like Lord Muck (*Brit*) (*umg*)
Pass [pas] **(-es, ¨-e)** *m* pass; (*Ausweis*) passport
passabel [pa'sa:bəl] *adj* passable, reasonable
Passage [pa'sa:ʒə] **(-, -n)** *f* passage; (*Ladenstraße*) arcade
Passagier [pasa'ʒi:r] **(-s, -e)** *m* passenger; **Passagierdampfer** *m* passenger steamer; **Passagierflugzeug** *nt* airliner
Passah ['pasa], **Passahfest** ['pasafɛst] *nt* (Feast of the) Passover
Passamt *nt* passport office
Passant, in [pa'sant(ɪn)] *m(f)* passer-by
Passbild *nt* passport photo(graph)
passé, passee [pa'se:] *adj*: **diese Mode ist längst ~** this fashion went out long ago
passen ['pasən] *vi* to fit; (*auf Frage, Karten*) to pass; **~ zu** (*Farbe etc*) to go with; **Sonntag passt uns nicht** Sunday is no good for us; **die Schuhe ~ (mir) gut** the shoes are a good fit (for me); **zu jdm ~** (*Mensch*) to suit sb; **das passt mir nicht** that doesn't suit me; **er passt nicht zu dir** he's not right for you; **das könnte dir so ~!** (*umg*) you'd like that, wouldn't you?
passend *adj* suitable; (*zusammenpassend*) matching; (*angebracht*) fitting; (*Zeit*) convenient; **haben Sie es ~?** (*Geld*) have you got the right money?
Passfoto *nt* passport photo(graph)
passierbar [pa'si:rba:r] *adj* passable; (*Fluss, Kanal*) negotiable
passieren *vt* to pass; (*durch Sieb*) to strain ▷ *vi* (*Hilfsverb sein*) to happen; **es ist ein Unfall passiert** there has been an accident
Passierschein *m* pass, permit
Passion [pasi'o:n] *f* passion
passioniert [pasio:'ni:rt] *adj* enthusiastic, passionate
Passionsfrucht *f* passion fruit
Passionsspiel *nt* Passion Play
Passionszeit *f* Passiontide
passiv ['pasi:f] *adj* passive; **~es Rauchen** passive smoking; **Passiv (-s, -e)** *nt* passive
Passiva [pa'si:va] *pl* (*Comm*) liabilities *pl*
Passivität [pasivi'tɛ:t] *f* passiveness
Passivposten *m* (*Comm*) debit entry
Pass- *zW*: **Passkontrolle** *f* passport control; **Passstelle** *f* passport office; **Passstraße** *f* (mountain) pass; **Passzwang** *m* requirement to carry a passport
Paste ['pastə] **(-, -n)** *f* paste
Pastell [pas'tɛl] **(-(e)s, -e)** *nt* pastel; **Pastellfarbe** *f* pastel colour (*Brit*) *od* color (*US*); **pastellfarben** *adj* pastel-colo(u)red
Pastete [pas'te:tə] **(-, -n)** *f* pie; (*Pastetchen*) vol-au-vent; (*: ungefüllt*) vol-au-vent case
pasteurisieren [pastøri'zi:rən] *vt* to pasteurize
Pastor ['pastɔr] *m* vicar; pastor, minister
Pate ['pa:tə] **(-n, -n)** *m* godfather; **bei etw ~ gestanden haben** (*fig*) to be the force behind sth
Patenkind *nt* godchild
Patenstadt *f* twin town (*Brit*)
patent [pa'tɛnt] *adj* clever
Patent (-(e)s, -e) *nt* patent; (*Mil*) commission; **etw als** *od* **zum ~ anmelden** to apply for a patent on sth
Patentamt *nt* patent office
patentieren [patɛn'ti:rən] *vt* to patent
Patent- *zW*: **Patentinhaber** *m* patentee; **Patentlösung** *f* (*fig*) patent remedy; **Patentschutz** *m* patent right; **Patenturkunde** *f* letters patent *pl*
Pater ['pa:tər] **(-s, -** *od* **Patres)** *m* Father
Paternoster [patər'nɔstər] **(-s, -)** *m* (*Aufzug*) paternoster
pathetisch [pa'te:tɪʃ] *adj* emotional

Pathologe [pato'lo:gə] (**-n, -n**) *m* pathologist
Pathologin [pato'lo:gɪn] *f* pathologist
pathologisch *adj* pathological
Pathos ['pa:tɔs] (**-**) *nt* pathos
Patience [pasi'ã:s] (**-, -n**) *f*: **~n legen** to play patience
Patient, in [patsi'ɛnt(ɪn)] *m(f)* patient
Patin ['pa:tɪn] *f* godmother
Patriarch [patri'arç] (**-en, -en**) *m* patriarch
patriarchalisch [patriar'ça:lɪʃ] *adj* patriarchal
Patriot, in [patri'o:t(ɪn)] (**-en, -en**) *m(f)* patriot; **patriotisch** *adj* patriotic
Patriotismus [patrio:'tɪsmʊs] *m* patriotism
Patron [pa'tro:n] (**-s, -e**) *m* patron; (*Eccl*) patron saint
Patrone (**-, -n**) *f* cartridge
Patronenhülse *f* cartridge case
Patronin *f* patroness; (*Eccl*) patron saint
Patrouille [pa'trʊljə] (**-, -n**) *f* patrol
patrouillieren [patrʊl'ji:rən] *vi* to patrol
patsch [patʃ] *interj* splash!
Patsche (**-, -n**) (*umg*) *f* (*Händchen*) paw; (*Fliegenpatsche*) swat; (*Feuerpatsche*) beater; (*Bedrängnis*) mess, jam
patschen *vi* to smack, slap; (*im Wasser*) to splash
patschnass *adj* soaking wet
Patt [pat] (**-s, -s**) *nt* (*lit, fig*) stalemate
patzen ['patsən] (*umg*) *vi* to boob (*Brit*), goof (*US*)
patzig ['patsɪç] (*umg*) *adj* cheeky, saucy
Pauke ['paʊkə] (**-, -n**) *f* kettledrum; **auf die ~ hauen** to live it up; **mit ~n und Trompeten durchfallen** (*umg*) to fail dismally
pauken *vt, vi* (*Sch*) to swot (*Brit*), cram
Pauker (**-s, -**) (*umg*) *m* teacher
pausbäckig ['paʊsbɛkɪç] *adj* chubby-cheeked
pauschal [paʊ'ʃa:l] *adj* (*Kosten*) inclusive; (*einheitlich*) flat-rate *attrib*; (*Urteil*) sweeping; **die Werkstatt berechnet ~ pro Inspektion 130 Euro** the garage has a flat rate of 130 euros per service
Pauschale (**-, -n**) *f* flat rate; (*vorläufig geschätzter Betrag*) estimated amount
Pauschal- *zW*: **Pauschalgebühr** *f* flat rate; **Pauschalpreis** *m* all-in price; **Pauschalreise** *f* package tour; **Pauschalsumme** *f* lump sum; **Pauschalversicherung** *f* comprehensive insurance
Pause ['paʊzə] (**-, -n**) *f* break; (*Theat*) interval; (*das Innehalten*) pause; (*Mus*) rest; (*Kopie*) tracing
pausen *vt* to trace
Pausen- *zW*: **Pausenbrot** *nt* sandwich (*to eat at break*); **Pausenhof** *m* playground, schoolyard (*US*); **pausenlos** *adj* nonstop; **Pausenzeichen** *nt* (*Rundf*) call sign; (*Mus*) rest
pausieren [paʊ'si:rən] *vi* to make a break
Pauspapier ['paʊspapi:r] *nt* tracing paper
Pavian ['pa:via:n] (**-s, -e**) *m* baboon
Paybackkarte ['pe:bɛkkartə] *f* loyalty card
Pay-per-Click ['pe:pərklɪk] (**-s**) *nt* pay-per-click
Pazifik [pa'tsi:fɪk] (**-s**) *m* Pacific
pazifisch *adj* Pacific; **der P~e Ozean** the Pacific (Ocean)
Pazifist, in [patsi'fɪst(ɪn)] *m(f)* pacifist; **pazifistisch** *adj* pacifist
PC *m abk* (*= Personal Computer*) PC
PDA *m abk* (*Comput: = personal digital assistant*) PDA
PDS *f abk* (*= Partei des Demokratischen Sozialismus*) *German Socialist Party*; *see culture note*

PDS

The *PDS* (Partei des Demokratischen Sozialismus) was founded in 1989 as the successor of the SED, the former East German Communist Party. Its aims are the establishment of a democratic socialist society and to hold a position in the German political scene left of the *SPD*.

Pech [pɛç] (**-s, -e**) *nt* pitch; (*fig*) bad luck; **~ haben** to be unlucky; **die beiden halten zusammen wie ~ und Schwefel** (*umg*) the two are inseparable; **~ gehabt!** tough! (*umg*); **pechschwarz** *adj* pitch-black; **Pechsträhne** (*umg*) *f* unlucky patch; **Pechvogel** (*umg*) *m* unlucky person
Pedal [pe'da:l] (**-s, -e**) *nt* pedal; **in die ~e treten** to pedal (hard)
Pedant [pe'dant] *m* pedant
Pedanterie [pedantə'ri:] *f* pedantry
pedantisch *adj* pedantic
Peddigrohr ['pɛdɪçro:r] *nt* cane
Pediküre [pedi'ky:rə] (**-, -n**) *f* (*Fußpflege*) pedicure; (*Fußpflegerin*) chiropodist
Pegel ['pe:gəl] (**-s, -**) *m* water gauge; (*Geräuschpegel*) noise level; **Pegelstand** *m* water level
peilen ['paɪlən] *vt* to get a fix on; **die Lage ~** (*umg*) to see how the land lies
Pein [paɪn] (**-**) *f* agony, suffering
peinigen *vt* to torture; (*plagen*) to torment
peinlich *adj* (*unangenehm*) embarrassing, awkward, painful; (*genau*) painstaking; **in seinem Zimmer herrschte ~e Ordnung** his room was meticulously tidy; **er vermied es ~st, davon zu sprechen** he was at pains not to talk about it; **Peinlichkeit** *f* painfulness, awkwardness; (*Genauigkeit*) scrupulousness
Peitsche ['paɪtʃə] (**-, -n**) *f* whip
peitschen *vt* to whip; (*Regen*) to lash
Peitschenhieb *m* lash
Pekinese [peki'ne:zə] (**-n, -n**) *m* Pekinese, peke (*umg*)
Peking ['pe:kɪŋ] (**-s**) *nt* Peking
Pelikan ['pe:lika:n] (**-s, -e**) *m* pelican
Pelle ['pɛlə] (**-, -n**) *f* skin; **der Chef sitzt mir auf der ~** (*umg*) I've got the boss on my back
pellen *vt* to skin, peel
Pellkartoffeln *pl* jacket potatoes *pl*
Pelz [pɛlts] (**-es, -e**) *m* fur
Pendel ['pɛndəl] (**-s, -**) *nt* pendulum
pendeln *vi* (*schwingen*) to swing (to and fro); (*Zug, Fähre etc*) to shuttle; (*Mensch*) to commute; (*fig*) to fluctuate
Pendelverkehr *m* shuttle service;

(*Berufsverkehr*) commuter traffic
Pendler, in ['pɛndlər(ɪn)] (**-s, -**) *m(f)* commuter
penetrant [pene'trant] *adj* sharp; (*Person*) pushing; **das schmeckt/riecht ~ nach Knoblauch** it has a very strong taste/smell of garlic
penibel [pe'niːbəl] *adj* pernickety (*Brit*) (*umg*), persnickety (*US*) (*umg*), precise
Penis ['peːnɪs] (**-, -se**) *m* penis
Pennbruder ['pɛnbruːdər] (*umg*) *m* tramp (*Brit*), hobo (*US*)
Penne (**-, -n**) (*umg*) *f* (*Sch*) school
pennen (*umg*) *vi* to kip
Penner (**-s, -**) (*pej*: *umg*) *m* tramp (*Brit*), hobo (*US*)
Pension [pɛnzi'oːn] *f* (*Geld*) pension; (*Ruhestand*) retirement; (*für Gäste*) boarding house, guesthouse; **halbe/volle ~** half/full board; **in ~ gehen** to retire
Pensionär, in [pɛnzio'nɛːr(ɪn)] (**-s, -e**) *m(f)* pensioner
Pensionat (**-(e)s, -e**) *nt* boarding school
pensionieren [pɛnzio'niːrən] *vt* to pension (off); **sich ~ lassen** to retire
pensioniert *adj* retired
Pensionierung *f* retirement
Pensions- *zW*: **pensionsberechtigt** *adj* entitled to a pension; **Pensionsfonds** *m* pension fund; **Pensionsgast** *m* boarder, paying guest; **pensionsreif** (*umg*) *adj* ready for retirement
Pensum ['pɛnzʊm] (**-s, Pensen**) *nt* quota; (*Sch*) curriculum
Peperoni [pepe'roːni] *pl* chillies *pl*
per [pɛr] *präp +akk* by, per; (*pro*) per; (*bis*) by; **~ Adresse** (*Comm*) care of, c/o; **mit jdm ~ du sein** (*umg*) to be on first-name terms with sb
Perfekt ['pɛrfɛkt] (**-(e)s, -e**) *nt* perfect
perfekt [pɛr'fɛkt] *adj* perfect; (*abgemacht*) settled; **die Sache ~ machen** to clinch the deal; **der Vertrag ist ~** the contract is all settled
perfektionieren [pɛrfɛktsio'niːrən] *vt* to perfect
Perfektionismus [pɛrfɛktsio'nɪsmʊs] *m* perfectionism
perforieren [pɛrfo'riːrən] *vt* to perforate
Pergament [pɛrga'mɛnt] *nt* parchment; **Pergamentpapier** *nt* greaseproof paper (*Brit*), wax(ed) paper (*US*)
Pergola ['pɛrgola] (**-, Pergolen**) *f* pergola, arbour (*Brit*), arbor (*US*)
Periode [peri'oːdə] (**-, -n**) *f* period; **0,33 ~** 0.33 recurring
periodisch [peri'oːdɪʃ] *adj* periodic; (*dezimal*) recurring
Peripherie [perife'riː] *f* periphery; (*um Stadt*) outskirts *pl*; (*Math*) circumference; **Peripheriegerät** *nt* (*Comput*) peripheral
Perle ['pɛrlə] (**-, -n**) *f* (*lit, fig*) pearl; (*Glasperle, Holzperle, Tropfen*) bead; (*veraltet*: *umg*: *Hausgehilfin*) maid
perlen *vi* to sparkle; (*Tropfen*) to trickle
Perlenkette *f* pearl necklace
Perlhuhn *nt* guinea fowl
Perlmutt ['pɛrlmʊt] (**-s**) *nt* mother-of-pearl
Perlon® ['pɛrlɔn] (**-s**) *nt* ≈ nylon
Perlwein *m* sparkling wine
perplex [pɛr'plɛks] *adj* dumbfounded
Perser ['pɛrzər] (**-s, -**) *m* (*Person*) Persian; (*umg*: *Teppich*) Persian carpet
Perserin *f* Persian
Persianer [pɛrzi'aːnər] (**-s, -**) *m* Persian lamb (coat)
Persien ['pɛrziən] (**-s**) *nt* Persia
Persiflage [pɛrzi'flaːʒə] (**-, -n**) *f*: **~ (***+gen od* **auf** *+akk***)** pastiche (of), satire (on)
persisch *adj* Persian; **P~er Golf** Persian Gulf
Person [pɛr'zoːn] (**-, -en**) *f* person; (*pej*: *Frau*) female; **sie ist Köchin und Haushälterin in einer ~** she is cook and housekeeper rolled into one; **ich für meine ~** personally I
Personal [pɛrzo'naːl] (**-s**) *nt* personnel; (*Bedienung*) servants *pl*; **Personalabbau** *m* staff cuts *pl*; **Personalakte** *f* personal file; **Personalangaben** *pl* particulars *pl*; **Personalausweis** *m* identity card; **Personalbogen** *m* personal record; **Personalbüro** *nt* personnel (department); **Personalchef** *m* personnel manager; **Personal Computer** *m* personal computer
Personalien [pɛrzo'naːliən] *pl* particulars *pl*
Personalität [pɛrzonali'tɛːt] *f* personality
Personal- *zW*: **Personalkosten** *pl* staff costs; **Personalmangel** *m* staff shortage; **Personalpronomen** *nt* personal pronoun; **Personalreduzierung** *f* staff reduction
personell [pɛrzo'nɛl] *adj* staff *attrib*; **~e Veränderungen** changes in personnel
Personen- *zW*: **Personenaufzug** *m* lift, elevator (*US*); **Personenbeschreibung** *f* (personal) description; **Personengedächtnis** *nt* memory for faces; **Personengesellschaft** *f* partnership; **Personenkraftwagen** *m* private motorcar, automobile (*US*); **Personenkreis** *m* group of people; **Personenkult** *m* personality cult; **Personennahverkehr** *m*: **öffentlicher Personennahverkehr** local public transport; **Personenschaden** *m* injury to persons; **Personenverkehr** *m* passenger services *pl*; **Personenwaage** *f* scales *pl*; **Personenzug** *m* stopping train; passenger train
personifizieren [pɛrzonifi'tsiːrən] *vt* to personify
persönlich [pɛr'zøːnlɪç] *adj* personal ▷ *adv* in person; personally; (*auf Briefen*) private (and confidential); **~ haften** (*Comm*) to be personally liable; **Persönlichkeit** *f* personality; **Persönlichkeiten des öffentlichen Lebens** public figures
Perspektive [pɛrspɛk'tiːvə] *f* perspective; **das eröffnet ganz neue ~n für uns** that opens new horizons for us
Pers. Ref. *abk* (= *Persönlicher Referent*) personal representative
Peru [pe'ruː] (**-s**) *nt* Peru
Peruaner, in [peru'aːnər(ɪn)] (**-s, -**) *m(f)* Peruvian

peruanisch *adj* Peruvian
Perücke [pe'rʏkə] (**-, -n**) *f* wig
pervers [pɛr'vɛrs] *adj* perverse
Perversität [pɛrvɛrzi'tɛ:t] *f* perversity
Pessar [pe'sa:r] (**-s, -e**) *nt* pessary; (*zur Empfängnisverhütung*) cap, diaphragm
Pessimismus [pɛsi'mɪsmʊs] *m* pessimism
Pessimist, in [pɛsi'mɪst(ɪn)] *m(f)* pessimist; **pessimistisch** *adj* pessimistic
Pest [pɛst] (-) *f* plague; **jdn/etw wie die ~ hassen** (*umg*) to loathe (and detest) sb/sth
Petersilie [petər'zi:liə] *f* parsley
Petrochemie [petro:çe'mi:] *f* petrochemistry
Petrodollar [petro'dɔlar] *m* petrodollar
Petroleum [pe'tro:leʊm] (**-s**) *nt* paraffin (*Brit*), kerosene (*US*)
petzen ['pɛtsən] (*umg*) *vi* to tell tales; **er petzt immer** he always tells
Pf. (*Hist*) *abk* = **Pfennig**
Pfad [pfa:t] (**-(e)s, -e**) *m* path; **Pfadfinder** *m* Boy Scout; **er ist bei den Pfadfindern** he's in the (Boy) Scouts; **Pfadfinderin** *f* Girl Guide
Pfaffe ['pfafə] (**-n, -n**) (*pej*) *m* cleric, parson
Pfahl [pfa:l] (**-(e)s, ¨-e**) *m* post, stake; **Pfahlbau** *m* pile dwelling
Pfalz [pfalts] (**-, -en**) *f* (*Geog*) Palatinate
Pfälzer, in ['pfɛltsər(ɪn)] (**-s, -**) *m(f)* person from the Palatinate
pfälzisch *adj* Palatine, of the (Rhineland) Palatinate
Pfand [pfant] (**-(e)s, ¨-er**) *nt* pledge, security; (*Flaschenpfand*) deposit; (*im Spiel*) forfeit; (*fig: der Liebe etc*) pledge; **Pfandbrief** *m* bond
pfänden ['pfɛndən] *vt* to seize, impound
Pfänderspiel *nt* game of forfeits
Pfand- *zW*: **Pfandhaus** *nt* pawnshop; **Pfandleiher** (**-s, -**) *m* pawnbroker; **Pfandrecht** *nt* lien; **Pfandschein** *m* pawn ticket
Pfändung ['pfɛndʊŋ] *f* seizure, distraint (*form*)
Pfanne ['pfanə] (**-, -n**) *f* (frying) pan; **jdn in die ~ hauen** (*umg*) to tear a strip off sb
Pfannkuchen *m* pancake; (*Berliner*) doughnut (*Brit*), donut (*US*)
Pfarrei [pfar'raɪ] *f* parish
Pfarrer (**-s, -**) *m* priest; (*evangelisch*) vicar; (*von Freikirchen*) minister
Pfarrhaus *nt* vicarage
Pfau [pfaʊ] (**-(e)s, -en**) *m* peacock
Pfauenauge *nt* peacock butterfly
Pfd. *abk* (= *Pfund*) ≈ lb.
Pfeffer ['pfɛfər] (**-s, -**) *m* pepper; **er soll bleiben, wo der ~ wächst!** (*umg*) he can take a running jump; **Pfefferkorn** *nt* peppercorn; **Pfefferkuchen** *m* gingerbread; **Pfefferminz** (**-es, -e**) *nt* peppermint; **Pfefferminze** *f* peppermint (plant); **Pfeffermühle** *f* pepper mill
pfeffern *vt* to pepper; (*umg: werfen*) to fling; **gepfefferte Preise/Witze** steep prices/spicy jokes
Pfeife ['pfaɪfə] (**-, -n**) *f* whistle; (*Tabakpfeife, Orgelpfeife*) pipe; **nach jds ~ tanzen** to dance to sb's tune
pfeifen *unreg vt, vi* to whistle; **auf dem letzten Loch ~** (*umg: erschöpft sein*) to be on one's last legs; (*: finanziell*) to be on one's beam ends; **ich pfeif(e) drauf!** (*umg*) I don't give a damn!; **Pfeifenstopfer** *m* tamper
Pfeifer (**-s, -**) *m* piper
Pfeifkonzert *nt* catcalls *pl*
Pfeil [pfaɪl] (**-(e)s, -e**) *m* arrow
Pfeiler ['pfaɪlər] (**-s, -**) *m* pillar, prop; (*Brückenpfeiler*) pier
Pfennig ['pfɛnɪç] (**-(e)s, -e**) *m* (*Hist*) pfennig (*one hundredth of a mark*); **Pfennigabsatz** *m* stiletto heel; **Pfennigfuchser** (**-s, -**) (*umg*) *m* skinflint
pferchen ['pfɛrçən] *vt* to cram, pack
Pferd [pfe:rt] (**-(e)s, -e**) *nt* horse; **wie ein ~ arbeiten** (*umg*) to work like a Trojan; **mit ihm kann man ~e stehlen** (*umg*) he's a great sport; **auf das falsche/richtige ~ setzen** (*lit, fig*) to back the wrong/right horse
Pferde- *zW*: **Pferdeäpfel** *pl* horse droppings *pl od* dung *sing*; **Pferdefuß** *m*: **die Sache hat aber einen Pferdefuß** there's just one snag; **Pferderennen** *nt* horse-race; (*Sportart*) horse-racing; **Pferdeschwanz** *m* (*Frisur*) ponytail; **Pferdestall** *m* stable; **Pferdestärke** *f* horsepower
Pfiff (**-(e)s, -e**) *m* whistle; (*Kniff*) trick
pfiff *etc* [pfɪf] *vb siehe* **pfeifen**
Pfifferling ['pfɪfərlɪŋ] *m* yellow chanterelle; **keinen ~ wert** not worth a thing
pfiffig *adj* smart
Pfingsten ['pfɪŋstən] (**-, -**) *nt* Whitsun
Pfingstrose *f* peony
Pfingstsonntag *m* Whit Sunday, Pentecost (*Rel*)
Pfirsich ['pfɪrzɪç] (**-s, -e**) *m* peach
Pflanze ['pflantsə] (**-, -n**) *f* plant
pflanzen *vt* to plant ▷ *vr* (*umg*) to plonk o.s.
Pflanzenfett *nt* vegetable fat
Pflanzenschutzmittel *nt* pesticide
pflanzlich *adj* vegetable
Pflanzung *f* plantation
Pflaster ['pflastər] (**-s, -**) *nt* plaster; (*Straßenpflaster*) pavement (*Brit*), sidewalk (*US*); **ein teures ~** (*umg*) a pricey place; **ein heißes ~** a dangerous *od* unsafe place; **pflastermüde** *adj* dead on one's feet
pflastern *vt* to pave
Pflasterstein *m* paving stone
Pflaume ['pflaʊmə] (**-, -n**) *f* plum; (*umg: Mensch*) twit (*Brit*)
Pflaumenmus *nt* plum jam
Pflege ['pfle:gə] (**-, -n**) *f* care; (*von Idee*) cultivation; (*Krankenpflege*) nursing; **jdn/etw in ~ nehmen** to look after sb/sth; **in ~ sein** (*Kind*) to be fostered out; **pflegebedürftig** *adj* needing care; **Pflegeeltern** *pl* foster parents *pl*; **Pflegefall** *m* case for nursing; **Pflegegeld** *nt* (*für Pflegekinder*) boarding-out allowance; (*für Kranke*) attendance allowance; **Pflegeheim** *nt* nursing home; **Pflegekind** *nt* foster child; **pflegeleicht** *adj* easy-care; **Pflegemutter** *f* foster mother

pflegen *vt* to look after; (*Kranke*) to nurse; (*Beziehungen*) to foster ▷ *vi* (*gewöhnlich tun*): **sie pflegte zu sagen** she used to say
Pfleger (**-s, -**) *m* (*im Krankenhaus*) orderly; (*voll qualifiziert*) male nurse; **Pflegerin** *f* nurse
Pflegesatz *m* hospital and nursing charges *pl*
Pflegevater *m* foster father
Pflegeversicherung *f* geriatric care insurance
Pflicht [pflɪçt] (**-, -en**) *f* duty; (*Sport*) compulsory section; **Rechte und ~en** rights and responsibilities; **pflichtbewusst** *adj* conscientious; **Pflichtbewusstsein** *nt* sense of duty; **Pflichtfach** *nt* (*Sch*) compulsory subject; **Pflichtgefühl** *nt* sense of duty; **pflichtgemäß** *adj* dutiful; **pflichtvergessen** *adj* irresponsible; **Pflichtversicherung** *f* compulsory insurance
Pflock [pflɔk] (**-(e)s, ¨-e**) *m* peg; (*für Tiere*) stake
pflog *etc* [pflo:k] *vb* (*veraltet*) *siehe* **pflegen**
pflücken ['pflʏkən] *vt* to pick
Pflug [pflu:k] (**-(e)s, ¨-e**) *m* plough (*Brit*), plow (*US*)
pflügen ['pfly:gən] *vt* to plough (*Brit*), plow (*US*)
Pflugschar *f* ploughshare (*Brit*), plowshare (*US*)
Pforte ['pfɔrtə] (**-, -n**) *f* (*Tor*) gate
Pförtner ['pfœrtnər] (**-s, -**) *m* porter, doorkeeper, doorman
Pförtnerin *f* doorkeeper, porter
Pfosten ['pfɔstən] (**-s, -**) *m* post; (*senkrechter Balken*) upright
Pfote ['pfo:tə] (**-, -n**) *f* paw; (*umg: Schrift*) scrawl
Pfropf [pfrɔpf] (**-(e)s, -e**) *m* (*Flaschenpfropf*) stopper; (*Blutpfropf*) clot
Pfropfen (**-s, -**) *m* = **Pfropf**
pfropfen *vt* (*stopfen*) to cram; (*Baum*) to graft; **gepfropft voll** crammed full
pfui [pfʊɪ] *interj* ugh!; (*na na*) tut tut!; (*Buhruf*) boo!; **~ Teufel!** (*umg*) ugh!, yuck!
Pfund [pfʊnt] (**-(e)s, -e**) *nt* (*Gewicht, Fin*) pound; **das ~ sinkt** sterling *od* the pound is falling
pfundig (*umg*) *adj* great
Pfundskerl ['pfʊntskɛrl] (*umg*) *m* great guy
pfundweise *adv* by the pound
pfuschen ['pfʊʃən] *vi* to bungle; (*einen Fehler machen*) to slip up
Pfuscher, in ['pfʊʃər(ɪn)] (**-s, -**) (*umg*) *m(f)* sloppy worker; (*Kurpfuscher*) quack
Pfuscherei [pfʊʃə'raɪ] (*umg*) *f* sloppy work; (*Kurpfuscherei*) quackery
Pfütze ['pfʏtsə] (**-, -n**) *f* puddle
PH (**-, -s**) *f abk* = **pädagogische Hochschule**
Phänomen [fɛno'me:n] (**-s, -e**) *nt* phenomenon; **phänomenal** [-'na:l] *adj* phenomenal
Phantasie *etc* [fanta'zi:] = **Fantasie** *etc*
phantasieren [fanta'zi:rən] *vi* = **fantasieren**
phantasievoll *adj* = **fantasievoll**
Phantast [fan'tast] (**-en, -en**) *m* = **Fantast**
phantastisch *adj* = **fantastisch**
Phantom [fan'to:m] (**-s, -e**) *nt* (*Trugbild*) phantom; **einem ~ nachjagen** (*fig*) to tilt at windmills; **Phantombild** *nt* Identikit® picture
Pharisäer [fari'zɛ:ər] (**-s, -**) *m* (*lit, fig*) pharisee
Pharmazeut, in [farma'tsɔʏt(ɪn)] (**-en, -en**) *m(f)* pharmacist
pharmazeutisch *adj* pharmaceutical
Pharmazie *f* pharmacy, pharmaceutics *sing*
Phase ['fa:zə] (**-, -n**) *f* phase
Philanthrop [filan'tro:p] (**-en, -en**) *m* philanthropist; **philanthropisch** *adj* philanthropic
Philatelist, in [filate'lɪst(ɪn)] (**-en, -en**) *m(f)* philatelist
Philharmoniker [fɪlhar'mo:nikər] (**-s, -**) *m*: **die ~** the philharmonic (orchestra) *sing*
Philippine [fɪlɪ'pi:nə] (**-n, -n**) *m* Filipino
Philippinen *pl* Philippines *pl*, Philippine Islands *pl*
Philippinin *f* Filipino
philippinisch *adj* Filipino
Philologe [filo'lo:gə] (**-n, -n**) *m* philologist
Philologie [filolo'gi:] *f* philology
Philologin *f* philologist
Philosoph, in [filo'zo:f(ɪn)] (**-en, -en**) *m(f)* philosopher
Philosophie [filozo'fi:] *f* philosophy
philosophieren [filozo'fi:rən] *vi*: **~ (über** *+akk***)** to philosophize (about)
philosophisch *adj* philosophical
Phlegma ['flɛgma] (**-s**) *nt* lethargy
phlegmatisch [flɛ'gma:tɪʃ] *adj* lethargic
Phobie [fo'bi:] *f*: **~ (vor** *+dat***)** phobia (about)
Phonetik [fo'ne:tɪk] *f* phonetics *sing*
phonetisch *adj* phonetic
Phonotypistin [fonoty'pɪstɪn] *f* audiotypist
Phosphat [fɔs'fa:t] (**-(e)s, -e**) *nt* phosphate
Phosphor ['fɔsfɔr] (**-s**) *m* phosphorus
phosphoreszieren [fɔsforɛs'tsi:rən] *vt* to phosphoresce
Photo *etc* ['fo:to] = **Foto** *etc*
Phrase ['fra:zə] (**-, -n**) *f* phrase; (*pej*) hollow phrase; **~n dreschen** (*umg*) to churn out one cliché after another
pH-Wert [pe:'ha:ve:rt] *m* pH value
Physik [fy'zi:k] *f* physics *sing*
physikalisch [fyzi'ka:lɪʃ] *adj* of physics
Physiker, in ['fy:zikər(ɪn)] (**-s, -**) *m(f)* physicist
Physikum ['fy:zikʊm] (**-s**) *nt* (*Univ*) *preliminary examination in medicine*
Physiologe [fyzio'lo:gə] (**-n, -n**) *m* physiologist
Physiologie [fyziolo'gi:] *f* physiology
Physiologin *f* physiologist
physisch ['fy:zɪʃ] *adj* physical
Pianist, in [pia'nɪst(ɪn)] *m(f)* pianist
Piccolo ['pɪkolo] (**-s, -s**) *m* trainee waiter; (*auch*: **Piccoloflasche**) *quarter bottle of champagne*; (*Mus*: *auch*: **Piccoloflöte**) piccolo
picheln ['pɪçəln] (*umg*) *vi* to booze
Pickel ['pɪkəl] (**-s, -**) *m* pimple; (*Werkzeug*) pickaxe; (*Bergpickel*) ice axe
pickelig, picklig *adj* pimply
picken ['pɪkən] *vt* to peck ▷ *vi*: **~ (nach)** to peck (at)
Picknick ['pɪknɪk] (**-s, -e** *od* **-s**) *nt* picnic; **~ machen** to have a picnic

piekfein ['pi:k'faɪn] (*umg*) *adj* posh
Piemont [pie'mɔnt] (**-s**) *nt* Piedmont
piepen ['pi:pən] *vi* to chirp; (*Funkgerät etc*) to bleep; **bei dir piepts wohl!** (*umg*) are you off your head?; **es war zum P~!** (*umg*) it was a scream!
piepsen ['pi:psən] *vi* = **piepen**
Piepser (*umg*) *m* pager, paging device
Piepsstimme *f* squeaky voice
Piepton *m* bleep
Pier [pi:ər] (**-s, -s** *od* **-e**) *m* jetty, pier
piesacken ['pi:zakən] (*umg*) *vt* to torment
Pietät [pie'tɛ:t] *f* piety; reverence; **pietätlos** *adj* impious, irreverent
Pigment [pɪg'mɛnt] (**-(e)s, -e**) *nt* pigment
Pik [pi:k] (**-s, -s**) *nt* (*Karten*) spades; **einen ~ auf jdn haben** (*umg*) to have it in for sb
pikant [pi'kant] *adj* spicy, piquant; (*anzüglich*) suggestive
Pike (**-, -n**) *f*: **etw von der ~ auf lernen** (*fig*) to learn sth from the bottom up
pikiert [pi'ki:rt] *adj* offended
Pikkolo ['pɪkolo] (**-s, -s**) *m* = **Piccolo**
Piktogramm [pɪkto'gram] *nt* pictogram
Pilger, in ['pɪlgər(ɪn)] (**-s, -**) *m(f)* pilgrim; **Pilgerfahrt** *f* pilgrimage
pilgern *vi* to make a pilgrimage; (*umg: gehen*) to wend one's way
Pille ['pɪlə] (**-, -n**) *f* pill
Pilot, in [pi'lo:t(ɪn)] (**-en, -en**) *m(f)* pilot; **Pilotenschein** *m* pilot's licence (*Brit*) *od* license (*US*)
Pils [pɪls] (**-, -**) *nt* Pilsner (lager)
Pilsener [pɪlzənər], **Pilsner** [pɪlznər] (**-s, -**) *nt* Pilsner (lager)
Pilz [pɪlts] (**-es, -e**) *m* fungus; (*essbar*) mushroom; (*giftig*) toadstool; **wie ~e aus dem Boden schießen** (*fig*) to mushroom; **Pilzkrankheit** *f* fungal disease
Pimmel ['pɪməl] (**-s, -**) (*umg*) *m* (*Penis*) willie
pingelig ['pɪŋəlɪç] (*umg*) *adj* fussy
Pinguin ['pɪŋgui:n] (**-s, -e**) *m* penguin
Pinie ['pi:niə] *f* pine
Pinkel (**-s, -**) (*umg*) *m*: **ein feiner** *od* **vornehmer ~** a swell, Lord Muck (*Brit*) (*umg*)
pinkeln ['pɪŋkəln] (*umg*) *vi* to pee
Pinnwand ['pɪnvant] *f* pinboard
Pinsel ['pɪnzəl] (**-s, -**) *m* paintbrush
pinseln (*umg*) *vt, vi* to paint; (*pej: malen*) to daub
Pinte ['pɪntə] (**-, -n**) (*umg*) *f* (*Lokal*) boozer (*Brit*)
Pinzette [pɪn'tsɛtə] *f* tweezers *pl*
Pionier [pio'ni:r] (**-s, -e**) *m* pioneer; (*Mil*) sapper, engineer; **Pionierarbeit** *f* pioneering work; **Pionierunternehmen** *nt* pioneer company
Pipi [pi'pi:] (**-s, -s**) *nt od m* (*Kindersprache*) wee(-wee)
Pirat [pi'ra:t] (**-en, -en**) *m* pirate
Piratensender *m* pirate radio station
Pirsch [pɪrʃ] (**-**) *f* stalking
PISA-Studie ['pi:za-] *f* (*Sch*) PISA study
pissen ['pɪsən] (*umg!*) *vi* to (have a) piss (*!*); (*regnen*) to piss down (*!*)
Pistazie [pɪs'ta:tsiə] (**-, -n**) *f* pistachio
Piste ['pɪstə] (**-, -n**) *f* (*Ski*) run, piste; (*Aviat*) runway
Pistole [pɪs'to:lə] (**-, -n**) *f* pistol; **wie aus der ~ geschossen** (*fig*) like a shot; **jdm die ~ auf die Brust setzen** (*fig*) to hold a pistol to sb's head
pitschenass ['pɪtʃə'nas], **pitschnass** ['pɪtʃnas] (*umg*) *adj* soaking (wet)
Pizza ['pɪtsa] (**-, -s**) *f* pizza
PKW, Pkw (**-(s), -(s)**) *m abk* = **Personenkraftwagen**
Pl. *abk* (= *Plural*) pl.; (= *Platz*) Sq.
Plackerei [plakə'raɪ] *f* drudgery
plädieren [plɛ'di:rən] *vi* to plead
Plädoyer [plɛdoa'je:] (**-s, -s**) *nt* speech for the defence; (*fig*) plea
Plage ['pla:gə] (**-, -n**) *f* plague; (*Mühe*) nuisance; **Plagegeist** *m* pest, nuisance
plagen *vt* to torment ▷ *vr* to toil, slave
Plagiat [plagi'a:t] (**-(e)s, -e**) *nt* plagiarism
Plakat [pla'ka:t] (**-(e)s, -e**) *nt* poster; (*aus Pappe*) placard
plakativ [plaka'ti:f] *adj* striking, bold
Plakatwand *f* hoarding, billboard (*US*)
Plakette [pla'kɛtə] (**-, -n**) *f* (*Abzeichen*) badge; (*Münze*) commemorative coin; (*an Wänden*) plaque
Plan [pla:n] (**-(e)s, ¨-e**) *m* plan; (*Karte*) map; **Pläne schmieden** to make plans; **nach ~ verlaufen** to go according to plan; **jdn auf den ~ rufen** (*fig*) to bring sb into the arena
Plane (**-, -n**) *f* tarpaulin
planen *vt* to plan; (*Mord etc*) to plot
Planer, in (**-s, -**) *m(f)* planner
Planet [pla'ne:t] (**-en, -en**) *m* planet
Planetenbahn *f* orbit (of a planet)
planieren [pla'ni:rən] *vt* to level off
Planierraupe *f* bulldozer
Planke ['plaŋkə] (**-, -n**) *f* plank
Plänkelei [plɛŋkə'laɪ] *f* skirmish(ing)
plänkeln ['plɛŋkəln] *vi* to skirmish
Plankton ['plaŋktɔn] (**-s**) *nt* plankton
planlos *adj* (*Vorgehen*) unsystematic; (*Umherlaufen*) aimless
planmäßig *adj* according to plan; (*methodisch*) systematic; (*Eisenb*) scheduled
Planschbecken, **Plantschbecken** ['planʃbɛkən] *nt* paddling pool
planschen, **plantschen** *vi* to splash
Plansoll *nt* output target
Planstelle *f* post
Plantage [plan'ta:ʒə] (**-, -n**) *f* plantation
Planung *f* planning
Planwagen *m* covered wagon
Planwirtschaft *f* planned economy
Plappermaul (*umg*) *nt* (*Kind*) chatterbox
plappern ['plapərn] *vi* to chatter
plärren ['plɛrən] *vi* (*Mensch*) to cry, whine; (*Radio*) to blare
Plasma ['plasma] (**-s, Plasmen**) *nt* plasma
Plastik¹ ['plastɪk] *f* sculpture
Plastik² ['plastɪk] (**-s**) *nt* (*Kunststoff*) plastic; **Plastikfolie** *f* plastic film; **Plastikgeschoss** *nt*

plastic bullet; **Plastiktüte** *f* plastic bag
Plastilin [plasti'li:n] (**-s**) *nt* Plasticine®
plastisch ['plastɪʃ] *adj* plastic; **stell dir das ~ vor!** just picture it!
Platane [pla'ta:nə] (**-, -n**) *f* plane (tree)
Platin ['pla:ti:n] (**-s**) *nt* platinum
Platitüde [plati'ty:də] (**-, -n**) *f* platitude
platonisch [pla'to:nɪʃ] *adj* platonic
platsch [platʃ] *interj* splash!
platschen *vi* to splash
plätschern ['plɛtʃərn] *vi* to babble
platschnass *adj* drenched
platt [plat] *adj* flat; (*umg: überrascht*) flabbergasted; (*fig: geistlos*) flat, boring; **einen P~en haben** to have a flat (*umg*), have a flat tyre (*Brit*) *od* tire (*US*)
plattdeutsch *adj* Low German
Platte (**-, -n**) *f* (*Speisenplatte, Phot, Tech*) plate; (*Steinplatte*) flag; (*Kachel*) tile; (*Schallplatte*) record; **kalte ~** cold dish; **die ~ kenne ich schon** (*umg*) I've heard all that before
Plätteisen *nt* iron
plätten *vt, vi* to iron
Platten- *zW*: **Plattenleger** (**-s, -**) *m* paver; **Plattenspieler** *m* record player; **Plattenteller** *m* turntable
Plattform *f* platform; (*fig: Grundlage*) basis
Plattfuß *m* flat foot; (*Reifen*) flat tyre (*Brit*) *od* tire (*US*)
Plattitüde [plati'ty:də] (**-, -n**) *f* platitude
Platz [plats] (**-es, ¨-e**) *m* place; (*Sitzplatz*) seat; (*Raum*) space, room; (*in Stadt*) square; (*Sportplatz*) playing field; **~ machen** to get out of the way; **~ nehmen** to take a seat; **jdm ~ machen** to make room for sb; **~ sparend** space-saving; **auf ~ zwei** in second place; **fehl am ~e sein** to be out of place; **seinen ~ behaupten** to stand one's ground; **das erste Hotel am ~** the best hotel in town; **auf die Plätze, fertig, los!** (*beim Sport*) on your marks, get set, go!; **einen Spieler vom ~ stellen** *od* **verweisen** (*Sport*) to send a player off; **Platzangst** *f* (*Med*) agoraphobia; (*umg*) claustrophobia; **Platzangst haben/bekommen** (*umg*) to feel/get claustrophobic; **Platzanweiser, in** (**-s, -**) *m(f)* usher(ette)
Plätzchen ['plɛtsçən] *nt* spot; (*Gebäck*) biscuit
platzen *vi* (*Hilfsverb sein*) to burst; (*Bombe*) to explode; (*Naht, Hose, Haut*) to split; (*umg: scheitern: Geschäft*) to fall through; (*: Freundschaft*) to break up; (*: Theorie, Verschwörung*) to collapse; (*: Wechsel*) to bounce; **vor Wut ~** (*umg*) to be bursting with anger
platzieren [pla'tsi:rən] *vt* to place ▷ *vr* (*Sport*) to be placed; (*Tennis*) to be seeded; (*umg: sich setzen, stellen*) to plant o.s.
Platz- *zW*: **Platzkarte** *f* seat reservation; **Platzkonzert** *nt* open-air concert; **Platzmangel** *m* lack of space; **Platzpatrone** *f* blank cartridge; **Platzregen** *m* downpour; **platzsparend** *adj* space-saving; **Platzverweis** *m* sending-off; **Platzwart** *m* (*Sport*) groundsman (*Brit*), groundskeeper (*US*); **Platzwunde** *f* cut
Plauderei [plaʊdə'raɪ] *f* chat, conversation
plaudern ['plaʊdərn] *vi* to chat, talk
Plausch [plaʊʃ] (**-(e)s, -e**) (*umg*) *m* chat
plausibel [plaʊ'zi:bəl] *adj* plausible
Play-back, **Playback** ['pleɪbæk] (**-s, -s**) *nt* (*Verfahren: Schallplatte*) double-tracking; (*TV*) miming
plazieren [pla'tsi:rən] *vt siehe* **platzieren**
Plebejer, in [ple'be:jər(ɪn)] (**-s, -**) *m(f)* plebeian
plebejisch [ple'be:jɪʃ] *adj* plebeian
pleite ['plaɪtə] (*umg*) *adj* broke; **Pleite** (**-, -n**) *f* bankruptcy; (*umg: Reinfall*) flop; **Pleite machen** to go bust
Pleitegeier (*umg*) *m* (*drohende Pleite*) vulture; (*Bankrotteur*) bankrupt
plemplem [plɛm'plɛm] (*umg*) *adj* nuts
Plenarsitzung [ple'na:rzɪtsʊŋ] *f* plenary session
Plenum ['ple:nʊm] (**-s, Plenen**) *nt* plenum
Pleuelstange ['plɔʏəlʃtaŋə] *f* connecting rod
Plissee [plɪ'se:] (**-s, -s**) *nt* pleat
Plombe ['plɔmbə] (**-, -n**) *f* lead seal; (*Zahnplombe*) filling
plombieren [plɔm'bi:rən] *vt* to seal; (*Zahn*) to fill
Plotter ['plɔtər] (**-s, -s**) *m* (*Comput*) plotter
plötzlich ['plœtslɪç] *adj* sudden ▷ *adv* suddenly; **~er Kindstod** SIDS
Pluderhose ['plu:dərho:zə] *f* harem trousers *pl*
plump [plʊmp] *adj* clumsy; (*Hände*) coarse; (*Körper*) shapeless; **~e Annäherungsversuche** very obvious advances
plumpsen (*umg*) *vi* to plump down, fall
Plumpsklo, **Plumpsklosett** (*umg*) *nt* earth closet
Plunder ['plʊndər] (**-s**) *m* junk, rubbish
Plundergebäck *nt* flaky pastry
plündern ['plʏndərn] *vt* to plunder; (*Stadt*) to sack ▷ *vi* to plunder
Plünderung ['plʏndərʊŋ] *f* plundering, sack, pillage
Plural ['plu:ra:l] (**-s, -e**) *m* plural; **im ~ stehen** to be (in the) plural
pluralistisch [plura'lɪstɪʃ] *adj* pluralistic
plus [plʊs] *adv* plus; **mit ~ minus null abschließen** (*Comm*) to break even; **Plus** (**-, -**) *nt* plus; (*Fin*) profit; (*Vorteil*) advantage
Plüsch [ply:ʃ] (**-(e)s, -e**) *m* plush; **Plüschtier** *nt* ≈ soft toy
Plus- *zW*: **Pluspol** *m* (*Elek*) positive pole; **Pluspunkt** *m* (*Sport*) point; (*fig*) point in sb's favour; **Plusquamperfekt** *nt* pluperfect
Plutonium [plu'to:niʊm] (**-s**) *nt* plutonium
PLZ *abk* = **Postleitzahl**
Pneu [pnɔʏ] (**-s, -s**) *m abk* (= *Pneumatik*) tyre (*Brit*), tire (*US*)
Po [po:] (**-s, -s**) (*umg*) *m* bum (*Brit*), fanny (*US*)
Pöbel ['pø:bəl] (**-s**) *m* mob, rabble
Pöbelei [pø:bə'laɪ] *f* vulgarity
pöbelhaft *adj* low, vulgar
pochen ['pɔxən] *vi* to knock; (*Herz*) to pound; **auf etw** *akk* **~** (*fig*) to insist on sth

Pocken ['pɔkən] *pl* smallpox *sing*
Pockenimpfung, **Pockenschutzimpfung** *f* smallpox vaccination
Podest [pɔ'dɛst] (**-(e)s, -e**) *nt od m* (*Sockel, fig*) pedestal; (*Podium*) platform
Podium ['po:diʊm] *nt* podium
Podiumsdiskussion *f* panel discussion
Poesie [poe'zi:] *f* poetry
Poet [po'e:t] (**-en, -en**) *m* poet; **poetisch** *adj* poetic
pofen ['po:fən] (*umg*) *vi* to kip (*Brit*), doss
Pointe [po'[˜ɛ]:tə] (**-, -n**) *f* point; (*eines Witzes*) punch line
pointiert [po[˜ɛ]'ti:rt] *adj* trenchant, pithy
Pokal [po'ka:l] (**-s, -e**) *m* goblet; (*Sport*) cup; **Pokalspiel** *nt* cup tie
Pökelfleisch ['pø:kəlflaɪʃ] *nt* salt meat
pökeln *vt* (*Fleisch, Fisch*) to pickle, salt
Poker ['po:kər] (**-s**) *nt* poker
pokern ['po:kərn] *vi* to play poker
Pol [po:l] (**-s, -e**) *m* pole; **der ruhende ~** (*fig*) the calming influence
pol. *abk* = **politisch; polizeilich**
polar [po'la:r] *adj* polar
polarisieren [polari'zi:rən] *vt, vr* to polarize
Polarkreis *m* polar circle; **nördlicher/ südlicher ~** Arctic/Antarctic Circle
Polarstern *m* Pole Star
Pole ['po:lə] (**-n, -n**) *m* Pole
Polemik [po'le:mɪk] *f* polemics *sing*
polemisch *adj* polemical
polemisieren [polemi'zi:rən] *vi* to polemicize
Polen ['po:lən] (**-s**) *nt* Poland
Polente (-) (*veraltet: umg*) *f* cops *pl*
Police [po'li:s(ə)] (**-, -n**) *f* insurance policy
Polier [po'li:r] (**-s, -e**) *m* foreman
polieren *vt* to polish
Poliklinik [poli'kli:nɪk] *f* outpatients (department) *sing*
Polin *f* Pole, Polish woman
Politesse [poli'tɛsə] (**-, -n**) *f* (*Frau*) ≈ traffic warden (*Brit*)
Politik [poli'ti:k] *f* politics *sing*; (*eine bestimmte*) policy; **in die ~ gehen** to go into politics; **eine ~ verfolgen** to pursue a policy
Politiker, in [po'li:tikər(ɪn)] (**-s, -**) *m(f)* politician
politisch [po'li:tɪʃ] *adj* political
politisieren [politi'zi:rən] *vi* to talk politics ▷ *vt* to politicize; **jdn ~** to make sb politically aware
Politur [poli'tu:r] *f* polish
Polizei [poli'tsaɪ] *f* police; **Polizeiaufsicht** *f*: **unter Polizeiaufsicht stehen** to have to report regularly to the police; **Polizeibeamte, r** *m* police officer; **polizeilich** *adj* police *attrib*; **sich polizeilich melden** to register with the police; **polizeiliches Führungszeugnis** *certificate of "no criminal record" issued by the police*; **Polizeipräsidium** *nt* police headquarters *pl*; **Polizeirevier** *nt* police station; **Polizeispitzel** *m* police spy, informer; **Polizeistaat** *m* police state; **Polizeistreife** *f* police patrol; **Polizeistunde** *f* closing time; **Polizeiwache** *f* police station; **polizeiwidrig** *adj* illegal
Polizist, in [poli'tsɪst(ɪn)] (**-en, -en**) *m(f)* policeman/-woman
Pollen ['pɔlən] (**-s, -**) *m* pollen
poln. *abk* = **polnisch**
polnisch ['pɔlnɪʃ] *adj* Polish
Polohemd ['po:lohɛmt] *nt* polo shirt
Polster ['pɔlstər] (**-s, -**) *nt* cushion; (*Polsterung*) upholstery; (*in Kleidung*) padding; (*fig: Geld*) reserves *pl*; **Polsterer** (**-s, -**) *m* upholsterer; **Polstergarnitur** *f* three-piece suite; **Polstermöbel** *pl* upholstered furniture *sing*
polstern *vt* to upholster; (*Kleidung*) to pad; **sie ist gut gepolstert** (*umg*) she's well padded; (*: finanziell*) she's not short of the odd penny
Polsterung *f* upholstery
Polterabend ['pɔltəra:bənt] *m party on the eve of a wedding*
poltern *vi* (*Krach machen*) to crash; (*schimpfen*) to rant
Polygamie [polyga'mi:] *f* polygamy
Polynesien [poly'ne:ziən] (**-s**) *nt* Polynesia
Polynesier, in [poly'ne:ziər(ɪn)] (**-s, -**) *m(f)* Polynesian
polynesisch *adj* Polynesian
Polyp [po'ly:p] (**-en, -en**) *m* polyp; (*umg*) cop; **Polypen** *pl* (*Med*) adenoids *pl*
Polytechnikum [poly'tɛçnikʊm] (**-s, Polytechnika**) *nt* polytechnic, poly (*umg*)
Pomade [po'ma:də] *f* pomade
Pommern ['pɔmərn] (**-s**) *nt* Pomerania
Pommes frites [pɔm'frɪt] *pl* chips *pl* (*Brit*), French fried potatoes *pl* (*Brit*), French fries *pl* (*US*)
Pomp [pɔmp] (**-(e)s**) *m* pomp
pompös [pɔm'pø:s] *adj* grandiose
Pontius ['pɔntsiʊs] *m*: **von ~ zu Pilatus** from pillar to post
Pony ['pɔni] (**-s, -s**) *m* (*Frisur*) fringe (*Brit*), bangs *pl* (*US*) ▷ *nt* (*Pferd*) pony
Pop [pɔp] (**-s**) *m* (*Mus*) pop; (*Kunst*) pop art
Popelin [popə'li:n] (**-s, -e**) *m* poplin
Popeline (**-, -n**) *f* poplin
Popkonzert *nt* pop concert
Popmusik *f* pop music
Popo [po'po:] (**-s, -s**) (*umg*) *m* bottom, bum (*Brit*)
populär [popu'lɛ:r] *adj* popular
Popularität [populari'tɛ:t] *f* popularity
populärwissenschaftlich *adj* popular science
Pore ['po:rə] (**-, -n**) *f* pore
Porno ['pɔrno] (**-s**, *no pl*) (*umg*) *m* porn
Pornografie [pɔrnogra'fi:] *f* pornography
pornografisch [pɔrno'gra:fɪʃ] *adj* pornographic
porös [po'rø:s] *adj* porous
Porree ['pɔre] (**-s, -s**) *m* leek
Portal [pɔr'ta:l] (**-s, -e**) *nt* portal
Portefeuille [pɔrt(ə)'fø:j] (**-s, -s**) *nt* (*Pol, Fin*) portfolio
Portemonnaie [pɔrtmɔ'nɛ:] (**-s, -s**) *nt* purse
Portier [pɔrti'e:] (**-s, -s**) *m* porter; (*Pförtner*) porter, doorkeeper, doorman
Portion [pɔrtsi'o:n] *f* portion, helping;

(*umg: Anteil*) amount; **eine halbe ~** (*fig: umg: Person*) a half-pint; **eine ~ Kaffee** a pot of coffee
Portmonee [pɔrtmɔ'nɛ:] (**-s, -s**) *nt* purse
Porto ['pɔrto] (**-s, -s** *od* **Porti**) *nt* postage; **~ zahlt Empfänger** postage paid; **portofrei** *adj* post-free, (postage) prepaid
Porträt [pɔr'trɛ:] (**-s, -s**) *nt* portrait
porträtieren [pɔrtrɛ'ti:rən] *vt* to paint (a portrait of); (*fig*) to portray
Portugal ['pɔrtugal] (**-s**) *nt* Portugal
Portugiese [pɔrtu'gi:zə] (**-n, -n**) *m* Portuguese
Portugiesin *f* Portuguese
portugiesisch *adj* Portuguese
Portwein ['pɔrtvaɪn] *m* port
Porzellan [pɔrtsɛ'la:n] (**-s, -e**) *nt* china, porcelain; (*Geschirr*) china
Posaune [po'zaʊnə] (**-, -n**) *f* trombone
Pose ['po:zə] (**-, -n**) *f* pose
posieren [po'zi:rən] *vi* to pose
Position [pozitsi'o:n] *f* position; (*Comm: auf Liste*) item
Positionslichter *pl* navigation lights *pl*
Positionspapier *nt* position paper
positiv ['po:ziti:f] *adj* positive; **~ zu etw stehen** to be in favour (*Brit*) *od* favor (*US*) of sth; **Positiv** (**-s, -e**) *nt* (*Phot*) positive
Positur [pozi'tu:r] *f* posture, attitude; **sich in ~ setzen** *od* **stellen** to adopt a posture
Posse ['pɔsə] (**-, -n**) *f* farce
possessiv ['pɔsɛsi:f] *adj* possessive; **Possessiv** (**-s, -e**) *nt* possessive pronoun; **Possessivpronomen** (**-s, -e**) *nt* possessive pronoun
possierlich [pɔ'si:rlɪç] *adj* funny
Post [pɔst] (**-, -en**) *f* post (office); (*Briefe*) post, mail; **ist ~ für mich da?** are there any letters for me?; **mit getrennter ~** under separate cover; **etw auf die ~ geben** to post (*Brit*) *od* mail sth; **auf die** *od* **zur ~ gehen** to go to the post office; **Postamt** *nt* post office; **Postanweisung** *f* postal order (*Brit*), money order; **Postbote** *m* postman (*Brit*), mailman (*US*)
Posten (**-s, -**) *m* post, position; (*Comm*) item; (*: Warenmenge*) quantity, lot; (*auf Liste*) entry; (*Mil*) sentry; (*Streikposten*) picket; **~ beziehen** to take up one's post; **nicht ganz auf dem ~ sein** (*nicht gesund sein*) to be off-colour (*Brit*) *od* off-color (*US*)
Poster ['pɔstər] (**-s, -(s)**) *nt* poster
Postf. *abk* (= *Postfach*) PO Box
Post- *zW*: **Postfach** *nt* post office box; **Postkarte** *f* postcard; **postlagernd** *adv* poste restante; **Postleitzahl** *f* postal code
postmodern [pɔstmo'dɛrn] *adj* postmodern
Post- *zW*: **Postscheckkonto** *nt* Post Office Giro account (*Brit*); **Postsparbuch** *nt* post office savings book (*Brit*); **Postsparkasse** *f* post office savings bank; **Poststempel** *m* postmark; **postwendend** *adv* by return (of post); **Postwertzeichen** *nt* (*form*) postage stamp; **Postwurfsendung** *f* direct mail advertising
potent [po'tɛnt] *adj* potent; (*fig*) high-powered
Potential [potɛntsi'a:l] (**-s, -e**) *nt* = **Potenzial**
potentiell [potɛntsi'ɛl] *adj* = **potenziell**
Potenz [po'tɛnts] *f* power; (*eines Mannes*) potency
Potenzial [potɛntsi'a:l] (**-s, -e**) *nt* potential
potenziell [potɛntsi'ɛl] *adj* potential
potenzieren [potɛn'tsi:rən] *vt* (*Math*) to raise to the power of
Potpourri ['pɔtpʊri] (**-s, -s**) *nt*: **~ (aus)** (*Mus*) medley (of); (*fig*) assortment (of)
Pott [pɔt] (**-(e)s, ¨-e**) (*umg*) *m* pot; **potthässlich** (*umg*) *adj* ugly as sin
pp., ppa. *abk* (= *per procura*) p.p.
Präambel [prɛ'|ambəl] (**-, -n**) *f* (*+gen*) preamble (to)
Pracht [praxt] (**-**) *f* splendour (*Brit*), splendor (*US*), magnificence; **es ist eine wahre ~** it's (really) marvellous; **Prachtexemplar** *nt* beauty (*umg*); (*fig: Mensch*) fine specimen
prächtig ['prɛçtɪç] *adj* splendid
Prachtstück *nt* showpiece
prachtvoll *adj* splendid, magnificent
prädestinieren [prɛdɛsti'ni:rən] *vt* to predestine
Prädikat [prɛdi'ka:t] (**-(e)s, -e**) *nt* title; (*Gram*) predicate; (*Zensur*) distinction; **Wein mit ~** special quality wine
Prag [pra:k] (**-s**) *nt* Prague
prägen ['prɛ:gən] *vt* to stamp; (*Münze*) to mint; (*Ausdruck*) to coin; (*Charakter*) to form; (*kennzeichnen: Stadtbild*) to characterize; **das Erlebnis prägte ihn** the experience left its mark on him
prägend *adj* having a forming *od* shaping influence
pragmatisch [pra'gma:tɪʃ] *adj* pragmatic
prägnant [prɛ'gnant] *adj* concise, terse
Prägnanz *f* conciseness, terseness
Prägung ['prɛ:gʊŋ] *f* minting; forming; (*Eigenart*) character, stamp
prahlen ['pra:lən] *vi* to boast, brag
Prahlerei [pra:lə'raɪ] *f* boasting
prahlerisch *adj* boastful
Praktik ['praktɪk] *f* practice
praktikabel [praktɪ'ka:bəl] *adj* practicable
Praktikant, in [praktɪ'kant(ɪn)] *m(f)* trainee
Praktikum (**-s, Praktika** *od* **Praktiken**) *nt* practical training
praktisch ['praktɪʃ] *adj* practical, handy; **~er Arzt** general practitioner; **~es Beispiel** concrete example
praktizieren [prakti'tsi:rən] *vt, vi* to practise (*Brit*), practice (*US*)
Praline [pra'li:nə] *f* chocolate
prall [pral] *adj* firmly rounded; (*Segel*) taut; (*Arme*) plump; (*Sonne*) blazing
prallen *vi* to bounce, rebound; (*Sonne*) to blaze
prallvoll *adj* full to bursting; (*Brieftasche*) bulging
Prämie ['prɛ:miə] *f* premium; (*Belohnung*) award, prize
prämienbegünstigt *adj* with benefit of premiums

prämiensparen *vi* to save in a bonus scheme
prämieren [prɛ'mi:rən] *vt* to give an award to
Pranger ['praŋər] (**-s, -**) *m* (*Hist*) pillory; **jdn an den ~ stellen** (*fig*) to pillory sb
Pranke ['praŋkə] (**-, -n**) *f* (*Tierpranke: umg: Hand*) paw
Präparat [prɛpa'ra:t] (**-(e)s, -e**) *nt* (*Biol*) preparation; (*Med*) medicine
präparieren *vt* (*konservieren*) to preserve; (*Med: zerlegen*) to dissect
Präposition [prɛpozitsi'o:n] *f* preposition
Prärie [prɛ'ri:] *f* prairie
Präs. *abk* = **Präsens; Präsident**
Präsens ['prɛ:zɛns] (**-**) *nt* present tense
präsent *adj*: **etw ~ haben** to have sth at hand
präsentieren [prɛzɛn'ti:rən] *vt* to present
Präsenzbibliothek *f* reference library
Präservativ [prɛzɛrva'ti:f] (**-s, -e**) *nt* condom, sheath
Präsident, in [prɛzi'dɛnt(ɪn)] *m(f)* president; **Präsidentschaft** *f* presidency; **Präsidentschaftskandidat** *m* presidential candidate
Präsidium [prɛ'zi:diʊm] *nt* presidency, chairmanship; (*Polizeipräsidium*) police headquarters *pl*
prasseln ['prasəln] *vi* (*Feuer*) to crackle; (*Hagel*) to drum; (*Wörter*) to rain down
prassen ['prasən] *vi* to live it up
Präteritum [prɛ'te:ritʊm] (**-s, Präterita**) *nt* preterite
Pratze ['pratsə] (**-, -n**) *f* paw
Präventiv- [prɛvɛn'ti:f] *in zw* preventive
Praxis ['praksɪs] (**-, Praxen**) *f* practice; (*Erfahrung*) experience; (*Behandlungsraum*) surgery; (*von Anwalt*) office; **die ~ sieht anders aus** the reality is different; **ein Beispiel aus der ~** an example from real life
Präzedenzfall [prɛtse:'dɛntsfal] *m* precedent
präzis [prɛ'tsi:s] *adj* precise
Präzision [prɛtsizi'o:n] *f* precision
PR-Chef *m* PR officer
predigen ['pre:dɪgən] *vt, vi* to preach
Prediger (**-s, -**) *m* preacher
Predigt ['pre:dɪçt] (**-, -en**) *f* sermon
Preis [praɪs] (**-es, -e**) *m* price; (*Siegespreis*) prize; (*Auszeichnung*) award; **um keinen ~** not at any price; **um jeden ~** at all costs; **Preisangebot** *nt* quotation; **Preisausschreiben** *nt* competition; **Preisbindung** *f* price-fixing; **Preisbrecher** *m* (*Firma*) undercutter
Preiselbeere *f* cranberry
preisempfindlich *adj* price-sensitive
preisen [praɪzən] *unreg vt* to praise; **sich glücklich ~** (*geh*) to count o.s. lucky
Preis- *zW*: **Preisentwicklung** *f* price trend; **Preiserhöhung** *f* price increase; **Preisfrage** *f* question of price; (*Wettbewerb*) prize question
preisgeben *unreg vt* to abandon; (*opfern*) to sacrifice; (*zeigen*) to expose
Preis- *zW*: **Preisgefälle** *nt* price gap; **preisgekrönt** *adj* prizewinning; **Preisgericht** *nt* jury; **preisgünstig** *adj* inexpensive; **Preisindex** *m* price index; **Preiskrieg** *m* price war; **Preislage** *f* price range; **preislich** *adj* price *attr*, in price; **Preisliste** *f* price list, tariff; **Preisnachlass** *m* discount; **Preisschild** *nt* price tag; **Preisspanne** *f* price range; **Preissturz** *m* slump; **Preisträger** *m* prizewinner; **preiswert** *adj* inexpensive
prekär [pre'kɛ:r] *adj* precarious
Prellbock [prɛlbɔk] *m* buffers *pl*
prellen *vt* to bruise; (*fig*) to cheat, swindle
Prellung *f* bruise
Premiere [prəmi'ɛ:rə] (**-, -n**) *f* premiere
Premierminister, in [prəmɪ'e:mɪnɪstər(ɪn)] *m(f)* prime minister, premier
Presse ['prɛsə] (**-, -n**) *f* press; **Presseagentur** *f* press *od* news agency; **Presseausweis** *m* press pass; **Presseerklärung** *f* press release; **Pressefreiheit** *f* freedom of the press; **Pressekonferenz** *f* press conference; **Pressemeldung** *f* press report
pressen *vt* to press
Presse- *zW*: **Pressesprecher, in** *m(f)* spokesperson, press officer; **Pressestelle** *f* press office; **Presseverlautbarung** *f* press release
pressieren [prɛ'si:rən] *vi* to be in a hurry; **es pressiert** it's urgent
Pressluft ['prɛslʊft] *f* compressed air; **Pressluftbohrer** *m* pneumatic drill
Prestige [prɛs'ti:ʒə] (**-s**) *nt* prestige; **Prestigeverlust** *m* loss of prestige
Preuße ['prɔʏsə] (**-n, -n**) *m* Prussian
Preußen (**-s**) *nt* Prussia
Preußin *f* Prussian
preußisch *adj* Prussian
prickeln ['prɪkəln] *vi* to tingle; (*kitzeln*) to tickle; (*Bläschen bilden*) to sparkle, bubble ▷ *vt* to tickle
pries *etc* [pri:s] *vb siehe* **preisen**
Priester ['pri:stər] (**-s, -**) *m* priest
Priesterin *f* priestess
Priesterweihe *f* ordination (to the priesthood)
Prima ['pri:ma] (**-, Primen**) *f* (*früher*) *eighth and ninth year of German secondary school*
prima *adj inv* first-class, excellent
primär [pri'mɛ:r] *adj* primary; **Primärdaten** *pl* primary data *pl*
Primel ['pri:məl] (**-, -n**) *f* primrose
primitiv [primi'ti:f] *adj* primitive
Primzahl ['pri:mtsa:l] *f* prime (number)
Prinz [prɪnts] (**-en, -en**) *m* prince
Prinzessin [prɪn'tsɛsɪn] *f* princess
Prinzip [prɪn'tsi:p] (**-s, -ien**) *nt* principle; **aus ~** on principle; **im ~** in principle
prinzipiell [prɪntsi'piɛl] *adj* on principle
prinzipienlos *adj* unprincipled
Priorität [priori'tɛ:t] *f* priority; **Prioritäten** *pl* (*Comm*) preference shares *pl*, preferred stock *sing* (*US*); **~en setzen** to establish one's priorities
Prise ['pri:zə] (**-, -n**) *f* pinch
Prisma ['prɪsma] (**-s, Prismen**) *nt* prism
privat [pri'va:t] *adj* private; **jdn ~ sprechen** to speak to sb in private; **Privatbesitz** *m* private

property; **Privatdozent** *m* outside lecturer; **Privatfernsehen** *nt* commercial television; **Privatgespräch** *nt* private conversation; (*am Telefon*) private call
privatisieren [privati'zi:rən] *vt* to privatize
Privatschule *f* private school
Privatvorsorge *f* (*fürs Alter*) private pension scheme; (*für Gesundheit*) health insurance scheme
Privatwirtschaft *f* private sector
Privileg [privi'le:k] (**-(e)s, -ien**) *nt* privilege
Pro [pro:] (**-**) *nt* pro
pro *präp +akk* per; **~ Stück** each, apiece
Probe ['pro:bə] (**-, -n**) *f* test; (*Teststück*) sample; (*Theat*) rehearsal; **jdn auf die ~ stellen** to put sb to the test; **er ist auf ~ angestellt** he's employed for a probationary period; **zur ~** to try out; **Probebohrung** *f* (*Öl*) exploration well; **Probeexemplar** *nt* specimen copy; **Probefahrt** *f* test drive; **Probelauf** *m* trial run
proben *vt* to try; (*Theat*) to rehearse
Probe- *zW*: **Probestück** *nt* specimen; **probeweise** *adv* on approval; **Probezeit** *f* probation period
probieren [pro'bi:rən] *vt* to try; (*Wein, Speise*) to taste, sample ▷ *vi* to try; to taste
Problem [pro'ble:m] (**-s, -e**) *nt* problem; **vor einem ~ stehen** to be faced with a problem
Problematik [proble:'ma:tɪk] *f* problem
problematisch [proble:'ma:tɪʃ] *adj* problematic
problemlos *adj* problem-free
Problemstellung *f* way of looking at a problem
Produkt [pro'dʊkt] (**-(e)s, -e**) *nt* product; (*Agr*) produce *no pl*
Produktentwicklung *f* product development
Produktion [prodʊktsi'o:n] *f* production
Produktionsleiter *m* production manager
Produktionsstätte *f* (*Halle*) shop floor
produktiv [prodʊk'ti:f] *adj* productive
Produktivität [prodʊktivi'tɛ:t] *f* productivity
Produzent [produ'tsɛnt] *m* manufacturer; (*Film*) producer
produzieren [produ'tsi:rən] *vt* to produce ▷ *vr* to show off
Prof. [prof] *abk* (= *Professor*) Prof
profan [pro'fa:n] *adj* (*weltlich*) secular, profane; (*gewöhnlich*) mundane
professionell [profɛsio'nɛl] *adj* professional
Professor, in [pro'fɛsɔr, profɛ'so:rɪn] *m(f)* professor; (*Österr: Gymnasiallehrer*) grammar school teacher (*Brit*), high school teacher (*US*)
Professur [profɛ'su:r] *f*: **~ (für)** chair (of)
Profi ['pro:fi] (**-s, -s**) *m abk* (= *Professional*) pro
Profil [pro'fi:l] (**-s, -e**) *nt* profile; (*fig*) image; (*Querschnitt*) cross section; (*Längsschnitt*) vertical section; (*von Reifen, Schuhsohle*) tread
profilieren [profi'li:rən] *vr* to create an image for o.s.
Profilsohle *f* sole with a tread
Profit [pro'fi:t] (**-(e)s, -e**) *m* profit
profitgeil *adj* (*umg*) profit-greedy
profitieren [profi'ti:rən] *vi*: **~ (von)** to profit (from)
Profitmacherei (*umg*) *f* profiteering
pro forma *adv* as a matter of form
Pro-forma-Rechnung *f* pro forma invoice
Prognose [pro'gno:zə] (**-, -n**) *f* prediction, prognosis
Programm [pro'gram] (**-s, -e**) *nt* programme (*Brit*), program (*US*); (*Comput*) program; (*TV: Sender*) channel; (*Kollektion*) range; **nach ~** as planned; **Programmfehler** *m* (*Comput*) bug; **programmgemäß** *adj* according to plan; **Programmhinweis** *m* (*Rundf, TV*) programme (*Brit*) *od* program (*US*) announcement
programmieren [progra'mi:rən] *vt* to programme (*Brit*), program (*US*); (*Comput*) to program; **auf etw** *akk* **programmiert sein** (*fig*) to be geared to sth
Programmierer, in (**-s, -**) *m(f)* programmer
Programmiersprache *f* (*Comput*) programming language
Programmierung *f* (*Comput*) programming
Programmvorschau *f* preview; (*Film*) trailer
progressiv [progrɛ'si:f] *adj* progressive
Projekt [pro'jɛkt] (**-(e)s, -e**) *nt* project
Projektleiter, in *m(f)* project manager(ess)
Projektor [pro'jɛktɔr] *m* projector
projizieren [proji'tsi:rən] *vt* to project
proklamieren [prokla'mi:rən] *vt* to proclaim
Pro-Kopf-Einkommen *nt* per capita income
Prokura [pro'ku:ra] (**-, Prokuren**) *f* (*form*) power of attorney
Prokurist, in [proku'rɪst(ɪn)] *m(f)* attorney
Prolet [pro'le:t] (**-en, -en**) *m* prole, pleb
Proletariat [proletari'a:t] (**-(e)s, -e**) *nt* proletariat
Proletarier [prole'ta:riər] (**-s, -**) *m* proletarian
Prolog [pro'lo:k] (**-(e)s, -e**) *m* prologue
Promenade [promə'na:də] (**-, -n**) *f* promenade
Promenadenmischung *f* (*hum*) mongrel
Promille [pro'mɪle] (**-(s), -**) (*umg*) *nt* alcohol level; **Promillegrenze** *f* legal (alcohol) limit
prominent [promi'nɛnt] *adj* prominent
Prominenz [promi'nɛnts] *f* VIPs *pl*
Promoter [pro'mo:tər] (**-s, -**) *m* promoter
Promotion [promotsi'o:n] *f* doctorate, Ph.D.
promovieren [promo'vi:rən] *vi* to receive a doctorate *etc*
prompt [prɔmpt] *adj* prompt
Pronomen [pro'no:mɛn] (**-s, -**) *nt* pronoun
Propaganda [propa'ganda] (**-**) *f* propaganda
propagieren [propa'gi:rən] *vt* to propagate
Propangas [pro'pa:nga:s] *nt* propane gas
Propeller [pro'pɛlər] (**-s, -**) *m* propeller
proper ['prɔpər] (*umg*) *adj* neat, tidy
Prophet, in [pro'fe:t(ɪn)] (**-en, -en**) *m(f)* prophet(ess)
prophezeien [profe'tsaɪən] *vt* to prophesy
Prophezeiung *f* prophecy
prophylaktisch [profy'laktɪʃ] *adj* prophylactic (*form*), preventive
Proportion [propɔrtsi'o:n] *f* proportion
proportional [propɔrtsio'na:l] *adj* proportional; **Proportionalschrift** *f* (*Comput*)

proportional printing
proportioniert [propɔrtsio'ni:rt] *adj*: **gut/schlecht ~** well/badly proportioned
Proporz [pro'pɔrts] (**-es, -e**) *m* proportional representation
Prosa ['pro:za] (**-**) *f* prose
prosaisch [pro'za:ɪʃ] *adj* prosaic
prosit ['pro:zɪt] *interj* cheers!; **~ Neujahr!** happy New Year!
Prospekt [pro'spɛkt] (**-(e)s, -e**) *m* leaflet, brochure
prost [pro:st] *interj* cheers!
Prostata ['prɔstata] (**-**) *f* prostate gland
Prostituierte [prostitu'i:rtə] (**-n, -n**) *f* prostitute
Prostitution [prostitutsi'o:n] *f* prostitution
prot. [prot] *abk* = **protestantisch**
Protektionismus [protɛktsio'nɪsmʊs] *m* protectionism
Protektorat [protɛkto'ra:t] (**-(e)s, -e**) *nt* (*Schirmherrschaft*) patronage; (*Schutzgebiet*) protectorate
Protest [pro'tɛst] (**-(e)s, -e**) *m* protest
Protestant, in [protɛs'tant(ɪn)] *m(f)* Protestant; **protestantisch** *adj* Protestant
Protestbewegung *f* protest movement
protestieren [protɛs'ti:rən] *vi* to protest
Protestkundgebung *f* (protest) rally
Protestpartei *f* protest party
Prothese [pro'te:zə] (**-, -n**) *f* artificial limb; (*Zahnprothese*) dentures *pl*
Protokoll [proto'kɔl] (**-s, -e**) *nt* register; (*Niederschrift*) record; (*von Sitzung*) minutes *pl*; (*diplomatisch*) protocol; (*Polizeiprotokoll*) statement; (*Strafzettel*) ticket; **(das) ~ führen** (*bei Sitzung*) to take the minutes; (*bei Gericht*) to make a transcript of the proceedings; **etw zu ~ geben** to have sth put on record; (*bei Polizei*) to say sth in one's statement; **Protokollführer** *m* secretary; (*Jur*) clerk (of the court)
protokollieren [protokɔ'li:rən] *vt* to take down; (*Bemerkung*) to enter in the minutes
Proton ['pro:tɔn] (**-s, -en**) *nt* proton
Prototyp *m* prototype
Protz ['prɔts] (**-es, -e**) *m* swank; **protzen** *vi* to show off
protzig *adj* ostentatious
Proviant [provi'ant] (**-s, -e**) *m* provisions *pl*, supplies *pl*
Provinz [pro'vɪnts] (**-, -en**) *f* province; **das ist finsterste ~** (*pej*) it's a cultural backwater
provinziell [provɪn'tsiɛl] *adj* provincial
Provision [provizi'o:n] *f* (*Comm*) commission
provisorisch [provi'zo:rɪʃ] *adj* provisional
Provisorium [provi'zo:riʊm] (**-s, -ien**) *nt* provisional arrangement
Provokation [provokatsi'o:n] *f* provocation
provokativ [provoka'ti:f] *adj* provocative, provoking
provokatorisch [provoka'to:rɪʃ] *adj* provocative, provoking
provozieren [provo'tsi:rən] *vt* to provoke
Proz. *abk* (= *Prozent*) pc
Prozedur [protse'du:r] *f* procedure; (*pej*) carry-on; **die ~ beim Zahnarzt** the ordeal at the dentist's
Prozent [pro'tsɛnt] (**-(e)s, -e**) *nt* per cent, percentage; **Prozentrechnung** *f* percentage calculation; **Prozentsatz** *m* percentage
prozentual [protsɛntu'a:l] *adj* percentage *attrib*
Prozess [pro'tsɛs] (**-es, -e**) *m* trial, case; (*Vorgang*) process; **es zum ~ kommen lassen** to go to court; **mit jdm/etw kurzen ~ machen** (*fig: umg*) to make short work of sb/sth; **Prozessanwalt** *m* barrister, counsel; **Prozessführung** *f* handling of a case
prozessieren [protsɛ'si:rən] *vi*: **~ (mit)** to bring an action (against), go to law (with *od* against)
Prozession [protsɛsi'o:n] *f* procession
Prozesskosten *pl* (legal) costs *pl*
prüde ['pry:də] *adj* prudish
Prüderie [pry:də'ri:] *f* prudery
prüfen ['pry:fən] *vt* to examine, test; (*nachprüfen*) to check; (*erwägen*) to consider; (*Geschäftsbücher*) to audit; (*mustern*) to scrutinize
Prüfer, in (**-s, -**) *m(f)* examiner
Prüfling *m* examinee
Prüfstein *m* touchstone
Prüfung *f* (*Sch, Univ*) examination, exam; (*Überprüfung*) checking; **eine ~ machen** to take *od* sit (*Brit*) an exam(ination); **durch eine ~ fallen** to fail an exam(ination)
Prüfungs- *zW*: **Prüfungsausschuss** *m* examining board; **Prüfungskommission** *f* examining board; **Prüfungsordnung** *f* exam(ination) regulations *pl*
Prügel ['pry:gəl] (**-s, -**) *m* cudgel ▷ *pl* beating *sing*
Prügelei [pry:gə'laɪ] *f* fight
Prügelknabe *m* scapegoat
prügeln *vt* to beat ▷ *vr* to fight
Prügelstrafe *f* corporal punishment
Prunk [prʊŋk] (**-(e)s**) *m* pomp, show; **prunkvoll** *adj* splendid, magnificent
prusten ['pru:stən] (*umg*) *vi* to snort
PS *abk* (= *Pferdestärke*) hp; (= *Postskript(um)*) PS
Psalm [psalm] (**-s, -en**) *m* psalm
pseudo- [psɔʏdo] *in zW* pseudo
Psychiater [psy'çia:tər] (**-s, -**) *m* psychiatrist
Psychiatrie [psyçia'tri:] *f* psychiatry
psychiatrisch [psy'çia:trɪʃ] *adj* psychiatric; **~e Klinik** mental *od* psychiatric hospital
psychisch ['psy:çɪʃ] *adj* psychological; **~ gestört** emotionally *od* psychologically disturbed
Psychoanalyse [psyçoana'ly:zə] *f* psychoanalysis
Psychologe [psyço'lo:gə] (**-n, -n**) *m* psychologist
Psychologie *f* psychology
Psychologin *f* psychologist
psychologisch *adj* psychological
Psychotherapie *f* psychotherapy
PTT (*Schweiz*) *abk* (= *Post, Telefon, Telegraf*) *postal and telecommunication services*
Pubertät [pubɛr'tɛ:t] *f* puberty
publik [pu'bli:k] *adj*: **~ werden** to become

public knowledge
Publikum ['pu:blikʊm] (**-s**) *nt* audience; (*Sport*) crowd; **das ~ in dieser Bar ist sehr gemischt** you get a very mixed group of people using this bar
Publikumserfolg *m* popular success
Publikumsverkehr *m*: **„heute kein ~"** "closed today for public business"
publizieren [publi'tsi:rən] *vt* to publish
Pudding ['pʊdɪŋ] (**-s, -e** *od* **-s**) *m* blancmange; **Puddingpulver** *nt* custard powder
Pudel ['pu:dəl] (**-s, -**) *m* poodle; **das also ist des ~s Kern** (*fig*) that's what it's really all about
pudelwohl (*umg*) *adj*: **sich ~ fühlen** to feel on top of the world
Puder ['pu:dər] (**-s, -**) *m* powder; **Puderdose** *f* powder compact
pudern *vt* to powder
Puderzucker *m* icing sugar (*Brit*), confectioner's sugar (*US*)
Puerto Ricaner, in [puɛrtori'ka:nər(ɪn)] (**-s, -**) *m(f)* Puerto Rican
puerto-ricanisch *adj* Puerto Rican
Puerto Rico [pu'ɛrto'ri:ko] (**-s**) *nt* Puerto Rico
Puff[1] [pʊf] (**-(e)s, -e**) *m* (*Wäschepuff*) linen basket; (*Sitzpuff*) pouf
Puff[2] (**-(e)s, ⸚e**) (*umg*) *m* (*Stoß*) push
Puff[3] (**-s, -s**) (*umg*) *m od nt* (*Bordell*) brothel
Puffer (**-s, -**) *m* (*auch Comput*) buffer; **Pufferspeicher** *m* (*Comput*) cache; **Pufferstaat** *m* buffer state; **Pufferzone** *f* buffer zone
Puffreis *m* puffed rice
Pulle ['pʊlə] (**-, -n**) (*umg*) *f* bottle; **volle ~ fahren** (*umg*) to drive flat out
Pulli ['pʊli] (**-s, -s**) (*umg*) *m* sweater, jumper (*Brit*)
Pullover [pʊ'lo:vər] (**-s, -**) *m* sweater, jumper (*Brit*)
Pullunder [pʊ'lʊndər] (**-s, -**) *m* slipover
Puls [pʊls] (**-es, -e**) *m* pulse; **Pulsader** *f* artery; **sich** *dat* **die Pulsader(n) aufschneiden** to slash one's wrists
pulsieren [pʊl'zi:rən] *vi* to throb, pulsate
Pult [pʊlt] (**-(e)s, -e**) *nt* desk
Pulver ['pʊlfər] (**-s, -**) *nt* powder; **Pulverfass** *nt* powder keg; **(wie) auf einem Pulverfass sitzen** (*fig*) to be sitting on (top of) a volcano
pulverig *adj* powdery
pulverisieren [pʊlveri'zi:rən] *vt* to pulverize
Pulverkaffee *m* instant coffee
Pulverschnee *m* powdery snow
pummelig ['pʊməlɪç] *adj* chubby
Pump (**-(e)s**) (*umg*) *m*: **auf ~ kaufen** to buy on tick (*Brit*) *od* credit
Pumpe ['pʊmpə] (**-, -n**) *f* pump; (*umg: Herz*) ticker
pumpen *vt* to pump; (*umg*) to lend; (*: entleihen*) to borrow
Pumphose *f* knickerbockers *pl*
puncto ['pʊŋkto] *präp +gen*: **in ~ X** where X is concerned
Punkt [pʊŋkt] (**-(e)s, -e**) *m* point; (*bei Muster*) dot; (*Satzzeichen*) full stop, period (*bes US*); **~ 12 Uhr** at 12 o'clock on the dot; **nun mach aber mal einen ~!** (*umg*) come off it!; **punktgleich** *adj* (*Sport*) level
punktieren [pʊŋk'ti:rən] *vt* to dot; (*Med*) to aspirate
pünktlich ['pʏŋktlɪç] *adj* punctual; **Pünktlichkeit** *f* punctuality
Punkt- *zW*: **Punktmatrix** *f* dot matrix; **Punktrichter** *m* (*Sport*) judge; **Punktsieg** *m* victory on points; **Punktwertung** *f* points system; **Punktzahl** *f* score
Punsch [pʊnʃ] (**-(e)s, -e**) *m* (hot) punch
Pupille [pu'pɪlə] (**-, -n**) *f* (*im Auge*) pupil
Puppe ['pʊpə] (**-, -n**) *f* doll; (*Marionette*) puppet; (*Insektenpuppe*) pupa, chrysalis; (*Schaufensterpuppe, Übungspuppe*) dummy; (*umg: Mädchen*) doll, bird (*bes Brit*)
Puppen- *zW*: **Puppenhaus** *nt* doll's house, dollhouse (*US*); **Puppenspieler** *m* puppeteer; **Puppenstube** *f* (single-room) doll's house *od* dollhouse (*US*); **Puppentheater** *nt* puppet theatre (*Brit*) *od* theater (*US*); **Puppenwagen** *m* doll's pram
pupsen ['pu:psən] (*umg*) *vi* to make a rude noise/smell
pur [pu:r] *adj* pure; (*völlig*) sheer; (*Whisky*) neat
Püree [py're:] (**-s, -s**) *nt* purée; (*Kartoffelpüree*) mashed potatoes *pl*
Purpur ['pʊrpʊr] (**-s**) *m* crimson
Purzelbaum ['pʊrtsəlbaʊm] *m* somersault
purzeln *vi* to tumble
Puste ['pu:stə] (**-**) (*umg*) *f* puff; (*fig*) steam
Pusteblume (*umg*) *f* dandelion
Pustel ['pʊstəl] (**-, -n**) *f* pustule
pusten ['pu:stən] (*umg*) *vi* to puff
Pute ['pu:tə] (**-, -n**) *f* turkey hen
Puter (**-s, -**) *m* turkey cock; **puterrot** *adj* scarlet
Putsch [pʊtʃ] (**-(e)s, -e**) *m* revolt, putsch; **putschen** *vi* to revolt; **Putschist** *m* rebel; **Putschversuch** *m* attempted coup (d'état)
Putte ['pʊtə] (**-, -n**) *f* (*Kunst*) cherub
Putz [pʊts] (**-es**) *m* (*Mörtel*) plaster, roughcast; **eine Mauer mit ~ verkleiden** to roughcast a wall
putzen *vt* to clean; (*Nase*) to wipe, blow ▷ *vr* to clean o.s.; (*veraltet: sich schmücken*) to dress o.s. up
Putzfrau *f* cleaning lady, charwoman (*Brit*)
putzig *adj* quaint, funny
Putzlappen *m* cloth
putzmunter (*umg*) *adj* full of beans
Putz- *zW*: **Putztag** *m* cleaning day; **Putzteufel** (*umg*) *m* maniac for housework; **Putzzeug** *nt* cleaning things *pl*
Puzzle ['pasəl] (**-s, -s**) *nt* jigsaw (puzzle)
PVC [pe:fau'tse:] (**-(s)**) *nt abk* PVC
Pygmäe [pʏ'gmɛ:ə] (**-n, -n**) *m* Pygmy
Pyjama [pi'dʒa:ma] (**-s, -s**) *m* pyjamas *pl* (*Brit*), pajamas *pl* (*US*)
Pyramide [pyra'mi:də] (**-, -n**) *f* pyramid
Pyrenäen [pyre'nɛ:ən] *pl*: **die ~** the Pyrenees *pl*
Python ['py:tɔn] (**-s, -s**) *m* python; **Pythonschlange** *f* python

Qq

Q, q [ku:] *nt* Q, q; **Q wie Quelle** ≈ Q for Queen
qcm *abk* (= *Quadratzentimeter*) cm^2
qkm *abk* (= *Quadratkilometer*) km^2
qm *abk* (= *Quadratmeter*) m^2
quabbelig ['kvabəlıç], **quabblig** ['kvablıç] *adj* wobbly; (*Frosch*) slimy
Quacksalber ['kvakzalbər] (**-s, -**) *m* quack (doctor)
Quader ['kva:dər] (**-s, -**) *m* square stone block; (*Math*) cuboid
Quadrat [kva'dra:t] (**-(e)s, -e**) *nt* square; **quadratisch** *adj* square; **Quadratlatschen** *pl* (*hum: umg: Schuhe*) clodhoppers *pl*; **Quadratmeter** *m* square metre (*Brit*) *od* meter (*US*)
quadrieren [kva'dri:rən] *vt* to square
quaken ['kva:kən] *vi* to croak; (*Ente*) to quack
quäken ['kvɛ:kən] *vi* to screech
quäkend *adj* screeching
Quäker, in (**-s, -**) *m(f)* Quaker
Qual [kva:l] (**-, -en**) *f* pain, agony; (*seelisch*) anguish; **er machte ihr das Leben zur ~** he made her life a misery
quälen ['kvɛ:lən] *vt* to torment ▷ *vr* (*sich abmühen*) to struggle; (*geistig*) to torment o.s.; **~de Ungewissheit** agonizing uncertainty
Quälerei [kvɛ:lə'raı] *f* torture, torment
Quälgeist (*umg*) *m* pest
Qualifikation [kvalifikatsi'o:n] *f* qualification
qualifizieren [kvalifi'tsi:rən] *vt* to qualify; (*einstufen*) to label ▷ *vr* to qualify
qualifiziert *adj* (*Arbeiter, Nachwuchs*) qualified; (*Arbeit*) professional; (*Pol: Mehrheit*) requisite
Qualität [kvali'tɛ:t] *f* quality; **von ausgezeichneter ~** (of) top quality
qualitativ [kvalita'ti:f] *adj* qualitative
Qualitätskontrolle *f* quality control
Qualitätsstandard *m* quality standard
Qualitätsware *f* article of high quality
Qualle ['kvalə] (**-, -n**) *f* jellyfish
Qualm [kvalm] (**-(e)s**) *m* thick smoke
qualmen *vt, vi* to smoke
qualvoll ['kva:lfɔl] *adj* painful; (*Schmerzen*) excruciating, agonizing
Quantensprung *m* quantum leap
Quantentheorie ['kvantənteori:] *f* quantum theory
Quantität [kvanti'tɛ:t] *f* quantity
quantitativ [kvantita'ti:f] *adj* quantitative
Quantum ['kvantʊm] (**-s, Quanten**) *nt* quantity, amount
Quarantäne [karan'tɛ:nə] (**-, -n**) *f* quarantine
Quark[1] [kvark] (**-s**) *m* curd cheese, quark; (*umg*) rubbish
Quark[2] [kvark] (**-s, -s**) *nt* (*Phys*) quark
Quarta ['kvarta] (**-, Quarten**) *f* (*früher*) *third year of German secondary school*
Quartal [kvar'ta:l] (**-s, -e**) *nt* quarter (year); **Kündigung zum ~** quarterly notice date
Quartett [kvar'tɛt] (**-(e)s, -e**) *nt* (*Mus*) quartet; (*Karten*) set of four cards; (*: Spiel*) ≈ happy families
Quartier [kvar'ti:r] (**-s, -e**) *nt* accommodation (*Brit*), accommodations *pl* (*US*); (*Mil*) quarters *pl*; (*Stadtquartier*) district
Quarz [kva:rts] (**-es, -e**) *m* quartz
quasi ['kva:zi] *adv* virtually ▷ *präf* quasi
quasseln ['kvasəln] (*umg*) *vi* to natter
Quaste ['kvastə] (**-, -n**) *f* (*Troddel*) tassel; (*von Pinsel*) bristles *pl*
Quästur [kvɛs'tu:r] *f* (*Univ*) bursary
Quatsch [kvatʃ] (**-es**) (*umg*) *m* rubbish, hogwash; **hört doch endlich auf mit dem ~!** stop being so stupid!; **~ machen** to mess about
quatschen *vi* to chat, natter
Quatschkopf (*umg*) *m* (*pej: Schwätzer*) windbag; (*Dummkopf*) twit (*Brit*)
Quecksilber ['kvɛkzılbər] *nt* mercury
Quelle ['kvɛlə] (**-, -n**) *f* spring; (*eines Flusses, Comput*) source; **an der ~ sitzen** (*fig*) to be well placed; **aus zuverlässiger ~** from a reliable source
quellen *vi* (*hervorquellen*) to pour *od* gush forth; (*schwellen*) to swell
Quellenangabe *f* reference
Quellsprache *f* source language
Quengelei [kvɛŋə'laı] (*umg*) *f* whining
quengelig (*umg*) *adj* whining
quengeln (*umg*) *vi* to whine
quer [kve:r] *adv* crossways, diagonally; (*rechtwinklig*) at right angles; **~ gestreift** horizontally striped; **~ auf dem Bett** across the bed; *siehe auch* **querlegen**; **Querbalken** *m* crossbeam; **Querdenker** *m* maverick
Quere ['kve:rə] (**-**) *f*: **jdm in die ~ kommen** to cross sb's path

quer- *zW:* **querfeldein** *adv* across country; **Querfeldeinrennen** *nt* cross-country; (*mit Motorrädern*) motocross; (*Radrennen*) cyclo-cross; **Querflöte** *f* flute; **Querformat** *nt* oblong format; **Querkopf** *m* awkward customer; **querlegen** *vr* (*fig: umg*) to be awkward; **Querschiff** *nt* transept; **Querschläger** (*umg*) *m* ricochet; **Querschnitt** *m* cross section; **querschnittsgelähmt** *adj* paraplegic, paralysed below the waist; **Querschnittslähmung** *f* paraplegia; **Querstraße** *f* intersecting road; **Querstrich** *m* (horizontal) stroke *od* line; **Quersumme** *f* (*Math*) sum of digits of a number; **Quertreiber** (**-s, -**) *m* obstructionist

Querulant, in [kveru'lant(ɪn)] (**-en, -en**) *m(f)* grumbler

Querverbindung *f* connection, link

Querverweis *m* cross-reference

quetschen ['kvɛtʃən] *vt* to squash, crush; (*Med*) to bruise ▷ *vr* (*sich klemmen*) to be caught; (*sich zwängen*) to squeeze (o.s.)

Quetschung *f* bruise, contusion (*form*)

Queue [kø:] (**-s, -s**) *nt* (*Billiard*) cue

quicklebendig ['kvɪkle'bɛndɪç] (*umg*) *adj* (*Kind*) lively, active; (*ältere Person*) spry

quieken ['kvi:kən] *vi* to squeak

quietschen ['kvi:tʃən] *vi* to squeak

quietschvergnügt ['kvi:tʃfɛrgny:kt] (*umg*) *adj* happy as a sandboy

quillt [kvɪlt] *vb siehe* **quellen**

Quinta ['kvɪnta] (**-, Quinten**) *f* (*früher*) *second year in German secondary school*

Quintessenz ['kvɪntɛsɛnts] *f* quintessence

Quintett [kvɪn'tɛt] (**-(e)s, -e**) *nt* quintet

Quirl [kvɪrl] (**-(e)s, -e**) *m* whisk

quirlig ['kvɪrlɪç] *adj* lively, frisky

quitt [kvɪt] *adj* quits, even

Quitte (**-, -n**) *f* quince

quittieren [kvɪ'ti:rən] *vt* to give a receipt for; (*Dienst*) to leave

Quittung *f* receipt; **er hat seine ~ bekommen** he's paid the penalty *od* price

Quiz [kvɪs] (**-, -**) *nt* quiz

quoll *etc* [kvɔl] *vb siehe* **quellen**

Quote ['kvo:tə] (**-, -n**) *f* proportion; (*Rate*) rate

Quotenbringer *m* (*TV: umg*) ratings booster

Quotenregelung *f* quota system (*for ensuring adequate representation of women*)

Quotierung [kvo'ti:rʊŋ] *f* (*Comm*) quotation

Rr

R¹, r *nt* R, r; **R wie Richard** ≈ R for Robert, R for Roger (*US*)
R², r *abk* (= *Radius*) r.
r. *abk* (= *rechts*) r.
Rabatt [ra'bat] (**-(e)s, -e**) *m* discount
Rabatte (**-, -n**) *f* flower bed, border
Rabattmarke *f* trading stamp
Rabatz [ra'bats] (**-es**) (*umg*) *m* row, din
Rabe ['ra:bə] (**-n, -n**) *m* raven
Rabenmutter *f* bad mother
rabenschwarz *adj* pitch-black
rabiat [rabi'a:t] *adj* furious
Rache ['raxə] (-) *f* revenge, vengeance
Rachen (**-s, -**) *m* throat
rächen ['rɛçən] *vt* to avenge, revenge ▷ *vr* to take (one's) revenge; **das wird sich ~** you'll pay for that
Rachitis [ra'xi:tɪs] (-) *f* rickets *sing*
Rachsucht *f* vindictiveness
rachsüchtig *adj* vindictive
Racker ['rakər] (**-s, -**) *m* rascal, scamp
Rad [ra:t] (**-(e)s, ¨er**) *nt* wheel; (*Fahrrad*) bike; **~ fahren** to cycle; **unter die Räder kommen** (*umg*) to fall into bad ways; **das fünfte ~ am Wagen sein** (*umg*) to be in the way
Radar ['ra:da:r] (**-s**) *m od nt* radar; **Radarfalle** *f* speed trap; **Radarkontrolle** *f* radar-controlled speed check
Radau [ra'daʊ] (**-s**) (*umg*) *m* row; **~ machen** to kick up a row; (*Unruhe stiften*) to cause trouble
Raddampfer *m* paddle steamer
radebrechen ['ra:dəbrɛçən] *vi untr*: **Deutsch** *etc* **~** to speak broken German *etc*
radeln *vi* (*Hilfsverb sein*) to cycle
Rädelsführer ['rɛ:dəlsfy:rər] (**-s, -**) *m* ringleader
Rad- *zW*: **Radfahrer** *m* cyclist; (*pej: umg*) crawler; **Radfahrweg** *m* cycle track *od* path
radieren [ra'di:rən] *vt* to rub out, erase; (*Art*) to etch
Radiergummi *m* rubber (*Brit*), eraser (*bes US*)
Radierung *f* etching
Radieschen [ra'di:sçən] *nt* radish
radikal [radi'ka:l] *adj* radical; **~ gegen etw vorgehen** to take radical steps against sth
Radikale, r *f(m)* radical
Radikalisierung [radikali'zi:rʊŋ] *f* radicalization
Radikalkur (*umg*) *f* drastic remedy
Radio ['ra:dio] (**-s, -s**) *nt* radio, wireless (*bes Brit*); **im ~** on the radio; **radioaktiv** *adj* radioactive; **radioaktiver Niederschlag** (radioactive) fallout; **Radioaktivität** *f* radioactivity; **Radioapparat** *m* radio (set); **Radiorekorder** *m* radio-cassette recorder
Radium ['ra:diʊm] (**-s**) *nt* radium
Radius ['ra:diʊs] (**-, Radien**) *m* radius
Radkappe *f* (*Aut*) hub cap
Radler, in (**-s, -**) *m(f)* cyclist
Rad- *zW*: **Radrennbahn** *f* cycling (race)track; **Radrennen** *nt* cycle race; (*Sportart*) cycle racing; **Radsport** *m* cycling
RAF (-) *f abk* (= *Rote Armee Fraktion*) Red Army Faction
raffen ['rafən] *vt* to snatch, pick up; (*Stoff*) to gather (up); (*Geld*) to pile up, rake in; (*umg: verstehen*) to catch on to
Raffgier *f* greed, avarice
Raffinade [rafi'na:də] *f* refined sugar
Raffinesse [rafi'nɛsə] (-) *f* (*Feinheit*) refinement; (*Schlauheit*) cunning
raffinieren [rafi'ni:rən] *vt* to refine
raffiniert *adj* crafty, cunning; (*Zucker*) refined
Rage ['ra:ʒə] (-) *f* (*Wut*) rage, fury
ragen ['ra:gən] *vi* to tower, rise
Rahm [ra:m] (**-s**) *m* cream
Rahmen (**-s, -**) *m* frame(work); **aus dem ~ fallen** to go too far; **im ~ des Möglichen** within the bounds of possibility; **rahmen** *vt* to frame; **Rahmenhandlung** *f* (*Liter*) background story; **Rahmenplan** *m* outline plan; **Rahmenrichtlinien** *pl* guidelines *pl*
rahmig *adj* creamy
räkeln ['rɛ:kln] *vr* = **rekeln**
Rakete [ra'ke:tə] (**-, -n**) *f* rocket; **ferngelenkte ~** guided missile
Raketenstützpunkt *m* missile base
Rallye ['rali] (**-, -s**) *f* rally
rammdösig ['ramdø:zɪç] (*umg*) *adj* giddy, dizzy
rammen ['ramən] *vt* to ram
Rampe ['rampə] (**-, -n**) *f* ramp
Rampenlicht *nt* (*Theat*) footlights *pl*; **sie möchte immer im ~ stehen** (*fig*) she always wants to be in the limelight
ramponieren [rampo'ni:rən] (*umg*) *vt* to damage

Ramsch [ramʃ] (**-(e)s, -e**) *m* junk
ran [ran] (*umg*) *adv* = **heran**
Rand [rant] (**-(e)s, ¨-er**) *m* edge; (*von Brille, Tasse etc*) rim; (*Hutrand*) brim; (*auf Papier*) margin; (*Schmutzrand, unter Augen*) ring; (*fig*) verge, brink; **außer ~ und Band** wild; **am ~e bemerkt** mentioned in passing; **am ~e der Stadt** on the outskirts of the town; **etw am ~e miterleben** to experience sth from the sidelines
randalieren [randa'li:rən] *vi* to (go on the) rampage
Rand- *zW*: **Randbemerkung** *f* marginal note; (*fig*) odd comment; **Randerscheinung** *f* unimportant side effect, marginal phenomenon; **Randfigur** *f* minor figure; **Randgebiet** *nt* (*Geog*) fringe; (*Pol*) border territory; (*fig*) subsidiary; **Randstreifen** *m* (*der Straße*) verge (*Brit*), berm (*US*); (*der Autobahn*) hard shoulder (*Brit*), shoulder (*US*); **randvoll** *adj* full to the brim
rang *etc* [raŋ] *vb siehe* **ringen**
Rang (**-(e)s, ¨-e**) *m* rank; (*Stand*) standing; (*Wert*) quality; (*Theat*) circle; **ein Mann ohne ~ und Namen** a man without any standing; **erster/zweiter ~** dress/upper circle
Rangabzeichen *nt* badge of rank
Rangälteste, r *m* senior officer
rangeln ['raŋəln] (*umg*) *vi* to scrap; (*um Posten*): **~ (um)** to wrangle (for)
Rangfolge *f* order of rank (*bes MIL*)
Rangierbahnhof [rã'ʒi:rba:nho:f] *m* marshalling yard
rangieren *vt* (*Eisenb*) to shunt, switch (*US*) ▷ *vi* to rank, be classed
Rangiergleis *nt* siding
Rangliste *f* (*Sport*) ranking list, rankings *pl*
Rangordnung *f* hierarchy; (*Mil*) rank
Rangunterschied *m* social distinction; (*Mil*) difference in rank
rank [raŋk] *adj*: **~ und schlank** (*liter*) slender and supple
Ranke ['raŋkə] (**-, -n**) *f* tendril, shoot
Ränke ['rɛŋkə] *pl* intrigues *pl*
ranken ['raŋkən] *vr* to trail, grow; **sich um etw ~** to twine around sth
Ränkeschmied *m* (*liter*) intriguer
ränkevoll *adj* scheming
ranklotzen ['ranklɔtsən] (*umg*) *vi* to put one's nose to the grindstone
ranlassen *unreg* (*umg*) *vt*: **jdn ~** to let sb have a go
rann *etc* [ran] *vb siehe* **rinnen**
rannte *etc* ['rantə] *vb siehe* **rennen**
Ranzen ['rantsən] (**-s, -**) *m* satchel; (*umg: Bauch*) belly, gut
ranzig ['rantsıç] *adj* rancid
Rappe ['rapə] (**-n, -n**) *m* black horse
Rappel ['rapəl] (**-s, -**) (*umg*) *m* (*Fimmel*) craze; (*Wutanfall*): **einen ~ kriegen** to throw a fit
Rappen ['rapən] (**-s, -**) (*Schweiz*) *m* (*Geld*) centime, rappen
Raps [raps] (**-es, -e**) *m* (*Bot*) rape; **Rapsöl** *nt* rapeseed oil
rar [ra:r] *adj* rare; *siehe auch* **rarmachen**
Rarität [rari'tɛ:t] *f* rarity; (*Sammelobjekt*) curio
rarmachen (*umg*) *vr* to stay away
rasant [ra'zant] *adj* quick, rapid
rasch [raʃ] *adj* quick
rascheln *vi* to rustle
rasen ['ra:zən] *vi* to rave; (*sich schnell bewegen*) to race
Rasen (**-s, -**) *m* grass; (*gepflegt*) lawn
rasend *adj* furious; **~e Kopfschmerzen** a splitting headache
Rasen- *zW*: **Rasenmäher** (**-s, -**) *m* lawnmower; **Rasenmähmaschine** *f* lawnmower; **Rasenplatz** *m* lawn; **Rasensprenger** *m* (lawn) sprinkler
Raserei [ra:zə'raı] *f* raving, ranting; (*Schnelle*) reckless speeding
Rasier- *zW*: **Rasierapparat** *m* shaver; **Rasiercreme** *f* shaving cream; **rasieren** *vt, vr* to shave; **Rasierklinge** *f* razor blade; **Rasiermesser** *nt* razor; **Rasierpinsel** *m* shaving brush; **Rasierseife** *f* shaving soap *od* stick; **Rasierwasser** *nt* aftershave
raspeln ['raspəln] *vt* to grate; (*Holz*) to rasp
Rasse ['rasə] (**-, -n**) *f* race; (*Tierrasse*) breed; **Rassehund** *m* thoroughbred dog
Rassel (**-, -n**) *f* rattle
rasseln *vi* to rattle, clatter
Rassenhass *m* race *od* racial hatred
Rassentrennung *f* racial segregation
rassig ['rasıç] *adj* (*Pferd, Auto*) sleek; (*Frau*) vivacious; (*Wein*) spirited, lively
Rassismus [ra'sısmʊs] (**-**) *m* racialism, racism
rassistisch [ra'sıstıʃ] *adj* racialist, racist
Rast [rast] (**-, -en**) *f* rest; **rasten** *vi* to rest
Raster ['rastər] (**-s, -**) *m* (*Archit*) grid; (*Phot: Gitter*) screen; (*TV*) raster; (*fig*) framework
Rast- *zW*: **Rasthaus** *nt* (*Aut*) service area, services *pl*; **Rasthof** *m* (motorway) motel; (*mit Tankstelle*) service area (*with a motel*); **rastlos** *adj* tireless; (*unruhig*) restless; **Rastplatz** *m* (*Aut*) lay-by (*Brit*); **Raststätte** *f* service area, services *pl*
Rasur [ra'zu:r] *f* shave; (*das Rasieren*) shaving
Rat [ra:t] (**-(e)s, -schläge**) *m* (piece of) advice; **jdm mit ~ und Tat zur Seite stehen** to support sb in (both) word and deed; **sich ~ suchend an jdn wenden** to turn to sb for advice; **(sich *dat*) keinen ~ wissen** not to know what to do; *siehe auch* **zurate**
rät [rɛ:t] *vb siehe* **raten**
Rate (**-, -n**) *f* instalment (*Brit*), installment (*US*); **auf ~n kaufen** to buy on hire purchase (*Brit*) *od* on the installment plan (*US*); **in ~n zahlen** to pay in instalments (*Brit*) *od* installments (*US*)
raten *unreg vt, vi* to guess; (*empfehlen*): **jdm ~** to advise sb; **dreimal darfst du ~** I'll give you three guesses (*auch ironisch*)
ratenweise *adv* by instalments (*Brit*) *od* installments (*US*)
Ratenzahlung *f* hire purchase (*Brit*),

installment plan (*US*)
Ratespiel *nt* guessing game; (*TV*) quiz; (: *Beruferaten etc*) panel game
Ratgeber (**-s, -**) *m* adviser
Rathaus *nt* town hall; (*einer Großstadt*) city hall (*bes US*)
ratifizieren [ratifi'tsi:rən] *vt* to ratify
Ratifizierung *f* ratification
Ration [ratsi'o:n] *f* ration
rational [ratsio'na:l] *adj* rational
rationalisieren [ratsionali'zi:rən] *vt* to rationalize
rationell [ratsio'nɛl] *adj* efficient
rationieren [ratsio'ni:rən] *vt* to ration
ratlos *adj* at a loss, helpless
Ratlosigkeit *f* helplessness
rätoromanisch [rɛtoro'ma:nɪʃ] *adj* Rhaetian
ratsam *adj* advisable
Ratschlag *m* (piece of) advice
Rätsel ['rɛ:tsəl] (**-s, -**) *nt* puzzle; (*Worträtsel*) riddle; **vor einem ~ stehen** to be baffled; **rätselhaft** *adj* mysterious; **es ist mir rätselhaft** it's a mystery to me; **rätseln** *vi* to puzzle; **Rätselraten** *nt* guessing game
Ratsherr *m* councillor (*Brit*), councilor (*US*)
Ratskeller *m* town-hall restaurant
Ratte ['ratə] (**-, -n**) *f* rat
Rattenfänger (**-s, -**) *m* rat-catcher
rattern ['ratərn] *vi* to rattle, clatter
rau [raʊ] *adj* rough, coarse; (*Wetter*) harsh; **in ~en Mengen** (*umg*) by the ton, galore
Raub [raʊp] (**-(e)s**) *m* robbery; (*Beute*) loot, booty; **Raubbau** *m* overexploitation; **Raubdruck** *m* pirate(d) edition
raubeinig *adj* rough-and-ready
rauben ['raʊbən] *vt* to rob; (*jdn*) to kidnap, abduct
Räuber ['rɔʏbər] (**-s, -**) *m* robber; **räuberisch** *adj* thieving
Raub- *zW*: **Raubfisch** *m* predatory fish; **raubgierig** *adj* rapacious; **Raubkassette** *f* pirate cassette; **Raubmord** *m* robbery with murder; **Raubtier** *nt* predator; **Raubüberfall** *m* robbery with violence; **Raubvogel** *m* bird of prey
Rauch [raʊx] (**-(e)s**) *m* smoke; **Rauchabzug** *m* smoke outlet
rauchen *vt, vi* to smoke; **mir raucht der Kopf** (*fig*) my head's spinning; **„R~ verboten"** "no smoking"
Raucher, in (**-s, -**) *m(f)* smoker; **Raucherabteil** *nt* (*Eisenb*) smoker
räuchern ['rɔʏçərn] *vt* to smoke, cure
Räucherspeck *m* ≈ smoked bacon
Räucherstäbchen *nt* joss stick
Rauch- *zW*: **Rauchfahne** *f* smoke trail; **Rauchfang** *m* chimney hood; **Rauchfleisch** *nt* smoked meat
rauchig *adj* smoky
Rauchschwaden *pl* drifts of smoke *pl*
räudig ['rɔʏdɪç] *adj* mangy
rauf [raʊf] (*umg*) *adv* = **herauf; hinauf**
Raufasertapete *f* woodchip paper
Raufbold (**-(e)s, -e**) *m* thug, hooligan
raufen *vt* (*Haare*) to pull out ▷ *vi, vr* to fight
Rauferei [raʊfə'raɪ] *f* brawl, fight
rauflustig *adj* ready for a fight, pugnacious
rauh *etc siehe* **rau** *etc*
rauhaarig *adj* wire-haired
Raum [raʊm] (**-(e)s, Räume**) *m* space; (*Zimmer, Platz*) room; (*Gebiet*) area; **~ sparend** space-saving; **eine Frage im ~ stehen lassen** to leave a question unresolved; **Raumausstatter, in** *m(f)* interior decorator
räumen ['rɔʏmən] *vt* to clear; (*Wohnung, Platz*) to vacate, move out of; (*verlassen: Gebäude, Gebiet*) to evacuate; (*wegbringen*) to shift, move; (*in Schrank etc*) to put away
Raum- *zW*: **Raumfähre** *f* space shuttle; **Raumfahrer** *m* astronaut; (*sowjetisch*) cosmonaut; **Raumfahrt** *f* space travel
Räumfahrzeug ['rɔʏmfa:rtsɔʏk] *nt* bulldozer; (*für Schnee*) snow-clearer
Rauminhalt *m* cubic capacity, volume
Raumkapsel *f* space capsule
räumlich ['rɔʏmlɪç] *adj* spatial; **Räumlichkeiten** *pl* premises *pl*
Raum- *zW*: **Raummangel** *m* lack of space; **Raummaß** *nt* unit of volume; cubic measurement; **Raummeter** *m* cubic metre (*Brit*) *od* meter (*US*); **Raumnot** *f* shortage of space; **Raumordnung** *f* environmental planning; **Raumpflegerin** *f* cleaner; **Raumschiff** *nt* spaceship; **Raumschifffahrt** *f* space travel; **Raumstation** *f* space station; **Raumtransporter** *m* space shuttle
Räumung ['rɔʏmʊŋ] *f* clearing (away); (*von Haus etc*) vacating; (*wegen Gefahr*) evacuation; (*unter Zwang*) eviction
Räumungs- *zW*: **Räumungsbefehl** *m* eviction order; **Räumungsklage** *f* action for eviction; **Räumungsverkauf** *m* clearance sale
raunen ['raʊnən] *vt, vi* to whisper
Raupe ['raʊpə] (**-, -n**) *f* caterpillar; (*Raupenkette*) (caterpillar) track
Raupenschlepper *m* caterpillar tractor
Raureif ['raʊraɪf] *m* hoarfrost
raus [raʊs] (*umg*) *adv* = **heraus; hinaus**
Rausch [raʊʃ] (**-(e)**, *pl* **Räusche**) *m* intoxication; **einen ~ haben** to be drunk
rauschen *vi* (*Wasser*) to rush; (*Baum*) to rustle; (*Radio etc*) to hiss; (*Mensch*) to sweep, sail
rauschend *adj* (*Beifall*) thunderous; (*Fest*) sumptuous
Rauschgift *nt* drug; **Rauschgifthandel** *m* drug traffic; **Rauschgifthändler, in** *m(f)* drug trafficker; **Rauschgiftsüchtige, r** *f(m)* drug addict
rausfliegen *unreg* (*umg*) *vi* to be chucked out
räuspern ['rɔʏspərn] *vr* to clear one's throat
Rausschmeißer ['raʊsʃmaɪsər] (**-s, -**) (*umg*) *m* bouncer
Raute ['raʊtə] (**-, -n**) *f* diamond; (*Math*) rhombus
rautenförmig *adj* rhombic
Razzia ['ratsia] (**-, Razzien**) *f* raid

Reagenzglas [rea'gɛntsglaːs] *nt* test tube
reagieren [rea'giːrən] *vi*: ~ **(auf** *+akk***)** to react (to)
Reaktion [reaktsi'oːn] *f* reaction
reaktionär [reaktsio'nɛːr] *adj* reactionary
Reaktionsfähigkeit *f* reactions *pl*
Reaktionsgeschwindigkeit *f* speed of reaction
Reaktor [re'aktɔr] *m* reactor; **Reaktorkern** *m* reactor core; **Reaktorunglück** *nt* nuclear accident
real [re'aːl] *adj* real, material; **Realeinkommen** *nt* real income
realisierbar [reali'ziːrbaːr] *adj* practicable, feasible
Realismus [rea'lɪsmʊs] *m* realism
Realist, in [rea'lɪst(ɪn)] *m(f)* realist; **realistisch** *adj* realistic
Realität [reali'tɛːt] *f* reality; **Realitäten** *pl* (*Gegebenheiten*) facts *pl*
realitätsfremd *adj* out of touch with reality
Realpolitik *f* political realism
Realschule *f* ≈ middle school (*Brit*), junior high school (*US*); *see culture note*

REALSCHULE

The *Realschule* is one of the choices of secondary schools available to a German schoolchild after the *Grundschule*. At the end of six years' schooling in the Realschule pupils gain the *mittlere Reife* and usually go on to some kind of training or to a college of further education.

Realzeit *f* real time
Rebe ['reːbə] (**-, -n**) *f* vine
Rebell, in [re'bɛl(ɪn)] (**-en, -en**) *m(f)* rebel
rebellieren [rebɛ'liːrən] *vi* to rebel
Rebellion [rebɛli'oːn] *f* rebellion
rebellisch [re'bɛlɪʃ] *adj* rebellious
Rebensaft *m* wine
Reb- [rɛp] *zW*: **Rebhuhn** *nt* partridge; **Reblaus** *f* vine pest; **Rebstock** *m* vine
Rechen ['rɛçən] (**-s, -**) *m* rake; **rechen** *vt, vi* to rake
Rechen- *zW*: **Rechenaufgabe** *f* sum, mathematical problem; **Rechenfehler** *m* miscalculation; **Rechenmaschine** *f* adding machine
Rechenschaft *f* account; **jdm über etw** *akk* **~ ablegen** to account to sb for sth; **jdn zur ~ ziehen (für)** to call sb to account (for *od* over); **jdm ~ schulden** to be accountable to sb
Rechenschaftsbericht *m* report
Rechenschieber *m* slide rule
Rechenzentrum *nt* computer centre (*Brit*) *od* center (*US*)
recherchieren [reʃɛr'ʃiːrən] *vt, vi* to investigate
rechnen ['rɛçnən] *vt, vi* to calculate; (*veranschlagen*) to estimate, reckon; **jdn/etw zu etw** ~ to count sb/sth among sth; **~ mit** to reckon with; **~ auf** *+akk* to count on
Rechnen *nt* arithmetic; (*bes Sch*) sums *pl*
Rechner (**-s, -**) *m* calculator; (*Comput*) computer; **rechnerfern** *adj* (*Comput*) remote; **rechnerisch** *adj* arithmetical
Rechnung *f* calculation(s); (*Comm*) bill (*Brit*), check (*US*); **auf eigene ~** on one's own account; **(jdm) etw in ~ stellen** to charge (sb) for sth; **jdm/etw ~ tragen** to take sb/sth into account
Rechnungs- *zW*: **Rechnungsbuch** *nt* account book; **Rechnungshof** *m* ≈ Auditor-General's office (*Brit*), audit division (*US*); **Rechnungsjahr** *nt* financial year; **Rechnungsprüfer** *m* auditor; **Rechnungsprüfung** *f* audit(ing)
recht [rɛçt] *adj* right ▷ *adv* (*vor Adjektiv*) really, quite; **das ist mir ~** that suits me; **jetzt erst** ~ now more than ever; **alles, was ~ ist** (*empört*) fair's fair; (*anerkennend*) you can't deny it; **nach dem R~en sehen** to see that everything's O.K.; **~ haben** to be right; **jdm ~ geben** to agree with sb, admit that sb is right; **du kommst gerade ~, um ...** you're just in time to ...; **gehe ich ~ in der Annahme, dass ...?** am I correct in assuming that ...?; **~ herzlichen Dank** thank you very much indeed
Recht (**-(e)s, -e**) *nt* right; (*Jur*) law; **~ sprechen** to administer justice; **mit** *od* **zu** ~ rightly, justly; **von ~s wegen** by rights; **zu seinem ~ kommen** (*lit*) to gain one's rights; (*fig*) to come into one's own; **gleiches ~ für alle!** equal rights for all!
Rechte *f* right (hand); (*Pol*) Right
Rechte, r, s *f(m)* (*Pol*) right-winger ▷ *nt* right thing; **etwas/nichts ~s** something/nothing proper
rechte, r, s *adj* right; (*Pol*) right-wing
recht- *zW*: **Rechteck** (**-(e)s, -e**) *nt* rectangle; **rechteckig** *adj* rectangular; **rechtfertigen** *vt untr* to justify ▷ *vr untr* to justify o.s.; **Rechtfertigung** *f* justification; **rechthaberisch** *adj* dogmatic; **rechtlich** *adj* legal, lawful; **rechtlich nicht zulässig** not permissible in law, illegal; **rechtmäßig** *adj* legal, lawful
rechts [rɛçts] *adv* on *od* to the right; **~ stehen** *od* **sein** (*Pol*) to be right-wing; **~ stricken** to knit (plain); **Rechtsabbieger** (**-s, -**) *m*: **die Spur für Rechtsabbieger** the right-hand turn-off lane; **Rechtsanspruch** *m*: **einen Rechtsanspruch auf etw** *akk* **haben** to be legally entitled to sth; **Rechtsanwalt** *m*, **Rechtsanwältin** *f* lawyer, barrister; **Rechtsaußen** (**-, -**) *m* (*Sport*) outside right; **Rechtsbeistand** *m* legal adviser
rechtschaffen *adj* upright
Rechtschreibung *f* spelling
Rechts- *zW*: **Rechtsdrehung** *f* clockwise rotation; **Rechtsextremismus** *m* right-wing extremism; **Rechtsextremist** *m* right-wing extremist; **Rechtsfall** *m* (law) case; **Rechtsfrage** *f* legal question; **rechtsgültig**

adj legally valid; **Rechtshänder, in (-s, -)** *m(f)* right-handed person; **rechtskräftig** *adj* valid, legal; **Rechtskurve** *f* right-hand bend; **Rechtslage** *f* legal position; **rechtslastig** *adj* listing to the right; *(fig)* leaning to the right; **Rechtspflege** *f* administration of justice; **Rechtspfleger** *m official with certain judicial powers*

Rechtsprechung ['rɛçtʃprɛçʊŋ] *f* *(Gerichtsbarkeit)* jurisdiction; *(richterliche Tätigkeit)* dispensation of justice

Rechts- *zW*: **rechtsradikal** *adj (Pol)* extreme right-wing; **Rechtsschutz** *m* legal protection; **Rechtsspruch** *m* verdict; **Rechtsstaat** *m* state under the rule of law; **Rechtsstreit** *m* lawsuit; **Rechtstitel** *m* title; **rechtsverbindlich** *adj* legally binding; **Rechtsverkehr** *m* driving on the right; **Rechtsweg** *m*: **der Rechtsweg ist ausgeschlossen** ≈ the judges' decision is final; **rechtswidrig** *adj* illegal; **Rechtswissenschaft** *f* jurisprudence

rechtwinklig *adj* right-angled

rechtzeitig *adj* timely ▷ *adv* in time

Reck [rɛk] **(-(e)s, -e)** *nt* horizontal bar

recken *vt, vr* to stretch

recyceln [ri:'saɪkəln] *vt* to recycle

Recycling [ri'saɪklɪŋ] **(-s)** *nt* recycling

Red. *abk* = **Redaktion**; (= *Redakteur(in)*) ed

Redakteur, in [redak'tø:r(ɪn)] *m(f)* editor

Redaktion [redaktsi'o:n] *f* editing; *(Leute)* editorial staff; *(Büro)* editorial office(s *pl*)

Redaktionsschluss *m* time of going to press; *(Einsendeschluss)* copy deadline

Rede ['re:də] **(-, -n)** *f* speech; *(Gespräch)* talk; **jdn zur ~ stellen** to take sb to task; **eine ~ halten** to make a speech; **das ist nicht der ~ wert** it's not worth mentioning; **davon kann keine ~ sein** it's out of the question; **Redefreiheit** *f* freedom of speech; **redegewandt** *adj* eloquent

Reden (-s) *nt* talking, speech

reden *vi* to talk, speak ▷ *vt* to say; *(Unsinn etc)* to talk; **(viel) von sich ~ machen** to become (very much) a talking point; **darüber lässt sich ~** that's a possibility; *(über Preis, Bedingungen)* I think we could discuss that; **er lässt mit sich ~** he could be persuaded; *(in Bezug auf Preis)* he's open to offers; *(gesprächsbereit)* he's open to discussion

Redensart *f* set phrase

Redeschwall *m* torrent of words

Redewendung *f* expression, idiom

redlich ['re:tlɪç] *adj* honest; **Redlichkeit** *f* honesty

Redner, in (-s, -) *m(f)* speaker, orator

redselig ['re:tze:lɪç] *adj* talkative, loquacious; **Redseligkeit** *f* talkativeness, loquacity

redundant [redʊn'dant] *adj* redundant

Redundanz [redʊn'dants] **(-)** *f* redundancy

reduzieren [redu'tsi:rən] *vt* to reduce

Reduzierung *f* reduction

Reede ['re:də] **(-, -n)** *f* protected anchorage

Reeder (-s, -) *m* shipowner

Reederei [re:də'raɪ] *f* shipping line *od* firm

reell [re'ɛl] *adj* fair, honest; *(Preis)* fair; *(Comm: Geschäft)* sound; *(Math)* real

Reetdach ['re:tdax] *nt* thatched roof

Ref. *abk* = **Referendar(in); Referent(in)**

Referat [refe'ra:t] **(-(e)s, -e)** *nt* report; *(Vortrag)* paper; *(Gebiet)* section; *(Verwaltung: Ressort)* department; **ein ~ halten** to present a seminar paper

Referendar, in [referɛn'dar(ɪn)] *m(f)* trainee (in civil service); *(Studienreferendar)* trainee teacher; *(Gerichtsreferendar)* articled clerk

Referendum [refe'rɛndʊm] **(-s, Referenden)** *nt* referendum

Referent, in [refe'rɛnt(ɪn)] *m(f)* speaker; *(Berichterstatter)* reporter; *(Sachbearbeiter)* expert

Referenz [refe'rɛnts] *f* reference

referieren [refe'ri:rən] *vi*: **~ über** *+akk* to speak *od* talk on

reflektieren [reflek'ti:rən] *vt, vi* to reflect; **~ auf** *+akk* to be interested in

Reflex [re'flɛks] **(-es, -e)** *m* reflex; **Reflexbewegung** *f* reflex action

reflexiv [reflɛ'ksi:f] *adj (Gram)* reflexive

Reform [re'fɔrm] **(-, -en)** *f* reform

Reformation [refɔrmatsi'o:n] *f* reformation

Reformator [refɔr'ma:tɔr] *m* reformer; **reformatorisch** *adj* reformatory, reforming

reform- *zW*: **reformbedürftig** *adj* in need of reform; **reformfreudig** *adj* avid for reform; **Reformhaus** *nt* health food shop

reformieren [refɔr'mi:rən] *vt* to reform

Refrain [rə'frɛ̃:] **(-s, -s)** *m* refrain, chorus

Reg. *abk* (= *Regierungs-*) gov.; (= *Register*) reg

Regal [re'ga:l] **(-s, -e)** *nt* (book)shelves *pl*, bookcase; *(Typ)* stand, rack

Regatta [re'gata] **(-, Regatten)** *f* regatta

Reg.-Bez. *abk* = **Regierungsbezirk**

rege ['re:gə] *adj* lively, active; *(Geschäft)* brisk

Regel ['re:gəl] **(-, -n)** *f* rule; *(Med)* period; **in der ~** as a rule; **nach allen ~n der Kunst** *(fig)* thoroughly; **sich** *dat* **etw zur ~ machen** to make a habit of sth; **regellos** *adj* irregular, unsystematic; **regelmäßig** *adj* regular; **Regelmäßigkeit** *f* regularity

regeln *vt* to regulate, control; *(Angelegenheit)* to settle ▷ *vr*: **sich von selbst ~** to take care of itself; **gesetzlich geregelt sein** to be laid down by law

regelrecht *adj* proper, thorough

Regelung *f* regulation; settlement

regelwidrig *adj* irregular, against the rules

regen ['re:gən] *vt* to move ▷ *vr* to move, stir

Regen (-s, -) *m* rain; **vom ~ in die Traufe kommen** *(Sprichwort)* to jump out of the frying pan into the fire *(Sprichwort)*

Regenbogen *m* rainbow; **Regenbogenhaut** *f (Anat)* iris; **Regenbogenpresse** *f* trashy magazines *pl*

regenerieren [regene'ri:rən] *vr (Biol)* to regenerate; *(fig)* to revitalize *od* regenerate o.s. *od* itself; *(nach Anstrengung, Schock etc)* to recover

Regen- *zW*: **Regenguss** *m* downpour;

Regenmantel *m* raincoat, mac(kintosh); **Regenmenge** *f* rainfall; **Regenschauer** *m* shower (of rain); **Regenschirm** *m* umbrella

Regent, in [re'gɛnt(ɪn)] *m(f)* regent

Regentag *m* rainy day

Regentropfen *m* raindrop

Regentschaft *f* regency

Regen- *zW*: **Regenwald** *m* (*Geog*) rain forest; **Regenwetter** *nt*: **er macht ein Gesicht wie drei** *od* **sieben Tage Regenwetter** (*umg*) he's got a face as long as a month of Sundays; **Regenwurm** *m* earthworm; **Regenzeit** *f* rainy season, rains *pl*

Regie [re'ʒi:] *f* (*Film etc*) direction; (*Theat*) production; **unter der ~ von** directed *od* produced by; **Regieanweisung** *f* (stage) direction

regieren [re'gi:rən] *vt, vi* to govern, rule

Regierung *f* government; (*Monarchie*) reign; **an die ~ kommen** to come to power

Regierungs- *zW*: **Regierungsbezirk** *m* ≈ county (*Brit, US*), ≈ region (*Scot*); **Regierungserklärung** *f* inaugural speech; (*in Großbritannien*) Queen's/King's Speech; **Regierungsmannschaft** *f* government team; **Regierungssprecher** *m* government spokesman; **Regierungsvorlage** *f* government bill; **Regierungswechsel** *m* change of government; **Regierungszeit** *f* period in government; (*von König*) reign

Regiment [regi'mɛnt] **(-s, -er)** *nt* regiment

Region [regi'o:n] *f* region

Regionalplanung [regio'na:lpla:nʊŋ] *f* regional planning

Regionalprogramm *nt* (*Rundf, TV*) regional programme (*Brit*) *od* program (*US*)

Regisseur, in [reʒɪ'sø:r(ɪn)] *m(f)* director; (*Theat*) (stage) producer

Register [re'gɪstər] **(-s, -)** *nt* register; (*in Buch*) table of contents, index; **alle ~ ziehen** (*fig*) to pull out all the stops; **Registerführer** *m* registrar

Registratur [regɪstra'tu:r] *f* registry, records office

registrieren [regɪs'tri:rən] *vt* to register; (*umg: zur Kenntnis nehmen*) to note

Registrierkasse *f* cash register

Regler ['re:glər] **(-s, -)** *m* regulator, governor

reglos ['re:klo:s] *adj* motionless

regnen ['re:gnən] *vi unpers* to rain ▷ *vt unpers*: **es regnet Glückwünsche** congratulations are pouring in; **es regnet in Strömen** it's pouring (with rain)

regnerisch *adj* rainy

Regress [re'grɛs] **(-es, -e)** *m* (*Jur*) recourse, redress; **Regressanspruch** *m* (*Jur*) claim for compensation

regsam ['re:kza:m] *adj* active

regulär [regu'lɛ:r] *adj* regular

regulieren [regu'li:rən] *vt* to regulate; (*Comm*) to settle; **sich von selbst ~** to be self-regulating

Regulierungsbehörde [regu'li:rəʊŋsbəhø:rdə] *f* regulatory body *od* authority

Regung ['re:gʊŋ] *f* motion; (*Gefühl*) feeling, impulse

regungslos *adj* motionless

Reh [re:] **(-(e)s, -e)** *nt* deer; (*weiblich*) roe deer

rehabilitieren [rehabili'ti:rən] *vt* to rehabilitate; (*Ruf, Ehre*) to vindicate ▷ *vr* to rehabilitate (*form*) *od* vindicate o.s.

Rehabilitierung *f* rehabilitation

Reh- *zW*: **Rehbock** *m* roebuck; **Rehbraten** *m* roast venison; **Rehkalb** *nt* fawn; **Rehkitz** *nt* fawn

Reibach ['raɪbax] **(-s)** *m*: **einen ~ machen** (*umg*) to make a killing

Reibe ['raɪbə] **(-, -n)** *f* grater

Reibeisen ['raɪp|aɪzən] *nt* grater

Reibekuchen *m* (*Koch*) ≈ potato waffle

reiben *unreg vt* to rub; (*Koch*) to grate

Reiberei [raɪbə'raɪ] *f* friction *no pl*

Reibfläche *f* rough surface

Reibung *f* friction

reibungslos *adj* smooth; **~ verlaufen** to go off smoothly

Reich [raɪç] **(-(e)s, -e)** *nt* empire, kingdom; (*fig*) realm; **das Dritte ~** the Third Reich

reich *adj* rich ▷ *adv*: **eine ~ ausgestattete Bibliothek** a well-stocked library

reichen *vi* to reach; (*genügen*) to be enough *od* sufficient ▷ *vt* to hold out; (*geben*) to pass, hand; (*anbieten*) to offer; **so weit das Auge reicht** as far as the eye can see; **jdm ~** (*genügen*) to be enough *od* sufficient for sb; **mir reichts!** I've had enough!

reich- *zW*: **reichhaltig** *adj* ample, rich; **reichlich** *adj* ample, plenty of; **Reichtum (-s, -tümer)** *m* wealth; **Reichweite** *f* range; **jd ist in Reichweite** sb is nearby

reif [raɪf] *adj* ripe; (*Mensch, Urteil*) mature; **für etw ~ sein** (*umg*) to be ready for sth

Reif[1] **(-(e)s)** *m* hoarfrost

Reif[2] **(-(e)s, -e)** *m* (*Ring*) ring, hoop

Reife (-) *f* ripeness; maturity; **mittlere ~** (*Sch*) *first public examination in secondary school*, ≈ O-Levels *pl* (*Brit*)

Reifen (-s, -) *m* ring, hoop; (*Fahrzeugreifen*) tyre (*Brit*), tire (*US*)

reifen *vi* to mature; (*Obst*) to ripen

Reifen- *zW*: **Reifendruck** *m* tyre (*Brit*) *od* tire (*US*) pressure; **Reifenpanne** *f* puncture, flat; **Reifenprofil** *nt* tyre (*Brit*) *od* tire (*US*) tread; **Reifenschaden** *m* puncture, flat

Reifeprüfung *f* school-leaving exam

Reifezeugnis *nt* school-leaving certificate

reiflich ['raɪflɪç] *adj* thorough, careful

Reihe ['raɪə] **(-, -n)** *f* row; (*von Tagen etc: umg: Anzahl*) series *sing*; **eine ganze ~ (von)** (*unbestimmte Anzahl*) a whole lot (of); **der ~ nach** in turn; **er ist an der ~** it's his turn; **an die ~ kommen** to have one's turn; **außer der ~** out of turn; (*ausnahmsweise*) out of the usual way of things; **aus der ~ tanzen** (*fig: umg*) to be different; (*gegen Konventionen verstoßen*) to step out of line; **ich kriege heute nichts auf die ~** I can't get my act together today

reihen *vt* to set in a row; to arrange in series; (*Perlen*) to string
Reihen- *zW*: **Reihenfolge** *f* sequence; **alphabetische Reihenfolge** alphabetical order; **Reihenhaus** *nt* terraced (*Brit*) *od* row (*US*) house; **Reihenuntersuchung** *f* mass screening; **reihenweise** *adv* (*in Reihen*) in rows; (*fig: in großer Anzahl*) by the dozen
Reiher (**-s, -**) *m* heron
reihum [raɪ'|ʊm] *adv*: **etw ~ gehen lassen** to pass sth around
Reim [raɪm] (**-(e)s, -e**) *m* rhyme; **sich** *dat* **einen ~ auf etw** *akk* **machen** (*umg*) to make sense of sth; **reimen** *vt* to rhyme
rein[1] [raɪn] (*umg*) *adv* = **herein; hinein**
rein[2] [raɪn] *adj* pure; (*sauber*) clean ▷ *adv* purely; **~ waschen** to clear o.s.; **das ist die ~ste Freude/der ~ste Hohn** *etc* it's pure *od* sheer joy/mockery *etc*; **etw ins R~e schreiben** to make a fair copy of sth; **etw ins R~e bringen** to clear sth up; **~en Tisch machen** (*fig*) to get things straight; **~ unmöglich** (*umg: ganz, völlig*) absolutely impossible
Rein- *in zw* (*Comm*) net(t)
Reinemachefrau *f* cleaning lady, charwoman (*Brit*)
reineweg (*umg*) *adv* completely, absolutely
rein- *zW*: **Reinfall** (*umg*) *m* let-down; (*Misserfolg*) flop; **reinfallen** *vi*: **auf jdn/etw reinfallen** to be taken in by sb/sth; **Reingewinn** *m* net profit; **Reinheit** *f* purity; cleanness
reinigen ['raɪnɪgən] *vt* to clean; (*Wasser*) to purify
Reiniger (**-s, -**) *m* cleaner
Reinigung *f* cleaning; purification; (*Geschäft*) cleaner's; **chemische ~** dry-cleaning; (*Geschäft*) dry-cleaner's
Reinigungsmittel *nt* cleansing agent
rein- *zW*: **reinlich** *adj* clean; **Reinlichkeit** *f* cleanliness; **Reinmachefrau** *f* = **Reinemachefrau**; **reinrassig** *adj* pedigree; **reinreiten** *unreg vt*: **jdn reinreiten** to get sb into a mess; **Reinschrift** *f* fair copy; **Reinvermögen** *nt* net assets *pl*
reinweg (*umg*) *adv* = **reineweg**
Reis[1] [raɪs] (**-es, -e**) *m* rice
Reis[2] [raɪs] (**-es, -er**) *nt* twig, sprig
Reise ['raɪzə] (**-, -n**) *f* journey; (*Schiffsreise*) voyage; **Reisen** *pl* travels *pl*; **gute ~!** bon voyage!, have a good journey!; **auf ~n sein** to be away (travelling (*Brit*) *od* traveling (*US*)); **er ist viel auf ~n** he does a lot of travelling (*Brit*) *od* traveling (*US*); **Reiseandenken** *nt* souvenir; **Reiseapotheke** *f* first-aid kit; **Reisebericht** *m* account of one's journey; (*Buch*) travel story; (*Film*) travelogue (*Brit*), travelog (*US*); **Reisebüro** *nt* travel agency; **Reisediplomatie** *f* shuttle diplomacy; **Reiseerleichterungen** *pl* easing *sing* of travel restrictions; **reisefertig** *adj* ready to start; **Reisefieber** *nt* (*fig*) travel nerves *pl*; **Reiseführer** *m* guide(book); (*Mensch*) (travel) guide; **Reisegepäck** *nt* luggage; **Reisegesellschaft** *f* party of travellers (*Brit*) *od* travelers (*US*); **Reisekosten** *pl* travelling (*Brit*) *od* traveling (*US*) expenses *pl*; **Reiseleiter** *m* courier; **Reiselektüre** *f* reading for the journey; **Reiselust** *f* wanderlust
reisen *vi* to travel; **~ nach** to go to
Reisende, r *f(m)* traveller (*Brit*), traveler (*US*)
Reise- *zW*: **Reisepass** *m* passport; **Reisepläne** *pl* plans *pl* for a *od* the journey; **Reiseproviant** *m* provisions *pl* for the journey; **Reiseroute** *f* itinerary; **Reisescheck** *m* traveller's cheque (*Brit*), traveler's check (*US*); **Reiseschreibmaschine** *f* portable typewriter; **Reisetasche** *f* travelling (*Brit*) *od* traveling (*US*) bag *od* case; **Reisethrombose** *f* deep vein thrombosis, economy-class syndrome (*umg*); **Reiseveranstalter** *m* tour operator; **Reiseverkehr** *m* tourist *od* holiday traffic; **Reisewetter** *nt* holiday weather; **Reiseziel** *nt* destination
Reisig ['raɪzɪç] (**-s**) *nt* brushwood
Reißaus *m*: **~ nehmen** to run away, flee
Reißbrett *nt* drawing board; **Reißbrettstift** *m* drawing pin (*Brit*), thumbtack (*US*)
reißen ['raɪsən] *unreg vt* to tear; (*ziehen*) to pull, drag; (*Witz*) to crack ▷ *vi* to tear; to pull, drag; **etw an sich ~** to snatch sth up; (*fig*) to take sth over; **sich um etw ~** to scramble for sth; **wenn alle Stricke ~** (*fig: umg*) if the worst comes to the worst; *siehe auch* **hingerissen**
Reißen *nt* (*Gewichtheben: Disziplin*) snatch; (*umg: Gliederreißen*) ache
reißend *adj* (*Fluss*) torrential; (*Comm*) rapid; **~en Absatz finden** to sell like hot cakes (*umg*)
Reißer (**-s, -**) (*umg*) *m* thriller; **reißerisch** *adj* sensational
Reiß- *zW*: **Reißleine** *f* (*Aviat*) ripcord; **Reißnagel** *m* drawing pin (*Brit*), thumbtack (*US*); **Reißschiene** *f* T-square; **Reißverschluss** *m* zip (fastener) (*Brit*), zipper (*US*); **Reißwolf** *m* shredder; **durch den Reißwolf geben** (*Dokumente*) to shred; **Reißzeug** *nt* geometry set; **Reißzwecke** *f* = **Reißnagel**
reiten ['raɪtən] *unreg vt, vi* to ride
Reiter (**-s, -**) *m* rider; (*Mil*) cavalryman, trooper
Reiterei [raɪtə'raɪ] *f* cavalry
Reiterin *f* rider
Reit- *zW*: **Reithose** *f* riding breeches *pl*; **Reitpferd** *nt* saddle horse; **Reitschule** *f* riding school; **Reitstiefel** *m* riding boot; **Reitturnier** *nt* horse show; **Reitweg** *m* bridle path; **Reitzeug** *nt* riding outfit
Reiz [raɪts] (**-es, -e**) *m* stimulus; (*angenehm*) charm; (*Verlockung*) attraction
reizbar *adj* irritable; **Reizbarkeit** *f* irritability
reizen *vt* to stimulate; (*unangenehm*) to irritate; (*verlocken*) to appeal to, attract; (*Karten*) to bid ▷ *vi*: **zum Widerspruch ~** to invite contradiction
reizend *adj* charming
Reiz- *zW*: **Reizgas** *nt* tear gas, CS gas; **Reizhusten** *m* chesty cough; **reizlos** *adj* unattractive; **reizvoll** *adj* attractive; **Reizwäsche** *f* sexy underwear; **Reizwort** *nt*

emotive word
rekapitulieren [rekapitu'li:rən] *vt* to recapitulate
rekeln ['re:kəln] *vr* to stretch out; (*lümmeln*) to lounge *od* loll about
Reklamation [reklamatsi'o:n] *f* complaint
Reklame [re'kla:mə] (**-, -n**) *f* advertising; (*Anzeige*) advertisement; **mit etw ~ machen** (*pej*) to show off about sth; **für etw ~ machen** to advertise sth; **Reklametrommel** *f*: **die Reklametrommel für jdn/etw rühren** (*umg*) to beat the (big) drum for sb/sth; **Reklamewand** *f* notice (*Brit*) *od* bulletin (*US*) board
reklamieren [rekla'mi:rən] *vi* to complain ▷ *vt* to complain about; (*zurückfordern*) to reclaim
rekonstruieren [rekɔnstru'i:rən] *vt* to reconstruct
Rekonvaleszenz [rekɔnvalɛs'tsɛnts] *f* convalescence
Rekord [re'kɔrt] (**-(e)s, -e**) *m* record; **Rekordleistung** *f* record performance
Rekrut [re'kru:t] (**-en, -en**) *m* recruit
rekrutieren [rekru'ti:rən] *vt* to recruit ▷ *vr* to be recruited
Rektor ['rɛktɔr] *m* (*Univ*) rector, vice-chancellor; (*Sch*) head teacher (*Brit*), principal (*US*)
Rektorat [rɛktɔ'rat] (**-(e)s, -e**) *nt* rectorate, vice-chancellorship; headship (*Brit*), principalship (*US*); (*Zimmer*) rector's *etc* office
Rektorin [rɛk'to:rɪn] *f* (*Sch*) head teacher (*Brit*), principal (*US*)
Rel. *abk* (= *Religion*) rel.
Relais [rə'lɛ:] (**-, -**) *nt* relay
Relation [relatsi'o:n] *f* relation
relativ [rela'ti:f] *adj* relative
Relativität [relativi'tɛ:t] *f* relativity
Relativpronomen *nt* (*Gram*) relative pronoun
relevant [rele'vant] *adj* relevant
Relevanz *f* relevance
Relief [reli'ɛf] (**-s, -s**) *nt* relief
Religion [religi'o:n] *f* religion
Religions- *zW*: **Religionsfreiheit** *f* freedom of worship; **Religionslehre** *f* religious education; **Religionsunterricht** *m* religious education
religiös [religi'ø:s] *adj* religious
Relikt [re'lɪkt] (**-(e)s, -e**) *nt* relic
Reling ['re:lɪŋ] (**-, -s**) *f* (*Naut*) rail
Reliquie [re'li:kviə] *f* relic
Reminiszenz [reminɪs'tsɛnts] *f* reminiscence, recollection
Remis [rə'mi:] (**-, -** *od* **-en**) *nt* (*Schach, Sport*) draw
Remittende [remɪ'tɛndə] (**-, -n**) *f* (*Comm*) return
Remittent *m* (*Fin*) payee
remittieren *vt* (*Comm: Waren*) to return; (*Geld*) to remit
Remmidemmi ['rɛmi'dɛmi] (**-s**) (*umg*) *nt* (*Krach*) row, rumpus; (*Trubel*) rave-up
Remoulade [remu'la:də] (**-, -n**) *f* remoulade
rempeln ['rɛmpəln] (*umg*) *vt* to jostle, elbow; (*Sport*) to barge into; (*foulen*) to push
Ren [re:n, rɛn] (**-s, -s** *od* **-e**) *nt* reindeer
Renaissance [rənɛ'sã:s] (**-, -n**) *f* (*Hist*) renaissance; (*fig*) revival, rebirth
Rendezvous [rãde'vu:] (**-, -**) *nt* rendezvous
Rendite [rɛn'di:tə] (**-, -n**) *f* (*Fin*) yield, return on capital
Rennbahn *f* racecourse; (*Aut*) circuit, racetrack
rennen ['rɛnən] *unreg vt, vi* to run, race; **um die Wette ~** to have a race; **Rennen** (**-s, -**) *nt* running; (*Wettbewerb*) race; **das Rennen machen** (*lit, fig*) to win (the race)
Renner (**-s, -**) (*umg*) *m* winner, worldbeater
Renn- *zW*: **Rennfahrer** *m* racing driver (*Brit*), race car driver (*US*); **Rennpferd** *nt* racehorse; **Rennplatz** *m* racecourse; **Rennrad** *nt* racing cycle; **Rennsport** *m* racing; **Rennwagen** *m* racing car (*Brit*), race car (*US*)
renommiert [renɔ'mi:rt] *adj*: **~ (wegen)** renowned (for), famous (for)
renovieren [reno'vi:rən] *vt* to renovate
Renovierung *f* renovation
rentabel [rɛn'ta:bəl] *adj* profitable, lucrative
Rentabilität [rɛntabili'tɛ:t] *f* profitability
Rente ['rɛntə] (**-, -n**) *f* pension
Renten- *zW*: **Rentenbasis** *f* annuity basis; **Rentenempfänger** *m* pensioner; **Rentenpapier** *nt* (*Fin*) fixed-interest security; **Rentenversicherung** *f* pension scheme; **Rentenversicherungsträger** *m* pension provider
Rentier ['rɛnti:r] *nt* reindeer
rentieren [rɛn'ti:rən] *vi, vr* to pay, be profitable; **das rentiert (sich) nicht** it's not worth it
Rentner, in ['rɛntnər(ɪn)] (**-s, -**) *m(f)* pensioner
Reparation [reparatsi'o:n] *f* reparation
Reparatur [repara'tu:r] *f* repairing; repair; **etw in ~ geben** to have sth repaired; **reparaturbedürftig** *adj* in need of repair; **Reparaturwerkstatt** *f* repair shop; (*Aut*) garage
reparieren [repa'ri:rən] *vt* to repair
Repertoire [repɛrto'a:r] (**-s, -s**) *nt* repertoire
Reportage [repɔr'ta:ʒə] (**-, -n**) *f* report
Reporter, in [re'pɔrtər(ɪn)] (**-s, -**) *m(f)* reporter, commentator
Repräsentant, in [reprɛzɛn'tant(ɪn)] *m(f)* representative
repräsentativ [reprɛzɛnta'ti:f] *adj* representative; (*Geschenk etc*) prestigious; **die ~en Pflichten eines Botschafters** the social duties of an ambassador
repräsentieren [reprɛzɛn'ti:rən] *vt* to represent ▷ *vi* to perform official duties
Repressalien [reprɛ'sa:liən] *pl* reprisals *pl*
reprivatisieren [reprivati'zi:rən] *vt* to denationalize
Reprivatisierung *f* denationalization
Reproduktion [reprodʊktsi'o:n] *f* reproduction
reproduzieren [reprodu'tsi:rən] *vt* to reproduce
Reptil [rɛp'ti:l] (**-s, -ien**) *nt* reptile
Republik [repu'bli:k] *f* republic

Republikaner [republi'ka:nər] (**-s, -**) *m* republican
republikanisch *adj* republican
Requisiten *pl* (*Theat*) props *pl*, properties *pl* (*form*)
Reservat [rezɛr'va:t] (**-(e)s, -e**) *nt* reservation
Reserve [re'zɛrvə] (**-, -n**) *f* reserve; **jdn aus der ~ locken** to bring sb out of his/her shell; **Reserverad** *nt* (*Aut*) spare wheel; **Reservespieler** *m* reserve; **Reservetank** *m* reserve tank
reservieren [rezɛr'vi:rən] *vt* to reserve
reserviert *adj* (*Platz, Mensch*) reserved
Reservist [rezɛr'vɪst] *m* reservist
Reservoir [rezɛrvo'a:r] (**-s, -e**) *nt* reservoir
Residenz [rezi'dɛnts] *f* residence, seat
residieren [rezi'di:rən] *vi* to reside
Resignation [rezɪgnatsi'o:n] *f* resignation
resignieren [rezɪ'gni:rən] *vi* to resign
resolut [rezo'lu:t] *adj* resolute
Resolution [rezolutsi'o:n] *f* resolution; (*Bittschrift*) petition
Resonanz [rezo'nants] *f* (*lit, fig*) resonance; **Resonanzboden** *m* sounding board; **Resonanzkasten** *m* soundbox
Resopal® [rezo'pa:l] (**-s**) *nt* Formica®
resozialisieren [rezotsiali'zi:rən] *vt* to rehabilitate
Resozialisierung *f* rehabilitation
Respekt [rɛ'spɛkt] (**-(e)s**) *m* respect; (*Angst*) fear; **bei allem ~ (vor jdm/etw)** with all due respect (to sb/for sth)
respektabel [rɛspɛk'ta:bəl] *adj* respectable
respektieren [rɛspɛk'ti:rən] *vt* to respect
respektlos *adj* disrespectful
Respektsperson *f* person commanding respect
respektvoll *adj* respectful
Ressentiment [rɛsãti'mã:] (**-s, -s**) *nt* resentment
Ressort [rɛ'so:r] (**-s, -s**) *nt* department; **in das ~ von jdm fallen** (*lit, fig*) to be sb's department
Ressourcen [rɛ'sʊrsən] *pl* resources *pl*
Rest [rɛst] (**-(e)s, -e**) *m* remainder, rest; (*Überrest*) remains *pl*; **Reste** *pl* (*Comm*) remnants *pl*; **das hat mir den ~ gegeben** (*umg*) that finished me off
Restaurant [rɛsto'rã:] (**-s, -s**) *nt* restaurant
Restauration [restaʊratsi'o:n] *f* restoration
restaurieren [restaʊ'ri:rən] *vt* to restore
Restaurierung *f* restoration
Rest- *zW*: **Restbetrag** *m* remainder, outstanding sum; **Restlaufzeit** *f* (*Wirts*) unexpired term; **restlich** *adj* remaining; **restlos** *adj* complete; **Restmüll** *m* non-recyclable waste; **Restposten** *m* (*Comm*) remaining stock
Resultat [rezʊl'ta:t] (**-(e)s, -e**) *nt* result
Retorte [re'tɔrtə] (**-, -n**) *f* retort; **aus der ~** (*umg*) synthetic
Retortenbaby *nt* test-tube baby
retour [re'tu:r] *adv* (*veraltet*) back
Retouren *pl* (*Waren*) returns *pl*
retten ['rɛtən] *vt* to save, rescue ▷ *vr* to escape; **bist du noch zu ~?** (*umg*) are you out of your mind?; **sich vor etw** *dat* **nicht mehr ~ können** (*fig*) to be swamped with sth
Retter, in (**-s, -**) *m(f)* rescuer, saviour (*Brit*), savior (*US*)
Rettich ['rɛtɪç] (**-s, -e**) *m* radish
Rettung *f* rescue; (*Hilfe*) help; **seine letzte ~** his last hope
Rettungs- *zW*: **Rettungsaktion** *f* rescue operation; **Rettungsboot** *nt* lifeboat; **Rettungsdienst** *m* rescue service; **Rettungsgürtel** *m* lifebelt, life preserver (*US*); **rettungslos** *adj* hopeless; **Rettungsring** *m* = **Rettungsgürtel**; **Rettungsschwimmer** *m* lifesaver; (*am Strand*) lifeguard; **Rettungswagen** *m* ambulance
Return-Taste [ri'tø:rntastə] *f* (*Comput*) return key
retuschieren [retʊ'ʃi:rən] *vt* (*Phot*) to retouch
Reue ['rɔʏə] (**-**) *f* remorse; (*Bedauern*) regret
reuen *vt*: **es reut ihn** he regrets it, he is sorry about it
reuig ['rɔʏɪç] *adj* penitent
reumütig *adj* remorseful; (*Sünder*) contrite
Reuse ['rɔʏzə] (**-, -n**) *f* fish trap
Revanche [re'vã:ʃə] (**-, -n**) *f* revenge; (*Sport*) return match
revanchieren [revã'ʃi:rən] *vr* (*sich rächen*) to get one's own back, have one's revenge; (*erwidern*) to reciprocate, return the compliment
Revers [re've:r] (**-, -**) *nt or m* lapel
revidieren [revi'di:rən] *vt* to revise; (*Comm*) to audit
Revier [re'vi:r] (**-s, -e**) *nt* district; (*Min: Kohlenrevier*) (coal)mine; (*Jagdrevier*) preserve; (*Polizeirevier*) police station, station house (*US*); (*Dienstbereich*) beat (*Brit*), precinct (*US*); (*Mil*) sick bay
Revision [revizi'o:n] *f* revision; (*Comm*) auditing; (*Jur*) appeal
Revisionsverhandlung *f* appeal hearing
Revisor [re'vi:zɔr] (**-s, -en**) *m* (*Comm*) auditor
Revolte [re'vɔltə] (**-, -n**) *f* revolt
Revolution [revolutsi'o:n] *f* revolution
revolutionär [revolutsio'nɛ:r] *adj* revolutionary
Revolutionär, in [revolutsio'nɛ:r(ɪn)] (**-s, -e**) *m(f)* revolutionary
revolutionieren [revolutsio'ni:rən] *vt* to revolutionize
Revoluzzer [revo'lʊtsər] (**-s, -**) (*pej*) *m* would-be revolutionary
Revolver [re'vɔlvər] (**-s, -**) *m* revolver
Revue [rə'vy:] (**-, -n**) *f*: **etw ~ passieren lassen** (*fig*) to pass sth in review
Reykjavik ['raɪkjavi:k] (**-s**) *nt* Reykjavik
Rezensent [retsɛn'zɛnt] *m* reviewer, critic
rezensieren [retsɛn'zi:rən] *vt* to review
Rezension *f* review
Rezept [re'tsɛpt] (**-(e)s, -e**) *nt* (*Koch*) recipe; (*Med*) prescription
Rezeption [retsɛptsi'o:n] *f* (*von Hotel: Empfang*)

reception
rezeptpflichtig *adj* available only on prescription
Rezession [retsɛsi'o:n] *f* (*Fin*) recession
rezitieren [retsi'ti:rən] *vt* to recite
R-Gespräch ['ɛrgəʃprɛ:ç] *nt* (*Tel*) reverse charge call (*Brit*), collect call (*US*)
Rh *abk* (= *Rhesus(faktor) positiv*) Rh positive
rh *abk* (= *Rhesus(faktor) negativ*) Rh negative
Rhabarber [ra'barbər] (**-s**) *m* rhubarb
Rhein [raɪn] (**-(e)s**) *m* Rhine
rhein. *abk* = **rheinisch**
Rheingau *m* *wine-growing area along the Rhine*
Rheinhessen *nt* *wine-growing area along the Rhine*
rheinisch *adj attrib* Rhenish, Rhineland
Rheinland *nt* Rhineland
Rheinländer, in *m(f)* Rhinelander
Rheinland-Pfalz *nt* Rhineland-Palatinate
Rhesusfaktor ['re:zusfaktɔr] *m* rhesus factor
Rhetorik [re'to:rɪk] *f* rhetoric
rhetorisch [re'to:rɪʃ] *adj* rhetorical
Rheuma ['rɔyma] (**-s**) *nt* rheumatism
Rheumatismus [rɔyma'tɪsmʊs] *m* rheumatism
Rhinozeros [ri'no:tserɔs] (*- od* **-ses, -se**) *nt* rhinoceros; (*umg: Dummkopf*) fool
Rhld. *abk* = **Rheinland**
Rhodesien [ro'de:ziən] (**-s**) *nt* Rhodesia
Rhodos ['ro:dɔs] (-) *nt* Rhodes
rhythmisch ['rytmɪʃ] *adj* rhythmical
Rhythmus *m* rhythm
RIAS ['ri:as] (-) *m abk* (= *Rundfunk im amerikanischen Sektor (Berlin)*) *broadcasting station in the former American sector of Berlin*
Richtantenne ['rɪçt|antɛnə] (**-, -n**) *f* directional aerial (*bes Brit*) *od* antenna
richten ['rɪçtən] *vt* to direct; (*Waffe*) to aim; (*einstellen*) to adjust; (*instand setzen*) to repair; (*zurechtmachen*) to prepare, get ready; (*adressieren: Briefe, Anfragen*) to address; (*Bitten, Forderungen*) to make; (*in Ordnung bringen*) to do, fix; (*bestrafen*) to pass judgement on ▷ *vr*: **sich ~ nach** to go by; **~ an** *+akk* to direct at; (*fig*) to direct to; (*Briefe etc*) to address to; (*Bitten etc*) to make to; **~ auf** *+akk* to aim at; **wir ~ uns ganz nach unseren Kunden** we are guided entirely by our customers' wishes
Richter, in (**-s, -**) *m(f)* judge; **sich zum ~ machen** (*fig*) to set (o.s.) up in judgement; **richterlich** *adj* judicial
Richtgeschwindigkeit *f* recommended speed
richtig *adj* right, correct; (*echt*) proper ▷ *adv* correctly, right; (*umg: sehr*) really; **der/die R~e** the right one *od* person; **das R~e** the right thing; **die Uhr geht ~** the clock is right; **Richtigkeit** *f* correctness; **das hat schon seine Richtigkeit** it's right enough; **richtigstellen** *vt* to correct; **Richtigstellung** *f* correction, rectification
Richt- *zW*: **Richtlinie** *f* guideline; **Richtpreis** *m* recommended price; **Richtschnur** *f* (*fig: Grundsatz*) guiding principle
Richtung *f* direction; (*Tendenz*) tendency, orientation; **in jeder ~** each way
Richtungsstreit *m* (*Pol*) factional dispute
richtungweisend *adj*: **~ sein** to point the way (ahead)
rieb *etc* [ri:p] *vb siehe* **reiben**
riechen ['ri:çən] *unreg vt, vi* to smell; **an etw** *dat* **~** to smell sth; **es riecht nach Gas** there's a smell of gas; **ich kann das/ihn nicht ~** (*umg*) I can't stand it/him; **das konnte ich doch nicht ~!** (*umg*) how was I (supposed) to know?
Riecher (**-s, -**) *m*: **einen guten** *od* **den richtigen ~ für etw haben** (*umg*) to have a nose for sth
Ried [ri:t] (**-(e)s, -e**) *nt* reed; (*Moor*) marsh
rief *etc* [ri:f] *vb siehe* **rufen**
Riege ['ri:gə] (**-, -n**) *f* team, squad
Riegel ['ri:gəl] (**-s, -**) *m* bolt, bar; **einer Sache** *dat* **einen ~ vorschieben** (*fig*) to clamp down on sth
Riemen ['ri:mən] (**-s, -**) *m* strap; (*Gürtel, Tech*) belt; (*Naut*) oar; **sich am ~ reißen** (*fig: umg*) to get a grip on o.s.; **Riemenantrieb** *m* belt drive
Riese ['ri:zə] (**-n, -n**) *m* giant
rieseln *vi* to trickle; (*Schnee*) to fall gently
Riesen- *zW*: **Riesenerfolg** *m* enormous success; **Riesengebirge** *nt* (*Geog*) Sudeten Mountains *pl*; **riesengroß** *adj*, **riesenhaft** *adj* colossal, gigantic, huge; **Riesenrad** *nt* big *od* Ferris wheel; **Riesenschritt** *m*: **sich mit Riesenschritten nähern** (*fig*) to be drawing on apace; **Riesenslalom** *m* (*Ski*) giant slalom
riesig ['ri:zɪç] *adj* enormous, huge, vast
Riesin *f* giantess
riet *etc* [ri:t] *vb siehe* **raten**
Riff [rɪf] (**-(e)s, -e**) *nt* reef
rigoros [rigo'ro:s] *adj* rigorous
Rille ['rɪlə] (**-, -n**) *f* groove
Rind [rɪnt] (**-(e)s, -er**) *nt* ox; (*Kuh*) cow; (*Koch*) beef; **Rinder** *pl* cattle *pl*; **vom ~** beef
Rinde ['rɪndə] (**-, -n**) *f* rind; (*Baumrinde*) bark; (*Brotrinde*) crust
Rinderbraten *m* roast beef
Rinderwahn ['rɪndərva:n] *m* mad cow disease
Rindfleisch *nt* beef
Rindvieh *nt* cattle *pl*; (*umg*) blockhead, stupid oaf
Ring [rɪŋ] (**-(e)s, -e**) *m* ring; **Ringbuch** *nt* ring binder
ringeln ['rɪŋəln] *vt* (*Pflanze*) to (en)twine; (*Schwanz etc*) to curl ▷ *vr* to go curly, curl; (*Rauch*) to curl up(wards)
Ringelnatter *f* grass snake
Ringeltaube *f* wood pigeon
ringen *unreg vi* to wrestle; **nach** *od* **um etw ~** (*streben*) to struggle for sth; **Ringen** (**-s**) *nt* wrestling
Ringer (**-s, -**) *m* wrestler
Ring- *zW*: **Ringfinger** *m* ring finger; **ringförmig** *adj* ring-shaped; **Ringkampf** *m* wrestling bout; **Ringrichter** *m* referee
rings *adv*: **~ um** round; **ringsherum** *adv* round about
Ringstraße *f* ring road

ringsum [rɪŋs'|ʊm], **ringsumher** ['rɪŋs-|ʊm'he:r] *adv* (*rundherum*) round about; (*überall*) all round
Rinne ['rɪnə] (**-, -n**) *f* gutter, drain
rinnen *unreg vi* to run, trickle
Rinnsal (**-s, -e**) *nt* trickle of water
Rinnstein *m* gutter
Rippchen ['rɪpçən] *nt* small rib; cutlet
Rippe ['rɪpə] (**-, -n**) *f* rib
Rippen- *zW*: **Rippenfellentzündung** *f* pleurisy; **Rippenspeer** *m od nt* (*Koch*): **Kasseler Rippenspeer** *slightly cured pork spare rib*; **Rippenstoß** *m* dig in the ribs
Risiko ['ri:ziko] (**-s, -s** *od* **Risiken**) *nt* risk; **risikobehaftet** *adj* fraught with risk; **Risikoinvestition** *f* sunk cost
riskant [rɪs'kant] *adj* risky, hazardous
riskieren [rɪs'ki:rən] *vt* to risk
riss *etc* [rɪs] *vb siehe* **reißen**
Riss (**-es, -e**) *m* tear; (*in Mauer, Tasse etc*) crack; (*in Haut*) scratch; (*Tech*) design
rissig ['rɪsɪç] *adj* torn; cracked; scratched
ritt *etc* [rɪt] *vb siehe* **reiten**
Ritt (**-(e)s, -e**) *m* ride
Ritter (**-s, -**) *m* knight; **jdn zum ~ schlagen** to knight sb; **arme ~** *pl* (*Koch*) *sweet French toast, made with bread soaked in milk*; **ritterlich** *adj* chivalrous; **Ritterschlag** *m* knighting; **Rittertum** (**-s**) *nt* chivalry; **Ritterzeit** *f* age of chivalry
rittlings *adv* astride
Ritual [ritu'a:l] (**-s, -e** *od* **-ien**) *nt* (*lit, fig*) ritual
rituell [ritu'ɛl] *adj* ritual
Ritus ['ri:tʊs] (**-, Riten**) *m* rite
Ritze ['rɪtsə] (**-, -n**) *f* crack, chink
ritzen *vt* to scratch; **die Sache ist geritzt** (*umg*) it's all fixed up
Rivale [ri'va:lə] (**-n, -n**) *m*, **Rivalin** *f* rival
rivalisieren [rivali'zi:rən] *vi*: **mit jdm ~** to compete with sb
Rivalität [rivali'tɛ:t] *f* rivalry
Riviera [rivi'e:ra] (**-**) *f* Riviera
Rizinusöl ['ri:tsinʊs|ø:l] *nt* castor oil
r.-k. *abk* (= *römisch-katholisch*) R.C.
Robbe ['rɔbə] (**-, -n**) *f* seal
robben ['rɔbən] *vi* (*Hilfsverb sein: auch Mil*) to crawl (*using elbows*)
Robbenfang *m* seal hunting
Robe ['ro:bə] (**-, -n**) *f* robe
Roboter ['rɔbɔtər] (**-s, -**) *m* robot; **Robotertechnik** *f* robotics *sing*
Robotik ['rɔbɔtɪk] *f* robotics *sing*
robust [ro'bʊst] *adj* (*Mensch, Gesundheit*) robust; (*Material*) tough
roch *etc* [rɔx] *vb siehe* **riechen**
Rochade [rɔ'xa:də] (**-, -n**) *f* (*Schach*): **die kleine/große ~** castling king's side/queen's side
röcheln ['rœçəln] *vi* to wheeze; (*Sterbender*) to give the death rattle
Rock[1] [rɔk] (**-(e)s, ¨-e**) *m* skirt; (*Jackett*) jacket; (*Uniformrock*) tunic
Rock[2] [rɔk] (**-(s), -(s)**) *m* (*Mus*) rock; **Rockmusik** *f* rock music
Rockzipfel *m*: **an Mutters ~ hängen** (*umg*) to cling to (one's) mother's skirts
Rodel ['ro:dəl] (**-s, -**) *m* toboggan; **Rodelbahn** *f* toboggan run
rodeln *vi* to toboggan
roden ['ro:dən] *vt, vi* to clear
Rogen ['ro:gən] (**-s, -**) *m* roe
Roggen ['rɔgən] (**-s, -**) *m* rye; **Roggenbrot** *nt* rye bread; (*Vollkornbrot*) black bread
roh [ro:] *adj* raw; (*Mensch*) coarse, crude; **~e Gewalt** brute force; **Rohbau** *m* shell of a building; **Roheisen** *nt* pig iron; **Rohfassung** *f* rough draft; **Rohkost** *f* raw fruit and vegetables *pl*; **Rohling** *m* ruffian; **Rohmaterial** *nt* raw material; **Rohöl** *nt* crude oil
Rohr [ro:r] (**-(e)s, -e**) *nt* pipe, tube; (*Bot*) cane; (*Schilf*) reed; (*Gewehrrohr*) barrel; **Rohrbruch** *m* burst pipe
Röhre ['rø:rə] (**-, -n**) *f* tube, pipe; (*Rundf etc*) valve; (*Backröhre*) oven
Rohr- *zW*: **Rohrgeflecht** *nt* wickerwork; **Rohrleger** (**-s, -**) *m* plumber; **Rohrleitung** *f* pipeline; **Rohrpost** *f* pneumatic post; **Rohrspatz** *m*: **schimpfen wie ein Rohrspatz** (*umg*) to curse and swear; **Rohrstock** *m* cane; **Rohrstuhl** *m* basket chair; **Rohrzucker** *m* cane sugar
Rohseide *f* raw silk
Rohstoff *m* raw material
Rokoko ['rɔkoko] (**-s**) *nt* rococo
Rolladen *m siehe* **Rollladen**
Rollbahn *f* (*Aviat*) runway
Rolle ['rɔlə] (**-, -n**) *f* roll; (*Theat, Soziologie*) role; (*Garnrolle etc*) reel, spool; (*Walze*) roller; (*Wäscherolle*) mangle, wringer; **bei** *od* **in etw** *dat* **eine ~ spielen** to play a part in sth; **aus der ~ fallen** (*fig*) to forget o.s.; **keine ~ spielen** not to matter
rollen *vi* to roll; (*Aviat*) to taxi ▷ *vt* to roll; (*Wäsche*) to mangle, put through the wringer; **den Stein ins R~ bringen** (*fig*) to start the ball rolling
Rollen- *zW*: **Rollenbesetzung** *f* (*Theat*) cast; **Rollenkonflikt** *m* (*Psych*) role conflict; **Rollenspiel** *nt* role-play; **Rollentausch** *m* exchange of roles; (*Soziologie*) role reversal
Roller (**-s, -**) *m* scooter; (*Welle*) roller
Roll- *zW*: **Rollfeld** *nt* runway; **Rollkragen** *m* roll *od* polo neck; **Rollladen** *m* shutter; **Rollmops** *m* pickled herring
Rollo ['rɔlo] (**-, -s**) *nt* (roller) blind
Roll- *zW*: **Rollschrank** *m* roll-fronted cupboard; **Rollschuh** *m* roller skate; **Rollschuhlaufen** *nt* roller skating; **Rollsplitt** *m* grit; **Rollstuhl** *m* wheelchair; **Rolltreppe** *f* escalator
Rom [ro:m] (**-s**) *nt* Rome; **das sind Zustände wie im alten ~** (*umg: unmoralisch*) it's disgraceful; (*: primitiv*) it's medieval (*umg*)
röm. *abk* = **römisch**
Roman [ro'ma:n] (**-s, -e**) *m* novel; **(jdm) einen ganzen ~ erzählen** (*umg*) to give (sb) a long rigmarole; **Romanheft** *nt* pulp novel
romanisch *adj* (*Volk, Sprache*) Romance; (*Kunst*)

Romanesque
Romanistik [roma'nɪstɪk] *f* (*Univ*) Romance languages and literature
Romanschreiber *m* novelist
Romanschriftsteller *m* novelist
Romantik [ro'mantɪk] *f* romanticism
Romantiker, in (**-s, -**) *m(f)* romanticist
romantisch *adj* romantic
Romanze [ro'mantsə] (**-, -n**) *f* romance
Römer ['rø:mər] (**-s, -**) *m* wineglass; (*Mensch*) Roman; **Römertopf®** *m* (*Koch*) ≈ (chicken) brick
römisch ['rø:mɪʃ] *adj* Roman; **römisch-katholisch** *adj* Roman Catholic
röm.-kath. *abk* (= *römisch-katholisch*) R.C.
Rommé, Rommee [rɔ'me:] (**-s, -s**) *nt* rummy
röntgen ['rœntgən] *vt* to X-ray; **Röntgenaufnahme** *f* X-ray; **Röntgenbild** *nt* X-ray; **Röntgenstrahlen** *pl* X-rays *pl*
rosa ['ro:za] *adj inv* pink, rose(-coloured)
Rose ['ro:zə] (**-, -n**) *f* rose
Rosé [ro'ze:] (**-s, -s**) *m* rosé
Rosenkohl *m* Brussels sprouts *pl*
Rosenkranz *m* rosary
Rosenmontag *m* Monday of Shrovetide; *siehe auch* **Karneval**
Rosette [ro'zɛtə] *f* rosette
rosig ['ro:zɪç] *adj* rosy
Rosine [ro'zi:nə] *f* raisin; **(große) ~n im Kopf haben** (*umg*) to have big ideas
Rosmarin ['ro:smari:n] (**-s**) *m* rosemary
Ross [rɔs] (**-es, -e**) *nt* horse, steed; **auf dem hohen ~ sitzen** (*fig*) to be on one's high horse; **Rosskastanie** *f* horse chestnut; **Rosskur** (*umg*) *f* kill-or-cure remedy
Rost [rɔst] (**-(e)s, -e**) *m* rust; (*Gitter*) grill, gridiron; (*Bettrost*) springs *pl*; **Rostbraten** *m* roast(ed) meat, roast; **Rostbratwurst** *f* grilled *od* barbecued sausage
rosten *vi* to rust
rösten ['rø:stən] *vt* to roast; (*Brot*) to toast
rostfrei *adj* (*Stahl*) stainless
rostig *adj* rusty
Röstkartoffeln *pl* fried potatoes *pl*
Rostschutz *m* rustproofing
rot [ro:t] *adj* red; **~ werden, einen roten Kopf bekommen** to blush, go red; **die R~e Armee** the Red Army; **das R~e Kreuz** the Red Cross; **das R~e Meer** the Red Sea
Rotation [rotatsi'o:n] *f* rotation
rot- *zW*: **rotbäckig** *adj* red-cheeked; **Rotbarsch** *m* rosefish; **rotblond** *adj* strawberry blond
Röte ['rø:tə] (**-**) *f* redness
Röteln *pl* German measles *sing*
röten *vt, vr* to redden
rothaarig *adj* red-haired
rotieren [ro'ti:rən] *vi* to rotate
Rot- *zW*: **Rotkäppchen** *nt* Little Red Riding Hood; **Rotkehlchen** *nt* robin; **Rotkohl** *m* red cabbage; **Rotkraut** *nt* red cabbage; **rotsehen** (*umg*: *unreg*: *vi* to see red, to become angry; **Rotstift** *m* red pencil; **Rotwein** *m* red wine
Rotz [rɔts] (**-es, -e**) (*umg*) *m* snot; **rotzfrech** (*umg*) *adj* cocky; **rotznäsig** (*umg*) *adj* snotty-nosed
Rouge [ru:ʒ] (**-s, -s**) *nt* rouge
Roulade [ru'la:də] (**-, -n**) *f* (*Koch*) beef olive
Roulette, Roulett [ru'lɛt] (**-s, -s**) *nt* roulette
Route ['ru:tə] (**-, -n**) *f* route
Routine [ru'ti:nə] *f* experience; (*Gewohnheit*) routine
routiniert [ruti'ni:ərt] *adj* experienced
Rowdy ['raʊdɪ] (**-s, -s**) *m* hooligan; (*zerstörerisch*) vandal; (*lärmend*) rowdy (type)
Ruanda [ru'anda] *nt* Rwanda
ruandisch *adj* Rwandan
rubbeln ['rʊbəln] (*umg*) *vt, vi* to rub
Rübe ['ry:bə] (**-, -n**) *f* turnip; **Gelbe ~** carrot; **Rote ~** beetroot (*Brit*), beet (*US*)
Rübenzucker *m* beet sugar
Rubin [ru'bi:n] (**-s, -e**) *m* ruby
Rubrik [ru'bri:k] *f* heading; (*Spalte*) column
Ruck [rʊk] (**-(e)s, -e**) *m* jerk, jolt; **sich** *dat* **einen ~ geben** (*fig*: *umg*) to make an effort
ruck *adv*: **das geht ~, zuck** it won't take a second
Rückantwort *f* reply, answer; **um ~ wird gebeten** please reply
ruckartig *adj*: **er stand ~ auf** he shot to his feet
Rück- *zW*: **Rückbesinnung** *f* recollection; **rückbezüglich** *adj* reflexive; **Rückblende** *f* flashback; **rückblenden** *vi* to flash back; **Rückblick** *m*: **im Rückblick auf etw** *akk* looking back on sth; **rückblickend** *adj* retrospective ▷ *adv* in retrospect; **rückdatieren** *vt* to backdate
Rücken (**-s, -**) *m* back; (*Bergrücken*) ridge; **jdm in den ~ fallen** (*fig*) to stab sb in the back
rücken *vt, vi* to move
Rücken- *zW*: **Rückendeckung** *f* backing; **Rückenlage** *f* supine position; **Rückenlehne** *f* back (of chair); **Rückenmark** *nt* spinal cord; **Rückenschwimmen** *nt* backstroke; **Rückenstärkung** *f* (*fig*) moral support; **Rückenwind** *m* following wind
Rück- *zW*: **Rückerstattung** *f* return, restitution; **Rückfahrkarte** *f* return ticket (*Brit*), round-trip ticket (*US*); **Rückfahrt** *f* return journey; **Rückfall** *m* relapse; **rückfällig** *adj* relapsed; **rückfällig werden** to relapse; **Rückflug** *m* return flight; **Rückfrage** *f* question; **nach Rückfrage bei der zuständigen Behörde ...** after checking this with the appropriate authority ...; **rückfragen** *vi* to inquire; (*nachprüfen*) to check; **Rückführung** *f* (*von Menschen*) repatriation, return; **Rückgabe** *f* return; **gegen Rückgabe (+gen)** on return (of); **Rückgang** *m* decline, fall; **rückgängig** *adj*: **etw rückgängig machen** (*widerrufen*) to undo sth; (*Bestellung*) to cancel sth; **Rückgewinnung** *f* recovery; (*von Land, Gebiet*) reclaiming; (*aus verbrauchten Stoffen*) recycling
Rückgrat *nt* spine, backbone
Rück- *zW*: **Rückgriff** *m* recourse; **Rückhalt** *m* backing; (*Einschränkung*) reserve; **rückhaltlos**

adj unreserved; **Rückhand** *f* (*Sport*) backhand; **rückkaufbar** *adj* redeemable; **Rückkehr** (**-, -en**) *f* return; **Rückkoppelung** *f* feedback; **Rücklage** *f* reserve, savings *pl*; **Rücklauf** *m* reverse running; (*beim Tonband*) rewind; (*von Maschinenteil*) return travel; **rückläufig** *adj* declining, falling; **eine rückläufige Entwicklung** a decline; **Rücklicht** *nt* rear light; **rücklings** *adv* from behind; (*rückwärts*) backwards; **Rückmeldung** *f* (*Univ*) reregistration; **Rücknahme** (**-, -n**) *f* taking back; **Rückporto** *nt* return postage; **Rückreise** *f* return journey; (*Naut*) home voyage; **Rückruf** *m* recall

Rucksack ['rʊkzak] *m* rucksack

Rück- *zW*: **Rückschau** *f* reflection; **rückschauend** *adj* = **rückblickend**; **Rückschlag** *m* setback; **Rückschluss** *m* conclusion; **Rückschritt** *m* retrogression; **rückschrittlich** *adj* reactionary; (*Entwicklung*) retrograde; **Rückseite** *f* back; (*von Münze etc*) reverse; **siehe Rückseite** see over(leaf); **rücksetzen** *vt* (*Comput*) to reset

Rücksicht *f* consideration; **~ nehmen auf** *+akk* to show consideration for; **Rücksichtnahme** *f* consideration

rücksichtslos *adj* inconsiderate; (*Fahren*) reckless; (*unbarmherzig*) ruthless

Rücksichtslosigkeit *f* lack of consideration; (*beim Fahren*) recklessness; (*Unbarmherzigkeit*) ruthlessness

rücksichtsvoll *adj* considerate

Rück- *zW*: **Rücksitz** *m* back seat; **Rückspiegel** *m* (*Aut*) rear-view mirror; **Rückspiel** *nt* return match; **Rücksprache** *f* further discussion *od* talk; **Rücksprache mit jdm nehmen** to confer with sb; **Rückstand** *m* arrears *pl*; (*Verzug*) delay; **rückständig** *adj* backward, out-of-date; (*Zahlungen*) in arrears; **Rückstau** *m* (*Aut*) tailback (*Brit*), line of cars; **Rückstoß** *m* recoil; **Rückstrahler** (**-s, -**) *m* rear reflector; **Rückstrom** *m* (*von Menschen, Fahrzeugen*) return; **Rücktaste** *f* (*an Schreibmaschine*) backspace key; **Rücktritt** *m* resignation; **Rücktrittbremse** *f* backpedal brake; **Rücktrittsklausel** *f* (*Vertrag*) escape clause; **Rückvergütung** *f* repayment; (*Comm*) refund; **rückversichern** *vt, vi* to reinsure ▷ *vr* to check (up *od* back); **Rückversicherung** *f* reinsurance; **rückwärtig** *adj* rear; **rückwärts** *adv* backward(s), back; **Rückwärtsgang** *m* (*Aut*) reverse gear; **im Rückwärtsgang fahren** to reverse; **Rückweg** *m* return journey, way back; **rückwirkend** *adj* retroactive; **Rückwirkung** *f* repercussion; **eine Zahlung mit Rückwirkung vom ...** a payment backdated to ...; **eine Gesetzesänderung mit Rückwirkung vom ...** an amendment made retrospective to ...; **Rückzahlung** *f* repayment; **Rückzieher** (*umg*) *m*: **einen Rückzieher machen** to back out; **Rückzug** *m* retreat; **Rückzugsgefecht** *nt* (*Mil, fig*) rearguard action

rüde ['ry:də] *adj* blunt, gruff

Rüde (**-n, -n**) *m* male dog

Rudel ['ru:dəl] (**-s, -**) *nt* pack; (*von Hirschen*) herd

Ruder ['ru:dər] (**-s, -**) *nt* oar; (*Steuer*) rudder; **das ~ fest in der Hand haben** (*fig*) to be in control of the situation; **Ruderboot** *nt* rowing boat; **Ruderer** (**-s, -**) *m* rower, oarsman

rudern *vt, vi* to row; **mit den Armen ~** (*fig*) to flail one's arms about

Ruf [ru:f] (**-(e)s, -e**) *m* call, cry; (*Ansehen*) reputation; (*Univ: Berufung*) offer of a chair

rufen *unreg vt, vi* to call; (*ausrufen*) to cry; **um Hilfe ~** to call for help; **das kommt mir wie ge~** that's just what I needed

Rüffel ['rʏfəl] (**-s, -**) (*umg*) *m* telling-off, ticking-off

Ruf- *zW*: **Rufmord** *m* character assassination; **Rufname** *m* usual (first) name; **Rufnummer** *f* (tele)phone number; **Rufsäule** *f* (*für Taxi*) telephone; (*an Autobahn*) emergency telephone; **Rufzeichen** *nt* (*Rundf*) call sign; (*Tel*) ringing tone

Rüge ['ry:gə] (**-, -n**) *f* reprimand, rebuke

rügen *vt* to reprimand

Ruhe ['ru:ə] (**-**) *f* rest; (*Ungestörtheit*) peace, quiet; (*Gelassenheit, Stille*) calm; (*Schweigen*) silence; **~!** be quiet!, silence!; **angenehme ~!** sleep well!; **~ bewahren** to stay cool *od* calm; **das lässt ihm keine ~** he can't stop thinking about it; **sich zur ~ setzen** to retire; **die ~ weghaben** (*umg*) to be unflappable; **immer mit der ~** (*umg*) don't panic; **die letzte ~ finden** (*liter*) to be laid to rest; **Ruhelage** *f* (*von Mensch*) reclining position; (*Med: bei Bruch*) immobile position; **ruhelos** *adj* restless

ruhen *vi* to rest; (*Verkehr*) to cease; (*Arbeit*) to stop, cease; (*Waffen*) to be laid down; (*begraben sein*) to lie, be buried

Ruhe- *zW*: **Ruhepause** *f* break; **Ruheplatz** *m* resting place; **Ruhestand** *m* retirement; **Ruhestätte** *f*: **letzte Ruhestätte** final resting place; **Ruhestörung** *f* breach of the peace; **Ruhetag** *m* closing day

ruhig ['ru:ɪç] *adj* quiet; (*bewegungslos*) still; (*Hand*) steady; (*gelassen, friedlich*) calm; (*Gewissen*) clear; **tu das ~** feel free to do that; **etw ~ mit ansehen** (*gleichgültig*) to stand by and watch sth; **du könntest ~ mal etwas für mich tun!** it's about time you did something for me!

Ruhm [ru:m] (**-(e)s**) *m* fame, glory

rühmen ['ry:mən] *vt* to praise ▷ *vr* to boast

rühmlich *adj* praiseworthy; (*Ausnahme*) notable

ruhmlos *adj* inglorious

ruhmreich *adj* glorious

Ruhr [ru:r] (**-**) *f* dysentery

Rührei ['ry:r|aɪ] *nt* scrambled egg

rühren *vt* (*lit, fig*) to move, stir (*auch Koch*) ▷ *vr* (*lit, fig*) to move, stir ▷ *vi*: **~ von** to come *od* stem from; **~ an** *+akk* to touch; (*fig*) to touch on

rührend *adj* touching, moving; **das ist ~ von Ihnen** that is sweet of you

Ruhrgebiet *nt* Ruhr (area)

rührig *adj* active, lively

rührselig *adj* sentimental, emotional
Rührung *f* emotion
Ruin [ru'i:n] (**-s**) *m* ruin; **vor dem ~ stehen** to be on the brink *od* verge of ruin
Ruine (**-, -n**) *f* (*lit, fig*) ruin
ruinieren [rui'ni:rən] *vt* to ruin
rülpsen ['rʏlpsən] *vi* to burp, belch
Rum [rʊm] (**-s, -s**) *m* rum
rum (*umg*) *adv* = **herum**
Rumäne [ru'mɛ:nə] (**-n, -n**) *m* Romanian
Rumänien (**-s**) *nt* Romania
Rumänin *f* Romanian
rumänisch *adj* Romanian
rumfuhrwerken ['rʊmfu:rvɛrkən] (*umg*) *vt* to bustle around
Rummel ['rʊməl] (**-s**) (*umg*) *m* hurly-burly; (*Jahrmarkt*) fair; **Rummelplatz** *m* fairground, fair
rumoren [ru'mo:rən] *vi* to be noisy, make a noise
Rumpelkammer ['rʊmpəlkamər] *f* junk room
rumpeln *vi* to rumble; (*holpern*) to jolt
Rumpf [rʊmpf] (**-(e)s, ⸚e**) *m* trunk, torso; (*Aviat*) fuselage; (*Naut*) hull
rümpfen ['rʏmpfən] *vt* (*Nase*) to turn up
Rumtopf *m soft fruit in rum*
rund [rʊnt] *adj* round ▷*adv* (*etwa*) around; **~ um etw** round sth; **jetzt gehts ~** (*umg*) this is where the fun starts; **wenn er das erfährt, gehts ~** (*umg*) there'll be a to-do when he finds out; **Rundbogen** *m* Norman *od* Romanesque arch; **Rundbrief** *m* circular
Runde ['rʊndə] (**-, -n**) *f* round; (*in Rennen*) lap; (*Gesellschaft*) circle; **die ~ machen** to do the rounds; (*herumgegeben werden*) to be passed round; **über die ~n kommen** (*Sport, fig*) to pull through; **eine ~ spendieren** *od* **schmeißen** (*umg*: *Getränke*) to stand a round
runden *vt* to make round ▷*vr* (*fig*) to take shape
rund- *zW*: **runderneuert** *adj* (*Reifen*) remoulded (*Brit*), remolded (*US*); **Rundfahrt** *f* (round) trip; **Rundfrage** *f*: **Rundfrage (unter** *+dat*) survey (of)
Rundfunk ['rʊntfʊŋk] (**-(e)s**) *m* broadcasting; (*bes Hörfunk*) radio; (*Rundfunkanstalt*) broadcasting corporation; **im ~** on the radio; **Rundfunkanstalt** *f* broadcasting corporation; **Rundfunkempfang** *m* reception; **Rundfunkgebühr** *f* licence (*Brit*), license (*US*); **Rundfunkgerät** *nt* radio set; **Rundfunksendung** *f* broadcast, radio programme (*Brit*) *od* program (*US*)
Rund- *zW*: **Rundgang** *m* (*Spaziergang*) walk; (*von Wachmann*) rounds *pl*; (*von Briefträger etc*) round; (*zur Besichtigung*): **Rundgang (durch)** tour (of); **rundheraus** *adv* straight out, bluntly; **rundherum** *adv* all round; (*fig*: *umg*: *völlig*) totally; **rundlich** *adj* plump, rounded; **Rundreise** *f* round trip; **Rundschreiben** *nt* (*Comm*) circular; **rundum** *adv* all around; (*fig*) completely
Rundung *f* curve, roundness
rundweg *adv* straight out
runter ['rʊntər] (*umg*) *adv* = **herunter; hinunter**; **runterwürgen** (*umg*) *vt* (*Ärger*) to swallow
Runzel ['rʊntsəl] (**-, -n**) *f* wrinkle
runzelig, runzlig *adj* wrinkled
runzeln *vt* to wrinkle; **die Stirn ~** to frown
Rüpel ['ry:pəl] (**-s, -**) *m* lout; **rüpelhaft** *adj* loutish
rupfen ['rʊpfən] *vt* to pluck
Rupfen (**-s, -**) *m* sackcloth
ruppig ['rʊpɪç] *adj* rough, gruff
Rüsche ['ry:ʃə] (**-, -n**) *f* frill
Ruß [ru:s] (**-es**) *m* soot
Russe ['rʊsə] (**-n, -n**) *m* Russian
Rüssel ['rʏsəl] (**-s, -**) *m* snout; (*Elefantenrüssel*) trunk
rußen *vi* to smoke; (*Ofen*) to be sooty
rußig *adj* sooty
Russin *f* Russian
russisch *adj* Russian; **~e Eier** (*Koch*) egg(s) mayonnaise
Russland (**-s**) *nt* Russia
rüsten ['rʏstən] *vt, vi, vr* to prepare; (*Mil*) to arm
rüstig ['rʏstɪç] *adj* sprightly, vigorous; **Rüstigkeit** *f* sprightliness, vigour (*Brit*), vigor (*US*)
rustikal [rʊsti'ka:l] *adj*: **sich ~ einrichten** to furnish one's home in a rustic style
Rüstung ['rʏstʊŋ] *f* preparation; (*Mil*) arming; (*Ritterrüstung*) armour (*Brit*), armor (*US*); (*Waffen etc*) armaments *pl*
Rüstungs- *zW*: **Rüstungsgegner** *m* opponent of the arms race; **Rüstungsindustrie** *f* armaments industry; **Rüstungskontrolle** *f* arms control; **Rüstungswettlauf** *m* arms race
Rüstzeug *nt* tools *pl*; (*fig*) capacity
Rute ['ru:tə] (**-, -n**) *f* rod, switch
Rutsch [rʊtʃ] (**-(e)s, -e**) *m* slide; (*Erdrutsch*) landslide; **guten ~!** (*umg*) have a good New Year!; **Rutschbahn** *f* slide
rutschen *vi* to slide; (*ausrutschen*) to slip; **auf dem Stuhl hin und her ~** to fidget around on one's chair
rutschfest *adj* non-slip
rutschig *adj* slippery
rütteln ['rʏtəln] *vt, vi* to shake, jolt; **daran ist nicht zu ~** (*fig*: *umg*: *an Grundsätzen*) there's no doubt about that
Rüttelschwelle *f* (*Aut*) rumble strips *pl*

Ss

S¹, s¹ [ɛs] *nt* S, s; **S wie Samuel** ≈ S for Sugar
S² [ɛs] *abk* (= *Süden*) S; (= *Seite*) p; (= *Schilling*) S
s² *abk* (= *Sekunde*) sec.; (= *siehe*) v., vid.
Sa. *abk* = **Samstag**
SA (-) *f abk* (= *Sturmabteilung*) SA
s. a. *abk* (= *siehe auch*) see also
Saal [za:l] (**-(e)s, Säle**) *m* hall; (*für Sitzungen etc*) room
Saarland ['za:rlant] (**-s**) *nt* Saarland
Saat [za:t] (**-, -en**) *f* seed; (*Pflanzen*) crop; (*Säen*) sowing; **Saatgut** *nt* seed(s *pl*)
Sabbat ['zabat] (**-s, -e**) *m* sabbath
sabbern ['zabərn] (*umg*) *vi* to dribble
Säbel ['zɛ:bəl] (**-s, -**) *m* sabre (*Brit*), saber (*US*); **Säbelrasseln** *nt* sabre-rattling
Sabotage [zabo'ta:ʒə] (**-, -n**) *f* sabotage
sabotieren [zabo'ti:rən] *vt* to sabotage
Saccharin, Sacharin [zaxa'ri:n] (**-s**) *nt* saccharin
Sachanlagen ['zax|anla:gən] *pl* tangible assets *pl*
Sachbearbeiter, in *m(f)*: ~ **(für)** (*Beamter*) official in charge (of)
Sachbuch *nt* non-fiction book
sachdienlich *adj* relevant, helpful
Sache ['zaxə] (**-, -n**) *f* thing; (*Angelegenheit*) affair, business; (*Frage*) matter; (*Pflicht*) task; (*Thema*) subject; (*Jur*) case; (*Aufgabe*) job; (*Ideal*) cause; (*umg: km/h*): **mit 60/100 ~n** ≈ at 40/60 (mph); **ich habe mir die ~ anders vorgestellt** I had imagined things differently; **er versteht seine ~** he knows what he's doing; **das ist so eine ~** (*umg*) it's a bit tricky; **mach keine ~n!** (*umg*) don't be daft!; **bei der ~ bleiben** (*bei Diskussion*) to keep to the point; **bei der ~ sein** to be with it (*umg*); **das ist ~ der Polizei** this is a matter for the police; **zur ~** to the point; **das ist eine runde ~** that is well-balanced *od* rounded-off
Sachertorte ['zaxərtɔrtə] *f rich chocolate cake*, sachertorte
Sach- *zW*: **sachgemäß** *adj* appropriate, suitable; **Sachkenntnis** *f* (*in Bezug auf Wissensgebiet*) knowledge of the/his *etc* subject; (*in Bezug auf Sachlage*) knowledge of the facts; **sachkundig** *adj* (well-)informed; **sich sachkundig machen** to inform oneself; **Sachlage** *f* situation, state of affairs; **Sachleistung** *f* payment in kind; **sachlich** *adj* matter-of-fact; (*Kritik etc*) objective; (*Irrtum, Angabe*) factual; **bleiben Sie bitte sachlich** don't get carried away (*umg*); (*nicht persönlich werden*) please stay objective
sächlich ['zɛxlɪç] *adj* neuter
Sachregister *nt* subject index
Sachschaden *m* material damage
Sachse ['zaksə] (**-n, -n**) *m* Saxon
Sachsen (**-s**) *nt* Saxony; **Sachsen-Anhalt** (**-s**) *nt* Saxony Anhalt
Sächsin ['zɛksɪn] *f* Saxon
sächsisch ['zɛksɪʃ] *adj* Saxon
sacht, sachte *adv* softly, gently
Sach- *zW*: **Sachverhalt** (**-(e)s, -e**) *m* facts *pl* (of the case); **sachverständig** *adj* (*Urteil*) expert; (*Publikum*) informed; **Sachverständige, r** *f(m)* expert; **Sachzwang** *m* force of circumstances
Sack [zak] (**-(e)s, ¨-e**) *m* sack; (*aus Papier, Plastik*) bag; (*Anat, Zool*) sac; (*umg!: Hoden*) balls *pl* (*!*); (*: Kerl, Bursche*) bastard (*!*); **mit ~ und Pack** (*umg*) with bag and baggage
sacken *vi* to sag, sink
Sackgasse *f* cul-de-sac, dead-end street (*US*)
Sackhüpfen *nt* sack race
Sadismus [za'dɪsmʊs] *m* sadism
Sadist, in [za'dɪst(ɪn)] *m(f)* sadist; **sadistisch** *adj* sadistic
Sadomasochismus [zadomazɔ'xɪsmʊs] *m* sadomasochism
säen ['zɛ:ən] *vt, vi* to sow; **dünn gesät** (*fig*) thin on the ground, few and far between
Safari [za'fa:ri] (**-, -s**) *f* safari
Safe [ze:f] (**-s, -s**) *m od nt* safe
Saft [zaft] (**-(e)s, ¨-e**) *m* juice; (*Bot*) sap; **ohne ~ und Kraft** (*fig*) wishy-washy (*umg*), effete
saftig *adj* juicy; (*Grün*) lush; (*umg: Rechnung, Ohrfeige*) hefty; (*Brief, Antwort*) hard-hitting
Saftladen (*pej: umg*) *m* rum joint
saftlos *adj* dry
Sage ['za:gə] (**-, -n**) *f* saga
Säge ['zɛ:gə] (**-, -n**) *f* saw; **Sägeblatt** *nt* saw blade; **Sägemehl** *nt* sawdust
sagen ['za:gən] *vt, vi*: **(jdm etw) ~** to say (sth to sb), tell (sb sth); **unter uns gesagt** between you and me (and the gatepost (*hum umg*)); **lass dir das gesagt sein** take it from me; **das hat nichts zu ~** that doesn't mean anything; **sagt**

dir der Name etwas? does the name mean anything to you?; **das ist nicht gesagt** that's by no means certain; **sage und schreibe** (whether you) believe it or not
sägen *vt, vi* to saw; (*hum: umg: schnarchen*) to snore, saw wood (*US*)
sagenhaft *adj* legendary; (*umg*) great, smashing
sagenumwoben *adj* legendary
Sägespäne *pl* wood shavings *pl*
Sägewerk *nt* sawmill
sah *etc* [za:] *vb siehe* **sehen**
Sahara [za'ha:ra] *f* Sahara (Desert)
Sahne ['za:nə] (-) *f* cream
Saison [zɛ'zõ:] (**-, -s**) *f* season
saisonal [zɛzo'na:l] *adj* seasonal
Saisonarbeiter *m* seasonal worker
saisonbedingt *adj* seasonal
Saite ['zaɪtə] (**-, -n**) *f* string; **andere ~n aufziehen** (*umg*) to get tough
Saiteninstrument *nt* string(ed) instrument
Sakko ['zako] (**-s, -s**) *m od nt* jacket
Sakrament [zakra'mɛnt] *nt* sacrament
Sakristei [zakrɪs'taɪ] *f* sacristy
Salami [za'la:mi] (**-, -s**) *f* salami
Salat [za'la:t] (**-(e)s, -e**) *m* salad; (*Kopfsalat*) lettuce; **da haben wir den ~!** (*umg*) now we're in a fine mess!; **Salatbesteck** *nt* salad servers *pl*; **Salatplatte** *f* salad; **Salatsoße** *f* salad dressing
Salbe ['zalbə] (**-, -n**) *f* ointment
Salbei ['zalbaɪ] (**-s**) *m* sage
salben *vt* to anoint
Salbung *f* anointing
salbungsvoll *adj* unctuous
saldieren [zal'di:rən] *vt* (*Comm*) to balance
Saldo ['zaldo] (**-s, Salden**) *m* balance; **Saldoübertrag** *m* balance brought *od* carried forward; **Saldovortrag** *m* balance brought *od* carried forward
Säle ['zɛ:lə] *pl von* **Saal**
Salmiak [zalmi'ak] (**-s**) *m* sal ammoniac; **Salmiakgeist** *m* liquid ammonia
Salmonellen [zalmo'nɛlən] *pl* salmonellae *pl*
Salon [za'lɔŋ, za'lõ:] (**-s, -s**) *m* salon; **Salonlöwe** *m* lounge lizard
salopp [za'lɔp] *adj* casual; (*Manieren*) slovenly; (*Sprache*) slangy
Salpeter [zal'pe:tər] (**-s**) *m* saltpetre (*Brit*), saltpeter (*US*); **Salpetersäure** *f* nitric acid
Salto ['zalto] (**-s, -s** *od* **Salti**) *m* somersault
Salut [za'lu:t] (**-(e)s, -e**) *m* salute
salutieren [zalu'ti:rən] *vi* to salute
Salve ['zalvə] (**-, -n**) *f* salvo
Salz [zalts] (**-es, -e**) *nt* salt; **salzarm** *adj* (*Koch*) low-salt; **Salzbergwerk** *nt* salt mine
salzen *unreg vt* to salt
salzig *adj* salty
Salz- *zW*: **Salzkartoffeln** *pl* boiled potatoes *pl*; **Salzsäule** *f*: **zur Salzsäule erstarren** (*fig*) to stand rooted to the spot; **Salzsäure** *f* hydrochloric acid; **Salzstange** *f* pretzel stick; **Salzstreuer** *m* salt cellar; **Salzwasser** *nt* salt water
Sambia ['zambia] (**-s**) *nt* Zambia
sambisch *adj* Zambian
Samen ['za:mən] (**-s, -**) *m* seed; (*Anat*) sperm; **Samenbank** *f* sperm bank; **Samenhandlung** *f* seed shop
sämig ['zɛ:mɪç] *adj* thick, creamy
Sammel- *zW*: **Sammelanschluss** *m* (*Tel*) private (branch) exchange; (*von Privathäusern*) party line; **Sammelantrag** *m* composite motion; **Sammelband** *m* anthology; **Sammelbecken** *nt* reservoir; (*fig*): **Sammelbecken (von)** melting pot (for); **Sammelbegriff** *m* collective term; **Sammelbestellung** *f* collective order; **Sammelbüchse** *f* collecting tin; **Sammelmappe** *f* folder
sammeln *vt* to collect ▷ *vr* to assemble, gather; (*sich konzentrieren*) to collect one's thoughts
Sammelname *m* collective term
Sammelnummer *f* (*Tel*) private exchange number, switchboard number
Sammelsurium [zaməl'zu:riʊm] *nt* hotchpotch (*Brit*), hodgepodge (*US*)
Sammler, in (**-s, -**) *m(f)* collector
Sammlung ['zamlʊŋ] *f* collection; (*Konzentration*) composure
Samstag ['zamsta:k] *m* Saturday; *siehe auch* **Dienstag**
samstags *adv* (on) Saturdays
samt [zamt] *präp +dat* (along) with, together with; **~ und sonders** each and every one (of them); **Samt** (**-(e)s, -e**) *m* velvet; **in Samt und Seide** (*liter*) in silks and satins
Samthandschuh *m*: **jdn mit ~en anfassen** (*umg*) to handle sb with kid gloves
sämtlich ['zɛmtlɪç] *adj* (*alle*) all (the); (*vollständig*) complete; **Schillers ~e Werke** the complete works of Schiller
Sanatorium [zana'to:riʊm] *nt* sanatorium (*Brit*), sanitarium (*US*)
Sand [zant] (**-(e)s, -e**) *m* sand; **das/die gibts wie ~ am Meer** (*umg*) there are piles of it/heaps of them; **im ~e verlaufen** to peter out
Sandale [zan'da:lə] (**-, -n**) *f* sandal
Sandbank *f* sandbank
Sandelholz ['zandəlhɔlts] (**-es**) *nt* sandalwood
sandig ['zandɪç] *adj* sandy
Sand- *zW*: **Sandkasten** *m* sandpit; **Sandkastenspiele** *pl* (*Mil*) sand-table exercises *pl*; (*fig*) tactical manoeuvrings *pl* (*Brit*) *od* maneuverings *pl* (*US*); **Sandkuchen** *m* Madeira cake; **Sandmann** *m*, **Sandmännchen** *nt* (*in Geschichten*) sandman; **Sandpapier** *nt* sandpaper; **Sandstein** *m* sandstone; **sandstrahlen** *vt, vi untr* to sandblast
sandte *etc* ['zantə] *vb siehe* **senden**
Sanduhr *f* hourglass; (*Eieruhr*) egg timer
sanft [zanft] *adj* soft, gentle; **sanftmütig** *adj* gentle, meek
sang *etc* [zaŋ] *vb siehe* **singen**
Sänger, in ['zɛŋər(ɪn)] (**-s, -**) *m(f)* singer
sang-und klanglos (*umg*) *adv* without any ado, quietly

Sani ['zani] (**-s, -s**) *(umg)* *m* = **Sanitäter**
sanieren [za'ni:rən] *vt* to redevelop; *(Betrieb)* to make financially sound; *(Haus)* to renovate ▷ *vr* to line one's pockets; *(Unternehmen)* to become financially sound
Sanierung *f* redevelopment; renovation
sanitär [zani'tɛ:r] *adj* sanitary; **~e Anlagen** sanitation *sing*
Sanitäter [zani'tɛ:tər] (**-s, -**) *m* first-aid attendant; *(in Krankenwagen)* ambulance man; *(Mil)* (medical) orderly
Sanitätsauto *nt* ambulance
sank *etc* [zaŋk] *vb siehe* **sinken**
Sanktion [zaŋktsi'o:n] *f* sanction
sanktionieren [zaŋktsio'ni:rən] *vt* to sanction
sann *etc* [zan] *vb siehe* **sinnen**
Saphir ['za:fi:r] (**-s, -e**) *m* sapphire
Sarde ['zardə] (**-n, -n**) *m* Sardinian
Sardelle [zar'dɛlə] *f* anchovy
Sardine [zar'di:nə] *f* sardine
Sardinien [zar'di:niən] (**-s**) *nt* Sardinia
Sardinier, in (**-s, -**) *m(f)* Sardinian
sardinisch *adj* Sardinian
sardisch *adj* Sardinian
Sarg [zark] (**-(e)s, ¨-e**) *m* coffin; **Sargnagel** *(umg)* *m* *(Zigarette)* coffin nail
Sarkasmus [zar'kasmʊs] *m* sarcasm
sarkastisch [zar'kastɪʃ] *adj* sarcastic
SARS, **Sars** [zars] *abk* (= *Schweres Akutes Respiratorisches Syndrom*) SARS
saß *etc* [zas] *vb siehe* **sitzen**
Satan ['za:tan] (**-s, -e**) *m* Satan; *(fig)* devil
Satansbraten *m* *(hum: umg)* young devil
Satellit [zatɛ'li:t] (**-en, -en**) *m* satellite
Satelliten- *zW*: **Satellitenantenne** *f* satellite dish; **Satellitenfernsehen** *nt* satellite television; **Satellitenfoto** *nt* satellite picture; **Satellitenschüssel** *f* satellite dish; **Satellitenstation** *f* space station
Satin [za'tɛ̃:] (**-s, -s**) *m* satin
Satire [za'ti:rə] (**-, -n**) *f*: **~ (auf** *+akk*) satire (on)
Satiriker [za'ti:rikər] (**-s, -**) *m* satirist
satirisch [za'ti:rɪʃ] *adj* satirical
satt [zat] *adj* full; *(Farbe)* rich, deep; *(blasiert, übersättigt)* well-fed; *(selbstgefällig)* smug; **jdn/etw ~ sein** to be fed-up with sb/sth; **sich ~ essen** to eat one's fill; **~ machen** to be filling; *siehe auch* **satthaben; satthören; sattsehen**
Sattel ['zatəl] (**-s, ¨**) *m* saddle; *(Berg)* ridge; **sattelfest** *adj (fig)* proficient
satteln *vt* to saddle
Sattelschlepper *m* articulated lorry *(Brit)*, artic *(Brit umg)*, semitrailer *(US)*, semi *(US umg)*
Satteltasche *f* saddlebag; *(Gepäcktasche am Fahrrad)* pannier
satthaben *unreg vt*: **jdn/etw ~** to be fed up with sb/sth
satthören *vr*: **sich ~ an** *+dat* to hear enough of
sättigen ['zɛtɪgən] *vt* to satisfy; *(Chem)* to saturate
Sattler (**-s, -**) *m* saddler; *(Polsterer)* upholsterer
sattsehen *unreg vt*: **sich ~ an** *+dat* to see enough of
Satz [zats] (**-es, ¨-e**) *m* *(Gram)* sentence; *(Nebensatz, Adverbialsatz)* clause; *(Theorem)* theorem; *(der gesetzte Text)* type; *(Mus)* movement; *(Comput)* record; *(Briefmarken, Zusammengehöriges, Tennis)* set; *(Kaffeesatz)* grounds *pl*; *(Bodensatz)* dregs *pl*; *(Spesensatz)* allowance; *(Comm)* rate; *(Sprung)* jump; **Satzbau** *m* sentence construction; **Satzgegenstand** *m* *(Gram)* subject; **Satzlehre** *f* syntax; **Satzteil** *m* constituent (of a sentence)
Satzung *f* statute, rule; *(Firma)* (memorandum and) articles of association
satzungsgemäß *adj* statutory
Satzzeichen *nt* punctuation mark
Sau [zaʊ] (**-, Säue**) *f* sow; *(umg)* dirty pig; **die ~ rauslassen** *(fig: umg)* to let it all hang out
sauber ['zaʊbər] *adj* clean; *(anständig)* honest, upstanding; *(umg: großartig)* fantastic, great; *(: ironisch)* fine; **~ sein** *(Kind)* to be (potty-)trained; *(Hund etc)* to be house-trained; **~ halten** to keep clean; **~ machen** to clean; **Sauberkeit** *f* cleanness; *(einer Person)* cleanliness
säuberlich ['zɔʏbərlɪç] *adv* neatly
säubern *vt* to clean; *(Pol etc)* to purge
Säuberung *f* cleaning; purge
Säuberungsaktion *f* cleaning-up operation; *(Pol)* purge
saublöd *(umg)* *adj* bloody *(Brit!)* *od* damn *(!)* stupid
Saubohne *f* broad bean
Sauce ['zo:sə] (**-, -n**) *f* = **Soße**
Sauciere [zosi'e:rə] (**-, -n**) *f* sauce boat
Saudi- [zaʊdi-] *zW*: **Saudi-Araber, in** *m(f)* Saudi; **Saudi-Arabien** (**-s**) *nt* Saudi Arabia; **saudi-arabisch** *adj* Saudi(-Arabian)
sauer ['zaʊər] *adj* sour; *(Chem)* acid; *(umg)* cross; **saurer Regen** acid rain; **~ werden** *(Milch, Sahne)* to go sour, turn; **jdm das Leben ~ machen** to make sb's life a misery; **Sauerbraten** *m braised beef (marinaded in vinegar)*, sauerbraten *(US)*
Sauerei [zaʊə'raɪ] *(umg)* *f* rotten state of affairs, scandal; *(Schmutz etc)* mess; *(Unanständigkeit)* obscenity
Sauerkirsche *f* sour cherry
Sauerkraut (**-(e)s**) *nt* sauerkraut, pickled cabbage
säuerlich ['zɔʏərlɪç] *adj* sourish, tart
Sauer- *zW*: **Sauermilch** *f* sour milk; **Sauerstoff** *m* oxygen; **Sauerstoffgerät** *nt* breathing apparatus; **Sauerteig** *m* leaven
saufen ['zaʊfən] *unreg (umg) vt, vi* to drink, booze; **wie ein Loch ~** *(umg)* to drink like a fish
Säufer, in ['zɔʏfər(ɪn)] (**-s, -**) *(umg)* *m(f)* boozer, drunkard
Sauferei [zaʊfə'raɪ] *f* drinking, boozing; *(Saufgelage)* booze-up
Saufgelage *(pej: umg)* *nt* drinking bout, booze-up
säuft [zɔʏft] *vb siehe* **saufen**
saugen ['zaʊgən] *unreg vt, vi* to suck

säugen ['zɔʏgən] *vt* to suckle
Sauger ['zaʊgər] (**-s, -**) *m* dummy (*Brit*), pacifier (*US*); (*auf Flasche*) teat; (*Staubsauger*) vacuum cleaner, hoover® (*Brit*)
Säugetier *nt* mammal
saugfähig *adj* absorbent
Säugling *m* infant, baby
Säuglingsschwester *f* infant nurse
Sau- *zW*: **Sauhaufen** (*umg*) *m* bunch of layabouts; **saukalt** (*umg*) *adj* bloody (*Brit!*) *od* damn (*!*) cold; **Sauklaue** (*umg*) *f* scrawl
Säule ['zɔʏlə] (**-, -n**) *f* column, pillar
Säulengang *m* arcade
Saum [zaʊm] (**-(e)s, Säume**) *m* hem; (*Naht*) seam
saumäßig (*umg*) *adj* lousy ▷ *adv* lousily
säumen ['zɔʏmən] *vt* to hem; to seam ▷ *vi* to delay, hesitate
säumig ['zɔʏmɪç] *adj* (*geh: Schuldner*) defaulting; (*Zahlung*) outstanding, overdue
Sauna ['zaʊna] (**-, -s**) *f* sauna
Säure ['zɔʏrə] (**-, -n**) *f* acid; (*Geschmack*) sourness, acidity; **säurebeständig** *adj* acid-proof
Saure-Gurken-Zeit (**-**) *f* (*hum: umg*) bad time *od* period; (*in den Medien*) silly season
säurehaltig *adj* acidic
Saurier ['zaʊriər] (**-s, -**) *m* dinosaur
Saus [zaʊs] (**-es**) *m*: **in ~ und Braus leben** to live like a lord
säuseln ['zɔʏzəln] *vi* to murmur; (*Blätter*) to rustle ▷ *vt* to murmur
sausen ['zaʊzən] *vi* to blow; (*umg: eilen*) to rush; (*Ohren*) to buzz; **etw ~ lassen** (*umg*) not to bother with sth
Sau- *zW*: **Saustall** (*umg*) *m* pigsty; **Sauwetter** (*umg*) *nt* bloody (*Brit!*) *od* damn (*!*) awful weather; **sauwohl** (*umg*) *adj*: **ich fühle mich sauwohl** I feel bloody (*Brit!*) *od* really good
Saxofon, Saxophon [zakso'fo:n] (**-s, -e**) *nt* saxophone
SB *abk* = **Selbstbedienung**
S-Bahn *f abk* (*= Schnellbahn*) *high-speed suburban railway or railroad* (*US*)
SBB *abk* (*= Schweizerische Bundesbahnen*) Swiss Railways
s. Br. *abk* (*= südlicher Breite*) southern latitude
Schabe ['ʃa:bə] (**-, -n**) *f* cockroach
schaben *vt* to scrape
Schaber (**-s, -**) *m* scraper
Schabernack (**-(e)s, -e**) *m* trick, prank
schäbig ['ʃɛ:bɪç] *adj* shabby; (*Mensch*) mean; **Schäbigkeit** *f* shabbiness
Schablone [ʃa'blo:nə] (**-, -n**) *f* stencil; (*Muster*) pattern; (*fig*) convention
schablonenhaft *adj* stereotyped, conventional
Schach [ʃax] (**-s, -s**) *nt* chess; (*Stellung*) check; **im ~ stehen** to be in check; **jdn in ~ halten** (*fig*) to stall sb; **Schachbrett** *nt* chessboard
schachern (*pej*) *vi*: **um etw ~** to haggle over sth
Schach- *zW*: **Schachfigur** *f* chessman; **schachmatt** *adj* checkmate; **jdn schachmatt setzen** (*lit*) to (check)mate sb; (*fig*) to snooker sb (*umg*); **Schachpartie** *f* game of chess; **Schachspiel** *nt* game of chess
Schacht [ʃaxt] (**-(e)s, ¨-e**) *m* shaft
Schachtel (**-, -n**) *f* box; (*pej: Frau*) bag, cow (*Brit*); **Schachtelsatz** *m* complicated *od* multi-clause sentence
Schachzug *m* (*auch fig*) move
schade ['ʃa:də] *adj* a pity *od* shame ▷ *interj* (what a) pity *od* shame; **sich** *dat* **für etw zu ~ sein** to consider o.s. too good for sth; **um sie ist es nicht ~** she's no great loss
Schädel ['ʃɛ:dəl] (**-s, -**) *m* skull; **einen dicken ~ haben** (*fig: umg*) to be stubborn; **Schädelbruch** *m* fractured skull
Schaden (**-s, ¨-**) *m* damage; (*Verletzung*) injury; (*Nachteil*) disadvantage; **zu ~ kommen** to suffer; (*physisch*) to be injured; **jdm ~ zufügen** to harm sb
schaden ['ʃa:dən] *vi +dat* to hurt; **einer Sache ~** to damage sth
Schaden- *zW*: **Schadenersatz** *m* compensation, damages *pl*; **Schadenersatz leisten** to pay compensation; **Schadenersatzanspruch** *m* claim for compensation; **schadenersatzpflichtig** *adj* liable for damages; **Schadenfreiheitsrabatt** *m* (*Versicherung*) no-claim(s) bonus; **Schadenfreude** *f* malicious delight; **schadenfroh** *adj* gloating
schadhaft ['ʃa:thaft] *adj* faulty, damaged
schädigen ['ʃɛdɪgən] *vt* to damage; (*Person*) to do harm to, harm
Schädigung *f* damage; harm
schädlich *adj*: **~ (für)** harmful (to); **Schädlichkeit** *f* harmfulness
Schädling *m* pest
Schädlingsbekämpfungsmittel *nt* pesticide
schadlos ['ʃa:tlos] *adj*: **sich ~ halten an** *+dat* to take advantage of
Schadstoff (**-(e)s, -e**) *m* pollutant; **schadstoffarm** *adj* low in pollutants; **schadstoffhaltig** *adj* containing pollutants
Schaf [ʃa:f] (**-(e)s, -e**) *nt* sheep; (*umg: Dummkopf*) twit (*Brit*), dope; **Schafbock** *m* ram
Schäfchen ['ʃɛ:fçən] *nt* lamb; **sein ~ ins Trockene bringen** (*Sprichwort*) to see o.s. all right (*umg*); **Schäfchenwolken** *pl* cirrus clouds *pl*
Schäfer ['ʃɛ:fər] (**-s, -**) *m* shepherd; **Schäferhund** *m* Alsatian (dog) (*Brit*), German shepherd (dog) (*US*); **Schäferin** *f* shepherdess
Schaffen ['ʃafən] (**-s**) *nt* (creative) activity
schaffen[1] *unreg vt* to create; (*Platz*) to make; **sich** *dat* **etw ~** to get o.s. sth; **dafür ist er wie ge~** he's just made for it
schaffen[2] ['ʃafən] *vt* (*erreichen*) to manage, do; (*erledigen*) to finish; (*Prüfung*) to pass; (*transportieren*) to take ▷ *vi* (*tun*) to do; (*umg: arbeiten*) to work; **das ist nicht zu ~** that can't be done; **das hat mich geschafft** it took it out of me; (*nervlich*) it got on top of me; **ich habe damit nichts zu ~** that has nothing to do with me; **jdm (schwer) zu ~**

machen (*zusetzen*) to cause sb (a lot of) trouble; (*bekümmern*) to worry sb (a lot); **sich** *dat* **an etw** *dat* **zu ~ machen** to busy o.s. with sth
Schaffensdrang *m* energy; (*von Künstler*) creative urge
Schaffenskraft *f* creativity
Schaffner, in ['ʃafnər(ɪn)] (**-s, -**) *m(f)* (*Busschaffner*) conductor, conductress; (*Eisenb*) guard (*Brit*), conductor (*US*)
Schaffung *f* creation
Schafskäse *m* sheep's *od* ewe's milk cheese
Schaft [ʃaft] (**-(e)s, ⸚e**) *m* shaft; (*von Gewehr*) stock; (*von Stiefel*) leg; (*Bot*) stalk; (*von Baum*) tree trunk; **Schaftstiefel** *m* high boot
Schakal [ʃa'ka:l] (**-s, -e**) *m* jackal
Schäker, in ['ʃɛ:kər(ɪn)] (**-s, -**) *m(f)* flirt; (*Witzbold*) joker
schäkern *vi* to flirt; to joke
Schal [ʃa:l] (**-s, -s** *od* **-e**) *m* scarf
schal *adj* flat; (*fig*) insipid
Schälchen ['ʃɛ:lçən] *nt* bowl
Schale ['ʃa:lə] (**-, -n**) *f* skin; (*abgeschält*) peel; (*Nussschale, Muschelschale, Eierschale*) shell; (*Geschirr*) dish, bowl; **sich in ~ werfen** (*umg*) to get dressed up
schälen ['ʃɛ:lən] *vt* to peel; to shell ▷ *vr* to peel
Schalk [ʃalk] (**-s, -e** *od* **⸚e**) *m* (*veraltet*) joker
Schall [ʃal] (**-(e)s, -e**) *m* sound; **Name ist ~ und Rauch** what's in a name?; **schalldämmend** *adj* sound-deadening; **Schalldämpfer** *m* (*Aut*) silencer (*Brit*), muffler (*US*); **schalldicht** *adj* soundproof
schallen *vi* to (re)sound
schallend *adj* resounding, loud
Schall- *zW*: **Schallgeschwindigkeit** *f* speed of sound; **Schallgrenze** *f* sound barrier; **Schallmauer** *f* sound barrier; **Schallplatte** *f* record
schalt *etc* [ʃalt] *vb siehe* **schelten**
Schaltbild *nt* circuit diagram
Schaltbrett *nt* switchboard
schalten ['ʃaltən] *vt* to switch, turn ▷ *vi* (*Aut*) to change (gear); (*umg: begreifen*) to catch on; (*reagieren*) to react; **in Reihe/parallel ~** (*Elek*) to connect in series/in parallel; **~ und walten** to do as one pleases
Schalter (**-s, -**) *m* counter; (*an Gerät*) switch; **Schalterbeamte, r** *m* counter clerk; **Schalterstunden** *pl* hours of business *pl*
Schalt- *zW*: **Schalthebel** *m* switch; (*Aut*) gear lever (*Brit*), gearshift (*US*); **Schaltjahr** *nt* leap year; **Schaltknüppel** *m* (*Aut*) gear lever (*Brit*), gearshift (*US*); (*Aviat, Comput*) joystick; **Schaltkreis** *m* (switching) circuit; **Schaltplan** *m* circuit diagram; **Schaltpult** *nt* control desk; **Schaltstelle** *f* (*fig*) coordinating point; **Schaltuhr** *f* time switch
Schaltung *f* switching; (*Elek*) circuit; (*Aut*) gear change
Scham [ʃa:m] (**-**) *f* shame; (*Schamgefühl*) modesty; (*Organe*) private parts *pl*
schämen ['ʃɛ:mən] *vr* to be ashamed
Scham- *zW*: **Schamgefühl** *nt* sense of shame; **Schamhaare** *pl* pubic hair *sing*; **schamhaft** *adj* modest; bashful; **Schamlippen** *pl* labia *pl*, lips *pl* of the vulva; **schamlos** *adj* shameless; (*unanständig*) indecent; (*Lüge*) brazen, barefaced
Schampus ['ʃampʊs] (**-,** *no pl*) (*umg*) *m* champagne, champers (*Brit*)
Schande ['ʃandə] (**-**) *f* disgrace; **zu meiner ~ muss ich gestehen, dass ...** to my shame I have to admit that ...
schänden ['ʃɛndən] *vt* to violate
Schandfleck ['ʃantflɛk] *m*: **er war der ~ der Familie** he was the disgrace of his family
schändlich ['ʃɛntlɪç] *adj* disgraceful, shameful; **Schändlichkeit** *f* disgracefulness, shamefulness
Schandtat (*umg*) *f* escapade, shenanigan
Schändung *f* violation, defilement
Schänke ['ʃɛŋkə] (**-, -n**) *f* = **Schenke**
Schank- *zW*: **Schankerlaubnis** *f*, **Schankkonzession** *f* (publican's) licence (*Brit*), excise license (*US*); **Schanktisch** *m* bar
Schanze ['ʃantsə] (**-, -n**) *f* (*Mil*) fieldwork, earthworks *pl*; (*Sprungschanze*) ski jump
Schar [ʃa:r] (**-, -en**) *f* band, company; (*Vögel*) flock; (*Menge*) crowd; **in ~en** in droves
Scharade [ʃa'ra:də] (**-, -n**) *f* charade
scharen *vr* to assemble, rally
scharenweise *adv* in droves
scharf [ʃarf] *adj* sharp; (*Verstand, Augen*) keen; (*Kälte, Wind*) biting; (*Protest*) fierce; (*Ton*) piercing, shrill; (*Essen*) hot, spicy; (*Munition*) live; (*Maßnahmen*) severe; (*Bewachung*) close, tight; (*Geruch, Geschmack*) pungent, acrid; (*umg: geil*) randy (*Brit*), horny; (*Film*) sexy, blue *attrib*; **~ nachdenken** to think hard; **~ aufpassen/zuhören** to pay close attention/listen closely; **etw ~ einstellen** (*Bild, Diaprojektor etc*) to bring sth into focus; **mit ~em Blick** (*fig*) with penetrating insight; **auf etw** *akk* **~ sein** (*umg*) to be keen on sth; **~e Sachen** (*umg*) hard stuff
Scharfblick *m* (*fig*) penetration
Schärfe ['ʃɛrfə] (**-, -n**) *f* sharpness; (*Strenge*) rigour (*Brit*), rigor (*US*); (*an Kamera, Fernsehen*) focus
schärfen *vt* to sharpen
Schärfentiefe *f* (*Phot*) depth of focus
Scharf- *zW*: **scharfmachen** (*umg*) *vt* to stir up; **Scharfrichter** *m* executioner; **Scharfschießen** *nt* shooting with live ammunition; **Scharfschütze** *m* marksman, sharpshooter; **Scharfsinn** *m* astuteness, shrewdness; **scharfsinnig** *adj* astute, shrewd
Scharlach ['ʃarlax] (**-s, -e**) *m* scarlet; (*Krankheit*) scarlet fever; **Scharlachfieber** *nt* scarlet fever
Scharlatan ['ʃarlatan] (**-s, -e**) *m* charlatan
Scharmützel [ʃar'mʏtsəl] (**-s, -**) *nt* skirmish
Scharnier [ʃar'ni:r] (**-s, -e**) *nt* hinge
Schärpe ['ʃɛrpə] (**-, -n**) *f* sash
scharren ['ʃarən] *vt, vi* to scrape, scratch
Scharte ['ʃartə] (**-, -n**) *f* notch, nick; (*Berg*) wind gap
schartig ['ʃartɪç] *adj* jagged

Schaschlik ['ʃaʃlɪk] (**-s, -s**) *m od nt* (shish) kebab
Schatten ['ʃatən] (**-s, -**) *m* shadow; (*schattige Stelle*) shade; **jdn/etw in den ~ stellen** (*fig*) to put sb/sth in the shade; **Schattenbild** *nt* silhouette; **schattenhaft** *adj* shadowy
Schattenmorelle (**-, -n**) *f* morello cherry
Schatten- *zW*: **Schattenriss** *m* silhouette; **Schattenseite** *f* shady side; (*von Planeten*) dark side; (*fig: Nachteil*) drawback; **Schattenwirtschaft** *f* black economy
schattieren [ʃa'ti:rən] *vt, vi* to shade
Schattierung *f* shading
schattig ['ʃatɪç] *adj* shady
Schatulle [ʃa'tʊlə] (**-, -n**) *f* casket; (*Geldschatulle*) coffer
Schatz [ʃats] (**-es, ¨-e**) *m* treasure; (*Person*) darling; **Schatzamt** *nt* treasury
schätzbar ['ʃɛtsba:r] *adj* assessable
Schätzchen *nt* darling, love
schätzen *vt* (*abschätzen*) to estimate; (*Gegenstand*) to value; (*würdigen*) to value, esteem; (*vermuten*) to reckon; **etw zu ~ wissen** to appreciate sth; **sich glücklich ~** to consider o.s. lucky; **~ lernen** to learn to appreciate
Schatzkammer *f* treasure chamber *od* vault
Schatzmeister *m* treasurer
Schätzung *f* estimate; estimation; valuation; **nach meiner ~ ...** I reckon that ...
schätzungsweise *adv* (*ungefähr*) approximately; (*so vermutet man*) it is thought
Schätzwert *m* estimated value
Schau [ʃaʊ] (**-**) *f* show; (*Ausstellung*) display, exhibition; **etw zur ~ stellen** to make a show of sth, show sth off; **eine ~ abziehen** (*umg*) to put on a show; **Schaubild** *nt* diagram
Schauder ['ʃaʊdər] (**-s, -**) *m* shudder; (*wegen Kälte*) shiver; **schauderhaft** *adj* horrible
schaudern *vi* to shudder; (*wegen Kälte*) to shiver
schauen ['ʃaʊən] *vi* to look; **da schau her!** well, well!
Schauer ['ʃaʊər] (**-s, -**) *m* (*Regenschauer*) shower; (*Schreck*) shudder; **Schauergeschichte** *f* horror story; **schauerlich** *adj* horrific, spine-chilling; **Schauermärchen** (*umg*) *nt* horror story
Schaufel ['ʃaʊfəl] (**-, -n**) *f* shovel; (*Kehrichtschaufel*) dustpan; (*von Turbine*) vane; (*Naut*) paddle; (*Tech*) scoop
schaufeln *vt* to shovel; (*Grab, Grube*) to dig ▷ *vi* to shovel
Schaufenster *nt* shop window; **Schaufensterauslage** *f* window display; **Schaufensterbummel** *m* window-shopping (expedition); **Schaufensterdekorateur, in** *m(f)* window dresser; **Schaufensterpuppe** *f* display dummy
Schaugeschäft *nt* show business
Schaukasten *m* showcase
Schaukel ['ʃaʊkəl] (**-, -n**) *f* swing
schaukeln *vi* to swing, rock ▷ *vt* to rock; **wir werden das Kind** *od* **das schon ~** (*fig: umg*) we'll manage it
Schaukelpferd *nt* rocking horse
Schaukelstuhl *m* rocking chair
Schaulustige, r ['ʃaʊlʊstɪgə(r)] *f(m)* onlooker
Schaum [ʃaʊm] (**-(e)s, Schäume**) *m* foam; (*Seifenschaum*) lather; (*von Getränken*) froth; (*von Bier*) head; **Schaumbad** *nt* bubble bath
schäumen ['ʃɔʏmən] *vi* to foam
Schaumgummi *m* foam (rubber)
schaumig *adj* frothy, foamy
Schaum- *zW*: **Schaumkrone** *f* whitecap; **Schaumschläger** *m* (*fig*) windbag; **Schaumschlägerei** *f* (*fig: umg*) hot air; **Schaumstoff** *m* foam material; **Schaumwein** *m* sparkling wine
Schauplatz *m* scene
Schauprozess *m* show trial
schaurig *adj* horrific, dreadful
Schauspiel *nt* spectacle; (*Theat*) play
Schauspieler, in *m(f)* actor, actress; **schauspielerisch** *adj* (*Können, Leistung*) acting
schauspielern *vi untr* to act
Schauspielhaus *nt* playhouse, theatre (*Brit*), theater (*US*)
Schauspielschule *f* drama school
Schausteller ['ʃaʊʃtɛlər] (**-s, -**) *m person who owns or runs a fairground ride/sideshow etc*
Scheck [ʃɛk] (**-s, -s**) *m* cheque (*Brit*), check (*US*); **Scheckbuch** *nt*, **Scheckheft** *nt* cheque book (*Brit*), check book (*US*)
scheckig *adj* dappled, piebald
Scheckkarte *f* cheque (*Brit*) *od* check (*US*) card, banker's card
scheel [ʃe:l] (*umg*) *adj* dirty; **jdn ~ ansehen** to give sb a dirty look
scheffeln ['ʃɛfəln] *vt* to amass
Scheibe ['ʃaɪbə] (**-, -n**) *f* disc (*Brit*), disk (*US*); (*Brot etc*) slice; (*Glasscheibe*) pane; (*Mil*) target; (*Eishockey*) puck; (*Töpferscheibe*) wheel; (*umg: Schallplatte*) disc (*Brit*), disk (*US*); **von ihm könntest du dir eine ~ abschneiden** (*fig: umg*) you could take a leaf out of his book
Scheiben- *zW*: **Scheibenbremse** *f* (*Aut*) disc brake; **Scheibenkleister** *interj* (*euph: umg*) sugar!; **Scheibenwaschanlage** *f* (*Aut*) windscreen (*Brit*) *od* windshield (*US*) washers *pl*; **Scheibenwischer** *m* (*Aut*) windscreen (*Brit*) *od* windshield (*US*) wiper
Scheich [ʃaɪç] (**-s, -e** *od* **-s**) *m* sheik(h)
Scheide ['ʃaɪdə] (**-, -n**) *f* sheath; (*Anat*) vagina
scheiden *unreg vt* to separate; (*Ehe*) to dissolve ▷ *vi* to depart; (*sich trennen*) to part ▷ *vr* (*Wege*) to divide; (*Meinungen*) to diverge; **sich ~ lassen** to get a divorce; **von dem Moment an waren wir (zwei) geschiedene Leute** (*umg*) after that it was the parting of the ways for us; **aus dem Leben ~** to depart this life
Scheideweg *m* (*fig*) crossroads *sing*
Scheidung *f* (*Ehescheidung*) divorce; **die ~ einreichen** to file a petition for divorce
Scheidungsgrund *m* grounds *pl* for divorce
Scheidungsklage *f* divorce suit
Schein [ʃaɪn] (**-(e)s, -e**) *m* light; (*Anschein*) appearance; (*Geldschein*) (bank)note; (*Bescheinigung*) certificate; **den ~ wahren** to keep up appearances; **etw zum ~ tun**

to pretend to do sth, make a pretence (*Brit*) *od* pretense (*US*) of doing sth; **scheinbar** *adj* apparent
scheinen *unreg vi* to shine; (*Anschein haben*) to seem
Schein- *zW*: **scheinheilig** *adj* hypocritical; **Scheintod** *m* apparent death; **Scheinwerfer** (**-s, -**) *m* floodlight; (*Theat*) spotlight; (*Suchscheinwerfer*) searchlight; (*Aut*) headlight
Scheiß [ʃaɪs] (**-,** *no pl*) (*umg*) *m* bullshit (*!*)
Scheiß- ['ʃaɪs-] (*umg*) *in zw* bloody (*Brit!*); **Scheißdreck** (*umg!*) *m* shit (*!*), crap (*!*); **das geht dich einen Scheißdreck an** it's got bugger-all to do with you (*!*)
Scheiße ['ʃaɪsə] (-) (*umg!*) *f* shit (*!*)
scheißegal (*umg!*) *adj*: **das ist mir doch ~!** I don't give a shit (*!*)
scheißen (*umg!*) *vi* to shit (*!*)
scheißfreundlich (*pej*: *umg*) *adj* as nice as pie (*ironisch*)
Scheißkerl (*umg!*) *m* bastard (*!*), son-of-a-bitch (*US!*)
Scheit [ʃaɪt] (**-(e)s, -e** *od* **-er**) *nt* log
Scheitel ['ʃaɪtəl] (**-s, -**) *m* top; (*Haar*) parting (*Brit*), part (*US*)
scheiteln *vt* to part
Scheitelpunkt *m* zenith, apex
Scheiterhaufen ['ʃaɪtərhaʊfən] *m* (funeral) pyre; (*Hist*: *zur Hinrichtung*) stake
scheitern ['ʃaɪtərn] *vi* to fail
Schelle ['ʃɛlə] (**-, -n**) *f* small bell
schellen *vi* to ring; **es hat geschellt** the bell has gone
Schellfisch ['ʃɛlfɪʃ] *m* haddock
Schelm [ʃɛlm] (**-(e)s, -e**) *m* rogue
Schelmenroman *m* picaresque novel
schelmisch *adj* mischievous, roguish
Schelte ['ʃɛltə] (**-, -n**) *f* scolding
schelten *unreg vt* to scold
Schema ['ʃe:ma] (**-s, -s** *od* **-ta**) *nt* scheme, plan; (*Darstellung*) schema; **nach ~ F** quite mechanically
schematisch [ʃe'ma:tɪʃ] *adj* schematic; (*pej*) mechanical
Schemel ['ʃe:məl] (**-s, -**) *m* (foot)stool
schemenhaft *adj* shadowy
Schenke (**-, -n**) *f* tavern, inn
Schenkel ['ʃɛŋkəl] (**-s, -**) *m* thigh; (*Math*: *von Winkel*) side
schenken ['ʃɛŋkən] *vt* (*lit, fig*) to give; (*Getränk*) to pour; **ich möchte nichts geschenkt haben!** (*lit*) I don't want any presents!; (*fig*: *bevorzugt werden*) I don't want any special treatment!; **sich** *dat* **etw ~** (*umg*) to skip sth; **jdm etw ~** (*erlassen*) to let sb off sth; **ihm ist nie etwas geschenkt worden** (*fig*) he never had it easy; **das ist geschenkt!** (*billig*) that's a giveaway!; (*nichts wert*) that's worthless!
Schenkung *f* gift
Schenkungsurkunde *f* deed of gift
scheppern ['ʃɛpərn] (*umg*) *vi* to clatter
Scherbe ['ʃɛrbə] (**-, -n**) *f* broken piece, fragment; (*archäologisch*) potsherd
Schere ['ʃe:rə] (**-, -n**) *f* scissors *pl*; (*groß*) shears *pl*; (*Zool*) pincer; (*von Hummer, Krebs etc*) pincer, claw; **eine ~** a pair of scissors
scheren *unreg vt* to cut; (*Schaf*) to shear; (*stören*) to bother ▷ *vr* (*sich kümmern*) to care; **scher dich (zum Teufel)!** get lost!
Scherenschleifer (**-s, -**) *m* knife grinder
Scherenschnitt *m* silhouette
Schererei [ʃe:rə'raɪ] (*umg*) *f* bother, trouble
Scherflein ['ʃɛrflaɪn] *nt* mite, bit
Scherz [ʃɛrts] (**-es, -e**) *m* joke; fun; **scherzen** *vi* to joke; (*albern*) to banter; **Scherzfrage** *f* conundrum; **scherzhaft** *adj* joking, jocular
Scheu [ʃɔʏ] (-) *f* shyness; (*Ehrfurcht*) awe; (*Angst*): **~ (vor** *+dat***)** fear (of)
scheu [ʃɔʏ] *adj* shy
Scheuche (**-, -n**) *f* scarecrow
scheuchen ['ʃɔʏçən] *vt* to scare (off)
scheuen *vr*: **sich ~ vor** *+dat* to be afraid of, shrink from ▷ *vt* to shun ▷ *vi* (*Pferd*) to shy; **weder Mühe noch Kosten ~** to spare neither trouble nor expense
Scheuer ['ʃɔʏər] (**-, -n**) *f* barn
Scheuer- *zW*: **Scheuerbürste** *f* scrubbing brush; **Scheuerlappen** *m* floorcloth (*Brit*), scrubbing rag (*US*); **Scheuerleiste** *f* skirting board
scheuern *vt* to scour; (*mit Bürste*) to scrub ▷ *vr*: **sich** *akk* **(wund) ~** to chafe o.s.; **jdm eine ~** (*umg*) to clout sb one
Scheuklappe *f* blinker
Scheune ['ʃɔynə] (**-, -n**) *f* barn
Scheunendrescher (**-s, -**) *m*: **er frisst wie ein ~** (*umg*) he eats like a horse
Scheusal ['ʃɔʏza:l] (**-s, -e**) *nt* monster
scheußlich ['ʃɔʏslɪç] *adj* dreadful, frightful; **Scheußlichkeit** *f* dreadfulness
Schi [ʃi:] *m* = **Ski**
Schicht [ʃɪçt] (**-, -en**) *f* layer; (*Klasse*) class, level; (*in Fabrik etc*) shift; **Schichtarbeit** *f* shift work
schichten *vt* to layer, stack
Schichtwechsel *m* change of shifts
schick [ʃɪk] *adj* = **chic**
schicken *vt* to send ▷ *vr*: **sich ~ (in** *+akk***)** to resign o.s. (to) ▷ *vb unpers* (*anständig sein*) to be fitting
Schickeria [ʃɪkə'ri:a] *f* (*ironisch*) in-people *pl*
Schicki ['ʃɪkɪ], **Schickimicki** ['ʃɪkɪ'mɪkɪ] (**-s, -s**) (*umg*) *m* trendy
schicklich *adj* proper, fitting
Schicksal (**-s, -e**) *nt* fate
schicksalhaft *adj* fateful
Schicksalsschlag *m* great misfortune, blow
Schickse ['ʃɪksə] (**-, -n**) (*umg*) *f* floozy, shiksa (*US*)
Schiebedach *nt* (*Aut*) sunroof, sunshine roof
schieben ['ʃi:bən] *unreg vt* (*auch Drogen*) to push; (*Schuld*) to put; (*umg*: *handeln mit*) to traffic in; **die Schuld auf jdn ~** to put the blame on (to) sb; **etw vor sich** *dat* **her ~** (*fig*) to put sth off
Schieber (**-s, -**) *m* slide; (*Besteckteil*) pusher; (*Person*) profiteer; (*umg*: *Schwarzhändler*) black marketeer; (*: Waffenschieber*) gunrunner;

(: *Drogenschieber*) pusher
Schiebetür *f* sliding door
Schieblehre *f* (*Math*) calliper (*Brit*) *od* caliper (*US*) rule
Schiebung *f* fiddle; **das war doch ~** (*umg*) that was rigged *od* a fix
schied *etc* [ʃi:t] *vb siehe* **scheiden**
Schieds- *zW*: **Schiedsgericht** *nt* court of arbitration; **Schiedsmann** (**-(e)s**, *pl* **-männer**) *m* arbitrator; **Schiedsrichter** *m* referee, umpire; (*Schlichter*) arbitrator; **schiedsrichtern** *vi untr* to referee, umpire; to arbitrate; **Schiedsspruch** *m* (arbitration) award; **Schiedsverfahren** *nt* arbitration
schief [ʃi:f] *adj* crooked; (*Ebene*) sloping; (*Turm*) leaning; (*Winkel*) oblique; (*Blick*) wry; (*Vergleich*) distorted ▷ *adv* crookedly; (*ansehen*) askance; **auf die ~e Bahn geraten** (*fig*) to leave the straight and narrow; **etw ~ stellen** to slope sth; *siehe auch* **schiefgehen; schiefliegen**
Schiefer ['ʃi:fər] (**-s, -**) *m* slate; **Schieferdach** *nt* slate roof; **Schiefertafel** *f* (child's) slate
schiefgehen (*umg*: *unreg*: *vi* to go wrong; **es wird schon ~!** (*hum*) it'll be OK
schieflachen (*umg*) *vr* to kill o.s. laughing
schiefliegen (*umg*: *unreg*: *vi* to be wrong, be on the wrong track (*umg*)
schielen ['ʃi:lən] *vi* to squint; **nach etw ~** (*fig*) to eye sth up
schien *etc* [ʃi:n] *vb siehe* **scheinen**
Schienbein *nt* shinbone
Schiene ['ʃi:nə] *f* rail; (*Med*) splint
schienen *vt* to put in splints
Schienenbus *m* railcar
Schienenstrang *m* (*Eisenb etc*) (section of) track
schier [ʃi:r] *adj* pure; (*fig*) sheer ▷ *adv* nearly, almost
Schießbude *f* shooting gallery
Schießbudenfigur (*umg*) *f* clown, ludicrous figure
schießen ['ʃi:sən] *unreg vi* to shoot; (*Salat etc*) to run to seed ▷ *vt* to shoot; (*Ball*) to kick; (*Geschoss*) to fire; **~ auf** *+akk* to shoot at; **aus dem Boden ~** (*lit, fig*) to spring *od* sprout up; **jdm durch den Kopf ~** (*fig*) to flash through sb's mind
Schießerei [ʃi:sə'raɪ] *f* shoot-out, gun battle
Schieß- *zW*: **Schießgewehr** *nt* (*hum*) gun; **Schießhund** *m*: **wie ein Schießhund aufpassen** (*umg*) to watch like a hawk; **Schießplatz** *m* firing range; **Schießpulver** *nt* gunpowder; **Schießscharte** *f* embrasure; **Schießstand** *m* rifle *od* shooting range
Schiff [ʃɪf] (**-(e)s, -e**) *nt* ship, vessel; (*Kirchenschiff*) nave
Schiffahrt *f siehe* **Schifffahrt**
Schiff- *zw***: **schiffbar** *adj* navigable; **Schiffbau** *m* shipbuilding; **Schiffbruch** *m* shipwreck; **Schiffbruch erleiden** (*lit*) to be shipwrecked; (*fig*) to fail; (*Unternehmen*) to founder; **schiffbrüchig** *adj* shipwrecked
Schiffchen *nt* small boat; (*Weben*) shuttle; (*Mütze*) forage cap
Schiffer (**-s, -**) *m* boatman, sailor; (*von Lastkahn*) bargee
Schiff- *zW*: **Schifffahrt** *f* shipping; (*Reise*) voyage; **Schifffahrtslinie** *f* shipping route; **Schiffschaukel** *f* swing boat
Schiffs- *zW*: **Schiffsjunge** *m* cabin boy; **Schiffskörper** *m* hull; **Schiffsladung** *f* cargo, shipload; **Schiffsplanke** *f* gangplank; **Schiffsschraube** *f* ship's propeller
Schiit [ʃi:it] (**-en, -en**) *m* Shiite; **schiitisch** *adj* Shiite
Schikane [ʃi'ka:nə] (**-, -n**) *f* harassment; dirty trick; **mit allen ~n** with all the trimmings; **das hat er aus reiner ~ gemacht** he did it out of sheer bloody-mindedness
schikanieren [ʃika'ni:rən] *vt* to harass; (*Ehepartner*) to mess around; (*Mitschüler*) to bully
schikanös [ʃika'nø:s] *adj* (*Mensch*) bloody-minded; (*Maßnahme etc*) harassing
Schild[1] [ʃɪlt] (**-(e)s, -e**) *m* shield; (*Mützenschild*) peak, visor; **etwas im ~e führen** to be up to something
Schild[2] [ʃɪlt] (**-(e)s, -er**) *nt* sign; (*Namensschild*) nameplate; (*an Monument, Haus, Grab*) plaque; (*Etikett*) label
Schildbürger *m* duffer, blockhead
Schilddrüse *f* thyroid gland
schildern ['ʃɪldərn] *vt* to describe; (*Menschen etc*) to portray; (*skizzieren*) to outline
Schilderung *f* description; portrayal
Schildkröte *f* tortoise; (*Wasserschildkröte*) turtle
Schildkrötensuppe *f* turtle soup
Schilf [ʃɪlf] (**-(e)s, -e**) *nt*, **Schilfrohr** *nt* (*Pflanze*) reed; (*Material*) reeds *pl*, rushes *pl*
Schillerlocke ['ʃɪlərlɔkə] *f* (*Gebäck*) cream horn; (*Räucherfisch*) *strip of smoked rock salmon*
schillern ['ʃɪlərn] *vi* to shimmer
schillernd *adj* iridescent; (*fig: Charakter*) enigmatic
Schilling ['ʃɪlɪŋ] (**-s, -** *od* (*Schillingstücke*) **-e**) (*Österr*) *m* schilling
schilt [ʃɪlt] *vb siehe* **schelten**
Schimmel ['ʃɪməl] (**-s, -**) *m* mould (*Brit*), mold (*US*); (*Pferd*) white horse
schimmelig *adj* mouldy (*Brit*), moldy (*US*)
schimmeln *vi* to go mouldy (*Brit*) *od* moldy (*US*)
Schimmer ['ʃɪmər] (**-s**) *m* glimmer; **keinen (blassen) ~ von etw haben** (*umg*) not to have the slightest idea about sth
schimmern *vi* to glimmer; (*Seide, Perlen*) to shimmer
schimmlig *adj* = **schimmelig**
Schimpanse [ʃɪm'panzə] (**-n, -n**) *m* chimpanzee
Schimpf [ʃɪmpf] (**-(e)s, -e**) *m* disgrace; **mit ~ und Schande** in disgrace
schimpfen *vi* (*sich beklagen*) to grumble; (*fluchen*) to curse
Schimpfkanonade *f* barrage of abuse
Schimpfwort *nt* term of abuse
Schindel ['ʃɪndəl] (**-, -n**) *f* shingle
schinden ['ʃɪndən] *unreg vt* to maltreat, drive

too hard ▷ *vr*: **sich ~ (mit)** to sweat and strain (at), toil away (at); **Eindruck ~** (*umg*) to create an impression

Schinder (**-s, -**) *m* knacker; (*fig*) slave driver

Schinderei [ʃındəˈraı] *f* grind, drudgery

Schindluder [ˈʃıntluːdər] *nt*: **mit etw ~ treiben** to muck *od* mess sth about; (*Vorrecht*) to abuse sth

Schinken [ˈʃıŋkən] (**-s, -**) *m* ham; (*gekocht und geräuchert*) gammon; (*pej: umg: Theaterstück etc*) hackneyed and clichéd play *etc*; **Schinkenspeck** *m* bacon

Schippe [ˈʃıpə] (**-, -n**) *f* shovel; **jdn auf die ~ nehmen** (*fig: umg*) to pull sb's leg

schippen *vt* to shovel

Schirm [ʃırm] (**-(e)s, -e**) *m* (*Regenschirm*) umbrella; (*Sonnenschirm*) parasol, sunshade; (*Wandschirm, Bildschirm*) screen; (*Lampenschirm*) (lamp)shade; (*Mützenschirm*) peak; (*Pilzschirm*) cap; **Schirmbildaufnahme** *f* X-ray; **Schirmherr, in** *m(f)* patron(ess); **Schirmherrschaft** *f* patronage; **Schirmmütze** *f* peaked cap; **Schirmständer** *m* umbrella stand

Schiss *m*: **~ haben** (*umg*) to be shit scared (*!*)

schiss *etc* [ʃıs] *vb siehe* **scheißen**

schizophren [ʃitsoˈfreːn] *adj* schizophrenic

Schizophrenie [ʃitsofreˈniː] *f* schizophrenia

schlabbern [ˈʃlabərn] (*umg*) *vt, vi* to slurp

Schlacht [ʃlaxt] (**-, -en**) *f* battle

schlachten *vt* to slaughter, kill

Schlachtenbummler (*umg*) *m* visiting football fan

Schlachter (**-s, -**) *m* butcher

Schlacht- *zW*: **Schlachtfeld** *nt* battlefield; **Schlachtfest** *nt country feast at which freshly slaughtered meat is served*; **Schlachthaus** *nt*, **Schlachthof** *m* slaughterhouse, abattoir (*Brit*); **Schlachtopfer** *nt* sacrifice; (*Mensch*) human sacrifice; **Schlachtplan** *m* battle plan; (*fig*) plan of action; **Schlachtruf** *m* battle cry, war cry; **Schlachtschiff** *nt* battleship; **Schlachtvieh** *nt* animals *pl* kept for meat

Schlacke [ˈʃlakə] (**-, -n**) *f* slag

schlackern (*umg*) *vi* to tremble; (*Kleidung*) to hang loosely, be baggy; **mit den Ohren ~** (*fig*) to be (left) speechless

Schlaf [ʃlaːf] (**-(e)s**) *m* sleep; **um seinen ~ kommen** *od* **gebracht werden** to lose sleep; **Schlafanzug** *m* pyjamas *pl* (*Brit*), pajamas *pl* (*US*)

Schläfchen [ˈʃlɛːfçən] *nt* nap

Schläfe (**-, -n**) *f* (*Anat*) temple

schlafen *unreg vi* to sleep; (*umg: nicht aufpassen*) to be asleep; **~ gehen** to go to bed; **bei jdm ~** to stay overnight with sb; **Schlafengehen** *nt* going to bed

Schlafenszeit *f* bedtime

Schläfer, in [ˈʃlɛːfər(ın)] (**-s, -**) *m(f)* sleeper

schlaff [ʃlaf] *adj* slack; (*Haut*) loose; (*Muskeln*) flabby; (*energielos*) limp; (*erschöpft*) exhausted; **Schlaffheit** *f* slackness; looseness; flabbiness; limpness; exhaustion

Schlafgelegenheit *f* place to sleep

Schlafittchen [ʃlaˈfıtçən] (*umg*) *nt*: **jdn am** *od* **beim ~ nehmen** to take sb by the scruff of the neck

Schlaf- *zW*: **Schlafkrankheit** *f* sleeping sickness; **Schlaflied** *nt* lullaby; **schlaflos** *adj* sleepless; **Schlaflosigkeit** *f* sleeplessness, insomnia; **Schlafmittel** *nt* sleeping drug; (*fig, ironisch*) soporific; **Schlafmütze** (*umg*) *f* dope

schläfrig [ˈʃlɛːfrıç] *adj* sleepy

Schlaf- *zW*: **Schlafrock** *m* dressing gown; **Apfel im Schlafrock** baked apple in puff pastry; **Schlafsaal** *m* dormitory; **Schlafsack** *m* sleeping bag

schläft [ʃlɛːft] *vb siehe* **schlafen**

Schlaf- *zW*: **Schlaftablette** *f* sleeping pill; **schlaftrunken** *adj* drowsy, half-asleep; **Schlafwagen** *m* sleeping car, sleeper; **schlafwandeln** *vi untr* to sleepwalk; **Schlafwandler, in** (**-s, -**) *m(f)* sleepwalker; **Schlafzimmer** *nt* bedroom

Schlag [ʃlaːk] (**-(e)s, ⸚e**) *m* (*lit, fig*) blow; (*auch Med*) stroke; (*Pulsschlag, Herzschlag*) beat; (*Elek*) shock; (*Blitzschlag*) bolt, stroke; (*Glockenschlag*) chime; (*Autotür*) car door; (*umg: Portion*) helping; (*: Art*) kind, type; **Schläge** *pl* (*Tracht Prügel*) beating *sing*; **~ acht Uhr** (*umg*) on the stroke of eight; **mit einem ~** all at once; **~ auf Schlag** in rapid succession; **die haben keinen ~ getan** (*umg*) they haven't done a stroke (of work); **ich dachte, mich trifft der ~** (*umg*) I was thunderstruck; **vom gleichen ~ sein** to be cast in the same mould (*Brit*) *od* mold (*US*); (*pej*) to be tarred with the same brush; **ein ~ ins Wasser** (*umg*) a wash-out; **Schlagabtausch** *m* (*Boxen*) exchange of blows; (*fig*) (verbal) exchange; **Schlagader** *f* artery; **Schlaganfall** *m* stroke; **schlagartig** *adj* sudden, without warning; **Schlagbaum** *m* barrier; **Schlagbohrer** *m* percussion drill

Schlägel [ˈʃlɛːgl] (**-s, -**) *m* drumstick; (*Hammer*) hammer

schlagen [ˈʃlaːgən] *unreg vt* to strike, hit; (*wiederholt schlagen, besiegen*) to beat; (*Glocke*) to ring; (*Stunde*) to strike; (*Kreis, Bogen*) to describe; (*Purzelbaum*) to do; (*Sahne*) to whip; (*Schlacht*) to fight; (*einwickeln*) to wrap ▷ *vi* to strike, hit; to beat; to ring; to strike ▷ *vr* to fight; **um sich ~** to lash out; **ein Ei in die Pfanne ~** to crack an egg into the pan; **eine ge~e Stunde** a full hour; **na ja, ehe ich mich ~ lasse!** (*hum: umg*) I suppose you could twist my arm; **nach jdm ~** (*fig*) to take after sb; **sich gut ~** (*fig*) to do well; **sich nach links/Norden ~** to strike out to the left/(for the) north; **sich auf jds Seite** *akk* **~** to side with sb; (*die Fronten wechseln*) to go over to sb

schlagend *adj* (*Beweis*) convincing; **~e Wetter** (*Min*) firedamp

Schlager [ˈʃlaːgər] (**-s, -**) *m* (*Mus, fig*) hit

Schläger [ˈʃlɛːgər] (**-s, -**) *m* brawler; (*Sport*) bat; (*Tennis etc*) racket; (*Golf*) club; (*Hockeyschläger*) hockey stick

Schlägerei [ʃlɛːgəˈraɪ] *f* fight, punch-up
Schlagersänger *m* pop singer
Schlägertyp (*umg*) *m* thug
Schlag- *zW*: **schlagfertig** *adj* quick-witted; **Schlagfertigkeit** *f* ready wit, quickness of repartee; **Schlaginstrument** *nt* percussion instrument; **Schlagkraft** *f* (*lit, fig*) power; (*Mil*) strike power; (*Boxen*) punch(ing power); **schlagkräftig** *adj* powerful; (*Beweise*) clear-cut; **Schlagloch** *nt* pothole; **Schlagobers** **(-, -)** (*Österr*) *nt*, **Schlagrahm** *m*, **Schlagsahne** *f* (whipped) cream; **Schlagseite** *f* (*Naut*) list; **Schlagstock** *m* (*form*) truncheon (*Brit*), nightstick (*US*)
schlägt [ʃlɛːkt] *vb siehe* **schlagen**
Schlag- *zW*: **Schlagwort** *nt* slogan, catch phrase; **Schlagzeile** *f* headline; **Schlagzeilen machen** (*umg*) to hit the headlines; **Schlagzeug** *nt* drums *pl*; (*in Orchester*) percussion; **Schlagzeuger** **(-s, -)** *m* drummer; percussionist
schlaksig [ˈʃlaːksɪç] (*umg*) *adj* gangling, gawky
Schlamassel [ʃlaˈmasəl] **(-s, -)** (*umg*) *m* mess
Schlamm [ʃlam] **(-(e)s, -e)** *m* mud
schlammig *adj* muddy
Schlampe [ˈʃlampə] **(-, -n)** (*umg*) *f* slattern, slut
schlampen (*umg*) *vi* to be sloppy
Schlamperei [ʃlampəˈraɪ] (*umg*) *f* disorder, untidiness; (*schlechte Arbeit*) sloppy work
schlampig (*umg*) *adj* slovenly, sloppy
schlang *etc* [ʃlaŋ] *vb siehe* **schlingen**
Schlange [ˈʃlaŋə] **(-, -n)** *f* snake; (*Menschenschlange*) queue (*Brit*), line (*US*); **~ stehen** to (form a) queue (*Brit*), stand in line (*US*); **eine falsche ~** a snake in the grass
schlängeln [ˈʃlɛŋəln] *vr* to twist, wind; (*Fluss*) to meander
Schlangen- *zW*: **Schlangenbiss** *m* snake bite; **Schlangengift** *nt* snake venom; **Schlangenlinie** *f* wavy line
schlank [ʃlaŋk] *adj* slim, slender; **Schlankheit** *f* slimness, slenderness; **Schlankheitskur** *f* diet
schlapp [ʃlap] *adj* limp; (*locker*) slack; (*umg: energielos*) listless; (*nach Krankheit etc*) run-down
Schlappe **(-, -n)** (*umg*) *f* setback
Schlappen **(-s, -)** (*umg*) *m* slipper
schlapp- *zW*: **Schlappheit** *f* limpness; slackness; **Schlapphut** *m* slouch hat; **schlappmachen** (*umg*) *vi* to wilt, droop; **Schlappschwanz** (*pej: umg*) *m* weakling, softy
Schlaraffenland [ʃlaˈrafənlant] *nt* land of milk and honey
schlau [ʃlaʊ] *adj* crafty, cunning; **ich werde nicht ~ aus ihm** I don't know what to make of him; **Schlauberger** **(-s, -)** (*umg*) *m* clever Dick
Schlauch [ʃlaʊx] **(-(e)s, Schläuche)** *m* hose; (*in Reifen*) inner tube; (*umg: Anstrengung*) grind; **auf dem ~ stehen** (*umg*) to be in a jam *od* fix; **Schlauchboot** *nt* rubber dinghy
schlauchen (*umg*) *vt* to tell on, exhaust
schlauchlos *adj* (*Reifen*) tubeless
Schläue [ˈʃlɔʏə] **(-)** *f* cunning
Schlaufe [ˈʃlaʊfə] **(-, -n)** *f* loop; (*Aufhänger*) hanger
Schlauheit *f* cunning
Schlaukopf *m* clever Dick
Schlawiner [ʃlaˈviːnər] **(-s, -)** *m* (*hum: umg*) villain, rogue
schlecht [ʃlɛçt] *adj* bad; (*ungenießbar*) bad, off (*Brit*) ▷ *adv*: **jdm geht es ~** sb is in a bad way; **heute geht es ~** today is not very convenient; **er kann ~ Nein sagen** he finds it hard to say no, he can't say no; **jdm ist ~** sb feels sick *od* ill; **~ und recht** after a fashion; **auf jdn ~ zu sprechen sein** not to have a good word to say for sb; **er hat nicht ~ gestaunt** (*umg*) he wasn't half surprised; *siehe auch* **schlechtmachen**
schlechterdings *adv* simply
Schlecht- *zW*: **Schlechtheit** *f* badness; **schlechthin** *adv* simply; **der Dramatiker schlechthin** THE playwright
Schlechtigkeit *f* badness; (*Tat*) bad deed
schlechtmachen *vt* to run down, denigrate
schlecken [ˈʃlɛkən] *vt, vi* to lick
Schlegel [ˈʃleːgəl] **(-s, -)** *m* (*Koch*) leg; *siehe auch* **Schlägel**
schleichen [ˈʃlaɪçən] *unreg vi* to creep, crawl
schleichend *adj* creeping; (*Krankheit, Gift*) insidious
Schleichweg *m*: **auf ~en** (*fig*) on the quiet
Schleichwerbung *f*: **eine ~** a plug
Schleie [ˈʃlaɪə] **(-, -n)** *f* tench
Schleier [ˈʃlaɪər] **(-s, -)** *m* veil; **Schleiereule** *f* barn owl; **schleierhaft** (*umg*) *adj*: **jdm schleierhaft sein** to be a mystery to sb
Schleife [ˈʃlaɪfə] **(-, -n)** *f* (*auch Comput*) loop; (*Band*) bow; (*Kranzschleife*) ribbon
schleifen[1] *vt* to drag; (*Mil: Festung*) to raze ▷ *vi* to drag; **die Kupplung ~ lassen** (*Aut*) to slip the clutch
schleifen[2] *unreg vt* to grind; (*Edelstein*) to cut; (*Mil: Soldaten*) to drill
Schleifmaschine *f* sander; (*in Fabrik*) grinding machine
Schleifstein *m* grindstone
Schleim [ʃlaɪm] **(-(e)s, -e)** *m* slime; (*Med*) mucus; (*Koch*) gruel; **Schleimhaut** *f* mucous membrane
schleimig *adj* slimy
schlemmen [ˈʃlɛmən] *vi* to feast
Schlemmer, in **(-s, -)** *m(f)* gourmet, bon vivant
Schlemmerei [ʃlɛməˈraɪ] *f* feasting
schlendern [ˈʃlɛndərn] *vi* to stroll
Schlendrian [ˈʃlɛndriaːn] **(-(e)s)** *m* sloppy way of working
Schlenker [ˈʃlɛŋkər] **(-s, -)** *m* swerve
schlenkern *vt, vi* to swing, dangle
Schleppe [ˈʃlɛpə] **(-, -n)** *f* train
schleppen *vt* to drag; (*Auto, Schiff*) to tow; (*tragen*) to lug
schleppend *adj* dragging; (*Bedienung, Abfertigung*) sluggish, slow
Schlepper **(-s, -)** *m* tractor; (*Schiff*) tug
Schleppkahn *m* (canal) barge

Schlepptau *nt* towrope; **jdn ins ~ nehmen** (*fig*) to take sb in tow
Schlesien ['ʃle:ziən] (**-s**) *nt* Silesia
Schlesier, in (**-s, -**) *m(f)* Silesian
schlesisch *adj* Silesian
Schleswig-Holstein ['ʃle:svıç'hɔlʃtaın] (**-s**) *nt* Schleswig-Holstein
Schleuder ['ʃlɔydər] (**-, -n**) *f* catapult; (*Wäscheschleuder*) spin-dryer; (*Zentrifuge*) centrifuge; **Schleuderhonig** *m* extracted honey
schleudern *vt* to hurl; (*Wäsche*) to spin-dry ▷ *vi* (*Aut*) to skid; **ins S~ kommen** (*Aut*) to go into a skid; (*fig: umg*) to run into trouble
Schleuder- *zW*: **Schleuderpreis** *m* give-away price; **Schleudersitz** *m* (*Aviat*) ejector seat; (*fig*) hot seat; **Schleuderware** *f* cut-price (*Brit*) *od* cut-rate (*US*) goods *pl*
schleunig ['ʃlɔynıç] *adj* prompt, speedy; (*Schritte*) quick
schleunigst *adv* straight away
Schleuse ['ʃlɔyzə] (**-, -n**) *f* lock; (*Schleusentor*) sluice
schleusen *vt* (*Schiffe*) to pass through a lock, lock; (*Wasser*) to channel; (*Menschen*) to filter; (*fig: heimlich*) to smuggle
Schlich (**-(e)s, -e**) *m* dodge, trick; **jdm auf die ~e kommen** to get wise to sb
schlich *etc* [ʃlıç] *vb siehe* **schleichen**
schlicht [ʃlıçt] *adj* simple, plain
schlichten *vt* to smooth; (*beilegen*) to settle; (*Streit: vermitteln*) to mediate, arbitrate
Schlichter, in (**-s, -**) *m(f)* mediator, arbitrator
Schlichtheit *f* simplicity, plainness
Schlichtung *f* settlement; arbitration
Schlick [ʃlık] (**-(e)s, -e**) *m* mud; (*Ölschlick*) slick
schlief *etc* [ʃli:f] *vb siehe* **schlafen**
Schließe ['ʃli:sə] (**-, -n**) *f* fastener
schließen ['ʃli:sən] *unreg vt* to close, shut; (*beenden*) to close; (*Freundschaft, Bündnis, Ehe*) to enter into; (*Comput: Datei*) to close; (*folgern*): **~ (aus)** to infer (from) ▷ *vi, vr* to close, shut; **auf etw** *akk* **~ lassen** to suggest sth; **jdn/etw in sein Herz ~** to take sb/sth to one's heart; **etw in sich ~** to include sth; **„geschlossen"** "closed"
Schließfach *nt* locker
schließlich *adv* finally; (*schließlich doch*) after all
Schliff (**-(e)s, -e**) *m* cut(ting); (*fig*) polish; **einer Sache den letzten ~ geben** (*fig*) to put the finishing touch(es) to sth
schliff *etc* [ʃlıf] *vb siehe* **schleifen**
schlimm [ʃlım] *adj* bad; **das war ~** that was terrible; **das ist halb so ~!** that's not so bad!; **schlimmer** *adj* worse; **schlimmste, r, s** *adj* worst
schlimmstenfalls *adv* at (the) worst
Schlinge ['ʃlıŋə] (**-, -n**) *f* loop; (*an Galgen*) noose; (*Falle*) snare; (*Med*) sling
Schlingel (**-s, -**) *m* rascal
schlingen *unreg vt* to wind ▷ *vi* (*essen*) to bolt one's food, gobble
schlingern *vi* to roll
Schlingpflanze *f* creeper
Schlips [ʃlıps] (**-es, -e**) *m* tie, necktie (*US*); **sich auf den ~ getreten fühlen** (*fig: umg*) to feel offended
Schlitten ['ʃlıtən] (**-s, -**) *m* sledge, sled; (*Pferdeschlitten*) sleigh; **mit jdm ~ fahren** (*umg*) to give sb a rough time; **Schlittenbahn** *f* toboggan run; **Schlittenfahren** (**-s**) *nt* tobogganing
schlittern ['ʃlıtərn] *vi* to slide; (*Wagen*) to skid
Schlittschuh ['ʃlıtʃu:] *m* skate; **~ laufen** to skate; **Schlittschuhbahn** *f* skating rink; **Schlittschuhläufer** *m* skater
Schlitz [ʃlıts] (**-es, -e**) *m* slit; (*für Münze*) slot; (*Hosenschlitz*) flies *pl*; **schlitzäugig** *adj* slant-eyed; **schlitzen** *vt* to slit; **Schlitzohr** *nt* (*fig*) sly fox
schlohweiß ['ʃlo:'vaıs] *adj* snow-white
Schlokal *nt* gourmet restaurant
Schloss (**-es, -"er**) *nt* lock, padlock; (*an Schmuck etc*) clasp; (*Bau*) castle; (*Palast*) palace; **ins ~ fallen** to lock (itself)
schloss *etc* [ʃlɔs] *vb siehe* **schließen**
Schlosser ['ʃlɔsər] (**-s, -**) *m* (*Autoschlosser*) fitter; (*für Schlüssel etc*) locksmith
Schlosserei [slɔsə'raı] *f* metal(working) shop
Schlosshund *m*: **heulen wie ein ~** to howl one's head off
Schlot [ʃlo:t] (**-(e)s, -e**) *m* chimney; (*Naut*) funnel
schlottern ['ʃlɔtərn] *vi* to shake; (*vor Angst*) to tremble; (*Kleidung*) to be baggy
Schlucht [ʃlʊxt] (**-, -en**) *f* gorge, ravine
schluchzen ['ʃlʊxtsən] *vi* to sob
Schluck [ʃlʊk] (**-(e)s, -e**) *m* swallow; (*größer*) gulp; (*kleiner*) sip; (*ein bisschen*) drop
Schluckauf (**-s**) *m* hiccups *pl*
schlucken *vt* to swallow; (*umg: Alkohol, Benzin*) to guzzle; (*: verschlingen*) to swallow up ▷ *vi* to swallow
Schlucker (**-s, -**) (*umg*) *m*: **armer ~** poor devil
Schluckimpfung *f* oral vaccination
schluderig ['ʃlu:dərıç], **schludrig** ['ʃlu:drıç] (*umg*) *adj* slipshod
schludern ['ʃlu:dərn] (*umg*) *vi* to do slipshod work
schlug *etc* [ʃlu:k] *vb siehe* **schlagen**
Schlummer ['ʃlʊmər] (**-s**) *m* slumber
schlummern *vi* to slumber
Schlund [ʃlʊnt] (**-(e)s, ¨-e**) *m* gullet; (*fig*) jaw
schlüpfen ['ʃlʏpfən] *vi* to slip; (*Vogel etc*) to hatch (out)
Schlüpfer ['ʃlʏpfər] (**-s, -**) *m* panties *pl*, knickers *pl*
Schlupfloch ['ʃlʊpflɔx] *nt* hole; (*Versteck*) hide-out; (*fig*) loophole
schlüpfrig ['ʃlʏpfrıç] *adj* slippery; (*fig*) lewd; **Schlüpfrigkeit** *f* slipperiness; lewdness
Schlupfwinkel *m* hiding place; (*fig*) quiet corner
schlurfen ['ʃlʊrfən] *vi* to shuffle
schlürfen ['ʃlʏrfən] *vt, vi* to slurp
Schluss [ʃlʊs] (**-es, -"e**) *m* end; (*Schlussfolgerung*)

conclusion; **am ~** at the end; **~ für heute!** that'll do for today; **~ jetzt!** that's enough now!; **~ machen mit** to finish with

Schlüssel ['ʃlʏsəl] (**-s, -**) *m* (*lit, fig*) key; (*Schraubschlüssel*) spanner, wrench; (*Mus*) clef; **Schlüsselbein** *nt* collarbone; **Schlüsselblume** *f* cowslip, primrose; **Schlüsselbund** *m* bunch of keys; **Schlüsselerlebnis** *nt* (*Psych*) crucial experience; **Schlüsselkind** *nt* latchkey child; **Schlüsselloch** *nt* keyhole; **Schlüsselposition** *f* key position; **Schlüsselwort** *nt* safe combination; (*Comput*) keyword

Schlussfolgerung *f* conclusion, inference

Schlussformel *f* (*in Brief*) closing formula; (*bei Vertrag*) final clause

schlüssig ['ʃlʏsɪç] *adj* conclusive; **sich** *dat* **(über etw** *akk***) ~ sein** to have made up one's mind (about sth)

Schluss- *zW*: **Schlusslicht** *nt* rear light (*Brit*), taillight (*US*); (*fig*) tail ender; **Schlussstrich** *m* (*fig*) final stroke; **einen Schlussstrich unter etw** *akk* **ziehen** to consider sth finished; **Schlussverkauf** *m* clearance sale; **Schlusswort** *nt* concluding words *pl*

Schmach [ʃma:x] (**-**) *f* disgrace, ignominy

schmachten ['ʃmaxtən] *vi* to languish; **nach jdm ~** to pine for sb

schmächtig ['ʃmɛçtɪç] *adj* slight

schmachvoll *adj* ignominious, humiliating

schmackhaft ['ʃmakhaft] *adj* tasty; **jdm etw ~ machen** (*fig*) to make sth palatable to sb

schmähen ['ʃmɛ:ən] *vt* to abuse, revile

schmählich *adj* ignominious, shameful

Schmähung *f* abuse

schmal [ʃma:l] *adj* narrow; (*Person, Buch etc*) slender, slim; (*karg*) meagre (*Brit*), meager (*US*); **schmalbrüstig** *adj* narrow-chested

schmälern ['ʃmɛ:lərn] *vt* to diminish; (*fig*) to belittle

Schmalfilm *m* cine (*Brit*) *od* movie (*US*) film

Schmalspur *f* narrow gauge

Schmalspur- (*pej*) *in zw* small-time

Schmalz [ʃmalts] (**-es, -e**) *nt* dripping; (*Schweineschmalz*) lard; (*fig*) sentiment, schmaltz

schmalzig *adj* (*fig*) schmaltzy, slushy

schmarotzen [ʃma'rɔtsən] *vi* (*Biol*) to be parasitic; (*fig*) to sponge

Schmarotzer (**-s, -**) *m* (*auch fig*) parasite

Schmarren ['ʃmarən] (**-s, -**) *m* (*Österr*) small pieces of pancake; (*fig*) rubbish, tripe

schmatzen ['ʃmatsən] *vi* to eat noisily

Schmaus [ʃmaʊs] (**-es, Schmäuse**) *m* feast; **schmausen** *vi* to feast

schmecken ['ʃmɛkən] *vt, vi* to taste; **es schmeckt ihm** he likes it; **schmeckt es Ihnen?** is it good?, are you enjoying your food *od* meal?; **das schmeckt nach mehr!** (*umg*) it's very moreish (*hum*); **es sich ~ lassen** to tuck in

Schmeichelei [ʃmaɪçə'laɪ] *f* flattery

schmeichelhaft ['ʃmaɪçəlhaft] *adj* flattering

schmeicheln *vi* to flatter

Schmeichler, in (**-s, -**) *m(f)* flatterer

schmeißen ['ʃmaɪsən] *unreg* (*umg*) *vt* to throw, chuck; (*spendieren*): **eine Runde** *od* **Lage ~** to stand a round

Schmeißfliege *f* bluebottle

Schmelz [ʃmɛlts] (**-es, -e**) *m* enamel; (*Glasur*) glaze; (*von Stimme*) melodiousness; **schmelzbar** *adj* fusible

schmelzen *unreg vt* to melt; (*Erz*) to smelt ▷ *vi* to melt

Schmelz- *zW*: **Schmelzhütte** *f* smelting works *pl*; **Schmelzkäse** *m* cheese spread; (*in Scheiben*) processed cheese; **Schmelzofen** *m* melting furnace; (*für Erze*) smelting furnace; **Schmelzpunkt** *m* melting point; **Schmelztiegel** *m* (*lit, fig*) melting pot; **Schmelzwasser** *nt* melted snow

Schmerbauch ['ʃme:rbaʊx] (*umg*) *m* paunch, potbelly

Schmerz [ʃmɛrts] (**-es, -en**) *m* pain; (*Trauer*) grief *no pl*; **~en haben** to be in pain; **schmerzempfindlich** *adj* sensitive to pain

schmerzen *vt, vi* to hurt

Schmerzensgeld *nt* compensation

Schmerz- *zW*: **schmerzhaft** *adj* painful; **schmerzlich** *adj* painful; **schmerzlindernd** *adj* pain-relieving; **schmerzlos** *adj* painless; **Schmerzmittel** *nt* painkiller, analgesic; **schmerzstillend** *adj* pain-killing, analgesic; **Schmerztablette** *f* pain-killing tablet

Schmetterling ['ʃmɛtərlɪŋ] *m* butterfly

Schmetterlingsstil *m* (*Schwimmen*) butterfly stroke

schmettern ['ʃmɛtərn] *vt* to smash; (*Melodie*) to sing loudly, bellow out ▷ *vi* to smash (*SPORT*); (*Trompete*) to blare

Schmied [ʃmi:t] (**-(e)s, -e**) *m* blacksmith

Schmiede ['ʃmi:də] (**-, -n**) *f* smithy, forge; **Schmiedeeisen** *nt* wrought iron

schmieden *vt* to forge; (*Pläne*) to devise, concoct

schmiegen ['ʃmi:gən] *vt* to press, nestle ▷ *vr*: **sich ~ an** *+akk* to cuddle up to, nestle up to

schmiegsam ['ʃmi:kza:m] *adj* flexible, pliable

Schmiere ['ʃmi:rə] *f* grease; (*Theat*) greasepaint, make-up; (*pej: schlechtes Theater*) fleapit; **~ stehen** (*umg*) to be the look-out

schmieren *vt* to smear; (*ölen*) to lubricate, grease; (*bestechen*) to bribe ▷ *vi* (*schreiben*) to scrawl; **es läuft wie geschmiert** it's going like clockwork; **jdm eine ~** (*umg*) to clout sb one

Schmierenkomödiant (*pej*) *m* ham (actor)

Schmier- *zW*: **Schmierfett** *nt* grease; **Schmierfink** *m* messy person; **Schmiergeld** *nt* bribe; **Schmierheft** *nt* jotter

schmierig *adj* greasy

Schmiermittel *nt* lubricant

Schmierseife *f* soft soap

schmilzt [ʃmɪltst] *vb siehe* **schmelzen**

Schminke ['ʃmɪŋkə] (**-, -n**) *f* make-up

schminken *vt, vr* to make up

schmirgeln ['ʃmɪrgəln] *vt* to sand (down)

Schmirgelpapier (**-s**) *nt* emery paper
Schmiss (**-es, -e**) *m* (*Narbe*) duelling (*Brit*) *od* dueling (*US*) scar; (*veraltet: Schwung*) dash, élan
schmiss *etc* [ʃmɪs] *vb siehe* **schmeißen**
Schmöker ['ʃmøːkər] (**-s, -**) (*umg*) *m* (trashy) old book
schmökern *vi* to bury o.s. in a book; (*umg*) to browse
schmollen ['ʃmɔlən] *vi* to pout; (*gekränkt*) to sulk
schmollend *adj* sulky
Schmollmund *m* pout
schmolz *etc* [ʃmɔlts] *vb siehe* **schmelzen**
Schmorbraten *m* stewed *od* braised meat
schmoren ['ʃmoːrən] *vt* to braise
Schmu [ʃmuː] (**-s**) (*umg*) *m* cheating
Schmuck [ʃmʊk] (**-(e)s, -e**) *m* jewellery (*Brit*), jewelry (*US*); (*Verzierung*) decoration
schmücken ['ʃmʏkən] *vt* to decorate
Schmuck- *zW*: **schmucklos** *adj* unadorned, plain; **Schmucklosigkeit** *f* simplicity; **Schmucksachen** *pl* jewels *pl*, jewellery *sing* (*Brit*), jewelry *sing* (*US*); **Schmuckstück** *nt* (*Ring etc*) piece of jewellery (*Brit*) *od* jewelry (*US*); (*fig: Prachtstück*) gem
schmuddelig ['ʃmʊdəlɪç], **schmuddlig** ['ʃmʊdlɪç] *adj* messy; (*schmutzig*) dirty; (*schmierig, unsauber*) filthy
Schmuggel ['ʃmʊgəl] (**-s**) *m* smuggling
schmuggeln *vt, vi* to smuggle
Schmuggelware *f* contraband
Schmuggler, in (**-s, -**) *m(f)* smuggler
schmunzeln ['ʃmʊntsəln] *vi* to smile benignly
schmusen ['ʃmuːzən] (*umg*) *vi* (*zärtlich sein*) to cuddle; **mit jdm ~** to cuddle sb
Schmutz [ʃmʊts] (**-es**) *m* dirt; (*fig*) filth; **schmutzen** *vi* to get dirty; **Schmutzfink** *m* filthy creature; **Schmutzfleck** *m* stain
schmutzig *adj* dirty; **~e Wäsche waschen** (*fig*) to wash one's dirty linen in public
Schnabel ['ʃnaːbəl] (**-s, ¨-**) *m* beak, bill; (*Ausguss*) spout; (*umg: Mund*) mouth; **reden, wie einem der ~ gewachsen ist** to say exactly what comes into one's head; (*unaffektiert*) to talk naturally
schnacken ['ʃnakən] (*Nordd: umg*) *vi* to chat
Schnake ['ʃnaːkə] (**-, -n**) *f* crane fly; (*Stechmücke*) gnat
Schnalle ['ʃnalə] (**-, -n**) *f* buckle; (*an Handtasche, Buch*) clasp
schnallen *vt* to buckle
schnalzen ['ʃnaltsən] *vi* to snap; (*mit Zunge*) to click
Schnäppchen ['ʃnɛpçən] (*umg*) *nt* bargain, snip
schnappen ['ʃnapən] *vt* to grab, catch; (*umg: ergreifen*) to snatch ▷ *vi* to snap
Schnappschloss *nt* spring lock
Schnappschuss *m* (*Phot*) snapshot
Schnaps [ʃnaps] (**-es, ¨-e**) *m* schnapps; (*umg: Branntwein*) spirits *pl*; **Schnapsidee** (*umg*) *f* crackpot idea; **Schnapsleiche** (*umg*) *f* drunk
schnarchen ['ʃnarçən] *vi* to snore
schnattern ['ʃnatərn] *vi* to chatter; (*zittern*) to shiver
schnauben ['ʃnaʊbən] *vi* to snort ▷ *vr* to blow one's nose
schnaufen ['ʃnaʊfən] *vi* to puff, pant
Schnaufer (**-s, -**) (*umg*) *m* breath
Schnauzbart ['ʃnaʊtsbaːrt] *m* moustache (*Brit*), mustache (*US*)
Schnauze (**-, -n**) *f* snout, muzzle; (*Ausguss*) spout; (*umg*) gob; **auf die ~ fallen** (*fig*) to come a cropper (*umg*); **etw frei nach ~ machen** to do sth any old how
schnäuzen ['ʃnɔʏtsn] *vr* to blow one's nose
Schnecke ['ʃnɛkə] (**-, -n**) *f* snail; (*Nacktschnecke*) slug; (*Koch: Gebäck*) ≈ Chelsea bun; **jdn zur ~ machen** (*umg*) to give sb a real bawling out
Schneckenhaus *nt* snail's shell
Schneckentempo (*umg*) *nt*: **im ~** at a snail's pace
Schnee [ʃneː] (**-s**) *m* snow; (*Eischnee*) beaten egg white; **~ von gestern** old hat; water under the bridge; **Schneeball** *m* snowball; **Schneebesen** *m* (*Koch*) whisk; **Schneefall** *m* snowfall; **Schneeflocke** *f* snowflake; **Schneegestöber** *nt* snowstorm; **Schneeglöckchen** *nt* snowdrop; **Schneegrenze** *f* snowline; **Schneekette** *f* (*Aut*) snow chain; **Schneekönig** *m*: **sich freuen wie ein Schneekönig** to be as pleased as Punch; **Schneemann** *m* snowman; **Schneepflug** *m* snowplough (*Brit*), snowplow (*US*); **Schneeregen** *m* sleet; **Schneeschmelze** *f* thaw; **Schneetreiben** *nt* driving snow; **Schneewehe** *f* snowdrift; **Schneewittchen** *nt* Snow White
Schneid [ʃnaɪt] (**-(e)s**) (*umg*) *m* pluck
Schneidbrenner (**-s, -**) *m* (*Tech*) oxyacetylene cutter
Schneide ['ʃnaɪdə] (**-, -n**) *f* edge; (*Klinge*) blade
schneiden *unreg vt* to cut; (*Film, Tonband*) to edit; (*kreuzen*) to cross, intersect ▷ *vr* to cut o.s.; (*umg: sich täuschen*): **da hat er sich aber geschnitten!** he's very much mistaken; **die Luft ist zum S~** (*fig: umg*) the air is very bad
schneidend *adj* cutting
Schneider (**-s, -**) *m* tailor; **frieren wie ein ~** (*umg*) to be frozen to the marrow; **aus dem ~ sein** (*fig*) to be out of the woods
Schneiderei [ʃnaɪdə'raɪ] *f* tailor's shop; (*einer Schneiderin*) dressmaker's shop
Schneiderin *f* dressmaker
schneidern *vt* to make ▷ *vi* to be a tailor
Schneidersitz (**-es**) *m*: **im ~ sitzen** to sit cross-legged
Schneidezahn *m* incisor
schneidig *adj* dashing; (*mutig*) plucky
schneien ['ʃnaɪən] *vi* to snow; **jdm ins Haus ~** (*umg: Besuch*) to drop in on sb; (*: Rechnung, Brief*) to come in the post (*Brit*) *od* mail (*US*)
Schneise ['ʃnaɪzə] (**-, -n**) *f* (*Waldschneise*) clearing
schnell [ʃnɛl] *adj* quick, fast ▷ *adv* quick(ly), fast; **das ging ~** that was quick; **Schnellboot** *nt* speedboat
Schnelle (**-**) *f*: **etw auf die ~ machen** to do sth in a rush

schnellen *vi* to shoot
Schnellgericht *nt* (*Jur*) summary court; (*Koch*) convenience food
Schnellhefter *m* loose-leaf binder
Schnelligkeit *f* speed
Schnell- *zW*: **Schnellimbiss** *m* (*Essen*) (quick) snack; (*Raum*) snack bar; **Schnellkochtopf** *m* (*Dampfkochtopf*) pressure cooker; **Schnellreinigung** *f* express cleaner's
schnellstens *adv* as quickly as possible
Schnellstraße *f* expressway
Schnellzug *m* fast *od* express train
schneuzen ['ʃnɔytsən] *vr siehe* **schnäuzen**
Schnickschnack ['ʃnɪkʃnak] (**-(e)s**) (*umg*) *m* twaddle
Schnippchen ['ʃnɪpçən] *nt*: **jdm ein ~ schlagen** to play a trick on sb
schnippeln ['ʃnɪpəln] (*umg*) *vt* to snip; (*mit Messer*) to hack ▷ *vi*: **~ an** *+dat* to snip at; to hack at
schnippen ['ʃnɪpən] *vi*: **mit den Fingern ~** to snap one's fingers
schnippisch ['ʃnɪpɪʃ] *adj* sharp-tongued
Schnipsel ['ʃnɪpsəl] (**-s, -**) (*umg*) *m od nt* scrap; (*Papierschnipsel*) scrap of paper
Schnitt (**-(e)s, -e**) *m* cut(ting); (*Schnittpunkt*) intersection; (*Querschnitt*) (cross) section; (*Durchschnitt*) average; (*Schnittmuster*) pattern; (*Ernte*) crop; (*an Buch*) edge; (*umg: Gewinn*) profit; **~: L. Schwarz** (*Film*) editor – L. Schwarz; **im ~** on average
schnitt *etc* [ʃnɪt] *vb siehe* **schneiden**
Schnittblumen *pl* cut flowers *pl*
Schnittbohnen *pl* French *od* green beans *pl*
Schnitte (**-, -n**) *f* slice; (*belegt*) sandwich
schnittfest *adj* (*Tomaten*) firm
Schnittfläche *f* section
schnittig ['ʃnɪtɪç] *adj* smart; (*Auto, Formen*) stylish
Schnitt- *zW*: **Schnittlauch** *m* chive; **Schnittmuster** *nt* pattern; **Schnittpunkt** *m* (point of) intersection; **Schnittstelle** *f* (*Comput*) interface; **Schnittwunde** *f* cut
Schnitzarbeit *f* wood carving
Schnitzel (**-s, -**) *nt* scrap; (*Koch*) escalope; **Schnitzeljagd** *f* paperchase
schnitzen ['ʃnɪtsən] *vt* to carve
Schnitzer (**-s, -**) *m* carver; (*umg*) blunder
Schnitzerei [ʃnɪtsə'raɪ] *f* wood carving
schnodderig ['ʃnɔdərɪç] (*umg*) *adj* snotty
schnöde ['ʃnøːdə] *adj* base, mean
Schnorchel ['ʃnɔrçəl] (**-s, -**) *m* snorkel
schnorcheln *vi* to go snorkelling
Schnörkel ['ʃnœrkəl] (**-s, -**) *m* flourish; (*Archit*) scroll
schnorren ['ʃnɔrən] *vt, vi* to cadge (*Brit*)
Schnorrer (**-s, -**) (*umg*) *m* cadger (*Brit*)
Schnösel ['ʃnøːzəl] (**-s, -**) (*umg*) *m* snotty(-nosed) little upstart
schnuckelig ['ʃnʊkəlɪç] (*umg*) *adj* (*gemütlich*) snug, cosy; (*Person*) sweet
schnüffeln ['ʃnʏfəln] *vi* to sniff; (*fig: umg: spionieren*) to snoop around; **Schnüffeln** *nt* (*von Klebstoff etc*) glue-sniffing *etc*
Schnüffler, in (**-s, -**) *m(f)* snooper
Schnuller ['ʃnʊlər] (**-s, -**) *m* dummy (*Brit*), pacifier (*US*)
Schnulze ['ʃnʊltsə] (**-, -n**) (*umg*) *f* schmaltzy film/book/song
Schnupfen ['ʃnʊpfən] (**-s, -**) *m* cold
Schnupftabak *m* snuff
schnuppe ['ʃnʊpə] (*umg*) *adj*: **jdm ~ sein** to be all the same to sb
schnuppern ['ʃnʊpərn] *vi* to sniff
Schnur [ʃnuːr] (**-, ⸚e**) *f* string; (*Kordel*) cord; (*Elek*) flex
Schnürchen ['ʃnyːrçən] *nt*: **es läuft** *od* **klappt (alles) wie am ~** everything's going like clockwork
schnüren ['ʃnyːrən] *vt* to tie
schnurgerade *adj* straight (as a die *od* an arrow)
Schnurrbart ['ʃnʊrbaːrt] *m* moustache (*Brit*), mustache (*US*)
schnurren ['ʃnʊrən] *vi* to purr; (*Kreisel*) to hum
Schnürschuh *m* lace-up (shoe)
Schnürsenkel *m* shoelace
schnurstracks *adv* straight (away); **~ auf jdn/etw zugehen** to make a beeline for sb/sth (*umg*)
schob *etc* [ʃoːp] *vb siehe* **schieben**
Schock [ʃɔk] (**-(e)s, -e**) *m* shock; **unter ~ stehen** to be in (a state of) shock
schocken (*umg*) *vt* to shock
Schocker (**-s, -**) (*umg*) *m* shocking film/novel, shocker
schockieren *vt* to shock, outrage
Schöffe ['ʃœfə] (**-n, -n**) *m* lay magistrate
Schöffengericht *nt* magistrates' court
Schöffin *f* lay magistrate
Schokolade [ʃoko'laːdə] (**-, -n**) *f* chocolate
scholl *etc* [ʃɔl] *vb siehe* **schallen**
Scholle ['ʃɔlə] (**-, -n**) *f* clod; (*Eisscholle*) ice floe; (*Fisch*) plaice
Scholli ['ʃɔlɪ] (*umg*) *m*: **mein lieber ~!** (*drohend*) now look here!

SCHLÜSSELWORT

schon [ʃoːn] *adv* **1** (*bereits*) already; **er ist schon da** he's there/here already, he's already there/here; **ist er schon da?** is he there/here yet?; **warst du schon einmal dort?** have you ever been there?; **ich war schon einmal dort** I've been there before; **das war schon immer so** that has always been the case; **hast du schon gehört?** have you heard?; **schon 1920** as early as 1920; **schon vor 100 Jahren** as far back as 100 years ago; **er wollte schon die Hoffnung aufgeben, als ...** he was just about to give up hope when ...; **wartest du schon lange?** have you been waiting (for) long?; **wie schon so oft** as so often (before); **was, schon wieder?** what – again?
2 (*bestimmt*) all right; **du wirst schon sehen** you'll see (all right); **das wird schon noch**

gut gehen that should turn out OK (in the end)
3 (*bloß*) just; **allein schon das Gefühl ...** just the very feeling ...; **schon der Gedanke** the mere *od* very thought; **wenn ich das schon höre** I only have to hear that
4 (*einschränkend*): **ja schon, aber ...** yes (well), but ...
5: das ist schon möglich that's quite possible; **schon gut** OK; **du weißt schon** you know; **komm schon** come on; **hör schon auf damit!** will you stop that!; **was macht das schon, wenn ...?** what does it matter if ...?; **und wenn schon!** (*umg*) so what?

schön [ʃøːn] *adj* beautiful; (*Mann*) handsome; (*nett*) nice ▷ *adv*: **sich ganz ~ ärgern** to be very angry; **da hast du etwas S~es angerichtet** you've made a fine *od* nice mess; **sich ~ machen** to make o.s. look nice; **~e Grüße** best wishes; **~en Dank** (many) thanks; **~ weich/warm** nice and soft/warm
schonen [ˈʃoːnən] *vt* to look after; (*jds Nerven*) to spare; (*Gegner, Kind*) to be easy on; (*Teppich, Füße*) to save ▷ *vr* to take it easy
schonend *adj* careful, gentle; **jdm etw ~ beibringen** to break sth to sb gently
Schoner [ˈʃoːnər] **(-s, -)** *m* (*Naut*) schooner; (*Sesselschoner*) cover
Schönfärberei *f* (*fig*) glossing things over
Schonfrist *f* period of grace
Schöngeist *m* cultured person, aesthete (*Brit*), esthete (*US*)
Schönheit *f* beauty
Schönheits- *zW*: **Schönheitsfehler** *m* blemish, flaw; **Schönheitsoperation** *f* cosmetic surgery; **Schönheitswettbewerb** *m* beauty contest
Schonkost (-) *f* light diet
Schönschrift *f*: **in ~** in one's best (hand)writing
schöntun *unreg vi*: **jdm ~** (*schmeicheln*) to flatter *od* soft-soap sb, play up to sb
Schonung *f* good care; (*Nachsicht*) consideration; (*Forst*) plantation of young trees
schonungslos *adj* ruthless, harsh
Schonzeit *f* close season
Schopf [ʃɔpf] **(-(e)s, ¨-e)** *m*: **eine Gelegenheit beim ~ ergreifen** *od* **fassen** to seize *od* grasp an opportunity with both hands
schöpfen [ˈʃœpfən] *vt* to scoop; (*Suppe*) to ladle; (*Mut*) to summon up; (*Luft*) to breathe in; (*Hoffnung*) to find
Schöpfer (-s, -) *m* creator; (*Gott*) Creator; (*umg: Schöpfkelle*) ladle; **schöpferisch** *adj* creative
Schöpfkelle *f* ladle
Schöpflöffel *m* skimmer, scoop
Schöpfung *f* creation
Schoppen [ˈʃɔpən] **(-s, -)** *m* (*Glas Wein*) glass of wine; **Schoppenwein** *m* wine by the glass
schor *etc* [ʃoːr] *vb siehe* **scheren**
Schorf [ʃɔrf] **(-(e)s, -e)** *m* scab
Schorle [ˈʃɔrlə] **(-, -n)** *f* spritzer, *wine and soda water or lemonade*
Schornstein [ˈʃɔrnʃtaɪn] *m* chimney; (*Naut*) funnel; **Schornsteinfeger (-s, -)** *m* chimney sweep
Schose [ˈʃoːzə] **(-, -n)** *f* = **Chose**
Schoß (-es, -¨e) *m* lap; (*Rockschoß*) coat tail; **im ~e der Familie** in the bosom of one's family
schoss *etc* [ʃɔs] *vb siehe* **schießen**
Schoßhund *m* lapdog
Schössling [ˈʃœslɪŋ] *m* (*Bot*) shoot
Schote [ˈʃoːtə] **(-, -n)** *f* pod
Schotte [ˈʃɔtə] **(-n, -n)** *m* Scot, Scotsman
Schottenrock [ˈʃɔtənrɔk] *m* kilt; (*für Frauen*) tartan skirt
Schotter [ˈʃɔtər] **(-s)** *m* gravel; (*im Straßenbau*) road metal; (*Eisenb*) ballast
Schottin [ˈʃɔtɪn] *f* Scot, Scotswoman
schottisch [ˈʃɔtɪʃ] *adj* Scottish, Scots; **das ~e Hochland** the Scottish Highlands *pl*
Schottland (-s) *nt* Scotland
schraffieren [ʃraˈfiːrən] *vt* to hatch
schräg [ʃrɛːk] *adj* slanting; (*schief, geneigt*) sloping; (*nicht gerade od parallel*) oblique ▷ *adv*: **~ gedruckt** in italics; **etw ~ stellen** to put sth at an angle; **~ gegenüber** diagonally opposite
Schräge [ˈʃrɛːgə] **(-, -n)** *f* slant
Schräg- *zW*: **Schrägkante** *f* bevelled (*Brit*) *od* beveled (*US*) edge; **Schrägschrift** *f* italics *pl*; **Schrägstreifen** *m* bias binding; **Schrägstrich** *m* oblique stroke
Schramme [ˈʃramə] **(-, -n)** *f* scratch
schrammen *vt* to scratch
Schrank [ʃraŋk] **(-(e)s, ¨-e)** *m* cupboard (*Brit*), closet (*US*); (*Kleiderschrank*) wardrobe
Schranke (-, -n) *f* barrier; (*fig: Grenze*) limit; (*: Hindernis*) barrier; **jdn in seine ~n (ver)weisen** (*fig*) to put sb in his place
schrankenlos *adj* boundless; (*zügellos*) unrestrained
Schrankenwärter *m* (*Eisenb*) level-crossing (*Brit*) *od* grade-crossing (*US*) attendant
Schrankkoffer *m* wardrobe trunk
Schrankwand *f* wall unit
Schraube [ˈʃraʊbə] **(-, -n)** *f* screw
schrauben *vt* to screw; **etw in die Höhe ~** (*fig: Preise, Rekorde*) to push sth up; (*: Ansprüche*) to raise sth
Schraubenschlüssel *m* spanner (*Brit*), wrench (*US*)
Schraubenzieher (-s, -) *m* screwdriver
Schraubstock [ˈʃraʊpʃtɔk] *m* (*Tech*) vice (*Brit*), vise (*US*)
Schrebergarten [ˈʃreːbərgartən] *m* allotment (*Brit*)
Schreck [ʃrɛk] **(-(e)s, -e)** *m* fright; **o ~ lass nach!** (*hum: umg*) for goodness' sake!
Schrecken (-s, -) *m* terror; (*Schreck*) fright; **schrecken** *vt* to frighten, scare ▷ *vi*: **aus dem Schlaf schrecken** to be startled out of one's sleep
schreckensbleich *adj* as white as a sheet *od*

ghost

Schreckensherrschaft *f* (reign of) terror

Schreck- *zW*: **Schreckgespenst** *nt* nightmare; **schreckhaft** *adj* jumpy, easily frightened; **schrecklich** *adj* terrible, dreadful; **schrecklich gerne!** (*umg*) I'd absolutely love to; **Schreckschraube** (*pej*: *umg*) *f* (old) battle-axe; **Schreckschuss** *m* shot fired in the air; **Schrecksekunde** *f* moment of shock

Schrei [ʃraɪ] (**-(e)s, -e**) *m* scream; (*Ruf*) shout; **der letzte ~** (*umg*) the latest thing, all the rage

Schreibbedarf *m* writing materials *pl*, stationery

Schreibblock *m* writing pad

schreiben ['ʃraɪbən] *unreg vt* to write; (*mit Schreibmaschine*) to type out; (*berichten*: *Zeitung etc*) to say; (*buchstabieren*) to spell ▷ *vi* to write; to type; to say; to spell ▷ *vr*: **wie schreibt sich das?** how is that spelt?; **Schreiben** (**-s, -**) *nt* letter, communication

Schreiber, in (**-s, -**) *m(f)* writer; (*Büroschreiber*) clerk

Schreib- *zW*: **schreibfaul** *adj* lazy about writing letters; **Schreibfehler** *m* spelling mistake; **Schreibkraft** *f* typist; **Schreibmaschine** *f* typewriter; **Schreibpapier** *nt* notepaper; **Schreibschrift** *f* running handwriting; (*Typ*) script; **Schreibschutz** *m* (*Comput*) write-protect; **Schreibstube** *f* orderly room; **Schreibtisch** *m* desk; **Schreibtischtäter** *m* wire *od* string puller

Schreibung *f* spelling

Schreib- *zW*: **Schreibunterlage** *f* pad; **Schreibwaren** *pl* stationery *sing*; **Schreibwarengeschäft** *nt* stationer's (shop) (*Brit*), stationery store (*US*); **Schreibweise** *f* spelling; (*Stil*) style; **schreibwütig** *adj* crazy about writing; **Schreibzentrale** *f* typing pool; **Schreibzeug** *nt* writing materials *pl*

schreien ['ʃraɪən] *unreg vt, vi* to scream; (*rufen*) to shout; **es war zum S~** (*umg*) it was a scream *od* a hoot; **nach etw ~** (*fig*) to cry out for sth

schreiend *adj* (*fig*) glaring; (: *Farbe*) loud

Schreihals (*umg*) *m* (*Baby*) bawler; (*Unruhestifter*) noisy troublemaker

Schreikrampf *m* screaming fit

Schreiner ['ʃraɪnər] (**-s, -**) *m* joiner; (*Zimmermann*) carpenter; (*Möbelschreiner*) cabinetmaker

Schreinerei [ʃraɪnə'raɪ] *f* joiner's workshop

schreiten ['ʃraɪtən] *unreg vi* to stride

schrie *etc* [ʃri:] *vb siehe* **schreien**

Schrieb (**-(e)s, -e**) (*umg*) *m* missive (*hum*)

schrieb *etc* [ʃri:p] *vb siehe* **schreiben**

Schrift [ʃrɪft] (**-, -en**) *f* writing; (*Handschrift*) handwriting; (*Schriftart*) script; (*Typ*) typeface; (*Buch*) work; **Schriftart** *f* (*Handschrift*) script; (*Typ*) typeface; **Schriftbild** *nt* script; (*Comput*) typeface; **Schriftdeutsch** *nt* written German; **Schrifterkennung** *f* optical character recognition, OCR; **Schriftführer** *m* secretary; **schriftlich** *adj* written ▷ *adv* in writing; **das kann ich Ihnen schriftlich geben** (*fig*: *umg*) I can tell you that for free; **Schriftprobe** *f* (*Handschrift*) specimen of one's handwriting; **Schriftsatz** *m* (*Typ*) fount (*Brit*), font (*US*); **Schriftsetzer** *m* compositor; **Schriftsprache** *f* written language

Schriftsteller, in (**-s, -**) *m(f)* writer; **schriftstellerisch** *adj* literary

Schrift- *zW*: **Schriftstück** *nt* document; **Schriftverkehr** *m* correspondence; **Schriftwechsel** *m* correspondence

schrill [ʃrɪl] *adj* shrill; **schrillen** *vi* (*Stimme*) to sound shrilly; (*Telefon*) to ring shrilly

Schritt (**-(e)s, -e**) *m* step; (*Gangart*) walk; (*Tempo*) pace; (*von Hose*) crotch, crutch (*Brit*); **auf ~ und Tritt** (*lit, fig*) wherever *od* everywhere one goes; **„~ fahren"** "dead slow"; **mit zehn ~en Abstand** at a distance of ten paces; **den ersten ~ tun** (*fig*) to make the first move; (: *etw beginnen*) to take the first step

schritt *etc* [ʃrɪt] *vb siehe* **schreiten**

Schritt- *zW*: **Schrittmacher** *m* pacemaker; **Schritttempo** *nt*: **im Schritttempo** at a walking pace; **schrittweise** *adv* gradually, little by little

schroff [ʃrɔf] *adj* steep; (*zackig*) jagged; (*fig*) brusque; (*ungeduldig*) abrupt

schröpfen ['ʃrœpfən] *vt* (*fig*) to fleece

Schrot [ʃro:t] (**-(e)s, -e**) *m od nt* (*Blei*) (small) shot; (*Getreide*) coarsely ground grain, groats *pl*; **Schrotflinte** *f* shotgun

Schrott [ʃrɔt] (**-(e)s, -e**) *m* scrap metal; **ein Auto zu ~ fahren** to write off a car; **Schrotthändler** *m* scrap merchant; **Schrotthaufen** *m* scrap heap; **schrottreif** *adj* ready for the scrap heap; **Schrottwert** *m* scrap value

schrubben ['ʃrʊbən] *vt* to scrub

Schrubber (**-s, -**) *m* scrubbing brush

Schrulle ['ʃrʊlə] (**-, -n**) *f* eccentricity, quirk

schrullig *adj* cranky

schrumpfen ['ʃrʊmpfən] *vi* (*Hilfsverb sein*) to shrink; (*Apfel*) to shrivel; (*Leber, Niere*) to atrophy

Schub [ʃu:p] (**-(e)s, ¨-e**) *m* (*Stoß*) push, shove; (*Gruppe, Anzahl*) batch; **Schubfach** *nt* drawer; **Schubkarren** *m* wheelbarrow; **Schublade** *f* drawer

Schubs [ʃu:ps] (**-es, -e**) (*umg*) *m* shove, push; **schubsen** (*umg*) *vt, vi* to shove, push

schüchtern ['ʃʏçtərn] *adj* shy; **Schüchternheit** *f* shyness

schuf *etc* [ʃu:f] *vb siehe* **schaffen**

Schuft [ʃʊft] (**-(e)s, -e**) *m* scoundrel

schuften (*umg*) *vi* to graft, slave away

Schuh [ʃu:] (**-(e)s, -e**) *m* shoe; **jdm etw in die ~e schieben** (*fig*: *umg*) to put the blame for sth on sb; **wo drückt der ~?** (*fig*) what's troubling you?; **Schuhband** *nt* shoelace; **Schuhcreme** *f* shoe polish; **Schuhgröße** *f* shoe size; **Schuhlöffel** *m* shoehorn; **Schuhmacher** *m* shoemaker; **Schuhwerk** *nt* footwear

Schukosteckdose® ['ʃʊkoʃtɛkdo:zə] *f* safety socket

Schukostecker® *m* safety plug
Schul- *zW*: **Schulaufgaben** *pl* homework *sing*; **Schulbank** *f*: **die Schulbank drücken** (*umg*) to go to school; **Schulbehörde** *f* education authority; **Schulbesuch** *m* school attendance; **Schulbuch** *nt* schoolbook; **Schulbuchverlag** *m* educational publisher
Schuld [ʃʊlt] (**-, -en**) *f* guilt; (*Fin*) debt; (*Verschulden*) fault; **~ haben (an** *+dat***)** to be to blame (for); **jdm (die) ~ geben, jdm die ~ zuschieben** to blame sb; **ich bin mir keiner ~ bewusst** I'm not aware of having done anything wrong; **~ und Sühne** crime and punishment; **ich stehe tief in seiner ~** (*fig*) I'm deeply indebted to him; **~en machen** to run up debts; *siehe auch* **zuschulden**; **schuld** *adj*: **schuld sein (an** *+dat***)** to be to blame (for); **er ist schuld** it's his fault
schuldbewusst *adj* (*Mensch*) feeling guilty; (*Miene*) guilty
schulden [ˈʃʊldən] *vt* to owe
schuldenfrei *adj* free from debt
Schuldgefühl *nt* feeling of guilt
schuldhaft *adj* (*Jur*) culpable
Schuldienst (**-(e)s**) *m* (school)teaching
schuldig *adj* guilty; (*gebührend*) due; **an etw** *dat* **~ sein** to be guilty of sth; **jdm etw ~ sein** *od* **bleiben** to owe sb sth; **jdn ~ sprechen** to find sb guilty; **~ geschieden sein** to be the guilty party in a divorce; **Schuldigkeit** *f* duty
schuldlos *adj* innocent, blameless
Schuldner, in (**-s, -**) *m(f)* debtor
Schuld- *zW*: **Schuldprinzip** *nt* (*Jur*) principle of the guilty party; **Schuldschein** *m* promissory note, IOU; **Schuldspruch** *m* verdict of guilty
Schule [ˈʃuːlə] (**-, -n**) *f* school; **auf** *od* **in der ~** at school; **in die ~ kommen/gehen** to start school/go to school; **~ machen** (*fig*) to become the accepted thing
schulen *vt* to train, school
Schüler, in [ˈʃyːlər(ɪn)] (**-s, -**) *m(f)* pupil; **Schülerausweis** *m* (school) student card; **Schülerlotse** *m pupil acting as a road-crossing warden*; **Schülermitverwaltung** *f* school *od* student council
Schul- *zW*: **Schulferien** *pl* school holidays *pl* (*Brit*) *od* vacation *sing* (*US*); **Schulfernsehen** *nt* schools' *od* educational television; **schulfrei** *adj*: **die Kinder haben morgen schulfrei** the children don't have to go to school tomorrow; **Schulfunk** *m* schools' broadcasts *pl*; **Schulgeld** *nt* school fees *pl*, tuition (*US*); **Schulheft** *nt* exercise book; **Schulhof** *m* playground, schoolyard
schulisch [ˈʃuːlɪʃ] *adj* (*Leistungen, Probleme*) at school; (*Angelegenheiten*) school *attrib*
Schul- *zW*: **Schuljahr** *nt* school year; **Schuljunge** *m* schoolboy; **Schulkind** *nt* schoolchild; **Schulleiter** *m* headmaster (*bes Brit*), principal; **Schulleiterin** *f* headmistress (*bes Brit*), principal; **Schulmädchen** *nt* schoolgirl; **Schulmedizin** *f* orthodox medicine; **Schulpflicht** *f* compulsory school attendance; **schulpflichtig** *adj* of school age; **Schulreife** *f*: **die Schulreife haben** to be ready to go to school; **Schulschiff** *nt* (*Naut*) training ship; **Schulsprecher, in** *m(f)* head boy/girl (*Brit*); **Schulstunde** *f* period, lesson; **Schultasche** *f* school bag
Schulter [ˈʃʊltər] (**-, -n**) *f* shoulder; **auf die leichte ~ nehmen** to take lightly; **Schulterblatt** *nt* shoulder blade
schultern *vt* to shoulder
Schultüte *f bag of sweets given to children on the first day at school*
Schulung *f* education, schooling
Schul- *zW*: **Schulverweigerer, in** *m(f)* school refuser; **Schulweg** *m* way to school; **Schulwesen** *nt* educational system; **Schulzeugnis** *nt* school report
schummeln [ˈʃʊməln] (*umg*) *vi*: **(bei etw) ~** to cheat (at sth)
schummerig [ˈʃʊmərɪç], **schummrig** [ˈʃʊmrɪç] *adj* (*Beleuchtung*) dim; (*Raum*) dimly-lit
Schund (**-(e)s**) *m* trash, garbage
schund *etc* [ʃʊnt] *vb siehe* **schinden**
Schundroman *m* trashy novel
Schupo [ˈʃuːpo] (**-s, -s**) *m abk* (*veraltet: = Schutzpolizist*) cop
Schuppe [ˈʃʊpə] (**-, -n**) *f* scale; **Schuppen** *pl* (*Haarschuppen*) dandruff
Schuppen (**-s, -**) *m* shed; (*umg: übles Lokal*) dive; *siehe auch* **Schuppe**
schuppen *vt* to scale ▷ *vr* to peel
schuppig [ˈʃʊpɪç] *adj* scaly
Schur [ʃuːr] (**-, -en**) *f* shearing
Schüreisen *nt* poker
schüren [ˈʃyːrən] *vt* to rake; (*fig*) to stir up
schürfen [ˈʃʏrfən] *vt, vi* to scrape, scratch; (*Min*) to prospect; to dig
Schürfung *f* abrasion; (*Min*) prospecting
Schürhaken *m* poker
Schurke [ˈʃʊrkə] (**-n, -n**) *m* rogue
Schurwolle *f*: **„reine ~"** "pure new wool"
Schurz [ʃʊrts] (**-es, -e**) *m* apron
Schürze [ˈʃʏrtsə] (**-, -n**) *f* apron
Schürzenjäger (*umg*) *m* philanderer, one for the girls
Schuss [ʃʊs] (**-es, -"e**) *m* shot; (*Fussball*) kick; (*Spritzer: von Wein, Essig etc*) dash; (*Weben*) weft; **(gut) in ~ sein** (*umg*) to be in good shape *od* nick; (*Mensch*) to be in form; **etw in ~ halten** to keep sth in good shape; **weitab vom ~ sein** (*fig: umg*) to be miles from where the action is; **der goldene ~** ≈ a lethal dose of a drug; **ein ~ in den Ofen** (*umg*) a complete waste of time, a failure; **Schussbereich** *m* effective range
Schüssel [ˈʃʏsəl] (**-, -n**) *f* bowl, basin; (*Servierschüssel, umg: Satellitenschüssel*) dish; (*Waschschüssel*) basin
schusselig [ˈʃʊsəlɪç] (*umg*) *adj* (*zerstreut*) scatterbrained, muddle-headed (*umg*)
Schuss- *zW*: **Schusslinie** *f* line of fire; **Schussverletzung** *f* bullet wound; **Schusswaffe** *f* firearm; **Schusswaffengebrauch** *m* (*form*) use of

firearms; **Schusswechsel** *m* exchange of shots; **Schussweite** *f* range (of fire)
Schuster ['ʃu:stər] **(-s, -)** *m* cobbler, shoemaker
Schutt [ʃʊt] **(-(e)s)** *m* rubbish; (*Bauschutt*) rubble; **„~ abladen verboten"** "no tipping"; **Schuttabladeplatz** *m* refuse dump
Schüttelfrost *m* shivering
schütteln ['ʃʏtəln] *vt* to shake ▷ *vr* to shake o.s.; **sich vor Kälte ~** to shiver with cold; **sich vor Ekel ~** to shudder with *od* in disgust
schütten ['ʃʏtən] *vt* to pour; (*Zucker, Kies etc*) to tip; (*verschütten*) to spill ▷ *vi unpers* to pour (down)
schütter *adj* (*Haare*) sparse, thin
Schutthalde *f* dump
Schutthaufen *m* heap of rubble
Schutz [ʃʊts] **(-es)** *m* protection; (*Unterschlupf*) shelter; **jdn in ~ nehmen** to stand up for sb; **Schutzanzug** *m* overalls *pl*; **schutzbedürftig** *adj* in need of protection; **Schutzbefohlene, r** *f(m)* charge; **Schutzblech** *nt* mudguard; **Schutzbrief** *m* (international) travel cover; **Schutzbrille** *f* goggles *pl*
Schütze ['ʃʏtsə] **(-n, -n)** *m* gunman; (*Gewehrschütze*) rifleman; (*Scharfschütze, Sportschütze*) marksman; (*Astrol*) Sagittarius
schützen ['ʃʏtsən] *vt* to protect ▷ *vr* to protect o.s.; **(sich) ~ vor** *+dat od* **gegen** to protect (o.s.) from *od* against; **gesetzlich geschützt** registered; **urheberrechtlich geschützt** protected by copyright; **vor Nässe ~!** keep dry
Schützenfest *nt fair featuring shooting matches*
Schutzengel *m* guardian angel
Schützen- *zW*: **Schützengraben** *m* trench; **Schützenhilfe** *f* (*fig*) support; **Schützenverein** *m* shooting club
Schutz- *zW*: **Schutzgebiet** *nt* protectorate; (*Naturschutzgebiet*) reserve; **Schutzgebühr** *f* (token) fee; **Schutzhaft** *f* protective custody; **Schutzheilige, r** *f(m)* patron saint; **Schutzhelm** *m* safety helmet; **Schutzimpfung** *f* immunization
Schützling ['ʃʏtslɪŋ] *m* protégé; (*bes Kind*) charge
Schutz- *zW*: **schutzlos** *adj* defenceless (*Brit*), defenseless (*US*); **Schutzmann** **(-(e)s,** *pl* **-leute** *od* **-männer)** *m* policeman; **Schutzmarke** *f* trademark; **Schutzmaßnahme** *f* precaution; **Schutzpatron** *m* patron saint; **Schutzschirm** *m* (*Tech*) protective screen; **Schutzumschlag** *m* (book) jacket; **Schutzverband** *m* (*Med*) protective bandage *od* dressing; **Schutzvorrichtung** *f* safety device
Schw. *abk* = **Schwester**
schwabbelig ['ʃvab(ə)lɪç] (*umg*) *adj* (*Körperteil*) flabby; (*: Gelee*) wobbly
Schwabe ['ʃva:bə] **(-n, -n)** *m* Swabian
Schwaben **(-s)** *nt* Swabia
Schwäbin ['ʃvɛ:bɪn] *f* Swabian
schwäbisch ['ʃvɛ:bɪʃ] *adj* Swabian
schwach [ʃvax] *adj* weak, feeble; (*Gedächtnis, Gesundheit*) poor; (*Hoffnung*) faint; **~ werden** to weaken; **das ist ein ~es Bild** (*umg*) *od* **eine ~e Leistung** (*umg*) that's a poor show; **ein ~er Trost** cold *od* small comfort; **mach mich nicht ~!** (*umg*) don't say that!; **auf ~en Beinen** *od* **Füßen stehen** (*fig*) to be on shaky ground; (*: Theorie*) to be shaky
Schwäche ['ʃvɛçə] **(-, -n)** *f* weakness
schwächen *vt* to weaken
schwach- *zW*: **Schwachheit** *f* weakness; **Schwachkopf** (*umg*) *m* dimwit, idiot; **schwachköpfig** *adj* silly, daft (*Brit*)
schwächlich *adj* weakly, delicate
Schwächling *m* weakling
Schwach- *zW*: **Schwachsinn** *m* (*Med*) mental deficiency, feeble-mindedness (*veraltet*); (*umg: Quatsch*) rubbish; (*fig: umg: unsinnige Tat*) idiocy; **schwachsinnig** *adj* mentally deficient; (*Idee*) idiotic; **Schwachstelle** *f* weak point; **Schwachstrom** *m* weak current
Schwächung ['ʃvɛçʊŋ] *f* weakening
Schwaden ['ʃva:dən] **(-s, -)** *m* cloud
schwafeln ['ʃva:fəln] (*umg*) *vi* to blather, drivel; (*in einer Prüfung*) to waffle
Schwager ['ʃva:gər] **(-s, ⸚)** *m* brother-in-law
Schwägerin ['ʃvɛ:gərɪn] *f* sister-in-law
Schwalbe ['ʃvalbə] **(-, -n)** *f* swallow
Schwall [ʃval] **(-(e)s, -e)** *m* surge; (*Worte*) flood, torrent
Schwamm **(-(e)s, ⸚e)** *m* sponge; (*Pilz*) fungus; **~ drüber!** (*umg*) (let's) forget it!
schwamm *etc* [ʃvam] *vb siehe* **schwimmen**
schwammig *adj* spongy; (*Gesicht*) puffy; (*vage: Begriff*) woolly (*Brit*), wooly (*US*)
Schwan [ʃva:n] **(-(e)s, ⸚e)** *m* swan
schwand *etc* [ʃvant] *vb siehe* **schwinden**
schwanen *vi unpers*: **jdm schwant es** sb has a foreboding *od* forebodings; **jdm schwant etwas** sb senses something might happen
schwang *etc* [ʃvaŋ] *vb siehe* **schwingen**
schwanger ['ʃvangər] *adj* pregnant
schwängern ['ʃvɛŋərn] *vt* to make pregnant
Schwangerschaft *f* pregnancy
Schwangerschaftsabbruch *m* termination of pregnancy, abortion
Schwank [ʃvaŋk] **(-(e)s, ⸚e)** *m* funny story; (*Liter*) merry *od* comical tale; (*Theat*) farce
schwanken *vi* to sway; (*taumeln*) to stagger, reel; (*Preise, Zahlen*) to fluctuate; (*zögern*) to hesitate; (*Überzeugung etc*) to begin to waver; **ins S~ kommen** (*Baum, Gebäude etc*) to start to sway; (*Preise, Kurs etc*) to start to fluctuate *od* vary
Schwankung *f* fluctuation
Schwanz [ʃvants] **(-es, ⸚e)** *m* tail; (*umg!: Penis*) prick (*!*); **kein ~** (*umg*) not a (blessed) soul
schwänzen ['ʃvɛntsən] (*umg*) *vt* (*Stunde, Vorlesung*) to skip ▷ *vi* to play truant
Schwänzer ['ʃvɛntsər] **(-s, -)** (*umg*) *m* truant
schwappen ['ʃvapən] *vi* (*überschwappen*) to splash, slosh
Schwarm [ʃvarm] **(-(e)s, ⸚e)** *m* swarm; (*umg*) heart-throb, idol
schwärmen ['ʃvɛrmən] *vi* to swarm; **~ für** to be mad *od* wild about

Schwärmerei [ʃvɛrmə'raɪ] *f* enthusiasm
schwärmerisch *adj* impassioned, effusive
Schwarte ['ʃvartə] (**-, -n**) *f* hard skin; (*Speckschwarte*) rind; (*umg: Buch*) tome (*hum*)
Schwartenmagen (**-s**) *m* (*Koch*) brawn
schwarz [ʃvarts] *adj* black; (*umg: ungesetzlich*) illicit; (*: katholisch*) Catholic, Papist (*pej*); (*Pol*) Christian Democrat; **ins S~e treffen** (*lit, fig*) to hit the bull's-eye; **das S~e Brett** the notice (*Brit*) *od* bulletin (*US*) board; **~e Liste** blacklist; **~es Loch** black hole; **das S~e Meer** the Black Sea; **S~er Peter** (*Karten*) *children's card game*; **jdm den ~en Peter zuschieben** (*fig: die Verantwortung abschieben*) to pass the buck to sb (*umg*); **dort wählen alle ~** they all vote conservative there; **in den ~en Zahlen** in the black; *siehe auch* **schwarzärgern; schwarzmalen; schwarzsehen**; **Schwarzarbeit** *f* illicit work, moonlighting; **Schwarzarbeiter** *m* moonlighter; **schwarzärgern** *vr* to get extremely annoyed; **Schwarzbrot** *nt* (*Pumpernickel*) black bread, pumpernickel; (*braun*) brown rye bread
Schwärze ['ʃvɛrtsə] (**-, -n**) *f* blackness; (*Farbe*) blacking; (*Druckerschwärze*) printer's ink
Schwarze, r *f(m)* (*Neger*) black; (*umg: Katholik*) Papist; (*Pol: umg*) Christian Democrat
schwärzen *vt* to blacken
Schwarz- *zW*: **schwarzfahren** *unreg vi* to travel without paying; (*ohne Führerschein*) to drive without a licence (*Brit*) *od* license (*US*); **Schwarzfahrer** *m* (*Bus etc*) fare dodger (*umg*); **Schwarzhandel** *m* black market (trade); **Schwarzhändler** *m* black-market operator; **schwarzhören** *vi* to listen to the radio without a licence (*Brit*) *od* license (*US*)
schwärzlich ['ʃvɛrtslɪç] *adj* blackish, darkish
Schwarz- *zW*: **schwarzmalen** *vi* to be pessimistic; **Schwarzmarkt** *m* black market; **schwarzsehen** *vi unreg* (*TV*) to watch TV without a licence (*Brit*) *od* license (*US*); (*umg*) to see the gloomy side of things; **Schwarzseher** *m* pessimist; (*TV*) viewer without a licence (*Brit*) *od* license (*US*); **Schwarzwald** *m* Black Forest; **Schwarzwälder Kirschtorte** *f* Black Forest gâteau; **schwarz-weiß, schwarzweiß** *adj* black and white; **Schwarzweiß-** *in zw* black and white; **Schwarzwurzel** *f* (*Koch*) salsify
Schwatz [ʃvats] (**-es, -e**) *m* chat
schwatzen ['ʃvatsən] *vi* to chat; (*schnell, unaufhörlich*) to chatter; (*über belanglose Dinge*) to prattle; (*Unsinn reden*) to blether (*umg*)
schwätzen ['ʃvɛtsən] *vi* = **schwatzen**
Schwätzer, in ['ʃvɛtsər(ɪn)] (**-s, -**) *m(f)* chatterbox; (*Schwafler*) gasbag (*umg*); (*Klatschbase*) gossip
schwatzhaft *adj* talkative, gossipy
Schwebe ['ʃve:bə] *f*: **in der ~** (*fig*) in abeyance; (*Jur, Comm*) pending
Schwebebahn *f* overhead railway (*Brit*) *od* railroad (*US*)
Schwebebalken *m* (*Sport*) beam
schweben *vi* to drift, float; (*hoch*) to soar; (*unentschieden sein*) to be in the balance; **es schwebte mir vor Augen** (*Bild*) I saw it in my mind's eye
schwebend *adj* (*Tech, Chem*) suspended; (*fig*) undecided, unresolved; **~es Verfahren** (*Jur*) pending case
schwed. *abk* = **schwedisch**
Schwede ['ʃve:də] (**-n, -n**) *m* Swede
Schweden (**-s**) *nt* Sweden
Schwedin ['ʃve:dɪn] *f* Swede
schwedisch *adj* Swedish
Schwefel ['ʃve:fəl] (**-s**) *m* sulphur (*Brit*), sulfur (*US*); **Schwefeldioxid** *nt* sulphur dioxide
schwefelig *adj* sulphurous (*Brit*), sulfurous (*US*)
Schwefelsäure *f* sulphuric (*Brit*) *od* sulfuric (*US*) acid
Schweif [ʃvaɪf] (**-(e)s, -e**) *m* tail
schweifen *vi* to wander, roam
Schweigegeld *nt* hush money
Schweigeminute *f* one minute('s) silence
schweigen ['ʃvaɪgən] *unreg vi* to be silent; (*still sein*) to keep quiet; **kannst du ~?** can you keep a secret?; **ganz zu ~ von ...** to say nothing of ...; **Schweigen** (**-s**) *nt* silence
schweigend *adj* silent
Schweigepflicht *f* pledge of secrecy; (*von Anwalt etc*) requirement of confidentiality
schweigsam ['ʃvaɪkza:m] *adj* silent; (*als Charaktereigenschaft*) taciturn; **Schweigsamkeit** *f* silence; taciturnity
Schwein [ʃvaɪn] (**-(e)s, -e**) *nt* pig; (*fig: umg*) (good) luck; **kein ~** (*umg*) nobody, not a single person
Schweine- *zW*: **Schweinebraten** *m* joint of pork; (*gekocht*) roast pork; **Schweinefleisch** *nt* pork; **Schweinegeld** (*umg*) *nt*: **ein Schweinegeld** a packet; **Schweinehund** (*umg*) *m* stinker, swine
Schweinerei [ʃvaɪnə'raɪ] *f* mess; (*Gemeinheit*) dirty trick; **so eine ~!** (*umg*) how disgusting!
Schweineschmalz *nt* dripping; (*als Kochfett*) lard
Schweinestall *m* pigsty
schweinisch *adj* filthy
Schweinsleder *nt* pigskin
Schweinsohr *nt* pig's ear; (*Gebäck*) (kidney-shaped) pastry
Schweiß [ʃvaɪs] (**-es**) *m* sweat, perspiration; **Schweißband** *nt* sweatband
Schweißbrenner (**-s, -**) *m* (*Tech*) welding torch
schweißen *vt, vi* to weld
Schweißer (**-s, -**) *m* welder
Schweiß- *zW*: **Schweißfüße** *pl* sweaty feet *pl*; **Schweißnaht** *f* weld; **schweißnass** *adj* sweaty
Schweiz [ʃvaɪts] *f*: **die ~** Switzerland
schweiz. *abk* = **schweizerisch**
Schweizer ['ʃvaɪtsər] (**-s, -**) *m* Swiss ▷ *adj attrib* Swiss; **Schweizerdeutsch** *nt* Swiss German; **Schweizerin** *f* Swiss; **schweizerisch** *adj* Swiss
schwelen ['ʃve:lən] *vi* to smoulder (*Brit*), smolder (*US*)
schwelgen ['ʃvɛlgən] *vi* to indulge o.s.; **~ in** *+dat* to indulge in

Schwelle [ˈʃvɛlə] **(-, -n)** *f (auch fig)* threshold; *(Eisenb)* sleeper *(Brit)*, tie *(US)*
schwellen *unreg vi* to swell
Schwellenland *nt* threshold country
Schwellung *f* swelling
Schwemme [ˈʃvɛmə] *f*: **eine ~ an** *+dat* a glut of
schwemmen [ˈʃvɛmən] *vt (treiben: Sand etc)* to wash
Schwengel [ˈʃvɛŋəl] **(-s, -)** *m* pump handle; *(Glockenschwengel)* clapper
Schwenk [ʃvɛŋk] **(-(e)s, -s)** *m (Film)* pan, panning shot
Schwenkarm *m* swivel arm
schwenkbar *adj* swivel-mounted
schwenken *vt* to swing; *(Kamera)* to pan; *(Fahne)* to wave; *(Kartoffeln)* to toss; *(abspülen)* to rinse ▷ *vi* to turn, swivel; *(Mil)* to wheel
Schwenkung *f* turn; *(Mil)* wheel
schwer [ʃveːr] *adj* heavy; *(schwierig)* difficult, hard; *(schlimm)* serious, bad ▷ *adv (sehr)* very (much); *(verletzt etc)* seriously, badly; **~ erziehbar** maladjusted; **jdm/sich etw ~ machen** to make sth difficult for sb/o.s.; **~ verdaulich** indigestible; *(fig)* heavy; **~ verdient** *(Geld)* hard-earned; **~ verletzt** seriously *od* badly injured; **~ verwundet** seriously wounded; **~ erkältet sein** to have a heavy cold; **er lernt ~** he's a slow learner; **er ist ~ in Ordnung** *(umg)* he's a good bloke *(Brit) od* guy; **~ hören** to be hard of hearing; *siehe auch* **schwerfallen; schwernehmen; schwertun; schwerwiegend**; **Schwerarbeiter** *m* labourer *(Brit)*, laborer *(US)*; **Schwerbehinderte, r** *f(m)*, **Schwerbeschädigte, r** *f(m) (veraltet)* severely handicapped person
Schwere **(-, -n)** *f* weight; heaviness; *(Phys)* gravity; **schwerelos** *adj* weightless; **Schwerelosigkeit** *f* weightlessness
schwer- *zW*: **schwerfallen** *unreg vi*: **jdm schwerfallen** to be difficult for sb; **schwerfällig** *adj (auch Stil)* ponderous; *(Gang)* clumsy, awkward; *(Verstand)* slow; **Schwergewicht** *nt* heavyweight; *(fig)* emphasis; **schwergewichtig** *adj* heavyweight; **schwerhörig** *adj* hard of hearing; **Schwerindustrie** *f* heavy industry; **Schwerkraft** *f* gravity; **Schwerkranke, r** *f(m)* person who is seriously ill; **schwerlich** *adv* hardly; **Schwermetall** *nt* heavy metal; **schwermütig** *adj* melancholy; **schwernehmen** *unreg vt* to take to heart; **Schwerpunkt** *m* centre *(Brit) od* center *(US)* of gravity; *(fig)* emphasis, crucial point; **Schwerpunktstreik** *m* pinpoint strike; **schwerreich** *(umg) adj attrib* stinking rich
Schwert [ʃveːrt] **(-(e)s, -er)** *nt* sword; **Schwertlilie** *f* iris
schwer- *zW*: **schwertun** *unreg vr*: **sich** *dat od akk* **schwertun** to have difficulties; **Schwerverbrecher** *m* criminal; **Schwerverletzte, r** *f(m)* serious casualty; **schwerwiegend** *adj* weighty, important
Schwester [ˈʃvɛstər] **(-, -n)** *f* sister; *(Med)* nurse; **schwesterlich** *adj* sisterly
schwieg *etc* [ʃviːk] *vb siehe* **schweigen**
Schwieger- *zW*: **Schwiegereltern** *pl* parents-in-law *pl*; **Schwiegermutter** *f* mother-in-law; **Schwiegersohn** *m* son-in-law; **Schwiegertochter** *f* daughter-in-law; **Schwiegervater** *m* father-in-law
Schwiele [ˈʃviːlə] **(-, -n)** *f* callus
schwierig [ˈʃviːrɪç] *adj* difficult, hard; **Schwierigkeit** *f* difficulty; **Schwierigkeitsgrad** *m* degree of difficulty
schwillt [ʃvɪlt] *vb siehe* **schwellen**
Schwimmbad *nt* swimming baths *pl*
Schwimmbecken *nt* swimming pool
schwimmen *unreg vi* to swim; *(treiben, nicht sinken)* to float; *(fig: unsicher sein)* to be all at sea; **im Geld ~** *(umg)* to be rolling in money; **mir schwimmt es vor den Augen** I feel dizzy
Schwimmer **(-s, -)** *m* swimmer; *(Angeln)* float
Schwimmerin *f* swimmer
Schwimm- *zW*: **Schwimmflosse** *f (von Taucher)* flipper; **Schwimmhaut** *f (Ornithologie)* web; **Schwimmlehrer** *m* swimming instructor; **Schwimmsport** *m* swimming; **Schwimmweste** *f* life jacket
Schwindel [ˈʃvɪndəl] **(-s)** *m* dizziness; *(Betrug)* swindle, fraud; *(Zeug)* stuff; **in ~ erregender Höhe** at a dizzy height; **schwindelfrei** *adj* free from giddiness
schwindeln *vi (umg: lügen)* to fib; **mir schwindelt** I feel dizzy; **jdm schwindelt es** sb feels dizzy
schwinden [ˈʃvɪndən] *unreg vi* to disappear; *(Kräfte)* to fade, fail; *(sich verringern)* to decrease
Schwindler **(-s, -)** *m* swindler; *(Hochstapler)* con man, fraud; *(Lügner)* liar
schwindlig *adj* dizzy; **mir ist ~** I feel dizzy
Schwindsucht *f (veraltet)* consumption
schwingen [ˈʃvɪŋən] *unreg vt* to swing; *(Waffe etc)* to brandish ▷ *vi* to swing; *(vibrieren)* to vibrate; *(klingen)* to sound
Schwinger **(-s, -)** *m (Boxen)* swing
Schwingtor *nt* up-and-over door
Schwingtür *f* swing door(s *pl*) *(Brit)*, swinging door(s *pl*) *(US)*
Schwingung *f* vibration; *(Phys)* oscillation
Schwips [ʃvɪps] **(-es, -e)** *m*: **einen ~ haben** to be tipsy
schwirren [ˈʃvɪrən] *vi* to buzz
Schwitze [ˈʃvɪtsə] **(-, -n)** *f (Koch)* roux
schwitzen *vi* to sweat, perspire
schwofen [ˈʃvoːfən] *(umg) vi* to dance
schwoll *etc* [ʃvɔl] *vb siehe* **schwellen**
schwören [ˈʃvøːrən] *unreg vt, vi* to swear; **auf jdn/etw ~** *(fig)* to swear by sb/sth
schwul [ʃvuːl] *(umg) adj* gay, queer *(pej)*
schwül [ʃvyːl] *adj* sultry, close
Schwule, r *(umg) m* gay, queer *(pej)*, fag *(US pej)*
Schwüle **(-)** *f* sultriness, closeness
Schwulität [ʃvuliˈtɛːt] *(umg) f* trouble, difficulty
Schwulst [ʃvʊlst] **(-(e)s)** *m* bombast

schwülstig ['ʃvylstɪç] *adj* pompous
Schwund [ʃvʊnt] (**-(e)s**) *m (+gen)* decrease (in), decline (in), dwindling (of); (*Med*) atrophy; (*Schrumpfen*) shrinkage
Schwung [ʃvʊŋ] (**-(e)s, ⸚e**) *m* swing; (*Triebkraft*) momentum; (*fig: Energie*) verve, energy; (*umg: Menge*) batch; **in ~ sein** (*fig*) to be in full swing; **~ in die Sache bringen** (*umg*) to liven things up; **schwunghaft** *adj* brisk, lively; **Schwungrad** *nt* flywheel; **schwungvoll** *adj* vigorous
Schwur (**-(e)s, ⸚e**) *m* oath
schwur *etc* [ʃvu:r] *vb siehe* **schwören**
Schwurgericht *nt* court with a jury
SDR (**-**) *m abk* (= *Süddeutscher Rundfunk*) South German Radio
sechs [zɛks] *num* six; **Sechseck** *nt* hexagon; **sechshundert** *num* six hundred
sechste, r, s *adj* sixth
Sechstel ['zɛkstəl] (**-s, -**) *nt* sixth
sechzehn ['zɛçtse:n] *num* sixteen
sechzig ['zɛçtsɪç] *num* sixty
See[1] [ze:] (**-, -n**) *f* sea; **an der ~** by the sea, at the seaside; **in ~ stechen** to put to sea; **auf hoher ~** on the high seas
See[2] [ze:] (**-s, -n**) *m* lake
See- *zW*: **Seebad** *nt* seaside resort; **Seebär** *m* (*hum: umg*) seadog; (*Zool*) fur seal; **Seefahrt** *f* seafaring; (*Reise*) voyage; **seefest** *adj* (*Mensch*) not subject to seasickness; **Seegang** *m* (motion of the) sea; **Seegras** *nt* seaweed; **Seehund** *m* seal; **Seeigel** *m* sea urchin; **Seekarte** *f* chart; **seekrank** *adj* seasick; **Seekrankheit** *f* seasickness; **Seelachs** *m* rock salmon
Seele ['ze:lə] (**-, -n**) *f* soul; (*Mittelpunkt*) life and soul; **jdm aus der ~ sprechen** to express exactly what sb feels; **das liegt mir auf der ~** it weighs heavily on my mind; **eine ~ von Mensch** an absolute dear
Seelen- *zW*: **Seelenamt** *nt* (*Rel*) requiem; **Seelenfriede**, **Seelenfrieden** *m* peace of mind; **Seelenheil** *nt* salvation of one's soul; (*fig*) spiritual welfare; **Seelenruhe** *f*: **in aller Seelenruhe** calmly; (*kaltblütig*) as cool as you please; **seelenruhig** *adv* calmly
Seeleute ['ze:lɔʏtə] *pl* seamen *pl*
Seel- *zW*: **seelisch** *adj* mental; (*Rel*) spiritual; (*Belastung*) emotional; **Seelsorge** *f* pastoral duties *pl*; **Seelsorger** (**-s, -**) *m* clergyman
See- *zW*: **Seemacht** *f* naval power; **Seemann** (**-(e)s**, *pl* **-leute**) *m* seaman, sailor; **Seemeile** *f* nautical mile
Seengebiet ['ze:əngəbi:t] *nt* lakeland district
See- *zW*: **Seenot** *f*: **in Seenot** (*Schiff etc*) in distress; **Seepferd**, **Seepferdchen** *nt* sea horse; **Seeräuber** *m* pirate; **Seerecht** *nt* maritime law; **Seerose** *f* waterlily; **Seestern** *m* starfish; **Seetang** *m* seaweed; **seetüchtig** *adj* seaworthy; **Seeversicherung** *f* marine insurance; **Seeweg** *m* sea route; **auf dem Seeweg** by sea; **Seezunge** *f* sole
Segel ['ze:gəl] (**-s, -**) *nt* sail; **mit vollen ~n** under full sail *od* canvas; (*fig*) with gusto; **die ~ streichen** (*fig*) to give in; **Segelboot** *nt* yacht; **Segelfliegen** (**-s**) *nt* gliding; **Segelflieger** *m* glider pilot; **Segelflugzeug** *nt* glider
segeln *vt, vi* to sail; **durch eine Prüfung ~** (*umg*) to flop in an exam, fail (in) an exam
Segel- *zW*: **Segelschiff** *nt* sailing vessel; **Segelsport** *m* sailing; **Segeltuch** *nt* canvas
Segen ['ze:gən] (**-s, -**) *m* blessing
segensreich *adj* beneficial
Segler ['ze:glər] (**-s, -**) *m* sailor, yachtsman; (*Boot*) sailing boat
Seglerin *f* yachtswoman
segnen ['ze:gnən] *vt* to bless
sehen ['ze:ən] *unreg vt, vi* to see; (*in bestimmte Richtung*) to look; (*Fernsehsendung*) to watch; **sieht man das?** does it show?; **da sieht man(s) mal wieder!** that's typical!; **du siehst das nicht richtig** you've got it wrong; **so ge~** looked at in this way; **sich ~ lassen** to put in an appearance, appear; **das neue Rathaus kann sich ~ lassen** the new town hall is certainly something to be proud of; **siehe oben/unten** see above/below; **da kann man mal ~** that just shows (you) *od* just goes to show (*umg*); **mal ~!** we'll see!; **darauf ~, dass ...** to make sure (that) ...; **jdn kommen ~** to see sb coming
sehenswert *adj* worth seeing
Sehenswürdigkeiten *pl* sights *pl* (of a town)
Seher (**-s, -**) *m* seer
Sehfehler *m* sight defect
Sehkraft *f* (eye)sight
Sehne ['ze:nə] (**-, -n**) *f* sinew; (*an Bogen*) string
sehnen *vr*: **sich ~ nach** to long *od* yearn for
Sehnenscheidenentzündung *f* (*Med*) tendinitis
Sehnerv *m* optic nerve
sehnig *adj* sinewy
sehnlich *adj* ardent
Sehnsucht *f* longing
sehnsüchtig *adj* longing; (*Erwartung*) eager
sehnsuchtsvoll *adv* longingly, yearningly
sehr [ze:r] *adv* (*vor adj, adv*) very; (*mit Verben*) a lot, (very) much; **zu ~** too much; **er ist ~ dafür/dagegen** he is all for it/very much against it; **wie ~ er sich auch bemühte ...** however much he tried ...
Sehvermögen ['ze:fɛrmø:gən] (**-s**) *nt* powers *pl* of vision
seicht [zaɪçt] *adj* (*lit, fig*) shallow
seid [zaɪt] *vb siehe* **sein**
Seide ['zaɪdə] (**-, -n**) *f* silk
Seidel (**-s, -**) *nt* tankard, beer mug
seiden *adj* silk; **Seidenpapier** *nt* tissue paper
seidig ['zaɪdɪç] *adj* silky
Seife ['zaɪfə] (**-, -n**) *f* soap
Seifen- *zW*: **Seifenblase** *f* soap bubble; (*fig*) bubble; **Seifenlauge** *f* soapsuds *pl*; **Seifenschale** *f* soap dish; **Seifenschaum** *m* lather
seifig ['zaɪfɪç] *adj* soapy
seihen ['zaɪən] *vt* to strain, filter

Seil [zaɪl] (**-(e)s, -e**) *nt* rope; (*Kabel*) cable; **Seilbahn** *f* cable railway; **Seilhüpfen** (**-s**) *nt* skipping; **Seilspringen** (**-s**) *nt* skipping; **Seiltänzer, in** *m(f)* tightrope walker; **Seilzug** *m* tackle

SCHLÜSSELWORT

sein [zaɪn] (*pt* **war**, *pp* **gewesen**) *vi* **1** to be; **ich bin** I am; **du bist** you are; **er/sie/es ist** he/she/it is; **wir sind/ihr seid/sie sind** we/you/they are; **wir waren** we were; **wir sind gewesen** we have been

2: seien Sie nicht böse don't be angry; **sei so gut und ...** be so kind as to ...; **das wäre gut** that would *od* that'd be a good thing; **wenn ich Sie wäre** if I were *od* was you; **das wärs** that's all, that's it; **morgen bin ich in Rom** tomorrow I'll *od* I will *od* I shall be in Rome; **waren Sie mal in Rom?** have you ever been to Rome?

3: wie ist das zu verstehen? how is that to be understood?; **er ist nicht zu ersetzen** he cannot be replaced; **mit ihr ist nicht zu reden** you can't talk to her

4: mir ist kalt I'm cold; **mir ist, als hätte ich ihn früher schon einmal gesehen** I've a feeling I've seen him before; **was ist?** what's the matter?, what is it?; **ist was?** is something the matter?; **es sei denn(, dass ...)** unless ...; **wie dem auch sei** be that as it may; **wie wäre es mit ...?** how *od* what about ...?; **etw sein lassen** (*aufhören*) to stop (doing) sth; (*nicht tun*) to drop sth, leave sth; **lass das sein!** stop that!; **es ist an dir, zu ...** it's up to you to ...; **was sind Sie (beruflich)?** what do you do?; **das kann schon sein** that may well be

▷ *pron* his; (*bei Dingen*) its

Sein (**-s**) *nt*: **~ oder Nichtsein** to be or not to be

seine, r, s *poss pron* his; its; **er ist gut ~ zwei Meter** (*umg*) he's a good two metres (*Brit*) *od* meters (*US*); **die S~n** (*geh*) his family, his people; **jedem das S~** to each his own

seiner *gen von* **er; es** ▷ *pron* of him; of it

seinerseits *adv* for his part

seinerzeit *adv* in those days, formerly

seinesgleichen *pron* people like him

seinetwegen *adv* (*für ihn*) for his sake; (*wegen ihm*) on his account; (*von ihm aus*) as far as he is concerned

seinetwillen *adv*: **um ~ = seinetwegen**

seinige *pron*: **der/die/das ~** his

Seismograf [zaɪsmo'gra:f] (**-en, -en**) *m* seismograph

seit [zaɪt] *präp +dat* since; (*Zeitdauer*) for, in (*bes US*) ▷ *konj* since; **er ist ~ einer Woche hier** he has been here for a week; **~ Langem** for a long time; **seitdem** *adv, konj* since

Seite ['zaɪtə] (**-, -n**) *f* side; (*Buchseite*) page; (*Mil*) flank; **~ an Seite** side by side; **jdm zur ~ stehen** (*fig*) to stand by sb's side; **jdn zur ~ nehmen** to take sb aside; **auf der einen ~ ... auf der anderen (~) ...** on the one hand ..., on the other (hand) ...; **einer Sache** *dat* **die beste ~ abgewinnen** to make the best *od* most of sth; *siehe auch* **aufseiten; vonseiten**

Seiten- *zW*: **Seitenairbag** *m* (*Aut*) side-impact airbag; **Seitenansicht** *f* side view; **Seitenhieb** *m* (*fig*) passing shot, dig; **seitenlang** *adj* several pages long, going on for pages; **Seitenruder** *nt* (*Aviat*) rudder

seitens *präp +gen* on the part of

Seiten- *zW*: **Seitenschiff** *nt* aisle; **Seitensprung** *m* extramarital escapade; **Seitenstechen** *nt* (a) stitch; **Seitenstraße** *f* side road; **Seitenstreifen** *m* (*der Straße*) verge (*Brit*), berm (*US*); (*der Autobahn*) hard shoulder (*Brit*), shoulder (*US*); **seitenverkehrt** *adj* the wrong way round; **Seitenwagen** *m* sidecar; **Seitenwind** *m* crosswind; **Seitenzahl** *f* page number; (*Gesamtzahl*) number of pages

seit- *zW*: **seither** [zaɪt'he:r] *adv, konj* since (then); **seitlich** *adv* on one/the side ▷ *adj* side *attrib*; **seitwärts** *adv* sideways

sek, Sek. *abk* (= *Sekunde*) sec.

Sekretär [zekre'tɛ:r] *m* secretary; (*Möbel*) bureau

Sekretariat [zekretari'a:t] (**-(e)s, -e**) *nt* secretary's office, secretariat

Sekretärin *f* secretary

Sekt [zɛkt] (**-(e)s, -e**) *m* sparkling wine

Sekte (**-, -n**) *f* sect

Sektor ['zɛktɔr] *m* sector; (*Sachgebiet*) field

Sekunda [ze'kʊnda] (**-, Sekunden**) *f* (*Sch: früher: Untersekunda/Obersekunda*) *sixth/seventh year of German secondary school*

sekundär [zekʊn'dɛ:r] *adj* secondary; **Sekundärliteratur** *f* secondary literature

Sekunde [ze'kʊndə] (**-, -n**) *f* second

Sekunden- *zW*: **Sekundenkleber** *m* superglue; **Sekundenschnelle** *f*: **in Sekundenschnelle** in a matter of seconds; **Sekundenzeiger** *m* second hand

sel. *abk* = **selig**

selber ['zɛlbər] *demon pron* = **selbst**; **Selbermachen** *nt* do-it-yourself, DIY (*Brit*); (*von Kleidern etc*) making one's own

Selbst [zɛlpst] (**-**) *nt* self

SCHLÜSSELWORT

selbst [zɛlpst] *pron* **1: ich/er/wir selbst** I myself/he himself/we ourselves; **sie ist die Tugend selbst** she's virtue itself; **er braut sein Bier selbst** he brews his own beer; **das muss er selbst wissen** it's up to him; **wie gehts? — gut, und selbst?** how are things? — fine, and yourself?

2 (*ohne Hilfe*) alone, on my/his/one's *etc* own; **von selbst** by itself; **er kam von selbst** he came of his own accord; **selbst ist der Mann/die Frau!** self-reliance is the name of the game (*umg*); **selbst gemacht** home-made; **selbst gestrickt** hand-knitted; (*umg: Methode etc*) homespun, amateurish; **selbst**

verdientes Geld money one has earned o.s. ▷ *adv* even; **selbst wenn** even if; **selbst Gott** even God (himself)

Selbstachtung *f* self-respect

selbständig *etc* ['zɛlpʃtɛndɪç] *adj* = **selbstständig** *etc*

Selbst- *zW*: **Selbstanzeige** *f*: **Selbstanzeige erstatten** to come forward oneself; **der Dieb hat Selbstanzeige erstattet** the thief has come forward; **Selbstauslöser** *m* (*Phot*) delayed-action shutter release; **Selbstbedienung** *f* self-service; **Selbstbedienungsmentalität** *f* self-service mentality; **Selbstbefriedigung** *f* masturbation; (*fig*) self-gratification; **Selbstbeherrschung** *f* self-control; **Selbstbestätigung** *f* self-affirmation; **selbstbewusst** *adj* self-confident; (*selbstsicher*) self-assured; **Selbstbewusstsein** *nt* self-confidence; **Selbstbildnis** *nt* self-portrait; **Selbsterhaltung** *f* self-preservation; **Selbsterkenntnis** *f* self-knowledge; **Selbstfahrer** *m* (*Aut*): **Autovermietung für Selbstfahrer** self-drive car hire (*Brit*) *od* rental; **selbstgefällig** *adj* smug, self-satisfied; **selbstgerecht** *adj* self-righteous; **Selbstgespräch** *nt* conversation with o.s.; **selbstgewiss** *adj* confident; **selbstherrlich** *adj* high-handed; (*selbstgerecht*) self-satisfied; **Selbsthilfe** *f* self-help; **zur Selbsthilfe greifen** to take matters into one's own hands; **selbstklebend** *adj* self-adhesive; **Selbstkostenpreis** *m* cost price; **selbstlos** *adj* unselfish, selfless; **Selbstmord** *m* suicide; **Selbstmordanschlag** *m* suicide attack; **Selbstmordattentäter, in** *m(f)* suicide bomber; **Selbstmörder, in** *m(f)* (*Person*) suicide; **selbstmörderisch** *adj* suicidal; **selbstsicher** *adj* self-assured; **Selbstsicherheit** *f* self-assurance; **selbstständig** ['zɛlpstʃtɛndɪç] *adj* independent; **sich selbstständig machen** (*beruflich*) to set up on one's own, start one's own business; **Selbstständigkeit** *f* independence; **Selbststudium** *nt* private study; **selbstsüchtig** *adj* selfish; **selbsttätig** *adj* automatic; **Selbstüberwindung** *f* willpower; **selbstvergessen** *adj* absent-minded; (*Blick*) faraway; **selbstverschuldet** *adj*: **wenn der Unfall selbstverschuldet ist** if there is personal responsibility for the accident; **Selbstversorger** *m*: **Selbstversorger sein** to be self-sufficient *od* self-reliant; **Urlaub für Selbstversorger** self-catering holiday

selbstverständlich *adj* obvious ▷ *adv* naturally; **ich halte das für ~** I take that for granted

Selbstverständlichkeit *f* (*Unbefangenheit*) naturalness; (*natürliche Voraussetzung*) matter of course

Selbst- *zW*: **Selbstverständnis** *nt*: **nach seinem eigenen Selbstverständnis** as he sees himself; **Selbstverteidigung** *f* self-defence (*Brit*), self-defense (*US*); **Selbstvertrauen** *nt* self-confidence; **Selbstverwaltung** *f* autonomy, self-government; **Selbstwählferndienst** *m* (*Tel*) automatic dialling service, subscriber trunk dialling (*Brit*), STD (*Brit*), direct distance dialing (*US*); **Selbstwertgefühl** *nt* feeling of one's own worth *od* value, self-esteem; **selbstzufrieden** *adj* self-satisfied; **Selbstzweck** *m* end in itself

selig ['ze:lɪç] *adj* happy, blissful; (*Rel*) blessed; (*tot*) late; **Seligkeit** *f* bliss

Sellerie ['zɛləri:] (**-s, -(s)** *od* **-, -n**) *m od f* celery

selten ['zɛltən] *adj* rare ▷ *adv* seldom, rarely; **Seltenheit** *f* rarity; **Seltenheitswert** (**-(e)s**) *m* rarity value

Selterswasser ['zɛltərsvasər] *nt* soda water

seltsam ['zɛltza:m] *adj* curious, strange

seltsamerweise *adv* curiously, strangely

Seltsamkeit *f* strangeness

Semester [ze'mɛstər] (**-s, -**) *nt* semester; **ein älteres ~** a senior student

Semi- [zemi] *in zw* semi-

Semikolon [-'ko:lɔn] (**-s, -s**) *nt* semicolon

Seminar [zemi'na:r] (**-s, -e**) *nt* seminary; (*Kurs*) seminar; (*Univ: Ort*) department building

semitisch [ze'mi:tɪʃ] *adj* Semitic

Semmel ['zɛməl] (**-, -n**) *f* roll; **Semmelbrösel**, **Semmelbröseln** *pl* breadcrumbs *pl*; **Semmelknödel** (*Südd, Österr*) *m* bread dumpling

sen. *abk* (= *senior*) sen.

Senat [ze'na:t] (**-(e)s, -e**) *m* senate

Sendebereich *m* transmission range

Sendefolge *f* (*Serie*) series

senden[1] *unreg vt* to send

senden[2] *vt, vi* (*Rundf, TV*) to transmit, broadcast

Sendenetz *nt* network

Sendepause *f* (*Rundf, TV*) interval

Sender (**-s, -**) *m* station; (*Anlage*) transmitter

Sende- *zW*: **Sendereihe** *f* series (of broadcasts); **Sendeschluss** *m* (*Rundf, TV*) closedown; **Sendestation** *f* transmitting station; **Sendestelle** *f* transmitting station; **Sendezeit** *f* broadcasting time, air time

Sendung ['zɛndʊŋ] *f* consignment; (*Aufgabe*) mission; (*Rundf, TV*) transmission; (*Programm*) programme (*Brit*), program (*US*)

Senegal ['ze:negal] (**-s**) *nt* Senegal

Senf [zɛnf] (**-(e)s, -e**) *m* mustard; **seinen ~ dazugeben** (*umg*) to put one's oar in; **Senfkorn** *nt* mustard seed

sengen ['zɛŋən] *vt* to singe ▷ *vi* to scorch

senil [ze'ni:l] (*pej*) *adj* senile

Senior ['ze:niɔr] (**-s, -en**) *m* (*Rentner*) senior citizen; (*Geschäftspartner*) senior partner

Seniorenpass [zeni'o:rənpas] *m* senior citizen's travel pass (*Brit*)

Senkblei ['zɛŋkblaɪ] *nt* plumb

Senke (**-, -n**) *f* depression

Senkel (**-s, -**) *m* (shoe)lace

senken *vt* to lower; (*Kopf*) to bow; (*Tech*) to sink

▷ *vr* to sink; (*Stimme*) to drop
Senk- *zW*: **Senkfuß** *m* flat foot; **Senkgrube** *f* cesspit; **senkrecht** *adj* vertical, perpendicular; **Senkrechte** *f* perpendicular; **Senkrechtstarter** *m* (*Aviat*) vertical takeoff plane; (*fig: Person*) high-flier
Senner, in ['zɛnər(ɪn)] (**-s, -**) *m(f)* (Alpine) dairyman, dairymaid
Sensation [zenzatsi'o:n] *f* sensation
sensationell [zɛnzatsio'nɛl] *adj* sensational
Sensationsblatt *nt* sensational paper
Sensationssucht *f* sensationalism
Sense ['zɛnzə] (**-, -n**) *f* scythe; **dann ist ~!** (*umg*) that's the end!
sensibel [zɛn'zi:bəl] *adj* sensitive
sensibilisieren [zɛnzibili'zi:rən] *vt* to sensitize
Sensibilität [zɛnzibili'tɛ:t] *f* sensitivity
sentimental [zɛntimɛn'ta:l] *adj* sentimental
Sentimentalität [zɛntimɛntali'tɛ:t] *f* sentimentality
separat [zepa'ra:t] *adj* separate; (*Wohnung, Zimmer*) self-contained
Sept. *abk* (= *September*) Sept.
September [zɛp'tɛmbər] (**-(s), -**) *m* September; **im ~** in September; **im Monat ~** in the month of September; **heute ist der zweite ~** today is the second of September *od* September second (*US*); (*geschrieben*) today is 2nd September; **in diesem ~** this September; **Anfang/Ende/Mitte ~** at the beginning/end/in the middle of September
septisch ['zɛptɪʃ] *adj* septic
sequentiell [zekvɛntsi'ɛl] *adj* = **sequenziell**
Sequenz [ze'kvɛnts] *f* sequence
sequenziell [zekvɛntsi'ɛl] *adj* (*Comput*) sequential; **~er Zugriff** sequential access
Serbe ['zɛrbə] (**-n, -n**) *m* Serbian
Serbien (**-s**) *nt* Serbia; **~ und Montenegro** Serbia and Montenegro
Serbin *f* Serbian
serbisch *adj* Serbian
Serbokroatisch, e *nt* Serbo-Croat
Serie ['ze:riə] *f* series
seriell [zeri'ɛl] *adj* (*Comput*) serial; **~e Daten** serial data *pl*; **~er Anschluss** serial port; **~er Drucker** serial printer
Serien- *zW*: **Serienanfertigung** *f*, **Serienherstellung** *f* series production; **serienmäßig** *adj* (*Ausstattung*) standard; (*Herstellung*) series *attrib* ▷ *adv* (*herstellen*) in series; **Seriennummer** *f* serial number; **serienweise** *adv* in series
seriös [zeri'ø:s] *adj* serious; (*anständig*) respectable
Serpentine [zɛrpɛn'ti:nə] *f* hairpin (bend)
Serum ['ze:rʊm] (**-s, Seren**) *nt* serum
Service[1] [zɛr'vi:s] (**-(s), -**) *nt* (*Gläserservice*) set; (*Geschirr*) service
Service[2] ['sə:vɪs] (**-, -s**) *m* (*Comm, Sport*) service
servieren [zɛr'vi:rən] *vt, vi* to serve
Serviererin [zɛr'vi:rərɪn] *f* waitress
Servierwagen *m* trolley
Serviette [zɛrvi'ɛtə] *f* napkin, serviette
Servolenkung *f* power steering
Servomotor *m* servo motor
Servus ['zɛrvʊs] (*Österr, Südd*) *interj* hello; (*beim Abschied*) goodbye, so long (*umg*)
Sesam ['ze:zam] (**-s, -s**) *m* sesame
Sessel ['zɛsəl] (**-s, -**) *m* armchair; **Sessellift** *m* chairlift
sesshaft ['zɛshaft] *adj* settled; (*ansässig*) resident
Set [zɛt] (**-s, -s**) *nt od m* set; (*Deckchen*) tablemat
setzen ['zɛtsən] *vt* to put, place, set; (*Baum etc*) to plant; (*Segel, Typ*) to set ▷ *vr* (*Platz nehmen*) to sit down; (*Kaffee, Tee*) to settle ▷ *vi* to leap; (*wetten*) to bet; (*Typ*) to set; **jdm ein Denkmal ~** to build a monument to sb; **sich zu jdm ~** to sit with sb
Setzer ['zɛtsər] (**-s, -**) *m* (*Typ*) typesetter
Setzerei [zɛtsə'raɪ] *f* caseroom; (*Firma*) typesetting firm
Setz- *zW*: **Setzkasten** *m* (*Typ*) case; (*an Wand*) ornament shelf; **Setzling** *m* young plant; **Setzmaschine** *f* (*Typ*) typesetting machine
Seuche ['zɔʏçə] (**-, -n**) *f* epidemic
Seuchengebiet *nt* infected area
seufzen ['zɔʏftsən] *vt, vi* to sigh
Seufzer ['zɔʏftsər] (**-s, -**) *m* sigh
Sex [zɛks] (**-(es)**) *m* sex
Sexta ['zɛksta] (**-, Sexten**) *f* (*früher*) *first year of German secondary school*
Sexualerziehung [zɛksu'a:lɛrtsi:ʊŋ] *f* sex education
Sexualität [zɛksuali'tɛ:t] *f* sex, sexuality
Sexual- *zW*: **Sexualkunde** [zɛksu'a:lkʊndə] *f* sex education; **Sexualleben** *nt* sex life; **Sexualobjekt** *nt* sex object
sexuell [zɛksu'ɛl] *adj* sexual
Seychellen [ze'ʃɛlən] *pl* Seychelles *pl*
sezieren [ze'tsi:rən] *vt* to dissect
SFB (**-**) *m abk* (= *Sender Freies Berlin*) Radio Free Berlin
Sfr, sFr. *abk* (= *Schweizer Franken*) sfr
Shampoo [ʃam'pu:] (**-s, -s**) *nt* shampoo
Shetlandinseln ['ʃɛtlant|ɪnzəln] *pl* Shetland, Shetland Isles *pl*
Shorts [ʃo:rts] *pl* shorts *pl*
Showmaster ['ʃoʊma:stər] (**-s, -**) *m* compère, MC
siamesisch [zia'me:zɪʃ] *adj*: **~e Zwillinge** Siamese twins
Siamkatze *f* Siamese (cat)
Sibirien [zi'bi:riən] (**-s**) *nt* Siberia
sibirisch *adj* Siberian

SCHLÜSSELWORT

sich [zɪç] *pron* **1** (*akk*): **er/sie/es ... sich** he/she/it ... himself/herself/itself; **sie** *pl*/**man ... sich** they/one ... themselves/oneself; **Sie ... sich** you ... yourself/yourselves *pl*; **sich wiederholen** to repeat oneself/itself
2 (*dat*): **er/sie/es ... sich** he/she/it ... to himself/herself/itself; **sie** *pl*/**man ... sich** they/one ... to themselves/oneself; **Sie ...**

sich you ... to yourself/yourselves *pl*; **sie hat sich einen Pullover gekauft** she bought herself a jumper; **sich die Haare waschen** to wash one's hair
3 (*mit Präposition*): **haben Sie Ihren Ausweis bei sich?** do you have your pass on you?; **er hat nichts bei sich** he's got nothing on him; **sie bleiben gern unter sich** they keep themselves to themselves
4 (*einander*) each other, one another; **sie bekämpfen sich** they fight each other *od* one another
5: dieses Auto fährt sich gut this car drives well; **hier sitzt es sich gut** it's good to sit here

Sichel ['zɪçəl] (**-, -n**) *f* sickle; (*Mondsichel*) crescent
sicher ['zɪçər] *adj* safe; (*gewiss*) certain; (*Hand, Job*) steady; (*zuverlässig*) secure, reliable; (*selbstsicher*) confident; (*Stellung*) secure ▷ *adv* (*natürlich*): **du hast dich ~ verrechnet** you must have counted wrongly; **vor jdm/etw ~ sein** to be safe from sb/sth; **sich** *dat* **einer Sache/jds ~ sein** to be sure of sth/sb; **~ ist sicher** you can't be too sure
sichergehen *unreg vi* to make sure
Sicherheit ['zɪçərhaɪt] *f* safety; (*auch Fin*) security; (*Gewissheit*) certainty; (*Selbstsicherheit*) confidence; **die öffentliche ~** public security; **~ im Straßenverkehr** road safety; **~ leisten** (*Comm*) to offer security
Sicherheits- *zW*: **Sicherheitsabstand** *m* safe distance; **Sicherheitsbestimmungen** *pl* safety regulations *pl*; (*betrieblich, Pol etc*) security controls *pl*; **Sicherheitseinrichtungen** *pl* security equipment *sing*, security devices *pl*; **Sicherheitsglas** *nt* safety glass; **Sicherheitsgurt** *m* seat belt; **sicherheitshalber** *adv* to be on the safe side; **Sicherheitsnadel** *f* safety pin; **Sicherheitsrat** *m* Security Council; **Sicherheitsschloss** *nt* safety lock; **Sicherheitsspanne** *f* (*Comm*) margin of safety; **Sicherheitsverschluss** *m* safety clasp; **Sicherheitsvorkehrung** *f* safety precaution
sicherlich *adv* certainly, surely
sichern *vt* to secure; (*schützen*) to protect; (*Bergsteiger etc*) to belay; (*Waffe*) to put the safety catch on; (*Comput: Daten*) to back up; **jdm/sich etw ~** to secure sth for sb/for o.s.
sicherstellen *vt* to impound; (*garantieren*) to guarantee
Sicherung *f* (*Sichern*) securing; (*Vorrichtung*) safety device; (*an Waffen*) safety catch; (*Elek*) fuse; **da ist (bei) ihm die ~ durchgebrannt** (*fig: umg*) he blew a fuse
Sicherungskopie *f* backup copy
Sicht [zɪçt] (**-**) *f* sight; (*Aussicht*) view; (*Sehweite*) visibility; **auf** *od* **nach ~** (*Fin*) at sight; **auf lange ~** on a long-term basis; **sichtbar** *adj* visible; **Sichtbarkeit** *f* visibility
sichten *vt* to sight; (*auswählen*) to sort out; (*ordnen*) to sift through
Sicht- *zW*: **sichtlich** *adj* evident, obvious; **Sichtverhältnisse** *pl* visibility *sing*; **Sichtvermerk** *m* visa; **Sichtweite** *f* visibility; **außer Sichtweite** out of sight
sickern ['zɪkərn] *vi* (*Hilfsverb sein*) to seep; (*in Tropfen*) to drip
Sie [zi:] *nom, akk pron* you
sie *pron* (*sing: nom*) she; (*: akk*) her; (*pl: nom*) they; (*: akk*) them
Sieb [zi:p] (**-(e)s, -e**) *nt* sieve; (*Koch*) strainer; (*Gemüsesieb*) colander
sieben[1] ['zi:bən] *vt* to sieve, sift; (*Flüssigkeit*) to strain ▷ *vi*: **bei der Prüfung wird stark gesiebt** (*fig: umg*) the exam will weed a lot of people out
sieben[2] ['zi:bən] *num* seven; **Siebengebirge** *nt*: **das Siebengebirge** the Seven Mountains *pl* (*near Bonn*); **siebenhundert** *num* seven hundred; **Siebenmeter** *m* (*Sport*) penalty; **Siebensachen** *pl* belongings *pl*; **Siebenschläfer** *m* (*Zool*) dormouse
siebte, r, s ['zi:ptə(r, s)] *adj* seventh
Siebtel (**-s, -**) *nt* seventh
siebzehn ['zi:ptse:n] *num* seventeen
siebzig ['zi:ptsɪç] *num* seventy
siedeln ['zi:dəln] *vi* to settle
sieden ['zi:dən] *vt, vi* to boil
Siedepunkt *m* boiling point
Siedler (**-s, -**) *m* settler
Siedlung *f* settlement; (*Häusersiedlung*) housing estate (*Brit*) *od* development (*US*)
Sieg [zi:k] (**-(e)s, -e**) *m* victory
Siegel ['zi:gəl] (**-s, -**) *nt* seal; **Siegellack** *m* sealing wax; **Siegelring** *m* signet ring
siegen ['zi:gən] *vi* to be victorious; (*Sport*) to win; **über jdn/etw ~** (*fig*) to triumph over sb/sth; (*in Wettkampf*) to beat sb/sth
Sieger, in (**-s, -**) *m(f)* victor; (*Sport etc*) winner; **Siegerehrung** *f* (*Sport*) presentation ceremony
siegessicher *adj* sure of victory
Siegeszug *m* triumphal procession
siegreich *adj* victorious
siehe ['zi:ə] *imperativ* see; (*siehe da*) behold
siehst [zi:st], **sieht** [zi:t] *vb siehe* **sehen**
Siel [zi:l] (**-(e)s, -e**) *nt od m* (*Schleuse*) sluice; (*Abwasserkanal*) sewer
siezen ['zi:tsən] *vt* to address as "Sie"; *siehe auch* **duzen**
Signal [zɪ'gna:l] (**-s, -e**) *nt* signal; **Signalanlage** *f* signals *pl*, set of signals
signalisieren [zɪgnali'zi:rən] *vt* (*lit, fig*) to signal
Signatur [zɪgna'tu:r] *f* signature; (*Bibliothekssignatur*) shelf mark
Silbe ['zɪlbə] (**-, -n**) *f* syllable; **er hat es mit keiner ~ erwähnt** he didn't say a word about it
Silber ['zɪlbər] (**-s**) *nt* silver; **Silberbergwerk** *nt* silver mine; **Silberblick** *m*: **einen Silberblick haben** to have a slight squint; **Silberhochzeit** *f* silver wedding
silbern *adj* silver
Silberpapier *nt* silver paper

Silhouette [zilu'ɛtə] *f* silhouette
Silikonchip [zili'ko:ntʃɪp] *m* silicon chip
Silo ['zi:lo] (**-s, -s**) *nt od m* silo
Silvester [zɪl'vɛstər] (**-s, -**) *m or nt* New Year's Eve, Hogmanay (*Scot*); *see culture note*

SILVESTER

Silvester is the German name for New Year's Eve. Although not an official holiday, most businesses close early and shops shut at midday. Most Germans celebrate in the evening and at midnight they let off fireworks and rockets; the revelry usually lasts until the early hours of the morning.

Simbabwe [zɪm'ba:bvə] (**-s**) *nt* Zimbabwe
SIM-Karte ['zɪm-] *f* SIM card
simpel ['zɪmpəl] *adj* simple; **Simpel** (**-s, -**) (*umg*) *m* simpleton
Sims [zɪms] (**-es, -e**) *nt od m* (*Kaminsims*) mantelpiece; (*Fenstersims*) (window)sill
simsen ['zɪmsən] (*umg*) *vti* to text
Simulant, in [zimu'lant(ɪn)] (**-en, -en**) *m(f)* malingerer
simulieren [zimu'li:rən] *vt* to simulate; (*vortäuschen*) to feign ▷ *vi* to feign illness
simultan [zimʊl'ta:n] *adj* simultaneous; **Simultandolmetscher** *m* simultaneous interpreter
sind [zɪnt] *vb siehe* **sein**
Sinfonie [zɪnfo'ni:] *f* symphony
Singapur ['zɪŋgapu:r] (**-s**) *nt* Singapore
singen ['zɪŋən] *unreg vt, vi* to sing
Single[1] ['sɪŋgəl] (**-s, -s**) *m* (*Alleinlebender*) single person
Single[2] ['sɪŋgəl] (**-, -s**) *f* (*Mus*) single
Singsang *m* (*Gesang*) monotonous singing
Singstimme *f* vocal part
Singular ['zɪŋgula:r] *m* singular
Singvogel ['zɪŋfo:gəl] *m* songbird
sinken ['zɪŋkən] *unreg vi* to sink; (*Boden, Gebäude*) to subside; (*Fundament*) to settle; (*Preise etc*) to fall, go down; **den Mut/die Hoffnung ~ lassen** to lose courage/hope
Sinn [zɪn] (**-(e)s, -e**) *m* mind; (*Wahrnehmungssinn*) sense; (*Bedeutung*) sense, meaning; **im ~e des Gesetzes** according to the spirit of the law; **~ für etw** sense of sth; **im ~e des Verstorbenen** in accordance with the wishes of the deceased; **von ~en sein** to be out of one's mind; **das ist nicht der ~ der Sache** that is not the point; **das hat keinen ~** there is no point in that; **Sinnbild** *nt* symbol; **sinnbildlich** *adj* symbolic
sinnen *unreg vi* to ponder; **auf etw** *akk* **~** to contemplate sth; **über etw** *akk* **~** to reflect on sth
Sinnenmensch *m* sensualist
Sinnes- *zW*: **Sinnesorgan** *nt* sense organ; **Sinnestäuschung** *f* illusion; **Sinneswandel** *m* change of mind
sinngemäß *adj* faithful; (*Wiedergabe*) in one's own words
sinnig *adj* apt; (*ironisch*) clever
Sinn- *zW*: **sinnlich** *adj* sensual, sensuous; (*Wahrnehmung*) sensory; **Sinnlichkeit** *f* sensuality; **sinnlos** *adj* senseless, meaningless; **sinnlos betrunken** blind drunk; **Sinnlosigkeit** *f* senselessness, meaninglessness; **sinnverwandt** *adj* synonymous; **sinnvoll** *adj* meaningful; (*vernünftig*) sensible
Sinologe [zino'lo:gə] (**-n, -n**) *m* Sinologist
Sinologie *f* Sinology
Sinologin *f* Sinologist
Sintflut ['zɪntflu:t] *f* Flood; **nach uns die ~** (*umg*) it doesn't matter what happens after we've gone; **sintflutartig** *adj*: **sintflutartige Regenfälle** torrential rain *sing*
Sinus ['zi:nʊs] (**-, - *od* -se**) *m* (*Anat*) sinus; (*Math*) sine
Siphon [zi'fõ:] (**-s, -s**) *m* siphon
Sippe ['zɪpə] (**-, -n**) *f* (extended) family; (*umg: Verwandtschaft*) clan
Sippschaft ['zɪpʃaft] (*pej*) *f* tribe; (*Bande*) gang
Sirene [zi're:nə] (**-, -n**) *f* siren
Sirup ['zi:rʊp] (**-s, -e**) *m* syrup
Sit-in [sɪt'|ɪn] (**-(s), -s**) *nt*: **ein ~ machen** to stage a sit-in
Sitte ['zɪtə] (**-, -n**) *f* custom; **Sitten** *pl* morals *pl*; **was sind denn das für ~n?** what sort of way is that to behave?
Sitten- *zW*: **Sittenpolizei** *f* vice squad; **Sittenstrolch** (*umg*) *m* sex fiend; **Sittenwächter** *m* (*ironisch*) guardian of public morals; **sittenwidrig** *adj* (*form*) immoral
Sittich ['zɪtɪç] (**-(e)s, -e**) *m* parakeet
Sitt- *zW*: **sittlich** *adj* moral; **Sittlichkeit** *f* morality; **Sittlichkeitsverbrechen** *nt* sex offence (*Brit*) *od* offense (*US*); **sittsam** *adj* modest, demure
Situation [zituatsi'o:n] *f* situation
situiert [zitu'i:rt] *adj*: **gut ~ sein** to be well off
Sitz [zɪts] (**-es, -e**) *m* seat; (*von Firma, Verwaltung*) headquarters *pl*; **der Anzug hat einen guten ~** the suit sits well
sitzen *unreg vi* to sit; (*Bemerkung, Schlag*) to strike home; (*Gelerntes*) to have sunk in; (*umg: im Gefängnis sitzen*) to be inside; **locker ~** to be loose; **einen ~ haben** (*umg*) to have had one too many; **er sitzt im Kultusministerium** (*umg: sein*) he's in the Ministry of Education; **~ bleiben** to remain seated; (*Sch*) to have to repeat a year; **auf etw** *dat* **~ bleiben** to be lumbered with sth; **~ lassen** (*Sch*) to keep down a year; (*Mädchen*) to jilt; (*Wartenden*) to stand up; **etw auf sich** *dat* **~ lassen** to take sth lying down
sitzend *adj* (*Tätigkeit*) sedentary
Sitz- *zW*: **Sitzfleisch** (*umg*) *nt*: **Sitzfleisch haben** to be able to sit still; **Sitzgelegenheit** *f* seats *pl*; **Sitzordnung** *f* seating plan; **Sitzplatz** *m* seat; **Sitzstreik** *m* sit-down strike
Sitzung *f* meeting
Sizilianer, in [zitsili'a:nər(ɪn)] (**-s, -**) *m(f)*

Sicilian
sizilianisch *adj* Sicilian
Sizilien [zi'tsi:liən] (**-s**) *nt* Sicily
Skala ['ska:la] (**-, Skalen**) *f* scale; (*fig*) range
Skalpell [skal'pɛl] (**-s, -e**) *nt* scalpel
skalpieren [skal'pi:rən] *vt* to scalp
Skandal [skan'da:l] (**-s, -e**) *m* scandal
skandalös [skanda'lø:s] *adj* scandalous
Skandinavien [skandi'na:viən] (**-s**) *nt* Scandinavia
Skandinavier, in (**-s, -**) *m(f)* Scandinavian
skandinavisch *adj* Scandinavian
Skat [ska:t] (**-(e)s, -e** *od* **-s**) *m* (*Karten*) skat
Skelett [ske'lɛt] (**-(e)s, -e**) *nt* skeleton
Skepsis ['skɛpsɪs] (**-**) *f* scepticism (*Brit*), skepticism (*US*)
skeptisch ['skɛptɪʃ] *adj* sceptical (*Brit*), skeptical (*US*)
Ski [ʃi:] (**-s, -er**) *m* ski; **~ laufen** *od* **fahren** to ski; **Skifahrer** *m* skier; **Skihütte** *f* ski hut; **Skiläufer** *m* skier; **Skilehrer** *m* ski instructor; **Skilift** *m* ski lift; **Skispringen** *nt* ski jumping; **Skistiefel** *m* ski boot; **Skistock** *m* ski pole
Skizze ['skɪtsə] (**-, -n**) *f* sketch
skizzieren [skɪ'tsi:rən] *vt* to sketch; (*fig: Plan etc*) to outline ▷ *vi* to sketch
Sklave ['skla:və] (**-n, -n**) *m* slave
Sklaventreiber (**-s, -**) (*pej*) *m* slave-driver
Sklaverei [skla:və'raɪ] *f* slavery
Sklavin *f* slave
sklavisch *adj* slavish
Skonto ['skɔnto] (**-s, -s**) *nt od m* discount
Skorbut [skɔr'bu:t] (**-(e)s**) *m* scurvy
Skorpion [skɔrpi'o:n] (**-s, -e**) *m* scorpion; (*Astrol*) Scorpio
Skrupel ['skru:pəl] (**-s, -**) *m* scruple; **skrupellos** *adj* unscrupulous
Skulptur [skʊlp'tu:r] *f* sculpture
skurril [skʊ'ri:l] *adj* (*geh*) droll, comical
Slalom ['sla:lɔm] (**-s, -s**) *m* slalom
Slawe ['sla:və] (**-n, -n**) *m* Slav
Slawin *f* Slav
slawisch *adj* Slavonic, Slavic
Slip [slɪp] (**-s, -s**) *m* (pair of) briefs *pl*
Slowake [slo'va:kə] (**-n, -n**) *m* Slovak
Slowakei [slova'kaɪ] *f* Slovakia
Slowakin *f* Slovak
Slowakisch [slo'va:kɪʃ] *nt* (*Ling*) Slovak; **slowakisch** *adj* Slovak
Slowenien [slo've:niən] (**-s**) *nt* Slovenia
slowenisch *adj* Slovene
Smaragd [sma'rakt] (**-(e)s, -e**) *m* emerald
Smoking ['smo:kɪŋ] (**-s, -s**) *m* dinner jacket (*Brit*), tuxedo (*US*)
SMS (**-, -**) *f abk* (= *Short Message Service*) SMS; **jdm eine ~ schicken** to send sb a text; **SMS-Nachricht** *f* text message
SMV (**-, -s**) *f abk* = **Schülermitverwaltung**
Snob [snɔp] (**-s, -s**) *m* snob
So. *abk* = **Sonntag**
SO *abk* (= *Südost(en)*) SE

SCHLÜSSELWORT

so [zo:] *adv* **1** (*so sehr*) so; **so groß/schön** *etc* so big/nice *etc*; **so groß/schön wie ...** as big/nice as ...; **das hat ihn so geärgert, dass ...** that annoyed him so much that ...
2 (*auf diese Weise*) like this; **so genannt** so-called; **mach es nicht so** don't do it like that; **so oder so** (in) one way or the other; **... oder so** something (like that); **und so weiter** and so on; **so viel (wie)** as much as; **rede nicht so viel** don't talk so much; **so weit sein** to be ready; **so weit wie** *od* **als möglich** as far as possible; **ich bin so weit zufrieden** by and large I'm quite satisfied; **es ist bald so weit** it's nearly time; **so wenig (wie)** no more (than), not any more (than); **so wenig wie möglich** as little as possible; **so ein ...** such a ...; **so einer wie ich** somebody like me; **so (et)was** something like this/that; **na so was!** well I never!; **das ist gut so** that's fine; **sie ist nun einmal so** that's just the way she is; **das habe ich nur so gesagt** I didn't really mean it
3 (*umg: umsonst*): **ich habe es so bekommen** I got it for nothing
4 (*als Füllwort: nicht übersetzt*): **so mancher** a number of people *pl*
▷ *konj*: **so wie es jetzt ist** as things are at the moment; *siehe auch* **sodass**
▷ *interj*: **so?** really?; **so, das wärs** right, that's it then

s. o. *abk* (= *siehe oben*) see above
sobald [zo'balt] *konj* as soon as
Söckchen [zœkçən] *nt* ankle sock
Socke ['zɔkə] (**-, -n**) *f* sock; **sich auf die ~n machen** (*umg*) to get going
Sockel ['zɔkəl] (**-s, -**) *m* pedestal, base
sodass [zo'das] *konj* so that
Sodawasser ['zo:davasər] *nt* soda water
Sodbrennen ['zo:tbrɛnən] (**-s**) *nt* heartburn
Sodomie [zodo'mi:] *f* bestiality
soeben [zo'|e:bən] *adv* just (now)
Sofa ['zo:fa] (**-s, -s**) *nt* sofa
Sofabett *nt* sofa bed, bed settee
sofern [zo'fɛrn] *konj* if, provided (that)
soff *etc* [zɔf] *vb siehe* **saufen**
sofort [zo'fɔrt] *adv* immediately, at once; **(ich) komme ~!** (I'm) just coming!; **Soforthilfe** *f* emergency relief *od* aid; **Soforthilfegesetz** *nt* law on emergency aid
sofortig *adj* immediate
Sofortmaßnahme *f* immediate measure
Softeis ['sɔft|aɪs] (**-es**) *nt* soft ice-cream
Softie ['zɔfti:] (**-s, -s**) (*umg*) *m* softy
Software ['zɔftwɛ:ər] (**-, -s**) *f* software; **softwarekompatibel** *adj* software compatible; **Softwarepaket** *nt* software package
Sog (**-(e)s, -e**) *m* suction; (*von Strudel*) vortex; (*fig*) maelstrom
sog *etc* [zo:k] *vb siehe* **saugen**
sog. *abk* = **sogenannt**

sogar [zo'ga:r] *adv* even
sogenannt ['zo:gənant] *adj attrib* so-called
sogleich [zo'glaıç] *adv* straight away, at once
Sogwirkung *f* suction; (*fig*) knock-on effect
Sohle ['zo:lə] (**-, -n**) *f* (*Fußsohle*) sole; (*Talsohle etc*) bottom; (*Min*) level; **auf leisen ~n** (*fig*) softly, noiselessly
Sohn [zo:n] (**-(e)s, ¨-e**) *m* son
Sojasoße ['zo:jazo:sə] *f* soy *od* soya sauce
solang, solange *konj* as *od* so long as
Solar- [zo'la:r] *in zw* solar; **Solarenergie** *f* solar energy
Solarium [zo'la:riʊm] *nt* solarium
Solbad ['zo:lba:t] *nt* saltwater bath
solch [zɔlç] *adj inv* such
solche, r, s *adj* such; **ein ~r Mensch** such a person
Sold [zɔlt] (**-(e)s, -e**) *m* pay
Soldat [zɔl'da:t] (**-en, -en**) *m* soldier; **soldatisch** *adj* soldierly
Söldner ['zœldnər] (**-s, -**) *m* mercenary
Sole ['zo:lə] (**-, -n**) *f* brine, salt water
Solei ['zo:laı] *nt* pickled egg
Soli ['zo:li] *pl von* **Solo**
solid [zo'li:d], **solide** [zo'li:də] *adj* solid; (*Arbeit, Wissen*) sound; (*Leben, Person*) staid, respectable
solidarisch [zoli'da:rıʃ] *adj* in *od* with solidarity; **sich ~ erklären** to declare one's solidarity
solidarisieren [zolidari'zi:rən] *vr*: **sich ~ mit** to show (one's) solidarity with
Solidarität [zolidari'tɛ:t] *f* solidarity
Solidaritätsstreik *m* sympathy strike
Solist, in [zo'lıst(ın)] *m(f)* (*Mus*) soloist
Soll [zɔl] (**-(s), -(s)**) *nt* (*Fin*) debit (side); (*Arbeitsmenge*) quota, target; **~ und Haben** debit and credit
soll *vb siehe* **sollen**

SCHLÜSSELWORT

sollen ['zɔlən] (*pt* **sollte**, *pp* **gesollt** *od* (*als Hilfsverb*) **sollen**) *hilfsverb* **1** (*Pflicht, Befehl*) be supposed to; **du hättest nicht gehen sollen** you shouldn't have gone, you oughtn't to have gone; **er sollte eigentlich morgen kommen** he was supposed to come tomorrow; **soll ich?** shall I?; **soll ich dir helfen?** shall I help you?; **sag ihm, er soll warten** tell him he's to wait; **was soll ich machen?** what should I do?; **mir soll es gleich sein** it's all the same to me; **er sollte sie nie wiedersehen** he was never to see her again
2 (*Vermutung*): **sie soll verheiratet sein** she's said to be married; **was soll das heißen?** what's that supposed to mean?; **man sollte glauben, dass ...** you would think that ...; **sollte das passieren, ...** if that should happen ...
▷ *vt, vi*: **was soll das?** what's all this about *od* in aid of?; **das sollst du nicht** you shouldn't do that; **was solls?** what the hell!

sollte *etc* ['zɔltə] *vb siehe* **sollen**
Solo ['zo:lo] (**-s, -s** *od* **Soli**) *nt* solo
solo *adv* (*Mus*) solo; (*fig: umg*) on one's own, alone
solvent [zɔl'vɛnt] *adj* (*Fin*) solvent
Solvenz [zɔl'vɛnts] *f* (*Fin*) solvency
Somalia [zo'ma:lia] (**-s**) *nt* Somalia
somit [zo'mıt] *konj* and so, therefore
Sommer ['zɔmər] (**-s, -**) *m* summer; **~ wie Winter** all year round; **Sommerferien** *pl* summer holidays *pl* (*Brit*) *od* vacation *sing* (*US*); (*Jur, Parl*) summer recess *sing*; **sommerlich** *adj* summer *attrib*; (*sommerartig*) summery; **Sommerloch** *nt* silly season; **Sommerreifen** *m* normal tyre (*Brit*) *od* tire (*US*); **Sommerschlussverkauf** *m* summer sale; **Sommersemester** *nt* (*Univ*) summer semester (*bes US*), ≈ summer term (*Brit*); **Sommersprossen** *pl* freckles *pl*; **Sommerzeit** *f* summertime
Sonate [zo'na:tə] (**-, -n**) *f* sonata
Sonde ['zɔndə] (**-, -n**) *f* probe
Sonder- ['zɔndər] *in zw* special; **Sonderanfertigung** *f* special model; **Sonderangebot** *nt* special offer; **Sonderausgabe** *f* special edition; **sonderbar** *adj* strange, odd; **Sonderbeauftragte, r** *f(m)* (*Pol*) special emissary; **Sonderbeitrag** *m* (special) feature; **Sonderfahrt** *f* special trip; **Sonderfall** *m* special case; **sondergleichen** *adj inv* without parallel, unparalleled; **eine Frechheit sondergleichen** the height of cheek; **sonderlich** *adj* particular; (*außergewöhnlich*) remarkable; (*eigenartig*) peculiar; **Sonderling** *m* eccentric; **Sondermarke** *f* special issue (stamp); **Sondermüll** *m* dangerous waste
sondern *konj* but ▷ *vt* to separate; **nicht nur ..., ~ auch** not only ..., but also
Sonder- *zW*: **Sonderpreis** *m* special price; **Sonderregelung** *f* special provision; **Sonderschule** *f* special school; **Sondervergünstigungen** *pl* perquisites *pl*, perks *pl* (*bes Brit*); **Sonderwünsche** *pl* special requests *pl*; **Sonderzug** *m* special train
sondieren [zɔn'di:rən] *vt* to suss out; (*Gelände*) to scout out
Sonett [zo'nɛt] (**-(e)s, -e**) *nt* sonnet
Sonnabend ['zɔn|a:bənt] *m* Saturday; *siehe auch* **Dienstag**
Sonne ['zɔnə] (**-, -n**) *f* sun; **an die ~ gehen** to go out in the sun
sonnen *vr* to sun o.s.; **sich in etw** *dat* **~** (*fig*) to bask in sth
Sonnen- *zW*: **Sonnenaufgang** *m* sunrise; **sonnenbaden** *vi* to sunbathe; **Sonnenblume** *f* sunflower; **Sonnenbrand** *m* sunburn; **Sonnenbrille** *f* sunglasses *pl*; **Sonnencreme** *f* suntan lotion; **Sonnenenergie** *f* solar energy; **Sonnenfinsternis** *f* solar eclipse; **Sonnenfleck** *m* sunspot; **sonnengebräunt** *adj* suntanned; **sonnenklar** *adj* crystal-clear; **Sonnenkollektor** *m* solar panel; **Sonnenkraftwerk** *nt* solar

power station; **Sonnenmilch** *f* suntan lotion; **Sonnenöl** *nt* suntan oil; **Sonnenschein** *m* sunshine; **Sonnenschirm** *m* sunshade; **Sonnenschutzmittel** *nt* sunscreen; **Sonnenstich** *m* sunstroke; **du hast wohl einen Sonnenstich!** (*hum: umg*) you must have been out in the sun too long!; **Sonnensystem** *nt* solar system; **Sonnenuhr** *f* sundial; **Sonnenuntergang** *m* sunset; **Sonnenwende** *f* solstice

sonnig ['zɔnɪç] *adj* sunny

Sonntag ['zɔnta:k] *m* Sunday; *siehe auch* **Dienstag**

sonntäglich *adj attrib*: ~ **gekleidet** dressed in one's Sunday best

sonntags *adv* (on) Sundays

Sonntagsdienst *m*: ~ **haben** (*Apotheke*) to be open on Sundays

Sonntagsfahrer (*pej*) *m* Sunday driver

sonst [zɔnst] *adv* otherwise; (*mit pron, in Fragen*) else; (*zu anderer Zeit*) at other times; (*gewöhnlich*) usually, normally ▷ *konj* otherwise; **er denkt, er ist ~ wer** (*umg*) he thinks he's somebody special; **~ gehts dir gut?** (*ironisch: umg*) are you feeling okay?; **wenn ich Ihnen ~ noch behilflich sein kann** if I can help you in any other way; ~ **noch etwas?** anything else?; ~ **nichts** nothing else; ~ **jemand** (*umg*) anybody (at all); **da kann ja ~ was passieren** (*umg*) anything could happen; ~ **wo** (*umg*) somewhere else; ~ **woher** (*umg*) from somewhere else; ~ **wohin** (*umg*) somewhere else

sonstig *adj* other; **„S~es"** "other"

sooft [zo'|ɔft] *konj* whenever

Sopran [zo'pra:n] (**-s, -e**) *m* soprano (voice)

Sopranistin [zopra'nɪstɪn] *f* soprano (singer)

Sorge ['zɔrgə] (**-, -n**) *f* care, worry; **dafür ~ tragen, dass ...** (*geh*) to see to it that ...

sorgen *vi*: **für jdn ~** to look after sb ▷ *vr*: **sich ~ (um)** to worry (about); **für etw ~** to take care of *od* see to sth; **dafür ~, dass ...** to see to it that ...; **dafür ist gesorgt** that's taken care of

Sorgen- *zW*: **sorgenfrei** *adj* carefree; **Sorgenkind** *nt* problem child; **sorgenvoll** *adj* troubled, worried

Sorgerecht (**-(e)s**) *nt* custody (of a child)

Sorgfalt ['zɔrkfalt] (**-**) *f* care(fulness); **viel ~ auf etw** *akk* **verwenden** to take a lot of care over sth

sorgfältig *adj* careful

sorglos *adj* careless; (*ohne Sorgen*) carefree

sorgsam *adj* careful

Sorte ['zɔrtə] (**-, -n**) *f* sort; (*Warensorte*) brand; **Sorten** *pl* (*Fin*) foreign currency *sing*

sortieren [zɔr'ti:rən] *vt* to sort (out); (*Comput*) to sort

Sortiermaschine *f* sorting machine

Sortiment [zɔrti'mɛnt] *nt* assortment

SOS [ɛs|o:'|ɛs] *nt abk* SOS

sosehr [zo'ze:r] *konj* as much as

soso [zo'zo:] *interj*: **~!** I see!; (*erstaunt*) well, well!; (*drohend*) well!

Soße ['zo:sə] (**-, -n**) *f* sauce; (*Bratensoße*) gravy

Souffleur [zu'flø:r] *m* prompter

Souffleuse [zu'flø:zə] *f* prompter

soufflieren [zu'fli:rən] *vt, vi* to prompt

soundso ['zo:|ʊnt'zo:] *adv*: ~ **lange** for such and such a time

soundsovielte, r, s *adj*: **am S~n** (*Datum*) on such and such a date

Souterrain [zutɛ'rɛ̃:] (**-s, -s**) *nt* basement

Souvenir [zuvə'ni:r] (**-s, -s**) *nt* souvenir

souverän [zuvə'rɛ:n] *adj* sovereign; (*überlegen*) superior; (*fig*) supremely good

soviel [zo'fi:l] *konj* as far as

sowenig [zo've:nɪç] *konj* however little

sowie [zo'vi:] *konj* (*sobald*) as soon as; (*ebenso*) as well as

sowieso [zovi'zo:] *adv* anyway

Sowjetbürger *m* (*früher*) Soviet citizen

sowjetisch [zɔ'vjɛtɪʃ] *adj* (*früher*) Soviet

Sowjet- *zW* (*früher*): **Sowjetrepublik** *f* Soviet Republic; **Sowjetrusse** *m* Soviet Russian; **Sowjetunion** *f* Soviet Union

sowohl [zo'vo:l] *konj*: **~ ... als** *od* **wie auch ...** both ... and ...

soz. *abk* = **sozial; sozialistisch**

sozial [zotsi'a:l] *adj* social; ~ **eingestellt** public-spirited; ~ **verträglich** socially acceptable; **~er Wohnungsbau** public-sector housing (programme); **Sozialabbau** *m* public-spending cuts *pl*; **Sozialabgaben** *pl* National Insurance contributions *pl* (*Brit*), Social Security contributions *pl* (*US*); **Sozialamt** *nt* (social) welfare office; **Sozialarbeiter** *m* social worker; **Sozialberuf** *m* caring profession; **Sozialdemokrat** *m* social democrat; **Sozialhilfe** *f* welfare (aid)

Sozialisation [zotsializatsi'o:n] *f* (*Psych, Soziologie*) socialization

sozialisieren [zotsiali'zi:rən] *vt* to socialize

Sozialismus [zotsia'lɪsmʊs] *m* socialism

Sozialist, in [zotsia'lɪst(ɪn)] *m(f)* socialist

sozialistisch *adj* socialist

Sozial- *zW*: **Sozialkunde** *f* social studies *sing*; **Sozialleistungen** *pl* social security contributions (*from the state and employer*); **Sozialplan** *m* redundancy payments scheme; **Sozialpolitik** *f* social welfare policy; **Sozialprodukt** *nt* (gross *od* net) national product; **Sozialstaat** *m* welfare state; **Sozialversicherung** *f* national insurance (*Brit*), social security (*US*); **sozialverträglich** *adj siehe* **sozial**; **Sozialwohnung** *f* ≈ council flat (*Brit*), state-subsidized apartment; *see culture note*

SOZIALWOHNUNG

A *Sozialwohnung* is a council house or flat let at a fairly low rent to people on low income. They are built from public funds. People applying for a Sozialwohnung have to prove their entitlement.

Soziologe [zotsio'lo:gə] (**-n, -n**) *m* sociologist
Soziologie [zotsiolo'gi:] *f* sociology
Soziologin [zotsio'lo:gɪn] *f* sociologist
soziologisch [zotsio'lo:gɪʃ] *adj* sociological
Sozius ['zo:tsiʊs] (**-, -se**) *m* (*Comm*) partner; (*Motorrad*) pillion rider; **Soziussitz** *m* pillion (seat)
sozusagen [zotsu'za:gən] *adv* so to speak
Spachtel ['ʃpaxtəl] (**-s, -**) *m* spatula
spachteln *vt* (*Mauerfugen, Ritzen*) to fill (in) ▷ *vi* (*umg: essen*) to tuck in
Spagat [ʃpa'ga:t] (**-s, -e**) *m od nt* splits *pl*
Spaghetti, **Spagetti** [ʃpa'gɛti] *pl* spaghetti *sing*
spähen ['ʃpɛ:ən] *vi* to peep, peek
Spalier [ʃpa'li:r] (**-s, -e**) *nt* (*Gerüst*) trellis; (*Leute*) guard of honour (*Brit*) *od* honor (*US*); **~ stehen, ein ~ bilden** to form a guard of honour (*Brit*) *od* honor (*US*)
Spalt [ʃpalt] (**-(e)s, -e**) *m* crack; (*Türspalt*) chink; (*fig: Kluft*) split
Spalte (**-, -n**) *f* crack, fissure; (*Gletscherspalte*) crevasse; (*in Text*) column
spalten *vt, vr* (*lit, fig*) to split
Spaltung *f* splitting
Spamfilter ['spɛmfɪltər] *m* spam filter *od* blocker
spammen ['spɛmən] *vt, vi* to spam
Span [ʃpa:n] (**-(e)s, ¨-e**) *m* shaving
Spanferkel *nt* sucking pig
Spange ['ʃpaŋə] (**-, -n**) *f* clasp; (*Haarspange*) hair slide; (*Schnalle*) buckle; (*Armspange*) bangle
Spaniel ['ʃpa:niəl] (**-s, -s**) *m* spaniel
Spanien ['ʃpa:niən] (**-s**) *nt* Spain
Spanier, in (**-s, -**) *m(f)* Spaniard
spanisch *adj* Spanish; **das kommt mir ~ vor** (*umg*) that seems odd to me; **~e Wand** (folding) screen
Spann (**-(e)s, -e**) *m* instep
spann *etc* [ʃpan] *vb siehe* **spinnen**
Spannbeton (**-s**) *m* prestressed concrete
Spanne (**-, -n**) *f* (*Zeitspanne*) space; (*Differenz*) gap; *siehe auch* **Spann**
spannen *vt* (*straffen*) to tighten, tauten; (*befestigen*) to brace ▷ *vi* to be tight
spannend *adj* exciting, gripping; **machs nicht so ~!** (*umg*) don't keep me *etc* in suspense!
Spanner (**-s, -**) (*umg*) *m* (*Voyeur*) peeping Tom
Spannkraft *f* elasticity; (*fig*) energy
Spannung *f* tension; (*Elek*) voltage; (*fig*) suspense; (*unangenehm*) tension
Spannungsgebiet *nt* (*Pol*) flashpoint, area of tension
Spannungsprüfer *m* voltage detector
Spannweite *f* (*von Flügeln, Aviat*) (wing)span
Spanplatte *f* chipboard
Sparbuch *nt* savings book
Sparbüchse *f* moneybox
sparen ['ʃpa:rən] *vt, vi* to save; **sich** *dat* **etw ~** to save o.s. sth; (*Bemerkung*) to keep sth to o.s.; **mit etw ~** to be sparing with sth; **an etw** *dat* **~** to economize on sth
Sparer, in (**-s, -**) *m(f)* (*bei Bank etc*) saver
Sparflamme *f* low flame; **auf ~** (*fig: umg*) just ticking over
Spargel ['ʃpargəl] (**-s, -**) *m* asparagus
Spar- *zW*: **Spargroschen** *m* nest egg; **Sparkasse** *f* savings bank; **Sparkonto** *nt* savings account
spärlich ['ʃpɛ:rlɪç] *adj* meagre (*Brit*), meager (*US*); (*Bekleidung*) scanty; (*Beleuchtung*) poor
Spar- *zW*: **Sparmaßnahme** *f* economy measure; **Sparpackung** *f* economy size; **sparsam** *adj* economical, thrifty; **sparsam im Verbrauch** economical; **Sparsamkeit** *f* thrift, economizing; **Sparschwein** *nt* piggy bank
Sparte ['ʃpartə] (**-, -n**) *f* field; (*Comm*) line of business; (*Presse*) column
Sparvertrag *m* savings agreement
Spaß [ʃpa:s] (**-es, ¨-e**) *m* joke; (*Freude*) fun; **~ muss sein** there's no harm in a joke; **jdm ~ machen** to be fun (for sb); **spaßen** *vi* to joke; **mit ihm ist nicht zu spaßen** you can't take liberties with him
spaßeshalber *adv* for the fun of it
spaßig *adj* funny, droll
Spaß- *zW*: **Spaßmacher** *m* joker, funny man; **Spaßverderber** (**-s, -**) *m* spoilsport; **Spaßvogel** *m* joker
Spastiker, in ['ʃpastikər(ɪn)] *m(f)* (*Med*) spastic
spät [ʃpɛ:t] *adj, adv* late; **heute Abend wird es ~** it'll be a late night tonight
Spaten ['ʃpa:tən] (**-s, -**) *m* spade; **Spatenstich** *m*: **den ersten Spatenstich tun** to turn the first sod
Spätentwickler *m* late developer
später *adj, adv* later; **an ~ denken** to think of the future; **bis ~!** see you later!
spätestens *adv* at the latest
Spätlese *f* late vintage
Spatz [ʃpats] (**-en, -en**) *m* sparrow
spazieren [ʃpa'tsi:rən] *vi* (*Hilfsverb sein*) to stroll; **~ fahren** to go for a drive; **~ gehen** to go for a walk
Spazier- *zW*: **Spaziergang** *m* walk; **einen Spaziergang machen** to go for a walk; **Spaziergänger, in** *m(f)* stroller; **Spazierstock** *m* walking stick; **Spazierweg** *m* path, walk
SPD (**-**) *f abk* (*= Sozialdemokratische Partei Deutschlands*) German Social Democratic Party; *see culture note*

SPD

The *SPD* (Sozialdemokratische Partei Deutschlands), the German Social Democratic Party, was newly formed in 1945. It is the largest political party in Germany.

Specht [ʃpɛçt] (**-(e)s, -e**) *m* woodpecker
Speck [ʃpɛk] (**-(e)s, -e**) *m* bacon; **mit ~ fängt man Mäuse** (*Sprichwort*) you need a sprat to catch a mackerel; **ran an den ~** (*umg*) let's get stuck in
Spediteur [ʃpedi'tø:r] *m* carrier; (*Möbelspediteur*) furniture remover
Spedition [ʃpeditsi'o:n] *f* carriage;

(*Speditionsfirma*) road haulage contractor; (*Umzugsfirma*) removal (*Brit*) *od* moving (*US*) firm

Speer [ʃpeːr] (**-(e)s, -e**) *m* spear; (*Sport*) javelin; **Speerwerfen** *nt*: **das Speerwerfen** throwing the javelin

Speiche [ˈʃpaɪçə] (**-, -n**) *f* spoke

Speichel [ˈʃpaɪçəl] (**-s**) *m* saliva, spit(tle); **Speichellecker** (*pej: umg*) *m* bootlicker

Speicher [ˈʃpaɪçər] (**-s, -**) *m* storehouse; (*Dachspeicher*) attic, loft; (*Kornspeicher*) granary; (*Wasserspeicher*) tank; (*Tech*) store; (*Comput*) memory; **Speicherauszug** *m* (*Comput*) dump

speichern *vt* (*auch Comput*) to store

speien [ˈʃpaɪən] *unreg vt, vi* to spit; (*erbrechen*) to vomit; (*Vulkan*) to spew

Speise [ˈʃpaɪzə] (**-, -n**) *f* food; **kalte und warme ~n** hot and cold meals; **Speiseeis** *nt* ice-cream; **Speisefett** *nt* cooking fat; **Speisekammer** *f* larder, pantry; **Speisekarte** *f* menu

speisen *vt* to feed; to eat ▷ *vi* to dine

Speise- *zW*: **Speiseöl** *nt* salad oil; (*zum Braten*) cooking oil; **Speiseröhre** *f* (*Anat*) gullet, oesophagus (*Brit*), esophagus (*US*); **Speisesaal** *m* dining room; **Speisewagen** *m* dining car; **Speisezettel** *m* menu

Spektakel [ʃpɛkˈtaːkəl] (**-s, -**) *m* (*umg: Lärm*) row ▷ *nt* (**-s, -**) spectacle

spektakulär [ʃpɛktakuˈlɛːr] *adj* spectacular

Spektrum [ˈʃpɛktrʊm] (**-s, -tren**) *nt* spectrum

Spekulant, in [ʃpekuˈlant(ɪn)] *m(f)* speculator

Spekulation [ʃpekulatsiˈoːn] *f* speculation

Spekulatius [ʃpekuˈlaːtsiʊs] (**-, -**) *m* spiced biscuit (*Brit*) *od* cookie (*US*)

spekulieren [ʃpekuˈliːrən] *vi* (*fig*) to speculate; **auf etw** *akk* ~ to have hopes of sth

Spelunke [ʃpeˈlʊŋkə] (**-, -n**) *f* dive

spendabel [ʃpɛnˈdaːbəl] (*umg*) *adj* generous, open-handed

Spende [ˈʃpɛndə] (**-, -n**) *f* donation

spenden *vt* to donate, give; **Spendenkonto** *nt* donations account; **Spendenwaschanlage** *f* donation-laundering organization

Spender, in (**-s, -**) *m(f)* donator; (*Med*) donor

spendieren [ʃpɛnˈdiːrən] *vt* to pay for, buy; **jdm etw** ~ to treat sb to sth, stand sb sth

Sperling [ˈʃpɛrlɪŋ] *m* sparrow

Sperma [ˈspɛrma] (**-s, Spermen**) *nt* sperm

sperrangelweit [ˈʃpɛrˈ|aŋəlˈvaɪt] *adj* wide-open

Sperrbezirk *m* no-go area

Sperre (**-, -n**) *f* barrier; (*Verbot*) ban; (*Polizeisperre*) roadblock

sperren [ˈʃpɛrən] *vt* to block; (*Comm: Konto*) to freeze; (*Comput: Daten*) to disable; (*Sport*) to suspend, bar; (*: vom Ball*) to obstruct; (*einschließen*) to lock; (*verbieten*) to ban ▷ *vr* to baulk, jibe, jib

Sperr- *zW*: **Sperrfeuer** *nt* (*Mil, fig*) barrage; **Sperrfrist** *f* (*auch Jur*) waiting period; (*Sport*) (period of) suspension; **Sperrgebiet** *nt* prohibited area; **Sperrgut** *nt* bulky freight; **Sperrholz** *nt* plywood

sperrig *adj* bulky

Sperr- *zW*: **Sperrkonto** *nt* blocked account; **Sperrmüll** *m* bulky refuse; **Sperrsitz** *m* (*Theat*) stalls *pl* (*Brit*), orchestra (*US*); **Sperrstunde** *f* closing time; **Sperrzeit** *f* closing time; **Sperrzone** *f* exclusion zone

Spesen [ˈʃpeːzən] *pl* expenses *pl*; **Spesenabrechnung** *f* expense account

Spessart [ˈʃpɛsart] (**-s**) *m* Spessart (Mountains *pl*)

Spezi [ˈʃpeːtsi] (**-s, -s**) (*umg*) *m* pal, mate (*Brit*)

Spezial- [ʃpetsiˈaːl] *in zW* special; **Spezialausbildung** *f* specialized training

spezialisieren [ʃpetsialiˈziːrən] *vr* to specialize

Spezialisierung *f* specialization

Spezialist, in [ʃpetsiaˈlɪst(ɪn)] *m(f)*: **~ (für)** specialist (in)

Spezialität [ʃpetsialiˈtɛːt] *f* speciality (*Brit*), specialty (*US*)

speziell [ʃpetsiˈɛl] *adj* special

Spezifikation [ʃpetsifikatsiˈoːn] *f* specification

spezifisch [ʃpeˈtsiːfɪʃ] *adj* specific

Sphäre [ˈsfɛːrə] (**-, -n**) *f* sphere

spicken [ˈʃpɪkən] *vt* to lard ▷ *vi* (*Sch*) to copy, crib

Spickzettel *m* (*Sch: umg*) crib

spie *etc* [ʃpiː] *vb siehe* **speien**

Spiegel [ˈʃpiːgəl] (**-s, -**) *m* mirror; (*Wasserspiegel*) level; (*Mil*) tab; **Spiegelbild** *nt* reflection; **spiegelbildlich** *adj* reversed

Spiegelei [ˈʃpiːgəl|aɪ] *nt* fried egg

spiegeln *vt* to mirror, reflect ▷ *vr* to be reflected ▷ *vi* to gleam; (*widerspiegeln*) to be reflective

Spiegelreflexkamera *f* reflex camera

Spiegelschrift *f* mirror writing

Spiegelung *f* reflection

spiegelverkehrt *adj* in mirror image

Spiel [ʃpiːl] (**-(e)s, -e**) *nt* game; (*Schauspiel*) play; (*Tätigkeit*) play(ing); (*Karten*) pack (*Brit*), deck (*US*); (*Tech*) (free) play; **leichtes ~ (bei** *od* **mit jdm) haben** to have an easy job of it (with sb); **die Hand** *od* **Finger im ~ haben** to have a hand in affairs; **jdn/etw aus dem ~ lassen** to leave sb/sth out of it; **auf dem ~(e) stehen** to be at stake; **Spielautomat** *m* gambling machine; (*zum Geldgewinnen*) fruit machine (*Brit*); **Spielbank** *f* casino; **Spieldose** *f* musical box (*Brit*), music box (*US*)

spielen *vt, vi* to play; (*um Geld*) to gamble; (*Theat*) to perform, act; **was wird hier gespielt?** (*umg*) what's going on here?

spielend *adv* easily

Spieler, in (**-s, -**) *m(f)* player; (*um Geld*) gambler

Spielerei [ʃpiːləˈraɪ] *f* (*Kinderspiel*) child's play

spielerisch *adj* playful; (*Leichtigkeit*) effortless; **~es Können** skill as a player; (*Theat*) acting ability

Spiel- *zW*: **Spielfeld** *nt* pitch, field; **Spielfilm** *m* feature film; **Spielgeld** *nt* (*Einsatz*) stake; (*unechtes Geld*) toy money; **Spielkarte** *f* playing card; **Spielkonsole** *f* play console; **Spielmannszug** *m* (brass) band; **Spielplan** *m* (*Theat*) programme (*Brit*), program (*US*); **Spielplatz** *m* playground; **Spielraum** *m* room to manoeuvre (*Brit*) *od* maneuver (*US*), scope; **Spielregel** *f* (*lit, fig*) rule of the game; **Spielsachen** *pl* toys *pl*; **Spielshow** *f* gameshow; **Spielstand** *m* score; **Spielstraße** *f* play street; **Spielsucht** *f* addiction to gambling; **Spielverderber** (**-s, -**) *m* spoilsport; **Spielwaren** *pl* toys *pl*; **Spielzeit** *f* (*Saison*) season; (*Spieldauer*) playing time; **Spielzeug** *nt* toy; (*Spielsachen*) toys *pl*

Spieß [ʃpiːs] (**-es, -e**) *m* spear; (*Bratspieß*) spit; (*Mil: umg*) sarge; **den ~ umdrehen** (*fig*) to turn the tables; **wie am ~(e) schreien** (*umg*) to squeal like a stuck pig; **Spießbraten** *m* joint roasted on a spit

Spießbürger (**-s, -**) *m* bourgeois

Spießer (**-s, -**) *m* bourgeois

Spikes [spaɪks] *pl* (*Sport*) spikes *pl*; (*Aut*) studs *pl*; **Spikesreifen** *m* studded tyre (*Brit*) *od* tire (*US*)

Spinat [ʃpiˈnaːt] (**-(e)s, -e**) *m* spinach

Spind [ʃpɪnt] (**-(e)s, -e**) *m od nt* locker

spindeldürr [ˈʃpɪndəlˈdʏr] (*pej*) *adj* spindly, thin as a rake

Spinne [ˈʃpɪnə] (**-, -n**) *f* spider; **spinnefeind** (*umg*) *adj*: **sich** *od* **einander** *dat* **spinnefeind sein** to be deadly enemies

spinnen *unreg vt* to spin ▷ *vi* (*umg*) to talk rubbish; (*verrückt*) to be crazy *od* mad; **ich denk ich spinne** (*umg*) I don't believe it

Spinnengewebe *nt* cobweb

Spinner, in (**-s, -**) *m(f)* (*fig: umg*) screwball, crackpot

Spinnerei [ʃpɪnəˈraɪ] *f* spinning mill

Spinn- *zW*: **Spinngewebe** *nt* cobweb; **Spinnrad** *nt* spinning wheel; **Spinnwebe** *f* cobweb

Spion [ʃpiˈoːn] (**-s, -e**) *m* spy; (*in Tür*) spyhole

Spionage [ʃpioˈnaːʒə] (**-**) *f* espionage; **Spionageabwehr** *f* counterintelligence; **Spionagesatellit** *m* spy satellite

spionieren [ʃpioˈniːrən] *vi* to spy

Spionin *f* (woman) spy

Spirale [ʃpiˈraːlə] (**-, -n**) *f* spiral; (*Med*) coil

Spirituosen [ʃpirituˈoːzən] *pl* spirits *pl*

Spiritus [ˈʃpiːritʊs] (**-, -se**) *m* (methylated) spirits *pl*; **Spirituskocher** *m* spirit stove

Spitz [ʃpɪts] (**-es, -e**) *m* (*Hund*) spitz

spitz *adj* pointed; (*Winkel*) acute; (*fig: Zunge*) sharp; (*: Bemerkung*) caustic

Spitz- *zW*: **spitzbekommen** *unreg vt*: **etw spitzbekommen** (*umg*) to get wise to sth; **Spitzbogen** *m* pointed arch; **Spitzbube** *m* rogue

Spitze (**-, -n**) *f* point, tip; (*Bergspitze*) peak; (*Bemerkung*) taunt; (*fig: Stichelei*) dig; (*erster Platz*) lead, top; (*meist pl: Gewebe*) lace; **etw auf die ~ treiben** to carry sth too far

spitze *adj inv* (*umg: prima*) great

Spitzel (**-s, -**) *m* police informer

spitzen *vt* to sharpen; (*Lippen, Mund*) to purse; (*lit, fig: Ohren*) to prick up

Spitzen- *in zw* top; **Spitzenleistung** *f* top performance; **Spitzenlohn** *m* top wages *pl*; **Spitzenmarke** *f* brand leader; **spitzenmäßig** *adj* really great; **Spitzenposition** *f* leading position; **Spitzenreiter** *m* (*Sport*) leader; (*fig: Kandidat*) front runner; (*Ware*) top seller; (*Schlager*) number one; **Spitzensportler** *m* top-class sportsman; **Spitzenverband** *m* leading organization; **Spitzenverdiener, in** *m(f)* top earner

Spitzer (**-s, -**) *m* sharpener

spitzfindig *adj* (over)subtle

Spitzmaus *f* shrew

Spitzname *m* nickname

Spleen [ʃpliːn] (**-s, -e** *od* **-s**) *m* (*Angewohnheit*) crazy habit; (*Idee*) crazy idea; (*Fimmel*) obsession

Splitt [ʃplɪt] (**-s, -e**) *m* stone chippings *pl*; (*Streumittel*) grit

Splitter (**-s, -**) *m* splinter; **Splittergruppe** *f* (*Pol*) splinter group; **splitternackt** *adj* stark naked

SPÖ (**-**) *f abk* (= *Sozialistische Partei Österreichs*) Austrian Socialist Party

sponsern [ˈʃpɔnzərn] *vt* to sponsor

Sponsor [ˈʃpɔnzɔr] (**-s, -en**) *m* sponsor

spontan [ʃpɔnˈtaːn] *adj* spontaneous

sporadisch [ʃpoˈraːdɪʃ] *adj* sporadic

Sporen [ˈʃpoːrən] *pl* (*auch Bot, Zool*) spurs *pl*

Sport [ʃpɔrt] (**-(e)s, -e**) *m* sport; (*fig*) hobby; **treiben Sie ~?** do you do any sport?; **Sportabzeichen** *nt* sports certificate; **Sportartikel** *pl* sports equipment *sing*; **Sportfest** *nt* sports gala; (*Sch*) sports day (*Brit*); **Sportgeist** *m* sportsmanship; **Sporthalle** *f* sports hall; **Sportklub** *m* sports club; **Sportlehrer** *m* games *od* P.E. teacher

Sportler, in (**-s, -**) *m(f)* sportsman, sportswoman

Sport- *zW*: **sportlich** *adj* sporting; (*Mensch*) sporty; (*durchtrainiert*) athletic; (*Kleidung*) smart but casual; **Sportmedizin** *f* sports medicine; **Sportplatz** *m* playing *od* sports field; **Sportschuh** *m* sports shoe; (*sportlicher Schuh*) casual shoe

Sportsfreund *m* (*fig: umg*) buddy

Sport- *zW*: **Sportverein** *m* sports club; **Sportwagen** *m* sports car; **Sportzeug** *nt* sports gear

Spot [spɔt] (**-s, -s**) *m* commercial, advertisement

Spott [ʃpɔt] (**-(e)s**) *m* mockery, ridicule; **spottbillig** *adj* dirt-cheap; **spotten** *vi* to mock; **spotten über** *+akk* to mock (at), ridicule; **das spottet jeder Beschreibung** that simply defies description

spöttisch [ˈʃpœtɪʃ] *adj* mocking

Spottpreis *m* ridiculously low price

sprach *etc* [ʃpraːx] *vb siehe* **sprechen**

sprachbegabt *adj* good at languages

Sprache (**-, -n**) *f* language; **heraus mit der ~!** (*umg*) come on, out with it!; **zur ~ kommen** to be mentioned; **in französischer ~** in French

Sprachenschule *f* language school

Sprach- *zW*: **Sprachfehler** *m* speech defect; **Sprachfertigkeit** *f* fluency; **Sprachführer** *m* phrase book; **Sprachgebrauch** *m* (linguistic) usage; **Sprachgefühl** *nt* feeling for language;

Sprachkenntnisse *pl*: **mit englischen Sprachkenntnissen** with a knowledge of English; **Sprachkurs** *m* language course; **Sprachlabor** *nt* language laboratory; **sprachlich** *adj* linguistic; **sprachlos** *adj* speechless; **Sprachrohr** *nt* megaphone; (*fig*) mouthpiece; **Sprachstörung** *f* speech disorder; **Sprachwissenschaft** *f* linguistics *sing*

sprang *etc* [ʃpraŋ] *vb siehe* **springen**

Spray [spre:] (**-s, -s**) *m od nt* spray; **Spraydose** *f* aerosol (can), spray

sprayen *vt, vi* to spray

Sprechanlage *f* intercom

Sprechblase *f* speech balloon

sprechen ['ʃprɛçən] *unreg vi* to speak, talk ▷ *vt* to say; (*Sprache*) to speak; (*Person*) to speak to; **mit jdm ~** to speak *od* talk to sb; **das spricht für ihn** that's a point in his favour; **frei ~** to extemporize; **nicht gut auf jdn zu ~ sein** to be on bad terms with sb; **es spricht vieles dafür, dass ...** there is every reason to believe that ...; **hier spricht man Spanisch** Spanish spoken; **wir ~ uns noch!** you haven't heard the last of this!

Sprecher, in (**-s, -**) *m(f)* speaker; (*für Gruppe*) spokesman, spokeswoman; (*Rundf, TV*) announcer

Sprech- *zW*: **Sprechfunkgerät** *nt* radio telephone; **Sprechrolle** *f* speaking part; **Sprechstunde** *f* consultation (hour); (*von Arzt*) (doctor's) surgery (*Brit*); **Sprechstundenhilfe** *f* (doctor's) receptionist; **Sprechzimmer** *nt* consulting room, surgery (*Brit*)

spreizen ['ʃpraɪtsən] *vt* to spread ▷ *vr* to put on airs

Sprengarbeiten *pl* blasting operations *pl*

sprengen ['ʃprɛŋən] *vt* to sprinkle; (*mit Sprengstoff*) to blow up; (*Gestein*) to blast; (*Versammlung*) to break up

Spreng- *zW*: **Sprengkopf** *m* warhead; **Sprengladung** *f* explosive charge; **Sprengsatz** *m* explosive device; **Sprengstoff** *m* explosive(s *pl*); **Sprengstoffanschlag** *m* bomb attack

Spreu [ʃprɔʏ] (**-**) *f* chaff

spricht [ʃprɪçt] *vb siehe* **sprechen**

Sprichwort *nt* proverb

sprichwörtlich *adj* proverbial

sprießen ['ʃpri:sən] *vi* (*aus der Erde*) to spring up; (*Knospen*) to shoot

Springbrunnen *m* fountain

springen ['ʃprɪŋən] *unreg vi* to jump, leap; (*Glas*) to crack; (*mit Kopfsprung*) to dive; **etw ~ lassen** (*umg*) to fork out sth

springend *adj*: **der ~e Punkt** the crucial point

Springer (**-s, -**) *m* jumper; (*Schach*) knight

Springreiten *nt* show jumping

Springseil *nt* skipping rope

Sprinkler ['ʃprɪŋklər] (**-s, -**) *m* sprinkler

Sprit [ʃprɪt] (**-(e)s, -e**) (*umg*) *m* petrol (*Brit*), gas(oline) (*US*), fuel

Spritzbeutel *m* icing bag

Spritze ['ʃprɪtsə] (**-, -n**) *f* syringe; (*Injektion*) injection; (*an Schlauch*) nozzle

spritzen *vt* to spray; (*Wein*) to dilute with soda water/lemonade; (*Med*) to inject ▷ *vi* to splash; (*heißes Fett*) to spit; (*herausspritzen*) to spurt; (*aus einer Tube etc*) to squirt; (*Med*) to give injections

Spritzer (**-s, -**) *m* (*Farbspritzer, Wasserspritzer*) splash

Spritzpistole *f* spray gun

Spritztour (*umg*) *f* spin

spröde ['ʃprø:də] *adj* brittle; (*Person*) reserved; (*Haut*) rough

Spross (**-es, -e**) *m* shoot

spross *etc* [ʃprɔs] *vb siehe* **sprießen**

Sprosse ['ʃprɔsə] (**-, -n**) *f* rung

Sprossenwand *f* (*Sport*) wall bars *pl*

Sprössling ['ʃprœslɪŋ] *m* offspring *no pl*

Spruch [ʃprʊx] (**-(e)s, ⸚e**) *m* saying, maxim; (*Jur*) judgement; **Sprüche klopfen** (*umg*) to talk fancy; **Spruchband** *nt* banner

Sprüchemacher ['ʃprʏçəmaxər] (*umg*) *m* patter-merchant

spruchreif *adj*: **die Sache ist noch nicht ~** it's not definite yet

Sprudel ['ʃpru:dəl] (**-s, -**) *m* mineral water; (*süß*) lemonade

sprudeln *vi* to bubble

Sprüh- *zW*: **Sprühdose** *f* aerosol (can); **sprühen** *vi* to spray; (*fig*) to sparkle ▷ *vt* to spray; **Sprühregen** *m* drizzle

Sprung [ʃprʊŋ] (**-(e)s, ⸚e**) *m* jump; (*schwungvoll, fig: Gedankensprung*) leap; (*Riss*) crack; **immer auf dem ~ sein** (*umg*) to be always on the go; **jdm auf die Sprünge helfen** (*wohlwollend*) to give sb a (helping) hand; **auf einen ~ bei jdm vorbeikommen** (*umg*) to drop in to see sb; **damit kann man keine großen Sprünge machen** (*umg*) you can't exactly live it up on that; **Sprungbrett** *nt* springboard; **Sprungfeder** *f* spring; **sprunghaft** *adj* erratic; (*Aufstieg*) rapid; **Sprungschanze** *f* ski jump; **Sprungturm** *m* diving platform

Spucke ['ʃpʊkə] (**-**) *f* spit

spucken *vt, vi* to spit; **in die Hände ~** (*fig*) to roll up one's sleeves

Spucknapf *m* spittoon

Spucktüte *f* sickbag

Spuk [ʃpu:k] (**-(e)s, -e**) *m* haunting; (*fig*) nightmare; **spuken** *vi* to haunt; **hier spukt es** this place is haunted

Spülbecken ['ʃpy:lbɛkən] *nt* sink

Spule ['ʃpu:lə] (**-, -n**) *f* spool; (*Elek*) coil

Spüle ['ʃpy:lə] (**-, -n**) *f* (kitchen) sink

spülen *vt* to rinse; (*Geschirr*) to wash, do; (*Toilette*) to flush ▷ *vi* to rinse; to wash up (*Brit*), do the dishes; to flush; **etw an Land ~** to wash sth ashore

Spül- *zW*: **Spülmaschine** *f* dishwasher; **Spülmittel** *nt* washing-up liquid (*Brit*), dish-washing liquid; **Spülstein** *m* sink

Spülung *f* rinsing; (*Wasserspülung*) flush; (*Med*) irrigation

Spund [ʃpʊnt] (**-(e)s, -e**) *m*: **junger ~**

(*veraltet: umg*) young pup
Spur [ʃpu:r] (**-, -en**) *f* trace; (*Fußspur, Radspur, Tonbandspur*) track; (*Fährte*) trail; (*Fahrspur*) lane; **jdm auf die ~ kommen** to get onto sb; **(seine) ~en hinterlassen** (*fig*) to leave its mark; **keine ~** (*umg*) not/nothing at all
spürbar *adj* noticeable, perceptible
spuren (*umg*) *vi* to obey; (*sich fügen*) to toe the line
spüren ['ʃpy:rən] *vt* to feel; **etw zu ~ bekommen** (*lit*) to feel sth; (*fig*) to feel the (full) force of sth
Spurenelement *nt* trace element
Spurensicherung *f* securing of evidence
Spürhund *m* tracker dog; (*fig*) sleuth
spurlos *adv* without (a) trace; **~ an jdm vorübergehen** to have no effect on sb
Spurt [ʃpʊrt] (**-(e)s, -s** *od* **-e**) *m* spurt
spurten *vi* (*Hilfsverb sein: Sport*) to spurt; (*umg: rennen*) to sprint
sputen ['ʃpu:tən] *vr* to make haste
Squash [skvɔʃ] (-) *nt* (*Sport*) squash
SS (-) *f abk* (= *Schutzstaffel*) SS ▷ *nt abk* = **Sommersemester**
s. S. *abk* (= *siehe Seite*) see p.
SSV *abk* = **Sommerschlussverkauf**
st *abk* (= *Stunde*) h.
St. *abk* = **Stück**; (= *Stunde*) h.; (= *Sankt*) St
Staat [ʃta:t] (**-(e)s, -en**) *m* state; (*Prunk*) show; (*Kleidung*) finery; **mit etw ~ machen** to show off *od* parade sth
staatenlos *adj* stateless
staatl. *abk* = **staatlich**
staatlich *adj* state *attrib*; state-run ▷ *adv*: **~ geprüft** state-certified
Staats- *zW*: **Staatsaffäre** *f* (*lit*) affair of state; (*fig*) major operation; **Staatsangehörige, r** *f(m)* national; **Staatsangehörigkeit** *f* nationality; **Staatsanleihe** *f* government bond; **Staatsanwalt** *m* public prosecutor; **Staatsbürger** *m* citizen; **Staatsbürgerschaft** *f* nationality; **doppelte Staatsbürgerschaft** dual nationality; **Staatsdienst** *m* civil service; **staatseigen** *adj* state-owned; **Staatseigentum** *nt* public ownership; **Staatsexamen** *nt* (*Univ*) degree; **staatsfeindlich** *adj* subversive; **Staatsgeheimnis** *nt* (*lit, fig hum*) state secret; **Staatshaushalt** *m* budget; **Staatskosten** *pl* public expenses *pl*; **Staatsmann** (**-(e)s**, *pl* **-männer**) *m* statesman; **staatsmännisch** *adj* statesmanlike; **Staatsoberhaupt** *nt* head of state; **Staatsschuld** *f* (*Fin*) national debt; **Staatssekretär** *m* secretary of state; **Staatsstreich** *m* coup (d'état); **Staatsverschuldung** *f* national debt
Stab [ʃta:p] (**-(e)s, ⸚e**) *m* rod; (*für Stabhochsprung*) pole; (*für Staffellauf*) baton; (*Gitterstab*) bar; (*Menschen*) staff; (*von Experten*) panel
Stäbchen ['ʃtɛ:pçən] *nt* (*Essstäbchen*) chopstick
Stabhochsprung *m* pole vault
stabil [ʃta'bi:l] *adj* stable; (*Möbel*) sturdy
Stabilisator [ʃtabili'za:tɔr] *m* stabilizer
stabilisieren [ʃtabili'zi:rən] *vt* to stabilize
Stabilisierung *f* stabilization
Stabilität [ʃtabili'tɛ:t] *f* stability
Stabreim *m* alliteration
Stabsarzt *m* (*Mil*) captain in the medical corps
stach *etc* [ʃta:x] *vb siehe* **stechen**
Stachel ['ʃtaxəl] (**-s, -n**) *m* spike; (*von Tier*) spine; (*von Insekten*) sting; **Stachelbeere** *f* gooseberry; **Stacheldraht** *m* barbed wire
stachelig, stachlig *adj* prickly
Stachelschwein *nt* porcupine
Stadion ['ʃta:diɔn] (**-s, Stadien**) *nt* stadium
Stadium ['ʃta:diʊm] *nt* stage, phase
Stadt [ʃtat] (**-, ⸚e**) *f* town; (*Großstadt*) city; (*Stadtverwaltung*) (town/city) council; **Stadtbad** *nt* municipal swimming baths *pl*; **stadtbekannt** *adj* known all over town; **Stadtbezirk** *m* municipal district
Städtchen ['ʃtɛ:tçən] *nt* small town
Städtebau (**-(e)s**) *m* town planning
Städter, in (**-s, -**) *m(f)* town/city dweller, townie
Stadtgespräch *nt*: **(das) ~ sein** to be the talk of the town
Stadtguerilla *f* urban guerrilla
städtisch *adj* municipal; (*nicht ländlich*) urban
Stadt- *zW*: **Stadtkasse** *f* town/city treasury; **Stadtkern** *m* = **Stadtzentrum**; **Stadtkreis** *m* town/city borough; **Stadtmauer** *f* city wall(s *pl*); **Stadtmitte** *f* town/city centre (*Brit*) *od* center (*US*); **Stadtpark** *m* municipal park; **Stadtplan** *m* street map; **Stadtrand** *m* outskirts *pl*; **Stadtrat** *m* (*Behörde*) (town/city) council; **Stadtstreicher** *m* street vagrant; **Stadtstreicherin** *f* bag lady; **Stadtteil** *m* district, part of town; **Stadtverwaltung** *f* (*Behörde*) municipal authority; **Stadtviertel** *m* district *od* part of a town; **Stadtzentrum** *nt* town/city centre (*Brit*) *od* center (*US*)
Staffel ['ʃtafəl] (**-, -n**) *f* rung; (*Sport*) relay (team); (*Aviat*) squadron
Staffelei [ʃtafə'laɪ] *f* easel
Staffellauf *m* relay race
staffeln *vt* to graduate
Staffelung *f* graduation
Stagnation [ʃtagnatsi'o:n] *f* stagnation
stagnieren [ʃta'gni:rən] *vi* to stagnate
Stahl (**-(e)s, ⸚e**) *m* steel
stahl *etc* [ʃta:l] *vb siehe* **stehlen**
Stahlhelm *m* steel helmet
stak *etc* [ʃta:k] *vb siehe* **stecken**
Stall [ʃtal] (**-(e)s, ⸚e**) *m* stable; (*Kaninchenstall*) hutch; (*Schweinestall*) sty; (*Hühnerstall*) henhouse
Stallung *f* stables *pl*
Stamm [ʃtam] (**-(e)s, ⸚e**) *m* (*Baumstamm*) trunk; (*Menschenstamm*) tribe; (*Gram*) stem; (*Bakterienstamm*) strain; **Stammaktie** *f* ordinary share, common stock (*US*); **Stammbaum** *m* family tree; (*von Tier*) pedigree; **Stammbuch** *nt book of family events with legal documents*
stammeln *vt, vi* to stammer
stammen *vi*: **~ von** *od* **aus** to come from

Stamm- *zW*: **Stammform** *f* base form; **Stammgast** *m* regular (customer); **Stammhalter** *m* son and heir
stämmig ['ʃtɛmɪç] *adj* sturdy; (*Mensch*) stocky; **Stämmigkeit** *f* sturdiness; stockiness
Stamm- *zW*: **Stammkapital** *nt* (*Fin*) ordinary share *od* common stock (*US*) capital; **Stammkunde** *m*, **Stammkundin** *f* regular (customer); **Stammlokal** *nt* favourite (*Brit*) *od* favorite (*US*) café/restaurant *etc*; (*Kneipe*) local (*Brit*); **Stammplatz** *m* usual seat; **Stammtisch** *m* (*Tisch in Gasthaus*) *table reserved for the regulars*; **Stammzelle** *f* stem cell; **embryonale Stammzellen** embryonic stem cells
stampfen ['ʃtampfən] *vi* to stamp; (*stapfen*) to tramp ▷ *vt* (*mit Stampfer*) to mash
Stampfer (**-s, -**) *m* (*Stampfgerät*) masher
Stand (**-(e)s, ¨-e**) *m* position; (*Wasserstand, Benzinstand etc*) level; (*Zählerstand etc*) reading; (*Stehen*) standing position; (*Zustand*) state; (*Spielstand*) score; (*Messestand etc*) stand; (*Klasse*) class; (*Beruf*) profession; **bei jdm** *od* **gegen jdn einen schweren ~ haben** (*fig*) to have a hard time of it with sb; **etw auf den neuesten ~ bringen** to bring sth up to date; *siehe auch* **außerstande; imstande; zustande**
stand *etc* [ʃtant] *vb siehe* **stehen**
Standard ['ʃtandart] (**-s, -s**) *m* standard; **Standardausführung** *f* standard design
standardisieren [ʃtandardi'zi:rən] *vt* to standardize
Standarte (**-, -n**) *f* (*Mil, Pol*) standard
Standbild *nt* statue
Ständchen ['ʃtɛntçən] *nt* serenade
Ständer (**-s, -**) *m* stand
Standes- *zW*: **Standesamt** *nt* registry office (*Brit*), city/county clerk's office (*US*); **standesamtlich** *adj*: **standesamtliche Trauung** registry office wedding (*Brit*), civil marriage ceremony; **Standesbeamte, r** *m* registrar; **Standesbewusstsein** *nt* status consciousness; **Standesdünkel** *m* snobbery; **standesgemäß** *adj, adv* according to one's social position; **Standesunterschied** *m* social difference
Stand- *zW*: **standfest** *adj* (*Tisch, Leiter*) stable, steady; (*fig*) steadfast; **standhaft** *adj* steadfast; **Standhaftigkeit** *f* steadfastness; **standhalten** *unreg vi*: **(jdm/etw) standhalten** to stand firm (against sb/sth), resist (sb/sth)
ständig ['ʃtɛndɪç] *adj* permanent; (*ununterbrochen*) constant, continual
Stand- *zW*: **Standlicht** *nt* sidelights *pl* (*Brit*), parking lights *pl* (*US*); **Standort** *m* location; (*Mil*) garrison; **Standpauke** (*umg*) *f*: **jdm eine Standpauke halten** to give sb a lecture; **Standpunkt** *m* standpoint; **standrechtlich** *adj*: **standrechtlich erschießen** to put before a firing squad; **Standspur** *f* (*Aut*) hard shoulder (*Brit*), berm (*US*)
Stange ['ʃtaŋə] (**-, -n**) *f* stick; (*Stab*) pole; (*Querstange*) bar; (*Zigaretten*) carton; **von der ~** (*Comm*) off the peg (*Brit*) *od* rack (*US*); **eine ~ Geld** quite a packet; **jdm die ~ halten** (*umg*) to stick up for sb; **bei der ~ bleiben** (*umg*) to stick at *od* to sth
Stängel ['ʃtɛŋl] (**-s, -**) *m* stalk; **vom ~ fallen** (*umg*: *überrascht sein*) to be staggered
Stangenbohne *f* runner bean
Stangenbrot *nt* French bread; (*Laib*) French stick (loaf)
stank *etc* [ʃtaŋk] *vb siehe* **stinken**
stänkern ['ʃtɛŋkərn] (*umg*) *vi* to stir things up
Stanniol [ʃtani'o:l] (**-s, -e**) *nt* tinfoil
Stanze ['ʃtantsə] (**-, -n**) *f* stanza; (*Tech*) stamp
stanzen *vt* to stamp; (*Löcher*) to punch
Stapel ['ʃta:pəl] (**-s, -**) *m* pile; (*Naut*) stocks *pl*; **Stapellauf** *m* launch
stapeln *vt* to pile (up)
Stapelverarbeitung *f* (*Comput*) batch processing
stapfen ['ʃtapfən] *vi* to trudge, plod
Star[1] [ʃta:r] (**-(e)s, -e**) *m* starling; **grauer/grüner ~** (*Med*) cataract/glaucoma
Star[2] [ʃta:r] (**-s, -s**) *m* (*Filmstar etc*) star
starb *etc* [ʃtarp] *vb siehe* **sterben**
stark [ʃtark] *adj* strong; (*heftig, groß*) heavy; (*Maßangabe*) thick; (*umg*: *hervorragend*) great ▷ *adv* very; (*beschädigt etc*) badly; (*vergrößert, verkleinert*) greatly; **das ist ein ~es Stück!** (*umg*) that's a bit much!; **er ist ~ erkältet** he has a bad cold; *siehe auch* **starkmachen**
Stärke ['ʃtɛrkə] (**-, -n**) *f* strength (*auch fig*); heaviness; thickness; (*von Mannschaft*) size; (*Wäschestärke, Koch*) starch; **Stärkemehl** *nt* (*Koch*) thickening agent
stärken *vt* (*lit, fig*) to strengthen; (*Wäsche*) to starch; (*Selbstbewusstsein*) to boost; (*Gesundheit*) to improve; (*erfrischen*) to fortify ▷ *vi* to be fortifying; **~des Mittel** tonic
starkmachen *vr*: **sich für etw ~** (*umg*) to stand up for sth
Starkstrom *m* heavy current
Stärkung ['ʃtɛrkʊŋ] *f* strengthening; (*Essen*) refreshment
Stärkungsmittel *nt* tonic
starr [ʃtar] *adj* stiff; (*unnachgiebig*) rigid; (*Blick*) staring
starren *vi* to stare; **~ vor** *+dat od* **von** (*voll von*) to be covered in; (*Waffen*) to be bristling with; **vor sich** *akk* **hin ~** to stare straight ahead
starr- *zW*: **Starrheit** *f* rigidity; **starrköpfig** *adj* stubborn; **Starrsinn** *m* obstinacy
Start [ʃtart] (**-(e)s, -e**) *m* start; (*Aviat*) takeoff; **Startautomatik** *f* (*Aut*) automatic choke; **Startbahn** *f* runway; **starten** *vi* to start; (*Aviat*) to take off ▷ *vt* to start; **Starter** (**-s, -**) *m* starter; **Starterlaubnis** *f* takeoff clearance; **Starthilfe** *f* (*Aviat*) rocket-assisted takeoff; (*fig*) initial aid; **jdm Starthilfe geben** to help sb get off the ground; **Starthilfekabel** *nt* jump leads *pl* (*Brit*), jumper cables *pl* (*US*); **startklar** *adj* (*Aviat*) clear for takeoff; (*Sport*) ready to start; **Startkommando** *nt* (*Sport*) starting signal; **Startzeichen** *nt* start signal
Stasi ['ʃta:zi] (**-**) (*umg*) *f abk*

(*früher: = Staatssicherheitsdienst der DDR*) Stasi; *see culture note*

STASI

Stasi, an abbreviation of Staatssicherheitsdienst, the DDR secret service, was founded in 1950 and disbanded in 1989. The Stasi organized an extensive spy network of full-time and part-time workers who often held positions of trust in both the DDR and the BRD. They held personal files on 6 million people.

Station [ʃtatsi'o:n] *f* station; (*Krankenstation*) hospital ward; (*Haltestelle*) stop; **~ machen** to stop off
stationär [ʃtatsio'nɛ:r] *adj* stationary; (*Med*) in-patient *attrib*
stationieren [ʃtatsio'ni:rən] *vt* to station; (*Atomwaffen etc*) to deploy
Stations- *zW*: **Stationsarzt** *m* ward doctor; **Stationsärztin** *f* ward doctor; **Stationsvorsteher** *m* (*Eisenb*) stationmaster
statisch ['ʃta:tɪʃ] *adj* static
Statist, in [ʃta'tɪst(ɪn)] *m(f)* (*Film*) extra; (*Theat*) supernumerary
Statistik *f* statistic; (*Wissenschaft*) statistics *sing*
Statistiker, in (**-s, -**) *m(f)* statistician
statistisch *adj* statistical
Stativ [ʃta'ti:f] (**-s, -e**) *nt* tripod
statt *konj* instead of ▷ *präp* (*+dat od gen*) instead of
stattdessen *adv* instead
Stätte ['ʃtɛtə] (**-, -n**) *f* place
statt- *zW*: **stattfinden** *unreg vi* to take place; **statthaft** *adj* admissible; **Statthalter** *m* governor; **stattlich** *adj* imposing, handsome; (*Bursche*) strapping; (*Sammlung*) impressive; (*Familie*) large; (*Summe*) handsome
Statue ['ʃta:tuə] (**-, -n**) *f* statue
Statur [ʃta'tu:r] *f* build
Status ['ʃta:tʊs] (**-, -**) *m* status; **Statussymbol** *nt* status symbol
Statuten [ʃta'tu:tən] *pl* by(e)-law(s *pl*)
Stau [ʃtaʊ] (**-(e)s, -e**) *m* blockage; (*Verkehrsstau*) (traffic) jam
Staub [ʃtaʊp] (**-(e)s**) *m* dust; **~ saugen** to vacuum; **~ wischen** to dust; **sich aus dem ~ machen** (*umg*) to clear off
stauben ['ʃtaʊbən] *vi* to be dusty
Staubfaden *m* (*Bot*) stamen
staubig ['staʊbɪç] *adj* dusty
Staub- *zW*: **Staublappen** *m* duster; **Staublunge** *f* (*Med*) dust on the lung; **staubsaugen** (*pp* **staubgesaugt**) *vi untr* to vacuum; **Staubsauger** *m* vacuum cleaner; **Staubtuch** *nt* duster
Staudamm *m* dam
Staude ['ʃtaʊdə] (**-, -n**) *f* shrub
stauen ['ʃtaʊən] *vt* (*Wasser*) to dam up; (*Blut*) to stop the flow of ▷ *vr* (*Wasser*) to become dammed up; (*Verkehr, Med*) to become congested; (*Menschen*) to collect together; (*Gefühle*) to build up
staunen ['ʃtaʊnən] *vi* to be astonished; **da kann man nur noch ~** it's just amazing; **Staunen** (**-s**) *nt* amazement
Stausee ['ʃtaʊze:] *m* reservoir; artificial lake
Stauung ['ʃtaʊʊŋ] *f* (*von Wasser*) damming-up; (*von Blut, Verkehr*) congestion
Std. *abk* (= *Stunde*) h.
stdl. *abk* = **stündlich**
Steak [ʃte:k] (**-s, -s**) *nt* steak
Stechen ['ʃtɛçən] (**-s, -**) *nt* (*Sport*) play-off; (*Springreiten*) jump-off; (*Schmerz*) sharp pain
stechen *unreg vt* (*mit Nadel etc*) to prick; (*mit Messer*) to stab; (*mit Finger*) to poke; (*Biene etc*) to sting; (*Mücke*) to bite; (*Karten*) to take; (*Kunst*) to engrave; (*Torf, Spargel*) to cut ▷ *vi* (*Sonne*) to beat down; (*mit Stechkarte*) to clock in ▷ *vr*: **sich** *akk od dat* **in den Finger ~** to prick one's finger; **es sticht** it is prickly; **in See ~** to put to sea
stechend *adj* piercing, stabbing; (*Geruch*) pungent
Stech- *zW*: **Stechginster** *m* gorse; **Stechkarte** *f* clocking-in card; **Stechmücke** *f* gnat; **Stechpalme** *f* holly; **Stechuhr** *f* time clock
Steck- *zW*: **Steckbrief** *m* "wanted" poster; **steckbrieflich** *adv*: **steckbrieflich gesucht werden** to be wanted; **Steckdose** *f* (wall) socket
stecken ['ʃtɛkən] *vt* to put; (*einführen*) to insert; (*Nadel*) to stick; (*Pflanzen*) to plant; (*beim Nähen*) to pin ▷ *vi* (*auch unreg*) to be; (*festsitzen*) to be stuck; (*Nadeln*) to stick; **etw in etw** *akk* **~** (*umg: Geld, Mühe*) to put sth into sth; (*: Zeit*) to devote sth to sth; **der Schlüssel steckt** the key is in the lock; **wo steckt er?** where has he got to?; **zeigen, was in einem steckt** to show what one is made of; **~ bleiben** to get stuck; **~ lassen** to leave in
Steckenpferd *nt* hobbyhorse
Stecker (**-s, -**) *m* (*Elek*) plug
Steck- *zW*: **Stecknadel** *f* pin; **Steckrübe** *f* swede, turnip; **Steckschlüssel** *m* box spanner (*Brit*) *od* wrench (*US*); **Steckzwiebel** *f* bulb
Steg [ʃte:k] (**-(e)s, -e**) *m* small bridge; (*Anlegesteg*) landing stage
Stegreif *m*: **aus dem ~** just like that
Stehaufmännchen ['ʃte:|aʊfmɛnçən] *nt* (*Spielzeug*) tumbler
stehen ['ʃte:ən] *unreg vi* to stand; (*sich befinden*) to be; (*in Zeitung*) to say; (*angehalten haben*) to have stopped ▷ *vi unpers*: **es steht schlecht um ...** things are bad for ... ▷ *vr*: **sich gut/schlecht ~** to be well-off/badly off; **zu jdm/etw ~** to stand by sb/sth; **jdm ~** to suit sb; **ich tue, was in meinen Kräften steht** I'll do everything I can; **es steht 2:1 für München** the score is 2-1 to Munich; **mit dem Dativ ~** (*Gram*) to take the dative; **auf Betrug steht eine Gefängnisstrafe** the penalty for fraud is imprisonment; **wie ~ Sie dazu?** what are your views on that?; **wie stehts?** how are things?;

(*Sport*) what's the score?; **wie steht es damit?** how about it?; **~ bleiben** (*Uhr*) to stop; (*Zeit*) to stand still; (*Auto, Zug*) to stand; (*Fehler*) to stay as it is; (*Verkehr, Produktion etc*) to come to a standstill *od* stop; **~ lassen** to leave; (*Bart*) to grow; **alles ~ und liegen lassen** to drop everything

stehend *adj attrib* (*Fahrzeug*) stationary; (*Gewässer*) stagnant; (*ständig: Heer*) regular

Stehlampe *f* standard lamp (*Brit*), floor lamp (*US*)

stehlen ['ʃte:lən] *unreg vt* to steal

Stehplatz *m*: **ein ~ kostet 15 Euro** a standing ticket costs 15 euros

Stehvermögen *nt* staying power, stamina

Steiermark ['ʃtaɪrmark] *f*: **die ~** Styria

steif [ʃtaɪf] *adj* stiff; **~ und fest auf etw** *dat* **beharren** to insist stubbornly on sth

Steifftier® ['ʃtaɪfti:r] *nt soft toy animal*

Steifheit *f* stiffness

Steigbügel ['ʃtaɪkby:gəl] *m* stirrup

Steigeisen *nt* crampon

steigen *unreg vi* to rise; (*klettern*) to climb ▷ *vt* (*Treppen, Stufen*) to climb (up); **das Blut stieg ihm in den Kopf** the blood rushed to his head; **~ in** *+akk***/auf** *+akk* to get in/on

Steiger (**-s, -**) *m* (*Min*) pit foreman

steigern *vt* to raise; (*Gram*) to compare ▷ *vi* (*Auktion*) to bid ▷ *vr* to increase

Steigerung *f* raising; (*Gram*) comparison

Steigung *f* incline, gradient, rise

steil [ʃtaɪl] *adj* steep; **Steilhang** *m* steep slope; **Steilpass** *m* (*Sport*) through ball

Stein [ʃtaɪn] (**-(e)s, -e**) *m* stone; (*in Uhr*) jewel; **mir fällt ein ~ vom Herzen!** (*fig*) that's a load off my mind!; **bei jdm einen ~ im Brett haben** (*fig: umg*) to be well in with sb; **jdm ~e in den Weg legen** to make things difficult for sb; **Steinadler** *m* golden eagle; **steinalt** *adj* ancient; **Steinbock** *m* (*Astrol*) Capricorn; **Steinbruch** *m* quarry

steinern *adj* (made of) stone; (*fig*) stony

Stein- *zW*: **Steinerweichen** *nt*: **zum Steinerweichen weinen** to cry heartbreakingly; **Steingarten** *m* rockery; **Steingut** *nt* stoneware; **steinhart** *adj* hard as stone

steinig *adj* stony

steinigen *vt* to stone

Stein- *zW*: **Steinkohle** *f* mineral coal; **Steinmetz** (**-es, -e**) *m* stonemason; **steinreich** (*umg*) *adj* stinking rich; **Steinschlag** *m*: **„Achtung Steinschlag"** "danger – falling stones"; **Steinwurf** *m* (*fig*) stone's throw; **Steinzeit** *f* Stone Age

Steiß [ʃtaɪs] (**-es, -e**) *m* rump; **Steißbein** *nt* (*Anat*) coccyx

Stelle ['ʃtɛlə] (**-, -n**) *f* place; (*Arbeit*) post, job; (*Amt*) office; (*Abschnitt*) passage; (*Textstelle, bes beim Zitieren*) reference; **drei ~n hinter dem Komma** (*Math*) three decimal places; **eine freie** *od* **offene ~** a vacancy; **an dieser ~** in this place, here; **an anderer ~** elsewhere; **nicht von der ~ kommen** not to make any progress; **auf der ~** (*fig: sofort*) on the spot; *siehe auch* **anstelle**

stellen *vt* to put; (*Uhr etc*) to set; (*zur Verfügung stellen*) to supply; (*fassen: Dieb*) to apprehend; (*Antrag, Forderung*) to make; (*Aufnahme*) to pose; (*arrangieren: Szene*) to arrange ▷ *vr* (*sich aufstellen*) to stand; (*sich einfinden*) to present o.s.; (*bei Polizei*) to give o.s. up; (*vorgeben*) to pretend (to be); **das Radio lauter/leiser ~** to turn the radio up/down; **auf sich** *akk* **selbst gestellt sein** (*fig*) to have to fend for o.s.; **sich hinter jdn/etw ~** (*fig*) to support sb/sth; **sich einer Herausforderung ~** to take up a challenge; **sich zu etw ~** to have an opinion of sth

Stellen- *zW*: **Stellenangebot** *nt* offer of a post; (*in Zeitung*): **„Stellenangebote"** "vacancies"; **Stellenanzeige** *f* job advertisement *od* ad (*umg*); **Stellengesuch** *nt* application for a post; **„Stellengesuche"** "situations wanted"; **Stellenmarkt** *m* job market; (*in Zeitung*) appointments section; **Stellennachweis** *m* employment agency; **Stellenvermittlung** *f* employment agency; **stellenweise** *adv* in places; **Stellenwert** *m* (*fig*) status

Stellung *f* position; (*Mil*) line; **~ nehmen zu** to comment on

Stellungnahme *f* comment

stellungslos *adj* unemployed

stellv. *abk* = **stellvertretend**

Stell- *zW*: **stellvertretend** *adj* deputy *attrib*, acting *attrib*; **Stellvertreter** *m* (*von Amts wegen*) deputy, representative; **Stellwerk** *nt* (*Eisenb*) signal box

Stelze ['ʃtɛltsə] (**-, -n**) *f* stilt

stelzen (*umg*) *vi* to stalk

Stemmbogen *m* (*Ski*) stem turn

Stemmeisen *nt* crowbar

stemmen ['ʃtɛmən] *vt* to lift (up); (*drücken*) to press; **sich ~ gegen** (*fig*) to resist, oppose

Stempel ['ʃtɛmpəl] (**-s, -**) *m* stamp; (*Poststempel*) postmark; (*Tech: Prägestempel*) die; (*Bot*) pistil; **Stempelgebühr** *f* stamp duty; **Stempelkissen** *nt* inkpad

stempeln *vt* to stamp; (*Briefmarke*) to cancel ▷ *vi* (*umg: Stempeluhr betätigen*) to clock in/out; **~ gehen** (*umg*) to be *od* go on the dole (*Brit*) *od* on welfare (*US*)

Stengel ['ʃtɛŋəl] (**-s, -**) *m siehe* **Stängel**

Steno ['ʃteno] (*umg*) *f* shorthand; **Stenograf, in** [-gra:f(ɪn)] *m(f)* (*im Büro*) shorthand secretary; **Stenografie** [-gra'fi:] *f* shorthand; **stenografieren** [-gra'fi:rən] *vt, vi* to write (in) shorthand; **Stenogramm** [-'gram] *nt* text in shorthand; **Stenotypist, in** [-ty'pɪst(ɪn)] *m(f)* shorthand typist (*Brit*), stenographer (*US*)

Steppdecke *f* quilt

Steppe (**-, -n**) *f* steppe

steppen ['ʃtɛpən] *vt* to stitch ▷ *vi* to tap-dance

Stepptanz *m* tap-dance

Sterbe- *zW*: **Sterbebett** *nt* deathbed; **Sterbefall** *m* death; **Sterbehilfe** *f* euthanasia; **Sterbekasse** *f* death benefit fund

sterben ['ʃtɛrbən] *unreg vi* to die; **an einer Krankheit/Verletzung ~** to die of an illness/from an injury; **er ist für mich gestorben** (*fig: umg*) he might as well be dead
Sterben *nt*: **im ~ liegen** to be dying
sterbenslangweilig (*umg*) *adj* deadly boring
Sterbenswörtchen (*umg*) *nt*: **er hat kein ~ gesagt** he didn't say a word
Sterbeurkunde *f* death certificate
sterblich ['ʃtɛrplɪç] *adj* mortal; **Sterblichkeit** *f* mortality; **Sterblichkeitsziffer** *f* death rate
stereo- ['ste:reo] *in zw* stereo(-); **Stereoanlage** *f* stereo unit; **stereotyp** *adj* stereotyped
steril [ʃte'ri:l] *adj* sterile
sterilisieren [ʃterili'zi:rən] *vt* to sterilize
Sterilisierung *f* sterilization
Stern [ʃtɛrn] (**-(e)s, -e**) *m* star; **das steht (noch) in den ~en** (*fig*) it's in the lap of the gods; **Sternbild** *nt* constellation; **Sternchen** *nt* asterisk; **Sternenbanner** *nt* Stars and Stripes *sing*; **sternhagelvoll** (*umg*) *adj* legless; **Sternschnuppe** (**-, -n**) *f* meteor, falling star; **Sternstunde** *f* historic moment; **Sternwarte** *f* observatory; **Sternzeichen** *nt* (*Astrol*) sign of the zodiac
stet [ʃte:t] *adj* steady
Stethoskop [ʃteto'sko:p] (**-(e)s, -e**) *nt* stethoscope
stetig *adj* constant, continual; (*Math: Funktion*) continuous
stets *adv* continually, always
Steuer[1] ['ʃtɔʏər] (**-s, -**) *nt* (*Naut*) helm; (*Steuerruder*) rudder; (*Aut*) steering wheel; **am ~ sitzen** (*Aut*) to be at the wheel; (*Aviat*) to be at the controls
Steuer[2] (**-, -n**) *f* tax
Steuer- *zW*: **Steuerbefreiung** *f* tax exemption; **steuerbegünstigt** *adj* (*Investitionen, Hypothek*) tax-deductible; (*Waren*) taxed at a lower rate; **Steuerberater, in** *m(f)* tax consultant; **Steuerbescheid** *m* tax assessment; **Steuerbord** *nt* starboard; **Steuererhöhung** *f* tax increase; **Steuererklärung** *f* tax return; **steuerfrei** *adj* tax-free; **Steuerfreibetrag** *m* tax allowance; **Steuerhinterziehung** *f* tax evasion; **Steuerjahr** *nt* fiscal *od* tax year; **Steuerkarte** *f* tax notice; **Steuerklasse** *f* tax group; **Steuerknüppel** *m* control column; (*Aviat, Comput*) joystick; **steuerlich** *adj* tax *attrib*; **Steuermann** (**-(e)s**, *pl* **-männer** *od* **-leute**) *m* helmsman
steuern *vt* to steer; (*Flugzeug*) to pilot; (*Entwicklung, Tonstärke*) to control ▷ *vi* to steer; (*in Flugzeug etc*) to be at the controls; (*bei Entwicklung etc*) to be in control
Steuer- *zW*: **Steuernummer** *f* ≈ National Insurance Number (*Brit*), ≈ Social Security Number (*US*); **Steuerparadies** *nt* tax haven; **steuerpflichtig** *adj* taxable; (*Person*) liable to pay tax; **Steuerprogression** *f* progressive taxation; **Steuerprüfung** *f* tax inspector's investigation; **Steuerrad** *nt* steering wheel; **Steuerrückvergütung** *f* tax rebate; **Steuersenkung** *f* tax cut
Steuerung *f* steering (*auch AUT*), piloting; control; (*Vorrichtung*) controls *pl*; **automatische ~** (*Aviat*) autopilot; (*Tech*) automatic steering (device)
Steuer- *zW*: **Steuervergünstigung** *f* tax relief; **Steuerzahler** *m* taxpayer; **Steuerzuschlag** *m* additional tax
Steward ['stju:ərt] (**-s, -s**) *m* steward
Stewardess ['stju:ərdɛs] (**-, -en**) *f* stewardess
StGB (**-s**) *nt abk* = **Strafgesetzbuch**
stibitzen [ʃti'bɪtsən] (*umg*) *vt* to pilfer, pinch (*umg*)
Stich [ʃtɪç] (**-(e)s, -e**) *m* (*Insektenstich*) sting; (*Messerstich*) stab; (*beim Nähen*) stitch; (*Färbung*) tinge; (*Karten*) trick; (*Art*) engraving; (*fig*) pang; **ein ~ ins Rote** a tinge of red; **einen ~ haben** (*umg: Esswaren*) to be bad *od* off (*Brit*); (*: Mensch: verrückt sein*) to be nuts; **jdn im ~ lassen** to leave sb in the lurch
Stichel (**-s, -**) *m* engraving tool, style
Stichelei [ʃtɪçə'laɪ] *f* jibe, taunt
sticheln *vi* (*fig*) to jibe; (*pej: umg*) to make snide remarks
Stich- *zW*: **Stichflamme** *f* tongue of flame; **stichhaltig** *adj* valid; (*Beweis*) conclusive; **Stichprobe** *f* spot check
sticht [ʃtɪçt] *vb siehe* **stechen**
Stichtag *m* qualifying date
Stichwahl *f* final ballot
Stichwort *nt* (*pl* **-worte**) cue; (*: für Vortrag*) note (*pl* **-wörter**) (*in Wörterbuch*) headword; **Stichwortkatalog** *m* classified catalogue (*Brit*) *od* catalog (*US*); **Stichwortverzeichnis** *nt* index
Stichwunde *f* stab wound
sticken ['ʃtɪkən] *vt, vi* to embroider
Stickerei [ʃtɪkə'raɪ] *f* embroidery
stickig *adj* stuffy, close
Stickstoff (**-(e)s**) *m* nitrogen
stieben ['ʃti:bən] *vi* (*geh: sprühen*) to fly
Stief- ['ʃti:f] *in zw* step-
Stiefel ['ʃti:fəl] (**-s, -**) *m* boot; (*Trinkgefäß*) *large boot-shaped beer glass*
Stief- *zW*: **Stiefkind** *nt* stepchild; (*fig*) Cinderella; **Stiefmutter** *f* stepmother; **Stiefmütterchen** *nt* pansy; **stiefmütterlich** *adj* (*fig*): **jdn/etw stiefmütterlich behandeln** to pay little attention to sb/sth; **Stiefvater** *m* stepfather
stieg *etc* [ʃti:k] *vb siehe* **steigen**
Stiege ['ʃti:gə] (**-, -n**) *f* staircase
Stieglitz ['ʃti:glɪts] (**-es, -e**) *m* goldfinch
stiehlt [ʃti:lt] *vb siehe* **stehlen**
Stiel [ʃti:l] (**-(e)s, -e**) *m* handle; (*Bot*) stalk
Stielaugen *pl* (*fig: umg*): **er machte ~** his eyes (nearly) popped out of his head
Stier (**-(e)s, -e**) *m* bull; (*Astrol*) Taurus
stier [ʃti:r] *adj* staring, fixed
stieren *vi* to stare
Stierkampf *m* bullfight
stieß *etc* [ʃti:s] *vb siehe* **stoßen**
Stift [ʃtɪft] (**-(e)s, -e**) *m* peg; (*Nagel*) tack; (*Buntstift*) crayon; (*Bleistift*) pencil;

(*umg: Lehrling*) apprentice (boy)
stiften *vt* to found; (*Unruhe*) to cause; (*spenden*) to contribute; **~ gehen** to hop it
Stifter, in (**-s, -**) *m(f)* founder
Stiftung *f* donation; (*Organisation*) foundation
Stiftzahn *m* post crown
Stil [ʃti:l] (**-(e)s, -e**) *m* style; (*Eigenart*) way, manner; **Stilblüte** *f* howler; **Stilbruch** *m* stylistic incongruity
stilistisch [ʃti'lɪstɪʃ] *adj* stylistic
still [ʃtɪl] *adj* quiet; (*unbewegt*) still; (*heimlich*) secret; **ich dachte mir im S~en** I thought to myself; **er ist ein ~es Wasser** he's a deep one; **~er Teilhaber** (*Comm*) sleeping (*Brit*) *od* silent (*US*) partner; **der S~e Ozean** the Pacific (Ocean); **~ stehen** (*unbewegt*) to stand still
Stille (**-, -n**) *f* quietness; stillness; **in aller ~** quietly
Stilleben *nt siehe* **Stillleben**
Stillegung *f siehe* **Stilllegung**
stillen *vt* to stop; (*befriedigen*) to satisfy; (*Säugling*) to breast-feed
still- *zW*: **stillgestanden** *interj* attention!; **Stillhalteabkommen** *nt* (*Fin, fig*) moratorium; **stillhalten** *unreg vi* to keep still; **Stillleben** *nt* still life; **stilllegen** *vt* to close down; **Stilllegung** *f* (*Betrieb*) shut-down, closure; **stillliegen** *unreg vi* (*außer Betrieb sein*) to be shut down; (*lahmgelegt sein*) to be at a standstill; **Stillschweigen** *nt* silence; **stillschweigen** *unreg vi* to be silent; **stillschweigend** *adj* silent; (*Einverständnis*) tacit ▷ *adv* silently; tacitly; **Stillstand** *m* standstill; **stillstehen** *unreg vi* to stand still
Stilmöbel *pl* reproduction *od* (*antik*) period furniture *sing*
stilvoll *adj* stylish
Stimm- *zW*: **Stimmabgabe** *f* voting; **Stimmbänder** *pl* vocal cords *pl*; **stimmberechtigt** *adj* entitled to vote; **Stimmbruch** *m*: **er ist im Stimmbruch** his voice is breaking
Stimme ['ʃtɪmə] (**-, -n**) *f* voice; (*Wahlstimme*) vote; (*Mus: Rolle*) part; **mit leiser/lauter ~** in a soft/loud voice; **seine ~ abgeben** to vote
stimmen *vi* (*richtig sein*) to be right; (*wählen*) to vote ▷ *vt* (*Instrument*) to tune; **stimmt so!** that's all right; **für/gegen etw ~** to vote for/against sth; **jdn traurig ~** to make sb feel sad
Stimmen- *zW*: **Stimmengewirr** *nt* babble of voices; **Stimmengleichheit** *f* tied vote; **Stimmenmehrheit** *f* majority (of votes)
Stimm- *zW*: **Stimmenthaltung** *f* abstention; **Stimmgabel** *f* tuning fork; **stimmhaft** *adj* voiced
stimmig *adj* harmonious
Stimm- *zW*: **stimmlos** *adj* (*Ling*) unvoiced; **Stimmrecht** *nt* right to vote; **stimmrechtslos** *adj*: **stimmrechtslose Aktien** "A" shares
Stimmung *f* mood; (*Atmosphäre*) atmosphere; (*Moral*) morale; **in ~ kommen** to liven up; **~ gegen/für jdn/etw machen** to stir up (public) opinion against/in favour of sb/sth
Stimmungs- *zW*: **Stimmungskanone** (*umg*) *f* life and soul of the party; **Stimmungsmache** (*pej*) *f* cheap propaganda; **stimmungsvoll** *adj* (*Atmosphäre*) enjoyable; (*Gedicht*) full of atmosphere
Stimmzettel *m* ballot paper
stinken ['ʃtɪŋkən] *unreg vi* to stink; **die Sache stinkt mir** (*umg*) I'm fed-up to the back teeth (with it)
Stink- *zW*: **stinkfaul** (*umg*) *adj* bone-lazy; **stinklangweilig** (*umg*) *adj* deadly boring; **Stinktier** *nt* skunk; **Stinkwut** (*umg*) *f*: **eine Stinkwut (auf jdn) haben** to be livid (with sb)
Stipendium [ʃti'pɛndiʊm] *nt* grant; (*als Auszeichnung*) scholarship
Stippvisite ['ʃtɪpvi'zi:tə] (*umg*) *f* flying visit
stirbt [ʃtɪrpt] *vb siehe* **sterben**
Stirn [ʃtɪrn] (**-, -en**) *f* forehead, brow; (*Frechheit*) impudence; **die ~ haben zu ...** to have the nerve to ...; **Stirnband** *nt* headband; **Stirnhöhle** *f* sinus; **Stirnrunzeln** (**-s**) *nt* frown
stob *etc* [ʃto:p] *vb siehe* **stieben**
stöbern ['ʃtøbərn] *vi* to rummage
stochern ['stɔxərn] *vi* to poke (about)
Stock[1] [ʃtɔk] (**-(e)s, ¨-e**) *m* stick; (*Rohrstock*) cane; (*Zeigestock*) pointer; (*Bot*) stock; **über ~ und Stein** up hill and down dale
Stock[2] [ʃtɔk] (**-(e)s, -** *od* **-werke**) *m* storey (*Brit*), story (*US*); **im ersten ~** on the first (*Brit*) *od* second (*US*) floor
stock- *in zw* (*vor adj: umg*) completely
Stöckelschuh ['ʃtœkəlʃu:] *m* stiletto-heeled shoe
stocken *vi* to stop, pause; (*Arbeit, Entwicklung*) to make no progress; (*im Satz*) to break off; (*Verkehr*) to be held up
stockend *adj* halting
stockfinster (*umg*) *adj* pitch-dark
Stockholm ['ʃtɔkhɔlm] (**-s**) *nt* Stockholm
stocksauer (*umg*) *adj* pissed-off (*!*)
stocktaub *adj* stone-deaf
Stockung *f* stoppage
Stockwerk *nt* storey (*Brit*), story (*US*), floor
Stoff [ʃtɔf] (**-(e)s, -e**) *m* (*Gewebe*) material, cloth; (*Materie*) matter; (*von Buch etc*) subject (matter); (*umg: Rauschgift*) dope
Stoffel (**-s, -**) (*pej: umg*) *m* lout, boor
Stoff- *zW*: **stofflich** *adj* with regard to subject matter; **Stoffrest** *m* remnant; **Stofftier** *nt* soft toy; **Stoffwechsel** *m* metabolism
stöhnen ['ʃtø:nən] *vi* to groan
stoisch ['ʃto:ɪʃ] *adj* stoical
Stola ['ʃto:la] (**-, Stolen**) *f* stole
Stollen ['ʃtɔlən] (**-s, -**) *m* (*Min*) gallery; (*Koch*) stollen, *cake eaten at Christmas*; (*von Schuhen*) stud
stolpern ['ʃtɔlpərn] *vi* to stumble, trip; (*fig: zu Fall kommen*) to come a cropper (*umg*)
stolz [ʃtɔlts] *adj* proud; (*imposant: Bauwerk*) majestic; (*ironisch: Preis*) princely; **Stolz** (**-es**) *m* pride
stolzieren [ʃtɔl'tsi:rən] *vi* to strut
stopfen ['ʃtɔpfən] *vt* (*hineinstopfen*) to stuff;

(*nähen*) to darn ▷ *vi* (*Med*) to cause constipation; **jdm das Maul ~** (*umg*) to silence sb
Stopfgarn *nt* darning thread
Stopp [ʃtɔp] (**-s, -s**) *m* stop, halt; (*Lohnstopp*) freeze
Stoppel [ˈʃtɔpəl] (**-, -n**) *f* stubble
stoppen *vt* to stop; (*mit Uhr*) to time ▷ *vi* to stop
Stoppschild *nt* stop sign
Stoppuhr *f* stopwatch
Stöpsel [ˈʃtœpsəl] (**-s, -**) *m* plug; (*für Flaschen*) stopper
Stör [ʃtøːr] (**-(e)s, -e**) *m* sturgeon
Störaktion *f* disruptive action
störanfällig *adj* susceptible to interference *od* breakdown
Storch [ʃtɔrç] (**-(e)s, ¨-e**) *m* stork
Store [ʃtoːr] (**-s, -s**) *m* net curtain
stören [ˈʃtøːrən] *vt* to disturb; (*behindern, Rundf*) to interfere with ▷ *vr*: **sich an etw** *dat* **~** to let sth bother one ▷ *vi* to get in the way; **was mich an ihm/daran stört** what I don't like about him/it; **stört es Sie, wenn ich rauche?** do you mind if I smoke?; **ich möchte nicht ~** I don't want to be in the way
störend *adj* disturbing, annoying
Störenfried (**-(e)s, -e**) *m* troublemaker
Störfall *m* (*in Kraftwerk etc*) malfunction, accident
stornieren [ʃtɔrˈniːrən] *vt* (*Comm: Auftrag*) to cancel; (*: Buchungsfehler*) to reverse
Storno [ˈʃtɔrno] (**-s**) *m od nt* (*Comm: von Buchungsfehler*) reversal; (*: von Auftrag*) cancellation (*Brit*), cancelation (*US*)
störrisch [ˈʃtœrɪʃ] *adj* stubborn, perverse
Störsender *m* jammer, jamming transmitter
Störung *f* disturbance; interference; (*Tech*) fault; (*Med*) disorder
Störungsstelle *f* (*Tel*) faults service
Stoß [ʃtoːs] (**-es, ¨-e**) *m* (*Schub*) push; (*leicht*) poke; (*Schlag*) blow; (*mit Schwert*) thrust; (*mit Ellbogen*) nudge; (*mit Fuß*) kick; (*Erdstoß*) shock; (*Haufen*) pile; **seinem Herzen einen ~ geben** to pluck up courage; **Stoßdämpfer** *m* shock absorber
Stößel [ˈʃtøːsəl] (**-s, -**) *m* pestle; (*Aut: Ventilstößel*) tappet
stoßen *unreg vt* (*mit Druck*) to shove, push; (*mit Schlag*) to knock, bump; (*mit Ellbogen*) to nudge; (*mit Fuß*) to kick; (*mit Schwert*) to thrust; (*anstoßen: Kopf etc*) to bump; (*zerkleinern*) to pulverize ▷ *vr* to get a knock ▷ *vi*: **~ an** *od* **auf** *+akk* to bump into; (*finden*) to come across; (*angrenzen*) to be next to; **sich ~ an** *+dat* (*fig*) to take exception to; **zu jdm ~** to meet up with sb
Stoßgebet *nt* quick prayer
Stoßstange *f* (*Aut*) bumper
stößt [ʃtøːst] *vb siehe* **stoßen**
Stoß- *zW*: **Stoßverkehr** *m* rush-hour traffic; **Stoßzahn** *m* tusk; **Stoßzeit** *f* (*im Verkehr*) rush hour; (*in Geschäft etc*) peak period
Stotterer (**-s, -**) *m* stutterer
Stotterin *f* stutterer
stottern [ˈʃtɔtərn] *vt, vi* to stutter
Stövchen [ˈʃtøːfçən] *nt* (teapot- *etc*) warmer
StPO *abk* = **Strafprozessordnung**
Str. *abk* (= *Straße*) St.
stracks [ʃtraks] *adv* straight
Straf- *zW*: **Strafanstalt** *f* penal institution; **Strafarbeit** *f* (*Sch*) lines *pl*, punishment exercise; **Strafbank** *f* (*Sport*) penalty bench; **strafbar** *adj* punishable; **sich strafbar machen** to commit an offence (*Brit*) *od* offense (*US*); **Strafbarkeit** *f* criminal nature
Strafe [ˈʃtraːfə] (**-, -n**) *f* punishment; (*Jur*) penalty; (*Gefängnisstrafe*) sentence; (*Geldstrafe*) fine; **... bei ~ verboten** ... forbidden; **100 Dollar ~ zahlen** to pay a $100 fine; **er hat seine ~ weg** (*umg*) he's had his punishment
strafen *vt, vi* to punish; **mit etw gestraft sein** to be cursed with sth
strafend *adj attrib* punitive; (*Blick*) reproachful
straff [ʃtraf] *adj* tight; (*streng*) strict; (*Stil etc*) concise; (*Haltung*) erect
straffällig [ˈʃtraːffɛlɪç] *adj*: **~ werden** to commit a criminal offence (*Brit*) *od* offense (*US*)
straffen *vt* to tighten
Straf- *zW*: **straffrei** *adj*: **straffrei ausgehen** to go unpunished; **Strafgefangene, r** *f(m)* prisoner, convict; **Strafgesetzbuch** *nt* penal code; **Strafkolonie** *f* penal colony
sträflich [ˈʃtrɛːflɪç] *adj* criminal ▷ *adv* (*vernachlässigen etc*) criminally
Sträfling *m* convict
Straf- *zW*: **Strafmandat** *nt* ticket; **Strafmaß** *nt* sentence; **strafmildernd** *adj* mitigating; **Strafporto** *nt* excess postage (charge); **Strafpredigt** *f* severe lecture; **Strafprozessordnung** *f* code of criminal procedure; **Strafraum** *m* (*Sport*) penalty area; **Strafrecht** *nt* criminal law; **strafrechtlich** *adj* criminal; **Strafstoß** *m* (*Sport*) penalty (kick); **Straftat** *f* punishable act; **strafversetzen** *vt untr* (*Beamte*) to transfer for disciplinary reasons; **Strafvollzug** *m* penal system; **Strafzettel** (*umg*) *m* ticket
Strahl [ʃtraːl] (**-(e)s, -en**) *m* ray, beam; (*Wasserstrahl*) jet
strahlen *vi* (*Kernreaktor*) to radiate; (*Sonne, Licht*) to shine; (*fig*) to beam
Strahlenbehandlung *f* radiotherapy
Strahlenbelastung *f* (effects of) radiation
strahlend *adj* (*Wetter*) glorious; (*Lächeln, Schönheit*) radiant
Strahlen- *zW*: **Strahlendosis** *f* radiation dose; **strahlengeschädigt** *adj* suffering from radiation damage; **Strahlenopfer** *nt* victim of radiation; **Strahlenschutz** *m* radiation protection; **Strahlentherapie** *f* radiotherapy
Strahlung *f* radiation
Strähnchen [ˈʃtrɛːnçən] *pl* strands (of hair); (*gefärbt*) highlights
Strähne [ˈstrɛːnə] (**-, -n**) *f* strand
strähnig *adj* (*Haar*) straggly
stramm [ʃtram] *adj* tight; (*Haltung*) erect; (*Mensch*) robust; **strammstehen** *unreg vi* (*Mil*) to stand to attention

Strampelhöschen *nt* rompers *pl*
strampeln ['ʃtrampəln] *vi* to kick (about), fidget
Strand [ʃtrant] **(-(e)s, ¨-e)** *m* shore; (*Meeresstrand*) beach; **am ~** on the beach; **Strandbad** *nt* open-air swimming pool; (*Badeort*) bathing resort
stranden ['ʃtrandən] *vi* to run aground; (*fig: Mensch*) to fail
Strandgut *nt* flotsam and jetsam
Strandkorb *m* beach chair
Strang [ʃtraŋ] **(-(e)s, ¨-e)** *m* (*Nervenstrang, Muskelstrang*) cord; (*Schienenstrang*) track; **über die Stränge schlagen** to run riot (*umg*); **an einem ~ ziehen** (*fig*) to act in concert
strangulieren [ʃtraŋgu'li:rən] *vt* to strangle
Strapaze [ʃtra'pa:tsə] **(-, -n)** *f* strain
strapazieren [ʃtrapa'tsi:rən] *vt* (*Material*) to be hard on, punish; (*jdn*) to be a strain on; (*erschöpfen*) to wear out, exhaust
strapazierfähig *adj* hard-wearing
strapaziös [ʃtrapatsi'ø:s] *adj* exhausting, tough
Straßburg ['ʃtra:sbʊrk] **(-s)** *nt* Strasbourg
Straße ['ʃtra:sə] **(-, -n)** *f* road; (*in Stadt, Dorf*) street; **auf der** ~ in the street; **auf der ~ liegen** (*fig: umg*) to be out of work; **auf die ~ gesetzt werden** (*umg*) to be turned out (onto the streets)
Straßen- *zW*: **Straßenbahn** *f* tram (*Brit*), streetcar (*US*); **Straßenbauarbeiten** *pl* roadworks *pl* (*Brit*), roadwork *sing* (*US*); **Straßenbeleuchtung** *f* street lighting; **Straßenfeger** **(-s, -)** *m* roadsweeper; **Straßenglätte** *f* slippery road surface; **Straßenjunge** (*pej*) *m* street urchin; **Straßenkarte** *f* road map; **Straßenkehrer** **(-s, -)** *m* roadsweeper; **Straßenkind** *nt* child of the streets; **Straßenkreuzer** (*umg*) *m* limousine; **Straßenmädchen** *nt* streetwalker; **Straßenrand** *m* road side; **Straßensperre** *f* roadblock; **Straßenüberführung** *f* footbridge; **Straßenverkehr** *m* road traffic; **Straßenverkehrsordnung** *f* Highway Code (*Brit*); **Straßenzustandsbericht** *m* road report
Stratege [ʃtra'te:gə] **(-n, -n)** *m* strategist
Strategie [ʃtrate'gi:] *f* strategy
strategisch *adj* strategic
Stratosphäre [ʃtrato'sfɛ:rə] **(-)** *f* stratosphere
sträuben ['ʃtrɔʏbən] *vt* to ruffle ▷ *vr* to bristle; (*Mensch*): **sich (gegen etw)** ~ to resist (sth)
Strauch [ʃtraʊx] **(-(e)s, Sträucher)** *m* bush, shrub
straucheln ['ʃtraʊxəln] *vi* to stumble, stagger
Strauß[1] [ʃtraʊs] **(-es, Sträuße)** *m* (*Blumenstrauß*) bouquet, bunch
Strauß[2] [ʃtraʊs] **(-es, -e)** *m* ostrich
Strebe ['ʃtre:bə] **(-, -n)** *f* strut
Strebebalken *m* buttress
streben *vi* to strive, endeavour (*Brit*), endeavor (*US*); **~ nach** to strive for; **~ zu** *od* **nach** (*sich bewegen*) to make for
Strebepfeiler *m* buttress
Streber **(-s, -)** *m* (*pej*) pushy person; (*Sch*) swot (*Brit*)
strebsam *adj* industrious; **Strebsamkeit** *f* industry
Strecke ['ʃtrɛkə] **(-, -n)** *f* stretch; (*Entfernung*) distance; (*Eisenb, Math*) line; **auf der ~ Paris-Brüssel** on the way from Paris to Brussels; **auf der ~ bleiben** (*fig*) to fall by the wayside; **zur ~ bringen** (*Jagd*) to bag
strecken *vt* to stretch; (*Waffen*) to lay down; (*Koch*) to eke out ▷ *vr* to stretch (o.s.)
streckenweise *adv* in parts
Streich [ʃtraiç] **(-(e)s, -e)** *m* trick, prank; (*Hieb*) blow; **jdm einen ~ spielen** (*Person*) to play a trick on sb
streicheln *vt* to stroke
streichen *unreg vt* (*berühren*) to stroke; (*auftragen*) to spread; (*anmalen*) to paint; (*durchstreichen*) to delete; (*nicht genehmigen*) to cancel; (*Schulden*) to write off; (*Zuschuss etc*) to cut ▷ *vi* (*berühren*) to brush past; (*schleichen*) to prowl; **etw glatt ~** to smooth sth (out)
Streicher *pl* (*Mus*) strings *pl*
Streich- *zW*: **Streichholz** *nt* match; **Streichholzschachtel** *f* matchbox; **Streichinstrument** *nt* string(ed) instrument; **Streichkäse** *m* cheese spread
Streifband *nt* wrapper; **Streifbandzeitung** *f* *newspaper sent at printed paper rate*
Streife **(-, -n)** *f* patrol
streifen ['ʃtraɪfən] *vt* (*leicht berühren*) to brush against, graze; (*Blick*) to skim over; (*Thema, Problem*) to touch on; (*abstreifen*) to take off ▷ *vi* (*gehen*) to roam
Streifen **(-s, -)** *m* (*Linie*) stripe; (*Stück*) strip; (*Film*) film
Streifendienst *m* patrol duty
Streifenwagen *m* patrol car
Streifschuss *m* graze, grazing shot
Streifzug *m* scouting trip; (*Bummel*) expedition; (*fig: kurzer Überblick*): **~ (durch)** brief survey (of)
Streik [ʃtraɪk] **(-(e)s, -s)** *m* strike; **in den ~ treten** to come out on strike, strike; **Streikbrecher** *m* blackleg (*Brit*), strikebreaker; **streiken** *vi* to strike; **der Computer streikt** the computer's packed up (*umg*), the computer's on the blink (*umg*); **da streike ich** (*umg*) I refuse!; **Streikkasse** *f* strike fund; **Streikmaßnahmen** *pl* industrial action *sing*; **Streikposten** *m* (peaceful) picket
Streit [ʃtraɪt] **(-(e)s, -e)** *m* argument; (*Auseinandersetzung*) dispute
streiten *unreg vi, vr* to argue; to dispute; **darüber lässt sich ~** that's debatable
Streitfrage *f* point at issue
Streitgespräch *nt* debate
streitig *adj*: **jdm etw ~ machen** to dispute sb's right to sth; **Streitigkeiten** *pl* quarrel *sing*, dispute *sing*
Streit- *zW*: **Streitkräfte** *pl* (*Mil*) armed forces *pl*; **streitlustig** *adj* quarrelsome; **Streitpunkt** *m* contentious issue; **Streitsucht**

f quarrelsomeness
streng [ʃtrɛŋ] *adj* severe; (*Lehrer, Maßnahme*) strict; (*Geruch etc*) sharp; **~ geheim** top-secret; **~ genommen** strictly speaking; **~ verboten!** strictly prohibited
Strenge (-) *f* severity; strictness; sharpness
strenggläubig *adj* strict
strengstens *adv* strictly
Stress [ʃtrɛs] (**-es, -e**) *m* stress
stressen *vt* to put under stress
stressfrei *adj* without stress
stressig *adj* stressful
Streu [ʃtrɔʏ] (**-, -en**) *f* litter, bed of straw
streuen *vt* to strew, scatter, spread ▷ *vi* (*mit Streupulver*) to grit; (*mit Salz*) to put down salt
Streuer (**-s, -**) *m* shaker; (*Salzstreuer*) cellar; (*Pfefferstreuer*) pot
Streufahrzeug *nt* gritter (*Brit*), sander
streunen *vi* to roam about; (*Hund, Katze*) to stray
Streupulver (**-s**) *nt* grit *od* sand for road
Streuselkuchen ['ʃtrɔʏzəlku:xən] *m cake with crumble topping*
Streuung *f* dispersion; (*Statistik*) mean variation; (*Phys*) scattering
Strich (**-(e)s, -e**) *m* (*Linie*) line; (*Federstrich, Pinselstrich*) stroke; (*von Geweben*) nap; (*von Fell*) pile; (*Querstrich*) dash; (*Schrägstrich*) oblique, slash (*bes US*); **einen ~ machen durch** (*lit*) to cross out; (*fig*) to foil; **jdm einen ~ durch die Rechnung machen** to thwart *od* foil sb's plans; **einen ~ unter etw** *akk* **machen** (*fig*) to forget sth; **nach ~ und Faden** (*umg*) good and proper; **auf den ~ gehen** (*umg*) to walk the streets; **jdm gegen den ~ gehen** to rub sb up the wrong way
strich *etc* [ʃtrɪç] *vb siehe* **streichen**
Strichcode *m* bar code (*Brit*), universal product code (*US*)
Stricheinteilung *f* calibration
stricheln ['ʃtrɪçəln] *vt*: **eine gestrichelte Linie** a broken line
Strich- *zW*: **Strichjunge** (*umg*) *m* male prostitute; **Strichkode** *m* = **Strichcode**; **Strichmädchen** *nt* streetwalker; **Strichpunkt** *m* semicolon; **strichweise** *adv* here and there; **strichweise Regen** (*Met*) rain in places
Strick [ʃtrɪk] (**-(e)s, -e**) *m* rope; **jdm aus etw einen ~ drehen** to use sth against sb
stricken *vt, vi* to knit
Strick- *zW*: **Strickjacke** *f* cardigan; **Strickleiter** *f* rope ladder; **Stricknadel** *f* knitting needle; **Strickwaren** *pl* knitwear *sing*
striegeln ['ʃtri:gəln] (*umg*) *vr* to spruce o.s. up
Strieme ['ʃtri:mə] (**-, -n**) *f* weal
strikt [strɪkt] *adj* strict
Strippe ['ʃtrɪpə] (**-, -n**) *f* (*Tel: umg*): **jdn an der ~ haben** to have sb on the line
Stripper, in (**-s, -**) *m(f)* stripper
stritt *etc* [ʃtrɪt] *vb siehe* **streiten**
strittig ['ʃtrɪtɪç] *adj* disputed, in dispute
Stroh [ʃtro:] (**-(e)s**) *nt* straw; **Strohblume** *f* everlasting flower; **Strohdach** *nt* thatched roof; **strohdumm** (*umg*) *adj* thick; **Strohfeuer** *nt*: **ein Strohfeuer sein** (*fig*) to be a passing fancy; **Strohhalm** *m* (drinking) straw; **Strohmann** (**-(e)s**, *pl* **-männer**) *m* (*Comm*) dummy; **Strohwitwe** *f* grass widow; **Strohwitwer** *m* grass widower
Strolch [ʃtrɔlç] (**-(e)s, -e**) (*pej*) *m* rogue, rascal
Strom [ʃtro:m] (**-(e)s, ¨-e**) *m* river; (*fig*) stream; (*Elek*) current; **unter ~ stehen** (*Elek*) to be live; (*fig*) to be excited; **der Wein floss in Strömen** the wine flowed like water; **in Strömen regnen** to be pouring with rain; **stromabwärts** *adv* downstream; **Stromanschluss** *m*: **Stromanschluss haben** to be connected to the electricity mains; **stromaufwärts** *adv* upstream; **Stromausfall** *m* power failure
strömen ['ʃtrø:mən] *vi* to stream, pour
Strom- *zW*: **Stromkabel** *nt* electric cable; **Stromkreis** *m* (electrical) circuit; **stromlinienförmig** *adj* streamlined; **Stromnetz** *nt* power supply system; **Stromrechnung** *f* electricity bill; **Stromschnelle** *f* rapids *pl*; **Stromsperre** *f* power cut; **Stromstärke** *f* amperage
Strömung ['ʃtrø:mʊŋ] *f* current
Stromzähler *m* electricity meter
Strophe ['ʃtro:fə] (**-, -n**) *f* verse
strotzen ['ʃtrɔtsən] *vi*: **~ vor** *+dat od* **von** to abound in, be full of
Strudel ['ʃtru:dəl] (**-s, -**) *m* whirlpool, vortex; (*Koch*) strudel
strudeln *vi* to swirl, eddy
Struktur [ʃtrʊk'tu:r] *f* structure
strukturell [ʃtrʊktu'rɛl] *adj* structural
strukturieren [ʃtrʊktu'ri:rən] *vt* to structure
Strumpf [ʃtrʊmpf] (**-(e)s, ¨-e**) *m* stocking; **Strumpfband** *nt* garter; **Strumpfhalter** *m* suspender (*Brit*), garter (*US*); **Strumpfhose** *f* (pair of) tights *pl* (*Brit*) *od* pantihose *pl* (*US*)
Strunk [ʃtrʊŋk] (**-(e)s, ¨-e**) *m* stump
struppig ['ʃtrʊpɪç] *adj* shaggy, unkempt
Stube ['ʃtu:bə] (**-, -n**) *f* room; **die gute ~** (*veraltet*) the parlour (*Brit*) *od* parlor (*US*)
Stuben- *zW*: **Stubenarrest** *m* confinement to one's room; (*Mil*) confinement to quarters; **Stubenfliege** *f* (common) housefly; **Stubenhocker** (*umg*) *m* stay-at-home; **stubenrein** *adj* house-trained
Stuck [ʃtʊk] (**-(e)s**) *m* stucco
Stück [ʃtʏk] (**-(e)s, -e**) *nt* piece; (*etwas*) bit; (*Theat*) play; **am ~** in one piece; **das ist ein starkes ~!** (*umg*) that's a bit much!; **große ~e auf jdn halten** to think highly of sb; **Stückarbeit** *f* piecework
Stuckateur [ʃtʊka'tø:r] *m* (ornamental) plasterer
Stück- *zw***: **Stückgut** *nt* (*Eisenb*) parcel service; **Stückkosten** *pl* unit cost *sing*; **Stücklohn** *m* piecework rates *pl*; **stückweise** *adv* bit by bit, piecemeal; (*Comm*) individually; **Stückwerk** *nt* bits and pieces *pl*
Student, in [ʃtu'dɛnt(ɪn)] *m(f)* student

Studenten- *zW*: **Studentenausweis** *m* student card; **Studentenfutter** *nt* nuts and raisins *pl*; **Studentenwerk** *nt* student administration; **Studentenwohnheim** *nt* hall of residence (Brit), dormitory (US)
studentisch *adj* student *attrib*
Studie ['ʃtu:diə] *f* study
Studien- *zW*: **Studienberatung** *f* course guidance service; **Studienbuch** *nt* (*Univ*) *book in which the courses one has attended are entered*; **Studienfahrt** *f* study trip; **Studienplatz** *m* university place; **Studienrat** *m*, **Studienrätin** *f* teacher at a secondary (Brit) *od* high (US) school; **Studienreform** *f* university course reform; **Studienzeitverkürzung** *f* shortening of the course of studies
studieren [ʃtu'di:rən] *vt, vi* to study; **bei jdm ~** to study under sb
Studio ['ʃtu:dio] **(-s, -s)** *nt* studio
Studium ['ʃtu:diʊm] *nt* studies *pl*
Stufe ['ʃtu:fə] **(-, -n)** *f* step; (*Entwicklungsstufe*) stage; (*Niveau*) level
Stufen- *zW*: **Stufenheck** *nt* (*Aut*) notchback; **Stufenleiter** *f* (*fig*) ladder; **stufenlos** *adj* (*Tech*) infinitely variable; **stufenlos verstellbar** continuously adjustable; **Stufenplan** *m* graduated plan; **Stufenschnitt** *m* (*Frisur*) layered cut; **stufenweise** *adv* gradually
Stuhl [ʃtu:l] **(-(e)s, ¨-e)** *m* chair; **zwischen zwei Stühlen sitzen** (*fig*) to fall between two stools
Stuhlgang *m* bowel movement
Stukkateur [ʃtʊka'tø:r] *m siehe* **Stuckateur**
stülpen ['ʃtʏlpən] *vt* (*bedecken*) to put; **etw über etw** *akk* **~** to put sth over sth; **den Kragen nach oben ~** to turn up one's collar
stumm [ʃtʊm] *adj* silent; (*Med*) dumb
Stummel (-s, -) *m* stump; (*Zigarettenstummel*) stub
Stummfilm *m* silent film (*Brit*) *od* movie (*US*)
Stümper, in ['ʃtʏmpər(ɪn)] **(-s, -)** *m(f)* incompetent, duffer; **stümperhaft** *adj* bungling, incompetent
stümpern (*umg*) *vi* to bungle
Stumpf [ʃtʊmpf] **(-(e)s, ¨-e)** *m* stump; **etw mit ~ und Stiel ausrotten** to eradicate sth root and branch
stumpf *adj* blunt; (*teilnahmslos, glanzlos*) dull; (*Winkel*) obtuse
Stumpfsinn (-(e)s) *m* tediousness
stumpfsinnig *adj* dull
Stunde ['ʃtʊndə] **(-, -n)** *f* hour; (*Augenblick, Zeitpunkt*) time; (*Sch*) lesson, period (*Brit*); **~ um Stunde** hour after hour; **80 Kilometer in der ~** ≈ 50 miles per hour
stunden *vt*: **jdm etw ~** to give sb time to pay sth
Stunden- *zW*: **Stundengeschwindigkeit** *f* average speed (per hour); **Stundenkilometer** *pl* kilometres (*Brit*) *od* kilometers (*US*) per hour; **stundenlang** *adj* for hours; **Stundenlohn** *m* hourly wage; **Stundenplan** *m* timetable; **stundenweise** *adv* by the hour; (*stündlich*) every hour
stündlich ['ʃtʏntlɪç] *adj* hourly
Stunk [ʃtʊŋk] **(-s,** *no pl***)** *m*: **~ machen** (*umg*) to kick up a stink
stupide [ʃtu'pi:də] *adj* mindless
Stups [ʃtʊps] **(-es, -e)** (*umg*) *m* push
stupsen *vt* to nudge
Stupsnase *f* snub nose
stur [ʃtu:r] *adj* obstinate, stubborn; (*Nein, Arbeiten*) dogged; **er fuhr ~ geradeaus** he just carried straight on; **sich ~ stellen, auf ~ stellen** (*umg*) to dig one's heels in; **ein ~er Bock** (*umg*) a pig-headed fellow
Sturm [ʃtʊrm] **(-(e)s, ¨-e)** *m* storm; (*Wind*) gale; (*Mil etc*) attack, assault; **~ läuten** to keep one's finger on the doorbell; **gegen etw ~ laufen** (*fig*) to be up in arms against sth
stürmen ['ʃtʏrmən] *vi* (*Wind*) to blow hard, to rage; (*rennen*) to storm ▷ *vt* (*Mil, fig*) to storm ▷ *vi unpers*: **es stürmt** there's a gale blowing
Stürmer (-s, -) *m* (*Sport*) forward
sturmfrei *adj* (*Mil*) unassailable; **eine ~e Bude** (*umg*) a room free from disturbance
stürmisch *adj* stormy; (*fig*) tempestuous; (*Entwicklung*) rapid; (*Liebhaber*) passionate; (*Beifall*) tumultuous; **nicht so ~** take it easy
Sturm- *zW*: **Sturmschritt** *m* (*Mil, fig*): **im Sturmschritt** at the double; **Sturmwarnung** *f* gale warning; **Sturmwind** *m* gale
Sturz [ʃtʊrts] **(-es, ¨-e)** *m* fall; (*Pol*) overthrow; (*in Temperatur, Preis*) drop
stürzen ['ʃtʏrtsən] *vt* (*werfen*) to hurl; (*Pol*) to overthrow; (*umkehren*) to overturn ▷ *vr* to rush; (*hineinstürzen*) to plunge ▷ *vi* to fall; (*Aviat*) to dive; (*rennen*) to dash; **jdn ins Unglück ~** to bring disaster upon sb; **„nicht ~"** "this side up"; **sich auf jdn/etw ~** to pounce on sb/sth; **sich in Unkosten ~** to go to great expense
Sturzflug *m* nose dive
Sturzhelm *m* crash helmet
Stuss [ʃtʊs] **(-es)** (*umg*) *m* nonsense, rubbish
Stute ['ʃtu:tə] **(-, -n)** *f* mare
Stuttgart ['ʃtʊtgart] **(-s)** *nt* Stuttgart
Stützbalken *m* brace, joist
Stütze ['ʃtʏtsə] **(-, -n)** *f* support; (*Hilfe*) help; **die ~n der Gesellschaft** the pillars of society
stutzen ['ʃtʊtsən] *vt* to trim; (*Ohr, Schwanz*) to dock; (*Flügel*) to clip ▷ *vi* to hesitate; (*argwöhnisch werden*) to become suspicious
stützen *vt* (*lit, fig*) to support; (*Ellbogen etc*) to prop up ▷ *vr*: **sich auf jdn/etw ~** (*lit*) to lean on sb/sth; (*Beweise, Theorie*) to be based on sb/sth
stutzig *adj* perplexed, puzzled; (*misstrauisch*) suspicious
Stützmauer *f* supporting wall
Stützpunkt *m* point of support; (*von Hebel*) fulcrum; (*Mil, fig*) base
Stützungskäufe *pl* (*Fin*) support buying *sing*
StVO *abk* = **Straßenverkehrsordnung**
stylen ['staɪlən] *vt* to style; (*Wohnung*) to design
Styling ['stailɪŋ] **(-s,** *no pl***)** *nt* styling
Styropor® [ʃtyro'po:r] **(-s)** *nt* (expanded) polystyrene

s. u. *abk* (= *siehe unten*) see below
Suaheli [zua'he:li] (**-(s)**) *nt* Swahili
Subjekt [zʊp'jɛkt] (**-(e)s, -e**) *nt* subject; (*pej: Mensch*) character (*umg*)
subjektiv [zʊpjɛk'ti:f] *adj* subjective
Subjektivität [zʊpjɛktivi'tɛ:t] *f* subjectivity
Subkultur ['zʊpkʊltu:r] *f* subculture
sublimieren [zubli'mi:rən] *vt* (*Chem, Psych*) to sublimate
Submissionsangebot [zʊpmɪsi'o:ns|angəbo:t] *nt* sealed-bid tender
Subroutine ['zʊpruti:nə] *f* (*Comput*) subroutine
Subskription [zʊpskrɪptsi'o:n] *f* subscription
Substantiv ['zʊpstanti:f] (**-s, -e**) *nt* noun
Substanz [zʊp'stants] *f* substance; **von der ~ zehren** to live on one's capital
subtil [zʊp'ti:l] *adj* subtle
subtrahieren [zʊptra'hi:rən] *vt* to subtract
subtropisch ['zʊptro:pɪʃ] *adj* subtropical
Subunternehmer *m* subcontractor
Subvention [zʊpvɛntsi'o:n] *f* subsidy
subventionieren [zʊpvɛntsio'ni:rən] *vt* to subsidize
subversiv [zʊpvɛr'zi:f] *adj* subversive
Suchaktion *f* search
Suchdienst *m* missing persons tracing service
Suche (**-, -n**) *f* search
suchen ['zu:xən] *vt* to look for, seek; (*versuchen*) to try ▷ *vi* to seek, search; **du hast hier nichts zu ~** you have no business being here; **nach Worten ~** to search for words; (*sprachlos sein*) to be at a loss for words; **such!** (*zu Hund*) seek!, find!; **~ und ersetzen** (*Comput*) search and replace
Sucher (**-s, -**) *m* seeker, searcher; (*Phot*) viewfinder
Suchmaschine *f* (*Comput*) search engine
Suchmeldung *f* missing *od* wanted person announcement
Suchscheinwerfer *m* searchlight
Sucht [zʊxt] (**-, ⸚e**) *f* mania; (*Med*) addiction; **Suchtdroge** *f* addictive drug; **suchterzeugend** *adj* addictive
süchtig ['zʏçtɪç] *adj* addicted
Süchtige, r *f(m)* addict
Süd [zy:t] (**-(e)s**) *m* south; **Südafrika** *nt* South Africa; **Südamerika** *nt* South America
Sudan [zu'da:n] (**-s**) *m*: **der ~** the Sudan
Sudanese [zuda'ne:zə] (**-n, -n**) *m* Sudanese
Sudanesin *f* Sudanese
südd. *abk* = **süddeutsch**
süddeutsch *adj* South German
Süddeutschland *nt* South(ern) Germany
Süden ['zy:dən] (**-s**) *m* south
Süd- *zW*: **Südeuropa** *nt* Southern Europe; **Südfrüchte** *pl* Mediterranean fruit; **Südkorea** *nt* South Korea; **südländisch** *adj* southern; (*italienisch, spanisch etc*) Latin; **südlich** *adj* southern; **südlich von** (to the) south of; **Südostasien** *nt* South-East Asia; **Südpol** *m* South Pole; **Südpolarmeer** *nt* Antarctic Ocean; **Südsee** *f* South Seas *pl*, South Pacific; **Südtirol** *nt* South Tyrol; **südwärts** *adv* southwards; **Südwestafrika** *nt* South West Africa, Namibia
Sueskanal ['zu:ɛskana:l] (**-s**) *m* Suez Canal
Suff [zʊf] *m*: **etw im ~ sagen** (*umg*) to say sth while under the influence
süffig ['zʏfɪç] *adj* (*Wein*) very drinkable
süffisant [zʏfi'zant] *adj* smug
suggerieren [zʊge'ri:rən] *vt* to suggest
Suggestivfrage [zʊgɛs'ti:ffra:gə] *f* leading question
suhlen ['zu:lən] *vr* (*lit, fig*) to wallow
Sühne ['zy:nə] (**-, -n**) *f* atonement, expiation
sühnen *vt* to atone for, expiate
Sühnetermin *m* (*Jur*) conciliatory hearing
Suite ['svi:tə] *f* suite
Sulfat [zʊl'fa:t] (**-(e)s, -e**) *nt* sulphate (*Brit*), sulfate (*US*)
Sultan ['zʊltan] (**-s, -e**) *m* sultan
Sultanine [zʊlta'ni:nə] *f* sultana
Sülze ['zʏltsə] (**-, -n**) *f* brawn (*Brit*), headcheese (*US*); (*Aspik*) aspic
summarisch [zʊ'ma:rɪʃ] *adj* summary
Sümmchen ['zʏmçən] *nt*: **ein hübsches ~** a tidy sum
Summe (**-, -n**) *f* sum, total
summen *vi* to buzz ▷ *vt* (*Lied*) to hum
Summer (**-s, -**) *m* buzzer
summieren [zʊ'mi:rən] *vt* to add up ▷ *vr* to mount up
Sumpf [zʊmpf] (**-(e)s, ⸚e**) *m* swamp, marsh
sumpfig *adj* marshy
Sund [zʊnt] (**-(e)s, -e**) *m* sound, straits *pl*
Sünde ['zʏndə] (**-, -n**) *f* sin
Sünden- *zW*: **Sündenbock** *m* (*fig*) scapegoat; **Sündenfall** *m* (*Rel*) Fall; **Sündenregister** *nt* (*fig*) list of sins
Sünder, in (**-s, -**) *m(f)* sinner
sündhaft *adj* (*lit*) sinful; (*fig: umg: Preise*) wicked
sündigen ['zʏndɪgən] *vi* to sin; (*hum*) to indulge; **~ an** *+dat* to sin against
Super ['zu:pər] (**-s**) *nt* (*Benzin*) four-star (petrol) (*Brit*), premium (*US*)
super (*umg*) *adj* super ▷ *adv* incredibly well
Superlativ ['zu:pərlati:f] (**-s, -e**) *m* superlative
Supermarkt *m* supermarket
Superstar *m* superstar
Suppe ['zʊpə] (**-, -n**) *f* soup; (*mit Einlage*) broth; (*klare Brühe*) bouillon; (*fig: umg: Nebel*) peasouper (*Brit*), pea soup (*US*); **jdm die ~ versalzen** (*umg*) to put a spoke in sb's wheel
Suppen- *zW*: **Suppenfleisch** *nt* meat for making soup; **Suppengrün** *nt herbs and vegetables for making soup*; **Suppenkasper** (*umg*) *m* poor eater; **Suppenteller** *m* soup plate
Surfbrett ['zø:rfbrɛt] *nt* surfboard
surfen ['zø:rfən] *vi* to surf
Surfer, in *m(f)* surfer
Surrealismus [zʊrea'lɪsmʊs] *m* surrealism
surren ['zʊrən] *vi* to buzz; (*Insekt*) to hum
Surrogat [zʊro'ga:t] (**-(e)s, -e**) *nt* substitute, surrogate
suspekt [zʊs'pɛkt] *adj* suspect
suspendieren [zʊspɛn'di:rən] *vt*: **~ (von)** to suspend (from)

Suspendierung *f* suspension
süß [zy:s] *adj* sweet
Süße (-) *f* sweetness
süßen *vt* to sweeten
Süßholz *nt*: ~ **raspeln** (*fig*) to turn on the blarney
Süßigkeit *f* sweetness; (*Bonbon etc*) sweet (*Brit*), candy (*US*)
süß- *zW*: **süßlich** *adj* sweetish; (*fig*) sugary; **süßsauer** *adj* sweet-and-sour; (*fig: gezwungen: Lächeln*) forced; (*Gurken etc*) pickled; (*Miene*) artificially friendly; **Süßspeise** *f* pudding, sweet (*Brit*); **Süßstoff** *m* sweetener; **Süßwaren** *pl* confectionery *sing*; **Süßwasser** *nt* fresh water
SV (-) *m abk* = **Sportverein**
SW *abk* (= *Südwest(en)*) SW
Swasiland ['sva:zilant] (**-s**) *nt* Swaziland
SWF (-) *m abk* (*früher*: = *Südwestfunk*) *South West German Radio*
Sylvester [zʏl'vɛstər] (**-s, -**) *nt* = **Silvester**
Symbol [zʏm'bo:l] (**-s, -e**) *nt* symbol
Symbolik *f* symbolism
symbolisch *adj* symbolic(al)
symbolisieren [zʏmboli'zi:rən] *vt* to symbolize
Symmetrie [zʏme'tri:] *f* symmetry; **Symmetrieachse** *f* symmetric axis
symmetrisch [zʏ'me:trɪʃ] *adj* symmetrical
Sympathie [zʏmpa'ti:] *f* liking; sympathy; **er hat sich** *dat* **alle ~(n) verscherzt** he has turned everyone against him; **Sympathiekundgebung** *f* demonstration of support; **Sympathiestreik** *m* sympathy strike
Sympathisant, in *m(f)* sympathizer
sympathisch [zʏm'pa:tɪʃ] *adj* likeable, congenial; **er ist mir ~** I like him
sympathisieren [zʏmpati'zi:rən] *vi* to sympathize
Symphonie [zʏmfo'ni:] *f* = **Sinfonie**
Symptom [zʏmp'to:m] (**-s, -e**) *nt* symptom
symptomatisch [zʏmpto'ma:tɪʃ] *adj* symptomatic
Synagoge [zʏna'go:gə] (**-, -n**) *f* synagogue
synchron [zʏn'kro:n] *adj* synchronous; **Synchrongetriebe** *nt* synchromesh gearbox (*Brit*) *od* transmission (*US*)
synchronisieren [zʏnkroni'zi:rən] *vt* to synchronize; (*Film*) to dub
Synchronschwimmen *nt* synchronized swimming
Syndikat [zʏndi'ka:t] (**-(e)s, -e**) *nt* combine, syndicate
Syndrom [zʏn'dro:m] (**-s, -e**) *nt* syndrome
Synkope [zʏn'ko:pə] (**-, -n**) *f* (*Mus*) syncopation
Synode [zʏ'no:də] (**-, -n**) *f* (*Rel*) synod
Synonym [zʏno'ny:m] (**-s, -e**) *nt* synonym; **synonym** *adj* synonymous
Syntax ['zʏntaks] (**-, -en**) *f* syntax
Synthese [zʏn'te:zə] (**-, -n**) *f* synthesis
synthetisch *adj* synthetic
Syphilis ['zy:filɪs] (-) *f* syphilis
Syrer, in ['zy:rər(ɪn)] (**-s, -**) *m(f)* Syrian
Syrien (**-s**) *nt* Syria
syrisch *adj* Syrian
System [zʏs'te:m] (**-s, -e**) *nt* system; **Systemanalyse** *f* systems analysis; **Systemanalytiker, in** *m(f)* systems analyst
Systematik *f* system
systematisch [zʏste'ma:tɪʃ] *adj* systematic
systematisieren [zʏstemati'zi:rən] *vt* to systematize
System- *zW*: **Systemkritiker** *m* critic of the system; **Systemplatte** *f* (*Comput*) system disk; **Systemvoraussetzung** *f* (*meist pl*) system requirement; **Systemzwang** *m* obligation to conform (to the system)
Szenarium [stse'na:riʊm] *nt* scenario
Szene ['stse:nə] (**-, -n**) *f* scene; **sich in der ~ auskennen** (*umg*) to know the scene; **sich in ~ setzen** to play to the gallery
Szenenwechsel *m* scene change
Szenerie [stsenə'ri:] *f* scenery

Tt

T, t[1] [teː] *nt* T, t; **T wie Theodor** ≈ T for Tommy
t[2] *abk* (= *Tonne*) t
Tabak ['taːbak] (**-s, -e**) *m* tobacco; **Tabakladen** *m* tobacconist's (*Brit*), tobacco store (*US*)
tabellarisch [tabɛ'laːrɪʃ] *adj* tabular
Tabelle (**-, -n**) *f* table
Tabellenführer *m* (*Sport*) top of the table, league leader
Tabernakel [tabɛr'naːkəl] (**-s, -**) *nt* tabernacle
Tabl. *abk* = **Tablette(n)**
Tablett (**-(e)s, -s** *od* **-e**) *nt* tray
Tablette [ta'blɛtə] (**-, -n**) *f* tablet, pill
Tabu [ta'buː] (**-s, -s**) *nt* taboo
tabuisieren [tabui'ziːrən] *vt* to make taboo
Tabulator [tabu'laːtɔr] *m* tabulator, tab (*umg*)
tabulieren *vt* to tab
Tacho ['taxo] (**-s, -s**) (*umg*) *m* speedo (*Brit*)
Tachometer [taxo'meːtər] (**-s, -**) *m* (*Aut*) speedometer
Tadel ['taːdəl] (**-s, -**) *m* censure, scolding; (*Fehler*) fault; (*Makel*) blemish; **tadellos** *adj* faultless, irreproachable
tadeln *vt* to scold
tadelnswert *adj* blameworthy
Tadschikistan [ta'dʒiːkistaːn] (**-s**) *nt* Tajikistan
Tafel ['taːfəl] (**-, -n**) *f* (*form: festlicher Speisetisch, Math*) table; (*Festmahl*) meal; (*Anschlagtafel*) board; (*Wandtafel*) blackboard; (*Schiefertafel*) slate; (*Gedenktafel*) plaque; (*Illustration*) plate; (*Schalttafel*) panel; (*Schokoladentafel etc*) bar; **tafelfertig** *adj* ready to serve
täfeln ['tɛːfəln] *vt* to panel
Tafelöl *nt* cooking oil; salad oil
Täfelung *f* panelling (*Brit*), paneling (*US*)
Tafelwasser *nt* table water
Taft [taft] (**-(e)s, -e**) *m* taffeta
Tag [taːk] (**-(e)s, -e**) *m* day; (*Tageslicht*) daylight; **am ~** during the day; **für** *od* **auf ein paar ~e** for a few days; **in den ~ hinein leben** to take each day as it comes; **bei ~(e)** (*ankommen*) while it's light; (*arbeiten, reisen*) during the day; **unter ~e** (*Min*) underground; **über ~e** (*Min*) on the surface; **an den ~ kommen** to come to light; **er legte großes Interesse an den ~** he showed great interest; **auf den ~ (genau)** to the day; **auf seine alten ~e** at his age; **guten ~!** good morning/afternoon!; *siehe auch* **zutage**; **tagaus** *adv*: **tagaus, tagein** day in, day out; **Tagdienst** *m* day duty
Tage- *zW*: **Tagebau** *m* (*Min*) open-cast mining; **Tagebuch** *nt* diary; **Tagedieb** *m* idler; **Tagegeld** *nt* daily allowance; **tagelang** *adv* for days
tagen *vi* to sit, meet ▷ *vi unpers*: **es tagt** dawn is breaking
Tages- *zW*: **Tagesablauf** *m* daily routine; **Tagesanbruch** *m* dawn; **Tagesausflug** *m* day trip; **Tagesdecke** *f* bedspread; **Tagesfahrt** *f* day trip; **Tageskarte** *f* (*Eintrittskarte*) day ticket; (*Speisekarte*) menu of the day; **Tageskasse** *f* (*Comm*) day's takings *pl*; (*Theat*) box office; **Tageslicht** *nt* daylight; **Tagesmutter** *f* child minder; **Tagesordnung** *f* agenda; **an der Tagesordnung sein** (*fig*) to be the order of the day; **Tagesrückfahrkarte** *f* day return (ticket); **Tagessatz** *m* daily rate; **Tagesschau** *f* (*TV*) television news (programme (*Brit*) *od* program (*US*)); **Tagesstätte** *f* day nursery (*Brit*), daycare center (*US*); **Tageswert** *m* (*Fin*) present value; **Tageszeit** *f* time of day; **zu jeder Tages- und Nachtzeit** at all hours of the day and night; **Tageszeitung** *f* daily (paper)
tägl. *abk* = **täglich**
täglich ['tɛːklɪç] *adj, adv* daily; **einmal ~** once a day
tags [taːks] *adv*: **~ darauf** *od* **danach** the next *od* following day; **tagsüber** *adv* during the day
tagtäglich *adj* daily ▷ *adv* every (single) day
Tagung *f* conference
Tagungsort *m* venue (of a conference)
Tahiti [ta'hiːti] (**-s**) *nt* Tahiti
Taifun [taɪ'fuːn] (**-s, -e**) *m* typhoon
Taille ['taljə] (**-, -n**) *f* waist
tailliert [ta'jiːrt] *adj* waisted, gathered at the waist
Taiwan ['taɪvan] (**-s**) *nt* Taiwan
Takel ['taːkəl] (**-s, -**) *nt* tackle
takeln ['taːkəln] *vt* to rig
Takt [takt] (**-(e)s, -e**) *m* tact; (*Mus*) time; **Taktgefühl** *nt* tact
Taktik *f* tactics *pl*
Taktiker, in *m(f)* tactician
taktisch *adj* tactical
Takt- *zW*: **taktlos** *adj* tactless; **Taktlosigkeit** *f* tactlessness; **Taktstock** *m* (conductor's) baton; **Taktstrich** *m* (*Mus*) bar (line); **taktvoll**

adj tactful
Tal [ta:l] (**-(e)s, ¨-er**) *nt* valley
Talar [ta'la:r] (**-s, -e**) *m* (*Jur*) robe; (*Univ*) gown
Talbrücke *f* bridge over a valley
Talent [ta'lɛnt] (**-(e)s, -e**) *nt* talent
talentiert [talɛn'ti:rt] *adj* talented, gifted
Talfahrt *f* descent; (*fig*) decline
Talg [talk] (**-(e)s, -e**) *m* tallow
Talgdrüse *f* sebaceous gland
Talisman ['ta:lɪsman] (**-s, -e**) *m* talisman
Tal- *zW*: **Talsohle** *f* bottom of a valley; **Talsperre** *f* dam; **talwärts** *adv* down to the valley
Tamburin [tambu'ri:n] (**-s, -e**) *nt* tambourine
Tamile [ta'mi:lə] (**-n, -n**) *m*, **Tamilin** *f* Tamil
tamilisch *adj* Tamil
Tampon ['tampɔn] (**-s, -s**) *m* tampon
Tamtam [tam'tam] (**-s, -s**) *nt* (*Mus*) tomtom; (*umg: Wirbel*) fuss, ballyhoo; (*Lärm*) din
Tang [taŋ] (**-(e)s, -e**) *m* seaweed
Tangente [taŋ'gɛntə] (**-, -n**) *f* tangent
Tanger ['taŋər] (**-s**) *nt* Tangier(s)
tangieren [taŋ'gi:rən] *vt* (*Problem*) to touch on; (*fig*) to affect
Tank [taŋk] (**-s, -s**) *m* tank
tanken *vt* (*Wagen etc*) to fill up with petrol (*Brit*) *od* gas (*US*); (*Benzin etc*) to fill up with; (*Aviat*) to (re)fuel; (*umg: frische Luft, neue Kräfte*) to get ▷ *vi* to fill up (with petrol *od* gas); to (re)fuel
Tanker (**-s, -**) *m* tanker
Tank- *zW*: **Tanklaster** *m* tanker; **Tankschiff** *nt* tanker; **Tankstelle** *f* petrol (*Brit*) *od* gas (*US*) station; **Tankuhr** *f* fuel gauge; **Tankverschluss** *m* fuel cap; **Tankwart** *m* petrol pump (*Brit*) *od* gas station (*US*) attendant
Tanne ['tanə] (**-, -n**) *f* fir
Tannenbaum *m* fir tree
Tannenzapfen *m* fir cone
Tansania [tan'za:nia] (**-s**) *nt* Tanzania
Tante ['tantə] (**-, -n**) *f* aunt; **Tante-Emma-Laden** (*umg*) *m* corner shop
Tantieme [tãti'e:mə] (**-, -n**) *f* fee; (*für Künstler etc*) royalty
Tanz [tants] (**-es, ¨-e**) *m* dance
tänzeln ['tɛntsəln] *vi* to dance along
tanzen *vt, vi* to dance
Tänzer, in (**-s, -**) *m(f)* dancer
Tanz- *zW*: **Tanzfläche** *f* (dance) floor; **Tanzlokal** *nt* café/restaurant with dancing; **Tanzschule** *f* dancing school
Tapet [ta'pe:t] (*umg*) *nt*: **etw aufs ~ bringen** to bring sth up
Tapete [ta'pe:tə] (**-, -n**) *f* wallpaper
Tapetenwechsel *m* (*fig*) change of scenery
tapezieren [tape'tsi:rən] *vt* to (wall)paper
Tapezierer (**-s, -**) *m* (interior) decorator
tapfer ['tapfər] *adj* brave; **sich ~ schlagen** (*umg*) to put on a brave show; **Tapferkeit** *f* courage, bravery
tappen ['tapən] *vi* to walk uncertainly *od* clumsily; **im Dunkeln ~** (*fig*) to grope in the dark
täppisch ['tɛpɪʃ] *adj* clumsy
Tara ['ta:ra] (**-, Taren**) *f* tare
Tarantel [ta'rantəl] (**-, -n**) *f*: **wie von der ~ gestochen** as if stung by a bee
Tarif [ta'ri:f] (**-s, -e**) *m* tariff, (scale of) fares/charges; **nach/über/unter ~ bezahlen** to pay according to/above/below the (union) rate(s); **Tarifautonomie** *f* free collective bargaining; **Tarifgruppe** *f* grade; **tariflich** *adj* agreed, union; **Tariflohn** *m* standard wage rate; **Tarifordnung** *f* wage *od* salary scale; **Tarifpartner** *m*: **die Tarifpartner** union and management; **Tarifvereinbarung** *f* labour (*Brit*) *od* labor (*US*) agreement; **Tarifverhandlungen** *pl* collective bargaining *sing*; **Tarifvertrag** *m* pay agreement
tarnen ['tarnən] *vt* to camouflage; (*Person, Absicht*) to disguise
Tarnfarbe *f* camouflage paint
Tarnmanöver *nt* (*lit, fig*) feint, covering ploy
Tarnung *f* camouflaging; disguising
Tarock [ta'rɔk] (**-s, s**) *m od nt* tarot
Tasche ['taʃə] (**-, -n**) *f* pocket; (*Handtasche*) handbag; **in die eigene ~ wirtschaften** to line one's own pockets; **jdm auf der ~ liegen** (*umg*) to live off sb
Taschen- *zW*: **Taschenbuch** *nt* paperback; **Taschendieb** *m* pickpocket; **Taschengeld** *nt* pocket money; **Taschenlampe** *f* (electric) torch, flashlight (*US*); **Taschenmesser** *nt* penknife; **Taschenrechner** *m* pocket calculator; **Taschenspieler** *m* conjurer; **Taschentuch** *nt* handkerchief
Tasmanien [tas'ma:niən] (**-s**) *nt* Tasmania
Tasse ['tasə] (**-, -n**) *f* cup; **er hat nicht alle ~n im Schrank** (*umg*) he's not all there
Tastatur [tasta'tu:r] *f* keyboard
Taste ['tastə] (**-, -n**) *f* push-button control; (*an Schreibmaschine*) key
tasten *vt* to feel, touch; (*drücken*) to press ▷ *vi* to feel, grope ▷ *vr* to feel one's way
Tastentelefon *nt* push-button telephone
Tastsinn *m* sense of touch
Tat (**-, -en**) *f* act, deed, action; **in der ~** indeed, as a matter of fact; **etw in die ~ umsetzen** to put sth into action
tat *etc* [ta:t] *vb siehe* **tun**
Tatbestand *m* facts *pl* of the case
Tatendrang *m* energy
tatenlos *adj* inactive
Täter, in ['tɛ:tər(ɪn)] (**-s, -**) *m(f)* perpetrator, culprit; **Täterschaft** *f* guilt
tätig *adj* active; **~er Teilhaber** active partner; **in einer Firma ~ sein** to work for a firm
tätigen *vt* (*Comm*) to conclude; (*geh: Einkäufe, Anruf*) to make
Tätigkeit *f* activity; (*Beruf*) occupation
Tätigkeitsbereich *m* field of activity
tatkräftig *adj* energetic; (*Hilfe*) active
tätlich *adj* violent; **Tätlichkeit** *f* violence; **es kam zu Tätlichkeiten** there were violent scenes
Tatort (**-(e)s, -e**) *m* scene of the crime
tätowieren [tɛto'vi:rən] *vt* to tattoo

Tätowierung *f* tattooing; (*Ergebnis*) tattoo
Tatsache *f* fact; **jdn vor vollendete ~n stellen** to present sb with a fait accompli
Tatsachenbericht *m* documentary (report)
tatsächlich *adj* actual ▷ *adv* really
tatverdächtig *adj* suspected
Tatze ['tatsə] (**-, -n**) *f* paw
Tau[1] [taʊ] (**-(e)s, -e**) *nt* rope
Tau[2] (**-(e)s**) *m* dew
taub [taʊp] *adj* deaf; (*Nuss*) hollow; **sich ~ stellen** to pretend not to hear
Taube ['taʊbə] (**-, -n**) *f* (*Zool*) pigeon; (*fig*) dove
Taubenschlag *m* dovecote; **hier geht es zu wie im ~** (*fig: umg*) it's like Waterloo Station here (*Brit*), it's like Grand Central Station here (*US*)
Taubheit *f* deafness
taubstumm *adj* deaf-mute
tauchen ['taʊxən] *vt* to dip ▷ *vi* to dive; (*Naut*) to submerge
Taucher (**-s, -**) *m* diver; **Taucheranzug** *m* diving suit
Tauchsieder (**-s, -**) *m* portable immersion heater
Tauchstation *f*: **auf ~ gehen** (*U-Boot*) to dive
tauen ['taʊən] *vt, vi* to thaw ▷ *vi unpers*: **es taut** it's thawing
Taufbecken *nt* font
Taufe ['taʊfə] (**-, -n**) *f* baptism
taufen *vt* to baptize; (*nennen*) to christen
Tauf- *zW*: **Taufname** *m* Christian name; **Taufpate** *m* godfather; **Taufpatin** *f* godmother; **Taufschein** *m* certificate of baptism
taugen ['taʊgən] *vi* to be of use; **~ für** to do *od* be good for; **nicht ~** to be no good *od* useless
Taugenichts (**-es, -e**) *m* good-for-nothing
tauglich ['taʊklɪç] *adj* suitable; (*Mil*) fit (for service); **Tauglichkeit** *f* suitability; fitness
Taumel ['taʊməl] (**-s**) *m* dizziness; (*fig*) frenzy
taumelig *adj* giddy, reeling
taumeln *vi* to reel, stagger
Taunus ['taʊnʊs] (**-**) *m* Taunus (Mountains *pl*)
Tausch [taʊʃ] (**-(e)s, -e**) *m* exchange; **einen guten/schlechten ~ machen** to get a good/bad deal
tauschen *vt* to exchange, swap ▷ *vi*: **ich möchte nicht mit ihm ~** I wouldn't like to be in his place
täuschen ['tɔʏʃən] *vt* to deceive ▷ *vi* to be deceptive ▷ *vr* to be wrong; **wenn mich nicht alles täuscht** unless I'm completely wrong
täuschend *adj* deceptive
Tauschhandel *m* barter
Täuschung *f* deception; (*optisch*) illusion
Täuschungsmanöver *nt* (*Sport*) feint; (*fig*) ploy
tausend ['taʊzənt] *num* a *od* one thousand; **Tausend** (**-, -en**) *f* (*Zahl*) thousand
Tausender (**-s, -**) *m* (*Geldschein*) thousand
Tausendfüßler (**-s, -**) *m* centipede
Tau- *zW*: **Tautropfen** *m* dew drop; **Tauwetter** *nt* thaw; **Tauziehen** *nt* tug-of-war
Taxe ['taksə] (**-, -n**) *f* taxi, cab
Taxi ['taksi] (**-(s), -(s)**) *nt* taxi, cab
taxieren [ta'ksi:rən] *vt* (*Preis, Wert*) to estimate; (*Haus, Gemälde*) to value; (*mustern*) to look up and down
Taxi- *zW*: **Taxifahrer** *m* taxi driver; **Taxistand** *m* taxi rank (*Brit*) *od* stand (*US*)
Tb, Tbc *f abk* (= *Tuberkulose*) TB
Teamarbeit ['ti:m|arbaɪt] *f* teamwork
Technik ['tɛçnɪk] *f* technology; (*Methode, Kunstfertigkeit*) technique
Techniker, in (**-s -**) *m(f)* technician
technisch *adj* technical; **~e Hochschule** ≈ polytechnic
Technologie [tɛçnolo'gi:] *f* technology
technologisch [tɛçno'lo:gɪʃ] *adj* technological
Techtelmechtel [tɛçtəl'mɛçtəl] (**-s, -**) (*umg*) *nt* (*Liebschaft*) affair, carry-on
TEE *abk* (= *Trans-Europ-Express*) Trans-Europe-Express
Tee [te:] (**-s, -s**) *m* tea; **Teebeutel** *m* tea bag; **Teekanne** *f* teapot; **Teelicht** *nt* night-light; **Teelöffel** *m* teaspoon; **Teemischung** *f* blend of tea
Teer [te:r] (**-(e)s, -e**) *m* tar; **teeren** *vt* to tar
Teesieb *nt* tea strainer
Teewagen *m* tea trolley
Teflon® ['tɛflo:n] (**-s**) *nt* Teflon®
Teheran ['te:həra:n] (**-s**) *nt* Teheran
Teich [taɪç] (**-(e)s, -e**) *m* pond
Teig [taɪk] (**-(e)s, -e**) *m* dough
teigig ['taɪgɪç] *adj* doughy
Teigwaren *pl* pasta *sing*
Teil [taɪl] (**-(e)s, -e**) *m od nt* part; (*Anteil*) share ▷ *nt* (*Bestandteil*) component, part; (*Ersatzteil*) spare (part); **zum ~** partly; **ich für mein(en) ~ ...** I, for my part ...; **sich** *dat* **sein ~ denken** (*umg*) to draw one's own conclusions; **er hat sein(en) ~ dazu beigetragen** he did his bit *od* share; **teilbar** *adj* divisible; **Teilbetrag** *m* instalment (*Brit*), installment (*US*); **Teilchen** *nt* (atomic) particle
teilen *vt* to divide; (*mit jdm*) to share ▷ *vr* to divide; (*in Gruppen*) to split up
Teil- *zW*: **teilentrahmt** *adj* semi-skimmed; **Teilgebiet** *nt* (*Bereich*) branch; (*räumlich*) area; **teilhaben** *unreg vi*: **an etw** *dat* **teilhaben** to share in sth; **Teilhaber** (**-s, -**) *m* partner; **Teilkaskoversicherung** *f* third party, fire and theft insurance
Teilnahme (**-, -n**) *f* participation; (*Mitleid*) sympathy; **jdm seine herzliche ~ aussprechen** to offer sb one's heartfelt sympathy
teilnahmslos *adj* disinterested, apathetic
teilnehmen *unreg vi*: **an etw** *dat* **~** to take part in sth
Teilnehmer, in (**-s, -**) *m(f)* participant
teils *adv* partly
Teilschaden *m* partial loss
Teilstrecke *f* stage; (*von Straße*) stretch; (*bei Bus etc*) fare stage
Teilung *f* division
Teil- *zW*: **teilweise** *adv* partially, in part;

Teilzahlung *f* payment by instalments (*Brit*) *od* installments (*US*); **Teilzeitarbeit** *f* part-time job *od* work; **Teilzeitbasis** *f*: **auf Teilzeitbasis arbeiten** to work part-time; **Teilzeitmodell** *nt* part-time working arrangements
Teint [tɛ̃ː] (**-s, -s**) *m* complexion
Telearbeit ['teːlearbaɪt] *f* teleworking
Telebanking ['teːlebɛŋkɪŋ] (**-s**) *nt* telebanking
Telebrief ['teːlebriːf] *m* facsimile, fax
Telefax ['teːlefaks] (-) *nt* telefax
Telefon [tele'foːn] (**-s, -e**) *nt* (tele)phone; **ans ~ gehen** to answer the phone; **Telefonamt** *nt* telephone exchange; **Telefonanruf** *m* (tele)phone call
Telefonat [telefo'naːt] (**-(e)s, -e**) *nt* (tele)phone call
Telefon- *zW*: **Telefonbuch** *nt* (tele)phone directory; **Telefongebühr** *f* call charge; (*Grundgebühr*) (tele)phone rental; **Telefongespräch** *nt* (tele)phone call; **Telefonhäuschen** (*umg*) *nt* = **Telefonzelle**
telefonieren [telefo'niːrən] *vi* to (tele)phone; **bei jdm ~** to use sb's phone; **mit jdm ~** to speak to sb on the phone
telefonisch [tele'foːnɪʃ] *adj* telephone; (*Benachrichtigung*) by telephone; **ich bin ~ zu erreichen** I can be reached by phone
Telefonist, in [telefo'nɪst(ɪn)] *m(f)* telephonist
Telefon- *zW*: **Telefonkarte** *f* phone card; **Telefonnummer** *f* (tele)phone number; **Telefonseelsorge** *f*: **die Telefonseelsorge** ≈ the Samaritans; **Telefonverbindung** *f* telephone connection; **Telefonzelle** *f* telephone box (*Brit*) *od* booth (*US*), callbox (*Brit*); **Telefonzentrale** *f* telephone exchange
Telegraf [tele'graːf] (**-en, -en**) *m* telegraph
Telegrafenleitung *f* telegraph line
Telegrafenmast *m* telegraph pole
Telegrafie [telegra'fiː] *f* telegraphy
telegrafieren [telegra'fiːrən] *vt, vi* to telegraph, cable, wire
telegrafisch [tele'graːfɪʃ] *adj* telegraphic; **jdm ~ Geld überweisen** to cable sb money
Telegramm [tele'gram] (**-s, -e**) *nt* telegram, cable; **Telegrammadresse** *f* telegraphic address; **Telegrammformular** *nt* telegram form
Telekolleg ['teːləkɔleːk] *nt* ≈ Open University (*Brit*)
Teleobjektiv ['teːlə|ɔpjɛktiːf] *nt* telephoto lens
Telepathie [telepa'tiː] *f* telepathy
telepathisch [tele'paːtɪʃ] *adj* telepathic
Teleskop [tele'skoːp] (**-s, -e**) *nt* telescope
Telespiel *nt* video game
Telex ['teːlɛks] (**-, -(e)**) *nt* telex
Teller ['tɛlər] (**-s, -**) *m* plate
Tempel ['tɛmpəl] (**-s, -**) *m* temple
Temperafarbe ['tɛmperafarbə] *f* distemper
Temperament [tɛmpera'mɛnt] *nt* temperament; (*Schwung*) vivacity, vitality; **sein ~ ist mit ihm durchgegangen** he went over the top; **temperamentlos** *adj* spiritless; **temperamentvoll** *adj* high-spirited, lively
Temperatur [tɛmpera'tuːr] *f* temperature; **erhöhte ~ haben** to have a temperature
Tempo¹ ['tɛmpo] (**-s, -s**) *nt* speed, pace; **~!** get a move on!
Tempo² ['tɛmpo] (**-s, Tempi**) *nt* (*Mus*) tempo; **das ~ angeben** (*fig*) to set the pace; **Tempolimit** *nt* speed limit
temporär [tɛmpo'rɛːr] *adj* temporary
Tempotaschentuch® *nt* paper handkerchief
Tendenz [tɛn'dɛnts] *f* tendency; (*Absicht*) intention
tendenziell [tɛndɛntsi'ɛl] *adj*: **nur ~e Unterschiede** merely differences in emphasis
tendenziös [tɛndɛntsi'øːs] *adj* bias(s)ed, tendentious
tendieren [tɛn'diːrən] *vi*: **zu etw ~** to show a tendency to(wards) sth, incline to(wards) sth
Teneriffa [tene'rɪfa] (**-s**) *nt* Tenerife
Tenne ['tɛnə] (**-, -n**) *f* threshing floor
Tennis ['tɛnɪs] (-) *nt* tennis; **Tennisplatz** *m* tennis court; **Tennisschläger** *m* tennis racket; **Tennisspieler** *m* tennis player
Tenor [te'noːr] (**-s, ¨-e**) *m* tenor
Teppich ['tɛpɪç] (**-s, -e**) *m* carpet; **Teppichboden** *m* wall-to-wall carpeting; **Teppichkehrmaschine** *f* carpet sweeper; **Teppichklopfer** *m* carpet beater
Termin [tɛr'miːn] (**-s, -e**) *m* (*Zeitpunkt*) date; (*Frist*) deadline; (*Arzttermin etc*) appointment; (*Jur: Verhandlung*) hearing; **sich** *dat* **einen ~ geben lassen** to make an appointment; **termingerecht** *adj* on schedule
terminieren [tɛrmi'niːrən] *vt* (*befristen*) to limit; (*festsetzen*) to set a date for
Terminkalender *m* diary, appointments book
Terminologie [tɛrminolo'giː] *f* terminology
Termite [tɛr'miːtə] (**-, -n**) *f* termite
Terpentin [tɛrpɛn'tiːn] (**-s, -e**) *nt* turpentine, turps *sing*
Terrain [tɛ'rɛ̃ː] (**-s, -s**) *nt* land, terrain; (*fig*) territory; **das ~ sondieren** (*Mil*) to reconnoitre the terrain; (*fig*) to see how the land lies
Terrasse [tɛ'rasə] (**-, -n**) *f* terrace
Terrine [tɛ'riːnə] *f* tureen
territorial [tɛritori'aːl] *adj* territorial
Territorium [tɛri'toːriʊm] *nt* territory
Terror ['tɛrɔr] (**-s**) *m* terror; (*Terrorherrschaft*) reign of terror; **blanker ~** sheer terror; **Terroranschlag** *m* terrorist attack
terrorisieren [tɛrori'ziːrən] *vt* to terrorize
Terrorismus [tɛro'rɪsmʊs] *m* terrorism
Terrorist, in *m(f)* terrorist
terroristisch *adj* terrorist *attr*
Terrornetz(werk) *nt* terrorist network
Terrororganisation *f* terrorist organization
Terrorzelle *f* terrorist cell
Tertia ['tɛrtsia] (**-, Tertien**) *f* (*Sch: früher: Untertertia/Obertertia*) *fourth/fifth year of German secondary school*
Terz [tɛrts] (**-, -en**) *f* (*Mus*) third
Terzett [tɛr'tsɛt] (**-(e)s, -e**) *nt* (*Mus*) trio
Tesafilm® ['teːzafɪlm] *m* Sellotape® (*Brit*), Scotch tape® (*US*)

Test [tɛst] (**-s, -s**) *m* test
Testament [tɛsta'mɛnt] *nt* will, testament; (*Rel*) Testament; **Altes/Neues ~** Old/New Testament
testamentarisch [tɛstamɛn'ta:rɪʃ] *adj* testamentary
Testamentsvollstrecker, in (**-s, -**) *m(f)* executor (of a will)
Testat [tɛs'ta:t] (**-(e)s, -e**) *nt* certificate
Testator [tɛs'ta:tɔr] *m* testator
Test- *zW*: **Testbild** *nt* (*TV*) test card; **testen** *vt* to test; **Testfall** *m* test case; **Testperson** *f* subject (of a test); **Teststoppabkommen** *nt* nuclear test ban agreement
Tetanus ['te:tanʊs] (**-**) *m* tetanus; **Tetanusimpfung** *f* (anti-)tetanus injection
teuer ['tɔʏər] *adj* dear, expensive; **teures Geld** good money; **das wird ihn ~ zu stehen kommen** (*fig*) that will cost him dear
Teuerung *f* increase in prices
Teuerungszulage *f* cost-of-living bonus
Teufel ['tɔʏfəl] (**-s, -**) *m* devil; **den ~ an die Wand malen** (*schwarzmalen*) to imagine the worst; (*Unheil heraufbeschwören*) to tempt fate *od* providence; **in ~s Küche kommen** to get into a mess; **jdn zum ~ jagen** (*umg*) to send sb packing
Teufelei [tɔʏfə'laɪ] *f* devilment
Teufels- *zW*: **Teufelsaustreibung** *f* exorcism; **Teufelsbrut** (*umg*) *f* devil's brood; **Teufelskreis** *m* vicious circle
teuflisch ['tɔʏflɪʃ] *adj* fiendish, diabolic
Text [tɛkst] (**-(e)s, -e**) *m* text; (*Liedertext*) words *pl*; (*: von Schlager*) lyrics *pl*; **Textdichter** *m* songwriter; **texten** *vi* to write the words
textil [tɛks'ti:l] *adj* textile; **Textilbranche** *f* textile trade
Textilien *pl* textiles *pl*
Textilindustrie *f* textile industry
Textilwaren *pl* textiles *pl*
Text- *zW*: **Textnachrichten** *pl* (*Tel*) text messaging; **Textstelle** *f* passage; **Textverarbeitungssystem** *nt* word processor
TH (**-, -s**) *f abk* (*= technische Hochschule*) *siehe* **technisch**
Thailand ['taɪlant] (**-s**) *nt* Thailand
Thailänder, in ['taɪlɛndər(ɪn)] (**-s, -**) *m(f)* Thai
Theater [te'a:tər] (**-s, -**) *nt* theatre (*Brit*), theater (*US*); (*umg*) fuss; **(ein) ~ machen** to make a (big) fuss; **~ spielen** to act; (*fig*) to put on an act; **Theaterbesucher** *m* playgoer; **Theaterkasse** *f* box office; **Theaterstück** *nt* (stage) play
theatralisch [tea'tra:lɪʃ] *adj* theatrical
Theke ['te:kə] (**-, -n**) *f* (*Schanktisch*) bar; (*Ladentisch*) counter
Thema ['te:ma] (**-s, Themen** *od* **-ta**) *nt* (*Leitgedanke, Mus*) theme; topic, subject; **beim ~ bleiben/vom ~ abschweifen** to stick to/ wander off the subject
thematisch [te'ma:tɪʃ] *adj* thematic
Themenkreis *m* topic
Themenpark *m* theme park
Themse ['tɛmzə] *f*: **die ~** the Thames
Theologe [teo'lo:gə] (**-n, -n**) *m* theologian
Theologie [teolo'gi:] *f* theology
Theologin *f* theologian
theologisch [teo'lo:gɪʃ] *adj* theological
Theoretiker, in [teo're:tikər(ɪn)] (**-s, -**) *m(f)* theorist
theoretisch *adj* theoretical; **~ gesehen** in theory, theoretically
Theorie [teo'ri:] *f* theory
Therapeut [tera'pɔʏt] (**-en, -en**) *m* therapist
therapeutisch *adj* therapeutic
Therapie [tera'pi:] *f* therapy
Thermalbad [tɛr'ma:lba:t] *nt* thermal bath; (*Badeort*) thermal spa
Thermalquelle *f* thermal spring
Thermometer [tɛrmo'me:tər] (**-s, -**) *nt* thermometer
Thermosflasche® ['tɛrmɔsflaʃə] *f* Thermos® flask
Thermostat [tɛrmo'sta:t] (**-(e)s** *od* **-en, -e(n)**) *m* thermostat
These ['te:zə] (**-, -n**) *f* thesis
Thrombose [trɔm'bo:sə] (**-, -n**) *f* thrombosis
Thron [tro:n] (**-(e)s, -e**) *m* throne; **Thronbesteigung** *f* accession (to the throne)
thronen *vi* to sit enthroned; (*fig*) to sit in state
Thronerbe *m* heir to the throne
Thronfolge *f* succession (to the throne)
Thunfisch ['tu:nfɪʃ] *m* tuna (fish)
Thüringen ['ty:rɪŋən] (**-s**) *nt* Thuringia
Thymian ['ty:mia:n] (**-s, -e**) *m* thyme
Tibet ['ti:bɛt] (**-s**) *nt* Tibet
Tick [tɪk] (**-(e)s, -s**) *m* tic; (*Eigenart*) quirk; (*Fimmel*) craze
ticken *vi* to tick; **nicht richtig ~** (*umg*) to be off one's rocker
Ticket ['tɪkət] (**-s, -s**) *nt* ticket
tief [ti:f] *adj* deep; (*tiefsinnig*) profound; (*Ausschnitt, Ton*) low; **~er Teller** soup plate; **~ greifend** far-reaching; **~ schürfend** profound; **bis ~ in die Nacht hinein** late into the night; **Tief** (**-s, -s**) *nt* (*Met*) depression; (*fig*) low; **Tiefbau** *m* civil engineering (*at or below ground level*); **Tiefdruck** *m* (*Met*) low pressure
Tiefe (**-, -n**) *f* depth
Tiefebene ['ti:f|e:bənə] *f* plain
Tiefenpsychologie *f* depth psychology
Tiefenschärfe *f* (*Phot*) depth of focus
tief- *zW*: **tiefernst** *adj* very grave *od* solemn; **Tiefflug** *m* low-level *od* low-altitude flight; **Tiefgang** *m* (*Naut*) draught (*Brit*), draft (*US*); (*geistig*) depth; **Tiefgarage** *f* underground car park (*Brit*) *od* parking lot (*US*); **tiefgekühlt** *adj* frozen; **Tiefkühlfach** *nt* freezer compartment; **Tiefkühlkost** *f* frozen food; **Tiefkühltruhe** *f* freezer, deep freeze (*US*); **Tieflader** (**-s, -**) *m* low-loader; **Tiefland** *nt* lowlands *pl*; **Tiefparterre** *f* basement; **Tiefpunkt** *m* low point; (*fig*) low ebb; **Tiefschlag** *m* (*Boxen, fig*) blow below the belt; **Tiefsee** *f* deep parts of the sea; **Tiefsinn** *m* profundity; **tiefsinnig** *adj* profound; (*umg*) melancholy; **Tiefstand**

m low level; **tiefstapeln** *vi* to be overmodest; **Tiefstart** *m* (*Sport*) crouch start
Tiefstwert *m* minimum *od* lowest value
Tiegel ['ti:gəl] (**-s, -**) *m* saucepan; (*Chem*) crucible
Tier [ti:r] (**-(e)s, -e**) *nt* animal; **Tierarzt** *m*, **Tierärztin** *f* vet(erinary surgeon) (*Brit*), veterinarian (*US*); **Tierfreund** *m* animal lover; **Tiergarten** *m* zoo, zoological gardens *pl*; **Tierhandlung** *f* pet shop (*Brit*) *od* store (*US*); **tierisch** *adj* animal *attrib*; (*lit, fig*) brutish; (*fig: Ernst etc*) deadly; **Tierkreis** *m* zodiac; **Tierkunde** *f* zoology; **tierlieb** *adj*, **tierliebend** *adj* fond of animals; **Tierquälerei** *f* cruelty to animals; **Tierreich** *nt* animal kingdom; **Tierschutz** *m* protection of animals; **Tierschutzverein** *m* society for the prevention of cruelty to animals; **Tierversuch** *m* animal experiment; **Tierwelt** *f* animal kingdom
Tiger ['ti:gər] (**-s, -**) *m* tiger; **Tigerin** *f* tigress
tilgen ['tɪlgən] *vt* to erase; (*Sünden*) to expiate; (*Schulden*) to pay off
Tilgung *f* erasing, blotting out; expiation; repayment
Tilgungsfonds *m* (*Comm*) sinking fund
tingeln ['tɪŋgəln] (*umg*) *vi* to appear in small night clubs
Tinktur [tɪŋk'tu:r] *f* tincture
Tinte ['tɪntə] (**-, -n**) *f* ink
Tinten- *zW*: **Tintenfass** *nt* inkwell; **Tintenfisch** *m* cuttlefish; (*achtarmig*) octopus; **Tintenfleck** *m* ink stain *od* blot; **Tintenstift** *m* indelible pencil; **Tintenstrahldrucker** *m* ink-jet printer
Tipp [tɪp] (**-s, -s**) *m* (*Sport, Börse*) tip; (*Andeutung*) hint; (*an Polizei*) tip-off
Tippelbruder (*umg*) *m* tramp, gentleman of the road (*Brit*), hobo (*US*)
tippen ['tɪpən] *vi* to tap, touch; (*umg: schreiben*) to type; (*im Lotto etc*) to bet ▷ *vt* to type; to bet; **auf jdn ~** (*umg: raten*) to tip sb, put one's money on sb (*fig*)
Tippfehler (*umg*) *m* typing error
Tippse (**-, -n**) (*umg*) *f* typist
tipptopp ['tɪp'tɔp] (*umg*) *adj* tiptop
Tippzettel *m* (pools) coupon
Tirade [ti'ra:də] (**-, -n**) *f* tirade
Tirol [ti'ro:l] (**-s**) *nt* the Tyrol
Tiroler, in (**-s, -**) *m(f)* Tyrolese, Tyrolean
tirolerisch *adj* Tyrolese, Tyrolean
Tisch [tɪʃ] (**-(e)s, -e**) *m* table; **bitte zu ~!** lunch *od* dinner is served; **bei ~** at table; **vor/nach ~** before/after eating; **unter den ~ fallen** (*fig*) to be dropped; **Tischdecke** *f* tablecloth
Tischler (**-s, -**) *m* carpenter, joiner
Tischlerei [tɪʃlə'raɪ] *f* joiner's workshop; (*Arbeit*) carpentry, joinery
Tischlerhandwerk *nt* cabinetmaking
tischlern *vi* to do carpentry *etc*
Tisch- *zW*: **Tischnachbar** *m* neighbour (*Brit*) *od* neighbor (*US*) (at table); **Tischrechner** *m* desk calculator; **Tischrede** *f* after-dinner speech; **Tischtennis** *nt* table tennis; **Tischtuch** *nt* tablecloth
Titel ['ti:təl] (**-s, -**) *m* title; **Titelanwärter** *m* (*Sport*) challenger; **Titelbild** *nt* cover (picture); (*von Buch*) frontispiece; **Titelgeschichte** *f* headline story; **Titelrolle** *f* title role; **Titelseite** *f* cover; (*Buchtitel*) title page; **Titelverteidiger** *m* defending champion, title holder
Titte ['tɪtə] (**-, -n**) (*umg*) *f* (*weibliche Brust*) boob, tit (*umg*)
titulieren [titu'li:rən] *vt* to entitle; (*anreden*) to address
tja [tja] *interj* well!
Toast [to:st] (**-(e)s, -s** *od* **-e**) *m* toast
toasten *vi* to drink a toast ▷ *vt* (*Brot*) to toast; **auf jdn ~** to toast sb, drink a toast to sb
Toaster (**-s, -**) *m* toaster
toben ['to:bən] *vi* to rage; (*Kinder*) to romp about
tob- *zW*: **Tobsucht** *f* raving madness; **tobsüchtig** *adj* maniacal; **Tobsuchtsanfall** *m* maniacal fit
Tochter ['tɔxtər] (**-, ⸗**) *f* daughter; **Tochtergesellschaft** *f* subsidiary (company)
Tod [to:t] (**-(e)s, -e**) *m* death; **zu ~e betrübt sein** to be in the depths of despair; **eines natürlichen/gewaltsamen ~es sterben** to die of natural causes/die a violent death; **todernst** (*umg*) *adj* deadly serious ▷ *adv* in dead earnest
Todes- *zW*: **Todesangst** *f* mortal fear; **Todesängste ausstehen** (*umg*) to be scared to death; **Todesanzeige** *f* obituary (notice); **Todesfall** *m* death; **Todeskampf** *m* death throes *pl*; **Todesopfer** *nt* death, casualty, fatality; **Todesqualen** *pl*: **Todesqualen ausstehen** (*fig*) to suffer agonies; **Todesstoß** *m* deathblow; **Todesstrafe** *f* death penalty; **Todestag** *m* anniversary of death; **Todesursache** *f* cause of death; **Todesurteil** *nt* death sentence; **Todesverachtung** *f* utter disgust
Todfeind *m* deadly *od* mortal enemy
todkrank *adj* dangerously ill
tödlich ['tø:tlɪç] *adj* fatal; (*Gift*) deadly, lethal
tod- *zW*: **todmüde** *adj* dead tired; **todschick** (*umg*) *adj* smart, classy; **todsicher** (*umg*) *adj* absolutely *od* dead certain; **Todsünde** *f* deadly sin; **todtraurig** *adj* extremely sad
Tofu ['to:fu] (**-(s)**) *m* tofu
Togo ['to:go] (**-s**) *nt* Togo
Toilette [toa'lɛtə] *f* toilet, lavatory (*Brit*), john (*US*); (*Frisiertisch*) dressing table; (*Kleidung*) outfit; **auf die ~ gehen/auf der ~ sein** to go to/be in the toilet
Toiletten- *zW*: **Toilettenartikel** *pl* toiletries *pl*, toilet articles *pl*; **Toilettenpapier** *nt* toilet paper; **Toilettentisch** *m* dressing table
toi, toi, toi ['tɔy'tɔy'tɔy] (*umg*) *interj* good luck; (*unberufen*) touch wood
Tokio ['to:kjo] (**-s**) *nt* Tokyo
tolerant [tole'rant] *adj* tolerant
Toleranz *f* tolerance
tolerieren [tole'ri:rən] *vt* to tolerate
toll [tɔl] *adj* mad; (*Treiben*) wild; (*umg*) terrific

tollen *vi* to romp
toll- *zW*: **Tollheit** *f* madness, wildness; **Tollkirsche** *f* deadly nightshade; **tollkühn** *adj* daring; **Tollwut** *f* rabies
Tölpel ['tœlpəl] (**-s, -**) *m* oaf, clod
Tomate [to'ma:tə] (**-, -n**) *f* tomato; **du treulose ~!** (*umg*) you're a fine friend!
Tomatenmark (**-(e)s**) *nt* tomato purée
Tombola ['tɔmbola] (**-, -s** *od* **Tombolen**) *f* tombola
Ton¹ [to:n] (**-(e)s, -e**) *m* (*Erde*) clay
Ton² [to:n] (**-(e)s, ¨-e**) *m* (*Laut*) sound; (*Mus*) note; (*Redeweise*) tone; (*Farbton, Nuance*) shade; (*Betonung*) stress; **keinen ~ herausbringen** not to be able to say a word; **den ~ angeben** (*Mus*) to give an A; (*fig: Mensch*) to set the tone; **Tonabnehmer** *m* pick-up; **tonangebend** *adj* leading; **Tonarm** *m* pick-up arm; **Tonart** *f* (musical) key; **Tonband** *nt* tape; **Tonbandaufnahme** *f* tape recording; **Tonbandgerät** *nt* tape recorder
tönen ['tø:nən] *vi* to sound ▷ *vt* to shade; (*Haare*) to tint
tönern ['tø:nərn] *adj* clay
Ton- *zW*: **Tonfall** *m* intonation; **Tonfilm** *m* sound film; **Tonhöhe** *f* pitch
Tonika ['to:nika] (**-, -iken**) *f* (*Mus*) tonic
Tonikum (**-s, -ika**) *nt* (*Med*) tonic
Ton- *zW*: **Toningenieur** *m* sound engineer; **Tonkopf** *m* recording head; **Tonkünstler** *m* musician; **Tonleiter** *f* (*Mus*) scale; **tonlos** *adj* soundless
Tonne ['tɔnə] (**-, -n**) *f* barrel; (*Maß*) ton
Ton- *zW*: **Tonspur** *f* soundtrack; **Tontaube** *f* clay pigeon; **Tonwaren** *pl* pottery *sing*, earthenware *sing*
Topf [tɔpf] (**-(e)s, ¨-e**) *m* pot; **alles in einen ~ werfen** (*fig*) to lump everything together; **Topfblume** *f* pot plant
Töpfer, in ['tœpfər(ɪn)] (**-s, -**) *m(f)* potter
Töpferei [tœpfə'raɪ] *f* (*Töpferware*) pottery; (*Werkstatt*) pottery, potter's workshop
töpfern *vi* to do pottery
Töpferscheibe *f* potter's wheel
topfit ['tɔp'fɪt] *adj* in top form
Topflappen *m* ovencloth
topografisch [topo'gra:fɪʃ] *adj* topographic
topp [tɔp] *interj* O.K.
Tor¹ [to:r] (**-en, -en**) *m* fool
Tor² (**-(e)s, -e**) *nt* gate; (*Sport*) goal; **Torbogen** *m* archway; **Toreinfahrt** *f* entrance gate
Toresschluss *m*: **(kurz) vor ~** right at the last minute
Torf [tɔrf] (**-(e)s**) *m* peat; **Torfstechen** *nt* peat-cutting
Torheit *f* foolishness; (*törichte Handlung*) foolish deed
Torhüter (**-s, -**) *m* goalkeeper
töricht ['tørɪçt] *adj* foolish
torkeln ['tɔrkəln] *vi* to stagger, reel
torpedieren [tɔrpe'di:rən] *vt* (*lit, fig*) to torpedo
Torpedo [tɔr'pe:do] (**-s, -s**) *m* torpedo
Torschlusspanik ['to:rʃlʊspa:nɪk] (*umg*) *f* (*von Unverheirateten*) *fear of being left on the shelf*
Torte ['tɔrtə] (**-, -n**) *f* cake; (*Obsttorte*) flan, tart
Tortenguss *m* glaze
Tortenheber *m* cake slice
Tortur [tɔr'tu:r] *f* ordeal
Torverhältnis *nt* goal average
Torwart (**-(e)s, -e**) *m* goalkeeper
tosen ['to:zən] *vi* to roar
Toskana [tɔs'ka:na] *f* Tuscany
tot [to:t] *adj* dead; **er war auf der Stelle ~** he died instantly; **~ geboren** stillborn; **sich ~ stellen** to pretend to be dead; **der ~e Winkel** the blind spot; **einen ~en Punkt haben** to be at one's lowest; **das T~e Meer** the Dead Sea
total [to'ta:l] *adj* total; **Totalausverkauf** *m* clearance sale
totalitär [totali'tɛ:r] *adj* totalitarian
Totaloperation *f* extirpation; (*von Gebärmutter*) hysterectomy
Totalschaden *m* (*Aut*) complete write-off
totarbeiten *vr* to work o.s. to death
totärgern (*umg*) *vr* to get really annoyed
Tote, r *f(m)* dead person
töten ['tøtən] *vt, vi* to kill
Toten- *zW*: **Totenbett** *nt* deathbed; **totenblass** *adj* deathly pale, white as a sheet; **Totengräber** (**-s, -**) *m* gravedigger; **Totenhemd** *nt* shroud; **Totenkopf** *m* skull; **Totenmesse** *f* requiem mass; **Totenschein** *m* death certificate; **Totenstille** *f* deathly silence; **Totentanz** *m* danse macabre; **Totenwache** *f* wake
tot- *zW*: **totfahren** *unreg vt* to run over; **totkriegen** (*umg*) *vt*: **nicht totzukriegen sein** to go on for ever; **totlachen** (*umg*) *vr* to laugh one's head off
Toto ['to:to] (**-s, -s**) *m od nt* ≈ pools *pl*; **Totoschein** *m* ≈ pools coupon
tot- *zW*: **totsagen** *vt*: **jdn totsagen** to say that sb is dead; **Totschlag** *m* (*Jur*) manslaughter, second degree murder (*US*); **totschlagen** *unreg vt* (*lit, fig*) to kill; **Totschläger** *m* (*Waffe*) cosh (*Brit*), blackjack (*US*); **totschweigen** *unreg vt* to hush up; **tottreten** *unreg vt* to trample to death
Tötung ['tø:tʊŋ] *f* killing
Toupet [tu'pe:] (**-s, -s**) *nt* toupee
toupieren [tu'pi:rən] *vt* to backcomb
Tour [tu:r] (**-, -en**) *f* tour, trip; (*Umdrehung*) revolution; (*Verhaltensart*) way; **auf ~en kommen** (*Aut*) to reach top speed; (*fig*) to get into top gear; **auf vollen ~en laufen** (*lit*) to run at full speed; (*fig*) to be in full swing; **auf die krumme ~** by dishonest means; **in einer ~** incessantly
Tourenzahl *f* number of revolutions
Tourenzähler *m* rev counter
Tourismus [tu'rɪsmʊs] *m* tourism
Tourist, in *m(f)* tourist
Touristenklasse *f* tourist class
Touristik [tu'rɪstɪk] *f* tourism
touristisch *adj* tourist *attr*
Tournee [tʊr'ne:] (**-, -s** *od* **-n**) *f* (*Theat etc*) tour;

auf ~ gehen to go on tour
Trab [tra:p] (**-(e)s**) *m* trot; **auf ~ sein** (*umg*) to be on the go
Trabant [tra'bant] *m* satellite
Trabantenstadt *f* satellite town
traben ['tra:bən] *vi* to trot
Tracht [traxt] (**-, -en**) *f* (*Kleidung*) costume, dress; **eine ~ Prügel** a sound thrashing
trachten *vi* to strive, endeavour (*Brit*), endeavor (*US*); **danach ~, etw zu tun** to strive to do sth; **jdm nach dem Leben ~** to seek to kill sb
trächtig ['trɛçtɪç] *adj* (*Tier*) pregnant
Tradition [traditsi'o:n] *f* tradition
traditionell [traditsio:'nɛl] *adj* traditional
traf *etc* [tra:f] *vb siehe* **treffen**
Tragbahre *f* stretcher
tragbar *adj* (*Gerät*) portable; (*Kleidung*) wearable; (*erträglich*) bearable
träge ['trɛ:gə] *adj* sluggish, slow; (*Phys*) inert
tragen ['tra:gən] *unreg vt* to carry; (*Kleidung, Brille*) to wear; (*Namen, Früchte*) to bear; (*erdulden*) to endure ▷ *vi* (*schwanger sein*) to be pregnant; (*Eis*) to hold; **schwer an etw** *dat* **~** (*lit*) to have a job carrying sth; (*fig*) to find sth hard to bear; **zum T~ kommen** to come to fruition; (*nützlich werden*) to come in useful
tragend *adj* (*Säule, Bauteil*) load-bearing; (*Idee, Motiv*) fundamental
Träger ['trɛ:gər] (**-s, -**) *m* carrier; wearer; bearer; (*Ordensträger*) holder; (*an Kleidung*) (shoulder) strap; (*Körperschaft etc*) sponsor; (*Holzträger, Betonträger*) (supporting) beam; (*Stahlträger, Eisenträger*) girder; (*Tech: Stütze von Brücken etc*) support
Trägerin *f* (*Person*) *siehe* **Träger**
Träger- *zW*: **Trägerkleid** *nt* pinafore dress (*Brit*), jumper (*US*); **Trägerrakete** *f* launch vehicle; **Trägerrock** *m* skirt with shoulder straps
Tragetasche *f* carrier bag (*Brit*), carry-all (*US*)
Trag- *zW*: **Tragfähigkeit** *f* load-bearing capacity; **Tragfläche** *f* (*Aviat*) wing; **Tragflügelboot** *nt* hydrofoil
Trägheit ['trɛ:khaɪt] *f* laziness; (*Phys*) inertia
Tragik ['tra:gɪk] *f* tragedy
tragikomisch [tragi'ko:mɪʃ] *adj* tragi-comic
tragisch *adj* tragic; **etw ~ nehmen** (*umg*) to take sth to heart
Traglast *f* load
Tragödie [tra'gø:diə] *f* tragedy
trägt [trɛ:kt] *vb siehe* **tragen**
Tragweite *f* range; (*fig*) scope; **von großer ~ sein** to have far-reaching consequences
Tragwerk *nt* wing assembly
Trainer, in ['trɛ:nər(ɪn)] (**-s, -**) *m(f)* (*Sport*) trainer, coach; (*Fussball*) manager
trainieren [trɛ'ni:rən] *vt* to train; (*Übung*) to practise (*Brit*), practice (*US*) ▷ *vi* to train; **Fußball ~** to do football practice
Training (**-s, -s**) *nt* training
Trainingsanzug *m* track suit
Trakt [trakt] (**-(e)s, -e**) *m* (*Gebäudeteil*) section; (*Flügel*) wing
Traktat [trak'ta:t] (**-(e)s, -e**) *m od nt* (*Abhandlung*) treatise; (*Flugschrift, religiöse Schrift*) tract
traktieren (*umg*) *vt* (*schlecht behandeln*) to maltreat; (*quälen*) to torment
Traktor ['traktɔr] *m* tractor; (*von Drucker*) tractor feed
trällern ['trɛlərn] *vt, vi* to warble; (*Vogel*) to trill, warble
trampeln ['trampəln] *vt* to trample; (*abschütteln*) to stamp ▷ *vi* to stamp
Trampelpfad *m* track, path
Trampeltier *nt* (*Zool*) (Bactrian) camel; (*fig: umg*) clumsy oaf
trampen ['trɛmpən] *vi* to hitchhike
Tramper, in [trɛmpər(ɪn)] (**-s, -**) *m(f)* hitchhiker
Trampolin [trampo'li:n] (**-s, -e**) *nt* trampoline
Tranchierbesteck *nt* pair of carvers, carvers *pl*
tranchieren [trã'ʃi:rən] *vt* to carve
Träne ['trɛ:nə] (**-, -n**) *f* tear
tränen *vi* to water
Tränengas *nt* tear gas
tranig ['tra:nɪç] (*umg*) *adj* slow, sluggish
trank *etc* [traŋk] *vb siehe* **trinken**
Tränke ['trɛŋkə] (**-, -n**) *f* watering place
tränken *vt* (*nass machen*) to soak; (*Tiere*) to water
Transaktion [trans|aktsi'o:n] *f* transaction
Transchierbesteck *nt* = **Tranchierbesteck**
transchieren *vt* = **tranchieren**
Transformator [transfɔr'ma:tɔr] *m* transformer
Transfusion [transfuzi'o:n] *f* transfusion
Transistor [tran'zistɔr] *m* transistor
transitiv ['tranziti:f] *adj* transitive
Transitverkehr [tran'zi:tfɛrke:r] *m* transit traffic
transparent [transpa'rɛnt] *adj* transparent; **Transparent** (**-(e)s, -e**) *nt* (*Bild*) transparency; (*Spruchband*) banner
transpirieren [transpi'ri:rən] *vi* to perspire
Transplantation [transplantatsi'o:n] *f* transplantation; (*Hauttransplantation*) graft(ing)
Transport [trans'pɔrt] (**-(e)s, -e**) *m* transport; (*Fracht*) consignment, shipment; **transportfähig** *adj* moveable
transportieren [transpɔr'ti:rən] *vt* to transport
Transport- *zW*: **Transportkosten** *pl* transport charges *pl*, carriage *sing*; **Transportmittel** *nt* means *sing* of transport; **Transportunternehmen** *nt* carrier
transsexuell [transzɛksu'ɛl] *adj* transsexual
transusig ['tra:nzu:zɪç] (*umg*) *adj* sluggish
Transvestit [transvɛs'ti:t] (**-en, -en**) *m* transvestite
Trapez [tra'pe:ts] (**-es, -e**) *nt* trapeze; (*Math*) trapezium
Trara [tra'ra:] (**-s**) *nt*: **mit viel ~ (um)** (*fig: umg*) with a great hullabaloo (about)
trat *etc* [tra:t] *vb siehe* **treten**
Tratsch [tra:tʃ] (**-(e)s**) (*umg*) *m* gossip
tratschen ['tra:tʃən] (*umg*) *vi* to gossip

Tratte ['tratə] (**-, -n**) *f* (*Fin*) draft
Traube ['traʊbə] (**-, -n**) *f* grape; (*ganze Frucht*) bunch (of grapes)
Traubenlese *f* grape harvest
Traubenzucker *m* glucose
trauen ['traʊən] *vi +dat* to trust ▷ *vr* to dare ▷ *vt* to marry; **jdm/etw ~** to trust sb/sth
Trauer ['traʊər] (-) *f* sorrow; (*für Verstorbenen*) mourning; **Trauerfall** *m* death, bereavement; **Trauerfeier** *f* funeral service; **Trauerflor** (**-s, -e**) *m* black ribbon; **Trauergemeinde** *f* mourners *pl*; **Trauermarsch** *m* funeral march
trauern *vi* to mourn; **um jdn ~** to mourn (for) sb
Trauer- *zW*: **Trauerrand** *m* black border; **Trauerspiel** *nt* tragedy; **Trauerweide** *f* weeping willow
Traufe ['traʊfə] (**-, -n**) *f* eaves *pl*
träufeln ['trɔʏfəln] *vt, vi* to drip
traulich ['traʊlɪç] *adj* cosy, intimate
Traum [traʊm] (**-(e)s, Träume**) *m* dream; **aus der ~!** it's all over!
Trauma (**-s, -men**) *nt* trauma
traumatisieren [traʊmati'zi:rən] *vt* to traumatize
Traumbild *nt* vision
Traumdeutung *f* interpretation of dreams
träumen ['trɔʏmən] *vt, vi* to dream; **das hätte ich mir nicht ~ lassen** I'd never have thought it possible
Träumer, in (**-s, -**) *m(f)* dreamer
Träumerei [trɔʏmə'raɪ] *f* dreaming
träumerisch *adj* dreamy
traumhaft *adj* dreamlike; (*fig*) wonderful
Traumtänzer *m* dreamer
traurig ['traʊrɪç] *adj* sad; **Traurigkeit** *f* sadness
Trauring *m* wedding ring
Trauschein *m* marriage certificate
Trauung *f* wedding ceremony
Trauzeuge *m* witness (to a marriage)
treffen ['trɛfən] *unreg vt* to strike, hit; (*Bemerkung*) to hurt; (*begegnen*) to meet; (*Entscheidung etc*) to make; (*Maßnahmen*) to take ▷ *vi* to hit ▷ *vr* to meet; **er hat es gut getroffen** he did well; **er fühlte sich getroffen** he took it personally; **~ auf** *+akk* to come across, meet; **es traf sich, dass ...** it so happened that ...; **es trifft sich gut** it's convenient
Treffen (**-s, -**) *nt* meeting
treffend *adj* pertinent, apposite
Treffer (**-s, -**) *m* hit; (*Tor*) goal; (*Los*) winner
trefflich *adj* excellent
Treffpunkt *m* meeting place
Treibeis *nt* drift ice
treiben ['traɪbən] *unreg vt* to drive; (*Studien etc*) to pursue; (*Sport*) to do, go in for ▷ *vi* (*Schiff etc*) to drift; (*Pflanzen*) to sprout; (*Koch: aufgehen*) to rise; (*Medikamente*) to be diuretic; **die ~de Kraft** (*fig*) the driving force; **Handel mit etw/jdm ~** to trade in sth/with sb; **es zu weit ~** to go too far; **Unsinn ~** to fool around; **Treiben** (**-s**) *nt* activity
Treib- *zW*: **Treibgut** *nt* flotsam and jetsam; **Treibhaus** *nt* greenhouse; **Treibhauseffekt** *m* greenhouse effect; **Treibhausgas** *nt* greenhouse gas; **Treibjagd** *f* shoot (*in which game is sent up*); (*fig*) witchhunt; **Treibsand** *m* quicksand; **Treibstoff** *m* fuel
Trend [trɛnt] (**-s, -s**) *m* trend; **Trendwende** *f* new trend
trennbar *adj* separable
trennen ['trɛnən] *vt* to separate; (*teilen*) to divide ▷ *vr* to separate; **sich ~ von** to part with
Trennschärfe *f* (*Rundf*) selectivity
Trennung *f* separation
Trennungsstrich *m* hyphen
Trennwand *f* partition (wall)
treppab *adv* downstairs
treppauf *adv* upstairs
Treppe ['trɛpə] (**-, -n**) *f* stairs *pl*, staircase; (*im Freien*) steps *pl*; **eine ~** a staircase, a flight of stairs *od* steps; **sie wohnt zwei ~n hoch/höher** she lives two flights up/higher up
Treppengeländer *nt* banister
Treppenhaus *nt* staircase
Tresen ['tre:zən] (**-s, -**) *m* (*Theke*) bar; (*Ladentisch*) counter
Tresor [tre'zo:r] (**-s, -e**) *m* safe
Tretboot *nt* pedal boat, pedalo
treten ['tre:tən] *unreg vi* to step; (*Tränen, Schweiß*) to appear ▷ *vt* (*mit Fußtritt*) to kick; (*niedertreten*) to tread, trample; **~ nach** to kick at; **~ in** *+akk* to step in(to); **in Verbindung ~** to get in contact; **in Erscheinung ~** to appear; **der Fluss trat über die Ufer** the river overflowed its banks; **in Streik ~** to go on strike
Treter ['tre:tər] (*umg*) *pl* (*Schuhe*) casual shoes *pl*
Tretmine *f* (*Mil*) (anti-personnel) mine
Tretmühle *f* (*fig*) daily grind
treu [trɔʏ] *adj* faithful, true; **treudoof** (*umg*) *adj* naïve
Treue (-) *f* loyalty, faithfulness
Treuhand (*umg*) *f*, **Treuhandanstalt** *f* trustee organization (*overseeing the privatization of former GDR state-owned firms*)
Treuhandanstalt *f see culture note*

TREUHANDANSTALT

The *Treuhandanstalt* is a now defunct organization set up in 1990 to take over the nationally-owned companies of the former DDR, to break them down into smaller units and to privatize them. It was based in Berlin and had nine branches. Many companies were closed down by the Treuhandanstalt because of their outdated equipment and inability to compete with the western firms. This resulted in a rise in unemployment.

Treuhänder (**-s, -**) *m* trustee
Treuhandgesellschaft *f* trust company
treu- *zW*: **treuherzig** *adj* innocent; **treulich** *adv* faithfully; **treulos** *adj* faithless; **treulos an**

jdm handeln to fail sb
Triathlon ['tri:atlɔn] (**-s, -s**) *nt* triathlon
Tribüne [tri'by:nə] (**-, -n**) *f* grandstand; (*Rednertribüne*) platform
Tribut [tri'bu:t] (**-(e)s, -e**) *m* tribute
Trichter ['trɪçtər] (**-s, -**) *m* funnel; (*Bombentrichter*) crater
Trick [trɪk] (**-s, -e** *od* **-s**) *m* trick; **Trickfilm** *m* cartoon
Trieb (**-(e)s, -e**) *m* urge, drive; (*Neigung*) inclination; (*Bot*) shoot
trieb *etc* [tri:p] *vb siehe* **treiben**
Trieb- *zW*: **Triebfeder** *f* (*fig*) motivating force; **triebhaft** *adj* impulsive; **Triebkraft** *f* (*fig*) drive; **Triebtäter** *m* sex offender; **Triebwagen** *m* (*Eisenb*) railcar; **Triebwerk** *nt* engine
triefen ['tri:fən] *vi* to drip
trifft [trɪft] *vb siehe* **treffen**
triftig ['trɪftɪç] *adj* convincing; (*Grund etc*) good
Trigonometrie [trigonome'tri:] *f* trigonometry
Trikot [tri'ko:] (**-s, -s**) *nt* vest; (*Sport*) shirt ▷ *m* (*Gewebe*) tricot
Triller ['trɪlər] (**-s, -**) *m* (*Mus*) trill
trillern *vi* to trill, warble
Trillerpfeife *f* whistle
Trilogie [trilo'gi:] *f* trilogy
Trimester [tri'mɛstər] (**-s, -**) *nt* term
Trimm-Aktion *f* keep-fit campaign
Trimm-dich-Pfad *m* keep-fit trail
trimmen *vt* (*Hund*) to trim; (*umg: Mensch, Tier*) to teach, train ▷ *vr* to keep fit
trinkbar *adj* drinkable
trinken ['trɪŋkən] *unreg vt, vi* to drink
Trinker, in (**-s, -**) *m(f)* drinker
Trink- *zW*: **trinkfest** *adj*: **ich bin nicht sehr trinkfest** I can't hold my drink very well; **Trinkgeld** *nt* tip; **Trinkhalle** *f* (*Kiosk*) refreshment kiosk; **Trinkhalm** *m* (drinking) straw; **Trinkmilch** *f* milk; **Trinkspruch** *m* toast; **Trinkwasser** *nt* drinking water
Trio ['tri:o] (**-s, -s**) *nt* trio
trippeln ['trɪpəln] *vi* to toddle
Tripper ['trɪpər] (**-s, -**) *m* gonorrhoea (*Brit*), gonorrhea (*US*)
trist [trɪst] *adj* dreary, dismal; (*Farbe*) dull
tritt [trɪt] *vb siehe* **treten**
Tritt (**-(e)s, -e**) *m* step; (*Fußtritt*) kick
Trittbrett *nt* (*Eisenb*) step; (*Aut*) running board
Trittleiter *f* stepladder
Triumph [tri'ʊmf] (**-(e)s, -e**) *m* triumph; **Triumphbogen** *m* triumphal arch
triumphieren [triʊm'fi:rən] *vi* to triumph; (*jubeln*) to exult
trivial [trivi'a:l] *adj* trivial; **Trivialliteratur** *f* light fiction
trocken ['trɔkən] *adj* dry; **sich ~ rasieren** to use an electric razor; **Trockenautomat** *m* tumble dryer; **Trockendock** *nt* dry dock; **Trockeneis** *nt* dry ice; **Trockenelement** *nt* dry cell; **Trockenhaube** *f* hair-dryer; **Trockenheit** *f* dryness; **trockenlegen** *vt* (*Sumpf*) to drain; (*Kind*) to put a clean nappy (*Brit*) *od* diaper (*US*) on; **Trockenmilch** *f* dried milk; **Trockenzeit** *f* (*Jahreszeit*) dry season
trocknen *vt, vi* to dry
Trockner (**-s, -**) *m* dryer
Troddel ['trɔdəl] (**-, -n**) *f* tassel
Trödel ['trø:dəl] (**-s**) (*umg*) *m* junk; **Trödelmarkt** *m* flea market
trödeln (*umg*) *vi* to dawdle
Trödler (**-s, -**) *m* secondhand dealer
Trog (**-(e)s, ¨-e**) *m* trough
trog *etc* [tro:k] *vb siehe* **trügen**
trollen ['trɔlən] (*umg*) *vr* to push off
Trommel ['trɔməl] (**-, -n**) *f* drum; **die ~ rühren** (*fig: umg*) to drum up support; **Trommelfell** *nt* eardrum; **Trommelfeuer** *nt* drumfire, heavy barrage
trommeln *vt, vi* to drum
Trommelrevolver *m* revolver
Trommelwaschmaschine *f* tumble-action washing machine
Trommler, in ['trɔmlər(ɪn)] (**-s, -**) *m(f)* drummer
Trompete [trɔm'pe:tə] (**-, -n**) *f* trumpet
Trompeter (**-s, -**) *m* trumpeter
Tropen ['tro:pən] *pl* tropics *pl*; **tropenbeständig** *adj* suitable for the tropics; **Tropenhelm** *m* topee, sun helmet
Tropf[1] [trɔpf] (**-(e)s, ¨-e**) (*umg*) *m* rogue; **armer ~** poor devil
Tropf[2] (**-(e)s**) (*umg*) *m* (*Med: Infusion*) drip (*umg*); **am ~ hängen** to be on a drip
tröpfeln ['trœpfəln] *vi* to drip, trickle
Tropfen (**-s, -**) *m* drop; **ein guter** *od* **edler ~** a good wine; **ein ~ auf den heißen Stein** (*fig: umg*) a drop in the ocean
tropfen *vt, vi* to drip ▷ *vi unpers*: **es tropft** a few raindrops are falling
tropfenweise *adv* in drops
tropfnass *adj* dripping wet
Tropfsteinhöhle *f* stalactite cave
Trophäe [tro'fɛ:ə] (**-, -n**) *f* trophy
tropisch ['tro:pɪʃ] *adj* tropical
Trost [tro:st] (**-es**) *m* consolation, comfort; **trostbedürftig** *adj* in need of consolation
trösten ['trø:stən] *vt* to console, comfort
Tröster, in (**-s, -**) *m(f)* comfort(er)
tröstlich *adj* comforting
trost- *zW*: **trostlos** *adj* bleak; (*Verhältnisse*) wretched; **Trostpflaster** *nt* (*fig*) consolation; **Trostpreis** *m* consolation prize; **trostreich** *adj* comforting
Tröstung ['trø:stʊŋ] *f* comfort, consolation
Trott [trɔt] (**-(e)s, -e**) *m* trot; (*Routine*) routine
Trottel (**-s, -**) (*umg*) *m* fool, dope
trotten *vi* to trot
Trottoir [trɔto'a:r] (**-s, -s** *od* **-e**) *nt* (*veraltet*) pavement (*Brit*), sidewalk (*US*)
trotz [trɔts] *präp* (*+gen od dat*) in spite of
Trotz (**-es**) *m* pig-headedness; **etw aus ~ tun** to do sth just to show them; **jdm zum ~** in defiance of sb
Trotzalter *nt* obstinate phase
trotzdem *adv* nevertheless ▷ *konj* although

trotzen *vi+dat* to defy; (*der Kälte, dem Klima etc*) to withstand; (*der Gefahr*) to brave; (*trotzig sein*) to be awkward
trotzig *adj* defiant; (*Kind*) difficult, awkward
Trotzkopf *m* obstinate child
Trotzreaktion *f* fit of pique
trüb [try:p] *adj* dull; (*Flüssigkeit, Glas*) cloudy; (*fig*) gloomy; **~e Tasse** (*umg*) drip
Trubel ['tru:bəl] (**-s**) *m* hurly-burly
trüben ['try:bən] *vt* to cloud ▷ *vr* to become clouded
Trübheit *f* dullness; cloudiness; gloom
Trübsal (**-, -e**) *f* distress; **~ blasen** (*umg*) to mope
trüb- *zW*: **trübselig** *adj* sad, melancholy; **Trübsinn** *m* depression; **trübsinnig** *adj* depressed, gloomy
trudeln ['tru:dəln] *vi* (*Aviat*) to (go into a) spin
Trüffel ['trʏfəl] (**-, -n**) *f* truffle
Trug (**-(e)s**) *m* (*liter*) deception; (*der Sinne*) illusion
trug *etc* [tru:k] *vb siehe* **tragen**
trügen ['try:gən] *unreg vt* to deceive ▷ *vi* to be deceptive; **wenn mich nicht alles trügt** unless I am very much mistaken
trügerisch *adj* deceptive
Trugschluss ['tru:gʃlʊs] *m* false conclusion
Truhe ['tru:ə] (**-, -n**) *f* chest
Trümmer ['trʏmər] *pl* wreckage *sing*; (*Bautrümmer*) ruins *pl*; **Trümmerfeld** *nt* expanse of rubble *od* ruins; (*fig*) scene of devastation; **Trümmerfrauen** *pl* (*German*) *women who cleared away the rubble after the war*; **Trümmerhaufen** *m* heap of rubble
Trumpf [trʊmpf] (**-(e)s, ¨-e**) *m* (*lit, fig*) trump; **trumpfen** *vt, vi* to trump
Trunk [trʊŋk] (**-(e)s, ¨-e**) *m* drink
trunken *adj* intoxicated; **Trunkenbold** (**-(e)s, -e**) *m* drunkard; **Trunkenheit** *f* intoxication; **Trunkenheit am Steuer** drink-driving
Trunksucht *f* alcoholism
Trupp [trʊp] (**-s, -s**) *m* troop
Truppe (**-, -n**) *f* troop; (*Waffengattung*) force; (*Schauspieltruppe*) troupe; **nicht von der schnellen ~ sein** (*umg*) to be slow
Truppen *pl* troops *pl*; **Truppenabbau** *m* cutback in troop numbers; **Truppenführer** *m* (military) commander; **Truppenteil** *m* unit; **Truppenübungsplatz** *m* training area
Trust [trast] (**-(e)s, -e** *od* **-s**) *m* trust
Truthahn ['tru:tha:n] *m* turkey
Tschad [tʃat] (**-s**) *m*: **der ~** Chad
Tscheche ['tʃɛçə] (**-n, -n**) *m*, **Tschechin** *f* Czech
tschechisch *adj* Czech; **die T~e Republik** the Czech Republic
Tschechoslowakei [tʃɛçoslova:'kai] *f* (*früher*): **die ~** Czechoslovakia
tschüss [tʃʏs] (*umg*) *interj* cheerio (*Brit*), so long (*US*)
T-Shirt ['ti:ʃə:t] (**-s, -s**) *nt* T-shirt
TU (**-**) *f abk* (*= technische Universität*) ≈ polytechnic
Tuba ['tu:ba] (**-, Tuben**) *f* (*Mus*) tuba
Tube ['tu:bə] (**-, -n**) *f* tube
Tuberkulose [tubɛrku'lo:zə] (**-, -n**) *f* tuberculosis
Tuch [tu:x] (**-(e)s, ¨-er**) *nt* cloth; (*Halstuch*) scarf; (*Kopftuch*) (head)scarf; (*Handtuch*) towel; **Tuchfühlung** *f* physical contact
tüchtig ['tʏçtɪç] *adj* efficient; (*fähig*) able, capable; (*umg: kräftig*) good, sound; **etwas T~es lernen/werden** (*umg*) to get a proper training/job; **Tüchtigkeit** *f* efficiency; ability
Tücke ['tʏkə] (**-, -n**) *f* (*Arglist*) malice; (*Trick*) trick; (*Schwierigkeit*) difficulty, problem; **seine ~n haben** to be temperamental
tückisch *adj* treacherous; (*böswillig*) malicious
tüfteln ['tʏftəln] (*umg*) *vi* to puzzle; (*basteln*) to fiddle about
Tugend ['tu:gənt] (**-, -en**) *f* virtue; **tugendhaft** *adj* virtuous
Tüll [tʏl] (**-s, -e**) *m* tulle
Tülle (**-, -n**) *f* spout
Tulpe ['tʊlpə] (**-, -n**) *f* tulip
tummeln ['tʊməln] *vr* to romp (about); (*sich beeilen*) to hurry
Tummelplatz *m* play area; (*fig*) hotbed
Tumor ['tu:mɔr] (**-s, -e**) *m* tumour (*Brit*), tumor (*US*)
Tümpel ['tʏmpəl] (**-s, -**) *m* pond
Tumult [tu'mʊlt] (**-(e)s, -e**) *m* tumult
tun [tu:n] *unreg vt* (*machen*) to do; (*legen*) to put ▷ *vi* to act ▷ *vr*: **es tut sich etwas/viel** something/a lot is happening; **jdm etw ~** to do sth to sb; **etw tut es auch** sth will do; **das tut nichts** that doesn't matter; **das tut nichts zur Sache** that's neither here nor there; **du kannst ~ und lassen, was du willst** you can do as you please; **so ~, als ob** to act as if; **zu ~ haben** (*beschäftigt sein*) to be busy, have things *od* something to do
Tünche ['tʏnçə] (**-, -n**) *f* whitewash
tünchen *vt* to whitewash
Tunesien [tu'ne:ziən] (**-s**) *nt* Tunisia
Tunesier, in (**-s, -**) *m(f)* Tunisian
tunesisch *adj* Tunisian
Tunfisch *m* = **Thunfisch**
Tunke ['tʊŋkə] (**-, -n**) *f* sauce
tunken *vt* to dip, dunk
tunlichst ['tu:nlɪçst] *adv* if at all possible; **~ bald** as soon as possible
Tunnel ['tʊnəl] (**-s, -s** *od* **-**) *m* tunnel
Tunte ['tʊntə] (**-, -n**) (*pej: umg*) *f* fairy (*pej*)
Tüpfel ['tʏpfəl] (**-s, -**) *m* dot; **Tüpfelchen** *nt* (small) dot
tüpfeln ['tʏpfəln] *vt* to dab
tupfen ['tʊpfən] *vt* to dab; (*mit Farbe*) to dot; **Tupfen** (**-s, -**) *m* dot, spot
Tupfer (**-s, -**) *m* swab
Tür [ty:r] (**-, -en**) *f* door; **an die ~ gehen** to answer the door; **zwischen ~ und Angel** in passing; **Weihnachten steht vor der ~** (*fig*) Christmas is just around the corner; **mit der ~ ins Haus fallen** (*umg*) to blurt it *od* things out; **Türangel** *f* (door) hinge
Turbine [tʊr'bi:nə] *f* turbine
turbulent [tʊrbu'lɛnt] *adj* turbulent

Türke ['tʏrkə] (**-n, -n**) *m* Turk
Türkei [tʏr'kaɪ] *f*: **die ~** Turkey
Türkin *f* Turk
Türkis [tʏr'ki:s] (**-es, -e**) *m* turquoise; **türkis** *adj* turquoise
türkisch *adj* Turkish
Türklinke *f* door handle
Turm [tʊrm] (**-(e)s, ¨-e**) *m* tower; (*Kirchturm*) steeple; (*Sprungturm*) diving platform; (*Schach*) castle, rook
türmen ['tʏrmən] *vr* to tower up ▷ *vt* to heap up ▷ *vi* (*umg*) to scarper, bolt
Turmuhr *f* clock (on a tower); (*Kirchturmuhr*) church clock
Turnanzug *m* gym costume
turnen ['tʊrnən] *vi* to do gymnastic exercises; (*herumklettern*) to climb about; (*Kind*) to romp ▷ *vt* to perform; **Turnen** (**-s**) *nt* gymnastics *sing*; (*Sch*) physical education, P.E.
Turner, in (**-s, -**) *m(f)* gymnast
Turnhalle *f* gym(nasium)
Turnhose *f* gym shorts *pl*
Turnier [tʊr'ni:r] (**-s, -e**) *nt* tournament
Turn- *zW*: **Turnlehrer, in** *m(f)* gym *od* PE teacher; **Turnschuh** *m* gym shoe; **Turnstunde** *f* gym *od* PE lesson
Turnus ['tʊrnʊs] (**-, -se**) *m* rota; **im ~** in rotation
Turnverein *m* gymnastics club
Turnzeug *nt* gym kit
Türöffner *m* buzzer
turteln ['tʊrtəln] (*umg*) *vi* to bill and coo; (*fig*) to whisper sweet nothings
Tusch [tʊʃ] (**-(e)s, -e**) *m* (*Mus*) flourish
Tusche ['tʊʃə] (**-, -n**) *f* Indian ink
tuscheln ['tʊʃəln] *vt, vi* to whisper
Tuschkasten *m* paintbox
Tussi ['tʊsɪ] (**-, -s**) (*umg*) *f* (*Frau, Freundin*) bird (*Brit*), chick (*US*)
tust [tu:st] *vb siehe* **tun**
tut [tu:t] *vb siehe* **tun**
Tüte ['ty:tə] (**-, -n**) *f* bag; **in die ~ blasen** (*umg*) to be breathalyzed; **das kommt nicht in die ~!** (*umg*) no way!
tuten ['tu:tən] *vi* (*Aut*) to hoot (*Brit*), honk (*US*); **von T~ und Blasen keine Ahnung haben** (*umg*) not to have a clue
TÜV [tʏf] *m abk* (= *Technischer Überwachungs-Verein*) ≈ MOT (*Brit*); **durch den ~ kommen** (*Aut*) to pass its test *od* MOT (*Brit*); *see culture note*

TÜV

The *TÜV* (Technischer Überwachungsverein) is the organization responsible for checking the safety of machinery, particularly vehicles. Cars over three years old have to be examined every two years for their safety and for their exhaust emissions. The *TÜV* is the German equivalent of the MOT.

TV (-) *nt abk* (= *Television*) TV ▷ *m abk* = **Turnverein**
Twen [tvɛn] (**-(s), -s**) *m person in his/her twenties*
Typ [ty:p] (**-s, -en**) *m* type
Type (**-, -n**) *f* (*Typ*) type
Typenrad *nt* (*Drucker*) daisywheel; **Typenraddrucker** *m* daisywheel printer
Typhus ['ty:fʊs] (-) *m* typhoid (fever)
typisch ['ty:pɪʃ] *adj*: **~ (für)** typical (of)
Tyrann [ty'ran] (**-en, -en**) *m(f)* tyrant
Tyrannei [tyra'naɪ] *f* tyranny
Tyrannin *f* tyrant
tyrannisch *adj* tyrannical
tyrannisieren [tyrani'zi:rən] *vt* to tyrannize
tyrrhenisch [ty're:nɪʃ] *adj* Tyrrhenian; **T~es Meer** Tyrrhenian Sea

Uu

U, u [uː] *nt* U, u; **U wie Ulrich** ≈ U for Uncle
u. *abk* = **und**
u. a. *abk* (= *und andere(s)*) and others; (= *unter anderem*) amongst other things
u. Ä. *abk* (= *und Ähnliche(s)*) and similar
u. A. w. g. *abk* (= *um Antwort wird gebeten*) R.S.V.P.
U-Bahn [ˈuːbaːn] *f abk* (= *Untergrundbahn*) underground (*Brit*), subway (*US*)
übel [ˈyːbəl] *adj* bad; **jdm ist ~** sb feels sick; **~ gelaunt** bad-tempered, sullen; **jdm eine Bemerkung** *etc* **~ nehmen** to be offended at sb's remark *etc*; *siehe auch* **übelwollend**; **Übel (-s, -)** *nt* evil; (*Krankheit*) disease; **zu allem Übel ...** to make matters worse ...; **Übelkeit** *f* nausea; **Übelstand** *m* bad state of affairs; **Übeltäter** *m* wrongdoer; **übelwollend** *adj* malevolent
üben [ˈyːbən] *vt, vi, vr* to practise (*Brit*), practice (*US*); (*Gedächtnis, Muskeln*) to exercise; **Kritik an etw** *dat* **~** to criticize sth

SCHLÜSSELWORT

über [ˈyːbər] *präp +dat* **1** (*räumlich*) over, above; **zwei Grad über null** two degrees above zero
2 (*zeitlich*) over; **über der Arbeit einschlafen** to fall asleep over one's work
▷ *präp +akk* **1** (*räumlich*) over; (*hoch über*) above; (*quer über*) across; **er lachte über das ganze Gesicht** he was beaming all over his face; **Macht über jdn haben** to have power over sb
2 (*zeitlich*) over; **über Weihnachten** over Christmas; **über kurz oder lang** sooner or later
3 (*auf dem Wege*) via; **nach Köln über Aachen** to Cologne via Aachen; **ich habe es über die Auskunft erfahren** I found out from information
4 (*betreffend*) about; **ein Buch über ...** a book about *od* on ...; **über jdn/etw lachen** to laugh about *od* at sb/sth; **ein Scheck über 200 Euro** a cheque for 200 euros
5: Fehler über Fehler mistake after mistake
▷ *adv* **1** (*mehr als*) over, more than; **Kinder über 12 Jahren** children over *od* above 12 years of age; **sie liebt ihn über alles** she loves him more than anything
2: über und über over and over; **den ganzen Tag/die ganze Zeit über** all day long/all the time; **jdm in etw** *dat* **über sein** to be superior to sb in sth

überall [yːbərˈ|al] *adv* everywhere; **überallhin** *adv* everywhere
überaltert [yːbərˈ|altərt] *adj* obsolete
Überangebot [ˈyːbər|angəboːt] *nt*: **~ (an** *+dat***)** surplus (of)
überanstrengen [yːbərˈ|anʃtrɛŋən] *vt untr* to overexert ▷ *vr untr* to overexert o.s.
überantworten [yːbərˈ|antvɔrtən] *vt untr* to hand over, deliver (up)
überarbeiten [yːbərˈ|arbaɪtən] *vt untr* to revise, rework ▷ *vr untr* to overwork (o.s.)
überaus [ˈyːbər|aʊs] *adv* exceedingly
überbacken [yːbərˈbakən] *unreg vt untr* to put in the oven/under the grill
Überbau [ˈyːbərbaʊ] *m* (*Gebäude, Philosophie*) superstructure
überbeanspruchen [ˈyːbərbə|anʃprʊxən] *vt untr* (*Menschen, Körper, Maschine*) to overtax
überbelichten [ˈyːbərbəlɪçtən] *vt untr* (*Phot*) to overexpose
Überbesetzung [ˈyːbərbəzɛtsʊŋ] *f* overmanning
überbewerten [ˈyːbərbəveːrtən] *vt untr* (*fig*) to overrate; (*Äußerungen*) to attach too much importance to
überbieten [yːbərˈbiːtən] *unreg vt untr* to outbid; (*übertreffen*) to surpass; (*Rekord*) to break ▷ *vr untr*: **sich in etw** *dat* **(gegenseitig) ~** to vie with each other in sth
Überbleibsel [ˈyːbərblaɪpsəl] **(-s, -)** *nt* residue, remainder
Überblick [ˈyːbərblɪk] *m* view; (*fig: Darstellung*) survey, overview; (*Fähigkeit*): **~ (über** *+akk***)** overall view (of), grasp (of); **den ~ verlieren** to lose track (of things); **sich** *dat* **einen ~ verschaffen** to get a general idea
überblicken [yːbərˈblɪkən] *vt untr* to survey; (*fig*) to see; (: *Lage etc*) to grasp
überbringen [yːbərˈbrɪŋən] *unreg vt untr* to deliver, hand over
Überbringer (-s, -) *m* bearer
Überbringung *f* delivery
überbrücken [yːbərˈbrʏkən] *vt untr* to bridge
Überbrückung *f*: **100 Euro zur ~** 100 euros to

tide me/him *etc* over
Überbrückungskredit *m* bridging loan
überbuchen ['y:bərbu:xən] *vt* to overbook
überdauern [y:bər'daʊərn] *vt untr* to outlast
überdenken [y:bər'dɛŋkən] *unreg vt untr* to think over
überdies [y:bər'di:s] *adv* besides
überdimensional ['y:bərdimɛnziona:l] *adj* oversize
Überdosis ['y:bərdo:zɪs] *f* overdose, OD (*umg*); (*zu große Zumessung*) excessive amount
überdrehen [y:bər'dre:ən] *vt untr* (*Uhr etc*) to overwind
überdreht *adj*: ~ **sein** (*fig*) to be hyped up, be overexcited
Überdruck ['y:bərdrʊk] *m* (*Tech*) excess pressure
Überdruss ['y:bərdrʊs] **(-es)** *m* weariness; **bis zum ~** ad nauseam
überdrüssig ['y:bərdrʏsɪç] *adj +gen* tired of, sick of
überdurchschnittlich ['y:bərdʊrçʃnɪtlɪç] *adj* above-average ▷ *adv* exceptionally
übereifrig ['y:bər|aɪfrɪç] *adj* overzealous
übereignen [y:bər'|aɪgnən] *vt untr*: **jdm etw ~** (*geh*) to make sth over to sb
übereilen [y:bər'|aɪlən] *vt untr* to hurry
übereilt *adj* (over)hasty
übereinander [y:bər|aɪ'nandər] *adv* one upon the other; (*sprechen*) about each other
übereinanderschlagen *unreg vt* (*Arme*) to fold; (*Beine*) to cross
übereinkommen [y:bər'|aɪnkɔmən] *unreg vi* to agree
Übereinkunft [y:bər'|aɪnkʊnft] **(-, -künfte)** *f* agreement
übereinstimmen [y:bər'|aɪnʃtɪmən] *vi* to agree; (*Angaben, Messwerte etc*) to tally; (*mit Tatsachen*) to fit
Übereinstimmung *f* agreement
überempfindlich ['y:bər|ɛmpfɪntlɪç] *adj* hypersensitive
überfahren¹ ['y:bərfa:rən] *unreg vt* to take across ▷ *vi* to cross, go across
überfahren² [y:bər'fa:rən] *unreg vt untr* (*Aut*) to run over; (*fig*) to walk all over
Überfahrt ['y:bərfa:rt] *f* crossing
Überfall ['y:bərfal] *m* (*Banküberfall, Mil*) raid; (*auf jdn*) assault
überfallen [y:bər'falən] *unreg vt untr* to attack; (*Bank*) to raid; (*besuchen*) to drop in on, descend (up)on
überfällig ['y:bərfɛlɪç] *adj* overdue
Überfallkommando *nt* flying squad
überfliegen [y:bər'fli:gən] *unreg vt untr* to fly over, overfly; (*Buch*) to skim through
Überflieger *m* (*fig*) high-flier
überflügeln [y:bər'fly:gəln] *vt untr* to outdo
Überfluss ['y:bərflʊs] *m*: **~ (an** *+dat***)** (super)abundance (of), excess (of); **zu allem** *od* **zum ~** (*unnötigerweise*) superfluously; (*obendrein*) to crown it all (*umg*); **Überflussgesellschaft** *f* affluent society
überflüssig ['y:bərflʏsɪç] *adj* superfluous
überfluten [y:bər'flu:tən] *vt untr* (*lit*) to flood; (*fig*) to flood, inundate
überfordern [y:bər'fɔrdərn] *vt untr* to demand too much of; (*Kräfte etc*) to overtax
überfragt [y:bər'fra:kt] *adj*: **da bin ich ~** there you've got me, you've got me there
überführen¹ ['y:bərfy:rən] *vt* to transfer; (*Leiche etc*) to transport
überführen² [y:bər'fy:rən] *vt untr* (*Täter*) to have convicted
Überführung *f* (*siehe vbs*) transfer; transport; conviction; (*Brücke*) bridge, overpass
überfüllt [y:bər'fʏlt] *adj* overcrowded; (*Kurs*) oversubscribed
Übergabe ['y:bərga:bə] *f* handing over; (*Mil*) surrender
Übergang ['y:bərgaŋ] *m* crossing; (*Wandel, Überleitung*) transition
Übergangs- *zW*: **Übergangserscheinung** *f* transitory phenomenon; **Übergangsfinanzierung** *f* (*Fin*) accommodation; **übergangslos** *adj* without a transition; **Übergangslösung** *f* provisional solution, stopgap; **Übergangsstadium** *nt* state of transition; **Übergangszeit** *f* transitional period
übergeben [y:bər'ge:bən] *unreg vt untr* to hand over; (*Mil*) to surrender ▷ *vr untr* to be sick; **dem Verkehr ~** to open to traffic
übergehen¹ ['y:bərge:ən] *unreg vi* (*Besitz*) to pass; (*zum Feind etc*) to go over, defect; (*überwechseln*): **(zu etw) ~** to go on (to sth); **~ in** *+akk* to turn into
übergehen² [y:bər'ge:ən] *unreg vt untr* to pass over, omit
übergeordnet ['y:bərgə|ɔrdnət] *adj* (*Behörde*) higher
Übergepäck ['y:bərgəpɛk] *nt* excess baggage
übergeschnappt ['y:bərgəʃnapt] (*umg*) *adj* crazy
Übergewicht ['y:bərgəvɪçt] *nt* excess weight; (*fig*) preponderance
übergießen [y:bər'gi:sən] *unreg vt untr* to pour over; (*Braten*) to baste
überglücklich ['y:bərglʏklɪç] *adj* overjoyed
übergreifen ['y:bərgraɪfən] *unreg vi*: **~ (auf** *+akk***)** (*auf Rechte etc*) to encroach (on); (*Feuer, Streik, Krankheit etc*) to spread (to); **ineinander ~** to overlap
übergroß ['y:bərgro:s] *adj* outsize, huge
Übergröße ['y:bərgrø:sə] *f* oversize
überhaben ['y:bərha:bən] *unreg* (*umg*) *vt* to be fed up with
überhandnehmen [y:bər'hant-] *unreg vi* to gain the ascendancy
überhängen ['y:bərhɛŋən] *unreg vi* to overhang
überhäufen [y:bər'hɔʏfən] *vt untr*: **jdn mit Geschenken/Vorwürfen ~** to heap presents/reproaches on sb
überhaupt [y:bər'haʊpt] *adv* at all; (*im Allgemeinen*) in general; (*besonders*) especially; **~ nicht** not at all; **wer sind Sie ~?** who do you

think you are?
überheblich [y:bər'he:plıç] *adj* arrogant; **Überheblichkeit** *f* arrogance
überhöht [y:bər'hø:t] *adj* (*Forderungen, Preise*) exorbitant, excessive
überholen [y:bər'ho:lən] *vt untr* to overtake; (*Tech*) to overhaul
Überholspur *f* overtaking lane
überholt *adj* out-of-date, obsolete
Überholverbot [y:bər'ho:lfɛrbo:t] *nt* overtaking (*Brit*) *od* passing ban
überhören [y:bər'hø:rən] *vt untr* to not hear; (*absichtlich*) to ignore; **das möchte ich überhört haben!** (I'll pretend) I didn't hear that!
Über-Ich, Überich ['y:bər|ıç] (**-s**) *nt* superego
überirdisch ['y:bər|ırdıʃ] *adj* supernatural, unearthly
überkapitalisieren ['y:bərkapitali'zi:rən] *vt untr* to overcapitalize
überkochen ['y:bərkɔxən] *vi* to boil over
überkompensieren ['y:bərkɔmpɛnzi:rən] *vt untr* to overcompensate for
überladen [y:bər'ladən] *unreg vt untr* to overload ▷ *adj* (*fig*) cluttered
überlassen [y:bər'lasən] *unreg vt untr*: **jdm etw ~** to leave sth to sb ▷ *vr untr*: **sich einer Sache** *dat* **~** to give o.s. over to sth; **das bleibt Ihnen ~** that's up to you; **jdn sich** *dat* **selbst ~** to leave sb to his/her own devices
überlasten [y:bər'lastən] *vt untr* to overload; (*jdn*) to overtax
überlaufen[1] ['y:bərlaʊfən] *unreg vi* (*Flüssigkeit*) to flow over; (*zum Feind etc*) to go over, defect
überlaufen[2] [y:bər'laʊfən] *unreg vt untr* (*Schauer etc*) to come over ▷ *adj* overcrowded; **~ sein** to be inundated *od* besieged
Überläufer ['y:bərlɔyfər] *m* deserter
überleben [y:bər'le:bən] *vt untr* to survive
Überlebende, r *f(m)* survivor
überlebensgroß *adj* larger-than-life
überlegen [y:bər'le:gən] *vt untr* to consider ▷ *adj* superior; **ich habe es mir anders** *od* **noch einmal überlegt** I've changed my mind; **Überlegenheit** *f* superiority
Überlegung *f* consideration, deliberation
überleiten ['y:bərlaıtən] *vt* (*Abschnitt etc*): **~ in** *+akk* to link up with
überlesen [y:bər'le:zən] *unreg vt untr* (*übersehen*) to overlook, miss
überliefern [y:bər'li:fərn] *vt untr* to hand down, transmit
Überlieferung *f* tradition; **schriftliche ~en** (written) records
überlisten [y:bər'lıstən] *vt untr* to outwit
überm ['y:bərm] = **über dem**
Übermacht ['y:bərmaxt] *f* superior force, superiority
übermächtig ['y:bərmɛçtıç] *adj* superior (in strength); (*Gefühl etc*) overwhelming
übermannen [y:bər'manən] *vt untr* to overcome
Übermaß ['ybərma:s] *nt*: **~ (an** *+dat***)** excess (of)
übermäßig ['y:bərmɛ:sıç] *adj* excessive
Übermensch ['y:bərmɛnʃ] *m* superman; **übermenschlich** *adj* superhuman
übermitteln [y:bər'mıtəln] *vt untr* to convey
übermorgen ['y:bərmɔrgən] *adv* the day after tomorrow
Übermüdung [y:bər'my:dʊŋ] *f* overtiredness
Übermut ['y:bərmu:t] *m* exuberance
übermütig ['y:bərmy:tıç] *adj* exuberant, high-spirited; **~ werden** to get overconfident
übernächste, r, s ['y:bərnɛ:çstə(r, s)] *adj* next … but one; (*Woche, Jahr etc*) after next
übernachten [y:bər'naxtən] *vi untr*: **(bei jdm) ~** to spend the night (at sb's place)
übernächtigt [y:bər'nɛçtıçt] *adj* sleepy, tired
Übernachtung *f*: **~ mit Frühstück** bed and breakfast
Übernahme ['y:bərna:mə] (**-, -n**) *f* taking over *od* on; (*von Verantwortung*) acceptance; **Übernahmeangebot** *nt* takeover bid
übernatürlich ['y:bərnaty:rlıç] *adj* supernatural
übernehmen [y:bər'ne:mən] *unreg vt untr* to take on, accept; (*Amt, Geschäft*) to take over ▷ *vr untr* to take on too much; (*sich überanstrengen*) to overdo it
überparteilich ['y:bərpartaılıç] *adj* (*Zeitung*) independent; (*Amt, Präsident etc*) above party politics
überprüfen [y:bər'pry:fən] *vt untr* to examine, check; (*Pol: jdn*) to screen
Überprüfung *f* examination
überqueren [y:bər'kve:rən] *vt untr* to cross
überragen [y:bər'ra:gən] *vt untr* to tower above; (*fig*) to surpass
überragend *adj* outstanding; (*Bedeutung*) paramount
überraschen [y:bər'raʃən] *vt untr* to surprise
Überraschung *f* surprise
überreden [y:bər're:dən] *vt untr* to persuade; **jdn zu etw ~** to talk sb into sth
Überredungskunst *f* powers *pl* of persuasion
überregional ['y:bərregiona:l] *adj* national; (*Zeitung, Sender*) nationwide
überreichen [y:bər'raıçən] *vt untr* to hand over; (*feierlich*) to present
überreichlich *adj* (more than) ample
überreizt [y:bər'raıtst] *adj* overwrought
Überreste ['y:bərrɛstə] *pl* remains *pl*, remnants *pl*
überrumpeln [y:bər'rʊmpəln] *vt untr* to take by surprise; (*umg: überwältigen*) to overpower
überrunden [y:bər'rʊndən] *vt untr* (*Sport*) to lap
übers ['y:bərs] = **über das**
übersättigen [y:bər'zɛtıgən] *vt untr* to satiate
Überschall- ['y:bərʃal] *in zw* supersonic; **Überschallflugzeug** *nt* supersonic jet; **Überschallgeschwindigkeit** *f* supersonic speed
überschatten [y:bər'ʃatən] *vt untr* to overshadow
überschätzen [y:bər'ʃɛtsən] *vt untr, vr untr* to overestimate

überschaubar [yːbərˈʃaʊbaːr] *adj* (*Plan*) easily comprehensible, clear
überschäumen [ˈyːbərʃɔymən] *vi* to froth over; (*fig*) to bubble over
überschlafen [yːbərˈʃlaːfən] *unreg vt untr* (*Problem*) to sleep on
Überschlag [ˈyːbərʃlaːk] *m* (*Fin*) estimate; (*Sport*) somersault
überschlagen[1] [yːbərˈʃlaːgən] *unreg vt untr* (*berechnen*) to estimate; (*auslassen: Seite*) to omit ▷ *vr untr* to somersault; (*Stimme*) to crack; (*Aviat*) to loop the loop ▷ *adj* lukewarm, tepid
überschlagen[2] [ˈyːbərʃlaːgən] *unreg vt* (*Beine*) to cross; (*Arme*) to fold ▷ *vi* (*Hilfsverb sein: Wellen*) to break; (*: Funken*) to flash over; **in etw** *akk* ~ (*Stimmung etc*) to turn into sth
überschnappen [ˈyːbərʃnapən] *vi* (*Stimme*) to crack; (*umg: Mensch*) to flip one's lid
überschneiden [yːbərˈʃnaɪdən] *unreg vr untr* (*lit, fig*) to overlap; (*Linien*) to intersect
überschreiben [yːbərˈʃraɪbən] *unreg vt untr* to provide with a heading; (*Comput*) to overwrite; **jdm etw** ~ to transfer *od* make over sth to sb
überschreiten [yːbərˈʃraɪtən] *unreg vt untr* to cross over; (*fig*) to exceed; (*verletzen*) to transgress
Überschrift [ˈyːbərʃrɪft] *f* heading, title
überschuldet [yːbərˈʃʊldət] *adj* heavily in debt; (*Grundstück*) heavily mortgaged
Überschuss [ˈyːbərʃʊs] *m*: ~ **(an** *+dat***)** surplus (of)
überschüssig [ˈyːbərʃʏsɪç] *adj* surplus, excess
überschütten [yːbərˈʃʏtən] *vt untr*: **jdn/etw mit etw** ~ (*lit*) to pour sth over sb/sth; **jdn mit etw** ~ (*fig*) to shower sb with sth
Überschwang [ˈyːbərʃvaŋ] *m* exuberance
überschwänglich [ˈyːbərʃvɛŋlɪç] *adj* effusive; **Überschwänglichkeit** *f* effusion
überschwappen [ˈyːbərʃvapən] *vi* to splash over
überschwemmen [yːbərˈʃvɛmən] *vt untr* to flood
Überschwemmung *f* flood
überschwenglich [ˈyːbərʃvɛŋlɪç] *adj siehe* **überschwänglich**
Übersee [ˈyːbərzeː] *f*: **nach/in** ~ overseas
überseeisch *adj* overseas
übersehbar [yːbərˈzeːbaːr] *adj* (*fig: Folgen, Zusammenhänge etc*) clear; (*Kosten, Dauer etc*) assessable
übersehen [yːbərˈzeːən] *unreg vt untr* to look (out) over; (*fig: Folgen*) to see, get an overall view of; (*: nicht beachten*) to overlook
übersenden [yːbərˈzɛndən] *unreg vt untr* to send, forward
übersetzen[1] [yːbərˈzɛtsən] *vt untr, vi untr* to translate
übersetzen[2] [ˈyːbərzɛtsən] *vi* (*Hilfsverb sein*) to cross
Übersetzer, in [yːbərˈzɛtsər(ɪn)] **(-s, -)** *m(f)* translator
Übersetzung [yːbərˈzɛtsʊŋ] *f* translation; (*Tech*) gear ratio
Übersicht [ˈyːbərzɪçt] *f* overall view; (*Darstellung*) survey; **die ~ verlieren** to lose track; **übersichtlich** *adj* clear; (*Gelände*) open; **Übersichtlichkeit** *f* clarity, lucidity
übersiedeln[1] [ˈyːbərziːdəln] *vi* to move
übersiedeln[2] [yːbərˈziːdəln] *vi untr* to move
überspannen [yːbərˈʃpanən] *vt untr* (*zu sehr spannen*) to overstretch; (*überdecken*) to cover
überspannt *adj* eccentric; (*Idee*) wild, crazy; **Überspanntheit** *f* eccentricity
überspielen [yːbərˈʃpiːlən] *vt untr* (*verbergen*) to cover (up); (*übertragen: Aufnahme*) to transfer
überspitzt [yːbərˈʃpɪtst] *adj* exaggerated
überspringen [yːbərˈʃprɪŋən] *unreg vt untr* to jump over; (*fig*) to skip
übersprudeln [ˈyːbərʃpruːdəln] *vi* to bubble over
überstehen[1] [yːbərˈʃteːən] *unreg vt untr* to overcome, get over; (*Winter etc*) to survive, get through
überstehen[2] [ˈyːbərʃteːən] *unreg vi* to project
übersteigen [yːbərˈʃtaɪgən] *unreg vt untr* to climb over; (*fig*) to exceed
übersteigert [yːbərˈʃtaɪgərt] *adj* excessive
überstimmen [yːberˈʃtɪmən] *vt untr* to outvote
überstrapazieren [ˈyːbərʃtrapatsiːrən] *vt untr* to wear out ▷ *vr* to wear o.s. out
überstreifen [ˈyːbərʃtraɪfən] *vt*: **(sich** *dat***) etw** ~ to slip sth on
überströmen[1] [yːbərˈʃtrøːmən] *vt untr*: **von Blut überströmt sein** to be streaming with blood
überströmen[2] [ˈyːbərʃtrøːmən] *vi* (*lit, fig*): ~ **(vor** *+dat***)** to overflow (with)
Überstunden [ˈyːbərʃtʊndən] *pl* overtime *sing*
überstürzen [yːbərˈʃtʏrtsən] *vt untr* to rush ▷ *vr untr* to follow (one another) in rapid succession
überstürzt *adj* (over)hasty
übertariflich [ˈyːbərtariflɪç] *adj, adv* above the agreed *od* union rate
übertölpeln [yːbərˈtœlpln] *vt untr* to dupe
übertönen [yːbərˈtøːnən] *vt untr* to drown (out)
Übertrag [ˈyːbərtraːk] **(-(e)s, -träge)** *m* (*Comm*) amount brought forward
übertragbar [yːbərˈtraːkbaːr] *adj* transferable; (*Med*) infectious
übertragen [yːbərˈtraːgən] *unreg vt untr* to transfer; (*Rundf*) to broadcast; (*anwenden: Methode*) to apply; (*übersetzen*) to render; (*Krankheit*) to transmit ▷ *vr untr* to spread ▷ *adj* figurative; **~ auf** *+akk* to transfer to; to apply to; **sich ~ auf** *+akk* to spread to; **jdm etw** ~ to assign sth to sb; (*Verantwortung etc*) to give sb sth *od* sth to sb
Übertragung *f* (*siehe vb*) transference; broadcast; rendering; transmission
übertreffen [yːbərˈtrɛfən] *unreg vt untr* to surpass
übertreiben [yːbərˈtraɪbən] *unreg vt untr* to exaggerate; **man kann es auch** ~ you can overdo things
Übertreibung *f* exaggeration

übertreten[1] [y:bər'tre:tən] *unreg vt untr* to cross; (*Gebot etc*) to break
übertreten[2] ['y:bərtre:tən] *unreg vi* (*über Linie, Gebiet*) to step (over); (*Sport*) to overstep; (*zu anderem Glauben*) to be converted; **~ (in** *+akk*): *Pol*) to go over (to)
Übertretung [y:bər'tre:tʊŋ] *f* violation, transgression
übertrieben [y:bər'tri:bən] *adj* exaggerated, excessive
Übertritt ['y:bərtrɪt] *m* (*zu anderem Glauben*) conversion; (*bes zu anderer Partei*) defection
übertrumpfen [y:bər'trʊmpfən] *vt untr* to outdo; (*Karten*) to overtrump
übertünchen [y:bər'tʏnçən] *vt untr* to whitewash; (*fig*) to cover up, whitewash
übervölkert [y:bər'fœlkərt] *adj* overpopulated
übervoll ['y:bərfɔl] *adj* overfull
übervorteilen [y:bər'fɔrtaɪlən] *vt untr* to dupe, cheat
überwachen [y:bər'vaxən] *vt untr* to supervise; (*Verdächtigen*) to keep under surveillance
Überwachung *f* supervision; surveillance
überwältigen [y:bər'vɛltɪgən] *vt untr* to overpower
überwältigend *adj* overwhelming
überwechseln ['y:bərvɛksəln] *vi*: **~ (in** *+akk***)** to move (to); (*zu Partei etc*): **~ (zu)** to go over (to)
überweisen [y:bər'vaɪzən] *unreg vt untr* to transfer; (*Patienten*) to refer
Überweisung *f* transfer; (*von Patient*) referral
überwerfen[1] ['y:bərvɛrfən] *unreg vt* (*Kleidungsstück*) to put on; (*sehr rasch*) to throw on
überwerfen[2] [y:bər'vɛrfən] *unreg vr untr*: **sich (mit jdm)** ~ to fall out (with sb)
überwiegen [y:bər'vi:gən] *unreg vi untr* to predominate
überwiegend *adj* predominant
überwinden [y:bər'vɪndən] *unreg vt untr* to overcome ▷ *vr untr*: **sich ~, etw zu tun** to make an effort to do sth, bring o.s. to do sth
Überwindung *f* overcoming; (*Selbstüberwindung*) effort of will
überwintern [y:bər'vɪntərn] *vi untr* to (spend the) winter; (*umg: Winterschlaf halten*) to hibernate
Überwurf ['y:bərvʊrf] *m* wrap
Überzahl ['y:bərtsa:l] *f* superior numbers *pl*, superiority; **in der ~ sein** to be numerically superior
überzählig ['y:bərtsɛ:lɪç] *adj* surplus
überzeugen [y:bər'tsɔygən] *vt untr* to convince
überzeugend *adj* convincing
überzeugt *adj attrib* (*Anhänger etc*) dedicated; (*Vegetarier*) strict; (*Christ, Moslem*) devout
Überzeugung *f* conviction; **zu der ~ gelangen, dass ...** to become convinced that ...
Überzeugungskraft *f* power of persuasion
überziehen[1] ['y:bərtsi:ən] *unreg vt* to put on
überziehen[2] [y:bər'tsi:ən] *unreg vt untr* to cover; (*Konto*) to overdraw; (*Redezeit etc*) to overrun ▷ *vr untr* (*Himmel*) to cloud over; **ein Bett frisch ~** to change a bed, change the sheets (on a bed)
Überziehungskredit *m* overdraft
überzüchten [y:bər'tsʏçtən] *vt untr* to overbreed
Überzug ['y:bərtsu:k] *m* cover; (*Belag*) coating
üblich ['y:plɪç] *adj* usual; **allgemein ~ sein** to be common practice
U-Boot ['u:bo:t] *nt* U-boat, submarine
übrig ['y:brɪç] *adj* remaining; **die Übrigen** the others; **das Übrige** the rest; **im Übrigen** besides; **~ bleiben** to remain, be left (over); **~ lassen** to leave (over); **einiges/viel zu wünschen ~ lassen** (*umg*) to leave something/ a lot to be desired; *siehe auch* **übrighaben**
übrigens ['y:brɪgəns] *adv* besides; (*nebenbei bemerkt*) by the way
übrighaben *unreg vi*: **für jdn etwas ~** (*umg*) to be fond of sb
Übung ['y:bʊŋ] *f* practice; (*Turnübung, Aufgabe etc*) exercise; **~ macht den Meister** (*Sprichwort*) practice makes perfect
Übungsarbeit *f* (*Sch*) mock test
Übungsplatz *m* training ground; (*Mil*) drill ground
u. d. M. *abk* (= *unter dem Meeresspiegel*) below sea level
ü. d. M. *abk* (= *über dem Meeresspiegel*) above sea level
u. E. *abk* (= *unseres Erachtens*) in our opinion
Ufer ['u:fər] **(-s, -)** *nt* bank; (*Meeresufer*) shore; **Uferbefestigung** *f* embankment
uferlos *adj* endless; (*grenzenlos*) boundless; **ins U~e gehen** (*Kosten*) to go up and up; (*Debatte etc*) to go on forever
UFO, Ufo ['u:fo] **(-(s), -s)** *nt abk* (= *unbekanntes Flugobjekt*) UFO, ufo
Uganda [u'ganda] **(-s)** *nt* Uganda
Ugander, in **(-s, -)** *m(f)* Ugandan
ugandisch *adj* Ugandan
U-Haft ['u:haft] *f abk* = **Untersuchungshaft**
Uhr [u:r] **(-, -en)** *f* clock; (*Armbanduhr*) watch; **wie viel ~ ist es?** what time is it?; **um wie viel ~?** at what time?; **1 ~** 1 o'clock; **20 ~** 8 o'clock, 20.00 (twenty hundred) hours; **Uhrband** *nt* watchstrap; **Uhrengehäuse, Uhrgehäuse** *nt* clock case; watch case; **Uhrkette** *f* watch chain; **Uhrmacher** *m* watchmaker; **Uhrwerk** *nt* (*auch fig*) clockwork mechanism; **Uhrzeiger** *m* hand; **Uhrzeigersinn** *m*: **im Uhrzeigersinn** clockwise; **entgegen dem Uhrzeigersinn** anticlockwise; **Uhrzeit** *f* time (of day)
Uhu ['u:hu] **(-s, -s)** *m* eagle owl
Ukraine [ukra'i:nə] *f* Ukraine
Ukrainer, in [ukra'i:nər(ɪn)] **(-s, -)** *m(f)* Ukrainian
ukrainisch *adj* Ukrainian
UKW *abk* (= *Ultrakurzwelle*) VHF
Ulk [ʊlk] **(-s, -e)** *m* lark
ulkig ['ʊlkɪç] *adj* funny
Ulme ['ʊlmə] **(-, -n)** *f* elm
Ulster ['ʊlstər] **(-s)** *nt* Ulster

Ultimatum [ʊlti'ma:tʊm] (**-s, Ultimaten**) *nt* ultimatum; **jdm ein ~ stellen** to give sb an ultimatum

Ultra- *zW*: **Ultrakurzwelle** *f* very high frequency; **Ultraleichtflugzeug** *nt* microlight; **Ultraschall** *m* (*Phys*) ultrasound; **ultraviolett** *adj* ultraviolet

SCHLÜSSELWORT

um [ʊm] *präp +akk* **1** (*um herum*) (a)round; **um Weihnachten** around Christmas; **er schlug um sich** he hit about him

2 (*mit Zeitangabe*) at; **um acht (Uhr)** at eight (o'clock)

3 (*mit Größenangabe*) by; **etw um 4 cm kürzen** to shorten sth by 4 cm; **um 10% teurer** 10% more expensive; **um vieles besser** better by far; **um nichts besser** not in the least bit better; *siehe auch* **umso**

4: der Kampf um den Titel the battle for the title; **um Geld spielen** to play for money; **es geht um das Prinzip** it's a question of principle; **Stunde um Stunde** hour after hour; **Auge um Auge** an eye for an eye

▷ *präp +gen*: **um ... willen** for the sake of ...; **um Gottes willen** for goodness *od* (*stärker*) God's sake

▷ *konj*: **um ... zu** (in order) to ...; **zu klug, um zu ...** too clever to ...; *siehe auch* **umso**

▷ *adv* **1** (*ungefähr*) about; **um (die) 30 Leute** about *od* around 30 people

2 (*vorbei*): **die zwei Stunden sind um** the two hours are up

umadressieren ['ʊm|adrɛsi:rən] *vt untr* to readdress

umändern ['ʊm|ɛndərn] *vt* to alter

Umänderung *f* alteration

umarbeiten ['ʊm|arbaɪtən] *vt* to remodel; (*Buch etc*) to revise, rework

umarmen [ʊm'|armən] *vt untr* to embrace

Umbau ['ʊmbaʊ] (**-(e)s, -e** *od* **-ten**) *m* reconstruction, alteration(s *pl*)

umbauen ['ʊmbaʊən] *vt* to rebuild, reconstruct

umbenennen ['ʊmbənɛnən] *unreg vt untr* to rename

umbesetzen ['ʊmbəzɛtsən] *vt untr* (*Theat*) to recast; (*Mannschaft*) to change; (*Posten, Stelle*) to find someone else for

umbiegen ['ʊmbi:gən] *unreg vt* to bend (over)

umbilden ['ʊmbɪldən] *vt* to reorganize; (*Pol: Kabinett*) to reshuffle

umbinden[1] ['ʊmbɪndən] *unreg vt* (*Krawatte etc*) to put on

umbinden[2] [ʊm'bɪndən] *unreg vt untr*: **etw mit etw ~** to tie sth round sth

umblättern ['ʊmblɛtərn] *vt* to turn over

umblicken ['ʊmblɪkən] *vr* to look around

umbringen ['ʊmbrɪŋən] *unreg vt* to kill

Umbruch ['ʊmbrʊx] *m* radical change; (*Typ*) make-up (into page)

umbuchen ['ʊmbu:xən] *vi* to change one's reservation *od* flight *etc* ▷ *vt* to change

umdenken ['ʊmdɛŋkən] *unreg vi* to adjust one's views

umdisponieren ['ʊmdɪsponi:rən] *vi untr* to change one's plans

umdrängen [ʊm'drɛŋən] *vt untr* to crowd round

umdrehen ['ʊmdre:ən] *vt* to turn (round); (*Hals*) to wring ▷ *vr* to turn (round); **jdm den Arm ~** to twist sb's arm

Umdrehung *f* turn; (*Phys*) revolution, rotation

umeinander [ʊm|aɪ'nandər] *adv* round one another; (*füreinander*) for one another

umerziehen ['ʊm|ɛrtsi:ən] *unreg vt* (*Pol: euph*): **jdn (zu etw) ~** to re-educate sb (to become sth)

umfahren[1] ['ʊmfa:rən] *unreg vt* to run over

umfahren[2] [ʊm'fa:rən] *unreg vt untr* to drive round; (*die Welt*) to sail round

umfallen ['ʊmfalən] *unreg vi* to fall down *od* over; (*fig: umg: nachgeben*) to give in

Umfang ['ʊmfaŋ] *m* extent; (*von Buch*) size; (*Reichweite*) range; (*Fläche*) area; (*Math*) circumference; **in großem ~** on a large scale; **umfangreich** *adj* extensive; (*Buch etc*) voluminous

umfassen [ʊm'fasən] *vt untr* to embrace; (*umgeben*) to surround; (*enthalten*) to include

umfassend *adj* comprehensive; (*umfangreich*) extensive

Umfeld ['ʊmfɛlt] *nt*: **zum ~ von etw gehören** to be associated with sth

umformatieren ['ʊmfɔrmati:rən] *vt untr* (*Comput*) to reformat

umformen ['ʊmfɔrmən] *vi* to transform

Umformer (**-s, -**) *m* (*Elek*) converter

umformulieren ['ʊmfɔrmuli:rən] *vt untr* to redraft

Umfrage ['ʊmfra:gə] *f* poll; **~ halten** to ask around

umfüllen ['ʊmfʏlən] *vt* to transfer; (*Wein*) to decant

umfunktionieren ['ʊmfʊŋktsioni:rən] *vt untr* to convert

Umgang ['ʊmgaŋ] *m* company; (*mit jdm*) dealings *pl*; (*Behandlung*) dealing

umgänglich ['ʊmgɛŋlɪç] *adj* sociable

Umgangs- *zW*: **Umgangsformen** *pl* manners *pl*; **Umgangssprache** *f* colloquial language; **umgangssprachlich** *adj* colloquial

umgeben [ʊm'ge:bən] *unreg vt untr* to surround

Umgebung *f* surroundings *pl*; (*Milieu*) environment; (*Personen*) people in one's circle; **in der näheren/weiteren ~ Münchens** on the outskirts/in the environs of Munich

umgehen[1] ['ʊmge:ən] *unreg vi* to go (a)round; **im Schlosse ~** to haunt the castle; **mit jdm/etw ~ können** to know how to handle sb/sth; **mit jdm grob** *etc* **~** to treat sb roughly *etc*; **mit Geld sparsam ~** to be careful with one's money

umgehen[2] [ʊm'ge:ən] *unreg vt untr* to bypass;

(*Mil*) to outflank; (*Gesetz, Vorschrift etc*) to circumvent; (*vermeiden*) to avoid
umgehend *adj* immediate
Umgehung *f* (*siehe vb*) bypassing; outflanking; circumvention; avoidance
Umgehungsstraße *f* bypass
umgekehrt ['ʊmgəke:rt] *adj* reverse(d); (*gegenteilig*) opposite ▷ *adv* the other way around; **und** ~ and vice versa
umgestalten ['ʊmgəʃtaltən] *vt untr* to alter; (*reorganisieren*) to reorganize; (*umordnen*) to rearrange
umgewöhnen ['ʊmgəvø:nən] *vr* to readapt
umgraben ['ʊmgra:bən] *unreg vt* to dig up
umgruppieren ['ʊmgrʊpi:rən] *vt untr* to regroup
Umhang ['ʊmhaŋ] *m* wrap, cape
umhängen ['ʊmhɛŋən] *vt* (*Bild*) to hang somewhere else; **jdm etw** ~ to put sth on sb
Umhängetasche *f* shoulder bag
umhauen ['ʊmhaʊən] *vt* to fell; (*fig*) to bowl over
umher [ʊm'he:r] *adv* about, around; **umhergehen** *unreg vi* to walk about; **umherirren** *vi* to wander around; (*Blick, Augen*) to roam about; **umherreisen** *vi* to travel about; **umherschweifen** *vi* to roam about; **umherziehen** *unreg vi* to wander from place to place
umhinkönnen [ʊm'hɪnkœnən] *unreg vi*: **ich kann nicht umhin, das zu tun** I can't help doing it
umhören ['ʊmhø:rən] *vr* to ask around
umkämpfen [ʊm'kɛmpfən] *vt untr* (*Entscheidung*) to dispute; (*Wahlkreis, Sieg*) to contest
Umkehr ['ʊmke:r] (-) *f* turning back; (*Änderung*) change
umkehren *vi* to turn back; (*fig*) to change one's ways ▷ *vt* to turn round, reverse; (*Tasche etc*) to turn inside out; (*Gefäß etc*) to turn upside down
umkippen ['ʊmkɪpən] *vt* to tip over ▷ *vi* to overturn; (*umg: ohnmächtig werden*) to keel over; (*fig: Meinung ändern*) to change one's mind
umklammern [ʊm'klamərn] *vt untr* (*mit Händen*) to clasp; (*festhalten*) to cling to
umklappen ['ʊmklapən] *vt* to fold down
Umkleidekabine ['ʊmklaɪdəkabi:nə] *f* changing cubicle (*Brit*), dressing room (*US*)
Umkleideraum ['ʊmklaɪdəraʊm] *m* changing room; (*US: Theat*) dressing room
umknicken ['ʊmknɪkən] *vt* (*Ast*) to snap; (*Papier*) to fold (over) ▷ *vi*: **mit dem Fuß** ~ to twist one's ankle
umkommen ['ʊmkɔmən] *unreg vi* to die, perish; (*Lebensmittel*) to go bad
Umkreis ['ʊmkraɪs] *m* neighbourhood (*Brit*), neighborhood (*US*); **im** ~ **von** within a radius of
umkreisen [ʊm'kraɪzən] *vt untr* to circle (round); (*Satellit*) to orbit
umkrempeln ['ʊmkrɛmpəln] *vt* to turn up; (*mehrmals*) to roll up; (*umg: Betrieb*) to shake up
umladen ['ʊmla:dən] *unreg vt* to transfer, reload
Umlage ['ʊmla:gə] *f* share of the costs
Umlauf *m* (*Geldumlauf*) circulation; (*von Gestirn*) revolution; (*Schreiben*) circular; **in ~ bringen** to circulate; **Umlaufbahn** *f* orbit
umlaufen ['ʊmlaʊfən] *unreg vi* to circulate
Umlaufkapital *nt* working capital
Umlaufvermögen *nt* current assets *pl*
Umlaut ['ʊmlaʊt] *m* umlaut
umlegen ['ʊmle:gən] *vt* to put on; (*verlegen*) to move, shift; (*Kosten*) to share out; (*umkippen*) to tip over; (*umg: töten*) to bump off
umleiten ['ʊmlaɪtən] *vt* to divert
Umleitung *f* diversion
umlernen ['ʊmlɛrnən] *vi* to learn something new; (*fig*) to adjust one's views
umliegend ['ʊmli:gənt] *adj* surrounding
ummelden ['ʊmmɛldən] *vt, vr*: **jdn/sich** ~ to notify (the police of) a change in sb's/one's address
Umnachtung [ʊm'naxtʊŋ] *f* mental derangement
umorganisieren ['ʊm|ɔrganizi:rən] *vt untr* to reorganize
umpflanzen ['ʊmpflantsən] *vt* to transplant
umquartieren ['ʊmkvarti:rən] *vt untr* to move; (*Truppen*) to requarter
umrahmen [ʊm'ra:mən] *vt untr* to frame
umranden [ʊm'randən] *vt untr* to border, edge
umräumen ['ʊmrɔʏmən] *vt* (*anders anordnen*) to rearrange ▷ *vi* to rearrange things, move things around
umrechnen ['ʊmrɛçnən] *vt* to convert
Umrechnung *f* conversion
Umrechnungskurs *m* rate of exchange
umreißen [ʊm'raɪsən] *unreg vt untr* to outline
umrennen ['ʊmrɛnən] *unreg vt* to (run into and) knock down
umringen [ʊm'rɪŋən] *vt untr* to surround
Umriss ['ʊmrɪs] *m* outline
umrühren ['ʊmry:rən] *vt, vi* to stir
umrüsten ['ʊmrʏstən] *vt* (*Tech*) to adapt; (*Mil*) to re-equip; ~ **auf** *+akk* to adapt to
ums [ʊms] = **um das**
umsatteln ['ʊmzatəln] (*umg*) *vi* to change one's occupation, switch jobs
Umsatz ['ʊmzats] *m* turnover; **Umsatzbeteiligung** *f* commission; **Umsatzeinbuße** *f* loss of profit; **Umsatzsteuer** *f* turnover tax
umschalten ['ʊmʃaltən] *vt* to switch ▷ *vi* to push/pull a lever; (*auf anderen Sender*): **~ (auf** *+akk***)** to change over (to); (*Aut*): **~ in** *+akk* to change (*Brit*) *od* shift into; **„wir schalten jetzt um nach Hamburg"** "and now we go over to Hamburg"
Umschalttaste *f* shift key
Umschau *f* look(ing) round; **~ halten nach** to look around for
umschauen ['ʊmʃaʊən] *vr* to look round
Umschlag ['ʊmʃla:k] *m* cover; (*Buchumschlag*) jacket, cover; (*Med*) compress; (*Briefumschlag*)

envelope; (*Gütermenge*) volume of traffic; (*Wechsel*) change; (*von Hose*) turn-up (*Brit*), cuff (*US*)
umschlagen ['ʊmʃla:gən] *unreg vi* to change; (*Naut*) to capsize ▷ *vt* to knock over; (*Ärmel*) to turn up; (*Seite*) to turn over; (*Waren*) to transfer
Umschlag- *zW*: **Umschlaghafen** *m* port of transshipment; **Umschlagplatz** *m* (*Comm*) distribution centre (*Brit*) *od* center (*US*); **Umschlagseite** *f* cover page
umschlingen [ʊm'ʃlɪŋən] *unreg vt untr* (*Pflanze*) to twine around; (*jdn*) to embrace
umschreiben¹ ['ʊmʃraɪbən] *unreg vt* (*neu umschreiben*) to rewrite; (*übertragen*) to transfer; ~ **auf** *+akk* to transfer to
umschreiben² [ʊm'ʃraɪbən] *unreg vt untr* to paraphrase; (*abgrenzen*) to circumscribe, define
Umschuldung ['ʊmʃʊldʊŋ] *f* rescheduling (of debts)
umschulen ['ʊmʃu:lən] *vt* to retrain; (*Kind*) to send to another school
umschwärmen [ʊm'ʃvɛrmən] *vt untr* to swarm round; (*fig*) to surround, idolize
Umschweife ['ʊmʃvaɪfə] *pl*: **ohne ~** without beating about the bush, straight out
umschwenken ['ʊmʃvɛnkən] *vi* (*Kran*) to swing out; (*fig*) to do an about-turn (*Brit*) *od* about-face (*US*); (*Wind*) to veer
Umschwung ['ʊmʃvʊŋ] *m* (*Gymnastik*) circle; (*fig: ins Gegenteil*) change (around)
umsegeln [ʊm'ze:gəln] *vt untr* to sail around; (*Erde*) to circumnavigate
umsehen ['ʊmze:ən] *unreg vr* to look around *od* about; (*suchen*): **sich ~ (nach)** to look out (for); **ich möchte mich nur mal ~** (*in Geschäft*) I'm just looking
umseitig ['ʊmzaɪtɪç] *adv* overleaf
umsetzen ['ʊmzɛtsən] *vt* (*Waren*) to turn over ▷ *vr* (*Schüler*) to change places; **etw in die Tat ~** to translate sth into action
Umsicht ['ʊmzɪçt] *f* prudence, caution
umsichtig *adj* prudent, cautious
umsiedeln ['ʊmzi:dəln] *vt* to resettle
Umsiedler, in (-s, -) *m(f)* resettler
umso ['ʊmzo] *konj*: **~ besser/schlimmer** so much the better/worse; **~ mehr, als ...** all the more considering ...
umsonst [ʊm'zɔnst] *adv* in vain; (*gratis*) for nothing
umspringen ['ʊmʃprɪŋən] *unreg vi* to change; **mit jdm ~** to treat sb badly
Umstand ['ʊmʃtant] *m* circumstance; **Umstände** *pl* (*fig: Schwierigkeiten*) fuss *sing*; **in anderen Umständen sein** to be pregnant; **Umstände machen** to go to a lot of trouble; **den Umständen entsprechend** much as one would expect (under the circumstances); **die näheren Umstände** further details; **unter Umständen** possibly; **mildernde Umstände** (*Jur*) extenuating circumstances
umständehalber *adv* owing to circumstances
umständlich ['ʊmʃtɛntlɪç] *adj* (*Methode*) cumbersome, complicated; (*Ausdrucksweise, Erklärung*) long-winded; (*ungeschickt*) ponderous; **etw ~ machen** to make heavy weather of (doing) sth
Umstandskleid *nt* maternity dress
Umstandswort *nt* adverb
umstehend ['ʊmʃte:ənt] *adj attrib* (*umseitig*) overleaf; **die U~en** *pl* the bystanders *pl*
Umsteigekarte *f* transfer ticket
umsteigen ['ʊmʃtaɪgən] *unreg vi* (*Eisenb*) to change; (*fig: umg*): **~ (auf** *+akk*) to change over (to), switch (over) (to)
umstellen¹ ['ʊmʃtɛlən] *vt* (*an anderen Ort*) to change round, rearrange; (*Tech*) to convert ▷ *vr*: **sich ~ (auf** *+akk*) to adapt o.s. (to)
umstellen² [ʊm'ʃtɛlən] *vt untr* to surround
Umstellung *f* change; (*Umgewöhnung*) adjustment; (*Tech*) conversion
umstimmen ['ʊmʃtɪmən] *vt* (*Mus*) to retune; **jdn ~** to make sb change his mind
umstoßen ['ʊmʃto:sən] *unreg vt* (*lit*) to overturn; (*Plan etc*) to change, upset
umstritten [ʊm'ʃtrɪtən] *adj* disputed; (*fraglich*) controversial
Umsturz ['ʊmʃtʊrts] *m* overthrow
umstürzen ['ʊmʃtʏrtsən] *vt* (*umwerfen*) to overturn ▷ *vi* to collapse, fall down; (*Wagen*) to overturn
umstürzlerisch *adj* revolutionary
Umtausch ['ʊmtaʊʃ] *m* exchange; **diese Waren sind vom ~ ausgeschlossen** these goods cannot be exchanged
umtauschen *vt* to exchange
Umtriebe ['ʊmtri:bə] *pl* machinations *pl*, intrigues *pl*
umtun ['ʊmtu:n] *unreg vr*: **sich nach etw ~** to look for sth
umverteilen ['ʊmfɛrtaɪlən] *vt untr* to redistribute
umwälzend ['ʊmvɛltsənt] *adj* (*fig*) radical; (*Veränderungen*) sweeping; (*Ereignisse*) revolutionary
Umwälzung *f* (*fig*) radical change
umwandeln ['ʊmvandəln] *vt* to change, convert; (*Elek*) to transform
umwechseln ['ʊmvɛksəln] *vt* to change
Umweg ['ʊmve:k] *m* detour; (*fig*) roundabout way
Umwelt ['ʊmvɛlt] *f* environment; **Umweltallergie** *f* environmental allergy; **Umweltauto** (*umg*) *nt* environment-friendly vehicle; **Umweltbelastung** *f* environmental pollution; **Umweltbewusstsein** *nt* environmental awareness; **umweltfreundlich** *adj* environment-friendly; **Umweltkrankheit** *f* environmental illness; **Umweltkriminalität** *f* crimes *pl* against the environment; **Umweltministerium** *nt* Ministry of the Environment; **umweltschädlich** *adj* harmful to the environment; **Umweltschutz** *m* environmental protection; **Umweltschützer (-s, -)** *m* environmentalist; **Umweltverschmutzung** *f* pollution (of the environment); **umweltverträglich**

adj not harmful to the environment; **Umweltverträglichkeit** *f* ecofriendliness
umwenden ['ʊmvɛndən] *unreg vt, vr* to turn (round)
umwerben [ʊm'vɛrbən] *unreg vt untr* to court, woo
umwerfen ['ʊmvɛrfən] *unreg vt* (*lit*) to upset, overturn; (*Mantel*) to throw on; (*fig: erschüttern*) to upset, throw
umwerfend (*umg*) *adj* fantastic
umziehen ['ʊmtsi:ən] *unreg vt, vr* to change ▷ *vi* to move
umzingeln [ʊm'tsɪŋəln] *vt untr* to surround, encircle
Umzug ['ʊmtsu:k] *m* procession; (*Wohnungsumzug*) move, removal
UN *pl abk* (*= United Nations*): **die UN** the UN *sing*
un- *zW*: **unabänderlich** *adj* irreversible, unalterable; **unabänderlich feststehen** to be absolutely certain; **unabdingbar** *adj* indispensable, essential; (*Recht*) inalienable; **unabhängig** *adj* independent; **Unabhängigkeit** *f* independence; **unabkömmlich** *adj* indispensable; **zur Zeit unabkömmlich** not free at the moment; **unablässig** *adj* incessant, constant; **unabsehbar** *adj* immeasurable; (*Folgen*) unforeseeable; (*Kosten*) incalculable; **unabsichtlich** *adj* unintentional; **unabwendbar** *adj* inevitable
unachtsam ['ʊn|axtza:m] *adj* careless; **Unachtsamkeit** *f* carelessness
un- *zW*: **unanfechtbar** *adj* indisputable; **unangebracht** *adj* uncalled-for; **unangefochten** *adj* unchallenged; (*Testament, Wahlkandidat, Urteil*) uncontested; **unangemeldet** *adj* unannounced; (*Besucher*) unexpected; **unangemessen** *adj* inadequate; **unangenehm** *adj* unpleasant; (*peinlich*) embarrassing; **unangepasst** *adj* nonconformist; **Unannehmlichkeit** *f* inconvenience; **Unannehmlichkeiten** *pl* trouble *sing*; **unansehnlich** *adj* unsightly; **unanständig** *adj* indecent, improper; **Unanständigkeit** *f* indecency, impropriety; **unantastbar** *adj* inviolable, sacrosanct
unappetitlich ['ʊn|apeti:tlɪç] *adj* unsavoury (*Brit*), unsavory (*US*)
Unart ['ʊn|a:rt] *f* bad manners *pl*; (*Angewohnheit*) bad habit
unartig *adj* naughty, badly behaved
un- *zW*: **unaufdringlich** *adj* unobtrusive; (*Parfüm*) discreet; (*Mensch*) unassuming; **unauffällig** *adj* unobtrusive; (*Kleidung*) inconspicuous; **unauffindbar** *adj* not to be found; **unaufgefordert** *adj* unsolicited ▷ *adv* unasked, spontaneously; **unaufgefordert zugesandte Manuskripte** unsolicited manuscripts; **unaufhaltsam** *adj* irresistible; **unaufhörlich** *adj* incessant, continuous; **unaufmerksam** *adj* inattentive; **unaufrichtig** *adj* insincere
un- *zW*: **unausbleiblich** *adj* inevitable, unavoidable; **unausgeglichen** *adj* volatile; **unausgegoren** *adj* immature; (*Idee, Plan*) half-baked; **unausgesetzt** *adj* incessant, constant; **unausgewogen** *adj* unbalanced; **unaussprechlich** *adj* inexpressible; **unausstehlich** *adj* intolerable; **unausweichlich** *adj* inescapable, ineluctable
unbändig ['ʊnbɛndɪç] *adj* extreme, excessive
unbarmherzig ['ʊnbarmhɛrtsɪç] *adj* pitiless, merciless
unbeabsichtigt ['ʊnbə|apzɪçtɪçt] *adj* unintentional
unbeachtet ['ʊnbə|axtət] *adj* unnoticed; (*Warnung*) ignored
unbedacht ['ʊnbədaxt] *adj* rash
unbedarft ['ʊnbədarft] (*umg*) *adj* clueless
unbedenklich ['ʊnbədɛŋklɪç] *adj* unhesitating; (*Plan*) unobjectionable ▷ *adv* without hesitation
unbedeutend ['ʊnbədɔʏtənt] *adj* insignificant, unimportant; (*Fehler*) slight
unbedingt ['ʊnbədɪŋt] *adj* unconditional ▷ *adv* absolutely; **musst du ~ gehen?** do you really have to go?; **nicht ~** not necessarily
unbefangen ['ʊnbəfaŋən] *adj* impartial, unprejudiced; (*ohne Hemmungen*) uninhibited; **Unbefangenheit** *f* impartiality; uninhibitedness
unbefriedigend ['ʊnbəfri:dɪgənd] *adj* unsatisfactory
unbefriedigt ['ʊnbəfri:dɪçt] *adj* unsatisfied; (*unzufrieden*) dissatisfied; (*unerfüllt*) unfulfilled
unbefristet ['ʊnbəfrɪstət] *adj* permanent
unbefugt ['ʊnbəfu:kt] *adj* unauthorized; **U~en ist der Eintritt verboten** no admittance to unauthorized persons
unbegabt ['ʊnbəga:pt] *adj* untalented
unbegreiflich [ʊnbə'graɪflɪç] *adj* inconceivable
unbegrenzt ['ʊnbəgrɛntst] *adj* unlimited
unbegründet ['ʊnbəgrʏndət] *adj* unfounded
Unbehagen ['ʊnbəha:gən] *nt* discomfort
unbehaglich ['ʊnbəha:klɪç] *adj* uncomfortable; (*Gefühl*) uneasy
unbeherrscht ['ʊnbəhɛrʃt] *adj* uncontrolled; (*Mensch*) lacking self-control
unbeholfen ['ʊnbəhɔlfən] *adj* awkward, clumsy; **Unbeholfenheit** *f* awkwardness, clumsiness
unbeirrt ['ʊnbə|ɪrt] *adj* imperturbable
unbekannt ['ʊnbəkant] *adj* unknown; **~e Größe** (*Math, fig*) unknown quantity
unbekannterweise *adv*: **grüß(e) sie ~ von mir** give her my regards although I don't know her
unbekümmert ['ʊnbəkʏmərt] *adj* unconcerned
unbelehrbar [ʊnbə'le:rba:r] *adj* fixed in one's views; (*Rassist etc*) dyed-in-the-wool *attrib*
unbeliebt ['ʊnbəli:pt] *adj* unpopular; **Unbeliebtheit** *f* unpopularity
unbemannt ['ʊnbəmant] *adj* (*Raumflug*) unmanned; (*Flugzeug*) pilotless
unbemerkt ['ʊnbəmɛrkt] *adj* unnoticed

unbenommen [ʊnbəˈnɔmən] *adj (form)*: **es bleibt** *od* **ist Ihnen ~, zu ...** you are at liberty to ...
unbequem [ˈʊnbəkveːm] *adj (Stuhl)* uncomfortable; *(Mensch)* bothersome; *(Regelung)* inconvenient
unberechenbar [ʊnbəˈrɛçənbaːr] *adj* incalculable; *(Mensch, Verhalten)* unpredictable
unberechtigt [ˈʊnbərɛçtɪçt] *adj* unjustified; *(nicht erlaubt)* unauthorized
unberücksichtigt [ʊnbəˈrʏkzɪçtɪçt] *adj*: **etw ~ lassen** not to consider sth
unberufen [ʊnbəˈruːfən] *interj* touch wood!
unberührt [ˈʊnbəryːrt] *adj* untouched; *(Natur)* unspoiled; **sie ist noch ~** she is still a virgin
unbeschadet [ʊnbəˈʃaːdət] *präp +gen (form)* regardless of
unbescheiden [ˈʊnbəʃaɪdən] *adj* presumptuous
unbescholten [ˈʊnbəʃɔltən] *adj* respectable; *(Ruf)* spotless
unbeschrankt [ˈʊnbəʃraŋkt] *adj (Bahnübergang)* unguarded
unbeschränkt [ʊnbəˈʃrɛŋkt] *adj* unlimited
unbeschreiblich [ʊnbəˈʃraɪplɪç] *adj* indescribable
unbeschwert [ˈʊnbəʃveːrt] *adj (sorgenfrei)* carefree; *(Melodien)* light
unbesehen [ʊnbəˈzeːən] *adv* indiscriminately; *(ohne es anzusehen)* without looking at it
unbesonnen [ˈʊnbəzɔnən] *adj* unwise, rash, imprudent
unbesorgt [ˈʊnbəzɔrkt] *adj* unconcerned; **Sie können ganz ~ sein** you can set your mind at rest
unbespielt [ˈʊnbəʃpiːlt] *adj (Kassette)* blank
unbest. *abk* = **unbestimmt**
unbeständig [ˈʊnbəʃtɛndɪç] *adj (Mensch)* inconstant; *(Wetter)* unsettled; *(Lage)* unstable
unbestechlich [ʊnbəˈʃtɛçlɪç] *adj* incorruptible
unbestimmt [ˈʊnbəʃtɪmt] *adj* indefinite; *(Zukunft)* uncertain; **Unbestimmtheit** *f* vagueness
unbestritten [ˈʊnbəʃtrɪtən] *adj* undisputed
unbeteiligt [ʊnbəˈtaɪlɪçt] *adj* unconcerned; *(uninteressiert)* indifferent
unbeugsam [ˈʊnbɔʏkzaːm] *adj* stubborn, inflexible; *(Wille)* unbending
unbewacht [ˈʊnbəvaxt] *adj* unguarded, unwatched
unbewaffnet [ˈʊnbəvafnət] *adj* unarmed
unbeweglich [ˈʊnbəveːklɪç] *adj* immovable
unbewegt *adj* motionless; *(fig: unberührt)* unmoved
unbewohnt [ˈʊnbəvoːnt] *adj (Gegend)* uninhabited; *(Haus)* unoccupied
unbewusst [ˈʊnbəvʊst] *adj* unconscious
unbezahlbar [ʊnbəˈtsaːlbaːr] *adj* prohibitively expensive; *(fig)* priceless; *(nützlich)* invaluable
unbezahlt [ˈʊnbətsaːlt] *adj* unpaid
unblutig [ˈʊnbluːtɪç] *adj* bloodless
unbrauchbar [ˈʊnbraʊxbaːr] *adj (nutzlos)* useless; *(Gerät)* unusable; **Unbrauchbarkeit** *f* uselessness
unbürokratisch [ˈʊnbyrokratɪʃ] *adj* without any red tape
und [ʊnt] *konj* and; **~ so weiter** and so on
Undank [ˈʊndaŋk] *m* ingratitude; **undankbar** *adj* ungrateful; **Undankbarkeit** *f* ingratitude
undefinierbar [ʊndefiˈniːrbaːr] *adj* indefinable
undenkbar [ʊnˈdɛŋkbaːr] *adj* inconceivable
undeutlich [ˈʊndɔʏtlɪç] *adj* indistinct; *(Schrift)* illegible; *(Ausdrucksweise)* unclear
undicht [ˈʊndɪçt] *adj* leaky
undifferenziert [ˈʊndɪfərɛntsiːrt] *adj* simplistic
Unding [ˈʊndɪŋ] *nt* absurdity
unduldsam [ˈʊnduldsaːm] *adj* intolerant
un- *zW*: **undurchdringlich** *adj (Urwald)* impenetrable; *(Gesicht)* inscrutable; **undurchführbar** *adj* impracticable; **undurchlässig** *adj* impervious; *(wasserundurchlässig)* waterproof, impermeable; **undurchschaubar** *adj* inscrutable; **undurchsichtig** *adj* opaque; *(Motive)* obscure; *(fig: pej: Mensch, Methoden)* devious
uneben [ˈʊn|eːbən] *adj* uneven
unecht [ˈʊn|ɛçt] *adj* artificial, fake; *(pej: Freundschaft, Lächeln)* false
unehelich [ˈʊn|eːəlɪç] *adj* illegitimate
uneigennützig [ˈʊn|aɪgənnʏtsɪç] *adj* unselfish
uneinbringlich [ʊn|aɪnˈbrɪŋlɪç] *adj*: **~e Forderungen** *(Comm)* bad debts *pl*
uneingeschränkt [ˈʊn|aɪngəʃrɛŋkt] *adj* absolute, total; *(Rechte, Handel)* unrestricted; *(Zustimmung)* unqualified
uneinig [ˈʊn|aɪnɪç] *adj* divided; **~ sein** to disagree; **Uneinigkeit** *f* discord, dissension
uneinnehmbar [ʊn|aɪnˈneːmbaːr] *adj* impregnable
uneins [ˈʊn|aɪns] *adj* at variance, at odds
unempfänglich [ˈʊn|ɛmpfɛŋlɪç] *adj*: **~ (für)** not susceptible (to)
unempfindlich [ˈʊn|ɛmpfɪntlɪç] *adj* insensitive; **Unempfindlichkeit** *f* insensitivity
unendlich [ʊnˈ|ɛntlɪç] *adj* infinite ▷ *adv* endlessly; *(fig: sehr)* terribly; **Unendlichkeit** *f* infinity
un- *zW*: **unentbehrlich** *adj* indispensable; **unentgeltlich** *adj* free (of charge); **unentschieden** *adj* undecided; **unentschieden enden** *(Sport)* to end in a draw; **unentschlossen** *adj* undecided; *(entschlusslos)* irresolute; **unentwegt** *adj* unswerving; *(unaufhörlich)* incessant
un- *zW*: **unerbittlich** *adj* unyielding, inexorable; **unerfahren** *adj* inexperienced; **unerfreulich** *adj* unpleasant; **Unerfreuliches** *(schlechte Nachrichten)* bad news *sing*; *(Übles)* bad things *pl*; **unerfüllt** *adj* unfulfilled; **unergiebig** *adj (Quelle, Thema)* unproductive; *(Ernte, Nachschlagewerk)* poor; **unergründlich** *adj* unfathomable; **unerheblich** *adj* unimportant; **unerhört** *adj* unheard-of; *(unverschämt)* outrageous; *(Bitte)* unanswered; **unerlässlich** *adj* indispensable; **unerlaubt**

adj unauthorized; **unerledigt** *adj* unfinished; (*Post*) unanswered; (*Rechnung*) outstanding; (*schwebend*) pending; **unermesslich** *adj* immeasurable, immense; **unermüdlich** *adj* indefatigable; **unersättlich** *adj* insatiable; **unerschlossen** *adj* (*Land*) undeveloped; (*Boden*) unexploited; (*Vorkommen, Markt*) untapped; **unerschöpflich** *adj* inexhaustible; **unerschrocken** *adj* intrepid, courageous; **unerschütterlich** *adj* unshakeable; **unerschwinglich** *adj* (*Preis*) prohibitive; **unersetzlich** *adj* irreplaceable; **unerträglich** *adj* unbearable; (*Frechheit*) insufferable; **unerwartet** *adj* unexpected; **unerwünscht** *adj* undesirable, unwelcome; **unerzogen** *adj* ill-bred, rude

unfähig ['ʊnfɛːɪç] *adj* incapable; (*attrib*) incompetent; **zu etw ~ sein** to be incapable of sth; **Unfähigkeit** *f* inability; incompetence

unfair ['ʊnfɛːr] *adj* unfair

Unfall ['ʊnfal] *m* accident; **Unfallflucht** *f* hit-and-run (driving); **Unfallopfer** *nt* casualty; **Unfallstation** *f* emergency ward; **Unfallstelle** *f* scene of the accident; **Unfallversicherung** *f* accident insurance; **Unfallwagen** *m car involved in an accident*; (*umg: Rettungswagen*) ambulance

unfassbar [ʊn'fasbaːr] *adj* inconceivable

unfehlbar [ʊn'feːlbaːr] *adj* infallible ▷ *adv* without fail; **Unfehlbarkeit** *f* infallibility

unfertig ['ʊnfɛrtɪç] *adj* unfinished, incomplete; (*Mensch*) immature

unflätig ['ʊnflɛːtɪç] *adj* rude

unfolgsam ['ʊnfɔlkzaːm] *adj* disobedient

unförmig ['ʊnfœrmɪç] *adj* (*formlos*) shapeless; (*groß*) cumbersome; (*Füße, Nase*) unshapely

unfrankiert ['ʊnfraŋkiːrt] *adj* unfranked

unfrei ['ʊnfraɪ] *adj* not free

unfreiwillig *adj* involuntary

unfreundlich ['ʊnfrɔʏntlɪç] *adj* unfriendly; **Unfreundlichkeit** *f* unfriendliness

Unfriede ['ʊnfriːdə], **Unfrieden** ['ʊnfriːdən] *m* dissension, strife

unfruchtbar ['ʊnfrʊxtbaːr] *adj* infertile; (*Gespräche*) fruitless; **Unfruchtbarkeit** *f* infertility; fruitlessness

Unfug ['ʊnfuːk] **(-s)** *m* (*Benehmen*) mischief; (*Unsinn*) nonsense; **grober ~** (*Jur*) gross misconduct

Ungar, in ['ʊŋgar(ɪn)] **(-n, -n)** *m(f)* Hungarian; **ungarisch** *adj* Hungarian

Ungarn **(-s)** *nt* Hungary

ungeachtet ['ʊngə|axtət] *präp +gen* notwithstanding

ungeahndet ['ʊngə|aːndət] *adj* (*Jur*) unpunished

ungeahnt ['ʊngə|aːnt] *adj* unsuspected, undreamt-of

ungebeten ['ʊngəbeːtən] *adj* uninvited

ungebildet ['ʊngəbɪldət] *adj* uncultured; (*ohne Bildung*) uneducated

ungeboren ['ʊngəboːrən] *adj* unborn

ungebräuchlich ['ʊngəbrɔʏçlɪç] *adj* unusual, uncommon

ungebraucht ['ʊngəbraʊxt] *adj* unused

ungebührlich ['ʊngəbyːrlɪç] *adj*: **sich ~ aufregen** to get unduly excited

ungebunden ['ʊngəbʊndən] *adj* (*Buch*) unbound; (*Leben*) (fancy-)free; (*ohne festen Partner*) unattached; (*Pol*) independent

ungedeckt ['ʊngədɛkt] *adj* (*schutzlos*) unprotected; (*Scheck*) uncovered

Ungeduld ['ʊngədʊlt] *f* impatience

ungeduldig ['ʊngədʊldɪç] *adj* impatient

ungeeignet ['ʊngə|aɪgnət] *adj* unsuitable

ungefähr ['ʊngəfɛːr] *adj* rough, approximate ▷ *adv* roughly, approximately; **so ~!** more or less!; **das kommt nicht von ~** that's hardly surprising

ungefährlich ['ʊngəfɛːrlɪç] *adj* not dangerous, harmless

ungehalten ['ʊngəhaltən] *adj* indignant

ungeheuer ['ʊngəhɔʏər] *adj* huge ▷ *adv* (*umg*) enormously; **Ungeheuer** **(-s, -)** *nt* monster; **ungeheuerlich** [ʊngə'hɔʏərlɪç] *adj* monstrous

ungehindert ['ʊngəhɪndərt] *adj* unimpeded

ungehobelt ['ʊngəhoːbəlt] *adj* (*fig*) uncouth

ungehörig ['ʊngəhøːrɪç] *adj* impertinent, improper; **Ungehörigkeit** *f* impertinence

ungehorsam ['ʊngəhoːrzaːm] *adj* disobedient; **Ungehorsam** *m* disobedience

ungeklärt ['ʊngəklɛːrt] *adj* not cleared up; (*Rätsel*) unsolved; (*Abwasser*) untreated

ungekürzt ['ʊngəkʏrtst] *adj* not shortened; (*Film*) uncut

ungeladen ['ʊngəlaːdən] *adj* not loaded; (*Elek*) uncharged; (*Gast*) uninvited

ungelegen ['ʊngəleːgən] *adj* inconvenient; **komme ich (Ihnen) ~?** is this an inconvenient time for you?

ungelernt ['ʊngəlɛrnt] *adj* unskilled

ungelogen ['ʊngəloːgən] *adv* really, honestly

ungemein ['ʊngəmaɪn] *adj* immense

ungemütlich ['ʊngəmyːtlɪç] *adj* uncomfortable; (*Person*) disagreeable; **er kann ~ werden** he can get nasty

ungenau ['ʊngənaʊ] *adj* inaccurate

Ungenauigkeit *f* inaccuracy

ungeniert ['ʊnʒeniːrt] *adj* free and easy; (*bedenkenlos, taktlos*) uninhibited ▷ *adv* without embarrassment, freely

ungenießbar ['ʊngəniːsbaːr] *adj* inedible; (*nicht zu trinken*) undrinkable; (*umg*) unbearable

ungenügend ['ʊngənyːgənt] *adj* insufficient, inadequate; (*Sch*) unsatisfactory

ungenutzt ['ʊngənʊtst] *adj*: **eine Chance ~ lassen** to miss an opportunity

ungepflegt ['ʊngəpfleːkt] *adj* (*Garten etc*) untended; (*Person*) unkempt; (*Hände*) neglected

ungerade ['ʊngəraːdə] *adj* odd, uneven (*US*)

ungerecht ['ʊngərɛçt] *adj* unjust

ungerechtfertigt *adj* unjustified

Ungerechtigkeit *f* unfairness, injustice

ungeregelt ['ʊngəreːgəlt] *adj* irregular

ungereimt ['ʊngəraɪmt] *adj* (*Verse*) unrhymed; (*fig*) inconsistent

ungern ['ʊngɛrn] *adv* unwillingly, reluctantly
ungerufen ['ʊngəru:fən] *adj* without being called
ungeschehen ['ʊngəʃe:ən] *adj*: **~ machen** to undo
Ungeschicklichkeit ['ʊngəʃɪklɪçkaɪt] *f* clumsiness
ungeschickt *adj* awkward, clumsy
ungeschliffen ['ʊngəʃlɪfən] *adj* (*Edelstein*) uncut; (*Messer etc*) blunt; (*fig: Benehmen*) uncouth
ungeschmälert ['ʊngəʃmɛ:lərt] *adj* undiminished
ungeschminkt ['ʊngəʃmɪŋkt] *adj* without make-up; (*fig*) unvarnished
ungeschoren ['ʊngəʃo:rən] *adj*: **jdn ~ lassen** (*umg*) to spare sb; (*ungestraft*) to let sb off
ungesetzlich ['ʊngəzɛtslɪç] *adj* illegal
ungestempelt ['ʊngəʃtɛmpəlt] *adj* (*Briefmarke*) unfranked, mint
ungestört ['ʊngəʃtø:rt] *adj* undisturbed
ungestraft ['ʊngəʃtra:ft] *adv* with impunity
ungestüm ['ʊngəʃty:m] *adj* impetuous; **Ungestüm** (**-(e)s**) *nt* impetuosity
ungesund ['ʊngəzʊnt] *adj* unhealthy
ungetrübt ['ʊngətry:pt] *adj* clear; (*fig*) untroubled; (*Freude*) unalloyed
Ungetüm ['ʊngəty:m] (**-(e)s, -e**) *nt* monster
ungeübt ['ʊngə|y:pt] *adj* unpractised (*Brit*), unpracticed (*US*); (*Mensch*) out of practice
ungewiss ['ʊngəvɪs] *adj* uncertain; **Ungewissheit** *f* uncertainty
ungewöhnlich ['ʊngəvø:nlɪç] *adj* unusual
ungewohnt ['ʊngəvo:nt] *adj* unusual
ungewollt ['ʊngəvɔlt] *adj* unintentional
Ungeziefer ['ʊngətsi:fər] (**-s**) *nt* vermin *pl*
ungezogen ['ʊngətso:gən] *adj* rude, impertinent; **Ungezogenheit** *f* rudeness, impertinence
ungezwungen ['ʊngətsvʊŋən] *adj* natural, unconstrained
ungläubig ['ʊnglɔʏbɪç] *adj* unbelieving; **ein ~er Thomas** a doubting Thomas; **die U~en** the infidel(s *pl*)
unglaublich [ʊn'glaʊplɪç] *adj* incredible
unglaubwürdig ['ʊnglaʊpvʏrdɪç] *adj* untrustworthy, unreliable; (*Geschichte*) improbable; **sich ~ machen** to lose credibility
ungleich ['ʊnglaɪç] *adj* dissimilar; (*Mittel, Waffen*) unequal ▷ *adv* incomparably; **ungleichartig** *adj* different; **Ungleichbehandlung** *f* (*von Frauen, Ausländern*) unequal treatment; **Ungleichheit** *f* dissimilarity; inequality; **ungleichmäßig** *adj* uneven; (*Atemzüge, Gesichtszüge, Puls*) irregular
Unglück ['ʊnglʏk] *nt* misfortune; (*Pech*) bad luck; (*Unglücksfall*) calamity, disaster; (*Verkehrsunglück*) accident; **zu allem ~** to make matters worse; **unglücklich** *adj* unhappy; (*erfolglos*) unlucky; (*unerfreulich*) unfortunate; **unglücklicherweise** *adv* unfortunately; **unglückselig** *adj* calamitous; (*Person*) unfortunate
Unglücksfall *m* accident, mishap
Unglücksrabe (*umg*) *m* unlucky thing
Ungnade ['ʊngna:də] *f*: **bei jdm in ~ fallen** to fall out of favour (*Brit*) *od* favor (*US*) with sb
ungültig ['ʊngʏltɪç] *adj* invalid; **etw für ~ erklären** to declare sth null and void; **Ungültigkeit** *f* invalidity
ungünstig ['ʊngʏnstɪç] *adj* unfavourable (*Brit*), unfavorable (*US*); (*Termin*) inconvenient; (*Augenblick, Wetter*) bad; (*nicht preiswert*) expensive
ungut ['ʊngu:t] *adj* (*Gefühl*) uneasy; **nichts für ~!** no offence!
unhaltbar ['ʊnhaltba:r] *adj* untenable
unhandlich ['ʊnhantlɪç] *adj* unwieldy
Unheil ['ʊnhaɪl] *nt* evil; (*Unglück*) misfortune; **~ anrichten** to cause mischief; **~ bringend** fatal, fateful
unheilbar [ʊn'haɪlbar] *adj* incurable
unheilvoll *adj* disastrous
unheimlich ['ʊnhaɪmlɪç] *adj* weird, uncanny ▷ *adv* (*umg*) tremendously; **das/er ist mir ~** it/he gives me the creeps (*umg*)
unhöflich ['ʊnhø:flɪç] *adj* impolite; **Unhöflichkeit** *f* impoliteness
unhörbar [ʊn'hø:rba:r] *adj* silent; (*Frequenzen*) inaudible
unhygienisch ['ʊnhygie:nɪʃ] *adj* unhygienic
Uni ['ʊni] (**-, -s**) (*umg*) *f* university
uni ['yni:] *adj* self-coloured (*Brit*), self-colored (*US*)
Uniform [uni'fɔrm] (**-, -en**) *f* uniform
uniformiert [unifɔr'mi:rt] *adj* uniformed
Unikum ['u:nɪkʊm] (**-s, -s** *od* **Unika**) (*umg*) *nt* real character
uninteressant ['ʊn|ɪntərɛsant] *adj* uninteresting
uninteressiert ['ʊn|ɪntərɛ'si:rt] *adj*: **~ (an** *+dat***)** uninterested (in), not interested (in)
Union [uni'o:n] *f* union
Unionsparteien *pl* (*BRD Pol*) CDU and CSU parties *pl*
universal [univɛr'za:l] *adj* universal
universell [univɛr'zɛl] *adj* universal
Universität [univɛrzi'tɛ:t] *f* university; **auf die ~ gehen, die ~ besuchen** to go to university
Universum [uni'vɛrzʊm] (**-s**) *nt* universe
unkenntlich ['ʊnkɛntlɪç] *adj* unrecognizable; **Unkenntlichkeit** *f*: **bis zur Unkenntlichkeit** beyond recognition
Unkenntnis ['ʊnkɛntnɪs] *f* ignorance
unklar ['ʊnkla:r] *adj* unclear; **im U~en sein über** *+akk* to be in the dark about; **Unklarheit** *f* unclarity; (*Unentschiedenheit*) uncertainty
unklug ['ʊnklu:k] *adj* unwise
unkompliziert ['ʊnkɔmplitsi:rt] *adj* straightforward, uncomplicated
unkontrolliert ['ʊnkɔntrɔli:rt] *adj* unchecked
unkonzentriert ['ʊnkɔntsɛntri:rt] *adj* lacking in concentration
Unkosten ['ʊnkɔstən] *pl* expense(s *pl*); **sich in ~ stürzen** (*umg*) to go to a lot of expense

Unkraut ['ʊnkraʊt] *nt* weed; weeds *pl*; **~ vergeht nicht** (*Sprichwort*) it would take more than that to finish me/him *etc* off; **Unkrautvertilgungsmittel** *nt* weedkiller
unlängst ['ʊnlɛŋst] *adv* not long ago
unlauter ['ʊnlaʊtər] *adj* unfair
unleserlich ['ʊnle:zərlɪç] *adj* illegible
unleugbar ['ʊnlɔʏkba:r] *adj* undeniable, indisputable
unlogisch ['ʊnlo:gɪʃ] *adj* illogical
unlösbar [ʊn'lø:sbar] *adj* insoluble
unlöslich [ʊn'lø:slɪç] *adj* insoluble
Unlust ['ʊnlʊst] *f* lack of enthusiasm
unlustig *adj* unenthusiastic ▷ *adv* without enthusiasm
unmännlich ['ʊnmɛnlɪç] *adj* unmanly
Unmasse ['ʊnmasə] (*umg*) *f* load
unmäßig ['ʊnmɛ:sɪç] *adj* immoderate
Unmenge ['ʊnmɛŋə] *f* tremendous number, vast number
Unmensch ['ʊnmɛnʃ] *m* ogre, brute; **unmenschlich** *adj* inhuman, brutal; (*ungeheuer*) awful
unmerklich [ʊn'mɛrklɪç] *adj* imperceptible
unmissverständlich ['ʊnmɪsfɛrʃtɛntlɪç] *adj* unmistakable
unmittelbar ['ʊnmɪtəlba:r] *adj* immediate; **~er Kostenaufwand** direct expense
unmöbliert ['ʊnmøbli:rt] *adj* unfurnished
unmöglich ['ʊnmø:klɪç] *adj* impossible; **ich kann es ~ tun** I can't possibly do it; **~ aussehen** (*umg*) to look ridiculous; **Unmöglichkeit** *f* impossibility
unmoralisch ['ʊnmora:lɪʃ] *adj* immoral
unmotiviert ['ʊnmotivi:rt] *adj* unmotivated
unmündig ['ʊnmʏndɪç] *adj* (*minderjährig*) underage
Unmut ['ʊnmu:t] *m* ill humour (*Brit*) *od* humor (*US*)
unnachahmlich ['ʊnna:x|a:mlɪç] *adj* inimitable
unnachgiebig ['ʊnna:xgi:bɪç] *adj* unyielding
unnahbar [ʊn'na:ba:r] *adj* unapproachable
unnatürlich ['ʊnnaty:rlɪç] *adj* unnatural
unnormal ['ʊnnɔrma:l] *adj* abnormal
unnötig ['ʊnnø:tɪç] *adj* unnecessary
unnötigerweise *adv* unnecessarily
unnütz ['ʊnnʏts] *adj* useless
UNO ['u:no] *f abk* (= *United Nations Organization*): **die ~** the UN
unordentlich ['ʊn|ɔrdəntlɪç] *adj* untidy
Unordnung ['ʊn|ɔrdnʊŋ] *f* disorder; (*Durcheinander*) mess
unorganisiert ['ʊn|ɔrganizi:rt] *adj* disorganized
unparteiisch ['ʊnpartaɪɪʃ] *adj* impartial
Unparteiische, r *f(m)* umpire; (*Fussball*) referee
unpassend ['ʊnpasənt] *adj* inappropriate; (*Zeit*) inopportune
unpässlich ['ʊnpɛslɪç] *adj* unwell
unpersönlich ['ʊnpɛrzø:nlɪç] *adj* impersonal
unpolitisch ['ʊnpoli:tɪʃ] *adj* apolitical
unpraktisch ['ʊnpraktɪʃ] *adj* impractical, unpractical
unproduktiv ['ʊnprodʊkti:f] *adj* unproductive
unproportioniert ['ʊnpropɔrtsioni:rt] *adj* out of proportion
unpünktlich ['ʊnpʏŋktlɪç] *adj* unpunctual
unqualifiziert ['ʊnkvalifitsi:rt] *adj* unqualified; (*Äußerung*) incompetent
unrasiert ['ʊnrazi:rt] *adj* unshaven
Unrat ['ʊnra:t] (**-(e)s**) *m* (*geh*) refuse; (*fig*) filth
unrationell ['ʊnratsionɛl] *adj* inefficient
unrecht ['ʊnrɛçt] *adj* wrong; **das ist mir gar nicht so ~** I don't really mind; **~ haben** to be wrong; **Unrecht** *nt* wrong; **zu Unrecht** wrongly; **nicht zu Unrecht** not without good reason; **im Unrecht sein** to be wrong
unrechtmäßig *adj* unlawful, illegal
unredlich ['ʊnre:tlɪç] *adj* dishonest; **Unredlichkeit** *f* dishonesty
unreell ['ʊnreɛl] *adj* unfair; (*unredlich*) dishonest; (*Preis*) unreasonable
unregelmäßig ['ʊnre:gəlmɛ:sɪç] *adj* irregular; **Unregelmäßigkeit** *f* irregularity
unreif ['ʊnraɪf] *adj* (*Obst*) unripe; (*fig*) immature
Unreife *f* immaturity
unrein ['ʊnraɪn] *adj* not clean; (*Ton, Gedanken, Taten*) impure; (*Atem, Haut*) bad
unrentabel ['ʊnrɛnta:bəl] *adj* unprofitable
unrichtig ['ʊnrɪçtɪç] *adj* incorrect, wrong
Unruh ['ʊnru:] (**-, -en**) *f* (*von Uhr*) balance
Unruhe (**-, -n**) *f* unrest; **Unruheherd** *m* trouble spot; **Unruhestifter** *m* troublemaker
unruhig *adj* restless; (*nervös*) fidgety; (*belebt*) noisy; (*Schlaf*) fitful; (*Zeit etc, Meer*) troubled
unrühmlich ['ʊnry:mlɪç] *adj* inglorious
uns [ʊns] *pron akk, dat von* **wir** us; (*reflexiv*) ourselves
unsachgemäß ['ʊnzaxgəmɛ:s] *adj* improper
unsachlich ['ʊnzaxlɪç] *adj* not to the point, irrelevant; (*persönlich*) personal
unsagbar [ʊn'za:kba:r] *adj* indescribable
unsäglich [ʊn'zɛ:klɪç] *adj* indescribable
unsanft ['ʊnzanft] *adj* rough
unsauber ['ʊnzaʊbər] *adj* (*schmutzig*) dirty; (*fig*) crooked; (*: Klang*) impure
unschädlich ['ʊnʃɛ:tlɪç] *adj* harmless; **jdn/etw ~ machen** to render sb/sth harmless
unscharf ['ʊnʃarf] *adj* indistinct; (*Bild etc*) out of focus, blurred
unschätzbar [ʊn'ʃɛtsba:r] *adj* incalculable; (*Hilfe*) invaluable
unscheinbar ['ʊnʃaɪnba:r] *adj* insignificant; (*Aussehen, Haus etc*) unprepossessing
unschlagbar [ʊn'ʃla:kba:r] *adj* invincible
unschlüssig ['ʊnʃlʏsɪç] *adj* undecided
unschön ['ʊnʃø:n] *adj* unsightly; (*lit, fig: Szene*) ugly; (*Vorfall*) unpleasant
Unschuld ['ʊnʃʊlt] *f* innocence
unschuldig ['ʊnʃʊldɪç] *adj* innocent
Unschuldsmiene *f* innocent expression
unschwer ['ʊnʃve:r] *adv* easily, without difficulty
unselbstständig ['ʊnzɛlpstʃtɛndɪç], **unselbständig** ['ʊnzɛlpʃtɛndɪç] *adj*

dependent, over-reliant on others
unselig ['ʊnze:lɪç] *adj* unfortunate; (*verhängnisvoll*) ill-fated
unser ['ʊnzər] *poss pron* our ▷ *pron gen von* **wir** of us
unsere, r, s *poss pron* ours; **wir tun das U~** (*geh*) we are doing our bit
unsereiner *pron* the likes of us
unsereins *pron* the likes of us
unsererseits ['ʊnzərər'zaɪts] *adv* on our part
unseresgleichen *pron* the likes of us
unserige, r, s *poss pron*: **der/die/das U~** ours
unseriös ['ʊnzeriø:s] *adj* (*unehrlich*) not straight, untrustworthy
unserseits ['ʊnzər'zaɪts] *adv* = **unsererseits**
unsertwegen ['ʊnzərt've:gən] *adv* (*für uns*) for our sake; (*wegen uns*) on our account
unsertwillen ['ʊnzərt'vɪlən] *adv*: **um ~** = **unsertwegen**
unsicher ['ʊnzɪçər] *adj* uncertain; (*Mensch*) insecure; **die Gegend ~ machen** (*fig: umg*) to knock about the district; **Unsicherheit** *f* uncertainty; insecurity
unsichtbar ['ʊnzɪçtba:r] *adj* invisible; **Unsichtbarkeit** *f* invisibility
Unsinn ['ʊnzɪn] *m* nonsense
unsinnig *adj* nonsensical
Unsitte ['ʊnzɪtə] *f* deplorable habit
unsittlich ['ʊnzɪtlɪç] *adj* indecent; **Unsittlichkeit** *f* indecency
unsolide ['ʊnzoli:də] *adj* (*Mensch, Leben*) loose; (*Firma*) unreliable
unsozial ['ʊnzotsia:l] *adj* (*Verhalten*) antisocial; (*Politik*) unsocial
unsportlich ['ʊnʃpɔrtlɪç] *adj* not sporty; (*Verhalten*) unsporting
unsre *etc* ['ʊnzrə] *poss pron* = **unsere** *etc*; *siehe auch* **unser**
unsrige, r, s ['ʊnzrɪgə(r, s)] *poss pron* = **unserige**
unsterblich ['ʊnʃtɛrplɪç] *adj* immortal; **Unsterblichkeit** *f* immortality
unstet ['ʊnʃte:t] *adj* (*Mensch*) restless; (*wankelmütig*) changeable; (*Leben*) unsettled
Unstimmigkeit ['ʊnʃtɪmɪçkaɪt] *f* inconsistency; (*Streit*) disagreement
Unsumme ['ʊnzʊmə] *f* vast sum
unsympathisch ['ʊnzʏmpa:tɪʃ] *adj* unpleasant; **er ist mir ~** I don't like him
untadelig ['ʊnta:dəlɪç], **untadlig** ['ʊnta:dlɪç] *adj* impeccable; (*Mensch*) beyond reproach
Untat ['ʊnta:t] *f* atrocity
untätig ['ʊntɛ:tɪç] *adj* idle
untauglich ['ʊntaʊklɪç] *adj* unsuitable; (*Mil*) unfit; **Untauglichkeit** *f* unsuitability; unfitness
unteilbar [ʊn'taɪlba:r] *adj* indivisible
unten ['ʊntən] *adv* below; (*im Haus*) downstairs; (*an der Treppe etc*) at the bottom; **~ genannt** undermentioned; **siehe ~** see below; **nach ~** down; **~ am Berg** *etc* at the bottom of the mountain *etc*; **er ist bei mir ~ durch** (*umg*) I'm through with him; **untenan** *adv* (*am unteren Ende*) at the far end; (*lit, fig*) at the bottom

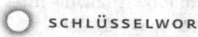

SCHLÜSSELWORT

unter ['ʊntər] *präp +dat* **1** (*räumlich*) under; (*drunter*) underneath, below
2 (*zwischen*) among(st); **sie waren unter sich** they were by themselves; **einer unter ihnen** one of them; **unter anderem** among other things; **unter der Hand** secretly; (*verkaufen*) privately
▷ *präp +akk* under, below
▷ *adv* (*weniger als*) under; **Mädchen unter 18 Jahren** girls under *od* less than 18 (years of age)

Unter- *zW*: **Unterabteilung** *f* subdivision; **Unterarm** *m* forearm; **unterbelegt** *adj* (*Kurs*) under-subscribed; (*Hotel etc*) not full
unterbelichten ['ʊntərbəlɪçtən] *vt untr* (*Phot*) to underexpose
Unterbeschäftigung ['ʊntərbəʃɛ:ftɪgʊŋ] *f* underemployment
unterbesetzt ['ʊntərbəzetst] *adj* understaffed
Unterbewusstsein ['ʊntərbəvʊstzaɪn] *nt* subconscious
unterbezahlt ['ʊntərbətsa:lt] *adj* underpaid
unterbieten [ʊntər'bi:tən] *unreg vt untr* (*Comm*) to undercut; (*fig*) to surpass
unterbinden [ʊntər'bɪndən] *unreg vt untr* to stop, call a halt to
unterbleiben [ʊntər'blaɪbən] *unreg vi untr* (*aufhören*) to stop; (*versäumt werden*) to be omitted
Unterbodenschutz [ʊntər'bo:dənʃʊts] *m* (*Aut*) underseal
unterbrechen [ʊntər'brɛçən] *unreg vt untr* to interrupt
Unterbrechung *f* interruption
unterbreiten [ʊntər'braɪtən] *vt untr* (*Plan*) to present
unterbringen ['ʊntərbrɪŋən] *unreg vt* (*in Koffer*) to stow; (*in Zeitung*) to place; (*Person: in Hotel etc*) to accommodate, put up; (*: beruflich*): **~ (bei)** to fix up (with)
unterbuttern ['ʊntərbʊtərn] (*umg*) *vt* (*zuschießen*) to throw in; (*unterdrücken*) to ride roughshod over
unterdessen [ʊntər'dɛsən] *adv* meanwhile
Unterdruck ['ʊntərdrʊk] *m* (*Tech*) below atmospheric pressure
unterdrücken [ʊntər'drʏkən] *vt untr* to suppress; (*Leute*) to oppress
untere, r, s ['ʊntərə(r, s)] *adj* lower
untereinander [ʊntər|aɪ'nandər] *adv* (*gegenseitig*) each other; (*miteinander*) among themselves *etc*
unterentwickelt ['ʊntər|ɛntvɪkəlt] *adj* underdeveloped
unterernährt ['ʊntər|ɛrnɛ:rt] *adj* undernourished
Unterernährung *f* malnutrition
Unterfangen [ʊntər'faŋən] *nt* undertaking
Unterführung [ʊntər|fy:rʊŋ] *f* subway,

underpass

Untergang ['ʊntərgaŋ] *m* (down)fall, decline; (*Naut*) sinking; (*von Gestirn*) setting; **dem ~ geweiht sein** to be doomed

untergeben [ʊntər'ge:bən] *adj* subordinate

Untergebene, r *f(m)* subordinate

untergehen ['ʊntərge:ən] *unreg vi* to go down; (*Sonne*) to set, go down; (*Staat*) to fall; (*Volk*) to perish; (*Welt*) to come to an end; (*im Lärm*) to be drowned

untergeordnet ['ʊntərgə|ɔrdnət] *adj* (*Dienststelle*) subordinate; (*Bedeutung*) secondary

Untergeschoss ['ʊntərgəʃɔs] *nt* basement

Untergewicht ['ʊntərgeviçt] *nt*: **(10 Kilo) ~ haben** to be (10 kilos) underweight

untergliedern [ʊntər'gli:dərn] *vt untr* to subdivide

untergraben [ʊntər'gra:bən] *unreg vt untr* to undermine

Untergrund ['ʊntərgrʊnt] *m* foundation; (*Pol*) underground; **Untergrundbahn** *f* underground (*Brit*), subway (*US*); **Untergrundbewegung** *f* underground (movement)

unterhaken ['ʊntərha:kən] *vr*: **sich bei jdm ~** to link arms with sb

unterhalb ['ʊntərhalp] *präp +gen* below ▷ *adv* below; **~ von** below

Unterhalt ['ʊntərhalt] *m* maintenance; **seinen ~ verdienen** to earn one's living

unterhalten [ʊntər'haltən] *unreg vt untr* to maintain; (*belustigen*) to entertain; (*versorgen*) to support; (*Geschäft, Kfz*) to run; (*Konto*) to have ▷ *vr untr* to talk; (*sich belustigen*) to enjoy o.s.

unterhaltend, unterhaltsam [ʊntər'haltza:m] *adj* entertaining

Unterhaltskosten *pl* maintenance costs *pl*

Unterhaltszahlung *f* maintenance payment

Unterhaltung *f* maintenance; (*Belustigung*) entertainment, amusement; (*Gespräch*) talk

Unterhaltungskosten *pl* running costs *pl*

Unterhaltungsmusik *f* light music

Unterhändler ['ʊntərhɛntlər] *m* negotiator

Unterhaus ['ʊntərhaus] *nt* House of Commons (*Brit*), House of Representatives (*US*), Lower House

Unterhemd ['ʊntərhɛmt] *nt* vest (*Brit*), undershirt (*US*)

unterhöhlen [ʊntər'hø:lən] *vt untr* (*lit, fig*) to undermine

Unterholz ['ʊntərhɔlts] *nt* undergrowth

Unterhose ['ʊntərho:zə] *f* underpants *pl*

unterirdisch ['ʊntər|ɪrdɪʃ] *adj* underground

unterjubeln ['ʊntərjubəln] (*umg*) *vt*: **jdm etw ~** to palm sth off on sb

unterkapitalisiert ['ʊntərkapitali'zi:rt] *adj* undercapitalized

unterkellern [ʊntər'kɛlərn] *vt untr* to build with a cellar

Unterkiefer ['ʊntərki:fər] *m* lower jaw

unterkommen ['ʊntərkɔmən] *unreg vi* to find shelter; (*Stelle finden*) to find work; **das ist mir noch nie untergekommen** I've never met with that; **bei jdm ~** to stay at sb's (place)

unterkriegen ['ʊntərkri:gən] (*umg*) *vt*: **sich nicht ~ lassen** not to let things get one down

unterkühlt [ʊntər'ky:lt] *adj* (*Körper*) affected by hypothermia; (*fig: Mensch, Atmosphäre*) cool

Unterkunft ['ʊntərkʊnft] (**-, -künfte**) *f* accommodation (*Brit*), accommodations *pl* (*US*); **~ und Verpflegung** board and lodging

Unterlage ['ʊntərla:gə] *f* foundation; (*Beleg*) document; (*Schreibunterlage etc*) pad

unterlassen [ʊntər'lasən] *unreg vt untr* (*versäumen*) to fail to do; (*sich enthalten*) to refrain from

unterlaufen [ʊntər'laufən] *unreg vi untr* to happen ▷ *adj*: **mit Blut ~** suffused with blood; (*Augen*) bloodshot; **mir ist ein Fehler ~** I made a mistake

unterlegen[1] ['ʊntərle:gən] *vt* to lay *od* put under

unterlegen[2] [ʊntər'le:gən] *adj* inferior; (*besiegt*) defeated

Unterleib ['ʊntərlaɪp] *m* abdomen

unterliegen [ʊntər'li:gən] *unreg vi untr +dat* to be defeated *od* overcome (by); (*unterworfen sein*) to be subject (to)

Unterlippe ['ʊntərlɪpə] *f* bottom *od* lower lip

unterm = **unter dem**

untermalen [ʊntər'ma:lən] *vt untr* (*mit Musik*) to provide with background music

Untermalung *f*: **musikalische ~** background music

untermauern [ʊntər'mauərn] *vt untr* (*Gebäude, fig*) to underpin

Untermiete ['ʊntərmi:tə] *f* subtenancy; **bei jdm zur ~ wohnen** to rent a room from sb

Untermieter, in *m(f)* lodger

untern = **unter den**

unternehmen [ʊntər'ne:mən] *unreg vt untr* to do; (*durchführen*) to undertake; (*Versuch, Reise*) to make; **Unternehmen** (**-s, -**) *nt* undertaking, enterprise (*auch COMM*); (*Firma*) business

unternehmend *adj* enterprising, daring

Unternehmensberater *m* management consultant

Unternehmensplanung *f* corporate planning, management planning

Unternehmer, in [ʊntər'ne:mər(ɪn)] (**-s, -**) *m(f)* (business) employer; (*alten Stils*) entrepreneur; **Unternehmerverband** *m* employers' association

Unternehmungsgeist *m* spirit of enterprise

unternehmungslustig *adj* enterprising

Unteroffizier ['ʊntər|ɔfɪtsi:r] *m* noncommissioned officer, NCO

unterordnen ['ʊntər|ɔrdnən] *vt*: **~ (+*dat*)** to subordinate (to)

Unterordnung *f* subordination

Unterprima ['ʊntərpri:ma] *f* (*früher*) *eighth year of German secondary school*

Unterprogramm ['ʊntərprogram] *nt* (*Comput*) subroutine

Unterredung [ʊntər're:dʊŋ] *f* discussion, talk

Unterricht ['ʊntərrɪçt] (**-(e)s**) *m* teaching; (*Stunden*) lessons *pl*; **jdm ~ (in etw** *dat*) **geben** to teach sb (sth)
unterrichten [ʊntər'rɪçtən] *vt untr* to instruct; (*Sch*) to teach ▷ *vr untr*: **sich ~ (über** *+akk*) to inform o.s. (about), obtain information (about)
Unterrichts- *zW*: **Unterrichtsgegenstand** *m* topic, subject; **Unterrichtsmethode** *f* teaching method; **Unterrichtsstoff** *m* teaching material; **Unterrichtsstunde** *f* lesson; **Unterrichtszwecke** *pl*: **zu Unterrichtszwecken** for teaching purposes
Unterrock ['ʊntərrɔk] *m* petticoat, slip
unters = **unter das**
untersagen [ʊntər'za:gən] *vt untr* to forbid; **jdm etw ~** to forbid sb to do sth
Untersatz ['ʊntərzats] *m* mat; (*für Blumentöpfe etc*) base
unterschätzen [ʊntər'ʃɛtsən] *vt untr* to underestimate
unterscheiden [ʊntər'ʃaɪdən] *unreg vt untr* to distinguish ▷ *vr untr* to differ
Unterscheidung *f* (*Unterschied*) distinction; (*Unterscheiden*) differentiation
Unterschenkel ['ʊntərʃɛŋkəl] *m* lower leg
Unterschicht ['ʊntərʃɪçt] *f* lower class
unterschieben ['ʊntərʃi:bən] *unreg vt* (*fig*): **jdm etw ~** to foist sth on sb
Unterschied ['ʊntərʃi:t] (**-(e)s, -e**) *m* difference, distinction; **im ~ zu** as distinct from; **unterschiedlich** *adj* varying, differing; (*diskriminierend*) discriminatory
unterschiedslos *adv* indiscriminately
unterschlagen [ʊntər'ʃlagən] *unreg vt untr* to embezzle; (*verheimlichen*) to suppress
Unterschlagung *f* embezzlement; (*von Briefen, Beweis*) withholding
Unterschlupf ['ʊntərʃlʊpf] (**-(e)s, -schlüpfe**) *m* refuge
unterschlüpfen ['ʊntərʃlʏpfən] (*umg*) *vi* to take cover *od* shelter; (*Versteck finden*): **(bei jdm) ~** to hide out (at sb's) (*umg*)
unterschreiben [ʊntər'ʃraɪbən] *unreg vt untr* to sign
Unterschrift ['ʊntərʃrɪft] *f* signature; (*Bildunterschrift*) caption
unterschwellig ['ʊntərʃvɛlɪç] *adj* subliminal
Unterseeboot ['ʊntərze:bo:t] *nt* submarine
Unterseite ['ʊntərzaɪtə] *f* underside
Untersekunda ['ʊntərzekunda] *f* (*früher*) *sixth year of German secondary school*
Untersetzer ['ʊntərzɛtsər] *m* tablemat; (*für Gläser*) coaster
untersetzt [ʊntər'zɛtst] *adj* stocky
unterste, r, s ['ʊntərstə(r, s)] *adj* lowest, bottom
unterstehen[1] [ʊntər'ʃte:ən] *unreg vi untr +dat* to be under ▷ *vr untr* to dare
unterstehen[2] ['ʊntərʃte:ən] *unreg vi* to shelter
unterstellen[1] [ʊntər'ʃtelən] *vt untr* to subordinate; (*fig*) to impute; **jdm/etw unterstellt sein** to be under sb/sth; (*in Firma*) to report to sb/sth
unterstellen[2] ['ʊntərʃtɛlən] *vt* (*Auto*) to garage, park ▷ *vr* to take shelter
Unterstellung *f* (*falsche Behauptung*) misrepresentation; (*Andeutung*) insinuation
unterstreichen [ʊntər'ʃtraɪçən] *unreg vt untr* (*lit, fig*) to underline
Unterstufe ['ʊntərʃtu:fə] *f* lower grade
unterstützen [ʊntər'ʃtʏtsən] *vt untr* to support
Unterstützung *f* support, assistance
untersuchen [ʊntər'zu:xən] *vt untr* (*Med*) to examine; (*Polizei*) to investigate; **sich ärztlich ~ lassen** to have a medical (*Brit*) *od* physical (*US*) (examination), have a check-up
Untersuchung *f* examination; investigation, inquiry
Untersuchungs- *zW*: **Untersuchungsausschuss** *m* committee of inquiry; **Untersuchungsergebnis** *nt* (*Jur*) findings *pl*; (*Med*) result of an examination; **Untersuchungshaft** *f* custody; **in Untersuchungshaft sein** to be remanded in custody; **Untersuchungsrichter** *m* examining magistrate
Untertagebau [ʊntər'ta:gəbau] *m* underground mining
Untertan ['ʊntərta:n] (**-s, -en**) *m* subject
untertänig ['ʊntərtɛ:nɪç] *adj* submissive, humble
Untertasse ['ʊntərtasə] *f* saucer
untertauchen ['ʊntərtaʊxən] *vi* to dive; (*fig*) to disappear, go underground
Unterteil ['ʊntərtaɪl] *nt od m* lower part, bottom
unterteilen [ʊntər'taɪlən] *vt untr* to divide up
Untertertia ['ʊntərtɛrtsia] *f* (*früher*) *fourth year of German secondary school*
Untertitel ['ʊntərti:təl] *m* subtitle; (*für Bild*) caption
unterwandern [ʊntər'vandərn] *vt untr* to infiltrate
Unterwäsche ['ʊntərvɛʃə] *f* underwear
unterwegs [ʊntər've:ks] *adv* on the way; (*auf Reisen*) away
unterweisen [ʊntər'vaɪzən] *unreg vt untr* to instruct
Unterwelt ['ʊntərvɛlt] *f* (*lit, fig*) underworld
unterwerfen [ʊntər'vɛrfən] *unreg vt untr* to subject; (*Volk*) to subjugate ▷ *vr untr* to submit
unterwürfig [ʊntər'vʏrfɪç] *adj* obsequious
unterzeichnen [ʊntər'tsaɪçnən] *vt untr* to sign
Unterzeichner *m* signatory
unterziehen [ʊntər'tsi:ən] *unreg vt untr +dat* to subject ▷ *vr untr +dat* to undergo; (*einer Prüfung*) to take
Untiefe ['ʊnti:fə] *f* shallow
Untier ['ʊnti:r] *nt* monster
untragbar [ʊn'tra:kba:r] *adj* intolerable, unbearable
untreu ['ʊntrɔʏ] *adj* unfaithful; **sich** *dat* **selbst ~ werden** to be untrue to o.s.
Untreue *f* unfaithfulness
untröstlich [ʊn'trø:stlɪç] *adj* inconsolable

Untugend ['ʊntu:gənt] *f* vice; (*Angewohnheit*) bad habit

un- *zW*: **unüberbrückbar** *adj* (*fig: Gegensätze etc*) irreconcilable; (*Kluft*) unbridgeable; **unüberlegt** *adj* ill-considered ▷ *adv* without thinking; **unübersehbar** *adj* (*Schaden etc*) incalculable; (*Menge*) vast, immense; (*auffällig: Fehler etc*) obvious; **unübersichtlich** *adj* (*Gelände*) broken; (*Kurve*) blind; (*System, Plan*) confused; **unübertroffen** *adj* unsurpassed

un- *zW*: **unumgänglich** *adj* indispensable, vital; **unumstößlich** *adj* (*Tatsache*) incontrovertible; (*Entschluss*) irrevocable; **unumstritten** *adj* undisputed; **unumwunden** [-ʊm'vʊndən] *adj* candid ▷ *adv* straight out

ununterbrochen ['ʊn|ʊntərbrɔxən] *adj* uninterrupted

un- *zW*: **unveränderlich** *adj* unchangeable; **unverantwortlich** *adj* irresponsible; (*unentschuldbar*) inexcusable; **unverarbeitet** *adj* (*lit, fig*) raw; **unveräußerlich** [-fɛr'ɔʏsərlich] *adj* inalienable; (*Besitz*) unmarketable; **unverbesserlich** *adj* incorrigible; **unverbindlich** *adj* not binding; (*Antwort*) curt ▷ *adv* (*Comm*) without obligation; **unverbleit** [-fɛrblaɪt] *adj* (*Benzin*) unleaded; **unverblümt** [-fɛr'bly:mt] *adj* plain, blunt ▷ *adv* plainly, bluntly; **unverdaulich** *adj* indigestible; **unverdorben** *adj* unspoilt; **unverdrossen** *adj* undeterred; (*unermüdlich*) untiring; **unvereinbar** *adj* incompatible; **unverfälscht** [-fɛrfɛlʃt] *adj* (*auch fig*) unadulterated; (*Dialekt*) pure; (*Natürlichkeit*) unaffected; **unverfänglich** *adj* harmless; **unverfroren** *adj* impudent; **unvergänglich** *adj* immortal; (*Eindruck, Erinnerung*) everlasting; **unvergesslich** *adj* unforgettable; **unvergleichlich** *adj* unique, incomparable; **unverhältnismäßig** *adv* disproportionately; (*übermäßig*) excessively; **unverheiratet** *adj* unmarried; **unverhofft** *adj* unexpected; **unverhohlen** [-fɛrho:lən] *adj* open, unconcealed; **unverkäuflich** *adj*: **„unverkäuflich"** "not for sale"; **unverkennbar** *adj* unmistakable; **unverletzlich** *adj* (*fig: Rechte*) inviolable; (*lit*) invulnerable; **unverletzt** *adj* uninjured; **unvermeidlich** *adj* unavoidable; **unvermittelt** *adj* (*plötzlich*) sudden, unexpected; **Unvermögen** *nt* inability; **unvermutet** *adj* unexpected; **unvernünftig** *adj* foolish; **unverrichtet** *adj*: **unverrichteter Dinge** empty-handed; **unverschämt** *adj* impudent; **Unverschämtheit** *f* impudence, insolence; **unverschuldet** *adj* occurring through no fault of one's own; **unversehens** *adv* all of a sudden; **unversehrt** [-fɛrze:rt] *adj* uninjured; **unversöhnlich** *adj* irreconcilable; **Unverstand** *m* lack of judgement; (*Torheit*) folly; **unverständlich** *adj* unintelligible; **unversucht** *adj*: **nichts unversucht lassen** to try everything; **unverträglich** *adj* quarrelsome; (*Meinungen, Med*) incompatible; **unverwechselbar** *adj* unmistakable, distinctive; **unverwüstlich** *adj* indestructible; (*Mensch*) irrepressible; **unverzeihlich** *adj* unpardonable; **unverzinslich** *adj* interest-free; **unverzüglich** [-fɛr'tsy:klɪç] *adj* immediate; **unvollendet** *adj* unfinished; **unvollkommen** *adj* imperfect; **unvollständig** *adj* incomplete; **unvorbereitet** *adj* unprepared; **unvoreingenommen** *adj* unbiased; **unvorhergesehen** *adj* unforeseen; **unvorsichtig** *adj* careless, imprudent; **unvorstellbar** *adj* inconceivable; **unvorteilhaft** *adj* disadvantageous

unwahr ['ʊnva:r] *adj* untrue; **unwahrhaftig** *adj* untruthful; **Unwahrheit** *f* untruth; **die Unwahrheit sagen** not to tell the truth; **unwahrscheinlich** *adj* improbable, unlikely ▷ *adv* (*umg*) incredibly; **Unwahrscheinlichkeit** *f* improbability, unlikelihood

unwegsam ['ʊnve:kza:m] *adj* (*Gelände etc*) rough

unweigerlich [ʊn'vaɪgərlɪç] *adj* unquestioning ▷ *adv* without fail

unweit ['ʊnvaɪt] *präp +gen* not far from ▷ *adv* not far

Unwesen ['ʊnve:zən] *nt* nuisance; (*Unfug*) mischief; **sein ~ treiben** to wreak havoc; (*Mörder etc*) to be at large

unwesentlich *adj* inessential, unimportant; **~ besser** marginally better

Unwetter ['ʊnvɛtər] *nt* thunderstorm

unwichtig ['ʊnvɪçtɪç] *adj* unimportant

un- *zW*: **unwiderlegbar** *adj* irrefutable; **unwiderruflich** *adj* irrevocable; **unwiderstehlich** [-vi:dər'ʃte:lɪç] *adj* irresistible

unwiederbringlich [ʊnvi:dər'brɪŋlɪç] *adj* (*geh*) irretrievable

Unwille ['ʊnvɪlə], **Unwillen** ['ʊnvɪlən] *m* indignation

unwillig *adj* indignant; (*widerwillig*) reluctant

unwillkürlich ['ʊnvɪlky:rlɪç] *adj* involuntary ▷ *adv* instinctively; (*lachen*) involuntarily

unwirklich ['ʊnvɪrklɪç] *adj* unreal

unwirksam ['ʊnvɪrkza:m] *adj* ineffective

unwirsch ['ʊnvɪrʃ] *adj* cross, surly

unwirtlich ['ʊnvɪrtlɪç] *adj* inhospitable

unwirtschaftlich ['ʊnvɪrtʃaftlɪç] *adj* uneconomical

unwissend ['ʊnvɪsənt] *adj* ignorant

Unwissenheit *f* ignorance

unwissenschaftlich *adj* unscientific

unwissentlich *adv* unwittingly, unknowingly

unwohl ['ʊnvo:l] *adj* unwell, ill; **Unwohlsein** (**-s**) *nt* indisposition

unwürdig ['ʊnvʏrdɪç] *adj* unworthy

Unzahl ['ʊntsa:l] *f*: **eine ~ von ...** a whole host of ...

unzählig [ʊn'tsɛ:lɪç] *adj* innumerable, countless

unzeitgemäß ['ʊntsaɪtgəmɛ:s] *adj* (*altmodisch*) old-fashioned

un- *zW*: **unzerbrechlich** *adj* unbreakable; **unzerreißbar** *adj* untearable; **unzerstörbar** *adj* indestructible; **unzertrennlich** *adj* inseparable

Unzucht ['ʊntsʊxt] *f* sexual offence
unzüchtig ['ʊntsʏçtɪç] *adj* immoral
un- *zW*: **unzufrieden** *adj* dissatisfied; **Unzufriedenheit** *f* discontent; **unzugänglich** *adj* (*Gegend*) inaccessible; (*Mensch*) inapproachable; **unzulänglich** *adj* inadequate; **unzulässig** *adj* inadmissible; **unzumutbar** *adj* unreasonable; **unzurechnungsfähig** *adj* irresponsible; **jdn für unzurechnungsfähig erklären lassen** (*Jur*) to have sb certified (insane); **unzusammenhängend** *adj* disconnected; (*Äußerung*) incoherent; **unzustellbar** *adj*: **falls unzustellbar, bitte an Absender zurück** if undelivered, please return to sender; **unzutreffend** *adj* incorrect; **„nzutreffendes bitte streichen"** "delete as applicable"; **unzuverlässig** *adj* unreliable
unzweckmäßig ['ʊntsvɛkmɛːsɪç] *adj* (*nicht ratsam*) inadvisable; (*unpraktisch*) impractical; (*ungeeignet*) unsuitable
unzweideutig ['ʊntsvaɪdɔʏtɪç] *adj* unambiguous
unzweifelhaft ['ʊntsvaɪfəlhaft] *adj* indubitable
üppig ['ʏpɪç] *adj* (*Frau*) curvaceous; (*Essen*) sumptuous, lavish; (*Vegetation*) luxuriant, lush; (*Haar*) thick
Ur- ['uːr] *in zw* original
Urabstimmung ['uːr|apʃtɪmʊŋ] *f* ballot
Ural [u'raːl] (**-s**) *m*: **der ~** the Ural mountains *pl*, the Urals *pl*; **Uralgebirge** *nt* Ural mountains
uralt ['uːr|alt] *adj* ancient, very old
Uran [u'raːn] (**-s**) *nt* uranium
Uraufführung *f* first performance
urbar *adj*: **die Wüste/Land ~ machen** to reclaim the desert/cultivate land
Urdu ['ʊrdu] (**-**) *nt* Urdu
Ur- *zW*: **Ureinwohner** *m* original inhabitant; **Ureltern** *pl* ancestors *pl*; **Urenkel, in** *m(f)* great-grandchild; **Urfassung** *f* original version; **Urgroßmutter** *f* great-grandmother; **Urgroßvater** *m* great-grandfather
Urheber (**-s, -**) *m* originator; (*Autor*) author; **Urheberrecht** *nt*: **Urheberrecht (an** *+dat*) copyright (on); **urheberrechtlich** *adv*: **urheberrechtlich geschützt** copyright
urig ['uːrɪç] (*umg*) *adj* (*Mensch, Atmosphäre*) earthy
Urin [u'riːn] (**-s, -e**) *m* urine
urkomisch *adj* incredibly funny
Urkunde *f* document; (*Kaufurkunde*) deed
urkundlich ['uːrkʊntlɪç] *adj* documentary
urladen ['uːrlaːdən] *vt* (*Comput*) to boot
Urlader *m* (*Comput*) bootstrap
Urlaub ['uːrlaʊp] (**-(e)s, -e**) *m* holiday(s *pl*) (*Brit*), vacation (*US*); (*Mil etc*) leave; **Urlauber** (**-s, -**) *m* holiday-maker (*Brit*), vacationer (*US*)
Urlaubs- *zW*: **Urlaubsgeld** *nt* holiday (*Brit*) *od* vacation (*US*) money; **Urlaubsort** *m* holiday (*Brit*) *od* vacation (*US*) resort; **urlaubsreif** *adj* in need of a holiday (*Brit*) *od* vacation (*US*)
Urmensch *m* primitive man
Urne ['ʊrnə] (**-, -n**) *f* urn; **zur ~ gehen** to go to the polls
urplötzlich ['uːr'plœtslɪç] (*umg*) *adv* all of a sudden
Ursache ['uːrzaxə] *f* cause; **keine ~!** (*auf Dank*) don't mention it, you're welcome; (*auf Entschuldigung*) that's all right
ursächlich ['uːrzɛçlɪç] *adj* causal
Urschrei ['uːrʃraɪ] *m* (*Psych*) primal scream
Ursprung ['uːrʃprʊŋ] *m* origin, source; (*von Fluss*) source
ursprünglich ['uːrʃprʏŋlɪç] *adj* original ▷ *adv* originally
Ursprungsland *nt* (*Comm*) country of origin
Ursprungszeugnis *nt* certificate of origin
Urteil ['ʊrtaɪl] (**-s, -e**) *nt* opinion; (*Jur*) sentence, judgement; **sich** *dat* **ein ~ über etw** *akk* **erlauben** to pass judgement on sth; **ein ~ über etw** *akk* **fällen** to pass judgement on sth; **urteilen** *vi* to judge
Urteilsbegründung *f* (*Jur*) opinion
Urteilsspruch *m* sentence; verdict
Uruguay [uru'guaːi] (**-s**) *nt* Uruguay
Uruguayer, in (**-s, -**) *m(f)* Uruguayan
uruguayisch *adj* Uruguayan
Ur- *zW*: **Urwald** *m* jungle; **urwüchsig** *adj* natural; (*Landschaft*) unspoilt; (*Humor*) earthy; **Urzeit** *f* prehistoric times *pl*
USA [uː'ɛs'|aː] *pl abk*: **die ~** the USA *sing*
USB *abk* (= *universal serial bus*) USB
Usbekistan [ʊs'beːkistaːn] (**-s**) *nt* Uzbekistan
usw. *abk* (= *und so weiter*) etc.
Utensilien [utɛn'ziːliən] *pl* utensils *pl*
Utopie [uto'piː] *f* pipe dream
utopisch [u'toːpɪʃ] *adj* utopian
u. U. *abk* (= *unter Umständen*) possibly
UV *abk* (= *ultraviolett*) U.V.
u. v. a. *abk* (= *und viele(s) andere*) and much/many more
u. v. a. m. *abk* (= *und viele(s) andere mehr*) and much/many more
u. W. *abk* (= *unseres Wissens*) to our knowledge
Ü-Wagen *m* (*Rundf, TV*) outside broadcast vehicle
uzen ['uːtsən] (*umg*) *vt, vi* to tease, kid
u. zw. *abk* = **und zwar**

Vv

V¹, v [faʊ] *nt* V, v; **V wie Viktor** ≈ V for Victor
V² [faʊ] *abk* (= *Volt*) v
VAE *pl abk* (= *Vereinigte Arabische Emirate*) UAE
vag, vage *adj* vague
Vagina [va'gi:na] (**-, Vaginen**) *f* vagina
Vakuum ['va:kuʊm] (**-s, Vakua** *od* **Vakuen**) *nt* vacuum; **vakuumverpackt** *adj* vacuum-packed
Vandalismus [vanda'lɪsmʊs] *m* vandalism
Vanille [va'nɪljə] (-) *f* vanilla; **Vanillezucker** *m* vanilla sugar
Vanillinzucker *m* vanilla sugar
variabel [vari'a:bəl] *adj*: **variable Kosten** variable costs
Variable [vari'a:blə] (**-, -n**) *f* variable
Variante [vari'antə] (**-, -n**) *f*: ~ **(zu)** variant (on)
Variation [variatsi'o:n] *f* variation
variieren [vari'i:rən] *vt, vi* to vary
Vase ['va:zə] (**-, -n**) *f* vase
Vater ['fa:tər] (**-s, ⸚**) *m* father; ~ **Staat** (*umg*) the State; **Vaterland** *nt* native country; (*bes Deutschland*) Fatherland; **Vaterlandsliebe** *f* patriotism
väterlich ['fɛ:tərlɪç] *adj* fatherly
väterlicherseits *adv* on the father's side
Vaterschaft *f* paternity
Vaterschaftsklage *f* paternity suit
Vaterstelle *f*: ~ **bei jdm vertreten** to take the place of sb's father
Vaterunser (**-s, -**) *nt* Lord's Prayer
Vati ['fa:ti] (**-s, -s**) (*umg*) *m* dad(dy)
Vatikan [vati'ka:n] (**-s**) *m* Vatican
V-Ausschnitt ['faʊ|aʊsʃnɪt] *m* V-neck
VB *abk* (= *Verhandlungsbasis*) o.i.r.o.
v. Chr. *abk* (= *vor Christus*) B.C.
Vegetarier, in [vege'ta:riər(ɪn)] (**-s, -**) *m(f)* vegetarian
vegetarisch *adj* vegetarian
Vegetation [vegetatsi'o:n] *f* vegetation
vegetativ [vegeta'ti:f] *adj* (*Biol*) vegetative; (*Med*) autonomic
vegetieren [vege'ti:rən] *vi* to vegetate; (*kärglich leben*) to eke out a bare existence
Vehikel [ve'hi:kəl] (**-s, -**) (*pej: umg*) *nt* boneshaker
Veilchen ['faɪlçən] *nt* violet; (*umg: blaues Auge*) shiner, black eye
Velours (**-, -**) *nt* suede; **Veloursleder** *nt* suede
Vene ['ve:nə] (**-, -n**) *f* vein
Venedig [ve'ne:dɪç] (**-s**) *nt* Venice
Venezianer, in [venetsi'a:nər(ɪn)] (**-s, -**) *m(f)* Venetian
venezianisch [venetsi'a:nɪʃ] *adj* Venetian
Venezolaner, in [venetso'la:nər(ɪn)] (**-s, -**) *m(f)* Venezuelan
venezolanisch *adj* Venezuelan
Venezuela [venetsu'e:la] (**-s**) *nt* Venezuela
Ventil [vɛn'ti:l] (**-s, -e**) *nt* valve
Ventilator [vɛnti'la:tɔr] *m* ventilator
verabreden [fɛr'|apre:dən] *vt* to arrange; (*Termin*) to agree upon ▷ *vr* to arrange to meet; **sich (mit jdm)** ~ to arrange to meet (sb); **schon verabredet sein** to have a prior engagement (*form*), have something else on
Verabredung *f* arrangement; (*Treffen*) appointment; **ich habe eine** ~ I'm meeting somebody
verabreichen [fɛr'|apraɪçən] *vt* (*Tracht Prügel etc*) to give; (*Arznei*) to administer (*form*)
verabscheuen [fɛr'|apʃɔyən] *vt* to detest, abhor
verabschieden [fɛr'|apʃi:dən] *vt* (*Gäste*) to say goodbye to; (*entlassen*) to discharge; (*Gesetz*) to pass ▷ *vr*: **sich ~ (von)** to take one's leave (of)
Verabschiedung *f* (*von Beamten etc*) discharge; (*von Gesetz*) passing
verachten [fɛr'|axtən] *vt* to despise; **nicht zu** ~ (*umg*) not to be scoffed at
verächtlich [fɛr'|ɛçtlɪç] *adj* contemptuous; (*verachtenswert*) contemptible; **jdn ~ machen** to run sb down
Verachtung *f* contempt; **jdn mit ~ strafen** to treat sb with contempt
veralbern [fɛr'|albərn] (*umg*) *vt* to make fun of
verallgemeinern [fɛr|algə'maɪnərn] *vt* to generalize
Verallgemeinerung *f* generalization
veralten [fɛr'|altən] *vi* to become obsolete *od* out-of-date
Veranda [ve'randa] (**-, Veranden**) *f* veranda
veränderlich [fɛr'|ɛndərlɪç] *adj* variable; (*Wetter*) changeable; **Veränderlichkeit** *f* variability; changeability
verändern *vt, vr* to change
Veränderung *f* change; **eine berufliche** ~ a change of job

verängstigen [fɛr'|ɛŋstɪgən] *vt* (*erschrecken*) to frighten; (*einschüchtern*) to intimidate
verankern [fɛr'|aŋkərn] *vt* (*Naut, Tech*) to anchor; (*fig*): **~ (in** *+dat***)** to embed (in)
veranlagen [fɛr'|anla:gən] *vt*: **etw ~ (mit)** to assess sth (at)
veranlagt *adj*: **praktisch ~ sein** to be practically-minded; **zu** *od* **für etw ~ sein** to be cut out for sth
Veranlagung *f* disposition, aptitude
veranlassen [fɛr'|anlasən] *vt* to cause; **Maßnahmen ~** to take measures; **sich veranlasst sehen** to feel prompted; **etw ~** to arrange for sth; (*befehlen*) to order sth
Veranlassung *f* cause; motive; **auf jds ~** *akk* **(hin)** at sb's instigation
veranschaulichen [fɛr'|anʃaʊlɪçən] *vt* to illustrate
veranschlagen [fɛr'|anʃla:gən] *vt* to estimate
veranstalten [fɛr'|anʃtaltən] *vt* to organize, arrange
Veranstalter, in (-s, -) *m(f)* organizer; (*Comm: von Konzerten etc*) promoter
Veranstaltung *f* (*Veranstalten*) organizing; (*Veranstaltetes*) event; (*feierlich, öffentlich*) function
verantworten [fɛr'|antvɔrtən] *vt* to accept responsibility for; (*Folgen etc*) to answer for ▹ *vr* to justify o.s.; **etw vor jdm ~** to answer to sb for sth
verantwortlich *adj* responsible
Verantwortung *f* responsibility; **jdn zur ~ ziehen** to call sb to account
verantwortungs- *zW*: **verantwortungsbewusst** *adj* responsible; **Verantwortungsgefühl** *nt* sense of responsibility; **verantwortungslos** *adj* irresponsible; **verantwortungsvoll** *adj* responsible
verarbeiten [fɛr'|arbaɪtən] *vt* to process; (*geistig*) to assimilate; (*Erlebnis etc*) to digest; **etw zu etw ~** to make sth into sth; **~de Industrie** processing industries *pl*
verarbeitet *adj*: **gut ~** (*Kleid etc*) well finished
Verarbeitung *f* processing; assimilation
verärgern [fɛr'|ɛrgərn] *vt* to annoy
verarmen [fɛr'|armən] *vi* (*lit, fig*) to become impoverished
verarschen [fɛr'|arʃən] (*umg!*) *vt*: **jdn ~** to take the mickey out of sb
verarzten [fɛr'|a:rtstən] *vt* to fix up (*umg*)
verausgaben [fɛr'|aʊsga:bən] *vr* to run out of money; (*fig*) to exhaust o.s.
veräußern [fɛr'|ɔʏsərn] *vt* (*form: verkaufen*) to dispose of
Verb [vɛrp] **(-s, -en)** *nt* verb
Verb. *abk* (*= Verband*) assoc.
Verband [fɛr'bant] **(-(e)s, ⸚e)** *m* (*Med*) bandage, dressing; (*Bund*) association, society; (*Mil*) unit
verband *etc vb siehe* **verbinden**
Verband- *zW*: **Verbandkasten**, **Verbandskasten** *m* medicine chest, first-aid box; **Verbandpäckchen**, **Verbandspäckchen** *nt* gauze bandage; **Verbandstoff** *m* bandage, dressing material; **Verbandzeug** *nt* bandage, dressing material
verbannen [fɛr'banən] *vt* to banish
Verbannung *f* exile
verbarrikadieren [fɛrbarika'di:rən] *vt* to barricade ▹ *vr* to barricade o.s. in
verbauen [fɛr'baʊən] *vt*: **sich** *dat* **alle Chancen ~** to spoil one's chances
verbergen [fɛr'bɛrgən] *unreg vt, vr*: **(sich) ~ (vor** *+dat***)** to hide (from)
verbessern [fɛr'bɛsərn] *vt* to improve; (*berichtigen*) to correct ▹ *vr* to improve; to correct o.s.
verbessert *adj* revised; improved; **eine neue, ~e Auflage** a new revised edition
Verbesserung *f* improvement; correction
verbeugen [fɛr'bɔʏgən] *vr* to bow
Verbeugung *f* bow
verbiegen [fɛr'bi:gən] *unreg vi* to bend
verbiestert [fɛr'bi:stərt] (*umg*) *adj* crotchety
verbieten [fɛr'bi:tən] *unreg vt* to forbid; (*amtlich*) to prohibit; (*Zeitung, Partei*) to ban; **jdm etw ~** to forbid sb to do sth
verbilligen [fɛr'bɪlɪgən] *vt* to reduce (the price of) ▹ *vr* to become cheaper, go down
verbinden [fɛr'bɪndən] *unreg vt* to connect; (*kombinieren*) to combine; (*Med*) to bandage ▹ *vr* to combine (*auch CHEM*), join (together); **jdm die Augen ~** to blindfold sb
verbindlich [fɛr'bɪntlɪç] *adj* binding; (*freundlich*) obliging; **~ zusagen** to accept definitely; **Verbindlichkeit** *f* obligation; (*Höflichkeit*) civility; **Verbindlichkeiten** *pl* (*Jur*) obligations *pl*; (*Comm*) liabilities *pl*
Verbindung *f* connection; (*Zusammensetzung*) combination; (*Chem*) compound; (*Univ*) club; (*Tel: Anschluss*) line; **mit jdm in ~ stehen** to be in touch *od* contact with sb; **~ mit jdm aufnehmen** to contact sb
Verbindungsmann (-(e)s, *pl* **-männer** *od* **-leute)** *m* intermediary; (*Agent*) contact
verbissen [fɛr'bɪsən] *adj* grim; (*Arbeiter*) dogged; **Verbissenheit** *f* grimness; doggedness
verbitten [fɛr'bɪtən] *unreg vt*: **sich** *dat* **etw ~** not to tolerate sth, not to stand for sth
verbittern [fɛr'bɪtərn] *vt* to embitter ▹ *vi* to get bitter
verblassen [fɛr'blasən] *vi* to fade
Verbleib [fɛr'blaɪp] **(-(e)s)** *m* whereabouts
verbleiben [fɛr'blaɪbən] *unreg vi* to remain; **wir sind so verblieben, dass wir ...** we agreed to ...
verbleit [fɛr'blaɪt] *adj* leaded
Verblendung [fɛr'blɛndʊŋ] *f* (*fig*) delusion
verblöden [fɛr'blø:dən] *vi* (*Hilfsverb sein*) to get stupid
verblüffen [fɛr'blʏfən] *vt* to amaze; (*verwirren*) to baffle
Verblüffung *f* stupefaction
verblühen [fɛr'bly:ən] *vi* to wither, fade
verbluten [fɛr'blu:tən] *vi* to bleed to death

verbohren [fɛrˈbo:rən] (*umg*) *vr*: **sich in etw** *akk* ~ to become obsessed with sth
verbohrt *adj* (*Haltung*) stubborn, obstinate
verborgen [fɛrˈbɔrgən] *adj* hidden; **~e Mängel** latent defects *pl*
Verbot [fɛrˈbo:t] (**-(e)s, -e**) *nt* prohibition, ban
verboten *adj* forbidden; **Rauchen ~!** no smoking; **er sah ~ aus** (*umg*) he looked a real sight
verbotenerweise *adv* though it is forbidden
Verbotsschild *nt* prohibitory sign
verbrämen [fɛrˈbrɛ:mən] *vt* (*fig*) to gloss over; (*Kritik*): ~ **(mit)** to veil (in)
Verbrauch [fɛrˈbraʊx] (**-(e)s**) *m* consumption
verbrauchen *vt* to use up; **der Wagen verbraucht 10 Liter Benzin auf 100 km** the car does 10 kms to the litre (*Brit*) *od* liter (*US*)
Verbraucher, in (**-s, -**) *m(f)* consumer; **Verbrauchermarkt** *m* hypermarket; **verbrauchernah** *adj* consumer-friendly; **Verbraucherschutz** *m* consumer protection; **Verbraucherverband** *m* consumer council
Verbrauchsgüter *pl* consumer goods *pl*
verbraucht *adj* used up, finished; (*Luft*) stale; (*Mensch*) worn-out
Verbrechen (**-s, -**) *nt* crime
Verbrecher, in (**-s, -**) *m(f)* criminal; **verbrecherisch** *adj* criminal; **Verbrecherkartei** *f* file of offenders, ≈ rogues' gallery; **Verbrechertum** (**-s**) *nt* criminality
verbreiten [fɛrˈbraɪtən] *vt* to spread; (*Licht*) to shed; (*Wärme, Ruhe*) to radiate ▷ *vr* to spread; **eine (weit) verbreitete Ansicht** a widely held opinion; **sich über etw** *akk* ~ to expound on sth
verbreitern [fɛrˈbraɪtərn] *vt* to broaden
Verbreitung *f* spread(ing); shedding; radiation
verbrennbar *adj* combustible
verbrennen [fɛrˈbrɛnən] *unreg vt* to burn; (*Leiche*) to cremate; (*versengen*) to scorch; (*Haar*) to singe; (*verbrühen*) to scald
Verbrennung *f* burning; (*in Motor*) combustion; (*von Leiche*) cremation
Verbrennungsanlage *f* incineration plant
Verbrennungsmotor *m* internal-combustion engine
verbriefen [fɛrˈbri:fən] *vt* to document
verbringen [fɛrˈbrɪŋən] *unreg vt* to spend
Verbrüderung [fɛrˈbry:dərʊŋ] *f* fraternization
verbrühen [fɛrˈbry:ən] *vt* to scald
verbuchen [fɛrˈbu:xən] *vt* (*Fin*) to register; (*Erfolg*) to enjoy; (*Misserfolg*) to suffer
verbummeln [fɛrˈbʊməln] (*umg*) *vt* (*verlieren*) to lose; (*Zeit*) to waste, fritter away; (*Verabredung*) to miss
verbunden [fɛrˈbʊndən] *adj* connected; **jdm ~ sein** to be obliged *od* indebted to sb; **ich/er** *etc* **war falsch ~** (*Tel*) it was a wrong number
verbünden [fɛrˈbʏndən] *vr* to form an alliance
Verbundenheit *f* bond, relationship
Verbündete, r *f(m)* ally
Verbundglas [fɛrˈbʊntgla:s] *nt* laminated glass
verbürgen [fɛrˈbʏrgən] *vr*: **sich ~ für** to vouch for; **ein verbürgtes Recht** an established right
verbüßen [fɛrˈby:sən] *vt*: **eine Strafe** ~ to serve a sentence
verchromt [fɛrˈkro:mt] *adj* chromium-plated
Verdacht [fɛrˈdaxt] (**-(e)s**) *m* suspicion; **~ schöpfen (gegen jdn)** to become suspicious (of sb); **jdn in ~ haben** to suspect sb; **es besteht ~ auf Krebs** *akk* cancer is suspected
verdächtig *adj* suspicious
verdächtigen [fɛrˈdɛçtɪgən] *vt* to suspect
Verdächtigung *f* suspicion
verdammen [fɛrˈdamən] *vt* to damn, condemn
Verdammnis (**-**) *f* perdition, damnation
verdammt (*umg*) *adj, adv* damned; **~ noch mal!** bloody hell (*!*), damn (*!*)
verdampfen [fɛrˈdampfən] *vt, vi* (*vi Hilfsverb sein*) to vaporize; (*Koch*) to boil away
verdanken [fɛrˈdaŋkən] *vt*: **jdm etw** ~ to owe sb sth
verdarb *etc* [fɛrˈdarp] *vb siehe* **verderben**
verdattert [fɛrˈdatərt] (*umg*) *adj, adv* flabbergasted
verdauen [fɛrˈdaʊən] *vt* (*lit, fig*) to digest ▷ *vi* (*lit*) to digest
verdaulich [fɛrˈdaʊlɪç] *adj* digestible; **das ist schwer ~** that is hard to digest
Verdauung *f* digestion
Verdauungsspaziergang *m* constitutional
Verdauungsstörung *f* indigestion
Verdeck [fɛrˈdɛk] (**-(e)s, -e**) *nt* (*Aut*) soft top; (*Naut*) deck
verdecken *vt* to cover (up); (*verbergen*) to hide
verdenken [fɛrˈdɛŋkən] *unreg vt*: **jdm etw ~** to blame sb for sth, hold sth against sb
verderben [fɛrˈdɛrbən] *unreg vt* to spoil; (*schädigen*) to ruin; (*moralisch*) to corrupt ▷ *vi* (*Essen*) to spoil, rot; (*Mensch*) to go to the bad; **es mit jdm ~** to get into sb's bad books
Verderben (**-s**) *nt* ruin
verderblich *adj* (*Einfluss*) pernicious; (*Lebensmittel*) perishable
verderbt *adj* (*veraltet*) depraved; **Verderbtheit** *f* depravity
verdeutlichen [fɛrˈdɔʏtlɪçən] *vt* to make clear
verdichten [fɛrˈdɪçtən] *vt* (*Phys, fig*) to compress ▷ *vr* to thicken; (*Verdacht, Eindruck*) to deepen
verdienen [fɛrˈdi:nən] *vt* to earn; (*moralisch*) to deserve ▷ *vi* (*Gewinn machen*): ~ **(an** *+dat***)** to make (a profit) (on)
Verdienst [fɛrˈdi:nst] (**-(e)s, -e**) *m* earnings *pl* ▷ *nt* merit; (*Dank*) credit; (*Leistung*): ~ **(um)** service (to), contribution (to); **verdienstvoll** *adj* commendable
verdient [fɛrˈdi:nt] *adj* well-earned; (*Person*) of outstanding merit; (*Lohn, Strafe*) rightful; **sich um etw ~ machen** to do a lot for sth
verdirbst [fɛrˈdɪrpst] *vb siehe* **verderben**
verdirbt [fɛrˈdɪrpt] *vb siehe* **verderben**
verdonnern [fɛrˈdɔnərn] (*umg*) *vt* (*zu Haft etc*): ~ **(zu)** to sentence (to); **jdn zu etw ~** to order sb

to do sth
verdoppeln [fɛr'dɔpəln] *vt* to double
Verdoppelung, Verdopplung *f* doubling
verdorben [fɛr'dɔrbən] *pp von* **verderben** ▷ *adj* spoilt; (*geschädigt*) ruined; (*moralisch*) corrupt
verdorren [fɛr'dɔrən] *vi* to wither
verdrängen [fɛr'drɛŋən] *vt* to oust; (*auch Phys*) to displace; (*Psych*) to repress
Verdrängung *f* displacement; (*Psych*) repression
verdrehen [fɛr'dre:ən] *vt* (*lit, fig*) to twist; (*Augen*) to roll; **jdm den Kopf ~** (*fig*) to turn sb's head
verdreht (*umg*) *adj* crazy; (*Bericht*) confused
verdreifachen [fɛr'draɪfaxən] *vt* to treble
verdrießen [fɛr'dri:sən] *unreg vt* to annoy
verdrießlich [fɛr'dri:slɪç] *adj* peevish, annoyed
verdross *etc* [fɛr'drɔs] *vb siehe* **verdrießen**
verdrossen [fɛr'drɔsən] *pp von* **verdrießen** ▷ *adj* cross, sulky
verdrücken [fɛr'drʏkən] (*umg*) *vt* to put away, eat ▷ *vr* to disappear
Verdruss [fɛr'drʊs] (**-es, -e**) *m* frustration; **zu jds ~** to sb's annoyance
verduften [fɛr'dʊftən] *vi* to evaporate; (*umg*) to disappear
verdummen [fɛr'dʊmən] *vt* to make stupid ▷ *vi* to grow stupid
verdunkeln [fɛr'dʊŋkəln] *vt* to darken; (*fig*) to obscure ▷ *vr* to darken
Verdunkelung, Verdunklung *f* blackout; (*fig*) obscuring
verdünnen [fɛr'dʏnən] *vt* to dilute
Verdünner (**-s, -**) *m* thinner
verdünnisieren [fɛrdʏni'zi:rən] (*umg*) *vr* to make o.s. scarce
verdunsten [fɛr'dʊnstən] *vi* to evaporate
verdursten [fɛr'dʊrstən] *vi* to die of thirst
verdutzt [fɛr'dʊtst] *adj* nonplussed (*Brit*), nonplused (*US*), taken aback
verebben [fɛr'|ɛbən] *vi* to subside
veredeln [fɛr'|e:dəln] *vt* (*Metalle, Erdöl*) to refine; (*Fasern*) to finish; (*Bot*) to graft
verehren [fɛr'|e:rən] *vt* to venerate, worship (*auch REL*); **jdm etw ~** to present sb with sth
Verehrer, in (**-s, -**) *m(f)* admirer, worshipper (*Brit*), worshiper (*US*)
verehrt *adj* esteemed; **(sehr) ~e Anwesende/ verehrtes Publikum** Ladies and Gentlemen
Verehrung *f* respect; (*Rel*) worship
vereidigen [fɛr'|aɪdɪgən] *vt* to put on oath; **jdn auf etw** *akk* **~** to make sb swear on sth
Vereidigung *f* swearing in
Verein [fɛr'|aɪn] (**-(e)s, -e**) *m* club, association; **ein wohltätiger ~** a charity
vereinbar *adj* compatible
vereinbaren [fɛr'|aɪnba:rən] *vt* to agree upon
Vereinbarkeit *f* compatibility
Vereinbarung *f* agreement
vereinfachen [fɛr'|aɪnfaxən] *vt* to simplify
Vereinfachung *f* simplification
vereinheitlichen [fɛr'|aɪnhaɪtlɪçən] *vt* to standardize
vereinigen [fɛr'|aɪnɪgən] *vt, vr* to unite
vereinigt *adj* united; **Vereinigte Arabische Emirate** *pl* United Arab Emirates; **Vereinigtes Königreich** *nt* United Kingdom; **Vereinigte Staaten** *pl* United States
Vereinigung *f* union; (*Verein*) association
vereinnahmen [fɛr'|aɪnna:mən] *vt* (*geh*) to take; **jdn ~** (*fig*) to make demands on sb
vereinsamen [fɛr'|aɪnza:mən] *vi* to become lonely
vereint [fɛr'|aɪnt] *adj* united; **Vereinte Nationen** *pl* United Nations
vereinzelt [fɛr'|aɪntsəlt] *adj* isolated
vereisen [fɛr'|aɪzən] *vi* to freeze, ice over ▷ *vt* (*Med*) to freeze
vereiteln [fɛr'|aɪtəln] *vt* to frustrate
vereitern [fɛr'|aɪtərn] *vi* to suppurate, fester
Verelendung [fɛr'|e:lɛndʊŋ] *f* impoverishment
verenden [fɛr'|ɛndən] *vi* to perish, die
verengen [fɛr'|ɛŋən] *vr* to narrow
vererben [fɛr'|ɛrbən] *vt* to bequeath; (*Biol*) to transmit ▷ *vr* to be hereditary
vererblich [fɛr'|ɛrplɪç] *adj* hereditary
Vererbung *f* bequeathing; (*Biol*) transmission; **das ist ~** (*umg*) it's hereditary
verewigen [fɛr'|e:vɪgən] *vt* to immortalize ▷ *vr* (*umg*) to leave one's name
Verf. *abk* = **Verfasser**
verfahren [fɛr'fa:rən] *unreg vi* to act ▷ *vr* to get lost ▷ *adj* tangled; **~ mit** to deal with
Verfahren (**-s, -**) *nt* procedure; (*Tech*) process; (*Jur*) proceedings *pl*
Verfahrenstechnik *f* (*Methode*) process
Verfahrensweise *f* procedure
Verfall [fɛr'fal] (**-(e)s**) *m* decline; (*von Haus*) dilapidation; (*Fin*) expiry
verfallen *unreg vi* to decline; (*Haus*) to be falling down; (*Fin*) to lapse ▷ *adj* (*Gebäude*) dilapidated, ruined; (*Karten, Briefmarken*) invalid; (*Strafe*) lapsed; (*Pass*) expired; **~ in** *+akk* to lapse into; **~ auf** *+akk* to hit upon; **einem Laster ~ sein** to be addicted to a vice; **jdm völlig ~ sein** to be completely under sb's spell
Verfallsdatum *nt* expiry date; (*der Haltbarkeit*) best-before date
verfänglich [fɛr'fɛŋlɪç] *adj* awkward, tricky; (*Aussage, Beweismaterial etc*) incriminating; (*gefährlich*) dangerous
verfärben [fɛr'fɛrbən] *vr* to change colour (*Brit*) *od* color (*US*)
verfassen [fɛr'fasən] *vt* to write; (*Gesetz, Urkunde*) to draw up
Verfasser, in (**-s, -**) *m(f)* author, writer
Verfassung *f* constitution (*auch POL*); (*körperlich*) state of health; (*seelisch*) state of mind; **sie ist in guter/schlechter ~** she is in good/bad shape
Verfassungs- *zW*: **verfassungsfeindlich** *adj* anticonstitutional; **Verfassungsgericht** *nt* constitutional court; **verfassungsmäßig** *adj* constitutional; **Verfassungsschutz** *m* (*Aufgabe*) defence of the constitution; (*Amt*)

office responsible for defending the constitution; **Verfassungsschützer, in** *m(f)* defender of the constitution; **verfassungswidrig** *adj* unconstitutional

verfaulen [fɛr'faʊlən] *vi* to rot

verfechten [fɛr'fɛçtən] *unreg vt* to defend; (*Lehre*) to advocate

Verfechter, in [fɛr'fɛçtər(ɪn)] **(-s, -)** *m(f)* champion; defender

verfehlen [fɛr'fe:lən] *vt* to miss; **das Thema ~** to be completely off the subject

verfehlt *adj* unsuccessful; (*unangebracht*) inappropriate; **etw für ~ halten** to regard sth as mistaken

Verfehlung *f* (*Vergehen*) misdemeanour (*Brit*), misdemeanor (*US*); (*Sünde*) transgression

verfeinern [fɛr'faɪnərn] *vt* to refine

Verfettung [fɛr'fɛtʊŋ] *f* (*von Organ, Muskeln*) fatty degeneration

verfeuern [fɛr'fɔʏərn] *vt* to burn; (*Munition*) to fire; (*umg*) to use up

verfilmen [fɛr'fɪlmən] *vt* to film, make a film of

Verfilmung *f* film (version)

Verfilzung [fɛr'fɪltsʊŋ] *f* (*fig: von Firmen, Parteien*) entanglements *pl*

verflachen [fɛr'flaxən] *vi* to flatten out; (*fig: Diskussion*) to become superficial

verfliegen [fɛr'fli:gən] *unreg vi* to evaporate; (*Zeit*) to pass, fly ▷ *vr* to stray (past)

verflixt [fɛr'flɪkst] (*umg*) *adj, adv* darned

verflossen [fɛr'flɔsən] *adj* past, former

verfluchen [fɛr'flu:xən] *vt* to curse

verflüchtigen [fɛr'flʏçtɪgən] *vr* to evaporate; (*Geruch*) to fade

verflüssigen [fɛr'flʏsɪgən] *vr* to become liquid

verfolgen [fɛr'fɔlgən] *vt* to pursue; (*gerichtlich*) to prosecute; (*grausam, bes Pol*) to persecute

Verfolger, in **(-s, -)** *m(f)* pursuer

Verfolgte, r *f(m)* (*politisch*) victim of persecution

Verfolgung *f* pursuit; persecution; **strafrechtliche ~** prosecution

Verfolgungswahn *m* persecution mania

verfrachten [fɛr'fraxtən] *vt* to ship

verfremden [fɛr'frɛmdən] *vt* to alienate, distance

verfressen [fɛr'frɛsən] (*umg*) *adj* greedy

verfrüht [fɛr'fry:t] *adj* premature

verfügbar *adj* available

verfügen [fɛr'fy:gən] *vt* to direct, order ▷ *vr* to proceed ▷ *vi*: **~ über** *+akk* to have at one's disposal; **über etw** *akk* **frei ~ können** to be able to do as one wants with sth

Verfügung *f* direction, order; (*Jur*) writ; **zur ~** at one's disposal; **jdm zur ~ stehen** to be available to sb

Verfügungsgewalt *f* (*Jur*) right of disposal

verführen [fɛr'fy:rən] *vt* to tempt; (*sexuell*) to seduce; (*die Jugend, das Volk etc*) to lead astray

Verführer *m* tempter; seducer

Verführerin *f* temptress; seductress

verführerisch *adj* seductive

Verführung *f* seduction; (*Versuchung*) temptation

Vergabe [fɛr'ga:bə] *f* (*von Arbeiten*) allocation; (*von Stipendium, Auftrag etc*) award

vergällen [fɛr'gɛlən] *vt* (*geh*): **jdm die Freude/das Leben ~** to spoil sb's fun/sour sb's life

vergaloppieren [fɛrgalɔ'pi:rən] (*umg*) *vr* (*sich irren*) to be on the wrong track

vergammeln [fɛr'gaməln] (*umg*) *vi* to go to seed; (*Nahrung*) to go off; (*Zeit*) to waste

vergangen [fɛr'gaŋən] *adj* past; **Vergangenheit** *f* past; **Vergangenheitsbewältigung** *f* coming to terms with the past

vergänglich [fɛr'gɛŋlɪç] *adj* transitory; **Vergänglichkeit** *f* transitoriness, impermanence

vergasen [fɛr'ga:zən] *vt* to gasify; (*töten*) to gas

Vergaser **(-s, -)** *m* (*Aut*) carburettor (*Brit*), carburetor (*US*)

vergaß *etc* [fɛr'ga:s] *vb siehe* **vergessen**

vergeben [fɛr'ge:bən] *unreg vt* to forgive; (*weggeben*) to give away; (*fig: Chance*) to throw away; (*Auftrag, Preis*) to award; (*Studienplätze, Stellen*) to allocate; **jdm (etw) ~** to forgive sb (sth); **~ an** *+akk* to award to; to allocate to; **~ sein** to be occupied; (*umg: Mädchen*) to be spoken for

vergebens *adv* in vain

vergeblich [fɛr'ge:plɪç] *adv* in vain ▷ *adj* vain, futile

Vergebung *f* forgiveness

vergegenwärtigen [fɛrge:gən'vɛrtɪgən] *vr*: **sich** *dat* **etw ~** to visualize sth; (*erinnern*) to recall sth

vergehen [fɛr'ge:ən] *unreg vi* to pass by *od* away ▷ *vr* to commit an offence (*Brit*) *od* offense (*US*); **vor Angst ~** to be scared to death; **jdm vergeht etw** sb loses sth; **sich an jdm ~** to (sexually) assault sb; **Vergehen** **(-s, -)** *nt* offence (*Brit*), offense (*US*)

vergeigen [fɛr'gaɪgən] (*umg*) *vt* to cock up

vergeistigt [fɛr'gaɪstɪçt] *adj* spiritual

vergelten [fɛr'gɛltən] *unreg vt*: **jdm etw ~** to pay sb back for sth, repay sb for sth

Vergeltung *f* retaliation, reprisal

Vergeltungsmaßnahme *f* retaliatory measure

Vergeltungsschlag *m* (*Mil*) reprisal

vergesellschaften [fɛrgə'zɛlʃaftən] *vt* (*Pol*) to nationalize

vergessen [fɛr'gɛsən] *unreg vt* to forget; **Vergessenheit** *f* oblivion; **in Vergessenheit geraten** to fall into oblivion

vergesslich [fɛr'gɛslɪç] *adj* forgetful; **Vergesslichkeit** *f* forgetfulness

vergeuden [fɛr'gɔʏdən] *vt* to squander, waste

vergewaltigen [fɛrgə'valtɪgən] *vt* to rape; (*fig*) to violate

Vergewaltigung *f* rape

vergewissern [fɛrgə'vɪsərn] *vr* to make sure; **sich einer Sache** *gen od* **über etw** *akk* **~** to make sure of sth

vergießen [fɛr'gi:sən] *unreg vt* to shed
vergiften [fɛr'gɪftən] *vt* to poison
Vergiftung *f* poisoning
vergilbt [fɛr'gɪlpt] *adj* yellowed
Vergissmeinnicht [fɛr'gɪsmaɪnnɪçt] **(-(e)s, -e)** *nt* forget-me-not
vergisst [fɛr'gɪst] *vb siehe* **vergessen**
vergittert [fɛr'gɪtərt] *adj*: **~e Fenster** barred windows
verglasen [fɛr'gla:zən] *vt* to glaze
Vergleich [fɛr'glaɪç] **(-(e)s, -e)** *m* comparison; *(Jur)* settlement; **einen ~ schließen** *(Jur)* to reach a settlement; **in keinem ~ zu etw stehen** to be out of all proportion to sth; **im ~ mit** *od* **zu** compared with *od* to; **vergleichbar** *adj* comparable
vergleichen *unreg vt* to compare ▷ *vr (Jur)* to reach a settlement
vergleichsweise *adv* comparatively
verglühen [fɛr'gly:ən] *vi (Feuer)* to die away; *(Draht)* to burn out; *(Raumkapsel, Meteor etc)* to burn up
vergnügen [fɛr'gny:gən] *vr* to enjoy *od* amuse o.s.; **Vergnügen (-s, -)** *nt* pleasure; **das war ein teures Vergnügen** *(umg)* that was an expensive bit of fun; **viel Vergnügen!** enjoy yourself!
vergnüglich *adj* enjoyable
vergnügt [fɛr'gny:kt] *adj* cheerful
Vergnügung *f* pleasure, amusement
Vergnügungs- *zW*: **Vergnügungspark** *m* amusement park; **vergnügungssüchtig** *adj* pleasure-loving; **Vergnügungsviertel** *nt* entertainments district
vergolden [fɛr'gɔldən] *vt* to gild
vergönnen [fɛr'gœnən] *vt* to grant
vergöttern [fɛr'gœtərn] *vt* to idolize
vergraben [fɛr'gra:bən] *unreg vt* to bury
vergrämt [fɛr'grɛ:mt] *adj (Gesicht)* troubled
vergreifen [fɛr'graɪfən] *unreg vr*: **sich an jdm ~** to lay hands on sb; **sich an etw** *dat* **~** to misappropriate sth; **sich im Ton ~** to say the wrong thing
vergriffen [fɛr'grɪfən] *adj (Buch)* out of print; *(Ware)* out of stock
vergrößern [fɛr'grø:sərn] *vt* to enlarge; *(mengenmäßig)* to increase; *(Lupe)* to magnify
Vergrößerung *f* enlargement; increase; magnification
Vergrößerungsglas *nt* magnifying glass
vergünstigt *adj (Lage)* improved; *(Preis)* reduced
Vergünstigung [fɛr'gʏnstɪgʊŋ] *f* concession; *(Vorteil)* privilege
vergüten [fɛr'gy:tən] *vt*: **jdm etw ~** to compensate sb for sth; *(Arbeit, Leistung)* to pay sb for sth
Vergütung *f* compensation; payment
verh. *abk* = **verheiratet**
verhaften [fɛr'haftən] *vt* to arrest
Verhaftete, r *f(m)* prisoner
Verhaftung *f* arrest
verhallen [fɛr'halən] *vi* to die away
verhalten [fɛr'haltən] *unreg vr (Sache)* to be, stand; *(sich benehmen)* to behave; *(Math)* to be in proportion to ▷ *vr unpers*: **wie verhält es sich damit?** *(wie ist die Lage?)* how do things stand?; *(wie wird das gehandhabt?)* how do you go about it? ▷ *adj* restrained; **sich ruhig ~** to keep quiet; *(sich nicht bewegen)* to keep still; **wenn sich das so verhält ...** if that is the case ...; **Verhalten (-s)** *nt* behaviour *(Brit)*, behavior *(US)*
Verhaltens- *zW*: **Verhaltensforschung** *f* behavioural *(Brit) od* behavioral *(US)* science; **verhaltensgestört** *adj* disturbed; **Verhaltensmaßregel** *f* rule of conduct
Verhältnis [fɛr'hɛltnɪs] **(-ses, -se)** *nt* relationship; *(Liebesverhältnis)* affair; *(Math)* proportion, ratio; *(Einstellung)*: **~ (zu)** attitude (to); **Verhältnisse** *pl (Umstände)* conditions *pl*; **aus was für ~sen kommt er?** what sort of background does he come from?; **für klare ~se sorgen, klare ~se schaffen** to get things straight; **über seine ~se leben** to live beyond one's means; **verhältnismäßig** *adj* relative, comparative ▷ *adv* relatively, comparatively; **Verhältniswahl** *f* proportional representation; **Verhältniswahlrecht** *nt* (system of) proportional representation
verhandeln [fɛr'handəln] *vi* to negotiate; *(Jur)* to hold proceedings ▷ *vt* to discuss; *(Jur)* to hear; **über etw** *akk* **~** to negotiate sth *od* about sth
Verhandlung *f* negotiation; *(Jur)* proceedings *pl*; **~en führen** to negotiate
Verhandlungspaket *nt (Comm)* package deal
Verhandlungstisch *m* negotiating table
verhangen [fɛr'haŋən] *adj* overcast
verhängen [fɛr'hɛŋən] *vt (fig)* to impose, inflict
Verhängnis [fɛr'hɛŋnɪs] **(-ses, -se)** *nt* fate; **jdm zum ~ werden** to be sb's undoing; **verhängnisvoll** *adj* fatal, disastrous
verharmlosen [fɛr'harmlo:zən] *vt* to make light of, play down
verharren [fɛr'harən] *vi* to remain; *(hartnäckig)* to persist
verhärten [fɛr'hɛrtən] *vr* to harden
verhaspeln [fɛr'haspəln] *(umg) vr* to get into a muddle *od* tangle
verhasst [fɛr'hast] *adj* odious, hateful
verhätscheln [fɛr'hɛ:tʃəln] *vt* to spoil, pamper
Verhau [fɛr'haʊ] **(-(e)s, -e)** *m (zur Absperrung)* barrier; *(Käfig)* coop
verhauen *unreg (umg) vt (verprügeln)* to beat up; *(Prüfung etc)* to muff
verheben [fɛr'he:bən] *unreg vr* to hurt o.s. lifting sth
verheerend [fɛr'he:rənt] *adj* disastrous, devastating
verhehlen [fɛr'he:lən] *vt* to conceal
verheilen [fɛr'haɪlən] *vi* to heal
verheimlichen [fɛr'haɪmlɪçən] *vt*: **(jdm) etw ~** to keep sth secret (from sb)
verheiratet [fɛr'haɪra:tət] *adj* married
verheißen [fɛr'haɪsən] *unreg vt*: **jdm etw ~** to

promise sb sth
verheißungsvoll *adj* promising
verheizen [fɛr'haɪtsən] *vt* to burn, use as fuel
verhelfen [fɛr'hɛlfən] *unreg vi*: **jdm zu etw ~** to help sb to get sth
verherrlichen [fɛr'hɛrlɪçən] *vt* to glorify
verheult [fɛr'hɔʏlt] *adj* (*Augen, Gesicht*) puffy (*from crying*)
verhexen [fɛr'hɛksən] *vt* to bewitch; **es ist wie verhext** it's jinxed
verhindern [fɛr'hɪndərn] *vt* to prevent; **verhindert sein** to be unable to make it; **das lässt sich leider nicht ~** it can't be helped, unfortunately; **ein verhinderter Politiker** (*umg*) a would-be politician
Verhinderung *f* prevention
verhöhnen [fɛr'hø:nən] *vt* to mock, sneer at
verhohnepipeln [fɛr'ho:nəpi:pəln] (*umg*) *vt* to send up (*Brit*), ridicule
verhökern [fɛr'hø:kərn] (*umg*) *vt* to turn into cash
Verhör [fɛr'hø:r] **(-(e)s, -e)** *nt* interrogation; (*gerichtlich*) (cross-)examination
verhören *vt* to interrogate; to (cross-)examine ▷ *vr* to mishear
verhüllen [fɛr'hʏlən] *vt* to veil; (*Haupt, Körperteil*) to cover
verhungern [fɛr'hʊŋərn] *vi* to starve, die of hunger
verhunzen [fɛr'hʊntsən] (*umg*) *vt* to ruin
verhüten [fɛr'hy:tən] *vt* to prevent, avert
Verhütung *f* prevention
Verhütungsmittel *nt* contraceptive
verifizieren [verifi'tsi:rən] *vt* to verify
verinnerlichen [fɛr'|ɪnərlɪçən] *vt* to internalize
verirren [fɛr'|ɪrən] *vr* to get lost, lose one's way; (*fig*) to go astray; (*Tier, Kugel*) to stray
verjagen [fɛr'ja:gən] *vt* to drive away *od* out
verjähren [fɛr'jɛ:rən] *vi* to come under the statute of limitations; (*Anspruch*) to lapse
Verjährungsfrist *f* limitation period
verjubeln [fɛr'ju:bəln] (*umg*) *vt* (*Geld*) to blow
verjüngen [fɛr'jʏŋən] *vt* to rejuvenate ▷ *vr* to taper
verkabeln [fɛr'ka:bəln] *vt* (*TV*) to link up to the cable network
Verkabelung *f* (*TV*) linking up to the cable network
verkalken [fɛr'kalkən] *vi* to calcify; (*umg*) to become senile
verkalkulieren [fɛrkalku'li:rən] *vr* to miscalculate
verkannt [fɛr'kant] *adj* unappreciated
verkatert [fɛr'ka:tərt] (*umg*) *adj* hung over
Verkauf [fɛr'kaʊf] *m* sale; **zum ~ stehen** to be up for sale
verkaufen *vt, vi* to sell; **„zu ~"** "for sale"
Verkäufer, in [fɛr'kɔʏfər(ɪn)] **(-s, -)** *m(f)* seller; (*im Außendienst*) salesman, saleswoman; (*in Laden*) shop assistant (*Brit*), sales clerk (*US*)
verkäuflich [fɛr'kɔʏflɪç] *adj* saleable
Verkaufs- *zW*: **Verkaufsabteilung** *f* sales department; **Verkaufsautomat** *m* slot machine; **Verkaufsbedingungen** *pl* (*Comm*) terms and conditions of sale; **Verkaufskampagne** *f* sales drive; **Verkaufsleiter** *m* sales manager; **verkaufsoffen** *adj*: **verkaufsoffener Samstag** *Saturday on which the shops are open all day*; **Verkaufsschlager** *m* big seller; **Verkaufsstelle** *f* outlet; **Verkaufstüchtigkeit** *f* salesmanship
Verkehr [fɛr'ke:r] **(-s, -e)** *m* traffic; (*Umgang, bes sexuell*) intercourse; (*Umlauf*) circulation; **aus dem ~ ziehen** to withdraw from service; **für den ~ freigeben** (*Straße etc*) to open to traffic; (*Transportmittel*) to bring into service
verkehren *vi* (*Fahrzeug*) to ply, run ▷ *vt, vr* to turn, transform; **~ mit** to associate with; **mit jdm brieflich** *od* **schriftlich ~** (*form*) to correspond with sb; **bei jdm ~** to visit sb regularly
Verkehrs- *zW*: **Verkehrsampel** *f* traffic lights *pl*; **Verkehrsamt** *nt* tourist (information) office; **Verkehrsaufkommen** *nt* volume of traffic; **verkehrsberuhigt** *adj* traffic-calmed; **Verkehrsberuhigung** *f* traffic-calming; **Verkehrsbetriebe** *pl* transport services *pl*; **Verkehrsdelikt** *nt* traffic offence (*Brit*) *od* violation (*US*); **Verkehrserziehung** *f* road safety training; **verkehrsgünstig** *adj* convenient; **Verkehrsinsel** *f* traffic island; **Verkehrsknotenpunkt** *m* traffic junction; **Verkehrsmittel** *nt*: **öffentliche/private Verkehrsmittel** public/private transport *sing*; **Verkehrsschild** *nt* road sign; **verkehrssicher** *adj* (*Fahrzeug*) roadworthy; **Verkehrssicherheit** *f* road safety; **Verkehrsstockung** *f* traffic jam, stoppage; **Verkehrssünder** (*umg*) *m* traffic offender; **Verkehrsteilnehmer** *m* road user; **verkehrstüchtig** *adj* (*Fahrzeug*) roadworthy; (*Mensch*) fit to drive; **Verkehrsunfall** *m* traffic accident; **Verkehrsverein** *m* tourist information office; **verkehrswidrig** *adj* contrary to traffic regulations; **Verkehrszeichen** *nt* road sign
verkehrt *adj* wrong; (*umgekehrt*) the wrong way round
verkennen [fɛr'kɛnən] *unreg vt* to misjudge; (*unterschätzen*) to underestimate
Verkettung [fɛr'kɛtʊŋ] *f*: **eine ~ unglücklicher Umstände** an unfortunate chain of events
verklagen [fɛr'kla:gən] *vt* to take to court
verklappen [fɛr'klapən] *vt* to dump (at sea)
verklären [fɛr'klɛ:rən] *vt* to transfigure; **verklärt lächeln** to smile radiantly
verklausulieren [fɛrklaʊzu'li:rən] *vt* (*Vertrag*) to hedge in with (restrictive) clauses
verkleben [fɛr'kle:bən] *vt* to glue up, stick ▷ *vi* to stick together
verkleiden [fɛr'klaɪdən] *vt* to disguise; (*kostümieren*) to dress up; (*Schacht, Tunnel*) to line; (*vertäfeln*) to panel; (*Heizkörper*) to cover in ▷ *vr* to disguise o.s.; to dress up
Verkleidung *f* disguise; (*Archit*) panelling (*Brit*), paneling (*US*)

verkleinern [fɛrˈklaɪnərn] *vt* to make smaller, reduce in size
verklemmt [fɛrˈklɛmt] *adj (fig)* inhibited
verklickern [fɛrˈklɪkərn] *(umg) vt:* **jdm etw ~** to make sth clear to sb
verklingen [fɛrˈklɪŋən] *unreg vi* to die away
verknacksen [fɛrˈknaksən] *(umg) vt:* **sich** *dat* **den Fuß ~** to twist one's ankle
verknallen [fɛrˈknalən] *(umg) vr:* **sich in jdn ~** to fall for sb
verkneifen [fɛrˈknaɪfən] *(umg) vt:* **sich** *dat* **etw ~** to stop o.s. from doing sth; **ich konnte mir das Lachen nicht ~** I couldn't help laughing
verknöchert [fɛrˈknœçərt] *adj (fig)* fossilized
verknüpfen [fɛrˈknʏpfən] *vt* to tie (up), knot; *(fig)* to connect
Verknüpfung *f* connection
verkochen [fɛrˈkɔxən] *vt, vi (Flüssigkeit)* to boil away
verkohlen [fɛrˈko:lən] *vi* to carbonize ▹*vt* to carbonize; *(umg)*: **jdn ~** to have sb on
verkommen [fɛrˈkɔmən] *unreg vi* to deteriorate, decay; *(Mensch)* to go downhill, come down in the world ▹*adj (moralisch)* dissolute, depraved; **Verkommenheit** *f* depravity
verkorksen [fɛrˈkɔrksən] *(umg) vt* to ruin, mess up
verkörpern [fɛrˈkœrpərn] *vt* to embody, personify
verköstigen [fɛrˈkœstɪgən] *vt* to feed
verkrachen [fɛrˈkraxən] *(umg) vr:* **sich (mit jdm) ~** to fall out (with sb)
verkracht *(umg) adj (Leben)* ruined
verkraften [fɛrˈkraftən] *vt* to cope with
verkrampfen [fɛrˈkrampfən] *vr (Muskeln)* to go tense
verkrampft [fɛrˈkrampft] *adj (fig)* tense
verkriechen [fɛrˈkri:çən] *unreg vr* to creep away, creep into a corner
verkrümeln [fɛrˈkry:məln] *(umg) vr* to disappear
verkrümmt [fɛrˈkrʏmt] *adj* crooked
Verkrümmung *f* bend, warp; *(Anat)* curvature
verkrüppelt [fɛrˈkrʏpəlt] *adj* crippled
verkrustet [fɛrˈkrʊstət] *adj* encrusted
verkühlen [fɛrˈky:lən] *vr* to get a chill
verkümmern [fɛrˈkʏmərn] *vi* to waste away; **emotionell/geistig ~** to become emotionally/intellectually stunted
verkünden [fɛrˈkʏndən] *vt* to proclaim; *(Urteil)* to pronounce
verkündigen [fɛrˈkʏndɪgən] *vt* to proclaim; *(ironisch)* to announce; *(Evangelium)* to preach
verkuppeln [fɛrˈkʊpəln] *vt:* **jdn an jdn ~** *(Zuhälter)* to procure sb for sb
verkürzen [fɛrˈkʏrtsən] *vt* to shorten; *(Wort)* to abbreviate; **sich** *dat* **die Zeit ~** to while away the time; **verkürzte Arbeitszeit** shorter working hours *pl*
Verkürzung *f* shortening; abbreviation
Verl. *abk (= Verlag)* publ.
verladen [fɛrˈla:dən] *unreg vt* to load
Verlag [fɛrˈla:k] **(-(e)s, -e)** *m* publishing firm
verlagern [fɛrˈla:gərn] *vt, vr (lit, fig)* to shift
Verlagsanstalt *f* publishing firm
Verlagswesen *nt* publishing
verlangen [fɛrˈlaŋən] *vt* to demand; *(wollen)* to want ▹*vi:* **~ nach** to ask for; **Sie werden am Telefon verlangt** you are wanted on the phone; **~ Sie Herrn X** ask for Mr X; **Verlangen (-s, -)** *nt:* **Verlangen (nach)** desire (for); **auf jds Verlangen** *akk* **(hin)** at sb's request
verlängern [fɛrˈlɛŋərn] *vt* to extend; *(länger machen)* to lengthen; *(zeitlich)* to prolong; *(Pass, Abonnement etc)* to renew; **ein verlängertes Wochenende** a long weekend
Verlängerung *f* extension; *(Sport)* extra time
Verlängerungsschnur *f* extension cable
verlangsamen [fɛrˈlaŋza:mən] *vt, vr* to decelerate, slow down
Verlass [fɛrˈlas] *m:* **auf ihn/das ist kein ~** he/it cannot be relied upon
verlassen [fɛrˈlasən] *unreg vt* to leave ▹*vr:* **sich ~ auf** *+akk* to depend on ▹*adj* desolate; *(Mensch)* abandoned; **einsam und ~** so all alone; **Verlassenheit** *f* loneliness *(Brit)*, lonesomeness *(US)*
verlässlich [fɛrˈlɛslɪç] *adj* reliable
Verlauf [fɛrˈlaʊf] *m* course; **einen guten/schlechten ~ nehmen** to go well/badly
verlaufen *unreg vi (zeitlich)* to pass; *(Farben)* to run ▹*vr* to get lost; *(Menschenmenge)* to disperse
Verlautbarung *f* announcement
verlauten [fɛrˈlaʊtən] *vi:* **etw ~ lassen** to disclose sth; **wie verlautet** as reported
verleben [fɛrˈle:bən] *vt* to spend
verlebt [fɛrˈle:pt] *adj* dissipated, worn-out
verlegen [fɛrˈle:gən] *vt* to move; *(verlieren)* to mislay; *(Kabel, Fliesen etc)* to lay; *(Buch)* to publish; *(verschieben)*: **~ (auf** *+akk***)** to postpone (until) ▹*vr:* **sich auf etw** *akk* **~** to resort to sth ▹*adj* embarrassed; **nicht ~ um** never at a loss for; **Verlegenheit** *f* embarrassment; *(Situation)* difficulty, scrape
Verleger [fɛrˈle:gər] **(-s, -)** *m* publisher
verleiden [fɛrˈlaɪdən] *vt:* **jdm etw ~** to put sb off sth
Verleih [fɛrˈlaɪ] **(-(e)s, -e)** *m* hire service; *(das Verleihen)* renting (out), hiring (out) *(Brit)*; *(Filmverleih)* distribution
verleihen *unreg vt:* **etw (an jdn) ~** to lend sth (to sb), lend (sb) sth; *(gegen Gebühr)* to rent sth (out) (to sb), hire sth (out) (to sb) *(Brit)*; *(Kraft, Anschein)* to confer sth (on sb), bestow sth (on sb); *(Preis, Medaille)* to award sth (to sb), award (sb) sth
Verleiher (-s, -) *m* hire *(Brit) od* rental firm; *(von Filmen)* distributor; *(von Büchern)* lender
Verleihung *f* lending; *(von Kraft etc)* bestowal; *(von Preis)* award
verleiten [fɛrˈlaɪtən] *vt* to lead astray; **~ zu** to talk into, tempt into
verlernen [fɛrˈlɛrnən] *vt* to forget, unlearn
verlesen [fɛrˈle:zən] *unreg vt* to read out; *(aussondern)* to sort out ▹*vr* to make a mistake in reading

verletzbar *adj* vulnerable
verletzen [fɛr'lɛtsən] *vt* (*lit, fig*) to injure, hurt; (*Gesetz etc*) to violate
verletzend *adj* (*fig: Worte*) hurtful
verletzlich *adj* vulnerable
Verletzte, r *f(m)* injured person
Verletzung *f* injury; (*Verstoß*) violation, infringement
verleugnen [fɛr'lɔʏgnən] *vt* to deny; (*Menschen*) to disown; **er lässt sich immer (vor ihr) ~** he always pretends not to be there (when she calls)
Verleugnung *f* denial
verleumden [fɛr'lɔʏmdən] *vt* to slander; (*schriftlich*) to libel
verleumderisch *adj* slanderous; libellous (*Brit*), libelous (*US*)
Verleumdung *f* slander; libel
verlieben *vr*: **sich ~ (in** *+akk***)** to fall in love (with)
verliebt [fɛr'li:pt] *adj* in love; **Verliebtheit** *f* being in love
verlieren [fɛr'li:rən] *unreg vt, vi* to lose ▷*vr* to get lost; (*verschwinden*) to disappear; **das/er hat hier nichts verloren** (*umg*) that/he has no business to be here
Verlierer, in (**-s, -**) *m(f)* loser
Verlies [fɛr'li:s] (**-es, -e**) *nt* dungeon
verloben [fɛr'lo:bən] *vr*: **sich ~ (mit)** to get engaged (to); **verlobt sein** to be engaged
Verlobte, r [fɛr'lo:ptə(r)] *f(m)*: **mein ~r** my fiancé; **meine ~** my fiancée
Verlobung *f* engagement
verlocken [fɛr'lɔkən] *vt* to entice, lure
verlockend *adj* (*Angebot, Idee*) tempting
Verlockung *f* temptation, attraction
verlogen [fɛr'lo:gən] *adj* untruthful; (*Komplimente, Versprechungen*) false; (*Moral, Gesellschaft*) hypocritical; **Verlogenheit** *f* untruthfulness
verlor *etc* [fɛr'lo:r] *vb siehe* **verlieren**
verloren *pp von* **verlieren** ▷*adj* lost; (*Eier*) poached; **der ~e Sohn** the prodigal son; **auf ~em Posten kämpfen** *od* **stehen** to be fighting a losing battle; **etw ~ geben** to give sth up for lost; **~ gehen** to get lost; **an ihm ist ein Sänger ~ gegangen** he would have made a (good) singer
verlöschen [fɛr'lœʃən] *vi* (*Hilfsverb sein*) to go out; (*Inschrift, Farbe, Erinnerung*) to fade
verlosen [fɛr'lo:zən] *vt* to raffle (off), draw lots for
Verlosung *f* raffle, lottery
verlottern [fɛr'lɔtərn] (*umg*) *vi* to go to the dogs
verludern [fɛr'lu:dərn] (*umg*) *vi* to go to the dogs
Verlust [fɛr'lʊst] (**-(e)s, -e**) *m* loss; (*Mil*) casualty; **mit ~ verkaufen** to sell at a loss; **Verlustanzeige** *f* "lost" notice; **Verlustgeschäft** *nt*: **das war ein Verlustgeschäft** I/he *etc* made a loss; **Verlustzeit** *f* (*Industrie*) waiting time
vermachen [fɛr'maxən] *vt* to bequeath, leave
Vermächtnis [fɛr'mɛçtnɪs] (**-ses, -se**) *nt* legacy
vermählen [fɛr'mɛ:lən] *vr* to marry
Vermählung *f* wedding, marriage
vermarkten [fɛr'marktən] *vt* to market; (*fig: Persönlichkeit*) to promote
Vermarktung [fɛr'marktʊŋ] *f* marketing
vermasseln [fɛr'masəln] (*umg*) *vt* to mess up
vermehren [fɛr'me:rən] *vt, vr* to multiply; (*Menge*) to increase
Vermehrung *f* multiplying; increase
vermeiden [fɛr'maɪdən] *unreg vt* to avoid
vermeidlich *adj* avoidable
vermeintlich [fɛr'maɪntlɪç] *adj* supposed
vermengen [fɛr'mɛŋən] *vt* to mix; (*fig*) to mix up, confuse
Vermenschlichung [fɛr'mɛnʃlɪçʊŋ] *f* humanization
Vermerk [fɛr'mɛrk] (**-(e)s, -e**) *m* note; (*in Ausweis*) endorsement
vermerken *vt* to note
vermessen [fɛr'mɛsən] *unreg vt* to survey ▷*vr* (*falsch messen*) to measure incorrectly ▷*adj* presumptuous, bold; **Vermessenheit** *f* presumptuousness
Vermessung *f* survey(ing)
Vermessungsamt *nt* land survey(ing) office
Vermessungsingenieur *m* land surveyor
vermiesen [fɛr'mi:zən] (*umg*) *vt* to spoil
vermieten [fɛr'mi:tən] *vt* to let (*Brit*), rent (out); (*Auto*) to hire out, rent
Vermieter, in (**-s, -**) *m(f)* landlord, landlady
Vermietung *f* letting, renting (out); (*von Autos*) hiring (out), rental
vermindern [fɛr'mɪndərn] *vt, vr* to lessen, decrease
Verminderung *f* reduction
verminen [fɛr'mi:nən] *vt* to mine
vermischen [fɛr'mɪʃən] *vt, vr* to mix; (*Teesorten etc*) to blend; **vermischte Schriften** miscellaneous writings
vermissen [fɛr'mɪsən] *vt* to miss; **vermisst sein, als vermisst gemeldet sein** to be reported missing; **wir haben dich bei der Party vermisst** we didn't see you at the party
Vermisste, r *f(m)* missing person
Vermisstenanzeige *f* missing persons report
vermitteln [fɛr'mɪtəln] *vi* to mediate ▷*vt* to arrange; (*Gespräch*) to connect; (*Stelle*) to find; (*Gefühl, Bild, Idee etc*) to convey; (*Wissen*) to impart; **~de Worte** conciliatory words; **jdm etw ~** to help sb to obtain sth; (*Stelle*) to find sth for sb
Vermittler, in [fɛr'mɪtlər(ɪn)] (**-s, -**) *m(f)* (*Comm*) agent; (*Schlichter*) mediator
Vermittlung *f* procurement; (*Stellenvermittlung*) agency; (*Tel*) exchange; (*Schlichtung*) mediation
Vermittlungsgebühr *f* commission
vermögen [fɛr'mø:gən] *unreg vt* to be capable of; **~ zu** to be able to; **Vermögen** (**-s, -**) *nt* wealth; (*Fähigkeit*) ability; **mein ganzes Vermögen besteht aus …** my entire assets consist of …; **ein Vermögen kosten** to cost a fortune

vermögend *adj* wealthy
Vermögens- *zW*: **Vermögenssteuer** *f* property tax, wealth tax; **Vermögenswert** *m* asset; **vermögenswirksam** *adj*: **sein Geld vermögenswirksam anlegen** to invest one's money profitably; **vermögenswirksame Leistungen** *employers' contributions to tax-deductible savings scheme*
vermummen [fɛr'mʊmən] *vr* to wrap up (warm); (*sich verkleiden*) to disguise
Vermummungsverbot (**-(e)s**) *nt law against disguising o.s. at demonstrations*
vermurksen [fɛr'mʊrksən] (*umg*) *vt* to make a mess of
vermuten [fɛr'mu:tən] *vt* to suppose; (*argwöhnen*) to suspect
vermutlich *adj* supposed, presumed ▷ *adv* probably
Vermutung *f* supposition; suspicion; **die ~ liegt nahe, dass ...** there are grounds for assuming that ...
vernachlässigen [fɛr'na:xlɛsɪgən] *vt* to neglect ▷ *vr* to neglect o.s. *od* one's appearance
Vernachlässigung *f* neglect
vernarben [fɛr'narbən] *vi* to heal up
vernarren [fɛr'narən] (*umg*) *vr*: **in jdn/etw vernarrt sein** to be crazy about sb/sth
vernaschen [fɛr'naʃən] *vt* (*Geld*) to spend on sweets; (*umg: Mädchen, Mann*) to make it with
vernehmen [fɛr'ne:mən] *unreg vt* to hear, perceive; (*erfahren*) to learn; (*Jur*) to (cross-)examine; (*Polizei*) to question; **Vernehmen** *nt*: **dem Vernehmen nach** from what I/we *etc* hear
vernehmlich *adj* audible
Vernehmung *f* (cross-)examination
vernehmungsfähig *adj* in a condition to be (cross-)examined
verneigen [fɛr'naɪgən] *vr* to bow
verneinen [fɛr'naɪnən] *vt* (*Frage*) to answer in the negative; (*ablehnen*) to deny; (*Gram*) to negate
verneinend *adj* negative
Verneinung *f* negation
vernichten [fɛr'nɪçtən] *vt* to destroy, annihilate
vernichtend *adj* (*fig*) crushing; (*Blick*) withering; (*Kritik*) scathing
Vernichtung *f* destruction, annihilation
Vernichtungsschlag *m* devastating blow
verniedlichen [fɛr'ni:tlɪçən] *vt* to play down
Vernunft [fɛr'nʊnft] (**-**) *f* reason; **~ annehmen** to see reason; **Vernunftehe** *f*, **Vernunftheirat** *f* marriage of convenience
vernünftig [fɛr'nʏnftɪç] *adj* sensible, reasonable
Vernunftmensch *m* rational person
veröden [fɛr'|ø:dən] *vi* to become desolate ▷ *vt* (*Med*) to remove
veröffentlichen [fɛr'|œfəntlɪçən] *vt* to publish
Veröffentlichung *f* publication
verordnen [fɛr'|ɔrdnən] *vt* (*Med*) to prescribe
Verordnung *f* order, decree; (*Med*) prescription
verpachten [fɛr'paxtən] *vt* to lease (out)
verpacken [fɛr'pakən] *vt* to pack; (*verbrauchergerecht*) to package; (*einwickeln*) to wrap
Verpackung *f* packing; packaging; wrapping
verpassen [fɛr'pasən] *vt* to miss; **jdm eine Ohrfeige ~** (*umg*) to give sb a clip round the ear
verpatzen [fɛr'patsən] (*umg*) *vt* to spoil, mess up
verpennen [fɛr'pɛnən] (*umg*) *vi, vr* to oversleep
verpesten [fɛr'pɛstən] *vt* to pollute
verpetzen [fɛr'pɛtsən] (*umg*) *vt*: **jdn ~ (bei)** to tell on sb (to)
verpfänden [fɛr'pfɛndən] *vt* to pawn; (*Jur*) to mortgage
verpfeifen [fɛr'pfaɪfən] *unreg* (*umg*) *vt*: **jdn ~ (bei)** to grass on sb (to)
verpflanzen [fɛr'pflantsən] *vt* to transplant
Verpflanzung *f* transplanting; (*Med*) transplant
verpflegen [fɛr'pfle:gən] *vt* to feed, cater for (*Brit*)
Verpflegung *f* catering; (*Kost*) food; (*in Hotel*) board
verpflichten [fɛr'pflɪçtən] *vt* to oblige, bind; (*anstellen*) to engage ▷ *vr* to undertake; (*Mil*) to sign on ▷ *vi* to carry obligations; **jdm verpflichtet sein** to be under an obligation to sb; **sich zu etw ~** to commit o.s. to doing sth; **jdm zu Dank verpflichtet sein** to be obliged to sb
verpflichtend *adj* (*Zusage*) binding
Verpflichtung *f* obligation; (*Aufgabe*) duty
verpfuschen [fɛr'pfʊʃən] (*umg*) *vt* to bungle, make a mess of
verplanen [fɛr'pla:nən] *vt* (*Zeit*) to book up; (*Geld*) to budget
verplappern [fɛr'plapərn] (*umg*) *vr* to open one's big mouth
verplempern [fɛr'plɛmpərn] (*umg*) *vt* to waste
verpönt [fɛr'pø:nt] *adj*: **~ (bei)** frowned upon (by)
verprassen [fɛr'prasən] *vt* to squander
verprügeln [fɛr'pry:gəln] (*umg*) *vt* to beat up
verpuffen [fɛr'pʊfən] *vi* to (go) pop; (*fig*) to fall flat
Verputz [fɛr'pʊts] *m* plaster; (*Rauputz*) roughcast; **verputzen** *vt* to plaster; (*umg: Essen*) to put away
verqualmen [fɛr'kvalmən] *vt* (*Zimmer*) to fill with smoke
verquollen [fɛr'kvɔlən] *adj* swollen; (*Holz*) warped
verrammeln [fɛr'raməln] *vt* to barricade
Verrat [fɛr'ra:t] (**-(e)s**) *m* treachery; (*Pol*) treason; **~ an jdm üben** to betray sb
verraten *unreg vt* to betray; (*fig: erkennen lassen*) to show; (*Geheimnis*) to divulge ▷ *vr* to give o.s. away
Verräter, in [fɛr'rɛ:tər(ɪn)] (**-s, -**) *m(f)* traitor, traitress; **verräterisch** *adj* treacherous
verrauchen [fɛr'raʊxən] *vi* (*fig: Zorn*) to blow over

verrechnen [fɛr'rɛçnən] *vt*: **~ mit** to set off against ▷ *vr* to miscalculate
Verrechnung *f*: **nur zur ~** (*auf Scheck*) a/c payee only
Verrechnungsscheck *m* crossed cheque (*Brit*)
verregnet [fɛr're:gnət] *adj* rainy, spoilt by rain
verreisen [fɛr'raɪzən] *vi* to go away (on a journey); **er ist geschäftlich verreist** he's away on business
verreißen [fɛr'raɪsən] *unreg vt* to pull to pieces
verrenken [fɛr'rɛŋkən] *vt* to contort; (*Med*) to dislocate; **sich** *dat* **den Knöchel ~** to sprain one's ankle
Verrenkung *f* contortion; (*Med*) dislocation
verrennen [fɛr'rɛnən] *unreg vr*: **sich in etw** *akk* **~** to get stuck on sth
verrichten [fɛr'rɪçtən] *vt* (*Arbeit*) to do, perform
verriegeln [fɛr'ri:gəln] *vt* to bolt
verringern [fɛr'rɪŋərn] *vt* to reduce ▷ *vr* to decrease
Verringerung *f* reduction; decrease
verrinnen [fɛr'rɪnən] *unreg vi* to run out *od* away; (*Zeit*) to elapse
Verriss [fɛr'rɪs] *m* slating review
verrohen [fɛr'ro:ən] *vi* to become brutalized
verrosten [fɛr'rɔstən] *vi* to rust
verrotten [fɛr'rɔtən] *vi* to rot
verrucht [fɛr'ru:xt] *adj* despicable; (*verrufen*) disreputable
verrücken [fɛr'rʏkən] *vt* to move, shift
verrückt *adj* crazy, mad; **Verrückte, r** *f(m)* lunatic; **Verrücktheit** *f* madness, lunacy
Verruf [fɛr'ru:f] *m*: **in ~ geraten/bringen** to fall/bring into disrepute
verrufen *adj* disreputable
verrutschen [fɛr'rʊtʃən] *vi* to slip
Vers [fɛrs] (**-es, -e**) *m* verse
versacken [fɛr'zakən] *vi* (*lit*) to sink; (*fig*: *umg*: *herunterkommen*) to go downhill; (: *lange zechen*) to get involved in a booze-up (*Brit*) *od* a drinking spree
versagen [fɛr'za:gən] *vt*: **jdm/sich etw ~** to deny sb/o.s. sth ▷ *vi* to fail; **Versagen** (**-s**) *nt* failure; **menschliches Versagen** human error
Versager (**-s, -**) *m* failure
versalzen [fɛr'zaltsən] *vt* to put too much salt in; (*fig*) to spoil
versammeln [fɛr'zaməln] *vt, vr* to assemble, gather
Versammlung *f* meeting, gathering
Versammlungsfreiheit *f* freedom of assembly
Versand [fɛr'zant] (**-(e)s**) *m* dispatch; (*Versandabteilung*) dispatch department; **Versandbahnhof** *m* dispatch station; **Versandhaus** *nt* mail-order firm; **Versandkosten** *pl* transport(ation) costs *pl*; **Versandweg** *m*: **auf dem Versandweg** by mail order
versäumen [fɛr'zɔʏmən] *vt* to miss; (*Pflicht*) to neglect; (*Zeit*) to lose
Versäumnis (**-ses, -se**) *nt* neglect; (*Unterlassung*) omission
verschachern [fɛr'ʃaxərn] (*umg*) *vt* to sell off
verschachtelt [fɛr'ʃaxtəlt] *adj* (*Satz*) complex
verschaffen [fɛr'ʃafən] *vt*: **jdm/sich etw ~** to get *od* procure sth for sb/o.s.
verschämt [fɛr'ʃɛ:mt] *adj* bashful
verschandeln [fɛr'ʃandəln] (*umg*) *vt* to spoil
verschanzen [fɛr'ʃantsən] *vr*: **sich hinter etw** *dat* **~** to dig in behind sth; (*fig*) to take refuge behind sth
verschärfen [fɛr'ʃɛrfən] *vt* to intensify; (*Lage*) to aggravate; (*strenger machen*: *Kontrollen, Gesetze*) to tighten up ▷ *vr* to intensify; to become aggravated; to become tighter
Verschärfung *f* intensification; (*der Lage*) aggravation; (*von Kontrollen etc*) tightening
verscharren [fɛr'ʃarən] *vt* to bury
verschätzen [fɛr'ʃɛtsən] *vr* to miscalculate
verschenken [fɛr'ʃɛŋkən] *vt* to give away
verscherzen [fɛr'ʃɛrtsən] *vt*: **sich** *dat* **etw ~** to lose sth, throw sth away
verscheuchen [fɛr'ʃɔʏçən] *vt* to frighten away
verschicken [fɛr'ʃɪkən] *vt* to send off; (*Sträfling*) to transport
verschieben [fɛr'ʃi:bən] *unreg vt* to shift; (*Eisenb*) to shunt; (*Termin*) to postpone; (*umg*: *Waren, Devisen*) to traffic in
Verschiebung *f* shift, displacement; shunting; postponement
verschieden [fɛr'ʃi:dən] *adj* different; **das ist ganz ~** (*wird verschieden gehandhabt*) that varies, that just depends; **sie sind ~ groß** they are of different sizes; **verschiedenartig** *adj* various, of different kinds; **zwei so verschiedenartige ...** two such differing ...; **Verschiedene** *pron pl* various people; various things *pl*; **Verschiedenes** *pron* various things *pl*; **etwas Verschiedenes** something different; **Verschiedenheit** *f* difference
verschiedentlich *adv* several times
verschiffen [fɛr'ʃɪfən] *vt* to ship; (*Sträfling*) to transport
verschimmeln [fɛr'ʃɪməln] *vi* (*Nahrungsmittel*) to go mouldy (*Brit*) *od* moldy (*US*); (*Leder, Papier etc*) to become mildewed
verschlafen [fɛr'ʃla:fən] *unreg vt* to sleep through; (*fig*: *versäumen*) to miss ▷ *vi, vr* to oversleep ▷ *adj* sleepy
Verschlag [fɛr'ʃla:k] *m* shed
verschlagen [fɛr'ʃla:gən] *unreg vt* to board up; (*Tennis*) to hit out of play; (*Buchseite*) to lose ▷ *adj* cunning; **jdm den Atem ~** to take sb's breath away; **an einen Ort ~ werden** to wind up in a place
verschlampen [fɛr'ʃlampən] *vi* (*Hilfsverb sein*: *Mensch*) to go to seed (*umg*) ▷ *vt* to lose, mislay
verschlechtern [fɛr'ʃlɛçtərn] *vt* to make worse ▷ *vr* to deteriorate, get worse; (*gehaltlich*) to take a lower-paid job
Verschlechterung *f* deterioration
Verschleierung [fɛr'ʃlaɪərʊŋ] *f* veiling; (*fig*) concealment; (*Mil*) screening
Verschleierungstaktik *f* smoke-screen tactics

pl
Verschleiß [fɛrˈʃlaɪs] (**-es, -e**) *m* wear and tear
verschleißen *unreg vt, vi, vr* to wear out
verschleppen [fɛrˈʃlɛpən] *vt* to carry off, abduct; (*zeitlich*) to drag out, delay; (*verbreiten: Seuche*) to spread
verschleudern [fɛrˈʃlɔydərn] *vt* to squander; (*Comm*) to sell dirt-cheap
verschließbar *adj* lockable
verschließen [fɛrˈʃliːsən] *unreg vt* to lock ▷ *vr*: **sich einer Sache** *dat* ~ to close one's mind to sth
verschlimmern [fɛrˈʃlɪmərn] *vt* to make worse, aggravate ▷ *vr* to get worse, deteriorate
Verschlimmerung *f* deterioration
verschlingen [fɛrˈʃlɪŋən] *unreg vt* to devour, swallow up; (*Fäden*) to twist
verschliss *etc* [fɛrˈʃlɪs] *vb siehe* **verschleißen**
verschlissen [fɛrˈʃlɪsən] *pp von* **verschleißen** ▷ *adj* worn(-out)
verschlossen [fɛrˈʃlɔsən] *adj* locked; (*fig*) reserved; (*schweigsam*) tight-lipped; **Verschlossenheit** *f* reserve
verschlucken [fɛrˈʃlʊkən] *vt* to swallow ▷ *vr* to choke
Verschluss [fɛrˈʃlʊs] *m* lock; (*von Kleid etc*) fastener; (*Phot*) shutter; (*Stöpsel*) plug; **unter ~ halten** to keep under lock and key
verschlüsseln [fɛrˈʃlʏsəln] *vt* to encode
verschmachten [fɛrˈʃmaxtən] *vi*: **~ (vor** *+dat*) to languish (for); **vor Durst ~** to be dying of thirst
verschmähen [fɛrˈʃmɛːən] *vt* to scorn
verschmelzen [fɛrˈʃmɛltsən] *unreg vt, vi* to merge, blend
verschmerzen [fɛrˈʃmɛrtsən] *vt* to get over
verschmiert [fɛrˈʃmiːrt] *adj* (*Hände*) smeary; (*Schminke*) smudged
verschmitzt [fɛrˈʃmɪtst] *adj* mischievous
verschmutzen [fɛrˈʃmʊtsən] *vt* to soil; (*Umwelt*) to pollute
Verschmutzung *f* pollution
verschnaufen [fɛrˈʃnaʊfən] (*umg*) *vi, vr* to have a breather
verschneiden [fɛrˈʃnaɪdən] *vt* (*Whisky etc*) to blend
verschneit [fɛrˈʃnaɪt] *adj* covered in snow, snowed up
Verschnitt [fɛrˈʃnɪt] *m* (*von Whisky etc*) blend
verschnörkelt [fɛrˈʃnœrkəlt] *adj* ornate
verschnupft [fɛrˈʃnʊpft] (*umg*) *adj*: **~ sein** to have a cold; (*beleidigt*) to be peeved (*umg*)
verschnüren [fɛrˈʃnyːrən] *vt* to tie up
verschollen [fɛrˈʃɔlən] *adj* lost, missing
verschonen [fɛrˈʃoːnən] *vt*: **jdn mit etw ~** to spare sb sth; **von etw verschont bleiben** to escape sth
verschönern [fɛrˈʃøːnərn] *vt* to decorate; (*verbessern*) to improve
verschossen [fɛrˈʃɔsən] *adj*: **~ sein** (*fig: umg*) to be in love
verschränken [fɛrˈʃrɛŋkən] *vt* to cross; (*Arme*) to fold
verschreckt [fɛrˈʃrɛkt] *adj* frightened, scared
verschreiben [fɛrˈʃraɪbən] *unreg vt* (*Papier*) to use up; (*Med*) to prescribe ▷ *vr* to make a mistake (in writing); **sich einer Sache** *dat* ~ to devote o.s. to sth
verschrieen [fɛrˈʃriːən], **verschrien** [fɛrˈʃriːn] *adj* notorious
verschroben [fɛrˈʃroːbən] *adj* eccentric, odd
verschrotten [fɛrˈʃrɔtən] *vt* to scrap
verschüchtert [fɛrˈʃʏçtərt] *adj* subdued, intimidated
verschulden [fɛrˈʃʊldən] *vt* to be guilty of ▷ *vi* (*in Schulden geraten*) to get into debt; **Verschulden** (**-s**) *nt* fault
verschuldet *adj* in debt
Verschuldung *f* debts *pl*
verschütten [fɛrˈʃʏtən] *vt* to spill; (*zuschütten*) to fill; (*unter Trümmer*) to bury
verschwand *etc* [fɛrˈʃvant] *vb siehe* **verschwinden**
verschweigen [fɛrˈʃvaɪgən] *unreg vt* to keep secret; **jdm etw ~** to keep sth from sb
verschwenden [fɛrˈʃvɛndən] *vt* to squander
Verschwender, in (**-s, -**) *m(f)* spendthrift; **verschwenderisch** *adj* wasteful; (*Leben*) extravagant
Verschwendung *f* waste
verschwiegen [fɛrˈʃviːgən] *adj* discreet; (*Ort*) secluded; **Verschwiegenheit** *f* discretion; seclusion; **zur Verschwiegenheit verpflichtet** bound to secrecy
verschwimmen [fɛrˈʃvɪmən] *unreg vi* to grow hazy, become blurred
verschwinden [fɛrˈʃvɪndən] *unreg vi* to disappear, vanish; **verschwinde!** clear off! (*umg*); **Verschwinden** (**-s**) *nt* disappearance
verschwindend *adj* (*Anzahl, Menge*) insignificant
verschwitzen [fɛrˈʃvɪtsən] *vt* to stain with sweat; (*umg*) to forget
verschwitzt *adj* (*Kleidung*) sweat-stained; (*Mensch*) sweaty
verschwommen [fɛrˈʃvɔmən] *adj* hazy, vague
verschworen [fɛrˈʃvoːrən] *adj* (*Gesellschaft*) sworn
verschwören [fɛrˈʃvøːrən] *unreg vr* to conspire, plot
Verschwörer, in (**-s, -**) *m(f)* conspirator
Verschwörung *f* conspiracy, plot
verschwunden [fɛrˈʃvʊndən] *pp von* **verschwinden** ▷ *adj* missing
versehen [fɛrˈzeːən] *unreg vt* to supply, provide; (*Pflicht*) to carry out; (*Amt*) to fill; (*Haushalt*) to keep ▷ *vr* (*fig*) to make a mistake; **ehe er (es) sich ~ hatte ...** before he knew it ...; **Versehen** (**-s, -**) *nt* oversight; **aus Versehen** by mistake
versehentlich *adv* by mistake
Versehrte, r [fɛrˈzeːrtə(r)] *f(m)* disabled person
verselbstständigen [fɛrˈzɛlpstʃtɛndɪgən], **verselbständigen** [fɛrˈzɛlpʃtɛndɪgən] *vr* to become independent
versenden [fɛrˈzɛndən] *unreg vt* to send; (*Comm*) to forward

versengen [fɛrˈzɛŋən] *vt* to scorch; (*Feuer*) to singe; (*umg: verprügeln*) to wallop
versenken [fɛrˈzɛŋkən] *vt* to sink ▷ *vr*: **sich ~ in** *+akk* to become engrossed in
versessen [fɛrˈzɛsən] *adj*: **~ auf** *+akk* mad about, hellbent on
versetzen [fɛrˈzɛtsən] *vt* to transfer; (*verpfänden*) to pawn; (*umg: vergeblich warten lassen*) to stand up; (*nicht geradlinig anordnen*) to stagger; (*Sch: in höhere Klasse*) to move up ▷ *vr*: **sich in jdn** *od* **in jds Lage ~** to put o.s. in sb's place; **jdm einen Tritt/Schlag ~** to kick/hit sb; **etw mit etw ~** to mix sth with sth; **jdm einen Stich ~** (*fig*) to cut sb to the quick, wound sb (deeply); **jdn in gute Laune ~** to put sb in a good mood
Versetzung *f* transfer; **seine ~ ist gefährdet** (*Sch*) he's in danger of having to repeat a year
verseuchen [fɛrˈzɔʏçən] *vt* to contaminate
Versicherer (**-s, -**) *m* insurer; (*bei Schiffen*) underwriter
versichern [fɛrˈzɪçərn] *vt* to assure; (*mit Geld*) to insure ▷ *vr*: **sich ~** *+gen* to make sure of
Versicherte, r *f(m)* insured
Versicherung *f* assurance; insurance
Versicherungs- *zW*: **Versicherungsbeitrag** *m* insurance premium; (*bei staatlicher Versicherung etc*) *social security contribution*; **Versicherungsgesellschaft** *f* insurance company; **Versicherungsnehmer** (**-s, -**) *m* (*form*) insured, policy holder; **Versicherungspolice** *f* insurance policy; **Versicherungsschutz** *m* insurance cover; **Versicherungssumme** *f* sum insured; **Versicherungsträger** *m* insurer
versickern [fɛrˈzɪkərn] *vi* to seep away; (*fig: Interesse etc*) to peter out
versiegeln [fɛrˈziːgəln] *vt* to seal (up)
versiegen [fɛrˈziːgən] *vi* to dry up
versiert [vɛrˈziːrt] *adj*: **in etw** *dat* **~ sein** to be experienced *od* well versed in sth
versilbert [fɛrˈzɪlbərt] *adj* silver-plated
versinken [fɛrˈzɪŋkən] *unreg vi* to sink; **ich hätte im Boden** *od* **vor Scham ~ mögen** I wished the ground would swallow me up
versinnbildlichen [fɛrˈzɪnbɪltlɪçən] *vt* to symbolize
Version [vɛrziˈoːn] *f* version
Versmaß [ˈfɛrsmaːs] *nt* metre (*Brit*), meter (*US*)
versohlen [fɛrˈzoːlən] (*umg*) *vt* to belt
versöhnen [fɛrˈzøːnən] *vt* to reconcile ▷ *vr* to become reconciled
versöhnlich *adj* (*Ton, Worte*) conciliatory; (*Ende*) happy
Versöhnung *f* reconciliation
versonnen [fɛrˈzɔnən] *adj* (*Gesichtsausdruck*) pensive, thoughtful; (*träumerisch: Blick*) dreamy
versorgen [fɛrˈzɔrgən] *vt* to provide, supply; (*Familie etc*) to look after ▷ *vr* to look after o.s.
Versorger, in (**-s, -**) *m(f)* (*Ernährer*) provider, breadwinner; (*Belieferer*) supplier
Versorgung *f* provision; (*Unterhalt*) maintenance; (*Altersversorgung etc*) benefit, assistance
Versorgungs- *zW*: **Versorgungsamt** *nt* pension office; **Versorgungsbetrieb** *m* public utility; **Versorgungsnetz** *nt* (*Wasserversorgung etc*) (supply) grid; (*von Waren*) supply network
verspannen [fɛrˈʃpanən] *vr* (*Muskeln*) to tense up
verspäten [fɛrˈʃpɛːtən] *vr* to be late
verspätet *adj* late
Verspätung *f* delay; **~ haben** to be late; **mit zwanzig Minuten ~** twenty minutes late
versperren [fɛrˈʃpɛrən] *vt* to bar, obstruct
verspielen [fɛrˈʃpiːlən] *vt, vi* to lose; **(bei jdm) verspielt haben** to have had it (as far as sb is concerned)
verspielt [fɛrˈʃpiːlt] *adj* playful
versponnen [fɛrˈʃpɔnən] *adj* crackpot
verspotten [fɛrˈʃpɔtən] *vt* to ridicule, scoff at
versprach *etc* [fɛrˈʃpraːx] *vb siehe* **versprechen**
versprechen [fɛrˈʃprɛçən] *unreg vt* to promise ▷ *vr* (*etwas Nichtgemeintes sagen*) to make a slip of the tongue; **sich** *dat* **etw von etw ~** to expect sth from sth; **Versprechen** (**-s, -**) *nt* promise
Versprecher (**-s, -**) (*umg*) *m* slip (of the tongue)
verspricht [fɛrˈʃprɪçt] *vb siehe* **versprechen**
verspüren [fɛrˈʃpyːrən] *vt* to feel, be conscious of
verstaatlichen [fɛrˈʃtaːtlɪçən] *vt* to nationalize
verstaatlicht *adj*: **~er Industriezweig** nationalized industry
Verstaatlichung *f* nationalization
Verstand [fɛrˈʃtant] *m* intelligence; (*Intellekt*) mind; (*Fähigkeit zu denken*) reason; **den ~ verlieren** to go out of one's mind; **über jds ~** *akk* **gehen** to be beyond sb
verstand *etc vb siehe* **verstehen**
verstanden [fɛrˈʃtandən] *pp von* **verstehen**
verstandesmäßig *adj* rational
verständig [fɛrˈʃtɛndɪç] *adj* sensible
verständigen [fɛrˈʃtɛndɪgən] *vt* to inform ▷ *vr* to communicate; (*sich einigen*) to come to an understanding
Verständigkeit *f* good sense
Verständigung *f* communication; (*Benachrichtigung*) informing; (*Einigung*) agreement
verständlich [fɛrˈʃtɛntlɪç] *adj* understandable, comprehensible; (*hörbar*) audible; **sich ~ machen** to make o.s. understood; (*sich klar ausdrücken*) to make o.s. clear
verständlicherweise *adv* understandably (enough)
Verständlichkeit *f* clarity, intelligibility
Verständnis (**-ses, -se**) *nt* understanding; **für etw kein ~ haben** to have no understanding *od* sympathy for sth; (*für Kunst etc*) to have no appreciation of sth; **verständnislos** *adj* uncomprehending; **verständnisvoll** *adj* understanding, sympathetic
verstärken [fɛrˈʃtɛrkən] *vt* to strengthen; (*Ton*) to amplify; (*erhöhen*) to intensify ▷ *vr* to intensify
Verstärker (**-s, -**) *m* amplifier

Verstärkung *f* strengthening; (*Hilfe*) reinforcements *pl*; (*von Ton*) amplification
verstaubt [fɛrˈʃtaʊpt] *adj* dusty; (*fig: Ansichten*) fuddy-duddy (*umg*)
verstauchen [fɛrˈʃtaʊxən] *vt* to sprain
verstauen [fɛrˈʃtaʊən] *vt* to stow away
Versteck [fɛrˈʃtɛk] **(-(e)s, -e)** *nt* hiding (place)
verstecken *vt, vr* to hide
versteckt *adj* hidden; (*Tür*) concealed; (*fig: Lächeln, Blick*) furtive; (*Andeutung*) veiled
verstehen [fɛrˈʃteːən] *unreg vt, vi* to understand; (*können, beherrschen*) to know ▷ *vr* (*auskommen*) to get on; **das ist nicht wörtlich zu ~** that isn't to be taken literally; **das versteht sich von selbst** that goes without saying; **die Preise ~ sich einschließlich Lieferung** prices are inclusive of delivery; **sich auf etw** *akk* **~** to be an expert at sth
versteifen [fɛrˈʃtaɪfən] *vt* to stiffen, brace ▷ *vr* (*fig*): **sich ~ auf** *+akk* to insist on
versteigen [fɛrˈʃtaɪgən] *unreg vr*: **sie hat sich zu der Behauptung verstiegen, dass ...** she presumed to claim that ...
versteigern [fɛrˈʃtaɪgərn] *vt* to auction
Versteigerung *f* auction
verstellbar *adj* adjustable, variable
verstellen [fɛrˈʃtɛlən] *vt* to move, shift; (*Uhr*) to adjust; (*versperren*) to block; (*fig*) to disguise ▷ *vr* to pretend, put on an act
Verstellung *f* pretence (*Brit*), pretense (*US*)
versteuern [fɛrˈʃtɔʏərn] *vt* to pay tax on; **zu ~** taxable
verstiegen [fɛrˈʃtiːgən] *adj* exaggerated
verstimmt [fɛrˈʃtɪmt] *adj* out of tune; (*fig*) cross, put out; (*: Magen*) upset
Verstimmung *f* (*fig*) disgruntled state, peevishness
verstockt [fɛrˈʃtɔkt] *adj* stubborn; **Verstocktheit** *f* stubbornness
verstohlen [fɛrˈʃtoːlən] *adj* stealthy
verstopfen [fɛrˈʃtɔpfən] *vt* to block, stop up; (*Med*) to constipate
Verstopfung *f* obstruction; (*Med*) constipation
verstorben [fɛrˈʃtɔrbən] *adj* deceased, late
Verstorbene, r *f(m)* deceased
verstört [fɛrˈʃtøːrt] *adj* (*Mensch*) distraught
Verstoß [fɛrˈʃtoːs] *m*: **~ (gegen)** infringement (of), violation (of)
verstoßen *unreg vt* to disown, reject ▷ *vi*: **~ gegen** to offend against
Verstrebung [fɛrˈʃtreːbʊŋ] *f* (*Strebebalken*) support(ing beam)
verstreichen [fɛrˈʃtraɪçən] *unreg vt* to spread ▷ *vi* to elapse; (*Zeit*) to pass (by); (*Frist*) to expire
verstreuen [fɛrˈʃtrɔʏən] *vt* to scatter (about)
verstricken [fɛrˈʃtrɪkən] *vt* (*fig*) to entangle, ensnare ▷ *vr*: **sich ~ in** *+akk* to get entangled in
verströmen [fɛrˈʃtrøːmən] *vt* to exude
verstümmeln [fɛrˈʃtʏməln] *vt* to maim, mutilate (*auch fig*)
verstummen [fɛrˈʃtʊmən] *vi* to go silent; (*Lärm*) to die away
Versuch [fɛrˈzuːx] **(-(e)s, -e)** *m* attempt; (*Chem etc*) experiment; **das käme auf einen ~ an** we'll have to have a try
versuchen *vt* to try; (*verlocken*) to tempt ▷ *vr*: **sich an etw** *dat* **~** to try one's hand at sth
Versuchs- *zW*: **Versuchsanstalt** *f* research institute; **Versuchsbohrung** *f* experimental drilling; **Versuchskaninchen** *nt* guinea pig; **Versuchsobjekt** *nt* test object; (*fig: Mensch*) guinea pig; **Versuchsreihe** *f* series of experiments; **versuchsweise** *adv* tentatively
Versuchung *f* temptation
versumpfen [fɛrˈzʊmpfən] *vi* (*Gebiet*) to become marshy; (*fig: umg*) to go to pot; (*lange zechen*) to get involved in a booze-up (*Brit*) *od* drinking spree (*US*)
versündigen [fɛrˈzʏndɪgən] *vr* (*geh*): **sich an jdm/etw ~** to sin against sb/sth
versunken [fɛrˈzʊŋkən] *adj* sunken; **~ sein in** *+akk* to be absorbed *od* engrossed in; **Versunkenheit** *f* absorption
versüßen [fɛrˈzyːsən] *vt*: **jdm etw ~** (*fig*) to make sth more pleasant for sb
vertagen [fɛrˈtaːgən] *vt, vi* to adjourn
Vertagung *f* adjournment
vertauschen [fɛrˈtaʊʃən] *vt* to exchange; (*versehentlich*) to mix up; **vertauschte Rollen** reversed roles
verteidigen [fɛrˈtaɪdɪgən] *vt* to defend ▷ *vr* to defend o.s.; (*vor Gericht*) to conduct one's own defence (*Brit*) *od* defense (*US*)
Verteidiger, in (-s, -) *m(f)* defender; (*Anwalt*) defence (*Brit*) *od* defense (*US*) lawyer
Verteidigung *f* defence (*Brit*), defense (*US*)
Verteidigungsfähigkeit *f* ability to defend
Verteidigungsminister *m* Minister of Defence (*Brit*), Defense Secretary (*US*)
verteilen [fɛrˈtaɪlən] *vt* to distribute; (*Rollen*) to assign; (*Salbe*) to spread
Verteiler (-s, -) *m* (*Comm, Aut*) distributor
Verteilung *f* distribution
Verteuerung [fɛrˈtɔʏərʊŋ] *f* increase in price
verteufeln [fɛrˈtɔʏfəln] *vt* to condemn
verteufelt (*umg*) *adj* awful, devilish ▷ *adv* awfully, devilishly
vertiefen [fɛrˈtiːfən] *vt* to deepen; (*Sch*) to consolidate ▷ *vr*: **sich in etw** *akk* **~** to become engrossed *od* absorbed in sth
Vertiefung *f* depression
vertikal [vɛrtiˈkaːl] *adj* vertical
vertilgen [fɛrˈtɪlgən] *vt* to exterminate; (*umg*) to eat up, consume
Vertilgungsmittel *nt* weedkiller; (*Insektenvertilgungsmittel*) pesticide
vertippen [fɛrˈtɪpən] *vr* to make a typing mistake
vertonen [fɛrˈtoːnən] *vt* to set to music; (*Film etc*) to add a soundtrack to
vertrackt [fɛrˈtrakt] *adj* awkward, tricky, complex
Vertrag [fɛrˈtraːk] **(-(e)s, ¨-e)** *m* contract, agreement; (*Pol*) treaty
vertragen [fɛrˈtraːgən] *unreg vt* to tolerate, stand ▷ *vr* to get along; (*sich aussöhnen*)

to become reconciled; **viel ~ können** (*umg*: *Alkohol*) to be able to hold one's drink; **sich mit etw ~** (*Nahrungsmittel, Farbe*) to go with sth; (*Aussage, Verhalten*) to be consistent with sth

vertraglich *adj* contractual

verträglich [fɛr'trɛ:klıç] *adj* good-natured; (*Speisen*) easily digested; (*Med*) easily tolerated; **Verträglichkeit** *f* good nature; digestibility

Vertrags- *zW*: **Vertragsbruch** *m* breach of contract; **vertragsbrüchig** *adj* in breach of contract; **vertragsfähig** *adj* (*Jur*) competent to contract; **vertragsmäßig** *adj, adv* (as) stipulated, according to contract; **Vertragspartner** *m* party to a contract; **Vertragsspieler** *m* (*Sport*) player under contract; **vertragswidrig** *adj, adv* contrary to contract

vertrauen [fɛr'traʊən] *vi*: **jdm ~** to trust sb; **~ auf** *+akk* to rely on; **Vertrauen (-s)** *nt* confidence; **jdn ins Vertrauen ziehen** to take sb into one's confidence; **Vertrauen zu jdm fassen** to gain confidence in sb; **vertrauenerweckend** *adj* inspiring trust

Vertrauens- *zW*: **Vertrauensmann (-(e)s,** *pl* **-männer** *od* **-leute)** *m* intermediary; **Vertrauenssache** *f* (*vertrauliche Angelegenheit*) confidential matter; (*Frage des Vertrauens*) question of trust; **vertrauensselig** *adj* trusting; **vertrauensvoll** *adj* trustful; **Vertrauensvotum** *nt* (*Parl*) vote of confidence; **vertrauenswürdig** *adj* trustworthy

vertraulich [fɛr'traʊlıç] *adj* familiar; (*geheim*) confidential; **Vertraulichkeit** *f* familiarity; confidentiality

verträumt [fɛr'trɔʏmt] *adj* dreamy; (*Städtchen etc*) sleepy

vertraut [fɛr'traʊt] *adj* familiar; **sich mit dem Gedanken ~ machen, dass ...** to get used to the idea that ...

Vertraute, r *f(m)* confidant(e), close friend

Vertrautheit *f* familiarity

vertreiben [fɛr'traıbən] *unreg vt* to drive away; (*aus Land*) to expel; (*Comm*) to sell; (*Zeit*) to pass

Vertreibung *f* expulsion

vertretbar *adj* justifiable; (*Theorie, Argument*) tenable

vertreten [fɛr'tre:tən] *unreg vt* to represent; (*Ansicht*) to hold, advocate; (*ersetzen*) to replace; (*Kollegen*) to cover for; (*Comm*) to be the agent for; **sich** *dat* **die Beine ~** to stretch one's legs

Vertreter, in (-s, -) *m(f)* representative; (*Verfechter*) advocate; (*Comm: Firma*) agent; **Vertreterprovision** *f* agent's commission

Vertretung *f* representation; advocacy; **die ~ übernehmen (für)** to stand in (for)

Vertretungsstunde *f* (*Sch*) cover lesson

Vertrieb [fɛr'tri:p] **(-(e)s, -e)** *m* marketing; **den ~ für eine Firma haben** to have the (selling) agency for a firm

Vertriebene, r [fɛr'tri:bənə(r)] *f(m)* exile

Vertriebskosten *pl* marketing costs *pl*

vertrocknen [fɛr'trɔknən] *vi* to dry up

vertrödeln [fɛr'trø:dəln] (*umg*) *vt* to fritter away

vertrösten [fɛr'trø:stən] *vt* to put off

vertun [fɛr'tu:n] *unreg vt* to waste ▷ *vr* (*umg*) to make a mistake

vertuschen [fɛr'tʊʃən] *vt* to hush *od* cover up

verübeln [fɛr'|y:bəln] *vt*: **jdm etw ~** to be cross *od* offended with sb on account of sth

verüben [fɛr'|y:bən] *vt* to commit

verulken [fɛr'|ʊlkən] (*umg*) *vt* to make fun of

verunglimpfen [fɛr'|ʊnglımpfən] *vt* to disparage

verunglücken [fɛr'|ʊnglʏkən] *vi* to have an accident; (*fig: umg: misslingen*) to go wrong; **tödlich ~** to be killed in an accident

Verunglückte, r *f(m)* accident victim

verunreinigen [fɛr'|ʊnraınıgən] *vt* to soil; (*Umwelt*) to pollute

verunsichern [fɛr'|ʊnzıçərn] *vt* to rattle (*fig*)

verunstalten [fɛr'|ʊnʃtaltən] *vt* to disfigure; (*Gebäude etc*) to deface

veruntreuen [fɛr'|ʊntrɔʏən] *vt* to embezzle

verursachen [fɛr'|u:rzaxən] *vt* to cause

verurteilen [fɛr'|u:rtaılən] *vt* to condemn; (*zu Strafe*) to sentence; (*für schuldig befinden*): **jdn ~ (für)** to convict sb (of)

Verurteilung *f* condemnation; (*Jur*) sentence; conviction

vervielfachen [fɛr'fi:lfaxən] *vt* to multiply

vervielfältigen [fɛr'fi:lfɛltıgən] *vt* to duplicate, copy

Vervielfältigung *f* duplication, copying

vervollkommnen [fɛr'fɔlkɔmnən] *vt* to perfect

vervollständigen [fɛr'fɔlʃtɛndıgən] *vt* to complete

verw. *abk* = **verwitwet**

verwachsen [fɛr'vaksən] *adj* (*Mensch*) deformed; (*verkümmert*) stunted; (*überwuchert*) overgrown

verwackeln [fɛr'vakəln] *vt* (*Foto*) to blur

verwählen [fɛr'vɛ:lən] *vr* (*Tel*) to dial the wrong number

verwahren [fɛr'va:rən] *vt* to keep (safe) ▷ *vr* to protest

verwahrlosen *vi* to become neglected; (*moralisch*) to go to the bad

verwahrlost *adj* neglected; (*moralisch*) wayward

Verwahrung *f* (*von Geld etc*) keeping; (*von Täter*) custody, detention; **jdn in ~ nehmen** to take sb into custody

verwaist [fɛr'vaıst] *adj* orphaned

verwalten [fɛr'valtən] *vt* to manage; (*Behörde*) to administer

Verwalter, in (-s, -) *m(f)* administrator; (*Vermögensverwalter*) trustee

Verwaltung *f* management; administration

Verwaltungs- *zW*: **Verwaltungsapparat** *m* administrative machinery; **Verwaltungsbezirk** *m* administrative district; **Verwaltungsgericht** *nt* Administrative Court

verwandeln [fɛr'vandəln] *vt* to change, transform ▷ *vr* to change

Verwandlung *f* change, transformation
verwandt [fɛr'vant] *adj*: ~ **(mit)** related (to); **geistig ~ sein** (*fig*) to be kindred spirits
Verwandte, r *f(m)* relative, relation
Verwandtschaft *f* relationship; (*Menschen*) relatives *pl*, relations *pl*; (*fig*) affinity
verwarnen [fɛr'varnən] *vt* to caution
Verwarnung *f* caution
verwaschen [fɛr'vaʃən] *adj* faded; (*fig*) vague
verwässern [fɛr'vɛsərn] *vt* to dilute, water down
verwechseln [fɛr'vɛksəln] *vt*: ~ **mit** to confuse with; **zum V~ ähnlich** as like as two peas
Verwechslung *f* confusion, mixing up; **das muss eine ~ sein** there must be some mistake
verwegen [fɛr've:gən] *adj* daring, bold; **Verwegenheit** *f* daring, audacity, boldness
verwehren [fɛr've:rən] *vt* (*geh*): **jdm etw ~** to refuse *od* deny sb sth
Verwehung [fɛr've:ʊŋ] *f* (*Schneeverwehung*) snowdrift; (*Sandverwehung*) sanddrift
verweichlichen [fɛr'vaiçlıçən] *vt* to mollycoddle
verweichlicht *adj* effeminate, soft
verweigern [fɛr'vaıgərn] *vt*: **jdm etw ~** to refuse sb sth; **den Gehorsam/die Aussage ~** to refuse to obey/testify
Verweigerung *f* refusal
verweilen [fɛr'vaılən] *vi* to stay; (*fig*): **~ bei** to dwell on
verweint [fɛr'vaınt] *adj* (*Augen*) swollen with tears *od* with crying; (*Gesicht*) tear-stained
Verweis [fɛr'vaıs] **(-es, -e)** *m* reprimand, rebuke; (*Hinweis*) reference
verweisen [fɛr'vaızən] *unreg vt* to refer; **jdn auf etw** *akk***/an jdn ~** (*hinweisen*) to refer sb to sth/sb; **jdn vom Platz** *od* **des Spielfeldes ~** (*Sport*) to send sb off; **jdn von der Schule ~** to expel sb (from school); **jdn des Landes ~** to deport sb
Verweisung *f* reference; (*Landesverweisung*) deportation
verwelken [fɛr'vɛlkən] *vi* to fade; (*Blumen*) to wilt
verweltlichen [fɛr'vɛltlıçən] *vt* to secularize
verwendbar [fɛr'vɛndba:r] *adj* usable
verwenden [fɛr'vɛndən] *unreg vt* to use; (*Mühe, Zeit, Arbeit*) to spend ▷ *vr* to intercede
Verwendung *f* use
Verwendungsmöglichkeit *f* (possible) use
verwerfen [fɛr'vɛrfən] *unreg vt* to reject; (*Urteil*) to quash; (*kritisieren: Handlungsweise*) to condemn
verwerflich [fɛr'vɛrflıç] *adj* reprehensible
verwertbar *adj* usable
verwerten [fɛr've:rtən] *vt* to utilize
Verwertung *f* utilization
verwesen [fɛr've:zən] *vi* to decay
Verwesung *f* decomposition
verwickeln [fɛr'vıkəln] *vt* to tangle (up); (*fig*) to involve ▷ *vr* to get tangled (up); **jdn ~ in** *+akk* to involve sb in, get sb involved in; **sich ~ in** *+akk* to get involved in
verwickelt *adj* involved
Verwicklung *f* entanglement, complication
verwildern [fɛr'vıldərn] *vi* to run wild
verwildert *adj* wild; (*Garten*) overgrown; (*jds Aussehen*) unkempt
verwinden [fɛr'vındən] *unreg vt* to get over
verwirken [fɛr'vırkən] *vt* (*geh*) to forfeit
verwirklichen [fɛr'vırklıçən] *vt* to realize, put into effect
Verwirklichung *f* realization
verwirren [fɛr'vırən] *vt* to tangle (up); (*fig*) to confuse
Verwirrspiel *nt* confusing tactics *pl*
Verwirrung *f* confusion
verwischen [fɛr'vıʃən] *vt* (*verschmieren*) to smudge; (*lit, fig: Spuren*) to cover over; (*fig: Erinnerungen*) to blur
verwittern [fɛr'vıtərn] *vi* to weather
verwitwet [fɛr'vıtvət] *adj* widowed
verwöhnen [fɛr'vø:nən] *vt* to spoil, pamper
Verwöhnung *f* spoiling, pampering
verworfen [fɛr'vɔrfən] *adj* depraved; **Verworfenheit** *f* depravity
verworren [fɛr'vɔrən] *adj* confused
verwundbar [fɛr'vʊntba:r] *adj* vulnerable
verwunden [fɛr'vʊndən] *vt* to wound
verwunderlich [fɛr'vʊndərlıç] *adj* surprising; (*stärker*) astonishing
verwundern *vt* to astonish ▷ *vr*: **sich ~ über** *+akk* to be astonished at
Verwunderung *f* astonishment
Verwundete, r *f(m)* injured person; **die ~n** the injured; (*Mil*) the wounded
Verwundung *f* wound, injury
verwünschen [fɛr'vʏnʃən] *vt* to curse
verwurzelt [fɛr'vʊrtsəlt] *adj*: **(fest) in etw** *dat* *od* **mit etw** ~ (*fig*) deeply rooted in sth
verwüsten [fɛr'vy:stən] *vt* to devastate
Verwüstung *f* devastation
Verz. *abk* = **Verzeichnis**
verzagen [fɛr'tsa:gən] *vi* to despair
verzagt [fɛr'tsa:kt] *adj* disheartened
verzählen [fɛr'tsɛ:lən] *vr* to miscount
verzahnen [fɛr'tsa:nən] *vt* to dovetail; (*Zahnräder*) to cut teeth in
verzapfen [fɛr'tsapfən] (*umg*) *vt*: **Unsinn ~** to talk nonsense
verzaubern [fɛr'tsaʊbərn] *vt* (*lit*) to cast a spell on; (*fig: jdn*) to enchant
verzehren [fɛr'tse:rən] *vt* to consume
verzeichnen [fɛr'tsaıçnən] *vt* to list; (*Niederlage, Verlust*) to register
Verzeichnis **(-ses, -se)** *nt* list, catalogue (*Brit*), catalog (*US*); (*in Buch*) index; (*Comput*) directory
verzeihen [fɛr'tsaıən] *unreg vt, vi* to forgive; **jdm etw ~** to forgive sb (for) sth; **~ Sie!** excuse me!
verzeihlich *adj* pardonable
Verzeihung *f* forgiveness, pardon; **~!** sorry!, excuse me!; **(jdn) um ~ bitten** to apologize (to sb)
verzerren [fɛr'tsɛrən] *vt* to distort; (*Sehne, Muskel*) to strain, pull

verzetteln [fɛr'tsɛtəln] *vr* to waste a lot of time
Verzicht [fɛr'tsɪçt] **(-(e)s, -e)** *m*: **~ (auf** *+akk***)** renunciation (of); **verzichten** *vi*: **verzichten auf** *+akk* to forego, give up
verziehen [fɛr'tsi:ən] *unreg vi (Hilfsverb sein)* to move ▷ *vt* to put out of shape; *(Kind)* to spoil; *(Pflanzen)* to thin out ▷ *vr* to go out of shape; *(Gesicht)* to contort; *(verschwinden)* to disappear; **verzogen** *(Vermerk)* no longer at this address; **keine Miene ~** not to turn a hair; **das Gesicht ~** to pull a face
verzieren [fɛr'tsi:rən] *vt* to decorate
Verzierung *f* decoration
verzinsen [fɛr'tsɪnzən] *vt* to pay interest on
verzinslich *adj*: **(fest)~ sein** to yield (a fixed rate of) interest
verzogen [fɛr'tso:gən] *adj (Kind)* spoilt; *siehe auch* **verziehen**
verzögern [fɛr'tsø:gərn] *vt* to delay
Verzögerung *f* delay
Verzögerungstaktik *f* delaying tactics *pl*
verzollen [fɛr'tsɔlən] *vt* to pay duty on; **haben Sie etwas zu ~?** have you anything to declare?
verzücken [fɛr'tsʏkən] *vt* to send into ecstasies, enrapture
Verzug [fɛr'tsu:k] *m* delay; *(Fin)* arrears *pl*; **mit etw in ~ geraten** to fall behind with sth
verzweifeln [fɛr'tsvaɪfəln] *vi* to despair
verzweifelt *adj* desperate
Verzweiflung *f* despair
verzweigen [fɛr'tsvaɪgən] *vr* to branch out
verzwickt [fɛr'tsvɪkt] *(umg) adj* awkward, complicated
Vesper ['fɛspər] **(-, -n)** *f* vespers *pl*
Vesuv [ve'zu:f] **(-(s))** *m* Vesuvius
Veto ['ve:to] **(-s, -s)** *nt* veto
Vetter ['fɛtər] **(-s, -n)** *m* cousin
vgl. *abk (= vergleiche)* cf
v. H. *abk (= vom Hundert)* pc
VHS (-) *f abk* = **Volkshochschule**
Viadukt [via'dʊkt] **(-(e)s, -e)** *m* viaduct
Vibrator [vi'bra:tɔr] *m* vibrator
vibrieren [vi'bri:rən] *vi* to vibrate
Video ['vi:deo] **(-s, -s)** *nt* video; **Videoaufnahme** *f* video (recording); **Videokamera** *f* video camera; **Videorekorder** *m* video recorder; **Videospiel** *nt* video game; **Videotext** *m* teletext
Vieh [fi:] **(-(e)s)** *nt* cattle *pl*; *(Nutztiere)* livestock; *(umg: Tier)* animal; **viehisch** *adj* bestial; **Viehzucht** *f* (live)stock *od* cattle breeding
viel [fi:l] *adj* a lot of, much ▷ *adv* a lot, much; **in ~em** in many respects; **noch (ein)mal so ~** *(Zeit etc)* as much (time *etc*) again; **einer zu ~** one too many; **~ zu wenig** much too little; **~ beschäftigt** very busy; **~ geprüft** *(hum)* sorely tried; **~ sagend** significant; **~ versprechend** promising; **viele** *pl* a lot of, many; **gleich viele (Angestellte/Anteile** *etc***)** the same number (of employees/shares *etc*)
vielerlei *adj* a great variety of
vielerorts *adv* in many places
viel- *zW*: **vielfach** *adj, adv* many times; **auf vielfachen Wunsch** at the request of many people; **Vielfache, s** *nt (Math)* multiple; **um ein Vielfaches** many times over; **Vielfalt** (-) *f* variety; **vielfältig** *adj* varied, many-sided; **Vielfraß** *m* glutton
vielleicht [fi'laɪçt] *adv* perhaps; *(in Bitten)* by any chance; **du bist ~ ein Idiot!** *(umg)* you really are an idiot!
viel- *zW*: **vielmal, vielmals** *adv* many times; **danke vielmals** many thanks; **ich bitte vielmals um Entschuldigung!** I do apologize!; **vielmehr** *adv* rather, on the contrary; **vielsagend** *adj* significant; **vielschichtig** *adj (fig)* complex; **vielseitig** *adj* many-sided; *(Ausbildung)* all-round *attr*; *(Interessen)* varied; *(Mensch, Gerät)* versatile; **vielversprechend** *adj* promising; **Vielvölkerstaat** *m* multinational state
vier [fi:r] *num* four; **alle ~e von sich strecken** *(umg)* to stretch out; **Vierbeiner** *m (hum)* four-legged friend; **Viereck (-(e)s, -e)** *nt* four-sided figure; *(gleichseitig)* square; **viereckig** *adj* four-sided; square; **vierhundert** *num* four hundred; **vierkant** *adj, adv (Naut)* square; **vierköpfig** *adj*: **eine vierköpfige Familie** a family of four; **Viermächteabkommen** *nt* four-power agreement
viert *adj*: **wir gingen zu ~** four of us went
Viertaktmotor *m* four-stroke engine
vierte, r, s ['fi:rtə(r, s)] *adj* fourth
vierteilen *vt* to quarter
Viertel ['fɪrtəl] **(-s, -)** *nt* quarter; **ein ~ Leberwurst** a quarter of liver sausage; **Viertelfinale** *nt* quarter finals *pl*; **Vierteljahr** *nt* three months *pl*, quarter *(COMM, FIN)*; **Vierteljahresschrift** *f* quarterly; **vierteljährlich** *adj* quarterly; **Viertelnote** *f* crotchet *(Brit)*, quarter note *(US)*; **Viertelstunde** *f* quarter of an hour
vier- *zW*: **viertürig** *adj* four-door *attr*; **Vierwaldstättersee** *m* Lake Lucerne; **vierzehn** ['fɪrtse:n] *num* fourteen; **in vierzehn Tagen** in a fortnight *(Brit)*, in two weeks *(US)*; **vierzehntägig** *adj* fortnightly; **vierzehnte, r, s** *adj* fourteenth
vierzig ['fɪrtsɪç] *num* forty; **Vierzigstundenwoche** *f* forty-hour week
Vierzimmerwohnung *f* four-room flat *(Brit) od* apartment *(US)*
Vietnam [viɛt'nam] **(-s)** *nt* Vietnam
Vietnamese [viɛtna'me:zə] **(-n, -n)** *m*, **Vietnamesin** *f* Vietnamese
vietnamesisch *adj* Vietnamese
Vikar [vi'ka:r] **(-s, -e)** *m* curate
Villa ['vɪla] **(-, Villen)** *f* villa
Villenviertel *nt* (prosperous) residential area
violett [vio'lɛt] *adj* violet
Violinbogen *m* violin bow
Violine [vio'li:nə] **(-, -n)** *f* violin
Violinkonzert *nt* violin concerto
Violinschlüssel *m* treble clef
virtuell [vɪrtu'ɛl] *adj (Comput)* virtual; **~e Realität** virtual reality

virtuos [vɪrtu'oːs] *adj* virtuoso *attrib*
Virtuose [vɪrtu'oːzə] (**-n, -n**) *m* virtuoso
Virtuosin [vɪrtu'oːzɪn] *f* virtuoso
Virtuosität [vɪrtuozi'tɛt] *f* virtuosity
Virus ['viːrʊs] (**-, Viren**) *m od nt* (*also Comput*) virus
Virus- *in zw* viral: **Virusinfektion** *f* virus infection
Visage [vi'zaːʒə] (**-, -n**) (*pej*) *f* face, (ugly) mug (*umg*)
Visagist, in [viza'ʒɪst(ɪn)] *m(f)* make-up artist
vis-à-vis, vis-a-vis [viza'viː] *adv* (*veraltet*): **~ (von)** opposite (to) ▷ *präp +dat* opposite (to)
Visier [vi'ziːr] (**-s, -e**) *nt* gunsight; (*am Helm*) visor
Vision [vizi'oːn] *f* vision
Visite [vi'ziːtə] (**-, -n**) *f* (*Med*) visit
Visitenkarte *f* visiting card
visuell [vizu'ɛl] *adj* visual
Visum ['viːzʊm] (**-s, Visa** *od* **Visen**) *nt* visa; **Visumzwang** *m* obligation to hold a visa
vital [vi'taːl] *adj* lively, full of life; (*lebenswichtig*) vital
Vitamin [vita'miːn] (**-s, -e**) *nt* vitamin; **Vitaminmangel** *m* vitamin deficiency
Vitrine [vi'triːnə] (**-, -n**) *f* (*Schrank*) glass cabinet; (*Schaukasten*) showcase, display case
Vivisektion [vivizɛktsi'oːn] *f* vivisection
Vize ['fiːtsə] *m* (*umg*) number two; (: *Vizemeister*) runner-up ▷ *in zw* vice-
v. J. *abk* (= *vorigen Jahres*) of the previous *od* last year
Vlies [fliːs] (**-es, -e**) *nt* fleece
v. M. *abk* (= *vorigen Monats*) ult.
V-Mann *m abk* = **Verbindungsmann; Vertrauensmann**
VN *pl abk* (= *Vereinte Nationen*) UN
VO *abk* = **Verordnung**
Vogel ['foːgəl] (**-s, ¨-**) *m* bird; **einen ~ haben** (*umg*) to have bats in the belfry; **den ~ abschießen** (*umg*) to surpass everyone (*ironisch*); **Vogelbauer** *nt* birdcage; **Vogelbeerbaum** *m* rowan (tree); **Vogeldreck** *m* bird droppings *pl*; **Vogelperspektive** *f* bird's-eye view; **Vogelschau** *f* bird's-eye view; **Vogelscheuche** *f* scarecrow; **Vogelschutzgebiet** *nt* bird sanctuary; **Vogel-Strauß-Politik** *f* head-in-the-sand policy
Vogesen [vo'geːzən] *pl* Vosges *pl*
Voicemail ['vɔismeːl] *f* (*Tel*) voice mail
Vokabel [vo'kaːbəl] (**-, -n**) *f* word
Vokabular [vokabu'laːr] (**-s, -e**) *nt* vocabulary
Vokal [vo'kaːl] (**-s, -e**) *m* vowel
Volk [fɔlk] (**-(e)s, ¨-er**) *nt* people; (*Nation*) nation; **etw unters ~ bringen** (*Nachricht*) to spread sth
Völker- *zW*: **Völkerbund** *m* League of Nations; **Völkerkunde** *f* ethnology; **Völkermord** *m* genocide; **Völkerrecht** *nt* international law; **völkerrechtlich** *adj* according to international law; **Völkerverständigung** *f* international understanding; **Völkerwanderung** *f* migration
Volks- *zW*: **Volksabstimmung** *f* referendum; **Volksarmee** *f* People's Army; **Volksbegehren** *nt* petition for a referendum; **Volksdeutsche, r** *f(m) dekl wie adj* ethnic German; **volkseigen** *adj* (DDR) nationally-owned; **Volksfeind** *m* enemy of the people; **Volksfest** *nt* popular festival; (*Jahrmarkt*) fair
Volkshochschule *f* adult education classes *pl*; *see culture note*

VOLKSHOCHSCHULE

The *Volkshochschule* (VHS) is an institution which offers Adult Education classes. No set qualifications are necessary to attend. For a small fee adults can attend both vocational and non-vocational classes in the day-time or evening.

Volks- *zW*: **Volkslauf** *m* fun run; **Volkslied** *nt* folk song; **Volksmund** *m* vernacular; **Volkspolizei** *f* (DDR) People's Police; **Volksrepublik** *f* people's republic; **Volksschule** *f* ≈ primary school (*Brit*), ≈ elementary school (*US*); **Volksseuche** *f* epidemic; **Volksstamm** *m* tribe; **Volksstück** *nt* folk play in dialect; **Volkstanz** *m* folk dance; **Volkstrauertag** *m* ≈ Remembrance Day (*Brit*), ≈ Memorial Day (*US*); **volkstümlich** *adj* popular; **Volkswirtschaft** *f* national economy; (*Fach*) economics *sing*, political economy; **Volkswirtschaftler** *m* economist; **Volkszählung** *f* (national) census
voll [fɔl] *adj* full ▷ *adv* fully; (*Tafel*) to cover (with writing); **jdn für ~ nehmen** (*umg*) to take sb seriously; **aus dem V~en schöpfen** to draw on unlimited resources; **in ~er Größe** (*Bild*) life-size(d); (*bei plötzlicher Erscheinung etc*) large as life; **~ sein** (*umg: satt*) to be full (up); (: *betrunken*) to be plastered; **~ und ganz** completely; *siehe auch* **vollmachen; vollschreiben; volltanken**
vollauf [fɔl'|aʊf] *adv* amply; **~ zu tun haben** to have quite enough to do
voll- *zW*: **Vollbad** *nt* (proper) bath; **Vollbart** *m* full beard; **Vollbeschäftigung** *f* full employment; **Vollbesitz** *m*: **im Vollbesitz** *+gen* in full possession of; **Vollblut** *nt* thoroughbred; **vollblütig** *adj* full-blooded; **Vollbremsung** *f* emergency stop; **vollbringen** *unreg vt untr* to accomplish; **Volldampf** *m* (*Naut*): **mit Volldampf** at full steam; **vollenden** *vt untr* to finish, complete; **vollendet** *adj* (*vollkommen*) perfect; (*Tänzer etc*) accomplished; **vollends** *adv* completely; **Vollendung** *f* completion
voller *adj* fuller; **~ Flecken/Ideen** full of stains/ideas
Völlerei [fœlə'raɪ] *f* gluttony
Volleyball ['vɔlibal] (**-(e)s**) *m* volleyball
voll- *zW*: **vollfett** *adj* full-fat; **Vollgas** *nt*: **mit Vollgas** at full throttle; **Vollgas geben** to step on it
völlig ['fœlɪç] *adj* complete ▷ *adv* completely

voll- *zW*: **volljährig** *adj* of age; **Vollkaskoversicherung** *f* fully comprehensive insurance; **vollkommen** *adj* perfect; (*völlig*) complete, absolute; **Vollkommenheit** *f* perfection; **Vollkornbrot** *nt* wholemeal (*Brit*) *od* whole-wheat (*US*) bread; **volllaufen** *unreg vi*: **etw volllaufen lassen** to fill sth up; **vollmachen** *vt* to fill (up); **Vollmacht** *f* authority, power of attorney; **Vollmatrose** *m* able-bodied seaman; **Vollmilch** *f* full-cream milk; **Vollmond** *m* full moon; **Vollnarkose** *f* general anaesthetic (*Brit*) *od* anesthetic (*US*); **Vollpension** *f* full board; **vollschlank** *adj* plump, stout; **vollschreiben** *unreg vt* (*Heft, Seite*) to fill; **vollständig** *adj* complete; **vollstrecken** *vt untr* to execute; **volltanken** *vt, vi* to fill up; **Volltreffer** *m* (*lit, fig*) bull's-eye; **Vollversammlung** *f* general meeting; **Vollwaise** *f* orphan; **vollwertig** *adj* full *attrib*; (*Stellung*) equal; **Vollwertkost** *f* wholefoods *pl*; **vollzählig** *adj* complete; (*anwesend*) in full number; **vollziehen** *unreg vt untr* to carry out ▷ *vr untr* to happen; **Vollzug** *m* execution

Volontär, in [volɔnˈtɛːr(ɪn)] (**-s, -e**) *m(f)* trainee

Volt [vɔlt] (**-** *od* **-(e)s, -**) *nt* volt

Volumen [voˈluːmən] (**-s, -** *od* **Volumina**) *nt* volume

vom [fɔm] = **von dem**

SCHLÜSSELWORT

von [fɔn] *präp +dat* **1** (*Ausgangspunkt*) from; **von ... bis** from ... to; **von morgens bis abends** from morning till night; **von ... nach ...** from ... to ...; **von ... an** from ...; **von ... aus** from ...; **von dort aus** from there; **etw von sich aus tun** to do sth of one's own accord; **von mir aus** (*umg*) if you like, I don't mind; **von wo/wann ...?** where/when ... from?

2 (*Ursache, im Passiv*) by; **ein Gedicht von Schiller** a poem by Schiller; **von etw müde** tired from sth

3 (*als Genitiv*) of; **ein Freund von mir** a friend of mine; **nett von dir** nice of you; **jeweils zwei von zehn** two out of every ten

4 (*über*) about; **er erzählte vom Urlaub** he talked about his holiday

5: von wegen! (*umg*) no way!

voneinander *adv* from each other

vonseiten, von Seiten [vɔnˈzaɪtn] *präp +gen* on the part of

vonstattengehen [fɔnˈʃtatən-] *unreg vi* to proceed, go

SCHLÜSSELWORT

vor [foːr] *präp +dat* **1** (*räumlich*) in front of

2 (*zeitlich, Reihenfolge*) before; **ich war vor ihm da** I was there before him; **X kommt vor Y** X comes before Y; **vor zwei Tagen** two days ago; **5 (Minuten) vor 4** 5 (minutes) to 4; **vor Kurzem** a little while ago

3 (*Ursache*) with; **vor Wut/Liebe** with rage/love; **vor Hunger sterben** to die of hunger; **vor lauter Arbeit** because of work

4: vor allem, vor allen Dingen above all

▷ *präp +akk* (*räumlich*) in front of; **vor sich hin summen** to hum to oneself

▷ *adv*: **vor und zurück** backwards and forwards

Vor- *zW*: **Vorabdruck** *m* preprint; **Vorabend** *m* evening before, eve; **Vorahnung** *f* presentiment, premonition

voran [foˈran] *adv* before, ahead; **voranbringen** *unreg vt* to make progress with; **vorangehen** *unreg vi* to go ahead; **einer Sache** *dat* **vorangehen** to precede sth; **vorangehend** *adj* previous; **vorankommen** *unreg vi* to make progress, come along

Voranschlag [ˈfoːr|anʃlaːk] *m* estimate

voranstellen [foˈranʃtɛlən] *vt +dat* to put in front (of); (*fig*) to give precedence (over)

Vorarbeiter [ˈfoːr|arbaɪtər] *m* foreman

voraus [foˈraʊs] *adv* ahead; (*zeitlich*) in advance; **jdm ~ sein** to be ahead of sb; **im V~** in advance; **vorausbezahlen** *vt* to pay in advance; **vorausgehen** *unreg vi* to go (on) ahead; (*fig*) to precede; **voraushaben** *unreg vt*: **jdm etw voraushaben** to have the edge on sb in sth; **Voraussage** *f* prediction; **voraussagen** *vt* to predict; **voraussehen** *unreg vt* to foresee; **voraussetzen** *vt* to assume; (*sicher annehmen*) to take for granted; (*erfordern: Kenntnisse, Geduld*) to require, demand; **vorausgesetzt, dass ...** provided that ...; **Voraussetzung** *f* requirement, prerequisite; **unter der Voraussetzung, dass ...** on condition that ...; **Voraussicht** *f* foresight; **aller Voraussicht nach** in all probability; **in der Voraussicht, dass ...** anticipating that ...; **voraussichtlich** *adv* probably; **Vorauszahlung** *f* advance payment

Vorbau [ˈfoːrbaʊ] (**-(e)s, -ten**) *m* porch; (*Balkon*) balcony

vorbauen [ˈfoːrbaʊən] *vt* to build up in front ▷ *vi +dat* to take precautions (against)

Vorbedacht [ˈfoːrbədaxt] *m*: **mit/ohne ~** (*Überlegung*) with/without due consideration; (*Absicht*) intentionally/unintentionally

Vorbedingung [ˈfoːrbədɪŋʊŋ] *f* precondition

Vorbehalt [ˈfoːrbəhalt] *m* reservation, proviso; **unter dem ~, dass ...** with the reservation that ...

vorbehalten *unreg vt*: **sich/jdm etw ~** to reserve sth (for o.s.)/for sb; **alle Rechte ~** all rights reserved

vorbehaltlich *präp +gen* (*form*) subject to

vorbehaltlos *adj* unconditional ▷ *adv* unconditionally

vorbei [fɔrˈbaɪ] *adv* by, past; **aus und ~** over and done with; **damit ist es nun ~** that's all over now; **vorbeibringen** *unreg* (*umg*) *vt* to drop off; **vorbeigehen** *unreg vi* to pass by,

go past; **vorbeikommen** *unreg vi*: **bei jdm vorbeikommen** to drop *od* call in on sb; **vorbeireden** *vi*: **an etw** *dat* **vorbeireden** to talk around sth
vorbelastet ['fo:rbəlastət] *adj (fig)* handicapped (*Brit*), handicaped (*US*)
Vorbemerkung ['fo:rbəmɛrkʊŋ] *f* introductory remark
vorbereiten ['fo:rbəraɪtən] *vt* to prepare
Vorbereitung *f* preparation
vorbestellen ['fo:rbəʃtɛlən] *vt* to book (in advance), reserve
Vorbestellung *f* advance booking
vorbestraft ['fo:rbəʃtraft] *adj* previously convicted, with a record
Vorbeugehaft *f* preventive custody
vorbeugen ['fo:rbɔʏgən] *vt, vr* to lean forward ▷ *vi +dat* to prevent
vorbeugend *adj* preventive
Vorbeugung *f* prevention; **zur ~ gegen** for the prevention of
Vorbild ['fo:rbɪlt] *nt* model; **sich** *dat* **jdn zum ~ nehmen** to model o.s. on sb; **vorbildlich** *adj* model, ideal
Vorbildung ['fo:rbɪldʊŋ] *f* educational background
Vorbote ['fo:rbo:tə] *m (fig)* herald
vorbringen ['fo:rbrɪŋən] *unreg vt* to voice; (*Meinung etc*) to advance, state; (*umg*: *nach vorne*) to bring to the front
vordatieren ['fo:rdati:rən] *vt (Schreiben)* to postdate
Vorder- *zW*: **Vorderachse** *f* front axle; **Vorderansicht** *f* front view; **Vorderasien** *nt* Near East
vordere, r, s *adj* front
Vorder- *zW*: **Vordergrund** *m* foreground; **im Vordergrund stehen** *(fig)* to be to the fore; **Vordergrundprogramm** *nt (Comput)* foreground program; **vorderhand** *adv* for the present; **Vordermann** (**-(e)s**, *pl* **-männer**) *m* man in front; **jdn auf Vordermann bringen** (*umg*) to get sb to shape up; **Vorderseite** *f* front (side); **Vordersitz** *m* front seat
vorderste, r, s *adj* front
vordrängen ['fo:rdrɛŋən] *vr* to push to the front
vordringen ['fo:rdrɪŋən] *unreg vi*: **bis zu jdm/etw ~** to get as far as sb/sth
vordringlich *adj* urgent
Vordruck ['fo:rdrʊk] *m* form
vorehelich ['fo:r|e:əlɪç] *adj* premarital
voreilig ['fo:r|aɪlɪç] *adj* hasty, rash; **~e Schlüsse ziehen** to jump to conclusions
voreinander [fo:r|aɪ'nandər] *adv (räumlich)* in front of each other; (*einander gegenüber*) face to face
voreingenommen ['fo:r|aɪngənɔmən] *adj* bias(s)ed; **Voreingenommenheit** *f* bias
voreingestellt ['fo:r|aɪngəʃtɛlt] *adj*: **~er Parameter** *(Comput)* default (parameter)
vorenthalten ['fo:r|ɛnthaltən] *unreg vt*: **jdm etw ~** to withhold sth from sb
Vorentscheidung ['fo:r|ɛntʃaɪdʊŋ] *f* preliminary decision
vorerst ['fo:r|e:rst] *adv* for the moment *od* present
Vorfahr ['fo:rfa:r] (**-en, -en**) *m* ancestor
vorfahren *unreg vi* to drive (on) ahead; (*vors Haus etc*) to drive up
Vorfahrt *f (Aut)* right of way; **„~ (be)achten"** "give way" (*Brit*), "yield" (*US*)
Vorfahrts- *zW*: **Vorfahrtsregel** *f* rule of right of way; **Vorfahrtsschild** *nt* "give way" (*Brit*) *od* "yield" (*US*) sign; **Vorfahrtsstraße** *f* major road
Vorfall ['fo:rfal] *m* incident
vorfallen *unreg vi* to occur
Vorfeld ['fo:rfɛlt] *nt (fig)*: **im ~ (***+gen***)** in the run-up (to)
Vorfilm ['fo:rfɪlm] *m* short
vorfinden ['fo:rfɪndən] *unreg vt* to find
Vorfreude ['fo:rfrɔʏdə] *f* anticipation
vorfühlen ['fo:rfy:lən] *vi (fig)* to put out feelers
vorführen ['fo:rfy:rən] *vt* to show, display; (*Theaterstück, Kunststücke*): **(jdm) etw ~** to perform sth (to *od* in front of sb); **dem Gericht ~** to bring before the court
Vorgabe ['fo:rga:bə] *f (Sport)* handicap
Vorgang ['fo:rgaŋ] *m (Ereignis)* event; (*Ablauf*) course of events; (*Chem etc*) process
Vorgänger, in ['fo:rgɛŋər(ɪn)] (**-s, -**) *m(f)* predecessor
vorgaukeln ['fo:rgaʊkəln] *vt*: **jdm etw ~** to lead sb to believe in sth
vorgeben ['fo:rge:bən] *unreg vt* to pretend, use as a pretext; (*Sport*) to give an advantage *od* a start of
Vorgebirge ['fo:rgəbɪrgə] *nt* foothills *pl*
vorgefasst ['fo:rgəfast] *adj* preconceived
vorgefertigt ['fo:rgəfɛrtɪçt] *adj* prefabricated
Vorgefühl ['fo:rgəfy:l] *nt* anticipation; (*etwas Böses*) presentiment
vorgehen ['fo:rge:ən] *unreg vi (voraus)* to go (on) ahead; (*nach vorn*) to go forward; (*handeln*) to act, proceed; (*Uhr*) to be fast; (*Vorrang haben*) to take precedence; (*passieren*) to go on
Vorgehen (**-s**) *nt* action
Vorgehensweise *f* proceedings *pl*
vorgerückt ['fo:rgərʏkt] *adj (Stunde)* late; (*Alter*) advanced
Vorgeschichte ['fo:rgəʃɪçtə] *f* prehistory; (*von Fall, Krankheit*) past history
Vorgeschmack ['fo:rgəʃmak] *m* foretaste
Vorgesetzte, r ['fo:rgəzɛtstə(r)] *f(m)* superior
vorgestern ['fo:rgɛstərn] *adv* the day before yesterday; **von ~** *(fig)* antiquated
vorgreifen ['fo:rgraɪfən] *unreg vi +dat* to anticipate; **jdm ~** to forestall sb
vorhaben ['fo:rha:bən] *unreg vt* to intend; **hast du schon was vor?** have you got anything on?
Vorhaben (**-s, -**) *nt* intention
Vorhalle ['fo:rhalə] *f (Diele)* entrance hall; (*von Parlament*) lobby
vorhalten ['fo:rhaltən] *unreg vt* to hold *od* put up ▷ *vi* to last; **jdm etw ~** to reproach sb for

sth
Vorhaltung *f* reproach
Vorhand ['fo:rhant] *f* forehand
vorhanden [fo:r'handən] *adj* existing; (*erhältlich*) available; **Vorhandensein** (**-s**) *nt* existence, presence
Vorhang ['fo:rhaŋ] *m* curtain
Vorhängeschloss ['fo:rhɛŋəʃlɔs] *nt* padlock
Vorhaut ['fo:rhaʊt] *f* (*Anat*) foreskin
vorher [fo:r'he:r] *adv* before(hand); **vorherbestimmen** *vt* (*Schicksal*) to preordain; **vorhergehen** *unreg vi* to precede
vorherig [fo:r'he:rɪç] *adj* previous
Vorherrschaft ['fo:rhɛrʃaft] *f* predominance, supremacy
vorherrschen *vi* to predominate
vorher- *zW*: **Vorhersage** *f* forecast; **vorhersagen** *vt* to forecast, predict; **vorhersehbar** *adj* predictable; **vorhersehen** *unreg vt* to foresee
vorhin [fo:r'hɪn] *adv* not long ago, just now
Vorhinein ['fo:rhɪnaɪn] *adv*: **im ~** beforehand
Vorhof ['fo:rho:f] *m* forecourt
vorig ['fo:rɪç] *adj* previous, last
Vorjahr ['fo:rja:r] *nt* previous year, year before
vorjährig ['fo:rjɛ:rɪç] *adj* of the previous year
vorjammern ['fo:rjamərn] *vt, vi*: **jdm (etwas) ~** to moan to sb (about sth)
Vorkämpfer, in ['fo:rkɛmpfər(ɪn)] *m(f)* pioneer
Vorkaufsrecht ['fo:rkaʊfsrɛçt] *nt* option to buy
Vorkehrung ['fo:rke:rʊŋ] *f* precaution
Vorkenntnis ['fo:rkɛntnɪs] *f* previous knowledge
vorknöpfen ['fo:rknœpfən] *vt* (*fig: umg*): **sich** *dat* **jdn ~** to take sb to task
vorkommen ['fo:rkɔmən] *unreg vi* to come forward; (*geschehen, sich finden*) to occur; (*scheinen*) to seem (to be); **so was soll ~!** that's life!; **sich** *dat* **dumm** *etc* **~** to feel stupid *etc*
Vorkommen *nt* occurrence; (*Min*) deposit
Vorkommnis ['fo:rkɔmnɪs] (**-ses, -se**) *nt* occurrence
Vorkriegs- ['fo:rkri:ks] *in zW* pre-war
vorladen ['fo:rla:dən] *unreg vt* (*bei Gericht*) to summons
Vorladung *f* summons
Vorlage ['fo:rla:gə] *f* model, pattern; (*das Vorlegen*) presentation; (*von Beweismaterial*) submission; (*Gesetzesvorlage*) bill; (*Sport*) pass
vorlassen ['fo:rlasən] *unreg vt* to admit; (*überholen lassen*) to let pass; (*vorgehen lassen*) to allow to go in front
Vorlauf ['fo:rlaʊf] *m* (preliminary) heat (*of running event*)
Vorläufer *m* forerunner
vorläufig ['fo:rlɔʏfɪç] *adj* temporary; (*provisorisch*) provisional
vorlaut ['fo:rlaʊt] *adj* impertinent, cheeky
Vorleben ['fo:rle:bən] *nt* past (life)
vorlegen ['fo:rle:gən] *vt* to put in front, present; (*Beweismaterial etc*) to produce, submit; **jdm etw ~** to put sth before sb
Vorleger (**-s, -**) *m* mat
Vorleistung ['fo:rlaɪstʊŋ] *f* (*Fin: Vorausbezahlung*) advance (payment); (*Vorarbeit*) preliminary work; (*Pol*) prior concession
vorlesen ['fo:rle:zən] *unreg vt* to read (out)
Vorlesung *f* (*Univ*) lecture
Vorlesungsverzeichnis *nt* lecture timetable
vorletzte, r, s ['fo:rlɛtstə(r, s)] *adj* last but one, penultimate
Vorliebe ['fo:rli:bə] *f* preference, special liking; **etw mit ~ tun** to particularly like doing sth
vorliebnehmen [fo:r'li:p-] *unreg vi*: **~ mit** to make do with
vorliegen ['fo:rli:gən] *unreg vi* to be (here); **etw liegt jdm vor** sb has sth; **etw liegt gegen jdn vor** sb is charged with sth
vorliegend *adj* present, at issue
vorm. *abk* (= *vormittags*) a.m.; (= *vormals*) formerly
vormachen ['fo:rmaxən] *vt*: **jdm etw ~** to show sb how to do sth; **jdm etwas ~** (*fig*) to fool sb; **mach mir doch nichts vor** don't try and fool me
Vormachtstellung ['fo:rmaxtʃtɛlʊŋ] *f* supremacy
vormals ['fo:rmals] *adv* formerly
Vormarsch ['fo:rmarʃ] *m* advance
vormerken ['fo:rmɛrkən] *vt* to book; (*notieren*) to make note of; (*bei Bestellung*) to take an order for
Vormittag ['fo:rmɪta:k] *m* morning; **am ~** in the morning
vormittags *adv* in the morning, before noon
Vormund ['fo:rmʊnt] (**-(e)s, -e** *od* **-münder**) *m* guardian
vorn [fɔrn] *adv* in front; **von ~ anfangen** to start at the beginning; **nach ~** to the front; **er betrügt sie von ~ bis hinten** he deceives her right, left and centre
Vorname ['fo:rna:mə] *m* first *od* Christian name
vornan [fɔrn'|an] *adv* at the front
vorne ['fɔrnə] = **vorn**
vornehm ['fo:rne:m] *adj* distinguished; (*Manieren etc*) refined; (*Kleid*) elegant; **in ~en Kreisen** in polite society
vornehmen *unreg vt* (*fig*) to carry out; **sich** *dat* **etw ~** to start on sth; (*beschließen*) to decide to do sth; **sich** *dat* **zu viel ~** to take on too much; **sich** *dat* **jdn ~** to tell sb off
vornehmlich *adv* chiefly, specially
vorneweg ['fɔrnəvɛk], **vornweg** ['fɔrnvɛk] *adv* in front; (*als Erstes*) first
vornherein ['fɔrnhɛraɪn] *adv*: **von ~** from the start
Vorort ['fo:r|ɔrt] *m* suburb; **Vorortzug** *m* commuter train
vorprogrammiert ['fo:rprogrami:rt] *adj* (*Erfolg, Antwort*) automatic
Vorrang ['fo:rraŋ] *m* precedence, priority
vorrangig *adj* of prime importance, primary
Vorrat ['fo:rra:t] *m* stock, supply; **solange der ~ reicht** (*Comm*) while stocks last
vorrätig ['fo:rrɛ:tɪç] *adj* in stock

Vorratskammer *f* store cupboard; (*für Lebensmittel*) larder
Vorraum *m* anteroom; (*Büro*) outer office
vorrechnen ['fo:rrɛçnən] *vt*: **jdm etw ~** to calculate sth for sb; (*als Kritik*) to point sth out to sb
Vorrecht ['fo:rrɛçt] *nt* privilege
Vorrede ['fo:rre:də] *f* introductory speech; (*Theat*) prologue (*Brit*), prolog (*US*)
Vorrichtung ['fo:rrɪçtʊŋ] *f* device, gadget
vorrücken ['fo:rrʏkən] *vi* to advance ▷ *vt* to move forward
Vorruhestand ['fo:rru:əʃtant] *m* early retirement
Vorrunde ['fo:rrʊndə] *f* (*Sport*) preliminary round
Vors. *abk* = **Vorsitzende(r)**
vorsagen ['fo:rza:gən] *vt* to recite; (*Sch: zuflüstern*) to tell secretly, prompt
Vorsaison ['fo:rzɛzõ:] *f* early season, low season
Vorsatz ['fo:rzats] *m* intention; (*Jur*) intent; **einen ~ fassen** to make a resolution
vorsätzlich ['fo:rzɛtslɪç] *adj* intentional; (*Jur*) premeditated ▷ *adv* intentionally
Vorschau ['fo:rʃaʊ] *f* (*Rundf, TV*) (programme (*Brit*) *od* program (*US*)) preview; (*Film*) trailer
Vorschein ['fo:rʃaɪn] *m*: **zum ~ kommen** (*lit: sichtbar werden*) to appear; (*fig: entdeckt werden*) to come to light
vorschieben ['fo:rʃi:bən] *unreg vt* to push forward; (*vor etw*) to push across; (*fig*) to put forward as an excuse; **jdn ~** to use sb as a front
vorschießen ['fo:rʃi:sən] *unreg* (*umg*) *vt*: **jdm Geld ~** to advance sb money
Vorschlag ['fo:rʃla:k] *m* suggestion, proposal
vorschlagen ['fo:rʃla:gən] *unreg vt* to suggest, propose
Vorschlaghammer *m* sledgehammer
vorschnell ['fo:rʃnɛl] *adj* hasty, too quick
vorschreiben ['fo:rʃraɪbən] *unreg vt* (*Dosis*) to prescribe; (*befehlen*) to specify; **(jdm) etw ~** (*lit*) to write sth out (for sb); **ich lasse mir nichts ~** I won't be dictated to
Vorschrift ['fo:rʃrɪft] *f* regulation(s *pl*), rule(s *pl*); (*Anweisungen*) instruction(s *pl*); **jdm ~en machen** to give sb orders; **Dienst nach ~** work-to-rule (*Brit*), slowdown (*US*)
vorschriftsmäßig *adv* as per regulations/instructions
Vorschub ['fo:rʃu:p] *m*: **jdm/einer Sache ~ leisten** to encourage sb/sth
Vorschule ['fo:rʃu:lə] *f* nursery school
vorschulisch ['fo:rʃu:lɪʃ] *adj* preschool *attr*
Vorschuss ['fo:rʃʊs] *m* advance
vorschützen ['fo:rʃʏtsən] *vt* to put forward as a pretext; (*Unwissenheit*) to plead
vorschweben ['fo:rʃve:bən] *vi*: **jdm schwebt etw vor** sb has sth in mind
vorsehen ['fo:rze:ən] *unreg vt* to provide for; (*planen*) to plan ▷ *vr* to take care, be careful
Vorsehung *f* providence
vorsetzen ['fo:rzɛtsən] *vt* to move forward; (*davor setzen*): **~ vor** +*akk* to put in front of; (*anbieten*): **jdm etw ~** to offer sb sth
Vorsicht ['fo:rzɪçt] *f* caution, care; **~!** look out!, take care!; (*auf Schildern*) caution!, danger!; **~ Stufe!** mind the step!; **etw mit ~ genießen** (*umg*) to take sth with a pinch of salt
vorsichtig *adj* cautious, careful
vorsichtshalber *adv* just in case
Vorsichtsmaßnahme *f* precaution
Vorsilbe ['fo:rzɪlbə] *f* prefix
vorsintflutlich ['fo:rzɪntflu:tlɪç] (*umg*) *adj* antiquated
Vorsitz ['fo:rzɪts] *m* chair(manship); **den ~ führen** to chair the meeting
Vorsitzende, r *f(m)* chairman/-woman, chair(person)
Vorsorge ['fo:rzɔrgə] *f* precaution(s *pl*); (*Fürsorge*) provision(s *pl*)
vorsorgen *vi*: **~ für** to make provision(s *pl*) for
Vorsorgeuntersuchung ['fo:rzɔrgə|ʊntərzu:xʊŋ] *f* medical check-up
vorsorglich ['fo:rzɔrklɪç] *adv* as a precaution
Vorspann ['vo:rʃpan] *m* (*Film, TV*) opening credits *pl*; (*Presse*) opening paragraph
vorspannen *vt* (*Pferde*) to harness
Vorspeise ['fo:rʃpaɪzə] *f* hors d'œuvre, starter
Vorspiegelung ['fo:rʃpi:gəlʊŋ] *f*: **das ist (eine) ~ falscher Tatsachen** it's all sham
Vorspiel ['fo:rʃpi:l] *nt* prelude; (*bei Geschlechtsverkehr*) foreplay
vorspielen *vt*: **jdm etw ~** (*Mus*) to play sth to sb; (*Theat*) to act sth to sb; (*fig*) to act out a sham of sth in front of sb
vorsprechen ['fo:rʃprɛçən] *unreg vt* to say out loud; (*vortragen*) to recite ▷ *vi* (*Theat*) to audition; **bei jdm ~** to call on sb
vorspringend ['fo:rʃprɪŋənt] *adj* projecting; (*Nase, Kinn*) prominent
Vorsprung ['fo:rʃprʊŋ] *m* projection; (*Felsvorsprung*) ledge; (*fig*) advantage, start
Vorstadt ['fo:rʃtat] *f* suburbs *pl*
Vorstand ['fo:rʃtant] *m* executive committee; (*Comm*) board (of directors); (*Person*) director; (*Leiter*) head
Vorstandssitzung *f* (*von Firma*) board meeting
Vorstandsvorsitzende, r *f(m)* chairperson
vorstehen ['fo:rʃte:ən] *unreg vi* to project; **einer Sache** *dat* **~** (*fig*) to be the head of sth
Vorsteher, in (-s, -) *m(f)* (*von Abteilung*) head; (*von Gefängnis*) governor; (*Bahnhofsvorsteher*) stationmaster
vorstellbar *adj* conceivable
vorstellen ['fo:rʃtɛlən] *vt* to put forward; (*vor etw*) to put in front; (*bekannt machen*) to introduce; (*darstellen*) to represent ▷ *vr* to introduce o.s.; (*bei Bewerbung*) to go for an interview; **sich** *dat* **etw ~** to imagine sth; **stell dir das nicht so einfach vor** don't think it's so easy
Vorstellung *f* (*Bekanntmachen*) introduction; (*Theat etc*) performance; (*Gedanke*) idea
Vorstellungsgespräch *nt* interview
Vorstellungsvermögen *nt* powers of

imagination *pl*
Vorstoß ['fo:ɐʃto:s] *m* advance; (*fig: Versuch*) attempt
vorstoßen *unreg vt, vi* to push forward
Vorstrafe ['fo:ɐʃtra:fə] *f* previous conviction
vorstrecken ['fo:ɐʃtrɛkən] *vt* to stretch out; (*Geld*) to advance
Vorstufe ['fo:ɐʃtu:fə] *f* first step(s *pl*)
Vortag ['fo:ɐta:k] *m*: **am ~ einer Sache** *gen* on the day before sth
Vortal ['fo:ɐta:l] *nt* (*Comput*) vortal
vortasten ['fo:ɐtastən] *vr*: **sich langsam zu etw ~** to approach sth carefully
vortäuschen ['fo:ɐtɔʏʃən] *vt* to pretend, feign
Vortäuschung *f*: **unter ~ falscher Tatsachen** under false pretences (*Brit*) *od* pretenses (*US*)
Vorteil ['fo:ɐtaɪl] (**-s, -e**) *m*: **~ (gegenüber)** advantage (over); **im ~ sein** to have the advantage; **die Vor- und Nachteile** the pros and cons; **vorteilhaft** *adj* advantageous; (*Kleider*) flattering; (*Geschäft*) lucrative
Vortr. *abk* = **Vortrag**
Vortrag ['fo:ɐtra:k] (**-(e)s, Vorträge**) *m* talk, lecture; (*Vortragsart*) delivery; (*von Gedicht*) rendering; (*Comm*) balance carried forward; **einen ~ halten** to give a lecture *od* talk
vortragen ['fo:ɐtra:gən] *unreg vt* to carry forward (*auch COMM*); (*fig*) to recite; (*Rede*) to deliver; (*Lied*) to perform; (*Meinung etc*) to express
Vortragsabend *m* lecture evening; (*mit Musik*) recital; (*mit Gedichten*) poetry reading
Vortragsreihe *f* series of lectures
vortrefflich [fo:ɐ'trɛflɪç] *adj* excellent
vortreten ['fo:ɐtre:tən] *unreg vi* to step forward; (*Augen etc*) to protrude
Vortritt ['fo:ɐtrɪt] *m*: **jdm den ~ lassen** (*lit, fig*) to let sb go first
vorüber [fo'ry:bər] *adv* past, over;
vorübergehen *unreg vi* to pass (by);
vorübergehen an *+dat* (*fig*) to pass over;
vorübergehend *adj* temporary, passing
Voruntersuchung ['fo:ɐ|ʊntərzu:xʊŋ] *f* (*Med*) preliminary examination; (*Jur*) preliminary investigation
Vorurteil ['fo:ɐ|ʊrtaɪl] *nt* prejudice
vorurteilsfrei *adj* unprejudiced, open-minded
Vorverkauf ['fo:ɐfɛrkaʊf] *m* advance booking
Vorverkaufsstelle *f* advance booking office
vorverlegen ['fo:ɐfɛrle:gən] *vt* (*Termin*) to bring forward
Vorw. *abk* = **Vorwort**
vorwagen ['fo:ɐva:gən] *vr* to venture forward
Vorwahl ['fo:ɐva:l] *f* preliminary election; (*Tel*) dialling (*Brit*) *od* area (*US*) code
Vorwand ['fo:ɐvant] (**-(e)s, Vorwände**) *m* pretext
Vorwarnung ['fo:ɐvarnʊŋ] *f* (advance) warning
vorwärts ['fo:ɐvɛrts] *adv* forward; **~!** (*umg*) let's go!; (*Mil*) forward march!; *siehe auch* **vorwärtsgehen; vorwärtskommen**;
Vorwärtsgang *m* (*Aut etc*) forward gear;
vorwärtsgehen *unreg vi* to progress;
vorwärtskommen *unreg vi* to get on, make progress
Vorwäsche *f* prewash
Vorwaschgang *m* prewash
vorweg [fo:ɐ'vɛk] *adv* in advance;
Vorwegnahme (**-, -n**) *f* anticipation;
vorwegnehmen *unreg vt* to anticipate
vorweisen ['fo:ɐvaɪzən] *unreg vt* to show, produce
vorwerfen ['fo:ɐvɛrfən] *unreg vt*: **jdm etw ~** to reproach sb for sth, accuse sb of sth; **sich** *dat* **nichts vorzuwerfen haben** to have nothing to reproach o.s. with; **das wirft er mir heute noch vor** he still holds it against me; **Tieren/Gefangenen etw ~** (*lit*) to throw sth down for the animals/prisoners
vorwiegend ['fo:ɐvi:gənt] *adj* predominant ▷ *adv* predominantly
vorwitzig *adj* saucy, cheeky
Vorwort ['fo:ɐvɔrt] (**-(e)s, -e**) *nt* preface
Vorwurf ['fo:ɐvʊrf] (**-(e)s, ¨-e**) *m* reproach; **jdm/sich Vorwürfe machen** to reproach sb/o.s.
vorwurfsvoll *adj* reproachful
Vorzeichen ['fo:ɐtsaɪçən] *nt* (*Omen*) omen; (*Med*) early symptom; (*Math*) sign
vorzeigen ['fo:ɐtsaɪgən] *vt* to show, produce
Vorzeit ['fo:ɐtsaɪt] *f* prehistoric times *pl*
vorzeitig *adj* premature
vorziehen ['fo:ɐtsi:ən] *unreg vt* to pull forward; (*Gardinen*) to draw; (*zuerst behandeln, abfertigen*) to give priority to; (*lieber haben*) to prefer
Vorzimmer ['fo:ɐtsɪmər] *nt* anteroom; (*Büro*) outer office
Vorzug ['fo:ɐtsu:k] *m* preference; (*gute Eigenschaft*) merit, good quality; (*Vorteil*) advantage; (*Eisenb*) relief train; **einer Sache** *dat* **den ~ geben** (*form*) to prefer sth; (*Vorrang geben*) to give sth precedence
vorzüglich [fo:ɐ'tsy:klɪç] *adj* excellent, first-rate
Vorzugsaktien *pl* preference shares (*Brit*), preferred stock (*US*)
vorzugsweise *adv* preferably; (*hauptsächlich*) chiefly
Votum ['vo:tʊm] (**-s, Voten**) *nt* vote
Voyeur [voa'jø:r] (**-s, -e**) *m* voyeur;
Voyeurismus [voajø'rɪsmʊs] *m* voyeurism
v. T. *abk* (= *vom Tausend*) per thousand
vulgär [vʊl'gɛ:r] *adj* vulgar
Vulkan [vʊl'ka:n] (**-s, -e**) *m* volcano;
Vulkanausbruch *m* volcanic eruption
vulkanisieren [vʊlkani'zi:rən] *vt* to vulcanize
v. u. Z. *abk* (= *vor unserer Zeitrechnung*) B.C.

Ww

W, w [ve:] *nt* W, w; **W wie Wilhelm** ≈ W for William
W. *abk* (= *West(en)*) W
w. *abk* = **wenden; werktags; westlich**; (= *weiblich*) f
Waage ['va:gə] (**-, -n**) *f* scales *pl*; (*Astrol*) Libra; **sich** *dat* **die ~ halten** (*fig*) to balance one another; **waagerecht** *adj* horizontal
Waagschale *f* (scale) pan; **(schwer) in die ~ fallen** (*fig*) to carry weight
wabbelig ['vabəlıç], **wabblig** ['vablıç] *adj* wobbly
Wabe ['va:bə] (**-, -n**) *f* honeycomb
wach [vax] *adj* awake; (*fig*) alert; **~ werden** to wake up
Wachablösung *f* changing of the guard; (*Mensch*) relief guard; (*fig: Regierungswechsel*) change of government
Wache (**-, -n**) *f* guard, watch; **~ halten** to keep watch; **~ stehen** *od* **schieben** (*umg*) to be on guard (duty)
wachen *vi* to be awake; (*Wache halten*) to keep watch; **bei jdm ~** to sit up with sb
wachhabend *adj attrib* duty
Wachhund *m* watchdog, guard dog; (*fig*) watchdog
Wacholder [va'xɔldər] (**-s, -**) *m* juniper
wachrütteln ['vaxrytəln] *vt* (*fig*) to (a)rouse
Wachs [vaks] (**-es, -e**) *nt* wax
wachsam ['vaxza:m] *adj* watchful, vigilant, alert; **Wachsamkeit** *f* vigilance
wachsen[1] *unreg vi* to grow
wachsen[2] *vt* (*Skier*) to wax
Wachsfigurenkabinett *nt* waxworks (exhibition)
Wachsmalstift, Wachsstift *m* wax crayon
wächst [vɛkst] *vb siehe* **wachsen**[1]
Wachstuch ['vakstu:x] *nt* oilcloth
Wachstum ['vakstu:m] (**-s**) *nt* growth
Wachstums- *zW*: **Wachstumsbranche** *f* growth industry; **Wachstumsgrenze** *f* limits of growth; **wachstumshemmend** *adj* growth-inhibiting; **Wachstumsrate** *f* growth rate; **Wachstumsschmerzen** *pl* growing pains; **Wachstumsstörung** *f* disturbance of growth
Wachtel ['vaxtəl] (**-, -n**) *f* quail
Wächter ['vɛçtər] (**-s, -**) *m* guard; (*Parkwächter*) warden, keeper; (*Museumswächter, Parkplatzwächter*) attendant
Wachtmeister *m* officer
Wachtposten *m* guard, sentry
Wachtturm, Wachturm *m* watchtower
Wach- und Schließgesellschaft *f* security corps
wackelig *adj* shaky, wobbly; **auf ~en Beinen stehen** to be wobbly on one's legs; (*fig*) to be unsteady
Wackelkontakt *m* loose connection
wackeln *vi* to shake; (*fig: Position*) to be shaky; **mit den Hüften/dem Schwanz ~** to wiggle one's hips/wag its tail
wacker ['vakər] *adj* valiant, stout; **sich ~ schlagen** (*umg*) to put up a brave fight
wacklig *adj* = **wackelig**
Wade ['va:də] (**-, -n**) *f* (*Anat*) calf
Waffe ['vafə] (**-, -n**) *f* weapon; **jdn mit seinen eigenen ~n schlagen** (*fig*) to beat sb at his own game
Waffel ['vafəl] (**-, -n**) *f* waffle; (*Eiswaffel*) wafer
Waffen- *zW*: **Waffengewalt** *f*: **mit Waffengewalt** by force of arms; **Waffenlager** *nt* (*von Armee*) ordnance depot; (*von Terroristen*) cache; **Waffenschein** *m* firearms *od* gun licence (*Brit*), firearms license (*US*); **Waffenschmuggel** *m* gunrunning, arms smuggling; **Waffenstillstand** *m* armistice, truce
Wagemut ['va:gəmu:t] *m* daring
Wagen ['va:gən] (**-s, -**) *m* vehicle; (*Auto*) car, automobile (*US*); (*Eisenb*) car, carriage (*Brit*); (*Pferdewagen*) wag(g)on, cart
wagen *vt* to venture, dare
Wagen- *zW*: **Wagenführer** *m* driver; **Wagenheber** (**-s, -**) *m* jack; **Wagenpark** *m* fleet of cars; **Wagenrückholtaste** *f* (*Schreibmaschine*) carriage return (key); **Wagenrücklauf** *m* carriage return
Waggon [va'gõ:] (**-s, -s**) *m* wag(g)on; (*Güterwaggon*) goods van (*Brit*), freight truck (*US*)
waghalsig ['va:khalzıç] *adj* foolhardy
Wagnis ['va:knıs] (**-ses, -se**) *nt* risk
Wagon (**-s, -s**) *m* = **Waggon**
Wahl [va:l] (**-, -en**) *f* choice; (*Pol*) election; **erste ~** (*Qualität*) top quality; (*Gemüse, Eier*) grade one; **zweite ~** (*Comm*) seconds *pl*; **aus freier ~** of

one's own free choice; **wer die ~ hat, hat die Qual** (*Sprichwort*) he is *od* you are *etc* spoilt for choice; **die ~ fiel auf ihn** he was chosen; **sich zur ~ stellen** (*Pol etc*) to stand (*Brit*) *od* run (for parliament *etc*)

wählbar *adj* eligible

Wahl- *zW*: **wahlberechtigt** *adj* entitled to vote; **Wahlbeteiligung** *f* poll, turnout; **Wahlbezirk** *m* (*Pol*) ward

wählen ['vɛːlən] *vt* to choose; (*Pol*) to elect, vote for; (*Tel*) to dial ▷ *vi* to choose; (*Pol*) to vote; (*Tel*) to dial

Wähler, in (**-s, -**) *m(f)* voter; **Wählerabwanderung** *f* voter drift; **wählerisch** *adj* fastidious, particular; **Wählerschaft** *f* electorate

Wahl- *zW*: **Wahlfach** *nt* optional subject; **wahlfrei** *adj*: **wahlfreier Zugriff** (*Comput*) random access; **Wahlgang** *m* ballot; **Wahlgeschenk** *nt pre-election vote-catching gimmick*; **Wahlheimat** *f* country of adoption; **Wahlhelfer** *m* (*im Wahlkampf*) election assistant; (*bei der Wahl*) polling officer; **Wahlkabine** *f* polling booth; **Wahlkampf** *m* election campaign; **Wahlkreis** *m* constituency; **Wahlleiter** *m* returning officer; **Wahlliste** *f* electoral register; **Wahllokal** *nt* polling station; **wahllos** *adv* at random; (*nicht wählerisch*) indiscriminately; **Wahlrecht** *nt* franchise; **allgemeines Wahlrecht** universal franchise; **das aktive Wahlrecht** the right to vote; **das passive Wahlrecht** eligibility (for political office); **Wahlspruch** *m* motto; **Wahlurne** *f* ballot box; **wahlweise** *adv* alternatively

Wählzeichen *nt* (*Tel*) dialling tone (*Brit*), dial tone (*US*)

Wahn [vaːn] (**-(e)s**) *m* delusion; **Wahnsinn** *m* madness; **wahnsinnig** *adj* insane, mad ▷ *adv* (*umg*) incredibly; **wahnwitzig** *adj* crazy *attrib* ▷ *adv* terribly

wahr [vaːr] *adj* true; **da ist (et)was W~es dran** there's some truth in that

wahren *vt* to maintain, keep

währen ['vɛːrən] *vi* to last

während *präp +gen* during ▷ *konj* while; **währenddessen** *adv* meanwhile

wahr- *zW*: **wahrhaben** *unreg vt*: **etw nicht wahrhaben wollen** to refuse to admit sth; **wahrhaft** *adv* (*tatsächlich*) truly; **wahrhaftig** *adj* true, real ▷ *adv* really

Wahrheit *f* truth; **die ~ sagen** to tell the truth

wahrheitsgetreu *adj* (*Bericht*) truthful; (*Darstellung*) faithful

wahrnehmen *unreg vt* to perceive; (*Frist*) to observe; (*Veränderungen etc*) to be aware of; (*Gelegenheit*) to take; (*Interessen, Rechte*) to look after

Wahrnehmung *f* perception; observing; awareness; taking; looking after

wahrsagen *vi* to predict the future, tell fortunes

Wahrsager *m* fortune-teller

wahrscheinlich [vaːr'ʃaɪnlɪç] *adj* probable ▷ *adv* probably; **Wahrscheinlichkeit** *f* probability; **aller Wahrscheinlichkeit nach** in all probability

Währung ['vɛːrʊŋ] *f* currency

Währungs- *zW*: **Währungseinheit** *f* monetary unit; **Währungspolitik** *f* monetary policy; **Währungsraum** *m* currency area; **Währungsreserven** *pl* official reserves *pl*; **Währungsunion** *f* monetary union

Wahrzeichen *nt* (*Gebäude, Turm etc*) symbol; (*von Stadt, Verein*) emblem

Waise ['vaɪzə] (**-, -n**) *f* orphan

Waisen- *zW*: **Waisenhaus** *nt* orphanage; **Waisenkind** *nt* orphan; **Waisenknabe** *m*: **gegen dich ist er ein Waisenknabe** (*umg*) he's no match for you; **Waisenrente** *f* orphan's allowance

Wal [vaːl] (**-(e)s, -e**) *m* whale

Wald [valt] (**-(e)s, ¨-er**) *m* wood(s *pl*); (*groß*) forest; **Waldbrand** *m* forest fire

Wäldchen ['vɛltçən] *nt* copse, grove

Waldhorn *nt* (*Mus*) French horn

waldig ['valdɪç] *adj* wooded

Wald- *zW*: **Waldlehrpfad** *m* nature trail; **Waldmeister** *m* (*Bot*) woodruff; **Waldsterben** *nt loss of trees due to pollution*

Wald- und Wiesen- (*umg*) *in zw* common-or-garden

Waldweg *m* woodland *od* forest path

Wales [weɪlz] *nt* Wales

Walfang ['vaːlfaŋ] *m* whaling

Walfisch ['valfɪʃ] *m* whale

Waliser, in [va'liːzər(ɪn)] (**-s, -**) *m(f)* Welshman, Welshwoman

walisisch *adj* Welsh

Walkman® ['wɔːkman] (**-s**) *m* Walkman®, personal stereo

Wall [val] (**-(e)s, ¨-e**) *m* embankment; (*Bollwerk*) rampart

wallfahren *vi untr* to go on a pilgrimage

Wallfahrer, in *m(f)* pilgrim

Wallfahrt *f* pilgrimage

Wallis ['valɪs] (**-**) *nt*: **das ~** Valais

Wallone [va'loːnə] (**-n, -n**) *m*, **Wallonin** *f* Walloon

Walnuss ['valnʊs] *f* walnut

Walross ['valrɔs] *nt* walrus

walten ['valtən] *vi* (*geh*): **Vernunft ~ lassen** to let reason prevail

Walzblech (**-(e)s**) *nt* sheet metal

Walze ['valtsə] (**-, -n**) *f* (*Gerät*) cylinder; (*Fahrzeug*) roller

walzen *vt* to roll (out)

wälzen ['vɛltsən] *vt* to roll (over); (*Bücher*) to hunt through; (*Probleme*) to deliberate on ▷ *vr* to wallow; (*vor Schmerzen*) to roll about; (*im Bett*) to toss and turn

Walzer ['valtsər] (**-s, -**) *m* waltz

Wälzer ['vɛltsər] (**-s, -**) (*umg*) *m* tome

Wampe ['vampə] (**-, -n**) (*umg*) *f* paunch

Wand (**-, ¨-e**) *f* wall; (*Trennwand*) partition; (*Bergwand*) precipice; (*Felswand*) (rock) face; (*fig*)

barrier; **weiß wie die ~** as white as a sheet; **jdn an die ~ spielen** to put sb in the shade; (*Sport*) to outplay sb
wand *etc* [vant] *vb siehe* **winden**
Wandel ['vandəl] (**-s**) *m* change; **wandelbar** *adj* changeable, variable
Wandelhalle *f* foyer
wandeln *vt, vr* to change ▷ *vi* (*gehen*) to walk
Wanderausstellung *f* touring exhibition
Wanderbühne *f* touring theatre (*Brit*) *od* theater (*US*)
Wanderer (**-s, -**) *m* hiker, rambler
Wanderin *f* hiker, rambler
Wanderkarte *f* hiker's map
Wanderlied *nt* hiking song
wandern *vi* to hike; (*Blick*) to wander; (*Gedanken*) to stray; (*umg: in den Papierkorb etc*) to land
Wanderpreis *m* challenge trophy
Wanderschaft *f* travelling (*Brit*), traveling (*US*)
Wanderung *f* walk, hike; (*von Tieren, Völkern*) migration
Wanderweg *m* trail, (foot)path
Wandgemälde *nt* mural
Wandlung *f* change; (*völlige Umwandlung*) transformation; (*Rel*) transubstantiation
Wand- *zW*: **Wandmalerei** *f* mural painting; **Wandschirm** *m* (folding) screen; **Wandschrank** *m* cupboard
wandte *etc* ['vantə] *vb siehe* **wenden**
Wandteppich *m* tapestry
Wandverkleidung *f* panelling
Wange ['vaŋə] (**-, -n**) *f* cheek
wankelmütig ['vaŋkəlmy:tɪç] *adj* fickle, inconstant
wanken ['vankən] *vi* to stagger; (*fig*) to waver
wann [van] *adv* when; **seit ~ bist/hast du ...?** how long have you been/have you had ...?
Wanne ['vanə] (**-, -n**) *f* tub
Wanze ['vantsə] (**-, -n**) *f* (*Abhörgerät, Zool*) bug
WAP *nt abk* (*Comput: = Wireless Application Protocol*) WAP
WAP-Handy *nt* WAP phone
Wappen ['vapən] (**-s, -**) *nt* coat of arms, crest; **Wappenkunde** *f* heraldry
wappnen *vr* (*fig*) to prepare o.s.; **gewappnet sein** to be forearmed
war *etc* [va:r] *vb siehe* **sein**
warb *etc* [varp] *vb siehe* **werben**
Ware ['va:rə] (**-, -n**) *f* ware; **Waren** *pl* goods *pl*
wäre *etc* ['vɛ:rə] *vb siehe* **sein**
Waren- *zW*: **Warenbestand** *m* stock; **Warenhaus** *nt* department store; **Warenlager** *nt* stock, store; **Warenmuster** *nt* sample; **Warenprobe** *f* sample; **Warenrückstände** *pl* backlog *sing*; **Warensendung** *f* trade sample (sent by post); **Warenzeichen** *nt* trademark
warf *etc* [varf] *vb siehe* **werfen**
warm [varm] *adj* warm; (*Essen*) hot; (*umg: homosexuell*) queer; **mir ist ~** I'm warm; **mit jdm ~ werden** (*umg*) to get close to sb; **~ laufen** (*Aut*) to warm up; *siehe auch* **warmhalten**
Wärme ['vɛrmə] (**-, -n**) *f* warmth; **10 Grad ~** 10 degrees above zero
wärmen *vt, vr* to warm (up), heat (up)
Wärmflasche *f* hot-water bottle
warm- *zW*: **Warmfront** *f* (*Met*) warm front; **warmhalten** *unreg vt*: **sich** *dat* **jdn warmhalten**: *fig*) to keep in with sb; **warmherzig** *adj* warm-hearted; **Warmwassertank** *m* hot-water tank
Warnblinkanlage *f* (*Aut*) hazard warning lights *pl*
Warndreieck *nt* warning triangle
warnen ['varnən] *vt* to warn
Warnstreik *m* token strike
Warnung *f* warning
Warschau ['varʃaʊ] (**-s**) *nt* Warsaw; **Warschauer Pakt** *m* Warsaw Pact
Warte (**-, -n**) *f* observation point; (*fig*) viewpoint
warten ['vartən] *vi* to wait ▷ *vt* (*Auto, Maschine*) to service; **~ auf** *+akk* to wait for; **auf sich ~ lassen** to take a long time; **warte mal!** wait a minute!; (*überlegend*) let me see; **mit dem Essen auf jdn ~** to wait for sb before eating
Wärter, in ['vɛrtər(ɪn)] (**-s, -**) *m(f)* attendant
Wartesaal *m* (*Eisenb*) waiting room
Wartezimmer *nt* waiting room
Wartung *f* (*von Auto, Maschine*) servicing; **~ und Instandhaltung** maintenance
warum [va'rʊm] *adv* why; **~ nicht gleich so!** that's better
Warze ['vartsə] (**-, -n**) *f* wart
was [vas] *pron* what; (*umg: etwas*) something; **das, ~ ...** that which ...; **~ für ...?** what sort *od* kind of ...?
Wasch- *zW*: **Waschanlage** *f* (*für Autos*) car wash; **waschbar** *adj* washable; **Waschbecken** *nt* washbasin
Wäsche ['vɛʃə] (**-, -n**) *f* wash(ing); (*Bettwäsche*) linen; (*Unterwäsche*) underwear; **dumm aus der ~ gucken** (*umg*) to look stupid
waschecht *adj* (*Farbe*) fast; (*fig*) genuine
Wäsche- *zW*: **Wäscheklammer** *f* clothes peg (*Brit*), clothespin (*US*); **Wäschekorb** *m* dirty clothes basket; **Wäscheleine** *f* washing line (*Brit*), clothes line (*US*)
waschen ['vaʃən] *unreg vt, vi* to wash ▷ *vr* to (have a) wash; **sich** *dat* **die Hände ~** to wash one's hands; **~ und legen** (*Haare*) to shampoo and set
Wäscherei [vɛʃə'raɪ] *f* laundry
Wäscheschleuder *f* spin-dryer
Wasch- *zW*: **Waschgang** *m* stage of the washing programme (*Brit*) *od* program (*US*); **Waschküche** *f* laundry room; **Waschlappen** *m* face cloth *od* flannel (*Brit*), washcloth (*US*); (*umg*) softy; **Waschmaschine** *f* washing machine; **Waschmittel** *nt* detergent; **Waschpulver** *nt* washing powder; **Waschsalon** *m* Launderette® (*Brit*), Laundromat® (*US*)
wäscht [vɛʃt] *vb siehe* **waschen**
Waschtisch *m* washstand

Washington ['wɔʃɪŋtən] **(-s)** *nt* Washington
Wasser[1] ['vasər] **(-s, -)** *nt* water; **~ abstoßend** water-repellent; **dort wird auch nur mit ~ gekocht** (*fig*) they're no different from anybody else (there); **ins ~ fallen** (*fig*) to fall through; **mit allen ~n gewaschen sein** (*umg*) to be a shrewd customer; **~ lassen** (*euph*) to pass water; **jdm das ~ abgraben** (*fig*) to take the bread from sb's mouth, take away sb's livelihood
Wasser[2] **(-s, ⸚)** *nt* (*Flüssigkeit*) water; (*Med*) lotion; (*Parfüm*) cologne; (*Mineralwasser*) mineral water
Wässerchen *nt*: **er sieht aus, als ob er kein ~ trüben könnte** he looks as if butter wouldn't melt in his mouth
Wasser- *zW*: **wasserdicht** *adj* watertight; (*Stoff, Uhr*) waterproof; **Wasserfall** *m* waterfall; **Wasserfarbe** *f* watercolour (*Brit*), watercolor (*US*); **wassergekühlt** *adj* (*Aut*) water-cooled; **Wassergraben** *m* (*Sport*) water jump; (*um Burg*) moat; **Wasserhahn** *m* tap, faucet (*US*)
wässerig ['vɛsərɪç] *adj* watery
Wasser- *zW*: **Wasserkessel** *m* kettle; (*Tech*) boiler; **Wasserkraftwerk** *nt* hydroelectric power station; **Wasserleitung** *f* water pipe; (*Anlagen*) plumbing; **Wassermann** *m* (*Astrol*) Aquarius
wassern *vi* to land on the water
wässern ['vɛsərn] *vt, vi* to water
Wasser- *zW*: **Wasserscheide** *f* watershed; **wasserscheu** *adj* afraid of water; **Wasserschutzpolizei** *f* (*auf Flüssen*) river police; (*im Hafen*) harbour (*Brit*) *od* harbor (*US*) police; (*auf der See*) coastguard service; **Wasserski** *nt* water-skiing; **Wasserspiegel** *m* (*Oberfläche*) surface of the water; (*Wasserstand*) water level; **Wasserstand** *m* water level; **Wasserstoff** *m* hydrogen; **Wasserstoffbombe** *f* hydrogen bomb; **Wasserverbrauch** *m* water consumption; **Wasserwaage** *f* spirit level; **Wasserwelle** *f* shampoo and set; **Wasserwerfer (-s, -)** *m* water cannon; **Wasserwerk** *nt* waterworks; **Wasserzeichen** *nt* watermark
waten ['va:tən] *vi* to wade
watscheln ['va:tʃəln] *vi* to waddle
Watt[1] [vat] **(-(e)s, -en)** *nt* mud flats *pl*
Watt[2] **(-s, -)** *nt* (*Elek*) watt
Watte (-, -n) *f* cotton wool (*Brit*), absorbent cotton (*US*)
Wattenmeer (-(e)s) *nt* mud flats *pl*
Wattestäbchen *nt* cotton(-wool) swab
wattieren [va'ti:rən] *vt* to pad
WC [ve:'tse:] **(-s, -s)** *nt abk* (= *Wasserklosett*) WC
Web [wɛb] *nt* (*Comput*): **das ~** the Web; **im ~** on the Web
weben ['ve:bən] *unreg vt* to weave
Weber, in (-s, -) *m(f)* weaver
Weberei [ve:bə'raɪ] *f* (*Betrieb*) weaving mill
Webpage ['wɛbpa:gə] *nt* web page
Webseite ['wɛbzaɪtə] *f* Web page, web site
Webstuhl ['ve:pʃtu:l] *m* loom
Wechsel ['vɛksəl] **(-s, -)** *m* change; (*Geldwechsel*) exchange; (*Comm*) bill of exchange; **Wechselbäder** *pl* alternating hot and cold baths *pl*; **Wechselbeziehung** *f* correlation; **Wechselforderungen** *pl* (*Comm*) bills receivable *pl*; **Wechselgeld** *nt* change; **wechselhaft** *adj* (*Wetter*) variable; **Wechselinhaber** *m* bearer; **Wechseljahre** *pl* change of life, menopause; **in die Wechseljahre kommen** to start the change; **Wechselkurs** *m* rate of exchange; **Wechselkursmechanismus** *m* Exchange Rate Mechanism, ERM
wechseln *vt* to change; (*Blicke*) to exchange ▷ *vi* to change; (*einander ablösen*) to alternate
wechselnd *adj* changing; (*Stimmungen*) changeable; (*Winde, Bewölkung*) variable
Wechsel- *zW*: **wechselseitig** *adj* reciprocal; **Wechselsprechanlage** *f* two-way intercom; **Wechselstrom** *m* alternating current; **Wechselstube** *f* currency exchange, bureau de change; **Wechselverbindlichkeiten** *pl* bills payable *pl*; **wechselweise** *adv* alternately; **Wechselwirkung** *f* interaction
wecken ['vɛkən] *vt* to wake (up); (*fig*) to arouse; (*Bedarf*) to create; (*Erinnerungen*) to revive
Wecker (-s, -) *m* alarm clock; **jdm auf den ~ fallen** (*umg*) to get on sb's nerves
Weckglas® *nt* preserving jar
Weckruf *m* (*Tel*) alarm call
wedeln ['ve:dəln] *vi* (*mit Schwanz*) to wag; (*mit Fächer*) to fan; (*Ski*) to wedel
weder ['ve:dər] *konj* neither; **~ ... noch ...** neither ... nor ...
Weg [ve:k] **(-(e)s, -e)** *m* way; (*Pfad*) path; (*Route*) route; **sich auf den ~ machen** to be on one's way; **jdm aus dem ~ gehen** to keep out of sb's way; **jdm nicht über den ~ trauen** (*fig*) not to trust sb an inch; **den ~ des geringsten Widerstandes gehen** to follow the line of least resistance; **etw in die ~e leiten** to arrange sth; **jdm Steine in den ~ legen** (*fig*) to put obstacles in sb's way; *siehe auch* **zuwege**
weg [vɛk] *adv* away, off; **über etw** *akk* **~ sein** to be over sth; **er war schon ~** he had already left; **nichts wie** *od* **nur ~ von hier!** let's get out of here!; **~ damit!** (*mit Schere etc*) put it/them away!; **Finger ~!** hands off!
Wegbereiter (-s, -) *m* pioneer
wegblasen *unreg vt* to blow away; **wie weggeblasen sein** (*fig*) to have vanished
wegbleiben *unreg vi* to stay away; **mir bleibt die Spucke weg!** (*umg*) I am absolutely flabbergasted!
wegen ['ve:gən] (*umg*) *präp +gen od +dat* because of; **von ~!** you must be joking!
weg- *zW*: **wegfahren** *unreg vi* to drive away; (*abfahren*) to leave; **Wegfahrsperre** *f* (*Aut*): **(elektronische) Wegfahrsperre** (electronic) immobilizer; **wegfallen** *unreg vi* to be left out; (*Ferien, Bezahlung*) to be cancelled; (*aufhören*) to cease; **weggehen** *unreg vi* to go away, leave; (*umg: Ware*) to sell; **weghören** *vi*

to turn a deaf ear; **wegjagen** *vt* to chase away; **wegkommen** *unreg vi*: **(bei etw) gut/schlecht wegkommen** (*umg*) to come off well/badly (with sth); **weglassen** *unreg vt* to leave out; **weglaufen** *unreg vi* to run away *od* off; **das läuft (dir) nicht weg!** (*fig hum*) that can wait; **weglegen** *vt* to put aside; **wegmachen** (*umg*) *vt* to get rid of; **wegmüssen** *unreg* (*umg*) *vi* to have to go; **wegnehmen** *unreg vt* to take away

Wegrand ['ve:krant] *m* wayside

weg- *zW*: **wegräumen** *vt* to clear away; **wegschaffen** *vt* to clear away; **wegschließen** *unreg vt* to lock away; **wegschnappen** *vt*: **(jdm) etw wegschnappen** to snatch sth away (from sb); **wegstecken** *vt* to put away; (*umg: verkraften*) to cope with; **wegtreten** *unreg vi* (*Mil*): **wegtreten!** dismiss!; **geistig weggetreten sein** (*umg: geistesabwesend*) to be away with the fairies; **wegtun** *unreg vt* to put away

wegweisend ['ve:gvaɪzənt] *adj* pioneering *attrib*, revolutionary

Wegweiser ['ve:gvaɪzər] **(-s, -)** *m* road sign, signpost; (*fig: Buch etc*) guide

Wegwerf- ['vɛkvɛrf] *in zw* disposable

weg- *zW*: **wegwerfen** *unreg vt* to throw away; **wegwerfend** *adj* disparaging; **Wegwerfgesellschaft** *f* throw-away society; **wegwollen** *unreg vi* (*verreisen*) to want to go away; **wegziehen** *unreg vi* to move away

weh [ve:] *adj* sore

Wehe ['ve:ə] **(-, -n)** *f* drift

wehe *interj*: **~, wenn du ...** you'll regret it if you ...; **~ dir!** you dare!

Wehen *pl* (*Med*) contractions *pl*; **in den ~ liegen** to be in labour (*Brit*) *od* labor (*US*)

wehen *vt, vi* to blow; (*Fahnen*) to flutter

weh- *zW*: **wehklagen** *vi untr* to wail; **wehleidig** *adj* oversensitive to pain; (*jammernd*) whiny, whining; **Wehmut** *f* melancholy; **wehmütig** *adj* melancholy

Wehr[1] [ve:r] **(-(e)s, -e)** *nt* weir

Wehr[2] [ve:r] **(-, -en)** *f* (*Feuerwehr*) fire brigade (*Brit*) *od* department (*US*) ▷ *in zw* defence (*Brit*), defense (*US*); **sich zur ~ setzen** to defend o.s.

Wehrdienst *m* military service; *see culture note*

WEHRDIENST

Wehrdienst is military service which is still compulsory in Germany. All young men receive their call-up papers at 18 and all who are pronounced physically fit are required to spend ten months in the *Bundeswehr*. Conscientious objectors are allowed to do *Zivildienst* as an alternative, on attending a hearing and presenting their case.

Wehrdienstverweigerer *m* ≈ conscientious objector

wehren *vr* to defend o.s.

Wehr- *zW*: **wehrlos** *adj* defenceless (*Brit*), defenseless (*US*); **jdm wehrlos ausgeliefert sein** to be at sb's mercy; **Wehrmacht** *f* armed forces *pl*; **Wehrpflicht** *f* conscription; **wehrpflichtig** *adj* liable for military service; **Wehrübung** *f* reserve duty training exercise

wehtun ['ve:tu:n] *unreg vt*: **jdm/sich ~** to hurt sb/o.s.

Wehwehchen (*umg*) *nt* (minor) complaint

Weib [vaɪp] **(-(e)s, -er)** *nt* woman, female (*pej*)

Weibchen *nt* (*Ehefrau*) little woman; (*Zool*) female

weibisch ['vaɪbɪʃ] *adj* effeminate

weiblich *adj* feminine

weich [vaɪç] *adj* soft; (*Ei*) soft-boiled; **~e Währung** soft currency

Weiche **(-, -n)** *f* (*Eisenb*) points *pl*; **die ~n stellen** (*lit*) to switch the points; (*fig*) to set the course

weichen *unreg vi* to yield, give way; **(nicht) von jdm** *od* **von jds Seite ~** (not) to leave sb's side

Weichensteller **(-s, -)** *m* pointsman

weich- *zW*: **Weichheit** *f* softness; **Weichkäse** *m* soft cheese; **weichlich** *adj* soft, namby-pamby; **Weichling** *m* wimp; **Weichspüler** **(-s, -)** *m* fabric conditioner; **Weichteile** *pl* soft parts *pl*; **Weichtier** *nt* mollusc (*Brit*), mollusk (*US*)

Weide ['vaɪdə] **(-, -n)** *f* (*Baum*) willow; (*Gras*) pasture

weiden *vi* to graze ▷ *vr*: **sich an etw** *dat* **~** to delight in sth

Weidenkätzchen *nt* willow catkin

weidlich ['vaɪtlɪç] *adv* thoroughly

weigern ['vaɪgərn] *vr* to refuse

Weigerung ['vaɪgərʊŋ] *f* refusal

Weihe ['vaɪə] **(-, -n)** *f* consecration; (*Priesterweihe*) ordination

weihen *vt* to consecrate; (*widmen*) to dedicate; **dem Untergang geweiht** (*liter*) doomed

Weiher **(-s, -)** *m* pond

Weihnachten **(-)** *nt* Christmas; **fröhliche ~!** happy *od* merry Christmas!; **weihnachten** *vi unpers*: **es weihnachtet sehr** (*poetisch, ironisch*) Christmas is very much in evidence

weihnachtlich *adj* Christmas(sy)

Weihnachts- *zW*: **Weihnachtsabend** *m* Christmas Eve; **Weihnachtsbaum** *m* Christmas tree; **Weihnachtsgeld** *nt* Christmas bonus; **Weihnachtsgeschenk** *nt* Christmas present; **Weihnachtslied** *nt* Christmas carol; **Weihnachtsmann** *m* Father Christmas (*Brit*), Santa Claus

Weihnachtsmarkt *m* Christmas fair; *see culture note*

WEIHNACHTSMARKT

The *Weihnachtsmarkt* is a market held in most large towns in Germany in the weeks prior to Christmas. People visit it to buy presents, toys and Christmas decorations, and to enjoy the festive atmosphere. Food and drink associated with the Christmas festivities can also be eaten and drunk there, for example, gingerbread and mulled wine.

Weihnachtstag *m*: **(erster) ~** Christmas day; **zweiter ~** Boxing Day (*Brit*)
Weihrauch *m* incense
Weihwasser *nt* holy water
weil [vaıl] *konj* because
Weile ['vaılə] (-) *f* while, short time
Weiler ['vaılər] **(-s, -)** *m* hamlet
Weimarer Republik ['vaımarər repu'bli:k] *f* Weimar Republic
Wein [vaın] **(-(e)s, -e)** *m* wine; (*Pflanze*) vine; **jdm reinen ~ einschenken** (*fig*) to tell sb the truth; **Weinbau** *m* cultivation of vines; **Weinbauer** *m* wine-grower; **Weinbeere** *f* grape; **Weinberg** *m* vineyard; **Weinbergschnecke** *f* snail; **Weinbrand** *m* brandy
weinen *vt, vi* to cry; **das ist zum W~** it's enough to make you cry *od* weep
weinerlich *adj* tearful
Wein- *zW*: **Weingegend** *f* wine-growing area; **Weingeist** *m* (ethyl) alcohol; **Weinglas** *nt* wine glass; **Weingut** *nt* wine-growing estate; **Weinkarte** *f* wine list
Weinkrampf *m* crying fit
Wein- *zW*: **Weinlese** *f* vintage; **Weinprobe** *f* wine tasting; **Weinrebe** *f* vine; **weinrot** *adj* (*Farbe*) claret; **weinselig** *adj* merry with wine; **Weinstein** *m* tartar; **Weinstock** *m* vine; **Weinstube** *f* wine bar; **Weintraube** *f* grape
weise ['vaızə] *adj* wise
Weise (-, -n) *f* manner, way; (*Lied*) tune; **auf diese ~** in this way
Weise, r *f(m)* wise man, wise woman, sage
weisen *unreg vt* to show; **etw (weit) von sich ~** (*fig*) to reject sth (emphatically)
Weisheit ['vaıshaıt] *f* wisdom
Weisheitszahn *m* wisdom tooth
weismachen ['vaısmaxən] *vt*: **er wollte uns ~, dass ...** he would have us believe that ...
weiß[1] [vaıs] *vb siehe* **wissen**
weiß[2] *adj* white; **Weißblech** *nt* tin plate; **Weißbrot** *nt* white bread; **weißen** *vt* to whitewash; **Weißglut** *f* (*Tech*) incandescence; **jdn zur Weißglut bringen** (*fig*) to make sb see red; **Weißkohl** *m* (white) cabbage
Weißrussland *nt* B(y)elorussia
weißt [vaıst] *vb siehe* **wissen**
Weiß- *zW*: **Weißwaren** *pl* linen *sing*; **Weißwein** *m* white wine; **Weißwurst** *f* veal sausage
Weisung ['vaızʊŋ] *f* instruction
weit [vaıt] *adj* wide; (*Begriff*) broad; (*Reise, Wurf*) long ▷ *adv* far; **~ blickend** far-seeing; **~ hergeholt** far-fetched; **~ reichend** (*fig*) far-reaching; **~ verbreitet** widespread; **~ verzweigt** = **weitverzweigt**; **in ~er Ferne** in the far distance; **wie ~ ist es ...?** how far is it ...?; **das geht zu ~** that's going too far; **~ und breit** for miles around; **~ gefehlt!** far from it!; **es so ~ bringen, dass ...** to bring it about that ...; **~ zurückliegen** to be far behind; **von W~em** from a long way off; **weitab** *adv*: **weitab von** far (away) from; **weitaus** *adv* by far; **Weitblick** *m* (*fig*) far-sightedness; **weitblickend** *adj* far-seeing
Weite (-, -n) *f* width; (*Raum*) space; (*von Entfernung*) distance
weiten *vt, vr* to widen
weiter ['vaıtər] *adj* wider; (*zusätzlich*) further ▷ *adv* further; **wenn es ~ nichts ist, ...** well, if that's all (it is), ...; **das hat ~ nichts zu sagen** that doesn't really matter; **immer ~** on and on; (*Anweisung*) keep on (going); **~ nichts/niemand** nothing/nobody else; **weiterarbeiten** *vi* to go on working; **weiterbilden** *vr* to continue one's studies; **Weiterbildung** *f* further education
Weitere, s *nt* further details *pl*; **bis auf ~s** for the time being; **ohne ~s** without further ado, just like that
weiter- *zW*: **weiterempfehlen** *unreg vt* to recommend (to others); **weitererzählen** *vt* (*Geheimnis*) to pass on; **Weiterfahrt** *f* continuation of the journey; **weiterführend** *adj* (*Schule*) secondary (*Brit*), high (*US*); **weitergehen** *unreg vi* to go on; **weiterhin** *adv*: **etw weiterhin tun** to go on doing sth; **weiterkommen** *unreg vi*: **nicht weiterkommen** (*fig*) to be bogged down; **weiterleiten** *vt* to pass on; **weitermachen** *vt, vi* to continue; **weiterreisen** *vi* to continue one's journey; **weitersagen** *vt*: **nicht weitersagen!** don't tell anyone!; **weitersehen** *unreg vi*: **dann sehen wir weiter** then we'll see; **weiterverarbeiten** *vt* to process; **weiterwissen** *unreg vi*: **nicht (mehr) weiterwissen** (*verzweifelt sein*) to be at one's wits' end
weit- *zW*: **weitgehend** *adj* considerable ▷ *adv* largely; **weithin** *adv* widely; (*weitgehend*) to a large extent; **weitläufig** *adj* (*Gebäude*) spacious; (*Erklärung*) lengthy; (*Verwandter*) distant; **weitreichend** *adj* (*fig*) far-reaching; **weitschweifig** *adj* long-winded; **weitsichtig** *adj* (*lit*) long-sighted (*Brit*), far-sighted (*US*); (*fig*) far-sighted; **Weitsprung** *m* long jump; **weitverbreitet** *adj* widespread; **weitverzweigt** *adj* (*Straßensystem*) extensive; **Weitwinkelobjektiv** *nt* (*Phot*) wide-angle lens
Weizen ['vaıtzən] **(-s, -)** *m* wheat; **Weizenbier** *nt light, fizzy wheat beer*; **Weizenkeime** *pl* (*Koch*) wheatgerm *sing*
welch [vɛlç] *pron*: **~ ein(e) ...** what a ...

SCHLÜSSELWORT

welche, r, s *interrog pron* which; **welcher von beiden?** which (one) of the two?; **welchen hast du genommen?** which (one) did you take?; **welche Freude!** what joy!
▷ *indef pron* some; (*in Fragen*) any; **ich habe welche** I have some; **haben Sie welche?** do you have any?
▷ *rel pron* (*bei Menschen*) who; (*bei Sachen*) which,

that; **welche(r, s) auch immer** whoever/whichever/whatever

welk [vɛlk] *adj* withered; **welken** *vi* to wither
Wellblech *nt* corrugated iron
Welle ['vɛlə] (**-, -n**) *f* wave; (*Tech*) shaft; **(hohe) ~n schlagen** (*fig*) to create (quite) a stir
Wellen- *zW*: **Wellenbereich** *m* waveband; **Wellenbrecher** *m* breakwater; **Wellengang** *m*: **starker Wellengang** heavy sea(s) *od* swell; **Wellenlänge** *f* (*lit, fig*) wavelength; **mit jdm auf einer Wellenlänge sein** (*fig*) to be on the same wavelength as sb; **Wellenlinie** *f* wavy line
Wellensittich *m* budgerigar
Wellpappe *f* corrugated cardboard
Welpe ['vɛlpə] (**-n, -n**) *m* pup, whelp; (*von Wolf etc*) cub
Welt [vɛlt] (**-, -en**) *f* world; **aus der ~ schaffen** to eliminate; **in aller ~** all over the world; **vor aller ~** in front of everybody; **auf die ~ kommen** to be born; **Weltall** *nt* universe; **Weltanschauung** *f* philosophy of life; **weltberühmt** *adj* world-famous; **weltbewegend** *adj* world-shattering; **Weltbild** *nt* conception of the world; (*jds Ansichten*) philosophy
Weltenbummler, in *m(f)* globetrotter
Weltergewicht ['vɛltərgəvɪçt] *nt* (*Sport*) welterweight
weltfremd *adj* unworldly
Weltgesundheitsorganisation *f* World Health Organization
Welt- *zW*: **weltgewandt** *adj* sophisticated; **Weltkirchenrat** *m* World Council of Churches; **Weltkrieg** *m* world war; **weltlich** *adj* worldly; (*nicht kirchlich*) secular; **Weltliteratur** *f* world literature; **Weltmacht** *f* world power; **weltmännisch** *adj* sophisticated; **Weltmeister** *m* world champion; **Weltmeisterschaft** *f* world *od* world's (*US*) championship; (*Fussball etc*) World Cup; **Weltrang** *m*: **von Weltrang** world-famous; **Weltraum** *m* space; **Weltraumforschung** *f* space research; **Weltraumstation** *f* space station; **Weltreise** *f* trip round the world; **Weltruf** *m* world-wide reputation; **Weltsicherheitsrat** *m* (*Pol*) United Nations Security Council; **Weltstadt** *f* metropolis; **Weltuntergang** *m* (*lit, fig*) end of the world; **weltweit** *adj* world-wide; **Weltwirtschaft** *f* world economy; **Weltwirtschaftskrise** *f* world economic crisis; **Weltwunder** *nt* wonder of the world
wem [veːm] *dat von* **wer** ▷ *pron* to whom
wen [veːn] *akk von* **wer** ▷ *pron* whom
Wende ['vɛndə] (**-, -n**) *f* turn; (*Veränderung*) change; **die ~** (*Pol*) (the) reunification (of Germany); **Wendekreis** *m* (*Geog*) tropic; (*Aut*) turning circle
Wendeltreppe *f* spiral staircase
wenden *unreg vt, vi, vr* to turn; **bitte ~!** please turn over; **sich an jdn ~** to go/come to sb
Wendepunkt *m* turning point
wendig *adj* (*lit, fig*) agile; (*Auto etc*) manoeuvrable (*Brit*), maneuverable (*US*)
Wendung *f* turn; (*Redewendung*) idiom
wenig ['veːnɪç] *adj, adv* little; **ein ~** a little; **er hat zu ~ Geld** he doesn't have enough money; **ein Exemplar zu ~** one copy too few
wenige ['veːnɪgə] *pl* few *pl*; **in ~n Tagen** in (just) a few days
weniger *adj* less; (*mit pl*) fewer ▷ *adv* less
Wenigkeit *f* trifle; **meine ~** (*umg*) little me
wenigste, r, s *adj* least
wenigstens *adv* at least
wenn [vɛn] *konj* if; (*zeitlich*) when; **~ auch ...** even if ...; **~ ich doch ...** if only I ...; **~ wir erst die neue Wohnung haben** once we get the new flat
Wenn *nt*: **ohne ~ und Aber** unequivocally
wennschon *adv*: **na ~!** so what?; **~, dennschon!** in for a penny, in for a pound!
wer [veːr] *pron* who
Werbe- *zW*: **Werbeagentur** *f* advertising agency; **Werbeaktion** *f* advertising campaign; **Werbeantwort** *f* business reply card; **Werbebanner** *nt* banner; **Werbefernsehen** *nt* commercial television; **Werbefilm** *m* promotional film; **Werbegeschenk** *nt* promotional gift, freebie (*umg*); (*zu Gekauftem*) free gift; **Werbegrafiker, in** *m(f)* commercial artist; **Werbekampagne** *f* advertising campaign
werben ['vɛrbən] *unreg vt* to win; (*Mitglied*) to recruit ▷ *vi* to advertise; **um jdn/etw ~** to try to win sb/sth; **für jdn/etw ~** to promote sb/sth
Werbe- *zW*: **Werbespot** *m* commercial; **Werbetexter** (**-s, -**) *m* copywriter; **Werbetrommel** *f*: **die Werbetrommel (für etw) rühren** (*umg*) to beat the big drum (for sth); **werbewirksam** *adj*: **werbewirksam sein** to be good publicity
Werbung *f* advertising; (*von Mitgliedern*) recruitment; (*TV etc: Werbeblock*) commercial break; **~ um jdn/etw** promotion of sb/sth
Werbungskosten *pl* professional *od* business expenses *pl*
Werdegang ['veːrdəgaŋ] *m* development; (*beruflich*) career

SCHLÜSSELWORT

werden ['veːrdən] *unreg* (*pt* **wurde**, *pp* **geworden** *od* **(bei Passiv) worden**) *vi* to become; **was ist aus ihm/aus der Sache geworden?** what became of him/it?; **es ist nichts/gut geworden** it came to nothing/turned out well; **es wird Nacht/Tage** it's getting dark/light; **es wird bald ein Jahr, dass ...** it's almost a year since ...; **er wird am 8. Mai 36** he will be 36 on the 8th May; **mir wird kalt** I'm getting cold; **mir wird schlecht** I feel ill; **Erster werden** to come *od* be first; **das muss anders werden** that will have to change; **rot/zu Eis werden** to turn red/to ice; **was**

willst du (mal) werden? what do you want to be?; **die Fotos sind gut geworden** the photos turned out well
▷ *hilfsverb* **1** (*bei Futur*): **er wird es tun** he will *od* he'll do it; **er wird das nicht tun** he will not *od* he won't do it; **es wird gleich regnen** it's going to rain any moment
2 (*bei Konjunktiv*): **ich würde ...** I would ...; **er würde gern ...** he would *od* he'd like to ...; **ich würde lieber ...** I would *od* I'd rather ...
3 (*bei Vermutung*): **sie wird in der Küche sein** she will be in the kitchen
4 (*bei Passiv*): **gebraucht werden** to be used; **er ist erschossen worden** he has *od* he's been shot; **mir wurde gesagt, dass ...** I was told that ...

werdend *adj*: **~e Mutter** expectant mother
werfen ['vɛrfən] *unreg vt* to throw ▷ *vi* (*Tier*) to have its young; **„nicht ~"** "handle with care"
Werft [vɛrft] (**-, -en**) *f* shipyard; (*für Flugzeuge*) hangar
Werk [vɛrk] (**-(e)s, -e**) *nt* work; (*Tätigkeit*) job; (*Fabrik, Mechanismus*) works *pl*; **ans ~ gehen** to set to work; **das ist sein** ~ this is his doing; **ab** ~ (*Comm*) ex works
werkeln ['vɛrkəln] (*umg*) *vi* to potter about (*Brit*), putter around (*US*)
Werken (**-s**) *nt* (*Sch*) handicrafts *pl*
Werkschutz *m* works security service
Werksgelände *nt* factory premises *pl*
Werk- *zW*: **Werkstatt** (**-, -stätten**) *f* workshop; (*Aut*) garage; **Werkstoff** *m* material; **Werkstudent** *m* self-supporting student; **Werktag** *m* working day; **werktags** *adv* on working days; **werktätig** *adj* working; **Werkzeug** *nt* tool; **Werkzeugkasten** *m* toolbox; **Werkzeugmaschine** *f* machine tool; **Werkzeugschrank** *m* tool chest
Wermut ['ve:rmu:t] (**-(e)s, -s**) *m* wormwood; (*Wein*) vermouth
Wermutstropfen *m* (*fig*) drop of bitterness
Wert [ve:rt] (**-(e)s, -e**) *m* worth; (*Fin*) value; **~ legen auf** *+akk* to attach importance to; **es hat doch keinen** ~ it's useless; **im ~e von** to the value of
wert [ve:rt] *adj* worth; (*geschätzt*) dear; (*würdig*) worthy; **das ist nichts/viel** ~ it's not worth anything/it's worth a lot; **das ist es/er mir** ~ it's/he's worth that to me; **ein Auto ist viel** ~ (*nützlich*) a car is very useful
Wertangabe *f* declaration of value
wertbeständig *adj* stable in value
werten *vt* to rate; (*beurteilen*) to judge; (*Sport: als gültig werten*) to allow; **~ als** to rate as; to judge to be
Wert- *zW*: **Wertgegenstand** *m* article of value; **wertlos** *adj* worthless; **Wertlosigkeit** *f* worthlessness; **Wertmaßstab** *m* standard; **Wertpapier** *nt* security; **Wertsteigerung** *f* appreciation
Wertung *f* (*Sport*) score
Wert- *zW*: **wertvoll** *adj* valuable; **Wertvorstellung** *f* moral concept; **Wertzuwachs** *m* appreciation
Wesen ['ve:zən] (**-s, -**) *nt* (*Geschöpf*) being; (*Natur, Character*) nature
wesentlich *adj* significant; (*beträchtlich*) considerable; **im W~en** essentially; (*im Großen*) in the main
weshalb [vɛs'halp] *adv* why
Wespe ['vɛspə] (**-, -n**) *f* wasp
wessen ['vɛsən] *gen von* **wer** ▷ *pron* whose
Wessi ['vɛsɪ] (**-s, -s**) (*umg*) *m* West German; *see culture note*

WESSI

A *Wessi* is a colloquial and often derogatory word used to describe a German from the former West Germany. The expression "Besserwessi" is used by East Germans to describe a West German who is considered to be a know-all.

West- *zW*: **westdeutsch** *adj* West German; **Westdeutsche, r** *f(m)* West German; **Westdeutschland** *nt* (*Pol: früher*) West Germany; (*Geog*) Western Germany
Weste ['vɛstə] (**-, -n**) *f* waistcoat, vest (*US*); **eine reine ~ haben** (*fig*) to have a clean slate
Westen (**-s**) *m* west
Westentasche *f*: **etw wie seine ~ kennen** (*umg*) to know sth like the back of one's hand
Westerwald ['vɛstərvalt] (**-s**) *m* Westerwald (Mountains *pl*)
Westeuropa *nt* Western Europe
westeuropäisch ['vɛst|ɔyro'pɛ:ɪʃ] *adj* West(ern) European; **~e Zeit** Greenwich Mean Time
Westfale [vɛst'fa:lə] (**-n, -n**) *m* Westphalian
Westfalen (**-s**) *nt* Westphalia
Westfälin [vɛst'fɛ:lɪn] *f* Westphalian
westfälisch *adj* Westphalian
Westindien ['vɛst|ɪndiən] (**-s**) *nt* West Indies *pl*
westindisch *adj* West Indian; **die W~en Inseln** the West Indies
west- *zW*: **westlich** *adj* western ▷ *adv* to the west; **Westmächte** *pl* (*Pol: früher*): **die Westmächte** the Western powers *pl*; **westwärts** *adv* westwards
weswegen [vɛs've:gən] *adv* why
wett [vɛt] *adj* even; **~ sein** to be quits
Wettbewerb *m* competition
Wettbewerbsbeschränkung *f* restraint of trade
wettbewerbsfähig *adj* competitive
Wette (**-, -n**) *f* bet, wager; **um die ~ laufen** to run a race (with each other)
Wetteifer *m* rivalry
wetteifern *vi untr*: **mit jdm um etw ~** to compete with sb for sth
wetten ['vɛtən] *vt, vi* to bet; **so haben wir nicht gewettet!** that's not part of the bargain!
Wetter ['vɛtər] (**-s, -**) *nt* weather; (*Min*) air; **Wetteramt** *nt* meteorological office; **Wetteraussichten** *pl* weather outlook

sing; **Wetterbericht** *m* weather report; **Wetterdienst** *m* meteorological service; **wetterfest** *adj* weatherproof; **wetterfühlig** *adj* sensitive to changes in the weather; **Wetterkarte** *f* weather chart; **Wetterlage** *f* (weather) situation

wettern ['vɛtərn] *vi* to curse and swear

Wetter- *zW*: **Wetterumschlag** *m* sudden change in the weather; **Wettervorhersage** *f* weather forecast; **Wetterwarte** *f* weather station; **wetterwendisch** *adj* capricious

Wett- *zW*: **Wettkampf** *m* contest; **Wettlauf** *m* race; **ein Wettlauf mit der Zeit** a race against time

wettmachen *vt* to make good

Wett- *zW*: **Wettrüsten** *nt* arms race; **Wettspiel** *nt* match; **Wettstreit** *m* contest

wetzen ['vɛtsən] *vt* to sharpen ▷ *vi* (*umg*) to scoot

WEU *f abk* (= *Westeuropäische Union*) WEU

WEZ *abk* (= *westeuropäische Zeit*) GMT

WG *abk* = **Wohngemeinschaft**

Whisky ['vɪski] (**-s, -s**) *m* whisky (*Brit*), whiskey (*US, Ireland*)

WHO (-) *f abk* (= *World Health Organization*) WHO

wich *etc* [vɪç] *vb siehe* **weichen**

wichsen ['vɪksən] *vt* (*Schuhe*) to polish ▷ *vi* (*umg!*: *onanieren*) to jerk *od* toss off (*!*)

Wichser (*umg!*) *m* wanker (*!*)

Wicht [vɪçt] (**-(e)s, -e**) *m* titch; (*pej*) worthless creature

wichtig *adj* important; **sich selbst/etw (zu) ~ nehmen** to take o.s./sth (too) seriously; **Wichtigkeit** *f* importance; **Wichtigtuer, in** (*pej*) *m(f)* pompous ass (*umg*)

Wicke ['vɪkə] (**-, -n**) *f* (*Bot*) vetch; (*Gartenwicke*) sweet pea

Wickelkleid *nt* wrap-around dress

wickeln ['vɪkəln] *vt* to wind; (*Haare*) to set; (*Kind*) to change; **da bist du schief gewickelt!** (*fig*: *umg*) you're very much mistaken; **jdn/etw in etw** *akk* **~** to wrap sb/sth in sth

Wickeltisch *m* baby's changing table

Widder ['vɪdər] (**-s, -**) *m* ram; (*Astrol*) Aries

wider ['vi:dər] *präp +akk* against

widerfahren *unreg vi untr*: **jdm ~** to happen to sb

Widerhaken ['vi:dərha:kən] *m* barb

Widerhall ['vi:dərhal] *m* echo; **keinen ~ (bei jdm) finden** (*Interesse*) to meet with no response (from sb)

widerlegen *vt untr* to refute

widerlich ['vi:dərlɪç] *adj* disgusting, repulsive; **Widerlichkeit** *f* repulsiveness

widerrechtlich *adj* unlawful

Widerrede *f* contradiction; **keine ~!** don't argue!

Widerruf ['vi:dərru:f] *m* retraction; countermanding; **bis auf ~** until revoked

widerrufen *unreg vt untr* to retract; (*Anordnung*) to revoke; (*Befehl*) to countermand

Widersacher, in ['vi:dərzaxər(ɪn)] (**-s, -**) *m(f)* adversary

widersetzen *vr untr*: **sich jdm ~** to oppose sb; (*der Polizei*) to resist sb; **sich einer Sache ~** to oppose sth; (*einem Befehl*) to refuse to comply with sth

widerspenstig ['vi:dərʃpɛnstɪç] *adj* wilful (*Brit*), willful (*US*); **Widerspenstigkeit** *f* wilfulness (*Brit*), willfulness (*US*)

widerspiegeln ['vi:dərʃpi:gəln] *vt* to reflect

widersprechen *unreg vi untr*: **jdm ~** to contradict sb

widersprechend *adj* contradictory

Widerspruch ['vi:dərʃprʊx] *m* contradiction; **ein ~ in sich** a contradiction in terms

widersprüchlich ['vi:dərʃprʏçlɪç] *adj* contradictory, inconsistent

widerspruchslos *adv* without arguing

Widerstand ['vi:dərʃtant] *m* resistance; **der Weg des geringsten ~es** the line of least resistance; **jdm/etw ~ leisten** to resist sb/sth

Widerstands- *zW*: **Widerstandsbewegung** *f* resistance (movement); **widerstandsfähig** *adj* resistant, tough; **widerstandslos** *adj* unresisting

widerstehen *unreg vi untr*: **jdm/etw ~** to withstand sb/sth

widerstreben *vi untr*: **es widerstrebt mir, so etwas zu tun** I am reluctant to do anything like that

widerstrebend *adj* reluctant; (*gegensätzlich*) conflicting

Wider- *zW*: **Widerstreit** *m* conflict; **widerwärtig** *adj* nasty, horrid; **Widerwille** *m*: **Widerwille (gegen)** aversion (to); (*Abneigung*) distaste (for); (*Widerstreben*) reluctance; **widerwillig** *adj* unwilling, reluctant; **Widerworte** *pl* answering back *sing*

widmen ['vɪtmən] *vt* to dedicate ▷ *vr* to devote o.s.

Widmung *f* dedication

widrig ['vi:drɪç] *adj* (*Umstände*) adverse; (*Mensch*) repulsive

SCHLÜSSELWORT

wie [vi:] *adv* how; **wie groß/schnell?** how big/fast?; **wie viel** how much; **wie viel Menschen** how many people; **wie wärs?** how about it?; **wie wärs mit einem Whisky?** (*umg*) how about a whisky?; **wie nennt man das?** what is that called?; **wie ist er?** what's he like?; **wie gut du das kannst!** you're very good at it; **wie bitte?** pardon? (*Brit*), pardon me? (*US*); (*entrüstet*) I beg your pardon!; **und wie!** and how!

▷ *konj* **1** (*bei Vergleichen*): **so schön wie ...** as beautiful as ...; **wie ich schon sagte** as I said; **wie noch nie** as never before; **wie du** like you; **singen wie ein ...** to sing like a ...; **wie (zum Beispiel)** such as (for example)

2 (*zeitlich*): **wie er das hörte, ging er** when he heard that he left; **er hörte, wie der Regen fiel** he heard the rain falling

wieder ['vi:dər] *adv* again; **~ da sein** to be back

(again); **gehst du schon ~?** are you off again?; **~ ein(e) ...** another ...; **das ist auch ~ wahr** that's true enough; **da sieht man mal ~ ...** it just shows ...; **~ finden, ~ gutmachen** *etc* = **wiederfinden, wiedergutmachen** *etc*

wieder- *zW*: **Wiederaufbau** [-'|aʊfbaʊ] *m* rebuilding; **wiederaufbereiten** *vt* to recycle; (*Atommüll*) to reprocess; **Wiederaufbereitungsanlage** *f* reprocessing plant; **Wiederaufnahme** [-'|aʊfna:mə] *f* resumption; **wiederaufnehmen** *unreg vt* to resume; (*Gedanken, Hobby*) to take up again; (*Thema*) to revert to; (*Jur: Verfahren*) to reopen; **wiederaufrollen** *vt* (*Fall, Prozess*) to reopen; **wiederbekommen** *unreg vt* to get back; **wiederbeleben** *unreg vt* to revive; **wiederbringen** *unreg vt* to bring back; **wiedererkennen** *unreg vt* to recognize; **Wiedererstattung** *f* reimbursement; **wiederfinden** *unreg vt* (*fig: Selbstachtung etc*) to regain

Wiedergabe *f* (*von Rede, Ereignis*) account; (*Wiederholung*) repetition; (*Darbietung*) performance; (*Reproduktion*) reproduction; **Wiedergabegerät** *nt* playback unit

wieder- *zW*: **wiedergeben** *unreg vt* (*zurückgeben*) to return; (*Erzählung etc*) to repeat; (*Gefühle etc*) to convey; **Wiedergeburt** *f* rebirth; **wiedergutmachen** *vt* to make up for; (*Fehler*) to put right; **Wiedergutmachung** *f* reparation; **wiederherstellen** *vt* (*Gesundheit, Gebäude, Ruhe*) to restore

wiederholen *vt untr* to repeat

wiederholt *adj*: **zum ~en Male** once again

Wiederholung *f* repetition

Wiederholungstäter, in *m(f)* (*Jur*) second-time offender; (*mehrmalig*) persistent offender

wieder- *zW*: **Wiederhören** *nt*: **auf Wiederhören** (*Tel*) goodbye; **wiederkäuen** *vi* to ruminate ▷ *vt* to ruminate; (*fig: umg*) to go over again and again; **Wiederkehr** (-) *f* return; (*von Vorfall*) repetition, recurrence; **wiederkehrend** *adj* recurrent; **Wiederkunft** (-, ¨-e) *f* return; **wiedersehen** *unreg vt* to see again; **auf Wiedersehen** goodbye; **wiederum** *adv* again; (*seinerseits etc*) in turn; (*andererseits*) on the other hand; **wiedervereinigen** *vt* to reunite; **Wiedervereinigung** *f* reunification; **Wiederverkäufer** *m* distributor; **Wiederwahl** *f* re-election

Wiege ['vi:ge] **(-, -n)** *f* cradle

wiegen[1] *vt* (*schaukeln*) to rock; (*Kopf*) to shake

wiegen[2] *unreg vt, vi* to weigh; **schwer ~** (*fig*) to carry a lot of weight; (*Irrtum*) to be serious

wiehern ['vi:ərn] *vi* to neigh, whinny

Wien [vi:n] **(-s)** *nt* Vienna

Wiener, in **(-s, -)** *m(f)* Viennese ▷ *adj attrib* Viennese; **~ Schnitzel** Wiener schnitzel

wies *etc* [vi:s] *vb siehe* **weisen**

Wiese ['vi:zə] **(-, -n)** *f* meadow

Wiesel ['vi:zəl] **(-s, -)** *nt* weasel; **schnell** *od* **flink wie ein ~** quick as a flash

wieso [vi:'zo:] *adv* why

wievielmal [vi:'fi:lma:l] *adv* how often

wievielte, r, s *adj*: **zum ~n Mal?** how many times?; **den W~n haben wir?** what's the date?; **an ~r Stelle?** in what place?; **der ~ Besucher war er?** how many visitors were there before him?

wieweit [vi:'vaɪt] *adv* to what extent

Wikinger ['vi:kɪŋər] **(-s, -)** *m* Viking

wild [vɪlt] *adj* wild; **~er Streik** unofficial strike; **in ~er Ehe leben** (*veraltet, hum*) to live in sin; **~ entschlossen** (*umg*) dead set

Wild **(-(e)s)** *nt* game

Wild- *zW*: **Wildbahn** *f*: **in freier Wildbahn** in the wild; **Wildbret** *nt* game; (*von Rotwild*) venison; **Wilddieb** *m* poacher

Wilde, r ['vɪldə(r)] *f(m)* savage

wildern ['vɪldərn] *vi* to poach

wild- *zW*: **Wildfang** *m* little rascal; **wildfremd** ['vɪlt'frɛmt] (*umg*) *adj* quite strange *od* unknown; **Wildheit** *f* wildness; **Wildleder** *nt* suede

Wildnis **(-, -se)** *f* wilderness

Wild- *zW*: **Wildschwein** *nt* (wild) boar; **Wildwechsel** *m*: **„Wildwechsel"** "wild animals"; **Wildwestroman** *m* western

will [vɪl] *vb siehe* **wollen**

Wille ['vɪlə] **(-ns, -n)** *m* will; **jdm seinen ~n lassen** to let sb have his own way; **seinen eigenen ~n haben** to be self-willed

willen *präp +gen*: **um ... ~** for the sake of ...

willenlos *adj* weak-willed

willens *adj* (*geh*): **~ sein** to be willing

willensstark *adj* strong-willed

willentlich ['vɪləntlɪç] *adj* wilful (*Brit*), willful (*US*), deliberate

willig *adj* willing

willkommen [vɪl'kɔmən] *adj* welcome; **jdn ~ heißen** to welcome sb; **herzlich ~ (in** *+dat***)** welcome (to); **Willkommen** **(-s, -)** *nt* welcome

willkürlich *adj* arbitrary; (*Bewegung*) voluntary

willst [vɪlst] *vb siehe* **wollen**

Wilna ['vɪlna] **(-s)** *nt* Vilnius

wimmeln ['vɪməln] *vi*: **~ (von)** to swarm (with)

wimmern ['vɪmərn] *vi* to whimper

Wimper ['vɪmpər] **(-, -n)** *f* eyelash; **ohne mit der ~ zu zucken** (*fig*) without batting an eyelid

Wimperntusche *f* mascara

Wind [vɪnt] **(-(e)s, -e)** *m* wind; **den Mantel** *od* **das Fähnchen nach dem ~ hängen** to trim one's sails to the wind; **etw in den ~ schlagen** to turn a deaf ear to sth

Windbeutel *m* cream puff; (*fig*) windbag

Winde ['vɪndə] **(-, -n)** *f* (*Tech*) winch, windlass; (*Bot*) bindweed

Windel ['vɪndəl] **(-, -n)** *f* nappy (*Brit*), diaper (*US*)

windelweich *adj*: **jdn ~ schlagen** (*umg*) to beat the living daylights out of sb

winden[1] ['vɪndən] *vi unpers* to be windy

winden[2] *unreg vt* to wind; (*Kranz*) to weave; (*entwinden*) to twist ▷ *vr* to wind; (*Person*) to writhe; (*fig: ausweichen*) to try to wriggle out

Windenergie *f* wind power

Windeseile *f*: **sich in** *od* **mit ~ verbreiten** to spread like wildfire
Windhose *f* whirlwind
Windhund *m* greyhound; (*Mensch*) fly-by-night
windig ['vɪndɪç] *adj* windy; (*fig*) dubious
Wind- *zW*: **Windjacke** *f* windcheater, windbreaker (*US*); **Windkanal** *m* (*Tech*) wind tunnel; **Windkraft** *f* wind power; **Windkraftanlage** *f* wind power station; **Windmühle** *f* windmill; **gegen Windmühlen (an)kämpfen** (*fig*) to tilt at windmills; **Windpark** *m* wind farm
Windpocken *pl* chickenpox *sing*
Wind- *zW*: **Windrose** *f* (*Naut*) compass card; (*Met*) wind rose; **Windschatten** *m* lee; (*von Fahrzeugen*) slipstream; **Windschutzscheibe** *f* (*Aut*) windscreen (*Brit*), windshield (*US*); **Windstärke** *f* wind force; **windstill** *adj* (*Tag*) windless; **es ist windstill** there's no wind; **Windstille** *f* calm; **Windstoß** *m* gust of wind; **Windsurfen** *nt* windsurfing
Windung *f* (*von Weg, Fluss etc*) meander; (*von Schlange, Spule*) coil; (*von Schraube*) thread
Wink [vɪŋk] **(-(e)s, -e)** *m* (*mit Kopf*) nod; (*mit Hand*) wave; (*Tipp, Hinweis*) hint; **ein ~ mit dem Zaunpfahl** a broad hint
Winkel ['vɪŋkəl] **(-s, -)** *m* (*Math*) angle; (*Gerät*) set square; (*in Raum*) corner; **Winkeladvokat** (*pej*) *m* incompetent lawyer; **Winkelmesser** *m* protractor; **Winkelzug** *m*: **mach keine Winkelzüge** stop evading the issue
winken ['vɪŋkən] *vt, vi* to wave; **dem Sieger winkt eine Reise nach Italien** the (lucky) winner will receive a trip to Italy
winseln ['vɪnzəln] *vi* to whine
Winter ['vɪntər] **(-s, -)** *m* winter; **Wintergarten** *m* conservatory; **winterlich** *adj* wintry; **Winterreifen** *m* winter tyre (*Brit*) *od* tire (*US*); **Winterschlaf** *m* (*Zool*) hibernation; **Winterschlussverkauf** *m* winter sale; **Wintersemester** *nt* (*Univ*) winter semester (*bes US*), ≈ autumn term (*Brit*); **Winterspiele** *pl*: **(Olympische) Winterspiele** Winter Olympics *pl*; **Wintersport** *m* winter sports *pl*
Winzer, in ['vɪntsər(ɪn)] **(-s, -)** *m(f)* wine-grower
winzig ['vɪntsɪç] *adj* tiny
Wipfel ['vɪpfəl] **(-s, -)** *m* treetop
Wippe ['vɪpə] **(-, -n)** *f* seesaw
wir [vi:r] *pron* we; **~ alle** all of us, we all
Wirbel ['vɪrbəl] **(-s, -)** *m* whirl, swirl; (*Trubel*) hurly-burly; (*Aufsehen*) fuss; (*Anat*) vertebra; **~ um jdn/etw machen** to make a fuss about sb/sth
wirbellos *adj* (*Zool*) invertebrate
wirbeln *vi* to whirl, swirl
Wirbel- *zW*: **Wirbelsäule** *f* spine; **Wirbeltier** *nt* vertebrate; **Wirbelwind** *m* whirlwind
wirbst *vb siehe* **werben**
wirbt [vɪrpt] *vb siehe* **werben**
wird [vɪrt] *vb siehe* **werden**
wirfst *vb siehe* **werfen**
wirft [vɪrft] *vb siehe* **werfen**
wirken ['vɪrkən] *vi* to have an effect; (*erfolgreich sein*) to work; (*scheinen*) to seem ▷ *vt* (*Wunder*) to work; **etw auf sich** *akk* **~ lassen** to take sth in
wirklich ['vɪrklɪç] *adj* real; **Wirklichkeit** *f* reality; **wirklichkeitsgetreu** *adj* realistic
wirksam ['vɪrkza:m] *adj* effective; **Wirksamkeit** *f* effectiveness
Wirkstoff *m* active substance
Wirkung ['vɪrkʊŋ] *f* effect
Wirkungs- *zW*: **Wirkungsbereich** *m* field (of activity *od* interest *etc*); (*Domäne*) domain; **wirkungslos** *adj* ineffective; **wirkungslos bleiben** to have no effect; **wirkungsvoll** *adj* effective
wirr [vɪr] *adj* confused; (*unrealistisch*) wild; (*Haare etc*) tangled
Wirren *pl* disturbances *pl*
Wirrwarr ['vɪrvar] **(-s)** *m* disorder, chaos; (*von Stimmen*) hubbub; (*von Fäden, Haaren etc*) tangle
Wirsing ['vɪrzɪŋ], **Wirsingkohl** ['vɪrzɪŋko:l] **(-s)** *m* savoy cabbage
wirst [vɪrst] *vb siehe* **werden**
Wirt, in [vɪrt(ɪn)] **(-(e)s, -e)** *m(f)* landlord, landlady
Wirtschaft ['vɪrtʃaft] *f* (*Gaststätte*) pub; (*Haushalt*) housekeeping; (*eines Landes*) economy; (*Geschäftsleben*) industry and commerce; (*umg: Durcheinander*) mess; **wirtschaften** *vi* (*sparsam sein*): **gut wirtschaften können** to be economical; **Wirtschafter** *m* (*Verwalter*) manager; **Wirtschafterin** *f* (*im Haushalt, Heim etc*) housekeeper; **wirtschaftlich** *adj* economical; (*Pol*) economic; **Wirtschaftlichkeit** *f* economy; (*von Betrieb*) viability
Wirtschafts- *zW*: **Wirtschaftsgeld** *nt* housekeeping (money); **Wirtschaftsgeografie** *f* economic geography; **Wirtschaftshilfe** *f* economic aid; **Wirtschaftskrise** *f* economic crisis; **Wirtschaftsminister** *m* minister of economic affairs; **Wirtschaftsordnung** *f* economic system; **Wirtschaftspolitik** *f* economic policy; **Wirtschaftsprüfer** *m* chartered accountant (*Brit*), certified public accountant (*US*); **Wirtschaftsspionage** *f* industrial espionage; **Wirtschaftswachstum** *nt* economic growth; **Wirtschaftswissenschaft** *f* economics *sing*; **Wirtschaftswunder** *nt* economic miracle; **Wirtschaftszweig** *m* branch of industry
Wirtshaus *nt* inn
Wisch [vɪʃ] **(-(e)s, -e)** *m* scrap of paper
wischen *vt* to wipe
Wischer **(-s, -)** *m* (*Aut*) wiper
Wischiwaschi [vɪʃi:'vaʃi:] **(-s)** (*pej: umg*) *nt* drivel
Wisent ['vi:zɛnt] **(-s, -e)** *m* bison
WiSo ['vɪzo] *abk* (= *Wirtschafts- und Sozialwissenschaften*) economics and social sciences
wispern ['vɪspərn] *vt, vi* to whisper
Wiss. *abk* = **Wissenschaft**
wiss. *abk* = **wissenschaftlich**

Wissbegier ['vɪsbəgiːr], **Wissbegierde** ['vɪsbəgiːrdə] *f* thirst for knowledge
wissbegierig *adj* eager for knowledge
wissen ['vɪsən] *unreg vt, vi* to know; **von jdm/etw nichts ~ wollen** not to be interested in sb/sth; **sie hält sich für wer weiß wie klug** (*umg*) she doesn't half think she's clever; **gewusst wie/wo!** *etc* sheer brilliance!; **ich weiß seine Adresse nicht mehr** (*sich erinnern*) I can't remember his address; **Wissen (-s)** *nt* knowledge; **etw gegen (sein) besseres Wissen tun** to do sth against one's better judgement; **nach bestem Wissen und Gewissen** to the best of one's knowledge and belief
Wissenschaft ['vɪsənʃaft] *f* science
Wissenschaftler, in (-s, -) *m(f)* scientist; (*Geisteswissenschaftler*) academic
wissenschaftlich *adj* scientific; **W~er Assistent** assistant lecturer
wissenswert *adj* worth knowing
wissentlich *adj* knowing
wittern ['vɪtərn] *vt* to scent; (*fig*) to suspect
Witterung *f* weather; (*Geruch*) scent
Witwe ['vɪtvə] **(-, -n)** *f* widow
Witwer (-s, -) *m* widower
Witz [vɪts] **(-es, -e)** *m* joke; **der ~ an der Sache ist, dass ...** the great thing about it is that ...; **Witzbold (-(e)s, -e)** *m* joker
witzeln *vi* to joke
witzig *adj* funny
witzlos (*umg*) *adj* (*unsinnig*) pointless, futile
WM (-) *f abk* = **Weltmeisterschaft**
wo [voː] *adv* where; (*umg: irgendwo*) somewhere ▷ *konj* (*wenn*) if; **im Augenblick, wo ...** the moment (that) ...; **die Zeit, wo ...** the time when ...
woanders [voː'|andərs] *adv* elsewhere
wob *etc* [voːp] *vb siehe* **weben**
wobei [voː'baɪ] *adv* (*rel*) ... in/by/with which; (*interrog*) how; what ... in/by/with; **~ mir gerade einfällt ...** which reminds me ...
Woche ['vɔxə] **(-, -n)** *f* week
Wochenbett *nt*: **im ~ sterben** to die in childbirth
Wochen- *zW*: **Wochenende** *nt* weekend; **Wochenendhaus** *nt* weekend house; **Wochenkarte** *f* weekly ticket; **wochenlang** *adj* lasting weeks ▷ *adv* for weeks; **Wochenschau** *f* newsreel; **Wochentag** *m* weekday
wöchentlich ['vœçəntlɪç] *adj, adv* weekly
Wochenzeitung *f* weekly (paper)
Wöchnerin ['vœçnərɪn] *f woman who has recently given birth*
Wodka ['vɔtka] **(-s, -s)** *m* vodka
wodurch [vo'dʊrç] *adv* (*rel*) through which; (*interrog*) what ... through
wofür [vo'fyːr] *adv* (*rel*) for which; (*interrog*) what ... for
wog *etc* [voːk] *vb siehe* **wiegen²**
Woge ['voːgə] **(-, -n)** *f* wave
wogegen [vo'geːgən] *adv* (*rel*) against which; (*interrog*) what ... against
wogen *vi* to heave, surge
woher [vo'heːr] *adv* where ... from; **~ kommt es eigentlich, dass ...?** how is it that ...?
wohin [vo'hɪn] *adv* where ... to; **~ man auch schaut** wherever you look
wohingegen *konj* whereas, while
Wohl (-(e)s) *nt* welfare; **zum ~!** cheers!

SCHLÜSSELWORT

wohl [voːl] *adv* **1** well; (*behaglich*) at ease, comfortable; **sich wohl fühlen** *siehe* **wohlfühlen**; **wohl gemeint** = **wohlgemeint**; **bei dem Gedanken ist mir nicht wohl** I'm not very happy at the thought; **wohl oder übel** whether one likes it or not; **er weiß das sehr wohl** he knows that perfectly well
2 (*wahrscheinlich*) probably; (*vermutlich*) I suppose; (*gewiss*) certainly; (*vielleicht*) perhaps; **sie ist wohl zu Hause** she's probably at home; **sie wird wohl das Haus verkaufen** I suppose *od* presumably she's going to sell the house; **das ist doch wohl nicht dein Ernst!** surely you're not serious!; **das mag wohl sein** that may well be; **ob das wohl stimmt?** I wonder if that's true; *siehe auch* **wohltun**

wohl- *zW*: **wohlauf** [voːl'|aʊf] *adj* well, in good health; **Wohlbefinden** *nt* well-being; **Wohlbehagen** *nt* comfort; **wohlbehalten** *adj* safe and sound; **Wohlergehen** *nt* welfare; **Wohlfahrt** *f* welfare; **Wohlfahrtsstaat** *m* welfare state; **wohlfühlen** *vr* (*zufrieden*) to feel happy; (*gesundheitlich*) to feel well; **Wohlgefallen** *nt*: **sich in Wohlgefallen auflösen** (*hum: Gegenstände, Probleme*) to vanish into thin air; (*zerfallen*) to fall apart; **wohlgemeint** *adj* well-intentioned; **wohlgemerkt** *adv* mark you; **wohlhabend** *adj* wealthy
wohlig *adj* contented; (*gemütlich*) comfortable
wohl- *zW*: **Wohlklang** *m* melodious sound; **wohlmeinend** *adj* well-meaning; **wohlschmeckend** *adj* delicious; **Wohlstand** *m* prosperity; **Wohlstandsgesellschaft** *f* affluent society; **Wohltat** *f* (*Gefallen*) favour (*Brit*), favor (*US*); (*gute Tat*) good deed; (*Erleichterung*) relief; **Wohltäter** *m* benefactor; **wohltätig** *adj* charitable; **Wohltätigkeit** *f* charity; **wohltuend** *adj* pleasant; **wohltun** *unreg vi*: **jdm wohltun** to do sb good; **wohlverdient** *adj* (*Ruhe*) well-earned; (*Strafe*) well-deserved; **wohlweislich** *adv* prudently; **Wohlwollen (-s)** *nt* good will; **wohlwollend** *adj* benevolent
Wohnblock ['voːnblɔk] **(-s, -s)** *m* block of flats (*Brit*), apartment house (*US*)
wohnen ['voːnən] *vi* to live
wohn- *zW*: **Wohnfläche** *f* living space; **Wohngeld** *nt* housing benefit; **Wohngemeinschaft** *f* people sharing a flat (*Brit*) *od* apartment (*US*); (*von Hippies*) commune; **wohnhaft** *adj* resident; **Wohnheim**

nt (*für Studenten*) hall (of residence), dormitory (*US*); (*für Senioren*) home; (*bes für Arbeiter*) hostel; **Wohnkomfort** *m*: **mit sämtlichem Wohnkomfort** with all mod cons (*Brit*); **wohnlich** *adj* comfortable; **Wohnmobil** *nt* motor caravan (*Brit*), motor home (*US*); **Wohnort** *m* domicile; **Wohnsilo** *nt* concrete block of flats (*Brit*) *od* apartment block (*US*); **Wohnsitz** *m* place of residence; **ohne festen Wohnsitz** of no fixed abode

Wohnung *f* house; (*Etagenwohnung*) flat (*Brit*), apartment (*US*)

Wohnungs- *zW*: **Wohnungsamt** *nt* housing office; **Wohnungsbau** *m* house-building; **Wohnungsmarkt** *m* housing market; **Wohnungsnot** *f* housing shortage

wohn- *zW*: **Wohnviertel** *nt* residential area; **Wohnwagen** *m* caravan (*Brit*), trailer (*US*); **Wohnzimmer** *nt* living room

wölben ['vœlbən] *vt, vr* to curve

Wölbung *f* curve

Wolf [vɔlf] (**-(e)s, ¨-e**) *m* wolf; (*Tech*) shredder; (*Fleischwolf*) mincer (*Brit*), grinder (*US*)

Wölfin ['vœlfɪn] *f* she-wolf

Wolke ['vɔlkə] (**-, -n**) *f* cloud; **aus allen ~n fallen** (*fig*) to be flabbergasted (*umg*)

Wolken- *zW*: **Wolkenbruch** *m* cloudburst; **wolkenbruchartig** *adj* torrential; **Wolkenkratzer** *m* skyscraper; **Wolkenkuckucksheim** *nt* cloud-cuckoo-land (*Brit*), cloudland (*US*); **wolkenlos** *adj* cloudless

wolkig ['vɔlkɪç] *adj* cloudy

Wolle ['vɔlə] (**-, -n**) *f* wool; **sich mit jdm in die ~ kriegen** (*fig: umg*) to start squabbling with sb

SCHLÜSSELWORT

wollen[1] ['vɔlən] *unreg* (*pt* **wollte**, *pp* **gewollt** *od* (*als Hilfsverb*) **wollen**) *vt, vi* to want; **ich will nach Hause** I want to go home; **er will nicht** he doesn't want to; **sie wollte das nicht** she didn't want it; **wenn du willst** if you like; **ich will, dass du mir zuhörst** I want you to listen to me; **oh, das hab ich nicht gewollt** oh, I didn't mean to do that; **ich weiß nicht, was er will** (*verstehe ihn nicht*) I don't know what he's on about

▷ *Hilfsverb*: **er will ein Haus kaufen** he wants to buy a house; **ich wollte, ich wäre ...** I wish I were ...; **etw gerade tun wollen** to be just about to *od* going to do sth; **und so jemand** *od* **etwas will Lehrer sein!** (*umg*) and he calls himself a teacher!; **das will alles gut überlegt sein** that needs a lot of thought

wollen[2] *adj* woollen (*Brit*), woolen (*US*)

Wollsachen *pl* wool(l)ens *pl*

wollüstig ['vɔlʏstɪç] *adj* lusty, sensual

wo- *zW*: **womit** [vo'mɪt] *adv* (*rel*) with which; (*interrog*) what ... with; **womit kann ich dienen?** what can I do for you?; **womöglich** [vo'mø:klɪç] *adv* probably, I suppose; **wonach** [vo'na:x] *adv* (*rel*) after/for which; (*interrog*) what ... after

Wonne ['vɔnə] (**-, -n**) *f* joy, bliss

woran [vo'ran] *adv* (*rel*) on/at which; (*interrog*) what ... on/at; **~ liegt das?** what's the reason for it?

worauf [vo'raʊf] *adv* (*rel*) on which; (*interrog*) what ... on; (*zeitlich*) whereupon; **~ du dich verlassen kannst** of that you can be sure

woraus [vo'raʊs] *adv* (*rel*) from/out of which; (*interrog*) what ... from/out of

worden ['vɔrdən] *vb siehe* **werden**

worin [vo'rɪn] *adv* (*rel*) in which; (*interrog*) what ... in

Wort [vɔrt] (**-(e)s, ¨-er** *od* **-e**) *nt* word; **jdn beim ~ nehmen** to take sb at his word; **ein ernstes ~ mit jdm reden** to have a serious talk with sb; **man kann sein eigenes ~ nicht (mehr) verstehen** you can't hear yourself speak; **jdm aufs ~ gehorchen** to obey sb's every word; **zu ~ kommen** to get a chance to speak; **jdm das ~ erteilen** to allow sb to speak; **Wortart** *f* (*Gram*) part of speech; **wortbrüchig** *adj* not true to one's word

Wörtchen *nt*: **da habe ich wohl ein ~ mitzureden** (*umg*) I think I have some say in that

Wörterbuch ['vœrtərbu:x] *nt* dictionary

Wort- *zW*: **Wortfetzen** *pl* snatches *pl* of conversation; **Wortführer** *m* spokesman; **wortgetreu** *adj* true to one's word; (*Übersetzung*) literal; **wortgewaltig** *adj* eloquent; **wortkarg** *adj* taciturn; **Wortlaut** *m* wording; **im Wortlaut** verbatim

wörtlich ['vœrtlɪç] *adj* literal

Wort- *zW*: **wortlos** *adj* mute; **Wortmeldung** *f*: **wenn es keine weiteren Wortmeldungen gibt, ...** if nobody else wishes to speak ...; **wortreich** *adj* wordy, verbose; **Wortschatz** *m* vocabulary; **Wortspiel** *nt* play on words, pun; **Wortwechsel** *m* dispute; **wortwörtlich** *adj* word-for-word ▷ *adv* quite literally

worüber [vo'ry:bər] *adv* (*rel*) over/about which; (*interrog*) what ... over/about

worum [vo'rʊm] *adv* (*rel*) about/round which; (*interrog*) what ... about/round; **~ handelt es sich?** what's it about?

worunter [vo'rʊntər] *adv* (*rel*) under which; (*interrog*) what ... under

wo- *zW*: **wovon** [vo'fɔn] *adv* (*rel*) from which; (*interrog*) what ... from; **wovor** [vo'fɔr] *adv* (*rel*) in front of/before which; (*interrog*) in front of/before what; **wozu** [vo'tsu] *adv* (*rel*) to/for which; (*interrog*) what ... for/to; (*warum*) why; **wozu soll das gut sein?** what's the point of that?

Wrack [vrak] (**-(e)s, -s**) *nt* wreck

wrang *etc* [vraŋ] *vb siehe* **wringen**

wringen ['vrɪŋən] *unreg vt* to wring

WS *abk* = **Wintersemester**

WSV *abk* = **Winterschlussverkauf**

Wucher ['vu:xər] (**-s**) *m* profiteering; **Wucherer** (**-s, -**) *m*, **Wucherin** *f* profiteer; **wucherisch** *adj* profiteering

wuchern *vi* (*Pflanzen*) to grow wild
Wucherpreis *m* exorbitant price
Wucherung *f* (*Med*) growth
Wuchs [vu:ks] (**-es**) *m* (*Wachstum*) growth; (*Statur*) build
wuchs *etc vb siehe* **wachsen¹**
Wucht [vʊxt] (**-**) *f* force
wuchtig *adj* massive, solid
wühlen ['vy:lən] *vi* to scrabble; (*Tier*) to root; (*Maulwurf*) to burrow; (*umg: arbeiten*) to slave away ▷ *vt* to dig
Wühlmaus *f* vole
Wühltisch *m* (*in Kaufhaus*) bargain counter
Wulst [vʊlst] (**-es, ¨-e**) *m* bulge; (*an Wunde*) swelling
wulstig *adj* bulging; (*Rand, Lippen*) thick
wund [vʊnt] *adj* sore; **sich** *dat* **die Füße ~ laufen** (*lit*) to get sore feet from walking; (*fig*) to walk one's legs off; **ein ~er Punkt** a sore point; **Wundbrand** *m* gangrene
Wunde ['vʊndə] (**-, -n**) *f* wound; **alte ~n wieder aufreißen** (*fig*) to open up old wounds
Wunder (**-s, -**) *nt* miracle; **es ist kein ~** it's no wonder; **meine Eltern denken ~ was passiert ist** my parents think goodness knows what has happened; **wunderbar** *adj* wonderful, marvellous (*Brit*), marvelous (*US*); **Wunderkerze** *f* sparkler; **Wunderkind** *nt* child prodigy; **wunderlich** *adj* odd, peculiar
wundern *vt* to surprise ▷ *vr*: **sich ~ über** *+akk* to be surprised at
Wunder- *zW*: **wunderschön** *adj* beautiful; **Wundertüte** *f* lucky bag; **wundervoll** *adj* wonderful
Wundfieber (**-s**) *nt* traumatic fever
Wundstarrkrampf ['vʊntʃtarkrampf] *m* tetanus, lockjaw
Wunsch [vʊnʃ] (**-(e)s, ¨-e**) *m* wish; **haben Sie (sonst) noch einen ~?** (*beim Einkauf etc*) is there anything else you'd like?; **auf jds (besonderen/ausdrücklichen) ~ hin** at sb's (special/express) request; **Wunschdenken** *nt* wishful thinking
Wünschelrute ['vʏnʃəlru:tə] *f* divining rod
wünschen ['vʏnʃən] *vt* to wish ▷ *vi*: **zu wünschen/viel zu ~ übrig lassen** to leave something/a great deal to be desired; **sich** *dat* **etw ~** to want sth, wish for sth; **was ~ Sie?** (*in Geschäft*) what can I do for you?; (*in Restaurant*) what would you like?
wünschenswert *adj* desirable
Wunsch- *zW*: **Wunschkind** *nt* planned child; **Wunschkonzert** *nt* (*Rundf*) musical request programme (*Brit*) *od* program (*US*); **wunschlos** *adj*: **wunschlos glücklich** perfectly happy; **Wunschtraum** *m* dream; (*unrealistisch*) pipe dream; **Wunschzettel** *m* list of things one would like
wurde *etc* ['vʊrdə] *vb siehe* **werden**
Würde ['vʏrdə] (**-, -n**) *f* dignity; (*Stellung*) honour (*Brit*), honor (*US*); **unter aller ~ sein** to be beneath contempt
Würdenträger *m* dignitary
würdevoll *adj* dignified
würdig ['vʏrdɪç] *adj* worthy; (*würdevoll*) dignified
würdigen ['vʏrdɪgən] *vt* to appreciate; **etw zu ~ wissen** to appreciate sth; **jdn keines Blickes ~** not to so much as look at sb
Wurf [vʊrf] (**-(e)s, ¨-e**) *m* throw; (*Junge*) litter
Würfel ['vʏrfəl] (**-s, -**) *m* dice; (*Math*) cube; **die ~ sind gefallen** the die is cast; **Würfelbecher** *m* (dice) cup
würfeln *vi* to play dice ▷ *vt* to dice
Würfelspiel *nt* game of dice
Würfelzucker *m* lump sugar
Wurf- *zW*: **Wurfgeschoss** *nt* projectile; **Wurfsendung** *f* circular; **Wurfsendungen** *pl* (*Reklame*) junk mail
Würgegriff (**-(e)s**) *m* (*lit, fig*) stranglehold
würgen ['vʏrgən] *vt, vi* to choke; **mit Hängen und W~** by the skin of one's teeth
Wurm [vʊrm] (**-(e)s, ¨-er**) *m* worm; **da steckt der ~ drin** (*fig: umg*) there's something wrong somewhere; (*verdächtig*) there's something fishy about it (*umg*)
wurmen (*umg*) *vt* to rile, nettle
Wurmfortsatz *m* (*Med*) appendix
wurmig *adj* worm-eaten
wurmstichig *adj* worm-ridden
Wurst [vʊrst] (**-, ¨-e**) *f* sausage; **das ist mir ~** (*umg*) I don't care, I don't give a damn; **jetzt geht es um die ~** (*fig: umg*) the moment of truth has come
Würstchen ['vʏrstçən] *nt* frankfurter, hot dog sausage; **Würstchenbude** *f*, **Würstchenstand** *m* hot dog stall
Württemberg ['vʏrtəmbɛrk] *nt* Württemberg
Würze ['vʏrtsə] (**-, -n**) *f* seasoning
Wurzel ['vʊrtsəl] (**-, -n**) *f* root; **~n schlagen** (*lit*) to root; (*fig*) to put down roots; **die ~ aus 4 ist 2** (*Math*) the square root of 4 is 2
würzen *vt* to season; (*würzig machen*) to spice
würzig *adj* spicy
wusch *etc* [vu:ʃ] *vb siehe* **waschen**
wusste *etc* ['vʊstə] *vb siehe* **wissen**
Wust [vu:st] (**-(e)s**) (*umg*) *m* (*Durcheinander*) jumble; (*Menge*) pile
wüst [vy:st] *adj* untidy, messy; (*ausschweifend*) wild; (*öde*) waste; (*umg: heftig*) terrible; **jdn ~ beschimpfen** to use vile language to sb
Wüste (**-, -n**) *f* desert; **die ~ Gobi** the Gobi Desert; **jdn in die ~ schicken** (*fig*) to send sb packing
Wut [vu:t] (**-**) *f* rage, fury; **eine ~ (auf jdn/etw) haben** to be furious (with sb/sth); **Wutanfall** *m* fit of rage
wüten ['vy:tən] *vi* to rage
wütend *adj* furious, enraged
wutentbrannt *adj* furious, enraged
Wz *abk* (= *Warenzeichen*) ®

Xx

X, **x** [ɪks] *nt* X, x; **X wie Xanthippe** ≈ X for Xmas; **jdm ein X für ein U vormachen** to put one over on sb (*umg*)
X-Beine ['ɪksbaɪnə] *pl* knock-knees *pl*
x-beliebig [ɪksbə'li:bɪç] *adj* any (... whatever)
Xerografie [kserogra'fi:] *f* xerography
xerokopieren [kseroko'pi:rən] *vt* to xerox, photocopy
x-fach ['ɪksfax] *adj*: **die ~e Menge** (*Math*) n times the amount
x-mal ['ɪksma:l] *adv* any number of times, n times
XML *abk* (*Comput: = extensible markup language*) XML
x-te ['ɪkstə] *adj* (*Math: umg*) nth; **zum ~n Male** (*umg*) for the nth *od* umpteenth time
Xylofon, **Xylophon** [ksylo'fo:n] (**-s, -e**) *nt* xylophone

Yy

Y, y ['ʏpsilɔn] *nt* Y, y; **Y wie Ypsilon** ≈ Y for Yellow, Y for Yoke (*US*)
Yen [jɛn] (**-(s), -(s)**) *m* yen
Yoga ['jo:ga] (**-(s)**) *m od nt* yoga
Ypsilon ['ʏpsilɔn] (**-(s), -s**) *nt* the letter Y

Zz

Z, z [tsɛt] *nt* Z, z; **Z wie Zacharias** ≈ Z for Zebra
Zack [tsak] *m*: **auf ~ sein** (*umg*) to be on the ball
Zacke ['tsakə] (**-, -n**) *f* point; (*Bergzacke*) jagged peak; (*Gabelzacke*) prong; (*Kammzacke*) tooth
zackig ['tsakıç] *adj* jagged; (*umg*) smart; (*: Tempo*) brisk
zaghaft ['tsa:khaft] *adj* timid
Zaghaftigkeit *f* timidity
Zagreb ['za:grɛp] (**-s**) *nt* Zagreb
zäh [tsɛ:] *adj* tough; (*Mensch*) tenacious; (*Flüssigkeit*) thick; (*schleppend*) sluggish; **zähflüssig** *adj* viscous; (*Verkehr*) slow-moving
Zähigkeit *f* toughness; tenacity
Zahl [tsa:l] (**-, -en**) *f* number
zahlbar *adj* payable
zahlen *vt, vi* to pay; **~ bitte!** the bill *od* check (*US*) please!
zählen ['tsɛ:lən] *vt* to count ▷ *vi* (*sich verlassen*): **~ auf** *+akk* to count on; **seine Tage sind gezählt** his days are numbered; **~ zu** to be numbered among
Zahlen- *zW*: **Zahlenangabe** *f* figure; **Zahlenkombination** *f* combination of figures; **zahlenmäßig** *adj* numerical; **Zahlenschloss** *nt* combination lock
Zahler (**-s, -**) *m* payer
Zähler (**-s, -**) *m* (*Tech*) meter; (*Math*) numerator; **Zählerstand** *m* meter reading
Zahl- *zW*: **Zahlgrenze** *f* fare stage; **Zahlkarte** *f* transfer form; **zahllos** *adj* countless; **Zahlmeister** *m* (*Naut*) purser; **zahlreich** *adj* numerous; **Zahltag** *m* payday
Zahlung *f* payment; **in ~ geben/nehmen** to give/take in part exchange
Zahlungs- *zW*: **Zahlungsanweisung** *f* transfer order; **Zahlungsaufforderung** *f* request for payment; **zahlungsfähig** *adj* solvent; **Zahlungsmittel** *nt* means *sing* of payment; (*Münzen, Banknoten*) currency; **Zahlungsrückstände** *pl* arrears *pl*; **zahlungsunfähig** *adj* insolvent; **Zahlungsverzug** *m* default
Zahlwort *nt* numeral
zahm [tsa:m] *adj* tame
zähmen ['tsɛ:mən] *vt* to tame; (*fig*) to curb
Zahn [tsa:n] (**-(e)s, ¨-e**) *m* tooth; **die dritten Zähne** (*umg*) false teeth *pl*; **einen ~ draufhaben** (*umg: Geschwindigkeit*) to be going like the clappers (*Brit*) *od* like crazy (*US*); **jdm auf den ~ fühlen** (*fig*) to sound sb out; **einen ~ zulegen** (*fig*) to get a move on; **Zahnarzt** *m*, **Zahnärztin** *f* dentist; **Zahnbelag** *m* plaque; **Zahnbürste** *f* toothbrush; **Zahncreme** *f* toothpaste; **zahnen** *vi* to teethe; **Zahnersatz** *m* denture; **Zahnfäule** (**-**) *f* tooth decay, caries *sing*; **Zahnfleisch** *nt* gums *pl*; **auf dem Zahnfleisch gehen** (*fig: umg*) to be all in, be at the end of one's tether; **zahnlos** *adj* toothless; **Zahnmedizin** *f* dentistry; **Zahnpasta** *f*, **Zahnpaste** *f* toothpaste; **Zahnrad** *nt* cog(wheel); **Zahnradbahn** *f* rack railway; **Zahnschmelz** *m* (tooth) enamel; **Zahnschmerzen** *pl* toothache *sing*; **Zahnseide** *f* dental floss; **Zahnspange** *f* brace; **Zahnstein** *m* tartar; **Zahnstocher** (**-s, -**) *m* toothpick; **Zahntechniker, in** *m(f)* dental technician; **Zahnweh** *nt* toothache
Zaire [za'i:r] (**-s**) *nt* Zaire
Zange ['tsaŋə] (**-, -n**) *f* pliers *pl*; (*Zuckerzange etc*) tongs *pl*; (*Beißzange, Zool*) pincers *pl*; (*Med*) forceps *pl*; **jdn in die ~ nehmen** (*fig*) to put the screws on sb (*umg*)
Zangengeburt *f* forceps delivery
Zankapfel *m* bone of contention
zanken ['tsaŋkən] *vi, vr* to quarrel
zänkisch ['tsɛŋkıʃ] *adj* quarrelsome
Zäpfchen ['tsɛpfçən] *nt* (*Anat*) uvula; (*Med*) suppository
Zapfen ['tsapfən] (**-s, -**) *m* plug; (*Bot*) cone; (*Eiszapfen*) icicle
zapfen *vt* to tap
Zapfenstreich *m* (*Mil*) tattoo
Zapfsäule *f* petrol (*Brit*) *od* gas (*US*) pump
zappelig ['tsapəlıç] *adj* wriggly; (*unruhig*) fidgety
zappeln ['tsapəln] *vi* to wriggle; to fidget; **jdn ~ lassen** (*fig: umg*) to keep sb in suspense
Zar [tsa:r] (**-en, -en**) *m* tzar, czar
zart [tsa:rt] *adj* (*weich, leise*) soft; (*Braten etc*) tender; (*fein, schwächlich*) delicate; **zartbesaitet** ['tsa:rtbəzaıtət] *adj* highly sensitive; **zartbitter** *adj* (*Schokolade*) plain (*Brit*), bittersweet (*US*); **Zartgefühl** *nt* tact; **Zartheit** *f* softness; tenderness; delicacy
zärtlich ['tsɛ:rtlıç] *adj* tender, affectionate; **Zärtlichkeit** *f* tenderness; **Zärtlichkeiten** *pl*

caresses *pl*
Zäsium ['tsɛːziʊm] *nt* = **Cäsium**
Zäsur [tsɛ'zuːr] *f* caesura; (*fig*) break
Zauber ['tsaʊbər] (**-s, -**) *m* magic; (*Zauberbann*) spell; **fauler ~** (*umg*) humbug
Zauberei [tsaʊbə'raɪ] *f* magic
Zauberer (**-s, -**) *m* magician; (*Zauberkünstler*) conjurer
Zauber- *zW*: **zauberhaft** *adj* magical, enchanting; **Zauberin** *f* magician; conjurer; **Zauberkünstler** *m* conjurer; **Zauberkunststück** *nt* conjuring trick; **Zaubermittel** *nt* magical cure; (*Trank*) magic potion
zaubern *vi* to conjure, do magic
Zauberspruch *m* (magic) spell
Zauberstab *m* magic wand
zaudern ['tsaʊdərn] *vi* to hesitate
Zaum [tsaʊm] (**-(e)s, Zäume**) *m* bridle; **etw im ~ halten** to keep sth in check
Zaun [tsaʊn] (**-(e)s, Zäune**) *m* fence; **vom ~(e) brechen** (*fig*) to start; **Zaungast** *m* (*Person*) mere onlooker; **Zaunkönig** *m* wren
z. B. *abk* (= *zum Beispiel*) e.g.
z. d. A. *abk* (= *zu den Akten*) to be filed
ZDF *nt see culture note*

ZDF

The ZDF (Zweites Deutsches Fernsehen) is the second German television channel. It was founded in 1961 and is based in Mainz. It is financed by licence fees and advertising. About 40% of its transmissions are news and educational programmes.

Zebra ['tseːbra] (**-s, -s**) *nt* zebra; **Zebrastreifen** *m* pedestrian crossing (*Brit*), crosswalk (*US*)
Zeche ['tsɛçə] (**-, -n**) *f* (*Rechnung*) bill, check (*US*); (*Bergbau*) mine
zechen *vi* to booze (*umg*)
Zechprellerei [tsɛçprɛlə'raɪ] *f skipping payment in restaurants etc*
Zecke ['tsɛkə] (**-, -n**) *f* tick
Zeder ['tseːdər] (**-, -n**) *f* cedar
Zeh [tseː] (**-s, -en**) *m* toe
Zehe ['tseːə] (**-, -n**) *f* toe; (*Knoblauchzehe*) clove
Zehenspitze *f*: **auf ~n** on tiptoe
zehn [tseːn] *num* ten
Zehnerpackung *f* packet of ten
Zehnfingersystem *nt* touch-typing method
Zehnkampf *m* (*Sport*) decathlon
zehnte, r, s *adj* tenth
Zehntel (**-s, -**) *nt* tenth (part)
zehren ['tseːrən] *vi*: **an jdm/etw ~** (*an Mensch, Kraft*) to wear sb/sth out
Zeichen ['tsaɪçən] (**-s, -**) *nt* sign; (*Comput*) character; **jdm ein ~ geben** to give sb a signal; **unser/Ihr ~** (*Comm*) our/your reference; **Zeichenblock** *m* sketch pad; **Zeichencode** *m* (*Comput*) character code; **Zeichenerklärung** *f* key; (*auf Karten*) legend; **Zeichenfolge** *f* (*Comput*) string; **Zeichenkette** *f* (*Comput*) character string; **Zeichensatz** *m* (*Comput*) character set; **Zeichensetzung** *f* punctuation; **Zeichentrickfilm** *m* (animated) cartoon
zeichnen *vt* to draw; (*kennzeichnen*) to mark; (*unterzeichnen*) to sign ▷ *vi* to draw; to sign
Zeichner, in (**-s, -**) *m(f)* artist; **technischer ~** draughtsman (*Brit*), draftsman (*US*)
Zeichnung *f* drawing; (*Markierung*) markings *pl*
zeichnungsberechtigt *adj* authorized to sign
Zeigefinger *m* index finger
zeigen ['tsaɪgən] *vt* to show ▷ *vi* to point ▷ *vr* to show o.s.; **~ auf** +*akk* to point to; **es wird sich ~** time will tell; **es zeigte sich, dass ...** it turned out that ...
Zeiger (**-s, -**) *m* pointer; (*Uhrzeiger*) hand
Zeile ['tsaɪlə] (**-, -n**) *f* line; (*Häuserzeile*) row
Zeilen- *zW*: **Zeilenabstand** *m* line spacing; **Zeilenausrichtung** *f* justification; **Zeilendrucker** *m* line printer; **Zeilenumbruch** *m* (*Comput*) wraparound; **Zeilenvorschub** *m* (*Comput*) line feed
zeit [tsaɪt] *präp* +*gen*: **~ meines Lebens** in my lifetime
Zeit (**-, -en**) *f* time; (*Gram*) tense; **sich** *dat* **~ lassen** to take one's time; **eine Stunde ~ haben** to have an hour (to spare); **sich** *dat* **für jdn/etw ~ nehmen** to devote time to sb/sth; **eine ~ lang** a while, a time; **von ~ zu Zeit** from time to time; **~ raubend** = **zeitraubend**; **in letzter ~** recently; **nach ~ bezahlt werden** to be paid by the hour; **zu der ~, als ...** (at the time) when ...; *siehe auch* **zurzeit**
Zeit- *zW*: **Zeitalter** *nt* age; **Zeitansage** *f* (*Rundf*) time check; (*Tel*) speaking clock; **Zeitarbeit** *f* temporary work; **Zeitaufwand** *m* time (*needed for a task*); **Zeitbombe** *f* time bomb; **Zeitdruck** *m*: **unter Zeitdruck stehen** to be under pressure; **Zeitgeist** *m* spirit of the times; **zeitgemäß** *adj* in keeping with the times; **Zeitgenosse** *m* contemporary; **zeitgenössisch** ['tsaɪtgənœsɪʃ] *adj* contemporary
zeitig *adj, adv* early
Zeit- *zW*: **Zeitkarte** *f* season ticket; **zeitkritisch** *adj* (*Aufsatz*) commenting on contemporary issues; **zeitlebens** *adv* all one's life; **zeitlich** *adj* temporal ▷ *adv*: **das kann sie zeitlich nicht einrichten** she can't find (the) time for that; **das Zeitliche segnen** (*euph*) to depart this life; **zeitlos** *adj* timeless; **Zeitlupe** *f* slow motion; **Zeitlupentempo** *nt*: **im Zeitlupentempo** at a snail's pace; **Zeitnot** *f*: **in Zeitnot geraten** to run short of time; **Zeitplan** *m* schedule; **Zeitpunkt** *m* moment, point in time; **Zeitraffer** (**-s**) *m* time-lapse photography; **zeitraubend** *adj* time-consuming; **Zeitraum** *m* period; **Zeitrechnung** *f* time, era; **nach/vor unserer Zeitrechnung** A.D./B.C.; **Zeitschrift** *f* periodical; **Zeittafel** *f* chronological table
Zeitung *f* newspaper
Zeitungs- *zW*: **Zeitungsanzeige** *f* newspaper advertisement; **Zeitungsausschnitt** *m* press cutting; **Zeitungshändler** *m* newsagent

(*Brit*), newsdealer (*US*); **Zeitungspapier** *nt* newsprint; **Zeitungsstand** *m* newsstand
Zeit- *zW*: **Zeitverschwendung** *f* waste of time; **Zeitvertreib** *m* pastime, diversion; **zeitweilig** *adj* temporary; **zeitweise** *adv* for a time; **Zeitwort** *nt* verb; **Zeitzeichen** *nt* (*Rundf*) time signal; **Zeitzone** *f* time zone; **Zeitzünder** *m* time fuse
Zelle ['tsɛlə] (**-, -n**) *f* cell; (*Telefonzelle*) callbox (*Brit*), booth
Zellkern *m* cell, nucleus
Zellophan [tsɛlo'fa:n] (**-s**) *nt* cellophane
Zellstoff *m* cellulose
Zelt [tsɛlt] (**-(e)s, -e**) *nt* tent; **seine ~e aufschlagen/abbrechen** to settle down/pack one's bags; **Zeltbahn** *f* groundsheet; **zelten** *vi* to camp; **Zeltlager** *nt* camp; **Zeltplatz** *m* camp site
Zement [tse'mɛnt] (**-(e)s, -e**) *m* cement
zementieren [tsemɛn'ti:rən] *vt* to cement
Zementmaschine *f* cement mixer
Zenit [tse'ni:t] (**-(e)s**) *m* (*lit, fig*) zenith
zensieren [tsɛn'zi:rən] *vt* to censor; (*Sch*) to mark
Zensur [tsɛn'zu:r] *f* censorship; (*Sch*) mark
Zensus ['tsɛnzʊs] (**-, -**) *m* census
Zentimeter [tsɛnti'me:tər] *m od nt* centimetre (*Brit*), centimeter (*US*); **Zentimetermaß** *nt* (metric) tape measure
Zentner ['tsɛntnər] (**-s, -**) *m* hundredweight
zentral [tsɛn'tra:l] *adj* central
Zentrale (**-, -n**) *f* central office; (*Tel*) exchange
Zentraleinheit *f* (*Comput*) central processing unit
Zentralheizung *f* central heating
zentralisieren [tsɛntrali'zi:rən] *vt* to centralize
Zentralverriegelung *f* (*Aut*) central locking
Zentrifugalkraft [tsɛntrifu'ga:lkraft] *f* centrifugal force
Zentrifuge [tsɛntri'fu:gə] (**-, -n**) *f* centrifuge; (*für Wäsche*) spin-dryer
Zentrum ['tsɛntrʊm] (**-s, Zentren**) *nt* centre (*Brit*), center (*US*)
Zepter ['tsɛptər] (**-s, -**) *nt* sceptre (*Brit*), scepter (*US*)
zerbrechen *unreg vt, vi* to break
zerbrechlich *adj* fragile
zerbröckeln [tsɛr'brœkəln] *vt, vi* to crumble (to pieces)
zerdeppern [tsɛr'dɛpərn] *vt* to smash
zerdrücken *vt* to squash; to crush; (*Kartoffeln*) to mash
Zeremonie [tseremo'ni:] *f* ceremony
Zeremoniell [tseremoni'ɛl] (**-s, -e**) *nt* ceremonial
zerfahren *adj* scatterbrained, distracted
Zerfall *m* decay, disintegration; (*von Kultur, Gesundheit*) decline; **zerfallen** *unreg vi* to disintegrate, decay; (*sich gliedern*): **zerfallen in** *+akk* to fall into
zerfetzen [tsɛr'fɛtsən] *vt* to tear to pieces
zerfleischen [tsɛr'flaɪʃən] *vt* to tear to pieces
zerfließen *unreg vi* to dissolve, melt away
zerfressen *unreg vt* to eat away; (*Motten, Mäuse etc*) to eat
zergehen *unreg vi* to melt, dissolve
zerkleinern [tsɛr'klaɪnərn] *vt* to reduce to small pieces
zerklüftet [tsɛr'klʏftət] *adj*: **tief ~es Gestein** deeply fissured rock
zerknirscht [tsɛr'knɪrʃt] *adj* overcome with remorse
zerknüllen [tsɛr'knʏlən] *vt* to crumple up
zerlaufen *unreg vi* to melt
zerlegbar [tsɛr'le:kba:r] *adj* able to be dismantled
zerlegen *vt* to take to pieces; (*Fleisch*) to carve; (*Satz*) to analyse
zerlumpt [tsɛr'lʊmpt] *adj* ragged
zermalmen [tsɛr'malmən] *vt* to crush
zermürben [tsɛr'mʏrbən] *vt* to wear down
zerpflücken *vt* (*lit, fig*) to pick to pieces
zerplatzen *vi* to burst
zerquetschen *vt* to squash
Zerrbild ['tsɛrbɪlt] *nt* (*fig*) caricature, distorted picture
zerreden *vt* (*Problem*) to flog to death
zerreiben *unreg vt* to grind down
zerreißen *unreg vt* to tear to pieces ▷ *vi* to tear, rip
Zerreißprobe *f* (*lit*) pull test; (*fig*) real test
zerren ['tsɛrən] *vt* to drag ▷ *vi*: **~ (an** *+dat***)** to tug (at)
zerrinnen *unreg vi* to melt away; (*Geld*) to disappear
zerrissen [tsɛr'rɪsən] *pp von* **zerreißen** ▷ *adj* torn, tattered; **Zerrissenheit** *f* tattered state; (*Pol*) disunion, discord; (*innere*) disintegration
Zerrspiegel ['tsɛrʃpi:gəl] *m* (*lit*) distorting mirror; (*fig*) travesty
Zerrung *f*: **eine** ~ a pulled ligament/muscle
zerrütten [tsɛr'rʏtən] *vt* to wreck, destroy
zerrüttet *adj* wrecked, shattered
Zerrüttungsprinzip *nt* (*bei Ehescheidung*) principle of irretrievable breakdown
zerschellen [tsɛr'ʃɛlən] *vi* (*Schiff, Flugzeug*) to be smashed to pieces
zerschießen *unreg vt* to shoot to pieces
zerschlagen *unreg vt* to shatter, smash; (*fig: Opposition*) to crush; (*: Vereinigung*) to break up ▷ *vr* to fall through
zerschleißen [tsɛr'ʃlaɪsən] *unreg vt, vi* to wear out
zerschmelzen *unreg vi* to melt
zerschmettern *unreg vt* to shatter; (*Feind*) to crush ▷ *vi* to shatter
zerschneiden *unreg vt* to cut up
zersetzen *vt, vr* to decompose, dissolve
zersetzend *adj* (*fig*) subversive
zersplittern [tsɛr'ʃplɪtərn] *vt, vi* to split (into pieces); (*Glas*) to shatter
zerspringen *unreg vi* to shatter ▷ *vi* (*fig*) to burst
zerstäuben [tsɛr'ʃtɔʏbən] *vt* to spray
Zerstäuber (**-s, -**) *m* atomizer
zerstören *vt* to destroy
Zerstörer (**-s, -**) *m* (*Naut*) destroyer

Zerstörung *f* destruction
Zerstörungswut *f* destructive mania
zerstoßen *unreg vt* to pound, pulverize
zerstreiten *unreg vr* to fall out, break up
zerstreuen *vt* to disperse, scatter; (*Zweifel etc*) to dispel ▷ *vr* (*sich verteilen*) to scatter; (*fig*) to be dispelled; (*sich ablenken*) to take one's mind off things
zerstreut *adj* scattered; (*Mensch*) absent-minded; **Zerstreutheit** *f* absent-mindedness
Zerstreuung *f* dispersion; (*Ablenkung*) diversion
zerstritten *adj*: **mit jdm ~ sein** to be on very bad terms with sb
zerstückeln [tsɛrˈʃtʏkəln] *vt* to cut into pieces
zerteilen *vt* to divide into parts
Zertifikat [tsɛrtifiˈkaːt] (**-(e)s, -e**) *nt* certificate
zertreten *unreg vt* to crush underfoot
zertrümmern [tsɛrˈtrʏmərn] *vt* to shatter; (*Gebäude etc*) to demolish
zerwühlen *vt* to ruffle up, tousle; (*Bett*) to rumple (up)
Zerwürfnis [tsɛrˈvʏrfnɪs] (**-ses, -se**) *nt* dissension, quarrel
zerzausen [tsɛrˈtsaʊzən] *vt* (*Haare*) to ruffle up, tousle
zetern [ˈtseːtərn] (*pej*) *vi* to clamour (*Brit*), clamor (*US*); (*keifen*) to scold
Zettel [ˈtsɛtəl] (**-s, -**) *m* piece *od* slip of paper; (*Notizzettel*) note; (*Formular*) form; **„~ ankleben verboten"** "stick no bills"; **Zettelkasten** *m* card index (box); **Zettelwirtschaft** (*pej*) *f*: **eine Zettelwirtschaft haben** to have bits of paper everywhere
Zeug [tsɔʏk] (**-(e)s, -e**) (*umg*) *nt* stuff; (*Ausrüstung*) gear; **dummes ~** (stupid) nonsense; **das ~ haben zu** to have the makings of; **sich ins ~ legen** to put one's shoulder to the wheel; **was das ~ hält** for all one is worth; **jdm am ~ flicken** to find fault with sb
Zeuge [ˈtsɔʏgə] (**-n, -n**) *m* witness
zeugen *vi* to bear witness, testify ▷ *vt* (*Kind*) to father; **es zeugt von ...** it testifies to ...
Zeugenaussage *f* evidence
Zeugenstand *m* witness box (*Brit*) *od* stand (*US*)
Zeugin *f* witness
Zeugnis [ˈtsɔʏgnɪs] (**-ses, -se**) *nt* certificate; (*Sch*) report; (*Referenz*) reference; (*Aussage*) evidence, testimony; **~ geben von** to be evidence of, testify to; **Zeugniskonferenz** *f* (*Sch*) *staff meeting to decide on marks etc*
Zeugung [ˈtsɔʏgʊŋ] *f* procreation
zeugungsunfähig *adj* sterile
ZH *abk* = **Zentralheizung**
z. H., z. Hd. *abk* (= *zu Händen*) att., attn.
Zicken [ˈtsɪkən] (*umg*) *pl*: **~ machen** to make trouble
zickig *adj* (*albern*) silly; (*prüde*) prudish
Zickzack [ˈtsɪktsak] (**-(e)s, -e**) *m* zigzag
Ziege [ˈtsiːgə] (**-, -n**) *f* goat; (*pej*: *umg*: *Frau*) cow (!)
Ziegel [ˈtsiːgəl] (**-s, -**) *m* brick; (*Dachziegel*) tile
Ziegelei [tsiːgəˈlaɪ] *f* brickworks
Ziegelstein *m* brick
Ziegenbock *m* billy goat
Ziegenleder *nt* kid
Ziegenpeter *m* mumps *sing*
Ziehbrunnen *m* well
ziehen [ˈtsiːən] *unreg vt* to draw; (*zerren*) to pull; (*Schach etc*) to move; (*züchten*) to rear ▷ *vi* to draw; (*umziehen, wandern*) to move; (*Rauch, Wolke etc*) to drift; (*reißen*) to pull ▷ *vb unpers*: **es zieht** there is a draught (*Brit*) *od* draft (*US*), it's draughty (*Brit*) *od* drafty (*US*) ▷ *vr* (*Gummi*) to stretch; (*Grenze etc*) to run; (*Gespräche*) to be drawn out; **etw nach sich ~** to lead to sth, entail sth; **etw ins Lächerliche ~** to ridicule sth; **so was zieht bei mir nicht** I don't like that sort of thing; **zu jdm ~** to move in with sb; **mir ziehts im Rücken** my back hurts; **Ziehen** (**-s, -**) *nt* (*Schmerz*) ache; (*im Unterleib*) dragging pain
Ziehharmonika [ˈtsiːharmoːnika] *f* concertina
Ziehung [ˈtsiːʊŋ] *f* (*Losziehung*) drawing
Ziel [tsiːl] (**-(e)s, -e**) *nt* (*einer Reise*) destination; (*Sport*) finish; (*Mil*) target; (*Absicht*) goal, aim; **jdm/sich ein ~ stecken** to set sb/o.s. a goal; **am ~ sein** to be at one's destination; (*fig*) to have reached one's goal; **über das ~ hinausschießen** (*fig*) to overshoot the mark; **zielbewusst** *adj* purposeful; **zielen** *vi*: **zielen (auf** *+akk***)** to aim (at); **Zielfernrohr** *nt* telescopic sight; **Zielfoto** *nt* (*Sport*) photo-finish, photograph; **Zielgruppe** *f* target group; **Ziellinie** *f* (*Sport*) finishing line; **ziellos** *adj* aimless; **Zielort** *m* destination; **Zielscheibe** *f* target; **zielstrebig** *adj* purposeful
ziemen [ˈtsiːmən] *vr unpers* (*geh*): **das ziemt sich nicht (für dich)** it is not proper (for you)
ziemlich [ˈtsiːmlɪç] *adj attrib* (*Anzahl*) fair ▷ *adv* quite, pretty (*umg*); (*beinahe*) almost, nearly; **eine ~e Anstrengung** quite an effort; **~ lange** quite a long time; **~ fertig** almost *od* nearly ready
Zierde [ˈtsiːrdə] (**-, -n**) *f* ornament, decoration; (*Schmuckstück*) adornment
zieren [ˈtsiːrən] *vr* to act coy
Zierleiste *f* border; (*an Wand, Möbeln*) moulding (*Brit*), molding (*US*); (*an Auto*) trim
zierlich *adj* dainty; **Zierlichkeit** *f* daintiness
Zierstrauch *m* flowering shrub
Ziffer [ˈtsɪfər] (**-, -n**) *f* figure, digit; **römische/arabische ~n** roman/arabic numerals; **Zifferblatt** *nt* dial, (clock *od* watch) face
zig [tsɪk] (*umg*) *adj* umpteen
Zigarette [tsigaˈrɛtə] *f* cigarette
Zigaretten- *zW*: **Zigarettenautomat** *m* cigarette machine; **Zigarettenpause** *f* break for a cigarette; **Zigarettenschachtel** *f* cigarette packet *od* pack (*US*); **Zigarettenspitze** *f* cigarette holder
Zigarillo [tsigaˈrɪlo] (**-s, -s**) *nt od m* cigarillo
Zigarre [tsiˈgarə] (**-, -n**) *f* cigar
Zigeuner, in [tsiˈgɔʏnər(ɪn)] (**-s, -**) *m(f)* gipsy; **Zigeunerschnitzel** *nt* (*Koch*) *cutlet served in a spicy*

sauce with green and red peppers; **Zigeunersprache** *f* Romany (language)
Zimmer ['tsɪmər] (**-s, -**) *nt* room; **Zimmerantenne** *f* indoor aerial; **Zimmerdecke** *f* ceiling; **Zimmerlautstärke** *f* reasonable volume; **Zimmermädchen** *nt* chambermaid; **Zimmermann** (**-(e)s**, *pl* **-leute**) *m* carpenter
zimmern *vt* to make from wood
Zimmer- *zW*: **Zimmernachweis** *m* accommodation service; **Zimmerpflanze** *f* indoor plant; **Zimmervermittlung** *f* accommodation (*Brit*) *od* accommodations (*US*) service
zimperlich ['tsɪmpərlɪç] *adj* squeamish; (*pingelig*) fussy, finicky
Zimt [tsɪmt] (**-(e)s, -e**) *m* cinnamon; **Zimtstange** *f* cinnamon stick
Zink [tsɪŋk] (**-(e)s**) *nt* zinc
Zinke (**-, -n**) *f* (*Gabelzinke*) prong; (*Kammzinke*) tooth
Zinken (**-s, -**) (*umg*) *m* (*Nase*) hooter
zinken *vt* (*Karten*) to mark
Zinksalbe *f* zinc ointment
Zinn [tsɪn] (**-(e)s**) *nt* (*Element*) tin; (*in Zinnwaren*) pewter; **Zinnbecher** *m* pewter tankard
zinnoberrot [tsɪ'no:bərrot] *adj* vermilion
Zinnsoldat *m* tin soldier
Zinnwaren *pl* pewter *sing*
Zins [tsɪns] (**-es, -en**) *m* interest
Zinseszins *m* compound interest
Zins- *zW*: **Zinsfuß** *m* rate of interest; **zinslos** *adj* interest-free; **Zinssatz** *m* rate of interest; **Zinssteuer** *f* tax on interest
Zionismus [tsio'nɪsmʊs] *m* Zionism
Zipfel ['tsɪpfəl] (**-s, -**) *m* corner; (*von Land*) tip; (*Hemdzipfel*) tail; (*Wurstzipfel*) end; **Zipfelmütze** *f* pointed cap
zirka ['tsɪrka] *adv* = **circa**
Zirkel ['tsɪrkəl] (**-s, -**) *m* circle; (*Math*) pair of compasses; **Zirkelkasten** *m* geometry set
zirkulieren [tsɪrku'li:rən] *vi* to circulate
Zirkus ['tsɪrkʊs] (**-, -se**) *m* circus; (*umg: Getue*) fuss, to-do
zirpen ['tsɪrpən] *vi* to chirp, cheep
Zirrhose [tsɪ'ro:zə] (**-, -n**) *f* cirrhosis
zischeln ['tsɪʃəln] *vt, vi* to whisper
zischen ['tsɪʃən] *vi* to hiss; (*Limonade*) to fizz; (*Fett*) to sizzle
Zitat [tsi'ta:t] (**-(e)s, -e**) *nt* quotation, quote
zitieren [tsi'ti:rən] *vt* to quote; (*vorladen, rufen*): **~ (vor** *+akk*) to summon (before)
Zitronat [tsitro'na:t] (**-(e)s, -e**) *nt* candied lemon peel
Zitrone [tsi'tro:nə] (**-, -n**) *f* lemon
Zitronen- *zW*: **Zitronenlimonade** *f* lemonade; **Zitronensaft** *m* lemon juice; **Zitronensäure** *f* citric acid; **Zitronenscheibe** *f* lemon slice
zitterig ['tsɪtərɪç], **zittrig** ['tsɪtrɪç] *adj* shaky
zittern ['tsɪtərn] *vi* to tremble; **vor jdm ~** to be terrified of sb
Zitze ['tsɪtsə] (**-, -n**) *f* teat, dug
Zivi ['tsivi] (**-s, -s**) *m abk* = **Zivildienstleistender**
zivil [tsi'vi:l] *adj* civilian; (*anständig*) civil; (*Preis*) moderate; **~er Ungehorsam** civil disobedience; **Zivil** (**-s**) *nt* plain clothes *pl*; (*Mil*) civilian clothing; **Zivilbevölkerung** *f* civilian population; **Zivilcourage** *f* courage of one's convictions
Zivildienst *m* *alternative service (for conscientious objectors)*; *see culture note*

ZIVILDIENST

A young German has to complete his 13 months' *Zivildienst* or community service if he has opted out of military service as a conscientious objector. This service is usually done in a hospital or old people's home. Many young Germans choose to do this as an alternative to the *Wehrdienst*, although it lasts three months longer.

Zivildienstleistender *m conscientious objector doing alternative community service*
Zivilisation [tsivilizatsi'o:n] *f* civilization
Zivilisationserscheinung *f* phenomenon of civilization
Zivilisationskrankheit *f* disease of civilized man
zivilisieren [tsivili'zi:rən] *vt* to civilize
zivilisiert *adj* civilized
Zivilist [tsivi'lɪst] *m* civilian
Zivilrecht *nt* civil law
ZK (**-s, -s**) *nt abk* (= *Zentralkomitee*) central committee
Zobel ['tso:bəl] (**-s, -**) *m* (*auch*: **Zobelpelz**) sable (fur)
Zofe ['tso:fə] (**-, -n**) *f* lady's maid; (*von Königin*) lady-in-waiting
zog *etc* [tso:k] *vb siehe* **ziehen**
zögern ['tsø:gərn] *vi* to hesitate
Zölibat [tsøli'ba:t] (**-(e)s**) *nt od m* celibacy
Zoll[1] [tsɔl] (**-(e)s, -**) *m* (*Maß*) inch
Zoll[2] (**-(e)s, ¨-e**) *m* customs *pl*; (*Abgabe*) duty; **Zollabfertigung** *f* customs clearance; **Zollamt** *nt* customs office; **Zollbeamte, r** *m* customs official; **Zollerklärung** *f* customs declaration; **zollfrei** *adj* duty-free; **Zollgutlager** *nt* bonded warehouse; **Zollkontrolle** *f* customs (check); **zollpflichtig** *adj* liable to duty, dutiable
Zollstock *m* inch rule
Zone ['tso:nə] (**-, -n**) *f* zone; (*von Fahrkarte*) fare stage
Zoo [tso:] (**-s, -s**) *m* zoo; **Zoohandlung** *f* pet shop
Zoologe [tsoo'lo:gə] (**-n, -n**) *m* zoologist
Zoologie *f* zoology
Zoologin *f* zoologist
zoologisch *adj* zoological
Zoom [zu:m] (**-s, -s**) *nt* zoom shot; (*Objektiv*) zoom lens
Zopf [tsɔpf] (**-(e)s, ¨-e**) *m* plait; pigtail; **alter ~** antiquated custom
Zorn [tsɔrn] (**-(e)s**) *m* anger
zornig *adj* angry

Zote ['tso:tə] (**-, -n**) *f* smutty joke/remark
zottig ['tsɔtɪç] *adj* shaggy
ZPO *abk* (= *Zivilprozessordnung*) ≈ General Practice Act (*US*)
z. T. *abk* = **zum Teil**

SCHLÜSSELWORT

zu [tsu:] *präp +dat* **1** (*örtlich*) to; **zum Bahnhof/Arzt gehen** to go to the station/doctor; **zur Schule/Kirche gehen** to go to school/church; **sollen wir zu Euch gehen?** shall we go to your place?; **sie sah zu ihm hin** she looked towards him; **zum Fenster herein** through the window; **zu meiner Linken** to *od* on my left
2 (*zeitlich*) at; **zu Ostern** at Easter; **bis zum 1. Mai** until May 1st; (*nicht später als*) by May 1st; **zu meiner Zeit** in my time
3 (*Zusatz*) with; **Wein zum Essen trinken** to drink wine with one's meal; **sich zu jdm setzen** to sit down beside sb; **setz dich doch zu uns** (come and) sit with us; **Anmerkungen zu etw** notes on sth
4 (*Zweck*) for; **Wasser zum Waschen** water for washing; **Papier zum Schreiben** paper to write on; **etw zum Geburtstag bekommen** to get sth for one's birthday; **es ist zu seinem Besten** it's for his own good
5 (*Veränderung*) into; **zu etw werden** to turn into sth; **jdn zu etw machen** to make sb (into) sth; **zu Asche verbrennen** to burn to ashes
6 (*mit Zahlen*): **3 zu 2** (*Sport*) 3-2; **das Stück zu 5 Euro** at 5 euros each; **zum ersten Mal** for the first time
7: zu meiner Freude *etc* to my joy *etc*; **zum Glück** luckily; **zu Fuß** on foot; **es ist zum Weinen** it's enough to make you cry
▷ *konj* to; **etw zu essen** sth to eat; **um besser sehen zu können** in order to see better; **ohne es zu wissen** without knowing it; **noch zu bezahlende Rechnungen** outstanding bills
▷ *adv* **1** (*allzu*) too; **zu sehr** too much; **zu viel** too much; (*umg: zu viele*) too many; **er kriegt zu viel** (*umg*) he gets annoyed; **zu wenig** too little; (*umg: zu wenige*) too few
2 (*örtlich*) toward(s); **er kam auf mich zu** he came towards *od* up to me
3 (*geschlossen*) shut; closed; **die Geschäfte haben zu** the shops are closed; **zu sein** to be closed; **auf/zu** (*Wasserhahn etc*) on/off
4 (*umg: los*): **nur zu!** just keep at it!; **mach zu!** hurry up!

zuallererst *adv* first of all
zuallerletzt *adv* last of all
zubauen ['tsu:baʊən] *vt* (*Lücke*) to fill in; (*Platz, Gebäude*) to build up
Zubehör ['tsu:bəhø:r] (**-(e)s, -e**) *nt* accessories *pl*
Zuber ['tsu:bər] (**-s, -**) *m* tub
zubereiten ['tsu:bəraɪtən] *vt* to prepare
zubilligen ['tsu:bɪlɪgən] *vt* to grant
zubinden ['tsu:bɪndən] *unreg vt* to tie up; **jdm die Augen ~** to blindfold sb
zubleiben ['tsu:blaɪbən] *unreg vi* to stay shut
zubringen ['tsu:brɪŋən] *unreg vt* to spend; (*herbeibringen*) to bring, take; (*umg: Tür*) to get shut
Zubringer (**-s, -**) *m* (*Tech*) feeder, conveyor; (*Verkehrsmittel*) shuttle; (*zum Flughafen*) airport bus; **Zubringerbus** *m* shuttle (bus); **Zubringerstraße** *f* slip road (*Brit*), entrance ramp (*US*)
Zucchini [tsʊ'ki:ni:] *pl* courgettes *pl* (*Brit*), zucchini(s) *pl* (*US*)
Zucht [tsʊxt] (**-, -en**) *f* (*von Tieren*) breeding; (*von Pflanzen*) cultivation; (*Rasse*) breed; (*Erziehung*) raising; (*Disziplin*) discipline; **Zuchtbulle** *m* breeding bull
züchten ['tsʏçtən] *vt* (*Tiere*) to breed; (*Pflanzen*) to cultivate, grow
Züchter, in (**-s, -**) *m(f)* breeder; grower
Zuchthaus *nt* prison, penitentiary (*US*)
Zuchthengst *m* stallion, stud
züchtig ['tsʏçtɪç] *adj* modest, demure
züchtigen ['tsʏçtɪgən] *vt* to chastise
Züchtigung *f* chastisement; **körperliche ~** corporal punishment
Zuchtperle *f* cultured pearl
Züchtung *f* (*von Tieren*) breeding; (*von Pflanzen*) cultivation; (*Zuchtart: von Tier*) breed; (*: von Pflanze*) strain
zucken ['tsʊkən] *vi* to jerk, twitch; (*Strahl etc*) to flicker ▷ *vt* to shrug; **der Schmerz zuckte (mir) durch den ganzen Körper** the pain shot right through my body
zücken ['tsʏkən] *vt* (*Schwert*) to draw; (*Geldbeutel*) to pull out
Zucker ['tsʊkər] (**-s, -**) *m* sugar; (*Med*) diabetes; **~ haben** (*umg*) to be a diabetic; **Zuckerdose** *f* sugar bowl; **Zuckererbse** *f* mangetout (*Brit*), sugar pea (*US*); **Zuckerguss** *m* icing; **Zuckerhut** *m* sugar loaf; **zuckerkrank** *adj* diabetic; **Zuckerkrankheit** *f* diabetes *sing*; **Zuckerlecken** *nt*: **das ist kein Zuckerlecken** it's no picnic
zuckern *vt* to sugar
Zucker- *zW*: **Zuckerrohr** *nt* sugar cane; **Zuckerrübe** *f* sugar beet; **Zuckerspiegel** *m* (*Med*) (blood) sugar level; **zuckersüß** *adj* sugary; **Zuckerwatte** *f* candy floss (*Brit*), cotton candy (*US*)
Zuckung *f* convulsion, spasm; (*leicht*) twitch
zudecken ['tsu:dɛkən] *vt* to cover (up); (*im Bett*) to tuck up *od* in
zudem [tsu'de:m] *adv* in addition (to this)
zudrehen ['tsu:dre:ən] *vt* to turn off
zudringlich ['tsu:drɪŋlɪç] *adj* forward, pushy; (*Nachbar etc*) intrusive; **~ werden** to make advances; **Zudringlichkeit** *f* forwardness; intrusiveness
zudrücken ['tsu:drʏkən] *vt* to close; **jdm die Kehle ~** to throttle sb; **ein Auge ~** to turn a blind eye

zueinander [tsu|aɪ'nandər] *adv* to one other; (*in Verbverbindung*) together
zuerkennen ['tsu:|ɛrkɛnən] *unreg vt*: **jdm etw ~** to award sth to sb, award sb sth
zuerst [tsu'|e:rst] *adv* first; (*zu Anfang*) at first; **~ einmal** first of all
Zufahrt ['tsu:fa:rt] *f* approach; **„keine ~ zum Krankenhaus"** "no access to hospital"
Zufahrtsstraße *f* approach road; (*von Autobahn etc*) slip road (*Brit*), entrance ramp (*US*)
Zufall ['tsu:fal] *m* chance; (*Ereignis*) coincidence; **durch ~** by accident; **so ein ~!** what a coincidence!
zufallen *unreg vi* to close, shut; (*Anteil, Aufgabe*): **jdm ~** to fall to sb
zufällig ['tsu:fɛlɪç] *adj* chance ▷ *adv* by chance; (*in Frage*) by any chance
Zufallstreffer *m* fluke
zufassen ['tsu:fasən] *vi* (*zugreifen*) to take hold (of it *od* them); (*fig: schnell handeln*) to seize the opportunity; (*helfen*) to lend a hand
zufliegen ['tsu:fli:gən] *unreg vi*: **ihm fliegt alles nur so zu** (*fig*) everything comes so easily to him
Zuflucht ['tsu:flʊxt] *f* recourse; (*Ort*) refuge; **zu etw ~ nehmen** (*fig*) to resort to sth
Zufluchtsort *m*, **Zufluchtsstätte** *f* place of refuge
Zufluss ['tsu:flʊs] *m* (*Zufließen*) inflow, influx; (*Geog*) tributary; (*Comm*) supply
zufolge [tsu'fɔlgə] *präp +dat od +gen* (*laut*) according to; (*aufgrund*) as a result of
zufrieden [tsu'fri:dən] *adj* content(ed); **er ist mit nichts ~** nothing pleases him; **zufriedengeben** *unreg vr*: **sich mit etw zufriedengeben** to be satisfied with sth; **Zufriedenheit** *f* contentedness; (*Befriedigtsein*) satisfaction; **zufriedenlassen** *unreg vt*: **lass mich damit zufrieden!** (*umg*) shut up about it!; **zufriedenstellen** *vt* to satisfy; **zufriedenstellend** *adj* satisfactory
zufrieren ['tsu:fri:rən] *unreg vi* to freeze up *od* over
zufügen ['tsu:fy:gən] *vt* to add; (*Leid etc*): **jdm etw ~** to cause sb sth
Zufuhr ['tsu:fu:r] **(-, -en)** *f* (*Herbeibringen*) supplying; (*Met*) influx; (*Mil*) supplies *pl*
zuführen ['tsu:fy:rən] *vt* (*bringen*) to bring; (*transportieren*) to convey; (*versorgen*) to supply ▷ *vi*: **auf etw** *akk* **~** to lead to sth
Zug [tsu:k] **(-(e)s, ⸗e)** *m* (*Eisenbahnzug*) train; (*Luftzug*) draught (*Brit*), draft (*US*); (*Ziehen*) pull(ing); (*Gesichtszug*) feature; (*Schach etc*) move; (*Klingelzug*) pull; (*Schriftzug, beim Schwimmen*) stroke; (*Atemzug*) breath; (*Charakterzug*) trait; (*an Zigarette*) puff, pull, drag; (*Schluck*) gulp; (*Menschengruppe*) procession; (*von Vögeln*) migration; (*Mil*) platoon; **etw in vollen Zügen genießen** to enjoy sth to the full; **in den letzten Zügen liegen** (*umg*) to be at one's last gasp; **im ~(e)** *+gen* (*im Verlauf*) in the course of; **~ um Zug** (*fig*) step by step; **zum ~(e) kommen** (*umg*) to get a look-in; **etw in groben Zügen darstellen** *od* **umreißen** to outline sth; **das war kein schöner ~ von dir** that wasn't nice of you
Zugabe ['tsu:ga:bə] *f* extra; (*in Konzert etc*) encore
Zugabteil *nt* train compartment
Zugang ['tsu:gaŋ] *m* entrance; (*Zutritt, fig*) access
zugänglich ['tsu:gɛŋlɪç] *adj* accessible; (*öffentliche Einrichtungen*) open; (*Mensch*) approachable
Zugangscode *m* (*Comput*) access code
Zugbegleiter *m* (*Eisenb*) guard (*Brit*), conductor (*US*)
Zugbrücke *f* drawbridge
zugeben ['tsu:ge:bən] *unreg vt* (*beifügen*) to add, throw in; (*zugestehen*) to admit; (*erlauben*) to permit; **zugegeben ...** granted ...
zugegebenermaßen ['tsu:gegə:bənər'ma:sən] *adv* admittedly
zugegen [tsu'ge:gən] *adv* (*geh*): **~ sein** to be present
zugehen ['tsu:ge:ən] *unreg vi* (*schließen*) to shut ▷ *vi unpers* (*sich ereignen*) to go on, happen; **auf jdn/etw ~** to walk towards sb/sth; **dem Ende ~** to be finishing; **er geht schon auf die siebzig zu** he's getting on for seventy; **hier geht es nicht mit rechten Dingen zu** there's something odd going on here; **dort geht es ... zu** things are ... there
Zugehörigkeit ['tsu:gəhø:rɪçkaɪt] *f*: **~ (zu)** membership (of), belonging (to)
Zugehörigkeitsgefühl *nt* feeling of belonging
zugeknöpft ['tsu:gəknœpft] (*umg*) *adj* reserved, stand-offish
Zügel ['tsy:gəl] **(-s, -)** *m* rein, reins *pl*; (*fig*) rein, curb; **die ~ locker lassen** to slacken one's hold on the reins; **die ~ locker lassen bei** (*fig*) to give free rein to
zugelassen ['tsu:gəlasən] *adj* authorized; (*Heilpraktiker*) registered; (*Kfz*) licensed
zügellos *adj* unrestrained; (*sexuell*) licentious
Zügellosigkeit *f* lack of restraint; licentiousness
zügeln *vt* to curb; (*Pferd*) to rein in
zugesellen *vr*: **sich jdm ~** to join sb, join up with sb
Zugeständnis ['tsu:gəʃtɛntnɪs] **(-ses, -se)** *nt* concession; **~se machen** to make allowances
zugestehen *unreg vt* to admit; (*Rechte*) to concede
zugetan ['tsu:gəta:n] *adj*: **jdm/etw ~ sein** to be fond of sb/sth
Zugewinn **(-(e)s)** *m* (*Jur*) *property acquired during marriage*
Zugezogene, r ['tsu:gətso:gənə(r)] *f(m)* newcomer
Zugführer *m* (*Eisenb*) chief guard (*Brit*) *od* conductor (*US*); (*Mil*) platoon commander
zugig *adj* draughty (*Brit*), drafty (*US*)
zügig ['tsy:gɪç] *adj* speedy, swift
zugkräftig *adj* (*fig: Werbetext, Titel*) eye-catching; (*Schauspieler*) crowd-pulling *attr*,

popular
zugleich [tsu'glaɪç] *adv* (*zur gleichen Zeit*) at the same time; (*ebenso*) both
Zugluft *f* draught (*Brit*), draft (*US*)
Zugmaschine *f* traction engine, tractor
zugreifen ['tsu:graɪfən] *unreg vi* to seize *od* grab it/them; (*helfen*) to help; (*beim Essen*) to help o.s.
Zugriff ['tsu:grɪf] *m* (*Comput*) access; **sich dem ~ der Polizei entziehen** (*fig*) to evade justice
zugrunde, zu Grunde [tsu'grʊndə] *adv*: **~ gehen** to collapse; (*Mensch*) to perish; **er wird daran nicht ~ gehen** he'll survive; (*finanziell*) it won't ruin him; **einer Sache** *dat* **etw ~ legen** to base sth on sth; **einer Sache** *dat* **~ liegen** to be based on sth; **~ richten** to ruin, destroy
zugunsten, zu Gunsten [tsu'gʊnstən] *präp +gen od +dat* in favour (*Brit*) *od* favor (*US*) of
zugutehalten [tsu'gu:təhaltən] *unreg vt*: **jdm etw ~** to concede sth to sb
zugutekommen [tsu'gu:təkɔmən] *unreg vt*: **jdm ~** to be of assistance to sb
Zug- *zW*: **Zugverbindung** *f* train connection; **Zugvogel** *m* migratory bird; **Zugzwang** *m* (*Schach*) zugzwang; **unter Zugzwang stehen** (*fig*) to be in a tight spot
zuhalten ['tsu:haltən] *unreg vt* to hold shut ▷ *vi*: **auf jdn/etw ~** to make for sb/sth; **sich** *dat* **die Nase ~** to hold one's nose
Zuhälter ['tsu:hɛltər] **(-s, -)** *m* pimp
zuhause [tsu'haʊzə] *adv* at home
Zuhause (-s) *nt* home
Zuhilfenahme [tsu'hɪlfəna:mə] *f*: **unter ~ von** with the help of
zuhören ['tsu:hø:rən] *vi* to listen
Zuhörer (-s, -) *m* listener; **Zuhörerschaft** *f* audience
zujubeln ['tsu:ju:bəln] *vi*: **jdm ~** to cheer sb
zukehren ['tsu:ke:rən] *vt* (*zuwenden*) to turn
zuklappen ['tsu:klapən] *vt* (*Buch, Deckel*) to close ▷ *vi* (*Hilfsverb sein: Tür etc*) to click shut
zukleben ['tsu:kle:bən] *vt* to paste up
zukneifen ['tsu:knaɪfən] *vt* (*Augen*) to screw up; (*Mund*) to shut tight(ly)
zuknöpfen ['tsu:knœpfən] *vt* to button (up), fasten (up)
zukommen ['tsu:kɔmən] *unreg vi* to come up; **auf jdn ~** to come up to sb; **jdm ~** (*sich gehören*) to be fitting for sb; **diesem Treffen kommt große Bedeutung zu** this meeting is of the utmost importance; **jdm etw ~ lassen** to give sb sth; **die Dinge auf sich** *akk* **~ lassen** to take things as they come
Zukunft ['tsu:kʊnft] **(-,** *no pl***)** *f* future
zukünftig ['tsu:kʏnftɪç] *adj* future ▷ *adv* in future; **mein ~er Mann** my husband-to-be
Zukunfts- *zW*: **Zukunftsaussichten** *pl* future prospects *pl*; **Zukunftsmusik** (*umg*) *f* wishful thinking; **Zukunftsroman** *m* science-fiction novel; **zukunftsträchtig** *adj* promising for the future; **zukunftsweisend** *adj* trend-setting
Zulage ['tsu:la:gə] *f* bonus
zulande [tsu'landə] *adv*: **bei uns ~** in our country
zulangen ['tsu:laŋən] (*umg*) *vi* (*Dieb, beim Essen*) to help o.s.
zulassen ['tsu:lasən] *unreg vt* (*hereinlassen*) to admit; (*erlauben*) to permit; (*Auto*) to license; (*umg: nicht öffnen*) to keep shut
zulässig ['tsu:lɛsɪç] *adj* permissible, permitted; **~e Höchstgeschwindigkeit** (upper) speed limit
Zulassung *f* (*amtlich*) authorization; (*von Kfz*) licensing; (*als praktizierender Arzt*) registration
Zulauf *m*: **großen ~ haben** (*Geschäft*) to be very popular
zulaufen ['tsu:laʊfən] *unreg vi*: **~ auf** *+akk* to run towards; **jdm ~** (*Tier*) to adopt sb; **spitz ~** to come to a point
zulegen ['tsu:le:gən] *vt* to add; (*Geld*) to put in; (*Tempo*) to accelerate, quicken; (*schließen*) to cover over; **sich** *dat* **etw ~** (*umg*) to get oneself sth
zuleide [tsu'laɪdə] *adj*: **jdm etw ~ tun** to harm sb
zuleiten ['tsu:laɪtən] *vt* (*Wasser*) to supply; (*schicken*) to send
Zuleitung *f* (*Tech*) supply
zuletzt [tsu'lɛtst] *adv* finally, at last; **wir blieben bis ~** we stayed to the very end; **nicht ~ wegen** not least because of
zuliebe [tsu'li:bə] *adv*: **jdm ~** (in order) to please sb
Zulieferbetrieb ['tsu:li:fərbətri:p] *m* (*Comm*) supplier
zum [tsʊm] = **zu dem**; **~ dritten Mal** for the third time; **~ Scherz** as a joke; **~ Trinken** for drinking; **bis ~ 15. April** until 15th April; (*nicht später als*) by 15th April; **~ ersten Mal(e)** for the first time; **es ist ~ Weinen** it's enough to make you (want to) weep; **~ Glück** luckily
zumachen ['tsu:maxən] *vt* to shut; (*Kleidung*) to do up, fasten ▷ *vi* to shut; (*umg*) to hurry up
zumal [tsu'ma:l] *konj* especially (as)
zumeist [tsu'maɪst] *adv* mostly
zumessen ['tsu:mɛsən] *unreg vt (+dat)* (*Zeit*) to allocate (for); (*Bedeutung*) to attach (to)
zumindest [tsu'mɪndəst] *adv* at least
zumutbar ['tsu:mu:tba:r] *adj* reasonable
zumute [tsu'mu:tə] *adv*: **wie ist ihm ~?** how does he feel?
zumuten ['tsu:mu:tən] *vt*: **(jdm) etw ~** to expect *od* ask sth (of sb); **sich** *dat* **zu viel ~** to take on too much
Zumutung *f* unreasonable expectation *od* demand; (*Unverschämtheit*) impertinence; **das ist eine ~!** that's a bit much!
zunächst [tsu'nɛ:çst] *adv* first of all; **~ einmal** to start with
zunageln ['tsu:na:gəln] *vt* (*Fenster etc*) to nail up; (*Kiste etc*) to nail down
zunähen ['tsu:nɛ:ən] *vt* to sew up
Zunahme ['tsu:na:mə] **(-, -n)** *f* increase
Zuname ['tsu:na:mə] *m* surname
zünden ['tsʏndən] *vi* (*Feuer*) to light, ignite;

(*Motor*) to fire; (*fig*) to kindle enthusiasm ▷ *vt* to ignite; (*Rakete*) to fire
zündend *adj* fiery
Zünder (**-s, -**) *m* fuse; (*Mil*) detonator
Zünd- *zW*: **Zündholz** *nt* match; **Zündkabel** *nt* (*Aut*) plug lead; **Zündkerze** *f* (*Aut*) spark(ing) plug; **Zündplättchen** *nt* cap; **Zündschlüssel** *m* ignition key; **Zündschnur** *f* fuse wire; **Zündstoff** *m* fuel; (*fig*) dynamite
Zündung *f* ignition
zunehmen ['tsu:ne:mən] *unreg vi* to increase, grow; (*Mensch*) to put on weight
zunehmend *adj*: **mit ~em Alter** with advancing age
zuneigen ['tsu:naɪgən] *vi* to incline, lean; **sich dem Ende ~** to draw to a close; **einer Auffassung ~** to incline towards a view; **jdm zugeneigt sein** to be attracted to sb
Zuneigung *f* affection
Zunft [tsʊnft] (**-, ¨-e**) *f* guild
zünftig ['tsʏnftɪç] *adj* (*Arbeit*) professional; (*umg: ordentlich*) proper, real
Zunge ['tsʊŋə] *f* tongue; (*Fisch*) sole; **böse ~n behaupten, ...** malicious gossip has it ...
züngeln ['tsʏŋəln] *vi* (*Flammen*) to lick
Zungenbrecher *m* tongue-twister
zungenfertig *adj* glib
Zünglein ['tsʏŋlaɪn] *nt*: **das ~ an der Waage sein** (*fig*) to tip the scales
zunichtemachen [tsu'nɪçtəmaxən] *vt* to ruin, destroy
zunichtewerden [tsu'nɪçtəve:rdən] *unreg vi* to come to nothing
zunutze [tsu'nʊtsə] *adv*: **sich** *dat* **etw ~ machen** to make use of sth
zuoberst [tsu'|o:bərst] *adv* at the top
zuordnen ['tsu:|ɔrdnən] *vt* to assign
zupacken ['tsu:pakən] (*umg*) *vi* (*zugreifen*) to make a grab for it; (*bei der Arbeit*) to get down to it; **mit ~** (*helfen*) to give me/them *etc* a hand
zupfen ['tsʊpfən] *vt* to pull, pick, pluck; (*Gitarre*) to pluck
zur [tsu:r] = **zu der**
zurate, zu Rate [tsu'ra:tə] *adv*: **jdn ~ ziehen** to consult sb
zurechnungsfähig ['tsu:reçnʊŋsfɛ:ɪç] *adj* (*Jur*) responsible, of sound mind; **Zurechnungsfähigkeit** *f* responsibility, accountability
zurecht- *zW*: **zurechtbiegen** *unreg vt* to bend into shape; (*fig*) to twist; **zurechtfinden** *unreg vr* to find one's way (about); **zurechtkommen** *unreg vi* (*rechtzeitig kommen*) to come in time; (*schaffen*) to cope; (*finanziell*) to manage; **zurechtlegen** *vt* to get ready; (*Ausrede etc*) to have ready; **zurechtmachen** *vt* to prepare ▷ *vr* to get ready; (*sich schminken*) to put on one's make-up; **zurechtweisen** *unreg vt* to reprimand; **Zurechtweisung** *f* reprimand, rebuff
zureden ['tsu:re:dən] *vi*: **jdm ~** to persuade sb, urge sb
zureiten ['tsuraɪtən] *unreg vt* (*Pferd*) to break in
Zürich ['tsy:rɪç] (**-s**) *nt* Zurich
zurichten ['tsu:rɪçtən] *vt* (*Essen*) to prepare; (*beschädigen*) to batter, bash up
zürnen ['tsʏrnən] *vi*: **jdm ~** to be angry with sb
zurück [tsu'rʏk] *adv* back; (*mit Zahlungen*) behind; (*fig: zurückgeblieben: von Kind*) backward; **~!** get back!; **zurückbehalten** *unreg vt* to keep back; **er hat Schäden zurückbehalten** he suffered lasting damage; **zurückbekommen** *unreg vt* to get back; **zurückbezahlen** *vt* to repay, pay back; **zurückbleiben** *unreg vi* (*Mensch*) to remain behind; (*nicht nachkommen*) to fall behind, lag; (*Schaden*) to remain; **zurückbringen** *unreg vt* to bring back; **zurückdatieren** *vt* to backdate; **zurückdrängen** *vt* (*Gefühle*) to repress; (*Feind*) to push back; **zurückdrehen** *vt* to turn back; **zurückerobern** *vt* to reconquer; **zurückerstatten** *vt* to refund; **zurückfahren** *unreg vi* to travel back; (*vor Schreck*) to recoil ▷ *vt* to drive back; **zurückfallen** *unreg vi* to fall back; (*in Laster*) to relapse; (*in Leistungen*) to fall behind; (*an Besitzer*): **zurückfallen an** *+akk* to revert to; **zurückfinden** *unreg vi* to find one's way back; **zurückfordern** *vt* to demand back; **zurückführen** *vt* to lead back; **etw auf etw** *akk* **zurückführen** to trace sth back to sth; **zurückgeben** *unreg vt* to give back; (*antworten*) to retort with; **zurückgeblieben** *adj* retarded; **zurückgehen** *unreg vi* to go back; (*fallen*) to go down, fall; (*zeitlich*): **zurückgehen (auf** *+akk***)** to date back (to); **Waren zurückgehen lassen** to send back goods; **zurückgezogen** *adj* retired, withdrawn; **zurückgreifen** *unreg vi*: **zurückgreifen (auf** *+akk***)** (*fig*) to fall back (upon); (*zeitlich*) to go back (to); **zurückhalten** *unreg vt* to hold back; (*Mensch*) to restrain; (*hindern*) to prevent ▷ *vr* (*reserviert sein*) to be reserved; (*im Essen*) to hold back; (*im Hintergrund bleiben*) to keep in the background; (*bei Verhandlung*) to keep a low profile; **zurückhaltend** *adj* reserved; **Zurückhaltung** *f* reserve; **zurückholen** *vt* (*Comput: Daten*) to retrieve; **zurückkehren** *vi* to return; **zurückkommen** *unreg vi* to come back; **auf etw** *akk* **zurückkommen** to return to sth; **zurücklassen** *unreg vt* to leave behind; **zurücklegen** *vt* to put back; (*Geld*) to put by; (*reservieren*) to keep back; (*Strecke*) to cover ▷ *vr* to lie back; **zurückliegen** *unreg vi*: **der Unfall liegt etwa eine Woche zurück** the accident was about a week ago; **zurücknehmen** *unreg vt* to take back; **zurückreichen** *vi* (*Tradition etc*): **zurückreichen (in** *+akk***)** to go back (to); **zurückrufen** *unreg vt, vi* to call back; **etw ins Gedächtnis zurückrufen** to recall sth; **zurückschrauben** *vt*: **seine Ansprüche zurückschrauben** to lower one's sights; **zurückschrecken** *vi*: **zurückschrecken vor** *+dat* to shrink from; **vor nichts zurückschrecken** to stop at nothing; **zurücksetzen** *vt* to put back; (*im Preis*) to reduce; (*benachteiligen*) to put at

a disadvantage ▷ *vi* (*mit Fahrzeug*) to reverse, back; **zurückstecken** *vt* to put back ▷ *vi* (*fig*) to moderate one's wishes; **zurückstellen** *vt* to put back, replace; (*aufschieben*) to put off, postpone; (*Mil*) to turn down; (*Interessen*) to defer; (*Ware*) to keep; **persönliche Interessen hinter etw** *dat* **zurückstellen** to put sth before one's personal interests; **zurückstoßen** *unreg vt* to repulse; **zurückstufen** *vt* to downgrade; **zurücktreten** *unreg vi* to step back; (*vom Amt*) to retire; (*von einem Vertrag etc*): **zurücktreten (von)** to withdraw (from); **gegenüber** *od* **hinter etw** *dat* **zurücktreten** to diminish in importance in view of sth; **bitte zurücktreten!** stand back, please!; **zurückverfolgen** *vt* (*fig*) to trace back; **zurückversetzen** *vt* (*in alten Zustand*): **zurückversetzen (in** *+akk***)** to restore (to) ▷ *vr*: **sich zurückversetzen (in** *+akk***)** to think back (to); **zurückweichen** *unreg vi*: **zurückweichen (vor** *+dat***)** to shrink back (from); **zurückweisen** *unreg vt* to turn down; (*Mensch*) to reject; **zurückwerfen** *unreg vt* (*Ball, Kopf*) to throw back; (*Strahlen, Schall*) to reflect; (*fig: Feind*) to repel; (*: wirtschaftlich*): **zurückwerfen (um)** to set back (by); **zurückzahlen** *vt* to pay back, repay; **Zurückzahlung** *f* repayment; **zurückziehen** *unreg vt* to pull back; (*Angebot*) to withdraw ▷ *vr* to retire

Zuruf ['tsu:ru:f] *m* shout, cry

zurzeit [tsʊr'tsaɪt] *adv* at the moment

zus. *abk* = **zusammen; zusätzlich**

Zusage ['tsu:za:gə] *f* promise; (*Annahme*) consent

zusagen *vt* to promise ▷ *vi* to accept; **jdm etw auf den Kopf ~** (*umg*) to tell sb sth outright; **jdm ~** (*gefallen*) to appeal to *od* please sb

zusammen [tsu'zamən] *adv* together; **Zusammenarbeit** *f* cooperation; **zusammenarbeiten** *vi* to cooperate; **Zusammenballung** *f* accumulation; **zusammenbauen** *vt* to assemble; **zusammenbeißen** *unreg vt* (*Zähne*) to clench; **zusammenbleiben** *unreg vi* to stay together; **zusammenbrauen** (*umg*) *vt* to concoct ▷ *vr* (*Gewitter, Unheil etc*) to be brewing; **zusammenbrechen** *unreg vi* (*Hilfsverb sein*) to collapse; (*Mensch*) to break down, collapse; (*Verkehr etc*) to come to a standstill; **zusammenbringen** *unreg vt* to bring *od* get together; (*Geld*) to get; (*Sätze*) to put together; **Zusammenbruch** *m* collapse; (*Comput*) crash; **zusammenfahren** *unreg vi* to collide; (*erschrecken*) to start; **zusammenfallen** *unreg vi* (*einstürzen*) to collapse; (*Ereignisse*) to coincide; **zusammenfassen** *vt* to summarize; (*vereinigen*) to unite; **zusammenfassend** *adj* summarizing ▷ *adv* to summarize; **Zusammenfassung** *f* summary, résumé; **zusammenfinden** *unreg vi, vr* to meet (together); **zusammenfließen** *unreg vi* to flow together, meet; **Zusammenfluss** *m* confluence; **zusammenfügen** *vt* to join (together), unite; **zusammenführen** *vt* to bring together; (*Familie*) to reunite; **zusammengehören** *vi* to belong together; (*Paar*) to match; **Zusammengehörigkeitsgefühl** *nt* sense of belonging; **zusammengesetzt** *adj* compound, composite; **zusammengewürfelt** *adj* motley; **zusammenhalten** *unreg vt* to hold together ▷ *vi* to hold together; (*Freunde, fig*) to stick together; **Zusammenhang** *m* connection; **im/aus dem Zusammenhang** in/out of context; **etw aus dem Zusammenhang reißen** to take sth out of its context; **zusammenhängen** *unreg vi* to be connected *od* linked; **zusammenhängend** *adj* (*Erzählung*) coherent; **zusammenhanglos, zusammenhangslos** *adj* incoherent; **zusammenklappbar** *adj* folding, collapsible; **zusammenklappen** *vt* (*Messer etc*) to fold ▷ *vi* (*umg: Mensch*) to flake out; **zusammenknüllen** *vt* to crumple up; **zusammenkommen** *unreg vi* to meet, assemble; (*sich ereignen*) to occur at once *od* together; **zusammenkramen** *vt* to gather (together); **Zusammenkunft (-, -künfte)** *f* meeting; **zusammenlaufen** *unreg vi* to run *od* come together; (*Straßen, Flüsse etc*) to converge, meet; (*Farben*) to run into one another; **zusammenlegen** *vt* to put together; (*stapeln*) to pile up; (*falten*) to fold; (*verbinden*) to combine, unite; (*Termine, Feste*) to combine; (*Geld*) to collect; **zusammennehmen** *unreg vt* to summon up ▷ *vr* to pull o.s. together; **alles zusammengenommen** all in all; **zusammenpassen** *vi* to go well together, match; **Zusammenprall** *m* (*lit*) collision; (*fig*) clash; **zusammenprallen** *vi* (*Hilfsverb sein*) to collide; **zusammenreimen** (*umg*) *vt*: **das kann ich mir nicht zusammenreimen** I can't make head nor tail of this; **zusammenreißen** *unreg vr* to pull o.s. together; **zusammenrotten** *unreg* (*pej*) *vr* to gang up; **zusammenschlagen** *unreg vt* (*jdn*) to beat up; (*Dinge*) to smash up; (*falten*) to fold; (*Hände*) to clap; (*Hacken*) to click; **zusammenschließen** *unreg vt, vr* to join (together); **Zusammenschluss** *m* amalgamation; **zusammenschmelzen** *unreg vi* (*verschmelzen*) to fuse; (*zerschmelzen*) to melt (away); (*Anzahl*) to dwindle; **zusammenschrecken** *unreg vi* to start; **zusammenschreiben** *unreg vt* to write together; (*Bericht*) to put together; **zusammenschrumpfen** *vi* (*Hilfsverb sein*) to shrink, shrivel up; **Zusammensein (-s)** *nt* get-together; **zusammensetzen** *vt* to put together ▷ *vr*: **sich zusammensetzen aus** to consist of; **Zusammensetzung** *f* composition; **Zusammenspiel** *nt* teamwork; (*von Kräften etc*) interaction; **zusammenstellen** *vt* to put together; **Zusammenstellung** *f* list; (*Vorgang*) compilation; **Zusammenstoß** *m* collision; **zusammenstoßen** *unreg vi* (*Hilfsverb sein*) to collide; **zusammenströmen** *vi* (*Hilfsverb sein: Menschen*) to flock together; **zusammentragen** *unreg vt* to collect;

Zusammentreffen *nt* meeting; (*Zufall*) coincidence; **zusammentreffen** *unreg vi* (*Hilfsverb sein*) to coincide; (*Menschen*) to meet; **zusammentreten** *unreg vi* (*Verein etc*) to meet; **zusammenwachsen** *unreg vi* to grow together; **zusammenwirken** *vi* to combine; **zusammenzählen** *vt* to add up; **zusammenziehen** *unreg vt* (*verengern*) to draw together; (*vereinigen*) to bring together; (*addieren*) to add up ▷ *vr* to shrink; (*sich bilden*) to form, develop; **zusammenzucken** *vi* (*Hilfsverb sein*) to start

Zusatz ['tsu:zats] *m* addition; **Zusatzantrag** *m* (*Pol*) amendment; **Zusatzgerät** *nt* attachment

zusätzlich ['tsu:zɛtslɪç] *adj* additional

Zusatzmittel *nt* additive

zuschauen ['tsu:ʃaʊən] *vi* to watch, look on

Zuschauer (**-s, -**) *m* spectator ▷ *pl* (*Theat*) audience *sing*

zuschicken ['tsu:ʃɪkən] *vt*: **jdm etw ~** to send *od* forward sth to sb

zuschießen ['tsu:ʃi:sən] *unreg vt* to fire; (*Geld*) to put in ▷ *vi*: **~ auf** *+akk* to rush towards

Zuschlag ['tsu:ʃla:k] *m* extra charge; (*Erhöhung*) surcharge; (*Eisenb*) supplement

zuschlagen ['tsu:ʃla:gən] *unreg vt* (*Tür*) to slam; (*Ball*) to hit; (*bei Auktion*) to knock down; (*Steine etc*) to knock into shape ▷ *vi* (*Fenster, Tür*) to shut; (*Mensch*) to hit, punch

zuschlagfrei *adj* (*Eisenb*) not subject to a supplement

zuschlagpflichtig *adj* subject to surcharge

Zuschlagskarte *f* (*Eisenb*) supplementary ticket

zuschließen ['tsu:ʃli:sən] *unreg vt* to lock (up)

zuschmeißen ['tsu:ʃmaɪsən] *unreg* (*umg*) *vt* to slam, bang shut

zuschmieren ['tsu:ʃmi:rən] *vt* to smear over; (*Löcher*) to fill in

zuschneiden ['tsu:ʃnaɪdən] *unreg vt* to cut to size; (*Nähen*) to cut out; **auf etw** *akk* **zugeschnitten sein** (*fig*) to be geared to sth

zuschnüren ['tsu:ʃny:rən] *vt* to tie up; **die Angst schnürte ihm die Kehle zu** (*fig*) he was choked with fear

zuschrauben ['tsu:ʃraʊbən] *vt* to screw shut

zuschreiben ['tsu:ʃraɪbən] *unreg vt* (*fig*) to ascribe, attribute; (*Comm*) to credit; **das hast du dir selbst zu~** you've only got yourself to blame

Zuschrift ['tsu:ʃrɪft] *f* letter, reply

zuschulden, zu Schulden [tsu'ʃʊldən] *adv*: **sich** *dat* **etw ~ kommen lassen** to make o.s. guilty of sth

Zuschuss ['tsu:ʃʊs] *m* subsidy

Zuschussbetrieb *m* loss-making concern

zuschütten ['tsu:ʃʏtən] *vt* to fill up

zusehen ['tsu:ze:ən] *unreg vi* to watch; (*dafür sorgen*) to take care; (*etw dulden*) to sit back (and watch); **jdm/etw ~** to watch sb/sth

zusehends *adv* visibly

zu sein ['tsu:zaɪn] *siehe* **zu**

zusenden ['tsu:zɛndən] *unreg vt* to forward, send on

zusetzen ['tsu:zɛtsən] *vt* (*beifügen*) to add; (*Geld*) to lose ▷ *vi*: **jdm ~** to harass sb; (*Krankheit*) to take a lot out of sb; (*unter Druck setzen*) to lean on sb (*umg*); (*schwer treffen*) to hit sb hard

zusichern ['tsu:zɪçərn] *vt*: **jdm etw ~** to assure sb of sth

Zusicherung *f* assurance

zusperren ['tsu:ʃpɛrən] *vt* to bar

zuspielen ['tsu:ʃpi:lən] *vt, vi* to pass; **jdm etw ~** to pass sth to sb; (*fig*) to pass sth on to sb; **etw der Presse ~** to leak sth to the press

zuspitzen ['tsu:ʃpɪtsən] *vt* to sharpen ▷ *vr* (*Lage*) to become critical

zusprechen ['tsu:ʃprɛçən] *unreg vt* (*zuerkennen*): **jdm etw ~** to award sb sth, award sth to sb ▷ *vi*: **jdm ~** to speak to sb; **jdm Trost ~** to comfort sb; **dem Essen/Alkohol ~** to eat/drink a lot

Zuspruch ['tsu:ʃprʊx] *m* encouragement; (*Anklang*) popularity

Zustand ['tsu:ʃtant] *m* state, condition; **in gutem/schlechtem ~** in good/poor condition; (*Haus*) in good/bad repair; **Zustände bekommen** *od* **kriegen** (*umg*) to have a fit

zustande, zu Stande [tsu'ʃtandə] *adv*: **~ bringen** to bring about; **~ kommen** to come about

zuständig ['tsu:ʃtɛndɪç] *adj* competent, responsible; **Zuständigkeit** *f* competence, responsibility; **Zuständigkeitsbereich** *m* area of responsibility

zustattenkommen [tsu'ʃtatənkɔmən] *unreg vi*: **jdm ~** (*geh*) to come in useful for sb

zustehen ['tsu:ʃte:ən] *unreg vi*: **jdm ~** to be sb's right

zusteigen ['tsu:ʃtaɪgən] *unreg vi*: **noch jemand zugestiegen?** (*in Zug*) any more tickets?

zustellen ['tsu:ʃtɛlən] *vt* (*verstellen*) to block; (*Post etc*) to send

Zustellung *f* delivery

zusteuern ['tsu:ʃtɔʏərn] *vi*: **auf etw** *akk* **~** to head for sth; (*beim Gespräch*) to steer towards sth ▷ *vt* (*beitragen*) to contribute

zustimmen ['tsu:ʃtɪmən] *vi* to agree

Zustimmung *f* agreement; (*Einwilligung*) consent; **allgemeine ~ finden** to meet with general approval

zustoßen ['tsu:ʃto:sən] *unreg vi* (*fig*): **jdm ~** to happen to sb

Zustrom ['tsu:ʃtro:m] *m* (*fig: Menschenmenge*) stream (of visitors *etc*); (*hineinströmend*) influx; (*Met*) inflow

zustürzen ['tsu:ʃtʏrtsən] *vi*: **auf jdn/etw ~** to rush up to sb/sth

zutage, zu Tage [tsu'ta:gə] *adv*: **~ bringen** to bring to light; **~ treten** to come to light

Zutaten ['tsu:ta:tən] *pl* ingredients *pl*; (*fig*) accessories *pl*

zuteilen ['tsu:taɪlən] *vt* to allocate, assign

zuteilwerden [tsu'taɪlve:rdən] *unreg vi* (*geh*): **jdm wird etw zuteil** sb is granted sth,

sth is granted to sb

zutiefst [tsu'ti:fst] *adv* deeply

zutragen ['tsu:tra:gən] *unreg vt*: **jdm etw ~** to bring sb sth, bring sth to sb ▷ *vt* (*Klatsch*) to tell sb sth ▷ *vr* to happen

zuträglich ['tsu:trɛ:klıç] *adj* beneficial

zutrauen ['tsu:traʊən] *vt*: **jdm etw ~** to credit sb with sth; **sich** *dat* **nichts ~** to have no confidence in o.s.; **jdm viel ~** to think a lot of sb; **jdm wenig ~** not to think much of sb; **Zutrauen (-s)** *nt*: **Zutrauen (zu)** trust (in); **zu jdm Zutrauen fassen** to begin to trust sb

zutraulich *adj* trusting; (*Tier*) friendly; **Zutraulichkeit** *f* trust

zutreffen ['tsu:trɛfən] *unreg vi* to be correct; (*gelten*) to apply

zutreffend *adj* (*richtig*) accurate; **Z~es bitte unterstreichen** please underline where applicable

zutrinken ['tsu:trıŋkən] *unreg vi*: **jdm ~** to drink to sb

Zutritt ['tsu:trıt] *m* access; (*Einlass*) admittance; **kein Zutritt, ~ verboten** no admittance

zutun ['tsu:tu:n] *unreg vt* to add; (*schließen*) to shut

Zutun (-s) *nt* assistance

zuunterst [tsu'|ʊntərst] *adv* right at the bottom

zuverlässig ['tsu:fɛrlɛsıç] *adj* reliable; **Zuverlässigkeit** *f* reliability

Zuversicht ['tsu:fɛrzıçt] **(-)** *f* confidence; **zuversichtlich** *adj* confident; **Zuversichtlichkeit** *f* confidence

zu viel [tsu'fi:l] *siehe* **zu**

zuvor [tsu'fo:r] *adv* before, previously

zuvorderst [tsu'fɔrdərst] *adv* right at the front

zuvorkommen *unreg vi +dat* to anticipate; (*Gefahr etc*) to forestall; **jdm ~** to beat sb to it

zuvorkommend *adj* courteous; (*gefällig*) obliging

Zuwachs ['tsu:vaks] **(-es)** *m* increase, growth; (*umg*) addition

zuwachsen *unreg vi* to become overgrown; (*Wunde*) to heal (up)

Zuwachsrate *f* rate of increase

zuwandern ['tsu:vandərn] *vi* to immigrate

zuwege, zu Wege [tsu've:gə] *adv*: **etw ~ bringen** to accomplish sth; **mit etw ~ kommen** to manage sth; **gut ~ sein** to be (doing) well

zuweilen [tsu'vaılən] *adv* at times, now and then

zuweisen ['tsu:vaızən] *unreg vt* to assign, allocate

zuwenden ['tsu:vɛndən] *unreg vt +dat* to turn towards ▷ *vr +dat* to turn to; (*sich widmen*) to devote o.s. to; **jdm seine Aufmerksamkeit ~** to give sb one's attention

Zuwendung *f* (*Geld*) financial contribution; (*Liebe*) love and care

zu wenig [tsu've:nıç] *siehe* **zu**

zuwerfen ['tsu:vɛrfən] *unreg vt*: **jdm etw ~** to throw sth to sb, throw sb sth

zuwider [tsu'vi:dər] *adv*: **etw ist jdm ~** sb loathes sth, sb finds sth repugnant ▷ *präp +dat* contrary to; **zuwiderhandeln** *vi +dat* to act contrary to; **einem Gesetz zuwiderhandeln** to contravene a law; **Zuwiderhandlung** *f* contravention; **zuwiderlaufen** *unreg vi*: **einer Sache** *dat* **zuwiderlaufen** to run counter to sth

zuz. *abk* = **zuzüglich**

zuzahlen ['tsu:tsa:lən] *vt*: **10 Euro ~** to pay another 10 euros

zuziehen ['tsu:tsi:ən] *unreg vt* (*schließen*: *Vorhang*) to draw, close; (*herbeirufen*: *Experten*) to call in ▷ *vi* to move in, come; **sich** *dat* **etw ~** (*Krankheit*) to catch sth; (*Zorn*) to incur sth; **sich** *dat* **eine Verletzung ~** (*form*) to sustain an injury

Zuzug ['tsu:tsuk] **(-(e)s)** *m* (*Zustrom*) influx; (*von Familie etc*): **~ nach** move to

zuzüglich ['tsu:tsy:klıç] *präp +gen* plus, with the addition of

zuzwinkern ['tsu:tsvınkərn] *vi*: **jdm ~** to wink at sb

ZVS *f abk* (*= Zentralstelle für die Vergabe von Studienplätzen*) *central body organizing the granting of places at university*

Zwang (-(e)s, ¨-e) *m* compulsion; (*Gewalt*) coercion; **gesellschaftliche Zwänge** social constraints; **tu dir keinen ~ an** don't feel you have to be polite

zwang *etc* [tsvaŋ] *vb siehe* **zwingen**

zwängen ['tsvɛŋən] *vt, vr* to squeeze

Zwang- *zW*: **zwanghaft** *adj* compulsive; **zwanglos** *adj* informal; **Zwanglosigkeit** *f* informality

Zwangs- *zW*: **Zwangsabgabe** *f* (*Comm*) compulsory levy; **Zwangsarbeit** *f* forced labour (*Brit*) *od* labor (*US*); **Zwangsernährung** *f* force-feeding; **Zwangsjacke** *f* straitjacket; **Zwangslage** *f* predicament, tight corner; **zwangsläufig** *adj* inevitable; **Zwangsmaßnahme** *f* compulsory measure; (*Pol*) sanction; **Zwangsvollstreckung** *f* execution; **Zwangsvorstellung** *f* (*Psych*) obsession; **zwangsweise** *adv* compulsorily

zwanzig ['tsvantsıç] *num* twenty

zwanzigste, r, s *adj* twentieth

zwar [tsva:r] *adv* to be sure, indeed; **das ist ~ ..., aber ...** that may be ... but ...; **und ~** in fact, actually; **und ~ am Sonntag** on Sunday to be precise; **und ~ so schnell, dass ...** in fact so quickly that ...

Zweck [tsvɛk] **(-(e)s, -e)** *m* purpose, aim; **es hat keinen ~, darüber zu reden** there is no point (in) talking about it; **zweckdienlich** *adj* practical; (*nützlich*) useful; **zweckdienliche Hinweise** (any) relevant information

Zwecke (-, -n) *f* hobnail; (*Heftzwecke*) drawing pin (*Brit*), thumbtack (*US*)

Zweck- *zW*: **zweckentfremden** *vt untr* to use for another purpose; **Zweckentfremdung** *f* misuse; **zweckfrei** *adj* (*Forschung etc*) pure; **zwecklos** *adj* pointless; **zweckmäßig** *adj*

suitable, appropriate; **Zweckmäßigkeit** *f* suitability
zwecks *präp+gen* (*form*) for (the purpose of)
zweckwidrig *adj* unsuitable
zwei [tsvaɪ] *num* two; **Zweibettzimmer** *nt* twin-bedded room; **zweideutig** *adj* ambiguous; (*unanständig*) suggestive; **Zweidrittelmehrheit** *f* (*Parl*) two-thirds majority; **zweieiig** *adj* (*Zwillinge*) non-identical
zweierlei ['tsvaɪər'laɪ] *adj* two kinds *od* sorts of; **~ Stoff** two different kinds of material; **~ zu tun haben** to have two different things to do
zweifach *adj* double
Zweifel ['tsvaɪfəl] (**-s, -**) *m* doubt; **ich bin mir darüber im ~** I'm in two minds about it; **zweifelhaft** *adj* doubtful, dubious; **zweifellos** *adj* doubtless
zweifeln *vi*: **(an etw** *dat***) ~** to doubt (sth)
Zweifelsfall *m*: **im ~** in case of doubt
Zweifrontenkrieg *m* war(fare) on two fronts
Zweig [tsvaɪk] (**-(e)s, -e**) *m* branch; **Zweiggeschäft** *nt* (*Comm*) branch
zweigleisig ['tsvaɪglaɪzɪç] *adj*: **~ argumentieren** to argue along two different lines
Zweigstelle *f* branch (office)
zwei- *zW*: **zweihändig** *adj* two-handed; (*Mus*) for two hands; **Zweiheit** *f* duality; **zweihundert** *num* two hundred; **Zweikampf** *m* duel; **zweimal** *adv* twice; **das lasse ich mir nicht zweimal sagen** I don't have to be told twice; **zweimotorig** *adj* twin-engined; **zweireihig** *adj* (*Anzug*) double-breasted; **Zweisamkeit** *f* togetherness; **zweischneidig** *adj* (*fig*) double-edged; **Zweisitzer** (**-s, -**) *m* two-seater; **zweisprachig** *adj* bilingual; **Zweispurgerät, Zweispurtonbandgerät** *nt* twin-track (tape) recorder; **zweispurig** *adj* (*Aut*) two-lane; **zweistellig** *adj* (*Zahl*) two-digit *attrib*, with two digits; **zweistimmig** *adj* for two voices
zweit [tsvaɪt] *adv*: **zu ~** (*in Paaren*) in twos
Zweitaktmotor *m* two-stroke engine
zweitbeste, r, s *adj* second best
zweite, r, s *adj* second; **Bürger ~r Klasse** second-class citizen(s *pl*)
zweiteilig ['tsvaɪtaɪlɪç] *adj* (*Buch, Film etc*) in two parts; (*Kleidung*) two-piece
zweitens *adv* secondly
zweit- *zW*: **zweitgrößte, r, s** *adj* second largest; **zweitklassig** *adj* second-class; **zweitletzte, r, s** *adj* last but one, penultimate; **zweitrangig** *adj* second-rate; **Zweitschlüssel** *m* duplicate key; **Zweitstimme** *f* second vote; *siehe auch* **Erststimme**
zweitürig ['tsvaɪtyrɪç] *adj* two-door
Zweitwagen *m* second car
Zweitwohnung *f* second home
zweizeilig *adj* two-lined; (*Typ: Abstand*) double-spaced
Zweizimmerwohnung *f* two-room(ed) flat (*Brit*) *od* apartment (*US*)
Zwerchfell ['tsvɛrçfɛl] *nt* diaphragm
Zwerg, in [tsvɛrk, 'tsvɛrgɪn] (**-(e)s, -e**) *m(f)* dwarf; (*fig: Knirps*) midget; **Zwergschule** (*umg*) *f* village school
Zwetsche ['tsvɛtʃə], **Zwetschge** ['tsvɛtʃgə] (**-, -n**) *f* plum
Zwickel ['tsvɪkəl] (**-s, -**) *m* gusset
zwicken ['tsvɪkən] *vt* to pinch, nip
Zwickmühle ['tsvɪkmy:lə] *f*: **in der ~ sitzen** (*fig*) to be in a dilemma
Zwieback ['tsvi:bak] (**-(e)s, -e** *od* **-bäcke**) *m* rusk
Zwiebel ['tsvi:bəl] (**-, -n**) *f* onion; (*Blumenzwiebel*) bulb; **zwiebelartig** *adj* bulbous; **Zwiebelturm** *m* (tower with an) onion dome
Zwie- *zW*: **Zwiegespräch** *nt* dialogue (*Brit*), dialog (*US*); **Zwielicht** *nt* twilight; **ins Zwielicht geraten sein** (*fig*) to appear in an unfavourable (*Brit*) *od* unfavorable (*US*) light; **zwielichtig** *adj* shady, dubious; **Zwiespalt** *m* conflict; (*zwischen Menschen*) rift, gulf; **zwiespältig** *adj* (*Gefühle*) conflicting; (*Charakter*) contradictory; **Zwietracht** *f* discord, dissension
Zwilling ['tsvɪlɪŋ] (**-s, -e**) *m* twin; **Zwillinge** *pl* (*Astrol*) Gemini
zwingen ['tsvɪŋən] *unreg vt* to force
zwingend *adj* (*Grund etc*) compelling; (*logisch notwendig*) necessary; (*Schluss, Beweis*) conclusive
Zwinger (**-s, -**) *m* (*Käfig*) cage; (*Hundezwinger*) run
zwinkern ['tsvɪŋkərn] *vi* to blink; (*absichtlich*) to wink
Zwirn [tsvɪrn] (**-(e)s, -e**) *m* thread
zwischen ['tsvɪʃən] *präp* (*+akk od dat*) between; (*bei mehreren*) among; **Zwischenaufenthalt** *m* stopover; **Zwischenbemerkung** *f* (incidental) remark; **Zwischenbilanz** *f* (*Comm*) interim balance; **zwischenblenden** *vt* (*Film, Rundf, TV*) to insert; **Zwischending** *nt* cross; **Zwischendividende** *f* interim dividend; **zwischendurch** *adv* in between; (*räumlich*) here and there; **Zwischenergebnis** *nt* intermediate result; **Zwischenfall** *m* incident; **Zwischenfrage** *f* question; **Zwischengröße** *f* in-between size; **Zwischenhandel** *m* wholesaling; **Zwischenhändler** *m* middleman, agent; **Zwischenlagerung** *f* temporary storage; **Zwischenlandung** *f* (*Aviat*) stopover; **Zwischenlösung** *f* temporary solution; **zwischenmahlzeit** *f* snack (*between meals*); **zwischenmenschlich** *adj* interpersonal; **Zwischenprüfung** *f* intermediate examination; **Zwischenraum** *m* gap, space; **Zwischenruf** *m* interjection, interruption; **Zwischenrufe** *pl* heckling *sing*; **Zwischensaison** *f* low season; **Zwischenspiel** *nt* (*Theat, fig*) interlude; (*Mus*) intermezzo; **zwischenstaatlich** *adj* interstate; (*international*) international; **Zwischenstation** *f* intermediate station; **Zwischenstecker** *m* (*Elek*) adapter; **Zwischenstück** *nt* connecting piece; **Zwischensumme** *f* subtotal; **Zwischenwand** *f* partition; **Zwischenzeit** *f* interval; **in der Zwischenzeit** in the interim,

meanwhile; **Zwischenzeugnis** *nt* (*Sch*) interim report
Zwist [tsvɪst] (**-es, -e**) *m* dispute
zwitschern ['tsvɪtʃərn] *vt, vi* to twitter, chirp; **einen ~** (*umg*) to have a drink
Zwitter ['tsvɪtər] (**-s, -**) *m* hermaphrodite
zwo [tsvo:] *num* (*Tel, Mil*) two
zwölf [tsvœlf] *num* twelve; **fünf Minuten vor ~** (*fig*) at the eleventh hour
Zwölffingerdarm (**-(e)s**) *m* duodenum
Zyankali [tsya:n'ka:li] (**-s**) *nt* (*Chem*) potassium cyanide
Zyklon [tsy'klo:n] (**-s, -e**) *m* cyclone
Zyklus ['tsy:klʊs] (**-, Zyklen**) *m* cycle
Zylinder [tsi'lɪndər] (**-s, -**) *m* cylinder; (*Hut*) top hat; **zylinderförmig** *adj* cylindrical
Zyniker, in ['tsy:nikər(ɪn)] (**-s, -**) *m(f)* cynic
zynisch ['tsy:nɪʃ] *adj* cynical
Zynismus [tsy'nɪsmʊs] *m* cynicism
Zypern ['tsy:pərn] (**-s**) *nt* Cyprus
Zypresse [tsy'prɛsə] (**-, -n**) *f* (*Bot*) cypress
Zypriot, in [tsypri'o:t(ɪn)] (**-en, -en**) *m(f)* Cypriot
zypriotisch *adj* Cypriot, Cyprian
zyprisch ['tsy:prɪʃ] *adj* Cypriot, Cyprian
Zyste ['tsʏstə] (**-, -n**) *f* cyst
zz., zzt. *abk* = **zurzeit**
z. Z., z. Zt. *abk* = **zur Zeit**

English–German
Englisch–Deutsch

Aa

A¹, a [eɪ] *n* (*letter*) A *nt*, a *nt*; (*Scol*) ≈ Eins *f*, sehr gut *nt*; **A for Andrew, A for Able** (*US*) ≈ A wie Anton; **A road** (*Brit: Aut*) Hauptverkehrsstraße *f*; **A shares** (*Brit: Stock Exchange*) stimmrechtslose Aktien *pl*
A² [eɪ] *n* (*Mus*) A *nt*, a *nt*

KEYWORD

a [ə] (*before vowel and silent h:* **an**) *indef art* **1** ein; (*before feminine noun*) eine; **a book** ein Buch; **a lamp** eine Lampe; **she's a doctor** sie ist Ärztin; **I haven't got a car** ich habe kein Auto; **a hundred/thousand** *etc* **pounds** einhundert/eintausend *etc* Pfund
2 (*in expressing ratios, prices etc*) pro; **3 a day/week** 3 pro Tag/Woche, 3 am Tag/in der Woche; **10 km an hour** 10 km pro Stunde

A2 (*Brit*) *n* (*Scol*) *Mit "A2" wird das zweite Jahr der britischen Sekundarstufe II bezeichnet, in dem die übrigen drei Wahlpflichtfächer unterrichtet und am Ende des Schuljahres geprüft werden. Die Note für den "A level" setzt sich aus den Noten der Jahre "AS" und "A2" zusammen*
AA *n abbr* (*Brit: = Automobile Association*) *Autofahrerorganisation*, ≈ ADAC *m*; (*US: = Associate in Art*) *akademischer Grad für Geisteswissenschaftler*; (*= Alcoholics Anonymous*) Anonyme Alkoholiker *pl*, AA *pl*
AAA *n abbr* (*= American Automobile Association*) *Autofahrerorganisation*, ≈ ADAC *m*; (*Brit: = Amateur Athletics Association*) *Leichtathletikverband der Amateure*
A&E *n abbr* (*= Accident and Emergency*): ~ **department** Notfallstation *f*, Notaufnahme *f*
abaci ['æbəsaɪ] *npl of* **abacus**
aback [ə'bæk] *adv*: **to be taken ~** verblüfft sein
abacus ['æbəkəs] (*pl* **abaci**) *n* Abakus *m*
abandon [ə'bændən] *vt* verlassen; (*child*) aussetzen; (*give up*) aufgeben ▷ *n* (*wild behaviour*): **with ~** selbstvergessen; **to ~ ship** das Schiff verlassen
abandoned [ə'bændənd] *adj* verlassen; (*child*) ausgesetzt; (*unrestrained*) selbstvergessen
abase [ə'beɪs] *vt*: **to ~ o.s.** sich erniedrigen; **to ~ o.s. so far as to do sth** sich dazu erniedrigen, etw zu tun
abashed [ə'bæʃt] *adj* verlegen
abate [ə'beɪt] *vi* nachlassen, sich legen
abatement [ə'beɪtmənt] *n*: **noise ~ society** Gesellschaft *f* zur Lärmbekämpfung
abattoir ['æbətwɑːʳ] (*Brit*) *n* Schlachthof *m*
abbey ['æbɪ] *n* Abtei *f*
abbot ['æbət] *n* Abt *m*
abbreviate [ə'briːvɪeɪt] *vt* abkürzen; (*essay etc*) kürzen
abbreviation [əbriːvɪ'eɪʃən] *n* Abkürzung *f*
ABC *n abbr* (*= American Broadcasting Companies*) *Fernsehsender*
abdicate ['æbdɪkeɪt] *vt* verzichten auf +*acc* ▷ *vi* (*monarch*) abdanken
abdication [æbdɪ'keɪʃən] *n* (*see vb*) Verzicht *m*; Abdankung *f*
abdomen ['æbdəmɛn] *n* Unterleib *m*
abdominal [æb'dɔmɪnl] *adj* (*pain etc*) Unterleibs-
abduct [æb'dʌkt] *vt* entführen
abduction [æb'dʌkʃən] *n* Entführung *f*
Aberdonian [æbə'dəunɪən] *adj* (*Geog*) Aberdeener *inv* ▷ *n* Aberdeener(in) *m(f)*
aberration [æbə'reɪʃən] *n* Anomalie *f*; **in a moment of mental ~** in einem Augenblick geistiger Verwirrung
abet [ə'bɛt] *vt see* **aid**
abeyance [ə'beɪəns] *n*: **in ~** (*law*) außer Kraft; (*matter*) ruhend
abhor [əb'hɔːʳ] *vt* verabscheuen
abhorrent [əb'hɔrənt] *adj* abscheulich
abide [ə'baɪd] *vt*: **I can't ~ it/him** ich kann es/ihn nicht ausstehen
▸ **abide by** *vt fus* sich halten an +*acc*
abiding [ə'baɪdɪŋ] *adj* (*memory, impression*) bleibend
ability [ə'bɪlɪtɪ] *n* Fähigkeit *f*; **to the best of my ~** so gut ich es kann
abject ['æbdʒɛkt] *adj* (*poverty*) bitter; (*apology*) demütig; (*coward*) erbärmlich
ablaze [ə'bleɪz] *adj* in Flammen; **~ with light** hell erleuchtet
able ['eɪbl] *adj* fähig; **to be ~ to do sth** etw tun können
able-bodied ['eɪbl'bɔdɪd] *adj* kräftig; **~ seaman** (*Brit*) Vollmatrose *m*

ablutions [ə'blu:ʃənz] *npl* Waschungen *pl*
ably ['eɪblɪ] *adv* gekonnt
ABM *n abbr (= antiballistic missile)* Anti-Raketen-Rakete *f*
abnormal [æb'nɔ:məl] *adj* abnorm; (*child*) anormal
abnormality [æbnɔ:'mælɪtɪ] *n* Abnormität *f*
aboard [ə'bɔ:d] *adv* (*Naut, Aviat*) an Bord ▷ *prep* an Bord *+gen*; **~ the train/bus** im Zug/Bus
abode [ə'bəud] *n* (*Law*): **of no fixed ~** ohne festen Wohnsitz
abolish [ə'bɔlɪʃ] *vt* abschaffen
abolition [æbə'lɪʃən] *n* Abschaffung *f*
abominable [ə'bɔmɪnəbl] *adj* scheußlich
abominably [ə'bɔmɪnəblɪ] *adv* scheußlich
Aborigine [æbə'rɪdʒɪnɪ] *n* Ureinwohner(in) *m(f)* Australiens
abort [ə'bɔ:t] *vt* abtreiben; (*Med: miscarry*) fehlgebären; (*Comput*) abbrechen
abortion [ə'bɔ:ʃən] *n* Abtreibung *f*; (*miscarriage*) Fehlgeburt *f*; **to have an ~** abtreiben lassen
abortionist [ə'bɔ:ʃənɪst] *n* Abtreibungshelfer(in) *m(f)*
abortive [ə'bɔ:tɪv] *adj* misslungen
abound [ə'baund] *vi* im Überfluss vorhanden sein; **to ~ in** *or* **with** reich sein an *+dat*

KEYWORD

about [ə'baut] *adv* **1** (*approximately*) etwa, ungefähr; **about a hundred/thousand** *etc* etwa hundert/tausend *etc*; **at about two o'clock** etwa um zwei Uhr; **I've just about finished** ich bin gerade fertig
2 (*referring to place*) herum; **to run/walk** *etc* **about** herumlaufen/-gehen *etc*; **is Paul about?** ist Paul da?
3: to be about to do sth im Begriff sein, etw zu tun; **he was about to cry** er fing fast an zu weinen; **she was about to leave/wash the dishes** sie wollte gerade gehen/das Geschirr spülen
▷ *prep* **1** (*relating to*) über *+acc*; **what is it about?** worum geht es?; (*book etc*) wovon handelt es?; **we talked about it** wir haben darüber geredet; **what** *or* **how about going to the cinema?** wollen wir ins Kino gehen?
2 (*referring to place*) um ... herum; **to walk about the town** durch die Stadt gehen; **her clothes were scattered about the room** ihre Kleider waren über das ganze Zimmer verstreut

about-face [ə'baut'feɪs] (*US*) *n* = **about-turn**
about-turn [ə'baut'tə:n] (*Brit*) *n* Kehrtwendung *f*
above [ə'bʌv] *adv* oben; (*greater, more*) darüber ▷ *prep* über *+dat*; **to cost ~ £10** mehr als £10 kosten; **mentioned ~** oben genannt; **he's not ~ a bit of blackmail** er ist sich *dat* nicht zu gut für eine kleine Erpressung; **~ all** vor allem
above board *adj* korrekt
abrasion [ə'breɪʒən] *n* Abschürfung *f*
abrasive [ə'breɪzɪv] *adj* (*substance*) Scheuer-; (*person, manner*) aggressiv
abreast [ə'brɛst] *adv* nebeneinander; **three ~** zu dritt nebeneinander; **to keep ~ of** (*fig*) auf dem Laufenden bleiben mit
abridge [ə'brɪdʒ] *vt* kürzen
abroad [ə'brɔ:d] *adv* (*be*) im Ausland; (*go*) ins Ausland; **there is a rumour ~ that ...** (*fig*) ein Gerücht geht um *or* kursiert, dass ...
abrupt [ə'brʌpt] *adj* abrupt; (*person, behaviour*) schroff
abruptly [ə'brʌptlɪ] *adv* abrupt
abscess ['æbsɪs] *n* Abszess *m*
abscond [əb'skɔnd] *vi*: **to ~ with** sich davonmachen mit; **to ~ (from)** fliehen (aus)
abseil ['æbseɪl] *vi* sich abseilen
absence ['æbsəns] *n* Abwesenheit *f*; **in the ~ of** (*person*) in Abwesenheit *+gen*; (*thing*) in Ermangelung *+gen*
absent ['æbsənt] *adj* abwesend, nicht da ▷ *vt*: **to ~ o.s. from** fernbleiben *+dat*; **to be ~** fehlen; **to be ~ without leave** (*Mil*) sich unerlaubt von der Truppe entfernen
absentee [æbsən'ti:] *n* Abwesende(r) *f(m)*
absenteeism [æbsən'ti:ɪzəm] *n* (*from school*) Schwänzen *nt*; (*from work*) Nichterscheinen *nt* am Arbeitsplatz
absent-minded ['æbsənt'maɪndɪd] *adj* zerstreut
absent-mindedly ['æbsənt'maɪndɪdlɪ] *adv* zerstreut; (*look*) abwesend
absent-mindedness ['æbsənt'maɪndɪdnɪs] *n* Zerstreutheit *f*
absolute ['æbsəlu:t] *adj* absolut; (*power*) uneingeschränkt
absolutely [æbsə'lu:tlɪ] *adv* absolut; (*agree*) vollkommen; **~!** genau!
absolution [æbsə'lu:ʃən] *n* Lossprechung *f*
absolve [əb'zɔlv] *vt*: **to ~ sb (from)** jdn lossprechen (von); (*responsibility*) jdn entbinden (von)
absorb [əb'zɔ:b] *vt* aufnehmen (*also fig*); (*light, heat*) absorbieren; (*group, business*) übernehmen; **to be ~ed in a book** in ein Buch vertieft sein
absorbent [əb'zɔ:bənt] *adj* saugfähig
absorbent cotton (*US*) *n* Watte *f*
absorbing [əb'zɔ:bɪŋ] *adj* saugfähig; (*book, film, work etc*) fesselnd
absorption [əb'sɔ:pʃən] *n* (*see vb*) Aufnahme *f*; Absorption *f*; Übernahme *f*; (*interest*) Faszination *f*
abstain [əb'steɪn] *vi* (*voting*) sich (der Stimme) enthalten; **to ~ (from)** (*eating, drinking etc*) sich enthalten (*+gen*)
abstemious [əb'sti:mɪəs] *adj* enthaltsam
abstention [əb'stɛnʃən] *n* (Stimm)enthaltung *f*
abstinence ['æbstɪnəns] *n* Enthaltsamkeit *f*
abstract ['æbstrækt] *adj* abstrakt ▷ *n* (*summary*) Zusammenfassung *f* ▷ *vt*: **to ~ sth (from)** (*summarize*) etw entnehmen (aus); (*remove*) etw entfernen (aus)

abstruse [æb'stru:s] *adj* abstrus
absurd [əb'sə:d] *adj* absurd
absurdity [əb'sə:dɪtɪ] *n* Absurdität *f*
ABTA ['æbtə] *n abbr (= Association of British Travel Agents) Verband der Reiseveranstalter*
Abu Dhabi ['æbu:'dɑ:bɪ] *n (Geog)* Abu Dhabi *nt*
abundance [ə'bʌndəns] *n* Reichtum *m*; **an ~ of** eine Fülle von; **in ~** in Hülle und Fülle
abundant [ə'bʌndənt] *adj* reichlich
abundantly [ə'bʌndəntlɪ] *adv* reichlich; **~ clear** völlig klar
abuse [ə'bju:s] *n (insults)* Beschimpfungen *pl*; *(ill-treatment)* Misshandlung *f*; *(misuse)* Missbrauch *m* ▷ *vt (see n)* beschimpfen; misshandeln; missbrauchen; **to be open to ~** sich leicht missbrauchen lassen
abuser [ə'bju:zə^r] *n (also:* **drug abuser***) jd, der Drogen missbraucht; (also:* **child abuser***) jd, der Kinder missbraucht oder misshandelt*
abusive [ə'bju:sɪv] *adj* beleidigend
abysmal [ə'bɪzməl] *adj* entsetzlich; *(ignorance etc)* grenzenlos
abysmally [ə'bɪzməlɪ] *adv (see adj)* entsetzlich; grenzenlos
abyss [ə'bɪs] *n* Abgrund *m*
AC *abbr* = **alternating current**; *(US: = athletic club)* ≈ SV *m*
a/c *abbr (Banking etc)* = **account**; *(= current account)* Girokonto *nt*
academic [ækə'dɛmɪk] *adj* akademisch *(also pej)*; *(work)* wissenschaftlich; *(person)* intellektuell ▷ *n* Akademiker(in) *m(f)*
academic year *n (university year)* Universitätsjahr *nt*; *(school year)* Schuljahr *nt*
academy [ə'kædəmɪ] *n* Akademie *f*; *(school)* Hochschule *f*; **~ of music** Musikhochschule *f*; **military/naval ~** Militär-/Marineakademie *f*
ACAS ['eɪkæs] *(Brit) n abbr (= Advisory Conciliation and Arbitration Service) Schlichtungsstelle für Arbeitskonflikte*
accede [æk'si:d] *vi*: **to ~ to** zustimmen *+dat*
accelerate [æk'sɛləreɪt] *vt* beschleunigen ▷ *vi (Aut)* Gas geben
acceleration [æksɛlə'reɪʃən] *n* Beschleunigung *f*
accelerator [æk'sɛləreɪtə^r] *n* Gaspedal *nt*
accent ['æksɛnt] *n* Akzent *m*; *(fig: emphasis, stress)* Betonung *f*; **to speak with an Irish ~** mit einem irischen Akzent sprechen; **to have a strong ~** einen starken Akzent haben
accentuate [æk'sɛntjueɪt] *vt* betonen; *(need, difference etc)* hervorheben
accept [ək'sɛpt] *vt* annehmen; *(fact, situation)* sich abfinden mit; *(risk)* in Kauf nehmen; *(responsibility)* übernehmen; *(blame)* auf sich *acc* nehmen
acceptable [ək'sɛptəbl] *adj* annehmbar
acceptance [ək'sɛptəns] *n* Annahme *f*; **to meet with general ~** allgemeine Anerkennung finden
access ['æksɛs] *n* Zugang *m* ▷ *vt (Comput)* zugreifen auf *+dat*; **the burglars gained ~ through a window** die Einbrecher gelangten durch ein Fenster hinein
accessible [æk'sɛsəbl] *adj* erreichbar; *(knowledge, art etc)* zugänglich
accession [æk'sɛʃən] *n* Antritt *m*; *(of monarch)* Thronbesteigung *f*; *(to library)* Neuanschaffung *f*
accessory [æk'sɛsərɪ] *n* Zubehörteil *nt*; *(Dress)* Accessoire *nt*; *(Law)*: **~ to** Mitschuldige(r) *f(m)* an *+dat*; **accessories** *npl* Zubehör *nt*; **toilet accessories** *(Brit)* Toilettenartikel *pl*
access road *n* Zufahrt(sstraße) *f*
access time *n (Comput)* Zugriffszeit *f*
accident ['æksɪdənt] *n* Zufall *m*; *(mishap, disaster)* Unfall *m*; **to meet with** *or* **to have an ~** einen Unfall haben, verunglücken; **~s at work** Arbeitsunfälle *pl*; **by ~** zufällig
accidental [æksɪ'dɛntl] *adj* zufällig; *(death, damage)* Unfall-
accidentally [æksɪ'dɛntəlɪ] *adv* zufällig
accident insurance *n* Unfallversicherung *f*
accident-prone ['æksɪdənt'prəun] *adj* vom Pech verfolgt
accident risk *n* Unfallrisiko *f*
acclaim [ə'kleɪm] *n* Beifall *m* ▷ *vt*: **to be ~ed for one's achievements** für seine Leistungen gefeiert werden
acclamation [æklə'meɪʃən] *n* Anerkennung *f*; *(applause)* Beifall *m*
acclimate [ə'klaɪmət] *(US) vt* = **acclimatize**
acclimatize [ə'klaɪmətaɪz], *(US)* **acclimate** *vt*: **to become ~d** sich akklimatisieren; **to become ~d to** sich gewöhnen an *+acc*
accolade ['ækəleɪd] *n (fig)* Auszeichnung *f*
accommodate [ə'kɔmədeɪt] *vt* unterbringen; *(subj: car, hotel etc)* Platz bieten *+dat*; *(oblige, help)* entgegenkommen *+dat*; **to ~ one's plans to** seine Pläne anpassen an *+acc*
accommodating [ə'kɔmədeɪtɪŋ] *adj* entgegenkommend
accommodation [əkɔmə'deɪʃən] *n* Unterkunft *f*; **accommodations** *(US) npl* Unterkunft *f*; **have you any ~?** haben Sie eine Unterkunft?; **"~ to let"** „Zimmer zu vermieten"; **they have ~ for 500** sie können 500 Personen unterbringen; **the hall has seating ~ for 600** *(Brit)* in dem Saal können 600 Personen sitzen
accompaniment [ə'kʌmpənɪmənt] *n* Begleitung *f*
accompanist [ə'kʌmpənɪst] *n* Begleiter(in) *m(f)*
accompany [ə'kʌmpənɪ] *vt* begleiten
accomplice [ə'kʌmplɪs] *n* Komplize *m*, Komplizin *f*
accomplish [ə'kʌmplɪʃ] *vt* vollenden; *(achieve)* erreichen
accomplished [ə'kʌmplɪʃt] *adj* ausgezeichnet
accomplishment [ə'kʌmplɪʃmənt] *n* Vollendung *f*; *(achievement)* Leistung *f*; *(skill: gen pl)* Fähigkeit *f*
accord [ə'kɔ:d] *n* Übereinstimmung *f*; *(treaty)* Vertrag *m* ▷ *vt* gewähren; **of his own ~** freiwillig; **with one ~** geschlossen; **to be in ~** übereinstimmen

accordance [əˈkɔːdəns] *n*: **in ~ with** in Übereinstimmung mit
according [əˈkɔːdɪŋ] *prep*: **~ to** zufolge *+dat*; **~ to plan** wie geplant
accordingly [əˈkɔːdɪŋlɪ] *adv* entsprechend; (*as a result*) folglich
accordion [əˈkɔːdɪən] *n* Akkordeon *nt*
accost [əˈkɔst] *vt* ansprechen
account [əˈkaunt] *n* (*Comm: bill*) Rechnung *f*; (*in bank, department store*) Konto *nt*; (*report*) Bericht *m*; **accounts** *npl* (*Comm*) Buchhaltung *f*; (*Bookkeeping*) (Geschäfts)bücher *pl*; **"~ payee only"** (*Brit*) „nur zur Verrechnung"; **to keep an ~ of** Buch führen über *+acc*; **to bring sb to ~ for sth/for having embezzled £50,000** jdn für etw/für die Unterschlagung von £50.000 zur Rechenschaft ziehen; **by all ~s** nach allem, was man hört; **of no ~** ohne Bedeutung; **on ~** auf Kredit; **to pay £5 on ~** eine Anzahlung von £5 leisten; **on no ~** auf keinen Fall; **on ~ of** wegen *+gen*; **to take into account, take ~ of** berücksichtigen
▸ **account for** *vt fus* erklären; (*expenditure*) Rechenschaft ablegen für; (*represent*) ausmachen; **all the children were ~ed for** man wusste, wo alle Kinder waren; **four people are still not ~ed for** vier Personen werden immer noch vermisst
accountability [əkauntəˈbɪlɪtɪ] *n* Verantwortlichkeit *f*
accountable [əˈkauntəbl] *adj*: **~ (to)** verantwortlich (gegenüber *+dat*); **to be held ~ for sth** für etw verantwortlich gemacht werden
accountancy [əˈkauntənsɪ] *n* Buchhaltung *f*
accountant [əˈkauntənt] *n* Buchhalter(in) *m(f)*
accounting [əˈkauntɪŋ] *n* Buchhaltung *f*
accounting period *n* Abrechnungszeitraum *m*
account number *n* Kontonummer *f*
accounts payable *npl* Verbindlichkeiten *pl*
accounts receivable *npl* Forderungen *pl*
accredited [əˈkrɛdɪtɪd] *adj* anerkannt
accretion [əˈkriːʃən] *n* Ablagerung *f*
accrue [əˈkruː] *vi* sich ansammeln; **to ~ to** zufließen *+dat*
accrued interest *n* aufgelaufene Zinsen *pl*
accumulate [əˈkjuːmjuleɪt] *vt* ansammeln ▹ *vi* sich ansammeln
accumulation [əkjuːmjuˈleɪʃən] *n* Ansammlung *f*
accuracy [ˈækjurəsɪ] *n* Genauigkeit *f*
accurate [ˈækjurɪt] *adj* genau
accurately [ˈækjurɪtlɪ] *adv* genau; (*answer*) richtig
accusation [ækjuˈzeɪʃən] *n* Vorwurf *m*; (*instance*) Beschuldigung *f*; (*Law*) Anklage *f*
accusative [əˈkjuːzətɪv] *n* Akkusativ *m*
accuse [əˈkjuːz] *vt*: **to ~ sb (of sth)** jdn (einer Sache *gen*) beschuldigen; (*Law*) jdn (wegen etw *dat*) anklagen
accused [əˈkjuːzd] *n* (*Law*): **the ~** der/die Angeklagte
accuser [əˈkjuːzə^r] *n* Ankläger(in) *m(f)*
accusing [əˈkjuːzɪŋ] *adj* anklagend
accustom [əˈkʌstəm] *vt* gewöhnen; **to ~ o.s. to sth** sich an etw *acc* gewöhnen
accustomed [əˈkʌstəmd] *adj* gewohnt; (*in the habit*): **~ to** gewohnt an *+acc*
AC/DC *abbr* (= *alternating current/direct current*) WS/GS
ACE [eɪs] *n abbr* (= *American Council on Education*) *akademischer Verband für das Erziehungswesen*
ace [eɪs] *n* As *nt*
acerbic [əˈsəːbɪk] *adj* scharf
acetate [ˈæsɪteɪt] *n* Acetat *nt*
ache [eɪk] *n* Schmerz *m* ▹ *vi* schmerzen, wehtun; (*yearn*): **to ~ to do sth** sich danach sehnen, etw zu tun; **I've got (a) stomach ~** ich habe Magenschmerzen; **I'm aching all over** mir tut alles weh; **my head ~s** mir tut der Kopf weh
achieve [əˈtʃiːv] *vt* (*aim, result*) erreichen; (*success*) erzielen; (*victory*) erringen
achievement [əˈtʃiːvmənt] *n* (*act of achieving*) Erreichen *nt*; (*success, feat*) Leistung *f*
Achilles heel [əˈkɪliːz-] *n* Achillesferse *f*
acid [ˈæsɪd] *adj* sauer ▹ *n* (*Chem*) Säure *f*; (*inf: LSD*) Acid *nt*
Acid House *n* Acid House *nt, elektronische Funk-Diskomusik*
acidic [əˈsɪdɪk] *adj* sauer
acidity [əˈsɪdɪtɪ] *n* Säure *f*
acid rain *n* saurer Regen *m*
acid test *n* (*fig*) Feuerprobe *f*
acknowledge [əkˈnɔlɪdʒ] *vt* (*also*: **acknowledge receipt of**) den Empfang *+gen* bestätigen; (*fact*) zugeben; (*situation*) zur Kenntnis nehmen; (*person*) grüßen
acknowledgement [əkˈnɔlɪdʒmənt] *n* Empfangsbestätigung *f*; **acknowledgements** *npl* (*in book*) ≈ Danksagung *f*
ACLU *n abbr* (= *American Civil Liberties Union*) *Bürgerrechtsverband*
acme [ˈækmɪ] *n* Gipfel *m*, Höhepunkt *m*
acne [ˈæknɪ] *n* Akne *f*
acorn [ˈeɪkɔːn] *n* Eichel *f*
acoustic [əˈkuːstɪk] *adj* akustisch
acoustic coupler *n* (*Comput*) Akustikkoppler *m*
acoustics [əˈkuːstɪks] *n* Akustik *f*
acoustic screen *n* Trennwand *f* zur Schalldämpfung
acquaint [əˈkweɪnt] *vt*: **to ~ sb with sth** jdn mit etw vertraut machen; **to be ~ed with** (*person*) bekannt sein mit; (*fact*) vertraut sein mit
acquaintance [əˈkweɪntəns] *n* Bekannte(r) *f(m)*; (*with person*) Bekanntschaft *f*; (*with subject*) Kenntnis *f*; **to make sb's ~** jds Bekanntschaft machen
acquiesce [ækwɪˈɛs] *vi* einwilligen; **to ~ (to)** (*demand, arrangement, request*) einwilligen (in *+acc*)
acquire [əˈkwaɪə^r] *vt* erwerben; (*interest*) entwickeln; (*habit*) annehmen
acquired [əˈkwaɪəd] *adj* erworben; **whisky is an ~ taste** man muss sich an Whisky erst

gewöhnen

acquisition [ækwɪ'zɪʃən] *n* (*see vb*) Erwerb *m*, Entwicklung *f*, Annahme *f*; (*thing acquired*) Errungenschaft *f*

acquisitive [ə'kwɪzɪtɪv] *adj* habgierig; **the ~ society** die Erwerbsgesellschaft

acquit [ə'kwɪt] *vt* freisprechen; **to ~ o.s. well** seine Sache gut machen

acquittal [ə'kwɪtl] *n* Freispruch *m*

acre ['eɪkəʳ] *n* Morgen *m*

acreage ['eɪkərɪdʒ] *n* Fläche *f*

acrid ['ækrɪd] *adj* bitter; (*smoke: fig*) beißend

acrimonious [ækrɪ'məunɪəs] *adj* bitter; (*dispute*) erbittert

acrimony ['ækrɪmənɪ] *n* Erbitterung *f*

acrobat ['ækrəbæt] *n* Akrobat(in) *m(f)*

acrobatic [ækrə'bætɪk] *adj* akrobatisch

acrobatics [ækrə'bætɪks] *npl* Akrobatik *f*

acronym ['ækrənɪm] *n* Akronym *nt*

Acropolis [ə'krɔpəlɪs] *n*: **the ~** (*Geog*) die Akropolis

across [ə'krɔs] *prep* über *+acc*; (*on the other side of*) auf der anderen Seite *+gen* ▷ *adv* (*direction*) hinüber, herüber; (*measurement*) breit; **to take sb ~ the road** jdn über die Straße bringen; **a road ~ the wood** eine Straße durch den Wald; **the lake is 12 km ~** der See ist 12 km breit; **~ from** gegenüber *+dat*; **to get sth ~ (to sb)** (jdm) etw klarmachen

acrylic [ə'krɪlɪk] *adj* (*acid, paint, blanket*) Acryl- ▷ *n* Acryl *nt*; **acrylics** *npl*: **he paints in ~s** er malt mit Acrylfarbe

ACT® *n abbr* (*= American College Test*) *Eignungstest für Studienbewerber*

act [ækt] *n* Tat *f*; (*of play*) Akt *m*; (*in a show etc*) Nummer *f*; (*Law*) Gesetz *nt* ▷ *vi* handeln; (*behave*) sich verhalten; (*have effect*) wirken; (*Theat*) spielen ▷ *vt* spielen; **it's only an ~** es ist nur Schau; **~ of God** (*Law*) höhere Gewalt *f*; **to be in the ~ of doing sth** dabei sein, etw zu tun; **to catch sb in the ~** jdn auf frischer Tat ertappen; **to ~ the fool** (*Brit*) herumalbern; **he is only ~ing** er tut (doch) nur so; **to ~ as** fungieren als; **it ~s as a deterrent** es dient zur Abschreckung

▸ **act on** *vt*: **to ~ on sth** (*take action*) auf etw *+acc* hin handeln

▸ **act out** *vt* (*event*) durchspielen; (*fantasies*) zum Ausdruck bringen

acting ['æktɪŋ] *adj* stellvertretend ▷ *n* (*profession*) Schauspielkunst *f*; (*activity*) Spielen *nt*; **~ in my capacity as chairman ...** in meiner Eigenschaft als Vorsitzender ...

action ['ækʃən] *n* Tat *f*; (*motion*) Bewegung *f*; (*Mil*) Kampf *m*, Gefecht *nt*; (*Law*) Klage *f*; **to bring an ~ against sb** (*Law*) eine Klage gegen jdn anstrengen; **killed in ~** (*Mil*) gefallen; **out of ~** (*person*) nicht einsatzfähig; (*thing*) außer Betrieb; **to take ~** etwas unternehmen; **to put a plan into ~** einen Plan in die Tat umsetzen

action replay *n* (*TV*) Wiederholung *f*

activate ['æktɪveɪt] *vt* in Betrieb setzen; (*Chem, Phys*) aktivieren

active ['æktɪv] *adj* aktiv; (*volcano*) tätig; **to play an ~ part in sth** sich aktiv an etw *dat* beteiligen

active duty (*US*) *n* (*Mil*) Einsatz *m*

actively ['æktɪvlɪ] *adv* aktiv; (*dislike*) offen

active partner *n* (*Comm*) aktiver Teilhaber *m*

active service (*Brit*) *n* (*Mil*) Einsatz *m*

active suspension *n* (*Aut*) aktives *or* computergesteuertes Fahrwerk *nt*

activist ['æktɪvɪst] *n* Aktivist(in) *m(f)*

activity [æk'tɪvɪtɪ] *n* Aktivität *f*; (*pastime, pursuit*) Betätigung *f*

activity holiday *n* Aktivurlaub *m*

actor ['æktəʳ] *n* Schauspieler *m*

actress ['æktrɪs] *n* Schauspielerin *f*

actual ['æktjuəl] *adj* wirklich; (*emphatic use*) eigentlich

actually ['æktjuəlɪ] *adv* wirklich; (*in fact*) tatsächlich; (*even*) sogar

actuary ['æktjuərɪ] *n* Aktuar *m*

actuate ['æktjueɪt] *vt* auslösen

acuity [ə'kjuːɪtɪ] *n* Schärfe *f*

acumen ['ækjumən] *n* Scharfsinn *m*; **business ~** Geschäftssinn *m*

acupuncture ['ækjupʌŋktʃəʳ] *n* Akupunktur *f*

acute [ə'kjuːt] *adj* akut; (*anxiety*) heftig; (*mind*) scharf; (*person*) scharfsinnig; (*Math: angle*) spitz; (*Ling*): **~ accent** Akut *m*

AD *adv abbr* (*= Anno Domini*) n. Chr. ▷ *n abbr* (*US: Mil*) = **active duty**

ad [æd] (*inf*) *n* = **advertisement**

adage ['ædɪdʒ] *n* Sprichwort *nt*

adamant ['ædəmənt] *adj*: **to be ~ that ...** darauf bestehen, dass ...; **to be ~ about sth** auf etw *dat* bestehen

Adam's apple ['ædəmz-] *n* Adamsapfel *m*

adapt [ə'dæpt] *vt* anpassen; (*novel etc*) bearbeiten ▷ *vi*: **to ~ (to)** sich anpassen (an *+acc*)

adaptability [ədæptə'bɪlɪtɪ] *n* Anpassungsfähigkeit *f*

adaptable [ə'dæptəbl] *adj* anpassungsfähig; (*device*) vielseitig

adaptation [ædæp'teɪʃən] *n* (*of novel etc*) Bearbeitung *f*; (*of machine etc*) Umstellung *f*

adapter [ə'dæptəʳ] *n* (*Elec*) Adapter *m*; (*: for several plugs*) Mehrfachsteckdose *f*

adaptor [ə'dæptəʳ] *n* = **adapter**

ADC *n abbr* (*Mil*) = **aide-de-camp**; (*US: = Aid to Dependent Children*) *Beihilfe für sozialschwache Familien*

add [æd] *vt* hinzufügen; (*figures: also:* **add up**) zusammenzählen ▷ *vi*: **to ~ to** (*increase*) beitragen zu

▸ **add on** *vt* (*amount*) dazurechnen; (*room*) anbauen

▸ **add up** *vt* (*figures*) zusammenzählen ▷ *vi* (*fig*): **it doesn't ~ up** es ergibt keinen Sinn; **it doesn't ~ up to much** (*fig*) das ist nicht berühmt (*inf*)

addenda [ə'dɛndə] *npl of* **addendum**

addendum [ə'dɛndəm] (*pl* **addenda**) *n*

Nachtrag *m*

adder ['ædəʳ] *n* Kreuzotter *f*, Viper *f*

addict ['ædɪkt] *n* Süchtige(r) *f(m)*; (*enthusiast*) Anhänger(in) *m(f)*

addicted [ə'dɪktɪd] *adj*: **to be ~ to drugs/drink** drogensüchtig/alkoholsüchtig sein; **to be ~ to football** (*fig*) ohne Fußball nicht mehr leben können

addiction [ə'dɪkʃən] *n* Sucht *f*

addictive [ə'dɪktɪv] *adj*: **to be ~** (*drug*) süchtig machen; (*activity*) zur Sucht werden können

adding machine ['ædɪŋ-] *n* Addiermaschine *f*

Addis Ababa ['ædɪs'æbəbə] *n* (*Geog*) Addis Abeba *nt*

addition [ə'dɪʃən] *n* (*adding up*) Zusammenzählen *nt*; (*thing added*) Zusatz *m*; (*: to payment, bill*) Zuschlag *m*; (*: to building*) Anbau *m*; **in ~ (to)** zusätzlich (zu)

additional [ə'dɪʃənl] *adj* zusätzlich

additive ['ædɪtɪv] *n* Zusatz *m*

addled ['ædld] *adj* (*Brit: egg*) faul; (*brain*) verwirrt

address [ə'drɛs] *n* Adresse *f*; (*speech*) Ansprache *f* ▷ *vt* adressieren; (*speak to: person*) ansprechen; (*: audience*) sprechen zu; **form of ~** (Form *f* der) Anrede *f*; **what form of ~ do you use for ...?** wie redet man ... an?; **absolute/relative ~** (*Comput*) absolute/relative Adresse; **to ~ (o.s. to)** (*problem*) sich befassen mit

address book *n* Adressbuch *nt*

addressee [ædrɛ'si:] *n* Empfänger(in) *m(f)*

Aden ['eɪdən] *n* (*Geog*): **Gulf of ~** Golf *m* von Aden

adenoids ['ædɪnɔɪdz] *npl* Rachenmandeln *pl*

adept ['ædɛpt] *adj*: **to be ~ at** gut sein in *+dat*

adequacy ['ædɪkwəsɪ] *n* (*of resources*) Adäquatheit *f*; (*of performance, proposals etc*) Angemessenheit *f*

adequate ['ædɪkwɪt] *adj* ausreichend, adäquat; (*satisfactory*) angemessen

adequately ['ædɪkwɪtlɪ] *adv* ausreichend; (*satisfactorily*) zufriedenstellend

adhere [əd'hɪəʳ] *vi*: **to ~ to** haften an *+dat*; (*fig: abide by*) sich halten an *+acc*; (*: hold to*) festhalten an *+dat*

adhesion [əd'hi:ʒən] *n* Haften *nt*, Haftung *f*

adhesive [əd'hi:zɪv] *adj* klebend, Klebe- ▷ *n* Klebstoff *m*

adhesive tape *n* (*Brit*) Klebstreifen *m*; (*US: Med*) Heftpflaster *nt*

ad hoc [æd'hɔk] *adj* (*committee, decision*) Ad-hoc- ▷ *adv* ad hoc

ad infinitum ['ædɪnfɪ'naɪtəm] *adv* ad infinitum

adjacent [ə'dʒeɪsənt] *adj*: **~ to** neben *+dat*

adjective ['ædʒɛktɪv] *n* Adjektiv *nt*, Eigenschaftswort *nt*

adjoin [ə'dʒɔɪn] *vt*: **the hotel ~ing the station** das Hotel neben dem Bahnhof

adjoining [ə'dʒɔɪnɪŋ] *adj* benachbart, Neben-

adjourn [ə'dʒə:n] *vt* vertagen ▷ *vi* sich vertagen; **to ~ a meeting till the following week** eine Besprechung auf die nächste Woche vertagen; **they ~ed to the pub** (*Brit: inf*) sie begaben sich in die Kneipe

adjournment [ə'dʒə:nmənt] *n* Unterbrechung *f*

Adjt. *abbr* (*Mil*) = **adjutant**

adjudicate [ə'dʒu:dɪkeɪt] *vt* (*contest*) Preisrichter sein bei; (*claim*) entscheiden ▷ *vi* entscheiden; **to ~ on** urteilen bei *+dat*

adjudication [ədʒu:dɪ'keɪʃən] *n* Entscheidung *f*

adjudicator [ə'dju:dɪkeɪtəʳ] *n* Schiedsrichter(in) *m(f)*; (*in contest*) Preisrichter(in) *m(f)*

adjust [ə'dʒʌst] *vt* anpassen; (*change*) ändern; (*clothing*) zurechtrücken; (*machine etc*) einstellen; (*Insurance*) regulieren ▷ *vi*: **to ~ (to)** sich anpassen (an *+acc*)

adjustable [ə'dʒʌstəbl] *adj* verstellbar

adjuster [ə'dʒʌstəʳ] *n see* **loss**

adjustment [ə'dʒʌstmənt] *n* Anpassung *f*; (*to machine*) Einstellung *f*

adjutant ['ædʒətənt] *n* Adjutant *m*

ad-lib [æd'lɪb] *vi, vt* improvisieren ▷ *adv*: **ad lib** aus dem Stegreif

adman ['ædmæn] (*inf: irreg: like* **man**) *n* Werbefachmann *m*

admin ['ædmɪn] (*inf*) *n* = **administration**

administer [əd'mɪnɪstəʳ] *vt* (*country, department*) verwalten; (*justice*) sprechen; (*oath*) abnehmen; (*Med: drug*) verabreichen

administration [ədmɪnɪs'treɪʃən] *n* (*management*) Verwaltung *f*; (*government*) Regierung *f*; **the A~** (*US*) die Regierung

administrative [əd'mɪnɪstrətɪv] *adj* (*department, reform etc*) Verwaltungs-

administrator [əd'mɪnɪstreɪtəʳ] *n* Verwaltungsbeamte(r) *f(m)*

admirable ['ædmərəbl] *adj* bewundernswert

admiral ['ædmərəl] *n* Admiral *m*

Admiralty ['ædmərəltɪ] (*Brit*) *n*: **the ~** (*also*: **the Admiralty Board**) das Marineministerium

admiration [ædmə'reɪʃən] *n* Bewunderung *f*; **to have great ~ for sb/sth** jdn/etw sehr bewundern

admire [əd'maɪəʳ] *vt* bewundern

admirer [əd'maɪərəʳ] *n* (*suitor*) Verehrer *m*; (*fan*) Bewunderer *m*, Bewunderin *f*

admiring [əd'maɪərɪŋ] *adj* bewundernd

admissible [əd'mɪsəbl] *adj* (*evidence, as evidence*) zulässig

admission [əd'mɪʃən] *n* (*admittance*) Zutritt *m*; (*to exhibition, night club etc*) Einlass *m*; (*to club, hospital*) Aufnahme *f*; (*entry fee*) Eintritt(spreis) *m*; (*confession*) Geständnis *nt*; **"~ free", "free admission"** „Eintritt frei"; **by his own ~** nach eigenem Eingeständnis

admit [əd'mɪt] *vt* (*confess*) gestehen; (*permit to enter*) einlassen; (*to club, hospital*) aufnehmen; (*responsibility etc*) anerkennen; **"children not ~ted"** „kein Zutritt für Kinder"; **this ticket ~s two** diese Karte ist für zwei Personen; **I must ~ that ...** ich muss zugeben, dass ...; **to ~ defeat** sich geschlagen geben

▶ **admit of** *vt fus* (*interpretation etc*) erlauben

▸ **admit to** *vt fus* (*murder etc*) gestehen
admittance [əd'mɪtəns] *n* Zutritt *m*; **"no ~"** „kein Zutritt"
admittedly [əd'mɪtɪdlɪ] *adv* zugegebenermaßen
admonish [əd'mɔnɪʃ] *vt* ermahnen
ad nauseam [æd'nɔːsɪæm] *adv* (*talk*) endlos; (*repeat*) bis zum Gehtnichtmehr (*inf*)
ado [ə'duː] *n*: **without (any) more ~** ohne weitere Umstände
adolescence [ædəu'lɛsns] *n* Jugend *f*
adolescent [ædəu'lɛsnt] *adj* heranwachsend; (*remark, behaviour*) pubertär ▹ *n* Jugendliche(r) *f(m)*
adopt [ə'dɔpt] *vt* adoptieren; (*Pol: candidate*) aufstellen; (*policy, attitude, accent*) annehmen
adopted [ə'dɔptɪd] *adj* (*child*) adoptiert
adoption [ə'dɔpʃən] *n* (*see vb*) Adoption *f*; Aufstellung *f*; Annahme *f*
adoptive [ə'dɔptɪv] *adj* (*parents etc*) Adoptiv-; **~ country** Wahlheimat *f*
adorable [ə'dɔːrəbl] *adj* entzückend
adoration [ædə'reɪʃən] *n* Verehrung *f*
adore [ə'dɔːʳ] *vt* (*person*) verehren; (*film, activity etc*) schwärmen für
adoring [ə'dɔːrɪŋ] *adj* (*fans etc*) ihn/sie bewundernd; (*husband/wife*) sie/ihn innig liebend
adoringly [ə'dɔːrɪŋlɪ] *adv* bewundernd
adorn [ə'dɔːn] *vt* schmücken
adornment [ə'dɔːnmənt] *n* Schmuck *m*
ADP *n abbr* = **automatic data processing**
adrenalin [ə'drɛnəlɪn] *n* Adrenalin *nt*; **it gets the ~ going** das bringt einen in Fahrt
Adriatic [eɪdrɪ'ætɪk] *n*: **the ~ (Sea)** (*Geog*) die Adria, das Adriatische Meer
adrift [ə'drɪft] *adv* (*Naut*) treibend; (*fig*) ziellos; **to be ~** (*Naut*) treiben; **to come ~** (*boat*) sich losmachen; (*fastening etc*) sich lösen
adroit [ə'drɔɪt] *adj* gewandt
adroitly [ə'drɔɪtlɪ] *adv* gewandt
ADT (*US*) *abbr* (= *Atlantic Daylight Time*) *atlantische Sommerzeit*
adulation [ædju'leɪʃən] *n* Verherrlichung *f*
adult ['ædʌlt] *n* Erwachsene(r) *f(m)* ▹ *adj* erwachsen; (*animal*) ausgewachsen; (*literature etc*) für Erwachsene
adult education *n* Erwachsenenbildung *f*
adulterate [ə'dʌltəreɪt] *vt* verunreinigen; (*with water*) panschen
adulterer [ə'dʌltərəʳ] *n* Ehebrecher *m*
adulteress [ə'dʌltərɪs] *n* Ehebrecherin *f*
adultery [ə'dʌltərɪ] *n* Ehebruch *m*
adulthood ['ædʌlthud] *n* Erwachsenenalter *nt*
advance [əd'vɑːns] *n* (*movement*) Vorrücken *nt*; (*progress*) Fortschritt *m*; (*money*) Vorschuss *m* ▹ *vt* (*money*) vorschießen; (*theory, idea*) vorbringen ▹ *vi* (*move forward*) vorrücken; (*make progress*) Fortschritte machen ▹ *adj*: **~ booking** Vorverkauf *m*; **to make ~s (to sb)** Annäherungsversuche (bei jdm) machen; **in ~** im Voraus; **to give sb ~ notice** jdm frühzeitig Bescheid sagen; **to give sb ~ warning** jdn vorwarnen
advanced [əd'vɑːnst] *adj* (*Scol: studies*) für Fortgeschrittene; (*country*) fortgeschritten; (*child*) weit entwickelt; (*ideas*) fortschrittlich; **~ in years** in fortgeschrittenem Alter
Advanced Higher (*Scot*) *n* (*Scol*) *Mit "Advanced Higher" wird das Ausbildungsjahr nach "Higher" bezeichnet, dessen erfolgreicher Abschluss eine Hochschulzugangsberechtigung darstellt*
advancement [əd'vɑːnsmənt] *n* (*improvement*) Förderung *f*; (*in job, rank*) Aufstieg *m*
advantage [əd'vɑːntɪdʒ] *n* Vorteil *m*; **to take ~ of** ausnutzen; (*opportunity*) nutzen; **it's to our ~ (to)** es ist für uns von Vorteil(, wenn wir)
advantageous [ædvən'teɪdʒəs] *adj*: **~ (to)** vorteilhaft (für), von Vorteil (für)
advent ['ædvənt] *n* (*of innovation*) Aufkommen *nt*; (*Rel*): **A~** Advent *m*
Advent calendar *n* Adventskalender *m*
adventure [əd'vɛntʃəʳ] *n* Abenteuer *nt*
adventure playground *n* Abenteuerspielplatz *m*
adventurous [əd'vɛntʃərəs] *adj* abenteuerlustig; (*bold*) mutig
adverb ['ædvəːb] *n* Adverb *nt*
adversarial [ædvə'sɛərɪəl] *adj* konfliktreich
adversary ['ædvəsərɪ] *n* Widersacher(in) *m(f)*
adverse ['ædvəːs] *adj* ungünstig; **in ~ circumstances** unter widrigen Umständen; **~ to** ablehnend gegenüber *+dat*
adversity [əd'vəːsɪtɪ] *n* Widrigkeit *f*
advert ['ædvəːt] (*Brit*) *n* = **advertisement**
advertise ['ædvətaɪz] *vi* (*Comm*) werben; (*in newspaper*) annoncieren, inserieren ▹ *vt* (*product, event*) werben für; (*job*) ausschreiben; **to ~ for** (*staff, accommodation etc*) (per Anzeige) suchen
advertisement [əd'vəːtɪsmənt] *n* (*Comm*) Werbung *f*, Reklame *f*; (*in classified ads*) Anzeige *f*, Inserat *nt*
advertiser ['ædvətaɪzəʳ] *n* (*in newspaper*) Inserent(in) *m(f)*; (*on television etc*) Firma, die im Fernsehen *etc* wirbt
advertising ['ædvətaɪzɪŋ] *n* Werbung *f*
advertising agency *n* Werbeagentur *f*
advertising campaign *n* Werbekampagne *f*
advice [əd'vaɪs] *n* Rat *m*; (*notification*) Benachrichtigung *f*, Avis *m or nt* (*Comm*); **a piece of ~** ein Rat(schlag); **to ask sb for ~** jdn um Rat fragen; **to take legal ~** einen Rechtsanwalt zurate ziehen
advice note (*Brit*) *n* (*Comm*) Avis *m or nt*
advisable [əd'vaɪzəbl] *adj* ratsam
advise [əd'vaɪz] *vt* (*person*) raten *+dat*; (*company etc*) beraten; **to ~ sb of sth** jdn von etw in Kenntnis setzen; **to ~ against sth** von etw abraten; **to ~ against doing sth** davon abraten, etw zu tun; **you would be well-/ill--d to go** Sie wären gut/schlecht beraten, wenn Sie gingen
advisedly [əd'vaɪzɪdlɪ] *adv* bewusst
adviser [əd'vaɪzəʳ] *n* Berater(in) *m(f)*
advisor [əd'vaɪzəʳ] *n* = **adviser**

advisory [əd'vaɪzərɪ] *adj* beratend, Beratungs-; **in an ~ capacity** in beratender Funktion
advocate ['ædvəkɪt] *vt* befürworten ▷ *n* (*Law*) (Rechts)anwalt *m*, (Rechts)anwältin *f*; (*supporter, upholder*): **~ of** Befürworter(in) *m(f)* *+gen*; **to be an ~ of sth** etw befürworten
advt. *abbr* = **advertisement**
AEA (*Brit*) *n abbr* (= *Atomic Energy Authority) britische Atomenergiebehörde*; (*Brit: Scol:* = *Advanced Extension Award) eine besondere Qualifikation für leistungsstarke Schüler des "A level"*
AEC (*US*) *n abbr* (= *Atomic Energy Commission) amerikanische Atomenergiebehörde*
AEEU (*Brit*) *n abbr* (= *Amalgamated Engineering and Electrical Union) Gewerkschaft der Ingenieure und Elektriker*
Aegean [iː'dʒiːən] *n*: **the ~ (Sea)** (*Geog*) die Ägäis, das Ägäische Meer
aegis ['iːdʒɪs] *n*: **under the ~ of** unter der Schirmherrschaft *+gen*
aeon ['iːən] *n* Äon *m*, Ewigkeit *f*
aerial ['ɛərɪəl] *n* Antenne *f* ▷ *adj* (*view, bombardment etc*) Luft-
aero... ['ɛərə(u)] *pref* Luft-
aerobatics ['ɛərəu'bætɪks] *npl* fliegerische Kunststücke *pl*
aerobics [ɛə'rəubɪks] *n* Aerobic *nt*
aerodrome ['ɛərədrəum] (*Brit*) *n* Flugplatz *m*
aerodynamic ['ɛərəudaɪ'næmɪk] *adj* aerodynamisch
aeronautics [ɛərə'nɔːtɪks] *n* Luftfahrt *f*, Aeronautik *f*
aeroplane ['ɛərəpleɪn] (*Brit*) *n* Flugzeug *nt*
aerosol ['ɛərəsɔl] *n* Sprühdose *f*
aerospace industry ['ɛərəuspeɪs-] *n* Raumfahrtindustrie *f*
aesthetic [iːs'θɛtɪk] *adj* ästhetisch
aesthetically [iːs'θɛtɪklɪ] *adv* ästhetisch
afar [ə'fɑːʳ] *adv*: **from ~** aus der Ferne
AFB (*US*) *n abbr* (= *Air Force Base*) Luftwaffenstützpunkt *m*
affable ['æfəbl] *adj* umgänglich, freundlich
affair [ə'fɛəʳ] *n* Angelegenheit *f*; (*romance: also:* **love affair**) Verhältnis *nt*; **affairs** *npl* Geschäfte *pl*
affect [ə'fɛkt] *vt* (*influence*) sich auswirken auf *+acc*; (*subj: disease*) befallen; (*move deeply*) bewegen; (*concern*) betreffen; (*feign*) vortäuschen; **to be ~ed by sth** von etw beeinflusst werden
affectation [æfɛk'teɪʃən] *n* Affektiertheit *f*
affected [ə'fɛktɪd] *adj* affektiert
affection [ə'fɛkʃən] *n* Zuneigung *f*
affectionate [ə'fɛkʃənɪt] *adj* liebevoll, zärtlich; (*animal*) anhänglich
affectionately [ə'fɛkʃənɪtlɪ] *adv* liebevoll, zärtlich
affidavit [æfɪ'deɪvɪt] *n* (*Law*) eidesstattliche Erklärung *f*
affiliated [ə'fɪlɪeɪtɪd] *adj* angeschlossen
affinity [ə'fɪnɪtɪ] *n*: **to have an ~ with** *or* **for** sich verbunden fühlen mit; (*resemblance*): **to have an ~ with** verwandt sein mit
affirm [ə'fəːm] *vt* versichern; (*profess*) sich bekennen zu
affirmation [æfə'meɪʃən] *n* (*of facts*) Bestätigung *f*; (*of beliefs*) Bekenntnis *nt*
affirmative [ə'fəːmətɪv] *adj* bejahend ▷ *n*: **to reply in the ~** mit „Ja" antworten
affix [ə'fɪks] *vt* aufkleben
afflict [ə'flɪkt] *vt* quälen; (*misfortune*) heimsuchen
affliction [ə'flɪkʃən] *n* Leiden *nt*
affluence ['æfluəns] *n* Wohlstand *m*
affluent ['æfluənt] *adj* wohlhabend; **the ~ society** die Wohlstandsgesellschaft
afford [ə'fɔːd] *vt* sich *dat* leisten; (*time*) aufbringen; (*provide*) bieten; **can we ~ a car?** können wir uns ein Auto leisten?; **I can't ~ the time** ich habe einfach nicht die Zeit
affordable [ə'fɔːdəbl] *adj* erschwinglich
affray [ə'freɪ] (*Brit*) *n* Schlägerei *f*
affront [ə'frʌnt] *n* Beleidigung *f*
affronted [ə'frʌntɪd] *adj* beleidigt
Afghan ['æfgæn] *adj* afghanisch ▷ *n* Afghane *m*, Afghanin *f*
Afghanistan [æf'gænɪstæn] *n* Afghanistan *nt*
afield [ə'fiːld] *adv*: **far ~** weit fort; **from far ~** aus weiter Ferne
AFL-CIO *n abbr* (= *American Federation of Labor and Congress of Industrial Organizations) amerikanischer Gewerkschafts-Dachverband*
afloat [ə'fləut] *adv* auf dem Wasser ▷ *adj*: **to be ~** schwimmen; **to stay ~** sich über Wasser halten; **to keep/get a business ~** ein Geschäft über Wasser halten/auf die Beine stellen
afoot [ə'fut] *adv*: **there is something ~** da ist etwas im Gang
aforementioned [ə'fɔːmɛnʃənd] *adj* oben erwähnt
aforesaid [ə'fɔːsɛd] *adj* = **aforementioned**
afraid [ə'freɪd] *adj* ängstlich; **to be ~ of** Angst haben vor *+dat*; **to be ~ of doing sth** *or* **to do sth** Angst davor haben, etw zu tun; **to be ~ to** sich scheuen, ...; **I am ~ that ...** leider ...; **I am ~ so/not** leider ja/nein
afresh [ə'frɛʃ] *adv* von Neuem, neu
Africa ['æfrɪkə] *n* Afrika *nt*
African ['æfrɪkən] *adj* afrikanisch ▷ *n* Afrikaner(in) *m(f)*
Afrikaans [æfrɪ'kɑːns] *n* Afrikaans *nt*
Afrikaner [æfrɪ'kɑːnəʳ] *n* Afrika(a)nder(in) *m(f)*
Afro-American ['æfrəuə'mɛrɪkən] *adj* afroamerikanisch
AFT (*US*) *n abbr* (= *American Federation of Teachers) Lehrergewerkschaft*
aft [ɑːft] *adv* (*be*) achtern; (*go*) nach achtern
after ['ɑːftəʳ] *prep* nach *+dat*; (*of place*) hinter *+dat* ▷ *adv* danach ▷ *conj* nachdem; **~ dinner** nach dem Essen; **the day ~ tomorrow** übermorgen; **what are you ~?** was willst du; **who are you ~?** wen suchst du?; **the police are ~ him** die Polizei ist hinter ihm her; **to name sb ~ sb** jdn nach jdm nennen; **it's twenty ~ eight** (*US*) es ist zwanzig nach acht;

to ask ~ sb nach jdm fragen; ~ all schließlich; ~ you! nach Ihnen!; ~ he left nachdem er gegangen war; ~ having shaved nachdem er sich rasiert hatte

afterbirth ['ɑːftəbəːθ] *n* Nachgeburt *f*

aftercare ['ɑːftəkeə^r] (*Brit*) *n* Nachbehandlung *f*

aftereffects ['ɑːftərɪfɛkts] *npl* Nachwirkungen *pl*

afterlife ['ɑːftəlaɪf] *n* Leben *nt* nach dem Tod

aftermath ['ɑːftəmɑːθ] *n* Auswirkungen *pl*; **in the ~ of** nach *+dat*

afternoon [ɑːftə'nuːn] *n* Nachmittag *m*

afternoon market *n* (*Econ*) Nachmittagsmarkt *m*

afters ['ɑːftəz] (*Brit: inf*) *n* Nachtisch *m*

after-sales service [ɑːftə'seɪlz-] (*Brit*) *n* Kundendienst *m*

aftershave ['ɑːftəʃeɪv], **aftershave lotion** *n* Rasierwasser *nt*

aftershock ['ɑːftəʃɔk] *n* Nachbeben *nt*

aftersun ['ɑːftəsʌn] *n* After-Sun-Lotion *f*

aftertaste ['ɑːftəteɪst] *n* Nachgeschmack *m*

afterthought ['ɑːftəθɔːt] *n*: **as an ~** nachträglich; **I had an ~** mir ist noch etwas eingefallen

afterwards, (*US*) **afterward** ['ɑːftəwəd(z)] *adv* danach

again [ə'gɛn] *adv* (*once more*) noch einmal; (*repeatedly*) wieder; **not him ~!** nicht schon wieder er!; **to do sth ~** etw noch einmal tun; **to begin ~** noch einmal anfangen; **to see ~** wiedersehen; **he's opened it ~** er hat er schon wieder geöffnet; **~ and again** immer wieder; **now and ~** ab und zu, hin und wieder

against [ə'gɛnst] *prep* gegen *+acc*; (*leaning on*) an *+acc*; (*compared to*) gegenüber *+dat*; **~ a blue background** vor einem blauen Hintergrund; **(as) ~** gegenüber *+dat*

age [eɪdʒ] *n* Alter *nt*; (*period*) Zeitalter *nt* ▷ *vi* altern, alt werden ▷ *vt* alt machen; **what ~ is he?** wie alt ist er?; **20 years of ~** 20 Jahre alt; **under ~** minderjährig; **to come of ~** mündig werden; **it's been ~s since ...** es ist ewig her, seit ...

aged[1] [eɪdʒd] *adj*: **~ ten** zehn Jahre alt, zehnjährig

aged[2] ['eɪdʒɪd] *npl*: **the ~** die Alten *pl*

age group *n* Altersgruppe *f*; **the 40 to 50 ~** die Gruppe der Vierzig- bis Fünfzigjährigen

ageing ['eɪdʒɪŋ] *adj* (*person, population*) alternd; (*thing*) älter werdend; (*system, technology*) veraltend

ageless ['eɪdʒlɪs] *adj* zeitlos

age limit *n* Altersgrenze *f*

agency ['eɪdʒənsɪ] *n* Agentur *f*; (*government body*) Behörde *f*; **through** *or* **by the ~ of** durch die Vermittlung von

agenda [ə'dʒɛndə] *n* Tagesordnung *f*

agent ['eɪdʒənt] *n* (*Comm*) Vertreter(in) *m(f)*; (*representative, spy*) Agent(in) *m(f)*; (*Chem*) Mittel *nt*; (*fig*) Kraft *f*

aggravate ['ægrəveɪt] *vt* verschlimmern; (*inf: annoy*) ärgern

aggravating ['ægrəveɪtɪŋ] (*inf*) *adj* ärgerlich

aggravation [ægrə'veɪʃən] (*inf*) *n* Ärger *m*

aggregate ['ægrɪgɪt] *n* Gesamtmenge *f* ▷ *vt* zusammenzählen; **on ~** (*Sport*) nach Toren

aggression [ə'grɛʃən] *n* Aggression *f*

aggressive [ə'grɛsɪv] *adj* aggressiv

aggressiveness [ə'grɛsɪvnɪs] *n* Aggressivität *f*

aggressor [ə'grɛsə^r] *n* Aggressor(in) *m(f)*, Angreifer(in) *m(f)*

aggrieved [ə'griːvd] *adj* verärgert

aggro ['ægrəu] (*Brit: inf*) *n* (*hassle*) Ärger *m*, Theater *nt*; (*aggressive behaviour*) Aggressivität *f*

aghast [ə'gɑːst] *adj* entsetzt

agile ['ædʒaɪl] *adj* beweglich, wendig

agility [ə'dʒɪlɪtɪ] *n* Beweglichkeit *f*, Wendigkeit *f*; (*of mind*) (geistige) Beweglichkeit *f*

agitate ['ædʒɪteɪt] *vt* aufregen; (*liquid: stir*) aufrühren; (*: shake*) schütteln ▷ *vi*: **to ~ for/against sth** für/gegen etw agitieren

agitated ['ædʒɪteɪtɪd] *adj* aufgeregt

agitator ['ædʒɪteɪtə^r] *n* Agitator(in) *m(f)*

AGM *n abbr* (*= annual general meeting*) JHV *f*

agnostic [æg'nɔstɪk] *n* Agnostiker(in) *m(f)*

ago [ə'gəu] *adv*: **two days ~** vor zwei Tagen; **not long ~** vor Kurzem; **as long ~ as 1980** schon 1980; **how long ~?** wie lange ist das her?

agog [ə'gɔg] *adj* gespannt

agonize ['ægənaɪz] *vi*: **to ~ over sth** sich *dat* den Kopf über etw *acc* zermartern

agonizing ['ægənaɪzɪŋ] *adj* qualvoll; (*pain etc*) quälend

agony ['ægənɪ] *n* (*pain*) Schmerz *m*; (*torment*) Qual *f*; **to be in ~** Qualen leiden

agony aunt (*Brit: inf*) *n* Briefkastentante *f*

agony column *n* Kummerkasten *m*

agree [ə'griː] *vt* (*price, date*) vereinbaren ▷ *vi* übereinstimmen; (*consent*) zustimmen; **to ~ with sb** (*subj: person*) jdm zustimmen; (*: food*) jdm bekommen; **to ~ to sth** einer Sache *dat* zustimmen; **to ~ to do sth** sich bereit erklären, etw zu tun; **to ~ on sth** sich auf etw *acc* einigen; **to ~ that** (*admit*) zugeben, dass; **garlic doesn't ~ with me** Knoblauch vertrage ich nicht; **it was ~d that ...** es wurde beschlossen, dass ...; **they ~d on this** sie haben sich in diesem Punkt geeinigt; **they ~d on going** sie einigten sich darauf, zu gehen; **they ~d on a price** sie vereinbarten einen Preis

agreeable [ə'griːəbl] *adj* angenehm; (*willing*) einverstanden; **are you ~ to this?** sind Sie hiermit einverstanden?

agreed [ə'griːd] *adj* vereinbart; **to be ~** sich *dat* einig sein

agreement [ə'griːmənt] *n* (*concurrence*) Übereinstimmung *f*; (*consent*) Zustimmung *f*; (*arrangement*) Abmachung *f*; (*contract*) Vertrag *m*; **to be in ~ (with sb)** (mit jdm) einer Meinung sein; **by mutual ~** in gegenseitigem Einverständnis

agricultural [ægrɪ'kʌltʃərəl] *adj* landwirtschaftlich; (*show*) Landwirtschafts-

agriculture ['ægrɪkʌltʃəʳ] *n* Landwirtschaft *f*
aground [ə'graund] *adv*: **to run ~** auf Grund laufen
ahead [ə'hɛd] *adv* vor uns/ihnen *etc*; **~ of** (*in advance of*) vor *+dat*; **to be ~ of sb** (*in progress, ranking*) vor jdm liegen; **to be ~ of schedule** schneller als geplant vorankommen; **~ of time** zeitlich voraus; **to arrive ~ of time** zu früh ankommen; **go right** *or* **straight ~** gehen/fahren Sie geradeaus; **go ~!** (*fig*) machen Sie nur!, nur zu!; **they were (right) ~ of us** sie waren (genau) vor uns
AI *n abbr* (*= Amnesty International*) AI *no art*; (*Comput*) = **artificial intelligence**
AID *n abbr* (*= artificial insemination by donor*) *künstliche Besamung durch Samenspender*; (US: *= Agency for International Development*) *Abteilung zur Koordination von Entwicklungshilfe und Außenpolitik*
aid [eɪd] *n* Hilfe *f*; (*to less developed country*) Entwicklungshilfe *f*; (*device*) Hilfsmittel *nt* ▷ *vt* (*help*) helfen, unterstützen; **with the ~ of** mithilfe von; **in ~ of** zugunsten *+gen*; **to ~ and abet** Beihilfe leisten; *see also* **hearing aid**
aide [eɪd] *n* Berater(in) *m(f)*; (*Mil*) Adjutant *m*
aide-de-camp ['eɪddə'kɔŋ] *n* (*Mil*) Adjutant *m*
AIDS [eɪdz] *n abbr* (*= acquired immune deficiency syndrome*) AIDS *nt*
AIH *n abbr* (*= artificial insemination by husband*) *künstliche Besamung durch den Ehemann/Partner*
ailing ['eɪlɪŋ] *adj* kränklich; (*economy, industry etc*) krank
ailment ['eɪlmənt] *n* Leiden *nt*
aim [eɪm] *vt*: **to ~ at** (*gun, missile, camera*) richten auf *+acc*; (*blow*) zielen auf *+acc*; (*remark*) richten an *+acc* ▷ *vi* (*also*: **take aim**) zielen ▷ *n* (*objective*) Ziel *nt*; (*in shooting*) Zielsicherheit *f*; **to ~ at** zielen auf *+acc*; (*objective*) anstreben *+acc*; **to ~ to do sth** vorhaben, etw zu tun
aimless ['eɪmlɪs] *adj* ziellos
aimlessly ['eɪmlɪslɪ] *adv* ziellos
ain't [eɪnt] (*inf*) = **am not; aren't; isn't**
air [ɛəʳ] *n* Luft *f*; (*tune*) Melodie *f*; (*appearance*) Auftreten *nt*; (*demeanour*) Haltung *f*; (*of house etc*) Atmosphäre *f* ▷ *vt* lüften; (*grievances, views*) Luft machen *+dat*; (*knowledge*) zur Schau stellen; (*ideas*) darlegen ▷ *cpd* Luft-; **into the ~** in die Luft; **by ~** mit dem Flugzeug; **to be on the ~** (*Radio, TV: programme*) gesendet werden; (*: station*) senden; (*: person*) auf Sendung sein
air base *n* Luftwaffenstützpunkt *m*
air bed (*Brit*) *n* Luftmatratze *f*
airborne ['ɛəbɔːn] *adj* in der Luft; (*plane, particles*) in der Luft befindlich; (*troops*) Luftlande-
air cargo *n* Luftfracht *f*
air-conditioned ['ɛəkən'dɪʃənd] *adj* klimatisiert
air conditioning *n* Klimaanlage *f*
air-cooled ['ɛəkuːld] *adj* (*engine*) luftgekühlt
aircraft ['ɛəkrɑːft] *n inv* Flugzeug *nt*
aircraft carrier *n* Flugzeugträger *m*
air cushion *n* Luftkissen *nt*
airfield ['ɛəfiːld] *n* Flugplatz *m*
Air Force *n* Luftwaffe *f*
air freight *n* Luftfracht *f*
air freshener *n* Raumspray *nt*
air gun *n* Luftgewehr *nt*
air hostess (*Brit*) *n* Stewardess *f*
airily ['ɛərɪlɪ] *adv* leichtfertig
airing ['ɛərɪŋ] *n*: **to give an ~ to** (*fig: ideas*) darlegen; (*: views*) Luft machen *+dat*
air letter (*Brit*) *n* Luftpostbrief *m*
airlift ['ɛəlɪft] *n* Luftbrücke *f*
airline ['ɛəlaɪn] *n* Fluggesellschaft *f*
airliner ['ɛəlaɪnəʳ] *n* Verkehrsflugzeug *nt*
airlock ['ɛəlɔk] *n* (*in pipe etc*) Luftblase *f*; (*compartment*) Luftschleuse *f*
air mail *n*: **by ~** per *or* mit Luftpost
air mattress *n* Luftmatratze *f*
airplane ['ɛəpleɪn] (*US*) *n* Flugzeug *nt*
air pocket *n* Luftloch *nt*
airport ['ɛəpɔːt] *n* Flughafen *m*
air raid *n* Luftangriff *m*
air rifle *n* Luftgewehr *nt*
airsick ['ɛəsɪk] *adj* luftkrank
airspace ['ɛəspeɪs] *n* Luftraum *m*
airspeed ['ɛəspiːd] *n* Fluggeschwindigkeit *f*
airstrip ['ɛəstrɪp] *n* Start-und-Lande-Bahn *f*
air terminal *n* Terminal *m or nt*
airtight ['ɛətaɪt] *adj* luftdicht
airtime ['ɛətaɪm] *n* (*Radio, TV*) Sendezeit *f*
air-traffic control ['ɛətræfɪk-] *n* Flugsicherung *f*
air-traffic controller ['ɛətræfɪk-] *n* Fluglotse *m*
air waybill *n* Luftfrachtbrief *m*
airy ['ɛərɪ] *adj* luftig; (*casual*) lässig
aisle [aɪl] *n* Gang *m*; (*section of church*) Seitenschiff *nt*
aisle seat *n* Sitz *m* am Gang
ajar [ə'dʒɑːʳ] *adj* angelehnt
AK (*US*) *abbr* (*Post*) = **Alaska**
a.k.a. *abbr* (*= also known as*) alias
akin [ə'kɪn] *adj*: **~ to** ähnlich *+dat*
AL (*US*) *abbr* (*Post*) = **Alabama**
ALA *n abbr* (*= American Library Association*) *akademischer Verband für das Bibliothekswesen*
Ala. (*US*) *abbr* (*Post*) = *Alabama*
alabaster ['æləbɑːstəʳ] *n* Alabaster *m*
à la carte *adv* à la carte
alacrity [ə'lækrɪtɪ] *n* Bereitwilligkeit *f*; **with ~** ohne zu zögern
alarm [ə'lɑːm] *n* (*anxiety*) Besorgnis *f*; (*in shop, bank*) Alarmanlage *f* ▷ *vt* (*worry*) beunruhigen; (*frighten*) erschrecken
alarm call *n* Weckruf *m*
alarm clock *n* Wecker *m*
alarmed [ə'lɑːmd] *adj* beunruhigt; **don't be ~** erschrecken Sie nicht
alarming [ə'lɑːmɪŋ] *adj* (*worrying*) beunruhigend; (*frightening*) erschreckend
alarmingly [ə'lɑːmɪŋlɪ] *adv* erschreckend
alarmist [ə'lɑːmɪst] *n* Panikmacher(in) *m(f)*
alas [ə'læs] *excl* leider
Alaska [ə'læskə] *n* Alaska *nt*
Albania [æl'beɪnɪə] *n* Albanien *nt*

Albanian [æl'beɪnɪən] *adj* albanisch ▷ *n* (*Ling*) Albanisch *nt*
albatross ['ælbətrɔs] *n* Albatros *m*
albeit [ɔ:l'bi:ɪt] *conj* wenn auch
album ['ælbəm] *n* Album *nt*
albumen ['ælbjumɪn] *n* Albumen *nt*
alchemy ['ælkɪmɪ] *n* Alchimie *f*, Alchemie *f*
alcohol ['ælkəhɔl] *n* Alkohol *m*
alcoholic [ælkə'hɔlɪk] *adj* alkoholisch ▷ *n* Alkoholiker(in) *m(f)*
alcoholism ['ælkəhɔlɪzəm] *n* Alkoholismus *m*
alcove ['ælkəuv] *n* Alkoven *m*, Nische *f*
Ald. *abbr* = **alderman**
alderman ['ɔ:ldəmən] (*irreg: like* **man**) *n* ≈ Stadtrat *m*
ale [eɪl] *n* Ale *nt*
alert [ə'lə:t] *adj* aufmerksam ▷ *n* Alarm *m* ▷ *vt* alarmieren; **to be ~ to** (*danger, opportunity*) sich *dat* bewusst sein *+gen*; **to be on the ~** wachsam sein; **to ~ sb (to sth)** jdn (vor etw *dat*) warnen
Aleutian Islands [ə'lu:ʃən-] *npl* Aleuten *pl*
A level (*Brit*) *n* ≈ Abschluss *m* der Sekundarstufe 2, ≈ Abitur *nt*
Alexandria [ælɪg'zɑ:ndrɪə] *n* Alexandria *nt*
alfresco [æl'frɛskəu] *adj, adv* im Freien
algebra ['ældʒɪbrə] *n* Algebra *f*
Algeria [æl'dʒɪərɪə] *n* Algerien *nt*
Algerian [æl'dʒɪərɪən] *adj* algerisch ▷ *n* Algerier(in) *m(f)*
Algiers [æl'dʒɪəz] *n* Algier *nt*
algorithm ['ælgərɪðəm] *n* Algorithmus *m*
alias ['eɪlɪəs] *adv* alias ▷ *n* Deckname *m*
alibi ['ælɪbaɪ] *n* Alibi *nt*
alien ['eɪlɪən] *n* Ausländer(in) *m(f)*; (*extraterrestrial*) außerirdisches Wesen *nt* ▷ *adj*: **~ (to)** fremd (*+dat*)
alienate ['eɪlɪəneɪt] *vt* entfremden; (*antagonize*) befremden
alienation [eɪlɪə'neɪʃən] *n* Entfremdung *f*
alight [ə'laɪt] *adj* brennend; (*eyes, expression*) leuchtend ▷ *vi* (*bird*) sich niederlassen; (*passenger*) aussteigen
align [ə'laɪn] *vt* ausrichten
alignment [ə'laɪnmənt] *n* Ausrichtung *f*; **it's out of ~ (with)** es ist nicht richtig ausgerichtet (nach)
alike [ə'laɪk] *adj* ähnlich ▷ *adv* (*similarly*) ähnlich; (*equally*) gleich; **to look ~** sich *dat* ähnlich sehen; **winter and summer ~** Sommer wie Winter
alimony ['ælɪmənɪ] *n* Unterhalt *m*
alive [ə'laɪv] *adj* (*living*) lebend; (*lively*) lebendig; (*active*) lebhaft; **~ with** erfüllt von; **to be ~ to sth** sich *dat* einer Sache *gen* bewusst sein
alkali ['ælkəlaɪ] *n* Base *f*, Lauge *f*
alkaline ['ælkəlaɪn] *adj* basisch, alkalisch

KEYWORD

all [ɔ:l] *adj* alle(r, s); **all day/night** den ganzen Tag/die ganze Nacht (über); **all men are equal** alle Menschen sind gleich; **all five came** alle fünf kamen; **all the books** die ganzen Bücher, alle Bücher; **all the food** das ganze Essen; **all the time** die ganze Zeit (über); **all his life** sein ganzes Leben (lang)
▷ *pron* **1** alles; **I ate it all, I ate all of it** ich habe alles gegessen; **all of us/the boys went** wir alle/alle Jungen gingen; **we all sat down** wir setzten uns alle; **is that all?** ist das alles?; (*in shop*) sonst noch etwas?
2 (*in phrases*): **above all** vor allem; **after all** schließlich; **all in all** alles in allem
▷ *adv* ganz; **all alone** ganz allein; **it's not as hard as all that** so schwer ist es nun auch wieder nicht; **all the more/the better** um so mehr/besser; **all but** (*all except for*) alle außer; (*almost*) fast; **the score is 2 all** der Spielstand ist 2 zu 2

allay [ə'leɪ] *vt* (*fears*) zerstreuen
all clear *n* Entwarnung *f*
allegation [ælɪ'geɪʃən] *n* Behauptung *f*
allege [ə'lɛdʒ] *vt* behaupten; **he is ~d to have said that ...** er soll angeblich gesagt haben, dass ...
alleged [ə'lɛdʒd] *adj* angeblich
allegedly [ə'lɛdʒɪdlɪ] *adv* angeblich
allegiance [ə'li:dʒəns] *n* Treue *f*
allegory ['ælɪgərɪ] *n* Allegorie *f*
all-embracing ['ɔ:lɪm'breɪsɪŋ] *adj* (all)umfassend
allergic [ə'lə:dʒɪk] *adj* (*rash, reaction*) allergisch; (*person*): **~ to** allergisch gegen
allergy ['ælədʒɪ] *n* Allergie *f*
alleviate [ə'li:vɪeɪt] *vt* lindern
alley ['ælɪ] *n* Gasse *f*
alleyway ['ælɪweɪ] *n* Durchgang *m*
alliance [ə'laɪəns] *n* Bündnis *nt*
allied ['ælaɪd] *adj* verbündet, alliiert; (*products, industries*) verwandt
alligator ['ælɪgeɪtə^r] *n* Alligator *m*
all-important ['ɔ:lɪm'pɔ:tənt] *adj* entscheidend, äußerst wichtig
all in (*Brit*) *adv* inklusive
all-in ['ɔ:lɪn] (*Brit*) *adj* (*price*) Inklusiv-
all-in wrestling *n* (*esp Brit*) Freistilringen *nt*
alliteration [əlɪtə'reɪʃən] *n* Alliteration *f*
all-night ['ɔ:l'naɪt] *adj* (*café, cinema*) die ganze Nacht geöffnet; (*party*) die ganze Nacht dauernd
allocate ['æləkeɪt] *vt* zuteilen
allocation [æləu'keɪʃən] *n* Verteilung *f*; (*of money, resources*) Zuteilung *f*
allot [ə'lɔt] *vt*: **to ~ (to)** zuteilen (*+dat*); **in the ~ted time** in der vorgesehenen Zeit
allotment [ə'lɔtmənt] *n* (*share*) Anteil *m*; (*garden*) Schrebergarten *m*
all-out ['ɔ:laut] *adj* (*effort, dedication etc*) äußerste(r, s); (*strike*) total ▷ *adv*: **all out** mit aller Kraft; **to go all out for** sein Letztes *or* Äußerstes geben für
allow [ə'lau] *vt* erlauben; (*behaviour*) zulassen; (*sum, time*) einplanen; (*claim, goal*) anerkennen; (*concede*): **to ~ that** annehmen, dass; **to ~ sb**

to do sth jdm erlauben, etw zu tun; **he is ~ed to ...** er darf ...; **smoking is not ~ed** Rauchen ist nicht gestattet; **we must ~ three days for the journey** wir müssen für die Reise drei Tage einplanen
▸ **allow for** *vt fus* einplanen, berücksichtigen
allowance [ə'lauəns] *n* finanzielle Unterstützung *f*; (*welfare payment*) Beihilfe *f*; (*pocket money*) Taschengeld *nt*; (*tax allowance*) Freibetrag *m*; **to make ~s for** (*person*) Zugeständnisse machen für; (*thing*) berücksichtigen
alloy ['ælɔɪ] *n* Legierung *f*
all right *adv* (*well*) gut; (*correctly*) richtig; (*as answer*) okay, in Ordnung
all-rounder [ɔ:l'raundəʳ] *n* Allrounder *m*; (*athlete etc*) Allroundsportler(in) *m(f)*
allspice ['ɔ:lspaɪs] *n* Piment *m or nt*
all-time ['ɔ:l'taɪm] *adj* aller Zeiten
allude [ə'lu:d] *vi*: **to ~ to** anspielen auf *+acc*
alluring [ə'ljuərɪŋ] *adj* verführerisch
allusion [ə'lu:ʒən] *n* Anspielung *f*
alluvium [ə'lu:vɪəm] *n* Anschwemmung *f*
ally ['ælaɪ] *n* Verbündete(r) *f(m)*; (*during wars*) Alliierte(r) *f(m)* ▹ *vt*: **to ~ o.s. with** sich verbünden mit
almighty [ɔ:l'maɪtɪ] *adj* allmächtig; (*tremendous*) mächtig
almond ['ɑ:mənd] *n* Mandel *f*; (*tree*) Mandelbaum *m*
almost ['ɔ:lməust] *adv* fast, beinahe; **he ~ fell** er wäre beinahe gefallen
alms [ɑ:mz] *npl* Almosen *pl*
aloft [ə'lɔft] *adv* (*hold, carry*) empor
alone [ə'ləun] *adj, adv* allein; **to leave sb ~** jdn in Ruhe lassen; **to leave sth ~** die Finger von etw lassen; **let ~ ...** geschweige denn ...
along [ə'lɔŋ] *prep* entlang *+acc* ▹ *adv*: **is he coming ~ with us?** kommt er mit?; **he was hopping/limping ~** er hüpfte/humpelte daher; **~ with** (*together with*) zusammen mit; **all ~** (*all the time*) die ganze Zeit
alongside [ə'lɔŋ'saɪd] *prep* neben *+dat*; (*ship*) längsseits *+gen* ▹ *adv* (*come*) nebendran; (*be*) daneben; **we brought our boat ~** wir brachten unser Boot heran; **a car drew up ~** ein Auto fuhr neben mich/ihn *etc* heran
aloof [ə'lu:f] *adj* unnahbar ▹ *adv*: **to stand ~** abseitsstehen
aloofness [ə'lu:fnɪs] *n* Unnahbarkeit *f*
aloud [ə'laud] *adv* laut
alphabet ['ælfəbɛt] *n* Alphabet *nt*
alphabetical [ælfə'bɛtɪkl] *adj* alphabetisch; **in ~ order** in alphabetischer Reihenfolge
alphanumeric ['ælfənju:'mɛrɪk] *adj* alphanumerisch
alpine ['ælpaɪn] *adj* alpin, Alpen-
Alps [ælps] *npl*: **the ~** die Alpen
already [ɔ:l'rɛdɪ] *adv* schon
alright ['ɔ:l'raɪt] (*Brit*) *adv* = **all right**
Alsace ['ælsæs] *n* Elsass *nt*
Alsatian [æl'seɪʃən] (*Brit*) *n* (*dog*) Schäferhund *m*
also ['ɔ:lsəu] *adv* (*too*) auch; (*moreover*) außerdem
altar ['ɔltəʳ] *n* Altar *m*
alter ['ɔltəʳ] *vt* ändern; (*clothes*) umändern ▹ *vi* sich (ver)ändern
alteration [ɔltə'reɪʃən] *n* Änderung *f*; (*to clothes*) Umänderung *f*; (*to building*) Umbau *m*; **alterations** *npl* (*Sewing*) Änderungen *pl*; (*Archit*) Umbau *m*
altercation [ɔltə'keɪʃən] *n* Auseinandersetzung *f*
alternate [*adj* ɔl'tə:nɪt, *vi* 'ɔltəneɪt] *adj* abwechselnd; (*US*: *alternative*: *plans etc*) Alternativ- ▹ *vi*: **to ~ (with)** sich abwechseln (mit); **on ~ days** jeden zweiten Tag
alternately [ɔl'tə:nɪtlɪ] *adv* abwechselnd
alternating current ['ɔltə:neɪtɪŋ-] *n* Wechselstrom *m*
alternative [ɔl'tə:nətɪv] *adj* alternativ; (*solution etc*) Alternativ- ▹ *n* Alternative *f*
alternative energy *n* Alternativenergie *f*
alternatively [ɔl'tə:nətɪvlɪ] *adv*: **~ one could ...** oder man könnte ...
alternative medicine *n* Alternativmedizin *f*
alternative society *n* Alternativgesellschaft *f*
alternator ['ɔltə:neɪtəʳ] *n* (*Aut*) Lichtmaschine *f*
although [ɔ:l'ðəu] *conj* obwohl
altitude ['æltɪtju:d] *n* Höhe *f*
alto ['æltəu] *n* Alt *m*
altogether [ɔ:ltə'gɛðəʳ] *adv* ganz; (*on the whole, in all*) im Ganzen, insgesamt; **how much is that ~?** was macht das zusammen?
altruism ['æltruɪzəm] *n* Altruismus *m*
altruistic [æltru'ɪstɪk] *adj* uneigennützig, altruistisch
aluminium [ælju'mɪnɪəm], (*US*) **aluminum** [ə'lu:mɪnəm] *n* Aluminium *nt*
always ['ɔ:lweɪz] *adv* immer; **we can ~ ...** (*if all else fails*) wir können ja auch ...
Alzheimer's ['æltshaɪməz], **Alzheimer's disease** *n* (*Med*) Alzheimerkrankheit *f*
AM *abbr* (= *amplitude modulation*) AM, ≈ MW ▹ *n abbr* (*Brit*: *in Wales*: *Pol*: = *Assembly Member*) Mitglied *nt* der walisischen Versammlung
am [æm] *vb see* **be**
a.m. *adv abbr* (= *ante meridiem*) morgens; (*later*) vormittags
AMA *n abbr* (= *American Medical Association*) *Medizinerverband*
amalgam [ə'mælgəm] *n* Amalgam *nt*; (*fig*) Mischung *f*
amalgamate [ə'mælgəmeɪt] *vi, vt* fusionieren
amalgamation [əmælgə'meɪʃən] *n* Fusion *f*
amass [ə'mæs] *vt* anhäufen; (*evidence*) zusammentragen
amateur ['æmətəʳ] *n* Amateur *m* ▹ *adj* (*Sport*) Amateur-; **~ dramatics** Laientheater *nt*
amateurish ['æmətərɪʃ] *adj* laienhaft; (*pej*) dilettantisch, stümperhaft
amaze [ə'meɪz] *vt* erstaunen; **to be ~d (at)** erstaunt sein (über *+acc*)
amazement [ə'meɪzmənt] *n* Erstaunen *nt*
amazing [ə'meɪzɪŋ] *adj* erstaunlich; (*bargain,*

offer) sensationell
amazingly [ə'meɪzɪŋlɪ] *adv* erstaunlich
Amazon ['æməzən] *n* (*river*) Amazonas *m*; **the ~ basin** das Amazonastiefland; **the ~ jungle** der Amazonas-Regenwald
Amazonian [æmə'zəunɪən] *adj* amazonisch
ambassador [æm'bæsədə^r] *n* Botschafter(in) *m(f)*
amber ['æmbə^r] *n* Bernstein *m*; **at ~** (*Brit: traffic lights*) auf Gelb; (*: move off*) bei Gelb
ambidextrous [æmbɪ'dɛkstrəs] *adj* beidhändig
ambience ['æmbɪəns] *n* Atmosphäre *f*
ambiguity [æmbɪ'gjuɪtɪ] *n* Zweideutigkeit *f*; (*lack of clarity*) Unklarheit *f*
ambiguous [æm'bɪgjuəs] *adj* zweideutig; (*not clear*) unklar
ambition [æm'bɪʃən] *n* Ehrgeiz *m*; (*desire*) Ambition *f*; **to achieve one's ~** seine Ambitionen erfüllen
ambitious [æm'bɪʃəs] *adj* ehrgeizig
ambivalence [æm'bɪvələns] *n* Ambivalenz *f*
ambivalent [æm'bɪvələnt] *adj* ambivalent
amble ['æmbl] *vi* schleudern
ambulance ['æmbjuləns] *n* Krankenwagen *m*
ambulanceman ['æmbjulənsmən] (*irreg: like* **man**) *n* Sanitäter *m*
ambush ['æmbuʃ] *n* Hinterhalt *m*; (*attack*) Überfall *m* aus dem Hinterhalt ▷ *vt* (aus dem Hinterhalt) überfallen
ameba [ə'mi:bə] (*US*) *n* = **amoeba**
ameliorate [ə'mi:lɪəreɪt] *vt* verbessern
amen ['ɑ:'mɛn] *excl* amen
amenable [ə'mi:nəbl] *adj*: **~ to** zugänglich *+dat*; (*to flattery etc*) empfänglich für; **~ to the law** dem Gesetz verantwortlich
amend [ə'mɛnd] *vt* ändern; (*habits, behaviour*) bessern
amendment [ə'mɛndmənt] *n* Änderung *f*; (*to law*) Amendement *nt*
amends [ə'mɛndz] *npl*: **to make ~** es wiedergutmachen; **to make ~ for sth** etw wiedergutmachen
amenities [ə'mi:nɪtɪz] *npl Einkaufs-, Unterhaltungs- und Transportmöglichkeiten*
amenity [ə'mi:nɪtɪ] *n* (Freizeit)einrichtung *f*
America [ə'mɛrɪkə] *n* Amerika *nt*
American [ə'mɛrɪkən] *adj* amerikanisch ▷ *n* Amerikaner(in) *m(f)*
Americanize [ə'mɛrɪkənaɪz] *vt* amerikanisieren
amethyst ['æmɪθɪst] *n* Amethyst *m*
Amex ['æmɛks] *n abbr* (*= American Stock Exchange*) *US-Börse*; (*= American Express®*) *Kreditkarte*
amiable ['eɪmɪəbl] *adj* liebenswürdig
amiably ['eɪmɪəblɪ] *adv* liebenswürdig
amicable ['æmɪkəbl] *adj* freundschaftlich; (*settlement*) gütlich
amicably ['æmɪkəblɪ] *adv* (*part, discuss*) in aller Freundschaft; (*settle*) gütlich
amid [ə'mɪd], **amidst** [ə'mɪdst] *prep* inmitten *+gen*
amiss [ə'mɪs] *adj, adv*: **to take sth ~** etw übel nehmen; **there's something ~** da stimmt irgendetwas nicht
ammeter ['æmɪtə^r] *n* Amperemeter *nt*
ammo ['æməu] (*inf*) *n* = **ammunition**
ammonia [ə'məunɪə] *n* Ammoniak *nt*
ammunition [æmju'nɪʃən] *n* Munition *f*
ammunition dump *n* Munitionslager *nt*
amnesia [æm'ni:zɪə] *n* Amnesie *f*, Gedächtnisschwund *m*
amnesty ['æmnɪstɪ] *n* Amnestie *f*; **to grant an ~ to** amnestieren
Amnesty International *n* Amnesty International *no art*
amoeba, (*US*) **ameba** [ə'mi:bə] *n* Amöbe *f*
amok [ə'mɔk] *adv*: **to run ~** Amok laufen
among [ə'mʌŋ], **amongst** [ə'mʌŋst] *prep* unter *+dat*
amoral [æ'mɔrəl] *adj* unmoralisch
amorous ['æmərəs] *adj* amourös
amorphous [ə'mɔ:fəs] *adj* formlos, gestaltlos
amortization [əmɔ:taɪ'zeɪʃən] *n* Amortisation *f*
amount [ə'maunt] *n* (*quantity*) Menge *f*; (*sum of money*) Betrag *m*; (*total*) Summe *f*; (*of bill etc*) Höhe *f* ▷ *vi*: **to ~ to** (*total*) sich belaufen auf *+acc*; (*be same as*) gleichkommen *+dat*; **the total ~** (*of money*) die Gesamtsumme
amp ['æmp], **ampère** ['æmpɛə^r] *n* Ampere *nt*; **a 3 ~(ère) fuse** eine Sicherung von 3 Ampere; **a 13 ~(ère) plug** ein Stecker mit einer Sicherung von 13 Ampere
ampersand ['æmpəsænd] *n* Et-Zeichen *nt*, Und-Zeichen *nt*
amphetamine [æm'fɛtəmi:n] *n* Amphetamin *nt*
amphibian [æm'fɪbɪən] *n* Amphibie *f*
amphibious [æm'fɪbɪəs] *adj* amphibisch; (*vehicle*) Amphibien-
amphitheatre, (*US*) **amphitheater** ['æmfɪθɪətə^r] *n* Amphitheater *nt*
ample ['æmpl] *adj* (*large*) üppig; (*abundant*) reichlich; (*enough*) genügend; **this is ~** das ist reichlich; **to have ~ time/room** genügend Zeit/Platz haben
amplifier ['æmplɪfaɪə^r] *n* Verstärker *m*
amplify ['æmplɪfaɪ] *vt* verstärken; (*expand: idea etc*) genauer ausführen
amply ['æmplɪ] *adv* reichlich
ampoule, (*US*) **ampule** ['æmpu:l] *n* Ampulle *f*
amputate ['æmpjuteɪt] *vt* amputieren
amputation [æmpju'teɪʃən] *n* Amputation *f*
amputee [æmpju'ti:] *n* Amputierte(r) *f(m)*
Amsterdam ['æmstədæm] *n* Amsterdam *nt*
amt *abbr* = **amount**
amuck [ə'mʌk] *adv* = **amok**
amuse [ə'mju:z] *vt* (*entertain*) unterhalten; (*make smile*) amüsieren, belustigen; **to ~ o.s. with sth/by doing sth** sich die Zeit mit etw vertreiben/damit vertreiben, etw zu tun; **to be ~d at** sich amüsieren über *+acc*; **he was not ~d** er fand das gar nicht komisch *or* zum Lachen
amusement [ə'mju:zmənt] *n* (*mirth*) Vergnügen *nt*; (*pleasure*) Unterhaltung *f*;

(*pastime*) Zeitvertreib *m*; **much to my ~** zu meiner großen Belustigung
amusement arcade *n* Spielhalle *f*
amusement park *n* Vergnügungspark *m*
amusing [ə'mju:zɪŋ] *adj* amüsant, unterhaltsam
an [æn, ən] *indef art see* **a**
ANA *n abbr (= American Newspaper Association) amerikanischer Zeitungsverband; (= American Nurses Association) Verband amerikanischer Krankenschwestern und Krankenpfleger*
anachronism [ə'nækrənɪzəm] *n* Anachronismus *m*
anaemia, (*US*) **anemia** [ə'ni:mɪə] *n* Anämie *f*
anaemic, (*US*) **anemic** [ə'ni:mɪk] *adj* blutarm
anaesthetic, (*US*) **anesthetic** [ænɪs'θɛtɪk] *n* Betäubungsmittel *nt*; **under (the) ~** unter Narkose; **local ~** örtliche Betäubung *f*; **general ~** Vollnarkose *f*
anaesthetist [æ'ni:sθɪtɪst] *n* Anästhesist(in) *m(f)*
anagram ['ænəgræm] *n* Anagramm *nt*
anal ['eɪnl] *adj* anal, Anal-
analgesic [ænæl'dʒi:sɪk] *adj* schmerzstillend ▷ *n* Schmerzmittel *nt*, schmerzstillendes Mittel *nt*
analogous [ə'næləgəs] *adj*: **~ (to** *or* **with)** analog (zu)
analogue, (*US*) **analog** ['ænəlɔg] *adj* (*watch, computer*) Analog-
analogy [ə'nælədʒɪ] *n* Analogie *f*; **to draw an ~ between** eine Analogie herstellen zwischen *+dat*; **by ~** durch einen Analogieschluss
analyse, (*US*) **analyze** ['ænəlaɪz] *vt* analysieren; (*Chem, Med*) untersuchen; (*person*) psychoanalytisch behandeln
analyses [ə'næləsi:z] *npl of* **analysis**
analysis [ə'næləsɪs] (*pl* **analyses**) *n* (*see vb*) Analyse *f*; Untersuchung *f*; Psychoanalyse *f*; **in the last ~** letzten Endes
analyst ['ænəlɪst] *n* Analytiker(in) *m(f)*; (US) Psychoanalytiker(in) *m(f)*
analytic [ænə'lɪtɪk], **analytical** [ænə'lɪtɪkəl] *adj* analytisch
analyze ['ænəlaɪz] (US) *vt* = **analyse**
anarchic [æ'nɑ:kɪk] *adj* anarchisch
anarchist ['ænəkɪst] *adj* anarchistisch ▷ *n* Anarchist(in) *m(f)*
anarchy ['ænəkɪ] *n* Anarchie *f*
anathema [ə'næθɪmə] *n*: **that is ~ to him** das ist ihm ein Gräuel
anatomical [ænə'tɔmɪkl] *adj* anatomisch
anatomy [ə'nætəmɪ] *n* Anatomie *f*; (*body*) Körper *m*
ANC *n abbr (= African National Congress)* ANC *m*
ancestor ['ænsɪstə^r] *n* Vorfahr(in) *m(f)*
ancestral [æn'sɛstrəl] *adj* angestammt; **~ home** Stammsitz *m*
ancestry ['ænsɪstrɪ] *n* Abstammung *f*
anchor ['æŋkə^r] *n* Anker *m* ▷ *vi* (*also*: **to drop anchor**) ankern, vor Anker gehen ▷ *vt* (*fig*) verankern; **to ~ sth to** etw verankern in *+dat*; **to weigh ~** den Anker lichten
anchorage ['æŋkərɪdʒ] *n* Ankerplatz *m*
anchorman [æŋkəmæn] (*irreg: like* **man**) *n* (*TV, Radio*) ≈ Moderator *m*
anchor store *n* (*attractive store*) ≈ Magnetbetrieb *m*
anchorwoman [æŋkəwʊmən] (*irreg: like* **woman**) *n* (*TV, Radio*) ≈ Moderatorin *f*
anchovy ['æntʃəvɪ] *n* Sardelle *f*, An(s)chovis *f*
ancient ['eɪnʃənt] *adj* alt; (*person, car*) uralt
ancient monument *n* historisches Denkmal *nt*
ancillary [æn'sɪlərɪ] *adj* Hilfs-
and [ænd] *conj* und; **~ so on** und so weiter; **try ~ come please** bitte versuche zu kommen; **better ~ better** immer besser
Andes ['ændi:z] *npl*: **the ~** die Anden *pl*
Andorra [æn'dɔ:rə] *n* Andorra *nt*
anecdote ['ænɪkdəut] *n* Anekdote *f*
anemia *etc* [ə'ni:mɪə] (US) = **anaemia** *etc*
anemone [ə'nɛmənɪ] *n* (*Bot*) Anemone *f*, Buschwindröschen *nt*
anesthetic *etc* [ænɪs'θɛtɪk] (US) = **anaesthetic** *etc*
anew [ə'nju:] *adv* von Neuem
angel ['eɪndʒəl] *n* Engel *m*
angel dust (*inf*) *n als halluzinogene Droge missbrauchtes Medikament*
angelic [æn'dʒɛlɪk] *adj* engelhaft
anger ['æŋgə^r] *n* Zorn *m* ▷ *vt* ärgern; (*enrage*) erzürnen; **red with ~** rot vor Wut
angina [æn'dʒaɪnə] *n* Angina pectoris *f*
angle ['æŋgl] *n* Winkel *m*; (*viewpoint*): **from their ~** von ihrem Standpunkt aus ▷ *vi*: **to ~ for** (*invitation*) aus sein auf *+acc*; (*compliments*) fischen nach ▷ *vt*: **to ~ sth towards** *or* **to** etw ausrichten auf *+acc*
angler ['æŋglə^r] *n* Angler(in) *m(f)*
Anglican ['æŋglɪkən] *adj* anglikanisch ▷ *n* Anglikaner(in) *m(f)*
anglicize ['æŋglɪsaɪz] *vt* anglisieren
angling ['æŋglɪŋ] *n* Angeln *nt*
Anglo- ['æŋgləu] *pref* Anglo-, anglo-
Anglo-German ['æŋgləu'dʒə:mən] *adj* englisch-deutsch
Anglo-Saxon ['æŋgləu'sæksən] *adj* angelsächsisch ▷ *n* Angelsachse *m*, Angelsächsin *f*
Angola [æŋ'gəulə] *n* Angola *nt*
Angolan [æŋ'gəulən] *adj* angolanisch ▷ *n* Angolaner(in) *m(f)*
angrily ['æŋgrɪlɪ] *adv* verärgert
angry ['æŋgrɪ] *adj* verärgert; (*wound*) entzündet; **to be ~ with sb** auf jdn böse sein; **to be ~ at sth** über etw *acc* verärgert sein; **to get ~** wütend werden; **to make sb ~** jdn wütend machen
anguish ['æŋgwɪʃ] *n* Qual *f*
anguished ['æŋgwɪʃt] *adj* gequält
angular ['æŋgjulə^r] *adj* eckig; (*features*) kantig
animal ['ænɪməl] *n* Tier *nt*; (*living creature*) Lebewesen *nt*; (*pej: person*) Bestie *f* ▷ *adj* tierhaft; (*attraction etc*) animalisch
animal spirits *npl* Vitalität *f*

animate [*vt* 'ænɪmeɪt, *adj* 'ænɪmɪt] *vt* beleben ▷ *adj* lebend
animated ['ænɪmeɪtɪd] *adj* lebhaft; (*film*) Zeichentrick-
animation [ænɪ'meɪʃən] *n* (*liveliness*) Lebhaftigkeit *f*; (*film*) Animation *f*
animosity [ænɪ'mɔsɪtɪ] *n* Feindseligkeit *f*
aniseed ['ænɪsi:d] *n* Anis *m*
Ankara ['æŋkərə] *n* Ankara *nt*
ankle ['æŋkl] *n* Knöchel *m*
ankle sock (*Brit*) *n* Söckchen *nt*
annex ['ænɛks] *n* (*also*: **annexe**: *Brit*) Anhang *m*; (*building*) Nebengebäude *nt*; (*extension*) Anbau *m* ▷ *vt* (*take over*) annektieren
annexation [ænɛk'seɪʃən] *n* Annexion *f*
annihilate [ə'naɪəleɪt] *vt* (*also fig*) vernichten
annihilation [ənaɪə'leɪʃən] *n* Vernichtung *f*
anniversary [ænɪ'vəːsərɪ] *n* Jahrestag *m*
anno Domini *adv* anno Domini, nach Christus
annotate ['ænəuteɪt] *vt* kommentieren
announce [ə'nauns] *vt* ankündigen; (*birth, death etc*) anzeigen; **he ~d that he wasn't going** er verkündete, dass er nicht gehen würde
announcement [ə'naunsmənt] *n* Ankündigung *f*; (*official*) Bekanntmachung *f*; (*of birth, death etc*) Anzeige *f*; **I'd like to make an ~** ich möchte etwas bekannt geben
announcer [ə'naunsəʳ] *n* Ansager(in) *m(f)*
annoy [ə'nɔɪ] *vt* ärgern; **to be ~ed (at sth/ with sb)** sich (über etw/jdn) ärgern; **don't get ~ed!** reg dich nicht auf!
annoyance [ə'nɔɪəns] *n* Ärger *m*
annoying [ə'nɔɪɪŋ] *adj* ärgerlich; (*person, habit*) lästig
annual ['ænjuəl] *adj* jährlich; (*income*) Jahres- ▷ *n* (*Bot*) einjährige Pflanze *f*; (*book*) Jahresband *m*
annual general meeting (*Brit*) *n* Jahreshauptversammlung *f*
annually ['ænjuəlɪ] *adv* jährlich
annual report *n* Geschäftsbericht *m*
annuity [ə'nju:ɪtɪ] *n* Rente *f*; **life ~** Rente *f* auf Lebenszeit
annul [ə'nʌl] *vt* annullieren; (*law*) aufheben
annulment [ə'nʌlmənt] *n* (*see vb*) Annullierung *f*; Aufhebung *f*
annum ['ænəm] *n see* **per**
Annunciation [ənʌnsɪ'eɪʃən] *n* Mariä Verkündigung *f*
anode ['ænəud] *n* Anode *f*
anodyne ['ænədaɪn] (*fig*) *n* Wohltat *f* ▷ *adj* schmerzlos
anoint [ə'nɔɪnt] *vt* salben
anomalous [ə'nɔmələs] *adj* anomal
anomaly [ə'nɔməlɪ] *n* Anomalie *f*
anon. [ə'nɔn] *abbr* = **anonymous**
anonymity [ænə'nɪmɪtɪ] *n* Anonymität *f*
anonymous [ə'nɔnɪməs] *adj* anonym
anorak ['ænəræk] *n* Anorak *m*
anorexia [ænə'rɛksɪə] *n* Magersucht *f*, Anorexie *f*
anorexic [ænə'rɛksɪk] *adj* magersüchtig
another [ə'nʌðəʳ] *pron* (*additional*) noch eine(r, s); (*different*) ein(e) andere(r, s) ▷ *adj*: **~ book** (*one more*) noch ein Buch; (*a different one*) ein anderes Buch; **~ drink?** noch etwas zu trinken?; **in ~ five years** in weiteren fünf Jahren; *see also* **one**
ANSI [eɪɛnɛs'aɪ] *n abbr* (= *American National Standards Institution*) *amerikanischer Normenausschuss*
answer ['ɑ:nsəʳ] *n* Antwort *f*; (*to problem*) Lösung *f* ▷ *vi* antworten; (*Tel*) sich melden ▷ *vt* (*reply to*: *person*) antworten *+dat*; (: *letter, question*) beantworten; (*problem*) lösen; (*prayer*) erhören; **in ~ to your letter** in Beantwortung Ihres Schreibens; **to ~ the phone** ans Telefon gehen; **to ~ the bell** *or* **the door** die Tür aufmachen
▶ **answer back** *vi* widersprechen; (*child*) frech sein
▶ **answer for** *vt fus* (*person*) verantwortlich sein für, sich verbürgen für
▶ **answer to** *vt fus* (*description*) entsprechen *+dat*
answerable ['ɑ:nsərəbl] *adj*: **to be ~ to sb for sth** jdm gegenüber für etw verantwortlich sein; **I am ~ to no-one** ich brauche mich vor niemandem zu verantworten
answering machine ['ɑ:nsərɪŋ-] *n* Anrufbeantworter *m*
ant [ænt] *n* Ameise *f*
antagonism [æn'tægənɪzəm] *n* Feindseligkeit *f*, Antagonismus *m*
antagonist [æn'tægənɪst] *n* Gegner(in) *m(f)*, Antagonist(in) *m(f)*
antagonistic [æntægə'nɪstɪk] *adj* feindselig
antagonize [æn'tægənaɪz] *vt* gegen sich aufbringen
Antarctic [ænt'ɑ:ktɪk] *n*: **the ~** die Antarktis
Antarctica [ænt'ɑ:ktɪkə] *n* Antarktik *f*
Antarctic Circle *n*: **the ~** der südliche Polarkreis
Antarctic Ocean *n*: **the ~** das Südpolarmeer
ante ['æntɪ] *n*: **to up the ~** den Einsatz erhöhen
ante ... ['æntɪ] *pref* vor-
anteater ['ænti:təʳ] *n* Ameisenbär *m*
antecedent [æntɪ'si:dənt] *n* Vorläufer *m*; (*of living creature*) Vorfahr *m*; **antecedents** *npl* Herkunft *f*
antechamber ['æntɪtʃeɪmbəʳ] *n* Vorzimmer *nt*
antelope ['æntɪləup] *n* Antilope *f*
antenatal ['æntɪ'neɪtl] *adj* vor der Geburt, Schwangerschafts-
antenatal clinic *n* Sprechstunde *f* für werdende Mütter
antenna [æn'tɛnə] (*pl* **~e**) *n* (*of insect*) Fühler *m*; (*Radio, TV*) Antenne *f*
antennae [æn'tɛni:] *npl of* **antenna**
anteroom ['æntɪrum] *n* Vorzimmer *nt*
anthem ['ænθəm] *n*: **national ~** Nationalhymne *f*
ant hill *n* Ameisenhaufen *m*
anthology [æn'θɔlədʒɪ] *n* Anthologie *f*
anthropologist [ænθrə'pɔlədʒɪst] *n* Anthropologe *m*, Anthropologin *f*

anthropology [ænθrəˈpɔlədʒɪ] *n* Anthropologie *f*
anti ... [ˈæntɪ] *pref* Anti-, anti-
anti-aircraft [ˈæntɪˈɛəkrɑːft] *adj (gun, rocket)* Flugabwehr-
anti-aircraft defence *n* Luftverteidigung *f*
antiballistic [ˈæntɪbəˈlɪstɪk] *adj (missile)* Anti-Raketen-
antibiotic [ˈæntɪbaɪˈɔtɪk] *n* Antibiotikum *nt*
antibody [ˈæntɪbɔdɪ] *n* Antikörper *m*
anticipate [ænˈtɪsɪpeɪt] *vt* erwarten; *(foresee)* vorhersehen; *(look forward to)* sich freuen auf *+acc*; *(forestall)* vorwegnehmen; **this is worse than I ~d** es ist schlimmer, als ich erwartet hatte; **as ~d** wie erwartet
anticipation [æntɪsɪˈpeɪʃən] *n* Erwartung *f*; *(eagerness)* Vorfreude *f*; **thanking you in ~** vielen Dank im Voraus
anticlimax [ˈæntɪˈklaɪmæks] *n* Enttäuschung *f*
anticlockwise [ˈæntɪˈklɔkwaɪz] *(Brit) adv* gegen den Uhrzeigersinn
antics [ˈæntɪks] *npl* Mätzchen *pl*; *(of politicians etc)* Gehabe *nt*
anticyclone [ˈæntɪˈsaɪkləun] *n* Hoch(druckgebiet) *nt*
antidote [ˈæntɪdəut] *n* Gegenmittel *nt*
antifreeze [ˈæntɪfriːz] *n* Frostschutzmittel *nt*
anti-globalist [æntɪˈgləubəlɪst] *n*, **anti-globalization protester** [æntɪgləublaɪˈzeɪʃn-] ▷ *n* Globalisierungsgegner(in) *m(f)*
antihistamine [ˈæntɪˈhɪstəmɪn] *n* Antihistamin *nt*
Antilles [ænˈtɪliːz] *npl*: **the ~** die Antillen *pl*
antipathy [ænˈtɪpəθɪ] *n* Antipathie *f*, Abneigung *f*
antiperspirant [ˈæntɪˈpəːspɪrənt] *n* Antitranspirant *nt*
Antipodean [æntɪpəˈdiːən] *adj* antipodisch
Antipodes [ænˈtɪpədiːz] *npl*: **the ~** Australien und Neuseeland *nt*
antiquarian [æntɪˈkwɛərɪən] *n (collector)* Antiquitätensammler(in) *m(f)*; *(seller)* Antiquitätenhändler(in) *m(f)* ▷ *adj*: **~ bookshop** Antiquariat *nt*
antiquated [ˈæntɪkweɪtɪd] *adj* antiquiert
antique [ænˈtiːk] *n* Antiquität *f* ▷ *adj* antik
antique dealer *n* Antiquitätenhändler(in) *m(f)*
antique shop *n* Antiquitätenladen *m*
antiquity [ænˈtɪkwɪtɪ] *n (period)* Antike *f*; **antiquities** *npl (objects)* Altertümer *pl*
anti-Semitic [ˈæntɪsɪˈmɪtɪk] *adj* antisemitisch
anti-Semitism [ˈæntɪˈsɛmɪtɪzəm] *n* Antisemitismus *m*
antiseptic [æntɪˈsɛptɪk] *n* Antiseptikum *nt* ▷ *adj* antiseptisch
antisocial [ˈæntɪˈsəuʃəl] *adj* unsozial; *(person)* ungesellig
antitank [ˈæntɪˈtæŋk] *adj (gun, fire)* Panzerabwehr-
antitheses [ænˈtɪθɪsiːz] *npl of* **antithesis**
antithesis [ænˈtɪθɪsɪs] *(pl* **antitheses***) n* Gegensatz *m*; **she's the ~ of a good cook** sie ist das genaue Gegenteil einer guten Köchin
antitrust [ˈæntɪˈtrʌst] *(US) adj*: **~ legislation** Kartellgesetzgebung *f*
anti-virus software [æntɪˈvaɪrəs-] *n* Antivirensoftware *f*
antlers [ˈæntləz] *npl* Geweih *nt*
Antwerp [ˈæntwəːp] *n* Antwerpen *nt*
anus [ˈeɪnəs] *n* After *m*
anvil [ˈænvɪl] *n* Amboss *m*
anxiety [æŋˈzaɪətɪ] *n (worry)* Sorge *f*; *(Med)* Angstzustand *m*; *(eagerness)*: **~ to do sth** Verlangen (danach), etw zu tun
anxious [ˈæŋkʃəs] *adj (worried)* besorgt; *(situation)* Angst einflößend; *(question, moments)* bang(e); *(keen)*: **to be ~ to do sth** etw unbedingt tun wollen; **I'm very ~ about you** ich mache mir große Sorgen um dich
anxiously [ˈæŋkʃəslɪ] *adv* besorgt

KEYWORD

any [ˈɛnɪ] *adj* **1** *(in questions etc)*: **have you any butter/children?** haben Sie Butter/Kinder?; **if there are any tickets left** falls noch Karten da sind
2 *(with negative)* kein(e); **I haven't any money/books** ich habe kein Geld/keine Bücher
3 *(no matter which)* irgendein(e); **choose any book you like** nehmen Sie irgendein Buch *or* ein beliebiges Buch
4 *(in phrases)*: **in any case** in jedem Fall; **any day now** jeden Tag; **at any moment** jeden Moment; **at any rate** auf jeden Fall; **any time** *(at any moment)* jeden Moment; *(whenever)* jederzeit
▷ *pron* **1** *(in questions etc)*: **have you got any?** haben Sie welche?; **can any of you sing?** kann (irgend)einer von euch singen?
2 *(with negative)*: **I haven't any (of them)** ich habe keine (davon)
3 *(no matter which one(s))* egal welche; **take any of those books (you like)** nehmen Sie irgendwelche von diesen Büchern
▷ *adv* **1** *(in questions etc)*: **do you want any more soup/sandwiches?** möchtest du noch Suppe/Butterbrote?; **are you feeling any better?** geht es Ihnen etwas besser?
2 *(with negative)*: **I can't hear him any more** ich kann ihn nicht mehr hören; **don't wait any longer** warte nicht noch länger

anybody [ˈɛnɪbɔdɪ] *pron* = **anyone**

KEYWORD

anyhow [ˈɛnɪhau] *adv* **1** *(at any rate)* sowieso, ohnehin; **I shall go anyhow** ich gehe auf jeden Fall
2 *(haphazard)*: **do it anyhow you like** machen Sie es, wie Sie wollen

KEYWORD

anyone ['ɛnɪwʌn] *pron* **1** *(in questions etc)* (irgend)jemand; **can you see anyone?** siehst du jemanden?
2 *(with negative)* keine(r); **I can't see anyone** ich kann keinen *or* niemanden sehen
3 *(no matter who)* jede(r); **anyone could do it** das kann jeder

anyplace ['ɛnɪpleɪs] *(US) adv* = **anywhere**

KEYWORD

anything ['ɛnɪθɪŋ] *pron* **1** *(in questions etc)* (irgend)etwas; **can you see anything?** kannst du etwas sehen?
2 *(with negative)* nichts; **I can't see anything** ich kann nichts sehen
3 *(no matter what)* irgendetwas; **you can say anything you like** du kannst sagen, was du willst; **anything between 15 and 20 pounds** (ungefähr) zwischen 15 und 20 Pfund

KEYWORD

anyway ['ɛnɪweɪ] *adv* **1** *(at any rate)* sowieso, ohnehin; **I shall go anyway** ich gehe auf jeden Fall
2 *(besides)*: **anyway, I can't come** jedenfalls kann ich nicht kommen; **why are you phoning, anyway?** warum rufst du überhaupt *or* eigentlich an?

KEYWORD

anywhere ['ɛnɪwɛəʳ] *adv* **1** *(in questions etc)* irgendwo; **can you see him anywhere?** kannst du ihn irgendwo sehen?
2 *(with negative)* nirgendwo, nirgends; **I can't see him anywhere** ich kann ihn nirgendwo *or* nirgends sehen
3 *(no matter where)* irgendwo; **put the books down anywhere** legen Sie die Bücher irgendwohin

Anzac ['ænzæk] *n abbr (= Australia-New Zealand Army Corps) (soldier)* australischer/neuseeländischer Soldat *m*; *siehe Info-Artikel*

ANZAC DAY

Anzac Day, der 25 April, ist in Australien und Neuseeland ein Feiertag zum Gedenken an die Landung der australischen und neuseeländischen Truppen in Gallipoli im Ersten Weltkrieg.

apace [ə'peɪs] *adv*: **to continue ~** *(negotiations, preparations etc)* rasch vorangehen
apart [ə'pɑːt] *adv (be)* entfernt; *(move)* auseinander; *(aside)* beiseite; *(separately)* getrennt; **10 miles ~** 10 Meilen voneinander entfernt; **a long way ~** weit auseinander; **they are living ~** sie leben getrennt; **with one's legs ~** mit gespreizten Beinen; **to take ~** auseinandernehmen; **~ from** *(excepting)* abgesehen von; *(in addition)* außerdem
apartheid [ə'pɑːteɪt] *n* Apartheid *f*
apartment [ə'pɑːtmənt] *n (US: flat)* Wohnung *f*; *(room)* Raum *m*, Zimmer *nt*
apartment building *(US) n* Wohnblock *m*
apathetic [æpə'θɛtɪk] *adj* apathisch, teilnahmslos
apathy ['æpəθɪ] *n* Apathie *f*, Teilnahmslosigkeit *f*
APB *(US) n abbr (= all points bulletin) polizeiliche Fahndung*
ape [eɪp] *n* (Menschen)affe *m* ▷ *vt* nachahmen
Apennines ['æpənaɪnz] *npl*: **the ~** die Apenninen *pl*, der Appenin
apéritif *n* Aperitif *m*
aperture ['æpətʃjuəʳ] *n* Öffnung *f*; *(Phot)* Blende *f*
APEX ['eɪpɛks] *n abbr (Aviat, Rail: = advance purchase excursion)* APEX
apex ['eɪpɛks] *n* Spitze *f*
aphid ['æfɪd] *n* Blattlaus *f*
aphorism ['æfərɪzəm] *n* Aphorismus *m*
aphrodisiac [æfrəu'dɪzɪæk] *adj* aphrodisisch ▷ *n* Aphrodisiakum *nt*
apiece [ə'piːs] *adv (each person)* pro Person; *(each thing)* pro Stück
aplomb [ə'plɔm] *n* Gelassenheit *f*
APO *(US) n abbr (= Army Post Office) Poststelle der Armee*
apocalypse [ə'pɔkəlɪps] *n* Apokalypse *f*
apolitical [eɪpə'lɪtɪkl] *adj* apolitisch
apologetic [əpɔlə'dʒɛtɪk] *adj* entschuldigend; **to be very ~ (about sth)** sich (wegen etw *gen*) sehr entschuldigen
apologize [ə'pɔlədʒaɪz] *vi*: **to ~ (for sth to sb)** sich (für etw bei jdm) entschuldigen
apology [ə'pɔlədʒɪ] *n* Entschuldigung *f*; **to send one's apologies** sich entschuldigen lassen; **please accept my apologies** ich bitte um Verzeihung
apoplectic [æpə'plɛktɪk] *adj (Med)* apoplektisch; *(fig)*: **to be ~ with rage** vor Wut fast platzen
apoplexy ['æpəplɛksɪ] *n* Schlaganfall *m*
apostle [ə'pɔsl] *n* Apostel *m*
apostrophe [ə'pɔstrəfɪ] *n* Apostroph *m*, Auslassungszeichen *nt*
apotheosis [əpɔθɪ'əusɪs] *n* Apotheose *f*
appal [ə'pɔːl] *vt* entsetzen; **to be ~led by** entsetzt sein über *+acc*
Appalachian Mountains [æpə'leɪʃən-] *npl*: **the ~** die Appalachen *pl*
appalling [ə'pɔːlɪŋ] *adj* entsetzlich; **she's an ~ cook** sie kann überhaupt nicht kochen
apparatus [æpə'reɪtəs] *n* Gerät *nt*; *(in gymnasium)* Geräte *pl*; *(of organization)* Apparat *m*; **a piece of ~** ein Gerät *nt*
apparel [ə'pærəl] *(US) n* Kleidung *f*

apparent [ə'pærənt] *adj* (*seeming*) scheinbar; (*obvious*) offensichtlich; **it is ~ that ...** es ist klar, dass ...
apparently [ə'pærəntlı] *adv* anscheinend
apparition [æpə'rıʃən] *n* Erscheinung *f*
appeal [ə'pi:l] *vi* (*Law*) Berufung einlegen ▷ *n* (*Law*) Berufung *f*; (*plea*) Aufruf *m*; (*charm*) Reiz *m*; **to ~ (to sb) for** (jdn) bitten um; **to ~ to** (*be attractive to*) gefallen *+dat*; **it doesn't ~ to me** es reizt mich nicht; **right of ~** (*Law*) Berufungsrecht *nt*; **on ~** (*Law*) in der Berufung
appealing [ə'pi:lıŋ] *adj* ansprechend; (*touching*) rührend
appear [ə'pıəʳ] *vi* erscheinen; (*seem*) scheinen; **to ~ on TV/in "Hamlet"** im Fernsehen/in „Hamlet" auftreten; **it would ~ that ...** anscheinend ...
appearance [ə'pıərəns] *n* Erscheinen *nt*; (*look*) Aussehen *nt*; (*in public, on TV*) Auftritt *m*; **to put in** *or* **make an ~** sich sehen lassen; **in** *or* **by order of ~** (*Theat etc*) in der Reihenfolge ihres Auftritts; **to keep up ~s** den (äußeren) Schein wahren; **to all ~s** allem Anschein nach
appease [ə'pi:z] *vt* beschwichtigen
appeasement [ə'pi:zmənt] *n* Beschwichtigung *f*
append [ə'pɛnd] *vt* (*Comput*) anhängen
appendage [ə'pɛndıdʒ] *n* Anhängsel *nt*
appendices [ə'pɛndısi:z] *npl of* **appendix**
appendicitis [əpɛndı'saıtıs] *n* Blinddarmentzündung *f*
appendix [ə'pɛndıks] (*pl* **appendices**) *n* (*Anat*) Blinddarm *m*; (*to publication*) Anhang *m*; **to have one's ~ out** sich *dat* den Blinddarm herausnehmen lassen
appetite ['æpıtaıt] *n* Appetit *m*; (*fig*) Lust *f*; **that walk has given me an ~** von dem Spaziergang habe ich Appetit bekommen
appetizer ['æpıtaızəʳ] *n* (*food*) Appetithappen *m*; (*drink*) appetitanregendes Getränk *nt*
appetizing ['æpıtaızıŋ] *adj* appetitanregend
applaud [ə'plɔ:d] *vi* applaudieren, klatschen ▷ *vt* (*actor etc*) applaudieren *+dat*, Beifall spenden *or* klatschen *+dat*; (*action, attitude*) loben; (*decision*) begrüßen
applause [ə'plɔ:z] *n* Applaus *m*, Beifall *m*
apple ['æpl] *n* Apfel *m*; **he's the ~ of her eye** er ist ihr Ein und Alles
apple tree *n* Apfelbaum *m*
apple turnover *n* Apfeltasche *f*
appliance [ə'plaıəns] *n* Gerät *nt*
applicable [ə'plıkəbl] *adj*: **~ (to)** anwendbar (auf *+acc*); (*on official forms*) zutreffend (auf *+acc*); **the law is ~ from January** das Gesetz gilt ab Januar
applicant ['æplıkənt] *n* Bewerber(in) *m(f)*
application [æplı'keıʃən] *n* (*for job*) Bewerbung *f*; (*for grant etc*) Antrag *m*; (*hard work*) Fleiß *m*; (*applying: of paint etc*) Auftragen *nt*; **on ~** auf Antrag
application form *n* (*for a job*) Bewerbungsformular *nt*; (*for a grant etc*) Antragsformular *nt*
application program *n* (*Comput*) Anwendungsprogramm *nt*
applications package *n* (*Comput*) Anwendungspaket *nt*
applied [ə'plaıd] *adj* angewandt
apply [ə'plaı] *vt* anwenden; (*paint etc*) auftragen ▷ *vi*: **to ~ (to)** (*be applicable*) gelten (für); **to ~ the brakes** die Bremse betätigen, bremsen; **to ~ o.s. to sth** sich bei etw anstrengen; **to ~ to** (*ask*) sich wenden an *+acc*; **to ~ for** (*permit, grant*) beantragen; (*job*) sich bewerben um
appoint [ə'pɔınt] *vt* ernennen; (*date, place*) festlegen, festsetzen
appointed [ə'pɔıntıd] *adj*: **at the ~ time** zur festgesetzten Zeit
appointee [əpɔın'ti:] *n* Ernannte(r) *f(m)*
appointment [ə'pɔıntmənt] *n* Ernennung *f*; (*post*) Stelle *f*; (*arranged meeting*) Termin *m*; **to make an ~ (with sb)** einen Termin (mit jdm) vereinbaren; **by ~** nach Anmeldung, mit Voranmeldung
apportion [ə'pɔ:ʃən] *vt* aufteilen; (*blame*) zuweisen; **to ~ sth to sb** jdm etw zuteilen
apposition [æpə'zıʃən] *n* Apposition *f*, Beifügung *f*; **A is in ~ to B** A ist eine Apposition zu B
appraisal [ə'preızl] *n* Beurteilung *f*
appraise [ə'preız] *vt* beurteilen
appreciable [ə'pri:ʃəbl] *adj* merklich, deutlich
appreciably [ə'pri:ʃəblı] *adv* merklich
appreciate [ə'pri:ʃıeıt] *vt* (*like*) schätzen; (*be grateful for*) zu schätzen wissen; (*understand*) verstehen; (*be aware of*) sich *dat* bewusst sein *+gen* ▷ *vi* (*Comm: currency, shares*) im Wert steigen; **I ~ your help** ich weiß Ihre Hilfe zu schätzen
appreciation [əpri:ʃı'eıʃən] *n* (*enjoyment*) Wertschätzung *f*; (*understanding*) Verständnis *nt*; (*gratitude*) Dankbarkeit *f*; (*Comm: in value*) (Wert)steigerung *f*
appreciative [ə'pri:ʃıətıv] *adj* dankbar; (*comment*) anerkennend
apprehend [æprı'hɛnd] *vt* (*arrest*) festnehmen; (*understand*) verstehen
apprehension [æprı'hɛnʃən] *n* (*fear*) Besorgnis *f*; (*arrest*) Festnahme *f*
apprehensive [æprı'hɛnsıv] *adj* ängstlich; **to be ~ about sth** sich *dat* Gedanken *or* Sorgen um etw machen
apprentice [ə'prɛntıs] *n* Lehrling *m*, Auszubildende(r) *f(m)* ▷ *vt*: **to be ~d to sb** bei jdm in der Lehre sein
apprenticeship [ə'prɛntısʃıp] *n* Lehre *f*, Lehrzeit *f*; **to serve one's ~** seine Lehre machen
appro ['æprəu] (*Brit: inf*) *abbr* (*Comm:* = *approval*): **on ~** zur Ansicht
approach [ə'prəutʃ] *vi* sich nähern; (*event*) nahen ▷ *vt* (*come to*) sich nähern *+dat*; (*ask, apply to: person*) herantreten an *+acc*, ansprechen; (*situation, problem*) herangehen an *+acc*, angehen ▷ *n* (*advance*) (Heran)nahen *nt*;

(*access*) Zugang *m*; (*: for vehicles*) Zufahrt *f*; (*to problem etc*) Ansatz *m*; **to ~ sb about sth** jdn wegen etw ansprechen
approachable [ə'prəutʃəbl] *adj* (*person*) umgänglich; (*place*) zugänglich
approach road *n* Zufahrtsstraße *f*
approbation [æprə'beɪʃən] *n* Zustimmung *f*
appropriate [*adj* ə'prəuprɪɪt, *vt* ə'prəuprɪeɪt] *adj* (*apt*) angebracht; (*relevant*) entsprechend ▷ *vt* sich *dat* aneignen; **it would not be ~ for me to comment** es wäre nicht angebracht, wenn ich mich dazu äußern würde
appropriately [ə'prəuprɪɪtlɪ] *adv* entsprechend
appropriation [əprəuprɪ'eɪʃən] *n* Zuteilung *f*, Zuweisung *f*
approval [ə'pru:vəl] *n* (*approbation*) Zustimmung *f*, Billigung *f*; (*permission*) Einverständnis *f*; **to meet with sb's ~** jds Zustimmung *or* Beifall finden; **on ~** (*Comm*) zur Probe
approve [ə'pru:v] *vt* billigen; (*motion, decision*) annehmen
▸ **approve of** *vt fus* etwas halten von; **I don't ~ of it/him** ich halte nichts davon/von ihm
approved school [ə'pru:vd-] (*Brit*) *n* Erziehungsheim *nt*
approvingly [ə'pru:vɪŋlɪ] *adv* zustimmend
approx. *abbr* = **approximately**
approximate [*adj* ə'prɔksɪmɪt, *vb* ə'prɔksɪmeɪt] *adj* ungefähr ▷ *vt, vi*: **to ~ (to)** nahe kommen *+dat*
approximately [ə'prɔksɪmɪtlɪ] *adv* ungefähr
approximation [ə'prɔksɪ'meɪʃən] *n* Annäherung *f*
APR *n abbr* (= *annual(ized) percentage rate*) Jahreszinssatz *m*
Apr. *abbr* = **April**
apricot ['eɪprɪkɔt] *n* Aprikose *f*
April ['eɪprəl] *n* April *m*; **~ fool!** April, April!; *see also* **July**
apron ['eɪprən] *n* Schürze *f*; (*Aviat*) Vorfeld *nt*
apse [æps] *n* Apsis *f*
Apt. *abbr* = **apartment**
apt [æpt] *adj* (*suitable*) passend, treffend; (*likely*): **to be ~ to do sth** dazu neigen, etw zu tun
aptitude ['æptɪtju:d] *n* Begabung *f*
aptitude test *n* Eignungstest *m*
aptly ['æptlɪ] *adv* passend, treffend
aqualung ['ækwəlʌŋ] *n* Tauchgerät *nt*
aquarium [ə'kwɛərɪəm] *n* Aquarium *nt*
Aquarius [ə'kwɛərɪəs] *n* Wassermann *m*; **to be ~** (ein) Wassermann sein
aquatic [ə'kwætɪk] *adj* (*plants etc*) Wasser-; (*life*) im Wasser
aqueduct ['ækwɪdʌkt] *n* Aquädukt *m or nt*
AR (*US*) *abbr* (*Post*) = **Arkansas**
ARA (*Brit*) *n abbr* (= *Associate of the Royal Academy*) *Qualifikationsnachweis im künstlerischen Bereich*
Arab ['ærəb] *adj* arabisch ▷ *n* Araber(in) *m(f)*
Arabia [ə'reɪbɪə] *n* Arabien *nt*
Arabian [ə'reɪbɪən] *adj* arabisch
Arabian Desert *n*: **the ~** die Arabische Wüste
Arabian Sea *n*: **the ~** das Arabische Meer
Arabic ['ærəbɪk] *adj* arabisch ▷ *n* (*Ling*) Arabisch *nt*
arable ['ærəbl] *adj* (*land*) bebaubar; **~ farm** *Bauernhof, der ausschließlich Ackerbau betreibt*
ARAM (*Brit*) *n abbr* (= *Associate of the Royal Academy of Music*) *Qualifikationsnachweis in Musik*
arbiter ['ɑ:bɪtə^r] *n* Vermittler *m*
arbitrary ['ɑ:bɪtrərɪ] *adj* willkürlich
arbitrate ['ɑ:bɪtreɪt] *vi* vermitteln
arbitration [ɑ:bɪ'treɪʃən] *n* Schlichtung *f*; **the dispute went to ~** der Streit wurde vor eine Schlichtungskommission gebracht
arbitrator ['ɑ:bɪtreɪtə^r] *n* Vermittler(in) *m(f)*; (*Industry*) Schlichter(in) *m(f)*
ARC *n abbr* (= *American Red Cross*) ≈ DRK *nt*
arc [ɑ:k] *n* Bogen *m*
arcade [ɑ:'keɪd] *n* Arkade *f*; (*shopping mall*) Passage *f*
arch [ɑ:tʃ] *n* Bogen *m*; (*of foot*) Gewölbe *nt* ▷ *vt* (*back*) krümmen ▷ *adj* schelmisch ▷ *pref* Erz-
archaeological [ɑ:kɪə'lɔdʒɪkl] *adj* archäologisch
archaeologist [ɑ:kɪ'ɔlədʒɪst] *n* Archäologe *m*, Archäologin *f*
archaeology, (*US*) **archeology** [ɑ:kɪ'ɔlədʒɪ] *n* Archäologie *f*
archaic [ɑ:'keɪɪk] *adj* altertümlich; (*language*) veraltet, archaisch
archangel ['ɑ:keɪndʒəl] *n* Erzengel *m*
archbishop [ɑ:tʃ'bɪʃəp] *n* Erzbischof *m*
archenemy ['ɑ:tʃ'ɛnəmɪ] *n* Erzfeind(in) *m(f)*
archeology *etc* [ɑ:kɪ'ɔlədʒɪ] (*US*) = **archaeology** *etc*
archery ['ɑ:tʃərɪ] *n* Bogenschießen *nt*
archetypal ['ɑ:kɪtaɪpəl] *adj* (arche)typisch
archetype ['ɑ:kɪtaɪp] *n* Urbild *nt*, Urtyp *m*
archipelago [ɑ:kɪ'pɛlɪgəu] *n* Archipel *m*
architect ['ɑ:kɪtɛkt] *n* Architekt(in) *m(f)*
architectural [ɑ:kɪ'tɛktʃərəl] *adj* architektonisch
architecture ['ɑ:kɪtɛktʃə^r] *n* Architektur *f*
archive file *n* (*Comput*) Archivdatei *f*
archives ['ɑ:kaɪvz] *npl* Archiv *nt*
archivist ['ɑ:kɪvɪst] *n* Archivar(in) *m(f)*
archway ['ɑ:tʃweɪ] *n* Torbogen *m*
ARCM (*Brit*) *n abbr* (= *Associate of the Royal College of Music*) *Qualifikationsnachweis in Musik*
Arctic ['ɑ:ktɪk] *adj* arktisch ▷ *n*: **the ~** die Arktis
Arctic Circle *n*: **the ~** der nördliche Polarkreis
Arctic Ocean *n*: **the ~** das Nordpolarmeer
ardent ['ɑ:dənt] *adj* leidenschaftlich; (*admirer*) glühend
ardour, (*US*) **ardor** ['ɑ:də^r] *n* Leidenschaft *f*
arduous ['ɑ:djuəs] *adj* mühsam
are [ɑ:^r] *vb see* **be**
area ['ɛərɪə] *n* Gebiet *nt*; (*Geom etc*) Fläche *f*; (*dining area etc*) Bereich *m*; **in the London ~** im Raum London
area code (*US*) *n* Vorwahl(nummer) *f*
arena [ə'ri:nə] *n* Arena *f*
aren't [ɑ:nt] = **are not**
Argentina [ɑ:dʒən'ti:nə] *n* Argentinien *nt*

Argentinian [ɑ:dʒən'tɪnɪən] *adj* argentinisch ▷ *n* Argentinier(in) *m(f)*
arguable ['ɑ:gjuəbl] *adj*: **it is ~ whether ...** es ist (noch) die Frage, ob ...; **it is ~ that ...** man kann (wohl) sagen, dass ...
arguably ['ɑ:gjuəblɪ] *adv* wohl; **it is ~ ...** es dürfte wohl ... sein
argue ['ɑ:gju:] *vi* (*quarrel*) sich streiten; (*reason*) diskutieren ▷ *vt* (*debate*) diskutieren, erörtern; **to ~ that ...** den Standpunkt vertreten, dass ...; **to ~ about sth** sich über etw *acc* streiten; **to ~ for/against sth** sich für/gegen etw aussprechen
argument ['ɑ:gjumənt] *n* (*reasons*) Argument *nt*; (*quarrel*) Streit *m*, Auseinandersetzung *f*; (*debate*) Diskussion *f*; **~ for/against** Argument für/gegen; **to have an ~** sich streiten
argumentative [ɑ:gju'mɛntətɪv] *adj* streitlustig
aria ['ɑ:rɪə] *n* Arie *f*
ARIBA [ə'ri:bə] (*Brit*) *n abbr* (= *Associate of the Royal Institute of British Architects*) *Qualifikationsnachweis in Architektur*
arid ['ærɪd] *adj* (*land*) dürr; (*subject*) trocken
aridity [ə'rɪdɪtɪ] *n* Dürre *f*, Trockenheit *f*
Aries ['ɛərɪz] *n* Widder *m*; **to be ~** (ein) Widder sein
arise [ə'raɪz] (*pt* **arose**, *pp* **~n**) *vi* (*difficulty etc*) sich ergeben; (*question*) sich stellen; **to ~ from** sich ergeben aus, herrühren von; **should the need ~** falls es nötig wird
arisen [ə'rɪzn] *pp of* **arise**
aristocracy [ærɪs'tɔkrəsɪ] *n* Aristokratie *f*, Adel *m*
aristocrat ['ærɪstəkræt] *n* Aristokrat(in) *m(f)*, Ad(e)lige(r) *f(m)*
aristocratic [ærɪstə'krætɪk] *adj* aristokratisch, ad(e)lig
arithmetic [ə'rɪθmətɪk] *n* Rechnen *nt*; (*calculation*) Rechnung *f*
arithmetical [ærɪθ'mɛtɪkl] *adj* rechnerisch, arithmetisch
Ariz. (*US*) *abbr* (*Post*) = *Arizona*
ark [ɑ:k] *n*: **Noah's A~** die Arche Noah
arm [ɑ:m] *n* Arm *m*; (*of clothing*) Ärmel *m*; (*of chair*) Armlehne *f*; (*of organization etc*) Zweig *m* ▷ *vt* bewaffnen; **arms** *npl* (*weapons*) Waffen *pl*; (*Heraldry*) Wappen *nt*
armaments ['ɑ:məmənts] *npl* (*weapons*) (Aus)rüstung *f*
armband ['ɑ:mbænd] *n* Armbinde *f*
armchair ['ɑ:mtʃɛəʳ] *n* Sessel *m*, Lehnstuhl *m*
armed [ɑ:md] *adj* bewaffnet; **the ~ forces** die Streitkräfte *pl*
armed robbery *n* bewaffneter Raubüberfall *m*
Armenia [ɑ:'mi:nɪə] *n* Armenien *nt*
Armenian [ɑ:'mi:nɪən] *adj* armenisch ▷ *n* Armenier(in) *m(f)*; (*Ling*) Armenisch *nt*
armful ['ɑ:mful] *n* Armvoll *m*
armistice ['ɑ:mɪstɪs] *n* Waffenstillstand *m*
armour, (*US*) **armor** ['ɑ:məʳ] *n* (*Hist*) Rüstung *f*; (*also*: **armour-plating**) Panzerplatte *f*; (*Mil: tanks*) Panzerfahrzeuge *pl*
armoured car ['ɑ:məd-] *n* Panzerwagen *m*
armoury ['ɑ:mərɪ] *n* (*storeroom*) Waffenlager *nt*
armpit ['ɑ:mpɪt] *n* Achselhöhle *f*
armrest ['ɑ:mrɛst] *n* Armlehne *f*
arms control [ɑ:mz-] *n* Rüstungskontrolle *f*
arms race [ɑ:mz-] *n*: **the ~** das Wettrüsten
army ['ɑ:mɪ] *n* Armee *f*, Heer *nt*; (*fig: host*) Heer
aroma [ə'rəumə] *n* Aroma *nt*, Duft *m*
aromatherapy [ərəumə'θɛrəpɪ] *n* Aromatherapie *f*
aromatic [ærə'mætɪk] *adj* aromatisch, duftend
arose [ə'rəuz] *pt of* **arise**
around [ə'raund] *adv* (*about*) herum; (*in the area*) in der Nähe ▷ *prep* (*encircling*) um ... herum; (*near*) in der Nähe von; (*fig: about: dimensions*) etwa; (*: time*) gegen; (*: date*) um; **is he ~?** ist er da?; **~ £5** um die £5, etwa £5; **~ 3 o'clock** gegen 3 Uhr
arousal [ə'rauzəl] *n* (*sexual*) Erregung *f*; (*of feelings, interest*) Weckung *f*
arouse [ə'rauz] *vt* (*feelings, interest*) wecken
arpeggio [ɑ:'pɛdʒɪəu] *n* Arpeggio *nt*
arrange [ə'reɪndʒ] *vt* (*meeting etc*) vereinbaren; (*tour etc*) planen; (*books etc*) anordnen; (*flowers*) arrangieren; (*Mus*) arrangieren, bearbeiten ▷ *vi*: **we have ~d for a car to pick you up** wir haben veranlasst, dass Sie mit dem Auto abgeholt werden; **it was ~d that ...** es wurde vereinbart, dass ...; **to ~ to do sth** vereinbaren *or* ausmachen, etw zu tun
arrangement [ə'reɪndʒmənt] *n* (*agreement*) Vereinbarung *f*; (*layout*) Anordnung *f*; (*Mus*) Arrangement *nt*, Bearbeitung *f*; **arrangements** *npl* Pläne *pl*; (*preparations*) Vorbereitungen *pl*; **to come to an ~ with sb** eine Regelung mit jdm treffen; **home deliveries by ~** nach Vereinbarung Lieferung ins Haus; **I'll make ~s for you to be met** ich werde veranlassen, dass Sie abgeholt werden
arrant ['ærənt] *adj* (*coward, fool etc*) Erz-; (*nonsense*) total
array [ə'reɪ] *n*: **an ~ of** (*things*) eine Reihe von; (*people*) Aufgebot an *+dat*; (*Math, Comput*) (Daten)feld *nt*
arrears [ə'rɪəz] *npl* Rückstand *m*; **to be in ~ with one's rent** mit seiner Miete im Rückstand sein
arrest [ə'rɛst] *vt* (*person*) verhaften; (*sb's attention*) erregen ▷ *n* Verhaftung *f*; **under ~** verhaftet
arresting [ə'rɛstɪŋ] *adj* (*fig*) atemberaubend
arrival [ə'raɪvl] *n* Ankunft *f*; (*Comm: of goods*) Sendung *f*; **new ~** (*person*) Neuankömmling *m*; (*baby*) Neugeborene(s) *nt*
arrive [ə'raɪv] *vi* ankommen
▸ **arrive at** *vt fus* (*fig: conclusion*) kommen zu; (*: situation*) es bringen zu
arrogance ['ærəgəns] *n* Arroganz *f*, Überheblichkeit *f*
arrogant ['ærəgənt] *adj* arrogant, überheblich
arrow ['ærəu] *n* Pfeil *m*
arse [ɑ:s] (*Brit: inf!*) *n* Arsch *m* (!)
arsenal ['ɑ:sɪnl] *n* Waffenlager *nt*; (*stockpile*)

Arsenal *nt*
arsenic ['ɑːsnɪk] *n* Arsen *nt*
arson ['ɑːsn] *n* Brandstiftung *f*
art [ɑːt] *n* Kunst *f*; **Arts** *npl* (*Scol*) Geisteswissenschaften *pl*; **work of ~** Kunstwerk *nt*
art and design (*Brit*) *n* (*Scol*) ≈ Kunst und Design
arterial [ɑː'tɪərɪəl] *adj* arteriell; **~ road** Fernverkehrsstraße *f*; **~ line** (*Rail*) Hauptstrecke *f*
artery ['ɑːtərɪ] *n* Arterie *f*, Schlagader *f*; (*fig*) Verkehrsader *f*
artful ['ɑːtful] *adj* raffiniert
art gallery *n* Kunstgalerie *f*
arthritic [ɑː'θrɪtɪk] *adj* arthritisch
arthritis [ɑː'θraɪtɪs] *n* Arthritis *f*
artichoke ['ɑːtɪtʃəuk] *n* (*also*: **globe artichoke**) Artischocke *f*; (*also*: **Jerusalem artichoke**) Topinambur *m*
article ['ɑːtɪkl] *n* Artikel *m*; (*object, item*) Gegenstand *m*; **articles** (*Brit*) *npl* (*Law*) (Rechts)referendarzeit *f*; **~ of clothing** Kleidungsstück *nt*
articles of association *npl* (*Comm*) Gesellschaftsvertrag *m*
articulate [*adj* ɑː'tɪkjulɪt, *vt, vi* ɑː'tɪkjuleɪt] *adj* (*speech, writing*) klar; (*speaker*) redegewandt ▷ *vt* darlegen ▷ *vi* artikulieren; **to be ~** (*person*) sich gut ausdrücken können
articulated lorry (*Brit*) *n* Sattelschlepper *m*
artifice ['ɑːtɪfɪs] *n* List *f*
artificial [ɑːtɪ'fɪʃəl] *adj* künstlich; (*manner*) gekünstelt; **to be ~** (*person*) gekünstelt *or* unnatürlich wirken
artificial insemination [-ɪnsɛmɪ'neɪʃən] *n* künstliche Besamung *f*
artificial intelligence *n* künstliche Intelligenz *f*
artificial respiration *n* künstliche Beatmung *f*
artillery [ɑː'tɪlərɪ] *n* Artillerie *f*
artisan ['ɑːtɪzæn] *n* Handwerker *m*
artist ['ɑːtɪst] *n* Künstler(in) *m(f)*
artistic [ɑː'tɪstɪk] *adj* künstlerisch
artistry ['ɑːtɪstrɪ] *n* künstlerisches Geschick *nt*
artless ['ɑːtlɪs] *adj* arglos
art school *n* Kunstakademie *f*, Kunsthochschule *f*
artwork ['ɑːtwəːk] *n* (*for advert etc, material for printing*) Druckvorlage *f*; (*in book*) Bildmaterial *nt*
ARV *n abbr* (*Bible: = American Revised Version*) *amerikanische revidierte Bibelübersetzung*
AS (*US*) *n abbr* (*= Associate in Science*) *akademischer Grad in Naturwissenschaften* ▷ *abbr* (*Post*) *= American Samoa*

KEYWORD

as [æz] *conj* **1** (*referring to time*) als; **as the years went by** mit den Jahren; **he came in as I was leaving** als er hereinkam, ging ich gerade; **as from tomorrow** ab morgen
2 (*in comparisons*): **as big as** so groß wie; **twice as big as** zweimal so groß wie; **as much/many as** so viel/so viele wie; **as soon as** sobald; **much as I admire her ...** sosehr ich sie auch bewundere ...
3 (*since, because*) da, weil; **as you can't come I'll go without you** da du nicht mitkommen kannst, gehe ich ohne dich
4 (*referring to manner, way*) wie; **do as you wish** mach, was du willst; **as she said** wie sie sagte; **he gave it to me as a present** er gab es mir als Geschenk; **as it were** sozusagen
5 (*in the capacity of*) als; **he works as a driver** er arbeitet als Fahrer
6 (*concerning*): **as for** *or* **to that** was das betrifft *or* angeht
7: **as if** *or* **though** als ob; *see also* **long; such; well**

ASA *n abbr* (*= American Standards Association*) *amerikanischer Normenausschuss*; (*Brit*) *= Advertising Standards Authority*
a.s.a.p. *adv abbr* (*= as soon as possible*) baldmöglichst
asbestos [æz'bɛstəs] *n* Asbest *m*
ascend [ə'sɛnd] *vt* hinaufsteigen; (*throne*) besteigen
ascendancy [ə'sɛndənsɪ] *n* Vormachtstellung *f*; **~ over sb** Vorherrschaft *f* über jdn
ascendant [ə'sɛndənt] *n*: **to be in the ~** im Aufstieg begriffen sein
ascension [ə'sɛnʃən] *n*: **the A~** (*Rel*) die Himmelfahrt *f* (Christi)
Ascension Island *n* Ascension *nt*
ascent [ə'sɛnt] *n* Aufstieg *m*
ascertain [æsə'teɪn] *vt* feststellen
ascetic [ə'sɛtɪk] *adj* asketisch
asceticism [ə'sɛtɪsɪzəm] *n* Askese *f*
ASCII ['æskiː] *n abbr* (*Comput: = American Standard Code for Information Interchange*) ASCII
ascribe [ə'skraɪb] *vt*: **to ~ sth to** etw zuschreiben *+dat*; (*cause*) etw zurückführen auf *+acc*
ASCU (*US*) *n abbr* (*= Association of State Colleges and Universities*) *Verband staatlicher Bildungseinrichtungen*
ASEAN ['æsɪæn] *n abbr* (*= Association of Southeast Asian Nations*) ASEAN *f* (*Gemeinschaft südostasiatischer Staaten*)
ASH [æʃ] (*Brit*) *n abbr* (*= Action on Smoking and Health*) *Antiraucherinitiative*
ash [æʃ] *n* Asche *f*; (*wood, tree*) Esche *f*
ashamed [ə'ʃeɪmd] *adj* beschämt; **to be ~ of** sich schämen für; **to be ~ of o.s. for having done sth** sich schämen, dass man etw getan hat
A shares *npl* stimmrechtslose Aktien *pl*
ashen ['æʃən] *adj* (*face*) aschfahl
ashore [ə'ʃɔːʳ] *adv* an Land
ashtray ['æʃtreɪ] *n* Aschenbecher *m*
Ash Wednesday *n* Aschermittwoch *m*
Asia ['eɪʃə] *n* Asien *nt*
Asia Minor *n* Kleinasien *nt*

Asian ['eɪʃən] *adj* asiatisch ▷*n* Asiat(in) *m(f)*
Asiatic [eɪsɪ'ætɪk] *adj* asiatisch
aside [ə'saɪd] *adv* zur Seite; (*take*) beiseite ▷*n* beiseite gesprochene Worte *pl*; **to brush objections ~** Einwände beiseiteschieben
aside from *prep* außer *+dat*
ask [ɑːsk] *vt* fragen; (*invite*) einladen; **to ~ sb to do sth** jdn bitten, etw zu tun; **to ~ (sb) sth** (jdn) etw fragen; **to ~ sb a question** jdm eine Frage stellen; **to ~ sb the time** jdn nach der Uhrzeit fragen; **to ~ sb about sth** jdn nach etw fragen; **to ~ sb out to dinner** jdn zum Essen einladen
▸ **ask after** *vt fus* fragen nach
▸ **ask for** *vt fus* bitten um; (*trouble*) haben wollen; **it's just ~ing for trouble/it** das kann ja nicht gut gehen
askance [ə'skɑːns] *adv*: **to look ~ at sb** jdn misstrauisch ansehen; **to look ~ at sth** etw mit Misstrauen betrachten
askew [ə'skjuː] *adv* schief
asking price ['ɑːskɪŋ-] *n*: **the ~** der geforderte Preis
asleep [ə'sliːp] *adj* schlafend; **to be ~** schlafen; **to fall ~** einschlafen
AS level *n abbr (= Advanced Subsidiary level) Mit "AS level" wird das erste Jahr der Sekundarstufe II bezeichnet, nach dessen Abschluss Prüfungen in drei der ingesamt sechs für den "A level" benötigten Wahlpflichtfächern abgehalten werden*
asp [æsp] *n* Natter *f*
asparagus [əs'pærəgəs] *n* Spargel *m*
asparagus tips *npl* Spargelspitzen *pl*
ASPCA *n abbr (= American Society for the Prevention of Cruelty to Animals) Tierschutzverein*
aspect ['æspɛkt] *n* (*of subject*) Aspekt *m*; (*of building etc*) Lage *f*; (*quality, air*) Erscheinung *f*; **to have a south-westerly ~** nach Südwesten liegen
aspersions [əs'pəːʃənz] *npl*: **to cast ~ on** sich abfällig äußern über *+acc*
asphalt ['æsfælt] *n* Asphalt *m*
asphyxiate [æs'fɪksɪeɪt] *vt* ersticken
asphyxiation [æsfɪksɪ'eɪʃən] *n* Erstickung *f*
aspirate ['æspəreɪt] *vt* aspirieren, behauchen
aspirations [æspə'reɪʃənz] *npl* Hoffnungen *pl*; **to have ~ to(wards) sth** etw anstreben
aspire [əs'paɪəʳ] *vi*: **to ~ to** streben nach
aspirin ['æsprɪn] *n* Kopfschmerztablette *f*, Aspirin® *nt*
aspiring [əs'paɪərɪŋ] *adj* aufstrebend
ass [æs] *n* (*also fig*) Esel *m*; (*US: inf!*) Arsch! *m*
assail [ə'seɪl] *vt* angreifen; (*fig*): **to be ~ed by doubts** von Zweifeln geplagt werden
assailant [ə'seɪlənt] *n* Angreifer(in) *m(f)*
assassin [ə'sæsɪn] *n* Attentäter(in) *m(f)*
assassinate [ə'sæsɪneɪt] *vt* ermorden, ein Attentat verüben auf *+acc*
assassination [əsæsɪ'neɪʃən] *n* Ermordung *f*, (geglücktes) Attentat *nt*
assault [ə'sɔːlt] *n* Angriff *m* ▷*vt* angreifen; (*sexually*) vergewaltigen; **~ and battery** (*Law*) Körperverletzung *f*
assemble [ə'sɛmbl] *vt* versammeln; (*car, machine*) montieren; (*furniture etc*) zusammenbauen ▷*vi* sich versammeln
assembly [ə'sɛmblɪ] *n* Versammlung *f*; (*of car, machine*) Montage *f*; (*of furniture*) Zusammenbau *m*
assembly language *n* (*Comput*) Assemblersprache *f*
assembly line *n* Fließband *nt*
assent [ə'sɛnt] *n* Zustimmung *f* ▷*vi*: **to ~ (to)** zustimmen (*+dat*)
assert [ə'səːt] *vt* behaupten; (*innocence*) beteuern; (*authority*) geltend machen; **to ~ o.s.** sich durchsetzen
assertion [ə'səːʃən] *n* Behauptung *f*
assertive [ə'səːtɪv] *adj* (*person*) selbstbewusst; (*manner*) bestimmt
assess [ə'sɛs] *vt* (*situation*) einschätzen; (*abilities etc*) beurteilen; (*tax*) festsetzen; (*damages, property etc*) schätzen
assessment [ə'sɛsmənt] *n* (*see vt*) Einschätzung *f*; Beurteilung *f*; Festsetzung *f*; Schätzung *f*
assessor [ə'sɛsəʳ] *n* (*Law*) Gutachter(in) *m(f)*
asset ['æsɛt] *n* Vorteil *m*; (*person*) Stütze *f*;
assets *npl* (*property, funds*) Vermögen *nt*; (*Comm*) Aktiva *pl*
asset-stripping ['æsɛt'strɪpɪŋ] *n* (*Comm*) *Aufkauf von finanziell gefährdeten Firmen und anschließender Verkauf ihrer Vermögenswerte*
assiduous [ə'sɪdjuəs] *adj* gewissenhaft
assign [ə'saɪn] *vt*: **to ~ (to)** (*date*) zuweisen (*+dat*); (*task*) übertragen (*+dat*); (*person*) einteilen (für); (*cause*) zuschreiben (*+dat*); (*meaning*) zuordnen (*+dat*); **to ~ sb to do sth** jdn damit beauftragen, etw zu tun
assignment [ə'saɪnmənt] *n* Aufgabe *f*
assimilate [ə'sɪmɪleɪt] *vt* aufnehmen; (*immigrants*) integrieren
assimilation [əsɪmɪ'leɪʃən] *n* (*see vt*) Aufnahme *f*; Integration *f*
assist [ə'sɪst] *vt* helfen; (*with money etc*) unterstützen
assistance [ə'sɪstəns] *n* Hilfe *f*; (*with money etc*) Unterstützung *f*
assistant [ə'sɪstənt] *n* Assistent(in) *m(f)*; (*Brit: also*: **shop assistant**) Verkäufer(in) *m(f)*
assistant manager *n* stellvertretender Geschäftsführer *m*, stellvertretende Geschäftsführerin *f*
assisted living [əsɪstd'lɪvɪŋ] *n* (*US*) betreutes Wohnen *nt*
associate [*adj, n* ə'səuʃɪɪt, *vt, vi* ə'səuʃɪeɪt] *adj* (*director*) assoziiert; (*member, professor*) außerordentlich ▷*n* (*at work*) Kollege *m*, Kollegin *f* ▷*vt* in Verbindung bringen ▷*vi*: **to ~ with sb** mit jdm verkehren
associated company [ə'səuʃɪeɪtɪd-] *n* Partnerfirma *f*
association [əsəusɪ'eɪʃən] *n* (*group*) Verband *m*; (*involvement*) Verbindung *f*; (*Psych*) Assoziation *f*; **in ~ with** in Zusammenarbeit mit
association football *n* Fußball *m*

assorted [ə'sɔːtɪd] *adj* gemischt; (*various*) diverse(r, s); **in ~ sizes** in verschiedenen Größen
assortment [ə'sɔːtmənt] *n* Mischung *f*; (*of books, people etc*) Ansammlung *f*
Asst *abbr* = **assistant**
assuage [ə'sweɪdʒ] *vt* (*grief, pain*) lindern; (*thirst, appetite*) stillen, befriedigen
assume [ə'sjuːm] *vt* annehmen; (*responsibilities etc*) übernehmen
assumed name [ə'sjuːmd-] *n* Deckname *m*
assumption [ə'sʌmpʃən] *n* Annahme *f*; (*of power etc*) Übernahme *f*; **on the ~ that ...** vorausgesetzt, dass ...
assurance [ə'ʃuərəns] *n* Versicherung *f*; (*promise*) Zusicherung *f*; (*confidence*) Zuversicht *f*; **I can give you no ~s** ich kann Ihnen nichts versprechen
assure [ə'ʃuəʳ] *vt* versichern; (*guarantee*) sichern
assured [ə'ʃuəd] *n* (*Brit*) Versicherte(r) *f(m)* ▷ *adj* sicher
AST (*US*) *abbr* (= *Atlantic Standard Time*) *Ortszeit in Ostkanada*
asterisk ['æstərɪsk] *n* Sternchen *nt*
astern [ə'stəːn] *adv* achtern
asteroid ['æstərɔɪd] *n* Asteroid *m*
asthma ['æsmə] *n* Asthma *nt*
asthmatic [æs'mætɪk] *adj* asthmatisch ▷ *n* Asthmatiker(in) *m(f)*
astigmatism [ə'stɪgmətɪzəm] *n* Astigmatismus *m*
astir [ə'stəːʳ] *adv*: **to be ~** (*out of bed*) auf sein
astonish [ə'stɔnɪʃ] *vt* erstaunen
astonishing [ə'stɔnɪʃɪŋ] *adj* erstaunlich; **I find it ~ that ...** es überrascht mich, dass ...
astonishingly [ə'stɔnɪʃɪŋlɪ] *adv* erstaunlich; **~, ...** erstaunlicherweise ...
astonishment [ə'stɔnɪʃmənt] *n* Erstaunen *nt*
astound [ə'staund] *vt* verblüffen, sehr erstaunen
astounded [ə'staundɪd] *adj* (höchst) erstaunt
astounding [ə'staundɪŋ] *adj* erstaunlich
astray [ə'streɪ] *adv*: **to go ~** (*letter*) verloren gehen; (*fig*) auf Abwege geraten; **to lead ~** auf Abwege bringen; **to go ~ in one's calculations** sich verrechnen
astride [ə'straɪd] *adv* (*sit, ride*) rittlings; (*stand*) breitbeinig ▷ *prep* rittlings auf +*dat*; breitbeinig über +*dat*
astringent [əs'trɪndʒənt] *adj* adstringierend; (*fig: caustic*) ätzend, beißend ▷ *n* Adstringens *nt*
astrologer [əs'trɔlədʒəʳ] *n* Astrologe *m*, Astrologin *f*
astrology [əs'trɔlədʒɪ] *n* Astrologie *f*
astronaut ['æstrənɔːt] *n* Astronaut(in) *m(f)*
astronomer [əs'trɔnəməʳ] *n* Astronom(in) *m(f)*
astronomical [æstrə'nɔmɪkl] *adj* (*also fig*) astronomisch
astronomy [əs'trɔnəmɪ] *n* Astronomie *f*
astrophysics ['æstrəu'fɪzɪks] *n* Astrophysik *f*
astute [əs'tjuːt] *adj* scharfsinnig; (*operator, behaviour*) geschickt
asunder [ə'sʌndəʳ] *adv*: **to tear ~** auseinanderreißen
ASV *n abbr* (*Bible:* = *American Standard Version*) *amerikanische Standard-Bibelübersetzung*
asylum [ə'saɪləm] *n* Asyl *nt*; (*mental hospital*) psychiatrische Klinik *f*; **to seek political ~** um (politisches) Asyl bitten
asymmetrical [eɪsɪ'mɛtrɪkl] *adj* asymmetrisch

KEYWORD

at [æt] *prep* **1** (*referring to position, direction*) an +*dat*, in +*dat*; **at the top** an der Spitze; **at home** zu Hause; **at school** in der Schule; **at the baker's** beim Bäcker; **to look at sth** auf etw *acc* blicken
2 (*referring to time*): **at four o'clock** um vier Uhr; **at night/dawn** bei Nacht/Tagesanbruch; **at Christmas** zu Weihnachten; **at times** zuweilen
3 (*referring to rates, speed etc*): **at £2 a kilo** zu £2 pro Kilo; **two at a time** zwei auf einmal; **at 50 km/h** mit 50 km/h
4 (*referring to activity*): **to be at work** (*in office etc*) auf der Arbeit sein; **to play at cowboys** Cowboy spielen; **to be good at sth** gut in etw *dat* sein
5 (*referring to cause*): **shocked/surprised/annoyed at sth** schockiert/überrascht/verärgert über etw *acc*; **I went at his suggestion** ich ging auf seinen Vorschlag hin
6: not at all (*in answer to question*) überhaupt nicht, ganz und gar nicht; (*in answer to thanks*) nichts zu danken, keine Ursache; **I'm not at all tired** ich bin überhaupt nicht müde; **anything at all** irgendetwas

ate [eɪt] *pt of* **eat**
atheism ['eɪθɪɪzəm] *n* Atheismus *m*
atheist ['eɪθɪɪst] *n* Atheist(in) *m(f)*
Athenian [ə'θiːnɪən] *adj* Athener ▷ *n* Athener(in) *m(f)*
Athens ['æθɪnz] *n* Athen *nt*
athlete ['æθliːt] *n* Athlet(in) *m(f)*
athletic [æθ'lɛtɪk] *adj* sportlich; (*muscular*) athletisch
athletics [æθ'lɛtɪks] *n* Leichtathletik *f*
Atlantic [ət'læntɪk] *adj* atlantisch; (*coast etc*) Atlantik- ▷ *n*: **the ~ (Ocean)** der Atlantik
atlas ['ætləs] *n* Atlas *m*
Atlas Mountains *npl*: **the ~** der Atlas, das Atlasgebirge
ATM *abbr* (= *automated teller machine*) Geldautomat *m*
atmosphere ['ætməsfɪəʳ] *n* Atmosphäre *f*; (*air*) Luft *f*
atmospheric [ætməs'fɛrɪk] *adj* atmosphärisch
atmospherics [ætməs'fɛrɪks] *npl* atmosphärische Störungen *pl*
atoll ['ætɔl] *n* Atoll *nt*
atom ['ætəm] *n* Atom *nt*
atom bomb *n* Atombombe *f*
atomic [ə'tɔmɪk] *adj* atomar; (*energy, weapons*) Atom-

atomic bomb *n* Atombombe *f*
atomizer [ˈætəmaɪzəʳ] *n* Zerstäuber *m*
atone [əˈtəun] *vi*: **to ~ for** büßen für
atonement [əˈtəunmənt] *n* Buße *f*
A to Z® *n* Stadtplan *m*
ATP *n abbr (= Association of Tennis Professionals)* *Tennis-Profiverband*
atrocious [əˈtrəuʃəs] *adj* grauenhaft
atrocity [əˈtrɔsɪtɪ] *n* Gräueltat *f*
atrophy [ˈætrəfɪ] *n* Schwund *m*, Atrophie *f* ▷ *vt* schwinden lassen ▷ *vi* schwinden, verkümmern
attach [əˈtætʃ] *vt* befestigen; *(document, letter)* anheften, beiheften; *(employee, troops)* zuteilen; *(importance etc)* beimessen; **to be ~ed to sb/sth** *(like)* an jdm/etw hängen; *(be connected with)* mit jdm/etw zu tun haben; **the ~ed letter** der beiliegende Brief
attaché [əˈtæʃeɪ] *n* Attaché *m*
attaché case *n* Aktenkoffer *m*
attachment [əˈtætʃmənt] *n (tool)* Zubehörteil *nt*; *(love)*: **~ (to sb)** Zuneigung *f* (zu jdm)
attack [əˈtæk] *vt* angreifen; *(subj: criminal)* überfallen; *(task, problem etc)* in Angriff nehmen ▷ *n (also fig)* Angriff *m*; *(on sb's life)* Anschlag *m*; *(of illness)* Anfall *m*; **heart ~** Herzanfall *m*, Herzinfarkt *m*
attacker [əˈtækəʳ] *n* Angreifer(in) *m(f)*
attain [əˈteɪn] *vt (also*: **attain to**) erreichen; *(knowledge)* erlangen
attainments [əˈteɪnmənts] *npl* Fähigkeiten *pl*
attempt [əˈtɛmpt] *n* Versuch *m* ▷ *vt* versuchen; **to make an ~ on sb's life** einen Anschlag auf jdn verüben
attempted [əˈtɛmptɪd] *adj* versucht; **~ murder/suicide** Mord-/Selbstmordversuch *m*; **~ theft** versuchter Diebstahl
attend [əˈtɛnd] *vt* besuchen; *(patient)* behandeln
▸ **attend to** *vt fus* sich kümmern um; *(needs)* nachkommen *+dat*; *(customer)* bedienen
attendance [əˈtɛndəns] *n* Anwesenheit *f*; *(people present)* Besucherzahl *f*; *(Sport)* Zuschauerzahl *f*
attendant [əˈtɛndənt] *n (helper)* Begleiter(in) *m(f)*; *(in garage)* Tankwart *m*; *(in museum)* Aufseher(in) *m(f)* ▷ *adj* damit verbunden
attention [əˈtɛnʃən] *n* Aufmerksamkeit *f*; *(care)* Fürsorge *f* ▷ *excl (Mil)* Achtung!; **attentions** *npl (acts of courtesy)* Aufmerksamkeiten *pl*; **for the ~ of ...** zu Händen von ...; **it has come to my ~ that ...** ich bin darauf aufmerksam geworden, dass ...; **to stand to** *or* **at ~** *(Mil)* stillstehen
attentive [əˈtɛntɪv] *adj* aufmerksam
attentively [əˈtɛntɪvlɪ] *adv* aufmerksam
attenuate [əˈtɛnjueɪt] *vt* abschwächen ▷ *vi* schwächer werden
attest [əˈtɛst] *vt, vi*: **to ~ (to)** bezeugen
attic [ˈætɪk] *n* Dachboden *m*
attire [əˈtaɪəʳ] *n* Kleidung *f*
attitude [ˈætɪtjuːd] *n (posture, manner)* Haltung *f*; *(mental)*: **~ to** *or* **towards** Einstellung *f* zu
attorney [əˈtəːnɪ] *n (US: lawyer)* (Rechts)anwalt *m*, (Rechts)anwältin *f*; *(having proxy)* Bevollmächtigte(r) *f(m)*; **power of ~** Vollmacht *f*
Attorney General *n (Brit)* ≈ Justizminister(in) *m(f)*; (US) ≈ Generalbundesanwalt *m*, ≈ Generalbundesanwältin *f*
attract [əˈtrækt] *vt (draw)* anziehen; *(interest)* auf sich *acc* lenken; *(attention)* erregen
attraction [əˈtrækʃən] *n* Anziehungskraft *f*; *(of house, city)* Reiz *m*; *(gen pl: amusements)* Attraktion *f*; *(fig)*: **to feel an ~ towards sb/sth** sich von jdm/etw angezogen fühlen
attractive [əˈtræktɪv] *adj* attraktiv; *(price, idea, offer)* verlockend, reizvoll
attribute [*n* ˈætrɪbjuːt, *vt* əˈtrɪbjuːt] *n* Eigenschaft *f* ▷ *vt*: **to ~ sth to** *(cause)* etw zurückführen auf *+acc*; *(poem, painting)* etw zuschreiben *+dat*; *(quality)* etw beimessen *+dat*
attribution [ætrɪˈbjuːʃən] *n (see vt)* Zurückführung *f*; Zuschreibung *f*; Beimessung *f*
attrition [əˈtrɪʃən] *n*: **war of ~** Zermürbungskrieg *m*
Atty. Gen. *abbr* = **Attorney General**
ATV *n abbr (= all-terrain vehicle)* Geländefahrzeug *nt*
atypical [eɪˈtɪpɪkl] *adj* atypisch
aubergine [ˈəubəʒiːn] *n* Aubergine *f*; *(colour)* Aubergine *nt*
auburn [ˈɔːbən] *adj* rotbraun
auction [ˈɔːkʃən] *n (also*: **sale by auction**) Versteigerung *f*, Auktion *f* ▷ *vt* versteigern
auctioneer [ɔːkʃəˈnɪəʳ] *n* Versteigerer *m*
auction room *n* Auktionssaal *m*
audacious [ɔːˈdeɪʃəs] *adj* wagemutig, kühn
audacity [ɔːˈdæsɪtɪ] *n* Kühnheit *f*, Verwegenheit *f*; *(pej: impudence)* Dreistigkeit *f*
audible [ˈɔːdɪbl] *adj* hörbar
audience [ˈɔːdɪəns] *n* Publikum *nt*; *(Radio)* Zuhörer *pl*; *(TV)* Zuschauer *pl*; *(with queen etc)* Audienz *f*
audiotypist [ˈɔːdɪəuˈtaɪpɪst] *n* Fonotypist(in) *m(f)*, Phonotypist(in) *m(f)*
audiovisual [ˈɔːdɪəuˈvɪzjuəl] *adj* audiovisuell
audiovisual aid *n* audiovisuelles Lehrmittel *nt*
audit [ˈɔːdɪt] *vt (Comm)* prüfen ▷ *n* Buchprüfung *f*, Rechnungsprüfung *f*
audition [ɔːˈdɪʃən] *n* Vorsprechprobe *f* ▷ *vi*: **to ~ (for)** vorsprechen (für)
auditor [ˈɔːdɪtəʳ] *n* Buchprüfer(in) *m(f)*, Rechnungsprüfer(in) *m(f)*
auditorium [ɔːdɪˈtɔːrɪəm] *n (building)* Auditorium *nt*; *(audience area)* Zuschauerraum *m*
AU *n abbr* = *African Union*
Aug. *abbr* = **August**
augment [ɔːgˈmɛnt] *vt* vermehren; *(income, diet)* verbessern
augur [ˈɔːgəʳ] *vi*: **it ~s well** das ist ein gutes Zeichen *or* Omen
August [ˈɔːgəst] *n* August *m*; *see also* **July**
august [ɔːˈgʌst] *adj* erhaben

aunt [ɑ:nt] *n* Tante *f*
auntie ['ɑ:ntɪ] *n dimin of* **aunt**
aunty ['ɑ:ntɪ] *n dimin of* **aunt**
au pair ['əu'pɛəʳ] *n* (*also*: **au pair girl**) Aupair(mädchen) *nt*, Au-pair(-Mädchen) *nt*
aura ['ɔ:rə] *n* Aura *f*
auspices ['ɔ:spɪsɪz] *npl*: **under the ~ of** unter der Schirmherrschaft *+gen*
auspicious [ɔ:s'pɪʃəs] *adj* verheißungsvoll; (*opening, start*) vielversprechend
austere [ɔs'tɪəʳ] *adj* streng; (*room, decoration*) schmucklos; (*person, lifestyle*) asketisch
austerity [ɔs'tɛrɪtɪ] *n* Strenge *f*; (*of room etc*) Schmucklosigkeit *f*; (*hardship*) Entbehrung *f*
Australasia [ɔ:strə'leɪzɪə] *n* Australien und Ozeanien *nt*
Australasian [ɔ:strə'leɪzɪən] *adj* ozeanisch, südwestpazifisch
Australia [ɔs'treɪlɪə] *n* Australien *nt*
Australian [ɔs'treɪlɪən] *adj* australisch ▷ *n* Australier(in) *m(f)*
Austria ['ɔstrɪə] *n* Österreich *nt*
Austrian ['ɔstrɪən] *adj* österreichisch ▷ *n* Österreicher(in) *m(f)*
AUT (*Brit*) *n abbr* (*= Association of University Teachers*) *Gewerkschaft der Universitätsdozenten*
authentic [ɔ:'θɛntɪk] *adj* authentisch
authenticate [ɔ:'θɛntɪkeɪt] *vt* beglaubigen
authenticity [ɔ:θɛn'tɪsɪtɪ] *n* Echtheit *f*
author ['ɔ:θəʳ] *n* (*of text*) Verfasser(in) *m(f)*; (*profession*) Autor(in) *m(f)*, Schriftsteller(in) *m(f)*; (*creator*) Urheber(in) *m(f)*; (*: of plan*) Initiator(in) *m(f)*
authoritarian [ɔ:θɔrɪ'tɛərɪən] *adj* autoritär
authoritative [ɔ:'θɔrɪtətɪv] *adj* (*person, manner*) bestimmt, entschieden; (*source, account*) zuverlässig; (*study, treatise*) maßgeblich, maßgebend
authority [ɔ:'θɔrɪtɪ] *n* Autorität *f*; (*government body*) Behörde *f*, Amt *nt*; (*official permission*) Genehmigung *f*; **the authorities** *npl* (*ruling body*) die Behörden *pl*; **to have the ~ to do sth** befugt sein, etw zu tun
authorization [ɔ:θəraɪ'zeɪʃən] *n* Genehmigung *f*
authorize ['ɔ:θəraɪz] *vt* genehmigen; **to ~ sb to do sth** jdn ermächtigen, etw zu tun
authorized capital ['ɔ:θəraɪzd-] *n* autorisiertes Aktienkapital *nt*
authorship ['ɔ:θəʃɪp] *n* Autorschaft *f*, Verfasserschaft *f*
autistic [ɔ:'tɪstɪk] *adj* autistisch
auto ['ɔ:təu] (*US*) *n* Auto *nt*, Wagen *m*
autobiographical ['ɔ:təbaɪə'græfɪkl] *adj* autobiografisch
autobiography [ɔ:təbaɪ'ɔgrəfɪ] *n* Autobiografie *f*
autocratic [ɔ:tə'krætɪk] *adj* autokratisch
Autocue® ['ɔ:təukju:] *n* Teleprompter *m*
autograph ['ɔ:təgrɑ:f] *n* Autogramm *nt* ▷ *vt* signieren
autoimmune [ɔ:təuɪ'mju:n] *adj* (*disease*) Autoimmun-
automat ['ɔ:təmæt] *n* Automat *m*; (*US*) Automatenrestaurant *nt*
automata [ɔ:'tɔmətə] *npl of* **automaton**
automate ['ɔ:təmeɪt] *vt* automatisieren
automatic [ɔ:tə'mætɪk] *adj* automatisch ▷ *n* (*gun*) automatische Waffe; (*washing machine*) Waschautomat *m*; (*car*) Automatikwagen *m*
automatically [ɔ:tə'mætɪklɪ] *adv* automatisch
automatic data processing *n* automatische Datenverarbeitung *f*
automation [ɔ:tə'meɪʃən] *n* Automatisierung *f*
automaton [ɔ:'tɔmətən] (*pl* **automata**) *n* Roboter *m*
automobile ['ɔ:təməbi:l] (*US*) *n* Auto(mobil) *nt*
autonomous [ɔ:'tɔnəməs] *adj* autonom
autonomy [ɔ:'tɔnəmɪ] *n* Autonomie *f*
autopsy ['ɔ:tɔpsɪ] *n* Autopsie *f*
autumn ['ɔ:təm] *n* Herbst *m*; **in ~** im Herbst
autumnal [ɔ:'tʌmnəl] *adj* herbstlich
auxiliary [ɔ:g'zɪlɪərɪ] *adj* (*tool, verb*) Hilfs- ▷ *n* (*assistant*) Hilfskraft *f*
AV *n abbr* (*Bible: = Authorized Version*) *englische Bibelübersetzung von 1611* ▷ *abbr* = **audiovisual**
avail [ə'veɪl] *vt*: **to ~ o.s. of** Gebrauch machen von ▷ *n*: **to no ~** vergeblich, erfolglos
availability [əveɪlə'bɪlɪtɪ] *n* Erhältlichkeit *f*; (*of staff*) Vorhandensein *nt*
available [ə'veɪləbl] *adj* erhältlich; (*person: unoccupied*) frei, abkömmlich; (*: unattached*) zu haben; (*time*) frei, verfügbar; **every ~ means** alle verfügbaren Mittel; **is the manager ~?** ist der Geschäftsführer zu sprechen?; **to make sth ~ to sb** jdm etw zur Verfügung stellen
avalanche ['ævəlɑ:nʃ] *n* (*also fig*) Lawine *f*
avant-garde ['ævɑ̃ŋ'gɑ:d] *adj* avantgardistisch
avarice ['ævərɪs] *n* Habsucht *f*
avaricious [ævə'rɪʃəs] *adj* habsüchtig
avdp. *abbr* (*= avoirdupois*) *Handelsgewicht*
Ave *abbr* = **avenue**
avenge [ə'vɛndʒ] *vt* rächen
avenue ['ævənju:] *n* Straße *f*; (*drive*) Auffahrt *f*; (*means*) Weg *m*
average ['ævərɪdʒ] *n* Durchschnitt *m* ▷ *adj* durchschnittlich, Durchschnitts- ▷ *vt* (*reach an average of*) einen Durchschnitt erreichen von; **on ~** im Durchschnitt, durchschnittlich; **above/below (the) ~** über/unter dem Durchschnitt
▸ **average out** *vi*: **to ~ out at** durchschnittlich ausmachen
averse [ə'və:s] *adj*: **to be ~ to sth/doing sth** eine Abneigung gegen etw haben/dagegen haben, etw zu tun; **I wouldn't be ~ to a drink** ich hätte nichts gegen einen Drink
aversion [ə'və:ʃən] *n* Abneigung *f*; **to have an ~ to sb/sth** eine Abneigung gegen jdn/etw haben
avert [ə'və:t] *vt* (*prevent*) verhindern; (*ward off*) abwehren; (*turn away*) abwenden
aviary ['eɪvɪərɪ] *n* Vogelhaus *nt*
aviation [eɪvɪ'eɪʃən] *n* Luftfahrt *f*
avid ['ævɪd] *adj* begeistert, eifrig

avidly ['ævɪdlɪ] *adv* begeistert, eifrig
avocado [ævə'kɑ:dəu] *(Brit) n (also:* **avocado pear***)* Avocado *f*
avoid [ə'vɔɪd] *vt (person, obstacle)* ausweichen *+dat*; *(trouble)* vermeiden; *(danger)* meiden
avoidable [ə'vɔɪdəbl] *adj* vermeidbar
avoidance [ə'vɔɪdəns] *n (of tax)* Umgehung *f*; *(of issue)* Vermeidung *f*
avowed [ə'vaud] *adj* erklärt
AVP *(US) n abbr (= assistant vice president) stellvertretender Vizepräsident*
avuncular [ə'vʌŋkjuləʳ] *adj* onkelhaft
AWACS ['eɪwæks] *n abbr (= airborne warning and control system)* AWACS
await [ə'weɪt] *vt* warten auf *+acc*; **~ing attention/delivery** zur Bearbeitung/ Lieferung bestimmt; **long ~ed** lang ersehnt
awake [ə'weɪk] *(pt* **awoke**, *pp* **awoken** *or* **~d***) adj* wach ▷ *vt* wecken ▷ *vi* erwachen, aufwachen; **~ to** sich *dat* bewusst werden *+gen*
awakening [ə'weɪknɪŋ] *n (also fig)* Erwachen *nt*
award [ə'wɔ:d] *n* Preis *m*; *(for bravery)* Auszeichnung *f*; *(damages)* Entschädigung(ssumme) *f* ▷ *vt (prize)* verleihen; *(damages)* zusprechen
aware [ə'wɛəʳ] *adj*: **~ (of)** bewusst *(+gen)*; **to become ~ of** sich *dat* bewusst werden *+gen*; **to become ~ that ...** sich *dat* bewusst werden, dass ...; **politically/socially ~** politik-/ sozialbewusst; **I am fully ~ that** es ist mir völlig klar *or* bewusst, dass
awareness [ə'wɛənɪs] *n* Bewusstsein *nt*; **to develop people's ~ of sth** den Menschen etw zu Bewusstsein bringen
awash [ə'wɔʃ] *adj (also fig)* überflutet
away [ə'weɪ] *adv* weg, fort; *(position)* entfernt; **two kilometres ~** zwei Kilometer entfernt; **two hours ~ by car** zwei Autostunden entfernt; **the holiday was two weeks ~** es war noch zwei Wochen bis zum Urlaub; **he's ~ for a week** er ist eine Woche nicht da; **he's ~ in Milan** er ist in Mailand; **to take ~ (from)** *(remove)* entfernen (von); *(subtract)* abziehen (von); **to work/pedal** *etc* **~** unablässig arbeiten/strampeln *etc*; **to fade ~** *(colour, light)* verblassen; *(sound)* verhallen; *(enthusiasm)* schwinden
away game *n* Auswärtsspiel *nt*
awe [ɔ:] *n* Ehrfurcht *f*
awe-inspiring ['ɔ:ɪnspaɪərɪŋ] *adj* Ehrfurcht gebietend
awesome ['ɔ:səm] *adj* Ehrfurcht gebietend; *(fig: inf)* überwältigend
awe-struck ['ɔ:strʌk] *adj* von Ehrfurcht ergriffen
awful ['ɔ:fəl] *adj* furchtbar, schrecklich; **an ~ lot (of)** furchtbar viel(e)
awfully ['ɔ:fəlɪ] *adv* furchtbar, schrecklich
awhile [ə'waɪl] *adv* eine Weile
awkward ['ɔ:kwəd] *adj (clumsy)* unbeholfen; *(inconvenient, difficult)* ungünstig; *(embarrassing)* peinlich
awkwardness ['ɔ:kwədnɪs] *n (see adj)* Unbeholfenheit *f*; Ungünstigkeit *f*; Peinlichkeit *f*
awl [ɔ:l] *n* Ahle *f*, Pfriem *m*
awning ['ɔ:nɪŋ] *n (of tent, caravan)* Vordach *nt*; *(of shop etc)* Markise *f*
awoke [ə'wəuk] *pt of* **awake**
awoken [ə'wəukən] *pp of* **awake**
AWOL ['eɪwɔl] *abbr (Mil: = absent without leave) see* **absent**
awry [ə'raɪ] *adv*: **to be ~** *(clothes)* schief sitzen; **to go ~** schiefgehen
axe, *(US)* **ax** [æks] *n* Axt *f*, Beil *nt* ▷ *vt (employee)* entlassen; *(project, jobs etc)* streichen; **to have an ~ to grind** *(fig)* ein persönliches Interesse haben
axes¹ ['æksɪz] *npl of* **axe**
axes² ['æksi:z] *npl of* **axis**
axiom ['æksɪəm] *n* Axiom *nt*, Grundsatz *m*
axiomatic [æksɪəu'mætɪk] *adj* axiomatisch
axis ['æksɪs] *(pl* **axes²***) n* Achse *f*
axle ['æksl] *n (also:* **axletree***)* Achse *f*
aye [aɪ] *excl (yes)* ja ▷ *n*: **the ~s** die Jastimmen *pl*
AYH *n abbr (= American Youth Hostels) Jugendherbergsverband*, ≈ DJHV *m*
AZ *(US) abbr (Post)* = **Arizona**
azalea [ə'zeɪlɪə] *n* Azalee *f*
Azerbaijan [æzəbaɪ'dʒɑ:n] *n* Aserbaidschan *nt*
Azerbaijani [æzəbaɪ'dʒɑ:nɪ], **Azeri** [ə'zeərɪ] *adj* aserbaidschanisch ▷ *n* Aserbaidschaner(in) *m(f)*
Azores [ə'zɔ:z] *npl*: **the ~** die Azoren *pl*
AZT *n abbr (= azidothymidine)* AZT *nt*
Aztec ['æztɛk] *adj* aztekisch ▷ *n* Azteke *m*, Aztekin *f*
azure ['eɪʒəʳ] *adj* azurblau, tiefblau

Bb

B¹, **b** [biː] *n* (*letter*) B *nt*, b *nt*; (*Scol*) ≈ Zwei *f*, ≈ Gut *nt*; **B for Benjamin, B for Baker** (*US*) ≈ B wie Bertha; **B road** (*Brit*) Landstraße *f*
B² [biː] *n* (*Mus*) H *nt*, h *nt*
b. *abbr* = **born**
BA *n abbr* (= *Bachelor of Arts*) *see* **bachelor**; (= *British Academy*) *Verband zur Förderung der Künste und Geisteswissenschaften*
babble [ˈbæbl] *vi* schwatzen; (*baby*) plappern; (*brook*) plätschern ▷ *n*: **a ~ of voices** ein Stimmengewirr *nt*
babe [beɪb] *n* (*liter*) Kindlein *nt*; (*esp US*: *address*) Schätzchen *nt*; **~ in arms** Säugling *m*
baboon [bəˈbuːn] *n* Pavian *m*
baby [ˈbeɪbɪ] *n* Baby *nt*; (*US*: *inf*: *darling*) Schatz *m*, Schätzchen *nt*
baby carriage (*US*) *n* Kinderwagen *m*
baby grand *n* (*also*: **baby grand piano**) Stutzflügel *m*
babyhood [ˈbeɪbɪhud] *n* frühe Kindheit *f*
babyish [ˈbeɪbɪɪʃ] *adj* kindlich
baby-minder [ˈbeɪbɪˈmaɪndəʳ] (*Brit*) *n* Tagesmutter *f*
baby-sit [ˈbeɪbɪsɪt] *vi* babysitten
baby-sitter [ˈbeɪbɪsɪtəʳ] *n* Babysitter(in) *m(f)*
baby wipe *n* Ölpflegetuch *nt*
bachelor [ˈbætʃələʳ] *n* Junggeselle *m*; **B~ of Arts/Science (degree)** ≈ Magister *m* der philosophischen Fakultät/der Naturwissenschaften
bachelorhood [ˈbætʃələhud] *n* Junggesellentum *nt*
bachelor party (*US*) *n* Junggesellenparty *f*

BACHELOR'S DEGREE

Bachelor's Degree ist der akademische Grad, den man nach drei- oder vierjährigem, erfolgreich abgeschlossenem Universitätsstudium erhält. Die am häufigsten verliehenen Grade sind *BA* (Bachelor of Arts = Magister der Geisteswissenschaften), *BSc* (Bachelor of Science = Magister der Naturwissenschaften), *BEd* (Bachelor of Education = Magister der Erziehungswissenschaften) und *LLB* (Bachelor of Laws = Magister der Rechtswissenschaften). Siehe auch *master's degree, doctorate*.

back [bæk] *n* Rücken *m*; (*of house, page*) Rückseite *f*; (*of chair*) (Rücken)lehne *f*; (*of train*) Ende *nt*; (*Football*) Verteidiger *m* ▷ *vt* (*candidate*: *also*: **back up**) unterstützen; (*horse*) setzen *or* wetten auf +*acc*; (*car*) zurücksetzen, zurückfahren ▷ *vi* (*also*: **back up**: *person*) rückwärtsgehen; (*car etc*) zurücksetzen, zurückfahren ▷ *cpd* (*payment, rent*) ausstehend ▷ *adv* hinten; **in the ~ (of the car)** hinten (im Auto); **at the ~ of the book/crowd/audience** hinten im Buch/in der Menge/im Publikum; **~ to front** verkehrt herum; **to break the ~ of a job** (*Brit*) mit einer Arbeit über den Berg sein; **to have one's ~ to the wall** (*fig*) in die Enge getrieben sein; **~ room** Hinterzimmer *nt*; **~ garden** Garten *m* (hinter dem Haus); **~ seat** (*Aut*) Rücksitz *m*; **to take a ~ seat** (*fig*) sich zurückhalten; **~ wheels** Hinterräder *pl*; **he's ~** er ist zurück *or* wieder da; **throw the ball ~** wirf den Ball zurück; **he called ~** er rief zurück; **he ran ~** er rannte zurück; **when will you be ~?** wann kommen Sie wieder?; **can I have it ~?** kann ich es zurückhaben *or* wiederhaben?
▸ **back down** *vi* nachgeben
▸ **back on to** *vt fus*: **the house ~s on to the golf course** das Haus grenzt hinten an den Golfplatz an
▸ **back out** *vi* (*of promise*) einen Rückzieher machen
▸ **back up** *vt* (*support*) unterstützen; (*Comput*) sichern
backache [ˈbækeɪk] *n* Rückenschmerzen *pl*

BACK BENCH

Back Bench bezeichnet im britischen Unterhaus die am weitesten vom Mittelgang entfernten Bänke, im Gegensatz zur *front bench*. Auf diesen hinteren Bänken sitzen diejenigen Unterhausabgeordneten (auch backbenchers genannt), die kein

Regierungsamt bzw. keine wichtige Stellung in der Opposition innehaben.

backbencher ['bæk'bɛntʃəʳ] (*Brit*) *n* Abgeordnete(r) *f(m)* (*in den hinteren Reihen im britischen Parlament*), Hinterbänkler(in) *m(f)* (*pej*); *see also* **back bench**
backbiting ['bækbaɪtɪŋ] *n* Lästern *nt*
backbone ['bækbəun] *n* (*also fig*) Rückgrat *nt*
backchat ['bæktʃæt] (*Brit: inf*) *n* Widerrede *f*
backcloth ['bækklɔθ] (*Brit*) *n* Hintergrund *m*
backcomb ['bækkəum] (*Brit*) *vt* toupieren
backdate [bæk'deɪt] *vt* (zu)rückdatieren; **~d pay rise** rückwirkend geltende Gehaltserhöhung *f*
backdrop ['bækdrɔp] *n* = **backcloth**
backer ['bækəʳ] *n* (*Comm*) Geldgeber *m*
backfire [bæk'faɪəʳ] *vi* (*Aut*) Fehlzündungen haben; (*plans*) ins Auge gehen
backgammon ['bækgæmən] *n* Backgammon *nt*
background ['bækgraund] *n* Hintergrund *m*; (*basic knowledge*) Grundkenntnisse *pl*; (*experience*) Erfahrung *f* ▷ *cpd* (*music*) Hintergrund-; **family ~** Herkunft *f*; **~ noise** Geräuschkulisse *f*; **~ reading** vertiefende Lektüre *f*
backhand ['bækhænd] *n* (*Tennis: also:* **backhand stroke**) Rückhand *f*
backhanded ['bæk'hændɪd] *adj* (*fig: compliment*) zweifelhaft
backhander ['bæk'hændəʳ] (*Brit*) *n* Schmiergeld *nt*
backing ['bækɪŋ] *n* (*Comm: fig*) Unterstützung *f*; (*Mus*) Begleitung *f*
backlash ['bæklæʃ] *n* (*fig*) Gegenreaktion *f*
backlog ['bæklɔg] *n*: **to have a ~ of work** mit der Arbeit im Rückstand sein
back number *n* alte Ausgabe *f or* Nummer *f*
backpack ['bækpæk] *n* Rucksack *m*
backpacker ['bækpækəʳ] *n* Rucksacktourist(in) *m(f)*
back pay *n* Nachzahlung *f*
back-pedal ['bækpɛdl] *vi* (*fig*) einen Rückzieher machen
back-seat driver *n Mitfahrer, der dem Fahrer dazwischenredet*
backside ['bæksaɪd] (*inf*) *n* Hintern *m*
backslash ['bækslæʃ] *n* Backslash *m*
backslide ['bækslaɪd] *vi* rückfällig werden
backspace ['bækspeɪs] *vi* (*in typing*) die Rücktaste betätigen
backstage [bæk'steɪdʒ] *adv* (*Theat*) hinter den Kulissen; (*: in dressing-room area*) in der Garderobe
backstreet ['bækstri:t] *n* Seitenstraße *f* ▷ *cpd*: **~ abortionist** Engelmacher(in) *m(f)*
backstroke ['bækstrəuk] *n* Rückenschwimmen *nt*
backtrack ['bæktræk] *vi* (*fig*) einen Rückzieher machen
backup ['bækʌp] *adj* (*train, plane*) Entlastungs-; (*Comput: copy etc*) Sicherungs- ▷ *n* (*support*) Unterstützung *f*; (*Comput: also:* **backup disk, backup file**) Sicherungskopie *f*, Back-up *nt*
backward ['bækwəd] *adj* (*movement*) Rückwärts-; (*person*) zurückgeblieben; (*country*) rückständig; **~ and forward movement** Vor- und Zurückbewegung *f*; **~ step/glance** Blick *m*/Schritt *m* zurück
backwards ['bækwədz] *adv* rückwärts; (*read*) von hinten nach vorne; (*fall*) nach hinten; (*in time*) zurück; **to know sth ~, to know sth ~ and forwards** (*US*) etw in- und auswendig kennen
backwater ['bækwɔ:təʳ] *n* (*fig*) Kaff *nt*
back yard *n* Hinterhof *m*
bacon ['beɪkən] *n* (Frühstücks)speck *m*, (Schinken)speck *m*
bacteria [bæk'tɪərɪə] *npl* Bakterien *pl*
bacteriology [bæktɪərɪ'ɔlədʒɪ] *n* Bakteriologie *f*
bad [bæd] *adj* schlecht; (*naughty*) unartig, ungezogen; (*mistake, accident, injury*) schwer; **his ~ leg** sein schlimmes Bein; **to go ~** verderben, schlecht werden; **to have a ~ time of it** es schwer haben; **I feel ~ about it** es tut mir leid; **in ~ faith** mit böser Absicht
bad debt *n* uneinbringliche Forderung *f*
baddy ['bædɪ] (*inf*) *n* Bösewicht *m*
bade [bæd] *pt of* **bid**
badge [bædʒ] *n* Plakette *f*; (*stick-on*) Aufkleber *m*; (*fig*) Merkmal *nt*
badger ['bædʒəʳ] *n* Dachs *m* ▷ *vt* zusetzen *+dat*
bad hair day *n* (*inf*) Scheißtag *f*, Tag *m*, an dem alles schiefgeht
badly ['bædlɪ] *adv* schlecht; **~ wounded** schwer verletzt; **he needs it ~** er braucht es dringend; **things are going ~** es sieht schlecht *or* nicht gut aus; **to be ~ off (for money)** wenig Geld haben
bad-mannered ['bæd'mænəd] *adj* ungezogen, unhöflich
badminton ['bædmɪntən] *n* Federball *m*
bad-tempered ['bæd'tɛmpəd] *adj* schlecht gelaunt; (*by nature*) übellaunig
baffle ['bæfl] *vt* verblüffen
baffling ['bæflɪŋ] *adj* rätselhaft, verwirrend
bag [bæg] *n* Tasche *f*; (*made of paper, plastic*) Tüte *f*; (*handbag*) (Hand)tasche *f*; (*satchel*) Schultasche *f*; (*case*) Reisetasche *f*; (*of hunter*) Jagdbeute *f*; (*pej: woman*) Schachtel *f*; **~s of** (*inf: lots of*) jede Menge; **to pack one's ~s** die Koffer packen; **~s under the eyes** Ringe *pl* unter den Augen
bagful ['bægful] *n*: **a ~ of** eine Tasche/Tüte voll
baggage ['bægɪdʒ] *n* Gepäck *nt*
baggage allowance *n* Freigepäck *nt*
baggage car (*US*) *n* Gepäckwagen *m*
baggage claim *n* Gepäckausgabe *f*
baggy ['bægɪ] *adj* weit; (*out of shape*) ausgebeult
Baghdad [bæg'dæd] *n* Bagdad *nt*
bag lady (*esp US*) *n* Stadtstreicherin *f*
bagpipes ['bægpaɪps] *npl* Dudelsack *m*
bag-snatcher ['bægsnætʃəʳ] (*Brit*) *n* Handtaschendieb(in) *m(f)*

Bahamas [bəˈhɑːməz] *npl*: **the ~** die Bahamas *pl*, die Bahamainseln *pl*
Bahrain [bɑːˈreɪn] *n* Bahrain *nt*
bail [beɪl] *n* (*Law: payment*) Kaution *f*; (*: release*) Freilassung *f* gegen Kaution ▷ *vt* (*prisoner*) gegen Kaution freilassen; (*boat: also*: **bail out**) ausschöpfen; **to be on ~** gegen Kaution freigelassen sein; **to be released on ~** gegen Kaution freigelassen werden; *see also* **bale**
▶ **bail out** *vt* (*prisoner*) gegen Kaution freibekommen; (*firm, friend*) aus der Patsche helfen *+dat*
bailiff [ˈbeɪlɪf] *n* (*Law: Brit*) Gerichtsvollzieher(in) *m(f)*; (*: US*) Gerichtsdiener(in) *m(f)*; (*Brit: factor*) (Guts)verwalter(in) *m(f)*
bait [beɪt] *n* Köder *m* ▷ *vt* (*hook, trap*) mit einem Köder versehen; (*tease*) necken
baize [beɪz] *n* Flausch *m*; **green ~** Billardtuch *nt*
bake [beɪk] *vt* backen; (*clay etc*) brennen ▷ *vi* backen
baked beans [beɪkt-] *npl* gebackene Bohnen *pl* (in Tomatensoße)
baked potato *n* in der Schale gebackene Kartoffel *f*
baker [ˈbeɪkəʳ] *n* Bäcker(in) *m(f)*
baker's dozen *n* dreizehn (Stück)
bakery [ˈbeɪkərɪ] *n* Bäckerei *f*
baking [ˈbeɪkɪŋ] *n* Backen *nt*; (*batch*) Ofenladung *f* ▷ *adj* (*inf: hot*) wie im Backofen
baking powder *n* Backpulver *nt*
baking tin *n* Backform *f*
baking tray *n* Backblech *nt*
balaclava [bæləˈklɑːvə] *n* (*also*: **balaclava helmet**) Kapuzenmütze *f*
balance [ˈbæləns] *n* (*equilibrium*) Gleichgewicht *nt*; (*Comm: sum*) Saldo *m*; (*remainder*) Restbetrag *m*; (*scales*) Waage *f* ▷ *vt* ausgleichen; (*Aut: wheels*) auswuchten; (*pros and cons*) (gegeneinander) abwägen; **on ~** alles in allem; **~ of trade/payments** Handels-/Zahlungsbilanz *f*; **~ carried forward** *or* **brought forward** (*Comm*) Saldovortrag *m*, Saldoübertrag *m*; **to ~ the books** (*Comm*) die Bilanz ziehen *or* machen
balanced [ˈbælənst] *adj* ausgeglichen; (*report*) ausgewogen
balance sheet *n* Bilanz *f*
balance wheel *n* Unruh *f*
balcony [ˈbælkənɪ] *n* Balkon *m*; (*in theatre*) oberster Rang *m*
bald [bɔːld] *adj* kahl; (*tyre*) abgefahren; (*statement*) knapp
baldness [ˈbɔːldnɪs] *n* Kahlheit *f*
bale [beɪl] *n* (*Agr*) Bündel *nt*; (*of papers etc*) Packen *m*
▶ **bale out** *vi* (*of a plane*) abspringen ▷ *vt* (*water*) schöpfen; (*boat*) ausschöpfen
Balearic Islands [bælɪˈærɪk-] *npl*: **the ~** die Balearen *pl*
baleful [ˈbeɪlful] *adj* böse
balk [bɔːk] *vi*: **to ~ (at)** (*subj: person*) zurückschrecken (vor *+dat*); (*: horse*) scheuen (vor *+dat*)
Balkan [ˈbɔːlkən] *adj* (*countries etc*) Balkan- ▷ *n*: **the ~s** der Balkan, die Balkanländer *pl*
ball [bɔːl] *n* Ball *m*; (*of wool, string*) Knäuel *m or nt*; **to set the ~ rolling** (*fig*) den Stein ins Rollen bringen; **to play ~ (with sb)** (*fig*) (mit jdm) mitspielen; **to be on the ~** (*fig: competent*) am Ball sein; (*: alert*) auf Draht *or* Zack sein; **the ~ is in their court** (*fig*) sie sind am Ball
ballad [ˈbæləd] *n* Ballade *f*
ballast [ˈbæləst] *n* Ballast *m*
ball bearing *npl* Kugellager *nt*; (*individual ball*) Kugellagerkugel *f*
ball cock *n* Schwimmerhahn *m*
ballerina [bæləˈriːnə] *n* Ballerina *f*
ballet [ˈbæleɪ] *n* Ballett *nt*
ballet dancer *n* Balletttänzer(in) *m(f)*
ballistic [bəˈlɪstɪk] *adj* ballistisch
ballistic missile *n* Raketengeschoss *nt*
ballistics [bəˈlɪstɪks] *n* Ballistik *f*
balloon [bəˈluːn] *n* (Luft)ballon *m*; (*hot air balloon*) Heißluftballon *m*; (*in comic strip*) Sprechblase *f*
balloonist [bəˈluːnɪst] *n* Ballonfahrer(in) *m(f)*
ballot [ˈbælət] *n* (geheime) Abstimmung *f*
ballot box *n* Wahlurne *f*
ballot paper *n* Stimmzettel *m*
ballpark [ˈbɔːlpɑːk] (*US*) *n* (*Sport*) Baseballstadion *nt*
ballpark figure (*inf*) *n* Richtzahl *f*
ballpoint [ˈbɔːlpɔɪnt], **ballpoint pen** *n* Kugelschreiber *m*
ballroom [ˈbɔːlrum] *n* Tanzsaal *m*
balls [bɔːlz] (*inf!*) *npl* (*testicles*) Eier *pl* (*!*); (*courage*) Schneid *m*, Mumm *m* ▷ *excl* red keinen Scheiß! (*!*)
balm [bɑːm] *n* Balsam *m*
balmy [ˈbɑːmɪ] *adj* (*breeze*) sanft; (*air*) lau, lind; (*Brit: inf*) = **barmy**
BALPA [ˈbælpə] *n abbr* (= *British Airline Pilots' Association*) *Flugpilotengewerkschaft*
balsa [ˈbɔːlsə], **balsa wood** *n* Balsaholz *nt*
balsam [ˈbɔːlsəm] *n* Balsam *m*
Baltic [ˈbɔːltɪk] *n*: **the ~ (Sea)** die Ostsee
balustrade [bæləsˈtreɪd] *n* Balustrade *f*
bamboo [bæmˈbuː] *n* Bambus *m*
bamboozle [bæmˈbuːzl] (*inf*) *vt* hereinlegen; **to ~ sb into doing sth** jdn durch Tricks dazu bringen, etw zu tun
ban [bæn] *n* Verbot *nt* ▷ *vt* verbieten; **he was ~ned from driving** (*Brit*) ihm wurde Fahrverbot erteilt
banal [bəˈnɑːl] *adj* banal
banana [bəˈnɑːnə] *n* Banane *f*
band [bænd] *n* (*group*) Gruppe *f*, Schar *f*; (*Mus: jazz, rock etc*) Band *f*; (*: military etc*) (Musik)kapelle *f*; (*strip, range*) Band *nt*; (*stripe*) Streifen *m*
▶ **band together** *vi* sich zusammenschließen
bandage [ˈbændɪdʒ] *n* Verband *m* ▷ *vt* verbinden
Band-Aid® [ˈbændeɪd] (*US*) *n* Heftpflaster *nt*
B&B *n abbr* = **bed and breakfast**

bandit ['bændɪt] *n* Bandit *m*
bandstand ['bændstænd] *n* Musikpavillion *m*
bandwagon ['bændwægən] *n*: **to jump on the ~** (*fig*) auf den fahrenden Zug aufspringen
bandy ['bændɪ] *vt* (*jokes*) sich erzählen; (*ideas*) diskutieren; (*insults*) sich an den Kopf werfen ▸ **bandy about** *vt* (*word, expression*) immer wieder gebrauchen; (*name*) immer wieder nennen
bandy-legged ['bændɪ'lɛgɪd] *adj* o-beinig
bane [beɪn] *n*: **it/he is the ~ of my life** das/er ist noch mal mein Ende
bang [bæŋ] *n* (*of door*) Knallen *nt*; (*of gun, exhaust*) Knall *m*; (*blow*) Schlag *m* ▹ *excl* peng ▹ *vt* (*door*) zuschlagen, zuknallen; (*one's head etc*) sich *dat* stoßen *+acc* ▹ *vi* knallen ▹ *adv*: **to be ~ on time** (*Brit: inf*) auf die Sekunde pünktlich sein; **to ~ at the door** gegen die Tür hämmern; **to ~ into sth** sich an etw *dat* stoßen
banger ['bæŋəʳ] (*Brit: inf*) *n* (*car: also:* **old banger**) Klapperkiste *f*; (*sausage*) Würstchen *nt*; (*firework*) Knallkörper *m*
Bangkok [bæŋ'kɔk] *n* Bangkok *nt*
Bangladesh [bæŋglə'dɛʃ] *n* Bangladesch *nt*
bangle ['bæŋgl] *n* Armreif(en) *m*
bangs [bæŋz] (*US*) *npl* (*fringe*) Pony *m*
banish ['bænɪʃ] *vt* verbannen
banister ['bænɪstəʳ] *n*, **banisters** ['bænɪstəz] ▹ *npl* Geländer *nt*
banjo ['bændʒəu] (*pl* **banjoes** *or* **~s**) *n* Banjo *nt*
bank [bæŋk] *n* Bank *f*; (*of river, lake*) Ufer *nt*; (*of earth*) Wall *m*; (*of switches*) Reihe *f* ▹ *vi* (*Aviat*) sich in die Kurve legen; (*Comm*): **they ~ with Pitt's** sie haben ihr Konto bei Pitt's ▸ **bank on** *vt fus* sich verlassen auf *+acc*
bank account *n* Bankkonto *nt*
bank balance *n* Kontostand *m*
bank card *n* Scheckkarte *f*
bank charges (*Brit*) *npl* Kontoführungsgebühren *pl*
bank draft *n* Bankanweisung *f*
banker ['bæŋkəʳ] *n* Bankier *m*
banker's card (*Brit*) *n* = **bank card**
banker's order (*Brit*) *n* Dauerauftrag *m*
bank giro *n* Banküberweisung *f*
bank holiday (*Brit*) *n* (öffentlicher) Feiertag *m*; *siehe Info-Artikel*

BANK HOLIDAY

Als *bank holiday* wird in Großbritannien ein gesetzlicher Feiertag bezeichnet, an dem die Banken geschlossen sind. Die meisten dieser Feiertage, abgesehen von Weihnachten und Ostern, fallen auf Montage im Mai und August. An diesen langen Wochenenden (bank holiday weekends) fahren viele Briten in Urlaub, sodass dann auf den Straßen, Flughäfen und bei der Bahn sehr viel Betrieb ist.

banking ['bæŋkɪŋ] *n* Bankwesen *nt*
banking hours *npl* Schalterstunden *pl*
bank loan *n* Bankkredit *m*
bank manager *n* Filialleiter(in) *m(f)* (einer Bank)
banknote ['bæŋknəut] *n* Geldschein *m*, Banknote *f*
bank rate *n* Diskontsatz *m*
bankrupt ['bæŋkrʌpt] *adj* bankrott ▹ *n* Bankrotteur(in) *m(f)*; **to go ~** Bankrott machen
bankruptcy ['bæŋkrʌptsɪ] *n* (*Comm: fig*) Bankrott *m*
bank statement *n* Kontoauszug *m*
banner ['bænəʳ] *n* Banner *nt*; (*in demonstration*) Spruchband *nt*
banner headline *n* Schlagzeile *f*
bannister ['bænɪstəʳ] *n*, **bannisters** ['bænɪstəz] ▹ *n(pl)* = **banister; banisters**
banns [bænz] *npl* Aufgebot *nt*
banquet ['bæŋkwɪt] *n* Bankett *nt*
bantamweight ['bæntəmweɪt] *n* Bantamgewicht *nt*
banter ['bæntəʳ] *n* Geplänkel *nt*
BAOR *n abbr* (*= British Army of the Rhine*) *britische Rheinarmee*
baptism ['bæptɪzəm] *n* Taufe *f*
Baptist ['bæptɪst] *n* Baptist(in) *m(f)*
baptize [bæp'taɪz] *vt* taufen
bar [bɑːʳ] *n* (*for drinking*) Lokal *nt*; (*counter*) Theke *f*; (*rod*) Stange *f*; (*on window etc*) (Gitter)stab *m*; (*slab: of chocolate*) Tafel *f*; (*fig: obstacle*) Hindernis *nt*; (*prohibition*) Verbot *nt*; (*Mus*) Takt *m* ▹ *vt* (*road*) blockieren, versperren; (*window*) verriegeln; (*person*) ausschließen; (*activity*) verbieten; **~ of soap** Stück *nt* Seife; **behind ~s** hinter Gittern; **the B~** (*Law*) die Anwaltschaft; **~ none** ohne Ausnahme
Barbados [bɑː'beɪdɔs] *n* Barbados *nt*
barbaric [bɑː'bærɪk] *adj* barbarisch
barbarous ['bɑːbərəs] *adj* barbarisch
barbecue ['bɑːbɪkjuː] *n* Grill *m*; (*meal, party*) Barbecue *nt*
barbed wire ['bɑːbd-] *n* Stacheldraht *m*
barber ['bɑːbəʳ] *n* (Herren)friseur *m*
barbiturate [bɑː'bɪtjurɪt] *n* Schlafmittel *nt*, Barbiturat *nt*
Barcelona [bɑːsə'ləunə] *n* Barcelona *nt*
bar chart *n* Balkendiagramm *nt*
bar code *n* Strichcode *m*
bare [bɛəʳ] *adj* nackt; (*trees, countryside*) kahl; (*minimum*) absolut ▹ *vt* entblößen; (*teeth*) blecken; **the ~ essentials, the ~ necessities** das Allernotwendigste; **to ~ one's soul** sein Innerstes entblößen
bareback ['bɛəbæk] *adv* ohne Sattel
barefaced ['bɛəfeɪst] *adj* (*fig*) unverfroren, schamlos
barefoot ['bɛəfut] *adj* barfüßig ▹ *adv* barfuß
bareheaded [bɛə'hɛdɪd] *adj* barhäuptig ▹ *adv* ohne Kopfbedeckung
barely ['bɛəlɪ] *adv* kaum
Barents Sea ['bærənts-] *n*: **the ~** die Barentssee
bargain ['bɑːgɪn] *n* (*deal*) Geschäft *nt*; (*transaction*) Handel *m*; (*good offer*)

Sonderangebot *nt*; (*good buy*) guter Kauf *m* ▷ *vi*: **to ~ (with sb)** (mit jdm) verhandeln; (*haggle*) (mit jdm) handeln; **into the ~** obendrein
▸ **bargain for** *vt fus*: **he got more than he ~ed for** er bekam mehr, als er erwartet hatte
bargaining ['bɑːɡənɪŋ] *n* Verhandeln *nt*
bargaining position *n* Verhandlungsposition *f*
barge [bɑːdʒ] *n* Lastkahn *m*, Frachtkahn *m*
▸ **barge in** *vi* (*enter*) hereinplatzen; (*interrupt*) unterbrechen
▸ **barge into** *vt fus* (*place*) hereinplatzen; (*person*) anrempeln
bargepole ['bɑːdʒpəul] *n*: **I wouldn't touch it with a ~** (*fig*) das würde ich nicht mal mit der Kneifzange anfassen
baritone ['bærɪtəun] *n* Bariton *m*
barium meal ['bɛərɪəm-] *n* Kontrastbrei *m*
bark [bɑːk] *n* (*of tree*) Rinde *f*; (*of dog*) Bellen *nt* ▷ *vi* bellen; **she's ~ing up the wrong tree** (*fig*) sie ist auf dem Holzweg
barley ['bɑːlɪ] *n* Gerste *f*
barley sugar *n* Malzbonbon *nt or m*
barmaid ['bɑːmeɪd] *n* Bardame *f*
barman ['bɑːmən] (*irreg: like* **man**) *n* Barmann *m*
barmy ['bɑːmɪ] (*Brit: inf*) *adj* bekloppt
barn [bɑːn] *n* Scheune *f*
barnacle ['bɑːnəkl] *n* Rankenfußkrebs *m*
barn owl *n* Schleiereule *f*
barometer [bə'rɔmɪtə^r] *n* Barometer *nt*
baron ['bærən] *n* Baron *m*; **industrial ~** Industriemagnat *m*; **press ~** Pressezar *m*
baroness ['bærənɪs] *n* (*baron's wife*) Baronin *f*; (*baron's daughter*) Baroness *f*, Baronesse *f*
baronet ['bærənɪt] *n* Baronet *m*
barracking ['bærəkɪŋ] *n* Buhrufe *pl*
barracks ['bærəks] *npl* Kaserne *f*
barrage ['bærɑːʒ] *n* (*Mil*) Sperrfeuer *nt*; (*dam*) Staustufe *f*; (*fig: of criticism, questions etc*) Hagel *m*
barrel ['bærəl] *n* Fass *nt*; (*of oil*) Barrel *nt*; (*of gun*) Lauf *m*
barrel organ *n* Drehorgel *f*
barren ['bærən] *adj* unfruchtbar
barricade [bærɪ'keɪd] *n* Barrikade *f* ▷ *vt* (*road, entrance*) verbarrikadieren; **to ~ o.s. (in)** sich verbarrikadieren
barrier ['bærɪə^r] *n* (*at frontier, entrance*) Schranke *f*; (*Brit: also:* **crash barrier**) Leitplanke *f*; (*fig*) Barriere *f*; (*: to progress etc*) Hindernis *nt*
barrier cream (*Brit*) *n* Hautschutzcreme *f*
barring ['bɑːrɪŋ] *prep* außer im Falle *+gen*
barrister ['bærɪstə^r] (*Brit*) *n* Rechtsanwalt *m*, Rechtsanwältin *f*; *siehe Info-Artikel*

BARRISTER

Barrister oder *barrister-at-law* ist in England die Bezeichnung für einen Rechtsanwalt, der seine Klienten vor allem vor Gericht vertritt; im Gegensatz zum *solicitor*, der nicht vor Gericht auftritt, sondern einen barrister mit dieser Aufgabe beauftragt.

barrow ['bærəu] *n* Schubkarre *f*, Schubkarren *m*; (*cart*) Karren *m*
bar stool *n* Barhocker *m*
Bart. (*Brit*) *abbr* = **baronet**
bartender ['bɑːtɛndə^r] (*US*) *n* Barmann *m*
barter ['bɑːtə^r] *n* Tauschhandel *m* ▷ *vt*: **to ~ sth for sth** etw gegen etw tauschen
barter exchange *n* Tauschbörse *f*
base [beɪs] *n* (*of tree etc*) Fuß *m*; (*of cup, box etc*) Boden *m*; (*foundation*) Grundlage *f*; (*centre*) Stützpunkt *m*, Standort *m*; (*for organization*) Sitz *m* ▷ *adj* gemein, niederträchtig ▷ *vt*: **to ~ sth on** etw gründen *or* basieren auf *+acc*; **to be ~d at** (*troops*) stationiert sein in *+dat*; (*employee*) arbeiten in *+dat*; **I'm ~d in London** ich wohne in London; **a Paris-~d firm** eine Firma mit Sitz in Paris; **coffee-~d** auf Kaffeebasis
baseball ['beɪsbɔːl] *n* Baseball *m*
baseboard ['beɪsbɔːd] (*US*) *n* Fußleiste *f*
base camp *n* Basislager *nt*, Versorgungslager *nt*
Basel [bɑːl] *n* = **Basle**
baseline ['beɪslaɪn] *n* (*Tennis*) Grundlinie *f*; (*fig: standard*) Ausgangspunkt *m*
basement ['beɪsmənt] *n* Keller *m*
base rate *n* Eckzins *m*, Leitzins *m*
bases[1] ['beɪsɪz] *npl of* **base**
bases[2] ['beɪsiːz] *npl of* **basis**
bash [bæʃ] (*inf*) *vt* schlagen, hauen ▷ *n*: **I'll have a ~ (at it)** (*Brit*) ich probier's mal
▸ **bash up** *vt* (*car*) demolieren; (*Brit: person*) vermöbeln
bashful ['bæʃful] *adj* schüchtern
bashing ['bæʃɪŋ] (*inf*) *n* Prügel *pl*; **Paki-/queer-~** Überfälle *pl* auf Pakistaner/Schwule
BASIC ['beɪsɪk] *n* (*Comput*) BASIC *nt*
basic ['beɪsɪk] *adj* (*method, needs etc*) Grund-; (*principles*) grundlegend; (*problem*) grundsätzlich; (*knowledge*) elementar; (*facilities*) primitiv
basically ['beɪsɪklɪ] *adv* im Grunde
basic rate *n* Eingangssteuersatz *m*
basics ['beɪsɪks] *npl*: **the ~** das Wesentliche
basil ['bæzl] *n* Basilikum *nt*
basin ['beɪsn] *n* Gefäß *nt*; (*Brit: for food*) Schüssel *f*; (*also:* **wash basin**) (Wasch)becken *nt*; (*of river, lake*) Becken *nt*
basis ['beɪsɪs] (*pl* **bases**) *n* Basis *f*, Grundlage *f*; **on a part-time ~** stundenweise; **on a trial ~** zur Probe; **on the ~ of what you've said** aufgrund dessen, was Sie gesagt haben
bask [bɑːsk] *vi*: **to ~ in the sun** sich sonnen
basket ['bɑːskɪt] *n* Korb *m*; (*smaller*) Körbchen *nt*
basketball ['bɑːskɪtbɔːl] *n* Basketball *m*
basketball player *n* Basketballspieler(in) *m(f)*
Basle [bɑːl] *n* Basel *nt*
basmati rice [bəz'mætɪ-] *n* Basmatireis *m*
Basque [bæsk] *adj* baskisch ▷ *n* Baske *m*, Baskin *f*
bass [beɪs] *n* Bass *m*
bass clef *n* Bassschlüssel *m*
bassoon [bə'suːn] *n* Fagott *nt*

bastard ['bɑːstəd] *n* uneheliches Kind *nt*; *(inf!)* Arschloch *nt (!)*
baste [beɪst] *vt (Culin)* (mit Fett und Bratensaft) begießen; *(Sewing)* heften, reihen
bastion ['bæstɪən] *n* Bastion *f*
bat [bæt] *n (Zool)* Fledermaus *f*; *(for cricket, baseball etc)* Schlagholz *nt*; *(Brit: for table tennis)* Schläger *m* ▷ *vt*: **he didn't ~ an eyelid** er hat nicht mit der Wimper gezuckt; **off one's own ~** auf eigene Faust
batch [bætʃ] *n (of bread)* Schub *m*; *(of letters, papers)* Stoß *m*, Stapel *m*; *(of applicants)* Gruppe *f*; *(of work)* Schwung *m*; *(of goods)* Ladung *f*, Sendung *f*
batch processing *n (Comput)* Stapelverarbeitung *f*
bated ['beɪtɪd] *adj*: **with ~ breath** mit angehaltenem Atem
bath [bɑːθ] *n* Bad *nt*; *(bathtub)* (Bade)wanne *f* ▷ *vt* baden; **to have a ~** baden, ein Bad nehmen; *see also* **baths**
bathe [beɪð] *vi, vt (also fig)* baden
bather ['beɪðəʳ] *n* Badende(r) *f(m)*
bathing ['beɪðɪŋ] *n* Baden *nt*
bathing cap *n* Bademütze *f*, Badekappe *f*
bathing costume, (US) **bathing suit** *n* Badeanzug *m*
bath mat *n* Badematte *f*, Badevorleger *m*
bathrobe ['bɑːθrəub] *n* Bademantel *m*
bathroom ['bɑːθrum] *n* Bad(ezimmer) *nt*
baths [bɑːðz] *npl (also:* **swimming baths***)* (Schwimm)bad *nt*
bath towel *n* Badetuch *nt*
bathtub ['bɑːθtʌb] *n* (Bade)wanne *f*
batman ['bætmən] *(irreg: like* **man***)* *(Brit) n (Mil)* (Offiziers)bursche *m*
baton ['bætən] *n (Mus)* Taktstock *m*; *(Athletics)* Staffelholz *nt*; *(policeman's)* Schlagstock *m*
battalion [bə'tælɪən] *n* Bataillon *nt*
batten ['bætn] *n* Leiste *f*, Latte *f*; *(Naut: on sail)* Segellatte *f*
▸ **batten down** *vt (Naut)*: **to ~ down the hatches** die Luken dicht machen
batter ['bætəʳ] *vt* schlagen, misshandeln; *(subj: rain)* schlagen; *(wind)* rütteln ▷ *n (Culin)* Teig *m*; *(for frying)* (Ausback)teig *m*
battered ['bætəd] *adj (hat, pan)* verbeult; **~ wife** misshandelte Ehefrau; **~ child** misshandeltes Kind
battering ram ['bætərɪŋ-] *n* Rammbock *m*
battery ['bætərɪ] *n* Batterie *f*; *(of tests, reporters)* Reihe *f*
battery charger *n* (Batterie)ladegerät *nt*
battery farming *n* Batteriehaltung *f*
battle ['bætl] *n (Mil)* Schlacht *f*; *(fig)* Kampf *m* ▷ *vi* kämpfen; **that's half the ~** damit ist schon viel gewonnen; **it's a losing ~, we're fighting a losing ~** *(fig)* es ist ein aussichtsloser Kampf
battledress ['bætldrɛs] *n* Kampfanzug *m*
battlefield ['bætlfiːld] *n* Schlachtfeld *nt*
battlements ['bætlmənts] *npl* Zinnen *pl*
battleship ['bætlʃɪp] *n* Schlachtschiff *nt*
batty ['bætɪ] *(inf) adj* verrückt
bauble ['bɔːbl] *n* Flitter *m*
baud [bɔːd] *n (Comput)* Baud *nt*
baud rate *n (Comput)* Baudrate *f*
baulk [bɔːlk] *vi* = **balk**
bauxite ['bɔːksaɪt] *n* Bauxit *m*
Bavaria [bə'vɛərɪə] *n* Bayern *nt*
Bavarian [bə'vɛərɪən] *adj* bay(e)risch ▷ *n* Bayer(in) *m(f)*
bawdy ['bɔːdɪ] *adj* derb, obszön
bawl [bɔːl] *vi* brüllen, schreien
bay [beɪ] *n* Bucht *f*; *(Brit: for parking)* Parkbucht *f*; *(: for loading)* Ladeplatz *m*; *(horse)* Braune(r) *m*; **to hold sb at ~** jdn in Schach halten
bay leaf *n* Lorbeerblatt *nt*
bayonet ['beɪənɪt] *n* Bajonett *nt*
bay tree *n* Lorbeerbaum *m*
bay window *n* Erkerfenster *nt*
bazaar [bə'zɑːʳ] *n* Basar *m*
bazooka [bə'zuːkə] *n* Panzerfaust *f*
BB *(Brit) n abbr (= Boys' Brigade) Jugendorganisation für Jungen*
BBB *(US) n abbr (= Better Business Bureau) amerikanische Verbraucherbehörde*
BBC *n abbr* BBC *f*; *siehe Info-Artikel*

BBC

BBC (Abkürzung für British Broadcasting Corporation) ist die staatliche britische Rundfunk- und Fernsehanstalt. Die Fernsehsender BBC1 und BBC2 bieten beide ein umfangsreiches Fernsehprogramm, wobei BBC1 mehr Sendungen von allgemeinem Interesse wie z.B. leichte Unterhaltung, Sport, Aktuelles, Kinderprogramme und Außenübertragungen zeigt. BBC2 berücksichtigt Reisesendungen, Drama, Musik und internationale Filme. Die 5 landesweiten Radiosender bieten von Popmusik bis Kricket etwas für jeden Geschmack; dazu gibt es noch 37 regionale Radiosender. Der BBC World Service ist auf der ganzen Welt auf Englisch oder in einer von 35 anderen Sprachen zu empfangen. Finanziert wird die BBC vor allem durch Fernsehgebühren und ins Ausland verkaufte Sendungen. Obwohl die BBC dem Parlament gegenüber verantwortlich ist, werden die Sendungen nicht vom Staat kontrolliert.

BC *adv abbr (= before Christ)* v. Chr. ▷ *abbr (Canada: = British Columbia)* Britisch-Kolumbien *nt*
BCG *n abbr (= bacille Calmette-Guérin)* BCG *m*
BD *n abbr (= Bachelor of Divinity) akademischer Grad in Theologie*
B/D *abbr* = **bank draft**
BDS *n abbr (= Bachelor of Dental Surgery) akademischer Grad in Zahnmedizin*
B/E *abbr* = **bill of exchange**

KEYWORD

be [biː] (*pt* **was, were**, *pp* **been**) *aux vb* **1** (*with present participle: forming continuous tenses*): **what are you doing?** was machst du?; **it is raining** es regnet; **have you been to Rome?** waren Sie schon einmal in Rom?
2 (*with pp: forming passives*) werden; **to be killed** getötet werden; **the box had been opened** die Kiste war geöffnet worden
3 (*in tag questions*): **he's good-looking, isn't he?** er sieht gut aus, nicht (wahr)?; **she's back again, is she?** sie ist wieder da, oder?
4 (*+ to + infinitive*): **the house is to be sold** das Haus soll verkauft werden; **he's not to open it** er darf es nicht öffnen
▷ *vb + complement* **1** sein; **I'm tired/English** ich bin müde/Engländer(in); **I'm hot/cold** mir ist heiß/kalt; **2 and 2 are 4** 2 und 2 ist *or* macht 4; **she's tall/pretty** sie ist groß/hübsch; **be careful/quiet** sei vorsichtig/ruhig
2 (*of health*): **how are you?** wie geht es Ihnen?
3 (*of age*): **how old are you?** wie alt bist du?; **I'm sixteen (years old)** ich bin sechzehn (Jahre alt)
4 (*cost*) kosten; **how much was the meal?** was hat das Essen gekostet?; **that'll be 5 pounds please** das macht 5 Pfund, bitte
▷ *vi* **1** (*exist, occur etc*) sein; **there is/are** es gibt; **is there a God?** gibt es einen Gott?; **be that as it may** wie dem auch sei; **so be it** gut (und schön)
2 (*referring to place*) sein, liegen; **Edinburgh is in Scotland** Edinburgh liegt *or* ist in Schottland; **I won't be here tomorrow** morgen bin ich nicht da
3 (*referring to movement*) sein; **where have you been?** wo warst du?
▷ *impers vb* **1** (*referring to time, distance, weather*) sein; **it's 5 o'clock** es ist 5 Uhr; **it's 10 km to the village** es sind 10 km bis zum Dorf; **it's too hot/cold** es ist zu heiß/kalt
2 (*emphatic*): **it's only me** ich bins nur; **it's only the postman** es ist nur der Briefträger

beach [biːtʃ] *n* Strand *m* ▷ *vt* (*boat*) auf (den) Strand setzen
beach buggy *n* Strandbuggy *m*
beachcomber [ˈbiːtʃkəuməʳ] *n* Strandgutsammler *m*
beachwear [ˈbiːtʃwɛəʳ] *n* Strandkleidung *f*
beacon [ˈbiːkən] *n* Leuchtfeuer *nt*; (*marker*) Bake *f*; (*also*: **radio beacon**) Funkfeuer *nt*
bead [biːd] *n* Perle *f*; **beads** *npl* (*necklace*) Perlenkette *f*
beady [ˈbiːdɪ] *adj*: **~ eyes** Knopfaugen *pl*
beagle [ˈbiːgl] *n* Beagle *m*
beak [biːk] *n* Schnabel *m*
beaker [ˈbiːkəʳ] *n* Becher *m*
beam [biːm] *n* (*Archit*) Balken *m*; (*of light*) Strahl *m*; (*Radio*) Leitstrahl *m* ▷ *vi* (*smile*) strahlen ▷ *vt* ausstrahlen, senden; **to ~ at sb** jdn anstrahlen; **to drive on full** *or* **main** *or* **high ~** mit Fernlicht fahren
beaming [ˈbiːmɪŋ] *adj* strahlend
bean [biːn] *n* Bohne *f*; **runner ~** Stangenbohne *f*; **broad ~** dicke Bohne; **coffee ~** Kaffeebohne *f*
beanpole [ˈbiːnpəul] *n* (*lit, fig*) Bohnenstange *f*
beanshoots [ˈbiːnʃuːts] *npl* Sojabohnensprossen *pl*
beansprouts [ˈbiːnsprauts] *npl* = **beanshoots**
bear [bɛəʳ] (*pt* **bore**, *pp* **borne**) *n* Bär *m*; (*Stock Exchange*) Baissier *m* ▷ *vt* tragen; (*tolerate, endure*) ertragen; (*examination*) standhalten *+dat*; (*traces, signs*) aufweisen, zeigen; (*Comm: interest*) tragen, bringen; (*produce: children*) gebären; (*: fruit*) tragen ▷ *vi*: **to ~ right/left** (*Aut*) sich rechts/links halten; **to ~ the responsibility of** die Verantwortung tragen für; **to ~ comparison with** einem Vergleich standhalten mit; **I can't ~ him** ich kann ihn nicht ausstehen; **to bring pressure to ~ on sb** Druck auf jdn ausüben
▸ **bear out** *vt* (*person, suspicions etc*) bestätigen
▸ **bear up** *vi* Haltung bewahren; **he bore up well** er hat sich gut gehalten
▸ **bear with** *vt fus* Nachsicht haben mit; **~ with me a minute** bitte gedulden Sie sich einen Moment
bearable [ˈbɛərəbl] *adj* erträglich
beard [bɪəd] *n* Bart *m*
bearded [ˈbɪədɪd] *adj* bärtig
bearer [ˈbɛərəʳ] *n* (*of letter, news*) Überbringer(in) *m(f)*; (*of cheque, passport, title etc*) Inhaber(in) *m(f)*
bearing [ˈbɛərɪŋ] *n* (*posture*) Haltung *f*; (*air*) Auftreten *nt*; (*connection*) Bezug *m*; (*Tech*) Lager *nt*; **bearings** *npl* (*also*: **ball bearings**) Kugellager *nt*; **to take a ~ with a compass** den Kompasskurs feststellen; **to get one's ~s** sich zurechtfinden
beast [biːst] *n* (*animal*) Tier *nt*; (*inf: person*) Biest *nt*
beastly [ˈbiːstlɪ] *adj* scheußlich
beat [biːt] (*pt* **~**, *pp* **~en**) *n* (*of heart*) Schlag *m*; (*Mus*) Takt *m*; (*of policeman*) Revier *nt* ▷ *vt* schlagen; (*record*) brechen ▷ *vi* schlagen; **to ~ time** den Takt schlagen; **to ~ it** (*inf*) abhauen, verschwinden; **that ~s everything** das ist doch wirklich der Gipfel *or* die Höhe; **to ~ about the bush** um den heißen Brei herumreden; **off the ~en track** abgelegen
▸ **beat down** *vt* (*door*) einschlagen; (*price*) herunterhandeln; (*seller*) einen niedrigeren Preis aushandeln mit ▷ *vi* (*rain*) herunterprasseln; (*sun*) herunterbrennen
▸ **beat off** *vt* (*attack, attacker*) abwehren
▸ **beat up** *vt* (*person*) zusammenschlagen; (*mixture, eggs*) schlagen
beater [ˈbiːtəʳ] *n* (*for eggs, cream*) Schneebesen *m*
beating [ˈbiːtɪŋ] *n* Schläge *pl*, Prügel *pl*; **to take a ~** (*fig*) eine Schlappe einstecken
beat-up [ˈbiːtˈʌp] (*inf*) *adj* zerbeult, ramponiert
beautician [bjuːˈtɪʃən] *n* Kosmetiker(in) *m(f)*
beautiful [ˈbjuːtɪful] *adj* schön

beautifully ['bju:tɪflɪ] *adv (play, sing, drive etc)* hervorragend; *(quiet, empty etc)* schön
beautify ['bju:tɪfaɪ] *vt* verschönern
beauty ['bju:tɪ] *n* Schönheit *f*; *(fig: attraction)* Schöne *nt*; **the ~ of it is that ...** das Schöne daran ist, dass ...
beauty contest *n* Schönheitswettbewerb *m*
beauty queen *n* Schönheitskönigin *f*
beauty salon *n* Kosmetiksalon *m*
beauty sleep *n* (Schönheits)schlaf *m*
beauty spot *(Brit) n* besonders schöner Ort *m*
beaver ['bi:vəʳ] *n* Biber *m*
becalmed [bɪ'kɑ:md] *adj*: **to be ~** *(sailing ship)* in eine Flaute geraten
became [bɪ'keɪm] *pt of* **become**
because [bɪ'kɔz] *conj* weil; **~ of** wegen *+gen or (inf) +dat*
beck [bɛk] *n*: **to be at sb's ~ and call** nach jds Pfeife tanzen
beckon ['bɛkən] *vt (also:* **beckon to***)* winken ▷ *vi* locken
become [bɪ'kʌm] *(irreg: like* **come***) vi* werden; **it became known that** es wurde bekannt, dass; **what has ~ of him?** was ist aus ihm geworden?
becoming [bɪ'kʌmɪŋ] *adj (behaviour)* schicklich; *(clothes)* kleidsam
BECTU ['bɛktu] *(Brit) n abbr (= Broadcasting, Entertainment, Cinematographic and Theatre Union) Gewerkschaft für Beschäftigte in der Unterhaltungsindustrie*
BEd *n abbr (= Bachelor of Education) akademischer Grad im Erziehungswesen*
bed [bɛd] *n* Bett *nt*; *(of coal)* Flöz *nt*; *(of clay)* Schicht *f*; *(of river)* (Fluss)bett *nt*; *(of sea)* (Meeres)boden *m*, (Meeres)grund *m*; *(of flowers)* Beet *nt*; **to go to ~** ins *or* zu Bett gehen
▸ **bed down** *vi* sein Lager aufschlagen
bed and breakfast *n (place)* (Frühstücks)pension *f*; *(terms)* Übernachtung *f* mit Frühstück; *siehe Info-Artikel*

BED AND BREAKFAST

Bed and breakfast bedeutet „Übernachtung mit Frühstück", wobei sich dies in Großbritannien nicht auf Hotels, sondern auf kleinere Pensionen, Privathäuser und Bauernhöfe bezieht, wo man wesentlich preisgünstiger übernachten kann als in Hotels. Oft wird für Bed and Breakfast, auch *B & B* genannt, durch ein entsprechendes Schild im Garten oder an der Einfahrt geworben.

bedbug ['bɛdbʌg] *n* Wanze *f*
bedclothes ['bɛdkləuðz] *npl* Bettzeug *nt*
bedding ['bɛdɪŋ] *n* Bettzeug *nt*
bedevil [bɪ'dɛvl] *vt (person)* heimsuchen; *(plans)* komplizieren; **to be ~led by misfortune/bad luck** vom Schicksal/Pech verfolgt sein
bedfellow ['bɛdfɛləu] *n*: **they are strange ~s** *(fig)* sie sind ein merkwürdiges Gespann
bedlam ['bɛdləm] *n* Chaos *nt*
bedpan ['bɛdpæn] *n* Bettpfanne *f*, Bettschüssel *f*
bedpost ['bɛdpəust] *n* Bettpfosten *m*
bedraggled [bɪ'drægld] *adj (wet)* triefnass, tropfnass; *(dirty)* verdreckt
bedridden ['bɛdrɪdn] *adj* bettlägerig
bedrock ['bɛdrɔk] *n (fig)* Fundament *nt*; *(Geog)* Grundgebirge *nt*, Grundgestein *nt*
bedroom ['bɛdrum] *n* Schlafzimmer *nt*
Beds [bɛdz] *(Brit) abbr (Post) = Bedfordshire*
bed settee *n* Sofabett *nt*
bedside ['bɛdsaɪd] *n*: **at sb's ~** an jds Bett; **~ lamp** Nachttischlampe *f*; **~ book** Bettlektüre *f*
bedsit ['bɛdsɪt], **bedsitter** ['bɛdsɪtəʳ] *(Brit) n* möbliertes Zimmer *nt*
bedspread ['bɛdsprɛd] *n* Tagesdecke *f*
bedtime ['bɛdtaɪm] *n* Schlafenszeit *f*; **it's ~** es ist Zeit, ins Bett zu gehen
bee [bi:] *n* Biene *f*; **to have a ~ in one's bonnet about cleanliness** einen Sauberkeitsfimmel *or* Sauberkeitstick haben
beech [bi:tʃ] *n* Buche *f*
beef [bi:f] *n* Rind(fleisch) *nt*; **roast ~** Rinderbraten *m*
▸ **beef up** *(inf) vt* aufmotzen; *(essay)* auswalzen
beefburger ['bi:fbə:gəʳ] *n* Hamburger *m*
beefeater ['bi:fi:təʳ] *n* Beefeater *m*
beehive ['bi:haɪv] *n* Bienenstock *m*
beekeeping ['bi:ki:pɪŋ] *n* Bienenzucht *f*, Imkerei *f*
beeline ['bi:laɪn] *n*: **to make a ~ for** schnurstracks zugehen auf *+acc*
been [bi:n] *pp of* **be**
beep [bi:p] *(inf) n* Tut(tut) *nt* ▷ *vi* tuten ▷ *vt*: **to ~ one's horn** hupen
beer [bɪəʳ] *n* Bier *nt*
beer belly *(inf) n* Bierbauch *m*
beer can *n* Bierdose *f*
beet [bi:t] *n* Rübe *f*; *(US: also:* **red beet***)* Rote Bete *f*
beetle ['bi:tl] *n* Käfer *m*
beetroot ['bi:tru:t] *(Brit) n* Rote Bete *f*
befall [bɪ'fɔ:l] *(irreg: like* **fall***) vi* sich zutragen ▷ *vt* widerfahren *+dat*
befit [bɪ'fɪt] *vt* sich gehören für
before [bɪ'fɔ:ʳ] *prep* vor *+dat*; *(with movement)* vor *+acc* ▷ *conj* bevor ▷ *adv (time)* vorher; *(space)* davor; **~ going** bevor er/sie *etc* geht/ging; **~ she goes** bevor sie geht; **the week ~** die Woche davor; **I've never seen it ~** ich habe es noch nie gesehen
beforehand [bɪ'fɔ:hænd] *adv* vorher
befriend [bɪ'frɛnd] *vt* sich annehmen *+gen*
befuddled [bɪ'fʌdld] *adj*: **to be ~** verwirrt sein
beg [bɛg] *vi* betteln ▷ *vt (food, money)* betteln um; *(favour, forgiveness etc)* bitten um; **to ~ for** *(food etc)* betteln um; *(forgiveness, mercy etc)* bitten um; **to ~ sb to do sth** jdn bitten, etw zu tun; **I ~ your pardon** *(apologizing)* entschuldigen Sie bitte; *(: not hearing)* (wie) bitte?; **to ~ the question** der Frage ausweichen; *see also* **pardon**

began [bɪ'gæn] *pt of* **begin**
beggar ['bɛgə^r] *n* Bettler(in) *m(f)*
begin [bɪ'gɪn] (*pt* **began**, *pp* **begun**) *vt, vi* beginnen, anfangen; **to ~ doing** *or* **to do sth** anfangen, etw zu tun; **~ning (from) Monday** ab Montag; **I can't ~ to thank you** ich kann Ihnen gar nicht genug danken; **we'll have soup to ~ with** als Vorspeise hätten wir gern Suppe; **to ~ with, I'd like to know ...** zunächst einmal möchte ich wissen, ...
beginner [bɪ'gɪnə^r] *n* Anfänger(in) *m(f)*
beginning [bɪ'gɪnɪŋ] *n* Anfang *m*; **right from the ~** von Anfang an
begrudge [bɪ'grʌdʒ] *vt*: **to ~ sb sth** jdm etw missgönnen *or* nicht gönnen
beguile [bɪ'gaɪl] *vt* betören
beguiling [bɪ'gaɪlɪŋ] *adj* (*charming*) verführerisch; (*deluding*) betörend
begun [bɪ'gʌn] *pp of* **begin**
behalf [bɪ'hɑ:f] *n*: **on ~ of, in ~ of** (*US: as representative of*) im Namen von; (*for benefit of*) zugunsten von; **on my/his ~** in meinem/seinem Namen; zu meinen/seinen Gunsten
behave [bɪ'heɪv] *vi* (*person*) sich verhalten, sich benehmen; (*thing*) funktionieren; (*also*: **behave o.s.**) sich benehmen
behaviour, (US) **behavior** [bɪ'heɪvjə^r] *n* Verhalten *nt*; (*manner*) Benehmen *nt*
behead [bɪ'hɛd] *vt* enthaupten
beheld [bɪ'hɛld] *pt, pp of* **behold**
behind [bɪ'haɪnd] *prep* hinter ▷ *adv* (*at/towards the back*) hinten ▷ *n* (*buttocks*) Hintern *m*, Hinterteil *nt*; **~ the scenes** (*fig*) hinter den Kulissen; **we're ~ them in technology** auf dem Gebiet der Technologie liegen wir hinter ihnen zurück; **to be ~** (*schedule*) im Rückstand *or* Verzug sein; **to leave/stay ~** zurücklassen/-bleiben
behold [bɪ'həuld] (*irreg: like* **hold**) *vt* sehen, erblicken
beige [beɪʒ] *adj* beige
Beijing ['beɪ'dʒɪŋ] *n* Peking *nt*
being ['bi:ɪŋ] *n* (*creature*) (Lebe)wesen *nt*; (*existence*) Leben *nt*, (Da)sein *nt*; **to come into ~** entstehen
Beirut [beɪ'ru:t] *n* Beirut *nt*
Belarus [bɛlə'rus] *n* Weißrussland *nt*
Belarussian *adj* belarussisch, weißrussisch ▷ *n* Weißrusse *m*, Weißrussin *f*; (*Ling*) Weißrussisch *nt*
belated [bɪ'leɪtɪd] *adj* verspätet
belch [bɛltʃ] *vi* rülpsen ▷ *vt* (*also*: **belch out**: *smoke etc*) ausstoßen
beleaguered [bɪ'li:gɪd] *adj* (*city*) belagert; (*army*) eingekesselt; (*fig*) geplagt
Belfast ['bɛlfɑ:st] *n* Belfast *nt*
belfry ['bɛlfrɪ] *n* Glockenstube *f*
Belgian ['bɛldʒən] *adj* belgisch ▷ *n* Belgier(in) *m(f)*
Belgium ['bɛldʒəm] *n* Belgien *nt*
Belgrade [bɛl'greɪd] *n* Belgrad *nt*
belie [bɪ'laɪ] *vt* (*contradict*) im Widerspruch stehen zu; (*give false impression of*) hinwegtäuschen über +*acc*; (*disprove*) widerlegen, Lügen strafen
belief [bɪ'li:f] *n* Glaube *m*; (*opinion*) Überzeugung *f*; **it's beyond ~** es ist unglaublich *or* nicht zu glauben; **in the ~ that** im Glauben, dass
believable [bɪ'li:vəbl] *adj* glaubhaft
believe [bɪ'li:v] *vt* glauben ▷ *vi* (an Gott) glauben; **he is ~d to be abroad** es heißt, dass er im Ausland ist; **to ~ in** (*God, ghosts*) glauben an +*acc*; (*method etc*) Vertrauen haben zu; **I don't ~ in corporal punishment** ich halte nicht viel von der Prügelstrafe
believer [bɪ'li:və^r] *n* (*in idea, activity*) Anhänger(in) *m(f)*; (*Rel*) Gläubige(r) *f(m)*; **she's a great ~ in healthy eating** sie ist sehr für eine gesunde Ernährung
belittle [bɪ'lɪtl] *vt* herabsetzen
Belize [bɛ'li:z] *n* Belize *nt*
bell [bɛl] *n* Glocke *f*; (*small*) Glöckchen *nt*, Schelle *f*; (*on door*) Klingel *f*; **that rings a ~** (*fig*) das kommt mir bekannt vor
bell-bottoms ['bɛlbɔtəmz] *npl* Hose *f* mit Schlag
bellboy ['bɛlbɔɪ] (*Brit*) *n* Page *m*, Hoteljunge *m*
bellhop ['bɛlhɔp] (*US*) *n* = **bellboy**
belligerence [bɪ'lɪdʒərəns] *n* Angriffslust *f*
belligerent [bɪ'lɪdʒərənt] *adj* angriffslustig
bellow ['bɛləu] *vi, vt* brüllen
bellows ['bɛləuz] *npl* Blasebalg *m*
bell push (*Brit*) *n* Klingel *f*
belly ['bɛlɪ] *n* Bauch *m*
bellyache ['bɛlɪeɪk] (*inf*) *n* Bauchschmerzen *pl* ▷ *vi* murren
bellybutton ['bɛlɪbʌtn] *n* Bauchnabel *m*
bellyful ['bɛlɪful] (*inf*) *n*: **I've had a ~ of that** davon habe ich die Nase voll
belong [bɪ'lɔŋ] *vi*: **to ~ to** (*person*) gehören +*dat*; (*club etc*) angehören +*dat*; **this book ~s here** dieses Buch gehört hierher
belongings [bɪ'lɔŋɪŋz] *npl* Sachen *pl*, Habe *f*; **personal ~** persönlicher Besitz *m*, persönliches Eigentum *nt*
Belorussia [bɛleu'rʌʃə] *n* Weißrussland *nt*
Belorussian [bɛleu'rʌʃən] *adj, n* = **Belarussian**
beloved [bɪ'lʌvɪd] *adj* geliebt ▷ *n* Geliebte(r) *f(m)*
below [bɪ'ləu] *prep* (*beneath*) unterhalb +*gen*; (*less than*) unter +*dat* ▷ *adv* (*beneath*) unten; **see ~** siehe unten; **temperatures ~ normal** Temperaturen unter dem Durchschnitt
belt [bɛlt] *n* Gürtel *m*; (*Tech*) (Treib)riemen *m* ▷ *vt* schlagen ▷ *vi* (*Brit: inf*): **to ~ along** rasen; **to ~ down/into** hinunter-/hineinrasen; **industrial ~** Industriegebiet *nt*
▸ **belt out** *vt* (*song*) schmettern
▸ **belt up** (*Brit: inf*) *vi* den Mund *or* die Klappe halten
beltway ['bɛltweɪ] (*US*) *n* Umgehungsstraße *f*, Ringstraße *f*; (*motorway*) Umgehungsautobahn *f*
bemoan [bɪ'məun] *vt* beklagen
bemused [bɪ'mju:zd] *adj* verwirrt

bench [bɛntʃ] *n* Bank *f*; (*work bench*) Werkbank *f*; **the B~** (*Law: judges*) die Richter *pl*, der Richterstand
benchmark ['bɛntʃmɑːk] *n* (*fig*) Maßstab *m*
bend [bɛnd] (*pt, pp* **bent**) *vt* (*leg, arm*) beugen; (*pipe*) biegen ▷ *vi* (*person*) sich beugen ▷ *n* (*Brit: in road*) Kurve *f*; (*in pipe, river*) Biegung *f*;
bends *npl* (*Med*): **the ~s** die Taucherkrankheit
▶ **bend down** *vi* sich bücken
▶ **bend over** *vi* sich bücken
beneath [bɪ'niːθ] *prep* unter *+dat* ▷ *adv* darunter
benefactor ['bɛnɪfæktə^r] *n* Wohltäter *m*
benefactress ['bɛnɪfæktrɪs] *n* Wohltäterin *f*
beneficial [bɛnɪ'fɪʃəl] *adj* (*effect*) nützlich; (*influence*) vorteilhaft; **~ (to)** gut (für)
beneficiary [bɛnɪ'fɪʃərɪ] *n* (*Law*) Nutznießer(in) *m(f)*
benefit ['bɛnɪfɪt] *n* (*advantage*) Vorteil *m*; (*money*) Beihilfe *f*; (*also*: **benefit concert, benefit match**) Benefizveranstaltung *f* ▷ *vt* nützen *+dat*, zugutekommen *+dat* ▷ *vi*: **he'll ~ from it** er wird davon profitieren
Benelux ['bɛnɪlʌks] *n* die Beneluxstaaten *pl*
benevolent [bɪ'nɛvələnt] *adj* wohlwollend; (*organization*) Wohltätigkeits-
BEng *n abbr* (*= Bachelor of Engineering*) *akademischer Grad für Ingenieure*
benign [bɪ'naɪn] *adj* gütig; (*Med*) gutartig
bent [bɛnt] *pt, pp of* **bend** ▷ *n* Neigung *f* ▷ *adj* (*wire, pipe*) gebogen; (*inf: dishonest*) korrupt; (*: pej: homosexual*) andersrum; **to be ~ on** entschlossen sein zu
bequeath [bɪ'kwiːð] *vt* vermachen
bequest [bɪ'kwɛst] *n* Vermächtnis *nt*, Legat *nt*
bereaved [bɪ'riːvd] *adj* leidtragend ▷ *npl*: **the ~** die Hinterbliebenen *pl*
bereavement [bɪ'riːvmənt] *n* schmerzlicher Verlust *m*
bereft [bɪ'rɛft] *adj*: **~ of** beraubt *+gen*
beret ['bɛreɪ] *n* Baskenmütze *f*
Bering Sea ['beɪrɪŋ-] *n*: **the ~** das Beringmeer
berk [bəːk] (*inf*) *n* Dussel *m*
Berks [bɑːks] (*Brit*) *abbr* (*Post*) *= Berkshire*
Berlin [bəː'lɪn] *n* Berlin *nt*; **East/West ~** (*formerly*) Ost-/Westberlin *nt*
berm [bəːm] (*US*) *n* Seitenstreifen *m*
Bermuda [bəː'mjuːdə] *n* Bermuda *nt*, die Bermudinseln *pl*
Bermuda shorts *npl* Bermudashorts *pl*
Bern [bəːn] *n* Bern *nt*
berry ['bɛrɪ] *n* Beere *f*
berserk [bə'səːk] *adj*: **to go ~** wild werden
berth [bəːθ] *n* (*bed*) Bett *nt*; (*on ship*) Koje *f*; (*on train*) Schlafwagenbett *nt*; (*for ship*) Liegeplatz *m* ▷ *vi* anlegen; **to give sb a wide ~** (*fig*) einen großen Bogen um jdn machen
beseech [bɪ'siːtʃ] (*pt, pp* **besought**) *vt* anflehen
beset [bɪ'sɛt] (*pt, pp* **~**) *vt* (*subj: difficulties*) bedrängen; (*: fears, doubts*) befallen; **~ with** (*problems, dangers etc*) voller *+dat*
beside [bɪ'saɪd] *prep* neben *+dat*; (*with movement*) neben *+acc*; **to be ~ o.s.** außer sich sein; **that's ~ the point** das hat damit nichts zu tun
besides [bɪ'saɪdz] *adv* außerdem ▷ *prep* außer *+dat*
besiege [bɪ'siːdʒ] *vt* belagern; (*fig*) belagern, bedrängen
besmirch [bɪ'sməːtʃ] *vt* besudeln
besotted [bɪ'sɔtɪd] (*Brit*) *adj*: **~ with** vernarrt in *+acc*
besought [bɪ'sɔːt] *pt, pp of* **beseech**
bespectacled [bɪ'spɛktɪkld] *adj* bebrillt
bespoke [bɪ'spəuk] (*Brit*) *adj* (*garment*) maßgeschneidert; (*suit*) Maß-; **~ tailor** Maßschneider *m*
best [bɛst] *adj* beste(r, s) ▷ *adv* am besten ▷ *n*: **at ~** bestenfalls; **the ~ thing to do is ...** das Beste ist ...; **the ~ part of** der größte Teil *+gen*; **to make the ~ of sth** das Beste aus etw machen; **to do one's ~** sein Bestes tun; **to the ~ of my knowledge** meines Wissens; **to the ~ of my ability** so gut ich kann; **he's not exactly patient at the ~ of times** er ist schon normalerweise ziemlich ungeduldig
best-before date *n* Mindesthaltbarkeitsdatum *nt*
bestial ['bɛstɪəl] *adj* bestialisch
best man *n* Trauzeuge *m* (*des Bräutigams*)
bestow [bɪ'stəu] *vt* schenken; **to ~ sth on sb** (*honour, praise*) jdm etw zuteilwerden lassen; (*title*) jdm etw verleihen
best seller *n* Bestseller *m*
bet [bɛt] (*pt, pp* **~** *or* **betted**) *n* Wette *f* ▷ *vi* wetten ▷ *vt*: **to ~ sb sth** mit jdm um etw wetten; **it's a safe ~** (*fig*) es ist so gut wie sicher; **to ~ money on sth** Geld auf etw *acc* setzen
Bethlehem ['bɛθlɪhɛm] *n* Bethlehem *nt*
betray [bɪ'treɪ] *vt* verraten; (*trust, confidence*) missbrauchen
betrayal [bɪ'treɪəl] *n* Verrat *m*
better ['bɛtə^r] *adj, adv* besser ▷ *vt* verbessern ▷ *n*: **to get the ~ of sb** jdn unterkriegen; (*curiosity*) über jdn siegen; **I had ~ go** ich gehe jetzt (wohl) besser; **you had ~ do it** tun Sie es lieber; **he thought ~ of it** er überlegte es sich *dat* anders; **to get ~** gesund werden; **that's ~!** so ist es besser!; **a change for the ~** eine Wendung zum Guten
better off *adj* (*wealthier*) bessergestellt; (*more comfortable etc*) besser dran; (*fig*): **you'd be ~ this way** so wäre es besser für Sie
betting ['bɛtɪŋ] *n* Wetten *nt*
betting shop (*Brit*) *n* Wettbüro *nt*
between [bɪ'twiːn] *prep* zwischen *+dat*; (*with movement*) zwischen *+acc*; (*amongst*) unter *+acc or dat* ▷ *adv* dazwischen; **the road ~ here and London** die Straße zwischen hier und London; **we only had £5 ~ us** wir hatten zusammen nur £5
bevel ['bɛvəl] *n* (*also*: **bevel edge**) abgeschrägte Kante *f*
bevelled ['bɛvəld] *adj*: **a ~ edge** eine Schrägkante, eine abgeschrägte Kante
beverage ['bɛvərɪdʒ] *n* Getränk *nt*
bevy ['bɛvɪ] *n*: **a ~ of** eine Schar *+gen*

bewail [bɪ'weɪl] *vt* beklagen
beware [bɪ'wɛəʳ] *vi*: **to ~ (of)** sich in Acht nehmen (vor *+dat*); **"~ of the dog"** „Vorsicht, bissiger Hund"
bewildered [bɪ'wɪldəd] *adj* verwirrt
bewildering [bɪ'wɪldrɪŋ] *adj* verwirrend
bewitching [bɪ'wɪtʃɪŋ] *adj* bezaubernd, hinreißend
beyond [bɪ'jɔnd] *prep (in space)* jenseits *+gen*; *(exceeding)* über *+acc* ... hinaus; *(after)* nach; *(above)* über *+dat* ▷ *adv (in space)* dahinter; *(in time)* darüber hinaus; **it is ~ doubt** es steht außer Zweifel; **~ repair** nicht mehr zu reparieren; **it is ~ my understanding** es übersteigt mein Begriffsvermögen; **it's ~ me** das geht über meinen Verstand
b/f *abbr (Comm: = brought forward)* Übertr.
BFPO *n abbr (= British Forces Post Office) Postbehörde der britischen Armee*
bhp *n abbr (Aut: = brake horsepower)* Bremsleistung *f*
bi ... [baɪ] *pref* Bi-, bi-
biannual [baɪ'ænjuəl] *adj* zweimal jährlich
bias ['baɪəs] *n (prejudice)* Vorurteil *nt*; *(preference)* Vorliebe *f*
biased, biassed ['baɪəst] *adj* voreingenommen; **to be bias(s)ed against** voreingenommen sein gegen
biathlon [baɪ'æθlən] *n* Biathlon *nt*
bib [bɪb] *n* Latz *m*
Bible ['baɪbl] *n* Bibel *f*
biblical ['bɪblɪkl] *adj* biblisch
bibliography [bɪblɪ'ɔgrəfɪ] *n* Bibliografie *f*
bicarbonate of soda [baɪ'kɑ:bənɪt-] *n* Natron *nt*
bicentenary [baɪsɛn'ti:nərɪ] *n* Zweihundertjahrfeier *f*
bicentennial [baɪsɛn'tɛnɪəl] *(US) n* = **bicentenary**
biceps ['baɪsɛps] *n* Bizeps *m*
bicker ['bɪkəʳ] *vi* sich zanken
bickering ['bɪkərɪŋ] *n* Zankerei *f*
bicycle ['baɪsɪkl] *n* Fahrrad *nt*
bicycle path *n* (Fahr)radweg *m*
bicycle pump *n* Luftpumpe *f*
bicycle track *n* (Fahr)radweg *m*
bid [bɪd] *(pt* **bade** *or* **~**, *pp* **bidden** *or* **~**) *n (at auction)* Gebot *nt*; *(in tender)* Angebot *nt*; *(attempt)* Versuch *m* ▷ *vi* bieten; *(Cards)* bieten, reizen ▷ *vt* bieten; **to ~ sb good day** jdm einen Guten Tag wünschen
bidder ['bɪdəʳ] *n*: **the highest** ~ der/die Höchstbietende *or* Meistbietende
bidding ['bɪdɪŋ] *n* Steigern *nt*, Bieten *nt*; *(order, command)*: **to do sb's** ~ tun, was jd einem sagt
bide [baɪd] *vt*: **to ~ one's time** den rechten Augenblick abwarten
bidet ['bi:deɪ] *n* Bidet *nt*
bidirectional ['baɪdɪ'rɛkʃənl] *adj (Comput)* bidirektional
biennial [baɪ'ɛnɪəl] *adj* zweijährlich ▷ *n* zweijährige Pflanze *f*
bifocals [baɪ'fəuklz] *npl* Bifokalbrille *f*
big [bɪg] *adj* groß; **to do things in a ~ way** alles im großen Stil tun
bigamist ['bɪgəmɪst] *n* Bigamist(in) *m(f)*
bigamous ['bɪgəməs] *adj* bigamistisch
bigamy ['bɪgəmɪ] *n* Bigamie *f*
big dipper [-'dɪpəʳ] *n* Achterbahn *f*
big end *n (Aut)* Pleuelfuß *m*, Schubstangenkopf *m*
biggish ['bɪgɪʃ] *adj* ziemlich groß
bigheaded ['bɪg'hɛdɪd] *adj* eingebildet
big-hearted ['bɪg'hɑ:tɪd] *adj* großherzig
bigot ['bɪgət] *n* Eiferer *m*; *(about religion)* bigotter Mensch *m*
bigoted ['bɪgətɪd] *adj (see n)* eifernd; bigott
bigotry ['bɪgətrɪ] *n (see n)* eifernde Borniertheit *f*; Bigotterie *f*
big toe *n* große Zehe *f*
big top *n* Zirkuszelt *nt*
big wheel *n* Riesenrad *nt*
bigwig ['bɪgwɪg] *(inf) n* hohes Tier *nt*
bike [baɪk] *n* (Fahr)rad *nt*; *(motorcycle)* Motorrad *nt*
bike lane *n* Fahrradspur *f*
bikini [bɪ'ki:nɪ] *n* Bikini *m*
bilateral [baɪ'lætərəl] *adj* bilateral
bile [baɪl] *n* Galle(nflüssigkeit) *f*; *(fig: invective)* Beschimpfungen *pl*
bilingual [baɪ'lɪŋgwəl] *adj* zweisprachig
bilious ['bɪlɪəs] *adj* unwohl; *(fig: colour)* widerlich; **he felt ~** ihm war schlecht *or* übel
bill [bɪl] *n* Rechnung *f*; *(Pol)* (Gesetz)entwurf *m*, (Gesetzes)vorlage *f*; *(US: banknote)* Banknote *f*, (Geld)schein *m*; *(of bird)* Schnabel *m* ▷ *vt (item)* in Rechnung stellen, berechnen; *(customer)* eine Rechnung ausstellen *+dat*; **"post no ~s"** „Plakate ankleben verboten"; **on the ~** *(Theat)* auf dem Programm; **to fit** *or* **fill the ~** *(fig)* der/die/das Richtige sein; **~ of exchange** Wechsel *m*, Tratte *f*; **~ of fare** Speisekarte *f*; **~ of lading** Seefrachtbrief *m*, Konnossement *nt*; **~ of sale** Verkaufsurkunde *f*
billboard ['bɪlbɔ:d] *n* Reklametafel *f*
billet ['bɪlɪt] *(Mil) n* Quartier *nt* ▷ *vt* einquartieren
billfold ['bɪlfəuld] *(US) n* Brieftasche *f*
billiards ['bɪljədz] *n* Billard *nt*
billion ['bɪljən] *n (Brit)* Billion *f*; *(US)* Milliarde *f*
billionaire [bɪljə'nɛəʳ] *n* Milliardär(in) *m(f)*
billow ['bɪləu] *n (of smoke)* Schwaden *m* ▷ *vi (smoke)* in Schwaden aufsteigen; *(sail)* sich blähen
billy goat ['bɪlɪ-] *n* Ziegenbock *m*
bimbo ['bɪmbəu] *(inf: pej) n (woman)* Puppe *f*, Häschen *nt*
bin [bɪn] *n (Brit)* Mülleimer *m*; *(container)* Behälter *m*
binary ['baɪnərɪ] *adj* binär
bind [baɪnd] *(pt, pp* **bound**) *vt* binden; *(tie together: hands and feet)* fesseln; *(constrain, oblige)* verpflichten ▷ *n (inf: nuisance)* Last *f*
▸ **bind over** *vt* rechtlich verpflichten
▸ **bind up** *vt (wound)* verbinden; **to be bound up in** sehr beschäftigt sein mit; **to be bound**

up with verbunden *or* verknüpft sein mit

binder ['baındəʳ] *n* (*file*) Hefter *m*; (*for magazines*) Mappe *f*

binding ['baındıŋ] *adj* bindend, verbindlich ▷ *n* (*of book*) Einband *m*

binge [bındʒ] (*inf*) *n*: **to go on a ~** auf eine Sauftour gehen

bingo ['bıŋgəu] *n* Bingo *nt*

bin liner *n* Müllbeutel *m*

binoculars [bı'nɔkjuləz] *npl* Fernglas *nt*

biochemistry [baıə'kɛmıstrı] *n* Biochemie *f*

biodegradable ['baıəudı'greıdəbl] *adj* biologisch abbaubar

biodiversity ['baıəudaı'və:sıtı] *n* biologische Vielfalt *f*

biofuel *n* Biotreibstoff *m*

biographer [baı'ɔgrəfəʳ] *n* Biograf(in) *m(f)*

biographic [baıə'græfık], **biographical** [baıə'græfıkl] *adj* biografisch

biography [baı'ɔgrəfı] *n* Biografie *f*

biological [baıə'lɔdʒıkl] *adj* biologisch

biological clock *n* biologische Uhr *f*

biological waste *n* Bioabfall *m*

biologist [baı'ɔlədʒıst] *n* Biologe *m*, Biologin *f*

biology [baı'ɔlədʒı] *n* Biologie *f*

biophysics ['baıəu'fızıks] *n* Biophysik *f*

biopic ['baıəupık] *n* Filmbiografie *f*

biopsy ['baıɔpsı] *n* Biopsie *f*

biosphere ['baıəsfıəʳ] *n* Biosphäre *f*

biotechnology ['baıəutɛk'nɔlədʒı] *n* Biotechnik *f*

biped ['baıpɛd] *n* Zweifüßer *m*

birch [bə:tʃ] *n* Birke *f*

bird [bə:d] *n* Vogel *m*; (*Brit*: *inf*: *girl*) Biene *f*

bird of prey *n* Raubvogel *m*

bird's-eye view ['bə:dzaı-] *n* Vogelperspektive *f*; (*overview*) Überblick *m*

bird-watcher ['bə:dwɔtʃəʳ] *n* Vogelbeobachter(in) *m(f)*

Biro® ['baıərəu] *n* Kugelschreiber *m*, Kuli *m* (*inf*)

birth [bə:θ] *n* Geburt *f*; **to give ~ to** (*subj*: *woman*) gebären, entbunden werden von; (: *animal*) werfen

birth certificate *n* Geburtsurkunde *f*

birth control *n* Geburtenkontrolle *f*, Geburtenregelung *f*

birthday ['bə:θdeı] *n* Geburtstag *m* ▷ *cpd* Geburtstags-; *see also* **happy**

birthmark ['bə:θmɑ:k] *n* Muttermal *nt*

birthplace ['bə:θpleıs] *n* Geburtsort *m*; (*house*) Geburtshaus *nt*; (*fig*) Entstehungsort *m*

birth rate ['bə:θreıt] *n* Geburtenrate *f*, Geburtenziffer *f*

Biscay ['bıskeı] *n*: **the Bay of ~** der Golf von Biskaya

biscuit ['bıskıt] *n* (*Brit*) Keks *m or nt*; (*US*) Brötchen *nt*

bisect [baı'sɛkt] *vt* halbieren

bisexual ['baı'sɛksjuəl] *adj* bisexuell ▷ *n* Bisexuelle(r) *f(m)*

bishop ['bıʃəp] *n* (*Rel*) Bischof *m*; (*Chess*) Läufer *m*

bistro ['bi:strəu] *n* Bistro *nt*

bit [bıt] *pt of* **bite** ▷ *n* (*piece*) Stück *nt*; (*of drill*) (Bohr)einsatz *m*, Bohrer *m*; (*of plane*) (Hobel)messer *nt*; (*Comput*) Bit *nt*; (*of horse*) Gebiss *nt*; (*US*): **two/four/six ~s** 25/50/75 Cent(s); **a ~ of** ein bisschen; **a ~ mad** ein bisschen verrückt; **a ~ dangerous** etwas gefährlich; **~ by bit** nach und nach; **to come to ~s** kaputtgehen; **bring all your ~s and pieces** bringen Sie Ihre (Sieben)sachen mit; **to do one's ~** sein(en) Teil tun *or* beitragen

bitch [bıtʃ] *n* (*dog*) Hündin *f*; (*inf!*: *woman*) Miststück *nt*

bite [baıt] (*pt* **bit**, *pp* **bitten**) *vt, vi* beißen; (*subj*: *insect etc*) stechen ▷ *n* (*insect bite*) Stich *m*; (*mouthful*) Bissen *m*; **to ~ one's nails** an seinen Nägeln kauen; **let's have a ~ (to eat)** (*inf*) lasst uns eine Kleinigkeit essen

biting ['baıtıŋ] *adj* (*wind*) schneidend; (*wit*) scharf

bit part *n* kleine Nebenrolle *f*

bitten ['bıtn] *pp of* **bite**

bitter ['bıtəʳ] *adj* bitter; (*person*) verbittert; (*wind, weather*) bitterkalt, eisig; (*criticism*) scharf ▷ *n* (*Brit*: *beer*) *halbdunkles obergäriges Bier*; **to the ~ end** bis zum bitteren Ende

bitterly ['bıtəlı] *adv* (*complain, weep*) bitterlich; (*oppose*) erbittert; (*criticize*) scharf; (*disappointed*) bitter; (*jealous*) sehr; **it's ~ cold** es ist bitterkalt

bitterness ['bıtənıs] *n* Bitterkeit *f*

bittersweet ['bıtəswi:t] *adj* bittersüß

bitty ['bıtı] (*Brit*: *inf*) *adj* zusammengestoppelt, zusammengestückelt

bitumen ['bıtjumın] *n* Bitumen *nt*

bivouac ['bıvuæk] *n* Biwak *nt*

bizarre [bı'zɑ:ʳ] *adj* bizarr

bk *abbr* = **bank; book**

BL *n abbr* (= *Bachelor of Law*) *akademischer Grad für Juristen*; (= *Bachelor of Letters*) *akademischer Grad für Literaturwissenschaftler*; (*US*: = *Bachelor of Literature*) *akademischer Grad für Literaturwissenschaftler*

B/L *abbr* = **bill of lading**

blab [blæb] (*inf*) *vi* quatschen

black [blæk] *adj* schwarz ▷ *vt* (*Brit*: *Industry*) boykottieren ▷ *n* Schwarz *nt*; (*person*): **B~** Schwarze(r) *f(m)*; **to give sb a ~ eye** jdm ein blaues Auge schlagen; **~ and blue** grün und blau; **there it is in ~ and white** (*fig*) da steht es schwarz auf weiß; **to be in the ~** in den schwarzen Zahlen sein

▸ **black out** *vi* (*faint*) ohnmächtig werden

black belt *n* (*US*) *Gebiet in den Südstaaten der USA, das vorwiegend von Schwarzen bewohnt wird*; (*Judo*) schwarzer Gürtel *m*

blackberry ['blækbərı] *n* Brombeere *f*

blackbird ['blækbə:d] *n* Amsel *f*

blackboard ['blækbɔ:d] *n* Tafel *f*

black box *n* (*Aviat*) Flugschreiber *m*

black coffee *n* schwarzer Kaffee *m*

Black Country (*Brit*) *n*: **the ~** *Industriegebiet in den englischen Midlands*

blackcurrant ['blæk'kʌrənt] *n* Johannisbeere *f*

black economy *n*: **the ~** die

Schattenwirtschaft
blacken ['blækn] *vt*: **to ~ sb's name/ reputation** *(fig)* jdn verunglimpfen
Black Forest *n*: **the ~** der Schwarzwald
blackhead ['blækhɛd] *n* Mitesser *m*
black hole *n* schwarzes Loch *nt*
black ice *n* Glatteis *nt*
blackjack ['blækdʒæk] *n (Cards)* Siebzehnundvier *nt*; *(US: truncheon)* Schlagstock *m*
blackleg ['blæklɛg] *(Brit) n* Streikbrecher(in) *m(f)*
blacklist ['blæklɪst] *n* schwarze Liste *f* ▷ *vt* auf die schwarze Liste setzen
blackmail ['blækmeɪl] *n* Erpressung *f* ▷ *vt* erpressen
blackmailer ['blækmeɪlə^r] *n* Erpresser(in) *m(f)*
black market *n* Schwarzmarkt *m*
blackout ['blækaut] *n (in wartime)* Verdunkelung *f*; *(power cut)* Stromausfall *m*; *(TV, Radio)* Ausfall *m*; *(faint)* Ohnmachtsanfall *m*
black pepper *n* schwarzer Pfeffer *m*
Black Sea *n*: **the ~** das Schwarze Meer
black sheep *n (fig)* schwarzes Schaf *nt*
blacksmith ['blæksmɪθ] *n* Schmied *m*
black spot *n (Aut)* Gefahrenstelle *f*; *(for unemployment etc) Gebiet, in dem ein Problem besonders ausgeprägt ist*
bladder ['blædə^r] *n* Blase *f*
blade [bleɪd] *n (of knife etc)* Klinge *f*; *(of oar, propeller)* Blatt *nt*; **a ~ of grass** ein Grashalm *m*
Blairite [blɛəraɪt] *(Pol) adj* blairistisch ▷ *n* Blair-Anhänger(in) *m(f)*
blame [bleɪm] *n* Schuld *f* ▷ *vt*: **to ~ sb for sth** jdm die Schuld an etw *dat* geben; **to be to ~** Schuld daran haben, schuld sein; **who's to ~?** wer hat Schuld *or* ist schuld?; **I'm not to ~** es ist nicht meine Schuld
blameless ['bleɪmlɪs] *adj* schuldlos
blanch [blɑːntʃ] *vi* blass werden ▷ *vt (Culin)* blanchieren
blancmange [blə'mɔnʒ] *n* Pudding *m*
bland [blænd] *adj (taste, food)* fade
blank [blæŋk] *adj (paper)* leer, unbeschrieben; *(look)* ausdruckslos ▷ *n (on form)* Lücke *f*; *(cartridge)* Platzpatrone *f*; **my mind was a ~** ich hatte ein Brett vor dem Kopf; **we drew a ~** *(fig)* wir hatten kein Glück
blank cheque *n* Blankoscheck *m*; **to give sb a ~ to do sth** *(fig)* jdm freie Hand geben, etw zu tun
blanket ['blæŋkɪt] *n* Decke *f* ▷ *adj (statement)* pauschal; *(agreement)* Pauschal-
blanket cover *n* umfassende Versicherung *f*
blare [blɛə^r] *vi (brass band)* schmettern; *(horn)* tuten; *(radio)* plärren
▶ **blare out** *vi (radio, stereo)* plärren
blasé ['blɑːzeɪ] *adj* blasiert
blaspheme [blæs'fiːm] *vi* Gott lästern
blasphemous ['blæsfɪməs] *adj* lästerlich, blasphemisch
blasphemy ['blæsfɪmɪ] *n* (Gottes)lästerung *f*, Blasphemie *f*
blast [blɑːst] *n (of wind)* Windstoß *m*; *(of whistle)* Trillern *nt*; *(shock wave)* Druckwelle *f*; *(of air, steam)* Schwall *m*; *(of explosive)* Explosion *f* ▷ *vt (blow up)* sprengen ▷ *excl (Brit: inf)* verdammt!, so ein Mist!; **at full ~** *(play music)* mit voller Lautstärke; *(move, work)* auf Hochtouren
▶ **blast off** *vi (Space)* abheben, starten
blast furnace *n* Hochofen *m*
blastoff ['blɑːstɔf] *n (Space)* Abschuss *m*
blatant ['bleɪtənt] *adj* offensichtlich
blatantly ['bleɪtəntlɪ] *adv (lie)* unverfroren; **it's ~ obvious** es ist überdeutlich
blaze [bleɪz] *n (fire)* Feuer *nt*, Brand *m*; *(fig: of colour)* Farbenpracht *f*; *(: of glory)* Glanz *m* ▷ *vi (fire)* lodern; *(guns)* feuern; *(fig: eyes)* glühen ▷ *vt*: **to ~ a trail** *(fig)* den Weg bahnen; **in a ~ of publicity** mit viel Publicity
blazer ['bleɪzə^r] *n* Blazer *m*
bleach [bliːtʃ] *n (also:* **household bleach***)* ≈ Reinigungsmittel *nt* ▷ *vt* bleichen
bleached [bliːtʃt] *adj* gebleicht
bleachers ['bliːtʃəz] *(US) npl* unüberdachte Zuschauertribüne *f*
bleak [bliːk] *adj (countryside)* öde; *(weather, situation)* trostlos; *(prospect)* trüb; *(expression, voice)* deprimiert
bleary-eyed ['blɪərɪ'aɪd] *adj* triefäugig
bleat [bliːt] *vi (goat)* meckern; *(sheep)* blöken ▷ *n* Meckern *nt*; Blöken *nt*
bled [blɛd] *pt, pp of* **bleed**
bleed [bliːd] *(pt, pp* **bled***) vi* bluten; *(colour)* auslaufen ▷ *vt (brakes, radiator)* entlüften; **my nose is ~ing** ich habe Nasenbluten
bleep [bliːp] *n* Piepton *m* ▷ *vi* piepen ▷ *vt (doctor etc)* rufen, anpiepen *(inf)*
bleeper ['bliːpə^r] *n* Piepser *m (inf)*, Funkrufempfänger *m*
blemish ['blɛmɪʃ] *n* Makel *m*
blend [blɛnd] *n* Mischung *f* ▷ *vt (Culin)* mischen, mixen; *(colours, styles, flavours etc)* vermischen ▷ *vi (colours etc: also:* **blend in***)* harmonieren
blender ['blɛndə^r] *n (Culin)* Mixer *m*
bless [blɛs] *(pt, pp* **~ed** *or* **blest***) vt* segnen; **to be ~ed with** gesegnet sein mit; **~ you!** *(after sneeze)* Gesundheit!
blessed ['blɛsɪd] *adj* heilig; *(happy)* selig; **it rains every ~ day** *(inf)* es regnet aber auch jeden Tag
blessing ['blɛsɪŋ] *n (approval)* Zustimmung *f*; *(Rel: fig)* Segen *m*; **to count one's ~s** von Glück sagen können; **it was a ~ in disguise** es war schließlich doch ein Segen
blew [bluː] *pt of* **blow**
blight [blaɪt] *vt* zerstören; *(hopes)* vereiteln; *(life)* verderben ▷ *n (of plants)* Brand *m*
blimey ['blaɪmɪ] *(Brit: inf) excl* Mensch!
blind [blaɪnd] *adj* blind ▷ *n (for window)* Rollo *nt*, Rouleau *nt*; *(also:* **Venetian blind***)* Jalousie *f* ▷ *vt* blind machen; *(dazzle)* blenden; *(deceive: with facts etc)* verblenden; **the blind** *npl (blind people)* die Blinden *pl*; **to turn a ~ eye (on** *or* **to)** ein

Auge zudrücken (bei); **to be ~ to sth** *(fig)* blind für etw sein
blind alley *n (fig)* Sackgasse *f*
blind corner *(Brit) n* unübersichtliche Ecke *f*
blind date *n* Rendezvous *nt* mit einem/einer Unbekannten
blinders ['blaɪndəz] *(US) npl* = **blinkers**
blindfold ['blaɪndfəuld] *n* Augenbinde *f* ▷ *adj, adv* mit verbundenen Augen ▷ *vt* die Augen verbinden *+dat*
blinding ['blaɪndɪŋ] *adj (dazzling)* blendend; *(remarkable)* bemerkenswert
blindly ['blaɪndlɪ] *adv (without seeing)* wie blind; *(without thinking)* blindlings
blindness ['blaɪndnɪs] *n* Blindheit *f*
blind spot *n (Aut)* toter Winkel *m*; *(fig: weak spot)* schwacher Punkt *m*
blink [blɪŋk] *vi* blinzeln; *(light)* blinken ▷ *n*: **the TV's on the ~** *(inf)* der Fernseher ist kaputt
blinkers ['blɪŋkəz] *npl* Scheuklappen *pl*
blinking ['blɪŋkɪŋ] *(Brit: inf) adj*: **this ~ ...** diese(r, s) verflixte ...
blip [blɪp] *n (on radar screen)* leuchtender Punkt *m*; *(in a straight line)* Ausschlag *m*; *(fig)* (zeitweilige) Abweichung *f*
bliss [blɪs] *n* Glück *nt*, Seligkeit *f*
blissful ['blɪsful] *adj (event, day)* herrlich; *(smile)* selig; **a ~ sigh** ein wohliger Seufzer *m*; **in ~ ignorance** in herrlicher Ahnungslosigkeit
blissfully ['blɪsfəlɪ] *adv* selig; **~ happy** überglücklich; **~ unaware of ...** ohne auch nur zu ahnen, dass ...
blister ['blɪstə^r] *n* Blase *f* ▷ *vi (paint)* Blasen werfen
BLit, BLitt *n abbr (= Bachelor of Literature; Bachelor of Letters) akademischer Grad für Literaturwissenschaftler*
blithely ['blaɪðlɪ] *adv (unconcernedly)* unbekümmert, munter; *(joyfully)* fröhlich
blithering ['blɪðərɪŋ] *(inf) adj*: **this ~ idiot** dieser Trottel
blitz [blɪts] *n (Mil)* Luftangriff *m*; **to have a ~ on sth** *(fig)* einen Großangriff auf etw *acc* starten
blizzard ['blɪzəd] *n* Schneesturm *m*
bloated ['bləutɪd] *adj* aufgedunsen; *(full)* (über)satt
blob [blɔb] *n* Tropfen *m*; *(sth indistinct)* verschwommener Fleck *m*
bloc [blɔk] *n* Block *m*; **the Eastern ~** *(Hist)* der Ostblock
block [blɔk] *n* Block *m*; *(toy)* Bauklotz *m*; *(in pipes)* Verstopfung *f* ▷ *vt* blockieren; *(progress)* aufhalten; *(Comput)* blocken; **~ of flats** *(Brit)* Wohnblock *m*; **3 ~s from here** 3 Blocks *or* Straßen weiter; **mental ~** geistige Sperre *f*, Mattscheibe *f (inf)*; **~ and tackle** Flaschenzug *m*
▸ **block up** *vt, vi* verstopfen
blockade [blɔ'keɪd] *n* Blockade *f* ▷ *vt* blockieren
blockage ['blɔkɪdʒ] *n* Verstopfung *f*
block booking *n* Gruppenbuchung *f*
blockbuster ['blɔkbʌstə^r] *n* Knüller *m*
block capitals *npl* Blockschrift *f*
blockhead ['blɔkhɛd] *(inf) n* Dummkopf *m*
block letters *npl* Blockschrift *f*
block release *(Brit) n blockweise Freistellung von Auszubildenden zur Weiterbildung*
block vote *(Brit) n* Stimmenblock *m*
bloke [bləuk] *(Brit: inf) n* Typ *m*
blond, blonde [blɔnd] *adj* blond ▷ *n*: **~(e)** *(woman)* Blondine *f*
blood [blʌd] *n* Blut *nt*; **new ~** *(fig)* frisches Blut *nt*
blood bank *n* Blutbank *f*
blood bath *n* Blutbad *nt*
blood count *n* Blutbild *nt*
bloodcurdling ['blʌdkə:dlɪŋ] *adj* grauenerregend
blood donor *n* Blutspender(in) *m(f)*
blood group *n* Blutgruppe *f*
bloodhound ['blʌdhaund] *n* Bluthund *m*
bloodless ['blʌdlɪs] *adj (victory)* unblutig; *(pale)* blutleer
blood-letting ['blʌdlɛtɪŋ] *n (also fig)* Aderlass *m*
blood poisoning *n* Blutvergiftung *f*
blood pressure *n* Blutdruck *m*; **to have high/low ~** hohen/niedrigen Blutdruck haben
bloodshed ['blʌdʃɛd] *n* Blutvergießen *nt*
bloodshot ['blʌdʃɔt] *adj (eyes)* blutunterlaufen
blood sport *n* Jagdsport *m (und andere Sportarten, bei denen Tiere getötet werden)*
bloodstained ['blʌdsteɪnd] *adj* blutbefleckt
bloodstream ['blʌdstri:m] *n* Blut *nt*, Blutkreislauf *m*
blood test *n* Blutprobe *f*
bloodthirsty ['blʌdθə:stɪ] *adj* blutrünstig
blood transfusion *n* Blutübertragung *f*, (Blut)transfusion *f*
blood type *n* Blutgruppe *f*
blood vessel *n* Blutgefäß *nt*
bloody ['blʌdɪ] *adj* blutig; *(Brit: inf!)*: **this ~ ...** diese(r, s) verdammte ...; **~ strong** *(inf!)* verdammt stark; **~ good** *(inf!)* echt gut
bloody-minded ['blʌdɪ'maɪndɪd] *(Brit: inf) adj* stur
bloom [blu:m] *n* Blüte *f* ▷ *vi* blühen; **to be in ~** in Blüte stehen
blooming ['blu:mɪŋ] *(Brit: inf) adj*: **this ~ ...** diese(r, s) verflixte ...
blossom ['blɔsəm] *n* Blüte *f* ▷ *vi* blühen; *(fig)*: **to ~ into** erblühen *or* aufblühen zu
blot [blɔt] *n* Klecks *m*; *(fig: on name etc)* Makel *m* ▷ *vt (liquid)* aufsaugen; *(make blot on)* beklecksen; **to be a ~ on the landscape** ein Schandfleck in der Landschaft sein; **to ~ one's copy book** *(fig)* sich unmöglich machen
▸ **blot out** *vt (view)* verdecken; *(memory)* auslöschen
blotchy ['blɔtʃɪ] *adj* fleckig
blotter ['blɔtə^r] *n* (Tinten)löscher *m*
blotting paper ['blɔtɪŋ-] *n* Löschpapier *nt*
blotto ['blɔtəu] *(inf) adj (drunk)* sternhagelvoll
blouse [blauz] *n* Bluse *f*
blow [bləu] *(pt* **blew**, *pp* **~n**) *n (also fig)* Schlag *m* ▷ *vi (wind)* wehen; *(person)* blasen ▷ *vt*

(*subj: wind*) wehen; (*instrument, whistle*) blasen; (*fuse*) durchbrennen lassen; **to come to ~s** handgreiflich werden; **to ~ off course** (*ship*) vom Kurs abgetrieben werden; **to ~ one's nose** sich *dat* die Nase putzen; **to ~ a whistle** pfeifen
▸ **blow away** *vt* wegblasen ▹ *vi* wegfliegen
▸ **blow down** *vt* umwehen
▸ **blow off** *vt* wegwehen ▹ *vi* wegfliegen
▸ **blow out** *vi* ausgehen
▸ **blow over** *vi* sich legen
▸ **blow up** *vi* ausbrechen ▹ *vt* (*bridge*) in die Luft jagen; (*tyre*) aufblasen; (*Phot*) vergrößern
blow-dry ['bləudraɪ] *vt* föhnen ▹ *n*: **to have a ~** sich föhnen lassen
blowlamp ['bləulæmp] (*Brit*) *n* Lötlampe *f*
blown [bləun] *pp of* **blow**
blowout ['bləʊaʊt] *n* Reifenpanne *f*; (*inf: big meal*) Schlemmerei *f*; (*of oil-well*) Ölausbruch *m*
blowtorch ['bləutɔ:tʃ] *n* = **blowlamp**
blow-up ['bləuʌp] *n* Vergrößerung *f*
blowzy ['blauzɪ] (*Brit*) *adj* schlampig
BLS (*US*) *n abbr* (*= Bureau of Labor Statistics*) *Amt für Arbeitsstatistik*
blubber ['blʌbə^r] *n* Walfischspeck *m* ▹ *vi* (*pej*) heulen
bludgeon ['blʌdʒən] *vt* niederknüppeln; (*fig*): **to ~ sb into doing sth** jdm so lange zusetzen, bis er etw tut
blue [blu:] *adj* blau; (*depressed*) deprimiert, niedergeschlagen ▹ *n*: **out of the ~** (*fig*) aus heiterem Himmel; **blues** *n* (*Mus*): **the ~s** der Blues; **~ film** Pornofilm *m*; **~ joke** schlüpfriger Witz *m*; **(only) once in a ~ moon** (nur) alle Jubeljahre einmal; **to have the ~s** deprimiert *or* niedergeschlagen sein
blue baby *n* Baby *nt* mit angeborenem Herzfehler
bluebell ['blu:bɛl] *n* Glockenblume *f*
bluebottle ['blu:bɔtl] *n* Schmeißfliege *f*
blue cheese *n* Blauschimmelkäse *m*
blue-chip ['blu:tʃɪp] *adj*: **~ investment** sichere Geldanlage *f*
blue-collar worker ['blu:kɔlə^r-] *n* Arbeiter(in) *m(f)*
blue jeans *npl* (Blue)jeans *pl*
blueprint ['blu:prɪnt] *n* (*fig*): **a ~ (for)** ein Plan *m or* Entwurf *m* (für)
bluff [blʌf] *vi* bluffen ▹ *n* Bluff *m*; (*cliff*) Klippe *f*; (*promontory*) Felsvorsprung *m*; **to call sb's ~** es darauf ankommen lassen
blunder ['blʌndə^r] *n* (dummer) Fehler *m* ▹ *vi* einen (dummen) Fehler machen; **to ~ into sb** mit jdm zusammenstoßen; **to ~ into sth** in etw *acc* (hinein)tappen
blunt [blʌnt] *adj* stumpf; (*person*) direkt; (*talk*) unverblümt ▹ *vt* stumpf machen; **~ instrument** (*Law*) stumpfer Gegenstand *m*
bluntly ['blʌntlɪ] *adv* (*speak*) unverblümt
bluntness ['blʌntnɪs] *n* (*of person*) Direktheit *f*
blur [blə:^r] *n* (*shape*) verschwommener Fleck *m*; (*scene etc*) verschwommenes Bild *nt*; (*memory*) verschwommene Erinnerung *f* ▹ *vt* (*vision*) trüben; (*distinction*) verwischen
blurb [blə:b] *n* Informationsmaterial *nt*
blurred [blə:d] *adj* (*photograph, TV picture etc*) verschwommen; (*distinction*) verwischt
blurt out [blə:t-] *vt* herausplatzen mit
blush [blʌʃ] *vi* erröten ▹ *n* Röte *f*
blusher ['blʌʃə^r] *n* Rouge *nt*
bluster ['blʌstə^r] *n* Toben *nt*, Geschrei *nt* ▹ *vi* toben
blustering ['blʌstərɪŋ] *adj* polternd
blustery ['blʌstərɪ] *adj* stürmisch
Blvd *abbr* = **boulevard**
BM *n abbr* (*= British Museum*) Britisches Museum *nt*; (*= Bachelor of Medicine*) *akademischer Grad für Mediziner*
BMA *n abbr* (*= British Medical Association*) *Dachverband der Ärzte*
BMJ *n abbr* (*= British Medical Journal*) *vom BMA herausgegebene Zeitschrift*
BMus *n abbr* (*= Bachelor of Music*) *akademischer Grad für Musikwissenschaftler*
BMX *n abbr* (*= bicycle motocross*): **~ bike** BMX-Rad *nt*
bn *abbr* = **billion**
BO *n abbr* (*inf: = body odour*) Körpergeruch *m*; = **box office**
boar [bɔ:^r] *n* (*male pig*) Eber *m*; (*wild pig*) Keiler *m*
board [bɔ:d] *n* Brett *nt*; (*cardboard*) Pappe *f*; (*committee*) Ausschuss *m*; (*in firm*) Vorstand *m* ▹ *vt* (*ship*) an Bord *+gen* gehen; (*train*) einsteigen in *+acc*; **on ~** (*Naut, Aviat*) an Bord; **full/half ~** (*Brit*) Voll-/Halbpension *f*; **~ and lodging** Unterkunft und Verpflegung *f*; **to go by the ~** (*fig*) unter den Tisch fallen; **above ~** (*fig*) korrekt; **across the ~** (*fig*) allgemein; (*: criticize, reject*) pauschal
▸ **board up** *vt* mit Brettern vernageln
boarder ['bɔ:də^r] *n* Internatsschüler(in) *m(f)*
board game *n* Brettspiel *nt*
boarding card ['bɔ:dɪŋ-] *n* (*Aviat, Naut*) = **boarding pass**
boarding house ['bɔ:dɪŋ-] *n* Pension *f*
boarding party ['bɔ:dɪŋ-] *n* (*Naut*) Enterkommando *nt*
boarding pass ['bɔ:dɪŋ-] *n* Bordkarte *f*
boarding school ['bɔ:dɪŋ-] *n* Internat *nt*
board meeting *n* Vorstandssitzung *f*
boardroom ['bɔ:dru:m] *n* Sitzungssaal *m*
boardwalk ['bɔ:dwɔ:k] (*US*) *n* Holzsteg *m*
boast [bəust] *vi* prahlen ▹ *vt* (*fig: possess*) sich rühmen *+gen*, besitzen; **to ~ about** *or* **of** prahlen mit
boastful ['bəustful] *adj* prahlerisch
boastfulness ['bəustfulnɪs] *n* Prahlerei *f*
boat [bəut] *n* Boot *nt*; (*ship*) Schiff *nt*; **to go by ~** mit dem Schiff fahren; **to be in the same ~** (*fig*) in einem Boot *or* im gleichen Boot sitzen
boater ['bəutə^r] *n* steifer Strohhut *m*, Kreissäge *f* (*inf*)
boating ['bəutɪŋ] *n* Bootfahren *nt*
boat people *npl* Bootsflüchtlinge *pl*
boatswain ['bəusn] *n* Bootsmann *m*
bob [bɔb] *vi* (*also*: **bob up and down**) sich auf

und ab bewegen ▷ *n* (*Brit: inf*) = **shilling**
▸ **bob up** *vi* auftauchen
bobbin ['bɔbɪn] *n* Spule *f*
bobby ['bɔbɪ] (*Brit: inf*) *n* Bobby *m*, Polizist *m*
bobsleigh ['bɔbsleɪ] *n* Bob *m*
bode [bəud] *vi*: **to ~ well/ill (for)** ein gutes/schlechtes Zeichen sein (für)
bodice ['bɔdɪs] *n* (*of dress*) Oberteil *nt*
bodily ['bɔdɪlɪ] *adj* körperlich; (*needs*) leiblich ▷ *adv* (*lift, carry*) mit aller Kraft
body ['bɔdɪ] *n* Körper *m*; (*corpse*) Leiche *f*; (*main part*) Hauptteil *m*; (*of car*) Karosserie *f*; (*of plane*) Rumpf *m*; (*group*) Gruppe *f*; (*organization*) Organ *nt*; **ruling ~** amtierendes Organ; **in a ~** geschlossen; **a ~ of facts** Tatsachenmaterial *nt*
body blow *n* (*fig: setback*) schwerer Schlag *m*
body building *n* Bodybuilding *nt*
body double *n* (*Film, TV*) *Double für Szenen, in denen Körperpartien in Nahaufnahme gezeigt werden*
bodyguard ['bɔdɪgɑːd] *n* (*group*) Leibwache *f*; (*one person*) Leibwächter *m*
body language *n* Körpersprache *f*
body repairs *npl* Karosseriearbeiten *pl*
body search *n* Leibesvisitation *f*
body stocking *n* Body(stocking) *m*
bodywork ['bɔdɪwəːk] *n* Karosserie *f*
boffin ['bɔfɪn] (*Brit*) *n* Fachidiot *m*
bog [bɔg] *n* Sumpf *m* ▷ *vt*: **to get ~ged down** (*fig*) sich verzetteln
bogey ['bəugɪ] *n* Schreckgespenst *nt*; (*also*: **bogeyman**) Butzemann *m*, schwarzer Mann *m*
boggle ['bɔgl] *vi*: **the mind ~s** das ist nicht *or* kaum auszumalen
bogie ['bəugɪ] *n* Drehgestell *nt*; (*trolley*) Draisine *f*
Bogotá [bəugə'tɑː] *n* Bogotá *nt*
bogus ['bəugəs] *adj* (*workman etc*) falsch; (*claim*) erfunden
Bohemia [bəu'hiːmɪə] *n* Böhmen *nt*
Bohemian [bəu'hiːmɪən] *adj* böhmisch ▷ *n* Böhme *m*, Böhmin *f*; (*also*: **bohemian**) Bohemien *m*
boil [bɔɪl] *vt, vi* kochen ▷ *n* (*Med*) Furunkel *nt or m*; **to come to the ~** (*Brit*): **to come to a ~** (*US*) zu kochen anfangen
▸ **boil down to** *vt fus* (*fig*) hinauslaufen auf *+acc*
▸ **boil over** *vi* überkochen
boiled egg [bɔɪld-] *n* gekochtes Ei *nt*
boiled potatoes *npl* Salzkartoffeln *pl*
boiler ['bɔɪlə^r] *n* Boiler *m*
boiler suit (*Brit*) *n* Overall *m*
boiling ['bɔɪlɪŋ] *adj*: **I'm ~ (hot)** (*inf*) mir ist fürchterlich heiß; **it's ~** es ist eine Affenhitze (*inf*)
boiling point *n* Siedepunkt *m*
boil-in-the-bag [bɔɪlɪnðə'bæg] *adj* (*meals*) Kochbeutel-
boisterous ['bɔɪstərəs] *adj* ausgelassen
bold [bəuld] *adj* (*brave*) mutig; (*pej: cheeky*) dreist; (*pattern, colours*) kräftig
boldly ['bəuldlɪ] *adv* (*see adj*) mutig; dreist; kräftig
boldness ['bəuldnɪs] *n* Mut *m*; (*cheekiness*) Dreistigkeit *f*
bold type *n* Fettdruck *m*
Bolivia [bə'lɪvɪə] *n* Bolivien *nt*
Bolivian [bə'lɪvɪən] *adj* bolivisch, bolivianisch ▷ *n* Bolivier(in) *m(f)*, Bolivianer(in) *m(f)*
bollard ['bɔləd] (*Brit*) *n* Poller *m*
bolshy ['bɔlʃɪ] (*Brit: inf*) *adj* (*stroppy*) pampig
bolster ['bəulstə^r] *n* Nackenrolle *f*
▸ **bolster up** *vt* stützen; (*case*) untermauern
bolt [bəult] *n* Riegel *m*; (*with nut*) Schraube *f*; (*of lightning*) Blitz(strahl) *m* ▷ *vt* (*door*) verriegeln; (*also*: **bolt together**) verschrauben; (*food*) hinunterschlingen ▷ *vi* (*run away: person*) weglaufen; (*: horse*) durchgehen ▷ *adv*: **~ upright** kerzengerade; **a ~ from the blue** (*fig*) ein Blitz *m* aus heiterem Himmel
bomb [bɔm] *n* Bombe *f* ▷ *vt* bombardieren; (*plant bomb in or near*) einen Bombenanschlag verüben auf *+acc*
bombard [bɔm'bɑːd] *vt* (*also fig*) bombardieren
bombardment [bɔm'bɑːdmənt] *n* Bombardierung *f*, Bombardement *nt*
bombastic [bɔm'bæstɪk] *adj* bombastisch
bomb disposal *n*: **~ unit** Bombenräumkommando *nt*; **~ expert** Bombenräumexperte *m*, Bombenräumexpertin *f*
bomber ['bɔmə^r] *n* Bomber *m*; (*terrorist*) Bombenattentäter(in) *m(f)*
bombing ['bɔmɪŋ] *n* Bombenangriff *m*
bomb scare *n* Bombenalarm *m*
bombshell ['bɔmʃɛl] *n* (*fig: revelation*) Bombe *f*
bomb site *n* Trümmergrundstück *nt*
bona fide ['bəunə'faɪdɪ] *adj* echt; **~ offer** Angebot *nt* auf Treu und Glauben
bonanza [bə'nænzə] *n* (*Econ*) Boom *m*
bond [bɔnd] *n* Band *nt*, Bindung *f*; (*Fin*) festverzinsliches Wertpapier *nt*, Bond *m*
bondage ['bɔndɪdʒ] *n* Sklaverei *f*
bonded warehouse ['bɔndɪd] *n* Zolllager *nt*
bone [bəun] *n* Knochen *m*; (*of fish*) Gräte *f* ▷ *vt* (*meat*) die Knochen herauslösen aus; (*fish*) entgräten; **I've got a ~ to pick with you** ich habe mit Ihnen (noch) ein Hühnchen zu rupfen
bone china *n* ≈ feines Porzellan *nt*
bone-dry ['bəun'draɪ] *adj* knochentrocken
bone idle *adj* stinkfaul
bone marrow *n* Knochenmark *nt*
boner ['bəunə^r] (*US*) *n* Schnitzer *m*
bonfire ['bɔnfaɪə^r] *n* Feuer *nt*
bonk [bɔŋk] (*inf*) *vt, vi* (*have sex (with)*) bumsen
bonkers ['bɔŋkəz] (*Brit: inf*) *adj* (*mad*) verrückt
Bonn [bɔn] *n* Bonn *nt*
bonnet ['bɔnɪt] *n* Haube *f*; (*for baby*) Häubchen *nt*; (*Brit: of car*) Motorhaube *f*
bonny ['bɔnɪ] (*Scot, Northern English*) *adj* schön, hübsch
bonus ['bəunəs] *n* Prämie *f*; (*on wages*) Zulage *f*; (*at Christmas*) Gratifikation *f*; (*fig: additional benefit*) Plus *nt*

bony ['bəunɪ] *adj* knochig; (*Med*) knöchern; (*tissue*) knochenartig; (*meat*) mit viel Knochen; (*fish*) mit viel Gräten
boo [bu:] *excl* buh ▷ *vt* auspfeifen, ausbuhen
boob [bu:b] (*inf*) *n* (*breast*) Brust *f*; (*Brit: mistake*) Schnitzer *m*
booby prize ['bu:bɪ-] *n* *Scherzpreis für den schlechtesten Teilnehmer*
booby trap ['bu:bɪ-] *n* versteckte Bombe *f*; (*fig: joke etc*) *als Schabernack versteckt angebrachte Falle*
booby-trapped ['bu:bɪtræpt] *adj*: **a ~ car** ein Auto *nt*, in dem eine Bombe versteckt ist
book [buk] *n* Buch *nt*; (*of stamps, tickets*) Heftchen *nt* ▷ *vt* bestellen; (*seat, room*) buchen, reservieren lassen; (*subj: traffic warden, policeman*) aufschreiben; (*: referee*) verwarnen; **books** *npl* (*Comm: accounts*) Bücher *pl*; **to keep the ~s** die Bücher führen; **by the ~** nach Vorschrift; **to throw the ~ at sb** jdn nach allen Regeln der Kunst fertig machen
▸ **book in** (*Brit*) *vi* sich eintragen
▸ **book up** *vt*: **all seats are ~ed up** es ist bis auf den letzten Platz ausverkauft; **the hotel is ~ed up** das Hotel ist ausgebucht
bookable ['bukəbl] *adj*: **all seats are ~** Karten für alle Plätze können vorbestellt werden
bookcase ['bukkeɪs] *n* Bücherregal *nt*
book ends *npl* Bücherstützen *pl*
booking ['bukɪŋ] (*Brit*) *n* Bestellung *f*; (*of seat, room*) Buchung *f*, Reservierung *f*
booking office (*Brit*) *n* (*Rail*) Fahrkartenschalter *m*; (*Theat*) Vorverkaufsstelle *f*, Vorverkaufskasse *f*
book-keeping ['buk'ki:pɪŋ] *n* Buchhaltung *f*, Buchführung *f*
booklet ['buklɪt] *n* Broschüre *f*
bookmaker ['bukmeɪkə^r] *n* Buchmacher *m*
bookmark ['bukmɑ:k] *n* Lesezeichen *nt*; (*Comput*) Bookmark *nt* ▷ *vt* (*Comput*) ein Bookmark einrichten für, bookmarken
bookseller ['buksɛlə^r] *n* Buchhändler(in) *m(f)*
bookshelf ['bukʃɛlf] *n* Bücherbord *nt*; **bookshelves** *npl* Bücherregal *nt*
bookshop ['bukʃɔp] *n* Buchhandlung *f*
bookstall ['bukstɔ:l] *n* Bücher- und Zeitungskiosk *m*
book store *n* = **bookshop**
book token *n* Buchgutschein *m*
book value *n* Buchwert *m*, Bilanzwert *m*
bookworm ['bukwə:m] *n* (*fig*) Bücherwurm *m*
boom [bu:m] *n* Donnern *nt*, Dröhnen *nt*; (*in prices, population etc*) rapider Anstieg *m*; (*Econ*) Hochkonjunktur *f*; (*busy period*) Boom *m* ▷ *vi* (*guns*) donnern; (*thunder*) hallen; (*voice*) dröhnen; (*business*) florieren
boomerang ['bu:məræŋ] *n* Bumerang *m* ▷ *vi* (*fig*) einen Bumerangeffekt haben
boom town *n* Goldgräberstadt *f*
boon [bu:n] *n* Segen *m*
boorish ['buərɪʃ] *adj* rüpelhaft
boost [bu:st] *n* Auftrieb *m* ▷ *vt* (*confidence*) stärken; (*sales, economy etc*) ankurbeln; **to give a ~ to sb/sb's spirits** jdm Auftrieb geben
booster ['bu:stə^r] *n* (*Med*) Wiederholungsimpfung *f*; (*TV*) Zusatzgleichrichter *m*; (*Elec*) Puffersatz *m*; (*also*: **booster rocket**) Booster *m*, Startrakete *f*
booster seat *n* (*Aut*) Sitzerhöhung *f*
boot [bu:t] *n* Stiefel *m*; (*ankle boot*) hoher Schuh *m*; (*Brit: of car*) Kofferraum *m* ▷ *vt* (*Comput*) laden; **... to ~** (*in addition*) obendrein ...; **to give sb the ~** (*inf*) jdn rauswerfen *or* rausschmeißen
booth [bu:ð] *n* (*at fair*) Bude *f*, Stand *m*; (*telephone booth*) Zelle *f*; (*voting booth*) Kabine *f*
bootleg ['bu:tlɛg] *adj* (*alcohol*) schwarzgebrannt; (*fuel*) schwarz hergestellt; (*tape etc*) schwarz mitgeschnitten
bootlegger ['bu:tlɛgə^r] *n* Bootlegger *m*, Schwarzhändler *m*
booty ['bu:tɪ] *n* Beute *f*
booze [bu:z] (*inf*) *n* Alkohol *m* ▷ *vi* saufen
boozer ['bu:zə^r] (*inf*) *n* (*person*) Säufer(in) *m(f)*; (*Brit: pub*) Kneipe *f*
border ['bɔ:də^r] *n* Grenze *f*; (*for flowers*) Rabatte *f*; (*on cloth etc*) Bordüre *f* ▷ *vt* (*road*) säumen; (*another country: also*: **border on**) grenzen an +*acc*; **Borders** *n*: **the B~s** *das Grenzgebiet zwischen England und Schottland*
▸ **border on** *vt fus* (*fig*) grenzen an +*acc*
borderline ['bɔ:dəlaɪn] *n* (*fig*): **on the ~** an der Grenze
borderline case *n* Grenzfall *m*
bore [bɔ:^r] *pt of* **bear** ▷ *vt* bohren; (*person*) langweilen ▷ *n* Langweiler *m*; (*of gun*) Kaliber *nt*; **to be ~d** sich langweilen; **he's ~d to tears** *or* **~d to death** *or* **~d stiff** er langweilt sich zu Tode
boredom ['bɔ:dəm] *n* Langeweile *f*; (*boring quality*) Langweiligkeit *f*
boring ['bɔ:rɪŋ] *adj* langweilig
born [bɔ:n] *adj*: **to be ~** geboren werden; **I was ~ in 1960** ich bin *or* wurde 1960 geboren; **~ blind** blind geboren, von Geburt (an) blind; **a ~ comedian** ein geborener Komiker
born-again [bɔ:nə'gɛn] *adj* wiedergeboren
borne [bɔ:n] *pp of* **bear**
Borneo ['bɔ:nɪəu] *n* Borneo *nt*
borough ['bʌrə] *n* Bezirk *m*, Stadtgemeinde *f*
borrow ['bɔrəu] *vt*: **to ~ sth** etw borgen, sich *dat* etw leihen; (*from library*) sich *dat* etw ausleihen; **may I ~ your car?** kann ich deinen Wagen leihen?
borrower ['bɔrəuə^r] *n* (*of loan etc*) Kreditnehmer(in) *m(f)*
borrowing ['bɔrəuɪŋ] *n* Kreditaufnahme *f*
borstal ['bɔ:stl] (*Brit*) *n* (*formerly*) Besserungsanstalt *f*
Bosnia ['bɔznɪə] *n* Bosnien *nt*
Bosnia-Herzegovina *n* Bosnien-Herzegowina *nt*
Bosnian ['bɔznɪən] *adj* bosnisch ▷ *n* Bosnier(in) *m(f)*
bosom ['buzəm] *n* Busen *m*; (*fig: of family*) Schoß *m*

bosom friend *n* Busenfreund(in) *m(f)*
boss [bɔs] *n* Chef(in) *m(f)*; (*leader*) Boss *m* ▹ *vt* (*also*: **boss around, boss about**) herumkommandieren; **stop ~ing everyone about!** hör auf mit dem ständigen Herumkommandieren!
bossy ['bɔsɪ] *adj* herrisch
bosun ['bəusn] *n* Bootsmann *m*
botanical [bə'tænɪkl] *adj* botanisch
botanist ['bɔtənɪst] *n* Botaniker(in) *m(f)*
botany ['bɔtənɪ] *n* Botanik *f*
botch [bɔtʃ] *vt* (*also*: **botch up**) verpfuschen
both [bəuθ] *adj* beide ▹ *pron* beide; (*two different things*) beides ▹ *adv*: **~ A and B** sowohl A als auch B; **~ (of them)** (alle) beide; **~ of us went, we ~ went** wir gingen beide; **they sell ~ the fabric and the finished curtains** sie verkaufen sowohl den Stoff als auch die fertigen Vorhänge
bother ['bɔðəʳ] *vt* Sorgen machen *+dat*; (*disturb*) stören ▹ *vi* (*also*: **bother o.s.**) sich *dat* Sorgen *or* Gedanken machen ▹ *n* (*trouble*) Mühe *f*; (*nuisance*) Plage *f* ▹ *excl* Mist! (*inf*); **don't ~ phoning** du brauchst nicht anzurufen; **I'm sorry to ~ you** es tut mir leid, dass ich Sie belästigen muss; **I can't be ~ed** ich habe keine Lust; **please don't ~** bitte machen Sie sich keine Umstände; **don't ~!** lass es!; **it is a ~ to have to shave every morning** es ist wirklich lästig, sich jeden Morgen rasieren zu müssen; **it's no ~** es ist kein Problem
Botswana [bɔt'swɑːnə] *n* Botswana *nt*
bottle ['bɔtl] *n* Flasche *f*; (*Brit*: *inf*: *courage*) Mumm *m* ▹ *vt* in Flaschen abfüllen; (*fruit*) einmachen; **a ~ of wine/milk** eine Flasche Wein/Milch; **wine/milk ~** Wein-/Milchflasche *f*
▸ **bottle up** *vt* in sich *dat* aufstauen
bottle bank *n* Altglascontainer *m*
bottle-fed ['bɔtlfɛd] *adj* mit der Flasche ernährt
bottleneck ['bɔtlnɛk] *n* (*also fig*) Engpass *m*
bottle-opener ['bɔtləupnəʳ] *n* Flaschenöffner *m*
bottom ['bɔtəm] *n* Boden *m*; (*buttocks*) Hintern *m*; (*of page, list*) Ende *nt*; (*of chair*) Sitz *m*; (*of mountain, tree*) Fuß *m* ▹ *adj* (*lower*) untere(r, s); (*last*) unterste(r, s); **at the ~ of** unten an/in *+dat*; **at the ~ of the page/list** unten auf der Seite/Liste; **to be at the ~ of the class** der/die Letzte in der Klasse sein; **to get to the ~ of sth** (*fig*) einer Sache *dat* auf den Grund kommen
bottomless ['bɔtəmlɪs] *adj* (*fig*) unerschöpflich
bottom line *n* (*of accounts*) Saldo *m*; (*fig*): **that's the ~ (of it)** (*what it amounts to*) darauf läuft es im Endeffekt hinaus
botulism ['bɔtjulɪzəm] *n* Botulismus *m*, Nahrungsmittelvergiftung *f*
bough [bau] *n* Ast *m*
bought [bɔːt] *pt, pp of* **buy**
boulder ['bəuldəʳ] *n* Felsblock *m*
boulevard ['buːləvɑːd] *n* Boulevard *m*
bounce [bauns] *vi* (auf)springen; (*cheque*) platzen ▹ *vt* (*ball*) (auf)springen lassen; (*signal*) reflektieren ▹ *n* Aufprall *m*; **he's got plenty of ~** (*fig*) er hat viel Schwung
bouncer ['baunsəʳ] (*inf*) *n* Rausschmeißer *m*
bouncy castle ['baunsɪ-] *n* Hüpfburg *f*
bound [baund] *pt, pp of* **bind** ▹ *n* Sprung *m*; (*gen pl*: *limit*) Grenze *f* ▹ *vi* springen ▹ *vt* begrenzen ▹ *adj*: **~ by** gebunden durch; **to be ~ to do sth** (*obliged*) verpflichtet sein, etw zu tun; (*very likely*) etw bestimmt tun; **he's ~ to fail** es kann ihm ja gar nicht gelingen; **~ for** nach; **the area is out of ~s** das Betreten des Gebiets ist verboten
boundary ['baundrɪ] *n* Grenze *f*
boundless ['baundlɪs] *adj* grenzenlos
bountiful ['bauntɪful] *adj* großzügig; (*God*) gütig; (*supply*) reichlich
bounty ['bauntɪ] *n* Freigebigkeit *f*; (*reward*) Kopfgeld *nt*
bounty hunter *n* Kopfgeldjäger *m*
bouquet ['bukeɪ] *n* (Blumen)strauß *m*; (*of wine*) Bukett *nt*, Blume *f*
bourbon ['buəbən] (*US*) *n* (*also*: **bourbon whiskey**) Bourbon *m*
bourgeois ['buəʒwɑː] *adj* bürgerlich, spießig (*pej*) ▹ *n* Bürger(in) *m(f)*, Bourgeois *m*
bout [baut] *n* Anfall *m*; (*Boxing etc*) Kampf *m*
boutique [buː'tiːk] *n* Boutique *f*
bow¹ [bəu] *n* Schleife *f*; (*weapon, Mus*) Bogen *m*
bow² [bau] *n* Verbeugung *f*; (*Naut*: *also*: **bows**) Bug *m* ▹ *vi* sich verbeugen; (*yield*): **to ~ to** *or* **before** sich beugen *+dat*; **to ~ to the inevitable** sich in das Unvermeidliche fügen
bowels ['bauəlz] *npl* Darm *m*; (*of the earth etc*) Innere *nt*
bowl [bəul] *n* Schüssel *f*; (*shallower*) Schale *f*; (*ball*) Kugel *f*; (*of pipe*) Kopf *m*; (*US*: *stadium*) Stadion *nt* ▹ *vi* werfen
▸ **bowl over** *vt* (*fig*) überwältigen
bow-legged ['bəu'lɛgɪd] *adj* o-beinig
bowler ['bəuləʳ] *n* Werfer(in) *m(f)*; (*Brit*: *also*: **bowler hat**) Melone *f*
bowling ['bəulɪŋ] *n* Kegeln *nt*; (*on grass*) Bowling *nt*
bowling alley *n* Kegelbahn *f*
bowling green *n* Bowlingrasen *m*
bowls [bəulz] *n* Bowling *nt*
bow tie [bəu-] *n* Fliege *f*
box [bɔks] *n* Schachtel *f*; (*cardboard box*) Karton *m*; (*crate*) Kiste *f*; (*Theat*) Loge *f*; (*Brit*: *Aut*) *gelb schraffierter Kreuzungsbereich*; (*on form*) Feld *nt* ▹ *vt* (in eine Schachtel *etc*) verpacken; (*fighter*) boxen ▹ *vi* boxen; **to ~ sb's ears** jdm eine Ohrfeige geben
▸ **box in** *vt* einkeilen
▸ **box off** *vt* abtrennen
boxer ['bɔksəʳ] *n* (*person, dog*) Boxer *m*
box file *n* Sammelordner *m*
boxing ['bɔksɪŋ] *n* Boxen *nt*
Boxing Day (*Brit*) *n* zweiter

Weihnachts(feier)tag *m*; *siehe Info-Artikel*

BOXING DAY

Boxing Day ist ein Feiertag in Großbritannien. Wenn Weihnachten auf ein Wochenende fällt, wird der Feiertag am nächsten darauffolgenden Wochentag nachgeholt. Der Name geht auf einen alten Brauch zurück; früher erhielten Händler und Lieferanten an diesem Tag ein Geschenk, die sogenannte Christmas Box.

boxing gloves *npl* Boxhandschuhe *pl*
boxing ring *n* Boxring *m*
box number *n* Chiffre *f*
box office *n* Kasse *f*
boxroom ['bɔksrum] *n* Abstellraum *m*
boy [bɔɪ] *n* Junge *m*
boycott ['bɔɪkɔt] *n* Boykott *m* ▷ *vt* boykottieren
boyfriend ['bɔɪfrɛnd] *n* Freund *m*
boyish ['bɔɪɪʃ] *adj* jungenhaft; (*woman*) knabenhaft
boy scout *n* Pfadfinder *m*
bp *abbr* = **bishop**
bra [brɑː] *n* BH *m*
brace [breɪs] *n* (*on teeth*) (Zahn)klammer *f*, (Zahn)spange *f*; (*tool*) (Hand)bohrer *m*; (*also*: **brace bracket**) geschweifte Klammer *f* ▷ *vt* spannen; **braces** *npl* (*Brit*) Hosenträger *pl*; **to ~ o.s.** (*for weight*) sich stützen; (*for shock*) sich innerlich vorbereiten
bracelet ['breɪslɪt] *n* Armband *nt*
bracing ['breɪsɪŋ] *adj* belebend
bracken ['brækən] *n* Farn *m*
bracket ['brækɪt] *n* Träger *m*; (*group, range*) Gruppe *f*; (*also*: **round bracket**) (runde) Klammer *f*; (*also*: **brace bracket**) geschweifte Klammer *f*; (*also*: **square bracket**) eckige Klammer *f* ▷ *vt* (*also*: **bracket together**) zusammenfassen; (*word, phrase*) einklammern; **income ~** Einkommensgruppe *f*; **in ~s** in Klammern
brackish ['brækɪʃ] *adj* brackig
brag [bræg] *vi* prahlen
braid [breɪd] *n* Borte *f*; (*of hair*) Zopf *m*
Braille [breɪl] *n* Blindenschrift *f*, Brailleschrift *f*
brain [breɪn] *n* Gehirn *nt*; **brains** *npl* (*Culin*) Hirn *nt*; (*intelligence*) Intelligenz *f*; **he's got ~s** er hat Köpfchen *or* Grips
brainchild ['breɪntʃaɪld] *n* Geistesprodukt *nt*
braindead ['breɪndɛd] *adj* hirntot; (*inf*) hirnlos
brain drain *n* Abwanderung *f* von Wissenschaftlern, Braindrain *m*
brainless ['breɪnlɪs] *adj* dumm
brainstorm ['breɪnstɔːm] *n* (*fig*) Anfall *m* geistiger Umnachtung; (*US: brain wave*) Geistesblitz *m*
brainwash ['breɪnwɔʃ] *vt* einer Gehirnwäsche *dat* unterziehen
brain wave *n* Geistesblitz *m*
brainy ['breɪnɪ] *adj* intelligent
braise [breɪz] *vt* schmoren
brake [breɪk] *n* Bremse *f* ▷ *vi* bremsen
brake fluid *n* Bremsflüssigkeit *f*
brake light *n* Bremslicht *nt*
brake pedal *n* Bremspedal *nt*
bramble ['bræmbl] *n* Brombeerstrauch *m*; (*fruit*) Brombeere *f*
bran [bræn] *n* Kleie *f*
branch [brɑːntʃ] *n* Ast *m*; (*of family, organization*) Zweig *m*; (*Comm*) Filiale *f*, Zweigstelle *f*; (*: bank, company etc*) Geschäftsstelle *f* ▷ *vi* sich gabeln
▶ **branch out** *vi* (*fig*): **to ~ out into** seinen (Geschäfts)bereich erweitern auf *+acc*
branch line *n* (*Rail*) Zweiglinie *f*, Nebenlinie *f*
branch manager *n* Zweigstellenleiter(in) *m(f)*, Filialleiter(in) *m(f)*
brand [brænd] *n* (*also*: **brand name**) Marke *f*; (*fig: type*) Art *f* ▷ *vt* mit einem Brandzeichen kennzeichnen; (*fig: pej*): **to ~ sb a communist** jdn als Kommunist brandmarken
brandish ['brændɪʃ] *vt* schwingen
brand name *n* Markenname *m*
brand-new ['brænd'njuː] *adj* nagelneu, brandneu
brandy ['brændɪ] *n* Weinbrand *m*
brash [bræʃ] *adj* dreist
Brasilia [brə'zɪlɪə] *n* Brasilia *nt*
brass [brɑːs] *n* Messing *nt*; **the ~** (*Mus*) die Blechbläser *pl*
brass band *n* Blaskapelle *f*
brassière ['bræsɪəʳ] *n* Büstenhalter *m*
brass tacks *npl*: **to get down to ~** zur Sache kommen
brassy ['brɑːsɪ] *adj* (*colour*) messingfarben; (*sound*) blechern; (*appearance, behaviour*) auffällig
brat [bræt] (*pej*) *n* Balg *m or nt*, Gör *nt*
bravado [brə'vɑːdəu] *n* Draufgängertum *nt*
brave [breɪv] *adj* mutig; (*attempt, smile*) tapfer ▷ *n* (indianischer) Krieger *m* ▷ *vt* trotzen *+dat*
bravely ['breɪvlɪ] *adv* (*see adj*) mutig; tapfer
bravery ['breɪvərɪ] *n* (*see adj*) Mut *m*; Tapferkeit *f*
bravo [brɑː'vəu] *excl* bravo
brawl [brɔːl] *n* Schlägerei *f* ▷ *vi* sich schlagen
brawn [brɔːn] *n* Muskeln *pl*; (*meat*) Schweinskopfsülze *f*
brawny ['brɔːnɪ] *adj* muskulös, kräftig
bray [breɪ] *vi* schreien ▷ *n* (Esels)schrei *m*
brazen ['breɪzn] *adj* unverschämt, dreist; (*lie*) schamlos ▷ *vt*: **to ~ it out** durchhalten
brazier ['breɪzɪəʳ] *n* (*container*) Kohlenbecken *nt*
Brazil [brə'zɪl] *n* Brasilien *nt*
Brazilian [brə'zɪljən] *adj* brasilianisch ▷ *n* Brasilianer(in) *m(f)*
Brazil nut *n* Paranuss *f*
breach [briːtʃ] *vt* (*defence*) durchbrechen; (*wall*) eine Bresche schlagen in *+acc* ▷ *n* (*gap*) Bresche *f*; (*estrangement*) Bruch *m*; (*breaking*): **~ of contract** Vertragsbruch *m*; **~ of the peace** öffentliche Ruhestörung *f*; **~ of trust** Vertrauensbruch *m*
bread [brɛd] *n* Brot *nt*; (*inf: money*) Moos *nt*, Kies *m*; **to earn one's daily ~** sein Brot verdienen;

to know which side one's ~ is buttered (on) wissen, wo etwas zu holen ist
bread and butter *n* Butterbrot *nt*; (*fig*) Broterwerb *m*
bread bin (*Brit*) *n* Brotkasten *m*
breadboard ['brɛdbɔːd] *n* Brot(schneide)brett *nt*; (*Comput*) Leiterplatte *f*
bread box (*US*) *n* Brotkasten *m*
breadcrumbs ['brɛdkrʌmz] *npl* Brotkrumen *pl*; (*Culin*) Paniermehl *nt*
breadline ['brɛdlaɪn] *n*: **to be on the ~** nur das Allernotwendigste zum Leben haben
breadth [brɛtθ] *n* (*also fig*) Breite *f*
breadwinner ['brɛdwɪnəʳ] *n* Ernährer(in) *m(f)*
break [breɪk] (*pt* **broke**, *pp* **broken**) *vt* zerbrechen; (*leg, arm*) sich *dat* brechen; (*promise, record*) brechen; (*law*) verstoßen gegen ▷ *vi* zerbrechen, kaputtgehen; (*storm*) losbrechen; (*weather*) umschlagen; (*dawn*) anbrechen; (*story, news*) bekannt werden ▷ *n* Pause *f*; (*gap*) Lücke *f*; (*fracture*) Bruch *m*; (*chance*) Chance *f*, Gelegenheit *f*; (*holiday*) Urlaub *m*; **to ~ the news to sb** es jdm sagen; **to ~ even** seine (Un)kosten decken; **to ~ with sb** mit jdm brechen, sich von jdm trennen; **to ~ free** *or* **loose** sich losreißen; **to take a ~** (eine) Pause machen; (*holiday*) Urlaub machen; **without a ~** ohne Unterbrechung *or* Pause, ununterbrochen; **a lucky ~** ein Durchbruch *m*
▸ **break down** *vt* (*figures, data*) aufschlüsseln; (*door etc*) einrennen ▷ *vi* (*car*) eine Panne haben; (*machine*) kaputtgehen; (*person, resistance*) zusammenbrechen; (*talks*) scheitern
▸ **break in** *vt* (*horse*) zureiten ▷ *vi* einbrechen; (*interrupt*) unterbrechen
▸ **break into** *vt fus* einbrechen in *+acc*
▸ **break off** *vi* abbrechen ▷ *vt* (*talks*) abbrechen; (*engagement*) lösen
▸ **break open** *vt, vi* aufbrechen
▸ **break out** *vi* ausbrechen; **to ~ out in spots/a rash** Pickel/einen Ausschlag bekommen
▸ **break through** *vi*: **the sun broke through** die Sonne kam durch ▷ *vt fus* durchbrechen
▸ **break up** *vi* (*ship*) zerbersten; (*crowd, meeting, partnership*) sich auflösen; (*marriage*) scheitern; (*friends*) sich trennen; (*Scol*) in die Ferien gehen ▷ *vt* zerbrechen; (*journey, fight etc*) unterbrechen; (*meeting*) auflösen; (*marriage*) zerstören
breakable ['breɪkəbl] *adj* zerbrechlich ▷ *n*: **~s** zerbrechliche Ware *f*
breakage ['breɪkɪdʒ] *n* Bruch *m*; **to pay for ~s** für zerbrochene Ware *or* für Bruch bezahlen
breakaway ['breɪkəweɪ] *adj* (*group etc*) Splitter-
break dancing *n* Breakdance *m*
breakdown ['breɪkdaun] *n* (*Aut*) Panne *f*; (*in communications*) Zusammenbruch *m*; (*of marriage*) Scheitern *nt*; (*also*: **nervous breakdown**) (Nerven)zusammenbruch *m*; (*of statistics*) Aufschlüsselung *f*
breakdown service (*Brit*) *n* Pannendienst *m*
breakdown van (*Brit*) *n* Abschleppwagen *m*
breaker ['breɪkəʳ] *n* (*wave*) Brecher *m*
breakeven ['breɪk'iːvn] *cpd*: **~ chart** Gewinnschwellendiagramm *nt*; **~ point** Gewinnschwelle *f*
breakfast ['brɛkfəst] *n* Frühstück *nt* ▷ *vi* frühstücken
breakfast cereal *n* Getreideflocken *pl*
break-in ['breɪkɪn] *n* Einbruch *m*
breaking and entering ['breɪkɪŋən'ɛntrɪŋ] *n* (*Law*) Einbruch *m*
breaking point ['breɪkɪŋ-] *n* (*fig*): **to reach ~** völlig am Ende sein
breakthrough ['breɪkθruː] *n* Durchbruch *m*
break-up ['breɪkʌp] *n* (*of partnership*) Auflösung *f*; (*of marriage*) Scheitern *nt*
break-up value *n* (*Comm*) Liquidationswert *m*
breakwater ['breɪkwɔːtəʳ] *n* Wellenbrecher *m*
breast [brɛst] *n* Brust *f*; (*of meat*) Brust *f*, Bruststück *nt*
breast-feed ['brɛstfiːd] (*irreg*: *like* **feed**) *vt, vi* stillen
breast pocket *n* Brusttasche *f*
breaststroke ['brɛststrəuk] *n* Brustschwimmen *nt*
breath [brɛθ] *n* Atem *m*; (*a breath*) Atemzug *m*; **to go out for a ~ of air** an die frische Luft gehen, frische Luft schnappen gehen; **out of ~** außer Atem, atemlos; **to get one's ~ back** wieder zu Atem kommen
breathalyse ['brɛθəlaɪz] *vt* blasen lassen (*inf*)
Breathalyser® ['brɛθəlaɪzəʳ] *n* Promillemesser *m*
breathe [briːð] *vt, vi* atmen; **I won't ~ a word about it** ich werde kein Sterbenswörtchen darüber sagen
▸ **breathe in** *vt, vi* einatmen
▸ **breathe out** *vt, vi* ausatmen
breather ['briːðəʳ] *n* Atempause *f*, Verschnaufpause *f*
breathing ['briːðɪŋ] *n* Atmung *f*
breathing space *n* (*fig*) Atempause *f*, Ruhepause *f*
breathless ['brɛθlɪs] *adj* atemlos, außer Atem; (*Med*) an Atemnot leidend; **I was ~ with excitement** die Aufregung verschlug mir den Atem
breathtaking ['brɛθteɪkɪŋ] *adj* atemberaubend
breath test *n* Atemalkoholtest *m*
bred [brɛd] *pt, pp of* **breed**
-bred *suff*: **well/ill-~** gut/schlecht erzogen
breed [briːd] (*pt, pp* **bred**) *vt* züchten; (*fig: give rise to*) erzeugen; (*: hate, suspicion*) hervorrufen ▷ *vi* Junge *pl* haben ▷ *n* Rasse *f*; (*type, class*) Art *f*
breeder ['briːdəʳ] *n* Züchter(in) *m(f)*; (*also*: **breeder reactor**) Brutreaktor *m*, Brüter *m*
breeding ['briːdɪŋ] *n* Erziehung *f*
breeding ground *n* (*also fig*) Brutstätte *f*
breeze [briːz] *n* Brise *f*
breeze block (*Brit*) *n* Ytong® *m*
breezy ['briːzɪ] *adj* (*manner, tone*) munter; (*weather*) windig
Breton ['brɛtən] *adj* bretonisch ▷ *n* Bretone *m*, Bretonin *f*
brevity ['brɛvɪtɪ] *n* Kürze *f*

brew [bru:] *vt* (*tea*) aufbrühen, kochen; (*beer*) brauen ▷ *vi* (*tea*) ziehen; (*beer*) gären; (*storm: fig*) sich zusammenbrauen
brewer ['bru:əʳ] *n* Brauer *m*
brewery ['bru:ərɪ] *n* Brauerei *f*
briar ['braɪəʳ] *n* Dornbusch *m*; (*wild rose*) wilde Rose *f*
bribe [braɪb] *n* Bestechungsgeld *nt* ▷ *vt* bestechen; **to ~ sb to do sth** jdn bestechen, damit er etw tut
bribery ['braɪbərɪ] *n* Bestechung *f*
bric-a-brac ['brɪkəbræk] *n* Nippes *pl*, Nippsachen *pl*
brick [brɪk] *n* Ziegelstein *m*, Backstein *m*; (*of ice cream*) Block *m*
bricklayer ['brɪkleɪəʳ] *n* Maurer(in) *m(f)*
brickwork ['brɪkwə:k] *n* Mauerwerk *nt*
bridal ['braɪdl] *adj* (*gown, veil etc*) Braut-
bride [braɪd] *n* Braut *f*
bridegroom ['braɪdgru:m] *n* Bräutigam *m*
bridesmaid ['braɪdzmeɪd] *n* Brautjungfer *f*
bridge [brɪdʒ] *n* Brücke *f*; (*Naut*) (Kommando)brücke *f*; (*of nose*) Sattel *m*; (*Cards*) Bridge *nt* ▷ *vt* (*river*) eine Brücke schlagen *or* bauen über +*acc*; (*fig*) überbrücken
bridging loan ['brɪdʒɪŋ-] (*Brit*) *n* Überbrückungskredit *m*
bridle ['braɪdl] *n* Zaum *m* ▷ *vt* aufzäumen ▷ *vi*: **to ~ (at)** sich entrüstet wehren (gegen)
bridle path *n* Reitweg *m*
brief [bri:f] *adj* kurz ▷ *n* (*Law*) Auftrag *m*; (*task*) Aufgabe *f* ▷ *vt* instruieren; (*Mil etc*): **to ~ sb (about)** jdn instruieren (über +*acc*); **briefs** *npl* Slip *m*; **in ~ ...** kurz (gesagt) ...
briefcase ['bri:fkeɪs] *n* Aktentasche *f*
briefing ['bri:fɪŋ] *n* Briefing *nt*, Lagebespechung *f*
briefly ['bri:flɪ] *adv* kurz; **to glimpse sth ~** einen flüchtigen Blick von etw erhaschen
Brig. *abbr* = **brigadier**
brigade [brɪ'geɪd] *n* Brigade *f*
brigadier [brɪgə'dɪəʳ] *n* Brigadegeneral *m*
bright [braɪt] *adj* (*light, room*) hell; (*weather*) heiter; (*clever*) intelligent; (*lively*) heiter, fröhlich; (*colour*) leuchtend; (*outlook, future*) glänzend; **to look on the ~ side** die Dinge von der positiven Seite betrachten
brighten ['braɪtn] (*also*: **brighten up**) *vt* aufheitern; (*event*) beleben ▷ *vi* (*weather, face*) sich aufheitern; (*person*) fröhlicher werden; (*prospects*) sich verbessern
brightly ['braɪtlɪ] *adv* (*shine*) hell; (*smile*) fröhlich; (*talk*) heiter
brill [brɪl] (*Brit: inf*) *adj* toll
brilliance ['brɪljəns] *n* Strahlen *nt*; (*of person*) Genialität *f*, Brillanz *f*; (*of talent, skill*) Großartigkeit *f*
brilliant ['brɪljənt] *adj* strahlend; (*person, idea*) genial, brillant; (*career*) großartig; (*inf: holiday etc*) fantastisch
brilliantly ['brɪljəntlɪ] *adv* (*see adj*) strahlend; genial, brillant; großartig; fantastisch
brim [brɪm] *n* Rand *m*; (*of hat*) Krempe *f*
brimful ['brɪm'ful] *adj*: **~ (of)** randvoll (mit); (*fig*) voll (von)
brine [braɪn] *n* Lake *f*
bring [brɪŋ] (*pt, pp* **brought**) *vt* bringen; (*with you*) mitbringen; **to ~ sth to an end** etw zu Ende bringen; **I can't ~ myself to fire him** ich kann es nicht über mich bringen, ihn zu entlassen
▸ **bring about** *vt* herbeiführen
▸ **bring back** *vt* (*restore*) wiedereinführen; (*return*) zurückbringen
▸ **bring down** *vt* (*government*) zu Fall bringen; (*plane*) herunterholen; (*price*) senken
▸ **bring forward** *vt* (*meeting*) vorverlegen; (*proposal*) vorbringen; (*Bookkeeping*) übertragen
▸ **bring in** *vt* (*money*) (ein)bringen; (*include*) einbeziehen; (*person*) einschalten; (*legislation*) einbringen; (*verdict*) fällen
▸ **bring off** *vt* (*plan*) durchführen; (*deal*) zustande bringen
▸ **bring out** *vt* herausholen; (*meaning, book, album*) herausbringen
▸ **bring round** *vt* (*after faint*) wieder zu Bewusstsein bringen
▸ **bring up** *vt* heraufbringen; (*educate*) erziehen; (*question, subject*) zur Sprache bringen; (*food*) erbrechen
bring-and-buy sale *n* Basar *m* (*wo mitgebrachte Sachen verkauft werden*)
brink [brɪŋk] *n* Rand *m*; **on the ~ of doing sth** nahe daran, etw zu tun; **she was on the ~ of tears** sie war den Tränen nahe
brisk [brɪsk] *adj* (*abrupt: person, tone*) forsch; (*pace*) flott; (*trade*) lebhaft, rege; **to go for a ~ walk** einen ordentlichen Spaziergang machen; **business is ~** das Geschäft ist rege
bristle ['brɪsl] *n* Borste *f*; (*of beard*) Stoppel *f* ▷ *vi* zornig werden; **bristling with** strotzend von
bristly ['brɪslɪ] *adj* borstig; (*chin*) stoppelig
Brit [brɪt] (*inf*) *n* (= *British person*) Brite *m*, Britin *f*
Britain ['brɪtən] *n* (*also*: **Great Britain**) Großbritannien *nt*
British ['brɪtɪʃ] *adj* britisch ▷ *npl*: **the ~** die Briten *pl*
British Isles *npl*: **the ~** die Britischen Inseln
British Rail *n* *britische Eisenbahngesellschaft*
British Summer Time *n* britische Sommerzeit *f*
Briton ['brɪtən] *n* Brite *m*, Britin *f*
Brittany ['brɪtənɪ] *n* die Bretagne
brittle ['brɪtl] *adj* spröde; (*glass*) zerbrechlich; (*bones*) schwach
broach [brəutʃ] *vt* (*subject*) anschneiden
broad [brɔ:d] *adj* breit; (*general*) allgemein; (*accent*) stark ▷ *n* (*US: inf*) Frau *f*; **in ~ daylight** am helllichten Tag; **~ hint** deutlicher Wink *m*
broadband ['brɔ:dbænd] (*Comput*) *adj* Breitband- ▷ *n* Breitband *nt*
broad bean *n* dicke Bohne *f*, Saubohne *f*
broadcast ['brɔ:dkɑ:st] (*pt, pp* **~**) *n* Sendung *f* ▷ *vt, vi* senden
broadcaster ['brɔ:dkɑ:stəʳ] *n* (*Radio, TV*) Rundfunk-/Fernsehpersönlichkeit *f*

broadcasting ['brɔ:dkɑ:stɪŋ] *n (Radio)* Rundfunk *m*; (TV) Fernsehen *nt*
broadcasting station *n (Radio)* Rundfunkstation *f*; (TV) Fernsehstation *f*
broaden ['brɔ:dn] *vt* erweitern ▷ *vi* breiter werden, sich verbreitern; **to ~ one's mind** seinen Horizont erweitern
broadly ['brɔ:dlɪ] *adv (in general terms)* in großen Zügen; **~ speaking** allgemein *or* generell gesagt
broad-minded ['brɔ:d'maɪndɪd] *adj* tolerant
broadsheet ['brɔ:dʃi:t] *n (newspaper)* *großformatige Zeitung*
broccoli ['brɔkəlɪ] *n* Brokkoli *pl*, Spargelkohl *m*
brochure ['brəuʃjuəʳ] *n* Broschüre *f*
brogue [brəug] *n* Akzent *m*; *(shoe)* fester Schuh *m*
broil [brɔɪl] (US) *vt* grillen
broiler ['brɔɪləʳ] *n* Brathähnchen *nt*
broke [brəuk] *pt of* **break** ▷ *adj (inf)* pleite; **to go ~** pleitegehen
broken ['brəukn] *pp of* **break** ▷ *adj* zerbrochen; *(machine: also:* **broken down***)* kaputt; *(promise, vow)* gebrochen; **a ~ leg** ein gebrochenes Bein; **a ~ marriage** eine gescheiterte Ehe; **a ~ home** zerrüttete Familienverhältnisse *pl*; **in ~ English/German** in gebrochenem Englisch/Deutsch
broken-down ['brəukn'daun] *adj* kaputt; *(house)* baufällig
brokenhearted [brəʊkn'ha:tɪd] *adj* untröstlich
broker ['brəukəʳ] *n* Makler(in) *m(f)*
brokerage ['brəukrɪdʒ] *n (commission)* Maklergebühr *f*; *(business)* Maklergeschäft *nt*
brolly ['brɔlɪ] *(Brit: inf) n* (Regen)schirm *m*
bronchitis [brɔŋ'kaɪtɪs] *n* Bronchitis *f*
bronze [brɔnz] *n* Bronze *f*
bronzed [brɔnzd] *adj* braun, (sonnen)gebräunt
brooch [brəutʃ] *n* Brosche *f*
brood [bru:d] *n* Brut *f* ▷ *vi (hen)* brüten; *(person)* grübeln
▸ **brood on** *vt fus* nachgrübeln über *+acc*
▸ **brood over** *vt fus* = **brood on**
broody ['bru:dɪ] *adj (person)* grüblerisch; *(hen)* brütig
brook [bruk] *n* Bach *m*
broom [brum] *n* Besen *m*; *(Bot)* Ginster *m*
broomstick ['brumstɪk] *n* Besenstiel *m*
bros., Bros. *abbr (Comm: = brothers)* Gebr.
broth [brɔθ] *n* Suppe *f*, Fleischbrühe *f*
brothel ['brɔθl] *n* Bordell *nt*
brother ['brʌðəʳ] *n* Bruder *m*; *(in trade union, society etc)* Kollege *m*
brotherhood ['brʌðəhud] *n* Brüderlichkeit *f*
brother-in-law ['brʌðərɪn'lɔ:] *n* Schwager *m*
brotherly ['brʌðəlɪ] *adj* brüderlich
brought [brɔ:t] *pt, pp of* **bring**
brought forward *adj (Comm)* vorgetragen
brow [brau] *n* Stirn *f*; *(eyebrow)* (Augen)braue *f*; *(of hill)* (Berg)kuppe *f*
browbeat ['braubi:t] *vt*: **to ~ sb (into doing sth)** jdn (so) unter Druck setzen(, dass er etw tut)
brown [braun] *adj* braun ▷ *n* Braun *nt* ▷ *vt (Culin)* (an)bräunen; **to go ~** braun werden
brown bread *n* Graubrot *nt*, Mischbrot *nt*
Brownie ['braunɪ] *n (also:* **Brownie Guide***)* Wichtel *m*
brownie ['braunɪ] (US) *n kleiner Schokoladenkuchen*
brown paper *n* Packpapier *nt*
brown rice *n* Naturreis *m*
brown sugar *n* brauner Zucker *m*
browse [brauz] *vi (in shop)* sich umsehen; *(animal)* weiden; *(: deer)* äsen ▷ *vti (Comput)* browsen ▷ *n*: **to have a ~ (around)** sich umsehen; **to ~ through a book** in einem Buch schmökern
browser ['brauzəʳ] *n (Comput)* Browser *m*
bruise [bru:z] *n* blauer Fleck *m*, Bluterguss *m*; *(on fruit)* Druckstelle *f* ▷ *vt (arm, leg etc)* sich *dat* stoßen; *(person)* einen blauen Fleck schlagen; *(fruit)* beschädigen ▷ *vi (fruit)* eine Druckstelle bekommen; **to ~ one's arm** sich *dat* den Arm stoßen, sich *dat* einen blauen Fleck am Arm holen
bruising ['bru:zɪŋ] *adj (experience, encounter)* schmerzhaft ▷ *n* Quetschung *f*
Brum [brʌm] *(Brit: inf) n abbr (= Birmingham)*
Brummie ['brʌmɪ] *(inf) n aus Birmingham stammende oder dort wohnhafte Person*, Birminghamer(in) *m(f)*
brunch [brʌntʃ] *n* Brunch *m*
brunette [bru:'nɛt] *n* Brünette *f*
brunt [brʌnt] *n*: **to bear the ~ of** die volle Wucht *+gen* tragen
brush [brʌʃ] *n* Bürste *f*; *(for painting, shaving etc)* Pinsel *m*; *(quarrel)* Auseinandersetzung *f* ▷ *vt* fegen; *(groom)* bürsten; *(teeth)* putzen; *(also:* **brush against***)* streifen; **to have a ~ with sb** *(verbally)* sich mit jdm streiten; *(physically)* mit jdm aneinandergeraten; **to have a ~ with the police** mit der Polizei aneinandergeraten
▸ **brush aside** *vt* abtun
▸ **brush past** *vt* streifen
▸ **brush up** *vt* auffrischen
brushed [brʌʃt] *adj (steel, chrome etc)* gebürstet; *(denim etc)* aufgeraut; **~ nylon** Nylonvelours *m*
brushoff ['brʌʃɔf] *(inf) n*: **to give sb the ~** jdm eine Abfuhr erteilen
brushwood ['brʌʃwud] *n* Reisig *nt*
brusque [bru:sk] *adj* brüsk; *(tone)* schroff
Brussels ['brʌslz] *n* Brüssel *nt*
Brussels sprouts *npl* Rosenkohl *m*
brutal ['bru:tl] *adj* brutal
brutality [bru:'tælɪtɪ] *n* Brutalität *f*
brutalize ['bru:təlaɪz] *vt* brutalisieren; *(ill-treat)* brutal behandeln
brute [bru:t] *n* brutaler Kerl *m*; *(animal)* Tier *nt* ▷ *adj*: **by ~ force** mit roher Gewalt
brutish ['bru:tɪʃ] *adj* tierisch
BS (US) *n abbr (= Bachelor of Science) akademischer Grad für Naturwissenschaftler*
BSA *n abbr (= Boy Scouts of America) amerikanische Pfadfinderorganisation*

BSc *abbr (= Bachelor of Science) akademischer Grad für Naturwissenschaftler*
BSE *n abbr (= bovine spongiform encephalopathy)* BSE *f*
BSI *n abbr (= British Standards Institution) britischer Normenausschuss*
BST *abbr* = **British Summer Time**
Bt (*Brit*) *abbr* = **baronet**
btu *n abbr (= British thermal unit) britische Wärmeeinheit*
bubble ['bʌbl] *n* Blase *f* ▷ *vi* sprudeln; (*sparkle*) perlen; (*fig: person*) übersprudeln
bubble bath *n* Schaumbad *nt*
bubble gum *n* Bubblegum *m*
bubble-jet printer *n* Bubblejetdrucker *m*, Bubble-Jet-Drucker *m*
bubble pack *n* (Klar)sichtpackung *f*
bubbly ['bʌblɪ] *adj* (*person*) lebendig; (*liquid*) sprudelnd ▷ *n* (*inf: champagne*) Schampus *m*
Bucharest [bu:kə'rɛst] *n* Bukarest *nt*
buck [bʌk] *n* (*rabbit*) Rammler *m*; (*deer*) Bock *m*; (*US: inf*) Dollar *m* ▷ *vi* bocken; **to pass the ~** die Verantwortung abschieben; **to pass the ~ to sb** jdm die Verantwortung zuschieben
▸ **buck up** *vi* (*cheer up*) aufleben ▷ *vt*: **to ~ one's ideas up** sich zusammenreißen
bucket ['bʌkɪt] *n* Eimer *m* ▷ *vi* (*Brit: inf*): **the rain is ~ing (down)** es gießt *or* schüttet (wie aus Kübeln)

BUCKINGHAM PALACE

Buckingham Palace ist die offizielle Londoner Residenz der britischen Monarchen und liegt am St James Park. Der Palast wurde 1703 für den Herzog von Buckingham erbaut, 1762 von Georg III. gekauft, zwischen 1821 und 1836 von John Nash umgebaut und Anfang des 20. Jahrhunderts teilweise neu gestaltet. Teile des Buckingham Palace sind heute der Öffentlichkeit zugänglich.

buckle ['bʌkl] *n* Schnalle *f* ▷ *vt* zuschnallen; (*wheel*) verbiegen ▷ *vi* sich verbiegen
▸ **buckle down** *vi* sich dahinter klemmen; **to ~ down to sth** sich hinter etw *acc* klemmen
Bucks [bʌks] (*Brit*) *abbr* (*Post*) = *Buckinghamshire*
bud [bʌd] *n* Knospe *f* ▷ *vi* knospen, Knospen treiben
Budapest [bju:də'pɛst] *n* Budapest *nt*
Buddha ['budə] *n* Buddha *m*
Buddhism ['budɪzəm] *n* Buddhismus *m*
Buddhist ['budɪst] *adj* buddhistisch ▷ *n* Buddhist(in) *m(f)*
budding ['bʌdɪŋ] *adj* angehend
buddy ['bʌdɪ] (*US*) *n* Kumpel *m*
budge [bʌdʒ] *vt* (von der Stelle) bewegen; (*fig*) zum Nachgeben bewegen ▷ *vi* sich von der Stelle rühren; (*fig*) nachgeben
budgerigar ['bʌdʒərɪgɑ:ʳ] *n* Wellensittich *m*
budget ['bʌdʒɪt] *n* Budget *nt*, Etat *m*, Haushalt *m* ▷ *vi* Haus halten, haushalten, wirtschaften; **I'm on a tight ~** ich habe nicht viel Geld zur Verfügung; **she works out her ~ every month** sie macht (sich *dat*) jeden Monat einen Haushaltsplan; **to ~ for sth** etw kostenmäßig einplanen
budgie ['bʌdʒɪ] *n* = **budgerigar**
Buenos Aires ['bweɪnɔs'aɪrɪz] *n* Buenos Aires *nt*
buff [bʌf] *adj* gelbbraun ▷ *n* (*inf*) Fan *m*
buffalo ['bʌfələu] (*pl* **~** *or* **buffaloes**) *n* (*Brit*) Büffel *m*; (*US*) Bison *m*
buffer ['bʌfəʳ] *n* (*Comput*) Puffer *m*, Pufferspeicher *m*; (*Rail*) Prellbock *m*; (*fig*) Polster *nt*
buffering ['bʌfərɪŋ] *n* (*Comput*) Pufferung *f*
buffer state *n* Pufferstaat *m*
buffer zone *n* Pufferzone *f*
buffet[1] ['bufeɪ] (*Brit*) *n* Büfett *nt*, Bahnhofsrestaurant *nt*; (*food*) kaltes Buffet *nt*
buffet[2] ['bʌfɪt] *vt* (*subj: sea*) hin und her werfen; (*: wind*) schütteln
buffet car (*Brit*) *n* Speisewagen *m*
buffet lunch *n* Buffet *nt*
buffoon [bə'fu:n] *n* Clown *m*
bug [bʌg] *n* (*esp US*) Insekt *nt*; (*Comput: of program*) Programmfehler *m*; (*: of equipment*) Fehler *m*; (*fig: germ*) Bazillus *m*; (*hidden microphone*) Wanze *f* ▷ *vt* (*inf*) nerven; (*telephone etc*) abhören; (*room*) verwanzen; **I've got the travel ~** (*fig*) mich hat die Reiselust gepackt
bugbear ['bʌgbɛəʳ] *n* Schreckgespenst *nt*
bugger ['bʌgəʳ] (*inf!*) *n* Scheißkerl *m*, Arschloch *nt* ▷ *vb*: **~ off!** hau ab!; **~ (it)!** Scheiße!
buggy ['bʌgɪ] *n* (*for baby*) Sportwagen *m*
bugle ['bju:gl] *n* Bügelhorn *nt*
build [bɪld] (*pt, pp* **built**) *n* Körperbau *m* ▷ *vt* bauen
▸ **build on** *vt fus* (*fig*) aufbauen auf *+dat*
▸ **build up** *vt* aufbauen; (*production*) steigern; (*morale*) stärken; (*stocks*) anlegen; **don't ~ your hopes up too soon** mach dir nicht zu früh Hoffnungen
builder ['bɪldəʳ] *n* Bauunternehmer *m*
building ['bɪldɪŋ] *n* (*industry*) Bauindustrie *f*; (*construction*) Bau *m*; (*structure*) Gebäude *nt*, Bau
building contractor *n* Bauunternehmer *m*
building industry *n* Bauindustrie *f*
building site *n* Baustelle *f*
building society (*Brit*) *n* Bausparkasse *f*
building trade *n* Baubranche *f or* -gewerbe *nt*
build-up ['bɪldʌp] *n* Ansammlung *f*; (*publicity*): **to give sb/sth a good ~** jdn/etw ganz groß herausbringen
built [bɪlt] *pt, pp of* **build** ▷ *adj*: **~-in** eingebaut, Einbau-; (*safeguards*) eingebaut; **well-~** gut gebaut
built-up area ['bɪltʌp-] *n* bebautes Gebiet *nt*
bulb [bʌlb] *n* (Blumen)zwiebel *f*; (*Elec*) (Glüh)birne *f*
bulbous ['bʌlbəs] *adj* knollig
Bulgaria [bʌl'gɛərɪə] *n* Bulgarien *nt*
Bulgarian [bʌl'gɛərɪən] *adj* bulgarisch ▷ *n* Bulgare *m*, Bulgarin *f*; (*Ling*) Bulgarisch *nt*
bulge [bʌldʒ] *n* Wölbung *f*; (*in birth rate, sales*) Zunahme *f* ▷ *vi* (*pocket*) prall gefüllt sein;

(*cheeks*) voll sein; (*file*) (zum Bersten) voll sein; **to be bulging with** prall gefüllt sein mit

bulimia [bəˈlɪmɪə] *n* Bulimie *f*

bulk [bʌlk] *n* (*of thing*) massige Form *f*; (*of person*) massige Gestalt *f*; **in ~** im Großen, en gros; **the ~ of** der Großteil *+gen*

bulk buying [-ˈbaɪɪŋ] *n* Mengeneinkauf *m*, Großeinkauf *m*

bulk carrier *n* Bulkcarrier *m*

bulkhead [ˈbʌlkhɛd] *n* Schott *nt*

bulky [ˈbʌlkɪ] *adj* sperrig

bull [bul] *n* Stier *m*; (*male elephant or whale*) Bulle *m*; (*Stock Exchange*) Haussier *m*, Haussespekulant *m*; (*Rel*) Bulle *f*

bulldog [ˈbuldɔg] *n* Bulldogge *f*

bulldoze [ˈbuldəuz] *vt* mit Bulldozern wegräumen; (*building*) mit Bulldozern abreißen; **I was ~d into it** (*fig: inf*) ich wurde gezwungen *or* unter Druck gesetzt, es zu tun

bulldozer [ˈbuldəuzəʳ] *n* Bulldozer *m*, Planierraupe *f*

bullet [ˈbulɪt] *n* Kugel *f*

bulletin [ˈbulɪtɪn] *n* (*TV etc*) Kurznachrichten *pl*; (*journal*) Bulletin *nt*

bulletin board *n* (*Comput*) Schwarzes Brett *nt*

bulletproof [ˈbulɪtpruːf] *adj* kugelsicher

bullfight [ˈbulfaɪt] *n* Stierkampf *m*

bullfighter [ˈbulfaɪtəʳ] *n* Stierkämpfer *m*

bullfighting [ˈbulfaɪtɪŋ] *n* Stierkampf *m*

bullion [ˈbuljən] *n*: **gold/silver ~** Barrengold *nt*/-silber *nt*

bullock [ˈbulək] *n* Ochse *m*

bullring [ˈbulrɪŋ] *n* Stierkampfarena *f*

bull's-eye [ˈbulzaɪ] *n* (*on a target*): **the ~** der Scheibenmittelpunkt, das Schwarze

bullshit [ˈbulʃɪt] (*inf!*) *n* Scheiß *m*, Quatsch *m* ▷ *vi* Scheiß erzählen; **~!** Quatsch!

bully [ˈbulɪ] *n* Tyrann *m* ▷ *vt* tyrannisieren; (*frighten*) einschüchtern

bullying [ˈbulɪɪŋ] *n* Tyrannisieren *nt*

bum [bʌm] (*inf*) *n* Hintern *m*; (*esp US: good-for-nothing*) Rumtreiber *m*; (*tramp*) Penner *m*

▸ **bum around** (*inf*) *vi* herumgammeln

bumblebee [ˈbʌmblbiː] *n* Hummel *f*

bumf [bʌmf] (*inf*) *n* Papierkram *m*

bump [bʌmp] *n* Zusammenstoß *m*; (*jolt*) Erschütterung *f*; (*swelling*) Beule *f*; (*on road*) Unebenheit *f* ▷ *vt* stoßen; (*car*) eine Delle fahren in *+acc*

▸ **bump along** *vi* entlangholpern

▸ **bump into** *vt fus* (*obstacle*) stoßen gegen; (*inf: person*) treffen

bumper [ˈbʌmpəʳ] *n* Stoßstange *f* ▷ *adj*: **~ crop, ~ harvest** Rekordernte *f*

bumper cars *npl* Autoskooter *pl*

bumper sticker *n* Aufkleber *m*

bumph [bʌmf] *n* = **bumf**

bumptious [ˈbʌmpʃəs] *adj* wichtigtuerisch

bumpy [ˈbʌmpɪ] *adj* holperig; **it was a ~ flight/ride** während des Fluges/auf der Fahrt wurden wir tüchtig durchgerüttelt

bun [bʌn] *n* Brötchen *nt*; (*of hair*) Knoten *m*

bunch [bʌntʃ] *n* Strauß *m*; (*of keys*) Bund *m*; (*of bananas*) Büschel *nt*; (*of people*) Haufen *m*; **bunches** *npl* (*in hair*) Zöpfe *pl*; **~ of grapes** Weintraube *f*

bundle [ˈbʌndl] *n* Bündel *nt* ▷ *vt* (*also*: **bundle up**) bündeln; (*put*): **to ~ sth into** etw stopfen *or* packen in *+acc*; **to ~ sb into** jdn schaffen in *+acc*

▸ **bundle off** *vt* schaffen

▸ **bundle out** *vt* herausschaffen

bun fight (*Brit: inf*) *n* Festivitäten *pl*; (*tea party*) Teegesellschaft *f*

bung [bʌŋ] *n* Spund *m*, Spundzapfen *m* ▷ *vt* (*Brit: inf: also*: **bung in**) schmeißen; (*also*: **bung up**) verstopfen; **my nose is ~ed up** meine Nase ist verstopft

bungalow [ˈbʌŋgələu] *n* Bungalow *m*

bungee jumping [ˈbʌndʒiːˈdʒʌmpɪŋ] *n* Bungeespringen *nt*

bungle [ˈbʌŋgl] *vt* verpfuschen

bunion [ˈbʌnjən] *n* entzündeter Ballen *m*

bunk [bʌŋk] *n* Bett *nt*, Koje *f*; **to do a ~** (*inf*) abhauen

▸ **bunk off** (*inf*) *vi* abhauen

bunk beds *npl* Etagenbett *nt*

bunker [ˈbʌŋkəʳ] *n* Kohlenbunker *m*; (*Mil, Golf*) Bunker *m*

bunny [ˈbʌnɪ] *n* (*also*: **bunny rabbit**) Hase *m*, Häschen *nt*

bunny girl (*Brit*) *n* Häschen *nt*

bunny hill (*US*) *n* (*Ski*) Anfängerhügel *m*

bunting [ˈbʌntɪŋ] *n* (*flags*) Wimpel *pl*, Fähnchen *pl*

buoy [bɔɪ] *n* Boje *f*

▸ **buoy up** *vt* (*fig*) Auftrieb geben *+dat*

buoyancy [ˈbɔɪənsɪ] *n* (*of ship, object*) Schwimmfähigkeit *f*

buoyant [ˈbɔɪənt] *adj* (*ship, object*) schwimmfähig; (*market*) fest; (*economy*) stabil; (*prices, currency*) fest, stabil; (*person, nature*) heiter

burden [ˈbəːdn] *n* Belastung *f*; (*load*) Last *f* ▷ *vt*: **to ~ sb with sth** jdn mit etw belasten; **to be a ~ to sb** jdm zur Last fallen

bureau [ˈbjuərəu] (*pl* **~x**) *n* (*Brit: writing desk*) Sekretär *m*; (*US: chest of drawers*) Kommode *f*; (*office*) Büro *nt*

bureaucracy [bjuəˈrɔkrəsɪ] *n* Bürokratie *f*

bureaucrat [ˈbjuərəkræt] *n* Bürokrat(in) *m(f)*

bureaucratic [bjuərəˈkrætɪk] *adj* bürokratisch

bureaux [ˈbjuərəuz] *npl of* **bureau**

burgeon [ˈbəːdʒən] *vi* hervorsprießen

burger [ˈbəːgəʳ] (*inf*) *n* Hamburger *m*

burglar [ˈbəːgləʳ] *n* Einbrecher(in) *m(f)*

burglar alarm *n* Alarmanlage *f*

burglarize [ˈbəːgləraɪz] (*US*) *vt* einbrechen in *+acc*

burglary [ˈbəːglərɪ] *n* Einbruch *m*

burgle [ˈbəːgl] *vt* einbrechen in *+acc*

Burgundy [ˈbəːgəndɪ] *n* Burgund *nt*

burial [ˈbɛrɪəl] *n* Beerdigung *f*

burial ground *n* Begräbnisstätte *f*

burlesque [bəːˈlɛsk] *n (parody)* Persiflage *f*; *(US: Theat)* Burleske *f*
burly [ˈbəːlɪ] *adj* kräftig, stämmig
Burma [ˈbəːmə] *n* Birma *nt*, Burma *nt*
Burmese [bəːˈmiːz] *adj* birmanisch, burmesisch ▷ *n inv* Birmane *m*, Burmese *m*, Birmanin *f*, Burmesin *f* ▷ *n (Ling)* Birmanisch *nt*, Burmesisch *nt*
burn [bəːn] *(pt, pp* **burned** *or* **~t**) *vt* verbrennen; *(fuel)* als Brennstoff verwenden; *(food)* anbrennen lassen; *(house etc)* niederbrennen ▷ *vi* brennen; *(food)* anbrennen ▷ *n* Verbrennung *f*; **the cigarette ~t a hole in her dress** die Zigarette brannte ein Loch in ihr Kleid; **I've ~t myself!** ich habe mich verbrannt!
▸ **burn down** *vt* abbrennen
▸ **burn out** *vt*: **to ~ o.s. out** *(writer etc)* sich völlig verausgaben; **the fire ~t itself out** das Feuer brannte aus
burner [ˈbəːnəʳ] *n* Brenner *m*
burning [ˈbəːnɪŋ] *adj* brennend; *(sand, desert)* glühend heiß
burnish [ˈbəːnɪʃ] *vt* polieren

BURNS' NIGHT

Burns' Night ist der am 25. Januar begangene Gedenktag für den schottischen Dichter Robert Burns (1759–1796). Wo Schotten leben, sei es in Schottland oder im Ausland, wird dieser Tag mit einem Abendessen gefeiert, bei dem es als Hauptgericht *haggis* gibt, der mit Dudelsackbegleitung aufgetischt wird. Dazu isst man Steckrüben- und Kartoffelpüree und trinkt Whisky. Während des Essens werden Burns' Gedichte vorgelesen, seine Lieder gesungen, bestimmte Reden gehalten und Trinksprüche ausgegeben.

burnt [bəːnt] *pt, pp of* **burn**
burnt sugar *(Brit) n* Karamell *m*
burp [bəːp] *(inf) n* Rülpser *m* ▷ *vt (baby)* aufstoßen lassen ▷ *vi* rülpsen
burrow [ˈbʌrəu] *n* Bau *m* ▷ *vi* graben; *(rummage)* wühlen
bursar [ˈbəːsəʳ] *n* Schatzmeister *m*, Finanzverwalter *m*
bursary [ˈbəːsərɪ] *(Brit) n* Stipendium *nt*
burst [bəːst] *(pt, pp* **~**) *vt* zum Platzen bringen, platzen lassen ▷ *vi* platzen ▷ *n* Salve *f*; *(also:* **burst pipe**) (Rohr)bruch *m*; **the river has ~ its banks** der Fluss ist über die Ufer getreten; **to ~ into flames** in Flammen aufgehen; **to ~ into tears** in Tränen ausbrechen; **to ~ out laughing** in Lachen ausbrechen; **~ blood vessel** geplatzte Ader *f*; **to be ~ing with** zum Bersten voll sein mit; *(pride)* fast platzen vor *+dat*; **to ~ open** aufspringen; **a ~ of energy** ein Ausbruch *m* von Energie; **a ~ of enthusiasm** ein Begeisterungsausbruch *m*; **a ~ of speed** ein Spurt *m*; **~ of laughter** Lachsalve *f*; **~ of applause** Beifallssturm *m*
▸ **burst in on** *vt fus*: **to ~ in on sb** bei jdm hereinplatzen
▸ **burst into** *vt fus (into room)* platzen in *+acc*
▸ **burst out of** *vt fus (of room)* stürmen *or* stürzen aus
bury [ˈbɛrɪ] *vt* begraben; *(at funeral)* beerdigen; **to ~ one's face in one's hands** das Gesicht in den Händen vergraben; **to ~ one's head in the sand** *(fig)* den Kopf in den Sand stecken; **to ~ the hatchet** *(fig)* das Kriegsbeil begraben
bus [bʌs] *n* (Auto)bus *m*, (Omni)bus *m*; *(double decker)* Doppeldecker *m (inf)*
bus boy *(US) n* Bedienungshilfe *f*
bush [buʃ] *n* Busch *m*, Strauch *m*; *(scrubland)* Busch; **to beat about the ~** um den heißen Brei herumreden
bushed [buʃt] *(inf) adj (exhausted)* groggy
bushel [ˈbuʃl] *n* Scheffel *m*
bushfire *n* Buschfeuer *nt*
bushy [ˈbuʃɪ] *adj* buschig
busily [ˈbɪzɪlɪ] *adv* eifrig; **to be ~ doing sth** eifrig etw tun
business [ˈbɪznɪs] *n (matter)* Angelegenheit *f*; *(trading)* Geschäft *nt*; *(firm)* Firma *f*, Betrieb *m*; *(occupation)* Beruf *m*; **to be away on ~** geschäftlich unterwegs sein; **I'm here on ~** ich bin geschäftlich hier; **he's in the insurance/transport ~** er arbeitet in der Versicherungs-/Transportbranche; **to do ~ with sb** Geschäfte *pl* mit jdm machen; **it's my ~ to ...** es ist meine Aufgabe, zu ...; **it's none of my ~** es geht mich nichts an; **he means ~** er meint es ernst
business address *n* Geschäftsadresse *f*
business card *n* (Visiten)karte *f*
businesslike [ˈbɪznɪslaɪk] *adj* geschäftsmäßig
businessman [ˈbɪznɪsmən] *(irreg: like* **man**) *n* Geschäftsmann *m*
business trip *n* Geschäftsreise *f*
businesswoman [ˈbɪznɪswumən] *(irreg: like* **woman**) *n* Geschäftsfrau *f*
busker [ˈbʌskəʳ] *(Brit) n* Straßenmusikant(in) *m(f)*
bus lane *(Brit) n* Busspur *f*
bus shelter *n* Wartehäuschen *nt*
bus station *n* Busbahnhof *m*
bus stop *n* Bushaltestelle *f*
bust [bʌst] *n* Busen *m*; *(measurement)* Oberweite *f*; *(sculpture)* Büste *f* ▷ *adj (inf)* kaputt ▷ *vt (inf)* verhaften; **to go ~** pleitegehen
bustle [ˈbʌsl] *n* Betrieb *m* ▷ *vi* eilig herumlaufen
bustling [ˈbʌslɪŋ] *adj* belebt
bust-up [ˈbʌstʌp] *(Brit: inf) n* Krach *m*
busty [ˈbʌstɪ] *adj (woman)* vollbusig
busy [ˈbɪzɪ] *adj (person)* beschäftigt; *(shop, street)* belebt; *(Tel, esp US)* besetzt ▷ *vt*: **to ~ o.s. with** sich beschäftigen mit; **he's a ~ man** er ist ein viel beschäftigter Mann; **he's ~** er hat (zurzeit) viel zu tun

busybody ['bɪzɪbɔdɪ] *n*: **to be a ~** sich ständig einmischen
busy signal (*US*) *n* (*Tel*) Besetztzeichen *nt*

KEYWORD

but [bʌt] *conj* **1** (*yet*) aber; **not blue but red** nicht blau, sondern rot; **he's not very bright, but he's hard-working** er ist nicht sehr intelligent, aber er ist fleißig
2 (*however*): **I'd love to come, but I'm busy** ich würde gern kommen, bin aber beschäftigt
3 (*showing disagreement, surprise etc*): **but that's far too expensive!** aber das ist viel zu teuer!; **but that's fantastic!** das ist doch toll!
▷ *prep* (*apart from, except*) außer *+dat*; **nothing but trouble** nichts als Ärger; **no-one but him can do it** keiner außer ihm kann es machen; **but for you** wenn Sie nicht gewesen wären; **but for your help** ohne Ihre Hilfe; **I'll do anything but that** ich mache alles, nur nicht das; **the last house but one** das vorletzte Haus; **the next street but one** die übernächste Straße
▷ *adv* (*just, only*) nur; **she's but a child** sie ist doch noch ein Kind; **I can but try** ich kann es ja versuchen

butane ['bju:teɪn] *n* (*also*: **butane gas**) Butan(gas) *nt*
butch [butʃ] (*inf*) *adj* maskulin
butcher ['butʃəʳ] *n* Fleischer *m*, Metzger *m*; (*pej*: *murderer*) Schlächter *m* ▷ *vt* schlachten; (*prisoners etc*) abschlachten
butcher's ['butʃəz], **butcher's shop** *n* Fleischerei *f*, Metzgerei *f*
butler ['bʌtləʳ] *n* Butler *m*
butt [bʌt] *n* großes Fass *nt*, Tonne *f*; (*thick end*) dickes Ende *nt*; (*of gun*) Kolben *m*; (*of cigarette*) Kippe *f*; (*Brit*: *fig*: *target*) Zielscheibe *f*; (*US*: *inf!*) Arsch *m* ▷ *vt* (*goat*) mit den Hörnern stoßen; (*person*) mit dem Kopf stoßen
▶ **butt in** *vi* sich einmischen, dazwischenfunken (*inf*)
butter ['bʌtəʳ] *n* Butter *f* ▷ *vt* buttern
buttercup ['bʌtəkʌp] *n* Butterblume *f*
butter dish *n* Butterdose *f*
butterfingers ['bʌtəfɪŋgəz] (*inf*) *n* Schussel *m*
butterfly ['bʌtəflaɪ] *n* Schmetterling *m*; (*Swimming*: *also*: **butterfly stroke**) Schmetterlingsstil *m*, Butterfly *m*
buttocks ['bʌtəks] *npl* Gesäß *nt*
button ['bʌtn] *n* Knopf *m*; (*US*: *badge*) Plakette *f* ▷ *vt* (*also*: **button up**) zuknöpfen ▷ *vi* geknöpft werden
buttonhole ['bʌtnhəul] *n* Knopfloch *nt*; (*flower*) Blume *f* im Knopfloch ▷ *vt* zu fassen bekommen, sich *dat* schnappen (*inf*)
buttress ['bʌtrɪs] *n* Strebepfeiler *m*
buxom ['bʌksəm] *adj* drall
buy [baɪ] (*pt, pp* **bought**) *vt* kaufen; (*company*) aufkaufen ▷ *n* Kauf *m*; **that was a good/bad ~** das war ein guter/schlechter Kauf; **to ~ sb sth** jdm etw kaufen; **to ~ sth from sb** etw bei jdm kaufen; (*from individual*) jdm etw abkaufen; **to ~ sb a drink** jdm einen ausgeben (*inf*)
▶ **buy back** *vt* zurückkaufen
▶ **buy in** (*Brit*) *vt* einkaufen
▶ **buy into** (*Brit*) *vt fus* sich einkaufen in *+acc*
▶ **buy off** *vt* kaufen
▶ **buy out** *vt* (*partner*) auszahlen; (*business*) aufkaufen
▶ **buy up** *vt* aufkaufen
buyer ['baɪəʳ] *n* Käufer(in) *m(f)*; (*Comm*) Einkäufer(in) *m(f)*
buyer's market ['baɪəz-] *n* Käufermarkt *m*
buyout ['baɪaʊt] *n* (*of firm*: *by workers, management*) Aufkauf *m*
buzz [bʌz] *vi* summen, brummen; (*saw*) kreischen ▷ *vt* rufen; (*with buzzer*) (mit dem Summer) rufen; (*Aviat*: *plane, building*) dicht vorbeifliegen an *+dat* ▷ *n* Summen *nt*, Brummen *nt*; (*inf*): **to give sb a ~** jdn anrufen; **my head is ~ing** mir schwirrt der Kopf
▶ **buzz off** (*inf*) *vi* abhauen
buzzard ['bʌzəd] *n* Bussard *m*
buzzer ['bʌzəʳ] *n* Summer *m*
buzz word (*inf*) *n* Modewort *nt*

KEYWORD

by [baɪ] *prep* **1** (*referring to cause, agent*) von *+dat*, durch *+acc*; **killed by lightning** vom Blitz *or* durch einen Blitz getötet; **a painting by Picasso** ein Bild von Picasso
2 (*referring to method, manner, means*): **by bus/car/train** mit dem Bus/Auto/Zug; **to pay by cheque** mit *or* per Scheck bezahlen; **by saving hard, he was able to ...** indem er eisern sparte, konnte er ...
3 (*via, through*) über *+acc*; **we came by Dover** wir sind über Dover gekommen
4 (*close to*) bei *+dat*, an *+dat*; **the house by the river** das Haus am Fluss
5 (*past*) an ... *dat* vorbei; **she rushed by me** sie eilte an mir vorbei
6 (*not later than*) bis *+acc*; **by 4 o'clock** bis 4 Uhr; **by this time tomorrow** morgen um diese Zeit
7 (*amount*): **by the kilo/metre** kilo-/meterweise; **to be paid by the hour** stundenweise bezahlt werden
8 (*Math, measure*): **to divide by 3** durch 3 teilen; **to multiply by 3** mit 3 malnehmen; **it missed me by inches** es hat mich um Zentimeter verfehlt
9 (*according to*): **to play by the rules** sich an die Regeln halten; **it's all right by me** von mir aus ist es in Ordnung
10: (all) by myself/himself *etc* (ganz) allein
11: by the way übrigens
▷ *adv* **1** *see* **go**, **pass** *etc*
2: by and by irgendwann
3: by and large im Großen und Ganzen

bye ['baɪ], **bye-bye** ['baɪ'baɪ] *excl* (auf) Wiedersehen, tschüss (*inf*)
bye-law ['baɪlɔː] *n see* **by-law**
by-election ['baɪɪlɛkʃən] (*Brit*) *n* Nachwahl *f*
Byelorussia [bjɛləu'rʌʃə] *n* = **Belorussia**
Byelorussian [bjɛləu'rʌʃən] *adj, n* = **Belarussian**
bygone ['baɪgɔn] *adj* (längst) vergangen ▷ *n*: **let ~s be ~s** wir sollten die Vergangenheit ruhen lassen
by-law ['baɪlɔː] *n* Verordnung *f*
bypass ['baɪpɑːs] *n* Umgehungsstraße *f*; (*Med*) Bypassoperation *f* ▷ *vt* (*also fig*) umgehen
by-product ['baɪprɔdʌkt] *n* Nebenprodukt *nt*
byre ['baɪəʳ] (*Brit*) *n* Kuhstall *m*
bystander ['baɪstændəʳ] *n* Zuschauer(in) *m(f)*
byte [baɪt] *n* (*Comput*) Byte *nt*
byway ['baɪweɪ] *n* Seitenweg *m*
byword ['baɪwəːd] *n*: **to be a ~ for** der Inbegriff *+gen* sein, gleichbedeutend sein mit
by-your-leave ['baɪjɔː'liːv] *n*: **without so much as a ~** ohne auch nur (um Erlaubnis) zu fragen

Cc

C[1], **c**[1] [si:] *n (letter)* C *nt*, c *nt*; *(Scol)* ≈ Drei *f*, ≈ Befriedigend *nt*; **C for Charlie** ≈ C wie Cäsar
C[2] [si:] *n (Mus)* C *nt*, c *nt*
C[3] [si:] *abbr* = **Celsius; centigrade**
c[2] *abbr* = **century**; (= *circa*) ca.; (*US etc*: = *cent(s)*) Cent
CA *n abbr (Brit)* = **chartered accountant** ▷ *abbr* = **Central America**; *(US: Post)* = *California*
C/A *abbr (Comm)* = **capital account; credit account; current account**
ca. *abbr* (= *circa*) ca.
CAA *n abbr (Brit)* = **Civil Aviation Authority**; (*US*: = *Civil Aeronautics Authority*) *Zivilluftfahrtbehörde*
CAB *(Brit) n abbr* = **Citizens' Advice Bureau**
cab [kæb] *n* Taxi *nt*; *(of truck, train etc)* Führerhaus *nt*; *(horse-drawn)* Droschke *f*
cabaret ['kæbəreɪ] *n* Kabarett *nt*
cabbage ['kæbɪdʒ] *n* Kohl *m*
cabbie, cabby ['kæbɪ] *n* Taxifahrer(in) *m(f)*
cab driver *n* Taxifahrer(in) *m(f)*
cabin ['kæbɪn] *n* Kabine *f*; *(house)* Hütte *f*
cabin cruiser *n* Kajütboot *nt*
cabinet ['kæbɪnɪt] *n* kleiner Schrank *m*; *(also:* **display cabinet**) Vitrine *f*; *(Pol)* Kabinett *nt*
cabinet-maker ['kæbɪnɪt'meɪkə^r] *n* Möbeltischler *m*
cabinet minister *n* Mitglied *nt* des Kabinetts, Minister(in) *m(f)*
cable ['keɪbl] *n* Kabel *nt* ▷ *vt* kabeln
cable car *n* (Draht)seilbahn *f*
cablegram ['keɪblgræm] *n* (Übersee)telegramm *nt*, Kabel *nt*
cable railway *n* Seilbahn *f*
cable television *n* Kabelfernsehen *nt*
cable TV *n* = **cable television**
cache [kæʃ] *n* Versteck *nt*, geheimes Lager *nt*; **a ~ of food** ein geheimes Proviantlager
cackle ['kækl] *vi (person: laugh)* meckernd lachen; *(hen)* gackern
cacti ['kæktaɪ] *npl of* **cactus**
cactus ['kæktəs] *(pl* **cacti**) *n* Kaktus *m*
CAD *n abbr (= computer-aided design)* CAD *nt*
caddie ['kædɪ] *n (Golf)* Caddie *m*
caddy ['kædɪ] *n* = **caddie**
cadence ['keɪdəns] *n (of voice)* Tonfall *m*
cadet [kə'dɛt] *n* Kadett *m*; **police ~** Polizeianwärter(in) *m(f)*
cadge [kædʒ] *(inf) vt*: **to ~ (from** *or* **off)** schnorren (bei *or* von *+dat*); **to ~ a lift with sb** von jdm mitgenommen werden
cadger ['kædʒə^r] *(Brit: inf) n* Schnorrer(in) *m(f)*
cadre ['kædrɪ] *n* Kader *m*
Caesarean [si:'zɛərɪən] *n*: **~ (section)** Kaiserschnitt *m*
CAF *(Brit) abbr (= cost and freight)* cf
café ['kæfeɪ] *n* Café *nt*
cafeteria [kæfɪ'tɪərɪə] *n* Cafeteria *f*
caffeine, caffein ['kæfi:n] *n* Koffein *nt*
cage [keɪdʒ] *n* Käfig *m*; *(of lift)* Fahrkorb *m* ▷ *vt* einsperren
cagey ['keɪdʒɪ] *(inf) adj* vorsichtig; *(evasive)* ausweichend
cagoule [kə'gu:l] *n* Regenjacke *f*
cahoots [kə'hu:ts] *(inf) n*: **to be in ~ with** unter einer Decke stecken mit
CAI *n abbr (= computer-aided instruction)* CAI *nt*
Cairo ['kaɪərəu] *n* Kairo *nt*
cajole [kə'dʒəul] *vt*: **to ~ sb into doing sth** jdn bereden, etw zu tun
cake [keɪk] *n* Kuchen *m*; *(small)* Gebäckstück *nt*; *(of soap)* Stück *nt*; **it's a piece of ~** *(inf)* das ist ein Kinderspiel *or* ein Klacks; **he wants to have his ~ and eat it (too)** *(fig)* er will das eine, ohne das andere zu lassen
caked [keɪkt] *adj*: **~ with** *(mud, blood)* verkrustet mit
cake shop *n* Konditorei *f*
Cal. *(US) abbr (Post)* = *California*
calamine lotion ['kæləmaɪn-] *n* Galmeilotion *f*
calamitous [kə'læmɪtəs] *adj* katastrophal
calamity [kə'læmɪtɪ] *n* Katastrophe *f*
calcium ['kælsɪəm] *n* Kalzium *nt*
calculate ['kælkjuleɪt] *vt (work out)* berechnen; *(estimate)* abschätzen
▸ **calculate on** *vt fus*: **to ~ on sth** mit etw rechnen; **to ~ on doing sth** damit rechnen, etw zu tun
calculated ['kælkjuleɪtɪd] *adj (insult)* bewusst; *(action)* vorsätzlich; **a ~ risk** ein kalkuliertes Risiko
calculating ['kælkjuleɪtɪŋ] *adj (scheming)* berechnend
calculation [kælkju'leɪʃən] *n (see vt)* Berechnung *f*; Abschätzung *f*; *(sum)* Rechnung

f

calculator ['kælkjuleɪtə^r] *n* Rechner *m*

calculus ['kælkjuləs] *n* Infinitesimalrechnung *f*; **integral/differential** ~ Integral-/ Differenzialrechnung *f*

calendar ['kæləndə^r] *n* Kalender *m*; (*timetable, schedule*) (Termin)kalender *m*

calendar month *n* Kalendermonat *m*

calendar year *n* Kalenderjahr *nt*

calf [kɑ:f] (*pl* **calves**) *n* Kalb *nt*; (*of elephant, seal etc*) Junge(s) *nt*; (*also*: **calfskin**) Kalb(s)leder *nt*; (*Anat*) Wade *f*

caliber ['kælɪbə^r] (*US*) *n* = **calibre**

calibrate ['kælɪbreɪt] *vt* (*gun etc*) kalibrieren; (*scale of measuring instrument*) eichen

calibre, (*US*) **caliber** ['kælɪbə^r] *n* Kaliber *nt*; (*of person*) Format *nt*

calico ['kælɪkəu] *n* (*Brit*) Kattun *m*, Kaliko *m*; (*US*) bedruckter Kattun

Calif. (*US*) *abbr* (*Post*) = *California*

California [kælɪ'fɔ:nɪə] *n* Kalifornien *nt*

calipers ['kælɪpəz] (*US*) *npl* = **callipers**

call [kɔ:l] *vt* (*name, consider*) nennen; (*shout out, summon*) rufen; (*Tel*) anrufen; (*witness, flight*) aufrufen; (*meeting*) einberufen; (*strike*) ausrufen ▷ *vi* rufen; (*Tel*) anrufen; (*visit*: *also*: **call in, call round**) vorbeigehen, vorbeikommen ▷ *n* Ruf *m*; (*Tel*) Anruf *m*; (*visit*) Besuch *m*; (*for a service etc*) Nachfrage *f*; (*for flight etc*) Aufruf *m*; (*fig*: *lure*) Ruf *m*, Verlockung *f*; **to be ~ed** (*named*) heißen; **who is ~ing?** (*Tel*) wer spricht da bitte?; **London ~ing** (*Radio*) hier ist London; **please give me a ~ at 7** rufen Sie mich bitte um 7 an; **to make a ~** ein (Telefon)gespräch führen; **to pay a ~ on sb** jdn besuchen; **on ~** dienstbereit; **to be on ~** einsatzbereit sein; (*doctor etc*) Bereitschaftsdienst haben; **there's not much ~ for these items** es besteht keine große Nachfrage nach diesen Dingen

▸ **call at** *vt fus* (*subj*: *ship*) anlaufen; (: *train*) halten in *+dat*

▸ **call back** *vi* (*return*) wiederkommen; (*Tel*) zurückrufen ▷ *vt* (*Tel*) zurückrufen

▸ **call for** *vt fus* (*demand*) fordern; (*fetch*) abholen

▸ **call in** *vt* (*doctor, expert, police*) zurate ziehen; (*books, cars, stock etc*) aus dem Verkehr ziehen ▷ *vi* vorbeigehen, vorbeikommen

▸ **call off** *vt* absagen

▸ **call on** *vt fus* besuchen; (*appeal to*) appellieren an *+acc*; **to ~ on sb to do sth** jdn bitten *or* auffordern, etw zu tun

▸ **call out** *vi* rufen ▷ *vt* rufen; (*police, troops*) alarmieren

▸ **call up** *vt* (*Mil*) einberufen; (*Tel*) anrufen

Callanetics® *n sing* Callanetics *f*

call box (*Brit*) *n* Telefonzelle *f*

call centre *n* Telefoncenter *nt*, Callcenter *nt*

caller ['kɔ:lə^r] *n* Besucher(in) *m(f)*; (*Tel*) Anrufer(in) *m(f)*; **hold the line, ~!** (*Tel*) bitte bleiben Sie am Apparat!

caller ID ['kɔ:lə^r aɪdi:] *n* (*Tel*) Anruferkennung *m*; (*of e-mail, text message*) Absenderkennung *m*

call girl *n* Callgirl *nt*

call-in ['kɔ:lɪn] (*US*) *n* (*Radio, TV*) Phone-in *nt*

calling ['kɔ:lɪŋ] *n* (*trade*) Beruf *m*; (*vocation*) Berufung *f*

calling card (*US*) *n* Visitenkarte *f*

callipers, (*US*) **calipers** ['kælɪpəz] *npl* (*Math*) Tastzirkel *m*; (*Med*) Schiene *f*

callous ['kæləs] *adj* herzlos

callousness ['kæləsnɪs] *n* Herzlosigkeit *f*

callow ['kæləu] *adj* unreif

calm [kɑ:m] *adj* ruhig; (*unworried*) gelassen ▷ *n* Ruhe *f* ▷ *vt* beruhigen; (*fears*) zerstreuen; (*grief*) lindern

▸ **calm down** *vt* beruhigen ▷ *vi* sich beruhigen

calmly ['kɑ:mlɪ] *adv* (*see adj*) ruhig; gelassen

calmness ['kɑ:mnɪs] *n* (*see adj*) Ruhe *f*; Gelassenheit *f*

Calor gas® ['kælə^r-] *n* Butangas *nt*

calorie ['kælərɪ] *n* Kalorie *f*; **low-~ product** kalorienarmes Produkt *nt*

calve [kɑ:v] *vi* kalben

calves [kɑ:vz] *npl of* **calf**

CAM *n abbr* (= *computer-aided manufacture*) CAM *nt*

camber ['kæmbə^r] *n* Wölbung *f*

Cambodia [kæm'bəudɪə] *n* Kambodscha *nt*

Cambodian [kæm'bəudɪən] *adj* kambodschanisch ▷ *n* Kambodschaner(in) *m(f)*

Cambs (*Brit*) *abbr* (*Post*) = *Cambridgeshire*

camcorder ['kæmkɔ:də^r] *n* Camcorder *m*, Kamerarekorder *m*

came [keɪm] *pt of* **come**

camel ['kæməl] *n* Kamel *nt*

cameo ['kæmɪəu] *n* Kamee *f*; (*Theat, Liter*) Miniatur *f*

camera ['kæmərə] *n* (*Cine, Phot*) Kamera *f*; (*also*: **cine camera, movie camera**) Filmkamera *f*; **35 mm ~** Kleinbildkamera *f*; **in ~** (*Law*) unter Ausschluss der Öffentlichkeit

cameraman ['kæmərəmæn] (*irreg*: *like* **man**) *n* Kameramann *m*

camera phone *n* Kameratelefon *nt*

Cameroon [kæmə'ru:n] *n* Kamerun *nt*

Cameroun [kæmə'ru:n] *n* = **Cameroon**

camomile ['kæməumaɪl] *n* Kamille *f*

camouflage ['kæməflɑ:ʒ] *n* Tarnung *f* ▷ *vt* tarnen

camp [kæmp] *n* Lager *nt*; (*barracks*) Kaserne *f* ▷ *vi* zelten ▷ *adj* (*effeminate*) tuntenhaft (*inf*)

campaign [kæm'peɪn] *n* (*Mil*) Feldzug *m*; (*Pol etc*) Kampagne *f* ▷ *vi* kämpfen; **to ~ for/against** sich einsetzen für/gegen

campaigner [kæm'peɪnə^r] *n*: **~ for** Befürworter(in) *m(f) +gen*; **~ against** Gegner(in) *m(f) +gen*

camp bed (*Brit*) *n* Campingliege *f*

camper ['kæmpə^r] *n* (*person*) Camper *m*; (*vehicle*) Wohnmobil *nt*

camping ['kæmpɪŋ] *n* Camping *nt*; **to go ~** zelten gehen, campen

camping site, **camp site** *n* Campingplatz *m*

campus ['kæmpəs] *n* (*Univ*)

Universitätsgelände *nt*, Campus *m*
camshaft ['kæmʃɑ:ft] *n* Nockenwelle *f*
can[1] [kæn] *n* Büchse *f*, Dose *f*; (*for oil, water*) Kanister *m* ▷ *vt* eindosen, in Büchsen *or* Dosen einmachen; **a ~ of beer** eine Dose Bier; **he had to carry the ~** (*Brit: inf*) er musste die Sache ausbaden

KEYWORD

can[2] (*negative* **cannot, can't**, *conditional and pt* **could**) *aux vb* **1** (*be able to, know how to*) können; **you can do it if you try** du kannst es, wenn du es nur versuchst; **I can't see you** ich kann dich nicht sehen; **I can swim/drive** ich kann schwimmen/Auto fahren; **can you speak English?** sprechen Sie Englisch?
2 (*may*) können, dürfen; **can I use your phone?** kann *or* darf ich Ihr Telefon benutzen?; **could I have a word with you?** könnte ich Sie mal sprechen?
3 (*expressing disbelief, puzzlement*): **it can't be true!** das darf doch nicht wahr sein!
4 (*expressing possibility, suggestion, etc*): **he could be in the library** er könnte in der Bibliothek sein

Canada ['kænədə] *n* Kanada *nt*
Canadian [kə'neɪdɪən] *adj* kanadisch ▷ *n* Kanadier(in) *m(f)*
canal [kə'næl] *n* (*also Anat*) Kanal *m*
Canaries [kə'nɛərɪz] *npl* = **Canary Islands**
canary [kə'nɛərɪ] *n* Kanarienvogel *m*
Canary Islands [kə'nɛərɪ 'aɪləndz] *npl*: **the ~** die Kanarischen Inseln *pl*
Canberra ['kænbərə] *n* Canberra *nt*
cancel ['kænsəl] *vt* absagen; (*reservation*) abbestellen; (*train, flight*) ausfallen lassen; (*contract*) annullieren; (*order*) stornieren; (*cross out*) durchstreichen; (*stamp*) entwerten; (*cheque*) ungültig machen
▸ **cancel out** *vt* aufheben; **they ~ each other out** sie heben sich gegenseitig auf
cancellation [kænsə'leɪʃən] *n* Absage *f*; (*of reservation*) Abbestellung *f*; (*of train, flight*) Ausfall *m*; (*Tourism*) Rücktritt *m*
cancer ['kænsə[r]] *n* (*also*: **Cancer**: *Astrol*) Krebs *m*; **to be C~** (ein) Krebs sein
cancerous ['kænsrəs] *adj* krebsartig
cancer patient *n* Krebskranke(r) *f(m)*
cancer research *n* Krebsforschung *f*
c and f (*Brit*) *abbr* (*Comm*: = *cost and freight*) cf
candid ['kændɪd] *adj* offen, ehrlich
candidacy ['kændɪdəsɪ] *n* Kandidatur *f*
candidate ['kændɪdeɪt] *n* Kandidat(in) *m(f)*; (*for job*) Bewerber(in) *m(f)*
candidature ['kændɪdətʃə[r]] (*Brit*) *n* = **candidacy**
candied ['kændɪd] *adj* kandiert; **~ apple** (*US*) kandierter Apfel *m*
candle ['kændl] *n* Kerze *f*; (*of tallow*) Talglicht *nt*
candleholder ['kændlhəuldə[r]] *n see* **candlestick**
candlelight ['kændllaɪt] *n*: **by ~** bei Kerzenlicht
candlestick ['kændlstɪk] *n* (*also, candleholder*) Kerzenhalter *m*; (*bigger, ornate*) Kerzenleuchter *m*
candour, (*US*) **candor** ['kændə[r]] *n* Offenheit *f*
C & W *n abbr* = **country and western**
candy ['kændɪ] *n* (*also*: **sugar-candy**) Kandis(zucker) *m*; (*US*) Bonbon *nt or m*
candyfloss ['kændɪflɔs] (*Brit*) *n* Zuckerwatte *f*
candy store (*US*) *n* Süßwarenhandlung *f*
cane [keɪn] *n* Rohr *nt*; (*stick*) Stock *m*; (: *for walking*) (Spazier)stock *m* ▷ *vt* (*Brit: Scol*) mit dem Stock schlagen
canine ['keɪnaɪn] *adj* (*species*) Hunde-
canister ['kænɪstə[r]] *n* Dose *f*; (*pressurized container*) Sprühdose *f*; (*of gas, chemicals etc*) Kanister *m*
cannabis ['kænəbɪs] *n* Haschisch *nt*; (*also*: **cannabis plant**) Hanf *m*, Cannabis *m*
canned [kænd] *adj* Dosen-; (*inf: music*) aus der Konserve; (*US: inf: worker*) entlassen, rausgeschmissen (*inf*)
cannibal ['kænɪbəl] *n* Kannibale *m*, Kannibalin *f*
cannibalism ['kænɪbəlɪzəm] *n* Kannibalismus *m*
cannibalization [kænɪbəlaɪ'zeɪʃn] *n* (*Econ*) Kannibalisierung *f*
cannon ['kænən] (*pl* **~** *or* **cannons**) *n* Kanone *f*
cannonball ['kænənbɔ:l] *n* Kanonenkugel *f*
cannon fodder *n* Kanonenfutter *nt*
cannot ['kænɔt] = **can not**
canny ['kænɪ] *adj* schlau
canoe [kə'nu:] *n* Kanu *nt*
canoeing [kə'nu:ɪŋ] *n* Kanusport *m*
canon ['kænən] *n* Kanon *m*; (*clergyman*) Kanoniker *m*, Kanonikus *m*
canonize ['kænənaɪz] *vt* kanonisieren, heiligsprechen
can-opener ['kænəupnə[r]] *n* Dosenöffner *m*, Büchsenöffner *m*
canopy ['kænəpɪ] *n* (*also fig*) Baldachin *m*
cant [kænt] *n* scheinheiliges Gerede *nt*
can't [kænt] = **can not**
Cantab. (*Brit*) *abbr* (*in degree titles*: = *Cantabrigiensis*) *der Universität Cambridge*
cantankerous [kæn'tæŋkərəs] *adj* mürrisch
canteen [kæn'ti:n] *n* (*in school, workplace*) Kantine *f*; (: *mobile*) Feldküche *f*; (*Brit: of cutlery*) Besteckkasten *m*
canter ['kæntə[r]] *vi* leicht galoppieren, kantern ▷ *n* leichter Galopp *m*, Kanter *m*
cantilever ['kæntɪli:və[r]] *n* Ausleger *m*
canvas ['kænvəs] *n* Leinwand *f*; (*painting*) Gemälde *nt*; (*Naut*) Segeltuch *nt*; **under ~** im Zelt
canvass ['kænvəs] *vt* (*opinions, views*) erforschen; (*person*) für seine Partei zu gewinnen suchen; (*place*) Wahlwerbung machen in +*dat* ▷ *vi*: **to ~ for ...** (*Pol*) um Stimmen für ... werben
canvasser ['kænvəsə[r]] *n* (*Pol*) Wahlhelfer(in) *m(f)*

canvassing ['kænvəsɪŋ] *n* (*Pol*) Wahlwerbung *f*
canyon ['kænjən] *n* Cañon *m*
CAP *n abbr* (*= Common Agricultural Policy*) gemeinsame Agrarpolitik *f* der EG
cap [kæp] *n* Mütze *f*, Kappe *f*; (*of pen*) (Verschluss)kappe *f*; (*of bottle*) Verschluss *m*, Deckel *m*; (*contraceptive*: *also*: **Dutch cap**) Pessar *nt*; (*for toy gun*) Zündplättchen *nt*; (*for swimming*) Bademütze *f*, Badekappe *f*; (*Sport*) *Ehrenkappe, die Nationalspielern verliehen wird* ▷ *vt* (*outdo*) überbieten; (*Sport*) für die Nationalmannschaft aufstellen; **~ped with ...** mit ... obendrauf; **and to ~ it all, ...** und obendrein ...
capability [keɪpə'bɪlɪtɪ] *n* Fähigkeit *f*; (*Mil*) Potenzial *nt*
capable ['keɪpəbl] *adj* fähig; **to be ~ of doing sth** etw tun können, fähig sein, etw zu tun; **to be ~ of sth** (*interpretation etc*) etw zulassen
capacious [kə'peɪʃəs] *adj* geräumig
capacity [kə'pæsɪtɪ] *n* Fassungsvermögen *nt*; (*of lift etc*) Höchstlast *f*; (*capability*) Fähigkeit *f*; (*position, role*) Eigenschaft *f*; (*of factory*) Kapazität *f*; **filled to ~** randvoll; (*stadium etc*) bis auf den letzten Platz besetzt; **in his ~ as ...** in seiner Eigenschaft als ...; **this work is beyond my ~** zu dieser Arbeit bin ich nicht fähig; **in an advisory ~** in beratender Funktion; **to work at full ~** voll ausgelastet sein
cape [keɪp] *n* Kap *nt*; (*cloak*) Cape *nt*, Umhang *m*
Cape of Good Hope *n*: **the ~** das Kap der guten Hoffnung
caper ['keɪpəʳ] *n* (*Culin*: *usu pl*) Kaper *f*; (*prank*) Eskapade *f*, Kapriole *f*
Cape Town *n* Kapstadt *nt*
capita ['kæpɪtə] *see* **per capita**
capital ['kæpɪtl] *n* (*also*: **capital city**) Hauptstadt *f*; (*money*) Kapital *nt*; (*also*: **capital letter**) Großbuchstabe *m*
capital account *n* Kapitalverkehrsbilanz *f*; (*of country*) Kapitalkonto *nt*
capital allowance *n* (Anlage)abschreibung *f*
capital assets *npl* Kapitalvermögen *nt*
capital expenditure *n* Kapitalaufwendungen *pl*
capital gains tax *n* Kapitalertragssteuer *f*
capital goods *npl* Investitionsgüter *pl*
capital-intensive ['kæpɪtlɪn'tɛnsɪv] *adj* kapitalintensiv
capitalism ['kæpɪtəlɪzəm] *n* Kapitalismus *m*
capitalist ['kæpɪtəlɪst] *adj* kapitalistisch ▷ *n* Kapitalist(in) *m(f)*
capitalize ['kæpɪtəlaɪz] *vt* (*Comm*) kapitalisieren ▷ *vi*: **to ~ on** Kapital schlagen aus
capital punishment *n* Todesstrafe *f*
capital transfer tax (*Brit*) *n* Erbschafts- und Schenkungssteuer *f*
Capitol ['kæpɪtl] *n*: **the ~** das Kapitol; *siehe Info-Artikel*

CAPITOL

Capitol ist das Gebäude in Washington auf dem Capitol Hill, in dem der Kongress der USA zusammentritt. Die Bezeichnung wird in vielen amerikanischen Bundesstaaten auch für das Parlamentsgebäude des jeweiligen Staates verwendet.

capitulate [kə'pɪtjuleɪt] *vi* kapitulieren
capitulation [kəpɪtju'leɪʃən] *n* Kapitulation *f*
capricious [kə'prɪʃəs] *adj* launisch
Capricorn ['kæprɪkɔːn] *n* (*Astrol*) Steinbock *m*; **to be ~** (ein) Steinbock sein
caps. [kæps] *abbr* (*= capital letters*) Großbuchstaben *pl*
capsize [kæp'saɪz] *vt* zum Kentern bringen ▷ *vi* kentern
capstan ['kæpstən] *n* Poller *m*
capsule ['kæpsjuːl] *n* Kapsel *f*
Capt. *abbr* (*Mil*) = **captain**
captain ['kæptɪn] *n* Kapitän *m*; (*of plane*) (Flug)kapitän *m*; (*in army*) Hauptmann *m* ▷ *vt* (*ship*) befehligen; (*team*) anführen
caption ['kæpʃən] *n* Bildunterschrift *f*
captivate ['kæptɪveɪt] *vt* fesseln
captive ['kæptɪv] *adj* gefangen ▷ *n* Gefangene(r) *f(m)*
captivity [kæp'tɪvɪtɪ] *n* Gefangenschaft *f*
captor ['kæptəʳ] *n*: **his ~s** diejenigen, die ihn gefangen nahmen
capture ['kæptʃəʳ] *vt* (*animal*) (ein)fangen; (*person*) gefangen nehmen; (*town, country, share of market*) erobern; (*attention*) erregen; (*Comput*) erfassen ▷ *n* (*of animal*) Einfangen *nt*; (*of person*) Gefangennahme *f*; (*of town etc*) Eroberung *f*; (*also*: **data capture**) Erfassung *f*
car [kɑːʳ] *n* Auto *nt*, Wagen *m*; (*Rail*) Wagen *m*; **by ~** mit dem Auto *or* Wagen
Caracas [kə'rækəs] *n* Caracas *nt*
carafe [kə'ræf] *n* Karaffe *f*
caramel ['kærəməl] *n* Karamelle *f*, Karamellbonbon *m or nt*; (*burnt sugar*) Karamell *m*
carat ['kærət] *n* Karat *nt*; **18 ~ gold** achtzehnkarätiges Gold
caravan ['kærəvæn] *n* (*Brit*) Wohnwagen *m*; (*in desert*) Karawane *f*
caravan site (*Brit*) *n* Campingplatz *m* für Wohnwagen
caraway seed *n* Kümmel *m*
carbohydrate [kɑːbəu'haɪdreɪt] *n* Kohle(n)hydrat *nt*
carbolic acid [kɑː'bɔlɪk-] *n* Karbolsäure *f*
car bomb *n* Autobombe *f*
carbon ['kɑːbən] *n* Kohlenstoff *m*
carbonated ['kɑːbəneɪtɪd] *adj* mit Kohlensäure (versetzt)
carbon copy *n* Durchschlag *m*
carbon dioxide *n* Kohlendioxid *nt*

carbon monoxide [mɔ'nɔksaɪd] *n* Kohlenmonoxid *nt*
carbon paper *n* Kohlepapier *nt*
carbon ribbon *n* Kohlefarbband *nt*
car-boot sale *n auf einem Parkplatz stattfindender Flohmarkt mit dem Kofferraum als Auslage*
carburettor, (US) **carburetor** [kɑːbju'rɛtəʳ] *n* Vergaser *m*
carcass ['kɑːkəs] *n* Kadaver *m*
carcinogenic [kɑːsɪnə'dʒɛnɪk] *adj* krebserregend, karzinogen
card [kɑːd] *n* Karte *f*; (*material*) (dünne) Pappe *f*, Karton *m*; (*also*: **record card, index card** *etc*) (Kartei)karte *f*; (*also*: **membership card**) (Mitglieds)ausweis *m*; (*also*: **playing card**) (Spiel)karte *f*; (*also*: **visiting card**) (Visiten)karte *f*; **to play ~s** Karten spielen
cardamom ['kɑːdəməm] *n* Kardamom *m*
cardboard ['kɑːdbɔːd] *n* Pappe *f*
cardboard box *n* (Papp)karton *m*
card-carrying ['kɑːd'kærɪɪŋ] *adj*: **~ member** eingetragenes Mitglied *nt*
card game *n* Kartenspiel *nt*
cardiac ['kɑːdɪæk] *adj* (*failure, patient*) Herz-
cardigan ['kɑːdɪgən] *n* Strickjacke *f*
cardinal ['kɑːdɪnl] *adj* (*principle, importance*) Haupt- ▷*n* Kardinal *m*; **~ number** Kardinalzahl *f*; **~ sin** Todsünde *f*
card index *n* Kartei *f*
cardphone *n* Kartentelefon *nt*
cardsharp ['kɑːdʃɑːp] *n* Falschspieler *m*
card vote (*Brit*) *n* Abstimmung *f* durch Wahlmänner
CARE [kɛəʳ] *n abbr* (= *Cooperative for American Relief Everywhere*) *karitative Organisation*
care [kɛəʳ] *n* (*attention*) Versorgung *f*; (*worry*) Sorge *f*; (*charge*) Obhut *f*, Fürsorge *f* ▷*vi*: **to ~ about** sich kümmern um; **~ of** bei; **"handle with ~"** „Vorsicht, zerbrechlich"; **in sb's ~** in jds *dat* Obhut; **to take ~** aufpassen; **to take ~ to do sth** sich bemühen, etw zu tun; **to take ~ of** sich kümmern um; **the child has been taken into ~** das Kind ist in Pflege genommen worden; **would you ~ to/for ...?** möchten Sie gerne ...?; **I wouldn't ~ to do it** ich möchte es nicht gern tun; **I don't ~** es ist mir egal *or* gleichgültig; **I couldn't ~ less** es ist mir völlig egal *or* gleichgültig
▸ **care for** *vt fus* (*look after*) sich kümmern um; (*like*) mögen
career [kə'rɪəʳ] *n* Karriere *f*; (*job, profession*) Beruf *m*; (*life*) Laufbahn *f* ▷*vi* (*also*: **career along**) rasen
career girl *n* Karrierefrau *f*
careers officer [kə'rɪəz-] *n* Berufsberater(in) *m(f)*
career woman *n* Karrierefrau *f*
carefree ['kɛəfriː] *adj* sorglos
careful ['kɛəful] *adj* vorsichtig; (*thorough*) sorgfältig; **(be) ~!** Vorsicht!, pass auf!; **to be ~ with one's money** sein Geld gut zusammenhalten
carefully ['kɛəfəlɪ] *adv* vorsichtig; (*methodically*) sorgfältig
careless ['kɛəlɪs] *adj* leichtsinnig; (*negligent*) nachlässig; (*remark*) gedankenlos
carelessly ['kɛəlɪslɪ] *adv* (*see adj*) leichtsinnig; nachlässig; gedankenlos
carelessness ['kɛəlɪsnɪs] *n* (*see adj*) Leichtsinn *m*; Nachlässigkeit *f*; Gedankenlosigkeit *f*
caress [kə'rɛs] *n* Streicheln *nt* ▷*vt* streicheln
caretaker ['kɛəteɪkəʳ] *n* Hausmeister(in) *m(f)*
caretaker government (*Brit*) *n* geschäftsführende Regierung *f*
car ferry *n* Autofähre *f*
cargo ['kɑːgəu] (*pl* **~es**) *n* Fracht *f*, Ladung *f*
cargo boat *n* Frachter *m*, Frachtschiff *nt*
cargo plane *n* Transportflugzeug *nt*
car hire (*Brit*) *n* Autovermietung *f*
Caribbean [kærɪ'biːən] *adj* karibisch ▷*n*: **the ~ (Sea)** die Karibik, das Karibische Meer
caricature ['kærɪkətjuəʳ] *n* Karikatur *f*
caring ['kɛərɪŋ] *adj* liebevoll; (*society, organization*) sozial; (*behaviour*) fürsorglich
carjacking *n Angriff durch Banditen, die gewaltsam in PKWs eindringen und den Wagen samt Insassen entführen*
carnage ['kɑːnɪdʒ] *n* (*Mil*) Blutbad *nt*, Gemetzel *nt*
carnal ['kɑːnl] *adj* fleischlich, sinnlich
carnation [kɑː'neɪʃən] *n* Nelke *f*
carnival ['kɑːnɪvl] *n* Karneval *m*; (*US: funfair*) Kirmes *f*
carnivorous [kɑː'nɪvərəs] *adj* fleischfressend
carol ['kærəl] *n*: **(Christmas) ~** Weihnachtslied *nt*
carouse [kə'rauz] *vi* zechen
carousel [kærə'sɛl] (*US*) *n* Karussell *nt*
carp [kɑːp] *n* Karpfen *m*
▸ **carp at** *vt fus* herumnörgeln an +*dat*
car park *n* Parkplatz *m*; (*building*) Parkhaus *nt*
car-park ticket *n* Parkschein *m*
carpenter ['kɑːpɪntəʳ] *n* Zimmermann *m*
carpentry ['kɑːpɪntrɪ] *n* Zimmerhandwerk *nt*; (*school subject, hobby*) Tischlern *nt*
carpet ['kɑːpɪt] *n* (*also fig*) Teppich *m* ▷*vt* (mit Teppichen/Teppichboden) auslegen; **fitted ~** (*Brit*) Teppichboden *m*
carpet bombing *n* Flächenbombardierung *f*
carpet slippers *npl* Pantoffeln *pl*
carpet-sweeper ['kɑːpɪtswiːpəʳ] *n* Teppichkehrer *m*
car phone *n* (*Telec*) Autotelefon *nt*
carport ['kɑːpɔːt] *n* Einstellplatz *m*
car rental *n* Autovermietung *f*
carriage ['kærɪdʒ] *n* (*Rail, of typewriter*) Wagen *m*; (*horse-drawn vehicle*) Kutsche *f*; (*of goods*) Beförderung *f*; (*transport costs*) Beförderungskosten *pl*; **~ forward** Fracht zahlt Empfänger; **~ free** frachtfrei; **~ paid** frei Haus
carriage return *n* (*on typewriter*) Wagenrücklauf *m*; (*Comput*) Return *nt*
carriageway ['kærɪdʒweɪ] (*Brit*) *n* Fahrbahn *f*
carrier ['kærɪəʳ] *n* Spediteur *m*, Transportunternehmer *m*; (*Med*) Überträger *m*

carrier bag (*Brit*) *n* Tragetasche *f*, Tragetüte *f*
carrier pigeon *n* Brieftaube *f*
carrion ['kærɪən] *n* Aas *nt*
carrot ['kærət] *n* Möhre *f*, Mohrrübe *f*, Karotte *f*; (*fig*) Köder *m*
carry ['kærɪ] *vt* tragen; (*transport*) transportieren; (*a motion, bill*) annehmen; (*responsibilities etc*) mit sich bringen; (*disease, virus*) übertragen ▷ *vi* (*sound*) tragen; **to get carried away** (*fig*) sich hinreißen lassen; **this loan carries 10% interest** dieses Darlehen wird mit 10% verzinst
▸ **carry forward** *vt* übertragen, vortragen
▸ **carry on** *vi* weitermachen; (*inf: make a fuss*) (ein) Theater machen ▷ *vt* fortführen; **to ~ on with sth** mit etw weitermachen; **to ~ on singing/eating** weitersingen/-essen
▸ **carry out** *vt* (*orders*) ausführen; (*investigation*) durchführen; (*idea*) in die Tat umsetzen; (*threat*) wahr machen
carrycot ['kærɪkɔt] (*Brit*) *n* Babytragetasche *f*
carry-on ['kærɪ'ɔn] (*inf*) *n* Theater *nt*
cart [kɑːt] *n* Wagen *m*, Karren *m*; (*for passengers*) Wagen *m*; (*handcart*) (Hand)wagen *m* ▷ *vt* (*inf*) mit sich herumschleppen
carte blanche ['kɑːt'blɔŋʃ] *n*: **to give sb ~** jdm Carte blanche *or* (eine) Blankovollmacht geben
cartel [kɑː'tɛl] *n* Kartell *nt*
cartilage ['kɑːtɪlɪdʒ] *n* Knorpel *m*
cartographer [kɑː'tɔgrəfəʳ] *n* Kartograf(in) *m(f)*
cartography [kɑː'tɔgrəfɪ] *n* Kartografie *f*
carton ['kɑːtən] *n* (Papp)karton *m*; (*of yogurt*) Becher *m*; (*of milk*) Tüte *f*; (*of cigarettes*) Stange *f*
cartoon [kɑː'tuːn] *n* (*drawing*) Karikatur *f*; (*Brit: comic strip*) Cartoon *m*; (*Cine*) Zeichentrickfilm *m*
cartoonist [kɑː'tuːnɪst] *n* Karikaturist(in) *m(f)*
cartridge ['kɑːtrɪdʒ] *n* (*for gun, pen*) Patrone *f*; (*music tape, for camera*) Kassette *f*; (*of record-player*) Tonabnehmer *m*
cartwheel ['kɑːtwiːl] *n* Rad *nt*; **to turn a ~** Rad schlagen
carve [kɑːv] *vt* (*meat*) (ab)schneiden; (*wood*) schnitzen; (*stone*) meißeln; (*initials, design*) einritzen
▸ **carve up** *vt* (*land etc*) aufteilen; (*meat*) aufschneiden
carving ['kɑːvɪŋ] *n* Skulptur *f*; (*in wood etc*) Schnitzerei *f*
carving knife *n* Tran(s)chiermesser *nt*
car wash *n* Autowaschanlage *f*
Casablanca [kæsə'blæŋkə] *n* Casablanca *nt*
cascade [kæs'keɪd] *n* Wasserfall *m*, Kaskade *f*; (*of money*) Regen *m*; (*of hair*) wallende Fülle *f* ▷ *vi* (in Kaskaden) herabfallen; (*hair etc*) wallen; (*people*) strömen
case [keɪs] *n* Fall *m*; (*for spectacles etc*) Etui *nt*; (*Brit: also*: **suitcase**) Koffer *m*; (*of wine, whisky etc*) Kiste *f*; (*Typ*): **lower/upper ~** klein-/großgeschrieben; **to have a good ~** gute Chancen haben, durchzukommen; **there's a strong ~ for reform** es spricht viel für eine Reform; **in ~ ...** falls ...; **in ~ of fire** bei Feuer; **in ~ of emergency** im Notfall; **in ~ he comes** falls er kommt; **in any ~** sowieso; **just in ~** für alle Fälle
case-hardened ['keɪshɑːdnd] *adj* (*fig*) abgebrüht (*inf*)
case history *n* (*Med*) Krankengeschichte *f*
case study *n* Fallstudie *f*
cash [kæʃ] *n* (Bar)geld *nt* ▷ *vt* (*cheque etc*) einlösen; **to pay (in) ~** bar bezahlen; **~ on delivery** per Nachnahme; **~ with order** zahlbar bei Bestellung
▸ **cash in** *vt* einlösen
▸ **cash in on** *vt fus* Kapital schlagen aus
cash account *n* Kassenbuch *nt*
cash-and-carry [kæʃən'kærɪ] *n* Abholmarkt *m*
cash-book ['kæʃbuk] *n* Kassenkonto *nt*
cash box *n* (Geld)kassette *f*
cash card (*Brit*) *n* (Geld)automatenkarte *f*
cash crop *n* zum Verkauf bestimmte Ernte *f*
cash desk (*Brit*) *n* Kasse *f*
cash discount *n* Skonto *m or nt*
cash dispenser (*Brit*) *n* Geldautomat *m*
cashew [kæ'ʃuː] *n* (*also*: **cashew nut**) Cashewnuss *f*
cash flow *n* Cashflow *m*
cashier [kæ'ʃɪəʳ] *n* Kassierer(in) *m(f)*
cashmere ['kæʃmɪəʳ] *n* Kaschmir *m*
cash point *n* Geldautomat *m*
cash price *n* Bar(zahlungs)preis *m*
cash register *n* Registrierkasse *f*
cash sale *n* Barverkauf *m*
casing ['keɪsɪŋ] *n* Gehäuse *nt*
casino [kə'siːnəu] *n* Kasino *nt*
cask [kɑːsk] *n* Fass *nt*
casket ['kɑːskɪt] *n* Schatulle *f*; (*US: coffin*) Sarg *m*
Caspian Sea ['kæspɪən-] *n*: **the ~** das Kaspische Meer
casserole ['kæsərəul] *n* Auflauf *m*; (*pot, container*) Kasserolle *f*
cassette [kæ'sɛt] *n* Kassette *f*
cassette deck *n* Kassettendeck *nt*
cassette player *n* Kassettenrekorder *m*
cassette recorder *n* Kassettenrekorder *m*
cast [kɑːst] (*pt, pp* **~**) *vt* werfen; (*net, fishing-line*) auswerfen; (*metal, statue*) gießen ▷ *vi* die Angel auswerfen ▷ *n* (*Theat*) Besetzung *f*; (*mould*) (Guss)form *f*; (*also*: **plaster cast**) Gipsverband *m*; **to ~ sb as Hamlet** (*Theat*) die Rolle des Hamlet mit jdm besetzen; **to ~ one's vote** seine Stimme abgeben; **to ~ one's eyes over sth** einen Blick auf etw *acc* werfen; **to ~ aspersions on sb/sth** abfällige Bemerkungen über jdn/etw machen; **to ~ doubts on sth** etw in Zweifel ziehen; **to ~ a spell on sb/sth** jdn/etw verzaubern; **to ~ its skin** sich häuten
▸ **cast aside** *vt* fallen lassen
▸ **cast off** *vi* (*Naut*) losmachen; (*Knitting*) abketten ▷ *vt* abketten
▸ **cast on** *vi, vt* (*Knitting*) anschlagen, aufschlagen
castaway ['kɑːstəweɪ] *n* Schiffbrüchige(r) *f(m)*

caste [kɑːst] *n* Kaste *f*; (*system*) Kastenwesen *nt*
caster sugar ['kɑːstə-] (*Brit*) *n* Raffinade *f*
casting vote ['kɑːstɪŋ-] (*Brit*) *n* ausschlaggebende Stimme *f*
cast iron *n* Gusseisen *nt* ▹ *adj*: **cast-iron** (*fig: will*) eisern; (*: alibi, excuse etc*) hieb- und stichfest
castle ['kɑːsl] *n* Schloss *nt*; (*manor*) Herrenhaus *nt*; (*fortified*) Burg *f*; (*Chess*) Turm *m*
cast off *n* abgelegtes Kleidungsstück *nt*
castor ['kɑːstəʳ] *n* Rolle *f*
castor oil *n* Rizinusöl *nt*
castrate [kæs'treɪt] *vt* kastrieren
casual ['kæʒjul] *adj* (*by chance*) zufällig; (*work etc*) Gelegenheits-; (*unconcerned*) lässig, gleichgültig; (*clothes*) leger; **~ wear** Freizeitkleidung *f*
casual labour *n* Gelegenheitsarbeit *f*
casually ['kæʒjulɪ] *adv* lässig; (*glance*) beiläufig; (*dress*) leger; (*by chance*) zufällig
casualty ['kæʒjultɪ] *n* (*of war etc*) Opfer *nt*; (*someone injured*) Verletzte(r) *f(m)*; (*someone killed*) Tote(r) *f(m)*; (*Med*) Unfallstation *f*; **heavy casualties** (*Mil*) schwere Verluste *pl*
casualty ward (*Brit*) *n* Unfallstation *f*
cat [kæt] *n* Katze *f*; (*lion etc*) (Raub)katze *f*
catacombs ['kætəkuːmz] *npl* Katakomben *pl*
catalogue, (*US*) **catalog** ['kætəlɔg] *n* Katalog *m* ▹ *vt* katalogisieren
catalyst ['kætəlɪst] *n* Katalysator *m*
catalytic converter [kætə'lɪtɪk kən'vəːtəʳ] *n* (*Aut*) Katalysator *m*
catapult ['kætəpʌlt] (*Brit*) *n* Schleuder *f*; (*Mil*) Katapult *nt or m* ▹ *vi* geschleudert *or* katapultiert werden ▹ *vt* schleudern, katapultieren
cataract ['kætərækt] *n* (*Med*) grauer Star *m*
catarrh [kə'tɑːʳ] *n* Katarrh *m*
catastrophe [kə'tæstrəfɪ] *n* Katastrophe *f*
catastrophic [kætə'strɔfɪk] *adj* katastrophal
catcalls ['kætkɔːlz] *npl* Pfiffe und Buhrufe *pl*
catch [kætʃ] (*pt, pp* **caught**) *vt* fangen; (*take: bus, train etc*) nehmen; (*arrest*) festnehmen; (*surprise*) erwischen, ertappen; (*breath*) holen; (*attention*) erregen; (*hit*) treffen; (*hear*) mitbekommen; (*illness*) sich *dat* zuziehen *or* holen; (*person: also:* **catch up**) einholen ▹ *vi* (*fire*) (anfangen zu) brennen; (*become trapped*) hängen bleiben ▹ *n* Fang *m*; (*trick, hidden problem*) Haken *m*; (*of lock*) Riegel *m*; (*game*) Fangen *nt*; **to ~ sb's attention/eye** jdn auf sich *acc* aufmerksam machen; **to ~ fire** Feuer fangen; **to ~ sight of** erblicken
▸ **catch on** *vi* (*grow popular*) sich durchsetzen; **to ~ on (to sth)** (etw) kapieren
▸ **catch out** (*Brit*) *vt* (*fig*) hereinlegen
▸ **catch up** *vi* (*fig: with person*) mitkommen; (*: on work*) aufholen ▹ *vt*: **to ~ sb up, to ~ up with sb** jdn einholen
catch-22 ['kætʃtwɛntɪ'tuː] *n*: **it's a ~ situation** es ist eine Zwickmühle
catching ['kætʃɪŋ] *adj* ansteckend
catchment area ['kætʃmənt-] (*Brit*) *n* Einzugsgebiet *nt*
catch phrase *n* Schlagwort *nt*, Slogan *m*
catchy ['kætʃɪ] *adj* (*tune*) eingängig
catechism ['kætɪkɪzəm] *n* Katechismus *m*
categoric [kætɪ'gɔrɪk], **categorical** [kætɪ'gɔrɪkəl] *adj* kategorisch
categorize ['kætɪgəraɪz] *vt* kategorisieren
category ['kætɪgərɪ] *n* Kategorie *f*
cater ['keɪtəʳ] *vi*: **to ~ (for)** die Speisen und Getränke liefern (für)
▸ **cater for** (*Brit*) *vt fus* (*needs, tastes*) gerecht werden *+dat*; (*readers, consumers*) eingestellt *or* ausgerichtet sein auf *+acc*
caterer ['keɪtərəʳ] *n* Lieferant(in) *m(f)* von Speisen und Getränken; (*company*) Lieferfirma *f* für Speisen und Getränke
catering ['keɪtərɪŋ] *n* Gastronomie *f*
caterpillar ['kætəpɪləʳ] *n* Raupe *f* ▹ *cpd* (*vehicle*) Raupen-
caterpillar track *n* Raupenkette *f*, Gleiskette *f*
cat flap *n* Katzentür *f*
cathedral [kə'θiːdrəl] *n* Kathedrale *f*, Dom *m*
cathode ['kæθəud] *n* Kat(h)ode *f*
cathode-ray tube [kæθəud'reɪ-] *n* Kat(h)odenstrahlröhre *f*
Catholic ['kæθəlɪk] *adj* katholisch ▹ *n* Katholik(in) *m(f)*
catholic ['kæθəlɪk] *adj* vielseitig
CAT scanner *n abbr* (*Med: = computerized axial tomography scanner*) CAT-Scanner *m*
Catseye® ['kæts'aɪ] (*Brit*) *n* Katzenauge *nt*
catsup ['kætsəp] (*US*) *n* Ket(s)chup *m or nt*
cattle ['kætl] *npl* Vieh *nt*
catty ['kætɪ] *adj* gehässig
catwalk ['kætwɔːk] *n* Steg *m*; (*for models*) Laufsteg *m*
Caucasian [kɔː'keɪzɪən] *adj* kaukasisch ▹ *n* Kaukasier(in) *m(f)*
Caucasus ['kɔːkəsəs] *n* Kaukasus *m*
caucus ['kɔːkəs] *n* (*group*) Gremium *nt*, Ausschuss *m*; (*US*) Parteiversammlung *f*; *siehe Info-Artikel*

CAUCUS

Caucus bedeutet vor allem in den USA ein privates Treffen von Parteifunktionären, bei dem z. B. Kandidaten ausgewählt oder Grundsatzentscheidungen getroffen werden. Meist wird ein solches Treffen vor einer öffentlichen Parteiversammlung abgehalten. Der Begriff bezieht sich im weiteren Sinne auch auf den kleinen, aber mächtigen Kreis von Parteifunktionären, der beim caucus zusammentrifft.

caught [kɔːt] *pt, pp of* **catch**
cauliflower ['kɔlɪflauəʳ] *n* Blumenkohl *m*
cause [kɔːz] *n* Ursache *f*; (*reason*) Grund *m*; (*aim*) Sache *f* ▹ *vt* verursachen; **there is no ~ for concern** es besteht kein Grund zur Sorge; **to ~ sth to be done** veranlassen, dass etw getan wird; **to ~ sb to do sth** jdn veranlassen, etw

zu tun
causeway ['kɔːzweɪ] *n* Damm *m*
caustic ['kɔːstɪk] *adj* ätzend, kaustisch; (*remark*) bissig
cauterize ['kɔːtəraɪz] *vt* kauterisieren
caution ['kɔːʃən] *n* Vorsicht *f*; (*warning*) Warnung *f*; (: *Law*) Verwarnung *f* ▷ *vt* warnen; (*Law*) verwarnen
cautious ['kɔːʃəs] *adj* vorsichtig
cautiously ['kɔːʃəslɪ] *adv* vorsichtig
cautiousness ['kɔːʃəsnɪs] *n* Vorsicht *f*
cavalier [kævə'lɪəʳ] *adj* unbekümmert
cavalry ['kævəlrɪ] *n* Kavallerie *f*
cave [keɪv] *n* Höhle *f* ▷ *vi*: **to go caving** auf Höhlenexpedition(en) gehen
▶ **cave in** *vi* einstürzen; (*to demands*) nachgeben
caveman ['keɪvmæn] (*irreg*: *like* **man**) *n* Höhlenmensch *m*
cavern ['kævən] *n* Höhle *f*
caviar, caviare ['kævɪɑːʳ] *n* Kaviar *m*
cavity ['kævɪtɪ] *n* Hohlraum *m*; (*in tooth*) Loch *nt*
cavity wall insulation *n* Schaumisolierung *f*
cavort [kə'vɔːt] *vi* tollen, toben
cayenne [keɪ'ɛn] *n* (*also*: **cayenne pepper**) Cayennepfeffer *m*
CB *n abbr* (= *Citizens' Band (Radio)*) CB-Funk *m*
CBC *n abbr* (= *Canadian Broadcasting Corporation*) *kanadische Rundfunkgesellschaft*
CBE (*Brit*) *n abbr* (= *Commander of (the Order of) the British Empire*) *britischer Ordenstitel*
CBI *n abbr* (= *Confederation of British Industry*) *britischer Unternehmerverband*, ≈ BDI *m*
CBS (*US*) *n abbr* (= *Columbia Broadcasting System*) *Rundfunkgesellschaft*
CC (*Brit*) *abbr* = **county council**
cc *abbr* (= *cubic centimetre*) ccm; = **carbon copy**
CCTV *n abbr* = **closed-circuit television**
CCU (*US*) *n abbr* (= *cardiac or coronary care unit*) *Intensivstation für Herzpatienten*
CD *abbr* (*Brit*: = *Corps Diplomatique*) CD ▷ *n abbr* (*Mil*: *Brit*: = *Civil Defence (Corps)*) Zivilschutz *m*; (: *US*: = *Civil Defense*) Zivilschutz *m*; (= *compact disc*) CD *f*; **CD player** CD-Spieler *m*
CDC (*US*) *n abbr* (= *Center for Disease Control*) *Seuchenkontrollbehörde*
Cdr *abbr* (*Mil*) = **commander**
CD-ROM *n abbr* (= *compact disc read-only memory*) CD-ROM *f*
CDT (*US*) *abbr* (= *Central Daylight Time*) *mittelamerikanische Sommerzeit*; (*Brit*: *Scol*: = *Craft, Design and Technology*) Arbeitslehre *f*
cease [siːs] *vt* beenden ▷ *vi* aufhören
ceasefire ['siːsfaɪəʳ] *n* Waffenruhe *f*
ceaseless ['siːslɪs] *adj* endlos, unaufhörlich
CED (*US*) *n abbr* (= *Committee for Economic Development*) *Komitee für wirtschaftliche Entwicklung*
cedar ['siːdəʳ] *n* Zeder *f*; (*wood*) Zedernholz *nt*
cede [siːd] *vt* abtreten
cedilla [sɪ'dɪlə] *n* Cedille *f*
CEEB (*US*) *n abbr* (= *College Entry Examination Board*) *akademische Zulassungsstelle*
ceilidh ['keɪlɪ] (*Scott*) *n Fest mit Volksmusik, Gesang und Tanz*
ceiling ['siːlɪŋ] *n* Decke *f*; (*upper limit*) Obergrenze *f*, Höchstgrenze *f*
celebrate ['sɛlɪbreɪt] *vt* feiern; (*mass*) zelebrieren ▷ *vi* feiern
celebrated ['sɛlɪbreɪtɪd] *adj* gefeiert
celebration [sɛlɪ'breɪʃən] *n* Feier *f*
celebrity [sɪ'lɛbrɪtɪ] *n* berühmte Persönlichkeit *f*
celeriac [sə'lɛrɪæk] *n* (Knollen)sellerie *f*
celery ['sɛlərɪ] *n* (Stangen)sellerie *f*
celestial [sɪ'lɛstɪəl] *adj* himmlisch
celibacy ['sɛlɪbəsɪ] *n* Zölibat *nt or m*
cell [sɛl] *n* Zelle *f*
cellar ['sɛləʳ] *n* Keller *m*; (*for wine*) (Wein)keller *m*
cellist ['tʃɛlɪst] *n* Cellist(in) *m(f)*
cello ['tʃɛləu] *n* Cello *nt*
cellophane ['sɛləfeɪn] *n* Cellophan *nt*
cellphone ['sɛlfəun] *n* Funktelefon *nt*
cell phone *n* Handy *nt*, Mobiltelefon *nt*
cellular ['sɛljuləʳ] *adj* (*Biol*) zellular, Zell-; (*fabrics*) aus porösem Material
Celluloid® ['sɛljulɔɪd] *n* Zelluloid *nt*
cellulose ['sɛljuləus] *n* Zellulose *f*, Zellstoff *m*
Celsius ['sɛlsɪəs] *adj* (*scale*) Celsius-
Celt [kɛlt] *n* Kelte *m*, Keltin *f*
Celtic ['kɛltɪk] *adj* keltisch ▷ *n* (*Ling*) Keltisch *nt*
cement [sə'mɛnt] *n* Zement *m*; (*concrete*) Beton *m*; (*glue*) Klebstoff *m* ▷ *vt* zementieren; (*stick, glue*) kleben; (*fig*) festigen
cement mixer *n* Betonmischmaschine *f*
cemetery ['sɛmɪtrɪ] *n* Friedhof *m*
cenotaph ['sɛnətɑːf] *n* Ehrenmal *nt*
censor ['sɛnsəʳ] *n* Zensor(in) *m(f)* ▷ *vt* zensieren
censorship ['sɛnsəʃɪp] *n* Zensur *f*
censure ['sɛnʃəʳ] *vt* tadeln ▷ *n* Tadel *m*
census ['sɛnsəs] *n* Volkszählung *f*
cent [sɛnt] *n* Cent *m*; *see also* **per cent**
centenary [sɛn'tiːnərɪ] *n* hundertster Jahrestag *m*
centennial [sɛn'tɛnɪəl] (*US*) *n* = **centenary**
center *etc* ['sɛntəʳ] (*US*) = **centre** *etc*
centigrade ['sɛntɪgreɪd] *adj* (*scale*) Celsius-
centilitre, (*US*) **centiliter** ['sɛntɪliːtəʳ] *n* Zentiliter *m or nt*
centimetre, (*US*) **centimeter** ['sɛntɪmiːtəʳ] *n* Zentimeter *m or nt*
centipede ['sɛntɪpiːd] *n* Tausendfüßler *m*
central ['sɛntrəl] *adj* zentral; (*committee, government*) Zentral-; (*idea*) wesentlich
Central African Republic *n* Zentralafrikanische Republik *f*
Central America *n* Mittelamerika *nt*
central heating *n* Zentralheizung *f*
centralize ['sɛntrəlaɪz] *vt* zentralisieren
central processing unit *n* (*Comput*) Zentraleinheit *f*
central reservation (*Brit*) *n* Mittelstreifen *m*
centre, (*US*) **center** ['sɛntəʳ] *n* Mitte *f*; (*health centre etc, town centre*) Zentrum *nt*; (*of attention, interest*) Mittelpunkt *m*; (*of action, belief etc*) Kern *m* ▷ *vt* zentrieren; (*ball*) zur Mitte spielen ▷ *vi*

(*concentrate*): **to ~ on** sich konzentrieren auf *+acc*
centrefold, (*US*) **centerfold** ['sɛntəfəuld] *n* *doppelseitiges Bild in der Mitte einer Zeitschrift*
centre forward *n* Mittelstürmer(in) *m(f)*
centre half *n* Stopper(in) *m(f)*
centrepiece, (*US*) **centerpiece** ['sɛntəpi:s] *n* Tafelaufsatz *m*; (*fig*) Kernstück *nt*
centre spread (*Brit*) *n* *Doppelseite in der Mitte einer Zeitschrift*
centre-stage [sɛntə'steɪdʒ] (*fig*) *adv*: **to be ~** im Mittelpunkt stehen ▷ *n*: **to take centre stage** in den Mittelpunkt rücken
centrifugal [sɛn'trɪfjugl] *adj* (*force*) Zentrifugal-
centrifuge ['sɛntrɪfju:ʒ] *n* Zentrifuge *f*, Schleuder *f*
century ['sɛntjurɪ] *n* Jahrhundert *nt*; (*Cricket*) Hundert *f*; **in the twentieth ~** im zwanzigsten Jahrhundert
CEO *n abbr* = **chief executive officer**
ceramic [sɪ'ræmɪk] *adj* keramisch; (*tiles*) Keramik-
ceramics [sɪ'ræmɪks] *npl* Keramiken *pl*
cereal ['si:rɪəl] *n* Getreide *nt*; (*food*) Getreideflocken *pl* (*Cornflakes etc*)
cerebral ['sɛrɪbrəl] *adj* (*Med*) zerebral; (*intellectual*) geistig
ceremonial [sɛrɪ'məunɪəl] *n* Zeremoniell *nt* ▷ *adj* zeremoniell
ceremony ['sɛrɪmənɪ] *n* Zeremonie *f*; (*behaviour*) Förmlichkeit *f*; **to stand on ~** förmlich sein
cert [sə:t] (*Brit: inf*) *n*: **it's a dead ~** es ist todsicher
certain ['sə:tən] *adj* sicher; **a ~ Mr Smith** ein gewisser Herr Smith; **~ days/places** bestimmte Tage/Orte; **a ~ coldness** eine gewisse Kälte; **to make ~ of** sich vergewissern *+gen*; **for ~** ganz sicher, ganz genau
certainly ['sə:tənlɪ] *adv* bestimmt; (*of course*) sicherlich; **~!** (aber) sicher!
certainty ['sə:təntɪ] *n* Sicherheit *f*; (*inevitability*) Gewissheit *f*
certificate [sə'tɪfɪkɪt] *n* Urkunde *f*; (*diploma*) Zeugnis *nt*
certified letter ['sə:tɪfaɪd-] (*US*) *n* Einschreibebrief *m*
certified mail (*US*) *n* Einschreiben *nt*
certified public accountant ['sə:tɪfaɪd-] (*US*) *n* geprüfter Buchhalter *m*, geprüfte Buchhalterin *f*
certify ['sə:tɪfaɪ] *vt* bescheinigen; (*award a diploma to*) ein Zeugnis verleihen *+dat*; (*declare insane*) für unzurechnungsfähig erklären ▷ *vi*: **to ~ to** sich verbürgen für
cervical ['sə:vɪkl] *adj*: **~ cancer** Gebärmutterhalskrebs *m*; **~ smear** Abstrich *m*
cervix ['sə:vɪks] *n* Gebärmutterhals *m*
Cesarean [sɪ'zɛərɪən] (*US*) *n* = **Caesarean**
cessation [sə'seɪʃən] *n* (*of hostilities etc*) Einstellung *f*, Ende *nt*
cesspit ['sɛspɪt] *n* (*sewage tank*) Senkgrube *f*
CET *abbr* (= *Central European Time*) MEZ
Ceylon [sɪ'lɔn] *n* Ceylon *nt*
cf. *abbr* (= *compare*) vgl.
c/f *abbr* (*Comm: = carried forward*) Übertr.
CFC *n abbr* (= *chlorofluorocarbon*) FCKW *m*
CG (*US*) *n abbr* = **coastguard**
cg *abbr* (= *centigram*) cg
CH (*Brit*) *n abbr* (= *Companion of Honour*) *britischer Ordenstitel*
ch. *abbr* (= *chapter*) Kap.
Chad [tʃæd] *n* Tschad *m*
chafe [tʃeɪf] *vt* (wund) reiben ▷ *vi* (*fig*): **to ~ against** sich ärgern über *+acc*
chaffinch ['tʃæfɪntʃ] *n* Buchfink *m*
chagrin ['ʃægrɪn] *n* Ärger *m*
chain [tʃeɪn] *n* Kette *f* ▷ *vt* (*also*: **chain up**: *prisoner*) anketten; (: *dog*) an die Kette legen
chain reaction *n* Kettenreaktion *f*
chain-smoke ['tʃeɪnsməuk] *vi* eine Zigarette nach der anderen rauchen
chain store *n* Kettenladen *m*
chair [tʃɛə^r] *n* Stuhl *m*; (*armchair*) Sessel *m*; (*of university*) Lehrstuhl *m*; (*of meeting, committee*) Vorsitz *m* ▷ *vt* den Vorsitz führen bei; **the ~** (*US*) der elektrische Stuhl
chair lift *n* Sessellift *m*
chairman ['tʃɛəmən] (*irreg: like* **man**) *n* Vorsitzende(r) *f(m)*; (*Brit: of company*) Präsident *m*
chairperson ['tʃɛəpə:sn] *n* Vorsitzende(r) *f(m)*
chairwoman ['tʃɛəwumən] (*irreg: like* **woman**) *n* Vorsitzende *f*
chalet ['ʃæleɪ] *n* Chalet *nt*
chalice ['tʃælɪs] *n* Kelch *m*
chalk [tʃɔ:k] *n* Kalkstein *m*, Kreide *f*; (*for writing*) Kreide *f*
▸ **chalk up** *vt* aufschreiben, notieren; (*fig: success etc*) verbuchen
challenge ['tʃælɪndʒ] *n* (*of new job*) Anforderungen *pl*; (*of unknown etc*) Reiz *m*; (*to authority etc*) Infragestellung *f*; (*dare*) Herausforderung *f* ▷ *vt* herausfordern; (*authority, right, idea etc*) infrage stellen; **to ~ sb to do sth** jdn dazu auffordern, etw zu tun; **to ~ sb to a fight/game** jdn zu einem Kampf/Spiel herausfordern
challenger ['tʃælɪndʒə^r] *n* Herausforderer *m*, Herausforderin *f*
challenging ['tʃælɪndʒɪŋ] *adj* (*career, task*) anspruchsvoll; (*tone, look etc*) herausfordernd
chamber ['tʃeɪmbə^r] *n* Kammer *f*; (*Brit: Law: gen pl: of barristers*) Kanzlei *f*; (: *of judge*) Amtszimmer *nt*; **~ of commerce** Handelskammer *f*
chambermaid ['tʃeɪmbəmeɪd] *n* Zimmermädchen *nt*
chamber music *n* Kammermusik *f*
chamber pot *n* Nachttopf *m*
chameleon [kə'mi:lɪən] *n* Chamäleon *nt*
chamois ['ʃæmwɑ:] *n* Gämse *f*; (*cloth*) Ledertuch *nt*, Fensterleder *nt*
chamois leather ['ʃæmɪ-] *n* Ledertuch *nt*, Fensterleder *nt*
champagne [ʃæm'peɪn] *n* Champagner *m*

champers ['ʃæmpəz] (*inf*) *n* (*champagne*) Schampus *m*
champion ['tʃæmpɪən] *n* Meister(in) *m(f)*; (*of cause, principle*) Verfechter(in) *m(f)*; (*of person*) Fürsprecher(in) *m(f)* ▷ *vt* eintreten für, sich engagieren für
championship ['tʃæmpɪənʃɪp] *n* Meisterschaft *f*; (*title*) Titel *m*
chance [tʃɑːns] *n* (*hope*) Aussicht *f*; (*likelihood, possibility*) Möglichkeit *f*; (*opportunity*) Gelegenheit *f*; (*risk*) Risiko *nt* ▷ *vt* riskieren ▷ *adj* zufällig; **the ~s are that ...** aller Wahrscheinlichkeit nach ..., wahrscheinlich ...; **there is little ~ of his coming** es ist unwahrscheinlich, dass er kommt; **to take a ~** es darauf ankommen lassen; **by ~** durch Zufall, zufällig; **it's the ~ of a lifetime** es ist eine einmalige Chance; **to ~ to do sth** zufällig etw tun; **to ~ it** es riskieren
▸ **chance (up)on** *vt fus* (*person*) zufällig begegnen *+dat*, zufällig treffen; (*thing*) zufällig stoßen auf *+acc*
chancel ['tʃɑːnsəl] *n* Altarraum *m*
chancellor ['tʃɑːnsələʳ] *n* Kanzler *m*
Chancellor of the Exchequer (*Brit*) *n* Schatzkanzler *m*, Finanzminister *m*
chancy ['tʃɑːnsɪ] *adj* riskant
chandelier [ʃændə'lɪəʳ] *n* Kronleuchter *m*
change [tʃeɪndʒ] *vt* ändern; (*wheel, job, money, baby's nappy*) wechseln; (*bulb*) auswechseln; (*baby*) wickeln ▷ *vi* sich verändern; (*traffic lights*) umspringen ▷ *n* Veränderung *f*; (*difference*) Abwechslung *f*; (*of government, climate, job*) Wechsel *m*; (*coins*) Kleingeld *nt*; (*money returned*) Wechselgeld *nt*; **to ~ sb into** jdn verwandeln in *+acc*; **to ~ gear** (*Aut*) schalten; **to ~ one's mind** seine Meinung ändern, es sich *dat* anders überlegen; **to ~ hands** den Besitzer wechseln; **to ~ (trains/buses/planes** *etc***)** umsteigen; **to ~ (one's clothes)** sich umziehen; **to ~ into** (*be transformed*) sich verwandeln in *+acc*; **she ~d into an old skirt** sie zog einen alten Rock an; **a ~ of clothes** Kleidung *f* zum Wechseln; **~ of government/climate/job** Regierungs-/Klima-/Berufswechsel *m*; **small ~** Kleingeld *nt*; **to give sb ~ for** *or* **of £10** jdm £10 wechseln; **keep the ~** das stimmt so, der Rest ist für Sie; **for a ~** zur Abwechslung
changeable ['tʃeɪndʒəbl] *adj* (*weather*) wechselhaft, veränderlich; (*mood*) wechselnd; (*person*) unbeständig
change machine *n* (Geld)wechselautomat *m*
changeover ['tʃeɪndʒəuvəʳ] *n* Umstellung *f*
changing ['tʃeɪndʒɪŋ] *adj* sich verändernd
changing room (*Brit*) *n* (Umkleide)kabine *f*; (*Sport*) Umkleideraum *m*
channel ['tʃænl] *n* (TV) Kanal *m*; (*of river, waterway*) (Fluss)bett *nt*; (*for boats*) Fahrrinne *f*; (*groove*) Rille *f*; (*fig: means*) Weg *m* ▷ *vt* leiten; (*fig*): **to ~ into** lenken auf *+acc*; **through the usual ~s** auf dem üblichen Wege; **green ~** (*Customs*) „nichts zu verzollen"; **red ~** (*Customs*) „Waren zu verzollen"; **the (English) C~** der Ärmelkanal; **the C~ Islands** die Kanalinseln *pl*
channel-hopping ['tʃænlhɔpɪŋ] *n* (TV) ständiges Umschalten
Channel Tunnel *n*: **the ~** der Kanaltunnel
chant [tʃɑːnt] *n* Sprechchor *m*; (*Rel*) Gesang *m* ▷ *vt* im (Sprech)chor rufen; (*Rel*) singen ▷ *vi* Sprechchöre anstimmen; (*Rel*) singen; **the demonstrators ~ed their disapproval** die Demonstranten machten ihrem Unmut in Sprechchören Luft
chaos ['keɪɔs] *n* Chaos *nt*, Durcheinander *nt*
chaos theory *n* Chaostheorie *f*
chaotic [keɪ'ɔtɪk] *adj* chaotisch
chap [tʃæp] (*Brit: inf*) *n* Kerl *m*, Typ *m*; **old ~** alter Knabe *or* Junge
chapel ['tʃæpl] *n* Kapelle *f*; (*Brit: non-conformist chapel*) Sektenkirche *f*; (*: of union*) *Betriebsgruppe innerhalb der Gewerkschaft der Drucker und Journalisten*
chaperone ['ʃæpərəun] *n* Anstandsdame *f* ▷ *vt* begleiten
chaplain ['tʃæplɪn] *n* Pfarrer(in) *m(f)*; (*Roman Catholic*) Kaplan *m*
chapped [tʃæpt] *adj* aufgesprungen, rau
chapter ['tʃæptəʳ] *n* Kapitel *nt*; **a ~ of accidents** eine Serie von Unfällen
char [tʃɑːʳ] *vt* verkohlen ▷ *vi* (*Brit*) putzen gehen ▷ *n* (*Brit*) = **charlady**
character ['kærɪktəʳ] *n* Charakter *m*; (*personality*) Persönlichkeit *f*; (*in novel, film*) Figur *f*, Gestalt *f*; (*eccentric*) Original *nt*; (*letter: also Comput*) Zeichen *nt*; **a person of good ~** ein guter Mensch
character code *n* (*Comput*) Zeichencode *m*
characteristic [kærɪktə'rɪstɪk] *n* Merkmal *nt* ▷ *adj*: **~ (of)** charakteristisch (für), typisch (für)
characterize ['kærɪktəraɪz] *vt* kennzeichnen, charakterisieren; (*describe the character of*): **to ~ (as)** beschreiben (als)
charade [ʃə'rɑːd] *n* Scharade *f*
charcoal ['tʃɑːkəul] *n* Holzkohle *f*; (*for drawing*) Kohle *f*, Kohlestift *m*
charge [tʃɑːdʒ] *n* (*fee*) Gebühr *f*; (*accusation*) Anklage *f*; (*responsibility*) Verantwortung *f*; (*attack*) Angriff *m* ▷ *vt* (*customer*) berechnen *+dat*; (*sum*) berechnen; (*battery*) (auf)laden; (*gun*) laden; (*enemy*) angreifen; (*sb with task*) beauftragen ▷ *vi* angreifen; (*usu with: up, along etc*) stürmen; **charges** *npl* Gebühren *pl*; **labour ~s** Arbeitskosten *pl*; **to reverse the ~s** (*Brit: Tel*) ein R-Gespräch führen; **is there a ~?** kostet das etwas?; **there's no ~** es ist umsonst, es kostet nichts; **at no extra ~** ohne Aufpreis; **free of ~** kostenlos, gratis; **to take ~ of** (*child*) sich kümmern um; (*company*) übernehmen; **to be in ~ of** die Verantwortung haben für; (*business*) leiten; **they ~d us £10 for the meal** das Essen kostete £10; **how much do you ~?** was verlangen Sie?; **to ~ an expense (up) to sb's**

account eine Ausgabe auf jds Rechnung *acc* setzen; **to ~ sb (with)** (*Law*) jdn anklagen (wegen)
charge account *n* Kunden(kredit)konto *nt*
charge card *n* Kundenkreditkarte *f*
chargé d'affaires *n* Chargé d'affaires *m*
charge hand (*Brit*) *n* Vorarbeiter(in) *m(f)*
charger ['tʃɑːdʒəʳ] *n* (*also*: **battery charger**) Ladegerät *nt*; (*warhorse*) (Schlacht)ross *nt*
chariot ['tʃærɪət] *n* (Streit)wagen *m*
charisma [kæ'rɪsmə] *n* Charisma *nt*
charitable ['tʃærɪtəbl] *adj* (*organization*) karitativ, Wohltätigkeits-; (*remark*) freundlich
charity ['tʃærɪtɪ] *n* (*organization*) karitative Organisation *f*, Wohltätigkeitsverein *m*; (*kindness, generosity*) Menschenfreundlichkeit *f*; (*money, gifts*) Almosen *nt*
charlady ['tʃɑːleɪdɪ] (*irreg: like* **lady**) (*Brit*) *n* Putzfrau *f*, Reinemachefrau *f*
charlatan ['ʃɑːlətən] *n* Scharlatan *m*
charm [tʃɑːm] *n* Charme *m*; (*to bring good luck*) Talisman *m*; (*on bracelet etc*) Anhänger *m* ▷ *vt* bezaubern
charm bracelet *n* Armband *nt* mit Anhängern
charming ['tʃɑːmɪŋ] *adj* reizend, charmant; (*place*) bezaubernd
chart [tʃɑːt] *n* Schaubild *nt*, Diagramm *nt*; (*map*) Karte *f*; (*also*: **weather chart**) Wetterkarte *f* ▷ *vt* (*course*) planen; (*progress*) aufzeichnen; **charts** *npl* (*hit parade*) Hitliste *f*
charter ['tʃɑːtəʳ] *vt* chartern ▷ *n* Charta *f*; (*of university, company*) Gründungsurkunde *f*; **on ~** gechartert
chartered accountant ['tʃɑːtəd-] (*Brit*) *n* Wirtschaftsprüfer(in) *m(f)*
charter flight *n* Charterflug *m*
charwoman ['tʃɑːwumən] (*irreg: like* **woman**) *n* Putzfrau *f*, Reinemachefrau *f*
chary ['tʃɛərɪ] *adj*: **to be ~ of doing sth** zögern, etw zu tun
chase [tʃeɪs] *vt* jagen, verfolgen; (*also*: **chase away**) wegjagen, vertreiben; (*business, job etc*) her sein hinter *+dat* (*inf*) ▷ *n* Verfolgungsjagd *f*
▸ **chase down** (*US*) *vt* = **chase up**
▸ **chase up** (*Brit*) *vt* (*person*) rankriegen (*inf*); (*information*) ranschaffen (*inf*)
chasm ['kæzəm] *n* Kluft *f*
chassis ['ʃæsɪ] *n* Fahrgestell *nt*
chaste [tʃeɪst] *adj* keusch
chastened ['tʃeɪsnd] *adj* zur Einsicht gebracht
chastening ['tʃeɪsnɪŋ] *adj* ernüchternd
chastise [tʃæs'taɪz] *vt* (*scold*) schelten
chastity ['tʃæstɪtɪ] *n* Keuschheit *f*
chat [tʃæt] *vi* (*also*: **have a chat**) plaudern, sich unterhalten ▷ *n* Plauderei *f*, Unterhaltung *f*
▸ **chat up** (*Brit: inf*) *vt* anmachen
chatline ['tʃætlaɪn] *n* *Telefondienst, der Anrufern die Teilnahme an einer Gesprächsrunde ermöglicht*
chatroom ['tʃætruːm] *n* (*Comput*) Chatroom *m*
chat show (*Brit*) *n* Talkshow *f*
chattel ['tʃætl] *n*: **goods and ~s** *see* **good**
chatter ['tʃætəʳ] *vi* schwatzen; (*monkey*) schnattern; (*teeth*) klappern ▷ *n* (*see vi*) Schwatzen *nt*; Schnattern *nt*; Klappern *nt*; **my teeth are ~ing** mir klappern die Zähne
chatterbox ['tʃætəbɔks] (*inf*) *n* Quasselstrippe *f*
chattering classes ['tʃætərɪŋ 'klɑːsɪz] *npl*: **the ~** die intellektuellen Schwätzer *pl*
chatty ['tʃætɪ] *adj* geschwätzig; (*letter*) im Plauderton
chauffeur ['ʃəufəʳ] *n* Chauffeur *m*, Fahrer *m*
chauvinism ['ʃəuvɪnɪzəm] *n* (*also*: **male chauvinism**) Chauvinismus *m*
chauvinist ['ʃəuvɪnɪst] *n* Chauvinist *m*
chauvinistic [ʃəuvɪ'nɪstɪk] *adj* chauvinistisch
ChE *abbr* (*= chemical engineer*) *Titel für Chemotechniker*
cheap [tʃiːp] *adj* billig; (*reduced*) ermäßigt; (*poor quality*) billig, minderwertig; (*behaviour, joke*) ordinär ▷ *adv*: **to buy/sell sth ~** etw billig kaufen/verkaufen
cheap day return *n* Tagesrückfahrkarte *f* (*zu einem günstigeren Tarif*)
cheapen ['tʃiːpn] *vt* entwürdigen
cheaper ['tʃiːpəʳ] *adj* billiger
cheaply ['tʃiːplɪ] *adv* billig
cheat [tʃiːt] *vi* mogeln (*inf*), schummeln (*inf*) ▷ *n* Betrüger(in) *m(f)* ▷ *vt*: **to ~ sb (out of sth)** jdn (um etw) betrügen; **to ~ on sb** (*inf*) jdn betrügen
cheating ['tʃiːtɪŋ] *n* Mogeln *nt* (*inf*), Schummeln *nt* (*inf*)
check [tʃɛk] *vt* überprüfen; (*passport, ticket*) kontrollieren; (*facts*) nachprüfen; (*enemy, disease*) aufhalten; (*impulse*) unterdrücken; (*person*) zurückhalten ▷ *vi* nachprüfen ▷ *n* Kontrolle *f*; (*curb*) Beschränkung *f*; (US) = **cheque**; (*: bill*) Rechnung *f*; (*pattern: gen pl*) Karo(muster) *nt* ▷ *adj* kariert; **to ~ o.s.** sich beherrschen; **to ~ with sb** bei jdm nachfragen; **to keep a ~ on sb/sth** jdn/etw kontrollieren
▸ **check in** *vi* (*at hotel*) sich anmelden; (*at airport*) einchecken ▷ *vt* (*luggage*) abfertigen lassen
▸ **check off** *vt* abhaken
▸ **check out** *vi* (*of hotel*) abreisen ▷ *vt* (*luggage*) abfertigen; (*investigate*) überprüfen
▸ **check up** *vi*: **to ~ up on sth** etw überprüfen; **to ~ up on sb** Nachforschungen über jdn anstellen
checkered ['tʃɛkəd] (US) *adj* = **chequered**
checkers ['tʃɛkəz] (*US*) *npl* Damespiel *nt*
check guarantee card (US) *n* Scheckkarte *f*
check-in ['tʃɛkɪn], **check-in desk** *n* (*at airport*) Abfertigung *f*, Abfertigungsschalter *m*
checking account ['tʃɛkɪŋ-] (US) *n* Girokonto *nt*
check list *n* Prüfliste *f*, Checkliste *f*
checkmate ['tʃɛkmeɪt] *n* Schachmatt *nt*
checkout ['tʃɛkaut] *n* Kasse *f*
checkpoint ['tʃɛkpɔɪnt] *n* Kontrollpunkt *m*
checkroom ['tʃɛkrum] (US) *n* (*left-luggage office*) Gepäckaufbewahrung *f*
checkup ['tʃɛkʌp] *n* Untersuchung *f*

cheek [tʃi:k] *n* Backe *f*; (*impudence*) Frechheit *f*; (*nerve*) Unverschämtheit *f*
cheekbone ['tʃi:kbəun] *n* Backenknochen *m*
cheeky ['tʃi:kɪ] *adj* frech
cheep [tʃi:p] *vi* (*bird*) piep(s)en ▷ *n* Piep(s) *m*, Piepser *m*
cheer [tʃɪəʳ] *vt* zujubeln *+dat*; (*gladden*) aufmuntern, aufheitern ▷ *vi* jubeln, Hurra rufen ▷ *n* (*gen pl*) Hurraruf *m*, Beifallsruf *m*; **cheers** *npl* Hurrageschrei *nt*, Jubel *m*; **~s!** prost!
▸ **cheer on** *vt* anspornen, anfeuern
▸ **cheer up** *vi* vergnügter *or* fröhlicher werden ▷ *vt* aufmuntern, aufheitern
cheerful ['tʃɪəful] *adj* fröhlich
cheerfulness ['tʃɪəfulnɪs] *n* Fröhlichkeit *f*
cheerio [tʃɪərɪ'əu] (*Brit*) *excl* tschüss (*inf*)
cheerleader ['tʃɪəli:dəʳ] *n jd, der bei Sportveranstaltungen etc die Zuschauer zu Beifallsrufen anfeuert*
cheerless ['tʃɪəlɪs] *adj* freudlos, trüb; (*room*) trostlos
cheese [tʃi:z] *n* Käse *m*
cheeseboard ['tʃi:zbɔ:d] *n* Käsebrett *nt*; (*with cheese on it*) Käseplatte *f*
cheeseburger ['tʃi:zbə:gəʳ] *n* Cheeseburger *m*
cheesecake ['tʃi:zkeɪk] *n* Käsekuchen *m*
cheetah ['tʃi:tə] *n* Gepard *m*
chef [ʃɛf] *n* Küchenchef(in) *m(f)*
chemical ['kɛmɪkl] *adj* chemisch ▷ *n* Chemikalie *f*
chemical engineering *n* Chemotechnik *f*
chemist ['kɛmɪst] *n* (*Brit: pharmacist*) Apotheker(in) *m(f)*; (*scientist*) Chemiker(in) *m(f)*
chemistry ['kɛmɪstrɪ] *n* Chemie *f*
chemist's ['kɛmɪsts]
chemist's shop (*Brit*) *n* Drogerie *f*; (*also*: **dispensing chemist's**) Apotheke *f*
chemotherapy [ki:məu'θɛrəpɪ] *n* Chemotherapie *f*
cheque [tʃɛk] (*Brit*) *n* Scheck *m*; **to pay by ~** mit (einem) Scheck bezahlen
chequebook ['tʃɛkbuk] *n* Scheckbuch *nt*
cheque card (*Brit*) *n* Scheckkarte *f*
chequered, (*US*) **checkered** ['tʃɛkəd] *adj* (*fig*) bewegt
cherish ['tʃɛrɪʃ] *vt* (*person*) liebevoll sorgen für; (*memory*) in Ehren halten; (*dream*) sich hingeben *+dat*; (*hope*) hegen
cheroot [ʃə'ru:t] *n* Stumpen *m*
cherry ['tʃɛrɪ] *n* Kirsche *f*; (*also*: **cherry tree**) Kirschbaum *m*
chervil ['tʃə:vɪl] *n* Kerbel *m*
Ches. (*Brit*) *abbr* (*Post*) = *Cheshire*
chess [tʃɛs] *n* Schach(spiel) *nt*
chessboard ['tʃɛsbɔ:d] *n* Schachbrett *nt*
chessman ['tʃɛsmən] (*irreg: like* **man**) *n* Schachfigur *f*
chess player *n* Schachspieler(in) *m(f)*
chest [tʃɛst] *n* Brust *f*, Brustkorb *m*; (*box*) Kiste *f*, Truhe *f*; **to get sth off one's ~** (*inf*) sich *dat* etw von der Seele reden
chest measurement *n* Brustweite *f*, Brustumfang *m*
chestnut ['tʃɛsnʌt] *n* Kastanie *f* ▷ *adj* kastanienbraun
chest of drawers *n* Kommode *f*
chesty ['tʃɛstɪ] *adj* (*cough*) tief sitzend
chew [tʃu:] *vt* kauen
chewing gum ['tʃu:ɪŋ-] *n* Kaugummi *m*
chic [ʃi:k] *adj* chic *inv*, schick
chick [tʃɪk] *n* Küken *nt*; (*inf: girl*) Mieze *f*
chicken ['tʃɪkɪn] *n* Huhn *nt*; (*meat*) Hähnchen *nt*; (*inf: coward*) Feigling *m*
▸ **chicken out** (*inf*) *vi*: **to ~ out of doing sth** davor kneifen, etw zu tun
chicken feed *n* (*inf: money*) ein paar Pfennige *pl* (*Hist*); (*as salary*) ein Hungerlohn *m*
chickenpox ['tʃɪkɪnpɔks] *n* Windpocken *pl*
chickpea ['tʃɪkpi:] *n* Kichererbse *f*
chicory ['tʃɪkərɪ] *n* (*in coffee*) Zichorie *f*; (*salad vegetable*) Chicorée *f or m*
chide [tʃaɪd] *vt*: **to ~ sb (for)** jdn schelten (wegen)
chief [tʃi:f] *n* Häuptling *m*; (*of organization, department*) Leiter(in) *m(f)*, Chef(in) *m(f)* ▷ *adj* Haupt-, wichtigste(r, s)
chief constable (*Brit*) *n* Polizeipräsident *m*, Polizeichef *m*
chief executive, (*US*) **chief executive officer** *n* Generaldirektor(in) *m(f)*
chiefly ['tʃi:flɪ] *adv* hauptsächlich
Chief of Staff *n* Stabschef *m*
chiffon ['ʃɪfɔn] *n* Chiffon *m*
chilblain ['tʃɪlbleɪn] *n* Frostbeule *f*
child [tʃaɪld] (*pl* **childen**) *n* Kind *nt*; **do you have any children?** haben Sie Kinder?
child benefit (*Brit*) *n* Kindergeld *nt*
childbirth ['tʃaɪldbə:θ] *n* Geburt *f*, Entbindung *f*
childhood ['tʃaɪldhud] *n* Kindheit *f*
childish ['tʃaɪldɪʃ] *adj* kindisch
childless ['tʃaɪldlɪs] *adj* kinderlos
childlike ['tʃaɪldlaɪk] *adj* kindlich
child minder (*Brit*) *n* Tagesmutter *f*
child prodigy *n* Wunderkind *nt*
children ['tʃɪldrən] *npl of* **child**
children's home ['tʃɪldrənz-] *n* Kinderheim *nt*
child's play ['tʃaɪldz-] *n*: **it was ~** es war ein Kinderspiel
Chile ['tʃɪlɪ] *n* Chile *nt*
Chilean ['tʃɪlɪən] *adj* chilenisch ▷ *n* Chilene *m*, Chilenin *f*
chill [tʃɪl] *n* Kühle *f*; (*illness*) Erkältung *f* ▷ *adj* kühl; (*fig: reminder*) erschreckend ▷ *vt* kühlen; (*person*) frösteln *or* frieren lassen; **"serve ~ed"** „gekühlt servieren"
chilli, (*US*) **chili** ['tʃɪlɪ] *n* Peperoni *pl*
chilling ['tʃɪlɪn] *adj* (*wind, morning*) eisig; (*fig: effect, prospect etc*) beängstigend
chill out (*inf*) *vi* sich entspannen, relaxen
chilly ['tʃɪlɪ] *adj* kühl; (*person, response, look*) kühl, frostig; **to feel ~** frösteln, frieren
chime [tʃaɪm] *n* Glockenspiel *nt* ▷ *vi* läuten
chimney ['tʃɪmnɪ] *n* Schornstein *m*
chimney sweep *n* Schornsteinfeger(in) *m(f)*
chimpanzee [tʃɪmpæn'zi:] *n* Schimpanse *m*

chin [tʃɪn] *n* Kinn *nt*
China ['tʃaɪnə] *n* China *nt*
china ['tʃaɪnə] *n* Porzellan *nt*
Chinese [tʃaɪ'ni:z] *adj* chinesisch ▷ *n inv* Chinese *m*, Chinesin *f*; (*Ling*) Chinesisch *nt*
chink [tʃɪŋk] *n* (*in door, wall etc*) Ritze *f*, Spalt *m*; (*of bottles etc*) Klirren *nt*
chintz [tʃɪnts] *n* Chintz *m*
chinwag ['tʃɪnwæg] (*Brit: inf*) *n* Schwatz *m*
chip [tʃɪp] *n* (*gen pl*) Pommes frites *pl*; (*US: also:* **potato chip**) Chip *m*; (*of wood*) Span *m*; (*of glass, stone*) Splitter *m*; (*in glass, cup etc*) abgestoßene Stelle *f*; (*in gambling*) Chip *m*, Spielmarke *f*; (*Comput: also:* **microchip**) Chip *m* ▷ *vt* (*cup, plate*) anschlagen; **when the ~s are down** (*fig*) wenn es drauf ankommt
▸ **chip in** (*inf*) *vi* (*contribute*) etwas beisteuern; (*interrupt*) sich einschalten
chipboard ['tʃɪpbɔ:d] *n* Spanplatte *f*
chipmunk ['tʃɪpmʌŋk] *n* Backenhörnchen *nt*
chippings ['tʃɪpɪŋz] *npl*: **loose ~** (*on road*) Schotter *m*

CHIP SHOP

Chip shop, auch „fish-and-chip shop", ist die traditionelle britische Imbissbude, in der vor allem frittierte Fischfilets und Pommes frites, aber auch andere einfache Mahlzeiten angeboten werden. Früher wurde das Essen zum Mitnehmen in Zeitungspapier verpackt. Manche chip shops haben auch einen Essraum.

chiropodist [kɪ'rɔpədɪst] (*Brit*) *n* Fußpfleger(in) *m(f)*
chiropody [kɪ'rɔpədɪ] (*Brit*) *n* Fußpflege *f*
chirp [tʃə:p] *vi* (*bird*) zwitschern; (*crickets*) zirpen
chirpy ['tʃə:pɪ] (*inf*) *adj* munter
chisel ['tʃɪzl] *n* (*for stone*) Meißel *m*; (*for wood*) Beitel *m*
chit [tʃɪt] *n* Zettel *m*
chitchat ['tʃɪttʃæt] *n* Plauderei *f*
chivalrous ['ʃɪvəlrəs] *adj* ritterlich
chivalry ['ʃɪvəlrɪ] *n* Ritterlichkeit *f*
chives [tʃaɪvz] *npl* Schnittlauch *m*
chloride ['klɔ:raɪd] *n* Chlorid *nt*
chlorinate ['klɔrɪneɪt] *vt* chloren
chlorine ['klɔ:ri:n] *n* Chlor *nt*
chock [tʃɔk] *n* Bremskeil *m*, Bremsklotz *m*
chock-a-block ['tʃɔkə'blɔk] *adj* gerammelt voll
chock-full [tʃɔk'ful] *adj* = **chock-a-block**
chocolate ['tʃɔklɪt] *n* Schokolade *f*; (*drink*) Kakao *m*, Schokolade *f*; (*sweet*) Praline *f* ▷ *cpd* Schokoladen-
choice [tʃɔɪs] *n* Auswahl *f*; (*option*) Möglichkeit *f*; (*preference*) Wahl *f* ▷ *adj* Qualitäts-, erstklassig; **I did it by** *or* **from ~** ich habe es mir so ausgesucht; **a wide ~** eine große Auswahl
choir ['kwaɪə'] *n* Chor *m*
choirboy ['kwaɪə'bɔɪ] *n* Chorknabe *m*
choke [tʃəuk] *vi* ersticken; (*with smoke, dust, anger etc*) keine Luft mehr bekommen ▷ *vt* erwürgen, erdrosseln ▷ *n* (*Aut*) Choke *m*, Starterklappe *f*; **to be ~d (with)** verstopft sein (mit)
cholera ['kɔlərə] *n* Cholera *f*
cholesterol [kə'lɛstərɔl] *n* Cholesterin *nt*
choose [tʃu:z] (*pt* **chose**, *pp* **chosen**) *vt* (aus)wählen; (*profession, friend*) sich *dat* aussuchen ▷ *vi*: **to ~ between** wählen zwischen *+dat*, eine Wahl treffen zwischen *+dat*; **to ~ from** wählen aus *or* unter *+dat*, eine Wahl treffen aus *or* unter *+dat*; **to ~ to do sth** beschließen, etw zu tun
choosy ['tʃu:zɪ] *adj* wählerisch
chop [tʃɔp] *vt* (*wood*) hacken; (*also:* **chop up**: *vegetables, fruit, meat*) klein schneiden ▷ *n* Kotelett *nt*; **chops** (*inf*) *npl* (*of animal*) Maul *nt*; (*of person*) Mund *m*; **to get the ~** (*Brit: inf: project*) dem Rotstift zum Opfer fallen; (*: be sacked*) rausgeschmissen werden
▸ **chop down** *vt* (*tree*) fällen
chopper ['tʃɔpə'] (*inf*) *n* Hubschrauber *m*
choppy ['tʃɔpɪ] *adj* (*sea*) kabbelig, bewegt
chopsticks ['tʃɔpstɪks] *npl* Stäbchen *pl*
choral ['kɔ:rəl] *adj* (*singing*) Chor-; (*society*) Gesang-
chord [kɔ:d] *n* Akkord *m*; (*Math*) Sehne *f*
chore [tʃɔ:'] *n* Hausarbeit *f*; (*routine task*) lästige Routinearbeit *f*; **household ~s** Hausarbeit
choreographer [kɔrɪ'ɔgrəfə'] *n* Choreograf(in) *m(f)*
choreography [kɔrɪ'ɔgrəfɪ] *n* Choreografie *f*
chorister ['kɔrɪstə'] *n* Chorsänger(in) *m(f)*
chortle ['tʃɔ:tl] *vi* glucksen
chorus ['kɔ:rəs] *n* Chor *m*; (*refrain*) Refrain *m*; (*of complaints*) Flut *f*
chose [tʃəuz] *pt of* **choose**
chosen ['tʃəuzn] *pp of* **choose**
chow [tʃau] *n* Chow-Chow *m*
chowder ['tʃaudə'] *n* (sämige) Fischsuppe *f*
Christ [kraɪst] *n* Christus *m*
christen ['krɪsn] *vt* taufen
christening ['krɪsnɪŋ] *n* Taufe *f*
Christian ['krɪstɪən] *adj* christlich ▷ *n* Christ(in) *m(f)*
Christianity [krɪstɪ'ænɪtɪ] *n* Christentum *nt*
Christian name *n* Vorname *m*
Christmas ['krɪsməs] *n* Weihnachten *nt*; **Happy** *or* **Merry ~!** frohe *or* fröhliche Weihnachten!
Christmas card *n* Weihnachtskarte *f*
Christmas Day *n* der erste Weihnachtstag
Christmas Eve *n* Heiligabend *m*
Christmas Island *n* Weihnachtsinsel *f*
Christmas tree *n* Weihnachtsbaum *m*, Christbaum *m*
chrome [krəum] *n* = **chromium**
chromium ['krəumɪəm] *n* Chrom *nt*; (*also:* **chromium plating**) Verchromung *f*
chromosome ['krəuməsəum] *n* Chromosom *nt*
chronic ['krɔnɪk] *adj* (*also fig*) chronisch; (*severe*) schlimm
chronicle ['krɔnɪkl] *n* Chronik *f*

chronological [krɔnə'lɔdʒɪkl] *adj* chronologisch
chrysanthemum [krɪ'sænθəməm] *n* Chrysantheme *f*
chubby ['tʃʌbɪ] *adj* pummelig; **~ cheeks** Pausbacken *pl*
chuck [tʃʌk] (*inf*) *vt* werfen, schmeißen; (*Brit: also:* **chuck up, chuck in**: *job*) hinschmeißen; (*: person*) Schluss machen mit
▸ **chuck out** *vt* (*person*) rausschmeißen; (*rubbish etc*) wegschmeißen
chuckle ['tʃʌkl] *vi* leise in sich *acc* hineinlachen
chuffed [tʃʌft] (*Brit: inf*) *adj* vergnügt und zufrieden; (*flattered*) gebauchpinselt
chug [tʃʌg] *vi* (*also:* **chug along**) tuckern
chum [tʃʌm] *n* Kumpel *m*
chump [tʃʌmp] (*inf*) *n* Trottel *m*
chunk [tʃʌŋk] *n* großes Stück *nt*
chunky ['tʃʌŋkɪ] *adj* (*furniture etc*) klobig; (*person*) stämmig, untersetzt; (*knitwear*) dick
church [tʃə:tʃ] *n* Kirche *f*; **the C~ of England** die anglikanische Kirche
churchyard ['tʃə:tʃjɑ:d] *n* Friedhof *m*
churlish ['tʃə:lɪʃ] *adj* griesgrämig; (*behaviour*) ungehobelt
churn [tʃə:n] *n* Butterfass *nt*; (*also:* **milk churn**) Milchkanne *f*
▸ **churn out** *vt* am laufenden Band produzieren
chute [ʃu:t] *n* (*also:* **rubbish chute**) Müllschlucker *m*; (*for coal, parcels etc*) Rutsche *f*; (*Brit: slide*) Rutschbahn *f*, Rutsche *f*
chutney ['tʃʌtnɪ] *n* Chutney *nt*
CIA (*US*) *n abbr* (*= Central Intelligence Agency*) CIA *f or m*
cicada [sɪ'kɑ:də] *n* Zikade *f*
CID (*Brit*) *n abbr* = **Criminal Investigation Department**
cider ['saɪdə^r] *n* Apfelwein *m*
c.i.f., CIF *abbr* (*Comm: = cost, insurance, and freight*) cif
cigar [sɪ'gɑ:^r] *n* Zigarre *f*
cigarette [sɪgə'rɛt] *n* Zigarette *f*
cigarette case *n* Zigarettenetui *nt*
cigarette end *n* Zigarettenstummel *m*
cigarette holder *n* Zigarettenspitze *f*
C in C *abbr* (*Mil*) = **commander in chief**
cinch [sɪntʃ] (*inf*) *n*: **it's a ~** das ist ein Kinderspiel *or* ein Klacks
Cinderella [sɪndə'rɛlə] *n* Aschenputtel *nt*, Aschenbrödel *nt*
cinders ['sɪndəz] *npl* Asche *f*
cine camera ['sɪnɪ-] (*Brit*) *n* (Schmal)filmkamera *f*
cine film (*Brit*) *n* Schmalfilm *m*
cinema ['sɪnəmə] *n* Kino *nt*; (*film-making*) Film *m*
cine projector (*Brit*) *n* Filmprojektor *m*
cinnamon ['sɪnəmən] *n* Zimt *m*
cipher ['saɪfə^r] *n* (*code*) Chiffre *f*; (*fig*) Niemand *m*; **in ~** chiffriert
circa ['sə:kə] *prep* circa
circle ['sə:kl] *n* Kreis *m*; (*in cinema, theatre*) Rang *m* ▸ *vi* kreisen ▸ *vt* kreisen um; (*surround*) umgeben
circuit ['sə:kɪt] *n* Runde *f*; (*Elec*) Stromkreis *m*; (*track*) Rennbahn *f*
circuit board *n* Platine *f*, Leiterplatte *f*
circuitous [sə:'kjuɪtəs] *adj* umständlich
circular ['sə:kjulə^r] *adj* rund; (*route*) Rund- ▸ *n* (*letter*) Rundschreiben *nt*, Rundbrief *m*; (*as advertisement*) Wurfsendung *f*; **~ argument** Zirkelschluss *m*
circulate ['sə:kjuleɪt] *vi* (*traffic*) fließen; (*blood, report*) zirkulieren; (*news, rumour*) kursieren, in Umlauf sein; (*person*) die Runde machen ▸ *vt* herumgehen *or* zirkulieren lassen
circulating capital [sə:kju'leɪtɪŋ-] *n* (*Comm*) flüssiges Kapital *nt*, Umlaufkapital *nt*
circulation [sə:kju'leɪʃən] *n* (*of traffic*) Fluss *m*; (*of air etc*) Zirkulation *f*; (*of newspaper*) Auflage *f*; (*Med: of blood*) Kreislauf *m*
circumcise ['sə:kəmsaɪz] *vt* beschneiden
circumference [sə'kʌmfərəns] *n* Umfang *m*; (*edge*) Rand *m*
circumflex ['sə:kəmflɛks] *n* (*also:* **circumflex accent**) Zirkumflex *m*
circumscribe ['sə:kəmskraɪb] *vt* (*Math*) einen Kreis umbeschreiben; (*fig*) eingrenzen
circumspect ['sə:kəmspɛkt] *adj* umsichtig
circumstances ['sə:kəmstənsɪz] *npl* Umstände *pl*; (*financial condition*) (finanzielle) Verhältnisse *pl*; **in the ~** unter diesen Umständen; **under no ~** unter (gar) keinen Umständen, auf keinen Fall
circumstantial [sə:kəm'stænʃl] *adj* ausführlich; **~ evidence** Indizienbeweis *m*
circumvent [sə:kəm'vɛnt] *vt* umgehen
circus ['sə:kəs] *n* Zirkus *m*; (*also:* **Circus**: *in place names*) Platz *m*
cirrhosis [sɪ'rəusɪs] *n* (*also:* **cirrhosis of the liver**) Leberzirrhose *f*
CIS *n abbr* (*= Commonwealth of Independent States*) GUS *f*
cissy ['sɪsɪ] *n, adj see* **sissy**
cistern ['sɪstən] *n* Zisterne *f*; (*of toilet*) Spülkasten *m*
citation [saɪ'teɪʃən] *n* Zitat *nt*; (*US*) Belobigung *f*; (*Law*) Vorladung *f* (vor Gericht)
cite [saɪt] *vt* zitieren; (*example*) anführen; (*Law*) vorladen
citizen ['sɪtɪzn] *n* Staatsbürger(in) *m(f)*; (*of town*) Bürger(in) *m(f)*
Citizens' Advice Bureau ['sɪtɪznz-] *n* ≈ Bürgerberatungsstelle *f*
citizenship ['sɪtɪznʃɪp] *n* Staatsbürgerschaft *f*; (*Brit: Scol*) Gesellschaftskunde *f*
citric acid ['sɪtrɪk-] *n* Zitronensäure *f*
citrus fruit ['sɪtrəs-] *n* Zitrusfrucht *f*
city ['sɪtɪ] *n* (Groß)stadt *f*; **the C~** (*Fin*) die City, das Londoner Banken- und Börsenviertel
city centre *n* Stadtzentrum *nt*, Innenstadt *f*
City Hall *n* Rathaus *nt*; (*US: municipal government*) Stadtverwaltung *f*
civic ['sɪvɪk] *adj* (*authorities etc*) Stadt-, städtisch; (*duties, pride*) Bürger-, bürgerlich

civic centre (*Brit*) *n* Stadtverwaltung *f*
civil ['sɪvɪl] *adj* (*disturbances, rights*) Bürger-; (*liberties, law*) bürgerlich; (*polite*) höflich
Civil Aviation Authority (*Brit*) *n* Behörde *f* für Zivilluftfahrt
civil defence *n* Zivilschutz *m*
civil disobedience *n* ziviler Ungehorsam *m*
civil engineer *n* Bauingenieur(in) *m(f)*
civil engineering *n* Hoch- und Tiefbau *m*
civilian [sɪ'vɪlɪən] *adj* (*population*) Zivil- ▷ *n* Zivilist *m*; **~ casualties** Verluste *pl* unter der Zivilbevölkerung
civilization [sɪvɪlaɪ'zeɪʃən] *n* Zivilisation *f*; (*a society*) Kultur *f*
civilized ['sɪvɪlaɪzd] *adj* zivilisiert; (*person*) kultiviert; (*place, experience*) gepflegt
civil law *n* Zivilrecht *nt*, bürgerliches Recht *nt*
civil liberties *n* (bürgerliche) Freiheitsrechte *pl*
civil rights *npl* Bürgerrechte *pl*
civil servant *n* (Staats)beamter *m*, (Staats)beamtin *f*
Civil Service *n* Beamtenschaft *f*
civil war *n* Bürgerkrieg *m*
civvies ['sɪvɪz] (*inf*) *npl* Zivilklamotten *pl*
cl *abbr* (= *centilitre*) cl
clad [klæd] *adj*: **~ (in)** gekleidet (in +*acc*)
claim [kleɪm] *vt* (*assert*) behaupten; (*responsibility*) übernehmen; (*credit*) in Anspruch nehmen; (*rights, inheritance*) Anspruch erheben auf +*acc*; (*expenses*) sich *dat* zurückerstatten lassen; (*compensation, damages*) verlangen ▷ *vi* (*for insurance*) Ansprüche geltend machen ▷ *n* (*assertion*) Behauptung *f*; (*for pension, wage rise, compensation*) Forderung *f*; (*right: to inheritance, land*) Anspruch *m*; (*for expenses*) Spesenabrechnung *f*; **(insurance) ~** (Versicherungs)anspruch *m*; **to put in a ~ for** beantragen
claimant ['kleɪmənt] *n* Antragsteller(in) *m(f)*
claim form *n* Antragsformular *nt*
clairvoyant [klɛə'vɔɪənt] *n* Hellseher(in) *m(f)*
clam [klæm] *n* Venusmuschel *f*
▸ **clam up** (*inf*) *vi* keinen Piep (mehr) sagen
clamber ['klæmbə^r] *vi* klettern
clammy ['klæmɪ] *adj* feucht
clamour, (*US*) **clamor** ['klæmə^r] *n* Lärm *m*; (*protest*) Protest *m*, Aufschrei *m* ▷ *vi*: **to ~ for** schreien nach
clamp [klæmp] *n* Schraubzwinge *f*, Klemme *f* ▷ *vt* (*two things*) zusammenklemmen; (*one thing on another*) klemmen; (*wheel*) krallen
▸ **clamp down on** *vt fus* rigoros vorgehen gegen
clampdown ['klæmpdaun] *n*: **~ (on)** hartes Durchgreifen *nt* (gegen)
clan [klæn] *n* Clan *m*
clandestine [klæn'dɛstɪn] *adj* geheim, Geheim-
clang [klæŋ] *vi* klappern; (*bell*) läuten ▷ *n* (*see vi*) Klappern *nt*; Läuten *nt*
clanger ['klæŋə^r] (*Brit: inf*) *n* Fauxpas *m*; **to drop a ~** ins Fettnäpfchen treten
clansman ['klænzmən] *n* (*irreg: like* **man**) Clanmitglied *nt*
clap [klæp] *vi* (Beifall) klatschen ▷ *vt*: **to ~ (one's hands)** (in die Hände) klatschen ▷ *n*: **a ~ of thunder** ein Donnerschlag *m*
clapping ['klæpɪŋ] *n* Beifall *m*
claptrap ['klæptræp] (*inf*) *n* Geschwafel *nt*
claret ['klærət] *n* roter Bordeaux(wein) *m*
clarification [klærɪfɪ'keɪʃən] *n* Klärung *f*
clarify ['klærɪfaɪ] *vt* klären
clarinet [klærɪ'nɛt] *n* Klarinette *f*
clarity ['klærɪtɪ] *n* Klarheit *f*
clash [klæʃ] *n* (*fight*) Zusammenstoß *m*; (*disagreement*) Streit *m*, Auseinandersetzung *f*; (*of beliefs, ideas, views*) Konflikt *m*; (*of colours, styles, personalities*) Unverträglichkeit *f*; (*of events, dates, appointments*) Überschneidung *f*; (*noise*) Klirren *nt* ▷ *vi* (*fight*) zusammenstoßen; (*disagree*) sich streiten, eine Auseinandersetzung haben; (*beliefs, ideas, views*) aufeinanderprallen; (*colours*) sich beißen; (*styles, personalities*) nicht zusammenpassen; (*two events, dates, appointments*) sich überschneiden; (*make noise*) klirrend aneinanderschlagen
clasp [klɑːsp] *n* Griff *m*; (*embrace*) Umklammerung *f*; (*of necklace, bag*) Verschluss *m* ▷ *vt* (er)greifen; (*embrace*) umklammern
class [klɑːs] *n* Klasse *f*; (*lesson*) (Unterrichts)stunde *f* ▷ *adj* (*struggle, distinction*) Klassen- ▷ *vt* einordnen, einstufen
class-conscious ['klɑːs'kɔnʃəs] *adj* klassenbewusst, standesbewusst
class-consciousness ['klɑːs'kɔnʃəsnɪs] *n* Klassenbewusstsein *nt*, Standesbewusstsein *nt*
classic ['klæsɪk] *adj* klassisch ▷ *n* Klassiker *m*; (*race*) *bedeutendes Pferderennen für dreijährige Pferde*;
classics *npl* (*Scol*) Altphilologie *f*
classical ['klæsɪkl] *adj* klassisch
classification [klæsɪfɪ'keɪʃən] *n* Klassifikation *f*; (*category*) Klasse *f*; (*system*) Einteilung *f*
classified ['klæsɪfaɪd] *adj* geheim
classified advertisement *n* Kleinanzeige *f*
classify ['klæsɪfaɪ] *vt* klassifizieren, (ein)ordnen
classless ['klɑːslɪs] *adj*: **~ society** klassenlose Gesellschaft *f*
classmate ['klɑːsmeɪt] *n* Klassenkamerad(in) *m(f)*
classroom ['klɑːsrum] *n* Klassenzimmer *nt*
classroom assistant *n* Assistenzlehrkraft *f*
classy ['klɑːsɪ] (*inf*) *adj* nobel, exklusiv; (*person*) todschick
clatter ['klætə^r] *n* Klappern *nt*; (*of hooves*) Trappeln *nt* ▷ *vi* (*see n*) klappern; trappeln
clause [klɔːz] *n* (*Law*) Klausel *f*; (*Ling*) Satz *m*
claustrophobia [klɔːstrə'fəubɪə] *n* Klaustrophobie *f*, Platzangst *f*
claustrophobic [klɔːstrə'fəubɪk] *adj* (*place, situation*) beengend; (*person*): **to be/feel ~** Platzangst haben/bekommen
claw [klɔː] *n* Kralle *f*; (*of lobster*) Schere *f*, Zange *f*
▸ **claw at** *vt fus* sich krallen an +*acc*

clay [kleɪ] *n* Ton *m*; (*soil*) Lehm *m*
clean [kli:n] *adj* sauber; (*fight*) fair; (*record, reputation*) einwandfrei; (*joke, story*) stubenrein, anständig; (*edge, fracture*) glatt ▷ *vt* sauber machen; (*car, hands, face etc*) waschen ▷ *adv*: **he ~ forgot** er hat es glatt(weg) vergessen; **to have a ~ driving licence, to have a ~ driving record** (*US*) keine Strafpunkte haben; **to ~ one's teeth** (*Brit*) sich *dat* die Zähne putzen; **the thief got ~ away** der Dieb konnte entkommen; **to come ~** (*inf*) auspacken
▸ **clean off** *vt* abwaschen, abwischen
▸ **clean out** *vt* gründlich sauber machen; (*inf: person*) ausnehmen
▸ **clean up** *vt* aufräumen; (*child*) sauber machen; (*fig*) für Ordnung sorgen in *+dat* ▷ *vi* aufräumen, sauber machen; (*inf: make profit*) absahnen
clean-cut ['kli:n'kʌt] *adj* gepflegt; (*situation*) klar
cleaner ['kli:nəʳ] *n* Raumpfleger(in) *m(f)*; (*woman*) Putzfrau *f*; (*substance*) Reinigungsmittel *nt*, Putzmittel *nt*
cleaner's ['kli:nəz] *n* (*also:* **dry cleaner's**) Reinigung *f*
cleaning ['kli:nɪŋ] *n* Putzen *nt*
cleaning lady *n* Putzfrau *f*, Reinemachefrau *f*
cleanliness ['klɛnlɪnɪs] *n* Sauberkeit *f*, Reinlichkeit *f*
cleanly ['kli:nlɪ] *adv* sauber
cleanse [klɛnz] *vt* (*purify*) läutern; (*face, cut*) reinigen
cleanser ['klɛnzəʳ] *n* (*for face*) Reinigungscreme *f*, Reinigungsmilch *f*
clean-shaven ['kli:n'ʃeɪvn] *adj* glatt rasiert
cleansing department ['klɛnzɪŋ-] (*Brit*) *n* ≈ Stadtreinigung *f*
clean sweep *n*: **to make a ~** (*Sport*) alle Preise einstecken
clean-up ['kli:nʌp] *n*: **to give sth a ~** etw gründlich sauber machen
clear [klɪəʳ] *adj* klar; (*footprint*) deutlich; (*photograph*) scharf; (*commitment*) eindeutig; (*glass, plastic*) durchsichtig; (*road, way, floor etc*) frei; (*conscience, skin*) rein ▷ *vt* (*room*) ausräumen; (*trees*) abholzen; (*weeds etc*) entfernen; (*slums etc, stock*) räumen; (*Law*) freisprechen; (*fence, wall*) überspringen; (*cheque*) verrechnen ▷ *vi* (*weather, sky*) aufklaren; (*fog, smoke*) sich auflösen; (*room etc*) sich leeren ▷ *adv*: **to be ~ of the ground** den Boden nicht berühren ▷ *n*: **to be in the ~** (*out of debt*) schuldenfrei sein; (*free of suspicion*) von jedem Verdacht frei sein; (*out of danger*) außer Gefahr sein; **~ profit** Reingewinn *m*; **I have a ~ day tomorrow** (*Brit*) ich habe morgen nichts vor; **to make o.s. ~** sich klar ausdrücken; **to make it ~ to sb that ...** es jdm (unmissverständlich) klarmachen, dass ...; **to ~ the table** den Tisch abräumen; **to ~ a space (for sth)** (für etw) Platz schaffen; **to ~ one's throat** sich räuspern; **to ~ a profit** einen Gewinn machen; **to keep ~ of sb** jdm aus dem Weg gehen; **to keep ~ of sth** etw meiden; **to keep ~ of trouble** allem Ärger aus dem Weg gehen
▸ **clear off** (*inf*) *vi* abhauen, verschwinden
▸ **clear up** *vt* aufräumen; (*mystery*) aufklären; (*problem*) lösen ▷ *vi* (*bad weather*) sich aufklären; (*illness*) sich bessern
clearance ['klɪərəns] *n* (*of slums*) Räumung *f*; (*of trees*) Abholzung *f*; (*permission*) Genehmigung *f*; (*free space*) lichte Höhe *f*
clearance sale *n* Räumungsverkauf *m*
clear-cut ['klɪə'kʌt] *adj* klar
clearing ['klɪərɪŋ] *n* Lichtung *f*; (*Brit: Banking*) Clearing *nt*
clearing bank (*Brit*) *n* Clearingbank *f*
clearing house *n* (*Comm*) Clearingstelle *f*
clearly ['klɪəlɪ] *adv* klar; (*obviously*) eindeutig
clearway ['klɪəweɪ] (*Brit*) *n* Straße *f* mit Halteverbot
cleavage ['kli:vɪdʒ] *n* (*of woman's breasts*) Dekolleté *nt*
cleaver ['kli:vəʳ] *n* Hackbeil *nt*
clef [klɛf] *n* (Noten)schlüssel *m*
cleft [klɛft] *n* Spalte *f*
cleft palate *n* (*Med*) Gaumenspalte *f*
clemency ['klɛmənsɪ] *n* Milde *f*
clement ['klɛmənt] *adj* mild
clench [klɛntʃ] *vt* (*fist*) ballen; (*teeth*) zusammenbeißen
clergy ['klə:dʒɪ] *n* Klerus *m*, Geistlichkeit *f*
clergyman ['klə:dʒɪmən] (*irreg: like* **man**) *n* Geistliche(r) *m*
clerical ['klɛrɪkl] *adj* (*job, worker*) Büro-; (*error*) Schreib-; (*Rel*) geistlich
clerk [klɑ:k, (*US*) klə:rk] *n* (*Brit*) Büroangestellte(r) *f(m)*; (*US: sales person*) Verkäufer(in) *m(f)*
Clerk of Court *n* Protokollführer(in) *m(f)*
clever ['klɛvəʳ] *adj* klug; (*deft, crafty*) schlau, clever (*inf*); (*device, arrangement*) raffiniert
cleverly ['klɛvəlɪ] *adv* geschickt
clew [klu:] (*US*) *n* = **clue**
cliché ['kli:ʃeɪ] *n* Klischee *nt*
click [klɪk] *vi* klicken ▷ *vt*: **to ~ one's tongue** mit der Zunge schnalzen; **to ~ one's heels** die Hacken zusammenschlagen
client ['klaɪənt] *n* Kunde *m*, Kundin *f*; (*of bank, lawyer*) Klient(in) *m(f)*; (*of restaurant*) Gast *m*
clientele [kli:ɑ̃:n'tɛl] *n* Kundschaft *f*
cliff [klɪf] *n* Kliff *nt*
cliffhanger ['klɪfhæŋəʳ] *n spannungsgeladene Szene am Ende einer Filmepisode*, Cliffhanger *m*
climactic [klaɪ'mæktɪk] *adj*: **~ point** Höhepunkt *m*
climate ['klaɪmɪt] *n* Klima *nt*
climate conference *n* (*Pol*) Klimakonferenz *f*
climax ['klaɪmæks] *n* (*sexual*) Höhepunkt *m*
climb [klaɪm] *vi* klettern; (*plane, sun, prices, shares*) steigen ▷ *vt* (*stairs, ladder*) hochsteigen, hinaufsteigen; (*tree*) klettern auf *+acc*; (*hill*) steigen auf *+acc* ▷ *n* Aufstieg *m*; (*of prices etc*) Anstieg *m*; **to ~ over a wall/into a car** über eine Mauer/in ein Auto steigen *or* klettern

▸ **climb down** (*Brit*) *vi* (*fig*) nachgeben
climb-down ['klaɪmdaun] *n* Nachgeben *nt*, Rückzieher *m* (*inf*)
climber ['klaɪmə^r] *n* Bergsteiger(in) *m(f)*; (*plant*) Kletterpflanze *f*
climbing ['klaɪmɪŋ] *n* Bergsteigen *nt*
clinch [klɪntʃ] *vt* (*deal*) perfekt machen; (*argument*) zum Abschluss bringen
clincher ['klɪntʃə^r] *n* ausschlaggebender Faktor *m*
cling [klɪŋ] (*pt, pp* **clung**) *vi*: **to ~ to** (*mother, support*) sich festklammern an *+dat*; (*idea, belief*) festhalten an *+dat*; (*subj: clothes, dress*) sich anschmiegen *+dat*
clingfilm ['klɪŋfɪlm] *n*, **clingwrap** ['klɪŋræp] *n* (*US*) Frischhaltefolie *f*
clinic ['klɪnɪk] *n* Klinik *f*; (*session*) Sprechstunde *f*; (: *Sport*) Trainingsstunde *f*
clinical ['klɪnɪkl] *adj* klinisch; (*fig*) nüchtern, kühl; (: *building, room*) steril
clink [klɪŋk] *vi* klirren
clip [klɪp] *n* (*also*: **paper clip**) Büroklammer *f*; (*Brit*: *also*: **bulldog clip**) Klammer *f*; (*holding wire, hose etc*) Klemme *f*; (*for hair*) Spange *f*; (*TV, Cine*) Ausschnitt *m* ▹ *vt* festklemmen; (*also*: **clip together**) zusammenheften; (*cut*) schneiden
clippers ['klɪpəz] *npl* (*for gardening*) Schere *f*; (*also*: **nail clippers**) Nagelzange *f*
clipping ['klɪpɪŋ] *n* (*from newspaper*) Ausschnitt *m*
clique [kli:k] *n* Clique *f*, Gruppe *f*
clitoris ['klɪtərɪs] *n* Klitoris *f*
cloak [kləuk] *n* Umhang *m* ▹ *vt* (*fig*) hüllen
cloakroom ['kləukrum] *n* Garderobe *f*; (*Brit*: WC) Toilette *f*
clobber ['klɔbə^r] (*inf*) *n* Klamotten *pl* ▹ *vt* (*hit*) hauen, schlagen; (*defeat*) in die Pfanne hauen
clock [klɔk] *n* Uhr *f*; **round the ~** rund um die Uhr; **30,000 on the ~** (*Brit*: *Aut*) ein Tachostand von 30.000; **to work against the ~** gegen die Uhr arbeiten
▸ **clock in** (*Brit*) *vi* (den Arbeitsbeginn) stempeln *or* stechen
▸ **clock off** (*Brit*) *vi* (das Arbeitsende) stempeln *or* stechen
▸ **clock on** (*Brit*) *vi* = **clock in**
▸ **clock out** (*Brit*) *vi* = **clock off**
▸ **clock up** *vt* (*miles*) fahren; (*hours*) arbeiten
clockwise ['klɔkwaɪz] *adv* im Uhrzeigersinn
clockwork ['klɔkwə:k] *n* Uhrwerk *nt* ▹ *adj* aufziehbar, zum Aufziehen; **like ~** wie am Schnürchen
clog [klɔg] *n* Clog *m*; (*wooden*) Holzschuh *m* ▹ *vt* verstopfen ▹ *vi* (*also*: **clog up**) verstopfen
cloister ['klɔɪstə^r] *n* Kreuzgang *m*
clone [kləun] *n* Klon *m*
close[1] [kləus] *adj* (*writing, friend, contact*) eng; (*texture*) dicht, fest; (*relative*) nahe; (*examination*) genau, gründlich; (*watch*) streng, scharf; (*contest*) knapp; (*weather*) schwül; (*room*) stickig ▹ *adv* nahe; **~ (to)** nahe (*+gen*); **~ to** in der Nähe *+gen*; **~ by, ~ at hand** in der Nähe; **how ~ is Edinburgh to Glasgow?** wie weit ist Edinburgh von Glasgow entfernt?; **a ~ friend** ein guter *or* enger Freund; **to have a ~ shave** (*fig*) gerade noch davonkommen; **at ~ quarters** aus der Nähe
close[2] [kləuz] *vt* schließen, zumachen; (*sale, deal, case*) abschließen; (*speech*) schließen, beenden ▹ *vi* schließen, zumachen; (*door, lid*) sich schließen, zugehen; (*end*) aufhören ▹ *n* Ende *nt*, Schlus *m*; **to bring sth to a ~** etw beenden
▸ **close down** *vi* (*factory*) stillgelegt werden; (*magazine etc*) eingestellt werden
▸ **close in** *vi* (*night*) hereinbrechen; (*fog*) sich verdichten; **to ~ in on sb/sth** jdm/etw auf den Leib rücken; **the days are closing in** die Tage werden kürzer
▸ **close off** *vt* (*area*) abriegeln; (*road*) sperren
closed [kləuzd] *adj* geschlossen; (*road*) gesperrt
closed-circuit television *n* Fernsehüberwachungsanlage *f*
closed shop *n* Betrieb *m* mit Gewerkschaftszwang
close-knit ['kləus'nɪt] *adj* eng zusammengewachsen
closely ['kləuslɪ] *adv* (*examine, watch*) genau; (*connected*) eng; (*related*) nah(e); (*resemble*) sehr; **we are ~ related** wir sind nah verwandt; **a ~ guarded secret** ein streng gehütetes Geheimnis
close season ['kləus-] *n* Schonzeit *f*; (*Sport*) Sommerpause *f*
closet ['klɔzɪt] *n* Wandschrank *m*
close-up ['kləusʌp] *n* Nahaufnahme *f*
closing ['kləuzɪŋ] *adj* (*stages*) Schluss-; (*remarks*) abschließend
closing price *n* (*Stock Exchange*) Schlusskurs *m*, Schlussnotierung *f*
closing time (*Brit*) *n* (*in pub*) Polizeistunde *f*, Sperrstunde *f*
closure ['kləuʒə^r] *n* (*of factory*) Stilllegung *f*; (*of magazine*) Einstellung *f*; (*of road*) Sperrung *f*; (*of border*) Schließung *f*
clot [klɔt] *n* (*blood clot*) (Blut)gerinnsel *nt*; (*inf: idiot*) Trottel *m* ▹ *vi* gerinnen; (*external bleeding*) zum Stillstand kommen
cloth [klɔθ] *n* (*material*) Stoff *m*, Tuch *nt*; (*rag*) Lappen *m*; (*Brit*: *also*: **teacloth**) (Spül)tuch *nt*; (*also*: **tablecloth**) Tischtuch *nt*, Tischdecke *f*
clothe [kləuð] *vt* anziehen, kleiden
clothes [kləuðz] *npl* Kleidung *f*, Kleider *pl*; **to put one's ~ on** sich anziehen; **to take one's ~ off** sich ausziehen
clothes brush *n* Kleiderbürste *f*
clothesline ['kləuðzlaɪn] *n* Wäscheleine *f*
clothes peg, (*US*) **clothes pin** *n* Wäscheklammer *f*
clothing ['kləuðɪŋ] *n* = **clothes**
clotted cream ['klɔtɪd-] (*Brit*) *n* *Sahne aus erhitzter Milch*
cloud [klaud] *n* Wolke *f* ▹ *vt* trüben; **every ~ has a silver lining** (*proverb*) auf Regen folgt Sonnenschein; **to ~ the issue** es unnötig kompliziert machen; (*deliberately*) die

Angelegenheit verschleiern
▸ **cloud over** *vi* (*sky*) sich bewölken, sich bedecken; (*face, eyes*) sich verfinstern
cloudburst ['klaudbə:st] *n* Wolkenbruch *m*
cloud-cuckoo-land [klaud'kuku:lænd] (*Brit*) *n* Wolkenkuckucksheim *nt*
cloudy ['klaudɪ] *adj* wolkig, bewölkt; (*liquid*) trüb
clout [klaut] *vt* schlagen, hauen ▹ *n* (*fig*) Schlagkraft *f*
clove [kləuv] *n* Gewürznelke *f*; **~ of garlic** Knoblauchzehe *f*
clover ['kləuvəʳ] *n* Klee *m*
cloverleaf ['kləuvəli:f] *n* Kleeblatt *nt*
clown [klaun] *n* Clown *m* ▹ *vi* (*also*: **clown about, clown around**) herumblödeln, herumkaspern
cloying ['klɔɪɪŋ] *adj* süßlich
club [klʌb] *n* Klub *m*, Verein *m*; (*weapon*) Keule *f*, Knüppel *m*; (*also*: **golf club**: *object*) Golfschläger *m* ▹ *vt* knüppeln ▹ *vi*: **to ~ together** zusammenlegen; **clubs** *npl* (*Cards*) Kreuz *nt*
club car (*US*) *n* Speisewagen *m*
club class *n* Klubklasse *f*, Businessklasse *f*
clubhouse ['klʌbhaus] *n* Klubhaus *nt*
club soda (*US*) *n* (*soda water*) Sodawasser *nt*
cluck [klʌk] *vi* glucken
clue [klu:] *n* Hinweis *m*, Anhaltspunkt *m*; (*in crossword*) Frage *f*; **I haven't a ~** ich habe keine Ahnung
clued-up ['klu:dʌp], (*US: inf*) **clued in** *adj*: **to be ~ on sth** über etw *acc* im Bilde sein
clueless ['klu:lɪs] *adj* ahnungslos, unbedarft
clump [klʌmp] *n* Gruppe *f*
clumsy ['klʌmzɪ] *adj* ungeschickt; (*object*) unförmig; (*effort, attempt*) plump
clung [klʌŋ] *pt, pp of* **cling**
cluster ['klʌstəʳ] *n* Gruppe *f* ▹ *vi* (*people*) sich scharen; (*houses*) sich drängen
clutch [klʌtʃ] *n* Griff *m*; (*Aut*) Kupplung *f* ▹ *vt* (*purse, hand*) umklammern; (*stick*) sich festklammern an *+dat* ▹ *vi*: **to ~ at** sich klammern an *+acc*
clutter ['klʌtəʳ] *vt* (*also*: **clutter up**: *room*) vollstopfen; (*: table*) vollstellen ▹ *n* Kram *m* (*inf*)
cm *abbr* (*= centimetre*) cm
CNAA (*Brit*) *n abbr* (*= Council for National Academic Awards*) *Zentralstelle zur Vergabe von Qualifikationsnachweisen*
CND (*Brit*) *n abbr* (*= Campaign for Nuclear Disarmament*) *Organisation für atomare Abrüstung*
CO *n abbr* = **commanding officer**; (*Brit: = Commonwealth Office*) *Regierungsstelle für Angelegenheiten des Commonwealth* ▹ *abbr* (*US: Post*) *= Colorado*
Co. *abbr* = **company; county**
c/o *abbr* (*= care of*) bei, c/o
coach [kəutʃ] *n* (Reise)bus *m*; (*horse-drawn*) Kutsche *f*; (*of train*) Wagen *m*; (*Sport*) Trainer *m*; (*Scol*) Nachhilfelehrer(in) *m(f)* ▹ *vt* trainieren; (*student*) Nachhilfeunterricht geben *+dat*
coach trip *n* Busfahrt *f*
coagulate [kəu'ægjuleɪt] *vi* (*blood*) gerinnen; (*paint etc*) eindicken ▹ *vt* (*blood*) gerinnen lassen; (*paint*) dick werden lassen
coal [kəul] *n* Kohle *f*
coalface ['kəulfeɪs] *n* Streb *m*
coalfield ['kəulfi:ld] *n* Kohlenrevier *nt*
coalition [kəuə'lɪʃən] *n* (*Pol*) Koalition *f*; (*of pressure groups etc*) Zusammenschluss *m*
coalman ['kəulmən] (*irreg: like* **man**) *n* Kohlenhändler *m*
coal merchant *n* = **coalman**
coal mine *n* Kohlenbergwerk *nt*, Zeche *f*
coal miner *n* Bergmann *m*, Kumpel *m* (*inf*)
coal mining *n* (Kohlen)bergbau *m*
coarse [kɔ:s] *adj* (*texture*) grob; (*vulgar*) gewöhnlich, derb; (*salt, sand etc*) grobkörnig
coast [kəust] *n* Küste *f* ▹ *vi* (im Leerlauf) fahren
coastal ['kəustl] *adj* Küsten-
coaster ['kəustəʳ] *n* (*Naut*) Küstenfahrzeug *nt*; (*for glass*) Untersetzer *m*
coastguard ['kəustgɑ:d] *n* (*officer*) Küstenwächter *m*; (*service*) Küstenwacht *f*
coastline ['kəustlaɪn] *n* Küste *f*
coat [kəut] *n* Mantel *m*; (*of animal*) Fell *nt*; (*layer*) Schicht *f*; (*: of paint*) Anstrich *m* ▹ *vt* überziehen
coat hanger *n* Kleiderbügel *m*
coating ['kəutɪŋ] *n* (*of chocolate etc*) Überzug *m*; (*of dust etc*) Schicht *f*
coat of arms *n* Wappen *nt*
coauthor ['kəu'ɔ:θəʳ] *n* Mitautor(in) *m(f)*, Mitverfasser(in) *m(f)*
coax [kəuks] *vt* (*person*) überreden
cob [kɔb] *n see* **corn**
cobbler ['kɔbləʳ] *n* Schuster *m*
cobbles ['kɔblz] *npl* Kopfsteinpflaster *nt*
cobblestones ['kɔblstəunz] *npl* = **cobbles**
COBOL ['kəubɔl] *n* COBOL *nt*
cobra ['kəubrə] *n* Kobra *f*
cobweb ['kɔbwɛb] *n* Spinnennetz *nt*
cocaine [kə'keɪn] *n* Kokain *nt*
cock [kɔk] *n* Hahn *m*; (*male bird*) Männchen *nt* ▹ *vt* (*gun*) entsichern; **to ~ one's ears** (*fig*) die Ohren spitzen
cock-a-hoop [kɔkə'hu:p] *adj* ganz aus dem Häuschen
cockerel ['kɔkərl] *n* junger Hahn *m*
cock-eyed ['kɔkaɪd] *adj* (*fig*) verrückt, widersinnig
cockle ['kɔkl] *n* Herzmuschel *f*
cockney ['kɔknɪ] *n* Cockney *m*, echter Londoner *m*; (*Ling*) Cockney *nt*
cockpit ['kɔkpɪt] *n* Cockpit *nt*
cockroach ['kɔkrəutʃ] *n* Küchenschabe *f*, Kakerlak *m*
cocktail ['kɔkteɪl] *n* Cocktail *m*; **fruit ~** Obstsalat *m*; **prawn ~** Krabbencocktail *m*
cocktail cabinet *n* Hausbar *f*
cocktail party *n* Cocktailparty *f*
cocktail shaker [-'ʃeɪkəʳ] *n* Mixbecher *m*
cock-up ['kɔkʌp] (*inf!*) *n* Schlamassel *m*
cocky ['kɔkɪ] *adj* großspurig
cocoa ['kəukəu] *n* Kakao *m*
coconut ['kəukənʌt] *n* Kokosnuss *f*

cocoon [kə'ku:n] *n* Puppe *f*, Kokon *m*; (*fig*) schützende Umgebung *f*
COD *abbr* (*Brit*) = **cash on delivery**; (*US*) = **collect on delivery**
cod [kɔd] *n* Kabeljau *m*
code [kəud] *n* (*cipher*) Chiffre *f*; (*also*: **dialling code**) Vorwahl *f*; (*also*: **post code**) Postleitzahl *f*; **~ of behaviour** Sittenkodex *m*; **~ of practice** Verfahrensregeln *pl*
codeine ['kəudi:n] *n* Codein *nt*
codger ['kɔdʒəʳ] (*inf*) *n*: **old ~** komischer Kauz *m*
codicil ['kɔdɪsɪl] *n* (*Law*) Kodizill *nt*
codify ['kəudɪfaɪ] *vt* kodifizieren
cod-liver oil ['kɔdlɪvə-] *n* Lebertran *m*
co-driver ['kəu'draɪvəʳ] *n* Beifahrer(in) *m(f)*
co-ed ['kəu'ɛd] (*Scol*) *adj abbr* = **coeducational** ▷ *n abbr* (*US: female pupil/student*) *Schülerin/Studentin an einer gemischten Schule/Universität*; (*Brit: school*) gemischte Schule *f*
coeducational ['kəuɛdju'keɪʃənl] *adj* (*school*) Koedukations-, gemischt
coerce [kəu'ə:s] *vt* zwingen
coercion [kəu'ə:ʃən] *n* Zwang *m*
coexistence ['kəuɪg'zɪstəns] *n* Koexistenz *f*
C of C *n abbr* = **chamber of commerce**
C of E *abbr* = **Church of England**
coffee ['kɔfɪ] *n* Kaffee *m*; **black ~** schwarzer Kaffee *m*; **white ~** Kaffee mit Milch; **~ with cream** Kaffee mit Sahne
coffee bar (*Brit*) *n* Café *nt*
coffee bean *n* Kaffeebohne *f*
coffee break *n* Kaffeepause *f*
coffee cake (*US*) *n* Kuchen *m* zum Kaffee
coffee cup *n* Kaffeetasse *f*
coffeepot ['kɔfɪpɔt] *n* Kaffeekanne *f*
coffee table *n* Couchtisch *m*
coffin ['kɔfɪn] *n* Sarg *m*
C of I *abbr* (*= Church of Ireland*) *anglikanische Kirche Irlands*
C of S *abbr* (*= Church of Scotland*) *presbyterianische Kirche in Schottland*
cog [kɔg] *n* (*wheel*) Zahnrad *nt*; (*tooth*) Zahn *m*
cogent ['kəudʒənt] *adj* stichhaltig, zwingend
cognac ['kɔnjæk] *n* Kognak *m*
cogwheel ['kɔgwi:l] *n* Zahnrad *nt*
cohabit [kəu'hæbɪt] *vi* (*formal*) in eheähnlicher Gemeinschaft leben; **to ~ (with sb)** (mit jdm) zusammenleben
coherent [kəu'hɪərənt] *adj* (*speech*) zusammenhängend; (*answer, theory*) schlüssig; (*person*) bei klarem Verstand
cohesion [kəu'hi:ʒən] *n* Geschlossenheit *f*
cohesive [kə'hi:sɪv] *adj* geschlossen
coil [kɔɪl] *n* Rolle *f*; (*one loop*) Windung *f*; (*of smoke*) Kringel *m*; (*Aut, Elec*) Spule *f*; (*contraceptive*) Spirale *f* ▷ *vt* aufrollen, aufwickeln
coin [kɔɪn] *n* Münze *f* ▷ *vt* prägen
coinage ['kɔɪnɪdʒ] *n* Münzen *pl*; (*Ling*) Prägung *f*
coin box (*Brit*) *n* Münzfernsprecher *m*
coincide [kəuɪn'saɪd] *vi* (*events*) zusammenfallen; (*ideas, views*) übereinstimmen
coincidence [kəu'ɪnsɪdəns] *n* Zufall *m*
coin-operated ['kɔɪn'ɔpəreɪtɪd] *adj* Münz-
Coke® [kəuk] *n* Coca-Cola® *nt or f*, Coke® *nt*
coke [kəuk] *n* Koks *m*
Col. *abbr* = **colonel**
COLA (*US*) *n abbr* (*= cost of living adjustment*) *Anpassung der Löhne und Gehälter an steigende Lebenshaltungskosten*
colander ['kɔləndəʳ] *n* Durchschlag *m*
cold [kəuld] *adj* kalt; (*unemotional*) kalt, kühl ▷ *n* Kälte *f*; (*Med*) Erkältung *f*; **it's ~** es ist kalt; **to be/feel ~** (*person*) frieren; (*object*) kalt sein; **in ~ blood** kaltblütig; **to have ~ feet** (*fig*) kalte Füße bekommen; **to give sb the ~ shoulder** jdm die kalte Schulter zeigen; **to catch ~, to catch a ~** sich erkälten
cold-blooded ['kəuld'blʌdɪd] *adj* kaltblütig
cold calling *n* (*Comm: on phone*) unaufgeforderte Telefonwerbung; (*: visit*) unaufgeforderter Vertreterbesuch
cold cream *n* (halbfette) Feuchtigkeitscreme *f*
coldly ['kəuldlɪ] *adv* kalt, kühl
cold-shoulder [kəuld'ʃəuldəʳ] *vt* die kalte Schulter zeigen *+dat*
cold sore *n* Bläschenausschlag *m*
cold sweat *n*: **to come out in a ~ (about sth)** (wegen etw) in kalten Schweiß ausbrechen
cold turkey *n*: **to do ~** Totalentzug machen
Cold War *n*: **the ~** der Kalte Krieg
coleslaw ['kəulslɔ:] *n* Krautsalat *m*
colic ['kɔlɪk] *n* Kolik *f*
colicky ['kɔlɪkɪ] *adj*: **to be ~** Kolik *f or* Leibschmerzen *pl* haben
collaborate [kə'læbəreɪt] *vi* zusammenarbeiten; (*with enemy*) kollaborieren
collaboration [kəlæbə'reɪʃən] *n* (*see vb*) Zusammenarbeit *f*; Kollaboration *f*
collaborator [kə'læbəreɪtəʳ] *n* (*see vb*) Mitarbeiter(in) *m(f)*; Kollaborateur(in) *m(f)*
collage [kɔ'lɑ:ʒ] *n* Collage *f*
collagen ['kɔlədʒən] *n* Kollagen *nt*
collapse [kə'læps] *vi* zusammenbrechen; (*building*) einstürzen; (*plans*) scheitern; (*government*) stürzen ▷ *n* (*see vb*) Zusammenbruch *m*; Einsturz *m*; Scheitern *nt*; Sturz *m*
collapsible [kə'læpsəbl] *adj* Klapp-, zusammenklappbar
collar ['kɔləʳ] *n* Kragen *m*; (*of dog, cat*) Halsband *nt*; (*Tech*) Bund *m* ▷ *vt* (*inf*) schnappen
collarbone ['kɔləbəun] *n* Schlüsselbein *nt*
collate [kɔ'leɪt] *vt* vergleichen
collateral [kə'lætərl] *n* (*Comm*) (zusätzliche) Sicherheit *f*
collateral damage *n* (*Mil*) Schäden *pl* in Wohngebieten; (*: casualties*) Opfer *pl* unter der Zivilbevölkerung
collation [kə'leɪʃən] *n* Vergleich *m*; (*Culin*): **a cold ~** ein kalter Imbiss *m*
colleague ['kɔli:g] *n* Kollege *m*, Kollegin *f*
collect [kə'lɛkt] *vt* sammeln; (*mail: Brit: fetch*) abholen; (*debts*) eintreiben; (*taxes*) einziehen

▷ *vi* sich ansammeln ▷ *adv* (*US: Tel*): **to call ~** ein R-Gespräch führen; **to ~ one's thoughts** seine Gedanken ordnen, sich sammeln; **~ on delivery** (*US: Comm*) per Nachnahme
collected [kə'lɛktɪd] *adj*: **~ works** gesammelte Werke *pl*
collection [kə'lɛkʃən] *n* Sammlung *f*; (*from place, person, of mail*) Abholung *f*; (*in church*) Kollekte *f*
collective [kə'lɛktɪv] *adj* kollektiv, gemeinsam ▷ *n* Kollektiv *nt*; **~ farm** landwirtschaftliche Produktionsgenossenschaft *f*
collective bargaining *n* Tarifverhandlungen *pl*
collector [kə'lɛktəʳ] *n* Sammler(in) *m(f)*; (*of taxes etc*) Einnehmer(in) *m(f)*; (*of rent, cash*) Kassierer(in) *m(f)*; **~'s item** *or* **piece** Sammlerstück *nt*, Liebhaberstück *nt*
college ['kɔlɪdʒ] *n* College *nt*; (*of agriculture, technology*) Fachhochschule *f*; **to go to ~** studieren; **~ of education** pädagogische Hochschule *f*
collide [kə'laɪd] *vi*: **to ~ (with)** zusammenstoßen (mit); (*fig: clash*) eine heftige Auseinandersetzung haben (mit)
collie ['kɔlɪ] *n* Collie *m*
colliery ['kɔlɪərɪ] (*Brit*) *n* (Kohlen)bergwerk *nt*, Zeche *f*
collision [kə'lɪʒən] *n* Zusammenstoß *m*; **to be on a ~ course** (*also fig*) auf Kollisionskurs sein
collision damage waiver *n* (*Insurance*) *Verzicht auf Haftungsbeschränkung bei Unfällen mit Mietwagen*
colloquial [kə'ləukwɪəl] *adj* umgangssprachlich
collusion [kə'lu:ʒən] *n* (geheime) Absprache *f*; **to be in ~ with** gemeinsame Sache machen mit
Colo. (*US*) *abbr* (*Post*) = *Colorado*
Cologne [kə'ləun] *n* Köln *nt*
cologne [kə'ləun] *n* (*also:* **eau de cologne**) Kölnischwasser *nt*, Eau de Cologne *nt*
Colombia [kə'lɔmbɪə] *n* Kolumbien *nt*
Colombian [kə'lɔmbɪən] *adj* kolumbianisch ▷ *n* Kolumbianer(in) *m(f)*
colon ['kəulən] *n* Doppelpunkt *m*; (*Anat*) Dickdarm *m*
colonel ['kə:nl] *n* Oberst *m*
colonial [kə'ləunɪəl] *adj* Kolonial-
colonize ['kɔlənaɪz] *vt* kolonisieren
colony ['kɔlənɪ] *n* Kolonie *f*
color *etc* ['kʌləʳ] (*US*) = **colour** *etc*
Colorado beetle [kɔlə'rɑ:dəu-] *n* Kartoffelkäfer *m*
colossal [kə'lɔsl] *adj* riesig, kolossal
colour, (*US*) **color** ['kʌləʳ] *n* Farbe *f*; (*skin colour*) Hautfarbe *f*; (*of spectacle etc*) Atmosphäre *f* ▷ *vt* bemalen; (*with crayons*) ausmalen; (*dye*) färben; (*fig*) beeinflussen ▷ *vi* (*blush*) erröten, rot werden ▷ *cpd* Farb-; **colours** *npl* (*of party, club etc*) Farben *pl*; **in ~** (*film*) in Farbe; (*illustrations*) bunt
▸ **colour in** *vt* ausmalen
colour bar *n* Rassenschranke *f*
colour-blind ['kʌləblaɪnd] *adj* farbenblind
coloured ['kʌləd] *adj* farbig; (*photo*) Farb-; (*illustration etc*) bunt
colour film *n* Farbfilm *m*
colourful ['kʌləful] *adj* bunt; (*account, story*) farbig, anschaulich; (*personality*) schillernd
colouring ['kʌlərɪŋ] *n* Gesichtsfarbe *f*, Teint *m*; (*in food*) Farbstoff *m*
colour scheme *n* Farbzusammenstellung *f*
colour supplement (*Brit*) *n* Farbbeilage *f*, Magazin *nt*
colour television *n* Farbfernsehen *nt*; (*set*) Farbfernseher *m*
colt [kəult] *n* Hengstfohlen *nt*
column ['kɔləm] *n* Säule *f*; (*of people*) Kolonne *f*; (*of print*) Spalte *f*; (*gossip/sports column*) Kolumne *f*; **the editorial ~** der Leitartikel
columnist ['kɔləmnɪst] *n* Kolumnist(in) *m(f)*
coma ['kəumə] *n* Koma *nt*; **to be in a ~** im Koma liegen
comb [kəum] *n* Kamm *m* ▷ *vt* kämmen; (*area*) durchkämmen
combat ['kɔmbæt] *n* Kampf *m* ▷ *vt* bekämpfen
combination [kɔmbɪ'neɪʃən] *n* Kombination *f*
combination lock *n* Kombinationsschloss *nt*
combine [*vti* kəm'baɪn, *n* 'kɔmbaɪn] *vt* verbinden ▷ *vi* sich zusammenschließen; (*Chem*) sich verbinden ▷ *n* Konzern *m*; (*Agr*) = **combine harvester**; **~d effort** vereintes Unternehmen
combine harvester *n* Mähdrescher *m*
combo ['kɔmbəu] *n* Combo *f*
combustible [kəm'bʌstɪbl] *adj* brennbar
combustion [kəm'bʌstʃən] *n* Verbrennung *f*

KEYWORD

come [kʌm] (*pt* **came**, *pp* **come**) *vi* **1** (*movement towards*) kommen; **come with me** kommen Sie mit mir; **to come running** angelaufen kommen; **coming!** ich komme!
2 (*arrive*) kommen; **they came to a river** sie kamen an einen Fluss; **to come home** nach Hause kommen
3 (*reach*): **to come to** kommen an *+acc*; **her hair came to her waist** ihr Haar reichte ihr bis zur Hüfte; **to come to a decision** zu einer Entscheidung kommen
4 (*occur*): **an idea came to me** mir kam eine Idee
5 (*be, become*) werden; **I've come to like him** mittlerweile mag ich ihn; **if it comes to it** wenn es darauf ankommt
▸ **come about** *vi* geschehen
▸ **come across** *vt fus* (*find: person, thing*) stoßen auf *+acc*
▷ *vi*: **to come across well/badly** (*idea etc*) gut/schlecht ankommen; (*meaning*) gut/schlecht verstanden werden
▸ **come along** *vi* (*arrive*) daherkommen; (*make progress*) vorankommen; **come along!** komm schon!

▸ **come apart** *vi* (*break in pieces*) auseinandergehen
▸ **come away** *vi* (*leave*) weggehen; (*become detached*) abgehen
▸ **come back** *vi* (*return*) zurückkommen; **to come back into fashion** wieder in Mode kommen
▸ **come by** *vt fus* (*acquire*) kommen zu
▸ **come down** *vi* (*price*) sinken, fallen; (*building: be demolished*) abgerissen werden; (*tree: during storm*) umstürzen
▸ **come forward** *vi* (*volunteer*) sich melden
▸ **come from** *vt fus* kommen von, stammen aus; (*person*) kommen aus
▸ **come in** *vi* (*enter*) hereinkommen; (*report, news*) eintreffen; (*on deal etc*) sich beteiligen; **come in!** herein!
▸ **come in for** *vt fus* (*criticism etc*) einstecken müssen
▸ **come into** *vt fus* (*inherit: money*) erben; **to come into fashion** in Mode kommen; **money doesn't come into it** Geld hat nichts damit zu tun
▸ **come off** *vi* (*become detached: button, handle*) sich lösen; (*succeed: attempt, plan*) klappen ▷ *vt fus* (*inf*): **come off it!** mach mal halblang!
▸ **come on** *vi* (*pupil, work, project*) vorankommen; (*lights etc*) angehen; **come on!** (*hurry up*) mach schon!; (*encouragement*) los!
▸ **come out** *vi* herauskommen; (*stain*) herausgehen; **to come out (on strike)** in den Streik treten
▸ **come over** *vt fus*: **I don't know what's come over him!** ich weiß nicht, was in ihn gefahren ist
▸ **come round** *vi* (*after faint, operation*) wieder zu sich kommen; (*visit*) vorbeikommen; (*agree*) zustimmen
▸ **come through** *vi* (*survive*) durchkommen; (*telephone call*) (durch)kommen ▷ *vt fus* (*illness etc*) überstehen
▸ **come to** *vi* (*regain consciousness*) wieder zu sich kommen ▷ *vt fus* (*add up to*): **how much does it come to?** was macht das zusammen?
▸ **come under** *vt fus* (*heading*) kommen unter +*acc*; (*criticism, pressure, attack*) geraten unter +*acc*
▸ **come up** *vi* (*approach*) herankommen; (*sun*) aufgehen; (*problem*) auftauchen; (*event*) bevorstehen; (*in conversation*) genannt werden; **something's come up** etwas ist dazwischengekommen
▸ **come up against** *vt fus* (*resistance, difficulties*) stoßen auf +*acc*
▸ **come upon** *vt fus* (*find*) stoßen auf +*acc*
▸ **come up to** *vt fus*: **the film didn't come up to our expectations** der Film entsprach nicht unseren Erwartungen; **it's coming up to 10 o'clock** es ist gleich 10 Uhr
▸ **come up with** *vt fus* (*idea*) aufwarten mit; (*money*) aufbringen

comeback ['kʌmbæk] *n* (*of film star etc*) Comeback *nt*; (*reaction, response*) Reaktion *f*
comedian [kə'mi:dɪən] *n* Komiker *m*
comedienne [kəmi:dɪ'ɛn] *n* Komikerin *f*
comedown ['kʌmdaun] (*inf*) *n* Enttäuschung *f*; (*professional*) Abstieg *m*
comedy ['kɔmɪdɪ] *n* Komödie *f*; (*humour*) Witz *m*
comet ['kɔmɪt] *n* Komet *m*
comeuppance [kʌm'ʌpəns] *n*: **to get one's ~** die Quittung bekommen
comfort ['kʌmfət] *n* (*physical*) Behaglichkeit *f*; (*material*) Komfort *m*; (*solace, relief*) Trost *m* ▷ *vt* trösten; **comforts** *npl* (*of home etc*) Komfort *m*, Annehmlichkeiten *pl*
comfortable ['kʌmfətəbl] *adj* bequem; (*room*) komfortabel; (*walk, climb etc*) geruhsam; (*income*) ausreichend; (*majority*) sicher; **to be ~** (*physically*) sich wohlfühlen; (*financially*) sehr angenehm leben; **the patient is ~** dem Patienten geht es den Umständen entsprechend gut; **I don't feel very ~ about it** mir ist nicht ganz wohl bei der Sache
comfortably ['kʌmfətəblɪ] *adv* (*sit*) bequem; (*live*) angenehm
comforter ['kʌmfətə^r] (*US*) *n* Schnuller *m*
comfort shopping *n* Frustkauf *m*
comfort station (*US*) *n* öffentliche Toilette *f*
comic ['kɔmɪk] *adj* (*also*: **comical**) komisch ▷ *n* Komiker(in) *m(f)*; (*Brit: magazine*) Comicheft *nt*
comical ['kɔmɪkl] *adj* komisch
comic strip *n* Comicstrip *m*
coming ['kʌmɪŋ] *n* Ankunft *f*, Kommen *nt* ▷ *adj* kommend; (*next*) nächste(r, s); **in the ~ weeks** in den nächsten Wochen
coming and going, *n*, **comings and goings** ▷ *npl* Kommen und Gehen *nt*
Comintern ['kɔmɪntə:n] *n* (*Pol*) Komintern *f*
comma ['kɔmə] *n* Komma *nt*
command [kə'mɑ:nd] *n* (*also Comput*) Befehl *m*; (*control, charge*) Führung *f*; (*Mil: authority*) Kommando *nt*, Befehlsgewalt *f*; (*mastery*) Beherrschung *f* ▷ *vt* (*troops*) befehligen, kommandieren; (*be able to get*) verfügen über +*acc*; (*deserve: respect, admiration etc*) verdient haben; **to be in ~ of** das Kommando *or* den (Ober)befehl haben über +*acc*; **to have ~ of** das Kommando haben über +*acc*; **to take ~ of** das Kommando übernehmen +*gen*; **to have at one's ~** verfügen über +*acc*; **to ~ sb to do sth** jdm befehlen, etw zu tun
commandant ['kɔməndænt] *n* Kommandant *m*
command economy *n* Kommandowirtschaft *f*
commandeer [kɔmən'dɪə^r] *vt* requirieren, beschlagnahmen; (*fig*) sich aneignen
commander [kə'mɑ:ndə^r] *n* Befehlshaber *m*, Kommandant *m*
commander in chief *n* Oberbefehlshaber *m*
commanding [kə'mɑ:ndɪŋ] *adj* (*appearance*) imposant; (*voice, tone*) gebieterisch; (*lead*) entscheidend; (*position*) vorherrschend

commanding officer *n* befehlshabender Offizier *m*
commandment [kə'mɑːndmənt] *n* Gebot *nt*
command module *n* Kommandokapsel *f*
commando [kə'mɑːndəu] *n* Kommando *nt*, Kommandotrupp *m*; (*soldier*) Angehörige(r) *m* eines Kommando(trupp)s
commemorate [kə'mɛməreɪt] *vt* gedenken *+gen*
commemoration [kəmɛmə'reɪʃən] *n* Gedenken *nt*
commemorative [kə'mɛmərətɪv] *adj* Gedenk-
commence [kə'mɛns] *vt, vi* beginnen
commend [kə'mɛnd] *vt* loben; **to ~ sth to sb** jdm etw empfehlen
commendable [kə'mɛndəbl] *adj* lobenswert
commendation [kɔmɛn'deɪʃən] *n* Auszeichnung *f*
commensurate [kə'mɛnʃərɪt] *adj*: **~ with** *or* **to** entsprechend *+dat*
comment ['kɔmɛnt] *n* Bemerkung *f*; (*on situation etc*) Kommentar *m* ▷ *vi*: **to ~ (on)** sich äußern (über *+acc or* zu); (*on situation etc*) einen Kommentar abgeben (zu); **"no ~"** „kein Kommentar!"; **to ~ that ...** bemerken, dass ...
commentary ['kɔməntərɪ] *n* Kommentar *m*; (*Sport*) Reportage *f*
commentator ['kɔmənteɪtə^r] *n* Kommentator(in) *m(f)*; (*Sport*) Reporter(in) *m(f)*
commerce ['kɔməːs] *n* Handel *m*
commercial [kə'məːʃəl] *adj* kommerziell; (*organization*) Wirtschafts- ▷ *n* (*advertisement*) Werbespot *m*
commercial bank *n* Handelsbank *f*
commercial break *n* Werbung *f*
commercial college *n* Fachschule *f* für kaufmännische Berufe
commercialism [kə'məːʃəlɪzəm] *n* Kommerzialisierung *f*
commercialize [kə'məːʃəlaɪz] *vt* kommerzialisieren
commercialized [kə'məːʃəlaɪzd] (*pej*) *adj* kommerzialisiert
commercial radio *n* kommerzielles Radio *nt*
commercial television *n* kommerzielles Fernsehen *nt*
commercial traveller *n* Handelsvertreter(in) *m(f)*
commercial vehicle *n* Lieferwagen *m*
commiserate [kə'mɪzəreɪt] *vi*: **to ~ with sb** jdm sein Mitgefühl zeigen
commission [kə'mɪʃən] *n* (*order for work*) Auftrag *m*; (*Comm*) Provision *f*; (*committee*) Kommission *f*; (*Mil*) Offizierspatent *nt* ▷ *vt* (*work of art*) in Auftrag geben; (*Mil*) (zum Offizier) ernennen; **out of ~** außer Betrieb; (*Naut*) nicht im Dienst; **I get 10% ~** ich bekomme 10% Provision; **~ of inquiry** Untersuchungsausschuss *m*, Untersuchungskommission *f*; **to ~ sb to do sth** jdn damit beauftragen, etw zu tun; **to ~ sth from sb** jdm etw in Auftrag geben
commissionaire [kəmɪʃə'nɛə^r] (*Brit*) *n* Portier *m*
commissioner [kə'mɪʃənə^r] *n* Polizeipräsident *m*
commit [kə'mɪt] *vt* (*crime*) begehen; (*money, resources*) einsetzen; (*to sb's care*) anvertrauen; **to ~ o.s.** sich festlegen; **to ~ o.s. to do sth** sich (dazu) verpflichten, etw zu tun; **to ~ suicide** Selbstmord begehen; **to ~ to writing** zu Papier bringen; **to ~ sb for trial** jdn einem Gericht überstellen
commitment [kə'mɪtmənt] *n* Verpflichtung *f*; (*to ideology, system*) Engagement *nt*
committed [kə'mɪtɪd] *adj* engagiert
committee [kə'mɪtɪ] *n* Ausschuss *m*, Komitee *nt*; **to be on a ~** in einem Ausschuss *or* Komitee sein *or* sitzen
committee meeting *n* Ausschusssitzung *f*
commodity [kə'mɔdɪtɪ] *n* Ware *f*; (*food*) Nahrungsmittel *nt*
common ['kɔmən] *adj* (*shared by all*) gemeinsam; (*good*) Gemein-; (*property*) Gemeinschafts-; (*usual, ordinary*) häufig; (*vulgar*) gewöhnlich ▷ *n* Gemeindeland *nt*; **the Commons** (*Brit: Pol*) *npl* das Unterhaus; **in ~ use** allgemein gebräuchlich; **it's ~ knowledge that** es ist allgemein bekannt, dass; **to the ~ good** für das Gemeinwohl; **to have sth in ~ (with sb)** etw (mit jdm) gemein haben
common cold *n* Schnupfen *m*
common denominator *n* (*Math: fig*) gemeinsamer Nenner *m*
commoner ['kɔmənə^r] *n* Bürgerliche(r) *f(m)*
common ground *n* (*fig*) gemeinsame Basis *f*
common land *n* Gemeindeland *nt*
common law *n* Gewohnheitsrecht *nt*
common-law ['kɔmənlɔː] *adj*: **she is his ~ wife** sie lebt mit ihm in eheähnlicher Gemeinschaft
commonly ['kɔmənlɪ] *adv* häufig
Common Market *n*: **the ~** der Gemeinsame Markt
commonplace ['kɔmənpleɪs] *adj* alltäglich
common room *n* Aufenthaltsraum *m*, Tagesraum *m*
common sense *n* gesunder Menschenverstand *m*
Commonwealth ['kɔmənwɛlθ] (*Brit*) *n*: **the ~** das Commonwealth; *siehe Info-Artikel*

COMMONWEALTH

Das *Commonwealth*, offiziell Commonwealth of Nations, ist ein lockerer Zusammenschluss aus souveränen Staaten, die früher unter britischer Regierung standen, und von Großbritannien abhängigen Gebieten. Die Mitgliedstaaten erkennen den britischen Monarchen als Oberhaupt des Commonwealth an. Bei der Commonwealth Conference, einem Treffen der Staatsoberhäupter der Commonwealthländer, werden Angelegenheiten von gemeinsamem Interesse diskutiert.

commotion [kə'məuʃən] *n* Tumult *m*
communal ['kɔmju:nl] *adj* gemeinsam, Gemeinschafts-; (*life*) Gemeinschafts-
commune [*n* 'kɔmju:n, *vi* kə'mju:n] *n* Kommune *f* ▷ *vi*: **to ~ with** Zwiesprache halten mit
communicate [kə'mju:nɪkeɪt] *vt* mitteilen; (*idea, feeling*) vermitteln ▷ *vi*: **to ~ (with)** (*by speech, gesture*) sich verständigen (mit); (*in writing*) in Verbindung *or* Kontakt stehen (mit)
communication [kəmju:nɪ'keɪʃən] *n* Kommunikation *f*; (*letter, call*) Mitteilung *f*
communication cord (*Brit*) *n* Notbremse *f*
communications network [kəmju:nɪ'keɪʃənz-] *n* Kommunikationsnetz *nt*
communications satellite *n* Kommunikationssatellit *m*, Nachrichtensatellit *m*
communicative [kə'mju:nɪkətɪv] *adj* gesprächig, mitteilsam
communion [kə'mju:nɪən] *n* (*also*: **Holy Communion**: *Catholic*) Kommunion *f*; (: *Protestant*) Abendmahl *nt*
communiqué [kə'mju:nɪkeɪ] *n* Kommuniqué *nt*, (amtliche) Verlautbarung *f*
communism ['kɔmjunɪzəm] *n* Kommunismus *m*
communist ['kɔmjunɪst] *adj* kommunistisch ▷ *n* Kommunist(in) *m(f)*
community [kə'mju:nɪtɪ] *n* Gemeinschaft *f*; (*within larger group*) Bevölkerungsgruppe *f*
community centre *n* Gemeindezentrum *nt*
community charge (*Brit*) *n* (*formerly*) Gemeindesteuer *f*
community chest (*US*) *n* Wohltätigkeitsfonds *m*, Hilfsfonds *m*
community health centre *n* Gemeinde-Ärztezentrum *nt*
community home (*Brit*) *n* Erziehungsheim *nt*
community service *n* Sozialdienst *m*
community spirit *n* Gemeinschaftssinn *m*
commutation ticket [kɔmju'teɪʃən-] (*US*) *n* Zeitkarte *f*
commute [kə'mju:t] *vi* pendeln ▷ *vt* (*Law, Math*) umwandeln
commuter [kə'mju:tə^r] *n* Pendler(in) *m(f)*
compact [*adj* kəm'pækt, *n* 'kɔmpækt] *adj* kompakt ▷ *n* (*also*: **powder compact**) Puderdose *f*
compact disc *n* Compact Disc *f*, CD *f*
compact disc player *n* CD-Spieler *m*
companion [kəm'pænjən] *n* Begleiter(in) *m(f)*
companionship [kəm'pænjənʃɪp] *n* Gesellschaft *f*
companionway [kəm'pænjənweɪ] *n* (*Naut*) Niedergang *m*
company ['kʌmpənɪ] *n* Firma *f*; (*Theat*) (Schauspiel)truppe *f*; (*Mil*) Kompanie *f*; (*companionship*) Gesellschaft *f*; **he's good ~** seine Gesellschaft ist angenehm; **to keep sb ~** jdm Gesellschaft leisten; **to part ~ with** sich trennen von; **Smith and C~** Smith & Co
company car *n* Firmenwagen *m*
company director *n* Direktor(in) *m(f)*, Firmenchef(in) *m(f)*
company secretary (*Brit*) *n* ≈ Prokurist(in) *m(f)*
comparable ['kɔmpərəbl] *adj* vergleichbar
comparative [kəm'pærətɪv] *adj* relativ; (*study, literature*) vergleichend; (*Ling*) komparativ
comparatively [kəm'pærətɪvlɪ] *adv* relativ
compare [kəm'pɛə^r] *vt*: **to ~ (with** *or* **to)** vergleichen (mit) ▷ *vi*: **to ~ (with)** sich vergleichen lassen (mit); **how do the prices ~?** wie lassen sich die Preise vergleichen?; **~d with** *or* **to** im Vergleich zu, verglichen mit
comparison [kəm'pærɪsn] *n* Vergleich *m*; **in ~ (with)** im Vergleich (zu)
compartment [kəm'pɑ:tmənt] *n* (*Rail*) Abteil *nt*; (*section*) Fach *nt*
compass ['kʌmpəs] *n* Kompass *m*; (*fig: scope*) Bereich *m*; **compasses** *npl* (*also*: **pair of compasses**) Zirkel *m*; **within the ~ of** im Rahmen *or* Bereich *+gen*; **beyond the ~ of** über den Rahmen *or* Bereich *+gen* hinaus
compassion [kəm'pæʃən] *n* Mitgefühl *nt*
compassionate [kəm'pæʃənɪt] *adj* mitfühlend; **on ~ grounds** aus familiären Gründen
compassionate leave *n* (*esp Mil*) *Beurlaubung wegen Krankheit oder Trauerfall in der Familie*
compatibility [kəmpætɪ'bɪlɪtɪ] *n* (*see adj*) Vereinbarkeit *f*; Zueinanderpassen *nt*; Kompatibilität *f*
compatible [kəm'pætɪbl] *adj* (*ideas etc*) vereinbar; (*people*) zueinanderpassend; (*Comput*) kompatibel
compel [kəm'pɛl] *vt* zwingen
compelling [kəm'pɛlɪŋ] *adj* zwingend
compendium [kəm'pɛndɪəm] *n* Kompendium *nt*
compensate ['kɔmpənseɪt] *vt* entschädigen ▷ *vi*: **to ~ for** (*loss*) ersetzen; (*disappointment, change etc*) (wieder) ausgleichen
compensation [kɔmpən'seɪʃən] *n* (*see vb*) Entschädigung *f*; Ersatz *m*; Ausgleich *m*; (*money*) Schaden(s)ersatz *m*
compère ['kɔmpɛə^r] *n* Conférencier *m*
compete [kəm'pi:t] *vi* (*in contest, game*) teilnehmen; (*two theories, statements*) unvereinbar sein; **to ~ (with)** (*companies, rivals*) konkurrieren (mit)
competence ['kɔmpɪtəns] *n* Fähigkeit *f*
competent ['kɔmpɪtənt] *adj* fähig
competing [kəm'pi:tɪŋ] *adj* konkurrierend
competition [kɔmpɪ'tɪʃən] *n* Konkurrenz *f*; (*contest*) Wettbewerb *m*; **in ~ with** im Wettbewerb mit
competitive [kəm'pɛtɪtɪv] *adj* (*industry, society*) wettbewerbsbetont, wettbewerbsorientiert; (*person*) vom Konkurrenzdenken geprägt; (*price, product*) wettbewerbsfähig, konkurrenzfähig;

(*sport*) (Wett)kampf-
competitive examination *n* (*for places*) Auswahlprüfung *f*; (*for prizes*) Wettbewerb *m*
competitor [kəm'pɛtɪtə^r] *n* Konkurrent(in) *m(f)*; (*participant*) Teilnehmer(in) *m(f)*
compilation [kɔmpɪ'leɪʃən] *n* Zusammenstellung *f*
compile [kəm'paɪl] *vt* zusammenstellen; (*book*) verfassen
complacency [kəm'pleɪsnsɪ] *n* Selbstzufriedenheit *f*, Selbstgefälligkeit *f*
complacent [kəm'pleɪsnt] *adj* selbstzufrieden, selbstgefällig
complain [kəm'pleɪn] *vi* (*protest*) sich beschweren; **to ~ (about)** sich beklagen (über *+acc*); **to ~ of** (*headache etc*) klagen über *+acc*
complaint [kəm'pleɪnt] *n* Klage *f*; (*in shop etc*) Beschwerde *f*; (*illness*) Beschwerden *pl*
complement ['kɔmplɪmənt] *n* Ergänzung *f*; (*esp ship's crew*) Besatzung *f* ▷ *vt* ergänzen; **to have a full ~ of ...** (*people*) die volle Stärke an ... *dat* haben; (*items*) die volle Zahl an ... *dat* haben
complementary [kɔmplɪ'mɛntərɪ] *adj* komplementär, einander ergänzend
complete [kəm'pli:t] *adj* (*total: silence*) vollkommen; (*: change*) völlig; (*: success*) voll; (*whole*) ganz; (*: set*) vollständig; (*: edition*) Gesamt-; (*finished*) fertig ▷ *vt* fertigstellen; (*task*) beenden; (*set, group etc*) vervollständigen; (*fill in*) ausfüllen; **it's a ~ disaster** es ist eine totale Katastrophe
completely [kəm'pli:tlɪ] *adv* völlig, vollkommen
completion [kəm'pli:ʃən] *n* Fertigstellung *f*; (*of contract*) Abschluss *m*; **to be nearing ~** kurz vor dem Abschluss sein *or* stehen; **on ~ of the contract** bei Vertragsabschluss
complex ['kɔmplɛks] *adj* kompliziert ▷ *n* Komplex *m*
complexion [kəm'plɛkʃən] *n* Teint *m*, Gesichtsfarbe *f*; (*of event etc*) Charakter *m*; (*political, religious*) Anschauung *f*; **to put a different ~ on sth** etw in einem anderen Licht erscheinen lassen
complexity [kəm'plɛksɪtɪ] *n* Kompliziertheit *f*
compliance [kəm'plaɪəns] *n* Fügsamkeit *f*; (*agreement*) Einverständnis *nt*; **~ with** Einverständnis mit, Zustimmung *f* zu; **in ~ with** gemäß *+dat*
compliant [kəm'plaɪənt] *adj* gefällig, entgegenkommend
complicate ['kɔmplɪkeɪt] *vt* komplizieren
complicated ['kɔmplɪkeɪtɪd] *adj* kompliziert
complication [kɔmplɪ'keɪʃən] *n* Komplikation *f*
complicity [kəm'plɪsɪtɪ] *n* Mittäterschaft *f*
compliment [*n* 'kɔmplɪmənt, *vt* 'kɔmplɪmɛnt] *n* Kompliment *nt* ▷ *vt* ein Kompliment/ Komplimente machen; **compliments** *npl* (*regards*) Grüße *pl*; **to pay sb a ~** jdm ein Kompliment machen; **to ~ sb (on sth)** jdm Komplimente (wegen etw) machen; **to ~ sb on doing sth** jdm Komplimente machen, dass er/sie etw getan hat
complimentary [kɔmplɪ'mɛntərɪ] *adj* schmeichelhaft; (*ticket, copy of book etc*) Frei-
compliments slip *n* Empfehlungszettel *m*
comply [kəm'plaɪ] *vi*: **to ~ with** (*law*) einhalten *+acc*; (*ruling*) sich richten nach
component [kəm'pəunənt] *adj* einzeln ▷ *n* Bestandteil *m*
compose [kəm'pəuz] *vt* (*music*) komponieren; (*poem*) verfassen; (*letter*) abfassen; **to be ~d of** bestehen aus; **to ~ o.s.** sich sammeln
composed [kəm'pəuzd] *adj* ruhig, gelassen
composer [kəm'pəuzə^r] *n* Komponist(in) *m(f)*
composite ['kɔmpəzɪt] *adj* zusammengesetzt; (*Bot*) Korbblütler-; (*Math*) teilbar; (*Bot*): **~ plant** Korbblütler *m*
composition [kɔmpə'zɪʃən] *n* Zusammensetzung *f*; (*essay*) Aufsatz *m*; (*Mus*) Komposition *f*
compositor [kəm'pɔzɪtə^r] *n* (Schrift)setzer(in) *m(f)*
compos mentis ['kɔmpɔs 'mɛntɪs] *adj* zurechnungsfähig
compost ['kɔmpɔst] *n* Kompost *m*; (*also*: **potting compost**) Blumenerde *f*
composure [kəm'pəuʒə^r] *n* Fassung *f*, Beherrschung *f*
compound [*n, adj* 'kɔmpaund, *vt* kəm'paund] *n* (*Chem*) Verbindung *f*; (*enclosure*) umzäuntes Gebiet *or* Gelände *nt*; (*Ling*) Kompositum *nt* ▷ *adj* zusammengesetzt; (*eye*) Facetten- ▷ *vt* verschlimmern, vergrößern
compound fracture *n* komplizierter Bruch *m*
compound interest *n* Zinseszins *m*
comprehend [kɔmprɪ'hɛnd] *vt* begreifen, verstehen
comprehension [kɔmprɪ'hɛnʃən] *n* Verständnis *nt*
comprehensive [kɔmprɪ'hɛnsɪv] *adj* umfassend; (*insurance*) Vollkasko- ▷ *n* = **comprehensive school**
comprehensive school (*Brit*) *n* Gesamtschule *f*; *siehe Info-Artikel*

COMPREHENSIVE SCHOOL

Comprehensive school ist in Großbritannien eine nicht selektive, weiterführende Schule, an der alle Kinder aus einem Einzugsgebiet gemeinsam unterrichtet werden. An einer solchen Gesamtschule können alle Schulabschlüsse gemacht werden. Die meisten staatlichen Schulen in Großbritannien sind comprehensive schools.

compress [*vt* kəm'prɛs, *n* 'kɔmprɛs] *vt* (*information etc*) verdichten; (*air*) komprimieren; (*cotton, paper etc*) zusammenpressen ▷ *n* (*Med*) Kompresse *f*
compressed air [kəm'prɛst-] *n* Druckluft *f*, Pressluft *f*

compression [kəm'prɛʃən] *n (see vb)* Verdichtung *f*; Kompression *f*; Zusammenpressen *nt*
comprise [kəm'praɪz] *vt (also:* **be comprised of***)* bestehen aus; *(constitute)* bilden, ausmachen
compromise ['kɔmprəmaɪz] *n* Kompromiss *m* ▷ *vt (beliefs, principles)* verraten; *(person)* kompromittieren ▷ *vi* Kompromisse schließen ▷ *cpd (solution etc)* Kompromiss-
compulsion [kəm'pʌlʃən] *n* Zwang *m*; *(force)* Druck *m*, Zwang *m*; **under ~** unter Druck *or* Zwang
compulsive [kəm'pʌlsɪv] *adj* zwanghaft; **it makes ~ viewing/reading** das muss man einfach sehen/lesen; **he's a ~ smoker** das Rauchen ist bei ihm zur Sucht geworden
compulsory [kəm'pʌlsərɪ] *adj* obligatorisch; *(retirement)* Zwangs-
compulsory purchase *n* Enteignung *f*
compunction [kəm'pʌŋkʃən] *n* Schuldgefühle *pl*, Gewissensbisse *pl*; **to have no ~ about doing sth** etw tun, ohne sich schuldig zu fühlen
computer [kəm'pju:tə^r] *n* Computer *m*, Rechner *m* ▷ *cpd* Computer-; **the process is done by ~** das Verfahren wird per Computer durchgeführt
computer game *n* Computerspiel *nt*
computerization [kəmpju:təraɪ'zeɪʃən] *n* Computerisierung *f*
computerize [kəm'pju:təraɪz] *vt* auf Computer umstellen; *(information)* computerisieren
computer literate *adj*: **to be ~** Computerkenntnisse haben
computer programmer *n* Programmierer(in) *m(f)*
computer programming *n* Programmieren *nt*
computer science *n* Informatik *f*
computer scientist *n* Informatiker(in) *m(f)*
computing [kəm'pju:tɪŋ] *n* Informatik *f*; *(activity)* Computerarbeit *f*
comrade ['kɔmrɪd] *n* Genosse *m*, Genossin *f*; *(friend)* Kamerad(in) *m(f)*
comradeship ['kɔmrɪdʃɪp] *n* Kameradschaft *f*
Comsat® ['kɔmsæt] *n abbr* = **communications satellite**
con [kɔn] *vt* betrügen; *(cheat)* hereinlegen ▷ *n* Schwindel *m*; **to ~ sb into doing sth** jdn durch einen Trick dazu bringen, dass er/sie etw tut
concave ['kɔnkeɪv] *adj* konkav
conceal [kən'si:l] *vt* verbergen; *(information)* verheimlichen
concede [kən'si:d] *vt* zugeben ▷ *vi* nachgeben; *(admit defeat)* sich geschlagen geben; **to ~ defeat** sich geschlagen geben; **to ~ a point to sb** jdm in einem Punkt recht geben
conceit [kən'si:t] *n* Einbildung *f*
conceited [kən'si:tɪd] *adj* eingebildet
conceivable [kən'si:vəbl] *adj* denkbar, vorstellbar; **it is ~ that ...** es ist denkbar, dass ...
conceivably [kən'si:vəblɪ] *adv*: **he may ~ be right** es ist durchaus denkbar, dass er recht hat
conceive [kən'si:v] *vt (child)* empfangen; *(plan)* kommen auf *+acc*; *(policy)* konzipieren ▷ *vi* empfangen; **to ~ of sth** sich *dat* etw vorstellen; **to ~ of doing sth** sich *dat* vorstellen, etw zu tun
concentrate ['kɔnsəntreɪt] *vi* sich konzentrieren ▷ *vt* konzentrieren
concentration [kɔnsən'treɪʃən] *n* Konzentration *f*
concentration camp *n* Konzentrationslager *nt*, KZ *nt*
concentric [kɔn'sɛntrɪk] *adj* konzentrisch
concept ['kɔnsɛpt] *n* Vorstellung *f*; *(principle)* Begriff *m*
conception [kən'sɛpʃən] *n* Vorstellung *f*; *(of child)* Empfängnis *f*
concern [kən'sə:n] *n* Angelegenheit *f*; *(anxiety, worry)* Sorge *f*; *(Comm)* Konzern *m* ▷ *vt* Sorgen machen *+dat*; *(involve)* angehen; *(relate to)* betreffen; **to be ~ed (about)** sich *dat* Sorgen machen (um); **"to whom it may ~"** *(on certificate)* „Bestätigung"; *(on reference)* „Zeugnis"; **as far as I am ~ed** was mich betrifft; **to be ~ed with** sich interessieren für; **the department ~ed** *(under discussion)* die betreffende Abteilung; *(involved)* die zuständige Abteilung
concerning [kən'sə:nɪŋ] *prep* bezüglich *+gen*, hinsichtlich *+gen*
concert ['kɔnsət] *n* Konzert *nt*; **in ~** *(Mus)* live; *(activities, actions etc)* gemeinsam
concerted [kən'sə:tɪd] *adj* gemeinsam
concert hall *n* Konzerthalle *f*, Konzertsaal *m*
concertina [kɔnsə'ti:nə] *n* Konzertina *f* ▷ *vi* sich wie eine Ziehharmonika zusammenschieben
concerto [kən'tʃə:təu] *n* Konzert *nt*
concession [kən'sɛʃən] *n* Zugeständnis *nt*, Konzession *f*; *(Comm)* Konzession; **tax ~** Steuervergünstigung *f*
concessionaire [kənsɛʃə'nɛə^r] *n* Konzessionär *m*
concessionary [kən'sɛʃənrɪ] *adj* ermäßigt
conciliation [kənsɪlɪ'eɪʃən] *n* Schlichtung *f*
conciliatory [kən'sɪlɪətrɪ] *adj* versöhnlich
concise [kən'saɪs] *adj* kurz gefasst, prägnant
conclave ['kɔnkleɪv] *n* Klausur *f*; *(Rel)* Konklave *f*
conclude [kən'klu:d] *vt* beenden, schließen; *(treaty, deal etc)* abschließen; *(decide)* schließen, folgern ▷ *vi* schließen; *(events)*: **to ~ (with)** enden (mit); **"That," he ~d, "is why we did it"** „Darum", schloss er, „haben wir es getan"; **I ~ that ...** ich komme zu dem Schluss, dass ...
concluding [kən'klu:dɪŋ] *adj (remarks etc)* abschließend, Schluss-
conclusion [kən'klu:ʒən] *n (see vb)* Ende *nt*; Schluss *m*; Abschluss *m*; Folgerung *f*; **to come to the ~ that ...** zu dem Schluss kommen, dass ...
conclusive [kən'klu:sɪv] *adj (evidence)* schlüssig;

(*defeat*) endgültig
concoct [kən'kɔkt] *vt* (*excuse etc*) sich *dat* ausdenken; (*meal, sauce*) improvisieren
concoction [kən'kɔkʃən] *n* Zusammenstellung *f*; (*drink*) Gebräu *nt*
concord ['kɔŋkɔ:d] *n* Eintracht *f*; (*treaty*) Vertrag *m*
concourse ['kɔŋkɔ:s] *n* (Eingangs)halle *f*; (*crowd*) Menge *f*
concrete ['kɔŋkri:t] *n* Beton *m* ▷ *adj* (*ceiling, block*) Beton-; (*proposal, idea*) konkret
concrete mixer *n* Betonmischmaschine *f*
concur [kən'kə:ʳ] *vi* übereinstimmen; **to ~ with** beipflichten *+dat*
concurrently [kən'kʌrntlɪ] *adv* gleichzeitig
concussion [kən'kʌʃən] *n* Gehirnerschütterung *f*
condemn [kən'dɛm] *vt* verurteilen; (*building*) für abbruchreif erklären
condemnation [kɔndɛm'neɪʃən] *n* Verurteilung *f*
condensation [kɔndɛn'seɪʃən] *n* Kondenswasser *nt*
condense [kən'dɛns] *vi* kondensieren, sich niederschlagen ▷ *vt* zusammenfassen
condensed milk [kən'dɛnst-] *n* Kondensmilch *f*, Büchsenmilch *f*
condescend [kɔndɪ'sɛnd] *vi* herablassend sein; **to ~ to do sth** sich dazu herablassen, etw zu tun
condescending [kɔndɪ'sɛndɪŋ] *adj* herablassend
condition [kən'dɪʃən] *n* Zustand *m*; (*requirement*) Bedingung *f*; (*illness*) Leiden *nt* ▷ *vt* konditionieren; (*hair*) in Form bringen;
conditions *npl* (*circumstances*) Verhältnisse *pl*; **in good/poor ~** (*person*) in guter/schlechter Verfassung; (*thing*) in gutem/schlechtem Zustand; **a heart ~** ein Herzleiden *nt*; **weather ~s** die Wetterlage; **on ~ that ...** unter der Bedingung, dass ...
conditional [kən'dɪʃənl] *adj* bedingt; **to be ~ upon** abhängen von
conditioner [kən'dɪʃənəʳ] *n* (*for hair*) Pflegespülung *f*; (*for fabrics*) Weichspüler *m*
condo ['kɔndəu] (*US: inf*) *n abbr* = **condominium**
condolences [kən'dəulənsɪz] *npl* Beileid *nt*
condom ['kɔndəm] *n* Kondom *m or nt*
condominium [kɔndə'mɪnɪəm] (*US*) *n* Haus *nt* mit Eigentumswohnungen; (*rooms*) Eigentumswohnung *f*
condone [kən'dəun] *vt* gutheißen
conducive [kən'dju:sɪv] *adj*: **~ to** förderlich *+dat*
conduct [*n* 'kɔndʌkt, *vt* kən'dʌkt] *n* Verhalten *nt* ▷ *vt* (*investigation etc*) durchführen; (*manage*) führen; (*orchestra, choir etc*) dirigieren; (*heat, electricity*) leiten; **to ~ o.s.** sich verhalten
conducted tour [kən'dʌktɪd-] *n* Führung *f*
conductor [kən'dʌktəʳ] *n* (*of orchestra*) Dirigent(in) *m(f)*; (*on bus*) Schaffner *m*; (*US: on train*) Zugführer(in) *m(f)*; (*Elec*) Leiter *m*
conductress [kən'dʌktrɪs] *n* (*on bus*) Schaffnerin *f*
conduit ['kɔndjuɪt] *n* (*Tech*) Leitungsrohr *nt*; (*Elec*) Isolierrohr *nt*
cone [kəun] *n* Kegel *m*; (*on road*) Leitkegel *m*; (*Bot*) Zapfen *m*; (*ice cream cornet*) (Eis)tüte *f*
confectioner [kən'fɛkʃənəʳ] *n* (*maker*) Süßwarenhersteller(in) *m(f)*; (*seller*) Süßwarenhändler(in) *m(f)*; (*of cakes*) Konditor(in) *m(f)*
confectioner's [kən'fɛkʃənəz], **confectioner's shop** *n* Süßwarenladen *m*; (*cake shop*) Konditorei *f*
confectionery [kən'fɛkʃənrɪ] *n* Süßwaren *pl*, Süßigkeiten *pl*; (*cakes*) Konditorwaren *pl*
confederate [kən'fɛdrɪt] *adj* verbündet ▷ *n* (*pej*) Komplize *m*, Komplizin *f*; (*US: Hist*): **the C~s** die Konföderierten *pl*
confederation [kənfɛdə'reɪʃən] *n* Bund *m*; (*Pol*) Bündnis *nt*; (*Comm*) Verband *m*
confer [kən'fə:ʳ] *vt*: **to ~ sth (on sb)** (jdm) etw verleihen ▷ *vi* sich beraten; **to ~ with sb about sth** sich mit jdm über etw *acc* beraten, etw mit jdm besprechen
conference ['kɔnfərəns] *n* Konferenz *f*; (*more informal*) Besprechung *f*; **to be in ~** in *or* bei einer Konferenz/Besprechung sein
conference room *n* Konferenzraum *m*; (*smaller*) Besprechungszimmer *nt*
confess [kən'fɛs] *vt* bekennen; (*sin*) beichten; (*crime*) zugeben, gestehen ▷ *vi* (*admit*) gestehen; **to ~ to sth** (*crime*) etw gestehen; (*weakness etc*) sich zu etw bekennen; **I must ~ that I didn't enjoy it at all** ich muss sagen, dass es mir überhaupt keinen Spaß gemacht hat
confession [kən'fɛʃən] *n* Geständnis *nt*; (*Rel*) Beichte *f*; **to make a ~** ein Geständnis ablegen
confessor [kən'fɛsəʳ] *n* Beichtvater *m*
confetti [kən'fɛtɪ] *n* Konfetti *nt*
confide [kən'faɪd] *vi*: **to ~ in** sich anvertrauen *+dat*
confidence ['kɔnfɪdns] *n* Vertrauen *nt*; (*self-assurance*) Selbstvertrauen *nt*; (*secret*) vertrauliche Mitteilung *f*, Geheimnis *nt*; **to have ~ in sb/sth** Vertrauen zu jdm/etw haben; **to have (every) ~ that ...** ganz zuversichtlich sein, dass ...; **motion of no ~** Misstrauensantrag *m*; **to tell sb sth in strict ~** jdm etw ganz im Vertrauen sagen; **in ~** vertraulich
confidence trick *n* Schwindel *m*
confident ['kɔnfɪdənt] *adj* (selbst)sicher; (*positive*) zuversichtlich
confidential [kɔnfɪ'dɛnʃəl] *adj* vertraulich; (*secretary*) Privat-
confidentiality [kɔnfɪdɛnʃɪ'ælɪtɪ] *n* Vertraulichkeit *f*
configuration [kənfɪgju'reɪʃən] *n* Anordnung *f*; (*Comput*) Konfiguration *f*
confine [kən'faɪn] *vt* (*shut up*) einsperren; **to ~ (to)** beschränken (auf *+acc*); **to ~ o.s. to sth** sich auf etw *acc* beschränken; **to ~ o.s. to doing sth** sich darauf beschränken, etw zu tun

confined [kən'faɪnd] *adj* begrenzt
confinement [kən'faɪnmənt] *n* Haft *f*
confines ['kɔnfaɪnz] *npl* Grenzen *pl*; (*of situation*) Rahmen *m*
confirm [kən'fə:m] *vt* bestätigen; **to be ~ed** (*Rel*) konfirmiert werden
confirmation [kɔnfə'meɪʃən] *n* Bestätigung *f*; (*Rel*) Konfirmation *f*
confirmed [kən'fə:md] *adj* (*bachelor*) eingefleischt; (*teetotaller*) überzeugt
confiscate ['kɔnfɪskeɪt] *vt* beschlagnahmen, konfiszieren
confiscation [kɔnfɪs'keɪʃən] *n* Beschlagnahme *f*, Konfiszierung *f*
conflagration [kɔnflə'greɪʃən] *n* Feuersbrunst *f*
conflict ['kɔnflɪkt] *n* Konflikt *m*; (*fighting*) Zusammenstoß *m*, Kampf *m* ▷ *vi*: **to ~ (with)** im Widerspruch stehen (zu)
conflicting [kən'flɪktɪŋ] *adj* widersprüchlich
conform [kən'fɔ:m] *vi* sich anpassen; **to ~ to** entsprechen *+dat*
conformist [kən'fɔ:mɪst] *n* Konformist(in) *m(f)*
confound [kən'faund] *vt* verwirren; (*amaze*) verblüffen
confounded [kən'faundɪd] *adj* verdammt, verflixt (*inf*)
confront [kən'frʌnt] *vt* (*problems, task*) sich stellen *+dat*; (*enemy, danger*) gegenübertreten *+dat*
confrontation [kɔnfrən'teɪʃən] *n* Konfrontation *f*
confuse [kən'fju:z] *vt* verwirren; (*mix up*) verwechseln; (*complicate*) durcheinanderbringen
confused [kən'fju:zd] *adj* (*person*) verwirrt; (*situation*) verworren, konfus; **to get ~** konfus werden
confusing [kən'fju:zɪŋ] *adj* verwirrend
confusion [kən'fju:ʒən] *n* (*mix-up*) Verwechslung *f*; (*perplexity*) Verwirrung *f*; (*disorder*) Durcheinander *nt*
congeal [kən'dʒi:l] *vi* (*blood*) gerinnen; (*sauce, oil*) erstarren
congenial [kən'dʒi:nɪəl] *adj* ansprechend, sympathisch; (*atmosphere, place, work, company*) angenehm
congenital [kən'dʒɛnɪtl] *adj* angeboren
conger eel ['kɔŋgər-] *n* Seeaal *m*
congested [kən'dʒɛstɪd] *adj* (*road*) verstopft; (*area*) überfüllt; (*nose*) verstopft; **his lungs are ~** in seiner Lunge hat sich Blut angestaut
congestion [kən'dʒɛstʃən] *n* (*Med*) Blutstau *m*; (*of road*) Verstopfung *f*; (*of area*) Überfüllung *f*
congestion charge *n* City-Maut *f*
conglomerate [kən'glɔmərɪt] *n* (*Comm*) Konglomerat *nt*
conglomeration [kənglɔmə'reɪʃən] *n* Ansammlung *f*
Congo ['kɔŋgəu] *n* (*state*) Kongo *m*
congratulate [kən'grætjuleɪt] *vt* gratulieren; **to ~ sb (on sth)** jdm (zu etw) gratulieren
congratulations [kəngrætju'leɪʃənz] *npl* Glückwunsch *m*, Glückwünsche *pl*; **~!** herzlichen Glückwunsch!; **~ on** Glückwünsche zu
congregate ['kɔŋgrɪgeɪt] *vi* sich versammeln
congregation [kɔŋgrɪ'geɪʃən] *n* Gemeinde *f*
congress ['kɔŋgrɛs] *n* Kongress *m*; (*US*): **C~** der Kongress; *siehe Info-Artikel*

CONGRESS

Der *Congress* ist die nationale gesetzgebende Versammlung der USA, die in Washington im *Capitol* zusammentritt. Der Kongress besteht aus dem Repräsentantenhaus (435 Abgeordnete, entsprechend den Bevölkerungszahlen auf die einzelnen Bundesstaaten verteilt und jeweils für 2 Jahre gewählt) und dem Senat (100 Senatoren, 2 für jeden Bundesstaat, für 6 Jahre gewählt, wobei ein Drittel alle zwei Jahre neu gewählt wird). Sowohl die Abgeordneten als auch die Senatoren werden in direkter Wahl vom Volk gewählt.

congressman ['kɔŋgrɛsmən] (*US*) *n* (*irreg: like* **man**) Kongressabgeordnete(r) *m*
congresswoman ['kɔŋgrɛswumən] (*US*) *n* (*irreg: like* **woman**) *n* Kongressabgeordnete *f*
conical ['kɔnɪkl] *adj* kegelförmig, konisch
conifer ['kɔnɪfə^r] *n* Nadelbaum *m*
coniferous [kə'nɪfərəs] *adj* Nadel-
conjecture [kən'dʒɛktʃə^r] *n* Vermutung *f*, Mutmaßung *f* ▷ *vi* vermuten, mutmaßen
conjugal ['kɔndʒugl] *adj* ehelich
conjugate ['kɔndʒugeɪt] *vt* konjugieren
conjugation [kɔndʒə'geɪʃən] *n* Konjugation *f*
conjunction [kən'dʒʌŋkʃən] *n* Konjunktion *f*; **in ~ with** zusammen mit, in Verbindung mit
conjunctivitis [kəndʒʌŋktɪ'vaɪtɪs] *n* Bindehautentzündung *f*
conjure ['kʌndʒə^r] *vi* zaubern ▷ *vt* (*also fig*) hervorzaubern
▸ **conjure up** *vt* (*ghost, spirit*) beschwören; (*memories*) heraufbeschwören
conjurer ['kʌndʒərə^r] *n* Zauberer *m*, Zauberkünstler(in) *m(f)*
conjuring trick ['kʌndʒərɪŋ-] *n* Zaubertrick *m*, Zauberkunststück *nt*
conker ['kɔŋkə^r] (*Brit*) *n* (Ross)kastanie *f*
conk out [kɔŋk-] (*inf*) *vi* den Geist aufgeben
con man *n* Schwindler *m*
Conn. (*US*) *abbr* (*Post*) = *Connecticut*
connect [kə'nɛkt] *vt* verbinden; (*Elec*) anschließen; (*Tel: caller*) verbinden; (*: subscriber*) anschließen; (*fig: associate*) in Zusammenhang bringen ▷ *vi*: **to ~ with** (*train, plane etc*) Anschluss haben an *+acc*; **to ~ sth to sth** etw mit einer Sache verbinden; **to be ~ed with** (*associated*) in einer Beziehung *or* in Verbindung stehen zu; (*have dealings with*) zu tun haben mit; **I am trying to ~ you** (*Tel*) ich versuche, Sie zu verbinden

connection [kəˈnɛkʃən] *n* Verbindung *f*; (*Elec*) Kontakt *m*; (*train, plane etc, Tel: subscriber*) Anschluss *m*; (*fig: association*) Beziehung *f*, Zusammenhang *m*; **in ~ with** in Zusammenhang mit; **what is the ~ between them?** welche Verbindung besteht zwischen ihnen?; **business ~s** Geschäftsbeziehungen *pl*; **to get/miss one's ~** seinen Anschluss erreichen/verpassen
connexion [kəˈnɛkʃən] (*Brit*) *n* = **connection**
conning tower [ˈkɔnɪŋ-] *n* Kommandoturm *m*
connive [kəˈnaɪv] *vi*: **to ~ at** stillschweigend dulden
connoisseur [kɔnɪˈsəːʳ] *n* Kenner(in) *m(f)*
connotation [kɔnəˈteɪʃən] *n* Konnotation *f*
connubial [kəˈnjuːbɪəl] *adj* ehelich
conquer [ˈkɔŋkəʳ] *vt* erobern; (*enemy, fear, feelings*) besiegen
conqueror [ˈkɔŋkərəʳ] *n* Eroberer *m*
conquest [ˈkɔŋkwɛst] *n* Eroberung *f*
cons [kɔnz] *npl see* **convenience**, **pro**
conscience [ˈkɔnʃəns] *n* Gewissen *nt*; **to have a guilty/clear ~** ein schlechtes/gutes Gewissen haben; **in all ~** allen Ernstes
conscientious [kɔnʃɪˈɛnʃəs] *adj* gewissenhaft
conscientious objector *n* Wehrdienst- *or* Kriegsdienstverweigerer *m* (*aus Gewissensgründen*)
conscious [ˈkɔnʃəs] *adj* bewusst; (*awake*) bei Bewusstsein; **to become ~ of sth** sich *dat* einer Sache *gen* bewusst werden; **to become ~ that ...** sich *dat* bewusst werden, dass ...
consciousness [ˈkɔnʃəsnɪs] *n* Bewusstsein *nt*; **to lose ~** bewusstlos werden; **to regain ~** wieder zu sich kommen
conscript [ˈkɔnskrɪpt] *n* Wehrpflichtige(r) *m*
conscription [kənˈskrɪpʃən] *n* Wehrpflicht *f*
consecrate [ˈkɔnsɪkreɪt] *vt* weihen
consecutive [kənˈsɛkjutɪv] *adj* aufeinanderfolgend; **on three ~ occasions** dreimal hintereinander
consensus [kənˈsɛnsəs] *n* Übereinstimmung *f*; **the ~ (of opinion)** die allgemeine Meinung
consent [kənˈsɛnt] *n* Zustimmung *f* ▷ *vi*: **to ~ to** zustimmen *+dat*; **age of ~** Ehemündigkeitsalter *nt*; **by common ~** auf allgemeinen Wunsch
consenting [kənˈsɛntɪŋ] *adj*: **between ~ adults** ≈ zwischen Erwachsenen
consequence [ˈkɔnsɪkwəns] *n* Folge *f*; **of ~** bedeutend, wichtig; **it's of little ~** es spielt kaum eine Rolle; **in ~** folglich
consequently [ˈkɔnsɪkwəntlɪ] *adv* folglich
conservation [kɔnsəˈveɪʃən] *n* Erhaltung *f*, Schutz *m*; (*of energy*) Sparen *nt*; (*also*: **nature conservation**) Umweltschutz *m*; (*of paintings, books*) Erhaltung *f*, Konservierung *f*; **energy ~** Energieeinsparung *f*
conservationist [kɔnsəˈveɪʃnɪst] *n* Umweltschützer(in) *m(f)*
conservative [kənˈsəːvətɪv] *adj* konservativ; (*cautious*) vorsichtig; (*Brit: Pol*): **C~** konservativ ▷ *n* (*Brit: Pol*): **C~** Konservative(r) *f(m)*
Conservative Party *n*: **the ~** die Konservative Partei *f*
conservatory [kənˈsəːvətrɪ] *n* Wintergarten *m*; (*Mus*) Konservatorium *nt*
conserve [kənˈsəːv] *vt* erhalten; (*supplies, energy*) sparen ▷ *n* Konfitüre *f*
consider [kənˈsɪdəʳ] *vt* (*study*) sich *dat* überlegen; (*take into account*) in Betracht ziehen; **to ~ that ...** der Meinung sein, dass ...; **to ~ sb/sth as ...** jdn/etw für ... halten; **to ~ doing sth** in Erwägung ziehen, etw zu tun; **they ~ themselves to be superior** sie halten sich für etwas Besseres; **she ~ed it a disaster** sie betrachtete es als eine Katastrophe; **~ yourself lucky** Sie können sich glücklich schätzen; **all things ~ed** alles in allem
considerable [kənˈsɪdərəbl] *adj* beträchtlich
considerably [kənˈsɪdərəblɪ] *adv* beträchtlich; (*bigger, smaller etc*) um einiges
considerate [kənˈsɪdərɪt] *adj* rücksichtsvoll
consideration [kənsɪdəˈreɪʃən] *n* Überlegung *f*; (*factor*) Gesichtspunkt *m*, Faktor *m*; (*thoughtfulness*) Rücksicht *f*; (*reward*) Entgelt *nt*; **out of ~ for** aus Rücksicht auf *+acc*; **to be under ~** geprüft werden; **my first ~ is my family** ich denke zuerst an meine Familie
considered [kənˈsɪdəd] *adj*: **~ opinion** ernsthafte Überzeugung *f*
considering [kənˈsɪdərɪŋ] *prep* in Anbetracht *+gen*; **~ (that)** wenn man bedenkt(, dass)
consign [kənˈsaɪn] *vt*: **to ~ to** (*object: to place*) verbannen in *+acc*; (*person: to sb's care*) anvertrauen *+dat*; (*: to poverty*) verurteilen zu; (*send*) versenden an *+acc*
consignment [kənˈsaɪnmənt] *n* Sendung *f*, Lieferung *f*
consignment note *n* Frachtbrief *m*
consist [kənˈsɪst] *vi*: **to ~ of** bestehen aus
consistency [kənˈsɪstənsɪ] *n* (*of actions etc*) Konsequenz *f*; (*of cream etc*) Konsistenz *f*, Dicke *f*
consistent [kənˈsɪstənt] *adj* konsequent; (*argument, idea*) logisch, folgerichtig; **to be ~ with** entsprechen *+dat*
consolation [kɔnsəˈleɪʃən] *n* Trost *m*
console [kənˈsəul] *vt* trösten ▷ *n* (*panel*) Schalttafel *f*
consolidate [kənˈsɔlɪdeɪt] *vt* festigen
consols [ˈkɔnsɔlz] (*Brit*) *npl* (*Stock Exchange*) Konsols *pl*, konsolidierte Staatsanleihen *pl*
consommé [kənˈsɔmeɪ] *n* Kraftbrühe *f*, Consommé *f*
consonant [ˈkɔnsənənt] *n* Konsonant *m*, Mitlaut *m*
consort [ˈkɔnsɔːt] *n* Gemahl(in) *m(f)*, Gatte *m*, Gattin *f* ▷ *vi*: **to ~ with sb** mit jdm verkehren; **prince ~** Prinzgemahl *m*
consortium [kənˈsɔːtɪəm] *n* Konsortium *nt*
conspicuous [kənˈspɪkjuəs] *adj* auffallend; **to make o.s. ~** auffallen
conspiracy [kənˈspɪrəsɪ] *n* Verschwörung *f*, Komplott *nt*
conspiratorial [kənspɪrəˈtɔːrɪəl] *adj* verschwörerisch

conspire [kən'spaɪəʳ] *vi* sich verschwören; (*events*) zusammenkommen
constable ['kʌnstəbl] (*Brit*) *n* Polizist *m*; **chief ~** Polizeipräsident *m*, Polizeichef *m*
constabulary [kən'stæbjulərɪ] (*Brit*) *n* Polizei *f*
constant ['kɔnstənt] *adj* dauernd, ständig; (*fixed*) konstant, gleichbleibend
constantly ['kɔnstəntlɪ] *adv* (an)dauernd, ständig
constellation [kɔnstə'leɪʃən] *n* Sternbild *nt*
consternation [kɔnstə'neɪʃən] *n* Bestürzung *f*
constipated ['kɔnstɪpeɪtɪd] *adj*: **to be ~** Verstopfung haben, verstopft sein
constipation [kɔnstɪ'peɪʃən] *n* Verstopfung *f*
constituency [kən'stɪtjuənsɪ] *n* (*Pol*) Wahlkreis *m*; (*electors*) Wähler *pl* (*eines Wahlkreises*)
constituency party *n Parteiorganisation in einem Wahlkreis*
constituent [kən'stɪtjuənt] *n* (*Pol*) Wähler(in) *m(f)*; (*component*) Bestandteil *m*
constitute ['kɔnstɪtju:t] *vt* (*represent*) darstellen; (*make up*) bilden, ausmachen
constitution [kɔnstɪ'tju:ʃən] *n* (*Pol*) Verfassung *f*; (*of club etc*) Satzung *f*; (*health*) Konstitution *f*, Gesundheit *f*; (*make-up*) Zusammensetzung *f*
constitutional [kɔnstɪ'tju:ʃənl] *adj* (*government*) verfassungsmäßig; (*reform etc*) Verfassungs-
constitutional monarchy *n* konstitutionelle Monarchie *f*
constrain [kən'streɪn] *vt* zwingen
constrained [kən'streɪnd] *adj* gezwungen
constraint [kən'streɪnt] *n* Beschränkung *f*, Einschränkung *f*; (*compulsion*) Zwang *m*; (*embarrassment*) Befangenheit *f*
constrict [kən'strɪkt] *vt* einschnüren; (*blood vessel*) verengen; (*limit, restrict*) einschränken
constriction [kən'strɪkʃən] *n* Einschränkung *f*; (*tightness*) Verengung *f*; (*squeezing*) Einschnürung *f*
construct [kən'strʌkt] *vt* bauen; (*machine*) konstruieren; (*theory, argument*) entwickeln
construction [kən'strʌkʃən] *n* Bau *m*; (*structure*) Konstruktion *f*; (*fig: interpretation*) Deutung *f*; **under ~** in *or* im Bau
construction industry *n* Bauindustrie *f*
constructive [kən'strʌktɪv] *adj* konstruktiv
construe [kən'stru:] *vt* auslegen, deuten
consul ['kɔnsl] *n* Konsul(in) *m(f)*
consulate ['kɔnsjulɪt] *n* Konsulat *nt*
consult [kən'sʌlt] *vt* (*doctor, lawyer*) konsultieren; (*friend*) sich beraten *or* besprechen mit; (*reference book*) nachschlagen in *+dat*; **to ~ sb (about sth)** jdn (wegen etw) fragen
consultancy [kən'sʌltənsɪ] *n* Beratungsbüro *nt or* -firma *f*; (*Med: job*) Facharztstelle *f*
consultant [kən'sʌltənt] *n* (*Med*) Facharzt *m*, Fachärztin *f*; (*other specialist*) Berater(in) *m(f)* ▷ *cpd*: **~ engineer** beratender Ingenieur *m*; **~ paediatrician** Facharzt/-ärztin *m/f* für Pädiatrie *or* Kinderheilkunde; **legal/management ~** Rechts-/ Unternehmensberater(in) *m(f)*; **consultants** *npl* Beratungsbüro *nt or* -firma *f*
consultation [kɔnsəl'teɪʃən] *n* (*Med, Law*) Konsultation *f*; (*discussion*) Beratung *f*, Besprechung *f*; **in ~ with** in gemeinsamer Beratung mit
consultative [kən'sʌltətɪv] *adj* beratend
consulting room [kən'sʌltɪŋ-] (*Brit*) *n* Sprechzimmer *nt*
consume [kən'sju:m] *vt* (*food, drink*) zu sich nehmen, konsumieren; (*fuel, energy*) verbrauchen; (*time*) in Anspruch nehmen; (*subj: emotion*) verzehren; (*: fire*) vernichten
consumer [kən'sju:məʳ] *n* Verbraucher(in) *m(f)*
consumer credit *n* Verbraucherkredit *m*
consumer durables *npl* (langlebige) Gebrauchsgüter *pl*
consumer goods *npl* Konsumgüter *pl*
consumerism [kən'sju:mərɪzəm] *n* Verbraucherschutz *m*
consumer society *n* Konsumgesellschaft *f*
consumer watchdog *n* Verbraucherschutzorganisation *f*
consummate ['kɔnsʌmeɪt] *vt* (*marriage*) vollziehen; (*ambition etc*) erfüllen
consumption [kən'sʌmpʃən] *n* Verbrauch *m*; (*of food*) Verzehr *m*; (*of drinks, buying*) Konsum *m*; (*Med*) Schwindsucht *f*; **not fit for human ~** zum Verzehr ungeeignet
cont. *abbr* (*= continued*) Forts.
contact ['kɔntækt] *n* Kontakt *m*; (*touch*) Berührung *f*; (*person*) Kontaktperson *f* ▷ *vt* sich in Verbindung setzen mit; **to be in ~ with sb/sth** mit jdm/etw in Verbindung *or* Kontakt stehen; (*touch*) jdn/etw berühren; **business ~s** Geschäftsverbindungen *pl*
contact lenses *npl* Kontaktlinsen *pl*
contagious [kən'teɪdʒəs] *adj* ansteckend
contain [kən'teɪn] *vt* enthalten; (*growth, spread*) in Grenzen halten; (*feeling*) beherrschen; **to ~ o.s.** an sich *acc* halten
container [kən'teɪnəʳ] *n* Behälter *m*; (*for shipping etc*) Container *m* ▷ *cpd* Container-
containerize [kən'teɪnəraɪz] *vt* in Container verpacken; (*port*) auf Container umstellen
container ship *n* Containerschiff *nt*
contaminate [kən'tæmɪneɪt] *vt* (*water, food*) verunreinigen; (*soil etc*) verseuchen
contamination [kəntæmɪ'neɪʃən] *n* (*see vb*) Verunreinigung *f*; Verseuchung *f*
cont'd *abbr* (*= continued*) Forts.
contemplate ['kɔntəmpleɪt] *vt* nachdenken über *+acc*; (*course of action*) in Erwägung ziehen; (*person, painting etc*) betrachten
contemplation [kɔntəm'pleɪʃən] *n* Betrachtung *f*
contemporary [kən'tɛmpərərɪ] *adj* zeitgenössisch; (*present-day*) modern ▷ *n* Altersgenosse *m*, Altersgenossin *f*; **Samuel Pepys and his contemporaries** Samuel Pepys und seine Zeitgenossen
contempt [kən'tɛmpt] *n* Verachtung *f*; **~ of court** (*Law*) Missachtung *f* (der Würde) des

Gerichts, Ungebühr *f* vor Gericht; **to have ~ for sb/sth** jdn/etw verachten; **to hold sb in ~** jdn verachten

contemptible [kən'tɛmptəbl] *adj* verachtenswert

contemptuous [kən'tɛmptjuəs] *adj* verächtlich, geringschätzig

contend [kən'tɛnd] *vt*: **to ~ that ...** behaupten, dass ...; **to ~ with** fertig werden mit; **to ~ for** kämpfen um; **to have to ~ with** es zu tun haben mit; **he has a lot to ~ with** er hat viel um die Ohren

contender [kən'tɛndə^r] *n* (*Sport*) Wettkämpfer(in) *m(f)*; (*for title*) Anwärter(in) *m(f)*; (*Pol*) Kandidat(in) *m(f)*

content [*adj, vt* kən'tɛnt, *n* 'kɔntɛnt] *adj* zufrieden ▷ *vt* zufriedenstellen ▷ *n* Inhalt *m*; (*fat content, moisture content etc*) Gehalt *m*; **contents** *npl* Inhalt; **(table of) ~s** Inhaltsverzeichnis *nt*; **to be ~ with** zufrieden sein mit; **to ~ o.s. with sth** sich mit etw zufriedengeben *or* begnügen; **to ~ o.s. with doing sth** sich damit zufriedengeben *or* begnügen, etw zu tun

contented [kən'tɛntɪd] *adj* zufrieden

contentedly [kən'tɛntɪdlɪ] *adv* zufrieden

contention [kən'tɛnʃən] *n* Behauptung *f*; (*disagreement, argument*) Streit *m*; **bone of ~** Zankapfel *m*

contentious [kən'tɛnʃəs] *adj* strittig, umstritten

contentment [kən'tɛntmənt] *n* Zufriedenheit *f*

contest [*n* 'kɔntɛst, *vt* kən'tɛst] *n* (*competition*) Wettkampf *m*; (*for control, power etc*) Kampf *m* ▷ *vt* (*election, competition*) teilnehmen an *+dat*; (*compete for*) kämpfen um; (*statement*) bestreiten; (*decision*) angreifen; (*Law*) anfechten

contestant [kən'tɛstənt] *n* (*in quiz*) Kandidat(in) *m(f)*; (*in competition*) Teilnehmer(in) *m(f)*; (*in fight*) Kämpfer(in) *m(f)*

context ['kɔntɛkst] *n* Zusammenhang *m*, Kontext *m*; **in ~** im Zusammenhang; **out of ~** aus dem Zusammenhang gerissen

continent ['kɔntɪnənt] *n* Kontinent *m*, Erdteil *m*; **the C~** (*Brit*) (Kontinental)europa *nt*; **on the C~** in (Kontinental)europa, auf dem Kontinent

continental [kɔntɪ'nɛntl] *adj* kontinental; (*European*) europäisch ▷ *n* (*Brit*) (Festlands)europäer(in) *m(f)*

continental breakfast *n* kleines Frühstück *nt*

continental quilt (*Brit*) *n* Steppdecke *f*

contingency [kən'tɪndʒənsɪ] *n* möglicher Fall *m*, Eventualität *f*

contingency plan *n* Plan *m* für den Eventualfall

contingent [kən'tɪndʒənt] *n* Kontingent *nt* ▷ *adj*: **to be ~ upon** abhängen von

continual [kən'tɪnjuəl] *adj* ständig; (*process*) ununterbrochen

continually [kən'tɪnjuəlɪ] *adv* (*see adj*) ständig; ununterbrochen

continuation [kəntɪnju'eɪʃən] *n* Fortsetzung *f*; (*extension*) Weiterführung *f*

continue [kən'tɪnju:] *vi* weitermachen, andauern; (*performance, road*) weitergehen; (*person: talking*) fortfahren ▷ *vt* fortsetzen; **to ~ to do sth/doing sth** etw weiter tun; **"to be ~d"** „Fortsetzung folgt"; **"~d on page 10"** „Fortsetzung auf Seite 10"

continuing education [kən'tɪnjuɪŋ-] *n* Erwachsenenbildung *f*

continuity [kɔntɪ'nju:ɪtɪ] *n* Kontinuität *f*; (*TV, Cine*) Anschluß *m* ▷ *cpd* (*TV*): **~ announcer** Ansager(in) *m(f)*; **~ studio** Ansagestudio *nt*

continuous [kən'tɪnjuəs] *adj* ununterbrochen; (*growth etc*) kontinuierlich; **~ form** (*Ling*) Verlaufsform *f*; **~ performance** (*Cine*) durchgehende Vorstellung *f*

continuously [kən'tɪnjuəslɪ] *adv* dauernd, ständig; (*uninterruptedly*) ununterbrochen

continuous stationery *n* (*Comput*) Endlospapier *nt*

contort [kən'tɔ:t] *vt* (*body*) verrenken, verdrehen; (*face*) verziehen

contortion [kən'tɔ:ʃən] *n* Verrenkung *f*

contortionist [kən'tɔ:ʃənɪst] *n* Schlangenmensch *m*

contour ['kɔntuə^r] *n* (*also*: **contour line**) Höhenlinie *f*; (*shape, outline*: *gen pl*) Kontur *f*, Umriss *m*

contraband ['kɔntrəbænd] *n* Schmuggelware *f* ▷ *adj* Schmuggel-

contraception [kɔntrə'sɛpʃən] *n* Empfängnisverhütung *f*

contraceptive [kɔntrə'sɛptɪv] *adj* empfängnisverhütend ▷ *n* Verhütungsmittel *nt*

contract [*n, cpd* 'kɔntrækt, *vb* kən'trækt] *n* Vertrag *m* ▷ *vi* schrumpfen; (*metal, muscle*) sich zusammenziehen ▷ *vt* (*illness*) erkranken an *+dat* ▷ *cpd* vertraglich festgelegt; (*work*) Auftrags-; **~ of employment/service** Arbeitsvertrag *m*; **to ~ to do sth** (*Comm*) sich vertraglich verpflichten, etw zu tun

▸ **contract in** (*Brit*) *vi* beitreten

▸ **contract out** (*Brit*) *vi* austreten

contraction [kən'trækʃən] *n* Zusammenziehen *nt*; (*Ling*) Kontraktion *f*; (*Med*) Wehe *f*

contractor [kən'træktə^r] *n* Auftragnehmer *m*; (*also*: **building contractor**) Bauunternehmer *m*

contractual [kən'træktʃuəl] *adj* vertraglich

contradict [kɔntrə'dɪkt] *vt* widersprechen *+dat*

contradiction [kɔntrə'dɪkʃən] *n* Widerspruch *m*; **to be in ~ with** im Widerspruch stehen zu; **a ~ in terms** ein Widerspruch in sich

contradictory [kɔntrə'dɪktərɪ] *adj* widersprüchlich

contralto [kən'træltəu] *n* (*Mus*) Altistin *f*; (*: voice*) Alt *m*

contraption [kən'træpʃən] (*pej*) *n* (*device*) Vorrichtung *f*; (*machine*) Gerät *nt*, Apparat *m*

contrary¹ ['kɔntrərɪ] *adj* entgegengesetzt;

(*ideas, opinions*) gegensätzlich; (*unfavourable*) widrig ▷ *n* Gegenteil *nt*; **~ to what we thought** im Gegensatz zu dem, was wir dachten; **on the ~** im Gegenteil; **unless you hear to the ~** sofern Sie nichts Gegenteiliges hören

contrary² [kən'trɛərɪ] *adj* widerspenstig

contrast ['kɔntrɑːst] *n* Gegensatz *m*, Kontrast *m* ▷ *vt* vergleichen, gegenüberstellen; **in ~ to** *or* **with** im Gegensatz zu

contrasting [kən'trɑːstɪŋ] *adj* (*colours*) kontrastierend; (*attitudes*) gegensätzlich

contravene [kɔntrə'viːn] *vt* verstoßen gegen

contravention [kɔntrə'vɛnʃən] *n* Verstoß *m*; **to be in ~ of sth** gegen etw verstoßen

contribute [kən'trɪbjuːt] *vi* beitragen ▷ *vt*: **to ~ £10/an article to** £10/einen Artikel beisteuern zu; **to ~ to** (*charity*) spenden für; (*newspaper*) schreiben für; (*discussion, problem etc*) beitragen zu

contribution [kɔntrɪ'bjuːʃən] *n* Beitrag *m*; (*donation*) Spende *f*

contributor [kən'trɪbjutəʳ] *n* (*to appeal*) Spender(in) *m(f)*; (*to newspaper*) Mitarbeiter(in) *m(f)*

contributory [kən'trɪbjutərɪ] *adj*: **a ~ cause** ein Faktor, der mit eine Rolle spielt; **it was a ~ factor in ...** es trug zu ... bei

contributory pension scheme (*Brit*) *n* beitragspflichtige Rentenversicherung *f*

contrite ['kɔntraɪt] *adj* zerknirscht

contrivance [kən'traɪvəns] *n* (*scheme*) List *f*; (*device*) Vorrichtung *f*

contrive [kən'traɪv] *vt* (*meeting*) arrangieren ▷ *vi*: **to ~ to do sth** es fertigbringen, etw zu tun

control [kən'trəul] *vt* (*country*) regieren; (*organization*) leiten; (*machinery, process*) steuern; (*wages, prices*) kontrollieren; (*temper*) zügeln; (*disease, fire*) unter Kontrolle bringen ▷ *n* (*of country*) Kontrolle *f*; (*of organization*) Leitung *f*; (*of oneself, emotions*) Beherrschung *f*; (*Sci*: *also*: **control group**) Kontrollgruppe *f*; **controls** *npl* (*of vehicle*) Steuerung *f*; (*on radio, television etc*) Bedienungsfeld *nt*; (*governmental*) Kontrolle *f*; **to ~ o.s.** sich beherrschen; **to take ~ of** die Kontrolle übernehmen über *+acc*; (*Comm*) übernehmen; **to be in ~ of** unter Kontrolle haben; (*in charge of*) unter sich *dat* haben; **out of/under ~** außer/unter Kontrolle; **everything is under ~** ich habe/wir haben *etc* die Sache im Griff (*inf*); **the car went out of ~** der Fahrer verlor die Kontrolle über den Wagen; **circumstances beyond our ~** unvorhersehbare Umstände

control key *n* (*Comput*) Controltaste *f*, Steuerungstaste *f*

controlled substance *n* veschreibungspflichtiges Medikament

controller [kən'trəuləʳ] *n* (*Radio, TV*) Intendant(in) *m(f)*

controlling interest [kən'trəulɪŋ-] *n* Mehrheitsanteil *m*

control panel *n* Schalttafel *f*; (*on television*) Bedienungsfeld *nt*

control point *n* Kontrollpunkt *m*, Kontrollstelle *f*

control room *n* (*Naut*) Kommandoraum *m*; (*Mil*) (Operations)zentrale *f*; (*Radio, TV*) Regieraum *m*

control tower *n* Kontrollturm *m*

control unit *n* (*Comput*) Steuereinheit *f*

controversial [kɔntrə'vəːʃl] *adj* umstritten, kontrovers

controversy ['kɔntrəvəːsɪ] *n* Streit *m*, Kontroverse *f*

conurbation [kɔnə'beɪʃən] *n* Ballungsgebiet *nt*, Ballungsraum *m*

convalesce [kɔnvə'lɛs] *vi* genesen

convalescence [kɔnvə'lɛsns] *n* Genesungszeit *f*

convalescent [kɔnvə'lɛsnt] *adj* (*leave etc*) Genesungs-, Kur- ▷ *n* Genesende(r) *f(m)*

convector [kən'vɛktəʳ] *n* Heizlüfter *m*

convene [kən'viːn] *vt* einberufen ▷ *vi* zusammentreten

convener [kən'viːnəʳ] *n* (*organizer*) Organisator(in) *m(f)*; (*chairperson*) Vorsitzende(r) *f(m)*

convenience [kən'viːnɪəns] *n* Annehmlichkeit *f*; (*suitability*): **the ~ of this arrangement/location** diese günstige Vereinbarung/Lage; **I like the ~ of having a shower** mir gefällt, wie angenehm es ist, eine Dusche zu haben; **I like the ~ of living in the city** mir gefällt, wie praktisch es ist, in der Stadt zu wohnen; **at your ~** wann es Ihnen passt; **at your earliest ~** möglichst bald, baldmöglichst; **with all modern ~s, with all mod cons** (*Brit*) mit allem modernen Komfort; *see also* **public convenience**

convenience foods *npl* Fertiggerichte *pl*

convenient [kən'viːnɪənt] *adj* günstig; (*handy*) praktisch; (*house etc*) günstig gelegen; **if it is ~ to you** wenn es Ihnen (so) passt, wenn es Ihnen keine Umstände macht

conveniently [kən'viːnɪəntlɪ] *adv* (*happen*) günstigerweise; (*situated*) günstig

convenor [kən'viːnəʳ] *n* = **convener**

convent ['kɔnvənt] *n* Kloster *nt*

convention [kən'vɛnʃən] *n* Konvention *f*; (*conference*) Tagung *f*, Konferenz *f*; (*agreement*) Abkommen *nt*

conventional [kən'vɛnʃənl] *adj* konventionell

convent school *n* Klosterschule *f*

converge [kən'vəːdʒ] *vi* (*roads*) zusammenlaufen ▷ *vi* sich einander annähern; **to ~ on sb/a place** (*people*) von überallher zu jdm/an einen Ort strömen

conversant [kən'vəːsnt] *adj*: **to be ~ with** vertraut sein mit

conversation [kɔnvə'seɪʃən] *n* Gespräch *nt*, Unterhaltung *f*

conversational [kɔnvə'seɪʃənl] *adj* (*tone, style*) Unterhaltungs-; (*language*) gesprochen; **~ mode** (*Comput*) Dialogbetrieb *m*

conversationalist [kɔnvəˈseɪʃnəlɪst] *n* Unterhalter(in) *m(f)*, Gesprächspartner(in) *m(f)*
converse [*n* ˈkɔnvəːs, *vi* kənˈvəːs] *n* Gegenteil *nt* ▷ *vi*: **to ~ (with sb) (about sth)** sich (mit jdm) (über etw) unterhalten
conversely [kɔnˈvəːslɪ] *adv* umgekehrt
conversion [kənˈvəːʃən] *n* Umwandlung *f*; (*of weights etc*) Umrechnung *f*; (*Rel*) Bekehrung *f*; (*Brit: of house*) Umbau *m*
conversion table *n* Umrechnungstabelle *f*
convert [*vt* kənˈvəːt, *n* ˈkɔnvəːt] *vt* umwandeln; (*person*) bekehren; (*building*) umbauen; (*vehicle*) umrüsten; (*Comm*) konvertieren; (*Rugby*) verwandeln ▷ *n* Bekehrte(r) *f(m)*
convertible [kənˈvəːtəbl] *adj* (*currency*) konvertierbar ▷ *n* (*Aut*) Kabriolett *nt*
convex [ˈkɔnvɛks] *adj* konvex
convey [kənˈveɪ] *vt* (*information etc*) vermitteln; (*cargo, traveller*) befördern; (*thanks*) übermitteln
conveyance [kənˈveɪəns] *n* Beförderung *f*, Spedition *f*; (*vehicle*) Gefährt *nt*
conveyancing [kənˈveɪənsɪŋ] *n* (Eigentums)übertragung *f*
conveyor belt *n* Fließband *nt*
convict [*vt* kənˈvɪkt, *n* ˈkɔnvɪkt] *vt* verurteilen ▷ *n* Sträfling *m*
conviction [kənˈvɪkʃən] *n* Überzeugung *f*; (*Law*) Verurteilung *f*
convince [kənˈvɪns] *vt* überzeugen; **to ~ sb (of sth)** jdn (von etw) überzeugen; **to ~ sb that ...** jdn davon überzeugen, dass ...
convinced [kənˈvɪnst] *adj*: **~ (of)** überzeugt (von); **~ that ...** überzeugt davon, dass ...
convincing [kənˈvɪnsɪŋ] *adj* überzeugend
convincingly [kənˈvɪnsɪŋlɪ] *adv* überzeugend
convivial [kənˈvɪvɪəl] *adj* freundlich; (*event*) gesellig
convoluted [ˈkɔnvəluːtɪd] *adj* verwickelt, kompliziert; (*shape*) gewunden
convoy [ˈkɔnvɔɪ] *n* Konvoi *m*
convulse [kənˈvʌls] *vt*: **to be ~d with laughter/pain** sich vor Lachen schütteln/Schmerzen krümmen
convulsion [kənˈvʌlʃən] *n* Schüttelkrampf *m*
coo [kuː] *vi* gurren
cook [kuk] *vt* kochen, zubereiten ▷ *vi* (*person, food*) kochen; (*fry, roast*) braten; (*pie*) backen ▷ *n* Koch *m*, Köchin *f*
▸ **cook up** (*inf*) *vt* sich *dat* einfallen lassen, zurechtbasteln
cookbook [ˈkukbuk] *n* Kochbuch *nt*
cook-chill [ˈkuktʃɪl] *adj* durch rasches Kühlen haltbar gemacht
cooker [ˈkukəʳ] *n* Herd *m*
cookery [ˈkukərɪ] *n* Kochen *nt*, Kochkunst *f*
cookery book (*Brit*) *n* = **cookbook**
cookie [ˈkukɪ] (*US*) *n* Keks *m or nt*, Plätzchen *nt*
cooking [ˈkukɪŋ] *n* Kochen *nt*; (*food*) Essen *nt* ▷ *cpd* Koch-; (*chocolate*) Block-
cookout [ˈkukaut] (*US*) *n* ≈ Grillparty *f*
cool [kuːl] *adj* kühl; (*dress, clothes*) leicht, luftig; (*person: calm*) besonnen; (*: unfriendly*) kühl ▷ *vt* kühlen ▷ *vi* abkühlen; **it's ~** es ist kühl; **to keep sth ~** *or* **in a ~ place** etw kühl aufbewahren; **to keep one's ~** die Ruhe bewahren
▸ **cool down** *vi* abkühlen; (*fig*) sich beruhigen
coolant [ˈkuːlənt] *n* Kühlflüssigkeit *f*
cool box *n* Kühlbox *f*
cooler [ˈkuːləʳ] (*US*) *n* = **cool box**
cooling [ˈkuːlɪŋ] *adj* (*drink, shower*) kühlend; (*feeling, emotion*) abkühlend
cooling tower [ˈkuːlɪŋ-] *n* Kühlturm *m*
coolly [ˈkuːlɪ] *adv* (*calmly*) besonnen, ruhig; (*in unfriendly way*) kühl
coolness [ˈkuːlnɪs] *n* (*see adj*) Kühle *f*; Leichtigkeit *f*, Luftigkeit *f*; Besonnenheit *f*
coop [kuːp] *n* (*for rabbits*) Kaninchenstall *m*; (*for poultry*) Hühnerstall *m* ▷ *vt*: **to ~ up** (*fig*) einsperren
co-op [ˈkəuɔp] *n abbr* (= *cooperative (society)*) Genossenschaft *f*
cooperate [kəuˈɔpəreɪt] *vi* zusammenarbeiten; (*assist*) mitmachen, kooperieren; **to ~ with sb** mit jdm zusammenarbeiten
cooperation [kəuɔpəˈreɪʃən] *n* (*see vb*) Zusammenarbeit *f*; Mitarbeit *f*, Kooperation *f*
cooperative [kəuˈɔpərətɪv] *adj* (*farm, business*) auf Genossenschaftsbasis; (*person*) kooperativ; (*: helpful*) hilfsbereit ▷ *n* Genossenschaft *f*, Kooperative *f*
coopt [kəuˈɔpt] *vt*: **to ~ sb onto a committee** jdn in ein Komitee hinzuwählen *or* kooptieren
coordinate [kəuˈɔːdɪneɪt] *vt* koordinieren ▷ *n* (*Math*) Koordinate *f*; **coordinates** *npl* (*clothes*) Kleidung *f* zum Kombinieren
coordination [kəuɔːdɪˈneɪʃən] *n* Koordinierung *f*, Koordination *f*
coownership [kəʊˈəʊnəʃɪp] *n* Mitbesitz *m*
cop [kɔp] (*inf*) *n* Polizist(in) *m(f)*, Bulle *m* (*pej*)
cope [kəup] *vi* zurechtkommen; **to ~ with** fertig werden mit
Copenhagen [ˈkəupnˈheɪgən] *n* Kopenhagen *nt*
copier [ˈkɔpɪəʳ] *n* (*also*: **photocopier**) Kopiergerät *nt*, Kopierer *m*
copilot [ˈkəupaɪlət] *n* Kopilot(in) *m(f)*
copious [ˈkəupɪəs] *adj* reichlich
copper [ˈkɔpəʳ] *n* Kupfer *nt*; (*Brit: inf*) Polizist(in) *m(f)*, Bulle *m* (*pej*); **coppers** *npl* (*small change, coins*) Kleingeld *nt*
coppice [ˈkɔpɪs] *n* Wäldchen *nt*
copse [kɔps] *n* = **coppice**
copulate [ˈkɔpjuleɪt] *vi* kopulieren
copy [ˈkɔpɪ] *n* Kopie *f*; (*of book, record, newspaper*) Exemplar *nt*; (*for printing*) Artikel *m* ▷ *vt* (*person*) nachahmen; (*idea etc*) nachmachen; (*something written*) abschreiben; **this murder story will make good ~** (*Press*) aus diesem Mord kann man etwas machen
▸ **copy out** *vt* abschreiben
copycat [ˈkɔpɪkæt] (*pej*) *n* Nachahmer(in) *m(f)*
copyright [ˈkɔpɪraɪt] *n* Copyright *nt*, Urheberrecht *nt*; **~ reserved** urheberrechtlich geschützt

copy typist *n* Schreibkraft *f* (*die mit Textvorlagen arbeitet*)
copywriter ['kɔpɪraɪtəʳ] *n* Werbetexter(in) *m(f)*
coral ['kɔrəl] *n* Koralle *f*
coral reef *n* Korallenriff *nt*
Coral Sea *n*: **the ~** das Korallenmeer
cord [kɔ:d] *n* Schnur *f*; (*string*) Kordel *f*; (*Elec*) Kabel *nt*, Schnur *f*; (*fabric*) Cord(samt) *m*; **cords** *npl* (*trousers*) Cordhosen *pl*
cordial ['kɔ:dɪəl] *adj* herzlich ▷ *n* (*Brit*) Fruchtsaftkonzentrat *nt*
cordless ['kɔ:dlɪs] *adj* schnurlos
cordon ['kɔ:dn] *n* Kordon *m*, Absperrkette *f* ▶ **cordon off** *vt* (*area*) absperren, abriegeln; (*crowd*) mit einer Absperrkette zurückhalten
corduroy ['kɔ:dərɔɪ] *n* Cord(samt) *m*
CORE [kɔ:ʳ] (*US*) *n abbr* (= *Congress of Racial Equality*) *Ausschuss für Rassengleichheit*
core [kɔ:ʳ] *n* Kern *m*; (*of fruit*) Kerngehäuse *nt* ▷ *vt* das Kerngehäuse ausschneiden aus; **rotten to the ~** durch und durch schlecht
core (business) activity *n* (*Econ*) Kerngeschäft *nt*
Corfu [kɔ:'fu:] *n* Korfu *nt*
coriander [kɔrɪ'ændəʳ] *n* Koriander *m*
cork [kɔ:k] *n* (*stopper*) Korken *m*; (*substance*) Kork *m*
corkage ['kɔ:kɪdʒ] *n* Korkengeld *nt*
corked [kɔ:kt] *adj*: **the wine is ~** der Wein schmeckt nach Kork
corkscrew ['kɔ:kskru:] *n* Korkenzieher *m*
corky ['kɔ:kɪ] (*US*) *adj* = **corked**
corm [kɔ:m] *n* Knolle *f*
cormorant ['kɔ:mərnt] *n* Kormoran *m*
corn [kɔ:n] *n* (*Brit*) Getreide *nt*, Korn *nt*; (*US*) Mais *m*; (*on foot*) Hühnerauge *nt*; **~ on the cob** Maiskolben *m*
cornea ['kɔ:nɪə] *n* Hornhaut *f*
corned beef ['kɔ:nd-] *n* Corned Beef *nt*
corner ['kɔ:nəʳ] *n* Ecke *f*; (*bend*) Kurve *f* ▷ *vt* in die Enge treiben; (*Comm: market*) monopolisieren ▷ *vi* (*in car*) die Kurve nehmen; **to cut ~s** (*fig*) das Verfahren abkürzen
corner flag *n* Eckfahne *f*
corner kick *n* Eckball *m*
cornerstone ['kɔ:nəstəun] *n* (*fig*) Grundstein *m*, Eckstein *m*
cornet ['kɔ:nɪt] *n* (*Mus*) Kornett *nt*; (*Brit: for ice cream*) Eistüte *f*
cornflakes ['kɔ:nfleɪks] *npl* Cornflakes *pl*
cornflour ['kɔ:nflauəʳ] (*Brit*) *n* Stärkemehl *nt*
cornice ['kɔ:nɪs] *n* (Ge)sims *nt*
Cornish ['kɔ:nɪʃ] *adj* kornisch, aus Cornwall
corn oil *n* (Mais)keimöl *nt*
cornstarch ['kɔ:nstɑ:tʃ] (*US*) *n* = **cornflour**
cornucopia [kɔ:nju'kəupɪə] *n* Fülle *f*
Cornwall ['kɔ:nwəl] *n* Cornwall *nt*
corny ['kɔ:nɪ] (*inf*) *adj* (*joke*) blöd
corollary [kə'rɔlərɪ] *n* (logische) Folge *f*
coronary ['kɔrənərɪ] *n* (*also*: **coronary thrombosis**) Herzinfarkt *m*
coronation [kɔrə'neɪʃən] *n* Krönung *f*
coroner ['kɔrənəʳ] *n Beamter, der Todesfälle untersucht, die nicht eindeutig eine natürliche Ursache haben*
coronet ['kɔrənɪt] *n* Krone *f*
Corp. *abbr* = **corporation**; (*Mil*) = **corporal**
corporal ['kɔ:pərl] *n* Stabsunteroffizier *m*
corporal punishment *n* Prügelstrafe *f*
corporate ['kɔ:pərɪt] *adj* (*organization*) körperschaftlich; (*action, effort, ownership*) gemeinschaftlich; (*finance*) Unternehmens-; (*image, identity*) Firmen-
corporate hospitality *n Empfänge, Diners etc auf Kosten der ausrichtenden Firma*
corporation [kɔ:pə'reɪʃən] *n* (*Comm*) Körperschaft *f*; (*of town*) Gemeinde *f*, Stadt *f*
corporation tax *n* Körperschaftssteuer *f*
corps [kɔ:ʳ] (*pl* **~**) *n* Korps *nt*; **the press ~** die Presse
corpse [kɔ:ps] *n* Leiche *f*
corpuscle ['kɔ:pʌsl] *n* Blutkörperchen *nt*
corral [kə'rɑ:l] *n* Korral *m*
correct [kə'rɛkt] *adj* richtig; (*proper*) korrekt ▷ *vt* korrigieren; (*mistake*) berichtigen, verbessern; **you are ~** Sie haben recht
correction [kə'rɛkʃən] *n* (*see vb*) Korrektur *f*; Berichtigung *f*, Verbesserung *f*
correctly [kə'rɛktlɪ] *adv* (*see adj*) richtig; korrekt
correlate ['kɔrɪleɪt] *vt* zueinander in Beziehung setzen ▷ *vi*: **to ~ with** in einer Beziehung stehen zu
correlation [kɔrɪ'leɪʃən] *n* Beziehung *f*, Zusammenhang *m*
correspond [kɔrɪs'pɔnd] *vi*: **to ~ (with)** (*write*) korrespondieren (mit); (*be in accordance*) übereinstimmen (mit); **to ~ to** (*be equivalent*) entsprechen *+dat*
correspondence [kɔrɪs'pɔndəns] *n* Korrespondenz *f*, Briefwechsel *m*; (*relationship*) Beziehung *f*
correspondence column *n* Leserbriefspalte *f*
correspondence course *n* Fernkurs *m*
correspondent [kɔrɪs'pɔndənt] *n* Korrespondent(in) *m(f)*
corresponding [kɔrɪs'pɔndɪŋ] *adj* entsprechend
corridor ['kɔrɪdɔ:ʳ] *n* Korridor *m*; (*in train*) Gang *m*
corroborate [kə'rɔbəreɪt] *vt* bestätigen
corrode [kə'rəud] *vt* zerfressen ▷ *vi* korrodieren
corrosion [kə'rəuʒən] *n* Korrosion *f*
corrosive [kə'rəuzɪv] *adj* korrosiv
corrugated ['kɔrəgeɪtɪd] *adj* (*roof*) gewellt; (*cardboard*) Well-
corrugated iron *n* Wellblech *nt*
corrupt [kə'rʌpt] *adj* korrupt; (*depraved*) verdorben ▷ *vt* korrumpieren; (*morally*) verderben; **~ practices** Korruption *f*
corruption [kə'rʌpʃən] *n* Korruption *f*
corset ['kɔ:sɪt] *n* Korsett *nt*; (*Med*) Stützkorsett *nt*
Corsica ['kɔ:sɪkə] *n* Korsika *nt*
Corsican ['kɔ:sɪkən] *adj* korsisch ▷ *n* Korse *m*, Korsin *f*

cortège [kɔːˈteɪʒ] *n* (*also*: **funeral cortège**) Leichenzug *m*
cortisone [ˈkɔːtɪzəun] *n* Kortison *nt*
coruscating [ˈkɔrəskeɪtɪŋ] *adj* sprühend
cosh [kɔʃ] (*Brit*) *n* Totschläger *m*
cosignatory [ˈkəuˈsɪgnətərɪ] *n* Mitunterzeichner(in) *m(f)*
cosiness [ˈkəuzɪnɪs] *n* Gemütlichkeit *f*, Behaglichkeit *f*
cos lettuce [ˈkɔs-] *n* römischer Salat *m*
cosmetic [kɔzˈmɛtɪk] *n* Kosmetikum *nt* ▷ *adj* kosmetisch; **~ surgery** (*Med*) kosmetische Chirurgie *f*
cosmic [ˈkɔzmɪk] *adj* kosmisch
cosmonaut [ˈkɔzmənɔːt] *n* Kosmonaut(in) *m(f)*
cosmopolitan [kɔzməˈpɔlɪtn] *adj* kosmopolitisch
cosmos [ˈkɔzmɔs] *n*: **the ~** der Kosmos
cosset [ˈkɔsɪt] *vt* verwöhnen
cost [kɔst] (*pt, pp* **~**) *n* Kosten *pl*; (*fig: loss, damage etc*) Preis *m* ▷ *vt* kosten; (*find out cost of*) (*pt, pp* **~ed**) veranschlagen; **costs** *npl* (*Comm, Law*) Kosten *pl*; **the ~ of living** die Lebenshaltungskosten *pl*; **at all ~s** um jeden Preis; **how much does it ~?** wie viel *or* was kostet es?; **it ~s £5/too much** es kostet £5/ist zu teuer; **what will it ~ to have it repaired?** wie viel kostet die Reparatur?; **to ~ sb time/effort** jdn Zeit/Mühe kosten; **it ~ him his life/job** es kostete ihn das Leben/seine Stelle
cost accountant *n* Kostenbuchhalter(in) *m(f)*
co-star [ˈkəustɑːʳ] *n* einer der Hauptdarsteller *m*, eine der Hauptdarstellerinnen *f*; **she was Sean Connery's ~ in ...** sie spielte neben Sean Connery in ...
Costa Rica [ˈkɔstəˈriːkə] *n* Costa Rica *nt*
cost centre *n* Kostenstelle *f*
cost control *n* Kostenkontrolle *f*
cost-effective [ˈkɔstɪˈfɛktɪv] *adj* rentabel; (*Comm*) kostengünstig
cost-effectiveness [ˈkɔstɪˈfɛktɪvnɪs] *n* Rentabilität *f*
costing [ˈkɔstɪŋ] *n* Kalkulation *f*
costly [ˈkɔstlɪ] *adj* teuer, kostspielig; (*in time, effort*) aufwendig
cost-of-living [ˈkɔstəvˈlɪvɪŋ] *adj* Lebenshaltungskosten-; (*index*) Lebenshaltungs-
cost price (*Brit*) *n* Selbstkostenpreis *m*; **to sell/buy at ~** zum Selbstkostenpreis verkaufen/kaufen
costume [ˈkɔstjuːm] *n* Kostüm *nt*; (*Brit: also*: **swimming costume**) Badeanzug *m*
costume jewellery *n* Modeschmuck *m*
cosy, (*US*) **cozy** [ˈkəuzɪ] *adj* gemütlich, behaglich; (*bed, scarf, gloves*) warm; (*chat, evening*) gemütlich; **I'm very ~ here** ich fühle mich hier sehr wohl, ich finde es hier sehr gemütlich
cot [kɔt] *n* (*Brit*) Kinderbett *nt*; (*US: campbed*) Feldbett *nt*
cot death *n* Krippentod *m*, plötzlicher Kindstod *m*
Cotswolds [ˈkɔtswəuldz] *npl*: **the ~** die Cotswolds *pl*
cottage [ˈkɔtɪdʒ] *n* Cottage *nt*, Häuschen *nt*
cottage cheese *n* Hüttenkäse *m*
cottage industry *n* Heimindustrie *f*
cottage pie *n Hackfleisch mit Kartoffelbrei überbacken*
cotton [ˈkɔtn] *n* (*fabric*) Baumwollstoff *m*; (*plant*) Baumwollstrauch *m*; (*thread*) (Baumwoll)garn *nt* ▷ *cpd* (*dress etc*) Baumwoll-
▸ **cotton on** (*inf*) *vi*: **to ~ on** es kapieren *or* schnallen; **to ~ on to sth** etw kapieren *or* schnallen
cotton candy (*US*) *n* Zuckerwatte *f*
cotton wool (*Brit*) *n* Watte *f*
couch [kautʃ] *n* Couch *f* ▷ *vt* formulieren
couchette [kuːˈʃɛt] *n* Liegewagen(platz) *m*
couch potato (*esp US: inf*) *n* Dauerglotzer(in) *m(f)*
cough [kɔf] *vi* husten; (*engine*) stottern ▷ *n* Husten *m*
cough drop *n* Hustenpastille *f*
cough mixture *n* Hustensaft *m*
cough syrup *n* = **cough mixture**
could [kud] *pt of* **can²**
couldn't [ˈkudnt] = **could not**
council [ˈkaunsl] *n* Rat *m*; **city/town ~** Stadtrat *m*; **C~ of Europe** Europarat *m*
council estate (*Brit*) *n* Siedlung *f* mit Sozialwohnungen
council house (*Brit*) *n* Sozialwohnung *f*
council housing *n* sozialer Wohnungsbau *m*; (*accommodation*) Sozialwohnungen *pl*
councillor [ˈkaunsləʳ] *n* Stadtrat *m*, Stadträtin *f*
council tax (*Brit*) *n* Gemeindesteuer *f*
counsel [ˈkaunsl] *n* Rat(schlag) *m*; (*lawyer*) Rechtsanwalt *m*, Rechtsanwältin *f* ▷ *vt* beraten; **to ~ sth** etw raten *or* empfehlen; **to ~ sb to do sth** jdm raten *or* empfehlen, etw zu tun; **~ for the defence** Verteidiger(in) *m(f)*; **~ for the prosecution** Vertreter(in) *m(f)* der Anklage
counsellor [ˈkaunsləʳ] *n* Berater(in) *m(f)*; (*US: lawyer*) Rechtsanwalt *m*, Rechtsanwältin *f*
count [kaunt] *vt* zählen; (*include*) mitrechnen, mitzählen ▷ *vi* zählen; (*be considered*) betrachtet *or* angesehen werden ▷ *n* Zählung *f*; (*level*) Zahl *f*; (*nobleman*) Graf *m*; **to ~ (up) to 10** bis 10 zählen; **not ~ing the children** die Kinder nicht mitgerechnet; **10 ~ing him** 10, wenn man ihn mitrechnet; **to ~ the cost of sth** die Folgen von etw abschätzen; **it ~s for very little** es zählt nicht viel; **~ yourself lucky** Sie können sich glücklich schätzen; **to keep ~ of sth** die Übersicht über etw *acc* behalten; **blood ~** Blutbild *nt*; **cholesterol/alcohol ~** Cholesterin-/Alkoholspiegel *m*
▸ **count on** *vt fus* rechnen mit; (*depend on*) sich verlassen auf *+acc*; **to ~ on doing sth** die feste Absicht haben, etw zu tun
▸ **count up** *vt* zusammenzählen, zusammenrechnen
countdown [ˈkauntdaun] *n* Countdown *m*

countenance ['kauntınəns] *n* Gesicht *nt* ▷ *vt* gutheißen
counter ['kauntə^r] *n* (*in shop*) Ladentisch *m*; (*in café*) Theke *f*; (*in bank, post office*) Schalter *m*; (*in game*) Spielmarke *f*; (*Tech*) Zähler *m* ▷ *vt* (*oppose: sth said, sth done*) begegnen +*dat*; (*blow*) kontern ▷ *adv*: **~ to** gegen +*acc*; **to buy sth under the ~** (*fig*) etw unter dem Ladentisch bekommen; **to ~ sth with sth** auf etw *acc* mit etw antworten; **to ~ sth by doing sth** einer Sache damit begegnen, dass man etw tut
counteract ['kauntər'ækt] *vt* entgegenwirken +*dat*; (*effect*) neutralisieren
counterattack ['kauntərə'tæk] *n* Gegenangriff *m* ▷ *vi* einen Gegenangriff starten
counterbalance ['kauntə'bæləns] *vt* Gegengewicht *nt*
counterclockwise ['kauntə'klɔkwaız] *adv* gegen den Uhrzeigersinn
counterespionage ['kauntər'ɛspıənɑ:ʒ] *n* Gegenspionage *f*, Spionageabwehr *f*
counterfeit ['kauntəfıt] *n* Fälschung *f* ▷ *vt* fälschen ▷ *adj* (*coin*) Falsch-
counterfoil ['kauntəfɔıl] *n* Kontrollabschnitt *m*
counterintelligence ['kauntərın'tɛlıdʒəns] *n* Gegenspionage *f*, Spionageabwehr *f*
countermand ['kauntəmɑ:nd] *vt* aufheben, widerrufen
countermeasure ['kauntəmɛʒə^r] *n* Gegenmaßnahme *f*
counteroffensive ['kauntərə'fɛnsıv] *n* Gegenoffensive *f*
counterpane ['kauntəpeın] *n* Tagesdecke *f*
counterpart ['kauntəpɑ:t] *n* Gegenüber *nt*; (*of document etc*) Gegenstück *nt*, Pendant *nt*
counterproductive ['kauntəprə'dʌktıv] *adj* widersinnig
counterproposal ['kauntəprə'pəuzl] *n* Gegenvorschlag *m*
countersign ['kauntəsaın] *vt* gegenzeichnen
countersink ['kauntəsıŋk] *vt* senken
countess ['kauntıs] *n* Gräfin *f*
countless ['kauntlıs] *adj* unzählig, zahllos
countrified ['kʌntrıfaıd] *adj* ländlich
country ['kʌntrı] *n* Land *nt*; (*native land*) Heimatland *nt*; **in the ~** auf dem Land; **mountainous ~** gebirgige Landschaft *f*
country and western, **country and western music** *n* Country-und-Western-Musik *f*
country dancing (*Brit*) *n* Volkstanz *m*
country house *n* Landhaus *nt*
countryman ['kʌntrımən] (*irreg: like* **man**) *n* (*compatriot*) Landsmann *m*; (*country dweller*) Landmann *m*
countryside ['kʌntrısaıd] *n* Land *nt*; (*scenery*) Landschaft *f*, Gegend *f*
country-wide ['kʌntrı'waıd] *adj, adv* landesweit
county ['kauntı] *n* (*Brit*) Grafschaft *f*; (*US*) (Verwaltungs)bezirk *m*
county council (*Brit*) *n* Gemeinderat *m* (*einer Grafschaft*)
county town (*Brit*) *n* *Hauptstadt einer Grafschaft*
coup [ku:] (*pl* **~s**) *n* (*also*: **coup d'état**) Staatsstreich *m*, Coup d'Etat *m*; (*achievement*) Coup *m*
coupé [ku:'peı] *n* Coupé *nt*
couple ['kʌpl] *n* Paar *nt*; (*also*: **married couple**) Ehepaar *nt* ▷ *vt* verbinden; (*vehicles*) koppeln; **a ~ of** (*two*) zwei; (*a few*) ein paar
couplet ['kʌplıt] *n* Verspaar *nt*
coupling ['kʌplıŋ] *n* Kupplung *f*
coupon ['ku:pɔn] *n* Gutschein *m*; (*detachable form*) Abschnitt *m*; (*Comm*) Coupon *m*
courage ['kʌrıdʒ] *n* Mut *m*
courageous [kə'reıdʒəs] *adj* mutig
courgette [kuə'ʒɛt] (*Brit*) *n* Zucchino *m*
courier ['kurıə^r] *n* (*messenger*) Kurier(in) *m(f)*; (*for tourists*) Reiseleiter(in) *m(f)*
course [kɔ:s] *n* (*Scol*) Kurs(us) *m*; (*of ship*) Kurs *m*; (*of life, events, time etc, of river*) Lauf *m*; (*of argument*) Richtung *f*; (*part of meal*) Gang *m*; (*for golf*) Platz *m*; **of ~** natürlich; **of ~!** (aber) natürlich!, (aber) selbstverständlich!; **(no) of ~ not!** natürlich nicht!; **in the ~ of the next few days** während *or* im Laufe der nächsten paar Tage; **in due ~** zu gegebener Zeit; **~ (of action)** Vorgehensweise *f*; **the best ~ would be to ...** das Beste wäre es, zu ...; **we have no other ~ but to ...** es bleibt uns nichts anderes übrig, als zu ...; **~ of lectures** Vorlesungsreihe *f*; **~ of treatment** (*Med*) Behandlung *f*; **first/last ~** erster/letzter Gang, Vor-/Nachspeise *f*
court [kɔ:t] *n* Hof *m*; (*Law*) Gericht *nt*; (*for tennis, badminton etc*) Platz *m* ▷ *vt* den Hof machen +*dat*; (*favour, popularity*) werben um; (*death, disaster*) herausfordern; **out of ~** (*Law*) außergerichtlich; **to take to ~** (*Law*) verklagen, vor Gericht bringen
courteous ['kə:tıəs] *adj* höflich
courtesan [kɔ:tı'zæn] *n* Kurtisane *f*
courtesy ['kə:təsı] *n* Höflichkeit *f*; **(by) ~ of** freundlicherweise zur Verfügung gestellt von
courtesy bus, **courtesy coach** *n* gebührenfreier Bus *m*
courtesy light *n* Innenleuchte *f*
court fine *n* Ordnungsgeld *nt*; **to issue/face a ~** ein Ordnungsgeld verhängen/zu zahlen haben
courthouse ['kɔ:thaus] (*US*) *n* Gerichtsgebäude *nt*
courtier ['kɔ:tıə^r] *n* Höfling *m*
court martial (*pl* **courts martial**) *n* Militärgericht *nt*
court of appeal (*pl* **courts of appeal**) *n* Berufungsgericht *nt*
court of inquiry (*pl* **courts of inquiry**) *n* Untersuchungskommission *f*
courtroom ['kɔ:trum] *n* Gerichtssaal *m*
court shoe *n* Pumps *m*
courtyard ['kɔ:tjɑ:d] *n* Hof *m*
cousin ['kʌzn] *n* (*male*) Cousin *m*, Vetter *m*; (*female*) Cousine *f*; **first ~** Cousin(e) ersten Grades
cove [kəuv] *n* (kleine) Bucht *f*

covenant ['kʌvənənt] *n* Schwur *m* ▷ *vt*: **to ~ £200 per year to a charity** sich vertraglich verpflichten, £200 im Jahr für wohltätige Zwecke zu spenden

Coventry ['kɔvəntrɪ] *n*: **to send sb to ~** *(fig)* jdn schneiden *(inf)*

cover ['kʌvəʳ] *vt* bedecken; *(distance)* zurücklegen; *(Insurance)* versichern; *(topic)* behandeln; *(include)* erfassen; *(Press: report on)* berichten über *+acc* ▷ *n (for furniture)* Bezug *m*; *(for typewriter, PC etc)* Hülle *f*; *(of book, magazine)* Umschlag *m*; *(shelter)* Schutz *m*; *(Insurance)* Versicherung *f*; *(fig: for illegal activities)* Tarnung *f*; **to be ~ed in** *or* **with** bedeckt sein mit; **£10 will ~ my expenses** £10 decken meine Unkosten; **to take ~** *(from rain)* sich unterstellen; **under ~** geschützt; **under ~ of darkness** im Schutz(e) der Dunkelheit; **under separate ~** getrennt

▸ **cover up** *vt* zudecken; *(fig: facts, feelings)* verheimlichen; *(: mistakes)* vertuschen ▷ *vi (fig)*: **to ~ up for sb** jdn decken

coverage ['kʌvərɪdʒ] *n* Berichterstattung *f*; **television ~ of the conference** Fernsehberichte *pl* über die Konferenz; **to give full ~ to** ausführlich berichten über *+acc*

coveralls ['kʌvərɔːlz] *(US) npl* Overall *m*

cover charge *n* Kosten *pl* für ein Gedeck

covering ['kʌvərɪŋ] *n* Schicht *f*; *(of snow, dust etc)* Decke *f*

covering letter, *(US)* **cover letter** *n* Begleitbrief *m*

cover note *n (Insurance)* Deckungszusage *f*

cover price *n* Einzel(exemplar)preis *m*

covert ['kʌvət] *adj* versteckt; *(glance)* verstohlen

cover-up ['kʌvərʌp] *n* Vertuschung *f*, Verschleierung *f*

covet ['kʌvɪt] *vt* begehren

cow [kau] *n (animal, inf!: woman)* Kuh *f* ▷ *cpd* Kuh- ▷ *vt* einschüchtern

coward ['kauəd] *n* Feigling *m*

cowardice ['kauədɪs] *n* Feigheit *f*

cowardly ['kauədlɪ] *adj* feige

cowboy ['kaubɔɪ] *n (in US)* Cowboy *m*; *(pej: tradesman)* Pfuscher *m*

cow elephant *n* Elefantenkuh *f*

cower ['kauəʳ] *vi* sich ducken; *(squatting)* kauern

cowshed ['kauʃɛd] *n* Kuhstall *m*

cowslip ['kauslɪp] *n* Schlüsselblume *f*

cox [kɔks] *n abbr* = **coxswain**

coxswain ['kɔksn] *n* Steuermann *m*; *(of ship)* Boot(s)führer *m*

coy [kɔɪ] *adj* verschämt

coyote [kɔɪ'əutɪ] *n* Kojote *m*

cozy ['kəuzɪ] *(US) adj* = **cosy**

CP *n abbr (= Communist Party)* KP *f*

cp. *abbr (= compare)* vgl.

CPA *(US) n abbr* = **certified public accountant**

CPI *n abbr (= Consumer Price Index)* (Verbraucher)preisindex *m*

Cpl *abbr (Mil)* = **corporal**

CP/M *n abbr (= Control Program for Microprocessors)* CP/M *nt*

cps *abbr (Comput, Typ: = characters per second)* cps, Zeichen *pl* pro Sekunde

CPSA *(Brit) n abbr (= Civil and Public Services Association) Gewerkschaft im öffentlichen Dienst*

CPU *n abbr (Comput)* = **central processing unit**

cr. *abbr* = **credit; creditor**

crab [kræb] *n* Krabbe *f*, Krebs *m*; *(meat)* Krabbe *f*

crab apple *n* Holzapfel *m*

crack [kræk] *n (noise)* Knall *m*; *(of wood breaking)* Knacks *m*; *(gap)* Spalte *f*; *(in bone, dish, glass)* Sprung *m*; *(in wall)* Riss *m*; *(joke)* Witz *m*; *(Drugs)* Crack *nt* ▷ *vt (whip)* knallen mit; *(twig)* knacken mit; *(dish, glass)* einen Sprung machen in *+acc*; *(bone)* anbrechen; *(nut, code)* knacken; *(wall)* rissig machen; *(problem)* lösen; *(joke)* reißen ▷ *adj* erstklassig; **to have a ~ at sth** *(inf)* etw mal probieren; **to ~ jokes** *(inf)* Witze reißen; **to get ~ing** *(inf)* loslegen

▸ **crack down on** *vt fus* hart durchgreifen gegen

▸ **crack up** *vi* durchdrehen, zusammenbrechen

crackdown ['krækdaun] *n*: **~ (on)** scharfes Durchgreifen *nt* (gegen)

cracked [krækt] *(inf) adj* übergeschnappt

cracker ['krækəʳ] *n (biscuit)* Cracker *m*; *(also:* **Christmas cracker***)* Knallbonbon *nt*; *(firework)* Knallkörper *m*, Kracher *m*; **a ~ of a ...** *(Brit: inf)* ein(e) tolle(r, s) ...; **he's ~s** *(Brit: inf)* er ist übergeschnappt

crackle ['krækl] *vi (fire)* knistern, prasseln; *(twig)* knacken

crackling ['kræklɪŋ] *n (of fire)* Knistern *nt*, Prasseln *nt*; *(of twig, on radio, telephone)* Knacken *nt*; *(of pork)* Kruste *f (des Schweinebratens)*

crackpot ['krækpɔt] *(inf) n* Spinner(in) *m(f)* ▷ *adj* verrückt

cradle ['kreɪdl] *n* Wiege *f* ▷ *vt* fest in den Armen halten

craft [krɑːft] *n (skill)* Geschicklichkeit *f*; *(art)* Kunsthandwerk *nt*; *(trade)* Handwerk *nt*; *(pl inv: boat)* Boot *nt*; *(pl inv: plane)* Flugzeug *nt*

craftsman ['krɑːftsmən] *(irreg: like* **man***) n* Handwerker *m*

craftsmanship ['krɑːftsmənʃɪp] *n* handwerkliche Ausführung *f*

crafty ['krɑːftɪ] *adj* schlau, clever

crag [kræg] *n* Fels *m*

craggy ['krægɪ] *adj (mountain)* zerklüftet; *(cliff)* felsig; *(face)* kantig

cram [kræm] *vt* vollstopfen ▷ *vi* pauken *(inf)*, büffeln *(inf)*; **to ~ with** vollstopfen mit; **to ~ sth into** etw hineinstopfen in *+acc*

cramming ['kræmɪŋ] *n (for exams)* Pauken *nt*, Büffeln *nt*

cramp [kræmp] *n* Krampf *m* ▷ *vt* hemmen

cramped [kræmpt] *adj* eng

crampon ['kræmpən] *n* Steigeisen *nt*

cranberry ['krænbərɪ] *n* Preiselbeere *f*

crane [kreɪn] *n* Kran *m*; *(bird)* Kranich *m* ▷ *vt*: **to ~ one's neck** den Hals recken ▷ *vi*: **to ~ forward** den Hals recken

crania ['kreɪnɪə] *npl of* **cranium**
cranium ['kreɪnɪəm] (*pl* **crania**) *n* Schädel *m*
crank [kræŋk] *n* Spinner(in) *m(f)*; (*handle*) Kurbel *f*
crankshaft ['kræŋkʃɑːft] *n* Kurbelwelle *f*
cranky ['kræŋkɪ] *adj* verrückt
cranny ['krænɪ] *n see* **nook**
crap [kræp] (*inf!*) *n* Scheiße *f* (*!*) ▷ *vi* scheißen (*!*); **to have a ~** scheißen (*!*)
crappy ['kræpɪ] (*inf!*) *adj* beschissen (*!*)
crash [kræʃ] *n* (*noise*) Krachen *nt*; (*of car*) Unfall *m*; (*of plane etc*) Unglück *nt*; (*collision*) Zusammenstoß *m*; (*of stock market, business etc*) Zusammenbruch *m* ▷ *vt* (*car*) einen Unfall haben mit; (*plane etc*) abstürzen mit ▷ *vi* (*plane*) abstürzen; (*car*) einen Unfall haben; (*two cars*) zusammenstoßen; (*market*) zusammenbrechen; (*firm*) Pleite machen; **to ~ into** krachen *or* knallen gegen; **he ~ed the car into a wall** er fuhr mit dem Auto gegen eine Mauer
crash barrier (*Brit*) *n* Leitplanke *f*
crash course *n* Schnellkurs *m*, Intensivkurs *m*
crash helmet *n* Sturzhelm *m*
crash-landing ['kræʃlændɪŋ] *n* Bruchlandung *f*
crass [kræs] *adj* krass; (*behaviour*) unfein, derb
crate [kreɪt] *n* (*also inf*) Kiste *f*; (*for bottles*) Kasten *m*
crater ['kreɪtəʳ] *n* Krater *m*
cravat [krə'væt] *n* Halstuch *nt*
crave [kreɪv] *vt, vi*: **to ~ (for)** sich sehnen nach
craven ['kreɪvən] *adj* feige
craving ['kreɪvɪŋ] *n*: **~ (for)** Verlangen *nt* (nach)
crawl [krɔːl] *vi* kriechen; (*child*) krabbeln ▷ *n* (*Swimming*) Kraulstil *m*, Kraul(en) *nt*; **to ~ to sb** (*inf*) vor jdm kriechen; **to drive along at a ~** im Schneckentempo *or* Kriechtempo vorankommen
crawler lane (*Brit*) *n* (*Aut*) Kriechspur *f*
crayfish ['kreɪfɪʃ] *n inv* (*freshwater*) Flusskrebs *m*; (*saltwater*) Languste *f*
crayon ['kreɪən] *n* Buntstift *m*
craze [kreɪz] *n* Fimmel *m*; **to be all the ~** große Mode sein
crazed [kreɪzd] *adj* wahnsinnig; (*pottery, glaze*) rissig
crazy ['kreɪzɪ] *adj* wahnsinnig, verrückt; **~ about sb/sth** (*inf*) verrückt *or* wild auf jdn/etw; **to go ~** wahnsinnig *or* verrückt werden
crazy paving (*Brit*) *n* Mosaikpflaster *nt*
creak [kriːk] *vi* knarren
cream [kriːm] *n* Sahne *f*, Rahm *m* (*Südd*); (*artificial cream, cosmetic*) Creme *f*; (*élite*) Creme *f*, Elite *f* ▷ *adj* cremefarben; **whipped ~** Schlagsahne *f*
▶ **cream off** *vt* absahnen (*inf*)
cream cake *n* Sahnetorte *f*; (*small*) Sahnetörtchen *nt*
cream cheese *n* (Doppelrahm)frischkäse *m*
creamery ['kriːmərɪ] *n* (*shop*) Milchgeschäft *nt*; (*factory*) Molkerei *f*
creamy ['kriːmɪ] *adj* (*colour*) cremefarben; (*taste*) sahnig
crease [kriːs] *n* Falte *f*; (*in trousers*) Bügelfalte *f* ▷ *vt* zerknittern; (*forehead*) runzeln ▷ *vi* knittern; (*forehead*) sich runzeln
crease-resistant ['kriːsrɪzɪstənt] *adj* knitterfrei
create [kriː'eɪt] *vt* schaffen; (*interest*) hervorrufen; (*problems*) verursachen; (*produce*) herstellen; (*design*) entwerfen, kreieren; (*impression, fuss*) machen
creation [kriː'eɪʃən] *n* (*see vb*) Schaffung *f*; Hervorrufen *nt*; Verursachung *f*; Herstellung *f*; Entwurf *m*, Kreation *f*; (*Rel*) Schöpfung *f*
creative [kriː'eɪtɪv] *adj* kreativ, schöpferisch
creativity [kriːeɪ'tɪvɪtɪ] *n* Kreativität *f*
creator [kriː'eɪtəʳ] *n* Schöpfer(in) *m(f)*
creature ['kriːtʃəʳ] *n* Geschöpf *nt*; (*living animal*) Lebewesen *nt*
creature comforts [-'kʌmfəts] *npl* Lebensgenüsse *pl*
crèche [krɛʃ] *n* (Kinder)krippe *f*; (*all day*) (Kinder)tagesstätte *f*
credence ['kriːdns] *n*: **to lend** *or* **give ~ to sth** etw glaubwürdig erscheinen lassen *or* machen
credentials [krɪ'dɛnʃlz] *npl* Referenzen *pl*, Zeugnisse *pl*; (*papers of identity*) (Ausweis)papiere *pl*
credibility [krɛdɪ'bɪlɪtɪ] *n* Glaubwürdigkeit *f*
credible ['krɛdɪbl] *adj* glaubwürdig
credit ['krɛdɪt] *n* (*loan*) Kredit *m*; (*recognition*) Anerkennung *f*; (*Scol*) Schein *m* ▷ *adj* (*Comm: terms etc*) Kredit- ▷ *vt* (*Comm*) gutschreiben; (*believe: also:* **give credit to**) glauben; **credits** *npl* (*Cine, TV: at beginning*) Vorspann *m*; (*: at end*) Nachspann *m*; **to be in ~** (*person*) Geld auf dem Konto haben; (*bank account*) im Haben sein; **on ~** auf Kredit; **it is to his ~ that ...** es ehrt ihn, dass ...; **to take the ~ for** das Verdienst in Anspruch nehmen für; **it does him ~** es spricht für ihn; **he's a ~ to his family** er macht seiner Familie Ehre; **to ~ sb with sth** (*fig*) jdm etw zuschreiben; **to ~ £5 to sb** jdm £5 gutschreiben
creditable ['krɛdɪtəbl] *adj* lobenswert, anerkennenswert
credit account *n* Kreditkonto *nt*
credit agency (*Brit*) *n* Kreditauskunftei *f*
credit balance *n* Kontostand *m*
credit bureau (*US*) *n* = **credit agency**
credit card *n* Kreditkarte *f*
credit control *n* Kreditüberwachung *f*
credit facilities *npl* (*Comm*) Kreditmöglichkeiten *pl*
credit limit *n* Kreditgrenze *f*
credit note (*Brit*) *n* Gutschrift *f*
creditor ['krɛdɪtəʳ] *n* Gläubiger *m*
credit transfer *n* Banküberweisung *f*
creditworthy ['krɛdɪt'wəːðɪ] *adj* kreditwürdig
credulity [krɪ'djuːlɪtɪ] *n* Leichtgläubigkeit *f*
creed [kriːd] *n* Glaubensbekenntnis *nt*
creek [kriːk] *n* (kleine) Bucht *f*; (*US: stream*) Bach *m*; **to be up the ~** (*inf*) in der Tinte sitzen
creel [kriːl] *n* (*also:* **lobster creel**) Hummer(fang)korb *m*

creep [kri:p] (*pt, pp* **crept**) *vi* schleichen; (*plant: horizontally*) kriechen; (*: vertically*) klettern ▷ *n* (*inf*) Kriecher *m*; **to ~ up on sb** sich an jdn heranschleichen; (*time etc*) langsam auf jdn zukommen; **he's a ~** er ist ein widerlicher *or* fieser Typ; **it gives me the ~s** davon kriege ich das kalte Grausen
creeper ['kri:pəʳ] *n* Kletterpflanze *f*
creepers ['kri:pəz] (US) *npl Schuhe mit weichen Sohlen*
creepy ['kri:pɪ] *adj* gruselig; (*experience*) unheimlich, gruselig
creepy-crawly ['kri:pɪ'krɔ:lɪ] (*inf*) *n* Krabbeltier *nt*
cremate [krɪ'meɪt] *vt* einäschern
cremation [krɪ'meɪʃən] *n* Einäscherung *f*, Kremation *f*
crematoria [krɛmə'tɔ:rɪə] *npl of* **crematorium**
crematorium [krɛmə'tɔ:rɪəm] (*pl* **crematoria**) *n* Krematorium *nt*
creosote ['krɪəsəut] *n* Kreosot *nt*
crepe [kreɪp] *n* Krepp *m*; (*rubber*) Krepp(gummi) *m*
crepe bandage (*Brit*) *n* elastische Binde *f*
crepe paper *n* Krepppapier *nt*
crepe sole *n* Kreppsohle *f*
crept [krɛpt] *pt, pp of* **creep**
crescendo [krɪ'ʃɛndəu] *n* Höhepunkt *m*; (*Mus*) Crescendo *nt*
crescent ['krɛsnt] *n* Halbmond *m*; (*street*) *halbkreisförmig verlaufende Straße*
cress [krɛs] *n* Kresse *f*
crest [krɛst] *n* (*of hill*) Kamm *m*; (*of bird*) Haube *f*; (*coat of arms*) Wappen *nt*
crestfallen ['krɛstfɔ:lən] *adj* niedergeschlagen
Crete [kri:t] *n* Kreta *nt*
crevasse [krɪ'væs] *n* Gletscherspalte *f*
crevice ['krɛvɪs] *n* Spalte *f*
crew [kru:] *n* Besatzung *f*; (*TV, Cine*) Crew *f*; (*gang*) Bande *f*
crew cut *n* Bürstenschnitt *m*
crew neck *n* runder (Hals)ausschnitt *m*
crib [krɪb] *n* Kinderbett *nt*; (*Rel*) Krippe *f* ▷ *vt* (*inf: copy*) abschreiben
cribbage ['krɪbɪdʒ] *n* Cribbage *nt*
crib death (US) *n* = **cot death**
crick [krɪk] *n* Krampf *m*
cricket ['krɪkɪt] *n* Kricket *nt*; (*insect*) Grille *f*
cricketer ['krɪkɪtəʳ] *n* Kricketspieler(in) *m(f)*
crime [kraɪm] *n* (*no pl: illegal activities*) Verbrechen *pl*; (*illegal action: fig*) Verbrechen *nt*; **minor ~** kleinere Vergehen *pl*
crime wave *n* Verbrechenswelle *f*
criminal ['krɪmɪnl] *n* Kriminelle(r) *f(m)*, Verbrecher(in) *m(f)* ▷ *adj* kriminell; **C~ Investigation Department** Kriminalpolizei *f*
criminal code *n* Strafgesetzbuch *nt*
criminal profile *n* Täterprofil *nt*
crimp [krɪmp] *vt* kräuseln; (*hair*) wellen
crimson ['krɪmzn] *adj* purpurrot
cringe [krɪndʒ] *vi* (*in fear*) zurückweichen; (*in embarrassment*) zusammenzucken
crinkle ['krɪŋkl] *vt* (zer)knittern
cripple ['krɪpl] *n* Krüppel *m* ▷ *vt* zum Krüppel machen; (*ship, plane*) aktionsunfähig machen; (*production, exports*) lahmlegen, lähmen; **~d with rheumatism** von Rheuma praktisch gelähmt
crippling ['krɪplɪŋ] *adj* (*disease*) schwer; (*taxation, debts*) erdrückend
crises ['kraɪsi:z] *npl of* **crisis**
crisis ['kraɪsɪs] (*pl* **crises**) *n* Krise *f*
crisp [krɪsp] *adj* (*vegetables etc*) knackig; (*bacon etc*) knusprig; (*weather*) frisch; (*manner, tone, reply*) knapp
crisps [krɪsps] (*Brit*) *npl* Chips *pl*
crisscross ['krɪskrɔs] *adj* (*pattern*) Kreuz- ▷ *vt* kreuz und quer durchziehen
criteria [kraɪ'tɪərɪə] *npl of* **criterion**
criterion [kraɪ'tɪərɪən] (*pl* **criteria**) *n* Kriterium *nt*
critic ['krɪtɪk] *n* Kritiker(in) *m(f)*
critical ['krɪtɪkl] *adj* kritisch; **to be ~ of sb/sth** jdn/etw kritisieren; **he is in a ~ condition** sein Zustand ist kritisch
critically ['krɪtɪklɪ] *adv* kritisch; (*ill*) schwer
criticism ['krɪtɪsɪzəm] *n* Kritik *f*
criticize ['krɪtɪsaɪz] *vt* kritisieren
critique [krɪ'ti:k] *n* Kritik *f*
croak [krəuk] *vi* (*frog*) quaken; (*bird, person*) krächzen
Croat *n* Kroate *m*, Kroatin *f*; (*Ling*) Kroatisch *nt*
Croatia [krəu'eɪʃə] *n* Kroatien *nt*
Croatian [krəu'eɪʃən] *adj* kroatisch
crochet ['krəuʃeɪ] *n* (*activity*) Häkeln *nt*; (*result*) Häkelei *f*
crock [krɔk] *n* Topf *m*; (*inf: also*: **old crock**: *vehicle*) Kiste *f*; (*: person*) Wrack *nt*
crockery ['krɔkərɪ] *n* Geschirr *nt*
crocodile ['krɔkədaɪl] *n* Krokodil *nt*
crocus ['krəukəs] *n* Krokus *m*
croft [krɔft] (*Brit*) *n* kleines Pachtgut *nt*
crofter ['krɔftəʳ] (*Brit*) *n* Kleinpächter(in) *m(f)*
crone [krəun] *n* alte Hexe *f*
crony ['krəunɪ] (*inf: pej*) *n* Kumpan(in) *m(f)*
crook [kruk] *n* (*criminal*) Gauner *m*; (*of shepherd*) Hirtenstab *m*; (*of arm*) Beuge *f*
crooked ['krukɪd] *adj* krumm; (*dishonest*) unehrlich
crop [krɔp] *n* (Feld)frucht *f*; (*amount produced*) Ernte *f*; (*riding crop*) Reitpeitsche *f*; (*of bird*) Kropf *m* ▷ *vt* (*hair*) stutzen; (*subj: animal: grass*) abfressen
▶ **crop up** *vi* aufkommen
cropper ['krɔpəʳ] (*inf*) *n*: **to come a ~** hinfallen; (*fig: fail*) auf die Nase fallen
crop spraying [-'spreɪɪŋ] *n* Schädlingsbekämpfung *f* (*durch Besprühen*)
croquet ['krəukeɪ] (*Brit*) *n* Krocket *nt*
croquette [krə'kɛt] *n* Krokette *f*
cross [krɔs] *n* Kreuz *nt*; (*Biol, Bot*) Kreuzung *f* ▷ *vt* (*street*) überqueren; (*room etc*) durchqueren; (*cheque*) zur Verrechnung ausstellen; (*arms*) verschränken; (*legs*) übereinanderschlagen; (*animal, plant*) kreuzen; (*thwart: person*) verärgern; (*: plan*) durchkreuzen ▷ *adj*

ärgerlich, böse ▷ *vi*: **the boat ~es from ... to ...** das Schiff fährt von ... nach ...; **to ~ o.s.** sich bekreuzigen; **we have a ~ed line** (*Brit*) es ist jemand in der Leitung; **they've got their lines** *or* **wires ~ed** (*fig*) sie reden aneinander vorbei; **to be/get ~ with sb (about sth)** mit jdm *or* auf jdn (wegen etw) böse sein/werden
▸ **cross out** *vt* streichen
▸ **cross over** *vi* hinübergehen

crossbar ['krɔsbɑːʳ] *n* (*Sport*) Querlatte *f*; (*of bicycle*) Stange *f*
crossbow *n* Armbrust *f*
crossbreed ['krɔsbriːd] *n* Kreuzung *f*
cross-Channel ferry ['krɔs'tʃænl-] *n* Kanalfähre *f*
crosscheck ['krɔstʃɛk] *n* Gegenprobe *f* ▷ *vt* überprüfen
cross-country ['krɔs'kʌntrɪ], **cross-country race** *n* Querfeldeinrennen *nt*
cross-dressing [krɔs'drɛsɪŋ] *n* (*transvestism*) Transvestismus *m*
cross-examination ['krɔsɪgzæmɪ'neɪʃən] *n* Kreuzverhör *nt*
cross-examine ['krɔsɪg'zæmɪn] *vt* ins Kreuzverhör nehmen
cross-eyed ['krɔsaɪd] *adj* schielend; **to be ~** schielen
crossfire ['krɔsfaɪəʳ] *n* Kreuzfeuer *nt*; **to get caught in the ~** (*also fig*) ins Kreuzfeuer geraten
crossing ['krɔsɪŋ] *n* Überfahrt *f*; (*also*: **pedestrian crossing**) Fußgängerüberweg *m*
crossing guard (*US*) *n* ≈ Schülerlotse *m*
crossing point *n* Übergangsstelle *f*
cross-purposes ['krɔs'pəːpəsɪz] *npl*: **to be at ~ with sb** jdn missverstehen; **we're (talking) at ~** wir reden aneinander vorbei
cross-question ['krɔs'kwɛstʃən] *vt* ins Kreuzverhör nehmen
cross-reference ['krɔs'rɛfrəns] *n* (Quer)verweis *m*
crossroads ['krɔsrəudz] *n* Kreuzung *f*
cross section *n* Querschnitt *m*
crosswalk ['krɔswɔːk] (*US*) *n* Fußgängerüberweg *m*
crosswind ['krɔswɪnd] *n* Seitenwind *m*
crosswise ['krɔswaɪz] *adv* quer
crossword ['krɔswəːd] *n* (*also*: **crossword puzzle**) Kreuzworträtsel *nt*
crotch [krɔtʃ] *n* Unterleib *m*; (*of garment*) Schritt *m*
crotchet ['krɔtʃɪt] *n* Viertelnote *f*
crotchety ['krɔtʃɪtɪ] *adj* reizbar
crouch [krautʃ] *vi* kauern
croup [kruːp] *n* (*Med*) Krupp *m*
croupier ['kruːpɪəʳ] *n* Croupier *m*
crouton ['kruːtɔn] *n* Crouton *m*
crow [krəu] *n* (*bird*) Krähe *f*; (*of cock*) Krähen *nt* ▷ *vi* krähen; (*fig*) sich brüsten, angeben
crowbar ['krəubɑːʳ] *n* Brechstange *f*
crowd [kraud] *n* (Menschen)menge *f* ▷ *vt* (*room, stadium*) füllen ▷ *vi*: **to ~ round** sich herumdrängen; **~s of people** Menschenmassen *pl*; **the/our ~** (*of friends*) die/unsere Clique *f*; **to ~ sb/sth in** jdn/etw hineinstopfen; **to ~ sb/sth into** jdn pferchen/etw stopfen in +*acc*; **to ~ in** sich hineindrängen
crowded ['kraudɪd] *adj* überfüllt; (*densely populated*) dicht besiedelt; **~ with** voll von
crowd scene *n* Massenszene *f*
crown [kraun] *n* (*also of tooth*) Krone *f*; (*of head*) Wirbel *m*; (*of hill*) Kuppe *f*; (*of hat*) Kopf *m* ▷ *vt* krönen; (*tooth*) überkronen; **the C~** die Krone; **and to ~ it all ...** (*fig*) und zur Krönung des Ganzen ...

CROWN COURT

Crown Court ist ein Strafgericht, das in etwa 90 verschiedenen Städten in England und Wales zusammentritt. Schwere Verbrechen wie Mord, Totschlag, Vergewaltigung und Raub werden nur vor dem crown court unter Vorsitz eines Richters mit Geschworenen verhandelt.

crowning ['kraunɪŋ] *adj* krönend
crown jewels *npl* Kronjuwelen *pl*
crown prince *n* Kronprinz *m*
crow's-feet ['krəuzfiːt] *npl* Krähenfüße *pl*
crow's-nest ['krəuznɛst] *n* Krähennest *nt*, Mastkorb *m*
crucial ['kruːʃl] *adj* (*decision*) äußerst wichtig; (*vote*) entscheidend; **~ to** äußerst wichtig für
crucifix ['kruːsɪfɪks] *n* Kruzifix *nt*
crucifixion [kruːsɪ'fɪkʃən] *n* Kreuzigung *f*
crucify ['kruːsɪfaɪ] *vt* kreuzigen; (*fig*) in der Luft zerreißen
crude [kruːd] *adj* (*oil, fibre*) Roh-; (*fig: basic*) primitiv; (*: vulgar*) ordinär ▷ *n* = **crude oil**
crude oil *n* Rohöl *nt*
cruel ['kruəl] *adj* grausam
cruelty ['kruəltɪ] *n* Grausamkeit *f*
cruet ['kruːɪt] *n* Gewürzständer *m*
cruise [kruːz] *n* Kreuzfahrt *f* ▷ *vi* (*ship*) kreuzen; (*car*) (mit Dauergeschwindigkeit) fahren; (*aircraft*) (mit Reisegeschwindigkeit) fliegen; (*taxi*) gemächlich fahren
cruise missile *n* Marschflugkörper *m*
cruiser ['kruːzəʳ] *n* Motorboot *nt*; (*warship*) Kreuzer *m*
cruising speed *n* Reisegeschwindigkeit *f*
crumb [krʌm] *n* Krümel *m*; (*fig: of information*) Brocken *m*; **a ~ of comfort** ein winziger Trost
crumble ['krʌmbl] *vt* (*bread*) zerbröckeln; (*biscuit etc*) zerkrümeln ▷ *vi* (*building, earth etc*) zerbröckeln; (*plaster*) abbröckeln; (*fig: opposition*) sich auflösen; (*: belief*) ins Wanken geraten
crumbly ['krʌmblɪ] *adj* krümelig
crummy ['krʌmɪ] (*inf*) *adj* mies
crumpet ['krʌmpɪt] *n* Teekuchen *m* (*zum Toasten*)
crumple ['krʌmpl] *vt* zerknittern

crunch [krʌntʃ] *vt* (*biscuit, apple etc*) knabbern; (*underfoot*) zertreten ▷ *n*: **the ~** der große Krach; **if it comes to the ~** wenn es wirklich dahin kommt; **when the ~ comes** wenn es hart auf hart geht
crunchy ['krʌntʃɪ] *adj* knusprig; (*apple etc*) knackig; (*gravel, snow etc*) knirschend
crusade [kru:'seɪd] *n* Feldzug *m* ▷ *vi*: **to ~ for/against sth** für/gegen etw zu Felde ziehen
crusader [kru:'seɪdəʳ] *n* Kreuzritter *m*; (*fig*): **~ (for)** Apostel *m* (*+gen*)
crush [krʌʃ] *n* (*crowd*) Gedränge *nt* ▷ *vt* quetschen; (*grapes*) zerquetschen; (*paper, clothes*) zerknittern; (*garlic, ice*) (zer)stoßen; (*defeat*) niederschlagen; (*devastate*) vernichten; **to have a ~ on sb** (*love*) für jdn schwärmen; **lemon ~** Zitronensaftgetränk *nt*
crush barrier (*Brit*) *n* Absperrung *f*
crushing ['krʌʃɪŋ] *adj* vernichtend
crust [krʌst] *n* Kruste *f*
crustacean [krʌs'teɪʃən] *n* Schalentier *nt*, Krustazee *f*
crusty ['krʌstɪ] *adj* knusprig
crutch [krʌtʃ] *n* Krücke *f*; (*support*) Stütze *f*; *see also* **crotch**
crux [krʌks] *n* Kern *m*
cry [kraɪ] *vi* weinen; (*also*: **cry out**) aufschreien ▷ *n* Schrei *m*; (*shout*) Ruf *m*; **what are you ~ing about?** warum weinst du?; **to ~ for help** um Hilfe rufen; **she had a good ~** sie hat sich (mal richtig) ausgeweint; **it's a far ~ from ...** (*fig*) das ist etwas ganz anderes als ...
▸ **cry off** (*inf*) *vi* absagen
crying ['kraɪɪŋ] *adj* (*fig: need*) dringend; **it's a ~ shame** es ist ein Jammer
crypt [krɪpt] *n* Krypta *f*
cryptic ['krɪptɪk] *adj* hintergründig, rätselhaft; (*clue*) verschlüsselt
crystal ['krɪstl] *n* Kristall *m*; (*glass*) Kristall(glas) *nt*
crystal clear *adj* glasklar
crystallize ['krɪstəlaɪz] *vt* (*opinion, thoughts*) (feste) Form geben *+dat* ▷ *vi* (*sugar etc*) kristallisieren; **~d fruits** (*Brit*) kandierte Früchte *pl*
CSA *n abbr* (*= Child Support Agency*) *Amt zur Regelung von Unterhaltszahlungen für Kinder*
CSC *n abbr* (*= Civil Service Commission*) *Einstellungsbehörde für den öffentlichen Dienst*
CSE (*Brit*) *n abbr* (*formerly: = Certificate of Secondary Education*) *Schulabschlusszeugnis*, ≈ mittlere Reife *f*
CS gas (*Brit*) *n* ≈ Tränengas *nt*
CST (*US*) *abbr* (*= Central Standard Time*) *mittelamerikanische Standardzeit*
CT (*US*) *abbr* (*Post*) = Connecticut
ct *abbr* = **cent; court**
CTC (*Brit*) *n abbr* = **city technology college**
CT scanner *n abbr* (*Med: = computerized tomography scanner*) CT-Scanner *m*
cu ['si:ju:] *abbr* (*= see you: in text messages*) bis dann, bis später
cu. *abbr* = **cubic**
cub [kʌb] *n* Junge(s) *nt*; (*also*: **cub scout**) Wölfling *m*
Cuba ['kju:bə] *n* Kuba *nt*
Cuban ['kju:bən] *adj* kubanisch ▷ *n* Kubaner(in) *m(f)*
cubbyhole ['kʌbɪhəul] *n* (*room*) Kabuff *nt*; (*space*) Eckchen *nt*
cube [kju:b] *n* Würfel *m*; (*Math: of number*) dritte Potenz *f* ▷ *vt* (*Math*) in die dritte Potenz erheben, hoch drei nehmen
cube farm *n* (*inf*) Großraumbüro *nt* (*mit Trennwänden*)
cube root *n* Kubikwurzel *f*
cubic ['kju:bɪk] *adj* (*volume*) Kubik-; **~ metre** *etc* Kubikmeter *m etc*
cubic capacity *n* Hubraum *m*
cubicle ['kju:bɪkl] *n* Kabine *f*; (*in hospital*) Bettnische *f*
cuckoo ['kuku:] *n* Kuckuck *m*
cuckoo clock *n* Kuckucksuhr *f*
cucumber ['kju:kʌmbəʳ] *n* Gurke *f*
cud [kʌd] *n*: **to chew the ~** (*animal*) wiederkäuen; (*fig: person*) vor sich *acc* hin grübeln
cuddle ['kʌdl] *vt* in den Arm nehmen, drücken ▷ *vi* schmusen
cuddly ['kʌdlɪ] *adj* (*toy*) zum Liebhaben *or* Drücken; (*person*) knuddelig (*inf*)
cudgel ['kʌdʒl] *n* Knüppel *m* ▷ *vt*: **to ~ one's brains** sich *dat* das (Ge)hirn zermartern
cue [kju:] *n* (*Sport*) Billardstock *m*, Queue *nt*; (*Theat: word*) Stichwort *nt*; (*: action*) (Einsatz)zeichen *nt*; (*Mus*) Einsatz *m*
cuff [kʌf] *n* (*of sleeve*) Manschette *f*; (*US: of trousers*) Aufschlag *m*; (*blow*) Klaps *m* ▷ *vt* einen Klaps geben *+dat*; **off the ~** aus dem Stegreif
cuff links *npl* Manschettenknöpfe *pl*
cu. in. *abbr* (*= cubic inches*) Kubikzoll
cuisine [kwɪ'zi:n] *n* Küche *f*
cul-de-sac ['kʌldəsæk] *n* Sackgasse *f*
culinary ['kʌlɪnərɪ] *adj* (*skill*) Koch-; (*delight*) kulinarisch
cull [kʌl] *vt* (zusammen)sammeln; (*animals*) ausmerzen ▷ *n* *Erlegen überschüssiger Tierbestände*
culminate ['kʌlmɪneɪt] *vi*: **to ~ in** gipfeln in *+dat*
culmination [kʌlmɪ'neɪʃən] *n* Höhepunkt *m*
culottes [kju:'lɔts] *npl* Hosenrock *m*
culpable ['kʌlpəbl] *adj* schuldig
culprit ['kʌlprɪt] *n* Täter(in) *m(f)*
cult [kʌlt] *n* Kult *m*
cult figure *n* Kultfigur *f*
cultivate ['kʌltɪveɪt] *vt* (*land*) bebauen, landwirtschaftlich nutzen; (*crop*) anbauen; (*feeling*) entwickeln; (*person*) sich *dat* warm halten (*inf*), die Beziehung pflegen zu
cultivation [kʌltɪ'veɪʃən] *n* (*of land*) Bebauung *f*, landwirtschaftliche Nutzung *f*; (*of crop*) Anbau *m*
cultural ['kʌltʃərəl] *adj* kulturell
culture ['kʌltʃəʳ] *n* Kultur *f*
cultured ['kʌltʃəd] *adj* kultiviert; (*pearl*) Zucht-
cumbersome ['kʌmbəsəm] *adj* (*suitcase etc*) sperrig, unhandlich; (*piece of machinery*) schwer

zu handhaben; (*clothing*) hinderlich; (*process*) umständlich

cumin ['kʌmɪn] *n* Kreuzkümmel *m*

cumulative ['kju:mjulətɪv] *adj* (*effect, result*) Gesamt-

cunning ['kʌnɪŋ] *n* Gerissenheit *f* ▷ *adj* gerissen; (*device, idea*) schlau

cunt [kʌnt] (*inf!*) *n* (*vagina*) Fotze *f* (*!*); (*term of abuse*) Arsch *m* (*!*)

cup [kʌp] *n* Tasse *f*; (*as prize*) Pokal *m*; (*of bra*) Körbchen *nt*; **a ~ of tea** eine Tasse Tee

cupboard ['kʌbəd] *n* Schrank *m*

cup final (*Brit*) *n* Pokalendspiel *nt*

cupful ['kʌpful] *n* Tasse *f*

Cupid ['kju:pɪd] *n* Amor *m*; (*figurine*) Amorette *f*

cupidity [kju:'pɪdɪtɪ] *n* Begierde *f*, Gier *f*

cupola ['kju:pələ] *n* Kuppel *f*

cuppa ['kʌpə] (*Brit: inf*) *n* Tasse *f* Tee

cup tie (*Brit*) *n* Pokalspiel *nt*

curable ['kjuərəbl] *adj* heilbar

curate ['kjuərɪt] *n* Vikar *m*

curator [kjuə'reɪtə^r] *n* Kustos *m*

curb [kə:b] *vt* einschränken; (*person*) an die Kandare nehmen ▷ *n* Einschränkung *f*; (*US: kerb*) Bordstein *m*

curd cheese *n* Weißkäse *m*

curdle ['kə:dl] *vi* gerinnen

curds [kə:dz] *npl* ≈ Quark *m*

cure [kjuə^r] *vt* heilen; (*Culin: salt*) pökeln; (*: smoke*) räuchern; (*: dry*) trocknen; (*problem*) abhelfen *+dat* ▷ *n* (*remedy*) (Heil)mittel *nt*; (*treatment*) Heilverfahren *nt*; (*solution*) Abhilfe *f*; **to be ~d of sth** von etw geheilt sein

cure-all ['kjuərɔ:l] *n* (*also fig*) Allheilmittel *nt*

curfew ['kə:fju:] *n* Ausgangssperre *f*; (*time*) Sperrstunde *f*

curio ['kjuərɪəu] *n* Kuriosität *f*

curiosity [kjuərɪ'ɔsɪtɪ] *n* (*see adj*) Wissbegier(de) *f*; Neugier *f*; Merkwürdigkeit *f*

curious ['kjuərɪəs] *adj* (*interested*) wissbegierig; (*nosy*) neugierig; (*strange, unusual*) sonderbar, merkwürdig; **I'm ~ about him** ich bin gespannt auf ihn

curiously ['kjuərɪəslɪ] *adv* neugierig; (*inquisitively*) wissbegierig; **~ enough, …** merkwürdigerweise …

curl [kə:l] *n* Locke *f*; (*of smoke etc*) Kringel *m* ▷ *vt* (*hair: loosely*) locken; (*: tightly*) kräuseln ▷ *vi* sich locken; sich kräuseln; (*smoke*) sich kringeln
▸ **curl up** *vi* sich zusammenrollen

curler ['kə:lə^r] *n* Lockenwickler *m*; (*Sport*) Curlingspieler(in) *m(f)*

curlew ['kə:lu:] *n* Brachvogel *m*

curling ['kə:lɪŋ] *n* (*Sport*) Curling *nt*

curling tongs, (*US*) **curling irons** *npl* Lockenschere *f*, Brennschere *f*

curly ['kə:lɪ] *adj* lockig; (*tightly curled*) kraus

currant ['kʌrnt] *n* Korinthe *f*; (*blackcurrant, redcurrant*) Johannisbeere *f*

currency ['kʌrnsɪ] *n* (*system*) Währung *f*; (*money*) Geld *nt*; **foreign ~** Devisen *pl*; **to gain ~** (*fig*) sich verbreiten, um sich greifen

current ['kʌrnt] *n* Strömung *f*; (*Elec*) Strom *m*; (*of opinion*) Tendenz *f*, Trend *m* ▷ *adj* gegenwärtig; (*expression*) gebräuchlich; (*idea, custom*) verbreitet; **direct/alternating ~** (*Elec*) Gleich-/Wechselstrom *m*; **the ~ issue of a magazine** die neueste *or* letzte Nummer einer Zeitschrift; **in ~ use** allgemein gebräuchlich

current account (*Brit*) *n* Girokonto *nt*

current affairs *npl* Tagespolitik *f*

current assets *npl* (*Comm*) Umlaufvermögen *nt*

current liabilities *npl* (*Comm*) kurzfristige Verbindlichkeiten *pl*

currently ['kʌrntlɪ] *adv* zurzeit

curricula [kə'rɪkjulə] *npl of* **curriculum**

curriculum [kə'rɪkjuləm] (*pl* **~s** *or* **curricula**) *n* Lehrplan *m*

curriculum vitae [-'vi:taɪ] *n* Lebenslauf *m*

curry ['kʌrɪ] *n* (*dish*) Currygericht *nt* ▷ *vt*: **to ~ favour with** sich einschmeicheln bei

curry powder *n* Curry *m or nt*, Currypulver *nt*

curse [kə:s] *vi* fluchen ▷ *vt* verfluchen ▷ *n* Fluch *m*

cursor ['kə:sə^r] *n* (*Comput*) Cursor *m*

cursory ['kə:sərɪ] *adj* flüchtig; (*examination*) oberflächlich

curt [kə:t] *adj* knapp, kurz angebunden

curtail [kə:'teɪl] *vt* einschränken; (*visit etc*) abkürzen

curtain ['kə:tn] *n* Vorhang *m*; (*net*) Gardine *f*; **to draw the ~s** (*together*) die Vorhänge zuziehen; (*apart*) die Vorhänge aufmachen

curtain call *n* (*Theat*) Vorhang *m*

curtsey, curtsy ['kə:tsɪ] *vi* knicksen ▷ *n* Knicks *m*

curvature ['kə:vətʃə^r] *n* Krümmung *f*

curve [kə:v] *n* Bogen *m*; (*in the road*) Kurve *f* ▷ *vi* einen Bogen machen; (*surface, arch*) sich wölben ▷ *vt* biegen

curved [kə:vd] *adj* (*line*) gebogen; (*table legs etc*) geschwungen; (*surface, arch, sides of ship*) gewölbt

cushion ['kuʃən] *n* Kissen *nt* ▷ *vt* dämpfen; (*seat*) polstern

cushy ['kuʃɪ] (*inf*) *adj*: **a ~ job** ein gemütlicher *or* ruhiger Job; **to have a ~ time** eine ruhige Kugel schieben

custard ['kʌstəd] *n* (*for pouring*) Vanillesoße *f*

custard powder (*Brit*) *n* Vanillesoßenpulver *nt*

custodial [kʌs'təudɪəl] *adj*: **~ sentence** Gefängnisstrafe *f*

custodian [kʌs'təudɪən] *n* Verwalter(in) *m(f)*; (*of museum etc*) Aufseher(in) *m(f)*, Wächter(in) *m(f)*

custody ['kʌstədɪ] *n* (*of child*) Vormundschaft *f*; (*for offenders*) (polizeilicher) Gewahrsam *m*, Haft *f*; **to take into ~** verhaften; **in the ~ of** unter der Obhut *+gen*; **the mother has ~ of the children** die Kinder sind der Mutter zugesprochen worden

custom ['kʌstəm] *n* Brauch *m*; (*habit*) (An)gewohnheit *f*; (*Law*) Gewohnheitsrecht *nt*; (*Comm*) Kundschaft *f*

customary ['kʌstəmərɪ] *adj* (*conventional*) üblich; (*habitual*) gewohnt; **it is ~ to do it** es

ist üblich, es zu tun
custom-built ['kʌstəm'bɪlt] *adj* speziell angefertigt
customer ['kʌstəməʳ] *n* Kunde *m*, Kundin *f*; **he's an awkward ~** (*inf*) er ist ein schwieriger Typ
customer profile *n* Kundenprofil *nt*
customized ['kʌstəmaɪzd] *adj* individuell aufgemacht
custom-made ['kʌstəm'meɪd] *adj* (*shirt etc*) maßgefertigt, nach Maß; (*car etc*) speziell angefertigt
customs ['kʌstəmz] *npl* Zoll *m*; **to go through (the) ~** durch den Zoll gehen
Customs and Excise (*Brit*) *n* die Zollbehörde *f*
customs duty *n* Zoll *m*
customs officer *n* Zollbeamte(r) *m*, Zollbeamtin *f*
cut [kʌt] (*pt, pp* **~**) *vt* schneiden; (*text, programme, spending*) kürzen; (*prices*) senken, heruntersetzen, herabsetzen; (*supply*) einschränken; (*cloth*) zuschneiden; (*road*) schlagen, hauen; (*inf: lecture, appointment*) schwänzen ▷ *vi* schneiden; (*lines*) sich schneiden ▷ *n* Schnitt *m*; (*in skin*) Schnittwunde *f*; (*in salary, spending etc*) Kürzung *f*; (*of meat*) Stück *nt*; (*of jewel*) Schnitt *m*, Schliff *m*; **to ~ a tooth** zahnen, einen Zahn bekommen; **to ~ one's finger/hand/knee** sich in den Finger/in die Hand/am Knie schneiden; **to get one's hair ~** sich *dat* die Haare schneiden lassen; **to ~ sth short** etw vorzeitig abbrechen; **to ~ sb dead** jdn wie Luft behandeln; **cold ~s** (*US*) Aufschnitt *m*; **power ~** Stromausfall *m*
▸ **cut back** *vt* (*plants*) zurückschneiden; (*production*) zurückschrauben; (*expenditure*) einschränken
▸ **cut down** *vt* (*tree*) fällen; (*consumption*) einschränken; **to ~ sb down to size** (*fig*) jdn auf seinen Platz verweisen
▸ **cut down on** *vt fus* einschränken
▸ **cut in** *vi* (*Aut*) sich direkt vor ein anderes Auto setzen; **to ~ in (on)** (*conversation*) sich einschalten (in *+acc*)
▸ **cut off** *vt* abschneiden; (*supply*) sperren; (*Tel*) unterbrechen; **we've been ~ off** (*Tel*) wir sind unterbrochen worden
▸ **cut out** *vt* ausschneiden; (*an activity etc*) aufhören mit; (*remove*) herausschneiden
▸ **cut up** *vt* klein schneiden; **it really ~ me up** (*inf*) es hat mich ziemlich mitgenommen; **to feel ~ up about sth** (*inf*) betroffen über etw *acc* sein
cut and dried *adj* (*also*: **cut-and-dry**: *answer*) eindeutig; (*: solution*) einfach
cutaway ['kʌtəweɪ] *n* (*coat*) Cut(away) *m*; (*drawing*) Schnittdiagramm *nt*; (*model*) Schnittmodell *nt*; (*Cine, TV*) Schnitt *m*
cutback ['kʌtbæk] *n* Kürzung *f*
cute [kju:t] *adj* süß, niedlich; (*clever*) schlau
cut glass *n* geschliffenes Glas *nt*
cuticle ['kju:tɪkl] *n* Nagelhaut *f*; **~ remover** Nagelhautentferner *m*
cutlery ['kʌtlərɪ] *n* Besteck *nt*
cutlet ['kʌtlɪt] *n* Schnitzel *nt*; (*also*: **vegetable cutlet, nut cutlet**) Bratling *m*
cutoff ['kʌtɔf] *n* (*also*: **cutoff point**) Trennlinie *f*
cutoff switch *n* Ausschaltmechanismus *m*
cutout ['kʌtaut] *n* (*switch*) Unterbrecher *m*; (*shape*) Ausschneidemodell *nt*; (*paper figure*) Ausschneidepuppe *f*
cut-price ['kʌt'praɪs] *adj* (*goods*) heruntergesetzt; (*offer*) Billig-
cut-rate ['kʌt'reɪt] (*US*) *adj* = **cut-price**
cutthroat ['kʌtθrəut] *n* Mörder(in) *m(f)* ▷ *adj* unbarmherzig, mörderisch
cutting ['kʌtɪŋ] *adj* (*edge, remark*) scharf ▷ *n* (*Brit: from newspaper*) Ausschnitt *m*; (*: Rail*) Durchstich *m*; (*from plant*) Ableger *m*
cutting edge *n* (*fig*) Spitzenstellung *f*; **on the ~ (of)** an der Spitze *+gen*
cuttlefish ['kʌtlfɪʃ] *n* Tintenfisch *m*
CV *n abbr* = **curriculum vitae**
c.w.o. *abbr* (*Comm*) = **cash with order**
cwt *abbr* = **hundredweight**
cyanide ['saɪənaɪd] *n* Zyanid *nt*
cybercafé ['saɪbəkæfeɪ] *n* Internetcafé *nt*
cybernetics [saɪbə'nɛtɪks] *n* Kybernetik *f*
cyclamen ['sɪkləmən] *n* Alpenveilchen *nt*
cycle ['saɪkl] *n* (*bicycle*) (Fahr)rad *nt*; (*series: of seasons, songs etc*) Zyklus *m*; (*: of events*) Gang *m*; (*: Tech*) Periode *f* ▷ *vi* Rad fahren
cycle lane, **cycle path** *n* (Fahr)radweg *m*
cycle race *n* Radrennen *nt*
cycle rack *n* Fahrradständer *m*
cycling ['saɪklɪŋ] *n* Radfahren *nt*; **to go on a ~ holiday** (*Brit*) Urlaub mit dem Fahrrad machen
cyclist ['saɪklɪst] *n* (Fahr)radfahrer(in) *m(f)*
cyclone ['saɪkləun] *n* Zyklon *m*
cygnet ['sɪgnɪt] *n* Schwanjunge(s) *nt*
cylinder ['sɪlɪndəʳ] *n* Zylinder *m*; (*of gas*) Gasflasche *f*
cylinder block *n* Zylinderblock *m*
cylinder head *n* Zylinderkopf *m*
cylinder-head gasket ['sɪlɪndəhɛd-] *n* Zylinderkopfdichtung *f*
cymbals ['sɪmblz] *npl* (*Mus*) Becken *nt*
cynic ['sɪnɪk] *n* Zyniker(in) *m(f)*
cynical ['sɪnɪkl] *adj* zynisch
cynicism ['sɪnɪsɪzəm] *n* Zynismus *m*
cypress ['saɪprɪs] *n* Zypresse *f*
Cypriot ['sɪprɪət] *adj* zypriotisch, zyprisch ▷ *n* Zypriot(in) *m(f)*
Cyprus ['saɪprəs] *n* Zypern *nt*
cyst [sɪst] *n* Zyste *f*
cystitis [sɪs'taɪtɪs] *n* Blasenentzündung *f*, Zystitis *f*
CZ (*US*) *n abbr* (*= Canal Zone*) *Bereich des Panamakanals*
czar [zɑ:ʳ] *n* = **tsar**
Czech [tʃɛk] *adj* tschechisch ▷ *n* Tscheche *m*, Tschechin *f*; (*language*) Tschechisch *nt*; **the ~ Republic** die Tschechische Republik *f*
Czechoslovak [tʃɛkə'sləuvæk] *adj, n* =

Czechoslovakian

Czechoslovakia [tʃɛkəslə'vækɪə] *n* (*formerly*) die Tschechoslowakei *f*

Czechoslovakian [tʃɛkəslə'vækɪən] (*formerly*) *adj* tschechoslowakisch ▷ *n* Tschechoslowake *m*, Tschechoslowakin *f*

Dd

D[1], d[1] [di:] *n (letter)* D *nt*, d *nt*; **D for David, D for Dog** *(US)* ≈ D wie Dora
D[2] [di:] *n (Mus)* D *nt*, d *nt*
D[3] [di:] *(US) abbr (Pol)* = **Democrat; Democratic**
d[2] *(Brit: formerly) abbr* = **penny**
d. *abbr (= died)*: **Henry Jones, d. 1754** Henry Jones, gest. 1754
DA *(US) n abbr* = **district attorney**
dab [dæb] *vt* betupfen; *(paint, cream)* tupfen ▷ *n* Tupfer *m*; **to be a ~ hand at sth** gut in etw *dat* sein; **to be a ~ hand at doing sth** sich darauf verstehen, etw zu tun
▶ **dab at** *vt* betupfen
dabble ['dæbl] *vi*: **to ~ in** sich (nebenbei) beschäftigen mit
dachshund ['dækshund] *n* Dackel *m*
dad [dæd] *(inf) n* Papa *m*, Vati *m*
daddy ['dædɪ] *(inf) n* = **dad**
daddy-longlegs [dædɪ'lɔŋlɛgz] *(inf) n* Schnake *f*
daffodil ['dæfədɪl] *n* Osterglocke *f*, Narzisse *f*
daft [dɑ:ft] *(inf) adj* doof *(inf)*, blöd *(inf)*; **to be ~ about sb/sth** verrückt nach jdm/etw sein
dagger ['dægə[r]] *n* Dolch *m*; **to be at ~s drawn with sb** mit jdm auf Kriegsfuß stehen; **to look ~s at sb** jdn mit Blicken durchbohren
dahlia ['deɪljə] *n* Dahlie *f*
daily ['deɪlɪ] *adj* täglich; *(wages)* Tages- ▷ *n* *(paper)* Tageszeitung *f*; *(Brit: also:* **daily help***)* Putzfrau *f* ▷ *adv* täglich; **twice ~** zweimal täglich *or* am Tag
dainty ['deɪntɪ] *adj* zierlich
dairy ['dɛərɪ] *n (Brit: shop)* Milchgeschäft *nt*; *(company)* Molkerei *f*; *(on farm)* Milchkammer *f* ▷ *cpd* Milch-; *(herd, industry, farming)* Milchvieh-
dairy farm *n auf Milchviehhaltung spezialisierter Bauernhof*
dairy products *npl* Milchprodukte *pl*, Molkereiprodukte *pl*
dairy store *(US) n* Milchgeschäft *nt*
dais ['deɪɪs] *n* Podium *nt*
daisy ['deɪzɪ] *n* Gänseblümchen *nt*
daisywheel ['deɪzɪwi:l] *n* Typenrad *nt*
daisywheel printer *n* Typenraddrucker *m*
Dakar ['dækə[r]] *n* Dakar *nt*
dale [deɪl] *(Brit) n* Tal *nt*
dally ['dælɪ] *vi* (herum)trödeln; **to ~ with** *(plan, idea)* spielen mit
dalmatian [dæl'meɪʃən] *n* Dalmatiner *m*
dam [dæm] *n* (Stau)damm *m*; *(reservoir)* Stausee *m* ▷ *vt* stauen
damage ['dæmɪdʒ] *n* Schaden *m* ▷ *vt* schaden *+dat*; *(spoil, break)* beschädigen; **damages** *npl (Law)* Schaden(s)ersatz *m*; **~ to property** Sachbeschädigung *f*; **to pay £5,000 in ~s** 5000 Pfund Schaden(s)ersatz (be)zahlen
damaging ['dæmɪdʒɪŋ] *adj*: **~ (to)** schädlich (für)
Damascus [də'mɑ:skəs] *n* Damaskus *nt*
dame [deɪm] *n* Dame *f*; *(US: inf)* Weib *nt*; *(Theat)* (komische) Alte *f (von einem Mann gespielt)*
damn [dæm] *vt* verfluchen; *(condemn)* verurteilen ▷ *adj (inf: also:* **damned***)* verdammt ▷ *n (inf)*: **I don't give a ~** das ist mir scheißegal *(!)*; **~ (it)!** verdammt (noch mal)!
damnable ['dæmnəbl] *adj* grässlich
damnation [dæm'neɪʃən] *n* Verdammnis *f* ▷ *excl (inf)* verdammt
damning ['dæmɪŋ] *adj* belastend
damp [dæmp] *adj* feucht ▷ *n* Feuchtigkeit *f* ▷ *vt (also:* **dampen***)* befeuchten, anfeuchten; *(enthusiasm etc)* dämpfen
dampcourse ['dæmpkɔ:s] *n* Dämmschicht *f*
damper ['dæmpə[r]] *n (Mus)* Dämpfer *m*; *(of fire)* (Luft)klappe *f*; **to put a ~ on** *(fig)* einen Dämpfer aufsetzen *+dat*
dampness ['dæmpnɪs] *n* Feuchtigkeit *f*
damson ['dæmzən] *n* Damaszenerpflaume *f*
dance [dɑ:ns] *n* Tanz *m*; *(social event)* Tanz(abend) *m* ▷ *vi* tanzen; **to ~ about** (herum)tänzeln
dance hall *n* Tanzsaal *m*
dancer ['dɑ:nsə[r]] *n* Tänzer(in) *m(f)*
dancing ['dɑ:nsɪŋ] *n* Tanzen *nt* ▷ *cpd (teacher, school, class etc)* Tanz-
D and C *n abbr (Med: = dilation and curettage)* Ausschabung *f*
dandelion ['dændɪlaɪən] *n* Löwenzahn *m*
dandruff ['dændrəf] *n* Schuppen *pl*
D and T *(Brit) n abbr (Scol)* = **Design and Technology**
dandy ['dændɪ] *n* Dandy *m* ▷ *adj (US: inf)* prima
Dane [deɪn] *n* Däne *m*, Dänin *f*
danger ['deɪndʒə[r]] *n* Gefahr *f*; **there is ~ of fire/poisoning** es besteht Feuer-/Vergiftungsgefahr; **there is a ~ of sth**

happening es besteht die Gefahr, dass etw geschieht; **"~!"** „Achtung!"; **in ~** in Gefahr; **to be in ~ of doing sth** Gefahr laufen, etw zu tun; **out of ~** außer Gefahr

danger list *n*: **on the ~** in Lebensgefahr

dangerous ['deɪndʒrəs] *adj* gefährlich

dangerously ['deɪndʒrəslɪ] *adv* gefährlich; (*close*) bedenklich; **~ ill** schwer krank

danger zone *n* Gefahrenzone *f*

dangle ['dæŋgl] *vt* baumeln lassen ▷ *vi* baumeln

Danish ['deɪnɪʃ] *adj* dänisch ▷ *n* (*Ling*) Dänisch *nt*

Danish pastry *n* Plundergebäck *nt*

dank [dæŋk] *adj* (unangenehm) feucht

Danube ['dænju:b] *n*: **the ~** die Donau

dapper ['dæpəʳ] *adj* gepflegt

Dardanelles [dɑ:də'nɛlz] *npl*: **the ~** die Dardanellen *pl*

dare [dɛəʳ] *vt*: **to ~ sb to do sth** jdn dazu herausfordern, etw zu tun ▷ *vi*: **to ~ (to) do sth** es wagen, etw zu tun; **I ~n't tell him** (*Brit*) ich wage nicht, es ihm zu sagen; **I ~ say** ich nehme an

daredevil ['dɛədɛvl] *n* Draufgänger *m*

Dar-es-Salaam ['dɑ:rɛssə'lɑ:m] *n* Daressalam *nt*

daring ['dɛərɪŋ] *adj* kühn, verwegen; (*bold*) gewagt ▷ *n* Kühnheit *f*

dark [dɑ:k] *adj* dunkel; (*look*) finster ▷ *n*: **in the ~** im Dunkeln; **to be in the ~ about** (*fig*) keine Ahnung haben von; **after ~** nach Einbruch der Dunkelheit; **it is/is getting ~** es ist/wird dunkel; **~ chocolate** Zartbitterschokolade *f*

Dark Ages *npl*: **the ~** das finstere Mittelalter

darken [dɑ:kn] *vt* dunkel machen ▷ *vi* sich verdunkeln

dark glasses *npl* Sonnenbrille *f*

dark horse *n* (*in competition*) Unbekannte(r) *f(m)* (mit Außenseiterchancen); (*quiet person*) stilles Wasser *nt*

darkly ['dɑ:klɪ] *adv* finster

darkness ['dɑ:knɪs] *n* Dunkelheit *f*, Finsternis *f*

darkroom ['dɑ:krum] *n* Dunkelkammer *f*

darling ['dɑ:lɪŋ] *adj* lieb ▷ *n* Liebling *m*; **to be the ~ of** der Liebling *+gen* sein; **she is a ~** sie ist ein Schatz

darn [dɑ:n] *vt* stopfen

dart [dɑ:t] *n* (*in game*) (Wurf)pfeil *m*; (*in sewing*) Abnäher *m* ▷ *vi*: **to ~ towards** (*also*: **make a dart towards**) zustürzen auf *+acc*; **to ~ away/along** davon-/entlangflitzen

dartboard ['dɑ:tbɔ:d] *n* Dartscheibe *f*

darts [dɑ:ts] *n* Darts *nt*, Pfeilwurfspiel *nt*

dash [dæʃ] *n* (*sign*) Gedankenstrich *m*; (*rush*) Jagd *f* ▷ *vt* (*throw*) schleudern; (*hopes*) zunichtemachen ▷ *vi*: **to ~ towards** zustürzen auf *+acc*; **a ~ of ...** (*small quantity*) etwas ..., ein Schuss *m* ...; **to make a ~ for sth** auf etw *acc* zustürzen; **we'll have to make a ~ for it** wir müssen rennen, so schnell wir können

▸ **dash away** *vi* losstürzen

▸ **dash off** *vi* = **dash away**

dashboard ['dæʃbɔ:d] *n* Armaturenbrett *nt*

dashing ['dæʃɪŋ] *adj* flott

dastardly ['dæstədlɪ] *adj* niederträchtig

DAT *n abbr* (= *digital audio tape*) DAT *nt*

data ['deɪtə] *npl* Daten *pl*

data analysis *n* Datenanalyse *f*

database ['deɪtəbeɪs] *n* Datenbank *f*

data capture *n* Datenerfassung *f*

data processing *n* Datenverarbeitung *f*

data projector *n* Beamer *m*

data transmission *n* Datenübertragung *f*

date [deɪt] *n* Datum *nt*; (*with friend*) Verabredung *f*; (*fruit*) Dattel *f* ▷ *vt* datieren; (*person*) ausgehen mit; **what's the ~ today?** der Wievielte ist heute?; **~ of birth** Geburtsdatum *nt*; **closing ~** Einsendeschluss *m*; **to ~** bis heute; **out of ~** altmodisch; (*expired*) abgelaufen; **up to ~** auf dem neuesten Stand; **to bring up to ~** auf den neuesten Stand bringen; (*person*) über den neuesten Stand der Dinge informieren; **a letter ~d 5 July** ein vom 5. Juli datierter Brief

dated ['deɪtɪd] *adj* altmodisch

dateline ['deɪtlaɪn] *n* (*Geog*) Datumsgrenze *f*; (*Press*) Datumszeile *f*

date rape *n* Vergewaltigung *f* einer Bekannten (*mit der der Täter eine Verabredung hatte*)

date stamp *n* Datumsstempel *m*

dative ['deɪtɪv] *n* Dativ *m*

daub [dɔ:b] *vt* schmieren; **to ~ with** beschmieren mit

daughter ['dɔ:təʳ] *n* Tochter *f*

daughter-in-law ['dɔ:tərɪnlɔ:] *n* Schwiegertochter *f*

daunt [dɔ:nt] *vt* entmutigen

daunting ['dɔ:ntɪŋ] *adj* entmutigend

dauntless ['dɔ:ntlɪs] *adj* unerschrocken, beherzt

dawdle ['dɔ:dl] *vi* trödeln; **to ~ over one's work** bei der Arbeit bummeln *or* trödeln

dawn [dɔ:n] *n* Tagesanbruch *m*, Morgengrauen *nt*; (*of period*) Anbruch *m* ▷ *vi* dämmern; (*fig*): **it ~ed on him that ...** es dämmerte ihm, dass ...; **from ~ to dusk** von morgens bis abends

dawn chorus (*Brit*) *n* Morgenkonzert *nt* der Vögel

day [deɪ] *n* Tag *m*; (*heyday*) Zeit *f*; **the ~ before/after** am Tag zuvor/danach; **the ~ after tomorrow** übermorgen; **the ~ before yesterday** vorgestern; **(on) the following ~** am Tag danach; **the ~ that ...** (am Tag,) als ...; **~ by day** jeden Tag, täglich; **by ~** tagsüber; **paid by the ~** tageweise bezahlt; **to work an eight hour ~** einen Achtstundentag haben; **these ~s, in the present ~** heute, heutzutage

daybook ['deɪbuk] (*Brit*) *n* Journal *nt*

dayboy ['deɪbɔɪ] *n* Externe(r) *m*

daybreak ['deɪbreɪk] *n* Tagesanbruch *m*

day-care centre ['deɪkɛə-] *n* (*for children*) (Kinder)tagesstätte *f*; (*for old people*) Altentagesstätte *f*

daydream ['deɪdri:m] *vi* (mit offenen Augen) träumen ▷ *n* Tagtraum *m*, Träumerei *f*

daygirl ['deɪgə:l] *n* Externe *f*
daylight ['deɪlaɪt] *n* Tageslicht *nt*
daylight robbery (*inf*) *n* Halsabschneiderei *f*
daylight-saving time (*US*) *n* Sommerzeit *f*
day release *n*: **to be on ~** tageweise (zur Weiterbildung) freigestellt sein
day return (*Brit*) *n* Tagesrückfahrkarte *f*
day shift *n* Tagschicht *f*
daytime ['deɪtaɪm] *n* Tag *m*; **in the ~** tagsüber, bei Tage
day-to-day ['deɪtə'deɪ] *adj* täglich, Alltags-; **on a ~ basis** tageweise
day trader *n* (*Stock Exchange*) Day-Trader(in) *m(f)*, Tageshändler(in) *m(f)*
day trip *n* Tagesausflug *m*
day-tripper ['deɪ'trɪpə^r] *n* Tagesausflügler(in) *m(f)*
daze [deɪz] *vt* benommen machen ▷ *n*: **in a ~** ganz benommen
dazed [deɪzd] *adj* benommen
dazzle ['dæzl] *vt* blenden
dazzling ['dæzlɪŋ] *adj* (*light*) blendend; (*smile*) strahlend; (*career, achievements*) glänzend
DC *abbr* = **direct current**
DCC *n abbr* (= *digital compact cassette*) DCC *f*
DD *n abbr* (= *Doctor of Divinity*) ≈ Dr. theol.
DD *abbr* = **direct debit**
D-day ['di:deɪ] *n* der Tag X
DDS (*US*) *n abbr* (= *Doctor of Dental Surgery*) ≈ Dr. med. dent.
DDT *n abbr* (= *dichlorodiphenyltrichloroethane*) DDT *nt*
deacon ['di:kən] *n* Diakon *m*
dead [dɛd] *adj* tot; (*flowers*) verwelkt; (*numb*) abgestorben, taub; (*battery*) leer; (*place*) wie ausgestorben ▷ *adv* total, völlig; (*directly, exactly*) genau ▷ *npl*: **the ~** die Toten *pl*; **to shoot sb ~** jdn erschießen; **~ silence** Totenstille *f*; **in the ~ centre (of)** genau in der Mitte (*+gen*); **the line has gone ~** (*Tel*) die Leitung ist tot; **~ on time** auf die Minute pünktlich; **~ tired** todmüde; **to stop ~** abrupt stehen bleiben
dead beat (*inf*) *adj* (*tired*) völlig kaputt
deaden [dɛdn] *vt* (*blow*) abschwächen; (*pain*) mildern; (*sound*) dämpfen
dead end *n* Sackgasse *f*
dead-end ['dɛdɛnd] *adj*: **a ~ job** ein Job *m* ohne Aufstiegsmöglichkeiten
dead heat *n*: **to finish in a ~** unentschieden ausgehen
dead letter office *n* Amt *nt* für unzustellbare Briefe
deadline ['dɛdlaɪn] *n* (letzter) Termin *m*; **to work to a ~** auf einen Termin hinarbeiten
deadlock ['dɛdlɔk] *n* Stillstand *m*; **the meeting ended in ~** die Verhandlung war festgefahren
dead loss (*inf*) *n*: **to be a ~** ein hoffnungsloser Fall sein
deadly ['dɛdlɪ] *adj* tödlich ▷ *adv*: **~ dull** todlangweilig
deadpan ['dɛdpæn] *adj* (*look*) unbewegt; (*tone*) trocken
Dead Sea *n*: **the ~** das Tote Meer
dead season *n* tote Saison *f*
deaf [dɛf] *adj* taub; (*partially*) schwerhörig; **to turn a ~ ear to sth** sich einer Sache *dat* gegenüber taub stellen
deaf aid (*Brit*) *n* Hörgerät *nt*
deaf-and-dumb ['dɛfən'dʌm] *adj* taubstumm; **~ alphabet** Taubstummensprache *f*
deafen ['dɛfn] *vt* taub machen
deafening ['dɛfnɪŋ] *adj* ohrenbetäubend
deaf-mute ['dɛfmju:t] *n* Taubstumme(r) *f(m)*
deafness ['dɛfnɪs] *n* Taubheit *f*
deal [di:l] (*pt, pp* **~t**) *n* Geschäft *nt*, Handel *m* ▷ *vt* (*blow*) versetzen; (*card*) geben, austeilen; **to strike a ~ with sb** ein Geschäft mit jdm abschließen; **it's a ~!** (*inf*) abgemacht!; **he got a fair/bad ~ from them** er ist von ihnen anständig/schlecht behandelt worden; **a good ~** (*a lot*) ziemlich viel; **a great ~ (of)** ziemlich viel
▸ **deal in** *vt fus* handeln mit
▸ **deal with** *vt fus* (*person*) sich kümmern um; (*problem*) sich befassen mit; (*successfully*) fertig werden mit; (*subject*) behandeln
dealer ['di:lə^r] *n* Händler(in) *m(f)*; (*in drugs*) Dealer *m*; (*Cards*) Kartengeber(in) *m(f)*
dealership ['di:ləʃɪp] *n* (Vertrags)händler *m*
dealings ['di:lɪŋz] *npl* Geschäfte *pl*; (*relations*) Beziehungen *pl*
dealt [dɛlt] *pt, pp of* **deal**
dean [di:n] *n* Dekan *m*; (*US: Scol: administrator*) *Schul- oder Collegeverwalter mit Beratungs- und Disziplinarfunktion*
dear [dɪə^r] *adj* lieb; (*expensive*) teuer ▷ *n*: **(my) ~** (mein) Liebling *m* ▷ *excl*: **~ me!** (ach) du liebe Zeit!; **D~ Sir/Madam** Sehr geehrte Damen und Herren; **D~ Mr/Mrs X** Sehr geehrter Herr/geehrte Frau X; (*less formal*) Lieber Herr/Liebe Frau X
dearly ['dɪəlɪ] *adv* (*love*) von ganzem Herzen; (*pay*) teuer
dear money *n* (*Comm*) teures Geld *nt*
dearth [də:θ] *n*: **a ~ of** ein Mangel *m* an *+dat*
death [dɛθ] *n* Tod *m*; (*fatality*) Tote(r) *f(m)*, Todesfall *m*
deathbed ['dɛθbɛd] *n*: **to be on one's ~** auf dem Sterbebett liegen
death certificate *n* Sterbeurkunde *f*, Totenschein *m*
deathly ['dɛθlɪ] *adj* (*silence*) eisig ▷ *adv* (*pale etc*) toten-
death penalty *n* Todesstrafe *f*
death rate *n* Sterbeziffer *f*
death row [-'rəu] (*US*) *n* Todestrakt *m*
death sentence *n* Todesurteil *nt*
death squad *n* Todeskommando *nt*
death toll *n* Zahl *f* der Todesopfer *or* Toten
deathtrap ['dɛθtræp] *n* Todesfalle *f*
deb [dɛb] (*inf*) *n abbr* = **debutante**
debacle [deɪ'bɑ:kl] *n* Debakel *nt*
debar [dɪ'bɑ:^r] *vt*: **to ~ sb from doing sth** jdn davon ausschließen, etw zu tun; **to ~ sb from**

a club jdn aus einem Klub ausschließen
debase [dɪˈbeɪs] *vt* (*value, quality*) mindern, herabsetzen; (*person*) erniedrigen, entwürdigen
debatable [dɪˈbeɪtəbl] *adj* fraglich
debate [dɪˈbeɪt] *n* Debatte *f* ▷ *vt* debattieren über *+acc*; (*course of action*) überlegen ▷ *vi*: **to ~ whether** hin und her überlegen, ob
debauchery [dɪˈbɔːtʃərɪ] *n* Ausschweifungen *pl*
debenture [dɪˈbɛntʃəʳ] *n* Schuldschein *m*
debilitate [dɪˈbɪlɪteɪt] *vt* schwächen
debilitating [dɪˈbɪlɪteɪtɪŋ] *adj* schwächend
debit [ˈdɛbɪt] *n* Schuldposten *m* ▷ *vt*: **to ~ a sum to sb/sb's account** jdn/jds Konto mit einer Summe belasten; *see also* **direct**
debit balance *n* Sollsaldo *nt*, Debetsaldo *nt*
debit note *n* Lastschriftanzeige *f*
debonair *adj* flott
debrief [diːˈbriːf] *vt* befragen
debriefing [diːˈbriːfɪŋ] *n* Befragung *f*
debris [ˈdɛbriː] *n* Trümmer *pl*, Schutt *m*
debt [dɛt] *n* Schuld *f*; (*state of owing money*) Schulden *pl*, Verschuldung *f*; **to be in ~** Schulden haben, verschuldet sein; **bad ~** uneinbringliche Forderung *f*
debt collector *n* Inkassobeauftragte(r) *f(m)*, Schuldeneintreiber(in) *m(f)*
debtor [ˈdɛtəʳ] *n* Schuldner(in) *m(f)*
debug [ˈdiːˈbʌg] *vt* (*Comput*) Fehler beseitigen in *+dat*
debunk [diːˈbʌŋk] *vt* (*myths, ideas*) bloßstellen; (*claim*) entlarven; (*person, institution*) vom Sockel stoßen
debut [ˈdeɪbjuː] *n* Debüt *nt*
debutante [ˈdɛbjutænt] *n* Debütantin *f*
Dec. *abbr* = **December**
decade [ˈdɛkeɪd] *n* Jahrzehnt *nt*
decadence [ˈdɛkədəns] *n* Dekadenz *f*
decadent [ˈdɛkədənt] *adj* dekadent
decaff [ˈdiːkæf] *n* koffeinfreier Kaffee *m*
decaffeinated [dɪˈkæfɪneɪtɪd] *adj* koffeinfrei
decamp [dɪˈkæmp] (*inf*) *vi* verschwinden, sich aus dem Staub machen
decant [dɪˈkænt] *vt* umfüllen
decanter [dɪˈkæntəʳ] *n* Karaffe *f*
decarbonize [diːˈkɑːbənaɪz] *vt* entkohlen
decathlon [dɪˈkæθlən] *n* Zehnkampf *m*
decay [dɪˈkeɪ] *n* Verfall *m*; (*of tooth*) Fäule *f* ▷ *vi* (*body*) verwesen; (*teeth*) faulen; (*leaves*) verrotten; (*fig: society etc*) verfallen
decease [dɪˈsiːs] *n* (*Law*): **upon your ~** bei Ihrem Ableben
deceased [dɪˈsiːst] *n*: **the ~** der/die Tote *or* Verstorbene
deceit [dɪˈsiːt] *n* Betrug *m*
deceitful [dɪˈsiːtful] *adj* betrügerisch
deceive [dɪˈsiːv] *vt* täuschen; (*husband, wife etc*) betrügen; **to ~ o.s.** sich *dat* etwas vormachen
decelerate [diːˈsɛləreɪt] *vi* (*car etc*) langsamer werden; (*driver*) die Geschwindigkeit herabsetzen
December [dɪˈsɛmbəʳ] *n* Dezember *m*; *see also* **July**
decency [ˈdiːsənsɪ] *n* (*propriety*) Anstand *m*; (*kindness*) Anständigkeit *f*
decent [ˈdiːsənt] *adj* anständig; **we expect you to do the ~ thing** wir erwarten, dass Sie die Konsequenzen ziehen; **they were very ~ about it** sie haben sich sehr anständig verhalten; **that was very ~ of him** das war sehr anständig von ihm; **are you ~?** (*dressed*) hast du etwas an?
decently [ˈdiːsəntlɪ] *adv* anständig
decentralization [ˈdiːsɛntrəlaɪˈzeɪʃən] *n* Dezentralisierung *f*
decentralize [diːˈsɛntrəlaɪz] *vt* dezentralisieren
deception [dɪˈsɛpʃən] *n* Täuschung *f*, Betrug *m*
deceptive [dɪˈsɛptɪv] *adj* irreführend, täuschend
decibel [ˈdɛsɪbɛl] *n* Dezibel *nt*
decide [dɪˈsaɪd] *vt* entscheiden; (*persuade*) veranlassen ▷ *vi* sich entscheiden; **to ~ to do sth/that** beschließen, etw zu tun/dass; **to ~ on sth** sich für etw entscheiden; **to ~ on/against doing sth** sich dafür/dagegen entscheiden, etw zu tun
decided [dɪˈsaɪdɪd] *adj* entschieden; (*character*) entschlossen; (*difference*) deutlich
decidedly [dɪˈsaɪdɪdlɪ] *adv* entschieden; (*emphatically*) entschlossen
deciding [dɪˈsaɪdɪŋ] *adj* entscheidend
deciduous [dɪˈsɪdjuəs] *adj* (*tree, woods*) Laub-
decimal [ˈdɛsɪməl] *adj* (*system, number*) Dezimal- ▷ *n* Dezimalzahl *f*; **to three ~ places** auf drei Dezimalstellen
decimalize [ˈdɛsɪməlaɪz] (*Brit*) *vt* auf das Dezimalsystem umstellen
decimal point *n* Komma *nt*
decimate [ˈdɛsɪmeɪt] *vt* dezimieren
decipher [dɪˈsaɪfəʳ] *vt* entziffern
decision [dɪˈsɪʒən] *n* Entscheidung *f*; (*decisiveness*) Bestimmtheit *f*, Entschlossenheit *f*; **to make a ~** eine Entscheidung treffen
decisive [dɪˈsaɪsɪv] *adj* (*action etc*) entscheidend; (*person*) entschlussfreudig; (*manner, reply*) bestimmt, entschlossen
deck [dɛk] *n* Deck *nt*; (*also*: **record deck**) Plattenspieler *m*; (*of cards*) Spiel *nt*; **to go up on ~** an Deck gehen; **below ~** unter Deck; **top ~** (*of bus*) Oberdeck *nt*; **cassette ~** Tapedeck *nt*
deck chair *n* Liegestuhl *m*
deck hand *n* Deckshelfer(in) *m(f)*
declaration [dɛkləˈreɪʃən] *n* Erklärung *f*
declare [dɪˈklɛəʳ] *vt* erklären; (*result*) bekannt geben, veröffentlichen; (*income etc*) angeben; (*goods at customs*) verzollen
declassify [diːˈklæsɪfaɪ] *vt* freigeben
decline [dɪˈklaɪn] *n* Rückgang *m*; (*decay*) Verfall *m* ▷ *vt* ablehnen ▷ *vi* (*strength*) nachlassen; (*business*) zurückgehen; (*old person*) abbauen; **~ in/of** Rückgang *m +gen*; **~ in living standards** Sinken *nt* des Lebensstandards
declutch [ˈdiːˈklʌtʃ] *vi* auskuppeln
decode [ˈdiːˈkəud] *vt* entschlüsseln
decoder [diːˈkəudəʳ] *n* Decoder *m*

decompose [diːkəm'pəuz] *vi* (*organic matter*) sich zersetzen; (*corpse*) verwesen
decomposition [diːkɔmpə'zɪʃən] *n* Zersetzung *f*
decompression [diːkəm'prɛʃən] *n* Dekompression *f*, Druckverminderung *f*
decompression chamber *n* Dekompressionskammer *f*
decongestant [diːkən'dʒɛstənt] *n* (*Med*) abschwellendes Mittel *nt*; (*: drops*) Nasentropfen *pl*
decontaminate [diːkən'tæmɪneɪt] *vt* entgiften
decontrol [diːkən'trəul] *vt* freigeben
décor ['deɪkɔːʳ] *n* Ausstattung *f*; (*Theat*) Dekor *m or nt*
decorate ['dɛkəreɪt] *vt*: **to ~ (with)** verzieren (mit); (*tree, building*) schmücken (mit) ▷ *vt* (*room, house: from bare walls*) anstreichen und tapezieren; (*: redecorate*) renovieren
decoration [dɛkə'reɪʃən] *n* Verzierung *f*; (*on tree, building*) Schmuck *m*; (*act: see verb*) Verzieren *nt*; Schmücken *nt*; (An)streichen *nt*; Tapezieren *nt*; (*medal*) Auszeichnung *f*
decorative ['dɛkərətɪv] *adj* dekorativ
decorator ['dɛkəreɪtəʳ] *n* Maler(in) *m(f)*, Anstreicher(in) *m(f)*
decorum [dɪ'kɔːrəm] *n* Anstand *m*
decoy ['diːkɔɪ] *n* Lockvogel *m*; (*object*) Köder *m*; **they used him as a ~ for the enemy** sie benutzten ihn dazu, den Feind anzulocken
decrease ['diːkriːs] *vt* verringern, reduzieren ▷ *vi* abnehmen, zurückgehen ▷ *n*: **~ (in)** Abnahme *f (+gen)*, Rückgang *m (+gen)*; **to be on the ~** abnehmen, zurückgehen
decreasing [diː'kriːsɪŋ] *adj* abnehmend, zurückgehend
decree [dɪ'kriː] *n* (*Admin, Law*) Verfügung *f*; (*Pol*) Erlass *m*; (*Rel*) Dekret *nt* ▷ *vt*: **to ~ (that)** verfügen(, dass), verordnen(, dass)
decree absolute *n* endgültiges Scheidungsurteil *nt*
decree nisi [-'naɪsaɪ] *n* vorläufiges Scheidungsurteil *nt*
decrepit [dɪ'krɛpɪt] *adj* (*shack*) baufällig; (*person*) klapprig (*inf*)
decry [dɪ'kraɪ] *vt* schlechtmachen
dedicate ['dɛdɪkeɪt] *vt*: **to ~ to** widmen *+dat*
dedicated ['dɛdɪkeɪtɪd] *adj* hingebungsvoll, engagiert; (*Comput*) dediziert; **~ word processor** dediziertes Textverarbeitungssystem *nt*
dedication [dɛdɪ'keɪʃən] *n* Hingabe *f*; (*in book, on radio*) Widmung *f*
deduce [dɪ'djuːs] *vt*: **to ~ (that)** schließen(, dass), folgern(, dass)
deduct [dɪ'dʌkt] *vt* abziehen; **to ~ sth (from)** etw abziehen (von); (*esp from wage etc*) etw einbehalten (von)
deduction [dɪ'dʌkʃən] *n* (*act of deducting*) Abzug *m*; (*act of deducing*) Folgerung *f*
deed [diːd] *n* Tat *f*; (*Law*) Urkunde *f*; **~ of covenant** Vertragsurkunde *f*
deem [diːm] *vt* (*formal*) erachten für, halten für; **to ~ it wise/helpful to do sth** es für klug/hilfreich halten, etw zu tun
deep [diːp] *adj* tief ▷ *adv*: **the spectators stood 20 ~** die Zuschauer standen in 20 Reihen hintereinander; **to be 4 metres ~** 4 Meter tief sein; **knee-~ in water** bis zu den Knien im Wasser; **he took a ~ breath** er holte tief Luft
deepen ['diːpn] *vt* vertiefen ▷ *vi* (*crisis*) sich verschärfen; (*mystery*) größer werden
deepfreeze ['diːp'friːz] *n* Tiefkühltruhe *f*
deep-fry ['diːp'fraɪ] *vt* frittieren
deeply ['diːplɪ] *adv* (*breathe*) tief; (*interested*) höchst; (*moved, grateful*) zutiefst
deep-rooted ['diːp'ruːtɪd] *adj* tief verwurzelt; (*habit*) fest eingefahren
deep-sea ['diːp'siː] *cpd* Tiefsee-; (*fishing*) Hochsee-
deep-seated ['diːp'siːtɪd] *adj* tief sitzend
deep-set ['diːpsɛt] *adj* tief liegend
deer [dɪəʳ] *n inv* Reh *nt*; (*male*) Hirsch *m*; **(red) ~** Rotwild *nt*; **(roe) ~** Reh *nt*; **(fallow) ~** Damwild *nt*
deerskin ['dɪəskɪn] *n* Hirschleder *nt*, Rehleder *nt*
deerstalker ['dɪəstɔːkəʳ] *n* ≈ Sherlock-Holmes-Mütze *f*
deface [dɪ'feɪs] *vt* (*with paint etc*) beschmieren; (*slash, tear*) zerstören
defamation [dɛfə'meɪʃən] *n* Diffamierung *f*, Verleumdung *f*
defamatory [dɪ'fæmətrɪ] *adj* diffamierend, verleumderisch
default [dɪ'fɔːlt] *n* (*also*: **default value**) Voreinstellung *f* ▷ *vi*: **to ~ on a debt** einer Zahlungsverpflichtung nicht nachkommen; **to win by ~** kampflos gewinnen
defaulter [dɪ'fɔːltəʳ] *n* säumiger Zahler *m*, säumige Zahlerin *f*
default option *n* Voreinstellung *f*
defeat [dɪ'fiːt] *vt* besiegen, schlagen ▷ *n* (*failure*) Niederlage *f*; (*of enemy*): **~ (of)** Sieg *m* (über *+acc*)
defeatism [dɪ'fiːtɪzəm] *n* Defätismus *m*
defeatist [dɪ'fiːtɪst] *adj* defätistisch ▷ *n* Defätist(in) *m(f)*
defect [*n* 'diːfɛkt, *vi* dɪ'fɛkt] *n* Fehler *m* ▷ *vi*: **to ~ to the enemy** zum Feind überlaufen; **physical/mental ~** körperlicher/geistiger Schaden *m or* Defekt *m*; **to ~ to the West** sich in den Westen absetzen
defective [dɪ'fɛktɪv] *adj* fehlerhaft
defector [dɪ'fɛktəʳ] *n* Überläufer(in) *m(f)*
defence, (*US*) **defense** [dɪ'fɛns] *n* Verteidigung *f*; (*justification*) Rechtfertigung *f*; **in ~ of** zur Verteidigung *+gen*; **witness for the ~** Zeuge *m*/Zeugin *f* der Verteidigung; **the Ministry of D~, the Department of Defense** (*US*) das Verteidigungsministerium
defenceless [dɪ'fɛnslɪs] *adj* schutzlos
defend [dɪ'fɛnd] *vt* verteidigen
defendant [dɪ'fɛndənt] *n* Angeklagte(r) *f(m)*; (*in civil case*) Beklagte(r) *f(m)*

defender [dɪ'fɛndəʳ] *n* Verteidiger(in) *m(f)*
defending champion [dɪ'fɛndɪŋ-] *n* (*Sport*) Titelverteidiger(in) *m(f)*
defending counsel [dɪ'fɛndɪŋ-] *n* Verteidiger(in) *m(f)*
defense [dɪ'fɛns] (*US*) *n* = **defence**
defensive [dɪ'fɛnsɪv] *adj* defensiv ▷ *n*: **on the ~** in der Defensive
defer [dɪ'fəːʳ] *vt* verschieben
deference ['dɛfərəns] *n* Achtung *f*, Respekt *m*; **out of** *or* **in ~ to** aus Rücksicht auf *+acc*
deferential [dɛfə'rɛnʃəl] *adj* ehrerbietig, respektvoll
defiance [dɪ'faɪəns] *n* Trotz *m*; **in ~ of sth** einer Sache *dat* zum Trotz, unter Missachtung einer Sache *gen*
defiant [dɪ'faɪənt] *adj* trotzig; (*challenging*) herausfordernd
defiantly [dɪ'faɪəntlɪ] *adv* (*see adj*) trotzig; herausfordernd
deficiency [dɪ'fɪʃənsɪ] *n* Mangel *m*; (*defect*) Unzulänglichkeit *f*; (*deficit*) Defizit *nt*
deficiency disease *n* Mangelkrankheit *f*
deficient [dɪ'fɪʃənt] *adj*: **sb/sth is ~ in sth** jdm/etw fehlt es an etw *dat*
deficit ['dɛfɪsɪt] *n* Defizit *nt*
defile [dɪ'faɪl] *vt* (*memory*) beschmutzen; (*statue etc*) schänden ▷ *n* Hohlweg *m*
define [dɪ'faɪn] *vt* (*limits, boundaries*) bestimmen, festlegen; (*word*) definieren
definite ['dɛfɪnɪt] *adj* definitiv; (*date etc*) fest; (*clear, obvious*) klar, eindeutig; (*certain*) bestimmt; **he was ~ about it** er war sich *dat* sehr sicher
definite article *n* bestimmter Artikel *m*
definitely ['dɛfɪnɪtlɪ] *adv* bestimmt; (*decide*) fest, definitiv
definition [dɛfɪ'nɪʃən] *n* (*of word*) Definition *f*; (*of photograph etc*) Schärfe *f*
definitive [dɪ'fɪnɪtɪv] *adj* (*account*) definitiv; (*version*) maßgeblich
deflate [diː'fleɪt] *vt* (*tyre, balloon*) die Luft ablassen aus; (*person*) einen Dämpfer versetzen *+dat*; (*Econ*) deflationieren
deflation [diː'fleɪʃən] *n* Deflation *f*
deflationary [diː'fleɪʃənrɪ] *adj* deflationistisch
deflect [dɪ'flɛkt] *vt* (*attention*) ablenken; (*criticism*) abwehren; (*shot*) abfälschen; (*light*) brechen, beugen
defog ['diː'fɔg] (*US*) *vt* von Beschlag freimachen
defogger ['diː'fɔgəʳ] (*US*) *n* Gebläse *nt*
deform [dɪ'fɔːm] *vt* deformieren, verunstalten
deformed [dɪ'fɔːmd] *adj* deformiert, missgebildet
deformity [dɪ'fɔːmɪtɪ] *n* Deformität *f*, Missbildung *f*
defraud [dɪ'frɔːd] *vt*: **to ~ sb (of sth)** jdn (um etw) betrügen
defray [dɪ'freɪ] *vt*: **to ~ sb's expenses** jds Unkosten tragen *or* übernehmen
defrost [diː'frɔst] *vt* (*fridge*) abtauen; (*windscreen*) entfrosten; (*food*) auftauen
defroster [diː'frɔstəʳ] (*US*) *n* (*Aut*) Gebläse *nt*
deft [dɛft] *adj* geschickt
defunct [dɪ'fʌŋkt] *adj* (*industry*) stillgelegt; (*organization*) nicht mehr bestehend
defuse [diː'fjuːz] *vt* entschärfen
defy [dɪ'faɪ] *vt* sich widersetzen *+dat*; (*challenge*) auffordern; **it defies description** es spottet jeder Beschreibung
degenerate [dɪ'dʒɛnəreɪt] *vi* degenerieren ▷ *adj* degeneriert
degradation [dɛgrə'deɪʃən] *n* Erniedrigung *f*
degrade [dɪ'greɪd] *vt* erniedrigen; (*reduce the quality of*) degradieren
degrading [dɪ'greɪdɪŋ] *adj* erniedrigend
degree [dɪ'griː] *n* Grad *m*; (*Scol*) akademischer Grad *m*; **10 ~s below (zero)** 10 Grad unter null; **6 ~s of frost** 6 Grad Kälte *or* unter null; **a considerable ~ of risk** ein gewisses Risiko; **a ~ in maths** ein Hochschulabschluss *m* in Mathematik; **by ~s** nach und nach; **to some ~, to a certain ~** einigermaßen, in gewissem Maße
dehydrated [diːhaɪ'dreɪtɪd] *adj* ausgetrocknet, dehydriert; (*milk, eggs*) pulverisiert, Trocken-
dehydration [diːhaɪ'dreɪʃən] *n* Austrocknung *f*, Dehydration *f*
de-ice ['diː'aɪs] *vt* enteisen
de-icer ['diː'aɪsəʳ] *n* Defroster *m*
deign [deɪn] *vi*: **to ~ to do sth** sich herablassen, etw zu tun
deity ['diːɪtɪ] *n* Gottheit *f*
dejected [dɪ'dʒɛktɪd] *adj* niedergeschlagen, deprimiert
dejection [dɪ'dʒɛkʃən] *n* Niedergeschlagenheit *f*, Depression *f*
Del. (*US*) *abbr* (*Post*) = *Delaware*
delay [dɪ'leɪ] *vt* (*decision, ceremony*) verschieben, aufschieben; (*person, plane, train*) aufhalten ▷ *vi* zögern ▷ *n* Verzögerung *f*; (*postponement*) Aufschub *m*; **to be ~ed** (*person*) sich verspäten; (*departure etc*) verspätet sein; (*flight etc*) Verspätung haben; **without ~** unverzüglich
delayed-action [dɪ'leɪd'ækʃən] *adj* (*bomb, mine*) mit Zeitzünder; (*Phot*): **~ shutter release** Selbstauslöser *m*
delectable [dɪ'lɛktəbl] *adj* (*person*) reizend; (*food*) köstlich
delegate ['dɛlɪgɪt] *n* Delegierte(r) *f(m)* ▷ *vt* delegieren; **to ~ sth to sb** jdm mit etw beauftragen; **to ~ sb to do sth** jdn damit beauftragen, etw zu tun
delegation [dɛlɪ'geɪʃən] *n* Delegation *f*; (*group*) Abordnung *f*, Delegation *f*
delete [dɪ'liːt] *vt* streichen; (*Comput*) löschen
Delhi ['dɛlɪ] *n* Delhi *nt*
deli ['dɛlɪ] *n* Feinkostgeschäft *nt*
deliberate [*adj* dɪ'lɪbərɪt, *vi* dɪ'lɪbəreɪt] *adj* absichtlich; (*action, insult*) bewusst; (*slow*) bedächtig ▷ *vi* überlegen
deliberately [dɪ'lɪbərɪtlɪ] *adv* absichtlich, bewusst; (*slowly*) bedächtig
deliberation [dɪlɪbə'reɪʃən] *n* Überlegung *f*; (*usu pl: discussions*) Beratungen *pl*

delicacy ['dɛlɪkəsɪ] *n* Feinheit *f*, Zartheit *f*; (*of problem*) Delikatheit *f*; (*choice food*) Delikatesse *f*
delicate ['dɛlɪkɪt] *adj* fein; (*colour, health*) zart; (*approach*) feinfühlig; (*problem*) delikat, heikel
delicately ['dɛlɪkɪtlɪ] *adv* zart, fein; (*act, express*) feinfühlig
delicatessen [dɛlɪkə'tɛsn] *n* Feinkostgeschäft *nt*
delicious [dɪ'lɪʃəs] *adj* köstlich; (*feeling, person*) herrlich
delight [dɪ'laɪt] *n* Freude *f* ▷ *vt* erfreuen; **sb takes (a) ~ in sth** etw bereitet jdm große Freude; **sb takes (a) ~ in doing sth** es bereitet jdm große Freude, etw zu tun; **to be the ~ of** die Freude *+gen* sein; **she was a ~ to interview** es war eine Freude, sie zu interviewen; **the ~s of country life** die Freuden des Landlebens
delighted [dɪ'laɪtɪd] *adj*: **~ (at** *or* **with)** erfreut (über *+acc*), entzückt (über *+acc*); **to be ~ to do sth** etw gern tun; **I'd be ~** ich würde mich sehr freuen
delightful [dɪ'laɪtful] *adj* reizend, wunderbar
delimit [diː'lɪmɪt] *vt* abgrenzen
delineate [dɪ'lɪnɪeɪt] *vt* (*fig*) beschreiben
delinquency [dɪ'lɪŋkwənsɪ] *n* Kriminalität *f*
delinquent [dɪ'lɪŋkwənt] *adj* straffällig ▷ *n* Delinquent(in) *m(f)*
delirious [dɪ'lɪrɪəs] *adj*: **to be ~** (*with fever*) im Delirium sein; (*with excitement*) im Taumel sein
delirium [dɪ'lɪrɪəm] *n* Delirium *nt*
deliver [dɪ'lɪvəʳ] *vt* liefern; (*letters, papers*) zustellen; (*hand over*) übergeben; (*message*) überbringen; (*speech*) halten; (*blow*) versetzen; (*Med: baby*) zur Welt bringen; (*warning*) geben; (*ultimatum*) stellen; (*free*): **to ~ (from)** befreien (von); **to ~ the goods** (*fig*) halten, was man versprochen hat
deliverance [dɪ'lɪvrəns] *n* Befreiung *f*
delivery [dɪ'lɪvərɪ] *n* Lieferung *f*; (*of letters, papers*) Zustellung *f*; (*of speaker*) Vortrag *m*; (*Med*) Entbindung *f*; **to take ~ of sth** etw in Empfang nehmen
delivery note *n* Lieferschein *m*
delivery van, (*US*) **delivery truck** *n* Lieferwagen *m*
delouse ['diː'laus] *vt* entlausen
delta ['dɛltə] *n* Delta *nt*
delude [dɪ'luːd] *vt* täuschen; **to ~ o.s.** sich *dat* etwas vormachen
deluge ['dɛljuːdʒ] *n* (*of rain*) Guss *m*; (*fig: of petitions, requests*) Flut *f*
delusion [dɪ'luːʒən] *n* Irrglaube *m*; **to have ~s of grandeur** größenwahnsinnig sein
de luxe [də'lʌks] *adj* (*hotel, model*) Luxus-
delve [dɛlv] *vi*: **to ~ into** (*subject*) sich eingehend befassen mit; (*cupboard, handbag*) tief greifen in *+acc*
Dem. (*US*) *abbr* (*Pol*) = **Democrat; Democratic**
demagogue ['dɛməgɔg] *n* Demagoge *m*, Demagogin *f*
demand [dɪ'mɑːnd] *vt* verlangen; (*rights*) fordern; (*need*) erfordern, verlangen ▷ *n* Verlangen *nt*; (*claim*) Forderung *f*; (*Econ*) Nachfrage *f*; **to ~ sth (from** *or* **of sb)** etw (von jdm) verlangen *or* fordern; **to be in ~** gefragt sein; **on ~** (*available*) auf Verlangen; (*payable*) bei Vorlage *or* Sicht
demand draft *n* Sichtwechsel *m*
demanding [dɪ'mɑːndɪŋ] *adj* anspruchsvoll; (*work, child*) anstrengend
demarcation [diːmɑː'keɪʃən] *n* (*of area, tasks*) Abgrenzung *f*
demarcation dispute *n* Streit *m* um den Zuständigkeitsbereich
demean [dɪ'miːn] *vt*: **to ~ o.s.** sich erniedrigen
demeanour, (*US*) **demeanor** [dɪ'miːnəʳ] *n* Benehmen *nt*, Auftreten *nt*
demented [dɪ'mɛntɪd] *adj* wahnsinnig
demerger [diː'məːdʒəʳ] *n* (*Comm*) Abspaltung *f*, Demerger *m*
demilitarized zone [diː'mɪlɪtəraɪzd-] *n* entmilitarisierte Zone *f*
demise [dɪ'maɪz] *n* Ende *nt*; (*death*) Tod *m*
demist [diː'mɪst] (*Brit*) *vt* (*Aut: windscreen*) von Beschlag freimachen
demister [diː'mɪstəʳ] (*Brit*) *n* (*Aut*) Gebläse *nt*
demo ['dɛməu] (*inf*) *n abbr* = **demonstration**
demob [diː'mɔb] (*inf*) *vt* = **demobilize**
demobilize [diː'məubɪlaɪz] *vt* aus dem Kriegsdienst entlassen, demobilisieren
democracy [dɪ'mɔkrəsɪ] *n* Demokratie *f*
democrat ['dɛməkræt] *n* Demokrat(in) *m(f)*
democratic [dɛmə'krætɪk] *adj* demokratisch
Democratic Party (*US*) *n*: **the ~** die Demokratische Partei
demography [dɪ'mɔgrəfɪ] *n* Demografie *f*
demolish [dɪ'mɔlɪʃ] *vt* abreißen, abbrechen; (*fig: argument*) widerlegen
demolition [dɛmə'lɪʃən] *n* Abriss *m*, Abbruch *m*; (*of argument*) Widerlegung *f*
demon ['diːmən] *n* Dämon *m* ▷ *adj* teuflisch gut
demonstrate ['dɛmənstreɪt] *vt* (*theory*) demonstrieren; (*skill*) zeigen, beweisen; (*appliance*) vorführen ▷ *vi*: **to ~ (for/against)** demonstrieren (für/gegen)
demonstration [dɛmən'streɪʃən] *n* Demonstration *f*; (*of gadget, machine etc*) Vorführung *f*; **to hold a ~** eine Demonstration veranstalten *or* durchführen
demonstrative [dɪ'mɔnstrətɪv] *adj* demonstrativ
demonstrator ['dɛmənstreɪtəʳ] *n* Demonstrant(in) *m(f)*; (*sales person*) Vorführer(in) *m(f)*; (*car*) Vorführwagen *m*; (*computer etc*) Vorführgerät *nt*
demoralize [dɪ'mɔrəlaɪz] *vt* entmutigen
demote [dɪ'məut] *vt* zurückstufen; (*Mil*) degradieren
demotion [dɪ'məuʃən] *n* Zurückstufung *f*; (*Mil*) Degradierung *f*
demur [dɪ'məːʳ] (*form*) *vi* Einwände *pl* erheben ▷ *n*: **without ~** widerspruchslos; **they ~red at the suggestion** sie erhoben Einwände gegen den Vorschlag
demure [dɪ'mjuəʳ] *adj* zurückhaltend; (*smile*)

höflich; (*dress*) schlicht
demurrage [dɪˈmʌrɪdʒ] *n* Liegegeld *nt*
den [dɛn] *n* Höhle *f*; (*of fox*) Bau *m*; (*room*) Bude *f*
denationalization [ˈdiːnæʃnəlaɪˈzeɪʃən] *n* Privatisierung *f*
denationalize [diːˈnæʃnəlaɪz] *vt* privatisieren
denatured alcohol [diːˈneɪtʃəd-] (US) *n* vergällter Alkohol *m*
denial [dɪˈnaɪəl] *n* Leugnen *nt*; (*of rights*) Verweigerung *f*
denier [ˈdɛnɪəʳ] *n* Denier *nt*
denigrate [ˈdɛnɪgreɪt] *vt* verunglimpfen
denim [ˈdɛnɪm] *n* Jeansstoff *m*; **denims** *npl* (Blue) Jeans *pl*
denim jacket *n* Jeansjacke *f*
denizen [ˈdɛnɪzn] *n* Bewohner(in) *m(f)*; (*person in town*) Einwohner(in) *m(f)*; (*foreigner*) eingebürgerter Ausländer *m*, eingebürgerte Ausländerin *f*
Denmark [ˈdɛnmɑːk] *n* Dänemark *nt*
denomination [dɪnɔmɪˈneɪʃən] *n* (*of money*) Nennwert *m*; (*Rel*) Konfession *f*
denominator [dɪˈnɔmɪneɪtəʳ] *n* Nenner *m*
denote [dɪˈnəut] *vt* (*indicate*) hindeuten auf *+acc*; (*represent*) bezeichnen
denounce [dɪˈnauns] *vt* (*person*) anprangern; (*action*) verurteilen
dense [dɛns] *adj* dicht; (*inf: person*) beschränkt
densely [ˈdɛnslɪ] *adv* dicht
density [ˈdɛnsɪtɪ] *n* Dichte *f*; **single/double-~ disk** (*Comput*) Diskette *f* mit einfacher/doppelter Dichte
dent [dɛnt] *n* Beule *f*; (*in pride, ego*) Knacks *m* ▷ *vt* (*also*: **make a dent in**) einbeulen; (*pride, ego*) anknacksen
dental [ˈdɛntl] *adj* (*filling, hygiene etc*) Zahn-; (*treatment*) zahnärztlich
dental floss [-flɔs] *n* Zahnseide *f*
dental surgeon *n* Zahnarzt *m*, Zahnärztin *f*
dentifrice [ˈdɛntɪfrɪs] *n* Zahnpasta *f*
dentist [ˈdɛntɪst] *n* Zahnarzt *m*, Zahnärztin *f*; (*also*: **dentist's (surgery)**) Zahnarzt *m*, Zahnarztpraxis *f*
dentistry [ˈdɛntɪstrɪ] *n* Zahnmedizin *f*
dentures [ˈdɛntʃəz] *npl* Zahnprothese *f*; (*full*) Gebiss *nt*
denuded [diːˈnjuːdɪd] *adj*: **~ of** entblößt von
denunciation [dɪnʌnsɪˈeɪʃən] *n* (*of person*) Anprangerung *f*; (*of action*) Verurteilung *f*
deny [dɪˈnaɪ] *vt* leugnen; (*involvement*) abstreiten; (*permission, chance*) verweigern; (*country, religion etc*) verleugnen; **he denies having said it** er leugnet *or* bestreitet, das gesagt zu haben
deodorant [diːˈəudərənt] *n* Deodorant *nt*
depart [dɪˈpɑːt] *vi* (*visitor*) abreisen; (*: on foot*) weggehen; (*bus, train*) abfahren; (*plane*) abfliegen; **to ~ from** (*fig*) abweichen von
departed [dɪˈpɑːtɪd] *adj*: **the (dear) ~** der/die (liebe) Verstorbene *m/f*, die (lieben) Verstorbenen *pl*
department [dɪˈpɑːtmənt] *n* Abteilung *f*; (*Scol*) Fachbereich *m*; (*Pol*) Ministerium *nt*; **that's not my ~** (*fig*) dafür bin ich nicht zuständig; **D~ of State** (US) Außenministerium *nt*
departmental [diːpɑːtˈmɛntl] *adj* (*budget, costs*) der Abteilung; (*level*) Abteilungs-; **~ manager** Abteilungsleiter(in) *m(f)*
department store *n* Warenhaus *nt*
departure [dɪˈpɑːtʃəʳ] *n* (*of visitor*) Abreise *f*; (*on foot, of employee etc*) Weggang *m*; (*of bus, train*) Abfahrt *f*; (*of plane*) Abflug *m*; (*fig*): **~ from** Abweichen *nt* von; **a new ~** ein neuer Weg *m*
departure lounge *n* Abflughalle *f*
depend [dɪˈpɛnd] *vi*: **to ~ on** abhängen von; (*rely on, trust*) sich verlassen auf *+acc*; (*financially*) abhängig sein von, angewiesen sein auf *+acc*; **it ~s** es kommt darauf an; **~ing on the result ...** je nachdem, wie das Ergebnis ausfällt, ...
dependable [dɪˈpɛndəbl] *adj* zuverlässig
dependant [dɪˈpɛndənt] *n* abhängige(r) (Familien)angehörige(r) *f(m)*
dependence [dɪˈpɛndəns] *n* Abhängigkeit *f*
dependent [dɪˈpɛndənt] *adj*: **to be ~ on** (*person*) abhängig sein von, angewiesen sein auf *+acc*; (*decision*) abhängen von ▷ *n* = **dependant**
depict [dɪˈpɪkt] *vt* (*in picture*) darstellen; (*describe*) beschreiben
depilatory [dɪˈpɪlətrɪ] *n* (*also*: **depilatory cream**) Enthaarungsmittel *nt*
depleted [dɪˈpliːtɪd] *adj* (*reserves*) aufgebraucht; (*stocks*) erschöpft
deplorable [dɪˈplɔːrəbl] *adj* bedauerlich
deplore [dɪˈplɔːʳ] *vt* verurteilen
deploy [dɪˈplɔɪ] *vt* einsetzen
depopulate [diːˈpɔpjuleɪt] *vt* entvölkern
depopulation [ˈdiːpɔpjuˈleɪʃən] *n* Entvölkerung *f*
deport [dɪˈpɔːt] *vt* (*criminal*) deportieren; (*illegal immigrant*) abschieben
deportation [diːpɔːˈteɪʃən] *n* (*see vb*) Deportation *f*; Abschiebung *f*
deportation order *n* Ausweisung *f*
deportee [diːpɔːˈtiː] *n* Deportierte(r) *f(m)*
deportment [dɪˈpɔːtmənt] *n* Benehmen *nt*
depose [dɪˈpəuz] *vt* absetzen
deposit [dɪˈpɔzɪt] *n* (*in account*) Guthaben *nt*; (*down payment*) Anzahlung *f*; (*for hired goods etc*) Sicherheit *f*, Kaution *f*; (*on bottle etc*) Pfand *nt*; (*Chem*) Ablagerung *f*; (*of ore, oil*) Lagerstätte *f* ▷ *vt* deponieren; (*subj: river: sand etc*) ablagern; **to put down a ~ of £50** eine Anzahlung von £50 machen
deposit account *n* Sparkonto *nt*
depositary [dɪˈpɔzɪtərɪ] *n* Treuhänder(in) *m(f)*
depositor [dɪˈpɔzɪtəʳ] *n* Deponent(in) *m(f)*, Einzahler(in) *m(f)*
depository [dɪˈpɔzɪtərɪ] *n* (*person*) Treuhänder(in) *m(f)*; (*place*) Lager(haus) *nt*
depot [ˈdɛpəu] *n* Lager(haus) *nt*; (*for vehicles*) Depot *nt*; (*US: station*) Bahnhof *m*; (*: bus station*) Busbahnhof *m*
depraved [dɪˈpreɪvd] *adj* verworfen
depravity [dɪˈprævɪtɪ] *n* Verworfenheit *f*
deprecate [ˈdɛprɪkeɪt] *vt* missbilligen

deprecating ['dɛprɪkeɪtɪŋ] *adj* (*disapproving*) missbilligend; (*apologetic*) entschuldigend
depreciate [dɪ'pri:ʃɪeɪt] *vi* an Wert verlieren; (*currency*) an Kaufkraft verlieren; (*value*) sinken
depreciation [dɪpri:ʃɪ'eɪʃən] *n* (*see vb*) Wertminderung *f*; Kaufkraftverlust *m*; Sinken *nt*
depress [dɪ'prɛs] *vt* deprimieren; (*price, wages*) drücken; (*press down*) herunterdrücken
depressant [dɪ'prɛsnt] *n* Beruhigungsmittel *nt*
depressed [dɪ'prɛst] *adj* deprimiert, niedergeschlagen; (*price*) gesunken; (*industry*) geschwächt; (*area*) Notstands-; **to get ~** deprimiert werden
depressing [dɪ'prɛsɪŋ] *adj* deprimierend
depression [dɪ'prɛʃən] *n* (*Psych*) Depressionen *pl*; (*Econ*) Wirtschaftskrise *f*; (*Met*) Tief(druckgebiet) *nt*; (*hollow*) Vertiefung *f*
deprivation [dɛprɪ'veɪʃən] *n* Entbehrung *f*, Not *f*; (*of freedom, rights etc*) Entzug *m*
deprive [dɪ'praɪv] *vt*: **to ~ sb of sth** (*liberty*) jdm etw entziehen; (*life*) jdm etw nehmen
deprived [dɪ'praɪvd] *adj* benachteiligt; (*area*) Not leidend
dept *abbr* = **department**
depth [dɛpθ] *n* Tiefe *f*; **in the ~s of** in den Tiefen *+gen*; **in the ~s of despair** in tiefster Verzweiflung; **in the ~s of winter** im tiefsten Winter; **at a ~ of 3 metres** in 3 Meter Tiefe; **to be out of one's ~** (*in water*) nicht mehr stehen können; (*fig*) überfordert sein; **to study sth in ~** etw gründlich *or* eingehend studieren
depth charge *n* Wasserbombe *f*
deputation [dɛpju'teɪʃən] *n* Abordnung *f*
deputize ['dɛpjutaɪz] *vi*: **to ~ for sb** jdn vertreten
deputy ['dɛpjutɪ] *cpd* stellvertretend ▷ *n* (Stell)vertreter(in) *m(f)*; (*Pol*) Abgeordnete(r) *f(m)*; (*US: also:* **deputy sheriff**) Hilfssheriff *m*; **~ head** (*Brit: Scol*) Konrektor(in) *m(f)*
derail [dɪ'reɪl] *vt*: **to be ~ed** entgleisen
derailment [dɪ'reɪlmənt] *n* Entgleisung *f*
deranged [dɪ'reɪndʒd] *adj*: **to be mentally ~** geistesgestört sein
derby ['də:rbɪ] *n* Derby *nt*; (*US: hat*) Melone *f*
deregulate [dɪ'rɛgjuleɪt] *vt* staatliche Kontrollen aufheben bei
deregulation [dɪ'rɛgju'leɪʃən] *n* Aufhebung *f* staatlicher Kontrollen
derelict ['dɛrɪlɪkt] *adj* verfallen
deride [dɪ'raɪd] *vt* sich lustig machen über *+acc*
derision [dɪ'rɪʒən] *n* Hohn *m*, Spott *m*
derisive [dɪ'raɪsɪv] *adj* spöttisch
derisory [dɪ'raɪsərɪ] *adj* spöttisch; (*sum*) lächerlich
derivation [dɛrɪ'veɪʃən] *n* Ableitung *f*
derivative [dɪ'rɪvətɪv] *n* (*Ling*) Ableitung *f*; (*Chem*) Derivat *nt* ▷ *adj* nachahmend
derive [dɪ'raɪv] *vt*: **to ~ (from)** gewinnen (aus); (*benefit*) ziehen (aus) ▷ *vi*: **to ~ from** (*originate in*) sich herleiten *or* ableiten von; **to ~ pleasure from** Freude haben an *+dat*
dermatitis [də:mə'taɪtɪs] *n* Hautentzündung *f*, Dermatitis *f*
dermatology [də:mə'tɔlədʒɪ] *n* Dermatologie *f*
derogatory [dɪ'rɔgətərɪ] *adj* abfällig
derrick ['dɛrɪk] *n* (*on ship*) Derrickkran *m*; (*on well*) Bohrturm *m*
derv [də:v] (*Brit*) *n* (*Aut*) Diesel(kraftstoff) *m*
desalination [di:sælɪ'neɪʃən] *n* Entsalzung *f*
descend [dɪ'sɛnd] *vt* hinuntergehen, hinuntersteigen; (*lift, vehicle*) hinunterfahren; (*road*) hinunterführen ▷ *vi* hinuntergehen; (*lift*) nach unten fahren; **to ~ from** abstammen von; **to ~ to** sich erniedrigen zu; **in ~ing order of importance** nach Wichtigkeit geordnet
▸ **descend on** *vt fus* überfallen; (*subj: misfortune*) hereinbrechen über *+acc*; (*: gloom*) befallen; (*: silence*) sich senken auf *+acc*; **visitors ~ed (up)on us** der Besuch hat uns überfallen
descendant [dɪ'sɛndənt] *n* Nachkomme *m*
descent [dɪ'sɛnt] *n* Abstieg *m*; (*origin*) Abstammung *f*
describe [dɪs'kraɪb] *vt* beschreiben
description [dɪs'krɪpʃən] *n* Beschreibung *f*; (*sort*): **of every ~** aller Art
descriptive [dɪs'krɪptɪv] *adj* deskriptiv
desecrate ['dɛsɪkreɪt] *vt* schänden
desegregate [di:'sɛgrɪgeɪt] *vt* die Rassentrennung aufheben in *+dat*
desert [*n* 'dɛzət, *vb* dɪ'zə:t] *n* Wüste *f* ▷ *vt* verlassen ▷ *vi* desertieren; *see also* **deserts**
deserter [dɪ'zə:tə^r] *n* Deserteur *m*
desertion [dɪ'zə:ʃən] *n* Desertion *f*, Fahnenflucht *f*; (*Law*) böswilliges Verlassen *nt*
desert island *n* einsame *or* verlassene Insel *f*
deserts [dɪ'zə:ts] *npl*: **to get one's just ~** bekommen, was man verdient
deserve [dɪ'zə:v] *vt* verdienen
deservedly [dɪ'zə:vɪdlɪ] *adv* verdientermaßen
deserving [dɪ'zə:vɪŋ] *adj* verdienstvoll
desiccated ['dɛsɪkeɪtɪd] *adj* vertrocknet; (*coconut*) getrocknet
design [dɪ'zaɪn] *n* Design *nt*; (*process*) Entwurf *m*, Gestaltung *f*; (*sketch*) Entwurf *m*; (*layout, shape*) Form *f*; (*pattern*) Muster *nt*; (*of car*) Konstruktion *f*; (*intention*) Plan *m*, Absicht *f* ▷ *vt* entwerfen; **to have ~s on** es abgesehen haben auf *+acc*; **well-~ed** mit gutem Design
design and technology (*Brit*) *n* (*Scol*) ≈ Design und Technologie
designate [*vt* 'dɛzɪgneɪt, *adj* 'dɛzɪgnɪt] *vt* bestimmen, ernennen ▷ *adj* designiert
designation [dɛzɪg'neɪʃən] *n* Bezeichnung *f*
designer [dɪ'zaɪnə^r] *n* Designer(in) *m(f)*; (*Tech*) Konstrukteur(in) *m(f)*; (*also:* **fashion designer**) Modeschöpfer(in) *m(f)* ▷ *adj* (*clothes etc*) Designer-
desirability [dɪzaɪərə'bɪlɪtɪ] *n*: **they discussed the ~ of the plan** sie besprachen, ob der Plan wünschenswert sei
desirable [dɪ'zaɪərəbl] *adj* (*proper*) wünschenswert; (*attractive*) reizvoll, attraktiv
desire [dɪ'zaɪə^r] *n* Wunsch *m*; (*sexual*) Verlangen *nt*, Begehren *nt* ▷ *vt* wünschen; (*lust after*)

begehren; **to ~ to do sth/that** wünschen, etw zu tun/dass
desirous [dɪ'zaɪərəs] *adj*: **to be ~ of doing sth** den Wunsch haben, etw zu tun
desist [dɪ'zɪst] *vi*: **to ~ (from)** absehen (von), Abstand nehmen (von)
desk [dɛsk] *n* Schreibtisch *m*; *(for pupil)* Pult *nt*; *(in hotel)* Empfang *m*; *(at airport)* Schalter *m*; *(Brit: in shop, restaurant)* Kasse *f*
desk job *n* Bürojob *m*
desktop ['dɛsktɔp] *n* Arbeitsfläche *f*
desktop publishing *n* Desktop-Publishing *nt*
desolate ['dɛsəlɪt] *adj* trostlos
desolation [dɛsə'leɪʃən] *n* Trostlosigkeit *f*
despair [dɪs'pɛəʳ] *n* Verzweiflung *f* ▷ *vi*: **to ~ of** alle Hoffnung aufgeben auf *+acc*; **to be in ~** verzweifelt sein
despatch [dɪs'pætʃ] *n, vt* = **dispatch**
desperate ['dɛspərɪt] *adj* verzweifelt; *(shortage)* akut; *(criminal)* zum Äußersten entschlossen; **to be ~ for sth/to do sth** etw dringend brauchen/unbedingt tun wollen
desperately ['dɛspərɪtlɪ] *adv* *(shout, struggle etc)* verzweifelt; *(ill)* schwer; *(unhappy etc)* äußerst
desperation [dɛspə'reɪʃən] *n* Verzweiflung *f*; **in (sheer) ~** aus (reiner) Verzweiflung
despicable [dɪs'pɪkəbl] *adj* *(action)* verabscheuungswürdig; *(person)* widerwärtig
despise [dɪs'paɪz] *vt* verachten
despite [dɪs'paɪt] *prep* trotz *+gen*
despondent [dɪs'pɔndənt] *adj* niedergeschlagen, mutlos
despot ['dɛspɔt] *n* Despot *m*
dessert [dɪ'zə:t] *n* Nachtisch *m*, Dessert *nt*
dessertspoon [dɪ'zə:tspu:n] *n* Dessertlöffel *m*
destabilize [di:'steɪbɪlaɪz] *vt* destabilisieren
destination [dɛstɪ'neɪʃən] *n* (Reise)ziel *nt*; *(of mail)* Bestimmungsort *m*
destined ['dɛstɪnd] *adj*: **to be ~ to do sth** dazu bestimmt *or* ausersehen sein, etw zu tun; **to be ~ for** bestimmt *or* ausersehen sein für
destiny ['dɛstɪnɪ] *n* Schicksal *nt*
destitute ['dɛstɪtju:t] *adj* mittellos
destroy [dɪs'trɔɪ] *vt* zerstören; *(animal)* töten
destroyer [dɪs'trɔɪəʳ] *n* Zerstörer *m*
destruction [dɪs'trʌkʃən] *n* Zerstörung *f*
destructive [dɪs'trʌktɪv] *adj* zerstörerisch; *(child, criticism etc)* destruktiv
desultory ['dɛsəltərɪ] *adj* flüchtig; *(conversation)* zwanglos
detach [dɪ'tætʃ] *vt* *(remove)* entfernen; *(unclip)* abnehmen; *(unstick)* ablösen
detachable [dɪ'tætʃəbl] *adj* abnehmbar
detached [dɪ'tætʃt] *adj* distanziert; *(house)* frei stehend, Einzel-
detachment [dɪ'tætʃmənt] *n* Distanz *f*; *(Mil)* Sonderkommando *nt*
detail ['di:teɪl] *n* Einzelheit *f*; *(no pl: in picture, one's work etc)* Detail *nt*; *(trifle)* unwichtige Einzelheit ▷ *vt* (einzeln) aufführen; **in ~** in Einzelheiten; **to go into ~s** auf Einzelheiten eingehen, ins Detail gehen
detailed ['di:teɪld] *adj* detailliert, genau
detain [dɪ'teɪn] *vt* aufhalten; *(in captivity)* in Haft halten; *(in hospital)* festhalten
detainee [di:teɪ'ni:] *n* Häftling *m*
detect [dɪ'tɛkt] *vt* wahrnehmen; *(Med, Tech)* feststellen; *(Mil)* ausfindig machen
detection [dɪ'tɛkʃən] *n* Entdeckung *f*, Feststellung *f*; **crime ~** Ermittlungsarbeit *f*; **to escape ~** *(criminal)* nicht gefasst werden; *(mistake)* der Aufmerksamkeit *dat* entgehen
detective [dɪ'tɛktɪv] *n* Kriminalbeamte(r) *m*; **private ~** Privatdetektiv *m*
detective story *n* Kriminalgeschichte *f*, Detektivgeschichte *f*
detector [dɪ'tɛktəʳ] *n* Detektor *m*
détente [deɪ'tɑ:nt] *n* Entspannung *f*, Détente *f*
detention [dɪ'tɛnʃən] *n* *(arrest)* Festnahme *f*; *(captivity)* Haft *f*; *(Scol)* Nachsitzen *nt*
deter [dɪ'tə:ʳ] *vt* *(discourage)* abschrecken; *(dissuade)* abhalten
detergent [dɪ'tə:dʒənt] *n* Reinigungsmittel *nt*; *(for clothes)* Waschmittel *nt*; *(for dishes)* Spülmittel *nt*
deteriorate [dɪ'tɪərɪəreɪt] *vi* sich verschlechtern
deterioration [dɪtɪərɪə'reɪʃən] *n* Verschlechterung *f*
determination [dɪtə:mɪ'neɪʃən] *n* Entschlossenheit *f*; *(establishment)* Festsetzung *f*
determine [dɪ'tə:mɪn] *vt* *(facts)* feststellen; *(limits etc)* festlegen; **to ~ that** beschließen, dass; **to ~ to do sth** sich entschließen, etw zu tun
determined [dɪ'tə:mɪnd] *adj* entschlossen; *(quantity)* bestimmt; **to be ~ to do sth** (fest) entschlossen sein, etw zu tun
deterrence [dɪ'tɛrəns] *n* Abschreckung *f*
deterrent [dɪ'tɛrənt] *n* Abschreckungsmittel *nt*; **to act as a ~** als Abschreckung(smittel) dienen
detest [dɪ'tɛst] *vt* verabscheuen
detestable [dɪ'tɛstəbl] *adj* abscheulich, widerwärtig
detonate ['dɛtəneɪt] *vi* detonieren ▷ *vt* zur Explosion bringen
detonator ['dɛtəneɪtəʳ] *n* Sprengkapsel *f*
detour ['di:tuəʳ] *n* Umweg *m*; *(US: Aut)* Umleitung *f*
detract [dɪ'trækt] *vi*: **to ~ from** schmälern; *(effect)* beeinträchtigen
detractor [dɪ'træktəʳ] *n* Kritiker(in) *m(f)*
detriment ['dɛtrɪmənt] *n*: **to the ~ of** zum Schaden *+gen*; **without ~ to** ohne Schaden für
detrimental [dɛtrɪ'mɛntl] *adj*: **to be ~ to** schaden *+dat*
deuce [dju:s] *n* *(Tennis)* Einstand *m*
devaluation [dɪvælju'eɪʃən] *n* Abwertung *f*
devalue ['di:'vælju:] *vt* abwerten
devastate ['dɛvəsteɪt] *vt* verwüsten; *(fig: shock)*: **to be ~d by** niedergeschmettert sein von
devastating ['dɛvəsteɪtɪŋ] *adj* verheerend; *(announcement, news)* niederschmetternd

devastation [dɛvəs'teɪʃən] *n* Verwüstung *f*
develop [dɪ'vɛləp] *vt* entwickeln; (*business*) erweitern, ausbauen; (*land, resource*) erschließen; (*disease*) bekommen ▷ *vi* sich entwickeln; (*facts*) an den Tag kommen; (*symptoms*) auftreten; **to ~ a taste for sth** Geschmack an etw finden; **the machine/car ~ed a fault/engine trouble** an dem Gerät/dem Wagen trat ein Defekt/ein Motorschaden auf; **to ~ into** sich entwickeln zu, werden
developer [dɪ'vɛləpə^r] *n* (*also:* **property developer**) *Bauunternehmer und Immobilienmakler*
developing country [dɪ'vɛləpɪŋ-] *n* Entwicklungsland *nt*
development [dɪ'vɛləpmənt] *n* Entwicklung *f*; (*of land*) Erschließung *f*
development area *n* Entwicklungsgebiet *nt*
deviant ['di:vɪənt] *adj* abweichend
deviate ['di:vɪeɪt] *vi*: **to ~ (from)** abweichen (von)
deviation [di:vɪ'eɪʃən] *n* Abweichung *f*
device [dɪ'vaɪs] *n* Gerät *nt*; (*ploy, stratagem*) Trick *m*; **explosive ~** Sprengkörper *m*
devil ['dɛvl] *n* Teufel *m*; **go on, be a ~!** nur zu, riskier mal was!; **talk of the ~!** wenn man vom Teufel spricht!
devilish ['dɛvlɪʃ] *adj* teuflisch
devil's advocate ['dɛvlz-] *n* Advocatus Diaboli *m*
devious ['di:vɪəs] *adj* (*person*) verschlagen; (*route, path*) gewunden
devise [dɪ'vaɪz] *vt* sich *dat* ausdenken; (*machine*) entwerfen
devoid [dɪ'vɔɪd] *adj*: **~ of** bar *+gen*, ohne *+acc*
devolution [di:və'lu:ʃən] *n* Dezentralisierung *f*
devolve [dɪ'vɔlv] *vt* übertragen ▷ *vi*: **to ~ (up)on** übergehen auf *+acc*
devote [dɪ'vəut] *vt*: **to ~ sth/o.s. to** etw/sich widmen *+dat*
devoted [dɪ'vəutɪd] *adj* treu; (*admirer*) eifrig; **to be ~ to sb** jdn innig lieben; **the book is ~ to politics** das Buch widmet sich ganz der Politik *dat*
devotee [dɛvəu'ti:] *n* (*fan*) Liebhaber(in) *m(f)*; (*Rel*) Anhänger(in) *m(f)*
devotion [dɪ'vəuʃən] *n* (*affection*) Ergebenheit *f*; (*dedication*) Hingabe *f*; (*Rel*) Andacht *f*
devour [dɪ'vauə^r] *vt* verschlingen
devout [dɪ'vaut] *adj* fromm
dew [dju:] *n* Tau *m*
dexterity [dɛks'tɛrɪtɪ] *n* Geschicklichkeit *f*; (*mental*) Gewandtheit *f*
dexterous, dextrous ['dɛkstrəs] *adj* geschickt
DfEE (*Brit*) *n abbr* (*= Department for Education and Employment*) ≈ Ministerium *nt* für Bildung und Arbeit
dg *abbr* (*= decigram*) dg
DHSS (*Brit*) *n abbr* (*formerly: = Department of Health and Social Security*) *Ministerium für Gesundheit und Sozialfürsorge*
diabetes [daɪə'bi:ti:z] *n* Zuckerkrankheit *f*
diabetic [daɪə'bɛtɪk] *adj* zuckerkrank; (*chocolate, jam*) Diabetiker- ▷ *n* Diabetiker(in) *m(f)*
diabolical [daɪə'bɔlɪkl] (*inf*) *adj* schrecklich, fürchterlich
diaeresis [daɪ'ɛrɪsɪs] *n* Diärese *f*
diagnose [daɪəg'nəuz] *vt* diagnostizieren
diagnoses [-si:z] *pl of* **diagnosis**
diagnosis [daɪəg'nəusɪs] (*pl* **diagnoses**) *n* Diagnose *f*
diagonal [daɪ'ægənl] *adj* diagonal ▷ *n* Diagonale *f*
diagram ['daɪəgræm] *n* Diagramm *nt*, Schaubild *nt*
dial ['daɪəl] *n* Zifferblatt *nt*; (*on radio set*) Einstellskala *f*; (*of phone*) Wählscheibe *f* ▷ *vt* wählen; **to ~ a wrong number** sich verwählen; **can I ~ London direct?** kann ich nach London durchwählen?
dial. *abbr* = **dialect**
dial code (*US*) *n* = **dialling code**
dialect ['daɪəlɛkt] *n* Dialekt *m*
dialling code ['daɪəlɪŋ-], (*US*) **dial code** *n* Vorwahl *f*
dialling tone, (*US*) **dial tone** *n* Amtszeichen *nt*
dialogue, (*US*) **dialog** ['daɪəlɔg] *n* Dialog *m*; (*conversation*) Gespräch *nt*, Dialog *m*
dial tone (*US*) *n* = **dialling tone**
dialysis [daɪ'ælɪsɪs] *n* Dialyse *f*
diameter [daɪ'æmɪtə^r] *n* Durchmesser *m*
diametrically [daɪə'mɛtrɪklɪ] *adv*: **~ opposed (to)** diametral entgegengesetzt (*+dat*)
diamond ['daɪəmənd] *n* Diamant *m*; (*shape*) Raute *f*; **diamonds** *npl* (*Cards*) Karo *nt*
diamond ring *n* Diamantring *m*
diaper ['daɪəpə^r] (*US*) *n* Windel *f*
diaphragm ['daɪəfræm] *n* Zwerchfell *nt*; (*contraceptive*) Pessar *nt*
diarrhoea, (*US*) **diarrhea** [daɪə'ri:ə] *n* Durchfall *m*
diary ['daɪərɪ] *n* (Termin)kalender *m*; (*daily account*) Tagebuch *nt*; **to keep a ~** Tagebuch führen
diatribe ['daɪətraɪb] *n* Schmährede *f*; (*written*) Schmähschrift *f*
dice [daɪs] *n inv* Würfel *m* ▷ *vt* in Würfel schneiden
dicey ['daɪsɪ] (*inf*) *adj* riskant
dichotomy [daɪ'kɔtəmɪ] *n* Dichotomie *f*, Kluft *f*
dickhead ['dɪkhɛd] (*inf*) *n* Knallkopf *m*
Dictaphone® ['dɪktəfəun] *n* Diktafon *nt*, Diktiergerät *nt*
dictate [dɪk'teɪt] *vt* diktieren ▷ *n* Diktat *nt*; (*principle*): **the ~s of** die Gebote *+gen* ▷ *vi*: **to ~ to** diktieren *+dat*; **I won't be ~d to** ich lasse mir keine Vorschriften machen
dictation [dɪk'teɪʃən] *n* Diktat *nt*; **at ~ speed** im Diktiertempo
dictator [dɪk'teɪtə^r] *n* Diktator *m*
dictatorship [dɪk'teɪtəʃɪp] *n* Diktatur *f*
diction ['dɪkʃən] *n* Diktion *f*
dictionary ['dɪkʃənrɪ] *n* Wörterbuch *nt*
did [dɪd] *pt of* **do**
didactic [daɪ'dæktɪk] *adj* didaktisch
diddle ['dɪdl] (*inf*) *vt* übers Ohr hauen

didn't ['dɪdnt] = **did not**

die [daɪ] *n* (*pl*: *dice*) Würfel *m*; (: *dies*) Gussform *f* ▷ *vi* sterben; (*plant*) eingehen; (*fig*: *noise*) aufhören; (: *smile*) vergehen; (*engine*) stehen bleiben; **to ~ of** *or* **from** sterben an *+dat*; **to be dying** im Sterben liegen; **to be dying for sth** etw unbedingt brauchen; **to be dying to do sth** darauf brennen, etw zu tun

▸ **die away** *vi* (*sound*) schwächer werden; (*light*) nachlassen

▸ **die down** *vi* (*wind*) sich legen; (*fire*) herunterbrennen; (*excitement, noise*) nachlassen

▸ **die out** *vi* aussterben

die-hard ['daɪhɑːd] *n* Ewiggestrige(r) *f(m)*

diesel ['diːzl] *n* (*vehicle*) Diesel *m*; (*also*: **diesel oil**) Diesel(kraftstoff) *m*

diesel engine *n* Dieselmotor *m*

diet ['daɪət] *n* Ernährung *f*; (*Med*) Diät *f*; (*when slimming*) Schlankheitskur *f* ▷ *vi* (*also*: **be on a diet**) eine Schlankheitskur machen; **to live on a ~ of** sich ernähren von, leben von

dietician [daɪə'tɪʃən] *n* Diätassistent(in) *m(f)*

differ ['dɪfəʳ] *vi* (*be different*): **to ~ (from)** sich unterscheiden (von); (*disagree*): **to ~ (about)** anderer Meinung sein (über *+acc*); **to agree to ~** sich *dat* verschiedene Meinungen zugestehen

difference ['dɪfrəns] *n* Unterschied *m*; (*disagreement*) Differenz *f*, Auseinandersetzung *f*; **it makes no ~ to me** das ist mir egal *or* einerlei; **to settle one's ~s** die Differenzen *or* Meinungsverschiedenheiten beilegen

different ['dɪfrənt] *adj* (*various people, things*) verschieden, unterschiedlich; **to be ~ (from)** anders sein (als)

differential [dɪfə'rɛnʃəl] *n* (*Math*) Differenzial *nt*; (*Brit*: *in wages*) (Einkommens)unterschied *m*

differentiate [dɪfə'rɛnʃɪeɪt] *vi*: **to ~ (between)** unterscheiden (zwischen) ▷ *vt*: **to ~ A from B** A von B unterscheiden

differently ['dɪfrəntlɪ] *adv* anders; (*shaped, designed*) verschieden, unterschiedlich

difficult ['dɪfɪkəlt] *adj* schwierig; (*task, problem*) schwer, schwierig; **~ to understand** schwer zu verstehen

difficulty ['dɪfɪkəltɪ] *n* Schwierigkeit *f*; **to be in/get into difficulties** in Schwierigkeiten sein/geraten

diffidence ['dɪfɪdəns] *n* Bescheidenheit *f*, Zurückhaltung *f*

diffident ['dɪfɪdənt] *adj* bescheiden, zurückhaltend

diffuse [dɪ'fjuːs] *adj* diffus ▷ *vt* verbreiten

dig [dɪg] (*pt, pp* **dug**) *vt* graben; (*garden*) umgraben ▷ *n* (*prod*) Stoß *m*; (*archaeological*) (Aus)grabung *f*; (*remark*) Seitenhieb *m*, spitze Bemerkung *f*; **to ~ one's nails into sth** seine Nägel in etw *acc* krallen

▸ **dig in** *vi* (*fig*: *inf*: *eat*) reinhauen ▷ *vt* (*compost*) untergraben, eingraben; (*knife*) hineinstoßen; (*claw*) festkrallen; **to ~ one's heels in** (*fig*) sich auf die Hinterbeine stellen (*inf*)

▸ **dig into** *vt fus* (*savings*) angreifen; (*snow, soil*) ein Loch graben in *+acc*; **to ~ into one's pockets for sth** in seinen Taschen nach etw suchen *or* wühlen

▸ **dig out** *vt* ausgraben

▸ **dig up** *vt* ausgraben

digest [daɪ'dʒɛst] *vt* verdauen ▷ *n* Digest *m or nt*, Auswahl *f*

digestible [dɪ'dʒɛstəbl] *adj* verdaulich

digestion [dɪ'dʒɛstʃən] *n* Verdauung *f*

digestive [dɪ'dʒɛstɪv] *adj* (*system, upsets*) Verdauungs- ▷ *n Keks aus Vollkornmehl*

digit ['dɪdʒɪt] *n* (*number*) Ziffer *f*; (*finger*) Finger *m*

digital ['dɪdʒɪtl] *adj* (*watch, display etc*) Digital-

digital computer *n* Digitalrechner *m*

digital projector *n* Beamer *m*

digital TV *n* Digitalfernsehen *nt*

dignified ['dɪgnɪfaɪd] *adj* würdevoll

dignitary ['dɪgnɪtərɪ] *n* Würdenträger(in) *m(f)*

dignity ['dɪgnɪtɪ] *n* Würde *f*

digress [daɪ'grɛs] *vi*: **to ~ (from)** abschweifen (von)

digression [daɪ'grɛʃən] *n* Abschweifung *f*

digs [dɪgz] (*Brit*: *inf*) *npl* Bude *f*

dike [daɪk] *n* = **dyke**

dilapidated [dɪ'læpɪdeɪtɪd] *adj* verfallen

dilate [daɪ'leɪt] *vi* sich weiten ▷ *vt* weiten

dilatory ['dɪlətərɪ] *adj* langsam

dilemma [daɪ'lɛmə] *n* Dilemma *nt*; **to be in a ~** sich in einem Dilemma befinden, in der Klemme sitzen (*inf*)

diligence ['dɪlɪdʒəns] *n* Fleiß *m*

diligent ['dɪlɪdʒənt] *adj* fleißig; (*research*) sorgfältig, genau

dill [dɪl] *n* Dill *m*

dilly-dally ['dɪlɪ'dælɪ] *vi* trödeln

dilute [daɪ'luːt] *vt* verdünnen; (*belief, principle*) schwächen ▷ *adj* verdünnt

dim [dɪm] *adj* schwach; (*outline, figure*) undeutlich, verschwommen; (*room*) dämmerig; (*future*) düster; (*prospects*) schlecht; (*inf*: *person*) schwer von Begriff ▷ *vt* (*light*) dämpfen; (*US*: *Aut*) abblenden; **to take a ~ view of sth** wenig *or* nicht viel von etw halten

dime [daɪm] (*US*) *n* Zehncentstück *nt*

dimension [daɪ'mɛnʃən] *n* (*aspect*) Dimension *f*; (*measurement*) Abmessung *f*, Maß *nt*; (*also pl*: *scale, size*) Ausmaß *nt*

-dimensional [dɪ'mɛnʃənl] *adj suff* -dimensional

diminish [dɪ'mɪnɪʃ] *vi* sich verringern ▷ *vt* verringern

diminished responsibility *n* verminderte Zurechnungsfähigkeit *f*

diminutive [dɪ'mɪnjutɪv] *adj* winzig ▷ *n* Verkleinerungsform *f*

dimly ['dɪmlɪ] *adv* schwach; (*see*) undeutlich, verschwommen

dimmer ['dɪməʳ] *n* (*also*: **dimmer switch**) Dimmer *m*; (*US*: *Aut*) Abblendschalter *m*

dimmer ['dɪmə]

dimmer switch *n* (*Elec*) Dimmer *m*; (*US*: *Aut*) Abblendschalter *m*

dimmers ['dɪməz] (US) *npl* (*Aut*: *dipped headlights*) Abblendlicht *nt*; (: *parking lights*) Parklicht *nt*
dimple ['dɪmpl] *n* Grübchen *nt*
dim-witted ['dɪm'wɪtɪd] (*inf*) *adj* dämlich
din [dɪn] *n* Lärm *m*, Getöse *nt* ▷ *vt* (*inf*): **to ~ sth into sb** jdm etw einbläuen
dine [daɪn] *vi* speisen
diner ['daɪnəʳ] *n* Gast *m*; (*US*: *restaurant*) Esslokal *nt*
dinghy ['dɪŋgɪ] *n* (*also*: **rubber dinghy**) Schlauchboot *nt*; (*also*: **sailing dinghy**) Dingi *nt*
dingy ['dɪndʒɪ] *adj* schäbig; (*clothes, curtains etc*) schmuddelig
dining car ['daɪnɪŋ-] (*Brit*) *n* Speisewagen *m*
dining room *n* Esszimmer *nt*; (*in hotel*) Speiseraum *m*
dinner ['dɪnəʳ] *n* (*evening meal*) Abendessen *nt*; (*lunch*) Mittagessen *nt*; (*banquet*) (Fest)essen *nt*
dinner jacket *n* Smokingjackett *nt*
dinner party *n* Abendgesellschaft *f* (mit Essen)
dinner service *n* Tafelservice *nt*
dinner time *n* Essenszeit *f*
dinosaur ['daɪnəsɔːʳ] *n* Dinosaurier *m*
dint [dɪnt] *n*: **by ~ of** durch *+acc*
diocese ['daɪəsɪs] *n* Diözese *f*
dioxide [daɪ'ɔksaɪd] *n* Dioxid *nt*
Dip. (*Brit*) *abbr* = **diploma**
dip [dɪp] *n* Senke *f*; (*in sea*) kurzes Bad *nt*; (*Culin*) Dip *m*; (*for sheep*) Desinfektionslösung *f* ▷ *vt* eintauchen; (*Brit*: *Aut*) abblenden ▷ *vi* abfallen
diphtheria [dɪf'θɪərɪə] *n* Diphtherie *f*
diphthong ['dɪfθɔŋ] *n* Diphthong *m*
diploma [dɪ'pləumə] *n* Diplom *nt*
diplomacy [dɪ'pləuməsɪ] *n* Diplomatie *f*
diplomat ['dɪpləmæt] *n* Diplomat(in) *m(f)*
diplomatic [dɪplə'mætɪk] *adj* diplomatisch; **to break off ~ relations (with)** die diplomatischen Beziehungen abbrechen (mit)
diplomatic corps *n* diplomatisches Korps *nt*
diplomatic immunity *n* Immunität *f*
dip rod ['dɪprɔd] (US) *n* Ölmessstab *m*
dipstick ['dɪpstɪk] (*Brit*) *n* Ölmessstab *m*
dip switch (*Brit*) *n* Abblendschalter *m*
dire [daɪəʳ] *adj* schrecklich
direct [daɪ'rɛkt] *adj, adv* direkt ▷ *vt* richten; (*company, project, programme etc*) leiten; (*play, film*) Regie führen bei; **to ~ sb to do sth** jdn anweisen, etw zu tun; **can you ~ me to ...?** können Sie mir den Weg nach ... sagen?
direct access *n* (*Comput*) Direktzugriff *m*
direct cost *n* direkte Kosten *pl*
direct current *n* Gleichstrom *m*
direct debit (*Brit*) *n* Einzugsauftrag *m*; (*transaction*) automatische Abbuchung *f*
direct dialling *n* Selbstwahl *f*
direct hit *n* Volltreffer *m*
direction [dɪ'rɛkʃən] *n* Richtung *f*; (TV, *Radio*) Leitung *f*; (*Cine*) Regie *f*; **directions** *npl* (*instructions*) Anweisungen *pl*; **sense of ~** Orientierungssinn *m*; **~s for use** Gebrauchsanweisung *f*, Gebrauchsanleitung *f*; **to ask for ~s** nach dem Weg fragen; **in the ~ of** in Richtung
directional [dɪ'rɛkʃənl] *adj* (*aerial*) Richt-
directive [dɪ'rɛktɪv] *n* Direktive *f*, Weisung *f*; **government ~** Regierungserlass *m*
direct labour *n* (*Comm*) Produktionsarbeit *f*; (*Brit*) eigene Arbeitskräfte *pl*
directly [dɪ'rɛktlɪ] *adv* direkt; (*at once*) sofort, gleich
direct mail *n* Werbebriefe *pl*
direct mailshot (*Brit*) *n* Direktwerbung *f* per Post
directness [daɪ'rɛktnɪs] *n* Direktheit *f*
director [dɪ'rɛktəʳ] *n* Direktor(in) *m(f)*; (*of project*, *TV*, *Radio*) Leiter(in) *m(f)*; (*Cine*) Regisseur(in) *m(f)*
Director of Public Prosecutions (*Brit*) *n* ≈ Generalstaatsanwalt *m*, ≈ Generalstaatsanwältin *f*
directory [dɪ'rɛktərɪ] *n* (*also*: **telephone directory**) Telefonbuch *nt*; (*also*: **street directory**) Einwohnerverzeichnis *nt*; (*Comput*) Verzeichnis *nt*; (*Comm*) Branchenverzeichnis *nt*
directory enquiries, (*US*) **directory assistance** *n* (Fernsprech)auskunft *f*
dirt [dəːt] *n* Schmutz *m*; (*earth*) Erde *f*; **to treat sb like ~** jdn wie (den letzten) Dreck behandeln
dirt-cheap ['dəːt'tʃiːp] *adj* spottbillig
dirt road *n* unbefestigte Straße *f*
dirty ['dəːtɪ] *adj* schmutzig; (*story*) unanständig ▷ *vt* beschmutzen
dirty bomb *n* schmutzige Bombe *f*
dirty trick *n* gemeiner Trick *m*
disability [dɪsə'bɪlɪtɪ] *n* Behinderung *f*
disability allowance *n* Behindertenbeihilfe *f*
disable [dɪs'eɪbl] *vt* zum Invaliden machen; (*tank, gun*) unbrauchbar machen
disabled [dɪs'eɪbld] *adj* behindert ▷ *npl*: **the ~** die Behinderten *pl*
disabuse [dɪsə'bjuːz] *vt*: **to ~ sb (of)** jdn befreien (von)
disadvantage [dɪsəd'vɑːntɪdʒ] *n* Nachteil *m*; (*detriment*) Schaden *m*; **to be at a ~** benachteiligt *or* im Nachteil sein
disadvantaged [dɪsəd'vɑːntɪdʒd] *adj* benachteiligt
disadvantageous [dɪsædvɑːn'teɪdʒəs] *adj* ungünstig
disaffected [dɪsə'fɛktɪd] *adj* entfremdet
disaffection [dɪsə'fɛkʃən] *n* Entfremdung *f*
disagree [dɪsə'griː] *vi* nicht übereinstimmen; (*to be against, think differently*): **to ~ (with)** nicht einverstanden sein (mit); **I ~ with you** ich bin anderer Meinung; **garlic ~s with me** ich vertrage keinen Knoblauch, Knoblauch bekommt mir nicht
disagreeable [dɪsə'griːəbl] *adj* unangenehm; (*person*) unsympathisch
disagreement [dɪsə'griːmənt] *n* Uneinigkeit *f*; (*argument*) Meinungsverschiedenheit *f*; **to have a ~ with sb** sich mit jdm nicht einig sein
disallow ['dɪsə'lau] *vt* (*appeal*) abweisen; (*goal*) nicht anerkennen, nicht geben

disappear [dɪsə'pɪə^r] *vi* verschwinden; (*custom etc*) aussterben
disappearance [dɪsə'pɪərəns] *n* (*see vi*) Verschwinden *nt*; Aussterben *nt*
disappoint [dɪsə'pɔɪnt] *vt* enttäuschen
disappointed [dɪsə'pɔɪntɪd] *adj* enttäuscht
disappointing [dɪsə'pɔɪntɪŋ] *adj* enttäuschend
disappointment [dɪsə'pɔɪntmənt] *n* Enttäuschung *f*
disapproval [dɪsə'pru:vəl] *n* Missbilligung *f*
disapprove [dɪsə'pru:v] *vi* dagegen sein; **to ~ of** missbilligen *+acc*
disapproving [dɪsə'pru:vɪŋ] *adj* missbilligend
disarm [dɪs'ɑ:m] *vt* entwaffnen; (*criticism*) zum Verstummen bringen ▷ *vi* abrüsten
disarmament [dɪs'ɑ:məmənt] *n* Abrüstung *f*
disarming [dɪs'ɑ:mɪŋ] *adj* entwaffnend
disarray [dɪsə'reɪ] *n*: **in ~** (*army, organization*) in Auflösung (begriffen); (*hair, clothes*) unordentlich; (*thoughts*) durcheinander; **to throw into ~** durcheinanderbringen
disaster [dɪ'zɑ:stə^r] *n* Katastrophe *f*; (*Aviat etc*) Unglück *nt*; (*fig: mess*) Fiasko *nt*
disaster area *n* Katastrophengebiet *nt*; (*fig: person*) Katastrophe *f*; **my office is a ~** in meinem Büro sieht es katastrophal aus
disastrous [dɪ'zɑ:strəs] *adj* katastrophal
disband [dɪs'bænd] *vt* auflösen ▷ *vi* sich auflösen
disbelief ['dɪsbə'li:f] *n* Ungläubigkeit *f*; **in ~** ungläubig
disbelieve ['dɪsbə'li:v] *vt* (*person*) nicht glauben *+dat*; (*story*) nicht glauben; **I don't ~ you** ich bezweifle nicht, was Sie sagen
disc [dɪsk] *n* (*Anat*) Bandscheibe *f*; (*record*) Platte *f*; (*Comput*) = **disk**
disc. *abbr* (*Comm*) = **discount**
discard [dɪs'kɑ:d] *vt* ausrangieren; (*fig: idea, plan*) verwerfen
disc brake *n* Scheibenbremse *f*
discern [dɪ'sə:n] *vt* wahrnehmen; (*identify*) erkennen
discernible [dɪ'sə:nəbl] *adj* erkennbar; (*object*) wahrnehmbar
discerning [dɪ'sə:nɪŋ] *adj* (*judgement*) scharfsinnig; (*look*) kritisch; (*listeners etc*) anspruchsvoll
discharge [dɪs'tʃɑ:dʒ] *vt* (*duties*) nachkommen *+dat*; (*debt*) begleichen; (*waste*) ablassen; (*Elec*) entladen; (*Med*) ausscheiden, absondern; (*patient, employee, soldier*) entlassen; (*defendant*) freisprechen ▷ *n* (*of gas*) Ausströmen *nt*; (*of liquid*) Ausfließen *nt*; (*Elec*) Entladung *f*; (*Med*) Ausfluss *m*; (*of patient, employee, soldier*) Entlassung *f*; (*of defendant*) Freispruch *m*; **to ~ a gun** ein Gewehr abfeuern
discharged bankrupt [dɪs'tʃɑ:dʒd-] *n* (*Law*) entlasteter Konkursschuldner *m*, entlastete Konkursschuldnerin *f*
disciple [dɪ'saɪpl] *n* Jünger *m*; (*fig: follower*) Schüler(in) *m(f)*
disciplinary ['dɪsɪplɪnərɪ] *adj* (*powers etc*) Disziplinar-; **to take ~ action against sb** ein Disziplinarverfahren gegen jdn einleiten
discipline ['dɪsɪplɪn] *n* Disziplin *f* ▷ *vt* disziplinieren; (*punish*) bestrafen; **to ~ o.s. to do sth** sich dazu anhalten *or* zwingen, etw zu tun
disc jockey *n* Discjockey *m*
disclaim [dɪs'kleɪm] *vt* (*knowledge*) abstreiten; (*responsibility*) von sich weisen
disclaimer [dɪs'kleɪmə^r] *n* Dementi *nt*; **to issue a ~** eine Gegenerklärung abgeben
disclose [dɪs'kləuz] *vt* enthüllen, bekannt geben
disclosure [dɪs'kləuʒə^r] *n* Enthüllung *f*
disco ['dɪskəu] *n* = **discotheque**
discolor *etc* [dɪs'kʌlə^r] (*US*) = **discolour** *etc*
discolour [dɪs'kʌlə^r] *vt* verfärben ▷ *vi* sich verfärben
discolouration [dɪskʌlə'reɪʃən] *n* Verfärbung *f*
discoloured [dɪs'kʌləd] *adj* verfärbt
discomfort [dɪs'kʌmfət] *n* (*unease*) Unbehagen *nt*; (*physical*) Beschwerden *pl*
disconcert [dɪskən'sə:t] *vt* beunruhigen, irritieren
disconcerting [dɪskən'sə:tɪŋ] *adj* beunruhigend, irritierend
disconnect [dɪskə'nɛkt] *vt* abtrennen; (*Elec, Radio*) abstellen; **I've been ~ed** (*Tel*) das Gespräch ist unterbrochen worden; (*supply, connection*) man hat mir das Telefon/den Strom/das Gas *etc* abgestellt
disconnected [dɪskə'nɛktɪd] *adj* unzusammenhängend
disconsolate [dɪs'kɔnsəlɪt] *adj* niedergeschlagen
discontent [dɪskən'tɛnt] *n* Unzufriedenheit *f*
discontented [dɪskən'tɛntɪd] *adj* unzufrieden
discontinue [dɪskən'tɪnju:] *vt* einstellen; **"~d"** (*Comm*) „ausgelaufene Serie"
discord ['dɪskɔ:d] *n* Zwietracht *f*; (*Mus*) Dissonanz *f*
discordant [dɪs'kɔ:dənt] *adj* unharmonisch
discotheque ['dɪskəutɛk] *n* Diskothek *f*
discount [*n* 'dɪskaunt, *vt* dɪs'kaunt] *n* Rabatt *m* ▷ *vt* nachlassen; (*idea, fact*) unberücksichtigt lassen; **to give sb a ~ on sth** jdm auf etw *acc* Rabatt geben; **~ for cash** Skonto *nt or m* (bei Barzahlung); **at a ~** mit Rabatt
discount house *n* Diskontbank *f*; (*also*: **discount store**) Diskontgeschäft *nt*
discount rate *n* Diskontsatz *m*
discourage [dɪs'kʌrɪdʒ] *vt* entmutigen; **to ~ sb from doing sth** jdm davon abraten, etw zu tun
discouragement [dɪs'kʌrɪdʒmənt] *n* Mutlosigkeit *f*; **to act as a ~ to sb** entmutigend für jdn sein
discouraging [dɪs'kʌrɪdʒɪŋ] *adj* entmutigend
discourteous [dɪs'kə:tɪəs] *adj* unhöflich
discover [dɪs'kʌvə^r] *vt* entdecken; (*missing person*) finden; **to ~ that ...** herausfinden, dass ...
discovery [dɪs'kʌvərɪ] *n* Entdeckung *f*
discredit [dɪs'krɛdɪt] *vt* in Misskredit bringen

▷ *n*: **to sb's ~** zu jds Schande
discreet [dɪˈkriːt] *adj* diskret; (*unremarkable*) dezent
discreetly [dɪˈkriːtlɪ] *adv* diskret; (*unremarkably*) dezent
discrepancy [dɪsˈkrɛpənsɪ] *n* Diskrepanz *f*
discretion [dɪsˈkrɛʃən] *n* Diskretion *f*; **at the ~ of** im Ermessen *+gen*; **use your own ~** Sie müssen nach eigenem Ermessen handeln
discretionary [dɪsˈkrɛʃənrɪ] *adj*: **~ powers** Ermessensspielraum *m*; **~ payments** Ermessenszahlungen *pl*
discriminate [dɪsˈkrɪmɪneɪt] *vi*: **to ~ between** unterscheiden zwischen *+dat*; **to ~ against** diskriminieren *+acc*
discriminating [dɪsˈkrɪmɪneɪtɪŋ] *adj* anspruchsvoll, kritisch; (*tax, duty*) Differenzial-
discrimination [dɪskrɪmɪˈneɪʃən] *n* Diskriminierung *f*; (*discernment*) Urteilsvermögen *nt*; **racial ~** Rassendiskriminierung *f*; **sexual ~** Diskriminierung aufgrund des Geschlechts
discus [ˈdɪskəs] *n* Diskus *m*; (*event*) Diskuswerfen *nt*
discuss [dɪsˈkʌs] *vt* besprechen; (*debate*) diskutieren; (*analyse*) erörtern, behandeln
discussion [dɪsˈkʌʃən] *n* Besprechung *f*; (*debate*) Diskussion *f*; **under ~** in der Diskussion
disdain [dɪsˈdeɪn] *n* Verachtung *f* ▷ *vt* verachten ▷ *vi*: **to ~ to do sth** es für unter seiner Würde halten, etw zu tun
disease [dɪˈziːz] *n* Krankheit *f*
diseased [dɪˈziːzd] *adj* krank; (*tree*) befallen
disembark [dɪsɪmˈbɑːk] *vt* ausschiffen ▷ *vi* (*passengers*) von Bord gehen
disembarkation [dɪsɛmbɑːˈkeɪʃən] *n* Ausschiffung *f*
disembodied [ˈdɪsɪmˈbɔdɪd] *adj* (*voice*) geisterhaft; (*hand*) körperlos
disembowel [ˈdɪsɪmˈbauəl] *vt* die Eingeweide herausnehmen *+dat*
disenchanted [ˈdɪsɪnˈtʃɑːntɪd] *adj*: **~ (with)** enttäuscht (von)
disenfranchise [ˈdɪsɪnˈfræntʃaɪz] *vt* (*Pol*) das Wahlrecht entziehen *+dat*; (*Comm*) die Konzession entziehen *+dat*
disengage [dɪsɪnˈgeɪdʒ] *vt* (*Tech*) ausrasten; **to ~ the clutch** auskuppeln
disengagement [dɪsɪnˈgeɪdʒmənt] *n* (*Pol*) Disengagement *nt*
disentangle [dɪsɪnˈtæŋgl] *vt* befreien; (*wool, wire*) entwirren
disfavour, (*US*) **disfavor** [dɪsˈfeɪvəʳ] *n* Missfallen *nt*; **to fall into ~ (with sb)** (bei jdm) in Ungnade fallen
disfigure [dɪsˈfɪgəʳ] *vt* entstellen; (*object, place*) verunstalten
disgorge [dɪsˈgɔːdʒ] *vt* (*liquid*) ergießen; (*people*) ausspeien
disgrace [dɪsˈgreɪs] *n* Schande *f*; (*scandal*) Skandal *m* ▷ *vt* Schande bringen über *+acc*
disgraceful [dɪsˈgreɪsful] *adj* skandalös
disgruntled [dɪsˈgrʌntld] *adj* verärgert
disguise [dɪsˈgaɪz] *n* Verkleidung *f* ▷ *vt*: **to ~ (as)** (*person*) verkleiden (als); (*object*) tarnen (als); **in ~** (*person*) verkleidet; **there's no disguising the fact that ...** es kann nicht geleugnet werden, dass ...; **to ~ o.s. as** sich verkleiden als
disgust [dɪsˈgʌst] *n* Abscheu *m* ▷ *vt* anwidern; **she walked off in ~** sie ging voller Empörung weg
disgusting [dɪsˈgʌstɪŋ] *adj* widerlich
dish [dɪʃ] *n* Schüssel *f*; (*flat*) Schale *f*; (*recipe, food*) Gericht *nt*; (*also*: **satellite dish**) Parabolantenne *f*, Schüssel (*inf*); **to do** *or* **wash the ~es** Geschirr spülen, abwaschen
▶ **dish out** *vt* verteilen; (*food, money*) austeilen; (*advice*) erteilen
▶ **dish up** *vt* (*food*) auftragen, servieren; (*facts, statistics*) auftischen (*inf*)
dishcloth [ˈdɪʃklɔθ] *n* Spültuch *nt*, Spüllappen *m*
dishearten [dɪsˈhɑːtn] *vt* entmutigen
dishevelled, (*US*) **disheveled** [dɪˈʃɛvəld] *adj* unordentlich; (*hair*) zerzaust
dishonest [dɪsˈɔnɪst] *adj* unehrlich; (*means*) unlauter
dishonesty [dɪsˈɔnɪstɪ] *n* Unehrlichkeit *f*
dishonor *etc* [dɪsˈɔnəʳ] (*US*) = **dishonour** *etc*
dishonour [dɪsˈɔnəʳ] *n* Schande *f*
dishonourable [dɪsˈɔnərəbl] *adj* unehrenhaft
dish soap (*US*) *n* Spülmittel *nt*
dishtowel [ˈdɪʃtauəl] (*US*) *n* Geschirrtuch *nt*
dishwasher [ˈdɪʃwɔʃəʳ] *n* (*machine*) (Geschirr)spülmaschine *f*
dishy [ˈdɪʃɪ] (*inf*: *Brit*) *adj* attraktiv
disillusion [dɪsɪˈluːʒən] *vt* desillusionieren ▷ *n* = **disillusionment**; **to become ~ed (with)** seine Illusionen (über *+acc*) verlieren
disillusionment [dɪsɪˈluːʒənmənt] *n* Desillusionierung *f*
disincentive [dɪsɪnˈsɛntɪv] *n* Entmutigung *f*; **it's a ~** es hält die Leute ab; **to be a ~ to sb** jdm keinen Anreiz bieten
disinclined [dɪsɪnˈklaɪnd] *adj*: **to be ~ to do sth** abgeneigt sein, etw zu tun
disinfect [dɪsɪnˈfɛkt] *vt* desinfizieren
disinfectant [dɪsɪnˈfɛktənt] *n* Desinfektionsmittel *nt*
disinflation [dɪsɪnˈfleɪʃən] *n* (*Econ*) Rückgang *m* einer inflationären Entwicklung
disinformation [dɪsɪnfəˈmeɪʃən] *n* Desinformation *f*
disingenuous [dɪsɪnˈdʒɛnjuəs] *adj* unaufrichtig
disinherit [dɪsɪnˈhɛrɪt] *vt* enterben
disintegrate [dɪsˈɪntɪgreɪt] *vi* zerfallen; (*marriage, partnership*) scheitern; (*organization*) sich auflösen
disinterested [dɪsˈɪntrəstɪd] *adj* (*advice*) unparteiisch, unvoreingenommen; (*help*) uneigennützig
disjointed [dɪsˈdʒɔɪntɪd] *adj* unzusammenhängend

disk [dɪsk] *n* Diskette *f*; **single-/double-sided ~** einseitige/zweiseitige Diskette
disk drive *n* Diskettenlaufwerk *nt*
diskette [dɪs'kɛt] (*US*) *n* = **disk**
disk operating system *n* Betriebssystem *nt*
dislike [dɪs'laɪk] *n* Abneigung *f* ▷ *vt* nicht mögen; **to take a ~ to sb/sth** eine Abneigung gegen jdn/etw entwickeln; **I ~ the idea** die Idee gefällt mir nicht; **he ~s it** er kann es nicht leiden, er mag es nicht
dislocate ['dɪsləkeɪt] *vt* verrenken, ausrenken; **he has ~d his shoulder** er hat sich *dat* den Arm ausgekugelt
dislodge [dɪs'lɔdʒ] *vt* verschieben
disloyal [dɪs'lɔɪəl] *adj* illoyal
dismal ['dɪzml] *adj* trübe, trostlos; (*song, person, mood*) trübsinnig; (*failure*) kläglich
dismantle [dɪs'mæntl] *vt* (*machine*) demontieren
dismast [dɪs'mɑːst] *vt* (*Naut*) entmasten
dismay [dɪs'meɪ] *n* Bestürzung *f* ▷ *vt* bestürzen; **much to my ~** zu meiner Bestürzung; **in ~** bestürzt
dismiss [dɪs'mɪs] *vt* entlassen; (*case*) abweisen; (*possibility, idea*) abtun
dismissal [dɪs'mɪsl] *n* Entlassung *f*
dismount [dɪs'maunt] *vi* absteigen
disobedience [dɪsə'biːdɪəns] *n* Ungehorsam *m*
disobedient [dɪsə'biːdɪənt] *adj* ungehorsam
disobey [dɪsə'beɪ] *vt* nicht gehorchen *+dat*; (*order*) nicht befolgen
disorder [dɪs'ɔːdəʳ] *n* Unordnung *f*; (*rioting*) Unruhen *pl*; (*Med*) (Funktions)störung *f*; **civil ~** öffentliche Unruhen *pl*
disorderly [dɪs'ɔːdəlɪ] *adj* unordentlich; (*meeting*) undiszipliniert; (*behaviour*) ungehörig
disorderly conduct *n* (*Law*) ungebührliches Benehmen *nt*
disorganize [dɪs'ɔːgənaɪz] *vt* durcheinanderbringen
disorganized [dɪs'ɔːgənaɪzd] *adj* chaotisch
disorientated [dɪs'ɔːrɪɛnteɪtɪd] *adj* desorientiert, verwirrt
disown [dɪs'əun] *vt* (*action*) verleugnen; (*child*) verstoßen
disparaging [dɪs'pærɪdʒɪŋ] *adj* (*remarks*) abschätzig, geringschätzig; **to be ~ about sb/sth** (*person*) abschätzig *or* geringschätzig über jdn/etw urteilen
disparate ['dɪspərɪt] *adj* völlig verschieden
disparity [dɪs'pærɪtɪ] *n* Unterschied *m*
dispassionate [dɪs'pæʃənət] *adj* nüchtern
dispatch [dɪs'pætʃ] *vt* senden, schicken; (*deal with*) erledigen; (*kill*) töten ▷ *n* Senden *nt*, Schicken *nt*; (*Press*) Bericht *m*; (*Mil*) Depesche *f*
dispatch department *n* Versandabteilung *f*
dispatch rider *n* (*Mil*) Meldefahrer *m*
dispel [dɪs'pɛl] *vt* (*myths*) zerstören; (*fears*) zerstreuen
dispensary [dɪs'pɛnsərɪ] *n* Apotheke *f*; (*in chemist's*) *Raum in einer Apotheke, wo Arzneimittel abgefüllt werden*
dispensation [dɪspən'seɪʃən] *n* (*of treatment*) Vergabe *f*; (*special permission*) Dispens *m*; **~ of justice** Rechtsprechung *f*
dispense [dɪs'pɛns] *vt* (*medicines*) abgeben; (*charity*) austeilen; (*advice*) erteilen
▸ **dispense with** *vt fus* verzichten auf *+acc*
dispenser [dɪs'pɛnsəʳ] *n* (*machine*) Automat *m*
dispensing chemist [dɪs'pɛnsɪŋ-] (*Brit*) *n* (*shop*) Apotheke *f*
dispersal [dɪs'pəːsl] *n* (*of objects*) Verstreuen *nt*; (*of group, crowd*) Auflösung *f*, Zerstreuen *nt*
disperse [dɪs'pəːs] *vt* (*objects*) verstreuen; (*crowd etc*) auflösen, zerstreuen; (*knowledge, information*) verbreiten ▷ *vi* (*crowd*) sich auflösen *or* zerstreuen
dispirited [dɪs'pɪrɪtɪd] *adj* entmutigt
displace [dɪs'pleɪs] *vt* ablösen
displaced person [dɪs'pleɪst-] *n* Verschleppte(r) *f(m)*
displacement [dɪs'pleɪsmənt] *n* Ablösung *f*; (*of people*) Vertreibung *f*; (*Phys*) Verdrängung *f*
display [dɪs'pleɪ] *n* (*in shop*) Auslage *f*; (*exhibition*) Ausstellung *f*; (*of feeling*) Zeigen *nt*; (*pej*) Zurschaustellung *f*; (*Comput, Tech*) Anzeige *f* ▷ *vt* zeigen; (*ostentatiously*) zur Schau stellen; (*results, departure times*) aushängen; **on ~** ausgestellt
display advertising *n* Displaywerbung *f*
displease [dɪs'pliːz] *vt* verstimmen, verärgern
displeased [dɪs'pliːzd] *adj*: **I am very ~ with you** ich bin sehr enttäuscht von dir
displeasure [dɪs'plɛʒəʳ] *n* Missfallen *nt*
disposable [dɪs'pəuzəbl] *adj* (*lighter*) Wegwerf-; (*bottle*) Einweg-; (*income*) verfügbar
disposable nappy (*Brit*) *n* Papierwindel *f*
disposal [dɪs'pəuzl] *n* (*of goods for sale*) Loswerden *nt*; (*of property, belongings: by selling*) Verkauf *m*; (*: by giving away*) Abgeben *nt*; (*of rubbish*) Beseitigung *f*; **at one's ~** zur Verfügung; **to put sth at sb's ~** jdm etw zur Verfügung stellen
dispose [dɪs'pəuz]: **~ of** *vt fus* (*body*) aus dem Weg schaffen; (*unwanted goods*) loswerden; (*problem, task*) erledigen; (*stock*) verkaufen
disposed [dɪs'pəuzd] *adj*: **to be ~ to do sth** (*inclined*) geneigt sein, etw zu tun; (*willing*) bereit sein, etw zu tun; **to be well ~ towards sb** jdm wohlwollen
disposition [dɪspə'zɪʃən] *n* (*nature*) Veranlagung *f*; (*inclination*) Neigung *f*
dispossess ['dɪspə'zɛs] *vt* enteignen; **to ~ sb of his/her land** jds Land enteignen
disproportion [dɪsprə'pɔːʃən] *n* Missverhältnis *nt*
disproportionate [dɪsprə'pɔːʃənət] *adj* unverhältnismäßig; (*amount*) unverhältnismäßig hoch/niedrig
disprove [dɪs'pruːv] *vt* widerlegen
dispute [dɪs'pjuːt] *n* Streit *m*; (*also*: **industrial dispute**) Auseinandersetzung *f* zwischen Arbeitgebern und Arbeitnehmern; (*Pol, Mil*) Streitigkeiten *pl* ▷ *vt* bestreiten; (*ownership etc*) anfechten; **to be in** *or* **under ~** umstritten sein

disqualification [dɪskwɔlɪfɪ'keɪʃən] *n*: **~ (from)** Ausschluss *m* (von); (*Sport*) Disqualifizierung *f* (von); **~ (from driving)** (*Brit*) Führerscheinentzug *m*
disqualify [dɪs'kwɔlɪfaɪ] *vt* disqualifizieren; **to ~ sb for sth** jdn für etw ungeeignet machen; **to ~ sb from doing sth** jdn ungeeignet machen, etw zu tun; **to ~ sb from driving** (*Brit*) jdm den Führerschein entziehen
disquiet [dɪs'kwaɪət] *n* Unruhe *f*
disquieting [dɪs'kwaɪətɪŋ] *adj* beunruhigend
disregard [dɪsrɪ'gɑːd] *vt* nicht beachten, ignorieren ▷ *n*: **~ (for)** Missachtung *f* (*+gen*); (*for danger, money*) Geringschätzung *f* (*+gen*)
disrepair ['dɪsrɪ'pɛəʳ] *n*: **to fall into ~** (*machine*) vernachlässigt werden; (*building*) verfallen
disreputable [dɪs'rɛpjutəbl] *adj* (*person*) unehrenhaft; (*behaviour*) unfein
disrepute ['dɪsrɪ'pjuːt] *n* schlechter Ruf *m*; **to bring/fall into ~** in Verruf bringen/kommen
disrespectful [dɪsrɪ'spɛktful] *adj* respektlos
disrupt [dɪs'rʌpt] *vt* (*plans*) durcheinanderbringen; (*conversation, proceedings*) unterbrechen
disruption [dɪs'rʌpʃən] *n* Unterbrechung *f*; (*disturbance*) Störung *f*
disruptive [dɪs'rʌptɪv] *adj* störend; (*action*) Stör-
dissatisfaction [dɪssætɪs'fækʃən] *n* Unzufriedenheit *f*
dissatisfied [dɪs'sætɪsfaɪd] *adj*: **~ (with)** unzufrieden (mit)
dissect [dɪ'sɛkt] *vt* sezieren
disseminate [dɪ'sɛmɪneɪt] *vt* verbreiten
dissent [dɪ'sɛnt] *n* abweichende Meinungen *pl*
dissenter [dɪ'sɛntəʳ] *n* Abweichler(in) *m(f)*
dissertation [dɪsə'teɪʃən] *n* (*speech*) Vortrag *m*; (*piece of writing*) Abhandlung *f*; (*for PhD*) Dissertation *f*
disservice [dɪs'səːvɪs] *n*: **to do sb a ~** jdm einen schlechten Dienst erweisen
dissident ['dɪsɪdnt] *adj* andersdenkend; (*voice*) kritisch ▷ *n* Dissident(in) *m(f)*
dissimilar [dɪ'sɪmɪləʳ] *adj*: **~ (to)** anders (als)
dissipate ['dɪsɪpeɪt] *vt* (*heat*) neutralisieren; (*clouds*) auflösen; (*money, effort*) verschwenden
dissipated ['dɪsɪpeɪtɪd] *adj* zügellos, ausschweifend
dissociate [dɪ'səuʃɪeɪt] *vt* trennen; **to ~ o.s. from** sich distanzieren von
dissolute ['dɪsəluːt] *adj* zügellos, ausschweifend
dissolution [dɪsə'luːʃən] *n* Auflösung *f*
dissolve [dɪ'zɔlv] *vt* auflösen ▷ *vi* sich auflösen; **to ~ in(to) tears** in Tränen zerfließen
dissuade [dɪ'sweɪd] *vt*: **to ~ sb (from sth)** jdn (von etw) abbringen
distaff ['dɪstɑːf] *n*: **the ~ side** die mütterliche Seite
distance ['dɪstns] *n* Entfernung *f*; (*in time*) Abstand *m*; (*reserve*) Abstand, Distanz *f* ▷ *vt*: **to ~ o.s. (from)** sich distanzieren (von); **in the ~** in der Ferne; **what's the ~ to London?** wie weit ist es nach London?; **it's within walking ~** es ist zu Fuß erreichbar; **at a ~ of 2 metres** in 2 Meter(n) Entfernung; **keep your ~!** halten Sie Abstand!
distant ['dɪstnt] *adj* (*place*) weit entfernt, fern; (*time*) weit zurückliegend; (*relative*) entfernt; (*manner*) distanziert, kühl
distaste [dɪs'teɪst] *n* Widerwille *m*
distasteful [dɪs'teɪstful] *adj* widerlich; **to be ~ to sb** jdm zuwider sein
Dist. Atty. (US) *abbr* = **district attorney**
distemper [dɪs'tɛmpəʳ] *n* (*paint*) Temperafarbe *f*; (*disease of dogs*) Staupe *f*
distend [dɪs'tɛnd] *vt* blähen ▷ *vi* sich blähen
distended [dɪs'tɛndɪd] *adj* aufgebläht
distil, (US) **distill** [dɪs'tɪl] *vt* destillieren; (*fig*) (heraus)destillieren
distillery [dɪs'tɪlərɪ] *n* Brennerei *f*
distinct [dɪs'tɪŋkt] *adj* deutlich, klar; (*possibility*) eindeutig; (*different*) verschieden; **as ~ from** im Unterschied zu
distinction [dɪs'tɪŋkʃən] *n* Unterschied *m*; (*honour*) Ehre *f*; (*in exam*) Auszeichnung *f*; **to draw a ~ between** einen Unterschied machen zwischen *+dat*; **a writer of ~** ein Schriftsteller von Rang
distinctive [dɪs'tɪŋktɪv] *adj* unverwechselbar
distinctly [dɪs'tɪŋktlɪ] *adv* deutlich, klar; (*tell*) ausdrücklich; (*unhappy*) ausgeprochen; (*better*) entschieden
distinguish [dɪs'tɪŋgwɪʃ] *vt* unterscheiden; (*details etc*) erkennen, ausmachen; **to ~ (between)** unterscheiden (zwischen *+dat*); **to ~ o.s.** sich hervortun
distinguished [dɪs'tɪŋgwɪʃt] *adj* von hohem Rang; (*career*) hervorragend; (*in appearance*) distinguiert
distinguishing [dɪs'tɪŋgwɪʃɪŋ] *adj* charakteristisch
distort [dɪs'tɔːt] *vt* verzerren; (*argument*) verdrehen
distortion [dɪs'tɔːʃən] *n* (*see vb*) Verzerrung *f*; Verdrehung *f*
distract [dɪs'trækt] *vt* ablenken
distracted [dɪs'træktɪd] *adj* unaufmerksam; (*anxious*) besorgt, beunruhigt
distraction [dɪs'trækʃən] *n* Unaufmerksamkeit *f*; (*confusion*) Verstörtheit *f*; (*sth which distracts*) Ablenkung *f*; (*amusement*) Zerstreuung *f*; **to drive sb to ~** jdn zur Verzweiflung treiben
distraught [dɪs'trɔːt] *adj* verzweifelt
distress [dɪs'trɛs] *n* Verzweiflung *f* ▷ *vt* Kummer machen *+dat*; **in ~** (*ship*) in Seenot; (*person*) verzweifelt; **~ed area** (*Brit*) Notstandsgebiet *nt*
distressing [dɪs'trɛsɪŋ] *adj* beunruhigend
distress signal *n* Notsignal *nt*
distribute [dɪs'trɪbjuːt] *vt* verteilen; (*profits*) aufteilen
distribution [dɪstrɪ'bjuːʃən] *n* Vertrieb *m*; (*of profits*) Aufteilung *f*
distribution costs *npl* Vertriebskosten *pl*
distribution management *n* (*Comm*)

Vertriebscontrolling *nt*
distributor [dɪs'trɪbjutər] *n (Comm)* Vertreiber(in) *m(f)*; *(Aut, Tech)* Verteiler *m*
district ['dɪstrɪkt] *n* Gebiet *nt*; *(of town)* Stadtteil *m*; *(Admin)* (Verwaltungs)bezirk *m*
district attorney *(US) n* Bezirksstaatsanwalt *m*, Bezirksstaatsanwältin *f*

DISTRICT COUNCIL

District Council heißt der in jedem der britischen *districts* (Bezirke) alle vier Jahre neu gewählte Bezirksrat, der für bestimmte Bereiche der Kommunalverwaltung (Gesundheitswesen, Wohnungsbeschaffung, Baugenehmigungen, Müllabfuhr) zuständig ist. Die district councils werden durch Kommunalabgaben und durch einen Zuschuss von der Regierung finanziert. Ihre Ausgaben werden von einer unabhängigen Prüfungskommission kontrolliert, und bei zu hohen Ausgaben wird der Regierungszuschuss gekürzt.

district nurse *(Brit) n* Gemeindeschwester *f*
distrust [dɪs'trʌst] *n* Misstrauen *nt* ▷ *vt* misstrauen *+dat*
distrustful [dɪs'trʌstful] *adj*: **~ (of)** misstrauisch (gegenüber *+dat*)
disturb [dɪs'tə:b] *vt* stören; *(upset)* beunruhigen; *(disorganize)* durcheinanderbringen; **sorry to ~ you** entschuldigen Sie bitte die Störung
disturbance [dɪs'tə:bəns] *n* Störung *f*; *(political etc)* Unruhe *f*; *(violent event)* Unruhen *pl*; *(by drunks etc)* (Ruhe)störung *f*; **to cause a ~** Unruhe/eine Ruhestörung verursachen; **~ of the peace** Ruhestörung
disturbed [dɪs'tə:bd] *adj* beunruhigt; *(childhood)* unglücklich; **mentally/emotionally ~** geistig/seelisch gestört
disturbing [dɪs'tə:bɪŋ] *adj* beunruhigend
disuse [dɪs'ju:s] *n*: **to fall into ~** nicht mehr benutzt werden
disused [dɪs'ju:zd] *adj (building)* leer stehend; *(airfield)* stillgelegt
ditch [dɪtʃ] *n* Graben *m* ▷ *vt (inf: partner)* sitzen lassen; *(: plan)* sausen lassen; *(: car etc)* loswerden
dither ['dɪðər] *(pej) vi* zaudern
ditto ['dɪtəu] *adv* dito, ebenfalls
divan [dɪ'væn] *n (also:* **divan bed***)* Polsterbett *nt*
dive [daɪv] *n* Sprung *m*; *(underwater)* Tauchen *nt*; *(of submarine)* Untertauchen *nt*; *(pej: place)* Spelunke *f (inf)* ▷ *vi* springen; *(under water)* tauchen; *(bird)* einen Sturzflug machen; *(submarine)* untertauchen; **to ~ into** *(bag, drawer etc)* greifen in *+acc*; *(shop, car etc)* sich stürzen in *+acc*
diver ['daɪvər] *n* Taucher(in) *m(f)*; *(also:* **deep-sea diver***)* Tiefseetaucher(in) *m(f)*
diverge [daɪ'və:dʒ] *vi* auseinandergehen
divergent [daɪ'və:dʒənt] *adj* unterschiedlich; *(views)* voneinander abweichend; *(interests)* auseinandergehend
diverse [daɪ'və:s] *adj* verschiedenartig
diversification [daɪvə:sɪfɪ'keɪʃən] *n* Diversifikation *f*
diversify [daɪ'və:sɪfaɪ] *vi* diversifizieren
diversion [daɪ'və:ʃən] *n (Brit: Aut)* Umleitung *f*; *(distraction)* Ablenkung *f*; *(of funds)* Umlenkung *f*
diversionary [daɪ'və:ʃənrɪ] *adj*: **~ tactics** Ablenkungsmanöver *pl*
diversity [daɪ'və:sɪtɪ] *n* Vielfalt *f*
divert [daɪ'və:t] *vt (sb's attention)* ablenken; *(funds)* umlenken; *(re-route)* umleiten
divest [daɪ'vɛst] *vt*: **to ~ sb of office/his authority** jdn seines Amtes entkleiden/seiner Macht entheben
divide [dɪ'vaɪd] *vt* trennen; *(Math)* dividieren, teilen; *(share out)* verteilen ▷ *vi* sich teilen; *(road)* sich gabeln; *(people, groups)* sich aufteilen ▷ *n* Kluft *f*; **to ~ (between** *or* **among)** aufteilen (unter *+dat*); **40 ~d by 5** 40 geteilt *or* dividiert durch 5
▶ **divide out** *vt*: **to ~ out (between** *or* **among)** aufteilen (unter *+dat*)
divided [dɪ'vaɪdɪd] *adj* geteilt; **to be ~ about** *or* **over sth** geteilter Meinung über etw *acc* sein
divided highway *(US) n* ≈ Schnellstraße *f*
dividend ['dɪvɪdɛnd] *n* Dividende *f*; *(fig)*: **to pay ~s** sich bezahlt machen
dividend cover *n (Comm)* Dividendendeckung *f*
dividers [dɪ'vaɪdəz] *npl (Math, Tech)* Stechzirkel *m*; *(between pages)* Register *nt*
divine [dɪ'vaɪn] *adj* göttlich ▷ *vt (future)* weissagen, prophezeien; *(truth)* erahnen; *(water, metal)* aufspüren
diving ['daɪvɪŋ] *n* Tauchen *nt*; *(Sport)* Kunstspringen *nt*
diving board *n* Sprungbrett *nt*
diving suit *n* Taucheranzug *m*
divinity [dɪ'vɪnɪtɪ] *n* Göttlichkeit *f*; *(god or goddess)* Gottheit *f*; *(Scol)* Theologie *f*
divisible [dɪ'vɪzəbl] *adj*: **~ (by)** teilbar (durch); **to be ~ into** teilbar sein in *+acc*
division [dɪ'vɪʒən] *n* Teilung *f*; *(Math)* Teilen *nt*, Division *f*; *(sharing out)* Verteilung *f*; *(disagreement)* Uneinigkeit *f*; *(Brit: Pol)* Abstimmung *f* durch Hammelsprung; *(Comm)* Abteilung *f*; *(Mil)* Division *f*; *(esp Football)* Liga *f*; **~ of labour** Arbeitsteilung *f*
divisive [dɪ'vaɪsɪv] *adj*: **to be ~** *(tactics)* auf Spaltung abzielen; *(system)* zu Feindseligkeit führen
divorce [dɪ'vɔ:s] *n* Scheidung *f* ▷ *vt* sich scheiden lassen von; *(dissociate)* trennen
divorced [dɪ'vɔ:st] *adj* geschieden
divorcee [dɪvɔ:'si:] *n* Geschiedene(r) *f(m)*
divot ['dɪvət] *n vom Golfschläger etc ausgehacktes Rasenstück*
divulge [daɪ'vʌldʒ] *vt* preisgeben
DIY *(Brit) n abbr* = **do-it-yourself**
dizziness ['dɪzɪnɪs] *n* Schwindel *m*

dizzy ['dɪzɪ] *adj* schwind(e)lig; (*turn, spell*) Schwindel-; (*height*) schwindelerregend; **I feel ~** mir ist *or* ich bin schwind(e)lig
DJ *n abbr* = **disc jockey**
dj *n abbr* = **dinner jacket**
Djakarta [dʒə'kɑːtə] *n* Jakarta *nt*
DJIA (*US*) *n abbr* (= *Dow-Jones Industrial Average*) Dow-Jones-Index *m*
dl *abbr* (= *decilitre*) dl
DLit, DLitt *n abbr* (= *Doctor of Literature, Doctor of Letters*) *akademischer Grad in Literaturwissenschaft*
dm *abbr* (= *decimetre*) dm
DMus *n abbr* (= *Doctor of Music*) *Doktor der Musikwissenschaft*
DMZ *n abbr* = **demilitarized zone**
DNA *n abbr* (= *deoxyribonucleic acid*) DNS *f*
DNA test *n* DNS-Test *m*

KEYWORD

do [duː] (*pt* **did**, *pp* **done**) *aux vb* **1** (*in negative constructions*): **I don't understand** ich verstehe nicht
2 (*to form questions*): **didn't you know?** wusstest du das nicht?; **what do you think?** was meinst du?
3 (*for emphasis*): **she does seem rather upset** sie scheint wirklich recht aufgeregt zu sein; **do sit down/help yourself** bitte nehmen Sie Platz/bedienen Sie sich; **oh do shut up!** halte endlich den Mund!
4 (*to avoid repeating vb*): **she swims better than I do** sie schwimmt besser als ich; **she lives in Glasgow — so do I** sie wohnt in Glasgow — ich auch; **who made this mess? — I did** wer hat dieses Durcheinander gemacht? — ich
5 (*in question tags*): **you like him, don't you?** du magst ihn, nicht wahr?; **I don't know him, do I?** ich kenne ihn nicht, oder?
▷ *vt* **1** (*carry out, perform*) tun, machen; **what are you doing tonight?** was machen Sie heute Abend?; **what do you do (for a living)?** was machen Sie beruflich?; **to do one's teeth/nails** sich *dat* die Zähne putzen/die Nägel schneiden
2 (*Aut etc*) fahren; **the car was doing 100** das Auto fuhr 100
▷ *vi* **1** (*act, behave*): **do as I do** mach es wie ich
2 (*get on, fare*): **he's doing well/badly at school** er ist gut/schlecht in der Schule; **the company is doing well** der Firma geht es gut; **how do you do?** guten Tag/Morgen/Abend!
3 (*suit, be sufficient*) reichen; **will that do?** reicht das?; **will this dress do for the party?** ist dieses Kleid gut genug für die Party?; **will £10 do?** reichen £10?; **that'll do** das reicht; (*in annoyance*) jetzt reichts aber!; **to make do with** auskommen mit
▷ *n* (*inf: party etc*) Party *f*, Fete *f*; **it was quite a do** es war ganz schön was los
▸ **do away with** *vt fus* (*get rid of*) abschaffen
▸ **do for** (*inf*) *vt fus*: **to be done for** erledigt sein
▸ **do in** (*inf*) *vt* (*kill*) umbringen
▸ **do out of** (*inf*) *vt* (*deprive*) bringen um
▸ **do up** *vt fus* (*laces, dress, buttons*) zumachen; (*renovate: room, house*) renovieren
▸ **do with** *vt fus* **1** (*need*) brauchen; **I could do with some help/a drink** ich könnte Hilfe/einen Drink gebrauchen
2: **it has to do with money** es hat mit Geld zu tun
▸ **do without** *vt fus* auskommen ohne

do. *abbr* = **ditto**
DOA *abbr* (= *dead on arrival*) bei Einlieferung ins Krankenhaus bereits tot
d.o.b. *abbr* = **date of birth**
doc [dɔk] (*inf*) *n* Doktor *m*
docile ['dəusaɪl] *adj* sanft(mütig)
dock [dɔk] *n* Dock *nt*; (*Law*) Anklagebank *f*; (*Bot*) Ampfer *m* ▷ *vi* anlegen; (*Space*) docken ▷ *vt*: **they ~ed a third of his wages** sie kürzten seinen Lohn um ein Drittel; **docks** *npl* (*Naut*) Hafen *m*
dock dues [-djuːz] *npl* Hafengebühr *f*
docker ['dɔkə^r] *n* Hafenarbeiter *m*, Docker *m*
docket ['dɔkɪt] *n* Inhaltserklärung *f*; (*on parcel etc*) Warenbegleitschein *m*, Laufzettel *m*
dockyard ['dɔkjɑːd] *n* Werft *f*
doctor ['dɔktə^r] *n* Arzt *m*, Ärztin *f*; (*PhD etc*) Doktor *m* ▷ *vt*: **to ~ a drink** *etc* einem Getränk *etc* etwas beimischen; **~'s office** (*US*) Sprechzimmer *nt*
doctorate ['dɔktərɪt] *n* Doktorwürde *f*; *siehe Info-Artikel*

DOCTORATE

Doctorate ist der höchste akademische Grad auf jedem Wissensgebiet und wird nach erfolgreicher Vorlage einer Doktorarbeit verliehen. Die Studienzeit (meist mindestens 3 Jahre) und Länge der Doktorarbeit ist je nach Hochschule verschieden. Am häufigsten wird der Titel *PhD* (Doctor of Philosophy) auf dem Gebiet der Geisteswissenschaften, Naturwissenschaften und des Ingenieurwesens verliehen, obwohl es auch andere Doktortitel (in Musik, Jura usw.) gibt. Siehe auch *Bachelor's degree*, *Master's degree*.

Doctor of Philosophy *n* Doktor *m* der Philosophie
doctrine ['dɔktrɪn] *n* Doktrin *f*
docudrama ['dɔkjudrɑːmə] *n* Dokumentarspiel *nt*
document ['dɔkjumənt] *n* Dokument *nt* ▷ *vt* dokumentieren
documentary [dɔkju'mɛntərɪ] *adj* dokumentarisch ▷ *n* Dokumentarfilm *m*
documentation [dɔkjumən'teɪʃən] *n* Dokumentation *f*
DOD (*US*) *n abbr* (= *Department of Defense*)

Verteidigungsministerium *nt*
doddering ['dɔdərɪŋ] *adj* (*shaky, unsteady*) zittrig
doddery ['dɔdərɪ] *adj* = **doddering**
doddle ['dɔdl] (*inf*) *n*: **a ~** ein Kinderspiel *nt*
Dodecanese [dəudɪkə'ni:z], **Dodecanese Islands** *npl*: **the ~ (Islands)** der Dodekanes
dodge [dɔdʒ] *n* Trick *m* ▹ *vt* ausweichen *+dat*; (*tax*) umgehen ▹ *vi* ausweichen; **to ~ out of the way** zur Seite springen; **to ~ through the traffic** sich durch den Verkehr schlängeln
dodgems ['dɔdʒəmz] (*Brit*) *npl* Autoskooter *pl*
dodgy ['dɔdʒɪ] (*inf*) *adj* (*person*) zweifelhaft; (*plan etc*) gewagt
DOE *n abbr* (*Brit*: = *Department of the Environment*) *Umweltministerium*; (*US*: = *Department of Energy*) *Energieministerium*
doe [dəu] *n* Reh *nt*, Ricke *f*; (*rabbit*) (Kaninchen)weibchen *nt*
does [dʌz] *vb see* **do**
doesn't ['dʌznt] = **does not**
dog [dɔg] *n* Hund *m* ▹ *vt* (*subj*: *person*) auf den Fersen bleiben *+dat*; (: *bad luck, memory etc*) verfolgen; **to go to the ~s** (*inf*) vor die Hunde gehen
dog biscuits *npl* Hundekuchen *pl*
dog collar *n* Hundehalsband *nt*; (*Rel*) Kragen *m* des Geistlichen
dog-eared ['dɔgɪəd] *adj* mit Eselsohren
dog food *n* Hundefutter *nt*
dogged ['dɔgɪd] *adj* beharrlich
doggy ['dɔgɪ] *n* Hündchen *nt*
doggy bag *n* *Tüte für Essensreste, die man nach Hause mitnehmen möchte*
dogma ['dɔgmə] *n* Dogma *nt*
dogmatic [dɔg'mætɪk] *adj* dogmatisch
do-gooder [du:'gudə^r] (*pej*) *n* Weltverbesserer(in) *m(f)*
dogsbody ['dɔgzbɔdɪ] (*Brit*: *inf*) *n* Mädchen *nt* für alles
doily ['dɔɪlɪ] *n* Deckchen *nt*
doing ['duɪŋ] *n*: **this is your ~** das ist dein Werk
doings ['duɪŋz] *npl* Treiben *nt*
do-it-yourself ['du:ɪtjɔ:'sɛlf] *n* Heimwerken *nt*, Do-it-yourself *nt*
doldrums ['dɔldrəmz] *npl*: **to be in the ~** (*person*) niedergeschlagen sein; (*business*) in einer Flaute stecken
dole [dəul] (*Brit*) *n* Arbeitslosenunterstützung *f*; **on the ~** arbeitslos
▸ **dole out** *vt* austeilen, verteilen
doleful ['dəulful] *adj* traurig
doll [dɔl] *n* (*toy, also US*: *inf*: *woman*) Puppe *f*
dollar ['dɔlə^r] (*US etc*) *n* Dollar *m*
dollar area *n* Dollarblock *m*
dolled up (*inf*) *adj* aufgedonnert
dollop ['dɔləp] (*inf*) *n* Schlag *m*
dolly ['dɔlɪ] (*inf*) *n* (*doll, woman*) Puppe *f*
Dolomites ['dɔləmaɪts] *npl*: **the ~** die Dolomiten *pl*
dolphin ['dɔlfɪn] *n* Delfin *m*
domain [də'meɪn] *n* Bereich *m*; (*empire*) Reich *nt*
dome [dəum] *n* Kuppel *f*
domestic [də'mɛstɪk] *adj* (*trade*) Innen-; (*situation*) innenpolitisch; (*news*) Inland-, aus dem Inland; (*tasks, appliances*) Haushalts-; (*animal*) Haus-; (*duty, happiness*) häuslich
domesticated [də'mɛstɪkeɪtɪd] *adj* (*animal*) zahm; (*person*) häuslich
domesticity [dəumɛs'tɪsɪtɪ] *n* häusliches Leben *nt*
domestic servant *n* Hausangestellte(r) *f(m)*
domicile ['dɔmɪsaɪl] *n* Wohnsitz *m*
dominant ['dɔmɪnənt] *adj* dominierend; (*share*) größte(r, s)
dominate ['dɔmɪneɪt] *vt* dominieren, beherrschen
domination [dɔmɪ'neɪʃən] *n* (Vor)herrschaft *f*
domineering [dɔmɪ'nɪərɪŋ] *adj* herrschsüchtig
Dominican Republic [də'mɪnɪkən-] *n*: **the ~** die Dominikanische Republik
dominion [də'mɪnɪən] *n* (*territory*) Herrschaftsgebiet *nt*; (*authority*): **to have ~ over** Macht haben über *+acc*
domino ['dɔmɪnəu] (*pl* **~es**) *n* (*block*) Domino(stein) *m*
domino effect *n* Dominoeffekt *m*
dominoes ['dɔmɪnəuz] *n* (*game*) Domino(spiel) *nt*
don [dɔn] *n* (*Brit*) (Universitäts)dozent *m* (*besonders in Oxford und Cambridge*) ▹ *vt* anziehen
donate [də'neɪt] *vt*: **to ~ (to)** (*organization, cause*) spenden (für)
donation [də'neɪʃən] *n* (*act of donating*) Spenden *nt*; (*contribution*) Spende *f*
done [dʌn] *pp of* **do**
donkey ['dɔŋkɪ] *n* Esel *m*
donkey-work ['dɔŋkɪwə:k] (*Brit*: *inf*) *n* Dreckarbeit *f*
donor ['dəunə^r] *n* Spender(in) *m(f)*
donor card *n* Organspenderausweis *m*
donor conference *n* (*Pol, Econ*) Geberkonferenz *f*
donor fatigue *n* Spendenmüdigkeit *f*
don't [dəunt] = **do not**
donut ['dəunʌt] (*US*) *n* = **doughnut**
doodle ['du:dl] *vi* Männchen malen ▹ *n* Kritzelei *f*
doom [du:m] *n* Unheil *nt* ▹ *vt*: **to be ~ed to failure** zum Scheitern verurteilt sein
doomsday ['du:mzdeɪ] *n* der Jüngste Tag
door [dɔ:^{r}] *n* Tür *f*; **to go from ~ to door** von Tür zu Tür gehen
door bell *n* Türklingel *f*
door handle *n* Türklinke *f*; (*of car*) Türgriff *m*
doorman ['dɔ:mən] (*irreg*: *like* **man**) *n* Portier *m*
doormat ['dɔ:mæt] *n* Fußmatte *f*; (*fig*) Fußabtreter *m*
doorpost ['dɔ:pəust] *n* Türpfosten *m*
doorstep ['dɔ:stɛp] *n* Eingangsstufe *f*, Türstufe *f*; **on the ~** vor der Haustür
door-to-door ['dɔ:tə'dɔ:^{r}] *adj* (*selling*) von Haus zu Haus; **~ salesman** Vertreter *m*
doorway ['dɔ:weɪ] *n* Eingang *m*
dope [dəup] *n* (*inf*) Stoff *m*, Drogen *pl*; (: *person*) Esel *m*, Trottel *m*; (: *information*) Informationen

pl ▹ *vt* dopen
dopey ['dəupɪ] (*inf*) *adj* (*groggy*) benebelt; (*stupid*) blöd, bekloppt
dormant ['dɔːmənt] *adj* (*plant*) ruhend; (*volcano*) untätig; (*idea, report etc*): **to lie ~** schlummern
dormer ['dɔːməʳ] *n* (*also*: **dormer window**) Mansardenfenster *nt*
dormice ['dɔːmaɪs] *npl of* **dormouse**
dormitory ['dɔːmɪtrɪ] *n* Schlafsaal *m*; (*US: building*) Wohnheim *nt*
dormouse ['dɔːmaus] (*pl* **dormice**) *n* Haselmaus *f*
DOS [dɔs] *n abbr* (*Comput*: = *disk operating system*) DOS
dosage ['dəusɪdʒ] *n* Dosis *f*; (*on label*) Dosierung *f*
dose [dəus] *n* Dosis *f*; (*Brit: bout*) Ration *f* ▹ *vt*: **to ~ o.s.** Medikamente nehmen; **a ~ of flu** eine Grippe
dosser ['dɔsəʳ] (*Brit: inf*) *n* Penner(in) *m(f)*
dosshouse ['dɔshaus] (*Brit: inf*) *n* Obdachlosenheim *nt*
dossier ['dɔsɪeɪ] *n* Dossier *nt*
DOT (*US*) *n abbr* (= *Department of Transportation*) ≈ Verkehrsministerium *nt*
dot [dɔt] *n* Punkt *m* ▹ *vt*: **~ted with** übersät mit; **on the ~** (auf die Minute) pünktlich
dote [dəut]: **~ on** *vt fus* abgöttisch lieben
dot-matrix printer [dɔt'meɪtrɪks-] *n* Nadeldrucker *m*
dotted line ['dɔtɪd-] *n* punktierte Linie *f*; **to sign on the ~** (*fig*) seine formelle Zustimmung geben
dotty ['dɔtɪ] (*inf*) *adj* schrullig
double ['dʌbl] *adj* doppelt; (*chin*) Doppel- ▹ *adv* (*cost*) doppelt so viel ▹ *n* Doppelgänger(in) *m(f)* ▹ *vt* verdoppeln; (*paper, blanket*) (einmal) falten ▹ *vi* sich verdoppeln; **~ five two six (5526)** (*Brit: Tel*) fünfundfünfzig sechsundzwanzig; **it's spelt with a ~ "l"** es wird mit zwei l geschrieben; **an egg with a ~ yolk** ein Ei mit zwei Dottern; **on the ~, at the ~** (*Brit: quickly*) schnell; (*immediately*) unverzüglich; **to ~ as ...** (*person*) auch als ... fungieren; (*thing*) auch als ... dienen
▸ **double back** *vi* kehrtmachen, zurückgehen/-fahren
▸ **double up** *vi* sich krümmen; (*share room*) sich ein Zimmer teilen
double bass *n* Kontrabass *m*
double bed *n* Doppelbett *nt*
double bend (*Brit*) *n* S-Kurve *f*
double-blind *adj*: **~ experiment** Doppelblindversuch *m*
double-breasted ['dʌbl'brɛstɪd] *adj* (*jacket, coat*) zweireihig
double-check ['dʌbl'tʃɛk] *vt* noch einmal (über)prüfen ▹ *vi* es noch einmal (über)prüfen
double-clutch ['dʌbl'klʌtʃ] (*US*) *vi* mit Zwischengas schalten
double cream (*Brit*) *n* Sahne *f* mit hohem Fettgehalt, ≈ Schlagsahne *f*
double-cross [dʌbl'krɔs] *vt* ein Doppelspiel treiben mit
double-decker [dʌbl'dɛkəʳ] *n* Doppeldecker *m*
double-declutch ['dʌbldiː'klʌtʃ] (*Brit*) *vi* mit Zwischengas schalten
double exposure *n* doppelt belichtetes Foto *nt*
double glazing [-'gleɪzɪŋ] (*Brit*) *n* Doppelverglasung *f*
double-page spread ['dʌblpeɪdʒ-] *n* Doppelseite *f*
double-parking [dʌbl'pɑːkɪŋ] *n* Parken *nt* in der zweiten Reihe
double room *n* Doppelzimmer *nt*
doubles ['dʌblz] *n* (*Tennis*) Doppel *nt*
double time *n* doppelter Lohn *m*
double whammy [-'wæmɪ] (*inf*) *n* Doppelschlag *m*
doubly ['dʌblɪ] *adv* (ganz) besonders
doubt [daut] *n* Zweifel *m* ▹ *vt* bezweifeln; **without (a) ~** ohne Zweifel; **to ~ sb** jdm nicht glauben; **I ~ it (very much)** das bezweifle ich (sehr), das möchte ich (stark) bezweifeln; **to ~ if** *or* **whether ...** bezweifeln, dass ...; **I don't ~ that ...** ich bezweifle nicht, dass ...
doubtful ['dautful] *adj* zweifelhaft; **to be ~ about sth** an etw *dat* zweifeln; **to be ~ about doing sth** Bedenken haben, ob man etw tun soll; **I'm a bit ~** ich bin nicht ganz sicher
doubtless ['dautlɪs] *adv* ohne Zweifel, sicherlich
dough [dəu] *n* Teig *m*; (*inf: money*) Kohle *f*, Knete *f*
doughnut, (*US*) **donut** ['dəunʌt] *n* ≈ Berliner (Pfannkuchen) *m*
dour [duəʳ] *adj* mürrisch, verdrießlich
douse [dauz] *vt* Wasser schütten über +*acc*; (*extinguish*) löschen; **to ~ with** übergießen mit
dove [dʌv] *n* Taube *f*
Dover ['dəuvəʳ] *n* Dover *nt*
dovetail ['dʌvteɪl] *vi* übereinstimmen ▹ *n* (*also*: **dovetail joint**) Schwalbenschwanzverbindung *f*
dowager ['dauədʒəʳ] *n* (adlige) Witwe *f*
dowdy ['daudɪ] *adj* ohne jeden Schick; (*clothes*) unmodern
Dow-Jones average ['dau'dʒəunz-] (*US*) *n* Dow-Jones-Index *m*
down [daun] *n* Daunen *pl* ▹ *adv* hinunter, herunter; (*on the ground*) unten ▹ *prep* hinunter, herunter; (*movement along*) entlang ▹ *vt* (*inf: drink*) runterkippen; **~ there/here** da/hier unten; **the price of meat is ~** die Fleischpreise sind gefallen; **I've got it ~ in my diary** ich habe es in meinem Kalender notiert; **to pay £2 ~** £2 anzahlen; **England is two goals ~** England liegt mit zwei Toren zurück; **to ~ tools** (*Brit*) die Arbeit niederlegen; **~ with ...!** nieder mit ...!
down-and-out ['daunəndaut] *n* Penner(in) *m(f)* (*inf*)
down-at-heel ['daunət'hiːl] *adj* (*appearance, person*) schäbig, heruntergekommen; (*shoes*) abgetreten
downbeat ['daunbiːt] *n* (*Mus*) erster betonter

Taktteil *m* ▷ *adj* zurückhaltend
downcast ['daunkɑːst] *adj* niedergeschlagen
downer ['daunəʳ] (*inf*) *n* (*drug*) Beruhigungsmittel *nt*; **to be on a ~** deprimiert sein
downfall ['daunfɔːl] *n* Ruin *m*; (*of dictator etc*) Sturz *m*, Fall *m*
downgrade ['daungreɪd] *vt* herunterstufen
downhearted ['daun'hɑːtɪd] *adj* niedergeschlagen, entmutigt
downhill ['daun'hɪl] *adv* bergab ▷ *n* (*Ski: also:* **downhill race**) Abfahrtslauf *m*; **to go ~** (*road*) bergab führen; (*person*) hinuntergehen, heruntergehen; (*car*) hinunterfahren, herunterfahren; (*fig*) auf dem absteigenden Ast sein

DOWNING STREET

Downing Street ist die Straße in London, die von Whitehall zum St James Park führt und in der sich der offizielle Wohnsitz des Premierministers (Nr. 10) und des Finanzministers (Nr. 11) befindet. Im weiteren Sinne bezieht sich der Begriff Downing Street auf die britische Regierung.

download ['daunləud] *vt* (*Comput*) herunterladen, downloaden ▷ *n* Download *m*
down-market ['daun'mɑːkɪt] *adj* (*product*) für den Massenmarkt
down payment *n* Anzahlung *f*
downplay ['daunpleɪ] (*US*) *vt* herunterspielen
downpour ['daunpɔːʳ] *n* Wolkenbruch *m*
downright ['daunraɪt] *adj* (*liar etc*) ausgesprochen; (*refusal, lie*) glatt
Downs [daunz] (*Brit*) *npl*: **the ~** die Downs *pl*, *Hügellandschaft in Südengland*
downscale ['daunskeɪl] *adj* (*US*) wenig anspruchsvoll; (*goods, products*) minderwertig; (*service*) mangelhaft; (*restaurant, hotel*) der unteren Preisklasse
downsize ['daun'saɪz] *vi* (*Econ: company*) sich verkleinern
Down's syndrome *n* (*Med*) Downsyndrom *nt*
downstairs ['daun'stɛəz] *adv* unten; (*downwards*) nach unten
downstream ['daunstriːm] *adv* flussabwärts, stromabwärts
downtime ['dauntaɪm] *n* Ausfallzeit *f*
down-to-earth ['dauntu'əːθ] *adj* (*person*) nüchtern; (*solution*) praktisch
downtown ['daun'taun] (*esp US*) *adv* im Zentrum, in der (Innen)stadt; (*go*) ins Zentrum, in die (Innen)stadt ▷ *adj*: **~ Chicago** das Zentrum von Chicago
downtrodden ['dauntrɔdn] *adj* unterdrückt, geknechtet
down under *adv* (*be*) in Australien/ Neuseeland; (*go*) nach Australien/Neuseeland
downward ['daunwəd] *adj, adv* nach unten; **a ~ trend** ein Abwärtstrend *m*
downwards ['daunwədz] *adv* = **downward**
dowry ['daurɪ] *n* Mitgift *f*
doz. *abbr* = **dozen**
doze [dəuz] *vi* ein Nickerchen *nt* machen
▶ **doze off** *vi* einschlafen, einnicken
dozen ['dʌzn] *n* Dutzend *nt*; **a ~ books** ein Dutzend Bücher; **80p a ~** 80 Pence das Dutzend; **~s of** Dutzende von
DPh *n abbr* (= *Doctor of Philosophy*) ≈ Dr. phil.
DPhil *n abbr* (= *Doctor of Philosophy*) ≈ Dr. phil.
DPP (*Brit*) *n abbr* (= *Director of Public Prosecutions*)
DPT *n abbr* (= *diphtheria, pertussis, tetanus*) Diphtherie, Keuchhusten und Tetanus
Dr *abbr* = **doctor**; (*in street names:* = *Drive*) ≈ Str.
dr *abbr* (*Comm*) = **debtor**
drab [dræb] *adj* trist
draft [drɑːft] *n* Entwurf *m*; (*also:* **bank draft**) Tratte *f*; (*US: call-up*) Einberufung *f* ▷ *vt* entwerfen; *see also* **draught**
draftsman *etc* ['drɑːftsmən] (*US*) *n* = **draughtsman** *etc*
drag [dræg] *vt* schleifen, schleppen; (*river*) absuchen ▷ *vi* sich hinziehen ▷ *n* (*Aviat*) Luftwiderstand *m*; (*Naut*) Wasserwiderstand *m*; (*inf*): **to be a ~** (*boring*) langweilig sein; (*a nuisance*) lästig sein; (*women's clothing*): **in ~** in Frauenkleidung
▶ **drag away** *vt*: **to ~ away (from)** wegschleppen *or* wegziehen (von)
▶ **drag on** *vi* sich hinziehen
dragnet ['drægnɛt] *n* Schleppnetz *nt*; (*fig*) groß angelegte Polizeiaktion *f*
dragon ['drægn] *n* Drache *m*
dragonfly ['drægənflaɪ] *n* Libelle *f*
dragoon [drə'guːn] *n* Dragoner *m* ▷ *vt*: **to ~ sb into doing sth** (*Brit*) jdn zwingen, etw zu tun
drain [dreɪn] *n* Belastung *f*; (*in street*) Gully *m* ▷ *vt* entwässern; (*pond*) trockenlegen; (*vegetables*) abgießen; (*glass, cup*) leeren ▷ *vi* ablaufen; **to feel ~ed (of energy/emotion)** sich ausgelaugt fühlen
drainage ['dreɪnɪdʒ] *n* Entwässerungssystem *nt*; (*process*) Entwässerung *f*
draining board ['dreɪnɪŋ-], (*US*) **drainboard** ['dreɪnbɔːd] *n* Ablaufbrett *nt*
drainpipe ['dreɪnpaɪp] *n* Abflussrohr *nt*
drake [dreɪk] *n* Erpel *m*, Enterich *m*
dram [dræm] (*Scot*) *n* (*drink*) Schluck *m*
drama ['drɑːmə] *n* Drama *nt*
drama festival *n* Theaterfestival *nt*
dramatic [drə'mætɪk] *adj* dramatisch; (*theatrical*) theatralisch
dramatically [drə'mætɪklɪ] *adv* dramatisch; (*say, announce, pause*) theatralisch
dramatist ['dræmətɪst] *n* Dramatiker(in) *m(f)*
dramatize ['dræmətaɪz] *vt* dramatisieren; (*for TV/cinema*) für das Fernsehen/den Film bearbeiten
drank [dræŋk] *pt of* **drink**
drape [dreɪp] *vt* drapieren
drapes [dreɪps] (*US*) *npl* Vorhänge *pl*
drastic ['dræstɪk] *adj* drastisch
drastically ['dræstɪklɪ] *adv* drastisch

draught, (*US*) **draft** [drɑ:ft] *n* (Luft)zug *m*; (*Naut*) Tiefgang *m*; (*of chimney*) Zug *m*; **on ~** vom Fass

draught beer *n* Bier *nt* vom Fass

draughtboard ['drɑ:ftbɔ:d] (*Brit*) *n* Damebrett *nt*

draughts [drɑ:fts] (*Brit*) *n* Damespiel *nt*

draughtsman, (*US*) **draftsman** ['drɑ:ftsmən] (*irreg: like* **man**) *n* Zeichner(in) *m(f)*; (*as job*) technischer Zeichner *m*, technische Zeichnerin *f*

draughtsmanship, (*US*) **draftsmanship** ['drɑ:ftsmənʃɪp] *n* zeichnerisches Können *nt*; (*art*) Zeichenkunst *f*

draw [drɔ:] (*pt* **drew**, *pp* **~n**) *vt* zeichnen; (*cart, gun, tooth, conclusion*) ziehen; (*curtain: open*) aufziehen; (*: close*) zuziehen; (*admiration, attention*) erregen; (*money*) abheben; (*wages*) bekommen ▷ *vi* (*Sport*) unentschieden spielen ▷ *n* (*Sport*) Unentschieden *nt*; (*lottery*) Lotterie *f*; (*: picking of ticket*) Ziehung *f*; **to ~ a comparison/distinction (between)** einen Vergleich ziehen/Unterschied machen (zwischen +*dat*); **to ~ near** näher kommen; (*event*) nahen; **to ~ to a close** zu Ende gehen

▶ **draw back** *vi*: **to ~ back (from)** zurückweichen (von)

▶ **draw in** *vi* (*Brit: car*) anhalten; (*: train*) einfahren; (*nights*) länger werden

▶ **draw on** *vt* (*resources*) zurückgreifen auf +*acc*; (*imagination*) zu Hilfe nehmen; (*person*) einsetzen

▶ **draw out** *vi* länger werden ▷ *vt* (*money*) abheben

▶ **draw up** *vi* (an)halten ▷ *vt* (*chair etc*) heranziehen; (*document*) aufsetzen

drawback ['drɔ:bæk] *n* Nachteil *m*

drawbridge ['drɔ:brɪdʒ] *n* Zugbrücke *f*

drawee [drɔ:'i:] *n* Bezogene(r) *f(m)*

drawer [drɔ:ʳ] *n* Schublade *f*

drawing ['drɔ:ɪŋ] *n* Zeichnung *f*; (*skill, discipline*) Zeichnen *nt*

drawing board *n* Reißbrett *nt*; **back to the ~** (*fig*) das muss noch einmal neu überdacht werden

drawing pin (*Brit*) *n* Reißzwecke *f*

drawing room *n* Salon *m*

drawl [drɔ:l] *n* schleppende Sprechweise *f* ▷ *vi* schleppend sprechen

drawn [drɔ:n] *pp of* **draw** ▷ *adj* abgespannt

drawstring ['drɔ:strɪŋ] *n* Kordel *f* zum Zuziehen

dread [drɛd] *n* Angst *f*, Furcht *f* ▷ *vt* große Angst haben vor +*dat*

dreadful ['drɛdful] *adj* schrecklich, furchtbar; **I feel ~!** (*ill*) ich fühle mich schrecklich; (*ashamed*) es ist mir schrecklich peinlich

dream [dri:m] (*pt, pp* **dreamed** *or* **~t**) *n* Traum *m* ▷ *vt, vi* träumen; **to have a ~ about sb/sth** von jdm/etw träumen; **sweet ~s!** träume süß!

▶ **dream up** *vt* sich *dat* einfallen lassen, sich *dat* ausdenken

dreamer ['dri:məʳ] *n* Träumer(in) *m(f)*

dreamt [drɛmt] *pt, pp of* **dream**

dream world *n* Traumwelt *f*

dreamy ['dri:mɪ] *adj* verträumt; (*music*) zum Träumen

dreary ['drɪərɪ] *adj* langweilig; (*weather*) trüb

dredge [drɛdʒ] *vt* ausbaggern

▶ **dredge up** *vt* ausbaggern; (*fig: unpleasant facts*) ausgraben

dredger ['drɛdʒəʳ] *n* (*ship*) Schwimmbagger *m*; (*machine*) Bagger *m*; (*Brit: also:* **sugar dredger**) Zuckerstreuer *m*

dregs [drɛgz] *npl* Bodensatz *m*; (*of humanity*) Abschaum *m*

drench [drɛntʃ] *vt* durchnässen; **~ed to the skin** nass bis auf die Haut

dress [drɛs] *n* Kleid *nt*; (*no pl: clothing*) Kleidung *f* ▷ *vt* anziehen; (*wound*) verbinden ▷ *vi* sich anziehen; **she ~es very well** sie kleidet sich sehr gut; **to ~ a shop window** ein Schaufenster dekorieren; **to get ~ed** sich anziehen

▶ **dress up** *vi* sich fein machen; (*in fancy dress*) sich verkleiden

dress circle (*Brit*) *n* (*Theat*) erster Rang *m*

dress designer *n* Modezeichner(in) *m(f)*

dresser ['drɛsəʳ] *n* (*Brit*) Anrichte *f*; (*US*) Kommode *f*; (*also:* **window dresser**) Dekorateur(in) *m(f)*

dressing ['drɛsɪŋ] *n* Verband *m*; (*Culin*) (Salat)soße *f*

dressing gown (*Brit*) *n* Morgenrock *m*

dressing room *n* Umkleidekabine *f*; (*Theat*) (Künstler)garderobe *f*

dressing table *n* Frisierkommode *f*

dressmaker ['drɛsmeɪkəʳ] *n* (Damen)schneider(in) *m(f)*

dressmaking ['drɛsmeɪkɪŋ] *n* Schneidern *nt*

dress rehearsal *n* Generalprobe *f*

dressy ['drɛsɪ] (*inf*) *adj* elegant

drew [dru:] *pt of* **draw**

dribble ['drɪbl] *vi* tropfen; (*baby*) sabbern; (*Football*) dribbeln ▷ *vt* (*ball*) dribbeln mit

dried [draɪd] *adj* (*fruit*) getrocknet, Dörr-; **~ egg** Trockenei *nt*, Eipulver *nt*; **~ milk** Trockenmilch *f*, Milchpulver *nt*

drier ['draɪəʳ] *n* = **dryer**

drift [drɪft] *n* Strömung *f*; (*of snow*) Schneewehe *f*; (*of questions*) Richtung *f* ▷ *vi* treiben; (*sand*) wehen; **to let things ~** die Dinge treiben lassen; **to ~ apart** sich auseinanderleben; **I get** *or* **catch your ~** ich verstehe, worauf Sie hinauswollen

drifter ['drɪftəʳ] *n*: **to be a ~** sich treiben lassen

driftwood ['drɪftwud] *n* Treibholz *nt*

drill [drɪl] *n* Bohrer *m*; (*machine*) Bohrmaschine *f*; (*Mil*) Drill *m* ▷ *vt* bohren; (*troops*) drillen ▷ *vi*: **to ~ (for)** bohren (nach); **to ~ pupils in grammar** mit den Schülern Grammatik pauken

drilling ['drɪlɪŋ] *n* Bohrung *f*

drilling rig *n* Bohrturm *m*; (*at sea*) Bohrinsel *f*

drily ['draɪlɪ] *adv* = **dryly**

drink [drɪŋk] (*pt* **drank**, *pp* **drunk**) *n* Getränk *nt*;

(*alcoholic*) Glas *nt*, Drink *m*; (*sip*) Schluck *m* ▷ *vt, vi* trinken; **to have a ~** etwas trinken; **a ~ of water** etwas Wasser; **we had ~s before lunch** vor dem Mittagessen gab es einen Drink; **would you like something to ~?** möchten Sie etwas trinken?
▸ **drink in** *vt* (*fresh air*) einatmen, einsaugen; (*story, sight*) (begierig) in sich aufnehmen

drinkable [ˈdrɪŋkəbl] *adj* trinkbar

drink-driving [ˈdrɪŋkˈdraɪvɪŋ] *n* Trunkenheit *f* am Steuer

drinker [ˈdrɪŋkəʳ] *n* Trinker(in) *m(f)*

drinking [ˈdrɪŋkɪŋ] *n* Trinken *nt*

drinking fountain *n* Trinkwasserbrunnen *m*

drinking water *n* Trinkwasser *nt*

drip [drɪp] *n* Tropfen *nt*; (*one drip*) Tropfen *m*; (*Med*) Tropf *m* ▷ *vi* tropfen; (*wall*) triefnass sein

drip-dry [ˈdrɪpˈdraɪ] *adj* bügelfrei

drip-feed [ˈdrɪpfiːd] *vt* künstlich ernähren ▷ *n*: **to be on a ~** künstlich ernährt werden

dripping [ˈdrɪpɪŋ] *n* Bratenfett *nt* ▷ *adj* triefend; **I'm ~** ich bin klatschnass (*inf*); **~ wet** triefnass

drive [draɪv] (*pt* **drove**, *pp* **~n**) *n* Fahrt *f*; (*also*: **driveway**) Einfahrt *f*; (: *longer*) Auffahrt *f*; (*energy*) Schwung *m*, Elan *m*; (*campaign*) Aktion *f*; (*Sport*) Treibschlag *m*; (*Comput*: *also*: **disk drive**) Laufwerk *nt* ▷ *vt* fahren; (*Tech*) antreiben ▷ *vi* fahren; **to go for a ~** ein bisschen (raus)fahren; **it's 3 hours' ~ from London** es ist drei Stunden Fahrt von London (entfernt); **left-/right-hand ~** Links-/Rechtssteuerung *f*; **front-/rear-wheel ~** Vorderrad-/Hinterradantrieb *m*; **he ~s a taxi** er ist Taxifahrer; **to ~ sth into sth** (*nail, stake etc*) etw in etw schlagen *acc*; (*animal*) treiben; (*ball*) weit schlagen; (*incite, encourage*: *also*: **drive on**) antreiben; **to ~ sb home/to the airport** jdn nach Hause/zum Flughafen fahren; **to ~ sb mad** jdn verrückt machen; **to ~ sb to (do) sth** jdn dazu treiben, etw zu tun; **to ~ at 50 km an hour** mit (einer Geschwindigkeit von) 50 Stundenkilometern fahren; **what are you driving at?** worauf wollen Sie hinaus?
▸ **drive off** *vt* vertreiben
▸ **drive out** *vt* (*evil spirit*) austreiben; (*person*) verdrängen

drive-by shooting [ˈdraɪvbaɪ-] *n* *Schusswaffenangriff aus einem vorbeifahrenden Wagen*

drive-in [ˈdraɪvɪn] (*esp US*) *adj, n*: **~ (cinema)** Autokino *nt*; **~ (restaurant)** Autorestaurant *nt*

drive-in window (*US*) *n* Autoschalter *m*

drivel [ˈdrɪvl] (*inf*) *n* Blödsinn *m*

driven [ˈdrɪvn] *pp of* **drive**

driver [ˈdraɪvəʳ] *n* Fahrer(in) *m(f)*; (*Rail*) Führer(in) *m(f)*

driver's license [ˈdraɪvəz-] (*US*) *n* Führerschein *m*

driveway [ˈdraɪvweɪ] *n* Einfahrt *f*; (*longer*) Auffahrt *f*

driving [ˈdraɪvɪŋ] *n* Fahren *nt* ▷ *adj*: **~ rain** strömender Regen *m*; **~ snow** Schneetreiben *nt*

driving belt *n* Treibriemen *m*

driving force *n* treibende Kraft *f*

driving instructor *n* Fahrlehrer(in) *m(f)*

driving lesson *n* Fahrstunde *f*

driving licence (*Brit*) *n* Führerschein *m*

driving mirror *n* Rückspiegel *m*

driving school *n* Fahrschule *f*

driving test *n* Fahrprüfung *f*

drizzle [ˈdrɪzl] *n* Nieselregen *m* ▷ *vi* nieseln

droll [drəul] *adj* drollig

dromedary [ˈdrɔmədərɪ] *n* Dromedar *nt*

drone [drəun] *n* Brummen *nt*; (*male bee*) Drohne *f* ▷ *vi* brummen; (*bee*) summen; (*also*: **drone on**) eintönig sprechen

drool [druːl] *vi* sabbern; **to ~ over sth/sb** etw/jdn sehnsüchtig anstarren

droop [druːp] *vi* (*flower*) den Kopf hängen lassen; **his shoulders/head ~ed** er ließ die Schultern/den Kopf herabhängen

drop [drɔp] *n* Tropfen *m*; (*lessening*) Rückgang *m*; (*distance*) Höhenunterschied *m*; (*in salary*) Verschlechterung *f*; (*also*: **parachute drop**) (Ab)sprung *m* ▷ *vt* fallen lassen; (*voice, eyes, price*) senken; (*set down from car*) absetzen; (*omit*) weglassen ▷ *vi* (herunter)fallen; (*wind*) sich legen; **drops** *npl* Tropfen *pl*; **a 300 ft ~** ein Höhenunterschied von 300 Fuß; **a ~ of 10%** ein Rückgang um 10%; **cough ~s** Hustentropfen *pl*; **to ~ anchor** ankern, vor Anker gehen; **to ~ sb a line** jdm ein paar Zeilen schreiben
▸ **drop in** (*inf*) *vi*: **to ~ in (on sb)** (bei jdm) vorbeikommen
▸ **drop off** *vi* einschlafen ▷ *vt* (*passenger*) absetzen
▸ **drop out** *vi* (*withdraw*) ausscheiden; (*student*) sein Studium abbrechen

droplet [ˈdrɔplɪt] *n* Tröpfchen *nt*

dropout [ˈdrɔpaut] *n* Aussteiger(in) *m(f)*; (*Scol*) Studienabbrecher(in) *m(f)*

dropper [ˈdrɔpəʳ] *n* Pipette *f*

droppings [ˈdrɔpɪŋz] *npl* Kot *m*

dross [drɔs] *n* Schlacke *f*; (*fig*) Schund *m*

drought [draut] *n* Dürre *f*

drove [drəuv] *pt of* **drive** ▷ *n*: **~s of people** Scharen *pl* von Menschen

drown [draun] *vt* ertränken; (*fig*: *also*: **drown out**) übertönen ▷ *vi* ertrinken

drowse [drauz] *vi* (vor sich *acc* hin) dösen *or* dämmern

drowsy [ˈdrauzɪ] *adj* schläfrig

drudge [drʌdʒ] *n* Arbeitstier *nt*

drudgery [ˈdrʌdʒərɪ] *n* (stumpfsinnige) Plackerei *f* (*inf*); **housework is sheer ~** Hausarbeit ist eine einzige Plackerei

drug [drʌg] *n* Medikament *nt*, Arzneimittel *nt*; (*narcotic*) Droge *f*, Rauschgift *nt* ▷ *vt* betäuben; **to be on ~s** drogensüchtig sein; **hard/soft ~s** harte/weiche Drogen *pl*

drug abuse *n* Drogenmissbrauch *m*; **~ prevention** Drogenprävention *f*

drug addict *n* Drogensüchtige(r) *f(m)*, Rauschgiftsüchtige(r) *f(m)*

druggist [ˈdrʌgɪst] (*US*) *n* Drogist(in) *m(f)*

drug peddler *n* Drogenhändler(in) *m(f)*, Dealer *m* (*inf*)
drugstore ['drʌgstɔːʳ] (*US*) *n* Drogerie *f*
drum [drʌm] *n* Trommel *f*; (*for oil, petrol*) Fass *nt* ▷ *vi* trommeln; **drums** *npl* (*kit*) Schlagzeug *nt* ▶ **drum up** *vt* (*enthusiasm*) erwecken; (*support*) auftreiben
drummer ['drʌməʳ] *n* Trommler(in) *m(f)*; (*in band, pop group*) Schlagzeuger(in) *m(f)*
drum roll *n* Trommelwirbel *m*
drumstick ['drʌmstɪk] *n* Trommelstock *m*; (*of chicken*) Keule *f*
drunk [drʌŋk] *pp of* **drink** ▷ *adj* betrunken ▷ *n* (*also*: **drunkard**) Trinker(in) *m(f)*; **to get ~** sich betrinken; **a ~ driving offence** Trunkenheit *f* am Steuer
drunken ['drʌŋkən] *adj* betrunken; (*party*) feucht-fröhlich; **~ driving** Trunkenheit *f* am Steuer
drunkenness ['drʌŋkənnɪs] *n* (*state*) Betrunkenheit *f*; (*habit*) Trunksucht *f*
dry [draɪ] *adj* trocken ▷ *vt, vi* trocknen; **on ~ land** auf festem Boden; **to ~ one's hands/ hair/eyes** sich *dat* die Hände (ab)trocknen/die Haare trocknen/die Tränen abwischen; **to ~ the dishes** (das Geschirr) abtrocknen ▶ **dry up** *vi* austrocknen; (*in speech*) den Faden verlieren
dry-clean ['draɪ'kliːn] *vt* chemisch reinigen
dry-cleaner ['draɪ'kliːnəʳ] *n* (*job*) Inhaber(in) *m(f)* einer chemischen Reinigung; (*shop*: *also*: **dry-cleaner's**) chemische Reinigung *f*
dry-cleaning ['draɪ'kliːnɪŋ] *n* (*process*) chemische Reinigung *f*
dry dock *n* Trockendock *nt*
dryer ['draɪəʳ] *n* Wäschetrockner *m*; (*US*: *spin-dryer*) Wäscheschleuder *f*
dry goods *npl* Kurzwaren *pl*
dry ice *n* Trockeneis *nt*
dryly ['draɪlɪ] *adv* (*say, remark*) trocken
dryness ['draɪnɪs] *n* Trockenheit *f*
dry rot *n* (Haus)schwamm *m*, (Holz)schwamm *m*
dry run *n* (*fig*) Probe *f*
dry ski slope *n* Trockenskipiste *f*
DSc *n abbr* (= *Doctor of Science*) ≈ Dr. rer. nat.
DSL *n abbr* (*Comput*: = *digital subscriber line*) DSL
DSL connection *n* (*Comput*) DSL-Anschluss *m*
DSS (*Brit*) *n abbr* (= *Department of Social Security*) *Ministerium für Sozialfürsorge*
DST *abbr* = **daylight-saving time**
DTI (*Brit*) *n abbr* (= *Department of Trade and Industry*) ≈ Wirtschaftsministerium *nt*
DTP *n abbr* (= *desktop publishing*) DTP *nt*; *see also* **desktop publishing**; (= *diphtheria, tetanus, pertussis*) Diphtherie, Tetanus und Keuchhusten
DT's (*inf*) *npl abbr* (= *delirium tremens*) Delirium tremens *nt*; **to have the ~** vom Trinken den Tatterich haben (*inf*)
dual ['djuəl] *adj* doppelt; (*personality*) gespalten
dual carriageway (*Brit*) *n* ≈ Schnellstraße *f*
dual nationality *n* doppelte Staatsangehörigkeit *f*
dual-purpose ['djuəl'pəːpəs] *adj* zweifach verwendbar
dubbed [dʌbd] *adj* synchronisiert; (*nicknamed*) getauft
dubious ['djuːbɪəs] *adj* zweifelhaft; **I'm very ~ about it** ich habe da (doch) starke Zweifel
Dublin ['dʌblɪn] *n* Dublin *nt*
Dubliner ['dʌblɪnəʳ] *n* Dubliner(in) *m(f)*
duchess ['dʌtʃɪs] *n* Herzogin *f*
duck [dʌk] *n* Ente *f* ▷ *vi* (*also*: **duck down**) sich ducken ▷ *vt* (*blow*) ausweichen *+dat*; (*duty, responsibility*) aus dem Weg gehen *+dat*
duckling ['dʌklɪŋ] *n* Entenküken *nt*; (*Culin*) (junge) Ente *f*
duct [dʌkt] *n* Rohr *nt*; (*Anat*) Röhre *f*; **tear ~** Tränenkanal *m*
dud [dʌd] *n* Niete *f* (*inf*); (*note*) Blüte *f* (*inf*) ▷ *adj*: **~ cheque** (*Brit*) ungedeckter Scheck *m*
due [djuː] *adj* fällig; (*attention etc*) gebührend; (*consideration*) reiflich ▷ *n*: **to give sb his/her ~** jdn gerecht behandeln ▷ *adv*: **~ north** direkt nach Norden; **dues** *npl* Beitrag *m*; (*in harbour*) Gebühren *pl*; **in ~ course** zu gegebener Zeit; (*eventually*) im Laufe der Zeit; **~ to** (*owing to*) wegen *+gen*, aufgrund *+gen*; **to be ~ to do sth** etw tun sollen; **the rent is ~ on the 30th** die Miete ist am 30. fällig; **the train is ~ at 8** der Zug soll (laut Fahrplan) um 8 ankommen; **she is ~ back tomorrow** sie müsste morgen zurück sein; **I am ~ 6 days' leave** mir stehen 6 Tage Urlaub zu
due date *n* Fälligkeitsdatum *nt*
duel ['djuəl] *n* Duell *nt*
duet [djuː'ɛt] *n* Duett *nt*
duff [dʌf] (*Brit*: *inf*) *adj* kaputt ▶ **duff up** *vt* vermöbeln
duffel bag ['dʌfl-] *n* Matchbeutel *m*
duffel coat *n* Dufflecoat *m*
duffer ['dʌfəʳ] (*inf*) *n* Versager *m*, Flasche *f*
dug [dʌg] *pt, pp of* **dig**
dugout ['dʌgaut] *n* (*canoe*) Einbaum *m*; (*shelter*) Unterstand *m*
duke [djuːk] *n* Herzog *m*
dull [dʌl] *adj* trüb; (*intelligence, wit*) schwerfällig, langsam; (*event*) langweilig; (*sound, pain*) dumpf ▷ *vt* (*pain, grief*) betäuben; (*mind, senses*) abstumpfen
duly ['djuːlɪ] *adv* (*properly*) gebührend; (*on time*) pünktlich
dumb [dʌm] *adj* stumm; (*pej*: *stupid*) dumm, doof (*inf*); **he was struck ~** es verschlug ihm die Sprache ▶ **dumb down** *vi* an Niveau *or* Qualität verlieren, verflachen ▷ *vt fus* verdummen, dumm machen
dumbbell ['dʌmbɛl] *n* Hantel *f*
dumbfounded [dʌm'faundɪd] *adj* verblüfft
dumbing down [dʌmiŋ'daʊn] *n* Verdummung *f*, Qualitätsverlust *m*
dummy ['dʌmɪ] *n* (Schneider)puppe *f*; (*mock-up*) Attrappe *f*; (*Sport*) Finte *f*; (*Brit*: *for baby*) Schnuller *m* ▷ *adj* (*firm*) fiktiv; **~ bullets**

Übungsmunition *f*
dummy run *n* Probe *f*
dump [dʌmp] *n* (*also*: **rubbish dump**) Abfallhaufen *m*; (*inf*: *place*) Müllkippe *f*; (*Mil*) Depot *nt* ▷ *vt* fallen lassen; (*get rid of*) abladen; (*car*) abstellen; (*Comput*: *data*) ausgeben; **to be down in the ~s** (*inf*) deprimiert *or* down sein; **"no ~ing"** „Schuttabladen verboten"
dumpling ['dʌmplɪŋ] *n* Kloß *m*, Knödel *m*
dumpy ['dʌmpɪ] *adj* pummelig
dunce [dʌns] *n* Niete *f*
dune [dju:n] *n* Düne *f*
dung [dʌŋ] *n* (*Agr*) Dünger *m*, Mist *m*; (*Zool*) Dung *m*
dungarees [dʌŋgə'ri:z] *npl* Latzhose *f*
dungeon ['dʌndʒən] *n* Kerker *m*, Verlies *nt*
dunk [dʌŋk] *vt* (ein)tunken
Dunkirk [dʌn'kə:k] *n* Dünkirchen *nt*
duo ['dju:əu] *n* Duo *nt*
duodenal [dju:əu'di:nl] *adj* Duodenal-; **~ ulcer** Zwölffingerdarmgeschwür *nt*
duodenum [dju:əu'di:nəm] *n* Zwölffingerdarm *m*
dupe [dju:p] *n* Betrogene(r) *f(m)* ▷ *vt* betrügen
duplex ['dju:plɛks] (US) *n* Zweifamilienhaus *nt*; (*apartment*) zweistöckige Wohnung *f*
duplicate [*n*, *adj* 'dju:plɪkət, *vt* 'dju:plɪkeɪt] *n* (*also*: **duplicate copy**) Duplikat *nt*, Kopie *f*; (*also*: **duplicate key**) Zweitschlüssel *m* ▷ *adj* doppelt ▷ *vt* kopieren; (*repeat*) wiederholen; **in ~** in doppelter Ausfertigung
duplicating machine ['dju:plɪkeɪtɪŋ-] *n* Vervielfältigungsapparat *m*
duplicator ['dju:plɪkeɪtə^r] *n* Vervielfältigungsapparat *m*
duplicity [dju:'plɪsɪtɪ] *n* Doppelspiel *nt*
Dur. (*Brit*) *abbr* (*Post*) = *Durham*
durability [djuərə'bɪlɪtɪ] *n* Haltbarkeit *f*
durable ['djuərəbl] *adj* haltbar
duration [djuə'reɪʃən] *n* Dauer *f*
duress [djuə'rɛs] *n*: **under ~** unter Zwang
Durex® ['djuərɛks] (*Brit*) *n* Gummi *m* (*inf*)
during ['djuərɪŋ] *prep* während *+gen*
dusk [dʌsk] *n* (Abend)dämmerung *f*
dusky ['dʌskɪ] *adj* (*room*) dunkel; (*light*) Dämmer-
dust [dʌst] *n* Staub *m* ▷ *vt* abstauben; (*cake etc*): **to ~ with** bestäuben mit
▶ **dust off** *vt* abwischen, wegwischen; (*fig*) hervorkramen
dustbin ['dʌstbɪn] (*Brit*) *n* Mülltonne *f*
dustbin liner (*Brit*) *n* Müllsack *m*
duster ['dʌstə^r] *n* Staubtuch *nt*
dust jacket *n* (Schutz)umschlag *m*
dustman ['dʌstmən] (*Brit*: *irreg*: *like* **man**) *n* Müllmann *m*
dustpan ['dʌstpæn] *n* Kehrschaufel *f*, Müllschaufel *f*
dusty ['dʌstɪ] *adj* staubig
Dutch [dʌtʃ] *adj* holländisch, niederländisch ▷ *n* Holländisch *nt*, Niederländisch *nt* ▷ *adv*: **to go ~** (*inf*) getrennte Kasse machen; **the Dutch** *npl* die Holländer *pl*, die Niederländer *pl*
Dutch auction *n* *Versteigerung mit stufenweise erniedrigtem Ausbietungspreis*
Dutchman ['dʌtʃmən] (*irreg*: *like* **man**) *n* Holländer *m*, Niederländer *m*
Dutchwoman ['dʌtʃwumən] (*irreg*: *like* **woman**) *n* Holländerin *f*, Niederländerin *f*
dutiable ['dju:tɪəbl] *adj* zollpflichtig
dutiful ['dju:tɪful] *adj* pflichtbewusst; (*son*, *daughter*) gehorsam
duty ['dju:tɪ] *n* Pflicht *f*; (*tax*) Zoll *m*; **duties** *npl* (*functions*) Aufgaben *pl*; **to make it one's ~ to do sth** es sich *dat* zur Pflicht machen, etw zu tun; **to pay ~ on sth** Zoll auf etw *acc* zahlen; **on/off ~** im/nicht im Dienst
duty-free ['dju:tɪ'fri:] *adj* zollfrei; **~ shop** Dutyfreeshop *m*, Duty-free-Shop *m*
duty officer *n* Offizier *m* vom Dienst
duvet ['du:veɪ] (*Brit*) *n* Federbett *nt*
DV *abbr* (= *Deo volente*) so Gott will
DVD *n abbr* (= *digital versatile or video disc*) DVD *f*
DVLA (*Brit*) *n abbr* (= *Driver and Vehicle Licensing Authority*) *Zulassungsbehörde für Kraftfahrzeuge*
DVM (*US*) *n abbr* (= *Doctor of Veterinary Medicine*) ≈ Dr. med. vet.
dwarf [dwɔ:f] (*pl* **dwarves**) *n* Zwerg(in) *m(f)* ▷ *vt*: **to be ~ed by sth** neben etw *dat* klein erscheinen
dwarves [dwɔ:vz] *npl of* **dwarf**
dwell [dwɛl] (*pt*, *pp* **dwelt**) *vi* wohnen, leben
▶ **dwell on** *vt fus* (in Gedanken) verweilen bei
dweller ['dwɛlə^r] *n* Bewohner(in) *m(f)*; **city ~** Stadtbewohner(in) *m(f)*
dwelling ['dwɛlɪŋ] *n* Wohnhaus *nt*
dwelt [dwɛlt] *pt*, *pp of* **dwell**
dwindle ['dwɪndl] *vi* abnehmen; (*interest*) schwinden; (*attendance*) zurückgehen
dwindling ['dwɪndlɪŋ] *adj* (*strength*, *interest*) schwindend; (*resources*, *supplies*) versiegend
dye [daɪ] *n* Farbstoff *m*; (*for hair*) Färbemittel *nt* ▷ *vt* färben
dyestuffs ['daɪstʌfs] *npl* Farbstoffe *pl*
dying ['daɪɪŋ] *adj* sterbend; (*moments*, *words*) letzte(r, s)
dyke [daɪk] *n* (*Brit*: *wall*) Deich *m*, Damm *m*; (*channel*) (Entwässerungs)graben *m*; (*causeway*) Fahrdamm *m*
dynamic [daɪ'næmɪk] *adj* dynamisch
dynamics [daɪ'næmɪks] *n or npl* Dynamik *f*
dynamite ['daɪnəmaɪt] *n* Dynamit *nt* ▷ *vt* sprengen
dynamo ['daɪnəməu] *n* Dynamo *m*; (*Aut*) Lichtmaschine *f*
dynasty ['dɪnəstɪ] *n* Dynastie *f*
dysentery ['dɪsntrɪ] *n* (*Med*) Ruhr *f*
dyslexia [dɪs'lɛksɪə] *n* Legasthenie *f*
dyslexic [dɪs'lɛksɪk] *adj* legasthenisch ▷ *n* Legastheniker(in) *m(f)*
dyspepsia [dɪs'pɛpsɪə] *n* Dyspepsie *f*, Verdauungsstörung *f*
dystrophy ['dɪstrəfɪ] *n* Dystrophie *f*, Ernährungsstörung *f*; **muscular ~** Muskelschwund *m*

Ee

E¹, e [iː] *n* (*letter*) E *nt*, e *nt*; **E for Edward, E for Easy** (*US*) E wie Emil
E² [iː] *n* (*Mus*) E *nt*, e *nt*
E³ [iː] *abbr* (= *east*) O ▷ *n abbr* (*drug*: = *Ecstasy*) Ecstasy *nt*
e- *pref* E-, elektronisch
E111 *n abbr* (*also*: **form E111**) E111-Formular *nt*
ea. *abbr* = **each**
each [iːtʃ] *adj, pron* jede(r, s); **~ other** sich, einander; **they hate ~ other** sie hassen sich *or* einander; **you are jealous of ~ other** ihr seid eifersüchtig aufeinander; **~ day** jeden Tag; **they have 2 books ~** sie haben je 2 Bücher; **they cost £5 ~** sie kosten 5 Pfund das Stück; **~ of us** jede(r, s) von uns
eager [ˈiːgəʳ] *adj* eifrig; **to be ~ to do sth** etw unbedingt tun wollen; **to be ~ for sth** auf etw *acc* erpicht *or* aus (*inf*) sein
eagerly [ˈiːgəlɪ] *adv* eifrig; (*awaited*) gespannt, ungeduldig
eagle [ˈiːgl] *n* Adler *m*
ear [ɪəʳ] *n* Ohr *nt*; (*of corn*) Ähre *f*; **to be up to one's ~s in debt/work** bis über beide Ohren in Schulden/Arbeit stecken; **to be up to one's ~s in paint/baking** mitten im Anstreichen/Backen stecken; **to give sb a thick ~** jdm ein paar hinter die Ohren geben; **we'll play it by ~** (*fig*) wir werden es auf uns zukommen lassen
earache [ˈɪəreɪk] *n* Ohrenschmerzen *pl*
eardrum [ˈɪədrʌm] *n* Trommelfell *nt*
earful [ˈɪəful] (*inf*) *n*: **to give sb an ~** jdm was erzählen; **to get an ~** was zu hören bekommen
earl [əːl] (*Brit*) *n* Graf *m*
earlier [ˈəːlɪəʳ] *adj, adv* früher; **I can't come any ~** ich kann nicht früher *or* eher kommen
early [ˈəːlɪ] *adv* früh; (*ahead of time*) zu früh ▷ *adj* früh; (*Christians*) Ur-; (*death, departure*) vorzeitig; (*reply*) baldig; **~ in the morning** früh am Morgen; **to have an ~ night** früh ins Bett gehen; **in the ~ hours** in den frühen Morgenstunden; **in the ~** *or* **~ in the spring/19th century** Anfang des Frühjahrs/des 19. Jahrhunderts; **take the ~ train** nimm den früheren Zug; **you're ~!** Sie sind früh dran!; **she's in her ~ forties** sie ist Anfang Vierzig; **at your earliest convenience** so bald wie möglich
early retirement *n*: **to take ~** vorzeitig in den Ruhestand gehen
early retirement benefits *npl* Vorruhestandsleistungen *pl*
early warning system *n* Frühwarnsystem *nt*
earmark [ˈɪəmɑːk] *vt*: **to ~ (for)** bestimmen (für), vorsehen (für)
earn [əːn] *vt* verdienen; (*interest*) bringen; **to ~ one's living** seinen Lebensunterhalt verdienen; **this ~ed him much praise, he ~ed much praise for this** das trug ihm viel Lob ein; **he's ~ed his rest/reward** er hat sich seine Pause/Belohnung verdient
earned income [əːnd-] *n* Arbeitseinkommen *nt*
earnest [ˈəːnɪst] *adj* ernsthaft; (*wish, desire*) innig ▷ *n* (*also*: **earnest money**) Angeld *nt*; **in ~** (*adv*) richtig; (*adj*): **to be in ~** es ernst meinen; **work on the tunnel soon began in ~** die Tunnelarbeiten begannen bald richtig; **is the Minister in ~ about these proposals?** meint der Minister diese Vorschläge ernst?
earnings [ˈəːnɪŋz] *npl* Verdienst *m*; (*of company etc*) Ertrag *m*
ear, nose and throat specialist *n* Hals-Nasen-Ohren-Arzt *m*, Hals-Nasen-Ohren-Ärztin *f*
earphones [ˈɪəfəunz] *npl* Kopfhörer *pl*
earplugs [ˈɪəplʌgz] *npl* Ohropax® *nt*
earring [ˈɪərɪŋ] *n* Ohrring *m*
earset [ˈɪəsɛt] *n* (*Tel*) Earset *nt*, Ohrhörer *m*
earshot [ˈɪəʃɔt] *n*: **within/out of ~** in/außer Hörweite
earth [əːθ] *n* Erde *f*; (*of fox*) Bau *m* ▷ *vt* (*Brit*: *Elec*) erden
earthenware [ˈəːθnwɛəʳ] *n* Tongeschirr *nt* ▷ *adj* Ton-
earthly [ˈəːθlɪ] *adj* irdisch; **~ paradise** Paradies *nt* auf Erden; **there is no ~ reason to think ...** es besteht nicht der geringste Grund für die Annahme ...
earthquake [ˈəːθkweɪk] *n* Erdbeben *nt*
earthshattering [ˈəːθʃætərɪŋ] *adj* (*fig*) weltbewegend
earth tremor *n* Erdstoß *m*
earthworks [ˈəːθwəːks] *npl* Erdarbeiten *pl*
earthworm [ˈəːθwəːm] *n* Regenwurm *m*

earthy ['ə:θɪ] *adj* (*humour*) derb
earwig ['ɪəwɪg] *n* Ohrwurm *m*
ease [i:z] *n* Leichtigkeit *f*; (*comfort*) Behagen *nt* ▷ *vt* (*problem*) vereinfachen; (*pain*) lindern; (*tension*) verringern; (*loosen*) lockern ▷ *vi* nachlassen; (*situation*) sich entspannen; **to ~ sth in/out** (*push/pull*) etw behutsam hineinschieben/herausziehen; **at ~!** (*Mil*) rührt euch!; **with ~** mit Leichtigkeit; **life of ~** Leben *nt* der Muße; **to ~ in the clutch** die Kupplung behutsam kommen lassen
▸ **ease off** *vi* nachlassen; (*slow down*) langsamer werden
▸ **ease up** *vi* = **ease off**
easel ['i:zl] *n* Staffelei *f*
easily ['i:zɪlɪ] *adv* (*see adj*) leicht; ungezwungen; bequem
easiness ['i:zɪnɪs] *n* Leichtigkeit *f*; (*of manner*) Ungezwungenheit *f*
east [i:st] *n* Osten *m* ▷ *adj* (*coast, Asia etc*) Ost- ▷ *adv* ostwärts, nach Osten; **the E~** der Osten
Easter ['i:stə^r] *n* Ostern *nt* ▷ *adj* (*holidays etc*) Oster-
Easter egg *n* Osterei *nt*
Easter Island *n* Osterinsel *f*
easterly ['i:stəlɪ] *adj* östlich; (*wind*) Ost-
Easter Monday *n* Ostermontag *m*
eastern ['i:stən] *adj* östlich; **E~ Europe** Osteuropa *nt*; **the E~ bloc** (*formerly*) der Ostblock
Easter Sunday *n* Ostersonntag *m*
East Germany *n* (*formerly*) die DDR *f*
eastward ['i:stwəd], **eastwards** ['i:stwədz] *adv* ostwärts, nach Osten
easy ['i:zɪ] *adj* leicht; (*relaxed*) ungezwungen; (*comfortable*) bequem ▷ *adv*: **to take it/things ~** (*go slowly*) sich *dat* Zeit lassen; (*not worry*) es nicht so schwernehmen; (*rest*) sich schonen; **payment on ~ terms** Zahlung zu günstigen Bedingungen; **that's easier said than done** das ist leichter gesagt als getan; **I'm ~** (*inf*) mir ist alles recht
easy chair *n* Sessel *m*
easy-going ['i:zɪ'gəuɪŋ] *adj* gelassen
easy touch (*inf*) *n*: **to be an ~** (*for money etc*) leicht anzuzapfen sein
eat [i:t] (*pt* **ate**, *pp* **~en**) *vt, vi* essen; (*animal*) fressen
▸ **eat away** *vt* (*subj: sea*) auswaschen; (*: acid*) zerfressen
▸ **eat away at** *vt fus* (*metal*) anfressen; (*savings*) angreifen
▸ **eat into** *vt fus* = **eat away at**
▸ **eat out** *vi* essen gehen
▸ **eat up** *vt* aufessen; **it ~s up electricity** es verbraucht viel Strom
eatable ['i:təbl] *adj* genießbar
eau de Cologne ['əudəkə'ləun] *n* Kölnischwasser *nt*, Eau de Cologne *nt*
eaves [i:vz] *npl* Dachvorsprung *m*
eavesdrop ['i:vzdrɔp] *vi* lauschen; **to ~ on** belauschen *+acc*
ebb [ɛb] *n* Ebbe *f* ▷ *vi* ebben; (*fig: also:* **ebb away**) dahinschwinden; (*: feeling*) abebben; **the ~ and flow** (*fig*) das Auf und Ab; **to be at a low ~** (*fig*) auf einem Tiefpunkt angelangt sein
ebb tide *n* Ebbe *f*
ebony ['ɛbənɪ] *n* Ebenholz *nt*
ebullient [ɪ'bʌlɪənt] *adj* überschäumend, übersprudelnd
EC *n abbr* (= *European Community*) EG *f*
e-card ['i:kɑ:d] *n abbr* (= *electronic card*) E-Card *nt*, *elektronische Grußkarte*
ECB *n abbr* (= *European Central Bank*) EZB *f*
eccentric [ɪk'sɛntrɪk] *adj* exzentrisch ▷ *n* Exzentriker(in) *m(f)*
ecclesiastic [ɪkli:zɪ'æstɪk], **ecclesiastical** [ɪkli:zɪ'æstɪkl] *adj* kirchlich
ECG *n abbr* (= *electrocardiogram*) EKG *nt*
echo ['ɛkəu] (*pl* **~es**) *n* Echo *nt* ▷ *vt* wiederholen ▷ *vi* widerhallen; (*place*) hallen
éclair [eɪ'klɛə^r] *n* Eclair *nt*
eclipse [ɪ'klɪps] *n* Finsternis *f* ▷ *vt* in den Schatten stellen
eco- ['i:kəu] *pref* Öko-, öko-
ecofriendly *adj* umweltfreundlich
ecological [i:kə'lɔdʒɪkəl] *adj* ökologisch; (*damage, disaster*) Umwelt-
ecologist [ɪ'kɔlədʒɪst] *n* Ökologe *m*, Ökologin *f*
ecology [ɪ'kɔlədʒɪ] *n* Ökologie *f*
e-commerce [i:'kɔmə:s] *n* E-Commerce *nt*, elektronischer Handel
economic [i:kə'nɔmɪk] *adj* (*system, policy etc*) Wirtschafts-; (*profitable*) wirtschaftlich
economical [i:kə'nɔmɪkl] *adj* wirtschaftlich; (*person*) sparsam
economically [i:kə'nɔmɪklɪ] *adv* wirtschaftlich; (*thriftily*) sparsam
economics [i:kə'nɔmɪks] *n* Wirtschaftswissenschaften *pl* ▷ *npl* Wirtschaftlichkeit *f*; (*of situation*) wirtschaftliche Seite *f*
economist [ɪ'kɔnəmɪst] *n* Wirtschaftswissenschaftler(in) *m(f)*
economize [ɪ'kɔnəmaɪz] *vi* sparen
economy [ɪ'kɔnəmɪ] *n* Wirtschaft *f*; (*financial prudence*) Sparsamkeit *f*; **economies of scale** (*Comm*) Einsparungen *pl* durch erhöhte Produktion
economy class *n* Touristenklasse *f*
economy size *n* Sparpackung *f*
ecosystem ['i:kəusɪstəm] *n* Ökosystem *nt*
ecotourism ['i:kəu'tuərɪzm] *n* Ökotourismus *m*
ECSC *n abbr* (= *European Coal and Steel Community*) *Europäische Gemeinschaft für Kohle und Stahl*
ecstasy ['ɛkstəsɪ] *n* Ekstase *f*; (*drug*) Ecstasy *nt*; **to go into ecstasies over** in Verzückung geraten über *+acc*; **in ~** verzückt
ecstatic [ɛks'tætɪk] *adj* ekstatisch
ECT *n abbr* = **electroconvulsive therapy**
Ecuador ['ɛkwədɔ:^r] *n* Ecuador *nt*, Ekuador *nt*
ecumenical [i:kju'mɛnɪkl] *adj* ökumenisch
eczema ['ɛksɪmə] *n* Ekzem *nt*
eddy ['ɛdɪ] *n* Strudel *m*
edge [ɛdʒ] *n* Rand *m*; (*of table, chair*) Kante *f*; (*of lake*) Ufer *nt*; (*of knife etc*) Schneide *f* ▷ *vt*

einfassen ▷ *vi*: **to ~ forward** sich nach vorne schieben; **on ~** (*fig*) = **edgy**; **to have the ~ on** überlegen sein *+dat*; **to ~ away from** sich allmählich entfernen von; **to ~ past** sich vorbeischieben, sich vorbeidrücken
edgeways ['ɛdʒweɪz] *adv*: **he couldn't get a word in ~** er kam überhaupt nicht zu Wort
edging ['ɛdʒɪŋ] *n* Einfassung *f*
edgy ['ɛdʒɪ] *adj* nervös
edible ['ɛdɪbl] *adj* essbar, genießbar
edict ['i:dɪkt] *n* Erlass *m*
edifice ['ɛdɪfɪs] *n* Gebäude *nt*
edifying ['ɛdɪfaɪɪŋ] *adj* erbaulich
Edinburgh ['ɛdɪnbərə] *n* Edinburg(h) *nt*
edit ['ɛdɪt] *vt* (*text*) redigieren; (*book*) lektorieren; (*film, broadcast*) schneiden, cutten; (*newspaper, magazine*) herausgeben; (*Comput*) editieren
edition [ɪ'dɪʃən] *n* Ausgabe *f*
editor ['ɛdɪtə^r] *n* Redakteur(in) *m(f)*; (*of newspaper, magazine*) Herausgeber(in) *m(f)*; (*of book*) Lektor(in) *m(f)*; (*Cine, Radio, TV*) Cutter(in) *m(f)*
editorial [ɛdɪ'tɔ:rɪəl] *adj* redaktionell; (*staff*) Redaktions- ▷ *n* Leitartikel *m*
EDP *n abbr* (*Comput: = electronic data processing*) EDV *f*
EDT (*US*) *abbr* (*= Eastern Daylight Time*) *ostamerikanische Sommerzeit*
educate ['ɛdjukeɪt] *vt* erziehen; **~d at ...** zur Schule/Universität gegangen in ...
educated ['ɛdjʊkeɪtɪd] *adj* gebildet
educated guess ['ɛdjukeɪtɪd-] *n* wohl begründete Vermutung *f*
education [ɛdju'keɪʃən] *n* Erziehung *f*; (*schooling*) Ausbildung *f*; (*knowledge, culture*) Bildung *f*; **primary ~, elementary ~** (*US*) Grundschul(aus)bildung *f*; **secondary ~** höhere Schul(aus)bildung *f*
educational [ɛdju'keɪʃənl] *adj* pädagogisch; (*experience*) lehrreich; (*toy*) pädagogisch wertvoll; **~ technology** Unterrichtstechnologie *f*
Edwardian [ɛd'wɔ:dɪən] *adj* aus der Zeit Edwards VII
EE *abbr* = **electrical engineer**
EEG *n abbr* (*= electroencephalogram*) EEG *nt*
eel [i:l] *n* Aal *m*
EEOC (*US*) *n abbr* (*= Equal Employment Opportunity Commission*) *Kommission für Gleichberechtigung am Arbeitsplatz*
eerie ['ɪərɪ] *adj* unheimlich
EET *abbr* (*= Eastern European Time*) OEZ *f*
efface [ɪ'feɪs] *vt* auslöschen; **to ~ o.s.** sich im Hintergrund halten
effect [ɪ'fɛkt] *n* Wirkung *f*, Effekt *m* ▷ *vt* bewirken; (*repairs*) durchführen; **effects** *npl* Effekten *pl*; (*Theat, Cine etc*) Effekte *pl*; **to take ~** (*law*) in Kraft treten; (*drug*) wirken; **to put into ~** in Kraft setzen; **to have an ~ on sb/sth** eine Wirkung auf jdn/etw haben; **in ~** eigentlich, praktisch; **his letter is to the ~ that ...** sein Brief hat zum Inhalt, dass ...
effective [ɪ'fɛktɪv] *adj* effektiv, wirksam; (*actual*) eigentlich, wirklich; **to become ~** in Kraft treten; **~ date** Zeitpunkt *m* des Inkrafttretens
effectively [ɪ'fɛktɪvlɪ] *adv* effektiv
effectiveness [ɪ'fɛktɪvnɪs] *n* Wirksamkeit *f*, Effektivität *f*
effeminate [ɪ'fɛmɪnɪt] *adj* feminin, effeminiert
effervescent [ɛfə'vɛsnt] *adj* sprudelnd
efficacy ['ɛfɪkəsɪ] *n* Wirksamkeit *f*
efficiency [ɪ'fɪʃənsɪ] *n* (*see adj*) Fähigkeit *f*, Tüchtigkeit *f*; Rationalität *f*; Leistungsfähigkeit *f*
efficiency apartment (*US*) *n* Einzimmerwohnung *f*
efficient [ɪ'fɪʃənt] *adj* fähig, tüchtig; (*organization*) rationell; (*machine*) leistungsfähig
efficiently [ɪ'fɪʃəntlɪ] *adv* gut, effizient
effigy ['ɛfɪdʒɪ] *n* Bildnis *nt*
effluent ['ɛfluənt] *n* Abwasser *nt*
effort ['ɛfət] *n* Anstrengung *f*; (*attempt*) Versuch *m*; **to make an ~ to do sth** sich bemühen, etw zu tun
effortless ['ɛfətlɪs] *adj* mühelos; (*style*) flüssig
effrontery [ɪ'frʌntərɪ] *n* Unverschämtheit *f*; **to have the ~ to do sth** die Frechheit besitzen, etw zu tun
effusive [ɪ'fju:sɪv] *adj* überschwänglich
EFL *n abbr* (*Scol: = English as a Foreign Language*) Englisch *nt* als Fremdsprache
EFTA ['ɛftə] *n abbr* (*= European Free Trade Association*) EFTA *f*
e.g. *adv abbr* (*= exempli gratia*) z. B.
egalitarian [ɪgælɪ'tɛərɪən] *adj* egalitär; (*principles*) Gleichheits- ▷ *n* Verfechter(in) *m(f)* des Egalitarismus
egg [ɛg] *n* Ei *nt*; **hard-boiled/soft-boiled ~** hart/weich gekochtes Ei *nt*
▶ **egg on** *vt* anstacheln
egg cup *n* Eierbecher *m*
eggplant ['ɛgplɑ:nt] *n* (*esp US*) Aubergine *f*
eggshell ['ɛgʃɛl] *n* Eierschale *f* ▷ *adj* eierschalenfarben
egg timer *n* Eieruhr *f*
egg white *n* Eiweiß *nt*
egg yolk *n* Eigelb *nt*
ego ['i:gəu] *n* (*self-esteem*) Selbstbewusstsein *nt*
egoism ['ɛgəuɪzəm] *n* Egoismus *m*
egoist ['ɛgəuɪst] *n* Egoist(in) *m(f)*
egotism ['ɛgəutɪzəm] *n* Ichbezogenheit *f*, Egotismus *m*
egotist ['ɛgəutɪst] *n* ichbezogener Mensch *m*, Egotist(in) *m(f)*
ego trip (*inf*) *n* Egotrip *m*
Egypt ['i:dʒɪpt] *n* Ägypten *nt*
Egyptian [ɪ'dʒɪpʃən] *adj* ägyptisch ▷ *n* Ägypter(in) *m(f)*
eiderdown ['aɪdədaun] *n* Federbett *nt*, Daunendecke *f*
eight [eɪt] *num* acht
eighteen [eɪ'ti:n] *num* achtzehn
eighteenth [eɪ'ti:nθ] *num* achtzehnte(r, s)

eighth [eɪtθ] *num* achte(r, s) ▷ *n* Achtel *nt*
eighty ['eɪtɪ] *num* achtzig
Eire ['ɛərə] *n* (Republik *f*) Irland *nt*
EIS *n abbr (= Educational Institute of Scotland) schottische Lehrergewerkschaft*
either ['aɪðəʳ] *adj (one or other)* eine(r, s) (von beiden); *(both, each)* beide *pl*, jede(r, s) ▷ *pron*: **~ (of them)** eine(r, s) (davon) ▷ *adv* auch nicht ▷ *conj*: **~ yes or no** entweder ja oder nein; **on ~ side** *(on both sides)* auf beiden Seiten; *(on one or other side)* auf einer der beiden Seiten; **I don't like ~** ich mag beide nicht *or* keinen von beiden; **no, I don't ~** nein, ich auch nicht; **I haven't seen ~ one or the other** ich habe weder den einen noch den anderen gesehen
ejaculation [ɪdʒækju'leɪʃən] *n* Ejakulation *f*, Samenerguss *m*
eject [ɪ'dʒɛkt] *vt* ausstoßen; *(tenant, gatecrasher)* hinauswerfen ▷ *vi* den Schleudersitz betätigen
ejector seat [ɪ'dʒɛktə-] *n* Schleudersitz *m*
eke out *vt (make last)* strecken
EKG (US) *n abbr* = **electrocardiogram**
el [ɛl] *(US: inf) n abbr* = **elevated railroad**
elaborate [*adj* ɪ'læbərɪt, *vb* ɪ'læbəreɪt] *adj* kompliziert; *(plan)* ausgefeilt ▷ *vt* näher ausführen; *(refine)* ausarbeiten ▷ *vi* mehr ins Detail gehen; **to ~ on** näher ausführen
elapse [ɪ'læps] *vi* vergehen, verstreichen
elastic [ɪ'læstɪk] *n* Gummi *nt* ▷ *adj* elastisch
elastic band *(Brit) n* Gummiband *nt*
elasticity [ɪlæs'tɪsɪtɪ] *n* Elastizität *f*
elated [ɪ'leɪtɪd] *adj*: **to be ~** hocherfreut *or* in Hochstimmung sein
elation [ɪ'leɪʃən] *n* große Freude *f*, Hochstimmung *f*
elbow ['ɛlbəu] *n* Ell(en)bogen *m* ▷ *vt*: **to ~ one's way through the crowd** sich durch die Menge boxen
elbow grease *(inf) n* Muskelkraft *f*
elbowroom ['ɛlbəurum] *n* Ellbogenfreiheit *f*
elder ['ɛldəʳ] *adj* älter ▷ *n (Bot)* Holunder *m*; *(older person: gen pl)* Ältere(r) *f(m)*
elderly ['ɛldəlɪ] *adj* ältere(r, s) ▷ *npl*: **the ~** ältere Leute *pl*
elder statesman *n* erfahrener Staatsmann *m*
eldest ['ɛldɪst] *adj* älteste(r, s) ▷ *n* Älteste(r) *f(m)*
elect [ɪ'lɛkt] *vt* wählen ▷ *adj*: **the president ~** der designierte *or* künftige Präsident; **to ~ to do sth** sich dafür entscheiden, etw zu tun
election [ɪ'lɛkʃən] *n* Wahl *f*; **to hold an ~** eine Wahl abhalten
election campaign *n* Wahlkampf *m*
election débâcle *n* Wahldebakel *nt*
electioneering [ɪlɛkʃə'nɪərɪŋ] *n* Wahlkampf *m*
elector [ɪ'lɛktəʳ] *n* Wähler(in) *m(f)*
electoral [ɪ'lɛktərəl] *adj* Wähler-
electoral college *n* Wahlmännergremium *nt*
electorate [ɪ'lɛktərɪt] *n* Wähler *pl*, Wählerschaft *f*
electric [ɪ'lɛktrɪk] *adj* elektrisch
electrical [ɪ'lɛktrɪkl] *adj* elektrisch; *(appliance)* Elektro-; *(failure)* Strom-
electrical engineer *n* Elektrotechniker *m*
electric blanket *n* Heizdecke *f*
electric chair (US) *n* elektrischer Stuhl *m*
electric cooker *n* Elektroherd *m*
electric current *n* elektrischer Strom *m*
electric fire *(Brit) n* elektrisches Heizgerät *nt*
electrician [ɪlɛk'trɪʃən] *n* Elektriker(in) *m(f)*
electricity [ɪlɛk'trɪsɪtɪ] *n* Elektrizität *f*; *(supply)* (elektrischer) Strom *m* ▷ *cpd* Strom-; **to switch on/off the ~** den Strom an-/abschalten
electricity board *(Brit) n* Elektrizitätswerk *nt*
electricity price *n* Strompreis *m*
electricity rate *n* Stromtarif *m*
electric light *n* elektrisches Licht *nt*
electric shock *n* elektrischer Schlag *m*, Stromschlag *m*
electrify [ɪ'lɛktrɪfaɪ] *vt (fence)* unter Strom setzen; *(rail network)* elektrifizieren; *(audience)* elektrisieren
electro ... [ɪ'lɛktrəu] *pref* Elektro-
electrocardiogram [ɪ'lɛktrə'kɑːdɪəgræm] *n* Elektrokardiogramm *nt*
electroconvulsive therapy [ɪ'lɛktrəkən'vʌlsɪv-] *n* Elektroschocktherapie *f*
electrocute [ɪ'lɛktrəkjuːt] *vt* durch einen Stromschlag töten; *(US: criminal)* auf dem elektrischen Stuhl hinrichten
electrode [ɪ'lɛktrəud] *n* Elektrode *f*
electroencephalogram [ɪ'lɛktrəuɛn'sɛfələgræm] *n* Elektroenzephalogramm *nt*
electrolysis [ɪlɛk'trɔlɪsɪs] *n* Elektrolyse *f*
electromagnetic [ɪ'lɛktrəmæg'nɛtɪk] *adj* elektromagnetisch
electron [ɪ'lɛktrɔn] *n* Elektron *nt*
electronic [ɪlɛk'trɔnɪk] *adj* elektronisch
electronic data processing *n* elektronische Datenverarbeitung *f*
electronic mail *n* elektronische Post *f*
electronics [ɪlɛk'trɔnɪks] *n* Elektronik *f*
electronic tag *n* elektronische Fußfessel *f*
electron microscope *n* Elektronenmikroskop *nt*
electroplated [ɪ'lɛktrə'pleɪtɪd] *adj* galvanisiert
electrotherapy [ɪ'lɛktrə'θɛrəpɪ] *n* Elektrotherapie *f*
elegance ['ɛlɪgəns] *n* Eleganz *f*
elegant ['ɛlɪgənt] *adj* elegant
element ['ɛlɪmənt] *n* Element *nt*; *(of heater, kettle etc)* Heizelement *nt*
elementary [ɛlɪ'mɛntərɪ] *adj* grundlegend; **~ school** Grundschule *f*; *siehe Info-Artikel*; **~ education** Elementarunterricht *m*; **~ maths/French** Grundbegriffe *pl* der Mathematik/des Französischen

ELEMENTARY SCHOOL

Elementary school ist in den USA und Kanada eine Grundschule, an der ein Kind die ersten sechs bis acht Schuljahre verbringt.

- In den USA heißt diese Schule auch „grade school" oder „grammar school". Siehe auch *high school*.

elephant ['ɛlɪfənt] *n* Elefant *m*
elevate ['ɛlɪveɪt] *vt* erheben; (*physically*) heben
elevated railroad ['ɛlɪveɪtɪd-] (*US*) *n* Hochbahn *f*
elevation [ɛlɪ'veɪʃən] *n* Erhebung *f*; (*height*) Höhe *f* über dem Meeresspiegel; (*Archit*) Aufriss *m*
elevator ['ɛlɪveɪtə^r] *n* (*US*) Aufzug *m*, Fahrstuhl *m*; (*in warehouse etc*) Lastenaufzug *m*
eleven [ɪ'lɛvn] *num* elf
elevenses [ɪ'lɛvnzɪz] (*Brit*) *npl* zweites Frühstück *nt*
eleventh [ɪ'lɛvnθ] *num* elfte(r, s); **at the ~ hour** (*fig*) in letzter Minute
elf [ɛlf] (*pl* **elves**) *n* Elf *m*, Elfe *f*; (*mischievous*) Kobold *m*
elicit [ɪ'lɪsɪt] *vt*: **to ~ (from sb)** (*information*) (aus jdm) herausbekommen; (*reaction, response*) (von jdm) bekommen
eligible ['ɛlɪdʒəbl] *adj* (*marriage partner*) begehrt; **to be ~ for sth** für etw infrage kommen; **to be ~ for a pension** pensionsberechtigt sein
eliminate [ɪ'lɪmɪneɪt] *vt* beseitigen; (*candidate etc*) ausschließen; (*team, contestant*) aus dem Wettbewerb werfen
elimination [ɪlɪmɪ'neɪʃən] *n* (*see vb*) Beseitigung *f*; Ausschluss *m*; Ausscheiden *nt*; **by process of ~** durch negative Auslese
élite [eɪ'li:t] *n* Elite *f*
élitist [eɪ'li:tɪst] (*pej*) *adj* elitär
elixir [ɪ'lɪksə^r] *n* Elixier *nt*
Elizabethan [ɪlɪzə'bi:θən] *adj* elisabethanisch
ellipse [ɪ'lɪps] *n* Ellipse *f*
elliptical [ɪ'lɪptɪkl] *adj* elliptisch
elm [ɛlm] *n* Ulme *f*
elocution [ɛlə'kju:ʃən] *n* Sprechtechnik *f*
elongated ['i:lɔŋgeɪtɪd] *adj* lang gestreckt; (*shadow*) verlängert
elope [ɪ'ləup] *vi* weglaufen
elopement [ɪ'ləupmənt] *n* Weglaufen *nt*
eloquence ['ɛləkwəns] *n* (*see adj*) Beredtheit *f*, Wortgewandtheit *f*; Ausdrucksfülle *f*
eloquent ['ɛləkwənt] *adj* beredt, wortgewandt; (*speech, description*) ausdrucksvoll
else [ɛls] *adv* andere(r, s); **something ~** etwas anderes; **somewhere ~** woanders, anderswo; **everywhere ~** sonst überall; **where ~?** wo sonst?; **is there anything ~ I can do?** kann ich sonst noch etwas tun?; **there was little ~ to do** es gab nicht viel anderes zu tun; **everyone ~** alle anderen; **nobody ~ spoke** niemand anders sagte etwas, sonst sagte niemand etwas
elsewhere [ɛls'wɛə^r] *adv* woanders, anderswo; (*go*) woandershin, anderswohin
ELT *n abbr* (*Scol*: = *English Language Teaching*) *Englisch als Unterrichtsfach*
elucidate [ɪ'lu:sɪdeɪt] *vt* erläutern
elude [ɪ'lu:d] *vt* (*captor*) entkommen *+dat*; (*capture*) sich entziehen *+dat*; **this fact/idea ~d him** diese Tatsache/Idee entging ihm
elusive [ɪ'lu:sɪv] *adj* schwer zu fangen; (*quality*) unerreichbar; **he's very ~** er ist sehr schwer zu erreichen
elves [ɛlvz] *npl of* **elf**
emaciated [ɪ'meɪsɪeɪtɪd] *adj* abgezehrt, ausgezehrt
E-mail ['i:meɪl] *n abbr* (= *electronic mail*) E-Mail *f* ▷ *vt* eine E-Mail schicken *+dat*
emanate ['ɛməneɪt] *vi*: **to ~ from** stammen von; (*sound, light etc*) ausgehen von
emancipate [ɪ'mænsɪpeɪt] *vt* (*women*) emanzipieren; (*poor*) befreien; (*slave*) freilassen
emancipation [ɪmænsɪ'peɪʃən] *n* (*see vb*) Emanzipation *f*; Befreiung *f*; Freilassung *f*
emasculate [ɪ'mæskjuleɪt] *vt* schwächen
embalm [ɪm'bɑ:m] *vt* einbalsamieren
embankment [ɪm'bæŋkmənt] *n* Böschung *f*; (*of railway*) Bahndamm *m*; (*of river*) Damm *m*
embargo [ɪm'bɑ:gəu] (*pl* **~es**) *n* Embargo *nt* ▷ *vt* mit einem Embargo belegen; **to put** *or* **impose** *or* **place an ~ on sth** ein Embargo über etw *acc* verhängen; **to lift an ~** ein Embargo aufheben
embark [ɪm'bɑ:k] *vt* einschiffen ▷ *vi*: **to ~ (on)** sich einschiffen (auf); **to ~ on** (*journey*) beginnen; (*task*) in Angriff nehmen; (*course of action*) einschlagen
embarkation [ɛmbɑ:'keɪʃən] *n* Einschiffung *f*
embarkation card *n* Bordkarte *f*
embarrass [ɪm'bærəs] *vt* in Verlegenheit bringen
embarrassed [ɪm'bærəst] *adj* verlegen
embarrassing [ɪm'bærəsɪŋ] *adj* peinlich
embarrassment [ɪm'bærəsmənt] *n* Verlegenheit *f*; (*embarrassing problem*) Peinlichkeit *f*
embassy ['ɛmbəsɪ] *n* Botschaft *f*; **the Swiss E~** die Schweizer Botschaft
embedded [ɪm'bɛdɪd] *adj* eingebettet; (*attitude, belief, feeling*) verwurzelt
embellish [ɪm'bɛlɪʃ] *vt* (*account*) ausschmücken; **to be ~ed with** geschmückt sein mit
embers ['ɛmbəz] *npl* Glut *f*
embezzle [ɪm'bɛzl] *vt* unterschlagen
embezzlement [ɪm'bɛzlmənt] *n* Unterschlagung *f*
embezzler [ɪm'bɛzlə^r] *n jd, der eine Unterschlagung begangen hat*
embitter [ɪm'bɪtə^r] *vt* verbittern
embittered [ɪm'bɪtəd] *adj* verbittert
emblem ['ɛmbləm] *n* Emblem *nt*; (*symbol*) Wahrzeichen *nt*
embodiment [ɪm'bɔdɪmənt] *n* Verkörperung *f*; **to be the ~ of ...** (*subj: thing*) ... verkörpern; (*: person*) ... in Person sein
embody [ɪm'bɔdɪ] *vt* verkörpern; (*include, contain*) enthalten
embolden [ɪm'bəuldn] *vt* ermutigen
embolism ['ɛmbəlɪzəm] *n* Embolie *f*
embossed [ɪm'bɔst] *adj* geprägt; **~ with a logo**

mit geprägtem Logo
embrace [ɪm'breɪs] *vt* umarmen; (*include*) umfassen ▷ *vi* sich umarmen ▷ *n* Umarmung *f*
embroider [ɪm'brɔɪdəʳ] *vt* (*cloth*) besticken; (*fig: story*) ausschmücken
embroidery [ɪm'brɔɪdərɪ] *n* Stickerei *f*; (*activity*) Sticken *nt*
embroil [ɪm'brɔɪl] *vt*: **to become ~ed (in sth)** (in etw *acc*) verwickelt *or* hineingezogen werden
embryo ['ɛmbrɪəu] *n* Embryo *m*; (*fig*) Keim *m*
emcee [ɛm'siː] *n* Conférencier *m*
emend [ɪ'mɛnd] *vt* verbessern, korrigieren
emerald ['ɛmərəld] *n* Smaragd *m*
emerge [ɪ'məːdʒ] *vi*: **to ~ (from)** auftauchen (aus); (*from sleep*) erwachen (aus); (*from imprisonment*) entlassen werden (aus); (*from discussion etc*) sich herausstellen (bei); (*new idea, industry, society*) entstehen (aus); **it ~s that** (*Brit*) es stellt sich heraus, dass
emergence [ɪ'məːdʒəns] *n* Entstehung *f*
emergency [ɪ'məːdʒənsɪ] *n* Notfall *m* ▷ *cpd* Not-; (*repair*) notdürftig; **in an ~** im Notfall; **state of ~** Notstand *m*
emergency cord (*US*) *n* Notbremse *f*
emergency exit *n* Notausgang *m*
emergency landing *n* Notlandung *f*
emergency lane (*US*) *n* Seitenstreifen *m*
emergency road service (*US*) *n* Pannendienst *m*
emergency services *npl*: **the ~** der Notdienst
emergency stop (*Brit*) *n* Vollbremsung *f*
emergent [ɪ'məːdʒənt] *adj* jung, aufstrebend
emeritus [ɪ'mɛrɪtəs] *adj* emeritiert
emery board ['ɛmərɪ-] *n* Papiernagelfeile *f*
emery paper ['ɛmərɪ-] *n* Schmirgelpapier *nt*
emetic [ɪ'mɛtɪk] *n* Brechmittel *nt*
emigrant ['ɛmɪgrənt] *n* Auswanderer *m*, Auswanderin *f*, Emigrant(in) *m(f)*
emigrate ['ɛmɪgreɪt] *vi* auswandern, emigrieren
emigration [ɛmɪ'greɪʃən] *n* Auswanderung *f*, Emigration *f*
émigré ['ɛmɪgreɪ] *n* Emigrant(in) *m(f)*
eminence ['ɛmɪnəns] *n* Bedeutung *f*
eminent ['ɛmɪnənt] *adj* bedeutend
eminently ['ɛmɪnəntlɪ] *adv* ausgesprochen
emirate ['ɛmɪrɪt] *n* Emirat *nt*
emission [ɪ'mɪʃən] *n* Emission *f*
emissions [ɪ'mɪʃənz] *npl* Emissionen *pl*
emit [ɪ'mɪt] *vt* abgeben; (*smell*) ausströmen; (*light, heat*) ausstrahlen
emolument [ɪ'mɔljumənt] *n* (*often pl*) Vergütung *f*; (*fee*) Honorar *nt*; (*salary*) Bezüge *pl*
emotion [ɪ'məuʃən] *n* Gefühl *nt*
emotional [ɪ'məuʃənl] *adj* emotional; (*exhaustion*) seelisch; (*scene*) ergreifend; (*speech*) gefühlsbetont
emotionally [ɪ'məuʃnəlɪ] *adv* emotional; (*be involved*) gefühlsmäßig; (*speak*) gefühlvoll; **~ disturbed** seelisch gestört
emotive [ɪ'məutɪv] *adj* emotional
empathy ['ɛmpəθɪ] *n* Einfühlungsvermögen *nt*; **to feel ~ with sb** sich in jdn einfühlen
emperor ['ɛmpərəʳ] *n* Kaiser *m*
emphases ['ɛmfəsiːz] *npl of* **emphasis**
emphasis ['ɛmfəsɪs] (*pl* **emphases**) *n* Betonung *f*; (*importance*) (Schwer)gewicht *nt*; **to lay** *or* **place ~ on sth** etw betonen; **the ~ is on reading** das Schwergewicht liegt auf dem Lesen
emphasize ['ɛmfəsaɪz] *vt* betonen; (*feature*) hervorheben; **I must ~ that ...** ich möchte betonen, dass ...
emphatic [ɛm'fætɪk] *adj* nachdrücklich; (*denial*) energisch; (*person, manner*) bestimmt, entschieden
emphatically [ɛm'fætɪklɪ] *adv* nachdrücklich; (*certainly*) eindeutig
emphysema [ɛmfɪ'siːmə] *n* Emphysem *nt*
empire ['ɛmpaɪəʳ] *n* Reich *nt*
empirical [ɛm'pɪrɪkl] *adj* empirisch
employ [ɪm'plɔɪ] *vt* beschäftigen; (*tool, weapon*) verwenden; **he's ~ed in a bank** er ist bei einer Bank angestellt
employee [ɪmplɔɪ'iː] *n* Angestellte(r) *f(m)*
employer [ɪm'plɔɪəʳ] *n* Arbeitgeber(in) *m(f)*
employment [ɪm'plɔɪmənt] *n* Arbeit *f*; **to find ~** Arbeit *or* eine (An)stellung finden; **without ~** stellungslos; **your place of ~** Ihre Arbeitsstätte *f*
employment agency *n* Stellenvermittlung *f*
employment exchange (*Brit*) *n* Arbeitsamt *nt*
empower [ɪm'pauəʳ] *vt*: **to ~ sb to do sth** jdn ermächtigen, etw zu tun
empress ['ɛmprɪs] *n* Kaiserin *f*
empties ['ɛmptɪz] *npl* Leergut *nt*
emptiness ['ɛmptɪnɪs] *n* Leere *f*
empty ['ɛmptɪ] *adj* leer; (*house, room*) leer stehend; (*space*) frei ▷ *vt* leeren; (*place, house etc*) räumen ▷ *vi* sich leeren; (*liquid*) abfließen; (*river*) münden; **on an ~ stomach** auf nüchternen Magen; **to ~ into** (*river*) münden *or* sich ergießen in +*acc*
empty-handed ['ɛmptɪ'hændɪd] *adj* mit leeren Händen; **he returned ~** er kehrte unverrichteter Dinge zurück
empty-headed ['ɛmptɪ'hɛdɪd] *adj* strohdumm
EMS *n abbr* (= *European Monetary System*) EWS *nt*
EMT (*US*) *n abbr* (= *emergency medical technician*) ≈ Sanitäter(in) *m(f)*
EMU *n abbr* (= *Economic and Monetary Union*) EWU *f*
emu ['iːmjuː] *n* Emu *m*
emulate ['ɛmjuleɪt] *vt* nacheifern +*dat*
emulsion [ɪ'mʌlʃən] *n* Emulsion *f*; (*also*: **emulsion paint**) Emulsionsfarbe *f*
enable [ɪ'neɪbl] *vt*: **to ~ sb to do sth** (*permit*) es jdm erlauben, etw zu tun; (*make possible*) es jdm ermöglichen, etw zu tun
enact [ɪ'nækt] *vt* (*law*) erlassen; (*play*) aufführen; (*role*) darstellen, spielen
enamel [ɪ'næməl] *n* Email *nt*, Emaille *f*; (*also*: **enamel paint**) Email(le)lack *m*; (*of tooth*) Zahnschmelz *m*
enamoured [ɪ'næməd] *adj*: **to be ~ of** (*person*) verliebt sein in +*acc*; (*pastime, idea, belief*)

angetan sein von
encampment [ɪn'kæmpmənt] *n* Lager *nt*
encased [ɪn'keɪst] *adj*: **~ in** (*shell*) umgeben von; **to be ~ in** (*limb*) in Gips liegen *or* sein
encash [ɪn'kæʃ] (*Brit*) *vt* einlösen
enchant [ɪn'tʃɑːnt] *vt* bezaubern
enchanted [ɪn'tʃɑːntɪd] *adj* verzaubert
enchanting [ɪn'tʃɑːntɪŋ] *adj* bezaubernd
encircle [ɪn'səːkl] *vt* umgeben; (*person*) umringen; (*building: police etc*) umstellen
encl. *abbr* (*on letters etc: = enclosed, enclosure*) Anl.
enclave ['ɛnkleɪv] *n*: **an ~ (of)** eine Enklave (*+gen*)
enclose [ɪn'kləuz] *vt* umgeben; (*land, space*) begrenzen; (*with fence*) einzäunen; (*letter etc*): **to ~ (with)** beilegen (*+dat*); **please find ~d** als Anlage übersenden wir Ihnen
enclosure [ɪn'kləuʒəʳ] *n* eingefriedeter Bereich *m*; (*in letter etc*) Anlage *f*
encoder [ɪn'kəudəʳ] *n* Codierer *m*
encompass [ɪn'kʌmpəs] *vt* umfassen
encore [ɔŋ'kɔːʳ] *excl* Zugabe! ▷ *n* Zugabe *f*
encounter [ɪn'kauntəʳ] *n* Begegnung *f* ▷ *vt* begegnen *+dat*; (*problem*) stoßen auf *+acc*
encourage [ɪn'kʌrɪdʒ] *vt* (*activity, attitude*) unterstützen; (*growth, industry*) fördern; **to ~ sb (to do sth)** jdn ermutigen(, etw zu tun)
encouragement [ɪn'kʌrɪdʒmənt] *n* (*see vb*) Unterstützung *f*; Förderung *f*; Ermutigung *f*
encouraging [ɪn'kʌrɪdʒɪŋ] *adj* ermutigend
encroach [ɪn'krəutʃ] *vi*: **to ~ (up)on** (*rights*) eingreifen in *+acc*; (*property*) eindringen in *+acc*; (*time*) in Anspruch nehmen
encrusted [ɪn'krʌstɪd] *adj*: **~ with** (*gems*) besetzt mit; (*snow, dirt*) verkrustet mit
encumber [ɪn'kʌmbəʳ] *vt*: **to be ~ed with** beladen sein mit; (*debts*) belastet sein mit
encyclopaedia, **encyclopedia** [ɛnsaɪkləu'piːdɪə] *n* Lexikon *nt*, Enzyklopädie *f*
end [ɛnd] *n* Ende *nt*; (*of film, book*) Schluss *m*, Ende *nt*; (*of table*) Schmalseite *f*; (*of pointed object*) Spitze *f*; (*aim*) Zweck *m*, Ziel *nt* ▷ *vt* (*also*: **bring to an end, put an end to**) beenden ▷ *vi* enden; **from ~ to end** von einem Ende zum anderen; **to come to an ~** zu Ende gehen; **to be at an ~** zu Ende sein; **in the ~** schließlich; **on ~** hochkant; **to stand on ~** (*hair*) zu Berge stehen; **for hours on ~** stundenlang ununterbrochen; **for 5 hours on ~** 5 Stunden ununterbrochen; **at the ~ of the street** am Ende der Straße; **at the ~ of the day** (*Brit: fig*) letztlich; **to this end, with this ~ in view** mit diesem Ziel vor Augen
▸ **end up** *vi*: **to ~ up in** (*place*) landen in *+dat*; **to ~ up in trouble** Ärger bekommen; **to ~ up doing sth** etw schließlich tun
endanger [ɪn'deɪndʒəʳ] *vt* gefährden; **an ~ed species** eine vom Aussterben bedrohte Art
endear [ɪn'dɪəʳ] *vt*: **to ~ o.s. to sb** sich bei jdm beliebt machen
endearing [ɪn'dɪərɪŋ] *adj* gewinnend
endearment [ɪn'dɪəmənt] *n*: **to whisper ~s** zärtliche Worte flüstern; **term of ~** Kosewort *nt*, Kosename *m*
endeavour, (*US*) **endeavor** [ɪn'dɛvəʳ] *n* Anstrengung *f*, Bemühung *f*; (*effort*) Bestrebung *f* ▷ *vi*: **to ~ to do sth** (*attempt*) sich anstrengen *or* bemühen, etw zu tun; (*strive*) bestrebt sein, etw zu tun
endemic [ɛn'dɛmɪk] *adj* endemisch, verbreitet
ending ['ɛndɪŋ] *n* Ende *nt*, Schluss *m*; (*Ling*) Endung *f*
endive ['ɛndaɪv] *n* Endivie *f*; (*chicory*) Chicorée *f or m*
endless ['ɛndlɪs] *adj* endlos; (*patience, resources, possibilities*) unbegrenzt
endorse [ɪn'dɔːs] *vt* (*cheque*) indossieren, auf der Rückseite unterzeichnen; (*proposal, plan*) billigen; (*candidate*) unterstützen
endorsee [ɪndɔː'siː] *n* Indossat *m*
endorsement [ɪn'dɔːsmənt] *n* Billigung *f*; (*of candidate*) Unterstützung *f*; (*Brit: on driving licence*) Strafvermerk *m*
endow [ɪn'dau] *vt* (*institution*) eine Stiftung machen an *+acc*; **to be ~ed with** besitzen
endowment [ɪn'daumənt] *n* Stiftung *f*; (*quality*) Begabung *f*
endowment assurance *n* Versicherung *f* auf den Erlebensfall, Erlebensversicherung *f*
endowment mortgage *n* Hypothek *f* mit Lebensversicherung
end product *n* Endprodukt *nt*; (*fig*) Produkt *nt*
end result *n* Endergebnis *nt*
endurable [ɪn'djuərəbl] *adj* erträglich
endurance [ɪn'djuərəns] *n* Durchhaltevermögen *nt*; (*patience*) Geduld *f*
endurance test *n* Belastungsprobe *f*
endure [ɪn'djuəʳ] *vt* ertragen ▷ *vi* Bestand haben
enduring [ɪn'djuərɪŋ] *adj* dauerhaft
end user *n* (*Comput*) Endbenutzer *m*
enema ['ɛnɪmə] *n* Klistier *nt*, Einlauf *m*
enemy ['ɛnəmɪ] *adj* feindlich; (*strategy*) des Feindes ▷ *n* Feind(in) *m(f)*; **to make an ~ of sb** sich *dat* jdn zum Feind machen
energetic [ɛnə'dʒɛtɪk] *adj* aktiv
energy ['ɛnədʒɪ] *n* Energie *f*; **Department of E~** Energieministerium *nt*
energy crisis *n* Energiekrise *f*
energy-saving ['ɛnədʒɪ'seɪvɪŋ] *adj* energiesparend; (*policy*) energiebewusst
enervating ['ɛnəveɪtɪŋ] *adj* strapazierend
enforce [ɪn'fɔːs] *vt* (*law, rule, decision*) Geltung verschaffen *+dat*
enforced [ɪn'fɔːst] *adj* erzwungen
enfranchise [ɪn'fræntʃaɪz] *vt* das Wahlrecht geben *or* erteilen *+dat*
engage [ɪn'geɪdʒ] *vt* in Anspruch nehmen; (*employ*) einstellen; (*lawyer*) sich *dat* nehmen; (*Mil*) angreifen ▷ *vi* (*Tech*) einrasten; **to ~ the clutch** einkuppeln; **to ~ sb in conversation** jdn in ein Gespräch verwickeln; **to ~ in** sich beteiligen an *+dat*; **to ~ in commerce** kaufmännisch tätig sein; **to ~ in study** studieren
engaged [ɪn'geɪdʒd] *adj* verlobt; (*Brit: busy,*

in use) besetzt; **to get** ~ sich verloben; **he is ~ in research/a survey** er ist mit Forschungsarbeit/einer Umfrage beschäftigt
engaged tone (*Brit*) *n* Besetztzeichen *nt*
engagement [ɪn'geɪdʒmənt] *n* Verabredung *f*; (*booking*) Engagement *nt*; (*to marry*) Verlobung *f*; (*Mil*) Gefecht *nt*, Kampf *m*; **I have a previous ~** ich habe schon eine Verabredung
engagement ring *n* Verlobungsring *m*
engaging [ɪn'geɪdʒɪŋ] *adj* einnehmend
engender [ɪn'dʒɛndəʳ] *vt* erzeugen
engine ['ɛndʒɪn] *n* Motor *m*; (*Rail*) Lok(omotive) *f*
engine driver *n* (*Rail*) Lok(omotiv)führer(in) *m(f)*
engineer [ɛndʒɪ'nɪəʳ] *n* Ingenieur(in) *m(f)*; (*Brit: for repairs*) Techniker(in) *m(f)*; (*US: Rail*) Lok(omotiv)führer(in) *m(f)*; (*on ship*) Maschinist(in) *m(f)*; **civil/mechanical ~** Bau-/Maschinenbauingenieur(in) *m(f)*
engineering [ɛndʒɪ'nɪərɪŋ] *n* Technik *f*; (*design, construction*) Konstruktion *f* ▷ *cpd*: **~ works** *or* **factory** Maschinenfabrik *f*
engine failure *n* Maschinenschaden *m*; (*Aut*) Motorschaden *m*
engine trouble *n* Maschinenschaden *m*; (*Aut*) Motorschaden *m*
England ['ɪŋglənd] *n* England *nt*
English ['ɪŋglɪʃ] *adj* englisch ▷ *n* Englisch *nt*; **the English** *npl* die Engländer *pl*; **an ~ speaker** *jd, der Englisch spricht*
English Channel *n*: **the ~** der Ärmelkanal
Englishman ['ɪŋglɪʃmən] (*irreg: like* **man**) *n* Engländer *m*
English-speaking ['ɪŋglɪʃspiːkɪŋ] *adj* (*country*) englischsprachig
Englishwoman ['ɪŋglɪʃwumən] (*irreg: like* **woman**) *n* Engländerin *f*
engrave [ɪn'greɪv] *vt* gravieren; (*name etc*) eingravieren; (*fig*) einprägen
engraving [ɪn'greɪvɪŋ] *n* Stich *m*
engrossed [ɪn'grəust] *adj*: **~ in** vertieft in *+acc*
engulf [ɪn'gʌlf] *vt* verschlingen; (*subj: panic, fear*) überkommen
enhance [ɪn'hɑːns] *vt* verbessern; (*enjoyment, beauty*) erhöhen
enigma [ɪ'nɪgmə] *n* Rätsel *nt*
enigmatic [ɛnɪg'mætɪk] *adj* rätselhaft
enjoy [ɪn'dʒɔɪ] *vt* genießen; (*health, fortune*) sich erfreuen *+gen*; (*success*) haben; **to ~ o.s.** sich amüsieren; **I ~ dancing** ich tanze gerne
enjoyable [ɪn'dʒɔɪəbl] *adj* nett, angenehm
enjoyment [ɪn'dʒɔɪmənt] *n* Vergnügen *nt*; (*activity*) Freude *f*
enlarge [ɪn'lɑːdʒ] *vt* vergrößern; (*scope*) erweitern ▷ *vi*: **to ~ on** weiter ausführen
enlarged [ɪn'lɑːdʒd] *adj* erweitert; (*Med*) vergrößert
enlargement [ɪn'lɑːdʒmənt] *n* Vergrößerung *f*
enlighten [ɪn'laɪtn] *vt* aufklären
enlightened [ɪn'laɪtnd] *adj* aufgeklärt
enlightening [ɪn'laɪtnɪŋ] *adj* aufschlussreich
enlightenment [ɪn'laɪtnmənt] *n* (*also Hist: Enlightenment*) Aufklärung *f*
enlist [ɪn'lɪst] *vt* anwerben; (*support, help*) gewinnen ▷ *vi*: **to ~ in** eintreten in *+acc*; **~ed man** (*US: Mil*) gemeiner Soldat *m*; (*US: in navy*) Matrose *m*
enliven [ɪn'laɪvn] *vt* beleben
enmity ['ɛnmɪtɪ] *n* Feindschaft *f*
ennoble [ɪ'nəubl] *vt* adeln; (*fig: dignify*) erheben
enormity [ɪ'nɔːmɪtɪ] *n* ungeheure Größe *f*
enormous [ɪ'nɔːməs] *adj* gewaltig, ungeheuer; (*pleasure, success etc*) riesig
enormously [ɪ'nɔːməslɪ] *adv* enorm; (*rich*) ungeheuer
enough [ɪ'nʌf] *adj* genug, genügend ▷ *pron* genug ▷ *adv*: **big ~** groß genug; **he has not worked ~** er hat nicht genug *or* genügend gearbeitet; **have you got ~?** haben Sie genug?; **~ to eat** genug zu essen; **will 5 be ~?** reichen 5?; **I've had ~!** jetzt reichts mir aber!; **it's hot ~ (as it is)** es ist heiß genug; **he was kind ~ to lend me the money** er war so gut und hat mir das Geld geliehen; **~!** es reicht!; **that's ~, thanks** danke, das reicht *or* ist genug; **I've had ~ of him** ich habe genug von ihm; **funnily/oddly ~** ... komischerweise ...
enquire [ɪn'kwaɪəʳ] *vt, vi* = **inquire**
enrage [ɪn'reɪdʒ] *vt* wütend machen
enrich [ɪn'rɪtʃ] *vt* bereichern
enrol, (*US*) **enroll** [ɪn'rəul] *vt* anmelden; (*at university*) einschreiben, immatrikulieren ▷ *vi* (*see vt*) sich anmelden; sich einschreiben, sich immatrikulieren
enrolment, (*US*) **enrollment** [ɪn'rəulmənt] *n* (*see vb*) Anmeldung *f*; Einschreibung *f*, Immatrikulation *f*
en route [ɔn'ruːt] *adv* unterwegs; **~ for** auf dem Weg nach; **~ from London to Berlin** auf dem Weg von London nach Berlin
ensconced [ɪn'skɔnst] *adj*: **she is ~ in ...** sie hat es sich *dat* in ... *dat* gemütlich gemacht
ensemble [ɔn'sɔmbl] *n* Ensemble *nt*
enshrine [ɪn'ʃraɪn] *vt* bewahren; **to be ~d in** verankert sein in *+dat*
ensue [ɪn'sjuː] *vi* folgen
ensuing [ɪn'sjuːɪŋ] *adj* folgend
ensure [ɪn'ʃuəʳ] *vt* garantieren; **to ~ that** sicherstellen, dass
ENT *n abbr* (*Med: = ear, nose, and throat*) HNO
entail [ɪn'teɪl] *vt* mit sich bringen
entangled [ɪn'tæŋgld] *adj*: **to become ~ (in)** sich verfangen (in *+dat*)
enter ['ɛntəʳ] *vt* betreten; (*club*) beitreten *+dat*; (*army*) gehen zu; (*profession*) ergreifen; (*race, contest*) sich beteiligen an *+dat*; (*sb for a competition*) anmelden; (*write down*) eintragen; (*Comput: data*) eingeben ▷ *vi* (*come in*) hereinkommen; (*go in*) hineingehen
▸ **enter for** *vt fus* anmelden für
▸ **enter into** *vt fus* (*discussion, negotiations*) aufnehmen; (*correspondence*) treten in *+acc*; (*agreement*) schließen
▸ **enter up** *vt* eintragen
▸ **enter (up)on** *vt fus* (*career, policy*) einschlagen

enteritis [ɛntəˈraɪtɪs] *n* Dünndarmentzündung *f*
enterprise [ˈɛntəpraɪz] *n* Unternehmen *nt*; *(initiative)* Initiative *f*; **free ~** freies Unternehmertum *nt*; **private ~** Privatunternehmertum *nt*
enterprising [ˈɛntəpraɪzɪŋ] *adj* einfallsreich
entertain [ɛntəˈteɪn] *vt* unterhalten; *(invite)* einladen; *(idea, plan)* erwägen
entertainer [ɛntəˈteɪnəʳ] *n* Unterhalter(in) *m(f)*, Entertainer(in) *m(f)*
entertaining [ɛntəˈteɪnɪŋ] *adj* amüsant ▷ *n*: **to do a lot of ~** sehr oft Gäste haben
entertainment [ɛntəˈteɪnmənt] *n* Unterhaltung *f*; *(show)* Darbietung *f*
entertainment allowance *n* Aufwandspauschale *f*
enthral [ɪnˈθrɔːl] *vt* begeistern; *(story)* fesseln
enthralled [ɪnˈθrɔːld] *adj* gefesselt; **he was ~ by** *or* **with the book** das Buch fesselte ihn
enthralling [ɪnˈθrɔːlɪŋ] *adj* fesselnd; *(details)* spannend
enthuse [ɪnˈθuːz] *vi*: **to ~ about** *or* **over** schwärmen von
enthusiasm [ɪnˈθuːzɪæzəm] *n* Begeisterung *f*
enthusiast [ɪnˈθuːzɪæst] *n* Enthusiast(in) *m(f)*; **he's a jazz/sports ~** er begeistert sich für Jazz/Sport
enthusiastic [ɪnθuːzɪˈæstɪk] *adj* begeistert; *(response, reception)* enthusiastisch; **to be ~ about** begeistert sein von
entice [ɪnˈtaɪs] *vt* locken; *(tempt)* verleiten
enticing [ɪnˈtaɪsɪŋ] *adj* verlockend
entire [ɪnˈtaɪəʳ] *adj* ganz
entirely [ɪnˈtaɪəlɪ] *adv* völlig
entirety [ɪnˈtaɪərətɪ] *n*: **in its ~** in seiner Gesamtheit
entitle [ɪnˈtaɪtl] *vt*: **to ~ sb to sth** jdn zu etw berechtigen; **to ~ sb to do sth** jdn dazu berechtigen, etw zu tun
entitled [ɪnˈtaɪtld] *adj*: **a book/film** *etc* **~ ...** ein Buch/Film *etc* mit dem Titel ...; **to be ~ to do sth** das Recht haben, etw zu tun
entity [ˈɛntɪtɪ] *n* Wesen *nt*
entourage [ɔntuˈrɑːʒ] *n* Gefolge *nt*
entrails [ˈɛntreɪlz] *npl* Eingeweide *pl*
entrance [*n* ˈɛntrns, *vt* ɪnˈtrɑːns] *n* Eingang *m*; *(arrival)* Ankunft *f*; *(on stage)* Auftritt *m* ▷ *vt* bezaubern; **to gain ~ to** *(building etc)* sich *dat* Zutritt verschaffen zu; *(university)* die Zulassung erhalten zu; *(profession etc)* Zugang erhalten zu
entrance examination *n* Aufnahmeprüfung *f*
entrance fee *n* Eintrittsgeld *nt*
entrance ramp *(US)* *n* Auffahrt *f*
entrancing [ɪnˈtrɑːnsɪŋ] *adj* bezaubernd
entrant [ˈɛntrnt] *n* Teilnehmer(in) *m(f)*; *(Brit: in exam)* Prüfling *m*
entreat [ɛnˈtriːt] *vt*: **to ~ sb to do sth** jdn anflehen, etw zu tun
entreaty [ɛnˈtriːtɪ] *n* (flehentliche) Bitte *f*
entrée [ˈɔntreɪ] *n* Hauptgericht *nt*
entrenched [ɛnˈtrɛntʃt] *adj* verankert; *(ideas)* festgesetzt
entrepreneur [ˈɔntrəprəˈnəːʳ] *n* Unternehmer(in) *m(f)*
entrepreneurial [ˈɔntrəprəˈnəːrɪəl] *adj* unternehmerisch
entrust [ɪnˈtrʌst] *vt*: **to ~ sth to sb** jdm etw anvertrauen; **to ~ sb with sth** *(task)* jdn mit etw betrauen; *(secret, valuables)* jdm etw anvertrauen
entry [ˈɛntrɪ] *n* Eingang *m*; *(in competition)* Meldung *f*; *(in register, account book, reference book)* Eintrag *m*; *(arrival)* Eintritt *m*; *(to country)* Einreise *f*; **"no ~"** „Zutritt verboten"; *(Aut)* „Einfahrt verboten"; **single/double ~ bookkeeping** einfache/doppelte Buchführung *f*
entry form *n* Anmeldeformular *nt*
entry phone *(Brit)* *n* Türsprechanlage *f*
entwine [ɪnˈtwaɪn] *vt* verflechten
enumerate [ɪˈnjuːməreɪt] *vt* aufzählen
enunciate [ɪˈnʌnsɪeɪt] *vt* artikulieren; *(principle, plan etc)* formulieren
envelop [ɪnˈvɛləp] *vt* einhüllen
envelope [ˈɛnvələup] *n* Umschlag *m*
enviable [ˈɛnvɪəbl] *adj* beneidenswert
envious [ˈɛnvɪəs] *adj* neidisch; **to be ~ of sth/sb** auf etw/jdn neidisch sein
environment [ɪnˈvaɪərnmənt] *n* Umwelt *f*; **Department of the E~** *(Brit)* Umweltministerium *nt*
environmental [ɪnvaɪərnˈmɛntl] *adj* *(problems, pollution etc)* Umwelt-; **~ expert** Umweltexperte *m*, Umweltexpertin *f*; **~ studies** Umweltkunde *f*
environmentalist [ɪnvaɪərnˈmɛntlɪst] *n* Umweltschützer(in) *m(f)*
Environmental Protection Agency *(US)* *n* *staatliche Umweltbehörde der USA*
environment-friendly *adj* umweltfreundlich
envisage [ɪnˈvɪzɪdʒ] *vt* sich *dat* vorstellen; **I ~ that ...** ich stelle mir vor, dass ...
envision [ɪnˈvɪʒən] *(US)* *vt* = **envisage**
envoy [ˈɛnvɔɪ] *n* Gesandte(r) *f(m)*
envy [ˈɛnvɪ] *n* Neid *m* ▷ *vt* beneiden; **to ~ sb sth** jdn um etw beneiden
enzyme [ˈɛnzaɪm] *n* Enzym *nt*
eon [ˈiːən] *n* Äon *m*, Ewigkeit *f*
EPA *(US)* *n abbr* = **Environmental Protection Agency**
ephemeral [ɪˈfɛmərl] *adj* kurzlebig
epic [ˈɛpɪk] *n* Epos *nt* ▷ *adj* *(journey)* lang und abenteuerlich
epicentre, *(US)* **epicenter** [ˈɛpɪsɛntəʳ] *n* Epizentrum *nt*
epidemic [ɛpɪˈdɛmɪk] *n* Epidemie *f*
epigram [ˈɛpɪgræm] *n* Epigramm *nt*
epilepsy [ˈɛpɪlɛpsɪ] *n* Epilepsie *f*
epileptic [ɛpɪˈlɛptɪk] *adj* epileptisch ▷ *n* Epileptiker(in) *m(f)*
epilogue [ˈɛpɪlɔg] *n* Epilog *m*, Nachwort *nt*
Epiphany [ɪˈpɪfənɪ] *n* Dreikönigsfest *nt*
episcopal [ɪˈpɪskəpl] *adj* bischöflich; **the E~ Church** die Episkopalkirche
episode [ˈɛpɪsəud] *n* Episode *f*; *(TV, Radio)*

Folge *f*
epistle [ɪ'pɪsl] *n* Epistel *f*; (*Rel*) Brief *m*
epitaph ['ɛpɪtɑːf] *n* Epitaph *nt*; (*on gravestone etc*) Grab(in)schrift *f*
epithet ['ɛpɪθɛt] *n* Beiname *m*
epitome [ɪ'pɪtəmɪ] *n* Inbegriff *m*
epitomize [ɪ'pɪtəmaɪz] *vt* verkörpern
epoch ['iːpɔk] *n* Epoche *f*
epoch-making ['iːpɔkmeɪkɪŋ] *adj* epochal; (*discovery*) epochemachend
eponymous [ɪ'pɔnɪməs] *adj* namengebend
equable ['ɛkwəbl] *adj* ausgeglichen; (*reply*) sachlich
equal ['iːkwl] *adj* gleich ▷ *n* Gleichgestellte(r) *f(m)* ▷ *vt* gleichkommen *+dat*; (*number*) gleich sein *+dat*; **they are roughly ~ in size** sie sind ungefähr gleich groß; **the number of exports should be ~ to imports** Export- und Importzahlen sollten gleich sein; **~ opportunities** Chancengleichheit *f*; **to be ~ to** (*task*) gewachsen sein *+dat*; **two times two ~s four** zwei mal zwei ist (gleich) vier
equality [iː'kwɔlɪtɪ] *n* Gleichheit *f*; **~ of opportunity** Chancengleichheit *f*
equalize ['iːkwəlaɪz] *vt* angleichen ▷ *vi* (*Sport*) ausgleichen
equally ['iːkwəlɪ] *adv* gleichmäßig; (*good, bad etc*) gleich; **they are ~ clever** sie sind beide gleich klug
Equal Opportunities Commission, (*US*) **Equal Employment Opportunity Commission** *n* Ausschuss *m* für Chancengleichheit am Arbeitsplatz
equal sign, **equals sign** *n* Gleichheitszeichen *nt*
equanimity [ɛkwə'nɪmɪtɪ] *n* Gleichmut *m*, Gelassenheit *f*
equate [ɪ'kweɪt] *vt*: **to ~ sth with** etw gleichsetzen mit ▷ *vt* (*compare*) auf die gleiche Stufe stellen; **to ~ A to B** A und B auf die gleiche Stufe stellen
equation [ɪ'kweɪʃən] *n* Gleichung *f*
equator [ɪ'kweɪtə^r] *n* Äquator *m*
equatorial [ɛkwə'tɔːrɪəl] *adj* äquatorial
Equatorial Guinea *n* Äquatorial-Guinea *nt*
equestrian [ɪ'kwɛstrɪən] *adj* (*sport, dress etc*) Reit-; (*statue*) Reiter- ▷ *n* Reiter(in) *m(f)*
equilibrium [iːkwɪ'lɪbrɪəm] *n* Gleichgewicht *nt*
equinox ['iːkwɪnɔks] *n* Tagundnachtgleiche *f*; **the spring/autumn ~** die Frühjahrs-/die Herbst-Tagundnachtgleiche *f*
equip [ɪ'kwɪp] *vt*: **to ~ (with)** (*person, army*) ausrüsten (mit); (*room, car etc*) ausstatten (mit); **to ~ sb for** jdn vorbereiten auf *+acc*; **to be well ~ped** gut ausgerüstet sein
equipment [ɪ'kwɪpmənt] *n* Ausrüstung *f*
equitable ['ɛkwɪtəbl] *adj* gerecht
equities ['ɛkwɪtɪz] (*Brit*) *npl* Stammaktien *pl*
equity ['ɛkwɪtɪ] *n* Gerechtigkeit *f*
equity capital *n* Eigenkapital *nt*
equivalent [ɪ'kwɪvələnt] *adj* gleich, gleichwertig ▷ *n* Gegenstück *nt*; **to be ~ to** *or* **the ~ of** entsprechen *+dat*
equivocal [ɪ'kwɪvəkl] *adj* vieldeutig; (*open to suspicion*) zweifelhaft
equivocate [ɪ'kwɪvəkeɪt] *vi* ausweichen, ausweichend antworten
equivocation [ɪkwɪvə'keɪʃən] *n* Ausflucht *f*, ausweichende Antwort *f*
ER (*Brit*) *abbr* (*= Elizabeth Regina*) *offizieller Namenszug der Königin*
ERA (*US*) *n abbr* (*Pol: = Equal Rights Amendment*) *Artikel der amerikanischen Verfassung zur Gleichberechtigung*; (*Baseball: = earned run average*) *durch Eigenleistung erzielte Läufe*
era ['ɪərə] *n* Ära *f*, Epoche *f*
eradicate [ɪ'rædɪkeɪt] *vt* ausrotten
erase [ɪ'reɪz] *vt* (*tape: Comput*) löschen; (*writing*) ausradieren; (*thought, feeling*) auslöschen
eraser [ɪ'reɪzə^r] *n* Radiergummi *m*
erect [ɪ'rɛkt] *adj* aufrecht; (*tail*) hoch erhoben; (*ears*) gespitzt ▷ *vt* bauen; (*assemble*) aufstellen
erection [ɪ'rɛkʃən] *n* Bauen *nt*; (*of statue*) Errichten *nt*; (*of tent, machinery etc*) Aufstellen *nt*; (*Physiol*) Erektion *f*
ergonomics [əːgə'nɔmɪks] *n sing* Ergonomie *f*, Ergonomik *f*
ERISA (*US*) *n abbr* (*= Employee Retirement Income Security Act*) *Gesetz zur Regelung der Rentenversicherung*
Eritrea *n* Eritrea *nt*
ERM *n abbr* (*= Exchange Rate Mechanism*) Wechselkursmechanismus *m*
ermine ['əːmɪn] *n* (*fur*) Hermelin *m*
Ernie, **Ernie** ['əːnɪ] (*Brit*) *n abbr* (*= Electronic Random Number Indicator Equipment*) *Gerät zur Ermittlung von Gewinnnummern für Prämiensparer*
erode [ɪ'rəud] *vt* erodieren, auswaschen; (*metal*) zerfressen; (*confidence, power*) untergraben
erogenous [ɪ'rɔdʒənəs] *adj* erogen
erosion [ɪ'rəuʒən] *n* (*see vb*) Erosion *f*, Auswaschen *nt*; Zerfressen *nt*; Untergraben *nt*
erotic [ɪ'rɔtɪk] *adj* erotisch
eroticism [ɪ'rɔtɪsɪzəm] *n* Erotik *f*
err [əː^r] *vi* sich irren; **to ~ on the side of caution/simplicity** (im Zweifelsfall) zur Vorsicht/Vereinfachung neigen
errand ['ɛrənd] *n* Besorgung *f*; (*to give a message etc*) Botengang *m*; **to run ~s** Besorgungen/ Botengänge machen; **~ of mercy** Rettungsaktion *f*
erratic [ɪ'rætɪk] *adj* unberechenbar; (*attempts*) unkoordiniert; (*noise*) unregelmäßig
erroneous [ɪ'rəunɪəs] *adj* irrig
error ['ɛrə^r] *n* Fehler *m*; **typing/spelling ~** Tipp-/Rechtschreibfehler *m*; **in ~** irrtümlicherweise; **~s and omissions excepted** Irrtum vorbehalten
error message *n* Fehlermeldung *f*
erstwhile ['əːstwaɪl] *adj* einstig, vormalig
erudite ['ɛrjudaɪt] *adj* gelehrt
erupt [ɪ'rʌpt] *vi* ausbrechen
eruption [ɪ'rʌpʃən] *n* Ausbruch *m*
ESA *n abbr* (*= European Space Agency*) Europäische Weltraumbehörde *f*

escalate ['ɛskəleɪt] *vi* eskalieren, sich ausweiten
escalation [ɛskə'leɪʃən] *n* Eskalation *f*
escalator ['ɛskəleɪtə^r] *n* Rolltreppe *f*
escalator clause *n* Gleitklausel *f*
escapade [ɛskə'peɪd] *n* Eskapade *f*
escape [ɪs'keɪp] *n* Flucht *f*; (*Tech: of liquid*) Ausfließen *nt*; (*of gas*) Ausströmen *nt*; (*of air, heat*) Entweichen *nt* ▷ *vi* entkommen; (*from prison*) ausbrechen; (*liquid*) ausfließen; (*gas*) ausströmen; (*air, heat*) entweichen ▷ *vt* (*pursuers etc*) entkommen *+dat*; (*punishment etc*) entgehen *+dat*; **his name ~s me** sein Name ist mir entfallen; **to ~ from** flüchten aus; (*prison*) ausbrechen aus; (*person*) entkommen *+dat*; **to ~ to Peru** nach Peru fliehen; **to ~ to safety** sich in Sicherheit bringen; **to ~ notice** unbemerkt bleiben
escape artist *n* Entfesselungskünstler(in) *m(f)*
escape clause *n* (*in contract*) Befreiungsklausel *f*
escapee [ɪskeɪ'pi:] *n* entwichener Häftling *m*
escape hatch *n* Notluke *f*
escape key *n* (*Comput*) Escape-Taste *f*
escape route *n* Fluchtweg *m*
escapism [ɪs'keɪpɪzəm] *n* Wirklichkeitsflucht *f*, Eskapismus *m*
escapist [ɪs'keɪpɪst] *adj* eskapistisch
escapologist [ɛskə'pɔlədʒɪst] (*Brit*) *n* = **escape artist**
escarpment [ɪs'kɑ:pmənt] *n* Steilhang *m*
eschew [ɪs'tʃu:] *vt* meiden
escort [*n* 'ɛskɔ:t, *vt* ɪs'kɔ:t] *n* Eskorte *f*; (*companion*) Begleiter(in) *m(f)* ▷ *vt* begleiten; **his ~** seine Begleiterin; **her ~** ihr Begleiter
escort agency *n* Agentur *f* für Begleiter(innen)
Eskimo ['ɛskɪməu] *n* Eskimo(frau) *m(f)*
ESL *n abbr* (*Scol: = English as a Second Language*) Englisch *nt* als Zweitsprache
esophagus [i:'sɔfəgəs] (*US*) *n* = **oesophagus**
esoteric [ɛsə'tɛrɪk] *adj* esoterisch
ESP *n abbr* = **extrasensory perception**; (*Scol: = English for Specific (or Special) Purposes*) *Englischunterricht für spezielle Fachbereiche*
esp. *abbr* = **especially**
especially [ɪs'pɛʃlɪ] *adv* besonders
espionage ['ɛspɪənɑ:ʒ] *n* Spionage *f*
esplanade [ɛsplə'neɪd] *n* Promenade *f*
espouse [ɪs'pauz] *vt* eintreten für
Esquire [ɪs'kwaɪə^r] *n* (*abbr Esq.*): **J. Brown, ~** Herrn J. Brown
essay ['ɛseɪ] *n* Aufsatz *m*; (*Liter*) Essay *m or nt*
essence ['ɛsns] *n* Wesen *nt*; (*Culin*) Essenz *f*; **in ~** im Wesentlichen; **speed is of the ~** Geschwindigkeit ist von entscheidender Bedeutung
essential [ɪ'sɛnʃl] *adj* notwendig; (*basic*) wesentlich ▷ *n* (*see adj*) Notwendigste(s) *nt*; Wesentliche(s) *nt*; **it is ~ that** es ist unbedingt *or* absolut erforderlich, dass
essentially [ɪ'sɛnʃəlɪ] *adv* im Grunde genommen
EST (*US*) *abbr* (*= Eastern Standard Time*) *ostamerikanische Standardzeit*
est. *abbr* = **established; estimate; estimated**
establish [ɪs'tæblɪʃ] *vt* gründen; (*facts*) feststellen; (*proof*) erstellen; (*relations, contact*) aufnehmen; (*reputation*) sich *dat* verschaffen
established [ɪs'tæblɪʃt] *adj* üblich; (*business*) eingeführt
establishment [ɪs'tæblɪʃmənt] *n* (*see vb*) Gründung *f*; Feststellung *f*; Erstellung *f*; Aufnahme *f*; (*of reputation*) Begründung *f*; (*shop etc*) Unternehmen *nt*; **the E~** das Establishment
estate [ɪs'teɪt] *n* Gut *nt*; (*Brit: also*: **housing estate**) Siedlung *f*; (*Law*) Nachlass *m*
estate agency (*Brit*) *n* Maklerbüro *nt*
estate agent (*Brit*) *n* Immobilienmakler(in) *m(f)*
estate car (*Brit*) *n* Kombiwagen *m*
esteem [ɪs'ti:m] *n*: **to hold sb in high ~** eine hohe Meinung von jdm haben
esthetic [ɪs'θɛtɪk] (*US*) *adj* = **aesthetic**
estimate ['ɛstɪmət] *n* Schätzung *f*; (*assessment*) Einschätzung *f*; (*Comm*) (Kosten)voranschlag *m* ▷ *vt* schätzen ▷ *vi* (*Brit: Comm*): **to ~ for** einen Kostenvoranschlag machen für; **to give sb an ~ of sth** jdm eine Vorstellung von etw geben; **to ~ for** einen Kostenvoranschlag machen für; **at a rough ~** grob geschätzt, über den Daumen gepeilt (*inf*); **I ~ that** ich schätze, dass
estimation [ɛstɪ'meɪʃən] *n* Schätzung *f*; (*opinion*) Einschätzung *f*; **in my ~** meiner Einschätzung nach
estimator ['ɛstɪmeɪtə^r] *n* Schätzer(in) *m(f)*
Estonia [ɛs'təunɪə] *n* Estland *nt*
Estonian [ɛs'təunɪən] *adj* estnisch ▷ *n* Este *m*, Estin *f*; (*Ling*) Estnisch *nt*
estranged [ɪs'treɪndʒd] *adj* entfremdet; (*from spouse*) getrennt; (*couple*) getrennt lebend
estrangement [ɪs'treɪndʒmənt] *n* Entfremdung *f*; (*from spouse*) Trennung *f*
estrogen ['i:strəudʒən] (*US*) *n* = **oestrogen**
estuary ['ɛstjuərɪ] *n* Mündung *f*
ET (*Brit*) *n abbr* (*= Employment Training*) *Ausbildungsmaßnahmen für Arbeitslose*
ETA *n abbr* (*= estimated time of arrival*) voraussichtliche Ankunftszeit *f*
et al. *abbr* (*= et alii*) u. a.
etc. *abbr* (*= et cetera*) etc.
etch [ɛtʃ] *vt* (*design, surface: with needle*) radieren; (*: with acid*) ätzen; (*: with chisel*) meißeln; **it will be ~ed on my memory** es wird sich tief in mein Gedächtnis eingraben
etching ['ɛtʃɪŋ] *n* Radierung *f*
ETD *n abbr* (*= estimated time of departure*) voraussichtliche Abflugzeit *f*
eternal [ɪ'tə:nl] *adj* ewig
eternity [ɪ'tə:nɪtɪ] *n* Ewigkeit *f*
ether ['i:θə^r] *n* Äther *m*
ethereal [ɪ'θɪərɪəl] *adj* ätherisch
ethical ['ɛθɪkl] *adj* ethisch
ethics ['ɛθɪks] *n* Ethik *f* ▷ *npl* (*morality*) Moral *f*
Ethiopia [i:θɪ'əupɪə] *n* Äthiopien *nt*
Ethiopian [i:θɪ'əupɪən] *adj* äthiopisch ▷ *n*

Äthiopier(in) *m(f)*
ethnic ['εθnɪk] *adj* ethnisch; (*music*) folkloristisch; (*culture etc*) urwüchsig
ethnic cleansing [-'klεnzɪŋ] *n* ethnische Säuberung *f*
ethnic minority *n* ethnische Minderheit *f*
ethnology [εθ'nɔlədʒɪ] *n* Ethnologie *f*, Völkerkunde *f*
ethos ['i:θɔs] *n* Ethos *nt*
e-ticket ['i:tɪkɪt] *n abbr* (= *electronic ticket*) E-Ticket *nt*, *elektronische Eintrittskarte/Fahrkarte etc*
etiquette ['εtɪkεt] *n* Etikette *f*
ETV (*US*) *n abbr* (= *educational television*) *Fernsehsender, der Bildungs- und Kulturprogramme ausstrahlt*
etymology [εtɪ'mɔlədʒɪ] *n* Etymologie *f*; (*of word*) Herkunft *f*
EU *n abbr* (= *European Union*) EU *f*
eucalyptus [ju:kə'lɪptəs] *n* Eukalyptus *m*
Eucharist ['ju:kərɪst] *n*: **the ~** die Eucharistie, das (heilige) Abendmahl
eulogy ['ju:lədʒɪ] *n* Lobrede *f*
euphemism ['ju:fəmɪzəm] *n* Euphemismus *m*
euphemistic [ju:fə'mɪstɪk] *adj* euphemistisch, verhüllend
euphoria [ju:'fɔ:rɪə] *n* Euphorie *f*
Eurasia [juə'reɪʃə] *n* Eurasien *nt*
Eurasian [juə'reɪʃən] *adj* eurasisch ▷ *n* Eurasier(in) *m(f)*
Euratom [juə'rætəm] *n abbr* (= *European Atomic Energy Community*) Euratom *f*
euro ['juərəu] *n* (*Fin*) Euro *m*
Euro- ['juərəu] *pref* Euro-
Eurocheque ['juərəutʃεk] *n* Eurocheque *m*
Eurocrat ['juərəukræt] *n* Eurokrat(in) *m(f)*
Eurodollar ['juərəudɔlə^r] *n* Eurodollar *m*
Euroland ['juərəulænd] *n* (*Fin*) Eurozone *f*
Europe ['juərəp] *n* Europa *nt*
European [juərə'pi:ən] *adj* europäisch ▷ *n* Europäer(in) *m(f)*
European Central Bank *n*: **the ~** die Europäische Zentralbank
European Community *n*: **the ~** die Europäische Gemeinschaft
European Convention *n* Europäische(r) Konvent *m*, EU-Konvent *m*
European Court of Justice *n*: **the ~** der Europäische Gerichtshof
European Economic Community *n* (*formerly*): **the ~** die Europäische Wirtschaftsgemeinschaft
Euro-sceptic ['juərəuskεptɪk] *n* Euroskeptiker(in) *m(f)*
euthanasia [ju:θə'neɪzɪə] *n* Euthanasie *f*
evacuate [ɪ'vækjueɪt] *vt* evakuieren; (*place*) räumen
evacuation [ɪvækju'eɪʃən] *n* (*see verb*) Evakuierung *f*; Räumung *f*
evacuee [ɪvækju'i:] *n* Evakuierte(r) *f(m)*
evade [ɪ'veɪd] *vt* (*person, question*) ausweichen *+dat*; (*tax*) hinterziehen; (*duty, responsibility*) sich entziehen *+dat*
evaluate [ɪ'væljueɪt] *vt* bewerten; (*situation*) einschätzen
evangelical [i:væn'dʒεlɪkl] *adj* evangelisch
evangelist [ɪ'vændʒəlɪst] *n* Evangelist(in) *m(f)*
evangelize [ɪ'vændʒəlaɪz] *vi* evangelisieren
evaporate [ɪ'væpəreɪt] *vi* verdampfen; (*feeling, attitude*) dahinschwinden
evaporated milk [ɪ'væpəreɪtɪd-] *n* Kondensmilch *f*, Büchsenmilch *f*
evaporation [ɪvæpə'reɪʃən] *n* Verdampfung *f*
evasion [ɪ'veɪʒən] *n* Ausweichen *nt*; (*of tax*) Hinterziehung *f*
evasive [ɪ'veɪsɪv] *adj* ausweichend; **to take ~ action** ein Ausweichmanöver machen
eve [i:v] *n*: **on the ~ of** am Tag vor *+dat*; **Christmas E~** Heiligabend *m*; **New Year's E~** Silvester *m or nt*
even ['i:vn] *adj* (*level*) eben; (*smooth*) glatt; (*equal*) gleich; (*number*) gerade ▷ *adv* sogar, selbst; (*introducing a comparison*) sogar noch; **~ if, ~ though** selbst wenn; **~ more** sogar noch mehr; **he loves her ~ more** er liebt sie umso mehr; **it's going ~ faster now** es fährt jetzt sogar noch schneller; **~ so** (aber) trotzdem; **not ~** nicht einmal; **~ he was there** sogar er war da; **to break ~** die Kosten decken; **to get ~ with sb** es jdm heimzahlen
▶ **even out** *vi* sich ausgleichen ▷ *vt* ausgleichen
even-handed ['i:vnhændɪd] *adj* gerecht
evening ['i:vnɪŋ] *n* Abend *m*; **in the ~** abends, am Abend; **this ~** heute Abend; **tomorrow/ yesterday ~** morgen/gestern Abend
evening class *n* Abendkurs *m*
evening dress *n* (*no pl*) Abendkleidung *f*; (*woman's*) Abendkleid *nt*
evenly ['i:vnlɪ] *adv* gleichmäßig
evensong ['i:vnsɔŋ] *n* Abendandacht *f*
event [ɪ'vεnt] *n* Ereignis *nt*; (*Sport*) Wettkampf *m*; **in the normal course of ~s** normalerweise; **in the ~ of** im Falle *+gen*; **in the ~** schließlich; **at all ~s** (*Brit*), **in any ~** auf jeden Fall
eventful [ɪ'vεntful] *adj* ereignisreich
eventing [ɪ'vεntɪŋ] *n* (*Horseriding*) Military *f*
eventual [ɪ'vεntʃuəl] *adj* schließlich; (*goal*) letztlich
eventuality [ɪvεntʃu'ælɪtɪ] *n* Eventualität *f*
eventually [ɪ'vεntʃuəlɪ] *adv* endlich; (*in time*) schließlich
ever ['εvə^r] *adv* immer; (*at any time*) je(mals); **why ~ not?** warum denn bloß nicht?; **the best ~** der/die/das Allerbeste; **have you ~ seen it?** haben Sie es schon einmal gesehen?; **for ~** für immer; **hardly ~** kaum je(mals); **better than ~** besser als je zuvor; **~ since** *adv* seitdem ▷ *conj* seit, seitdem; **~ so pretty** unheimlich hübsch (*inf*); **thank you ~ so much** ganz herzlichen Dank; **yours ~** (*Brit: in letters*) alles Liebe
Everest ['εvərɪst] *n* (*also*: **Mount Everest**) Mount Everest *m*

evergreen ['ɛvəgri:n] *n* (*tree/bush*) immergrüner Baum/Strauch *m*
everlasting [ɛvə'lɑ:stɪŋ] *adj* ewig

KEYWORD

every ['ɛvrɪ] *adj* **1** jede(r, s); **every one of them** (*persons*) jede(r) (Einzelne) von ihnen; (*objects*) jedes einzelne Stück; **every day** jeden Tag; **every week** jede Woche; **every other car** jedes zweite Auto; **every other/third day** alle zwei/drei Tage; **every shop in the town was closed** alle Geschäfte der Stadt waren geschlossen; **every now and then** ab und zu, hin und wieder
2 (*all possible*): **I have every confidence in him** ich habe volles Vertrauen in ihn; **we wish you every success** wir wünschen Ihnen alles Gute

everybody ['ɛvrɪbɔdɪ] *pron* jeder, alle *pl*; **~ knows about it** alle wissen es; **~ else** alle anderen *pl*
everyday ['ɛvrɪdeɪ] *adj* täglich; (*usual, common*) alltäglich; (*life, language*) Alltags-
everyone ['ɛvrɪwʌn] *pron* = **everybody**
everything ['ɛvrɪθɪŋ] *pron* alles; **he did ~ possible** er hat sein Möglichstes getan
everywhere ['ɛvrɪwɛəʳ] *adv* überall; (*wherever*) wo auch *or* immer; **~ you go you meet ...** wo man auch *or* wo immer man hingeht, trifft man ...
evict [ɪ'vɪkt] *vt* zur Räumung zwingen
eviction [ɪ'vɪkʃən] *n* Ausweisung *f*
eviction notice *n* Räumungskündigung *f*
eviction order *n* Räumungsbefehl *m*
evidence ['ɛvɪdns] *n* Beweis *m*; (*of witness*) Aussage *f*; (*sign, indication*) Zeichen *nt*, Spur *f*; **to give ~** (als Zeuge) aussagen; **to show ~ of** zeigen; **in ~** sichtbar
evident ['ɛvɪdnt] *adj* offensichtlich
evidently ['ɛvɪdntlɪ] *adv* offensichtlich
evil ['i:vl] *adj* böse; (*influence*) schlecht ▷ *n* Böse(s) *nt*; (*unpleasant situation or activity*) Übel *nt*
evocative [ɪ'vɔkətɪv] *adj* evokativ
evoke [ɪ'vəuk] *vt* hervorrufen; (*memory*) wecken
evolution [i:və'lu:ʃən] *n* Evolution *f*; (*development*) Entwicklung *f*
evolve [ɪ'vɔlv] *vt* entwickeln ▷ *vi* sich entwickeln
ewe [ju:] *n* Mutterschaf *nt*
ewer ['ju:əʳ] *n* (Wasser)krug *m*
ex- [ɛks] *pref* Ex-, frühere(r, s); **the price ex works** der Preis ab Werk
exacerbate [ɛks'æsəbeɪt] *vt* verschärfen; (*pain*) verschlimmern
exact [ɪg'zækt] *adj* genau; (*word*) richtig ▷ *vt*: **to ~ sth (from)** etw verlangen (von); (*payment*) etw eintreiben (von)
exacting [ɪg'zæktɪŋ] *adj* anspruchsvoll
exactly [ɪg'zæktlɪ] *adv* genau; **~!** (ganz) genau!; **not ~** (*hardly*) nicht gerade
exaggerate [ɪg'zædʒəreɪt] *vt, vi* übertreiben
exaggerated [ɪg'zædʒəreɪtɪd] *adj* übertrieben
exaggeration [ɪgzædʒə'reɪʃən] *n* Übertreibung *f*
exalt [ɪg'zɔ:lt] *vt* preisen
exalted [ɪg'zɔ:ltɪd] *adj* hoch; (*elated*) exaltiert
exam [ɪg'zæm] *n abbr* = **examination**
examination [ɪgzæmɪ'neɪʃən] *n* (*see vb*) Untersuchung *f*; Prüfung *f*; Verhör *nt*; **to take an ~, to sit an ~** (*Brit*) eine Prüfung machen; **the matter is under ~** die Angelegenheit wird geprüft *or* untersucht
examine [ɪg'zæmɪn] *vt* untersuchen; (*accounts, candidate*) prüfen; (*witness*) verhören
examiner [ɪg'zæmɪnəʳ] *n* Prüfer(in) *m(f)*
example [ɪg'zɑ:mpl] *n* Beispiel *nt*; **for ~** zum Beispiel; **to set a good/bad ~** ein gutes/schlechtes Beispiel geben
exasperate [ɪg'zɑ:spəreɪt] *vt* (*annoy*) verärgern; (*frustrate*) zur Verzweiflung bringen; **~d by** *or* **with** verärgert/verzweifelt über *+acc*
exasperating [ɪg'zɑ:spəreɪtɪŋ] *adj* ärgerlich; (*job*) leidig
exasperation [ɪgzɑ:spə'reɪʃən] *n* Verzweiflung *f*; **in ~** verzweifelt
excavate ['ɛkskəveɪt] *vt* ausgraben; (*hole*) graben ▷ *vi* Ausgrabungen machen
excavation [ɛkskə'veɪʃən] *n* Ausgrabung *f*
excavator ['ɛkskəveɪtəʳ] *n* Bagger *m*
exceed [ɪk'si:d] *vt* übersteigen; (*hopes*) übertreffen; (*limit, budget, powers*) überschreiten
exceedingly [ɪk'si:dɪŋlɪ] *adv* äußerst
excel [ɪk'sɛl] *vt* übertreffen ▷ *vi*: **to ~ (in** *or* **at)** sich auszeichnen (in *+dat*); **to ~ o.s.** (*Brit*) sich selbst übertreffen
excellence ['ɛksələns] *n* hervorragende Leistung *f*
Excellency ['ɛksələnsɪ] *n*: **His ~** Seine Exzellenz
excellent ['ɛksələnt] *adj* ausgezeichnet, hervorragend
except [ɪk'sɛpt] *prep* (*also*: **except for**) außer *+dat* ▷ *vt*: **to ~ sb (from)** jdn ausnehmen (bei); **~ if, ~ when** außer wenn; **~ that** nur dass
excepting [ɪk'sɛptɪŋ] *prep* außer *+dat*, mit Ausnahme *+gen*
exception [ɪk'sɛpʃən] *n* Ausnahme *f*; **to take ~ to** Anstoß nehmen an *+dat*; **with the ~ of** mit Ausnahme von
exceptional [ɪk'sɛpʃənl] *adj* außergewöhnlich
excerpt ['ɛksə:pt] *n* Auszug *m*
excess [ɪk'sɛs] *n* Übermaß *nt*; (*Insurance*) Selbstbeteiligung *f*; **excesses** *npl* Exzesse *pl*; **an ~ of £15, a £15 excess** eine Selbstbeteiligung von £15; **in ~ of** über *+dat*
excess baggage *n* Übergepäck *nt*
excess fare (*Brit*) *n* Nachlösegebühr *f*
excessive [ɪk'sɛsɪv] *adj* übermäßig
excess supply *n* Überangebot *nt*
exchange [ɪks'tʃeɪndʒ] *n* Austausch *m*; (*conversation*) Wortwechsel *m*; (*also*: **telephone exchange**) Fernsprechamt *nt* ▷ *vt*: **to ~ (for)** tauschen (gegen); (*in shop*) umtauschen (gegen); **in ~ for** für; **foreign ~** Devisenhandel *m*; (*money*) Devisen *pl*
exchange control *n* Devisenkontrolle *f*

exchange market *n* Devisenmarkt *m*
exchange rate *n* Wechselkurs *m*
Exchequer [ɪks'tʃɛkəʳ] (*Brit*) *n*: **the ~** das Finanzministerium
excisable [ɪk'saɪzəbl] *adj* steuerpflichtig
excise ['ɛksaɪz] *n* Verbrauchssteuer *f* ▷ *vt* entfernen
excise duties *npl* Verbrauchssteuern *pl*
excitable [ɪk'saɪtəbl] *adj* (leicht) erregbar
excite [ɪk'saɪt] *vt* aufregen; (*arouse*) erregen; **to get ~d** sich aufregen
excitement [ɪk'saɪtmənt] *n* Aufregung *f*; (*exhilaration*) Hochgefühl *nt*
exciting [ɪk'saɪtɪŋ] *adj* aufregend
excl. *abbr* = **excluding; exclusive (of)**
exclaim [ɪks'kleɪm] *vi* aufschreien
exclamation [ɛksklə'meɪʃən] *n* Ausruf *m*; **~ of joy** Freudenschrei *m*
exclamation mark *n* Ausrufezeichen *nt*
exclude [ɪks'klu:d] *vt* ausschließen
excluding [ɪks'klu:dɪŋ] *prep*: **~ VAT** ohne Mehrwertsteuer
exclusion [ɪks'klu:ʒən] *n* Ausschluss *m*; **to concentrate on sth to the ~ of everything else** sich ausschließlich auf etw *dat* konzentrieren
exclusion clause *n* Freizeichnungsklausel *f*
exclusion zone *n* Sperrzone *f*
exclusive [ɪks'klu:sɪv] *adj* exklusiv; (*story, interview*) Exklusiv-; (*use*) ausschließlich ▷ *n* Exklusivbericht *m* ▷ *adv*: **from 1st to 15th March ~** vom 1. bis zum 15. März ausschließlich; **~ of postage** ohne *or* exklusive Porto; **~ of tax** ausschließlich *or* exklusive Steuern; **to be mutually ~** sich *or* einander ausschließen
exclusively [ɪks'klu:sɪvlɪ] *adv* ausschließlich
exclusive rights *npl* Exklusivrechte *pl*
excommunicate [ɛkskə'mju:nɪkeɪt] *vt* exkommunizieren
excrement ['ɛkskrəmənt] *n* Kot *m*, Exkremente *pl*
excruciating [ɪks'kru:ʃɪeɪtɪŋ] *adj* grässlich, fürchterlich; (*noise, embarrassment*) unerträglich
excursion [ɪks'kə:ʃən] *n* Ausflug *m*
excursion ticket *n* verbilligte Fahrkarte *f*
excusable [ɪks'kju:zəbl] *adj* verzeihlich, entschuldbar
excuse [*n* ɪks'kju:s, *vb* ɪks'kju:z] *n* Entschuldigung *f* ▷ *vt* entschuldigen; (*forgive*) verzeihen; **to ~ sb from sth** jdm etw erlassen; **to ~ sb from doing sth** jdn davon befreien, etw zu tun; **~ me!** entschuldigen Sie!, Entschuldigung!; **if you will ~ me ...** entschuldigen Sie mich bitte ...; **to ~ o.s. for sth** sich für *or* wegen etw entschuldigen; **to ~ o.s. for doing sth** sich entschuldigen, dass man etw tut; **to make ~s for sb** jdn entschuldigen; **that's no ~!** das ist keine Ausrede!
ex-directory ['ɛksdɪ'rɛktərɪ] (*Brit*) *adj* (*number*) geheim; **she's ~** sie steht nicht im Telefonbuch
execrable ['ɛksɪkrəbl] *adj* scheußlich; (*manners*) abscheulich
execute ['ɛksɪkju:t] *vt* ausführen; (*person*) hinrichten
execution [ɛksɪ'kju:ʃən] *n* (*see vb*) Ausführung *f*; Hinrichtung *f*
executioner [ɛksɪ'kju:ʃnəʳ] *n* Scharfrichter *m*
executive [ɪg'zɛkjutɪv] *n* leitende(r) Angestellte(r) *f(m)*; (*committee*) Vorstand *m* ▷ *adj* geschäftsführend; (*role*) führend; (*secretary*) Chef-; (*car, chair*) für gehobene Ansprüche; (*toys*) Manager-; (*plane*) ≈ Privat-
executive director *n* leitender Direktor *m*, leitende Direktorin *f*
executor [ɪg'zɛkjutəʳ] *n* Testamentsvollstrecker(in) *m(f)*
exemplary [ɪg'zɛmplərɪ] *adj* vorbildlich, beispielhaft; (*punishment*) exemplarisch
exemplify [ɪg'zɛmplɪfaɪ] *vt* verkörpern; (*illustrate*) veranschaulichen
exempt [ɪg'zɛmpt] *adj*: **~ from** befreit von ▷ *vt*: **to ~ sb from** jdn befreien von
exemption [ɪg'zɛmpʃən] *n* Befreiung *f*
exercise ['ɛksəsaɪz] *n* Übung *f*; (*no pl: keep-fit*) Gymnastik *f*; (*: energetic movement*) Bewegung *f*; (*: of authority etc*) Ausübung *f* ▷ *vt* (*patience*) üben; (*right*) ausüben; (*dog*) ausführen; (*mind*) beschäftigen ▷ *vi* (*also*: **to take exercise**) Sport treiben
exercise book *n* (Schul)heft *nt*
exert [ɪg'zə:t] *vt* (*influence*) ausüben; (*authority*) einsetzen; **to ~ o.s.** sich anstrengen
exertion [ɪg'zə:ʃən] *n* Anstrengung *f*
ex gratia ['ɛks'greɪʃə] *adj*: **~ payment** freiwillige Zahlung *f*
exhale [ɛks'heɪl] *vt, vi* ausatmen
exhaust [ɪg'zɔ:st] *n* (*also*: **exhaust pipe**) Auspuff *m*; (*fumes*) Auspuffgase *pl* ▷ *vt* erschöpfen; (*money*) aufbrauchen; (*topic*) erschöpfend behandeln; **to ~ o.s.** sich verausgaben
exhausted [ɪg'zɔ:stɪd] *adj* erschöpft
exhausting [ɪg'zɔ:stɪŋ] *adj* anstrengend
exhaustion [ɪg'zɔ:stʃən] *n* Erschöpfung *f*; **nervous ~** nervöse Erschöpfung
exhaustive [ɪg'zɔ:stɪv] *adj* erschöpfend
exhibit [ɪg'zɪbɪt] *n* Ausstellungsstück *nt*; (*Law*) Beweisstück *nt* ▷ *vt* zeigen, an den Tag legen; (*paintings*) ausstellen
exhibition [ɛksɪ'bɪʃən] *n* Ausstellung *f*; **to make an ~ of o.s.** sich unmöglich aufführen; **an ~ of bad manners** schlechte Manieren *pl*; **an ~ of draughtsmanship** zeichnerisches Können *nt*
exhibitionist [ɛksɪ'bɪʃənɪst] *n* Exhibitionist(in) *m(f)*
exhibitor [ɪg'zɪbɪtəʳ] *n* Aussteller(in) *m(f)*
exhilarating [ɪg'zɪləreɪtɪŋ] *adj* erregend, berauschend; (*news*) aufregend
exhilaration [ɪgzɪlə'reɪʃən] *n* Hochgefühl *nt*
exhort [ɪg'zɔ:t] *vt*: **to ~ sb to do sth** jdn ermahnen, etw zu tun

exile [ˈɛksaɪl] *n* Exil *nt*; *(person)* Verbannte(r) *f(m)* ▷ *vt* verbannen; **in ~** im Exil
exist [ɪgˈzɪst] *vi* existieren
existence [ɪgˈzɪstəns] *n* Existenz *f*; **to be in ~** existieren
existentialism [ɛgzɪsˈtɛnʃlɪzəm] *n* Existenzialismus *m*
existing [ɪgˈzɪstɪŋ] *adj* bestehend
exit [ˈɛksɪt] *n* Ausgang *m*; *(from motorway)* Ausfahrt *f*; *(departure)* Abgang *m* ▷ *vi (Theat)* abgehen; *(Comput: from program/file etc)* das Programm/die Datei *etc* verlassen; **to ~ from** hinausgehen aus; *(motorway etc)* abfahren von
exit poll *n bei Wählern unmittelbar nach Verlassen der Wahllokale durchgeführte Umfrage*
exit ramp *(US) n* Ausfahrt *f*
exit visa *n* Ausreisevisum *nt*
exodus [ˈɛksədəs] *n* Auszug *m*; **the ~ to the cities** die Abwanderung in die Städte
ex officio [ˈɛksəˈfɪʃɪəu] *adj* von Amts wegen ▷ *adv* kraft seines Amtes
exonerate [ɪgˈzɔnəreɪt] *vt*: **to ~ from** entlasten von
exorbitant [ɪgˈzɔːbɪtnt] *adj (prices, rents)* astronomisch, unverschämt; *(demands)* maßlos, übertrieben
exorcize [ˈɛksɔːsaɪz] *vt* exorzieren; *(spirit)* austreiben
exotic [ɪgˈzɔtɪk] *adj* exotisch
expand [ɪksˈpænd] *vt* erweitern; *(staff, numbers etc)* vergrößern; *(influence)* ausdehnen ▷ *vi* expandieren; *(population)* wachsen; *(gas, metal)* sich ausdehnen; **to ~ on** weiter ausführen
expanse [ɪksˈpæns] *n* Weite *f*
expansion [ɪksˈpænʃən] *n* Expansion *f*; *(of population)* Wachstum *nt*; *(of gas, metal)* Ausdehnung *f*
expansionism [ɪksˈpænʃənɪzəm] *n* Expansionspolitik *f*
expansionist [ɪksˈpænʃənɪst] *adj* Expansions-, expansionistisch
expatriate [ɛksˈpætrɪət] *n* im Ausland Lebende(r) *f(m)*
expect [ɪksˈpɛkt] *vt* erwarten; *(suppose)* denken, glauben; *(count on)* rechnen mit ▷ *vi*: **to be ~ing** ein Kind erwarten; **to ~ sb to do sth** erwarten, dass jd etw tut; **to ~ to do sth** vorhaben, etw zu tun; **as ~ed** wie erwartet; **I ~ so** ich glaube schon
expectancy [ɪksˈpɛktənsɪ] *n* Erwartung *f*; **life ~** Lebenserwartung *f*
expectant [ɪksˈpɛktənt] *adj* erwartungsvoll
expectantly [ɪksˈpɛktəntlɪ] *adv* erwartungsvoll
expectant mother *n* werdende Mutter *f*
expectation [ɛkspɛkˈteɪʃən] *n* Erwartung *f*; *(hope)* Hoffnung *f*; **in ~ of** in Erwartung *+gen*; **against** *or* **contrary to all ~(s)** wider Erwarten; **to come** *or* **live up to sb's ~s** jds Erwartungen *dat* entsprechen
expedience [ɪksˈpiːdɪəns] *n* = **expediency**
expediency [ɪksˈpiːdɪənsɪ] *n* Zweckmäßigkeit *f*; **for the sake of ~** aus Gründen der Zweckmäßigkeit
expedient [ɪksˈpiːdɪənt] *adj* zweckmäßig ▷ *n* Hilfsmittel *nt*
expedite [ˈɛkspədaɪt] *vt* beschleunigen
expedition [ɛkspəˈdɪʃən] *n* Expedition *f*; *(for shopping etc)* Tour *f*
expeditionary force [ɛkspəˈdɪʃənrɪ-] *n* Expeditionskorps *nt*
expeditious [ɛkspəˈdɪʃəs] *adj* schnell
expel [ɪksˈpɛl] *vt (from school)* verweisen; *(from organization)* ausschließen; *(from place)* vertreiben; *(gas, liquid)* ausstoßen
expend [ɪksˈpɛnd] *vt* ausgeben; *(time, energy)* aufwenden
expendable [ɪksˈpɛndəbl] *adj* entbehrlich
expenditure [ɪksˈpɛndɪtʃə^r] *n* Ausgaben *pl*; *(of energy, time)* Aufwand *m*
expense [ɪksˈpɛns] *n* Kosten *pl*; *(expenditure)* Ausgabe *f*; **expenses** *npl* Spesen *pl*; **at the ~ of** auf Kosten *+gen*; **to go to the ~ of buying a new car** (viel) Geld für ein neues Auto anlegen; **at great/little ~** mit hohen/geringen Kosten
expense account *n* Spesenkonto *nt*
expensive [ɪksˈpɛnsɪv] *adj* teuer; **to have ~ tastes** einen teuren Geschmack haben
experience [ɪksˈpɪərɪəns] *n* Erfahrung *f*; *(event, activity)* Erlebnis *nt* ▷ *vt* erleben; **by** *or* **from ~** aus Erfahrung; **to learn by ~** durch eigene Erfahrung lernen
experienced [ɪksˈpɪərɪənst] *adj* erfahren
experiment [ɪksˈpɛrɪmənt] *n* Experiment *nt*, Versuch *m* ▷ *vi*: **to ~ (with/on)** experimentieren (mit/an *+dat*); **to perform** *or* **carry out an ~** einen Versuch *or* ein Experiment durchführen; **as an ~** versuchsweise
experimental [ɪkspɛrɪˈmɛntl] *adj* experimentell; **at the ~ stage** im Versuchsstadium
expert [ˈɛkspəːt] *adj* ausgezeichnet, geschickt; *(opinion, help etc)* eines Fachmanns ▷ *n* Fachmann *m*, Fachfrau *f*, Experte *m*, Expertin *f*; **to be ~ in** *or* **at doing sth** etw ausgezeichnet können; **an ~ on sth/on the subject of sth** ein Experte für etw/auf dem Gebiet einer Sache *gen*; **~ witness** *(Law)* sachverständiger Zeuge *m*
expertise [ɛkspəːˈtiːz] *n* Sachkenntnis *f*
expire [ɪksˈpaɪə^r] *vi* ablaufen
expiry [ɪksˈpaɪərɪ] *n* Ablauf *m*
expiry date *n* Ablauftermin *m*; *(of voucher, special offer etc)* Verfallsdatum *nt*
explain [ɪksˈpleɪn] *vt* erklären
▸ **explain away** *vt* eine Erklärung finden für
explanation [ɛkspləˈneɪʃən] *n* Erklärung *f*; **to find an ~ for sth** eine Erklärung für etw finden
explanatory [ɪksˈplænətrɪ] *adj* erklärend
expletive [ɪksˈpliːtɪv] *n* Kraftausdruck *m*
explicable [ɪksˈplɪkəbl] *adj* erklärbar; **for no ~ reason** aus unerfindlichen Gründen
explicit [ɪksˈplɪsɪt] *adj* ausdrücklich; *(sex,*

violence) deutlich, unverhüllt; **to be ~** (*frank*) sich deutlich ausdrücken
explode [ɪks'pləud] *vi* explodieren; (*population*) sprunghaft ansteigen ▷ *vt* zur Explosion bringen; (*myth, theory*) zu Fall bringen
exploit ['ɛksplɔɪt] *n* Heldentat *f* ▷ *vt* ausnutzen; (*workers etc*) ausbeuten; (*resources*) nutzen
exploitation [ɛksplɔɪ'teɪʃən] *n* (*see vb*) Ausnutzung *f*; Ausbeutung *f*; Nutzung *f*
exploration [ɛksplə'reɪʃən] *n* (*see vb*) Erforschung *f*; Erkundung *f*; Untersuchung *f*
exploratory [ɪks'plɔrətrɪ] *adj* exploratorisch; (*expedition*) Forschungs-; **~ operation** (*Med*) Explorationsoperation *f*; **~ talks** Sondierungsgespräche *pl*
explore [ɪks'plɔːʳ] *vt* erforschen; (*with hands etc, idea*) untersuchen
explorer [ɪks'plɔːrəʳ] *n* Forschungsreisende(r) *f(m)*; (*of place*) Erforscher(in) *m(f)*
explosion [ɪks'pləuʒən] *n* Explosion *f*; (*outburst*) Ausbruch *m*
explosive [ɪks'pləusɪv] *adj* explosiv; (*device*) Spreng-; (*temper*) aufbrausend ▷ *n* Sprengstoff *m*; (*device*) Sprengkörper *m*
exponent [ɪks'pəunənt] *n* Vertreter(in) *m(f)*, Exponent(in) *m(f)*; (*Math*) Exponent *m*
exponential [ɛkspəu'nɛnʃl] *adj* exponentiell; (*Math: function etc*) Exponential-
export [ɛks'pɔːt] *vt* exportieren, ausführen; (*ideas, values*) verbreiten ▷ *n* Export *m*, Ausfuhr *f*; (*product*) Exportgut *nt* ▷ *cpd* Export-, Ausfuhr-
exportation [ɛkspɔː'teɪʃən] *n* Export *m*, Ausfuhr *f*
exporter [ɛks'pɔːtəʳ] *n* Exporteur *m*
expose [ɪks'pəuz] *vt* freilegen; (*to heat, radiation*) aussetzen; (*unmask*) entlarven; **to ~ o.s.** sich entblößen
exposé [ɪk'spəuzeɪ] *n* Enthüllung *f*
exposed [ɪks'pəuzd] *adj* ungeschützt; (*wire*) bloßliegend; **to be ~ to** (*radiation, heat etc*) ausgesetzt sein *+dat*
exposition [ɛkspə'zɪʃən] *n* Erläuterung *f*; (*exhibition*) Ausstellung *f*
exposure [ɪks'pəuʒəʳ] *n* (*to heat, radiation*) Aussetzung *f*; (*publicity*) Publicity *f*; (*of person*) Entlarvung *f*; (*Phot*) Belichtung *f*; (*: shot*) Aufnahme *f*; **to be suffering from ~** an Unterkühlung leiden; **to die from ~** erfrieren
exposure meter *n* Belichtungsmesser *m*
expound [ɪks'paund] *vt* darlegen, erläutern
express [ɪks'prɛs] *adj* ausdrücklich; (*intention*) bestimmt; (*Brit: letter etc*) Express-, Eil- ▷ *n* (*train*) Schnellzug *m*; (*bus*) Schnellbus *m* ▷ *adv* (*send*) per Express ▷ *vt* ausdrücken; (*view, emotion*) zum Ausdruck bringen; **to ~ o.s.** sich ausdrücken
expression [ɪks'prɛʃən] *n* Ausdruck *m*; (*on face*) (Gesichts)ausdruck *m*
expressionism [ɪks'prɛʃənɪzəm] *n* Expressionismus *m*
expressive [ɪks'prɛsɪv] *adj* ausdrucksvoll; **~ ability** Ausdrucksfähigkeit *f*
expressly [ɪks'prɛslɪ] *adv* ausdrücklich; (*intentionally*) absichtlich
expressway [ɪks'prɛsweɪ] (*US*) *n* Schnellstraße *f*
expropriate [ɛks'prəuprɪeɪt] *vt* enteignen
expulsion [ɪks'pʌlʃən] *n* (*Scol*) Verweisung *f*; (*Pol*) Ausweisung *f*; (*of gas, liquid etc*) Ausstoßen *nt*
expurgate ['ɛkspəːgeɪt] *vt* zensieren; **the ~d version** die zensierte *or* bereinigte Fassung
exquisite [ɛks'kwɪzɪt] *adj* exquisit, erlesen; (*keenly felt*) köstlich
exquisitely [ɛks'kwɪzɪtlɪ] *adv* exquisit; (*carved*) kunstvoll; (*polite, sensitive*) äußerst
ex-serviceman ['ɛks'səːvɪsmən] (*irreg: like* **man**) *n* ehemaliger Soldat *m*
ext. *abbr* (*Tel*) = **extension**
extemporize [ɪks'tɛmpəraɪz] *vi* improvisieren
extend [ɪks'tɛnd] *vt* verlängern; (*building*) anbauen an *+acc*; (*offer, invitation*) aussprechen; (*arm, hand*) ausstrecken; (*deadline*) verschieben ▷ *vi* sich erstrecken; (*period*) dauern
extension [ɪks'tɛnʃən] *n* Verlängerung *f*; (*of building*) Anbau *m*; (*of time*) Aufschub *m*; (*of campaign, rights*) Erweiterung *f*; (*Tel*) (Neben)anschluss *m*; **~ 3718** (*Tel*) Apparat 3718
extension cable *n* Verlängerungskabel *nt*
extension lead *n* Verlängerungsschnur *f*
extensive [ɪks'tɛnsɪv] *adj* ausgedehnt; (*effect*) weitreichend; (*damage*) beträchtlich; (*coverage, discussion*) ausführlich; (*inquiries*) umfangreich; (*use*) häufig
extensively [ɪks'tɛnsɪvlɪ] *adv*: **he's travelled ~** er ist viel gereist
extent [ɪks'tɛnt] *n* Ausdehnung *f*; (*of problem, damage, loss etc*) Ausmaß *nt*; **to some ~** bis zu einem gewissen Grade; **to a certain ~** in gewissem Maße; **to a large ~** in hohem Maße; **to the ~ of …** (*debts*) in Höhe von …; **to go to the ~ of doing sth** so weit gehen, etw zu tun; **to such an ~ that …** dermaßen, dass …; **to what ~?** inwieweit?
extenuating [ɪks'tɛnjueɪtɪŋ] *adj*: **~ circumstances** mildernde Umstände *pl*
exterior [ɛks'tɪərɪəʳ] *adj* (*surface, angle, world*) Außen- ▷ *n* Außenseite *f*; (*appearance*) Äußere(s) *nt*
exterminate [ɪks'təːmɪneɪt] *vt* ausrotten
extermination [ɪkstəːmɪ'neɪʃən] *n* Ausrottung *f*
external [ɛks'təːnl] *adj* (*wall etc*) Außen-; (*use*) äußerlich; (*evidence*) unabhängig; (*examiner, auditor*) extern ▷ *n*: **the ~s** die Äußerlichkeiten *pl*; **for ~ use only** nur äußerlich (anzuwenden); **~ affairs** (*Pol*) auswärtige Angelegenheiten *pl*
externally [ɛks'təːnəlɪ] *adv* äußerlich
extinct [ɪks'tɪŋkt] *adj* ausgestorben; (*volcano*) erloschen
extinction [ɪks'tɪŋkʃən] *n* Aussterben *nt*
extinguish [ɪks'tɪŋgwɪʃ] *vt* löschen; (*hope*) zerstören
extinguisher [ɪks'tɪŋgwɪʃəʳ] *n* (*also*: **fire**

extinguisher) Feuerlöscher *m*
extol, (*US*) **extoll** [ɪks'təul] *vt* preisen, rühmen
extort [ɪks'tɔːt] *vt* erpressen; (*confession*) erzwingen
extortion [ɪks'tɔːʃən] *n* (*see vb*) Erpressung *f*; Erzwingung *f*
extortionate [ɪks'tɔːʃnɪt] *adj* überhöht; (*price*) Wucher-
extra ['ɛkstrə] *adj* zusätzlich ▷ *adv* extra ▷ *n* Extra *nt*; (*surcharge*) zusätzliche Kosten *pl*; (*Cine, Theat*) Statist(in) *m(f)*; **wine will cost ~** Wein wird extra berechnet
extra ... ['ɛkstrə] *pref* außer-, extra-
extract [*vt* ɪks'trækt, *n* 'ekstrækt] *vt* (*tooth*) ziehen; (*mineral*) gewinnen ▷ *n* Auszug *m*; (*also*: **malt extract, vanilla extract** *etc*) Extrakt *m*; **to ~ (from)** (*object*) herausziehen (aus); (*money*) herausholen (aus); (*promise*) abringen *+dat*
extraction [ɪks'trækʃən] *n* (*see vb*) Ziehen *nt*; Gewinnung *f*; Herausziehen *nt*; Herausholen *nt*; Abringen *nt*; (*Dentistry*) Extraktion *f*; (*descent*) Herkunft *f*, Abstammung *f*; **to be of Scottish ~, to be Scottish by ~** schottischer Herkunft *or* Abstammung sein
extractor fan [ɪks'træktə-] *n* Sauglüfter *m*
extracurricular ['ɛkstrəkə'rɪkjuləʳ] *adj* außerhalb des Lehrplans
extradite ['ɛkstrədaɪt] *vt* ausliefern
extradition [ɛkstrə'dɪʃən] *n* Auslieferung *f* ▷ *cpd* Auslieferungs-
extramarital ['ɛkstrə'mærɪtl] *adj* außerehelich
extramural ['ɛkstrə'mjuərl] *adj* außerhalb der Universität; **~ classes** von der Universität veranstaltete Teilzeitkurse *pl*
extraneous [ɛks'treɪnɪəs] *adj* unwesentlich
extraordinary [ɪks'trɔːdnrɪ] *adj* ungewöhnlich; (*special*) außerordentlich; **the ~ thing is that ...** das Merkwürdige ist, dass ...
extraordinary general meeting *n* außerordentliche Hauptversammlung *f*
extrapolation [ɛkstræpə'leɪʃən] *n* Extrapolation *f*
extrasensory perception ['ɛkstrə'sɛnsərɪ-] *n* außersinnliche Wahrnehmung *f*
extra time *n* (*Football*) Verlängerung *f*
extravagance [ɪks'trævəgəns] *n* (*no pl*) Verschwendungssucht *f*; (*example of spending*) Luxus *m*
extravagant [ɪks'trævəgənt] *adj* extravagant; (*tastes, gift*) teuer; (*wasteful*) verschwenderisch; (*praise*) übertrieben; (*ideas*) ausgefallen
extreme [ɪks'triːm] *adj* extrem; (*point, edge, poverty*) äußerste(r, s) ▷ *n* Extrem *nt*; **the ~ right/left** (*Pol*) die äußerste *or* extreme Rechte/Linke; **~s of temperature** extreme Temperaturen *pl*
extremely [ɪks'triːmlɪ] *adv* äußerst, extrem
extremist [ɪks'triːmɪst] *n* Extremist(in) *m(f)* ▷ *adj* extremistisch
extremities [ɪks'trɛmɪtɪz] *npl* Extremitäten *pl*
extremity [ɪks'trɛmɪtɪ] *n* Rand *m*; (*end*) äußerstes Ende *nt*; (*of situation*) Ausmaß *nt*
extricate ['ɛkstrɪkeɪt] *vt*: **to ~ sb/sth (from)** jdn/etw befreien (aus)
extrovert ['ɛkstrəvəːt] *n* extravertierter Mensch *m*
exuberance [ɪg'zjuːbərns] *n* Überschwänglichkeit *f*
exuberant [ɪg'zjuːbərnt] *adj* überschwänglich; (*imagination etc*) lebhaft
exude [ɪg'zjuːd] *vt* ausstrahlen; (*liquid*) absondern; (*smell*) ausströmen
exult [ɪg'zʌlt] *vi*: **to ~ (in)** jubeln (über *+acc*)
exultant [ɪg'zʌltənt] *adj* jubelnd; (*shout*) Jubel-; **to be ~** jubeln
exultation [ɛgzʌl'teɪʃən] *n* Jubel *m*
eye [aɪ] *n* Auge *nt*; (*of needle*) Öhr *nt* ▷ *vt* betrachten; **to keep an ~ on** aufpassen auf *+acc*; **as far as the ~ can see** so weit das Auge reicht; **in the public ~** im Blickpunkt der Öffentlichkeit; **to have an ~ for sth** einen Blick für etw haben; **with an ~ to doing sth** (*Brit*) mit der Absicht, etw zu tun; **there's more to this than meets the ~** da steckt mehr dahinter(, als man auf den ersten Blick meint)
eyeball ['aɪbɔːl] *n* Augapfel *m*
eyebath ['aɪbɑːθ] (*Brit*) *n* Augenbadewanne *f*
eyebrow ['aɪbrau] *n* Augenbraue *f*
eyebrow pencil *n* Augenbrauenstift *m*
eye-catching ['aɪkætʃɪŋ] *adj* auffallend
eyecup ['aɪkʌp] (*US*) *n* = **eyebath**
eye drops *npl* Augentropfen *pl*
eyeful ['aɪful] *n*: **to get an ~ of sth** (*lit*) etw ins Auge bekommen; (*fig: have a good look*) einiges von etw zu sehen bekommen; **she's quite an ~** sie hat allerhand zu bieten
eyeglass ['aɪglɑːs] *n* Augenglas *nt*
eyelash ['aɪlæʃ] *n* Augenwimper *f*
eyelet ['aɪlɪt] *n* Öse *f*
eye level *n*: **at ~** in Augenhöhe
eyelevel ['aɪlɛvl] *adj* in Augenhöhe
eyelid ['aɪlɪd] *n* Augenlid *nt*
eyeliner ['aɪlaɪnəʳ] *n* Eyeliner *m*
eye-opener ['aɪəupnəʳ] *n* Überraschung *f*; **to be an ~ to sb** jdm die Augen öffnen
eye shadow *n* Lidschatten *m*
eyesight ['aɪsaɪt] *n* Sehvermögen *nt*
eyesore ['aɪsɔːʳ] *n* Schandfleck *m*
eyestrain ['aɪstreɪn] *n*: **to get ~** seine Augen überanstrengen
eyetooth ['aɪtuːθ] (*pl* **eyeteeth**) *n* Eckzahn *m*, Augenzahn *m*; **to give one's eyeteeth for sth** alles für etw geben; **to give one's eyeteeth to do sth** alles darum geben, etw zu tun
eyewash ['aɪwɔʃ] *n* Augenwasser *nt*; (*fig*) Gewäsch *nt*
eyewitness ['aɪwɪtnɪs] *n* Augenzeuge *m*, Augenzeugin *f*
eyrie ['ɪərɪ] *n* Horst *m*

Ff

F[1], **f** [ɛf] *n (letter)* F *nt*, f *nt*; **F for Frederick, F for Fox** *(US)* ≈ F wie Friedrich
F[2] [ɛf] *n (Mus)* F *nt*, f *nt*
F[3] [ɛf] *abbr (= Fahrenheit)* F
FA *(Brit) n abbr (= Football Association) englischer Fußball-Dachverband,* ≈ DFB *m*
FAA *(US) n abbr (= Federal Aviation Administration) amerikanische Luftfahrtbehörde*
fable ['feɪbl] *n* Fabel *f*
fabric ['fæbrɪk] *n* Stoff *m*; *(of society)* Gefüge *nt*; *(of building)* Bausubstanz *f*
fabricate ['fæbrɪkeɪt] *vt* herstellen; *(story)* erfinden; *(evidence)* fälschen
fabrication [fæbrɪ'keɪʃən] *n* Herstellung *f*; *(lie)* Erfindung *f*
fabric ribbon *n (for typewriter)* Gewebefarbband *nt*
fabulous ['fæbjuləs] *adj* fabelhaft, toll *(inf)*; *(extraordinary)* sagenhaft; *(mythical)* legendär
façade [fə'sɑːd] *n* Fassade *f*
face [feɪs] *n* Gesicht *nt*; *(expression)* Gesichtsausdruck *m*; *(grimace)* Grimasse *f*; *(of clock)* Zifferblatt *nt*; *(of mountain, cliff)* (Steil)wand *f*; *(of building)* Fassade *f*; *(side, surface)* Seite *f* ▷ *vt (subj: person)* gegenübersitzen/-stehen *+dat etc*; *(: building, street etc)* liegen zu; *(: north, south etc)* liegen nach; *(unpleasant situation)* sich gegenübersehen *+dat*; *(facts)* ins Auge sehen *+dat*; **~ down** mit dem Gesicht nach unten; *(card)* mit der Bildseite nach unten; *(object)* mit der Vorderseite nach unten; **to lose/save ~** das Gesicht verlieren/wahren; **to make** *or* **pull a ~** das Gesicht verziehen; **in the ~ of** trotz *+gen*; **on the ~ of it** so, wie es aussieht; **to come ~ to ~ with sb** jdn treffen; **to come ~ to ~ with a problem** einem Problem gegenüberstehen; **to ~ each other** einander gegenüberstehen/-liegen/-sitzen *etc*; **to ~ the fact that ...** der Tatsache ins Auge sehen, dass ...; **the man facing me** der Mann mir gegenüber
▸ **face up to** *vt fus (obligations, difficulty)* auf sich *acc* nehmen; *(situation, possibility)* sich abfinden mit; *(danger, fact)* ins Auge sehen *+dat*
face cloth *(Brit) n* Waschlappen *m*
face cream *n* Gesichtscreme *f*
faceless ['feɪslɪs] *adj (fig)* anonym
face-lift ['feɪslɪft] *n* Facelifting *nt*; *(of building etc)* Verschönerung *f*
face powder *n* Gesichtspuder *m*
face-saving ['feɪs'seɪvɪŋ] *adj*: **a ~ excuse/tactic** eine Entschuldigung/Taktik, um das Gesicht zu wahren
facet ['fæsɪt] *n* Seite *f*, Aspekt *m*; *(of gem)* Facette *f*
face time *n (US) Zeit, die man mit jemandem im direkten persönlichen Gespräch verbringt*
facetious [fə'siːʃəs] *adj* witzelnd
face-to-face [feɪstə'feɪs] *adj* persönlich; *(confrontation)* direkt
face value *n* Nennwert *m*; **to take sth at ~** *(fig)* etw für bare Münze nehmen
facia ['feɪʃə] *n* = **fascia**
facial ['feɪʃl] *adj (expression, massage etc)* Gesichts- ▷ *n* kosmetische Gesichtsbehandlung *f*
facile ['fæsaɪl] *adj* oberflächlich; *(comment)* nichtssagend
facilitate [fə'sɪlɪteɪt] *vt* erleichtern
facilities [fə'sɪlɪtɪz] *npl* Einrichtungen *pl*; **cooking ~** Kochgelegenheit *f*; **credit ~** Kreditmöglichkeiten *pl*
facility [fə'sɪlɪtɪ] *n* Einrichtung *f*; **to have a ~ for** *(skill, aptitude)* eine Begabung haben für
facing ['feɪsɪŋ] *prep* gegenüber *+dat* ▷ *n (Sewing)* Besatz *m*
facsimile [fæk'sɪmɪlɪ] *n* Faksimile *nt*; *(also:* **facsimile machine***)* Fernkopierer *m*, (Tele)faxgerät *nt*; *(transmitted document)* Fernkopie *f*, (Tele)fax *nt*
fact [fækt] *n* Tatsache *f*; *(truth)* Wirklichkeit *f*; **in ~** eigentlich; *(in reality)* tatsächlich, in Wirklichkeit; **to know for a ~ that ...** ganz genau wissen, dass ...; **the ~ (of the matter) is that ...** die Sache ist die, dass ...; **it's a ~ of life that ...** es ist eine Tatsache, dass ...; **to tell sb the ~s of life** *(sex)* jdn aufklären
fact-finding ['fæktfaɪndɪŋ] *adj*: **a ~ tour** *or* **mission** eine Informationstour *f*
faction ['fækʃən] *n* Fraktion *f*
factional ['fækʃənl] *adj (dispute, system)* Fraktions-
factor ['fæktəʳ] *n* Faktor *m*; *(Comm)* Kommissionär *m*; *(: agent)* Makler *m*; **safety ~** Sicherheitsfaktor *m*; **human ~** menschlicher Faktor

factory ['fæktərɪ] *n* Fabrik *f*
factory farming *(Brit) n* industriell betriebene Viehzucht *f*
factory floor *n*: **the ~** *(workers)* die Fabrikarbeiter *pl*; **on the ~** bei *or* unter den Fabrikarbeitern
factory ship *n* Fabrikschiff *nt*
factual ['fæktjuəl] *adj* sachlich; *(information)* Sach-
faculty ['fækəltɪ] *n* Vermögen *nt*, Kraft *f*; *(ability)* Talent *nt*; *(of university)* Fakultät *f*; *(US: teaching staff)* Lehrkörper *m*
fad [fæd] *n* Fimmel *m*, Tick *m*
fade [feɪd] *vi* verblassen; *(light)* nachlassen; *(sound)* schwächer werden; *(flower)* verblühen; *(hope)* zerrinnen; *(smile)* verschwinden
▸ **fade in** *vt sep* allmählich einblenden
▸ **fade out** *vt sep* ausblenden
faeces, (US) **feces** ['fi:si:z] *npl* Kot *m*
fag [fæg] *n (Brit: inf: cigarette)* Glimmstängel *m*; *(: chore)* Schinderei *f (inf)*, Plackerei *f (inf)*; *(US: inf: homosexual)* Schwule(r) *m*
fail [feɪl] *vt (exam)* nicht bestehen; *(candidate)* durchfallen lassen; *(subj: courage)* verlassen; *(: leader, memory)* im Stich lassen ▷ *vi (candidate)* durchfallen; *(attempt)* fehlschlagen; *(brakes)* versagen; *(also:* **be failing**: *health)* sich verschlechtern; *(: eyesight, light)* nachlassen; **to ~ to do sth** etw nicht tun; *(neglect)* (es) versäumen, etw zu tun; **without ~** ganz bestimmt
failing ['feɪlɪŋ] *n* Schwäche *f*, Fehler *m* ▷ *prep* in Ermangelung *+gen*; **~ that** (oder) sonst, und wenn das nicht möglich ist
fail-safe ['feɪlseɪf] *adj* (ab)gesichert
failure ['feɪljə^r] *n* Misserfolg *m*; *(person)* Versager(in) *m(f)*; *(of brakes, heart)* Versagen *nt*; *(of engine, power)* Ausfall *m*; *(of crops)* Missernte *f*; *(in exam)* Durchfall *m*; **his ~ to turn up meant that we had to ...** weil er nicht kam, mussten wir ...; **it was a complete ~** es war ein totaler Fehlschlag
faint [feɪnt] *adj* schwach; *(breeze, trace)* leicht ▷ *n* Ohnmacht *f* ▷ *vi* ohnmächtig werden, in Ohnmacht fallen; **she felt ~** ihr wurde schwach
faintest ['feɪntɪst] *adj, n*: **I haven't the ~ (idea)** ich habe keinen blassen Schimmer
faint-hearted ['feɪnt'hɑ:tɪd] *adj* zaghaft
faintly ['feɪntlɪ] *adv* schwach
fair [fɛə^r] *adj* gerecht, fair; *(size, number)* ansehnlich; *(chance, guess)* recht gut; *(hair)* blond; *(skin, complexion)* hell; *(weather)* schön ▷ *adv*: **to play ~** fair spielen ▷ *n (also:* **trade fair**) Messe *f*; *(Brit: funfair)* Jahrmarkt *m*, Rummel *m*; **it's not ~!** das ist nicht fair!; **a ~ amount of** ziemlich viel
fair copy *n* Reinschrift *f*
fair game *n*: **to be ~ (for)** *(for attack, criticism)* Freiwild *nt* sein (für)
fairground ['fɛəgraund] *n* Rummelplatz *m*
fair-haired [fɛə'hɛəd] *adj* blond
fairly ['fɛəlɪ] *adv* gerecht; *(quite)* ziemlich; **I'm ~ sure** ich bin (mir) ziemlich sicher
fairness ['fɛənɪs] *n* Gerechtigkeit *f*; **in all ~** gerechterweise, fairerweise
fair play *n* faires Verhalten *nt*, Fair Play *nt*
fairway ['fɛəweɪ] *n (Golf)*: **the ~** das Fairway
fairy ['fɛərɪ] *n* Fee *f*
fairy godmother *n* gute Fee *f*
fairy lights *(Brit) npl* bunte Lichter *pl*
fairy tale *n* Märchen *nt*
faith [feɪθ] *n* Glaube *m*; *(trust)* Vertrauen *nt*; **to have ~ in sb** jdm vertrauen; **to have ~ in sth** Vertrauen in etw *acc* haben
faithful ['feɪθful] *adj (account)* genau; **~ (to)** *(person)* treu *+dat*
faithfully ['feɪθfəlɪ] *adv (see adj)* genau; treu
faith healer *n* Gesundbeter(in) *m(f)*
fake [feɪk] *n* Fälschung *f*; *(person)* Schwindler(in) *m(f)* ▷ *adj* gefälscht ▷ *vt* fälschen; *(illness, emotion)* vortäuschen; **his illness is a ~** er simuliert seine Krankheit nur
falcon ['fɔ:lkən] *n* Falke *m*
Falkland Islands ['fɔ:klənd-] *npl*: **the ~** die Falklandinseln *pl*
fall [fɔ:l] *(pt* **fell**, *pp* **~en**) *n* Fall *m*; *(of price, temperature)* Sinken *nt*; *(: sudden)* Sturz *m*; *(US: autumn)* Herbst *m* ▷ *vi* fallen; *(night, darkness)* hereinbrechen; *(silence)* eintreten; **falls** *npl (waterfall)* Wasserfall *m*; **a ~ of snow** ein Schneefall *m*; **a ~ of earth** ein Erdrutsch *m*; **to ~ flat** auf die Nase fallen; *(plan)* ins Wasser fallen; *(joke)* nicht ankommen; **to ~ in love (with sb/sth)** sich (in jdn/etw) verlieben; **to ~ short of sb's expectations** jds Erwartungen nicht erfüllen
▸ **fall apart** *vi* auseinanderfallen, kaputtgehen; *(inf: emotionally)* durchdrehen
▸ **fall back** *vi* zurückweichen
▸ **fall back on** *vi* zurückgreifen auf *+acc*; **to have sth to ~ back on** auf etw *acc* zurückgreifen können
▸ **fall behind** *vi* zurückbleiben; *(fig: with payment)* in Rückstand geraten
▸ **fall down** *vi* hinfallen; *(building)* einstürzen
▸ **fall for** *vt fus (trick, story)* hereinfallen auf *+acc*; *(person)* sich verlieben in *+acc*
▸ **fall in** *vi* einstürzen; *(Mil)* antreten
▸ **fall in with** *vt fus* eingehen auf *+acc*
▸ **fall off** *vi* herunterfallen; *(takings, attendance)* zurückgehen
▸ **fall out** *vi (hair, teeth)* ausfallen; **to ~ out with sb** sich mit jdm zerstreiten
▸ **fall over** *vi* hinfallen; *(object)* umfallen ▷ *vt*: **to ~ over o.s. to do sth** sich *dat* die größte Mühe geben, etw zu tun
▸ **fall through** *vi (plan, project)* ins Wasser fallen
fallacy ['fæləsɪ] *n* Irrtum *m*
fall-back ['fɔ:lbæk] *adj*: **~ position** Rückzugsbasis *f*
fallen ['fɔ:lən] *pp of* **fall**
fallible ['fæləbl] *adj* fehlbar
falling ['fɔ:lɪŋ] *adj*: **~ market** *(Comm)* Baissemarkt *m*
falling off *n* Rückgang *m*

falling-out ['fɔːlɪŋ'aut] *n* (*break-up*) Bruch *m*
Fallopian tube [fə'ləupɪən-] *n* Eileiter *m*
fallout ['fɔːlaut] *n* radioaktiver Niederschlag *m*
fallout shelter *n* Atombunker *m*
fallow ['fæləu] *adj* brach(liegend)
false [fɔːls] *adj* falsch; (*imprisonment*) widerrechtlich
false alarm *n* falscher *or* blinder Alarm *m*
falsehood ['fɔːlshud] *n* Unwahrheit *f*
falsely ['fɔːlslɪ] *adv* (*accuse*) zu Unrecht
false pretences *npl*: **under ~** unter Vorspiegelung falscher Tatsachen
false teeth (*Brit*) *npl* Gebiss *nt*
falsify ['fɔːlsɪfaɪ] *vt* fälschen
falter ['fɔːltəʳ] *vi* stocken; (*hesitate*) zögern
fame [feɪm] *n* Ruhm *m*
familiar [fə'mɪlɪəʳ] *adj* vertraut; (*intimate*) vertraulich; **to be ~ with** vertraut sein mit; **to make o.s. ~ with sth** sich mit etw vertraut machen; **to be on ~ terms with sb** mit jdm auf vertrautem Fuß stehen
familiarity [fəmɪlɪ'ærɪtɪ] *n* (*see adj*) Vertrautheit *f*; Vertraulichkeit *f*
familiarize [fə'mɪlɪəraɪz] *vt*: **to ~ o.s. with sth** sich mit etw vertraut machen
family ['fæmɪlɪ] *n* Familie *f*; (*relations*) Verwandtschaft *f*
family business, **family company** *n* Familienunternehmen *nt or* -betrieb *m*
family credit *n Beihilfe für einkommensschwache Familien*
family doctor *n* Hausarzt *m*, Hausärztin *f*
family life *n* Familienleben *nt*
family man *n* (*home-loving*) häuslich veranlagter Mann *m*; (*with a family*) Familienvater *m*
family planning *n* Familienplanung *f*; **~ clinic** ≈ Familienberatungsstelle *f*
family tree *n* Stammbaum *m*
famine ['fæmɪn] *n* Hungersnot *f*
famished ['fæmɪʃt] (*inf*) *adj* ausgehungert; **I'm ~** ich sterbe vor Hunger
famous ['feɪməs] *adj* berühmt
famously ['feɪməslɪ] *adv* (*get on*) prächtig
fan [fæn] *n* (*person*) Fan *m*; (*object: folding*) Fächer *m*; (*: Elec*) Ventilator *m* ▷ *vt* fächeln; (*fire*) anfachen; (*quarrel*) schüren
▸ **fan out** *vi* ausschwärmen; (*unfurl*) sich fächerförmig ausbreiten
fanatic [fə'nætɪk] *n* Fanatiker(in) *m(f)*; (*enthusiast*) Fan *m*
fanatical [fə'nætɪkl] *adj* fanatisch
fan belt *n* (*Aut*) Keilriemen *m*
fanciful ['fænsɪful] *adj* (*idea*) abstrus, seltsam; (*design, name*) fantasievoll; (*object*) reich verziert
fan club *n* Fanklub *m*
fancy ['fænsɪ] *n* Laune *f*; (*imagination*) Fantasie *f*; (*fantasy*) Fantasievorstellung *f* ▷ *adj* (*clothes, hat*) toll, chic *inv*; (*hotel*) fein, vornehm; (*food*) ausgefallen ▷ *vt* mögen; (*imagine*) sich *dat* einbilden; (*think*) glauben; **to take a ~ to sth** Lust auf etw *acc* bekommen; **when the ~ takes him** wenn ihm gerade danach ist; **it took** *or* **caught my ~** es gefiel mir; **to ~ that ...** meinen, dass ...; **~ that!** (nein) so was!; **he fancies her** (*inf*) sie gefällt ihm
fancy dress *n* Verkleidung *f*, (Masken)kostüm *nt*
fancy-dress ball ['fænsɪdrɛs-] *n* Maskenball *m*
fancy goods *npl* Geschenkartikel *pl*
fanfare ['fænfɛəʳ] *n* Fanfare *f*
fanfold paper ['fænfəuld-] *n* Endlospapier *nt*
fang [fæŋ] *n* (*tooth*) Fang *m*; (*: of snake*) Giftzahn *m*
fan heater (*Brit*) *n* Heizlüfter *m*
fanlight ['fænlaɪt] *n* Oberlicht *nt*
fanny ['fænɪ] *n* (*US: inf: bottom*) Po *m*; (*Brit: inf!: genitals*) Möse *f* (*!*)
fantasize ['fæntəsaɪz] *vi* fantasieren
fantastic [fæn'tæstɪk] *adj* fantastisch
fantasy ['fæntəsɪ] *n* Fantasie *f*; (*dream*) Traum *m*
fanzine ['fænziːn] *n* Fanmagazin *nt*
FAO *n abbr* (*= Food and Agriculture Organization*) FAO *f*
FAQ *abbr* (*Comput: = frequently-asked questions*) FAQ *pl*
far [fɑːʳ] *adj*: **at the ~ side** auf der anderen Seite ▷ *adv* weit; **at the ~ end** am anderen Ende; **the ~ left/right** die extreme Linke/Rechte; **~ away, ~ off** weit entfernt *or* weg; **her thoughts were ~ away** sie war mit ihren Gedanken weit weg; **~ from** (*fig*) alles andere als; **by ~** bei Weitem; **is it ~ to London?** ist es weit bis nach London?; **it's not ~ from here** es ist nicht weit von hier; **go as ~ as the church** gehen/fahren Sie bis zur Kirche; **as ~ back as the 13th century** schon im 13. Jahrhundert; **as ~ as I know** soweit ich weiß; **as ~ as possible** so weit wie möglich; **how ~?** wie weit?; **how ~ have you got with your work?** wie weit sind Sie mit Ihrer Arbeit (gekommen)?
faraway ['fɑːrəweɪ] *adj* weit entfernt; (*look, voice*) abwesend
farce [fɑːs] *n* Farce *f*
farcical ['fɑːsɪkl] *adj* absurd, grotesk
fare [fɛəʳ] *n* Fahrpreis *m*; (*money*) Fahrgeld *nt*; (*passenger*) Fahrgast *m*; (*food*) Kost *f* ▷ *vi*: **he ~d well/badly** es ging ihm gut/schlecht; **half/full ~** halber/voller Fahrpreis; **how did you ~?** wie ist es Ihnen ergangen?; **they ~d badly in the recent elections** sie haben bei den letzten Wahlen schlecht abgeschnitten
Far East *n*: **the ~** der Ferne Osten
farewell [fɛə'wɛl] *excl* lebe/lebt *etc* wohl! ▷ *n* Abschied *m* ▷ *cpd* Abschieds-
far-fetched ['fɑː'fɛtʃt] *adj* weit hergeholt
farm [fɑːm] *n* Bauernhof *m* ▷ *vt* bebauen
▸ **farm out** *vt* (*work etc*) vergeben
farmer ['fɑːməʳ] *n* Bauer *m*, Bäu(e)rin *f*, Landwirt(in) *m(f)*
farm hand *n* Landarbeiter(in) *m(f)*
farmhouse ['fɑːmhaus] *n* Bauernhaus *nt*
farming ['fɑːmɪŋ] *n* Landwirtschaft *f*; (*of crops*) Ackerbau *m*; (*of animals*) Viehzucht *f*;

sheep ~ Schafzucht *f*; **intensive** ~ (*of crops*) Intensivanbau *m*; (*of animals*) Intensivhaltung *f*
farm labourer *n* = **farm hand**
farmland ['fɑːmlænd] *n* Ackerland *nt*
farm produce *n* landwirtschaftliche Produkte *pl*
farm worker *n* = **farm hand**
farmyard ['fɑːmjɑːd] *n* Hof *m*
Faroe Islands ['fɛərəu-] *npl*: **the** ~ die Färöer *pl*
Faroes ['fɛərəuz] *npl* = **Faroe Islands**
far-reaching ['fɑː'riːtʃɪŋ] *adj* weitreichend
far-sighted ['fɑː'saɪtɪd] *adj* weitsichtig; (*fig*) weitblickend
fart [fɑːt] *vi* furzen (*inf!*) ▷ *n* Furz *m* (*inf!*)
farther ['fɑːðəʳ] *adv* weiter ▷ *adj* weiter entfernt
farthest ['fɑːðɪst] *superl of* **far**
FAS, f.a.s. (*Brit*) *abbr* (= *free alongside ship*) frei Kai
fascia ['feɪʃə] *n* (*Aut*) Armaturenbrett *nt*
fascinate ['fæsɪneɪt] *vt* faszinieren
fascinating ['fæsɪneɪtɪŋ] *adj* faszinierend
fascination [fæsɪ'neɪʃən] *n* Faszination *f*
fascism ['fæʃɪzəm] *n* Faschismus *m*
fascist ['fæʃɪst] *adj* faschistisch ▷ *n* Faschist(in) *m(f)*
fashion ['fæʃən] *n* Mode *f*; (*manner*) Art *f* ▷ *vt* formen; **in** ~ modern; **out of** ~ unmodern; **after a** ~ recht und schlecht; **in the Greek** ~ im griechischen Stil
fashionable ['fæʃnəbl] *adj* modisch, modern; (*subject*) Mode-; (*club, writer*) in Mode
fashion designer *n* Modezeichner(in) *m(f)*
fashion show *n* Modenschau *f*
fashion victim *n* Modesklave *m*, Modesklavin *f*
fast [fɑːst] *adj* schnell; (*dye, colour*) farbecht ▷ *adv* schnell; (*stuck, held*) fest ▷ *n* Fasten *nt*; (*period of fasting*) Fastenzeit *f* ▷ *vi* fasten; **my watch is (5 minutes)** ~ meine Uhr geht (5 Minuten) vor; **to be** ~ **asleep** tief *or* fest schlafen; **as** ~ **as I can** so schnell ich kann; **to make a boat** ~ (*Brit*) ein Boot festmachen
fasten ['fɑːsn] *vt* festmachen; (*coat, belt etc*) zumachen ▷ *vi* (*see vt*) festgemacht werden; zugemacht werden
▸ **fasten (up)on** *vt fus* sich *dat* in den Kopf setzen
fastener ['fɑːsnəʳ] *n* Verschluss *m*
fastening ['fɑːsnɪŋ] *n* = **fastener**
fast food *n* Fast Food *nt*, Schnellgerichte *pl*
fast-food ['fɑːstfuːd] *cpd* (*industry, chain*) Fast-Food-; ~ **restaurant** Schnellimbiss *m*
fastidious [fæs'tɪdɪəs] *adj* penibel
fast lane *n* (*Aut*): **the** ~ die Überholspur
fat [fæt] *adj* dick; (*person*) dick, fett (*pej*); (*animal*) fett; (*profit*) üppig ▷ *n* Fett *nt*; **that's a** ~ **lot of use** (*inf*) das hilft herzlich wenig; **to live off the** ~ **of the land** wie Gott in Frankreich *or* wie die Made im Speck leben
fatal ['feɪtl] *adj* tödlich; (*mistake*) verhängnisvoll
fatalistic [feɪtə'lɪstɪk] *adj* fatalistisch
fatality [fə'tælɪtɪ] *n* Todesopfer *nt*
fatally ['feɪtəlɪ] *adv* (*see adj*) tödlich; verhängnisvoll
fate [feɪt] *n* Schicksal *nt*; **to meet one's** ~ vom Schicksal ereilt werden
fated ['feɪtɪd] *adj* (*person*) unglückselig; (*project*) zum Scheitern verurteilt; (*governed by fate*) vorherbestimmt
fateful ['feɪtful] *adj* schicksalhaft
fat-free ['fæt'friː] *adj* fettfrei
father ['fɑːðəʳ] *n* Vater *m*
Father Christmas *n* der Weihnachtsmann
fatherhood ['fɑːðəhud] *n* Vaterschaft *f*
father-in-law ['fɑːðərənlɔː] *n* Schwiegervater *m*
fatherland ['fɑːðəlænd] *n* Vaterland *nt*
fatherly ['fɑːðəlɪ] *adj* väterlich
fathom ['fæðəm] *n* (*Naut*) Faden *m* ▷ *vt* (*also*: **fathom out**) verstehen
fatigue [fə'tiːg] *n* Erschöpfung *f*; **fatigues** *npl* (*Mil*) Arbeitsanzug *m*; **metal** ~ Metallermüdung *f*
fatness ['fætnɪs] *n* Dicke *f*
fatten ['fætn] *vt* mästen ▷ *vi* (*person*) dick werden; (*animal*) fett werden; **chocolate is** ~**ing** Schokolade macht dick
fatty ['fætɪ] *adj* fett ▷ *n* (*inf*) Dickerchen *nt*
fatuous ['fætjuəs] *adj* albern, töricht
faucet ['fɔːsɪt] (*US*) *n* (Wasser)hahn *m*
fault [fɔːlt] *n* Fehler *m*; (*blame*) Schuld *f*; (*in machine*) Defekt *m*; (*Geog*) Verwerfung *f* ▷ *vt* (*also*: **find fault with**) etwas auszusetzen haben an *+dat*; **it's my** ~ es ist meine Schuld; **at** ~ im Unrecht; **generous to a** ~ übermäßig großzügig
faultless ['fɔːltlɪs] *adj* fehlerlos
faulty ['fɔːltɪ] *adj* defekt
fauna ['fɔːnə] *n* Fauna *f*
faux pas ['fəu'pɑː] *n inv* Fauxpas *m*
favor *etc* (*US*) = **favour** *etc*
favour, (*US*) **favor** ['feɪvəʳ] *n* (*approval*) Wohlwollen *nt*; (*help*) Gefallen *m* ▷ *vt* bevorzugen; (*be favourable for*) begünstigen; **to ask a** ~ **of sb** jdn um einen Gefallen bitten; **to do sb a** ~ jdm einen Gefallen tun; **to find** ~ **with sb** bei jdm Anklang finden; **in** ~ **of** (*biased*) zugunsten von; (*rejected*) zugunsten *+gen*; **to be in** ~ **of sth** für etw sein; **to be in** ~ **of doing sth** dafür sein, etw zu tun
favourable ['feɪvrəbl] *adj* günstig; (*reaction*) positiv; (*comparison*) vorteilhaft
favourably ['feɪvrəblɪ] *adv* (*react*) positiv; (*compare*) vorteilhaft
favourite ['feɪvrɪt] *adj* Lieblings- ▷ *n* Liebling *m*; (*in race*) Favorit(in) *m(f)*
favouritism ['feɪvrɪtɪzəm] *n* Günstlingswirtschaft *f*
fawn [fɔːn] *n* Rehkitz *nt* ▷ *adj* (*also*: **fawn-coloured**) hellbraun ▷ *vi*: **to** ~ **(up)on** sich einschmeicheln bei
fax [fæks] *n* Fax *nt*; (*machine*) Fax(gerät) *nt* ▷ *vt* faxen
FBI (*US*) *n abbr* (= *Federal Bureau of Investigation*) FBI *nt*

FCC (*US*) *n abbr* (= *Federal Communications Commission*) *Aufsichtsbehörde im Medienbereich*
FCO (*Brit*) *n abbr* (= *Foreign and Commonwealth Office*) ≈ Auswärtiges Amt *nt*
FD (*US*) *n abbr* = **fire department**
FDA (*US*) *n abbr* (= *Food and Drug Administration*) *Nahrungs- und Arzneimittelbehörde*
fear [fɪəʳ] *n* Furcht *f*, Angst *f* ▷ *vt* fürchten, Angst haben vor +*dat*; (*be worried about*) befürchten ▷ *vi* sich fürchten; **~ of heights** Höhenangst *f*; **for ~ of doing sth** aus Angst, etw zu tun; **to ~ for** fürchten um; **to ~ that ...** befürchten, dass ...
fearful ['fɪəful] *adj* (*frightening*) furchtbar, schrecklich; (*apprehensive*) ängstlich; **to be ~ of** Angst haben vor +*dat*
fearfully ['fɪəfəlɪ] *adv* ängstlich; (*inf: very*) furchtbar, schrecklich
fearless ['fɪəlɪs] *adj* furchtlos
fearsome ['fɪəsəm] *adj* furchterregend
feasibility [fiːzə'bɪlɪtɪ] *n* Durchführbarkeit *f*
feasibility study *n* Machbarkeits- *or* Durchführbarkeitsstudie *f*
feasible ['fiːzəbl] *adj* machbar; (*proposal, plan*) durchführbar
feast [fiːst] *n* Festmahl *nt*; (*Rel*: *also*: **feast day**) Festtag *m*, Feiertag *m* ▷ *vi* schlemmen; **to ~ on** sich gütlich tun an +*dat*
feat [fiːt] *n* Leistung *f*
feather ['fɛðəʳ] *n* Feder *f* ▷ *cpd* Feder-; (*mattress*) Federkern- ▷ *vt*: **to ~ one's nest** (*fig*) sein Schäfchen ins Trockene bringen
featherweight ['fɛðəweɪt] *n* Leichtgewicht *nt*; (*Boxing*) Federgewicht *nt*
feature ['fiːtʃəʳ] *n* Merkmal *nt*; (*Press, TV*) Feature *nt* ▷ *vt*: **the film ~s Marlon Brando** Marlon Brando spielt in dem Film mit ▷ *vi*: **to ~ in** vorkommen in +*dat*; (*film*) mitspielen in +*dat*; **features** *npl* (*of face*) (Gesichts)züge *pl*; **it ~d prominently in** es spielte eine große Rolle in +*dat*; **a special ~ on sth/sb** ein Sonderbeitrag *m* über etw/jdn
feature film *n* Spielfilm *m*
featureless ['fiːtʃəlɪs] *adj* (*landscape*) eintönig
Feb. *abbr* (= *February*) Feb.
February ['fɛbruərɪ] *n* Februar *m*; *see also* **July**
feces ['fiːsiːz] (*US*) *npl* = **faeces**
feckless ['fɛklɪs] *adj* nutzlos
Fed [fɛd] (*US: inf*) *n abbr*: **the ~** = **Federal Reserve Board**
Fed. (*US*) *abbr* = **federal; federation**
fed [fɛd] *pt, pp of* **feed**
federal ['fɛdərəl] *adj* föderalistisch
Federal Republic of Germany *n* Bundesrepublik *f* Deutschland
Federal Reserve Board (*US*) *n Kontrollorgan der US-Zentralbank*
Federal Trade Commission (*US*) *n Handelskontrollbehörde*
federation [fɛdə'reɪʃən] *n* Föderation *f*, Bund *m*
fed up *adj*: **to be ~ with** die Nase vollhaben von
fee [fiː] *n* Gebühr *f*; (*of doctor, lawyer*) Honorar *nt*; **school ~s** Schulgeld *nt*; **entrance ~** Eintrittsgebühr *f*; **membership ~** Mitgliedsbeitrag *m*; **for a small ~** gegen eine geringe Gebühr
feeble ['fiːbl] *adj* schwach; (*joke*) lahm
feeble-minded ['fiːbl'maɪndɪd] *adj* dümmlich
feed [fiːd] (*pt, pp* **fed**) *n* Mahlzeit *f*; (*of animal*) Fütterung *f*; (*on printer*) Papiervorschub *m* ▷ *vt* füttern; (*family etc*) ernähren; (*machine*) versorgen; **to ~ sth into sth** etw in etw *acc* einfüllen *or* eingeben; (*data, information*) etw in etw *acc* eingeben; **to ~ material into sth** Material in etw *acc* eingeben
▸ **feed back** *vt* zurückleiten
▸ **feed on** *vt fus* sich nähren von
feedback ['fiːdbæk] *n* Feedback *nt*, Rückmeldung *f*; (*from person*) Reaktion *f*
feeder ['fiːdəʳ] *n* (*road*) Zubringer *m*; (*railway line, air route*) Zubringerlinie *f*; (*baby's bottle*) Flasche *f*
feeding bottle ['fiːdɪŋ-] (*Brit*) *n* Flasche *f*
feel [fiːl] (*pt, pp* **felt**) *n* (*sensation, touch*) Gefühl *nt*; (*impression*) Atmosphäre *f* ▷ *vt* (*object*) fühlen; (*desire, anger, grief*) empfinden; (*pain*) spüren; (*cold*) leiden unter +*dat*; (*think, believe*): **I ~ that you ought to do it** ich meine *or* ich bin der Meinung, dass Sie es tun sollten; **it has a soft ~** es fühlt sich weich an; **I ~ hungry** ich habe Hunger; **I ~ cold** mir ist kalt; **to ~ lonely/better** sich einsam/besser fühlen; **I don't ~ well** mir geht es nicht gut; **I ~ sorry for him** er tut mir leid; **it ~s soft** es fühlt sich weich an; **it ~s colder here** es kommt mir hier kälter vor; **it ~s like velvet** es fühlt sich wie Samt an; **to ~ like** (*desire*) Lust haben auf +*acc*; **to ~ like doing sth** Lust haben, etw zu tun; **to get the ~ of sth** ein Gefühl für etw bekommen; **I'm still ~ing my way** ich versuche noch, mich zu orientieren
▸ **feel about** *vi* umhertasten; **to ~ about** *or* **around in one's pocket for** in seiner Tasche herumsuchen nach
▸ **feel around** *vi* = **feel about**
feelbad factor ['fiːlbæd-] *n* (*inf*) Frustfaktor *m*
feeler ['fiːləʳ] *n* Fühler *m*; **to put out a ~** *or* **feelers** (*fig*) seine Fühler ausstrecken
feelgood ['fiːlgʊd] *adj* (*film, song*) Feelgood-
feeling ['fiːlɪŋ] *n* Gefühl *nt*; (*impression*) Eindruck *m*; **~s ran high about it** man ereiferte sich sehr darüber; **what are your ~s about the matter?** was meinen Sie dazu?; **I have a ~ that ...** ich habe das Gefühl, dass ...; **my ~ is that ...** meine Meinung ist, dass ...; **to hurt sb's ~s** jdn verletzen
fee-paying ['fiːpeɪɪŋ] *adj* (*school*) Privat-; **~ pupils** *Schüler, deren Eltern Schulgeld zahlen*
feet [fiːt] *npl of* **foot**
feign [feɪn] *vt* vortäuschen
feigned [feɪnd] *adj* vorgetäuscht
feint [feɪnt] *n* fein liniertes Papier *nt*
felicitous [fɪ'lɪsɪtəs] *adj* glücklich
feline ['fiːlaɪn] *adj* (*eyes etc*) Katzen-; (*features, grace*) katzenartig
fell [fɛl] *pt of* **fall** ▷ *vt* fällen; (*opponent*) niederstrecken ▷ *n* (*Brit: mountain*) Berg *m*;

(: *moorland*): **the ~s** das Moor(land) ▷ *adj*: **in one ~ swoop** auf einen Schlag

fellow ['fɛləu] *n* Mann *m*, Typ *m* (*inf*); (*comrade*) Kamerad *m*; (*of learned society*) Mitglied *nt*; (*of university*) Fellow *m*; **their ~ prisoners/ students** ihre Mitgefangenen/Kommilitonen (und Kommilitoninnen); **his ~ workers** seine Kollegen (und Kolleginnen)

fellow citizen *n* Mitbürger(in) *m(f)*

fellow countryman (*irreg: like* **man**) *n* Landsmann *m*, Landsmännin *f*

fellow men *npl* Mitmenschen *pl*

fellowship ['fɛləuʃɪp] *n* Kameradschaft *f*; (*society*) Gemeinschaft *f*; (*Scol*) Forschungsstipendium *nt*

fell-walking ['fɛlwɔːkɪŋ] (*Brit*) *n* Bergwandern *nt*

felon ['fɛlən] *n* (*Law*) (Schwer)verbrecher *m*

felony ['fɛlənɪ] *n* (*Law*) (schweres) Verbrechen *nt*

felt [fɛlt] *pt, pp of* **feel** ▷ *n* Filz *m*

felt-tip pen ['fɛlttɪp-] *n* Filzstift *m*

female ['fiːmeɪl] *n* Weibchen *nt*; (*pej: woman*) Frau *f*, Weib *nt* (*pej*) ▷ *adj* weiblich; (*vote etc*) Frauen-; (*Elec: connector, plug*) Mutter-, Innen-; **male and ~ students** Studenten und Studentinnen

Femidom® ['fɛmɪdɔm] *n* Kondom *nt* für die Frau, Femidom® *nt*

feminine ['fɛmɪnɪn] *adj* weiblich, feminin ▷ *n* Femininum *nt*

femininity [fɛmɪ'nɪnɪtɪ] *n* Weiblichkeit *f*

feminism ['fɛmɪnɪzəm] *n* Feminismus *m*

feminist ['fɛmɪnɪst] *n* Feminist(in) *m(f)*

fen [fɛn] (*Brit*) *n*: **the F~s** *die Niederungen in East Anglia*

fence [fɛns] *n* Zaun *m*; (*Sport*) Hindernis *nt* ▷ *vt* (*also*: **fence in**) einzäunen ▷ *vi* (*Sport*) fechten; **to sit on the ~** (*fig*) neutral bleiben, nicht Partei ergreifen

fencing ['fɛnsɪŋ] *n* (*Sport*) Fechten *nt*

fend [fɛnd] *vi*: **to ~ for o.s.** für sich (selbst) sorgen, sich allein durchbringen

▸ **fend off** *vt* abwehren

fender ['fɛndəʳ] *n* Kamingitter *nt*; (*on boat*) Fender *m*; (*US: of car*) Kotflügel *m*

fennel ['fɛnl] *n* Fenchel *m*

ferment [*vi* fə'mɛnt, *n* 'fəːmɛnt] *vi* gären ▷ *n* (*fig: unrest*) Unruhe *f*

fermentation [fəːmɛn'teɪʃən] *n* Gärung *f*

fern [fəːn] *n* Farn *m*

ferocious [fə'rəuʃəs] *adj* wild; (*behaviour*) heftig; (*competition*) scharf

ferocity [fə'rɔsɪtɪ] *n* (*see adj*) Wildheit *f*; Heftigkeit *f*; Schärfe *f*

ferret ['fɛrɪt] *n* Frettchen *nt*

▸ **ferret about** *vi* herumstöbern

▸ **ferret around** *vi* = **ferret about**

▸ **ferret out** *vt* aufspüren

ferry ['fɛrɪ] *n* (*also*: **ferryboat**) Fähre *f* ▷ *vt* transportieren; **to ~ sth/sb across** *or* **over** jdn/etw übersetzen

ferryman ['fɛrɪmən] (*irreg: like* **man**) *n* Fährmann *m*

fertile ['fəːtaɪl] *adj* fruchtbar; **~ period** fruchtbare Tage *pl*

fertility [fə'tɪlɪtɪ] *n* Fruchtbarkeit *f*

fertility drug *n* Fruchtbarkeitsmedikament *nt*

fertilization [fəːtɪlaɪ'zeɪʃən] *n* (*Biol*) Befruchtung *f*

fertilize ['fəːtɪlaɪz] *vt* düngen; (*Biol*) befruchten

fertilizer ['fəːtɪlaɪzəʳ] *n* Dünger *m*

fervent ['fəːvənt] *adj* leidenschaftlich; (*admirer*) glühend

fervour, (US) **fervor** ['fəːvəʳ] *n* Leidenschaft *f*

fester ['fɛstəʳ] *vi* (*wound*) eitern; (*insult*) nagen; (*row*) sich verschlimmern

festival ['fɛstɪvəl] *n* Fest *nt*; (*Art, Mus*) Festival *nt*, Festspiele *pl*

festive ['fɛstɪv] *adj* festlich; **the ~ season** (*Brit: Christmas and New Year*) die Festzeit *f*

festivities [fɛs'tɪvɪtɪz] *npl* Feierlichkeiten *pl*

festoon [fɛs'tuːn] *vt*: **to ~ with** schmücken mit

fetch [fɛtʃ] *vt* holen; (*sell for*) (ein)bringen; **would you ~ me a glass of water please?** kannst du mir bitte ein Glas Wasser bringen?; **how much did it ~?** wie viel hat es eingebracht?

▸ **fetch up** (*inf*) *vi* landen (*inf*)

fetching ['fɛtʃɪŋ] *adj* bezaubernd, reizend

fête [feɪt] *n* Fest *nt*

fetid ['fɛtɪd] *adj* übel riechend

fetish ['fɛtɪʃ] *n* Fetisch *m*

fetter ['fɛtəʳ] *vt* fesseln; (*horse*) anpflocken; (*fig*) in Fesseln legen

fetters ['fɛtəz] *npl* Fesseln *pl*

fettle ['fɛtl] (*Brit*) *n*: **in fine ~** in bester Form

fetus ['fiːtəs] (*US*) *n* = **foetus**

feud [fjuːd] *n* Streit *m* ▷ *vi* im Streit liegen; **a family ~** ein Familienstreit *m*

feudal ['fjuːdl] *adj* (*society etc*) Feudal-

feudalism ['fjuːdlɪzəm] *n* Feudalismus *m*

fever ['fiːvəʳ] *n* Fieber *nt*; **he has a ~** er hat Fieber

feverish ['fiːvərɪʃ] *adj* fiebrig; (*activity, emotion*) fieberhaft

few [fjuː] *adj* wenige; **a ~** (*adj*) ein paar, einige; (*pron*) ein paar; **a ~ more (days)** noch ein paar (Tage); **they were ~** sie waren nur wenige; **~ succeed** nur wenigen gelingt es; **very ~ survive** nur sehr wenige überleben; **I know a ~** ich kenne einige; **a good ~, quite a ~** ziemlich viele; **in the next/past ~ days** in den nächsten/letzten paar Tagen; **every ~ days/months** alle paar Tage/Monate

fewer ['fjuːəʳ] *adj* weniger; **there are ~ buses on Sundays** Sonntags fahren weniger Busse

fewest ['fjuːɪst] *adj* die wenigsten

FHA (*US*) *n abbr* (= *Federal Housing Administration*): **~ loan** Baudarlehen *nt*

fiancé [fɪ'ɑ̃ːŋseɪ] *n* Verlobte(r) *m*

fiancée [fɪ'ɑ̃ːŋseɪ] *n* Verlobte *f*

fiasco [fɪ'æskəu] *n* Fiasko *nt*

fib [fɪb] *n* Flunkerei *f* (*inf*)

fibre, (US) **fiber** ['faɪbəʳ] *n* Faser *f*; (*cloth*) (Faser)stoff *m*; (*roughage*) Ballaststoffe *pl*;

(*Anat: tissue*) Gewebe *nt*
fibreboard, (*US*) **fiberboard** ['faɪbəbɔːd] *n* Faserplatte *f*
fibreglass, (*US*) **fiberglass** ['faɪbəglɑːs] *n* Fiberglas *nt*
fibrositis [faɪbrə'saɪtɪs] *n* Bindegewebsentzündung *f*
FICA (*US*) *n abbr* (= *Federal Insurance Contributions Act*) *Abgabe zur Sozialversicherung*
fickle ['fɪkl] *adj* unbeständig; (*weather*) wechselhaft
fiction ['fɪkʃən] *n* Erfindung *f*; (*Liter*) Erzählliteratur *f*, Prosaliteratur *f*
fictional ['fɪkʃənl] *adj* erfunden
fictionalize ['fɪkʃnəlaɪz] *vt* fiktionalisieren
fictitious [fɪk'tɪʃəs] *adj* (*false*) falsch; (*invented*) fiktiv, frei erfunden
fiddle ['fɪdl] *n* Fiedel *f* (*inf*), Geige *f*; (*fraud, swindle*) Schwindelei *f* ▷ *vt* (*Brit: accounts*) frisieren (*inf*); **tax ~** Steuermanipulation *f*; **to work a ~** ein krummes Ding drehen (*inf*)
▸ **fiddle with** *vt fus* herumspielen mit
fiddler ['fɪdləʳ] *n* Geiger(in) *m(f)*
fiddly ['fɪdlɪ] *adj* knifflig (*inf*); (*object*) fummelig
fidelity [fɪ'dɛlɪtɪ] *n* Treue *f*; (*accuracy*) Genauigkeit *f*
fidget ['fɪdʒɪt] *vi* zappeln
fidgety ['fɪdʒɪtɪ] *adj* zappelig
fiduciary [fɪ'djuːʃɪərɪ] *n* (*Law*) Treuhänder *m*
field [fiːld] *n* Feld *nt*; (*Sport: ground*) Platz *m*; (*subject, area of interest*) Gebiet *nt*; (*Comput*) Datenfeld *nt* ▷ *cpd* Feld-; **to lead the ~** das Feld anführen; **~ trip** Exkursion *f*
field day *n*: **to have a ~** einen herrlichen Tag haben
field glasses *npl* Feldstecher *m*
field hospital *n* Feldlazarett *nt*
field marshal *n* Feldmarschall *m*
field work *n* Feldforschung *f*; (*Archaeology, Geog*) Arbeit *f* im Gelände
fiend [fiːnd] *n* Teufel *m*
fiendish ['fiːndɪʃ] *adj* teuflisch; (*problem*) verzwickt
fierce [fɪəs] *adj* wild; (*look*) böse; (*fighting, wind*) heftig; (*loyalty*) leidenschaftlich; (*enemy*) erbittert; (*heat*) glühend
fiery ['faɪərɪ] *adj* glühend; (*temperament*) feurig, hitzig
FIFA ['fiːfə] *n abbr* (= *Fédération Internationale de Football Association*) FIFA *f*
fifteen [fɪf'tiːn] *num* fünfzehn
fifteenth [fɪf'tiːnθ] *num* fünfzehnte(r, s)
fifth [fɪfθ] *num* fünfte(r, s) ▷ *n* Fünftel *nt*
fiftieth ['fɪftɪɪθ] *num* fünfzigste(r, s)
fifty ['fɪftɪ] *num* fünfzig
fifty-fifty ['fɪftɪ'fɪftɪ] *adj, adv* halbe-halbe, fifty-fifty; **to go/share ~ with sb** mit jdm halbe-halbe *or* fifty-fifty machen; **we have a ~ chance (of success)** unsere Chancen stehen fifty-fifty
fig [fɪg] *n* Feige *f*
fight [faɪt] (*pt, pp* **fought**) *n* Kampf *m*; (*quarrel*) Streit *m*; (*punch-up*) Schlägerei *f* ▷ *vt* kämpfen mit *or* gegen; (*prejudice etc*) bekämpfen; (*election*) kandidieren bei; (*emotion*) ankämpfen gegen; (*Law: case*) durchkämpfen, durchfechten ▷ *vi* kämpfen; (*quarrel*) sich streiten; (*punch-up*) sich schlagen; **to put up a ~** sich zur Wehr setzen; **to ~ one's way through a crowd/the undergrowth** sich *dat* einen Weg durch die Menge/das Unterholz bahnen; **to ~ against** bekämpfen; **to ~ for one's rights** für seine Rechte kämpfen
▸ **fight back** *vi* zurückschlagen; (*Sport*) zurückkämpfen; (*after illness*) zu Kräften kommen ▷ *vt fus* unterdrücken
▸ **fight down** *vt* unterdrücken
▸ **fight off** *vt* abwehren; (*sleep, urge*) ankämpfen gegen
▸ **fight out** *vt*: **to ~ it out** es untereinander ausfechten
fighter ['faɪtəʳ] *n* Kämpfer(in) *m(f)*; (*plane*) Jagdflugzeug *nt*; (*fig*) Kämpfernatur *f*
fighter pilot *n* Jagdflieger *m*
fighting ['faɪtɪŋ] *n* Kämpfe *pl*; (*brawl*) Schlägereien *pl*
figment ['fɪgmənt] *n*: **a ~ of the imagination** ein Hirngespinst *nt*, pure Einbildung *f*
figurative ['fɪgjurətɪv] *adj* bildlich, übertragen; (*style*) gegenständlich
figure ['fɪgəʳ] *n* Figur *f*; (*illustration*) Abbildung *f*; (*number, statistic, cipher*) Zahl *f*; (*person*) Gestalt *f*; (*personality*) Persönlichkeit *f* ▷ *vt* (*esp US*) glauben, schätzen ▷ *vi* eine Rolle spielen; **to put a ~ on sth** eine Zahl für etw angeben; **public ~** Persönlichkeit *f* des öffentlichen Lebens
▸ **figure out** *vt* ausrechnen
figurehead ['fɪgəhɛd] *n* Galionsfigur *f*
figure of speech *n* Redensart *f*, Redewendung *f*
figure skating *n* Eiskunstlaufen *nt*
Fiji ['fiːdʒiː] *n*, **Fiji Islands** *npl* Fidschi-Inseln *pl*
filament ['fɪləmənt] *n* Glühfaden *m*; (*Bot*) Staubfaden *m*
filch [fɪltʃ] (*inf*) *vt* filzen
file [faɪl] *n* Akte *f*; (*folder*) (Akten)ordner *m*; (*for loose leaf*) (Akten)mappe *f*; (*Comput*) Datei *f*; (*row*) Reihe *f*; (*tool*) Feile *f* ▷ *vt* ablegen, abheften; (*claim*) einreichen; (*wood, metal, fingernails*) feilen ▷ *vi*: **to ~ in/out** nacheinander hereinkommen/hinausgehen; **to ~ a suit against sb** eine Klage gegen jdn erheben; **to ~ past** in einer Reihe vorbeigehen; **to ~ for divorce** die Scheidung einreichen
filename ['faɪlneɪm] *n* (*Comput*) Dateiname *m*
filibuster ['fɪlɪbʌstəʳ] (*esp US: Pol*) *n* (*also*: **filibusterer**) Dauerredner(in) *m(f)* ▷ *vi* filibustern, Obstruktion betreiben
filing ['faɪlɪŋ] *n* Ablegen *nt*, Abheften *nt*
filing cabinet *n* Aktenschrank *m*
filing clerk *n* Angestellte(r) *f(m)* in der Registratur
Filipino [fɪlɪ'piːnəu] *n* Filipino *m*, Filipina *f*; (*Ling*) Philippinisch *nt*

fill [fɪl] *vt* füllen; (*space, area*) ausfüllen; (*tooth*) plombieren; (*need*) erfüllen ▷ *vi* sich füllen ▷ *n*: **to eat one's ~** sich satt essen; **we've already ~ed that vacancy** wir haben diese Stelle schon besetzt
▶ **fill in** *vt* füllen; (*time*) überbrücken; (*form*) ausfüllen ▷ *vi*: **to ~ in for sb** für jdn einspringen; **to ~ sb in on sth** (*inf*) jdn über etw *acc* ins Bild setzen
▶ **fill out** *vt* ausfüllen
▶ **fill up** *vt* füllen ▷ *vi* (*Aut*) tanken; **~ it up, please** (*Aut*) bitte volltanken
fillet ['fɪlɪt] *n* Filet *nt* ▷ *vt* filetieren
fillet steak *n* Filetsteak *nt*
filling ['fɪlɪŋ] *n* Füllung *f*; (*for tooth*) Plombe *f*
filling station *n* Tankstelle *f*
fillip ['fɪlɪp] *n* (*stimulus*) Ansporn *m*
filly ['fɪlɪ] *n* Stutfohlen *nt*
film [fɪlm] *n* Film *m*; (*of powder etc*) Schicht *f*; (*for wrapping*) Plastikfolie *f* ▷ *vt, vi* filmen
film star *n* Filmstar *m*
film strip *n* Filmstreifen *m*
film studio *n* Filmstudio *nt*
Filofax® ['faɪləufæks] *n* Filofax® *nt*, Terminplaner *m*
filter ['fɪltəʳ] *n* Filter *m* ▷ *vt* filtern
▶ **filter in** *vi* durchsickern
▶ **filter through** *vi* = **filter in**
filter coffee *n* Filterkaffee *m*
filter lane (*Brit*) *n* Abbiegespur *f*
filter tip *n* Filter *m*
filter-tipped ['fɪltə'tɪpt] *adj* (*cigarette*) Filter-
filth [fɪlθ] *n* Dreck *m*, Schmutz *m*
filthy ['fɪlθɪ] *adj* dreckig, schmutzig; (*language*) unflätig
fin [fɪn] *n* Flosse *f*; (*Tech*) Seitenflosse *f*
final ['faɪnl] *adj* letzte(r, s); (*ultimate*) letztendlich; (*definitive*) endgültig ▷ *n* Finale *nt*, Endspiel *nt*; **finals** *npl* (*Univ*) Abschlussprüfung *f*
final demand *n* letzte Zahlungsaufforderung *f*
finale [fɪ'nɑːlɪ] *n* Finale *nt*; (*Theat*) Schlussszene *f*
finalist ['faɪnəlɪst] *n* Endrundenteilnehmer(in) *m(f)*, Finalist(in) *m(f)*
finality [faɪ'nælɪtɪ] *n* Endgültigkeit *f*; **with an air of ~** mit Bestimmtheit
finalize ['faɪnəlaɪz] *vt* endgültig festlegen
finally ['faɪnəlɪ] *adv* endlich, schließlich; (*lastly*) schließlich, zum Schluss; (*irrevocably*) endgültig
finance [faɪ'næns] *n* Geldmittel *pl*; (*money management*) Finanzwesen *nt* ▷ *vt* finanzieren; **finances** *npl* (*personal*) Finanzen *pl*, Finanzlage *f*
financial [faɪ'nænʃəl] *adj* finanziell; **~ statement** Bilanz *f*
financially [faɪ'nænʃəlɪ] *adv* finanziell
financial year *n* Geschäftsjahr *nt*
financier [faɪ'nænsɪəʳ] *n* Finanzier *m*
find [faɪnd] (*pt, pp* **found**) *vt* finden; (*discover*) entdecken ▷ *n* Fund *m*; **to ~ sb guilty** jdn für schuldig befinden; **to ~ (some) difficulty in doing sth** (einige) Schwierigkeiten haben, etw zu tun
▶ **find out** *vt* herausfinden; (*person*) erwischen ▷ *vi*: **to ~ out about** etwas herausfinden über *+acc*; (*by chance*) etwas erfahren über *+acc*
findings ['faɪndɪŋz] *npl* (*Law*) Urteil *nt*; (*of report*) Ergebnis *nt*
fine [faɪn] *adj* fein; (*excellent*) gut; (*thin*) dünn ▷ *adv* gut; (*small*) fein ▷ *n* Geldstrafe *f* ▷ *vt* mit einer Geldstrafe belegen; **he's ~** es geht ihm gut; **the weather is ~** das Wetter ist schön; **that's cutting it (a bit) ~** das ist aber (ein bisschen) knapp; **you're doing ~** das machen Sie gut
fine arts *npl* schöne Künste *pl*
finely ['faɪnlɪ] *adv* schön; (*chop*) klein; (*slice*) dünn; (*adjust*) fein
fine print *n*: **the ~** das Kleingedruckte
finery ['faɪnərɪ] *n* (*of dress*) Staat *m*
finesse [fɪ'nɛs] *n* Geschick *nt*
fine-tooth comb ['faɪntuːθ-] *n*: **to go through sth with a ~** (*fig*) etw genau unter die Lupe nehmen
finger ['fɪŋgəʳ] *n* Finger *m* ▷ *vt* befühlen; **little ~** kleiner Finger; **index ~** Zeigefinger *m*
fingernail ['fɪŋgəneɪl] *n* Fingernagel *m*
fingerprint ['fɪŋgəprɪnt] *n* Fingerabdruck *m* ▷ *vt* Fingerabdrücke abnehmen *+dat*
fingerstall ['fɪŋgəstɔːl] *n* Fingerling *m*
fingertip ['fɪŋgətɪp] *n* Fingerspitze *f*; **to have sth at one's ~s** (*to hand*) etw parat haben; (*know well*) etw aus dem Effeff kennen (*inf*)
finicky ['fɪnɪkɪ] *adj* pingelig
finish ['fɪnɪʃ] *n* Schluss *m*, Ende *nt*; (*Sport*) Finish *nt*; (*polish etc*) Verarbeitung *f* ▷ *vt* fertig sein mit; (*work*) erledigen; (*book*) auslesen; (*use up*) aufbrauchen ▷ *vi* enden; (*person*) fertig sein; **to ~ doing sth** mit etw fertig werden; **to ~ third** als Dritter durchs Ziel gehen; **to have ~ed with sth** mit etw fertig sein; **she's ~ed with him** sie hat mit ihm Schluss gemacht
▶ **finish off** *vt* fertig machen; (*kill*) den Gnadenstoß geben
▶ **finish up** *vt* (*food*) aufessen; (*drink*) austrinken ▷ *vi* (*end up*) landen
finished ['fɪnɪʃt] *adj* fertig; (*performance*) ausgereift; (*inf: tired*) erledigt
finishing line ['fɪnɪʃɪŋ-] *n* Ziellinie *f*
finishing school *n* höhere Mädchenschule *f* (*in der auch Etikette und gesellschaftliches Verhalten gelehrt wird*)
finishing touches *npl*: **the ~** der letzte Schliff
finite ['faɪnaɪt] *adj* begrenzt; (*verb*) finit
Finland ['fɪnlənd] *n* Finnland *nt*
Finn [fɪn] *n* Finne *m*, Finnin *f*
Finnish ['fɪnɪʃ] *adj* finnisch ▷ *n* (*Ling*) Finnisch *nt*
fiord [fjɔːd] *n* = **fjord**
fir [fəːʳ] *n* Tanne *f*
fire ['faɪəʳ] *n* Feuer *nt*; (*in hearth*) (Kamin)feuer *nt*; (*accidental fire*) Brand *m* ▷ *vt* abschießen; (*imagination*) beflügeln; (*enthusiasm*) befeuern; (*inf: dismiss*) feuern ▷ *vi* feuern, schießen; **to ~ a gun** ein Gewehr abschießen; **to be**

on ~ brennen; **to set ~ to sth, set sth on ~** etw anzünden; **insured against ~** feuerversichert; **electric/gas ~** Elektro-/Gasofen *m*; **to come/be under ~ (from)** unter Beschuss (von) geraten/stehen
fire alarm *n* Feuermelder *m*
firearm ['faɪərɑːm] *n* Feuerwaffe *f*, Schusswaffe *f*
fire brigade *n* Feuerwehr *f*
fire chief *n* Branddirektor *m*
fire department (*US*) *n* Feuerwehr *f*
fire door *n* Feuertür *f*
fire drill *n* Probealarm *m*
fire engine *n* Feuerwehrauto *nt*
fire escape *n* Feuertreppe *f*
fire-extinguisher ['faɪərɪk'stɪŋgwɪʃəʳ] *n* Feuerlöscher *m*
fireguard ['faɪəgɑːd] (*Brit*) *n* (Schutz)gitter *nt* (*vor dem Kamin*)
fire hazard *n*: **that's a ~** das ist feuergefährlich
fire hydrant *n* Hydrant *m*
fire insurance *n* Feuerversicherung *f*
fireman ['faɪəmən] (*irreg: like* **man**) *n* Feuerwehrmann *m*
fireplace ['faɪəpleɪs] *n* Kamin *m*
fireplug ['faɪəplʌg] (*US*) *n* = **fire hydrant**
fire practice *n* = **fire drill**
fireproof ['faɪəpruːf] *adj* feuerfest
fire regulations *npl* Brandschutzbestimmungen *pl*
fire screen *n* Ofenschirm *m*
fireside ['faɪəsaɪd] *n*: **by the ~** am Kamin
fire station *n* Feuerwache *f*
firewood ['faɪəwud] *n* Brennholz *nt*
fireworks ['faɪəwəːks] *npl* Feuerwerkskörper *pl*; (*display*) Feuerwerk *nt*
firing line ['faɪərɪŋ-] *n* Feuerlinie *f*, Schusslinie *f*; **to be in the ~** (*fig*) in der Schusslinie sein
firing squad *n* Exekutionskommando *nt*
firm [fəːm] *adj* fest; (*mattress*) hart; (*measures*) durchgreifend ▷ *n* Firma *f*; **to be a ~ believer in sth** fest von etw überzeugt sein
firmly ['fəːmlɪ] *adv* (*see adj*) fest; hart; (*definitely*) entschlossen
firmness ['fəːmnɪs] *n* (*see adj*) Festigkeit *f*; Härte *f*; (*definiteness*) Entschlossenheit *f*
first [fəːst] *adj* erste(r, s) ▷ *adv* als Erste(r, s); (*before other things*) zuerst; (*when listing reasons etc*) erstens; (*for the first time*) zum ersten Mal ▷ *n* Erste(r, s); (*Aut: also:* **first gear**) der erste Gang; (*Brit: Scol*) ≈ Eins *f*; **the ~ of January** der erste Januar; **at ~** zuerst, zunächst; **~ of all** vor allem; **in the ~ instance** zuerst *or* zunächst einmal; **I'll do it ~ thing (tomorrow)** ich werde es (morgen) als Erstes tun; **from the very ~** gleich von Anfang an
first aid *n* erste Hilfe *f*
first-aid kit [fəːst'eɪd-] *n* Erste-Hilfe-Ausrüstung *f*
first-class ['fəːst'klɑːs] *adj* erstklassig; (*carriage, ticket*) Erste(r)-Klasse-; (*post*) bevorzugt befördert ▷ *adv* (*travel, send*) erster Klasse
first-hand ['fəːst'hænd] *adj* aus erster Hand
first lady (*US*) *n* First Lady *f*; **the ~ of jazz** die Königin des Jazz
firstly ['fəːstlɪ] *adv* erstens, zunächst einmal
first name *n* Vorname *m*
first night *n* Premiere *f*
first-rate ['fəːst'reɪt] *adj* erstklassig
first-time buyer ['fəːsttaɪm-] *n jd, der zum ersten Mal ein Haus/eine Wohnung kauft*
fir tree *n* Tannenbaum *m*
fiscal ['fɪskl] *adj* (*year*) Steuer-; (*policies*) Finanz-
fish [fɪʃ] *n inv* Fisch *m* ▷ *vt* (*area*) fischen in *+dat*; (*river*) angeln in *+dat* ▷ *vi* fischen; (*as sport, hobby*) angeln; **to go ~ing** fischen/angeln gehen
▸ **fish out** *vt* herausfischen
fish bone *n* (Fisch)gräte *f*
fish cake *n* Fischfrikadelle *f*
fisherman ['fɪʃəmən] (*irreg: like* **man**) *n* Fischer *m*
fishery ['fɪʃərɪ] *n* Fischereigebiet *nt*
fish factory (*Brit*) *n* Fischfabrik *f*
fish farm *n* Fischzucht(anlage) *f*
fishfingers [fɪʃ'fɪŋgəz] (*Brit*) *npl* Fischstäbchen *pl*
fish-hook ['fɪʃhuk] *n* Angelhaken *m*
fishing boat ['fɪʃɪŋ-] *n* Fischerboot *nt*
fishing line *n* Angelschnur *f*
fishing net *n* Fischnetz *nt*
fishing rod *n* Angelrute *f*
fishing tackle *n* Angelgeräte *pl*
fish market *n* Fischmarkt *m*
fishmonger ['fɪʃmʌŋgəʳ] (*esp Brit*) *n* Fischhändler(in) *m(f)*
fishmonger's ['fɪʃmʌŋgəz], **fishmonger's shop** (*esp Brit*) *n* Fischgeschäft *nt*
fish slice (*Brit*) *n* Fischvorlegemesser *nt*
fish sticks (*US*) *npl* = **fishfingers**
fishy ['fɪʃɪ] (*inf*) *adj* verdächtig, faul
fission ['fɪʃən] *n* Spaltung *f*; **atomic** *or* **nuclear ~** Atomspaltung *f*, Kernspaltung *f*
fissure ['fɪʃəʳ] *n* Riss *m*, Spalte *f*
fist [fɪst] *n* Faust *f*
fist fight *n* Faustkampf *m*
fit [fɪt] *adj* geeignet; (*healthy*) gesund; (*Sport*) fit ▷ *vt* passen *+dat*; (*adjust*) anpassen; (*match*) entsprechen *+dat*; (*be suitable for*) passen auf *+acc*; (*put in*) einbauen; (*attach*) anbringen; (*equip*) ausstatten ▷ *vi* passen; (*parts*) zusammenpassen; (*in space, gap*) hineinpassen ▷ *n* (*Med*) Anfall *m*; **to ~ the description** der Beschreibung entsprechen; **~ to** bereit zu; **~ to eat** essbar; **~ to drink** trinkbar; **to be ~ to keep** es wert sein, aufbewahrt zu werden; **~ for** geeignet für; **~ for work** arbeitsfähig; **to keep ~** sich fit halten; **do as you think** *or* **see ~** tun Sie, was Sie für richtig halten; **a ~ of anger** ein Wutanfall *m*; **a ~ of pride** eine Anwandlung von Stolz; **to have a ~** einen Anfall haben; (*inf, fig*) einen Anfall kriegen; **this dress is a good ~** dieses Kleid sitzt *or* passt gut; **by ~s and starts** unregelmäßig
▸ **fit in** *vi* (*person*) sich einfügen; (*object*)

hineinpassen ▷ *vt* (*fig*: *appointment*) unterbringen, einschieben; (*visitor*) Zeit finden für; **to ~ in with sb's plans** sich mit jds Plänen vereinbaren lassen
fitful ['fɪtful] *adj* unruhig
fitment ['fɪtmənt] *n* Einrichtungsgegenstand *m*
fitness ['fɪtnɪs] *n* Gesundheit *f*; (*Sport*) Fitness *f*
fitness instructor *n* Fitnesstrainer(in) *m(f)*
fitted carpet ['fɪtɪd-] *n* Teppichboden *m*
fitted cupboards *npl* Einbauschränke *pl*
fitted kitchen (*Brit*) *n* Einbauküche *f*
fitter ['fɪtə^r] *n* Monteur *m*; (*for machines*) (Maschinen)schlosser *m*
fitting ['fɪtɪŋ] *adj* passend; (*thanks*) gebührend ▷ *n* (*of dress*) Anprobe *f*; (*of piece of equipment*) Installation *f*; **fittings** *npl* Ausstattung *f*
fitting room *n* Anprobe(kabine) *f*
five [faɪv] *num* fünf
five-day week ['faɪvdeɪ-] *n* Fünftagewoche *f*
fiver ['faɪvə^r] (*inf*) *n* (*Brit*) Fünfpfundschein *m*; (*US*) Fünfdollarschein *m*
fix [fɪks] *vt* (*attach*) befestigen; (*arrange*) festsetzen, festlegen; (*mend*) reparieren; (*meal, drink*) machen; (*inf*) manipulieren ▷ *n*: **to be in a ~** in der Patsche *or* Klemme sitzen; **to ~ sth to/on sth** etw an/auf etw *dat* befestigen; **to ~ one's eyes/attention on** seinen Blick/seine Aufmerksamkeit richten auf *+acc*; **the fight was a ~** (*inf*) der Kampf war eine abgekartete Sache
▸ **fix up** *vt* arrangieren; **to ~ sb up with sth** jdm etw besorgen
fixation [fɪk'seɪʃən] *n* Fixierung *f*
fixative ['fɪksətɪv] *n* Fixativ *nt*
fixed [fɪkst] *adj* fest; (*ideas*) fix; (*smile*) starr; **~ charge** Pauschale *f*; **how are you ~ for money?** wie sieht es bei dir mit dem Geld aus?
fixed assets *npl* Anlagevermögen *nt*
fixture ['fɪkstʃə^r] *n* Ausstattungsgegenstand *m*; (*Football etc*) Spiel *nt*; (*Athletics etc*) Veranstaltung *f*
fizz [fɪz] *vi* sprudeln; (*firework*) zischen
fizzle out ['fɪzl-] *vi* (*plan*) im Sande verlaufen; (*interest*) sich verlieren
fizzy ['fɪzɪ] *adj* sprudelnd
fjord [fjɔ:d] *n* Fjord *m*
FL, Fla. (*US*) *abbr* (*Post*) = *Florida*
flabbergasted ['flæbəgɑ:stɪd] *adj* verblüfft
flabby ['flæbɪ] *adj* schwammig, wabbelig (*inf*)
flag [flæg] *n* Fahne *f*; (*of country*) Flagge *f*; (*for signalling*) Signalflagge *f*; (*also*: **flagstone**) (Stein)platte *f* ▷ *vi* erlahmen; **~ of convenience** Billigflagge *f*; **to ~ down** anhalten
flagon ['flægən] *n* Flasche *f*; (*jug*) Krug *m*
flagpole ['flægpəul] *n* Fahnenstange *f*
flagrant ['fleɪgrənt] *adj* flagrant; (*injustice*) himmelschreiend
flagship ['flægʃɪp] *n* Flaggschiff *nt*
flagstone ['flægstəun] *n* (Stein)platte *f*
flag stop (*US*) *n* Bedarfshaltestelle *f*
flair [flɛə^r] *n* Talent *nt*; (*style*) Flair *nt*
flak [flæk] *n* Flakfeuer *nt*; **to get a lot of ~ (for sth)** (*inf*: *criticism*) (wegen etw) unter Beschuss geraten
flake [fleɪk] *n* Splitter *m*; (*of snow, soap powder*) Flocke *f* ▷ *vi* (*also*: **flake off**) abblättern, absplittern
▸ **flake out** (*inf*) *vi* aus den Latschen kippen; (*go to sleep*) einschlafen
flaky ['fleɪkɪ] *adj* brüchig; (*skin*) schuppig
flaky pastry *n* Blätterteig *m*
flamboyant [flæm'bɔɪənt] *adj* extravagant
flame [fleɪm] *n* Flamme *f*; **to burst into ~s** in Flammen aufgehen; **an old ~** (*inf*) eine alte Flamme
flaming ['fleɪmɪŋ] (*inf!*) *adj* verdammt
flamingo [flə'mɪŋgəu] *n* Flamingo *m*
flammable ['flæməbl] *adj* leicht entzündbar
flan [flæn] *n* Kuchen *m*; **~ case** Tortenboden *m*
Flanders ['flɑ:ndəz] *n* Flandern *nt*
flange [flændʒ] *n* Flansch *m*
flank [flæŋk] *n* Flanke *f* ▷ *vt* flankieren
flannel ['flænl] *n* Flanell *m*; (*Brit*: *also*: **face flannel**) Waschlappen *m*; (: *inf*) Geschwafel *nt*; **flannels** *npl* (*trousers*) Flanellhose *f*
flannelette [flænə'lɛt] *n* Baumwollflanell *m*, Biber *m or nt*
flap [flæp] *n* Klappe *f*; (*of envelope*) Lasche *f* ▷ *vt* schlagen mit ▷ *vi* flattern; (*inf*: *also*: **be in a flap**) in heller Aufregung sein
flapjack ['flæpdʒæk] *n* (*US*: *pancake*) Pfannkuchen *m*; (*Brit*: *biscuit*) Haferkeks *m*
flare [flɛə^r] *n* Leuchtsignal *nt*; (*in skirt etc*) Weite *f*
▸ **flare up** *vi* auflodern; (*person*) aufbrausen; (*fighting, violence, trouble*) ausbrechen; *see also* **flared**
flared ['flɛəd] *adj* (*trousers*) mit Schlag; (*skirt*) ausgestellt
flash [flæʃ] *n* Aufblinken *nt*; (*also*: **newsflash**) Eilmeldung *f*; (*Phot*) Blitz *m*, Blitzlicht *nt*; (*US*: *torch*) Taschenlampe *f* ▷ *vt* aufleuchten lassen; (*news, message*) durchgeben; (*look, smile*) zuwerfen ▷ *vi* aufblinken; (*light on ambulance*) blinken; (*eyes*) blitzen; **in a ~** im Nu; **quick as a ~** blitzschnell; **~ of inspiration** Geistesblitz *m*; **to ~ one's headlights** die Lichthupe betätigen; **the thought ~ed through his mind** der Gedanke schoss ihm durch den Kopf; **to ~ by** *or* **past** vorbeiflitzen (*inf*)
flashback ['flæʃbæk] *n* Rückblende *f*
flashbulb ['flæʃbʌlb] *n* Blitzbirne *f*
flash card *n* Leselernkarte *f*
flashcube ['flæʃkju:b] *n* Blitzwürfel *m*
flasher ['flæʃə^r] *n* (*Aut*) Lichthupe *f*; (*inf!*: *man*) Exhibitionist *m*
flashlight ['flæʃlaɪt] *n* Blitzlicht *nt*
flash point *n* (*fig*): **to be at ~** auf dem Siedepunkt sein
flashy ['flæʃɪ] (*pej*) *adj* auffällig, protzig
flask [flɑ:sk] *n* Flakon *m*; (*Chem*) Glaskolben *m*; (*also*: **vacuum flask**) Thermosflasche® *f*
flat [flæt] *adj* flach; (*surface*) eben; (*tyre*) platt; (*battery*) leer; (*beer*) schal; (*refusal, denial*)

glatt; (*note, voice*) zu tief; (*rate, fee*) Pauschal- ▷ *n* (*Brit: apartment*) Wohnung *f*; (*Aut*) (Reifen)panne *f*; (*Mus*) Erniedrigungszeichen *nt*; **to work ~ out** auf Hochtouren arbeiten; **~ rate of pay** Pauschallohn *m*
flat-footed ['flæt'futɪd] *adj*: **to be ~** Plattfüße *pl* haben
flatly ['flætlɪ] *adv* (*refuse, deny*) glatt, kategorisch
flatmate ['flætmeɪt] (*Brit*) *n* Mitbewohner(in) *m(f)*
flatness ['flætnɪs] *n* Flachheit *f*
flat screen *n* Flachbildschirm *m*
flat-screen monitor *n* Flachbildschirm *m*
flatten ['flætn] *vt* (*also*: **flatten out**) (ein)ebnen; (*paper, fabric etc*) glätten; (*building, city*) dem Erdboden gleichmachen; (*crop*) zu Boden drücken; (*inf: person*) umhauen; **to ~ o.s. against a wall/door** *etc* sich platt gegen *or* an eine Wand/Tür *etc* drücken
flatter ['flætə^r] *vt* schmeicheln *+dat*
flatterer ['flætərə^r] *n* Schmeichler(in) *m(f)*
flattering ['flætərɪŋ] *adj* schmeichelhaft; (*dress etc*) vorteilhaft
flattery ['flætərɪ] *n* Schmeichelei *f*
flatulence ['flætjuləns] *n* Blähungen *pl*
flaunt [flɔ:nt] *vt* zur Schau stellen, protzen mit
flavour, (*US*) **flavor** ['fleɪvə^r] *n* Geschmack *m*; (*of ice-cream etc*) Geschmacksrichtung *f* ▷ *vt* Geschmack verleihen *+dat*; **to give** *or* **add ~ to** Geschmack verleihen *+dat*; **music with an African ~** (*fig*) Musik mit einer afrikanischen Note; **strawberry-~ed** mit Erdbeergeschmack
flavouring ['fleɪvərɪŋ] *n* Aroma *nt*
flaw [flɔ:] *n* Fehler *m*
flawless ['flɔ:lɪs] *adj* (*performance*) fehlerlos; (*complexion*) makellos
flax [flæks] *n* Flachs *m*
flaxen ['flæksən] *adj* (*hair*) flachsblond
flea [fli:] *n* Floh *m*
flea market *n* Flohmarkt *m*
fleck [flɛk] *n* Tupfen *m*, Punkt *m*; (*of dust*) Flöckchen *nt*; (*of mud, paint, colour*) Fleck(en) *m* ▷ *vt* bespritzen; **brown ~ed with white** braun mit weißen Punkten
fled [flɛd] *pt, pp of* **flee**
fledgeling, **fledgling** ['flɛdʒlɪŋ] *n* Jungvogel *m* ▷ *adj* (*inexperienced: actor etc*) Nachwuchs-; (*newly started: business etc*) jung
flee [fli:] (*pt, pp* **fled**) *vt* fliehen *or* flüchten vor *+dat*; (*country*) fliehen *or* flüchten aus ▷ *vi* fliehen, flüchten
fleece [fli:s] *n* Schafwolle *f*; (*sheep's coat*) Schaffell *nt*, Vlies *nt* ▷ *vt* (*inf: cheat*) schröpfen
fleecy ['fli:sɪ] *adj* flauschig; (*cloud*) Schäfchen-
fleet [fli:t] *n* Flotte *f*; (*of lorries, cars*) Fuhrpark *m*
fleeting ['fli:tɪŋ] *adj* flüchtig
Flemish ['flɛmɪʃ] *adj* flämisch ▷ *n* (*Ling*) Flämisch *nt*; **the Flemish** *npl* die Flamen
flesh [flɛʃ] *n* Fleisch *nt*; (*of fruit*) Fruchtfleisch *nt*
▸ **flesh out** *vt* ausgestalten
flesh wound [-wu:nd] *n* Fleischwunde *f*
flew [flu:] *pt of* **fly**
flex [flɛks] *n* Kabel *nt* ▷ *vt* beugen; (*muscles*) spielen lassen
flexibility [flɛksɪ'bɪlɪtɪ] *n* (*see adj*) Flexibilität *f*; Biegsamkeit *f*
flexible ['flɛksəbl] *adj* flexibel; (*material*) biegsam
flexitime ['flɛksɪtaɪm] *n* gleitende Arbeitszeit *f*, Gleitzeit *f*
flick [flɪk] *n* (*of finger*) Schnipsen *nt*; (*of hand*) Wischen *nt*; (*of whip*) Schnalzen *nt*; (*of towel etc*) Schlagen *nt*; (*of switch*) Knipsen *nt* ▷ *vt* schnipsen; (*with hand*) wischen; (*whip*) knallen mit; (*switch*) knipsen; **flicks** (*inf*) *npl* Kino *nt*; **to ~ a towel at sb** mit einem Handtuch nach jdm schlagen
▸ **flick through** *vt fus* durchblättern
flicker ['flɪkə^r] *vi* flackern; (*eyelids*) zucken ▷ *n* Flackern *nt*; (*of pain, fear*) Aufflackern *nt*; (*of smile*) Anflug *m*; (*of eyelid*) Zucken *nt*
flick knife (*Brit*) *n* Klappmesser *nt*
flier ['flaɪə^r] *n* Flieger(in) *m(f)*
flight [flaɪt] *n* Flug *m*; (*escape*) Flucht *f*; (*also*: **flight of steps**) Treppe *f*; **to take ~** die Flucht ergreifen; **to put to ~** in die Flucht schlagen
flight attendant (*US*) *n* Flugbegleiter(in) *m(f)*
flight crew *n* Flugbesatzung *f*
flight deck *n* (*Aviat*) Cockpit *nt*; (*Naut*) Flugdeck *nt*
flight path *n* Flugbahn *f*
flight recorder *n* Flugschreiber *m*
flimsy ['flɪmzɪ] *adj* leicht, dünn; (*building*) leicht gebaut; (*excuse*) fadenscheinig; (*evidence*) nicht stichhaltig
flinch [flɪntʃ] *vi* zusammenzucken; **to ~ from** zurückschrecken vor *+dat*
fling [flɪŋ] (*pt, pp* **flung**) *vt* schleudern; (*arms*) werfen; (*oneself*) stürzen ▷ *n* (flüchtige) Affäre *f*
flint [flɪnt] *n* Feuerstein *m*
flip [flɪp] *vt* (*switch*) knipsen; (*coin*) werfen; (*US: pancake*) umdrehen ▷ *vi*: **to ~ for sth** (*US*) um etw mit einer Münze knobeln
▸ **flip through** *vt fus* durchblättern; (*records etc*) durchgehen
flippant ['flɪpənt] *adj* leichtfertig
flipper ['flɪpə^r] *n* Flosse *f*; (*for swimming*) (Schwimm)flosse *f*
flip side *n* (*of record*) B-Seite *f*
flirt [flə:t] *vi* flirten; (*with idea*) liebäugeln ▷ *n*: **he/she is a ~** er/sie flirtet gern
flirtation [flə:'teɪʃən] *n* Flirt *m*
flit [flɪt] *vi* flitzen; (*expression, smile*) huschen
float [fləut] *n* Schwimmkork *m*; (*for fishing*) Schwimmer *m*; (*lorry*) Festwagen *m*; (*money*) Wechselgeld *nt* ▷ *vi* schwimmen; (*swimmer*) treiben; (*through air*) schweben; (*currency*) floaten ▷ *vt* (*currency*) freigeben, floaten lassen; (*company*) gründen; (*idea, plan*) in den Raum stellen
▸ **float around** *vi* im Umlauf sein; (*person*) herumschweben (*inf*); (*object*) herumfliegen (*inf*)
flock [flɔk] *n* Herde *f*; (*of birds*) Schwarm *m*

▹ *vi*: **to ~ to** (*place*) strömen nach; (*event*) in Scharen kommen zu

floe [fləu] *n* (*also*: **ice floe**) Eisscholle *f*

flog [flɔg] *vt* auspeitschen; (*inf*: *sell*) verscherbeln

flood [flʌd] *n* Überschwemmung *f*; (*of letters, imports etc*) Flut *f* ▹ *vt* überschwemmen; (*Aut*) absaufen lassen (*inf*) ▹ *vi* überschwemmt werden; **to be in ~** Hochwasser führen; **to ~ the market** den Markt überschwemmen; **to ~ into Hungary/the square/the palace** nach Ungarn/auf den Platz/in den Palast strömen

flooding ['flʌdɪŋ] *n* Überschwemmung *f*

floodlight ['flʌdlaɪt] *n* Flutlicht *nt* ▹ *vt* (mit Flutlicht) beleuchten; (*building*) anstrahlen

floodlit ['flʌdlɪt] *pt, pp of* **floodlight** ▹ *adj* (mit Flutlicht) beleuchtet; (*building*) angestrahlt

flood tide *n* Flut *f*

floodwater ['flʌdwɔːtəʳ] *n* Hochwasser *nt*

floor [flɔːʳ] *n* (Fuß)boden *m*; (*storey*) Stock *nt*; (*of sea, valley*) Boden *m* ▹ *vt* (*subj*: *blow*) zu Boden werfen; (: *question, remark*) die Sprache verschlagen *+dat*; **on the ~** auf dem Boden; **ground ~** (*Brit*), **first ~** (*US*) Erdgeschoss *nt*, Erdgeschoß *nt* (*Österr*); **first ~** (*Brit*), **second ~** (*US*) erster Stock *m*; **top ~** oberstes Stockwerk *nt*; **to have the ~** (*speaker*: *at meeting*) das Wort haben

floorboard ['flɔːbɔːd] *n* Diele *f*

flooring ['flɔːrɪŋ] *n* (Fuß)boden *m*; (*covering*) Fußbodenbelag *m*

floor lamp (*US*) *n* Stehlampe *f*

floor show *n* Show *f*, Vorstellung *f*

floorwalker ['flɔːwɔːkəʳ] (*esp US*) *n* Ladenaufsicht *f*

floozy ['fluːzɪ] (*inf*) *n* Flittchen *nt*

flop [flɔp] *n* Reinfall *m* ▹ *vi* (*play, book*) durchfallen; (*fall*) sich fallen lassen; (*scheme*) ein Reinfall sein

floppy ['flɔpɪ] *adj* schlaff, schlapp ▹ *n* (*also*: **floppy disk**) Diskette *f*, Floppy Disk *f*; **~ hat** Schlapphut *m*

floppy disk *n* Diskette *f*, Floppy Disk *f*

flora ['flɔːrə] *n* Flora *f*

floral ['flɔːrl] *adj* geblümt

Florence ['flɔrəns] *n* Florenz *nt*

Florentine ['flɔrəntaɪn] *adj* florentinisch

florid ['flɔrɪd] *adj* (*style*) blumig; (*complexion*) kräftig

florist ['flɔrɪst] *n* Blumenhändler(in) *m(f)*

florist's ['flɔrɪsts], **florist's shop** *n* Blumengeschäft *nt*

flotation [fləu'teɪʃən] *n* (*of shares*) Auflegung *f*; (*of company*) Umwandlung *f* in eine Aktiengesellschaft

flotsam ['flɔtsəm] *n* (*also*: **flotsam and jetsam**) Strandgut *nt*; (*floating*) Treibgut *nt*

flounce [flauns] *n* Volant *m*

▸ **flounce out** *vi* hinausstolzieren

flounder ['flaundəʳ] *vi* sich abstrampeln; (*fig*: *speaker*) ins Schwimmen kommen; (*economy*) in Schwierigkeiten geraten ▹ *n* Flunder *f*

flour ['flauəʳ] *n* Mehl *nt*

flourish ['flʌrɪʃ] *vi* gedeihen; (*business*) blühen, florieren ▹ *vt* schwenken ▹ *n* (*in writing*) Schnörkel *m*; (*bold gesture*): **with a ~** mit einer schwungvollen Bewegung

flourishing ['flʌrɪʃɪŋ] *adj* gut gehend, florierend

flout [flaut] *vt* sich hinwegsetzen über *+acc*

flow [fləu] *n* Fluss *m*; (*of sea*) Flut *f* ▹ *vi* fließen; (*clothes, hair*) wallen

flow chart *n* Flussdiagramm *nt*

flow diagram *n* = **flow chart**

flower ['flauəʳ] *n* Blume *f*; (*blossom*) Blüte *f* ▹ *vi* blühen; **to be in ~** blühen

flowerbed ['flauəbɛd] *n* Blumenbeet *nt*

flowerpot ['flauəpɔt] *n* Blumentopf *m*

flowery ['flauərɪ] *adj* blumig; (*pattern*) Blumen-

flown [fləun] *pp of* **fly**

flu [fluː] *n* Grippe *f*

fluctuate ['flʌktjueɪt] *vi* schwanken; (*opinions, attitudes*) sich ändern

fluctuation [flʌktju'eɪʃən] *n*: **~ (in)** Schwankung *f* (*+gen*)

flue [fluː] *n* Rauchfang *m*, Rauchabzug *m*

fluency ['fluːənsɪ] *n* Flüssigkeit *f*; **his ~ in German** sein flüssiges Deutsch

fluent ['fluːənt] *adj* flüssig; **he speaks ~ German, he's ~ in German** er spricht fließend Deutsch

fluently ['fluːəntlɪ] *adv* flüssig; (*speak a language*) fließend

fluff [flʌf] *n* Fussel *m*; (*fur*) Flaum *m* ▹ *vt* (*inf*: *do badly*) verpatzen; (*also*: **fluff out**) aufplustern

fluffy ['flʌfɪ] *adj* flaumig; (*jacket etc*) weich, kuschelig; **~ toy** Kuscheltier *nt*

fluid ['fluːɪd] *adj* fließend; (*situation, arrangement*) unklar ▹ *n* Flüssigkeit *f*

fluid ounce (*Brit*) *n* flüssige Unze *f* (= 28 ml)

fluke [fluːk] (*inf*) *n* Glücksfall *m*; **by a ~** durch einen glücklichen Zufall

flummox ['flʌməks] *vt* verwirren, durcheinanderbringen

flung [flʌŋ] *pt, pp of* **fling**

flunky ['flʌŋkɪ] *n* Lakai *m*

fluorescent [fluə'rɛsnt] *adj* fluoreszierend; (*paint*) Leucht-; (*light*) Neon-

fluoride ['fluəraɪd] *n* Fluorid *nt*

fluorine ['fluəriːn] *n* Fluor *nt*

flurry ['flʌrɪ] *n* (*of snow*) Gestöber *nt*; **a ~ of activity/excitement** hektische Aktivität/Aufregung

flush [flʌʃ] *n* Röte *f*; (*fig*: *of beauty etc*) Blüte *f* ▹ *vt* (durch)spülen, (aus)spülen ▹ *vi* erröten ▹ *adj*: **~ with** auf gleicher Ebene mit; **~ against** direkt an *+dat*; **in the first ~ of youth** in der ersten Jugendblüte; **in the first ~ of freedom** im ersten Freiheitstaumel; **hot ~es** (*Brit*) Hitzewallungen *pl*; **to ~ the toilet** spülen, die Wasserspülung betätigen

▸ **flush out** *vt* aufstöbern

flushed [flʌʃt] *adj* rot

fluster ['flʌstəʳ] *n*: **in a ~** nervös; (*confused*)

durcheinander ▷ *vt* nervös machen; (*confuse*) durcheinanderbringen
flustered ['flʌstəd] *adj* nervös; (*confused*) durcheinander
flute [flu:t] *n* Querflöte *f*
fluted ['flu:tɪd] *adj* gerillt; (*column*) kanneliert
flutter ['flʌtəʳ] *n* Flattern *nt*; (*of panic, nerves*) kurzer Anfall *m*; (*of excitement*) Beben *nt* ▷ *vi* flattern; (*person*) tänzeln; **to have a ~** (*Brit: inf: gamble*) sein Glück (beim Wetten) versuchen
flux [flʌks] *n*: **in a state of ~** im Fluss
fly [flaɪ] (*pt* **flew**, *pp* **flown**) *n* Fliege *f*; (*on trousers: also:* **flies**) (Hosen)schlitz *m* ▷ *vt* fliegen; (*kite*) steigen lassen ▷ *vi* fliegen; (*escape*) fliehen; (*flag*) wehen; **to ~ open** auffliegen; **to ~ off the handle** an die Decke gehen (*inf*); **pieces of metal went ~ing everywhere** überall flogen Metallteile herum; **she came ~ing into the room** sie kam ins Zimmer gesaust; **her glasses flew off** die Brille flog ihr aus dem Gesicht
▸ **fly away** *vi* wegfliegen
▸ **fly in** *vi* einfliegen; **he flew in yesterday** er ist gestern mit dem Flugzeug gekommen
▸ **fly off** *vi* = **fly away**
▸ **fly out** *vi* ausfliegen; **he flew out yesterday** er ist gestern hingeflogen
fly-fishing ['flaɪfɪʃɪŋ] *n* Fliegenfischen *nt*
flying ['flaɪɪŋ] *n* Fliegen *nt* ▷ *adj*: **a ~ visit** ein Blitzbesuch *m*; **he doesn't like ~** er fliegt nicht gerne; **with ~ colours** mit fliegenden Fahnen
flying buttress *n* Strebebogen *m*
flying picket *n* mobiler Streikposten *m*
flying saucer *n* fliegende Untertasse *f*
flying squad *n* mobiles Einsatzkommando *nt*
flying start *n*: **to get off to a ~** (*Sport*) hervorragend wegkommen; (*fig*) einen glänzenden Start haben
flyleaf ['flaɪli:f] *n* Vorsatzblatt *nt*
flyover ['flaɪəuvəʳ] *n* (*Brit*) Überführung *f*; (*US*) Luftparade *f*
fly-past ['flaɪpɑ:st] *n* Luftparade *f*
flysheet ['flaɪʃi:t] *n* (*for tent*) Überzelt *nt*
flyweight ['flaɪweɪt] *n* Fliegengewicht *nt*
flywheel ['flaɪwi:l] *n* Schwungrad *nt*
FM *abbr* (*Brit: Mil*) = **field marshal**; (*Radio: = frequency modulation*) FM, ≈ UKW
FMB (*US*) *n abbr* (*= Federal Maritime Board*) *Dachausschuss der Handelsmarine*
FMCS (*US*) *n abbr* (*= Federal Mediation and Conciliation Service*) *Schlichtungsstelle für Arbeitskonflikte*
FO (*Brit*) *n abbr* = **Foreign Office**
foal [fəul] *n* Fohlen *nt*
foam [fəum] *n* Schaum *m*; (*also:* **foam rubber**) Schaumgummi *m* ▷ *vi* schäumen
fob [fɔb] *vt*: **to ~ sb off** jdn abspeisen ▷ *n* (*also:* **watch fob**) Uhrkette *f*
f.o.b. *abbr* (*Comm: = free on board*) frei Schiff
foc (*Brit*) *abbr* (*Comm: = free of charge*) gratis
focal point ['fəukl-] *n* Mittelpunkt *m*; (*of camera, telescope etc*) Brennpunkt *m*
focus ['fəukəs] (*pl* **~es**) *n* Brennpunkt *m*; (*of storm*) Zentrum *nt* ▷ *vt* einstellen; (*light rays*) bündeln ▷ *vi*: **to ~ (on)** (*with camera*) klar *or* scharf einstellen *+acc*; (*person*) sich konzentrieren (auf *+acc*); **in/out of ~** (*camera etc*) scharf/unscharf eingestellt; (*photograph*) scharf/unscharf
focus group *n* (*Pol*) Fokusgruppe *f*
fodder ['fɔdəʳ] *n* Futter *nt*
FoE *n abbr* (*= Friends of the Earth*) *Umweltschutzorganisation*
foe [fəu] *n* Feind(in) *m(f)*
foetus, (*US*) **fetus** ['fi:təs] *n* Fötus *m*, Fetus *m*
fog [fɔg] *n* Nebel *m*
fogbound ['fɔgbaund] *adj* (*airport*) wegen Nebel geschlossen
foggy ['fɔgɪ] *adj* neb(e)lig
fog lamp, (*US*) **fog light** *n* (*Aut*) Nebelscheinwerfer *m*
foible ['fɔɪbl] *n* Eigenheit *f*
foil [fɔɪl] *vt* vereiteln ▷ *n* Folie *f*; (*complement*) Kontrast *m*; (*Fencing*) Florett *nt*; **to act as a ~ to** einen Kontrast darstellen zu
foist [fɔɪst] *vt*: **to ~ sth on sb** (*goods*) jdm etw andrehen; (*task*) etw an jdn abschieben; (*ideas, views*) jdm etw aufzwingen
fold [fəuld] *n* Falte *f*; (*Agr*) Pferch *m*; (*fig*) Schoß *m* ▷ *vt* (zusammen)falten; (*arms*) verschränken ▷ *vi* (*business*) eingehen (*inf*)
▸ **fold up** *vi* sich zusammenfalten lassen; (*bed, table*) sich zusammenklappen lassen; (*business*) eingehen (*inf*) ▷ *vt* zusammenfalten
folder ['fəuldəʳ] *n* Aktenmappe *f*; (*binder*) Hefter *m*; (*brochure*) Informationsblatt *nt*
folding ['fəuldɪŋ] *adj* (*chair, bed*) Klapp-
foliage ['fəulɪɪdʒ] *n* Laubwerk *nt*
folk [fəuk] *npl* Leute *pl* ▷ *cpd* Volks-; **my ~s** (*parents*) meine alten Herrschaften
folklore ['fəuklɔ:ʳ] *n* Folklore *f*
folk music *n* Volksmusik *f*; (*contemporary*) Folk *m*
folk song *n* Volkslied *nt*; (*contemporary*) Folksong *m*
follow ['fɔləu] *vt* folgen *+dat*; (*with eyes*) verfolgen; (*advice, instructions*) befolgen ▷ *vi* folgen; **to ~ in sb's footsteps** in jds Fußstapfen *acc* treten; **I don't quite ~ you** ich kann Ihnen nicht ganz folgen; **it ~s that** daraus folgt, dass; **to ~ suit** (*fig*) jds Beispiel *dat* folgen
▸ **follow on** *vi* (*continue*): **to ~ on from** aufbauen auf *+dat*
▸ **follow out** *vt* (*idea, plan*) zu Ende verfolgen
▸ **follow through** *vt* = **follow out**
▸ **follow up** *vt* nachgehen *+dat*; (*offer*) aufgreifen; (*case*) weiterverfolgen
follower ['fɔləuəʳ] *n* Anhänger(in) *m(f)*
following ['fɔləuɪŋ] *adj* folgend ▷ *n* Anhängerschaft *f*
follow-up ['fɔləuʌp] *n* Weiterführung *f* ▷ *adj*: **~ treatment** Nachbehandlung *f*
folly ['fɔlɪ] *n* Torheit *f*; (*building*) exzentrisches Bauwerk *nt*

fond [fɔnd] *adj* liebevoll; (*memory*) lieb; (*hopes, dreams*) töricht; **to be ~ of** mögen; **she's ~ of swimming** sie schwimmt gerne
fondle ['fɔndl] *vt* streicheln
fondly ['fɔndlı] *adv* liebevoll; (*naïvely*) törichterweise; **he ~ believed that ...** er war so naiv zu glauben, dass ...
fondness ['fɔndnıs] *n* (*for things*) Vorliebe *f*; (*for people*) Zuneigung *f*; **a special ~ for** eine besondere Vorliebe für/Zuneigung zu
font [fɔnt] *n* Taufbecken *nt*; (*Typ*) Schrift *f*
food [fu:d] *n* Essen *nt*; (*for animals*) Futter *nt*; (*nourishment*) Nahrung *f*; (*groceries*) Lebensmittel *pl*
food chain *n* Nahrungskette *f*
food combining *n* Trennkost *f*
food mixer *n* Küchenmixer *m*
food poisoning *n* Lebensmittelvergiftung *f*
food processor *n* Küchenmaschine *f*
food stamp *n* Lebensmittelmarke *f*
foodstuffs ['fu:dstʌfs] *npl* Lebensmittel *pl*
fool [fu:l] *n* Dummkopf *m*; (*Culin*) *Sahnespeise aus Obstpüree* ▷ *vt* hereinlegen, täuschen ▷ *vi* herumalbern; **to make a ~ of sb** jdn lächerlich machen; (*trick*) jdn hereinlegen; **to make a ~ of o.s.** sich blamieren; **you can't ~ me** du kannst mich nicht zum Narren halten
▸ **fool about** (*pej*) *vi* herumtrödeln; (*behave foolishly*) herumalbern
▸ **fool around** *vi* = **fool about**
foolhardy ['fu:lhɑ:dı] *adj* tollkühn
foolish ['fu:lıʃ] *adj* dumm
foolishly ['fu:lıʃlı] *adv* dumm; **~, I forgot ...** dummerweise habe ich ... vergessen
foolishness ['fu:lıʃnıs] *n* Dummheit *f*
foolproof ['fu:lpru:f] *adj* idiotensicher
foolscap ['fu:lskæp] *n* ≈ Kanzleipapier *nt*
foot [fut] (*pl* **feet**) *n* Fuß *m*; (*of animal*) Pfote *f* ▷ *vt* (*bill*) bezahlen; **on ~** zu Fuß; **to find one's feet** sich eingewöhnen; **to put one's ~ down** (*Aut*) Gas geben; (*say no*) ein Machtwort sprechen
footage ['futıdʒ] *n* Filmmaterial *nt*
foot-and-mouth [futənd'mauθ], **foot-and-mouth disease** *n* Maul- und Klauenseuche *f*
football ['futbɔ:l] *n* Fußball *m*; (*US*) Football *m*, amerikanischer Fußball *m*
footballer ['futbɔ:ləʳ] (*Brit*) *n* Fußballspieler(in) *m(f)*
football ground *n* Fußballplatz *m*
football match (*Brit*) *n* Fußballspiel *nt*
football player *n* (*Brit*) Fußballspieler(in) *m(f)*; (*US*) Footballspieler(in) *m(f)*

FOOTBALL POOLS

Football pools, umgangssprachlich auch *the pools* genannt, ist das in Großbritannien sehr beliebte Fußballtoto, bei dem auf die Ergebnisse der samstäglichen Fußballspiele gewettet wird. Die Gewinne können sehr hoch sein und gelegentlich Millionen von Pfund betragen.

foot brake *n* Fußbremse *f*
footbridge ['futbrıdʒ] *n* Fußgängerbrücke *f*
foothills ['futhılz] *npl* (Gebirgs)ausläufer *pl*
foothold ['futhəuld] *n* Halt *m*; **to get a ~** Fuß fassen
footing ['futıŋ] *n* Stellung *f*; (*relationship*) Verhältnis *nt*; **to lose one's ~** den Halt verlieren; **on an equal ~** auf gleicher Basis
footlights ['futlaıts] *npl* Rampenlicht *nt*
footman ['futmən] (*irreg: like* **man**) *n* Lakai *m*
footnote ['futnəut] *n* Fußnote *f*
footpath ['futpɑ:θ] *n* Fußweg *m*; (*in street*) Bürgersteig *m*
footprint ['futprınt] *n* Fußabdruck *m*; (*of animal*) Spur *f*
footrest ['futrɛst] *n* Fußstütze *f*
Footsie ['futsı] (*inf*) *n* = **FTSE 100 Index**
footsie ['futsı] (*inf*) *n*: **to play ~ with sb** mit jdm füßeln
footsore ['futsɔ:ʳ] *adj*: **to be ~** wunde Füße haben
footstep ['futstɛp] *n* Schritt *m*; (*footprint*) Fußabdruck *m*; **to follow in sb's ~s** in jds Fußstapfen *acc* treten
footwear ['futwɛəʳ] *n* Schuhe *pl*, Schuhwerk *nt*

KEYWORD

for [fɔ:ʳ] *prep* **1** für *+acc*; **is this for me?** ist das für mich?; **the train for London** der Zug nach London; **it's time for lunch** es ist Zeit zum Mittagessen; **what's it for?** wofür ist das?; **he works for the government/a local firm** er arbeitet für die Regierung/eine Firma am Ort; **he's mature for his age** er ist reif für sein Alter; **I sold it for £20** ich habe es für £20 verkauft; **I'm all for it** ich bin ganz dafür; **G for George** ≈ G wie Gustav
2 (*because of*): **for this reason** aus diesem Grund; **for fear of being criticised** aus Angst, kritisiert zu werden
3 (*referring to distance*): **there are roadworks for 5 km** die Straßenbauarbeiten erstrecken sich über 5 km; **we walked for miles** wir sind meilenweit gelaufen
4 (*referring to time*): **he was away for 2 years** er war 2 Jahre lang weg; **I have known her for years** ich kenne sie bereits seit Jahren
5 (*with infinitive clause*): **it is not for me to decide** es liegt nicht an mir, das zu entscheiden; **for this to be possible ...** um dies möglich zu machen, ...
6 (*in spite of*) trotz *+gen or dat*; **for all his complaints, he is very fond of her** trotz seiner vielen Klagen mag er sie sehr
▷ *conj* (*form: since, as*) denn; **she was very angry, for he was late again** sie war sehr böse, denn er kam wieder zu spät

f.o.r. *abbr* (*Comm: = free on rail*) frei Bahn
forage ['fɔrıdʒ] *n* Futter *nt* ▷ *vi* herumstöbern; **to ~ (for food)** nach Futter suchen
forage cap *n* Schiffchen *nt*

foray ['fɔreɪ] *n* (Raub)überfall *m*
forbad, forbade [fə'bæd] *pt of* **forbid**
forbearing [fɔː'bɛərɪŋ] *adj* geduldig
forbid [fə'bɪd] (*pt* **forbade**, *pp* **~den**) *vt* verbieten; **to ~ sb to do sth** jdm verbieten, etw zu tun
forbidden [fə'bɪdn] *pp of* **forbid** ▷ *adj* verboten
forbidding [fə'bɪdɪŋ] *adj* (*look*) streng; (*prospect*) grauenhaft
force [fɔːs] *n* Kraft *f*; (*violence*) Gewalt *f*; (*of blow, impact*) Wucht *f*; (*influence*) Macht *f* ▷ *vt* zwingen; (*push*) drücken; (*: person*) drängen; (*lock, door*) aufbrechen; **the Forces** (*Brit*) *npl* die Streitkräfte *pl*; **in ~** (*law etc*) geltend; (*people: arrive etc*) zahlreich; **to come into ~** in Kraft treten; **to join ~s** sich zusammentun; **a ~ 5 wind** Windstärke 5; **the sales ~** das Verkaufspersonal; **to ~ o.s./sb to do sth** sich/jdn zwingen, etw zu tun
▸ **force back** *vt* zurückdrängen; (*tears*) unterdrücken
▸ **force down** *vt* (*food*) hinunterwürgen (*inf*)
forced [fɔːst] *adj* gezwungen; **~ labour** Zwangsarbeit *f*; **~ landing** Notlandung *f*
force-feed ['fɔːsfiːd] *vt* zwangsernähren; (*animal*) stopfen
forceful ['fɔːsful] *adj* energisch; (*attack*) wirkungsvoll; (*point*) überzeugend
forceps ['fɔːsɛps] *npl* Zange *f*
forcible ['fɔːsəbl] *adj* gewaltsam; (*reminder, lesson*) eindringlich
forcibly ['fɔːsəblɪ] *adv* mit Gewalt; (*express*) eindringlich
ford [fɔːd] *n* Furt *f* ▷ *vt* durchqueren; (*on foot*) durchwaten
fore [fɔːʳ] *n*: **to come to the ~** ins Blickfeld geraten
forearm ['fɔːrɑːm] *n* Unterarm *m*
forebear ['fɔːbɛəʳ] *n* Vorfahr(in) *m(f)*, Ahn(e) *m(f)*
foreboding [fɔː'bəudɪŋ] *n* Vorahnung *f*
forecast ['fɔːkɑːst] (*irreg: like* **cast**) *n* Prognose *f*; (*of weather*) (Wetter)vorhersage *f* ▷ *vt* voraussagen
foreclose [fɔː'kləuz] *vt* (*Law: also:* **foreclose on**) kündigen; **to ~ sb** (*on loan/mortgage*) jds Darlehen/Hypothek kündigen
foreclosure [fɔː'kləuʒəʳ] *n* Zwangsvollstreckung *f*
forecourt ['fɔːkɔːt] *n* Vorplatz *m*
forefathers ['fɔːfɑːðəz] *npl* Vorfahren *pl*
forefinger ['fɔːfɪŋgəʳ] *n* Zeigefinger *m*
forefront ['fɔːfrʌnt] *n*: **in the ~ of** an der Spitze *+gen*
forego [fɔː'gəu] (*irreg: like* **go**) *vt* verzichten auf *+acc*
foregoing ['fɔːgəuɪŋ] *adj* vorhergehend ▷ *n*: **the ~** das Vorhergehende
foregone ['fɔːgɔn] *pp of* **forego** ▷ *adj*: **it's a ~ conclusion** es steht von vornherein fest
foreground ['fɔːgraund] *n* Vordergrund *m*
forehand ['fɔːhænd] *n* (*Tennis*) Vorhand *f*
forehead ['fɔrɪd] *n* Stirn *f*
foreign ['fɔrɪn] *adj* ausländisch; (*holiday*) im Ausland; (*customs, appearance*) fremdartig; (*trade, policy*) Außen-; (*correspondent*) Auslands-; (*object, matter*) fremd; **goods from ~ countries/a ~ country** Waren aus dem Ausland
foreign body *n* Fremdkörper *m*
foreign currency *n* Devisen *pl*
foreigner ['fɔrɪnəʳ] *n* Ausländer(in) *m(f)*
foreign exchange *n* Devisenhandel *m*; (*money*) Devisen *pl*
foreign exchange market *n* Devisenmarkt *m*
foreign exchange rate *n* Devisenkurs *m*
foreign investment *n* Auslandsinvestition *f*
foreign minister *n* Außenminister(in) *m(f)*
Foreign Office (*Brit*) *n* Außenministerium *nt*
Foreign Secretary (*Brit*) *n* Außenminister(in) *m(f)*
foreleg ['fɔːlɛg] *n* Vorderbein *nt*
foreman ['fɔːmən] (*irreg: like* **man**) *n* Vorarbeiter *m*; (*of jury*) Obmann *m*
foremost ['fɔːməust] *adj* führend ▷ *adv*: **first and ~** zunächst, vor allem
forename ['fɔːneɪm] *n* Vorname *m*
forensic [fə'rɛnsɪk] *adj* (*test*) forensisch; (*medicine*) Gerichts-; (*expert*) Spurensicherungs-
foreplay ['fɔːpleɪ] *n* Vorspiel *nt*
forerunner ['fɔːrʌnəʳ] *n* Vorläufer *m*
foresee [fɔː'siː] (*irreg: like* **see**) *vt* vorhersehen
foreseeable [fɔː'siːəbl] *adj* vorhersehbar; **in the ~ future** in absehbarer Zeit
foreseen [fɔː'siːn] *pp of* **foresee**
foreshadow [fɔː'ʃædəu] *vt* andeuten
foreshore ['fɔːʃɔːʳ] *n* Strand *m*
foreshorten [fɔː'ʃɔːtn] *vt* perspektivisch verkürzen
foresight ['fɔːsaɪt] *n* Voraussicht *f*, Weitblick *m*
foreskin ['fɔːskɪn] *n* (*Anat*) Vorhaut *f*
forest ['fɔrɪst] *n* Wald *m*
forestall [fɔː'stɔːl] *vt* zuvorkommen *+dat*; (*discussion*) im Keim ersticken
forestry ['fɔrɪstrɪ] *n* Forstwirtschaft *f*
foretaste ['fɔːteɪst] *n*: **a ~ of** ein Vorgeschmack von
foretell [fɔː'tɛl] (*irreg: like* **tell**) *vt* vorhersagen
forethought ['fɔːθɔːt] *n* Vorbedacht *m*
foretold [fɔː'təuld] *pt, pp of* **foretell**
forever [fə'rɛvəʳ] *adv* für immer; (*endlessly*) ewig; (*consistently*) dauernd, ständig; **you're ~ finding difficulties** du findest ständig *or* dauernd neue Schwierigkeiten
forewarn [fɔː'wɔːn] *vt* vorwarnen
forewent [fɔː'wɛnt] *pt of* **forego**
forewoman ['fɔːwumən] (*irreg: like* **woman**) *n* Vorarbeiterin *f*; (*of jury*) Obmännin *f*
foreword ['fɔːwəːd] *n* Vorwort *nt*
forfeit ['fɔːfɪt] *n* Strafe *f*, Buße *f* ▷ *vt* (*right*) verwirken; (*friendship etc*) verlieren; (*one's happiness, health*) einbüßen
forgave [fə'geɪv] *pt of* **forgive**
forge [fɔːdʒ] *n* Schmiede *f* ▷ *vt* fälschen; (*wrought iron*) schmieden
▸ **forge ahead** *vi* große *or* schnelle Fortschritte

machen
forger ['fɔːdʒəʳ] *n* Fälscher(in) *m(f)*
forgery ['fɔːdʒərɪ] *n* Fälschung *f*
forget [fə'gɛt] (*pt* **forgot**, *pp* **forgotten**) *vt* vergessen ▷ *vi* es vergessen; **to ~ o.s.** sich vergessen
forgetful [fə'gɛtful] *adj* vergesslich; **~ of sth** (*of duties etc*) nachlässig gegenüber etw
forgetfulness [fə'gɛtfulnɪs] *n* Vergesslichkeit *f*; (*oblivion*) Vergessenheit *f*
forget-me-not [fə'gɛtmɪnɔt] *n* Vergissmeinnicht *nt*
forgive [fə'gɪv] (*pt* **forgave**, *pp* **~n**) *vt* verzeihen *+dat*, vergeben *+dat*; **to ~ sb for sth** jdm etw verzeihen *or* vergeben; **to ~ sb for doing sth** jdm verzeihen *or* vergeben, dass er etw getan hat; **~ me, but ...** entschuldigen Sie, aber ...; **they could be ~n for thinking that ...** es ist verständlich, wenn sie denken, dass ...
forgiveness [fə'gɪvnɪs] *n* Verzeihung *f*
forgiving [fə'gɪvɪŋ] *adj* versöhnlich
forgo [fɔː'gəu] (*pt* **forwent**, *pp* **~ne**) *vt* = **forego**
forgot [fə'gɔt] *pt of* **forget**
forgotten [fə'gɔtn] *pp of* **forget**
fork [fɔːk] *n* Gabel *f*; (*in road, river, railway*) Gabelung *f* ▷ *vi* (*road*) sich gabeln
▸ **fork out** (*inf*) *vt*, *vi* (*pay*) blechen
forked [fɔːkt] *adj* (*lightning*) zickzackförmig
fork-lift truck ['fɔːklɪft-] *n* Gabelstapler *m*
forlorn [fə'lɔːn] *adj* verlassen; (*person*) einsam und verlassen; (*attempt*) verzweifelt; (*hope*) schwach
form [fɔːm] *n* Form *f*; (*Scol*) Klasse *f*; (*questionnaire*) Formular *nt* ▷ *vt* formen, gestalten; (*queue, organization, group*) bilden; (*idea, habit*) entwickeln; **in the ~ of** in Form von *or +gen*; **in the ~ of Peter** in Gestalt von Peter; **to be in good ~** gut in Form sein; **in top ~** in Hochform; **on ~** in Form; **to ~ part of sth** Teil von etw sein
formal ['fɔːməl] *adj* offiziell; (*person, behaviour*) förmlich, formell; (*occasion, dinner*) feierlich; (*clothes*) Gesellschafts-; (*garden*) formell angelegt; (*Art, Philosophy*) formal; **~ dress** Gesellschaftskleidung *f*
formalities [fɔː'mælɪtɪz] *npl* Formalitäten *pl*
formality [fɔː'mælɪtɪ] *n* Förmlichkeit *f*; (*procedure*) Formalität *f*
formalize ['fɔːməlaɪz] *vt* formell machen
formally ['fɔːməlɪ] *adv* (*see adj*) offiziell; förmlich, formell; feierlich; **to be ~ invited** ausdrücklich eingeladen sein
format ['fɔːmæt] *n* Format *nt*; (*form, style*) Aufmachung *f* ▷ *vt* (*Comput*) formatieren
formation [fɔː'meɪʃən] *n* Bildung *f*; (*of theory*) Entstehung *f*; (*of business*) Gründung *f*; (*pattern: of rocks, clouds*) Formation *f*
formative ['fɔːmətɪv] *adj* (*influence*) prägend; (*years*) entscheidend
former ['fɔːməʳ] *adj* früher; **the ~ ... the latter ...** Erstere(r, s) ... Letztere(r, s); **the ~ president** der ehemalige Präsident; **the ~ East Germany** die ehemalige DDR
formerly ['fɔːməlɪ] *adv* früher
form feed *n* (*on printer*) Papiervorschub *m*
Formica® [fɔː'maɪkə] *n* Resopal® *nt*
formidable ['fɔːmɪdəbl] *adj* (*task*) gewaltig, enorm; (*opponent*) furchterregend
formula ['fɔːmjulə] (*pl* **formulae** *or* **~s**) *n* Formel *f*; **F~ One** (*Aut*) Formel Eins
formulate ['fɔːmjuleɪt] *vt* formulieren
fornicate ['fɔːnɪkeɪt] *vi* Unzucht treiben
forsake [fə'seɪk] (*pt* **forsook**, *pp* **~n**) *vt* im Stich lassen; (*belief*) aufgeben
forsook [fə'suk] *pt of* **forsake**
fort [fɔːt] *n* Fort *nt*; **to hold the ~** die Stellung halten
forte ['fɔːtɪ] *n* Stärke *f*, starke Seite *f*
forth [fɔːθ] *adv* aus; **back and ~** hin und her; **to go back and ~** auf und ab gehen; **to bring ~** hervorbringen; **and so ~** und so weiter
forthcoming [fɔːθ'kʌmɪŋ] *adj* (*event*) bevorstehend; (*person*) mitteilsam; **to be ~** (*help*) erfolgen; (*evidence*) geliefert werden
forthright ['fɔːθraɪt] *adj* offen
forthwith ['fɔːθ'wɪθ] *adv* umgehend
fortieth ['fɔːtɪɪθ] *num* vierzigste(r, s)
fortification [fɔːtɪfɪ'keɪʃən] *n* Befestigung *f*, Festungsanlage *f*
fortified wine ['fɔːtɪfaɪd-] *n* weinhaltiges Getränk *nt* (*Sherry, Portwein etc*)
fortify ['fɔːtɪfaɪ] *vt* (*city*) befestigen; (*person*) bestärken; (*: subj: food, drink*) stärken
fortitude ['fɔːtɪtjuːd] *n* innere Kraft *or* Stärke *f*
fortnight ['fɔːtnaɪt] (*Brit*) *n* vierzehn Tage *pl*, zwei Wochen *pl*; **it's a ~ since ...** es ist vierzehn Tage *or* zwei Wochen her, dass ...
fortnightly ['fɔːtnaɪtlɪ] *adj* vierzehntägig, zweiwöchentlich ▷ *adv* alle vierzehn Tage, alle zwei Wochen
FORTRAN ['fɔːtræn] *n* FORTRAN *nt*
fortress ['fɔːtrɪs] *n* Festung *f*
fortuitous [fɔː'tjuːɪtəs] *adj* zufällig
fortunate ['fɔːtʃənɪt] *adj* glücklich; **to be ~** Glück haben; **he is ~ to have ...** er kann sich glücklich schätzen, ... zu haben; **it is ~ that ...** es ist ein Glück, dass ...
fortunately ['fɔːtʃənɪtlɪ] *adv* glücklicherweise, zum Glück
fortune ['fɔːtʃən] *n* Glück *nt*; (*wealth*) Vermögen *nt*; **to make a ~** ein Vermögen machen; **to tell sb's ~** jdm wahrsagen
fortune-teller ['fɔːtʃəntɛləʳ] *n* Wahrsager(in) *m(f)*
forty ['fɔːtɪ] *num* vierzig
forum ['fɔːrəm] *n* Forum *nt*
forward ['fɔːwəd] *adj* vordere(r, s); (*movement*) Vorwärts-; (*not shy*) dreist; (*Comm: buying, price*) Termin- ▷ *adv* nach vorn; (*movement*) vorwärts; (*in time*) voraus ▷ *n* (*Sport*) Stürmer *m* ▷ *vt* (*letter etc*) nachsenden; (*career, plans*) voranbringen; **~ planning** Vorausplanung *f*; **to move ~** vorwärtskommen; **"please ~"** „bitte nachsenden"
forwards ['fɔːwədz] *adv* nach vorn; (*movement*) vorwärts; (*in time*) voraus

fossil ['fɔsl] *n* Fossil *nt*
fossil fuel *n* fossiler Brennstoff *m*
foster ['fɔstəʳ] *vt* (*child*) in Pflege nehmen; (*idea, activity*) fördern
foster child *n* Pflegekind *nt*
foster mother *n* Pflegemutter *f*
fought [fɔ:t] *pt, pp of* **fight**
foul [faul] *adj* abscheulich; (*taste, smell, temper*) übel; (*water*) faulig; (*air*) schlecht; (*language*) unflätig ▷ *n* (*Sport*) Foul *nt* ▷ *vt* beschmutzen; (*Sport*) foulen; (*entangle*) sich verheddern in *+dat*
foul play *n* unnatürlicher *or* gewaltsamer Tod *m*; **~ is not suspected** es besteht kein Verdacht auf ein Verbrechen
found [faund] *pt, pp of* **find** ▷ *vt* gründen
foundation [faun'deɪʃən] *n* Gründung *f*; (*base: also: fig*) Grundlage *f*; (*organization*) Stiftung *f*; (*also:* **foundation cream**) Grundierungscreme *f*; **foundations** *npl* (*of building*) Fundament *nt*; **the rumours are without ~** die Gerüchte entbehren jeder Grundlage; **to lay the ~s** (*fig*) die Grundlagen schaffen
foundation stone *n* Grundstein *m*
founder ['faundəʳ] *n* Gründer(in) *m(f)* ▷ *vi* (*ship*) sinken
founder member *n* Gründungsmitglied *nt*
founding ['faundɪŋ] *adj*: **~ fathers** (*esp US*) Väter *pl*
foundry ['faundrɪ] *n* Gießerei *f*
fount [faunt] *n* Quelle *f*; (*Typ*) Schrift *f*
fountain ['fauntɪn] *n* Brunnen *m*
fountain pen *n* Füllfederhalter *m*, Füller *m*
four [fɔ:ʳ] *num* vier; **on all ~s** auf allen vieren
four-letter word ['fɔ:lɛtə-] *n* Vulgärausdruck *m*
four-poster ['fɔ:'pəustəʳ] *n* (*also:* **four-poster bed**) Himmelbett *nt*
foursome ['fɔ:səm] *n* Quartett *nt*; **in** *or* **as a ~** zu viert
fourteen ['fɔ:'ti:n] *num* vierzehn
fourteenth ['fɔ:'ti:nθ] *num* vierzehnte(r, s)
fourth [fɔ:θ] *num* vierte(r, s) ▷ *n* (*Aut: also:* **fourth gear**) der vierte (Gang)
four-wheel drive ['fɔ:wi:l-] *n* (*Aut*): **with ~** mit Vierradantrieb *m*
fowl [faul] *n* Vogel *m* (*besonders Huhn, Gans, Ente etc*)
fox [fɔks] *n* Fuchs *m* ▷ *vt* verblüffen
foxglove ['fɔksglʌv] *n* (*Bot*) Fingerhut *m*
fox-hunting ['fɔkshʌntɪŋ] *n* Fuchsjagd *f*
foxtrot ['fɔkstrɔt] *n* Foxtrott *m*
foyer ['fɔɪeɪ] *n* Foyer *nt*
FPA (*Brit*) *n abbr* (= *Family Planning Association*) *Organisation für Familienplanung*
Fr. *abbr* (*Rel*) = **father; friar**
fr. *abbr* (= *franc*) Fr.
fracas ['fræka:] *n* Aufruhr *m*, Tumult *m*
fraction ['frækʃən] *n* Bruchteil *m*; (*Math*) Bruch *m*
fractionally ['frækʃnəlɪ] *adv* geringfügig
fractious ['frækʃəs] *adj* verdrießlich
fracture ['fræktʃəʳ] *n* Bruch *m* ▷ *vt* brechen
fragile ['frædʒaɪl] *adj* zerbrechlich; (*economy*) schwach; (*health*) zart; (*person*) angeschlagen
fragment [*n* 'frægmənt, *vb* fræg'mɛnt] *n* Stück *nt* ▷ *vt* aufsplittern ▷ *vi* sich aufsplittern
fragmentary ['frægməntərɪ] *adj* fragmentarisch, bruchstückhaft
fragrance ['freɪgrəns] *n* Duft *m*
fragrant ['freɪgrənt] *adj* duftend
frail [freɪl] *adj* schwach, gebrechlich; (*structure*) zerbrechlich
frame [freɪm] *n* Rahmen *m*; (*of building*) (Grund)gerippe *nt*; (*of human, animal*) Gestalt *f*; (*of spectacles: also:* **frames**) Gestell *nt* ▷ *vt* (*picture*) rahmen; (*reply*) formulieren; (*law, theory*) entwerfen; **~ of mind** Stimmung *f*, Laune *f*; **to ~ sb** (*inf*) jdm etwas anhängen
framework ['freɪmwə:k] *n* Rahmen *m*
France [fra:ns] *n* Frankreich *nt*
franchise ['fræntʃaɪz] *n* Wahlrecht *nt*; (*Comm*) Konzession *f*, Franchise *f*
franchisee [fræntʃaɪ'zi:] *n* Franchisenehmer(in) *m(f)*
franchiser ['fræntʃaɪzəʳ] *n* Franchisegeber(in) *m(f)*
frank [fræŋk] *adj* offen ▷ *vt* (*letter*) frankieren
Frankfurt ['fræŋkfə:t] *n* Frankfurt *nt*
frankfurter ['fræŋkfə:təʳ] *n* (Frankfurter) Würstchen *nt*
franking machine ['fræŋkɪŋ-] *n* Frankiermaschine *f*
frankly ['fræŋklɪ] *adv* ehrlich gesagt; (*candidly*) offen
frankness ['fræŋknɪs] *n* Offenheit *f*
frantic ['fræntɪk] *adj* verzweifelt; (*hectic*) hektisch; (*desperate*) übersteigert
frantically ['fræntɪklɪ] *adv* verzweifelt; (*hectically*) hektisch
fraternal [frə'tə:nl] *adj* brüderlich
fraternity [frə'tə:nɪtɪ] *n* Brüderlichkeit *f*; (*US: Univ*) Verbindung *f*; **the legal/medical/golfing ~** die Juristen/Mediziner/Golfer *pl*
fraternize ['frætənaɪz] *vi* Umgang haben
fraud [frɔ:d] *n* Betrug *m*; (*person*) Betrüger(in) *m(f)*
fraudulent ['frɔ:djulənt] *adj* betrügerisch
fraught [frɔ:t] *adj* (*person*) nervös; **to be ~ with danger/problems** voller Gefahren/Probleme sein
fray [freɪ] *n*: **the ~** der Kampf ▷ *vi* (*cloth*) ausfransen; (*rope*) sich durchscheuern; **to return to the ~** sich wieder ins Getümmel stürzen; **tempers were ~ed** die Gemüter erhitzten sich; **her nerves were ~ed** sie war mit den Nerven am Ende
FRB (*US*) *n abbr* = **Federal Reserve Board**
FRCM (*Brit*) *n abbr* (= *Fellow of the Royal College of Music*) *Qualifikationsnachweis in Musik*
FRCO (*Brit*) *n abbr* (= *Fellow of the Royal College of Organists*) *Qualifikationsnachweis für Organisten*
FRCP (*Brit*) *n abbr* (= *Fellow of the Royal College of Physicians*) *Qualifikationsnachweis für Ärzte*
FRCS (*Brit*) *n abbr* (= *Fellow of the Royal College of*

Surgeons) Qualifikationsnachweis für Chirurgen
freak [fri:k] *n* Irre(r) *f(m)*; *(in appearance)* Missgeburt *f*; *(event, accident)* außergewöhnlicher Zufall *m*; *(pej: fanatic)*: **health ~** Gesundheitsapostel *m* ▸ **freak out** *(inf) vi* aussteigen; *(on drugs)* ausflippen
freakish ['fri:kɪʃ] *adj* verrückt
freckle ['frɛkl] *n* Sommersprosse *f*
freckled ['frɛkld] *adj* sommersprossig
free [fri:] *adj* frei; *(costing nothing)* kostenlos, gratis ▹ *vt* freilassen, frei lassen; *(jammed object)* lösen; **to give sb a ~ hand** jdm freie Hand lassen; **~ and easy** ungezwungen; **admission ~** Eintritt frei; **~ (of charge), for free** umsonst, gratis
free agent *n*: **to be a ~** sein eigener Herr sein
freebie ['fri:bɪ] *(inf) n (promotional gift)* Werbegeschenk *nt*
freedom ['fri:dəm] *n* Freiheit *f*
freedom fighter *n* Freiheitskämpfer(in) *m(f)*
free enterprise *n* freies Unternehmertum *nt*
Freefone® ['fri:fəun] *n*: **call ~ 0800** rufen Sie gebührenfrei 0800 an
free-for-all ['fri:fərɔ:l] *n* Gerangel *nt*; **the fight turned into a ~** schließlich beteiligten sich alle an der Schlägerei
free gift *n* Werbegeschenk *nt*
freehold ['fri:həuld] *n (of property)* Besitzrecht *nt*
free kick *n* Freistoß *m*
freelance ['fri:lɑ:ns] *adj (journalist etc)* frei(schaffend), freiberuflich tätig
freelance work *n* freiberufliche Arbeit *f*
freeloader ['fri:ləudə^r] *(pej) n* Schmarotzer(in) *m(f)*
freely ['fri:lɪ] *adv* frei; *(spend)* mit vollen Händen; *(liberally)* großzügig; **drugs are ~ available in the city** Drogen sind in der Stadt frei erhältlich
free-market economy ['fri:'mɑ:kɪt-] *n* freie Marktwirtschaft *f*
Freemason ['fri:meɪsn] *n* Freimaurer *m*
Freemasonry ['fri:meɪsnrɪ] *n* Freimaurerei *f*
Freepost® ['fri:pəust] *n* ≈ „Gebühr zahlt Empfänger"
free-range ['fri:'reɪndʒ] *adj (eggs)* von frei laufenden Hühnern
free sample *n* Gratisprobe *f*
freesia ['fri:zɪə] *n* Freesie *f*
free speech *n* Redefreiheit *f*
freestyle ['fri:staɪl] *n* Freistil *m*
free trade *n* Freihandel *m*
freeway ['fri:weɪ] *(US) n* Autobahn *f*
freewheel [fri:'wi:l] *vi* im Freilauf fahren
free will *n* freier Wille *m*; **of one's own ~** aus freien Stücken
freeze [fri:z] *(pt* **froze**, *pp* **frozen**) *vi* frieren; *(liquid)* gefrieren; *(pipe)* einfrieren; *(person: stop moving)* erstarren ▹ *vt* einfrieren; *(water, lake)* gefrieren ▹ *n* Frost *m*; *(on arms, wages)* Stopp *m* ▸ **freeze over** *vi (river)* überfrieren; *(windscreen, windows)* vereisen ▸ **freeze up** *vi* zufrieren
freeze-dried ['fri:zdraɪd] *adj* gefriergetrocknet
freezer ['fri:zə^r] *n* Tiefkühltruhe *f*; *(upright)* Gefrierschrank *m*; *(in fridge: also:* **freezer compartment**) Gefrierfach *nt*
freezing ['fri:zɪŋ] *adj*: **~ (cold)** eiskalt ▹ *n*: **3 degrees below ~** 3 Grad unter null; **I'm ~** mir ist eiskalt
freezing point *n* Gefrierpunkt *m*
freight [freɪt] *n* Fracht *f*; *(money charged)* Frachtkosten *pl*; **~ forward** Fracht gegen Nachnahme; **~ inward** Eingangsfracht *f*
freight car *(US) n* Güterwagen *m*
freighter ['freɪtə^r] *n (Naut)* Frachter *m*, Frachtschiff *nt*; *(Aviat)* Frachtflugzeug *nt*
freight forwarder [-'fɔ:wədə^r] *n* Spediteur *m*
freight train *(US) n* Güterzug *m*
French [frɛntʃ] *adj* französisch ▹ *n (Ling)* Französisch *nt*; **the French** *npl* die Franzosen *pl*
French bean *(Brit) n* grüne Bohne *f*
French Canadian *adj* frankokanadisch ▹ *n* Frankokanadier(in) *m(f)*
French dressing *n* Vinaigrette *f*
French fried potatoes *npl* Pommes frites *pl*
French fries [-fraɪz] *(US) npl* = **French fried potatoes**
French Guiana [-gaɪ'ænə] *n* Französisch-Guyana *nt*
Frenchman ['frɛntʃmən] *(irreg: like* **man**) *n* Franzose *m*
French Riviera *n*: **the ~** die französische Riviera
French stick *n* Stangenbrot *nt*
French window *n* Verandatür *f*
Frenchwoman ['frɛntʃwumən] *(irreg: like* **woman**) *n* Französin *f*
frenetic [frə'nɛtɪk] *adj* frenetisch, rasend
frenzied ['frɛnzɪd] *adj* rasend
frenzy ['frɛnzɪ] *n* Raserei *f*; *(of joy, excitement)* Taumel *m*; **to drive sb into a ~** jdn zum Rasen bringen; **to be in a ~** in wilder Aufregung sein
frequency ['fri:kwənsɪ] *n* Häufigkeit *f*; *(Radio)* Frequenz *f*
frequency modulation *n* Frequenzmodulation *f*
frequent [*adj* 'fri:kwənt, *vt* frɪ'kwɛnt] *adj* häufig ▹ *vt (pub, restaurant)* oft *or* häufig besuchen
frequently ['fri:kwəntlɪ] *adv* oft, häufig
fresco ['frɛskəu] *n* Fresko *nt*
fresh [frɛʃ] *adj* frisch; *(instructions, approach, start)* neu; *(cheeky)* frech; **to make a ~ start** einen neuen Anfang machen
freshen ['frɛʃən] *vi (wind)* auffrischen; *(air)* frisch werden ▸ **freshen up** *vi* sich frisch machen
freshener ['frɛʃnə^r] *n*: **skin ~** Gesichtswasser *nt*; **air ~** Raumspray *m or nt*
fresher ['frɛʃə^r] *(Brit: inf) n* Erstsemester(in) *m(f)*
freshly ['frɛʃlɪ] *adv* frisch
freshman ['frɛʃmən] *(US: irreg: like* **man**) *n* = **fresher**

freshness ['frɛʃnɪs] *n* Frische *f*
freshwater ['frɛʃwɔːtəʳ] *adj* (*fish etc*) Süßwasser-
fret [frɛt] *vi* sich *dat* Sorgen machen
fretful ['frɛtful] *adj* (*child*) quengelig
Freudian ['frɔɪdɪən] *adj* freudianisch, freudsch; **~ slip** freudscher Versprecher *m*
FRG *n abbr* (*Hist*: = *Federal Republic of Germany*) BRD *f*
Fri. *abbr* (= *Friday*) Fr.
friar ['fraɪəʳ] *n* Mönch *m*, (Ordens)bruder *m*
friction ['frɪkʃən] *n* Reibung *f*; (*between people*) Reibereien *pl*
friction feed *n* (*on printer*) Friktionsvorschub *m*
Friday ['fraɪdɪ] *n* Freitag *m*; *see also* **Tuesday**
fridge [frɪdʒ] (*Brit*) *n* Kühlschrank *m*
fridge-freezer ['frɪdʒ'friːzəʳ] *n* Kühl- und Gefrierkombination *f*
fried [fraɪd] *pt, pp of* **fry** ▷ *adj* gebraten; **~ egg** Spiegelei *nt*; **~ fish** Bratfisch *m*
friend [frɛnd] *n* Freund(in) *m(f)*; (*less intimate*) Bekannte(r) *f(m)*; **to make ~s with** sich anfreunden mit
friendliness ['frɛndlɪnɪs] *n* Freundlichkeit *f*
friendly ['frɛndlɪ] *adj* freundlich; (*government*) befreundet; (*game, match*) Freundschafts- ▷ *n* (*also*: **friendly match**) Freundschaftsspiel *nt*; **to be ~ with** befreundet sein mit; **to be ~ to** freundlich *or* nett sein zu
friendly fire *n* Beschuss *m* durch die eigene Seite
friendly society *n* Versicherungsverein *m* auf Gegenseitigkeit
friendship ['frɛndʃɪp] *n* Freundschaft *f*
frieze [friːz] *n* Fries *m*
frigate ['frɪgɪt] *n* Fregatte *f*
fright [fraɪt] *n* Schreck(en) *m*; **to take ~** es mit der Angst zu tun bekommen; **she looks a ~** sie sieht verboten *or* zum Fürchten aus (*inf*)
frighten ['fraɪtn] *vt* erschrecken
▸ **frighten away** *or* **off** *vt* verscheuchen
frightened ['fraɪtnd] *adj* ängstlich; **to be ~ (of)** Angst haben (vor +*dat*)
frightening ['fraɪtnɪŋ] *adj* furchterregend
frightful ['fraɪtful] *adj* schrecklich, furchtbar
frightfully ['fraɪtfəlɪ] *adv* schrecklich, furchtbar; **I'm ~ sorry** es tut mir schrecklich leid
frigid ['frɪdʒɪd] *adj* frigide
frigidity [frɪ'dʒɪdɪtɪ] *n* Frigidität *f*
frill [frɪl] *n* Rüsche *f*; **without ~s** (*fig*) schlicht
fringe [frɪndʒ] *n* (*Brit*: *of hair*) Pony *m*; (*decoration*) Fransen *pl*; (*edge*: *also*: *fig*) Rand *m*
fringe benefits *npl* zusätzliche Leistungen *pl*
fringe theatre *n* avantgardistisches Theater *nt*
Frisbee® ['frɪzbɪ] *n* Frisbee® *nt*
frisk [frɪsk] *vt* durchsuchen, filzen (*inf*) ▷ *vi* umhertollen
frisky ['frɪskɪ] *adj* lebendig, ausgelassen
fritter ['frɪtəʳ] *n* Schmalzgebackenes *nt no pl* mit Füllung
▸ **fritter away** *vt* vergeuden
frivolity [frɪ'vɔlɪtɪ] *n* Frivolität *f*
frivolous ['frɪvələs] *adj* frivol; (*activity*) leichtfertig
frizzy ['frɪzɪ] *adj* kraus
fro [frəu] *adv*: **to and ~** hin und her; (*walk*) auf und ab
frock [frɔk] *n* Kleid *nt*
frog [frɔg] *n* Frosch *m*; **to have a ~ in one's throat** einen Frosch im Hals haben
frogman ['frɔgmən] (*irreg*: *like* **man**) *n* Froschmann *m*
frogmarch ['frɔgmɑːtʃ] (*Brit*) *vt*: **to ~ sb in/out** jdn herein-/herausschleppen
frolic ['frɔlɪk] *vi* umhertollen ▷ *n* Ausgelassenheit *f*; (*fun*) Spaß *m*

KEYWORD

from [frɔm] *prep* **1** (*indicating starting place, origin*) von +*dat*; **where do you come from?** woher kommen Sie?; **from London to Glasgow** von London nach Glasgow; **a letter/telephone call from my sister** ein Brief/Anruf von meiner Schwester; **to drink from the bottle** aus der Flasche trinken
2 (*indicating time*) von (... an); **from one o'clock to** *or* **until** *or* **till now** von ein Uhr bis jetzt; **from January (on)** von Januar an, ab Januar
3 (*indicating distance*) von ... entfernt; **the hotel is 1 km from the beach** das Hotel ist 1 km vom Strand entfernt
4 (*indicating price, number etc*): **trousers from £20** Hosen ab £20; **prices range from £10 to £50** die Preise liegen zwischen £10 und £50
5 (*indicating difference*): **he can't tell red from green** er kann Rot und Grün nicht unterscheiden; **to be different from sb/sth** anders sein als jd/etw
6 (*because of, on the basis of*): **from what he says** nach dem, was er sagt; **to act from conviction** aus Überzeugung handeln; **weak from hunger** schwach vor Hunger

frond [frɔnd] *n* Wedel *m*
front [frʌnt] *n* Vorderseite *f*; (*of dress*) Vorderteil *nt*; (*promenade*: *also*: **sea front**) Strandpromenade *f*; (*Mil, Met*) Front *f*; (*fig*: *appearances*) Fassade *f* ▷ *adj* vorderste(r, s); (*wheel, tooth, view*) Vorder- ▷ *vi*: **to ~ onto sth** (*house*) auf etw *acc* hinausliegen; (*window*) auf etw *acc* hinausgehen; **in ~** vorne; **in ~ of** vor; **at the ~ of the coach/train/car** vorne im Bus/Zug/Auto; **on the political ~, little progress has been made** an der politischen Front sind kaum Fortschritte gemacht worden
frontage ['frʌntɪdʒ] *n* Vorderseite *f*, Front *f*; (*of shop*) Front
frontal ['frʌntl] *adj* (*attack etc*) Frontal-
front bench (*Brit*) *n* (*Pol*) vorderste *or* erste Reihe *f*

FRONT BENCH

Front Bench bezeichnet im britischen Unterhaus die vorderste Bank auf der

Regierungs- und Oppositionsseite zur Rechten und Linken des Sprechers. Im weiteren Sinne bezieht sich front bench auf die Spitzenpolitiker der verschiedenen Parteien, die auf dieser Bank sitzen (auch „frontbenchers" genannt), d. h. die Minister auf der einen Seite und die Mitglieder des Schattenkabinetts auf der anderen.

front desk (*US*) *n* Rezeption *f*
front door *n* Haustür *f*
frontier ['frʌntɪəʳ] *n* Grenze *f*
frontispiece ['frʌntɪspi:s] *n* zweite Titelseite *f*, Frontispiz *nt*
front page *n* erste Seite *f*, Titelseite *f*
front room (*Brit*) *n* Wohnzimmer *nt*
frontrunner ['frʌntrʌnəʳ] *n* Spitzenreiter *m*
front-wheel drive ['frʌntwi:l-] *n* (*Aut*) Vorderradantrieb *m*
frost [frɔst] *n* Frost *m*; (*also:* **hoarfrost**) Raureif *m*
frostbite ['frɔstbaɪt] *n* Erfrierungen *pl*
frosted ['frɔstɪd] *adj* (*glass*) Milch-; (*esp US*) glasiert, mit Zuckerguss überzogen
frosting ['frɔstɪŋ] (*esp US*) *n* Zuckerguss *m*
frosty ['frɔstɪ] *adj* frostig; (*look*) eisig; (*window*) bereift
froth [frɔθ] *n* Schaum *m*
frothy ['frɔθɪ] *adj* schäumend
frown [fraun] *n* Stirnrunzeln *nt* ▷ *vi* die Stirn runzeln
▶ **frown on** *vt fus* missbilligen
froze [frəuz] *pt of* **freeze**
frozen ['frəuzn] *pp of* **freeze** ▷ *adj* tiefgekühlt; (*food*) Tiefkühl-; (*Comm*) eingefroren
FRS *n abbr* (*Brit: = Fellow of the Royal Society*) *Auszeichnung für Naturwissenschaftler*; (*US: = Federal Reserve System*) *amerikanische Zentralbank*
frugal ['fru:gl] *adj* genügsam; (*meal*) einfach
fruit [fru:t] *n inv* Frucht *f*; (*collectively*) Obst *nt*; (*fig: results*) Früchte *pl*
fruiterer ['fru:tərəʳ] (*esp Brit*) *n* Obsthändler(in) *m(f)*
fruit fly *n* Fruchtfliege *f*
fruitful ['fru:tful] *adj* fruchtbar
fruition [fru:'ɪʃən] *n*: **to come to ~** (*plan*) Wirklichkeit werden; (*efforts*) Früchte tragen; (*hope*) in Erfüllung gehen
fruit juice *n* Fruchtsaft *m*
fruitless ['fru:tlɪs] *adj* fruchtlos, ergebnislos
fruit machine (*Brit*) *n* Spielautomat *m*
fruit salad *n* Obstsalat *m*
fruity ['fru:tɪ] *adj* (*taste, smell etc*) Frucht-, Obst-; (*wine*) fruchtig; (*voice, laugh*) volltönend
frump [frʌmp] *n*: **to feel a ~** sich *dat* wie eine Vogelscheuche vorkommen
frustrate [frʌs'treɪt] *vt* frustrieren; (*attempt*) vereiteln; (*plan*) durchkreuzen
frustrated [frʌs'treɪtɪd] *adj* frustriert
frustrating [frʌs'treɪtɪŋ] *adj* frustrierend
frustration [frʌs'treɪʃən] *n* Frustration *f*; (*of attempt*) Vereitelung *f*; (*of plan*) Zerschlagung *f*
fry [fraɪ] (*pt, pp* **fried**) *vt* braten; *see also* **small**
frying pan ['fraɪɪŋ-] *n* Bratpfanne *f*
FT (*Brit*) *n abbr* (*= Financial Times*) *Wirtschaftszeitung*; **the FT index** der Aktienindex der „Financial Times"
ft. *abbr* = **foot; feet**
FTC (*US*) *n abbr* = **Federal Trade Commission**
FTSE 100 Index *n Aktienindex der "Financial Times"*
fuchsia ['fju:ʃə] *n* Fuchsie *f*
fuck [fʌk] (*inf!*) *vt, vi* ficken (*!*); **~ off!** (*inf!*) verpiss dich! (*!*)
fuddled ['fʌdld] *adj* verwirrt
fuddy-duddy ['fʌdɪdʌdɪ] (*pej*) *n* Langweiler *m*
fudge [fʌdʒ] *n* Fondant *m* ▷ *vt* (*issue, problem*) ausweichen *+dat*, aus dem Weg gehen *+dat*
fuel ['fjuəl] *n* Brennstoff *m*; (*for vehicle*) Kraftstoff *m*; (*: petrol*) Benzin *nt*; (*for aircraft, rocket*) Treibstoff *m* ▷ *vt* (*furnace etc*) betreiben; (*aircraft, ship etc*) antreiben
fuel oil *n* Gasöl *nt*
fuel pump *n* (*Aut*) Benzinpumpe *f*
fuel tank *n* Öltank *m*; (*in vehicle*) (Benzin)tank *m*
fug [fʌg] (*Brit: inf*) *n* Mief *m* (*inf*)
fugitive ['fju:dʒɪtɪv] *n* Flüchtling *m*
fulfil, (*US*) **fulfill** [ful'fɪl] *vt* erfüllen; (*order*) ausführen
fulfilled [ful'fɪld] *adj* ausgefüllt
fulfilment, (*US*) **fulfillment** [ful'fɪlmənt] *n* Erfüllung *f*
full [ful] *adj* voll; (*complete*) vollständig; (*skirt*) weit; (*life*) ausgefüllt ▷ *adv*: **to know ~ well that ...** sehr wohl wissen, dass ...; **~ up** (*hotel etc*) ausgebucht; **I'm ~ (up)** ich bin satt; **a ~ two hours** volle zwei Stunden; **~ marks** die beste Note, ≈ eine Eins; (*fig*) höchstes Lob *nt*; **at ~ speed** in voller Fahrt; **in ~** ganz, vollständig; **to pay in ~** den vollen Betrag bezahlen; **to write one's name** *etc* **in ~** seinen Namen *etc* ausschreiben
fullback ['fulbæk] *n* (*Rugby, Football*) Verteidiger *m*
full-blooded ['ful'blʌdɪd] *adj* (*vigorous*) kräftig; (*virile*) vollblütig
full board *n* Vollpension *f*
full-cream ['ful'kri:m] *adj*: **~ milk** (*Brit*) Vollmilch *f*
full employment *n* Vollbeschäftigung *f*
full grown *adj* ausgewachsen
full-length ['ful'lɛŋθ] *adj* (*film*) abendfüllend; (*coat*) lang; (*portrait*) lebensgroß; (*mirror*) groß; **~ novel** Roman *m*
full moon *n* Vollmond *m*
fullness ['fulnɪs] *n*: **in the ~ of time** zu gegebener Zeit
full-page ['fulpeɪdʒ] *adj* ganzseitig
full-scale ['fulskeɪl] *adj* (*war*) richtig; (*attack*) Groß-; (*model*) in Originalgröße; (*search*) groß angelegt
full-sized ['ful'saɪzd] *adj* lebensgroß
full stop *n* Punkt *m*
full-time ['ful'taɪm] *adj* (*work*) Ganztags-; (*study*) Voll- ▷ *adv* ganztags
fully ['fulɪ] *adv* völlig; **~ as big as** mindestens

so groß wie

fully fledged [-'flɛdʒd] *adj* richtiggehend; (*doctor etc*) voll qualifiziert; (*member*) Voll-; (*bird*) flügge

fulsome ['fulsəm] (*pej*) *adj* übertrieben

fumble ['fʌmbl] *vi*: **to ~ with** herumfummeln an *+dat* ▷ *vt* (*ball*) nicht sicher fangen

fume [fju:m] *vi* wütend sein, kochen (*inf*)

fumes [fju:mz] *npl* (*of fire*) Rauch *m*; (*of fuel*) Dämpfe *pl*; (*of car*) Abgase *pl*

fumigate ['fju:mɪgeɪt] *vt* ausräuchern

fun [fʌn] *n* Spaß *m*; **he's good ~ (to be with)** es macht viel Spaß, mit ihm zusammen zu sein; **for ~** aus *or* zum Spaß; **it's not much ~** es macht keinen Spaß; **to make ~ of, to poke ~ at** sich lustig machen über *+acc*

function ['fʌŋkʃən] *n* Funktion *f*; (*social occasion*) Veranstaltung *f*, Feier *f* ▷ *vi* funktionieren; **to ~ as** (*thing*) dienen als; (*person*) fungieren als

functional ['fʌŋkʃənl] *adj* (*operational*) funktionsfähig; (*practical*) funktionell, zweckmäßig

functional food *adj* Functional Food *nt*, Funktionsnahrung *f*

function key *n* (*Comput*) Funktionstaste *f*

fund [fʌnd] *n* (*of money*) Fonds *m*; (*source, store*) Schatz *m*, Vorrat *m*; **funds** *npl* (*money*) Mittel *pl*, Gelder *pl*

fundamental [fʌndə'mɛntl] *adj* fundamental, grundlegend

fundamentalism [fʌndə'mɛntəlɪzəm] *n* Fundamentalismus *m*

fundamentalist [fʌndə'mɛntəlɪst] *n* Fundamentalist(in) *m(f)*

fundamentally [fʌndə'mɛntəlɪ] *adv* im Grunde; (*radically*) von Grund auf

fundamentals [fʌndə'mɛntlz] *npl* Grundbegriffe *pl*

funding ['fʌndɪŋ] *n* Finanzierung *f*

fund-raising ['fʌndreɪzɪŋ] *n* Geldbeschaffung *f*

funeral ['fju:nərəl] *n* Beerdigung *f*

funeral director *n* Beerdigungsunternehmer(in) *m(f)*

funeral parlour *n* Leichenhalle *f*

funeral service *n* Trauergottesdienst *m*

funereal [fju:'nɪərɪəl] *adj* traurig, trübselig

funfair ['fʌnfɛəʳ] (*Brit*) *n* Jahrmarkt *m*

fungi ['fʌŋgaɪ] *npl of* **fungus**

fungus ['fʌŋgəs] (*pl* **fungi**) *n* Pilz *m*; (*mould*) Schimmel(pilz) *m*

funicular [fju:'nɪkjuləʳ] *n* (*also*: **funicular railway**) Seilbahn *f*

funky ['fʌŋkɪ] *adj* (*music*) Funk-

funnel ['fʌnl] *n* Trichter *m*; (*of ship*) Schornstein *m*

funnily ['fʌnɪlɪ] *adv* komisch; **~ enough** komischerweise

funny ['fʌnɪ] *adj* komisch; (*strange*) seltsam, komisch

funny bone *n* Musikantenknochen *m*

fun run *n* ≈ Volkslauf *m*

fur [fə:ʳ] *n* Fell *nt*, Pelz *m*; (*Brit: in kettle etc*) Kesselstein *m*

fur coat *n* Pelzmantel *m*

furious ['fjuərɪəs] *adj* wütend; (*exchange, argument*) heftig; (*effort*) riesig; (*speed*) rasend; **to be ~ with sb** wütend auf jdn sein

furiously ['fjuərɪəslɪ] *adv* (*see adj*) wütend; (*struggle etc*) heftig; (*run*) schnell

furl [fə:l] *vt* (*Naut*) einrollen

furlong ['fə:lɔŋ] *n* Achtelmeile *f* (*= 201,17 m*)

furlough ['fə:ləu] *n* (*Mil*) Urlaub *m*

furnace ['fə:nɪs] *n* (*in foundry*) Schmelzofen *m*; (*in power plant*) Hochofen *m*

furnish ['fə:nɪʃ] *vt* einrichten; (*room*) möblieren; **to ~ sb with sth** jdm etw liefern; **~ed flat, ~ed apartment** (*US*) möblierte Wohnung *f*

furnishings ['fə:nɪʃɪŋz] *npl* Einrichtung *f*

furniture ['fə:nɪtʃəʳ] *n* Möbel *pl*; **piece of ~** Möbelstück *nt*

furniture polish *n* Möbelpolitur *f*

furore [fjuə'rɔ:rɪ] *n* (*protests*) Proteste *pl*; (*enthusiasm*) Furore *f or nt*

furrier ['fʌrɪəʳ] *n* Kürschner(in) *m(f)*

furrow ['fʌrəu] *n* Furche *f*; (*in skin*) Runzel *f* ▷ *vt* (*brow*) runzeln

furry ['fə:rɪ] *adj* (*coat, tail*) flauschig; (*animal*) Pelz-; (*toy*) Plüsch-

further ['fə:ðəʳ] *adj* weitere(r, s) ▷ *adv* weiter; (*moreover*) darüber hinaus ▷ *vt* fördern; **until ~ notice** bis auf Weiteres; **how much ~ is it?** wie weit ist es noch?; **~ to your letter of ...** (*Comm*) Bezug nehmend auf Ihr Schreiben vom ...

further education (*Brit*) *n* Weiterbildung *f*, Fortbildung *f*

furthermore [fə:ðə'mɔ:ʳ] *adv* außerdem

furthermost ['fə:ðəməust] *adj* äußerste(r, s)

furthest ['fə:ðɪst] *superl of* **far**

furtive ['fə:tɪv] *adj* verstohlen

furtively ['fə:tɪvlɪ] *adv* verstohlen

fury ['fjuərɪ] *n* Wut *f*; **to be in a ~** in Rage sein

fuse, (*US*) **fuze** [fju:z] *n* (*Elec*) Sicherung *f*; (*for bomb etc*) Zündschnur *f* ▷ *vt* (*pieces of metal*) verschmelzen; (*fig*) vereinigen ▷ *vi* (*pieces of metal*) sich verbinden; (*fig*) sich vereinigen; **to ~ the lights** (*Brit*) die Sicherung durchbrennen lassen; **a ~ has blown** eine Sicherung ist durchgebrannt

fuse box *n* Sicherungskasten *m*

fuselage ['fju:zəlɑ:ʒ] *n* Rumpf *m*

fuse wire *n* Schmelzdraht *m*

fusillade [fju:zɪ'leɪd] *n* Salve *f*

fusion ['fju:ʒən] *n* Verschmelzung *f*; (*also*: **nuclear fusion**) Kernfusion *f*

fuss [fʌs] *n* Theater *nt* (*inf*) ▷ *vi* sich (unnötig) aufregen ▷ *vt* keine Ruhe lassen *+dat*; **to make a ~** Krach schlagen (*inf*); **to make a ~ of sb** viel Getue um jdn machen (*inf*)
▶ **fuss over** *vt fus* bemuttern

fusspot ['fʌspɔt] *n* Nörgler(in) *m(f)*

fussy ['fʌsɪ] *adj* kleinlich, pingelig (*inf*); (*clothes, room etc*) verspielt; **I'm not ~** es ist mir egal

fusty ['fʌstɪ] *adj* muffig

futile ['fju:taɪl] *adj* vergeblich; (*existence*)

sinnlos; (*comment*) zwecklos
futility [fjuːˈtɪlɪtɪ] *n* (*see adj*) Vergeblichkeit *f*; Sinnlosigkeit *f*; Zwecklosigkeit *f*
futon [ˈfuːtɔn] *n* Futon *m*
future [ˈfjuːtʃəʳ] *adj* zukünftig ▷ *n* Zukunft *f*; (*Ling*) Futur *nt*; **futures** *npl* (*Comm*) Termingeschäfte *pl*; **in (the) ~** in Zukunft; **in the near ~** in der nahen Zukunft; **in the immediate ~** sehr bald
futuristic [fjuːtʃəˈrɪstɪk] *adj* futuristisch
fuze [fjuːz] (*US*) *n, vt, vi* = **fuse**
fuzz [fʌz] (*inf*) *n* (*police*): **the ~** die Bullen *pl*
fuzzy [ˈfʌzɪ] *adj* verschwommen; (*hair*) kraus; (*thoughts*) verworren
fwd. *abbr* = **forward**
fwy (*US*) *abbr* = **freeway**
FYI *abbr* (*= for your information*) zu Ihrer Information

Gg

G[1], g[1] [dʒiː] *n* (*letter*) G *nt*, g *nt*; **G for George** ≈ G wie Gustav
G[2] [dʒiː] *n* (*Mus*) G *nt*, g *nt*
G[3] [dʒiː] *n abbr* (*Brit: Scol*) = **good**; (*US: Cine: = general (audience)) Klassifikation für jugendfreie Filme*; (*Phys*): **G-force** g-Druck *m*
g[2] *abbr* (= *gram(me)*) g; (*Phys*) = **gravity**
G8 *n abbr* (*Pol: = Group of Eight*) G8 *f*
GA (*US*) *n abbr* (*Post*) = *Georgia*
gab [gæb] (*inf*) *n*: **to have the gift of the ~** reden können, nicht auf den Mund gefallen sein
gabble ['gæbl] *vi* brabbeln (*inf*)
gaberdine [gæbə'diːn] *n* Gabardine *m*
gable ['geɪbl] *n* Giebel *m*
Gabon [gə'bɔn] *n* Gabun *nt*
gad about [gæd-] (*inf*) *vi* herumziehen
gadget ['gædʒɪt] *n* Gerät *nt*
gadgetry ['gædʒɪtrɪ] *n* Geräte *pl*
Gaelic ['geɪlɪk] *adj* gälisch ▷ *n* (*Ling*) Gälisch *nt*
gaffe [gæf] *n* Fauxpas *m*
gaffer ['gæfər] (*Brit: inf*) *n* (*boss*) Chef *m*; (*foreman*) Vorarbeiter *m*; (*old man*) Alte(r) *m*
gag [gæg] *n* Knebel *m*; (*joke*) Gag *m* ▷ *vt* knebeln ▷ *vi* würgen
gaga ['gɑːgɑː] (*inf*) *adj*: **to go ~** verkalken
gage [geɪdʒ] (*US*) *n, vt* = **gauge**
gaiety ['geɪɪtɪ] *n* Fröhlichkeit *f*
gaily ['geɪlɪ] *adv* fröhlich; **~ coloured** farbenfroh, farbenprächtig
gain [geɪn] *n* Gewinn *m* ▷ *vt* gewinnen ▷ *vi* (*clock, watch*) vorgehen; **to do sth for ~** etw aus Berechnung tun; (*for money*) etw des Geldes wegen tun; **~ (in)** (*increase*) Zunahme *f* (an *+dat*); (*in rights, conditions*) Verbesserung *f +gen*; **to ~ ground** (an) Boden gewinnen; **to ~ speed** schneller werden; **to ~ weight** zunehmen; **to ~ 3lbs (in weight)** 3 Pfund zunehmen; **to ~ (in) confidence** sicherer werden; **to ~ from sth** von etw profitieren; **to ~ in strength** stärker werden; **to ~ by doing sth** davon profitieren, etw zu tun; **to ~ on sb** jdn einholen
gainful ['geɪnful] *adj*: **~ employment** Erwerbstätigkeit *f*
gainfully ['geɪnfəlɪ] *adv*: **~ employed** erwerbstätig
gainsay [geɪn'seɪ] (*irreg: like* **say**) *vt* widersprechen *+dat*; (*fact*) leugnen
gait [geɪt] *n* Gang *m*; **to walk with a slow/confident ~** mit langsamen Schritten/selbstbewusst gehen
gal. *abbr* = **gallon**
gala ['gɑːlə] *n* Galaveranstaltung *f*; **swimming ~** großes Schwimmfest *nt*
Galapagos [gə'læpəgəs], **Galapagos Islands** *npl*: **(the) Galapagos (Islands)** die Galapagosinseln *pl*
galaxy ['gæləksɪ] *n* Galaxis *f*, Sternsystem *nt*
gale [geɪl] *n* Sturm *m*; **~ force 10** Sturmstärke 10
gall [gɔːl] *n* Galle *f*; (*fig: impudence*) Frechheit *f* ▷ *vt* maßlos ärgern
gall. *abbr* = **gallon**
gallant ['gælənt] *adj* tapfer; (*polite*) galant
gallantry ['gæləntrɪ] *n* (*see adj*) Tapferkeit *f*; Galanterie *f*
gall bladder *n* Gallenblase *f*
galleon ['gælɪən] *n* Galeone *f*
gallery ['gælərɪ] *n* (*also*: **art gallery**) Galerie *f*, Museum *nt*; (*private*) (Privat)galerie *f*; (*in hall, church*) Galerie *f*; (*in theatre*) oberster Rang *m*, Balkon *m*
galley ['gælɪ] *n* Kombüse *f*; (*ship*) Galeere *f*; (*also*: **galley proof**) Fahne *f*, Fahnenabzug *m*
Gallic ['gælɪk] *adj* gallisch; (*French*) französisch
galling ['gɔːlɪŋ] *adj* äußerst ärgerlich
gallon ['gæln] *n* Gallone *f* (*Brit = 4,5 l, US = 3,8 l*)
gallop ['gæləp] *n* Galopp *m* ▷ *vi* galoppieren; **~ing inflation** galoppierende Inflation *f*
gallows ['gæləuz] *n* Galgen *m*
gallstone ['gɔːlstəun] *n* Gallenstein *m*
Gallup poll ['gæləp-] *n* Meinungsumfrage *f*
galore [gə'lɔːr] *adv* in Hülle und Fülle
galvanize ['gælvənaɪz] *vt* (*fig*) mobilisieren; **to ~ sb into action** jdn plötzlich aktiv werden lassen
galvanized ['gælvənaɪzd] *adj* (*metal*) galvanisiert
Gambia ['gæmbɪə] *n* Gambia *nt*
gambit ['gæmbɪt] *n*: **(opening) ~** (einleitender) Schachzug *m*; (*in conversation*) (einleitende) Bemerkung *f*
gamble ['gæmbl] *n* Risiko *nt* ▷ *vt* einsetzen ▷ *vi* ein Risiko eingehen; (*bet*) spielen; (*on horses etc*) wetten; **to ~ on the Stock Exchange** an

der Börse spekulieren; **to ~ on sth** (*horses, race*) auf etw *acc* wetten; (*success, outcome etc*) sich auf etw *acc* verlassen
gambler ['gæmbləʳ] *n* Spieler(in) *m(f)*
gambling ['gæmblɪŋ] *n* Spielen *nt*; (*on horses etc*) Wetten *nt*
gambol ['gæmbl] *vi* herumtollen
game [geɪm] *n* Spiel *nt*; (*sport*) Sport *m*; (*strategy, scheme*) Vorhaben *nt*; (*Culin, Hunting*) Wild *nt* ▹ *adj*: **to be ~ (for)** mitmachen (bei); **games** *npl* (*Scol*) Sport *m*; **to play a ~ of football/tennis** Fußball/(eine Partie) Tennis spielen; **big ~** Großwild *nt*
game bird *n* Federwild *nt no pl*
gamekeeper ['geɪmkiːpəʳ] *n* Wildhüter(in) *m(f)*
gamely ['geɪmlɪ] *adv* mutig
game reserve *n* Wildschutzreservat *nt*
games console ['geɪmz-] *n* (*Comput*) Gameboy® *m*, Konsole *f*
game show *n* (TV) Spielshow *f*
gamesmanship ['geɪmzmənʃɪp] *n* Gerissenheit *f* beim Spiel
gaming ['geɪmɪŋ] *n* (*gambling*) Spielen *nt*
gammon ['gæmən] *n* Schinken *m*
gamut ['gæmət] *n* Skala *f*; **to run the ~ of** die ganze Skala *+gen* durchlaufen
gander ['gændəʳ] *n* Gänserich *m*
gang [gæŋ] *n* Bande *f*; (*of friends*) Haufen *m*; (*of workmen*) Kolonne *f*
▸ **gang up** *vi*: **to ~ up on sb** sich gegen jdn zusammentun
Ganges ['gændʒiːz] *n*: **the ~** der Ganges
gangland ['gæŋlænd] *adj* (*killer, boss*) Unterwelt-
gangling ['gæŋglɪŋ] *adj* schlaksig, hoch aufgeschossen
gangly ['gæŋglɪ] *adj* schlaksig
gangplank ['gæŋplæŋk] *n* Laufplanke *f*
gangrene ['gæŋgriːn] *n* (*Med*) Brand *m*
gangster ['gæŋstəʳ] *n* Gangster *m*
gangway ['gæŋweɪ] *n* Laufplanke *f*, Gangway *f*; (*in cinema, bus, plane etc*) Gang *m*
gantry ['gæntrɪ] *n* (*for crane*) Portal *nt*; (*for railway signal*) Signalbrücke *f*; (*for rocket*) Abschussrampe *f*
GAO (US) *n abbr* (*= General Accounting Office*) *Rechnungshof der USA*
gaol [dʒeɪl] (*Brit*) *n, vt* = **jail**
gap [gæp] *n* Lücke *f*; (*in time*) Pause *f*; (*difference*): **~ (between)** Kluft *f* (zwischen *+dat*)
gape [geɪp] *vi* starren, gaffen; (*hole*) gähnen; (*shirt*) offen stehen
gaping ['geɪpɪŋ] *adj* (*hole*) gähnend; (*shirt*) offen
garage ['gærɑːʒ] *n* Garage *f*; (*for car repairs*) (Reparatur)werkstatt *f*; (*petrol station*) Tankstelle *f*
garb [gɑːb] *n* Gewand *nt*, Kluft *f*
garbage ['gɑːbɪdʒ] *n* (*US: rubbish*) Abfall *m*, Müll *m*; (*inf: nonsense*) Blödsinn *m*, Quatsch *m*; (*fig: film, book*) Schund *m*
garbage can (US) *n* Mülleimer *m*, Abfalleimer *m*
garbage collector (US) *n* Müllmann *m*
garbage disposal, **garbage disposal unit** *n* Müllschlucker *m*
garbage truck (US) *n* Müllwagen *m*
garbled ['gɑːbld] *adj* (*account*) wirr; (*message*) unverständlich
garden ['gɑːdn] *n* Garten *m* ▹ *vi* gärtnern; **gardens** *npl* (*public park*) Park *m*; (*private*) Gartenanlagen *pl*; **she was ~ing** sie arbeitete im Garten
garden centre *n* Gartencenter *nt*
garden city *n* Gartenstadt *f*
gardener ['gɑːdnəʳ] *n* Gärtner(in) *m(f)*
gardening ['gɑːdnɪŋ] *n* Gartenarbeit *f*
gargle ['gɑːgl] *vi* gurgeln ▹ *n* Gurgelwasser *nt*
gargoyle ['gɑːgɔɪl] *n* Wasserspeier *m*
garish ['gɛərɪʃ] *adj* grell
garland ['gɑːlənd] *n* Kranz *m*
garlic ['gɑːlɪk] *n* Knoblauch *m*
garment ['gɑːmənt] *n* Kleidungsstück *nt*
garner ['gɑːnəʳ] *vt* sammeln
garnish ['gɑːnɪʃ] *vt* garnieren
garret ['gærɪt] *n* Dachkammer *f*, Mansarde *f*
garrison ['gærɪsn] *n* Garnison *f*
garrulous ['gærulәs] *adj* geschwätzig
garter ['gɑːtəʳ] *n* Strumpfband *nt*; (*US: suspender*) Strumpfhalter *m*
garter belt (US) *n* Strumpfgürtel *m*, Hüftgürtel *m*
gas [gæs] *n* Gas *nt*; (*US: gasoline*) Benzin *nt* ▹ *vt* mit Gas vergiften; (*Mil*) vergasen; **to be given ~** (*as anaesthetic*) Lachgas bekommen
gas cooker (*Brit*) *n* Gasherd *m*
gas cylinder *n* Gasflasche *f*
gaseous ['gæsɪəs] *adj* gasförmig
gas fire (*Brit*) *n* Gasofen *m*
gas-fired ['gæsfaɪəd] *adj* (*heater etc*) Gas-
gash [gæʃ] *n* klaffende Wunde *f*; (*tear*) tiefer Schlitz *m* ▹ *vt* aufschlitzen
gasket ['gæskɪt] *n* Dichtung *f*
gas mask *n* Gasmaske *f*
gas meter *n* Gaszähler *m*
gasoline ['gæsəliːn] (US) *n* Benzin *nt*
gasp [gɑːsp] *n* tiefer Atemzug *m* ▹ *vi* keuchen; (*in surprise*) nach Luft schnappen; **to give a ~ (of shock/horror)** (vor Schreck/Entsetzen) die Luft anhalten; **to be ~ing for** sich sehnen nach *+dat*
▸ **gasp out** *vt* hervorstoßen
gas permeable *adj* (*lenses*) luftdurchlässig
gas ring *n* Gasbrenner *m*
gas station (US) *n* Tankstelle *f*
gas stove *n* (*cooker*) Gasherd *m*; (*for camping*) Gaskocher *m*
gassy ['gæsɪ] *adj* (*drink*) kohlensäurehaltig
gas tank *n* Benzintank *m*
gastric ['gæstrɪk] *adj* (*upset, ulcer etc*) Magen-
gastric flu *n* Darmgrippe *f*
gastroenteritis ['gæstrəuɛntə'raɪtɪs] *n* Magen-Darm-Katarrh *m*
gastronomy [gæs'trɔnəmɪ] *n* Gastronomie *f*
gasworks ['gæswəːks] *n* Gaswerk *nt*
gate [geɪt] *n* (*of garden*) Pforte *f*; (*of field*) Gatter

nt; (*of building*) Tor *nt*; (*at airport*) Flugsteig *m*; (*of level crossing*) Schranke *f*; (*of lock*) Tor *nt*

gateau ['gætəu] (*pl* **~x**) *n* Torte *f*

gate-crash ['geɪtkræʃ] (*Brit*) *vt* (*party*) ohne Einladung besuchen; (*concert*) eindringen in *+acc* ▷ *vi* ohne Einladung hingehen; eindringen

gate-crasher ['geɪtkræʃəʳ] *n* ungeladener Gast *m*

gatehouse ['geɪthaus] *n* Pförtnerhaus *nt*

gateway ['geɪtweɪ] *n* (*also fig*) Tor *nt*

gather ['gæðəʳ] *vt* sammeln; (*flowers, fruit*) pflücken; (*understand*) schließen; (*Sewing*) kräuseln ▷ *vi* (*assemble*) sich versammeln; (*dust*) sich ansammeln; (*clouds*) sich zusammenziehen; **to ~ (from)** schließen (aus); **to ~ (that)** annehmen(, dass); **as far as I can ~** so wie ich es sehe; **to ~ speed** schneller werden

gathering ['gæðərɪŋ] *n* Versammlung *f*

GATT [gæt] *n abbr* (*= General Agreement on Tariffs and Trade*) GATT *nt*

gauche [gəuʃ] *adj* linkisch

gaudy ['gɔːdɪ] *adj* knallig

gauge, (US) **gage** [geɪdʒ] *n* Messgerät *nt*, Messinstrument *nt*; (*Rail*) Spurweite *f* ▷ *vt* messen; (*fig*) beurteilen; **petrol ~, fuel ~, gas gage** (US) Benzinuhr *f*; **to ~ the right moment** den richtigen Moment abwägen

Gaul [gɔːl] *n* Gallien *nt*; (*person*) Gallier(in) *m(f)*

gaunt [gɔːnt] *adj* (*haggard*) hager; (*bare, stark*) öde

gauntlet ['gɔːntlɪt] *n* (Stulpen)handschuh *m*; (*fig*): **to run the ~** Spießruten laufen; **to throw down the ~** den Fehdehandschuh hinwerfen

gauze [gɔːz] *n* Gaze *f*

gave [geɪv] *pt of* **give**

gavel ['gævl] *n* Hammer *m*

gawk [gɔːk] (*inf*) *vi* gaffen, glotzen

gawky ['gɔːkɪ] *adj* schlaksig

gawp [gɔːp] *vi*: **to ~ at** angaffen, anglotzen (*inf*)

gay [geɪ] *adj* (*homosexual*) schwul; (*cheerful*) fröhlich; (*dress*) bunt

gay marriage *adj* gleichgeschlechtliche Ehe *f*, Homoehe *f* (*inf*)

gaze [geɪz] *n* Blick *m* ▷ *vi*: **to ~ at sth** etw anstarren

gazelle [gə'zɛl] *n* Gazelle *f*

gazette [gə'zɛt] *n* Zeitung *f*; (*official*) Amtsblatt *nt*

gazetteer [gæzə'tɪəʳ] *n* alphabetisches Ortsverzeichnis *nt*

gazump [gə'zʌmp] (*Brit*) *vt*: **to be ~ed** *ein mündlich zugesagtes Haus an einen Höherbietenden verlieren*

GB *abbr* (*= Great Britain*) GB

GBH (*Brit*) *n abbr* (*Law*) = **grievous bodily harm**

GC (*Brit*) *n abbr* (*= George Cross*) *britische Tapferkeitsmedaille*

GCE (*Brit*) *n abbr* (*= General Certificate of Education*) *Schulabschlusszeugnis*, ≈ Abitur *nt*

GCHQ (*Brit*) *n abbr* (*= Government Communications Headquarters*) *Zentralstelle des britischen Nachrichtendienstes*

GCSE (*Brit*) *n abbr* (*= General Certificate of Secondary Education*) *Schulabschlusszeugnis*, ≈ mittlere Reife *f*

Gdns *abbr* (*in street names: = Gardens*) ≈ Str.

GDP *n abbr* = **gross domestic product**

GDR *n abbr* (*Hist: = German Democratic Republic*) DDR *f*

gear [gɪəʳ] *n* (*equipment*) Ausrüstung *f*; (*belongings*) Sachen *pl*; (*Tech*) Getriebe *nt*; (*Aut*) Gang *m*; (*on bicycle*) Gangschaltung *f* ▷ *vt* (*fig: adapt*): **to ~ sth to** etw ausrichten auf *+acc*; **top/low/bottom ~, high/low/bottom ~** (US) hoher/niedriger/erster Gang; **to put a car into ~** einen Gang einlegen; **to leave the car in ~** den Gang eingelegt lassen; **to leave out of ~** im Leerlauf lassen; **our service is ~ed to meet the needs of the disabled** unser Betrieb ist auf die Bedürfnisse von Behinderten eingerichtet
▶ **gear up** *vt, vi*: **to ~ (o.s.) up (to)** sich vorbereiten (auf *+acc*) ▷ *vt*: **to ~ o.s. up to do sth** sich darauf vorbereiten, etw zu tun

gearbox ['gɪəbɔks] *n* Getriebe *nt*

gear lever, (US) **gear shift** *n* Schalthebel *m*

GED (US) *n abbr* (*Scol: = general educational development*) *allgemeine Lernentwicklung*

geek-speak ['giːkspiːk] *n* (*US: inf*) Fachchinesisch *nt*

geese [giːs] *npl of* **goose**

geezer ['giːzəʳ] (*inf*) *n* Kerl *m*, Typ *m*

Geiger counter ['gaɪgə-] *n* Geigerzähler *m*

gel [dʒɛl] *n* Gel *nt*

gelatin, gelatine ['dʒɛlətiːn] *n* Gelatine *f*

gelignite ['dʒɛlɪgnaɪt] *n* Plastiksprengstoff *m*

gem [dʒɛm] *n* Edelstein *m*; **she/the house is a ~** (*fig*) sie/das Haus ist ein Juwel; **a ~ of an idea** eine ausgezeichnete Idee

Gemini ['dʒɛmɪnaɪ] *n* (*Astrol*) Zwillinge *pl*; **to be ~** (ein) Zwilling sein

gen [dʒɛn] (*Brit: inf*) *n*: **to give sb the ~ on sth** jdn über etw *acc* informieren

Gen. *abbr* (*Mil: = General*) Gen.

gen. *abbr* = **general, generally**

gender ['dʒɛndəʳ] *n* Geschlecht *nt*

gene [dʒiːn] *n* Gen *nt*

genealogy [dʒiːnɪ'ælədʒɪ] *n* Genealogie *f*, Stammbaumforschung *f*; (*family history*) Stammbaum *m*

general ['dʒɛnərl] *n* General *m* ▷ *adj* allgemein; (*widespread*) weitverbreitet; (*non-specific*) generell; **in ~** im Allgemeinen; **the ~ public** die Öffentlichkeit, die Allgemeinheit; **~ audit** (*Comm*) Jahresabschlussprüfung *f*

general anaesthetic *n* Vollnarkose *f*

general delivery (US) *n*: **to send sth ~** etw postlagernd schicken

general election *n* Parlamentswahlen *pl*

generalization ['dʒɛnrəlaɪ'zeɪʃən] *n* Verallgemeinerung *f*

generalize ['dʒɛnrəlaɪz] *vi* verallgemeinern

generally ['dʒɛnrəlɪ] *adv* im Allgemeinen

general manager *n* Hauptgeschäftsführer(in)

m(f)
general practitioner *n* praktischer Arzt *m*, praktische Ärztin *f*
general strike *n* Generalstreik *m*
generate ['dʒɛnəreɪt] *vt* erzeugen; *(jobs)* schaffen; *(profits)* einbringen
generation [dʒɛnə'reɪʃən] *n* Generation *f*; *(of electricity etc)* Erzeugung *f*
generator ['dʒɛnəreɪtə^r] *n* Generator *m*
generic [dʒɪ'nɛrɪk] *adj* allgemein; **~ term** Oberbegriff *m*
generosity [dʒɛnə'rɔsɪtɪ] *n* Großzügigkeit *f*
generous ['dʒɛnərəs] *adj* großzügig; *(measure, remuneration)* reichlich
genesis ['dʒɛnɪsɪs] *n* Entstehung *f*
genetic [dʒɪ'nɛtɪk] *adj* genetisch
genetically *adv* genetisch; **~ modified** genmanipuliert
genetic engineering *n* Gentechnologie *f*
genetic fingerprint *n* genetischer Fingerabdruck *m*
genetics [dʒɪ'nɛtɪks] *n* Genetik *f*
Geneva [dʒɪ'niːvə] *n* Genf *nt*
genial ['dʒiːnɪəl] *adj* freundlich; *(climate)* angenehm
genitals ['dʒɛnɪtlz] *npl* Genitalien *pl*, Geschlechtsteile *pl*
genitive ['dʒɛnɪtɪv] *n* Genitiv *m*
genius ['dʒiːnɪəs] *n* Talent *nt*; *(person)* Genie *nt*
Genoa ['dʒɛnəuə] *n* Genua *nt*
genocide ['dʒɛnəusaɪd] *n* Völkermord *m*
Genoese [dʒɛnəu'iːz] *adj* genuesisch ▷ *n inv* Genuese *m*, Genuesin *f*
gent [dʒɛnt] *(Brit: inf)* *n abbr* = **gentleman**
genteel [dʒɛn'tiːl] *adj* vornehm, fein
gentle ['dʒɛntl] *adj* sanft; *(movement, breeze)* leicht; **a ~ hint** ein zarter Hinweis
gentleman ['dʒɛntlmən] *(irreg: like* **man***)* *n* Herr *m*; *(referring to social position or good manners)* Gentleman *m*; **~'s agreement** Vereinbarung *f* auf Treu und Glauben
gentlemanly ['dʒɛntlmənlɪ] *adj* zuvorkommend
gentleness ['dʒɛntlnɪs] *n* *(see adj)* Sanftheit *f*; Leichtheit *f*; Zartheit *f*
gently ['dʒɛntlɪ] *adv* *(see adj)* sanft; leicht; zart
gentry ['dʒɛntrɪ] *n inv*: **the ~** die Gentry, der niedere Adel
gents [dʒɛnts] *n*: **the ~** die Herrentoilette
genuine ['dʒɛnjuɪn] *adj* echt; *(person)* natürlich, aufrichtig
genuinely ['dʒɛnjuɪnlɪ] *adv* wirklich
geographer [dʒɪ'ɔgrəfə^r] *n* Geograf(in) *m(f)*
geographic [dʒɪə'græfɪk], **geographical** [dʒɪə'græfɪkl] *adj* geografisch
geography [dʒɪ'ɔgrəfɪ] *n* Geografie *f*; *(Scol)* Erdkunde *f*
geological [dʒɪə'lɔdʒɪkl] *adj* geologisch
geologist [dʒɪ'ɔlədʒɪst] *n* Geologe *m*, Geologin *f*
geology [dʒɪ'ɔlədʒɪ] *n* Geologie *f*
geometric [dʒɪə'mɛtrɪk], **geometrical** [dʒɪə'mɛtrɪkl] *adj* geometrisch
geometry [dʒɪ'ɔmətrɪ] *n* Geometrie *f*
Geordie ['dʒɔːdɪ] *(inf)* *n aus dem Gebiet von Newcastle stammende oder dort wohnhafte Person*
Georgia ['dʒɔːdʒə] *n* *(in Eastern Europe)* Georgien *nt*
Georgian ['dʒɔːdʒən] *adj* georgisch ▷ *n* Georgier(in) *m(f)*; *(Ling)* Georgisch *nt*
geranium [dʒɪ'reɪnɪəm] *n* Geranie *f*
geriatric [dʒɛrɪ'ætrɪk] *adj* geriatrisch ▷ *n* Greis(in) *m(f)*
germ [dʒəːm] *n* Bazillus *m*; *(Biol: fig)* Keim *m*
German ['dʒəːmən] *adj* deutsch ▷ *n* Deutsche(r) *f(m)*; *(Ling)* Deutsch *nt*
German Democratic Republic *n* *(formerly)* Deutsche Demokratische Republik *f*
germane [dʒəː'meɪn] *adj*: **~ (to)** von Belang (für)
German measles *(Brit)* *n* Röteln *pl*
German Shepherd, German Shepherd dog *(esp US)* *n* Schäferhund *m*
Germany ['dʒəːmənɪ] *n* Deutschland *nt*
germinate ['dʒəːmɪneɪt] *vi* keimen; *(fig)* aufkeimen
germination [dʒəːmɪ'neɪʃən] *n* Keimung *f*
germ warfare *n* biologische Kriegsführung *f*, Bakterienkrieg *m*
gerrymandering ['dʒɛrɪmændərɪŋ] *n* Wahlkreisschiebungen *pl*
gestation [dʒɛs'teɪʃən] *n* *(of animals)* Trächtigkeit *f*; *(of humans)* Schwangerschaft *f*
gesticulate [dʒɛs'tɪkjuleɪt] *vi* gestikulieren
gesture ['dʒɛstjə^r] *n* Geste *f*; **as a ~ of friendship** als Zeichen der Freundschaft

KEYWORD

get [gɛt] *(pt, pp* **got***, US pp* **gotten***)* *vi* **1** *(become, be)* werden; **to get old/tired/cold** alt/müde/kalt werden; **to get dirty** sich schmutzig machen; **to get killed** getötet werden; **to get married** heiraten
2 *(go)*: **to get (from ...) to ...** (von ...) nach ... kommen; **how did you get here?** wie sind Sie hierhin gekommen?
3 *(begin)*: **to get to know sb** jdn kennenlernen; **let's get going** *or* **started** fangen wir an!
▷ *modal aux vb*: **you've got to do it** du musst es tun
▷ *vt* **1**: **to get sth done** *(do oneself)* etw gemacht bekommen; *(have done)* etw machen lassen; **to get one's hair cut** sich *dat* die Haare schneiden lassen; **to get the car going** *or* **to go** das Auto in Gang bringen; **to get sb to do sth** etw von jdm machen lassen; *(persuade)* jdn dazu bringen, etw zu tun
2 *(obtain: money, permission, results)* erhalten; *(find: job, flat)* finden; *(fetch: person, doctor, object)* holen; **to get sth for sb** jdm etw besorgen; **can I get you a drink?** kann ich Ihnen etwas zu trinken anbieten?
3 *(receive, acquire: present, prize)* bekommen; **how much did you get for the painting?** wie viel haben Sie für das Bild bekommen?
4 *(catch)* bekommen, kriegen *(inf)*; *(hit: target*

etc) treffen; **to get sb by the arm/throat** jdm am Arm/Hals packen; **the bullet got him in the leg** die Kugel traf ihn ins Bein
5 (*take, move*) bringen; **to get sth to sb** jdm etw zukommen lassen
6 (*plane, bus etc: take*) nehmen; (*: catch*) bekommen
7 (*understand: joke etc*) verstehen; **I get it** ich verstehe
8 (*have, possess*): **to have got** haben; **how many have you got?** wie viele hast du?
▸ **get about** *vi* (*person*) herumkommen; (*news, rumour*) sich verbreiten
▸ **get across** *vt* (*message, meaning*) klarmachen
▸ **get along** *vi* (*be friends*) (miteinander) auskommen; (*depart*) sich auf den Weg machen
▸ **get around** *vt fus* = **get round**
▸ **get at** *vt fus* (*attack, criticize*) angreifen; (*reach*) herankommen an *+acc*; **what are you getting at?** worauf willst du hinaus?
▸ **get away** *vi* (*leave*) wegkommen; (*on holiday*) verreisen; (*escape*) entkommen
▸ **get away with** *vt fus* (*stolen goods*) entkommen mit; **he'll never get away with it!** damit kommt er nicht durch
▸ **get back** *vi* (*return*) zurückkommen
▹ *vt* (*regain*) zurückbekommen; **get back!** zurück!
▸ **get back at** (*inf*) *vt fus*: **to get back at sb for sth** jdm etw heimzahlen
▸ **get back to** *vt fus* (*return to*) zurückkehren zu; (*contact again*) zurückkommen auf *+acc*; **to get back to sleep** wieder einschlafen
▸ **get by** *vi* (*pass*) vorbeikommen; (*manage*) zurechtkommen; **I can get by in German** ich kann mich auf Deutsch verständlich machen
▸ **get down** *vi* (*from tree, ladder etc*) heruntersteigen; (*from horse*) absteigen; (*leave table*) aufstehen; (*bend down*) sich bücken; (*duck*) sich ducken
▹ *vt* (*depress: person*) fertigmachen; (*write*) aufschreiben
▸ **get down to** *vt fus*: **to get down to sth** (*work*) etw in Angriff nehmen; (*find time*) zu etw kommen; **to get down to business** (*fig*) zur Sache kommen
▸ **get in** *vi* (*be elected: candidate, party*) gewählt werden; (*arrive*) ankommen
▹ *vt* (*bring in: harvest*) einbringen; (*: shopping, supplies*) (herein)holen
▸ **get into** *vt fus* (*conversation, argument, fight*) geraten in *+acc*; (*vehicle*) einsteigen in *+acc*; (*clothes*) hineinkommen in *+acc*; **to get into bed** ins Bett gehen; **to get into the habit of doing sth** sich *dat* angewöhnen, etw zu tun
▸ **get off** *vi* (*from train etc*) aussteigen; (*escape punishment*) davonkommen
▹ *vt* (*remove: clothes*) ausziehen; (*: stain*) herausbekommen
▹ *vt fus* (*leave: train, bus*) aussteigen aus; **we get 3 days off at Christmas** zu Weihnachten bekommen wir 3 Tage frei; **to get off to a good start** (*fig*) einen guten Anfang machen
▸ **get on** *vi* (*be friends*) (miteinander) auskommen
▹ *vt fus* (*bus, train*) einsteigen in *+acc*; **how are you getting on?** wie kommst du zurecht?; **time is getting on** es wird langsam spät
▸ **get on to** (*Brit*) *vt fus* (*subject, topic*) übergehen zu; (*contact: person*) sich in Verbindung setzen mit
▸ **get on with** *vt fus* (*person*) auskommen mit; (*meeting, work etc*) weitermachen mit
▸ **get out** *vi* (*leave: on foot*) hinausgehen; (*of vehicle*) aussteigen; (*news etc*) herauskommen
▹ *vt* (*take out: book etc*) herausholen; (*remove: stain*) herausbekommen
▸ **get out of** *vt fus* (*money: bank etc*) abheben von; (*avoid: duty etc*) herumkommen um
▹ *vt* (*extract: confession etc*) herausbekommen aus; (*derive: pleasure*) haben an *+dat*; (*: benefit*) haben von
▸ **get over** *vt fus* (*overcome*) überwinden; (*: illness*) sich erholen von; (*communicate: idea etc*) verständlich machen
▹ *vt*: **to get it over with** (*finish*) es hinter sich *acc* bringen
▸ **get round** *vt fus* (*law, rule*) umgehen; (*person*) herumkriegen
▸ **get round to** *vt fus*: **to get round to doing sth** dazu kommen, etw zu tun
▸ **get through** *vi* (*Tel*) durchkommen
▹ *vt fus* (*finish: work*) schaffen; (*: book*) lesen
▸ **get through to** *vt fus* (*Tel*) durchkommen zu; (*make o.s. understood*) durchdringen zu
▸ **get together** *vi* (*people*) zusammenkommen
▹ *vt* (*people*) zusammenbringen; (*project, plan etc*) zusammenstellen
▸ **get up** *vi* (*rise*) aufstehen
▹ *vt*: **to get up enthusiasm for sth** Begeisterung für etw aufbringen
▸ **get up to** *vt fus* (*prank etc*) anstellen

getaway ['gɛtəweɪ] *n*: **to make a/one's ~** sich davonmachen
getaway car *n* Fluchtauto *nt*
get-together ['gɛttəgɛðə^r] *n* Treffen *nt*; (*party*) Party *f*
get-up ['gɛtʌp] (*inf*) *n* Aufmachung *f*
get-well card [gɛt'wɛl-] *n* Karte *f* mit Genesungswünschen
geyser ['gi:zə^r] *n* Geiser *m*; (*Brit: water heater*) Durchlauferhitzer *m*
Ghana ['gɑ:nə] *n* Ghana *nt*
Ghanaian [gɑ:'neɪən] *adj* ghanaisch ▹ *n* Ghanaer(in) *m(f)*
ghastly ['gɑ:stlɪ] *adj* grässlich; (*complexion*) totenblass; **you look ~!** (*ill*) du siehst grässlich aus!
gherkin ['gə:kɪn] *n* Gewürzgurke *f*
ghetto ['gɛtəu] *n* G(h)etto *nt*
ghetto blaster [-'blɑ:stə^r] (*inf*) *n* Gettoblaster *m*
ghost [gəust] *n* Geist *m*, Gespenst *nt* ▹ *vt* für jdn (als Ghostwriter) schreiben; **to give up the ~**

den Geist aufgeben
ghost town *n* Geisterstadt *f*
ghostwriter ['gəustraɪtəʳ] *n* Ghostwriter(in) *m(f)*
ghoul [gu:l] *n* böser Geist *m*
ghoulish ['gu:lɪʃ] *adj* makaber
GHQ *n abbr* (*Mil: = General Headquarters*) Hauptquartier *nt*
GHz *abbr* (*= gigahertz*) GHz
GI (*US: inf*) *n abbr* (*= government issue*) GI *m*
giant ['dʒaɪənt] *n* (*also fig*) Riese *m* ▷ *adj* riesig, riesenhaft; **~ (size) packet** Riesenpackung *f*
giant killer *n* (*fig*) Goliathbezwinger(in) *m(f)*
gibber ['dʒɪbəʳ] *vi* brabbeln
gibberish ['dʒɪbərɪʃ] *n* Quatsch *m*
gibe [dʒaɪb] *n* spöttische Bemerkung *f* ▷ *vi*: **to ~ at** spöttische Bemerkungen machen über *+acc*
giblets ['dʒɪblɪts] *npl* Geflügelinnereien *pl*
Gibraltar [dʒɪ'brɔ:ltəʳ] *n* Gibraltar *nt*
giddiness ['gɪdɪnɪs] *n* Schwindelgefühl *nt*
giddy ['gɪdɪ] *adj*: **I am/feel ~** mir ist schwind(e)lig; (*height*) schwindelerregend; **~ with excitement** vor Aufregung ganz ausgelassen
gift [gɪft] *n* Geschenk *nt*; (*donation*) Spende *f*; (*Comm: also*: **free gift**) (Werbe)geschenk *nt*; (*ability*) Gabe *f*; **to have a ~ for sth** ein Talent für etw haben
gift card *n* (*US*) elektronische Guthabenkarte *f*, Gift Card *f* (*häufig in Form eines Gutscheins*)
gifted ['gɪftɪd] *adj* begabt
gift token *n* Geschenkgutschein *m*
gift voucher *n* = **gift token**
gig [gɪg] (*inf*) *n* Konzert *nt*
gigabyte ['dʒɪgəbaɪt] *n* Gigabyte *nt*
gigantic [dʒaɪ'gæntɪk] *adj* riesig, riesengroß
giggle ['gɪgl] *vi* kichern ▷ *n* Spaß *m*; **to do sth for a ~** etw aus Spaß tun
GIGO ['gaɪgəu] (*inf*) *abbr* (*Comput: = garbage in, garbage out*) GIGO
gild [gɪld] *vt* vergolden
gill [dʒɪl] *n* Gill *nt* (*Brit = 15 cl, US = 12 cl*)
gills [gɪlz] *npl* Kiemen *pl*
gilt [gɪlt] *adj* vergoldet ▷ *n* Vergoldung *f*; **gilts** *npl* (*Comm*) mündelsichere Wertpapiere *pl*
gilt-edged ['gɪltɛdʒd] *adj* (*stocks, securities*) mündelsicher
gimlet ['gɪmlɪt] *n* Handbohrer *m*
gimmick ['gɪmɪk] *n* Gag *m*; **sales ~** Verkaufsmasche *f*, Verkaufstrick *m*
gin [dʒɪn] *n* Gin *m*
ginger ['dʒɪndʒəʳ] *n* Ingwer *m* ▷ *adj* (*hair*) rötlich; (*cat*) rötlich gelb
ginger ale *n* Gingerale *nt*
ginger beer *n* Ingwerbier *nt*
gingerbread ['dʒɪndʒəbrɛd] *n* (*cake*) Ingwerkuchen *m*; (*biscuit*) ≈ Pfefferkuchen *m*
ginger group (*Brit*) *n* Aktionsgruppe *f*
gingerly ['dʒɪndʒəlɪ] *adv* vorsichtig
gingham ['gɪŋəm] *n* Gingan *m*, Gingham *m*
ginseng ['dʒɪnsɛŋ] *n* Ginseng *m*
gipsy ['dʒɪpsɪ] *n* Zigeuner(in) *m(f)*
gipsy caravan *n* Zigeunerwagen *m*
giraffe [dʒɪ'rɑ:f] *n* Giraffe *f*
girder ['gə:dəʳ] *n* Träger *m*
girdle ['gə:dl] *n* Hüftgürtel *m*, Hüfthalter *m* ▷ *vt* (*fig*) umgeben
girl [gə:l] *n* Mädchen *nt*; (*young unmarried woman*) (junges) Mädchen *nt*; (*daughter*) Tochter *f*; **this is my little ~** das ist mein Töchterchen; **an English ~** eine Engländerin
girlfriend ['gə:lfrɛnd] *n* Freundin *f*
Girl Guide *n* Pfadfinderin *f*
girlish ['gə:lɪʃ] *adj* mädchenhaft
Girl Scout (*US*) *n* Pfadfinderin *f*
Giro ['dʒaɪrəu] *n*: **the National ~** (*Brit*) der Postscheckdienst
giro ['dʒaɪrəu] *n* Giro *nt*, Giroverkehr *m*; (*post office giro*) Postscheckverkehr *m*; (*Brit: welfare cheque*) Sozialhilfescheck *m*
girth [gə:θ] *n* Umfang *m*; (*of horse*) Sattelgurt *m*
gist [dʒɪst] *n* Wesentliche(s) *nt*

KEYWORD

give [gɪv] (*pt* **gave**, *pp* **given**) *vt* **1** (*hand over*): **to give sb sth, give sth to sb** jdm etw geben; **I'll give you £5 for it** ich gebe dir £5 dafür
2 (*used with noun to replace a verb*): **to give a sigh/cry/laugh** *etc* seufzen/schreien/lachen *etc*; **to give a speech/a lecture** eine Rede/einen Vortrag halten; **to give three cheers** ein dreifaches Hoch ausbringen
3 (*tell, deliver: news, message etc*) mitteilen; (*: advice, answer*) geben
4 (*supply, provide: opportunity, job etc*) geben; (*: surprise*) bereiten; (*bestow: title, honour, right*) geben, verleihen; **that's given me an idea** dabei kommt mir eine Idee
5 (*devote: time, one's life*) geben; (*: attention*) schenken
6 (*organize: party, dinner etc*) geben
▷ *vi* **1** (*also*: **give way**: *break, collapse*) nachgeben
2 (*stretch: fabric*) sich dehnen
▸ **give away** *vt* (*money, opportunity*) verschenken; (*secret, information*) verraten; (*bride*) zum Altar führen; **that immediately gave him away** dadurch verriet er sich sofort
▸ **give back** *vt* (*money, book etc*) zurückgeben
▸ **give in** *vi* (*yield*) nachgeben
▷ *vt* (*essay etc*) abgeben
▸ **give off** *vt* (*heat, smoke*) abgeben
▸ **give out** *vt* (*prizes, books, drinks etc*) austeilen
▷ *vi* (*be exhausted: supplies*) zu Ende gehen; (*fail*) versagen
▸ **give up** *vt, vi* aufgeben; **to give up smoking** das Rauchen aufgeben; **to give o.s. up** sich stellen; (*after siege etc*) sich ergeben
▸ **give way** *vi* (*yield, collapse*) nachgeben; (*Brit: Aut*) die Vorfahrt achten

give-and-take ['gɪvənd'teɪk] *n* (gegenseitiges) Geben und Nehmen *nt*
giveaway ['gɪvəweɪ] (*inf*) *n*: **her expression was a ~** ihr Gesichtsausdruck verriet alles; **the exam was a ~!** die Prüfung war

geschenkt!; ~ **prices** Schleuderpreise *pl*
given ['gɪvn] *pp of* **give** ▷ *adj* (*time, amount*) bestimmt ▷ *conj*: **~ the circumstances ...** unter den Umständen ...; **~ that ...** angesichts der Tatsache, dass ...
glacial ['gleɪsɪəl] *adj* (*landscape etc*) Gletscher-; (*fig*) eisig
glacier ['glæsɪəʳ] *n* Gletscher *m*
glad [glæd] *adj* froh; **to be ~ about sth** sich über etw *acc* freuen; **to be ~ that** sich freuen, dass; **I was ~ of his help** ich war froh über seine Hilfe
gladden ['glædn] *vt* erfreuen
glade [gleɪd] *n* Lichtung *f*
gladioli [glædɪ'əulaɪ] *npl* Gladiolen *pl*
gladly ['glædlɪ] *adv* gern(e)
glamorous ['glæmərəs] *adj* reizvoll; (*model etc*) glamourös
glamour ['glæməʳ] *n* Glanz *m*, Reiz *m*
glance [glɑːns] *n* Blick *m* ▷ *vi*: **to ~ at** einen Blick werfen auf *+acc*
▸ **glance off** *vt fus* abprallen von
glancing ['glɑːnsɪŋ] *adj*: **to strike sth a ~ blow** etw streifen
gland [glænd] *n* Drüse *f*
glandular fever ['glændjulə-] (*Brit*) *n* Drüsenfieber *nt*
glare [glɛəʳ] *n* wütender Blick *m*; (*of light*) greller Schein *m*; (*of publicity*) grelles Licht *nt* ▷ *vi* (*light*) grell scheinen; **to ~ at** (wütend) anstarren
glaring ['glɛərɪŋ] *adj* eklatant
glasnost ['glæznɔst] *n* Glasnost *f*
glass [glɑːs] *n* Glas *nt*; **glasses** *npl* (*spectacles*) Brille *f*
glass-blowing ['glɑːsbləuɪŋ] *n* Glasbläserei *f*
glass ceiling *n* (*fig*) gläserne Decke *f*
glass fibre *n* Glasfaser *f*
glasshouse ['glɑːshaus] *n* Gewächshaus *nt*
glassware ['glɑːswɛəʳ] *n* Glaswaren *pl*
glassy ['glɑːsɪ] *adj* glasig
Glaswegian [glæs'wiːdʒən] *adj* Glasgower ▷ *n* Glasgower(in) *m(f)*
glaze [gleɪz] *vt* (*door, window*) verglasen; (*pottery*) glasieren ▷ *n* Glasur *f*
glazed [gleɪzd] *adj* (*eyes*) glasig; (*pottery, tiles*) glasiert
glazier ['gleɪzɪəʳ] *n* Glaser(in) *m(f)*
gleam [gliːm] *vi* (*light*) schimmern; (*polished surface, eyes*) glänzen ▷ *n*: **a ~ of hope** ein Hoffnungsschimmer *m*
gleaming ['gliːmɪŋ] *adj* schimmernd, glänzend
glean [gliːn] *vt* (*information*) herausbekommen, ausfindig machen
glee [gliː] *n* Freude *f*
gleeful ['gliːful] *adj* fröhlich
glen [glɛn] *n* Tal *nt*
glib [glɪb] *adj* (*person*) glatt; (*promise, response*) leichthin gemacht
glibly ['glɪblɪ] *adv* (*talk*) gewandt; (*answer*) leichthin
glide [glaɪd] *vi* gleiten ▷ *n* Gleiten *nt*
glider ['glaɪdəʳ] *n* Segelflugzeug *nt*
gliding ['glaɪdɪŋ] *n* Segelfliegen *nt*
glimmer ['glɪməʳ] *n* Schimmer *m*; (*of interest, hope*) Funke *m* ▷ *vi* schimmern
glimpse [glɪmps] *n* Blick *m* ▷ *vt* einen Blick werfen auf *+acc*; **to catch a ~ (of)** einen flüchtigen Blick erhaschen (von *+dat*)
glint [glɪnt] *vi* glitzern; (*eyes*) funkeln ▷ *n* (*see vb*) Glitzern *nt*; Funkeln *nt*
glisten ['glɪsn] *vi* glänzen
glitter ['glɪtəʳ] *vi* glitzern; (*eyes*) funkeln ▷ *n* (*see vb*) Glitzern *nt*; Funkeln *nt*
glittering ['glɪtərɪŋ] *adj* glitzernd; (*eyes*) funkelnd; (*career*) glänzend
glitz [glɪts] (*inf*) *n* Glanz *m*
gloat [gləut] *vi*: **to ~ (over)** (*own success*) sich brüsten (mit); (*sb's failure*) sich hämisch freuen (über *+acc*)
global ['gləubl] *adj* global
globalization [gləublaɪ'zeɪʃn] *n* (*Pol, Econ*) Globalisierung *f*
global player *n* (*Econ*) Weltfirma *f*, Global Player *m*
global warming [-'wɔːmɪŋ] *n* Erwärmung *f* der Erdatmosphäre
globe [gləub] *n* Erdball *m*; (*model*) Globus *m*; (*shape*) Kugel *f*
globetrotter ['gləubtrɔtəʳ] *n* Globetrotter(in) *m(f)*, Weltenbummler(in) *m(f)*
globule ['glɔbjuːl] *n* Tröpfchen *nt*
gloom [gluːm] *n* Düsterkeit *f*; (*sadness*) düstere *or* gedrückte Stimmung *f*
gloomily ['gluːmɪlɪ] *adv* düster
gloomy ['gluːmɪ] *adj* düster; (*person*) bedrückt; (*situation*) bedrückend
glorification [glɔːrɪfɪ'keɪʃən] *n* Verherrlichung *f*
glorify ['glɔːrɪfaɪ] *vt* verherrlichen
glorious ['glɔːrɪəs] *adj* herrlich; (*victory*) ruhmreich; (*future*) glanzvoll
glory ['glɔːrɪ] *n* Ruhm *m*; (*splendour*) Herrlichkeit *f* ▷ *vi*: **to ~ in** sich sonnen in *+dat*
glory hole (*inf*) *n* Rumpelkammer *f*
Glos (*Brit*) *abbr* (*Post*) = *Gloucestershire*
gloss [glɔs] *n* Glanz *m*; (*also*: **gloss paint**) Lack *m*, Lackfarbe *f*
▸ **gloss over** *vt fus* vom Tisch wischen
glossary ['glɔsərɪ] *n* Glossar *nt*
glossy ['glɔsɪ] *adj* glänzend; (*photograph, magazine*) Hochglanz- ▷ *n* (*also*: **glossy magazine**) (Hochglanz)magazin *nt*
glove [glʌv] *n* Handschuh *m*
glove compartment *n* Handschuhfach *nt*
glow [gləu] *vi* glühen; (*stars, eyes*) leuchten ▷ *n* (*see vb*) Glühen *nt*; Leuchten *nt*
glower ['glauəʳ] *vi*: **to ~ at sb** jdn finster ansehen
glowing ['gləuɪŋ] *adj* glühend; (*complexion*) blühend; (*fig: report, description etc*) begeistert
glow-worm ['gləuwəːm] *n* Glühwürmchen *nt*
glucose ['gluːkəus] *n* Traubenzucker *m*
glue [gluː] *n* Klebstoff *m* ▷ *vt*: **to ~ sth onto sth** etw an etw *acc* kleben; **to ~ sth into place** etw festkleben

glue-sniffing ['glu:snɪfɪŋ] *n* (Klebstoff-)Schnüffeln *nt*
glum [glʌm] *adj* bedrückt, niedergeschlagen
glut [glʌt] *n*: **~ (of)** Überangebot *nt* (an *+dat*) ▷ *vt*: **to be ~ted (with)** überschwemmt sein (mit); **a ~ of pears** eine Birnenschwemme
glutinous ['glu:tɪnəs] *adj* klebrig
glutton ['glʌtn] *n* Vielfraß *m*; **a ~ for work** ein Arbeitstier *nt*; **a ~ for punishment** ein Masochist *m*
gluttonous ['glʌtənəs] *adj* gefräßig
gluttony ['glʌtənɪ] *n* Völlerei *f*
glycerin, glycerine ['glɪsəri:n] *n* Glyzerin *nt*
GM *abbr* = **genetically modified**
gm *abbr* (= *gram(me)*) g
GMAT (*US*) *n abbr* (= *Graduate Management Admissions Test*) *Zulassungsprüfung für Handelsschulen*
GMT *abbr* (= *Greenwich Mean Time*) WEZ *f*
gnarled [nɑ:ld] *adj* (*tree*) knorrig; (*hand*) knotig
gnash [næʃ] *vt*: **to ~ one's teeth** mit den Zähnen knirschen
gnat [næt] *n* (Stech)mücke *f*
gnaw [nɔ:] *vt* nagen an *+dat* ▷ *vi* (*fig*): **to ~ at** quälen
gnome [nəum] *n* Gnom *m*; (*in garden*) Gartenzwerg *m*
GNP *n abbr* (= *gross national product*) BSP *nt*
GNVQ (*Brit*) *n abbr* (= *General National Vocational Qualification*) *allgemeine, auf die Arbeitswelt bezogene Qualifikation*

go [gəu] (*pt* **went**, *pp* **gone**) *vi* **1** gehen; (*travel*) fahren; **a car went by** ein Auto fuhr vorbei
2 (*depart*) gehen; **"I must go," she said** „ich muss gehen", sagte sie; **she has gone to Sheffield/Australia** (*permanently*) sie ist nach Sheffield/Australien gegangen
3 (*attend, take part in activity*) gehen; **she went to university in Oxford** sie ist in Oxford zur Universität gegangen; **to go for a walk** spazieren gehen; **to go dancing** tanzen gehen
4 (*work*) funktionieren; **the tape recorder was still going** das Tonband lief noch
5 (*become*): **to go pale/mouldy** blass/schimmelig werden
6 (*be sold*): **to go for £100** für £100 weggehen *or* verkauft werden
7 (*be about to, intend to*): **we're going to stop in an hour** wir hören in einer Stunde auf; **are you going to come?** kommst du?, wirst du kommen?
8 (*time*) vergehen
9 (*event, activity*) ablaufen; **how did it go?** wie wars?
10 (*be given*): **the job is to go to someone else** die Stelle geht an jemand anders
11 (*break etc*) kaputtgehen; **the fuse went** die Sicherung ist durchgebrannt
12 (*be placed*) hingehören; **the milk goes in the fridge** die Milch kommt in den Kühlschrank
▷ *n* **1** (*try*): **to have a go at sth** etw versuchen; **I'll have a go at mending it** ich will versuchen, es zu reparieren; **to have a go** es versuchen
2 (*turn*): **whose go is it?** wer ist dran *or* an der Reihe?
3 (*move*): **to be on the go** auf Trab sein
▶ **go about** *vi* (*also*: **go around**: *rumour*) herumgehen
▷ *vt fus*: **how do I go about this?** wie soll ich vorgehen?; **to go about one's business** seinen eigenen Geschäften nachgehen
▶ **go after** *vt fus* (*pursue*: *person*) nachgehen *+dat*; (: *job etc*) sich bemühen um; (: *record*) erreichen wollen
▶ **go against** *vt fus* (*be unfavourable to*) ungünstig verlaufen für; (*disregard*: *advice, wishes etc*) handeln gegen
▶ **go ahead** *vi* (*proceed*) weitergehen; **to go ahead with** weitermachen mit
▶ **go along** *vi* gehen
▶ **go along with** *vt fus* (*agree with*) zustimmen *+dat*; (*accompany*) mitgehen mit
▶ **go away** *vi* (*leave*) weggehen
▶ **go back** *vi* zurückgehen
▶ **go back on** *vt fus* (*promise*) zurücknehmen
▶ **go by** *vi* (*years, time*) vergehen
▷ *vt fus* (*rule etc*) sich richten nach
▶ **go down** *vi* (*descend*) hinuntergehen; (*ship, sun*) untergehen; (*price, level*) sinken
▷ *vt fus* (*stairs, ladder*) hinuntergehen; **his speech went down well** seine Rede kam gut an
▶ **go for** *vt fus* (*fetch*) holen (gehen); (*like*) mögen; (*attack*) losgehen auf *+acc*; (*apply to*) gelten für
▶ **go in** *vi* (*enter*) hineingehen
▶ **go in for** *vt fus* (*competition*) teilnehmen an *+dat*; (*favour*) stehen auf *+acc*
▶ **go into** *vt fus* (*enter*) hineingehen in *+acc*; (*investigate*) sich befassen mit; (*career*) gehen in *+acc*
▶ **go off** *vi* (*leave*) weggehen; (*food*) schlecht werden; (*bomb, gun*) losgehen; (*event*) verlaufen; (*lights etc*) ausgehen
▷ *vt fus* (*inf*): **I've gone off it/him** ich mache mir nichts mehr daraus/aus ihm; **the gun went off** das Gewehr ging los; **to go off to sleep** einschlafen; **the party went off well** die Party verlief gut
▶ **go on** *vi* (*continue*) weitergehen; (*happen*) vor sich gehen; (*lights*) angehen
▷ *vt fus* (*be guided by*) sich stützen auf *+acc*; **to go on doing sth** mit etw weitermachen; **what's going on here?** was geht hier vor?, was ist hier los?
▶ **go on at** (*inf*) *vt fus* (*nag*) herumnörgeln an *+dat*
▶ **go on with** *vt fus* weitermachen mit
▶ **go out** *vt fus* (*leave*) hinausgehen
▷ *vi* (*for entertainment*) ausgehen; (*fire, light*) ausgehen; (*couple*): **they went out for 3 years** sie gingen 3 Jahre lang miteinander
▶ **go over** *vi* hinübergehen

▹ *vt* (*check*) durchgehen; **to go over sth in one's mind** etw überdenken
▸ **go round** *vi* (*circulate*: *news, rumour*) umgehen; (*revolve*) sich drehen; (*suffice*) ausreichen; (*visit*): **to go round (to sb's)** (bei jdm) vorbeigehen; **there's not enough to go round** es reicht nicht (für alle)
▸ **go through** *vt fus* (*place*) gehen durch; (*by car*) fahren durch; (*undergo*) durchmachen; (*search through*: *files, papers*) durchsuchen; (*describe*: *list, book, story*) durchgehen; (*perform*) durchgehen
▸ **go through with** *vt fus* (*plan, crime*) durchziehen; **I couldn't go through with it** ich brachte es nicht fertig
▸ **go under** *vi* (*sink*: *person*) untergehen; (*fig*: *business, project*) scheitern
▸ **go up** *vi* (*ascend*) hinaufgehen; (*price, level*) steigen; **to go up in flames** in Flammen aufgehen
▸ **go with** *vt fus* (*suit*) passen zu
▸ **go without** *vt fus* (*food, treats*) verzichten auf *+acc*

goad [gəud] *vt* aufreizen
▸ **goad on** *vt* anstacheln
go-ahead ['gəuəhɛd] *adj* zielstrebig; (*firm*) fortschrittlich ▹ *n* grünes Licht *nt*; **to give sb the ~** jdm grünes Licht geben
goal [gəul] *n* Tor *nt*; (*aim*) Ziel *nt*; **to score a ~** ein Tor schießen *or* erzielen
goal difference *n* Tordifferenz *f*
goalie ['gəulɪ] (*inf*) *n* Tormann *m*
goalkeeper ['gəulki:pəʳ] *n* Torwart *m*
goal post *n* Torpfosten *m*
goat [gəut] *n* Ziege *f*
gobble ['gɔbl] *vt* (*also*: **gobble down, gobble up**) verschlingen
go-between ['gəubɪtwi:n] *n* Vermittler(in) *m(f)*
Gobi Desert ['gəubɪ-] *n*: **the ~** die Wüste Gobi
goblet ['gɔblɪt] *n* Pokal *m*
goblin ['gɔblɪn] *n* Kobold *m*
go-cart ['gəukɑ:t] *n* Gokart *m*
God [gɔd] *n* Gott *m* ▹ *excl* o Gott!
god [gɔd] *n* Gott *m*
god-awful [gɔd'ɔ:fəl] (*inf*) *adj* beschissen (*!*)
godchild ['gɔdtʃaɪld] *n* Patenkind *nt*
goddamn ['gɔddæm], **goddamned** ['gɔddæmd] (*US*: *inf*) *adj* gottverdammt
goddaughter ['gɔddɔ:təʳ] *n* Patentochter *f*
goddess ['gɔdɪs] *n* Göttin *f*
godfather ['gɔdfɑ:ðəʳ] *n* Pate *m*
God-fearing ['gɔdfɪərɪŋ] *adj* gottesfürchtig
godforsaken ['gɔdfəseɪkən] *adj* gottverlassen
godmother ['gɔdmʌðəʳ] *n* Patin *f*
godparent ['gɔdpɛərənt] *n* Pate *m*, Patin *f*
godsend ['gɔdsɛnd] *n* Geschenk *nt* des Himmels
godson ['gɔdsʌn] *n* Patensohn *m*
goes [gəuz] *vb see* **go**
gofer ['gəufəʳ] (*inf*) *n* Mädchen *nt* für alles
go-getter ['gəugɛtəʳ] (*inf*) *n* Ellbogentyp (*pej, inf*) *m*
goggle ['gɔgl] (*inf*) *vi*: **to ~ at** anstarren, anglotzen
goggles ['gɔglz] *npl* Schutzbrille *f*
going ['gəuɪŋ] *n*: **it was slow/hard ~** (*fig*) es ging nur langsam/schwer voran ▹ *adj*: **the ~ rate** der gängige Preis; **when the ~ gets tough** wenn es schwierig wird; **a ~ concern** ein gut gehendes Unternehmen
going-over [gəuɪŋ'əuvəʳ] (*inf*) *n* (*check*) Untersuchung *f*; (*beating-up*) Abreibung *f*; **to give sb a good ~** jdm eine tüchtige Abreibung verpassen
goings-on ['gəuɪŋz'ɔn] (*inf*) *npl* Vorgänge *pl*, Dinge *pl*
go-kart ['gəukɑ:t] *n* = **go-cart**
gold [gəuld] *n* Gold *nt*; (*also*: **gold medal**) Gold *nt*, Goldmedaille *f* ▹ *adj* golden; (*reserves, jewellery, tooth*) Gold-
golden ['gəuldən] *adj* (*also fig*) golden
golden age *n* Blütezeit *f*
golden handshake (*Brit*) *n* Abstandssumme *f*
golden rule *n* goldene Regel *f*
goldfish ['gəuldfɪʃ] *n* Goldfisch *m*
gold leaf *n* Blattgold *nt*
gold medal *n* Goldmedaille *f*
gold mine *n* (*also fig*) Goldgrube *f*
gold-plated ['gəuld'pleɪtɪd] *adj* vergoldet
goldsmith ['gəuldsmɪθ] *n* Goldschmied(in) *m(f)*
gold standard *n* Goldstandard *m*
golf [gɔlf] *n* Golf *nt*
golf ball *n* (*for game*) Golfball *m*; (*on typewriter*) Kugelkopf *m*
golf club *n* Golfklub *m*; (*stick*) Golfschläger *m*
golf course *n* Golfplatz *m*
golfer ['gɔlfəʳ] *n* Golfspieler(in) *m(f)*, Golfer(in) *m(f)*
golfing ['gɔlfɪŋ] *n* Golf(spielen) *nt*; **he does a lot of ~** er spielt viel Golf ▹ *cpd* Golf-
gondola ['gɔndələ] *n* Gondel *f*
gondolier [gɔndə'lɪəʳ] *n* Gondoliere *m*
gone [gɔn] *pp of* **go** ▹ *adj* weg; (*days*) vorbei
goner ['gɔnəʳ] (*inf*) *n*: **to be a ~** hinüber sein
gong [gɔŋ] *n* Gong *m*
good [gud] *adj* gut; (*well-behaved*) brav, lieb ▹ *n* (*virtue, morality*) Gute(s) *nt*; (*benefit*) Wohl *nt*; **goods** *npl* (*Comm*) Güter *pl*; **to have a ~ time** sich (gut) amüsieren; **to be ~ at sth** (*swimming, talking etc*) etw gut können; (*science, sports etc*) gut in etw *dat* sein; **to be ~ for sb/sth** gut für jdn/zu etw *dat* sein; **it's ~ for you** das tut dir gut; **it's a ~ thing you were there** gut, dass Sie da waren; **she is ~ with children** sie kann gut mit Kindern umgehen; **she is ~ with her hands** sie ist geschickt; **to feel ~** sich wohlfühlen; **it's ~ to see you** (es ist) schön, Sie zu sehen; **would you be ~ enough to ...?** könnten Sie bitte ...?; **that's very ~ of you** das ist wirklich nett von Ihnen; **a ~ deal (of)** ziemlich viel; **a ~ many** ziemlich viele; **take a ~ look** sieh dir das genau *or* gut an; **a ~ while ago** vor einiger Zeit; **to make ~** (*damage*) wiedergutmachen; (*loss*) ersetzen;

it's no ~ complaining es ist sinnlos *or* es nützt nichts, sich zu beklagen; **~ morning/afternoon/evening!** guten Morgen/Tag/Abend!; **~ night!** gute Nacht!; **he's up to no ~** er führt nichts Gutes im Schilde; **for the common ~** zum Wohle aller; **is this any ~?** (*will it help you?*) können Sie das gebrauchen?; (*is it good enough?*) reicht das?; **is the book/film any ~?** was halten Sie von dem Buch/Film?; **for ~** für immer; **~s and chattels** Hab und Gut *nt*

goodbye [gud'baɪ] *excl* auf Wiedersehen!; **to say ~** sich verabschieden

good-for-nothing ['gudfənʌθɪŋ] *adj* nichtsnutzig

Good Friday *n* Karfreitag *m*

good-humoured ['gud'hjuːməd] *adj* gut gelaunt; (*good-natured*) gutmütig; (*remark, joke*) harmlos

good-looking ['gud'lukɪŋ] *adj* gut aussehend

good-natured ['gud'neɪtʃəd] *adj* gutmütig; (*discussion*) freundlich

goodness ['gudnɪs] *n* Güte *f*; **for ~ sake!** um Himmels willen!; **~ gracious!** ach du liebe *or* meine Güte!

goods train (*Brit*) *n* Güterzug *m*

goodwill [gud'wɪl] *n* Wohlwollen *nt*; (*Comm*) Goodwill *m*

goody ['gudɪ] (*inf*) *n* Gute(r) *m*, Held *m*

goody-goody ['gudɪgudɪ] (*pej*) *n* Tugendlamm *nt*, Musterkind (*inf*) *nt*

gooey ['guːɪ] (*inf*) *adj* (*sticky*) klebrig; (*cake*) üppig; (*fig: sentimental*) rührselig

goose [guːs] (*pl* **geese**) *n* Gans *f*

gooseberry ['guzbərɪ] *n* Stachelbeere *f*; **to play ~** (*Brit*) das fünfte Rad am Wagen sein

goose flesh *n* = **goose pimples**

goose pimples *npl* Gänsehaut *f*

goose step *n* Stechschritt *m*

GOP (*US: inf*) *n abbr* (*Pol: = Grand Old Party*) *Republikanische Partei*

gopher ['gəufə^r] *n* (*Zool*) Taschenratte *f*

gore [gɔː^r] *vt* aufspießen ▷ *n* Blut *nt*

gorge [gɔːdʒ] *n* Schlucht *f* ▷ *vt*: **to ~ o.s. (on)** sich vollstopfen (mit)

gorgeous ['gɔːdʒəs] *adj* herrlich; (*person*) hinreißend

gorilla [gə'rɪlə] *n* Gorilla *m*

gormless ['gɔːmlɪs] (*Brit: inf*) *adj* doof

gorse [gɔːs] *n* Stechginster *m*

gory ['gɔːrɪ] *adj* blutig

go-slow ['gəu'sləu] (*Brit*) *n* Bummelstreik *m*

gospel ['gɔspl] *n* Evangelium *nt*; (*doctrine*) Lehre *f*

gossamer ['gɔsəmə^r] *n* Spinnfäden *pl*; (*light fabric*) hauchdünne Gaze *f*

gossip ['gɔsɪp] *n* (*rumours*) Klatsch *m*, Tratsch *m*; (*chat*) Schwatz *m*; (*person*) Klatschbase *f* ▷ *vi* schwatzen; **a piece of ~** eine Neuigkeit

gossip column *n* Klatschkolumne *f*, Klatschspalte *f*

got [gɔt] *pt, pp of* **get**

Gothic ['gɔθɪk] *adj* gotisch

gotten ['gɔtn] (*US*) *pp of* **get**

gouge [gaudʒ] *vt* (*also*: **gouge out**: *hole etc*) bohren; (*: initials*) eingravieren; **to ~ sb's eyes out** jdm die Augen ausstechen

gourd [guəd] *n* (*container*) Kürbisflasche *f*

gourmet ['guəmeɪ] *n* Feinschmecker(in) *m(f)*, Gourmet *m*

gout [gaut] *n* Gicht *f*

govern ['gʌvən] *vt* (*also Ling*) regieren; (*event, conduct*) bestimmen

governess ['gʌvənɪs] *n* Gouvernante *f*

governing ['gʌvənɪŋ] *adj* (*Pol*) regierend

governing body *n* Vorstand *m*

government ['gʌvnmənt] *n* Regierung *f* ▷ *cpd* Regierungs-; **local ~** Kommunalverwaltung *f*, Gemeindeverwaltung *f*

governmental [gʌvn'mɛntl] *adj* Regierungs-

government stocks *npl* Staatspapiere *pl*, Staatsanleihen *pl*

governor ['gʌvənə^r] *n* Gouverneur(in) *m(f)*; (*of bank, hospital, Brit: of prison*) Direktor(in) *m(f)*; (*of school*) ≈ Mitglied *nt* des Schulbeirats

Govt *abbr* = **government**

gown [gaun] *n* (Abend)kleid *nt*; (*of teacher, Brit: of judge*) Robe *f*

GP *n abbr* = **general practitioner**

GPMU (*Brit*) *n abbr* (*= Graphical Paper and Media Union*) *Mediengewerkschaft*

GPO *n abbr* (*Brit: formerly: = general post office*) Postbehörde *f*; (*US: = Government Printing Office*) *regierungsamtliche Druckanstalt*

gr. *abbr* (*Comm*) = **gross**; (*= gram(me)*) g

grab [græb] *vt* packen; (*chance, opportunity*) (beim Schopf) ergreifen ▷ *vi*: **to ~ at** greifen *or* grapschen nach *+dat*; **to ~ some food** schnell etwas essen; **to ~ a few hours sleep** ein paar Stunden schlafen

grace [greɪs] *n* Gnade *f*; (*gracefulness*) Anmut *f* ▷ *vt* (*honour*) beehren; (*adorn*) zieren; **5 days' ~** 5 Tage Aufschub; **with (a) good ~** anstandslos; **with (a) bad ~** widerwillig; **his sense of humour is his saving ~** was einen mit ihm versöhnt, ist sein Sinn für Humor; **to say ~** das Tischgebet sprechen

graceful ['greɪsful] *adj* anmutig; (*style, shape*) gefällig; (*refusal, behaviour*) charmant

gracious ['greɪʃəs] *adj* (*kind, courteous*) liebenswürdig; (*compassionate*) gnädig; (*smile*) freundlich; (*house, mansion etc*) stilvoll; (*living etc*) kultiviert ▷ *excl*: **(good) ~!** (ach) du meine Güte!, (ach du) lieber Himmel!

gradation [grə'deɪʃən] *n* Abstufung *f*

grade [greɪd] *n* (*Comm*) (Güte)klasse *f*; (*in hierarchy*) Rang *m*; (*Scol: mark*) Note *f*; (*US: school class*) Klasse *f*; (*: gradient: upward*) Neigung *f*, Steigung *f*; (*: downward*) Neigung *f*, Gefälle *nt* ▷ *vt* klassifizieren; (*work, student*) einstufen; **to make the ~** (*fig*) es schaffen

grade crossing (*US*) *n* Bahnübergang *m*

grade school (*US*) *n* Grundschule *f*

gradient ['greɪdɪənt] *n* (*upward*) Neigung *f*, Steigung *f*; (*downward*) Neigung, Gefälle *nt*; (*Geom*) Gradient *m*

gradual ['grædjuəl] *adj* allmählich
gradually ['grædjuəlı] *adv* allmählich
graduate [*n* 'grædjuıt, *vi* 'grædjueıt] *n* (*of university*) Hochschulabsolvent(in) *m(f)*; (*US: of high school*) Schulabgänger(in) *m(f)* ▷ *vi* (*from university*) graduieren; (*US*) die (Schul)abschlussprüfung bestehen
graduated pension ['grædjueıtıd-] *n* gestaffelte Rente *f*
graduation [grædju'eıʃən] *n* (Ab)schlussfeier *f*
graffiti [grə'fi:tı] *n, npl* Graffiti *pl*
graft [grɑ:ft] *n* (*Agr*) (Pfropf)reis *nt*; (*Med*) Transplantat *nt*; (*Brit: inf: hard work*) Schufterei *f*; (*bribery*) Schiebung *f* ▷ *vt*: **to ~ (onto)** (*Agr*) (auf)pfropfen (auf +*acc*); (*Med*) übertragen (auf +*acc*), einpflanzen (in +*acc*); (*fig*) aufpfropfen +*dat*
grain [greın] *n* Korn *nt*; (*no pl: cereals*) Getreide *nt*; (*US: corn*) Getreide *nt*, Korn; (*of wood*) Maserung *f*; **it goes against the ~** (*fig*) es geht einem gegen den Strich
gram [græm] *n* Gramm *nt*
grammar ['græmə^r] *n* Grammatik *f*, Sprachlehre *f*
grammar school (*Brit*) *n* ≈ Gymnasium *nt*
grammatical [grə'mætıkl] *adj* grammat(ikal)isch
gramme [græm] *n* = **gram**
gramophone ['græməfəun] (*Brit*) *n* Grammofon *nt*
granary ['grænərı] *n* Kornspeicher *m*; **G~® bread/loaf** Körnerbrot *nt*
grand [grænd] *adj* großartig; (*inf: wonderful*) fantastisch ▷ *n* (*inf*) ≈ Riese *m* (*1000 Pfund/Dollar*)
grandchild ['græntʃaıld] (*irreg: like* **child**) *n* Enkelkind *nt*, Enkel(in) *m(f)*
granddad ['grændæd] (*inf*) *n* Opa *m*
granddaughter ['grændɔ:tə^r] *n* Enkelin *f*
grandeur ['grændjə^r] *n* (*of scenery etc*) Erhabenheit *f*; (*of building*) Vornehmheit *f*
grandfather ['grændfɑ:ðə^r] *n* Großvater *m*
grandiose ['grændıəus] (*also pej*) *adj* grandios
grand jury (*US*) *n* Großes Geschworenengericht *nt*
grandma ['grænmɑ:] (*inf*) *n* Oma *f*
grandmother ['grænmʌðə^r] *n* Großmutter *f*
grandpa ['grænpɑ:] (*inf*) *n* Opa *m*
grandparents ['grændpɛərənts] *npl* Großeltern *pl*
grand piano *n* Flügel *m*
Grand Prix ['grɑ̃:'pri:] *n* (*Aut*) Grand Prix *m*
grandson ['grænsʌn] *n* Enkel *m*
grandstand ['grændstænd] *n* Haupttribüne *f*
grand total *n* Gesamtsumme *f*, Endsumme *f*
granite ['grænıt] *n* Granit *m*
granny ['grænı] (*inf*) *n* Oma *f*
grant [grɑ:nt] *vt* (*money*) bewilligen; (*request etc*) gewähren; (*visa*) erteilen; (*admit*) zugeben ▷ *n* Stipendium *nt*; (*subsidy*) Subvention *f*; **to take sth for ~ed** etw für selbstverständlich halten; **to take sb for ~ed** jdn als selbstverständlich hinnehmen; **to ~ that** zugeben, dass
granulated sugar ['grænjuleıtıd-] *n* (Zucker)raffinade *f*
granule ['grænju:l] *n* Körnchen *nt*
grape [greıp] *n* (Wein)traube *f*; **a bunch of ~s** eine (ganze) Weintraube
grapefruit ['greıpfru:t] (*pl* ~ *or* **grapefruits**) *n* Pampelmuse *f*, Grapefruit *f*
grapevine ['greıpvaın] *n* Weinstock *m*; **I heard it on the ~** (*fig*) es ist mir zu Ohren gekommen
graph [grɑ:f] *n* (*diagram*) grafische Darstellung *f*, Schaubild *nt*
graphic ['græfık] *adj* plastisch, anschaulich; (*art, design*) grafisch; *see also* **graphics**
graphic designer *n* Grafiker(in) *m(f)*
graphic equalizer [-i:kwəlaızə^r] *n* (Graphic) Equalizer *m*
graphics ['græfıks] *n* Grafik *f* ▷ *npl* (*drawings*) Zeichnungen *pl*, grafische Darstellungen *pl*
graphite ['græfaıt] *n* Grafit *m*
graph paper *n* Millimeterpapier *nt*
grapple ['græpl] *vi*: **to ~ with sb/sth** mit jdm/etw kämpfen; **to ~ with a problem** sich mit einem Problem herumschlagen
grasp [grɑ:sp] *vt* (*seize*) ergreifen; (*hold*) festhalten; (*understand*) begreifen ▷ *n* Griff *m*; (*understanding*) Verständnis *nt*; **it slipped from my ~** es entglitt mir; **to have sth within one's ~** etw in greifbarer Nähe haben; **to have a good ~ of sth** (*fig*) etw gut beherrschen
▶ **grasp at** *vt fus* greifen nach; (*fig: opportunity*) ergreifen
grasping ['grɑ:spıŋ] *adj* habgierig
grass [grɑ:s] *n* Gras *nt*; (*lawn*) Rasen *m*; (*Brit: inf: informer*) (Polizei)spitzel *m*
grasshopper ['grɑ:shɔpə^r] *n* Grashüpfer *m*, Heuschrecke *f*
grass-roots ['grɑ:sru:ts] *npl* (*of party etc*) Basis *f* ▷ *adj* (*opinion*) des kleinen Mannes; **at ~ level** an der Basis
grass snake *n* Ringelnatter *f*
grassy ['grɑ:sı] *adj* Gras-, grasig
grate [greıt] *n* (Feuer)rost *m* ▷ *vt* reiben; (*carrots etc*) raspeln ▷ *vi*: **to ~ (on)** kratzen (auf +*dat*)
grateful ['greıtful] *adj* dankbar; (*thanks*) aufrichtig
gratefully ['greıtfəlı] *adv* dankbar
grater ['greıtə^r] *n* Reibe *f*
gratification [grætıfı'keıʃən] *n* (*pleasure*) Genugtuung *f*; (*satisfaction*) Befriedigung *f*
gratify ['grætıfaı] *vt* (*please*) erfreuen; (*satisfy*) befriedigen
gratifying ['grætıfaııŋ] *adj* (*see vt*) erfreulich; befriedigend
grating ['greıtıŋ] *n* Gitter *nt* ▷ *adj* (*noise*) knirschend; (*voice*) schrill
gratitude ['grætıtju:d] *n* Dankbarkeit *f*
gratuitous [grə'tju:ıtəs] *adj* unnötig
gratuity [grə'tju:ıtı] *n* Trinkgeld *nt*
grave [greıv] *n* Grab *nt* ▷ *adj* (*decision, mistake*) schwer (wiegend), schwerwiegend; (*expression, person*) ernst
grave digger *n* Totengräber *m*
gravel ['grævl] *n* Kies *m*
gravely ['greıvlı] *adv* (*see adj*) schwer, ernst; ~

ill schwer krank
gravestone ['greɪvstəun] *n* Grabstein *m*
graveyard ['greɪvjɑːd] *n* Friedhof *m*
gravitas ['grævɪtæs] *n* Seriosität *f*
gravitate ['grævɪteɪt] *vi*: **to ~ towards** angezogen werden von
gravity ['grævɪtɪ] *n* Schwerkraft *f*; (*seriousness*) Ernst *m*, Schwere *f*
gravy ['greɪvɪ] *n* (*juice*) (Braten)saft *m*; (*sauce*) (Braten)soße *f*
gravy boat *n* Sauciere *f*, Soßenschüssel *f*
gravy train (*inf*) *n*: **to ride the ~** leichtes Geld machen
gray [greɪ] (*US*) *adj* = **grey**
graze [greɪz] *vi* grasen, weiden ▷ *vt* streifen; (*scrape*) aufschürfen ▷ *n* (*Med*) Abschürfung *f*
grazing ['greɪzɪŋ] *n* Weideland *nt*
grease [griːs] *n* (*lubricant*) Schmiere *f*; (*fat*) Fett *nt* ▷ *vt* (*see n*) schmieren; fetten; **to ~ the skids** (*US: fig*) die Maschinerie in Gang halten
grease gun *n* Fettspritze *f*, Fettpresse *f*
greasepaint ['griːspeɪnt] *n* (Fett)schminke *f*
greaseproof paper ['griːspruːf-] (*Brit*) *n* Pergamentpapier *nt*
greasy ['griːsɪ] *adj* fettig; (*food: containing grease*) fett; (*tools*) schmierig, ölig; (*clothes*) speckig; (*Brit: road, surface*) glitschig, schlüpfrig
great [greɪt] *adj* groß; (*city*) bedeutend; (*inf: terrific*) prima, toll; **they're ~ friends** sie sind gute Freunde; **we had a ~ time** wir haben uns glänzend amüsiert; **it was ~!** es war toll!; **the ~ thing is that ...** das Wichtigste ist, dass ...
Great Barrier Reef *n*: **the ~** das Große Barriereriff
Great Britain *n* Großbritannien *nt*
greater ['greɪtəʳ] *adj* (*see* **great**) größer; bedeutender; **people in G~ Calcutta** die Leute in Kalkutta und Umgebung; **G~ Manchester** Groß-Manchester *nt*
great-grandchild [greɪt'grænt∫aɪld] (*irreg: like* **child**) *n* Urenkel(in) *m(f)*
great-grandfather [greɪt'grænfɑːðəʳ] *n* Urgroßvater *m*
great-grandmother [greɪt'grænmʌðəʳ] *n* Urgroßmutter *f*
Great Lakes *npl*: **the ~** die Großen Seen *pl*
greatly ['greɪtlɪ] *adv* sehr; (*influenced*) stark
greatness ['greɪtnɪs] *n* Bedeutung *f*
Grecian ['griːʃən] *adj* griechisch
Greece [griːs] *n* Griechenland *nt*
greed [griːd] *n* (*also*: **greediness**): **~ for** Gier *f* nach; **~ for power** Machtgier *f*; **~ for money** Geldgier *f*
greedily ['griːdɪlɪ] *adv* gierig
greedy ['griːdɪ] *adj* gierig
Greek [griːk] *adj* griechisch ▷ *n* Grieche *m*, Griechin *f*; (*Ling*) Griechisch *nt*; **ancient/ modern ~** Alt-/Neugriechisch *nt*
green [griːn] *adj* (*also ecological*) grün ▷ *n* (*also Golf*) Grün *nt*; (*stretch of grass*) Rasen *m*, Grünfläche *f*; (*also*: **village green**) Dorfwiese *f*, Anger *m*; **greens** *npl* (*vegetables*) Grüngemüse *nt*; (*Pol*): **the G~s** die Grünen *pl*; **to have ~ fingers, to have a ~ thumb** (*US*) eine Hand für Pflanzen haben; **to give sb the ~ light** jdm grünes Licht geben
green belt *n* Grüngürtel *m*
green card *n* (*Aut*) grüne (Versicherungs)karte *f*; (*US*) ≈ Aufenthaltserlaubnis *f*
greenery ['griːnərɪ] *n* Grün *nt*
greenfly ['griːnflaɪ] (*Brit*) *n* Blattlaus *f*
greengage ['griːngeɪdʒ] *n* Reneklode *f*
greengrocer ['griːngrəusəʳ] (*Brit*) *n* Obst- und Gemüsehändler(in) *m(f)*
greenhouse ['griːnhaus] *n* Gewächshaus *nt*, Treibhaus *nt*; **~ effect** Treibhauseffekt *m*; **~ gas** Treibhausgas *nt*
greenish ['griːnɪʃ] *adj* grünlich
Greenland ['griːnlənd] *n* Grönland *nt*
Greenlander ['griːnləndəʳ] *n* Grönländer(in) *m(f)*
green light *n* grünes Licht *nt*; **to give sb the ~** jdm grünes Licht *or* freie Fahrt geben
Green Party *n* (*Pol*): **the ~** die Grünen *pl*
green pepper *n* grüne Paprikaschote *f*
green pound *n* grünes Pfund *nt*
greet [griːt] *vt* begrüßen; (*news*) aufnehmen
greeting ['griːtɪŋ] *n* Gruß *m*; (*welcome*) Begrüßung *f*; **Christmas ~s** Weihnachtsgrüße *pl*; **birthday ~s** Geburtstagsglückwünsche *pl*; **Season's ~s** frohe Weihnachten und ein glückliches neues Jahr
greeting card, greetings card *n* Grußkarte *f*; (*congratulating*) Glückwunschkarte *f*
gregarious [grə'gɛərɪəs] *adj* gesellig
grenade [grə'neɪd] *n* (*also*: **hand grenade**) (Hand)granate *f*
grew [gruː] *pt of* **grow**
grey, (*US*) **gray** [greɪ] *adj* grau; (*dismal*) trüb, grau; **to go ~** grau werden
grey-haired [greɪ'hɛəd] *adj* grauhaarig
greyhound ['greɪhaund] *n* Windhund *m*
grid [grɪd] *n* Gitter *nt*; (*Elec*) (Verteiler)netz *nt*; (*US: Aut: intersection*) Kreuzung *f*
griddle [grɪdl] *n gusseiserne Pfanne zum Braten und Pfannkuchenbacken*
gridiron ['grɪdaɪən] *n* Bratrost *m*
gridlock ['grɪdlɔk] *n* (*esp US: on road*) totaler Stau *m*; (*stalemate*) Patt *nt* ▷ *vt*: **to be ~ed** (*roads*) total verstopft sein; (*talks etc*) festgefahren sein
grief [griːf] *n* Kummer *m*, Trauer *f*; **to come to ~** (*plan*) scheitern; (*person*) zu Schaden kommen; **good ~!** ach du liebe Gute!
grievance ['griːvəns] *n* Beschwerde *f*; (*feeling of resentment*) Groll *m*
grieve [griːv] *vi* trauern ▷ *vt* Kummer bereiten *+dat*, betrüben; **to ~ for** trauern um
grievous ['griːvəs] *adj* (*mistake*) schwer; (*situation*) betrüblich; **~ bodily harm** (*Law*) schwere Körperverletzung *f*
grill [grɪl] *n* Grill *m*; (*grilled food: also*: **mixed grill**) Grillgericht *nt*; (*restaurant*) = **grillroom** ▷ *vt* (*Brit*) grillen; (*inf: question*) in die Zange

nehmen, ausquetschen

grille [grɪl] *n* (*screen*) Gitter *nt*; (*Aut*) Kühlergrill *m*

grillroom ['grɪlrum] *n* Grillrestaurant *nt*

grim [grɪm] *adj* trostlos; (*serious, stern*) grimmig

grimace [grɪ'meɪs] *n* Grimasse *f* ▷ *vi* Grimassen schneiden

grime [graɪm] *n* Dreck *m*, Schmutz *m*

grimy ['graɪmɪ] *adj* dreckig, schmutzig

grin [grɪn] *n* Grinsen *nt* ▷ *vi* grinsen; **to ~ at sb** jdn angrinsen

grind [graɪnd] (*pt, pp* **ground**) *vt* zerkleinern; (*coffee, pepper etc*) mahlen; (*US: meat*) hacken, durch den Fleischwolf drehen; (*knife*) schleifen, wetzen; (*gem, lens*) schleifen ▷ *vi* (*car gears*) knirschen ▷ *n* (*work*) Schufterei *f*; **to ~ one's teeth** mit den Zähnen knirschen; **to ~ to a halt** (*vehicle*) quietschend zum Stehen kommen; (*fig: talks, scheme*) sich festfahren; (*work*) stocken; (*production*) zum Erliegen kommen; **the daily ~** (*inf*) der tägliche Trott

grinder ['graɪndə^r] *n* (*for coffee*) Kaffemühle *f*; (*for waste disposal etc*) Müllzerkleinerungsanlage *f*

grindstone ['graɪndstəun] *n*: **to keep one's nose to the ~** hart arbeiten

grip [grɪp] *n* Griff *m*; (*of tyre, shoe*) Halt *m*; (*holdall*) Reisetasche *f* ▷ *vt* packen; (*audience, attention*) fesseln; **to come to ~s with sth** etw in den Griff bekommen; **to lose one's ~** den Halt verlieren; (*fig*) nachlassen; **to ~ the road** (*car*) gut auf der Straße liegen

gripe [graɪp] (*inf*) *n* (*complaint*) Meckerei *f* ▷ *vi* meckern; **the ~s** (*Med*) Kolik *f*, Bauchschmerzen *pl*

gripping ['grɪpɪŋ] *adj* fesselnd, packend

grisly ['grɪzlɪ] *adj* grässlich, grausig

grist [grɪst] *n* (*fig*): **it's all ~ to the mill** das kann man alles verwerten

gristle ['grɪsl] *n* Knorpel *m*

grit [grɪt] *n* (*for icy roads: sand*) Sand *m*; (*crushed stone*) Splitt *m*; (*determination, courage*) Mut *m* ▷ *vt* (*road*) streuen; **grits** *npl* (*US*) Grütze *f*; **I've got a piece of ~ in my eye** ich habe ein Staubkorn im Auge; **to ~ one's teeth** die Zähne zusammenbeißen

grizzle ['grɪzl] (*Brit*) *vi* quengeln

grizzly ['grɪzlɪ] *n* (*also*: **grizzly bear**) Grizzlybär *m*

groan [grəun] *n* Stöhnen *nt* ▷ *vi* stöhnen; (*tree, floorboard etc*) ächzen, knarren

grocer ['grəusə^r] *n* Lebensmittelhändler(in) *m(f)*

groceries ['grəusərɪz] *npl* Lebensmittel *pl*

grocer's, grocer's shop *n* Lebensmittelgeschäft *nt*

grog [grɔg] *n* Grog *m*

groggy ['grɔgɪ] *adj* angeschlagen

groin [grɔɪn] *n* Leistengegend *f*

groom [gru:m] *n* Stallbursche *m*; (*also*: **bridegroom**) Bräutigam *m* ▷ *vt* (*horse*) striegeln; (*fig*): **to ~ sb for** (*job*) jdn aufbauen für; **well-~ed** gepflegt

groove [gru:v] *n* Rille *f*

grope [grəup] *vi*: **to ~ for** tasten nach; (*fig: try to think of*) suchen nach

grosgrain ['grəugreɪn] *n* grob gerippter Stoff *m*

gross [grəus] *adj* (*neglect*) grob; (*injustice*) krass; (*behaviour, speech*) grob, derb; (*Comm: income, weight*) Brutto- ▷ *n inv* Gros *nt* ▷ *vt*: **to ~ £500,000** £500 000 brutto einnehmen

gross domestic product *n* Bruttoinlandsprodukt *nt*

grossly ['grəuslɪ] *adv* äußerst; (*exaggerated*) grob

gross national product *n* Bruttosozialprodukt *nt*

grotesque [grə'tɛsk] *adj* grotesk

grotto ['grɔtəu] *n* Grotte *f*

grotty ['grɔtɪ] (*inf*) *adj* mies

grouch [grautʃ] (*inf*) *vi* schimpfen ▷ *n* (*person*) Miesepeter *m*, Muffel *m*

ground [graund] *pt, pp of* **grind** ▷ *n* Boden *m*, Erde *f*; (*land*) Land *nt*; (*Sport*) Platz *m*, Feld *nt*; (*US: Elec: also* **ground wire**) Erde *f*; (*reason: gen pl*) Grund *m* ▷ *vt* (*plane*) aus dem Verkehr ziehen; (*US: Elec*) erden ▷ *adj* (*coffee etc*) gemahlen ▷ *vi* (*ship*) auflaufen; **grounds** *npl* (*of coffee etc*) Satz *m*; (*gardens etc*) Anlagen *pl*; **below ~** unter der Erde; **to gain/lose ~** Boden gewinnen/verlieren; **common ~** Gemeinsame(s) *nt*; **on the ~s that** mit der Begründung, dass

ground cloth (*US*) *n* = **groundsheet**

ground control *n* (*Aviat, Space*) Bodenkontrolle *f*

ground floor *n* Erdgeschoss *nt*, Erdgeschoß *nt* (*Österr*)

grounding ['graundɪŋ] *n* (*in education*) Grundwissen *nt*

groundless ['graundlɪs] *adj* grundlos, unbegründet

groundnut ['graundnʌt] *n* Erdnuss *f*

ground rent (*Brit*) *n* Erbbauzins *m*

ground rule *n* Grundregel *f*

groundsheet ['graundʃi:t] (*Brit*) *n* Zeltboden *m*

groundskeeper ['graundzki:pə^r] (*US*) *n* = **groundsman**

groundsman ['graundzmən] (*irreg: like* **man**) *n* (*Sport*) Platzwart *m*

ground staff *n* (*Aviat*) Bodenpersonal *nt*

groundswell *n*: **there was a ~ of public opinion against him** die Öffentlichkeit wandte sich gegen ihn

ground-to-air missile ['graundtə'ɛə^r-] *n* Boden-Luft-Rakete *f*

ground-to-ground missile ['graundtə'graund-] *n* Boden-Boden-Rakete *f*

groundwork ['graundwə:k] *n* Vorarbeit *f*

group [gru:p] *n* Gruppe *f*; (*Comm*) Konzern *m* ▷ *vt* (*also*: **group together**: *in one group*) zusammentun; (*: in several groups*) in Gruppen einteilen ▷ *vi* (*also*: **group together**) sich zusammentun

groupie ['gru:pɪ] (*inf*) *n* Groupie *nt*

group therapy *n* Gruppentherapie *f*

grouse [graus] *n inv* schottisches Moorhuhn *nt* ▷ *vi* (*complain*) schimpfen

grove [grəuv] *n* Hain *m*, Wäldchen *nt*
grovel ['grɔvl] *vi* (*crawl*) kriechen; (*fig*): **to ~ (before)** kriechen (vor *+dat*)
grow [grəu] (*pt* **grew**, *pp* **~n**) *vi* wachsen; (*increase*) zunehmen; (*become*) werden ▷ *vt* (*roses*) züchten; (*vegetables*) anbauen, ziehen; (*beard*) sich *dat* wachsen lassen; **to ~ tired of waiting** das Warten leid sein; **to ~ (out of** *or* **from)** (*develop*) entstehen (aus)
▸ **grow apart** *vi* (*fig*) sich auseinanderentwickeln
▸ **grow away from** *vt fus* (*fig*) sich entfremden *+dat*
▸ **grow on** *vt fus*: **that painting is ~ing on me** allmählich finde ich Gefallen an dem Bild
▸ **grow out of** *vt fus* (*clothes*) herauswachsen aus; (*habit*) ablegen; **he'll ~ out of it** diese Phase geht auch vorbei
▸ **grow up** *vi* aufwachsen; (*mature*) erwachsen werden; (*idea, friendship*) entstehen
grower ['grəuə[r]] *n* (*Bot*) Züchter(in) *m(f)*; (*Agr*) Pflanzer(in) *m(f)*
growing ['grəuɪŋ] *adj* wachsend; (*number*) zunehmend; **~ pains** Wachstumsschmerzen *pl*; (*fig*) Kinderkrankheiten *pl*, Anfangsschwierigkeiten *pl*
growl [graul] *vi* knurren
grown [grəun] *pp of* **grow**
grown-up [grəun'ʌp] *n* Erwachsene(r) *f(m)*
growth [grəuθ] *n* Wachstum *nt*; (*what has grown*: *of weeds, beard etc*) Wuchs *m*; (*of person, character*) Entwicklung *f*; (*Med*) Gewächs *nt*, Wucherung *f*
growth rate *n* Wachstumsrate *f*, Zuwachsrate *f*
grub [grʌb] *n* (*larva*) Larve *f*; (*inf*: *food*) Fressalien *pl*, Futter *nt* ▷ *vi*: **to ~ about** *or* **around (for)** (herum)wühlen (nach)
grubby ['grʌbɪ] *adj* (*dirty*) schmuddelig; (*fig*) schmutzig
grudge [grʌdʒ] *n* Groll *m* ▷ *vt*: **to ~ sb sth** jdm etw nicht gönnen; **to bear sb a ~** jdm böse sein, einen Groll gegen jdn hegen
grudging ['grʌdʒɪŋ] *adj* widerwillig
grudgingly ['grʌdʒɪŋlɪ] *adv* widerwillig
gruelling, (US) **grueling** ['gruəlɪŋ] *adj* (*encounter*) aufreibend; (*trip, journey*) äußerst strapaziös
gruesome ['gru:səm] *adj* grauenhaft
gruff [grʌf] *adj* barsch, schroff
grumble ['grʌmbl] *vi* murren, schimpfen
grumpy ['grʌmpɪ] *adj* mürrisch, brummig
grunge [grʌndʒ] (*inf*) *n* Grunge *nt*
grunt [grʌnt] *vi* grunzen ▷ *n* Grunzen *nt*
G-string ['dʒi:strɪŋ] *n* Minislip *m*, Tangaslip *m*
GT *abbr* (*Aut*: = *gran turismo*) GT
GU (US) *abbr* (*Post*) = *Guam*
guarantee [gærən'ti:] *n* Garantie *f* ▷ *vt* garantieren; **he can't ~ (that) he'll come** er kann nicht dafür garantieren, dass er kommt
guarantor [gærən'tɔ:[r]] *n* (*Comm*) Bürge *m*
guard [gɑ:d] *n* Wache *f*; (*Boxing, Fencing*) Deckung *f*; (*Brit*: *Rail*) Schaffner(in) *m(f)*; (*on machine*) Schutz *m*, Schutzvorrichtung *f*; (*also*: **fireguard**) (Schutz)gitter *nt* ▷ *vt* (*prisoner*) bewachen; (*protect*): **to ~ (against)** (be)schützen (vor *+dat*); (*secret*) hüten (vor *+dat*); **to be on one's ~** auf der Hut sein
▸ **guard against** *vt fus* (*disease*) vorbeugen *+dat*; (*damage, accident*) verhüten
guard dog *n* Wachhund *m*
guarded ['gɑ:dɪd] *adj* vorsichtig, zurückhaltend
guardian ['gɑ:dɪən] *n* Vormund *m*; (*defender*) Hüter *m*
guardrail ['gɑ:dreɪl] *n* (Schutz)geländer *nt*
guard's van (*Brit*) *n* (*Rail*) Schaffnerabteil *nt*, Dienstwagen *m*
Guatemala [gwɑ:tɪ'mɑ:lə] *n* Guatemala *nt*
Guatemalan [gwɑ:tɪ'mɑ:lən] *adj* guatemaltekisch, aus Guatemala
Guernsey ['gə:nzɪ] *n* Guernsey *nt*
guerrilla [gə'rɪlə] *n* Guerilla *m*, Guerillakämpfer(in) *m(f)*
guerrilla warfare *n* Guerillakrieg *m*
guess [gɛs] *vt* schätzen; (*answer*) (er)raten; (*US*: *think*) schätzen (*inf*) ▷ *vi* (*see vt*) schätzen; raten ▷ *n* Vermutung *f*; **I ~ you're right** da haben Sie wohl recht; **to keep sb ~ing** jdn im Ungewissen lassen; **to take** *or* **have a ~** raten; (*estimate*) schätzen; **my ~ is that ...** ich schätze *or* vermute, dass ...
guesstimate ['gɛstɪmɪt] (*inf*) *n* grobe Schätzung *f*
guesswork ['gɛswə:k] *n* Vermutungen *pl*; **I got the answer by ~** ich habe die Antwort nur geraten
guest [gɛst] *n* Gast *m*; **be my ~** (*inf*) nur zu!
guesthouse ['gɛsthaus] *n* Pension *f*
guest room *n* Gästezimmer *nt*
guff [gʌf] (*inf*) *n* Quatsch *m*, Käse *m*
guffaw [gʌ'fɔ:] *vi* schallend lachen ▷ *n* schallendes Lachen *nt*
guidance ['gaɪdəns] *n* Rat *m*, Beratung *f*; **under the ~ of** unter der Leitung von; **vocational ~** Berufsberatung *f*; **marriage ~** Eheberatung *f*
guide [gaɪd] *n* (*person*) Führer(in) *m(f)*; (*book*) Führer *m*; (*Brit*: *also* **girl guide**) Pfadfinderin *f* ▷ *vt* führen; (*direct*) lenken; **to be ~d by sb/sth** sich von jdm/etw leiten lassen
guidebook ['gaɪdbuk] *n* Führer *m*
guided missile *n* Lenkwaffe *f*
guide dog *n* Blindenhund *m*
guidelines ['gaɪdlaɪnz] *npl* Richtlinien *pl*
guild [gɪld] *n* Verein *m*
guildhall ['gɪldhɔ:l] (*Brit*) *n* Gildehaus *nt*
guile [gaɪl] *n* Arglist *f*
guileless ['gaɪllɪs] *adj* arglos
guillotine ['gɪləti:n] *n* Guillotine *f*, Fallbeil *nt*; (*for paper*) (Papier)schneidemaschine *f*
guilt [gɪlt] *n* Schuld *f*; (*remorse*) Schuldgefühl *nt*
guilty ['gɪltɪ] *adj* schuldig; (*expression*) schuldbewusst; (*secret*) dunkel; **to plead ~/not ~** sich schuldig/nicht schuldig bekennen; **to feel ~ about doing sth** ein schlechtes

Gewissen haben, etw zu tun
Guinea ['gɪnɪ] *n*: **Republic of ~** Guinea *nt*
guinea ['gɪnɪ] *(Brit) n (old)* Guinee *f*
guinea pig *n* Meerschweinchen *nt*; *(fig: person)* Versuchskaninchen *nt*
guise [gaɪz] *n*: **in** *or* **under the ~ of** in der Form *+gen*, in Gestalt *+gen*
guitar [gɪ'tɑːʳ] *n* Gitarre *f*
guitarist [gɪ'tɑːrɪst] *n* Gitarrist(in) *m(f)*
gulch [gʌltʃ] *(US) n* Schlucht *f*
gulf [gʌlf] *n* Golf *m*; *(abyss)* Abgrund *m*; *(fig: difference)* Kluft *f*; **the (Persian) G~** der (Persische) Golf
Gulf States *npl*: **the ~** die Golfstaaten *pl*
Gulf Stream *n*: **the ~** der Golfstrom
Gulf War *n*: **the ~** der Golfkrieg
gull [gʌl] *n* Möwe *f*
gullet ['gʌlɪt] *n* Speiseröhre *f*
gullibility [gʌlɪ'bɪlɪtɪ] *n* Leichtgläubigkeit *f*
gullible ['gʌlɪbl] *adj* leichtgläubig
gully ['gʌlɪ] *n* Schlucht *f*
gulp [gʌlp] *vi* schlucken ▷ *vt (also:* **gulp down***)* hinunterschlucken ▷ *n*: **at one ~** mit einem Schluck
gum [gʌm] *n (Anat)* Zahnfleisch *nt*; *(glue)* Klebstoff *m*; *(also:* **gumdrop***)* Weingummi *nt*; *(also:* **chewing-gum***)* Kaugummi *m* ▷ *vt*: **to ~ (together)** (zusammen)kleben
▸ **gum up** *vt*: **to ~ up the works** *(inf)* alles vermasseln
gumboots ['gʌmbuːts] *(Brit) npl* Gummistiefel *pl*
gumption ['gʌmpʃən] *n* Grips *m (inf)*
gumtree ['gʌmtriː] *n*: **to be up a ~** *(fig: inf)* aufgeschmissen sein
gun [gʌn] *n (small)* Pistole *f*; *(medium-sized)* Gewehr *nt*; *(large)* Kanone *f* ▷ *vt (also:* **gun down***)* erschießen; **to stick to one's ~s** *(fig)* nicht nachgeben, festbleiben
gunboat ['gʌnbəut] *n* Kanonenboot *nt*
gun dog *n* Jagdhund *m*
gunfire ['gʌnfaɪəʳ] *n* Geschützfeuer *nt*
gunge [gʌndʒ] *(inf) n* Schmiere *f*
gung ho ['gʌŋ'həu] *(inf) adj* übereifrig
gunman ['gʌnmən] *(irreg: like* **man***) n* bewaffneter Verbrecher *m*
gunner ['gʌnəʳ] *n* Kanonier *m*, Artillerist *m*
gunpoint ['gʌnpɔɪnt] *n*: **at ~** mit vorgehaltener Pistole; mit vorgehaltenem Gewehr
gunpowder ['gʌnpaudəʳ] *n* Schießpulver *nt*
gunrunner ['gʌnrʌnəʳ] *n* Waffenschmuggler(in) *m(f)*, Waffenschieber(in) *m(f)*
gunrunning ['gʌnrʌnɪŋ] *n* Waffenschmuggel *m*, Waffenschieberei *f*
gunshot ['gʌnʃɔt] *n* Schuss *m*
gunsmith ['gʌnsmɪθ] *n* Büchsenmacher *m*
gurgle ['gəːgl] *vi (baby)* glucksen; *(water)* gluckern
guru ['guruː] *n* Guru *m*
gush [gʌʃ] *vi* hervorquellen, hervorströmen; *(person)* schwärmen ▷ *n* Strahl *m*
gushing ['gʌʃɪŋ] *adj (fig)* überschwänglich
gusset ['gʌsɪt] *n* Keil *m*, Zwickel *m*
gust [gʌst] *n* Windstoß *m*, Bö(e) *f*; *(of smoke)* Wolke *f*
gusto ['gʌstəu] *n*: **with ~** mit Genuss, mit Schwung
gusty ['gʌstɪ] *adj (wind)* böig; *(day)* stürmisch
gut [gʌt] *n (Anat)* Darm *m*; *(for violin, racket)* Darmsaiten *pl* ▷ *vt (poultry, fish)* ausnehmen; *(building)* ausräumen; *(by fire)* ausbrennen;
guts *npl (Anat)* Eingeweide *pl*; *(inf: courage)* Mumm *m*; **to hate sb's ~s** jdn auf den Tod nicht ausstehen können
gut reaction *n* rein gefühlsmäßige Reaktion *f*
gutsy ['gʌtsɪ] *(inf) adj (vivid)* rasant; *(courageous)* mutig
gutter ['gʌtəʳ] *n (in street)* Gosse *f*, Rinnstein *m*; *(of roof)* Dachrinne *f*
gutter press *n* Boulevardpresse *f*
guttural ['gʌtərl] *adj* guttural
guy [gaɪ] *n (inf: man)* Typ *m*, Kerl *m*; *(also:* **guyrope***)* Haltetau *nt*, Halteseil *nt*; *(for Guy Fawkes' night)* (Guy-Fawkes-)Puppe *f*

GUY FAWKES' NIGHT

Guy Fawkes' Night, auch „bonfire night" genannt, erinnert an den „Gunpowder Plot", einen Attentatsversuch auf James I. und sein Parlament am 5. November 1605. Einer der Verschwörer, Guy Fawkes, wurde auf frischer Tat ertappt, als er das Parlamentsgebäude in die Luft sprengen wollte. Vor der Guy Fawkes' Night basteln Kinder in Großbritannien eine Puppe des Guy Fawkes, mit der sie Geld für Feuerwerkskörper von Passanten erbetteln, und die dann am 5. November auf einem Lagerfeuer mit Feuerwerk verbrannt wird.

Guyana [gaɪ'ænə] *n* Guyana *nt*
guzzle ['gʌzl] *vt (food)* futtern; *(drink)* saufen *(inf)*
gym [dʒɪm] *n (also:* **gymnasium***)* Turnhalle *f*; *(also:* **gymnastics***)* Gymnastik *f*, Turnen *nt*
gymkhana [dʒɪm'kɑːnə] *n* Reiterfest *nt*
gymnasium [dʒɪm'neɪzɪəm] *n* Turnhalle *f*
gymnast ['dʒɪmnæst] *n* Turner(in) *m(f)*
gymnastics [dʒɪm'næstɪks] *n* Gymnastik *f*, Turnen *nt*
gym shoes *npl* Turnschuhe *pl*
gymslip ['dʒɪmslɪp] *(Brit) n* (Schul)trägerrock *m*
gynaecologist, *(US)* **gynecologist** [gaɪnɪ'kɔlədʒɪst] *n* Gynäkologe *m*, Gynäkologin *f*, Frauenarzt *m*, Frauenärztin *f*
gynaecology, *(US)* **gynecology** [gaɪnɪ'kɔlədʒɪ] *n* Gynäkologie *f*, Frauenheilkunde *f*
gypsy ['dʒɪpsɪ] *n* = **gipsy**
gyrate [dʒaɪ'reɪt] *vi* kreisen, sich drehen
gyroscope ['dʒaɪərəskəup] *n* Gyroskop *nt*

Hh

H, h [eɪtʃ] *n* (*letter*) H, h *nt*; **H for Harry, H for How** (*US*) ≈ H wie Heinrich
habeas corpus ['heɪbɪəs'kɔ:pəs] *n* Habeaskorpusakte *f*
haberdashery [hæbə'dæʃərɪ] (*Brit*) *n* Kurzwaren *pl*
habit ['hæbɪt] *n* Gewohnheit *f*; (*esp undesirable*) Angewohnheit *f*; (*addiction*) Sucht *f*; (*Rel*) Habit *m or nt*; **to get out of/into the ~ of doing sth** sich abgewöhnen/angewöhnen, etw zu tun; **to be in the ~ of doing sth** die (An)gewohnheit haben, etw zu tun
habitable ['hæbɪtəbl] *adj* bewohnbar
habitat ['hæbɪtæt] *n* Heimat *f*; (*of animals*) Lebensraum *m*, Heimat *f*
habitation [hæbɪ'teɪʃən] *n* Wohnstätte *f*; **fit for human ~** für Wohnzwecke geeignet, bewohnbar
habitual [hə'bɪtjuəl] *adj* (*action*) gewohnt; (*drinker*) Gewohnheits-; (*liar*) gewohnheitsmäßig
habitually [hə'bɪtjuəlɪ] *adv* ständig
hack [hæk] *vt, vi* (*also Comput*) hacken ▷ *n* (*pej: writer*) Schreiberling *m*; (*horse*) Mietpferd *nt*
hacker ['hækəʳ] *n* (*Comput*) Hacker *m*
hackles ['hæklz] *npl*: **to make sb's ~ rise** (*fig*) jdn auf die Palme bringen (*inf*)
hackney cab ['hæknɪ-] *n* Taxi *nt*
hackneyed ['hæknɪd] *adj* abgedroschen
hacksaw ['hæksɔ:] *n* Metallsäge *f*
had [hæd] *pt, pp of* **have**
haddock ['hædək] (*pl* **~** *or* **haddocks**) *n* Schellfisch *m*
hadn't ['hædnt] = **had not**
haematology, (*US*) **hematology** ['hi:mə'tɔlədʒɪ] *n* Hämatologie *f*
haemoglobin, (*US*) **hemoglobin** ['hi:mə'gləubɪn] *n* Hämoglobin *nt*
haemophilia, (*US*) **hemophilia** ['hi:mə'fɪlɪə] *n* Bluterkrankheit *f*
haemorrhage, (*US*) **hemorrhage** ['hɛmərɪdʒ] *n* Blutung *f*
haemorrhoids, (*US*) **hemorrhoids** ['hɛmərɔɪdz] *npl* Hämorr(ho)iden *pl*
hag [hæg] *n* alte Hexe *f*; (*witch*) Hexe *f*
haggard ['hægəd] *adj* ausgezehrt; (*from worry*) abgehärmt; (*from tiredness*) abgespannt
haggis ['hægɪs] (*Scot*) *n* *Gericht aus gehackten Schafsinnereien und Haferschrot, im Schafsmagen gekocht*
haggle ['hægl] *vi*: **to ~ (over)** feilschen (um)
haggling ['hæglɪŋ] *n* Feilschen *nt*
Hague [heɪg] *n*: **The ~** Den Haag *m*
hail [heɪl] *n* Hagel *m* ▷ *vt* (*person*) zurufen *+dat*; (*taxi*) herbeiwinken, anhalten; (*acclaim: person*) zujubeln *+dat*; (*: event etc*) bejubeln ▷ *vi* hageln; **he ~s from Scotland** er kommt *or* stammt aus Schottland
hailstone ['heɪlstəun] *n* Hagelkorn *nt*
hailstorm ['heɪlstɔ:m] *n* Hagelschauer *m*
hair [hɛəʳ] *n* (*collectively: of person*) Haar *nt*, Haare *pl*; (*: of animal*) Fell *nt*; (*single hair*) Haar *nt*; **to do one's ~** sich frisieren; **by a ~'s breadth** um Haaresbreite
hairbrush ['hɛəbrʌʃ] *n* Haarbürste *f*
haircut ['hɛəkʌt] *n* Haarschnitt *m*; (*style*) Frisur *f*
hairdo ['hɛədu:] *n* Frisur *f*
hairdresser ['hɛədrɛsəʳ] *n* Friseur *m*, Friseuse *f*
hairdresser's ['hɛədrɛsəz] *n* Friseursalon *m*
hair dryer *n* Haartrockner *m*, Föhn *f*, Fön® *m*
-haired [hɛəd] *suff*: **fair-~** blond; **long-~** langhaarig
hairgrip ['hɛəgrɪp] *n* Haarklemme *f*
hairline ['hɛəlaɪn] *n* Haaransatz *m*
hairline fracture *n* Haarriss *m*
hairnet ['hɛənɛt] *n* Haarnetz *nt*
hair oil *n* Haaröl *nt*
hairpiece ['hɛəpi:s] *n* Haarteil *nt*; (*for men*) Toupet *nt*
hairpin ['hɛəpɪn] *n* Haarnadel *f*
hairpin bend, (*US*) **hairpin curve** *n* Haarnadelkurve *f*
hair-raising ['hɛəreɪzɪŋ] *adj* haarsträubend
hair remover *n* Enthaarungscreme *f*
hair slide *n* Haarspange *f*
hair spray *n* Haarspray *nt*
hairstyle ['hɛəstaɪl] *n* Frisur *f*
hairy ['hɛərɪ] *adj* behaart; (*inf: situation*) brenzlig, haarig
Haiti ['heɪtɪ] *n* Haiti *nt*
hake [heɪk] (*pl* **~** *or* **hakes**) *n* Seehecht *m*
halcyon ['hælsɪən] *adj* glücklich
hale [heɪl] *adj*: **~ and hearty** gesund und munter
half [hɑ:f] (*pl* **halves**) *n* Hälfte *f*; (*of beer etc*)

kleines Bier *nt etc*; (*Rail, bus*) Fahrkarte *f* zum halben Preis ▷ *adj, adv* halb; **first/second ~** (*Sport*) erste/zweite Halbzeit *f*; **two and a ~** zweieinhalb; **~-an-hour** eine halbe Stunde; **~ a dozen/pound** ein halbes Dutzend/Pfund; **a week and a ~** eineinhalb *or* anderthalb Wochen; **~ (of it)** die Hälfte; **~ (of)** die Hälfte (von *or* +*gen*); **~ the amount of** die halbe Menge an +*dat*; **to cut sth in ~** etw halbieren; **~ past three** halb vier; **to go halves (with sb)** (mit jdm) halbe-halbe machen; **she never does things by halves** sie macht keine halben Sachen; **he's too clever by ~** er ist ein richtiger Schlaumeier; **~ empty** halb leer; **~ closed** halb geschlossen

half-baked ['hɑːf'beɪkt] *adj* blödsinnig (*inf*)

half board *n* Halbpension *f*

half-breed ['hɑːfbriːd] *n* (*pej*) = **half-caste**

half-brother ['hɑːfbrʌðəʳ] *n* Halbbruder *m*

half-caste ['hɑːfkɑːst] *n* (*pej*) Mischling *m*

half-day [hɑːf'deɪ] *n* halber freier Tag *m*

half-hearted ['hɑːf'hɑːtɪd] *adj* halbherzig, lustlos

half-hour [hɑːf'auəʳ] *n* halbe Stunde *f*

half-life ['hɑːflaɪf] *n* (*Tech*) Halbwertszeit *f*

half-mast ['hɑːf'mɑːst]: **at ~** *adv* (auf) halbmast

halfpenny ['heɪpnɪ] (*Brit*) *n* halber Penny *m*

half-price ['hɑːf'praɪs] *adj, adv* zum halben Preis

half-sister ['hɑːfsɪstəʳ] *n* Halbschwester *f*

half term (*Brit*) *n* kleine Ferien *pl* (*in der Mitte des Trimesters*)

half-timbered [hɑːf'tɪmbəd] *adj* (*house*) Fachwerk-

half-time [hɑːf'taɪm] *n* (*Sport*) Halbzeit *f*

halfway ['hɑːf'weɪ] *adv*: **~ to** auf halbem Wege nach; **~ through** mitten in +*dat*; **to meet sb ~** (*fig*) jdm auf halbem Wege entgegenkommen

halfway house *n* (*hostel*) offene Anstalt *f*; (*fig*) Zwischending *nt*; (: *compromise*) Kompromiss *m*

halfwit ['hɑːfwɪt] *n* Schwachsinnige(r) *f(m)*; (*fig: inf*) Schwachkopf *m*

half-yearly [hɑːf'jɪəlɪ] *adv* halbjährlich, jedes halbe Jahr ▷ *adj* halbjährlich

halibut ['hælɪbət] *n inv* Heilbutt *m*

halitosis [hælɪ'təusɪs] *n* schlechter Atem *m*, Mundgeruch *m*

hall [hɔːl] *n* Diele *f*, (Haus)flur *m*; (*corridor*) Korridor *m*, Flur *m*; (*mansion*) Herrensitz *m*, Herrenhaus *nt*; (*for concerts etc*) Halle *f*; **to live in ~** (*Brit*) im Wohnheim wohnen

hallmark ['hɔːlmɑːk] *n* (*on gold, silver*) (Feingehalts)stempel *m*; (*of writer, artist etc*) Kennzeichen *nt*

hallo [hə'ləu] *excl* = **hello**

hall of residence (*pl* **halls of residence**) (*Brit*) *n* Studentenwohnheim *nt*

hallowed ['hæləud] *adj* (*ground*) heilig; (*fig: respected, revered*) geheiligt

Hallowe'en ['hæləu'iːn] *n* der Tag vor Allerheiligen

HALLOWE'EN

Hallowe'en ist der 31. Oktober, der Vorabend von Allerheiligen und nach altem Glauben der Abend, an dem man Geister und Hexen sehen kann. In Großbritannien und vor allem in den USA feiern die Kinder Hallowe'en, indem sie sich verkleiden und mit selbst gemachten Laternen aus Kürbissen von Tür zu Tür ziehen.

hallucination [həluːsɪ'neɪʃən] *n* Halluzination *f*

hallucinogenic [həluːsɪnəu'dʒenɪk] *adj* (*drug*) halluzinogen ▷ *n* Halluzinogen *nt*

hallway ['hɔːlweɪ] *n* Diele *f*, (Haus)flur *m*

halo ['heɪləu] *n* Heiligenschein *m*; (*circle of light*) Hof *m*

halt [hɔːlt] *vt* anhalten; (*progress etc*) zum Stillstand bringen ▷ *vi* anhalten, zum Stillstand kommen ▷ *n*: **to come to a ~** zum Stillstand kommen; **to call a ~ to sth** (*fig*) einer Sache *dat* ein Ende machen

halter ['hɔːltəʳ] *n* Halfter *nt*

halter-neck ['hɔːltənɛk] *adj* (*dress*) rückenfrei mit Nackenverschluss

halve [hɑːv] *vt* halbieren

halves [hɑːvz] *pl of* **half**

ham [hæm] *n* Schinken *m*; (*inf: also*: **radio ham**) Funkamateur *m*; (: *actor*) Schmierenkomödiant(in) *m(f)*

Hamburg ['hæmbəːg] *n* Hamburg *nt*

hamburger ['hæmbəːgəʳ] *n* Hamburger *m*

ham-fisted ['hæm'fɪstɪd], (*US*) **ham-handed** ['hæm'hændɪd] *adj* ungeschickt

hamlet ['hæmlɪt] *n* Weiler *m*, kleines Dorf *nt*

hammer ['hæməʳ] *n* Hammer *m* ▷ *vt* hämmern; (*fig: criticize*) vernichtend kritisieren; (: *defeat*) vernichtend schlagen ▷ *vi* hämmern; **to ~ sth into sb, to ~ sth across to sb** jdm etw einhämmern *or* einbläuen

▸ **hammer out** *vt* hämmern; (*solution, agreement*) ausarbeiten

hammock ['hæmək] *n* Hängematte *f*

hamper ['hæmpəʳ] *vt* behindern ▷ *n* Korb *m*

hamster ['hæmstəʳ] *n* Hamster *m*

hamstring ['hæmstrɪŋ] *n* Kniesehne *f* ▷ *vt* einengen

hand [hænd] *n* Hand *f*; (*of clock*) Zeiger *m*; (*handwriting*) Hand(schrift) *f*; (*worker*) Arbeiter(in) *m(f)*; (*of cards*) Blatt *nt*; (*measurement: of horse*) ≈ 10 cm ▷ *vt* geben, reichen; **to give** *or* **lend sb a ~** jdm helfen; **at ~** (*place*) in der Nähe; (*time*) unmittelbar bevorstehend; **by ~** von Hand; **in ~** (*time*) zur Verfügung; (*job*) anstehend; (*situation*) unter Kontrolle; **we have the matter in ~** wir haben die Sache im Griff; **on ~** zur Verfügung; **out of ~** *adj* außer Kontrolle ▷ *adv* (*reject etc*) rundweg; **to ~** zur Hand; **on the one ~ ..., on the other ~ ...** einerseits ... andererseits ...;

to force sb's ~ jdn zwingen; **to have a free ~** freie Hand haben; **to change ~s** den Besitzer wechseln; **to have in one's ~** (*also fig*) in der Hand halten; **"~s off!"** „Hände weg!"
▸ **hand down** *vt* (*knowledge*) weitergeben; (*possessions*) vererben; (*Law: judgement, sentence*) fällen
▸ **hand in** *vt* abgeben, einreichen
▸ **hand out** *vt* verteilen; (*information*) austeilen; (*punishment*) verhängen
▸ **hand over** *vt* übergeben
▸ **hand round** *vt* (*Brit*) verteilen; (*chocolates etc*) herumreichen

handbag ['hændbæg] *n* Handtasche *f*
hand baggage *n* Handgepäck *nt*
handball ['hændbɔːl] *n* Handball *m*
hand basin *n* Handwaschbecken *nt*
handbook ['hændbuk] *n* Handbuch *nt*
handbrake ['hændbreɪk] *n* Handbremse *f*
h & c (*Brit*) *abbr* (= *hot and cold (water)*) h. u. k.
hand cream *n* Handcreme *f*
handcuff ['hændkʌf] *vt* Handschellen anlegen *+dat*
handcuffs ['hændkʌfs] *npl* Handschellen *pl*
handful ['hændful] *n* Handvoll *f*
hand-held ['hænd'hɛld] *adj* (*camera*) Hand-
handicap ['hændɪkæp] *n* Behinderung *f*; (*disadvantage*) Nachteil *m*; (*Sport*) Handicap *nt* ▹ *vt* benachteiligen; **mentally/physically ~ped** geistig/körperlich behindert
handicraft ['hændɪkrɑːft] *n* Kunsthandwerk *nt*; (*object*) Kunsthandwerksarbeit *f*
handiwork ['hændɪwəːk] *n* Arbeit *f*; **this looks like his ~** (*pej*) das sieht nach seiner Arbeit aus
handkerchief ['hæŋkətʃɪf] *n* Taschentuch *nt*
handle ['hændl] *n* Griff *m*; (*of door*) Klinke *f*; (*of cup*) Henkel *m*; (*of broom, brush etc*) Stiel *m*; (*for winding*) Kurbel *f*; (*CB Radio: name*) Sendezeichen *nt* ▹ *vt* anfassen, berühren; (*problem etc*) sich befassen mit; (*: successfully*) fertig werden mit; (*people*) umgehen mit; **"~ with care"** „Vorsicht – zerbrechlich"; **to fly off the ~** an die Decke gehen; **to get a ~ on a problem** (*inf*) ein Problem in den Griff bekommen
handlebar ['hændlbɑːʳ] *n*, **handlebars** ['hændlbɑːz] ▹ *npl* Lenkstange *f*
handling ['hændlɪŋ] *n*: **~ (of)** (*of plant, animal, issue etc*) Behandlung *f +gen*; (*of person, tool, machine etc*) Umgang *m* (mit); (*Admin*) Bearbeitung *f +gen*
handling charges *npl* Bearbeitungsgebühr *f*; (*Banking*) Kontoführungsgebühr *f*
hand luggage *n* Handgepäck *nt*
handmade ['hænd'meɪd] *adj* handgearbeitet
hand-out ['hændaut] *n* (*money, food etc*) Unterstützung *f*; (*publicity leaflet*) Flugblatt *nt*; (*summary*) Informationsblatt *nt*
hand-picked ['hænd'pɪkt] *adj* von Hand geerntet; (*staff etc*) handverlesen
handrail ['hændreɪl] *n* Geländer *nt*
handset ['hændsɛt] *n* (*Tel*) Hörer *m*
hands-free ['hændzfriː] *adj* (*telephone, microphone*) Freisprech-
handshake ['hændʃeɪk] *n* Händedruck *m*
handsome ['hænsəm] *adj* gut aussehend; (*building*) schön; (*gift*) großzügig; (*profit, return*) ansehnlich
hands-on ['hændz'ɔn] *adj* (*training*) praktisch; (*approach etc*) aktiv; **~ experience** praktische Erfahrung
handstand ['hændstænd] *n*: **to do a ~** einen Handstand machen
hand-to-mouth ['hændtə'mauθ] *adj*: **to lead a ~ existence** von der Hand in den Mund leben
handwriting ['hændraɪtɪŋ] *n* Handschrift *f*
handwritten ['hændrɪtn] *adj* handgeschrieben
handy ['hændɪ] *adj* praktisch; (*skilful*) geschickt; (*close at hand*) in der Nähe; **to come in ~** sich als nützlich erweisen
handyman ['hændɪmæn] (*irreg: like* **man**) *n* (*at home*) Heimwerker *m*; (*in hotel etc*) Faktotum *nt*
hang [hæŋ] (*pt, pp* **hung**) *vt* aufhängen; (*criminal: pt, pp* **~ed**) hängen; (*head*) hängen lassen ▹ *vi* hängen; (*hair, drapery*) fallen ▹ *n*: **to get the ~ of sth** (*inf*) den richtigen Dreh (bei etw) herauskriegen
▸ **hang about** *vi* herumlungern
▸ **hang around** *vi* = **hang about**
▸ **hang back** *vi*: **to ~ back (from doing sth)** zögern(, etw zu tun)
▸ **hang on** *vi* warten ▹ *vt fus* (*depend on*) abhängen von; **to ~ on to** festhalten; (*for protection, support*) sich festhalten an *+dat*; (*hope, position*) sich klammern an *+acc*; (*ideas*) festhalten an *+dat*; (*keep*) behalten
▸ **hang out** *vt* draußen aufhängen ▹ *vi* heraushängen; (*inf: live*) wohnen
▸ **hang together** *vi* (*argument*) folgerichtig *or* zusammenhängend sein; (*story, explanation*) zusammenhängend sein; (*statements*) zusammenpassen
▸ **hang up** *vt* aufhängen ▹ *vi* (*Tel*): **to ~ up (on sb)** einfach auflegen

hangar ['hæŋəʳ] *n* Hangar *m*, Flugzeughalle *f*
hangdog ['hæŋdɔg] *adj* zerknirscht
hanger ['hæŋəʳ] *n* Bügel *m*
hanger-on [hæŋər'ɔn] *n* (*parasite*) Trabant *m* (*inf*); **the hangers-on** der Anhang
hang-glide ['hæŋglaɪd] *vi* drachenfliegen
hang-glider ['hæŋglaɪdəʳ] *n* (Flug)drachen *m*
hang-gliding ['hæŋglaɪdɪŋ] *n* Drachenfliegen *nt*
hanging ['hæŋɪŋ] *n* (*execution*) Hinrichtung *f* durch den Strang; (*for wall*) Wandbehang *m*
hangman ['hæŋmən] (*irreg: like* **man**) *n* Henker *m*
hangover ['hæŋəuvəʳ] *n* Kater *m*; (*from past*) Überbleibsel *nt*
hang-up ['hæŋʌp] *n* Komplex *m*
hank [hæŋk] *n* Strang *m*
hanker ['hæŋkəʳ] *vi*: **to ~ after** sich sehnen nach
hankering ['hæŋkərɪŋ] *n*: **~ (for)** Verlangen *nt* (nach)
hankie, hanky ['hæŋkɪ] (*pl* **~s**) *n* = **handkerchief**

haphazard [hæp'hæzəd] *adj* planlos, wahllos
hapless ['hæplɪs] *adj* glücklos
happen ['hæpən] *vi* geschehen; **to ~ to do sth** zufällig(erweise) etw tun; **as it ~s** zufälligerweise; **what's ~ing?** was ist los?; **she ~ed to be free** sie hatte zufällig(erweise) gerade Zeit; **if anything ~ed to him** wenn ihm etwas zustoßen *or* passieren sollte
▸ **happen (up)on** *vt fus* zufällig stoßen auf *+acc*; (*person*) zufällig treffen
happening ['hæpnɪŋ] *n* Ereignis *nt*, Vorfall *m*
happily ['hæpɪlɪ] *adv* (*luckily*) glücklicherweise; (*cheerfully*) fröhlich
happiness ['hæpɪnɪs] *n* Glück *nt*
happy ['hæpɪ] *adj* glücklich; (*cheerful*) fröhlich; **to be ~ (with)** zufrieden sein (mit); **to be ~ to do sth** etw gerne tun; **~ birthday!** herzlichen Glückwunsch zum Geburtstag!
happy-go-lucky ['hæpɪgəu'lʌkɪ] *adj* unbekümmert
happy hour *n Zeit, in der Bars, Pubs usw Getränke zu ermäßigten Preisen anbieten*
harangue [hə'ræŋ] *vt* predigen *+dat* (*inf*)
harass ['hærəs] *vt* schikanieren
harassed ['hærəst] *adj* geplagt
harassment ['hærəsmənt] *n* Schikanierung *f*; **sexual ~** sexuelle Belästigung *f*
harbour, (*US*) **harbor** ['hɑːbəʳ] *n* Hafen *m* ▷ *vt* (*hope, fear, grudge etc*) hegen; (*criminal, fugitive*) Unterschlupf gewähren *+dat*
harbour dues *npl* Hafengebühren *pl*
harbour master *n* Hafenmeister *m*
hard [hɑːd] *adj* hart; (*question, problem*) schwierig; (*evidence*) gesichert ▷ *adv* (*work*) hart, schwer; (*think*) scharf; (*try*) sehr; **~ luck!** Pech!; **no ~ feelings!** ich nehme es dir nicht übel; **to be ~ of hearing** schwerhörig sein; **to be ~ done by** ungerecht behandelt werden; **I find it ~ to believe that ...** ich kann es kaum glauben, dass ...; **to look ~ at sth** (*object*) sich *+dat* etw genau ansehen; (*idea*) etw gründlich prüfen
hard-and-fast ['hɑːdən'fɑːst] *adj* fest
hardback ['hɑːdbæk] *n* gebundene Ausgabe *f*
hardboard ['hɑːdbɔːd] *n* Hartfaserplatte *f*
hard-boiled egg ['hɑːd'bɔɪld-] *n* hart gekochtes Ei *nt*
hard cash *n* Bargeld *nt*
hard copy *n* (*Comput*) Ausdruck *m*
hard core *n* harter Kern *m*
hard-core ['hɑːd'kɔːʳ] *adj* (*pornography*) hart; (*supporters*) zum harten Kern gehörend
hard court *n* (*Tennis*) Hartplatz *m*
hard disk *n* (*Comput*) Festplatte *f*
harden ['hɑːdn] *vt* härten; (*attitude, person*) verhärten ▷ *vi* hart werden, sich verhärten
hardened ['hɑːdnd] *adj* (*criminal*) Gewohnheits-; **to be ~ to sth** gegen etw abgehärtet sein
hardening ['hɑːdnɪŋ] *n* Verhärtung *f*
hard graft *n*: **by sheer ~** durch harte Arbeit
hard-headed ['hɑːd'hɛdɪd] *adj* nüchtern
hardhearted ['hɑːd'hɑːtɪd] *adj* hartherzig
hard-hitting ['hɑːd'hɪtɪŋ] *adj* (*fig: speech, journalist etc*) knallhart
hard labour *n* Zwangsarbeit *f*
hardliner [hɑːd'laɪnəʳ] *n* Vertreter(in) *m(f)* der harten Linie
hard-luck story ['hɑːdlʌk-] *n* Leidensgeschichte *f*
hardly ['hɑːdlɪ] *adv* kaum; (*harshly*) hart, streng; **it's ~ the case** (*ironic*) das ist wohl kaum der Fall; **I can ~ believe it** ich kann es kaum glauben
hard-nosed [hɑːd'nəuzd] *adj* abgebrüht
hard-pressed [hɑːd'prɛst] *adj*: **to be ~** unter Druck sein; **~ for money** in Geldnot
hard sell *n* aggressive Verkaufstaktik *f*
hardship ['hɑːdʃɪp] *n* Not *f*
hard shoulder (*Brit*) *n* (*Aut*) Seitenstreifen *m*
hard up (*inf*) *adj* knapp bei Kasse
hardware ['hɑːdwɛəʳ] *n* Eisenwaren *pl*; (*household goods*) Haushaltswaren *pl*; (*Comput*) Hardware *f*; (*Mil*) Waffen *pl*
hardware shop *n* Eisenwarenhandlung *f*
hard-wearing [hɑːd'wɛərɪŋ] *adj* strapazierfähig
hard-won [hɑːd'wʌn] *adj* schwer erkämpft
hard-working [hɑːd'wəːkɪŋ] *adj* fleißig
hardy ['hɑːdɪ] *adj* (*animals*) zäh; (*people*) abgehärtet; (*plant*) winterhart
hare [hɛəʳ] *n* Hase *m*
harebrained ['hɛəbreɪnd] *adj* verrückt
harelip ['hɛəlɪp] *n* Hasenscharte *f*
harem [hɑː'riːm] *n* Harem *m*
hark back [hɑːk-] *vi*: **to ~ to** zurückkommen auf *+acc*
harm [hɑːm] *n* Schaden *m*; (*injury*) Verletzung *f* ▷ *vt* schaden *+dat*; (*person: physically*) verletzen; **to mean no ~** es nicht böse meinen; **out of ~'s way** in Sicherheit; **there's no ~ in trying** es kann nicht schaden, es zu versuchen
harmful ['hɑːmful] *adj* schädlich
harmless ['hɑːmlɪs] *adj* harmlos
harmonic [hɑː'mɔnɪk] *adj* harmonisch
harmonica [hɑː'mɔnɪkə] *n* Harmonika *f*
harmonics [hɑː'mɔnɪks] *npl* Harmonik *f*
harmonious [hɑː'məunɪəs] *adj* harmonisch
harmonium [hɑː'məunɪəm] *n* Harmonium *nt*
harmonize ['hɑːmənaɪz] *vi* (*Mus*) mehrstimmig singen/spielen; (*: one person*) die zweite Stimme singen/spielen; (*colours, ideas*) harmonieren
harmony ['hɑːmənɪ] *n* Einklang *m*; (*Mus*) Harmonie *f*
harness ['hɑːnɪs] *n* (*for horse*) Geschirr *nt*; (*for child*) Laufgurt *m*; (*also*: **safety harness**) Sicherheitsgurt *m* ▷ *vt* (*resources, energy etc*) nutzbar machen; (*horse, dog*) anschirren
harp [hɑːp] *n* Harfe *f* ▷ *vi*: **to ~ on about** (*pej*) herumreiten auf *+dat*
harpist ['hɑːpɪst] *n* Harfenspieler(in) *m(f)*
harpoon [hɑː'puːn] *n* Harpune *f*
harpsichord ['hɑːpsɪkɔːd] *n* Cembalo *nt*
harried ['hærɪd] *adj* bedrängt
harrow ['hærəu] *n* Egge *f*
harrowing ['hærəuɪŋ] *adj* (*film*) erschütternd;

(*experience*) grauenhaft
harry ['hærɪ] *vt* bedrängen, zusetzen *+dat*
harsh [hɑːʃ] *adj* (*sound, light*) grell; (*judge, winter*) streng; (*criticism, life*) hart
harshly ['hɑːʃlɪ] *adv* (*judge*) streng; (*say*) barsch; (*criticize*) hart
harshness ['hɑːʃnɪs] *n* (*see adj*) Grelle *f*; Strenge *f*; Härte *f*
harvest ['hɑːvɪst] *n* Ernte *f* ▷ *vt* ernten
harvester ['hɑːvɪstəʳ] *n* (*also*: **combine harvester**) Mähdrescher *m*
has [hæz] *vb see* **have**
has-been ['hæzbiːn] (*inf*) *n*: **he's/she's a ~** er/sie ist eine vergangene *or* vergessene Größe
hash [hæʃ] *n* (*Culin*) Haschee *nt*; (*fig*): **to make a ~ of sth** etw verpfuschen (*inf*); (*inf*) ▷ *n abbr* (= *hashish*) Hasch *nt*
hashish ['hæʃɪʃ] *n* Haschisch *nt*
hasn't ['hæznt] = **has not**
hassle ['hæsl] (*inf*) *n* (*bother*) Theater *nt* ▷ *vt* schikanieren
haste [heɪst] *n* Hast *f*; (*speed*) Eile *f*; **in ~** in Eile; **to make ~ (to do sth)** sich beeilen(, etw zu tun)
hasten ['heɪsn] *vt* beschleunigen ▷ *vi*: **to ~ to do sth** sich beeilen, etw zu tun; **I ~ to add ...** ich muss allerdings hinzufügen, ...; **she ~ed back to the house** sie eilte zum Haus zurück
hastily ['heɪstɪlɪ] *adv* (*see adj*) hastig, eilig; vorschnell
hasty ['heɪstɪ] *adj* hastig, eilig; (*rash*) vorschnell
hat [hæt] *n* Hut *m*; **to keep sth under one's ~** etw für sich behalten
hatbox ['hætbɔks] *n* Hutschachtel *f*
hatch [hætʃ] *n* (*Naut*: *also*: **hatchway**) Luke *f*; (*also*: **service hatch**) Durchreiche *f* ▷ *vi* (*bird*) ausschlüpfen ▷ *vt* ausbrüten; **the eggs ~ed after 10 days** nach 10 Tagen schlüpften die Jungen aus
hatchback ['hætʃbæk] *n* (*Aut*: *car*) Heckklappenmodell *nt*
hatchet ['hætʃɪt] *n* Beil *nt*; **to bury the ~** das Kriegsbeil begraben
hatchet job (*inf*) *adj*: **to do a ~ on sb** jdn fertigmachen
hatchet man (*inf*) *n* (*fig*) Vollstrecker *m*
hate [heɪt] *vt* hassen ▷ *n* Hass *m*; **I ~ him/milk** ich kann ihn/ Milch nicht ausstehen; **to ~ to do/doing sth** es hassen, etw zu tun; (*weaker*) etw ungern tun; **I ~ to trouble you, but ...** es ist mir sehr unangenehm, dass ich Sie belästigen muss, aber ...
hateful ['heɪtful] *adj* abscheulich
hatred ['heɪtrɪd] *n* Hass *m*; (*dislike*) Abneigung *f*
hat trick *n* Hattrick *m*
haughty ['hɔːtɪ] *adj* überheblich
haul [hɔːl] *vt* ziehen; (*by lorry*) transportieren; (*Naut*) den Kurs ändern *+gen* ▷ *n* Beute *f*; (*of fish*) Fang *m*; **he ~ed himself out of the pool** er stemmte sich aus dem Schwimmbecken
haulage ['hɔːlɪdʒ] *n* (*cost*) Transportkosten *pl*; (*business*) Transport *m*
haulage contractor (*Brit*) *n* Transportunternehmen *nt*, Spedition *f*; (*person*) Transportunternehmer(in) *m(f)*, Spediteur *m*
hauler ['hɔːləʳ] (*US*) *n* Transportunternehmer(in) *m(f)*, Spediteur *m*
haulier ['hɔːlɪəʳ] (*Brit*) *n* Transportunternehmer(in) *m(f)*, Spediteur *m*
haunch [hɔːntʃ] *n* Hüftpartie *f*; (*of meat*) Keule *f*
haunt [hɔːnt] *vt* (*place*) spuken in *+dat*, umgehen in *+dat*; (*person, fig*) verfolgen ▷ *n* Lieblingsplatz *m*; (*of crooks etc*) Treffpunkt *m*
haunted ['hɔːntɪd] *adj* (*expression*) gehetzt, gequält; **this building/room is ~** in diesem Gebäude/Zimmer spukt es
haunting ['hɔːntɪŋ] *adj* (*music*) eindringlich; **a ~ sight** ein Anblick, der einen nicht loslässt
Havana [hə'vænə] *n* Havanna *nt*

KEYWORD

have [hæv] (*pt, pp* **had**) *aux vb* **1** haben; (*with verbs of motion*) sein; **to have arrived/gone** angekommen/gegangen sein; **to have eaten/slept** gegessen/geschlafen haben; **he has been promoted** er ist befördert worden; **having eaten** *or* **when he had eaten, he left** nachdem er gegessen hatte, ging er
2 (*in tag questions*): **you've done it, haven't you?** du hast es gemacht, nicht wahr?; **he hasn't done it, has he?** er hat es nicht gemacht, oder?
3 (*in short answers and questions*): **you've made a mistake — no I haven't/so I have** du hast einen Fehler gemacht — nein(, das habe ich nicht)/ja, stimmt; **we haven't paid — yes we have!** wir haben nicht bezahlt — doch!; **I've been there before — have you?** ich war schon einmal da — wirklich *or* tatsächlich?
▷ *modal aux vb* (*be obliged*): **to have (got) to do sth** etw tun müssen; **this has (got) to be a mistake** das muss ein Fehler sein
▷ *vt* **1** (*possess*) haben; **she has (got) blue eyes/dark hair** sie hat blaue Augen/dunkle Haare; **I have (got) an idea** ich habe eine Idee
2 (*referring to meals etc*): **to have breakfast** frühstücken; **to have lunch/dinner** zu Mittag/Abend essen; **to have a drink** etwas trinken; **to have a cigarette** eine Zigarette rauchen
3 (*receive, obtain etc*) haben; **may I have your address?** kann ich Ihre Adresse haben *or* bekommen?; **to have a baby** ein Kind bekommen
4 (*allow*): **I won't have this nonsense** dieser Unsinn kommt nicht infrage!; **we can't have that** das kommt nicht infrage
5: to have sth done etw machen lassen; **to have one's hair cut** sich *dat* die Haare schneiden lassen; **to have sb do sth** (*order*) jdn etw tun lassen; **he soon had them all laughing/working** bald hatte er alle zum Lachen/Arbeiten gebracht

6 (*experience, suffer*): **to have a cold/flu** eine Erkältung/die Grippe haben; **she had her bag stolen** ihr *dat* wurde die Tasche gestohlen
7 (*+ noun: take, hold etc*): **to have a swim** schwimmen gehen; **to have a walk** spazieren gehen; **to have a rest** sich ausruhen; **to have a meeting** eine Besprechung haben; **to have a party** eine Party geben
8 (*inf: dupe*): **you've been had** man hat dich hereingelegt
▸ **have in** (*inf*) *vt*: **to have it in for sb** jdn auf dem Kieker haben
▸ **have on** *vt* (*wear*) anhaben; (*Brit: inf: tease*) auf den Arm nehmen; **I don't have any money on me** ich habe kein Geld bei mir; **do you have** *or* **have you anything on tomorrow?** haben Sie morgen etwas vor?
▸ **have out** *vt*: **to have it out with sb** (*settle a problem etc*) ein Wort mit jdm reden

haven ['heɪvn] *n* Hafen *m*; (*safe place*) Zufluchtsort *m*
haven't ['hævnt] = **have not**
haversack ['hævəsæk] *n* Rucksack *m*
haves [hævz] (*inf*) *npl*: **the ~ and the have-nots** die Betuchten und die Habenichtse
havoc ['hævək] *n* Verwüstung *f*; (*confusion*) Chaos *nt*; **to play ~ with sth** (*disrupt*) etw völlig durcheinanderbringen
Hawaii [hə'waɪi:] *n* Hawaii *nt*
Hawaiian [hə'waɪjən] *adj* hawaiisch ▹ *n* Hawaiianer(in) *m(f)*; (*Ling*) Hawaiisch *nt*
hawk [hɔ:k] *n* Habicht *m*
hawker ['hɔ:kəʳ] *n* Hausierer(in) *m(f)*
hawkish ['hɔ:kɪʃ] *adj* (*person, approach*) knallhart
hawthorn ['hɔ:θɔ:n] *n* Weißdorn *m*, Rotdorn *m*
hay [heɪ] *n* Heu *nt*
hay fever *n* Heuschnupfen *m*
haystack ['heɪstæk] *n* Heuhaufen *m*; **like looking for a needle in a ~** als ob man eine Stecknadel im Heuhaufen suchte
haywire ['heɪwaɪəʳ] (*inf*) *adj*: **to go ~** (*machine*) verrücktspielen; (*plans etc*) über den Haufen geworfen werden
hazard ['hæzəd] *n* Gefahr *f* ▹ *vt* riskieren; **to be a health/fire ~** eine Gefahr für die Gesundheit/feuergefährlich sein; **to ~ a guess** (es) wagen, eine Vermutung anzustellen
hazard lights, hazard warning lights *npl* (*Aut*) Warnblinkanlage *f*
hazardous ['hæzədəs] *adj* gefährlich
hazard pay (*US*) *n* Gefahrenzulage *f*
haze [heɪz] *n* Dunst *m*
hazel ['heɪzl] *n* Hasel(nuss)strauch *m*, Haselbusch *m* ▹ *adj* haselnussbraun
hazelnut ['heɪzlnʌt] *n* Haselnuss *f*
hazy ['heɪzɪ] *adj* dunstig, diesig; (*idea, memory*) unklar, verschwommen; **I'm rather ~ about the details** an die Einzelheiten kann ich mich nur vage *or* verschwommen erinnern; (*ignorant*) die genauen Einzelheiten sind mir nicht bekannt
H-bomb ['eɪtʃbɔm] *n* H-Bombe *f*
HE *abbr* (*Rel, Diplomacy: = His/Her Excellency*) Seine/Ihre Exzellenz; (*= high explosive*) hochexplosiver Sprengstoff *m*
he [hi:] *pron* er ▹ *pref* männlich; **he who ...** wer ...
head [hɛd] *n* Kopf *m*; (*of table*) Kopfende *nt*; (*of queue*) Spitze *f*; (*of company, organization*) Leiter(in) *m(f)*; (*of school*) Schulleiter(in) *m(f)*; (*on coin*) Kopfseite *f*; (*on tape recorder*) Tonkopf *m* ▹ *vt* anführen, an der Spitze stehen von; (*group, company*) leiten; (*Football: ball*) köpfen; **~s (or tails)** Kopf (oder Zahl); **~ over heels** Hals über Kopf; (*in love*) bis über beide Ohren; **£10 a** *or* **per ~** 10 Pfund pro Kopf; **at the ~ of the list** oben auf der Liste; **to have a ~ for business** einen guten Geschäftssinn haben; **to have no ~ for heights** nicht schwindelfrei sein; **to come to a ~** sich zuspitzen; **they put their ~s together** sie haben sich zusammengesetzt; **off the top of my** *etc* **~** ohne lange zu überlegen; **on your own ~ be it!** auf Ihre eigene Verantwortung *or* Kappe (*inf*)!; **to bite** *or* **snap sb's ~ off** jdn grob anfahren; **he won't bite your ~ off** er wird dir schon nicht den Kopf abreißen; **it went to my ~** es ist mir in den Kopf *or* zu Kopf gestiegen; **to lose/keep one's ~** den Kopf verlieren/nicht verlieren; **I can't make ~ nor tail of this** hieraus werde ich nicht schlau; **he's off his ~!** (*inf*) er ist nicht (ganz) bei Trost!
▸ **head for** *vt fus* (*on foot*) zusteuern auf *+acc*; (*by car*) in Richtung ... fahren; (*plane, ship*) Kurs nehmen auf *+acc*; **you are ~ing for trouble** du wirst Ärger bekommen
▸ **head off** *vt* abwenden
headache ['hɛdeɪk] *n* Kopfschmerzen *pl*, Kopfweh *nt*; (*fig*) Problem *nt*; **to have a ~** Kopfschmerzen *or* Kopfweh haben
headband ['hɛdbænd] *n* Stirnband *nt*
headboard ['hɛdbɔ:d] *n* Kopfteil *nt*
head cold *n* Kopfgrippe *f*
headdress ['hɛddrɛs] (*Brit*) *n* Kopfschmuck *m*
headed notepaper ['hɛdɪd-] *n* Schreibpapier *nt* mit Briefkopf
header ['hɛdəʳ] (*Brit: inf*) *n* (*Football*) Kopfball *m*
headfirst ['hɛd'fə:st] *adv* (*lit*) kopfüber; (*fig*) Hals über Kopf
headgear ['hɛdgɪəʳ] *n* Kopfbedeckung *f*
head-hunt ['hɛdhʌnt] *vt* abwerben
head-hunter ['hɛdhʌntəʳ] *n* (*Comm*) Kopfjäger(in) *m(f)*
heading ['hɛdɪŋ] *n* Überschrift *f*
headlamp ['hɛdlæmp] (*Brit*) *n* = **headlight**
headland ['hɛdlənd] *n* Landspitze *f*
headlight ['hɛdlaɪt] *n* Scheinwerfer *m*
headline ['hɛdlaɪn] *n* Schlagzeile *f*; (*Radio, TV*): **(news) ~s** Nachrichtenüberblick *m*
headlong ['hɛdlɔŋ] *adv* kopfüber; (*rush*) Hals über Kopf
headmaster [hɛd'mɑ:stəʳ] *n* Schulleiter *m*
headmistress [hɛd'mɪstrɪs] *n* Schulleiterin *f*
head office *n* Zentrale *f*

head of state (*pl* **heads of state**) *n* Staatsoberhaupt *nt*
head-on ['hɛd'ɔn] *adj* (*collision*) frontal; (*confrontation*) direkt
headphones ['hɛdfəunz] *npl* Kopfhörer *pl*
headquarters ['hɛdkwɔːtəz] *npl* Zentrale *f*; (*Mil*) Hauptquartier *nt*
headrest ['hɛdrɛst] *n* (*Aut*) Kopfstütze *f*
headroom ['hɛdrum] *n* (*in car*) Kopfraum *m*; (*under bridge*) lichte Höhe *f*
headscarf ['hɛdskɑːf] *n* Kopftuch *nt*
headset ['hɛdsɛt] *n* = **headphones**
head start *n* Vorsprung *m*
headstone ['hɛdstəun] *n* Grabstein *m*
headstrong ['hɛdstrɔŋ] *adj* eigensinnig
head waiter *n* Oberkellner *m*
headway ['hɛdweɪ] *n*: **to make ~** vorankommen
headwind ['hɛdwɪnd] *n* Gegenwind *m*
heady ['hɛdɪ] *adj* (*experience etc*) aufregend; (*drink, atmosphere*) berauschend
heal [hiːl] *vt, vi* heilen
health [hɛlθ] *n* Gesundheit *f*
health care *n* Gesundheitsfürsorge *f*
health centre (*Brit*) *n* Ärztezentrum *nt*
health food *n* Reformkost *f*, Naturkost *f*
health food shop *n* Reformhaus *nt*, Naturkostladen *m*
health hazard *n* Gefahr *f* für die Gesundheit
health service (*Brit*) *n*: **the Health Service** das Gesundheitswesen
healthy ['hɛlθɪ] *adj* gesund; (*profit*) ansehnlich
heap [hiːp] *n* Haufen *m* ▷ *vt*: **to ~ (up)** (auf)häufen; **~s of** (*inf*) jede Menge; **to ~ sth with** etw beladen mit; **to ~ sth on** etw häufen auf *+acc*; **to ~ favours/gifts** *etc* **on sb** jdn mit Gefälligkeiten/Geschenken *etc* überhäufen; **to ~ praises on sb** jdn mit Lob überschütten
hear [hɪəʳ] (*pt, pp* **~d**) *vt* hören; (*Law: case*) verhandeln; (*: witness*) vernehmen; **to ~ about** hören von; **to ~ from sb** von jdm hören; **I've never ~d of that book** von dem Buch habe ich noch nie etwas gehört; **I wouldn't ~ of it!** davon will ich nichts hören
▸ **hear out** *vt* ausreden lassen
heard [həːd] *pt, pp of* **hear**
hearing ['hɪərɪŋ] *n* Gehör *nt*; (*of facts, by committee*) Anhörung *f*; (*of witnesses*) Vernehmung *f*; (*of a case*) Verhandlung *f*; **to give sb a ~** (*Brit*) jdn anhören
hearing aid *n* Hörgerät *nt*
hearsay ['hɪəseɪ] *n* Gerüchte *pl*; **by ~** vom Hörensagen
hearse [həːs] *n* Leichenwagen *m*
heart [hɑːt] *n* Herz *nt*; (*of problem*) Kern *m*; **hearts** *npl* (*Cards*) Herz *nt*; **to lose ~** den Mut verlieren; **to take ~** Mut fassen; **at ~** im Grunde; **by ~** auswendig; **to set one's ~ on sth** sein Herz an etw *acc* hängen; **to set one's ~ on doing sth** alles daransetzen, etw zu tun; **the ~ of the matter** der Kern der Sache
heartache ['hɑːteɪk] *n* Kummer *m*
heart attack *n* Herzanfall *m*
heartbeat ['hɑːtbiːt] *n* Herzschlag *m*
heartbreak ['hɑːtbreɪk] *n* großer Kummer *m*, Leid *nt*
heartbreaking ['hɑːtbreɪkɪŋ] *adj* herzzerreißend
heartbroken ['hɑːtbrəukən] *adj*: **to be ~** todunglücklich sein
heartburn ['hɑːtbəːn] *n* Sodbrennen *nt*
-hearted ['hɑːtɪd] *suff*: **kind-~** gutherzig
heartening ['hɑːtnɪŋ] *adj* ermutigend
heart failure *n* Herzversagen *nt*
heartfelt ['hɑːtfɛlt] *adj* tief empfunden
hearth [hɑːθ] *n* ≈ Kamin *m*
heartily ['hɑːtɪlɪ] *adv* (*see adj*) (laut und) herzlich; herzhaft; tief; ungeteilt
heartland ['hɑːtlænd] *n* Herz *nt*; **Britain's industrial ~** Großbritanniens Industriezentrum *nt*
heartless ['hɑːtlɪs] *adj* herzlos
heartstrings ['hɑːtstrɪŋz] *npl*: **to tug at sb's ~** bei jdm auf die Tränendrüsen drücken
heart-throb ['hɑːtθrɔb] (*inf*) *n* Schwarm *m*
heart-to-heart ['hɑːt'tə'hɑːt] *adj, adv* ganz im Vertrauen
heart transplant *n* Herztransplantation *f*, Herzverpflanzung *f*
heart-warming ['hɑːtwɔːmɪŋ] *adj* herzerfreuend
hearty ['hɑːtɪ] *adj* (*person*) laut und herzlich; (*laugh, appetite*) herzhaft; (*welcome*) herzlich; (*dislike*) tief; (*support*) ungeteilt
heat [hiːt] *n* Hitze *f*; (*warmth*) Wärme *f*; (*temperature*) Temperatur *f*; (*Sport: also:* **qualifying heat**) Vorrunde *f* ▷ *vt* erhitzen, heiß machen; (*room, house*) heizen; **in ~, on ~** (*Brit: Zool*) brünstig, läufig
▸ **heat up** *vi* sich erwärmen, warm werden ▷ *vt* aufwärmen; (*water, room*) erwärmen
heated ['hiːtɪd] *adj* geheizt; (*pool*) beheizt; (*argument*) hitzig
heater ['hiːtəʳ] *n* (Heiz)ofen *m*; (*in car*) Heizung *f*
heath [hiːθ] (*Brit*) *n* Heide *f*
heathen ['hiːðn] *n* Heide *m*, Heidin *f*
heather ['hɛðəʳ] *n* Heidekraut *nt*, Erika *f*
heating ['hiːtɪŋ] *n* Heizung *f*
heat-resistant ['hiːtrɪzɪstənt] *adj* hitzebeständig
heat-seeking ['hiːtsiːkɪŋ] *adj* Wärme suchend
heatstroke ['hiːtstrəuk] *n* Hitzschlag *m*
heat wave *n* Hitzewelle *f*
heave [hiːv] *vt* (*pull*) ziehen; (*push*) schieben; (*lift*) (hoch)heben ▷ *vi* sich heben und senken; (*retch*) sich übergeben ▷ *n* (*see vt*) Zug *m*; Stoß *m*; Heben *nt*; **to ~ a sigh** einen Seufzer ausstoßen
▸ **heave to** (*pt, pp* **hove**) *vi* (*Naut*) beidrehen
heaven ['hɛvn] *n* Himmel *m*; **thank ~!** Gott sei Dank!; **~ forbid!** bloß nicht!; **for ~'s sake!** um Himmels *or* Gottes willen!
heavenly ['hɛvnlɪ] *adj* himmlisch
heaven-sent [hɛvn'sɛnt] *adj* ideal
heavily ['hɛvɪlɪ] *adv* schwer; (*drink, smoke, depend, rely*) stark; (*sleep, sigh*) tief; (*say*) mit schwerer Stimme

heavy ['hɛvɪ] *adj* schwer; (*clothes*) dick; (*rain, snow, drinker, smoker*) stark; (*build, frame*) kräftig; (*breathing, sleep*) tief; (*schedule, week*) anstrengend; (*weather*) drückend, schwül; **the conversation was ~ going** die Unterhaltung war mühsam; **the book was ~ going** das Buch las sich schwer
heavy cream (*US*) *n Sahne mit hohem Fettgehalt*, ≈ Schlagsahne *f*
heavy-duty ['hɛvɪ'dju:tɪ] *adj* strapazierfähig
heavy goods vehicle *n* Lastkraftwagen *m*
heavy-handed ['hɛvɪ'hændɪd] *adj* schwerfällig, ungeschickt
heavy industry *n* Schwerindustrie *f*
heavy metal *n* (*Mus*) Heavymetal *nt*
heavyset ['hɛvɪ'sɛt] (*esp US*) *adj* kräftig gebaut
heavyweight ['hɛvɪweɪt] *n* (*Sport*) Schwergewicht *nt*
Hebrew ['hi:bru:] *adj* hebräisch ▷ *n* (*Ling*) Hebräisch *nt*
Hebrides ['hɛbrɪdi:z] *npl*: **the ~** die Hebriden *pl*
heck [hɛk] (*inf*) *interj*: **oh ~!** zum Kuckuck! ▷ *n*: **a ~ of a lot** irrsinnig viel
heckle ['hɛkl] *vt* durch Zwischenrufe stören
heckler ['hɛkləʳ] *n* Zwischenrufer(in) *m(f)*, Störer(in) *m(f)*
hectare ['hɛktɑ:ʳ] (*Brit*) *n* Hektar *nt or m*
hectic ['hɛktɪk] *adj* hektisch
hector ['hɛktəʳ] *vt* tyrannisieren
he'd [hi:d] = **he would; he had**
hedge [hɛdʒ] *n* Hecke *f* ▷ *vi* ausweichen, sich nicht festlegen ▷ *vt*: **to ~ one's bets** (*fig*) sich absichern; **as a ~ against inflation** als Absicherung *or* Schutz gegen die Inflation
▸ **hedge in** *vt* (*person*) (in seiner Freiheit) einschränken; (*proposals etc*) behindern
hedgehog ['hɛdʒhɔg] *n* Igel *m*
hedgerow ['hɛdʒrəu] *n* Hecke *f*
hedonism ['hi:dənɪzəm] *n* Hedonismus *m*
heed [hi:d] *vt* (*also*: **take heed of**) beachten ▷ *n*: **to pay (no) ~ to, take (no) ~ of** (nicht) beachten
heedless ['hi:dlɪs] *adj* achtlos; **~ of sb/sth** ohne auf jdn/etw zu achten
heel [hi:l] *n* Ferse *f*; (*of shoe*) Absatz *m* ▷ *vt* (*shoe*) mit einem neuen Absatz versehen; **to bring to ~** (*dog*) bei Fuß gehen lassen; (*fig: person*) an die Kandare nehmen; **to take to one's ~s** (*inf*) sich aus dem Staub machen
hefty ['hɛftɪ] *adj* kräftig; (*parcel etc*) schwer; (*profit*) ansehnlich
heifer ['hɛfəʳ] *n* Färse *f*
height [haɪt] *n* Höhe *f*; (*of person*) Größe *f*; (*fig: of luxury, good taste etc*) Gipfel *m*; **what ~ are you?** wie groß bist du?; **of average ~** durchschnittlich groß; **to be afraid of ~s** nicht schwindelfrei sein; **it's the ~ of fashion** das ist die neueste Mode; **at the ~ of the tourist season** in der Hauptsaison
heighten ['haɪtn] *vt* erhöhen
heinous ['heɪnəs] *adj* abscheulich, verabscheuungswürdig
heir [ɛəʳ] *n* Erbe *m*; **the ~ to the throne** der Thronfolger
heir apparent *n* gesetzlicher Erbe *m*
heiress ['ɛərɛs] *n* Erbin *f*
heirloom ['ɛəlu:m] *n* Erbstück *nt*
heist [haɪst] (*US: inf*) *n* Raubüberfall *m*
held [hɛld] *pt, pp of* **hold**
helicopter ['hɛlɪkɔptəʳ] *n* Hubschrauber *m*
heliport ['hɛlɪpɔ:t] *n* Hubschrauberflugplatz *m*, Heliport *m*
helium ['hi:lɪəm] *n* Helium *nt*
hell [hɛl] *n* Hölle *f*; **~!** (*inf!*) verdammt! (*inf!*); **a ~ of a lot** (*inf*) verdammt viel (*inf*); **a ~ of a mess** (*inf*) ein wahnsinniges Chaos (*inf*); **a ~ of a noise** (*inf*) ein Höllenlärm *m*; **a ~ of a nice guy** ein wahnsinnig netter Typ
he'll [hi:l] = **he will; he shall**
hellbent [hɛl'bɛnt] *adj*: **~ (on)** versessen (auf +*acc*)
hellish ['hɛlɪʃ] (*inf*) *adj* höllisch
hello [hə'ləu] *excl* hallo; (*expressing surprise*) nanu, he
Hell's Angels *npl* Hell's Angels *pl*
helm [hɛlm] *n* Ruder *nt*, Steuer *nt*; **at the ~** am Ruder
helmet ['hɛlmɪt] *n* Helm *m*
helmsman ['hɛlmzmən] (*irreg: like* **man**) *n* Steuermann *m*
help [hɛlp] *n* Hilfe *f*; (*charwoman*) (Haushalts)hilfe *f* ▷ *vt* helfen +*dat*; **with the ~ of** (*person*) mit (der) Hilfe +*gen*; (*tool etc*) mithilfe +*gen*; **to be of ~ to sb** jdm behilflich sein, jdm helfen; **can I ~ you?** (*in shop*) womit kann ich Ihnen dienen?; **~ yourself** bedienen Sie sich; **he can't ~ it** er kann nichts dafür; **I can't ~ thinking that ...** ich kann mir nicht helfen, ich glaube, dass ...
helper ['hɛlpəʳ] *n* Helfer(in) *m(f)*
helpful ['hɛlpful] *adj* hilfsbereit; (*advice, suggestion*) nützlich, hilfreich
helping ['hɛlpɪŋ] *n* Portion *f*
helping hand *n*: **to give** *or* **lend sb a ~** jdm behilflich sein
helpless ['hɛlplɪs] *adj* hilflos
helplessly ['hɛlplɪslɪ] *adv* hilflos
helpline ['hɛlplaɪn] *n* (*for emergencies*) Notruf *m*; (*for information*) Informationsdienst *m*
Helsinki ['hɛlsɪŋkɪ] *n* Helsinki *nt*
helter-skelter ['hɛltə'skɛltəʳ] (*Brit*) *n* Rutschbahn *f*
hem [hɛm] *n* Saum *m* ▷ *vt* säumen
▸ **hem in** *vt* einschließen, umgeben; **to feel ~med in** (*fig*) sich eingeengt fühlen
hematology ['hi:mə'tɔlədʒɪ] (*US*) *n* = **haematology**
hemisphere ['hɛmɪsfɪəʳ] *n* Hemisphäre *f*; (*of sphere*) Halbkugel *f*
hemlock ['hɛmlɔk] *n* Schierling *m*
hemoglobin ['hi:mə'gləubɪn] (*US*) *n* = **haemoglobin**
hemophilia ['hi:mə'fɪlɪə] (*US*) *n* = **haemophilia**
hemorrhage ['hɛmərɪdʒ] (*US*) *n* = **haemorrhage**
hemorrhoids ['hɛmərɔɪdz] (*US*) *npl* =

haemorrhoids
hemp [hɛmp] *n* Hanf *m*
hen [hɛn] *n* Henne *f*, Huhn *nt*; (*female bird*) Weibchen *nt*
hence [hɛns] *adv* daher; **2 years ~** in zwei Jahren
henceforth [hɛns'fɔːθ] *adv* von nun an; (*from that time on*) von da an
henchman ['hɛntʃmən] (*irreg: like* **man**) (*pej*) *n* Spießgeselle *m*
henna ['hɛnə] *n* Henna *nt*
hen night, hen party (*inf*) *n* Damenkränzchen *nt*; *siehe Info-Artikel*

HEN NIGHT

Als *hen night* bezeichnet man eine feuchtfröhliche Frauenparty, die kurz vor einer Hochzeit von der Braut und ihren Freundinnen meist in einem Gasthaus oder Nachtklub abgehalten wird und bei der die Freundinnen dafür sorgen, dass vor allem die Braut große Mengen an Alkohol konsumiert. Siehe auch *stag night*.

henpecked ['hɛnpɛkt] *adj*: **to be ~** unter dem Pantoffel stehen; **~ husband** Pantoffelheld *m*
hepatitis [hɛpə'taɪtɪs] *n* Hepatitis *f*
her [həːʳ] *pron* sie; (*indirect*) ihr ▷ *adj* ihr; **I see ~** ich sehe sie; **give ~ a book** gib ihr ein Buch; **after ~** nach ihr; *see also* **me; my**
herald ['hɛrəld] *n* (Vor)bote *m* ▷ *vt* ankündigen
heraldic [hɛ'rældɪk] *adj* heraldisch, Wappen-
heraldry ['hɛrəldrɪ] *n* Wappenkunde *f*, Heraldik *f*; (*coats of arms*) Wappen *pl*
herb [həːb] *n* Kraut *nt*
herbaceous [həː'beɪʃəs] *adj*: **~ border** Staudenrabatte *f*; **~ plant** Staude *f*
herbal ['həːbl] *adj* (*tea, medicine*) Kräuter-
herbicide ['həːbɪsaɪd] *n* Unkraut-vertilgungsmittel *nt*, Herbizid *nt*
herd [həːd] *n* Herde *f*; (*of wild animals*) Rudel *nt* ▷ *vt* treiben; (*gather*) zusammentreiben; **~ed together** zusammengetrieben
here [hɪəʳ] *adv* hier; **she left ~ yesterday** sie ist gestern von hier abgereist; **~ is/are ...** hier ist/sind ...; **~ you are** (*giving*) (hier,) bitte; **~ we are!** (*finding sth*) da ist es ja!; **~ she is!** da ist sie ja!; **~ she comes** da kommt sie ja; **come ~!** komm hierher *or* hierhin!; **~ and there** hier und da; **"~'s to ..."** „auf ... *acc*"
hereabouts ['hɪərə'bauts] *adv* hier
hereafter [hɪər'ɑːftəʳ] *adv* künftig
hereby [hɪə'baɪ] *adv* hiermit
hereditary [hɪ'rɛdɪtrɪ] *adj* erblich, Erb-
heredity [hɪ'rɛdɪtɪ] *n* Vererbung *f*
heresy ['hɛrəsɪ] *n* Ketzerei *f*
heretic ['hɛrətɪk] *n* Ketzer(in) *m(f)*
heretical [hɪ'rɛtɪkl] *adj* ketzerisch
herewith [hɪə'wɪð] *adv* hiermit
heritage ['hɛrɪtɪdʒ] *n* Erbe *nt*; **our national ~** unser nationales Erbe
hermetically [həː'mɛtɪklɪ] *adv*: **~ sealed** hermetisch verschlossen
hermit ['həːmɪt] *n* Einsiedler(in) *m(f)*
hernia ['həːnɪə] *n* Bruch *m*
hero ['hɪərəu] (*pl* **~es**) *n* Held *m*; (*idol*) Idol *nt*
heroic [hɪ'rəuɪk] *adj* heroisch; (*figure, person*) heldenhaft
heroin ['hɛrəuɪn] *n* Heroin *nt*
heroin addict *n* Heroinsüchtige(r) *f(m)*
heroine ['hɛrəuɪn] *n* Heldin *f*; (*idol*) Idol *nt*
heroism ['hɛrəuɪzəm] *n* Heldentum *nt*
heron ['hɛrən] *n* Reiher *m*
hero worship *n* Heldenverehrung *f*
herring ['hɛrɪŋ] *n* Hering *m*
hers [həːz] *pron* ihre(r, s); **a friend of ~** ein Freund von ihr; **this is ~** das gehört ihr; *see also* **mine**
herself [həː'sɛlf] *pron* sich; (*emphatic*) (sie) selbst; *see also* **oneself**
Herts [hɑːts] (*Brit*) *abbr* (*Post*) = *Hertfordshire*
he's [hiːz] = **he is; he has**
hesitant ['hɛzɪtənt] *adj* zögernd; **to be ~ about doing sth** zögern, etw zu tun
hesitate ['hɛzɪteɪt] *vi* zögern; (*be unwilling*) Bedenken haben; **to ~ about** Bedenken haben wegen; **don't ~ to see a doctor if you are worried** gehen Sie ruhig zum Arzt, wenn Sie sich Sorgen machen
hesitation [hɛzɪ'teɪʃən] *n* Zögern *nt*; Bedenken *pl*; **to have no ~ in saying sth** etw ohne Weiteres sagen können
hessian ['hɛsɪən] *n* Sackleinwand *f*, Rupfen *m*
heterogenous [hɛtə'rɔdʒɪnəs] *adj* heterogen
heterosexual ['hɛtərəu'sɛksjuəl] *adj* heterosexuell ▷ *n* Heterosexuelle(r) *f(m)*
het up [hɛt-] (*inf*) *adj*: **to get ~ (about)** sich aufregen (über +*acc*)
HEW (*US*) *n abbr* (= *Department of Health, Education and Welfare*) *Ministerium für Gesundheit, Erziehung und Sozialfürsorge*
hew [hjuː] (*pt, pp* **hewed** *or* **~n**) *vt* (*stone*) behauen; (*wood*) hacken
hex [hɛks] (*US*) *n* Fluch *m* ▷ *vt* verhexen
hexagon ['hɛksəgən] *n* Sechseck *nt*
hexagonal [hɛk'sægənl] *adj* sechseckig
hey [heɪ] *excl* he; (*to attract attention*) he du/Sie
heyday ['heɪdeɪ] *n*: **the ~ of** (*person*) die Glanzzeit +*gen*; (*nation, group etc*) die Blütezeit +*gen*
HF *n abbr* (= *high frequency*) HF
HGV (*Brit*) *n abbr* (*Hist*: = *heavy goods vehicle*) Lkw *m*
HI (*US*) *abbr* (*Post*) = *Hawaii*
hi [haɪ] *excl* hallo
hiatus [haɪ'eɪtəs] *n* Unterbrechung *f*
hibernate ['haɪbəneɪt] *vi* Winterschlaf halten *or* machen
hibernation [haɪbə'neɪʃən] *n* Winterschlaf *m*
hiccough ['hɪkʌp] *vi* hicksen
hiccoughs ['hɪkʌps] *npl* Schluckauf *m*; **to have (the) ~** den Schluckauf haben
hiccup ['hɪkʌp] *vi* = **hiccough**
hiccups ['hɪkʌps] *npl* = **hiccoughs**
hick [hɪk] (*US: inf*) *n* Hinterwäldler *m*
hid [hɪd] *pt of* **hide**

hidden ['hɪdn] *pp of* **hide** ▷ *adj* (*advantage, danger*) unsichtbar; (*place*) versteckt; **there are no ~ extras** es gibt keine versteckten Extrakosten
hide [haɪd] (*pt* **hid**, *pp* **hidden**) *n* Haut *f*, Fell *nt*; (*of birdwatcher etc*) Versteck *nt* ▷ *vt* verstecken; (*feeling, information*) verbergen; (*obscure*) verdecken ▷ *vi*: **to ~ (from sb)** sich (vor jdm) verstecken; **to ~ sth (from sb)** etw (vor jdm) verstecken
hide-and-seek ['haɪdən'si:k] *n* Versteckspiel *nt*; **to play ~** Verstecken spielen
hideaway ['haɪdəweɪ] *n* Zufluchtsort *m*
hideous ['hɪdɪəs] *adj* scheußlich; (*conditions*) furchtbar
hideously ['hɪdɪəslɪ] *adv* furchtbar
hide-out ['haɪdaut] *n* Versteck *nt*
hiding ['haɪdɪŋ] *n* Tracht *f* Prügel; **to be in ~** (*concealed*) sich versteckt halten
hiding place *n* Versteck *nt*
hierarchy ['haɪərɑ:kɪ] *n* Hierarchie *f*
hieroglyphics [haɪərə'glɪfɪks] *npl* Hieroglyphen *pl*
hi-fi ['haɪfaɪ] *n abbr* (= *high fidelity*) Hi-Fi *nt* ▷ *adj* (*equipment etc*) Hi-Fi-
higgledy-piggledy ['hɪgldɪ'pɪgldɪ] *adj* durcheinander
high [haɪ] *adj* hoch; (*wind*) stark; (*risk*) groß; (*quality*) gut; (*inf: on drugs*) high; (*: on drink*) blau; (*Brit: food*) schlecht; (*: game*) anbrüchig ▷ *adv* hoch ▷ *n*: **exports have reached a new ~** der Export hat einen neuen Höchststand erreicht; **to pay a ~ price for sth** etw teuer bezahlen; **it's ~ time you did it** es ist *or* wird höchste Zeit, dass du es machst; **~ in the air** hoch oben in der Luft
highball ['haɪbɔ:l] (*US*) *n* Highball *m*
highboy ['haɪbɔɪ] (*US*) *n* hohe Kommode *f*
highbrow ['haɪbrau] *adj* intellektuell; (*book, discussion etc*) anspruchsvoll
highchair ['haɪtʃɛəʳ] *n* Hochstuhl *m*
high-class ['haɪ'klɑ:s] *adj* erstklassig; (*neighbourhood*) vornehm

HIGH COURT

High Court ist in England und Wales die Kurzform für „High Court of Justice" und bildet zusammen mit dem Berufungsgericht den Obersten Gerichtshof. In Schottland ist es die Kurzform für „High Court of Justiciary", das höchste Strafgericht in Schottland, das in Edinburgh und anderen Großstädten (immer mit Richter und Geschworenen) zusammentritt und für Verbrechen wie Mord, Vergewaltigung und Hochverrat zuständig ist. Weniger schwere Verbrechen werden vor dem „sheriff court" verhandelt und leichtere Vergehen vor dem „district court".

higher ['haɪəʳ] *adj* (*form of study, life etc*) höher (entwickelt) ▷ *adv* höher ▷ *n* (*Scot: Scol*): **H~** *mit „Higher" wird die vorgeschrittenenstufe des „Scottish certificate of education" und auch der Abschluss dieses Ausbildungsjahr bezeichnet*
higher education *n* Hochschulbildung *f*
highfalutin [haɪfə'lu:tɪn] (*inf*) *adj* hochtrabend
high finance *n* Hochfinanz *f*
high-flier, high-flyer [haɪ'flaɪəʳ] *n* Senkrechtstarter(in) *m(f)*
high-flying [haɪ'flaɪɪŋ] *adj* (*person*) erfolgreich; (*lifestyle*) exklusiv
high-handed [haɪ'hændɪd] *adj* eigenmächtig
high-heeled [haɪ'hi:ld] *adj* hochhackig
high heels *npl* hochhackige Schuhe *pl*
high jump *n* Hochsprung *m*
Highlands ['haɪləndz] *npl*: **the ~** das Hochland
high-level ['haɪlɛvl] *adj* (*talks etc*) auf höchster Ebene; **~ language** (*Comput*) höhere Programmiersprache *f*
highlight ['haɪlaɪt] *n* (*of event*) Höhepunkt *m*; (*in hair*) Strähnchen *nt* ▷ *vt* (*problem, need*) ein Schlaglicht werfen auf *+acc*
highlighter ['haɪlaɪtəʳ] *n* Textmarker *m*
highly ['haɪlɪ] *adv* hoch-; **to speak ~ of** sich sehr positiv äußern über *+acc*; **to think ~ of** eine hohe Meinung haben von
highly strung *adj* nervös
High Mass *n* Hochamt *nt*
highness ['haɪnɪs] *n*: **Her/His/Your H~** Ihre/Seine/Eure Hoheit *f*
high-pitched [haɪ'pɪtʃt] *adj* hoch
high point *n* Höhepunkt *m*
high-powered ['haɪ'pauəd] *adj* (*engine*) Hochleistungs-; (*job*) Spitzen-; (*businessman*) dynamisch; (*person*) äußerst fähig; (*course*) anspruchsvoll
high-pressure ['haɪprɛʃəʳ] *adj* (*area, system*) Hochdruck-; (*inf: sales technique*) aggressiv
high-rise ['haɪraɪz] *adj* (*apartment, block*) Hochhaus-; **~ building/flats** Hochhaus *nt*
high school *n* ≈ Oberschule *f*

HIGH SCHOOL

High school ist eine weiterführende Schule in den USA. Man unterscheidet zwischen „junior high school" (im Anschluss an die Grundschule, umfasst das 7., 8. und 9. Schuljahr) und „senior high school" (10., 11. und 12. Schuljahr, mit akademischen und berufsbezogenen Fächern). Weiterführende Schulen in Großbritannien werden manchmal auch als high school bezeichnet. Siehe auch *„elementary school"*.

high season (*Brit*) *n* Hochsaison *f*
high spirits *npl* Hochstimmung *f*
high street (*Brit*) *n* Hauptstraße *f*
high strung (*US*) *adj* = **highly strung**
high tide *n* Flut *f*
highway ['haɪweɪ] (*US*) *n* Straße *f*; (*between towns, states*) Landstraße *f*; **information ~** Datenautobahn *f*

Highway Code (*Brit*) *n* Straßenverkehrsordnung *f*
highwayman ['haɪweɪmən] (*irreg: like* **man**) *n* Räuber *m*, Wegelagerer *m*
hijack ['haɪdʒæk] *vt* entführen ▷ *n* (*also*: **hijacking**) Entführung *f*
hijacker ['haɪdʒækəʳ] *n* Entführer(in) *m(f)*
hike [haɪk] *vi* wandern ▷ *n* Wanderung *f*; (*inf: in prices etc*) Erhöhung *f* ▷ *vt* (*inf*) erhöhen
hiker ['haɪkəʳ] *n* Wanderer *m*, Wanderin *f*
hiking ['haɪkɪŋ] *n* Wandern *nt*
hilarious [hɪ'lɛərɪəs] *adj* urkomisch
hilarity [hɪ'lærɪtɪ] *n* übermütige Ausgelassenheit *f*
hill [hɪl] *n* Hügel *m*; (*fairly high*) Berg *m*; (*slope*) Hang *m*; (*on road*) Steigung *f*
hillbilly ['hɪlbɪlɪ] (*US*) *n* Hillbilly *m*; (*pej*) Hinterwäldler(in) *m(f)*, Landpomeranze *f*
hillock ['hɪlək] *n* Hügel *m*, Anhöhe *f*
hillside ['hɪlsaɪd] *n* Hang *m*
hill start *n* (*Aut*) Anfahren *nt* am Berg
hilltop ['hɪltɔp] *n* Gipfel *m*
hill walking *n* Bergwandern *nt*
hilly ['hɪlɪ] *adj* hügelig
hilt [hɪlt] *n* (*of sword, knife*) Heft *nt*; **to the ~** voll und ganz
him [hɪm] *pron* ihn; (*indirect*) ihm; *see also* **me**
Himalayas [hɪmə'leɪəz] *npl*: **the ~** der Himalaja
himself [hɪm'sɛlf] *pron* sich; (*emphatic*) (er) selbst; *see also* **oneself**
hind [haɪnd] *adj* (*legs*) Hinter- ▷ *n* (*female deer*) Hirschkuh *f*
hinder ['hɪndəʳ] *vt* behindern; **to ~ sb from doing sth** jdn daran hindern, etw zu tun
hindquarters ['haɪnd'kwɔːtəz] *npl* Hinterteil *nt*
hindrance ['hɪndrəns] *n* Behinderung *f*
hindsight ['haɪndsaɪt] *n*: **with ~** im Nachhinein
Hindu ['hɪnduː] *adj* hinduistisch, Hindu-
hinge [hɪndʒ] *n* (*on door*) Angel *f* ▷ *vi*: **to ~ on** anhängen von
hint [hɪnt] *n* Andeutung *f*; (*advice*) Tipp *m*; (*sign, glimmer*) Spur *f* ▷ *vt*: **to ~ that** andeuten, dass ▷ *vi*: **to ~ at** andeuten; **to drop a ~** eine Andeutung machen; **give me a ~** geben Sie mir einen Hinweis; **white with a ~ of pink** weiß mit einem Hauch von Rosa
hip [hɪp] *n* Hüfte *f*
hip flask *n* Taschenflasche *f*, Flachmann *m* (*inf*)
hip-hop ['hɪphɔp] *n* Hip-Hop *nt*
hippie ['hɪpɪ] *n* Hippie *m*
hippo ['hɪpəu] *n* Nilpferd *nt*
hip pocket *n* Gesäßtasche *f*
hippopotamus [hɪpə'pɔtəməs] (*pl* **~es** *or* **hippopotami**) *n* Nilpferd *nt*
hippy ['hɪpɪ] *n* = **hippie**
hire ['haɪəʳ] *vt* (*Brit*) mieten; (*worker*) einstellen ▷ *n* (*Brit*) Mieten *nt*; **for ~** (*taxi*) frei; (*boat*) zu vermieten; **on ~** gemietet
▸ **hire out** *vt* vermieten
hire car, **hired car** (*Brit*) *n* Mietwagen *m*, Leihwagen *m*
hire-purchase [haɪə'pəːtʃɪs] (*Brit*) *n* Ratenkauf *m*; **to buy sth on ~** etw auf Raten kaufen
his [hɪz] *pron* seine(r, s) ▷ *adj* sein; *see also* **my; mine²**
hiss [hɪs] *vi* zischen; (*cat*) fauchen ▷ *n* Zischen *nt*; (*of cat*) Fauchen *nt*
histogram ['hɪstəgræm] *n* Histogramm *nt*
historian [hɪ'stɔːrɪən] *n* Historiker(in) *m(f)*
historic [hɪ'stɔrɪk] *adj* historisch
historical [hɪ'stɔrɪkl] *adj* historisch
history ['hɪstərɪ] *n* Geschichte *f*; **there's a ~ of heart disease in his family** Herzleiden liegen bei ihm in der Familie; **medical ~** Krankengeschichte *f*
hit [hɪt] (*pt, pp* **~**) *vt* schlagen; (*reach, affect*) treffen; (*vehicle: another vehicle*) zusammenstoßen mit; (*: wall, tree*) fahren gegen; (*: more violently*) prallen gegen; (*: person*) anfahren ▷ *n* Schlag *m*; (*success*) Erfolg *m*; (*song*) Hit *m*; **to ~ it off with sb** sich gut mit jdm verstehen; **to ~ the headlines** Schlagzeilen machen; **to ~ the road** (*inf*) sich auf den Weg *or* die Socken (*inf*) machen; **to ~ the roof** (*inf*) an die Decke *or* in die Luft gehen
▸ **hit back** *vi*: **to ~ back at sb** jdn zurückschlagen; (*fig*) jdm Kontra geben
▸ **hit out at** *vt fus* auf jdn losschlagen; (*fig*) jdn scharf angreifen
▸ **hit (up)on** *vt fus* stoßen auf +*acc*, finden
hit-and-miss ['hɪtən'mɪs] *adj* = **hit-or-miss**
hit-and-run driver ['hɪtən'rʌn-] *n* unfallflüchtiger Fahrer *m*, unfallflüchtige Fahrerin *f*
hitch [hɪtʃ] *vt* festmachen, anbinden; (*also*: **hitch up**: *trousers, skirt*) hochziehen ▷ *n* Schwierigkeit *f*, Problem *nt*; **to ~ a lift** trampen, per Anhalter fahren; **technical ~** technische Panne *f*
▸ **hitch up** *vt* anspannen; *see also* **hitch**
hitchhike ['hɪtʃhaɪk] *vi* trampen, per Anhalter fahren
hitchhiker ['hɪtʃhaɪkəʳ] *n* Tramper(in) *m(f)*, Anhalter(in) *m(f)*
hi-tech ['haɪ'tɛk] *adj* Hightech-, hoch technisiert ▷ *n* Hightech *nt*, Hochtechnologie *f*
hitherto [hɪðə'tuː] *adv* bisher, bis jetzt
hit list *n* Abschussliste *f*
hit man (*inf*) *n* Killer *m*
hit-or-miss ['hɪtə'mɪs] *adj* ungeplant; **to be a ~ affair** eine unsichere Sache sein; **it's ~ whether ...** es ist nicht zu sagen, ob ...
hit parade *n* Hitparade *f*
hits counter *n* (*on website*) Zugriffs- *or* Besucherzähler *m*, Counter *m*
HIV *n abbr* (= *human immunodeficiency virus*) HIV; **~-negative** HIV-negativ; **~-positive** HIV-positiv
hive [haɪv] *n* Bienenkorb *m*; **to be a ~ of activity** einem Bienenhaus gleichen
▸ **hive off** (*inf*) *vt* ausgliedern, abspalten
hl *abbr* (= *hectolitre*) hl
HM *abbr* (= *His/Her Majesty*) S./I.M.
HMG (*Brit*) *abbr* (= *His/Her Majesty's Government*)

die Regierung Seiner/Ihrer Majestät

HMI (*Brit*) *n abbr* (*Scol*: = *His/Her Majesty's Inspector*) *regierungsamtlicher Schulaufsichtsbeauftragter*

HMO (*US*) *n abbr* (= *Health Maintenance Organization*) *Organisation zur Gesundheitsfürsorge*

HMS (*Brit*) *abbr* (= *His* (*or Her*) *Majesty's Ship*) *Namensteil von Schiffen der Kriegsmarine*

HNC (*Brit*) *n abbr* (= *Higher National Certificate*) *Berufsschulabschluss*

HND (*Brit*) *n abbr* (= *Higher National Diploma*) *Qualifikationsnachweis in technischen Fächern*

hoard [hɔːd] *n* (*of food*) Vorrat *m*; (*of money, treasure*) Schatz *m* ▷ *vt* (*food*) hamstern; (*money*) horten

hoarding ['hɔːdɪŋ] (*Brit*) *n* Plakatwand *f*

hoarfrost ['hɔːfrɔst] *n* (Rau)reif *m*

hoarse [hɔːs] *adj* heiser

hoax [həuks] *n* (*false alarm*) blinder Alarm *m*

hob [hɔb] *n* Kochmulde *f*

hobble ['hɔbl] *vi* humpeln

hobby ['hɔbɪ] *n* Hobby *nt*, Steckenpferd *nt*

hobbyhorse ['hɔbɪhɔːs] *n* (*fig*) Lieblingsthema *nt*

hobnail boot ['hɔbneɪl-] *n* Nagelschuh *m*

hobnob ['hɔbnɔb] *vi*: **to ~ with** auf Du und Du stehen mit

hobo ['həubəu] (*US*) *n* Penner *m* (*inf*)

hock [hɔk] *n* (*Brit*) weißer Rheinwein *m*; (*of animal*) Sprunggelenk *nt*; (*US*: *Culin*) Gelenkstück *nt*; (*inf*): **to be in ~** (*person*: *in debt*) in Schulden stecken; (*object*) verpfändet *or* im Leihhaus sein

hockey ['hɔkɪ] *n* Hockey *nt*

hocus-pocus ['həukəs'pəukəs] *n* Hokuspokus *m*; (*trickery*) faule Tricks *pl*; (*jargon*) Jargon *m*

hod [hɔd] *n* (*for bricks etc*) Tragemulde *f*

hodgepodge ['hɔdʒpɔdʒ] (*US*) *n* = **hotchpotch**

hoe [həu] *n* Hacke *f* ▷ *vt* hacken

hog [hɔg] *n* (Mast)schwein *nt* ▷ *vt* (*road*) für sich beanspruchen; (*telephone etc*) in Beschlag nehmen; **to go the whole ~** Nägel mit Köpfen machen

Hogmanay [hɔgmə'neɪ] (*Scot*) *n* Silvester *nt*

hogwash ['hɔgwɔʃ] (*inf*) *n* (*nonsense*) Quatsch *m*

ho hum ['həu'hʌm] *interj* na gut

hoist [hɔɪst] *n* Hebevorrichtung *f* ▷ *vt* hochheben; (*flag, sail*) hissen

hoity-toity [hɔɪtɪ'tɔɪtɪ] (*inf*: *pej*) *adj* hochnäsig

hold [həuld] (*pt, pp* **held**) *vt* halten; (*contain*) enthalten; (*power, qualification*) haben; (*opinion*) vertreten; (*meeting*) abhalten; (*conversation*) führen; (*prisoner, hostage*) festhalten ▷ *vi* halten; (*be valid*) gelten; (*weather*) sich halten ▷ *n* (*grasp*) Griff *m*; (*of ship, plane*) Laderaum *m*; **to ~ one's head up** den Kopf hochhalten; **to ~ sb responsible/liable** *etc* jdn verantwortlich/haftbar *etc* machen; **~ the line!** (*Tel*) bleiben Sie am Apparat!; **~ it!** Moment mal!; **to ~ one's own** sich behaupten; **he ~s the view that ...** er ist der Meinung *or* er vertritt die Ansicht, dass ...; **to ~ firm** *or* **fast** halten; **~ still!, ~ steady!** stillhalten!; **his luck held** das Glück blieb ihm treu; **I don't ~ with ...** ich bin gegen ...; **to catch** *or* **get (a) ~ of** sich festhalten an *+dat*; **to get ~ of** (*fig*) finden, auftreiben; **to get ~ of o.s.** sich in den Griff bekommen; **to have a ~ over** in der Hand haben

▸ **hold back** *vt* zurückhalten; (*tears, laughter*) unterdrücken; (*secret*) verbergen; (*information*) geheim halten

▸ **hold down** *vt* niederhalten; (*job*) sich halten in *+dat*

▸ **hold forth** *vi*: **to ~ forth (about)** sich ergehen *or* sich auslassen (über *+acc*)

▸ **hold off** *vt* abwehren ▷ *vi*: **if the rain ~s off** wenn es nicht regnet

▸ **hold on** *vi* sich festhalten; (*wait*) warten; **~ on!** (*Tel*) einen Moment bitte!

▸ **hold on to** *vt fus* sich festhalten an; (*keep*) behalten

▸ **hold out** *vt* (*hand*) ausstrecken; (*hope*) haben; (*prospect*) bieten ▷ *vi* nicht nachgeben

▸ **hold over** *vt* vertagen

▸ **hold up** *vt* hochheben; (*support*) stützen; (*delay*) aufhalten; (*rob*) überfallen

holdall ['həuldɔːl] (*Brit*) *n* Tasche *f*; (*for clothes*) Reisetasche *f*

holder ['həuldəʳ] *n* Halter *m*; (*of ticket, record, office, title etc*) Inhaber(in) *m(f)*

holding ['həuldɪŋ] *n* (*share*) Anteil *m*; (*small farm*) Gut *nt* ▷ *adj* (*operation, tactic*) zur Schadensbegrenzung

holding company *n* Dachgesellschaft *f*, Holdinggesellschaft *f*

hold-up ['həuldʌp] *n* bewaffneter Raubüberfall *m*; (*delay*) Verzögerung *f*; (*Brit*: *in traffic*) Stockung *f*

hole [həul] *n* Loch *nt*; (*unpleasant town*) Kaff *nt* (*inf*) ▷ *vt* (*ship*) leckschlagen; (*building etc*) durchlöchern; **~ in the heart** Loch im Herz(en); **to pick ~s** (*fig*) (über)kritisch sein; **to pick ~s in sth** (*fig*) an etw *dat* herumkritisieren

▸ **hole up** *vi* sich verkriechen

holiday ['hɔlɪdeɪ] *n* (*Brit*) Urlaub *m*; (*Scol*) Ferien *pl*; (*day off*) freier Tag *m*; (*also*: **public holiday**) Feiertag *m*; **on ~** im Urlaub, in den Ferien

holiday camp (*Brit*) *n* (*also*: **holiday centre**) Feriendorf *nt*

holiday-maker ['hɔlɪdɪmeɪkəʳ] (*Brit*) *n* Urlauber(in) *m(f)*

holiday pay *n* *Lohn-/Gehaltsfortzahlung während des Urlaubs*

holiday resort *n* Ferienort *m*

holiday season *n* Urlaubszeit *f*

holiness ['həulɪnɪs] *n* Heiligkeit *f*

holistic [həu'lɪstɪk] *adj* holistisch

Holland ['hɔlənd] *n* Holland *nt*

holler ['hɔləʳ] (*inf*) *vi* brüllen ▷ *n* Schrei *m*

hollow ['hɔləu] *adj* hohl; (*eyes*) tief liegend; (*laugh*) unecht; (*sound*) dumpf; (*fig*) leer; (: *victory, opinion*) wertlos ▷ *n* Vertiefung *f* ▷ *vt*: **to ~ out** aushöhlen

holly ['hɔlɪ] *n* Stechpalme *f*, Ilex *m*; (*leaves*) Stechpalmenzweige *pl*

hollyhock ['hɔlɪhɔk] *n* Malve *f*
holocaust ['hɔləkɔːst] *n* Inferno *nt*; (*in Third Reich*) Holocaust *m*
hologram ['hɔləgræm] *n* Hologramm *nt*
hols [hɔlz] (*inf*) *npl* Ferien *pl*
holster ['həulstəʳ] *n* Pistolenhalfter *m or nt*
holy ['həulɪ] *adj* heilig
Holy Communion *n* heilige Kommunion *f*
Holy Father *n* Heiliger Vater *m*
Holy Ghost *n* Heiliger Geist *m*
Holy Land *n*: **the ~** das Heilige Land
holy orders *npl* Priesterweihe *f*
Holy Spirit *n* Heiliger Geist *m*
homage ['hɔmɪdʒ] *n* Huldigung *f*; **to pay ~ to** huldigen *+dat*
home [həum] *n* Heim *nt*; (*house, flat*) Zuhause *nt*; (*area, country*) Heimat *f*; (*institution*) Anstalt *f* ▷ *cpd* Heim-; (*Econ, Pol*) Innen- ▷ *adv* (*go etc*) nach Hause, heim; **at ~** zu Hause (*Österr, Schweiz*); (*in country*) im Inland; **to be** *or* **feel at ~** (*fig*) sich wohlfühlen; **make yourself at ~** machen Sie es sich *dat* gemütlich *or* bequem; **to make one's ~ somewhere** sich irgendwo niederlassen; **the ~ of free enterprise/jazz** *etc* die Heimat des freien Unternehmertums/Jazz *etc*; **when will you be ~?** wann bist du wieder zu Hause?; **a ~ from home** ein zweites Zuhause *nt*; **~ and dry** aus dem Schneider; **to drive a nail ~** einen Nagel einschlagen; **to bring sth ~ to sb** jdm etw klarmachen
▶ **home in on** *vt fus* (*missiles*) sich ausrichten auf *+acc*
home address *n* Heimatanschrift *f*
home-brew [həum'bruː] *n* selbst gebrautes Bier *nt*
homecoming ['həumkʌmɪŋ] *n* Heimkehr *f*
home computer *n* Heimcomputer *m*
Home Counties (*Brit*) *npl*: **the ~** *die Grafschaften, die an London angrenzen*
home economics *n* Hauswirtschaft(slehre) *f*
home ground *n* (*Sport*) eigener Platz *m*; **to be on ~** (*fig*) sich auf vertrautem Terrain bewegen
home-grown ['həumgrəun] *adj* (*not foreign*) einheimisch; (*from garden*) selbst gezogen
home help *n* Haushaltshilfe *f*
homeland ['həumlænd] *n* Heimat *f*, Heimatland *nt*
homeless ['həumlɪs] *adj* obdachlos; (*refugee*) heimatlos
home loan *n* Hypothek *f*
homely ['həumlɪ] *adj* einfach; (*US: plain*) unscheinbar
home-made [həum'meɪd] *adj* selbst gemacht
Home Office (*Brit*) *n* Innenministerium *nt*
homeopath ['həumɪəupæθ] (*US*) *n* = **homoeopath**
homeopathy [həumɪ'ɔpəθɪ] (*US*) *n* = **homoeopathy**
home page *n* (*Comput*) Homepage *f*
home rule *n* Selbstbestimmung *f*, Selbstverwaltung *f*
Home Secretary (*Brit*) *n* Innenminister(in) *m(f)*
homesick ['həumsɪk] *adj* heimwehkrank; **to be ~** Heimweh haben
homestead ['həumstɛd] *n* Heimstätte *f*; (*farm*) Gehöft *nt*
home town *n* Heimatstadt *f*
home truth *n* bittere Wahrheit *f*; **to tell sb some ~s** jdm deutlich die Meinung sagen
homeward ['həumwəd] *adj* (*journey*) Heim- ▷ *adv* = **homewards**
homewards ['həumwədz] *adv* nach Hause, heim
homework ['həumwəːk] *n* Hausaufgaben *pl*
homicidal [hɔmɪ'saɪdl] *adj* gemeingefährlich
homicide ['hɔmɪsaɪd] (*US*) *n* Mord *m*
homily ['hɔmɪlɪ] *n* Predigt *f*
homing ['həumɪŋ] *adj* (*device, missile*) mit Zielsucheinrichtung; **~ pigeon** Brieftaube *f*
homoeopath, (*US*) **homeopath** ['həumɪəupæθ] *n* Homöopath(in) *m(f)*
homoeopathy, (*US*) **homeopathy** [həumɪ'ɔpəθɪ] *n* Homöopathie *f*
homogeneous [hɔməu'dʒiːnɪəs] *adj* homogen
homogenize [hə'mɔdʒənaɪz] *vt* homogenisieren
homosexual [hɔməu'sɛksjuəl] *adj* homosexuell ▷ *n* Homosexuelle(r) *f(m)*
Hon. *abbr* = **honourable; honorary**
Honduras [hɔn'djuərəs] *n* Honduras *nt*
hone [həun] *n* Schleifstein *m* ▷ *vt* schleifen; (*fig: groom*) erziehen
honest ['ɔnɪst] *adj* ehrlich; (*trustworthy*) redlich; (*sincere*) aufrichtig; **to be quite ~ with you ...** um ehrlich zu sein, ...
honestly ['ɔnɪstlɪ] *adv* (*see adj*) ehrlich; redlich; aufrichtig
honesty ['ɔnɪstɪ] *n* (*see adj*) Ehrlichkeit *f*; Redlichkeit *f*; Aufrichtigkeit *f*
honey ['hʌnɪ] *n* Honig *m*; (*US: inf*) Schätzchen *nt*
honeycomb ['hʌnɪkəum] *n* Bienenwabe *f*; (*pattern*) Wabe *f* ▷ *vt*: **to ~ with** durchlöchern mit
honeymoon ['hʌnɪmuːn] *n* Flitterwochen *pl*; (*trip*) Hochzeitsreise *f*
honeysuckle ['hʌnɪsʌkl] *n* Geißblatt *nt*
Hong Kong ['hɔŋ'kɔŋ] *n* Hongkong *nt*
honk [hɔŋk] *vi* (*Aut*) hupen
Honolulu [hɔnə'luːluː] *n* Honolulu *nt*
honor *etc* ['ɔnəʳ] (*US*) = **honour** *etc*
honorary ['ɔnərərɪ] *adj* ehrenamtlich; (*title, degree*) Ehren-
honour, (*US*) **honor** ['ɔnəʳ] *vt* ehren; (*commitment, promise*) stehen zu ▷ *n* Ehre *f*; (*tribute*) Auszeichnung *f*; **in ~ of** zu Ehren von *or +gen*
honourable ['ɔnərəbl] *adj* (*person*) ehrenwert; (*action, defeat*) ehrenvoll
honour-bound ['ɔnə'baund] *adj*: **to be ~ to do sth** moralisch verpflichtet sein, etw zu tun
honours degree ['ɔnəz-] *n akademischer Grad mit*

Prüfung im Spezialfach; siehe Info-Artikel

HONOURS DEGREE

Honours degree ist ein Universitätsabschluss mit einer guten Note, also der Note I (first class), II:1 (upper second class), II:2 (lower second class), oder III (third class). Wer ein honours degree erhalten hat, darf die Abkürzung *Hons* nach seinem Namen und Titel führen, z. B. Mary Smith MA Hons. Heute sind fast alle Universitätsabschlusse in Großbritannien honours degrees. Siehe auch *ordinary degree*.

honours list *n Liste verliehener/zu verleihender Ehrentitel; siehe Info-Artikel*

HONOURS LIST

Honours list ist eine Liste von Adelstiteln und Orden, die der britische Monarch zweimal jährlich (zu Neujahr und am offiziellen Geburtstag des Monarchen) an Bürger in Großbritannien und im Commonwealth verleiht. Die Liste wird vom Premierminister zusammengestellt, aber drei Orden (der Hosenbandorden, der Verdienstorden und der Victoria-Orden) werden vom Monarchen persönlich vergeben. Erfolgreiche Geschäftsleute, Militärangehörige, Sportler und andere Prominente, aber auch im sozialen Bereich besonders aktive Bürger werden auf diese Weise geehrt.

Hons. *abbr* (*Univ*) = **Honours degree**
hood [hud] *n* (*of coat etc*) Kapuze *f*; (*of cooker*) Abzugshaube *f*; (*Aut: Brit: folding roof*) Verdeck *nt*; (*: US: bonnet*) (Motor)haube *f*
hooded ['hudɪd] *adj* maskiert; (*jacket etc*) mit Kapuze
hoodlum ['hu:dləm] *n* Gangster *m*
hoodwink ['hudwɪŋk] *vt* (he)reinlegen
hoof [hu:f] (*pl* **hooves**) *n* Huf *m*
hook [huk] *n* Haken *m* ▷ *vt* festhaken; (*fish*) an die Angel bekommen; **by ~ or by crook** auf Biegen und Brechen; **to be ~ed on** (*inf: film, exhibition, etc*) fasziniert sein von; (*: drugs*) abhängig sein von; (*: person*) stehen auf *+acc*
▶ **hook up** *vt* (*Radio, TV etc*) anschließen
hook and eye (*pl* **hooks and eyes**) *n* Haken und Öse *pl*
hooligan ['hu:lɪgən] *n* Rowdy *m*
hooliganism ['hu:lɪgənɪzəm] *n* Rowdytum *nt*
hoop [hu:p] *n* Reifen *m*; (*for croquet: arch*) Tor *nt*
hooray [hu:'reɪ] *excl* = **hurrah**
hoot [hu:t] *vi* hupen; (*siren*) heulen; (*owl*) schreien, rufen; (*person*) johlen ▷ *vt* (*horn*) drücken auf *+acc* ▷ *n* (*see vi*) Hupen *nt*; Heulen *nt*; Schreien *nt*, Rufen *nt*; Johlen *nt*; **to ~ with laughter** in johlendes Gelächter ausbrechen
hooter ['hu:tə^r] *n* (*Brit: Aut*) Hupe *f*; (*Naut, of factory*) Sirene *f*
Hoover® ['hu:və^r] (*Brit*) *n* Staubsauger *m* ▷ *vt*: **hoover** (*carpet*) saugen
hooves [hu:vz] *npl of* **hoof**
hop [hɔp] *vi* hüpfen ▷ *n* Hüpfer *m*; *see also* **hops**
hope [həup] *vi* hoffen ▷ *n* Hoffnung *f* ▷ *vt*: **to ~ that** hoffen, dass; **I ~ so** ich hoffe es, hoffentlich; **I ~ not** ich hoffe nicht, hoffentlich nicht; **to ~ for the best** das Beste hoffen; **to have no ~ of sth/doing sth** keine Hoffnung auf etw *+acc* haben/darauf haben, etw zu tun; **in the ~ of/that** in der Hoffnung auf/, dass; **to ~ to do sth** hoffen, etw zu tun
hopeful ['həupful] *adj* hoffnungsvoll; (*situation*) vielversprechend; **I'm ~ that she'll manage** ich hoffe, dass sie es schafft
hopefully ['həupfulɪ] *adv* hoffnungsvoll; (*one hopes*) hoffentlich; **~, he'll come back** hoffentlich kommt er wieder
hopeless ['həuplɪs] *adj* hoffnungslos; (*situation*) aussichtslos; (*useless*): **to be ~ at sth** etw überhaupt nicht können
hopper ['hɔpə^r] *n* Einfülltrichter *m*
hops [hɔps] *npl* Hopfen *m*
horde [hɔ:d] *n* Horde *f*
horizon [hə'raɪzn] *n* Horizont *m*
horizontal [hɔrɪ'zɔntl] *adj* horizontal
hormone ['hɔ:məun] *n* Hormon *nt*
hormone replacement therapy *n* Hormonersatztherapie *f*
horn [hɔ:n] *n* Horn *nt*; (*Aut*) Hupe *f*
horned [hɔ:nd] *adj* (*animal*) mit Hörnern
hornet ['hɔ:nɪt] *n* Hornisse *f*
horn-rimmed ['hɔ:n'rɪmd] *adj* (*spectacles*) Horn-
horny ['hɔ:nɪ] (*inf*) *adj* (*aroused*) scharf, geil
horoscope ['hɔrəskəup] *n* Horoskop *nt*
horrendous [hə'rɛndəs] *adj* abscheulich, entsetzlich
horrible ['hɔrɪbl] *adj* fürchterlich, schrecklich; (*scream, dream*) furchtbar
horrid ['hɔrɪd] *adj* entsetzlich, schrecklich
horrific [hɔ'rɪfɪk] *adj* entsetzlich, schrecklich
horrify ['hɔrɪfaɪ] *vt* entsetzen
horrifying ['hɔrɪfaɪɪŋ] *adj* schrecklich, fürchterlich, entsetzlich
horror ['hɔrə^r] *n* Entsetzen *nt*, Grauen *nt*; **~ (of sth)** (*abhorrence*) Abscheu *m* (vor etw *dat*); **the ~s of war** die Schrecken *pl* des Krieges
horror film *n* Horrorfilm *m*
horror-stricken ['hɔrəstrɪkn] *adj* = **horror-struck**
horror-struck ['hɔrəstrʌk] *adj* von Entsetzen *or* Grauen gepackt
hors d'œuvre [ɔ:'də:vrə] *n* Hors d'œuvre *nt*, Vorspeise *f*
horse [hɔ:s] *n* Pferd *nt*
horseback ['hɔ:sbæk]: **on ~** *adj, adv* zu Pferd
horsebox ['hɔ:sbɔks] *n* Pferdetransporter *m*
horse chestnut *n* Rosskastanie *f*
horse-drawn ['hɔ:sdrɔ:n] *adj* von Pferden gezogen
horsefly ['hɔ:sflaɪ] *n* (Pferde)bremse *f*
horseman ['hɔ:smən] (*irreg: like* **man**) *n*

Reiter *m*
horsemanship ['hɔːsmənʃɪp] *n* Reitkunst *f*
horseplay ['hɔːspleɪ] *n* Alberei *f*, Balgerei *f*
horsepower ['hɔːspauəʳ] *n* Pferdestärke *f*
horse racing *n* Pferderennen *nt*
horseradish ['hɔːsrædɪʃ] *n* Meerrettich *m*
horseshoe ['hɔːsʃuː] *n* Hufeisen *nt*
horse show *n* Reitturnier *nt*
horse trading *n* Kuhhandel *m*
horse trials *npl* = **horse show**
horsewhip ['hɔːswɪp] *n* Reitpeitsche *f* ▷ *vt* auspeitschen
horsewoman ['hɔːswumən] (*irreg: like* **woman**) *n* Reiterin *f*
horsey ['hɔːsɪ] *adj* pferdenärrisch; (*appearance*) pferdeähnlich
horticulture ['hɔːtɪkʌltʃəʳ] *n* Gartenbau *m*
hose [həuz] *n* (*also*: **hose pipe**) Schlauch *m*
▸ **hose down** *vt* abspritzen
hosiery ['həuzɪərɪ] *n* Strumpfwaren *pl*
hospice ['hɔspɪs] *n* Pflegeheim *nt* (*für unheilbar Kranke*)
hospitable ['hɔspɪtəbl] *adj* gastfreundlich; (*climate*) freundlich
hospital ['hɔspɪtl] *n* Krankenhaus *nt*; **in ~, in the ~** (US) im Krankenhaus
hospitality [hɔspɪ'tælɪtɪ] *n* Gastfreundschaft *f*
hospitalize ['hɔspɪtəlaɪz] *vt* ins Krankenhaus einweisen
host [həust] *n* Gastgeber *m*; (*Rel*) Hostie *f* ▷ *adj* Gast- ▷ *vt* Gastgeber sein bei; **a ~ of** eine Menge
hostage ['hɔstɪdʒ] *n* Geisel *f*; **to be taken/held ~** als Geisel genommen/festgehalten werden
hostel ['hɔstl] *n* (Wohn)heim *nt*; (*also*: **youth hostel**) Jugendherberge *f*
hostelling ['hɔstlɪŋ] *n*: **to go (youth) ~** in Jugendherbergen übernachten
hostess ['həustɪs] *n* Gastgeberin *f*; (*Brit: also*: **air hostess**) Stewardess *f*; (*in night-club*) Hostess *f*
hostile ['hɔstaɪl] *adj* (*conditions*) ungünstig; (*environment*) unwirtlich; (*person*): **~ (to** *or* **towards)** feindselig (gegenüber +*dat*)
hostility [hɔ'stɪlɪtɪ] *n* Feindseligkeit *f*; **hostilities** *npl* (*fighting*) Feindseligkeiten *pl*
hot [hɔt] *adj* heiß; (*moderately hot*) warm; (*spicy*) scharf; (*temper*) hitzig; **I am** *or* **feel ~** mir ist heiß; **to be ~ on sth** (*knowledgeable etc*) sich gut mit etw auskennen; (*strict*) sehr auf etw *acc* achten
▸ **hot up** (*Brit: inf*) *vi* (*situation*) sich verschärfen *or* zuspitzen; (*party*) in Schwung kommen ▷ *vt* (*pace*) steigern; (*engine*) frisieren
hot air *n* leeres Gerede *nt*
hot-air balloon [hɔt'ɛəʳ-] *n* Heißluftballon *m*
hotbed ['hɔtbɛd] *n* (*fig*) Brutstätte *f*
hot-blooded [hɔt'blʌdɪd] *adj* heißblütig
hotchpotch ['hɔtʃpɔtʃ] (*Brit*) *n* Durcheinander *nt*, Mischmasch *m*
hot dog *n* Hotdog *m or nt*
hotel [həu'tɛl] *n* Hotel *nt*
hotelier [həu'tɛlɪəʳ] *n* Hotelier(in) *m(f)*
hotel industry *n* Hotelgewerbe *nt*
hotel room *n* Hotelzimmer *nt*
hot flash (*US*) *n* = **hot flush**
hot flush *n* (*Med*) Hitzewallung *f*
hotfoot ['hɔtfut] *adv* eilends
hothead ['hɔthɛd] *n* Hitzkopf *m*
hot-headed [hɔt'hɛdɪd] *adj* hitzköpfig
hothouse ['hɔthaus] *n* Treibhaus *nt*
hot line *n* (*Pol*) heißer Draht *m*
hotly ['hɔtlɪ] *adv* (*contest*) heiß; (*speak, deny*) heftig
hotplate ['hɔtpleɪt] *n* Kochplatte *f*
hotpot ['hɔtpɔt] (*Brit*) *n* Fleischeintopf *m*
hot potato (*fig: inf*) *n* heißes Eisen *nt*; **to drop sb like a ~** jdn wie eine heiße Kartoffel fallen lassen
hot seat *n*: **to be in the ~** auf dem Schleudersitz sitzen
hot spot *n* (*fig*) Krisenherd *m*
hot spring *n* heiße Quelle *f*, Thermalquelle *f*
hot stuff *n* große Klasse *f*
hot-tempered ['hɔt'tɛmpəd] *adj* leicht aufbrausend, jähzornig
hot-water bottle [hɔt'wɔːtəʳ-] *n* Wärmflasche *f*
hot-wire (*inf*) *vt* (*car*) kurzschließen
hound [haund] *vt* hetzen, jagen ▷ *n* Jagdhund *m*; **the ~s** die Meute
hour ['auəʳ] *n* Stunde *f*; (*time*) Zeit *f*; **at 60 miles an ~** mit 60 Meilen in der Stunde; **lunch ~** Mittagspause *f*; **to pay sb by the ~** jdn stundenweise bezahlen
hourly ['auəlɪ] *adj* stündlich; (*rate*) Stunden- ▷ *adv* stündlich, jede Stunde; (*soon*) jederzeit
house [haus] *n* Haus *nt*; (*household*) Haushalt *m*; (*dynasty*) Geschlecht *nt*, Haus *nt*; (*Theat: performance*) Vorstellung *f* ▷ *vt* unterbringen; **at my ~** bei mir (zu Hause); **to my ~** zu mir (nach Hause); **on the ~** (*fig*) auf Kosten des Hauses; **the H~ (of Commons)** (*Brit*) das Unterhaus; **the H~ (of Lords)** (*Brit*) das Oberhaus; **the H~ (of Representatives)** (US) das Repräsentantenhaus; *siehe Info-Artikel*
house arrest *n* Hausarrest *m*
houseboat ['hausbəut] *n* Hausboot *nt*
housebound ['hausbaund] *adj* ans Haus gefesselt
housebreaking ['hausbreɪkɪŋ] *n* Einbruch *m*
house-broken ['hausbrəukn] (US) *adj* = **house-trained**
housecoat ['hauskəut] *n* Morgenrock *m*
household ['haushəuld] *n* Haushalt *m*; **to be a ~ name** ein Begriff sein
householder ['haushəuldəʳ] *n* Hausinhaber(in) *m(f)*; (*of flat*) Wohnungsinhaber(in) *m(f)*
house-hunting ['haushʌntɪŋ] *n*: **to go ~** nach einem Haus suchen
housekeeper ['hauskiːpəʳ] *n* Haushälterin *f*
housekeeping ['hauskiːpɪŋ] *n* Hauswirtschaft *f*; (*money*) Haushaltsgeld *nt*, Wirtschaftsgeld *nt*
houseman ['hausmən] (*Brit: irreg: like* **man**) *n*

(*Med*) Assistenzarzt *m*, Assistenzärztin *f*

HOUSE OF COMMONS

Das *House of Commons* ist das Unterhaus des britischen Parlaments, mit 651 Abgeordneten, die in Wahlkreisen in allgemeiner Wahl gewählt werden. Das Unterhaus hat die Regierungsgewalt inne und tagt etwa 175 Tage im Jahr unter Vorsitz des Sprechers. Als *House of Lords* wird das Oberhaus des britischen Parlaments bezeichnet. Die Mitglieder sind nicht gewählt, sondern werden auf Lebenszeit ernannt („life peers") oder sie haben ihren Oberhaussitz geerbt („hereditary peers"). Das *House of Lords* setzt sich aus Kirchenmännern und Adeligen zusammen („Lords Spiritual/Temporal"). Es hat im Grunde keine Regierungsgewalt, kann aber vom Unterhaus erlassene Gesetze abändern und ist das oberste Berufungsgericht in Großbritannien (außer Schottland).

HOUSE OF REPRESENTATIVES

Das *House of Representatives* bildet zusammen mit dem Senat die amerikanische gesetzgebende Versammlung (den Kongress). Es besteht aus 435 Abgeordneten, die entsprechend den Bevölkerungszahlen auf die einzelnen Bundesstaaten verteilt sind und jeweils für 2 Jahre direkt vom Volk gewählt werden. Es tritt im „Capitol" in Washington zusammen. Siehe auch „Congress".

house owner *n* Hausbesitzer(in) *m(f)*
house party *n* mehrtägige Einladung *f*; (*people*) Gesellschaft *f*
house plant *n* Zimmerpflanze *f*
house-proud ['hauspraud] *adj* auf Ordnung und Sauberkeit im Haushalt bedacht
house-to-house ['haustə'haus] *adj* von Haus zu Haus
house-trained ['haustreɪnd] (*Brit*) *adj* (*animal*) stubenrein
house-warming ['hauswɔ:mɪŋ], **house-warming party** *n* Einzugsparty *f*
housewife ['hauswaɪf] (*irreg: like* **wife**) *n* Hausfrau *f*
housework ['hauswə:k] *n* Hausarbeit *f*
housing ['hauzɪŋ] *n* Wohnungen *pl*; (*provision*) Wohnungsbeschaffung *f* ▷ *cpd* Wohnungs-
housing association *n* Wohnungsbaugesellschaft *f*
housing benefit *n* ≈ Wohngeld *nt*
housing conditions *npl* Wohnbedingungen *pl*, Wohnverhältnisse *pl*
housing development *n* (Wohn)siedlung *f*
housing estate *n* (Wohn)siedlung *f*
hovel ['hɔvl] *n* (armselige) Hütte *f*
hover ['hɔvə^r] *vi* schweben; (*person*) herumstehen; **to ~ round sb** jdm nicht von der Seite weichen
hovercraft ['hɔvəkrɑ:ft] *n* Hovercraft *nt*, Luftkissenfahrzeug *nt*
hoverport ['hɔvəpɔ:t] *n* Anlegestelle *f* für Hovercrafts

KEYWORD

how [hau] *adv* **1** (*in what way*) wie; **how was the film?** wie war der Film?; **how is school?** was macht die Schule?; **how are you?** wie geht es Ihnen?
2 (*to what degree*): **how much milk?** wie viel Milch?; **how many people?** wie viele Leute?; **how long have you been here?** wie lange sind Sie schon hier?; **how old are you?** wie alt bist du?; **how lovely/awful!** wie schön/furchtbar!

however [hau'ɛvə^r] *conj* jedoch, aber ▷ *adv* wie ... auch; (*in questions*) wie ... bloß *or* nur
howl [haul] *vi* heulen; (*animal*) jaulen; (*baby, person*) schreien ▷ *n* (*see vb*) Heulen *nt*; Jaulen *nt*; Schreien *nt*
howler ['haulə^r] (*inf*) *n* (*mistake*) Schnitzer *m*
howling ['haulɪŋ] *adj* (*wind, gale*) heulend
HP (*Brit*) *n abbr* = **hire-purchase**
h.p. *abbr* (*Aut*: = *horsepower*) PS
HQ *abbr* = **headquarters**
HR (*US*) *n abbr* (*Pol*: = *House of Representatives*) Repräsentantenhaus *nt*; = *Human Resources*
hr *abbr* (= *hour*) Std.
HRH (*Brit*) *abbr* (= *His/Her Royal Highness*) Seine/Ihre Königliche Hoheit
hrs *abbr* (= *hours*) Std.
HST (*US*) *abbr* (= *Hawaiian Standard Time*) *Normalzeit in Hawaii*
HTML (*Comput*) *abbr* (= *hypertext markup language*) HTML *f*
hub [hʌb] *n* (Rad)nabe *f*; (*fig: centre*) Mittelpunkt *m*, Zentrum *nt*
hubbub ['hʌbʌb] *n* Lärm *m*; (*commotion*) Tumult *m*
hubcap ['hʌbkæp] *n* Radkappe *f*
HUD (*US*) *n abbr* (= *Department of Housing and Urban Development*) *Ministerium für Wohnungsbau und Stadtentwicklung*
huddle ['hʌdl] *vi*: **to ~ together** sich zusammendrängen ▷ *n*: **in a ~** dicht zusammengedrängt
hue [hju:] *n* Farbton *m*
hue and cry *n* großes Geschrei *nt*
huff [hʌf] *n*: **in a ~** beleidigt, eingeschnappt ▷ *vi*: **to ~ and puff** sich aufregen
huffy ['hʌfɪ] (*inf*) *adj* beleidigt
hug [hʌg] *vt* umarmen; (*thing*) umklammern ▷ *n* Umarmung *f*; **to give sb a ~** jdn umarmen
huge [hju:dʒ] *adj* riesig
hugely ['hju:dʒlɪ] *adv* ungeheuer

hulk [hʌlk] *n* (*wrecked ship*) Wrack *nt*; (*person, building etc*) Klotz *m*
hulking ['hʌlkɪŋ] *adj*: **~ great** massig
hull [hʌl] *n* Schiffsrumpf *m*; (*of nuts*) Schale *f*; (*of fruit*) Blättchen *nt* ▷ *vt* (*fruit*) entstielen
hullaballoo [hʌləbə'lu:] (*inf*) *n* Spektakel *m*
hullo [hə'ləu] *excl* = **hello**
hum [hʌm] *vt* summen ▷ *vi* summen; (*machine*) brummen ▷ *n* Summen *nt*; (*of traffic*) Brausen *nt*; (*of machines*) Brummen *nt*; (*of voices*) Gemurmel *nt*
human ['hju:mən] *adj* menschlich ▷ *n* (*also*: **human being**) Mensch *m*
humane [hju:'meɪn] *adj* human
humanism ['hju:mənɪzəm] *n* Humanismus *m*
humanitarian [hju:mænɪ'tɛərɪən] *adj* humanitär
humanity [hju:'mænɪtɪ] *n* Menschlichkeit *f*; (*mankind*) Menschheit *f*; (*humaneness*) Humanität *f*; **humanities** *npl* (*Scol*): **the humanities** die Geisteswissenschaften *pl*
humanly ['hju:mənlɪ] *adv* menschlich; **if (at all) ~ possible** wenn es irgend möglich ist
humanoid ['hju:mənɔɪd] *adj* menschenähnlich ▷ *n* menschenähnliches Wesen *nt*
human rights *npl* Menschenrechte *pl*
humble ['hʌmbl] *adj* bescheiden ▷ *vt* demütigen
humbly ['hʌmblɪ] *adv* bescheiden
humbug ['hʌmbʌg] *n* Humbug *m*, Mumpitz *m*; (*Brit*: *sweet*) Pfefferminzbonbon *m or nt*
humdrum ['hʌmdrʌm] *adj* eintönig, langweilig
humid ['hju:mɪd] *adj* feucht
humidifier [hju:'mɪdɪfaɪə^r] *n* Luftbefeuchter *m*
humidity [hju:'mɪdɪtɪ] *n* Feuchtigkeit *f*
humiliate [hju:'mɪlɪeɪt] *vt* demütigen
humiliating [hju:'mɪlɪeɪtɪŋ] *adj* demütigend
humiliation [hju:mɪlɪ'eɪʃən] *n* Demütigung *f*
humility [hju:'mɪlɪtɪ] *n* Bescheidenheit *f*
humor *etc* (*US*) = **humour** *etc*
humorist ['hju:mərɪst] *n* Humorist(in) *m(f)*
humorous ['hju:mərəs] *adj* (*remark*) witzig; (*book*) lustig; (*person*) humorvoll
humour, (*US*) **humor** ['hju:mə^r] *n* Humor *m*; (*mood*) Stimmung *f* ▷ *vt* seinen Willen lassen *+dat*; **sense of ~** (Sinn *m* für) Humor; **to be in good/bad ~** gute/schlechte Laune haben
humourless ['hju:məlɪs] *adj* humorlos
hump [hʌmp] *n* Hügel *m*; (*of camel*) Höcker *m*; (*deformity*) Buckel *m*
humpbacked ['hʌmpbækt] *adj*: **~ bridge** gewölbte Brücke *f*
humus ['hju:məs] *n* Humus *m*
hunch [hʌntʃ] *n* Gefühl *nt*, Ahnung *f*; **I have a ~ that ...** ich habe den (leisen) Verdacht, dass ...
hunchback ['hʌntʃbæk] *n* Bucklige(r) *f(m)*
hunched [hʌntʃt] *adj* gebeugt; (*shoulders*) hochgezogen; (*back*) krumm
hundred ['hʌndrəd] *num* hundert; **a** *or* **one ~ books/people/dollars** (ein)hundert Bücher/Personen/Dollar; **~s of** Hunderte von; **I'm a ~ per cent sure** ich bin absolut sicher
hundredth ['hʌndrədθ] *num* hundertste(r, s)
hundredweight ['hʌndrɪdweɪt] *n* *Gewichtseinheit* (*Brit* = *50,8 kg*; *US* = *45,3 kg*) ≈ Zentner *m*
hung [hʌŋ] *pt, pp of* **hang**
Hungarian [hʌŋ'gɛərɪən] *adj* ungarisch ▷ *n* Ungar(in) *m(f)*; (*Ling*) Ungarisch *nt*
Hungary ['hʌŋgərɪ] *n* Ungarn *nt*
hunger ['hʌŋgə^r] *n* Hunger *m* ▷ *vi*: **to ~ for** hungern nach
hunger strike *n* Hungerstreik *m*
hung over (*inf*) *adj* verkatert
hungrily ['hʌŋgrəlɪ] *adv* hungrig
hungry ['hʌŋgrɪ] *adj* hungrig; **to be ~** Hunger haben; **to be ~ for** hungern nach; (*news*) sehnsüchtig warten auf; **to go ~** hungern
hung up (*inf*) *adj*: **to be ~ on** (*person*) ein gestörtes Verhältnis haben zu; **to be ~ about** nervös sein wegen
hunk [hʌŋk] *n* großes Stück *nt*; (*inf*: *man*) (großer, gut aussehender) Mann *m*
hunt [hʌnt] *vt* jagen; (*criminal, fugitive*) fahnden nach ▷ *vi* (*Sport*) jagen ▷ *n* (*see vb*) Jagd *f*; Fahndung *f*; (*search*) Suche *f*; **to ~ for** (*search*) suchen (nach)
▸ **hunt down** *vt* Jagd machen auf *+acc*
hunter ['hʌntə^r] *n* Jäger(in) *m(f)*
hunting ['hʌntɪŋ] *n* Jagd *f*, Jagen *nt*
hurdle ['hə:dl] *n* Hürde *f*
hurl [hə:l] *vt* schleudern; **to ~ sth at sb** (*also fig*) jdm etw entgegenschleudern
hurling ['hə:lɪŋ] *n* (*Sport*) Hurling *nt*, *irische Hockeyart*
hurly-burly ['hə:lɪ'bə:lɪ] *n* Rummel *m*
hurrah [hu'rɑ:] *n* Hurra *nt* ▷ *excl* hurra
hurray [hu'reɪ] *n* = **hurrah**
hurricane ['hʌrɪkən] *n* Orkan *m*
hurried ['hʌrɪd] *adj* eilig; (*departure*) überstürzt
hurriedly ['hʌrɪdlɪ] *adv* eilig
hurry ['hʌrɪ] *n* Eile *f* ▷ *vi* eilen; (*to do sth*) sich beeilen ▷ *vt* (zur Eile) antreiben; (*work*) beschleunigen; **to be in a ~** es eilig haben; **to do sth in a ~** etw schnell tun; **there's no ~** es eilt nicht; **what's the ~?** warum so eilig?; **they hurried to help him** sie eilten ihm zu Hilfe; **to ~ home** nach Hause eilen
▸ **hurry along** *vi* sich beeilen
▸ **hurry away** *vi* schnell weggehen, forteilen
▸ **hurry off** *vi* = **hurry away**
▸ **hurry up** *vt* (zur Eile) antreiben ▷ *vi* sich beeilen
hurt [hə:t] (*pt, pp* **~**) *vt* wehtun *+dat*; (*injure, fig*) verletzen ▷ *vi* wehtun ▷ *adj* verletzt; **I've ~ my arm** ich habe mir am Arm wehgetan; (*injured*) ich habe mir den Arm verletzt; **where does it ~?** wo tut es weh?
hurtful ['hə:tful] *adj* verletzend
hurtle ['hə:tl] *vi*: **to ~ past** vorbeisausen; **to ~ down** (*fall*) hinunterfallen
husband ['hʌzbənd] *n* (Ehe)mann *m*
hush [hʌʃ] *n* Stille *f* ▷ *vt* zum Schweigen

bringen; **~!** pst!
▸ **hush up** *vt* vertuschen
hushed [hʌʃt] *adj* still; (*voice*) gedämpft
hush-hush [hʌʃ'hʌʃ] (*inf*) *adj* streng geheim
husk [hʌsk] *n* Schale *f*; (*of wheat*) Spelze *f*; (*of maize*) Hüllblatt *nt*
husky ['hʌskɪ] *adj* (*voice*) rau ▷ *n* Schlittenhund *m*
hustings ['hʌstɪŋz] (*Brit*) *npl* (*Pol*) Wahlkampf *m*
hustle ['hʌsl] *vt* drängen ▷ *n*: **~ and bustle** Geschäftigkeit *f*
hut [hʌt] *n* Hütte *f*
hutch [hʌtʃ] *n* (Kaninchen)stall *m*
hyacinth ['haɪəsɪnθ] *n* Hyazinthe *f*
hybrid ['haɪbrɪd] *n* (*plant, animal*) Kreuzung *f*; (*mixture*) Mischung *f* ▷ *adj* Misch-
hybrid car, hybrid vehicle *n* Hybridfahrzeug *nt or* -auto *nt*
hydrant ['haɪdrənt] *n* (*also*: **fire hydrant**) Hydrant *m*
hydraulic [haɪ'drɔːlɪk] *adj* hydraulisch
hydraulics [haɪ'drɔːlɪks] *n* Hydraulik *f*
hydrochloric acid ['haɪdrəu'klɔrɪk-] *n* Salzsäure *f*
hydroelectric ['haɪdrəuɪ'lɛktrɪk] *adj* hydroelektrisch
hydrofoil ['haɪdrəfɔɪl] *n* Tragflächenboot *nt*, Tragflügelboot *nt*
hydrogen ['haɪdrədʒən] *n* Wasserstoff *m*
hydrogen bomb *n* Wasserstoffbombe *f*
hydrophobia ['haɪdrə'fəubɪə] *n* Hydrophobie *f*, Wasserscheu *f*
hydroplane ['haɪdrəpleɪn] *n* Gleitboot *nt*; (*plane*) Wasserflugzeug *nt* ▷ *vi* (*boat*) abheben
hyena [haɪ'iːnə] *n* Hyäne *f*
hygiene ['haɪdʒiːn] *n* Hygiene *f*
hygienic [haɪ'dʒiːnɪk] *adj* hygienisch
hymn [hɪm] *n* Kirchenlied *nt*
hype [haɪp] (*inf*) *n* Rummel *m*
hyperactive ['haɪpər'æktɪv] *adj* überaktiv
hyperinflation ['haɪpərɪn'fleɪʃən] *n* galoppierende Inflation *f*
hypermarket ['haɪpəmɑːkɪt] (*Brit*) *n* Verbrauchermarkt *m*
hypertension ['haɪpə'tɛnʃən] *n* Hypertonie *f*, Bluthochdruck *m*
hypertext ['haɪpətɛkst] *n* (*Comput*) Hypertext *m*
hyphen ['haɪfn] *n* Bindestrich *m*; (*at end of line*) Trennungsstrich *m*
hyphenated ['haɪfəneɪtɪd] *adj* mit Bindestrich (geschrieben)
hypnosis [hɪp'nəusɪs] *n* Hypnose *f*
hypnotic [hɪp'nɔtɪk] *adj* hypnotisierend; (*trance*) hypnotisch
hypnotism ['hɪpnətɪzəm] *n* Hypnotismus *m*
hypnotist ['hɪpnətɪst] *n* Hypnotiseur *m*, Hypnotiseuse *f*
hypnotize ['hɪpnətaɪz] *vt* hypnotisieren
hypoallergenic ['haɪpəuælə'dʒɛnɪk] *adj* für äußerst empfindliche Haut
hypochondriac [haɪpə'kɔndrɪæk] *n* Hypochonder *m*
hypocrisy [hɪ'pɔkrɪsɪ] *n* Heuchelei *f*
hypocrite ['hɪpəkrɪt] *n* Heuchler(in) *m(f)*
hypocritical [hɪpə'krɪtɪkl] *adj* heuchlerisch
hypodermic [haɪpə'dəːmɪk] *adj* (*injection*) subkutan ▷ *n* (Injektions)spritze *f*
hypotenuse [haɪ'pɔtɪnjuːz] *n* Hypotenuse *f*
hypothermia [haɪpə'θəːmɪə] *n* Unterkühlung *f*
hypothesis [haɪ'pɔθɪsɪs] (*pl* **hypotheses**) *n* Hypothese *f*
hypothesize [haɪ'pɔθɪsaɪz] *vi* Hypothesen aufstellen ▷ *vt* annehmen
hypothetic [haɪpəu'θɛtɪk], **hypothetical** [haɪpəu'θɛtɪkl] *adj* hypothetisch
hysterectomy [hɪstə'rɛktəmɪ] *n* Hysterektomie *f*
hysteria [hɪ'stɪərɪə] *n* Hysterie *f*
hysterical [hɪ'stɛrɪkl] *adj* hysterisch; (*situation*) wahnsinnig komisch; **to become ~** hysterisch werden
hysterically [hɪ'stɛrɪklɪ] *adv* hysterisch; **~ funny** wahnsinnig komisch
hysterics [hɪ'stɛrɪks] *npl*: **to be in** *or* **to have** ~ einen hysterischen Anfall haben; (*laughter*) einen Lachanfall haben
Hz *abbr* (= *hertz*) Hz.

Ii

I¹, i [aɪ] *n* (*letter*) I *nt*, i *nt*; **I for Isaac, I for Item** (*US*) ≈ I wie Ida
I² [aɪ] *pron* ich
I. *abbr* = **island; isle**
IA (*US*) *abbr* (*Post*) = *Iowa*
IAEA *n abbr* = **International Atomic Energy Agency**
ib *abbr* (= *ibidem*) ib(id).
Iberian [aɪ'bɪərɪən] *adj*: **the ~ Peninsula** die Iberische Halbinsel
ibid *abbr* (= *ibidem*) ib(id).
i/c (*Brit*) *abbr* (= *in charge (of)*) *see* **charge**
ICBM *n abbr* (= *intercontinental ballistic missile*) Interkontinentalrakete *f*
ICC *n abbr* = **International Chamber of Commerce**; (*US*: = *Interstate Commerce Commission*) *Kommission zur Regelung des Warenverkehrs zwischen den US-Bundesstaaten*
ice [aɪs] *n* Eis *nt*; (*on road*) Glatteis *nt* ▷ *vt* (*cake*) mit Zuckerguss überziehen, glasieren ▷ *vi* (*also*: **ice over, ice up**) vereisen; (*puddle etc*) zufrieren; **to put sth on ~** (*fig*) etw auf Eis legen
Ice Age *n* Eiszeit *f*
ice axe *n* Eispickel *m*
iceberg ['aɪsbəːg] *n* Eisberg *m*; **the tip of the ~** (*fig*) die Spitze des Eisbergs
icebox ['aɪsbɔks] *n* (*US*: *fridge*) Kühlschrank *m*; (*Brit*: *compartment*) Eisfach *nt*; (*insulated box*) Kühltasche *f*
icebreaker ['aɪsbreɪkə^r] *n* Eisbrecher *m*
ice bucket *n* Eiskühler *m*
icecap ['aɪskæp] *n* Eisdecke *f*; (*polar*) Eiskappe *f*
ice-cold ['aɪs'kəuld] *adj* eiskalt
ice cream *n* Eis *nt*
ice-cream soda ['aɪskriːm-] *n* *Eisbecher mit Sirup und Sodawasser*
ice cube *n* Eiswürfel *m*
iced [aɪst] *adj* (*cake*) mit Zuckerguss überzogen, glasiert; (*beer etc*) eisgekühlt; (*tea, coffee*) Eis-
ice hockey *n* Eishockey *nt*
Iceland ['aɪslənd] *n* Island *nt*
Icelander ['aɪsləndə^r] *n* Isländer(in) *m(f)*
Icelandic [aɪs'lændɪk] *adj* isländisch ▷ *n* (*Ling*) Isländisch *nt*
ice lolly (*Brit*) *n* Eis *nt* am Stiel
ice pick *n* Eispickel *m*
ice rink *n* (Kunst)eisbahn *f*, Schlittschuhbahn *f*
ice skate *n* Schlittschuh *m*
ice-skate ['aɪsskeɪt] *vi* Schlittschuh laufen
ice-skating ['aɪsskeɪtɪŋ] *n* Eislauf *m*, Schlittschuhlaufen *nt*
icicle ['aɪsɪkl] *n* Eiszapfen *m*
icing ['aɪsɪŋ] *n* (*Culin*) Zuckerguss *m*; (*Aviat etc*) Vereisung *f*
icing sugar (*Brit*) *n* Puderzucker *m*
ICJ *n abbr* = **International Court of Justice**
icon ['aɪkɔn] *n* Ikone *f*; (*Comput*) Ikon *nt*
ICR (*US*) *n abbr* (= *Institute for Cancer Research*) *Krebsforschungsinstitut*
ICT (*Brit*) *n abbr* (*Scol*) = **information and communication technology**
ICU *n abbr* (*Med*) = **intensive care unit**
icy ['aɪsɪ] *adj* eisig; (*road*) vereist
ID, Ida. (*US*) *abbr* (*Post*) = *Idaho*; = *identification (document)*
I'd [aɪd] = **I would**; **I had**
ID card *n* = **identity card**
IDD (*Brit*) *n abbr* (*Tel*: = *international direct dialling*) *Selbstwählferndienst ins Ausland*
idea [aɪ'dɪə] *n* Idee *f*; (*opinion*) Ansicht *f*; (*notion*) Vorstellung *f*; (*objective*) Ziel *nt*; **good ~!** gute Idee!; **to have a good ~ that** sich *dat* ziemlich sicher sein, dass; **I haven't the least ~** ich habe nicht die leiseste Ahnung
ideal [aɪ'dɪəl] *n* Ideal *nt* ▷ *adj* ideal
idealist [aɪ'dɪəlɪst] *n* Idealist(in) *m(f)*
ideally [aɪ'dɪəlɪ] *adv* ideal; **~ the book should ...** idealerweise *or* im Idealfall sollte das Buch ...; **she's ~ suited for ...** sie eignet sich hervorragend für ...
identical [aɪ'dɛntɪkl] *adj* identisch; (*twins*) eineiig
identification [aɪdɛntɪfɪ'keɪʃən] *n* Identifizierung *f*; **(means of) ~** Ausweispapiere *pl*
identify [aɪ'dɛntɪfaɪ] *vt* (*recognize*) erkennen; (*distinguish*) identifizieren; **to ~ sb/sth with** jdn/etw identifizieren mit
Identikit® [aɪ'dɛntɪkɪt] *n*: **~ (picture)** Phantombild *nt*
identity [aɪ'dɛntɪtɪ] *n* Identität *f*
identity card *n* (Personal)ausweis *m*
identity papers *npl* Ausweispapiere *pl*
identity parade (*Brit*) *n* Gegenüberstellung *f*
ideological [aɪdɪə'lɔdʒɪkl] *adj* ideologisch,

weltanschaulich
ideology [aɪdɪ'ɔlədʒɪ] *n* Ideologie *f*, Weltanschauung *f*
idiocy ['ɪdɪəsɪ] *n* Idiotie *f*, Dummheit *f*
idiom ['ɪdɪəm] *n* (*style*) Ausdrucksweise *f*; (*phrase*) Redewendung *f*
idiomatic [ɪdɪə'mætɪk] *adj* idiomatisch
idiosyncrasy [ɪdɪəu'sɪŋkrəsɪ] *n* Eigenheit *f*, Eigenart *f*
idiosyncratic [ɪdɪəusɪŋ'krætɪk] *adj* eigenartig; (*way, method, style*) eigen
idiot ['ɪdɪət] *n* Idiot(in) *m(f)*, Dummkopf *m*
idiotic [ɪdɪ'ɔtɪk] *adj* idiotisch, blöd(sinnig)
idle ['aɪdl] *adj* untätig; (*lazy*) faul; (*unemployed*) unbeschäftigt; (*machinery, factory*) stillstehend; (*question*) müßig; (*conversation, pleasure*) leer ▷ *vi* leerlaufen, im Leerlauf sein; **to lie ~** (*machinery*) außer Betrieb sein; (*factory*) die Arbeit eingestellt haben
▶ **idle away** *vt* (*time*) vertrödeln, verbummeln
idleness ['aɪdlnɪs] *n* Untätigkeit *f*; (*laziness*) Faulheit *f*
idler ['aɪdlə^r] *n* Faulenzer(in) *m(f)*
idle time *n* (*Comm*) Leerlaufzeit *f*
idly ['aɪdlɪ] *adv* untätig; (*glance*) abwesend
idol ['aɪdl] *n* Idol *nt*; (*Rel*) Götzenbild *nt*
idolize ['aɪdəlaɪz] *vt* vergöttern
idyllic [ɪ'dɪlɪk] *adj* idyllisch
i.e. *abbr* (= *id est*) d. h.

KEYWORD

if [ɪf] *conj* **1** (*given that, providing that etc*) wenn, falls; **if anyone comes in** wenn *or* falls jemand hereinkommt; **if necessary** wenn *or* falls nötig; **if I were you** wenn ich Sie wäre, an Ihrer Stelle
2 (*whenever*) wenn
3 (*although*): **(even) if** auch *or* selbst wenn; **I like it, (even) if you don't** mir gefällt es, auch wenn du es nicht magst
4 (*whether*) ob; **ask him if he can come** frag ihn, ob er kommen kann
5: if so/not falls ja/nein; **if only** wenn nur; *see also* **as**

iffy ['ɪfɪ] (*inf*) *adj* (*uncertain*) unsicher; (*plan, proposal*) fragwürdig; **he was a bit ~ about it** er hat sich sehr vage ausgedrückt
igloo ['ɪglu:] *n* Iglu *m or nt*
ignite [ɪg'naɪt] *vt* entzünden ▷ *vi* sich entzünden
ignition [ɪg'nɪʃən] *n* (*Aut*) Zündung *f*
ignition key *n* (*Aut*) Zündschlüssel *m*
ignoble [ɪg'nəubl] *adj* schändlich, unehrenhaft
ignominious [ɪgnə'mɪnɪəs] *adj* schmachvoll
ignoramus [ɪgnə'reɪməs] *n* Ignorant(in) *m(f)*
ignorance ['ɪgnərəns] *n* Unwissenheit *f*, Ignoranz *f*; **to keep sb in ~ of sth** jdn in Unkenntnis über etw *acc* lassen
ignorant ['ɪgnərənt] *adj* unwissend, ignorant; **to be ~ of** (*subject*) sich nicht auskennen in *+dat*; (*events*) nicht informiert sein über *+acc*
ignore [ɪg'nɔ:^r] *vt* ignorieren; (*fact*) außer Acht lassen
ikon ['aɪkɔn] *n* = **icon**
IL (*US*) *abbr* (*Post*) = *Illinois*
I'll [aɪl] = **I will; I shall**
ill [ɪl] *adj* krank; (*effects*) schädlich ▷ *n* Übel *nt*; (*trouble*) Schlechte(s) *nt* ▷ *adv*: **to speak ~ of sb** Schlechtes über jdn sagen; **to be taken ~** krank werden; **to think ~ of sb** schlecht von jdm denken
ill-advised [ɪləd'vaɪzd] *adj* unklug; (*person*) schlecht beraten
ill at ease *adj* unbehaglich
ill-considered [ɪlkən'sɪdəd] *adj* unüberlegt
ill-disposed [ɪldɪs'pəuzd] *adj*: **to be ~ toward sb/sth** jdm/etw nicht wohlgesinnt sein
illegal [ɪ'li:gl] *adj* illegal
illegally [ɪ'li:gəlɪ] *adv* illegal
illegible [ɪ'lɛdʒɪbl] *adj* unleserlich
illegitimate [ɪlɪ'dʒɪtɪmət] *adj* (*child*) unehelich; (*activity, treaty*) unzulässig
ill-fated [ɪl'feɪtɪd] *adj* unglückselig
ill-favoured, (*US*) **ill-favored** [ɪl'feɪvəd] *adj* ungestalt (*liter*), hässlich
ill feeling *n* Verstimmung *f*
ill-gotten ['ɪlgɔtn] *adj*: **~ gains** unrechtmäßig erworbener Gewinn *m*
ill health *n* schlechter Gesundheitszustand *m*
illicit [ɪ'lɪsɪt] *adj* verboten
ill-informed [ɪlɪn'fɔ:md] *adj* (*judgement*) wenig sachkundig; (*person*) schlecht informiert *or* unterrichtet
illiterate [ɪ'lɪtərət] *adj* (*person*) des Lesens und Schreibens unkundig; (*letter*) voller Fehler
ill-mannered [ɪl'mænəd] *adj* unhöflich
illness ['ɪlnɪs] *n* Krankheit *f*
illogical [ɪ'lɔdʒɪkl] *adj* unlogisch
ill-suited [ɪl'su:tɪd] *adj* nicht zusammenpassend; **he is ~ to the job** er ist für die Stelle ungeeignet
ill-timed [ɪl'taɪmd] *adj* ungelegen, unpassend
ill-treat [ɪl'tri:t] *vt* misshandeln
ill-treatment [ɪl'tri:tmənt] *n* Misshandlung *f*
illuminate [ɪ'lu:mɪneɪt] *vt* beleuchten
illuminated sign [ɪ'lu:mɪneɪtɪd-] *n* Leuchtzeichen *nt*
illuminating [ɪ'lu:mɪneɪtɪŋ] *adj* aufschlussreich
illumination [ɪlu:mɪ'neɪʃən] *n* Beleuchtung *f*; **illuminations** *npl* (*decorative lights*) festliche Beleuchtung *f*, Illumination *f*
illusion [ɪ'lu:ʒən] *n* Illusion *f*; (*trick*) (Zauber)trick *m*; **to be under the ~ that ...** sich *dat* einbilden, dass ...
illusive [ɪ'lu:sɪv] *adj* = **illusory**
illusory [ɪ'lu:sərɪ] *adj* illusorisch, trügerisch
illustrate ['ɪləstreɪt] *vt* veranschaulichen; (*book*) illustrieren
illustration [ɪlə'streɪʃən] *n* Illustration *f*; (*example*) Veranschaulichung *f*
illustrator ['ɪləstreɪtə^r] *n* Illustrator(in) *m(f)*
illustrious [ɪ'lʌstrɪəs] *adj* (*career*) glanzvoll; (*predecessor*) berühmt

ill will *n* böses Blut *nt*
ILO *n abbr* = **International Labour Organization**
I'm [aɪm] = **I am**
image ['ɪmɪdʒ] *n* Bild *nt*; *(public face)* Image *nt*; *(reflection)* Abbild *nt*
image-building campaign ['ɪmɪdʒbɪldɪŋ-] *n* Imagekampagne *f*
imagery ['ɪmɪdʒərɪ] *n (in writing)* Metaphorik *f*; *(in painting etc)* Symbolik *f*
imaginable [ɪ'mædʒɪnəbl] *adj* vorstellbar, denkbar; **we've tried every ~ solution** wir haben jede denkbare Lösung ausprobiert; **she had the prettiest hair ~** sie hatte das schönste Haar, das man sich vorstellen kann
imaginary [ɪ'mædʒɪnərɪ] *adj* erfunden; *(being)* Fantasie-; *(danger)* eingebildet
imagination [ɪmædʒɪ'neɪʃən] *n* Fantasie *f*; *(illusion)* Einbildung *f*; **it's just your ~** das bildest du dir nur ein
imaginative [ɪ'mædʒɪnətɪv] *adj* fantasievoll; *(solution)* einfallsreich
imagine [ɪ'mædʒɪn] *vt* sich *dat* vorstellen; *(dream)* sich *dat* träumen lassen; *(suppose)* vermuten
imbalance [ɪm'bæləns] *n* Unausgeglichenheit *f*
imbecile ['ɪmbəsi:l] *n* Schwachkopf *m*, Idiot *m*
imbue [ɪm'bju:] *vt*: **to ~ sb/sth with** jdn/etw durchdringen mit
IMF *n abbr (= International Monetary Fund)* IWF *m*
imitate ['ɪmɪteɪt] *vt* imitieren; *(mimic)* nachahmen
imitation [ɪmɪ'teɪʃən] *n* Imitation *f*, Nachahmung *f*
imitator ['ɪmɪteɪtə^r] *n* Imitator(in) *m(f)*, Nachahmer(in) *m(f)*
immaculate [ɪ'mækjulət] *adj* makellos; *(appearance, piece of work)* tadellos; *(Rel)* unbefleckt
immaterial [ɪmə'tɪərɪəl] *adj* unwichtig, unwesentlich
immature [ɪmə'tjuə^r] *adj* unreif; *(organism)* noch nicht voll entwickelt
immaturity [ɪmə'tjuərɪtɪ] *n* Unreife *f*
immeasurable [ɪ'mɛʒrəbl] *adj* unermesslich groß
immediacy [ɪ'mi:dɪəsɪ] *n* Unmittelbarkeit *f*, Direktheit *f*; *(of needs)* Dringlichkeit *f*
immediate [ɪ'mi:dɪət] *adj* sofortig; *(need)* dringend; *(neighbourhood, family)* nächste(r, s)
immediately [ɪ'mi:dɪətlɪ] *adv* sofort; *(directly)* unmittelbar; **~ next to** direkt neben
immense [ɪ'mɛns] *adj* riesig, enorm
immensely [ɪ'mɛnslɪ] *adv* unheimlich; *(grateful, complex etc)* äußerst
immensity [ɪ'mɛnsɪtɪ] *n* ungeheure Größe *f*, Unermesslichkeit *f*; *(of problems etc)* gewaltiges Ausmaß *nt*
immerse [ɪ'mə:s] *vt* eintauchen; **to ~ sth in** etw tauchen in *+acc*; **to be ~d in** *(fig)* vertieft sein in *+acc*
immersion heater [ɪ'mə:ʃən-] *(Brit) n* elektrischer Heißwasserboiler *m*
immigrant ['ɪmɪgrənt] *n* Einwanderer *m*, Einwanderin *f*
immigration [ɪmɪ'greɪʃən] *n* Einwanderung *f*; *(at airport etc)* Einwanderungsstelle *f* ▷ *cpd* Einwanderungs-
imminent ['ɪmɪnənt] *adj* bevorstehend
immobile [ɪ'məubaɪl] *adj* unbeweglich
immobilize [ɪ'məubɪlaɪz] *vt (person)* handlungsunfähig machen; *(machine)* zum Stillstand bringen
immobilizer [ɪ'məubɪlaɪzə^r] *n (Aut)* Wegfahrsperre *f*
immoderate [ɪ'mɔdərət] *adj* unmäßig; *(opinion, reaction)* extrem; *(demand)* maßlos
immodest [ɪ'mɔdɪst] *adj* unanständig; *(boasting)* unbescheiden
immoral [ɪ'mɔrl] *adj* unmoralisch; *(behaviour)* unsittlich
immorality [ɪmɔ'rælɪtɪ] *n (see adj)* Unmoral *f*; Unsittlichkeit *f*
immortal [ɪ'mɔ:tl] *adj* unsterblich
immortality [ɪmɔ:'tælɪtɪ] *n* Unsterblichkeit *f*
immortalize [ɪ'mɔ:tlaɪz] *vt* unsterblich machen
immovable [ɪ'mu:vəbl] *adj* unbeweglich; *(person, opinion)* fest
immune [ɪ'mju:n] *adj*: **~ (to)** *(disease)* immun (gegen); *(flattery)* unempfänglich (für); *(criticism)* unempfindlich (gegen); *(attack)* sicher (vor *+dat*)
immune system *n* Immunsystem *nt*
immunity [ɪ'mju:nɪtɪ] *n (see adj)* Immunität *f*; Unempfänglichkeit *f*; Unempfindlichkeit *f*; Sicherheit *f*; *(of diplomat, from prosecution)* Immunität *f*
immunization [ɪmjunaɪ'zeɪʃən] *n* Immunisierung *f*
immunize ['ɪmjunaɪz] *vt*: **to ~ (against)** immunisieren (gegen)
imp [ɪmp] *n* Kobold *m*; *(child)* Racker *m (inf)*
impact ['ɪmpækt] *n* Aufprall *m*; *(of crash)* Wucht *f*; *(of law, measure)* (Aus)wirkung *f*
impair [ɪm'pɛə^r] *vt* beeinträchtigen
impaired [ɪm'pɛəd] *adj* beeinträchtigt; *(hearing)* schlecht; **~ vision** schlechte Augen *pl*
impale [ɪm'peɪl] *vt*: **to ~ sth (on)** etw aufspießen (auf *+dat*)
impart [ɪm'pɑ:t] *vt*: **to ~ (to)** *(information)* mitteilen *+dat*; *(flavour)* verleihen *+dat*
impartial [ɪm'pɑ:ʃl] *adj* unparteiisch
impartiality [ɪmpɑ:ʃɪ'ælɪtɪ] *n* Unparteilichkeit *f*
impassable [ɪm'pɑ:səbl] *adj* unpassierbar
impasse [æm'pɑ:s] *n* Sackgasse *f*
impassive [ɪm'pæsɪv] *adj* gelassen
impatience [ɪm'peɪʃəns] *n* Ungeduld *f*
impatient [ɪm'peɪʃənt] *adj* ungeduldig; **to get** *or* **grow ~** ungeduldig werden; **to be ~ to do sth** es nicht erwarten können, etw zu tun
impatiently [ɪm'peɪʃəntlɪ] *adv* ungeduldig
impeach [ɪm'pi:tʃ] *vt* anklagen; *(public official)* eines Amtsvergehens anklagen
impeachment [ɪm'pi:tʃmənt] *n* Anklage *f*

wegen eines Amtsvergehens, Impeachment *nt*
impeccable [ɪm'pɛkəbl] *adj* (*dress*) untadelig; (*manners*) tadellos
impecunious [ɪmpɪ'kjuːnɪəs] *adj* mittellos
impede [ɪm'piːd] *vt* behindern
impediment [ɪm'pɛdɪmənt] *n* Hindernis *nt*; (*also*: **speech impediment**) Sprachfehler *m*
impel [ɪm'pɛl] *vt*: **to ~ sb to do sth** jdn (dazu) nötigen, etw zu tun
impending [ɪm'pɛndɪŋ] *adj* bevorstehend; (*catastrophe*) drohend
impenetrable [ɪm'pɛnɪtrəbl] *adj* undurchdringlich; (*fig*) unergründlich
imperative [ɪm'pɛrətɪv] *adj* dringend; (*tone*) Befehls- ▷ *n* (*Ling*) Imperativ *m*, Befehlsform *f*
imperceptible [ɪmpə'sɛptɪbl] *adj* nicht wahrnehmbar, unmerklich
imperfect [ɪm'pəːfɪkt] *adj* mangelhaft; (*goods*) fehlerhaft ▷ *n* (*Ling*: *also*: **imperfect tense**) Imperfekt *nt*, Vergangenheit *f*
imperfection [ɪmpəː'fɛkʃən] *n* Fehler *m*
imperial [ɪm'pɪərɪəl] *adj* kaiserlich; (*Brit*: *measure*) britisch
imperialism [ɪm'pɪərɪəlɪzəm] *n* Imperialismus *m*
imperil [ɪm'pɛrɪl] *vt* gefährden
imperious [ɪm'pɪərɪəs] *adj* herrisch, gebieterisch
impersonal [ɪm'pəːsənl] *adj* unpersönlich
impersonate [ɪm'pəːsəneɪt] *vt* sich ausgeben als; (*Theat*) imitieren
impersonation [ɪmpəːsə'neɪʃən] *n* (*Theat*) Imitation *f*; **~ of** (*Law*) Auftreten *nt* als
impertinent [ɪm'pəːtɪnənt] *adj* unverschämt
imperturbable [ɪmpə'təːbəbl] *adj* unerschütterlich
impervious [ɪm'pəːvɪəs] *adj*: **~ to** (*criticism, pressure*) unberührt von; (*charm, influence*) unempfänglich für
impetuous [ɪm'pɛtjuəs] *adj* ungestüm, stürmisch; (*act*) impulsiv
impetus ['ɪmpətəs] *n* Schwung *m*; (*fig*: *driving force*) treibende Kraft *f*
impinge [ɪm'pɪndʒ]: **to ~ on** *vt fus* sich auswirken auf *+acc*; (*rights*) einschränken
impish ['ɪmpɪʃ] *adj* schelmisch
implacable [ɪm'plækəbl] *adj* unerbittlich, erbittert
implant [ɪm'plɑːnt] *vt* (*Med*) einpflanzen; (*fig*: *idea, principle*) einimpfen
implausible [ɪm'plɔːzɪbl] *adj* unglaubwürdig
implement [*n* 'ɪmplɪmənt, *vt* 'ɪmplɪmɛnt] *n* Gerät *nt*, Werkzeug *nt* ▷ *vt* durchführen
implicate ['ɪmplɪkeɪt] *vt* verwickeln
implication [ɪmplɪ'keɪʃən] *n* Auswirkung *f*; (*involvement*) Verwicklung *f*; **by ~** implizit
implicit [ɪm'plɪsɪt] *adj* (*inferred*) implizit, unausgesprochen; (*unquestioning*) absolut
implicitly [ɪm'plɪsɪtlɪ] *adv* (*see adj*) implizit; absolut
implore [ɪm'plɔːʳ] *vt* anflehen
imply [ɪm'plaɪ] *vt* andeuten; (*mean*) bedeuten
impolite [ɪmpə'laɪt] *adj* unhöflich
imponderable [ɪm'pɔndərəbl] *adj* unberechenbar ▷ *n* unberechenbare Größe *f*
import [*vt* ɪm'pɔːt, *n* 'ɪmpɔːt] *vt* importieren, einführen ▷ *n* Import *m*, Einfuhr *f*; (*article*) Importgut *nt* ▷ *cpd* Import-, Einfuhr-
importance [ɪm'pɔːtns] *n* (*see adj*) Wichtigkeit *f*; Bedeutung *f*; **to be of little/great ~** nicht besonders wichtig/sehr wichtig sein
important [ɪm'pɔːtənt] *adj* wichtig; (*influential*) bedeutend; **it's not ~** es ist unwichtig
importantly [ɪm'pɔːtəntlɪ] *adv* wichtigtuerisch; **but more ~ ...** aber was noch wichtiger ist, ...
importation [ɪmpɔː'teɪʃən] *n* Import *m*, Einfuhr *f*
imported [ɪm'pɔːtɪd] *adj* importiert, eingeführt
importer [ɪm'pɔːtəʳ] *n* Importeur *m*
impose [ɪm'pəuz] *vt* auferlegen; (*sanctions*) verhängen ▷ *vi*: **to ~ on sb** jdm zur Last fallen
imposing [ɪm'pəuzɪŋ] *adj* eindrucksvoll
imposition [ɪmpə'zɪʃən] *n* (*of tax etc*) Auferlegung *f*; **to be an ~ on** eine Zumutung sein für
impossibility [ɪmpɔsə'bɪlɪtɪ] *n* Unmöglichkeit *f*
impossible [ɪm'pɔsɪbl] *adj* unmöglich; **it's ~ for me to leave now** ich kann jetzt unmöglich gehen
impossibly [ɪm'pɔsɪblɪ] *adv* unmöglich
imposter [ɪm'pɔstəʳ] *n* = **impostor**
impostor [ɪm'pɔstəʳ] *n* Hochstapler(in) *m(f)*
impotence ['ɪmpətns] *n* (*see adj*) Machtlosigkeit *f*; Impotenz *f*
impotent ['ɪmpətnt] *adj* machtlos; (*Med*) impotent
impound [ɪm'paund] *vt* beschlagnahmen
impoverished [ɪm'pɔvərɪʃt] *adj* verarmt
impracticable [ɪm'præktɪkəbl] *adj* (*idea*) undurchführbar; (*solution*) unbrauchbar
impractical [ɪm'præktɪkl] *adj* (*plan*) undurchführbar; (*person*) unpraktisch
imprecise [ɪmprɪ'saɪs] *adj* ungenau
impregnable [ɪm'prɛgnəbl] *adj* uneinnehmbar; (*fig*) unerschütterlich
impregnate ['ɪmprɛgneɪt] *vt* tränken
impresario [ɪmprɪ'sɑːrɪəu] *n* (*Theat*) Impresario *m*
impress [ɪm'prɛs] *vt* beeindrucken; (*mark*) aufdrücken; **to ~ sth on sb** jdm etw einschärfen
impression [ɪm'prɛʃən] *n* Eindruck *m*; (*of stamp, seal*) Abdruck *m*; (*imitation*) Nachahmung *f*, Imitation *f*; **to make a good/bad ~ on sb** einen guten/schlechten Eindruck auf jdn machen; **to be under the ~ that ...** den Eindruck haben, dass ...
impressionable [ɪm'prɛʃnəbl] *adj* leicht zu beeindrucken
impressionist [ɪm'prɛʃənɪst] *n* Impressionist(in) *m(f)*; (*entertainer*) Imitator(in) *m(f)*
impressive [ɪm'prɛsɪv] *adj* beeindruckend
imprint ['ɪmprɪnt] *n* (*of hand etc*) Abdruck *m*;

(*Publishing*) Impressum *nt*
imprinted [ɪm'prɪntɪd] *adj*: **it is ~ on my memory/mind** es hat sich mir eingeprägt
imprison [ɪm'prɪzn] *vt* inhaftieren, einsperren
imprisonment [ɪm'prɪznmənt] *n* Gefangenschaft *f*; **three years' ~** drei Jahre Gefängnis *or* Freiheitsstrafe
improbable [ɪm'prɔbəbl] *adj* unwahrscheinlich
impromptu [ɪm'prɔmptju:] *adj* improvisiert
improper [ɪm'prɔpə^r] *adj* ungehörig; (*procedure*) unrichtig; (*dishonest*) unlauter
impropriety [ɪmprə'praɪətɪ] *n* (*see adj*) Ungehörigkeit *f*; Unrichtigkeit *f*; Unlauterkeit *f*
improve [ɪm'pru:v] *vt* verbessern ▷*vi* sich bessern; **the patient is improving** dem Patienten geht es besser
▸ **improve (up)on** *vt fus* verbessern
improvement [ɪm'pru:vmənt] *n*: **~ (in)** Verbesserung *f* (*+gen*); **to make ~s to** Verbesserungen durchführen an *+dat*
improvisation [ɪmprəvaɪ'zeɪʃən] *n* Improvisation *f*
improvise ['ɪmprəvaɪz] *vt, vi* improvisieren
imprudence [ɪm'pru:dns] *n* Unklugheit *f*
imprudent [ɪm'pru:dnt] *adj* unklug
impudent ['ɪmpjudnt] *adj* unverschämt
impugn [ɪm'pju:n] *vt* angreifen; (*sincerity, motives, reputation*) in Zweifel ziehen
impulse ['ɪmpʌls] *n* Impuls *m*; (*urge*) Drang *m*; **to act on ~** aus einem Impuls heraus handeln
impulse buy *n* Impulsivkauf *m*
impulsive [ɪm'pʌlsɪv] *adj* impulsiv, spontan; (*purchase*) Impulsiv-
impunity [ɪm'pju:nɪtɪ] *n*: **with ~** ungestraft
impure [ɪm'pjuə^r] *adj* unrein; (*adulterated*) verunreinigt
impurity [ɪm'pjuərɪtɪ] *n* Verunreinigung *f*
IN (*US*) *abbr* (*Post*) = *Indiana*

KEYWORD

in [ɪn] *prep* **1** (*indicating place, position*) in *+dat*; (*with motion*) in *+acc*; **in the house/garden** im Haus/Garten; **in town** in der Stadt; **in the country** auf dem Land; **in here** hierin; **in there** darin
2 (*with place names: of town, region, country*) in *+dat*; **in London/Bavaria** in London/Bayern
3 (*indicating time*) in *+dat*; **in spring/summer/May** im Frühling/Sommer/Mai; **in 1994** 1994; **in the afternoon** am Nachmittag; **at 4 o'clock in the afternoon** um 4 Uhr nachmittags; **I did it in 3 hours/days** ich habe es in 3 Stunden/Tagen gemacht; **in 2 weeks** *or* **2 weeks' time** in 2 Wochen
4 (*indicating manner, circumstances, state*) in *+dat*; **in a loud/soft voice** mit lauter/weicher Stimme; **in English/German** auf Englisch/Deutsch; **in the sun** in der Sonne; **in the rain** im Regen; **in good condition** in guter Verfassung
5 (*with ratios, numbers*): **1 in 10** eine(r, s) von 10; **20 pence in the pound** 20 Pence pro Pfund; **they lined up in twos** sie stellten sich in Zweierreihen auf
6 (*referring to people, works*): **the disease is common in children** die Krankheit ist bei Kindern verbreitet; **in (the works of) Dickens** bei Dickens; **they have a good leader in him** in ihm haben sie einen guten Führer
7 (*indicating profession etc*): **to be in teaching/the army** Lehrer(in)/beim Militär sein
8 (*with present participle*): **in saying this, I ...** wenn ich das sage, ...
▷*adv*: **to be in** (*person: at home, work*) da sein; (*train, ship, plane*) angekommen sein; (*in fashion*) in sein; **to ask sb in** jdn hereinbitten; **to run/limp** *etc* **in** hereinlaufen/-humpeln *etc*
▷*n*: **the ins and outs** (*of proposal, situation etc*) die Einzelheiten *pl*

in. *abbr* = **inch**
inability [ɪnə'bɪlɪtɪ] *n* Unfähigkeit *f*
inaccessible [ɪnək'sɛsɪbl] *adj* unzugänglich
inaccuracy [ɪn'ækjurəsɪ] *n* (*see adj*) Ungenauigkeit *f*; Unrichtigkeit *f*; (*mistake*) Fehler *m*
inaccurate [ɪn'ækjurət] *adj* ungenau; (*not correct*) unrichtig
inaction [ɪn'ækʃən] *n* Untätigkeit *f*
inactive [ɪn'æktɪv] *adj* untätig
inactivity [ɪnæk'tɪvɪtɪ] *n* Untätigkeit *f*
inadequacy [ɪn'ædɪkwəsɪ] *n* Unzulänglichkeit *f*
inadequate [ɪn'ædɪkwət] *adj* unzulänglich
inadmissible [ɪnəd'mɪsəbl] *adj* unzulässig
inadvertently [ɪnəd'və:tntlɪ] *adv* ungewollt
inadvisable [ɪnəd'vaɪzəbl] *adj* unratsam; **it is ~ to ...** es ist nicht ratsam, zu ...
inane [ɪ'neɪn] *adj* dumm
inanimate [ɪn'ænɪmət] *adj* unbelebt
inapplicable [ɪn'æplɪkəbl] *adj* unzutreffend
inappropriate [ɪnə'prəuprɪət] *adj* unpassend; (*word, expression*) unangebracht
inapt [ɪn'æpt] *adj* unpassend
inarticulate [ɪnɑ:'tɪkjulət] *adj* (*speech*) unverständlich; **he is ~** er kann sich nur schlecht ausdrücken
inasmuch as [ɪnəz'mʌtʃ-] *adv* da, weil; (*in so far as*) insofern als
inattention [ɪnə'tɛnʃən] *n* Unaufmerksamkeit *f*
inattentive [ɪnə'tɛntɪv] *adj* unaufmerksam
inaudible [ɪn'ɔ:dɪbl] *adj* unhörbar
inaugural [ɪ'nɔ:gjurəl] *adj* (*speech, meeting*) Eröffnungs-
inaugurate [ɪ'nɔ:gjureɪt] *vt* einführen; (*president, official*) (feierlich) in sein/ihr Amt einführen
inauguration [ɪnɔ:gju'reɪʃən] *n* (*see vb*) Einführung *f*; (feierliche) Amtseinführung *f*
inauspicious [ɪnɔ:s'pɪʃəs] *adj* Unheil verheißend

in-between [ɪnbɪ'twiːn] *adj* Mittel-, Zwischen-
inborn [ɪn'bɔːn] *adj* angeboren
inbred [ɪn'brɛd] *adj* angeboren; **an ~ family** eine Familie, in der Inzucht herrscht
inbreeding [ɪn'briːdɪŋ] *n* Inzucht *f*
in-built ['ɪnbɪlt] *adj* (*quality*) ihm/ihr *etc* eigen; (*feeling etc*) angeboren
Inc. *abbr* = **incorporated company**
Inca ['ɪŋkə] *adj* (*also*: **Incan**) Inka-, inkaisch ▷ *n* Inka *mf*
incalculable [ɪn'kælkjuləbl] *adj* (*effect*) unabsehbar; (*loss*) unermesslich
incapable [ɪn'keɪpəbl] *adj* hilflos; **to be ~ of sth** unfähig zu etw sein; **to be ~ of doing sth** unfähig sein, etw zu tun
incapacitate [ɪnkə'pæsɪteɪt] *vt*: **to ~ sb** jdn unfähig machen
incapacitated [ɪnkə'pæsɪteɪtɪd] *adj* (*Law*) entmündigt
incapacity [ɪnkə'pæsɪtɪ] *n* Hilflosigkeit *f*; (*inability*) Unfähigkeit *f*
incarcerate [ɪn'kɑːsəreɪt] *vt* einkerkern
incarnate [ɪn'kɑːnɪt] *adj* leibhaftig, in Person; **evil ~** das leibhaftige Böse
incarnation [ɪnkɑː'neɪʃən] *n* Inbegriff *m*; (*Rel*) Menschwerdung *f*
incendiary [ɪn'sɛndɪərɪ] *adj* (*bomb*) Brand-; **~ device** Brandsatz *m*
incense [*n* 'ɪnsɛns, *vt* ɪn'sɛns] *n* Weihrauch *m*; (*perfume*) Duft *m* ▷ *vt* wütend machen
incense burner *n* Weihrauchschwenker *m*
incentive [ɪn'sɛntɪv] *n* Anreiz *m*
inception [ɪn'sɛpʃən] *n* Beginn *m*, Anfang *m*
incessant [ɪn'sɛsnt] *adj* unablässig
incessantly [ɪn'sɛsntlɪ] *adv* unablässig
incest ['ɪnsɛst] *n* Inzest *m*
inch [ɪntʃ] *n* Zoll *m*; **to be within an ~ of sth** kurz vor etw *dat* stehen; **he didn't give an ~** (*fig*) er gab keinen Fingerbreit nach
▸ **inch forward** *vi* sich millimeterweise vorwärtsschieben
incidence ['ɪnsɪdns] *n* Häufigkeit *f*
incident ['ɪnsɪdnt] *n* Vorfall *m*; (*diplomatic etc*) Zwischenfall *m*
incidental [ɪnsɪ'dɛntl] *adj* zusätzlich; (*unimportant*) nebensächlich; **~ to** verbunden mit; **~ expenses** Nebenkosten *pl*
incidentally [ɪnsɪ'dɛntəlɪ] *adv* übrigens
incidental music *n* Begleitmusik *f*
incident room *n* Einsatzzentrale *f*
incinerate [ɪn'sɪnəreɪt] *vt* verbrennen
incinerator [ɪn'sɪnəreɪtə^r] *n* (*for waste, refuse*) (Müll)verbrennungsanlage *f*
incipient [ɪn'sɪpɪənt] *adj* einsetzend
incision [ɪn'sɪʒən] *n* Einschnitt *m*
incisive [ɪn'saɪsɪv] *adj* treffend
incisor [ɪn'saɪzə^r] *n* Schneidezahn *m*
incite [ɪn'saɪt] *vt* (*rioters*) aufhetzen; (*violence, hatred*) schüren
incl. *abbr* = **including; inclusive (of)**
inclement [ɪn'klɛmənt] *adj* (*weather*) rau, unfreundlich
inclination [ɪnklɪ'neɪʃən] *n* Neigung *f*
incline [*n* 'ɪnklaɪn, *vb* ɪn'klaɪn] *n* Abhang *m* ▷ *vt* neigen ▷ *vi* sich neigen; **to be ~d to** neigen zu; **to be well ~d towards sb** jdm geneigt *or* gewogen sein
include [ɪn'kluːd] *vt* einbeziehen; (*in price*) einschließen; **the tip is not ~d in the price** Trinkgeld ist im Preis nicht inbegriffen
including [ɪn'kluːdɪŋ] *prep* einschließlich; **~ service charge** inklusive Bedienung
inclusion [ɪn'kluːʒən] *n* (*see vb*) Einbeziehung *f*; Einschluss *m*
inclusive [ɪn'kluːsɪv] *adj* (*terms*) inklusive; (*price*) Inklusiv-, Pauschal-; **~ of** einschließlich *+gen*
incognito [ɪnkɔg'niːtəu] *adv* inkognito
incoherent [ɪnkəu'hɪərənt] *adj* zusammenhanglos; (*speech*) wirr; (*person*) sich unklar *or* undeutlich ausdrückend
income ['ɪnkʌm] *n* Einkommen *nt*; (*from property, investment, pension*) Einkünfte *pl*; **gross/net ~** Brutto-/Nettoeinkommen *nt*; **~ and expenditure account** Gewinn- und Verlustrechnung *f*; **~ bracket** Einkommensklasse *f*
income support *n* ≈ Sozialhilfe *f*
income tax *n* Einkommenssteuer *f* ▷ *cpd* Steuer-
incoming ['ɪnkʌmɪŋ] *adj* (*passenger*) ankommend; (*flight*) landend; (*call, mail*) eingehend; (*government, official*) neu; (*wave*) hereinbrechend; **~ tide** Flut *f*
incommunicado ['ɪnkəmjunɪ'kɑːdəu] *adj*: **to hold sb ~** jdn ohne jede Verbindung zur Außenwelt halten
incomparable [ɪn'kɔmpərəbl] *adj* unvergleichlich
incompatible [ɪnkəm'pætɪbl] *adj* unvereinbar
incompetence [ɪn'kɔmpɪtns] *n* Unfähigkeit *f*
incompetent [ɪn'kɔmpɪtnt] *adj* unfähig; (*job*) unzulänglich
incomplete [ɪnkəm'pliːt] *adj* unfertig; (*partial*) unvollständig
incomprehensible [ɪnkɔmprɪ'hɛnsɪbl] *adj* unverständlich
inconceivable [ɪnkən'siːvəbl] *adj*: **it is ~ (that ...)** es ist unvorstellbar *or* undenkbar(, dass ...)
inconclusive [ɪnkən'kluːsɪv] *adj* (*experiment, discussion*) ergebnislos; (*evidence, argument*) nicht überzeugend; (*result*) unbestimmt
incongruous [ɪn'kɔŋgruəs] *adj* (*strange*) absurd; (*inappropriate*) unpassend
inconsequential [ɪnkɔnsɪ'kwɛnʃl] *adj* unbedeutend, unwichtig
inconsiderable [ɪnkən'sɪdərəbl] *adj*: **not ~** beachtlich; (*sum*) nicht unerheblich
inconsiderate [ɪnkən'sɪdərət] *adj* rücksichtslos
inconsistency [ɪnkən'sɪstənsɪ] *n* (*see adj*) Widersprüchlichkeit *f*; Inkonsequenz *f*; Unbeständigkeit *f*
inconsistent [ɪnkən'sɪstnt] *adj* widersprüchlich; (*person*) inkonsequent; (*work*)

unbeständig; **to be ~ with** im Widerspruch stehen zu
inconsolable [ɪnkən'səuləbl] *adj* untröstlich
inconspicuous [ɪnkən'spɪkjuəs] *adj* unauffällig; **to make o.s. ~** sich unauffällig benehmen
incontinence [ɪn'kɔntɪnəns] *n* (*Med*) Unfähigkeit *f*, Stuhl und/oder Harn zurückzuhalten, Inkontinenz *f*
incontinent [ɪn'kɔntɪnənt] *adj* (*Med*) unfähig, Stuhl und/oder Harn zurückzuhalten, inkontinent
inconvenience [ɪnkən'vi:njəns] *n* Unannehmlichkeit *f*; (*trouble*) Umstände *pl* ▷ *vt* Umstände bereiten *+dat*; **don't ~ yourself** machen Sie sich keine Umstände
inconvenient [ɪnkən'vi:njənt] *adj* (*time, place*) ungünstig; (*house*) unbequem, unpraktisch; (*visitor*) ungelegen
incorporate [ɪn'kɔ:pəreɪt] *vt* aufnehmen; (*contain*) enthalten; **safety features have been ~d in the design** in der Konstruktion sind auch Sicherheitsvorkehrungen enthalten
incorporated company [ɪn'kɔ:pəreɪtɪd-] (*US*) *n* eingetragene Gesellschaft *f*
incorrect [ɪnkə'rɛkt] *adj* falsch
incorrigible [ɪn'kɔrɪdʒɪbl] *adj* unverbesserlich
incorruptible [ɪnkə'rʌptɪbl] *adj* unbestechlich
increase [*vb* ɪn'kri:s, *n* 'ɪnkri:s] *vi* (*level etc*) zunehmen; (*price*) steigen; (*in size*) sich vergrößern; (*in number, quantity*) sich vermehren ▷ *vt* vergrößern; (*price*) erhöhen ▷ *n*: **~ (in)** Zunahme *f* (*+gen*); (*in wages, spending etc*) Erhöhung *f* (*+gen*); **an ~ of 5%** eine Erhöhung von 5%, eine Zunahme um 5%; **to be on the ~** zunehmen
increasing [ɪn'kri:sɪŋ] *adj* zunehmend
increasingly [ɪn'kri:sɪŋlɪ] *adv* zunehmend
incredible [ɪn'krɛdɪbl] *adj* unglaublich; (*amazing, wonderful*) unwahrscheinlich (*inf*), sagenhaft (*inf*)
incredulity [ɪnkrɪ'dju:lɪtɪ] *n* Ungläubigkeit *f*
incredulous [ɪn'krɛdjuləs] *adj* ungläubig
increment ['ɪnkrɪmənt] *n* (*in salary*) Erhöhung *f*, Zulage *f*
incriminate [ɪn'krɪmɪneɪt] *vt* belasten
incriminating [ɪn'krɪmɪneɪtɪŋ] *adj* belastend
incrusted [ɪn'krʌstɪd] *adj* = **encrusted**
incubate ['ɪnkjubeɪt] *vt* ausbrüten ▷ *vi* ausgebrütet werden; (*disease*) zum Ausbruch kommen
incubation [ɪnkju'beɪʃən] *n* Ausbrüten *nt*; (*of illness*) Inkubation *f*
incubation period *n* Inkubationszeit *f*
incubator ['ɪnkjubeɪtəʳ] *n* (*for babies*) Brutkasten *m*, Inkubator *m*
inculcate ['ɪnkʌlkeɪt] *vt*: **to ~ sth in(to) sb** jdm etw einprägen
incumbent [ɪn'kʌmbənt] *n* Amtsinhaber(in) *m(f)* ▷ *adj*: **it is ~ on him to ...** es obliegt ihm *or* es ist seine Pflicht, zu ...
incur [ɪn'kə:ʳ] *vt* (*expenses, debt*) machen; (*loss*) erleiden; (*disapproval, anger*) sich *dat* zuziehen
incurable [ɪn'kjuərəbl] *adj* unheilbar
incursion [ɪn'kə:ʃən] *n* (*Mil*) Einfall *m*
Ind. (*US*) *abbr* (*Post*) = *Indiana*
indebted [ɪn'dɛtɪd] *adj*: **to be ~ to sb** jdm (zu Dank) verpflichtet sein
indecency [ɪn'di:snsɪ] *n* Unanständigkeit *f*, Anstößigkeit *f*
indecent [ɪn'di:snt] *adj* unanständig, anstößig; (*haste*) ungebührlich
indecent assault (*Brit*) *n* Sexualverbrechen *nt*
indecent exposure *n* Erregung *f* öffentlichen Ärgernisses
indecipherable [ɪndɪ'saɪfərəbl] *adj* unleserlich; (*expression, glance etc*) unergründlich
indecision [ɪndɪ'sɪʒən] *n* Unentschlossenheit *f*
indecisive [ɪndɪ'saɪsɪv] *adj* unentschlossen
indeed [ɪn'di:d] *adv* aber sicher; (*in fact*) tatsächlich, in der Tat; (*furthermore*) sogar; **yes ~!** oh ja!, das kann man wohl sagen!
indefatigable [ɪndɪ'fætɪgəbl] *adj* unermüdlich
indefensible [ɪndɪ'fɛnsɪbl] *adj* (*conduct*) unentschuldbar
indefinable [ɪndɪ'faɪnəbl] *adj* undefinierbar
indefinite [ɪn'dɛfɪnɪt] *adj* unklar, vage; (*period, number*) unbestimmt
indefinite article *n* (*Ling*) unbestimmter Artikel *m*
indefinitely [ɪn'dɛfɪnɪtlɪ] *adv* (*continue*) endlos; (*wait*) unbegrenzt (lange); (*postpone*) auf unbestimmte Zeit
indelible [ɪn'dɛlɪbl] *adj* (*mark, stain*) nicht zu entfernen; **~ pen** Tintenstift *m*; **~ ink** Wäschetinte *f*
indelicate [ɪn'dɛlɪkɪt] *adj* taktlos; (*not polite*) ungehörig
indemnify [ɪn'dɛmnɪfaɪ] *vt* entschädigen
indemnity [ɪn'dɛmnɪtɪ] *n* (*insurance*) Versicherung *f*; (*compensation*) Entschädigung *f*
indent [ɪn'dɛnt] *vt* (*text*) einrücken, einziehen
indentation [ɪndɛn'teɪʃən] *n* Einkerbung *f*; (*Typ*) Einrückung *f*, Einzug *m*; (*on metal*) Delle *f*
indenture [ɪn'dɛntʃəʳ] *n* Ausbildungsvertrag *m*, Lehrvertrag *m*
independence [ɪndɪ'pɛndns] *n* Unabhängigkeit *f*

INDEPENDENCE DAY

Independence Day (der 4. Juli) ist in den USA ein gesetzlicher Feiertag zum Gedenken an die Unabhängigkeitserklärung vom 4. Juli 1776, mit der die 13 amerikanischen Kolonien ihre Freiheit und Unabhängigkeit von Großbritannien erklärten.

independent [ɪndɪ'pɛndnt] *adj* unabhängig
independently [ɪndɪ'pɛndntlɪ] *adv* unabhängig
in-depth ['ɪndɛpθ] *adj* eingehend
indescribable [ɪndɪs'kraɪbəbl] *adj* unbeschreiblich

indestructible [ɪndɪs'trʌktəbl] *adj* unzerstörbar
indeterminate [ɪndɪ'tə:mɪnɪt] *adj* unbestimmt
index ['ɪndɛks] (*pl* **~es**) *n* (*in book*) Register *nt*; (*in library etc*) Katalog *m*; (*also*: **card index**) Kartei *f* (*pl* **indices**: *ratio*) Index *m*; (: *sign*) (An)zeichen *nt*
index card *n* Karteikarte *f*
indexed ['ɪndɛkst] (*US*) *adj* = **index-linked**
index finger *n* Zeigefinger *m*
index-linked ['ɪndɛks'lɪŋkt] *adj* der Inflationsrate *dat* angeglichen
India ['ɪndɪə] *n* Indien *nt*
Indian ['ɪndɪən] *adj* indisch; (*American Indian*) indianisch ▷ *n* Inder(in) *m(f)*; **American ~** Indianer(in) *m(f)*
Indian Ocean *n*: **the ~** der Indische Ozean
Indian summer *n* Altweibersommer *m*
India paper *n* Dünndruckpapier *nt*
India rubber *n* Gummi *m*, Kautschuk *m*
indicate ['ɪndɪkeɪt] *vt* (an)zeigen; (*point to*) deuten auf *+acc*; (*mention*) andeuten ▷ *vi* (*Brit*: *Aut*): **to ~ left/right** links/rechts blinken
indication [ɪndɪ'keɪʃən] *n* (An)zeichen *nt*
indicative [ɪn'dɪkətɪv] *n* (*Ling*) Indikativ *m*, Wirklichkeitsform *f* ▷ *adj*: **to be ~ of sth** auf etw *acc* schließen lassen
indicator ['ɪndɪkeɪtə^r] *n* (*instrument, gauge*) Anzeiger *m*; (*fig*) (An)zeichen *nt*; (*Aut*) Richtungsanzeiger *m*, Blinker *m*
indices ['ɪndɪsi:z] *npl of* **index**
indict [ɪn'daɪt] *vt* anklagen
indictable [ɪn'daɪtəbl] *adj* (*person*) strafrechtlich verfolgbar; **~ offence** strafbare Handlung *f*
indictment [ɪn'daɪtmənt] *n* Anklage *f*; **to be an ~ of sth** (*fig*) ein Armutszeugnis *nt* für etw sein
indifference [ɪn'dɪfrəns] *n* Gleichgültigkeit *f*
indifferent [ɪn'dɪfrənt] *adj* gleichgültig; (*mediocre*) mittelmäßig
indigenous [ɪn'dɪdʒɪnəs] *adj* einheimisch
indigestible [ɪndɪ'dʒɛstɪbl] *adj* unverdaulich
indigestion [ɪndɪ'dʒɛstʃən] *n* Magenverstimmung *f*
indignant [ɪn'dɪgnənt] *adj*: **to be ~ at sth/with sb** entrüstet über etw/jdn sein
indignation [ɪndɪg'neɪʃən] *n* Entrüstung *f*
indignity [ɪn'dɪgnɪtɪ] *n* Demütigung *f*
indigo ['ɪndɪgəu] *n* Indigo *nt or m*
indirect [ɪndɪ'rɛkt] *adj* indirekt; **~ way** *or* **route** Umweg *m*
indirectly [ɪndɪ'rɛktlɪ] *adv* indirekt
indiscreet [ɪndɪs'kri:t] *adj* indiskret
indiscretion [ɪndɪs'krɛʃən] *n* Indiskretion *f*
indiscriminate [ɪndɪs'krɪmɪnət] *adj* wahllos; (*taste*) unkritisch
indispensable [ɪndɪs'pɛnsəbl] *adj* unentbehrlich
indisposed [ɪndɪs'pəuzd] *adj* unpässlich
indisputable [ɪndɪs'pju:təbl] *adj* unbestreitbar
indistinct [ɪndɪs'tɪŋkt] *adj* undeutlich; (*image*) verschwommen; (*noise*) schwach
indistinguishable [ɪndɪs'tɪŋgwɪʃəbl] *adj*: **~ from** nicht zu unterscheiden von
individual [ɪndɪ'vɪdjuəl] *n* Individuum *nt*, Einzelne(r) *f(m)* ▷ *adj* eigen; (*single*) einzeln; (*case, portion*) Einzel-; (*particular*) individuell
individualist [ɪndɪ'vɪdjuəlɪst] *n* Individualist(in) *m(f)*
individuality [ɪndɪvɪdju'ælɪtɪ] *n* Individualität *f*
individually [ɪndɪ'vɪdjuəlɪ] *adv* einzeln, individuell
indivisible [ɪndɪ'vɪzɪbl] *adj* unteilbar
Indochina [ɪndəu'tʃaɪnə] *n* Indochina *nt*
indoctrinate [ɪn'dɔktrɪneɪt] *vt* indoktrinieren
indoctrination [ɪndɔktrɪ'neɪʃən] *n* Indoktrination *f*
indolence ['ɪndələns] *n* Trägheit *f*
indolent ['ɪndələnt] *adj* träge
Indonesia [ɪndə'ni:zɪə] *n* Indonesien *nt*
Indonesian [ɪndə'ni:zɪən] *adj* indonesisch ▷ *n* Indonesier(in) *m(f)*; (*Ling*) Indonesisch *nt*
indoor ['ɪndɔ:^r] *adj* (*plant, aerial*) Zimmer-; (*clothes, shoes*) Haus-; (*swimming pool, sport*) Hallen-; (*games*) im Haus
indoors [ɪn'dɔ:z] *adv* drinnen; **to go ~** hineingehen
indubitable [ɪn'dju:bɪtəbl] *adj* unzweifelhaft
indubitably [ɪn'dju:bɪtəblɪ] *adv* zweifellos
induce [ɪn'dju:s] *vt* herbeiführen; (*persuade*) dazu bringen; (*Med*: *birth*) einleiten; **to ~ sb to do sth** jdn dazu bewegen *or* bringen, etw zu tun
inducement [ɪn'dju:smənt] *n* Anreiz *m*; (*pej*: *bribe*) Bestechung *f*
induct [ɪn'dʌkt] *vt* (in sein/ihr *etc* Amt) einführen
induction [ɪn'dʌkʃən] *n* (*Med*: *of birth*) Einleitung *f*
induction course (*Brit*) *n* Einführungskurs *m*
indulge [ɪn'dʌldʒ] *vt* nachgeben *+dat*; (*person, child*) verwöhnen ▷ *vi*: **to ~ in** sich hingeben *+dat*
indulgence [ɪn'dʌldʒəns] *n* (*pleasure*) Luxus *m*; (*leniency*) Nachgiebigkeit *f*
indulgent [ɪn'dʌldʒənt] *adj* nachsichtig
industrial [ɪn'dʌstrɪəl] *adj* industriell; (*accident*) Arbeits-; (*city*) Industrie-
industrial action *n* Arbeitskampfmaßnahmen *pl*
industrial design *n* Industriedesign *nt*
industrial estate (*Brit*) *n* Industriegebiet *nt*
industrialist [ɪn'dʌstrɪəlɪst] *n* Industrielle(r) *f(m)*
industrialize [ɪn'dʌstrɪəlaɪz] *vt* industrialisieren
industrial park (*US*) *n* = **industrial estate**
industrial relations *npl Beziehungen zwischen Arbeitgebern, Arbeitnehmern und Gewerkschaften*
industrial tribunal (*Brit*) *n* Arbeitsgericht *nt*
industrial unrest (*Brit*) *n* Arbeitsunruhen *pl*
industrious [ɪn'dʌstrɪəs] *adj* fleißig
industry ['ɪndəstrɪ] *n* Industrie *f*; (*diligence*) Fleiß *m*
inebriated [ɪ'ni:brɪeɪtɪd] *adj* betrunken

inedible [ɪn'ɛdɪbl] *adj* ungenießbar
ineffective [ɪnɪ'fɛktɪv] *adj* wirkungslos; (*government*) unfähig
ineffectual [ɪnɪ'fɛktʃuəl] *adj* = **ineffective**
inefficiency [ɪnɪ'fɪʃənsɪ] *n* (*see adj*) Ineffizienz *f*; Leistungsunfähigkeit *f*
inefficient [ɪnɪ'fɪʃənt] *adj* ineffizient; (*machine*) leistungsunfähig
inelegant [ɪn'ɛlɪgənt] *adj* unelegant
ineligible [ɪn'ɛlɪdʒɪbl] *adj* (*candidate*) nicht wählbar; **to be ~ for sth** zu etw nicht berechtigt sein
inept [ɪ'nɛpt] *adj* (*politician*) unfähig; (*management*) stümperhaft
ineptitude [ɪ'nɛptɪtju:d] *n* (*see adj*) Unfähigkeit *f*; Stümperhaftigkeit *f*
inequality [ɪnɪ'kwɔlɪtɪ] *n* Ungleichheit *f*
inequitable [ɪn'ɛkwɪtəbl] *adj* ungerecht
inert [ɪ'nə:t] *adj* unbeweglich; **~ gas** Edelgas *nt*
inertia [ɪ'nə:ʃə] *n* Trägheit *f*
inertia-reel seat belt [ɪ'nə:ʃə'ri:l-] *n* Automatikgurt *m*
inescapable [ɪnɪ'skeɪpəbl] *adj* unvermeidlich; (*conclusion*) zwangsläufig
inessential [ɪnɪ'sɛnʃl] *adj* unwesentlich; (*furniture etc*) entbehrlich
inessentials [ɪnɪ'sɛnʃlz] *npl* Nebensächlichkeiten *pl*
inestimable [ɪn'ɛstɪməbl] *adj* unschätzbar
inevitability [ɪnɛvɪtə'bɪlɪtɪ] *n* Unvermeidlichkeit *f*; **it is an ~** es ist nicht zu vermeiden
inevitable [ɪn'ɛvɪtəbl] *adj* unvermeidlich; (*result*) zwangsläufig
inevitably [ɪn'ɛvɪtəblɪ] *adv* zwangsläufig; **~, he was late** es konnte ja nicht ausbleiben, dass er zu spät kam; **as ~ happens ...** wie es immer so ist ...
inexact [ɪnɪg'zækt] *adj* ungenau
inexcusable [ɪnɪks'kju:zəbl] *adj* unentschuldbar, unverzeihlich
inexhaustible [ɪnɪg'zɔ:stɪbl] *adj* unerschöpflich
inexorable [ɪn'ɛksərəbl] *adj* unaufhaltsam
inexpensive [ɪnɪk'spɛnsɪv] *adj* preisgünstig
inexperience [ɪnɪk'spɪərɪəns] *n* Unerfahrenheit *f*
inexperienced [ɪnɪk'spɪərɪənst] *adj* unerfahren; (*swimmer etc*) ungeübt; **to be ~ in sth** wenig Erfahrung mit etw haben
inexplicable [ɪnɪk'splɪkəbl] *adj* unerklärlich
inexpressible [ɪnɪk'sprɛsɪbl] *adj* unbeschreiblich
inextricable [ɪnɪk'strɪkəbl] *adj* unentwirrbar; (*dilemma*) unlösbar
inextricably [ɪnɪk'strɪkəblɪ] *adv* unentwirrbar; (*linked*) untrennbar
infallibility [ɪnfælə'bɪlɪtɪ] *n* Unfehlbarkeit *f*
infallible [ɪn'fælɪbl] *adj* unfehlbar
infamous ['ɪnfəməs] *adj* niederträchtig
infamy ['ɪnfəmɪ] *n* Verrufenheit *f*
infancy ['ɪnfənsɪ] *n* frühe Kindheit *f*; (*of movement, firm*) Anfangsstadium *nt*
infant ['ɪnfənt] *n* Säugling *m*; (*young child*) Kleinkind *nt* ▷ *cpd* Säuglings-
infantile ['ɪnfəntaɪl] *adj* kindisch, infantil; (*disease*) Kinder-
infantry ['ɪnfəntrɪ] *n* Infanterie *f*
infantryman ['ɪnfəntrɪmən] (*irreg: like* **man**) *n* Infanterist *m*
infant school (*Brit*) *n* Grundschule *f* (*für die ersten beiden Jahrgänge*)
infatuated [ɪn'fætjueɪtɪd] *adj*: **~ with** vernarrt in *+acc*; **to become ~ with** sich vernarren in *+acc*
infatuation [ɪnfætju'eɪʃən] *n* Vernarrtheit *f*
infect [ɪn'fɛkt] *vt* anstecken (*also fig*), infizieren; (*food*) verseuchen; **to become ~ed** (*wound*) sich entzünden
infection [ɪn'fɛkʃən] *n* Infektion *f*, Entzündung *f*; (*contagion*) Ansteckung *f*
infectious [ɪn'fɛkʃəs] *adj* ansteckend
infer [ɪn'fə:ʳ] *vt* schließen; (*imply*) andeuten
inference ['ɪnfərəns] *n* (*see vb*) Schluss *m*; Andeutung *f*
inferior [ɪn'fɪərɪəʳ] *adj* (*in rank*) untergeordnet, niedriger; (*in quality*) minderwertig; (*in quantity, number*) geringer ▷ *n* Untergebene(r) *f(m)*; **to feel ~ (to sb)** sich (jdm) unterlegen fühlen
inferiority [ɪnfɪərɪ'ɔrətɪ] *n* (*see adj*) untergeordnete Stellung *f*, niedriger Rang *m*; Minderwertigkeit *f*; geringere Zahl *f*
inferiority complex *n* Minderwertigkeitskomplex *m*
infernal [ɪn'fə:nl] *adj* höllisch; (*temper*) schrecklich
inferno [ɪn'fə:nəu] *n* (*blaze*) Flammenmeer *nt*
infertile [ɪn'fə:taɪl] *adj* unfruchtbar
infertility [ɪnfə:'tɪlɪtɪ] *n* Unfruchtbarkeit *f*
infested [ɪn'fɛstɪd] *adj*: **~ (with)** verseucht (mit)
infidelity [ɪnfɪ'dɛlɪtɪ] *n* Untreue *f*
infighting ['ɪnfaɪtɪŋ] *n* interne Machtkämpfe *pl*
infiltrate ['ɪnfɪltreɪt] *vt* (*organization etc*) infiltrieren, unterwandern; (*: to spy*) einschleusen
infinite ['ɪnfɪnɪt] *adj* unendlich; (*time, money*) unendlich viel
infinitely ['ɪnfɪnɪtlɪ] *adv* unendlich viel
infinitesimal [ɪnfɪnɪ'tɛsɪməl] *adj* unendlich klein, winzig
infinitive [ɪn'fɪnɪtɪv] *n* (*Ling*) Infinitiv *m*, Grundform *f*
infinity [ɪn'fɪnɪtɪ] *n* Unendlichkeit *f*; (*Math, Phot*) Unendliche *nt*; **an ~ of ...** unendlich viel(e) ...
infirm [ɪn'fə:m] *adj* schwach, gebrechlich
infirmary [ɪn'fə:mərɪ] *n* Krankenhaus *nt*
infirmity [ɪn'fə:mɪtɪ] *n* Schwäche *f*, Gebrechlichkeit *f*
inflame [ɪn'fleɪm] *vt* aufbringen
inflamed [ɪn'fleɪmd] *adj* entzündet
inflammable [ɪn'flæməbl] *adj* feuergefährlich
inflammation [ɪnflə'meɪʃən] *n* Entzündung *f*

inflammatory [ɪn'flæmətərɪ] *adj (speech)* aufrührerisch, Hetz-
inflatable [ɪn'fleɪtəbl] *adj* aufblasbar; *(dinghy)* Schlauch-
inflate [ɪn'fleɪt] *vt* aufpumpen; *(balloon)* aufblasen; *(price)* hochtreiben; *(expectation)* steigern; *(position, ideas etc)* hochspielen
inflated [ɪn'fleɪtɪd] *adj (value, price)* überhöht
inflation [ɪn'fleɪʃən] *n* Inflation *f*
inflationary [ɪn'fleɪʃənərɪ] *adj* inflationär; *(spiral)* Inflations-
inflexible [ɪn'flɛksɪbl] *adj* inflexibel; *(rule)* starr
inflict [ɪn'flɪkt] *vt*: **to ~ sth on sb** *(damage, suffering, wound)* jdm etw zufügen; *(punishment)* jdm etw auferlegen; *(fig: problems)* jdn mit etw belasten
infliction [ɪn'flɪkʃən] *n (see vb)* Zufügen *nt*; Auferlegung *f*; Belastung *f*
in-flight ['ɪnflaɪt] *adj* während des Fluges
inflow ['ɪnfləu] *n* Zustrom *m*
influence ['ɪnfluəns] *n* Einfluss *m* ▷ *vt* beeinflussen; **under the ~ of alcohol** unter Alkoholeinfluss
influential [ɪnflu'ɛnʃl] *adj* einflussreich
influenza [ɪnflu'ɛnzə] *n (Med)* Grippe *f*
influx ['ɪnflʌks] *n (of refugees)* Zustrom *m*; *(of funds)* Zufuhr *f*
inform [ɪn'fɔ:m] *vt*: **to ~ sb of sth** jdn von etw unterrichten, jdn über etw *acc* informieren ▷ *vi*: **to ~ on sb** jdn denunzieren
informal [ɪn'fɔ:ml] *adj* ungezwungen; *(manner, clothes)* leger; *(unofficial)* inoffiziell; *(announcement, invitation)* informell
informality [ɪnfɔ:'mælɪtɪ] *n (see adj)* Ungezwungenheit *f*; legere Art *f*; inoffizieller Charakter *m*; informeller Charakter *m*
informally [ɪn'fɔ:məlɪ] *adv (see adj)* ungezwungen; leger; inoffiziell; informell
informant [ɪn'fɔ:mənt] *n* Informant(in) *m(f)*
information [ɪnfə'meɪʃən] *n* Informationen *pl*, Auskunft *f*; *(knowledge)* Wissen *nt*; **to get ~ on** sich informieren über *+acc*; **a piece of ~** eine Auskunft *or* Information; **for your ~** zu Ihrer Information
information and communication technology *(Brit) n (Scol)* ≈ Informations- und Kommunikationstechnologie
information bureau *n* Auskunftsbüro *nt*
information desk *n* Auskunftsschalter *m*
information office *n* Auskunftsbüro *nt*
information processing *n* Informationsverarbeitung *f*
information retrieval *n* Informationsabruf *m*, Datenabruf *m*
information science *n* Informatik *f*
information superhighway *n (Comput)* Datenautobahn *f*
information technology *n* Informationstechnik *f*
informative [ɪn'fɔ:mətɪv] *adj* aufschlussreich
informed [ɪn'fɔ:md] *adj* informiert; *(guess, opinion)* wohlbegründet; **to be well/better ~** gut/besser informiert sein
informer [ɪn'fɔ:məʳ] *n* Informant(in) *m(f)*; *(also:* **police informer**) Polizeispitzel *m*
infra dig ['ɪnfrə'dɪg] *(inf) adj abbr (= infra dignitatem)* unter meiner/seiner *etc* Würde
infrared [ɪnfrə'rɛd] *adj* infrarot
infrastructure ['ɪnfrəstrʌktʃəʳ] *n* Infrastruktur *f*
infrequent [ɪn'fri:kwənt] *adj* selten
infringe [ɪn'frɪndʒ] *vt (law)* verstoßen gegen, übertreten ▷ *vi*: **to ~ on** *(rights)* verletzen
infringement [ɪn'frɪndʒmənt] *n (see vb)* Verstoß *m*, Übertretung *f*; Verletzung *f*
infuriate [ɪn'fjuərɪeɪt] *vt* wütend machen
infuriating [ɪn'fjuərɪeɪtɪŋ] *adj* äußerst ärgerlich
infuse [ɪn'fju:z] *vt (tea etc)* aufgießen; **to ~ sb with sth** *(fig)* jdm etw einflößen
infusion [ɪn'fju:ʒən] *n (tea etc)* Aufguss *m*
ingenious [ɪn'dʒi:njəs] *adj* genial
ingenuity [ɪndʒɪ'nju:ɪtɪ] *n* Einfallsreichtum *m*; *(skill)* Geschicklichkeit *f*
ingenuous [ɪn'dʒɛnjuəs] *adj* offen, aufrichtig; *(innocent)* naiv
ingot ['ɪŋgət] *n* Barren *m*
ingrained [ɪn'greɪnd] *adj (habit)* fest; *(belief)* unerschütterlich
ingratiate [ɪn'greɪʃɪeɪt] *vt*: **to ~ o.s. with sb** sich bei jdm einschmeicheln
ingratiating [ɪn'greɪʃɪeɪtɪŋ] *adj* schmeichlerisch
ingratitude [ɪn'grætɪtju:d] *n* Undank *m*
ingredient [ɪn'gri:dɪənt] *n (of cake etc)* Zutat *f*; *(of situation)* Bestandteil *m*
ingrowing ['ɪngrəuɪŋ] *adj*: **~ toenail** eingewachsener Zehennagel *m*
inhabit [ɪn'hæbɪt] *vt* bewohnen, wohnen in *+dat*
inhabitant [ɪn'hæbɪtnt] *n* Einwohner(in) *m(f)*; *(of street, house)* Bewohner(in) *m(f)*
inhale [ɪn'heɪl] *vt* einatmen ▷ *vi* einatmen; *(when smoking)* inhalieren
inhaler [ɪn'heɪləʳ] *n* Inhalationsapparat *m*
inherent [ɪn'hɪərənt] *adj*: **~ in** *or* **to** eigen *+dat*
inherently [ɪn'hɪərəntlɪ] *adv* von Natur aus
inherit [ɪn'hɛrɪt] *vt* erben
inheritance [ɪn'hɛrɪtəns] *n* Erbe *nt*
inhibit [ɪn'hɪbɪt] *vt* hemmen
inhibited [ɪn'hɪbɪtɪd] *adj* gehemmt
inhibiting [ɪn'hɪbɪtɪŋ] *adj* hemmend; **~ factor** Hemmnis *nt*
inhibition [ɪnhɪ'bɪʃən] *n* Hemmung *f*
inhospitable [ɪnhɔs'pɪtəbl] *adj* ungastlich; *(place, climate)* unwirtlich
in-house ['ɪn'haus] *adj, adv* hausintern
inhuman [ɪn'hju:mən] *adj (behaviour)* unmenschlich; *(appearance)* nicht menschlich
inhumane [ɪnhju:'meɪn] *adj* inhuman; *(treatment)* menschenunwürdig
inimitable [ɪ'nɪmɪtəbl] *adj* unnachahmlich
iniquitous [ɪ'nɪkwɪtəs] *adj (unfair)* ungerecht
iniquity [ɪ'nɪkwɪtɪ] *n* Ungerechtigkeit *f*; *(wickedness)* Ungeheuerlichkeit *f*
initial [ɪ'nɪʃl] *adj* anfänglich; *(stage)* Anfangs-

▷*n* Initiale *f*, Anfangsbuchstabe *m* ▷*vt* (*document*) abzeichnen; **initials** *npl* Initialen *pl*; (*as signature*) Namenszeichen *nt*
initialize [ɪ'nɪʃəlaɪz] *vt* initialisieren
initially [ɪ'nɪʃəlɪ] *adv* zu Anfang; (*first*) zuerst
initiate [ɪ'nɪʃɪeɪt] *vt* (*talks*) eröffnen; (*process*) einleiten; (*new member*) feierlich aufnehmen; **to ~ sb into a secret** jdn in ein Geheimnis einweihen; **to ~ proceedings against sb** (*Law*) einen Prozess gegen jdn anstrengen
initiation [ɪnɪʃɪ'eɪʃən] *n* (*beginning*) Einführung *f*; (*into secret etc*) Einweihung *f*
initiative [ɪ'nɪʃətɪv] *n* Initiative *f*; **to take the ~** die Initiative ergreifen
inject [ɪn'dʒɛkt] *vt* (ein)spritzen; (*fig: funds*) hineinpumpen; **to ~ sb with sth** jdm etw spritzen *or* injizieren; **to ~ money into sth** (*fig*) Geld in etw *acc* pumpen
injection [ɪn'dʒɛkʃən] *n* Spritze *f*, Injektion *f*; **to give/have an ~** eine Spritze *or* Injektion geben/bekommen; **an ~ of money/funds** (*fig*) eine Finanzspritze
injudicious [ɪndʒu'dɪʃəs] *adj* unklug
injunction [ɪn'dʒʌŋkʃən] *n* (*Law*) gerichtliche Verfügung *f*
injure ['ɪndʒə^r] *vt* verletzen; (*reputation*) schaden *+dat*; **to ~ o.s.** sich verletzen
injured ['ɪndʒəd] *adj* verletzt; (*tone*) gekränkt; **~ party** (*Law*) Geschädigte(r) *f(m)*
injurious [ɪn'dʒuərɪəs] *adj*: **to be ~ to** schaden *+dat*, schädlich sein *+dat*
injury ['ɪndʒərɪ] *n* Verletzung *f*; **to escape without ~** unverletzt davonkommen
injury time *n* (*Sport*) Nachspielzeit *f*; **to play ~** nachspielen
injustice [ɪn'dʒʌstɪs] *n* Ungerechtigkeit *f*; **you do me an ~** Sie tun mir unrecht
ink [ɪŋk] *n* Tinte *f*; (*in printing*) Druckfarbe *f*
ink-jet printer ['ɪŋkdʒɛt-] *n* Tintenstrahldrucker *m*
inkling ['ɪŋklɪŋ] *n* (dunkle) Ahnung *f*; **to have an ~ of** ahnen
ink pad *n* Stempelkissen *nt*
inky ['ɪŋkɪ] *adj* tintenschwarz; (*fingers*) tintenbeschmiert
inlaid ['ɪnleɪd] *adj* eingelegt
inland ['ɪnlənd] *adj* (*port, sea, waterway*) Binnen- ▷*adv* (*travel*) landeinwärts
Inland Revenue (*Brit*) *n* ≈ Finanzamt *nt*
in-laws ['ɪnlɔːz] *npl* (*parents-in-law*) Schwiegereltern *pl*; (*other relatives*) angeheiratete Verwandte *pl*
inlet ['ɪnlɛt] *n* (schmale) Bucht *f*
inlet pipe *n* Zuleitung *f*, Zuleitungsrohr *nt*
inmate ['ɪnmeɪt] *n* Insasse *m*, Insassin *f*
inmost ['ɪnməust] *adj* innerst
inn [ɪn] *n* Gasthaus *nt*
innards ['ɪnədz] (*inf*) *npl* Innereien *pl*
innate [ɪ'neɪt] *adj* angeboren
inner ['ɪnə^r] *adj* innere(r, s); (*courtyard*) Innen-
inner city *n* Innenstadt *f*
innermost ['ɪnəməust] *adj* = **inmost**
inner tube *n* (*of tyre*) Schlauch *m*
innings ['ɪnɪŋz] *n* (*Cricket*) Innenrunde *f*; **he's had a good ~** (*fig*) er kann auf ein langes, ausgefülltes Leben zurückblicken
innocence ['ɪnəsns] *n* Unschuld *f*
innocent ['ɪnəsnt] *adj* unschuldig
innocuous [ɪ'nɔkjuəs] *adj* harmlos
innovation [ɪnəu'veɪʃən] *n* Neuerung *f*
innuendo [ɪnju'ɛndəu] (*pl* **~es**) *n* versteckte Andeutung *f*
innumerable [ɪ'njuːmrəbl] *adj* unzählig
inoculate [ɪ'nɔkjuleɪt] *vt*: **to ~ sb against sth** jdn gegen etw impfen; **to ~ sb with sth** jdm etw einimpfen
inoculation [ɪnɔkju'leɪʃən] *n* Impfung *f*
inoffensive [ɪnə'fɛnsɪv] *adj* harmlos
inopportune [ɪn'ɔpətjuːn] *adj* unangebracht; (*moment*) ungelegen
inordinate [ɪ'nɔːdɪnət] *adj* (*thirst etc*) unmäßig; (*amount, pleasure*) ungeheuer
inordinately [ɪ'nɔːdɪnətlɪ] *adv* (*proud*) unmäßig; (*long, large etc*) ungeheuer
inorganic [ɪnɔː'gænɪk] *adj* anorganisch
inpatient ['ɪnpeɪʃənt] *n* stationär behandelter Patient *m*, stationär behandelte Patientin *f*
input ['ɪnput] *n* (*of capital, manpower*) Investition *f*; (*of energy*) Zufuhr *f*; (*Comput*) Eingabe *f*, Input *m or nt* ▷*vt* (*Comput*) eingeben
inquest ['ɪnkwɛst] *n* gerichtliche Untersuchung *f* der Todesursache
inquire [ɪn'kwaɪə^r] *vi*: **to ~ about** sich erkundigen nach, fragen nach ▷*vt* sich erkundigen nach, fragen nach; **to ~ when/where/whether** fragen *or* sich erkundigen, wann/wo/ob
▸ **inquire after** *vt fus* sich erkundigen nach
▸ **inquire into** *vt fus* untersuchen
inquiring [ɪn'kwaɪərɪŋ] *adj* wissensdurstig
inquiry [ɪn'kwaɪərɪ] *n* Untersuchung *f*; (*question*) Anfrage *f*; **to hold an ~ into sth** eine Untersuchung *+gen* durchführen
inquiry desk (*Brit*) *n* Auskunft *f*, Auskunftsschalter *m*
inquiry office (*Brit*) *n* Auskunft *f*, Auskunftsbüro *nt*
inquisition [ɪnkwɪ'zɪʃən] *n* Untersuchung *f*; (*Rel*): **the I~** die Inquisition
inquisitive [ɪn'kwɪzɪtɪv] *adj* neugierig
inroads ['ɪnrəudz] *npl*: **to make ~ into** (*savings, supplies*) angreifen
ins *abbr* (*= inches*) *see* **inch**
insane [ɪn'seɪn] *adj* wahnsinnig; (*Med*) geisteskrank
insanitary [ɪn'sænɪtərɪ] *adj* unhygienisch
insanity [ɪn'sænɪtɪ] *n* Wahnsinn *m*; (*Med*) Geisteskrankheit *f*
insatiable [ɪn'seɪʃəbl] *adj* unersättlich
inscribe [ɪn'skraɪb] *vt* (*on ring*) eingravieren; (*on stone*) einmeißeln; (*on banner*) schreiben; **to ~ a ring/stone/banner with sth** etw in einen Ring eingravieren/in einen Stein einmeißeln/auf ein Spruchband schreiben; **to ~ a book** eine Widmung in ein Buch schreiben

inscription [ɪn'skrɪpʃən] *n* Inschrift *f*; (*in book*) Widmung *f*
inscrutable [ɪn'skruːtəbl] *adj* (*comment*) unergründlich; (*expression*) undurchdringlich
inseam measurement ['ɪnsiːm-] (*US*) *n* innere Beinlänge *f*
insect ['ɪnsɛkt] *n* Insekt *nt*
insect bite *n* Insektenstich *m*
insecticide [ɪn'sɛktɪsaɪd] *n* Insektizid *nt*, Insektengift *nt*
insect repellent *n* Insektenbekämpfungsmittel *nt*
insecure [ɪnsɪ'kjuəʳ] *adj* unsicher
insecurity [ɪnsɪ'kjuərɪtɪ] *n* Unsicherheit *f*
insemination [ɪnsɛmɪ'neɪʃən] *n*: **artificial ~** künstliche Besamung *f*
insensible [ɪn'sɛnsɪbl] *adj* bewusstlos; **~ to** unempfindlich gegen; **~ of** nicht bewusst *+gen*
insensitive [ɪn'sɛnsɪtɪv] *adj* gefühllos
insensitivity [ɪnsɛnsɪ'tɪvɪtɪ] *n* Gefühllosigkeit *f*
inseparable [ɪn'sɛprəbl] *adj* untrennbar; (*friends*) unzertrennlich
insert [*vt* ɪn'səːt, *n* 'ɪnsəːt] *vt* einfügen; (*into sth*) hineinstecken ▷ *n* (*in newspaper etc*) Beilage *f*; (*in shoe*) Einlage *f*
insertion [ɪn'səːʃən] *n* Hineinstecken *nt*; (*of needle*) Einstechen *nt*; (*of comment*) Einfügen *nt*
in-service ['ɪn'səːvɪs] *adj*: **~ training** (berufsbegleitende) Fortbildung *f*; **~ course** Fortbildungslehrgang *m*
inshore ['ɪn'ʃɔːʳ] *adj* (*fishing, waters*) Küsten- ▷ *adv* in Küstennähe; (*move*) auf die Küste zu
inside ['ɪn'saɪd] *n* Innere(s) *nt*, Innenseite *f*; (*of road: in Britain*) linke Spur *f*; (*: in US, Europe etc*) rechte Spur *f* ▷ *adj* innere(r, s); (*pocket, cabin, light*) Innen- ▷ *adv* (*go*) nach innen, hinein; (*be*) drinnen ▷ *prep* (*location*) in *+dat*; (*motion*) in *+acc*; **~ 10 minutes** innerhalb von 10 Minuten; **insides** *npl* (*inf*) Bauch *m*; (*innards*) Eingeweide *pl*
inside forward *n* (*Sport*) Halbstürmer *m*
inside information *n* Insiderinformation *f*
inside knowledge *n* Insiderwissen *nt*
inside lane *n* (*Brit*) linke Spur *f*; (*in US, Europe etc*) rechte Spur *f*
inside leg measurement (*Brit*) *n* innere Beinlänge *f*
inside out *adv* (*know*) in- und auswendig; (*piece of clothing: be*) links *or* verkehrt herum; (*: turn*) nach links
insider [ɪn'saɪdəʳ] *n* Insider *m*, Eingeweihte(r) *f(m)*
insider dealing, insider trading *n* (*Stock Exchange*) Insiderhandel *m or* -geschäfte *pl*
inside story *n* Insidestory *f*, Inside Story *f*
insidious [ɪn'sɪdɪəs] *adj* heimtückisch
insight ['ɪnsaɪt] *n* Verständnis *nt*; **to gain (an) ~ into** einen Einblick gewinnen in *+acc*
insignia [ɪn'sɪgnɪə] *npl* Insignien *pl*
insignificant [ɪnsɪg'nɪfɪknt] *adj* belanglos
insincere [ɪnsɪn'sɪəʳ] *adj* unaufrichtig, falsch
insincerity [ɪnsɪn'sɛrɪtɪ] *n* Unaufrichtigkeit *f*, Falschheit *f*
insinuate [ɪn'sɪnjueɪt] *vt* anspielen auf *+acc*
insinuation [ɪnsɪnju'eɪʃən] *n* Anspielung *f*
insipid [ɪn'sɪpɪd] *adj* fad(e); (*person*) geistlos; (*colour*) langweilig
insist [ɪn'sɪst] *vi* bestehen; **to ~ on** bestehen auf *+dat*; **to ~ that** darauf bestehen, dass; (*claim*) behaupten, dass
insistence [ɪn'sɪstəns] *n* (*determination*) Bestehen *nt*
insistent [ɪn'sɪstənt] *adj* (*determined*) hartnäckig; (*continual*) andauernd, penetrant (*pej*)
in so far as *adv* insofern als
insole ['ɪnsəul] *n* Einlegesohle *f*
insolence ['ɪnsələns] *n* Frechheit *f*, Unverschämtheit *f*
insolent ['ɪnsələnt] *adj* frech, unverschämt
insoluble [ɪn'sɔljubl] *adj* unlösbar
insolvency [ɪn'sɔlvənsɪ] *n* Zahlungsunfähigkeit *f*
insolvent [ɪn'sɔlvənt] *adj* zahlungsunfähig
insomnia [ɪn'sɔmnɪə] *n* Schlaflosigkeit *f*
insomniac [ɪn'sɔmnɪæk] *n*: **to be an ~** an Schlaflosigkeit leiden
inspect [ɪn'spɛkt] *vt* kontrollieren; (*examine*) prüfen; (*troops*) inspizieren
inspection [ɪn'spɛkʃən] *n* (*see vb*) Kontrolle *f*; Prüfung *f*; Inspektion *f*
inspector [ɪn'spɛktəʳ] *n* Inspektor(in) *m(f)*; (*Brit: on buses, trains*) Kontrolleur(in) *m(f)*; (*: Police*) Kommissar(in) *m(f)*
inspiration [ɪnspə'reɪʃən] *n* Inspiration *f*; (*idea*) Eingebung *f*
inspire [ɪn'spaɪəʳ] *vt* inspirieren; (*confidence, hope etc*) (er)wecken
inspired [ɪn'spaɪəd] *adj* genial; **in an ~ moment** in einem Augenblick der Inspiration
inspiring [ɪn'spaɪərɪŋ] *adj* inspirierend
inst. (*Brit*) *abbr* (*Comm: = instant*): **of the 16th ~** vom 16. d. M.
instability [ɪnstə'bɪlɪtɪ] *n* Instabilität *f*; (*of person*) Labilität *f*
install [ɪn'stɔːl] *vt* installieren; (*telephone*) anschließen; (*official*) einsetzen; **to ~ o.s.** sich niederlassen
installation [ɪnstə'leɪʃən] *n* Installation *f*; (*of telephone*) Anschluss *m*; (*Industry, Mil: plant*) Anlage *f*
installment plan (*US*) *n* Ratenzahlung *f*
instalment, (US) installment [ɪn'stɔːlmənt] *n* Rate *f*; (*of story*) Fortsetzung *f*; (*of TV serial etc*) (Sende)folge *f*; **in ~s** in Raten
instance ['ɪnstəns] *n* Beispiel *nt*; **for ~** zum Beispiel; **in that ~** in diesem Fall; **in many ~s** in vielen Fällen; **in the first ~** zuerst *or* zunächst (einmal)
instant ['ɪnstənt] *n* Augenblick *m* ▷ *adj* (*reaction*) unmittelbar; (*success*) sofortig; **~ food** Schnellgerichte *pl*; **~ coffee** Instantkaffee *m*; **the 10th ~** (*Comm, Admin*) der 10. dieses Monats
instantaneous [ɪnstən'teɪnɪəs] *adj*

unmittelbar
instantly ['ɪnstəntlɪ] *adv* sofort
instant replay *n* (*TV*) Wiederholung *f*
instead [ɪn'stɛd] *adv* stattdessen; **~ of** statt *+gen*; **~ of sb** an jds Stelle *dat*; **~ of doing sth** anstatt *or* anstelle etw zu tun
instep ['ɪnstɛp] *n* (*of foot*) Spann *m*; (*of shoe*) Blatt *nt*
instigate ['ɪnstɪgeɪt] *vt* anstiften, anzetteln; (*talks etc*) initiieren
instigation [ɪnstɪ'geɪʃən] *n* (*see vb*) Anstiftung *f*, Anzettelung *f*; Initiierung *f*; **at sb's ~** auf jds Betreiben *acc*
instil [ɪn'stɪl] *vt*: **to ~ sth into sb** (*confidence, fear etc*) jdm etw einflößen
instinct ['ɪnstɪŋkt] *n* Instinkt *m*; (*reaction, inclination*) instinktive Reaktion *f*
instinctive [ɪn'stɪŋktɪv] *adj* instinktiv
instinctively [ɪn'stɪŋktɪvlɪ] *adv* instinktiv
institute ['ɪnstɪtju:t] *n* Institut *nt*; (*for teaching*) Hochschule *f*; (*professional body*) Bund *m*, Verband *m* ▷ *vt* einführen; (*inquiry, course of action*) einleiten; (*proceedings*) anstrengen
institution [ɪnstɪ'tju:ʃən] *n* Einführung *f*; (*organization*) Institution *f*, Einrichtung *f*; (*hospital, mental home*) Anstalt *f*, Heim *nt*
institutional [ɪnstɪ'tju:ʃənl] *adj* (*education*) institutionell; (*value, quality etc*) institutionalisiert; **~ care** Unterbringung *f* in einem Heim *or* einer Anstalt; **to be in ~ care** in einem Heim *or* einer Anstalt sein
instruct [ɪn'strʌkt] *vt*: **to ~ sb in sth** jdn in etw *dat* unterrichten; **to ~ sb to do sth** jdn anweisen, etw zu tun
instruction [ɪn'strʌkʃən] *n* Unterricht *m*; **instructions** *npl* (*orders*) Anweisungen *pl*; **~s (for use)** Gebrauchsanweisung *f*, Gebrauchsanleitung *f*; **~ book/manual/leaflet** *etc* Bedienungsanleitung *f*
instructive [ɪn'strʌktɪv] *adj* lehrreich; (*response*) aufschlussreich
instructor [ɪn'strʌktəʳ] *n* Lehrer(in) *m(f)*
instrument ['ɪnstrumənt] *n* Instrument *nt*; (*Mus*) (Musik)instrument *nt*
instrumental [ɪnstru'mɛntl] *adj* (*Mus: music, accompaniment*) Instrumental-; **to be ~ in** eine bedeutende Rolle spielen bei
instrumentalist [ɪnstru'mɛntəlɪst] *n* Instrumentalist(in) *m(f)*
instrument panel *n* Armaturenbrett *nt*
insubordination [ɪnsəbɔ:dɪ'neɪʃən] *n* Gehorsamsverweigerung *f*
insufferable [ɪn'sʌfrəbl] *adj* unerträglich
insufficient [ɪnsə'fɪʃənt] *adj* unzureichend
insufficiently [ɪnsə'fɪʃəntlɪ] *adv* unzureichend
insular ['ɪnsjuləʳ] *adj* engstirnig
insulate ['ɪnsjuleɪt] *vt* isolieren; (*person, group*) abschirmen
insulating tape ['ɪnsjuleɪtɪŋ-] *n* Isolierband *nt*
insulation [ɪnsju'leɪʃən] *n* (*see vb*) Isolierung *f*; Abschirmung *f*
insulator ['ɪnsjuleɪtəʳ] *n* Isolierstoff *m*
insulin ['ɪnsjulɪn] *n* Insulin *nt*
insult [*n* 'ɪnsʌlt, *vt* ɪn'sʌlt] *n* Beleidigung *f* ▷ *vt* beleidigen
insulting [ɪn'sʌltɪŋ] *adj* beleidigend
insuperable [ɪn'sju:prəbl] *adj* unüberwindlich
insurance [ɪn'ʃuərəns] *n* Versicherung *f*; **fire/life ~** Brand-/Lebensversicherung *f*; **to take out ~ (against)** eine Versicherung abschließen (gegen)
insurance agent *n* Versicherungsvertreter(in) *m(f)*
insurance broker *n* Versicherungsmakler(in) *m(f)*
insurance policy *n* Versicherungspolice *f*
insurance premium *n* Versicherungsprämie *f*
insure [ɪn'ʃuəʳ] *vt* versichern; **to ~ o.s./sth against sth** sich/etw gegen etw versichern; **to ~ o.s.** *or* **one's life** eine Lebensversicherung abschließen; **to ~ (o.s.) against sth** (*fig*) sich gegen etw absichern; **to be ~d for £5,000** für £5000 versichert sein
insured [ɪn'ʃuəd] *n*: **the ~** der/die Versicherte
insurer [ɪn'ʃuərəʳ] *n* Versicherer *m*
insurgent [ɪn'sə:dʒənt] *adj* aufständisch ▷ *n* Aufständische(r) *f(m)*
insurmountable [ɪnsə'mauntəbl] *adj* unüberwindlich
insurrection [ɪnsə'rɛkʃən] *n* Aufstand *m*
intact [ɪn'tækt] *adj* intakt; (*whole*) ganz; (*unharmed*) unversehrt
intake ['ɪnteɪk] *n* (*of food*) Aufnahme *f*; (*of air*) Zufuhr *f*; (*Brit: Scol*): **an ~ of 200 a year** 200 neue Schüler pro Jahr
intangible [ɪn'tændʒɪbl] *adj* unbestimmbar; (*idea*) vage; (*benefit*) immateriell
integer ['ɪntɪdʒəʳ] *n* (*Math*) ganze Zahl *f*
integral ['ɪntɪgrəl] *adj* wesentlich
integrate ['ɪntɪgreɪt] *vt* integrieren ▷ *vi* sich integrieren
integrated circuit ['ɪntɪgreɪtɪd-] *n* (*Comput*) integrierter Schaltkreis *m*
integration [ɪntɪ'greɪʃən] *n* Integration *f*; **racial ~** Rassenintegration *f*
integrity [ɪn'tɛgrɪtɪ] *n* Integrität *f*; (*of group*) Einheit *f*; (*of culture, text*) Unversehrtheit *f*
intellect ['ɪntəlɛkt] *n* Intellekt *m*
intellectual [ɪntə'lɛktjuəl] *adj* intellektuell, geistig ▷ *n* Intellektuelle(r) *f(m)*
intelligence [ɪn'tɛlɪdʒəns] *n* Intelligenz *f*; (*information*) Informationen *pl*
intelligence quotient *n* Intelligenzquotient *m*
intelligence service *n* Nachrichtendienst *m*, Geheimdienst *m*
intelligence test *n* Intelligenztest *m*
intelligent [ɪn'tɛlɪdʒənt] *adj* intelligent; (*decision*) klug
intelligently [ɪn'tɛlɪdʒəntlɪ] *adv* intelligent
intelligentsia [ɪntɛlɪ'dʒɛntsɪə] *n*: **the ~** die Intelligenz
intelligible [ɪn'tɛlɪdʒɪbl] *adj* verständlich
intemperate [ɪn'tɛmpərət] *adj* unmäßig; (*remark*) überzogen
intend [ɪn'tɛnd] *vt*: **to be ~ed for sb** für jdn gedacht sein; **to ~ to do sth** beabsichtigen,

etw zu tun
intended [ɪn'tɛndɪd] *adj* *(effect, victim)* beabsichtigt; *(journey)* geplant; *(insult)* absichtlich
intense [ɪn'tɛns] *adj* intensiv; *(anger, joy)* äußerst groß; *(person)* ernsthaft
intensely [ɪn'tɛnslɪ] *adv* äußerst; **I dislike him ~** ich verabscheue ihn
intensify [ɪn'tɛnsɪfaɪ] *vt* intensivieren, verstärken
intensity [ɪn'tɛnsɪtɪ] *n* Intensität *f*; *(of anger)* Heftigkeit *f*
intensive [ɪn'tɛnsɪv] *adj* intensiv
intensive care *n*: **to be in ~** auf der Intensivstation sein
intensive care unit *n* Intensivstation *f*
intent [ɪn'tɛnt] *n* Absicht *f* ▷ *adj* *(attentive)* aufmerksam; *(absorbed)*: **~ (on)** versunken (in *+acc*); **to all ~s and purposes** im Grunde; **to be ~ on doing sth** entschlossen sein, etw zu tun
intention [ɪn'tɛnʃən] *n* Absicht *f*
intentional [ɪn'tɛnʃənl] *adj* absichtlich
intentionally [ɪn'tɛnʃnəlɪ] *adv* absichtlich
intently [ɪn'tɛntlɪ] *adv* konzentriert
inter [ɪn'tə:ʳ] *vt* bestatten
interact [ɪntər'ækt] *vi* *(people)* interagieren; *(things)* aufeinander einwirken; *(ideas)* sich gegenseitig beeinflussen; **to ~ with** interagieren mit; einwirken auf *+acc*; beeinflussen
interaction [ɪntər'ækʃən] *n* *(see vb)* Interaktion *f*; gegenseitige Einwirkung *f*; gegenseitige Beeinflussung *f*
interactive [ɪntər'æktɪv] *adj* *(also Comput)* interaktiv
intercede [ɪntə'si:d] *vi*: **to ~ (with sb/on behalf of sb)** sich (bei jdm/für jdn) einsetzen
intercept [ɪntə'sɛpt] *vt* abfangen
interception [ɪntə'sɛpʃən] *n* Abfangen *nt*
interchange ['ɪntətʃeɪndʒ] *n* Austausch *m*; *(on motorway)* (Autobahn)kreuz *nt*
interchangeable [ɪntə'tʃeɪndʒəbl] *adj* austauschbar
intercity [ɪntə'sɪtɪ] *adj*: **~ train** Intercityzug *m*
intercom ['ɪntəkɔm] *n* (Gegen)sprechanlage *f*
interconnect [ɪntəkə'nɛkt] *vi* *(rooms)* miteinander verbunden sein
intercontinental ['ɪntəkɔntɪ'nɛntl] *adj* *(flight, missile)* Interkontinental-
intercourse ['ɪntəkɔ:s] *n* *(sexual)* (Geschlechts)verkehr *m*; *(social, verbal)* Verkehr *m*
intercultural [ɪntə'kʌltʃərəl] *adj* interkulturell
interdependence [ɪntədɪ'pɛndəns] *n* gegenseitige Abhängigkeit *f*
interdependent [ɪntədɪ'pɛndənt] *adj* voneinander abhängig
interest ['ɪntrɪst] *n* Interesse *nt*; *(Comm: in company)* Anteil *m*; *(: sum of money)* Zinsen *pl* ▷ *vt* interessieren; **compound ~** Zinseszins *m*; **simple ~** einfache Zinsen; **British ~s in the Middle East** britische Interessen im Nahen Osten; **his main ~ is ...** er interessiert sich hauptsächlich für ...
interested ['ɪntrɪstɪd] *adj* interessiert; *(party, body etc)* beteiligt; **to be ~ in sth** sich für etw interessieren; **to be ~ in doing sth** daran interessiert sein, etw zu tun
interest-free ['ɪntrɪst'fri:] *adj, adv* zinslos
interesting ['ɪntrɪstɪŋ] *adj* interessant
interest rate *n* Zinssatz *m*
interface ['ɪntəfeɪs] *n* Verbindung *f*; *(Comput)* Schnittstelle *f*
interfere [ɪntə'fɪəʳ] *vi*: **to ~ in** sich einmischen in *+acc*; **to ~ with** *(object)* sich zu schaffen machen an *+dat*; *(plans)* durchkreuzen; *(career, duty, decision)* beeinträchtigen; **don't ~** misch dich nicht ein
interference [ɪntə'fɪərəns] *n* Einmischung *f*; *(Radio, TV)* Störung *f*
interfering [ɪntə'fɪərɪŋ] *adj* *(person)* sich ständig einmischend
interim ['ɪntərɪm] *adj* *(agreement, government etc)* Übergangs- ▷ *n*: **in the ~** in der Zwischenzeit
interim dividend *n* *(Comm)* Abschlagsdividende *f*
interior [ɪn'tɪərɪəʳ] *n* Innere(s) *nt*; *(decor etc)* Innenausstattung *f* ▷ *adj* Innen-
interior decorator *n* Innenausstatter(in) *m(f)*
interior designer *n* Innenarchitekt(in) *m(f)*
interjection [ɪntə'dʒɛkʃən] *n* Einwurf *m*; *(Ling)* Interjektion *f*
interlock [ɪntə'lɔk] *vi* ineinandergreifen
interloper ['ɪntələupəʳ] *n* Eindringling *m*
interlude ['ɪntəlu:d] *n* Unterbrechung *f*, Pause *f*; *(Theat)* Zwischenspiel *nt*
intermarry [ɪntə'mærɪ] *vi* untereinander heiraten
intermediary [ɪntə'mi:dɪərɪ] *n* Vermittler(in) *m(f)*
intermediate [ɪntə'mi:dɪət] *adj* *(stage)* Zwischen-; **an ~ student** ein fortgeschrittener Anfänger
interment [ɪn'tə:mənt] *n* Bestattung *f*
interminable [ɪn'tə:mɪnəbl] *adj* endlos
intermission [ɪntə'mɪʃən] *n* Pause *f*
intermittent [ɪntə'mɪtnt] *adj* *(noise)* periodisch auftretend; *(publication)* in unregelmäßigen Abständen veröffentlicht
intermittently [ɪntə'mɪtntlɪ] *adv* *(see adj)* periodisch; in unregelmäßigen Abständen
intern [*vt* ɪn'tə:n, *n* 'ɪntə:n] *vt* internieren ▷ *n* *(US)* Assistenzarzt *m*, Assistenzärztin *f*
internal [ɪn'tə:nl] *adj* innere(r, s); *(pipes)* im Haus; *(politics)* Innen-; *(dispute, reform, memo, structure etc)* intern
internally [ɪn'tə:nəlɪ] *adv*: **"not to be taken ~"** „nicht zum Einnehmen"
Internal Revenue Service *(US) n* ≈ Finanzamt *nt*
international [ɪntə'næʃənl] *adj* international ▷ *n* *(Brit: Sport)* Länderspiel *nt*
International Atomic Energy Agency *n* *Internationale Atomenergiebehörde*
International Chamber of Commerce *n*

Internationale Handelskammer *f*
International Court of Justice *n* Internationaler Gerichtshof *m*
international date line *n* Datumsgrenze *f*
International Labour Organization *n* Internationale Arbeitsorganisation *f*
internationally [ɪntəˈnæʃnəlɪ] *adv* international
International Monetary Fund *n* Internationaler Währungsfonds *m*
international relations *npl* zwischenstaatliche Beziehungen *pl*
internecine [ɪntəˈniːsaɪn] *adj* mörderisch; (*war*) Vernichtungs-
internee [ɪntəːˈniː] *n* Internierte(r) *f(m)*
Internet [ˈɪntənɛt] *n* Internet *nt*
Internet café *n* Internetcafé *nt*
internment [ɪnˈtəːnmənt] *n* Internierung *f*
interplay [ˈɪntəpleɪ] *n*: **~ (of** *or* **between)** Zusammenspiel *nt* (von)
Interpol [ˈɪntəpɔl] *n* Interpol *f*
interpret [ɪnˈtəːprɪt] *vt* auslegen, interpretieren; (*translate*) dolmetschen ▷ *vi* dolmetschen
interpretation [ɪntəːprɪˈteɪʃən] *n* (*see vb*) Auslegung *f*, Interpretation *f*; Dolmetschen *nt*
interpreter [ɪnˈtəːprɪtəʳ] *n* Dolmetscher(in) *m(f)*
interpreting [ɪnˈtəːprɪtɪŋ] *n* Dolmetschen *nt*
interrelated [ɪntərɪˈleɪtɪd] *adj* zusammenhängend
interrogate [ɪnˈtɛrəugeɪt] *vt* verhören; (*witness*) vernehmen
interrogation [ɪntɛrəuˈgeɪʃən] *n* (*see vb*) Verhör *nt*; Vernehmung *f*
interrogative [ɪntəˈrɔgətɪv] *adj* (*Ling: pronoun*) Interrogativ-, Frage-
interrogator [ɪnˈtɛrəgeɪtəʳ] *n* (*Police*) Vernehmungsbeamte(r) *m*; **the hostage's ~** derjenige, der die Geisel verhörte
interrupt [ɪntəˈrʌpt] *vt, vi* unterbrechen
interruption [ɪntəˈrʌpʃən] *n* Unterbrechung *f*
intersect [ɪntəˈsɛkt] *vi* sich kreuzen ▷ *vt* durchziehen; (*Math*) schneiden
intersection [ɪntəˈsɛkʃən] *n* Kreuzung *f*; (*Math*) Schnittpunkt *m*
intersperse [ɪntəˈspəːs] *vt*: **to be ~d with** durchsetzt sein mit; **he ~d his lecture with ...** er spickte seine Rede mit ...
intertwine [ɪntəˈtwaɪn] *vi* sich ineinander verschlingen
interval [ˈɪntəvl] *n* Pause *f*; (*Mus*) Intervall *nt*; **bright ~s** (*in weather*) Aufheiterungen *pl*; **at ~s** in Abständen
intervene [ɪntəˈviːn] *vi* eingreifen; (*event*) dazwischenkommen; (*time*) dazwischenliegen
intervening [ɪntəˈviːnɪŋ] *adj* (*period, years*) dazwischenliegend
intervention [ɪntəˈvɛnʃən] *n* Eingreifen *nt*
interview [ˈɪntəvjuː] *n* (*for job*) Vorstellungsgespräch *nt*; (*for place at college etc*) Auswahlgespräch *nt*; (*Radio, TV etc*) Interview *nt* ▷ *vt* (*see n*) ein Vorstellungsgespräch/Auswahlgespräch führen mit; interviewen
interviewee [ɪntəvjuˈiː] *n* (*for job*) Stellenbewerber(in) *m(f)*; (*TV etc*) Interviewgast *m*
interviewer [ˈɪntəvjuəʳ] *n* Leiter(in) *m(f)* des Vorstellungsgesprächs/Auswahlgesprächs; (*Radio, TV etc*) Interviewer(in) *m(f)*
intestate [ɪnˈtɛsteɪt] *adv*: **to die ~** ohne Testament sterben
intestinal [ɪnˈtɛstɪnl] *adj* (*infection etc*) Darm-
intestine [ɪnˈtɛstɪn] *n* Darm *m*
intimacy [ˈɪntɪməsɪ] *n* Vertrautheit *f*
intimate [*adj* ˈɪntɪmət, *vt* ˈɪntɪmeɪt] *adj* eng; (*sexual, also restaurant, dinner, atmosphere*) intim; (*conversation, matter, detail*) vertraulich; (*knowledge*) gründlich ▷ *vt* andeuten; (*make known*) zu verstehen geben
intimately [ˈɪntɪmətlɪ] *adv* (*see adj*) eng; intim; vertraulich; gründlich
intimation [ɪntɪˈmeɪʃən] *n* Andeutung *f*
intimidate [ɪnˈtɪmɪdeɪt] *vt* einschüchtern
intimidation [ɪntɪmɪˈdeɪʃən] *n* Einschüchterung *f*

KEYWORD

into [ˈɪntu] *prep* **1** (*indicating motion or direction*) in +*acc*; **to go into town** in die Stadt gehen; **he worked late into the night** er arbeitete bis spät in die Nacht; **the car bumped into the wall** der Wagen fuhr gegen die Mauer
2 (*indicating change of condition, result*): **it broke into pieces** es zerbrach in Stücke; **she translated into English** sie übersetzte ins Englische; **to change pounds into dollars** Pfund in Dollar wechseln; **5 into 25** 25 durch 5

intolerable [ɪnˈtɔlərəbl] *adj* unerträglich
intolerance [ɪnˈtɔlərns] *n* Intoleranz *f*
intolerant [ɪnˈtɔlərnt] *adj*: **~ (of)** intolerant (gegenüber)
intonation [ɪntəuˈneɪʃən] *n* Intonation *f*
intoxicated [ɪnˈtɔksɪkeɪtɪd] *adj* betrunken; (*fig*) berauscht
intoxication [ɪntɔksɪˈkeɪʃən] *n* (Be)trunkenheit *f*; (*fig*) Rausch *m*
intractable [ɪnˈtræktəbl] *adj* hartnäckig; (*child*) widerspenstig; (*temper*) unbeugsam
intranet [ˈɪntrənɛt] *n* (*Comput*) Intranet *nt*
intransigence [ɪnˈtrænsɪdʒəns] *n* Unnachgiebigkeit *f*
intransigent [ɪnˈtrænsɪdʒənt] *adj* unnachgiebig
intransitive [ɪnˈtrænsɪtɪv] *adj* (*Ling*) intransitiv
intrauterine device [ˈɪntrəˈjuːtəraɪn-] *n* (*Med*) Intrauterinpessar *nt*, Spirale *f* (*inf*)
intravenous [ɪntrəˈviːnəs] *adj* intravenös
in-tray [ˈɪntreɪ] *n* Ablage *f* für Eingänge
intrepid [ɪnˈtrɛpɪd] *adj* unerschrocken
intricacy [ˈɪntrɪkəsɪ] *n* Kompliziertheit *f*
intricate [ˈɪntrɪkət] *adj* kompliziert
intrigue [ɪnˈtriːg] *n* Intrigen *pl* ▷ *vt* faszinieren

intriguing [ɪn'tri:gɪŋ] *adj* faszinierend
intrinsic [ɪn'trɪnsɪk] *adj* wesentlich
introduce [ɪntrə'dju:s] *vt* (*sth new*) einführen; (*speaker, TV show etc*) ankündigen; **to ~ sb (to sb)** jdn (jdm) vorstellen; **to ~ sb to** (*pastime, technique*) jdn einführen in *+acc*; **may I ~ ...?** darf ich ... vorstellen?
introduction [ɪntrə'dʌkʃən] *n* Einführung *f*; (*of person*) Vorstellung *f*; (*to book*) Einleitung *f*; **a letter of ~** ein Einführungsschreiben *nt*
introductory [ɪntrə'dʌktərɪ] *adj* Einführungs-; **~ remarks** einführende Bemerkungen *pl*; **~ offer** Einführungsangebot *nt*
introspection [ɪntrəu'spɛkʃən] *n* Selbstbeobachtung *f*, Introspektion *f*
introspective [ɪntrəu'spɛktɪv] *adj* in sich gekehrt
introvert ['ɪntrəuvə:t] *n* Introvertierte(r) *f(m)* ▷ *adj* (*also*: **introverted**) introvertiert
intrude [ɪn'tru:d] *vi* eindringen; **to ~ on** stören; (*conversation*) sich einmischen in *+acc*; **am I intruding?** störe ich?
intruder [ɪn'tru:dər] *n* Eindringling *m*
intrusion [ɪn'tru:ʒən] *n* Eindringen *nt*
intrusive [ɪn'tru:sɪv] *adj* aufdringlich
intuition [ɪntju:'ɪʃən] *n* Intuition *f*
intuitive [ɪn'tju:ɪtɪv] *adj* intuitiv; (*feeling*) instinktiv
inundate ['ɪnʌndeɪt] *vt*: **to ~ with** überschwemmen mit
inure [ɪn'juər] *vt*: **to ~ o.s. to** sich gewöhnen an *+acc*
invade [ɪn'veɪd] *vt* einfallen in *+acc*; (*fig*) heimsuchen
invader [ɪn'veɪdər] *n* Invasor *m*
invalid [*n* 'ɪnvəlɪd, *adj* ɪn'vælɪd] *n* Kranke(r) *f(m)*; (*disabled*) Invalide *m* ▷ *adj* ungültig
invalidate [ɪn'vælɪdeɪt] *vt* entkräften; (*law, marriage, election*) ungültig machen
invaluable [ɪn'væljuəbl] *adj* unschätzbar
invariable [ɪn'vɛərɪəbl] *adj* unveränderlich
invariably [ɪn'vɛərɪəblɪ] *adv* ständig, unweigerlich; **she is ~ late** sie kommt immer zu spät
invasion [ɪn'veɪʒən] *n* Invasion *f*; **an ~ of privacy** ein Eingriff *m* in die Privatsphäre
invective [ɪn'vɛktɪv] *n* Beschimpfungen *pl*
inveigle [ɪn'vi:gl] *vt*: **to ~ sb into sth/doing sth** jdn zu etw verleiten/dazu verleiten, etw zu tun
invent [ɪn'vɛnt] *vt* erfinden
invention [ɪn'vɛnʃən] *n* Erfindung *f*
inventive [ɪn'vɛntɪv] *adj* erfinderisch
inventiveness [ɪn'vɛntɪvnɪs] *n* Einfallsreichtum *m*
inventor [ɪn'vɛntər] *n* Erfinder(in) *m(f)*
inventory ['ɪnvəntrɪ] *n* Inventar *nt*
inventory control *n* (*Comm*) Bestandskontrolle *f*
inverse [ɪn'və:s] *adj* umgekehrt; **in ~ proportion (to)** im umgekehrten Verhältnis (zu)
invert [ɪn'və:t] *vt* umdrehen
invertebrate [ɪn'və:tɪbrət] *n* wirbelloses Tier *nt*
inverted commas [ɪn'və:tɪd-] (*Brit*) *npl* Anführungszeichen *pl*
invest [ɪn'vɛst] *vt* investieren ▷ *vi*: **~ in** investieren in *+acc*; (*fig*) sich *dat* anschaffen; **to ~ sb with sth** jdm etw verleihen
investigate [ɪn'vɛstɪgeɪt] *vt* untersuchen
investigation [ɪnvɛstɪ'geɪʃən] *n* Untersuchung *f*
investigative [ɪn'vɛstɪgeɪtɪv] *adj*: **~ journalism** Enthüllungsjournalismus *m*
investigator [ɪn'vɛstɪgeɪtər] *n* Ermittler(in) *m(f)*; **private ~** Privatdetektiv(in) *m(f)*
investiture [ɪn'vɛstɪtʃər] *n* (*of chancellor*) Amtseinführung *f*; (*of prince*) Investitur *f*
investment [ɪn'vɛstmənt] *n* Investition *f*
investment income *n* Kapitalerträge *pl*
investment trust *n* Investmenttrust *m*
investor [ɪn'vɛstər] *n* (Kapital)anleger(in) *m(f)*
inveterate [ɪn'vɛtərət] *adj* unverbesserlich
invidious [ɪn'vɪdɪəs] *adj* (*task, job*) unangenehm; (*comparison, decision*) ungerecht
invigilator [ɪn'vɪdʒɪleɪtər] *n* Aufsicht *f*
invigorating [ɪn'vɪgəreɪtɪŋ] *adj* belebend; (*experience etc*) anregend
invincible [ɪn'vɪnsɪbl] *adj* unbesiegbar; (*belief, conviction*) unerschütterlich
inviolate [ɪn'vaɪələt] *adj* sicher; (*truth*) unantastbar
invisible [ɪn'vɪzɪbl] *adj* unsichtbar
invisible mending *n* Kunststopfen *nt*
invitation [ɪnvɪ'teɪʃən] *n* Einladung *f*; **by ~ only** nur auf Einladung; **at sb's ~** auf jds Aufforderung *acc* (hin)
invite [ɪn'vaɪt] *vt* einladen; (*discussion*) auffordern zu; (*criticism*) herausfordern; **to ~ sb to do sth** jdn auffordern, etw zu tun; **to ~ sb to dinner** jdn zum Abendessen einladen
▸ **invite out** *vt* einladen
inviting [ɪn'vaɪtɪŋ] *adj* einladend; (*desirable*) verlockend
invoice ['ɪnvɔɪs] *n* Rechnung *f* ▷ *vt* in Rechnung stellen; **to ~ sb for goods** jdm für Waren eine Rechnung ausstellen
invoke [ɪn'vəuk] *vt* anrufen; (*feelings, memories etc*) heraufbeschwören
involuntary [ɪn'vɔləntrɪ] *adj* unbeabsichtigt; (*reflex*) unwillkürlich
involve [ɪn'vɔlv] *vt* (*person*) beteiligen; (*thing*) verbunden sein mit; (*concern, affect*) betreffen; **to ~ sb in sth** jdn in etw *acc* verwickeln
involved [ɪn'vɔlvd] *adj* kompliziert; **the work/problems ~** die damit verbundene Arbeit/verbundenen Schwierigkeiten; **to be ~ in** beteiligt sein an *+dat*; (*be engrossed*) engagiert sein in *+dat*; **to become ~ with sb** Umgang mit jdm haben; (*emotionally*) mit jdm eine Beziehung anfangen
involvement [ɪn'vɔlvmənt] *n* Engagement *nt*; (*participation*) Beteiligung *f*
invulnerable [ɪn'vʌlnərəbl] *adj* unverwundbar; (*ship, building etc*) uneinnehmbar
inward ['ɪnwəd] *adj* innerste(r, s); (*movement*)

nach innen ▷ *adv* nach innen
inwardly ['ɪnwədlɪ] *adv* innerlich
inwards ['ɪnwədz] *adv* nach innen
I/O *abbr* (*Comput*: = *input/output*) E/A
IOC *n abbr* (= *International Olympic Committee*) IOC *nt*, IOK *nt*
iodine ['aɪəudi:n] *n* Jod *nt*
IOM (*Brit*) *abbr* (*Post*) = *Isle of Man*
ion ['aɪən] *n* Ion *nt*
Ionian Sea [aɪ'əunɪən-] *n*: **the ~** das Ionische Meer
ionizer ['aɪənaɪzə^r] *n* Ionisator *m*
iota [aɪ'əutə] *n* Jota *nt*
IOU *n abbr* (= *I owe you*) Schuldschein *m*
IOW (*Brit*) *abbr* (*Post*) = *Isle of Wight*
IP *abbr* (*Comput*: = *Internet Protocol*) IP
IPA *n abbr* (= *International Phonetic Alphabet*) internationale Lautschrift *f*
IQ *n abbr* (= *intelligence quotient*) IQ *m*
IRA *n abbr* (= *Irish Republican Army*) IRA *f*; (*US*: = *individual retirement account*) *privates Rentensparkonto*
Iran [ɪ'rɑ:n] *n* (der) Iran
Iranian [ɪ'reɪnɪən] *adj* iranisch ▷ *n* Iraner(in) *m(f)*; (*Ling*) Iranisch *nt*
Iraq [ɪ'rɑ:k] *n* (der) Irak
Iraqi [ɪ'rɑ:kɪ] *adj* irakisch ▷ *n* Iraker(in) *m(f)*
irascible [ɪ'ræsɪbl] *adj* jähzornig
irate [aɪ'reɪt] *adj* zornig
Ireland ['aɪələnd] *n* Irland *nt*; **the Republic of ~** die Republik Irland
iris ['aɪrɪs] (*pl* **~es**) *n* (*Anat*) Iris *f*, Regenbogenhaut *f*; (*Bot*) Iris, Schwertlilie *f*
Irish ['aɪrɪʃ] *adj* irisch ▷ *npl*: **the ~** die Iren *pl*, die Irländer *pl*
Irishman ['aɪrɪʃmən] (*irreg*: *like* **man**) *n* Ire *m*, Irländer *m*
Irish Sea *n*: **the ~** die Irische See
Irishwoman ['aɪrɪʃwumən] (*irreg*: *like* **woman**) *n* Irin *f*, Irländerin *f*
irk [ə:k] *vt* ärgern
irksome ['ə:ksəm] *adj* lästig
IRN *n abbr* (= *Independent Radio News*) *Nachrichtendienst des kommerziellen Rundfunks*
iron ['aɪən] *n* Eisen *nt*; (*for clothes*) Bügeleisen *nt* ▷ *cpd* Eisen-; (*will, discipline etc*) eisern ▷ *vt* bügeln
▸ **iron out** *vt* (*fig*) aus dem Weg räumen
Iron Curtain *n*: **the ~** der Eiserne Vorhang
ironic [aɪ'rɔnɪk], **ironical** [aɪ'rɔnɪkl] *adj* ironisch; (*situation*) paradox, witzig
ironically [aɪ'rɔnɪklɪ] *adv* ironisch; **~, the intelligence chief was the last to find out** witzigerweise war der Geheimdienstchef der Letzte, der es erfuhr
ironing ['aɪənɪŋ] *n* Bügeln *nt*; (*clothes*) Bügelwäsche *f*
ironing board *n* Bügelbrett *nt*
iron lung *n* (*Med*) eiserne Lunge *f*
ironmonger ['aɪənmʌŋgə^r] (*Brit*) *n* Eisen- und Haushaltswarenhändler(in) *m(f)*
ironmonger's ['aɪənmʌŋgəz], **ironmonger's shop** (*Brit*) *n* Eisen- und Haushaltswarenhandlung *f*
iron ore *n* Eisenerz *nt*
irons ['aɪəns] *npl* Hand- und Fußschellen *pl*; **to clap sb in ~** jdn in Eisen legen
irony ['aɪrənɪ] *n* Ironie *f*; **the ~ of it is that ...** das Ironische daran ist, dass ...
irrational [ɪ'ræʃənl] *adj* irrational
irreconcilable [ɪrɛkən'saɪləbl] *adj* unvereinbar
irredeemable [ɪrɪ'di:məbl] *adj* (*Comm*) nicht einlösbar; (*loan*) unkündbar; (*fault, character*) unverbesserlich
irrefutable [ɪrɪ'fju:təbl] *adj* unwiderlegbar
irregular [ɪ'rɛgjulə^r] *adj* unregelmäßig; (*surface*) uneben; (*behaviour*) ungehörig
irregularity [ɪrɛgju'lærɪtɪ] *n* (*see adj*) Unregelmäßigkeit *f*; Unebenheit *f*; Ungehörigkeit *f*
irrelevance [ɪ'rɛləvəns] *n* Irrelevanz *f*
irrelevant [ɪ'rɛləvənt] *adj* unwesentlich, irrelevant
irreligious [ɪrɪ'lɪdʒəs] *adj* unreligiös
irreparable [ɪ'rɛprəbl] *adj* nicht wiedergutzumachen
irreplaceable [ɪrɪ'pleɪsəbl] *adj* unersetzlich
irrepressible [ɪrɪ'prɛsəbl] *adj* (*good humour*) unerschütterlich; (*enthusiasm etc*) unbändig; (*person*) nicht unterzukriegen
irreproachable [ɪrɪ'prəutʃəbl] *adj* untadelig
irresistible [ɪrɪ'zɪstɪbl] *adj* unwiderstehlich
irresolute [ɪ'rɛzəlu:t] *adj* unentschlossen
irrespective [ɪrɪ'spɛktɪv]: **~ of** *prep* ungeachtet *+gen*
irresponsible [ɪrɪ'spɔnsɪbl] *adj* verantwortungslos; (*action*) unverantwortlich
irretrievable [ɪrɪ'tri:vəbl] *adj* (*object*) nicht mehr wiederzubekommen; (*loss*) unersetzlich; (*damage*) nicht wiedergutzumachen
irreverent [ɪ'rɛvərnt] *adj* respektlos
irrevocable [ɪ'rɛvəkəbl] *adj* unwiderruflich
irrigate ['ɪrɪgeɪt] *vt* bewässern
irrigation [ɪrɪ'geɪʃən] *n* Bewässerung *f*
irritable ['ɪrɪtəbl] *adj* reizbar
irritant ['ɪrɪtənt] *n* Reizerreger *m*; (*situation etc*) Ärgernis *nt*
irritate ['ɪrɪteɪt] *vt* ärgern, irritieren; (*Med*) reizen
irritating ['ɪrɪteɪtɪŋ] *adj* ärgerlich, irritierend; **he is ~** er kann einem auf die Nerven gehen
irritation [ɪrɪ'teɪʃən] *n* Ärger *m*; (*Med*) Reizung *f*; (*annoying thing*) Ärgernis *nt*
IRS (*US*) *n abbr* (= *Internal Revenue Service*) *Steuereinzugsbehörde*
is [ɪz] *vb see* **be**
ISA ['aɪsə] *n abbr* (= *individual savings account*) *steuerfreies Sparsystem mit begrenzter Einlagenhöhe*
ISBN *n abbr* (= *International Standard Book Number*) ISBN *f*
ISDN *n abbr* (= *Integrated Services Digital Network*) ISDN *nt*
Islam ['ɪzlɑ:m] *n* der Islam; (*Islamic countries*) die islamischen Länder *pl*
Islamic [ɪz'læmɪk] *adj* islamisch
island ['aɪlənd] *n* Insel *f*; (*also*: **traffic island**)

Verkehrsinsel *f*
islander ['aɪləndəʳ] *n* Inselbewohner(in) *m(f)*
isle [aɪl] *n* Insel *f*
isn't ['ɪznt] = **is not**
isobar ['aɪsəubɑːʳ] *n* Isobare *f*
isolate ['aɪsəleɪt] *vt* isolieren
isolated ['aɪsəleɪtɪd] *adj* isoliert; (*place*) abgelegen; **~ incident** Einzelfall *m*
isolation [aɪsə'leɪʃən] *n* Isolierung *f*
isolationism [aɪsə'leɪʃənɪzəm] *n* Isolationismus *m*
isotope ['aɪsəutəup] *n* Isotop *nt*
ISP (*Comput*) *n abbr* (*= Internet Service Provider*) Provider *m*
Israel ['ɪzreɪl] *n* Israel *nt*
Israeli [ɪz'reɪlɪ] *adj* israelisch ▷ *n* Israeli *mf*
issue ['ɪʃjuː] *n* Frage *f*; (*subject*) Thema *nt*; (*problem*) Problem *nt*; (*of book, stamps etc*) Ausgabe *f*; (*offspring*) Nachkommenschaft *f* ▷ *vt* ausgeben; (*statement*) herausgeben; (*documents*) ausstellen ▷ *vi*: **to ~ (from)** dringen (aus); (*liquid*) austreten (aus); **the point at ~** der Punkt, um den es geht; **to avoid the ~** ausweichen; **to confuse** *or* **obscure the ~** es unnötig kompliziert machen; **to ~ sth to sb** *or* **~ sb with sth** jdm etw geben; (*documents*) jdm etw ausstellen; (*gun etc*) jdn mit etw ausstatten; **to take ~ with sb (over)** jdm widersprechen (in *+dat*); **to make an ~ of sth** etw aufbauschen
isthmus ['ɪsməs] *n* Landenge *f*, Isthmus *m*
IT *n abbr* = **information technology**

KEYWORD

it [ɪt] *pron* **1** (*specific: subject*) er/sie/es; (*: direct object*) ihn/sie/es; (*: indirect object*) ihm/ihr/ihm; **it's on the table** es ist auf dem Tisch; **I can't find it** ich kann es nicht finden; **give it to me** gib es mir; **about it** darüber; **from it** davon; **in it** darin; **of it** davon; **what did you learn from it?** was hast du daraus gelernt?; **I'm proud of it** ich bin stolz darauf
2 (*impersonal*) es; **it's raining** es regnet; **it's Friday tomorrow** morgen ist Freitag; **who is it? — it's me** wer ist da? — ich bins

ITA, (*Brit*) **i.t.a.** *n abbr* (*= initial teaching alphabet*) *Alphabet zum Lesenlernen*
Italian [ɪ'tæljən] *adj* italienisch ▷ *n* Italiener(in) *m(f)*; (*Ling*) Italienisch *nt*; **the ~s** die Italiener *pl*
italics [ɪ'tælɪks] *npl* Kursivschrift *f*
Italy ['ɪtəlɪ] *n* Italien *nt*
ITC (*Brit*) *n abbr* (*= Independent Television Commission*) *Fernseh-Aufsichtsgremium*
itch [ɪtʃ] *n* Juckreiz *m* ▷ *vi* jucken; **I am ~ing all over** mich juckt es überall; **to ~ to do sth** darauf brennen, etw zu tun
itchy ['ɪtʃɪ] *adj* juckend; **my back is ~** mein Rücken juckt
it'd ['ɪtd] = **it would; it had**
item ['aɪtəm] *n* Punkt *m*; (*of collection*) Stück *nt*; (*also*: **news item**) Meldung *f*; (*: in newspaper*) Zeitungsnotiz *f*; **~s of clothing** Kleidungsstücke *pl*
itemize ['aɪtəmaɪz] *vt* einzeln aufführen
itemized bill ['aɪtəmaɪzd-] *n Rechnung, auf der die Posten einzeln aufgeführt sind*
itinerant [ɪ'tɪnərənt] *adj* (*labourer, priest etc*) Wander-; (*salesman*) reisend
itinerary [aɪ'tɪnərərɪ] *n* Reiseroute *f*
it'll ['ɪtl] = **it will; it shall**
ITN (*Brit*) *n abbr* (TV: *= Independent Television News*) *Nachrichtendienst des kommerziellen Fernsehens*
its [ɪts] *adj* sein(e), ihr(e) ▷ *pron* seine(r, s), ihre(r, s)
it's [ɪts] = **it is; it has**
itself [ɪt'sɛlf] *pron* sich; (*emphatic*) selbst
ITV (*Brit*) *n abbr* (TV: *= Independent Television*) *kommerzieller Fernsehsender; siehe Info-Artikel*

ITV

ITV steht für „Independent Television" und ist ein landesweiter privater Fernsehsender in Großbritannien. Unter der Oberaufsicht einer unabhängigen Rundfunkbehörde produzieren Privatfirmen die Programme für die verschiedenen Sendegebiete. *ITV*, das seit 1955 Programme ausstrahlt, wird ganz durch Werbung finanziert und bietet etwa ein Drittel Informationssendungen (Nachrichten, Dokumentarfilme, Aktuelles) und ansonsten Unterhaltung (Sport, Komödien, Drama, Spielshows, Filme).

IUD *n abbr* = **intrauterine device**
I've [aɪv] = **I have**
ivory ['aɪvərɪ] *n* Elfenbein *nt*
Ivory Coast *n* Elfenbeinküste *f*
ivory tower *n* (*fig*) Elfenbeinturm *m*
ivy ['aɪvɪ] *n* Efeu *m*
Ivy League (*US*) *n Eliteuniversitäten der USA*

IVY LEAGUE

Als *Ivy League* bezeichnet man die acht renommiertesten Universitäten im Nordosten der Vereinigten Staaten (Brown, Columbia, Cornell, Dartmouth College, Harvard, Princeton, University of Pennsylvania, Yale), die untereinander Sportwettkämpfe austragen. Der Name bezieht sich auf die efeubewachsenen Mauern der Universitätsgebäude.

Jj

J, j [dʒeɪ] *n* (*letter*) J *nt*, j *nt*; **J for Jack, J for Jig** (*US*) ≈ J wie Julius
JA *n abbr* = **judge advocate; joint account**
J/A *abbr* = **joint account**
jab [dʒæb] *vt* stoßen; (*with finger, needle*) stechen ▹ *n* (*inf*) Spritze *f* ▹ *vi*: **to ~ at** einstechen auf +*acc*; **to ~ sth into sth** etw in etw *acc* stoßen/stechen
jack [dʒæk] *n* (*Aut*) Wagenheber *m*; (*Bowls*) Zielkugel *f*; (*Cards*) Bube *m*
▸ **jack in** (*inf*) *vt* aufgeben
▸ **jack up** *vt* (*Aut*) aufbocken
jackal ['dʒækl] *n* Schakal *m*
jackass ['dʒækæs] (*inf*) *n* (*person*) Esel *m*
jackdaw ['dʒækdɔː] *n* Dohle *f*
jacket ['dʒækɪt] *n* Jackett *nt*; (*of book*) Schutzumschlag *m*; **potatoes in their ~s, ~ potatoes** in der Schale gebackene Kartoffeln *pl*
jack-in-the-box ['dʒækɪnðəbɔks] *n* Schachtelteufel *m*, Kastenteufel *m*
jack-knife ['dʒæknaɪf] *n* Klappmesser *nt* ▹ *vi*: **the lorry ~d** der Anhänger (des Lastwagens) hat sich quer gestellt
jack-of-all-trades ['dʒækəv'ɔːltreɪdz] *n* Alleskönner *m*
jack plug *n* Bananenstecker *m*
jackpot ['dʒækpɔt] *n* Hauptgewinn *m*; **to hit the ~** (*fig*) das große Los ziehen
Jacuzzi® [dʒə'kuːzɪ] *n* Whirlpool *m*
jade [dʒeɪd] *n* Jade *m or f*
jaded ['dʒeɪdɪd] *adj* abgespannt; **to get ~** die Nase vollhaben
JAG *n abbr* = **Judge Advocate General**
jagged ['dʒægɪd] *adj* gezackt
jaguar ['dʒægjuəʳ] *n* Jaguar *m*
jail [dʒeɪl] *n* Gefängnis *nt* ▹ *vt* einsperren
jailbird ['dʒeɪlbəːd] *n* Knastbruder *m* (*inf*)
jailbreak ['dʒeɪlbreɪk] *n* (Gefängnis)ausbruch *m*
jalopy [dʒə'lɔpɪ] (*inf*) *n* alte (Klapper)kiste *f or* Mühle *f*
jam [dʒæm] *n* Marmelade *f*, Konfitüre *f*; (*also*: **traffic jam**) Stau *m*; (*inf*: *difficulty*) Klemme *f* ▹ *vt* blockieren; (*mechanism, drawer etc*) verklemmen; (*Radio*) stören ▹ *vi* klemmen; (*gun*) Ladehemmung haben; **I'm in a real ~** (*inf*) ich stecke wirklich in der Klemme; **to get sb out of a ~** (*inf*) jdm aus der Klemme helfen; **to ~ sth into sth** etw in etw *acc* stopfen; **the telephone lines are ~med** die Leitungen sind belegt
Jamaica [dʒə'meɪkə] *n* Jamaika *nt*
Jamaican [dʒə'meɪkən] *adj* jamaikanisch ▹ *n* Jamaikaner(in) *m(f)*
jamb [dʒæm] *n* (*of door*) (Tür)pfosten *m*; (*of window*) (Fenster)pfosten *m*
jamboree [dʒæmbə'riː] *n* Fest *nt*
jam-packed [dʒæm'pækt] *adj*: **~ (with)** vollgestopft (mit)
jam session *n* (*Mus*) Jamsession *f*
Jan. *abbr* (= *January*) Jan.
jangle ['dʒæŋgl] *vi* klimpern
janitor ['dʒænɪtəʳ] *n* Hausmeister(in) *m(f)*
January ['dʒænjuərɪ] *n* Januar *m*; *see also* **July**
Japan [dʒə'pæn] *n* Japan *nt*
Japanese [dʒæpə'niːz] *adj* japanisch ▹ *n inv* Japaner(in) *m(f)*; (*Ling*) Japanisch *nt*
jar [dʒɑːʳ] *n* Topf *m*, Gefäß *nt*; (*glass*) Glas *nt* ▹ *vi* (*sound*) gellen; (*colours*) nicht harmonieren, sich beißen ▹ *vt* erschüttern; **to ~ on sb** jdm auf die Nerven gehen
jargon ['dʒɑːgən] *n* Jargon *m*
jarring ['dʒɑːrɪŋ] *adj* (*sound*) gellend, schrill; (*colour*) schreiend
jasmine ['dʒæzmɪn] *n* Jasmin *m*
jaundice ['dʒɔːndɪs] *n* Gelbsucht *f*
jaundiced ['dʒɔːndɪst] *adj* (*view, attitude*) zynisch
jaunt [dʒɔːnt] *n* Spritztour *f*
jaunty ['dʒɔːntɪ] *adj* munter; (*step*) schwungvoll
Java ['dʒɑːvə] *n* Java *nt*
javelin ['dʒævlɪn] *n* Speer *m*
jaw [dʒɔː] *n* Kiefer *m*
jawbone ['dʒɔːbəun] *n* Kieferknochen *m*
jay [dʒeɪ] *n* Eichelhäher *m*
jaywalker ['dʒeɪwɔːkəʳ] *n* unachtsamer Fußgänger *m*, unachtsame Fußgängerin *f*
jazz [dʒæz] *n* Jazz *m*
▸ **jazz up** *vt* aufpeppen (*inf*)
jazz band *n* Jazzband *f*
JCB® *n* Erdräummaschine *f*
JCS (*US*) *n abbr* (= *Joint Chiefs of Staff*) Stabschefs *pl*
JD (*US*) *n abbr* (= *Doctor of Laws*) ≈ Dr. jur.; (= *Justice Department*), ≈ Justizministerium *nt*
jealous ['dʒɛləs] *adj* eifersüchtig; (*envious*)

neidisch
jealously ['dʒɛləslɪ] *adv* eifersüchtig; (*enviously*) neidisch; (*watchfully*) sorgsam
jealousy ['dʒɛləsɪ] *n* Eifersucht *f*; (*envy*) Neid *m*
jeans [dʒi:nz] *npl* Jeans *pl*
Jeep® [dʒi:p] *n* Jeep® *m*
jeer [dʒɪəʳ] *vi* höhnische Bemerkungen machen; **to ~ at** verhöhnen
jeering ['dʒɪərɪŋ] *adj* höhnisch; (*crowd*) johlend ▹ *n* Johlen *nt*
jeers ['dʒɪəz] *npl* Buhrufe *pl*
jelly ['dʒɛlɪ] *n* Götterspeise *f*; (*jam*) Gelee *m or nt*
jelly baby (*Brit*) *n* Gummibärchen *nt*
jellyfish ['dʒɛlɪfɪʃ] *n* Qualle *f*
jeopardize ['dʒɛpədaɪz] *vt* gefährden
jeopardy ['dʒɛpədɪ] *n*: **to be in ~** gefährdet sein
jerk [dʒə:k] *n* Ruck *m*; (*inf: idiot*) Trottel *m* ▹ *vt* reißen ▹ *vi* (*vehicle*) ruckeln
jerkin ['dʒə:kɪn] *n* Wams *nt*
jerky ['dʒə:kɪ] *adj* ruckartig
jerry-built ['dʒɛrɪbɪlt] *adj* schlampig gebaut
jerry can ['dʒɛrɪ-] *n* großer Blechkanister *m*
Jersey ['dʒə:zɪ] *n* Jersey *nt*
jersey ['dʒə:zɪ] *n* Pullover *m*; (*fabric*) Jersey *m*
Jerusalem [dʒə'ru:sləm] *n* Jerusalem *nt*
jest [dʒɛst] *n* Scherz *m*
jester ['dʒɛstəʳ] *n* Narr *m*
Jesus ['dʒi:zəs] *n* Jesus *m*; **~ Christ** Jesus Christus *m*
jet [dʒɛt] *n* Strahl *m*; (*Aviat*) Düsenflugzeug *nt*; (*Mineralogy, Jewellery*) Jett *m or nt*, Gagat *m*
jet-black ['dʒɛt'blæk] *adj* pechschwarz
jet engine *n* Düsentriebwerk *nt*
jet lag *n* Jetlag *nt*
jet-propelled ['dʒɛtprə'pɛld] *adj* Düsen-, mit Düsenantrieb
jetsam ['dʒɛtsəm] *n* Strandgut *nt*; (*floating*) Treibgut *nt*
jet-setter ['dʒɛtsɛtəʳ] *n*: **to be a ~** zum Jetset gehören
jettison ['dʒɛtɪsn] *vt* abwerfen; (*from ship*) über Bord werfen
jetty ['dʒɛtɪ] *n* Landesteg *m*, Pier *m*
Jew [dʒu:] *n* Jude *m*, Jüdin *f*
jewel ['dʒu:əl] *n* Edelstein *m*, Juwel *nt* (*also fig*); (*in watch*) Stein *m*
jeweller, (*US*) **jeweler** ['dʒu:ələʳ] *n* Juwelier *m*
jeweller's, jeweller's shop *n* Juwelier *m*, Juweliergeschäft *nt*
jewellery, (*US*) **jewelry** ['dʒu:əlrɪ] *n* Schmuck *m*
Jewess ['dʒu:ɪs] *n* Jüdin *f*
Jewish ['dʒu:ɪʃ] *adj* jüdisch
JFK (*US*) *n abbr* (= *John Fitzgerald Kennedy International Airport*) John-F.-Kennedy-Flughafen *m*
jib [dʒɪb] *n* (*Naut*) Klüver *m*; (*of crane*) Ausleger *m* ▹ *vi* (*horse*) scheuen, bocken; **to ~ at doing sth** sich dagegen sträuben, etw zu tun
jibe [dʒaɪb] *n* = **gibe**
jiffy ['dʒɪfɪ] (*inf*) *n*: **in a ~** sofort
jig [dʒɪg] *n* *lebhafter Volkstanz*
jigsaw ['dʒɪgsɔ:] *n* (*also*: **jigsaw puzzle**) Puzzle(spiel) *nt*; (*tool*) Stichsäge *f*
jilt [dʒɪlt] *vt* sitzen lassen
jingle ['dʒɪŋgl] *n* (*tune*) Jingle *m* ▹ *vi* (*bracelets*) klimpern; (*bells*) bimmeln
jingoism ['dʒɪŋgəuɪzəm] *n* Hurrapatriotismus *m*
jinx [dʒɪŋks] (*inf*) *n* Fluch *m*; **there's a ~ on it** es ist verhext
jitters ['dʒɪtəz] (*inf*) *npl*: **to get the ~** das große Zittern bekommen
jittery ['dʒɪtərɪ] (*inf*) *adj* nervös, rappelig
jiujitsu [dʒu:'dʒɪtsu:] *n* Jiu-Jitsu *nt*
job [dʒɔb] *n* Arbeit *f*; (*post, employment*) Stelle *f*, Job *m*; **it's not my ~** es ist nicht meine Aufgabe; **a part-time ~** eine Teilzeitbeschäftigung; **a full-time ~** eine Ganztagsstelle; **he's only doing his ~** er tut nur seine Pflicht; **it's a good ~ that ...** nur gut, dass ...; **just the ~!** genau das Richtige!
jobber ['dʒɔbəʳ] (*Brit*) *n* Börsenhändler *m*
jobbing ['dʒɔbɪŋ] (*Brit*) *adj* Gelegenheits-
job centre (*Brit*) *n* Arbeitsamt *nt*
job creation scheme *n* Arbeitsbeschaffungsmaßnahmen *pl*
job description *n* Tätigkeitsbeschreibung *f*
job interview *n* Vorstellungs- *or* Bewerbungsgespräch *nt*
jobless ['dʒɔblɪs] *adj* arbeitslos ▹ *npl*: **the ~** die Arbeitslosen *pl*
job lot *n* (Waren)posten *m*
job satisfaction *n* Zufriedenheit *f* am Arbeitsplatz
job security *n* Sicherheit *f* des Arbeitsplatzes
job sharing *n* Jobsharing *nt*, Arbeitsplatzteilung *f*
job specification *n* Tätigkeitsbeschreibung *f*
Jock [dʒɔk] (*inf*) *n* Schotte *m*
jockey ['dʒɔkɪ] *n* Jockey *m* ▹ *vi*: **to ~ for position** um eine gute Position rangeln
jockey box (*US*) *n* (*Aut*) Handschuhfach *nt*
jocular ['dʒɔkjuləʳ] *adj* spaßig, witzig
jog [dʒɔg] *vt* (an)stoßen ▹ *vi* joggen, Dauerlauf machen; **to ~ sb's memory** jds Gedächtnis *dat* nachhelfen
▸**jog along** *vi* entlangzuckeln (*inf*)
jogger ['dʒɔgəʳ] *n* Jogger(in) *m(f)*
jogging ['dʒɔgɪŋ] *n* Jogging *nt*, Joggen *nt*
john [dʒɔn] (*US: inf*) *n* (*toilet*) Klo *nt*
join [dʒɔɪn] *vt* (*club, party*) beitreten *+dat*; (*queue*) sich stellen in *+acc*; (*things, places*) verbinden; (*group of people*) sich anschließen *+dat* ▹ *vi* (*roads*) sich treffen; (*rivers*) zusammenfließen ▹ *n* Verbindungsstelle *f*; **to ~ forces (with)** (*fig*) sich zusammentun (mit); **will you ~ us for dinner?** wollen Sie mit uns zu Abend essen?; **I'll ~ you later** ich komme später
▸**join in** *vi* mitmachen ▹ *vt fus* sich beteiligen an *+dat*
▸**join up** *vi* sich treffen; (*Mil*) zum Militär gehen
joiner ['dʒɔɪnəʳ] (*Brit*) *n* Schreiner(in) *m(f)*
joinery ['dʒɔɪnərɪ] (*Brit*) *n* Schreinerei *f*
joint [dʒɔɪnt] *n* (*in woodwork*) Fuge *f*; (*in pipe*

etc) Verbindungsstelle *f*; (*Anat*) Gelenk *nt*; (*Brit: Culin*) Braten *m*; (*inf: place*) Laden *m*; (: *of cannabis*) Joint *m* ▷ *adj* gemeinsam; (*combined*) vereint

joint account *n* gemeinsames Konto *nt*

jointly ['dʒɔɪntlɪ] *adv* gemeinsam

joint ownership *n* Miteigentum *nt*

joint-stock company ['dʒɔɪnt'stɔk-] *n* Aktiengesellschaft *f*

joint venture *n* Gemeinschaftsunternehmen *nt*, Joint Venture *nt*

joist [dʒɔɪst] *n* Balken *m*, Träger *m*

joke [dʒəuk] *n* Witz *m*; (*also*: **practical joke**) Streich *m* ▷ *vi* Witze machen; **to play a ~ on sb** jdm einen Streich spielen

joker ['dʒəukəʳ] *n* (*Cards*) Joker *m*

joking ['dʒəukɪŋ] *adj* scherzhaft

jokingly ['dʒəukɪŋlɪ] *adv* scherzhaft, im Spaß

jollity ['dʒɔlɪtɪ] *n* Fröhlichkeit *f*

jolly ['dʒɔlɪ] *adj* fröhlich; (*enjoyable*) lustig ▷ *adv* (*Brit: inf: very*) ganz (schön) ▷ *vt* (*Brit*): **to ~ sb along** jdm aufmunternd zureden; **~ good!** prima!

jolt [dʒəult] *n* Ruck *m*; (*shock*) Schock *m* ▷ *vt* schütteln; (*subj: bus etc*) durchschütteln; (*emotionally*) aufrütteln

Jordan ['dʒɔːdən] *n* Jordanien *nt*; (*river*) Jordan *m*

Jordanian [dʒɔː'deɪnɪən] *adj* jordanisch ▷ *n* Jordanier(in) *m(f)*

joss stick [dʒɔs-] *n* Räucherstäbchen *nt*

jostle ['dʒɔsl] *vt* anrempeln ▷ *vi* drängeln

jot [dʒɔt] *n*: **not one ~** kein bisschen

▸ **jot down** *vt* notieren

jotter ['dʒɔtəʳ] (*Brit*) *n* Notizbuch *nt*; (*pad*) Notizblock *m*

journal ['dʒəːnl] *n* Zeitschrift *f*; (*diary*) Tagebuch *nt*

journalese [dʒəːnə'liːz] (*pej*) *n* Pressejargon *m*

journalism ['dʒəːnəlɪzəm] *n* Journalismus *m*

journalist ['dʒəːnəlɪst] *n* Journalist(in) *m(f)*

journey ['dʒəːnɪ] *n* Reise *f* ▷ *vi* reisen; **a 5-hour ~** eine Fahrt von 5 Stunden; **return ~** Rückreise *f*; (*both ways*) Hin- und Rückreise *f*

jovial ['dʒəuvɪəl] *adj* fröhlich; (*atmosphere*) freundlich, herzlich

jowl [dʒaul] *n* Backe *f*

joy [dʒɔɪ] *n* Freude *f*

joyful ['dʒɔɪful] *adj* freudig

joyride ['dʒɔɪraɪd] *n* *Spritztour in einem gestohlenen Auto*

joyrider ['dʒɔɪraɪdəʳ] *n* *Autodieb, der den Wagen nur für eine Spritztour benutzt*

joystick ['dʒɔɪstɪk] *n* (*Aviat*) Steuerknüppel *m*; (*Comput*) Joystick *m*

JP *n abbr* = **Justice of the Peace**

Jr *abbr* (*in names*: = *junior*) jun.

JTPA (*US*) *n abbr* (= *Job Training Partnership Act*) *Arbeitsbeschaffungsprogramm für benachteiligte Bevölkerungsteile und Minderheiten*

jubilant ['dʒuːbɪlnt] *adj* überglücklich

jubilation [dʒuːbɪ'leɪʃən] *n* Jubel *m*

jubilee ['dʒuːbɪliː] *n* Jubiläum *nt*; **silver ~** 25-jähriges Jubiläum; **golden ~** 50-jähriges Jubiläum

judge [dʒʌdʒ] *n* Richter(in) *m(f)*; (*in competition*) Preisrichter(in) *m(f)*; (*fig: expert*) Kenner(in) *m(f)* ▷ *vt* (*Law: person*) die Verhandlung führen über +*acc*; (: *case*) verhandeln; (*competition*) Preisrichter(in) sein bei; (*person etc*) beurteilen; (*consider*) halten für; (*estimate*) einschätzen ▷ *vi*: **judging by** *or* **to ~ by his expression** seinem Gesichtsausdruck nach zu urteilen; **she's a good ~ of character** sie ist ein guter Menschenkenner; **I'll be the ~ of that** das müssen Sie mich schon selbst beurteilen lassen; **as far as I can ~** soweit ich es beurteilen kann; **I ~d it necessary to inform him** ich hielt es für nötig, ihn zu informieren

judge advocate *n* (*Mil*) Beisitzer(in) *m(f)* bei einem Kriegsgericht

Judge Advocate General *n* (*Mil*) *Vorsitzender des obersten Militärgerichts*

judgment, judgement ['dʒʌdʒmənt] *n* Urteil *nt*; (*Rel*) Gericht *nt*; (*view, opinion*) Meinung *f*; (*discernment*) Urteilsvermögen *nt*; **in my ~** meiner Meinung nach; **to pass ~ (on)** (*Law*) das Urteil sprechen (über +*acc*); (*fig*) ein Urteil fällen (über +*acc*)

judicial [dʒuː'dɪʃl] *adj* gerichtlich, Justiz-; (*fig*) kritisch; **~ review** gerichtliche Überprüfung *f*

judiciary [dʒuː'dɪʃɪərɪ] *n*: **the ~** die Gerichtsbehörden *pl*

judicious [dʒuː'dɪʃəs] *adj* klug

judo ['dʒuːdəu] *n* Judo *nt*

jug [dʒʌg] *n* Krug *m*

jugged hare ['dʒʌgd-] (*Brit*) *n* ≈ Hasenpfeffer *m*

juggernaut ['dʒʌgənɔːt] (*Brit*) *n* Fernlastwagen *m*

juggle ['dʒʌgl] *vi* jonglieren

juggler ['dʒʌgləʳ] *n* Jongleur *m*

Jugoslav *etc* ['juːgəu'slɑːv] = **Yugoslav** *etc*

jugular ['dʒʌgjuləʳ] *adj*: **~ (vein)** Drosselvene *f*

juice [dʒuːs] *n* Saft *m*; (*inf: petrol*): **we've run out of ~** wir haben keinen Sprit mehr

juicy ['dʒuːsɪ] *adj* saftig

jukebox ['dʒuːkbɔks] *n* Musikbox *f*

Jul. *abbr* = **July**

July [dʒuː'laɪ] *n* Juli *m*; **the first of ~** der erste Juli; **on the eleventh of ~** am elften Juli; **in the month of ~** im (Monat) Juli; **at the beginning/end of ~** Anfang/Ende Juli; **in the middle of ~** Mitte Juli; **during ~** im Juli; **in ~ of next year** im Juli nächsten Jahres; **each** *or* **every ~** jedes Jahr im Juli; **~ was wet this year** der Juli war dieses Jahr ein nasser Monat

jumble ['dʒʌmbl] *n* Durcheinander *nt*; (*items for sale*) gebrauchte Sachen *pl*; *siehe Info-Artikel* ▷ *vt* (*also*: **jumble up**) durcheinanderbringen

JUMBLE SALE

Jumble sale ist ein Wohltätigkeitsbasar, meist in einer Aula oder einem Gemeindehaus abgehalten, bei dem alle möglichen Gebrauchtwaren (vor allem Kleidung, Spielzeug, Bücher,

Geschirr und Möbel) verkauft werden. Der Erlös fließt entweder einer Wohltätigkeitsorganisation zu oder wird für örtliche Zwecke verwendet, z. B. die Pfadfinder, die Grundschule, Reparatur der Kirche usw.

jumbo ['dʒʌmbəu]
jumbo jet *n* Jumbo(jet) *m*
jumbo-size ['dʒʌmbəusaɪz] *adj* (*packet etc*) Riesen-
jump [dʒʌmp] *vi* springen; (*with fear, surprise*) zusammenzucken; (*increase*) sprunghaft ansteigen ▷ *vt* springen über +*acc* ▷ *n* (*see vb*) Sprung *m*; Zusammenzucken *nt*; sprunghafter Anstieg *m*; **to ~ the queue** (*Brit*) sich vordrängeln
▸**jump about** *vi* herumspringen
▸**jump at** *vt fus* (*idea*) sofort aufgreifen; (*chance*) sofort ergreifen; **he ~ed at the offer** er griff bei dem Angebot sofort zu
▸**jump down** *vi* herunterspringen
▸**jump up** *vi* hochspringen; (*from seat*) aufspringen
jumped-up ['dʒʌmptʌp] (*Brit: pej*) *adj* eingebildet
jumper ['dʒʌmpəʳ] *n* (*Brit*) Pullover *m*; (*US: dress*) Trägerkleid *nt*; (*Sport*) Springer(in) *m(f)*
jumper cables (*US*) *npl* = **jump leads**
jumping jack *n* Knallfrosch *m*
jump jet *n* Senkrechtstarter *m*
jump leads (*Brit*) *npl* Starthilfekabel *nt*
jump-start ['dʒʌmpstɑːt] *vt* (*Aut: engine*) durch Anschieben des Wagens in Gang bringen
jump suit *n* Overall *m*
jumpy ['dʒʌmpɪ] *adj* nervös
Jun. *abbr* = **June**
junction ['dʒʌŋkʃən] (*Brit*) *n* Kreuzung *f*; (*Rail*) Gleisanschluss *m*
juncture ['dʒʌŋktʃəʳ] *n*: **at this ~** zu diesem Zeitpunkt
June [dʒuːn] *n* Juni *m*; *see also* **July**
jungle ['dʒʌŋgl] *n* Urwald *m*, Dschungel *m* (*also fig*)
junior ['dʒuːnɪəʳ] *adj* jünger; (*subordinate*) untergeordnet ▷ *n* Jüngere(r) *f(m)*; (*young person*) Junior *m*; **he's ~ to me (by 2 years), he's my ~ (by 2 years)** (*younger*) er ist (2 Jahre) jünger als ich; **he's ~ to me** (*subordinate*) er steht unter mir
junior executive *n* Zweiter Geschäftsführer *m*, Zweite Geschäftsführerin *f*
junior high school (*US*) *n* ≈ Mittelschule *f*
junior minister (*Brit*) *n* Staatssekretär(in) *m(f)*
junior partner *n* Juniorpartner(in) *m(f)*
junior school (*Brit*) *n* ≈ Grundschule *f*
junior sizes *npl* (*Comm*) Kindergrößen *pl*
juniper ['dʒuːnɪpəʳ] *n*: **~ berry** Wacholderbeere *f*
junk [dʒʌŋk] *n* (*rubbish*) Gerümpel *nt*; (*cheap goods*) Ramsch *m*; (*ship*) Dschunke *f* ▷ *vt* (*inf*) ausrangieren
junk bond *n* (*Fin*) *niedrig eingestuftes Wertpapier mit hohen Ertragschancen bei erhöhtem Risiko*
junket ['dʒʌŋkɪt] *n* Dickmilch *f*; (*inf: pej: free trip*): **to go on a ~** eine Reise auf Kosten des Steuerzahlers machen
junk food *n* ungesundes Essen *nt*
junkie ['dʒʌŋkɪ] (*inf*) *n* Fixer(in) *m(f)*
junk mail *n* (Post)wurfsendungen *pl*
junk room *n* Rumpelkammer *f*
junk shop *n* Trödelladen *m*
Junr *abbr* (*in names: = junior*) jun.
junta ['dʒʌntə] *n* Junta *f*
Jupiter ['dʒuːpɪtəʳ] *n* Jupiter *m*
jurisdiction [dʒuərɪs'dɪkʃən] *n* Gerichtsbarkeit *f*; (*Admin*) Zuständigkeit *f*, Zuständigkeitsbereich *m*; **it falls** *or* **comes within/outside my ~** dafür bin ich zuständig/nicht zuständig
jurisprudence [dʒuərɪs'pruːdəns] *n* Jura *no art*, Rechtswissenschaft *f*
juror ['dʒuərəʳ] *n* Schöffe *m*, Schöffin *f*; (*for capital crimes*) Geschworene(r) *f(m)*; (*in competition*) Preisrichter(in) *m(f)*
jury ['dʒuərɪ] *n*: **the ~** die Schöffen *pl*; (*for capital crimes*) die Geschworenen *pl*; (*for competition*) die Jury, das Preisgericht
jury box *n* Schöffenbank *f*; Geschworenenbank *f*
juryman ['dʒuərɪmən] (*irreg: like* **man**) *n* = **juror**
just [dʒʌst] *adj* gerecht ▷ *adv* (*exactly*) genau; (*only*) nur; **he's ~ done it/left** er hat es gerade getan/ist gerade gegangen; **~ as I expected** genau wie ich erwartet habe; **~ right** genau richtig; **~ two o'clock** erst zwei Uhr; **we were ~ going** wir wollten gerade gehen; **I was ~ about to phone** ich wollte gerade anrufen; **she's ~ as clever as you** sie ist genauso klug wie du; **it's ~ as well (that ...)** nur gut, dass ...; **~ as he was leaving** gerade als er gehen wollte; **~ before** gerade noch; **~ enough** gerade genug; **~ here** genau hier, genau an dieser Stelle; **he ~ missed** er hat genau danebengetroffen; **it's ~ me** ich bins nur; **it's ~ a mistake** es ist nur ein Fehler; **~ listen** hör mal; **~ ask someone the way** frage doch einfach jemanden nach dem Weg; **not ~ now** nicht gerade jetzt; **~ a minute!, ~ one moment!** einen Moment, bitte!
justice ['dʒʌstɪs] *n* Justiz *f*; (*of cause, complaint*) Berechtigung *f*; (*fairness*) Gerechtigkeit *f*; (*US: judge*) Richter(in) *m(f)*; **Lord Chief J~** (*Brit*) *oberster Richter in Großbritannien*; **to do ~ to** (*fig*) gerecht werden +*dat*
Justice of the Peace *n* Friedensrichter(in) *m(f)*
justifiable [dʒʌstɪ'faɪəbl] *adj* gerechtfertigt, berechtigt
justifiably [dʒʌstɪ'faɪəblɪ] *adv* zu Recht, berechtigterweise
justification [dʒʌstɪfɪ'keɪʃən] *n* Rechtfertigung *f*; (*Typ*) Justierung *f*
justify ['dʒʌstɪfaɪ] *vt* rechtfertigen; (*text*) justieren; **to be justified in doing sth** etw zu *or* mit Recht tun

justly ['dʒʌstlɪ] *adv* zu *or* mit Recht; (*deservedly*) gerecht
jut [dʒʌt] *vi* (*also*: **jut out**) vorstehen
jute [dʒu:t] *n* Jute *f*
juvenile ['dʒu:vənaɪl] *adj* (*crime, offenders*) Jugend-; (*humour, mentality*) kindisch, unreif ▷ *n* Jugendliche(r) *f(m)*
juvenile delinquency *n* Jugendkriminalität *f*
juvenile delinquent *n* jugendlicher Straftäter *m*, jugendliche Straftäterin *f*
juxtapose ['dʒʌkstəpəuz] *vt* nebeneinanderstellen
juxtaposition ['dʒʌkstəpə'zɪʃən] *n* Nebeneinanderstellung *f*

Kk

K[1], **k** [keɪ] *n* (*letter*) K *nt*, k *nt*; **K for King** ≈ K wie Kaufmann
K[2] [keɪ] *abbr* (= *one thousand*) K; (*Comput*: = *kilobyte*) KB; (*Brit*: *in titles*) = **knight**
kaftan ['kæftæn] *n* Kaftan *m*
Kalahari Desert [kælə'hɑːrɪ-] *n*: **the ~** die Kalahari
kale [keɪl] *n* Grünkohl *m*
kaleidoscope [kə'laɪdəskəup] *n* Kaleidoskop *nt*
kamikaze ['kæmɪ'kɑːzɪ] *adj* (*mission etc*) Kamikaze-, Selbstmord-
Kampala [kæm'pɑːlə] *n* Kampala *nt*
Kampuchea [kæmpu'tʃɪə] *n* Kampuchea *nt*
Kampuchean [kæmpu'tʃɪən] *adj* kampucheanisch
kangaroo [kæŋgə'ruː] *n* Känguru *nt*
Kans. (*US*) *abbr* (*Post*) = *Kansas*
kaput [kə'put] (*inf*) *adj*: **to be ~** kaputt sein
karaoke [kɑːrə'əukɪ] *n* Karaoke *nt*
karate [kə'rɑːtɪ] *n* Karate *nt*
Kashmir [kæʃmɪəʳ] *n* Kaschmir *nt*
kayak ['kaɪæk] *n* Kajak *m or nt*
Kazakhstan [kæzæk'stɑːn] *n* Kasachstan *nt*
KC (*Brit*) *n abbr* (*Law*: = *King's Counsel*) Kronanwalt *m*
kebab [kə'bæb] *n* Kebab *m*
keel [kiːl] *n* Kiel *m*; **on an even ~** (*fig*) stabil
▸**keel over** *vi* kentern; (*person*) umkippen
keen [kiːn] *adj* begeistert, eifrig; (*interest*) groß; (*desire*) heftig; (*eye, intelligence, competition, edge*) scharf; **to be ~ to do** *or* **on doing sth** scharf darauf sein, etw zu tun (*inf*); **to be ~ on sth** an etw *dat* sehr interessiert sein; **to be ~ on sb** von jdm sehr angetan sein; **I'm not ~ on going** ich brenne nicht gerade darauf, zu gehen
keenly ['kiːnlɪ] *adv* (*enthusiastically*) begeistert; (*feel*) leidenschaftlich; (*look*) aufmerksam
keenness ['kiːnnɪs] *n* Begeisterung *f*, Eifer *m*; **his ~ to go is suspicious** dass er so unbedingt gehen will, ist verdächtig
keep [kiːp] (*pt, pp* **kept**) *vt* behalten; (*preserve, store*) aufbewahren; (*house, shop, accounts, diary*) führen; (*garden etc*) pflegen; (*chickens, bees, promise*) halten; (*family etc*) versorgen, unterhalten; (*detain*) aufhalten; (*prevent*) abhalten ▹ *vi* (*remain*) bleiben; (*food*) sich halten ▹ *n* (*food etc*) Unterhalt *m*; (*of castle*) Bergfried *m*; **to ~ doing sth** etw immer wieder tun; **to ~ sb happy** jdn zufriedenstellen; **to ~ a room tidy** ein Zimmer in Ordnung halten; **to ~ sb waiting** jdn warten lassen; **to ~ an appointment** eine Verabredung einhalten; **to ~ a record of sth** über etw *acc* Buch führen; **to ~ sth to o.s.** etw für sich behalten; **to ~ sth (back) from sb** etw vor jdm geheim halten; **to ~ sb from doing sth** jdn davon abhalten, etw zu tun; **to ~ sth from happening** etw verhindern; **to ~ time** (*clock*) genau gehen; **enough for his ~** genug für seinen Unterhalt
▸**keep away** *vt* fernhalten ▹ *vi*: **to ~ away (from)** wegbleiben (von)
▸**keep back** *vt* zurückhalten; (*tears*) unterdrücken; (*money*) einbehalten ▹ *vi* zurückbleiben
▸**keep down** *vt* (*prices*) niedrig halten; (*spending*) einschränken; (*food*) bei sich behalten ▹ *vi* unten bleiben
▸**keep in** *vt* im Haus behalten; (*at school*) nachsitzen lassen ▹ *vi* (*inf*): **to ~ in with sb** sich mit jdm gut stellen
▸**keep off** *vt* fernhalten ▹ *vi* wegbleiben; **"~ off the grass"** „Betreten des Rasens verboten"; **~ your hands off** Hände weg
▸**keep on** *vi*: **to ~ on doing sth** (*continue*) etw weiter tun; **to ~ on (about sth)** unaufhörlich (von etw) reden
▸**keep out** *vt* fernhalten; **"~ out"** „Zutritt verboten"
▸**keep up** *vt* (*payments*) weiterbezahlen; (*standards etc*) aufrechterhalten ▹ *vi*: **to ~ up (with)** mithalten können (mit)
keeper ['kiːpəʳ] *n* Wärter(in) *m(f)*
keep fit *n* Fitnesstraining *nt*
keeping ['kiːpɪŋ] *n* (*care*) Obhut *f*; **in ~ with** in Übereinstimmung mit; **out of ~ with** nicht im Einklang mit; **I'll leave this in your ~** ich vertraue dies deiner Obhut an
keeps [kiːps] *n*: **for ~** (*inf*) für immer
keepsake ['kiːpseɪk] *n* Andenken *nt*
keg [kɛg] *n* Fässchen *nt*; **~ beer** Bier *nt* vom Fass
Ken. (*US*) *abbr* (*Post*) = *Kentucky*
kennel ['kɛnl] *n* Hundehütte *f*
kennels ['kɛnlz] *n* Hundeheim *nt*; **we had to leave our dog in ~ over Christmas** wir mussten unseren Hund über Weihnachten in

ein Heim geben
Kenya ['kɛnjə] *n* Kenia *nt*
Kenyan ['kɛnjən] *adj* kenianisch ▷ *n* Kenianer(in) *m(f)*
kept [kɛpt] *pt, pp of* **keep**
kerb [kə:b] *(Brit) n* Bordstein *m*
kerb crawler [-'krɔ:ləʳ] *(inf) n* Freier *m* im Autostrich
kernel ['kə:nl] *n* Kern *m*
kerosene ['kɛrəsi:n] *n* Kerosin *nt*
kestrel ['kɛstrəl] *n* Turmfalke *m*
ketchup ['kɛtʃəp] *n* Ket(s)chup *m or nt*
kettle ['kɛtl] *n* Kessel *m*
kettledrum ['kɛtldrʌm] *n* (Kessel)pauke *f*
key [ki:] *n* Schlüssel *m*; *(Mus)* Tonart *f*; *(of piano, computer, typewriter)* Taste *f* ▷ *cpd (issue etc)* Schlüssel- ▷ *vt (also:* **key in***)* eingeben
keyboard ['ki:bɔ:d] *n* Tastatur *f*
keyboarder ['ki:bɔ:dəʳ] *n* Datentypist(in) *m(f)*
keyed up [ki:d-] *adj*: **to be (all) ~** (ganz) aufgedreht sein *(inf)*
keyhole ['ki:həul] *n* Schlüsselloch *nt*
keyhole surgery *n* Schlüssellochchirurgie *f*, minimal invasive Chirurgie *f*
keynote ['ki:nəut] *n* Grundton *m*; *(of speech)* Leitgedanke *m*
keypad ['ki:pæd] *n* Tastenfeld *nt*
key ring *n* Schlüsselring *m*
keystroke ['ki:strəuk] *n* Anschlag *m*
kg *abbr (= kilogram)* kg
KGB *n abbr (Pol: formerly)* KGB *m*
khaki ['kɑ:kɪ] *n* K(h)aki *nt*
kHz *abbr (= kilohertz)* kHz
kibbutz [kɪ'buts] *n* Kibbuz *m*
kick [kɪk] *vt* treten; *(table, ball)* treten gegen *+acc*; *(inf: habit)* ablegen; *(: addiction)* wegkommen von ▷ *vi (horse)* ausschlagen ▷ *n* Tritt *m*; *(to ball)* Schuss *m*; *(of rifle)* Rückstoß *m*; *(thrill)*: **he does it for ~s** er macht es zum Spaß
▸ **kick around** *(inf) vi (person)* rumhängen; *(thing)* rumliegen
▸ **kick off** *vi (Sport)* anstoßen
kickoff ['kɪkɔf] *n (Sport)* Anstoß *m*
kick start *n (Aut: also:* **kick starter***)* Kickstarter *m*
kid [kɪd] *n (inf: child)* Kind *nt*; *(animal)* Kitz *nt*; *(leather)* Ziegenleder *nt*, Glacéleder *nt* ▷ *vi (inf)* Witze machen; **~ brother** kleiner Bruder *m*; **~ sister** kleine Schwester *f*
kid gloves *npl*: **to treat sb with ~** *(fig)* jdn mit Samthandschuhen anfassen
kidnap ['kɪdnæp] *vt* entführen, kidnappen
kidnapper ['kɪdnæpəʳ] *n* Entführer(in) *m(f)*, Kidnapper(in) *m(f)*
kidnapping ['kɪdnæpɪŋ] *n* Entführung *f*, Kidnapping *nt*
kidney ['kɪdnɪ] *n* Niere *f*
kidney bean *n* Gartenbohne *f*
kidney machine *n (Med)* künstliche Niere *f*
Kilimanjaro [kɪlɪmən'dʒɑ:rəu] *n*: **Mount ~** der Kilimandscharo
kill [kɪl] *vt* töten; *(murder)* ermorden, umbringen; *(plant)* eingehen lassen; *(proposal)* zu Fall bringen; *(rumour)* ein Ende machen *+dat* ▷ *n* Abschuss *m*; **to ~ time** die Zeit totschlagen; **to ~ o.s. to do sth** *(fig)* sich fast umbringen, um etw zu tun; **to ~ o.s. (laughing)** *(fig)* sich totlachen
▸ **kill off** *vt* abtöten; *(fig: romance)* beenden
killer ['kɪləʳ] *n* Mörder(in) *m(f)*
killer instinct *n (fig)* Tötungsinstinkt *m*
killing ['kɪlɪŋ] *n* Töten *nt*; *(instance)* Mord *m*; **to make a ~** *(inf)* einen Riesengewinn machen
killjoy ['kɪldʒɔɪ] *n* Spielverderber(in) *m(f)*
kiln [kɪln] *n* Brennofen *m*
kilo ['ki:ləu] *n* Kilo *nt*
kilobyte ['ki:ləubaɪt] *n* Kilobyte *nt*
kilogram, **kilogramme** ['kɪləugræm] *n* Kilogramm *nt*
kilohertz ['kɪləuhə:ts] *n inv* Kilohertz *nt*
kilometre, *(US)* **kilometer** ['kɪləmi:təʳ] *n* Kilometer *m*
kilowatt ['kɪləuwɔt] *n* Kilowatt *nt*
kilt [kɪlt] *n* Kilt *m*, Schottenrock *m*
kilter ['kɪltəʳ] *n*: **out of ~** nicht in Ordnung
kimono [kɪ'məunəu] *n* Kimono *m*
kin [kɪn] *n see* **kith; next**
kind [kaɪnd] *adj* freundlich ▷ *n* Art *f*; *(sort)* Sorte *f*; **would you be ~ enough to ...?, would you be so ~ as to ...?** wären Sie (vielleicht) so nett und ...?; **it's very ~ of you (to do ...)** es ist wirklich nett von Ihnen(, ... zu tun); **in ~** *(Comm)* in Naturalien; **a ~ of ...** eine Art ...; **they are two of a ~** sie sind beide von der gleichen Art; *(people)* sie sind vom gleichen Schlag
kindergarten ['kɪndəgɑ:tn] *n* Kindergarten *m*
kind-hearted [kaɪnd'hɑ:tɪd] *adj* gutherzig
kindle ['kɪndl] *vt* anzünden; *(emotion)* wecken
kindling ['kɪndlɪŋ] *n* Anzündholz *nt*
kindly ['kaɪndlɪ] *adj, adv* freundlich, nett; **will you ~ ...** würden Sie bitte ...; **he didn't take it ~** er konnte sich damit nicht anfreunden
kindness ['kaɪndnɪs] *n* Freundlichkeit *f*
kindred ['kɪndrɪd] *adj*: **~ spirit** Gleichgesinnte(r) *f(m)*
kinetic [kɪ'nɛtɪk] *adj* kinetisch
king [kɪŋ] *n (also fig)* König *m*
kingdom ['kɪŋdəm] *n* Königreich *nt*
kingfisher ['kɪŋfɪʃəʳ] *n* Eisvogel *m*
kingpin ['kɪŋpɪn] *n (Tech)* Bolzen *m*; *(Aut)* Achsschenkelbolzen *m*; *(fig)* wichtigste Stütze *f*
king-size ['kɪŋsaɪz], **king-sized** ['kɪŋsaɪzd] *adj* extragroß; *(cigarette)* Kingsize-
kink [kɪŋk] *n* Knick *m*; *(in hair)* Welle *f*; *(fig)* Schrulle *f*
kinky ['kɪŋkɪ] *(pej) adj* schrullig; *(sexually)* abartig
kinship ['kɪnʃɪp] *n* Verwandtschaft *f*
kinsman ['kɪnzmən] *(irreg: like* **man***) n* Verwandte(r) *m*
kinswoman ['kɪnzwumən] *(irreg: like* **woman***) n* Verwandte *f*
kiosk ['ki:ɔsk] *n* Kiosk *m*; *(Brit)* (Telefon)zelle *f*; *(also:* **newspaper kiosk***)* (Zeitungs)kiosk *m*

kipper ['kɪpəʳ] *n* Räucherhering *m*
Kirghizia [kəː'gɪzɪə] *n* Kirgistan *nt*
kiss [kɪs] *n* Kuß *m* ▷ *vt* küssen ▷ *vi* sich küssen; **to ~ (each other)** sich küssen; **to ~ sb goodbye** jdm einen Abschiedskuss geben
kissagram ['kɪsəgræm] *n durch eine(n) Angestellte(n) einer Agentur persönlich übermittelter Kuss*
kiss of life (*Brit*) *n*: **the ~** Mund-zu-Mund-Beatmung *f*
kit [kɪt] *n* Zeug *nt*, Sachen *pl*; (*equipment, also Mil*) Ausrüstung *f*; (*set of tools*) Werkzeug *nt*; (*for assembly*) Bausatz *m*
▸ **kit out** (*Brit*) *vt* ausrüsten, ausstatten
kitbag ['kɪtbæg] *n* Seesack *m*
kitchen ['kɪtʃɪn] *n* Küche *f*
kitchen garden *n* Küchengarten *m*
kitchen sink *n* Spüle *f*
kitchen unit (*Brit*) *n* Küchenschrank *m*
kitchenware ['kɪtʃɪnwɛəʳ] *n* Küchengeräte *pl*
kite [kaɪt] *n* Drachen *m*; (*Zool*) Milan *m*
kith [kɪθ] *n*: **~ and kin** Freunde und Verwandte *pl*
kitten ['kɪtn] *n* Kätzchen *nt*
kitty ['kɪtɪ] *n* (gemeinsame) Kasse *f*
kiwi ['kiːwiː], **kiwi fruit** *n* Kiwi(frucht) *f*
KKK (*US*) *n abbr* (*= Ku Klux Klan*) Ku-Klux-Klan *m*
Kleenex® ['kliːnɛks] *n* Tempo(taschentuch)® *nt*
kleptomaniac [klɛptəu'meɪnɪæk] *n* Kleptomane *m*, Kleptomanin *f*
km *abbr* (*= kilometre*) km
km/h *abbr* (*= kilometres per hour*) km/h
knack [næk] *n*: **to have the ~ of doing sth** es heraushaben, wie man etw macht; **there's a ~ to doing this** da ist ein Trick *or* Kniff dabei
knackered ['nækəd] (*Brit: inf*) *adj* kaputt
knapsack ['næpsæk] *n* Rucksack *m*
knead [niːd] *vt* kneten
knee [niː] *n* Knie *nt*
kneecap ['niːkæp] *n* Kniescheibe *f*
kneecapping ['niːkæpɪŋ] *n* Durchschießen *nt* der Kniescheibe
knee-deep ['niː'diːp] *adj, adv*: **the water was ~** das Wasser ging mir *etc* bis zum Knie; **~ in mud** knietief *or* bis zu den Knien im Schlamm
kneejerk reaction ['niːdʒəːk-] *n* (*fig*) instinktive Reaktion *f*
kneel [niːl] (*pt, pp* **knelt**) *vi* knien; (*also*: **kneel down**) niederknien
kneepad ['niːpæd] *n* Knieschützer *m*
knell [nɛl] *n* Totengeläut(e) *nt*; (*fig*) Ende *nt*
knelt [nɛlt] *pt, pp of* **kneel**
knew [njuː] *pt of* **know**
knickers ['nɪkəz] (*Brit*) *npl* Schlüpfer *m*
knick-knacks ['nɪknæks] *npl* Nippsachen *pl*
knife [naɪf] (*pl* **knives**) *n* Messer *nt* ▷ *vt* (*injure, attack*) einstechen auf *+acc*; **~, fork and spoon** Messer, Gabel und Löffel
knife edge *n*: **to be balanced on a ~** (*fig*) auf Messers Schneide stehen
knight [naɪt] *n* (*Brit*) Ritter *m*; (*Chess*) Springer *m*, Pferd *nt*
knighthood ['naɪthud] (*Brit*) *n*: **to get a ~** in den Adelsstand erhoben werden
knit [nɪt] *vt* stricken ▷ *vi* stricken; (*bones*) zusammenwachsen; **to ~ one's brows** die Stirn runzeln
knitted ['nɪtɪd] *adj* gestrickt, Strick-
knitting ['nɪtɪŋ] *n* Stricken *nt*; (*garment being made*) Strickzeug *nt*
knitting machine *n* Strickmaschine *f*
knitting needle *n* Stricknadel *f*
knitting pattern *n* Strickmuster *nt*
knitwear ['nɪtwɛəʳ] *n* Strickwaren *pl*
knives [naɪvz] *npl of* **knife**
knob [nɔb] *n* Griff *m*; (*of stick*) Knauf *m*; (*on radio, TV etc*) Knopf *m*; **a ~ of butter** (*Brit*) ein Stückchen *nt* Butter
knobbly ['nɔblɪ], (*US*) **knobby** *adj* (*wood*) knorrig; (*surface*) uneben; **~ knees** Knubbelknie *pl* (*inf*)
knock [nɔk] *vt* schlagen; (*bump into*) stoßen gegen *+acc*; (*inf: criticize*) runtermachen ▷ *vi* klopfen ▷ *n* Schlag *m*; (*bump*) Stoß *m*; (*on door*) Klopfen *nt*; **to ~ a nail into sth** einen Nagel in etw *acc* schlagen; **to ~ some sense into sb** jdn zur Vernunft bringen; **to ~ at/on** klopfen an/auf *+acc*; **he ~ed at the door** er klopfte an, er klopfte an die Tür
▸ **knock about** (*inf*) *vt* schlagen, verprügeln ▷ *vi* rumziehen; **~ about with** sich rumtreiben mit
▸ **knock around** *vt, vi* = **knock about**
▸ **knock back** (*inf*) *vt* (*drink*) sich *dat* hinter die Binde kippen
▸ **knock down** *vt* anfahren; (*fatally*) überfahren; (*building etc*) abreißen; (*price: buyer*) herunterhandeln; (*: seller*) heruntergehen mit
▸ **knock off** *vi* (*inf*) Feierabend machen ▷ *vt* (*from price*) nachlassen; (*inf: steal*) klauen; **to ~ off £10** £10 nachlassen
▸ **knock out** *vt* bewusstlos schlagen; (*subj: drug*) bewusstlos werden lassen; (*Boxing*) k. o. schlagen; (*in game, competition*) besiegen
▸ **knock over** *vt* umstoßen; (*with car*) anfahren
knockdown ['nɔkdaun] *adj*: **~ price** Schleuderpreis *m*
knocker ['nɔkəʳ] *n* Türklopfer *m*
knock-for-knock ['nɔkfə'nɔk] (*Brit*) *adj*: **~ agreement** *Vereinbarung, bei der jede Versicherungsgesellschaft den Schaden am von ihr versicherten Fahrzeug übernimmt*
knocking ['nɔkɪŋ] *n* Klopfen *nt*
knock-kneed [nɔk'niːd] *adj* x-beinig; **to be ~** X-Beine haben
knockout ['nɔkaut] *n* (*Boxing*) K.-o.-Schlag *m*, Ko.-Schlag *m* ▷ *cpd* (*competition etc*) Ausscheidungs-
knock-up ['nɔkʌp] *n* (*Tennis*): **to have a ~** ein paar Bälle schlagen
knot [nɔt] *n* Knoten *m*; (*in wood*) Ast *m* ▷ *vt* einen Knoten machen in *+acc*; (*knot together*) verknoten; **to tie a ~** einen Knoten machen
knotty ['nɔtɪ] *adj* (*fig: problem*) verwickelt
know [nəu] (*pt* **knew**, *pp* **~n**) *vt* kennen; (*facts*)

wissen; (*language*) können ▷ *vi*: **to ~ about** *or* **of sth/sb** von etw/jdm gehört haben; **to ~ how to swim** schwimmen können; **to get to ~ sth** etw erfahren; (*place*) etw kennenlernen; **I don't ~ him** ich kenne ihn nicht; **to ~ right from wrong** Gut und Böse unterscheiden können; **as far as I ~** soviel ich weiß; **yes, I ~** ja, ich weiß; **I don't ~** ich weiß (es) nicht
know-all ['nəuɔːl] (*Brit: pej*) *n* Alleswisser *m*
know-how ['nəuhau] *n* Know-how *nt*, Sachkenntnis *f*
knowing ['nəuɪŋ] *adj* wissend
knowingly ['nəuɪŋlɪ] *adv* (*purposely*) bewusst; (*smile, look*) wissend
know-it-all ['nəuɪtɔːl] (*US*) *n* = **know-all**
knowledge ['nɔlɪdʒ] *n* Wissen *nt*, Kenntnis *f*; (*learning, things learnt*) Kenntnisse *pl*; **to have no ~ of** nichts wissen von; **not to my ~** nicht, dass ich wüsste; **without my ~** ohne mein Wissen; **it is common ~ that ...** es ist allgemein bekannt, dass ...; **it has come to my ~ that ...** ich habe erfahren, dass ...; **to have a working ~ of French** Grundkenntnisse in Französisch haben
knowledgeable ['nɔlɪdʒəbl] *adj* informiert
known [nəun] *pp of* **know** ▷ *adj* bekannt; (*expert*) anerkannt
knuckle ['nʌkl] *n* (Finger)knöchel *m*
▸ **knuckle down** (*inf*) *vi* sich dahinter klemmen; **to ~ down to work** sich an die Arbeit machen
▸ **knuckle under** (*inf*) *vi* sich fügen, spuren
knuckle-duster ['nʌkl'dʌstəʳ] *n* Schlagring *m*
KO *n abbr* (= *knockout*) K. o. *m* ▷ *vt* k. o. schlagen
koala [kəu'ɑːlə] *n* (*also*: **koala bear**) Koala(bär) *m*
kook [kuːk] (*US: inf*) *n* Spinner *m*
Koran [kɔ'rɑːn] *n*: **the ~** der Koran
Korea [kə'rɪə] *n* Korea *nt*; **North ~** Nordkorea *nt*; **South ~** Südkorea *nt*
Korean [kə'rɪən] *adj* koreanisch ▷ *n* Koreaner(in) *m(f)*
kosher ['kəuʃəʳ] *adj* koscher
kowtow ['kau'tau] *vi*: **to ~ to sb** vor jdm dienern *or* einen Kotau machen
Kremlin ['krɛmlɪn] *n*: **the ~** der Kreml
KS (*US*) *abbr* (*Post*) = *Kansas*
Kt (*Brit*) *abbr* (*in titles*) = **knight**
Kuala Lumpur ['kwɑːlə'lumpuəʳ] *n* Kuala Lumpur *nt*
kudos ['kjuːdɔs] *n* Ansehen *nt*, Ehre *f*
Kurd [kəːd] *n* Kurde *m*, Kurdin *f*
Kuwait [ku'weɪt] *n* Kuwait *nt*
Kuwaiti [ku'weɪtɪ] *adj* kuwaitisch ▷ *n* Kuwaiter(in) *m(f)*
kW *abbr* (= *kilowatt*) kW
KY (*US*) *abbr* (*Post*) = *Kentucky*

Ll

L[1], **l**[1] [ɛl] *n* (*letter*) L *nt*, l *nt*; **L for Lucy, L for Love** (*US*) ≈ L wie Ludwig
L[2] [ɛl] *abbr* (*Brit: Aut:* = *learner*) *am Auto angebrachtes Kennzeichen für Fahrschüler*; = **lake**; (= *large*) gr.; (= *left*) l.
l[2] *abbr* (= *litre*) l
LA (*US*) *n abbr* = *Los Angeles* ▷ *abbr* (*Post*) = *Louisiana*
La. (*US*) *abbr* (*Post*) = *Louisiana*
lab [læb] *n abbr* = **laboratory**
label ['leɪbl] *n* Etikett *nt*; (*brand: of record*) Label *nt* ▷ *vt* etikettieren; (*fig: person*) abstempeln
labor *etc* ['leɪbə^r^] (*US*) *n* = **labour** *etc*
laboratory [lə'bɔrətərɪ] *n* Labor *nt*

LABOR DAY

Labor Day ist in den USA und Kanada der Name für den Tag der Arbeit. Er wird dort als gesetzlicher Feiertag am ersten Montag im September begangen.

laborious [lə'bɔːrɪəs] *adj* mühsam
labor union (*US*) *n* Gewerkschaft *f*
labour, (*US*) **labor** ['leɪbə^r^] *n* Arbeit *f*; (*work force*) Arbeitskräfte *pl*; (*Med*): **to be in ~** in den Wehen liegen ▷ *vi*: **to ~ (at sth)** sich (mit etw) abmühen ▷ *vt*: **to ~ a point** auf einem Thema herumreiten; **L~, the ~ Party** (*Brit*) die Labour Party; **hard ~** Zwangsarbeit *f*
labour camp *n* Arbeitslager *nt*
labour cost *n* Lohnkosten *pl*
labour dispute *n* Arbeitskampf *m*
laboured ['leɪbəd] *adj* (*breathing*) schwer; (*movement, style*) schwerfällig
labourer ['leɪbərə^r^] *n* Arbeiter(in) *m(f)*; **farm ~** Landarbeiter(in) *m(f)*
labour force *n* Arbeiterschaft *f*
labour intensive *adj* arbeitsintensiv
labour market *n* Arbeitsmarkt *m*
labour pains *npl* Wehen *pl*
labour relations *npl* Beziehungen *pl* zwischen Arbeitnehmern, Arbeitgebern und Gewerkschaften
labour-saving ['leɪbəseɪvɪŋ] *adj* arbeitsparend
laburnum [lə'bəːnəm] *n* (*Bot*) Goldregen *m*
labyrinth ['læbɪrɪnθ] *n* Labyrinth *nt*
lace [leɪs] *n* (*fabric*) Spitze *f*; (*of shoe etc*) (Schuh)band *nt*, Schnürsenkel *m* ▷ *vt* (*also*: **lace up**) (zu)schnüren; **to ~ a drink** einen Schuss Alkohol in ein Getränk geben
lacemaking ['leɪsmeɪkɪŋ] *n* Klöppelei *f*
lacerate ['læsəreɪt] *vt* zerschneiden
laceration [læsə'reɪʃən] *n* Schnittwunde *f*
lace-up ['leɪsʌp] *adj* (*shoes etc*) Schnür-
lack [læk] *n* Mangel *m* ▷ *vt, vi*: **sb ~s sth, sb is ~ing in sth** jdm fehlt es an etw *dat*; **through** *or* **for ~ of** aus Mangel an +*dat*; **to be ~ing** fehlen
lackadaisical [lækə'deɪzɪkl] *adj* lustlos
lackey ['lækɪ] (*pej*) *n* Lakai *m*
lacklustre, (*US*) **lackluster** ['læklʌstə^r^] *adj* farblos, langweilig
laconic [lə'kɔnɪk] *adj* lakonisch
lacquer ['lækə^r^] *n* Lack *m*; (*also*: **hair lacquer**) Haarspray *nt*
lacrosse [lə'krɔs] *n* Lacrosse *nt*
lacy ['leɪsɪ] *adj* Spitzen-; (*like lace*) spitzenartig
lad [læd] *n* Junge *m*
ladder ['lædə^r^] *n* (*also fig*) Leiter *f*; (*Brit: in tights*) Laufmasche *f* ▷ *vt* (*Brit*) Laufmaschen bekommen in +*dat* ▷ *vi* (*Brit*) Laufmaschen bekommen
laden ['leɪdn] *adj*: **~ (with)** beladen (mit); **fully ~** vollbeladen
ladle ['leɪdl] *n* Schöpflöffel *m*, (Schöpf)kelle *f* ▷ *vt* schöpfen
▸ **ladle out** *vt* (*fig*) austeilen
lady ['leɪdɪ] *n* (*woman*) Frau *f*; (*: dignified, graceful etc*) Dame *f*; (*Brit: title*) Lady *f*; **ladies and gentlemen ...** meine Damen und Herren ...; **young ~** junge Dame; **the ladies' (room)** die Damentoilette
ladybird ['leɪdɪbəːd], (*US*) **ladybug** *n* Marienkäfer *m*
lady-in-waiting ['leɪdɪɪn'weɪtɪŋ] *n* Hofdame *f*
lady-killer ['leɪdɪkɪlə^r^] *n* Herzensbrecher *m*
ladylike ['leɪdɪlaɪk] *adj* damenhaft
ladyship ['leɪdɪʃɪp] *n*: **your L~** Ihre Ladyschaft
lag [læg] *n* (*period of time*) Zeitabstand *m* ▷ *vi* (*also*: **lag behind**) zurückbleiben; (*trade, investment etc*) zurückgehen ▷ *vt* (*pipes etc*) isolieren; **old ~** (*inf: prisoner*) (ehemaliger) Knacki *m*
lager ['lɑːgə^r^] *n* helles Bier *nt*
lager lout (*Brit: inf*) *n* betrunkener Rowdy *m*
lagging ['lægɪŋ] *n* Isoliermaterial *nt*

lagoon [lə'gu:n] *n* Lagune *f*
Lagos ['leɪgɔs] *n* Lagos *nt*
laid [leɪd] *pt, pp of* **lay**
laid-back [leɪd'bæk] (*inf*) *adj* locker
laid up *adj*: **to be ~ (with)** im Bett liegen (mit)
lain [leɪn] *pp of* **lie**
lair [lɛəʳ] *n* Lager *nt*; (*cave*) Höhle *f*; (*den*) Bau *m*
laissez faire [lɛseɪ'fɛəʳ] *n* Laisser-faire *nt*
laity ['leɪətɪ] *n or npl* Laien *pl*
lake [leɪk] *n* See *m*
Lake District (*Brit*) *n*: **the ~** der Lake Distrikt, *Seengebiet im NW Englands*
lamb [læm] *n* Lamm *nt*; (*meat*) Lammfleisch *nt*
lamb chop *n* Lammkotelett *nt*
lambskin ['læmskɪn] *n* Lammfell *nt*
lamb's wool *n* Lammwolle *f*
lame [leɪm] *adj* lahm; (*argument, answer*) schwach
lame duck *n* (*person*) Niete *f*; (*business*) unwirtschaftliche Firma *f*
lamely ['leɪmlɪ] *adv* lahm
lament [lə'mɛnt] *n* Klage *f* ▷ *vt* beklagen
lamentable ['læməntəbl] *adj* beklagenswert
laminated ['læmɪneɪtɪd] *adj* laminiert; (*metal*) geschichtet; **~ glass** Verbundglas *nt*; **~ wood** Sperrholz *nt*
lamp [læmp] *n* Lampe *f*
lamplight ['læmplaɪt] *n*: **by ~** bei Lampenlicht
lampoon [læm'pu:n] *n* Schmähschrift *f* ▷ *vt* verspotten
lamppost ['læmppəust] (*Brit*) *n* Laternenpfahl *m*
lampshade ['læmpʃeɪd] *n* Lampenschirm *m*
lance [lɑ:ns] *n* Lanze *f* ▷ *vt* (*Med*) aufschneiden
lance corporal (*Brit*) *n* Obergefreite(r) *m*
lancet ['lɑ:nsɪt] *n* (*Med*) Lanzette *f*
Lancs [læŋks] (*Brit*) *abbr* (*Post*) = *Lancashire*
land [lænd] *n* Land *nt*; (*as property*) Grund und Boden *m* ▷ *vi* (*Aviat, fig*) landen; (*from ship*) an Land gehen ▷ *vt* (*passengers*) absetzen; (*goods*) an Land bringen; **to own ~** Land besitzen; **to go** *or* **travel by ~** auf dem Landweg reisen; **to ~ on one's feet** (*fig*) auf die Füße fallen; **to ~ sb with sth** (*inf*) jdm etw aufhalsen
▸ **land up** *vi*: **to ~ up in/at** landen in *+dat*
landed gentry ['lændɪd-] *n* Landadel *m*
landfill site ['lændfɪl-] *n* ≈ Mülldeponie *f*
landing ['lændɪŋ] *n* (*of house*) Flur *m*; (*outside flat door*) Treppenabsatz *m*; (*Aviat*) Landung *f*
landing card *n* Einreisekarte *f*
landing craft *n inv* Landungsboot *nt*
landing gear *n* (*Aviat*) Fahrgestell *nt*
landing stage *n* Landesteg *m*
landing strip *n* Landebahn *f*
landlady ['lændleɪdɪ] *n* Vermieterin *f*; (*of pub*) Wirtin *f*
landlocked ['lændlɔkt] *adj* von Land eingeschlossen; **~ country** Binnenstaat *m*
landlord ['lændlɔ:d] *n* Vermieter *m*; (*of pub*) Wirt *m*
landlubber ['lændlʌbəʳ] (*old*) *n* Landratte *f*
landmark ['lændmɑ:k] *n* Orientierungspunkt *m*; (*famous building*) Wahrzeichen *nt*; (*fig*) Meilenstein *m*
landowner ['lændəunəʳ] *n* Grundbesitzer(in) *m(f)*
landscape ['lændskeɪp] *n* Landschaft *f* ▷ *vt* landschaftlich *or* gärtnerisch gestalten
landscape architect *n* Landschaftsarchitekt(in) *m(f)*
landscape gardener *n* Landschaftsgärtner(in) *m(f)*
landscape painting *n* Landschaftsmalerei *f*
landslide ['lændslaɪd] *n* Erdrutsch *m*; (*fig: electoral*) Erdrutschsieg *m*
lane [leɪn] *n* (*in country*) Weg *m*; (*in town*) Gasse *f*; (*of carriageway*) Spur *f*; (*of race course, swimming pool*) Bahn *f*; **shipping ~** Schifffahrtsweg *m*
language ['læŋgwɪdʒ] *n* Sprache *f*; **bad ~** Kraftausdrücke *pl*
language laboratory *n* Sprachlabor *nt*
languid ['læŋgwɪd] *adj* träge, matt
languish ['læŋgwɪʃ] *vi* schmachten; (*project, case*) erfolglos bleiben
lank [læŋk] *adj* (*hair*) strähnig
lanky ['læŋkɪ] *adj* schlaksig
lanolin, lanoline ['lænəlɪn] *n* Lanolin *nt*
lantern ['læntən] *n* Laterne *f*
Laos [laus] *n* Laos *nt*
lap [læp] *n* Schoß *m*; (*in race*) Runde *f* ▷ *vt* (*also*: **lap up**) aufschlecken ▷ *vi* (*water*) plätschern
▸ **lap up** *vt* (*fig*) genießen
lapdog ['læpdɔg] (*pej*) *n* (*fig*) Schoßhund *m*
lapel [lə'pɛl] *n* Aufschlag *m*, Revers *nt or m*
Lapland ['læplænd] *n* Lappland *nt*
Lapp [læp] *adj* lappländisch ▷ *n* Lappe *m*, Lappin *f*; (*Ling*) Lappländisch *nt*
lapse [læps] *n* (*bad behaviour*) Fehltritt *m*; (*of memory etc*) Schwäche *f*; (*of time*) Zeitspanne *f* ▷ *vi* ablaufen; (*law*) ungültig werden; **to ~ into bad habits** in schlechte Gewohnheiten verfallen
laptop ['læptɔp] (*Comput*) *n* Laptop *m* ▷ *cpd* Laptop-
larceny ['lɑ:sənɪ] *n* Diebstahl *m*
larch [lɑ:tʃ] *n* Lärche *f*
lard [lɑ:d] *n* Schweineschmalz *nt*
larder ['lɑ:dəʳ] *n* Speisekammer *f*; (*cupboard*) Speiseschrank *m*
large [lɑ:dʒ] *adj* groß; (*person*) korpulent; **to make ~r** vergrößern; **a ~ number of people** eine große Anzahl von Menschen; **on a ~ scale** im großen Rahmen; (*extensive*) weitreichend; **at ~** (*as a whole*) im Allgemeinen; (*at liberty*) auf freiem Fuß; **by and ~** im Großen und Ganzen
large goods vehicle *n* Lastkraftwagen *m*
largely ['lɑ:dʒlɪ] *adv* (*mostly*) zum größten Teil; (*mainly*) hauptsächlich
large-scale ['lɑ:dʒ'skeɪl] *adj* im großen Rahmen; (*extensive*) weitreichend; (*map, diagram*) in einem großen Maßstab
largesse [lɑ:'ʒɛs] *n* Großzügigkeit *f*
lark [lɑ:k] *n* (*bird*) Lerche *f*; (*joke*) Spaß *m*, Jux *m*
▸ **lark about** *vi* herumalbern

larva ['lɑːvə] (*pl* **~e**) *n* Larve *f*
larvae ['lɑːviː] *npl of* **larva**
laryngitis [lærɪn'dʒaɪtɪs] *n* Kehlkopfentzündung *f*
larynx ['lærɪŋks] *n* Kehlkopf *m*
lasagne [lə'zænjə] *n* Lasagne *pl*
lascivious [lə'sɪvɪəs] *adj* lüstern
laser ['leɪzəʳ] *n* Laser *m*
laser beam *n* Laserstrahl *m*
laser printer *n* Laserdrucker *m*
lash [læʃ] *n* (*also*: **eyelash**) Wimper *f*; (*blow with whip*) Peitschenhieb *m* ▷ *vt* peitschen; (*rain, wind*) peitschen gegen; (*tie*): **to ~ to** festbinden an *+dat*; **to ~ together** zusammenbinden
▸ **lash down** *vt* festbinden ▷ *vi* (*rain*) niederprasseln
▸ **lash out** *vi* um sich schlagen; **to ~ out at sb** auf jdn losschlagen; **to ~ out at** *or* **against sb** (*criticize*) gegen jdn wettern
lashing ['læʃɪŋ] *n*: **~s of** (*Brit: inf*) massenhaft
lass [læs] (*Brit*) *n* Mädchen *nt*
lasso [læ'suː] *n* Lasso *nt* ▷ *vt* mit dem Lasso einfangen
last [lɑːst] *adj* letzte(r, s) ▷ *adv* (*most recently*) zuletzt, das letzte Mal; (*finally*) als Letztes ▷ *vi* (*continue*) dauern; (*: in good condition*) sich halten; (*money, commodity*) reichen; **~ week** letzte Woche; **~ night** gestern Abend; **~ but one** vorletzte(r, s); **the ~ time** das letzte Mal; **at ~** endlich; **it ~s (for) 2 hours** es dauert 2 Stunden
last-ditch ['lɑːst'dɪtʃ] *adj* (*attempt*) allerletzte(r, s)
lasting ['lɑːstɪŋ] *adj* dauerhaft
lastly ['lɑːstlɪ] *adv* (*finally*) schließlich; (*last of all*) zum Schluss
last-minute ['lɑːstmɪnɪt] *adj* in letzter Minute
latch [lætʃ] *n* Riegel *m*; **to be on the ~** nur eingeklinkt sein
▸ **latch on to** *vt fus* (*person*) sich anschließen *+dat*; (*idea*) abfahren auf *+acc* (*inf*)
latchkey ['lætʃkiː] *n* Hausschlüssel *m*
latchkey child *n* Schlüsselkind *nt*
late [leɪt] *adj* spät; (*not on time*) verspätet ▷ *adv* spät; (*behind time*) zu spät; (*recently*): **~ of Glasgow** bis vor Kurzem in Glasgow wohnhaft; **the ~ Mr X** (*deceased*) der verstorbene Herr X; **in ~ May** Ende Mai; **to be (10 minutes) ~** (10 Minuten) zu spät kommen; (*train etc*) (10 Minuten) Verspätung haben; **to work ~** länger arbeiten; **~ in life** relativ spät (im Leben); **of ~** in letzter Zeit
latecomer ['leɪtkʌməʳ] *n* Nachzügler(in) *m(f)*
lately ['leɪtlɪ] *adv* in letzter Zeit
lateness ['leɪtnɪs] *n* (*of person*) Zuspätkommen *nt*; (*of train, event*) Verspätung *f*
latent ['leɪtnt] *adj* (*energy*) ungenutzt; (*skill, ability*) verborgen
later ['leɪtəʳ] *adj, adv* später; **~ on** nachher
lateral ['lætərəl] *adj* seitlich; **~ thinking** kreatives Denken *nt*
latest ['leɪtɪst] *adj* neueste(r, s) ▷ *n*: **at the ~** spätestens
latex ['leɪtɛks] *n* Latex *m*
lathe [leɪð] *n* Drehbank *f*
lather ['lɑːðəʳ] *n* (Seifen)schaum *m* ▷ *vt* einschäumen
Latin ['lætɪn] *n* Latein *nt*; (*person*) Südländer(in) *m(f)* ▷ *adj* lateinisch; (*temperament etc*) südländisch
Latin America *n* Lateinamerika *nt*
Latin American *adj* lateinamerikanisch ▷ *n* Lateinamerikaner(in) *m(f)*
Latino [læ'tiːnəu] (*US*) *adj* aus Lateinamerika stammend ▷ *n* Latino *mf, in den USA lebende(r) Lateinamerikaner(in)*
latitude ['lætɪtjuːd] *n* (*Geog*) Breite *f*; (*fig: freedom*) Freiheit *f*
latrine [lə'triːn] *n* Latrine *f*
latter ['lætəʳ] *adj* (*of two*) letztere(r, s); (*later*) spätere(r, s); (*second part of period*) zweite(r, s); (*recent*) letzte(r, s) ▷ *n*: **the ~** der/die/das Letztere, die Letzteren
latter-day ['lætədeɪ] *adj* modern
latterly ['lætəlɪ] *adv* in letzter Zeit
lattice ['lætɪs] *n* Gitter *nt*
lattice window *n* Gitterfenster *nt*
Latvia ['lætvɪə] *n* Lettland *nt*
Latvian ['lætvɪən] *adj* lettisch ▷ *n* Lette *m*, Lettin *f*; (*Ling*) Lettisch *nt*
laudable ['lɔːdəbl] *adj* lobenswert
laudatory ['lɔːdətrɪ] *adj* (*comments*) lobend; (*speech*) Lob-
laugh [lɑːf] *n* Lachen *nt* ▷ *vi* lachen; **(to do sth) for a ~** (etw) aus Spaß (tun)
▸ **laugh at** *vt fus* lachen über *+acc*
▸ **laugh off** *vt* mit einem Lachen abtun
laughable ['lɑːfəbl] *adj* lächerlich, lachhaft
laughing gas ['lɑːfɪŋ-] *n* Lachgas *nt*
laughing matter *n*: **this is no ~** das ist nicht zum Lachen
laughing stock *n*: **to be the ~ of** zum Gespött *+gen* werden
laughter ['lɑːftəʳ] *n* Lachen *nt*, Gelächter *nt*
launch [lɔːntʃ] *n* (*of rocket, missile*) Abschuss *m*; (*of satellite*) Start *m*; (*Comm: of product*) Einführung *f*; (*: with publicity*) Lancierung *f*; (*motorboat*) Barkasse *f* ▷ *vt* (*ship*) vom Stapel lassen; (*rocket, missile*) abschießen; (*satellite*) starten; (*fig: start*) beginnen mit; (*Comm*) auf den Markt bringen; (*: with publicity*) lancieren
▸ **launch into** *vt fus* (*speech*) vom Stapel lassen; (*activity*) in Angriff nehmen
▸ **launch out** *vi*: **to ~ out (into)** beginnen (mit)
launching ['lɔːntʃɪŋ] *n* (*of ship*) Stapellauf *m*; (*of rocket, missile*) Abschuss *m*; (*of satellite*) Start *m*; (*fig: start*) Beginn *m*; (*Comm: of product*) Einführung *f*; (*: with publicity*) Lancierung *f*
launching pad, launch pad *n* Startrampe *f*, Abschussrampe *f*
launder ['lɔːndəʳ] *vt* waschen und bügeln; (*pej: money*) waschen
laundrette [lɔːn'drɛt] (*Brit*) *n* Waschsalon *m*
Laundromat® ['lɔːndrəmæt] (*US*) *n* Waschsalon *m*

laundry ['lɔːndrɪ] *n* Wäsche *f*; (*dirty*) (schmutzige) Wäsche; (*business*) Wäscherei *f*; (*room*) Waschküche *f*; **to do the ~** (Wäsche) waschen
laureate ['lɔːrɪət] *adj see* **poet laureate**
laurel ['lɔrl] *n* (*tree*) Lorbeer(baum) *m*; **to rest on one's ~s** sich auf seinen Lorbeeren ausruhen
Lausanne [ləu'zæn] *n* Lausanne *nt*
lava ['lɑːvə] *n* Lava *f*
lavatory ['lævətərɪ] *n* Toilette *f*
lavatory paper *n* Toilettenpapier *nt*
lavender ['lævəndəʳ] *n* Lavendel *m*
lavish ['lævɪʃ] *adj* großzügig; (*meal*) üppig; (*surroundings*) feudal; (*wasteful*) verschwenderisch ▷ *vt*: **to ~ sth on sb** jdn mit etw überhäufen
lavishly ['lævɪʃlɪ] *adv* (*generously*) großzügig; (*sumptuously*) aufwendig
law [lɔː] *n* Recht *nt*; (*a rule: also of nature, science*) Gesetz *nt*; (*professions connected with law*) Rechtswesen *nt*; (*Scol*) Jura *no art*; **against the ~** rechtswidrig; **to study ~** Jura *or* Recht(swissenschaft) studieren; **to go to ~** vor Gericht gehen; **to break the ~** gegen das Gesetz verstoßen
law-abiding ['lɔːəbaɪdɪŋ] *adj* gesetzestreu
law and order *n* Ruhe und Ordnung *f*
lawbreaker ['lɔːbreɪkəʳ] *n* Rechtsbrecher(in) *m(f)*
law court *n* Gerichtshof *m*, Gericht *nt*
lawful ['lɔːful] *adj* rechtmäßig
lawfully ['lɔːfəlɪ] *adv* rechtmäßig
lawless ['lɔːlɪs] *adj* gesetzwidrig
Law Lord (*Brit*) *n Mitglied des Oberhauses mit besonderem Verantwortungsbereich in Rechtsfragen*
lawn [lɔːn] *n* Rasen *m*
lawn mower *n* Rasenmäher *m*
lawn tennis *n* Rasentennis *nt*
law school (*US*) *n* juristische Hochschule *f*
law student *n* Jurastudent(in) *m(f)*
lawsuit ['lɔːsuːt] *n* Prozess *m*
lawyer ['lɔːjəʳ] *n* (Rechts)anwalt *m*, (Rechts)anwältin *f*
lax [læks] *adj* lax
laxative ['læksətɪv] *n* Abführmittel *nt*
laxity ['læksɪtɪ] *n* Laxheit *f*; **moral ~** lockere *or* laxe Moral *f*
lay [leɪ] (*pt, pp* **laid**) *pt of* **lie** ▷ *adj* (*Rel: preacher etc*) Laien- ▷ *vt* legen; (*table*) decken; (*carpet, cable etc*) verlegen; (*plans*) schmieden; (*trap*) stellen; **the ~ person** (*not expert*) der Laie; **to ~ facts/proposals before sb** jdm Tatsachen vorlegen/Vorschläge unterbreiten; **to ~ one's hands on sth** (*fig*) etw in die Finger bekommen; **to get laid** (*inf!*) bumsen (!)
▸ **lay aside** *vt* weglegen, zur Seite legen
▸ **lay by** *vt* beiseitelegen, auf die Seite legen
▸ **lay down** *vt* hinlegen; (*rules, laws etc*) festlegen; **to ~ down the law** Vorschriften machen; **to ~ down one's life** sein Leben geben
▸ **lay in** *vt* (*supply*) anlegen
▸ **lay into** *vt fus* losgehen auf *+acc*; (*criticize*) herunterputzen
▸ **lay off** *vt* (*workers*) entlassen
▸ **lay on** *vt* (*meal*) auftischen; (*entertainment etc*) sorgen für; (*water, gas*) anschließen; (*paint*) auftragen
▸ **lay out** *vt* ausbreiten; (*inf: spend*) ausgeben
▸ **lay up** *vt* (*illness*) außer Gefecht setzen; *see also* **lay by**
layabout ['leɪəbaut] (*inf: pej*) *n* Faulenzer *m*
lay-by ['leɪbaɪ] (*Brit*) *n* Parkbucht *f*
lay days *npl* Liegezeit *f*
layer ['leɪəʳ] *n* Schicht *f*
layette [leɪ'ɛt] *n* Babyausstattung *f*
layman ['leɪmən] (*irreg: like* **man**) *n* Laie *m*
lay-off ['leɪɔf] *n* Entlassung *f*
layout ['leɪaut] *n* (*of garden*) Anlage *f*; (*of building*) Aufteilung *f*; (*Typ*) Layout *nt*
laze [leɪz] *vi* (*also:* **laze about**) (herum)faulenzen
laziness ['leɪzɪnɪs] *n* Faulheit *f*
lazy ['leɪzɪ] *adj* faul; (*movement, action*) langsam, träge
LB (*Canada*) *abbr* = *Labrador*
lb *abbr* (= *pound (weight)*) *britisches Pfund (0,45 kg)*, ≈ Pfd.
lbw *abbr* (*Cricket:* = *leg before wicket*) *Regelverletzung beim Kricket*
LC (*US*) *n abbr* (= *Library of Congress*) *Bibliothek des US-Parlaments*
L/C *abbr* = **letter of credit**
lc *abbr* (*Typ:* = *lower case*) *see* **case**
lcd, LCD *n abbr* (= *liquid-crystal display*) LCD *nt*
Ld (*Brit*) *abbr* (*in titles*) = **lord**
LDS *n abbr* (*Brit:* = *Licentiate in Dental Surgery*) ≈ Dr. med. dent. ▷ *n abbr* (= *Latter-day Saints*) Heilige *pl* der Letzten Tage
LEA (*Brit*) *n abbr* (= *Local Education Authority*) *örtliche Schulbehörde*
lead¹ [liːd] (*pt, pp* **led**) *n* (*Sport, fig*) Führung *f*; (*clue*) Spur *f*; (*in play, film*) Hauptrolle *f*; (*for dog*) Leine *f*; (*Elec*) Kabel *nt* ▷ *vt* anführen; (*guide*) führen; (*organization, orchestra*) leiten ▷ *vi* führen; **to be in the ~** (*Sport, fig*) in Führung liegen; **to take the ~** (*Sport*) in Führung gehen; **to ~ the way** vorangehen; **to ~ sb astray** jdn vom rechten Weg abführen; (*mislead*) jdn irreführen; **to ~ sb to believe that ...** jdm den Eindruck vermitteln, dass ...; **to ~ sb to do sth** jdn dazu bringen, etw zu tun
▸ **lead away** *vt* wegführen; (*prisoner etc*) abführen
▸ **lead back** *vt* zurückführen
▸ **lead off** *vi* (*in conversation etc*) den Anfang machen; (*room, road*) abgehen ▷ *vt fus* abgehen von
▸ **lead on** *vt* (*tease*) aufziehen
▸ **lead to** *vt fus* führen zu
▸ **lead up to** *vt fus* (*events*) vorangehen *+dat*; (*in conversation*) hinauswollen auf *+acc*
lead² [lɛd] *n* Blei *nt*; (*in pencil*) Mine *f*
leaded ['lɛdɪd] *adj* (*window*) bleiverglast; (*petrol*) verbleit

leaden ['lɛdn] *adj* (*sky, sea*) bleiern; (*movements*) bleischwer
leader ['li:dəʳ] *n* Führer(in) *m(f)*; (*Sport*) Erste(r) *f(m)*; (*in newspaper*) Leitartikel *m*; **the L~ of the House (of Commons/of Lords)** (*Brit*) der Führer des Unterhauses/des Oberhauses
leadership ['li:dəʃɪp] *n* Führung *f*; (*position*) Vorsitz *m*; (*quality*) Führungsqualitäten *pl*
lead-free ['lɛdfri:] (*old*) *adj* bleifrei
leading ['li:dɪŋ] *adj* führend; (*role*) Haupt-; (*first, front*) vorderste(r, s)
leading lady *n* (*Theat*) Hauptdarstellerin *f*
leading light *n* führende Persönlichkeit *f*
leading man *n* (*Theat*) Hauptdarsteller *m*
leading question *n* Suggestivfrage *f*
lead pencil [lɛd-] *n* Bleistift *m*
lead poisoning [lɛd-] *n* Bleivergiftung *f*
lead singer [li:d-] *n* Leadsänger(in) *m(f)*
lead time [li:d-] *n* (*Comm: for production*) Produktionszeit *f*; (*: for delivery*) Lieferzeit *f*
lead-up ['li:dʌp] *n*: **the ~ to sth** die Zeit vor etw *dat*
leaf [li:f] (*pl* **leaves**) *n* Blatt *nt*; (*of table*) Ausziehplatte *f*; **to turn over a new ~** einen neuen Anfang machen; **to take a ~ out of sb's book** sich *dat* von jdm eine Scheibe abschneiden
▸ **leaf through** *vt fus* durchblättern
leaflet ['li:flɪt] *n* Informationsblatt *nt*
leafy ['li:fɪ] *adj* (*tree, branch*) belaubt; (*lane, suburb*) grün
league [li:g] *n* (*of people, clubs*) Verband *m*; (*of countries*) Bund *m*; (*Football*) Liga *f*; **to be in ~ with sb** mit jdm gemeinsame Sache machen
league table *n* Tabelle *f*
leak [li:k] *n* Leck *nt*; (*in roof, pipe etc*) undichte Stelle *f*; (*piece of information*) zugespielte Information *f* ▹ *vi* (*shoes, roof, pipe*) undicht sein; (*ship*) lecken; (*liquid*) auslaufen; (*gas*) ausströmen ▹ *vt* (*information*) durchsickern lassen; **to ~ sth to sb** jdm etw zuspielen
▸ **leak out** *vi* (*liquid*) auslaufen; (*news, information*) durchsickern
leakage ['li:kɪdʒ] *n* (*of liquid*) Auslaufen *nt*; (*of gas*) Ausströmen *nt*
leaky ['li:kɪ] *adj* (*roof, container*) undicht
lean [li:n] (*pt, pp* **leaned** *or* **~t**) *adj* (*person*) schlank; (*meat, time*) mager ▹ *vt*: **to ~ sth on sth** etw an etw *acc* lehnen; (*rest*) etw auf etw *acc* stützen ▹ *vi* (*slope*) sich neigen; **to ~ against** sich lehnen gegen; **to ~ on** sich stützen auf +*acc*; **to ~ forward/back** sich vorbeugen/zurücklehnen; **to ~ towards** tendieren zu
▸ **lean out** *vi* sich hinauslehnen
▸ **lean over** *vi* sich vorbeugen
leaning ['li:nɪŋ] *n* Hang *m*, Neigung *f*
leant [lɛnt] *pt, pp of* **lean**
lean-to ['li:ntu:] *n* Anbau *m*
leap [li:p] (*pt, pp* **leaped** *or* **~t**) *n* Sprung *m*; (*in price, number etc*) sprunghafter Anstieg *m* ▹ *vi* springen; (*price, number etc*) sprunghaft (an)steigen
▸ **leap at** *vt fus* (*offer*) sich stürzen auf +*acc*; (*opportunity*) beim Schopf ergreifen
▸ **leap up** *vi* aufspringen
leapfrog ['li:pfrɔg] *n* Bockspringen *nt*
leapt [lɛpt] *pt, pp of* **leap**
leap year *n* Schaltjahr *nt*
learn [lə:n] (*pt, pp* **learned** *or* **~t**) *vt* lernen; (*facts*) erfahren ▹ *vi* lernen; **to ~ about** *or* **of sth** von etw erfahren; **to ~ about sth** (*study*) etw lernen; **to ~ that ...** (*hear, read*) erfahren, dass ...; **to ~ to do sth** etw lernen
learned ['lə:nɪd] *adj* gelehrt; (*book, paper*) wissenschaftlich
learner ['lə:nəʳ] (*Brit*) *n* (*also*: **learner driver**) Fahrschüler(in) *m(f)*
learning ['lə:nɪŋ] *n* Gelehrsamkeit *f*
learnt [lə:nt] *pt, pp of* **learn**
lease [li:s] *n* Pachtvertrag *m* ▹ *vt*: **to ~ sth (to sb)** etw (an jdn) verpachten; **on ~ (to)** verpachtet (an +*acc*); **to ~ sth (from sb)** etw (von jdm) pachten
▸ **lease back** *vt* rückmieten
leaseback ['li:sbæk] *n* Verkauf und Rückmiete *pl*
leasehold ['li:shəuld] *n* Pachtbesitz *m* ▹ *adj* gepachtet
leash [li:ʃ] *n* Leine *f*
least [li:st] *adv* am wenigsten ▹ *adj*: **the ~** (+*noun*) der/die/das wenigste; (*: slightest*) der/die/das geringste; **the ~ expensive car** das billigste Auto; **at ~** mindestens; (*still, rather*) wenigstens; **you could at ~ have written** du hättest wenigstens schreiben können; **not in the ~** nicht im Geringsten; **it was the ~ I could do** das war das wenigste, was ich tun konnte
leather ['lɛðəʳ] *n* Leder *nt*
leave [li:v] (*pt, pp* **left**) *vt* verlassen; (*leave behind*) zurücklassen; (*mark, stain*) hinterlassen; (*object: accidentally*) liegen lassen, stehen lassen; (*food*) übrig lassen; (*space, time etc*) lassen ▹ *vi* (*go away*) (weg)gehen; (*bus, train*) abfahren ▹ *n* Urlaub *m*; **to ~ sth to sb** (*money etc*) jdm etw hinterlassen; **to ~ sb with sth** (*impose*) jdm etw aufhalsen; (*possession*) jdm etw lassen; **they were left with nothing** ihnen blieb nichts; **to be left** übrig sein; **to be left over** (*remain*) übrig (geblieben) sein; **to ~ for** gehen/fahren nach; **to take one's ~ of sb** sich von jdm verabschieden; **on ~** auf Urlaub
▸ **leave behind** *vt* zurücklassen; (*object: accidentally*) liegen lassen, stehen lassen
▸ **leave off** *vt* (*cover, lid*) ablassen; (*heating, light*) auslassen ▹ *vi* (*inf: stop*) aufhören
▸ **leave on** *vt* (*light, heating*) anlassen
▸ **leave out** *vt* auslassen
leave of absence *n* Beurlaubung *f*
leaves [li:vz] *npl of* **leaf**
Lebanese [lɛbə'ni:z] *adj* libanesisch ▹ *n inv* Libanese *m*, Libanesin *f*
Lebanon ['lɛbənən] *n* Libanon *m*
lecherous ['lɛtʃərəs] (*pej*) *adj* lüstern

lectern ['lɛktə:n] *n* Rednerpult *nt*
lecture ['lɛktʃə^r] *n* Vortrag *m*; *(Univ)* Vorlesung *f* ▷ *vi* Vorträge/Vorlesungen halten ▷ *vt* *(scold)*: **to ~ sb on** *or* **about sth** jdm wegen etw eine Strafpredigt halten; **to give a ~ on** einen Vortrag/eine Vorlesung halten über *+acc*
lecture hall *n* Hörsaal *m*
lecturer ['lɛktʃərə^r] *(Brit) n* Dozent(in) *m(f)*; *(speaker)* Redner(in) *m(f)*
LED *n abbr (Elec: = light-emitting diode)* LED *f*
led [lɛd] *pt, pp of* **lead'**
ledge [lɛdʒ] *n (of mountain)* (Fels)vorsprung *m*; *(of window)* Fensterbrett *nt*; *(on wall)* Leiste *f*
ledger ['lɛdʒə^r] *n (Comm)* Hauptbuch *nt*
lee [li:] *n* Windschatten *m*; *(Naut)* Lee *f*
leech [li:tʃ] *n* Blutegel *m*; *(fig)* Blutsauger *m*
leek [li:k] *n* Porree *m*, Lauch *m*
leer [lɪə^r] *vi*: **to ~ at sb** jdm lüsterne Blicke zuwerfen
leeward ['li:wəd] *(Naut) adj (side etc)* Lee- ▷ *adv* leewärts ▷ *n*: **to ~** an der Leeseite; *(direction)* nach der Leeseite
leeway ['li:weɪ] *n (fig)*: **to have some ~** etwas Spielraum haben; **there's a lot of ~ to make up** ein großer Rückstand muss aufgeholt werden
left [lɛft] *pt, pp of* **leave** ▷ *adj (remaining)* übrig; *(of position)* links; *(of direction)* nach links ▷ *n* linke Seite *f* ▷ *adv* links; nach links; **on the ~, to the ~** links; **the L~** *(Pol)* die Linke
left-click ['lɛftklɪk] *(Comput) vt* links klicken ▷ *vi* links klicken auf *+acc*
left-hand drive ['lɛfthænd-] *adj* mit Linkssteuerung
left-handed [lɛft'hændɪd] *adj* linkshändig
left-hand side ['lɛfthænd-] *n* linke Seite *f*
leftie ['lɛftɪ] *(inf) n* Linke(r) *f(m)*
leftist ['lɛftɪst] *(Pol) n* Linke(r) *f(m)* ▷ *adj* linke(r, s)
left-luggage [lɛft'lʌgɪdʒ], **left-luggage office** *(Brit) n* Gepäckaufbewahrung *f*
leftovers ['lɛftəuvəz] *npl* Reste *pl*
left-wing ['lɛft'wɪŋ] *adj (Pol)* linke(r, s)
left-winger ['lɛft'wɪŋgə^r] *n (Pol)* Linke(r) *f(m)*
lefty ['lɛftɪ] *n* = **leftie**
leg [lɛg] *n* Bein *nt*; *(Culin)* Keule *f*; *(Sport)* Runde *f*; *(: of relay race)* Teilstrecke *f*; *(of journey etc)* Etappe *f*; **to stretch one's ~s** sich *dat* die Beine vertreten; **to get one's ~ over** *(inf)* bumsen
legacy ['lɛgəsɪ] *n* Erbschaft *f*; *(fig)* Erbe *nt*
legal ['li:gl] *adj (requirement)* rechtlich, gesetzlich; *(system)* Rechts-; *(allowed by law)* legal, rechtlich zulässig; **to take ~ action** *or* **proceedings against sb** jdn verklagen
legal adviser *n* juristischer Berater *m*
legal holiday *(US) n* gesetzlicher Feiertag *m*
legality [lɪ'gælɪtɪ] *n* Legalität *f*
legalize ['li:gəlaɪz] *vt* legalisieren
legally ['li:gəlɪ] *adv* rechtlich, gesetzlich; *(in accordance with the law)* rechtmäßig; **~ binding** rechtsverbindlich
legal tender *n* gesetzliches Zahlungsmittel *nt*
legation [lɪ'geɪʃən] *n* Gesandtschaft *f*
legend ['lɛdʒənd] *n* Legende *f*, Sage *f*; *(fig: person)* Legende *f*
legendary ['lɛdʒəndərɪ] *adj* legendär; *(very famous)* berühmt
-legged ['lɛgɪd] *suff* -beinig
leggings ['lɛgɪŋz] *npl* Leggings *pl*, Leggins *pl*
leggy ['lɛgɪ] *adj* langbeinig
legibility [lɛdʒɪ'bɪlɪtɪ] *n* Lesbarkeit *f*
legible ['lɛdʒəbl] *adj* leserlich
legibly ['lɛdʒəblɪ] *adv* leserlich
legion ['li:dʒən] *n* Legion *f* ▷ *adj* zahlreich
legionnaire [li:dʒə'nɛə^r] *n* Legionär *m*
legionnaire's disease *n* Legionärskrankheit *f*
legislate ['lɛdʒɪsleɪt] *vi* Gesetze/ein Gesetz erlassen
legislation [lɛdʒɪs'leɪʃən] *n* Gesetzgebung *f*; *(laws)* Gesetze *pl*
legislative ['lɛdʒɪslətɪv] *adj* gesetzgebend; **~ reforms** Gesetzesreformen *pl*
legislator ['lɛdʒɪsleɪtə^r] *n* Gesetzgeber *m*
legislature ['lɛdʒɪslətʃə^r] *n* Legislative *f*
legitimacy [lɪ'dʒɪtɪməsɪ] *n (validity)* Berechtigung *f*; *(legality)* Rechtmäßigkeit *f*
legitimate [lɪ'dʒɪtɪmət] *adj (reasonable)* berechtigt; *(excuse)* begründet; *(legal)* rechtmäßig
legitimize [lɪ'dʒɪtɪmaɪz] *vt* legitimieren
legless ['lɛglɪs] *(inf) adj (drunk)* sternhagelvoll
legroom ['lɛgru:m] *n* Beinfreiheit *f*
Leics *(Brit) abbr (Post) = Leicestershire*
leisure ['lɛʒə^r] *n* Freizeit *f*; **at ~** in Ruhe
leisure centre *n* Freizeitzentrum *nt*
leisurely ['lɛʒəlɪ] *adj* geruhsam
leisure suit *n* Freizeitanzug *m*
lemon ['lɛmən] *n* Zitrone *f*; *(colour)* Zitronengelb *nt*
lemonade [lɛmə'neɪd] *n* Limonade *f*
lemon cheese *n* = **lemon curd**
lemon curd *n zähflüssiger Brotaufstrich mit Zitronengeschmack*
lemon juice *n* Zitronensaft *m*
lemon squeezer *n* Zitronenpresse *f*
lemon tea *n* Zitronentee *m*
lend [lɛnd] *(pt, pp* **lent***) vt*: **to ~ sth to sb** jdm etw leihen; **to ~ sb a hand (with sth)** jdm (bei etw) helfen; **it ~s itself to ...** es eignet sich für ...
lender ['lɛndə^r] *n* Verleiher(in) *m(f)*
lending library ['lɛndɪŋ-] *n* Leihbücherei *f*
length [lɛŋθ] *n* Länge *f*; *(piece)* Stück *nt*; *(amount of time)* Dauer *f*; **the ~ of the island** *(all along)* die ganze Insel entlang; **2 metres in ~** 2 Meter lang; **at ~** *(at last)* schließlich; *(for a long time)* lange; **to go to great ~s to do sth** sich *dat* sehr viel Mühe geben, etw zu tun; **to fall full-~** lang hinfallen; **to lie full-~** in voller Länge daliegen
lengthen ['lɛŋθn] *vt* verlängern ▷ *vi* länger werden
lengthways ['lɛŋθweɪz] *adv* der Länge nach
lengthy ['lɛŋθɪ] *adj* lang
leniency ['li:nɪənsɪ] *n* Nachsicht *f*

lenient ['li:nɪənt] *adj* nachsichtig
leniently ['li:nɪəntlɪ] *adv* nachsichtig
lens [lɛnz] *n* (*of spectacles*) Glas *nt*; (*of camera*) Objektiv *nt*; (*of telescope*) Linse *f*
Lent [lɛnt] *n* Fastenzeit *f*
lent [lɛnt] *pt, pp of* **lend**
lentil ['lɛntɪl] *n* Linse *f*
Leo ['li:əu] *n* Löwe *m*; **to be ~** Löwe sein
leopard ['lɛpəd] *n* Leopard *m*
leotard ['li:əta:d] *n* Gymnastikanzug *m*
leper ['lɛpə^r] *n* Leprakranke(r) *f(m)*
leper colony *n* Leprasiedlung *f*
leprosy ['lɛprəsɪ] *n* Lepra *f*
lesbian ['lɛzbɪən] *adj* lesbisch ▷ *n* Lesbierin *f*
lesion ['li:ʒən] *n* Verletzung *f*
Lesotho [lɪ'su:tu:] *n* Lesotho *nt*
less [lɛs] *adj, pron, adv* weniger ▷ *prep*: **~ tax/10% discount** abzüglich Steuer/10% Rabatt; **~ than half** weniger als die Hälfte; **~ than ever** weniger denn je; **~ and less** immer weniger; **the ~ he works ...** je weniger er arbeitet ...; **the Prime Minister, no ~** kein Geringerer als der Premierminister
lessee [lɛ'si:] *n* Pächter(in) *m(f)*
lessen ['lɛsn] *vi* nachlassen, abnehmen ▷ *vt* verringern
lesser ['lɛsə^r] *adj* geringer; **to a ~ extent** in geringerem Maße
lesson ['lɛsn] *n* (*class*) Stunde *f*; (*example, warning*) Lehre *f*; **to teach sb a ~** (*fig*) jdm eine Lektion erteilen
lessor ['lɛsɔ:^{r}] *n* Verpächter(in) *m(f)*
lest [lɛst] *conj* damit ... nicht
let [lɛt] (*pt, pp* **~**) *vt* (*allow*) lassen; (*Brit: lease*) vermieten; **to ~ sb do sth** jdn etw tun lassen, jdm erlauben, etw zu tun; **to ~ sb know sth** jdn etw wissen lassen; **~'s go** gehen wir!; **~ him come** lassen Sie ihn kommen; **"to ~"** „zu vermieten"
▸ **let down** *vt* (*tyre etc*) die Luft herauslassen aus; (*person*) im Stich lassen; (*dress etc*) länger machen; (*hem*) auslassen; **to ~ one's hair down** (*fig*) aus sich herausgehen
▸ **let go** *vi* loslassen ▷ *vt* (*release*) freilassen; **to ~ go of** loslassen; **to ~ o.s. go** aus sich herausgehen; (*neglect o.s.*) sich gehen lassen
▸ **let in** *vt* hereinlassen; (*water*) durchlassen
▸ **let off** *vt* (*culprit*) laufen lassen; (*firework, bomb*) hochgehen lassen; (*gun*) abfeuern; **to ~ sb off sth** (*excuse*) jdm etw erlassen; **to ~ off steam** (*inf: fig*) sich abreagieren
▸ **let on** *vi* verraten
▸ **let out** *vt* herauslassen; (*sound*) ausstoßen; (*house, room*) vermieten
▸ **let up** *vi* (*cease*) aufhören; (*diminish*) nachlassen
letdown ['lɛtdaun] *n* Enttäuschung *f*
lethal ['li:θl] *adj* tödlich
lethargic [lɛ'θa:dʒɪk] *adj* träge, lethargisch
lethargy ['lɛθədʒɪ] *n* Trägheit *f*, Lethargie *f*
letter ['lɛtə^r] *n* Brief *m*; (*of alphabet*) Buchstabe *m*; **small/capital ~** Klein-/Großbuchstabe *m*
letter bomb *n* Briefbombe *f*
letter box (*Brit*) *n* Briefkasten *m*
letterhead ['lɛtəhɛd] *n* Briefkopf *m*
lettering ['lɛtərɪŋ] *n* Beschriftung *f*
letter of credit *n* Akkreditiv *nt*
letter opener *n* Brieföffner *m*
letterpress ['lɛtəprɛs] *n* Hochdruck *m*
letter-quality printer ['lɛtəkwɔlɪtɪ-] *n* Schönschreibdrucker *m*
letters patent *npl* Patent *nt*, Patenturkunde *f*
lettuce ['lɛtɪs] *n* Kopfsalat *m*
let-up ['lɛtʌp] *n* Nachlassen *nt*; **there was no ~** es ließ nicht nach
leukaemia, (*US*) **leukemia** [lu:'ki:mɪə] *n* Leukämie *f*
level ['lɛvl] *adj* eben ▷ *n* (*on scale, of liquid*) Stand *m*; (*of lake, river*) Wasserstand *m*; (*height*) Höhe *f*; (*fig: standard*) Niveau *nt*; (*also:* **spirit level**) Wasserwaage *f* ▷ *vt* (*building*) abreißen; (*forest etc*) einebnen ▷ *vi*: **to ~ with sb** (*inf*) ehrlich mit jdm sein ▷ *adv*: **to draw ~ with** einholen; **to be ~ with** auf gleicher Höhe sein mit; **to do one's ~ best** sein Möglichstes tun; **"A" ~s** (*Brit*) ≈ Abitur *nt*; **"O" ~s** (*Brit*) ≈ mittlere Reife *f*; **on the ~** (*fig: honest*) ehrlich, reell; **to ~ a gun at sb** ein Gewehr auf jdn richten; **to ~ an accusation at** *or* **against sb** eine Anschuldigung gegen jdn erheben; **to ~ a criticism at** *or* **against sb** Kritik an jdm üben
▸ **level off** *vi* (*prices etc*) sich beruhigen
▸ **level out** *vi* = **level off**
level crossing (*Brit*) *n* (beschrankter) Bahnübergang *m*
level-headed [lɛvl'hɛdɪd] *adj* (*calm*) ausgeglichen
levelling ['lɛvlɪŋ] *n* Nivellierung *f*
level playing field *n* Chancengleichheit *f*; **to compete on a ~** unter gleichen Bedingungen antreten
lever ['li:və^r] *n* Hebel *m*; (*bar*) Brechstange *f*; (*fig*) Druckmittel *nt* ▷ *vt*: **to ~ up** hochhieven; **to ~ out** heraushieven
leverage ['li:vərɪdʒ] *n* Hebelkraft *f*; (*fig: influence*) Einfluss *m*
levity ['lɛvɪtɪ] *n* Leichtfertigkeit *f*
levy ['lɛvɪ] *n* (*tax*) Steuer *f*; (*charge*) Gebühr *f* ▷ *vt* erheben
lewd [lu:d] *adj* (*look etc*) lüstern; (*remark*) anzüglich
lexicographer [lɛksɪ'kɔgrəfə^r] *n* Lexikograf(in) *m(f)*
lexicography [lɛksɪ'kɔgrəfɪ] *n* Lexikografie *f*
LGV (*Brit*) *n abbr* (= *large goods vehicle*) Lkw *m*
LI (*US*) *abbr* = *Long Island*
liability [laɪə'bɪlətɪ] *n* Belastung *f*; (*Law*) Haftung *f*; **liabilities** *npl* (*Comm*) Verbindlichkeiten *pl*
liable ['laɪəbl] *adj*: **to be ~ to** (*subject to*) unterliegen *+dat*; (*prone to*) anfällig sein für; **~ for** (*responsible*) haftbar für; **to be ~ to do sth** dazu neigen, etw zu tun
liaise [li:'eɪz] *vi*: **to ~ (with)** sich in Verbindung setzen (mit)
liaison [li:'eɪzɔn] *n* Zusammenarbeit *f*; (*sexual*

relationship) Liaison *f*
liar ['laɪəʳ] *n* Lügner(in) *m(f)*
libel ['laɪbl] *n* Verleumdung *f* ▷ *vt* verleumden
libellous, (*US*) **libelous** ['laɪbləs] *adj* verleumderisch
liberal ['lɪbərl] *adj* (*Pol*) liberal; (*tolerant*) aufgeschlossen; (*generous*: *offer*) großzügig; (: *amount etc*) reichlich ▷ *n* (*tolerant person*) liberal eingestellter Mensch *m*; (*Pol*): **L~** Liberale(r) *f(m)*; **~ with** großzügig mit
Liberal Democrat *n* Liberaldemokrat(in) *m(f)*
liberalize ['lɪbərəlaɪz] *vt* liberalisieren
liberally ['lɪbrəlɪ] *adv* großzügig
liberal-minded ['lɪbərl'maɪndɪd] *adj* liberal (eingestellt)
liberate ['lɪbəreɪt] *vt* befreien
liberation [lɪbə'reɪʃən] *n* Befreiung *f*
liberation theology *n* Befreiungstheologie *f*
Liberia [laɪ'bɪərɪə] *n* Liberia *nt*
Liberian [laɪ'bɪərɪən] *adj* liberianisch ▷ *n* Liberianer(in) *m(f)*
liberty ['lɪbətɪ] *n* Freiheit *f*; **to be at ~** (*criminal*) auf freiem Fuß sein; **to be at ~ to do sth** etw tun dürfen; **to take the ~ of doing sth** sich *dat* erlauben, etw zu tun
libido [lɪ'bi:dəu] *n* Libido *f*
Libra ['li:brə] *n* Waage *f*; **to be ~** Waage sein
librarian [laɪ'brɛərɪən] *n* Bibliothekar(in) *m(f)*
library ['laɪbrərɪ] *n* Bibliothek *f*; (*institution*) Bücherei *f*
library book *n* Buch *nt* aus der Bücherei
libretto [lɪ'brɛtəu] *n* Libretto *nt*
Libya ['lɪbɪə] *n* Libyen *nt*
Libyan ['lɪbɪən] *adj* libysch ▷ *n* Libyer(in) *m(f)*
lice [laɪs] *npl of* **louse**
licence, (*US*) **license** ['laɪsns] *n* (*document*) Genehmigung *f*; (*also*: **driving licence**) Führerschein *m*; (*Comm*) Lizenz *f*; (*excessive freedom*) Zügellosigkeit *f*; **to get a TV ~** ≈ Fernsehgebühren bezahlen; **under ~** (*Comm*) in Lizenz
license ['laɪsns] *n* (*US*) = **licence** ▷ *vt* (*person, organization*) eine Lizenz vergeben an *+acc*; (*activity*) eine Genehmigung erteilen für
licensed ['laɪsnst] *adj*: **the car is ~** die Kfz-Steuer für das Auto ist bezahlt; **~ hotel/restaurant** Hotel/Restaurant mit Schankerlaubnis
licensee [laɪsən'si:] *n* (*of bar*) Inhaber(in) *m(f)* einer Schankerlaubnis
license plate (*US*) *n* Nummernschild *nt*
licensing hours ['laɪsnsɪŋ-] (*Brit*) *npl* Ausschankzeiten *pl*
licentious [laɪ'sɛnʃəs] *adj* ausschweifend, zügellos
lichen ['laɪkən] *n* Flechte *f*
lick [lɪk] *vt* lecken; (*stamp etc*) lecken an *+dat*; (*inf*: *defeat*) in die Pfanne hauen ▷ *n* Lecken *nt*; **to ~ one's lips** sich *dat* die Lippen lecken; (*fig*) sich *dat* die Finger lecken; **a ~ of paint** ein Anstrich *m*
licorice ['lɪkərɪs] (*US*) *n* = **liquorice**
lid [lɪd] *n* Deckel *m*; (*eyelid*) Lid *nt*; **to take the ~ off sth** (*fig*) etw enthüllen *or* aufdecken
lido ['laɪdəu] (*Brit*) *n* Freibad *nt*
lie¹ [laɪ] (*pt, pp* **~d**) *vi* lügen ▷ *n* Lüge *f*; **to tell ~s** lügen
lie² [laɪ] (*pt* **lay**, *pp* **lain**) *vi* (*lit, fig*) liegen; **to ~ low** (*fig*) untertauchen
▸ **lie about** *vi* herumliegen
▸ **lie around** *vi* = **lie about**
▸ **lie back** *vi* sich zurücklehnen; (*fig*: *accept the inevitable*) sich fügen
▸ **lie down** *vi* sich hinlegen
▸ **lie up** *vi* (*hide*) untertauchen; (*rest*) im Bett bleiben
Liechtenstein ['lɪktənstaɪn] *n* Liechtenstein *nt*
lie detector *n* Lügendetektor *m*
lie-down ['laɪdaun] (*Brit*) *n*: **to have a ~** ein Schläfchen machen
lie-in ['laɪɪn] (*Brit*) *n*: **to have a ~** (sich) ausschlafen
lieu [lu:]: **in ~ of** *prep* anstelle von, anstatt *+gen*
Lieut. *abbr* (*Mil*: = *lieutenant*) Lt.
lieutenant [lɛf'tɛnənt, (*US*) lu:'tɛnənt] *n* Leutnant *m*
lieutenant colonel *n* Oberstleutnant *m*
life [laɪf] (*pl* **lives**) *n* Leben *nt*; (*of machine etc*) Lebensdauer *f*; **true to ~** lebensecht; **painted from ~** aus dem Leben gegriffen; **to be sent to prison for ~** zu einer lebenslänglichen Freiheitsstrafe verurteilt werden; **such is ~** so ist das Leben; **to come to ~** (*fig*: *person*) munter werden; (: *party etc*) in Schwung kommen
life annuity *n* Leibrente *f*
life assurance (*Brit*) *n* = **life insurance**
life belt (*Brit*) *n* Rettungsgürtel *m*
lifeblood ['laɪfblʌd] *n* (*fig*) Lebensnerv *m*
lifeboat ['laɪfbəut] *n* Rettungsboot *nt*
life buoy *n* Rettungsring *m*
life expectancy *n* Lebenserwartung *f*
lifeguard ['laɪfgɑ:d] *n* (*at beach*) Rettungsschwimmer(in) *m(f)*; (*at swimming pool*) Bademeister(in) *m(f)*
life imprisonment *n* lebenslängliche Freiheitsstrafe *f*
life insurance *n* Lebensversicherung *f*
life jacket *n* Schwimmweste *f*
lifeless ['laɪflɪs] *adj* leblos; (*fig*: *person, party etc*) langweilig
lifelike ['laɪflaɪk] *adj* lebensecht; (*painting*) naturgetreu
lifeline ['laɪflaɪn] *n* (*fig*) Rettungsanker *m*; (*rope*) Rettungsleine *f*
lifelong ['laɪflɔŋ] *adj* lebenslang
life preserver (*US*) *n* = **life belt; life jacket**
lifer ['laɪfəʳ] (*inf*) *n* Lebenslängliche(r) *f(m)*
life raft *n* Rettungsfloß *nt*
life-saver ['laɪfseɪvəʳ] *n* Lebensretter(in) *m(f)*
life sciences *npl* Biowissenschaften *pl*
life sentence *n* lebenslängliche Freiheitsstrafe *f*
life-size ['laɪfsaɪz], **life-sized** ['laɪfsaɪzd] *adj* in Lebensgröße
life span *n* Lebensdauer *f*; (*of person*) Lebenszeit *f*

life style ['laɪfstaɪl] *n* Lebensstil *m*
life-support system ['laɪfsəpɔːt-] *n* (*Med*) Lebenserhaltungssystem *nt*
lifetime ['laɪftaɪm] *n* Lebenszeit *f*; (*of thing*) Lebensdauer *f*; (*of parliament*) Legislaturperiode *f*; **in my ~** während meines Lebens; **the chance of a ~** eine einmalige Chance
lift [lɪft] *vt* (*raise*) heben; (*end: ban etc*) aufheben; (*plagiarize*) abschreiben; (*inf: steal*) mitgehen lassen, klauen ▷ *vi* (*fog*) sich auflösen ▷ *n* (*Brit*) Aufzug *m*, Fahrstuhl *m*; **to take the ~** mit dem Aufzug *or* Fahrstuhl fahren; **to give sb a ~** (*Brit*) jdn (im Auto) mitnehmen
▸ **lift off** *vi* abheben
▸ **lift up** *vt* hochheben
liftoff ['lɪftɔf] *n* Abheben *nt*
ligament ['lɪgəmənt] *n* (*Anat*) Band *nt*
light [laɪt] (*pt, pp* **lit**) *n* Licht *nt* ▷ *vt* (*candle, cigarette, fire*) anzünden; (*room*) beleuchten ▷ *adj* leicht; (*pale, bright*) hell; (*traffic etc*) gering; (*music*) Unterhaltungs- ▷ *adv*: **to travel ~** mit leichtem Gepäck reisen; **lights** *npl* (*Aut: also*: **traffic lights**) Ampel *f*; **the ~s** (*of car*) die Beleuchtung; **have you got a ~?** haben Sie Feuer?; **to turn the ~ on/off** das Licht an-/ausmachen; **to come to ~** ans Tageslicht kommen; **to cast** *or* **shed** *or* **throw ~ on** (*fig*) Licht bringen in *+acc*; **in the ~ of** angesichts *+gen*; **to make ~ of sth** (*fig*) etw auf die leichte Schulter nehmen; **~ blue/green** *etc* hellblau/-grün *etc*
▸ **light up** *vi* (*face*) sich erhellen ▷ *vt* (*illuminate*) beleuchten, erhellen
light bulb *n* Glühbirne *f*
lighten ['laɪtn] *vt* (*make less heavy*) leichter machen ▷ *vi* (*become less dark*) sich aufhellen
lighter ['laɪtəʳ] *n* (*also*: **cigarette lighter**) Feuerzeug *nt*
light-fingered [laɪt'fɪŋgəd] (*inf*) *adj* langfingerig
light-headed [laɪt'hɛdɪd] *adj* (*dizzy*) benommen; (*excited*) ausgelassen
light-hearted [laɪt'hɑːtɪd] *adj* unbeschwert; (*question, remark etc*) scherzhaft
lighthouse ['laɪthaus] *n* Leuchtturm *m*
lighting ['laɪtɪŋ] *n* Beleuchtung *f*
lighting-up time [laɪtɪŋ'ʌp-] *n Zeitpunkt, zu dem die Fahrzeugbeleuchtung eingeschaltet werden muss*
lightly ['laɪtlɪ] *adv* leicht; (*not seriously*) leichthin; **to get off ~** glimpflich davonkommen
light meter *n* Belichtungsmesser *m*
lightness ['laɪtnɪs] *n* (*in weight*) Leichtigkeit *f*
lightning ['laɪtnɪŋ] *n* Blitz *m* ▷ *adj* (*attack etc*) Blitz-; **with ~ speed** blitzschnell
lightning conductor *n* Blitzableiter *m*
lightning rod (*US*) *n* = **lightning conductor**
light pen *n* Lichtstift *m*, Lichtgriffel *m*
lightship ['laɪtʃɪp] *n* Feuerschiff *nt*
lightweight ['laɪtweɪt] *adj* leicht ▷ *n* (*Boxing*) Leichtgewichtler *m*
light year *n* Lichtjahr *nt*
like [laɪk] *vt* mögen ▷ *prep* wie; (*such as*) wie (zum Beispiel) ▷ *n*: **and the ~** und dergleichen; **I would ~, I'd ~** ich hätte *or* möchte gern; **would you ~ a coffee?** möchten Sie einen Kaffee?; **if you ~** wenn Sie wollen; **to be/look ~ sb/sth** jdm/etw ähnlich sein/sehen; **something ~ that** so etwas Ähnliches; **what does it look/taste/sound ~?** wie sieht es aus/schmeckt es/hört es sich an?; **what's he/the weather ~?** wie ist er/das Wetter?; **I feel ~ a drink** ich möchte gerne etwas trinken; **there's nothing ~ ...** es geht nichts über *+acc*; **that's just ~ him** das sieht ihm ähnlich; **do it ~ this** mach es so; **it is nothing ~** (*+noun*) es ist ganz anders als; (*+adj*) es ist alles andere als; **it is nothing ~ as ...** es ist bei Weitem nicht so ...; **his ~s and dislikes** seine Vorlieben und Abneigungen
likeable ['laɪkəbl] *adj* sympathisch
likelihood ['laɪklɪhud] *n* Wahrscheinlichkeit *f*; **there is every ~ that ...** es ist sehr wahrscheinlich, dass ...; **in all ~** aller Wahrscheinlichkeit nach
likely ['laɪklɪ] *adj* wahrscheinlich; **to be ~ to do sth** wahrscheinlich etw tun; **not ~!** (*inf*) wohl kaum!
like-minded ['laɪk'maɪndɪd] *adj* gleich gesinnt
liken ['laɪkən] *vt*: **to ~ sth to sth** etw mit etw vergleichen
likeness ['laɪknɪs] *n* Ähnlichkeit *f*; **that's a good ~** (*photo, portrait*) das ist ein gutes Bild von ihm/ihr *etc*
likewise ['laɪkwaɪz] *adv* ebenso; **to do ~** das Gleiche tun
liking ['laɪkɪŋ] *n*: **~ (for)** (*person*) Zuneigung *f* (zu); (*thing*) Vorliebe *f* (für); **to be to sb's ~** nach jds Geschmack sein; **to take a ~ to sb** an jdm Gefallen finden
lilac ['laɪlək] *n* (*Bot*) Flieder *m* ▷ *adj* fliederfarben, (zart)lila
Lilo® ['laɪləu] *n* Luftmatratze *f*
lilt [lɪlt] *n* singender Tonfall *m*
lilting ['lɪltɪŋ] *adj* singend
lily ['lɪlɪ] *n* Lilie *f*
lily of the valley *n* Maiglöckchen *nt*
Lima ['liːmə] *n* Lima *nt*
limb [lɪm] *n* Glied *nt*; (*of tree*) Ast *m*; **to be out on a ~** (*fig*) (ganz) allein (da)stehen
limber up ['lɪmbəʳ-] *vi* Lockerungsübungen machen
limbo ['lɪmbəu] *n*: **to be in ~** (*fig: plans etc*) in der Schwebe sein; (*: person*) in der Luft hängen (*inf*)
lime [laɪm] *n* (*fruit*) Limone *f*; (*tree*) Linde *f*; (*also*: **lime juice**) Limonensaft *m*; (*for soil*) Kalk *m*; (*rock*) Kalkstein *m*
limelight ['laɪmlaɪt] *n*: **to be in the ~** im Rampenlicht stehen
limerick ['lɪmərɪk] *n* Limerick *m*
limestone ['laɪmstəun] *n* Kalkstein *m*
limit ['lɪmɪt] *n* Grenze *f*; (*restriction*) Beschränkung *f* ▷ *vt* begrenzen, einschränken; **within ~s** innerhalb gewisser Grenzen

limitation [lɪmɪ'teɪʃən] *n* Einschränkung *f*; **limitations** *npl* (*shortcomings*) Grenzen *pl*
limited ['lɪmɪtɪd] *adj* begrenzt, beschränkt; **to be ~ to** beschränkt sein auf *+acc*
limited edition *n* beschränkte Ausgabe *f*
limited company, limited liability company (*Brit*) *n* ≈ Gesellschaft *f* mit beschränkter Haftung
limitless ['lɪmɪtlɪs] *adj* grenzenlos
limousine ['lɪməzi:n] *n* Limousine *f*
limp [lɪmp] *adj* schlaff; (*material etc*) weich ▷ *vi* hinken ▷ *n*: **to have a ~** hinken
limpet ['lɪmpɪt] *n* Napfschnecke *f*
limpid ['lɪmpɪd] *adj* klar
limply ['lɪmplɪ] *adv* schlaff
linchpin ['lɪntʃpɪn] *n* (*fig*) wichtigste Stütze *f*
Lincs [lɪŋks] (*Brit*) *abbr* (*Post*) = *Lincolnshire*
line [laɪn] *n* Linie *f*; (*written, printed*) Zeile *f*; (*wrinkle*) Falte *f*; (*row: of people*) Schlange *f*; (*: of things*) Reihe *f*; (*for fishing, washing*) Leine *f*; (*wire, Tel*) Leitung *f*; (*railway track*) Gleise *pl*; (*fig: attitude*) Standpunkt *m*; (*: business*) Branche *f*; (*Comm: of product(s)*) Art *f* ▷ *vt* (*road*) säumen; (*container*) auskleiden; (*clothing*) füttern; **hold the ~ please!** (*Tel*) bleiben Sie am Apparat!; **to cut in ~** (*US*) sich vordrängeln; **in ~** in einer Reihe; **in ~ with** im Einklang mit, in Übereinstimmung mit; **to be in ~ for sth** mit etw an der Reihe sein; **to bring sth into ~ with sth** etw auf die gleiche Linie wie etw *acc* bringen; **on the right ~s** auf dem richtigen Weg; **I draw the ~ at that** da mache ich nicht mehr mit; **to ~ sth with sth** etw mit etw auskleiden; (*drawers etc*) etw mit etw auslegen; **to ~ the streets** die Straßen säumen
▸ **line up** *vi* sich aufstellen ▷ *vt* (*in a row*) aufstellen; (*engage*) verpflichten; (*prepare*) arrangieren; **to have sb ~d up** jdn verpflichtet haben; **to have sth ~d up** etw geplant haben
linear ['lɪnɪə^r] *adj* linear; (*shape, form*) gerade
lined [laɪnd] *adj* (*face*) faltig; (*paper*) liniert; (*skirt, jacket*) gefüttert
line editing *n* (*Comput*) zeilenweise Aufbereitung *f*
line feed *n* (*Comput*) Zeilenvorschub *m*
lineman ['laɪnmən] (*US: irreg: like* **man**) *n* (*Football*) Stürmer *m*
linen ['lɪnɪn] *n* (*cloth*) Leinen *nt*; (*tablecloths, sheets etc*) Wäsche *f*
line printer *n* (*Comput*) Zeilendrucker *m*
liner ['laɪnə^r] *n* (*ship*) Passagierschiff *nt*; (*also*: **bin liner**) Müllbeutel *m*
linesman ['laɪnzmən] (*irreg: like* **man**) *n* (*Sport*) Linienrichter *m*
line-up ['laɪnʌp] *n* (*US: queue*) Schlange *f*; (*Sport*) Aufstellung *f*; (*at concert etc*) Künstleraufgebot *nt*; (*identity parade*) Gegenüberstellung *f*
linger ['lɪŋgə^r] *vi* (*smell*) sich halten; (*tradition etc*) fortbestehen; (*person*) sich aufhalten
lingerie ['lænʒəri:] *n* (Damen)unterwäsche *f*
lingering ['lɪŋgərɪŋ] *adj* bleibend
lingo ['lɪŋgəu] (*pl* **~es**) (*inf*) *n* Sprache *f*
linguist ['lɪŋgwɪst] *n* (*person who speaks several languages*) Sprachkundige(r) *f(m)*
linguistic [lɪŋ'gwɪstɪk] *adj* sprachlich
linguistics [lɪŋ'gwɪstɪks] *n* Sprachwissenschaft *f*
liniment ['lɪnɪmənt] *n* Einreibemittel *nt*
lining ['laɪnɪŋ] *n* (*cloth*) Futter *nt*; (*Anat: of stomach*) Magenschleimhaut *f*; (*Tech*) Auskleidung *f*; (*of brakes*) (Brems)belag *m*
link [lɪŋk] *n* Verbindung *f*, Beziehung *f*; (*communications link*) Verbindung; (*of a chain*) Glied *nt*; (*Comput*) Link *m* ▷ *vi* (*Comput*): **to ~ to a site** einen Link zu einer Website haben ▷ *vt* (*join*) verbinden; (*Comput*) per Link verbinden; **links** *npl* (*Golf*) Golfplatz *m*; **rail ~** Bahnverbindung *f*
▸ **link up** *vt* verbinden ▷ *vi* verbunden werden
linkup ['lɪŋkʌp] *n* Verbindung *f*; (*of spaceships*) Koppelung *f*
lino ['laɪnəu] *n* = **linoleum**
linoleum [lɪ'nəulɪəm] *n* Linoleum *nt*
linseed oil ['lɪnsi:d-] *n* Leinöl *nt*
lint [lɪnt] *n* Mull *m*
lintel ['lɪntl] *n* (*Archit*) Sturz *m*
lion ['laɪən] *n* Löwe *m*
lion cub *n* Löwenjunge(s) *nt*
lioness ['laɪənɪs] *n* Löwin *f*
lip [lɪp] *n* (*Anat*) Lippe *f*; (*of cup etc*) Rand *m*; (*inf: insolence*) Frechheiten *pl*
liposuction ['lɪpəusʌkʃən] *n* Liposuktion *f*
lip-read ['lɪpri:d] *vi* von den Lippen ablesen
lip salve *n* Fettstift *m*
lip service (*pej*) *n*: **to pay ~ to sth** ein Lippenbekenntnis *nt* zu etw ablegen
lipstick ['lɪpstɪk] *n* Lippenstift *m*
liquefy ['lɪkwɪfaɪ] *vt* verflüssigen ▷ *vi* sich verflüssigen
liqueur [lɪ'kjuə^r] *n* Likör *m*
liquid ['lɪkwɪd] *adj* flüssig ▷ *n* Flüssigkeit *f*
liquid assets *npl* flüssige Vermögenswerte *pl*
liquidate ['lɪkwɪdeɪt] *vt* liquidieren
liquidation [lɪkwɪ'deɪʃən] *n* Liquidation *f*
liquidation sale (*US*) *n* Verkauf *m* wegen Geschäftsaufgabe
liquidator ['lɪkwɪdeɪtə^r] *n* Liquidator *m*
liquid-crystal display ['lɪkwɪd'krɪstl-] *n* Flüssigkristallanzeige *f*
liquidity [lɪ'kwɪdɪtɪ] *n* Liquidität *f*
liquidize ['lɪkwɪdaɪz] *vt* (im Mixer) pürieren
liquidizer ['lɪkwɪdaɪzə^r] *n* Mixer *m*
liquor ['lɪkə^r] *n* Spirituosen *pl*, Alkohol *m*; **hard ~** harte Drinks *pl*
liquorice ['lɪkərɪs] (*Brit*) *n* Lakritze *f*
liquor store (*US*) *n* Spirituosengeschäft *nt*
Lisbon ['lɪzbən] *n* Lissabon *nt*
lisp [lɪsp] *n* Lispeln *nt* ▷ *vi* lispeln
list [lɪst] *n* Liste *f* ▷ *vt* aufführen; (*Comput*) auflisten; (*write down*) aufschreiben ▷ *vi* (*ship*) Schlagseite haben
listed building ['lɪstɪd-] (*Brit*) *n* unter Denkmalschutz stehendes Gebäude *nt*
listed company *n* börsennotierte Firma *f*
listen ['lɪsn] *vi* hören; **to ~ (out) for** horchen

auf *+acc*; **to ~ to sb** jdm zuhören; **to ~ to sth** etw hören; **~!** hör zu!
listener ['lɪsnəʳ] *n* Zuhörer(in) *m(f)*; (*Radio*) Hörer(in) *m(f)*
listeria [lɪs'tɪərɪə] *n* Listeriose *f*
listing ['lɪstɪŋ] *n* Auflistung *f*; (*entry*) Eintrag *m*
listless ['lɪstlɪs] *adj* lustlos
listlessly ['lɪstlɪslɪ] *adv* lustlos
list price *n* Listenpreis *m*
lit [lɪt] *pt, pp of* **light**
litany ['lɪtənɪ] *n* Litanei *f*
liter ['li:təʳ] (US) *n* = **litre**
literacy ['lɪtərəsɪ] *n* die Fähigkeit, lesen und schreiben zu können
literacy campaign *n* Kampagne *f* gegen das Analphabetentum
literal ['lɪtərəl] *adj* wörtlich, eigentlich; (*translation*) (wort)wörtlich
literally ['lɪtrəlɪ] *adv* buchstäblich
literary ['lɪtərərɪ] *adj* literarisch
literate ['lɪtərət] *adj* (*educated*) gebildet; **to be ~** lesen und schreiben können
literature ['lɪtrɪtʃəʳ] *n* Literatur *f*; (*printed information*) Informationsmaterial *nt*
lithe [laɪð] *adj* gelenkig; (*animal*) geschmeidig
lithography [lɪ'θɔgrəfɪ] *n* Lithografie *f*
Lithuania [lɪθju'eɪnɪə] *n* Litauen *nt*
Lithuanian [lɪθju'eɪnɪən] *adj* litauisch ▷ *n* Litauer(in) *m(f)*; (*Ling*) Litauisch *nt*
litigation [lɪtɪ'geɪʃən] *n* Prozess *m*
litmus paper ['lɪtməs-] *n* Lackmuspapier *nt*
litre, (*US*) **liter** ['li:təʳ] *n* Liter *m or nt*
litter ['lɪtəʳ] *n* (*rubbish*) Abfall *m*; (*young animals*) Wurf *m*
litter bin (*Brit*) *n* Abfalleimer *m*
litterbug ['lɪtəbʌg] *n* Dreckspatz *m*
littered ['lɪtəd] *adj*: **~ with** (*scattered*) übersät mit
litter lout *n* Dreckspatz *m*
little ['lɪtl] *adj* klein; (*short*) kurz ▷ *adv* wenig; **a ~** ein wenig, ein bisschen; **a ~ bit** ein kleines bisschen; **to have ~ time/money** wenig Zeit/Geld haben; **~ by little** nach und nach
little finger *n* kleiner Finger *m*
little-known ['lɪtl'nəun] *adj* wenig bekannt
liturgy ['lɪtədʒɪ] *n* Liturgie *f*
live [*vi* lɪv, *adj* laɪv] *vi* leben; (*in house, town*) wohnen ▷ *adj* lebend; (*TV, Radio*) live; (*performance, pictures etc*) Live-; (*Elec*) Strom führend; (*bullet, bomb etc*) scharf; **to ~ with sb** mit jdm zusammenleben
▸ **live down** *vt* hinwegkommen über *+acc*
▸ **live for** *vt* leben für
▸ **live in** *vi* (*student/servant*) im Wohnheim/Haus wohnen
▸ **live off** *vt fus* leben von; (*parents etc*) auf Kosten *+gen* leben
▸ **live on** *vt fus* leben von
▸ **live out** *vi* (*Brit: student/servant*) außerhalb (des Wohnheims/Hauses) wohnen ▷ *vt*: **to ~ out one's days** *or* **life** sein Leben verbringen
▸ **live together** *vi* zusammenleben
▸ **live up** *vt*: **to ~ it up** einen draufmachen (*inf*)
▸ **live up to** *vt fus* erfüllen, entsprechen *+dat*
live-in ['lɪvɪn] *adj* (*cook, maid*) im Haus wohnend; **her ~ lover** ihr Freund, der bei ihr wohnt
livelihood ['laɪvlɪhud] *n* Lebensunterhalt *m*
liveliness ['laɪvlɪnɪs] *n* (*see adj*) Lebhaftigkeit *f*; Lebendigkeit *f*
lively ['laɪvlɪ] *adj* lebhaft; (*place, event, book etc*) lebendig
liven up ['laɪvn-] *vt* beleben, Leben bringen in *+acc*; (*person*) aufmuntern ▷ *vi* (*person*) aufleben; (*discussion, evening etc*) in Schwung kommen
liver ['lɪvəʳ] *n* (*Anat, Culin*) Leber *f*
liverish ['lɪvərɪʃ] *adj*: **to be ~** sich unwohl fühlen
Liverpudlian [lɪvə'pʌdlɪən] *adj* Liverpooler ▷ *n* Liverpooler(in) *m(f)*
livery ['lɪvərɪ] *n* Livree *f*
lives [laɪvz] *npl of* **life**
livestock ['laɪvstɔk] *n* Vieh *nt*
live wire (*inf*) *n* (*person*) Energiebündel *nt*
livid ['lɪvɪd] *adj* (*colour*) bleifarben; (*inf: furious*) fuchsteufelswild
living ['lɪvɪŋ] *adj* lebend ▷ *n*: **to earn** *or* **make a ~** sich *dat* seinen Lebensunterhalt verdienen; **within ~ memory** seit Menschengedenken; **the cost of ~** die Lebenshaltungskosten *pl*
living conditions *npl* Wohnverhältnisse *pl*
living expenses *npl* Lebenshaltungskosten *pl*
living room *n* Wohnzimmer *nt*
living standards *npl* Lebensstandard *m*
living wage *n* ausreichender Lohn *m*
lizard ['lɪzəd] *n* Eidechse *f*
llama ['lɑ:mə] *n* Lama *nt*
LLB *n abbr* (*= Bachelor of Laws*) *akademischer Grad für Juristen*
LLD *n abbr* (*= Doctor of Laws*) ≈ Dr. jur.
LMT (*US*) *abbr* (*= Local Mean Time*) *Ortszeit*
load [ləud] *n* Last *f*; (*of vehicle*) Ladung *f*; (*weight, Elec*) Belastung *f* ▷ *vt* (*also:* **load up**) beladen; (*gun, program, data*) laden; **that's a ~ of rubbish** (*inf*) das ist alles Blödsinn; **~s of, a ~ of** (*fig*) jede Menge; **to ~ a camera** einen Film einlegen
loaded ['ləudɪd] *adj* (*inf: rich*) steinreich; (*dice*) präpariert; (*vehicle*): **to be ~ with** beladen sein mit; **a ~ question** eine Fangfrage
loading bay ['ləudɪŋ-] *n* Ladeplatz *m*
loaf [ləuf] (*pl* **loaves**) *n* Brot *nt*, Laib *m* ▷ *vi* (*also:* **loaf about, loaf around**) faulenzen; **use your ~!** (*inf*) streng deinen Grips an!
loam [ləum] *n* Lehmerde *f*
loan [ləun] *n* Darlehen *nt* ▷ *vt*: **to ~ sth to sb** jdm etw leihen; **on ~** geliehen
loan account *n* Darlehenskonto *nt*
loan capital *n* Anleihekapital *nt*
loan shark (*inf*) *n* Kredithai *m*
loath [ləuθ] *adj*: **to be ~ to do sth** etw ungern tun
loathe [ləuð] *vt* verabscheuen
loathing ['ləuðɪŋ] *n* Abscheu *m*
loathsome ['ləuðsəm] *adj* abscheulich

loaves [ləuvz] *npl of* **loaf**
lob [lɔb] *vt* (*ball*) lobben
lobby ['lɔbɪ] *n* (*of building*) Eingangshalle *f*; (*Pol: pressure group*) Interessenverband *m* ▷ *vt* Einfluss nehmen auf *+acc*
lobbyist ['lɔbɪɪst] *n* Lobbyist(in) *m(f)*
lobe [ləub] *n* Ohrläppchen *nt*
lobster ['lɔbstəʳ] *n* Hummer *m*
lobster pot *n* Hummer(fang)korb *m*
local ['ləukl] *adj* örtlich; (*council*) Stadt-, Gemeinde-; (*paper*) Lokal- ▷ *n* (*pub*) Stammkneipe *f*; **the locals** *npl* (*local inhabitants*) die Einheimischen *pl*
local anaesthetic *n* örtliche Betäubung *f*
local authority *n* Gemeindeverwaltung *f*, Stadtverwaltung *f*
local call *n* Ortsgespräch *nt*
locale [ləu'kɑːl] *n* Umgebung *f*
local government *n* Kommunalverwaltung *f*
locality [ləu'kælɪtɪ] *n* Gegend *f*
localize ['ləukəlaɪz] *vt* lokalisieren
locally ['ləukəlɪ] *adv* am Ort
lo-carb [ləu'kɑːb] *adj* = **low-carb**
locate [ləu'keɪt] *vt* (*find*) ausfindig machen; **to be ~d in** sich befinden in *+dat*
location [ləu'keɪʃən] *n* Ort *m*; (*position*) Lage *f*; (*Cine*) Drehort *m*; **he's on ~ in Mexico** er ist bei Außenaufnahmen in Mexiko; **to be filmed on ~** als Außenaufnahme gedreht werden
loch [lɔx] (*Scot*) *n* See *m*
lock [lɔk] *n* (*of door etc*) Schloss *nt*; (*on canal*) Schleuse *f*; (*also*: **lock of hair**) Locke *f* ▷ *vt* (*door etc*) abschließen; (*steering wheel*) sperren; (*Comput: keyboard*) verriegeln ▷ *vi* (*door etc*) sich abschließen lassen; (*wheels, mechanism etc*) blockieren; **on full ~** (*Aut*) voll eingeschlagen; **~, stock and barrel** mit allem Drum und Dran; **his jaw ~ed** er hatte Mundsperre
▸ **lock away** *vt* wegschließen; (*criminal*) einsperren
▸ **lock in** *vt* einschließen
▸ **lock out** *vt* aussperren
▸ **lock up** *vt* (*criminal etc*) einsperren; (*house*) abschließen ▷ *vi* abschließen
locker ['lɔkəʳ] *n* Schließfach *nt*
locker room *n* Umkleideraum *m*
locket ['lɔkɪt] *n* Medaillon *nt*
lockjaw ['lɔkdʒɔː] *n* Wundstarrkrampf *m*
lockout ['lɔkaut] *n* Aussperrung *f*
locksmith ['lɔksmɪθ] *n* Schlosser *m*
lockup ['lɔkʌp] *n* (*US: inf: jail*) Gefängnis *nt*; (*also*: **lock-up garage**) Garage *f*
locomotive [ləukə'məutɪv] *n* Lokomotive *f*
locum ['ləukəm] *n* (*Med*) Vertreter(in) *m(f)*
locust ['ləukəst] *n* Heuschrecke *f*
lodge [lɔdʒ] *n* Pförtnerhaus *nt*; (*also*: **hunting lodge**) Hütte *f*; (*Freemasonry*) Loge *f* ▷ *vt* (*complaint, protest etc*) einlegen ▷ *vi* (*bullet*) stecken bleiben; (*person*): **to ~ (with)** zur Untermiete wohnen (bei)
lodger ['lɔdʒəʳ] *n* Untermieter(in) *m(f)*
lodging ['lɔdʒɪŋ] *n* Unterkunft *f*
lodging house *n* Pension *f*
lodgings ['lɔdʒɪŋz] *npl* möbliertes Zimmer *nt*; (*several rooms*) Wohnung *f*
loft [lɔft] *n* Boden *m*, Speicher *m*
lofty ['lɔftɪ] *adj* (*noble*) hoch(fliegend); (*self-important*) hochmütig; (*high*) hoch
log [lɔg] *n* (*of wood*) Holzblock *m*, Holzklotz *m*; (*written account*) Log *nt* ▷ *n abbr* (*Math*: = *logarithm*) log ▷ *vt* (ins Logbuch) eintragen
▸ **log in** *vi* (*Comput*) sich anmelden
▸ **log into** *vt fus* (*Comput*) sich anmelden bei
▸ **log off** *vi* (*Comput*) sich abmelden
▸ **log on** *vi* (*Comput*) = **log in**
▸ **log out** *vi* (*Comput*) = **log off**
logarithm ['lɔgərɪðm] *n* Logarithmus *m*
logbook ['lɔgbuk] *n* (*Naut*) Logbuch *nt*; (*Aviat*) Bordbuch *nt*; (*of car*) Kraftfahrzeugbrief *m*; (*of lorry driver*) Fahrtenbuch *nt*; (*of events*) Tagebuch *nt*; (*of movement of goods etc*) Dienstbuch *nt*
log fire *n* Holzfeuer *nt*
logger ['lɔgəʳ] *n* (*lumberjack*) Holzfäller *m*
loggerheads ['lɔgəhɛdz] *npl*: **to be at ~** Streit haben
logic ['lɔdʒɪk] *n* Logik *f*
logical ['lɔdʒɪkl] *adj* logisch
logically ['lɔdʒɪkəlɪ] *adv* logisch; (*reasonably*) logischerweise
logistics [lɔ'dʒɪstɪks] *n* Logistik *f*
log jam *n* (*fig*) Blockierung *f*; **to break the ~** freie Bahn schaffen
logo ['ləugəu] *n* Logo *nt*
loin [lɔɪn] *n* Lende *f*
loincloth ['lɔɪnklɔθ] *n* Lendenschurz *m*
loiter ['lɔɪtəʳ] *vi* sich aufhalten
loll [lɔl] *vi* (*also*: **loll about**: *person*) herumhängen; (*head*) herunterhängen; (*tongue*) heraushängen
lollipop ['lɔlɪpɔp] *n* Lutscher *m*
lollipop lady (*Brit*) *n* ≈ Schülerlotsin *f*
lollipop man (*Brit*) *n* ≈ Schülerlotse *m*; *siehe Info-Artikel*

LOLLIPOP MAN/LADY

Lollipop man/lady heißen in Großbritannien die Männer bzw. Frauen, die mithilfe eines runden Stoppschildes den Verkehr anhalten, damit Schulkinder die Straße gefahrlos überqueren können. Der Name bezieht sich auf die Form des Schildes, die an einen Lutscher erinnert.

lollop ['lɔləp] *vi* zockeln
lolly ['lɔlɪ] (*inf*) *n* (*lollipop*) Lutscher *m*; (*money*) Mäuse *pl*
London ['lʌndən] *n* London *nt*
Londoner ['lʌndənəʳ] *n* Londoner(in) *m(f)*
lone [ləun] *adj* einzeln, einsam; (*only*) einzig
loneliness ['ləunlɪnɪs] *n* Einsamkeit *f*
lonely ['ləunlɪ] *adj* einsam
lonely hearts *adj*: **~ ad** Kontaktanzeige *f*; **the ~ column** die Kontaktanzeigen *pl*
lone parent *n* Alleinerziehende(r) *f(m)*
loner ['ləunəʳ] *n* Einzelgänger(in) *m(f)*

long [lɔŋ] *adj* lang ▷ *adv* lang(e) ▷ *vi*: **to ~ for sth** sich nach etw sehnen; **in the ~ run** auf die Dauer; **how ~ is the lesson?** wie lange dauert die Stunde?; **6 metres/months ~** 6 Meter/Monate lang; **so** *or* **as ~ as** (*on condition that*) solange; (*while*) während; **don't be ~!** bleib nicht so lange!; **all night ~** die ganze Nacht; **he no ~er comes** er kommt nicht mehr; **~ ago** vor langer Zeit; **~ before/after** lange vorher/danach; **before ~** bald; **at ~ last** schließlich und endlich; **the ~ and the short of it is that ...** kurz gesagt, ...
long-distance [lɔŋ'dɪstəns] *adj* (*travel, phone call*) Fern-; (*race*) Langstrecken-
longevity [lɔn'dʒɛvɪtɪ] *n* Langlebigkeit *f*
long-haired ['lɔŋ'hɛəd] *adj* langhaarig; (*animal*) Langhaar-
longhand ['lɔŋhænd] *n* Langschrift *f*
longing ['lɔŋɪŋ] *n* Sehnsucht *f*
longingly ['lɔŋɪŋlɪ] *adv* sehnsüchtig
longitude ['lɔŋgɪtjuːd] *n* Länge *f*
long johns [-dʒɔnz] *npl* lange Unterhose *f*
long jump *n* Weitsprung *m*
long-life ['lɔŋlaɪf] *adj* (*batteries etc*) mit langer Lebensdauer; **~ milk** H-Milch *f*
long-lost ['lɔŋlɔst] *adj* verloren geglaubt
long-playing record ['lɔŋpleɪɪŋ-] *n* Langspielplatte *f*
long-range ['lɔŋ'reɪndʒ] *adj* (*plan, forecast*) langfristig; (*missile, plane etc*) Langstrecken-
longshoreman ['lɔŋʃɔːmən] (*US: irreg: like* **man**) *n* Hafenarbeiter *m*
long-sighted ['lɔŋ'saɪtɪd] *adj* weitsichtig
long-standing ['lɔŋ'stændɪŋ] *adj* langjährig
long-suffering [lɔŋ'sʌfərɪŋ] *adj* schwer geprüft
long-term ['lɔŋtəːm] *adj* langfristig
long wave *n* Langwelle *f*
long-winded [lɔŋ'wɪndɪd] *adj* umständlich, langatmig
loo [luː] (*Brit: inf*) *n* Klo *nt*
loofah ['luːfə] *n* Luffa(schwamm) *m*
look [luk] *vi* sehen, schauen, gucken (*inf*); (*seem, appear*) aussehen ▷ *n* (*glance*) Blick *m*; (*appearance*) Aussehen *nt*; (*expression*) Miene *f*; (*Fashion*) Look *m*; **looks** *npl* (*good looks*) (gutes) Aussehen; **to ~ (out) onto the sea/south** (*building etc*) Blick aufs Meer/nach Süden haben; **~ (here)!** (*expressing annoyance*) hör (mal) zu!; **~!** (*expressing surprise*) sieh mal!; **to ~ like sb/sth** wie jd/etw aussehen; **it ~s like him** es sieht ihm ähnlich; **it ~s about 4 metres long** es scheint etwa 4 Meter lang zu sein; **it ~s all right to me** es scheint mir in Ordnung zu sein; **to ~ ahead** vorausschauen; **to have a ~ at sth** sich *dat* etw ansehen; **let me have a ~** lass mich mal sehen; **to have a ~ for sth** nach etw suchen
▸ **look after** *vt fus* sich kümmern um
▸ **look at** *vt fus* ansehen; (*read quickly*) durchsehen; (*study, consider*) betrachten
▸ **look back** *vi*: **to ~ back (on)** zurückblicken (auf *+acc*); **to ~ back at sth/sb** sich nach jdm/etw umsehen
▸ **look down on** *vt fus* (*fig*) herabsehen auf *+acc*
▸ **look for** *vt fus* suchen
▸ **look forward to** *vt fus* sich freuen auf *+acc*; **we ~ forward to hearing from you** (*in letters*) wir hoffen, bald von Ihnen zu hören
▸ **look in** *vi*: **to ~ in on sb** bei jdm vorbeikommen
▸ **look into** *vt fus* (*investigate*) untersuchen
▸ **look on** *vi* (*watch*) zusehen
▸ **look out** *vi* (*beware*) aufpassen
▸ **look out for** *vt fus* Ausschau halten nach
▸ **look over** *vt* (*essay etc*) durchsehen; (*house, town etc*) sich *dat* ansehen; (*person*) mustern
▸ **look round** *vi* sich umsehen
▸ **look through** *vt fus* durchsehen
▸ **look to** *vt fus* (*rely on*) sich verlassen auf *+acc*
▸ **look up** *vi* aufsehen; (*situation*) sich bessern ▷ *vt* (*word etc*) nachschlagen; **things are ~ing up** es geht bergauf
▸ **look up to** *vt fus* aufsehen zu
lookalike ['lukəlaɪk] *n* Doppelgänger(in) *m(f)*
look-in ['lukɪn] *n*: **to get a ~** (*inf*) eine Chance haben
lookout ['lukaut] *n* (*tower etc*) Ausguck *m*; (*person*) Wachtposten *m*; **to be on the ~ for sth** nach etw Ausschau halten
loom [luːm] *vi* (*also*: **loom up**: *object, shape*) sich abzeichnen; (*event*) näher rücken ▷ *n* Webstuhl *m*
loony ['luːnɪ] (*inf*) *adj* verrückt ▷ *n* Verrückte(r) *f(m)*
loop [luːp] *n* Schlaufe *f*; (*Comput*) Schleife *f* ▷ *vt*: **to ~ sth around sth** etw um etw schlingen
loophole ['luːphəul] *n* Hintertürchen *nt*; **a ~ in the law** eine Lücke im Gesetz
loose [luːs] *adj* lose, locker; (*clothes etc*) weit; (*long hair*) offen; (*not strictly controlled, promiscuous*) locker; (*definition*) ungenau; (*translation*) frei ▷ *vt* (*animal*) loslassen; (*prisoner*) freilassen; (*set off, unleash*) entfesseln ▷ *n*: **to be on the ~** frei herumlaufen
loose change *n* Kleingeld *nt*
loose chippings *npl* Schotter *m*
loose end *n*: **to be at a ~, to be at ~s** (*US*) nichts mit sich *dat* anzufangen wissen; **to tie up ~s** die offenstehenden Probleme lösen
loose-fitting ['luːsfɪtɪŋ] *adj* weit
loose-leaf ['luːsliːf] *adj* Loseblatt-; **~ binder** Ringbuch *nt*
loose-limbed [luːs'lɪmd] *adj* gelenkig, beweglich
loosely ['luːslɪ] *adv* lose, locker
loosely-knit ['luːslɪ'nɪt] *adj* (*fig*) locker
loosen ['luːsn] *vt* lösen, losmachen; (*clothing, belt etc*) lockern
loosen up *vi* (*before game*) sich auflockern; (*relax*) auftauen
loot [luːt] *n* (*inf*) Beute *f* ▷ *vt* plündern
looter ['luːtə^r] *n* Plünderer *m*
looting ['luːtɪŋ] *n* Plünderung *f*
lop off [lɔp-] *vt* abhacken
lopsided ['lɔp'saɪdɪd] *adj* schief

lord [lɔ:d] *n* *(Brit)* Lord *m*; **L~ Smith** Lord Smith; **the L~** *(Rel)* der Herr; **my ~** *(to bishop)* Exzellenz; *(to noble)* Mylord; *(to judge)* Euer Ehren; **good L~!** ach, du lieber Himmel!; **the (House of) L~s** *(Brit)* das Oberhaus
lordly ['lɔ:dlɪ] *adj* hochmütig
lordship ['lɔ:dʃɪp] *n*: **your L~** Eure Lordschaft
lore [lɔ:ʳ] *n* Überlieferungen *pl*
lorry ['lɔrɪ] *(Brit)* *n* Lastwagen *m*, Lkw *m*
lorry driver *(Brit)* *n* Lastwagenfahrer *m*
lose [lu:z] *(pt, pp* **lost***)* *vt* verlieren; *(opportunity)* verpassen; *(pursuers)* abschütteln ▷ *vi* verlieren; **to ~ (time)** *(clock)* nachgehen; **to ~ weight** abnehmen; **to ~ 5 pounds** 5 Pfund abnehmen; **to ~ sight of sth** *(also fig)* etw aus den Augen verlieren
loser ['lu:zəʳ] *n* Verlierer(in) *m(f)*; *(inf: failure)* Versager *m*; **to be a good/bad ~** ein guter/schlechter Verlierer sein
loss [lɔs] *n* Verlust *m*; **to make a ~ (of £1,000)** (1000 Pfund) Verlust machen; **to sell sth at a ~** etw mit Verlust verkaufen; **heavy ~es** schwere Verluste *pl*; **to cut one's ~es** aufgeben, bevor es noch schlimmer wird; **to be at a ~** nicht mehr weiterwissen
loss adjuster *n* Schadenssachverständige(r) *f(m)*
loss leader *n* *(Comm)* Lockvogelangebot *nt*
lost [lɔst] *pt, pp of* **lose** ▷ *adj* *(person, animal)* vermisst; *(object)* verloren; **to be ~** sich verlaufen/verfahren haben; **to get ~** sich verlaufen/verfahren; **get ~!** *(inf)* verschwinde!; **~ in thought** in Gedanken verloren
lost and found *(US)* *n* = **lost property**
lost cause *n* aussichtslose Sache *f*
lost property *(Brit)* *n* Fundsachen *pl*; *(also:* **lost property office***)* Fundbüro *nt*
lot [lɔt] *n* *(kind)* Art *f*; *(group)* Gruppe *f*; *(at auctions, destiny)* Los *nt*; **to draw ~s** losen, Lose ziehen; **the ~** alles; **a ~ (of)** *(a large number (of))* viele; *(a great deal (of))* viel; **~s of** viele; **I read a ~** ich lese viel; **this happens a ~** das kommt oft vor
loth [ləuθ] *adj* = **loath**
lotion ['ləuʃən] *n* Lotion *f*
lottery ['lɔtərɪ] *n* Lotterie *f*
loud [laud] *adj* laut; *(clothes)* schreiend ▷ *adv* laut; **to be ~ in one's support of sb/sth** jdn/etw lautstark unterstützen; **out ~** *(read, laugh etc)* laut
loud-hailer [laud'heɪləʳ] *(Brit)* *n* Megafon *nt*
loudly ['laudlɪ] *adv* laut
loudmouthed ['laudmauθt] *adj* großmäulig
loudspeaker [laud'spi:kəʳ] *n* Lautsprecher *m*
lounge [laundʒ] *n* *(in house)* Wohnzimmer *nt*; *(in hotel)* Lounge *f*; *(at airport, station)* Wartehalle *f*; *(Brit: also:* **lounge bar***)* Salon *m* ▷ *vi* faulenzen
▶ **lounge about** *vi* herumliegen, herumsitzen, herumstehen
▶ **lounge around** *vi* = **lounge about**
lounge suit *(Brit)* *n* Straßenanzug *m*
louse [laus] *(pl* **lice***)* *n* Laus *f*
▶ **louse up** *(inf)* *vt* vermasseln
lousy ['lauzɪ] *(inf)* *adj* *(bad-quality)* lausig, mies; *(despicable)* fies, gemein; *(ill)*: **to feel ~** sich miserabel *or* elend fühlen
lout [laut] *n* Lümmel *m*, Flegel *m*
louvre, *(US)* **louver** ['lu:vəʳ] *adj* *(door, window)* Lamellen-
lovable ['lʌvəbl] *adj* liebenswert
love [lʌv] *n* Liebe *f* ▷ *vt* lieben; *(thing, activity etc)* gern mögen; **"~ (from) Anne"** *(on letter)* „mit herzlichen Grüßen, Anne"; **to be in ~ with** verliebt sein in *+acc*; **to fall in ~ with** sich verlieben in *+acc*; **to make ~** sich lieben; **~ at first sight** Liebe auf den ersten Blick; **to send one's ~ to sb** jdn grüßen lassen; **"fifteen ~"** *(Tennis)* „fünfzehn null"; **to ~ doing sth** etw gern tun; **I'd ~ to come** ich würde sehr gerne kommen; **I ~ chocolate** ich esse Schokolade liebend gern
love affair *n* Verhältnis *nt*, Liebschaft *f*
love child *n* uneheliches Kind *nt*, Kind *nt* der Liebe
loved ones ['lʌvdwʌnz] *npl* enge Freunde und Verwandte *pl*
love-hate relationship ['lʌvheɪt-] *n* Hassliebe *f*
love letter *n* Liebesbrief *m*
love life *n* Liebesleben *nt*
lovely ['lʌvlɪ] *adj* *(beautiful)* schön; *(delightful)* herrlich; *(person)* sehr nett
lover ['lʌvəʳ] *n* Geliebte(r) *f(m)*; *(person in love)* Liebende(r) *f(m)*; **~ of art/music** Kunst-/Musikliebhaber(in) *m(f)*; **to be ~s** ein Liebespaar sein
lovesick ['lʌvsɪk] *adj* liebeskrank
love song *n* Liebeslied *nt*
loving ['lʌvɪŋ] *adj* liebend; *(actions)* liebevoll
low [ləu] *adj* niedrig; *(bow, curtsey)* tief; *(quality)* schlecht; *(sound: deep)* tief; *(: quiet)* leise; *(depressed)* niedergeschlagen, bedrückt ▷ *adv* *(sing)* leise; *(fly)* tief ▷ *n* *(Met)* Tief *nt*; **to be/run ~** knapp sein/werden; **sb is running ~ on sth** jdm wird etw knapp; **to reach a new** *or* **an all-time ~** einen neuen Tiefstand erreichen
low-alcohol ['ləu'ælkəhɔl] *adj* alkoholarm
lowbrow ['ləubrau] *adj* (geistig) anspruchslos
low-calorie ['ləu'kælərɪ] *adj* kalorienarm
low-carb [ləu'kɑ:b] *adj* low-carb, kohlenhydratarm; **~ bread** kohlenhydratarmes Brot
low-cut ['ləukʌt] *adj* *(dress)* tief ausgeschnitten
lowdown ['ləudaun] *(inf)* *n*: **he gave me the ~ on it** er hat mich darüber informiert
lower ['ləuəʳ] *adj* untere(r, s); *(lip, jaw, arm)* Unter- ▷ *vt* senken
low-fat ['ləu'fæt] *adj* fettarm
low-key ['ləu'ki:] *adj* zurückhaltend; *(not obvious)* unaufdringlich
lowlands ['ləuləndz] *npl* Flachland *nt*
low-level language ['ləulɛvl-] *n* *(Comput)* niedere Programmiersprache *f*
low-loader ['ləu'ləudəʳ] *n* Tieflader *m*
lowly ['ləulɪ] *adj* *(position)* niedrig; *(origin)*

bescheiden
low-lying [ləu'laııŋ] *adj* tief gelegen
low-paid [ləu'peıd] *adj* schlecht bezahlt
low-rise ['ləuraız] *adj* niedrig (gebaut)
low-tech ['ləutɛk] *adj* nicht mit Hightech ausgestattet
loyal ['lɔıəl] *adj* treu; (*support*) loyal
loyalist ['lɔıəlıst] *n* Loyalist(in) *m(f)*
loyalty ['lɔıəltı] *n* (*see adj*) Treue *f*; Loyalität *f*
loyalty card (*Brit*) *n* (*Comm*) Paybackkarte *f*
lozenge ['lɔzındʒ] *n* Pastille *f*; (*shape*) Raute *f*
LP *n abbr* (= *long player*) LP *f*; *see also* **long-playing record**
LPG *n abbr* (= *liquefied petroleum gas*) Flüssiggas *nt*

L-PLATES

Als *L-plates* werden in Großbritannien die weißen Schilder mit einem roten „L" bezeichnet, die vorne und hinten an jedem von einem Fahrschüler geführten Fahrzeug befestigt werden müssen. Fahrschüler müssen einen vorläufigen Führerschein beantragen und dürfen damit unter der Aufsicht eines erfahrenen Autofahrers auf allen Straßen außer Autobahnen fahren.

LPN (*US*) *n abbr* (= *Licensed Practical Nurse*) staatlich anerkannte Krankenschwester *f*, staatlich anerkannter Krankenpfleger *m*
LRAM (*Brit*) *n abbr* (= *Licentiate of the Royal Academy of Music*) *Qualifikationsnachweis in Musik*
LSAT (*US*) *n abbr* (= *Law School Admissions Test*) *Zulassungsprüfung für juristische Hochschulen*
LSD *n abbr* (= *lysergic acid diethylamide*) LSD *nt*; (*Brit: also:* **L.S.D.**: = *pounds, shillings and pence*) *früheres britisches Währungssystem*
LSE (*Brit*) *n abbr* (= *London School of Economics*) *Londoner Wirtschaftshochschule*
Lt *abbr* (*Mil:* = *lieutenant*) Lt.
Ltd *abbr* (*Comm:* = *limited (liability)*) ≈ GmbH *f*
lubricant ['lu:brıkənt] *n* Schmiermittel *nt*
lubricate ['lu:brıkeıt] *vt* schmieren, ölen
lucid ['lu:sıd] *adj* klar; (*person*) bei klarem Verstand
lucidity [lu:'sıdıtı] *n* Klarheit *f*
luck [lʌk] *n* (*esp good luck*) Glück *nt*; **bad ~** Unglück *nt*; **good ~!** viel Glück!; **bad** *or* **hard** *or* **tough ~!** so ein Pech!; **hard** *or* **tough ~!** (*showing no sympathy*) Pech gehabt!; **to be in ~** Glück haben; **to be out of ~** kein Glück haben
luckily ['lʌkılı] *adv* glücklicherweise
luckless ['lʌklıs] *adj* glücklos
lucky ['lʌkı] *adj* (*situation, event*) glücklich; (*object*) Glück bringend; (*person*): **to be ~** Glück haben; **to have a ~ escape** noch einmal davonkommen; **~ charm** Glücksbringer *m*
lucrative ['lu:krətıv] *adj* einträglich
ludicrous ['lu:dıkrəs] *adj* grotesk
ludo ['lu:dəu] *n* Mensch, ärgere dich nicht *nt*
lug [lʌg] (*inf*) *vt* schleppen
luggage ['lʌgıdʒ] *n* Gepäck *nt*
luggage car (*US*) *n* = **luggage van**
luggage rack *n* Gepäckträger *m*; (*in train*) Gepäckablage *f*
luggage van (*Brit*) *n* (*Rail*) Gepäckwagen *m*
lugubrious [lu'gu:brıəs] *adj* schwermütig
lukewarm ['lu:kwɔ:m] *adj* lauwarm; (*fig: person, reaction etc*) lau
lull [lʌl] *n* Pause *f* ▷ *vt*: **to ~ sb to sleep** jdn einlullen *or* einschläfern; **to be ~ed into a false sense of security** in trügerische Sicherheit gewiegt werden
lullaby ['lʌləbaı] *n* Schlaflied *nt*
lumbago [lʌm'beıgəu] *n* Hexenschuss *m*
lumber ['lʌmbər] *n* (*wood*) Holz *nt*; (*junk*) Gerümpel *nt* ▷ *vi*: **to ~ about/along** herum-/entlangtapsen
▸ **lumber with** *vt*: **to be/get ~ed with sth** etw am Hals haben/aufgehalst bekommen
lumberjack ['lʌmbədʒæk] *n* Holzfäller *m*
lumber room (*Brit*) *n* Rumpelkammer *f*
lumberyard ['lʌmbəjɑ:d] (*US*) *n* Holzlager *nt*
luminous ['lu:mınəs] *adj* leuchtend, Leucht-
lump [lʌmp] *n* Klumpen *m*; (*on body*) Beule *f*; (*in breast*) Knoten *m*; (*also:* **sugar lump**) Stück *nt* (Zucker) ▷ *vt*: **to ~ together** in einen Topf werfen; **a ~ sum** eine Pauschalsumme
lumpy ['lʌmpı] *adj* klumpig
lunacy ['lu:nəsı] *n* Wahnsinn *m*
lunar ['lu:nər] *adj* Mond-
lunatic ['lu:nətık] *adj* wahnsinnig ▷ *n* Wahnsinnige(r) *f(m)*, Irre(r) *f(m)*
lunatic asylum *n* Irrenanstalt *f*
lunatic fringe *n*: **the ~** die Extremisten *pl*
lunch [lʌntʃ] *n* Mittagessen *nt*; (*time*) Mittagszeit *f* ▷ *vi* zu Mittag essen
lunch break *n* Mittagspause *f*
luncheon ['lʌntʃən] *n* Mittagessen *nt*
luncheon meat *n* Frühstücksfleisch *nt*
luncheon voucher (*Brit*) *n* Essensmarke *f*
lunch hour *n* Mittagspause *f*
lunch time *n* Mittagszeit *f*
lung [lʌŋ] *n* Lunge *f*
lunge [lʌndʒ] *vi* (*also:* **lunge forward**) sich nach vorne stürzen; **to ~ at** sich stürzen auf *+acc*
lupin ['lu:pın] *n* Lupine *f*
lurch [lə:tʃ] *vi* ruckeln; (*person*) taumeln ▷ *n* Ruck *m*; (*of person*) Taumeln *nt*; **to leave sb in the ~** jdn im Stich lassen
lure [luər] *n* Verlockung *f* ▷ *vt* locken
lurid ['luərıd] *adj* (*story etc*) reißerisch; (*pej: brightly coloured*) grell, in grellen Farben
lurk [lə:k] *vi* (*also fig*) lauern
luscious ['lʌʃəs] *adj* (*attractive*) fantastisch; (*food*) köstlich, lecker
lush [lʌʃ] *adj* (*fields*) saftig; (*gardens*) üppig; (*luxurious*) luxuriös
lust [lʌst] (*pej*) *n* (*sexual*) (sinnliche) Begierde *f*; (*for money, power etc*) Gier *f*
▸ **lust after** *vt fus* (*sexually*) begehren; (*crave*) gieren nach
▸ **lust for** *vt fus* = **lust after**
lustful ['lʌstful] *adj* lüstern
lustre, (*US*) **luster** ['lʌstər] *n* Schimmer *m*,

Glanz *m*
lusty ['lʌstɪ] *adj* gesund und munter
lute [lu:t] *n* Laute *f*
luvvie, luvvy ['lʌvɪ] (*inf*) *n* Schätzchen *nt*
Luxembourg ['lʌksəmbə:g] *n* Luxemburg *nt*
luxuriant [lʌg'zjuərɪənt] *adj* üppig
luxuriate [lʌg'zjuərɪeɪt] *vi*: **to ~ in sth** sich in etw *dat* aalen
luxurious [lʌg'zjuərɪəs] *adj* luxuriös
luxury ['lʌkʃərɪ] *n* Luxus *m* (*no pl*) ▷ *cpd* (*hotel, car etc*) Luxus-; **little luxuries** kleine Genüsse
LV (*Brit*) *n abbr* = **luncheon voucher**
LW *abbr* (*Radio*: = *long wave*) LW
Lycra® ['laɪkrə] *n* Lycra *nt*
lying ['laɪɪŋ] *n* Lügen *nt* ▷ *adj* verlogen
lynch [lɪntʃ] *vt* lynchen
lynx [lɪŋks] *n* Luchs *m*
lyric ['lɪrɪk] *adj* lyrisch
lyrical ['lɪrɪkl] *adj* lyrisch; (*fig: praise etc*) schwärmerisch
lyricism ['lɪrɪsɪzəm] *n* Lyrik *f*
lyrics ['lɪrɪks] *npl* (*of song*) Text *m*

Mm

M¹, **m¹** [ɛm] *n* (*letter*) M *nt*, m *nt*; **M for Mary, M for Mike** (*US*) ≈ M wie Martha
M² [ɛm] *n abbr* (*Brit*: = *motorway*): **the M8** ≈ die A8 ▷ *abbr* = **medium**
m² *abbr* (= *metre*) m; = **mile**; (= *million*) Mio.
MA *n abbr* (= *Master of Arts*) *akademischer Grad für Geisteswissenschaftler*; (= *military academy*) Militärakademie *f* ▷ *abbr* (*US*: *Post*) = *Massachusetts*
mac [mæk] (*Brit*) *n* Regenmantel *m*
macabre [mə'kɑːbrə] *adj* makaber
macaroni [mækə'rəunɪ] *n* Makkaroni *pl*
macaroon [mækə'ruːn] *n* Makrone *f*
mace [meɪs] *n* (*weapon*) Keule *f*; (*ceremonial*) Amtsstab *m*; (*spice*) Muskatblüte *f*
Macedonia [mæsɪ'dəunɪə] *n* Makedonien *nt*
Macedonian [mæsɪ'dəunɪən] *adj* makedonisch ▷ *n* Makedonier(in) *m(f)*; (*Ling*) Makedonisch *nt*
machinations [mækɪ'neɪʃənz] *npl* Machenschaften *pl*
machine [mə'ʃiːn] *n* Maschine *f*; (*fig*: *party machine etc*) Apparat *m* ▷ *vt* (*Tech*) maschinell herstellen *or* bearbeiten; (*dress etc*) mit der Maschine nähen
machine code *n* Maschinencode *m*
machine gun *n* Maschinengewehr *nt*
machine language *n* Maschinensprache *f*
machine-readable [mə'ʃiːnriːdəbl] *adj* maschinenlesbar
machinery [mə'ʃiːnərɪ] *n* Maschinen *pl*; (*fig*: *of government*) Apparat *m*
machine shop *n* Maschinensaal *m*
machine tool *n* Werkzeugmaschine *f*
machine washable *adj* waschmaschinenfest
machinist [mə'ʃiːnɪst] *n* Maschinist(in) *m(f)*
macho ['mætʃəu] *adj* Macho-; **a ~ man** ein Macho *m*
mackerel ['mækrl] *n inv* Makrele *f*
mackintosh ['mækɪntɔʃ] (*Brit*) *n* Regenmantel *m*
macro ... ['mækrəu] *pref* Makro-, makro-
macroeconomics ['mækrəuiːkə'nɔmɪks] *npl* Makroökonomie *f*
mad [mæd] *adj* wahnsinnig, verrückt; (*angry*) böse, sauer (*inf*); **to be ~ about** verrückt sein auf +*acc*; **to be ~ at sb** böse *or* sauer auf jdn sein; **to go ~** (*insane*) verrückt *or* wahnsinnig werden; (*angry*) böse *or* sauer werden
madam ['mædəm] *n* gnädige Frau *f*; **yes, ~** ja(wohl); **M~ Chairman** Frau Vorsitzende
madcap ['mædkæp] *adj* (*idea*) versponnen; (*tricks*) toll
mad cow disease *n* Rinderwahn *m*
madden ['mædn] *vt* ärgern, fuchsen (*inf*)
maddening ['mædnɪŋ] *adj* unerträglich
made [meɪd] *pt, pp of* **make**
Madeira [mə'dɪərə] *n* Madeira *nt*; (*wine*) Madeira *m*
made-to-measure ['meɪdtə'mɛʒəʳ] (*Brit*) *adj* maßgeschneidert
madhouse ['mædhaus] *n* (*also fig*) Irrenhaus *nt*
madly ['mædlɪ] *adv* wie verrückt; **~ in love** bis über beide Ohren verliebt
madman ['mædmən] (*irreg*: *like* **man**) *n* Verrückte(r) *m*, Irre(r) *m*
madness ['mædnɪs] *n* Wahnsinn *m*
Madrid [mə'drɪd] *n* Madrid *nt*
Mafia ['mæfɪə] *n* Mafia *f*
mag [mæg] (*Brit*: *inf*) *n* = **magazine**
magazine [mægə'ziːn] *n* Zeitschrift *f*; (*Radio, TV*) Magazin *nt*; (*Radio, TV, of firearm*) Magazin *nt*; (*Mil*: *store*) Depot *nt*
maggot ['mægət] *n* Made *f*
magic ['mædʒɪk] *n* Magie *f*; (*conjuring*) Zauberei *f* ▷ *adj* magisch; (*formula*) Zauber-; (*fig*: *place, moment etc*) zauberhaft
magical ['mædʒɪkl] *adj* magisch; (*experience, evening*) zauberhaft
magician [mə'dʒɪʃən] *n* (*wizard*) Magier *m*; (*conjurer*) Zauberer *m*
magistrate ['mædʒɪstreɪt] *n* Friedensrichter(in) *m(f)*
magnanimous [mæg'nænɪməs] *adj* großmütig
magnate ['mægneɪt] *n* Magnat *m*
magnesium [mæg'niːzɪəm] *n* Magnesium *nt*
magnet ['mægnɪt] *n* Magnet *m*
magnetic [mæg'nɛtɪk] *adj* magnetisch; (*field, compass, pole etc*) Magnet-; (*personality*) anziehend
magnetic disk *n* (*Comput*) Magnetplatte *f*
magnetic tape *n* Magnetband *nt*
magnetism ['mægnɪtɪzəm] *n* Magnetismus *m*; (*of person*) Anziehungskraft *f*
magnetize ['mægnɪtaɪz] *vt* magnetisieren
magnification [mægnɪfɪ'keɪʃən] *n*

Vergrößerung *f*
magnificence [mæg'nɪfɪsns] *n* Großartigkeit *f*; (*of robes*) Pracht *f*
magnificent [mæg'nɪfɪsnt] *adj* großartig; (*robes*) prachtvoll
magnify ['mægnɪfaɪ] *vt* vergrößern; (*sound*) verstärken; (*fig: exaggerate*) aufbauschen
magnifying glass ['mægnɪfaɪɪŋ-] *n* Vergrößerungsglas *nt*, Lupe *f*
magnitude ['mægnɪtju:d] *n* (*size*) Ausmaß *nt*, Größe *f*; (*importance*) Bedeutung *f*
magnolia [mæg'nəulɪə] *n* Magnolie *f*
magpie ['mægpaɪ] *n* Elster *f*
mahogany [mə'hɔgənɪ] *n* Mahagoni *nt* ▷ *cpd* Mahagoni-
maid [meɪd] *n* Dienstmädchen *nt*; **old ~** (*pej*) alte Jungfer
maiden ['meɪdn] *n* (*liter*) Mädchen *nt* ▷ *adj* unverheiratet; (*speech, voyage*) Jungfern-
maiden name *n* Mädchenname *m*
mail [meɪl] *n* Post *f* ▷ *vt* aufgeben; **by ~** mit der Post
mailbox ['meɪlbɔks] *n* (*US*) Briefkasten *m*; (*Comput*) Mailbox *f*, elektronischer Briefkasten *m*
mailing list ['meɪlɪŋ-] *n* Anschriftenliste *f*
mailman ['meɪlmæn] (*US: irreg: like* **man**) *n* Briefträger *m*, Postbote *m*
mail order *n* (*system*) Versand *m* ▷ *cpd*: **mail-order firm** *or* **business** Versandhaus *nt*; **mail-order catalogue** Versandhauskatalog *m*; **by ~** durch Bestellung per Post
mailshot ['meɪlʃɔt] (*Brit*) *n* Werbebrief *m*
mail train *n* Postzug *m*
mail truck (*US*) *n* Postauto *nt*
mail van (*Brit*) *n* (*Aut*) Postauto *nt*; (*Rail*) Postwagen *m*
maim [meɪm] *vt* verstümmeln
main [meɪn] *adj* Haupt-, wichtigste(r, s); (*door, entrance, meal*) Haupt- ▷ *n* Hauptleitung *f*; **the mains** *npl* (*Elec*) das Stromnetz; (*gas, water*) die Hauptleitung; **in the ~** im Großen und Ganzen
main course *n* (*Culin*) Hauptgericht *nt*
mainframe ['meɪnfreɪm] *n* (*Comput*) Großrechner *m*
mainland ['meɪnlənd] *n* Festland *nt*
mainline ['meɪnlaɪn] *adj*: **~ station** Fernbahnhof *m* ▷ *vt* (*drugs slang*) spritzen ▷ *vi* (*drugs slang*) fixen
main line *n* Hauptstrecke *f*
mainly ['meɪnlɪ] *adv* hauptsächlich
main road *n* Hauptstraße *f*
mainstay ['meɪnsteɪ] *n* (*foundation*) (wichtigste) Stütze *f*; (*chief constituent*) Hauptbestandteil *m*
mainstream ['meɪnstri:m] *n* Hauptrichtung *f* ▷ *adj* (*cinema etc*) populär; (*politics*) der Mitte
maintain [meɪn'teɪn] *vt* (*preserve*) aufrechterhalten; (*keep up*) beibehalten; (*provide for*) unterhalten; (*look after: building*) instand halten; (*: equipment*) warten; (*affirm: opinion*) vertreten; (*: innocence*) beteuern; **to ~ that ...** behaupten, dass ...
maintenance ['meɪntənəns] *n* (*of building*) Instandhaltung *f*; (*of equipment*) Wartung *f*; (*preservation*) Aufrechterhaltung *f*; (*Law: alimony*) Unterhalt *m*
maintenance contract *n* Wartungsvertrag *m*
maintenance order *n* (*Law*) Unterhaltsurteil *nt*
maisonette [meɪzə'nɛt] (*Brit*) *n* Maisonettewohnung *f*
maize [meɪz] *n* Mais *m*
Maj. *abbr* (*Mil*) = **major**
majestic [mə'dʒɛstɪk] *adj* erhaben
majesty ['mædʒɪstɪ] *n* (*title*): **Your M~** Eure Majestät; (*splendour*) Erhabenheit *f*
major ['meɪdʒə^r] *n* Major *m* ▷ *adj* bedeutend; (*Mus*) Dur ▷ *vi* (*US*): **to ~ in French** Französisch als Hauptfach belegen; **a ~ operation** eine größere Operation
Majorca [mə'jɔ:kə] *n* Mallorca *nt*
major general *n* Generalmajor *m*
majority [mə'dʒɔrɪtɪ] *n* Mehrheit *f* ▷ *cpd* (*verdict, holding*) Mehrheits-
make [meɪk] (*pt, pp* **made**) *vt* machen; (*clothes*) nähen; (*cake*) backen; (*speech*) halten; (*manufacture*) herstellen; (*earn*) verdienen; (*cause to be*): **to ~ sb sad** jdn traurig machen; (*force*): **to ~ sb do sth** jdn zwingen, etw zu tun; (*cause*) jdn dazu bringen, etw zu tun; (*equal*): **2 and 2 ~ 4** 2 und 2 ist *or* macht 4 ▷ *n* Marke *f*, Fabrikat *nt*; **to ~ a fool of sb** jdn lächerlich machen; **to ~ a profit/loss** Gewinn/Verlust machen; **to ~ it** (*arrive*) es schaffen; (*succeed*) Erfolg haben; **what time do you ~ it?** wie spät hast du?; **to ~ good** erfolgreich sein; (*threat*) wahr machen; (*promise*) einlösen; (*damage*) wiedergutmachen; (*loss*) ersetzen; **to ~ do with** auskommen mit
▸ **make for** *vt fus* (*place*) zuhalten auf +*acc*
▸ **make off** *vi* sich davonmachen
▸ **make out** *vt* (*decipher*) entziffern; (*understand*) verstehen; (*see*) ausmachen; (*write: cheque*) ausstellen; (*claim, imply*) behaupten; (*pretend*) so tun, als ob; **to ~ out a case for sth** für etw argumentieren
▸ **make over** *vt*: **to ~ over (to)** überschreiben (+*dat*)
▸ **make up** *vt* (*constitute*) bilden; (*invent*) erfinden; (*prepare: bed*) zurechtmachen; (*: parcel*) zusammenpacken ▷ *vi* (*after quarrel*) sich versöhnen; (*with cosmetics*) sich schminken; **to ~ up one's mind** sich entscheiden; **to be made up of** bestehen aus
▸ **make up for** *vt fus* (*loss*) ersetzen; (*disappointment etc*) ausgleichen
make-believe ['meɪkbɪli:v] *n* Fantasie *f*; **a world of ~** eine Fantasiewelt; **it's just ~** es ist nicht wirklich
maker ['meɪkə^r] *n* Hersteller *m*; **film ~** Filmemacher(in) *m(f)*
makeshift ['meɪkʃɪft] *adj* behelfsmäßig
make-up ['meɪkʌp] *n* Make-up *nt*, Schminke *f*
make-up bag *n* Kosmetiktasche *f*
make-up remover *n* Make-up-Entferner *m*

making ['meɪkɪŋ] *n (fig)*: **in the ~** im Entstehen; **to have the ~s of** das Zeug haben zu
maladjusted [mælə'dʒʌstɪd] *adj* verhaltensgestört
maladroit [mælə'drɔɪt] *adj* ungeschickt
malaise [mæ'leɪz] *n* Unbehagen *nt*
malaria [mə'lɛərɪə] *n* Malaria *f*
Malawi [mə'lɑ:wɪ] *n* Malawi *nt*
Malay [mə'leɪ] *adj* malaiisch ▷ *n* Malaie *m*, Malaiin *f*; *(Ling)* Malaiisch *nt*
Malaya [mə'leɪə] *n* Malaya *nt*
Malayan [mə'leɪən] *adj, n* = **Malay**
Malaysia [mə'leɪzɪə] *n* Malaysia *nt*
Malaysian [mə'leɪzɪən] *adj* malaysisch ▷ *n* Malaysier(in) *m(f)*
Maldives ['mɔ:ldi:vz] *npl* Malediven *pl*
male [meɪl] *n (animal)* Männchen *nt*; *(man)* Mann *m* ▷ *adj* männlich; *(Elec)*: **~ plug** Stecker *m*; **because he is ~** weil er ein Mann/Junge ist; **~ and female students** Studenten und Studentinnen; **a ~ child** ein Junge
male chauvinist *n* Chauvinist *m*
male nurse *n* Krankenpfleger *m*
malevolence [mə'lɛvələns] *n* Boshaftigkeit *f*; *(of action)* Böswilligkeit *f*
malevolent [mə'lɛvələnt] *adj* boshaft; *(intention)* böswillig
malfunction [mæl'fʌŋkʃən] *n (of computer)* Funktionsstörung *f*; *(of machine)* Defekt *m* ▷ *vi (computer)* eine Funktionsstörung haben; *(machine)* defekt sein
malice ['mælɪs] *n* Bosheit *f*
malicious [mə'lɪʃəs] *adj* boshaft; *(Law)* böswillig
malign [mə'laɪn] *vt* verleumden ▷ *adj (influence)* schlecht; *(interpretation)* böswillig
malignant [mə'lɪgnənt] *adj* bösartig; *(intention)* böswillig
malingerer [mə'lɪŋgərə^r] *n* Simulant(in) *m(f)*
mall [mɔ:l] *n (also:* **shopping mall***)* Einkaufszentrum *nt*
malleable ['mælɪəbl] *adj (lit, fig)* formbar
mallet ['mælɪt] *n* Holzhammer *m*
malnutrition [mælnju:'trɪʃən] *n* Unterernährung *f*
malpractice [mæl'præktɪs] *n* Berufsvergehen *nt*
malt [mɔ:lt] *n* Malz *nt*; *(also:* **malt whisky***)* Malt Whisky *m*
Malta ['mɔ:ltə] *n* Malta *nt*
Maltese [mɔ:l'ti:z] *adj* maltesisch ▷ *n inv* Malteser(in) *m(f)*; *(Ling)* Maltesisch *nt*
maltreat [mæl'tri:t] *vt* schlecht behandeln; *(violently)* misshandeln
mammal ['mæml] *n* Säugetier *nt*
mammoth ['mæməθ] *n* Mammut *nt* ▷ *adj (task)* Mammut-
man [mæn] *(pl* **men***)* *n* Mann *m*; *(mankind)* der Mensch, die Menschen *pl*; *(Chess)* Figur *f* ▷ *vt (ship)* bemannen; *(gun, machine)* bedienen; *(post)* besetzen; **~ and wife** Mann und Frau
manage ['mænɪdʒ] *vi*: **to ~ to do sth** es schaffen, etw zu tun; *(get by financially)* zurechtkommen ▷ *vt (business, organization)* leiten; *(control)* zurechtkommen mit; **to ~ without sb/sth** ohne jdn/etw auskommen; **well ~d** *(business, shop etc)* gut geführt
manageable ['mænɪdʒəbl] *adj (task)* zu bewältigen; *(number)* überschaubar
management ['mænɪdʒmənt] *n* Leitung *f*, Führung *f*; *(persons)* Unternehmensleitung *f*; **"under new ~"** „unter neuer Leitung"
management accounting *n* Kosten- und Leistungsrechnung *f*
management consultant *n* Unternehmensberater(in) *m(f)*
manager ['mænɪdʒə^r] *n (of business)* Geschäftsführer(in) *m(f)*; *(of institution etc)* Direktor(in) *m(f)*; *(of department)* Leiter(in) *m(f)*; *(of pop star)* Manager(in) *m(f)*; *(Sport)* Trainer(in) *m(f)*; **sales ~** Verkaufsleiter(in) *m(f)*
manageress [mænɪdʒə'rɛs] *n (of shop, business)* Geschäftsführerin *f*; *(of office, department etc)* Leiterin *f*
managerial [mænɪ'dʒɪərɪəl] *adj (role, post)* leitend; *(decisions)* geschäftlich; **~ staff/skills** Führungskräfte *pl*/-qualitäten *pl*
managing director ['mænɪdʒɪŋ-] *n* Geschäftsführer(in) *m(f)*
Mancunian [mæŋ'kju:nɪən] *n* Bewohner(in) *m(f)* Manchesters
mandarin ['mændərɪn] *n (also:* **mandarin orange***)* Mandarine *f*; *(official: Chinese)* Mandarin *m*; *(: gen)* Funktionär *m*
mandate ['mændeɪt] *n* Mandat *nt*; *(task)* Auftrag *m*
mandatory ['mændətərɪ] *adj* obligatorisch
mandolin, **mandoline** ['mændəlɪn] *n* Mandoline *f*
mane [meɪn] *n* Mähne *f*
maneuver *etc* [mə'nu:və^r] *(US)* = **manoeuvre** *etc*
manfully ['mænfəlɪ] *adv* mannhaft, beherzt
manganese [mæŋgə'ni:z] *n* Mangan *nt*
mangetout ['mɔnʒ'tu:] *(Brit) n* Zuckererbse *f*
mangle ['mæŋgl] *vt* (übel) zurichten ▷ *n* Mangel *f*
mango ['mæŋgəu] *(pl* **~es***)* *n* Mango *f*
mangrove ['mæŋgrəuv] *n* Mangrove(n)baum *m*
mangy ['meɪndʒɪ] *adj (animal)* räudig
manhandle ['mænhændl] *vt (mistreat)* grob behandeln; *(move by hand)* (von Hand) befördern
manhole ['mænhəul] *n* Kanalschacht *m*
manhood ['mænhud] *n* Mannesalter *nt*
man-hour ['mænauə^r] *n* Arbeitsstunde *f*
manhunt ['mænhʌnt] *n* Fahndung *f*
mania ['meɪnɪə] *n* Manie *f*; *(craze)* Sucht *f*; **persecution ~** Verfolgungswahn *m*
maniac ['meɪnɪæk] *n* Wahnsinnige(r) *f(m)*, Verrückte(r) *f(m)*; *(fig)* Fanatiker(in) *m(f)*
manic ['mænɪk] *adj (behaviour)* manisch; *(activity)* rasend
manic-depressive ['mænɪkdɪ'prɛsɪv] *n* Manisch-Depressive(r) *f(m)* ▷ *adj* manisch-

depressiv
manicure ['mænɪkjuəʳ] *n* Maniküre *f* ▷ *vt* maniküren
manicure set *n* Nageletui *nt*, Maniküreetui *nt*
manifest ['mænɪfɛst] *vt* zeigen, bekunden ▷ *adj* offenkundig ▷ *n* Manifest *nt*
manifestation [mænɪfɛs'teɪʃən] *n* Anzeichen *nt*
manifesto [mænɪ'fɛstəu] *n* Manifest *nt*
manifold ['mænɪfəuld] *adj* vielfältig ▷ *n*: **exhaust ~** Auspuffkrümmer *m*
Manila [mə'nɪlə] *n* Manila *nt*
manila [mə'nɪlə] *adj*: **~ envelope** brauner Briefumschlag *m*
manipulate [mə'nɪpjuleɪt] *vt* manipulieren
manipulation [mənɪpju'leɪʃən] *n* Manipulation *f*
mankind [mæn'kaɪnd] *n* Menschheit *f*
manliness ['mænlɪnɪs] *n* Männlichkeit *f*
manly ['mænlɪ] *adj* männlich
man-made ['mæn'meɪd] *adj* künstlich; (*fibre*) synthetisch
manna ['mænə] *n* Manna *nt*
mannequin ['mænɪkɪn] *n* (*dummy*) Schaufensterpuppe *f*; (*fashion model*) Mannequin *nt*
manner ['mænəʳ] *n* (*way*) Art *f*, Weise *f*; (*behaviour*) Art *f*; (*type, sort*): **all ~ of things** die verschiedensten Dinge; **manners** *npl* (*conduct*) Manieren *pl*, Umgangsformen *pl*; **bad ~s** schlechte Manieren; **that's bad ~s** das gehört sich nicht
mannerism ['mænərɪzəm] *n* Eigenheit *f*
mannerly ['mænəlɪ] *adj* wohlerzogen
manning ['mænɪŋ] *n* Besatzung *f*
manoeuvrable, (*US*) **maneuverable** [mə'nu:vrəbl] *adj* manövrierfähig
manoeuvre, (*US*) **maneuver** [mə'nu:vəʳ] *vt* manövrieren; (*situation*) manipulieren ▷ *vi* manövrieren ▷ *n* (*skilful move*) Manöver *nt*; **manoeuvres** *npl* (*Mil*) Manöver *nt*, Truppenübungen *pl*; **to ~ sb into doing sth** jdn dazu bringen, etw zu tun
manor ['mænəʳ] *n* (*also*: **manor house**) Herrenhaus *nt*
manpower ['mænpauəʳ] *n* Personal *nt*, Arbeitskräfte *pl*
Manpower Services Commission (*Brit*) *n* *Behörde für Arbeitsbeschaffung, Arbeitsvermittlung und Berufsausbildung*
manservant ['mænsə:vənt] (*pl* **menservants**) *n* Diener *m*
mansion ['mænʃən] *n* Villa *f*
manslaughter ['mænslɔ:təʳ] *n* Totschlag *m*
mantelpiece ['mæntlpi:s] *n* Kaminsims *nt or m*
mantle ['mæntl] *n* Decke *f*; (*fig*) Deckmantel *m*
man-to-man ['mæntə'mæn] *adj, adv* von Mann zu Mann
manual ['mænjuəl] *adj* manuell, Hand-; (*controls*) von Hand ▷ *n* Handbuch *nt*
manufacture [mænju'fæktʃəʳ] *vt* herstellen ▷ *n* Herstellung *f*
manufactured goods *npl* Fertigerzeugnisse *pl*
manufacturer [mænju'fæktʃərəʳ] *n* Hersteller *m*
manufacturing [mænju'fæktʃərɪŋ] *n* Herstellung *f*
manure [mə'njuəʳ] *n* Dung *m*
manuscript ['mænjuskrɪpt] *n* Manuskript *nt*; (*old document*) Handschrift *f*
many ['mɛnɪ] *adj, pron* viele; **a great ~** eine ganze Reihe; **how ~?** wie viele?; **too ~ difficulties** zu viele Schwierigkeiten; **twice as ~** doppelt so viele; **~ a time** so manches Mal
Maori ['maurɪ] *adj* maorisch ▷ *n* Maori *mf*
map [mæp] *n* (Land)karte *f*; (*of town*) Stadtplan *m* ▷ *vt* eine Karte anfertigen von
▶ **map out** *vt* planen; (*plan*) entwerfen; (*essay*) anlegen
maple ['meɪpl] *n* (*tree, wood*) Ahorn *m*
Mar. *abbr* = **March**
mar [mɑ:ʳ] *vt* (*appearance*) verunstalten; (*day*) verderben; (*event*) stören
marathon ['mærəθən] *n* Marathon *m* ▷ *adj*: **a ~ session** eine Marathonsitzung
marathon runner *n* Marathonläufer(in) *m(f)*
marauder [mə'rɔ:dəʳ] *n* (*robber*) Plünderer *m*; (*killer*) Mörder *m*
marble ['mɑ:bl] *n* Marmor *m*; (*toy*) Murmel *f*
marbles ['mɑ:blz] *n* (*game*) Murmeln *pl*
March [mɑ:tʃ] *n* März *m*; *see also* **July**
march [mɑ:tʃ] *vi* marschieren; (*protesters*) ziehen ▷ *n* Marsch *m*; (*demonstration*) Demonstration *f*; **to ~ out of/into** (heraus)marschieren aus *+dat*/ (herein)marschieren in *+acc*
marcher ['mɑ:tʃəʳ] *n* Demonstrant(in) *m(f)*
marching orders ['mɑ:tʃɪŋ-] *npl*: **to give sb his/her ~** (*employee*) jdn entlassen; (*lover*) jdm den Laufpass geben
march past *n* Vorbeimarsch *m*
mare [mɛəʳ] *n* Stute *f*
margarine [mɑ:dʒə'ri:n] *n* Margarine *f*
marge [mɑ:dʒ] (*Brit: inf*) *n* = **margarine**
margin ['mɑ:dʒɪn] *n* Rand *m*; (*of votes*) Mehrheit *f*; (*for safety, error etc*) Spielraum *m*; (*Comm*) Gewinnspanne *f*
marginal ['mɑ:dʒɪnl] *adj* geringfügig; (*note*) Rand-
marginally ['mɑ:dʒɪnəlɪ] *adv* nur wenig, geringfügig
marginal (seat) *n* (*Pol*) *mit knapper Mehrheit gewonnener Wahlkreis*
marigold ['mærɪgəuld] *n* Ringelblume *f*
marijuana [mærɪ'wɑ:nə] *n* Marihuana *nt*
marina [mə'ri:nə] *n* Jachthafen *m*
marinade [mærɪ'neɪd] *n* Marinade *f* ▷ *vt* = **marinate**
marinate ['mærɪneɪt] *vt* marinieren
marine [mə'ri:n] *adj* (*plant, biology*) Meeres- ▷ *n* (*Brit: soldier*) Marineinfanterist *m*; (*US: sailor*) Marinesoldat *m*; **~ engineer** Schiff(s)bauingenieur *m*; **~ engineering** Schiff(s)bau *m*
marine insurance *n* Seeversicherung *f*
marital ['mærɪtl] *adj* ehelich; (*problem*) Ehe-;

~ status Familienstand *m*
maritime ['mærɪtaɪm] *adj (nation)* Seefahrer-; *(museum)* Seefahrts-; *(law)* See-
marjoram ['mɑːdʒərəm] *n* Majoran *m*
mark [mɑːk] *n* Zeichen *nt*; *(stain)* Fleck *m*; *(in snow, mud etc)* Spur *f*; *(Brit: Scol)* Note *f*; *(level, point)*: **the halfway ~** die Hälfte *f*; *(currency)* Mark *f*; *(Brit: Tech)*: **M~ 2/3** Version *f* 2/3 ▷ *vt (with pen)* beschriften; *(with shoes etc)* schmutzig machen; *(with tyres etc)* Spuren hinterlassen auf *+dat*; *(damage)* beschädigen; *(stain)* Flecken machen auf *+dat*; *(indicate)* markieren; *(: price)* auszeichnen; *(commemorate)* begehen; *(characterize)* kennzeichnen; *(Brit: Scol)* korrigieren (und benoten); *(Sport: player)* decken; **punctuation ~s** Satzzeichen *pl*; **to be quick off the ~ (in doing sth)** *(fig)* blitzschnell reagieren (und etw tun); **to be up to the ~** den Anforderungen entsprechen; **to ~ time** auf der Stelle treten
▸ **mark down** *vt (prices, goods)* herabsetzen, heruntersetzen
▸ **mark off** *vt (tick off)* abhaken
▸ **mark out** *vt* markieren; *(person)* auszeichnen
▸ **mark up** *vt (price)* heraufsetzen
marked [mɑːkt] *adj* deutlich
markedly ['mɑːkɪdlɪ] *adv* deutlich
marker ['mɑːkə^r] *n* Markierung *f*; *(bookmark)* Lesezeichen *nt*
market ['mɑːkɪt] *n* Markt *m* ▷ *vt (sell)* vertreiben; *(new product)* auf den Markt bringen; **to be on the ~** auf dem Markt sein; **on the open ~** auf dem freien Markt; **to play the ~** *(Stock Exchange)* an der Börse spekulieren
marketable ['mɑːkɪtəbl] *adj* marktfähig
market analysis *n* Marktanalyse *f*
market day *n* Markttag *m*
market demand *n* Marktbedarf *m*
market economy *n* Marktwirtschaft *f*
market expert *n* Marktexperte *m*, Marktexpertin *f*
market forces *npl* Marktkräfte *pl*
market garden *(Brit) n* Gemüseanbaubetrieb *m*
marketing ['mɑːkɪtɪŋ] *n* Marketing *nt*
marketing manager *n* Marketingmanager(in) *m(f)*
marketplace ['mɑːkɪtpleɪs] *n* Marktplatz *m*; *(Comm)* Markt *m*
market price *n* Marktpreis *m*
market research *n* Marktforschung *f*
market sector *n* Marktsegment *nt or* -sektor *m*
market value *n* Marktwert *m*
marking ['mɑːkɪŋ] *n (on animal)* Zeichnung *f*; *(on road)* Markierung *f*
marksman ['mɑːksmən] *(irreg: like* **man***) n* Scharfschütze *m*
marksmanship ['mɑːksmənʃɪp] *n* Treffsicherheit *f*
mark-up ['mɑːkʌp] *n (Comm: margin)* Handelsspanne *f*; *(: increase)* (Preis)aufschlag *m*
marmalade ['mɑːməleɪd] *n* Orangenmarmelade *f*
maroon [mə'ruːn] *vt*: **to be ~ed** festsitzen ▷ *adj* kastanienbraun
marquee [mɑː'kiː] *n* Festzelt *nt*
marquess, **marquis** ['mɑːkwɪs] *n* Marquis *m*
Marrakech, **Marrakesh** [mærə'kɛʃ] *n* Marrakesch *nt*
marriage ['mærɪdʒ] *n* Ehe *f*; *(institution)* die Ehe; *(wedding)* Hochzeit *f*; **~ of convenience** Vernunftehe *f*
marriage bureau *n* Ehevermittlung *f*
marriage certificate *n* Heiratsurkunde *f*
marriage guidance, *(US)* **marriage counseling** *n* Eheberatung *f*
married ['mærɪd] *adj* verheiratet; *(life)* Ehe-; *(love)* ehelich; **to get ~** heiraten
marrow ['mærəu] *n (vegetable)* Kürbis *m*; *(also:* **bone marrow***)* (Knochen)mark *nt*
marry ['mærɪ] *vt* heiraten; *(father)* verheiraten; *(priest)* trauen ▷ *vi* heiraten
Mars [mɑːz] *n* Mars *m*
Marseilles [mɑː'seɪlz] *n* Marseilles *nt*
marsh [mɑːʃ] *n* Sumpf *m*; *(also:* **salt marsh***)* Salzsumpf *m*
marshal ['mɑːʃl] *n (Mil: also:* **field marshal***)* (Feld)marschall *m*; *(official)* Ordner *m*; *(US: of police)* Bezirkspolizeichef *m* ▷ *vt (thoughts)* ordnen; *(support)* auftreiben; *(soldiers)* aufstellen
marshalling yard ['mɑːʃlɪŋ-] *n (Rail)* Rangierbahnhof *m*
marshmallow [mɑːʃ'mæləu] *n (Bot)* Eibisch *m*; *(sweet)* Marshmallow *nt*
marshy ['mɑːʃɪ] *adj* sumpfig
marsupial [mɑː'suːpɪəl] *n* Beuteltier *nt*
martial ['mɑːʃl] *adj* kriegerisch
martial arts *npl* Kampfsport *m*; **the ~** die Kampfkunst *sing*
martial law *n* Kriegsrecht *nt*
Martian ['mɑːʃən] *n* Marsmensch *m*
martin ['mɑːtɪn] *n (also:* **house martin***)* Schwalbe *f*
martyr ['mɑːtə^r] *n* Märtyrer(in) *m(f)* ▷ *vt* martern
martyrdom ['mɑːtədəm] *n* Martyrium *nt*
marvel ['mɑːvl] *n* Wunder *nt* ▷ *vi*: **to ~ (at)** staunen (über *+acc*)
marvellous, *(US)* **marvelous** ['mɑːvləs] *adj* wunderbar
Marxism ['mɑːksɪzəm] *n* Marxismus *m*
Marxist ['mɑːksɪst] *adj* marxistisch ▷ *n* Marxist(in) *m(f)*
marzipan ['mɑːzɪpæn] *n* Marzipan *nt*
mascara [mæs'kɑːrə] *n* Wimperntusche *f*
mascot ['mæskət] *n* Maskottchen *nt*
masculine ['mæskjulɪn] *adj* männlich; *(atmosphere, woman)* maskulin; *(Ling)* männlich, maskulin
masculinity [mæskju'lɪnɪtɪ] *n* Männlichkeit *f*
MASH [mæʃ] *(US) n abbr (= mobile army surgical hospital)* mobiles Lazarett *nt*
mash [mæʃ] *vt* zerstampfen
mashed potatoes [mæʃt-] *npl* Kartoffelpüree

nt, Kartoffelbrei *m*

mask [mɑːsk] *n* Maske *f* ▷ *vt* (*cover*) verdecken; (*hide*) verbergen; **surgical ~** Mundschutz *m*

masking tape ['mɑːskɪŋ-] *n* Abdeckband *nt*

masochism ['mæsəukɪzəm] *n* Masochismus *m*

masochist ['mæsəukɪst] *n* Masochist(in) *m(f)*

mason ['meɪsn] *n* (*also*: **stone mason**) Steinmetz *m*; (*also*: **freemason**) Freimaurer *m*

masonic [mə'sɔnɪk] *adj* (*lodge etc*) Freimaurer-

masonry ['meɪsnrɪ] *n* Mauerwerk *nt*

masquerade [mæskə'reɪd] *vi*: **to ~ as** sich ausgeben als ▷ *n* Maskerade *f*

Mass. (*US*) *abbr* (*Post*) = *Massachusetts*

mass [mæs] *n* Masse *f*; (*of people*) Menge *f*; (*large amount*) Fülle *f*; (*Rel*): **M~** Messe *f* ▷ *cpd* Massen- ▷ *vi* (*troops*) sich massieren; (*protesters*) sich versammeln; **the masses** *npl* (*ordinary people*) die Masse, die Massen *pl*; **to go to M~** zur Messe gehen; **~es of** (*inf*) massenhaft, jede Menge

massacre ['mæsəkə[r]] *n* Massaker *nt* ▷ *vt* massakrieren

massage ['mæsɑːʒ] *n* Massage *f* ▷ *vt* massieren

masseur [mæ'səː[r]] *n* Masseur *m*

masseuse [mæ'səːz] *n* Masseurin *f*

massive ['mæsɪv] *adj* (*furniture, person*) wuchtig; (*support*) massiv; (*changes, increase*) enorm

mass market *n* Massenmarkt *m*

mass media *npl* Massenmedien *pl*

mass meeting *n* Massenveranstaltung *f*; (*of everyone concerned*) Vollversammlung *f*; (*Pol*) Massenkundgebung *f*

mass-produce ['mæsprə'djuːs] *vt* in Massenproduktion herstellen

mass-production ['mæsprə'dʌkʃən] *n* Massenproduktion *f*

mast [mɑːst] *n* (*Naut*) Mast *m*; (*Radio etc*) Sendeturm *m*

mastectomy [mæs'tɛktəmɪ] *n* Brustamputation *f*

master ['mɑːstə[r]] *n* Herr *m*; (*teacher*) Lehrer *m*; (*title*): **M~ X** (der junge) Herr X; (*Art, Mus, of craft etc*) Meister *m* ▷ *cpd*: **~ baker/plumber** *etc* Bäcker-/Klempnermeister *etc m* ▷ *vt* meistern; (*feeling*) unter Kontrolle bringen; (*skill, language*) beherrschen

master disk *n* (*Comput*) Stammdiskette *f*

masterful ['mɑːstəful] *adj* gebieterisch; (*skilful*) meisterhaft

master key *n* Hauptschlüssel *m*

masterly ['mɑːstəlɪ] *adj* meisterhaft

mastermind ['mɑːstəmaɪnd] *n* (führender) Kopf *m* ▷ *vt* planen und ausführen

Master of Arts *n* Magister *m* der philosophischen Fakultät

Master of Ceremonies *n* Zeremonienmeister *m*; (*for variety show etc*) Conférencier *m*

Master of Science *n* Magister *m* der naturwissenschaftlichen Fakultät

masterpiece ['mɑːstəpiːs] *n* Meisterwerk *nt*

master plan *n* kluger Plan *m*

MASTER'S DEGREE

Master's Degree ist ein höherer akademischer Grad, den man in der Regel nach dem *bachelor's degree* erwerben kann. Je nach Universität erhält man ein master's degree nach einem entsprechenden Studium und/oder einer Dissertation. Die am häufigsten verliehenen Grade sind *MA* (= Master of Arts) und *MSc* (= Master of Science), die beide Studium und Dissertation erfordern, während für *MLitt* (= Master of Letters) und *MPhil* (= Master of Philosophy) meist nur eine Dissertation nötig ist. Siehe auch *bachelor's degree, doctorate*.

masterstroke ['mɑːstəstrəuk] *n* Meisterstück *nt*

mastery ['mɑːstərɪ] *n* (*of language etc*) Beherrschung *f*; (*skill*) (meisterhaftes) Können *nt*

mastiff ['mæstɪf] *n* Dogge *f*

masturbate ['mæstəbeɪt] *vi* masturbieren, onanieren

masturbation [mæstə'beɪʃən] *n* Masturbation *f*, Onanie *f*

mat [mæt] *n* Matte *f*; (*also*: **doormat**) Fußmatte *f*; (*also*: **table mat**) Untersetzer *m*; (: *of cloth*) Deckchen *nt* ▷ *adj* = **matt**

match [mætʃ] *n* Wettkampf *m*; (*team game*) Spiel *nt*; (*Tennis*) Match *nt*; (*for lighting fire etc*) Streichholz *nt*; (*equivalent*): **to be a good/perfect ~** gut/perfekt zusammenpassen ▷ *vt* (*go well with*) passen zu; (*equal*) gleichkommen *+dat*; (*correspond to*) entsprechen *+dat*; (*suit*) sich anpassen *+dat*; (*also*: **match up**: *pair*) passend zusammenbringen ▷ *vi* zusammenpassen; **to be no ~ for** sich nicht messen können mit; **with shoes to ~** mit (dazu) passenden Schuhen

▶ **match up** *vi* zusammenpassen

matchbox ['mætʃbɔks] *n* Streichholzschachtel *f*

matching ['mætʃɪŋ] *adj* (dazu) passend

matchless ['mætʃlɪs] *adj* unvergleichlich

mate [meɪt] *n* (*inf: friend*) Freund(in) *m(f)*, Kumpel *m*; (*animal*) Männchen *nt*, Weibchen *nt*; (*assistant*) Gehilfe *m*, Gehilfin *f*; (*in merchant navy*) Maat *m* ▷ *vi* (*animals*) sich paaren

material [mə'tɪərɪəl] *n* Material *nt*; (*cloth*) Stoff *m* ▷ *adj* (*possessions, existence*) materiell; (*relevant*) wesentlich; **materials** *npl* (*equipment*) Material *nt*

materialistic [mətɪərɪə'lɪstɪk] *adj* materialistisch

materialize [mə'tɪərɪəlaɪz] *vi* (*event*) zustande kommen; (*plan*) verwirklicht werden; (*hope*) sich verwirklichen; (*problem*) auftreten; (*crisis, difficulty*) eintreten

maternal [mə'təːnl] *adj* mütterlich, Mutter-

maternity [mə'tə:nɪtɪ] *n* Mutterschaft *f* ▷ *cpd* (*ward etc*) Entbindungs-; (*care*) für werdende und junge Mütter
maternity benefit *n* Mutterschaftsgeld *nt*
maternity dress *n* Umstandskleid *nt*
maternity hospital *n* Entbindungsheim *nt*
maternity leave *n* Mutterschaftsurlaub *m*
matey ['meɪtɪ] (*Brit: inf*) *adj* kumpelhaft
math [mæθ] (*US*) *n* = **maths**
mathematical [mæθə'mætɪkl] *adj* mathematisch
mathematician [mæθəmə'tɪʃən] *n* Mathematiker(in) *m(f)*
mathematics [mæθə'mætɪks] *n* Mathematik *f*
maths [mæθs], (*US*) **math** [mæθ] *n* Mathe *f*
matinée ['mætɪneɪ] *n* Nachmittagsvorstellung *f*
mating ['meɪtɪŋ] *n* Paarung *f*
mating call *n* Lockruf *m*
mating season *n* Paarungszeit *f*
matriarchal [meɪtrɪ'ɑ:kl] *adj* matriarchalisch
matrices ['meɪtrɪsi:z] *npl of* **matrix**
matriculation [mətrɪkju'leɪʃən] *n* Immatrikulation *f*
matrimonial [mætrɪ'məunɪəl] *adj* Ehe-
matrimony ['mætrɪmənɪ] *n* Ehe *f*
matrix ['meɪtrɪks] (*pl* **matrices**) *n* (*Math*) Matrix *f*; (*framework*) Gefüge *nt*
matron ['meɪtrən] *n* (*in hospital*) Oberschwester *f*; (*in school*) Schwester *f*
matronly ['meɪtrənlɪ] *adj* matronenhaft
matt [mæt] *adj* matt; (*paint*) Matt-
matted ['mætɪd] *adj* verfilzt
matter ['mætə^r] *n* (*event, situation*) Sache *f*, Angelegenheit *f*; (*Phys*) Materie *f*; (*substance, material*) Stoff *m*; (*Med: pus*) Eiter *m* ▷ *vi* (*be important*) wichtig sein; **matters** *npl* (*affairs*) Angelegenheiten *pl*, Dinge *pl*; (*situation*) Lage *f*; **what's the ~?** was ist los?; **no ~ what** egal was (passiert); **that's another ~** das ist etwas anderes; **as a ~ of course** selbstverständlich; **as a ~ of fact** eigentlich; **it's a ~ of habit** es ist eine Gewohnheitssache; **vegetable ~** pflanzliche Stoffe *pl*; **printed ~** Drucksachen *pl*; **reading ~** (*Brit*) Lesestoff *m*; **it doesn't ~** es macht nichts
matter-of-fact ['mætərəv'fækt] *adj* sachlich
matting ['mætɪŋ] *n* Matten *pl*; **rush ~** Binsenmatten *pl*
mattress ['mætrɪs] *n* Matratze *f*
mature [mə'tjuə^r] *adj* reif; (*wine*) ausgereift ▷ *vi* reifen; (*Comm*) fällig werden
mature student *n* älterer Student *m*, ältere Studentin *f*
maturity [mə'tjuərɪtɪ] *n* Reife *f*; **to have reached ~** (*person*) erwachsen sein; (*animal*) ausgewachsen sein
maudlin ['mɔ:dlɪn] *adj* gefühlsselig
maul [mɔ:l] *vt* (anfallen und) übel zurichten
Mauritania [mɔ:rɪ'teɪnɪə] *n* Mauritanien *nt*
Mauritius [mə'rɪʃəs] *n* Mauritius *nt*
mausoleum [mɔ:sə'lɪəm] *n* Mausoleum *nt*
mauve [məuv] *adj* mauve
maverick ['mævrɪk] *n* (*dissenter*) Abtrünnige(r) *m*; (*independent thinker*) Querdenker *m*
mawkish ['mɔ:kɪʃ] *adj* rührselig
max. *abbr* = **maximum**
maxim ['mæksɪm] *n* Maxime *f*
maxima ['mæksɪmə] *npl of* **maximum**
maximize ['mæksɪmaɪz] *vt* maximieren
maximum ['mæksɪməm] (*pl* **maxima** *or* **~s**) *adj* (*amount, speed etc*) Höchst-; (*efficiency*) maximal ▷ *n* Maximum *nt*
May [meɪ] *n* Mai *m*; *see also* **July**
may [meɪ] (*conditional* **might**) *vi* (*be possible*) können; (*have permission*) dürfen; **he ~ come** vielleicht kommt er; **~ I smoke?** darf ich rauchen?; **~ God bless you!** (*wish*) Gott segne dich!; **~ I sit here?** kann ich mich hier hinsetzen?; **he might be there** er könnte da sein; **you might like to try** vielleicht möchten Sie es mal versuchen; **you ~ as well go** Sie können ruhig gehen
maybe ['meɪbi:] *adv* vielleicht; **~ he'll ...** es kann sein, dass er ...; **~ not** vielleicht nicht
Mayday ['meɪdeɪ] *n* Maydaysignal *nt*, ≈ SOS-Ruf *m*
May Day *n* der 1. Mai
mayhem ['meɪhɛm] *n* Chaos *nt*
mayonnaise [meɪə'neɪz] *n* Mayonnaise *f*
mayor [mɛə^r] *n* Bürgermeister *m*
mayoress ['mɛərɛs] *n* Bürgermeisterin *f*; (*partner*) Frau *f* des Bürgermeisters
maypole ['meɪpəul] *n* Maibaum *m*
maze [meɪz] *n* Irrgarten *m*; (*fig*) Wirrwarr *m*
MB *abbr* (*Comput*: = *megabyte*) MB; (*Canada*) = *Manitoba*
MBA *n abbr* (= *Master of Business Administration*) *akademischer Grad in Betriebswirtschaft*
MBE (*Brit*) *n abbr* (= *Member of (the Order of) the British Empire*) *britischer Ordenstitel*
MC *n abbr* = **Master of Ceremonies**
MCAT (*US*) *n abbr* (= *Medical College Admissions Test*) *Zulassungsprüfung für medizinische Fachschulen*
m-commerce ['ɛm'kɔmə:s] *n* (*Comm*) M-Commerce *m*, mobiler Handel *m*
MD *n abbr* (= *Doctor of Medicine*) ≈ Dr. med.; (*Comm*) = **managing director** ▷ *abbr* (*US: Post*) = *Maryland*
MDT (*US*) *abbr* (= *Mountain Daylight Time*) *amerikanische Sommerzeitzone*
ME *n abbr* (*US*) = **medical examiner**; (*Med*: = *myalgic encephalomyelitis*) *krankhafter Energiemangel (oft nach Viruserkrankungen)* ▷ *abbr* (*US: Post*) = *Maine*

KEYWORD

me [mi:] *pron* **1** (*direct*) mich; **can you hear me?** können Sie mich hören?; **it's me** ich bins
2 (*indirect*) mir; **he gave me the money, he gave the money to me** er gab mir das Geld
3 (*after prep*): **it's for me** es ist für mich; **with me** mit mir; **give them to me** gib sie mir; **without me** ohne mich

meadow ['mɛdəu] *n* Wiese *f*
meagre, (*US*) **meager** ['mi:gəʳ] *adj* (*amount*) kläglich; (*meal*) dürftig
meal [mi:l] *n* Mahlzeit *f*; (*food*) Essen *nt*; (*flour*) Schrotmehl *nt*; **to go out for a ~** essen gehen; **to make a ~ of sth** (*fig*) etw auf sehr umständliche Art machen
meals on wheels *n sing* Essen *nt* auf Rädern
mealtime ['mi:ltaɪm] *n* Essenszeit *f*
mealy-mouthed ['mi:lɪmauðd] *adj* unaufrichtig; (*politician*) schönfärberisch
mean [mi:n] (*pt, pp* **~t**) *adj* (*with money*) geizig; (*unkind*) gemein; (*US: inf: animal*) bösartig; (*shabby*) schäbig; (*average*) Durchschnitts-, mittlere(r, s) ▷ *vt* (*signify*) bedeuten; (*refer to*) meinen; (*intend*) beabsichtigen ▷ *n* (*average*) Durchschnitt *m*; **means** *npl* (*way*) Möglichkeit *f*; (*money*) Mittel *pl*; **by ~s of** durch; **by all ~s!** aber natürlich *or* selbstverständlich!; **do you ~ it?** meinst du das ernst?; **what do you ~?** was willst du damit sagen?; **to be ~t for sb/sth** für jdn/etw bestimmt sein; **to ~ to do sth** etw tun wollen
meander [mɪ'ændəʳ] *vi* (*river*) sich schlängeln; (*person: walking*) schlendern; (*: talking*) abschweifen
meaning ['mi:nɪŋ] *n* Sinn *m*; (*of word, gesture*) Bedeutung *f*
meaningful ['mi:nɪŋful] *adj* sinnvoll; (*glance, remark*) vielsagend, bedeutsam; (*relationship*) tiefer gehend
meaningless ['mi:nɪŋlɪs] *adj* sinnlos; (*word, song*) bedeutungslos
meanness ['mi:nnɪs] *n* (*with money*) Geiz *m*; (*unkindness*) Gemeinheit *f*; (*shabbiness*) Schäbigkeit *f*
means test [mi:nz-] *n* Überprüfung *f* der Einkommens- und Vermögensverhältnisse
means-tested ['mi:nztɛstɪd] *adj* von den Einkommens- und Vermögensverhältnissen abhängig
meant [mɛnt] *pt, pp of* **mean**
meantime ['mi:ntaɪm] *adv* (*also*: **in the meantime**) inzwischen
meanwhile ['mi:nwaɪl] *adv* = **meantime**
measles ['mi:zlz] *n* Masern *pl*
measly ['mi:zlɪ] (*inf*) *adj* mick(e)rig
measurable ['mɛʒərəbl] *adj* messbar
measure ['mɛʒəʳ] *vt, vi* messen ▷ *n* (*amount*) Menge *f*; (*ruler*) Messstab *m*; (*of achievement*) Maßstab *m*; (*action*) Maßnahme *f*; **a litre ~** ein Messbecher *m*, der einen Liter fasst; **a/some ~ of** ein gewisses Maß an *+dat*; **to take ~s to do sth** Maßnahmen ergreifen, um etw zu tun ▸ **measure up** *vi*: **to ~ up to** herankommen an *+acc*
measured ['mɛʒəd] *adj* (*tone*) bedächtig; (*step*) gemessen
measurement ['mɛʒəmənt] *n* (*measure*) Maß *nt*; (*act*) Messung *f*; **chest/hip ~** Brust-/Hüftumfang *m*
measurements ['mɛʒəmənts] *npl* Maße *pl*; **to take sb's ~** bei jdm Maß nehmen
meat [mi:t] *n* Fleisch *nt*; **cold ~s** (*Brit*) Aufschnitt *m*; **crab ~** Krabbenfleisch *nt*
meatball ['mi:tbɔ:l] *n* Fleischkloß *m*
meat pie *n* Fleischpastete *f*
meaty ['mi:tɪ] *adj* (*meal, dish*) mit viel Fleisch; (*fig: satisfying: book etc*) gehaltvoll; (*: brawny: person*) kräftig (gebaut)
Mecca ['mɛkə] *n* (*Geog, fig*) Mekka *nt*
mechanic [mɪ'kænɪk] *n* Mechaniker(in) *m(f)*
mechanical [mɪ'kænɪkl] *adj* mechanisch
mechanical engineering *n* Maschinenbau *m*
mechanics [mɪ'kænɪks] *n* (*Phys*) Mechanik *f* ▷ *npl* (*of reading etc*) Technik *f*; (*of government etc*) Mechanismus *m*
mechanism ['mɛkənɪzəm] *n* Mechanismus *m*
mechanization [mɛkənaɪ'zeɪʃən] *n* Mechanisierung *f*
mechanize ['mɛkənaɪz] *vt, vi* mechanisieren
MEd *n abbr* (*= Master of Education*) *akademischer Grad für Lehrer*
medal ['mɛdl] *n* Medaille *f*; (*decoration*) Orden *m*
medallion [mɪ'dælɪən] *n* Medaillon *nt*
medallist, (*US*) **medalist** ['mɛdlɪst] *n* Medaillengewinner(in) *m(f)*
meddle ['mɛdl] *vi*: **to ~ (in)** sich einmischen (in *+acc*); **to ~ with sb** sich mit jdm einlassen; **to ~ with sth** (*tamper*) sich *dat* an etw *dat* zu schaffen machen
meddlesome ['mɛdlsəm], **meddling** ['mɛdlɪŋ] *adj* sich ständig einmischend
media ['mi:dɪə] *npl* Medien *pl*
media bashing (*inf*) *n* Medienschelte *f*
media circus *n* Medienrummel *m*
mediaeval [mɛdɪ'i:vl] *adj* = **medieval**
median ['mi:dɪən] (*US*) *n* (*also*: **median strip**) Mittelstreifen *m*
mediate ['mi:dɪeɪt] *vi* vermitteln
mediation [mi:dɪ'eɪʃən] *n* Vermittlung *f*
mediator ['mi:dɪeɪtəʳ] *n* Vermittler(in) *m(f)*
Medicaid ['mɛdɪkeɪd] (*US*) *n staatliche Krankenversicherung und Gesundheitsfürsorge für Einkommensschwache*
medical ['mɛdɪkl] *adj* (*care*) medizinisch; (*treatment*) ärztlich ▷ *n* (ärztliche) Untersuchung *f*
medical certificate *n* (*confirming health*) ärztliches Gesundheitszeugnis *nt*; (*confirming illness*) ärztliches Attest *nt*
medical examiner (*US*) *n* ≈ Gerichtsmediziner(in) *m(f)*; (*performing autopsy*) Leichenbeschauer *m*
medical student *n* Medizinstudent(in) *m(f)*
Medicare ['mɛdɪkɛəʳ] (*US*) *n staatliche Krankenversicherung und Gesundheitsfürsorge für ältere Bürger*
medicated ['mɛdɪkeɪtɪd] *adj* medizinisch
medication [mɛdɪ'keɪʃən] *n* Medikamente *pl*
medicinal [mɛ'dɪsɪnl] *adj* (*substance*) Heil-; (*qualities*) heilend; (*purposes*) medizinisch
medicine ['mɛdsɪn] *n* Medizin *f*; (*drug*) Arznei *f*
medicine ball *n* Medizinball *m*
medicine chest *n* Hausapotheke *f*
medicine man *n* Medizinmann *m*

medieval [mɛdɪ'i:vl] *adj* mittelalterlich
mediocre [mi:dɪ'əukə^r] *adj* mittelmäßig
mediocrity [mi:dɪ'ɔkrɪtɪ] *n* Mittelmäßigkeit *f*
meditate ['mɛdɪteɪt] *vi* nachdenken; *(Rel)* meditieren
meditation [mɛdɪ'teɪʃən] *n* Nachdenken *nt*; *(Rel)* Meditation *f*
Mediterranean [mɛdɪtə'reɪnɪən] *adj (country, climate etc)* Mittelmeer-; **the ~ (Sea)** das Mittelmeer
medium ['mi:dɪəm] *(pl* **media** *or* **~s***) adj* mittlere(r, s) ▷ *n (means)* Mittel *nt*; *(substance, material)* Medium *nt (pl* **~s***) (person)* Medium *nt*; **of ~ height** mittelgroß; **to strike a happy ~** den goldenen Mittelweg finden
medium-dry ['mi:dɪəm'draɪ] *adj (wine, sherry)* halbtrocken
medium-sized ['mi:dɪəm'saɪzd] *adj* mittelgroß
medium wave *n (Radio)* Mittelwelle *f*
medley ['mɛdlɪ] *n* Gemisch *nt*; *(Mus)* Medley *nt*
meek [mi:k] *adj* sanft(mütig), duldsam
meet [mi:t] *(pt, pp* **met***) vt (encounter)* treffen; *(by arrangement)* sich treffen mit; *(for the first time)* kennenlernen; *(go and fetch)* abholen; *(opponent)* treffen auf *+acc*; *(condition, standard)* erfüllen; *(need, expenses)* decken; *(problem)* stoßen auf *+acc*; *(challenge)* begegnen *+dat*; *(bill)* begleichen; *(join: line)* sich schneiden mit; *(: road etc)* treffen auf *+acc* ▷ *vi (encounter)* sich begegnen; *(by arrangement)* sich treffen; *(for the first time)* sich kennenlernen; *(for talks etc)* zusammenkommen; *(committee)* tagen; *(join: lines)* sich schneiden; *(: roads etc)* aufeinandertreffen ▷ *n (Brit: Hunting)* Jagd *f*; *(US: Sport)* Sportfest *nt*; **pleased to ~ you!** (sehr) angenehm!
▸ **meet up** *vi*: **to ~ up with sb** sich mit jdm treffen
▸ **meet with** *vt fus (difficulty, success)* haben
meeting ['mi:tɪŋ] *n (assembly, people assembling)* Versammlung *f*; *(Comm, of committee etc)* Sitzung *f*; *(also:* **business meeting***)* Besprechung *f*; *(encounter)* Begegnung *f*; *(: arranged)* Treffen *nt*; *(Pol)* Gespräch *nt*; *(Sport)* Veranstaltung *f*; **she's at** *or* **in a ~** *(Comm)* sie ist bei einer Besprechung; **to call a ~** eine Sitzung/Versammlung einberufen
meeting-place ['mi:tɪŋpleɪs] *n* Treffpunkt *m*
megabyte ['mɛgəbaɪt] *n* Megabyte *nt*
megalomaniac [mɛgələ'meɪnɪæk] *n* Größenwahnsinnige(r) *f(m)*
megaphone ['mɛgəfəun] *n* Megafon *nt*
megawatt ['mɛgəwɔt] *n* Megawatt *nt*
melancholy ['mɛlənkəlɪ] *n* Melancholie *f*, Schwermut *f* ▷ *adj* melancholisch, schwermütig
mellow ['mɛləu] *adj (sound)* voll, weich; *(light, colour, stone)* warm; *(weathered)* verwittert; *(person)* gesetzt; *(wine)* ausgereift ▷ *vi (person)* gesetzter werden
melodious [mɪ'ləudɪəs] *adj* melodisch
melodrama ['mɛləudrɑ:mə] *n* Melodrama *nt*
melodramatic [mɛlədrə'mætɪk] *adj* melodramatisch
melody ['mɛlədɪ] *n* Melodie *f*
melon ['mɛlən] *n* Melone *f*
melt [mɛlt] *vi (lit, fig)* schmelzen ▷ *vt* schmelzen; *(butter)* zerlassen
▸ **melt down** *vt* einschmelzen
meltdown ['mɛltdaun] *n (in nuclear reactor)* Kernschmelze *f*
melting point ['mɛltɪŋ-] *n* Schmelzpunkt *m*
melting pot *n (lit, fig)* Schmelztiegel *m*; **to be in the ~** in der Schwebe sein
member ['mɛmbə^r] *n* Mitglied *nt*; *(Anat)* Glied *nt* ▷ *cpd*: **~ country** Mitgliedsland *nt*; **~ state** Mitgliedsstaat *m*; **M~ of Parliament** *(Brit)* Abgeordnete(r) *f(m)* (des Unterhauses); **M~ of the European Parliament** *(Brit)* Abgeordnete(r) *f(m)* des Europaparlaments
membership ['mɛmbəʃɪp] *n* Mitgliedschaft *f*; *(members)* Mitglieder *pl*; *(number of members)* Mitgliederzahl *f*
membership card *n* Mitgliedsausweis *m*
membrane ['mɛmbreɪn] *n* Membran(e) *f*
memento [mə'mɛntəu] *n* Andenken *nt*
memo ['mɛməu] *n* Memo *nt*, Mitteilung *f*
memoir ['mɛmwɑ:^r] *n* Kurzbiografie *f*
memoirs ['mɛmwɑ:z] *npl* Memoiren *pl*
memo pad *n* Notizblock *m*
memorable ['mɛmərəbl] *adj* denkwürdig; *(unforgettable)* unvergesslich
memorandum [mɛmə'rændəm] *(pl* **memoranda***) n* Mitteilung *f*
memorial [mɪ'mɔ:rɪəl] *n* Denkmal *nt* ▷ *adj (service, prize)* Gedenk-
Memorial Day *(US) n* ≈ Volkstrauertag *m*; *siehe Info-Artikel*

MEMORIAL DAY

Memorial Day ist in den USA ein gesetzlicher Feiertag am letzten Montag im Mai zum Gedenken an die in allen Kriegen gefallenen amerikanischen Soldaten. Siehe auch *Remembrance Sunday*

memorize ['mɛməraɪz] *vt* sich *dat* einprägen
memory ['mɛmərɪ] *n* Gedächtnis *nt*; *(sth remembered)* Erinnerung *f*; *(Comput)* Speicher *m*; **in ~ of** zur Erinnerung an *+acc*; **to have a good/bad ~** ein gutes/schlechtes Gedächtnis haben; **loss of ~** Gedächtnisschwund *m*
memory stick *n (Comput)* Memorystick® *nt*
men [mɛn] *npl of* **man**
menace ['mɛnɪs] *n* Bedrohung *f*; *(nuisance)* (Land)plage *f* ▷ *vt* bedrohen; **a public ~** eine Gefahr für die Öffentlichkeit
menacing ['mɛnɪsɪŋ] *adj* drohend
mend [mɛnd] *vt* reparieren; *(darn)* flicken ▷ *n*: **to be on the ~** auf dem Wege der Besserung sein; **to ~ one's ways** sich bessern
mending ['mɛndɪŋ] *n* Reparaturen *pl*; *(clothes)* Flickarbeiten *pl*
menial ['mi:nɪəl] *(often pej) adj* niedrig, untergeordnet

meningitis [mɛnɪn'dʒaɪtɪs] *n* Hirnhautentzündung *f*
menopause ['mɛnəupɔːz] *n*: **the ~** die Wechseljahre *pl*
menservants ['mɛnsəːvənts] *npl of* **manservant**
men's room (*US*) *n* Herrentoilette *f*
menstrual ['mɛnstruəl] *adj* (*Biol: cycle etc*) Menstruations-; **~ period** Monatsblutung *f*
menstruate ['mɛnstrueɪt] *vi* die Menstruation haben
menstruation [mɛnstru'eɪʃən] *n* Menstruation *f*
menswear ['mɛnzwɛəʳ] *n* Herren(be)kleidung *f*
mental ['mɛntl] *adj* geistig; (*illness*) Geistes-; **~ arithmetic** Kopfrechnen *nt*
mental hospital *n* psychiatrische Klinik *f*
mentality [mɛn'tælɪtɪ] *n* Mentalität *f*
mentally ['mɛntlɪ] *adv*: **to be ~ handicapped** geistig behindert sein
menthol ['mɛnθɔl] *n* Menthol *nt*
mention ['mɛnʃən] *n* Erwähnung *f* ▷ *vt* erwähnen; **don't ~ it!** (bitte,) gern geschehen!; **not to ~ ...** von ... ganz zu schweigen
mentor ['mɛntɔːʳ] *n* Mentor *m*
menu ['mɛnjuː] *n* Menü *nt*; (*printed*) Speisekarte *f*
menu-driven ['mɛnjuːdrɪvn] *adj* (*Comput*) menügesteuert
MEP (*Brit*) *n abbr* (= *Member of the European Parliament*) Abgeordnete(r) *f(m)* des Europaparlaments
mercantile ['məːkəntaɪl] *adj* (*class, society*) Handel treibend; (*law*) Handels-
mercenary ['məːsɪnərɪ] *adj* (*person*) geldgierig ▷ *n* Söldner *m*
merchandise ['məːtʃəndaɪz] *n* Ware *f*
merchandiser ['məːtʃəndaɪzəʳ] *n* Verkaufsförderungsexperte *m*
merchant ['məːtʃənt] *n* Kaufmann *m*; **timber/wine ~** Holz-/Weinhändler *m*
merchant bank (*Brit*) *n* Handelsbank *f*
merchantman ['məːtʃəntmən] (*irreg: like* **man**) *n* Handelsschiff *nt*
merchant navy, (*US*) **merchant marine** *n* Handelsmarine *f*
merciful ['məːsɪful] *adj* gnädig; **a ~ release** eine Erlösung
mercifully ['məːsɪflɪ] *adv* glücklicherweise
merciless ['məːsɪlɪs] *adj* erbarmungslos
mercurial [məː'kjuərɪəl] *adj* (*unpredictable*) sprunghaft, wechselhaft; (*lively*) quecksilbrig
mercury ['məːkjurɪ] *n* Quecksilber *nt*
mercy ['məːsɪ] *n* Gnade *f*; **to have ~ on sb** Erbarmen mit jdm haben; **at the ~ of** ausgeliefert *+dat*
mercy killing *n* Euthanasie *f*
mere [mɪəʳ] *adj* bloß; **his ~ presence irritates her** schon *or* allein seine Anwesenheit ärgert sie; **she is a ~ child** sie ist noch ein Kind; **it's a ~ trifle** es ist eine Lappalie; **by ~ chance** rein durch Zufall
merely ['mɪəlɪ] *adv* lediglich, bloß
merge [məːdʒ] *vt* (*combine*) vereinen; (*Comput: files*) mischen ▷ *vi* (*Comm*) fusionieren; (*colours, sounds, shapes*) ineinander übergehen; (*roads*) zusammenlaufen
merger ['məːdʒəʳ] *n* (*Comm*) Fusion *f*
meridian [mə'rɪdɪən] *n* Meridian *m*
meringue [mə'ræŋ] *n* Baiser *nt*
merit ['mɛrɪt] *n* (*worth, value*) Wert *m*; (*advantage*) Vorzug *m*; (*achievement*) Verdienst *nt* ▷ *vt* verdienen
meritocracy [mɛrɪ'tɔkrəsɪ] *n* Leistungsgesellschaft *f*
mermaid ['məːmeɪd] *n* Seejungfrau *f*, Meerjungfrau *f*
merrily ['mɛrɪlɪ] *adv* vergnügt
merriment ['mɛrɪmənt] *n* Heiterkeit *f*
merry ['mɛrɪ] *adj* vergnügt; (*music*) fröhlich; **M~ Christmas!** fröhliche *or* frohe Weihnachten!
merry-go-round ['mɛrɪgəuraund] *n* Karussell *nt*
mesh [mɛʃ] *n* Geflecht *nt*; **wire ~** Maschendraht *m*
mesmerize ['mɛzməraɪz] *vt* (*fig*) faszinieren
mess [mɛs] *n* Durcheinander *nt*; (*dirt*) Dreck *m*; (*Mil*) Kasino *nt*; **to be in a ~** (*untidy*) unordentlich sein; (*in difficulty*) in Schwierigkeiten stecken; **to be a ~** (*fig: life*) verkorkst sein; **to get o.s. in a ~** in Schwierigkeiten geraten
▸ **mess about** (*inf*) *vi* (*fool around*) herumalbern
▸ **mess about with** (*inf*) *vt fus* (*play around with*) herumfummeln an *+dat*
▸ **mess around** (*inf*) *vi* = **mess about**
▸ **mess around with** (*inf*) *vt fus* = **mess about with**
▸ **mess up** *vt* durcheinanderbringen; (*dirty*) verdrecken
message ['mɛsɪdʒ] *n* Mitteilung *f*, Nachricht *f*; (*meaning*) Aussage *f*; **to get the ~** (*inf: fig*) kapieren
message switching [-'swɪtʃɪŋ] *n* (*Comput*) Speichervermittlung *f*
messenger ['mɛsɪndʒəʳ] *n* Bote *m*
Messiah [mɪ'saɪə] *n* Messias *m*
Messrs ['mɛsəz] *abbr* (*on letters:* = *messieurs*) An (die Herren)
messy ['mɛsɪ] *adj* (*dirty*) dreckig; (*untidy*) unordentlich
Met [mɛt] (*US*) *n abbr* (= *Metropolitan Opera*) Met *f*
met [mɛt] *pt, pp of* **meet**
met. *adj abbr* (= *meteorological*): **the M~ Office** das Wetteramt
metabolism [mɛ'tæbəlɪzəm] *n* Stoffwechsel *m*
metal ['mɛtl] *n* Metall *nt*
metal fatigue *n* Metallermüdung *f*
metalled ['mɛtld] *adj* (*road*) asphaltiert
metallic [mɪ'tælɪk] *adj* metallisch; (*made of metal*) aus Metall
metallurgy [mɛ'tælədʒɪ] *n* Metallurgie *f*
metalwork ['mɛtlwəːk] *n* Metallarbeit *f*
metamorphosis [mɛtə'mɔːfəsɪs] (*pl*

metamorphoses) *n* Verwandlung *f*
metaphor ['mɛtəfəʳ] *n* Metapher *f*
metaphorical [mɛtə'fɔrɪkl] *adj* metaphorisch
metaphysics [mɛtə'fɪzɪks] *n* Metaphysik *f*
meteor ['mi:tɪəʳ] *n* Meteor *m*
meteoric [mi:tɪ'ɔrɪk] *adj (fig)* kometenhaft
meteorite ['mi:tɪəraɪt] *n* Meteorit *m*
meteorological [mi:tɪərə'lɔdʒɪkl] *adj (conditions, office etc)* Wetter-
meteorology [mi:tɪə'rɔlədʒɪ] *n* Wetterkunde *f*, Meteorologie *f*
mete out [mi:t-] *vt* austeilen; **to ~ justice** Recht sprechen
meter ['mi:təʳ] *n* Zähler *m*; *(also:* **water meter**) Wasseruhr *f*; *(also:* **parking meter**) Parkuhr *f*; *(US: unit)* = **metre**
methane ['mi:θeɪn] *n* Methan *nt*
method ['mɛθəd] *n* Methode *f*; **~ of payment** Zahlungsweise *f*
methodical [mɪ'θɔdɪkl] *adj* methodisch
Methodist ['mɛθədɪst] *n* Methodist(in) *m(f)*
methodology [mɛθə'dɔlədʒɪ] *n* Methodik *f*
meths [mɛθs] *(Brit) n* = **methylated spirit**
methylated spirit ['mɛθɪleɪtɪd-] *(Brit) n* (Brenn)spiritus *m*
meticulous [mɪ'tɪkjuləs] *adj* sorgfältig; *(detail)* genau
metre, (US) **meter** ['mi:təʳ] *n* Meter *m or nt*
metric ['mɛtrɪk] *adj* metrisch; **to go ~** auf das metrische Maßsystem umstellen
metrical ['mɛtrɪkl] *adj* metrisch
metrication [mɛtrɪ'keɪʃən] *n* Umstellung *f* auf das metrische Maßsystem
metric system *n* metrisches Maßsystem *nt*
metric ton *n* Metertonne *f*
metronome ['mɛtrənəum] *n* Metronom *nt*
metropolis [mɪ'trɔpəlɪs] *n* Metropole *f*
metropolitan [mɛtrə'pɔlɪtn] *adj* großstädtisch
Metropolitan Police *(Brit) n*: **the ~** die Londoner Polizei
mettle ['mɛtl] *n*: **to be on one's ~** auf dem Posten sein
mew [mju:] *vi* miauen
mews [mju:z] *(Brit) n* Gasse *f* mit ehemaligen Kutscherhäuschen
Mexican ['mɛksɪkən] *adj* mexikanisch ▷ *n* Mexikaner(in) *m(f)*
Mexico ['mɛksɪkəu] *n* Mexiko *nt*
Mexico City *n* Mexico City *f*
mezzanine ['mɛtsəni:n] *n* Mezzanin *nt*
MFA *(US) n abbr (= Master of Fine Arts) akademischer Grad in Kunst*
mfr *abbr* = **manufacture; manufacturer**
mg *abbr (= milligram(me))* mg
Mgr *abbr (= Monseigneur, Monsignor)* Mgr.; *(Comm)* = **manager**
MHR *(US, Australia) n abbr (= Member of the House of Representatives)* Abgeordnete(r) *f(m)* des Repräsentantenhauses
MHz *abbr (= megahertz)* MHz
MI *(US) abbr (Post) = Michigan*
MI5 *(Brit) n abbr (= Military Intelligence, section five) britischer Spionageabwehrdienst*
MI6 *(Brit) n abbr (= Military Intelligence, section six) britischer Geheimdienst*
MIA *abbr (Mil: = missing in action)* vermisst
miaow [mi:'au] *vi* miauen
mice [maɪs] *npl of* **mouse**
Mich. *(US) abbr (Post) = Michigan*
micro ['maɪkrəu] *n* = **microcomputer**
micro ... ['maɪkrəu] *pref* mikro-, Mikro-
microbe ['maɪkrəub] *n* Mikrobe *f*
microbiology [maɪkrəubaɪ'ɔlədʒɪ] *n* Mikrobiologie *f*
microchip ['maɪkrəutʃɪp] *n* Mikrochip *m*
microcomputer ['maɪkrəukəm'pju:təʳ] *n* Mikrocomputer *m*
microcosm ['maɪkrəukɔzəm] *n* Mikrokosmos *m*
microeconomics ['maɪkrəui:kə'nɔmɪks] *n* Mikroökonomie *f*
microelectronics ['maɪkrəuɪlɛk'trɔnɪks] *n* Mikroelektronik *f*
microfiche ['maɪkrəufi:ʃ] *n* Mikrofiche *m or nt*
microfilm ['maɪkrəufɪlm] *n* Mikrofilm *m*
microlight ['maɪkrəulaɪt] *n* Ultraleichtflugzeug *nt*
micrometer [maɪ'krɔmɪtəʳ] *n* Messschraube *f*
microphone ['maɪkrəfəun] *n* Mikrofon *nt*
microprocessor ['maɪkrəu'prəusɛsəʳ] *n* Mikroprozessor *m*
microscope ['maɪkrəskəup] *n* Mikroskop *nt*; **under the ~** unter dem Mikroskop
microscopic [maɪkrə'skɔpɪk] *adj* mikroskopisch; *(creature)* mikroskopisch klein
microwave ['maɪkrəuweɪv] *n* Mikrowelle *f*; *(also:* **microwave oven**) Mikrowellenherd *m*
mid [mɪd] *adj*: **in ~May** Mitte Mai; **in ~afternoon** (mitten) am Nachmittag; **in ~air** (mitten) in der Luft; **he's in his ~thirties** er ist Mitte dreißig
midday [mɪd'deɪ] *n* Mittag *m*
middle ['mɪdl] *n* Mitte *f* ▷ *adj* mittlere(r, s); **in the ~ of the night** mitten in der Nacht; **I'm in the ~ of reading it** ich bin mittendrin; **a ~ course** ein Mittelweg *m*
middle age *n* mittleres Lebensalter *nt*
middle-aged [mɪdl'eɪdʒd] *adj* mittleren Alters
Middle Ages *npl* Mittelalter *nt*
middle-class [mɪdl'klɑ:s] *adj* mittelständisch
middle class(es) *n(pl)* Mittelstand *m*
Middle East *n* Naher Osten *m*
middleman ['mɪdlmæn] *(irreg: like* **man**) *n* Zwischenhändler *m*
middle management *n* mittleres Management *nt*
middle name *n* zweiter Vorname *m*
middle-of-the-road ['mɪdləvðə'rəud] *adj* gemäßigt; *(politician)* der Mitte; *(Mus)* leicht
middleweight ['mɪdlweɪt] *n (Boxing)* Mittelgewicht *nt*
middling ['mɪdlɪŋ] *adj* mittelmäßig
Middx *(Brit) abbr (Post) = Middlesex*
midge [mɪdʒ] *n* Mücke *f*
midget ['mɪdʒɪt] *n* Liliputaner(in) *m(f)*
midi system ['mɪdɪ-] *n* Midi-System *nt*

Midlands ['mɪdləndz] (*Brit*) *npl*: **the ~** Mittelengland *nt*
midnight ['mɪdnaɪt] *n* Mitternacht *f* ▷ *cpd* Mitternachts-; **at ~** um Mitternacht
midriff ['mɪdrɪf] *n* Taille *f*
midst [mɪdst] *n*: **in the ~ of** mitten in +*dat*; **to be in the ~ of doing sth** mitten dabei sein, etw zu tun
midsummer [mɪd'sʌmər] *n* Hochsommer *m*; **M~('s) Day** Sommersonnenwende *f*
midway [mɪd'weɪ] *adj*: **we have reached the ~ point** wir haben die Hälfte hinter uns *dat* ▷ *adv* auf halbem Weg; **~ between** (*in space*) auf halbem Weg zwischen; **~ through** (*in time*) mitten in +*dat*
midweek [mɪd'wi:k] *adv* mitten in der Woche ▷ *adj* Mitte der Woche
midwife ['mɪdwaɪf] (*pl* **midwives**) *n* Hebamme *f*
midwifery ['mɪdwɪfərɪ] *n* Geburtshilfe *f*
midwinter [mɪd'wɪntər] *n*: **in ~** im tiefsten Winter
miffed [mɪft] (*inf*) *adj*: **to be ~** eingeschnappt sein
might [maɪt] *vb see* **may** ▷ *n* Macht *f*; **with all one's ~** mit aller Kraft
mighty ['maɪtɪ] *adj* mächtig
migraine ['mi:greɪn] *n* Migräne *f*
migrant ['maɪgrənt] *adj* (*bird*) Zug-; (*worker*) Wander- ▷ *n* (*bird*) Zugvogel *m*; (*worker*) Wanderarbeiter(in) *m(f)*
migrate [maɪ'greɪt] *vi* (*bird*) ziehen; (*person*) abwandern
migration [maɪ'greɪʃən] *n* Wanderung *f*; (*to cities*) Abwanderung *f*; (*of birds*) (Vogel)zug *m*
mike [maɪk] *n* = **microphone**
Milan [mɪ'læn] *n* Mailand *nt*
mild [maɪld] *adj* mild; (*gentle*) sanft; (*slight: infection etc*) leicht; (*: interest*) gering
mildew ['mɪldju:] *n* Schimmel *m*
mildly ['maɪldlɪ] *adv* (*say*) sanft; (*slight*) leicht; **to put it ~** gelinde gesagt
mildness ['maɪldnɪs] *n* Milde *f*; (*gentleness*) Sanftheit *f*; (*of infection etc*) Leichtigkeit *f*
mile [maɪl] *n* Meile *f*; **to do 30 ~s per gallon** ≈ 9 Liter auf 100 km verbrauchen
mileage ['maɪlɪdʒ] *n* Meilenzahl *f*; (*fig*) Nutzen *m*; **to get a lot of ~ out of sth** etw gründlich ausnutzen; **there is a lot of ~ in the idea** aus der Idee lässt sich viel machen
mileage allowance *n* ≈ Kilometergeld *nt*
mileometer [maɪ'lɔmɪtər] *n* ≈ Kilometerzähler *m*
milestone ['maɪlstəun] *n* (*lit, fig*) Meilenstein *m*
milieu ['mi:ljə:] *n* Milieu *nt*
militant ['mɪlɪtnt] *adj* militant ▷ *n* Militante(r) *f(m)*
militarism ['mɪlɪtərɪzəm] *n* Militarismus *m*
militaristic [mɪlɪtə'rɪstɪk] *adj* militaristisch
military ['mɪlɪtərɪ] *adj* (*history, leader etc*) Militär- ▷ *n*: **the ~** das Militär
military police *n* Militärpolizei *f*
military service *n* Militärdienst *m*
militate ['mɪlɪteɪt] *vi*: **to ~ against** negative Auswirkungen haben auf +*acc*
militia [mɪ'lɪʃə] *n* Miliz *f*
milk [mɪlk] *n* Milch *f* ▷ *vt* (*lit, fig*) melken
milk chocolate *n* Vollmilchschokolade *f*
milk float (*Brit*) *n* Milchwagen *m*
milking ['mɪlkɪŋ] *n* Melken *nt*
milkman ['mɪlkmən] (*irreg: like* **man**) *n* Milchmann *m*
milk shake *n* Milchmixgetränk *nt*
milk tooth *n* Milchzahn *m*
milk truck (*US*) *n* = **milk float**
milky ['mɪlkɪ] *adj* milchig; (*drink*) mit viel Milch; **~ coffee** Milchkaffee *m*
Milky Way *n* Milchstraße *f*
mill [mɪl] *n* Mühle *f*; (*factory*) Fabrik *f*; (*woollen mill*) Spinnerei *f* ▷ *vt* mahlen ▷ *vi* (*also:* **mill about**) umherlaufen
millennium [mɪ'lɛnɪəm] (*pl* **~s** *or* **millennia**) *n* Jahrtausend *nt*
millennium bug *n* (*Comput*) Jahrtausendfehler *m*
miller ['mɪlər] *n* Müller *m*
millet ['mɪlɪt] *n* Hirse *f*
milli... ['mɪlɪ] *pref* Milli-
milligram, milligramme ['mɪlɪgræm] *n* Milligramm *nt*
millilitre, (*US*) **milliliter** ['mɪlɪli:tər] *n* Milliliter *m or nt*
millimetre, (*US*) **millimeter** ['mɪlɪmi:tər] *n* Millimeter *m or nt*
millinery ['mɪlɪnərɪ] *n* Hüte *pl*
million ['mɪljən] *n* Million *f*; **a ~ times** (*fig*) tausend Mal, x-mal
millionaire [mɪljə'nɛər] *n* Millionär *m*
millipede ['mɪlɪpi:d] *n* Tausendfüßler *m*
millstone ['mɪlstəun] *n* (*fig*): **it's a ~ round his neck** es ist für ihn ein Klotz am Bein
millwheel ['mɪlwi:l] *n* Mühlrad *nt*
milometer [maɪ'lɔmɪtər] *n* = **mileometer**
mime [maɪm] *n* Pantomime *f*; (*actor*) Pantomime *m* ▷ *vt* pantomimisch darstellen
mimic ['mɪmɪk] *n* Imitator *m* ▷ *vt* (*for amusement*) parodieren; (*animal, person*) imitieren, nachahmen
mimicry ['mɪmɪkrɪ] *n* Nachahmung *f*
Min. (*Brit*) *abbr* (*Pol*) = **ministry**
min. *abbr* (= *minute*) Min. = **minimum**
minaret [mɪnə'rɛt] *n* Minarett *nt*
mince [mɪns] *vt* (*meat*) durch den Fleischwolf drehen ▷ *vi* (*in walking*) trippeln ▷ *n* (*Brit: meat*) Hackfleisch *nt*; **he does not ~ (his) words** er nimmt kein Blatt vor den Mund
mincemeat ['mɪnsmi:t] *n süße Gebäckfüllung aus Dörrobst und Sirup*; (*US: meat*) Hackfleisch *nt*; **to make ~ of sb** (*inf*) Hackfleisch aus jdm machen
mince pie *n mit Mincemeat gefülltes Gebäck*
mincer ['mɪnsər] *n* Fleischwolf *m*
mincing ['mɪnsɪŋ] *adj* (*walk*) trippelnd; (*voice*) geziert
mind [maɪnd] *n* Geist *m*, Verstand *m*; (*thoughts*) Gedanken *pl*; (*memory*) Gedächtnis *nt* ▷ *vt*

aufpassen auf *+acc*; (*office etc*) nach dem Rechten sehen in *+dat*; (*object to*) etwas haben gegen; **to my ~** meiner Meinung nach; **to be out of one's ~** verrückt sein; **it is on my ~** es beschäftigt mich; **to keep** *or* **bear sth in ~** etw nicht vergessen, an etw denken; **to make up one's ~** sich entscheiden; **to change one's ~** es sich *dat* anders überlegen; **to be in two ~s about sth** sich *dat* über etw *acc* nicht im Klaren sein; **to have it in ~ to do sth** die Absicht haben, etw zu tun; **to have sb/sth in ~** an jdn/etw denken; **it slipped my ~** ich habe es vergessen; **to bring** *or* **call sth to ~** etw in Erinnerung rufen; **I can't get it out of my ~** es geht mir nicht aus dem Kopf; **his ~ was on other things** er war mit den Gedanken woanders; **"~ the step"** „Vorsicht Stufe"; **do you ~ if ...?** macht es Ihnen etwas aus, wenn ...?; **I don't ~** es ist mir egal; **~ you, ...** allerdings ...; **never ~!** (*it makes no odds*) ist doch egal!; (*don't worry*) macht nichts!

mind-boggling ['maındbɔglıŋ] (*inf*) *adj* atemberaubend

-minded ['maındıd] *adj*: **fair~** gerecht; **an industrially~ nation** ein auf Industrie ausgerichtetes Land

minder ['maındə^r] *n* Betreuer(in) *m(f)*; (*inf: bodyguard*) Aufpasser(in) *m(f)*

mindful ['maındful] *adj*: **~ of** unter Berücksichtigung *+gen*

mindless ['maındlıs] *adj* (*violence*) sinnlos; (*work*) geistlos

mine¹ [maın] *n* (*also*: **coal mine, gold mine**) Bergwerk *nt*; (*bomb*) Mine *f* ▷ *vt* (*coal*) abbauen; (*beach etc*) verminen; (*ship*) eine Mine befestigen an *+dat*

mine² [maın] *pron* meine(r, s); **that book is ~** das Buch ist mein(e)s, das Buch gehört mir; **this is ~** das ist meins; **a friend of ~** ein Freund/eine Freundin von mir

mine detector *n* Minensuchgerät *nt*

minefield ['maınfi:ld] *n* Minenfeld *nt*; (*fig*) brisante Situation *f*

miner ['maınə^r] *n* Bergmann *m*, Bergarbeiter *m*

mineral ['mınərəl] *adj* (*deposit, resources*) Mineral- ▷ *n* Mineral *nt*; **minerals** *npl* (*Brit: soft drinks*) Erfrischungsgetränke *pl*

mineralogy [mınə'rælədʒı] *n* Mineralogie *f*

mineral water *n* Mineralwasser *nt*

minesweeper ['maınswi:pə^r] *n* Minensuchboot *nt*

mingle ['mıŋgl] *vi*: **to ~ (with)** sich vermischen (mit); **to ~ with** (*people*) Umgang haben mit; (*at party etc*) sich unterhalten mit; **you should ~ a bit** du solltest dich unter die Leute mischen

mingy ['mındʒı] (*inf*) *adj* knick(e)rig; (*amount*) mick(e)rig

mini... ['mını] *pref* Mini-

miniature ['mınətʃə^r] *adj* winzig; (*version etc*) Miniatur- ▷ *n* Miniatur *f*; **in ~** im Kleinen, im Kleinformat

minibus ['mınıbʌs] *n* Kleinbus *m*

minicab ['mınıkæb] *n* Kleintaxi *nt*

minicomputer ['mınıkəm'pju:tə^r] *n* Minicomputer *m*

minim ['mınım] *n* (*Mus*) halbe Note *f*

minima ['mınımə] *npl of* **minimum**

minimal ['mınıml] *adj* minimal

minimalist ['mınıməlıst] *adj* minimalistisch

minimize ['mınımaız] *vt* auf ein Minimum reduzieren; (*play down*) herunterspielen

minimum ['mınıməm] (*pl* **minima**) *n* Minimum *nt* ▷ *adj* (*income, speed*) Mindest-; **to reduce to a ~** auf ein Mindestmaß reduzieren; **~ wage** Mindestlohn *m*

minimum lending rate *n* Diskontsatz *m*

mining ['maınıŋ] *n* Bergbau *m* ▷ *cpd* Bergbau-

minion ['mınjən] (*pej*) *n* Untergebene(r) *f(m)*

miniseries ['mınısıəri:z] *n* Miniserie *f*

miniskirt ['mınıskə:t] *n* Minirock *m*

minister ['mınıstə^r] *n* (*Brit: Pol*) Minister(in) *m(f)*; (*Rel*) Pfarrer *m* ▷ *vi*: **to ~ to** sich kümmern um; (*needs*) befriedigen

ministerial [mınıs'tıərıəl] (*Brit*) *adj* (*Pol*) ministeriell

ministry ['mınıstrı] *n* (*Brit: Pol*) Ministerium *nt*; **to join the ~** (*Rel*) Geistliche(r) werden

Ministry of Defence (*Brit*) *n* Verteidigungsministerium *nt*

mink [mıŋk] (*pl* **minks** *or* **~**) *n* Nerz *m*

mink coat *n* Nerzmantel *m*

Minn. (*US*) *abbr* (*Post*) = *Minnesota*

minnow ['mınəu] *n* Elritze *f*

minor ['maınə^r] *adj* kleinere(r, s); (*poet*) unbedeutend; (*planet*) klein; (*Mus*) Moll ▷ *n* Minderjährige(r) *f(m)*

Minorca [mı'nɔ:kə] *n* Menorca *nt*

minority [maı'nɔrıtı] *n* Minderheit *f*; **to be in a ~** in der Minderheit sein

minster ['mınstə^r] *n* Münster *nt*

minstrel ['mınstrəl] *n* Spielmann *m*

mint [mınt] *n* Minze *f*; (*sweet*) Pfefferminz(bonbon) *nt*; (*place*): **the M~** die Münzanstalt ▷ *vt* (*coins*) prägen; **in ~ condition** neuwertig

mint sauce *n* Minzsoße *f*

minuet [mınju'ɛt] *n* Menuett *nt*

minus ['maınəs] *n* (*also*: **minus sign**) Minuszeichen *nt* ▷ *prep* minus, weniger; **~ 24°C** 24 Grad unter null

minuscule ['mınəskju:l] *adj* winzig

minute¹ [maı'nju:t] *adj* winzig; (*search*) peinlich genau; (*detail*) kleinste(r, s); **in ~ detail** in allen Einzelheiten

minute² ['mınıt] *n* Minute *f*; (*fig*) Augenblick *m*, Moment *m*; **minutes** *npl* (*of meeting*) Protokoll *nt*; **it is 5 ~s past 3** es ist 5 Minuten nach 3; **wait a ~!** einen Augenblick *or* Moment!; **up-to-the-~** (*news*) hochaktuell; (*technology*) allerneueste(r, s); **at the last ~** in letzter Minute

minute book *n* Protokollbuch *nt*

minute hand *n* Minutenzeiger *m*

minutely [maı'nju:tlı] *adv* (*in detail*) genauestens; (*by a small amount*) ganz

geringfügig
minutiae [mɪ'nju:ʃii:] *npl* Einzelheiten *pl*
miracle ['mɪrəkl] *n* (*Rel, fig*) Wunder *nt*
miraculous [mɪ'rækjuləs] *adj* wunderbar; (*powers, effect, cure*) Wunder-; (*success, change*) unglaublich; **to have a ~ escape** wie durch ein Wunder entkommen
mirage ['mɪrɑ:ʒ] *n* Fata Morgana *f*; (*fig*) Trugbild *nt*
mire ['maɪə^r] *n* Morast *m*
mirror ['mɪrə^r] *n* Spiegel *m* ▷ *vt* (*lit, fig*) widerspiegeln
mirror image *n* Spiegelbild *nt*
mirth [mə:θ] *n* Heiterkeit *f*
misadventure [mɪsəd'vɛntʃə^r] *n* Missgeschick *nt*; **death by ~** (*Brit*) Tod *m* durch Unfall
misanthropist [mɪ'zænθrəpɪst] *n* Misanthrop *m*, Menschenfeind *m*
misapply [mɪsə'plaɪ] *vt* (*term*) falsch verwenden; (*rule*) falsch anwenden
misapprehension ['mɪsæprɪ'hɛnʃən] *n* Missverständnis *nt*; **you are under a ~** Sie befinden sich im Irrtum
misappropriate [mɪsə'prəuprɪeɪt] *vt* veruntreuen
misappropriation ['mɪsəprəuprɪ'eɪʃən] *n* Veruntreuung *f*
misbehave [mɪsbɪ'heɪv] *vi* sich schlecht benehmen
misbehaviour, (*US*) **misbehavior** [mɪsbɪ'heɪvjə^r] *n* schlechtes Benehmen *nt*
misc. *abbr* = **miscellaneous**
miscalculate [mɪs'kælkjuleɪt] *vt* falsch berechnen; (*misjudge*) falsch einschätzen
miscalculation ['mɪskælkju'leɪʃən] *n* Rechenfehler *m*; (*misjudgement*) Fehleinschätzung *f*
miscarriage ['mɪskærɪdʒ] *n* (*Med*) Fehlgeburt *f*; **~ of justice** (*Law*) Justizirrtum *m*
miscarry [mɪs'kærɪ] *vi* (*Med*) eine Fehlgeburt haben; (*fail: plans*) fehlschlagen
miscellaneous [mɪsɪ'leɪnɪəs] *adj* verschieden; (*subjects, items*) divers; **~ expenses** sonstige Unkosten *pl*
mischance [mɪs'tʃɑ:ns] *n* unglücklicher Zufall *m*
mischief ['mɪstʃɪf] *n* (*bad behaviour*) Unfug *m*; (*playfulness*) Verschmitztheit *f*; (*harm*) Schaden *m*; (*pranks*) Streiche *pl*; **to get into ~** etwas anstellen; **to do sb a ~** jdm etwas antun
mischievous ['mɪstʃɪvəs] *adj* (*naughty*) ungezogen; (*playful*) verschmitzt
misconception ['mɪskən'sɛpʃən] *n* fälschliche Annahme *f*
misconduct [mɪs'kɔndʌkt] *n* Fehlverhalten *nt*; **professional ~** Berufsvergehen *nt*
misconstrue [mɪskən'stru:] *vt* missverstehen
miscount [mɪs'kaunt] *vt* falsch zählen ▷ *vi* sich verzählen
misdemeanour, (*US*) **misdemeanor** [mɪsdɪ'mi:nə^r] *n* Vergehen *nt*
misdirect [mɪsdɪ'rɛkt] *vt* (*person*) in die falsche Richtung schicken; (*talent*) vergeuden
miser ['maɪzə^r] *n* Geizhals *m*
miserable ['mɪzərəbl] *adj* (*unhappy*) unglücklich; (*wretched*) erbärmlich, elend; (*unpleasant: weather*) trostlos; (*: person*) gemein; (*contemptible: offer, donation*) armselig; (*: failure*) kläglich; **to feel ~** sich elend fühlen
miserably ['mɪzərəblɪ] *adv* (*fail*) kläglich; (*live*) elend; (*smile, speak*) unglücklich; (*small*) jämmerlich
miserly ['maɪzəlɪ] *adj* geizig; (*amount*) armselig
misery ['mɪzərɪ] *n* (*unhappiness*) Kummer *m*; (*wretchedness*) Elend *nt*; (*inf: person*) Miesepeter *m*
misfire [mɪs'faɪə^r] *vi* (*plan*) fehlschlagen; (*car engine*) fehlzünden
misfit ['mɪsfɪt] *n* Außenseiter(in) *m(f)*
misfortune [mɪs'fɔ:tʃən] *n* Pech *nt*, Unglück *nt*
misgiving [mɪs'gɪvɪŋ] *n* Bedenken *pl*; **to have ~s about sth** sich bei etw nicht wohlfühlen
misguided [mɪs'gaɪdɪd] *adj* töricht; (*opinion, view*) irrig; (*misplaced*) unangebracht
mishandle [mɪs'hændl] *vt* falsch handhaben
mishap ['mɪshæp] *n* Missgeschick *nt*
mishear [mɪs'hɪə^r] (*irreg: like* **hear**) *vt* falsch hören ▷ *vi* sich verhören
misheard [mɪs'hə:d] *pt, pp of* **mishear**
mishmash ['mɪʃmæʃ] (*inf*) *n* Mischmasch *m*
misinform [mɪsɪn'fɔ:m] *vt* falsch informieren
misinterpret [mɪsɪn'tə:prɪt] *vt* (*gesture, situation*) falsch auslegen; (*comment*) falsch auffassen
misinterpretation ['mɪsɪntə:prɪ'teɪʃən] *n* falsche Auslegung *f*
misjudge [mɪs'dʒʌdʒ] *vt* falsch einschätzen
mislay [mɪs'leɪ] (*irreg: like* **lay**) *vt* verlegen
mislead [mɪs'li:d] (*irreg: like* **lead**) *vt* irreführen
misleading [mɪs'li:dɪŋ] *adj* irreführend
misled [mɪs'lɛd] *pt, pp of* **mislead**
mismanage [mɪs'mænɪdʒ] *vt* (*business*) herunterwirtschaften; (*institution*) schlecht führen
mismanagement [mɪs'mænɪdʒmənt] *n* Misswirtschaft *f*
misnomer [mɪs'nəumə^r] *n* unzutreffende Bezeichnung *f*
misogynist [mɪ'sɔdʒɪnɪst] *n* Frauenfeind *m*
misplaced [mɪs'pleɪst] *adj* (*misguided*) unangebracht; (*wrongly positioned*) an der falschen Stelle
misprint ['mɪsprɪnt] *n* Druckfehler *m*
mispronounce [mɪsprə'nauns] *vt* falsch aussprechen
misquote ['mɪs'kwəut] *vt* falsch zitieren
misread [mɪs'ri:d] (*irreg: like* **read**) *vt* falsch lesen; (*misinterpret*) falsch verstehen
misrepresent [mɪsrɛprɪ'zɛnt] *vt* falsch darstellen; **he was ~ed** seine Worte wurden verfälscht wiedergegeben
Miss [mɪs] *n* Fräulein *nt*; **Dear ~ Smith** Liebe Frau Smith
miss [mɪs] *vt* (*train etc, chance, opportunity*) verpassen; (*target*) verfehlen; (*notice loss of, regret absence of*) vermissen; (*class, meeting*) fehlen bei ▷ *vi* danebentreffen; (*missile, object*) danebengehen ▷ *n* Fehltreffer *m*; **you can't ~**

it du kannst es nicht verfehlen; **the bus just ~ed the wall** der Bus wäre um ein Haar gegen die Mauer gefahren; **you're ~ing the point** das geht an der Sache vorbei
▸ **miss out** (*Brit*) *vt* auslassen
▸ **miss out on** *vt fus* (*party*) verpassen; (*fun*) zu kurz kommen bei

missal ['mɪsl] *n* Messbuch *nt*
misshapen [mɪs'ʃeɪpən] *adj* missgebildet
missile ['mɪsaɪl] *n* (*Mil*) Rakete *f*; (*object thrown*) (Wurf)geschoss *nt*, (Wurf)geschoß *nt* (*Österr*)
missile base *n* Raketenbasis *f*
missile launcher [-'lɔ:ntʃə^r] *n* Startrampe *f*
missing ['mɪsɪŋ] *adj* (*lost: person*) vermisst; (*: object*) verschwunden; (*absent, removed*) fehlend; **to be ~** fehlen; **to go ~** verschwinden; **~ person** Vermisste(r) *f(m)*
mission ['mɪʃən] *n* (*task*) Mission *f*, Auftrag *m*; (*representatives*) Gesandtschaft *f*; (*Mil*) Einsatz *m*; (*Rel*) Mission *f*; **on a ~ to ...** (*to place/people*) im Einsatz in *+dat*/bei ...
missionary ['mɪʃənrɪ] *n* Missionar(in) *m(f)*
missive ['mɪsɪv] (*form*) *n* Schreiben *nt*
misspell ['mɪs'spɛl] (*irreg: like* **spell**) *vt* falsch schreiben
misspent ['mɪs'spɛnt] *adj* (*youth*) vergeudet
mist [mɪst] *n* Nebel *m*; (*light*) Dunst *m* ▹ *vi* (*also:* **mist over**: *eyes*) sich verschleiern; (*Brit: also:* **mist over, mist up**: *windows*) beschlagen
mistake [mɪs'teɪk] (*irreg: like* **take**) *n* Fehler *m* ▹ *vt* sich irren in *+dat*; (*intentions*) falsch verstehen; **by ~** aus Versehen; **to make a ~** (*in writing, calculation*) sich vertun; **to make a ~ (about sb/sth)** sich (in jdm/etw) irren; **to ~ A for B** A mit B verwechseln
mistaken [mɪs'teɪkən] *pp of* **mistake** ▹ *adj* falsch; **to be ~** sich irren
mistaken identity *n* Verwechslung *f*
mistakenly [mɪs'teɪkənlɪ] *adv* irrtümlicherweise
mister ['mɪstə^r] (*inf*) *n* (*sir*) *not translated*; *see* **Mr**
mistletoe ['mɪsltəu] *n* Mistel *f*
mistook [mɪs'tuk] *pt of* **mistake**
mistranslation [mɪstræns'leɪʃən] *n* falsche Übersetzung *f*
mistreat [mɪs'tri:t] *vt* schlecht behandeln
mistress ['mɪstrɪs] *n* (*lover*) Geliebte *f*; (*of house, servant, situation*) Herrin *f*; (*Brit: teacher*) Lehrerin *f*
mistrust [mɪs'trʌst] *vt* misstrauen *+dat* ▹ *n*: **~ (of)** Misstrauen *nt* (gegenüber)
mistrustful [mɪs'trʌstful] *adj*: **~ (of)** misstrauisch (gegenüber)
misty ['mɪstɪ] *adj* (*day etc*) neblig; (*glasses, windows*) beschlagen
misty-eyed ['mɪstɪ'aɪd] *adj* mit verschleiertem Blick
misunderstand [mɪsʌndə'stænd] (*irreg: like* **understand**) *vt* missverstehen, falsch verstehen ▹ *vi* es falsch verstehen
misunderstanding ['mɪsʌndə'stændɪŋ] *n* Missverständnis *nt*; (*disagreement*) Meinungsverschiedenheit *f*
misunderstood [mɪsʌndə'stud] *pt, pp of* **misunderstand**
misuse [*n* mɪs'ju:s, *vt* mɪs'ju:z] *n* Missbrauch *m* ▹ *vt* missbrauchen; (*word*) falsch gebrauchen
MIT (*US*) *n abbr* (*= Massachusetts Institute of Technology*) *private technische Fachhochschule*
mite [maɪt] *n* (*small quantity*) bisschen *nt*; (*Brit: small child*) Würmchen *nt*
miter ['maɪtə^r] (*US*) *n* = **mitre**
mitigate ['mɪtɪgeɪt] *vt* mildern; **mitigating circumstances** mildernde Umstände *pl*
mitigation [mɪtɪ'geɪʃən] *n* Milderung *f*
mitre, (*US*) **miter** ['maɪtə^r] *n* (*of bishop*) Mitra *f*; (*Carpentry*) Gehrung *f*
mitt ['mɪt], **mitten** ['mɪtn] *n* Fausthandschuh *m*
mix [mɪks] *vt* mischen; (*drink*) mixen; (*sauce, cake*) zubereiten; (*ingredients*) verrühren ▹ *vi*: **to ~ (with)** verkehren (mit) ▹ *n* Mischung *f*; **to ~ sth with sth** etw mit etw vermischen; **to ~ business with pleasure** das Angenehme mit dem Nützlichen verbinden; **cake ~** Backmischung *f*
▸ **mix in** *vt* (*eggs etc*) unterrühren
▸ **mix up** *vt* (*people*) verwechseln; (*things*) durcheinanderbringen; **to be ~ed up in sth** in etw *acc* verwickelt sein

mixed [mɪkst] *adj* gemischt; **~ marriage** Mischehe *f*
mixed-ability ['mɪkstə'bɪlɪtɪ] *adj* (*group etc*) mit unterschiedlichen Fähigkeiten
mixed bag *n* (*of things, problems*) Sammelsurium *nt*; (*of people*) gemischter Haufen *m*
mixed blessing *n*: **it's a ~** das ist ein zweischneidiges Schwert
mixed doubles *npl* gemischtes Doppel *nt*
mixed economy *n* gemischte Wirtschaftsform *f*
mixed grill (*Brit*) *n* Grillteller *m*
mixed-up [mɪkst'ʌp] *adj* durcheinander
mixer ['mɪksə^r] *n* (*for food*) Mixer *m*; (*drink*) *Tonic etc zum Auffüllen von alkoholischen Mixgetränken*; **to be a good ~** (*sociable person*) kontaktfreudig sein
mixer tap *n* Mischbatterie *f*
mixture ['mɪkstʃə^r] *n* Mischung *f*; (*Culin*) Gemisch *nt*; (*: for cake*) Teig *m*; (*Med*) Mixtur *f*
mix-up ['mɪksʌp] *n* Durcheinander *nt*
MK (*Brit*) *abbr* (*Tech*) = **mark**
mkt *abbr* = **market**
MLA (*Brit*) *n abbr* (*Pol: = Member of the Legislative Assembly (of Northern Ireland)*) Abgeordnete(r) *f(m)* der gesetzgebenden Versammlung
MLitt *n abbr* (*= Master of Literature, Master of Letters*) *akademischer Grad in Literaturwissenschaft*
MLR (*Brit*) *n abbr* = **minimum lending rate**
mm *abbr* (*= millimetre*) mm
MMS *n abbr* (*= Multimedia Messaging Service*) MMS® *m*
MN *abbr* (*Brit*) = **merchant navy**; (*US: Post*) = *Minnesota*
MO *n abbr* (*= medical officer*) Sanitätsoffizier *m*;

(*US: inf*) = **modus operandi**
moan [məun] *n* Stöhnen *nt* ▷ *vi* stöhnen; (*inf: complain*): **to ~ (about)** meckern (über +*acc*)
moaner ['məunə^r] (*inf*) *n* Miesmacher(in) *m(f)*
moat [məut] *n* Wassergraben *m*
mob [mɔb] *n* Mob *m*; (*organized*) Bande *f* ▷ *vt* herfallen über +*acc*
mobile ['məubaɪl] *adj* beweglich; (*workforce, society*) mobil ▷ *n* (*decoration*) Mobile *nt*; **applicants must be ~** Bewerber müssen motorisiert sein
mobile home *n* Wohnwagen *m*
mobile (phone) *n* Funktelefon *nt*, Handy *nt*
mobility [məu'bɪlɪtɪ] *n* Beweglichkeit *f*; (*of workforce etc*) Mobilität *f*
mobility allowance *n Beihilfe für Gehbehinderte*
mobilize ['məubɪlaɪz] *vt* mobilisieren; (*Mil*) mobil machen ▷ *vi* (*Mil*) mobil machen
moccasin ['mɔkəsɪn] *n* Mokassin *m*
mock [mɔk] *vt* sich lustig machen über +*acc* ▷ *adj* (*fake: Elizabethan etc*) Pseudo-; (*exam*) Probe-; (*battle*) Schein-
mockery ['mɔkərɪ] *n* Spott *m*; **to make a ~ of sb** jdn zum Gespött machen; **to make a ~ of sth** etw zur Farce machen
mocking ['mɔkɪŋ] *adj* spöttisch
mockingbird ['mɔkɪŋbəːd] *n* Spottdrossel *f*
mock-up ['mɔkʌp] *n* Modell *nt*
MOD (*Brit*) *n abbr* = **Ministry of Defence**
mod cons ['mɔd'kɔnz] (*Brit*) *npl* (= *modern conveniences*) Komfort *m*
mode [məud] *n* Form *f*; (*Comput, Tech*) Betriebsart *f*; **~ of life** Lebensweise *f*; **~ of transport** Transportmittel *nt*
model ['mɔdl] *n* Modell *nt*; (*also:* **fashion model**) Mannequin *nt*; (*example*) Muster *nt* ▷ *adj* (*excellent*) vorbildlich; (*small scale: railway etc*) Modell- ▷ *vt* (*clothes*) vorführen; (*with clay etc*) modellieren, formen ▷ *vi* (*for designer, photographer etc*) als Modell arbeiten; **to ~ o.s. on sb** sich *dat* jdn zum Vorbild nehmen
modeller, (*US*) **modeler** ['mɔdlə^r] *n* Modellbauer *m*
model railway *n* Modelleisenbahn *f*
modem ['məudɛm] *n* Modem *nt*
moderate [*adj* 'mɔdərət, *vb* 'mɔdəreɪt] *adj* gemäßigt; (*amount*) nicht allzu groß; (*change*) leicht ▷ *n* Gemäßigte(r) *f(m)* ▷ *vi* (*storm, wind etc*) nachlassen ▷ *vt* (*tone, demands*) mäßigen
moderately ['mɔdərətlɪ] *adv* mäßig; (*expensive, difficult*) nicht allzu; (*pleased, happy*) einigermaßen; **~ priced** nicht allzu teuer
moderation [mɔdə'reɪʃən] *n* Mäßigung *f*; **in ~** in *or* mit Maßen
moderator ['mɔdəreɪtə^r] *n* (*Eccl*) Synodalpräsident *m*
modern ['mɔdən] *adj* modern; **~ languages** moderne Fremdsprachen *pl*
modernization [mɔdənaɪ'zeɪʃən] *n* Modernisierung *f*
modernize ['mɔdənaɪz] *vt* modernisieren
modest ['mɔdɪst] *adj* bescheiden; (*chaste*) schamhaft
modestly ['mɔdɪstlɪ] *adv* bescheiden; (*behave*) schamhaft; (*to a moderate extent*) mäßig
modesty ['mɔdɪstɪ] *n* Bescheidenheit *f*; (*chastity*) Schamgefühl *nt*
modicum ['mɔdɪkəm] *n*: **a ~ of** ein wenig *or* bisschen
modification [mɔdɪfɪ'keɪʃən] *n* Änderung *f*; (*to policy etc*) Modifizierung *f*; **to make ~s to** (Ver)änderungen vornehmen an +*dat*, modifizieren
modify ['mɔdɪfaɪ] *vt* (ver)ändern; (*policy etc*) modifizieren
modish ['məudɪʃ] *adj* (*fashionable*) modisch
Mods [mɔdz] (*Brit*) *n abbr* (*Scol*: = (*Honour*) *Moderations*) *akademische Prüfung an der Universität Oxford*
modular ['mɔdjulə^r] *adj* (*unit, furniture*) aus Bauelementen (zusammengesetzt); (*Comput*) modular
modulate ['mɔdjuleɪt] *vt* modulieren; (*process, activity*) umwandeln
modulation [mɔdju'leɪʃən] *n* Modulation *f*; (*modification*) Veränderung *f*
module ['mɔdjuːl] *n* (Bau)element *nt*; (*Space*) Raumkapsel *f*; (*Scol*) Kurs *m*
modus operandi ['məudəsɔpə'rændiː] *n* Modus Operandi *m*
Mogadishu [mɔgə'dɪʃuː] *n* Mogadischu *nt*
mogul ['məugl] *n* (*fig*) Mogul *m*
MOH (*Brit*) *n abbr* (= *Medical Officer of Health*) Amtsarzt *m*, Amtsärztin *f*
mohair ['məuhɛə^r] *n* Mohair *m*
Mohammed [mə'hæmɛd] *n* Mohammed *m*
moist [mɔɪst] *adj* feucht
moisten ['mɔɪsn] *vt* anfeuchten
moisture ['mɔɪstʃə^r] *n* Feuchtigkeit *f*
moisturize ['mɔɪstʃəraɪz] *vt* (*skin*) mit einer Feuchtigkeitscreme behandeln
moisturizer ['mɔɪstʃəraɪzə^r] *n* Feuchtigkeitscreme *f*
molar ['məulə^r] *n* Backenzahn *m*
molasses [mə'læsɪz] *n* Melasse *f*
mold *etc* [məuld] (*US*) *n, vt* = **mould** *etc*
Moldavia [mɔl'deɪvɪə] *n* Moldawien *nt*
Moldavian [mɔl'deɪvɪən] *adj* moldawisch
Moldova [mɔl'dəuvə] *n* Moldawien *nt*
Moldovan *adj* moldawisch
mole [məul] *n* (*on skin*) Leberfleck *m*; (*Zool*) Maulwurf *m*; (*fig: spy*) Spion(in) *m(f)*
molecular [məu'lɛkjulə^r] *adj* molekular; (*biology*) Molekular-
molecule ['mɔlɪkjuːl] *n* Molekül *nt*
molehill ['məulhɪl] *n* Maulwurfshaufen *m*
molest [mə'lɛst] *vt* (*assault sexually*) sich vergehen an +*dat*; (*harass*) belästigen
mollusc ['mɔləsk] *n* Weichtier *nt*
mollycoddle ['mɔlɪkɔdl] *vt* verhätscheln
Molotov cocktail ['mɔlətɔf-] *n* Molotowcocktail *m*
molt [məult] (*US*) *vi* = **moult**
molten ['məultən] *adj* geschmolzen, flüssig
mom [mɔm] (*US*) *n* = **mum**
moment ['məumənt] *n* Moment *m*,

Augenblick *m*; (*importance*) Bedeutung *f*; **for a ~** (für) einen Moment *or* Augenblick; **at that ~** in diesem Moment *or* Augenblick; **at the ~** momentan; **for the ~** vorläufig; **in a ~** gleich; **"one ~ please"** (*Tel*) „bleiben Sie am Apparat"

momentarily ['məumәntrılı] *adv* für einen Augenblick *or* Moment; (*US: very soon*) jeden Augenblick *or* Moment

momentary ['məuməntərı] *adj* (*brief*) kurz

momentous [məu'mɛntəs] *adj* (*occasion*) bedeutsam; (*decision*) von großer Tragweite

momentum [məu'mɛntəm] *n* (*Phys*) Impuls *m*; (*fig: of movement*) Schwung *m*; (*: of events, change*) Dynamik *f*; **to gather ~** schneller werden; (*fig*) richtig in Gang kommen

mommy ['mɔmı] (*US*) *n* = **mummy**

Mon. *abbr* (= *Monday*) Mo.

Monaco ['mɔnəkəu] *n* Monaco *nt*

monarch ['mɔnək] *n* Monarch(in) *m(f)*

monarchist ['mɔnəkıst] *n* Monarchist(in) *m(f)*

monarchy ['mɔnəkı] *n* Monarchie *f*; **the M~** (*royal family*) die königliche Familie

monastery ['mɔnəstərı] *n* Kloster *nt*

monastic [mə'næstık] *adj* Kloster-, klösterlich; (*fig*) mönchisch, klösterlich einfach

Monday ['mʌndı] *n* Montag *m*; *see also* **Tuesday**

Monegasque [mɔnə'gæsk] *adj* monegassisch ▷ *n* Monegasse *m*, Monegassin *f*

monetarist ['mʌnıtərıst] *n* Monetarist(in) *m(f)* ▷ *adj* monetaristisch

monetary ['mʌnıtərı] *adj* (*system, union*) Währungs-

money ['mʌnı] *n* Geld *nt*; **to make ~** (*person*) Geld verdienen; (*business*) etwas einbringen; **danger ~** (*Brit*) Gefahrenzulage *f*; **I've got no ~ left** ich habe kein Geld mehr

moneyed ['mʌnıd] (*form*) *adj* begütert

moneylender ['mʌnılɛndə^r] *n* Geldverleiher(in) *m(f)*

moneymaker ['mʌnımeıkə^r] *n* (*person*) Finanzgenie *nt*; (*idea*) einträgliche Sache *f*; (*product*) Verkaufserfolg *m*

moneymaking ['mʌnımeıkıŋ] *adj* einträglich

money market *n* Geldmarkt *m*

money order *n* Zahlungsanweisung *f*

money-spinner ['mʌnıspınə^r] (*inf*) *n* Verkaufsschlager *m*; (*person, business*) Goldgrube *f*

money supply *n* Geldvolumen *nt*

Mongol ['mɔŋgəl] *n* Mongole *m*, Mongolin *f*; (*Ling*) Mongolisch *nt*

mongol ['mɔŋgəl] (*offensive*) *n* Mongoloide(r) *f(m)*

Mongolia [mɔŋ'gəulıə] *n* die Mongolei

Mongolian [mɔŋ'gəulıən] *adj* mongolisch ▷ *n* Mongole *m*, Mongolin *f*; (*Ling*) Mongolisch *nt*

mongoose ['mɔŋgu:s] *n* Mungo *m*

mongrel ['mʌŋgrəl] *n* Promenadenmischung *f*

monitor ['mɔnıtə^r] *n* Monitor *m* ▷ *vt* überwachen; (*broadcasts*) mithören

monk [mʌŋk] *n* Mönch *m*

monkey ['mʌŋkı] *n* Affe *m*

monkey business (*inf*) *n* faule Sachen *pl*

monkey nut (*Brit*) *n* Erdnuss *f*

monkey tricks *npl* = **monkey business**

monkey wrench *n* verstellbarer Schraubenschlüssel *m*

mono ['mɔnəu] *adj* (*recording etc*) Mono-

monochrome ['mɔnəkrəum] *adj* (*photograph, television*) Schwarzweiß-; (*Comput: screen*) Monochrom-

monogamous [mə'nɔgəməs] *adj* monogam

monogamy [mə'nɔgəmı] *n* Monogamie *f*

monogram ['mɔnəgræm] *n* Monogramm *nt*

monolith ['mɔnəlıθ] *n* Monolith *m*

monolithic [mɔnə'lıθık] *adj* monolithisch

monologue ['mɔnəlɔg] *n* Monolog *m*

monoplane ['mɔnəpleın] *n* Eindecker *m*

monopolize [mə'nɔpəlaız] *vt* beherrschen; (*person*) mit Beschlag belegen; (*conversation*) an sich *acc* reißen

monopoly [mə'nɔpəlı] *n* Monopol *nt*; **to have a ~ on** *or* **of sth** (*fig: domination*) etw für sich gepachtet haben; **Monopolies and Mergers Commission** (*Brit*) ≈ Kartellamt *nt*

monorail ['mɔnəureıl] *n* Einschienenbahn *f*

monosodium glutamate [mɔnə'səudıəm-'glu:təmeıt] *n* Glutamat *nt*

monosyllabic [mɔnəsı'læbık] *adj* einsilbig

monosyllable ['mɔnəsıləbl] *n* einsilbiges Wort *nt*

monotone ['mɔnətəun] *n*: **in a ~** monoton

monotonous [mə'nɔtənəs] *adj* monoton, eintönig

monotony [mə'nɔtənı] *n* Monotonie *f*, Eintönigkeit *f*

monsoon [mɔn'su:n] *n* Monsun *m*

monster ['mɔnstə^r] *n* Ungetüm *nt*, Monstrum *nt*; (*imaginary creature*) Ungeheuer *nt*, Monster *nt*; (*person*) Unmensch *m*

monstrosity [mɔn'strɔsıtı] *n* Ungetüm *nt*, Monstrum *nt*

monstrous ['mɔnstrəs] *adj* (*huge*) riesig; (*ugly*) abscheulich; (*atrocious*) ungeheuerlich

Mont. (*US*) *abbr* (*Post*) = *Montana*

montage [mɔn'tɑ:ʒ] *n* Montage *f*

Mont Blanc [mɔ̃'blɑ̃] *n* Montblanc *m*

month [mʌnθ] *n* Monat *m*; **every ~** jeden Monat; **300 dollars a ~** 300 Dollar im Monat

monthly ['mʌnθlı] *adj* monatlich; (*ticket, magazine*) Monats- ▷ *adv* monatlich; **twice ~** zweimal im Monat

Montreal [mɔntrı'ɔ:l] *n* Montreal *nt*

monument ['mɔnjumənt] *n* Denkmal *nt*

monumental [mɔnju'mɛntl] *adj* (*building, statue*) gewaltig, monumental; (*book, piece of work*) unsterblich; (*storm, row*) ungeheuer

moo [mu:] *vi* muhen

mood [mu:d] *n* Stimmung *f*; (*of person*) Laune *f*, Stimmung *f*; **to be in a good/bad ~** gut/schlecht gelaunt sein; **to be in the ~ for** aufgelegt sein zu

moodily ['mu:dılı] *adv* launisch; (*sullenly*) schlecht gelaunt

moody ['mu:dı] *adj* launisch; (*sullen*) schlecht gelaunt

moon [muːn] *n* Mond *m*
moonlight ['muːnlaɪt] *n* Mondschein *m* ▷ *vi* (*inf*) schwarzarbeiten
moonlighting ['muːnlaɪtɪŋ] (*inf*) *n* Schwarzarbeit *f*
moonlit ['muːnlɪt] *adj* (*night*) mondhell
moonshot ['muːnʃɔt] *n* Mondflug *m*
moor [muəʳ] *n* (Hoch)moor *nt*, Heide *f* ▷ *vt* vertäuen ▷ *vi* anlegen
mooring ['muərɪŋ] *n* Anlegeplatz *m*; **moorings** *npl* (*chains*) Verankerung *f*
Moorish ['muərɪʃ] *adj* maurisch
moorland ['muələnd] *n* Moorlandschaft *f*, Heidelandschaft *f*
moose [muːs] *n inv* Elch *m*
moot [muːt] *vt*: **to be ~ed** vorgeschlagen werden ▷ *adj*: **it's a ~ point** das ist fraglich
mop [mɔp] *n* (*for floor*) Mop *m*; (*for dishes*) Spülbürste *f*; (*of hair*) Mähne *f* ▷ *vt* (*floor*) wischen; (*face*) abwischen; (*eyes*) sich *dat* wischen; **to ~ the sweat from one's brow** sich *dat* den Schweiß von der Stirn wischen
▸ **mop up** *vt* aufwischen
mope [məup] *vi* Trübsal blasen
▸ **mope about** *vi* mit einer Jammermiene herumlaufen
▸ **mope around** *vi* = **mope about**
moped ['məupɛd] *n* Moped *nt*
moquette [mɔ'kɛt] *n* Mokett *m*
MOR *adj abbr* (*Mus*) = **middle-of-the-road**
moral ['mɔrl] *adj* moralisch; (*welfare, values*) sittlich; (*behaviour*) moralisch einwandfrei ▷ *n* Moral *f*; **morals** *npl* (*principles, values*) Moralvorstellungen *pl*; **~ support** moralische Unterstützung *f*
morale [mɔ'rɑːl] *n* Moral *f*
morality [mə'rælɪtɪ] *n* Sittlichkeit *f*; (*system of morals*) Moral *f*, Ethik *f*; (*correctness*) moralische Richtigkeit *f*
moralize ['mɔrəlaɪz] *vi* moralisieren; **to ~ about** sich moralisch entrüsten über *+acc*
morally ['mɔrəlɪ] *adv* moralisch; (*live, behave*) moralisch einwandfrei
moral victory *n* moralischer Sieg *m*
morass [mə'ræs] *n* Morast *m*, Sumpf *m*, Sumpf *m* (*also fig*)
moratorium [mɔrə'tɔːrɪəm] *n* Stopp *m*; Moratorium *nt*
morbid ['mɔːbɪd] *adj* (*imagination*) krankhaft; (*interest*) unnatürlich; (*comments, behaviour*) makaber

KEYWORD

more [mɔːʳ] *adj* **1** (*greater in number etc*) mehr; **more people/work/letters than we expected** mehr Leute/Arbeit/Briefe, als wir erwarteten; **I have more wine/money than you** ich habe mehr Wein/Geld als du
2 (*additional*): **do you want (some) more tea?** möchten Sie noch mehr Tee?; **is there any more wine?** ist noch Wein da?; **I have no more money, I don't have any more money** ich habe kein Geld mehr
▷ *pron* **1** (*greater amount*) mehr; **more than 10** mehr als 10; **it cost more than we expected** es kostete mehr, als wir erwarteten
2 (*further or additional amount*): **is there any more?** gibt es noch mehr?; **there's no more** es ist nichts mehr da; **many/much more** viel mehr
▷ *adv* mehr; **more dangerous/difficult/easily** *etc* **(than)** gefährlicher/schwerer/leichter *etc* (als); **more and more** mehr und mehr, immer mehr; **more and more excited/expensive** immer aufgeregter/teurer; **more or less** mehr oder weniger; **more than ever** mehr denn je, mehr als jemals zuvor; **more beautiful than ever** schöner denn je; **no more, not any more** nicht mehr

moreover [mɔː'rəuvəʳ] *adv* außerdem, zudem
morgue [mɔːg] *n* Leichenschauhaus *nt*
MORI ['mɔːrɪ] (*Brit*) *n abbr* (*= Market and Opinion Research Institute*) *Markt- und Meinungsforschungsinstitut*
moribund ['mɔrɪbʌnd] *adj* dem Untergang geweiht
Mormon ['mɔːmən] *n* Mormone *m*, Mormonin *f*
morning ['mɔːnɪŋ] *n* Morgen *m*; (*as opposed to afternoon*) Vormittag *m* ▷ *cpd* Morgen-; **in the ~** morgens; vormittags; (*tomorrow*) morgen früh; **7 o'clock in the ~** 7 Uhr morgens; **this ~** heute Morgen
morning-after pill ['mɔːnɪŋ'ɑːftə-] *n* Pille *f* danach
morning market *n* (*Econ*) Vormittagsmarkt *m*
morning sickness *n* (Schwangerschafts)übelkeit *f*
Moroccan [mə'rɔkən] *adj* marokkanisch ▷ *n* Marokkaner(in) *m(f)*
Morocco [mə'rɔkəu] *n* Marokko *nt*
moron ['mɔːrɔn] (*inf*) *n* Schwachkopf *m*
moronic [mə'rɔnɪk] (*inf*) *adj* schwachsinnig
morose [mə'rəus] *adj* missmutig
morphine ['mɔːfiːn] *n* Morphium *nt*
morris dancing ['mɔrɪs-] *n* Moriskentanz *m*, *alter englischer Volkstanz*
Morse [mɔːs] *n* (*also*: **Morse code**) Morsealphabet *nt*
morsel ['mɔːsl] *n* Stückchen *nt*
mortal ['mɔːtl] *adj* sterblich; (*wound, combat*) tödlich; (*danger*) Todes-; (*sin, enemy*) Tod- ▷ *n* (*human being*) Sterbliche(r) *f(m)*
mortality [mɔː'tælɪtɪ] *n* Sterblichkeit *f*; (*number of deaths*) Todesfälle *pl*
mortality rate *n* Sterblichkeitsziffer *f*
mortar ['mɔːtəʳ] *n* (*Mil*) Minenwerfer *m*; (*Constr*) Mörtel *m*; (*Culin*) Mörser *m*
mortgage ['mɔːgɪdʒ] *n* Hypothek *f* ▷ *vt* mit einer Hypothek belasten; **to take out a ~** eine Hypothek aufnehmen
mortgage company (*US*) *n* Hypothekenbank *f*
mortgagee [mɔːgə'dʒiː] *n* Hypotheken-

gläubiger *m*
mortgagor ['mɔːgədʒəʳ] *n* Hypothekenschuldner *m*
mortician [mɔːˈtɪʃən] (US) *n* Bestattungsunternehmer *m*
mortified ['mɔːtɪfaɪd] *adj*: **he was ~** er empfand das als beschämend; *(embarrassed)* es war ihm schrecklich peinlich
mortify ['mɔːtɪfaɪ] *vt* beschämen
mortise lock ['mɔːtɪs-] *n* Einsteckschloss *nt*
mortuary ['mɔːtjuərɪ] *n* Leichenhalle *f*
mosaic [məu'zeɪɪk] *n* Mosaik *nt*
Moscow ['mɔskəu] *n* Moskau *nt*
Moslem ['mɔzləm] *adj, n* = **Muslim**
mosque [mɔsk] *n* Moschee *f*
mosquito [mɔs'kiːtəu] (*pl* **~es**) *n* Stechmücke *f*; *(in tropics)* Moskito *m*
mosquito net *n* Moskitonetz *nt*
moss [mɔs] *n* Moos *nt*
mossy ['mɔsɪ] *adj* bemoost

KEYWORD

most [məust] *adj* **1** *(almost all: people, things etc)* meiste(r, s); **most people** die meisten Leute
2 *(largest, greatest: interest, money etc)* meiste(r, s); **who has (the) most money?** wer hat das meiste Geld?
▷ *pron (greatest quantity, number)* der/die/das meiste; **most of it** das meiste (davon); **most of them** die meisten von ihnen; **most of the time/work** die meiste Zeit/Arbeit; **most of the time he's very helpful** er ist meistens sehr hilfsbereit; **to make the most of sth** das Beste aus etw machen; **at the (very) most** (aller)höchstens
▷ *adv (+ vb: spend, eat, work etc)* am meisten; *(+ adv: carefully, easily etc)* äußerst; *(very: polite, interesting etc)* höchst; *(+ adj)*: **the most intelligent/expensive** *etc* der/die/das intelligenteste/teuerste *etc*; **a most interesting book** ein höchst interessantes Buch

mostly ['məustlɪ] *adv (chiefly)* hauptsächlich; *(usually)* meistens
MOT *(Brit) n abbr (= Ministry of Transport)*: **~ (test)** ≈ TÜV *m*; **the car failed its ~** das Auto ist nicht durch den TÜV gekommen
motel [məu'tɛl] *n* Motel *nt*
moth [mɔθ] *n* Nachtfalter *m*; *(also:* **clothes moth**) Motte *f*
mothball ['mɔθbɔːl] *n* Mottenkugel *f*
moth-eaten ['mɔθiːtn] *(pej) adj* mottenzerfressen
mother ['mʌðəʳ] *n* Mutter *f* ▷ *adj (country)* Heimat-; *(company)* Mutter- ▷ *vt* großziehen; *(pamper, protect)* bemuttern
motherboard ['mʌðəbɔːd] *n (Comput)* Hauptplatine *f*
motherhood ['mʌðəhud] *n* Mutterschaft *f*
mother-in-law ['mʌðərɪnlɔː] *n* Schwiegermutter *f*
motherly ['mʌðəlɪ] *adj* mütterlich
mother-of-pearl ['mʌðərəv'pəːl] *n* Perlmutt *nt*
mother's help *n* Haushaltshilfe *f*
mother-to-be ['mʌðətə'biː] *n* werdende Mutter *f*
mother tongue *n* Muttersprache *f*
mothproof ['mɔθpruːf] *adj* mottenfest
motif [məu'tiːf] *n* Motiv *nt*
motion ['məuʃən] *n* Bewegung *f*; *(proposal)* Antrag *m*; *(Brit: also:* **bowel motion**) Stuhlgang *m* ▷ *vt, vi*: **to ~ (to) sb to do sth** jdm ein Zeichen geben, dass er/sie etw tun solle; **to be in ~** *(vehicle)* fahren; **to set in ~** in Gang bringen; **to go through the ~s (of doing sth)** *(fig)* etw der Form halber tun; *(pretend)* so tun, als ob (man etw täte)
motionless ['məuʃənlɪs] *adj* reg(ungs)los
motion picture *n* Film *m*
motivate ['məutɪveɪt] *vt* motivieren
motivated ['məutɪveɪtɪd] *adj* motiviert; **~ by** getrieben von
motivation [məutɪ'veɪʃən] *n* Motivation *f*
motive ['məutɪv] *n* Motiv *nt*, Beweggrund *m* ▷ *adj (power, force)* Antriebs-; **from the best (of) ~s** mit den besten Absichten
motley ['mɔtlɪ] *adj* bunt (gemischt)
motor ['məutəʳ] *n* Motor *m*; *(Brit: inf: car)* Auto *nt* ▷ *cpd (industry, trade)* Auto(mobil)-
motorbike ['məutəbaɪk] *n* Motorrad *nt*
motorboat ['məutəbəut] *n* Motorboot *nt*
motorcade ['məutəkeɪd] *n* Fahrzeugkolonne *f*
motorcar ['məutəkɑː] *(Brit) n* (Personenkraft)wagen *m*
motorcoach ['məutəkəutʃ] *(Brit) n* Reisebus *m*
motorcycle ['məutəsaɪkl] *n* Motorrad *nt*
motorcycle racing *n* Motorradrennen *nt*
motorcyclist ['məutəsaɪklɪst] *n* Motorradfahrer(in) *m(f)*
motoring ['məutərɪŋ] *(Brit) n* Autofahren *nt* ▷ *cpd* Auto-; *(offence, accident)* Verkehrs-
motorist ['məutərɪst] *n* Autofahrer(in) *m(f)*
motorized ['məutəraɪzd] *adj* motorisiert
motor oil *n* Motorenöl *nt*
motor racing *(Brit) n* Autorennen *nt*
motor scooter *n* Motorroller *m*
motor vehicle *n* Kraftfahrzeug *nt*
motorway ['məutəweɪ] *(Brit) n* Autobahn *f*
mottled ['mɔtld] *adj* gesprenkelt
motto ['mɔtəu] (*pl* **~es**) *n* Motto *nt*
mould, (US) **mold** [məuld] *n (cast)* Form *f*; *(: for metal)* Gussform *f*; *(mildew)* Schimmel *m* ▷ *vt (lit, fig)* formen
moulder, (US) **molder** ['məuldəʳ] *vi (decay)* vermodern
moulding, (US) **molding** ['məuldɪŋ] *n (Archit)* Zierleiste *f*
mouldy, (US) **moldy** ['məuldɪ] *adj* schimmelig; *(smell)* moderig
moult, (US) **molt** [məult] *vi (animal)* sich haaren; *(bird)* sich mausern
mound [maund] *n (of earth)* Hügel *m*; *(heap)* Haufen *m*
mount [maunt] *n (in proper names)*: **M~ Carmel**

der Berg Karmel; (*horse*) Pferd *nt*; (*for picture*) Passepartout *nt* ▷ *vt* (*horse*) besteigen; (*exhibition etc*) vorbereiten; (*jewel*) (ein)fassen; (*picture*) mit einem Passepartout versehen; (*staircase*) hochgehen; (*stamp*) aufkleben; (*attack, campaign*) organisieren ▷ *vi* (*increase*) steigen; (: *problems*) sich häufen; (*on horse*) aufsitzen
▸ **mount up** *vi* (*costs, savings*) sich summieren, sich zusammenläppern (*inf*)
mountain ['mauntın] *n* Berg *m* ▷ *cpd* (*road, stream*) Gebirgs-; **to make a ~ out of a molehill** aus einer Mücke einen Elefanten machen
mountain bike *n* Mountainbike *nt*
mountaineer [mauntı'nıəʳ] *n* Bergsteiger(in) *m(f)*
mountaineering [mauntı'nıərıŋ] *n* Bergsteigen *nt*; **to go ~** bergsteigen gehen
mountainous ['mauntınəs] *adj* gebirgig
mountain range *n* Gebirgskette *f*
mountain rescue team *n* Bergwacht *f*
mountainside ['mauntınsaıd] *n* (Berg)hang *m*
mounted ['mauntıd] *adj* (*police*) beritten
Mount Everest *n* Mount Everest *m*
mourn [mɔːn] *vt* betrauern ▷ *vi*: **to ~ (for)** trauern (um)
mourner ['mɔːnəʳ] *n* Trauernde(r) *f(m)*
mournful ['mɔːnful] *adj* traurig
mourning ['mɔːnıŋ] *n* Trauer *f*; **to be in ~** trauern; (*wear special clothes*) Trauer tragen
mouse [maus] (*pl* **mice**) *n* (*Zool, Comput*) Maus *f*; (*fig: person*) schüchternes Mäuschen *nt*
mouse potato *n* (*inf*) Computerjunkie *m*, Mouse Potato *f*
mousetrap ['maustræp] *n* Mausefalle *f*
moussaka [mu'sɑːkə] *n* Moussaka *f*
mousse [muːs] *n* (*Culin*) Mousse *f*; (*cosmetic*) Schaumfestiger *m*
moustache, (*US*) **mustache** [məs'tɑːʃ] *n* Schnurrbart *m*
mousy ['mausı] *adj* (*hair*) mausgrau
mouth [mauθ] (*pl* **~s**) *n* Mund *m*; (*of cave, hole, bottle*) Öffnung *f*; (*of river*) Mündung *f*
mouthful ['mauθful] *n* (*of food*) Bissen *m*; (*of drink*) Schluck *m*
mouth organ *n* Mundharmonika *f*
mouthpiece ['mauθpiːs] *n* Mundstück *nt*; (*spokesman*) Sprachrohr *nt*
mouth-to-mouth ['mauθtə'mauθ] *adj*: **~ resuscitation** Mund-zu-Mund-Beatmung *f*
mouthwash ['mauθwɔʃ] *n* Mundwasser *nt*
mouth-watering ['mauθwɔːtərıŋ] *adj* appetitlich
movable ['muːvəbl] *adj* beweglich; **~ feast** beweglicher Feiertag *m*
move [muːv] *n* (*movement*) Bewegung *f*; (*in game*) Zug *m*; (*change: of house*) Umzug *m*; (: *of job*) Stellenwechsel *m* ▷ *vt* bewegen; (*furniture*) (ver)rücken; (*car*) umstellen; (*in game*) ziehen mit; (*emotionally*) bewegen, ergreifen; (*Pol: resolution etc*) beantragen ▷ *vi* sich bewegen; (*traffic*) vorankommen; (*in game*) ziehen; (*also*: **move house**) umziehen; (*develop*) sich entwickeln; **it's my ~** ich bin am Zug; **to get a ~ on** sich beeilen; **to ~ sb to do sth** jdn (dazu) veranlassen, etw zu tun; **to ~ towards** sich nähern +*dat*
▸ **move about** *vi* sich (hin- und her)bewegen; (*travel*) unterwegs sein; (*from place to place*) umherziehen; (*change residence*) umziehen; (*change job*) die Stelle wechseln; **I can hear him moving about** ich höre ihn herumlaufen
▸ **move along** *vi* weitergehen
▸ **move around** *vi* = **move about**
▸ **move away** *vi* (*from town, area*) wegziehen
▸ **move back** *vi* (*return*) zurückkommen
▸ **move forward** *vi* (*advance*) vorrücken
▸ **move in** *vi* (*to house*) einziehen; (*police, soldiers*) anrücken
▸ **move off** *vi* (*car*) abfahren
▸ **move on** *vi* (*leave*) weitergehen; (*travel*) weiterfahren ▷ *vt* (*onlookers*) zum Weitergehen auffordern
▸ **move out** *vi* (*of house*) ausziehen
▸ **move over** *vi* (*to make room*) (zur Seite) rücken
▸ **move up** *vi* (*employee*) befördert werden; (*pupil*) versetzt werden; (*deputy*) aufrücken
moveable ['muːvəbl] *adj* = **movable**
movement ['muːvmənt] *n* (*action, group*) Bewegung *f*; (*freedom to move*) Bewegungsfreiheit *f*; (*transportation*) Beförderung *f*; (*shift*) Trend *m*; (*Mus*) Satz *m*; (*Med: also*: **bowel movement**) Stuhlgang *m*
mover ['muːvəʳ] *n* (*of proposal*) Antragsteller(in) *m(f)*
movie ['muːvı] *n* Film *m*; **to go to the ~s** ins Kino gehen
movie camera *n* Filmkamera *f*
moviegoer ['muːvıgəuəʳ] (*US*) *n* Kinogänger(in) *m(f)*
moving ['muːvıŋ] *adj* beweglich; (*emotional*) ergreifend; (*instigating*): **the ~ spirit/force** die treibende Kraft
mow [məu] (*pt* **~ed**, *pp* **mowed** *or* **~n**) *vt* mähen
▸ **mow down** *vt* (*kill*) niedermähen
mower ['məuəʳ] *n* (*also*: **lawnmower**) Rasenmäher *m*
Mozambique [məuzəm'biːk] *n* Mosambik *nt*
MP *n abbr* (= *Member of Parliament*) ≈ MdB; = **military police**; (*Canada*: = *Mounted Police*) berittene Polizei *f*
MP3 *abbr* (*Comput*) MP3
MP3 player *n* (*Comput*) MP3-Spieler *m*
mpg *n abbr* (= *miles per gallon*) *see* **mile**
mph *abbr* (= *miles per hour*) Meilen pro Stunde
MPhil *n abbr* (= *Master of Philosophy*) ≈ M.A.
MPS (*Brit*) *n abbr* (= *Member of the Pharmaceutical Society*) *Qualifikationsnachweis für Pharmazeuten*
Mr, (*US*) **Mr.** ['mıstəʳ] *n*: **Mr Smith** Herr Smith
MRC (*Brit*) *n abbr* (= *Medical Research Council*) *medizinischer Forschungsausschuss*
MRCP (*Brit*) *n abbr* (= *Member of the Royal College of Physicians*) *höchster akademischer Grad in Medizin*
MRCS (*Brit*) *n abbr* (= *Member of the Royal College of*

Surgeons) höchster akademischer Grad für Chirurgen

MRCVS (*Brit*) *n abbr* (*= Member of the Royal College of Veterinary Surgeons) höchster akademischer Grad für Tiermediziner*

Mrs, (*US*) **Mrs.** ['mɪsɪz] *n*: ~ **Smith** Frau Smith

MS *n abbr* (*= multiple sclerosis*) MS *f*; (*US*: *= Master of Science) akademischer Grad in Naturwissenschaften* ▷ *abbr* (*US*: *Post*) *= Mississippi*

MS. (*pl* **MSS.**) *n abbr* (*= manuscript*) Ms.

Ms, (*US*) **Ms.** [mɪz] *n* (*= Miss or Mrs*): **Ms Smith** Frau Smith

MSA (*US*) *n abbr* (*= Master of Science in Agriculture*) *akademischer Grad in Agronomie*

MSc *n abbr* (*= Master of Science*) *akademischer Grad in Naturwissenschaften*

MSG *n abbr* = **monosodium glutamate**

MSP (*Brit*) *n abbr* (*Pol*: *= Member of the Scottish Parliament*) Abgeordnete(r) *f*(*m*) des schottischen Parlaments

MST (*US*) *abbr* (*= Mountain Standard Time*) *amerikanische Standardzeitzone*

MSW (*US*) *n abbr* (*= Master of Social Work*) *akademischer Grad in Sozialwissenschaft*

MT *n abbr* (*Comput*, *Ling*: *= machine translation*) maschinelle Übersetzung *f*

Mt *abbr* (*Geog*) = **mount**

MTV (*esp US*) *n abbr* (*= music television*) MTV *nt*

KEYWORD

much [mʌtʃ] *adj* (*time, money, effort*) viel; **how much money/time do you need?** wie viel Geld/Zeit brauchen Sie?; **he's done so much work for us** er hat so viel für uns gearbeitet; **as much as** so viel wie; **I have as much money/intelligence as you** ich besitze genauso viel Geld/Intelligenz wie du
▷ *pron* viel; **how much is it?** was kostet es?
▷ *adv* **1** (*greatly, a great deal*) sehr; **thank you very much** vielen Dank, danke sehr; **I read as much as I can** ich lese so viel wie ich kann
2 (*by far*) viel; **I'm much better now** mir geht es jetzt viel besser
3 (*almost*) fast; **how are you feeling? — much the same** wie fühlst du dich? — fast genauso; **the two books are much the same** die zwei Bücher sind sich sehr ähnlich

muck [mʌk] *n* (*dirt*) Dreck *m*
▸ **muck about** (*inf*) *vi* (*fool about*) herumalbern ▷ *vt*: **to ~ sb about** mit jdm beliebig umspringen
▸ **muck around** *vi*, *vt* = **muck about**
▸ **muck in** (*Brit*: *inf*) *vi* mit anpacken
▸ **muck out** *vt* (*stable*) ausmisten
▸ **muck up** (*inf*) *vt* (*exam etc*) verpfuschen

muckraking ['mʌkreɪkɪŋ] (*fig*: *inf*) *n* Sensationsmache *f* ▷ *adj* sensationslüstern

mucky ['mʌkɪ] *adj* (*dirty*) dreckig; (*field*) matschig

mucus ['mju:kəs] *n* Schleim *m*

mud [mʌd] *n* Schlamm *m*

muddle ['mʌdl] *n* (*mess*) Durcheinander *nt*; (*confusion*) Verwirrung *f* ▷ *vt* (*person*) verwirren; (*also*: **muddle up**) durcheinanderbringen; **to be in a ~** völlig durcheinander sein; **to get in a ~** (*person*) konfus werden; (*things*) durcheinandergeraten
▸ **muddle along** *vi* vor sich *acc* hin wursteln
▸ **muddle through** *vi* (*get by*) sich durchschlagen

muddle-headed [mʌdl'hɛdɪd] *adj* zerstreut

muddy ['mʌdɪ] *adj* (*floor*) schmutzig; (*field*) schlammig

mud flats *npl* Watt(enmeer) *nt*

mudguard ['mʌdgɑ:d] (*Brit*) *n* Schutzblech *nt*

mudpack ['mʌdpæk] *n* Schlammpackung *f*

mud-slinging ['mʌdslɪŋɪŋ] *n* (*fig*) Schlechtmacherei *f*

muesli ['mju:zlɪ] *n* Müsli *nt*

muffin ['mʌfɪn] *n* (*Brit*) *weiches, flaches Milchbrötchen, meist warm gegessen*; (*US*) *kleiner runder Rührkuchen*

muffle ['mʌfl] *vt* (*sound*) dämpfen; (*against cold*) einmummeln

muffled ['mʌfld] *adj* (*see vt*) gedämpft; eingemummelt

muffler ['mʌflə^r] *n* (*US*: *Aut*) Auspufftopf *m*; (*scarf*) dicker Schal *m*

mufti ['mʌftɪ] *n*: **in ~** in Zivil

mug [mʌg] *n* (*cup*) Becher *m*; (*for beer*) Krug *m*; (*inf*: *face*) Visage *f*; (: *fool*) Trottel *m* ▷ *vt* (auf der Straße) überfallen; **it's a ~'s game** (*Brit*) das ist doch Schwachsinn
▸ **mug up** (*Brit*: *inf*) *vt* (*also*: **mug up on**) pauken

mugger ['mʌgə^r] *n* Straßenräuber *m*

mugging ['mʌgɪŋ] *n* Straßenraub *m*

muggins ['mʌgɪnz] (*Brit*: *inf*) *n* Dummkopf *m*; **... and ~ does all the work** ... und ich bin mal wieder der/die Dumme und mache die ganze Arbeit

muggy ['mʌgɪ] *adj* (*weather, day*) schwül

mug shot (*inf*) *n* (*of criminal*) Verbrecherfoto *nt*; (*for passport*) Passbild *nt*

mulatto [mju:'lætəu] (*pl* **~es**) *n* Mulatte *m*, Mulattin *f*

mulberry ['mʌlbrɪ] *n* (*fruit*) Maulbeere *f*; (*tree*) Maulbeerbaum *m*

mule [mju:l] *n* Maultier *nt*

mulled [mʌld] *adj*: **~ wine** Glühwein *m*

mullioned ['mʌlɪənd] *adj* (*windows*) längs unterteilt

mull over [mʌl-] *vt* sich *dat* durch den Kopf gehen lassen

multi... ['mʌltɪ] *pref* multi-, Multi-

multi-access ['mʌltɪ'æksɛs] *adj* (*Comput*: *system etc*) Mehrplatz-

multicoloured, (*US*) **multicolored** ['mʌltɪkʌləd] *adj* mehrfarbig

multifarious [mʌltɪ'fɛərɪəs] *adj* vielfältig

multifocals ['mʌltɪfəuklz] *npl* Gleitsichtgläser *pl*

multilateral [mʌltɪ'lætərl] *adj* multilateral

multi-level ['mʌltɪlɛvl] (*US*) *adj* = **multistorey**

multimillionaire [mʌltɪmɪljəˈnɛəʳ] *n* Multimillionär *m*
multinational [mʌltɪˈnæʃənl] *adj* multinational ▷ *n* multinationaler Konzern *m*, Multi *m* (*inf*)
multiple [ˈmʌltɪpl] *adj* (*injuries*) mehrfach; (*interests, causes*) vielfältig ▷ *n* Vielfache(s) *nt*; **~ collision** Massenkarambolage *f*
multiple-choice [ˈmʌltɪpltʃɔɪs] *adj* (*question etc*) Multiple-Choice-
multiple sclerosis *n* multiple Sklerose *f*
multiplex [ˈmʌltɪplɛks] *n*: **~ transmitter** Multiplexsender *m*; **~ (cinema)** Multiplexkino *nt* ▷ *adj* (*Tech*) Mehrfach- ▷ *vt* (*Tel*) gleichzeitig senden
multiplication [mʌltɪplɪˈkeɪʃən] *n* Multiplikation *f*; (*increase*) Vervielfachung *f*
multiplication table *n* Multiplikationstabelle *f*
multiplicity [mʌltɪˈplɪsɪtɪ] *n*: **a ~ of** eine Vielzahl von
multiply [ˈmʌltɪplaɪ] *vt* multiplizieren ▷ *vi* (*increase: problems*) stark zunehmen; (*: number*) sich vervielfachen; (*breed*) sich vermehren
multiracial [mʌltɪˈreɪʃl] *adj* gemischtrassig; (*school*) ohne Rassentrennung; **~ policy** Politik *f* der Rassenintegration
multistorey [mʌltɪˈstɔːrɪ] (*Brit*) *adj* (*building, car park*) mehrstöckig
multitude [ˈmʌltɪtjuːd] *n* Menge *f*; **a ~ of** eine Vielzahl von, eine Menge
mum [mʌm] (*Brit: inf*) *n* Mutti *f*, Mama *f* ▷ *adj*: **to keep ~** den Mund halten; **~'s the word** nichts verraten!
mumble [ˈmʌmbl] *vt, vi* (*indistinctly*) nuscheln; (*quietly*) murmeln
mumbo jumbo [ˈmʌmbəu-] *n* (*nonsense*) Geschwafel *nt*
mummify [ˈmʌmɪfaɪ] *vt* mumifizieren
mummy [ˈmʌmɪ] *n* (*Brit: mother*) Mami *f*; (*embalmed body*) Mumie *f*
mumps [mʌmps] *n* Mumps *m or f*
munch [mʌntʃ] *vt, vi* mampfen
mundane [mʌnˈdeɪn] *adj* (*life*) banal; (*task*) stumpfsinnig
Munich [ˈmjuːnɪk] *n* München *nt*
municipal [mjuːˈnɪsɪpl] *adj* städtisch, Stadt-; (*elections, administration*) Kommunal-
municipality [mjuːnɪsɪˈpælɪtɪ] *n* Gemeinde *f*, Stadt *f*
munitions [mjuːˈnɪʃənz] *npl* Munition *f*
mural [ˈmjuərl] *n* Wandgemälde *nt*
murder [ˈməːdəʳ] *n* Mord *m* ▷ *vt* ermorden; (*spoil: piece of music, language*) verhunzen; **to commit ~** einen Mord begehen
murderer [ˈməːdərəʳ] *n* Mörder *m*
murderess [ˈməːdərɪs] *n* Mörderin *f*
murderous [ˈməːdərəs] *adj* blutrünstig; (*attack*) Mord-; (*fig: look, attack*) vernichtend; (*: pace, heat*) mörderisch
murk [məːk] *n* Düsternis *f*
murky [ˈməːkɪ] *adj* düster; (*water*) trübe
murmur [ˈməːməʳ] *n* (*of voices*) Murmeln *nt*; (*of wind, waves*) Rauschen *nt* ▷ *vt, vi* murmeln; **heart ~** Herzgeräusche *pl*
MusB, MusBac *n abbr* (= *Bachelor of Music*) *akademischer Grad in Musikwissenschaft*
muscle [ˈmʌsl] *n* Muskel *m*; (*fig: strength*) Macht *f*
▶ **muscle in** *vi*: **to ~ in (on sth)** (bei etw) mitmischen
muscular [ˈmʌskjuləʳ] *adj* (*pain, dystrophy*) Muskel-; (*person, build*) muskulös
muscular dystrophy *n* Muskeldystrophie *f*
MusD, MusDoc *n abbr* (= *Doctor of Music*) *Doktorat in Musikwissenschaft*
muse [mjuːz] *vi* nachgrübeln ▷ *n* Muse *f*
museum [mjuːˈzɪəm] *n* Museum *nt*
mush [mʌʃ] *n* Brei *m*; (*pej*) Schmalz *m*
mushroom [ˈmʌʃrum] *n* (*edible*) (essbarer) Pilz *m*; (*poisonous*) Giftpilz *m*; (*button mushroom*) Champignon *m* ▷ *vi* (*fig: buildings etc*) aus dem Boden schießen; (*: town, organization*) explosionsartig wachsen
mushroom cloud *n* Atompilz *m*
mushy [ˈmʌʃɪ] *adj* matschig; (*consistency*) breiig; (*inf: sentimental*) rührselig; **~ peas** Erbsenbrei *m*
music [ˈmjuːzɪk] *n* Musik *f*; (*written music, score*) Noten *pl*
musical [ˈmjuːzɪkl] *adj* musikalisch; (*sound, tune*) melodisch ▷ *n* Musical *nt*
musical box *n* = **music box**
musical chairs *n* die Reise *f* nach Jerusalem
musical instrument *n* Musikinstrument *nt*
music box *n* Spieldose *f*
music centre *n* Musikcenter *nt*
music hall *n* Varieté *nt*
musician [mjuːˈzɪʃən] *n* Musiker(in) *m(f)*
music stand *n* Notenständer *m*
musk [mʌsk] *n* Moschus *m*
musket [ˈmʌskɪt] *n* Muskete *f*
muskrat [ˈmʌskræt] *n* Bisamratte *f*
musk rose *n* Moschusrose *f*
Muslim [ˈmʌzlɪm] *adj* moslemisch ▷ *n* Moslem *m*, Moslime *f*
muslin [ˈmʌzlɪn] *n* Musselin *m*
musquash [ˈmʌskwɔʃ] *n* Bisamratte *f*; (*fur*) Bisam *m*
mussel [ˈmʌsl] *n* (Mies)muschel *f*
must [mʌst] *aux vb* müssen; (*in negative*) dürfen ▷ *n* Muss *nt*; **I ~ do it** ich muss es tun; **you ~ not do that** das darfst du nicht tun; **he ~ be there by now** jetzt müsste er schon dort sein; **you ~ come and see me soon** Sie müssen mich bald besuchen; **why ~ he behave so badly?** warum muss er sich so schlecht benehmen?; **I ~ have made a mistake** ich muss mich geirrt haben; **the film is a ~** den Film muss man unbedingt gesehen haben
mustache [ˈmʌstæʃ] (*US*) *n* = **moustache**
mustard [ˈmʌstəd] *n* Senf *m*
mustard gas *n* (*Mil*) Senfgas *nt*
muster [ˈmʌstəʳ] *vt* (*support*) zusammenbekommen; (*also:* **muster**

up: *energy, strength, courage*) aufbringen; (*troops, members*) antreten lassen ▷*n*: **to pass ~** den Anforderungen genügen
mustiness ['mʌstɪnɪs] *n* Muffigkeit *f*
mustn't ['mʌsnt] = **must not**
musty ['mʌstɪ] *adj* muffig; (*building*) moderig
mutant ['mju:tənt] *n* Mutante *f*
mutate [mju:'teɪt] *vi* (*Biol*) mutieren
mutation [mju:'teɪʃən] *n* (*Biol*) Mutation *f*; (*alteration*) Veränderung *f*
mute [mju:t] *adj* stumm
muted ['mju:tɪd] *adj* (*colour*) gedeckt; (*reaction, criticism*) verhalten; (*sound, trumpet, Mus*) gedämpft
mutilate ['mju:tɪleɪt] *vt* verstümmeln
mutilation [mju:tɪ'leɪʃən] *n* Verstümmelung *f*
mutinous ['mju:tɪnəs] *adj* meuterisch; (*attitude*) rebellisch
mutiny ['mju:tɪnɪ] *n* Meuterei *f* ▷*vi* meutern
mutter ['mʌtəʳ] *vt, vi* murmeln
mutton ['mʌtn] *n* Hammelfleisch *nt*
mutual ['mju:tʃuəl] *adj* (*feeling, attraction*) gegenseitig; (*benefit*) beiderseitig; (*interest, friend*) gemeinsam; **the feeling was ~** das beruhte auf Gegenseitigkeit
mutually ['mju:tʃuəlɪ] *adv* (*beneficial, satisfactory*) für beide Seiten; (*accepted*) von beiden Seiten; **to be ~ exclusive** einander ausschließen; **~ incompatible** nicht miteinander vereinbar
Muzak® ['mju:zæk] *n* Berieselungsmusik *f* (*inf*)
muzzle ['mʌzl] *n* (*of dog*) Maul *nt*; (*of gun*) Mündung *f*; (*guard: for dog*) Maulkorb *m* ▷*vt* (*dog*) einen Maulkorb anlegen +*dat*; (*fig: press, person*) mundtot machen
MV *abbr* (= *motor vessel*) MS
MVP (*US*) *n abbr* (*Sport*: = *most valuable player*) wertvollster Spieler *m*, wertvollste Spielerin *f*
MW *abbr* (*Radio*: = *medium wave*) MW

KEYWORD

my [maɪ] *adj* mein(e); **this is my brother/sister/house** das ist mein Bruder/meine Schwester/mein Haus; **I've washed my hair/cut my finger** ich habe mir die Haare gewaschen/mir *or* mich in den Finger geschnitten; **is this my pen or yours?** ist das mein Stift oder deiner?

Myanmar ['maɪænma:ʳ] *n* Myanmar *nt*
myopic [maɪ'ɔpɪk] *adj* (*Med, fig*) kurzsichtig
myriad ['mɪrɪəd] *n* Unzahl *f*
myrrh [mə:ʳ] *n* Myrr(h)e *f*
myself [maɪ'sɛlf] *pron* (*acc*) mich; (*dat*) mir; (*emphatic*) selbst; *see also* **oneself**
mysterious [mɪs'tɪərɪəs] *adj* geheimnisvoll, mysteriös
mysteriously [mɪs'tɪərɪəslɪ] *adv* auf mysteriöse Weise; (*smile*) geheimnisvoll
mystery ['mɪstərɪ] *n* (*puzzle*) Rätsel *nt*; (*strangeness*) Rätselhaftigkeit *f* ▷*cpd* (*guest, voice*) mysteriös; **~ tour** Fahrt *f* ins Blaue
mystery caller *n* Testanrufer(in) *m(f)*
mystery calling *n* Testanruf *m*
mystery shopper *n* Testkäufer(in) *m(f)*
mystery story *n* Kriminalgeschichte *f*
mystery visitor *n* Testbesucher(in) *m(f)*
mystic ['mɪstɪk] *n* Mystiker(in) *m(f)* ▷*adj* mystisch
mystical ['mɪstɪkl] *adj* mystisch
mystify ['mɪstɪfaɪ] *vt* vor ein Rätsel stellen
mystique [mɪs'ti:k] *n* geheimnisvoller Nimbus *m*
myth [mɪθ] *n* Mythos *m*; (*fallacy*) Märchen *nt*
mythical ['mɪθɪkl] *adj* mythisch; (*jobs, opportunities etc*) fiktiv
mythological [mɪθə'lɔdʒɪkl] *adj* mythologisch
mythology [mɪ'θɔlədʒɪ] *n* Mythologie *f*

Nn

N[1], **n** [ɛn] *n* (*letter*) N *nt*, n *nt*; **N for Nellie, N for Nan** (*US*) ≈ N wie Nordpol

N[2] [ɛn] *abbr* (= *north*) N

NA (*US*) *n abbr* (= *Narcotics Anonymous*) *Hilfsorganisation für Drogensüchtige*; (= *National Academy*) *Dachverband verschiedener Forschungsunternehmen*

n/a *abbr* (= *not applicable*) entf.

NAACP (*US*) *n abbr* (= *National Association for the Advancement of Colored People*) *Vereinigung zur Förderung Farbiger*

NAAFI ['næfɪ] (*Brit*) *n abbr* (= *Navy, Army, & Air Force Institutes*) *Laden für britische Armeeangehörige*

NACU (*US*) *n abbr* (= *National Association of Colleges and Universities*) *Fachhochschul- und Universitätsverband*

nadir ['neɪdɪə^r] *n* (*fig*) Tiefstpunkt *m*; (*Astron*) Nadir *m*

NAFTA *n abbr* (= *North Atlantic Free Trade Agreement*) *amerikanische Freihandelszone*

nag [næg] *vt* herumnörgeln an +*dat* ▷ *vi* nörgeln ▷ *n* (*pej*: *horse*) Gaul *m*; (: *person*) Nörgler(in) *m*(*f*); **to ~ at sb** jdn plagen, jdm keine Ruhe lassen

nagging ['nægɪŋ] *adj* (*doubt, suspicion*) quälend; (*pain*) dumpf

nail [neɪl] *n* Nagel *m* ▷ *vt* (*inf*: *thief etc*) drankriegen; (: *fraud*) aufdecken; **to ~ sth to sth** etw an etw *acc* nageln; **to ~ sb down (to sth)** jdn (auf etw *acc*) festnageln

nailbrush ['neɪlbrʌʃ] *n* Nagelbürste *f*

nailfile ['neɪlfaɪl] *n* Nagelfeile *f*

nail polish *n* Nagellack *m*

nail polish remover *n* Nagellackentferner *m*

nail scissors *npl* Nagelschere *f*

nail varnish (*Brit*) *n* = **nail polish**

Nairobi [naɪ'rəubɪ] *n* Nairobi *nt*

naive [nɑː'iːv] *adj* naiv

naïveté [nɑːiːv'teɪ] *n* = **naivety**

naivety [naɪ'iːvtɪ] *n* Naivität *f*

naked ['neɪkɪd] *adj* nackt; (*flame, light*) offen; **with the ~ eye** mit bloßem Auge; **to the ~ eye** für das bloße Auge

nakedness ['neɪkɪdnɪs] *n* Nacktheit *f*

NAM (*US*) *n abbr* (= *National Association of Manufacturers*) *nationaler Verband der verarbeitenden Industrie*

name [neɪm] *n* Name *m* ▷ *vt* nennen; (*ship*) taufen; (*identify*) (beim Namen) nennen; (*date etc*) bestimmen, festlegen; **what's your ~?** wie heißen Sie?; **my ~ is Peter** ich heiße Peter; **by ~** mit Namen; **in the ~ of** im Namen +*gen*; **to give one's ~ and address** Namen und Adresse angeben; **to make a ~ for o.s.** sich *dat* einen Namen machen; **to give sb a bad ~** jdn in Verruf bringen; **to call sb ~s** jdn beschimpfen; **to be ~d after sb/sth** nach jdm/etw benannt werden

name-dropping ['neɪmdrɔpɪŋ] *n* Angeberei *f* mit berühmten Namen

nameless ['neɪmlɪs] *adj* namenlos; **who/which shall remain ~** der/die/das ungenannt bleiben soll

namely ['neɪmlɪ] *adv* nämlich

nameplate ['neɪmpleɪt] *n* Namensschild *nt*

namesake ['neɪmseɪk] *n* Namensvetter(in) *m*(*f*)

nan bread [nɑːn-] *n* Nan-Brot *nt*, *fladenförmiges Weißbrot als Beilage zu indischen Gerichten*

nanny ['nænɪ] *n* Kindermädchen *nt*

nanny-goat ['nænɪgəut] *n* Geiß *f*

nap [næp] *n* Schläfchen *nt*; (*of fabric*) Strich *m* ▷ *vi*: **to be caught ~ping** (*fig*) überrumpelt werden; **to have a ~** ein Schläfchen *or* ein Nickerchen (*inf*) machen

NAPA (*US*) *n abbr* (= *National Association of Performing Artists*) *Künstlergewerkschaft*

napalm ['neɪpɑːm] *n* Napalm *nt*

nape [neɪp] *n*: **the ~ of the neck** der Nacken

napkin ['næpkɪn] *n* (*also*: **table napkin**) Serviette *f*

Naples ['neɪplz] *n* Neapel *nt*

Napoleonic [nəpəulɪ'ɔnɪk] *adj* napoleonisch

nappy ['næpɪ] (*Brit*) *n* Windel *f*

nappy liner (*Brit*) *n* Windeleinlage *f*

nappy rash *n* Wundsein *nt*

narcissistic [nɑːsɪ'sɪstɪk] *adj* narzisstisch

narcissus [nɑː'sɪsəs] (*pl* **narcissi**) *n* Narzisse *f*

narcotic [nɑː'kɔtɪk] *adj* narkotisch ▷ *n* Narkotikum *nt*; **narcotics** *npl* (*drugs*) Drogen *pl*; **~ drug** Rauschgift *nt*

nark [nɑːk] (*Brit*: *inf*) *vt*: **to be ~ed at sth** sauer über etw *acc* sein

narrate [nə'reɪt] *vt* erzählen; (*film, programme*) kommentieren

narration [nə'reɪʃən] *n* Kommentar *m*

narrative ['nærətɪv] *n* Erzählung *f*; (*of journey etc*) Schilderung *f*
narrator [nə'reɪtəʳ] *n* Erzähler(in) *m(f)*; (*in film etc*) Kommentator(in) *m(f)*
narrow ['nærəu] *adj* eng; (*ledge etc*) schmal; (*majority, advantage, victory, defeat*) knapp; (*ideas, view*) engstirnig ▷ *vi* sich verengen; (*gap, difference*) sich verringern ▷ *vt* (*gap, difference*) verringern; (*eyes*) zusammenkneifen; **to have a ~ escape** mit knapper Not davonkommen; **to ~ sth down (to sth)** etw (auf etw *acc*) beschränken
narrow gauge ['nærəugeɪdʒ] *adj* (*Rail*) Schmalspur-
narrowly ['nærəulɪ] *adv* knapp; (*escape*) mit knapper Not
narrow-minded [nærəu'maɪndɪd] *adj* engstirnig
NAS (*US*) *n abbr* (*= National Academy of Sciences*) *Akademie der Wissenschaften*
NASA ['næsə] (*US*) *n abbr* (*= National Aeronautics and Space Administration*) NASA *f*
nasal ['neɪzl] *adj* Nasen-; (*voice*) näselnd
Nassau ['næsɔ:] *n* Nassau *nt*
nastily ['nɑ:stɪlɪ] *adv* gemein; (*say*) gehässig
nastiness ['nɑ:stɪnɪs] *n* Gemeinheit *f*; (*of remark*) Gehässigkeit *f*; (*of smell, taste etc*) Ekelhaftigkeit *f*
nasturtium [nəs'tə:ʃəm] *n* Kapuzinerkresse *f*
nasty ['nɑ:stɪ] *adj* (*remark*) gehässig; (*person*) gemein; (*taste, smell*) ekelhaft; (*wound, disease, accident, shock*) schlimm; (*problem, question*) schwierig; (*weather, temper*) abscheulich; **to turn ~** unangenehm werden; **it's a ~ business** es ist schrecklich; **he's got a ~ temper** mit ihm ist nicht gut Kirschen essen
NAS/UWT (*Brit*) *n abbr* (*= National Association of Schoolmasters/Union of Women Teachers*) *Lehrergewerkschaft*
nation ['neɪʃən] *n* Nation *f*; (*people*) Volk *nt*
national ['næʃənl] *adj* (*character, flag*) National-; (*interests*) Staats-; (*newspaper*) überregional ▷ *n* Staatsbürger(in) *m(f)*; **foreign ~** Ausländer(in) *m(f)*
national anthem *n* Nationalhymne *f*
National Curriculum *n zentraler Lehrplan für Schulen in England und Wales*
national debt *n* Staatsverschuldung *f*
national dress *n* Nationaltracht *f*
National Guard (*US*) *n* Nationalgarde *f*
National Health Service (*Brit*) *n* Staatlicher Gesundheitsdienst *m*
National Insurance (*Brit*) *n* Sozialversicherung *f*
nationalism ['næʃnəlɪzəm] *n* Nationalismus *m*
nationalist ['næʃnəlɪst] *adj* nationalistisch ▷ *n* Nationalist(in) *m(f)*
nationality [næʃə'nælɪtɪ] *n* Staatsangehörigkeit *f*, Nationalität *f*
nationalization [næʃnəlaɪ'zeɪʃən] *n* Verstaatlichung *f*
nationalize ['næʃnəlaɪz] *vt* verstaatlichen
National Lottery *n* ≈ Lotto *nt*
nationally ['næʃnəlɪ] *adv* landesweit
national park *n* Nationalpark *m*
national press *n* überregionale Presse *f*
National Security Council (*US*) *n* Nationaler Sicherheitsrat *m*
national service *n* Wehrdienst *m*
National Trust (*Brit*) *n Organisation zum Schutz historischer Bauten und Denkmäler sowie zum Landschaftsschutz; siehe Info-Artikel*

NATIONAL TRUST

Der *National Trust* ist ein 1895 gegründeter Natur- und Denkmalschutzverband in Großbritannien, der Gebäude und Gelände von besonderem historischem oder ästhetischem Interesse erhält und der Öffentlichkeit zugänglich macht. Viele Gebäude im Besitz des National Trust sind (z. T. gegen ein Eintrittsgeld) zu besichtigen.

nationwide ['neɪʃənwaɪd] *adj, adv* landesweit
native ['neɪtɪv] *n* Einheimische(r) *f(m)* ▷ *adj* einheimisch; (*country*) Heimat-; (*language*) Mutter-; (*innate*) angeboren; **a ~ of Germany, a ~ German** ein gebürtiger Deutscher, eine gebürtige Deutsche; **~ to** beheimatet in *+dat*
Native American *adj* indianisch, der Ureinwohner Amerikas ▷ *n* Ureinwohner(in) *m(f)* Amerikas
native speaker *n* Muttersprachler(in) *m(f)*
Nativity [nə'tɪvɪtɪ] *n*: **the ~** Christi Geburt *f*
nativity play *n* Krippenspiel *nt*
NATO ['neɪtəu] *n abbr* (*= North Atlantic Treaty Organization*) NATO *f*
natter ['nætəʳ] (*Brit*) *vi* quatschen (*inf*) ▷ *n*: **to have a ~** einen Schwatz halten
natural ['nætʃrəl] *adj* natürlich; (*disaster*) Natur-; (*innate*) angeboren; (*born*) geboren; (*Mus*) ohne Vorzeichen; **to die of ~ causes** eines natürlichen Todes sterben; **~ foods** Naturkost *f*; **she played F ~ not F sharp** sie spielte f statt fis
natural childbirth *n* natürliche Geburt *f*
natural gas *n* Erdgas *nt*
natural history *n* Naturkunde *f*; **the ~ of England** die Naturgeschichte Englands
naturalist ['nætʃrəlɪst] *n* Naturforscher(in) *m(f)*
naturalize ['nætʃrəlaɪz] *vt*: **to become ~d** eingebürgert werden
naturally ['nætʃrəlɪ] *adv* natürlich; (*happen*) auf natürlichem Wege; (*die*) eines natürlichen Todes; (*cheerful, talented, blonde*) von Natur aus
naturalness ['nætʃrəlnɪs] *n* Natürlichkeit *f*
natural resources *npl* Naturschätze *pl*
natural selection *n* natürliche Auslese *f*
natural wastage *n* natürliche Personalreduzierung *f*
nature ['neɪtʃəʳ] *n* (*Nature*) Natur *f*; (*kind, sort*) Art *f*; (*character*) Wesen *nt*; **by ~** von Natur aus; **by its (very) ~** naturgemäß; **documents of a**

confidential ~ Unterlagen vertraulicher Art
-natured ['neɪtʃəd] *suff*: **good-~** gutmütig; **ill-~** bösartig
nature reserve (*Brit*) *n* Naturschutzgebiet *nt*
nature trail *n* Naturlehrpfad *m*
naturist ['neɪtʃərɪst] *n* Anhänger(in) *m(f)* der Freikörperkultur
naught [nɔ:t] *n* = **nought**
naughtiness ['nɔ:tɪnɪs] *n* (*see adj*) Unartigkeit *f*, Ungezogenheit *f*; Unanständigkeit *f*
naughty ['nɔ:tɪ] *adj* (*child*) unartig, ungezogen; (*story, film, words*) unanständig
nausea ['nɔ:sɪə] *n* Übelkeit *f*
nauseate ['nɔ:sɪeɪt] *vt* Übelkeit verursachen *+dat*; (*fig*) anwidern
nauseating ['nɔ:sɪeɪtɪŋ] *adj* ekelerregend; (*fig*) widerlich
nauseous ['nɔ:sɪəs] *adj* ekelhaft; **I feel ~** mir ist übel
nautical ['nɔ:tɪkl] *adj* (*chart*) See-; (*uniform*) Seemanns-
nautical mile *n* Seemeile *f*
naval ['neɪvl] *adj* Marine-; (*battle, forces*) See-
naval officer *n* Marineoffizier *m*
nave [neɪv] *n* Hauptschiff *nt*, Mittelschiff *nt*
navel ['neɪvl] *n* Nabel *m*
navel piercing ['neɪvl] *n* Nabelpiercing *nt*
navigable ['nævɪgəbl] *adj* schiffbar
navigate ['nævɪgeɪt] *vt* (*river*) befahren; (*path*) begehen ▷ *vi* navigieren; (*Aut*) den Fahrer dirigieren
navigation [nævɪ'geɪʃən] *n* Navigation *f*
navigator ['nævɪgeɪtə^r] *n* (*Naut*) Steuermann *m*; (*Aviat*) Navigator(in) *m(f)*; (*Aut*) Beifahrer(in) *m(f)*
navvy ['nævɪ] (*Brit*) *n* Straßenarbeiter *m*
navy ['neɪvɪ] *n* (Kriegs)marine *f*; (*ships*) (Kriegs)flotte *f* ▷ *adj* marineblau; **Department of the N~** (*US*) Marineministerium *nt*
navy-blue ['neɪvɪ'blu:] *adj* marineblau
Nazareth ['næzərɪθ] *n* Nazareth *nt*
Nazi ['nɑ:tsɪ] *n* Nazi *m*
NB *abbr* (= *nota bene*) NB; (*Canada*) = *New Brunswick*
NBA (*US*) *n abbr* (= *National Basketball Association*) *Basketball-Dachverband*; (= *National Boxing Association*) *Boxsport-Dachverband*
NBC (*US*) *n abbr* (= *National Broadcasting Company*) *Fernsehsender*
NBS (*US*) *n abbr* (= *National Bureau of Standards*) *amerikanischer Normenausschuss*
NC *abbr* (*Comm etc*: = *no charge*) frei; (*US: Post*) = *North Carolina*
NCC (*US*) *n abbr* (= *National Council of Churches*) *Zusammenschluss protestantischer und orthodoxer Kirchen*
NCCL (*Brit*) *n abbr* (= *National Council for Civil Liberties*) *Organisation zum Schutz von Freiheitsrechten*
NCO *n abbr* (*Mil*: = *noncommissioned officer*) Uffz.
ND (*US*) *abbr* (*Post*) = *North Dakota*
N.Dak. (*US*) *abbr* (*Post*) = *North Dakota*
NE *abbr* = **north-east**; (*US: Post*) = *New England*; *Nebraska*
NEA (*US*) *n abbr* (= *National Education Association*) *Verband für das Erziehungswesen*
neap [ni:p] *n* (*also*: **neap tide**) Nippflut *f*
Neapolitan [nɪə'pɔlɪtən] *adj* neapolitanisch ▷ *n* Neapolitaner(in) *m(f)*
near [nɪə^r] *adj* nahe ▷ *adv* nahe; (*almost*) fast, beinahe ▷ *prep* (*also*: **near to**: *in space*) nahe an *+dat*; (: *in time*) um *acc* ... herum; (: *in situation, in intimacy*) nahe *+dat* ▷ *vt* sich nähern *+dat*; (*state, situation*) kurz vor *+dat* stehen; **Christmas is ~** bald ist Weihnachten; **£25,000 or ~est offer** (*Brit*) £25.000 oder das nächstbeste Angebot; **in the ~ future** in naher Zukunft, bald; **in ~ darkness** fast im Dunkeln; **a ~ tragedy** beinahe eine Tragödie; **~ here/there** hier/dort in der Nähe; **to be ~ (to) doing sth** nahe daran sein, etw zu tun; **the building is ~ing completion** der Bau steht kurz vor dem Abschluss
nearby [nɪə'baɪ] *adj* nahe gelegen ▷ *adv* in der Nähe
Near East *n*: **the ~** der Nahe Osten
nearer ['nɪərə^r] *adj comp, adv comp of* **near**
nearest ['nɪərəst] *adj superl, adv superl of* **near**
nearly ['nɪəlɪ] *adv* fast; **I ~ fell** ich wäre beinahe gefallen; **it's not ~ big enough** es ist bei Weitem nicht groß genug; **she was ~ crying** sie war den Tränen nahe
near miss *n* Beinahezusammenstoß *m*; **that was a ~** (*shot*) das war knapp daneben
nearness ['nɪənɪs] *n* Nähe *f*
nearside ['nɪəsaɪd] (*Aut*) *adj* (*when driving on left*) linksseitig; (*when driving on right*) rechtsseitig ▷ *n*: **the ~** (*when driving on left*) die linke Seite; (*when driving on right*) die rechte Seite
near-sighted [nɪə'saɪtɪd] *adj* kurzsichtig
neat [ni:t] *adj* ordentlich; (*handwriting*) sauber; (*plan, solution*) elegant; (*description*) prägnant; (*spirits*) pur; **I drink it ~** ich trinke es pur
neatly ['ni:tlɪ] *adv* ordentlich; (*conveniently*) sauber
neatness ['ni:tnɪs] *n* Ordentlichkeit *f*; (*of solution, plan*) Sauberkeit *f*
Nebr. (*US*) *abbr* (*Post*) = *Nebraska*
nebulous ['nɛbjuləs] *adj* vage, unklar
necessarily ['nɛsɪsrɪlɪ] *adv* notwendigerweise; **not ~** nicht unbedingt
necessary ['nɛsɪsrɪ] *adj* notwendig, nötig; (*inevitable*) unausweichlich; **if ~** wenn nötig, nötigenfalls; **it is ~ to ...** man muss ...
necessitate [nɪ'sɛsɪteɪt] *vt* erforderlich machen
necessity [nɪ'sɛsɪtɪ] *n* Notwendigkeit *f*; **of ~** notgedrungen; **out of ~** aus Not; **the necessities (of life)** das Notwendigste (zum Leben)
neck [nɛk] *n* Hals *m*; (*of shirt, dress, jumper*) Ausschnitt *m* ▷ *vi* (*inf*) knutschen; **~ and neck** Kopf an Kopf; **to stick one's ~ out** (*inf*) seinen Kopf riskieren
necklace ['nɛklɪs] *n* (Hals)kette *f*
neckline ['nɛklaɪn] *n* Ausschnitt *m*

necktie ['nɛktaɪ] *(esp US) n* Krawatte *f*
nectar ['nɛktəʳ] *n* Nektar *m*
nectarine ['nɛktərɪn] *n* Nektarine *f*
née [neɪ] *prep*: **~ Scott** geborene Scott
need [ni:d] *n* Bedarf *m*; *(necessity)* Notwendigkeit *f*; *(requirement)* Bedürfnis *nt*; *(poverty)* Not *f* ▷ *vt* brauchen; *(could do with)* nötig haben; **in ~** bedürftig; **to be in ~ of sth** etw nötig haben; **£10 will meet my immediate ~s** mit £ 10 komme ich erst einmal aus; **(there's) no ~** (das ist) nicht nötig; **there's no ~ to get so worked up about it** du brauchst dich darüber nicht so aufzuregen; **he had no ~ to work** er hatte es nicht nötig zu arbeiten; **I ~ to do it** ich muss es tun; **you don't ~ to go, you needn't go** du brauchst nicht zu gehen; **a signature is ~ed** das bedarf einer Unterschrift *gen*
needle ['ni:dl] *n* Nadel *f* ▷ *vt (fig: inf: goad)* ärgern, piesacken
needless ['ni:dlɪs] *adj* unnötig; **~ to say** natürlich
needlessly ['ni:dlɪslɪ] *adv* unnötig
needlework ['ni:dlwə:k] *n* Handarbeit *f*
needn't ['ni:dnt] = **need not**
needy ['ni:dɪ] *adj* bedürftig ▷ *npl*: **the ~** die Bedürftigen *pl*
negation [nɪ'geɪʃən] *n* Verweigerung *f*
negative ['nɛgətɪv] *adj* negativ; *(answer)* abschlägig ▷ *n (Phot)* Negativ *nt*; *(Ling)* Verneinungswort *nt*, Negation *f*; **to answer in the ~** eine verneinende Antwort geben
negative equity *n Differenz zwischen gefallenem Wert und hypothekarischer Belastung eines Wohnungseigentums*
neglect [nɪ'glɛkt] *vt* vernachlässigen; *(writer, artist)* unterschätzen ▷ *n* Vernachlässigung *f*
neglected [nɪ'glɛktɪd] *adj* vernachlässigt; *(writer, artist)* unterschätzt
neglectful [nɪ'glɛktful] *adj* nachlässig; *(father)* pflichtvergessen; **to be ~ of sth** etw vernachlässigen
negligee ['nɛglɪʒeɪ] *n* Negligee *nt*, Negligé *nt*
negligence ['nɛglɪdʒəns] *n* Nachlässigkeit *f*; *(Law)* Fahrlässigkeit *f*
negligent ['nɛglɪdʒənt] *adj* nachlässig; *(Law)* fahrlässig; *(casual)* lässig
negligently ['nɛglɪdʒəntlɪ] *adv (see adj)* nachlässig; fahrlässig; lässig
negligible ['nɛglɪdʒɪbl] *adj* geringfügig
negotiable [nɪ'gəuʃɪəbl] *adj* verhandlungsfähig; *(path, river)* passierbar; **not ~** *(on cheque etc)* nicht übertragbar
negotiate [nɪ'gəuʃɪeɪt] *vi* verhandeln ▷ *vt* aushandeln; *(obstacle, hill)* überwinden; *(bend)* nehmen; **to ~ with sb (for sth)** mit jdm (über etw *acc*) verhandeln
negotiating table [nɪ'gəuʃɪeɪtɪŋ-] *n* Verhandlungstisch *m*
negotiation [nɪgəuʃɪ'eɪʃən] *n* Verhandlung *f*; **the matter is still under ~** über die Sache wird noch verhandelt
negotiator [nɪ'gəuʃɪeɪtəʳ] *n* Unterhändler(in) *m(f)*
Negress ['ni:grɪs] *(pej) n* Negerin *f*
Negro ['ni:grəu] *(pl* **N~es**; *pej) adj (boy, slave)* Neger- ▷ *n* Neger *m*
neigh [neɪ] *vi* wiehern
neighbour, *(US)* **neighbor** ['neɪbəʳ] *n* Nachbar(in) *m(f)*
neighbourhood ['neɪbəhud] *n (place)* Gegend *f*; *(people)* Nachbarschaft *f*; **in the ~ of ...** in der Nähe von ...; *(sum of money)* so um die ...
neighbourhood watch *n Vereinigung von Bürgern, die Straßenwachen etc zur Unterstützung der Polizei bei der Verbrechensbekämpfung organisiert*
neighbouring ['neɪbərɪŋ] *adj* benachbart, Nachbar-
neighbourly ['neɪbəlɪ] *adj* nachbarlich
neither ['naɪðəʳ] *conj*: **I didn't move and ~ did John** ich bewegte mich nicht und John auch nicht ▷ *pron* keine(r, s) (von beiden) ▷ *adv*: **~ ... nor ...** weder ... noch ...; **~ story is true** keine der beiden Geschichten stimmt; **~ is true** beides stimmt nicht; **~ do I/have I** ich auch nicht
neo ... ['ni:əu] *pref* neo-, Neo-
neolithic [ni:ə'lɪθɪk] *adv* jungsteinzeitlich, neolithisch
neologism [nɪ'ɔlədʒɪzəm] *n* (Wort)neubildung *f*, Neologismus *m*
neon ['ni:ɔn] *n* Neon *nt*
neon light *n* Neonlampe *f*
neon sign *n* Neonreklame *f*
Nepal [nɪ'pɔ:l] *n* Nepal *nt*
nephew ['nɛvju:] *n* Neffe *m*
nepotism ['nɛpətɪzəm] *n* Vetternwirtschaft *f*
nerd [nə:d] *(inf) n* Schwachkopf *m*
nerve [nə:v] *n (Anat)* Nerv *m*; *(courage)* Mut *m*; *(impudence)* Frechheit *f*; **nerves** *npl (anxiety)* Nervosität *f*; *(emotional strength)* Nerven *pl*; **he gets on my ~s** er geht mir auf die Nerven; **to lose one's ~** die Nerven verlieren
nerve-centre, *(US)* **nerve-center** ['nə:vsɛntəʳ] *n (fig)* Schaltzentrale *f*
nerve gas *n* Nervengas *nt*
nerve-racking ['nə:vrækɪŋ] *adj* nervenaufreibend
nervous ['nə:vəs] *adj* Nerven-, nervlich; *(anxious)* nervös; **to be ~ of/about** Angst haben vor *+dat*
nervous breakdown *n* Nervenzusammenbruch *m*
nervously ['nə:vəslɪ] *adv* nervös
nervousness ['nə:vəsnɪs] *n* Nervosität *f*
nervous system *n* Nervensystem *nt*
nervous wreck *(inf) n* Nervenbündel *nt*; **to be a ~** mit den Nerven völlig am Ende sein
nervy ['nə:vɪ] *(inf) adj (Brit: tense)* nervös; *(US: cheeky)* dreist
nest [nɛst] *n* Nest *nt* ▷ *vi* nisten; **a ~ of tables** ein Satz Tische *or* von Tischen
nest egg *n* Notgroschen *m*
nestle ['nɛsl] *vi* sich kuscheln; *(house)* eingebettet sein
nestling ['nɛstlɪŋ] *n* Nestling *m*

Net [nɛt] *n*: **the ~** (*Comput*) das Internet
net [nɛt] *n* Netz *nt*; (*fabric*) Tüll *m* ▷ *adj* (*Comm*) Netto-; (*final: result, effect*) End- ▷ *vt* (mit einem Netz) fangen; (*profit*) einbringen; (*deal, sale, fortune*) an Land ziehen; **~ of tax** steuerfrei; **he earns £10,000 ~ per year** er verdient £ 10.000 netto im Jahr; **it weighs 250g ~** es wiegt 250 g netto
netball ['nɛtbɔ:l] *n* Netzball *m*
net curtains *npl* Gardinen *pl*, Stores *pl*
Netherlands ['nɛðələndz] *npl*: **the ~** die Niederlande *pl*
nett [nɛt] *adj* = **net**
netting ['nɛtɪŋ] *n* (*for fence etc*) Maschendraht *m*; (*fabric*) Netzgewebe *nt*, Tüll *m*
nettle ['nɛtl] *n* Nessel *f*; **to grasp the ~** (*fig*) in den sauren Apfel beißen
network ['nɛtwə:k] *n* Netz *nt*; (*TV, Radio*) Sendenetz *nt* ▷ *vt* (*Radio, TV*) im ganzen Netzbereich ausstrahlen; (*computers*) in einem Netzwerk zusammenschließen
neuralgia [njuə'rældʒə] *n* Neuralgie *f*, Nervenschmerzen *pl*
neurological [njuərə'lɔdʒɪkl] *adj* neurologisch
neurotic [njuə'rɔtɪk] *adj* neurotisch ▷ *n* Neurotiker(in) *m(f)*
neuter ['nju:tə^r] *adj* (*Ling*) sächlich ▷ *vt* kastrieren; (*female*) sterilisieren
neutral ['nju:trəl] *adj* neutral ▷ *n* (*Aut*) Leerlauf *m*
neutrality [nju:'trælɪtɪ] *n* Neutralität *f*
neutralize ['nju:trəlaɪz] *vt* neutralisieren, aufheben
neutron ['nju:trɔn] *n* Neutron *nt*
neutron bomb *n* Neutronenbombe *f*
Nev. (*US*) *abbr* (*Post*) = *Nevada*
never ['nɛvə^r] *adv* nie; (*not*) nicht; **~ in my life** noch nie; **~ again** nie wieder; **well I ~!** nein, so was!; *see also* **mind**
never-ending [nɛvər'ɛndɪŋ] *adj* endlos
nevertheless [nɛvəðə'lɛs] *adv* trotzdem, dennoch
new [nju:] *adj* neu; (*mother*) jung; **as good as ~** so gut wie neu; **to be ~ to sb** jdm neu sein
New Age *n* New Age *nt*
newborn ['nju:bɔ:n] *adj* neugeboren
newcomer ['nju:kʌmə^r] *n* Neuankömmling *m*; (*in job*) Neuling *m*
new-fangled ['nju:'fæŋgld] (*pej*) *adj* neumodisch
new-found ['nju:faund] *adj* neu entdeckt; (*confidence*) neu geschöpft
Newfoundland ['nju:fənlənd] *n* Neufundland *nt*
New Guinea *n* Neuguinea *nt*
newly ['nju:lɪ] *adv* neu
newly-weds ['nju:lɪwɛdz] *npl* Neuvermählte *pl*, Frischvermählte *pl*
new moon *n* Neumond *m*
newness ['nju:nɪs] *n* Neuheit *f*; (*of cheese, bread etc*) Frische *f*
New Orleans [-'ɔ:li:ənz] *n* New Orleans *nt*
news [nju:z] *n* Nachricht *f*; **a piece of ~** eine Neuigkeit; **the ~** (*Radio, TV*) die Nachrichten *pl*; **good/bad ~** gute/schlechte Nachrichten
news agency *n* Nachrichtenagentur *f*
newsagent ['nju:zeɪdʒənt] (*Brit*) *n* Zeitungshändler(in) *m(f)*
news bulletin *n* Bulletin *nt*
newscaster ['nju:zkɑ:stə^r] *n* Nachrichtensprecher(in) *m(f)*
newsdealer ['nju:zdi:lə^r] (*US*) *n* = **newsagent**
newsflash ['nju:zflæʃ] *n* Kurzmeldung *f*
newsletter ['nju:zlɛtə^r] *n* Rundschreiben *nt*, Mitteilungsblatt *nt*
newspaper ['nju:zpeɪpə^r] *n* Zeitung *f*; **daily/weekly ~** Tages-/Wochenzeitung *f*
newsprint ['nju:zprɪnt] *n* Zeitungspapier *nt*
newsreader ['nju:zri:də^r] *n* = **newscaster**
newsreel ['nju:zri:l] *n* Wochenschau *f*
newsroom ['nju:zru:m] *n* Nachrichtenredaktion *f*; (*Radio, TV*) Nachrichtenstudio *nt*
newsstand ['nju:zstænd] *n* Zeitungsstand *m*
newsworthy ['nju:zwə:ðɪ] *adj*: **to be ~** Neuigkeitswert haben
newt [nju:t] *n* Wassermolch *m*
new town (*Brit*) *n neue, teilweise mit Regierungsgeldern errichtete städtische Siedlung*
New Year *n* neues Jahr *nt*; (*New Year's Day*) Neujahr *nt*; **Happy ~!** (ein) glückliches *or* frohes neues Jahr!
New Year's Day *n* Neujahr *nt*, Neujahrstag *m*
New Year's Eve *n* Silvester *nt*
New York [-'jɔ:k] *n* New York *nt*; (*also:* **New York State**) der Staat New York
New Zealand [-'zi:lənd] *n* Neuseeland *nt* ▷ *adj* neuseeländisch
New Zealander [-'zi:ləndə^r] *n* Neuseeländer(in) *m(f)*
next [nɛkst] *adj* nächste(r, s); (*room*) Neben- ▷ *adv* dann; (*do, happen*) als Nächstes; (*afterwards*) danach; **the ~ day** am nächsten *or* folgenden Tag; **~ time** das nächste Mal; **~ year** nächstes Jahr; **~ please!** der Nächste bitte!; **who's ~?** wer ist der Nächste?; **"turn to the ~ page"** „bitte umblättern"; **the week after ~** übernächste Woche; **the ~ on the right/left** der/die/das Nächste rechts/links; **the ~ thing I knew** das Nächste, woran ich mich erinnern konnte; **~ to** neben *+dat*; **~ to nothing** so gut wie nichts; **when do we meet ~?** wann treffen wir uns wieder *or* das nächste Mal?; **the ~ best** der/die/das Nächstbeste
next door *adv* nebenan ▷ *adj*: **next-door** nebenan; **the house ~** das Nebenhaus; **to go ~** nach nebenan gehen; **my next-door neighbour** mein direkter Nachbar
next-of-kin ['nɛkstəv'kɪn] *n* nächster Verwandter *m*, nächste Verwandte *f*
NF *n abbr* (*Brit: Pol: = National Front*) *rechtsradikale Partei* ▷ *abbr* (*Canada*) = *Newfoundland*
NFL (*US*) *n abbr* (*= National Football League*) *Fußball-Nationalliga*
NG (*US*) *abbr* = **National Guard**
NGO *n abbr* (*= nongovernmental organization*)

nichtstaatliche Organisation
NH (*US*) *abbr* (*Post*) = *New Hampshire*
NHL (*US*) *n abbr* (= *National Hockey League*) *Hockey-Nationalliga*
NHS (*Brit*) *n abbr* = **National Health Service**
NI *abbr* = **Northern Ireland**; (*Brit*) = **National Insurance**
Niagara Falls [naɪ'ægərə-] *npl* Niagarafälle *pl*
nib [nɪb] *n* Feder *f*
nibble ['nɪbl] *vt* knabbern; (*bite*) knabbern an *+dat* ▷*vi*: **to ~ at** knabbern an *+dat*
Nicaragua [nɪkə'rægjuə] *n* Nicaragua *nt*
Nicaraguan [nɪkə'rægjuən] *adj* nicaraguanisch ▷*n* Nicaraguaner(in) *m(f)*
Nice [ni:s] *n* Nizza *nt*
nice [naɪs] *adj* nett; (*holiday, weather, picture etc*) schön; (*taste*) gut; (*person, clothes etc*) hübsch
nicely ['naɪslɪ] *adv* (*attractively*) hübsch; (*politely*) nett; (*satisfactorily*) gut; **that will do ~** das reicht (vollauf)
niceties ['naɪsɪtɪz] *npl*: **the ~** die Feinheiten *pl*
niche [ni:ʃ] *n* Nische *f*; (*job, position*) Plätzchen *nt*
nick [nɪk] *n* Kratzer *m*; (*in metal, wood etc*) Kerbe *f* ▷*vt* (*Brit*: *inf*: *steal*) klauen; (: *arrest*) einsperren, einlochen; (*cut*): **to ~ o.s.** sich schneiden; **in good ~** (*Brit*: *inf*) gut in Schuss; **in the ~** (*Brit*: *inf*: *in prison*) im Knast; **in the ~ of time** gerade noch rechtzeitig
nickel ['nɪkl] *n* Nickel *nt*; (US) Fünfcentstück *nt*
nickname ['nɪkneɪm] *n* Spitzname *m* ▷*vt* betiteln, taufen (*inf*)
Nicosia [nɪkə'si:ə] *n* Nikosia *nt*
nicotine ['nɪkəti:n] *n* Nikotin *nt*
nicotine patch *n* Nikotinpflaster *nt*
niece [ni:s] *n* Nichte *f*
nifty ['nɪftɪ] (*inf*) *adj* flott; (*gadget, tool*) schlau
Niger ['naɪdʒər] *n* Niger *m*
Nigeria [naɪ'dʒɪərɪə] *n* Nigeria *nt*
Nigerian [naɪ'dʒɪərɪən] *adj* nigerianisch ▷*n* Nigerianer(in) *m(f)*
niggardly ['nɪgədlɪ] *adj* knauserig; (*allowance, amount*) armselig
nigger [nɪgər] (*inf*) *n* Nigger *m* (*inf!*)
niggle ['nɪgl] *vt* plagen, zu schaffen machen *+dat* ▷*vi* herumkritisieren
niggling ['nɪglɪŋ] *adj* quälend; (*pain, ache*) bohrend
night [naɪt] *n* Nacht *f*; (*evening*) Abend *m*; **the ~ before last** vorletzte Nacht, vorgestern Abend; **at ~, by ~** nachts, abends; **nine o'clock at ~** neun Uhr abends; **in the ~, during the ~** in der Nacht; **~ and day** Tag und Nacht
nightcap ['naɪtkæp] *n* Schlaftrunk *m*
nightclub ['naɪtklʌb] *n* Nachtlokal *nt*
nightdress ['naɪtdrɛs] *n* Nachthemd *nt*
nightfall ['naɪtfɔ:l] *n* Einbruch *m* der Dunkelheit
nightgown ['naɪtgaun] *n* = **nightdress**
nightie ['naɪtɪ] *n* = **nightdress**
nightingale ['naɪtɪŋgeɪl] *n* Nachtigall *f*
nightlife ['naɪtlaɪf] *n* Nachtleben *nt*
nightly ['naɪtlɪ] *adj* (all)nächtlich, Nacht-; (*every evening*) (all)abendlich, Abend- ▷*adv* jede Nacht; (*every evening*) jeden Abend
nightmare ['naɪtmɛər] *n* Albtraum *m*
night porter *n* Nachtportier *m*
night safe *n* Nachtsafe *m*
night school *n* Abendschule *f*
nightshade ['naɪtʃeɪd] *n*: **deadly ~** Tollkirsche *f*
night shift *n* Nachtschicht *f*
night-time ['naɪttaɪm] *n* Nacht *f*
night watchman *n* Nachtwächter *m*
nihilism ['naɪɪlɪzəm] *n* Nihilismus *m*
nil [nɪl] *n* Nichts *nt*; (*Brit*: *Sport*) Null *f*
Nile [naɪl] *n*: **the ~** der Nil
nimble ['nɪmbl] *adj* flink; (*mind*) beweglich
nine [naɪn] *num* neun
nineteen ['naɪn'ti:n] *num* neunzehn
nineteenth [naɪn'ti:nθ] *num* neunzehnte(r, s)
ninety ['naɪntɪ] *num* neunzig
ninth [naɪnθ] *num* neunte(r, s) ▷*n* Neuntel *nt*
nip [nɪp] *vt* zwicken ▷*n* Biss *m*; (*drink*) Schlückchen *nt* ▷*vi* (*Brit*: *inf*): **to ~ out/down/up** kurz raus-/runter-/raufgehen; **to ~ into a shop** (*Brit*: *inf*) kurz in einen Laden gehen
nipple ['nɪpl] *n* (*Anat*) Brustwarze *f*
nippy ['nɪpɪ] (*Brit*) *adj* (*quick*: *person*) flott; (: *car*) spritzig; (*cold*) frisch
nit [nɪt] *n* Nisse *f*; (*inf*: *idiot*) Dummkopf *m*
nitpicking ['nɪtpɪkɪŋ] (*inf*) *n* Kleinigkeitskrämerei *f*
nitrogen ['naɪtrədʒən] *n* Stickstoff *m*
nitroglycerin, nitroglycerine ['naɪtrəu'glɪsəri:n] *n* Nitroglyzerin *nt*
nitty-gritty ['nɪtɪ'grɪtɪ] (*inf*) *n*: **to get down to the ~** zur Sache kommen
nitwit ['nɪtwɪt] (*inf*) *n* Dummkopf *m*
NJ (*US*) *abbr* (*Post*) = *New Jersey*
NLF *n abbr* (= *National Liberation Front*) *vietnamesische Befreiungsbewegung während des Vietnamkrieges*
NLRB (*US*) *n abbr* (= *National Labor Relations Board*) *Ausschuss zur Regelung der Beziehungen zwischen Arbeitgebern und Arbeitnehmern*
NM, N.Mex. (*US*) *abbr* (*Post*) = *New Mexico*

KEYWORD

no [nəu] (*pl* **noes**) *adv* (*opposite of "yes"*) nein; **no thank you** nein danke
▷*adj* (*not any*) kein(e); **I have no money/time/books** ich habe kein Geld/keine Zeit/keine Bücher; **"no entry"** „kein Zutritt"; **"no smoking"** „Rauchen verboten"
▷*n* Nein *nt*; **there were 20 noes and one abstention** es gab 20 Neinstimmen und eine Enthaltung; **I won't take no for an answer** ich bestehe darauf

no. *abbr* (= *number*) Nr.
nobble [nɔbl] (*Brit*: *inf*) *vt* (*bribe*) (sich *dat*) kaufen; (*grab*) sich *dat* schnappen; (*Racing*: *horse, dog*) lahmlegen
Nobel Prize [nəu'bɛl-] *n* Nobelpreis *m*
nobility [nəu'bɪlɪtɪ] *n* Adel *m*; (*quality*) Edelmut

m

noble ['nəubl] *adj* edel, nobel; (*aristocratic*) ad(e)lig; (*impressive*) prächtig

nobleman ['nəublmən] (*irreg: like* **man**) *n* Ad(e)lige(r) *f(m)*

nobly ['nəublɪ] *adv* edel

nobody ['nəubədɪ] *pron* niemand, keiner ▷ *n*: **he's a ~** er ist ein Niemand *m*

no-claims bonus [nəu'kleɪmz-] *n* Schadenfreiheitsrabatt *m*

nocturnal [nɔk'tə:nl] *adj* nächtlich; (*animal*) Nacht-

nod [nɔd] *vi* nicken; (*fig: flowers etc*) wippen ▷ *vt*: **to ~ one's head** mit dem Kopf nicken ▷ *n* Nicken *nt*; **they ~ded their agreement** sie nickten zustimmend
▶ **nod off** *vi* einnicken

no-fly zone [nəu'flaɪ-] *n* Sperrzone *f* für den Flugverkehr

noise [nɔɪz] *n* Geräusch *nt*; (*din*) Lärm *m*

noiseless ['nɔɪzlɪs] *adj* geräuschlos

noisily ['nɔɪzɪlɪ] *adv* laut

noisy ['nɔɪzɪ] *adj* laut

nomad ['nəumæd] *n* Nomade *m*, Nomadin *f*

nomadic [nəu'mædɪk] *adj* Nomaden-, nomadisch

no-man's-land ['nəumænzlænd] *n* Niemandsland *nt*

nominal ['nɔmɪnl] *adj* nominell

nominate ['nɔmɪneɪt] *vt* nominieren; (*appoint*) ernennen

nomination [nɔmɪ'neɪʃən] *n* Nominierung *f*; (*appointment*) Ernennung *f*

nominee [nɔmɪ'ni:] *n* Kandidat(in) *m(f)*

non- [nɔn] *pref* nicht-, Nicht-

non-alcoholic [nɔnælkə'hɔlɪk] *adj* alkoholfrei

non-aligned [nɔnə'laɪnd] *adj* blockfrei

non-breakable [nɔn'breɪkəbl] *adj* unzerbrechlich

nonce word ['nɔns-] *n* Ad-hoc-Bildung *f*

nonchalant ['nɔnʃələnt] *adj* lässig, nonchalant

noncommissioned officer [nɔnkə'mɪʃənd-] *n* Unteroffizier *m*

non-committal [nɔnkə'mɪtl] *adj* zurückhaltend; (*answer*) unverbindlich

nonconformist [nɔnkən'fɔ:mɪst] *n* Nonkonformist(in) *m(f)* ▷ *adj* nonkonformistisch

non-cooperation ['nɔnkəuɔpə'reɪʃən] *n* unkooperative Haltung *f*

nondescript ['nɔndɪskrɪpt] *adj* unauffällig; (*colour*) unbestimmbar

none [nʌn] *pron* (*not one*) kein(e, er, es); (*not any*) nichts; **~ of us** keiner von uns; **I've ~ left** (*not any*) ich habe nichts übrig; (*not one*) ich habe kein(e, en, es) übrig; **~ at all** (*not any*) überhaupt nicht; (*not one*) überhaupt kein(e, er, es); **I was ~ the wiser** ich war auch nicht klüger; **she would have ~ of it** sie wollte nichts davon hören; **it was ~ other than X** es war kein anderer als X

nonentity [nɔ'nɛntɪtɪ] *n* (*person*) Nichts *nt*, unbedeutende Figur *f*

non-essential [nɔnɪ'sɛnʃl] *adj* unnötig ▷ *n*: **~s** nicht (lebens)notwendige Dinge *pl*

nonetheless ['nʌnðə'lɛs] *adv* nichtsdestoweniger, trotzdem

nonevent [nɔnɪ'vɛnt] *n* Reinfall *m*

non-existent [nɔnɪg'zɪstənt] *adj* nicht vorhanden

non-fiction [nɔn'fɪkʃən] *n* Sachbücher *pl* ▷ *adj* (*book*) Sach-; (*prize*) Sachbuch-

non-flammable [nɔn'flæməbl] *adj* nicht entzündbar

non-intervention ['nɔnɪntə'vɛnʃən] *n* Nichteinmischung *f*, Nichteingreifen *nt*

no-no ['nəunəu] *n*: **it's a ~** (*inf*) das kommt nicht infrage

non obst. *abbr* (= *non obstante*) dennoch

no-nonsense [nəu'nɔnsəns] *adj* (*approach, look*) nüchtern

non-payment [nɔn'peɪmənt] *n* Nichtzahlung *f*, Zahlungsverweigerung *f*

nonplussed [nɔn'plʌst] *adj* verdutzt, verblüfft

non-profit making ['nɔn'prɔfɪt-] *adj* (*organization*) gemeinnützig

nonreturnable [nɔnrə'tə:nəbl] *adj*: **~ bottle** Einwegflasche *f*

nonsense ['nɔnsəns] *n* Unsinn *m*; **~!** Unsinn!, Quatsch!; **it is ~ to say that ...** es ist dummes Gerede zu sagen, dass ...; **to make (a) ~ of sth** etw ad absurdum führen

nonsensical [nɔn'sɛnsɪkl] *adj* (*idea, action etc*) unsinnig

non-shrink [nɔn'ʃrɪŋk] (*Brit*) *adj* nicht einlaufend

non-smoker ['nɔn'sməukə^r] *n* Nichtraucher(in) *m(f)*

nonstarter [nɔn'stɑ:tə^r] *n* (*fig*): **it's a ~** (*idea etc*) es hat keine Erfolgschance

non-stick ['nɔn'stɪk] *adj* kunststoffbeschichtet, Teflon-®

non-stop ['nɔn'stɔp] *adj* ununterbrochen; (*flight*) Nonstop-, Non-Stop- ▷ *adv* ununterbrochen; (*fly*) nonstop

non-taxable [nɔn'tæksəbl] *adj* nicht steuerpflichtig

non-U [nɔn'ju:] (*Brit: inf*) *adj abbr* (= *non-upper class*) nicht vornehm

non-white ['nɔn'waɪt] *adj* farbig ▷ *n* Farbige(r) *f(m)*

noodles ['nu:dlz] *npl* Nudeln *pl*

nook [nuk] *n*: **every ~ and cranny** jeder Winkel

noon [nu:n] *n* Mittag *m*

no-one ['nəuwʌn] *pron* = **nobody**

noose [nu:s] *n* Schlinge *f*

nor [nɔ:^r] *conj, adv* = **neither**

Norf (*Brit*) *abbr* (*Post*) = *Norfolk*

norm [nɔ:m] *n* Norm *f*

normal ['nɔ:məl] *adj* normal ▷ *n*: **to return to ~** sich wieder normalisieren

normality [nɔ:'mælɪtɪ] *n* Normalität *f*

normally ['nɔ:məlɪ] *adv* normalerweise; (*act, behave*) normal

Normandy ['nɔ:məndɪ] *n* Normandie *f*

north [nɔːθ] *n* Norden *m* ▷ *adj* nördlich, Nord- ▷ *adv* nach Norden; **~ of** nördlich von
North Africa *n* Nordafrika *nt*
North African *adj* nordafrikanisch ▷ *n* Nordafrikaner(in) *m(f)*
North America *n* Nordamerika *nt*
North American *adj* nordamerikanisch ▷ *n* Nordamerikaner(in) *m(f)*
Northants [nɔː'θænts] *(Brit) abbr (Post)* = *Northamptonshire*
northbound ['nɔːθbaund] *adj* in Richtung Norden; *(carriageway)* nach Norden (führend)
Northd *(Brit) abbr (Post)* = *Northumberland*
north-east [nɔːθ'iːst] *n* Nordosten *m* ▷ *adj* nordöstlich, Nordost- ▷ *adv* nach Nordosten; **~ of** nordöstlich von
northerly ['nɔːðəlɪ] *adj* nördlich
northern ['nɔːðən] *adj* nördlich, Nord-
Northern Ireland *n* Nordirland *nt*
North Korea *n* Nordkorea *nt*
North Pole *n*: **the ~** der Nordpol
North Sea *n*: **the ~** die Nordsee *f*
North Sea oil *n* Nordseeöl *nt*
northward ['nɔːθwəd], **northwards** ['nɔːθwədz] *adv* nach Norden, nordwärts
north-west [nɔːθ'wɛst] *n* Nordwesten *m* ▷ *adj* nordwestlich, Nordwest- ▷ *adv* nach Nordwesten; **~ of** nordwestlich von
Norway ['nɔːweɪ] *n* Norwegen *nt*
Norwegian [nɔː'wiːdʒən] *adj* norwegisch ▷ *n* Norweger(in) *m(f)*; *(Ling)* Norwegisch *nt*
nos. *abbr (= numbers)* Nrn.
nose [nəuz] *n* Nase *f*; *(of car)* Schnauze *f* ▷ *vi (also:* **nose one's way**) sich schieben; **to follow one's ~** immer der Nase nach gehen; **to get up one's ~** *(inf)* auf die Nerven gehen *+dat*; **to have a (good) ~ for sth** eine (gute) Nase für etw haben; **to keep one's ~ clean** *(inf)* eine saubere Weste behalten; **to look down one's ~ at sb/sth** *(inf)* auf jdn/etw herabsehen; **to pay through the ~ (for sth)** *(inf)* (für etw) viel blechen; **to rub sb's ~ in sth** *(inf)* jdm etw unter die Nase reiben; **to turn one's ~ up at sth** *(inf)* die Nase über etw *acc* rümpfen; **under sb's ~** vor jds Augen
▸ **nose about** *vi* herumschnüffeln
▸ **nose around** *vi* = **nose about**
nosebleed ['nəuzbliːd] *n* Nasenbluten *nt*
nose-dive ['nəuzdaɪv] *n (of plane)* Sturzflug *m* ▷ *vi (plane)* im Sturzflug herabgehen
nose drops *npl* Nasentropfen *pl*
nosey ['nəuzɪ] *(inf) adj* = **nosy**
nostalgia [nɔs'tældʒɪə] *n* Nostalgie *f*
nostalgic [nɔs'tældʒɪk] *adj* nostalgisch
nostril ['nɔstrɪl] *n* Nasenloch *nt*; *(of animal)* Nüster *f*
nosy ['nəuzɪ] *(inf) adj* neugierig

KEYWORD

not [nɔt] *adv* nicht; **he is not** *or* **isn't here** er ist nicht hier; **you must not** *or* **you mustn't do that** das darfst du nicht tun; **it's too late, isn't it?** es ist zu spät, nicht wahr?; **not that I don't like him** nicht, dass ich ihn nicht mag; **not yet** noch nicht; **not now** nicht jetzt; *see also* **all; only**

notable ['nəutəbl] *adj* bemerkenswert
notably ['nəutəblɪ] *adv* hauptsächlich; *(markedly)* bemerkenswert
notary ['nəutərɪ] *n (also:* **notary public**) Notar(in) *m(f)*
notation [nəu'teɪʃən] *n* Notation *f*; *(Mus)* Notenschrift *f*
notch [nɔtʃ] *n* Kerbe *f*; *(in blade, saw)* Scharte *f*; *(fig)* Klasse *f*
▸ **notch up** *vt* erzielen; *(victory)* erringen
note [nəut] *n* Notiz *f*; *(of lecturer)* Manuskript *nt*; *(of student etc)* Aufzeichnung *f*; *(in book etc)* Anmerkung *f*; *(letter)* paar Zeilen *pl*; *(banknote)* Note *f*, Schein *m*; *(Mus: sound)* Ton *m*; *(: symbol)* Note *f*; *(tone)* Ton *m*, Klang *m* ▷ *vt* beachten; *(point out)* anmerken; *(also:* **note down**) notieren; **of ~** bedeutend; **to make a ~ of sth** sich *dat* etw notieren; **to take ~s** Notizen machen, mitschreiben; **to take ~ of sth** etw zur Kenntnis nehmen
notebook ['nəutbuk] *n* Notizbuch *nt*; *(for shorthand)* Stenoblock *m*
notecase ['nəutkeɪs] *(Brit) n* Brieftasche *f*
noted ['nəutɪd] *adj* bekannt
notepad ['nəutpæd] *n* Notizblock *m*
notepaper ['nəutpeɪpə^r] *n* Briefpapier *nt*
noteworthy ['nəutwəːðɪ] *adj* beachtenswert
nothing ['nʌθɪŋ] *n* nichts; **~ new/worse** *etc* nichts Neues/Schlimmeres *etc*; **~ much** nicht viel; **~ else** sonst nichts; **for ~** umsonst; **~ at all** überhaupt nichts
notice ['nəutɪs] *n* Bekanntmachung *f*; *(sign)* Schild *nt*; *(warning)* Ankündigung *f*; *(dismissal)* Kündigung *f*; *(Brit: review)* Kritik *f*, Rezension *f* ▷ *vt* bemerken; **to bring sth to sb's ~** jdn auf etw *acc* aufmerksam machen; **to take no ~ of** ignorieren, nicht beachten; **to escape sb's ~** jdm entgehen; **it has come to my ~ that ...** es ist mir zu Ohren gekommen, dass ...; **to give sb ~ of sth** jdm von etw Bescheid geben; **without ~** ohne Ankündigung; **advance ~** Vorankündigung *f*; **at short/a moment's ~** kurzfristig/innerhalb kürzester Zeit; **until further ~** bis auf Weiteres; **to hand in one's ~** kündigen; **to be given one's ~** gekündigt werden *+dat*
noticeable ['nəutɪsəbl] *adj* deutlich
noticeboard ['nəutɪsbɔːd] *(Brit) n* Anschlagbrett *nt*
notification [nəutɪfɪ'keɪʃən] *n* Benachrichtigung *f*
notify ['nəutɪfaɪ] *vt*: **to ~ sb (of sth)** jdn (von etw) benachrichtigen
notion ['nəuʃən] *n* Vorstellung *f*; **notions** *(US) npl (haberdashery)* Kurzwaren *pl*
notoriety [nəutə'raɪətɪ] *n* traurige Berühmtheit *f*
notorious [nəu'tɔːrɪəs] *adj* berüchtigt

notoriously [nəu'tɔ:rɪəslɪ] *adv* notorisch
Notts [nɔts] (*Brit*) *abbr* (*Post*) = *Nottinghamshire*
notwithstanding [nɔtwɪθ'stændɪŋ] *adv* trotzdem ▷ *prep* trotz +*dat*
nougat ['nu:gɑ:] *n* Nugat *m*
nought [nɔ:t] *n* Null *f*
noughties ['nɔ:tɪz] *npl* (*inf*) *das erste Jahrzehnt des dritten Jahrtausends*, Nullerjahre *pl*
noun [naun] *n* Hauptwort *nt*, Substantiv *nt*
nourish ['nʌrɪʃ] *vt* nähren
nourishing ['nʌrɪʃɪŋ] *adj* nahrhaft
nourishment ['nʌrɪʃmənt] *n* Nahrung *f*
Nov. *abbr* (= *November*) Nov.
Nova Scotia ['nəuvə'skəuʃə] *n* Neuschottland *nt*
novel ['nɔvl] *n* Roman *m* ▷ *adj* neu(artig)
novelist ['nɔvəlɪst] *n* Romanschriftsteller(in) *m(f)*
novelty ['nɔvəltɪ] *n* Neuheit *f*; (*object*) Kleinigkeit *f*
November [nəu'vɛmbəʳ] *n* November *m*; *see also* **July**
novice ['nɔvɪs] *n* Neuling *m*, Anfänger(in) *m(f)*; (*Rel*) Novize *m*, Novizin *f*
NOW [nau] (*US*) *n abbr* (= *National Organization for Women*) *Frauenvereinigung*
now [nau] *adv* jetzt; (*these days*) heute ▷ *conj*: ~ **(that)** jetzt, wo; **right** ~ gleich, sofort; **by** ~ inzwischen, mittlerweile; **that's the fashion just** ~ das ist gerade modern; **I saw her just** ~ ich habe sie gerade gesehen; **(every)** ~ **and then, (every)** ~ **and again** ab und zu, gelegentlich; **from** ~ **on** von nun an; **in 3 days from** ~ (heute) in 3 Tagen; **between** ~ **and Monday** bis Montag; **that's all for** ~ das ist erst einmal alles; **any day** ~ jederzeit; ~ **then** also
nowadays ['nauədeɪz] *adv* heute
nowhere ['nəuwɛəʳ] *adv* (*be*) nirgends, nirgendwo; (*go*) nirgendwohin; ~ **else** nirgendwo anders
no-win situation [nəu'wɪn-] *n* aussichtslose Lage *f*
noxious ['nɔkʃəs] *adj* (*gas, fumes*) schädlich; (*smell*) übel
nozzle ['nɔzl] *n* Düse *f*
NP *n abbr* (*Law*) = **notary public**
NS (*Canada*) *abbr* = *Nova Scotia*
NSC (*US*) *n abbr* = **National Security Council**
NSF (*US*) *n abbr* (= *National Science Foundation*) *Organisation zur Förderung der Wissenschaft*
NSPCC (*Brit*) *n abbr* (= *National Society for the Prevention of Cruelty to Children*) Kinderschutzbund *m*
NSW (*Australia*) *abbr* (*Post*) = *New South Wales*
NT *n abbr* (*Bible*: = *New Testament*) NT
nth [ɛnθ] (*inf*) *adj*: **to the** ~ **degree** in der n-ten Potenz
nuance ['nju:ɑ̃:ns] *n* Nuance *f*
nubile ['nju:baɪl] *adj* gut entwickelt
nuclear ['nju:klɪəʳ] *adj* (*bomb, industry etc*) Atom-; ~ **physics** Kernphysik *f*; ~ **war** Atomkrieg *m*
nuclear disarmament *n* nukleare *or* atomare Abrüstung *f*
nuclear family *n* Kleinfamilie *f*, Kernfamilie *f*
nuclear-free zone ['nju:klɪə'fri:-] *n* atomwaffenfreie Zone *f*
nuclei ['nju:klɪaɪ] *npl of* **nucleus**
nucleus ['nju:klɪəs] (*pl* **nuclei**) *n* Kern *m*
NUCPS (*Brit*) *n abbr* (= *National Union of Civil and Public Servants*) *Gewerkschaft für Beschäftigte im öffentlichen Dienst*
nude [nju:d] *adj* nackt ▷ *n* (*Art*) Akt *m*; **in the** ~ nackt
nudge [nʌdʒ] *vt* anstoßen
nudist ['nju:dɪst] *n* Nudist(in) *m(f)*
nudist colony *n* FKK-Kolonie *f*
nudity ['nju:dɪtɪ] *n* Nacktheit *f*
nugget ['nʌgɪt] *n* (*of gold*) Klumpen *m*; (*fig*: *of information*) Brocken *m*
nuisance ['nju:sns] *n*: **to be a** ~ lästig sein; (*situation*) ärgerlich sein; **he's a** ~ er geht einem auf die Nerven; **what a ~!** wie ärgerlich/lästig!
NUJ (*Brit*) *n abbr* (= *National Union of Journalists*) *Journalistengewerkschaft*
null [nʌl] *adj*: ~ **and void** null und nichtig
nullify ['nʌlɪfaɪ] *vt* zunichtemachen; (*claim, law*) für null und nichtig erklären
NUM (*Brit*) *n abbr* (= *National Union of Mineworkers*) *Bergarbeitergewerkschaft*
numb [nʌm] *adj* taub, gefühllos; (*fig*: *with fear etc*) wie betäubt ▷ *vt* taub *or* gefühllos machen; (*pain, mind*) betäuben
number ['nʌmbəʳ] *n* Zahl *f*; (*quantity*) (An)zahl *f*; (*of house, bank account, bus etc*) Nummer *f* ▷ *vt* (*pages etc*) nummerieren; (*amount to*) zählen; **a** ~ **of** einige; **any** ~ **of** beliebig viele; (*reasons*) alle möglichen; **wrong** ~ (*Tel*) falsch verbunden; **to be ~ed among** zählen zu
number plate (*Brit*) *n* (*Aut*) Nummernschild *nt*
Number Ten (*Brit*) *n* (*Pol*: = *10 Downing Street*) Nummer zehn *f* (Downing Street)
numbness ['nʌmnɪs] *n* Taubheit *f*, Starre *f*; (*fig*) Benommenheit *f*, Betäubung *f*
numbskull ['nʌmskʌl] *n* = **numskull**
numeral ['nju:mərəl] *n* Ziffer *f*
numerate ['nju:mərɪt] (*Brit*) *adj*: **to be** ~ rechnen können
numerical [nju:'mɛrɪkl] *adj* numerisch
numerous ['nju:mərəs] *adj* zahlreich
numskull ['nʌmskʌl] (*inf*) *n* Holzkopf *m*
nun [nʌn] *n* Nonne *f*
nunnery ['nʌnərɪ] *n* (Nonnen)kloster *nt*
nuptial ['nʌpʃəl] *adj* (*feast, celebration*) Hochzeits-; ~ **bliss** Eheglück *nt*
nurse [nə:s] *n* Krankenschwester *f*; (*also*: **nursemaid**) Kindermädchen *nt* ▷ *vt* pflegen; (*cold, toothache etc*) auskurieren; (*baby*) stillen; (*fig*: *desire, grudge*) hegen
nursery ['nə:sərɪ] *n* Kindergarten *m*; (*room*) Kinderzimmer *nt*; (*for plants*) Gärtnerei *f*
nursery rhyme *n* Kinderreim *m*
nursery school *n* Kindergarten *m*
nursery slope (*Brit*) *n* (*Ski*) Anfängerhügel *m*
nursing ['nə:sɪŋ] *n* Krankenpflege *f*; (*care*)

Pflege *f*
nursing home *n* Pflegeheim *nt*
nursing mother *n* stillende Mutter *f*
nurture ['nə:tʃə^r] *vt* hegen und pflegen; (*fig: ideas, creativity*) fördern
NUS (*Brit*) *n abbr* (= *National Union of Students*) *Studentengewerkschaft*
NUT (*Brit*) *n abbr* (= *National Union of Teachers*) *Lehrergewerkschaft*
nut [nʌt] *n* (*Tech*) (Schrauben)mutter *f*; (*Bot*) Nuss *f*; (*inf: lunatic*) Spinner(in) *m(f)*
nutcase ['nʌtkeɪs] (*inf*) *n* Spinner(in) *m(f)*
nutcrackers ['nʌtkrækəz] *npl* Nussknacker *m*
nutmeg ['nʌtmɛg] *n* Muskat *m*, Muskatnuss *f*
nutrient ['nju:trɪənt] *n* Nährstoff *m*
nutrition [nju:'trɪʃən] *n* Ernährung *f*; (*nourishment*) Nahrung *f*
nutritionist [nju:'trɪʃənɪst] *n* Ernährungswiss enschaftler(in) *m(f)*
nutritious [nju:'trɪʃəs] *adj* nahrhaft
nuts [nʌts] (*inf*) *adj* verrückt; **he's ~** er spinnt
nutshell ['nʌtʃɛl] *n* Nussschale *f*; **in a ~** (*fig*) kurz gesagt
nutty ['nʌtɪ] *adj* (*flavour*) Nuss-; (*inf: idea etc*) bekloppt
nuzzle ['nʌzl] *vi*: **to ~ up to** sich drücken *or* schmiegen an *+acc*
NV (*US*) *abbr* (*Post*) = *Nevada*
NVQ *n abbr* (= *National Vocational Qualification*) *Qualifikation für berufsbegleitende Ausbildungsinhalte*
NW *abbr* = **north-west**
NY (*US*) *abbr* (*Post*) = *New York*
nylon ['naɪlɔn] *n* Nylon *nt* ▷ *adj* Nylon-; **nylons** *npl* (*stockings*) Nylonstrümpfe *pl*
nymph [nɪmf] *n* Nymphe *f*
nymphomaniac ['nɪmfəu'meɪnɪæk] *n* Nymphomanin *f*
NYSE (*US*) *n abbr* (= *New York Stock Exchange*) *New Yorker Börse*
NZ *abbr* = **New Zealand**

Oo

O, o [əu] *n* (*letter*) O *nt*, o *nt*; (*US*: *Scol*: *outstanding*) ≈ Eins *f*; (*Tel etc*) Null *f*; **O for Olive, O for Oboe** (*US*) ≈ O wie Otto
oaf [əuf] *n* Trottel *m*
oak [əuk] *n* (*tree, wood*) Eiche *f* ▷ *adj* (*furniture, door*) Eichen-
O&M *n abbr* (= *organization and method*) Organisation und Arbeitsweise *pl*
OAP (*Brit*) *n abbr* = **old age pensioner**
oar [ɔːʳ] *n* Ruder *nt*; **to put** *or* **shove one's ~ in** (*inf*: *fig*) mitmischen, sich einmischen
oarsman ['ɔːzmən] (*irreg*: *like* **man**) *n* Ruderer *m*
oarswoman ['ɔːzwumən] (*irreg*: *like* **woman**) *n* Ruderin *f*
OAS *n abbr* (= *Organization of American States*) OAS *f*
oasis [əu'eɪsɪs] (*pl* **oases**) *n* (*lit, fig*) Oase *f*
oath [əuθ] *n* (*promise*) Eid *m*, Schwur *m*; (*swear word*) Fluch *m*; **on ~** (*Brit*): **under ~** unter Eid; **to take the ~** (*Law*) vereidigt werden
oatmeal ['əutmiːl] *n* Haferschrot *m*; (*colour*) Hellbeige *nt*
oats [əuts] *npl* Hafer *m*; **he's getting his ~** (*Brit*: *inf*: *fig*) er kommt im Bett auf seine Kosten
obdurate ['ɔbdjurɪt] *adj* unnachgiebig
OBE (*Brit*) *n abbr* (= *Officer of (the order of) the British Empire*) *britischer Ordenstitel*
obedience [ə'biːdɪəns] *n* Gehorsam *m*; **in ~ to** gemäß *+dat*
obedient [ə'biːdɪənt] *adj* gehorsam; **to be ~ to sb** jdm gehorchen
obelisk ['ɔbɪlɪsk] *n* Obelisk *m*
obese [əu'biːs] *adj* fettleibig
obesity [əu'biːsɪtɪ] *n* Fettleibigkeit *f*
obey [ə'beɪ] *vt* (*person*) gehorchen *+dat*, folgen *+dat*; (*orders, law*) befolgen ▷ *vi* gehorchen
obituary [ə'bɪtjuərɪ] *n* Nachruf *m*
object [*n* 'ɔbdʒɪkt, *vi* əb'dʒɛkt] *n* (*also Ling*) Objekt *nt*; (*aim, purpose*) Ziel *nt*, Zweck *m* ▷ *vi* dagegen sein; **to be an ~ of ridicule** (*person*) sich lächerlich machen; (*thing*) lächerlich wirken; **money is no ~** Geld spielt keine Rolle; **he ~ed that ...** er wandte ein, dass ...; **I ~!** ich protestiere!; **do you ~ to my smoking?** haben Sie etwas dagegen, wenn ich rauche?
objection [əb'dʒɛkʃən] *n* (*argument*) Einwand *m*; **I have no ~ to ...** ich habe nichts dagegen, dass ...; **if you have no ~** wenn Sie nichts dagegen haben; **to raise** *or* **voice an ~** einen Einwand erheben *or* vorbringen
objectionable [əb'dʒɛkʃənəbl] *adj* (*language, conduct*) anstößig; (*person*) unausstehlich
objective [əb'dʒɛktɪv] *adj* objektiv ▷ *n* Ziel *nt*
objectively [əb'dʒɛktɪvlɪ] *adv* objektiv
objectivity [ɔbdʒɪk'tɪvɪtɪ] *n* Objektivität *f*
object lesson *n*: **an ~ in** ein Paradebeispiel *nt* für
objector [əb'dʒɛktəʳ] *n* Gegner(in) *m(f)*
obligation [ɔblɪ'geɪʃən] *n* Pflicht *f*; **to be under an ~ to do sth** verpflichtet sein, etw zu tun; **to be under an ~ to sb** jdm verpflichtet sein; **"no ~ to buy"** (*Comm*) „kein Kaufzwang"
obligatory [ə'blɪgətərɪ] *adj* obligatorisch
oblige [ə'blaɪdʒ] *vt* (*compel*) zwingen; (*do a favour for*) einen Gefallen tun *+dat*; **I felt ~d to invite him in** ich fühlte mich verpflichtet, ihn hereinzubitten; **to be ~d to sb for sth** (*grateful*) jdm für etw dankbar sein; **anything to ~!** (*inf*) stets zu Diensten!
obliging [ə'blaɪdʒɪŋ] *adj* entgegenkommend
oblique [ə'bliːk] *adj* (*line, angle*) schief; (*reference, compliment*) indirekt, versteckt ▷ *n* (*Brit*: *also*: **oblique stroke**) Schrägstrich *m*
obliterate [ə'blɪtəreɪt] *vt* (*village etc*) vernichten; (*fig*: *memory, error*) auslöschen
oblivion [ə'blɪvɪən] *n* (*unconsciousness*) Bewusstlosigkeit *f*; (*being forgotten*) Vergessenheit *f*; **to sink into ~** (*event etc*) in Vergessenheit geraten
oblivious [ə'blɪvɪəs] *adj*: **he was ~ of** *or* **to it** er war sich dessen nicht bewusst
oblong ['ɔblɔŋ] *adj* rechteckig ▷ *n* Rechteck *nt*
obnoxious [əb'nɔkʃəs] *adj* widerwärtig, widerlich
o.b.o. (*US*) *abbr* (*in classified ads*: = *or best offer*) bzw. Höchstgebot
oboe ['əubəu] *n* Oboe *f*
obscene [əb'siːn] *adj* obszön; (*fig*: *wealth*) unanständig; (*income etc*) unverschämt
obscenity [əb'sɛnɪtɪ] *n* Obszönität *f*
obscure [əb'skjuəʳ] *adj* (*little known*) unbekannt, obskur; (*difficult to understand*) unklar ▷ *vt* (*obstruct, conceal*) verdecken
obscurity [əb'skjuərɪtɪ] *n* (*of person, book*) Unbekanntheit *f*; (*of remark etc*) Unklarheit *f*
obsequious [əb'siːkwɪəs] *adj* unterwürfig

observable [əb'zə:vəbl] *adj* wahrnehmbar; (*noticeable*) erkennbar
observance [əb'zə:vəns] *n* (*of law etc*) Befolgung *f*; **religious ~s** religiöse Feste *pl*
observant [əb'zə:vənt] *adj* aufmerksam
observation [ɔbzə'veɪʃən] *n* (*remark*) Bemerkung *f*; (*act of observing, Med*) Beobachtung *f*; **she's in hospital under ~** sie ist zur Beobachtung im Krankenhaus
observation post *n* Beobachtungsposten *m*
observatory [əb'zə:vətrɪ] *n* Observatorium *nt*
observe [əb'zə:v] *vt* (*watch*) beobachten; (*notice, comment*) bemerken; (*abide by: rule etc*) einhalten
observer [əb'zə:vəʳ] *n* Beobachter(in) *m(f)*
obsess [əb'sɛs] *vt* verfolgen; **to be ~ed by** *or* **with sb/sth** von jdm/etw besessen sein
obsession [əb'sɛʃən] *n* Besessenheit *f*
obsessive [əb'sɛsɪv] *adj* (*person*) zwanghaft; (*interest, hatred, tidiness*) krankhaft; **to be ~ about cleaning/tidying up** einen Putz-/Ordnungsfimmel haben (*inf*)
obsolescence [ɔbsə'lɛsns] *n* Veralten *nt*; **built-in** *or* **planned ~** (*Comm*) geplanter Verschleiß *m*
obsolete ['ɔbsəli:t] *adj* veraltet
obstacle ['ɔbstəkl] *n* (*lit, fig*) Hindernis *nt*
obstacle race *n* Hindernisrennen *nt*
obstetrician [ɔbstə'trɪʃən] *n* Geburtshelfer(in) *m(f)*
obstetrics [ɔb'stɛtrɪks] *n* Geburtshilfe *f*
obstinacy ['ɔbstɪnəsɪ] *n* (*of person*) Starrsinn *m*
obstinate ['ɔbstɪnɪt] *adj* (*person*) starrsinnig, stur; (*refusal, cough etc*) hartnäckig
obstruct [əb'strʌkt] *vt* (*road, path*) blockieren; (*traffic, fig*) behindern
obstruction [əb'strʌkʃən] *n* (*object*) Hindernis *nt*; (*of plan, law*) Behinderung *f*
obstructive [əb'strʌktɪv] *adj* hinderlich, obstruktiv (*esp Pol*); **she's being ~** sie macht Schwierigkeiten
obtain [əb'teɪn] *vt* erhalten, bekommen ▷ *vi* (*form: exist, be the case*) gelten
obtainable [əb'teɪnəbl] *adj* erhältlich
obtrusive [əb'tru:sɪv] *adj* aufdringlich; (*conspicuous*) auffällig
obtuse [əb'tju:s] *adj* (*person, remark*) einfältig; (*Math*) stumpf
obverse ['ɔbvə:s] *n* (*of situation, argument*) Kehrseite *f*
obviate ['ɔbvɪeɪt] *vt* (*need, problem etc*) vorbeugen *+dat*
obvious ['ɔbvɪəs] *adj* offensichtlich; (*lie*) klar; (*predictable*) naheliegend
obviously ['ɔbvɪəslɪ] *adv* (*clearly*) offensichtlich; (*of course*) natürlich; **~!** selbstverständlich!; **~ not** offensichtlich nicht; **he was ~ not drunk** er war natürlich nicht betrunken; **he was not ~ drunk** offenbar war er nicht betrunken
OCAS *n abbr* (*= Organization of Central American States*) *mittelamerikanischer Staatenbund*
occasion [ə'keɪʒən] *n* Gelegenheit *f*; (*celebration etc*) Ereignis *nt* ▷ *vt* (*form: cause*) verursachen; **on ~** (*sometimes*) gelegentlich; **on that ~** bei der Gelegenheit; **to rise to the ~** sich der Lage gewachsen zeigen
occasional [ə'keɪʒənl] *adj* gelegentlich; **he likes the ~ cigar** er raucht gelegentlich gern eine Zigarre
occasionally [ə'keɪʒənəlɪ] *adv* gelegentlich; **very ~** sehr selten
occasional table *n* Beistelltisch *m*
occult [ɔ'kʌlt] *n*: **the ~** der Okkultismus ▷ *adj* okkult
occupancy ['ɔkjupənsɪ] *n* (*of room etc*) Bewohnen *nt*
occupant ['ɔkjupənt] *n* (*of house etc*) Bewohner(in) *m(f)*; (*temporary: of car*) Insasse *m*, Insassin *f*; **the ~ of this table/office** derjenige, der an diesem Tisch sitzt/in diesem Büro arbeitet
occupation [ɔkju'peɪʃən] *n* (*job*) Beruf *m*; (*pastime*) Beschäftigung *f*; (*of building, country etc*) Besetzung *f*
occupational guidance [ɔkju'peɪʃənl-] (*Brit*) *n* Berufsberatung *f*
occupational hazard *n* Berufsrisiko *nt*
occupational pension scheme *n* betriebliche Altersversorgung *f*
occupational therapy *n* Beschäftigungstherapie *f*
occupier ['ɔkjupaɪəʳ] *n* Bewohner(in) *m(f)*
occupy ['ɔkjupaɪ] *vt* (*house, office*) bewohnen; (*place etc*) belegen; (*building, country etc*) besetzen; (*time, attention*) beanspruchen; (*position, space*) einnehmen; **to ~ o.s. (in** *or* **with sth)** sich (mit etw) beschäftigen; **to ~ o.s. in** *or* **with doing sth** sich damit beschäftigen, etw zu tun; **to be occupied in** *or* **with sth** mit etw beschäftigt sein; **to be occupied in** *or* **with doing sth** damit beschäftigt sein, etw zu tun
occur [ə'kə:ʳ] *vi* (*take place*) geschehen, sich ereignen; (*exist*) vorkommen; **to ~ to sb** jdm einfallen
occurrence [ə'kʌrəns] *n* (*event*) Ereignis *nt*; (*incidence*) Auftreten *nt*
ocean ['əuʃən] *n* Ozean *m*, Meer *nt*; **~s of** (*inf*) jede Menge
ocean bed *n* Meeresgrund *m*
ocean-going ['əuʃəngəuɪŋ] *adj* (*ship, vessel*) Hochsee-
Oceania [əuʃɪ'eɪnɪə] *n* Ozeanien *nt*
ocean liner *n* Ozeandampfer *m*
ochre, (*US*) **ocher** ['əukəʳ] *adj* ockerfarben
o'clock [ə'klɔk] *adv*: **it is 5 ~** es ist 5 Uhr
OCR *n abbr* (*Comput*) = **optical character reader; optical character recogniton**
Oct. *abbr* (*= October*) Okt.
octagonal [ɔk'tægənl] *adj* achteckig
octane ['ɔkteɪn] *n* Oktan *nt*; **high-~ petrol, high-~ gas** (*US*) Benzin *nt* mit hoher Oktanzahl
octave ['ɔktɪv] *n* Oktave *f*
October [ɔk'təubəʳ] *n* Oktober *m*; *see also* **July**
octogenarian ['ɔktəudʒɪ'nɛərɪən] *n* Achtzigjährige(r) *f(m)*

octopus ['ɔktəpəs] *n* Tintenfisch *m*
odd [ɔd] *adj (person)* sonderbar, komisch; *(behaviour, shape)* seltsam; *(number)* ungerade; *(sock, shoe etc)* einzeln; *(occasional)* gelegentlich; **60-~** etwa 60; **at ~ times** ab und zu; **to be the ~ one out** der Außenseiter/die Außenseiterin sein; **add meat or the ~ vegetable to the soup** fügen Sie der Suppe Fleisch oder auch etwas Gemüse bei
oddball ['ɔdbɔ:l] *(inf) n* komischer Kauz *m*
oddity ['ɔdɪtɪ] *n (person)* Sonderling *m*; *(thing)* Merkwürdigkeit *f*
odd-job man [ɔd'dʒɔb-] *n* Mädchen *nt* für alles
odd jobs *npl* Gelegenheitsarbeiten *pl*
oddly ['ɔdlɪ] *adv (behave, dress)* seltsam; *see also* **enough**
oddments ['ɔdmənts] *npl (Comm)* Restposten *m*
odds [ɔdz] *npl (in betting)* Gewinnquote *f*; *(fig)* Chancen *pl*; **the ~ are in favour of/against his coming** es sieht so aus, als ob er kommt/nicht kommt; **to succeed against all the ~** allen Erwartungen zum Trotz erfolgreich sein; **it makes no ~** es spielt keine Rolle; **to be at ~ (with)** *(in disagreement)* uneinig sein (mit); *(at variance)* sich nicht vertragen (mit)
odds and ends *npl* Kleinigkeiten *pl*
odds-on [ɔdz'ɔn] *adj*: **the ~ favourite** der klare Favorit ▷ *adv*: **it's ~ that she'll win** es ist so gut wie sicher, dass sie gewinnt
ode [əud] *n* Ode *f*
odious ['əudɪəs] *adj* widerwärtig
odometer [ɔ'dɔmɪtə^r] *(US) n* Tacho(meter) *m*
odor *etc (US)* = **odour** *etc*
odour, *(US)* **odor** ['əudə^r] *n* Geruch *m*
odourless ['əudəlɪs] *adj* geruchlos
OECD *n abbr (= Organization for Economic Cooperation and Development)* OECD *f*
oesophagus, *(US)* **esophagus** [i:'sɔfəgəs] *n* Speiseröhre *f*
oestrogen, *(US)* **estrogen** ['i:strəudʒən] *n* Östrogen *nt*

KEYWORD

of [ɔv] *prep* **1** von; **the history of Germany** die Geschichte Deutschlands; **a friend of ours** ein Freund von uns; **a boy of ten** ein Junge von zehn Jahren, ein zehnjähriger Junge; **that was kind of you** das war nett von Ihnen; **the city of New York** die Stadt New York
2 *(expressing quantity, amount, dates etc)*: **a kilo of flour** ein Kilo Mehl; **how much of this do you need?** wie viel brauchen Sie davon?; **3 of them** *(people)* 3 von ihnen; *(objects)* 3 davon; **a cup of tea** eine Tasse Tee; **a vase of flowers** eine Vase mit Blumen; **the 5th of July** der 5. Juli
3 *(from, out of)* aus; **a bracelet of solid gold** ein Armband aus massivem Gold; **made of wood** aus Holz (gemacht)

Ofcom ['ɔfkɔm] *(Brit) n abbr (= Office of Communications Regulation) Regulierungsbehörde für die Kommunikationsindustrie*

KEYWORD

off [ɔf] *adv* **1** *(referring to distance, time)*: **it's a long way off** es ist sehr weit weg; **the game is 3 days off** es sind noch 3 Tage bis zum Spiel
2 *(departure)*: **to go off to Paris/Italy** nach Paris/Italien fahren; **I must be off** ich muss gehen
3 *(removal)*: **to take off one's coat/clothes** seinen Mantel/sich ausziehen; **the button came off** der Knopf ging ab; **10 % off** *(Comm)* 10% Nachlass
4: to be off *(on holiday)* im Urlaub sein; *(due to sickness)* krank sein; **I'm off on Fridays** freitags habe ich frei; **he was off on Friday** Freitag war er nicht da; **to have a day off** *(from work)* einen Tag freihaben; **to be off sick** wegen Krankheit fehlen
▷ *adj* **1** *(not turned on: machine, light, engine etc)* aus; *(: water, gas)* abgedreht; *(: tap)* zu
2: to be off *(meeting, match)* ausfallen; *(agreement)* nicht mehr gelten
3 *(Brit: not fresh)* verdorben, schlecht
4: on the off chance that ... für den Fall, dass ...; **to have an off day** *(not as good as usual)* nicht in Form sein; **to be badly off** sich schlecht stehen
▷ *prep* **1** *(indicating motion, removal etc)* von *+dat*; **to fall off a cliff** von einer Klippe fallen; **to take a picture off the wall** ein Bild von der Wand nehmen
2 *(distant from)*: **5 km off the main road** 5 km von der Hauptstraße entfernt; **an island off the coast** eine Insel vor der Küste
3: I'm off meat/beer *(no longer eat/drink it)* ich esse kein Fleisch/trinke kein Bier mehr; *(no longer like it)* ich kann kein Fleisch/Bier *etc* mehr sehen

offal ['ɔfl] *n (Culin)* Innereien *pl*
off-beat ['ɔfbi:t] *adj (clothes, ideas)* ausgefallen
off-centre, *(US)* **off-center** [ɔf'sɛntə^r] *adj* nicht genau in der Mitte, links/rechts von der Mitte ▷ *adv* asymmetrisch
off-colour ['ɔf'kʌlə^r] *(Brit) adj (ill)* unpässlich; **to feel ~** sich unwohl fühlen
offence, *(US)* **offense** [ə'fɛns] *n (crime)* Vergehen *nt*; *(insult)* Beleidigung *f*, Kränkung *f*; **to commit an ~** eine Straftat begehen; **to take ~ (at)** Anstoß nehmen (an *+dat*); **to give ~ (to)** Anstoß erregen (bei); **"no ~"** „nichts für ungut"
offend [ə'fɛnd] *vt (upset)* kränken; **to ~ against** *(law, rule)* verstoßen gegen
offender [ə'fɛndə^r] *n* Straftäter(in) *m(f)*
offending [ə'fɛndɪŋ] *adj (item etc)* anstoßerregend
offense [ə'fɛns] *(US) n* = **offence**
offensive [ə'fɛnsɪv] *adj (remark, behaviour)* verletzend; *(smell etc)* übel; *(weapon)* Angriffs- ▷ *n (Mil)* Offensive *f*

offer ['ɔfəʳ] *n* Angebot *nt* ▷ *vt* anbieten; (*money, opportunity, service*) bieten; (*reward*) aussetzen; **to make an ~ for sth** ein Angebot für etw machen; **on ~** (*Comm: available*) erhältlich; (*: cheaper*) im Angebot; **to ~ sth to sb** jdm etw anbieten; **to ~ to do sth** anbieten, etw zu tun
offering ['ɔfərɪŋ] *n* Darbietung *f*; (*Rel*) Opfergabe *f*
off-hand [ɔf'hænd] *adj* (*casual*) lässig; (*impolite*) kurz angebunden ▷ *adv* auf Anhieb; **I can't tell you ~** das kann ich Ihnen auf Anhieb nicht sagen
office ['ɔfɪs] *n* Büro *nt*; (*position*) Amt *nt*; **doctor's ~** (*US*) Praxis *f*; **to take ~** das Amt antreten; **in ~** (*minister etc*) im Amt; **through his good ~s** durch seine guten Dienste; **O~ of Fair Trading** (*Brit*) Behörde *f* gegen unlauteren Wettbewerb
office block, (*US*) **office building** *n* Bürogebäude *nt*
office boy *n* Bürogehilfe *m*
office holder *n* Amtsinhaber(in) *m(f)*
office hours *npl* (*Comm*) Bürostunden *pl*; (*US: Med*) Sprechstunde *f*
office manager *n* Büroleiter(in) *m(f)*
officer ['ɔfɪsəʳ] *n* (*Mil etc*) Offizier *m*; (*also:* **police officer**) Polizeibeamte(r) *m*, Polizeibeamtin *f*; (*of organization*) Funktionär *m*
office work *n* Büroarbeit *f*
office worker *n* Büroangestellte(r) *f(m)*
official [ə'fɪʃl] *adj* offiziell ▷ *n* (*in government*) Beamte(r) *m*, Beamtin *f*; (*in trade union etc*) Funktionär *m*
officialdom [ə'fɪʃldəm] (*pej*) *n* Bürokratie *f*
officially [ə'fɪʃəlɪ] *adv* offiziell
official receiver *n* (*Comm*) Konkursverwalter *m*
officiate [ə'fɪʃɪeɪt] *vi* amtieren; **to ~ at a marriage** eine Trauung vornehmen
officious [ə'fɪʃəs] *adj* übereifrig
offing ['ɔfɪŋ] *n*: **in the ~** in Sicht
off-key [ɔf'ki:] *adj* (*Mus: sing, play*) falsch; (*instrument*) verstimmt
off-licence ['ɔflaɪsns] (*Brit*) *n* ≈ Wein- und Spirituosenhandlung *f*; *siehe Info-Artikel*

OFF-LICENCE

Off-licence ist ein Geschäft (oder eine Theke in einer Gaststätte), wo man alkoholische Getränke kaufen kann, die aber anderswo konsumiert werden müssen. In solchen Geschäften, die oft von landesweiten Ketten betrieben werden, kann man auch andere Getränke, Süßigkeiten, Zigaretten und Knabbereien kaufen.

off-limits [ɔf'lɪmɪts] *adj* verboten
off-line [ɔf'laɪn] (*Comput*) *adj* Offline- ▷ *adv* offline; (*switched off*) abgetrennt
off-load ['ɔfləud] *vt* abladen
off-peak ['ɔf'pi:k] *adj* (*heating*) Nachtspeicher-; (*electricity*) Nacht-; (*train*) außerhalb der Stoßzeit; **~ ticket** Fahrkarte *f* zur Fahrt außerhalb der Stoßzeit
off-putting ['ɔfputɪŋ] (*Brit*) *adj* (*remark, behaviour*) abstoßend
off-season ['ɔf'si:zn] *adj, adv* außerhalb der Saison
offset ['ɔfsɛt] (*irreg: like* **set**) *vt* (*counteract*) ausgleichen
offshoot ['ɔfʃu:t] *n* (*Bot, fig*) Ableger *m*
offshore [ɔf'ʃɔ:ʳ] *adj* (*breeze*) ablandig; (*oil rig, fishing*) küstennah
offside ['ɔf'saɪd] *adj* (*Sport*) im Abseits; (*Aut: when driving on left*) rechtsseitig; (*: when driving on right*) linksseitig ▷ *n*: **the ~** (*Aut: when driving on left*) die rechte Seite; (*: when driving on right*) die linke Seite
offspring ['ɔfsprɪŋ] *n inv* Nachwuchs *m*
offstage [ɔf'steɪdʒ] *adv* hinter den Kulissen
off-the-cuff [ɔfðə'kʌf] *adj* (*remark*) aus dem Stegreif
off-the-job ['ɔfðə'dʒɔb] *adj*: **~ training** außerbetriebliche Weiterbildung *f*
off-the-peg ['ɔfðə'pɛg], (*US*) **off-the-rack** ['ɔfðə'ræk] *adv* von der Stange
off-the-record ['ɔfðə'rɛkɔ:d] *adj* (*conversation, briefing*) inoffiziell; **that's strictly ~** das ist ganz im Vertrauen
off-white ['ɔfwaɪt] *adj* gebrochen weiß
Ofgem ['ɔfgɛm] *n Überwachungsgremium zum Verbraucherschutz nach Privatisierung der Stromindustrie*
often ['ɔfn] *adv* oft; **how ~?** wie oft?; **more ~ than not** meistens; **as ~ as not** ziemlich oft; **every so ~** ab und zu
Ofwat ['ɔfwɔt] *n Überwachungsgremium zum Verbraucherschutz nach Privatisierung der Wasserindustrie*
ogle ['əugl] *vt* schielen nach, begaffen (*pej*)
ogre ['əugəʳ] *n* (*monster*) Menschenfresser *m*
OH (*US*) *abbr* (*Post*) = *Ohio*
oh [əu] *excl* oh
ohm [əum] *n* Ohm *nt*
OHMS (*Brit*) *abbr* (= *On His/Her Majesty's Service*) *Aufdruck auf amtlichen Postsendungen*
oil [ɔɪl] *n* Öl *nt*; (*petroleum*) (Erd)öl *nt* ▷ *vt* ölen
oilcan ['ɔɪlkæn] *n* Ölkanne *f*
oil change *n* Ölwechsel *m*
oilcloth ['ɔɪlklɔθ] *n* Wachstuch *nt*
oilfield ['ɔɪlfi:ld] *n* Ölfeld *nt*
oil filter *n* Ölfilter *m*
oil-fired ['ɔɪlfaɪəd] *adj* (*boiler, central heating*) Öl-
oil gauge *n* Ölstandsmesser *m*
oil painting *n* Ölgemälde *nt*
oil refinery *n* Ölraffinerie *f*
oil rig *n* Ölförderturm *m*; (*at sea*) Bohrinsel *f*
oilskins ['ɔɪlskɪnz] *npl* Ölzeug *nt*
oil slick *n* Ölteppich *m*
oil tanker *n* (*ship*) (Öl)tanker *m*; (*truck*) Tankwagen *m*
oil well *n* Ölquelle *f*
oily ['ɔɪlɪ] *adj* (*substance*) ölig; (*rag*) öldurchtränkt; (*food*) fettig
ointment ['ɔɪntmənt] *n* Salbe *f*
OK (*US*) *abbr* (*Post*) = *Oklahoma*

O.K. ['əu'keɪ] (*inf*) *excl* okay; (*granted*) gut ▷ *adj* (*average*) einigermaßen; (*acceptable*) in Ordnung ▷ *vt* genehmigen ▷ *n*: **to give sb/sth the ~** jdm/etw seine Zustimmung geben; **is it ~?** ist es in Ordnung?; **are you ~?** bist du in Ordnung?; **are you ~ for money?** hast du (noch) genug Geld?; **it's ~ with** *or* **by me** mir ist es recht
okay ['əu'keɪ] *excl* = **O.K.**
Okla. (US) *abbr* (*Post*) = *Oklahoma*
old [əuld] *adj* alt; **how ~ are you?** wie alt bist du?; **he's 10 years ~** er ist 10 Jahre alt; **~er brother** ältere(r) Bruder; **any ~ thing will do for him** ihm ist alles recht
old age *n* Alter *nt*
old age pension *n* Rente *f*
old age pensioner (*Brit*) *n* Rentner(in) *m(f)*
old-fashioned ['əuld'fæʃnd] *adj* altmodisch
old hand *n* alter Hase *m*
old hat *adj*: **to be ~** ein alter Hut sein
old maid *n* alte Jungfer *f*
old people's home *n* Altersheim *nt*
old-style ['əuldstaɪl] *adj* im alten Stil
old-time dancing ['əuldtaɪm-] *n* Tänze *pl* im alten Stil
old-timer [əuld'taɪməʳ] (*esp US*) *n* Veteran *m*
old wives' tale *n* Ammenmärchen *nt*
oleander [əulɪ'ændəʳ] *n* Oleander *m*
O level (*Brit*) *n* (*formerly*) ≈ Abschluss *m* der Sekundarstufe 1 ≈ mittlere Reife *f*
olive ['ɔlɪv] *n* Olive *f*; (*tree*) Olivenbaum *m* ▷ *adj* (*also*: **olive-green**) olivgrün; **to offer an ~ branch to sb** (*fig*) jdm ein Friedensangebot machen
olive oil *n* Olivenöl *nt*
Olympic [əu'lɪmpɪk] *adj* olympisch
Olympic Games *npl*: **the ~** (*also*: **the Olympics**) die Olympischen Spiele *pl*
OM (*Brit*) *n abbr* (= *Order of Merit*) *britischer Verdienstorden*
Oman [əu'mɑːn] *n* Oman *nt*
OMB (*US*) *n abbr* (= *Office of Management and Budget*) *Regierungsbehörde für Verwaltung und Etat*
ombudsman ['ɔmbudzmən] *n* Ombudsmann *m*
omelette, (US) **omelet** ['ɔmlɪt] *n* Omelett *nt*; **ham/cheese omelet(te)** Schinken-/Käseomelett *nt*
omen ['əumən] *n* Omen *nt*
ominous ['ɔmɪnəs] *adj* (*silence, warning*) ominös; (*clouds, smoke*) bedrohlich
omission [əu'mɪʃən] *n* (*thing omitted*) Auslassung *f*; (*act of omitting*) Auslassen *nt*
omit [əu'mɪt] *vt* (*deliberately*) unterlassen; (*by mistake*) auslassen ▷ *vi*: **to ~ to do sth** es unterlassen, etw zu tun
omnivorous [ɔm'nɪvrəs] *adj*: **to be ~** Allesfresser sein
ON (*Canada*) *abbr* = *Ontario*

KEYWORD

on [ɔn] *prep* **1** (*indicating position*) auf +*dat*; (*with vb of motion*) auf +*acc*; **it's on the table** es ist auf dem Tisch; **she put the book on the table** sie legte das Buch auf den Tisch; **on the left** links; **on the right** rechts; **the house is on the main road** das Haus liegt an der Hauptstraße
2 (*indicating means, method, condition etc*): **on foot** (*go, be*) zu Fuß; **to be on the train/plane** im Zug/Flugzeug sein; **to go on the train/plane** mit dem Zug/Flugzeug reisen; **(to be wanted) on the telephone** am Telefon (verlangt werden); **on the radio/television** im Radio/Fernsehen; **to be on drugs** Drogen nehmen; **to be on holiday** im Urlaub sein; **I'm here on business** ich bin geschäftlich hier
3 (*referring to time*): **on Friday** am Freitag; **on Fridays** freitags; **on June 20th** am 20. Juni; **on Friday, June 20th** am Freitag, dem 20. Juni; **a week on Friday** Freitag in einer Woche; **on (his) arrival he went straight to his hotel** bei seiner Ankunft ging er direkt in sein Hotel; **on seeing this he ...** als er das sah, ... er ...
4 (*about, concerning*) über +*acc*; **a book on physics** ein Buch über Physik
▷ *adv* **1** (*referring to dress*): **to have one's coat on** seinen Mantel anhaben; **what's she got on?** was hat sie an?
2 (*referring to covering*): **screw the lid on tightly** dreh den Deckel fest zu
3 (*further, continuously*): **to walk/drive/read on** weitergehen/-fahren/-lesen
▷ *adj* **1** (*functioning, in operation: machine, radio, TV, light*) an; (*: tap*) auf; (*: handbrake*) angezogen; **there's a good film on at the cinema** im Kino läuft ein guter Film
2: that's not on! (*inf: of behaviour*) das ist nicht drin!

once [wʌns] *adv* (*on one occasion*) einmal; (*formerly*) früher; (*a long time ago*) früher einmal ▷ *conj* (*as soon as*) sobald; **at ~** (*immediately*) sofort; (*simultaneously*) gleichzeitig; **~ a week** einmal pro Woche; **~ more** *or* **again** noch einmal; **~ and for all** ein für alle Mal; **~ upon a time** es war einmal; **~ in a while** ab und zu; **all at ~** (*suddenly*) plötzlich; **for ~** ausnahmsweise (einmal); **~ or twice** ein paarmal; **~ he had left** sobald er gegangen war; **~ it was done** nachdem es getan war
oncoming ['ɔnkʌmɪŋ] *adj* (*traffic etc*) entgegenkommend

KEYWORD

one [wʌn] *num* ein(e); (*counting*) eins; **one hundred and fifty** (ein)hundert(und)fünfzig; **one day there was a sudden knock at the door** eines Tages klopfte es plötzlich an der Tür; **one by one** einzeln
▷ *adj* **1** (*sole*) einzige(r, s); **the one book which ...** das einzige Buch, das ...
2 (*same*): **they came in the one car** sie kamen

in demselben Wagen; **they all belong to the one family** sie alle gehören zu ein und derselben Familie
▷ *pron* **1: this one** diese(r, s); **that one** der/die/das (da); **which one?** welcher/welche/welches?; **he is one of us** er ist einer von uns; **I've already got one/a red one** ich habe schon eins/ein rotes
2: one another einander; **do you two ever see one another?** seht ihr zwei euch jemals?
3 (*impersonal*) man; **one never knows** man weiß nie; **to cut one's finger** sich *dat* in den Finger schneiden

one-day excursion ['wʌndeɪ-] (*US*) *n* (*day return*) Tagesrückfahrkarte *f*
one-man ['wʌn'mæn] *adj* (*business, show*) Einmann-
one-man band *n* Einmannkapelle *f*
one-off [wʌn'ɔf] (*Brit: inf*) *n* einmaliges Ereignis *nt*
one-parent family ['wʌnpɛərənt-] *n* Familie *f* mit nur einem Elternteil
one-piece ['wʌnpi:s] *adj*: **~ swimsuit** einteiliger Badeanzug *m*
onerous ['ɔnərəs] *adj* (*duty etc*) schwer

KEYWORD

oneself [wʌn'sɛlf] *pron* (*reflexive: after prep*) sich; (*emphatic*) selbst; **to hurt oneself** sich *dat* wehtun; **to keep sth for oneself** etw für sich behalten; **to talk to oneself** Selbstgespräche führen

one-shot ['wʌnʃɔt] (*US*) *n* = **one-off**
one-sided [wʌn'saɪdɪd] *adj* einseitig
one-time ['wʌntaɪm] *adj* ehemalig
one-to-one ['wʌntəwʌn] *adj* (*relationship, tuition*) Einzel-
one-upmanship [wʌn'ʌpmənʃɪp] *n*: **the art of ~** die Kunst, anderen um einen Schritt voraus zu sein
one-way ['wʌnweɪ] *adj* (*street, traffic*) Einbahn-; (*ticket*) Einzel-
ongoing ['ɔngəuɪŋ] *adj* (*project*) laufend; (*situation etc*) andauernd
onion ['ʌnjən] *n* Zwiebel *f*
on-line ['ɔnlaɪn] (*Comput*) *adj* (*printer, database*) Online-; (*switched on*) gekoppelt ▷ *adv* online
onlooker ['ɔnlukər] *n* Zuschauer(in) *m(f)*
only ['əunlɪ] *adv* nur ▷ *adj* einzige(r, s) ▷ *conj* nur, bloß; **I ~ took one** ich nahm nur eins; **I saw her ~ yesterday** ich habe sie erst gestern gesehen; **I'd be ~ too pleased to help** ich würde allzu gern helfen; **not ~ ... but (also) ...** nicht nur ..., sondern auch ...; **an ~ child** ein Einzelkind *nt*; **I would come, ~ I'm too busy** ich würde kommen, wenn ich nicht so viel zu tun hätte
ono (*Brit*) *abbr* (*in classified ads: = or near(est) offer*) *see* **near**
onset ['ɔnsɛt] *n* Beginn *m*
onshore ['ɔnʃɔ:r] *adj* (*wind*) auflandig, See-
onslaught ['ɔnslɔ:t] *n* Attacke *f*
on-the-job ['ɔnðə'dʒɔb] *adj*: **~ training** Ausbildung *f* am Arbeitsplatz
onto ['ɔntu] *prep* = **on to**
onus ['əunəs] *n* Last *f*, Pflicht *f*; **the ~ is on him to prove it** er trägt die Beweislast
onward ['ɔnwəd], **onwards** ['ɔnwədz] *adv* weiter; **from that time ~(s)** von der Zeit an ▷ *adj* fortschreitend
onyx ['ɔnɪks] *n* Onyx *m*
ooze [u:z] *vi* (*mud, water etc*) triefen
opacity [əu'pæsɪtɪ] *n* (*of substance*) Undurchsichtigkeit *f*
opal ['əupl] *n* Opal *m*
opaque [əu'peɪk] *adj* (*substance*) undurchsichtig, trüb
OPEC ['əupɛk] *n abbr* (*= Organization of Petroleum-Exporting Countries*) OPEC *f*
open ['əupn] *adj* offen; (*packet, shop, museum*) geöffnet; (*view*) frei; (*meeting, debate*) öffentlich; (*ticket, return*) unbeschränkt; (*vacancy*) verfügbar ▷ *vt* öffnen, aufmachen; (*book, paper etc*) aufschlagen; (*account*) eröffnen; (*blocked road*) frei machen ▷ *vi* (*door, eyes, mouth*) sich öffnen; (*shop, bank etc*) aufmachen; (*commence*) beginnen; (*film, play*) Premiere haben; (*flower*) aufgehen; **in the ~ (air)** im Freien; **the ~ sea** das offene Meer; **to have an ~ mind on sth** etw *dat* aufgeschlossen gegenüberstehen; **to be ~ to** (*ideas etc*) offen sein für; **to be ~ to criticism** der Kritik *dat* ausgesetzt sein; **to be ~ to the public** für die Öffentlichkeit zugänglich sein; **to ~ one's mouth** (*speak*) den Mund aufmachen
▸ **open on to** *vt fus* (*room, door*) führen auf *+acc*
▸ **open up** *vi* (*unlock*) aufmachen; (*confide*) sich äußern
open-air [əupn'ɛər] *adj* im Freien; **~ concert** Open-Air-Konzert *nt*; **~ swimming pool** Freibad *nt*
open-and-shut ['əupnən'ʃʌt] *adj*: **~ case** klarer Fall *m*
open day *n* Tag *m* der offenen Tür
open-ended [əupn'ɛndɪd] *adj* (*question etc*) mit offenem Ausgang; (*contract*) unbefristet
opener ['əupnər] *n* (*also*: **tin opener, can opener**) Dosenöffner *m*
open-heart [əupn'hɑ:t] *adj*: **~ surgery** Eingriff *m* am offenen Herzen
opening ['əupnɪŋ] *adj* (*commencing: stages, scene*) erste(r, s); (*remarks, ceremony etc*) Eröffnungs- ▷ *n* (*gap, hole*) Öffnung *f*; (*of play etc*) Anfang *m*; (*of new building etc*) Eröffnung *f*; (*opportunity*) Gelegenheit *f*
opening hours *npl* Öffnungszeiten *pl*
opening night *n* (*Theat*) Eröffnungsabend *m*
open learning *n* *Weiterbildungssystem auf Teilzeitbasis*
openly ['əupnlɪ] *adv* offen
open-minded [əupn'maɪndɪd] *adj* aufgeschlossen
open-necked ['əupnnɛkt] *adj* (*shirt*) mit

offenem Kragen
openness ['əupnnɪs] *n* *(frankness)* Offenheit *f*
open-plan ['əupn'plæn] *adj* *(office)* Großraum-
open prison *n* offenes Gefängnis *nt*
open sandwich *n* belegtes Brot *nt*
open shop *n* *Unternehmen ohne Gewerkschaftszwang*
Open University *(Brit)* *n* ≈ Fernuniversität *f*; *siehe Info-Artikel*

OPEN UNIVERSITY

Open University ist eine 1969 in Großbritannien gegründete Fernuniversität für Spätstudierende. Der Unterricht findet durch Fernseh- und Radiosendungen statt, schriftliche Arbeiten werden mit der Post verschickt, und der Besuch von Sommerkursen ist Pflicht. Die Studenten müssen eine bestimmte Anzahl von Unterrichtseinheiten in einem bestimmten Zeitraum absolvieren und für die Verleihung eines akademischen Grades eine Mindestzahl von Scheinen machen.

open verdict *n* *(Law)* *Todesfeststellung ohne Angabe der Todesursache*
opera ['ɔpərə] *n* Oper *f*
opera glasses *npl* Opernglas *nt*
opera house *n* Opernhaus *nt*
opera singer *n* Opernsänger(in) *m(f)*
operate ['ɔpəreɪt] *vt* *(machine etc)* bedienen ▷ *vi* *(machine etc)* funktionieren; *(company)* arbeiten; *(laws, forces)* wirken; *(Med)* operieren; **to ~ on sb** jdn operieren
operatic [ɔpə'rætɪk] *adj* *(singer etc)* Opern-
operating room ['ɔpəreɪtɪŋ-] (US) *n* Operationssaal *m*
operating system *n* *(Comput)* Betriebssystem *nt*
operating table *n* *(Med)* Operationstisch *m*
operating theatre *n* *(Med)* Operationssaal *m*
operation [ɔpə'reɪʃən] *n* *(activity)* Unternehmung *f*; *(of machine etc)* Betrieb *m*; *(Mil, Med)* Operation *f*; *(Comm)* Geschäft *nt*; **to be in ~** *(law, scheme)* in Kraft sein; **to have an ~** *(Med)* operiert werden; **to perform an ~** *(Med)* eine Operation vornehmen
operational [ɔpə'reɪʃənl] *adj* *(machine etc)* einsatzfähig
operative ['ɔpərətɪv] *adj* *(measure, system)* wirksam; *(law)* gültig ▷ *n* *(in factory)* Maschinenarbeiter(in) *m(f)*; **the ~ word** das entscheidende Wort
operator ['ɔpəreɪtə^r] *n* *(Tel)* Vermittlung *f*; *(of machine)* Bediener(in) *m(f)*
operetta [ɔpə'rɛtə] *n* Operette *f*
ophthalmic [ɔf'θælmɪk] *adj* *(department)* Augen-
ophthalmic optician *n* Augenoptiker(in) *m(f)*
ophthalmologist [ɔfθæl'mɔlədʒɪst] *n* Augenarzt *m*, Augenärztin *f*
opinion [ə'pɪnjən] *n* Meinung *f*; **in my ~** meiner Meinung nach; **to have a good/high ~ of sb/o.s.** eine gute/hohe Meinung von jdm/sich haben; **to be of the ~ that ...** der Ansicht *or* Meinung sein, dass ...; **to get a second ~** *(Med etc)* ein zweites Gutachten einholen
opinionated [ə'pɪnjəneɪtɪd] *(pej)* *adj* rechthaberisch
opinion poll *n* Meinungsumfrage *f*
opium ['əupɪəm] *n* Opium *nt*
opponent [ə'pəunənt] *n* Gegner(in) *m(f)*
opportune ['ɔpətju:n] *adj* *(moment)* günstig
opportunism [ɔpə'tju:nɪsəm] *(pej)* *n* Opportunismus *m*
opportunist [ɔpə'tju:nɪst] *(pej)* *n* Opportunist(in) *m(f)*
opportunity [ɔpə'tju:nɪtɪ] *n* Gelegenheit *f*, Möglichkeit *f*; *(prospects)* Chance *f*; **to take the ~ of doing sth** die Gelegenheit ergreifen, etw zu tun
oppose [ə'pəuz] *vt* *(opinion, plan)* ablehnen; **to be ~d to sth** gegen etw sein; **as ~d to** im Gegensatz zu
opposing [ə'pəuzɪŋ] *adj* *(side, team)* gegnerisch; *(ideas, tendencies)* entgegengesetzt
opposite ['ɔpəzɪt] *adj* *(house, door)* gegenüberliegend; *(end, direction)* entgegengesetzt; *(point of view, effect)* gegenteilig ▷ *adv* gegenüber ▷ *prep* *(in front of)* gegenüber; *(next to: on list, form etc)* neben ▷ *n*: **the ~** das Gegenteil; **the ~ sex** das andere Geschlecht; **"see ~ page"** „siehe gegenüber"
opposite number *n* *(person)* Gegenspieler(in) *m(f)*
opposition [ɔpə'zɪʃən] *n* *(resistance)* Widerstand *m*; *(Sport)* Gegner *pl*; **the O~** *(Pol)* die Opposition
oppress [ə'prɛs] *vt* unterdrücken
oppressed [ə'prɛst] *adj* unterdrückt
oppression [ə'prɛʃən] *n* Unterdrückung *f*
oppressive [ə'prɛsɪv] *adj* *(weather, heat)* bedrückend; *(political regime)* repressiv
opprobrium [ə'prəubrɪəm] *n* *(form)* Schande *f*, Schmach *f*
opt [ɔpt] *vi*: **to ~ for** sich entscheiden für; **to ~ to do sth** sich entscheiden, etw zu tun
▸ **opt out (of)** *vi* *(not participate)* sich nicht beteiligen (an+*dat*); *(of insurance scheme etc)* kündigen; **to ~ out (of local authority control)** *(Pol: hospital, school)* aus der Kontrolle der Gemeindeverwaltung austreten
optical ['ɔptɪkl] *adj* optisch
optical character reader *n* optischer Klarschriftleser *m*
optical character recognition *n* optische Zeichenerkennung *f*
optical illusion *n* optische Täuschung *f*
optician [ɔp'tɪʃən] *n* Optiker(in) *m(f)*
optics ['ɔptɪks] *n* Optik *f*
optimism ['ɔptɪmɪzəm] *n* Optimismus *m*
optimist ['ɔptɪmɪst] *n* Optimist(in) *m(f)*
optimistic [ɔptɪ'mɪstɪk] *adj* optimistisch

optimum ['ɔptɪməm] *adj* optimal
option ['ɔpʃən] *n* *(choice)* Möglichkeit *f*; *(Scol)* Wahlfach *nt*; *(Comm)* Option *f*; **to keep one's ~s open** sich *dat* alle Möglichkeiten offenhalten; **to have no ~** keine (andere) Wahl haben
optional ['ɔpʃənl] *adj* freiwillig; **~ extras** *(Comm)* Extras *pl*
opulence ['ɔpjuləns] *n* Reichtum *m*
opulent ['ɔpjulənt] *adj* *(very wealthy)* reich, wohlhabend
OR *(US)* *abbr* *(Post)* = *Oregon*
or [ɔːʳ] *conj* oder; **he hasn't seen or heard anything** er hat weder etwas gesehen noch gehört; **or else** *(otherwise)* sonst; **fifty or sixty people** fünfzig bis sechzig Leute
oracle ['ɔrəkl] *n* Orakel *nt*
oral ['ɔːrəl] *adj* *(test, report)* mündlich; *(Med: vaccine, contraceptive)* zum Einnehmen ▷ *n* *(exam)* mündliche Prüfung *f*
orange ['ɔrɪndʒ] *n* Orange *f*, Apfelsine *f* ▷ *adj* *(colour)* orange
orangeade [ɔrɪndʒ'eɪd] *n* Orangenlimonade *f*
oration [ɔː'reɪʃən] *n* Ansprache *f*
orator ['ɔrətəʳ] *n* Redner(in) *m(f)*
oratorio [ɔrə'tɔːrɪəu] *n* *(Mus)* Oratorium *nt*
orb [ɔːb] *n* Kugel *f*
orbit ['ɔːbɪt] *n* *(of planet etc)* Umlaufbahn *f* ▷ *vt* umkreisen
orbital motorway ['ɔːbɪtəl-] *n* Ringautobahn *f*
orchard ['ɔːtʃəd] *n* Obstgarten *m*; **apple ~** Obstgarten mit Apfelbäumen
orchestra ['ɔːkɪstrə] *n* Orchester *nt*; *(US: stalls)* Parkett *nt*
orchestral [ɔː'kɛstrəl] *adj* *(piece, musicians)* Orchester-
orchestrate ['ɔːkɪstreɪt] *vt* orchestrieren
orchid ['ɔːkɪd] *n* Orchidee *f*
ordain [ɔː'deɪn] *vt* *(Rel)* ordinieren; *(decree)* verfügen
ordeal [ɔː'diːl] *n* Qual *f*
order ['ɔːdəʳ] *n* *(command)* Befehl *m*; *(Comm, in restaurant)* Bestellung *f*; *(sequence)* Reihenfolge *f*; *(discipline, organization)* Ordnung *f*; *(Rel)* Orden *m* ▷ *vt* *(command)* befehlen; *(Comm, in restaurant)* bestellen; *(also:* **put in order***)* ordnen; **in ~** *(permitted)* in Ordnung; **in (working) ~** betriebsfähig; **in ~ to do sth** um etw zu tun; **in ~ of size** nach Größe (geordnet); **on ~** *(Comm)* bestellt; **out of ~** *(not working)* außer Betrieb; *(in the wrong sequence)* durcheinander; *(motion, proposal)* nicht zulässig; **to place an ~ for sth with sb** eine Bestellung für etw bei jdm aufgeben; **made to ~** *(Comm)* auf Bestellung (gemacht); **to be under ~s to do sth** die Anweisung haben, etw zu tun; **to take ~s** Befehle entgegennehmen; **a point of ~** *(in debate etc)* eine Verfahrensfrage; **"pay to the ~ of ..."** „zahlbar an *+dat* ..."; **of** *or* **in the ~ of** in der Größenordnung von; **to ~ sb to do sth** jdn anweisen, etw zu tun
▸ **order around** *vt* *(also:* **order about***)* herumkommandieren
order book *n* *(Comm)* Auftragsbuch *nt*
order form *n* Bestellschein *m*
orderly ['ɔːdəlɪ] *n* *(Mil)* Offiziersbursche *m*; *(Med)* Pfleger(in) *m(f)* ▷ *adj* *(manner)* ordentlich; *(sequence, system)* geordnet
order number *n* *(Comm)* Bestellnummer *f*
ordinal ['ɔːdɪnl] *adj*: **~ number** Ordinalzahl *f*
ordinarily ['ɔːdnrɪlɪ] *adv* normalerweise
ordinary ['ɔːdnrɪ] *adj* *(everyday)* gewöhnlich, normal; *(pej: mediocre)* mittelmäßig; **out of the ~** außergewöhnlich

ORDINARY DEGREE

Ordinary degree ist ein Universitätsabschluss, der an Studenten vergeben wird, die entweder die für ein *honours degree* nötige Note nicht erreicht haben, aber trotzdem nicht durchgefallen sind, oder die sich nur für ein ordinary degree eingeschrieben haben, wobei das Studium meist kürzer ist.

ordinary seaman *(Brit)* *n* Leichtmatrose *m*
ordinary shares *npl* Stammaktien *pl*
ordination [ɔːdɪ'neɪʃən] *n* *(Rel)* Ordination *f*
ordnance ['ɔːdnəns] *n* *(unit)* Technische Truppe *f* ▷ *adj* *(factory, supplies)* Munitions-
Ordnance Survey *(Brit)* *n* Landesvermessung *f*
ore [ɔːʳ] *n* Erz *nt*
Ore. *(US)* *abbr* *(Post)* = *Oregon*
organ ['ɔːgən] *n* *(Anat)* Organ *nt*; *(Mus)* Orgel *f*
organic [ɔː'gænɪk] *adj* organisch
organism ['ɔːgənɪzəm] *n* Organismus *m*
organist ['ɔːgənɪst] *n* Organist(in) *m(f)*
organization [ɔːgənaɪ'zeɪʃən] *n* Organisation *f*
organization chart *n* Organisationsplan *m*
organize ['ɔːgənaɪz] *vt* organisieren; **to get ~d** sich fertig machen
organized crime *n* organisiertes Verbrechen *nt*
organized labour *n* organisierte Arbeiterschaft *f*
organizer ['ɔːgənaɪzəʳ] *n* *(of conference etc)* Organisator *m*, Veranstalter *m*
orgasm ['ɔːgæzəm] *n* Orgasmus *m*
orgy ['ɔːdʒɪ] *n* Orgie *f*; **an ~ of destruction** eine Zerstörungsorgie
Orient ['ɔːrɪənt] *n*: **the ~** der Orient
orient ['ɔːrɪənt] *vt*: **to ~ o.s. (to)** sich orientieren (in *+dat*); **to be ~ed towards** ausgerichtet sein auf *+acc*
oriental [ɔːrɪ'ɛntl] *adj* orientalisch
orientate ['ɔːrɪənteɪt] *vt*: **to ~ o.s.** sich orientieren; *(fig)* sich zurechtfinden; **to be ~d towards** ausgerichtet sein auf *+acc*
orifice ['ɔrɪfɪs] *n* *(Anat)* Öffnung *f*
origin ['ɔrɪdʒɪn] *n* Ursprung *m*; *(of person)* Herkunft *f*; **country of ~** Herkunftsland *nt*
original [ə'rɪdʒɪnl] *adj* *(first)* ursprünglich; *(genuine)* original; *(imaginative)* originell ▷ *n* Original *nt*

originality [ərɪdʒɪˈnælɪtɪ] *n* Originalität *f*
originally [əˈrɪdʒɪnəlɪ] *adv* (*at first*) ursprünglich
originate [əˈrɪdʒɪneɪt] *vi*: **to ~ in** (*idea, custom etc*) entstanden sein in *+dat*; **to ~ with** *or* **from** stammen von
originator [əˈrɪdʒɪneɪtəʳ] *n* (*of idea, custom*) Urheber(in) *m(f)*
Orkneys [ˈɔːknɪz] *npl*: **the ~** (*also*: **the Orkney Islands**) die Orkneyinseln *pl*
ornament [ˈɔːnəmənt] *n* (*object*) Ziergegenstand *m*; (*decoration*) Verzierungen *pl*
ornamental [ɔːnəˈmɛntl] *adj* (*garden, pond*) Zier-
ornamentation [ɔːnəmɛnˈteɪʃən] *n* Verzierungen *pl*
ornate [ɔːˈneɪt] *adj* (*necklace, design*) kunstvoll
ornithologist [ɔːnɪˈθɔlədʒɪst] *n* Ornithologe *m*, Ornithologin *f*
ornithology [ɔːnɪˈθɔlədʒɪ] *n* Ornithologie *f*, Vogelkunde *f*
orphan [ˈɔːfn] *n* Waise *f*, Waisenkind *nt* ▹ *vt*: **to be ~ed** zur Waise werden
orphanage [ˈɔːfənɪdʒ] *n* Waisenhaus *nt*
orthodox [ˈɔːθədɔks] *adj* orthodox; **~ medicine** die konventionelle Medizin
orthodoxy [ˈɔːθədɔksɪ] *n* Orthodoxie *f*
orthopaedic, (*US*) **orthopedic** [ɔːθəˈpiːdɪk] *adj* orthopädisch
OS *abbr* (*Brit*) = **Ordnance Survey**; (*Naut*) = **ordinary seaman**; (*Dress*) = **outsize**
o.s. *abbr* (*Comm*: = *out of stock*) nicht auf Lager
Oscar [ˈɔskəʳ] *n* Oscar *m*
oscillate [ˈɔsɪleɪt] *vi* (*Elec, Phys*) schwingen, oszillieren; (*fig*) schwanken
OSHA (*US*) *n abbr* (= *Occupational Safety and Health Administration*) *Regierungsstelle für Arbeitsschutzvorschriften*
Oslo [ˈɔzləu] *n* Oslo *nt*
OST *n abbr* (= *Office of Science and Technology*) *Ministerium für Wissenschaft und Technologie*
ostensible [ɔsˈtɛnsɪbl] *adj* vorgeblich, angeblich
ostensibly [ɔsˈtɛnsɪblɪ] *adv* angeblich
ostentation [ɔstɛnˈteɪʃən] *n* Pomp *m*, Protz *m*
ostentatious [ɔstɛnˈteɪʃəs] *adj* (*building, car etc*) pompös; (*person*) protzig
osteopath [ˈɔstɪəpæθ] *n* Osteopath(in) *m(f)*
ostracize [ˈɔstrəsaɪz] *vt* ächten
ostrich [ˈɔstrɪtʃ] *n* Strauß *m*
OT *abbr* (*Bible*: = *Old Testament*) AT
OTB (*US*) *n abbr* (= *offtrack betting*) *Wetten außerhalb des Rennbahngeländes*
OTE *abbr* (*Comm*: = *on-target earnings*) Einkommensziel *nt*
other [ˈʌðəʳ] *adj* andere(r, s) ▹ *pron*: **the ~ (one)** der/die/das andere; **~s** andere *pl*; **the ~s** die anderen *pl*; **~ than** (*apart from*) außer; **the ~ day** (*recently*) neulich; **some actor or ~** irgendein Schauspieler; **somebody or ~** irgendjemand; **the car was none ~ than Robert's** das Auto gehörte keinem anderen als Robert
otherwise [ˈʌðəwaɪz] *adv* (*differently*) anders; (*apart from that, if not*) sonst, ansonsten; **an ~ good piece of work** eine im Übrigen gute Arbeit
OTT (*inf*) *abbr* (= *over the top*) *see* **top**
otter [ˈɔtəʳ] *n* Otter *m*
OU (*Brit*) *n abbr* = **Open University**
ouch [autʃ] *excl* autsch
ought [ɔːt] (*pt* **~**) *aux vb*: **I ~ to do it** ich sollte es tun; **this ~ to have been corrected** das hätte korrigiert werden müssen; **he ~ to win** (*he probably will win*) er dürfte wohl gewinnen; **you ~ to go and see it** das solltest du dir ansehen
ounce [auns] *n* Unze *f*; (*fig*: *small amount*) bisschen *nt*
our [ˈauəʳ] *adj* unsere(r, s); *see also* **my**
ours [auəz] *pron* unsere(r, s); *see also* **mine¹**
ourselves [auəˈsɛlvz] *pron pl* uns (selbst); (*emphatic*) selbst; **we did it (all) by ~** wir haben alles selbst gemacht; *see also* **oneself**
oust [aust] *vt* (*forcibly remove*) verdrängen

KEYWORD

out¹ [aut] *adv* **1** (*not in*) draußen; **out in the rain/snow** draußen im Regen/Schnee; **out here** hier; **out there** dort; **to go/come** *etc* **out** hinausgehen/-kommen *etc*; **to speak out loud** laut sprechen
2 (*not at home, absent*) nicht da
3 (*indicating distance*): **the boat was 10 km out** das Schiff war 10 km weit draußen; **3 days out from Plymouth** 3 Tage nach dem Auslaufen von Plymouth
4 (*Sport*) aus; **the ball is out/has gone out** der Ball ist aus
▹ *adj* **1: to be out** (*person*: *unconscious*) bewusstlos sein; (: *out of game*) ausgeschieden sein; (*out of fashion*: *style, singer*) out sein
2 (*have appeared*: *flowers*) da; (: *news, secret*) heraus
3 (*extinguished, finished*: *fire, light, gas*) aus; **before the week was out** ehe die Woche zu Ende war
4: to be out to do sth (*intend*) etw tun wollen
5 (*wrong*): **to be out in one's calculations** sich in seinen Berechnungen irren

out² [aut] *vt* (*inf*: *expose as homosexual*) outen
outage [ˈautɪdʒ] (*esp US*) *n* (*power failure*) Stromausfall *m*
out-and-out [ˈautəndaut] *adj* (*liar, thief etc*) ausgemacht
outback [ˈautbæk] *n* (*in Australia*): **the ~** das Hinterland
outbid [autˈbɪd] *vt* überbieten
outboard [ˈautbɔːd] *n* (*also*: **outboard motor**) Außenbordmotor *m*
outbound [ˈautbaund] *adj* (*ship*) auslaufend
outbreak [ˈautbreɪk] *n* (*of war, disease etc*) Ausbruch *m*
outbuilding [ˈautbɪldɪŋ] *n* Nebengebäude *nt*
outburst [ˈautbəːst] *n* (*of anger etc*) Gefühlsausbruch *m*
outcast [ˈautkɑːst] *n* Ausgestoßene(r) *f(m)*
outclass [autˈklɑːs] *vt* deklassieren
outcome [ˈautkʌm] *n* Ergebnis *nt*, Resultat *nt*

outcrop ['autkrɔp] *n* (*of rock*) Block *m*
outcry ['autkraɪ] *n* Aufschrei *m*
outdated [aut'deɪtɪd] *adj* (*custom, idea*) veraltet
outdo [aut'du:] (*irreg: like* **do**) *vt* übertreffen
outdoor [aut'dɔ:ʳ] *adj* (*activities*) im Freien; (*clothes*) für draußen; **~ swimming pool** Freibad *nt*; **she's an ~ person** sie liebt die freie Natur
outdoors [aut'dɔ:z] *adv* (*play, sleep*) draußen, im Freien
outer ['autəʳ] *adj* äußere(r, s); **~ suburbs** (äußere) Vorstädte *pl*; **the ~ office** das Vorzimmer
outer space *n* der Weltraum
outfit ['autfɪt] *n* (*clothes*) Kleidung *f*; (*inf: team*) Verein *m*
outfitter's ['autfɪtəz] (*Brit*) *n* (*shop*) Herrenausstatter *m*
outgoing ['autgəuɪŋ] *adj* (*extrovert*) kontaktfreudig; (*retiring: president etc*) scheidend; (*mail etc*) ausgehend
outgoings ['autgəuɪŋz] (*Brit*) *npl* Ausgaben *pl*
outgrow [aut'grəu] (*irreg: like* **grow**) *vt* (*clothes*) herauswachsen aus; (*habits etc*) ablegen
outhouse ['authaus] *n* Nebengebäude *nt*
outing ['autɪŋ] *n* Ausflug *m*
outlandish [aut'lændɪʃ] *adj* eigenartig, seltsam
outlast [aut'lɑ:st] *vt* überleben
outlaw ['autlɔ:] *n* Geächtete(r) *f(m)* ▷ *vt* verbieten
outlay ['autleɪ] *n* Auslagen *pl*
outlet ['autlɛt] *n* (*hole, pipe*) Abfluss *m*; (*US: Elec*) Steckdose *f*; (*Comm: also:* **retail outlet**) Verkaufsstelle *f*; (*fig: for grief, anger etc*) Ventil *nt*
outline ['autlaɪn] *n* (*shape*) Umriss *m*; (*brief explanation*) Abriss *m*; (*rough sketch*) Skizze *f* ▷ *vt* (*fig: theory, plan etc*) umreißen, skizzieren
outlive [aut'lɪv] *vt* (*survive*) überleben
outlook ['autluk] *n* (*attitude*) Einstellung *f*; (*prospects*) Aussichten *pl*; (*for weather*) Vorhersage *f*
outlying ['autlaɪɪŋ] *adj* (*area, town etc*) entlegen
outmanoeuvre, (*US*) **outmaneuver** [autmə'nu:vəʳ] *vt* ausmanövrieren
outmoded [aut'məudɪd] *adj* veraltet
outnumber [aut'nʌmbəʳ] *vt* zahlenmäßig überlegen sein *+dat*; **to be ~ed (by) 5 to 1** im Verhältnis 5 zu 1 in der Minderheit sein

KEYWORD

out of *prep* **1** (*outside, beyond: position*) nicht in *+dat*; (*: motion*) aus *+dat*; **to look out of the window** aus dem Fenster blicken; **to be out of danger** außer Gefahr sein
2 (*cause, origin*) aus *+dat*; **out of curiosity/fear/greed** aus Neugier/Angst/Habgier; **to drink sth out of a cup** etw aus einer Tasse trinken
3 (*from among*) von *+dat*; **one out of every three smokers** einer von drei Rauchern
4 (*without*): **to be out of sugar/milk/petrol** *etc* keinen Zucker/keine Milch/kein Benzin *etc* mehr haben

out of bounds *adj*: **to be ~** verboten sein
out-of-court [autəv'kɔ:t] *adj* (*settlement*) außergerichtlich; *see also* **court**
out-of-date [autəv'deɪt] *adj* (*passport, ticket etc*) abgelaufen; (*clothes, idea*) veraltet
out-of-doors [autəv'dɔ:z] *adv* (*play, stay etc*) im Freien
out-of-the-way ['autəvðə'weɪ] *adj* (*place*) entlegen; (*pub, restaurant etc*) kaum bekannt
out-of-work ['autəvwə:k] *adj* arbeitslos
outpatient ['autpeɪʃənt] *n* ambulanter Patient *m*, ambulante Patientin *f*
outpost ['autpəust] *n* (*Mil, Comm*) Vorposten *m*
outpouring ['autpɔ:rɪŋ] *n* (*of emotion etc*) Erguss *m*
output ['autput] *n* (*production: of factory, writer etc*) Produktion *f*; (*Comput*) Output *m*, Ausgabe *f* ▷ *vt* (*Comput*) ausgeben
outrage ['autreɪdʒ] *n* (*scandal*) Skandal *m*; (*atrocity*) Verbrechen *nt*, Ausschreitung *f*; (*anger*) Empörung *f* ▷ *vt* (*shock, anger*) empören
outrageous [aut'reɪdʒəs] *adj* (*remark etc*) empörend; (*clothes*) unmöglich; (*scandalous*) skandalös
outrider ['autraɪdəʳ] *n* (*on motorcycle*) Kradbegleiter *m*
outright [aut'raɪt] *adv* (*kill*) auf der Stelle; (*win*) überlegen; (*buy*) auf einen Schlag; (*ask, refuse*) ohne Umschweife ▷ *adj* (*winner, victory*) unbestritten; (*refusal, hostility*) total
outrun [aut'rʌn] (*irreg: like* **run**) *vt* schneller laufen als
outset ['autsɛt] *n* Anfang *m*, Beginn *m*; **from the ~** von Anfang an; **at the ~** am Anfang
outshine [aut'ʃaɪn] (*irreg: like* **shine**) *vt* (*fig*) in den Schatten stellen
outside [aut'saɪd] *n* (*of building etc*) Außenseite *f* ▷ *adj* (*wall, lavatory*) Außen- ▷ *adv* (*be, wait*) draußen; (*go*) nach draußen ▷ *prep* außerhalb *+gen*; (*door etc*) vor *+dat*; **at the ~** (*at the most*) höchstens; (*at the latest*) spätestens; **an ~ chance** eine geringe Chance
outside broadcast *n* außerhalb des Studios produzierte Sendung *f*
outside lane *n* Überholspur *f*
outside line *n* (*Tel*) Amtsanschluss *m*
outsider [aut'saɪdəʳ] *n* (*stranger*) Außenstehende(r) *f(m)*; (*odd one out, in race etc*) Außenseiter(in) *m(f)*
outsize ['autsaɪz] *adj* (*clothes*) übergroß
outskirts ['autskə:ts] *npl* (*of town*) Stadtrand *m*
outsmart [aut'smɑ:t] *vt* austricksen (*inf*)
outspoken [aut'spəukən] *adj* offen
outspread [aut'sprɛd] *adj* (*wings, arms etc*) ausgebreitet
outstanding [aut'stændɪŋ] *adj* (*exceptional*) hervorragend; (*remaining*) ausstehend; **your account is still ~** Ihr Konto weist noch Außenstände auf
outstay [aut'steɪ] *vt*: **to ~ one's welcome** länger bleiben als erwünscht
outstretched [aut'strɛtʃt] *adj* ausgestreckt

outstrip [aut'strɪp] *vt* (*competitors, supply*): **to ~ (in)** übertreffen (an *+dat*)
out tray *n* Ablage *f* für Ausgänge
outvote [aut'vəut] *vt* überstimmen
outward ['autwəd] *adj* (*sign, appearances*) äußere(r, s) ▷ *adv* (*move, face*) nach außen; **~ journey** Hinreise *f*
outwardly ['autwədlɪ] *adv* (*on the surface*) äußerlich
outwards ['autwədz] *adv* (*move, face*) nach außen
outweigh [aut'weɪ] *vt* schwerer wiegen als
outwit [aut'wɪt] *vt* überlisten
ova ['əuvə] *npl of* **ovum**
oval ['əuvl] *adj* oval ▷ *n* Oval *nt*

OVAL OFFICE

Oval Office, ein großer ovaler Raum im Weißen Haus, ist das private Büro des amerikanischen Präsidenten. Im weiteren Sinne bezieht sich dieser Begriff oft auf die Präsidentschaft selbst.

ovarian [əu'vɛərɪən] *adj* (*Anat*) des Eierstocks/der Eierstöcke; **~ cyst** Zyste *f* im Eierstock
ovary ['əuvərɪ] *n* (*Anat, Med*) Eierstock *m*
ovation [əu'veɪʃən] *n* Ovation *f*
oven ['ʌvn] *n* (*Culin*) Backofen *m*
ovenproof ['ʌvnpru:f] *adj* (*dish etc*) feuerfest
oven-ready ['ʌvnrɛdɪ] *adj* backfertig
ovenware ['ʌvnwɛə^r] *n* feuerfestes Geschirr *nt*

KEYWORD

over ['əuvə^r] *adv* **1** (*across: walk, jump, fly etc*) hinüber; **over here** hier; **over there** dort (drüben); **to ask sb over** (*to one's house*) jdn zu sich einladen
2 (*indicating movement*): **to fall over** (*person*) hinfallen; (*object*) umfallen; **to knock sth over** etw umstoßen; **to turn over** (*in bed*) sich umdrehen; **to bend over** sich bücken
3 (*finished*): **to be over** (*game, life, relationship etc*) vorbei sein, zu Ende sein
4 (*excessively: clever, rich, fat etc*) übermäßig
5 (*remaining: money, food etc*) übrig; **is there any cake (left) over?** ist noch Kuchen übrig?
6: all over (*everywhere*) überall
7 (*repeatedly*): **over and over (again)** immer (und immer) wieder; **five times over** fünfmal
▷ *prep* **1** (*on top of, above*) über *+dat*; (*with vb of motion*) über *+acc*; **to spread a sheet over sth** ein Laken über etw *acc* breiten
2 (*on the other side of*): **the pub over the road** die Kneipe gegenüber; **he jumped over the wall** er sprang über die Mauer
3 (*more than*) über *+acc*; **over 200 people** über 200 Leute; **over and above my normal duties** über meine normalen Pflichten hinaus; **over and above that** darüber hinaus
4 (*during*) während; **let's discuss it over dinner** wir sollten es beim Abendessen besprechen

over ... ['əuvə^r] *pref* über-
overact [əuvər'ækt] *vi* übertreiben
overall ['əuvərɔ:l] *adj* (*length, cost etc*) Gesamt-; (*impression, view*) allgemein ▷ *adv* (*measure, cost*) insgesamt; (*generally*) im Allgemeinen ▷ *n* (*Brit*) Kittel *m*; **overalls** *npl* Overall *m*
overall majority *n* absolute Mehrheit *f*
overanxious [əuvər'æŋkʃəs] *adj* überängstlich
overawe [əuvər'ɔ:] *vt*: **to be ~d (by)** überwältigt sein (von)
overbalance [əuvə'bæləns] *vi* das Gleichgewicht verlieren
overbearing [əuvə'bɛərɪŋ] *adj* (*person, manner*) aufdringlich
overboard ['əuvəbɔ:d] *adv* (*Naut*) über Bord; **to go ~** (*fig*) es übertreiben, zu weit gehen
overbook [əuvə'buk] *vt* überbuchen
overcame [əuvə'keɪm] *pt of* **overcome**
overcapitalize [əuvə'kæpɪtəlaɪz] *vt* überkapitalisieren
overcast ['əuvəka:st] *adj* (*day, sky*) bedeckt
overcharge [əuvə'tʃa:dʒ] *vt* zu viel berechnen *+dat*
overcoat ['əuvəkəut] *n* Mantel *m*
overcome [əuvə'kʌm] (*irreg: like* **come**) *vt* (*problem, fear*) überwinden ▷ *adj* überwältigt; **she was ~ with grief** der Schmerz übermannte sie
overconfident [əuvə'kɔnfɪdənt] *adj* zu selbstsicher
overcrowded [əuvə'kraudɪd] *adj* überfüllt
overcrowding [əuvə'kraudɪŋ] *n* Überfüllung *f*
overdo [əuvə'du:] (*irreg: like* **do**) *vt* übertreiben; **to ~ it** es übertreiben
overdose ['əuvədəus] *n* Überdosis *f*
overdraft ['əuvədra:ft] *n* Kontoüberziehung *f*; **to have an ~** sein Konto überziehen
overdrawn [əuvə'drɔ:n] *adj* (*account*) überzogen; **I am ~** ich habe mein Konto überzogen
overdrive ['əuvədraɪv] *n* (*Aut*) Schongang *m*
overdue [əuvə'dju:] *adj* überfällig; **that change was long ~** diese Änderung war schon lange fällig
overemphasis [əuvər'ɛmfəsɪs] *n*: **~ on** Überbetonung *+gen*
overestimate [əuvər'ɛstɪmeɪt] *vt* überschätzen
overexcited [əuvərɪk'saɪtɪd] *adj* ganz aufgeregt
overexertion [əuvərɪg'zə:ʃən] *n* Überanstrengung *f*
overexpose [əuvərɪk'spəuz] *vt* (*Phot*) überbelichten
overflow [əuvə'fləu] *vi* (*river*) über die Ufer treten; (*bath, jar etc*) überlaufen ▷ *n* (*also:* **overflow pipe**) Überlaufrohr *nt*
overgenerous [əuvə'dʒɛnərəs] *adj* allzu großzügig

overgrown [əuvə'grəun] *adj* (*garden*) verwildert; **he's just an ~ schoolboy** er ist nur ein großes Kind
overhang ['əuvə'hæŋ] (*irreg: like* **hang**) *vt* herausragen über *+acc* ▷ *vi* überhängen ▷ *n* Überhang *m*
overhaul [əuvə'hɔ:l] *vt* (*equipment, car etc*) überholen ▷ *n* Überholung *f*
overhead [əuvə'hɛd] *adv* (*above*) oben; (*in the sky*) in der Luft ▷ *adj* (*lighting*) Decken-; (*cables, wires*) Überland- ▷ *n* (*US*) = **overheads**
overheads *npl* allgemeine Unkosten *pl*
overhear [əuvə'hɪəʳ] (*irreg: like* **hear**) *vt* (zufällig) mit anhören
overheat [əuvə'hi:t] *vi* (*engine*) heißlaufen
overjoyed [əuvə'dʒɔɪd] *adj* überglücklich; **to be ~ (at)** überglücklich sein (über *+acc*)
overkill ['əuvəkɪl] *n* (*fig*): **it would be ~** das wäre zu viel des Guten
overland ['əuvəlænd] *adj* (*journey*) Überland- ▷ *adv* (*travel*) über Land
overlap [əuvə'læp] *vi* (*figures, ideas etc*) sich überschneiden
overleaf [əuvə'li:f] *adv* umseitig, auf der Rückseite
overload [əuvə'ləud] *vt* (*vehicle*) überladen; (*Elec*) überbelasten; (*fig: with work etc*) überlasten
overlook [əuvə'luk] *vt* (*have view over*) überblicken; (*fail to notice*) übersehen; (*excuse, forgive*) hinwegsehen über *+acc*
overlord ['əuvəlɔ:d] *n* oberster Herr *m*
overmanning [əuvə'mænɪŋ] *n* Überbesetzung *f*
overnight [əuvə'naɪt] *adv* über Nacht ▷ *adj* (*bag, clothes*) Reise-; (*accommodation, stop*) für die Nacht; **to travel ~** nachts reisen; **he'll be away ~** (*tonight*) er kommt erst morgen zurück; **to stay ~** über Nacht bleiben; **~ stay** Übernachtung *f*
overpass ['əuvəpɑ:s] (*esp US*) *n* Überführung *f*
overpay [əuvə'peɪ] *vt*: **to ~ sb by £50** jdm £ 50 zu viel bezahlen
overplay [əuvə'pleɪ] *vt* (*overact*) übertrieben darstellen; **to ~ one's hand** den Bogen überspannen
overpower [əuvə'pauəʳ] *vt* überwältigen
overpowering [əuvə'pauərɪŋ] *adj* (*heat*) unerträglich; (*stench*) durchdringend; (*feeling, desire*) überwältigend
overproduction ['əuvəprə'dʌkʃən] *n* Überproduktion *f*
overrate [əuvə'reɪt] *vt* überschätzen
overreach [əuvə'ri:tʃ] *vt*: **to ~ o.s.** sich übernehmen
overreact [əuvəri:'ækt] *vi* übertrieben reagieren
override [əuvə'raɪd] (*irreg: like* **ride**) *vt* (*order etc*) sich hinwegsetzen über *+acc*
overriding [əuvə'raɪdɪŋ] *adj* vorrangig
overrule [əuvə'ru:l] *vt* (*claim, person*) zurückweisen; (*decision*) aufheben
overrun [əuvə'rʌn] (*irreg: like* **run**) *vt* (*country, continent*) einfallen in *+acc* ▷ *vi* (*meeting etc*) zu lange dauern; **the town is ~ with tourists** die Stadt ist von Touristen überlaufen
overseas [əuvə'si:z] *adv* (*live, work*) im Ausland; (*travel*) ins Ausland ▷ *adj* (*market, trade*) Übersee-; (*student, visitor*) aus dem Ausland
oversee [əuvə'si:] *vt* (*supervise*) beaufsichtigen, überwachen
overseer ['əuvəsɪəʳ] *n* Aufseher(in) *m(f)*
overshadow [əuvə'ʃædəu] *vt* (*place, building etc*) überschatten; (*fig*) in den Schatten stellen
overshoot [əuvə'ʃu:t] (*irreg: like* **shoot**) *vt* (*target, runway*) hinausschießen über *+acc*
oversight ['əuvəsaɪt] *n* Versehen *nt*; **due to an ~** aus Versehen
oversimplify [əuvə'sɪmplɪfaɪ] *vt* zu stark vereinfachen
oversleep [əuvə'sli:p] (*irreg: like* **sleep**) *vi* verschlafen
overspend [əuvə'spɛnd] (*irreg: like* **spend**) *vi* zu viel ausgeben; **we have overspent by 5,000 dollars** wir haben 5000 Dollar zu viel ausgegeben
overspill ['əuvəspɪl] *n* (*excess population*) Bevölkerungsüberschuss *m*
overstaffed [əuvə'stɑ:ft] *adj*: **to be ~** überbesetzt sein
overstate [əuvə'steɪt] *vt* (*exaggerate*) zu sehr betonen
overstatement [əuvə'steɪtmənt] *n* Übertreibung *f*
overstay [əuvə'steɪ] *vt see* **outstay**
overstep [əuvə'stɛp] *vt*: **to ~ the mark** zu weit gehen
overstock [əuvə'stɔk] *vt* zu große Bestände anlegen in *+dat*
overstretched [əuvə'strɛtʃt] *adj* (*person, resources*) überfordert
overstrike ['əuvəstraɪk] (*irreg: like* **strike**) *n* (*on printer*) Mehrfachdruck *m* ▷ *vt* mehrfachdrucken
oversubscribed [əuvəsəb'skraɪbd] *adj* (*Comm etc*) überzeichnet
overt [əu'və:t] *adj* offen
overtake [əuvə'teɪk] (*irreg: like* **take**) *vt* (*Aut*) überholen; (*event, change*) hereinbrechen über *+acc*; (*emotion*) befallen ▷ *vi* (*Aut*) überholen
overtaking [əuvə'teɪkɪŋ] *n* (*Aut*) Überholen *nt*
overtax [əuvə'tæks] *vt* (*Econ*) zu hoch besteuern; (*strength, patience*) überfordern; **to ~ o.s.** sich übernehmen
overthrow [əuvə'θrəu] (*irreg: like* **throw**) *vt* (*government etc*) stürzen
overtime ['əuvətaɪm] *n* Überstunden *pl*; **to do** *or* **work ~** Überstunden machen
overtime ban *n* Überstundenverbot *nt*
overtone ['əuvətəun] *n* (*fig: also:* **overtones**): **~s of** Untertöne *pl* von
overture ['əuvətʃuəʳ] *n* (*Mus*) Ouvertüre *f*; (*fig*) Annäherungsversuch *m*
overturn [əuvə'tə:n] *vt* (*car, chair*) umkippen; (*fig: decision*) aufheben; (*: government*) stürzen ▷ *vi* (*train etc*) umkippen; (*car*) sich

überschlagen; (*boat*) kentern
overview ['əuvəvju:] *n* Überblick *m*
overweight [əuvə'weɪt] *adj* (*person*) übergewichtig
overwhelm [əuvə'wɛlm] *vt* überwältigen
overwhelming [əuvə'wɛlmɪŋ] *adj* überwältigend; **one's ~ impression is of heat/noise** man bemerkt vor allem die Hitze/den Lärm
overwhelmingly [əuvə'wɛlmɪŋlɪ] *adv* (*vote, reject*) mit überwältigender Mehrheit; (*appreciative, generous etc*) über alle Maßen; (*opposed etc*) überwiegend
overwork [əuvə'wə:k] *n* Überarbeitung *f* ▷ *vt* (*person*) (mit Arbeit) überlasten; (*cliché etc*) überstrapazieren ▷ *vi* sich überarbeiten
overwrite [əuvə'raɪt] *vt* (*Comput*) überschreiben
overwrought [əuvə'rɔ:t] *adj* (*person*) überreizt
ovulate ['ɔvjuleɪt] *vi* ovulieren
ovulation [ɔvju'leɪʃən] *n* Eisprung *m*, Ovulation *f*
ovum ['əuvəm] (*pl* **ova**) *n* Eizelle *f*
owe [əu] *vt*: **to ~ sb sth, to ~ sth to sb** (*lit, fig*) jdm etw schulden; (*life, talent, good looks etc*) jdm etw verdanken
owing to ['əuɪŋ-] *prep* (*because of*) wegen *+gen*, aufgrund *+gen*
owl [aul] *n* Eule *f*
own [əun] *vt* (*possess*) besitzen ▷ *vi* (*Brit: form*): **to ~ up to sth** etw zugeben ▷ *adj* eigen; **a room of my ~** mein eigenes Zimmer; **to get one's ~ back** (*take revenge*) sich rächen; **on one's ~** allein; **to come into one's ~** sich entfalten
▸ **own up** *vi* gestehen, es zugeben
own brand *n* (*Comm*) Hausmarke *f*
owner ['əunəʳ] *n* Besitzer(in) *m(f)*, Eigentümer(in) *m(f)*
owner-occupier ['əunər'ɔkjupaɪəʳ] *n* (*Admin, Law*) Bewohner(in) *m(f)* im eigenen Haus
ownership ['əunəʃɪp] *n* Besitz *m*; **under new ~** (*shop etc*) unter neuer Leitung
own goal *n* (*also fig*) Eigentor *nt*
ox [ɔks] (*pl* **oxen**) *n* Ochse *m*

OXBRIDGE

Oxbridge, eine Mischung aus Ox(ford) und (Cam)bridge, bezieht sich auf die traditionsreichen Universitäten von Oxford und Cambridge. Dieser Begriff ist oft wertend und bringt das Prestige und die Privilegien zum Ausdruck, die traditionellerweise mit diesen Universitäten in Verbindung gebracht werden.

OXFAM (*Brit*) *n abbr* (*= Oxford Committee for Famine Relief*) *karitative Vereinigung zur Hungerhilfe*
oxide ['ɔksaɪd] *n* Oxid *nt*
oxidize ['ɔksɪdaɪz] *vi* oxidieren
Oxon. ['ɔksn] (*Brit*) *abbr* (*Post*) *= Oxfordshire*; (*in degree titles: = Oxoniensis*) *der Universität Oxford*
oxtail ['ɔksteɪl] *n*: **~ soup** Ochsenschwanzsuppe *f*
oxyacetylene ['ɔksɪə'sɛtɪli:n] *adj* (*flame*) Azetylensauerstoff-; **~ burner** Schweißbrenner *m*; **~ welding** Autogenschweißen *nt*
oxygen ['ɔksɪdʒən] *n* Sauerstoff *m*
oxygen mask *n* Sauerstoffmaske *f*
oxygen tent *n* Sauerstoffzelt *nt*
oyster ['ɔɪstəʳ] *n* Auster *f*
oz *abbr* = **ounce**
ozone ['əuzəun] *n* Ozon *nt*
ozone hole *n* Ozonloch *nt*
ozone layer *n*: **the ~** die Ozonschicht

Pp

P, **p**[1] [piː] *n* (*letter*) P *nt*, p *nt*; **P for Peter** ≈ P wie Paula
P. *abbr* = **president; prince**
p[2] (*Brit*) *abbr* = **penny; pence**
p. *abbr* (= *page*) S.
PA *n abbr* = **personal assistant; public-address system** ▷ *abbr* (*US: Post*) = *Pennsylvania*
pa [pɑː] (*inf*) *n* Papa *m*
p.a. *abbr* (= *per annum*) p.a.
PAC (*US*) *n abbr* (= *political action committee*) *politisches Aktionskomitee*
pace [peɪs] *n* (*step*) Schritt *m*; (*speed*) Tempo *nt* ▷ *vi*: **to ~ up and down** auf und ab gehen; **to keep ~ with** Schritt halten mit; **to set the ~** das Tempo angeben; **to put sb through his/her ~s** (*fig*) jdn auf Herz und Nieren prüfen
pacemaker [ˈpeɪsmeɪkəʳ] *n* (*Med*) (Herz)schrittmacher *m*; (*Sport: pacesetter*) Schrittmacher *m*
pacesetter [ˈpeɪssɛtəʳ] *n* (*Sport*) = **pacemaker**
Pacific [pəˈsɪfɪk] *n* (*Geog*): **the ~ (Ocean)** der Pazifik, der Pazifische Ozean
pacific [pəˈsɪfɪk] *adj* (*intentions etc*) friedlich
pacifier [ˈpæsɪfaɪəʳ] (*US*) *n* (*dummy*) Schnuller *m*
pacifist [ˈpæsɪfɪst] *n* Pazifist(in) *m(f)*
pacify [ˈpæsɪfaɪ] *vt* (*person, fears*) beruhigen
pack [pæk] *n* (*packet*) Packung *f*; (*US: of cigarettes*) Schachtel *f*; (*of people, hounds*) Meute *f*; (*also*: **back pack**) Rucksack *m*; (*of cards*) (Karten)spiel *nt* ▷ *vt* (*clothes etc*) einpacken; (*suitcase etc, Comput*) packen; (*press down*) pressen ▷ *vi* packen; **to ~ one's bags** (*fig*) die Koffer packen; **to ~ into** (*cram: people, objects*) hineinstopfen in +*acc*; **to send sb ~ing** (*inf*) jdn kurz abfertigen
▸ **pack in** (*Brit: inf*) *vt* (*job*) hinschmeißen; **~ it in!** hör auf!
▸ **pack off** *vt* schicken
▸ **pack up** *vi* (*Brit: inf: machine*) den Geist aufgeben; (*: person*) Feierabend machen ▷ *vt* (*belongings*) zusammenpacken
package [ˈpækɪdʒ] *n* (*parcel, Comput*) Paket *nt*; (*also*: **package deal**) Pauschalangebot *nt* ▷ *vt* verpacken
package holiday (*Brit*), **package tour** (*US*) *n* Pauschalreise *f*
packaging [ˈpækɪdʒɪŋ] *n* Verpackung *f*
packaging industry *n* Verpackungsindustrie *f*
packed [pækt] *adj* (*crowded*) randvoll
packed lunch (*Brit*) *n* Lunchpaket *nt*
packer [ˈpækəʳ] *n* Packer(in) *m(f)*
packet [ˈpækɪt] *n* Packung *f*; (*of cigarettes*) Schachtel *m*; **to make a ~** (*Brit: inf*) einen Haufen Geld verdienen
packet switching *n* (*Comput*) Paketvermittlung *f*
pack ice [ˈpækaɪs] *n* Packeis *nt*
packing [ˈpækɪŋ] *n* (*act*) Packen *nt*; (*material*) Verpackung *f*
packing case *n* Kiste *f*
pact [pækt] *n* Pakt *m*
pad [pæd] *n* (*paper*) Block *m*; (*to prevent damage*) Polster *nt*; (*inf: home*) Bude *f* ▷ *vt* (*upholstery etc*) polstern ▷ *vi*: **to ~ about/in** herum-/hereintrotten
padded cell [ˈpædɪd-] *n* Gummizelle *f*
padding [ˈpædɪŋ] *n* (*material*) Polsterung *f*; (*fig*) Füllwerk *nt*
paddle [ˈpædl] *n* (*oar*) Paddel *nt*; (*US: for table tennis*) Schläger *m* ▷ *vt* paddeln ▷ *vi* (*at seaside*) plan(t)schen
paddle steamer *n* Raddampfer *m*
paddling pool [ˈpædlɪŋ-] (*Brit*) *n* Plan(t)schbecken *nt*
paddock [ˈpædək] *n* (*small field*) Koppel *f*; (*at race course*) Sattelplatz *m*
paddy field [ˈpædɪ-] *n* Reisfeld *nt*
padlock [ˈpædlɔk] *n* Vorhängeschloss *nt* ▷ *vt* (mit einem Vorhängeschloss) verschließen
padre [ˈpɑːdrɪ] *n* (*Rel*) Feldgeistliche(r) *m*
paediatrician [piːdɪəˈtrɪʃən] *n* Kinderarzt *m*, Kinderärztin *f*
paediatrics, (US) **pediatrics** [piːdɪˈætrɪks] *n* Kinderheilkunde *f*, Pädiatrie *f*
paedophile [ˈpiːdəufaɪl] *n* Pädophile(r) *f(m)* ▷ *adj* pädophil
paedophilia [piːdəuˈfɪlɪə] *n* Pädophilie *f*
pagan [ˈpeɪgən] *adj* heidnisch ▷ *n* Heide *m*, Heidin *f*
page [peɪdʒ] *n* (*of book etc*) Seite *f*; (*also*: **pageboy**: *in hotel*) Page *m* ▷ *vt* (*in hotel etc*) ausrufen lassen
pageant [ˈpædʒənt] *n* (*historical procession*) Festzug *m*; (*show*) Historienspiel *nt*
pageantry [ˈpædʒəntrɪ] *n* Prunk *m*
pageboy [ˈpeɪdʒbɔɪ] *n see* **page**

pager ['peɪdʒəʳ] *n* Funkrufempfänger *m*, Piepser *m* (*inf*)
paginate ['pædʒɪneɪt] *vt* paginieren
pagination [pædʒɪ'neɪʃən] *n* Paginierung *f*
pagoda [pə'gəudə] *n* Pagode *f*
paid [peɪd] *pt, pp of* **pay** ▷ *adj* bezahlt; **to put ~ to** (*Brit*) zunichtemachen
paid-in ['peɪdɪn] (*US*) *adj* = **paid-up**
paid-up ['peɪdʌp], (*US*) **paid-in** *adj* (*member*) zahlend; (*Comm: shares*) eingezahlt; **~ capital** eingezahltes Kapital *nt*
pail [peɪl] *n* Eimer *m*
pain [peɪn] *n* Schmerz *m*; (*also*: **pain in the neck**: *inf: nuisance*) Plage *f*; **to have a ~ in the chest/arm** Schmerzen in der Brust/im Arm haben; **to be in ~** Schmerzen haben; **to take ~s to do sth** (*make an effort*) sich *dat* Mühe geben, etw zu tun; **on ~ of death** bei Todesstrafe; **he is/it is a right ~ (in the neck)** (*inf*) er/das geht einem auf den Wecker
pained [peɪnd] *adj* (*expression*) gequält
painful ['peɪnful] *adj* (*back, injury etc*) schmerzhaft; (*sight, decision etc*) schmerzlich; (*laborious*) mühsam; (*embarrassing*) peinlich
painfully ['peɪnfəlɪ] *adv* (*fig: extremely*) furchtbar
painkiller ['peɪnkɪləʳ] *n* schmerzstillendes Mittel *nt*
painless ['peɪnlɪs] *adj* schmerzlos
painstaking ['peɪnzteɪkɪŋ] *adj* (*work, person*) gewissenhaft
paint [peɪnt] *n* Farbe *f* ▷ *vt* (*door, house etc*) anstreichen; (*person, picture*) malen; (*fig*) zeichnen; **a tin of ~** eine Dose Farbe; **to ~ the door blue** die Tür blau streichen; **to ~ in oils** in Öl malen
paintbox ['peɪntbɔks] *n* Farbkasten *m*, Malkasten *m*
paintbrush ['peɪntbrʌʃ] *n* Pinsel *m*
painter ['peɪntəʳ] *n* (*artist*) Maler(in) *m(f)*; (*decorator*) Anstreicher(in) *m(f)*
painting ['peɪntɪŋ] *n* (*activity: of artist*) Malerei *f*; (*: of decorator*) Anstreichen *nt*; (*picture*) Bild *nt*, Gemälde *nt*
paint stripper *n* Abbeizmittel *nt*
paintwork ['peɪntwəːk] *n* (*of wall etc*) Anstrich *m*; (*of car*) Lack *m*
pair [pɛəʳ] *n* Paar *nt*; **a ~ of scissors** eine Schere; **a ~ of trousers** eine Hose
▶ **pair off** *vi*: **to ~ off with sb** sich jdm anschließen
pajamas [pə'dʒɑːməz] (*US*) *npl* Schlafanzug *m*, Pyjama *m*
Pakistan [pɑːkɪ'stɑːn] *n* Pakistan *nt*
Pakistani [pɑːkɪ'stɑːnɪ] *adj* pakistanisch ▷ *n* Pakistani *m*, Pakistaner(in) *m(f)*
PAL *n abbr* (TV: = *phase alternation line*) PAL *nt*
pal [pæl] (*inf*) *n* (*friend*) Kumpel *m*, Freund(in) *m(f)*
palace ['pæləs] *n* Palast *m*
palaeontology [pælɪɔn'tɔlədʒɪ] *n* Paläontologie *f*
palatable ['pælɪtəbl] *adj* (*food, drink*) genießbar; (*fig: idea, fact etc*) angenehm
palate ['pælɪt] *n* (*Anat*) Gaumen *m*; (*sense of taste*) Geschmackssinn *m*
palatial [pə'leɪʃəl] *adj* (*residence etc*) prunkvoll
palaver [pə'lɑːvəʳ] (*inf*) *n* (*fuss*) Theater *nt*
pale [peɪl] *adj* blass; (*light*) fahl ▷ *vi* erblassen ▷ *n*: **beyond the ~** (*unacceptable: behaviour*) indiskutabel; **to grow** *or* **turn ~** erblassen, blass werden; **~ blue** zartblau; **to ~ into insignificance (beside)** zur Bedeutungslosigkeit herabsinken (gegenüber +*dat*)
paleness ['peɪlnɪs] *n* Blässe *f*
Palestine ['pælɪstaɪn] *n* Palästina *nt*
Palestinian [pælɪs'tɪnɪən] *adj* palästinensisch ▷ *n* Palästinenser(in) *m(f)*
palette ['pælɪt] *n* Palette *f*
palings ['peɪlɪŋz] *npl* (*fence*) Lattenzaun *m*
palisade [pælɪ'seɪd] *n* Palisade *f*
pall [pɔːl] *n* (*cloud of smoke*) (Rauch)wolke *f* ▷ *vi* an Reiz verlieren
pallet ['pælɪt] *n* (*for goods*) Palette *f*
palliative ['pælɪətɪv] *n* (*Med*) Linderungsmittel *nt*; (*fig*) Beschönigung *f*
pallid ['pælɪd] *adj* bleich
pallor ['pæləʳ] *n* Bleichheit *f*
pally ['pælɪ] (*inf*) *adj*: **they're very ~** sie sind dicke Freunde
palm [pɑːm] *n* (*also*: **palm tree**) Palme *f*; (*of hand*) Handteller *m* ▷ *vt*: **to ~ sth off on sb** (*inf*) jdm etw andrehen
palmistry ['pɑːmɪstrɪ] *n* Handlesekunst *f*
Palm Sunday *n* Palmsonntag *m*
palpable ['pælpəbl] *adj* (*obvious*) offensichtlich
palpitations [pælpɪ'teɪʃənz] *npl* (*Med*) Herzklopfen *nt*
paltry ['pɔːltrɪ] *adj* (*amount, wage*) armselig
pamper ['pæmpəʳ] *vt* verwöhnen
pamphlet ['pæmflət] *n* Broschüre *f*; (*political*) Flugschrift *f*
pan [pæn] *n* (*also*: **saucepan**) Topf *m*; (*also*: **frying pan**) Pfanne *f* ▷ *vi* (*Cine, TV*) schwenken ▷ *vt* (*inf: book, film*) verreißen; **to ~ for gold** Gold waschen
panacea [pænə'sɪə] *n* Allheilmittel *nt*
panache [pə'næʃ] *n* Elan *m*, Schwung *m*
Panama ['pænəmɑː] *n* Panama *nt*
panama [pænə'mɑː] *n* (*also*: **panama hat**) Panamahut *m*
Panama Canal *n*: **the ~** der Panamakanal
Panamanian [pænə'meɪnɪən] *adj* panamaisch ▷ *n* Panamaer(in) *m(f)*
pancake ['pænkeɪk] *n* Pfannkuchen *m*
Pancake Day (*Brit*) *n* Fastnachtsdienstag *m*
pancake roll *n* *gefüllte Pfannkuchenrolle*
pancreas ['pæŋkrɪəs] *n* Bauchspeicheldrüse *f*
panda ['pændə] *n* Panda *m*
panda car (*Brit*) *n* Streifenwagen *m*
pandemonium [pændɪ'məunɪəm] *n* Chaos *nt*
pander ['pændəʳ] *vi*: **to ~ to** (*person, desire etc*) sich richten nach, entgegenkommen +*dat*
p&h (*US*) *abbr* (= *postage and handling*) Porto und Bearbeitungsgebühr
P&L *abbr* (= *profit and loss*) Gewinn und Verlust;

see also **profit**

p & p *(Brit) abbr (= postage and packing)* Porto und Verpackung

pane [peɪn] *n (of glass)* Scheibe *f*

panel ['pænl] *n (wood, metal, glass etc)* Platte *f*, Tafel *f*; *(group of experts etc)* Diskussionsrunde *f*; **~ of judges** Jury *f*

panel game *(Brit) n* Ratespiel *nt*

panelling, (US) **paneling** ['pænəlɪŋ] *n* Täfelung *f*

panellist, (US) **panelist** ['pænəlɪst] *n* Diskussionsteilnehmer(in) *m(f)*

pang [pæŋ] *n*: **to have** *or* **feel a ~ of regret** Reue empfinden; **hunger ~s** quälender Hunger *m*; **~s of conscience** Gewissensbisse *pl*

panhandler ['pænhændləʳ] *(US: inf) n* Bettler(in) *m(f)*

panic ['pænɪk] *n* Panik *f* ▷ *vi* in Panik geraten

panic buying [-baɪɪŋ] *n* Panikkäufe *pl*

panicky ['pænɪkɪ] *adj (person)* überängstlich; *(feeling)* Angst-; *(reaction)* Kurzschluss-

panic-stricken ['pænɪkstrɪkən] *adj (person, face)* von Panik erfasst

pannier ['pænɪəʳ] *n (on bicycle)* Satteltasche *f*; *(on animal)* (Trage)korb *m*

panorama [pænə'rɑːmə] *n (view)* Panorama *nt*

panoramic [pænə'ræmɪk] *adj (view)* Panorama-

pansy ['pænzɪ] *n (Bot)* Stiefmütterchen *nt*; *(inf: pej: sissy)* Tunte *f*

pant [pænt] *vi (person)* keuchen; *(animal)* hecheln

pantechnicon [pæn'tɛknɪkən] *(Brit) n* Möbelwagen *m*

panther ['pænθəʳ] *n* Pant(h)er *m*

panties ['pæntɪz] *npl* Höschen *nt*

panto ['pæntəu] *n*, **pantomime** ['pæntəumaɪm] *n siehe Info-Artikel*

PANTOMIME

Pantomime oder umgangssprächlich *panto* ist in Großbritannien ein zur Weihnachtszeit aufgeführtes Märchenspiel mit possenhaften Elementen, Musik, Standardrollen (ein als Frau verkleideter Mann, ein Junge, ein Bösewicht) und aktuellen Witzen. Publikumsbeteiligung wird gern gesehen (z. B. warnen die Kinder den Helden mit dem Ruf „He's behind you" vor einer drohenden Gefahr), und viele der Witze sprechen vor allem Erwachsene an, sodass pantomimes Unterhaltung für die ganze Familie bieten.

pantry ['pæntrɪ] *n (cupboard)* Vorratsschrank *m*; *(room)* Speisekammer *f*

pants [pænts] *npl (Brit: woman's)* Höschen *nt*; *(: man's)* Unterhose *f*; *(US: trousers)* Hose *f*

panty hose *(US) npl* Strumpfhose *f*

papacy ['peɪpəsɪ] *n* Papsttum *nt*; **during the ~ of Paul VI** während der Amtszeit von Papst Paul VI

papal ['peɪpəl] *adj* päpstlich

paparazzi [pæpə'rætsiː] *npl* Pressefotografen *pl*, Paparazzi *pl*

paper ['peɪpəʳ] *n* Papier *nt*; *(also:* **newspaper***)* Zeitung *f*; *(exam)* Arbeit *f*; *(academic essay)* Referat *nt*; *(document)* Dokument *nt*, Papier; *(wallpaper)* Tapete *f* ▷ *adj (made from paper: hat, plane etc)* Papier-, aus Papier ▷ *vt (room)* tapezieren; **papers** *npl (also:* **identity papers***)* Papiere *pl*; **a piece of ~** *(odd bit)* ein Stück *nt* Papier, ein Zettel *m*; *(sheet)* ein Blatt *nt* Papier; **to put sth down on ~** etw schriftlich festhalten

paper advance *n (on printer)* Papiervorschub *m*

paperback ['peɪpəbæk] *n* Taschenbuch *nt*, Paperback *nt* ▷ *adj*: **~ edition** Taschenbuchausgabe *f*

paper bag *n* Tüte *f*

paperboy ['peɪpəbɔɪ] *n* Zeitungsjunge *m*

paperclip ['peɪpəklɪp] *n* Büroklammer *f*

paper hankie *n* Tempotaschentuch® *nt*

paper mill *n* Papierfabrik *f*

paper money *n* Papiergeld *nt*

paper shop *n* Zeitungsladen *m*

paperweight ['peɪpəweɪt] *n* Briefbeschwerer *m*

paperwork ['peɪpəwəːk] *n* Schreibarbeit *f*

papier-mâché [pæpjeɪ'mæʃeɪ] *n* Papiermaschee *nt*

paprika ['pæprɪkə] *n* Paprika *m*

Pap Smear, **Pap Test** *n (Med)* Abstrich *m*

par [pɑːʳ] *n (Golf)* Par *nt*; **to be on a ~ with** sich messen können mit; **at ~** *(Comm)* zum Nennwert; **above/below ~** *(Comm)* über/unter dem Nennwert; **above** *or* **over ~** *(Golf)* über dem Par; **below** *or* **under ~** *(Golf)* unter dem Par; **to feel below** *or* **under ~** sich nicht auf der Höhe fühlen; **to be ~ for the course** *(fig)* zu erwarten sein

parable ['pærəbl] *n* Gleichnis *nt*

parabola [pə'ræbələ] *n (Math)* Parabel *f*

parachute ['pærəʃuːt] *n* Fallschirm *m*

parachute jump *n* Fallschirmabsprung *m*

parachutist ['pærəʃuːtɪst] *n* Fallschirmspringer(in) *m(f)*

parade [pə'reɪd] *n (procession)* Parade *f*; *(ceremony)* Zeremonie *f* ▷ *vt (people)* aufmarschieren lassen; *(wealth, knowledge etc)* zur Schau stellen ▷ *vi (Mil)* aufmarschieren; **fashion ~** Modenschau *f*

parade ground *n* Truppenübungsplatz *m*, Exerzierplatz *m*

paradise ['pærədaɪs] *n (also fig)* Paradies *nt*

paradox ['pærədɔks] *n* Paradox *nt*

paradoxical [pærə'dɔksɪkl] *adj (situation)* paradox

paradoxically [pærə'dɔksɪklɪ] *adv* paradoxerweise

paraffin ['pærəfɪn] *(Brit) n (also:* **paraffin oil***)* Petroleum *nt*; **liquid ~** Paraffinöl *nt*

paraffin heater *(Brit) n* Petroleumofen *m*

paraffin lamp *(Brit) n* Petroleumlampe *f*

paragon ['pærəgən] *n*: **a ~ of** *(honesty, virtue etc)* ein Muster *nt* an *+dat*

paragraph ['pærəgrɑ:f] *n* Absatz *m*, Paragraf *m*; **to begin a new ~** einen neuen Absatz beginnen
parallel ['pærəlɛl] *adj* (*also Comput*) parallel; (*fig: similar*) vergleichbar ▷ *n* Parallele *f*; (*Geog*) Breitenkreis *m*; **to run ~ (with** *or* **to)** (*lit, fig*) parallel verlaufen (zu); **to draw ~s between/ with** Parallelen ziehen zwischen/mit; **in ~** (*Elec*) parallel
paralyse ['pærəlaɪz] (*Brit*) *vt* (*also fig*) lähmen
paralysis [pə'rælɪsɪs] (*pl* **paralyses**) *n* Lähmung *f*
paralytic [pærə'lɪtɪk] *adj* paralytisch, Lähmungs-; (*Brit: inf: drunk*) sternhagelvoll
paralyze ['pærəlaɪz] (*US*) *vt* = **paralyse**
paramedic [pærə'mɛdɪk] *n* Sanitäter(in) *m(f)*; (*in hospital*) medizinisch-technischer Assistent *m*, medizinisch-technische Assistentin *f*
parameter [pə'ræmɪtə^r] *n* (*Math*) Parameter *m*; (*fig: factor*) Faktor *m*; (*: limit*) Rahmen *m*
paramilitary [pærə'mɪlɪtərɪ] *adj* paramilitärisch
paramount ['pærəmaunt] *adj* vorherrschend; **of ~ importance** von höchster *or* größter Wichtigkeit
paranoia [pærə'nɔɪə] *n* Paranoia *f*
paranoid ['pærənɔɪd] *adj* paranoid
paranormal [pærə'nɔ:ml] *adj* übersinnlich, paranormal ▷ *n*: **the ~** das Übersinnliche
parapet ['pærəpɪt] *n* Brüstung *f*
paraphernalia [pærəfə'neɪlɪə] *n* Utensilien *pl*
paraphrase ['pærəfreɪz] *vt* umschreiben
paraplegic [pærə'pli:dʒɪk] *n* Paraplegiker(in) *m(f)*, doppelseitig Gelähmte(r) *f(m)*
parapsychology [pærəsaɪ'kɔlədʒɪ] *n* Parapsychologie *f*
parasite ['pærəsaɪt] *n* (*also fig*) Parasit *m*
parasol ['pærəsɔl] *n* Sonnenschirm *m*
paratrooper ['pærətru:pə^r] *n* Fallschirmjäger *m*
parcel ['pɑ:sl] *n* Paket *nt* ▷ *vt* (*also:* **parcel up**) verpacken
▸ **parcel out** *vt* aufteilen
parcel bomb (*Brit*) *n* Paketbombe *f*
parcel post *n* Paketpost *f*
parch [pɑ:tʃ] *vt* ausdörren, austrocknen
parched [pɑ:tʃt] *adj* ausgetrocknet; **I'm ~** (*inf: thirsty*) ich bin am Verdursten
parchment ['pɑ:tʃmənt] *n* Pergament *nt*
pardon ['pɑ:dn] *n* (*Law*) Begnadigung *f* ▷ *vt* (*forgive*) verzeihen *+dat*, vergeben *+dat*; (*Law*) begnadigen; **~ me!, I beg your pardon!** (*I'm sorry!*) verzeihen Sie bitte!; **(I beg your) ~?, ~ me?** (*US: what did you say?*) bitte?
pare [pɛə^r] *vt* (*Brit: nails*) schneiden; (*fruit etc*) schälen; (*fig: costs etc*) reduzieren
parent ['pɛərənt] *n* (*mother*) Mutter *f*; (*father*) Vater *m*; **parents** *npl* (*mother and father*) Eltern *pl*
parentage ['pɛərəntɪdʒ] *n* Herkunft *f*; **of unknown ~** unbekannter Herkunft
parental [pə'rɛntl] *adj* (*love, control etc*) elterlich
parent company *n* Mutterunternehmen *nt*
parentheses [pə'rɛnθɪsi:z] *npl of* **parenthesis**
parenthesis [pə'rɛnθɪsɪs] (*pl* **parentheses**) *n* Klammer *f*; **in ~** in Klammern
parenthood ['pɛərənthud] *n* Elternschaft *f*
parenting ['pɛərəntɪŋ] *n* elterliche Pflege *f*
Paris ['pærɪs] *n* Paris *nt*
parish ['pærɪʃ] *n* Gemeinde *f*
parish council (*Brit*) *n* Gemeinderat *m*
parishioner [pə'rɪʃənə^r] *n* Gemeindemitglied *nt*
Parisian [pə'rɪzɪən] *adj* Pariser *inv*, paris(er)isch ▷ *n* Pariser(in) *m(f)*
parity ['pærɪtɪ] *n* (*equality*) Gleichstellung *f*
park [pɑ:k] *n* Park *m* ▷ *vt, vi* (*Aut*) parken
parka ['pɑ:kə] *n* Parka *m*
parking ['pɑ:kɪŋ] *n* Parken *nt*; **"no ~"** „Parken verboten"
parking lights *npl* Parklicht *nt*
parking lot (*US*) *n* Parkplatz *m*
parking meter *n* Parkuhr *f*
parking offence (*Brit*) *n* Parkvergehen *nt*
parking place *n* Parkplatz *m*
parking ticket *n* Strafzettel *m*
parking violation (*US*) *n* = **parking offence**
Parkinson's ['pɑ:kɪnsənz], **Parkinson's disease** *n* parkinsonsche Krankheit *f*
parkway ['pɑ:kweɪ] (*US*) *n* Allee *f*
parlance ['pɑ:ləns] *n*: **in common/modern ~** im allgemeinen/modernen Sprachgebrauch
parliament ['pɑ:ləmənt] *n* Parlament *nt*

PARLIAMENT

Parliament ist die höchste gesetzgebende Versammlung in Großbritannien und tritt im Parlamentsgebäude in London zusammen. Die Legislaturperiode beträgt normalerweise 5 Jahre von einer Wahl zur nächsten. Das Parlament besteht aus zwei Kammern, dem Oberhaus (siehe *House of Lords* und dem Unterhaus (siehe *House of Commons*).

parliamentary [pɑ:lə'mɛntərɪ] *adj* parlamentarisch
parlour, (*US*) **parlor** ['pɑ:lə^r] *n* Salon *m*
parlous ['pɑ:ləs] *adj* (*state*) prekär
Parmesan [pɑ:mɪ'zæn] *n* (*also:* **Parmesan cheese**) Parmesan(käse) *m*
parochial [pə'rəukɪəl] (*pej*) *adj* (*person, attitude*) engstirnig
parody ['pærədɪ] *n* Parodie *f* ▷ *vt* parodieren
parole [pə'rəul] *n* (*Law*) Bewährung *f*; **on ~** auf Bewährung
paroxysm ['pærəksɪzəm] *n* (*also Med*) Anfall *m*
parquet ['pɑ:keɪ] *n* (*also:* **parquet floor(ing)**) Parkettboden *m*
parrot ['pærət] *n* Papagei *m*
parrot-fashion ['pærətfæʃən] *adv* (*say, learn*) mechanisch; (*repeat*) wie ein Papagei
parry ['pærɪ] *vt* (*blow, argument*) parieren, abwehren
parsimonious [pɑ:sɪ'məunɪəs] *adj* geizig
parsley ['pɑ:slɪ] *n* Petersilie *f*
parsnip ['pɑ:snɪp] *n* Pastinake *f*

parson ['pɑːsn] *n* Pfarrer *m*
part [pɑːt] *n* Teil *m*; (*Tech*) Teil *nt*; (*Theat, Cine etc: role*) Rolle *f*; (*US: in hair*) Scheitel *m*; (*Mus*) Stimme *f* ▷ *adv* = **partly** ▷ *vt* (*separate*) trennen; (*hair*) scheiteln ▷ *vi* (*roads, people*) sich trennen; (*crowd*) sich teilen; **to take ~ in** teilnehmen an *+dat*; **to take sth in good ~** etw nicht übel nehmen; **to take sb's ~** (*support*) sich auf jds Seite *acc* stellen; **on his ~** seinerseits; **for my ~** für meinen Teil; **for the most ~** (*generally*) zumeist; **for the better** *or* **best ~ of the day** die meiste Zeit des Tages; **to be ~ and parcel of** dazugehören zu; **~ of speech** (*Ling*) Wortart *f*
▸ **part with** *vt fus* sich trennen von
partake [pɑː'teɪk] (*irreg: like* **take**) *vi* (*form*): **to ~ of sth** etw zu sich nehmen
part exchange (*Brit*) *n*: **to give/take sth in ~** etw in Zahlung geben/nehmen
partial ['pɑːʃl] *adj* (*victory, solution*) Teil-; (*support*) teilweise; (*biassed*) parteiisch; **to be ~ to** (*person, drink etc*) eine Vorliebe haben für
partially ['pɑːʃəlɪ] *adv* (*to some extent*) teilweise, zum Teil
participant [pɑː'tɪsɪpənt] *n* Teilnehmer(in) *m(f)*
participate [pɑː'tɪsɪpeɪt] *vi* sich beteiligen; **to ~ in** teilnehmen an *+dat*
participation [pɑːtɪsɪ'peɪʃən] *n* Teilnahme *f*
participle ['pɑːtɪsɪpl] *n* Partizip *nt*
particle ['pɑːtɪkl] *n* Teilchen *nt*, Partikel *f*
particular [pə'tɪkjuləʳ] *adj* (*distinct: person, time, place etc*) bestimmt, speziell; (*special*) speziell, besondere(r, s) ▷ *n*: **in ~** im Besonderen, besonders; **particulars** *npl* Einzelheiten *pl*; (*name, address etc*) Personalien *pl*; **to be very ~ about sth** (*fussy*) in Bezug auf etw *acc* sehr eigen sein
particularly [pə'tɪkjuləlɪ] *adv* besonders
parting ['pɑːtɪŋ] *n* (*action*) Teilung *f*; (*farewell*) Abschied *m*; (*Brit: in hair*) Scheitel *m* ▷ *adj* (*words, gift etc*) Abschieds-; **his ~ shot was ...** (*fig*) seine Bemerkung zum Abschied war ...
partisan [pɑːtɪ'zæn] *adj* (*politics, views*) voreingenommen ▷ *n* (*supporter*) Anhänger(in) *m(f)*; (*fighter*) Partisan *m*
partition [pɑː'tɪʃən] *n* (*wall, screen*) Trennwand *f*; (*of country*) Teilung *f* ▷ *vt* (*room, office*) aufteilen; (*country*) teilen
partly ['pɑːtlɪ] *adv* teilweise, zum Teil
partner ['pɑːtnəʳ] *n* Partner(in) *m(f)*; (*Comm*) Partner(in), Teilhaber(in) *m(f)* ▷ *vt* (*at dance, cards etc*) als Partner(in) haben
partnership ['pɑːtnəʃɪp] *n* (*Pol etc*) Partnerschaft *f*; (*Comm*) Teilhaberschaft *f*; **to go into ~ (with sb), form a ~ (with sb)** (mit jdm) eine Partnerschaft eingehen
part payment *n* Anzahlung *f*
partridge ['pɑːtrɪdʒ] *n* Rebhuhn *nt*
part-time ['pɑː't'taɪm] *adj* (*work, staff*) Teilzeit-, Halbtags- ▷ *adv*: **to work ~** Teilzeit arbeiten; **to study ~** Teilzeitstudent(in) *m(f)* sein
part-timer [pɑː't'taɪməʳ] *n* (*also*: **part-time worker**) Teilzeitbeschäftigte(r) *f(m)*
party ['pɑːtɪ] *n* (*Pol, Law*) Partei *f*; (*celebration, social event*) Party *f*, Fete *f*; (*group of people*) Gruppe *f*, Gesellschaft *f* ▷ *cpd* (*Pol*) Partei-; **dinner ~** Abendgesellschaft *f*; **to give** *or* **throw a ~** eine Party geben, eine Fete machen; **we're having a ~ next Saturday** bei uns ist nächsten Samstag eine Party; **our son's birthday ~** die Geburtstagsfeier unseres Sohnes; **to be a ~ to a crime** an einem Verbrechen beteiligt sein
party dress *n* Partykleid *nt*
party line *n* (*Tel*) Gemeinschaftsanschluss *m*; (*Pol*) Parteilinie *f*
party piece (*inf*) *n*: **to do one's ~** auf einer Party etwas zum Besten geben
party political *adj* parteipolitisch
party political broadcast *n* parteipolitische Sendung *f*
par value *n* (*Comm: of share, bond*) Nennwert *m*
pass [pɑːs] *vt* (*spend: time*) verbringen; (*hand over*) reichen, geben; (*go past*) vorbeikommen an *+dat*; (*: in car*) vorbeifahren an *+dat*; (*overtake*) überholen; (*fig: exceed*) übersteigen; (*exam*) bestehen; (*law, proposal*) genehmigen ▷ *vi* (*go past*) vorbeigehen; (*: in car*) vorbeifahren; (*in exam*) bestehen ▷ *n* (*permit*) Ausweis *m*; (*in mountains, Sport*) Pass *m*; **to ~ sth through sth** etw durch etw führen; **to ~ the ball to** den Ball zuspielen *+dat*; **could you ~ the vegetables round?** könnten Sie das Gemüse herumreichen?; **to get a ~ in ...** (*Scol*) die Prüfung in ... bestehen; **things have come to a pretty ~ when ...** (*Brit: inf*) so weit ist es schon gekommen, dass ...; **to make a ~ at sb** (*inf*) jdn anmachen
▸ **pass away** *vi* (*die*) dahinscheiden
▸ **pass by** *vi* (*go past*) vorbeigehen; (*: in car*) vorbeifahren ▷ *vt* (*ignore*) vorbeigehen an *+dat*
▸ **pass down** *vt* (*customs, inheritance*) weitergeben
▸ **pass for** *vt*: **she could ~ for 25** sie könnte für 25 durchgehen
▸ **pass on** *vi* (*die*) verscheiden ▷ *vt*: **to ~ on (to)** weitergeben (an *+acc*)
▸ **pass out** *vi* (*faint*) ohnmächtig werden; (*Brit: Mil*) die Ausbildung beenden
▸ **pass over** *vt* (*ignore*) übergehen ▷ *vi* (*die*) entschlafen
▸ **pass up** *vt* (*opportunity*) sich *dat* entgehen lassen
passable ['pɑːsəbl] *adj* (*road*) passierbar; (*acceptable*) passabel
passage ['pæsɪdʒ] *n* Gang *m*; (*in book*) Passage *f*; (*way through crowd etc, Anat*) Weg *m*; (*act of passing: of train etc*) Durchfahrt *f*; (*journey: on boat*) Überfahrt *f*
passageway ['pæsɪdʒweɪ] *n* Gang *m*
passenger ['pæsɪndʒəʳ] *n* (*in boat, plane*) Passagier *m*; (*in car*) Fahrgast *m*
passer-by [pɑːsə'baɪ] (*pl* **passers-by**) *n* Passant(in) *m(f)*
passing ['pɑːsɪŋ] *adj* (*moment, thought etc*)

flüchtig; **in ~** *(incidentally)* beiläufig, nebenbei; **to mention sth in ~** etw beiläufig *or* nebenbei erwähnen
passing place *n (Aut)* Ausweichstelle *f*
passion ['pæʃən] *n* Leidenschaft *f*; **to have a ~ for sth** eine Leidenschaft für etw haben
passionate ['pæʃənɪt] *adj* leidenschaftlich
passion fruit *n* Passionsfrucht *f*, Maracuja *f*
Passion play *n* Passionsspiel *nt*
passive ['pæsɪv] *adj* passiv; *(Ling)* Passiv- ▷ *n (Ling)* Passiv *nt*
passive smoking *n* passives Rauchen, Passivrauchen *nt*
passkey ['pɑːskiː] *n* Hauptschlüssel *m*
Passover ['pɑːsəuvə^r] *n* Passah(fest) *nt*
passport ['pɑːspɔːt] *n* Pass *m*; *(fig: to success etc)* Schlüssel *m*
passport control *n* Passkontrolle *f*
passport office *n* Passamt *nt*
password ['pɑːswəːd] *n* Kennwort *nt*; *(Comput)* Passwort *nt*
past [pɑːst] *prep (in front of)* vorbei an *+dat*; *(beyond)* hinter *+dat*; *(later than)* nach ▷ *adj (government etc)* früher, ehemalig; *(week, month etc)* vergangen ▷ *n* Vergangenheit *f* ▷ *adv*: **to run ~** vorbeilaufen; **he's ~ 40** er ist über 40; **it's ~ midnight** es ist nach Mitternacht; **ten/quarter ~ eight** zehn/Viertel nach acht; **he ran ~ me** er lief an mir vorbei; **I'm ~ caring** es kümmert mich nicht mehr; **to be ~ it** *(Brit: inf: person)* es nicht mehr bringen; **for the ~ few/3 days** während der letzten Tage/3 Tage; **in the ~** *(also Ling)* in der Vergangenheit
pasta ['pæstə] *n* Nudeln *pl*
paste [peɪst] *n (wet mixture)* Teig *m*; *(glue)* Kleister *m*; *(jewellery)* Strass *m*; *(fish, tomato paste)* Paste *f* ▷ *vt (stick)* kleben
pastel ['pæstl] *adj (colour)* Pastell-
pasteurized ['pæstʃəraɪzd] *adj* pasteurisiert
pastille ['pæstɪl] *n* Pastille *f*
pastime ['pɑːstaɪm] *n* Zeitvertreib *m*, Hobby *nt*
past master *(Brit) n*: **to be a ~ at sth** ein Experte *m* in etw *dat* sein
pastor ['pɑːstə^r] *n* Pastor(in) *m(f)*
pastoral ['pɑːstərl] *adj (Rel: duties etc)* als Pastor
pastry ['peɪstrɪ] *n (dough)* Teig *m*; *(cake)* Gebäckstück *nt*
pasture ['pɑːstʃə^r] *n* Weide *f*
pasty [*n* 'pæstɪ, *adj* 'peɪstɪ] *n (pie)* Pastete *f* ▷ *adj (complexion)* bläßlich
pat [pæt] *vt (with hand)* tätscheln ▷ *adj (answer, remark)* glatt ▷ *n*: **to give sb/o.s. a ~ on the back** *(fig)* jdm/sich auf die Schulter klopfen; **he knows it off ~, he has it down ~** *(US)* er kennt das in- und auswendig
patch [pætʃ] *n (piece of material)* Flicken *m*; *(also:* **eye patch***)* Augenklappe *f*; *(damp, bald etc)* Fleck *m*; *(of land)* Stück *nt*; *(: for growing vegetables etc)* Beet *nt* ▷ *vt (clothes)* flicken; **(to go through) a bad ~** eine schwierige Zeit (durchmachen)
▸ **patch up** *vt (clothes etc)* flicken; *(quarrel)* beilegen
patchwork ['pætʃwəːk] *n (Sewing)* Patchwork *nt*
patchy ['pætʃɪ] *adj (colour)* ungleichmäßig; *(information, knowledge etc)* lückenhaft
pate [peɪt] *n*: **a bald ~** eine Glatze
pâté ['pæteɪ] *n* Pastete *f*
patent ['peɪtnt] *n* Patent *nt* ▷ *vt* patentieren lassen ▷ *adj (obvious)* offensichtlich
patent leather *n* Lackleder *nt*
patently ['peɪtntlɪ] *adv (obvious, wrong)* vollkommen
patent medicine *n* patentrechtlich geschütztes Arzneimittel *nt*
Patent Office *n* Patentamt *nt*
paternal [pə'təːnl] *adj* väterlich; **my ~ grandmother** meine Großmutter väterlicherseits
paternalistic [pətəːnə'lɪstɪk] *adj* patriarchalisch
paternity [pə'təːnɪtɪ] *n* Vaterschaft *f*
paternity leave *n* Vaterschaftsurlaub *m*
paternity suit *n* Vaterschaftsprozess *m*
path [pɑːθ] *n (also fig)* Weg *m*; *(trail, track)* Pfad *m*; *(trajectory: of bullet, aircraft, planet)* Bahn *f*
pathetic [pə'θɛtɪk] *adj (pitiful)* mitleiderregend; *(very bad)* erbärmlich
pathological [pæθə'lɔdʒɪkl] *adj (liar, hatred)* krankhaft; *(Med)* pathologisch
pathologist [pə'θɔlədʒɪst] *n* Pathologe *m*, Pathologin *f*
pathology [pə'θɔlədʒɪ] *n* Pathologie *f*
pathos ['peɪθɔs] *n* Pathos *nt*
pathway ['pɑːθweɪ] *n* Pfad *m*, Weg *m*; *(fig)* Weg
patience ['peɪʃns] *n* Geduld *f*; *(Brit: Cards)* Patience *f*; **to lose (one's) ~** die Geduld verlieren
patient ['peɪʃnt] *n* Patient(in) *m(f)* ▷ *adj* geduldig; **to be ~ with sb** Geduld mit jdm haben
patiently ['peɪʃntlɪ] *adv* geduldig
patio ['pætɪəu] *n* Terrasse *f*
patriot ['peɪtrɪət] *n* Patriot(in) *m(f)*
patriotic [pætrɪ'ɔtɪk] *adj* patriotisch
patriotism ['pætrɪətɪzəm] *n* Patriotismus *m*
patrol [pə'trəul] *n (Mil)* Patrouille *f*; *(Police)* Streife *f* ▷ *vt (Mil, Police: city, streets etc)* patrouillieren; **to be on ~** *(Mil)* auf Patrouille sein; *(Police)* auf Streife sein
patrol boat *n* Patrouillenboot *nt*
patrol car *n* Streifenwagen *m*
patrolman [pə'trəulmən] *(US: irreg: like* **man***) n (Police)* (Streifen)polizist *m*
patron ['peɪtrən] *n (customer)* Kunde *m*, Kundin *f*; *(benefactor)* Förderer *m*; **~ of the arts** Kunstmäzen *m*
patronage ['pætrənɪdʒ] *n (of artist, charity etc)* Förderung *f*
patronize ['pætrənaɪz] *vt (pej: look down on)* von oben herab behandeln; *(artist etc)* fördern; *(shop, club)* besuchen
patronizing ['pætrənaɪzɪŋ] *adj* herablassend
patron saint *n* Schutzheilige(r) *f(m)*
patter ['pætə^r] *n (of feet)* Trappeln *nt*; *(of rain)* Prasseln *nt*; *(sales talk etc)* Sprüche *pl* ▷ *vi*

(*footsteps*) trappeln; (*rain*) prasseln

pattern ['pætən] *n* Muster *nt*; (*Sewing*) Schnittmuster *nt*; **behaviour ~s** Verhaltensmuster *pl*

patterned ['pætənd] *adj* gemustert; **~ with flowers** mit Blumenmuster

paucity ['pɔːsɪtɪ] *n*: **a ~ of** ein Mangel *m* an *+dat*

paunch [pɔːntʃ] *n* Bauch *m*, Wanst *m*

pauper ['pɔːpəʳ] *n* Arme(r) *f(m)*; **~'s grave** Armengrab *nt*

pause [pɔːz] *n* Pause *f* ▷ *vi* eine Pause machen; (*hesitate*) innehalten; **to ~ for breath** eine Verschnaufpause einlegen

pave [peɪv] *vt* (*street, yard etc*) pflastern; **to ~ the way for** (*fig*) den Weg bereiten *or* bahnen für

pavement ['peɪvmənt] *n* (*Brit*) Bürgersteig *m*; (*US: roadway*) Straße *f*

pavilion [pə'vɪlɪən] *n* (*Sport*) Klubhaus *nt*

paving ['peɪvɪŋ] *n* (*material*) Straßenbelag *m*

paving stone *n* Pflasterstein *m*

paw [pɔː] *n* (*of cat, dog etc*) Pfote *f*; (*of lion, bear etc*) Tatze *f*, Pranke *f* ▷ *vt* (*pej: touch*) betatschen; **to ~ the ground** (*animal*) scharren

pawn [pɔːn] *n* (*Chess*) Bauer *m*; (*fig*) Schachfigur *f* ▷ *vt* versetzen

pawnbroker ['pɔːnbrəukəʳ] *n* Pfandleiher *m*

pawnshop ['pɔːnʃɔp] *n* Pfandhaus *nt*

pay [peɪ] (*pt, pp* **paid**) *n* (*wage*) Lohn *m*; (*salary*) Gehalt *nt* ▷ *vt* (*sum of money, wage*) zahlen; (*bill, person*) bezahlen ▷ *vi* (*be profitable*) sich bezahlt machen; (*fig*) sich lohnen; **how much did you ~ for it?** wie viel hast du dafür bezahlt?; **I paid 10 pounds for that book** ich habe 10 Pfund für das Buch bezahlt, das Buch hat mich 10 Pfund gekostet; **to ~ one's way** seinen Beitrag leisten; **to ~ dividends** (*fig*) sich bezahlt machen; **to ~ the price/penalty for sth** (*fig*) den Preis/die Strafe für etw zahlen; **to ~ sb a compliment** jdm ein Kompliment machen; **to ~ attention (to)** achtgeben (auf *+acc*); **to ~ sb a visit** jdn besuchen; **to ~ one's respects to sb** jdm seine Aufwartung machen

▸ **pay back** *vt* zurückzahlen; **I'll ~ you back next week** ich gebe dir das Geld nächste Woche zurück

▸ **pay for** *vt fus* (*also fig*) (be)zahlen für

▸ **pay in** *vt* einzahlen

▸ **pay off** *vt* (*debt*) abbezahlen; (*person*) auszahlen; (*creditor*) befriedigen; (*mortgage*) tilgen ▷ *vi* sich auszahlen; **to ~ sth off in instalments** etw in Raten (ab)zahlen

▸ **pay out** *vt* (*money*) ausgeben; (*rope*) ablaufen lassen

▸ **pay up** *vi* zahlen

payable ['peɪəbl] *adj* zahlbar; **to make a cheque ~ to sb** einen Scheck auf jdn ausstellen

pay award *n* Lohn-/Gehaltserhöhung *f*

payday ['peɪdeɪ] *n* Zahltag *m*

PAYE (*Brit*) *n abbr* (*= pay as you earn*) *Lohnsteuerabzugsverfahren*

payee [peɪ'iː] *n* Zahlungsempfänger *m*

pay envelope (*US*) *n* = **pay packet**

paying guest ['peɪɪŋ-] *n* zahlender Gast *m*

payload ['peɪləud] *n* Nutzlast *f*

payment ['peɪmənt] *n* (*act*) Zahlung *f*, Bezahlung *f*; (*of bill*) Begleichung *f*; (*sum of money*) Zahlung *f*; **advance ~** (*part sum*) Anzahlung *f*; (*total sum*) Vorauszahlung *f*; **deferred payment, ~ by instalments** Ratenzahlung *f*; **monthly ~** (*sum of money*) Monatsrate *f*; **on ~ of** gegen Zahlung von

pay packet (*Brit*) *n* Lohntüte *f*

pay-per-click ['peɪpəː'klɪk] *n* (*Comput*) Pay-per-Click *nt*

payphone ['peɪfəun] *n* Münztelefon *nt*; (*card phone*) Kartentelefon *nt*

payroll ['peɪrəul] *n* Lohnliste *f*; **to be on a firm's ~** bei einer Firma beschäftigt sein

pay slip (*Brit*) *n see* **pay** Lohnstreifen *m*; Gehaltsstreifen *m*

pay station (*US*) *n* = **payphone**

PBS (*US*) *n abbr* (*= Public Broadcasting Service*) *öffentliche Rundfunkanstalt*

PC *n abbr* (*= personal computer*) PC *m*; (*Brit*) = **police constable** ▷ *adj abbr* = **politically correct** ▷ *abbr* (*Brit*) = **Privy Councillor**

pc *abbr* = **per cent; postcard**

p/c *abbr* = **petty cash**

PCB *n abbr* (*Elec, Comput*) = **printed circuit board**; (*= polychlorinated biphenyl*) PCB *nt*

pcm *abbr* (*= per calendar month*) pro Monat

PD (*US*) *n abbr* = **police department**

pd *abbr* (*= paid*) bez.

PDA *abbr* (*Comput*) *of* **personal digital assistant** PDA *m*

pdq (*inf*) *adv abbr* (*= pretty damn quick*) verdammt schnell

PDSA (*Brit*) *n abbr* (*= People's Dispensary for Sick Animals*) *kostenloses Behandlungszentrum für Haustiere*

PDT (*US*) *abbr* (*= Pacific Daylight Time*) *pazifische Sommerzeit*

PE *n abbr* (*Scol*) = **physical education**

pea [piː] *n* Erbse *f*

peace [piːs] *n* Frieden *m*; **to be at ~ with sb/sth** mit jdm/etw in Frieden leben; **to keep the ~** (*policeman*) die öffentliche Ordnung aufrechterhalten; (*citizen*) den Frieden wahren

peaceable ['piːsəbl] *adj* friedlich

peaceful ['piːsful] *adj* friedlich

peacekeeper ['piːskiːpəʳ] *n* Friedenswächter(in) *m(f)*

peacekeeping force ['piːskiːpɪŋ-] *n* Friedenstruppen *pl*

peace offering *n* Friedensangebot *nt*

peach [piːtʃ] *n* Pfirsich *m*

peacock ['piːkɔk] *n* Pfau *m*

peak [piːk] *n* (*of mountain*) Spitze *f*, Gipfel *m*; (*of cap*) Schirm *m*; (*fig*) Höhepunkt *m*

peak hours *npl* Stoßzeit *f*

peak period *n* Spitzenzeit *f*, Stoßzeit *f*

peak rate *n* Höchstrate *f*

peaky ['piːkɪ] (*Brit: inf*) *adj* blass

peal [piːl] *n* (*of bells*) Läuten *nt*; **~s of laughter** schallendes Gelächter *nt*
peanut ['piːnʌt] *n* Erdnuss *f*
peanut butter *n* Erdnussbutter *f*
pear [pɛəʳ] *n* Birne *f*
pearl [pəːl] *n* Perle *f*
peasant ['pɛznt] *n* Bauer *m*
peat [piːt] *n* Torf *m*
pebble ['pɛbl] *n* Kieselstein *m*
peck [pɛk] *vt* (*bird*) picken; (*also*: **peck at**) picken an *+dat* ▷ *n* (*of bird*) Schnabelhieb *m*; (*kiss*) Küsschen *nt*
pecking order ['pɛkɪŋ-] *n* (*fig*) Hackordnung *f*
peckish ['pɛkɪʃ] (*Brit*: *inf*) *adj* (*hungry*) leicht hungrig; **I'm feeling ~** ich könnte was zu essen gebrauchen
peculiar [pɪ'kjuːlɪəʳ] *adj* (*strange*) seltsam; **~ to** (*exclusive to*) charakteristisch für
peculiarity [pɪkjuːlɪ'ærɪtɪ] *n* (*strange habit*) Eigenart *f*; (*distinctive feature*) Besonderheit *f*, Eigentümlichkeit *f*
peculiarly [pɪ'kjuːlɪəlɪ] *adv* (*oddly*) seltsam; (*distinctively*) unverkennbar
pecuniary [pɪ'kjuːnɪərɪ] *adj* finanziell
pedal ['pɛdl] *n* Pedal *nt* ▷ *vi* in die Pedale treten
pedal bin (*Brit*) *n* Treteimer *m*
pedant ['pɛdənt] *n* Pedant(in) *m(f)*
pedantic [pɪ'dæntɪk] *adj* pedantisch
peddle ['pɛdl] *vt* (*goods*) feilbieten, verkaufen; (*drugs*) handeln mit; (*gossip*) verbreiten
peddler ['pɛdləʳ] *n* (*also*: **drug peddler**) Pusher *m*
pedestal ['pɛdəstl] *n* Sockel *m*
pedestrian [pɪ'dɛstrɪən] *n* Fußgänger(in) *m(f)* ▷ *adj* Fußgänger-; (*fig*) langweilig
pedestrian crossing (*Brit*) *n* Fußgängerüberweg *m*
pedestrian mall (*US*) *n* Fußgängerzone *f*
pedestrian precinct (*Brit*) *n* Fußgängerzone *f*
pediatrics [piːdɪ'ætrɪks] (*US*) *n* = **paediatrics**
pedigree ['pɛdɪgriː] *n* (*of animal*) Stammbaum *m*; (*fig*: *background*) Vorgeschichte *f* ▷ *cpd* (*dog*) Rasse-, reinrassig
pee [piː] (*inf*) *vi* pinkeln
peek [piːk] *vi*: **to ~ at/over/into** *etc* gucken nach/über *+acc*/in *+acc etc* ▷ *n*: **to have** *or* **take a ~ (at)** einen (kurzen) Blick werfen (auf *+acc*)
peel [piːl] *n* Schale *f* ▷ *vt* schälen ▷ *vi* (*paint*) abblättern; (*wallpaper*) sich lösen; (*skin, back etc*) sich schälen
▸ **peel back** *vt* abziehen
peeler ['piːləʳ] *n* (*potato peeler etc*) Schälmesser *nt*
peelings ['piːlɪŋz] *npl* Schalen *pl*
peep [piːp] *n* (*look*) kurzer Blick *m*; (*sound*) Pieps *m* ▷ *vi* (*look*) gucken; **to have** *or* **take a ~ (at)** einen kurzen Blick werfen (auf *+acc*)
▸ **peep out** *vi* (*be visible*) hervorgucken
peephole ['piːphəul] *n* Guckloch *nt*
peer [pɪəʳ] *n* (*noble*) Peer *m*; (*equal*) Gleichrangige(r) *f(m)*; (*contemporary*) Gleichaltrige(r) *f(m)* ▷ *vi*: **to ~ at** starren auf *+acc*
peerage ['pɪərɪdʒ] *n* (*title*) Adelswürde *f*; (*position*) Adelsstand *m*; **the ~** (*all the peers*) der Adel
peerless ['pɪəlɪs] *adj* unvergleichlich
peeved [piːvd] *adj* verärgert, sauer (*inf*)
peevish ['piːvɪʃ] *adj* (*bad-tempered*) mürrisch
peg [pɛg] *n* (*hook, knob*) Haken *m*; (*Brit*: *also*: **clothes peg**) Wäscheklammer *f*; (*also*: **tent peg**) Zeltpflock *m*, Hering *m* ▷ *vt* (*washing*) festklammern; (*prices*) festsetzen; **off the ~** von der Stange
pejorative [pɪ'dʒɔrətɪv] *adj* abwertend
Pekin [piː'kɪn] *n* = **Peking**
Pekinese [piːkɪ'niːz] *n* = **Pekingese**
Peking [piː'kɪŋ] *n* Peking *nt*
Pekingese [piːkɪ'niːz] *n* (*dog*) Pekinese *m*
pelican ['pɛlɪkən] *n* Pelikan *m*
pelican crossing (*Brit*) *n* (*Aut*) Fußgängerüberweg *m* mit Ampel
pellet ['pɛlɪt] *n* (*of paper etc*) Kügelchen *nt*; (*of mud etc*) Klümpchen *nt*; (*for shotgun*) Schrotkugel *f*
pell-mell ['pɛl'mɛl] *adv* in heillosem Durcheinander
pelmet ['pɛlmɪt] *n* (*wooden*) Blende *f*; (*fabric*) Querbehang *m*
pelt [pɛlt] *vi* (*rain*: *also*: **pelt down**) niederprasseln; (*inf*: *run*) rasen ▷ *n* (*animal skin*) Pelz *m*, Fell *nt* ▷ *vt*: **to ~ sb with sth** jdn mit etw bewerfen
pelvis ['pɛlvɪs] *n* Becken *nt*
pen [pɛn] *n* (*also*: **fountain pen**) Füller *m*; (*also*: **ballpoint pen**) Kugelschreiber *m*; (*also*: **felt-tip pen**) Filzstift *m*; (*enclosure*: *for sheep, pigs etc*) Pferch *m*; (*US*: *inf*: *prison*) Knast *m*; **to put ~ to paper** zur Feder greifen
penal ['piːnl] *adj* (*Law*: *colony, institution*) Straf-; (: *system, reform*) Strafrechts-; **~ code** Strafgesetzbuch *nt*
penalize ['piːnəlaɪz] *vt* (*punish*) bestrafen; (*fig*) benachteiligen
penal servitude [-'səːvɪtjuːd] *n* Zwangsarbeit *f*
penalty ['pɛnltɪ] *n* Strafe *f*; (*Sport*) Strafstoß *m*; (: *Football*) Elfmeter *m*
penalty area (*Brit*) *n* (*Sport*) Strafraum *m*
penalty clause *n* Strafklausel *f*
penalty kick *n* (*Rugby*) Strafstoß *m*; (*Football*) Elfmeter *m*
penalty shoot-out [-'ʃuːtaut] *n* (*Football*) Elfmeterschießen *nt*
penance ['pɛnəns] *n* (*Rel*): **to do ~ for one's sins** für seine Sünden Buße tun
pence [pɛns] *npl of* **penny**
penchant ['pɑ̃ːʃɑ̃ːŋ] *n* Vorliebe *f*, Schwäche *f*; **to have a ~ for** eine Schwäche haben für
pencil ['pɛnsl] *n* Bleistift *m* ▷ *vt*: **to ~ sb/sth in** jdn/etw vormerken
pencil case *n* Federmäppchen *nt*
pencil sharpener *n* Bleistiftspitzer *m*
pendant ['pɛndnt] *n* Anhänger *m*
pending ['pɛndɪŋ] *adj* anstehend ▷ *prep*: **~ his return** bis zu seiner Rückkehr; **~ a decision** bis eine Entscheidung getroffen ist
pendulum ['pɛndjuləm] *n* Pendel *nt*
penetrate ['pɛnɪtreɪt] *vt* (*person*: *territory etc*)

durchdringen; (*light, water, sound*) eindringen in *+acc*
penetrating ['pɛnɪtreɪtɪŋ] *adj* (*sound, gaze*) durchdringend; (*mind, observation*) scharf
penetration [pɛnɪ'treɪʃən] *n* Durchdringen *nt*
pen friend (*Brit*) *n* Brieffreund(in) *m(f)*
penguin ['pɛŋgwɪn] *n* Pinguin *m*
penicillin [pɛnɪ'sɪlɪn] *n* Penizillin *nt*
peninsula [pə'nɪnsjulə] *n* Halbinsel *f*
penis ['pi:nɪs] *n* Penis *m*
penitence ['pɛnɪtns] *n* Reue *f*
penitent ['pɛnɪtnt] *adj* reuig
penitentiary [pɛnɪ'tɛnʃərɪ] (*US*) *n* Gefängnis *nt*
penknife ['pɛnnaɪf] *n* Taschenmesser *nt*
Penn. (*US*) *abbr* (*Post*) = *Pennsylvania*
pen name *n* Pseudonym *nt*
pennant ['pɛnənt] *n* (*Naut*) Wimpel *m*
penniless ['pɛnɪlɪs] *adj* mittellos
Pennines ['pɛnaɪnz] *npl*: **the ~** die Pennines *pl*
penny ['pɛnɪ] (*Brit*) (*pl* **pence**) *n* Penny *m*; (*US*) Cent *m*; **it was worth every ~** es war jeden Pfennig wert; **it won't cost you a ~** es kostet dich keinen Pfennig
pen pal *n* Brieffreund(in) *m(f)*
penpusher ['pɛnpuʃəʳ] *n* Schreiberling *m*
pension ['pɛnʃən] *n* Rente *f*
▸ **pension off** *vt* (vorzeitig) pensionieren
pensionable ['pɛnʃnəbl] *adj* (*age*) Pensions-; (*job*) mit Pensionsberechtigung
pensioner ['pɛnʃənəʳ] (*Brit*) *n* Rentner(in) *m(f)*
pension scheme *n* Rentenversicherung *f*
pensive ['pɛnsɪv] *adj* nachdenklich
pentagon ['pɛntəgən] (*US*) *n*: **the P~** das Pentagon; *siehe Info-Artikel*

PENTAGON

Pentagon heißt das fünfeckige Gebäude in Arlington, Virginia, in dem das amerikanische Verteidigungsministerium untergebracht ist. Im weiteren Sinne bezieht sich dieses Wort auf die amerikanische Militärführung.

Pentecost ['pɛntɪkɔst] *n* (*in Judaism*) Erntefest *nt*; (*in Christianity*) Pfingsten *nt*
penthouse ['pɛnthaus] *n* Penthouse *nt*
pent-up ['pɛntʌp] *adj* (*feelings*) aufgestaut
penultimate [pɛ'nʌltɪmət] *adj* vorletzte(r, s)
penury ['pɛnjurɪ] *n* Armut *f*, Not *f*
people ['pi:pl] *npl* (*persons*) Leute *pl*; (*inhabitants*) Bevölkerung *f* ▹ *n* (*nation, race*) Volk *nt*; **old ~** alte Menschen *or* Leute; **young ~** junge Leute; **the room was full of ~** das Zimmer war voller Leute *or* Menschen; **several ~ came** mehrere (Leute) kamen; **~ say that ...** man sagt, dass ...; **the ~** (*Pol*) das Volk; **a man of the ~** ein Mann des Volkes
PEP *n abbr* (= *personal equity plan*) *steuerbegünstigte Kapitalinvestition*
pep [pɛp] (*inf*) *n* Schwung *m*, Pep *m*
▸ **pep up** *vt* (*person*) aufmöbeln; (*food*) pikanter machen

pepper ['pɛpəʳ] *n* (*spice*) Pfeffer *m*; (*vegetable*) Paprika *m* ▹ *vt*: **to ~ with** (*fig*) übersäen mit; **two ~s** zwei Paprikaschoten
peppercorn ['pɛpəkɔ:n] *n* Pfefferkorn *nt*
pepper mill *n* Pfeffermühle *f*
peppermint ['pɛpəmɪnt] *n* (*sweet*) Pfefferminz *nt*; (*plant*) Pfefferminze *f*
pepperoni [pɛpə'rəunɪ] *n* ≈ Pfeffersalami *f*
pepper pot *n* Pfefferstreuer *m*
pep talk (*inf*) *n* aufmunternde Worte *pl*
per [pə:ʳ] *prep* (*for each*) pro; **~ day/person/kilo** pro Tag/Person/Kilo; **~ annum** pro Jahr; **as ~ your instructions** gemäß Ihren Anweisungen
per capita [-'kæpɪtə] *adj* (*income*) Pro-Kopf- ▹ *adv* pro Kopf
perceive [pə'si:v] *vt* (*see*) wahrnehmen; (*view, understand*) verstehen
per cent *n* Prozent *nt*; **a 20 ~ discount** 20 Prozent Rabatt
percentage [pə'sɛntɪdʒ] *n* Prozentsatz *m*; **on a ~ basis** auf Prozentbasis
percentage point *n* Prozent *nt*
perceptible [pə'sɛptɪbl] *adj* (*difference, change*) wahrnehmbar, merklich
perception [pə'sɛpʃən] *n* (*insight*) Einsicht *f*; (*opinion, understanding*) Erkenntnis *f*; (*faculty*) Wahrnehmung *f*
perceptive [pə'sɛptɪv] *adj* (*person*) aufmerksam; (*analysis etc*) erkenntnisreich
perch [pə:tʃ] *n* (*for bird*) Stange *f*; (*fish*) Flussbarsch *m* ▹ *vi*: **to ~ (on)** (*bird*) sitzen (auf *+dat*); (*person*) hocken (auf *+dat*)
percolate ['pə:kəleɪt] *vt* (*coffee*) (mit einer Kaffeemaschine) zubereiten ▹ *vi* (*coffee*) durchlaufen; **to ~ through/into** (*idea, light etc*) durchsickern durch/in *+acc*
percolator ['pə:kəleɪtəʳ] *n* (*also*: **coffee percolator**) Kaffeemaschine *f*
percussion [pə'kʌʃən] *n* (*Mus*) Schlagzeug *nt*
peremptory [pə'rɛmptərɪ] (*pej*) *adj* (*person*) herrisch; (*order*) kategorisch
perennial [pə'rɛnɪəl] *adj* (*plant*) mehrjährig; (*fig: problem, feature etc*) immer wiederkehrend ▹ *n* (*Bot*) mehrjährige Pflanze *f*
perfect [*adj, n* 'pə:fɪkt, *vt* pə'fɛkt] *adj* perfekt; (*nonsense, idiot etc*) ausgemacht ▹ *vt* (*technique*) perfektionieren ▹ *n*: **the ~** (*also*: **the perfect tense**) das Perfekt; **he's a ~ stranger to me** er ist mir vollkommen fremd
perfection [pə'fɛkʃən] *n* Perfektion *f*, Vollkommenheit *f*
perfectionist [pə'fɛkʃənɪst] *n* Perfektionist(in) *m(f)*
perfectly ['pə:fɪktlɪ] *adv* vollkommen; (*faultlessly*) perfekt; **I'm ~ happy with the situation** ich bin mit der Lage vollkommen zufrieden; **you know ~ well that ...** Sie wissen ganz genau, dass ...
perforate ['pə:fəreɪt] *vt* perforieren
perforated ulcer ['pə:fəreɪtəd-] *n* durchgebrochenes Geschwür *nt*
perforation [pə:fə'reɪʃən] *n* (*small hole*) Loch *nt*;

(*line of holes*) Perforation *f*
perform [pəˈfɔːm] *vt* (*operation, ceremony etc*) durchführen; (*task*) erfüllen; (*piece of music, play etc*) aufführen ▷ *vi* auftreten; **to ~ well/badly** eine gute/schlechte Leistung zeigen
performance [pəˈfɔːməns] *n* Leistung *f*; (*of play, show*) Vorstellung *f*; **the team put up a good ~** die Mannschaft zeigte eine gute Leistung
performer [pəˈfɔːməʳ] *n* Künstler(in) *m(f)*
performing [pəˈfɔːmɪŋ] *adj* (*animal*) dressiert
performing arts *npl*: **the ~** die darstellenden Künste *pl*
perfume [ˈpəːfjuːm] *n* Parfüm *nt*; (*fragrance*) Duft *m* ▷ *vt* parfümieren
perfunctory [pəˈfʌŋktərɪ] *adj* flüchtig
perhaps [pəˈhæps] *adv* vielleicht; **~ he'll come** er kommt vielleicht; **~ not** vielleicht nicht
peril [ˈpɛrɪl] *n* Gefahr *f*
perilous [ˈpɛrɪləs] *adj* gefährlich
perilously [ˈpɛrɪləslɪ] *adv*: **they came ~ close to being caught** sie wären um ein Haar gefangen worden
perimeter [pəˈrɪmɪtəʳ] *n* Umfang *m*
perimeter fence *n* Umzäunung *f*
period [ˈpɪərɪəd] *n* (*length of time*) Zeitraum *m*, Periode *f*; (*era*) Zeitalter *nt*; (*Scol*) Stunde *f*; (*esp US: full stop*) Punkt *m*; (*Med: also:* **menstrual period**) Periode ▷ *adj* (*costume etc*) zeitgenössisch; **for a ~ of 3 weeks** für eine Dauer *or* einen Zeitraum von 3 Wochen; **the holiday ~** (*Brit*) die Urlaubszeit; **I won't do it. P~.** ich mache das nicht, und damit basta!
periodic [pɪərɪˈɔdɪk] *adj* periodisch
periodical [pɪərɪˈɔdɪkl] *n* Zeitschrift *f* ▷ *adj* periodisch
periodically [pɪərɪˈɔdɪklɪ] *adv* periodisch
period pains (*Brit*) *npl* Menstruationsschmerzen *pl*
peripatetic [pɛrɪpəˈtɛtɪk] *adj* (*Brit: teacher*) an mehreren Schulen tätig; **~ life** Wanderleben *nt*
peripheral [pəˈrɪfərəl] *adj* (*feature, issue*) Rand-, nebensächlich; (*vision*) peripher ▷ *n* (*Comput*) Peripheriegerät *nt*
periphery [pəˈrɪfərɪ] *n* Peripherie *f*
periscope [ˈpɛrɪskəup] *n* Periskop *nt*
perish [ˈpɛrɪʃ] *vi* (*die*) umkommen; (*rubber, leather etc*) verschleißen
perishable [ˈpɛrɪʃəbl] *adj* (*food*) leicht verderblich
perishables [ˈpɛrɪʃəblz] *npl* leicht verderbliche Waren *pl*
perishing [ˈpɛrɪʃɪŋ] (*Brit: inf*) *adj*: **it's ~ (cold)** es ist eisig kalt
peritonitis [pɛrɪtəˈnaɪtɪs] *n* Bauchfellentzündung *f*
perjure [ˈpəːdʒəʳ] *vt*: **to ~ o.s.** einen Meineid leisten
perjury [ˈpəːdʒərɪ] *n* (*in court*) Meineid *m*; (*breach of oath*) Eidesverletzung *f*
perks [pəːks] (*inf*) *npl* (*extras*) Vergünstigungen *pl*
perk up *vi* (*cheer up*) munter werden
perky [ˈpəːkɪ] *adj* (*cheerful*) munter
perm [pəːm] *n* Dauerwelle *f* ▷ *vt*: **to have one's hair ~ed** sich *dat* eine Dauerwelle machen lassen
permanence [ˈpəːmənəns] *n* Dauerhaftigkeit *f*
permanent [ˈpəːmənənt] *adj* dauerhaft; (*job, position*) fest; **~ address** ständiger Wohnsitz *m*; **I'm not ~ here** ich bin hier nicht fest angestellt
permanently [ˈpəːmənəntlɪ] *adv* (*damage*) dauerhaft; (*stay, live*) ständig; (*locked, open, frozen etc*) dauernd
permeable [ˈpəːmɪəbl] *adj* durchlässig
permeate [ˈpəːmɪeɪt] *vt* durchdringen ▷ *vi*: **to ~ through** dringen durch
permissible [pəˈmɪsɪbl] *adj* zulässig
permission [pəˈmɪʃən] *n* Erlaubnis *f*, Genehmigung *f*; **to give sb ~ to do sth** jdm die Erlaubnis geben, etw zu tun
permissive [pəˈmɪsɪv] *adj* permissiv
permit [*n* ˈpəːmɪt, *vt* pəˈmɪt] *n* Genehmigung *f* ▷ *vt* (*allow*) erlauben; (*make possible*) gestatten; **fishing ~** Angelschein *m*; **to ~ sb to do sth** jdm erlauben, etw zu tun; **weather ~ting** wenn das Wetter es zulässt
permutation [pəːmjuˈteɪʃən] *n* Permutation *f*; (*fig*) Variation *f*
pernicious [pəːˈnɪʃəs] *adj* (*lie, nonsense*) bösartig; (*effect*) schädlich
pernickety [pəˈnɪkɪtɪ] (*inf*) *adj* pingelig
perpendicular [pəːpənˈdɪkjuləʳ] *adj* senkrecht ▷ *n*: **the ~** die Senkrechte; **~ to** senkrecht zu
perpetrate [ˈpəːpɪtreɪt] *vt* (*crime*) begehen
perpetual [pəˈpɛtjuəl] *adj* ständig, dauernd
perpetuate [pəˈpɛtjueɪt] *vt* (*custom, belief etc*) bewahren; (*situation*) aufrechterhalten
perpetuity [pəːpɪˈtjuːɪtɪ] *n*: **in ~** auf ewig
perplex [pəˈplɛks] *vt* verblüffen
perplexing [pəːˈplɛksɪŋ] *adj* verblüffend
perquisites [ˈpəːkwɪzɪts] (*form*) *npl* Vergünstigungen *pl*
per se [-seɪ] *adv* an sich
persecute [ˈpəːsɪkjuːt] *vt* verfolgen
persecution [pəːsɪˈkjuːʃən] *n* Verfolgung *f*
perseverance [pəːsɪˈvɪərns] *n* Beharrlichkeit *f*, Ausdauer *f*
persevere [pəːsɪˈvɪəʳ] *vi* durchhalten, beharren
Persia [ˈpəːʃə] *n* Persien *nt*
Persian [ˈpəːʃən] *adj* persisch ▷ *n* (*Ling*) Persisch *nt*; **the (persian) Gulf** der (Persische) Golf
Persian cat *n* Perserkatze *f*
persist [pəˈsɪst] *vi*: **to ~ (with** *or* **in)** beharren (auf +*dat*), festhalten (an +*dat*); **to ~ in doing sth** darauf beharren, etw zu tun
persistence [pəˈsɪstəns] *n* Beharrlichkeit *f*
persistent [pəˈsɪstənt] *adj* (*person, noise*) beharrlich; (*smell, cough etc*) hartnäckig; (*lateness, rain*) andauernd; **~ offender** Wiederholungstäter(in) *m(f)*
persnickety [pəˈsnɪkɪtɪ] (*US: inf*) *adj* = **pernickety**
person [ˈpəːsn] *n* Person *f*, Mensch *m*; **in ~**

persönlich; **on** *or* **about one's ~** bei sich; **~ to ~ call** (*Tel*) Gespräch *nt* mit Voranmeldung
personable ['pə:snəbl] *adj* von angenehmer Erscheinung
personal ['pə:snl] *adj* persönlich; (*life*) Privat-; **nothing ~!** nehmen Sie es nicht persönlich!
personal allowance *n* (*Tax*) persönlicher Steuerfreibetrag *m*
personal assistant *n* persönlicher Referent *m*, persönliche Referentin *f*
personal column *n* private Kleinanzeigen *pl*
personal computer *n* Personal Computer *m*
personal details *npl* Personalien *pl*
personal hygiene *n* Körperhygiene *f*
personal identification number *n* Geheimnummer *f*, PIN-Nummer *f*
personality [pə:sə'nælɪtɪ] *n* (*character, person*) Persönlichkeit *f*
personal loan *n* Personaldarlehen *nt*
personally ['pə:snəlɪ] *adv* persönlich; **to take sth ~** etw persönlich nehmen
personal organizer *n* Terminplaner *m*
personal, social and health education (*Brit*) *n* (*Scol*) ≈ persönlichkeits-, gesellschafts- und gesundheitsbezogene Erziehung
personal stereo *n* Walkman® *m*
personal trainer *n* (persönlicher) Fitnesstrainer *m*, (persönliche) Fitnesstrainerin *f*
personify [pə:'sɔnɪfaɪ] *vt* personifizieren; (*embody*) verkörpern
personnel [pə:sə'nɛl] *n* Personal *nt*
personnel department *n* Personalabteilung *f*
personnel manager *n* Personalleiter(in) *m(f)*
perspective [pə'spɛktɪv] *n* (*also fig*) Perspektive *f*; **to get sth into ~** (*fig*) etw in Relation zu anderen Dingen sehen
Perspex® ['pə:spɛks] *n* Acrylglas *nt*
perspicacity [pə:spɪ'kæsɪtɪ] *n* Scharfsinn *m*
perspiration [pə:spɪ'reɪʃən] *n* Transpiration *f*
perspire [pə'spaɪə^r] *vi* transpirieren
persuade [pə'sweɪd] *vt*: **to ~ sb to do sth** jdn dazu überreden, etw zu tun; **to ~ sb that** jdn davon überzeugen, dass; **to be ~d of sth** von etw überzeugt sein
persuasion [pə'sweɪʒən] *n* (*act*) Überredung *f*; (*creed*) Überzeugung *f*
persuasive [pə'sweɪsɪv] *adj* (*person, argument*) überzeugend
pert [pə:t] *adj* (*person*) frech; (*nose, buttocks*) keck; (*hat*) kess
pertaining [pə:'teɪnɪŋ]: **~ to** *prep* betreffend *+acc*
pertinent ['pə:tɪnənt] *adj* relevant
perturb [pə'tə:b] *vt* beunruhigen
Peru [pə'ru:] *n* Peru *nt*
perusal [pə'ru:zl] *n* Durchsicht *f*
peruse [pə'ru:z] *vt* durchsehen
Peruvian [pə'ru:vjən] *adj* peruanisch ▷ *n* Peruaner(in) *m(f)*
pervade [pə'veɪd] *vt* (*smell, feeling*) erfüllen
pervasive [pə'veɪzɪv] *adj* (*smell*) durchdringend; (*influence*) weitreichend; (*mood, atmosphere*) allumfassend
perverse [pə'və:s] *adj* (*person*) borniert; (*behaviour*) widernatürlich, pervers
perversion [pə'və:ʃən] *n* (*sexual*) Perversion *f*; (*of truth, justice*) Verzerrung *f*, Pervertierung *f*
perversity [pə'və:sɪtɪ] *n* Widernatürlichkeit *f*
pervert [*n* 'pə:və:t, *vt* pə'və:t] *n* (*sexual deviant*) perverser Mensch *m* ▷ *vt* (*person, mind*) verderben; (*distort: truth, custom*) verfälschen
pessimism ['pɛsɪmɪzəm] *n* Pessimismus *m*
pessimist ['pɛsɪmɪst] *n* Pessimist(in) *m(f)*
pessimistic [pɛsɪ'mɪstɪk] *adj* pessimistisch
pest [pɛst] *n* (*insect*) Schädling *m*; (*fig: nuisance*) Plage *f*
pest control *n* Schädlingsbekämpfung *f*
pester ['pɛstə^r] *vt* belästigen
pesticide ['pɛstɪsaɪd] *n* Schädlingsbekämpfungsmittel *nt*, Pestizid *nt*
pestilence ['pɛstɪləns] *n* Pest *f*
pestle ['pɛsl] *n* Stößel *m*
pet [pɛt] *n* (*animal*) Haustier *nt* ▷ *adj* (*theory etc*) Lieblings- ▷ *vt* (*stroke*) streicheln ▷ *vi* (*inf: sexually*) herumknutschen; **teacher's ~** (*favourite*) Lehrers Liebling *m*; **a ~ rabbit/snake** *etc* ein Kaninchen/eine Schlange *etc* (als Haustier); **that's my ~ hate** das hasse ich besonders
petal ['pɛtl] *n* Blütenblatt *nt*
peter out ['pi:tə-] *vi* (*road etc*) allmählich aufhören, zu Ende gehen; (*conversation, meeting*) sich totlaufen
petite [pə'ti:t] *adj* (*woman*) zierlich
petition [pə'tɪʃən] *n* (*signed document*) Petition *f*; (*Law*) Klage *f* ▷ *vt* ersuchen ▷ *vi*: **to ~ for divorce** die Scheidung einreichen
pet name (*Brit*) *n* Kosename *m*
petrified ['pɛtrɪfaɪd] *adj* (*fig: terrified*) starr vor Angst
petrify ['pɛtrɪfaɪ] *vt* (*fig: terrify*) vor Angst erstarren lassen
petrochemical [pɛtrə'kɛmɪkl] *adj* petrochemisch
petrodollars ['pɛtrəudɔləz] *npl* Petrodollar *pl*
petrol ['pɛtrəl] (*Brit*) *n* Benzin *nt*; **two-star ~** Normalbenzin *nt*; **four-star ~** Super(benzin) *nt*; **unleaded ~** bleifreies *or* unverbleites Benzin
petrol bomb *n* Benzinbombe *f*
petrol can (*Brit*) *n* Benzinkanister *m*
petrol engine (*Brit*) *n* Benzinmotor *m*
petroleum [pə'trəulɪəm] *n* Petroleum *nt*
petroleum jelly *n* Vaseline *f*
petrol pump (*Brit*) *n* (*in garage*) Zapfsäule *f*; (*in engine*) Benzinpumpe *f*
petrol station (*Brit*) *n* Tankstelle *f*
petrol tank (*Brit*) *n* Benzintank *m*
petticoat ['pɛtɪkəut] *n* (*underskirt: full-length*) Unterkleid *nt*; (*: waist*) Unterrock *m*
pettifogging ['pɛtɪfɔgɪŋ] *adj* kleinlich
pettiness ['pɛtɪnɪs] *n* Kleinlichkeit *f*
petty ['pɛtɪ] *adj* (*trivial*) unbedeutend; (*small-minded*) kleinlich; (*crime*) geringfügig; (*official*) untergeordnet; (*excuse*) billig; (*remark*) spitz

petty cash *n* (*in office*) Portokasse *f*
petty officer *n* Maat *m*
petulant ['pɛtjulənt] *adj* (*person, expression*) gereizt
pew [pju:] *n* (*in church*) Kirchenbank *f*
pewter ['pju:tə^r] *n* Zinn *nt*
PG *n abbr* (*Cine: = parental guidance*) *Klassifikation für Filme, die Kinder nur in Begleitung Erwachsener sehen dürfen*
PGA *n abbr* (*= Professional Golfers' Association*) *Golf-Profiverband*
PGA 13 (*US*) *abbr* (*Cine: = Parental Guidance 13*) *Klassifikation für Kinofilme, welche Kinder unter 13 Jahren nur in Begleitung Erwachsener sehen dürfen*
pH *n abbr* (*= potential of hydrogen*) pH
PHA (*US*) *n abbr* (*= Public Housing Administration*) *Regierungsbehörde für sozialen Wohnungsbau*
phallic ['fælɪk] *adj* phallisch; (*symbol*) Phallus-
phantom ['fæntəm] *n* Phantom *nt* ▷ *adj* (*fig*) Phantom-
Pharaoh ['fɛərəu] *n* Pharao *m*
pharmaceutical [fɑ:mə'sju:tɪkl] *adj* pharmazeutisch
pharmaceuticals [fɑ:mə'sju:tɪklz] *npl* Arzneimittel *pl*, Pharmaka *pl*
pharmacist ['fɑ:məsɪst] *n* Apotheker(in) *m(f)*
pharmacy ['fɑ:məsɪ] *n* (*shop*) Apotheke *f*; (*science*) Pharmazie *f*
phase [feɪz] *n* Phase *f* ▷ *vt*: **to ~ sth in/out** etw stufenweise einführen/abschaffen
phat [fæt] *adj* (*inf*) abgefahren, geil
PhD *n abbr* (*= Doctor of Philosophy*) ≈ Dr. phil.
pheasant ['fɛznt] *n* Fasan *m*
phenomena [fə'nɔmɪnə] *npl of* **phenomenon**
phenomenal [fə'nɔmɪnl] *adj* phänomenal
phenomenon [fə'nɔmɪnən] (*pl* **phenomena**) *n* Phänomen *nt*
phew [fju:] *excl* puh!
phial ['faɪəl] *n* Fläschchen *nt*
philanderer [fɪ'lændərə^r] *n* Schwerenöter *m*
philanthropic [fɪlən'θrɔpɪk] *adj* philanthropisch
philanthropist [fɪ'lænθrəpɪst] *n* Philanthrop(in) *m(f)*
philatelist [fɪ'lætəlɪst] *n* Philatelist(in) *m(f)*
philately [fɪ'lætəlɪ] *n* Philatelie *f*
Philippines ['fɪlɪpi:nz] *npl*: **the ~** die Philippinen *pl*
Philistine ['fɪlɪstaɪn] *n* (*boor*) Banause *m*
philosopher [fɪ'lɔsəfə^r] *n* Philosoph(in) *m(f)*
philosophical [fɪlə'sɔfɪkl] *adj* philosophisch; (*fig: calm, resigned*) gelassen
philosophize [fɪ'lɔsəfaɪz] *vi* philosophieren
philosophy [fɪ'lɔsəfɪ] *n* Philosophie *f*
phlegm [flɛm] *n* (*Med*) Schleim *m*
phlegmatic [flɛg'mætɪk] *adj* phlegmatisch
phobia ['fəubjə] *n* Phobie *f*
phone [fəun] *n* Telefon *nt* ▷ *vt* anrufen ▷ *vi* anrufen, telefonieren; **to be on the ~** (*possess a phone*) Telefon haben; (*be calling*) telefonieren
▶ **phone back** *vt, vi* zurückrufen
▶ **phone up** *vt, vi* anrufen
phone book *n* Telefonbuch *nt*
phone booth *n* Telefonzelle *f*
phone box (*Brit*) *n* Telefonzelle *f*
phone call *n* Anruf *m*
phonecard ['fəunkɑ:d] *n* Telefonkarte *f*
phone-in ['fəunɪn] (*Brit*) *n* (*Radio, TV*) *Radio-/Fernsehsendung mit Hörer-/Zuschauerbeteiligung per Telefon*, Phone-in *nt* ▷ *adj* mit Hörer-/Zuschaueranrufen
phone tapping [-tæpɪŋ] *n* Abhören *nt* von Telefonleitungen
phonetics [fə'nɛtɪks] *n* Phonetik *f*
phoney ['fəunɪ] *adj* (*address*) falsch; (*accent*) unecht; (*person*) unaufrichtig
phonograph ['fəunəgrɑ:f] (*US*) *n* Grammofon *nt*
phony ['fəunɪ] *adj* = **phoney**
phosphate ['fɔsfeɪt] *n* Phosphat *nt*
phosphorus ['fɔsfərəs] *n* Phosphor *m*
photo ['fəutəu] *n* Foto *nt*
photo ... ['fəutəu] *pref* Foto-
photocopier ['fəutəukɔpɪə^r] *n* Fotokopierer *m*
photocopy ['fəutəukɔpɪ] *n* Fotokopie *f* ▷ *vt* fotokopieren
photoelectric [fəutəuɪ'lɛktrɪk] *adj* (*effect*) fotoelektrisch; (*cell*) Photo-
photo finish *n* Fotofinish *nt*
Photofit® ['fəutəufɪt] *n*, **Photofit® picture** ▷ *n* Phantombild *nt*
photogenic [fəutəu'dʒɛnɪk] *adj* fotogen
photograph ['fəutəgræf] *n* Fotografie *f* ▷ *vt* fotografieren; **to take a ~ of sb** jdn fotografieren
photographer [fə'tɔgrəfə^r] *n* Fotograf(in) *m(f)*
photographic [fəutə'græfɪk] *adj* (*equipment etc*) fotografisch, Foto-
photography [fə'tɔgrəfɪ] *n* Fotografie *f*
photo opportunity *n* Fototermin *m*; (*accidental*) Fotogelegenheit *f*
photostat ['fəutəustæt] *n* Fotokopie *f*
photosynthesis [fəutəu'sɪnθəsɪs] *n* Fotosynthese *f*
phrase [freɪz] *n* Satz *m*; (*Ling*) Redewendung *f*; (*Mus*) Phrase *f* ▷ *vt* ausdrücken; (*letter*) formulieren
phrase book *n* Sprachführer *m*
physical ['fɪzɪkl] *adj* (*bodily*) körperlich; (*geography, properties*) physikalisch; (*law, explanation*) natürlich; **~ examination** ärztliche Untersuchung *f*; **the ~ sciences** die Naturwissenschaften
physical education *n* Sportunterricht *m*
physically ['fɪzɪklɪ] *adv* (*fit, attractive*) körperlich
physician [fɪ'zɪʃən] *n* Arzt *m*, Ärztin *f*
physicist ['fɪzɪsɪst] *n* Physiker(in) *m(f)*
physics ['fɪzɪks] *n* Physik *f*
physiological ['fɪzɪə'lɔdʒɪkl] *adj* physiologisch
physiology [fɪzɪ'ɔlədʒɪ] *n* Physiologie *f*
physiotherapist [fɪzɪəu'θɛrəpɪst] *n* Physiotherapeut(in) *m(f)*
physiotherapy [fɪzɪəu'θɛrəpɪ] *n* Physiotherapie *f*
physique [fɪ'zi:k] *n* Körperbau *m*

pianist ['pi:ənɪst] *n* Pianist(in) *m(f)*
piano [pɪ'ænəu] *n* Klavier *nt*, Piano *nt*
piano accordion (*Brit*) *n* Akkordeon *nt*
piccolo ['pɪkələu] *n* Piccoloflöte *f*
pick [pɪk] *n* (*also*: **pickaxe**) Spitzhacke *f* ▷ *vt* (*select*) aussuchen; (*gather*: *fruit, mushrooms*) sammeln; (: *flowers*) pflücken; (*remove, take out*) herausnehmen; (*lock*) knacken; (*scab, spot*) kratzen an *+dat*; **take your ~** (*choose*) Sie haben die Wahl; **the ~ of** (*best*) das Beste *+gen*; **to ~ one's nose** in der Nase bohren; **to ~ one's teeth** in den Zähnen stochern; **to ~ sb's brains** jdn als Informationsquelle nutzen; **to ~ sb's pocket** jdn bestehlen; **to ~ a quarrel (with sb)** einen Streit (mit jdm) anfangen
▸ **pick at** *vt fus* (*food*) herumstochern in *+dat*
▸ **pick off** *vt* (*shoot*) abschießen
▸ **pick on** *vt fus* (*criticize*) herumhacken auf *+dat*
▸ **pick out** *vt* (*distinguish*) ausmachen; (*select*) aussuchen
▸ **pick up** *vi* (*health*) sich verbessern; (*economy*) sich erholen ▷ *vt* (*from floor etc*) aufheben; (*arrest*) festnehmen; (*collect*: *person, parcel etc*) abholen; (*hitchhiker*) mitnehmen; (*for sexual encounter*) aufreißen; (*learn*: *skill etc*) mitbekommen; (*Radio*) empfangen; **to ~ up where one left off** da weitermachen, wo man aufgehört hat; **to ~ up speed** schneller werden; **to ~ o.s. up** (*after falling etc*) sich aufrappeln
pickaxe, (*US*) **pickax** ['pɪkæks] *n* Spitzhacke *f*
picket ['pɪkɪt] *n* (*in strike*) Streikposten *m* ▷ *vt* (*factory etc*) Streikposten aufstellen vor *+dat*
picketing ['pɪkɪtɪŋ] *n* Aufstellen *nt* von Streikposten
picket line *n* Streikpostenkette *f*
pickings ['pɪkɪŋz] *npl*: **there are rich ~ to be had here** hier ist die Ausbeute gut
pickle ['pɪkl] *n* (*also*: **pickles**: *as condiment*) Pickles *pl* ▷ *vt* einlegen; **to be in a ~** in der Klemme sitzen; **to get in a ~** in eine Klemme geraten
pick-me-up ['pɪkmi:ʌp] *n* Muntermacher *m*
pickpocket ['pɪkpɔkɪt] *n* Taschendieb(in) *m(f)*
pick-up ['pɪkʌp] *n* (*also*: **pick-up truck**) offener Kleintransporter *m*; (*Brit*: *on record player*) Tonabnehmer *m*
picnic ['pɪknɪk] *n* Picknick *nt* ▷ *vi* picknicken
picnicker ['pɪknɪkə^r] *n* Picknicker(in) *m(f)*
pictorial [pɪk'tɔ:rɪəl] *adj* (*record, coverage etc*) bildlich
picture ['pɪktʃə^r] *n* Bild *nt*; (*film*) Film *m* ▷ *vt* (*imagine*) sich *dat* vorstellen; **the ~s** (*Brit*: *inf*: *the cinema*) das Kino; **to take a ~ of sb** ein Bild von jdm machen; **to put sb in the ~** jdn ins Bild setzen
picture book *n* Bilderbuch *nt*
picture messaging *n* Picture Messaging *nt*
picturesque [pɪktʃə'rɛsk] *adj* malerisch
picture window *n* Aussichtsfenster *nt*
piddling ['pɪdlɪŋ] (*inf*) *adj* lächerlich
pidgin ['pɪdʒɪn] *adj*: **~ English** Pidginenglisch *nt*
pie [paɪ] *n* (*vegetable, meat*) Pastete *f*; (*fruit*) Torte *f*
piebald ['paɪbɔ:ld] *adj* (*horse*) scheckig
piece [pi:s] *n* Stück *nt*; (*Draughts etc*) Stein *m*; (*Chess*) Figur *f*; **in ~s** (*broken*) kaputt; (*taken apart*) auseinandergenommen, in Einzelteilen; **a ~ of clothing/furniture/music** ein Kleidungs-/Möbel-/Musikstück *nt*; **a ~ of machinery** eine Maschine; **a ~ of research** eine Forschungsarbeit; **a ~ of advice** ein Rat *m*; **to take sth to ~s** etw auseinandernehmen; **in one ~** (*object*) unbeschädigt; (*person*) wohlbehalten; **a 10p ~** (*Brit*) ein 10-Pence-Stück *nt*; **~ by piece** Stück für Stück; **a six-~ band** eine sechsköpfige Band; **let her say her ~** lass sie ausreden
▸ **piece together** *vt* zusammenfügen
piecemeal ['pi:smi:l] *adv* stückweise, Stück für Stück
piecework ['pi:swə:k] *n* Akkordarbeit *f*
pie chart *n* Tortendiagramm *nt*
pier [pɪə^r] *n* Pier *m*
pierce [pɪəs] *vt* durchstechen; **to have one's ears ~d** sich *dat* die Ohrläppchen durchstechen lassen
piercing ['pɪəsɪŋ] *adj* (*fig*: *cry, eyes, stare*) durchdringend; (*wind*) schneidend
piety ['paɪətɪ] *n* Frömmigkeit *f*
piffling ['pɪflɪŋ] (*inf*) *adj* lächerlich
pig [pɪg] *n* (*also pej*) Schwein *nt*; (*greedy person*) Vielfraß *m*
pigeon ['pɪdʒən] *n* Taube *f*
pigeonhole ['pɪdʒənhəul] *n* (*for letters etc*) Fach *nt*; (*fig*) Schublade *f* ▷ *vt* (*fig*: *person*) in eine Schublade stecken
pigeon-toed ['pɪdʒəntəud] *adj* mit einwärtsgerichteten Zehen
piggy bank ['pɪgɪ-] *n* Sparschwein *nt*
pig-headed ['pɪg'hɛdɪd] (*pej*) *adj* dickköpfig
piglet ['pɪglɪt] *n* Schweinchen *nt*, Ferkel *nt*
pigment ['pɪgmənt] *n* Pigment *nt*
pigmentation [pɪgmən'teɪʃən] *n* Pigmentierung *f*, Färbung *f*
pigmy ['pɪgmɪ] *n* = **pygmy**
pigskin ['pɪgskɪn] *n* Schweinsleder *nt*
pigsty ['pɪgstaɪ] *n* (*also fig*) Schweinestall *m*
pigtail ['pɪgteɪl] *n* Zopf *m*
pike [paɪk] *n* (*fish*) Hecht *m*; (*spear*) Spieß *m*
pilchard ['pɪltʃəd] *n* Sardine *f*
pile [paɪl] *n* (*heap*) Haufen *m*; (*stack*) Stapel *m*; (*of carpet, velvet*) Flor *m*; (*pillar*) Pfahl *m* ▷ *vt* (*also*: **pile up**) (auf)stapeln; **in a ~** in einem Haufen; **to ~ into/out of** (*vehicle*) sich drängen in *+acc*/aus
▸ **pile on** *vt*: **to ~ it on** (*inf*) zu dick auftragen
▸ **pile up** *vi* sich stapeln
piles [paɪlz] *npl* (*Med*) Hämorr(ho)iden *pl*
pile-up ['paɪlʌp] *n* (*Aut*) Massenkarambolage *f*
pilfer ['pɪlfə^r] *vt, vi* stehlen
pilfering ['pɪlfərɪŋ] *n* Diebstahl *m*
pilgrim ['pɪlgrɪm] *n* Pilger(in) *m(f)*
pilgrimage ['pɪlgrɪmɪdʒ] *n* Pilgerfahrt *f*, Wallfahrt *f*
pill [pɪl] *n* Tablette *f*, Pille *f*; **the ~** (*contraceptive*) die Pille; **to be on the ~** die Pille nehmen

pillage ['pɪlɪdʒ] *n* Plünderung *f* ▹ *vt* plündern
pillar ['pɪləʳ] *n* Säule *f*; **a ~ of society** (*fig*) eine Säule *or* Stütze der Gesellschaft
pillar box (*Brit*) *n* Briefkasten *m*
pillion ['pɪljən] *n*: **to ride ~** (*on motorcycle*) auf dem Soziussitz mitfahren; (*on horse*) hinten auf dem Pferd mitreiten
pillory ['pɪlərɪ] *vt* (*criticize*) anprangern ▹ *n* Pranger *m*
pillow ['pɪləu] *n* (Kopf)kissen *nt*
pillowcase ['pɪləukeɪs] *n* (Kopf)kissenbezug *m*
pillowslip ['pɪləuslɪp] *n* = **pillowcase**
pilot ['paɪlət] *n* (*Aviat*) Pilot(in) *m(f)*; (*Naut*) Lotse *m* ▹ *adj* (*scheme, study etc*) Pilot- ▹ *vt* (*aircraft*) steuern; (*fig: new law, scheme*) sich zum Fürsprecher machen *+gen*
pilot boat *n* Lotsenboot *nt*
pilot light *n* (*on cooker, boiler*) Zündflamme *f*
pilot test *n* (*Test*) Pilot- *od* Modellversuch *m*
pimento [pɪ'mɛntəu] *n* (*spice*) Piment *nt*
pimp [pɪmp] *n* Zuhälter *m*
pimple ['pɪmpl] *n* Pickel *m*
pimply ['pɪmplɪ] *adj* pick(e)lig
PIN *n abbr* (= *personal identification number*) PIN; **~ number** PIN-Nummer *f*
pin [pɪn] *n* (*metal: for clothes, papers*) Stecknadel *f*; (*Tech*) Stift *m*; (*Brit: also*: **drawing pin**) Heftzwecke *f*; (*in grenade*) Sicherungsstift *m*; (*Brit: Elec*) Pol *m* ▹ *vt* (*fasten with pin*) feststecken; **~s and needles** (*in arms, legs etc*) Kribbeln *nt*; **to ~ sb against/to sth** jdn gegen/an etw *acc* pressen; **to ~ sth on sb** (*fig*) jdm etw anhängen
▸ **pin down** *vt* (*fig: person*) festnageln; **there's something strange here but I can't quite ~ it down** hier stimmt etwas nicht, aber ich weiß nicht genau was
pinafore ['pɪnəfɔːʳ] (*Brit*) *n* (*also*: **pinafore dress**) Trägerkleid *nt*
pinball ['pɪnbɔːl] *n* (*game*) Flippern *nt*; (*machine*) Flipper *m*
pincers ['pɪnsəz] *npl* (*tool*) Kneifzange *f*; (*of crab, lobster etc*) Schere *f*
pinch [pɪntʃ] *n* (*of salt etc*) Prise *f* ▹ *vt* (*with finger and thumb*) zwicken, kneifen; (*inf: steal*) klauen ▹ *vi* (*shoe*) drücken; **at a ~** zur Not; **to feel the ~** (*fig*) die schlechte Lage zu spüren bekommen
pinched [pɪntʃt] *adj* (*face*) erschöpft; **~ with cold** verfroren
pincushion ['pɪnkuʃən] *n* Nadelkissen *nt*
pine [paɪn] *n* (*also*: **pine tree**) Kiefer *f*; (*wood*) Kiefernholz *nt* ▹ *vi*: **to ~ for** sich sehnen nach
▸ **pine away** *vi* sich (vor Kummer) verzehren
pineapple ['paɪnæpl] *n* Ananas *f*
pine cone *n* Kiefernzapfen *m*
pine needles *npl* Kiefernnadeln *pl*
ping [pɪŋ] *n* (*noise*) Klingeln *nt*
Ping-Pong® ['pɪŋpɔŋ] *n* Pingpong *nt*
pink [pɪŋk] *adj* rosa *inv* ▹ *n* (*colour*) Rosa *nt*; (*Bot*) Gartennelke *f*
pinking shears *npl* Zickzackschere *f*
pin money (*Brit: inf*) *n* Nadelgeld *nt*
pinnacle ['pɪnəkl] *n* (*of building, mountain*) Spitze *f*; (*fig*) Gipfel *m*
pinpoint ['pɪnpɔɪnt] *vt* (*identify*) genau festlegen, identifizieren; (*position of sth*) genau aufzeigen
pinstripe ['pɪnstraɪp] *adj*: **~ suit** Nadelstreifenanzug *m*
pint [paɪnt] *n* (*Brit: = 568 cc*) (britisches) Pint *nt*; (*US: = 473 cc*) (amerikanisches) Pint; **a ~** (*Brit: inf: of beer*) ≈ eine Halbe
pin-up ['pɪnʌp] *n* (*picture*) Pin-up-Foto *nt*
pioneer [paɪə'nɪəʳ] *n* (*lit, fig*) Pionier *m* ▹ *vt* (*invention etc*) Pionierarbeit leisten für
pious ['paɪəs] *adj* fromm
pip [pɪp] *n* (*of apple, orange*) Kern *m* ▹ *vt*: **to be ~ped at the post** (*Brit: fig*) um Haaresbreite geschlagen werden; **the pips** *npl* (*Brit: Radio*) das Zeitzeichen
pipe [paɪp] *n* (*for water, gas*) Rohr *nt*; (*for smoking*) Pfeife *f*; (*Mus*) Flöte *f* ▹ *vt* (*water, gas, oil*) (durch Rohre) leiten; **pipes** *npl* (*also*: **bagpipes**) Dudelsack *m*
▸ **pipe down** (*inf*) *vi* (*be quiet*) ruhig sein
pipe cleaner *n* Pfeifenreiniger *m*
piped music [paɪpt-] *n* Berieselungsmusik *f*
pipe dream *n* Hirngespinst *nt*
pipeline ['paɪplaɪn] *n* Pipeline *f*; **it's in the ~** (*fig*) es ist in Vorbereitung
piper ['paɪpəʳ] *n* (*bagpipe player*) Dudelsackspieler(in) *m(f)*
pipe tobacco *n* Pfeifentabak *m*
piping ['paɪpɪŋ] *adv*: **~ hot** kochend heiß
piquant ['piːkənt] *adj* (*also fig*) pikant
pique ['piːk] *n*: **in a fit of ~** eingeschnappt, pikiert
piracy ['paɪərəsɪ] *n* Piraterie *f*, Seeräuberei *f*; (*Comm*): **to commit ~** ein Plagiat *nt* begehen
pirate ['paɪərət] *n* Pirat *m*, Seeräuber *m* ▹ *vt* (*Comm: video tape, cassette etc*) illegal herstellen
pirate radio station (*Brit*) *n* Piratensender *m*
pirouette [pɪru'ɛt] *n* Pirouette *f* ▹ *vi* Pirouetten drehen
Pisces ['paɪsiːz] *n* Fische *pl*; **to be ~** Fische *or* (ein) Fisch sein
piss [pɪs] (*inf!*) *vi* pissen ▹ *n* Pisse *f*; **~ off!** verpiss dich!; **to be ~ed off (with sb/sth)** (von jdm/etw) die Schnauze vollhaben; **it's ~ing down** (*Brit: raining*) es schifft; **to take the ~ out of sb** (*Brit*) jdn verarschen
pissed [pɪst] (*inf!*) *adj* (*drunk*) besoffen
pistol ['pɪstl] *n* Pistole *f*
piston ['pɪstən] *n* Kolben *m*
pit [pɪt] *n* Grube *f*; (*in surface of road*) Schlagloch *nt*; (*coal mine*) Zeche *f*; (*also*: **orchestra pit**) Orchestergraben *m* ▹ *vt*: **to ~ one's wits against sb** seinen Verstand mit jdm messen; **the pits** *npl* (*Aut*) die Box; **to ~ o.s. against sth** den Kampf gegen etw aufnehmen; **to ~ sb against sb** jdn gegen jdn antreten lassen; **the ~ of one's stomach** die Magengrube
pitapat ['pɪtə'pæt] (*Brit*) *adv*: **to go ~** (*heart*) pochen, klopfen; (*rain*) prasseln
pitch [pɪtʃ] *n* (*Brit: Sport: field*) Spielfeld *nt*; (*Mus*) Tonhöhe *f*; (*fig: level, degree*) Grad *m*; (*tar*) Pech

nt; (*also*: **sales pitch**) Verkaufsmasche *f*; (*Naut*) Stampfen *nt* ▷ *vt* (*throw*) werfen, schleudern; (*set*: *price, message*) ansetzen ▷ *vi* (*fall forwards*) hinschlagen; (*Naut*) stampfen; **to ~ a tent** ein Zelt aufschlagen; **to be ~ed forward** vornüber geworfen werden

pitch-black [ˈpɪtʃˈblæk] *adj* pechschwarz

pitched battle [pɪtʃt-] *n* offene Schlacht *f*

pitcher [ˈpɪtʃəʳ] *n* (*jug*) Krug *m*; (*US*: *Baseball*) Werfer *m*

pitchfork [ˈpɪtʃfɔːk] *n* Heugabel *f*

piteous [ˈpɪtɪəs] *adj* kläglich, erbärmlich

pitfall [ˈpɪtfɔːl] *n* Falle *f*

pith [pɪθ] *n* (*of orange etc*) weiße Haut *f*; (*of plant*) Mark *nt*; (*fig*) Kern *m*

pithead [ˈpɪthɛd] *n* Schachtanlagen *pl* über Tage

pithy [ˈpɪθɪ] *adj* (*comment etc*) prägnant

pitiable [ˈpɪtɪəbl] *adj* mitleiderregend

pitiful [ˈpɪtɪful] *adj* (*sight etc*) mitleiderregend; (*excuse, attempt*) jämmerlich, kläglich

pitifully [ˈpɪtɪfəlɪ] *adv* (*thin, frail*) jämmerlich; (*inadequate, ill-equipped*) fürchterlich

pitiless [ˈpɪtɪlɪs] *adj* mitleidlos

pittance [ˈpɪtns] *n* Hungerlohn *m*

pitted [ˈpɪtɪd] *adj*: **~ with** übersät mit; **~ with rust** voller Rost

pity [ˈpɪtɪ] *n* Mitleid *nt* ▷ *vt* bemitleiden, bedauern; **what a ~!** wie schade!; **it is a ~ that you can't come** schade, dass du nicht kommen kannst; **to take ~ on sb** Mitleid mit jdm haben

pitying [ˈpɪtɪɪŋ] *adj* mitleidig

pivot [ˈpɪvət] *n* (*Tech*) Drehpunkt *m*; (*fig*) Dreh- und Angelpunkt *m* ▷ *vi* sich drehen
▸ **pivot on** (*depend on*) abhängen von

pixel [ˈpɪksl] *n* (*Comput*) Pixel *nt*

pixie [ˈpɪksɪ] *n* Elf *m*, Elfe *f*

pizza [ˈpiːtsə] *n* Pizza *f*

placard [ˈplækɑːd] *n* Plakat *nt*, Aushang *m*; (*in march etc*) Transparent *nt*

placate [pləˈkeɪt] *vt* beschwichtigen, besänftigen

placatory [pləˈkeɪtərɪ] *adj* beschwichtigend, besänftigend

place [pleɪs] *n* Platz *m*; (*position*) Stelle *f*, Ort *m*; (*seat*: *on committee etc*) Sitz *m*; (*home*) Wohnung *f*; (*in street names*) ≈ Straße *f* ▷ *vt* (*put*: *object*) stellen, legen; (*identify*: *person*) unterbringen; **~ of birth** Geburtsort *m*; **to take ~** (*happen*) geschehen, passieren; **at/to his ~** (*home*) bei/zu ihm; **from ~ to place** von Ort zu Ort; **all over the ~** überall; **in ~s** stellenweise; **in sb's/sth's ~** anstelle von jdm/etw; **to take sb's/sth's ~** an die Stelle von jdm/etw treten, jdn/etw ersetzen; **out of ~** (*inappropriate*) unangebracht; **I feel out of ~ here** ich fühle mich hier fehl am Platze; **in the first ~** (*first of all*) erstens; **to change ~s with sb** mit jdm den Platz tauschen; **to put sb in his ~** (*fig*) jdn in seine Schranken weisen; **he's going ~s** er bringt es noch mal weit; **it's not my ~ to do it** es ist nicht an mir, das zu tun; **to be ~d** (*in race, exam*) platziert sein; **to be ~d third** den dritten Platz belegen; **to ~ an order with sb (for sth)** eine Bestellung bei jdm (für etw) aufgeben; **how are you ~d next week?** wie sieht es bei Ihnen nächste Woche aus?

placebo [pləˈsiːbəu] *n* Placebo *nt*; (*fig*) Beruhigungsmittel *nt*

place mat *n* Set *nt or m*

placement [ˈpleɪsmənt] *n* Platzierung *f*

place name *n* Ortsname *m*

placenta [pləˈsɛntə] *n* Plazenta *f*

place setting *n* Gedeck *nt*

placid [ˈplæsɪd] *adj* (*person*) ruhig, gelassen; (*place, river etc*) friedvoll

plagiarism [ˈpleɪdʒjərɪzəm] *n* Plagiat *nt*

plagiarist [ˈpleɪdʒjərɪst] *n* Plagiator(in) *m(f)*

plagiarize [ˈpleɪdʒjəraɪz] *vt* (*idea, work*) kopieren, plagiieren

plague [pleɪg] *n* (*Med*) Seuche *f*; (*fig*: *of locusts etc*) Plage *f* ▷ *vt* (*fig*: *problems etc*) plagen; **to ~ sb with questions** jdn mit Fragen quälen

plaice [pleɪs] *n inv* Scholle *f*

plaid [plæd] *n* Plaid *nt*

plain [pleɪn] *adj* (*unpatterned*) einfarbig; (*simple*) einfach, schlicht; (*clear, easily understood*) klar; (*not beautiful*) unattraktiv; (*frank*) offen ▷ *adv* (*wrong, stupid etc*) einfach ▷ *n* (*area of land*) Ebene *f*; (*Knitting*) rechte Masche *f*; **to make sth ~ to sb** jdm etw klarmachen

plain chocolate *n* Bitterschokolade *f*

plain-clothes [ˈpleɪnkləuðz] *adj* (*police officer*) in Zivil

plainly [ˈpleɪnlɪ] *adv* (*obviously*) eindeutig; (*clearly*) deutlich, klar

plainness [ˈpleɪnnɪs] *n* (*of person*) Reizlosigkeit *f*

plain speaking *n* Offenheit *f*; **a bit of ~** ein paar offene Worte

plain-spoken [ˈpleɪnˈspəukn] *adj* offen

plaintiff [ˈpleɪntɪf] *n* Kläger(in) *m(f)*

plaintive [ˈpleɪntɪv] *adj* (*cry, voice*) klagend; (*song*) schwermütig; (*look*) traurig

plait [plæt] *n* (*of hair*) Zopf *m*; (*of rope, leather*) Geflecht *nt* ▷ *vt* flechten

plan [plæn] *n* Plan *m* ▷ *vt* planen; (*building, schedule*) entwerfen ▷ *vi* planen; **to ~ to do sth** planen *or* vorhaben, etw zu tun; **how long do you ~ to stay?** wie lange haben Sie vor, zu bleiben?; **to ~ for** *or* **on** (*expect*) sich einstellen auf *+acc*; **to ~ on doing sth** vorhaben, etw zu tun

plane [pleɪn] *n* (*Aviat*) Flugzeug *nt*; (*Math*) Ebene *f*; (*fig*: *level*) Niveau *nt*; (*tool*) Hobel *m*; (*also*: **plane tree**) Platane *f* ▷ *vt* (*wood*) hobeln ▷ *vi* (*Naut, Aut*) gleiten

planet [ˈplænɪt] *n* Planet *m*

planetarium [plænɪˈtɛərɪəm] *n* Planetarium *nt*

plank [plæŋk] *n* (*of wood*) Brett *nt*; (*fig*: *of policy etc*) Schwerpunkt *m*

plankton [ˈplæŋktən] *n* Plankton *nt*

planned economy [ˈplænd-] *n* Planwirtschaft *f*

planner [ˈplænəʳ] *n* Planer(in) *m(f)*

planning [ˈplænɪŋ] *n* Planung *f*

planning permission (*Brit*) *n* Baugenehmigung *f*
plant [plɑ:nt] *n* (*Bot*) Pflanze *f*; (*machinery*) Maschinen *pl*; (*factory*) Anlage *f* ▷ *vt* (*seed, plant, crops*) pflanzen; (*field, garden*) bepflanzen; (*microphone, bomb etc*) anbringen; (*incriminating evidence*) schleusen; (*fig: object*) stellen; (*: kiss*) drücken
plantation [plæn'teɪʃən] *n* Plantage *f*; (*wood*) Anpflanzung *f*
plant pot (*Brit*) *n* Blumentopf *m*
plaque [plæk] *n* (*on building etc*) Tafel *f*, Plakette *f*; (*on teeth*) Zahnbelag *m*
plasma ['plæzmə] *n* Plasma *nt*
plaster ['plɑ:stəʳ] *n* (*for walls*) Putz *m*; (*also*: **plaster of Paris**) Gips *m*; (*Brit*: *also*: **sticking plaster**) Pflaster *nt* ▷ *vt* (*wall, ceiling*) verputzen; **in ~** (*Brit*) in Gips; **to ~ with** (*cover*) bepflastern mit
plasterboard ['plɑ:stəbɔ:d] *n* Gipskarton *m*
plaster cast *n* (*Med*) Gipsverband *m*; (*model, statue*) Gipsform *f*
plastered ['plɑ:stəd] (*inf*) *adj* (*drunk*) sturzbesoffen
plasterer ['plɑ:stərəʳ] *n* Gipser *m*
plastic ['plæstɪk] *n* Plastik *nt* ▷ *adj* (*bucket, cup etc*) Plastik-; (*flexible*) formbar; **the ~ arts** die bildende Kunst
plastic bag *n* Plastiktüte *f*
plastic bullet *n* Plastikgeschoss *nt*
plastic explosive *n* Plastiksprengstoff *m*
Plasticine® ['plæstɪsi:n] *n* Plastilin *nt*
plastic surgery *n* plastische Chirurgie *f*
plate [pleɪt] *n* Teller *m*; (*metal cover*) Platte *f*; (*Typ*) Druckplatte *f*; (*Aut*) Nummernschild *nt*; (*in book: picture*) Tafel *f*; (*also*: **dental plate**) Gaumenplatte *f*; (*on door*) Schild *nt*; **gold/silver ~** vergoldeter/versilberter Artikel *m*; **that necklace is just ~** die Halskette ist nur vergoldet/versilbert
plateau ['plætəu] (*pl* **plateaus** *or* **~x**) *n* (*Geog*) Plateau *nt*, Hochebene *f*; (*fig*) stabiler Zustand *m*
plateful ['pleɪtful] *n* Teller *m*
plate glass *n* Tafelglas *nt*
platen ['plætən] *n* (*on typewriter, printer*) (Schreib)walze *f*
plate rack *n* Geschirrständer *m*
platform ['plætfɔ:m] *n* (*stage*) Podium *nt*; (*for landing, loading on etc, Brit: of bus*) Plattform *f*; (*Rail*) Bahnsteig *m*; (*Pol*) Programm *nt*; **the train leaves from ~ 7** der Zug fährt von Gleis 7 ab
platform ticket (*Brit*) *n* (*Rail*) Bahnsteigkarte *f*
platinum ['plætɪnəm] *n* Platin *nt*
platitude ['plætɪtju:d] *n* Plattitüde *f*, Gemeinplatz *m*
platonic [plə'tɔnɪk] *adj* (*relationship*) platonisch
platoon [plə'tu:n] *n* Zug *m*
platter ['plætəʳ] *n* Platte *f*
plaudits ['plɔ:dɪts] *npl* Ovationen *pl*
plausible ['plɔ:zɪbl] *adj* (*theory, excuse*) plausibel; (*liar etc*) glaubwürdig
play [pleɪ] *n* (*Theat*) (Theater)stück *nt*; (*TV*) Fernsehspiel *nt*; (*Radio*) Hörspiel *nt*; (*activity*) Spiel *nt* ▷ *vt* spielen; (*team, opponent*) spielen gegen ▷ *vi* spielen; **to bring into ~** ins Spiel bringen; **a ~ on words** ein Wortspiel *nt*; **to ~ a trick on sb** jdn hereinlegen; **to ~ a part** *or* **role in sth** (*fig*) eine Rolle bei etw spielen; **to ~ for time** (*fig*) auf Zeit spielen, Zeit gewinnen wollen; **to ~ safe** auf Nummer sicher gehen; **to ~ into sb's hands** jdm in die Hände spielen
▸ **play about with** *vt fus* = **play around with**
▸ **play along with** *vt fus* (*person*) sich richten nach; (*plan, idea*) eingehen auf *+acc*
▸ **play around with** *vt fus* (*fiddle with*) herumspielen mit
▸ **play at** *vt fus* (*do casually*) spielen mit; **to ~ at being sb/sth** jdn/etw spielen
▸ **play back** *vt* (*recording*) abspielen
▸ **play down** *vt* herunterspielen
▸ **play on** *vt fus* (*sb's feelings etc*) ausnutzen; **to ~ on sb's mind** jdm im Kopf herumgehen
▸ **play up** *vi* (*machine, knee etc*) Schwierigkeiten machen; (*children*) frech werden
play-act ['pleɪækt] *vi* Theater spielen
playboy ['pleɪbɔɪ] *n* Playboy *m*
player ['pleɪəʳ] *n* (*Sport, Mus*) Spieler(in) *m(f)*; (*Theat*) Schauspieler(in) *m(f)*
playful ['pleɪful] *adj* (*person, gesture*) spielerisch; (*animal*) verspielt
playgoer ['pleɪgəuəʳ] *n* Theaterbesucher(in) *m(f)*
playground ['pleɪgraund] *n* (*in park*) Spielplatz *m*; (*in school*) Schulhof *m*
playgroup ['pleɪgru:p] *n* Spielgruppe *f*
playing card ['pleɪɪŋ-] *n* Spielkarte *f*
playing field *n* Sportplatz *m*
playmaker ['pleɪmeɪkəʳ] *n* (*Sport*) Spielmacher(in) *m(f)*
playmate ['pleɪmeɪt] *n* Spielkamerad(in) *m(f)*
play-off ['pleɪɔf] *n* Ausscheidungsspiel *nt*, Play-off *nt*
playpen ['pleɪpɛn] *n* Laufstall *m*
playroom ['pleɪru:m] *n* Spielzimmer *nt*
playschool ['pleɪsku:l] *n* = **playgroup**
plaything ['pleɪθɪŋ] *n* (*also fig*) Spielzeug *nt*
playtime ['pleɪtaɪm] *n* (kleine) Pause *f*
playwright ['pleɪraɪt] *n* Dramatiker(in) *m(f)*
plc (*Brit*) *n abbr* (= *public limited company*) ≈ AG *f*
plea [pli:] *n* (*request*) Bitte *f*; (*Law*): **to enter a ~ of guilty/not guilty** sich schuldig/unschuldig erklären; (*excuse*) Vorwand *m*
plea bargaining *n* *Verhandlungen zwischen Anklage und Verteidigung mit dem Ziel, bestimmte Anklagepunkte fallen zu lassen, wenn der Angeklagte sich in anderen Punkten schuldig bekennt*
plead [pli:d] *vi* (*Law*) *vor Gericht eine Schuld-/Unschuldserklärung abgeben* ▷ *vt* (*Law*): **to ~ sb's case** jdn vertreten; (*give as excuse: ignorance, ill health etc*) vorgeben, sich berufen auf *+acc*; **to ~ with sb** (*beg*) jdn inständig bitten; **to ~ for sth** um etw nachsuchen; **to ~ guilty/not guilty** sich schuldig/nicht schuldig bekennen
pleasant ['plɛznt] *adj* angenehm; (*smile*)

freundlich
pleasantly ['plɛzntlɪ] *adv* (*surprised*) angenehm; (*say, behave*) freundlich
pleasantries ['plɛzntrɪz] *npl* Höflichkeiten *pl*, Nettigkeiten *pl*
please [pli:z] *excl* bitte ▷ *vt* (*satisfy*) zufriedenstellen ▷ *vi* (*give pleasure*) gefällig sein; **~ Miss/Sir!** (*to attract teacher's attention*) ≈ Frau/Herr X!; **yes, ~** ja, bitte; **my bill, ~** die Rechnung, bitte; **~ don't cry!** bitte wein doch nicht!; **~ yourself!** (*inf*) wie du willst!; **do as you ~** machen Sie, was Sie für richtig halten
pleased [pli:zd] *adj* (*happy*) erfreut; (*satisfied*) zufrieden; **~ to meet you** freut mich(, Sie kennenzulernen); **~ with** zufrieden mit; **we are ~ to inform you that ...** wir freuen uns, Ihnen mitzuteilen, dass ...
pleasing ['pli:zɪŋ] *adj* (*remark, picture etc*) erfreulich; (*person*) sympathisch
pleasurable ['plɛʒərəbl] *adj* angenehm
pleasure ['plɛʒə^r] *n* (*happiness, satisfaction*) Freude *f*; (*fun, enjoyable experience*) Vergnügen *nt*; **it's a ~, my ~** gern geschehen; **with ~** gern, mit Vergnügen; **is this trip for business or ~?** ist diese Reise geschäftlich oder zum Vergnügen?
pleasure boat *n* Vergnügungsschiff *nt*
pleasure cruise *n* Vergnügungsfahrt *f*
pleat [pli:t] *n* Falte *f*
pleb [plɛb] (*inf: pej*) *n* Prolet *m*
plebiscite ['plɛbɪsɪt] *n* Volksentscheid *m*, Plebiszit *nt*
plectrum ['plɛktrəm] *n* Plektron *nt*, Plektrum *nt*
pledge [plɛdʒ] *n* (*promise*) Versprechen *nt* ▷ *vt* (*promise*) versprechen; **to ~ sb to secrecy** jdn zum Schweigen verpflichten
plenary ['pli:nərɪ] *adj* (*powers*) unbeschränkt; **~ session** Plenarsitzung *f*; **~ meeting** Vollversammlung *f*
plentiful ['plɛntɪful] *adj* reichlich
plenty ['plɛntɪ] *n* (*lots*) eine Menge; (*sufficient*) reichlich; **~ of** eine Menge; **we've got ~ of time to get there** wir haben jede Menge Zeit, dorthin zu kommen
plethora ['plɛθərə] *n*: **a ~ of** eine Fülle von, eine Unmenge an *+dat*
pleurisy ['pluərɪsɪ] *n* Rippenfellentzündung *f*
Plexiglas® ['plɛksɪglɑ:s] (US) *n* Plexiglas® *nt*
pliable ['plaɪəbl] *adj* (*material*) biegsam; (*fig: person*) leicht beeinflussbar
pliant ['plaɪənt] *adj* = **pliable**
pliers ['plaɪəz] *npl* Zange *f*
plight [plaɪt] *n* (*of person, country*) Not *f*
plimsolls ['plɪmsəlz] (*Brit*) *npl* Turnschuhe *pl*
plinth [plɪnθ] *n* Sockel *m*
PLO *n abbr* (*= Palestine Liberation Organization*) PLO *f*
plod [plɔd] *vi* (*walk*) trotten; (*fig*) sich abplagen
plodder ['plɔdə^r] (*pej*) *n* (*slow worker*) zäher Arbeiter *m*, zähe Arbeiterin *f*
plonk [plɔŋk] (*inf*) *n* (*Brit: wine*) (billiger) Wein *m* ▷ *vt*: **to ~ sth down** etw hinknallen
plot [plɔt] *n* (*secret plan*) Komplott *nt*, Verschwörung *f*; (*of story, play, film*) Handlung *f* ▷ *vt* (*sb's downfall etc*) planen; (*on chart, graph*) markieren ▷ *vi* (*conspire*) sich verschwören; **a ~ of land** ein Grundstück *nt*; **a vegetable ~** (*Brit*) ein Gemüsebeet *nt*
plotter ['plɔtə^r] *n* (*instrument, Comput*) Plotter *m*
plough, (US) **plow** [plau] *n* Pflug *m* ▷ *vt* pflügen; **to ~ money into sth** (*project etc*) Geld in etw *acc* stecken
▸ **plough back** *vt* (*Comm*) reinvestieren
▸ **plough into** *vt fus* (*crowd*) rasen in *+acc*
ploughman, (US) **plowman** ['plaumən] (*irreg: like* **man**) *n* Pflüger *m*
ploughman's lunch ['plaumənz-] (*Brit*) *n* *Imbiss aus Brot, Käse und Pickles*
plow *etc* (US) = **plough** *etc*
ploy [plɔɪ] *n* Trick *m*
pls *abbr* (*= please*) b.
pluck [plʌk] *vt* (*fruit, flower, leaf*) pflücken; (*musical instrument, eyebrows*) zupfen; (*bird*) rupfen ▷ *n* (*courage*) Mut *m*; **to ~ up courage** allen Mut zusammennehmen
plucky ['plʌkɪ] (*inf*) *adj* (*person*) tapfer
plug [plʌg] *n* (*Elec*) Stecker *m*; (*stopper*) Stöpsel *m*; (*Aut: also:* **spark(ing) plug**) Zündkerze *f* ▷ *vt* (*hole*) zustopfen; (*inf: advertise*) Reklame machen für; **to give sb/sth a ~** für jdn/etw Reklame machen
▸ **plug in** *vt* (*Elec*) einstöpseln, anschließen ▷ *vi* angeschlossen werden
plughole ['plʌghəul] (*Brit*) *n* Abfluss *m*
plum [plʌm] *n* (*fruit*) Pflaume *f* ▷ *adj* (*inf*): **a ~ job** ein Traumjob *m*
plumage ['plu:mɪdʒ] *n* Gefieder *nt*
plumb [plʌm] *vt*: **to ~ the depths of despair/humiliation** die tiefste Verzweiflung/Erniedrigung erleben
▸ **plumb in** *vt* anschließen, installieren
plumber ['plʌmə^r] *n* Installateur *m*, Klempner *m*
plumbing ['plʌmɪŋ] *n* (*piping*) Installationen *pl*, Rohrleitungen *pl*; (*trade*) Klempnerei *f*; (*work*) Installationsarbeiten *pl*
plumb line *n* Lot *nt*, Senkblei *nt*
plume [plu:m] *n* (*of bird*) Feder *f*; (*on helmet, horse's head*) Federbusch *m*; **~ of smoke** Rauchfahne *f*
plummet ['plʌmɪt] *vi* (*bird, aircraft*) (hinunter)stürzen; (*price, rate*) rapide absacken
plump [plʌmp] *adj* (*person*) füllig, mollig
▸ **plump for** (*inf*) *vt fus* sich entscheiden für
▸ **plump up** *vt* (*cushion*) aufschütteln
plunder ['plʌndə^r] *n* (*activity*) Plünderung *f*; (*stolen things*) Beute *f* ▷ *vt* (*city, tomb*) plündern
plunge [plʌndʒ] *n* (*of bird, person*) Sprung *m*; (*fig: of prices, rates etc*) Sturz *m* ▷ *vt* (*hand, knife*) stoßen ▷ *vi* (*thing*) stürzen; (*bird, person*) sich stürzen; (*fig: prices, rates etc*) abfallen, stürzen; **to take the ~** (*fig*) den Sprung wagen; **the room was ~d into darkness** das Zimmer war in Dunkelheit getaucht
plunger ['plʌndʒə^r] *n* (*for sink*) Sauger *m*
plunging ['plʌndʒɪŋ] *adj*: **~ neckline** tiefer

Ausschnitt *m*
pluperfect [plu:'pə:fɪkt] *n*: **the** ~ das Plusquamperfekt
plural ['pluərl] *adj* Plural- ▷ *n* Plural *m*, Mehrzahl *f*
plus [plʌs] *n* (*also*: **plus sign**) Pluszeichen *nt* ▷ *prep, adj* plus; **it's a** ~ (*fig*) es ist ein Vorteil *or* ein Pluspunkt; **ten/twenty** ~ (*more than*) über zehn/zwanzig; **B** ~ (*Scol*) ≈ Zwei plus
plus fours *npl* Überfallhose *f*
plush [plʌʃ] *adj* (*car, hotel etc*) feudal ▷ *n* (*fabric*) Plüsch *m*
plutonium [plu:'təuniəm] *n* Plutonium *nt*
ply [plaɪ] *vt* (*a trade*) ausüben, nachgehen +*dat*; (*tool*) gebrauchen, anwenden ▷ *vi* (*ship*) verkehren ▷ *n* (*of wool, rope*) Stärke *f*; (*also*: **plywood**) Sperrholz *nt*; **to ~ sb with drink** jdn ausgiebig bewirten; **to ~ sb with questions** jdm viele Fragen stellen; **two-/three-~ wool** zwei-/dreifädige Wolle
plywood ['plaɪwud] *n* Sperrholz *nt*
PM (*Brit*) *abbr* = **Prime Minister**
p.m. *adv abbr* (= *post meridiem*) nachmittags; (*later*) abends
PMT *abbr* = **premenstrual tension**
pneumatic [nju:'mætɪk] *adj* pneumatisch
pneumatic drill *n* Pressluftbohrer *m*
pneumonia [nju:'məuniə] *n* Lungenentzündung *f*
PO *n abbr* = **Post Office**; (*Mil*) = **petty officer**
p.o. *abbr* = **postal order**
POA (*Brit*) *n abbr* (= *Prison Officers' Association*) *Gewerkschaft der Gefängnisbeamten*
poach [pəutʃ] *vt* (*steal: fish, animals, birds*) illegal erbeuten, wildern; (*Culin: egg*) pochieren; (*: fish*) dünsten ▷ *vi* (*steal*) wildern
poached [pəutʃt] *adj*: ~ **eggs** verlorene Eier
poacher ['pəutʃə^r] *n* Wilderer *m*
PO Box *n abbr* (= *Post Office Box*) Postf.
pocket ['pɔkɪt] *n* Tasche *f*; (*fig: small area*) vereinzelter Bereich *m* ▷ *vt* (*put in one's pocket, steal*) einstecken; **to be out of** ~ (*Brit*) Verlust machen; ~ **of resistance** Widerstandsnest *nt*
pocketbook ['pɔkɪtbuk] *n* (*notebook*) Notizbuch *nt*; (US: *wallet*) Brieftasche *f*; (: *handbag*) Handtasche *f*
pocket calculator *n* Taschenrechner *m*
pocketknife ['pɔkɪtnaɪf] *n* Taschenmesser *nt*
pocket money *n* Taschengeld *nt*
pocket-sized ['pɔkɪtsaɪzd] *adj* im Taschenformat
pockmarked ['pɔkmɑ:kt] *adj* (*face*) pockennarbig
pod [pɔd] *n* Hülse *f*
podgy ['pɔdʒɪ] (*inf*) *adj* rundlich, pummelig
podiatrist [pɔ'di:ətrɪst] (US) *n* Fußspezialist(in) *m(f)*
podiatry [pɔ'di:ətrɪ] (US) *n* Fußpflege *f*
podium ['pəudiəm] *n* Podium *nt*
POE *n abbr* (= *port of embarkation*) Ausgangshafen *m*; (= *port of entry*) Eingangshafen *m*
poem ['pəuɪm] *n* Gedicht *nt*
poet ['pəuɪt] *n* Dichter(in) *m(f)*
poetic [pəu'ɛtɪk] *adj* poetisch, dichterisch; (*fig*) malerisch
poetic justice *n* ausgleichende Gerechtigkeit *f*
poetic licence *n* dichterische Freiheit *f*
poet laureate *n* Hofdichter *m*; *siehe Info-Artikel*

POET LAUREATE

Poet laureate ist in Großbritannien ein Dichter, der ein Gehalt als Hofdichter bezieht und kraft seines Amtes ein lebenslanges Mitglied des britischen Königshofes ist. Der Poet Laureate schrieb traditionellerweise ausführliche Gedichte zu Staatsanlässen; ein Brauch, der heute kaum noch befolgt wird. Der erste Poet Laureate 1616 war Ben Jonson.

poetry ['pəuɪtrɪ] *n* (*poems*) Gedichte *pl*; (*writing*) Poesie *f*
poignant ['pɔɪnjənt] *adj* ergreifend; (*situation*) herzzerreißend
point [pɔɪnt] *n* Punkt *m*; (*of needle, knife etc*) Spitze *f*; (*purpose*) Sinn *m*, Zweck *m*; (*significant part*) Entscheidende(s) *nt*; (*moment*) Zeitpunkt *m*; (*Elec: also*: **power point**) Steckdose *f*; (*also*: **decimal point**) ≈ Komma *nt* ▷ *vt* (*show, mark*) deuten auf +*acc* ▷ *vi* (*with finger, stick etc*) zeigen, deuten; **points** *npl* (*Aut*) (Unterbrecher)kontakte *pl*; (*Rail*) Weichen *pl*; **two ~ five** (= 2.5) zwei Komma fünf; **good/bad ~s** (*of person*) gute/schlechte Seiten *or* Eigenschaften; **the train stops at Carlisle and all ~s south** der Zug hält in Carlisle und allen Orten weiter südlich; **to be on the ~ of doing sth** im Begriff sein, etw zu tun; **to make a ~ of doing sth** besonders darauf achten, etw zu tun; (*make a habit of*) Wert darauf legen, etw zu tun; **to get/miss the ~** verstehen/nicht verstehen, worum es geht; **to come** *or* **get to the** ~ zur Sache kommen; **to make one's** ~ seinen Standpunkt klarmachen; **that's the whole ~!** darum geht es ja gerade!; **what's the ~?** was solls?; **to be beside the** ~ unwichtig *or* irrelevant sein; **there's no ~ talking to you** es ist sinnlos, mit dir zu reden; **you've got a ~ there!** da könnten Sie recht haben!; **in ~ of fact** in Wirklichkeit; **~ of sale** (*Comm*) Verkaufsstelle *f*; **to ~ sth at sb** (*gun etc*) etw auf jdn richten; (*finger*) mit etw auf jdn *acc* zeigen; **to ~ at** zeigen auf +*acc*; **to ~ to** zeigen auf +*acc*; (*fig*) hinweisen auf +*acc*
▸ **point out** *vt* hinweisen auf +*acc*
▸ **point to** *vt fus* hindeuten auf +*acc*
point-blank ['pɔɪnt'blæŋk] *adv* (*say, ask*) direkt; (*refuse*) glatt; (*also*: **at point-blank range**) aus unmittelbarer Entfernung
point duty (*Brit*) *n*: **to be on** ~ Verkehrsdienst haben
pointed ['pɔɪntɪd] *adj* spitz; (*fig: remark*) spitz, scharf
pointedly ['pɔɪntɪdlɪ] *adv* (*ask, reply etc*) spitz,

scharf
pointer ['pɔɪntəʳ] *n* (*on chart, machine*) Zeiger *m*; (*fig: piece of information or advice*) Hinweis *m*; (*stick*) Zeigestock *m*; (*dog*) Pointer *m*
pointing ['pɔɪntɪŋ] *n* (*Constr*) Ausfugung *f*
pointless ['pɔɪntlɪs] *adj* sinnlos, zwecklos
point of view *n* Ansicht *f*, Standpunkt *m*; **from a practical ~** von einem praktischen Standpunkt aus
poise [pɔɪz] *n* (*composure*) Selbstsicherheit *f*; (*balance*) Haltung *f* ▷ *vt*: **to be ~d for sth** (*fig*) bereit zu etw sein
poison ['pɔɪzn] *n* Gift *nt* ▷ *vt* vergiften
poisoning ['pɔɪznɪŋ] *n* Vergiftung *f*
poisonous ['pɔɪznəs] *adj* (*animal, plant*) Gift-; (*fumes, chemicals etc*) giftig; (*fig: rumours etc*) zersetzend
poison-pen letter [pɔɪzn'pɛn] *n* anonymer Brief *m* (*mit Indiskretionen*)
poke [pəuk] *vt* (*with finger, stick etc*) stoßen; (*fire*) schüren ▷ *n* (*jab*) Stoß *m*, Schubs *m* (*inf*); **to ~ sth in(to)** (*put*) etw stecken in *+acc*; **to ~ one's head out of the window** seinen Kopf aus dem Fenster strecken; **to ~ fun at sb** sich über jdn lustig machen
▸ **poke about** *vi* (*search*) herumstochern
▸ **poke out** *vi* (*stick out*) vorstehen
poker ['pəukəʳ] *n* (*metal bar*) Schürhaken *m*; (*Cards*) Poker *nt*
poker-faced ['pəukə'feɪst] *adj* mit unbewegter Miene, mit Pokergesicht
poky ['pəukɪ] (*pej*) *adj* (*room, house*) winzig
Poland ['pəulənd] *n* Polen *nt*
polar ['pəuləʳ] *adj* (*icecap*) polar; (*region*) Polar-
polar bear *n* Eisbär *m*
polarize ['pəuləraɪz] *vt* polarisieren
Pole [pəul] *n* Pole *m*, Polin *f*
pole [pəul] *n* (*post, stick*) Stange *f*; (*flag pole, telegraph pole etc*) Mast *m*; (*Geog, Elec*) Pol *m*; **to be ~s apart** (*fig*) durch Welten (voneinander) getrennt sein
poleaxe, (*US*) **poleax** ['pəulæks] *vt* (*fig*) umhauen
pole bean (*US*) *n* (*runner bean*) Stangenbohne *f*
polecat ['pəulkæt] *n* Iltis *m*
Pol. Econ. ['pɔlɪkɔn] *n abbr* (*= political economy*) Volkswirtschaft *f*
polemic [pɔ'lɛmɪk] *n* Polemik *f*
Pole Star *n* Polarstern *m*
pole vault ['pəulvɔːlt] *n* Stabhochsprung *m*
police [pə'liːs] *npl* (*organization*) Polizei *f*; (*members*) Polizisten *pl*, Polizeikräfte *pl* ▷ *vt* (*street, area, town*) kontrollieren; **a large number of ~ were hurt** viele Polizeikräfte wurden verletzt
police car *n* Polizeiauto *nt*
police constable (*Brit*) *n* Polizist(in) *m(f)*, Polizeibeamte(r) *m*, Polizeibeamtin *f*
police department (*US*) *n* Polizei *f*
police force *n* Polizei *f*
policeman [pə'liːsmən] (*irreg: like* **man**) *n* Polizist *m*
police officer *n* = **police constable**
police record *n*: **to have a ~** vorbestraft sein
police state *n* (*Pol*) Polizeistaat *m*
police station *n* Polizeiwache *f*
policewoman [pə'liːswumən] (*irreg: like* **woman**) *n* Polizistin *f*
policy ['pɔlɪsɪ] *n* (*Pol, Econ*) Politik *f*; (*also*: **insurance policy**) (Versicherungs)police *f*; (*of newspaper*) Grundsatz *m*; **to take out a ~** (*Insurance*) eine Versicherung abschließen
policyholder ['pɔlɪsɪ'həuldəʳ] *n* (*Insurance*) Versicherungsnehmer(in) *m(f)*
policy making *n* Strategieplanung *f*
polio ['pəulɪəu] *n* Kinderlähmung *f*, Polio *f*
Polish ['pəulɪʃ] *adj* polnisch ▷ *n* (*Ling*) Polnisch *nt*
polish ['pɔlɪʃ] *n* (*for shoes*) Creme *f*; (*for furniture*) Politur *f*; (*for floors*) Bohnerwachs *nt*; (*shine: on shoes, floor etc*) Glanz *m*; (*fig: refinement*) Schliff *m* ▷ *vt* (*shoes*) putzen; (*floor, furniture etc*) polieren
▸ **polish off** *vt* (*work*) erledigen; (*food*) verputzen
polished ['pɔlɪʃt] *adj* (*fig: person*) mit Schliff; (*: style*) geschliffen
polite [pə'laɪt] *adj* höflich; (*company, society*) fein; **it's not ~ to do that** es gehört sich nicht, das zu tun
politely [pə'laɪtlɪ] *adv* höflich
politeness [pə'laɪtnɪs] *n* Höflichkeit *f*
politic ['pɔlɪtɪk] *adj* klug, vernünftig
political [pə'lɪtɪkl] *adj* politisch
political asylum *n* politisches Asyl *nt*
politically [pə'lɪtɪklɪ] *adv* politisch; **~ correct** politisch korrekt
politician [pɔlɪ'tɪʃən] *n* Politiker(in) *m(f)*
politics ['pɔlɪtɪks] *n* Politik *f* ▷ *npl* (*beliefs, opinions*) politische Ansichten *pl*
polka ['pɔlkə] *n* Polka *f*
poll [pəul] *n* (*also*: **opinion poll**) (Meinungs)umfrage *f*; (*election*) Wahl *f* ▷ *vt* (*in opinion poll*) befragen; (*number of votes*) erhalten; **to go to the ~s** (*voters*) zur Wahl gehen; (*government*) sich den Wählern stellen
pollen ['pɔlən] *n* Pollen *m*, Blütenstaub *m*
pollen count *n* Pollenkonzentration *f*
pollinate ['pɔlɪneɪt] *vt* bestäuben
polling booth ['pəulɪŋ-] (*Brit*) *n* Wahlkabine *f*
polling day (*Brit*) *n* Wahltag *m*
polling station (*Brit*) *n* Wahllokal *nt*
pollster ['pəulstəʳ] *n* Meinungsforscher(in) *m(f)*
poll tax *n* Kopfsteuer *f*
pollutant [pə'luːtənt] *n* Schadstoff *m*
pollute [pə'luːt] *vt* verschmutzen
pollution [pə'luːʃən] *n* (*process*) Verschmutzung *f*; (*substances*) Schmutz *m*
polo ['pəuləu] *n* Polo *nt*
polo neck *n* (*jumper*) Rollkragenpullover *m*
polo-necked ['pəuləunɛkt] *adj* (*jumper, sweater*) Rollkragen-
poltergeist ['pɔːltəgaɪst] *n* Poltergeist *m*
poly ['pɔlɪ] (*Brit*) *n* = **polytechnic**
poly bag (*inf*) *n* Plastiktüte *f*
polyester [pɔlɪ'ɛstəʳ] *n* Polyester *m*

polygamy [pəˈlɪgəmɪ] *n* Polygamie *f*
polygraph [ˈpɔlɪgrɑːf] (*US*) *n* (*lie detector*) Lügendetektor *m*
Polynesia [pɔlɪˈniːzɪə] *n* Polynesien *nt*
Polynesian [pɔlɪˈniːzɪən] *adj* polynesisch ▷ *n* Polynesier(in) *m(f)*
polyp [ˈpɔlɪp] *n* Polyp *m*
polystyrene [pɔlɪˈstaɪriːn] *n* ≈ Styropor® *nt*
polytechnic [pɔlɪˈtɛknɪk] *n* technische Hochschule *f*
polythene [ˈpɔlɪθiːn] *n* Polyäthylen *nt*
polythene bag *n* Plastiktüte *f*
polyurethane [pɔlɪˈjuərɪθeɪn] *n* Polyurethan *nt*
pomegranate [ˈpɔmɪgrænɪt] *n* Granatapfel *m*
pommel [ˈpɔml] *n* (*on saddle*) Sattelknopf *m* ▷ *vt* (*US*) = **pummel**
po-mo [ˈpəʊməʊ] *abbr* (= *postmodern*) postmodern; (= *postmodernism*) Postmoderne *f*
pomp [pɔmp] *n* Pomp *m*, Prunk *m*
pompom [ˈpɔmpɔm] *n* Troddel *f*
pompous [ˈpɔmpəs] (*pej*) *adj* (*person*) aufgeblasen; (*piece of writing*) geschwollen
pond [pɔnd] *n* Teich *m*
ponder [ˈpɔndəʳ] *vt* nachdenken über *+acc* ▷ *vi* nachdenken
ponderous [ˈpɔndərəs] *adj* (*style, language*) schwerfällig
pong [pɔŋ] (*Brit: inf*) *n* Gestank *m* ▷ *vi* stinken
pontiff [ˈpɔntɪf] *n* Papst *m*
pontificate [pɔnˈtɪfɪkeɪt] *vi* dozieren
pontoon [pɔnˈtuːn] *n* (*floating platform*) Ponton *m*; (*Cards*) Siebzehnundvier *nt*
pony [ˈpəunɪ] *n* Pony *nt*
ponytail [ˈpəunɪteɪl] *n* Pferdeschwanz *m*; **to have one's hair in a ~** einen Pferdeschwanz tragen
pony trekking (*Brit*) *n* Ponytrecken *nt*
poodle [ˈpuːdl] *n* Pudel *m*
pooh-pooh [ˈpuːˈpuː] *vt* verächtlich abtun
pool [puːl] *n* (*pond*) Teich *m*; (*also*: **swimming pool**) Schwimmbad *nt*; (*of blood*) Lache *f*; (*Sport*) Poolbillard *nt*; (*of cash, workers*) Bestand *m*; (*Cards: kitty*) Kasse *f*; (*Comm: consortium*) Interessengemeinschaft *f* ▷ *vt* (*money*) zusammenlegen; (*knowledge, resources*) vereinigen; **pools** *npl* (*also*: **football pools**) ≈ Fußballtoto *nt*; **a ~ of sunlight/shade** eine sonnige/schattige Stelle; **car ~** Fahrgemeinschaft *f*; **typing ~, secretary ~** (*US*) Schreibzentrale *f*; **to do the (football) ~s** ≈ im Fußballtoto spielen
poor [puəʳ] *adj* arm; (*bad*) schlecht ▷ *npl*: **the ~** die Armen *pl*; **~ in** (*resources etc*) arm an *+dat*; **~ Bob** der arme Bob
poorly [ˈpuəlɪ] *adj* (*ill*) elend, krank ▷ *adv* (*badly: designed, paid, furnished*) schlecht
pop [pɔp] *n* (*Mus*) Pop *m*; (*fizzy drink*) Limonade *f*; (*US: inf: father*) Papa *m*; (*sound*) Knall *m* ▷ *vi* (*balloon*) platzen; (*cork*) knallen ▷ *vt*: **to ~ sth into/onto sth** etw schnell in etw *acc* stecken/auf etw *acc* legen; **his eyes ~ped out of his head** (*inf*) ihm fielen fast die Augen aus dem Kopf; **she ~ped her head out of the window** sie streckte den Kopf aus dem Fenster
▸ **pop in** *vi* vorbeikommen
▸ **pop out** *vi* kurz weggehen
▸ **pop up** *vi* auftauchen; (*Comput: window*) aufpoppen
popcorn [ˈpɔpkɔːn] *n* Popcorn *nt*
pope [pəup] *n* Papst *m*
poplar [ˈpɔpləʳ] *n* Pappel *f*
poplin [ˈpɔplɪn] *n* Popeline *f*
popper [ˈpɔpəʳ] (*Brit: inf*) *n* (*for fastening*) Druckknopf *m*
poppy [ˈpɔpɪ] *n* Mohn *m*
poppycock [ˈpɔpɪkɔk] (*inf*) *n* Humbug *m*, dummes Zeug *nt*
Popsicle® [ˈpɔpsɪkl] (*US*) *n* Eis *nt* am Stiel
pop star *n* Popstar *m*
populace [ˈpɔpjuləs] *n*: **the ~** die Bevölkerung, das Volk
popular [ˈpɔpjuləʳ] *adj* (*well-liked, fashionable*) beliebt, populär; (*general, non-specialist*) allgemein; (*idea*) weitverbreitet; (*Pol: movement*) Volks-; (*: cause*) des Volkes; **to be ~ with** beliebt sein bei; **the ~ press** die Boulevardpresse
popularity [pɔpjuˈlærɪtɪ] *n* Beliebtheit *f*, Popularität *f*
popularize [ˈpɔpjuləraɪz] *vt* (*sport, music, fashion*) populär machen; (*science, ideas*) popularisieren
popularly [ˈpɔpjuləlɪ] *adv* (*commonly*) allgemein
population [pɔpjuˈleɪʃən] *n* Bevölkerung *f*; (*of a species*) Zahl *f*, Population *f*; **a prison ~ of 44,000** (eine Zahl von) 44.000 Gefängnisinsassen; **the civilian ~** die Zivilbevölkerung
population explosion *n* Bevölkerungsexplosion *f*
populous [ˈpɔpjuləs] *adj* dicht besiedelt
pop-up window [ˈpɔpʌp-] *n* (*Comput*) Popup-Fenster *nt*
porcelain [ˈpɔːslɪn] *n* Porzellan *nt*
porch [pɔːtʃ] *n* (*entrance*) Vorbau *m*; (*US*) Veranda *f*
porcupine [ˈpɔːkjupaɪn] *n* Stachelschwein *nt*
pore [pɔːʳ] *n* Pore *f* ▷ *vi*: **to ~ over** (*book etc*) gründlich studieren
pork [pɔːk] *n* Schweinefleisch *nt*
pork chop *n* Schweinekotelett *nt*
porn [pɔːn] (*inf*) *n* Porno *m*; **~ channel/magazine/shop** Pornokanal *m*/-magazin *nt*/-laden *m*
pornographic [pɔːnəˈgræfɪk] *adj* pornografisch
pornography [pɔːˈnɔgrəfɪ] *n* Pornografie *f*
porous [ˈpɔːrəs] *adj* porös
porpoise [ˈpɔːpəs] *n* Tümmler *m*
porridge [ˈpɔrɪdʒ] *n* Haferbrei *m*, Porridge *nt*
port [pɔːt] *n* (*harbour*) Hafen *m*; (*Naut: left side*) Backbord *nt*; (*wine*) Portwein *m*; (*Comput*) Port *m* ▷ *adj* (*Naut*) Backbord-; **to ~** (*Naut*) an Backbord; **~ of call** (*Naut*) Anlaufhafen *nt*
portable [ˈpɔːtəbl] *adj* (*television, typewriter etc*) tragbar, portabel

portal ['pɔːtl] *n* Portal *nt*
portaloo ['pɔːtəluː] *n* Mobiltoilette *f*
portcullis [pɔːt'kʌlɪs] *n* Fallgitter *nt*
portend [pɔː'tɛnd] *vt* hindeuten auf *+acc*
portent ['pɔːtɛnt] *n* Vorzeichen *nt*
porter ['pɔːtə^r] *n* (*for luggage*) Gepäckträger *m*; (*doorkeeper*) Pförtner *m*; (*US: Rail*) Schlafwagenschaffner(in) *m(f)*
portfolio [pɔːt'fəulɪəu] *n* (*case*) Aktenmappe *f*; (*Pol*) Geschäftsbereich *m*; (*Fin*) Portefeuille *nt*; (*of artist*) Kollektion *f*
porthole ['pɔːthəul] *n* Bullauge *nt*
portico ['pɔːtɪkəu] *n* Säulenhalle *f*
portion ['pɔːʃən] *n* (*part*) Teil *m*; (*helping of food*) Portion *f*
portly ['pɔːtlɪ] *adj* beleibt, korpulent
portrait ['pɔːtreɪt] *n* Porträt *nt*
portray [pɔː'treɪ] *vt* darstellen
portrayal [pɔː'treɪəl] *n* Darstellung *f*
Portugal ['pɔːtjugl] *n* Portugal *nt*
Portuguese [pɔːtju'giːz] *adj* portugiesisch ▷ *n inv* (*person*) Portugiese *m*, Portugiesin *f*; (*Ling*) Portugiesisch *nt*
Portuguese man-of-war [-mænəv'wɔː^r] *n* (*Zool*) Röhrenqualle *f*, Portugiesische Galeere *f*
pose [pəuz] *n* Pose *f* ▷ *vt* (*question, problem*) aufwerfen; (*danger*) mit sich bringen ▷ *vi*: **to ~ as** (*pretend*) sich ausgeben als; **to strike a ~** sich in Positur werfen; **to ~ for** (*painting etc*) Modell sitzen für, posieren für
poser ['pəuzə^r] *n* (*problem, puzzle*) harte Nuss *f* (*inf*); (*person*) = **poseur**
poseur [pəu'zəː^r] (*pej*) *n* Angeber(in) *m(f)*
posh [pɔʃ] (*inf*) *adj* vornehm; **to talk ~** vornehm daherreden
position [pə'zɪʃən] *n* (*place: of thing, person*) Position *f*, Lage *f*; (*of person's body*) Stellung *f*; (*job*) Stelle *f*; (*in race etc*) Platz *m*; (*attitude*) Haltung *f*, Standpunkt *m*; (*situation*) Lage ▷ *vt* (*person, thing*) stellen; **to be in a ~ to do sth** in der Lage sein, etw zu tun
positive ['pɔzɪtɪv] *adj* positiv; (*certain*) sicher; (*decisive: action, policy*) konstruktiv
positively ['pɔzɪtɪvlɪ] *adv* (*emphatic: rude, stupid etc*) eindeutig; (*encouragingly, Elec*) positiv; **the body has been ~ identified** die Leiche ist eindeutig identifiziert worden
posse ['pɔsɪ] (*US*) *n* (Polizei)truppe *f*
possess [pə'zɛs] *vt* besitzen; (*subj: feeling, belief*) Besitz ergreifen von; **like a man ~ed** wie besessen; **whatever ~ed you to do it?** was ist in dich gefahren, das zu tun?
possession [pə'zɛʃən] *n* Besitz *m*; **possessions** *npl* (*belongings*) Besitz *m*; **to take ~ of** Besitz ergreifen von
possessive [pə'zɛsɪv] *adj* (*nature etc*) besitzergreifend; (*Ling: pronoun*) Possessiv-; (*: adjective*) besitzanzeigend; **to be ~ about sb/sth** Besitzansprüche an jdn/etw *acc* stellen
possessiveness [pə'zɛsɪvnɪs] *n* besitzergreifende Art *f*
possessor [pə'zɛsə^r] *n* Besitzer(in) *m(f)*
possibility [pɔsɪ'bɪlɪtɪ] *n* Möglichkeit *f*
possible ['pɔsɪbl] *adj* möglich; **it's ~** (*may be true*) es ist möglich, es kann sein; **it's ~ to do it** es ist machbar *or* zu machen; **as far as ~** so weit wie möglich; **if ~** falls *or* wenn möglich; **as soon as ~** so bald wie möglich
possibly ['pɔsɪblɪ] *adv* (*perhaps*) möglicherweise, vielleicht; (*conceivably*) überhaupt; **if you ~ can** falls überhaupt möglich; **what could they ~ want?** was um alles in der Welt wollen sie?; **I cannot ~ come** ich kann auf keinen Fall kommen
post [pəust] *n* (*Brit*) Post *f*; (*pole, goal post*) Pfosten *m*; (*job*) Stelle *f*; (*Mil*) Posten *m*; (*also*: **trading post**) Handelsniederlassung *f* ▷ *vt* (*Brit: letter*) aufgeben; (*Mil*) aufstellen; **by ~** (*Brit*) per Post; **by return of ~** (*Brit*) postwendend, umgehend; **to keep sb ~ed** (*informed*) jdn auf dem Laufenden halten; **to ~ sb to** (*town, country*) jdn versetzen nach; (*embassy, office*) jdn versetzen zu; (*Mil*) jdn abkommandieren nach
▸ **post up** *vt* anschlagen
post ... [pəust] *pref* Post-, post-; **~-1990** nach 1990
postage ['pəustɪdʒ] *n* Porto *nt*
postage stamp *n* Briefmarke *f*
postal ['pəustl] *adj* (*charges, service*) Post-
postal order (*Brit*) *n* Postanweisung *f*
postbag ['pəustbæg] (*Brit*) *n* Postsack *m*; (*letters*) Posteingang *m*
postbox ['pəustbɔks] *n* Briefkasten *m*
postcard ['pəustkɑːd] *n* Postkarte *f*
postcode ['pəustkəud] (*Brit*) *n* Postleitzahl *f*
postdate ['pəust'deɪt] *vt* (*cheque*) vordatieren
poster ['pəustə^r] *n* Poster *nt*, Plakat *nt*
poste restante [pəust'rɛstɑ̃ːnt] (*Brit*) *n* Stelle *f* für postlagernde Sendungen ▷ *adv* postlagernd
posterior [pɔs'tɪərɪə^r] (*hum*) *n* Allerwerteste(r) *m*
posterity [pɔs'tɛrɪtɪ] *n* die Nachwelt
poster paint *n* Plakatfarbe *f*
post exchange (*US*) *n* (*Mil*) *Laden für US-Militärpersonal*
post-free [pəust'friː] (*Brit*) *adj, adv* portofrei
postgraduate ['pəust'grædjuət] *n* Graduierte(r) *f(m)* (*im Weiterstudium*)
posthumous ['pɔstjuməs] *adj* posthum
posthumously ['pɔstjuməslɪ] *adv* posthum
posting ['pəustɪŋ] *n* (*job*) Stelle *f*
postman ['pəustmən] (*irreg: like* **man**) *n* Briefträger *m*, Postbote *m*
postmark ['pəustmɑːk] *n* Poststempel *m*
postmaster ['pəustmɑːstə^r] *n* Postmeister *m*
Postmaster General *n* ≈ Postminister(in) *m(f)*
postmistress ['pəustmɪstrɪs] *n* Postmeisterin *f*
postmortem [pəust'mɔːtəm] *n* (*Med*) Obduktion *f*; (*fig*) nachträgliche Erörterung *f*
postnatal ['pəust'neɪtl] *adj* nach der Geburt, postnatal
post office *n* (*building*) Post *f*, Postamt *nt*; **the Post Office** (*organization*) die Post
Post Office Box *n* Postfach *nt*

post-paid ['pəust'peɪd] *adj, adv* = **post-free**
postpone [pəus'pəun] *vt* verschieben
postponement [pəus'pəunmənt] *n* Aufschub *m*
postscript ['pəustskrɪpt] *n* (*to letter*) Nachschrift *f*, PS *nt*
postulate ['pɔstjuleɪt] *vt* ausgehen von, postulieren
posture ['pɔstʃəʳ] *n* (*also fig*) Haltung *f* ▷ *vi* (*pej*) posieren
postwar [pəust'wɔːʳ] *adj* Nachkriegs-
posy ['pəuzɪ] *n* Blumensträußchen *nt*
pot [pɔt] *n* Topf *m*; (*teapot, coffee pot, potful*) Kanne *f*; (*inf: marijuana*) Pot *nt* ▷ *vt* (*plant*) eintopfen; **to go to ~** (*inf*) auf den Hund kommen; **~s of** (*Brit: inf*) jede Menge
potash ['pɔtæʃ] *n* Pottasche *f*
potassium [pə'tæsɪəm] *n* Kalium *nt*
potato [pə'teɪtəu] (*pl* **~es**) *n* Kartoffel *f*
potato chips (US) *npl* = **potato crisps**
potato crisps *npl* Kartoffelchips *pl*
potato flour *n* Kartoffelmehl *nt*
potato peeler *n* Kartoffelschäler *m*
potbellied ['pɔtbɛlɪd] *adj* (*from overeating*) dickbäuchig; (*from malnutrition*) blähbäuchig
potency ['pəutnsɪ] *n* (*sexual*) Potenz *f*; (*of drink, drug*) Stärke *f*
potent ['pəutnt] *adj* (*powerful*) stark; (*sexually*) potent
potentate ['pəutnteɪt] *n* Machthaber *m*, Potentat *m*
potential [pə'tɛnʃl] *adj* potenziell ▷ *n* Potenzial *nt*; **to have ~** (*person, machine*) Fähigkeiten *or* Potenzial haben; (*idea, plan*) ausbaufähig sein
potentially [pə'tɛnʃəlɪ] *adv* potentziell; **it's ~ dangerous** es könnte gefährlich sein
pothole ['pɔthəul] *n* (*in road*) Schlagloch *nt*; (*cave*) Höhle *f*
potholing ['pɔthəulɪŋ] (*Brit*) *n*: **to go ~** Höhlenforschung betreiben
potion ['pəuʃən] *n* Elixier *nt*
potluck [pɔt'lʌk] *n*: **to take ~** sich überraschen lassen
potpourri [pəu'puriː] *n* (*dried petals*) Duftsträußchen *nt*; (*fig*) Sammelsurium *nt*
pot roast *n* Schmorbraten *m*
pot shot *n*: **to take a ~ at** aufs Geratewohl schießen auf *+acc*
potted ['pɔtɪd] *adj* (*food*) eingemacht; (*plant*) Topf-; (*abbreviated: history etc*) Kurz-, kurz gefasst
potter ['pɔtəʳ] *n* Töpfer(in) *m(f)* ▷ *vi*: **to ~ around, ~ about** (*Brit*) herumhantieren; **to ~ around the house** im Haus herumwerkeln
potter's wheel *n* Töpferscheibe *f*
pottery ['pɔtərɪ] *n* (*pots, dishes etc*) Keramik *f*, Töpferwaren *pl*; (*work, hobby*) Töpfern *nt*; (*factory, workshop*) Töpferei *f*; **a piece of ~** ein Töpferstück *nt*
potty ['pɔtɪ] *adj* (*inf: mad*) verrückt ▷ *n* (*for child*) Töpfchen *nt*
potty-training ['pɔtɪtreɪnɪŋ] *n* Entwöhnung *f* vom Windeltragen
pouch [pautʃ] *n* Beutel *m* (*also Zool*)
pouf, **pouffe** [puːf] *n* (*stool*) gepolsterter Hocker *m*
poultice ['pəultɪs] *n* Umschlag *m*
poultry ['pəultrɪ] *n* Geflügel *nt*
poultry farm *n* Geflügelfarm *f*
poultry farmer *n* Geflügelzüchter(in) *m(f)*
pounce [pauns] *vi*: **to ~ on** (*also fig*) sich stürzen auf *+acc*
pound [paund] *n* (*unit of money*) Pfund *nt*; (*unit of weight*) (britisches) Pfund (*= 453,6g*); (*for dogs*) Zwinger *m*; (*for cars*) Abholstelle *f* (*für abgeschleppte Fahrzeuge*) ▷ *vt* (*beat: table, wall etc*) herumhämmern auf *+dat*; (*crush: grain, spice etc*) zerstoßen; (*bombard*) beschießen ▷ *vi* (*heart*) klopfen, pochen; (*head*) dröhnen; **half a ~ of butter** ein halbes Pfund Butter; **a five-~ note** ein Fünfpfundschein *m*
pounding ['paundɪŋ] *n*: **to take a ~** (*fig*) schwer angegriffen werden; (*team*) eine Schlappe einstecken müssen
pound sterling *n* Pfund *nt* Sterling
pour [pɔːʳ] *vt* (*tea, wine etc*) gießen; (*cereal etc*) schütten ▷ *vi* strömen; **to ~ sb a glass of wine/a cup of tea** jdm ein Glas Wein/eine Tasse Tee einschenken; **to ~ with rain** in Strömen gießen
▸ **pour away** *vt* wegschütten
▸ **pour in** *vi* (*people*) hereinströmen; (*letters etc*) massenweise eintreffen
▸ **pour out** *vi* (*people*) herausströmen ▷ *vt* (*tea, wine etc*) eingießen; (*fig: thoughts, feelings, etc*) freien Lauf lassen *+dat*
pouring ['pɔːrɪŋ] *adj*: **~ rain** strömender Regen *m*
pout [paut] *vi* einen Schmollmund ziehen
poverty ['pɔvətɪ] *n* Armut *f*
poverty line *n* Armutsgrenze *f*
poverty risk *n* Armutsrisiko *f*
poverty-stricken ['pɔvətɪstrɪkn] *adj* verarmt, Not leidend
poverty trap (*Brit*) *n* *gleichbleibend schlechte wirtschaftliche Situation aufgrund des Wegfalls von Sozialleistungen bei verbessertem Einkommen*, Armutsfalle *f*
POW *n abbr* = **prisoner of war**
powder ['paudəʳ] *n* Pulver *nt* ▷ *vt*: **to ~ one's face** sich *dat* das Gesicht pudern; **to ~ one's nose** (*euph*) kurz mal verschwinden
powder compact *n* Puderdose *f*
powdered milk ['paudəd-] *n* Milchpulver *nt*
powder keg *n* (*also fig*) Pulverfass *nt*
powder puff *n* Puderquaste *f*
powder room (*euph*) *n* Damentoilette *f*
power ['pauəʳ] *n* (*control, legal right*) Macht *f*; (*ability*) Fähigkeit *f*; (*of muscles, ideas, words*) Kraft *f*; (*of explosion, engine*) Gewalt *f*; (*electricity*) Strom *m*; **2 to the ~ (of) 3** (*Math*) 2 hoch 3; **to do everything in one's ~ to help** alles in seiner Macht Stehende tun, um zu helfen; **a world ~** eine Weltmacht; **the ~s that be** (*authority*) diejenigen, die das Sagen haben; **~ of attorney** Vollmacht *f*; **to be in ~** (*Pol etc*) an

der Macht sein

powerboat ['pauəbəut] *n* schnelles Motorboot *nt*, Rennboot *nt*

power cut *n* Stromausfall *m*

powered ['pauəd] *adj*: **~ by** angetrieben von; **nuclear-~ submarine** atomgetriebenes U-Boot

power failure *n* Stromausfall *m*

powerful ['pauəful] *adj* (*person, organization*) mächtig; (*body, voice, blow etc*) kräftig; (*engine*) stark; (*unpleasant: smell*) streng; (*emotion*) überwältigend; (*argument, evidence*) massiv

powerhouse ['pauəhaus] *n*: **he is a ~ of ideas** er hat ständig neue Ideen

powerless ['pauəlɪs] *adj* machtlos; **to be ~ to do sth** nicht die Macht haben, etw zu tun

power line *n* Stromkabel *nt*

power point (*Brit*) *n* Steckdose *f*

power station *n* Kraftwerk *nt*

power steering *n* (*Aut*) Servolenkung *f*

powwow ['pauwau] *n* Besprechung *f*

pp *abbr* (= *per procurationem*) ppa.

pp. *abbr* (= *pages*) S.

PPE (*Brit*) *n abbr* (*Univ*: = *philosophy, politics, and economics*) *Studiengang bestehend aus Philosophie, Politologie und Volkswirtschaft*

PPS *n abbr* (= *post postscriptum*) PPS; (*Brit*: = *parliamentary private secretary*) *Privatsekretär eines Ministers*

PQ (*Canada*) *abbr* (= *Province of Quebec*)

PR *n abbr* = **public relations**; (*Pol*) = **proportional representation** ▷ *abbr* (*US*: *Post*) = *Puerto Rico*

Pr. *abbr* = **prince**

practicability [præktɪkə'bɪlɪtɪ] *n* Durchführbarkeit *f*

practicable ['præktɪkəbl] *adj* (*scheme, idea*) durchführbar

practical ['præktɪkl] *adj* praktisch; (*person: good with hands*) praktisch veranlagt; (*ideas, methods*) praktikabel

practicality [præktɪ'kælɪtɪ] *n* (*of person*) praktische Veranlagung *f*; **practicalities** *npl* (*of situation etc*) praktische Einzelheiten *pl*

practical joke *n* Streich *m*

practically ['præktɪklɪ] *adv* praktisch

practice ['præktɪs] *n* (*also Med, Law*) Praxis *f*; (*custom*) Brauch *m*; (*exercise*) Übung *f* ▷ *vt, vi* (*US*) = **practise**; **in ~** in der Praxis; **out of ~** aus der Übung; **2 hours' piano ~** 2 Stunden Klavierübungen; **it's common** *or* **standard ~** es ist allgemein üblich; **to put sth into ~** etw in die Praxis umsetzen; **target ~** Zielschießen *nt*

practice match *n* Übungsspiel *nt*

practise, (*US*) **practice** ['præktɪs] *vt* (*train at*) üben; (*carry out: custom*) pflegen; (*: activity etc*) ausüben; (*profession*) praktizieren ▷ *vi* (*train*) üben; (*lawyer, doctor etc*) praktizieren

practised ['præktɪst] (*Brit*) *adj* (*person, liar*) geübt; (*performance*) gekonnt; **with a ~ eye** mit geschultem Auge

practising ['præktɪsɪŋ] *adj* praktizierend

practitioner [præk'tɪʃənəʳ] *n*: **medical ~** praktischer Arzt *m*, praktische Ärztin *f*; **legal ~** Rechtsanwalt *m*, Rechtsanwältin *f*

pragmatic [præg'mætɪk] *adj* pragmatisch

pragmatism ['prægmətɪzəm] *n* Pragmatismus *m*

Prague [prɑːg] *n* Prag *nt*

prairie ['prɛərɪ] *n* (Gras)steppe *f*; **the ~s** (*US*) die Prärien

praise [preɪz] *n* Lob *nt* ▷ *vt* loben; (*Rel*) loben, preisen

praiseworthy ['preɪzwəːðɪ] *adj* lobenswert

pram [præm] (*Brit*) *n* Kinderwagen *m*

prance [prɑːns] *vi* (*horse*) tänzeln; **to ~ about/in/out** (*person*) herum-/hinein-/hinausstolzieren

prank [præŋk] *n* Streich *m*

prat [præt] (*Brit: inf*) *n* (*idiot*) Trottel *m*

prattle ['prætl] *vi*: **to ~ on (about)** pausenlos plappern (über +*acc*)

prawn [prɔːn] *n* (*Culin, Zool*) Garnele *f*, Krabbe *f*; **~ cocktail** Krabbencocktail *m*

pray [preɪ] *vi* beten; **to ~ for sb/sth** (*Rel, fig*) für jdn/um etw beten

prayer [prɛəʳ] *n* Gebet *nt*; **to say one's ~s** beten

prayer book *n* Gebetbuch *nt*

pre ... [priː] *pref* Prä-, prä-; **~-1970** vor 1970

preach [priːtʃ] *vi* (*Rel*) predigen; (*pej: moralize*) Predigten halten ▷ *vt* (*sermon*) direkt halten; (*fig: advocate*) predigen, verkünden; **to ~ at sb** (*fig*) jdm Moralpredigten halten; **to ~ to the converted** (*fig*) offene Türen einrennen

preacher ['priːtʃəʳ] *n* Prediger(in) *m(f)*

preamble [prɪ'æmbl] *n* Vorbemerkung *f*

prearranged [priːə'reɪndʒd] *adj* (vorher) vereinbart

precarious [prɪ'kɛərɪəs] *adj* prekär

precaution [prɪ'kɔːʃən] *n* Vorsichtsmaßnahme *f*; **to take ~s** Vorsichtsmaßnahmen treffen

precautionary [prɪ'kɔːʃənrɪ] *adj* (*measure*) vorbeugend, Vorsichts-

precede [prɪ'siːd] *vt* (*event*) vorausgehen +*dat*; (*person*) vorangehen +*dat*; (*words, sentences*) vorangestellt sein +*dat*

precedence ['prɛsɪdəns] *n* (*priority*) Vorrang *m*; **to take ~ over** Vorrang haben vor +*dat*

precedent ['prɛsɪdənt] *n* (*Law*) Präzedenzfall *m*; **without ~** noch nie da gewesen; **to establish** *or* **set a ~** einen Präzedenzfall schaffen

preceding [prɪ'siːdɪŋ] *adj* vorhergehend

precept ['priːsɛpt] *n* Grundsatz *m*, Regel *f*

precinct ['priːsɪŋkt] *n* (*US: part of city*) Bezirk *m*; **precincts** *npl* (*of cathedral, palace*) Gelände *nt*; **shopping ~** (*Brit*) Einkaufsviertel *nt*; (*under cover*) Einkaufscenter *nt*

precious ['prɛʃəs] *adj* wertvoll, kostbar; (*pej: person, writing*) geziert; (*ironic: damned*) heiß geliebt, wundervoll ▷ *adv* (*inf*): **~ little/few** herzlich wenig/wenige

precious stone *n* Edelstein *m*

precipice ['prɛsɪpɪs] *n* (*also fig*) Abgrund *m*

precipitate [*vt* prɪ'sɪpɪteɪt, *adj* prɪ'sɪpɪtɪt] *vt* (*event*) heraufbeschwören ▷ *adj* (*hasty*) überstürzt, übereilt

precipitation [prɪsɪpɪˈteɪʃən] *n* (*rain*) Niederschlag *m*
precipitous [prɪˈsɪpɪtəs] *adj* (*steep*) steil; (*hasty*) übereilt
précis [ˈpreɪsiː] *n inv* Zusammenfassung *f*
precise [prɪˈsaɪs] *adj* genau, präzise; **at 4 o'clock to be ~** um 4 Uhr, um genau zu sein
precisely [prɪˈsaɪslɪ] *adv* genau, exakt; (*emphatic*) ganz genau; **~!** genau!
precision [prɪˈsɪʒən] *n* Genauigkeit *f*, Präzision *f*
preclude [prɪˈkluːd] *vt* ausschließen; **to ~ sb from doing sth** jdn daran hindern, etw zu tun
precocious [prɪˈkəuʃəs] *adj* (*child, behaviour*) frühreif
preconceived [priːkənˈsiːvd] *adj* (*idea*) vorgefasst
preconception [ˈpriːkənˈsɛpʃən] *n* vorgefasste Meinung *f*
precondition [ˈpriːkənˈdɪʃən] *n* Vorbedingung *f*
precursor [priːˈkəːsə^r] *n* Vorläufer *m*
predate [ˈpriːˈdeɪt] *vt* (*precede*) vorausgehen *+dat*
predator [ˈprɛdətə^r] *n* (*Zool*) Raubtier *nt*; (*fig*) Eindringling *m*
predatory [ˈprɛdətərɪ] *adj* (*animal*) Raub-; (*person, organization*) auf Beute lauernd
predecessor [ˈpriːdɪsɛsə^r] *n* Vorgänger(in) *m(f)*
predestination [priːdɛstɪˈneɪʃən] *n* Vorherbestimmung *f*
predetermine [priːdɪˈtəːmɪn] *vt* vorherbestimmen
predicament [prɪˈdɪkəmənt] *n* Notlage *f*, Dilemma *nt*; **to be in a ~** in einer Notlage *or* einem Dilemma stecken
predicate [ˈprɛdɪkɪt] *n* (*Ling*) Prädikat *nt*
predict [prɪˈdɪkt] *vt* vorhersagen
predictable [prɪˈdɪktəbl] *adj* vorhersagbar
predictably [prɪˈdɪktəblɪ] *adv* (*behave, react*) wie vorherzusehen; **~ she didn't come** wie vorherzusehen war, kam sie nicht
prediction [prɪˈdɪkʃən] *n* Voraussage *f*
predispose [ˈpriːdɪsˈpəuz] *vt*: **to ~ sb to sth** jdn zu etw veranlassen; **to be ~d to do sth** geneigt sein, etw zu tun
predominance [prɪˈdɔmɪnəns] *n* Vorherrschaft *f*
predominant [prɪˈdɔmɪnənt] *adj* vorherrschend; **to become ~** vorherrschend werden
predominantly [prɪˈdɔmɪnəntlɪ] *adv* überwiegend
predominate [prɪˈdɔmɪneɪt] *vi* (*in number, size*) vorherrschen; (*in strength, influence*) überwiegen
pre-eminent [priːˈɛmɪnənt] *adj* herausragend
pre-empt [priːˈɛmt] *vt* zuvorkommen *+dat*
pre-emptive [priːˈɛmtɪv] *adj*: **~ strike** Präventivschlag *m*
preen [priːn] *vt*: **to ~ itself** (*bird*) sich putzen; **to ~ o.s.** sich herausputzen
prefab [ˈpriːfæb] *n* Fertighaus *nt*
prefabricated [priːˈfæbrɪkeɪtɪd] *adj* vorgefertigt
preface [ˈprɛfəs] *n* Vorwort *nt* ▷ *vt*: **to ~ with/by** (*speech, action*) einleiten mit/durch
prefect [ˈpriːfɛkt] (*Brit*) *n* (*in school*) Aufsichtsschüler(in) *m(f)*
prefer [prɪˈfəː^r] *vt* (*like better*) vorziehen; **to ~ charges** (*Law*) Anklage erheben; **to ~ doing** *or* **to do sth** (es) vorziehen, etw zu tun; **I ~ tea to coffee** ich mag lieber Tee als Kaffee
preferable [ˈprɛfrəbl] *adj*: **to be ~ (to)** vorzuziehen sein (*+dat*)
preferably [ˈprɛfrəblɪ] *adv* vorzugsweise, am besten
preference [ˈprɛfrəns] *n*: **to have a ~ for** (*liking*) eine Vorliebe haben für; **I drink beer in ~ to wine** ich trinke lieber Bier als Wein; **to give ~ to** (*priority*) vorziehen, Vorrang einräumen *+dat*
preference shares (*Brit*) *npl* (*Comm*) Vorzugsaktien *pl*
preferential [prɛfəˈrɛnʃəl] *adj*: **~ treatment** bevorzugte Behandlung *f*; **to give sb ~ treatment** jdn bevorzugt behandeln
preferred stock [prɪˈfəd-] (*US*) *npl* = **preference shares**
prefix [ˈpriːfɪks] *n* (*Ling*) Präfix *nt*
pregnancy [ˈprɛgnənsɪ] *n* (*of woman*) Schwangerschaft *f*; (*of female animal*) Trächtigkeit *f*
pregnancy test *n* Schwangerschaftstest *m*
pregnant [ˈprɛgnənt] *adj* (*woman*) schwanger; (*female animal*) trächtig; (*fig: pause, remark*) bedeutungsschwer; **3 months ~** im vierten Monat (schwanger)
prehistoric [ˈpriːhɪsˈtɔrɪk] *adj* prähistorisch, vorgeschichtlich
prehistory [priːˈhɪstərɪ] *n* Vorgeschichte *f*
prejudge [priːˈdʒʌdʒ] *vt* vorschnell beurteilen
prejudice [ˈprɛdʒudɪs] *n* (*bias against*) Vorurteil *nt*; (*bias in favour*) Voreingenommenheit *f* ▷ *vt* beeinträchtigen; **without ~ to** (*form*) unbeschadet *+gen*, ohne Beeinträchtigung *+gen*; **to ~ sb in favour of/against sth** jdn für/gegen etw einnehmen
prejudiced [ˈprɛdʒudɪst] *adj* (*person, view*) voreingenommen
prelate [ˈprɛlət] *n* Prälat *m*
preliminaries [prɪˈlɪmɪnərɪz] *npl* Vorbereitungen *pl*; (*of competition*) Vorrunde *f*
preliminary [prɪˈlɪmɪnərɪ] *adj* (*step, arrangements*) vorbereitend; (*remarks*) einleitend
pre-loaded [prɪˈləudɪd] *adj* (*Comput: program etc*) vorinstalliert
prelude [ˈprɛljuːd] *n* (*Mus*) Präludium *nt*; (*: as introduction*) Vorspiel *nt*; **a ~ to** (*fig*) ein Vorspiel *or* ein Auftakt zu
premarital [ˈpriːˈmærɪtl] *adj* vorehelich
premature [ˈprɛmətʃuə^r] *adj* (*earlier than expected*) vorzeitig; (*too early*) verfrüht; **you are being a little ~** Sie sind etwas voreilig; **~ baby** Frühgeburt *f*
premeditated [priːˈmɛdɪteɪtɪd] *adj* vorsätzlich
premeditation [priːmɛdɪˈteɪʃən] *n* Vorsatz *m*

premenstrual tension [priːˈmɛnstruəl-] *n* prämenstruelles Syndrom *nt*
premier [ˈprɛmɪəʳ] *adj* (*best*) beste(r, s), bedeutendste(r, s) ▷ *n* (*Pol*) Premierminister(in) *m(f)*
premiere [ˈprɛmɪɛəʳ] *n* Premiere *f*
premise [ˈprɛmɪs] *n* (*of argument*) Voraussetzung *f*; **premises** *npl* (*of business etc*) Räumlichkeiten *pl*; **on the ~s** im Hause
premium [ˈpriːmɪəm] *n* (*Comm, Insurance*) Prämie *f*; **to be at a ~** (*expensive*) zum Höchstpreis gehandelt werden; (*hard to get*) Mangelware sein
premium bond (*Brit*) *n* Prämienanleihe *f*; *siehe Info-Artikel*

PREMIUM BONDS

Premium bonds, eigentlich *premium savings bonds*, sind Lotterieaktien, die seit 1956 vom britischen Finanzministerium ausgegeben werden und keine Zinsen bringen, sondern stattdessen an einer monatlichen Auslosung teilnehmen. Die Gewinnnummern für die verschiedenen Geldpreise werden in Blackpool von einem Computer namens „ERNIE" (Electronic Random Number Indicator Equipment) ermittelt.

premium gasoline (*US*) *n* Super(benzin) *nt*
premonition [prɛməˈnɪʃən] *n* Vorahnung *f*
preoccupation [priːɔkjuˈpeɪʃən] *n*: **~ with** (vorrangige) Beschäftigung mit
preoccupied [priːˈɔkjupaɪd] *adj* (*thoughtful*) gedankenverloren; (*with work, family*) beschäftigt
prep [prɛp] (*Scol*) *adj* (*= preparatory*) *see* **prep school** ▷ *n* (*= preparation*) Hausaufgaben *pl*
prepaid [priːˈpeɪd] *adj* (*paid in advance*) im Voraus bezahlt; (*envelope*) frankiert
preparation [prɛpəˈreɪʃən] *n* Vorbereitung *f*; (*food, medicine, cosmetic*) Zubereitung *f*; **preparations** *npl* Vorbereitungen *pl*; **in ~ for sth** als Vorbereitung für etw
preparatory [prɪˈpærətərɪ] *adj* vorbereitend; **~ to sth/to doing sth** als Vorbereitung für etw/, um etw zu tun
prepare [prɪˈpɛəʳ] *vt* vorbereiten; (*food, meal*) zubereiten ▷ *vi*: **to ~ for** sich vorbereiten auf *+acc*
prepared [prɪˈpɛəd] *adj*: **to be ~ to do sth** (*willing*) bereit sein, etw zu tun; **to be ~ for sth** (*ready*) auf etw *acc* vorbereitet sein
preponderance [prɪˈpɔndərns] *n* Übergewicht *nt*
preposition [prɛpəˈzɪʃən] *n* Präposition *f*
prepossessing [priːpəˈzɛsɪŋ] *adj* von angenehmer Erscheinung
preposterous [prɪˈpɔstərəs] *adj* grotesk, widersinnig
prep school *n* = **prep(aratory) school**; *siehe Info-Artikel*

PREP(ARATORY) SCHOOL

Prep(aratory) school ist in Großbritannien eine meist private Schule für Kinder im Alter von 7 bis 13 Jahren, die auf eine weiterführende Privatschule vorbereiten soll.

prerecorded [ˈpriːrɪˈkɔːdɪd] *adj* (*broadcast*) aufgezeichnet; (*cassette, video*) bespielt
prerequisite [priːˈrɛkwɪzɪt] *n* Vorbedingung *f*, Grundvoraussetzung *f*
prerogative [prɪˈrɔgətɪv] *n* Vorrecht *nt*, Privileg *nt*
Presbyterian [prɛzbɪˈtɪərɪən] *adj* presbyterianisch ▷ *n* Presbyterianer(in) *m(f)*
presbytery [ˈprɛzbɪtərɪ] *n* Pfarrhaus *nt*
preschool [ˈpriːˈskuːl] *adj* (*age, child, education*) Vorschul-
prescribe [prɪˈskraɪb] *vt* (*Med*) verschreiben; (*demand*) anordnen, vorschreiben
prescribed *adj* (*duties, period*) vorgeschrieben
prescription [prɪˈskrɪpʃən] *n* (*Med: slip of paper*) Rezept *nt*; (*: medicine*) Medikament *nt*; **to make up a ~, to fill a ~** (*US*) ein Medikament zubereiten; **"only available on ~"** „rezeptpflichtig"
prescription charges (*Brit*) *npl* Rezeptgebühr *f*
prescriptive [prɪˈskrɪptɪv] *adj* normativ
presence [ˈprɛzns] *n* Gegenwart *f*, Anwesenheit *f*; (*fig: personality*) Ausstrahlung *f*; (*spirit, invisible influence*) Erscheinung *f*; **in sb's ~** in jds *dat* Gegenwart *or* Beisein; **~ of mind** Geistesgegenwart *f*
present [*adj, n* ˈprɛznt, *vt* prɪˈzɛnt] *adj* (*current*) gegenwärtig, derzeitig; (*in attendance*) anwesend ▷ *n* (*gift*) Geschenk *nt*; (*Ling: also:* **present tense**) Präsens *nt*, Gegenwart *f* ▷ *vt* (*give: prize etc*) überreichen; (*plan, report*) vorlegen; (*cause, provide, portray*) darstellen; (*information, view*) darlegen; (*Radio, TV*) leiten; **to be ~ at** anwesend *or* zugegen sein bei; **those ~** die Anwesenden; **to give sb a ~** jdm ein Geschenk geben; **the ~** (*actuality*) die Gegenwart; **at ~** gegenwärtig, im Augenblick; **to ~ sth to sb, ~ sb with sth** jdm etw übergeben *or* überreichen; **to ~ sb (to)** (*formally: introduce*) jdn vorstellen *+dat*; **to ~ itself** (*opportunity*) sich bieten
presentable [prɪˈzɛntəbl] *adj* (*person*) präsentabel, ansehnlich
presentation [prɛznˈteɪʃən] *n* (*of prize*) Überreichung *f*; (*of plan, report etc*) Vorlage *f*; (*appearance*) Erscheinungsbild *nt*; (*talk*) Vortrag *m*; **on ~ of** (*voucher etc*) gegen Vorlage *+gen*
present-day [ˈprɛzntdeɪ] *adj* heutig, gegenwärtig
presenter [prɪˈzɛntəʳ] *n* (*on radio, TV*) Moderator(in) *m(f)*
presently [ˈprɛzntlɪ] *adv* (*soon after*) gleich darauf; (*soon*) bald, in Kürze; (*currently*) derzeit,

gegenwärtig
present participle *n* Partizip *nt* Präsens
preservation [prɛzəˈveɪʃən] *n* (*of peace, standards etc*) Erhaltung *f*; (*of furniture, building*) Konservierung *f*
preservative [prɪˈzəːvətɪv] *n* Konservierungsmittel *nt*
preserve [prɪˈzəːv] *vt* erhalten; (*peace*) wahren; (*wood*) schützen; (*food*) konservieren ▷ *n* (*often pl: jam, chutney etc*) Eingemachte(s) *nt*; (*for game, fish*) Revier *nt*; **a male ~** (*fig*) eine männliche Domäne; **a working class ~** (*fig*) eine Domäne der Arbeiterklasse
preshrunk [ˈpriːˈʃrʌŋk] *adj* (*jeans etc*) vorgewaschen
preside [prɪˈzaɪd] *vi*: **to ~ over** (*meeting etc*) vorsitzen +*dat*, den Vorsitz haben bei
presidency [ˈprɛzɪdənsɪ] *n* (*Pol*) Präsidentschaft *f*; (*US: of company*) Vorsitz *m*
president [ˈprɛzɪdənt] *n* (*Pol*) Präsident(in) *m(f)*; (*of organization*) Vorsitzende(r) *f(m)*
presidential [prɛzɪˈdɛnʃl] *adj* (*election, campaign etc*) Präsidentschafts-; (*adviser, representative etc*) des Präsidenten
press [prɛs] *n* (*also*: **printing press**) Presse *f*; (*of switch, bell*) Druck *m*; (*for wine*) Kelter *f* ▷ *vt* drücken, pressen; (*button, sb's hand etc*) drücken; (*iron: clothes*) bügeln; (*put pressure on: person*) drängen; (*pursue: idea, claim*) vertreten ▷ *vi* (*squeeze*) drücken, pressen; **the P~** (*newspapers, journalists*) die Presse; **to go to ~** (*newspaper*) in Druck gehen; **to be in ~** (*at the printer's*) im Druck sein; **to be in the ~** (*in the newspapers*) in der Zeitung stehen; **at the ~ of a button** auf Knopfdruck; **to ~ sth (up)on sb** (*force*) jdm etw aufdrängen; **we are ~ed for time/money** wir sind in Geldnot/Zeitnot; **to ~ sb for an answer** auf jds *acc* Antwort drängen; **to ~ sb to do** *or* **into doing sth** jdn drängen, etw zu tun; **to ~ charges (against sb)** (*Law*) Klage (gegen jdn) erheben; **to ~ for** (*changes etc*) drängen auf +*acc*
▸ **press ahead** *vi* weitermachen; **to ~ ahead with sth** etw durchziehen
▸ **press on** *vi* weitermachen
press agency *n* Presseagentur *f*
press clipping *n* Zeitungsausschnitt *m*
press conference *n* Pressekonferenz *f*
press cutting *n* = **press clipping**
press-gang [ˈprɛsgæŋ] *vt*: **to ~ sb into doing sth** jdn bedrängen, etw zu tun
pressing [ˈprɛsɪŋ] *adj* (*urgent*) dringend
press officer *n* Pressesprecher(in) *m(f)*
press release *n* Pressemitteilung *f*
press stud (*Brit*) *n* Druckknopf *m*
press-up [ˈprɛsʌp] (*Brit*) *n* Liegestütz *m*
pressure [ˈprɛʃə^r] *n* (*also fig*) Druck *m* ▷ *vt*: **to ~ sb to do sth** jdn dazu drängen, etw zu tun; **to put ~ on sb (to do sth)** Druck auf jdn ausüben(, etw zu tun); **high/low ~** (*Tech, Met*) Hoch-/Tiefdruck *m*
pressure cooker *n* Schnellkochtopf *m*
pressure gauge *n* Druckmesser *m*, Manometer *nt*
pressure group *n* Interessenverband *m*, Pressuregroup *f*
pressurize [ˈprɛʃəraɪz] *vt*: **to ~ sb (to do sth** *or* **into doing sth)** jdn unter Druck setzen(, etw zu tun)
pressurized [ˈprɛʃəraɪzd] *adj* (*cabin, container etc*) Druck-
Prestel® [ˈprɛstɛl] *n* ≈ Bildschirmtext *m*, Btx *nt*
prestige [prɛsˈtiːʒ] *n* Prestige *nt*
prestigious [prɛsˈtɪdʒəs] *adj* (*institution, appointment*) mit hohem Prestigewert
presumably [prɪˈzjuːməblɪ] *adv* vermutlich; **~ he did it** vermutlich *or* wahrscheinlich hat er es getan
presume [prɪˈzjuːm] *vt*: **to ~ (that)** (*assume*) annehmen(, dass); **to ~ to do sth** (*dare*) sich anmaßen, etw zu tun; **I ~ so** das nehme ich an
presumption [prɪˈzʌmpʃən] *n* (*supposition*) Annahme *f*; (*audacity*) Anmaßung *f*
presumptuous [prɪˈzʌmpʃəs] *adj* anmaßend
presuppose [priːsəˈpəuz] *vt* voraussetzen
presupposition [priːsʌpəˈzɪʃən] *n* Voraussetzung *f*
pretax [priːˈtæks] *adj* (*profit*) vor (Abzug der) Steuern
pretence, (*US*) **pretense** [prɪˈtɛns] *n* (*false appearance*) Vortäuschung *f*; **under false ~s** unter Vorspiegelung falscher Tatsachen; **she is devoid of all ~** sie ist völlig natürlich; **to make a ~ of doing sth** vortäuschen, etw zu tun
pretend [prɪˈtɛnd] *vt* (*feign*) vorgeben ▷ *vi* (*feign*) sich verstellen, so tun, als ob; **I don't ~ to understand it** (*claim*) ich erhebe nicht den Anspruch, es zu verstehen
pretense [prɪˈtɛns] (*US*) *n* = **pretence**
pretentious [prɪˈtɛnʃəs] *adj* anmaßend
preterite [ˈprɛtərɪt] *n* Imperfekt *nt*, Präteritum *nt*
pretext [ˈpriːtɛkst] *n* Vorwand *m*; **on** *or* **under the ~ of doing sth** unter dem Vorwand, etw zu tun
pretty [ˈprɪtɪ] *adj* hübsch, nett ▷ *adv*: **~ clever** ganz schön schlau; **~ good** ganz gut
prevail [prɪˈveɪl] *vi* (*be current*) vorherrschen; (*triumph*) siegen; **to ~ (up)on sb to do sth** (*persuade*) jdn dazu bewegen *or* überreden, etw zu tun
prevailing [prɪˈveɪlɪŋ] *adj* (*wind, fashion etc*) vorherrschend
prevalent [ˈprɛvələnt] *adj* (*belief, custom*) vorherrschend
prevaricate [prɪˈværɪkeɪt] *vi* (*by saying sth*) Ausflüchte machen; (*by doing sth*) Ausweichmanöver machen
prevarication [prɪværɪˈkeɪʃən] *n* (*see vi*) Ausflucht *f*; Ausweichmanöver *nt*
prevent [prɪˈvɛnt] *vt* verhindern; **to ~ sb from doing sth** jdn daran hindern, etw zu tun; **to ~ sth from happening** verhindern, dass etw geschieht
preventable [prɪˈvɛntəbl] *adj* verhütbar,

vermeidbar

preventative [prɪ'vɛntətɪv] *adj* = **preventive**

prevention [prɪ'vɛnʃən] *n* Verhütung *f*

preventive [prɪ'vɛntɪv] *adj* (*measures, medicine*) vorbeugend

preview ['pri:vju:] *n* (*of film*) Vorpremiere *f*; (*of exhibition*) Vernissage *f*

previous ['pri:vɪəs] *adj* (*earlier*) früher; (*preceding*) vorhergehend; **~ to** vor *+dat*

previously ['pri:vɪəslɪ] *adv* (*before*) zuvor; (*formerly*) früher

prewar [pri:'wɔ:ʳ] *adj* (*period*) Vorkriegs-

prey [preɪ] *n* Beute *f*; **to fall ~ to** (*fig*) zum Opfer fallen *+dat*
▸ **prey on** *vt fus* (*animal*) Jagd machen auf *+acc*; **it was ~ing on his mind** es ließ ihn nicht los

price [praɪs] *n* (*also fig*) Preis *m* ▹ *vt* (*goods*) auszeichnen; **what is the ~ of ...?** was kostet ...?; **to go up** *or* **rise in ~** im Preis steigen, teurer werden; **to put a ~ on sth** (*also fig*) einen Preis für etw festsetzen; **what ~ his promises now?** wie steht es jetzt mit seinen Versprechungen?; **he regained his freedom, but at a ~** er hat seine Freiheit wieder, aber zu welchem Preis!; **to be ~d at £30** £30 kosten; **to ~ o.s. out of the market** durch zu hohe Preise konkurrenzunfähig werden

price control *n* Preiskontrolle *f*

price-cutting ['praɪskʌtɪŋ] *n* Preissenkungen *pl*

priceless ['praɪslɪs] *adj* (*diamond, painting*) von unschätzbarem Wert; (*inf: amusing*) unbezahlbar, köstlich

price list *n* Preisliste *f*

price range *n* Preisklasse *f*; **it's within my ~** ich kann es mir leisten

price tag *n* Preisschild *nt*; (*fig*) Preis *m*

price war *n* Preiskrieg *m*

pricey ['praɪsɪ] (*inf*) *adj* kostspielig

prick [prɪk] *n* (*sting*) Stich *m*; (*inf!: penis*) Schwanz *m*; (*: idiot*) Arsch *m* ▹ *vt* stechen; (*sausage, balloon*) einstechen; **to ~ up one's ears** die Ohren spitzen

prickle ['prɪkl] *n* (*of plant*) Dorn *m*, Stachel *m*; (*sensation*) Prickeln *nt*

prickly ['prɪklɪ] *adj* (*plant*) stachelig; (*fabric*) kratzig

prickly heat *n* Hitzebläschen *pl*

prickly pear *n* Feigenkaktus *m*

pride [praɪd] *n* Stolz *m*; (*pej: arrogance*) Hochmut *m* ▹ *vt*: **to ~ o.s. on** sich rühmen *+gen*; **to take (a) ~ in** stolz sein auf *+acc*; **to take a ~ in doing sth** etw mit Stolz tun; **to have** *or* **take ~ of place** (*Brit*) die Krönung sein

priest [pri:st] *n* Priester *m*

priestess ['pri:stɪs] *n* Priesterin *f*

priesthood ['pri:sthud] *n* Priestertum *nt*

prig [prɪg] *n*: **he's a ~** er hält sich für ein Tugendlamm

prim [prɪm] (*pej*) *adj* (*person*) etepetete

primacy ['praɪməsɪ] *n* (*supremacy*) Vorrang *m*; (*position*) Vorrangstellung *f*

prima-facie ['praɪmə'feɪʃɪ] *adj*: **to have a ~ case** (*Law*) eine gute Beweisgrundlage haben

primal ['praɪməl] *adj* ursprünglich; **~ scream** Urschrei *m*

primarily ['praɪmərɪlɪ] *adv* in erster Linie, hauptsächlich

primary ['praɪmərɪ] *adj* (*principal*) Haupt-, hauptsächlich; (*education, teacher*) Grundschul- ▹ *n* (*US: election*) Vorwahl *f*; *siehe Info-Artikel*

PRIMARY

Als *primary* wird im amerikanischen Präsidentschaftswahlkampf eine Vorwahl bezeichnet, die mitentscheidet, welche Präsidentschaftskandidaten die beiden großen Parteien aufstellen. Vorwahlen werden nach komplizierten Regeln von Februar (New Hampshire) bis Juni in etwa 35 Staaten abgehalten. Der von den Kandidaten in den primaries erzielte Stimmenanteil bestimmt, wie viele Abgeordnete bei der endgültigen Auswahl der demokratischen bzw. republikanischen Kandidaten auf den nationalen Parteitagen im Juli/August für sie stimmen.

primary colour *n* Primärfarbe *f*

primary school (*Brit*) *n* Grundschule *f*; *siehe Info-Artikel*

PRIMARY SCHOOL

Primary school ist in Großbritannien eine Grundschule für Kinder im Alter von 5 bis 11 Jahren. Oft wird sie aufgeteilt in „infant school" (5 bis 7 Jahre) und „junior school" (7 bis 11 Jahre). Siehe auch *secondary school*.

primate ['praɪmɪt] *n* (*Zool*) Primat *m*; (*Rel*) Primas *m*

prime [praɪm] *adj* (*most important*) oberste(r, s); (*best quality*) erstklassig ▹ *n* (*of person's life*) die besten Jahre *pl* ▹ *vt* (*wood*) grundieren; (*fig: person*) informieren; (*gun*) schussbereit machen; (*pump*) auffüllen; **~ example** erstklassiges Beispiel; **in the ~ of life** im besten Alter

Prime Minister *n* Premierminister(in) *m(f)*

primer ['praɪməʳ] *n* (*paint*) Grundierung *f*; (*book*) Einführung *f*

prime time *n* (*Radio, TV*) Hauptsendezeit *f*

primeval [praɪ'mi:vl] *adj* (*beast*) urzeitlich; (*fig: feelings*) instinktiv; **~ forest** Urwald *m*

primitive ['prɪmɪtɪv] *adj* (*tribe, tool, conditions etc*) primitiv; (*life form, machine etc*) frühzeitlich; (*man*) der Urzeit

primrose ['prɪmrəuz] *n* Primel *f*, gelbe Schlüsselblume *f*

primula ['prɪmjulə] *n* Primel *f*

Primus® ['praɪməs], **Primus stove** (*Brit*) *n* Primuskocher *m*

prince [prɪns] *n* Prinz *m*

Prince Charming *(hum)* *n* Märchenprinz *m*
princess [prɪn'sɛs] *n* Prinzessin *f*
principal ['prɪnsɪpl] *adj* *(most important)* Haupt-, wichtigste(r, s) ▷ *n* *(of school, college)* Rektor(in) *m(f)*; *(Theat)* Hauptdarsteller(in) *m(f)*; *(Fin)* Kapitalsumme *f*
principality [prɪnsɪ'pælɪtɪ] *n* Fürstentum *nt*
principally ['prɪnsɪplɪ] *adv* vornehmlich
principle ['prɪnsɪpl] *n* Prinzip *nt*; **in ~** im Prinzip, prinzipiell; **on ~** aus Prinzip
print [prɪnt] *n* *(Art)* Druck *m*; *(Phot)* Abzug *m*; *(fabric)* bedruckter Stoff *m* ▷ *vt* *(produce)* drucken; *(publish)* veröffentlichen; *(cloth, pattern)* bedrucken; *(write in capitals)* in Druckschrift schreiben; **prints** *npl* *(fingerprints etc)* Abdrücke *pl*; **out of ~** vergriffen; **in ~** erhältlich; **the fine** *or* **small ~** das Kleingedruckte
▸ **print out** *vt* *(Comput)* ausdrucken
printed circuit ['prɪntɪd-] *n* gedruckte Schaltung *f*
printed circuit board *n* Leiterplatte *f*
printed matter *n* Drucksache *f*
printer ['prɪntə[r]] *n* *(person)* Drucker(in) *m(f)*; *(firm)* Druckerei *f*; *(machine)* Drucker *m*
printhead ['prɪnthɛd] *n* Druckkopf *m*
printing ['prɪntɪŋ] *n* *(activity)* Drucken *nt*
printing press *n* Druckerpresse *f*
print-out ['prɪntaut] *(Comput)* *n* Ausdruck *m*
print run *n* Auflage *f*
printwheel ['prɪntwi:l] *n* *(Comput)* Typenrad *nt*
prior ['praɪə[r]] *adj* *(previous: knowledge, warning)* vorherig; *(: engagement)* früher; *(more important: claim, duty)* vorrangig ▷ *n* *(Rel)* Prior *m*; **without ~ notice** ohne vorherige Ankündigung; **to have a ~ claim on sth** ein Vorrecht auf etw *acc* haben; **~ to** vor *+dat*
priority [praɪ'ɔrɪtɪ] *n* vorrangige Angelegenheit *f*; **priorities** *npl* Prioritäten *pl*; **to take** *or* **have ~ (over sth)** Vorrang (vor etw *dat*) haben; **to give ~ to sb/sth** jdm/etw Vorrang einräumen
priory ['praɪərɪ] *n* Kloster *nt*
prise [praɪz] *(Brit)* *vt*: **to ~ open** aufbrechen
prism ['prɪzəm] *n* Prisma *nt*
prison ['prɪzn] *n* Gefängnis *nt* ▷ *cpd* *(officer, food, cell etc)* Gefängnis-
prison camp *n* Gefangenenlager *nt*
prisoner ['prɪznə[r]] *n* Gefangene(r) *f(m)*; **the ~ at the bar** *(Law)* der/die Angeklagte; **to take sb ~** jdn gefangen nehmen
prisoner of war *n* Kriegsgefangene(r) *f(m)*
prissy ['prɪsɪ] *(pej)* *adj* zimperlich
pristine ['prɪsti:n] *adj* makellos; **in ~ condition** in makellosem Zustand
privacy ['prɪvəsɪ] *n* Privatsphäre *f*
private ['praɪvɪt] *adj* privat; *(life)* Privat-; *(thoughts, plans etc)* persönlich; *(place)* abgelegen; *(secretive: person)* verschlossen ▷ *n* *(Mil)* Gefreite(r) *m*; **"~"** *(on envelope)* „vertraulich"; *(on door)* „privat"; **in ~** privat; **in (his) ~ life** in seinem Privatleben; **to be in ~ practice** *(Med)* Privatpatienten haben; **~ hearing** *(Law)* nicht öffentliche Verhandlung *f*
private enterprise *n* Privatunternehmen *nt*
private eye *n* Privatdetektiv *m*
private limited company *(Brit)* *n* *(Comm)* ≈ Aktiengesellschaft *f*
privately ['praɪvɪtlɪ] *adv* privat; *(secretly)* insgeheim; **a ~ owned company** eine Firma im Privatbesitz
private parts *npl* *(Anat)* Geschlechtsteile *pl*
private property *n* Privatbesitz *m*
private school *n* *(fee-paying)* Privatschule *f*
privation [praɪ'veɪʃən] *n* Not *f*
privatize ['praɪvɪtaɪz] *vt* privatisieren
privet ['prɪvɪt] *n* Liguster *m*
privilege ['prɪvɪlɪdʒ] *n* *(advantage)* Privileg *nt*; *(honour)* Ehre *f*
privileged ['prɪvɪlɪdʒd] *adj* privilegiert; **to be ~ to do sth** das Privileg *or* die Ehre haben, etw zu tun
privy ['prɪvɪ] *adj*: **to be ~ to** eingeweiht sein in *+acc*

PRIVY COUNCIL

Privy Council ist eine Gruppe von königlichen Beratern, die ihren Ursprung im normannischen England hat. Heute hat dieser Rat eine rein formale Funktion. Kabinettsmitglieder und andere bedeutende politische, kirchliche oder juristische Persönlichkeiten sind automatisch Mitglieder.

Privy Councillor *(Brit)* *n* Geheimer Rat *m*
prize [praɪz] *n* Preis *m* ▷ *adj* *(prize-winning)* preisgekrönt; *(classic: example)* erstklassig ▷ *vt* schätzen; **~ idiot** *(inf)* Vollidiot *m*
prizefighter ['praɪzfaɪtə[r]] *n* Preisboxer *m*
prizegiving ['praɪzgɪvɪŋ] *n* Preisverleihung *f*
prize money *n* Geldpreis *m*
prizewinner ['praɪzwɪnə[r]] *n* Preisträger(in) *m(f)*
prizewinning ['praɪzwɪnɪŋ] *adj* preisgekrönt
PRO *n abbr* = **public relations officer**
pro [prəu] *n* *(Sport)* Profi *m* ▷ *prep* *(in favour of)* pro *+acc*, für *+acc*; **the ~s and cons** das Für und Wider
pro- [prəu] *pref* *(in favour of)* Pro-, pro-; **~disarmament campaign** Kampagne *f* für Abrüstung
proactive [prəu'æktɪv] *adj* proaktiv
probability [prɔbə'bɪlɪtɪ] *n* Wahrscheinlichkeit *f*; **in all ~** aller Wahrscheinlichkeit nach
probable ['prɔbəbl] *adj* wahrscheinlich; **it seems ~ that ...** es ist wahrscheinlich, dass ...
probably ['prɔbəblɪ] *adv* wahrscheinlich
probate ['prəubɪt] *n* gerichtliche Testamentsbestätigung *f*
probation [prə'beɪʃən] *n*: **on ~** *(lawbreaker)* auf Bewährung; *(employee)* auf Probe
probationary [prə'beɪʃənrɪ] *adj* *(period)* Probe-

probationer [prəˈbeɪʃənəʳ] *n* (*nurse*: *female*) Lernschwester *f*; (: *male*) Lernpfleger *m*
probation officer *n* Bewährungshelfer(in) *m(f)*
probe [prəub] *n* (*Med, Space*) Sonde *f*; (*enquiry*) Untersuchung *f* ▷ *vt* (*investigate*) untersuchen; (*poke*) bohren in *+dat*
probity [ˈprəubɪtɪ] *n* Rechtschaffenheit *f*
problem [ˈprɔbləm] *n* Problem *nt*; **to have ~s with the car** Probleme *or* Schwierigkeiten mit dem Auto haben; **what's the ~?** wo fehlts?; **I had no ~ finding her** ich habe sie ohne Schwierigkeiten gefunden; **no ~!** kein Problem!
problematic [prɔbləˈmætɪk], **problematical** [prɔbləˈmætɪkl] *adj* problematisch
problem-solving [ˈprɔbləmsɔlvɪŋ] *adj* (*skills, ability*) zur Problemlösung ▷ *n* Problemlösung *f*
procedural [prəˈsiːdjurəl] *adj* (*agreement, problem*) verfahrensmäßig
procedure [prəˈsiːdʒəʳ] *n* Verfahren *nt*
proceed [prəˈsiːd] *vi* (*carry on*) fortfahren; (*person*: *go*) sich bewegen; **to ~ to do sth** etw tun; **to ~ with** fortfahren mit; **I am not sure how to ~** ich bin nicht sicher über die weitere Vorgehensweise; **to ~ against sb** (*Law*) gegen jdn gerichtlich vorgehen
proceedings [prəˈsiːdɪŋz] *npl* (*organized events*) Vorgänge *pl*; (*Law*) Verfahren *nt*; (*records*) Protokoll *nt*
proceeds [ˈprəusiːdz] *npl* Erlös *m*
process [ˈprəusɛs] *n* (*series of actions*) Verfahren *nt*; (*Biol, Chem*) Prozess *m* ▷ *vt* (*raw materials, food, Comput*: *data*) verarbeiten; (*application*) bearbeiten; (*Phot*) entwickeln; **in the ~** dabei; **to be in the ~ of doing sth** (gerade) dabei sein, etw zu tun
processed cheese [ˈprəusɛst-], (*US*) **process cheese** *n* Schmelzkäse *m*
processing [ˈprəusɛsɪŋ] *n* (*Phot*) Entwickeln *nt*
procession [prəˈsɛʃən] *n* Umzug *m*, Prozession *f*; **wedding/funeral ~** Hochzeits-/Trauerzug *m*
proclaim [prəˈkleɪm] *vt* verkünden, proklamieren
proclamation [prɔkləˈmeɪʃən] *n* Proklamation *f*
proclivity [prəˈklɪvɪtɪ] (*form*) *n* Vorliebe *f*
procrastinate [prəuˈkræstɪneɪt] *vi* zögern, zaudern
procrastination [prəukræstɪˈneɪʃən] *n* Zögern *nt*, Zaudern *nt*
procreation [prəukrɪˈeɪʃən] *n* Fortpflanzung *f*
procurator fiscal [ˈprɔkjureɪtə-] *n* (*pl* **procurators fiscal**) (*Scot*) ≈ Staatsanwalt *m*, ≈ Staatsanwältin *f*
procure [prəˈkjuəʳ] *vt* (*obtain*) beschaffen
procurement [prəˈkjuəmənt] *n* (*Comm*) Beschaffung *f*
prod [prɔd] *vt* (*push*: *with finger, stick etc*) stoßen, stupsen (*inf*); (*fig*: *urge*) anspornen ▷ *n* (*with finger, stick etc*) Stoß *m*, Stups *m* (*inf*); (*fig*: *reminder*) mahnender Hinweis *m*
prodigal [ˈprɔdɪgl] *adj*: **~ son** verlorener Sohn *m*
prodigious [prəˈdɪdʒəs] *adj* (*cost, memory*) ungeheuer
prodigy [ˈprɔdɪdʒɪ] *n* (*person*) Naturtalent *nt*; **child ~** Wunderkind *nt*
produce [*n* ˈprɔdjuːs, *vt* prəˈdjuːs] *n* (*Agr*) (Boden)produkte *pl* ▷ *vt* (*result etc*) hervorbringen; (*goods, commodity*) produzieren, herstellen; (*Biol, Chem*) erzeugen; (*fig*: *evidence etc*) liefern; (: *passport etc*) vorlegen; (*play, film, programme*) produzieren
producer [prəˈdjuːsəʳ] *n* (*person*) Produzent(in) *m(f)*; (*country, company*) Produzent *m*, Hersteller *m*
product [ˈprɔdʌkt] *n* Produkt *nt*
production [prəˈdʌkʃən] *n* Produktion *f*; (*Theat*) Inszenierung *f*; **to go into ~** (*goods*) in Produktion gehen; **on ~ of** gegen Vorlage *+gen*
production agreement (*US*) *n* Produktivitätsabkommen *nt*
production line *n* Fließband *nt*, Fertigungsstraße *f*
production manager *n* Produktionsleiter(in) *m(f)*
productive [prəˈdʌktɪv] *adj* produktiv
productivity [prɔdʌkˈtɪvɪtɪ] *n* Produktivität *f*
productivity agreement (*Brit*) *n* Produktivitätsabkommen *nt*
productivity bonus *n* Leistungszulage *f*
Prof. *n abbr* (= *professor*) Prof.
profane [prəˈfeɪn] *adj* (*language etc*) profan; (*secular*) weltlich
profess [prəˈfɛs] *vt* (*claim*) vorgeben; (*express*: *feeling, opinion*) zeigen, bekunden; **I do not ~ to be an expert** ich behaupte nicht, ein Experte zu sein
professed [prəˈfɛst] *adj* (*self-declared*) erklärt
profession [prəˈfɛʃən] *n* Beruf *m*; (*people*) Berufsstand *m*; **the ~s** die gehobenen Berufe
professional [prəˈfɛʃənl] *adj* (*organization, musician etc*) Berufs-; (*misconduct, advice*) beruflich; (*skilful*) professionell ▷ *n* (*doctor, lawyer, teacher etc*) Fachmann *m*, Fachfrau *f*; (*Sport*) Profi *m*; (*skilled person*) Experte *m*, Expertin *f*; **to seek ~ advice** fachmännischen Rat einholen
professionalism [prəˈfɛʃnəlɪzəm] *n* fachliches Können *nt*
professionally [prəˈfɛʃnəlɪ] *adv* beruflich; (*for a living*) berufsmäßig; **I only know him ~** ich kenne ihn nur beruflich
professor [prəˈfɛsəʳ] *n* (*Brit*) Professor(in) *m(f)*; (*US, Canada*) Dozent(in) *m(f)*
professorship [prəˈfɛsəʃɪp] *n* Professur *f*
proffer [ˈprɔfəʳ] *vt* (*advice, drink, one's hand*) anbieten; (*apologies*) aussprechen; (*plate etc*) hinhalten
proficiency [prəˈfɪʃənsɪ] *n* Können *nt*, Fertigkeiten *pl*
proficient [prəˈfɪʃənt] *adj* fähig; **to be ~ at** *or* **in** gut sein in *+dat*
profile [ˈprəufaɪl] *n* (*of person's face*) Profil *nt*; (*fig*: *biography*) Porträt *nt*; **to keep a low ~** (*fig*)

sich zurückhalten; **to have a high ~** (*fig*) eine große Rolle spielen

profit ['prɔfɪt] *n* (*Comm*) Gewinn *m*, Profit *m* ▷ *vi*: **to ~ by** *or* **from** (*fig*) profitieren von; **~ and loss account** Gewinn-und-Verlust-Rechnung; **to make a ~** einen Gewinn machen; **to sell (sth) at a ~** (etw) mit Gewinn verkaufen

profitability [prɔfɪtə'bɪlɪtɪ] *n* Rentabilität *f*

profitable ['prɔfɪtəbl] *adj* (*business, deal*) rentabel, einträglich; (*fig: useful*) nützlich

profit centre *n* Bilanzabteilung *f*

profiteering [prɔfɪ'tɪərɪŋ] (*pej*) *n* Profitmacherei *f*

profit-making ['prɔfɪtmeɪkɪŋ] *adj* (*organization*) gewinnorientiert

profit margin *n* Gewinnspanne *f*

profit-sharing ['prɔfɪtʃɛərɪŋ] *n* Gewinnbeteiligung *f*

profits tax (*Brit*) *n* Ertragssteuer *f*

profligate ['prɔflɪgɪt] *adj* (*person, spending*) verschwenderisch; (*waste*) sinnlos; **~ with** (*extravagant*) verschwenderisch mit

pro forma ['prəu'fɔːmə] *adj*: **~ invoice** Pro-forma-Rechnung *f*

profound [prə'faund] *adj* (*shock*) schwer, tief; (*effect, differences*) weitreichend; (*idea, book*) tief schürfend

profuse [prə'fjuːs] *adj* (*apologies*) überschwänglich

profusely [prə'fjuːslɪ] *adv* (*apologise, thank*) vielmals; (*sweat, bleed*) stark

profusion [prə'fjuːʒən] *n* Überfülle *f*

progeny ['prɔdʒɪnɪ] *n* Nachkommenschaft *f*

prognoses [prɔg'nəusiːz] *npl of* **prognosis**

prognosis [prɔg'nəusɪs] (*pl* **prognoses**) *n* (*Med, fig*) Prognose *f*

program ['prəugræm] (*Comput*) *n* Programm *nt* ▷ *vt* programmieren

programme, (*US*) **program** ['prəugræm] *n* Programm *nt* ▷ *vt* (*machine, system*) programmieren

programmer ['prəugræməʳ] *n* Programmierer(in) *m(f)*

programming, (*US*) **programing** ['prəugræmɪŋ] *n* Programmierung *f*

programming language *n* Programmiersprache *f*

progress [*n* 'prəugrɛs, *vi* prə'grɛs] *n* Fortschritt *m*; (*improvement*) Fortschritte *pl* ▷ *vi* (*advance*) vorankommen; (*become higher in rank*) aufsteigen; (*continue*) sich fortsetzen; **in ~** (*meeting, battle, match*) im Gange; **to make ~** Fortschritte machen

progression [prə'grɛʃən] *n* (*development*) Fortschritt *m*, Entwicklung *f*; (*series*) Folge *f*

progressive [prə'grɛsɪv] *adj* (*enlightened*) progressiv, fortschrittlich; (*gradual*) fortschreitend

progressively [prə'grɛsɪvlɪ] *adv* (*gradually*) zunehmend

progress report *n* (*Med*) Fortschrittsbericht *m*; (*Admin*) Tätigkeitsbericht *m*

prohibit [prə'hɪbɪt] *vt* (*ban*) verbieten; **to ~ sb from doing sth** jdm verbieten *or* untersagen, etw zu tun; **"smoking ~ed"** „Rauchen verboten"

prohibition [prəuɪ'bɪʃən] *n* Verbot *nt*; **P~** (*US*) Prohibition *f*

prohibitive [prə'hɪbɪtɪv] *adj* (*cost etc*) untragbar

project [*n* 'prɔdʒɛkt, *vt, vi* prə'dʒɛkt] *n* (*plan, scheme*) Projekt *nt*; (*Scol*) Referat *nt* ▷ *vt* (*plan*) planen; (*estimate*) schätzen, voraussagen; (*light, film, picture*) projizieren ▷ *vi* (*stick out*) hervorragen

projectile [prə'dʒɛktaɪl] *n* Projektil *nt*, Geschoss *nt*, Geschoß *nt* (*Österr*)

projection [prə'dʒɛkʃən] *n* (*estimate*) Schätzung *f*, Voraussage *f*; (*overhang*) Vorsprung *m*; (*Cine*) Projektion *f*

projectionist [prə'dʒɛkʃənɪst] *n* Filmvorführer(in) *m(f)*

projection room *n* Vorführraum *m*

projector [prə'dʒɛktəʳ] *n* Projektor *m*

proletarian [prəulɪ'tɛərɪən] *adj* proletarisch

proletariat [prəulɪ'tɛərɪət] *n*: **the ~** das Proletariat

proliferate [prə'lɪfəreɪt] *vi* sich vermehren

proliferation [prəlɪfə'reɪʃən] *n* Vermehrung *f*, Verbreitung *f*

prolific [prə'lɪfɪk] *adj* (*artist, writer*) produktiv

prologue, (*US*) **prolog** ['prəulɔg] *n* (*of play, book*) Prolog *m*

prolong [prə'lɔŋ] *vt* verlängern

prom [prɔm] *n abbr* = **promenade**; (*Mus*) = **promenade concert**; (*US: college ball*) Studentenball *m*; *siehe Info-Artikel*

PROM

Prom (promenade concert) ist in Großbritannien ein Konzert, bei dem ein Teil der Zuhörer steht (ursprünglich spazieren ging). Die seit 1895 alljährlich stattfindenden Proms (seit 1941 immer in der Londoner Royal Albert Hall) zählen zu den bedeutendsten Musikereignissen in England. Der letzte Abend der Proms steht ganz im Zeichen des Patriotismus und gipfelt im Singen des Lieds „Land of Hope and Glory". In den USA und Kanada steht das Wort für *promenade*, ein Ball an einer *high school* oder einem *college*.

promenade [prɔmə'nɑːd] *n* Promenade *f*

promenade concert (*Brit*) *n* Promenadenkonzert *nt*

promenade deck *n* Promenadendeck *nt*

prominence ['prɔmɪnəns] *n* (*importance*) Bedeutung *f*; **to rise to ~** bekannt werden

prominent ['prɔmɪnənt] *adj* (*person*) prominent; (*thing*) bedeutend; (*very noticeable*) herausragend; **he is ~ in the field of science** er ist eine führende Persönlichkeit im naturwissenschaftlichen Bereich

prominently ['prɔmɪnəntlɪ] *adv* (*display, set*)

deutlich sichtbar; **he figured ~ in the case** er spielte in dem Fall eine bedeutende Rolle

promiscuity [prɔmɪs'kju:ɪtɪ] *n* Promiskuität *f*

promiscuous [prə'mɪskjuəs] *adj* promisk

promise ['prɔmɪs] *n* (*vow*) Versprechen *nt*; (*potential, hope*) Hoffnung *f* ▷ *vi* versprechen ▷ *vt*: **to ~ sb sth, ~ sth to sb** jdm etw versprechen; **to make/break/keep a ~** ein Versprechen geben/brechen/halten; **a young man of ~** ein vielversprechender junger Mann; **she shows ~** sie gibt zu Hoffnungen Anlass; **it ~s to be lively** es verspricht lebhaft zu werden; **to ~ (sb) to do sth** (jdm) versprechen, etw zu tun

promising ['prɔmɪsɪŋ] *adj* vielversprechend

promissory note ['prɔmɪsərɪ-] *n* Schuldschein *m*

promontory ['prɔməntrɪ] *n* Felsvorsprung *m*

promote [prə'məut] *vt* (*employee*) befördern; (*advertise*) werben für; (*encourage: peace etc*) fördern; **the team was ~d to the first division** (*Brit: Football*) die Mannschaft stieg in die erste Division auf

promoter [prə'məutə^r] *n* (*of concert, event*) Veranstalter(in) *m(f)*; (*of cause, idea*) Förderer *m*, Förderin *f*

promotion [prə'məuʃən] *n* (*at work*) Beförderung *f*; (*of product, event*) Werbung *f*; (*of idea*) Förderung *f*; (*publicity campaign*) Werbekampagne *f*

prompt [prɔmpt] *adj* prompt, sofortig ▷ *adv* (*exactly*) pünktlich ▷ *n* (*Comput*) Prompt *m* ▷ *vt* (*cause*) veranlassen; (*when talking*) auf die Sprünge helfen *+dat*; (*Theat*) soufflieren *+dat*; **they're very ~** (*punctual*) sie sind sehr pünktlich; **he was ~ to accept** er nahm unverzüglich an; **at 8 o'clock ~** (um) Punkt 8 Uhr; **to ~ sb to do sth** jdn dazu veranlassen, etw zu tun

prompter ['prɔmptə^r] *n* (*Theat*) Souffleur *m*, Souffleuse *f*

promptly ['prɔmptlɪ] *adv* (*immediately*) sofort; (*exactly*) pünktlich

promptness ['prɔmptnɪs] *n* Promptheit *f*

promulgate ['prɔməlgeɪt] *vt* (*policy*) bekannt machen, verkünden; (*idea*) verbreiten

prone [prəun] *adj* (*face down*) in Bauchlage; **to be ~ to sth** zu etw neigen; **she is ~ to burst into tears if ...** sie neigt dazu, in Tränen auszubrechen, wenn ...

prong [prɔŋ] *n* (*of fork*) Zinke *f*

pronoun ['prəunaun] *n* Pronomen *nt*, Fürwort *nt*

pronounce [prə'nauns] *vt* (*word*) aussprechen; (*give verdict, opinion*) erklären ▷ *vi*: **to ~ (up)on** sich äußern zu; **they ~d him dead/unfit to drive** sie erklärten ihn für tot/fahruntüchtig

pronounced [prə'naunst] *adj* (*noticeable*) ausgeprägt, deutlich

pronouncement [prə'naunsmənt] *n* Erklärung *f*

pronto ['prɔntəu] (*inf*) *adv* fix

pronunciation [prənʌnsɪ'eɪʃən] *n* Aussprache *f*

proof [pru:f] *n* (*evidence*) Beweis *m*; (*Typ*) (Korrektur)fahne *f* ▷ *adj*: **~ against** sicher vor *+dat*; **to be 70 % ~** (*alcohol*) ≈ einen Alkoholgehalt von 40% haben

proofreader ['pru:fri:də^r] *n* Korrektor(in) *m(f)*

Prop. *abbr* (*Comm: = proprietor*) Inh.

prop [prɔp] *n* (*support*) Stütze *f* ▷ *vt* (*lean*): **to ~ sth against sth** etw an etw *acc* lehnen

▶ **prop up** *vt sep* (*thing*) (ab)stützen; (*fig: government, industry*) unterstützen

propaganda [prɔpə'gændə] *n* Propaganda *f*

propagate ['prɔpəgeɪt] *vt* (*plants*) züchten; (*ideas etc*) propagieren ▷ *vi* (*plants, animals*) sich fortpflanzen

propagation [prɔpə'geɪʃən] *n* (*of ideas etc*) Propagierung *f*; (*of plants, animals*) Fortpflanzung *f*

propel [prə'pɛl] *vt* (*vehicle, machine*) antreiben; (*person*) schubsen; (*fig: person*) treiben

propeller [prə'pɛlə^r] *n* Propeller *m*

propelling pencil [prə'pɛlɪŋ-] (*Brit*) *n* Drehbleistift *m*

propensity [prə'pɛnsɪtɪ] *n*: **a ~ for** *or* **to sth** ein Hang *m or* eine Neigung zu etw; **to have a ~ to do sth** dazu neigen, etw zu tun

proper ['prɔpə^r] *adj* (*genuine, correct*) richtig; (*socially acceptable*) schicklich; (*inf: real*) echt; **the town/city ~** die Stadt selbst; **to go through the ~ channels** den Dienstweg einhalten

properly ['prɔpəlɪ] *adv* (*eat, work*) richtig; (*behave*) anständig

proper noun *n* Eigenname *m*

property ['prɔpətɪ] *n* (*possessions*) Eigentum *nt*; (*building and its land*) Grundstück *nt*; (*quality*) Eigenschaft *f*; **it's their ~** es gehört ihnen

property developer *n* ≈ Grundstücksmakler(in) *m(f)*

property market *n* Immobilienmarkt *m*

property owner *n* Grundbesitzer(in) *m(f)*

property tax *n* Vermögenssteuer *f*

prophecy ['prɔfɪsɪ] *n* Prophezeiung *f*

prophesy ['prɔfɪsaɪ] *vt* prophezeien ▷ *vi* Prophezeiungen machen

prophet ['prɔfɪt] *n* Prophet *m*; **~ of doom** Unheilsprophet(in) *m(f)*

prophetic [prə'fɛtɪk] *adj* prophetisch

proportion [prə'pɔ:ʃən] *n* (*part*) Teil *m*; (*number: of people, things*) Anteil *m*; (*ratio*) Verhältnis *nt*; **in ~ to** im Verhältnis zu; **to be out of all ~ to sth** in keinem Verhältnis zu etw stehen; **to get sth in/out of ~** etw im richtigen/falschen Verhältnis sehen; **a sense of ~** (*fig*) ein Sinn für das Wesentliche

proportional [prə'pɔ:ʃənl] *adj*: **~ to** proportional zu

proportional representation *n* Verhältniswahlrecht *nt*

proportionate [prə'pɔ:ʃənɪt] *adj* = **proportional**

proposal [prə'pəuzl] *n* (*plan*) Vorschlag *m*; **~ (of marriage)** Heiratsantrag *m*

propose [prə'pəuz] *vt* (*plan, idea*) vorschlagen; (*motion*) einbringen; (*toast*) ausbringen ▷ *vi*

(*offer marriage*) einen Heiratsantrag machen; **to ~ to do sth** *or* **doing sth** (*intend*) die Absicht haben, etw zu tun
proposer [prəˈpəuzəʳ] *n* (*of motion etc*) Antragsteller(in) *m(f)*
proposition [prɔpəˈzɪʃən] *n* (*statement*) These *f*; (*offer*) Angebot *nt*; **to make sb a ~** jdm ein Angebot machen
propound [prəˈpaund] *vt* (*idea etc*) darlegen
proprietary [prəˈpraɪətərɪ] *adj* (*brand, medicine*) Marken-; (*tone, manner*) besitzergreifend
proprietor [prəˈpraɪətəʳ] *n* (*of hotel, shop etc*) Inhaber(in) *m(f)*; (*of newspaper*) Besitzer(in) *m(f)*
propriety [prəˈpraɪətɪ] *n* (*seemliness*) Schicklichkeit *f*
props [prɔps] *npl* (*Theat*) Requisiten *pl*
propulsion [prəˈpʌlʃən] *n* Antrieb *m*
pro rata [prəuˈrɑːtə] *adj, adv* anteilmäßig; **on a ~ basis** anteilmäßig
prosaic [prəuˈzeɪɪk] *adj* prosaisch, nüchtern
Pros. Atty. (*US*) *abbr* = **prosecuting attorney**
proscribe [prəˈskraɪb] (*form*) *vt* verbieten, untersagen
prose [prəuz] *n* (*not poetry*) Prosa *f*; (*Brit: Scol: translation*) Übersetzung *f* in die Fremdsprache
prosecute [ˈprɔsɪkjuːt] *vt* (*Law: person*) strafrechtlich verfolgen; (*: case*) die Anklage vertreten in *+dat*
prosecuting attorney [ˈprɔsɪkjuːtɪŋ-] (*US*) *n* Staatsanwalt *m*, Staatsanwältin *f*
prosecution [prɔsɪˈkjuːʃən] *n* (*Law: action*) strafrechtliche Verfolgung *f*; (*: accusing side*) Anklage(vertretung) *f*
prosecutor [ˈprɔsɪkjuːtəʳ] *n* Anklagevertreter(in) *m(f)*; (*also*: **public prosecutor**) Staatsanwalt *m*, Staatsanwältin *f*
prospect [*n* ˈprɔspɛkt, *vi* prəˈspɛkt] *n* Aussicht *f* ▷ *vi*: **to ~ (for)** suchen (nach); **prospects** *npl* (*for work etc*) Aussichten *pl*, Chancen *pl*; **we are faced with the ~ of higher unemployment** wir müssen mit der Möglichkeit rechnen, dass die Arbeitslosigkeit steigt
prospecting [ˈprɔspɛktɪŋ] *n* (*for gold, oil etc*) Suche *f*
prospective [prəˈspɛktɪv] *adj* (*son-in-law*) zukünftig; (*customer, candidate*) voraussichtlich
prospectus [prəˈspɛktəs] *n* (*of college, company*) Prospekt *m*
prosper [ˈprɔspəʳ] *vi* (*person*) Erfolg haben; (*business, city etc*) gedeihen, florieren
prosperity [prɔˈspɛrɪtɪ] *n* Wohlstand *m*
prosperous [ˈprɔspərəs] *adj* (*person*) wohlhabend; (*business, city etc*) blühend
prostate [ˈprɔsteɪt] *n* (*also*: **prostate gland**) Prostata *f*
prostitute [ˈprɔstɪtjuːt] *n* (*female*) Prostituierte *f*; (*male*) männliche(r) Prostituierte(r) *m*, Strichjunge *m* (*inf*) ▷ *vt*: **to ~ o.s.** (*fig*) sich prostituieren, sich unter Wert verkaufen
prostitution [prɔstɪˈtjuːʃən] *n* Prostitution *f*
prostrate [ˈprɔstreɪt] *adj* (*face down*) ausgestreckt (liegend); (*fig*) niedergeschmettert ▷ *vt*: **to ~ o.s. before** sich zu Boden werfen vor *+dat*
protagonist [prəˈtægənɪst] *n* (*of idea, movement*) Verfechter(in) *m(f)*; (*Theat, Liter*) Protagonist(in) *m(f)*
protect [prəˈtɛkt] *vt* schützen
protection [prəˈtɛkʃən] *n* Schutz *m*; **police ~** Polizeischutz *m*
protectionism [prəˈtɛkʃənɪzəm] *n* Protektionismus *m*
protection racket *n* Organisation *f* zur Erpressung von Schutzgeld
protective [prəˈtɛktɪv] *adj* (*clothing, layer etc*) Schutz-; (*person*) fürsorglich; **~ custody** Schutzhaft *f*
protector [prəˈtɛktəʳ] *n* (*person*) Beschützer(in) *m(f)*; (*device*) Schutz *m*
protégé, protégée [ˈprəutɪʒeɪ] *n* Schützling *m*
protein [ˈprəutiːn] *n* Protein *nt*, Eiweiß *nt*
pro tem [prəuˈtɛm] *adv abbr* (= *pro tempore*) vorläufig
protest [*n* ˈprəutɛst, *vi, vt* prəˈtɛst] *n* Protest *m* ▷ *vi*: **to ~ about** *or* **against** *or* **at sth** gegen etw protestieren ▷ *vt*: **to ~ (that)** (*insist*) beteuern(, dass)
Protestant [ˈprɔtɪstənt] *adj* protestantisch ▷ *n* Protestant(in) *m(f)*
protester [prəˈtɛstəʳ] *n* (*in demonstration*) Demonstrant(in) *m(f)*
protest march *n* Protestmarsch *m*
protestor [prəˈtɛstəʳ] *n* = **protester**
protocol [ˈprəutəkɔl] *n* Protokoll *nt*
prototype [ˈprəutətaɪp] *n* Prototyp *m*
protracted [prəˈtræktɪd] *adj* (*meeting etc*) langwierig, sich hinziehend; (*absence*) länger
protractor [prəˈtræktəʳ] *n* (*Geom*) Winkelmesser *m*
protrude [prəˈtruːd] *vi* (*rock, ledge, teeth*) vorstehen
protuberance [prəˈtjuːbərəns] *n* Auswuchs *m*
proud [praud] *adj* stolz; (*arrogant*) hochmütig; **~ of sb/sth** stolz auf jdn/etw; **to be ~ to do sth** stolz (darauf) sein, etw zu tun; **to do sb/o.s. ~** (*inf*) jdn/sich verwöhnen
proudly [ˈpraudlɪ] *adv* stolz
prove [pruːv] *vt* beweisen ▷ *vi*: **to ~ (to be) correct** sich als richtig herausstellen *or* erweisen; **to ~ (o.s./itself) (to be) useful** sich als nützlich erweisen; **he was ~d right in the end** er hat schließlich recht behalten
proverb [ˈprɔvəːb] *n* Sprichwort *nt*
proverbial [prəˈvəːbɪəl] *adj* sprichwörtlich
provide [prəˈvaɪd] *vt* (*food, money, shelter etc*) zur Verfügung stellen; (*answer, example etc*) liefern; **to ~ sb with sth** jdm etw zur Verfügung stellen
▸ **provide for** *vt fus* (*person*) sorgen für; (*future event*) vorsorgen für
provided [prəˈvaɪdɪd] *conj*: **~ (that)** vorausgesetzt(, dass)
Providence [ˈprɔvɪdəns] *n* die Vorsehung
providing [prəˈvaɪdɪŋ] *conj*: **~ (that)** vorausgesetzt(, dass)

province ['prɔvɪns] *n (of country)* Provinz *f*; *(responsibility etc)* Bereich *m*, Gebiet *nt*; **provinces** *npl*: **the ~s** *außerhalb der Hauptstadt liegende Landesteile*, Provinz *f*
provincial [prə'vɪnʃəl] *adj (town, newspaper etc)* Provinz-; *(pej: parochial)* provinziell
provision [prə'vɪʒən] *n (supplying)* Bereitstellung *f*; *(preparation)* Vorsorge *f*, Vorkehrungen *pl*; *(stipulation, clause)* Bestimmung *f*; **provisions** *npl (food)* Proviant *m*; **to make ~ for** vorsorgen für; *(for people)* sorgen für; **there's no ~ for this in the contract** dies ist im Vertrag nicht vorgesehen
provisional [prə'vɪʒənl] *adj* vorläufig, provisorisch ▷ *n*: **P~** *(Irish: Pol) Mitglied der provisorischen Irisch-Republikanischen Armee*
provisional licence *(Brit) n (Aut)* vorläufige Fahrerlaubnis *f*
provisionally [prə'vɪʒnəlɪ] *adv* vorläufig
proviso [prə'vaɪzəu] *n* Vorbehalt *m*; **with the ~ that ...** unter dem Vorbehalt, dass ...
Provo ['prɔvəu] *(Irish: inf) n abbr (Pol)* = **Provisional**
provocation [prɔvə'keɪʃən] *n* Provokation *f*, Herausforderung *f*; **to be under ~** provoziert werden
provocative [prə'vɔkətɪv] *adj* provozierend, herausfordernd; *(sexually stimulating)* aufreizend
provoke [prə'vəuk] *vt (person)* provozieren, herausfordern; *(fight)* herbeiführen; *(reaction etc)* hervorrufen; **to ~ sb to do** *or* **into doing sth** jdn dazu provozieren, etw zu tun
provost ['prɔvəst] *n (Brit: of university)* Dekan *m*; *(Scot)* Bürgermeister(in) *m(f)*
prow [prau] *n (of boat)* Bug *m*
prowess ['prauɪs] *n* Können *nt*, Fähigkeiten *pl*; **his ~ as a footballer** sein fußballerisches Können
prowl [praul] *vi (also:* **prowl about, prowl around***)* schleichen ▷ *n*: **on the ~** auf Streifzug
prowler ['praulə^r] *n* Herumtreiber *m*
proximity [prɔk'sɪmɪtɪ] *n* Nähe *f*
proxy ['prɔksɪ] *n*: **by ~** durch einen Stellvertreter
prude [pru:d] *n*: **to be a ~** prüde sein
prudence ['pru:dns] *n* Klugheit *f*, Umsicht *f*
prudent ['pru:dnt] *adj (sensible)* klug
prudish ['pru:dɪʃ] *adj* prüde
prune [pru:n] *n* Backpflaume *f* ▷ *vt (plant)* stutzen, beschneiden
pry [praɪ] *vi*: **to ~ (into)** seine Nase hineinstecken (in *+acc*), herumschnüffeln (in *+dat*)
PS *abbr (= postscript)* PS
psalm [sɑ:m] *n* Psalm *m*
PSAT® *(US) n abbr (= Preliminary Scholastic Aptitude Test) Schuleignungstest*
PSBR *(Brit) n abbr (Econ: = public sector borrowing requirement)* staatlicher Kreditbedarf *m*
pseud [sju:d] *(Brit: inf: pej) n* Angeber(in) *m(f)*
pseudo- ['sju:dəu] *pref* Pseudo-
pseudonym ['sju:dənɪm] *n* Pseudonym *nt*
PSHE *(Brit) n abbr (Scol)* = **personal, social and health education**
PST *(US) abbr (= Pacific Standard Time) pazifische Standardzeit*
psyche ['saɪkɪ] *n* Psyche *f*
psychedelic [saɪkə'dɛlɪk] *adj (drug)* psychedelisch; *(clothes, colours)* in psychedelischen Farben
psychiatric [saɪkɪ'ætrɪk] *adj* psychiatrisch
psychiatrist [saɪ'kaɪətrɪst] *n* Psychiater(in) *m(f)*
psychiatry [saɪ'kaɪətrɪ] *n* Psychiatrie *f*
psychic ['saɪkɪk] *adj (person)* übersinnlich begabt; *(damage, disorder)* psychisch ▷ *n* Mensch *m* mit übersinnlichen Fähigkeiten
psycho ['saɪkəu] *(US: inf) n* Verrückte(r) *f(m)*
psychoanalyse [saɪkəu'ænəlaɪz] *vt* psychoanalytisch behandeln, psychoanalysieren
psychoanalysis [saɪkəuə'nælɪsɪs] *n* Psychoanalyse *f*
psychoanalyst [saɪkəu'ænəlɪst] *n* Psychoanalytiker(in) *m(f)*
psychological [saɪkə'lɔdʒɪkl] *adj* psychologisch
psychologist [saɪ'kɔlədʒɪst] *n* Psychologe *m*, Psychologin *f*
psychology [saɪ'kɔlədʒɪ] *n (science)* Psychologie *f*; *(character)* Psyche *f*
psychopath ['saɪkəupæθ] *n* Psychopath(in) *m(f)*
psychoses [saɪ'kəusi:z] *npl of* **psychosis**
psychosis [saɪ'kəusɪs] *(pl* **psychoses***) n* Psychose *f*
psychosomatic ['saɪkəusə'mætɪk] *adj* psychosomatisch
psychotherapy [saɪkəu'θɛrəpɪ] *n* Psychotherapie *f*
psychotic [saɪ'kɔtɪk] *adj* psychotisch
PT *(Brit) n abbr (Scol: = physical training)* Turnen *nt*
Pt *abbr (in place names: = Point)* Pt.
pt *abbr* = **pint; point**
PTA *n abbr (= Parent-Teacher Association) Lehrer- und Elternverband*
Pte *(Brit) abbr (Mil)* = **private**
PTO *abbr (= please turn over)* b. w.
PTV *(US) n abbr (= pay television)* Pay-TV *nt*; *(= public television)* öffentliches Fernsehen *nt*
pub [pʌb] *n* = **public house**; *siehe Info-Artikel*

PUB

Pub ist ein Gasthaus mit einer Lizenz zum Ausschank von alkoholischen Getränken. Ein Pub besteht meist aus verschiedenen gemütlichen (lounge, snug) oder einfacheren Räumen (public bar), in der oft auch Spiele wie Darts, Domino und Poolbillard zur Verfügung stehen. In Pubs werden vor allem mittags oft auch Mahlzeiten angeboten. Pubs sind normalerweise von 11 bis 23 Uhr geöffnet, aber manchmal nachmittags geschlossen.

pub-crawl ['pʌbkrɔːl] (*inf*) *n*: **to go on a ~** eine Kneipentour machen
puberty ['pjuːbətɪ] *n* Pubertät *f*
pubic ['pjuːbɪk] *adj* (*hair*) Scham-; **~ bone** Schambein *nt*
public ['pʌblɪk] *adj* öffentlich ▷ *n*: **the ~** (*in general*) die Öffentlichkeit; (*particular set of people*) das Publikum; **to be ~ knowledge** allgemein bekannt sein; **to make sth ~** etw bekannt machen; **to go ~** (*Comm*) in eine Aktiengesellschaft umgewandelt werden; **in ~** in aller Öffentlichkeit; **the general ~** die Allgemeinheit
public-address system [pʌblɪkə'drɛs-] *n* Lautsprecheranlage *f*
publican ['pʌblɪkən] *n* Gastwirt(in) *m(f)*
publication [pʌblɪ'keɪʃən] *n* Veröffentlichung *f*
public company *n* Aktiengesellschaft *f*
public convenience (*Brit*) *n* öffentliche Toilette *f*
public holiday *n* gesetzlicher Feiertag *m*
public house (*Brit*) *n* Gaststätte *f*
publicity [pʌb'lɪsɪtɪ] *n* (*information*) Werbung *f*; (*attention*) Publicity *f*
publicity tour *n* Werbetour *f*; **to be on a ~** auf Werbetour sein
publicize ['pʌblɪsaɪz] *vt* (*fact*) bekannt machen; (*event*) Publicity machen für
public limited company *n* ≈ Aktiengesellschaft *f*
publicly ['pʌblɪklɪ] *adv* öffentlich; **to be ~ owned** (*Comm*) in Staatsbesitz sein
public opinion *n* die öffentliche Meinung
public ownership *n*: **to be taken into ~** verstaatlicht werden
Public Prosecutor *n* Staatsanwalt *m*, Staatsanwältin *f*
public relations *n* Public Relations *pl*, Öffentlichkeitsarbeit *f*
public relations officer *n* Beauftragte(r) *f(m)* für Öffentlichkeitsarbeit
public school *n* (*Brit*) Privatschule *f*; (*US*) staatliche Schule *f*; *siehe Info-Artikel*

PUBLIC SCHOOL

Public school bezeichnet vor allem in England eine weiterführende Privatschule, meist eine Internatsschule mit hohem Prestige, an die oft auch eine *preparatory school* angeschlossen ist. Public schools werden von einem Schulbeirat verwaltet und durch Stiftungen und Schulgelder, die an den bekanntesten Schulen wie Eton, Harrow und Westminster sehr hoch sein konnen, finanziert. Die meisten Schüler einer public school gehen zur Universität, oft nach Oxford oder Cambridge. Viele Industrielle, Abgeordnete und hohe Beamte haben eine public school besucht. In Schottland und den USA bedeutet public school eine öffentliche, vom Steuerzahler finanzierte Schule.

public sector *n*: **the ~** der öffentliche Sektor
public-service vehicle [pʌblɪk'səːvɪs-] (*Brit*) *n* öffentliches Verkehrsmittel *nt*
public-spirited [pʌblɪk'spɪrɪtɪd] *adj* gemeinsinnig
public transport *n* öffentliche Verkehrsmittel *pl*
public utility *n* öffentlicher Versorgungsbetrieb *m*
public works *npl* öffentliche Bauprojekte *pl*
publish ['pʌblɪʃ] *vt* veröffentlichen
publisher ['pʌblɪʃəʳ] *n* (*person*) Verleger(in) *m(f)*; (*company*) Verlag *m*
publishing ['pʌblɪʃɪŋ] *n* (*profession*) das Verlagswesen
publishing company *n* Verlag *m*, Verlagshaus *nt*
pub lunch *n* *in Pubs servierter Imbiss*
puce [pjuːs] *adj* (*face*) hochrot
puck [pʌk] *n* (*Ice Hockey*) Puck *m*
pucker ['pʌkəʳ] *vi* (*lips, face*) sich verziehen; (*fabric etc*) Falten werfen ▷ *vt* (*lips, face*) verziehen; (*fabric etc*) Falten machen in *+acc*
pudding ['pudɪŋ] *n* (*cooked sweet food*) Süßspeise *f*; (*Brit: dessert*) Nachtisch *m*; **rice ~** Milchreis *m*; **black ~, blood ~** (*US*) ≈ Blutwurst *f*
puddle ['pʌdl] *n* (*of rain*) Pfütze *f*; (*of blood*) Lache *f*
puerile ['pjuəraɪl] *adj* kindisch
Puerto Rico ['pwəːtəu'riːkəu] *n* Puerto Rico *nt*
puff [pʌf] *n* (*of cigarette, pipe*) Zug *m*; (*gasp*) Schnaufer *m*; (*of air*) Stoß *m*; (*of smoke*) Wolke *f* ▷ *vt* (*also*: **puff on, puff at**: *cigarette, pipe*) ziehen an *+dat* ▷ *vi* (*gasp*) keuchen, schnaufen
▸ **puff out** *vt* (*one's chest*) herausdrücken; (*one's cheeks*) aufblasen
puffed [pʌft] (*inf*) *adj* außer Puste
puffin ['pʌfɪn] *n* Papageientaucher *m*
puff pastry, (*US*) **puff paste** *n* Blätterteig *m*
puffy ['pʌfɪ] *adj* (*eye*) geschwollen; (*face*) aufgedunsen
pugnacious [pʌg'neɪʃəs] *adj* (*person*) streitsüchtig
pull [pul] *vt* (*rope, handle etc*) ziehen an *+dat*; (*cart etc*) ziehen; (*close: curtain*) zuziehen; (*: blind*) herunterlassen; (*inf: attract: people*) anlocken; (*: sexual partner*) aufreißen; (*pint of beer*) zapfen ▷ *vi* ziehen ▷ *n* (*also fig: attraction*) Anziehungskraft *f*; **to ~ the trigger** abdrücken; **to ~ a face** ein Gesicht schneiden; **to ~ a muscle** sich *dat* einen Muskel zerren; **not to ~ one's** *or* **any punches** (*fig*) sich *dat* keine Zurückhaltung auferlegen; **to ~ to pieces** (*fig*) zerreißen; **to ~ one's weight** (*fig*) sich ins Zeug legen; **to ~ o.s. together** sich zusammenreißen; **to ~ sb's leg** (*fig*) jdn auf den Arm nehmen; **to ~ strings (for sb)** seine Beziehungen (für jdn) spielen lassen; **to give sth a ~** an etw *dat* ziehen

▸ **pull apart** *vt* (*separate*) trennen
▸ **pull away** *vi* (*Aut*) losfahren
▸ **pull back** *vi* (*retreat*) sich zurückziehen; (*fig*) einen Rückzieher machen (*inf*)
▸ **pull down** *vt* (*building*) abreißen
▸ **pull in** *vi* (*Aut: at kerb*) anhalten; (*Rail*) einfahren ▹ *vt* (*inf: money*) einsacken; (*crowds, people*) anlocken; (*police: suspect*) sich *dat* schnappen (*inf*)
▸ **pull off** *vt* (*clothes etc*) ausziehen; (*fig: difficult thing*) schaffen, bringen (*inf*)
▸ **pull out** *vi* (*Aut: from kerb*) losfahren; (*: when overtaking*) ausscheren; (*Rail*) ausfahren; (*withdraw*) sich zurückziehen ▹ *vt* (*extract*) herausziehen
▸ **pull over** *vi* (*Aut*) an den Straßenrand fahren
▸ **pull through** *vi* (*Med*) durchkommen
▸ **pull up** *vi* (*Aut, Rail: stop*) anhalten ▹ *vt* (*raise*) hochziehen; (*uproot*) herausreißen; (*chair*) heranrücken

pullback ['pulbæk] *n* (*retreat*) Rückzug *m*
pulley ['pulı] *n* Flaschenzug *m*
pull-out ['pulaut] *n* (*in magazine*) Beilage *f* (*zum Heraustrennen*)
pullover ['puləuvəʳ] *n* Pullover *m*
pulp [pʌlp] *n* (*of fruit*) Fruchtfleisch *nt*; (*for paper*) (Papier)brei *m*; (*Liter: pej*) Schund *m* ▹ *adj* (*pej: magazine, novel*) Schund-; **to reduce sth to a ~** etw zu Brei machen
pulpit ['pulpıt] *n* Kanzel *f*
pulsate [pʌl'seıt] *vi* (*heart*) klopfen; (*music*) pulsieren
pulse [pʌls] *n* (*Anat*) Puls *m*; (*rhythm*) Rhythmus *m*; **pulses** *npl* (*Bot*) Hülsenfrüchte *pl*; (*Tech*) Impuls *m* ▹ *vi* pulsieren; **to take** *or* **feel sb's ~** jdm den Puls fühlen; **to have one's finger on the ~ (of sth)** (*fig*) den Finger am Puls (einer Sache *gen*) haben
pulverize ['pʌlvəraız] *vt* pulverisieren; (*fig: destroy*) vernichten
puma ['pju:mə] *n* Puma *m*
pumice ['pʌmıs] *n* (*also*: **pumice stone**) Bimsstein *m*
pummel ['pʌml] *vt* mit Faustschlägen bearbeiten
pump [pʌmp] *n* Pumpe *f*; (*also*: **petrol pump**) Zapfsäule *f*; (*shoe*) Turnschuh *m* ▹ *vt* pumpen; **to ~ sb for information** jdn aushorchen; **she had her stomach ~ed** ihr wurde der Magen ausgepumpt
▸ **pump up** *vt* (*inflate*) aufpumpen
pumpkin ['pʌmpkın] *n* Kürbis *m*
pun [pʌn] *n* Wortspiel *nt*
punch [pʌntʃ] *n* (*blow*) Schlag *m*; (*fig: force*) Schlagkraft *f*; (*tool*) Locher *m*; (*drink*) Bowle *f*, Punsch *m* ▹ *vt* (*hit*) schlagen; (*make a hole in*) lochen; **to ~ a hole in sth** ein Loch in etw *acc* stanzen
▸ **punch in** (US) *vi* (bei Arbeitsbeginn) stempeln
▸ **punch out** (US) *vi* (bei Arbeitsende) stempeln
Punch and Judy show *n* ≈ Kasper(le)theater *nt*
punch card, (US) **punched card** [pʌntʃt-] *n* Lochkarte *f*
punch-drunk ['pʌntʃdrʌŋk] (*Brit*) *adj* (*boxer*) angeschlagen
punch line *n* Pointe *f*
punch-up ['pʌntʃʌp] (*Brit: inf*) *n* Schlägerei *f*
punctual ['pʌŋktjuəl] *adj* pünktlich
punctuality [pʌŋktju'ælıtı] *n* Pünktlichkeit *f*
punctually ['pʌŋktjuəlı] *adv* pünktlich; **it will start ~ at 6** es beginnt um Punkt 6 *or* pünktlich um 6
punctuation [pʌŋktju'eıʃən] *n* Zeichensetzung *f*
punctuation mark *n* Satzzeichen *nt*
puncture ['pʌŋktʃəʳ] *n* (*Aut*) Reifenpanne *f* ▹ *vt* durchbohren; **I have a ~** ich habe eine Reifenpanne
pundit ['pʌndıt] *n* Experte *m*, Expertin *f*
pungent ['pʌndʒənt] *adj* (*smell, taste*) scharf; (*fig: speech, article etc*) spitz, scharf
punish ['pʌnıʃ] *vt* bestrafen; **to ~ sb for sth** jdn für etw bestrafen; **to ~ sb for doing sth** jdn dafür bestrafen, dass er etw getan hat
punishable ['pʌnıʃəbl] *adj* strafbar
punishing ['pʌnıʃıŋ] *adj* (*fig: exercise, ordeal*) hart
punishment ['pʌnıʃmənt] *n* (*act*) Bestrafung *f*; (*way of punishing*) Strafe *f*; **to take a lot of ~** (*fig: car, person etc*) viel abbekommen
punitive ['pju:nıtıv] *adj* (*action*) Straf-, zur Strafe; (*measure*) (extrem) hart
punk [pʌŋk] *n* (*also*: **punk rocker**) Punker(in) *m(f)*; (*also*: **punk rock**) Punk *m*; (*US: inf: hoodlum*) Gangster *m*
punnet ['pʌnıt] *n* (*of raspberries etc*) Körbchen *nt*
punt¹ [pʌnt] *n* (*boat*) Stechkahn *m* ▹ *vi* mit dem Stechkahn fahren
punt² [pʌnt] (*Irish*) *n* (*currency*) irisches Pfund *nt*
punter ['pʌntəʳ] (*Brit*) *n* (*gambler*) Wetter(in) *m(f)*; **the ~s** (*inf: customers*) die Leute; **the average ~** (*inf*) Otto Normalverbraucher
puny ['pju:nı] *adj* (*person, arms etc*) schwächlich; (*efforts*) kläglich, kümmerlich
pup [pʌp] *n* (*young dog*) Welpe *m*, junger Hund *m*; **seal ~** Welpenjunge(s) *nt*
pupil ['pju:pl] *n* (*Scol*) Schüler(in) *m(f)*; (*of eye*) Pupille *f*
puppet ['pʌpıt] *n* Handpuppe *f*; (*with strings, fig: person*) Marionette *f*
puppet government *n* Marionettenregierung *f*
puppy ['pʌpı] *n* (*young dog*) Welpe *m*, junger Hund *m*
purchase ['pə:tʃıs] *n* Kauf *m*; (*grip*) Halt *m* ▹ *vt* kaufen; **to get** *or* **gain (a) ~ on** (*grip*) Halt finden an *+dat*
purchase order *n* Bestellung *f*
purchase price *n* Kaufpreis *m*
purchaser ['pə:tʃısəʳ] *n* Käufer(in) *m(f)*
purchase tax *n* Kaufsteuer *f*
purchasing power ['pə:tʃısıŋ-] *n* Kaufkraft *f*
pure [pjuəʳ] *adj* rein; **a ~ wool jumper** ein Pullover aus reiner Wolle; **it's laziness ~ and simple** es ist nichts als reine Faulheit

purebred ['pjuəbrɛd] *adj* reinrassig
puree ['pjʊəreɪ] *n* Püree *nt*
purely ['pjuəlɪ] *adv* rein
purgatory ['pəːgətərɪ] *n* (*Rel*) das Fegefeuer; (*fig*) die Hölle
purge [pəːdʒ] *n* (*Pol*) Säuberung *f* ▷ *vt* (*Pol*: *organization*) säubern; (: *extremists etc*) entfernen; (*fig*: *thoughts, mind etc*) befreien
purification [pjuərɪfɪ'keɪʃən] *n* Reinigung *f*
purify ['pjuərɪfaɪ] *vt* reinigen
purist ['pjuərɪst] *n* Purist(in) *m(f)*
puritan ['pjuərɪtən] *n* Puritaner(in) *m(f)*
puritanical [pjuərɪ'tænɪkl] *adj* puritanisch
purity ['pjuərɪtɪ] *n* Reinheit *f*
purl [pəːl] (*Knitting*) *n* linke Masche *f* ▷ *vt* links stricken
purloin [pəː'lɔɪn] (*form*) *vt* entwenden
purple ['pəːpl] *adj* violett
purport [pəː'pɔːt] *vi*: **to ~ to be/do sth** vorgeben, etw zu sein/tun
purpose ['pəːpəs] *n* (*reason*) Zweck *m*; (*aim*) Ziel *nt*, Absicht *f*; **on ~** absichtlich; **for illustrative ~s** zu Illustrationszwecken; **for all practical ~s** praktisch (gesehen); **for the ~s of this meeting** zum Zweck dieses Treffens; **to little ~** mit wenig Erfolg; **to no ~** ohne Erfolg; **a sense of ~** ein Zielbewusstsein *nt*
purpose-built ['pəːpəs'bɪlt] (*Brit*) *adj* speziell angefertigt, Spezial-
purposeful ['pəːpəsful] *adj* entschlossen
purposely ['pəːpəslɪ] *adv* absichtlich, bewusst
purr [pəːʳ] *vi* (*cat*) schnurren
purse [pəːs] *n* (*Brit*: *for money*) Geldbörse *f*, Portemonnaie *nt*; (*US*: *handbag*) Handtasche *f* ▷ *vt* (*lips*) kräuseln
purser ['pəːsəʳ] *n* (*Naut*) Zahlmeister *m*
purse-snatcher ['pəːssnætʃəʳ] (*US*) *n* Handtaschendieb *m*
pursue [pə'sjuː] *vt* (*person, vehicle, plan, aim*) verfolgen; (*fig*: *interest etc*) nachgehen *+dat*
pursuer [pə'sjuːəʳ] *n* Verfolger(in) *m(f)*
pursuit [pə'sjuːt] *n* (*chase*) Verfolgung *f*; (*pastime*) Beschäftigung *f*; (*fig*): **~ of** (*of happiness etc*) Streben *nt* nach; **in ~ of** (*person, car etc*) auf der Jagd nach; (*fig*: *happiness etc*) im Streben nach
purveyor [pə'veɪəʳ] (*form*) *n* (*of goods etc*) Lieferant *m*
pus [pʌs] *n* Eiter *m*
push [puʃ] *n* Stoß *m*, Schub *m* ▷ *vt* (*press*) drücken; (*shove*) schieben; (*fig*: *put pressure on*: *person*) bedrängen; (: *promote*: *product*) werben für; (*inf*: *sell*: *drugs*) pushen ▷ *vi* (*press*) drücken; (*shove*) schieben; **at the ~ of a button** auf Knopfdruck; **at a ~** (*Brit*: *inf*) notfalls; **to ~ a door open/shut** eine Tür auf-/zudrücken; **"~"** (*on door*) „drücken"; (*on bell*) „klingeln"; **to be ~ed for time/money** (*inf*) in Zeitnot/Geldnot sein; **she is ~ing fifty** (*inf*) sie geht auf die fünfzig zu; **to ~ for** (*demand*) drängen auf *+acc*
▸ **push around** *vt* (*bully*) herumschubsen
▸ **push aside** *vt* beiseiteschieben
▸ **push in** *vi* sich dazwischendrängeln
▸ **push off** (*inf*) *vi* abhauen
▸ **push on** *vi* (*continue*) weitermachen
▸ **push over** *vt* umstoßen
▸ **push through** *vt* (*measure etc*) durchdrücken
▸ **push up** *vt* (*total, prices*) hochtreiben
push-bike ['puʃbaɪk] (*Brit*) *n* Fahrrad *nt*
push-button ['puʃbʌtn] *adj* (*machine, calculator*) Drucktasten-
pushchair ['puʃtʃɛəʳ] (*Brit*) *n* Sportwagen *m*
pusher ['puʃəʳ] *n* (*drug dealer*) Pusher *m*
pushover ['puʃəuvəʳ] (*inf*) *n*: **it's a ~** das ist ein Kinderspiel
push-up ['puʃʌp] (*US*) *n* Liegestütz *m*
pushy ['puʃɪ] (*pej*) *adj* aufdringlich
puss [pus] (*inf*) *n* Mieze *f*
pussy ['pusɪ], **pussycat** ['pusɪkæt] (*inf*) *n* Mieze(katze) *f*
put [put] (*pt, pp* **~**) *vt* (*thing*) tun; (: *upright*) stellen; (: *flat*) legen; (*person*: *in room, institution etc*) stecken; (: *in state, situation*) versetzen; (*express*: *idea etc*) ausdrücken; (*present*: *case, view*) vorbringen; (*ask*: *question*) stellen; (*classify*) einschätzen; (*write, type*) schreiben; **to ~ sb in a good/bad mood** jdn gut/schlecht stimmen; **to ~ sb to bed** jdn ins Bett bringen; **to ~ sb to a lot of trouble** jdm viele Umstände machen; **how shall I ~ it?** wie soll ich es sagen *or* ausdrücken?; **to ~ a lot of time into sth** viel Zeit auf etw *acc* verwenden; **to ~ money on a horse** Geld auf ein Pferd setzen; **the cost is now ~ at 2 million pounds** die Kosten werden jetzt auf 2 Millionen Pfund geschätzt; **I ~ it to you that ...** (*Brit*) ich behaupte, dass ...; **to stay ~** (an Ort und Stelle) bleiben
▸ **put about** *vi* (*Naut*) den Kurs ändern ▷ *vt* (*rumour*) verbreiten
▸ **put across** *vt* (*ideas etc*) verständlich machen
▸ **put around** *vt* = **put about**
▸ **put aside** *vt* (*work*) zur Seite legen; (*idea, problem*) unbeachtet lassen; (*sum of money*) zurücklegen
▸ **put away** *vt* (*store*) wegräumen; (*inf*: *consume*) verdrücken; (*save*: *money*) zurücklegen; (*imprison*) einsperren
▸ **put back** *vt* (*replace*) zurücktun; (: *upright*) zurückstellen; (: *flat*) zurücklegen; (*postpone*) verschieben; (*delay*) zurückwerfen
▸ **put by** *vt* (*money, supplies etc*) zurücklegen
▸ **put down** *vt* (*upright*) hinstellen; (*flat*) hinlegen; (*cup, glass*) absetzen; (*in writing*) aufschreiben; (*riot, rebellion*) niederschlagen; (*humiliate*) demütigen; (*kill*) töten
▸ **put down to** *vt* (*attribute*) zurückführen auf *+acc*
▸ **put forward** *vt* (*ideas etc*) vorbringen; (*watch, clock*) vorstellen; (*date, meeting*) vorverlegen
▸ **put in** *vt* (*application, complaint*) einreichen; (*time, effort*) investieren; (*gas, electricity etc*) installieren ▷ *vi* (*Naut*) einlaufen
▸ **put in for** *vt fus* (*promotion*) sich bewerben um; (*leave*) beantragen

▸ **put off** *vt* (*delay*) verschieben; (*distract*) ablenken; **to ~ sb off sth** (*discourage*) jdn von etw abbringen
▸ **put on** *vt* (*clothes, brake*) anziehen; (*glasses, kettle*) aufsetzen; (*make-up, ointment etc*) auftragen; (*light*, TV) anmachen; (*play etc*) aufführen; (*record, tape, video*) auflegen; (*dinner etc*) aufsetzen; (*assume*: *look, behaviour etc*) annehmen; (*inf*: *tease*) auf den Arm nehmen; (*extra bus, train etc*) einsetzen; **to ~ on airs** sich zieren; **to ~ on weight** zunehmen
▸ **put on to** *vt* (*tell about*) vermitteln
▸ **put out** *vt* (*fire, light*) ausmachen; (*take out*: *rubbish*) herausbringen; (: *cat etc*) vor die Tür setzen; (*one's hand*) ausstrecken; (*story, announcement*) verbreiten; (*Brit*: *dislocate*: *shoulder etc*) verrenken; (*inf*: *inconvenience*) Umstände machen *+dat* ▹ *vi* (*Naut*): **to ~ out to sea** in See stechen; **to ~ out from Plymouth** von Plymouth auslaufen
▸ **put through** *vt* (*Tel*: *person*) verbinden; (: *call*) durchstellen; (*plan, agreement*) durchbringen; **~ me through to Ms Blair** verbinden Sie mich mit Frau Blair
▸ **put together** *vt* (*furniture etc*) zusammenbauen; (*plan, campaign*) ausarbeiten; **more than the rest of them ~ together** mehr als alle anderen zusammen
▸ **put up** *vt* (*fence, building*) errichten; (*tent*) aufstellen; (*umbrella*) aufspannen; (*hood*) hochschlagen; (*poster, sign etc*) anbringen; (*price, cost*) erhöhen; (*accommodate*) unterbringen; **to ~ up resistance** Widerstand leisten; **to ~ up a fight** sich zur Wehr setzen; **to ~ sb up to sth** jdn zu etw anstiften; **to ~ sb up to doing sth** jdn dazu anstiften, etw zu tun; **to ~ sth up for sale** etw zum Verkauf anbieten
▸ **put upon** *vt fus*: **to be ~ upon** (*imposed on*) ausgenutzt werden
▸ **put up with** *vt fus* sich abfinden mit

putative ['pju:tətɪv] *adj* mutmaßlich
putrid ['pju:trɪd] *adj* (*mess, meat*) faul
putt [pʌt] *n* Putt *m*
putter ['pʌtə^r] *n* (*Golf*) Putter *m* ▹ *vi* (*US*) = **potter**
putting green ['pʌtɪŋ-] *n* kleiner Golfplatz *m* zum Putten
putty ['pʌtɪ] *n* Kitt *m*
put-up ['putʌp] *adj*: **a ~ job** ein abgekartetes Spiel *nt*
puzzle ['pʌzl] *n* (*game, toy*) Geschicklichkeitsspiel *nt*; (*mystery*) Rätsel *nt* ▹ *vt* verwirren ▹ *vi*: **to ~ over sth** sich *dat* über etw *acc* den Kopf zerbrechen; **to be ~d as to why ...** vor einem Rätsel stehen, warum ...
puzzling ['pʌzlɪŋ] *adj* verwirrend; (*mysterious*) rätselhaft
PVC *n abbr* (= *polyvinyl chloride*) PVC *nt*
Pvt. (*US*) *abbr* (*Mil*) = **private**
p.w. *abbr* (= *per week*) pro Woche
pygmy ['pɪgmɪ] *n* Pygmäe *m*
pyjamas, (*US*) **pajamas** [pə'dʒɑ:məz] *npl* Pyjama *m*, Schlafanzug *m*; **a pair of ~** ein Schlafanzug
pylon ['paɪlən] *n* Mast *m*
pyramid ['pɪrəmɪd] *n* Pyramide *f*
Pyrenean [pɪrə'ni:ən] *adj* pyrenäisch
Pyrenees [pɪrə'ni:z] *npl*: **the ~** die Pyrenäen *pl*
Pyrex® ['paɪrɛks] *n* ≈ Jenaer Glas® *nt* ▹ *adj* (*dish, bowl*) aus Jenaer Glas®
python ['paɪθən] *n* Pythonschlange *f*

Qq

Q, **q** [kjuː] *n* (*letter*) Q *nt*, q *nt*; **Q for Queen** ≈ Q wie Quelle
Qatar [kæ'tɑːʳ] *n* Katar *nt*
QC (*Brit*) *n abbr* (*Law*: *= Queen's Counsel*) Kronanwalt *m*; *siehe Info-Artikel*

> **QC**
>
> QC (kurz für Queen's Counsel, bzw. KC für King's Counsel) ist in Großbritannien ein hochgestellter *barrister*, der auf Empfehlung des Lordkanzlers ernannt wird und zum Zeichen seines Amtes einen seidenen Umhang trägt und daher auch als *silk* bezeichnet wird. Ein QC muss vor Gericht in Begleitung eines rangniedrigeren Anwaltes erscheinen.

QCA (*Brit*) *n abbr* (*= Qualifications and Curriculum Authority*) *Behörde, die in England für die Entwicklung von Lehrplänen und deren Beachtung zuständig ist*
QED *abbr* (*= quod erat demonstrandum*) q. e. d.
QM *n abbr* (*Mil*) = **quartermaster**
q.t. (*inf*) *n abbr* (*= quiet*): **on the ~** heimlich
quack [kwæk] *n* (*of duck*) Schnattern *nt*, Quaken *nt*; (*inf*: *pej*: *doctor*) Quacksalber *m* ▷ *vi* schnattern, quaken
quad [kwɔd] *abbr* = **quadrangle**; (*= quadruplet*) Vierling *m*
quadrangle ['kwɔdræŋgl] *n* (*courtyard*) Innenhof *m*
quadrilateral [kwɔdrɪ'lætərəl] *n* Viereck *nt*
quadruped ['kwɔdrupɛd] *n* Vierfüßer *m*
quadruple [kwɔ'druːpl] *vt* vervierfachen ▷ *vi* sich vervierfachen
quadruplets [kwɔ'druːplɪts] *npl* Vierlinge *pl*
quagmire ['kwægmaɪəʳ] *n* (*also fig*) Sumpf *m*
quail [kweɪl] *n* Wachtel *f* ▷ *vi*: **he ~ed at the thought/before her anger** ihm schauderte bei dem Gedanken/vor ihrem Zorn
quaint [kweɪnt] *adj* (*house, village*) malerisch; (*ideas, customs*) urig, kurios
quake [kweɪk] *vi* beben, zittern ▷ *n* = **earthquake**
Quaker ['kweɪkəʳ] *n* Quäker(in) *m(f)*
qualification [kwɔlɪfɪ'keɪʃən] *n* (*often pl*: *degree etc*) Qualifikation *f*; (*attribute*) Voraussetzung *f*; (*reservation*) Vorbehalt *m*; **what are your ~s?** welche Qualifikationen haben Sie?
qualified ['kwɔlɪfaɪd] *adj* (*trained*: *doctor etc*) qualifiziert, ausgebildet; (*limited*: *agreement, praise*) bedingt; **to be/feel ~ to do sth** (*fit, competent*) qualifiziert sein/sich qualifiziert fühlen, etw zu tun; **it was a ~ success** es war kein voller Erfolg; **he's not ~ for the job** ihm fehlen die Qualifikationen für die Stelle
qualify ['kwɔlɪfaɪ] *vt* (*entitle*) qualifizieren; (*modify*: *statement*) einschränken ▷ *vi* (*pass examination*) sich qualifizieren; **to ~ for** (*be eligible*) die Berechtigung erlangen für; (*in competition*) sich qualifizieren für; **to ~ as an engineer** die Ausbildung zum Ingenieur abschließen
qualifying ['kwɔlɪfaɪɪŋ] *adj*: **~ exam** Auswahlprüfung *f*; **~ game** Vorrunden- *or* Qualifikationsspiel *f*; **~ group** Vorrunden- *or* Qualifikationsgruppe *f*; **~ round** Qualifikationsrunde *f*
qualitative ['kwɔlɪtətɪv] *adj* qualitativ
quality ['kwɔlɪtɪ] *n* Qualität *f*; (*characteristic*) Eigenschaft *f* ▷ *cpd* Qualitäts-; **of good/poor ~** von guter/schlechter Qualität; **~ of life** Lebensqualität *f*
quality control *n* Qualitätskontrolle *f*
quality papers (*Brit*) *npl*: **the ~** die seriösen Zeitungen *pl*; *siehe Info-Artikel*

> **QUALITY PRESS**
>
> *Quality press* bezeichnet die seriösen Tages- und Wochenzeitungen im Gegensatz zu den Massenblättern. Diese Zeitungen sind fast alle großformatig und wenden sich an den anspruchsvolleren Leser, der voll informiert sein möchte und bereit ist, für die Zeitungslektüre viel Zeit aufzuwenden. Siehe auch *tabloid press*.

qualm [kwɑːm] *n* Bedenken *pl*; **to have ~s about sth** Bedenken wegen etw haben
quandary ['kwɔndrɪ] *n*: **to be in a ~** in einem Dilemma sein
quango ['kwæŋgəu] (*Brit*) *n abbr* (*= quasi-autonomous nongovernmental organization*) ≈ (regierungsunabhängige) Kommission *f*
quantifiable ['kwɔntɪfaɪəbl] *adj*

quantifizierbar

quantitative ['kwɔntɪtətɪv] *adj* quantitativ

quantity ['kwɔntɪtɪ] *n* (*amount*) Menge *f*; **in large/small quantities** in großen/kleinen Mengen; **in ~** (*in bulk*) in großen Mengen; **an unknown ~** (*fig*) eine unbekannte Größe

quantity surveyor *n* Baukostenkalkulator(in) *m(f)*

quantum leap ['kwɔntəm-] *n* (*Phys*) Quantensprung *m*; (*fig*) Riesenschritt *m*

quarantine ['kwɔrnti:n] *n* Quarantäne *f*; **in ~** in Quarantäne

quark [kwɑ:k] *n* (*cheese*) Quark *m*; (*Phys*) Quark *nt*

quarrel ['kwɔrl] *n* (*argument*) Streit *m* ▷ *vi* sich streiten; **to have a ~ with sb** sich mit jdm streiten; **I've no ~ with him** ich habe nichts gegen ihn; **I can't ~ with that** dagegen kann ich nichts einwenden

quarrelsome ['kwɔrəlsəm] *adj* streitsüchtig

quarry ['kwɔrɪ] *n* (*for stone*) Steinbruch *m*; (*prey*) Beute *f* ▷ *vt* (*marble etc*) brechen

quart [kwɔ:t] *n* Quart *nt*

quarter ['kwɔ:tə^r] *n* Viertel *nt*; (*US: coin*) 25-Cent-Stück *nt*; (*of year*) Quartal *nt*; (*district*) Viertel *nt* ▷ *vt* (*divide*) vierteln; (*Mil: lodge*) einquartieren; **quarters** *npl* (*Mil*) Quartier *nt*; (*also*: **living quarters**) Unterkünfte *pl*; **a ~ of an hour** eine viertel Stunde; **it's a ~ to three, it's a ~ of three** (US) es ist Viertel vor drei; **it's a ~ past three, it's a ~ after three** (*US*) es ist Viertel nach drei; **from all ~s** aus allen Richtungen; **at close ~s** aus unmittelbarer Nähe

quarterback ['kwɔ:təbæk] *n* (*American Football*) Quarterback *m*

quarterdeck ['kwɔ:tədɛk] *n* (*Naut*) Quarterdeck *nt*

quarterfinal ['kwɔ:tə'faɪnl] *n* Viertelfinale *nt*

quarterly ['kwɔ:təlɪ] *adj, adv* vierteljährlich ▷ *n* Vierteljahresschrift *f*

quartermaster ['kwɔ:təmɑ:stə^r] *n* (*Mil*) Quartiermeister *m*

quartet [kwɔ:'tɛt] *n* (*Mus*) Quartett *nt*

quarto ['kwɔ:təu] *n* (*size of paper*) Quartformat *nt*; (*book*) im Quartformat

quartz [kwɔ:ts] *n* Quarz *m* ▷ *cpd* (*watch, clock*) Quarz-

quash [kwɔʃ] *vt* (*verdict*) aufheben

quasi- ['kweɪzaɪ] *pref* quasi-

quaver ['kweɪvə^r] *n* (*Brit: Mus*) Achtelnote *f* ▷ *vi* (*voice*) beben, zittern

quay [ki:] *n* Kai *m*

quayside ['ki:saɪd] *n* Kai *m*

queasiness ['kwi:zɪnɪs] *n* Übelkeit *f*

queasy ['kwi:zɪ] *adj* (*nauseous*) übel; **I feel ~** mir ist übel *or* schlecht

Quebec [kwɪ'bɛk] *n* Quebec *nt*

queen [kwi:n] *n* (*also Zool*) Königin *f*; (*Cards, Chess*) Dame *f*

queen mother *n* Königinmutter *f*

Queen's speech (*Brit*) *n* ≈ Regierungserklärung *f*; *siehe Info-Artikel*

QUEEN'S SPEECH

Queen's Speech (bzw. *King's Speech*) ist eine vom britischen Monarchen bei der alljährlichen feierlichen Parlamentseröffnung im Oberhaus vor dem versammelten Ober- und Unterhaus verlesene Rede. Sie wird vom Premierminister in Zusammenarbeit mit dem Kabinett verfasst und enthält die Regierungserklärung.

queer [kwɪə^r] *adj* (*odd*) sonderbar, seltsam ▷ *n* (*inf!: pej: male homosexual*) Schwule(r) *m*; **I feel ~** (*Brit: unwell*) mir ist ganz komisch

quell [kwɛl] *vt* (*riot*) niederschlagen; (*fears*) überwinden

quench [kwɛntʃ] *vt*: **to ~ one's thirst** seinen Durst stillen

querulous ['kwɛruləs] *adj* nörglerisch

query ['kwɪərɪ] *n* Anfrage *f* ▷ *vt* (*check*) nachfragen bezüglich *+gen*; (*express doubt about*) bezweifeln

quest [kwɛst] *n* Suche *f*

question ['kwɛstʃən] *n* Frage *f* ▷ *vt* (*interrogate*) befragen; (*doubt*) bezweifeln; **to ask sb a question, put a ~ to sb** jdm eine Frage stellen; **to bring** *or* **call sth into ~** etw infrage stellen; **the ~ is ...** die Frage ist ...; **there's no ~ of him playing for England** es ist ausgeschlossen, dass er für England spielt; **the person/night in ~** die fragliche Person/Nacht; **to be beyond ~** außer Frage stehen; **to be out of the ~** nicht infrage kommen

questionable ['kwɛstʃənəbl] *adj* fraglich

questioner ['kwɛstʃənə^r] *n* Fragesteller(in) *m(f)*

questioning ['kwɛstʃənɪŋ] *adj* (*look*) fragend; (*mind*) forschend ▷ *n* (*Police*) Vernehmung *f*

question mark *n* Fragezeichen *nt*

questionnaire [kwɛstʃə'nɛə^r] *n* Fragebogen *m*

queue [kju:] (*Brit*) *n* Schlange *f* ▷ *vi* (*also*: **queue up**) Schlange stehen

quibble ['kwɪbl] *vi*: **to ~ about** *or* **over** sich streiten über *+acc*; **to ~ with** herumnörgeln an *+dat* ▷ *n* Krittelei *f*

quiche [ki:ʃ] *n* Quiche *f*

quick [kwɪk] *adj* schnell; (*mind, wit*) wach; (*look, visit*) flüchtig ▷ *adv* schnell ▷ *n*: **to cut sb to the ~** (*fig*) jdn tief verletzen; **be ~!** mach schnell!; **to be ~ to act** schnell handeln; **she was ~ to see that ...** sie begriff schnell, dass ...; **she has a ~ temper** sie wird leicht hitzig

quicken ['kwɪkən] *vt* beschleunigen ▷ *vi* schneller werden, sich beschleunigen

quick-fire ['kwɪkfaɪə^r] *adj* (*questions*) wie aus der Pistole

quick fix *n* Sofortlösung *f*

quicklime ['kwɪklaɪm] *n* ungelöschter Kalk *m*

quickly ['kwɪklɪ] *adv* schnell

quickness ['kwɪknɪs] *n* Schnelligkeit *f*; **~ of mind** Scharfsinn *m*

quicksand ['kwɪksænd] *n* Treibsand *m*
quickstep ['kwɪkstɛp] *n* Quickstepp *m*
quick-tempered [kwɪk'tɛmpəd] *adj* hitzig, leicht erregbar
quick-witted [kwɪk'wɪtɪd] *adj* schlagfertig
quid [kwɪd] (*Brit: inf*) *n inv* Pfund *nt*
quid pro quo ['kwɪdprəu'kwəu] *n* Gegenleistung *f*
quiet ['kwaɪət] *adj* leise; (*place*) ruhig, still; (*silent, reserved*) still; (*business, day*) ruhig; (*without fuss etc: wedding*) in kleinem Rahmen ▷ *n* (*peacefulness*) Stille *f*, Ruhe *f*; (*silence*) Ruhe *f* ▷ *vt, vi* (*US*) = **quieten**; **keep** *or* **be ~!** sei still!; **I'll have a ~ word with him** ich werde mal unter vier Augen mit ihm reden; **on the ~** (*in secret*) heimlich
quieten ['kwaɪətn] (*Brit: also:* **quieten down**) *vi* ruhiger werden ▷ *vt* (*person, animal*) beruhigen
quietly ['kwaɪətlɪ] *adv* leise; (*silently*) still; (*calmly*) ruhig; **~ confident** insgeheim sicher
quietness ['kwaɪətnɪs] *n* (*peacefulness*) Ruhe *f*; (*silence*) Stille *f*
quill [kwɪl] *n* (*pen*) Feder *f*; (*of porcupine*) Stachel *m*
quilt [kwɪlt] *n* Decke *f*; (*also:* **continental quilt**) Federbett *nt*
quin [kwɪn] (*Brit*) *n abbr* (= *quintuplet*) Fünfling *m*
quince [kwɪns] *n* Quitte *f*
quinine [kwɪ'ni:n] *n* Chinin *nt*
quintet [kwɪn'tɛt] *n* (*Mus*) Quintett *nt*
quintuplets [kwɪn'tju:plɪts] *npl* Fünflinge *pl*
quip [kwɪp] *n* witzige *or* geistreiche Bemerkung *f* ▷ *vt* witzeln
quire ['kwaɪəʳ] *n* (*of paper*) 24 Bogen Papier
quirk [kwə:k] *n* Marotte *f*; **a ~ of fate** eine Laune des Schicksals
quit [kwɪt] (*pt, pp* **~** *or* **quitted**) *vt* (*smoking*) aufgeben; (*job*) kündigen; (*premises*) verlassen ▷ *vi* (*give up*) aufgeben; (*resign*) kündigen; **to ~ doing sth** aufhören, etw zu tun; **~ stalling!** (*US: inf*) weichen Sie nicht ständig aus!; **notice to ~** (*Brit*) Kündigung *f*
quite [kwaɪt] *adv* (*rather*) ziemlich; (*entirely*) ganz; **not ~** nicht ganz; **I ~ like it** ich mag es ganz gern; **I ~ understand** ich verstehe; **I don't ~ remember** ich erinnere mich nicht genau; **not ~ as many as the last time** nicht ganz so viele wie das letzte Mal; **that meal was ~ something!** das Essen konnte sich sehen lassen!; **it was ~ a sight** das war vielleicht ein Anblick; **~ a few of them** eine ganze Reihe von Ihnen; **~ (so)!** ganz recht!
quits [kwɪts] *adj*: **we're ~** wir sind quitt; **let's call it ~** lassen wirs dabei
quiver ['kwɪvəʳ] *vi* zittern
quiz [kwɪz] *n* (*game*) Quiz *nt* ▷ *vt* (*question*) befragen
quizzical ['kwɪzɪkl] *adj* (*look, smile*) wissend
quoits [kwɔɪts] *npl* (*game*) *Wurfspiel mit Ringen*
quorum ['kwɔ:rəm] *n* Quorum *nt*
quota ['kwəutə] *n* (*allowance*) Quote *f*
quotation [kwəu'teɪʃən] *n* (*from book etc*) Zitat *nt*; (*estimate*) Preisangabe *f*; (*Comm*) Kostenvoranschlag *m*
quotation marks *npl* Anführungszeichen *pl*
quote [kwəut] *n* (*from book etc*) Zitat *nt*; (*estimate*) Kostenvoranschlag *m* ▷ *vt* zitieren; (*fact, example*) anführen; (*price*) nennen; **quotes** *npl* (*quotation marks*) Anführungszeichen *pl*; **in ~s** in Anführungszeichen; **the figure ~d for the repairs** die für die Reparatur genannte Summe; **~ ... unquote** Zitat Anfang ... Zitat Ende
quotient ['kwəuʃənt] *n* Quotient *m*
qv *abbr* (= *quod vide*) s.d.
qwerty keyboard ['kwə:tɪ-] *n* Qwerty-Tastatur *f*

Rr

R¹, **r** [ɑːʳ] *n* (*letter*) R *nt*, r *nt*; **R for Robert, R for Roger** (*US*) ≈ R wie Richard
R² [ɑːʳ] *abbr* (= *Réaumur (scale)*) R; (*US: Cine:* = *restricted*) *Klassifikation für nicht jugendfreie Filme*
R. *abbr* (= *right*) r. = **river**; (*US: Pol*) = **republican**; (*Brit:* = *Rex*) *König*; (= *Regina*) *Königin*
RA *abbr* (*Mil*) = **rear admiral** ▷ *n abbr* (*Brit:* = *Royal Academy*) *Gesellschaft zur Förderung der Künste*; (= *Royal Academician*) *Mitglied der Royal Academy*
RAAF *n abbr* (*Mil:* = *Royal Australian Air Force*) australische Luftwaffe *f*
Rabat [rəˈbɑːt] *n* Rabat *nt*
rabbi [ˈræbaɪ] *n* Rabbi *m*
rabbit [ˈræbɪt] *n* Kaninchen *nt* ▷ *vi* (*Brit: inf: also:* **to rabbit on**) quatschen, schwafeln
rabbit hole *n* Kaninchenbau *m*
rabbit hutch *n* Kaninchenstall *m*
rabble [ˈræbl] (*pej*) *n* Pöbel *m*
rabid [ˈræbɪd] *adj* (*animal*) tollwütig; (*fig: fanatical*) fanatisch
rabies [ˈreɪbiːz] *n* Tollwut *f*
RAC (*Brit*) *n abbr* (= *Royal Automobile Club*) *Autofahrerorganisation*, ≈ ADAC *m*
raccoon [rəˈkuːn] *n* Waschbär *m*
race [reɪs] *n* (*species*) Rasse *f*; (*competition*) Rennen *nt*; (*for power, control*) Wettlauf *m* ▷ *vt* (*horse, pigeon*) an Wettbewerben teilnehmen lassen; (*car etc*) ins Rennen schicken; (*person*) um die Wette laufen mit ▷ *vi* (*compete*) antreten; (*hurry*) rennen; (*pulse, heart*) rasen; (*engine*) durchdrehen; **the human ~** die Menschheit; **a ~ against time** ein Wettlauf mit der Zeit; **he ~d across the road** er raste über die Straße; **to ~ in/out** hinein-/hinausstürzen
race car (*US*) *n* = **racing car**
race car driver (*US*) *n* = **racing driver**
racecourse [ˈreɪskɔːs] *n* Rennbahn *f*
racehorse [ˈreɪshɔːs] *n* Rennpferd *nt*
race meeting *n* Rennveranstaltung *f*
race relations *npl* Beziehungen *pl* zwischen den Rassen
racetrack [ˈreɪstræk] *n* Rennbahn *f*; (*US*) = **racecourse**
racial [ˈreɪʃl] *adj* Rassen-
racialism [ˈreɪʃlɪzəm] *n* Rassismus *m*
racialist [ˈreɪʃlɪst] *adj* rassistisch ▷ *n* (*pej*) Rassist(in) *m(f)*
racing [ˈreɪsɪŋ] *n* (*also:* **horse racing**) Pferderennen *nt*; (*also:* **motor racing**) Rennsport *m*
racing car (*Brit*) *n* Rennwagen *m*
racing driver (*Brit*) *n* Rennfahrer(in) *m(f)*
racism [ˈreɪsɪzəm] *n* Rassismus *m*
racist [ˈreɪsɪst] *adj* rassistisch ▷ *n* (*pej*) Rassist(in) *m(f)*
rack [ræk] *n* (*also:* **luggage rack**) Gepäckablage *f*; (*also:* **roof rack**) Dachgepäckträger *m*; (*for dresses etc*) Ständer *m*; (*for dishes*) Gestell *nt* ▷ *vt*: **~ed by** (*pain etc*) gemartert von; **magazine/toast ~** Zeitungs-/Toastständer *m*; **to ~ one's brains** sich *dat* den Kopf zerbrechen; **to go to ~ and ruin** (*building*) zerfallen; (*business, country*) herunterkommen
racket [ˈrækɪt] *n* (*for tennis etc*) Schläger *m*; (*noise*) Krach *m*, Radau *m*; (*swindle*) Schwindel *m*
racketeer [rækɪˈtɪəʳ] (*esp US*) *n* Gangster *m*
racoon [rəˈkuːn] *n* = **raccoon**
racquet [ˈrækɪt] *n* (*for tennis etc*) Schläger *m*
racy [ˈreɪsɪ] *adj* (*book, story*) rasant
RADA [rɑːdə] (*Brit*) *n abbr* (= *Royal Academy of Dramatic Art*) *Schauspielschule*
radar [ˈreɪdɑːʳ] *n* Radar *m or nt* ▷ *cpd* Radar-
radar trap *n* Radarfalle *f*
radial [ˈreɪdɪəl] *adj* (*roads*) strahlenförmig verlaufend; (*pattern*) strahlenförmig ▷ *n* (*also:* **radial tyre**) Gürtelreifen *m*
radiance [ˈreɪdɪəns] *n* Glanz *m*
radiant [ˈreɪdɪənt] *adj* strahlend; (*Phys: heat*) Strahlungs-
radiate [ˈreɪdɪeɪt] *vt* (*lit, fig*) ausstrahlen ▷ *vi* (*lines, roads*) strahlenförmig verlaufen
radiation [reɪdɪˈeɪʃən] *n* (*radioactivity*) radioaktive Strahlung *f*; (*from sun etc*) Strahlung *f*
radiation sickness *n* Strahlenkrankheit *f*
radiator [ˈreɪdɪeɪtəʳ] *n* (*heater*) Heizkörper *m*; (*Aut*) Kühler *m*
radiator cap *n* (*Aut*) Kühlerdeckel *m*
radiator grill *n* (*Aut*) Kühlergrill *m*
radical [ˈrædɪkl] *adj* radikal ▷ *n* (*person*) Radikale(r) *f(m)*
radii [ˈreɪdɪaɪ] *npl of* **radius**
radio [ˈreɪdɪəu] *n* (*broadcasting*) Radio *nt*, Rundfunk *m*; (*device: for receiving broadcasts*)

Radio *nt*; (*: for transmitting and receiving*) Funkgerät *nt* ▷ *vi*: **to ~ to sb** mit jdm per Funk sprechen ▷ *vt* (*person*) per Funk verständigen; (*message, position*) per Funk durchgeben; **on the ~** im Radio

radio ... ['reɪdɪəu] *pref* Radio ..., radio ...

radioactive ['reɪdɪəu'æktɪv] *adj* radioaktiv

radioactivity ['reɪdɪəuæk'tɪvɪtɪ] *n* Radioaktivität *f*

radio announcer *n* Rundfunksprecher(in) *m(f)*

radio-controlled ['reɪdɪəukən'trəuld] *adj* ferngesteuert

radiographer [reɪdɪ'ɔgrəfəʳ] *n* Röntgenologe *m*, Röntgenologin *f*

radiography [reɪdɪ'ɔgrəfɪ] *n* Röntgenografie *f*

radiologist [reɪdɪ'ɔlədʒɪst] *n* Radiologe *m*, Radiologin *f*

radiology [reɪdɪ'ɔlədʒɪ] *n* Radiologie *f*

radio station *n* Radiosender *m*

radio taxi *n* Funktaxi *nt*

radiotelephone ['reɪdɪəu'tɛlɪfəun] *n* Funksprechgerät *nt*

radio telescope *n* Radioteleskop *nt*

radiotherapist ['reɪdɪəu'θɛrəpɪst] *n* Strahlentherapeut(in) *m(f)*

radiotherapy ['reɪdɪəu'θɛrəpɪ] *n* Strahlentherapie *f*

radish ['rædɪʃ] *n* Radieschen *nt*; (*long white variety*) Rettich *m*

radium ['reɪdɪəm] *n* Radium *nt*

radius ['reɪdɪəs] (*pl* **radii**) *n* Radius *m*; (*area*) Umkreis *m*; **within a ~ of 50 miles** in einem Umkreis von 50 Meilen

RAF (*Brit*) *n abbr* = **Royal Air Force**

raffia ['ræfɪə] *n* Bast *m*

raffish ['ræfɪʃ] *adj* (*person*) verwegen; (*place*) verkommen

raffle ['ræfl] *n* Verlosung *f*, Tombola *f* ▷ *vt* (*prize*) verlosen; **~ ticket** Los *nt*

raft [rɑ:ft] *n* Floß *nt*; (*also*: **life raft**) Rettungsfloß *nt*

rafter ['rɑ:ftəʳ] *n* Dachsparren *m*

rag [ræg] *n* (*piece of cloth*) Lappen *m*; (*torn cloth*) Fetzen *m*; (*pej: newspaper*) Käseblatt *nt*; (*Brit: Univ*) *studentische Wohltätigkeitsveranstaltung* ▷ *vt* (*Brit: tease*) aufziehen; **rags** *npl* (*torn clothes*) Lumpen *pl*; **in ~s** (*person*) zerlumpt; **his was a ~s-to-riches story** er brachte es vom Tellerwäscher zum Millionär

rag-and-bone man [rægən'bəun-] (*Brit*) *n* Lumpensammler *m*

ragbag ['rægbæg] *n* (*assortment*) Sammelsurium *nt*

RAG DAY/WEEK

Rag Day/Week heißt der Tag bzw. die Woche, wenn Studenten Geld für wohltätige Zwecke sammeln. Diverse gesponserte Aktionen wie Volksläufe, Straßentheater und Kneipentouren werden zur Unterhaltung der Studenten und der Bevölkerung organisiert. Studentenzeitschriften mit schlüpfrigen Witzen werden auf der Straße verkauft, und fast alle Universitäten und Colleges halten einen Ball ab. Der Erlös aller Veranstaltungen fließt Wohltätigkeitsorganisationen zu.

rag doll *n* Stoffpuppe *f*

rage [reɪdʒ] *n* (*fury*) Wut *f*, Zorn *m* ▷ *vi* toben, wüten; **it's all the ~** (*fashionable*) es ist der letzte Schrei; **to fly into a ~** einen Wutanfall bekommen

ragged ['rægɪd] *adj* (*jagged*) zackig; (*clothes, person*) zerlumpt; (*beard*) ausgefranst

raging ['reɪdʒɪŋ] *adj* (*sea, storm, torrent*) tobend, tosend; (*fever*) heftig; (*thirst*) brennend; (*toothache*) rasend

rag trade (*inf*) *n*: **the ~** die Modebranche *f*

raid [reɪd] *n* (*Mil*) Angriff *m*, Überfall *m*; (*by police*) Razzia *f*; (*by criminal: forcefully*) Überfall *m*; (*: secretly*) Einbruch *m* ▷ *vt* (*Mil*) angreifen, überfallen; (*police*) stürmen; (*criminal: forcefully*) überfallen; (*: secretly*) einbrechen in *+acc*

rail [reɪl] *n* Geländer *nt*; (*on deck of ship*) Reling *f*; **rails** *npl* (*for train*) Schienen *pl*; **by ~** mit der Bahn

railcard ['reɪlkɑ:d] (*Brit*) *n* (*for young people*) ≈ Juniorenpass *m*; (*for pensioners*) ≈ Seniorenpass *m*

railing ['reɪlɪŋ] *n*, **railings** ['reɪlɪŋz] ▷ *npl* (*fence*) Zaun *m*

railroad ['reɪlrəud] (*US*) *n* = **railway**

railway ['reɪlweɪ] (*Brit*) *n* Eisenbahn *f*; (*track*) Gleis *nt*; (*company*) Bahn *f*

railway engine (*Brit*) *n* Lokomotive *f*

railway line (*Brit*) *n* Bahnlinie *f*; (*track*) Gleis *nt*

railwayman ['reɪlweɪmən] (*irreg: like* **man**); (*Brit*) *n* Eisenbahner *m*

railway station (*Brit*) *n* Bahnhof *m*

rain [reɪn] *n* Regen *m* ▷ *vi* regnen; **in the ~** im Regen; **as right as ~** voll auf der Höhe; **it's ~ing** es regnet; **it's ~ing cats and dogs** es regnet in Strömen

rainbow ['reɪnbəu] *n* Regenbogen *m*

rainbow family *n gleichgeschlechtliches Paar mit Kind/Kindern*, Regenbogenfamilie *f*

rainbow flag *n* Regenbogenfahne *f or* -flagge *f*

rain check (*US*) *n*: **to take a ~ on sth** sich *dat* etw noch einmal überlegen

raincoat ['reɪnkəut] *n* Regenmantel *m*

raindrop ['reɪndrɔp] *n* Regentropfen *m*

rainfall ['reɪnfɔ:l] *n* Niederschlag *m*

rainforest ['reɪnfɔrɪst] *n* Regenwald *m*

rainproof ['reɪnpru:f] *adj* wasserfest

rainstorm ['reɪnstɔ:m] *n* schwere Regenfälle *pl*

rainwater ['reɪnwɔ:təʳ] *n* Regenwasser *nt*

rainy ['reɪnɪ] *adj* (*day*) regnerisch, verregnet; (*area*) regenreich; **~ season** Regenzeit *f*; **to save sth for a ~ day** etw für schlechte Zeiten aufheben

raise [reɪz] *n* (*pay rise*) Gehaltserhöhung *f* ▷ *vt* (*lift: hand*) hochheben; (*: window*) hochziehen; (*siege*) beenden; (*embargo*) aufheben; (*increase*) erhöhen; (*improve*) verbessern; (*question etc*) zur Sprache bringen; (*doubts etc*) vorbringen; (*child, cattle*) aufziehen; (*crop*) anbauen; (*army*) aufstellen; (*funds*) aufbringen; (*loan*) aufnehmen; **to ~ a glass to sb/sth** das Glas auf jdn/etw erheben; **to ~ one's voice** die Stimme erheben; **to ~ sb's hopes** jdm Hoffnungen machen; **to ~ a laugh/smile** Gelächter/ein Lächeln hervorrufen; **this ~s the question ...** das wirft die Frage auf ...

raisin ['reɪzn] *n* Rosine *f*

Raj [rɑːdʒ] *n*: **the ~** *britische Regierung in Indien vor 1947*

rajah ['rɑːdʒə] *n* Radscha *m*

rake [reɪk] *n* Harke *f*; (*old: person*) Schwerenöter *m* ▷ *vt* harken; (*light, gun: area*) bestreichen; **he's raking it in** (*inf*) er scheffelt das Geld nur so

rake-off ['reɪkɔf] (*inf*) *n* Anteil *m*

rally ['rælɪ] *n* (*Pol etc*) Kundgebung *f*; (*Aut*) Rallye *f*; (*Tennis etc*) Ballwechsel *m* ▷ *vt* (*support*) sammeln ▷ *vi* (*sick person, Stock Exchange*) sich erholen

▶ **rally round** *vi* sich zusammentun ▷ *vt fus* zu Hilfe kommen *+dat*

rallying point ['rælɪɪŋ-] *n* Sammelstelle *f*

RAM [ræm] *n abbr* (*Comput: = random access memory*) RAM

ram [ræm] *n* Widder *m* ▷ *vt* rammen

ramble ['ræmbl] *n* Wanderung *f* ▷ *vi* wandern; (*also*: **ramble on**: *talk*) schwafeln

rambler ['ræmblə^r] *n* Wanderer *m*, Wanderin *f*; (*Bot*) Kletterrose *f*

rambling ['ræmblɪŋ] *adj* (*speech, letter*) weitschweifig; (*house*) weitläufig; (*Bot*) rankend, Kletter-

rambunctious [ræm'bʌŋkʃəs] (*US*) *adj* = **rumbustious**

RAMC (*Brit*) *n abbr* (*= Royal Army Medical Corps*) *Verband zur Versorgung der Armee mit Stabsärzten und Sanitätern*

ramifications [ræmɪfɪ'keɪʃənz] *npl* Auswirkungen *pl*

ramp [ræmp] *n* Rampe *f*; (*in garage*) Hebebühne *f*; **on ~** (*US: Aut*) Auffahrt *f*; **off ~** (*US: Aut*) Ausfahrt *f*

rampage [ræm'peɪdʒ] *n*: **to be/go on the ~** randalieren ▷ *vi*: **they went rampaging through the town** sie zogen randalierend durch die Stadt

rampant ['ræmpənt] *adj*: **to be ~** (*crime, disease etc*) wild wuchern

rampart ['ræmpɑːt] *n* Schutzwall *m*

ram raiding [-reɪdɪŋ] *n Einbruchdiebstahl, wobei die Diebe mit einem Wagen in die Schaufensterfront eines Ladens eindringen*

ramshackle ['ræmʃækl] *adj* (*house*) baufällig; (*cart*) klapprig; (*table*) altersschwach

RAN *n abbr* (*= Royal Australian Navy*) australische Marine *f*

ran [ræn] *pt of* **run**

ranch [rɑːntʃ] *n* Ranch *f*

rancher ['rɑːntʃə^r] *n* Rancher(in) *m(f)*; (*worker*) Farmhelfer(in) *m(f)*

rancid ['rænsɪd] *adj* ranzig

rancour, (*US*) **rancor** ['ræŋkə^r] *n* Verbitterung *f*

R&B *n abbr* (*= rhythm and blues*) R & B

R&D *n abbr* = **research and development**

random ['rændəm] *adj* (*arrangement*) willkürlich; (*selection*) zufällig; (*Comput*) wahlfrei; (*Math*) Zufalls- ▷ *n*: **at ~** aufs Geratewohl

random access *n* (*Comput*) wahlfreier Zugriff *m*

random access memory *n* (*Comput*) Schreib-Lese-Speicher *m*

R&R (*US*) *n abbr* (*Mil: = rest and recreation*) Urlaub *m*

randy ['rændɪ] (*Brit: inf*) *adj* geil, scharf

rang [ræŋ] *pt of* **ring**

range [reɪndʒ] *n* (*of mountains*) Kette *f*; (*of missile*) Reichweite *f*; (*of voice*) Umfang *m*; (*series*) Reihe *f*; (*of products*) Auswahl *f*; (*Mil: also*: **rifle range**) Schießstand *m*; (*also*: **kitchen range**) Herd *m* ▷ *vt* (*place in a line*) anordnen ▷ *vi*: **to ~ over** (*extend*) sich erstrecken über *+acc*; **price ~** Preisspanne *f*; **do you have anything else in this price ~?** haben Sie noch etwas anderes in dieser Preisklasse?; **within (firing) ~** in Schussweite; **at close ~** aus unmittelbarer Entfernung; **~d left/right** (*text*) links-/rechtsbündig; **to ~ from ... to ...** sich zwischen ... und ... bewegen

ranger ['reɪndʒə^r] *n* Förster(in) *m(f)*

Rangoon [ræŋ'guːn] *n* Rangun *nt*

rank [ræŋk] *n* (*row*) Reihe *f*; (*Mil*) Rang *m*; (*social class*) Schicht *f*; (*Brit: also*: **taxi rank**) Taxistand *m* ▷ *vi*: **to ~ as/among** zählen zu ▷ *vt*: **he is ~ed third in the world** er steht weltweit an dritter Stelle ▷ *adj* (*stinking*) stinkend; (*sheer: hypocrisy etc*) rein; **the ranks** *npl* (*Mil*) die Mannschaften *pl*; **the ~ and file** (*ordinary members*) die Basis *f*; **to close ~s** (*Mil, fig*) die Reihen schließen

rankle ['ræŋkl] *vi* (*insult*) nachwirken; **to ~ with sb** jdn wurmen

rank outsider *n* totaler Außenseiter *m*, totale Außenseiterin *f*

ransack ['rænsæk] *vt* (*search*) durchwühlen; (*plunder*) plündern

ransom ['rænsəm] *n* (*money*) Lösegeld *nt*; **to hold sb to ~** (*hostage*) jdn als Geisel halten; (*fig*) jdn erpressen

rant [rænt] *vi* schimpfen, wettern; **to ~ and rave** herumwettern

ranting ['ræntɪŋ] *n* Geschimpfe *nt*

rap [ræp] *vi* klopfen ▷ *vt*: **to ~ sb's knuckles** jdm auf die Finger klopfen ▷ *n* (*at door*) Klopfen *nt*; (*also*: **rap music**) Rap *m*

rape [reɪp] *n* Vergewaltigung *f*; (*Bot*) Raps *m* ▷ *vt* vergewaltigen

rape oil, rapeseed oil ['reɪpsiːd-] *n* Rapsöl *nt*

rapid ['ræpɪd] *adj* schnell; (*growth, change*) schnell, rapide

rapidity [rə'pɪdɪtɪ] *n* Schnelligkeit *f*

rapidly ['ræpɪdlɪ] *adv* schnell; (*grow, change*) schnell, rapide

rapids ['ræpɪdz] *npl* Stromschnellen *pl*
rapist ['reɪpɪst] *n* Vergewaltiger *m*
rapport [ræ'pɔːʳ] *n* enges Verhältnis *nt*
rapprochement [ræ'prɔʃmɑ̃ːŋ] *n* Annäherung *f*
rapt [ræpt] *adj* (*attention*) gespannt; **to be ~ in thought** in Gedanken versunken sein
rapture ['ræptʃəʳ] *n* Entzücken *nt*; **to go into ~s over** ins Schwärmen geraten über *+acc*
rapturous ['ræptʃərəs] *adj* (*applause, welcome*) stürmisch
rare [rɛəʳ] *adj* selten; (*steak*) nur angebraten, englisch (gebraten); **it is ~ to find that ...** es kommt nur selten vor, dass ...
rarebit ['rɛəbɪt] *n see* **Welsh rarebit**
rarefied ['rɛərɪfaɪd] *adj* (*air, atmosphere*) dünn; (*fig*) exklusiv
rarely ['rɛəlɪ] *adv* selten
raring ['rɛərɪŋ] *adj*: **~ to go** (*inf*) in den Startlöchern
rarity ['rɛərɪtɪ] *n* Seltenheit *f*
rascal ['rɑːskl] *n* (*child*) Frechdachs *m*; (*rogue*) Schurke *m*
rash [ræʃ] *adj* (*person*) unbesonnen; (*promise, act*) übereilt ▷ *n* (*Med*) Ausschlag *m*; (*of events etc*) Flut *f*; **to come out in a ~** einen Ausschlag bekommen
rasher ['ræʃəʳ] *n* (*of bacon*) Scheibe *f*
rashly ['ræʃlɪ] *adv* (*promise etc*) voreilig
rasp [rɑːsp] *n* (*tool*) Raspel *f*; (*sound*) Kratzen *nt* ▷ *vt, vi* krächzen
raspberry ['rɑːzbərɪ] *n* Himbeere *f*; **~ bush** Himbeerstrauch *m*; **to blow a ~** (*inf*) verächtlich schnauben
rasping ['rɑːspɪŋ] *adj*: **a ~ noise** ein kratzendes Geräusch
Rastafarian *n* Rastafarier *m*
rat [ræt] *n* Ratte *f*
ratable ['reɪtəbl] *adj* = **rateable**
ratchet ['rætʃɪt] *n* Sperrklinke *f*; **~ wheel** Sperrrad *nt*
rate [reɪt] *n* (*speed: of change etc*) Tempo *nt*; (*of inflation, unemployment etc*) Rate *f*; (*of interest, taxation*) Satz *m*; (*price*) Preis *m* ▷ *vt* einschätzen; **rates** *npl* (*Brit: property tax*) Kommunalabgaben *pl*; **at a ~ of 60 kph** mit einem Tempo von 60 km/h; **~ of growth** (*Econ*) Wachstumsrate *f*; **~ of return** (*Fin*) Rendite *f*; **pulse ~** Pulszahl *f*; **at this/that ~** wenn es so weitergeht; **at any ~** auf jeden Fall; **to ~ sb/sth as** jdn/etw einschätzen als; **to ~ sb/sth among** jdn/etw zählen zu; **to ~ sb/sth highly** jdn/etw hoch einschätzen
rateable ['reɪtəbl] *adj*: **~ value** (*Brit*) ▷ *n* steuerbarer Wert *m*
ratepayer ['reɪtpeɪəʳ] (*Brit*) *n* Steuerzahler(in) *m(f)*
rather ['rɑːðəʳ] *adv* (*somewhat*) etwas; (*very*) ziemlich; **~ a lot** ziemlich *or* recht viel; **I would ~ go** ich würde lieber gehen; **~ than** (*instead of*) anstelle von; **or ~** (*more accurately*) oder vielmehr; **I'd ~ not say** das möchte ich lieber nicht sagen; **I ~ think he won't come** ich glaube eher, dass er nicht kommt
ratification [rætɪfɪ'keɪʃən] *n* Ratifikation *f*
ratify ['rætɪfaɪ] *vt* (*treaty etc*) ratifizieren
rating ['reɪtɪŋ] *n* (*score*) Rate *f*; (*assessment*) Beurteilung *f*; (*Naut: Brit: sailor*) Matrose *m*; **ratings** *npl* (*Radio, TV*) Einschaltquote *f*; **~s hit** Quotenhit *m*
ratio ['reɪʃɪəu] *n* Verhältnis *nt*; **a ~ of 5 to 1** ein Verhältnis von 5 zu 1
ration ['ræʃən] *n* Ration *f* ▷ *vt* rationieren; **rations** *npl* (*Mil*) Rationen *pl*
rational ['ræʃənl] *adj* rational, vernünftig
rationale [ræʃə'nɑːl] *n* Grundlage *f*
rationalization [ræʃnəlaɪ'zeɪʃən] *n* (*justification*) Rechtfertigung *f*; (*of company, system*) Rationalisierung *f*
rationalize ['ræʃnəlaɪz] *vt* (*see n*) rechtfertigen, rationalisieren
rationally ['ræʃnəlɪ] *adv* vernünftig, rational
rationing ['ræʃnɪŋ] *n* Rationierung *f*
ratpack (*Brit: inf*) *n* (*reporters*) Pressemeute *f*
rat poison *n* Rattengift *nt*
rat race *n*: **the ~** der ständige *or* tägliche Konkurrenzkampf *m*
rattan [ræ'tæn] *n* Rattan *nt*, Peddigrohr *nt*
rattle ['rætl] *n* (*of door, window, snake*) Klappern *nt*; (*of train, car etc*) Rattern *nt*; (*of chain*) Rasseln *nt*; (*toy*) Rassel *f* ▷ *vi* (*chains*) rasseln; (*windows*) klappern; (*bottles*) klirren ▷ *vt* (*shake noisily*) rütteln an *+dat*; (*fig: unsettle*) nervös machen; **to ~ along** (*car, bus*) dahinrattern
rattlesnake ['rætlsneɪk] *n* Klapperschlange *f*
ratty ['rætɪ] (*inf*) *adj* gereizt
raucous ['rɔːkəs] *adj* (*voice etc*) rau
raucously ['rɔːkəslɪ] *adv* rau
raunchy ['rɔːntʃɪ] *adj* (*voice, song*) lüstern, geil
ravage ['rævɪdʒ] *vt* verwüsten
ravages ['rævɪdʒɪz] *npl* (*of war*) Verwüstungen *pl*; (*of weather*) zerstörende Auswirkungen *pl*; (*of time*) Spuren *pl*
rave [reɪv] *vi* (*in anger*) toben ▷ *adj* (*inf: review*) glänzend; (*scene, culture*) Rave- ▷ *n* (*Brit: inf: party*) Rave *m*, Fete *f*
▸ **rave about** schwärmen von
raven ['reɪvən] *n* Rabe *m*
ravenous ['rævənəs] *adj* (*person*) ausgehungert; (*appetite*) unersättlich
ravine [rə'viːn] *n* Schlucht *f*
raving ['reɪvɪŋ] *adj*: **a ~ lunatic** ein total verrückter Typ
ravings ['reɪvɪŋz] *npl* Fantastereien *pl*
ravioli [rævɪ'əulɪ] *n* Ravioli *pl*
ravishing ['rævɪʃɪŋ] *adj* hinreißend
raw [rɔː] *adj* roh; (*sore*) wund; (*inexperienced*) unerfahren; (*weather, day*) rau; **to get a ~ deal** ungerecht behandelt werden
Rawalpindi [rɔːl'pɪndɪ] *n* Rawalpindi *nt*
raw material *n* Rohmaterial *nt*
ray [reɪ] *n* Strahl *m*; **~ of hope** Hoffnungsschimmer *m*
rayon ['reɪɔn] *n* Reyon *nt*
raze [reɪz] *vt* (*also:* **to raze to the ground**) dem Erdboden gleichmachen

razor ['reɪzəʳ] *n* Rasierapparat *m*; (*open razor*) Rasiermesser *nt*
razor blade *n* Rasierklinge *f*
razzle ['ræzl] (*Brit: inf*) *n*: **to be/go on the ~** einen draufmachen
razzmatazz ['ræzmə'tæz] (*inf*) *n* Trubel *m*
RC *abbr* (= *Roman Catholic*) r.-k.
RCAF *n abbr* (= *Royal Canadian Air Force*) kanadische Luftwaffe *f*
RCMP *n abbr* (= *Royal Canadian Mounted Police*) *kanadische berittene Polizei*
RCN *n abbr* (= *Royal Canadian Navy*) kanadische Marine
RD (*US*) *abbr* (*Post*) = *rural delivery* Landpostzustellung *f*
Rd *abbr* (= *road*) Str.
RDC (*Brit*) *n abbr* = **rural district council**
RE (*Brit*) *n abbr* (*Scol*) = **religious education** (*Mil*: = *Royal Engineers*) *Königliches Pionierkorps*
re [ri:] *prep* (*with regard to*) bezüglich *+gen*
reach [ri:tʃ] *n* (*range*) Reichweite *f* ▷ *vt* erreichen; (*conclusion, decision*) kommen zu; (*be able to touch*) kommen an *+acc* ▷ *vi* (*stretch out one's arm*) langen; **reaches** *npl* (*of river*) Gebiete *pl*; **within/out of ~** in/außer Reichweite; **within easy ~ of the supermarket/station** ganz in der Nähe des Supermarkts/Bahnhofs; **beyond the ~ of sb/sth** außerhalb der Reichweite von jdm/etw; **"keep out of the ~ of children"** „von Kindern fernhalten"; **can I ~ you at your hotel?** kann ich Sie in Ihrem Hotel erreichen?
▸ **reach out** *vt* (*hand*) ausstrecken ▷ *vi* die Hand ausstrecken; **to ~ out for sth** nach etw greifen
react [ri:'ækt] *vi*: **to ~ (to)** (*also Med*) reagieren (auf *+acc*); (*Chem*): **to ~ (with)** reagieren (mit); **to ~ (against)** (*rebel*) sich wehren (gegen)
reaction [ri:'ækʃən] *n* Reaktion *f*; **reactions** *npl* (*reflexes*) Reaktionen *pl*; **a ~ against sth** Widerstand gegen etw
reactionary [ri:'ækʃənrɪ] *adj* reaktionär ▷ *n* Reaktionär(in) *m(f)*
reactor [ri:'æktəʳ] *n* (*also*: **nuclear reactor**) Kernreaktor *m*
read [ri:d] (*pt, pp* **~**) [rɛd] *vi* lesen; (*piece of writing etc*) sich lesen ▷ *vt* lesen; (*meter, thermometer etc*) ablesen; (*understand: mood, thoughts*) sich versetzen in *+acc*; (*meter, thermometer etc: measurement*) anzeigen; (*study*) studieren; **to ~ sb's lips** jdm von den Lippen ablesen; **to ~ sb's mind** jds Gedanken lesen; **to ~ between the lines** zwischen den Zeilen lesen; **to take sth as ~** (*self-evident*) etw für selbstverständlich halten; **you can take it as ~ that ...** Sie können davon ausgehen, dass ...; **do you ~ me?** (*Tel*) verstehen Sie mich?; **to ~ sth into sb's remarks** etw in jds Bemerkungen hineininterpretieren
▸ **read out** *vt* vorlesen
▸ **read over** *vt* durchlesen
▸ **read through** *vt* durchlesen
▸ **read up on** *vt fus* sich informieren über *+acc*
readable ['ri:dəbl] *adj* (*legible*) lesbar; (*book, author etc*) lesenswert
reader ['ri:dəʳ] *n* (*person*) Leser(in) *m(f)*; (*book*) Lesebuch *nt*; (*Brit: at university*) ≈ Dozent(in) *m(f)*; **to be an avid/slow ~** eifrig/langsam lesen
readership ['ri:dəʃɪp] *n* (*of newspaper etc*) Leserschaft *f*
readily ['rɛdɪlɪ] *adv* (*without hesitation*) bereitwillig; (*easily*) ohne Weiteres
readiness ['rɛdɪnɪs] *n* Bereitschaft *f*; **in ~ for** bereit für
reading ['ri:dɪŋ] *n* Lesen *nt*; (*understanding*) Verständnis *nt*; (*from bible, of poetry etc*) Lesung *f*; (*on meter, thermometer etc*) Anzeige *f*
reading lamp *n* Leselampe *f*
reading matter *n* Lesestoff *m*
reading room *n* Lesesaal *m*
readjust [ri:ə'dʒʌst] *vt* (*position, knob, instrument etc*) neu einstellen ▷ *vi*: **to ~ (to)** sich anpassen (an *+acc*)
readjustment [ri:ə'dʒʌstmənt] *n* (*fig*) Neuorientierung *f*
ready ['rɛdɪ] *adj* (*prepared*) bereit, fertig; (*willing*) bereit; (*easy*) leicht; (*available*) fertig ▷ *n*: **at the ~** (*Mil*) einsatzbereit; (*fig*) griffbereit; **~ for use** gebrauchsfertig; **to be ~ to do sth** bereit sein, etw zu tun; **to get ~** sich fertig machen; **to get sth ~** etw bereitmachen
ready cash *n* Bargeld *nt*
ready-cooked ['rɛdɪkukt] *adj* vorgekocht
ready-made ['rɛdɪ'meɪd] *adj* (*clothes*) von der Stange, Konfektions-; **~ meal** Fertiggericht *nt*
ready-mix ['rɛdɪmɪks] *n* (*for cakes etc*) Backmischung *f*; (*concrete*) Fertigbeton *m*
ready money *n* = **ready cash**
ready reckoner [-'rɛkənəʳ] (*Brit*) *n* Rechentabelle *f*
ready-to-wear ['rɛdɪtə'wɛəʳ] *adj* (*clothes*) von der Stange, Konfektions-
reaffirm [ri:ə'fə:m] *vt* bestätigen
reagent [ri:'eɪdʒənt] *n*: **chemical ~** Reagens *nt*, Reagenz *nt*
real [rɪəl] *adj* (*reason, result etc*) wirklich; (*leather, gold etc*) echt; (*life, feeling*) wahr; (*for emphasis*) echt ▷ *adv* (*US: inf: very*) echt; **in ~ life** im wahren *or* wirklichen Leben; **in ~ terms** effektiv
real ale *n* Real Ale *nt*
real estate *n* Immobilien *pl* ▷ *cpd* (*US: agent, business etc*) Immobilien-
realign *vt* neu ausrichten
realism ['rɪəlɪzəm] *n* (*also Art*) Realismus *m*
realist ['rɪəlɪst] *n* Realist(in) *m(f)*
realistic [rɪə'lɪstɪk] *adj* realistisch
reality [ri:'ælɪtɪ] *n* Wirklichkeit *f*, Realität *f*; **in ~** in Wirklichkeit
realization [rɪəlaɪ'zeɪʃən] *n* (*understanding*) Erkenntnis *f*; (*fulfilment*) Verwirklichung *f*, Realisierung *f*; (*Fin: of asset*) Realisation *f*
realize ['rɪəlaɪz] *vt* (*understand*) verstehen; (*fulfil*) verwirklichen, realisieren; (*Fin: amount, profit*) realisieren; **I ~ that ...** es ist mir klar, dass ...

really ['rɪəlɪ] *adv* wirklich; **what ~ happened** was wirklich geschah; **~?** wirklich?; **~!** (*indicating annoyance*) also wirklich!
realm [rɛlm] *n* (*fig: field*) Bereich *m*; (*kingdom*) Reich *nt*
real-time ['ri:ltaɪm] *adj* (*Comput: processing etc*) Echtzeit-
Realtor® ['rɪəltɔ:ʳ] (*US*) *n* Immobilienmakler(in) *m(f)*
ream [ri:m] *n* (*of paper*) Ries *nt*; **reams** (*inf: fig*) Bände *pl*
reap [ri:p] *vt* (*crop*) einbringen, ernten; (*fig: benefits*) ernten; (*: rewards*) bekommen
reaper ['ri:pəʳ] *n* (*machine*) Mähdrescher *m*
reappear [ri:ə'pɪəʳ] *vi* wieder auftauchen
reappearance [ri:ə'pɪərəns] *n* Wiederauftauchen *nt*
reapply [ri:ə'plaɪ] *vi*: **to ~ for** sich erneut bewerben um
reappoint [ri:ə'pɔɪnt] *vt* (*to job*) wiedereinstellen
reappraisal [ri:ə'preɪzl] *n* (*of idea etc*) Neubeurteilung *f*
rear [rɪəʳ] *adj* hintere(r, s); (*wheel etc*) Hinter- ▷ *n* Rückseite *f*; (*buttocks*) Hinterteil *nt* ▷ *vt* (*family, animals*) aufziehen ▷ *vi* (*also*: **rear up**: *horse*) sich aufbäumen
rear admiral *n* Konteradmiral *m*
rear-engined ['rɪər'ɛndʒɪnd] *adj* mit Heckmotor
rearguard ['rɪəgɑ:d] *n* (*Mil*) Nachhut *f*; **to fight a ~ action** (*fig*) sich erbittert wehren
rearm [ri:'ɑ:m] *vi* (*country*) wiederaufrüsten ▷ *vt* wiederbewaffnen
rearmament [ri:'ɑ:məmənt] *n* Wiederaufrüstung *f*
rearrange [ri:ə'reɪndʒ] *vt* (*furniture*) umstellen; (*meeting*) den Termin ändern *+gen*
rear-view mirror ['rɪəvju:-] *n* Rückspiegel *m*
reason ['ri:zn] *n* (*cause*) Grund *m*; (*rationality*) Verstand *m*; (*common sense*) Vernunft *f* ▷ *vi*: **to ~ with sb** vernünftig mit jdm reden; **the ~ for/why** der Grund für/, warum; **we have ~ to believe that ...** wir haben Grund zu der Annahme, dass ...; **it stands to ~ that ...** es ist zu erwarten, dass ...; **she claims with good ~ that ...** sie behauptet mit gutem Grund *or* mit Recht, dass ...; **all the more ~ why ...** ein Grund mehr, warum ...; **yes, but within ~** ja, solange es sich im Rahmen hält
reasonable ['ri:znəbl] *adj* vernünftig; (*number, amount*) angemessen; (*not bad*) ganz ordentlich; **be ~!** sei doch vernünftig!
reasonably ['ri:znəblɪ] *adv* (*fairly*) ziemlich; (*sensibly*) vernünftig; **one could ~ assume that ...** man könnte durchaus annehmen, dass ...
reasoned ['ri:znd] *adj* (*argument*) durchdacht
reasoning ['ri:znɪŋ] *n* Argumentation *f*
reassemble [ri:ə'sɛmbl] *vt* (*machine*) wieder zusammensetzen ▷ *vi* sich wieder versammeln
reassert [ri:ə'sə:t] *vt*: **to ~ oneself/one's authority** seine Autorität wieder geltend machen
reassurance [ri:ə'ʃuərəns] *n* (*comfort*) Beruhigung *f*; (*guarantee*) Bestätigung *f*
reassure [ri:ə'ʃuəʳ] *vt* beruhigen
reassuring [ri:ə'ʃuərɪŋ] *adj* beruhigend
reawakening [ri:ə'weɪknɪŋ] *n* Wiedererwachen *nt*
rebate ['ri:beɪt] *n* (*on tax etc*) Rückerstattung *f*; (*discount*) Ermäßigung *f*
rebel ['rɛbl] *n* Rebell(in) *m(f)* ▷ *vi* rebellieren
rebellion [rɪ'bɛljən] *n* Rebellion *f*
rebellious [rɪ'bɛljəs] *adj* rebellisch
rebirth [ri:'bə:θ] *n* Wiedergeburt *f*
rebound [rɪ'baund] *vi* (*ball*) zurückprallen ▷ *n*: **on the ~** (*fig*) als Tröstung
rebuff [rɪ'bʌf] *n* Abfuhr *f* ▷ *vt* zurückweisen
rebuild [ri:'bɪld] (*irreg: like* **build**) *vt* wiederaufbauen; (*confidence*) wiederherstellen
rebuke [rɪ'bju:k] *vt* zurechtweisen, tadeln ▷ *n* Zurechtweisung *f*, Tadel *m*
rebut [rɪ'bʌt] (*form*) *vt* widerlegen
rebuttal [rɪ'bʌtl] (*form*) *n* Widerlegung *f*
recalcitrant [rɪ'kælsɪtrənt] *adj* aufsässig
recall [rɪ'kɔ:l] *vt* (*remember*) sich erinnern an *+acc*; (*ambassador*) abberufen; (*product*) zurückrufen ▷ *n* (*of memories*) Erinnerung *f*; (*of ambassador*) Abberufung *f*; (*of product*) Rückruf *m*; **beyond ~** unwiederbringlich
recant [rɪ'kænt] *vi* widerrufen
recap ['ri:kæp] *vt, vi* zusammenfassen ▷ *n* Zusammenfassung *f*
recapitulate [ri:kə'pɪtjuleɪt] *vt, vi* = **recap**
recapture [ri:'kæptʃəʳ] *vt* (*town*) wiedereinnehmen; (*prisoner*) wiederergreifen; (*atmosphere etc*) heraufbeschwören
rec'd *abbr* (*Comm: = received*) erh.
recede [rɪ'si:d] *vi* (*tide*) zurückgehen; (*lights etc*) verschwinden; (*memory, hope*) schwinden; **his hair is beginning to ~** er bekommt eine Stirnglatze
receding [rɪ'si:dɪŋ] *adj* (*hairline*) zurückweichend; (*chin*) fliehend
receipt [rɪ'si:t] *n* (*document*) Quittung *f*; (*act of receiving*) Erhalt *m*; **receipts** *npl* (*Comm*) Einnahmen *pl*; **on ~ of** bei Erhalt *+gen*; **to be in ~ of sth** etw erhalten
receivable [rɪ'si:vəbl] *adj* (*Comm*) zulässig; (*owing*) ausstehend
receive [rɪ'si:v] *vt* erhalten, bekommen; (*injury*) erleiden; (*treatment*) erhalten; (*visitor, guest*) empfangen; **to be on the receiving end of sth** der/die Leidtragende von etw sein; **"~d with thanks"** (*Comm*) „dankend erhalten"

RECEIVED PRONUNCIATION

Received Pronunciation oder *RP* ist die hochsprachliche Standardaussprache des britischen Englisch, die bis vor Kurzem in der Ober- und Mittelschicht vorherrschte und auch noch großes Ansehen unter höheren Beamten genießt.

receiver [rɪ'siːvə^r] *n* (*Tel*) Hörer *m*; (*Radio, TV*) Empfänger *m*; (*of stolen goods*) Hehler(in) *m(f)*; (*Comm*) Empfänger(in) *m(f)*
receivership [rɪ'siːvəʃɪp] *n*: **to go into ~** in Konkurs gehen
recent ['riːsnt] *adj* (*event*) kürzlich; (*times*) letzte(r, s); **in ~ years** in den letzten Jahren
recently ['riːsntlɪ] *adv* (*not long ago*) kürzlich; (*lately*) in letzter Zeit; **as ~ as** erst; **until ~** bis vor Kurzem
receptacle [rɪ'sɛptɪkl] *n* Behälter *m*
reception [rɪ'sɛpʃən] *n* (*in hotel, office etc*) Rezeption *f*; (*party, Radio, TV*) Empfang *m*; (*welcome*) Aufnahme *f*
reception centre (*Brit*) *n* Aufnahmelager *nt*
reception desk *n* Rezeption *f*
receptionist [rɪ'sɛpʃənɪst] *n* (*in hotel*) Empfangschef *m*, Empfangsdame *f*; (*in doctor's surgery*) Sprechstundenhilfe *f*
receptive [rɪ'sɛptɪv] *adj* aufnahmebereit
recess [rɪ'sɛs] *n* (*in room*) Nische *f*; (*secret place*) Winkel *m*; (*Pol etc: holiday*) Ferien *pl*; (*US: Law: short break*) Pause *f*; (*esp US: Scol*) Pause *f*
recession [rɪ'sɛʃən] *n* (*Econ*) Rezession *f*
recharge [riː'tʃɑːdʒ] *vt* (*battery*) aufladen
rechargeable [riː'tʃɑːdʒəbl] *adj* (*battery*) aufladbar
recipe ['rɛsɪpɪ] *n* Rezept *nt*; **a ~ for success** ein Erfolgsrezept *nt*; **to be a ~ for disaster** in die Katastrophe führen
recipient [rɪ'sɪpɪənt] *n* Empfänger(in) *m(f)*
reciprocal [rɪ'sɪprəkl] *adj* gegenseitig
reciprocate [rɪ'sɪprəkeɪt] *vt* (*invitation, feeling*) erwidern ▷ *vi* sich revanchieren
recital [rɪ'saɪtl] *n* (*concert*) Konzert *nt*
recitation [rɛsɪ'teɪʃən] *n* (*of poem etc*) Vortrag *m*
recite [rɪ'saɪt] *vt* (*poem*) vortragen; (*complaints etc*) aufzählen
reckless ['rɛkləs] *adj* (*driving, driver*) rücksichtslos; (*spending*) leichtsinnig
recklessly ['rɛkləslɪ] *adv* (*drive*) rücksichtslos; (*spend, gamble*) leichtsinnig
reckon ['rɛkən] *vt* (*consider*) halten für; (*calculate*) berechnen ▷ *vi*: **he is somebody to be ~ed with** mit ihm muss man rechnen; **I ~ that ...** (*think*) ich schätze, dass ...; **to ~ without sb/sth** nicht mit jdm/etw rechnen
▸ **reckon on** *vt fus* rechnen mit
reckoning ['rɛknɪŋ] *n* (*calculation*) Berechnung *f*; **the day of ~** der Tag der Abrechnung
reclaim [rɪ'kleɪm] *vt* (*luggage*) abholen; (*tax etc*) zurückfordern; (*land*) gewinnen; (*waste materials*) zur Wiederverwertung sammeln
reclamation [rɛklə'meɪʃən] *n* (*of land*) Gewinnung *f*
recline [rɪ'klaɪn] *vi* (*sit or lie back*) zurückgelehnt sitzen
reclining [rɪ'klaɪnɪŋ] *adj* (*seat*) Liege-
recluse [rɪ'kluːs] *n* Einsiedler(in) *m(f)*
recognition [rɛkəg'nɪʃən] *n* (*of person, place*) Erkennen *nt*; (*of problem, fact*) Erkenntnis *f*; (*of achievement*) Anerkennung *f*; **in ~ of** in Anerkennung *+gen*; **to gain ~** Anerkennung finden; **she had changed beyond ~** sie war nicht wieder zu erkennen
recognizable ['rɛkəgnaɪzəbl] *adj* erkennbar
recognize ['rɛkəgnaɪz] *vt* (*person, place, voice*) wiedererkennen; (*sign, problem*) erkennen; (*qualifications, government, achievement*) anerkennen; **to ~ sb by/as** jdn erkennen an *+dat*/als
recoil [rɪ'kɔɪl] *vi* (*person*): **to ~ from** zurückweichen vor *+dat*; (*fig*) zurückschrecken vor *+dat* ▷ *n* (*of gun*) Rückstoß *m*
recollect [rɛkə'lɛkt] *vt* (*remember*) sich erinnern an *+acc*
recollection [rɛkə'lɛkʃən] *n* Erinnerung *f*; **to the best of my ~** soweit ich mich erinnern *or* entsinnen kann
recommend [rɛkə'mɛnd] *vt* empfehlen; **she has a lot to ~ her** es spricht sehr viel für sie
recommendation [rɛkəmɛn'deɪʃən] *n* Empfehlung *f*; **on the ~ of** auf Empfehlung *+gen*
recommended retail price (*Brit*) *n* (*Comm*) unverbindlicher Richtpreis *m*
recompense ['rɛkəmpɛns] *n* (*reward*) Belohnung *f*; (*compensation*) Entschädigung *f*
reconcilable ['rɛkənsaɪləbl] *adj* (*ideas*) (miteinander) vereinbar
reconcile ['rɛkənsaɪl] *vt* (*people*) versöhnen; (*facts, beliefs*) (miteinander) vereinbaren, in Einklang bringen; **to ~ o.s. to sth** sich mit etw abfinden
reconciliation [rɛkənsɪlɪ'eɪʃən] *n* (*of people*) Versöhnung *f*; (*of facts, beliefs*) Vereinbarung *f*
recondite [rɪ'kɔndaɪt] *adj* obskur
recondition [riːkən'dɪʃən] *vt* (*machine*) überholen
reconditioned [riːkən'dɪʃənd] *adj* (*engine, TV*) generalüberholt
reconnaissance [rɪ'kɔnɪsns] *n* (*Mil*) Aufklärung *f*
reconnoitre, (*US*) **reconnoiter** [rɛkə'nɔɪtə^r] *vt* (*Mil*) erkunden
reconsider [riːkən'sɪdə^r] *vt* (noch einmal) überdenken ▷ *vi* es sich *dat* noch einmal überlegen
reconstitute [riː'kɔnstɪtjuːt] *vt* (*organization*) neu bilden; (*food*) wiederherstellen
reconstruct [riːkən'strʌkt] *vt* (*building*) wiederaufbauen; (*policy, system*) neu organisieren; (*event, crime*) rekonstruieren
reconstruction [riːkən'strʌkʃən] *n* Wiederaufbau *m*; (*of crime*) Rekonstruktion *f*
reconvene [riːkən'viːn] *vi* (*meet again*) wieder zusammenkommen ▷ *vt* (*meeting etc*) wiedereinberufen
record ['rɛkɔːd] *n* (*written account*) Aufzeichnung *f*; (*of meeting*) Protokoll *nt*; (*of decision*) Beleg *m*; (*Comput*) Datensatz *m*; (*file*) Akte *f*; (*Mus: disc*) Schallplatte *f*; (*history*) Vorgeschichte *f*; (*also*: **criminal record**) Vorstrafen *pl*; (*Sport*) Rekord *m* ▷ *vt* aufzeichnen; (*song etc*) aufnehmen; (*temperature, speed etc*) registrieren ▷ *adj* (*sales, profits*) Rekord-; **~ of attendance**

Anwesenheitsliste *f*; **public ~s** Urkunden *pl* des Nationalarchivs; **to keep a ~ of sth** etw schriftlich festhalten; **to have a good/poor ~** gute/schlechte Leistungen vorzuweisen haben; **to have a (criminal) ~** vorbestraft sein; **to set** *or* **put the ~ straight** *(fig)* Klarheit schaffen; **he is on ~ as saying that ...** er hat nachweislich gesagt, dass ...; **off the ~** *(remark)* inoffiziell ▷ *adv (speak)* im Vertrauen; **in ~ time** in Rekordzeit

recorded delivery [rɪ'kɔːdɪd-] *(Brit) n (Post)* Einschreiben *nt*; **to send sth (by) ~** etw per Einschreiben senden

recorder [rɪ'kɔːdəʳ] *n (Mus)* Blockflöte *f*; *(Law) nebenamtlich als Richter tätiger Rechtsanwalt*

record holder *n (Sport)* Rekordinhaber(in) *m(f)*

recording [rɪ'kɔːdɪŋ] *n* Aufnahme *f*

recording studio *n* Aufnahmestudio *nt*

record library *n* Schallplattenverleih *m*

record player *n* Plattenspieler *m*

recount [rɪ'kaunt] *vt (story etc)* erzählen

re-count ['riːkaunt] *n (of votes)* Nachzählung *f* ▷ *vt (votes)* nachzählen

recoup [rɪ'kuːp] *vt*: **to ~ one's losses** seine Verluste ausgleichen

recourse [rɪ'kɔːs] *n*: **to have ~ to sth** Zuflucht zu etw nehmen

recover [rɪ'kʌvəʳ] *vt (get back)* zurückbekommen; *(stolen goods)* sicherstellen; *(wreck, body)* bergen; *(financial loss)* ausgleichen ▷ *vi* sich erholen

re-cover [riː'kʌvəʳ] *vt (chair etc)* neu beziehen

recovery [rɪ'kʌvərɪ] *n (from illness etc)* Erholung *f*; *(in economy)* Aufschwung *m*; *(of lost items)* Wiederfinden *nt*; *(of stolen goods)* Sicherstellung *f*; *(of wreck, body)* Bergung *f*; *(of financial loss)* Ausgleich *m*

re-create [riːkrɪ'eɪt] *vt (atmosphere, situation)* wiederherstellen

recreation [rɛkrɪ'eɪʃən] *n (leisure)* Erholung *f*, Entspannung *f*

recreational [rɛkrɪ'eɪʃənl] *adj (facilities etc)* Freizeit-

recreational drug *n* Freizeitdroge *f*

recreational vehicle *(US) n* Caravan *m*

recrimination [rɪkrɪmɪ'neɪʃən] *n* gegenseitige Anschuldigungen *pl*

recruit [rɪ'kruːt] *n (Mil)* Rekrut *m*; *(in company)* neuer Mitarbeiter *m*, neue Mitarbeiterin *f* ▷ *vt (Mil)* rekrutieren; *(staff, new members)* anwerben

recruiting office [rɪ'kruːtɪŋ-] *n (Mil)* Rekrutierungsbüro *nt*

recruitment [rɪ'kruːtmənt] *n (of staff)* Anwerbung *f*

rectangle ['rɛktæŋgl] *n* Rechteck *nt*

rectangular [rɛk'tæŋgjuləʳ] *adj (shape)* rechteckig

rectify ['rɛktɪfaɪ] *vt (mistake etc)* korrigieren

rector ['rɛktəʳ] *n (Rel)* Pfarrer(in) *m(f)*

rectory ['rɛktərɪ] *n* Pfarrhaus *nt*

rectum ['rɛktəm] *n* Rektum *nt*, Mastdarm *m*

recuperate [rɪ'kjuːpəreɪt] *vi (recover)* sich erholen

recur [rɪ'kəːʳ] *vi (error, event)* sich wiederholen; *(pain etc)* wiederholt auftreten

recurrence [rɪ'kəːrns] *n (see vi)* Wiederholung *f*; wiederholtes Auftreten *nt*

recurrent [rɪ'kəːrnt] *adj (see vi)* sich wiederholend; wiederholt auftretend

recurring [rɪ'kəːrɪŋ] *adj (problem, dream)* sich wiederholend; *(Math)*: **six point five four ~** sechs Komma fünf Periode vier

recycle [riː'saɪkl] *vt (waste, paper etc)* recyceln, wiederverwerten

recycling [riː'saɪklɪŋ] *n* Recycling *nt*; **~ site** Recycling- *or* Wertstoffhof *m*

red [rɛd] *n* Rot *nt*; *(pej, Pol)* Rote(r) *f(m)* ▷ *adj* rot; **to be in the ~** *(business etc)* in den roten Zahlen sein

red alert *n*: **to be on ~** in höchster Alarmbereitschaft sein

red-blooded ['rɛd'blʌdɪd] *adj* heißblütig

REDBRICK UNIVERSITY

Als *redbrick university* werden die jüngeren britischen Universitäten bezeichnet, die im späten 19. und Anfang des 20. Jh. in Städten wie Manchester, Liverpool und Bristol gegründet wurden. Der Name steht im Gegensatz zu Oxford und Cambridge und bezieht sich auf die roten Backsteinmauern der Universitätsgebäude.

red carpet treatment *n*: **to give sb the ~** den roten Teppich für jdn ausrollen

Red Cross *n* Rotes Kreuz *nt*

redcurrant ['rɛdkʌrənt] *n* Rote Johannisbeere *f*

redden ['rɛdn] *vt* röten ▷ *vi (blush)* erröten

reddish ['rɛdɪʃ] *adj* rötlich

redecorate [riː'dɛkəreɪt] *vt, vi* renovieren

redecoration [riːdɛkə'reɪʃən] *n* Renovierung *f*

redeem [rɪ'diːm] *vt (situation etc)* retten; *(voucher, sth in pawn)* einlösen; *(loan)* abzahlen; *(Rel)* erlösen; **to ~ oneself for sth** etw wiedergutmachen

redeemable [rɪ'diːməbl] *adj (voucher etc)* einlösbar

redeeming [rɪ'diːmɪŋ] *adj (feature, quality)* versöhnend

redefine [riːdɪ'faɪn] *vt* neu definieren

redemption [rɪ'dɛmʃən] *n (Rel)* Erlösung *f*; **past** *or* **beyond ~** nicht mehr zu retten

redeploy [riːdɪ'plɔɪ] *vt (resources, staff)* umverteilen; *(Mil)* verlegen

redeployment [riːdɪ'plɔɪmənt] *n (see vt)* Umverteilung *f*; Verlegung *f*

redevelop [riːdɪ'vɛləp] *vt (area)* sanieren

redevelopment [riːdɪ'vɛləpmənt] *n* Sanierung *f*

red-handed [rɛd'hændɪd] *adj*: **to be caught ~** auf frischer Tat ertappt werden

redhead ['rɛdhɛd] *n* Rotschopf *m*

red herring *n (fig)* falsche Spur *f*

red-hot [rɛd'hɔt] *adj (metal)* rot glühend

redirect [riːdaɪˈrɛkt] *vt* (*mail*) nachsenden; (*traffic*) umleiten
rediscover [riːdɪsˈkʌvəʳ] *vt* wiederentdecken
redistribute [riːdɪsˈtrɪbjuːt] *vt* umverteilen
red-letter day [ˈrɛdlɛtə-] *n* besonderer Tag *m*
red light *n* (*Aut*): **to go through a ~** eine Ampel bei Rot überfahren
red-light district [ˈrɛdlaɪt-] *n* Rotlichtviertel *nt*
red meat *n Rind- und Lammfleisch*
redness [ˈrɛdnɪs] *n* Röte *f*
redo [riːˈduː] (*irreg: like* **do**) *vt* noch einmal machen
redolent [ˈrɛdələnt] *adj*: **to be ~ of sth** nach etw riechen; (*fig*) an etw erinnern
redouble [riːˈdʌbl] *vt*: **to ~ one's efforts** seine Anstrengungen verdoppeln
redraft [riːˈdrɑːft] *vt* (*agreement*) neu abfassen
redraw [riːˈdrɔː] *vt* neu zeichnen
redress [rɪˈdrɛs] *n* (*compensation*) Wiedergutmachung *f* ▷ *vt* (*error etc*) wiedergutmachen; **to ~ the balance** das Gleichgewicht wiederherstellen
Red Sea *n*: **the ~** das Rote Meer
redskin [ˈrɛdskɪn] (*old: offensive*) *n* Rothaut *f*
red tape *n* (*fig*) Bürokratie *f*
reduce [rɪˈdjuːs] *vt* (*spending, numbers, risk etc*) vermindern, reduzieren; **to ~ sth by/to 5%** etw um/auf 5% *acc* reduzieren; **to ~ sb to tears/silence** jdn zum Weinen/Schweigen bringen; **to ~ sb to begging/stealing** jdn zur Bettelei/zum Diebstahl zwingen; **"~ speed now"** (*Aut*) „langsam fahren"
reduced [rɪˈdjuːst] *adj* (*goods, ticket etc*) ermäßigt; **"greatly ~ prices"** „Preise stark reduziert"
reduction [rɪˈdʌkʃən] *n* (*in price etc*) Ermäßigung, Reduzierung *f*; (*in numbers*) Verminderung *f*
redundancy [rɪˈdʌndənsɪ] (*Brit*) *n* (*dismissal*) Entlassung *f*; (*unemployment*) Arbeitslosigkeit *f*; **compulsory ~** Entlassung *f*; **voluntary ~** freiwilliger Verzicht *m* auf den Arbeitsplatz
redundancy payment (*Brit*) *n* Abfindung *f*
redundant [rɪˈdʌndnt] *adj* (*Brit: worker*) arbeitslos; (*word, object*) überflüssig; **to be made ~** (*worker*) den Arbeitsplatz verlieren
reed [riːd] *n* (*Bot*) Schilf *nt*; (*Mus: of clarinet etc*) Rohrblatt *nt*
re-educate [riːˈɛdjukeɪt] *vt* umerziehen
reedy [ˈriːdɪ] *adj* (*voice*) Fistel-
reef [riːf] *n* (*at sea*) Riff *nt*
reek [riːk] *vi*: **to ~ (of)** (*lit, fig*) stinken (nach)
reel [riːl] *n* (*of thread etc, on fishing-rod*) Rolle *f*; (*Cine: scene*) Szene *f*; (*of film, tape*) Spule *f*; (*dance*) Reel *m* ▷ *vi* (*sway*) taumeln; **my head is ~ing** mir dreht sich der Kopf
▸ **reel in** *vt* (*fish, line*) einholen
▸ **reel off** *vt* (*say*) herunterrasseln
re-election [riːɪˈlɛkʃən] *n* Wiederwahl *f*
re-enter [riːˈɛntəʳ] *vt* (*country*) wieder einreisen in *+acc*; (*Space*) wieder eintreten in *+acc*
re-entry [riːˈɛntrɪ] *n* Wiedereinreise *f*; (*Space*) Wiedereintritt *m*
re-examine [riːɪɡˈzæmɪn] *vt* (*proposal etc*) nochmals prüfen; (*witness*) nochmals vernehmen
re-export [ˈriːɪksˈpɔːt] *vt* wiederausführen ▷ *n* Wiederausfuhr *f*; (*commodity*) wiederausgeführte Ware *f*
ref [rɛf] (*inf*) *n abbr* (*Sport*) = **referee**
ref. *abbr* (*Comm: = with reference to*) betr.; **your ~** Ihr Zeichen:
refectory [rɪˈfɛktərɪ] *n* (*in university*) Mensa *f*
refer [rɪˈfəːʳ] *vt*: **to ~ sb to** (*book etc*) jdn verweisen auf *+acc*; (*doctor, hospital*) jdn überweisen zu; **to ~ sth to** (*task, problem*) etw übergeben an *+acc*; **he ~red me to the manager** er verwies mich an den Geschäftsführer
▸ **refer to** *vt fus* (*mention*) erwähnen; (*relate to*) sich beziehen auf *+acc*; (*consult*) hinzuziehen
referee [rɛfəˈriː] *n* (*Sport*) Schiedsrichter(in) *m(f)*; (*Brit: for job application*) Referenz *f* ▷ *vt* als Schiedsrichter(in) leiten
reference [ˈrɛfrəns] *n* (*mention*) Hinweis *m*; (*in book, article*) Quellenangabe *f*; (*for job application, person*) Referenz *f*; **with ~ to** mit Bezug auf *+acc*; **"please quote this ~"** (*Comm*) „bitte dieses Zeichen angeben"
reference book *n* Nachschlagewerk *nt*
reference library *n* Präsenzbibliothek *f*
reference number *n* Aktenzeichen *nt*
referenda [rɛfəˈrɛndə] *npl of* **referendum**
referendum [rɛfəˈrɛndəm] (*pl* **referenda**) *n* Referendum *nt*, Volksentscheid *m*
referral [rɪˈfəːrəl] *n* (*of matter, problem*) Weiterleitung *f*; (*to doctor, specialist*) Überweisung *f*
refill [riːˈfɪl] *vt* nachfüllen ▷ *n* (*for pen etc*) Nachfüllmine *f*; (*drink*) Nachfüllung *f*
refine [rɪˈfaɪn] *vt* (*sugar, oil*) raffinieren; (*theory, idea*) verfeinern
refined [rɪˈfaɪnd] *adj* (*person*) kultiviert; (*taste*) fein, vornehm; (*sugar, oil*) raffiniert
refinement [rɪˈfaɪnmənt] *n* (*of person*) Kultiviertheit *f*; (*of system, ideas*) Verfeinerung *f*
refinery [rɪˈfaɪnərɪ] *n* (*for oil etc*) Raffinerie *f*
refit [riːˈfɪt] (*Naut*) *n* Überholung *f* ▷ *vt* (*ship*) überholen
reflate [riːˈfleɪt] *vt* (*economy*) ankurbeln
reflation [riːˈfleɪʃən] *n* (*Econ*) Reflation *f*
reflationary [riːˈfleɪʃənrɪ] *adj* (*Econ*) reflationär
reflect [rɪˈflɛkt] *vt* reflektieren; (*fig*) widerspiegeln ▷ *vi* (*think*) nachdenken
▸ **reflect on** *vt fus* (*discredit*) ein schlechtes Licht werfen auf *+acc*
reflection [rɪˈflɛkʃən] *n* (*image*) Spiegelbild *nt*; (*of light, heat*) Reflexion *f*; (*fig*) Widerspiegelung *f*; (*: thought*) Gedanke *m*; **on ~** nach genauerer Überlegung; **this is a ~ on ...** (*criticism*) das sagt einiges über ...
reflector [rɪˈflɛktəʳ] *n* (*Aut etc*) Rückstrahler *m*; (*for light, heat*) Reflektor *m*
reflex [ˈriːflɛks] *adj* Reflex-; **reflexes** *npl* (*Physiol, Psych*) Reflexe *pl*
reflexive [rɪˈflɛksɪv] *adj* (*Ling*) reflexiv

reform [rɪ'fɔ:m] *n* Reform *f* ▷ *vt* reformieren ▷ *vi* (*criminal etc*) sich bessern
reformat [ri:'fɔ:mæt] *vt* (*Comput*) neu formatieren
Reformation [rɛfə'meɪʃən] *n*: **the ~** die Reformation
reformatory [rɪ'fɔ:mətərɪ] (*US*) *n* Besserungsanstalt *f*
reformed [rɪ'fɔ:md] *adj* (*character, alcoholic*) gewandelt
refrain [rɪ'freɪn] *vi*: **to ~ from doing sth** etw unterlassen ▷ *n* (*of song*) Refrain *m*
refresh [rɪ'frɛʃ] *vt* erfrischen; **to ~ one's memory** sein Gedächtnis auffrischen
refresher course [rɪ'frɛʃə-] *n* Auffrischungskurs *m*
refreshing [rɪ'frɛʃɪŋ] *adj* erfrischend; (*sleep*) wohltuend; (*idea etc*) angenehm
refreshment [rɪ'frɛʃmənt] *n* Erfrischung *f*
refreshments [rɪ'frɛʃmənts] *npl* (*food and drink*) Erfrischungen *pl*
refrigeration [rɪfrɪdʒə'reɪʃən] *n* Kühlung *f*
refrigerator [rɪ'frɪdʒəreɪtə^r] *n* Kühlschrank *m*
refuel [ri:'fjuəl] *vt, vi* auftanken
refuelling [ri:'fjuəlɪŋ] *n* Auftanken *nt*
refuge ['rɛfju:dʒ] *n* Zuflucht *f*; **to seek/take ~ in** Zuflucht suchen/nehmen in *+dat*
refugee [rɛfju'dʒi:] *n* Flüchtling *m*; **a political ~** ein politischer Flüchtling
refugee camp *n* Flüchtlingslager *nt*
refund ['ri:fʌnd] *n* Rückerstattung *f* ▷ *vt* (*money*) zurückerstatten
refurbish [ri:'fə:bɪʃ] *vt* (*shop etc*) renovieren
refurbishment [ri:fə:bɪʃmənt] *n* (*of shop etc*) Renovierung *f*
refurnish [ri:'fə:nɪʃ] *vt* neu möblieren
refusal [rɪ'fju:zəl] *n* Ablehnung *f*; **a ~ to do sth** eine Weigerung, etw zu tun; **to give sb first ~ on sth** jdm etw zuerst anbieten
refuse[1] [rɪ'fju:z] *vt* (*request, offer etc*) ablehnen; (*gift*) zurückweisen; (*permission*) verweigern ▷ *vi* ablehnen; (*horse*) verweigern; **to ~ to do sth** sich weigern, etw zu tun
refuse[2] ['rɛfju:s] *n* (*rubbish*) Abfall *m*, Müll *m*
refuse collection *n* Müllabfuhr *f*
refuse disposal *n* Müllbeseitigung *f*
refusenik [rɪ'fju:znɪk] *n* (*inf*) Verweigerer(in) *m(f)*; (*in former USSR*) *sowjetischer Jude, dem die Emigration nach Israel verweigert wurde*
refute [rɪ'fju:t] *vt* (*argument*) widerlegen
regain [rɪ'geɪn] *vt* wiedererlangen
regal ['ri:gl] *adj* königlich
regale [rɪ'geɪl] *vt*: **to ~ sb with sth** jdn mit etw verwöhnen
regalia [rɪ'geɪlɪə] *n* (*costume*) Amtstracht *f*
regard [rɪ'gɑ:d] *n* (*esteem*) Achtung *f* ▷ *vt* (*consider*) ansehen, betrachten; (*view*) betrachten; **to give one's ~s to sb** jdm Grüße bestellen; **"with kindest ~s"** „mit freundlichen Grüßen"; **as regards, with ~ to** bezüglich *+gen*
regarding [rɪ'gɑ:dɪŋ] *prep* bezüglich *+gen*
regardless [rɪ'gɑ:dlɪs] *adv* trotzdem ▷ *adj*: **~ of** ohne Rücksicht auf *+acc*
regatta [rɪ'gætə] *n* Regatta *f*
regency ['ri:dʒənsɪ] *n* Regentschaft *f* ▷ *adj*: **R~** (*furniture etc*) Regency-
regenerate [rɪ'dʒɛnəreɪt] *vt* (*inner cities, arts*) erneuern; (*person, feelings*) beleben ▷ *vi* (*Biol*) sich regenerieren
regent ['ri:dʒənt] *n* Regent(in) *m(f)*
reggae ['rɛgeɪ] *n* Reggae *m*
regime [reɪ'ʒi:m] *n* (*government*) Regime *nt*; (*diet etc*) Kur *f*
regiment ['rɛdʒɪmənt] *n* (*Mil*) Regiment *nt* ▷ *vt* reglementieren
regimental [rɛdʒɪ'mɛntl] *adj* Regiments-
regimentation [rɛdʒɪmɛn'teɪʃən] *n* Reglementierung *f*
region ['ri:dʒən] *n* (*of land*) Gebiet *nt*; (*of body*) Bereich *m*; (*administrative division of country*) Region *f*; **in the ~ of** (*approximately*) im Bereich von
regional ['ri:dʒənl] *adj* regional
regional development *n* regionale Entwicklung *f*
regionalize ['ri:dʒənəlaɪz] *vt* regionalisieren
register ['rɛdʒɪstə^r] *n* (*list, Mus*) Register *nt*; (*also*: **electoral register**) Wählerverzeichnis *nt*; (*Scol*) Klassenbuch *nt* ▷ *vt* registrieren; (*car*) anmelden; (*letter*) als Einschreiben senden; (*amount, measurement*) verzeichnen ▷ *vi* (*person*) sich anmelden; (*: at doctor's*) sich (als Patient) eintragen; (*amount etc*) registriert werden; (*make impression*) (einen) Eindruck machen; **to ~ a protest** Protest anmelden
registered ['rɛdʒɪstəd] *adj* (*letter, parcel*) eingeschrieben; (*drug addict, childminder etc*) (offiziell) eingetragen
registered company *n* eingetragene Gesellschaft *f*
registered nurse (*US*) *n* staatlich geprüfte Krankenschwester *f*, staatlich geprüfter Krankenpfleger *m*
registered trademark *n* eingetragenes Warenzeichen *nt*
register office *n* = **registry office**
registrar ['rɛdʒɪstrɑ:^{r}] *n* (*in registry office*) Standesbeamte(r) *m*, Standesbeamtin *f*; (*in college etc*) Kanzler *m*; (*Brit: in hospital*) Krankenhausarzt *m*, Krankenhausärztin *f*
registration [rɛdʒɪs'treɪʃən] *n* Registrierung *f*; (*of students, unemployed etc*) Anmeldung *f*
registration number (*Brit*) *n* (*Aut*) polizeiliches Kennzeichen *nt*
registry ['rɛdʒɪstrɪ] *n* Registratur *f*
registry office (*Brit*) *n* Standesamt *nt*; **to get married in a ~** standesamtlich heiraten
regret [rɪ'grɛt] *n* Bedauern *nt* ▷ *vt* bedauern; **with ~** mit Bedauern; **to have no ~s** nichts bereuen; **we ~ to inform you that ...** wir müssen Ihnen leider mitteilen, dass ...
regretfully [rɪ'grɛtfəlɪ] *adv* mit Bedauern
regrettable [rɪ'grɛtəbl] *adj* bedauerlich
regrettably [rɪ'grɛtəblɪ] *adv* bedauerlicherweise; **~, he said ...**

bedauerlicherweise sagte er ...
Regt *abbr* (*Mil*: = *regiment*) Rgt.
regular ['rɛgjuləʳ] *adj* (*also Ling*) regelmäßig; (*usual*: *time, doctor*) üblich; (: *customer*) Stamm-; (*soldier*) Berufs-; (*Comm*: *size*) normal ▷ *n* (*client*) Stammkunde *m*, Stammkundin *f*
regularity [rɛgju'lærɪtɪ] *n* Regelmäßigkeit *f*
regularly ['rɛgjuləlɪ] *adv* regelmäßig; (*breathe, beat*: *evenly*) gleichmäßig
regulate ['rɛgjuleɪt] *vt* regulieren
regulation [rɛgju'leɪʃən] *n* Regulierung *f*; (*rule*) Vorschrift *f*
regulatory [rɛgju'leɪtrɪ] *adj* (*system*) Regulierungs-; (*body, agency*) Überwachungs-
rehabilitate [ri:ə'bɪlɪteɪt] *vt* (*criminal, drug addict*) (in die Gesellschaft) wiedereingliedern; (*invalid*) rehabilitieren
rehabilitation ['ri:əbɪlɪ'teɪʃən] *n* (*see vt*) Wiedereingliederung *f* (in die Gesellschaft); Rehabilitation *f*
rehash [ri:'hæʃ] (*inf*) *vt* (*idea etc*) aufwärmen
rehearsal [rɪ'hə:səl] *n* (*Theat*) Probe *f*; **dress ~** Generalprobe *f*
rehearse [rɪ'hə:s] *vt* (*play, speech etc*) proben
rehouse [ri:'hauz] *vt* neu unterbringen
reign [reɪn] *n* (*lit, fig*) Herrschaft *f* ▷ *vi* (*lit, fig*) herrschen
reigning ['reɪnɪŋ] *adj* regierend; (*champion*) amtierend
reimburse [ri:ɪm'bə:s] *vt* die Kosten erstatten *+dat*
rein [reɪn] *n* Zügel *m*; **to give sb free ~** (*fig*) jdm freie Hand lassen; **to keep a tight ~ on sth** (*fig*) bei etw die Zügel kurz halten
reincarnation [ri:ɪnkɑ:'neɪʃən] *n* (*belief*) die Wiedergeburt *f*; (*person*) Reinkarnation *f*
reindeer ['reɪndɪəʳ] *n inv* Ren(tier) *nt*
reinforce [ri:ɪn'fɔ:s] *vt* (*strengthen*) verstärken; (*support*: *idea etc*) stützen; (: *prejudice*) stärken
reinforced concrete *n* Stahlbeton *m*
reinforcement [ri:ɪn'fɔ:smənt] *n* (*strengthening*) Verstärkung *f*; (*of attitude etc*) Stärkung *f*; **reinforcements** *npl* (*Mil*) Verstärkung *f*
reinstate [ri:ɪn'steɪt] *vt* (*employee*) wiedereinstellen; (*tax, law*) wiedereinführen; (*text*) wiedereinfügen
reinstatement [ri:ɪn'steɪtmənt] *n* (*of employee*) Wiedereinstellung *f*
reissue [ri:'ɪʃju:] *vt* neu herausgeben
reiterate [ri:'ɪtəreɪt] *vt* wiederholen
reject ['ri:dʒɛkt] *n* (*Comm*) Ausschuss *m no pl* ▷ *vt* ablehnen; (*admirer*) abweisen; (*goods*) zurückweisen; (*machine*: *coin*) nicht annehmen; (*Med*: *heart, kidney*) abstoßen
rejection [rɪ'dʒɛkʃən] *n* Ablehnung *f*; (*of admirer*) Abweisung *f*; (*Med*) Abstoßung *f*
rejoice [rɪ'dʒɔɪs] *vi*: **to ~ at** *or* **over** jubeln über *+acc*
rejoinder [rɪ'dʒɔɪndəʳ] *n* Erwiderung *f*
rejuvenate [rɪ'dʒu:vəneɪt] *vt* (*person*) verjüngen; (*organization etc*) beleben
rekindle [ri:'kɪndl] *vt* (*interest, emotion etc*) wiedererwecken
relapse [rɪ'læps] *n* (*Med*) Rückfall *m* ▷ *vi*: **to ~ into** zurückfallen in *+acc*
relate [rɪ'leɪt] *vt* (*tell*) berichten; (*connect*) in Verbindung bringen ▷ *vi*: **to ~ to** (*empathize with*: *person, subject*) eine Beziehung finden zu; (*connect with*) zusammenhängen mit
related [rɪ'leɪtɪd] *adj*: **to be ~** (miteinander) verwandt sein; (*issues etc*) zusammenhängen
relating to [rɪ'leɪtɪŋ-] *prep* bezüglich *+gen*, mit Bezug auf *+acc*
relation [rɪ'leɪʃən] *n* (*member of family*) Verwandte(r) *f(m)*; (*connection*) Beziehung *f*; **relations** *npl* (*contact*) Beziehungen *pl*; **diplomatic/international ~s** diplomatische/internationale Beziehungen; **in ~ to** im Verhältnis zu; **to bear no ~ to** in keinem Verhältnis stehen zu
relationship [rɪ'leɪʃənʃɪp] *n* Beziehung *f*; (*between countries*) Beziehungen *pl*; (*affair*) Verhältnis *nt*; **they have a good ~** sie haben ein gutes Verhältnis zueinander
relative ['rɛlətɪv] *n* Verwandte(r) *f(m)* ▷ *adj* relativ; **all her ~s** ihre ganze Verwandtschaft; **~ to** im Vergleich zu; **it's all ~** es ist alles relativ
relatively ['rɛlətɪvlɪ] *adv* relativ
relative pronoun *n* Relativpronomen *nt*
relax [rɪ'læks] *vi* (*person, muscle*) sich entspannen; (*calm down*) sich beruhigen ▷ *vt* (*one's grip*) lockern; (*mind, person*) entspannen; (*control etc*) lockern
relaxation [ri:læk'seɪʃən] *n* Entspannung *f*; (*of control etc*) Lockern *nt*
relaxed [rɪ'lækst] *adj* (*person, atmosphere*) entspannt; (*discussion*) locker
relaxing [rɪ'læksɪŋ] *adj* entspannend
relay ['ri:leɪ] *n* (*race*) Staffel *f*, Staffellauf *m* ▷ *vt* (*message etc*) übermitteln; (*broadcast*) übertragen
release [rɪ'li:s] *n* (*from prison*) Entlassung *f*; (*from obligation, situation*) Befreiung *f*; (*of documents, funds etc*) Freigabe *f*; (*of gas etc*) Freisetzung *f*; (*of film, book, record*) Herausgabe *f*; (*record, film*) Veröffentlichung *f*; (*Tech*: *device*) Auslöser *m* ▷ *vt* (*from prison*) entlassen; (*person*: *from obligation, from wreckage*) befreien; (*gas etc*) freisetzen; (*Tech, Aut*: *catch, brake etc*) lösen; (*record, film*) herausbringen; (*news, figures*) bekannt geben; **on general ~** (*film*) überall in den Kinos; *see also* **press release**
relegate ['rɛləgeɪt] *vt* (*downgrade*) herunterstufen; (*Brit*: *Sport*): **to be ~d** absteigen
relent [rɪ'lɛnt] *vi* (*give in*) nachgeben
relentless [rɪ'lɛntlɪs] *adj* (*heat, noise*) erbarmungslos; (*enemy etc*) unerbittlich
relevance ['rɛləvəns] *n* Relevanz *f*, Bedeutung *f*; **the ~ of religion to society** die Relevanz *or* Bedeutung der Religion für die Gesellschaft
relevant ['rɛləvənt] *adj* relevant; (*chapter, area*) entsprechend; **~ to** relevant für
reliability [rɪlaɪə'bɪlɪtɪ] *n* Zuverlässigkeit *f*
reliable [rɪ'laɪəbl] *adj* zuverlässig

reliably [rɪ'laɪəblɪ] *adv*: **to be ~ informed that ...** zuverlässige Informationen darüber haben, dass ...
reliance [rɪ'laɪəns] *n*: **~ (on)** *(person)* Angewiesenheit *f* (auf *+acc*); *(drugs, financial support)* Abhängigkeit *f* (von)
reliant [rɪ'laɪənt] *adj*: **to be ~ on sth/sb** auf etw/jdn angewiesen sein
relic ['rɛlɪk] *n (Rel)* Reliquie *f*; *(of the past)* Relikt *nt*
relief [rɪ'li:f] *n (from pain etc)* Erleichterung *f*; *(aid)* Hilfe *f*; *(Art, Geog)* Relief *nt* ▷ *cpd (bus)* Entlastungs-; *(driver)* zur Ablösung; **light ~** leichte Abwechslung *f*
relief map *n* Reliefkarte *f*
relief road *(Brit) n* Entlastungsstraße *f*
relieve [rɪ'li:v] *vt (pain)* lindern; *(fear, worry)* mildern; *(take over from)* ablösen; **to ~ sb of sth** *(load)* jdm etw abnehmen; *(duties, post)* jdn einer Sache *gen* entheben; **to ~ o.s.** *(euphemism)* sich erleichtern
relieved [rɪ'li:vd] *adj* erleichtert; **I'm ~ to hear it** es erleichtert mich, das zu hören
religion [rɪ'lɪdʒən] *n* Religion *f*
religious [rɪ'lɪdʒəs] *adj* religiös
religious education *n* Religionsunterricht *m*
religiously [rɪ'lɪdʒəslɪ] *adv (regularly, thoroughly)* gewissenhaft
relinquish [rɪ'lɪŋkwɪʃ] *vt (control etc)* aufgeben; *(claim)* verzichten auf *+acc*
relish ['rɛlɪʃ] *n (Culin)* würzige Soße *f*, Relish *nt*; *(enjoyment)* Genuss *m* ▷ *vt (enjoy)* genießen; **to ~ doing sth** etw mit Genuss tun
relive [ri:'lɪv] *vt* noch einmal durchleben
reload [ri:'ləud] *vt (gun)* neu laden
relocate [ri:ləu'keɪt] *vt* verlegen ▷ *vi* den Standort wechseln; **to ~ in** seinen Standort verlegen nach
reluctance [rɪ'lʌktəns] *n* Widerwille *m*
reluctant [rɪ'lʌktənt] *adj* unwillig, widerwillig; **I'm ~ to do that** es widerstrebt mir, das zu tun
reluctantly [rɪ'lʌktəntlɪ] *adv* widerwillig, nur ungern
rely on [rɪ'laɪ-] *vt fus (be dependent on)* abhängen von; *(trust)* sich verlassen auf *+acc*
remain [rɪ'meɪn] *vi* bleiben; *(survive)* übrig bleiben; **to ~ silent** weiterhin schweigen; **to ~ in control** die Kontrolle behalten; **much ~s to be done** es ist noch viel zu tun; **the fact ~s that ...** Tatsache ist und bleibt, dass ...; **it ~s to be seen whether ...** es bleibt abzuwarten, ob ...
remainder [rɪ'meɪndəʳ] *n* Rest *m* ▷ *vt (Comm)* zu ermäßigtem Preis anbieten
remaining [rɪ'meɪnɪŋ] *adj* übrig
remains [rɪ'meɪnz] *npl (of meal)* Überreste *pl*; *(of building etc)* Ruinen *pl*; *(of body)* sterbliche Überreste *pl*
remand [rɪ'mɑ:nd] *n*: **to be on ~** in Untersuchungshaft sein ▷ *vt*: **to be ~ed in custody** in Untersuchungshaft bleiben müssen
remand home *(formerly: Brit) n* Untersuchungsgefängnis *nt* für Jugendliche
remark [rɪ'mɑ:k] *n* Bemerkung *f* ▷ *vt* bemerken ▷ *vi*: **to ~ on sth** Bemerkungen über etw *acc* machen; **to ~ that** die Bemerkung machen, dass
remarkable [rɪ'mɑ:kəbl] *adj* bemerkenswert
remarry [ri:'mærɪ] *vi* wieder heiraten
remedial [rɪ'mi:dɪəl] *adj (tuition, classes)* Förder-; **~ exercise** Heilgymnastik *f*
remedy ['rɛmədɪ] *n (lit, fig)* (Heil)mittel *nt* ▷ *vt (mistake, situation)* abhelfen *+dat*
remember [rɪ'mɛmbəʳ] *vt (call back to mind)* sich erinnern an *+acc*; *(bear in mind)* denken an *+acc*; **~ me to him** *(send greetings)* grüße ihn von mir; **I ~ seeing it, I ~ having seen it** ich erinnere mich (daran), es gesehen zu haben; **she ~ed to do it** sie hat daran gedacht, es zu tun
remembrance [rɪ'mɛmbrəns] *n* Erinnerung *f*; **in ~ of sb/sth** im Gedenken an *+acc*
Remembrance Sunday *(Brit) n* ≈ Volkstrauertag *m*; *siehe Info-Artikel*

REMEMBRANCE SUNDAY

Remembrance Sunday oder *Remembrance Day* ist der britische Gedenktag für die Gefallenen der beiden Weltkriege und anderer Konflikte. Er fällt auf einen Sonntag vor oder nach dem 11. November (am 11. November 1918 endete der Erste Weltkrieg) und wird mit einer Schweigeminute, Kranzniederlegungen an Kriegerdenkmälern und dem Tragen von Anstecknadeln in Form einer Mohnblume begangen.

remind [rɪ'maɪnd] *vt*: **to ~ sb to do sth** jdn daran erinnern, etw zu tun; **to ~ sb of sth** jdn an etw *acc* erinnern; **to ~ sb that ...** jdn daran erinnern, dass ...; **she ~s me of her mother** sie erinnert mich an ihre Mutter; **that ~s me!** dabei fällt mir etwas ein!
reminder [rɪ'maɪndəʳ] *n (of person, place etc)* Erinnerung *f*; *(letter)* Mahnung *f*
reminisce [rɛmɪ'nɪs] *vi*: **to ~ (about)** sich in Erinnerungen ergehen (über *+acc*)
reminiscences [rɛmɪ'nɪsnsɪz] *npl* Erinnerungen *pl*
reminiscent [rɛmɪ'nɪsnt] *adj*: **to be ~ of sth** an etw *acc* erinnern
remiss [rɪ'mɪs] *adj* nachlässig; **it was ~ of him** es war nachlässig von ihm
remission [rɪ'mɪʃən] *n (of sentence)* Straferlass *m*; *(Med)* Remission *f*; *(Rel)* Erlass *m*
remit [rɪ'mɪt] *vt (money)* überweisen ▷ *n (of official etc)* Aufgabenbereich *m*
remittance [rɪ'mɪtns] *n* Überweisung *f*
remnant ['rɛmnənt] *n* Überrest *m*; *(Comm: of cloth)* Rest *m*
remonstrate ['rɛmənstreɪt] *vi*: **to ~ (with sb about sth)** sich beschweren (bei jdm wegen etw)

remorse [rɪ'mɔ:s] *n* Reue *f*
remorseful [rɪ'mɔ:sful] *adj* reumütig
remorseless [rɪ'mɔ:slɪs] *adj* (*noise, pain*) unbarmherzig
remote [rɪ'məut] *adj* (*distant: place, time*) weit entfernt; (*aloof*) distanziert; (*slight: chance etc*) entfernt; **there is a ~ possibility that ...** es besteht eventuell die Möglichkeit, dass ...
remote control *n* Fernsteuerung *f*; (*TV etc*) Fernbedienung *f*
remote-controlled [rɪ'məutkən'trəuld] *adj* ferngesteuert
remotely [rɪ'məutlɪ] *adv* (*slightly*) entfernt
remoteness [rɪ'məutnɪs] *n* (*of place*) Entlegenheit *f*; (*of person*) Distanziertheit *f*
remould ['ri:məuld] (*Brit*) *n* (*Aut*) runderneuerter Reifen *m*
removable [rɪ'mu:vəbl] *adj* (*detachable*) abnehmbar
removal [rɪ'mu:vəl] *n* (*of object etc*) Entfernung *f*; (*of threat etc*) Beseitigung *f*; (*Brit: from house*) Umzug *m*; (*dismissal*) Entlassung *f*; (*Med: of kidney etc*) Entfernung *f*
removal man (*Brit*) *n* Möbelpacker *m*
removal van (*Brit*) *n* Möbelwagen *m*
remove [rɪ'mu:v] *vt* entfernen; (*clothing*) ausziehen; (*bandage etc*) abnehmen; (*employee*) entlassen; (*name: from list*) streichen; (*doubt, threat, obstacle*) beseitigen; **my first cousin once ~d** mein Vetter ersten Grades
remover [rɪ'mu:vəʳ] *n* (*for paint, varnish*) Entferner *m*; **stain ~** Fleckentferner *m*; **make-up ~** Make-up-Entferner *m*
remunerate [rɪ'mju:nəreɪt] *vt* vergüten
remuneration [rɪmju:nə'reɪʃən] *n* Vergütung *f*
Renaissance [rɪ'neɪsɑ̃:s] *n*: **the ~** die Renaissance
renal ['ri:nl] *adj* (*Med*) Nieren-
renal failure *n* Nierenversagen *nt*
rename [ri:'neɪm] *vt* umbenennen
rend [rɛnd] (*pt, pp* **rent**) *vt* (*air, silence*) zerreißen
render ['rɛndəʳ] *vt* (*give: assistance, aid*) leisten; (*cause to become: unconscious, harmless, useless*) machen; (*submit*) vorlegen
rendering ['rɛndərɪŋ] (*Brit*) *n* = **rendition**
rendezvous ['rɔndɪvu:] *n* (*meeting*) Rendezvous *nt*; (*place*) Treffpunkt *m* ▷ *vi* (*people*) sich treffen; (*spacecraft*) ein Rendezvousmanöver durchführen; **to ~ with sb** sich mit jdm treffen
rendition [rɛn'dɪʃən] *n* (*of song etc*) Vortrag *m*
renegade ['rɛnɪgeɪd] *n* Renegat(in) *m(f)*, Überläufer(in) *m(f)*
renew [rɪ'nju:] *vt* erneuern; (*attack, negotiations*) wiederaufnehmen; (*loan, contract etc*) verlängern; (*relationship etc*) wiederaufleben lassen
renewables *npl* erneuerbare Energien *pl*
renewal [rɪ'nju:əl] *n* Erneuerung *f*; (*of conflict*) Wiederaufnahme *f*; (*of contract etc*) Verlängerung *f*
renounce [rɪ'nauns] *vt* verzichten auf +*acc*; (*belief*) aufgeben
renovate ['rɛnəveɪt] *vt* (*building*) restaurieren; (*machine*) überholen
renovation [rɛnə'veɪʃən] *n* (*see vb*) Restaurierung *f*; Überholung *f*
renown [rɪ'naun] *n* Ruf *m*
renowned [rɪ'naund] *adj* berühmt
rent [rɛnt] *pt, pp of* **rend** ▷ *n* (*for house*) Miete *f* ▷ *vt* mieten; (*also*: **rent out**) vermieten
rental ['rɛntl] *n* (*for television, car*) Mietgebühr *f*
rent boy (*inf*) *n* Strichjunge *m*
rent strike *n* Mietstreik *m*
renunciation [rɪnʌnsɪ'eɪʃən] *n* Verzicht *m*; (*of belief*) Aufgabe *f*; (*self-denial*) Selbstverleugnung *f*
reopen [ri:'əupən] *vt* (*shop etc*) wiedereröffnen; (*negotiations, legal case etc*) wiederaufnehmen
reopening [ri:'əupnɪŋ] *n* (*see vt*) Wiedereröffnung *f*; Wiederaufnahme *f*
reorder [ri:'ɔ:dəʳ] *vt* (*rearrange*) umordnen
reorganization ['ri:ɔ:gənaɪ'zeɪʃən] *n* Umorganisation *f*
reorganize [ri:'ɔ:gənaɪz] *vt* umorganisieren
Rep. (*US*) *abbr* (*Pol*) = **representative; Republican**
rep [rɛp] *n abbr* (*Comm*) = **representative**; (*Theat*) = **repertory**
repair [rɪ'pɛəʳ] *n* Reparatur *f* ▷ *vt* reparieren; (*clothes, road*) ausbessern; **in good/bad ~** in gutem/schlechtem Zustand; **beyond ~** nicht mehr zu reparieren; **to be under ~** (*road*) ausgebessert werden
repair kit *n* (*for bicycle*) Flickzeug *nt*
repair man *n* Handwerker *m*
repair shop *n* Reparaturwerkstatt *f*
repartee [rɛpɑ:'ti:] *n* (*exchange*) Schlagabtausch *m*; (*reply*) schlagfertige Bemerkung *f*
repast [rɪ'pɑ:st] (*form*) *n* Mahl *nt*
repatriate [ri:'pætrɪeɪt] *vt* repatriieren
repay [ri:'peɪ] (*irreg: like* **pay**) *vt* zurückzahlen; (*sb's efforts, attention*) belohnen; (*favour*) erwidern; **I'll ~ you next week** ich zahle es dir nächste Woche zurück
repayment [ri:'peɪmənt] *n* Rückzahlung *f*
repeal [rɪ'pi:l] *n* (*of law*) Aufhebung *f* ▷ *vt* (*law*) aufheben
repeat [rɪ'pi:t] *n* (*Radio, TV*) Wiederholung *f* ▷ *vt, vi* wiederholen ▷ *cpd* (*performance*) Wiederholungs-; (*order*) Nach-; **to ~ o.s./itself** sich wiederholen; **to ~ an order for sth** etw nachbestellen
repeatedly [rɪ'pi:tɪdlɪ] *adv* wiederholt
repel [rɪ'pɛl] *vt* (*drive away*) zurückschlagen; (*disgust*) abstoßen
repellent [rɪ'pɛlənt] *adj* abstoßend ▷ *n*: **insect ~** Insekten(schutz)mittel *nt*
repent [rɪ'pɛnt] *vi*: **to ~ of sth** etw bereuen
repentance [rɪ'pɛntəns] *n* Reue *f*
repercussions [ri:pə'kʌʃənz] *npl* Auswirkungen *pl*
repertoire ['rɛpətwɑ:ʳ] *n* (*Mus, Theat*) Repertoire *nt*; (*fig*) Spektrum *nt*
repertory ['rɛpətərɪ] *n* (*also*: **repertory theatre**) Repertoiretheater *nt*

repertory company *n* Repertoire-Ensemble *nt*
repetition [rɛpɪ'tɪʃən] *n* (*repeat*) Wiederholung *f*
repetitious [rɛpɪ'tɪʃəs] *adj* (*speech etc*) voller Wiederholungen
repetitive [rɪ'pɛtɪtɪv] *adj* eintönig, monoton
replace [rɪ'pleɪs] *vt* (*put back: upright*) zurückstellen; (*: flat*) zurücklegen; (*take the place of*) ersetzen; **to ~ X with Y** X durch Y ersetzen; **"~ the receiver"** (*Tel*) „Hörer auflegen"
replacement [rɪ'pleɪsmənt] *n* Ersatz *m*
replacement part *n* Ersatzteil *nt*
replay ['ri:pleɪ] *n* (*of match*) Wiederholungsspiel *nt* ▷ *vt* (*match*) wiederholen; (*track, song: on tape*) nochmals abspielen
replenish [rɪ'plɛnɪʃ] *vt* (*glass, stock etc*) auffüllen
replete [rɪ'pli:t] *adj* (*after meal*) gesättigt; **~ with** reichlich ausgestattet mit
replica ['rɛplɪkə] *n* (*of object*) Nachbildung *f*
reply [rɪ'plaɪ] *n* Antwort *f* ▷ *vi*: **to ~ (to sb/sth)** (jdm/auf etw *acc*) antworten; **in ~ to** als Antwort auf *+acc*; **there's no ~** (*Tel*) es meldet sich niemand
reply coupon *n* Antwortschein *m*
report [rɪ'pɔ:t] *n* Bericht *m*; (*Brit: also:* **school report**) Zeugnis *nt*; (*of gun*) Knall *m* ▷ *vt* berichten; (*casualties, damage, theft etc*) melden; (*person: to police*) anzeigen ▷ *vi* (*make a report*) Bericht erstatten; **to ~ to sb** (*present o.s. to*) sich bei jdm melden; (*be responsible to*) jdm unterstellt sein; **to ~ on sth** über etw *acc* Bericht erstatten; **to ~ sick** sich krankmelden; **it is ~ed that** es wird berichtet *or* gemeldet, dass ...
report card (*US, Scot*) *n* Zeugnis *nt*
reportedly [rɪ'pɔ:tɪdlɪ] *adv*: **she is ~ living in Spain** sie lebt angeblich in Spanien
reported speech *n* (*Ling*) indirekte Rede *f*
reporter [rɪ'pɔ:təʳ] *n* Reporter(in) *m(f)*
repose [rɪ'pəuz] *n*: **in ~** in Ruhestellung
repository [rɪ'pɔzɪtərɪ] *n* (*person: of knowledge*) Quelle *f*; (*place: of collection etc*) Lager *nt*
repossess ['ri:pə'zɛs] *vt* (wieder) in Besitz nehmen
repossession order [ri:pə'zɛʃən-] *n* Beschlagnahmungsverfügung *f*
reprehensible [rɛprɪ'hɛnsɪbl] *adj* verwerflich
represent [rɛprɪ'zɛnt] *vt* (*person, nation*) vertreten; (*show: view, opinion*) darstellen; (*symbolize: idea*) symbolisieren, verkörpern; **to ~ sth as** (*describe*) etw darstellen als
representation [rɛprɪzɛn'teɪʃən] *n* (*state of being represented*) Vertretung *f*; (*picture etc*) Darstellung *f*; **representations** *npl* (*protest*) Proteste *pl*
representative [rɛprɪ'zɛntətɪv] *n* (*also Comm*) Vertreter(in) *m(f)*; (*US: Pol*) Abgeordnete(r) *f(m)* des Repräsentantenhauses ▷ *adj* repräsentativ; **~ of** repräsentativ für
repress [rɪ'prɛs] *vt* unterdrücken
repression [rɪ'prɛʃən] *n* Unterdrückung *f*
repressive [rɪ'prɛsɪv] *adj* repressiv
reprieve [rɪ'pri:v] *n* (*cancellation*) Begnadigung *f*; (*postponement*) Strafaufschub *m*; (*fig*) Gnadenfrist *f* ▷ *vt*: **he was ~d** (*see n*) er wurde begnadigt; ihm wurde Strafaufschub gewährt
reprimand ['rɛprɪmɑ:nd] *n* Tadel *m* ▷ *vt* tadeln
reprint ['ri:prɪnt] *n* Nachdruck *m* ▷ *vt* nachdrucken
reprisal [rɪ'praɪzl] *n* Vergeltung *f*; **reprisals** *npl* Repressalien *pl*; (*in war*) Vergeltungsaktionen *pl*; **to take ~s** zu Repressalien greifen; (*in war*) Vergeltungsaktionen durchführen
reproach [rɪ'prəutʃ] *n* (*rebuke*) Vorwurf *m* ▷ *vt*: **to ~ sb for sth** jdm etw zum Vorwurf machen; **beyond ~** über jeden Vorwurf erhaben; **to ~ sb with sth** jdm etw vorwerfen
reproachful [rɪ'prəutʃful] *adj* vorwurfsvoll
reproduce [ri:prə'dju:s] *vt* reproduzieren ▷ *vi* (*Biol*) sich vermehren
reproduction [ri:prə'dʌkʃən] *n* Reproduktion *f*; (*Biol*) Fortpflanzung *f*
reproductive [ri:prə'dʌktɪv] *adj* (*system, organs*) Fortpflanzungs-
reproof [rɪ'pru:f] *n* (*rebuke*) Tadel *m*; **with ~** tadelnd
reprove [rɪ'pru:v] *vt* tadeln; **to ~ sb for sth** jdn wegen etw tadeln
reproving [rɪ'pru:vɪŋ] *adj* tadelnd
reptile ['rɛptaɪl] *n* Reptil *nt*
Repub. (*US*) *abbr* (*Pol*) = **Republican**
republic [rɪ'pʌblɪk] *n* Republik *f*
republican [rɪ'pʌblɪkən] *adj* republikanisch ▷ *n* Republikaner(in) *m(f)*; **the R~s** (*US: Pol*) die Republikaner
repudiate [rɪ'pju:dɪeɪt] *vt* (*accusation*) zurückweisen; (*violence*) ablehnen; (*old: friend, wife etc*) verstoßen
repugnance [rɪ'pʌgnəns] *n* Abscheu *m*
repugnant [rɪ'pʌgnənt] *adj* abstoßend
repulse [rɪ'pʌls] *vt* (*attack etc*) zurückschlagen; (*sight, picture etc*) abstoßen
repulsion [rɪ'pʌlʃən] *n* Abscheu *m*
repulsive [rɪ'pʌlsɪv] *adj* widerwärtig, abstoßend
reputable ['rɛpjutəbl] *adj* (*make, company etc*) angesehen
reputation [rɛpju'teɪʃən] *n* Ruf *m*; **to have a ~ for** einen Ruf haben für; **he has a ~ for being awkward** er gilt als schwierig
repute [rɪ'pju:t] *n*: **of ~** angesehen; **to be held in high ~** in hohem Ansehen stehen
reputed [rɪ'pju:tɪd] *adj* angeblich; **he is ~ to be rich** er ist angeblich reich
reputedly [rɪ'pju:tɪdlɪ] *adv* angeblich
request [rɪ'kwɛst] *n* (*polite*) Bitte *f*; (*formal*) Ersuchen *nt*; (*Radio*) Musikwunsch *m* ▷ *vt* (*politely*) bitten um; (*formally*) ersuchen; **at the ~ of** auf Wunsch von; **"you are ~ed not to smoke"** „bitte nicht rauchen"
request stop (*Brit*) *n* Bedarfshaltestelle *f*
requiem ['rɛkwɪəm] *n* (*Rel: also:* **requiem mass**) Totenmesse *f*; (*Mus*) Requiem *nt*
require [rɪ'kwaɪəʳ] *vt* (*need*) benötigen; (*: situation*) erfordern; (*demand*) verlangen; **to ~ sb to do sth** von jdm verlangen, etw zu tun;

if ~d falls nötig; **what qualifications are ~d?** welche Qualifikationen werden verlangt?; **~d by law** gesetzlich vorgeschrieben

required [rɪ'kwaɪəd] *adj* erforderlich

requirement [rɪ'kwaɪəmənt] *n* (*need*) Bedarf *m*; (*condition*) Anforderung *f*; **to meet sb's ~s** jds Anforderungen erfüllen

requisite ['rɛkwɪzɪt] *adj* erforderlich; **requisites** *npl*: **toilet/travel ~s** Toiletten-/Reiseartikel *pl*

requisition [rɛkwɪ'zɪʃən] *n*: **~ (for)** (*demand*) Anforderung *f* (von) ▷ *vt* (*Mil*) beschlagnahmen

reroute [riː'ruːt] *vt* (*train etc*) umleiten

resale [riː'seɪl] *n* Weiterverkauf *m*; **"not for ~"** „nicht zum Weiterverkauf bestimmt"

resale price maintenance *n* Preisbindung *f*

rescind [rɪ'sɪnd] *vt* (*law, order*) aufheben; (*decision*) rückgängig machen; (*agreement*) widerrufen

rescue ['rɛskjuː] *n* Rettung *f* ▷ *vt* retten; **to come to sb's ~** jdm zu Hilfe kommen

rescue party *n* Rettungsmannschaft *f*

rescuer ['rɛskjuəʳ] *n* Retter(in) *m(f)*

research [rɪ'səːtʃ] *n* Forschung *f* ▷ *vt* erforschen ▷ *vi*: **to ~ into sth** etw erforschen; **to do ~** Forschung betreiben; **a piece of ~** eine Forschungsarbeit; **~ and development** Forschung und Entwicklung

researcher [rɪ'səːtʃəʳ] *n* Forscher(in) *m(f)*

research work *n* Forschungsarbeit *f*

research worker *n* = **researcher**

resell [riː'sɛl] (*irreg: like* **sell**) *vt* weiterverkaufen

resemblance [rɪ'zɛmbləns] *n* Ähnlichkeit *f*; **to bear a strong ~ to** starke Ähnlichkeit haben mit; **it bears no ~ to ...** es hat keine Ähnlichkeit mit ...

resemble [rɪ'zɛmbl] *vt* ähneln *+dat*, gleichen *+dat*

resent [rɪ'zɛnt] *vt* (*attitude, treatment*) missbilligen; (*person*) ablehnen

resentful [rɪ'zɛntful] *adj* (*person*) gekränkt; (*attitude*) missbilligend

resentment [rɪ'zɛntmənt] *n* Verbitterung *f*

reservation [rɛzə'veɪʃən] *n* (*booking*) Reservierung *f*; (*doubt*) Vorbehalt *m*; (*land*) Reservat *nt*; **to make a ~** (*in hotel etc*) eine Reservierung vornehmen; **with ~(s)** (*doubts*) unter Vorbehalt

reservation desk *n* Reservierungsschalter *m*

reserve [rɪ'zəːv] *n* Reserve *f*, Vorrat *m*; (*fig: of talent etc*) Reserve *f*; (*Sport*) Reservespieler(in) *m(f)*; (*also*: **nature reserve**) Naturschutzgebiet *nt*; (*restraint*) Zurückhaltung *f* ▷ *vt* reservieren; (*table, ticket*) reservieren lassen; **reserves** *npl* (*Mil*) Reserve *f*; **in ~** in Reserve

reserve currency *n* Reservewährung *f*

reserved [rɪ'zəːvd] *adj* (*restrained*) zurückhaltend; (*seat*) reserviert

reserve price (*Brit*) *n* Mindestpreis *m*

reserve team (*Brit*) *n* Reservemannschaft *f*

reservist [rɪ'zəːvɪst] *n* (*Mil*) Reservist *m*

reservoir ['rɛzəvwɑːʳ] *n* (*lit, fig*) Reservoir *nt*

reset [riː'sɛt] (*irreg: like* **set**) *vt* (*watch*) neu stellen; (*broken bone*) wieder einrichten; (*Comput*) zurückstellen

reshape [riː'ʃeɪp] *vt* (*policy, view*) umgestalten

reshuffle [riː'ʃʌfl] *n*: **cabinet ~** Kabinettsumbildung *f*

reside [rɪ'zaɪd] *vi* (*live: person*) seinen/ihren Wohnsitz haben

▸ **reside in** *vt fus* (*exist*) liegen in *+dat*

residence ['rɛzɪdəns] *n* (*form: home*) Wohnsitz *m*; (*length of stay*) Aufenthalt *m*; **to take up ~** sich niederlassen; **in ~** (*queen etc*) anwesend; **writer/artist in ~** *Schriftsteller/Künstler, der in einer Ausbildungsstätte bei freier Unterkunft lehrt und arbeitet*

residence permit (*Brit*) *n* Aufenthaltserlaubnis *f*

resident ['rɛzɪdənt] *n* (*of country, town*) Einwohner(in) *m(f)*; (*in hotel*) Gast *m* ▷ *adj* (*in country, town*) wohnhaft; (*population*) ansässig; (*doctor*) hauseigen; (*landlord*) im Hause wohnend

residential [rɛzɪ'dɛnʃəl] *adj* (*area*) Wohn-; (*course*) mit Wohnung am Ort; (*staff*) im Hause wohnend

residue ['rɛzɪdjuː] *n* (*Chem*) Rückstand *m*; (*fig*) Überrest *m*

resign [rɪ'zaɪn] *vt* (*one's post*) zurücktreten von ▷ *vi* (*from post*) zurücktreten; **to ~ o.s. to** (*situation etc*) sich abfinden mit

resignation [rɛzɪg'neɪʃən] *n* (*from post*) Rücktritt *m*; (*state of mind*) Resignation *f*; **to tender one's ~** seine Kündigung einreichen

resigned [rɪ'zaɪnd] *adj*: **to be ~ to sth** sich mit etw abgefunden haben

resilience [rɪ'zɪlɪəns] *n* (*of material*) Widerstandsfähigkeit *f*; (*of person*) Unverwüstlichkeit *f*

resilient [rɪ'zɪlɪənt] *adj* (*see n*) widerstandsfähig; unverwüstlich

resin ['rɛzɪn] *n* Harz *nt*

resist [rɪ'zɪst] *vt* (*change, demand*) sich widersetzen *+dat*; (*attack etc*) Widerstand leisten *+dat*; (*urge etc*) widerstehen *+dat*; **I couldn't ~ (doing) it** ich konnte nicht widerstehen(, es zu tun)

resistance [rɪ'zɪstəns] *n* (*also Elec*) Widerstand *m*; (*to illness*) Widerstandsfähigkeit *f*

resistant [rɪ'zɪstənt] *adj*: **~ (to)** (*to change etc*) widerstandsfähig (gegenüber); (*to antibiotics etc*) resistent (gegen)

resolute ['rɛzəluːt] *adj* (*person*) entschlossen, resolut; (*refusal*) entschieden

resolution [rɛzə'luːʃən] *n* (*decision*) Beschluss *m*; (*determination*) Entschlossenheit *f*; (*of problem*) Lösung *f*; **to make a ~** einen Entschluss fassen

resolve [rɪ'zɔlv] *n* (*determination*) Entschlossenheit *f* ▷ *vt* (*problem*) lösen; (*difficulty*) beseitigen ▷ *vi*: **to ~ to do sth** beschließen, etw zu tun

resolved [rɪ'zɔlvd] *adj* (*determined*) entschlossen

resonance ['rɛzənəns] *n* Resonanz *f*

resonant ['rɛzənənt] *adj* (*sound, voice*) volltönend; (*place*) widerhallend
resort [rɪ'zɔːt] *n* (*town*) Urlaubsort *m*; (*recourse*) Zuflucht *f* ▷ *vi*: **to ~ to** Zuflucht nehmen zu; **seaside ~** Seebad *nt*; **winter sports ~** Wintersportort *m*; **as a last ~** als letzter Ausweg; **in the last ~** schlimmstenfalls
resound [rɪ'zaund] *vi*: **to ~ (with)** widerhallen (von)
resounding [rɪ'zaundɪŋ] *adj* (*noise*) widerhallend; (*voice*) schallend; (*fig: success*) durchschlagend; (*: victory*) überlegen
resource [rɪ'sɔːs] *n* (*raw material*) Bodenschatz *m*; **resources** *npl* (*coal, oil etc*) Energiequellen *pl*; (*money*) Mittel *pl*, Ressourcen *pl*; **natural ~s** Naturschätze *pl*
resourceful [rɪ'sɔːsful] *adj* einfallsreich
resourcefulness [rɪ'sɔːsfulnɪs] *n* Einfallsreichtum *m*
respect [rɪs'pɛkt] *n* (*consideration, esteem*) Respekt *m* ▷ *vt* respektieren; **respects** *npl* (*greetings*) Grüße *pl*; **to have ~ for sb/sth** Respekt vor jdm/etw haben; **to show sb/sth ~** Respekt vor jdm/etw zeigen; **out of ~ for** aus Rücksicht auf *+acc*; **with ~ to, in ~ of** in Bezug auf *+acc*; **in this ~** in dieser Hinsicht; **in some/many ~s** in gewisser/vielfacher Hinsicht; **with (all due) ~** bei allem Respekt
respectability [rɪspɛktə'bɪlɪtɪ] *n* Anständigkeit *f*
respectable [rɪs'pɛktəbl] *adj* anständig; (*amount, income*) ansehnlich; (*standard, mark etc*) ordentlich
respected [rɪs'pɛktɪd] *adj* angesehen
respectful [rɪs'pɛktful] *adj* respektvoll
respectfully [rɪs'pɛktfəlɪ] *adv* (*behave*) respektvoll
respective [rɪs'pɛktɪv] *adj* jeweilig
respectively [rɪs'pɛktɪvlɪ] *adv* beziehungsweise; **Germany and Britain were 3rd and 4th ~** Deutschland und Großbritannien belegten den 3. beziehungsweise 4. Platz
respiration [rɛspɪ'reɪʃən] *n* see **artificial**
respirator ['rɛspɪreɪtə^r] *n* Respirator *m*, Beatmungsgerät *nt*
respiratory ['rɛspərətərɪ] *adj* (*system, failure*) Atmungs-
respite ['rɛspaɪt] *n* (*rest*) Ruhepause *f*
resplendent [rɪs'plɛndənt] *adj* (*clothes*) prächtig
respond [rɪs'pɔnd] *vi* (*answer*) antworten; (*react*) reagieren
respondent [rɪs'pɔndənt] *n* (*Law*) Beklagte(r) *f(m)*
response [rɪs'pɔns] *n* (*to question*) Antwort *f*; (*to event etc*) Reaktion *f*; **in ~ to** als Antwort/Reaktion auf *+acc*
responsibility [rɪspɔnsɪ'bɪlɪtɪ] *n* Verantwortung *f*; **to take ~ for sth/sb** die Verantwortung für etw/jdn übernehmen
responsible [rɪs'pɔnsɪbl] *adj* verantwortlich; (*reliable, important*) verantwortungsvoll; **to be ~ for sth** für etw verantwortlich sein; **to be ~ for doing sth** dafür verantwortlich sein, etw zu tun; **to be ~ to sb** jdm gegenüber verantwortlich sein
responsibly [rɪs'pɔnsɪblɪ] *adv* verantwortungsvoll
responsive [rɪs'pɔnsɪv] *adj* (*person*) ansprechbar
rest [rɛst] *n* (*relaxation*) Ruhe *f*; (*pause*) Ruhepause *f*; (*remainder*) Rest *m*; (*support*) Stütze *f*; (*Mus*) Pause *f* ▷ *vi* (*relax*) sich ausruhen ▷ *vt* (*eyes, legs etc*) ausruhen; **the ~ of them** die Übrigen; **to put** *or* **set sb's mind at ~** jdn beruhigen; **to come to ~** (*object*) zum Stillstand kommen; **to lay sb to ~** jdn zur letzten Ruhe betten; **to ~ on sth** (*lit, fig*) sich auf etw *acc* stützen; **to let the matter ~** die Sache auf sich beruhen lassen; **~ assured that ...** seien Sie versichert, dass ...; **I won't ~ until ...** ich werde nicht ruhen, bis ...; **may he/she ~ in peace** möge er/sie in Frieden ruhen; **to ~ sth on/against sth** (*lean*) etw an *acc*/gegen etw lehnen; **to ~ one's eyes** *or* **gaze on sth** den Blick auf etw heften; **I ~ my case** mehr brauche ich dazu wohl nicht zu sagen
restart [riː'stɑːt] *vt* (*engine*) wieder anlassen; (*work*) wiederaufnehmen
restaurant ['rɛstərɔŋ] *n* Restaurant *nt*
restaurant car (*Brit*) *n* (*Rail*) Speisewagen *m*
rest cure *n* Erholung *f*
restful ['rɛstful] *adj* (*music*) ruhig; (*lighting*) beruhigend; (*atmosphere*) friedlich
rest home *n* Pflegeheim *nt*
restitution [rɛstɪ'tjuːʃən] *n*: **to make ~ to sb of sth** jdm etw zurückerstatten; (*as compensation*) jdn für etw entschädigen
restive ['rɛstɪv] *adj* (*person, crew*) unruhig; (*horse*) störrisch
restless ['rɛstlɪs] *adj* rastlos; (*audience*) unruhig; **to get ~** unruhig werden
restlessly ['rɛstlɪslɪ] *adv* (*walk around*) rastlos; (*turn over*) unruhig
restock [riː'stɔk] *vt* (*shop, freezer*) wieder auffüllen; (*lake, river: with fish*) wieder besetzen
restoration [rɛstə'reɪʃən] *n* (*of painting etc*) Restauration *f*; (*of law and order, health, sight etc*) Wiederherstellung *f*; (*of land, rights*) Rückgabe *f*; (*Hist*): **the R~** die Restauration
restorative [rɪ'stɔrətɪv] *adj* (*power, treatment*) stärkend ▷ *n* (*old: drink*) Stärkungsmittel *nt*
restore [rɪ'stɔː^r] *vt* (*painting etc*) restaurieren; (*law and order, faith, health etc*) wiederherstellen; (*property*) zurückgeben; **to ~ sth to** (*to former state*) etw zurückverwandeln in *+acc*; **to ~ sb to power** jdn wieder an die Macht bringen
restorer [rɪ'stɔːrə^r] *n* (*Art etc*) Restaurator(in) *m(f)*
restrain [rɪs'treɪn] *vt* (*person*) zurückhalten; (*feeling*) unterdrücken; (*growth, inflation*) dämpfen; **to ~ sb from doing sth** jdn davon abhalten, etw zu tun; **to ~ o.s. from doing sth** sich beherrschen, etw nicht zu tun
restrained [rɪs'treɪnd] *adj* (*person*) beherrscht; (*style etc*) zurückhaltend

restraint [rɪs'treɪnt] *n* (*restriction*) Einschränkung *f*; (*moderation*) Zurückhaltung *f*; **wage ~** Zurückhaltung *f* bei Lohnforderungen
restrict [rɪs'trɪkt] *vt* beschränken
restricted area (*Brit*) *n* (*Aut*) Bereich *m* mit Geschwindigkeitsbeschränkung
restriction [rɪs'trɪkʃən] *n* Beschränkung *f*
restrictive [rɪs'trɪktɪv] *adj* (*law, measure*) restriktiv; (*clothing*) beengend
restrictive practices (*Brit*) *npl* (*Industry*) wettbewerbshemmende Geschäftspraktiken *pl*
rest room (*US*) *n* Toilette *f*
restructure [ri:'strʌktʃə^r] *vt* umstrukturieren
result [rɪ'zʌlt] *n* Resultat *nt*; (*of match, election, exam etc*) Ergebnis *nt* ▷ *vi*: **to ~ in** führen zu; **as a ~ of the accident** als Folge des Unfalls; **he missed the train as a ~ of sleeping in** er verpasste den Zug, weil er verschlafen hatte; **to ~ from** resultieren *or* sich ergeben aus; **as a ~ it is too expensive** folglich ist es zu teuer
resultant [rɪ'zʌltənt] *adj* resultierend, sich ergebend
resume [rɪ'zju:m] *vt* (*work, journey*) wiederaufnehmen; (*seat*) wieder einnehmen ▷ *vi* (*start again*) von Neuem beginnen
résumé ['reɪsju:meɪ] *n* Zusammenfassung *f*; (*US: curriculum vitae*) Lebenslauf *m*
resumption [rɪ'zʌmpʃən] *n* (*of work etc*) Wiederaufnahme *f*
resurgence [rɪ'sə:dʒəns] *n* Wiederaufleben *nt*
resurrection [rɛzə'rɛkʃən] *n* (*of hopes, fears*) Wiederaufleben *nt*; (*of custom etc*) Wiederbelebung *f*; (*Rel*): **the R~** die Auferstehung *f*
resuscitate [rɪ'sʌsɪteɪt] *vt* (*Med, fig*) wiederbeleben
resuscitation [rɪsʌsɪ'teɪʃən] *n* Wiederbelebung *f*
retail ['ri:teɪl] *adj* (*trade, department*) Verkaufs-; (*shop, goods*) Einzelhandels- ▷ *adv* im Einzelhandel ▷ *vt* (*sell*) (im Einzelhandel) verkaufen ▷ *vi*: **to ~ at** (im Einzelhandel) kosten; **this product ~s at £25** dieses Produkt kostet im Laden £25
retailer ['ri:teɪlə^r] *n* Einzelhändler(in) *m(f)*
retail outlet *n* Einzelhandelsverkaufsstelle *f*
retail price *n* Einzelhandelspreis *m*
retail price index *n* Einzelhandelspreisindex *m*
retain [rɪ'teɪn] *vt* (*keep*) behalten; (*: heat, moisture*) zurückhalten
retainer [rɪ'teɪnə^r] *n* (*fee*) Vorauszahlung *f*
retaliate [rɪ'tælɪeɪt] *vi* Vergeltung üben
retaliation [rɪtælɪ'eɪʃən] *n* Vergeltung *f*; **in ~ for** als Vergeltung für
retaliatory [rɪ'tælɪətərɪ] *adj* (*move, attack*) Vergeltungs-
retarded [rɪ'tɑ:dɪd] *adj* zurückgeblieben; **mentally ~** geistig zurückgeblieben
retch [rɛtʃ] *vi* würgen
retention [rɪ'tɛnʃən] *n* (*of tradition etc*) Beibehaltung *f*; (*of land, memories*) Behalten *nt*; (*of heat, fluid etc*) Zurückhalten *nt*
retentive [rɪ'tɛntɪv] *adj* (*memory*) merkfähig
rethink ['ri:'θɪŋk] *vt* noch einmal überdenken
reticence ['rɛtɪsns] *n* Zurückhaltung *f*
reticent ['rɛtɪsnt] *adj* zurückhaltend
retina ['rɛtɪnə] *n* Netzhaut *f*
retinue ['rɛtɪnju:] *n* Gefolge *nt*
retire [rɪ'taɪə^r] *vi* (*give up work*) in den Ruhestand treten; (*withdraw, go to bed*) sich zurückziehen
retired [rɪ'taɪəd] *adj* (*person*) im Ruhestand
retirement [rɪ'taɪəmənt] *n* (*state*) Ruhestand *m*; (*act*) Pensionierung *f*
retirement age *n* Rentenalter *nt*
retiring [rɪ'taɪərɪŋ] *adj* (*leaving*) ausscheidend; (*shy*) zurückhaltend
retort [rɪ'tɔ:t] *vi* erwidern ▷ *n* (*reply*) Erwiderung *f*
retrace [ri:'treɪs] *vt*: **to ~ one's steps** (*lit, fig*) seine Schritte zurückverfolgen
retract [rɪ'trækt] *vt* (*promise*) zurücknehmen; (*confession*) zurückziehen; (*claws, undercarriage*) einziehen
retractable [rɪ'træktəbl] *adj* (*undercarriage, aerial*) einziehbar
retrain [ri:'treɪn] *vt* umschulen ▷ *vi* umgeschult werden
retraining [ri:'treɪnɪŋ] *n* Umschulung *f*
retread ['ri:trɛd] *n* (*tyre*) runderneuerter Reifen *m*
retreat [rɪ'tri:t] *n* (*place*) Zufluchtsort *m*; (*withdrawal, also Mil*) Rückzug *m* ▷ *vi* sich zurückziehen; **to beat a hasty ~** schleunigst den Rückzug antreten
retrial [ri:'traɪəl] *n* erneute Verhandlung *f*
retribution [rɛtrɪ'bju:ʃən] *n* Strafe *f*
retrieval [rɪ'tri:vəl] *n* (*of object*) Zurückholen *nt*; (*Comput*) Abruf *m*
retrieve [rɪ'tri:v] *vt* (*object*) zurückholen; (*situation*) retten; (*error*) wiedergutmachen; (*dog*) apportieren; (*Comput*) abrufen
retriever [rɪ'tri:və^r] *n* (*dog*) Apportierhund *m*
retroactive [rɛtrəu'æktɪv] *adj* rückwirkend
retrograde ['rɛtrəgreɪd] *adj* (*step*) Rück-
retrospect ['rɛtrəspɛkt] *n*: **in ~** rückblickend, im Rückblick
retrospective [rɛtrə'spɛktɪv] *adj* (*opinion etc*) im Nachhinein; (*law, tax*) rückwirkend ▷ *n* (*Art*) Retrospektive *f*
return [rɪ'tə:n] *n* (*going or coming back*) Rückkehr *f*; (*of sth stolen etc*) Rückgabe *f*; (*also*: **return ticket**: *Brit*) Rückfahrkarte *f*; (*Fin: from investment etc*) Ertrag *m*; (*of merchandise*) Rücksendung *f*; (*official report*) Erklärung *f* ▷ *cpd* (*journey*) Rück- ▷ *vi* (*person etc: come or go back*) zurückkehren; (*feelings, symptoms etc*) wiederkehren ▷ *vt* (*favour, greetings etc*) erwidern; (*sth stolen etc*) zurückgeben; (*Law: verdict*) fällen; (*Pol: candidate*) wählen; (*ball*) zurückspielen; **returns** *npl* (*Comm*) Gewinne *pl*; **in ~ (for)** als Gegenleistung (für); **by ~ of post** postwendend; **many happy ~s (of the day)!** herzlichen Glückwunsch zum

Geburtstag!; ~ **match** Rückspiel *nt*
▸ **return to** *vt fus* (*regain: consciousness, power*) wiedererlangen
returnable [rɪ'tə:nəbl] *adj* (*bottle etc*) Mehrweg-
returner *n jd, der nach längerer Abwesenheit wieder in die Arbeitswelt zurückkehrt*
returning officer [rɪ'tə:nɪŋ-] (*Brit*) *n* Wahlleiter(in) *m(f)*
return key *n* (*Comput*) Return-Taste *f*
reunion [ri:'ju:nɪən] *n* Treffen *nt*; (*after long separation*) Wiedervereinigung *f*
reunite [ri:ju:'naɪt] *vt* wiedervereinigen
Rev. *abbr* (*Rel*) = **Reverend**
rev [rɛv] *n abbr* (*Aut: = revolution per minute*) Umdrehung *f* pro Minute, U/min. ▹ *vt* (*also*: **rev up**: *engine*) aufheulen lassen
revaluation [ri:vælju'eɪʃən] *n* (*of property*) Neuschätzung *f*; (*of currency*) Aufwertung *f*; (*of attitudes*) Neubewertung *f*
revamp [ri:'væmp] *vt* (*company, system*) auf Vordermann bringen
rev counter (*Brit*) *n* (*Aut*) Drehzahlmesser *m*
Revd. *abbr* (*Rel*) = **Reverend**
reveal [rɪ'vi:l] *vt* (*make known*) enthüllen; (*make visible*) zum Vorschein bringen
revealing [rɪ'vi:lɪŋ] *adj* (*comment, action*) aufschlussreich; (*dress*) tief ausgeschnitten
reveille [rɪ'vælɪ] *n* (*Mil*) Wecksignal *nt*
revel ['rɛvl] *vi*: **to ~ in sth** in etw schwelgen; **to ~ in doing sth** es genießen, etw zu tun
revelation [rɛvə'leɪʃən] *n* (*disclosure*) Enthüllung *f*
reveller ['rɛvlə^r] *n* Zecher(in) *m(f)*
revelry ['rɛvlrɪ] *n* Gelage *nt*
revenge [rɪ'vɛndʒ] *n* (*for insult etc*) Rache *f* ▹ *vt* rächen; **to get one's ~ (for sth)** seine Rache (für etw) bekommen; **to ~ o.s.** *or* **take one's ~ (on sb)** sich (an jdm) rächen
revengeful [rɪ'vɛndʒful] *adj* rachsüchtig
revenue ['rɛvənju:] *n* (*of person, company*) Einnahmen *pl*; (*of government*) Staatseinkünfte *pl*
reverberate [rɪ'və:bəreɪt] *vi* (*sound etc*) widerhallen; (*fig: shock etc*) Nachwirkungen haben
reverberation [rɪvə:bə'reɪʃən] *n* (*of sound*) Widerhall *m*; (*fig: of event etc*) Nachwirkungen *pl*
revere [rɪ'vɪə^r] *vt* verehren
reverence ['rɛvərəns] *n* Ehrfurcht *f*
Reverend ['rɛvərənd] *adj* (*in titles*) Pfarrer; **the ~ John Smith** Pfarrer John Smith
reverent ['rɛvərənt] *adj* ehrfürchtig
reverie ['rɛvərɪ] *n* Träumerei *f*
reversal [rɪ'və:sl] *n* (*of policy, trend*) Umkehr *f*; **a ~ of roles** ein Rollentausch *m*
reverse [rɪ'və:s] *n* (*opposite*) Gegenteil *nt*; (*back: of cloth*) linke Seite *f*; (: *of coin, paper*) Rückseite *f*; (*Aut: also*: **reverse gear**) Rückwärtsgang *m*; (*setback*) Rückschlag *m* ▹ *adj* (*side*) Rück-; (*process*) umgekehrt ▹ *vt* (*position, trend etc*) umkehren; (*Law: verdict*) revidieren; (*roles*) vertauschen; (*car*) zurücksetzen ▹ *vi* (*Brit: Aut*) zurücksetzen; **in ~** umgekehrt; **to go into ~** den Rückwärtsgang einlegen; **in ~ order** in umgekehrter Reihenfolge; **to ~ direction** sich um 180 Grad drehen
reverse-charge call [rɪ'və:stʃɑ:dʒ-] (*Brit*) *n* R-Gespräch *nt*
reverse video *n* (*Comput*) invertierte Darstellung *f*
reversible [rɪ'və:səbl] *adj* (*garment*) auf beiden Seiten tragbar; (*decision, operation*) umkehrbar
reversing lights [rɪ'və:sɪŋ-] (*Brit*) *npl* Rückfahrscheinwerfer *m*
reversion [rɪ'və:ʃən] *n*: ~ **to** Rückfall in *+acc*; (*Zool*) Rückentwicklung *f*
revert [rɪ'və:t] *vi*: **to ~ to** (*former state*) zurückkehren zu, zurückfallen in *+acc*; (*Law: money, property*) zurückfallen an *+acc*
review [rɪ'vju:] *n* (*magazine*) Zeitschrift *f*; (*Mil*) Inspektion *f*; (*of book, film etc*) Kritik *f*, Besprechung *f*, Rezension *f*; (*of policy etc*) Überprüfung *f* ▹ *vt* (*Mil: troops*) inspizieren; (*book, film etc*) besprechen, rezensieren; (*policy etc*) überprüfen; **to be/come under ~** überprüft werden
reviewer [rɪ'vju:ə^r] *n* Kritiker(in) *m(f)*, Rezensent(in) *m(f)*
revile [rɪ'vaɪl] *vt* schmähen
revise [rɪ'vaɪz] *vt* (*manuscript*) überarbeiten, revidieren; (*opinion etc*) ändern; (*price, procedure*) revidieren ▹ *vi* (*study*) wiederholen; **~d edition** überarbeitete Ausgabe
revision [rɪ'vɪʒən] *n* (*of manuscript, law etc*) Überarbeitung *f*, Revision *f*; (*for exam*) Wiederholung *f*
revitalize [ri:'vaɪtəlaɪz] *vt* neu beleben
revival [rɪ'vaɪvəl] *n* (*recovery*) Aufschwung *m*; (*of interest, faith*) Wiederaufleben *nt*; (*Theat*) Wiederaufnahme *f*
revive [rɪ'vaɪv] *vt* (*person*) wiederbeleben; (*economy etc*) Auftrieb geben *+dat*; (*custom*) wiederaufleben lassen; (*hope, interest etc*) neu beleben; (*play*) wiederaufnehmen ▹ *vi* (*person*) wieder zu sich kommen; (*activity, economy etc*) wieder aufblühen; (*hope, interest etc*) wiedererweckt werden
revoke [rɪ'vəuk] *vt* (*law etc*) aufheben; (*title, licence*) entziehen *+dat*; (*promise, decision*) widerrufen
revolt [rɪ'vəult] *n* Revolte *f*, Aufstand *m* ▹ *vi* rebellieren ▹ *vt* abstoßen; **to ~ against sb/sth** gegen jdn/etw rebellieren
revolting [rɪ'vəultɪŋ] *adj* (*disgusting*) abscheulich, ekelhaft
revolution [rɛvə'lu:ʃən] *n* (*Pol etc*) Revolution *f*; (*rotation*) Umdrehung *f*
revolutionary [rɛvə'lu:ʃənrɪ] *adj* revolutionär; (*leader, army*) Revolutions- ▹ *n* Revolutionär(in) *m(f)*
revolutionize [rɛvə'lu:ʃənaɪz] *vt* revolutionieren
revolve [rɪ'vɔlv] *vi* sich drehen; **to ~ (a)round** sich drehen um
revolver [rɪ'vɔlvə^r] *n* Revolver *m*

revolving [rɪ'vɔlvɪŋ] *adj (chair)* Dreh-; *(sprinkler etc)* drehbar
revolving door *n* Drehtür *f*
revue [rɪ'vjuː] *n (Theat)* Revue *f*
revulsion [rɪ'vʌlʃən] *n (disgust)* Abscheu *m*, Ekel *m*
reward [rɪ'wɔːd] *n* Belohnung *f*; *(satisfaction)* Befriedigung *f* ▷ *vt* belohnen
reward card *n* Kundenkarte *f*, Pay-back-Karte® *f*
rewarding [rɪ'wɔːdɪŋ] *adj* lohnend; **financially ~** einträglich
rewind [riː'waɪnd] *(irreg: like* **wind***)* *vt (tape etc)* zurückspulen
rewire [riː'waɪəʳ] *vt* neu verkabeln
reword [riː'wəːd] *vt (message, note)* umformulieren
rework [riː'wəːk] *vt (use again: theme etc)* wiederverarbeiten; *(revise)* neu fassen
rewrite [riː'raɪt] *(irreg: like* **write***)* *vt* neu schreiben
Reykjavik ['reɪkjəviːk] *n* Reykjavik *nt*
RFD *(US) abbr (Post: = rural free delivery) freie Landpostzustellung*
RGN *(Brit) n abbr (= Registered General Nurse)* staatlich geprüfte Krankenschwester *f*, staatlich geprüfter Krankenpfleger *m*
Rh *abbr (Med: = rhesus)* Rh.
rhapsody ['ræpsədɪ] *n (Mus)* Rhapsodie *f*
rhesus negative *adj* Rhesus negativ
rhesus positive *adj* Rhesus positiv
rhetoric ['rɛtərɪk] *n* Rhetorik *f*
rhetorical [rɪ'tɔrɪkl] *adj* rhetorisch
rheumatic [ruː'mætɪk] *adj* rheumatisch
rheumatism ['ruːmətɪzəm] *n* Rheuma *nt*, Rheumatismus *m*
rheumatoid arthritis ['ruːmətɔɪd-] *n* Gelenkrheumatismus *m*
Rhine [raɪn] *n*: **the ~** der Rhein
rhinestone ['raɪnstəun] *n* Rheinkiesel *m*
rhinoceros [raɪ'nɔsərəs] *n* Rhinozeros *nt*
Rhodes [rəudz] *n* Rhodos *nt*
Rhodesia [rəu'diːʒə] *(formerly) n (Geog)* Rhodesien *nt*
rhododendron [rəudə'dɛndrən] *n* Rhododendron *m or nt*
Rhone [rəun] *n*: **the ~** die Rhone
rhubarb ['ruːbɑːb] *n* Rhabarber *m*
rhyme [raɪm] *n* Reim *m*; *(verse)* Verse *pl* ▷ *vi*: **to ~ (with)** sich reimen (mit); **without ~ or reason** ohne Sinn und Verstand
rhythm ['rɪðm] *n* Rhythmus *m*
rhythmic ['rɪðmɪk], **rhythmical** ['rɪðmɪkl] *adj* rhythmisch
rhythmically ['rɪðmɪklɪ] *adv (move, beat)* rhythmisch, im Rhythmus
rhythm method *n* Knaus-Ogino-Methode *f*
RI *n abbr (Brit: Scol: = religious instruction)* Religionsunterricht *m* ▷ *abbr (US: Post) = Rhode Island*
rib [rɪb] *n* Rippe *f* ▷ *vt (mock)* aufziehen
ribald ['rɪbəld] *adj (laughter, joke)* rüde; *(person)* anzüglich
ribbed [rɪbd] *adj (socks, sweater)* gerippt
ribbon ['rɪbən] *n (for hair, decoration)* Band *nt*; *(of typewriter)* Farbband *nt*; **in ~s** *(torn)* in Fetzen
rice [raɪs] *n* Reis *m*
ricefield ['raɪsfiːld] *n* Reisfeld *nt*
rice pudding *n* Milchreis *m*
rich [rɪtʃ] *adj* reich; *(soil)* fruchtbar; *(food)* schwer; *(diet)* reichhaltig; *(colour)* satt; *(voice)* volltönend; *(tapestries, silks)* prächtig ▷ *npl*: **the ~** die Reichen; **~ in** reich an *+dat*
riches ['rɪtʃɪz] *npl* Reichtum *m*
richly ['rɪtʃlɪ] *adv (decorated, carved)* reich; *(reward, benefit)* reichlich; **~ deserved/earned** wohlverdient
richness ['rɪtʃnɪs] *n (wealth)* Reichtum *m*; *(of life, culture, food)* Reichhaltigkeit *f*; *(of soil)* Fruchtbarkeit *f*; *(of costumes, furnishings)* Pracht *f*
rickets ['rɪkɪts] *n* Rachitis *f*
rickety ['rɪkɪtɪ] *adj (chair etc)* wackelig
rickshaw ['rɪkʃɔː] *n* Rikscha *f*
ricochet ['rɪkəʃeɪ] *vi* abprallen ▷ *n* Abpraller *m*
rid [rɪd] *(pt, pp* **~***)* *vt*: **to ~ sb/sth of** jdn/etw befreien von; **to get ~ of** loswerden; *(inhibitions, illusions etc)* sich befreien von
riddance ['rɪdns] *n*: **good ~!** gut, dass wir den/die/das los sind!
ridden ['rɪdn] *pp of* **ride**
riddle ['rɪdl] *n* Rätsel *nt* ▷ *vt*: **to be ~d with** *(guilt, doubts)* geplagt sein von; *(holes, corruption)* durchsetzt sein von
ride [raɪd] *(pt* **rode**, *pp* **ridden***)* *n (in car, on bicycle)* Fahrt *f*; *(on horse)* Ritt *m*; *(path)* Reitweg *m* ▷ *vi (on horse)* reiten; *(on bicycle, bus etc)* fahren ▷ *vt (see vi)* reiten; fahren; **car ~** Autofahrt *f*; **to go for a ~** eine Fahrt/einen Ausritt machen; **to take sb for a ~** *(fig)* jdn hereinlegen; **we rode all day/all the way** wir sind den ganzen Tag/den ganzen Weg geritten/gefahren; **to ~ at anchor** *(Naut)* vor Anker liegen; **can you ~ a bike?** kannst du Fahrrad fahren?
▶ **ride out** *vt*: **to ~ out the storm** *(fig)* den Sturm überstehen
rider ['raɪdəʳ] *n (on horse)* Reiter(in) *m(f)*; *(on bicycle etc)* Fahrer(in) *m(f)*; *(in document etc)* Zusatz *m*
ridge [rɪdʒ] *n (of hill)* Grat *m*; *(of roof)* First *m*; *(in sand etc)* Rippelmarke *f*
ridicule ['rɪdɪkjuːl] *n* Spott *m* ▷ *vt (person)* verspotten; *(proposal, system etc)* lächerlich machen; **she was the object of ~** alle machten sich über sie lustig
ridiculous [rɪ'dɪkjuləs] *adj* lächerlich
riding ['raɪdɪŋ] *n* Reiten *nt*
riding school *n* Reitschule *f*
rife [raɪf] *adj*: **to be ~** *(corruption, disease etc)* grassieren; **to be ~ with** *(rumours etc)* durchsetzt sein von
riffraff ['rɪfræf] *n* Gesindel *nt*
rifle ['raɪfl] *n (gun)* Gewehr *nt* ▷ *vt (wallet etc)* plündern
▶ **rifle through** *vt fus (papers etc)* durchwühlen
rifle range *n* Schießstand *m*
rift [rɪft] *n* Spalt *m*; *(fig)* Kluft *f*

rig [rɪg] *n* (*also*: **oil rig**: *at sea*) Bohrinsel *f*; (: *on land*) Bohrturm *m* ▷ *vt* (*election, game etc*) manipulieren
▸ **rig out** (*Brit*) *vt*: **to ~ sb out as/in** jdn ausstaffieren als/in +*dat*
▸ **rig up** *vt* (*device*) montieren
rigging ['rɪgɪŋ] *n* (*Naut*) Takelage *f*
right [raɪt] *adj* (*correct*) richtig; (*not left*) rechte(r, s) ▷ *n* Recht *nt* ▷ *adv* (*correctly, properly*) richtig; (*directly, exactly*) genau; (*not on the left*) rechts ▷ *vt* (*ship, car etc*) aufrichten; (*fault, situation*) korrigieren, berichtigen ▷ *excl* okay; **the ~ time** (*exact*) die genaue Zeit; (*most suitable*) die richtige Zeit; **to be ~** (*person*) recht haben; (*answer, fact*) richtig sein; (*clock*) genau gehen; (*reading etc*) korrekt sein; **to get sth ~** etw richtig machen; **let's get it ~ this time!** diesmal machen wir es richtig!; **you did the ~ thing** du hast das Richtige getan; **to put sth ~** (*mistake etc*) etw berichtigen; **on/to the ~** rechts; **the R~** (*Pol*) die Rechte; **by ~s** richtig genommen; **to be in the ~** im Recht sein; **you're within your ~s (to do that)** es ist dein gutes Recht(, das zu tun); **he is a well-known author in his own ~** er ist selbst auch ein bekannter Autor; **film ~s** Filmrechte *pl*; **~ now** im Moment; **~ before/after the party** gleich vor/nach der Party; **~ against the wall** unmittelbar an der Wand; **~ ahead** geradeaus; **~ away** (*immediately*) sofort; **~ in the middle** genau in der Mitte; **he went ~ to the end of the road** er ging bis ganz ans Ende der Straße
right angle *n* rechter Winkel *m*
right-click ['raɪtklɪk] (*Comput*) *vi* rechts klicken ▷ *vt* rechts klicken auf +*acc*
righteous ['raɪtʃəs] *adj* (*person*) rechtschaffen; (*indignation*) gerecht
righteousness ['raɪtʃəsnɪs] *n* Rechtschaffenheit *f*
rightful ['raɪtful] *adj* rechtmäßig
rightfully ['raɪtfəlɪ] *adv* von Rechts wegen
right-hand drive *adj* (*vehicle*) mit Rechtssteuerung
right-handed [raɪt'hændɪd] *adj* rechtshändig
right-hand man *n* rechte Hand *f*
right-hand side *n* rechte Seite *f*
rightly ['raɪtlɪ] *adv* (*with reason*) zu Recht; **if I remember ~** (*Brit*) wenn ich mich recht entsinne
right-minded [raɪt'maɪndɪd] *adj* vernünftig
right of way *n* (*on path etc*) Durchgangsrecht *f*; (*Aut*) Vorfahrt *f*
rights issue *n* (*Stock Exchange*) Bezugsrechtsemission *f*
right wing *n* (*Pol, Sport*) rechter Flügel *m*
right-wing [raɪt'wɪŋ] *adj* (*Pol*) rechtsgerichtet
right-winger [raɪt'wɪŋəʳ] *n* (*Pol*) Rechte(r) *f*(*m*); (*Sport*) Rechtsaußen *m*
rigid ['rɪdʒɪd] *adj* (*structure, views*) starr; (*principle, control etc*) streng
rigidity [rɪ'dʒɪdɪtɪ] *n* (*of structure etc*) Starrheit *f*; (*of attitude, views etc*) Strenge *f*
rigidly ['rɪdʒɪdlɪ] *adv* (*hold, fix etc*) starr; (*control, interpret*) streng
rigmarole ['rɪgmərəul] *n* Gedöns *nt* (*inf*)
rigor ['rɪgəʳ] (*US*) *n* = **rigour**
rigor mortis ['rɪgə'mɔːtɪs] *n* Totenstarre *f*
rigorous ['rɪgərəs] *adj* (*control etc*) streng; (*training*) gründlich
rigorously ['rɪgərəslɪ] *adv* (*test, assess etc*) streng
rigour, (*US*) **rigor** ['rɪgəʳ] *n* (*of argument, law*) Strenge *f*; (*of research*) Gründlichkeit; **the ~s of life/winter** die Härten des Lebens/des Winters
rig-out ['rɪgaut] (*Brit*: *inf*) *n* Aufzug *m*
rile [raɪl] *vt* ärgern
rim [rɪm] *n* (*of glass, spectacles*) Rand *m*; (*of wheel*) Felge *f*, Radkranz *m*
rimless ['rɪmlɪs] *adj* (*spectacles*) randlos
rimmed [rɪmd] *adj*: **~ with** umrandet von; **gold-~ spectacles** Brille *f* mit Goldfassung *or* Goldrand
rind [raɪnd] *n* (*of bacon*) Schwarte *f*; (*of lemon, melon*) Schale *f*; (*of cheese*) Rinde *f*
ring [rɪŋ] (*pt* **rang**, *pp* **rung**) *n* Ring *m*; (*of people, objects*) Kreis *m*; (*of circus*) Manege *f*; (*bullring*) Arena *f*; (*sound of telephone*) Klingeln *nt*; (*sound of bell*) Läuten *nt*; (*on cooker*) Kochstelle *m* ▷ *vi* (*Tel*: *person*) anrufen; (*telephone, doorbell*) klingeln; (*bell*) läuten; (*also*: **ring out**) ertönen ▷ *vt* (*Brit*: *Tel*) anrufen; (*bell etc*) läuten; (*encircle*) einen Kreis machen um; **to give sb a ~** (*Brit*: *Tel*) jdn anrufen; **that has a ~ of truth about it** das könnte stimmen; **to run ~s round sb** (*inf*: *fig*) jdn in die Tasche stecken; **to ~ true/false** wahr/falsch klingen; **my ears are ~ing** mir klingen die Ohren; **to ~ the doorbell** klingeln; **the name doesn't ~ a bell (with me)** der Name sagt mir nichts
▸ **ring back** (*Brit*) *vt, vi* (*Tel*) zurückrufen
▸ **ring off** (*Brit*) *vi* (*Tel*) (den Hörer) auflegen
▸ **ring up** (*Brit*) *vt* (*Tel*) anrufen
ring binder *n* Ringbuch *nt*
ring finger *n* Ringfinger *m*
ringing ['rɪŋɪŋ] *n* (*of telephone*) Klingeln *nt*; (*of bell*) Läuten *nt*; (*in ears*) Klingen *nt*
ringing tone (*Brit*) *n* (*Tel*) Rufzeichen *nt*
ringleader ['rɪŋliːdəʳ] *n* Rädelsführer(in) *m*(*f*)
ringlets ['rɪŋlɪts] *npl* Ringellocken *pl*; **in ~** in Ringellocken
ring road (*Brit*) *n* Ringstraße *f*
ringtone ['rɪŋtəun] *n* (*of mobile phone*) Klingelton *m*
rink [rɪŋk] *n* (*also*: **ice rink**) Eisbahn *f*; (*also*: **roller skating rink**) Rollschuhbahn *f*
rinse [rɪns] *n* Spülen *nt*; (*of hands*) Abspülen *nt*; (*hair dye*) Tönung *f* ▷ *vt* spülen; (*hands*) abspülen; (*also*: **rinse out**: *clothes*) auswaschen; (: *mouth*) ausspülen; **to give sth a ~** etw spülen; (*dishes*) etw abspülen
Rio ['riːəu], **Rio de Janeiro** ['riːəudədʒə'nɪərəu] *n* Rio (de Janeiro) *nt*
riot ['raɪət] *n* (*disturbance*) Aufruhr *m* ▷ *vi* randalieren; **a ~ of colours** ein Farbenmeer *nt*; **to run ~** randalieren

rioter ['raɪətəʳ] *n* Randalierer *m*
riot gear *n* Schutzausrüstung *f*
riotous ['raɪətəs] *adj (crowd)* randalierend; *(nights, party)* ausschweifend; *(welcome etc)* tumultartig
riotously ['raɪətəslɪ] *adv*: **~ funny** *or* **comic** urkomisch
riot police *n* Bereitschaftspolizei *f*; **hundreds of ~** Hunderte von Bereitschaftspolizisten
RIP *abbr (= requiescat or requiescant in pace)* R.I.P.
rip [rɪp] *n (tear)* Riss *m* ▷ *vt* zerreißen ▷ *vi* reißen
▸ **rip off** *vt (clothes)* herunterreißen; *(inf: swindle)* übers Ohr hauen
▸ **rip up** *vt* zerreißen
ripcord ['rɪpkɔːd] *n* Reißleine *f*
ripe [raɪp] *adj* reif; **to be ~ for sth** *(fig)* reif für etw sein; **he lived to a ~ old age** er erreichte ein stolzes Alter
ripen ['raɪpn] *vt* reifen lassen ▷ *vi* reifen
ripeness ['raɪpnɪs] *n* Reife *f*
rip-off ['rɪpɔf] *(inf) n*: **it's a ~!** das ist Wucher!
riposte [rɪ'pɔst] *n* scharfe Entgegnung *f*
ripple ['rɪpl] *n (wave)* kleine Welle *f*; *(of laughter, applause)* Welle *f* ▷ *vi (water)* sich kräuseln; *(muscles)* spielen ▷ *vt (surface)* kräuseln
rise [raɪz] *(pt* **rose**, *pp* **~n**) *n (incline)* Steigung *f*; *(Brit: salary increase)* Gehaltserhöhung *f*; *(in prices, temperature etc)* Anstieg *m*; *(fig: to fame etc)* Aufstieg *m* ▷ *vi (prices, water)* steigen; *(sun, moon)* aufgehen; *(wind)* aufkommen; *(from bed, chair)* aufstehen; *(sound, voice)* ansteigen; *(also:* **rise up**: *tower, rebel)* sich erheben; *(in rank)* aufsteigen; **to give ~ to** Anlass geben zu; **to ~ to power** an die Macht kommen
risen [rɪzn] *pp of* **rise**
rising ['raɪzɪŋ] *adj (increasing)* steigend; *(up-and-coming)* aufstrebend
rising damp *n* aufsteigende Feuchtigkeit *f*
rising star *n (fig: person)* Aufsteiger(in) *m(f)*
risk [rɪsk] *n (danger, chance)* Gefahr *f*; *(deliberate)* Risiko *nt* ▷ *vt* riskieren; **to take a ~** ein Risiko eingehen; **to run the ~ of sth** etw zu fürchten haben; **to run the ~ of doing sth** Gefahr laufen, etw zu tun; **at ~** in Gefahr; **at one's own ~** auf eigene Gefahr; **at the ~ of sounding rude ...** auf die Gefahr hin, unhöflich zu klingen, ...; **it's a fire/health ~** es ist ein Feuer-/Gesundheitsrisiko; **I'll ~ it** ich riskiere es
risk capital *n* Risikokapital *nt*
risky ['rɪskɪ] *adj* riskant
risqué ['riːskeɪ] *adj (joke)* gewagt
rissole ['rɪsəul] *n (of meat, fish etc)* Frikadelle *f*
rite [raɪt] *n* Ritus *m*; **last ~s** *(Rel)* Letzte Ölung *f*
ritual ['rɪtjuəl] *adj (law, murder)* Ritual-; *(dance)* rituell ▷ *n* Ritual *nt*
rival ['raɪvl] *n* Rivale *m*, Rivalin *f* ▷ *adj (firm, newspaper etc)* Konkurrenz-; *(teams, groups etc)* rivalisierend ▷ *vt (match)* sich messen können mit; **to ~ sth/sb in sth** sich mit etw/jdm in Bezug auf etw messen können
rivalry ['raɪvlrɪ] *n* Rivalität *f*
river ['rɪvəʳ] *n* Fluss *m*; *(fig: of blood etc)* Strom *m* ▷ *cpd (port, traffic)* Fluss-; **up/down ~** flussaufwärts/-abwärts
river bank *n* Flussufer *nt*
river bed *n* Flussbett *nt*
riverside ['rɪvəsaɪd] *n* = **river bank**
rivet ['rɪvɪt] *n* Niete *f* ▷ *vt (fig: attention)* fesseln; *(: eyes)* heften
riveting ['rɪvɪtɪŋ] *adj (fig)* fesselnd
Riviera [rɪvɪ'ɛərə] *n*: **the (French) ~** die (französische) Riviera; **the Italian ~** die italienische Riviera
Riyadh [rɪ'jɑːd] *n* Riad *nt*
RMT *n abbr (= National Union of Rail, Maritime and Transport Workers) Gewerkschaft der Eisenbahner, Seeleute und Transportarbeiter*
RN *n abbr (Brit)* = **Royal Navy**; *(US)* = **registered nurse**
RNA *n abbr (= ribonucleic acid)* RNS *f*
RNLI *(Brit) n abbr (= Royal National Lifeboat Institution) durch Spenden finanzierter Seenot-Rettungsdienst*, ≈ DLRG *f*
RNZAF *n abbr (= Royal New Zealand Air Force)* neuseeländische Luftwaffe *f*
RNZN *n abbr (= Royal New Zealand Navy)* neuseeländische Marine *f*
road [rəud] *n* Straße *f*; *(fig)* Weg *m* ▷ *cpd (accident, sense)* Verkehrs-; **main ~** Hauptstraße *f*; **it takes four hours by ~** man braucht vier Stunden mit dem Auto; **let's hit the ~** machen wir uns auf den Weg!; **to be on the ~** *(salesman etc)* unterwegs sein; *(pop group etc)* auf Tournee sein; **on the ~ to success** auf dem Weg zum Erfolg; **major/minor ~** Haupt-/Nebenstraße *f*
road accident *n* Verkehrsunfall *m*
roadblock ['rəudblɔk] *n* Straßensperre *f*
road haulage *n* Spedition *f*
roadhog ['rəudhɔg] *n* Verkehrsrowdy *m*
road map *n* Straßenkarte *f*
road rage *n* Aggressivität *f* im Straßenverkehr
road safety *n* Verkehrssicherheit *f*
roadside ['rəudsaɪd] *n* Straßenrand *m* ▷ *cpd (building, sign etc)* am Straßenrand; **by the ~** am Straßenrand
road sign *n* Verkehrszeichen *nt*
roadsweeper ['rəudswiːpəʳ] *(Brit) n (person)* Straßenkehrer(in) *m(f)*; *(vehicle)* Straßenkehrmaschine *f*
road user *n* Verkehrsteilnehmer(in) *m(f)*
roadway ['rəudweɪ] *n* Fahrbahn *f*
road works *npl* Straßenbauarbeiten *pl*
roadworthy ['rəudwəːðɪ] *adj* verkehrstüchtig
roam [rəum] *vi* wandern, streifen ▷ *vt (streets, countryside)* durchstreifen
roar [rɔːʳ] *n (of animal, crowd)* Brüllen *nt*; *(of vehicle)* Getöse *nt*; *(of storm)* Heulen *nt* ▷ *vi (animal, person)* brüllen; *(engine, wind etc)* heulen; **~s of laughter** brüllendes Gelächter; **to ~ with laughter** vor Lachen brüllen
roaring ['rɔːrɪŋ] *adj*: **a ~ fire** ein prasselndes Feuer; **a ~ success** ein Bombenerfolg *m*; **to do a ~ trade (in sth)** ein Riesengeschäft (mit etw) machen

roast [rəust] *n* Braten *m* ▷ *vt* (*meat, potatoes*) braten; (*coffee*) rösten
roast beef *n* Roastbeef *nt*
roasting ['rəustıŋ] (*inf*) *adj* (*hot*) knallheiß ▷ *n* (*criticism*) Verriss *m*; (*telling-off*) Standpauke *f*; **to give sb a ~** (*criticize*) jdn verreißen; (*scold*) jdm eine Standpauke halten
rob [rɔb] *vt* (*person*) bestehlen; (*house, bank*) ausrauben; **to ~ sb of sth** jdm etw rauben; (*fig: deprive*) jdm etw vorenthalten
robber ['rɔbəʳ] *n* Räuber(in) *m(f)*
robbery ['rɔbərı] *n* Raub *m*
robe [rəub] *n* (*for ceremony etc*) Gewand *nt*; (*also*: **bath robe**) Bademantel *m*; (*US*) Morgenrock *m* ▷ *vt*: **to be ~d in** (*form*) (festlich) in etw *acc* gekleidet sein
robin ['rɔbın] *n* Rotkehlchen *nt*
robot ['rəubɔt] *n* Roboter *m*
robotics [rə'bɔtıks] *n* Robotik *f*
robust [rəu'bʌst] *adj* robust; (*appetite*) gesund
rock [rɔk] *n* (*substance*) Stein *m*; (*boulder*) Felsen *m*; (*US: small stone*) Stein *m*; (*Brit: sweet*) ≈ Zuckerstange *f*; (*Mus: also*: **rock music**) Rock *m*, Rockmusik *f* ▷ *vt* (*swing gently: cradle*) schaukeln; (*: child*) wiegen; (*shake: also fig*) erschüttern ▷ *vi* (*object*) schwanken; (*person*) schaukeln; **on the ~s** (*drink*) mit Eis; (*ship*) (auf Felsen) aufgelaufen; (*marriage etc*) gescheitert; **to ~ the boat** (*fig*) Unruhe stiften
rock and roll *n* Rock and Roll *m*
rock bottom ['rɔk'bɔtəm] *adj* (*prices*) Tiefst- ▷ *n*: **to reach** *or* **touch** *or* **hit ~** (*person, prices*) den Tiefpunkt erreichen
rock cake *n* ≈ Rosinenbrötchen *nt*
rock climber *n* Felsenkletterer(in) *m(f)*
rock climbing *n* Felsenklettern *nt*
rockery ['rɔkərı] *n* Steingarten *m*
rocket ['rɔkıt] *n* Rakete *f* ▷ *vi* (*prices*) in die Höhe schießen
rocket launcher *n* Raketenwerfer *m*
rock face *n* Felswand *f*
rock fall *n* Steinschlag *m*
rocking chair ['rɔkıŋ-] *n* Schaukelstuhl *m*
rocking horse *n* Schaukelpferd *nt*
rocky ['rɔkı] *adj* (*path, ground*) felsig; (*fig: business, marriage*) wackelig
Rocky Mountains *npl*: **the ~** die Rocky Mountains *pl*
rod [rɔd] *n* (*also Tech*) Stange *f*; (*also*: **fishing rod**) Angelrute *f*
rode [rəud] *pt of* **ride**
rodent ['rəudnt] *n* Nagetier *nt*
rodeo ['rəudıəu] (*US*) *n* Rodeo *nt*
roe [rəu] *n* (*Culin*): **hard ~** Rogen *m*; **soft ~** Milch *f*
roe deer *n inv* Reh *nt*
rogue [rəug] *n* Gauner *m*
roguish ['rəugıʃ] *adj* schelmisch
role [rəul] *n* Rolle *f*
role model *n* Rollenmodell *nt*
role play *n* Rollenspiel *nt*
roll [rəul] *n* (*of paper*) Rolle *f*; (*of cloth*) Ballen *m*; (*of banknotes*) Bündel *nt*; (*also*: **bread roll**) Brötchen *nt*; (*register, list*) Verzeichnis *nt*; (*of drums etc*) Wirbel *m* ▷ *vt* rollen; (*also*: **roll up**: *string*) aufrollen; (*: sleeves*) aufkrempeln; (*cigarette*) drehen; (*also*: **roll out**: *pastry*) ausrollen; (*flatten: lawn, road*) walzen ▷ *vi* rollen; (*drum*) wirbeln; (*thunder*) grollen; (*ship*) schlingern; (*tears, sweat*) fließen; (*camera, printing press*) laufen; **cheese/ham ~** Käse-/Schinkenbrötchen *nt*; **he's ~ing in it** (*inf: rich*) er schwimmt im Geld
▸ **roll about** *vi* sich wälzen
▸ **roll around** *vi* = **roll about**
▸ **roll in** *vi* (*money, invitations*) hereinströmen
▸ **roll over** *vi* sich umdrehen
▸ **roll up** *vi* (*inf: arrive*) aufkreuzen ▷ *vt* (*carpet, umbrella etc*) aufrollen; **to ~ o.s. up into a ball** sich zusammenrollen
roll call *n* namentlicher Aufruf *m*
rolled gold [rəuld-] *n* Doublégold *nt*
roller ['rəuləʳ] *n* Rolle *f*; (*for lawn, road*) Walze *f*; (*for hair*) Lockenwickler *m*
Rollerblades® *npl* Rollerblades *pl*
roller blind *n* Rollo *nt*
roller coaster *n* Achterbahn *f*
roller skates *npl* Rollschuhe *pl*
rollicking ['rɔlıkıŋ] *adj* toll, Mords-; **to have a ~ time** sich ganz toll amüsieren
rolling ['rəulıŋ] *adj* (*hills*) wellig
rolling mill *n* Walzwerk *nt*
rolling pin *n* Nudelholz *nt*
rolling stock *n* (*Rail*) Fahrzeuge *pl*
roll-on-roll-off ['rəulɔn'rəulɔf] (*Brit*) *adj* (*ferry*) Roll-on-roll-off-
roly-poly ['rəulı'pəulı] (*Brit*) *n* ≈ Strudel *m*
ROM [rɔm] *n abbr* (*Comput*: = *read only memory*) ROM
Roman ['rəumən] *adj* römisch ▷ *n* (*person*) Römer(in) *m(f)*
Roman Catholic *adj* römisch-katholisch ▷ *n* Katholik(in) *m(f)*
romance [rə'mæns] *n* (*love affair*) Romanze *f*; (*romanticism*) Romantik *f*; (*novel*) fantastische Erzählung *f*
Romanesque [rəumə'nɛsk] *adj* romanisch
Romania [rəu'meınıə] *n* Rumänien *nt*
Romanian [rəu'meınıən] *adj* rumänisch ▷ *n* (*person*) Rumäne *m*, Rumänin *f*; (*Ling*) Rumänisch *nt*
Roman numeral *n* römische Ziffer *f*
romantic [rə'mæntık] *adj* romantisch
romanticism [rə'mæntısızəm] *n* (*also Art, Liter*) Romantik *f*
Romany ['rɔmənı] *adj* Roma- ▷ *n* (*person*) Roma *mf*; (*Ling*) Romani *nt*
Rome [rəum] *n* Rom *nt*
romp [rɔmp] *n* Klamauk *m* ▷ *vi* (*also*: **romp about**) herumtollen; **to ~ home** (*horse*) spielend gewinnen
rompers ['rɔmpəz] *npl* (*clothing*) *einteiliger Spielanzug für Babys*
rondo ['rɔndəu] *n* (*Mus*) Rondo *nt*
roof [ru:f] (*pl* **~s**) *n* Dach *nt* ▷ *vt* (*house etc*) überdachen; **the ~ of the mouth** der Gaumen

roof garden *n* Dachgarten *m*
roofing ['ru:fɪŋ] *n* Deckung *f*; **~ felt** Dachpappe *f*
roof rack *n* Dachgepäckträger *m*
rook [ruk] *n* (*bird*) Saatkrähe *f*; (*Chess*) Turm *m*
rookie ['ruki:] (*inf*) *n* (*esp Mil*) Grünschnabel *m*
room [ru:m] *n* (*in house, hotel*) Zimmer *nt*; (*space*) Raum *m*, Platz *m*; (*scope: for change etc*) Raum *m* ▷ *vi*: **to ~ with sb** (*esp US*) ein Zimmer mit jdm teilen; **rooms** *npl* (*lodging*) Zimmer *pl*; **"~s to let", "~s for rent"** (*US*) „Zimmer zu vermieten"; **single/double ~** Einzel-/Doppelzimmer *nt*; **is there ~ for this?** ist dafür Platz vorhanden?; **to make ~ for sb** für jdn Platz machen; **there is ~ for improvement** es gibt Möglichkeiten zur Verbesserung
rooming house ['ru:mɪŋ-] (*US*) *n* Mietshaus *nt*
roommate ['ru:mmeɪt] *n* Zimmergenosse *m*, Zimmergenossin *f*
room service *n* Zimmerservice *m*
room temperature *n* Zimmertemperatur *f*
roomy ['ru:mɪ] *adj* (*building, car*) geräumig
roost [ru:st] *vi* (*birds*) sich niederlassen
rooster ['ru:stə^r] (*esp US*) *n* Hahn *m*
root [ru:t] *n* (*also Math*) Wurzel *f* ▷ *vi* (*plant*) Wurzeln schlagen ▷ *vt*: **to be ~ed in** verwurzelt sein in *+dat*; **roots** *npl* (*family origins*) Wurzeln *pl*; **to take ~** (*plant, idea*) Wurzeln schlagen; **the ~ cause of the problem** die Wurzel des Problems
▸ **root about** *vi* (*search*) herumwühlen
▸ **root for** *vt fus* (*support*) anfeuern
▸ **root out** *vt* ausrotten
root beer (*US*) *n* *kohlensäurehaltiges Getränk aus Wurzel- und Kräuterextrakten*
rope [rəup] *n* Seil *nt*; (*Naut*) Tau *nt* ▷ *vt* (*tie*) festbinden; (*also*: **rope together**) zusammenbinden; **to know the ~s** (*fig*) sich auskennen
▸ **rope in** *vt* (*fig: person*) einspannen
▸ **rope off** *vt* (*area*) mit einem Seil absperren
rope ladder *n* Strickleiter *f*
ropey, ropy ['rəupɪ] (*inf*) *adj* (*ill, poor quality*) miserabel
rosary ['rəuzərɪ] *n* Rosenkranz *m*
rose [rəuz] *pt of* **rise** ▷ *n* (*flower*) Rose *f*; (*also*: **rosebush**) Rosenstrauch *m*; (*on watering can*) Brause *f* ▷ *adj* rosarot
rosé ['rəuzeɪ] *n* (*wine*) Rosé *m*
rosebed ['rəuzbɛd] *n* Rosenbeet *nt*
rosebud ['rəuzbʌd] *n* Rosenknospe *f*
rosebush ['rəuzbuʃ] *n* Rosenstrauch *m*
rosemary ['rəuzmərɪ] *n* Rosmarin *m*
rosette [rəu'zɛt] *n* Rosette *f*
ROSPA ['rɔspə] (*Brit*) *n abbr* (= *Royal Society for the Prevention of Accidents*) *Verband, der Maßnahmen zur Unfallverhütung propagiert*
roster ['rɔstə^r] *n*: **duty ~** Dienstplan *m*
rostrum ['rɔstrəm] *n* Rednerpult *nt*
rosy ['rəuzɪ] *adj* (*colour*) rosarot; (*face, situation*) rosig; **a ~ future** eine rosige Zukunft
rot [rɔt] *n* (*decay*) Fäulnis *f*; (*fig: rubbish*) Quatsch *m* ▷ *vt* verfaulen lassen ▷ *vi* (*teeth, wood, fruit etc*) verfaulen; **to stop the ~** (*Brit: fig*) den Verfall stoppen; **dry ~** Holzschwamm *m*; **wet ~** Nassfäule *f*
rota ['rəutə] *n* Dienstplan *m*; **on a ~ basis** reihum nach Plan
rotary ['rəutərɪ] *adj* (*cutter*) rotierend; (*motion*) Dreh-
rotate [rəu'teɪt] *vt* (*spin*) drehen, rotieren lassen; (*crops*) im Wechsel anbauen; (*jobs*) turnusmäßig wechseln ▷ *vi* (*revolve*) rotieren, sich drehen
rotating [rəu'teɪtɪŋ] *adj* (*revolving*) rotierend; (*drum, mirror*) Dreh-
rotation [rəu'teɪʃən] *n* (*of planet, drum etc*) Rotation *f*, Drehung *f*; (*of crops*) Wechsel *m*; (*of jobs*) turnusmäßiger Wechsel *m*; **in ~** der Reihe nach
rote [rəut] *n*: **by ~** auswendig
rotor ['rəutə^r] *n* (*also*: **rotor blade**) Rotor *m*
rotten ['rɔtn] *adj* (*decayed*) faul, verfault; (*inf: person, situation*) gemein; (*: film, weather, driver etc*) mies; **to feel ~** sich elend fühlen
rotund [rəu'tʌnd] *adj* (*person*) rundlich
rouble, (*US*) **ruble** ['ru:bl] *n* Rubel *m*
rouge [ru:ʒ] *n* Rouge *nt*
rough [rʌf] *adj* rau; (*terrain, road*) uneben; (*person, plan, drawing, guess*) grob; (*life, conditions, journey*) hart; (*sea, crossing*) stürmisch ▷ *n* (*Golf*): **in the ~** im Rough ▷ *vt*: **to ~ it** primitiv *or* ohne Komfort leben; **the sea is ~ today** die See ist heute stürmisch; **to have a ~ time** eine harte Zeit durchmachen; **can you give me a ~ idea of the cost?** können Sie mir eine ungefähre Vorstellung von den Kosten geben?; **to feel ~** (*Brit*) sich elend fühlen; **to sleep ~** (*Brit*) im Freien übernachten; **to play ~** (*fig*) auf die grobe Tour kommen
▸ **rough out** *vt* (*drawing, idea etc*) skizzieren
roughage ['rʌfɪdʒ] *n* Ballaststoffe *pl*
rough-and-ready ['rʌfən'rɛdɪ] *adj* provisorisch
rough-and-tumble ['rʌfən'tʌmbl] *n* (*fighting*) Balgerei *f*; (*fig*) Schlachtfeld *nt*
roughcast ['rʌfkɑ:st] *n* Rauputz *m*
rough copy *n* Entwurf *m*
rough draft *n* = **rough copy**
rough justice *n* Justizwillkür *f*
roughly ['rʌflɪ] *adv* grob; (*approximately*) ungefähr; **~ speaking** grob gesagt
roughness ['rʌfnɪs] *n* Rauheit *f*; (*of manner*) Grobheit *f*
roughshod ['rʌfʃɔd] *adv*: **to ride ~ over** sich rücksichtslos hinwegsetzen über *+acc*
roulette [ru:'lɛt] *n* Roulette *nt*
Roumania *etc* [ru:'meɪnɪə] *n* = **Romania** *etc*
round [raund] *adj* rund ▷ *n* Runde *f*; (*of ammunition*) Ladung *f* ▷ *vt* (*corner*) biegen um; (*cape*) umrunden ▷ *prep* um ▷ *adv*: **all ~** rundherum; **in ~ figures** rund gerechnet; **the daily ~** (*fig*) der tägliche Trott; **a ~ of applause** Beifall *m*; **a ~ (of drinks)** eine Runde; **a ~ of sandwiches** ein Butterbrot; **a ~ of toast** (*Brit*) eine Scheibe Toast; **it's just ~ the corner** (*fig*)

es steht vor der Tür; **to go ~ the back** hinten herum gehen; **to go ~ (an obstacle)** (um ein Hindernis) herumgehen; **~ the clock** rund um die Uhr; **~ his neck/the table** um seinen Hals/den Tisch; **to sail ~ the world** die Welt umsegeln; **to walk ~ the room/park** im Zimmer/Park herumgehen; **~ about 300** *(approximately)* ungefähr 300; **the long way ~** auf Umwegen; **all (the) year ~** das ganze Jahr über; **the wrong way ~** falsch herum; **to ask sb ~** jdn zu sich einladen; **I'll be ~ at 6 o'clock** ich komme um 6 Uhr; **to go ~** *(rotate)* sich drehen; **to go ~ to sb's (house)** jdn (zu Hause) besuchen; **enough to go ~** genug für alle

▸ **round off** *vt* abrunden

▸ **round up** *vt* *(cattle etc)* zusammentreiben; *(people)* versammeln; *(figure)* aufrunden

roundabout ['raundəbaut] *(Brit)* *n* *(Aut)* Kreisverkehr *m*; *(at fair)* Karussell *nt* ▹ *adj*: **by a ~ route** auf Umwegen; **in a ~ way** auf Umwegen

rounded ['raundɪd] *adj* *(hill, figure etc)* rundlich

rounders ['raundəz] *n* ≈ Schlagball *m*

roundly ['raundlɪ] *adv* *(fig: criticize etc)* nachdrücklich

round robin *(esp US)* *n* *(Sport)* *Wettkampf, bei dem jeder gegen jeden spielt*

round-shouldered ['raund'ʃəuldəd] *adj* mit runden Schultern

round trip *n* Rundreise *f*

roundup ['raundʌp] *n* *(of news etc)* Zusammenfassung *f*; *(of animals)* Zusammentreiben *nt*; *(of criminals)* Aufgreifen *nt*; **a ~ of the latest news** ein Nachrichtenüberblick *m*

rouse [rauz] *vt* *(wake up)* aufwecken; *(stir up)* reizen

rousing ['rauzɪŋ] *adj* *(speech)* mitreißend; *(welcome)* stürmisch

rout [raut] *(Mil)* *n* totale Niederlage *f* ▹ *vt* *(defeat)* vernichtend schlagen

route [ru:t] *n* Strecke *f*; *(of bus, train, shipping)* Linie *f*; *(of procession, fig)* Weg *m*; **"all ~s"** *(Aut)* „alle Richtungen"; **the best ~ to London** der beste Weg nach London

route map *(Brit)* *n* Streckenkarte *f*

routine [ru:'ti:n] *adj* *(work, check etc)* Routine- ▹ *n* *(habits)* Routine *f*; *(drudgery)* Stumpfsinn *m*; *(Theat)* Nummer *f*; **~ procedure** Routinesache *f*

rove [rəuv] *vt* *(area, streets)* ziehen durch

roving reporter ['rəuvɪŋ-] *n* Reporter(in) *m(f)* im Außendienst

row¹ [rəu] *n* *(line)* Reihe *f* ▹ *vi* *(in boat)* rudern ▹ *vt* *(boat)* rudern; **three times in a ~** dreimal hintereinander

row² [rau] *n* *(din)* Krach *m*, Lärm *m*; *(dispute)* Streit *m* ▹ *vi* *(argue)* sich streiten; **to have a ~** sich streiten

rowboat ['rəubəut] *(US)* *n* = **rowing boat**

rowdiness ['raudɪnɪs] *n* Rowdytum *nt*

rowdy ['raudɪ] *adj* *(person)* rüpelhaft; *(party etc)* lärmend

rowdyism ['raudɪɪzəm] *n* = **rowdiness**

rowing ['rəuɪŋ] *n* *(sport)* Rudern *nt*

rowing boat *(Brit)* *n* Ruderboot *nt*

rowlock ['rɔlək] *(Brit)* *n* Dolle *f*

royal ['rɔɪəl] *adj* königlich; **the ~ family** die königliche Familie

ROYAL ACADEMY

Die *Royal Academy* oder *Royal Academy of Arts*, eine Akademie zur Förderung der Malerei, Bildhauerei und Architektur, wurde 1768 unter der Schirmherrschaft von George II. gegründet und befindet sich seit 1869 in Burlington House, Piccadilly, London. Jeden Sommer findet dort eine Ausstellung mit Werken zeitgenössischer Künstler statt. Die Royal Academy unterhält auch Schulen, an denen Malerei, Bildhauerei und Architektur unterrichtet wird.

Royal Air Force *(Brit)* *n*: **the ~** die Königliche Luftwaffe

royal blue *adj* königsblau

royalist ['rɔɪəlɪst] *n* Royalist(in) *m(f)* ▹ *adj* royalistisch

Royal Navy *(Brit)* *n*: **the ~** die Königliche Marine

royalty ['rɔɪəltɪ] *n* *(royal persons)* die königliche Familie; **royalties** *npl* *(to author)* Tantiemen *pl*; *(to inventor)* Honorar *nt*

RP *(Brit)* *n abbr* *(= received pronunciation)* *Standardaussprache des Englischen*; *see also* **receive**

rpm *abbr* *(= revolutions per minute)* U/min.

RR *(US)* *abbr* = **railroad**

RRP *(Brit)* *n abbr* = **recommended retail price**

RSA *(Brit)* *n abbr* *(= Royal Society of Arts)* *akademischer Verband zur Vergabe von Diplomen*; *(= Royal Scottish Academy) Kunstakademie*

RSI *n abbr* *(Med: = repetitive strain injury)* RSI *nt*, *Schmerzempfindung durch ständige Wiederholung bestimmter Bewegungen*

RSPB *(Brit)* *n abbr* *(= Royal Society for the Protection of Birds)* *Vogelschutzorganisation*

RSPCA *(Brit)* *n abbr* *(= Royal Society for the Prevention of Cruelty to Animals)* Tierschutzverein *m*

RSVP *abbr* *(= répondez s'il vous plaît)* u. A. w. g.

RTA *n abbr* *(= road traffic accident)* Verkehrsunfall *m*

Rt Hon. *(Brit)* *abbr* *(= Right Honourable)* *Titel für Abgeordnete des Unterhauses*

Rt Rev. *abbr* *(Rel: = Right Reverend)* *Titel für Bischöfe*

rub [rʌb] *vt* reiben ▹ *n*: **to give sth a ~** *(polish)* etw polieren; **he ~bed his hands together** er rieb sich *dat* die Hände; **to ~ sb up the wrong way, to ~ sb the wrong way** *(US)* bei jdm anecken

▸ **rub down** *vt* *(body, horse)* abreiben

▸ **rub in** *vt* *(ointment)* einreiben; **don't ~ it in!** *(fig)* reite nicht so darauf herum!

▸ **rub off** *vi* *(paint)* abfärben

▸ **rub off on** *vt fus* abfärben auf *+acc*

▸ **rub out** *vt* (*with eraser*) ausradieren
rubber ['rʌbər] *n* (*also inf: condom*) Gummi *nt or m*; (*Brit: eraser*) Radiergummi *m*
rubber band *n* Gummiband *nt*
rubber bullet *n* Gummigeschoss *nt*
rubber plant *n* Gummibaum *m*
rubber ring *n* (*for swimming*) Schwimmreifen *m*
rubber stamp *n* Stempel *m*
rubber-stamp [rʌbə'stæmp] *vt* (*fig: decision*) genehmigen
rubbery ['rʌbərɪ] *adj* (*material*) gummiartig; (*meat, food*) wie Gummi
rubbish ['rʌbɪʃ] (*Brit*) *n* (*waste*) Abfall *m*; (*fig: junk*) Schrott *m*; (*: pej: nonsense*) Quatsch *m* ▹*vt* (*inf*) heruntermachen; **~!** Quatsch!
rubbish bin (*Brit*) *n* Abfalleimer *m*
rubbish dump (*Brit*) *n* Müllabladeplatz *m*
rubbishy ['rʌbɪʃɪ] (*Brit: inf*) *adj* miserabel, mies
rubble ['rʌbl] *n* (*debris*) Trümmer *pl*; (*Constr*) Schutt *m*
ruble ['ru:bl] (*US*) *n* = **rouble**
ruby ['ru:bɪ] *n* (*gem*) Rubin *m* ▹*adj* (*red*) rubinrot
RUC (*Brit*) *n abbr* (= *Royal Ulster Constabulary*) *nordirische Polizeibehörde*
rucksack ['rʌksæk] *n* Rucksack *m*
ructions ['rʌkʃənz] (*inf*) *npl* Krach *m*, Ärger *m*
rudder ['rʌdər] *n* (*of ship, plane*) Ruder *nt*
ruddy ['rʌdɪ] *adj* (*complexion etc*) rötlich; (*inf: damned*) verdammt
rude [ru:d] *adj* (*impolite*) unhöflich; (*naughty*) unanständig; (*unexpected: shock etc*) böse; (*crude: table, shelter etc*) primitiv; **to be ~ to sb** unhöflich zu jdm sein; **a ~ awakening** ein böses Erwachen
rudely ['ru:dlɪ] *adv* (*interrupt*) unhöflich; (*say, push*) grob
rudeness ['ru:dnɪs] *n* (*impoliteness*) Unhöflichkeit *f*
rudimentary [ru:dɪ'mɛntərɪ] *adj* (*equipment*) primitiv; (*knowledge*) Grund-
rudiments ['ru:dɪmənts] *npl* Grundlagen *pl*
rue [ru:] *vt* bereuen
rueful ['ru:ful] *adj* (*expression, person*) reuevoll
ruff [rʌf] *n* (*collar*) Halskrause *f*
ruffian ['rʌfɪən] *n* Rüpel *m*
ruffle ['rʌfl] *vt* (*hair, feathers*) zerzausen; (*water*) kräuseln; (*fig: person*) aus der Fassung bringen
rug [rʌg] *n* (*on floor*) Läufer *m*; (*Brit: blanket*) Decke *f*
rugby ['rʌgbɪ] *n* (*also:* **rugby football**) Rugby *nt*
rugged ['rʌgɪd] *adj* (*landscape*) rau; (*man*) robust; (*features, face*) markig; (*determination, independence*) wild
rugger ['rʌgər] (*Brit: inf*) *n* Rugby *nt*
ruin ['ru:ɪn] *n* (*destruction, downfall*) Ruin *m*; (*remains*) Ruine *f* ▹*vt* ruinieren; (*building*) zerstören; (*clothes, carpet etc*) verderben; **ruins** *npl* (*of castle*) Ruinen *pl*; (*of building*) Trümmer *pl*; **in ~s** (*lit, fig*) in Trümmern
ruination [ru:ɪ'neɪʃən] *n* (*of building etc*) Zerstörung *f*; (*of person, life*) Ruinierung *f*
ruinous ['ru:ɪnəs] *adj* (*expense, interest*) ruinös
rule [ru:l] *n* (*norm*) Regel *f*; (*regulation*) Vorschrift *f*; (*government*) Herrschaft *f*; (*ruler*) Lineal *nt* ▹*vt* (*country, people*) herrschen über *+acc* ▹*vi* (*monarch etc*) herrschen; **it's against the ~s** das ist nicht gestattet; **as a ~ of thumb** als Faustregel; **under British ~** unter britischer Herrschaft; **as a ~** in der Regel; **to ~ in favour of/against/on sth** (*Law*) für/gegen/über etw *acc* entscheiden; **to ~ that ...** (*umpire, judge etc*) entscheiden, dass ...
▸ **rule out** *vt* (*possibility etc*) ausschließen; **murder cannot be ~d out** Mord ist nicht auszuschließen
ruled [ru:ld] *adj* (*paper*) liniert
ruler ['ru:lər] *n* (*sovereign*) Herrscher(in) *m(f)*; (*for measuring*) Lineal *nt*
ruling ['ru:lɪŋ] *adj* (*party*) Regierungs-; (*body*) maßgebend ▹*n* (*Law*) Entscheidung *f*; **the ~ class** die herrschende Klasse
rum [rʌm] *n* Rum *m* ▹*adj* (*Brit: inf: peculiar*) komisch
Rumania *etc n* = **Romania** *etc*
rumble ['rʌmbl] *n* (*of thunder*) Grollen *nt*; (*of traffic*) Rumpeln *nt*; (*of guns*) Donnern *nt*; (*of voices*) Gemurmel *nt* ▹*vi* (*stomach*) knurren; (*thunder*) grollen; (*traffic*) rumpeln; (*guns*) donnern
rumbustious [rʌm'bʌstʃəs] *adj* (*person*) ungebärdig
ruminate ['ru:mɪneɪt] *vi* (*person*) grübeln; (*cow, sheep etc*) wiederkäuen
rummage ['rʌmɪdʒ] *vi* herumstöbern
rummage sale (*US*) *n* Trödelmarkt *m*
rumour, (*US*) **rumor** ['ru:mər] *n* Gerücht *nt* ▹*vt*: **it is ~ed that ...** man sagt, dass ...
rump [rʌmp] *n* (*of animal*) Hinterteil *nt*; (*of group etc*) Rumpf *m*
rumple ['rʌmpl] *vt* (*clothes etc*) zerknittern; (*hair*) zerzausen
rump steak *n* Rumpsteak *nt*
rumpus ['rʌmpəs] *n* Krach *m*; **to kick up a ~** Krach schlagen
run [rʌn] (*pt* **ran**, *pp* **~**) *n* (*as exercise, sport*) Lauf *m*; (*in car, train etc*) Fahrt *f*; (*series*) Serie *f*; (*Ski*) Abfahrt *f*; (*Cricket, Baseball*) Run *m*; (*Theat*) Spielzeit *f*; (*in tights etc*) Laufmasche *f* ▹*vt* (*race, distance*) laufen, rennen; (*operate: business*) leiten; (*: hotel, shop*) führen; (*: competition, course*) durchführen; (*Comput: program*) laufen lassen; (*hand, fingers*) streichen mit; (*water, bath*) einlaufen lassen; (*Press: feature, article*) bringen ▹*vi* laufen, rennen; (*flee*) weglaufen; (*bus, train*) fahren; (*river, tears*) fließen; (*colours*) auslaufen; (*jumper*) färben; (*in election*) antreten; (*road, railway etc*) verlaufen; **to go for a ~** (*as exercise*) einen Dauerlauf machen; **to break into a ~** zu laufen *or* rennen beginnen; **a ~ of good/bad luck** eine Glücks-/Pechsträhne; **to have the ~ of sb's house** jds Haus zur freien Verfügung haben; **there was a ~ on ...** (*meat, tickets*) es gab einen Ansturm auf *+acc*; **in the long ~** langfristig; **in the short ~** kurzfristig; **to make a ~ for it** die Beine in die Hand nehmen; **on the ~** (*fugitive*)

auf der Flucht; **I'll ~ you to the station** ich fahre dich zum Bahnhof; **to ~ the risk of doing sth** Gefahr laufen, etw zu tun; **she ran her finger down the list** sie ging die Liste mit dem Finger durch; **it's very cheap to ~** (*car, machine*) es ist sehr billig im Verbrauch; **to ~ a bath** das Badewasser einlaufen lassen; **to be ~ off one's feet** (*Brit*) ständig auf Trab sein; **the baby's nose was ~ning** dem Baby lief die Nase; **the train ~s between Gatwick and Victoria** der Zug verkehrt zwischen Gatwick und Victoria; **the bus ~s every 20 minutes** der Bus fährt alle 20 Minuten; **to ~ on petrol/off batteries** mit Benzin/auf Batterie laufen; **to ~ for president** für das Amt des Präsidenten kandidieren; **to ~ dry** (*well etc*) austrocknen; **tempers were ~ning high** alle waren sehr erregt; **unemployment is ~ning at 20 per cent** die Arbeitslosigkeit beträgt 20 Prozent; **blonde hair ~s in the family** blonde Haare liegen in der Familie

▸ **run across** *vt fus* (*find*) stoßen auf *+acc*

▸ **run after** *vt fus* nachlaufen *+dat*

▸ **run away** *vi* weglaufen

▸ **run down** *vt* (*production*) verringern; (*factory*) allmählich stilllegen; (*Aut: person*) überfahren; (*criticize*) schlechtmachen ▹ *vi* (*battery*) leer werden

▸ **run in** (*Brit*) *vt* (*car*) einfahren

▸ **run into** *vt fus* (*meet: person*) begegnen *+dat*; (*: trouble etc*) bekommen; (*collide with*) laufen/fahren gegen; **to ~ into debt** in Schulden geraten; **their losses ran into millions** ihre Schulden gingen in die Millionen

▸ **run off** *vt* (*liquid*) ablassen; (*copies*) machen ▹ *vi* weglaufen

▸ **run out** *vi* (*time, passport*) ablaufen; (*money*) ausgehen; (*luck*) zu Ende gehen

▸ **run out of** *vt fus*: **we're ~ning out of money/petrol** uns geht das Geld/das Benzin aus; **we're ~ning out of time** wir haben keine Zeit mehr

▸ **run over** *vt* (*Aut*) überfahren ▹ *vt fus* (*repeat*) durchgehen ▹ *vi* (*bath, water*) überlaufen

▸ **run through** *vt fus* (*instructions, lines*) durchgehen

▸ **run up** *vt* (*debt*) anhäufen

▸ **run up against** *vt fus* (*difficulties*) stoßen auf *+acc*

runabout ['rʌnəbaut] *n* (*Aut*) Flitzer *m*

run-around ['rʌnəraund] (*inf*) *n*: **to give sb the ~** jdn an der Nase herumführen

runaway ['rʌnəweɪ] *adj* (*horse*) ausgerissen; (*truck, train*) außer Kontrolle geraten; (*child, slave*) entlaufen; (*fig: inflation*) unkontrollierbar; (*: success*) überwältigend

rundown ['rʌndaun] *n* (*of industry etc*) allmähliche Stillegung *f* ▹ *adj*: **to be run-down** (*person*) total erschöpft sein; (*building, area*) heruntergekommen

rung [rʌŋ] *pp of* **ring** ▹ *n* (*also fig*) Sprosse *f*

run-in ['rʌnɪn] (*inf*) *n* Auseinandersetzung *f*

runner ['rʌnə^r^] *n* Läufer(in) *m(f)*; (*horse*) Rennpferd *nt*; (*on sledge, drawer etc*) Kufe *f*

runner bean (*Brit*) *n* Stangenbohne *f*

runner-up [rʌnər'ʌp] *n* Zweitplatzierte(r) *f(m)*

running ['rʌnɪŋ] *n* (*sport*) Laufen *nt*; (*of business etc*) Leitung *f*; (*of machine etc*) Betrieb *m* ▹ *adj* (*water, stream*) laufend; **to be in/out of the ~ for sth** bei etw im Rennen liegen/aus dem Rennen sein; **to make the ~** (*in race, fig*) das Rennen machen; **6 days ~** 6 Tage hintereinander; **to have a ~ battle with sb** ständig im Streit mit jdm liegen; **to give a ~ commentary on sth** etw fortlaufend kommentieren; **a ~ sore** eine nässende Wunde

running costs *npl* (*of car, machine*) Unterhaltskosten *pl*

running head *n* (*Typ, Comput*) Kolumnentitel *m*

running mate (*US*) *n* (*Pol*) Vizepräsidentschaftskandidat *m*

runny ['rʌnɪ] *adj* (*egg, butter*) dünnflüssig; (*nose, eyes*) triefend

run-off ['rʌnɔf] *n* (*in contest, election*) Entscheidungsrunde *f*; (*extra race*) Entscheidungsrennen *nt*

run-of-the-mill ['rʌnəvðə'mɪl] *adj* gewöhnlich

runt [rʌnt] *n* (*animal*) *kleinstes und schwächstes Tier eines Wurfs*; (*pej: person*) Zwerg *m*

run-through ['rʌnθru:] *n* (*rehearsal*) Probe *f*

run-up ['rʌnʌp] *n*: **the ~ to** (*election etc*) die Zeit vor *+dat*

runway ['rʌnweɪ] *n* (*Aviat*) Start- und Landebahn *f*

rupee [ru:'pi:] *n* Rupie *f*

rupture ['rʌptʃə^r^] *n* (*Med*) Bruch *m*; (*conflict*) Spaltung *f* ▹ *vt*: **to ~ o.s.** (*Med*) sich *dat* einen Bruch zuziehen

rural ['ruərl] *adj* ländlich; (*crime*) auf dem Lande

rural district council (*Brit*) *n* Landbezirksverwaltung *f*

ruse [ru:z] *n* List *f*

rush [rʌʃ] *n* (*hurry*) Eile *f*, Hetze *f*; (*Comm: sudden demand*) starke Nachfrage *f*; (*of water, air*) Stoß *m*; (*of feeling*) Woge *f* ▹ *vt* (*lunch, job etc*) sich beeilen bei; (*person, supplies etc*) schnellstens bringen ▹ *vi* (*person*) sich beeilen; (*air, water*) strömen; **rushes** *npl* (*Bot*) Schilf *nt*; (*for chair, basket etc*) Binsen *pl*; **is there any ~ for this?** eilt das?; **we've had a ~ of orders** wir hatten einen Zustrom von Bestellungen; **I'm in a ~ (to do sth)** ich habe es eilig (, etw zu tun); **gold ~** Goldrausch *m*; **don't ~ me!** drängen Sie mich nicht!; **to ~ sth off** (*send*) etw schnellstens abschicken; **to ~ sb into doing sth** jdn dazu drängen, etw zu tun

▸ **rush through** *vt* (*order, application*) schnellstens erledigen

rush hour *n* Hauptverkehrszeit *f*, Rushhour *f*

rush job *n* Eilauftrag *m*

rush matting *n* Binsenmatte *f*

rusk [rʌsk] *n* Zwieback *m*

Russia ['rʌʃə] *n* Russland *nt*

Russian ['rʌʃən] *adj* russisch ▹ *n* (*person*) Russe

m, Russin *f*; *(Ling)* Russisch *nt*

rust [rʌst] *n* Rost *m* ▷ *vi* rosten

rustic ['rʌstɪk] *adj (style, furniture)* rustikal ▷ *n (pej: person)* Bauer *m*

rustle ['rʌsl] *vi (paper, leaves)* rascheln ▷ *vt (paper)* rascheln mit; *(US: cattle)* stehlen

rustproof ['rʌstpru:f] *adj* nicht rostend

rustproofing ['rʌstpru:fɪŋ] *n* Rostschutz *m*

rusty ['rʌstɪ] *adj (car)* rostig; *(fig: skill etc)* eingerostet

rut [rʌt] *n (in path etc)* Furche *f*; *(Zool: season)* Brunft *f*, Brunst *f*; **to be in a ~** *(fig)* im Trott stecken

rutabaga [ru:tə'beɪgə] *(US) n* Steckrübe *f*

ruthless ['ru:θlɪs] *adj* rücksichtslos

ruthlessness ['ru:θlɪsnɪs] *n* Rücksichtslosigkeit *f*

RV *abbr (Bible: = revised version) englische Bibelübersetzung von 1885* ▷ *n abbr* (US) = **recreational vehicle**

Rwanda [ru'ændə] *n* Ruanda *nt*

Rwandan [ru'ændən] *adj* ruandisch

rye [raɪ] *n (cereal)* Roggen *m*

rye bread *n* Roggenbrot *nt*

Ss

S¹, **s** [ɛs] *n* *(letter)* S *nt*, s *nt*; *(US: Scol: satisfactory)* ≈ 3; **S for sugar** ≈ S wie Samuel
S² [ɛs] *abbr* *(= saint)* St.; *(= small)* kl.; *(= south)* S
SA *abbr* = **South Africa; South America**; *(= South Australia)* Südaustralien *nt*
Sabbath ['sæbəθ] *n* *(Jewish)* Sabbat *m*; *(Christian)* Sonntag *m*
sabbatical [sə'bætɪkl] *n* *(also:* **sabbatical year***)* Forschungsjahr *nt*
sabotage ['sæbətɑːʒ] *n* Sabotage *f* ▷ *vt* einen Sabotageakt verüben auf *+acc*; *(plan, meeting)* sabotieren
sabre ['seɪbəʳ] *n* Säbel *m*
sabre-rattling ['seɪbərætlɪŋ] *n* Säbelrasseln *nt*
saccharin, saccharine ['sækərɪn] *n* Sa(c)charin *nt* ▷ *adj* *(fig)* zuckersüß
sachet ['sæʃeɪ] *n* *(of shampoo)* Beutel *m*; *(of sugar etc)* Tütchen *nt*
sack [sæk] *n* Sack *m* ▷ *vt* *(dismiss)* entlassen; *(plunder)* plündern; **to get the ~** rausfliegen *(inf)*; **to give sb the ~** jdn rausschmeißen *(inf)*
sackful ['sækful] *n*: **a ~ of** ein Sack
sacking ['sækɪŋ] *n* *(dismissal)* Entlassung *f*; *(material)* Sackleinen *nt*
sacrament ['sækrəmənt] *n* Sakrament *nt*
sacred ['seɪkrɪd] *adj* heilig; *(music, history)* geistlich; *(memory)* geheiligt; *(building)* sakral
sacred cow *n* *(lit, fig)* heilige Kuh *f*
sacrifice ['sækrɪfaɪs] *n* Opfer *nt* ▷ *vt* opfern; **to make ~s (for sb)** (für jdn) Opfer bringen
sacrilege ['sækrɪlɪdʒ] *n* Sakrileg *nt*; **that would be ~** das wäre ein Sakrileg
sacrosanct ['sækrəusæŋkt] *adj* *(lit, fig)* sakrosankt
sad [sæd] *adj* traurig; **he was ~ to see her go** er war traurig (darüber), dass sie wegging
sadden ['sædn] *vt* betrüben
saddle ['sædl] *n* Sattel *m* ▷ *vt* *(horse)* satteln; **to be ~d with sb/sth** *(inf)* jdn/etw am Hals haben
saddlebag ['sædlbæg] *n* Satteltasche *f*
sadism ['seɪdɪzəm] *n* Sadismus *m*
sadist ['seɪdɪst] *n* Sadist(in) *m(f)*
sadistic [sə'dɪstɪk] *adj* sadistisch
sadly ['sædlɪ] *adv* traurig, betrübt; *(unfortunately)* leider, bedauerlicherweise; *(seriously)* schwer; **he is ~ lacking in humour** ihm fehlt leider jeglicher Humor
sadness ['sædnɪs] *n* Traurigkeit *f*
sadomasochism [seɪdəu'mæsəkɪzəm] *n* Sadomasochismus *m*
s.a.e. *(Brit)* *abbr* *(= stamped addressed envelope)* *see* **stamp**
safari [sə'fɑːrɪ] *n* Safari *f*; **to go on ~** auf Safari gehen
safari park *n* Safaripark *m*
safe [seɪf] *adj* sicher; *(out of danger)* in Sicherheit ▷ *n* Safe *m or nt*, Tresor *m*; **~ from** sicher vor *+dat*; **~ and sound** gesund und wohlbehalten; **(just) to be on the ~ side** (nur) um sicherzugehen; **to play ~** auf Nummer sicher gehen *(inf)*; **it is ~ to say that ...** man kann wohl sagen, dass ...; **~ journey!** gute Fahrt *or* Reise!
safe bet *n*: **it's a ~ that ...** es ist sicher, dass ...
safe-breaker ['seɪfbreɪkəʳ] *(Brit)* *n* Safeknacker *m* *(inf)*
safe-conduct [seɪf'kɔndʌkt] *n* freies *or* sicheres Geleit *nt*
safe-cracker ['seɪfkrækəʳ] *n* = **safe-breaker**
safe-deposit ['seɪfdɪpɔzɪt] *n* *(vault)* Tresorraum *m*; *(also:* **safe-deposit box***)* Banksafe *m*
safeguard ['seɪfgɑːd] *n* Schutz *m* ▷ *vt* schützen; *(interests)* wahren; *(future)* sichern; **as a ~ against** zum Schutz gegen
safe haven *n* Zufluchtsort *m*
safe house *n* geheimer Unterschlupf *m*
safekeeping ['seɪf'kiːpɪŋ] *n* sichere Aufbewahrung *f*
safely ['seɪflɪ] *adv* sicher; *(assume, say)* wohl, ruhig; *(arrive)* wohlbehalten; **I can ~ say ...** ich kann wohl sagen ...
safe passage *n* sichere Durchreise *f*
safe sex *n* Safer Sex *m*
safety ['seɪftɪ] *n* Sicherheit *f*; **~ first!** Sicherheit geht vor!
safety belt *n* Sicherheitsgurt *m*
safety catch *n* *(on gun)* Sicherung *f*; *(on window, door)* Sperre *f*
safety net *n* Sprungnetz *nt*, Sicherheitsnetz *nt*; *(fig)* Sicherheitsvorkehrung *f*
safety pin *n* Sicherheitsnadel *f*
safety valve *n* Sicherheitsventil *nt*
saffron ['sæfrən] *n* Safran *m*
sag [sæg] *vi* durchhängen; *(breasts)* hängen; *(fig: spirits, demand)* sinken

saga ['sɑ:gə] *n* Saga *f*; *(fig)* Geschichte *f*
sage [seɪdʒ] *n* *(herb)* Salbei *m*; *(wise man)* Weise(r) *m*
Sagittarius [sædʒɪ'tɛərɪəs] *n* Schütze *m*; **to be ~** Schütze sein
sago ['seɪgəu] *n* Sago *m*
Sahara [sə'hɑ:rə] *n*: **the ~ (Desert)** die (Wüste) Sahara
Sahel [sæ'hɛl] *n* Sahel *m*, Sahelzone *f*
said [sɛd] *pt, pp of* **say**
Saigon [saɪ'gɔn] *n* Saigon *nt*
sail [seɪl] *n* Segel *nt* ▷ *vt* segeln ▷ *vi* fahren; *(Sport)* segeln; *(begin voyage: ship)* auslaufen; *(: passenger)* abfahren; *(fig: ball etc)* fliegen, segeln; **to go for a ~** segeln gehen; **to set ~** losfahren, abfahren
▶ **sail through** *vt fus* *(fig: exam etc)* spielend schaffen
sailboat ['seɪlbəut] *(US)* *n* = **sailing boat**
sailing ['seɪlɪŋ] *n* *(Sport)* Segeln *nt*; *(voyage)* Überfahrt *f*; **to go ~** segeln gehen
sailing boat *n* Segelboot *nt*
sailing ship *n* Segelschiff *nt*
sailor ['seɪlə^r] *n* Seemann *m*, Matrose *m*
saint [seɪnt] *n* *(lit, fig)* Heilige(r) *f(m)*
saintly ['seɪntlɪ] *adj* heiligmäßig; *(expression)* fromm
sake [seɪk] *n*: **for the ~ of sb/sth, for sb's/sth's sake** um jds/einer Sache *gen* willen; *(out of consideration for)* jdm/etw zuliebe; **he enjoys talking for talking's ~** er redet gerne, nur damit etwas gesagt wird; **for the ~ of argument** rein theoretisch; **art for art's ~** Kunst um der Kunst willen; **for heaven's ~!** um Gottes willen!
salad ['sæləd] *n* Salat *m*; **tomato ~** Tomatensalat *m*; **green ~** grüner Salat *m*
salad bowl *n* Salatschüssel *f*
salad cream *(Brit)* *n* ≈ Mayonnaise *f*
salad dressing *n* Salatsoße *f*
salami [sə'lɑ:mɪ] *n* Salami *f*
salaried ['sælərɪd] *adj*: **~ staff** Gehaltsempfänger *pl*
salary ['sælərɪ] *n* Gehalt *nt*
salary scale *n* Gehaltsskala *f*
sale [seɪl] *n* Verkauf *m*; *(at reduced prices)* Ausverkauf *m*; *(auction)* Auktion *f*; **sales** *npl* *(total amount sold)* Absatz *m* ▷ *cpd* *(campaign)* Verkaufs-; *(conference)* Vertreter-; *(figures)* Absatz-; **"for ~"** „zu verkaufen"; **on ~** im Handel; **on ~ or return** auf Kommissionsbasis; **closing-down ~, liquidation ~** *(US)* Räumungsverkauf *m*
sale and lease back *n* *(Comm)* Verkauf *m* mit Rückmiete
saleroom ['seɪlru:m] *n* Auktionsraum *m*
sales assistant, *(US)* **sales clerk** [seɪlz-] *n* Verkäufer(in) *m(f)*
sales force *n* Vertreterstab *m*
salesman ['seɪlzmən] *(irreg: like* **man***)* *n* Verkäufer *m*; *(representative)* Vertreter *m*
sales manager *n* Verkaufsleiter *m*
salesmanship ['seɪlzmənʃɪp] *n* Verkaufstechnik *f*
sales tax *(US)* *n* Verkaufssteuer *f*
saleswoman ['seɪlzwumən] *(irreg: like* **woman***)* *n* Verkäuferin *f*; *(representative)* Vertreterin *f*
salient ['seɪlɪənt] *adj* *(features)* hervorstechend; *(points)* Haupt-
saline ['seɪlaɪn] *adj* *(solution etc)* Salz-
saliva [sə'laɪvə] *n* Speichel *m*
sallow ['sæləu] *adj* *(complexion)* fahl
sally forth ['sælɪ-] *(old)* *vi* sich aufmachen
sally out *vi* = **sally forth**
salmon ['sæmən] *n inv* Lachs *m*
salmon trout *n* Lachsforelle *f*
salon ['sælɔn] *n* Salon *m*
saloon [sə'lu:n] *n* *(US: bar)* Saloon *m*; *(Brit: Aut)* Limousine *f*; *(ship's lounge)* Salon *m*
SALT [sɔ:lt] *n abbr* *(= Strategic Arms Limitation Talks/Treaty)* SALT
salt [sɔ:lt] *n* Salz *nt* ▷ *vt* *(preserve)* einsalzen; *(put salt on)* salzen; *(road)* mit Salz streuen ▷ *cpd* Salz-; *(pork, beef)* gepökelt; **the ~ of the earth** *(fig)* das Salz der Erde; **to take sth with a pinch** *or* **grain of ~** *(fig)* etw nicht ganz so ernst nehmen
salt cellar *n* Salzstreuer *m*
salt-free ['sɔ:lt'fri:] *adj* salzlos
salt mine *n* Salzbergwerk *nt*
saltwater ['sɔ:lt'wɔ:tə^r] *adj* *(fish, plant)* Meeres-
salty ['sɔ:ltɪ] *adj* salzig
salubrious [sə'lu:brɪəs] *adj* *(district etc)* fein; *(air, living conditions)* gesund
salutary ['sæljutərɪ] *adj* heilsam
salute [sə'lu:t] *n* *(Mil, greeting)* Gruß *m*; *(Mil: with guns)* Salut *m* ▷ *vt* *(Mil)* grüßen, salutieren vor *+dat*; *(fig)* begrüßen
salvage ['sælvɪdʒ] *n* Bergung *f*; *(things saved)* Bergungsgut *nt* ▷ *vt* bergen; *(fig)* retten
salvage vessel *n* Bergungsschiff *nt*
salvation [sæl'veɪʃən] *n* *(Rel)* Heil *nt*; *(economic etc)* Rettung *f*
Salvation Army *n* Heilsarmee *f*
salver ['sælvə^r] *n* Tablett *nt*
salvo ['sælvəu] *(pl* **~es***)* *n* Salve *f*
Samaritan [sə'mærɪtən] *n*: **the ~s** ≈ die Telefonseelsorge
same [seɪm] *adj* *(similar)* gleiche(r, s); *(identical)* selbe(r, s) ▷ *pron*: **the ~** *(similar)* der/die/das Gleiche; *(identical)* derselbe/dieselbe/dasselbe; **the ~ book as** das gleiche Buch wie; **they are the ~ age** sie sind gleichaltrig; **they are exactly the ~** sie sind genau gleich; **on the ~ day** am gleichen *or* selben Tag; **at the ~ time** *(simultaneously)* gleichzeitig, zur gleichen Zeit; *(yet)* doch; **they're one and the ~** *(person)* das ist doch ein und derselbe/dieselbe; *(thing)* das ist doch dasselbe; **~ again** *(in bar etc)* das Gleiche noch mal; **all** *or* **just the ~** trotzdem; **to do the ~ (as sb)** das Gleiche (wie jd) tun; **the ~ to you!** (danke) gleichfalls!; **~ here!** ich/wir *etc* auch!; **thanks all the ~** trotzdem vielen Dank; **it's all the ~ to me** es ist mir egal
same-sex marriage ['seɪmsɛks-] *n*

gleichgeschlechtliche Ehe *f*, Homoehe *f* (*inf*)
same-sex relationship ['seɪmsɛks-] *n* gleichgeschlechtliche Beziehung *f*
sample ['sɑːmpl] *n* Probe *f*; (*of merchandise*) Probe *f*, Muster *nt* ▷ *vt* probieren; **to take a ~** eine Stichprobe machen; **free ~** kostenlose Probe
sanatorium [sænə'tɔːrɪəm] (*pl* **sanatoria**) *n* Sanatorium *nt*
sanctify ['sæŋktɪfaɪ] *vt* heiligen
sanctimonious [sæŋktɪ'məunɪəs] *adj* scheinheilig
sanction ['sæŋkʃən] *n* Zustimmung *f* ▷ *vt* sanktionieren; **sanctions** *npl* (*Pol*) Sanktionen *pl*; **to impose economic ~s on** *or* **against** Wirtschaftssanktionen verhängen gegen
sanctity ['sæŋktɪtɪ] *n* (*holiness*) Heiligkeit *f*; (*inviolability*) Unantastbarkeit *f*
sanctuary ['sæŋktjuərɪ] *n* (*for birds/animals*) Schutzgebiet *nt*; (*place of refuge*) Zuflucht *f*; (*Rel: in church*) Altarraum *m*
sand [sænd] *n* Sand *m* ▷ *vt* (*also:* **sand down**) abschmirgeln; *see also* **sands**
sandal ['sændl] *n* Sandale *f*
sandbag ['sændbæg] *n* Sandsack *m*
sandblast ['sændblɑːst] *vt* sandstrahlen
sandbox ['sændbɔks] (*US*) *n* Sandkasten *m*; (*Comput: antivirus software*) Sandbox *f*
sandcastle ['sændkɑːsl] *n* Sandburg *f*
sand dune *n* Sanddüne *f*
sander ['sændə^r] *n* (*tool*) Schleifmaschine *f*
S & M (*US*) *n abbr* (= *sadomasochism*) S/M
sandpaper ['sændpeɪpə^r] *n* Schmirgelpapier *nt*
sandpit ['sændpɪt] *n* Sandkasten *m*; (*Comput: antivirus software*) Sandbox *f*
sands [sændz] *npl* (*beach*) Sandstrand *m*
sandstone ['sændstəun] *n* Sandstein *m*
sandstorm ['sændstɔːm] *n* Sandsturm *m*
sandwich ['sændwɪtʃ] *n* Sandwich *nt* ▷ *vt*: **~ed between** eingequetscht zwischen; **cheese/ham ~** Käse-/Schinkenbrot *nt*
sandwich board *n* Reklametafel *f*
sandwich course (*Brit*) *n Ausbildungsgang, bei dem sich Theorie und Praxis abwechseln*
sandwich man *n* Sandwichmann *m*, Plakatträger *m*
sandy ['sændɪ] *adj* sandig; (*beach*) Sand-; (*hair*) rotblond
sane [seɪn] *adj* geistig gesund; (*sensible*) vernünftig
sang [sæŋ] *pt of* **sing**
sanguine ['sæŋgwɪn] *adj* zuversichtlich
sanitarium [sænɪ'tɛərɪəm] (*US*) (*pl* **sanitaria**) *n* = **sanatorium**
sanitary ['sænɪtərɪ] *adj* hygienisch; (*facilities*) sanitär; (*inspector*) Gesundheits-
sanitary towel, (*US*) **sanitary napkin** *n* Damenbinde *f*
sanitation [sænɪ'teɪʃən] *n* Hygiene *f*; (*toilets etc*) sanitäre Anlagen *pl*; (*drainage*) Kanalisation *f*
sanitation department (*US*) *n* Stadtreinigung *f*
sanity ['sænɪtɪ] *n* geistige Gesundheit *f*; (*common sense*) Vernunft *f*
sank [sæŋk] *pt of* **sink**
Santa Claus [sæntə'klɔːz] *n* ≈ der Weihnachtsmann
Santiago [sæntɪ'ɑːgəu] *n* (*also:* **Santiago de Chile**) Santiago (de Chile) *nt*
sap [sæp] *n* Saft *m* ▷ *vt* (*strength*) zehren an +*dat*; (*confidence*) untergraben
sapling ['sæplɪŋ] *n* junger Baum *m*
sapphire ['sæfaɪə^r] *n* Saphir *m*
sarcasm ['sɑːkæzm] *n* Sarkasmus *m*
sarcastic [sɑː'kæstɪk] *adj* sarkastisch
sarcophagus [sɑː'kɔfəgəs] (*pl* **sarcophagi**) *n* Sarkophag *m*
sardine [sɑː'diːn] *n* Sardine *f*
Sardinia [sɑː'dɪnɪə] *n* Sardinien *nt*
Sardinian [sɑː'dɪnɪən] *adj* sardinisch, sardisch ▷ *n* (*person*) Sardinier(in) *m(f)*; (*Ling*) Sardinisch *nt*
sardonic [sɑː'dɔnɪk] *adj* (*smile*) süffisant
sari ['sɑːrɪ] *n* Sari *m*
SARS [sɑːz] *n abbr* (= *severe acute respiratory syndrome*) SARS *nt*
sartorial [sɑː'tɔːrɪəl] *adj*: **his ~ elegance** seine elegante Art, sich zu kleiden
SAS (*Brit*) *n abbr* (*Mil:* = *Special Air Service*) *Spezialeinheit der britischen Armee*
SASE (*US*) *n abbr* (= *self-addressed stamped envelope*) frankierter Rückumschlag *m*
sash [sæʃ] *n* Schärpe *f*; (*of window*) Fensterrahmen *m*
sash window *n* Schiebefenster *nt*
SAT (*US*) *n abbr* (= *Scholastic Aptitude Test*) *Hochschulaufnahmeprüfung*
sat [sæt] *pt, pp of* **sit**
Sat. *abbr* (= *Saturday*) Sa.
Satan ['seɪtn] *n* Satan *m*
satanic [sə'tænɪk] *adj* satanisch
satanism ['seɪtnɪzəm] *n* Satanismus *m*
satchel ['sætʃl] *n* (*child's*) Schultasche *f*
sated ['seɪtɪd] *adj* gesättigt; **to be ~ with sth** (*fig*) von etw übersättigt sein
satellite ['sætəlaɪt] *n* Satellit *m*; (*also:* **satellite state**) Satellitenstaat *m*
satellite dish *n* Satellitenantenne *f*, Parabolantenne *f*
satellite receiver *n* Satellitenempfänger *m*
satellite television *n* Satellitenfernsehen *nt*
satiate ['seɪʃɪeɪt] *vt* (*food*) sättigen; (*fig: pleasure etc*) übersättigen
satin ['sætɪn] *n* Satin *m* ▷ *adj* (*dress etc*) Satin-; **with a ~ finish** mit Seidenglanz
satire ['sætaɪə^r] *n* Satire *f*
satirical [sə'tɪrɪkl] *adj* satirisch
satirist ['sætɪrɪst] *n* Satiriker(in) *m(f)*
satirize ['sætɪraɪz] *vt* satirisch darstellen
satisfaction [sætɪs'fækʃən] *n* Befriedigung *f*; **to get ~ from sb** (*refund, apology etc*) Genugtuung von jdm erhalten; **has it been done to your ~?** sind Sie damit zufrieden?
satisfactorily [sætɪs'fæktərɪlɪ] *adv* zufriedenstellend
satisfactory [sætɪs'fæktərɪ] *adj*

zufriedenstellend
satisfied ['sætɪsfaɪd] *adj* zufrieden
satisfy ['sætɪsfaɪ] *vt* zufriedenstellen; (*needs, demand*) befriedigen; (*requirements, conditions*) erfüllen; **to ~ sb/o.s. that ...** jdn/sich davon überzeugen, dass ...
satisfying ['sætɪsfaɪɪŋ] *adj* befriedigend; (*meal*) sättigend
satsuma [sæt'su:mə] *n* Satsuma *f*
saturate ['sætʃəreɪt] *vt*: **to ~ (with)** durchnässen (mit); (*Chem: market*) sättigen; (*fig: area etc*) überschwemmen
saturated fat ['sætʃəreɪtɪd-] *n* gesättigtes Fett *nt*
saturation [sætʃə'reɪʃən] *n* (*Chem*) Sättigung *f*; **~ advertising** flächendeckende Werbung *f*; **~ bombing** Flächenbombardierung *f*
Saturday ['sætədɪ] *n* Samstag *m*; *see also* **Tuesday**
sauce [sɔ:s] *n* Soße *f*
saucepan ['sɔ:spən] *n* Kochtopf *m*
saucer ['sɔ:səʳ] *n* Untertasse *f*
saucy ['sɔ:sɪ] *adj* frech
Saudi ['saudi-] *adj* (*also*: **Saudi Arabian**) saudisch, saudi-arabisch
Saudi Arabia ['saudɪ-] *n* Saudi-Arabien *nt*
sauna ['sɔ:nə] *n* Sauna *f*
saunter ['sɔ:ntəʳ] *vi* schlendern
sausage ['sɔsɪdʒ] *n* Wurst *f*
sausage roll *n* Wurst *f* im Schlafrock
sauté ['səʊteɪ] *vt* kurz anbraten ▷ *adj*: **~ed potatoes** Bratkartoffeln *pl*
savage ['sævɪdʒ] *adj* (*attack etc*) brutal; (*dog*) gefährlich; (*criticism*) schonungslos ▷ *n* (*old: pej*) Wilde(r) *f(m)* ▷ *vt* (*maul*) zerfleischen; (*fig: criticize*) verreißen
savagely ['sævɪdʒlɪ] *adv* (*attack etc*) brutal; (*criticize*) schonungslos
savagery ['sævɪdʒrɪ] *n* (*of attack*) Brutalität *f*
save [seɪv] *vt* (*rescue*) retten; (*money, time*) sparen; (*food etc*) aufheben; (*work, trouble*) (er)sparen; (*keep: receipts etc*) aufbewahren; (*: seat etc*) frei halten; (*Comput: file*) abspeichern; (*Sport: shot, ball*) halten ▷ *vi* (*also*: **save up**) sparen ▷ *n* (*Sport*) (Ball)abwehr *f* ▷ *prep* (*form*) außer *+dat*; **it will ~ me an hour** dadurch spare ich eine Stunde; **to ~ face** das Gesicht wahren; **God ~ the Queen!** Gott schütze die Königin!
saving ['seɪvɪŋ] *n* (*on price etc*) Ersparnis *f* ▷ *adj*: **the ~ grace of sth** das einzig Gute an etw *dat*; **savings** *npl* (*money*) Ersparnisse *pl*; **to make ~s** sparen
savings account *n* Sparkonto *nt*
savings bank *n* Sparkasse *f*
saviour, (*US*) **savior** ['seɪvjəʳ] *n* Retter(in) *m(f)*; (*Rel*) Erlöser *m*
savoir-faire ['sævwɑ:fɛəʳ] *n* Gewandtheit *f*
savour, (*US*) **savor** ['seɪvəʳ] *vt* genießen ▷ *n* (*of food*) Geschmack *m*
savoury, (*US*) **savory** ['seɪvərɪ] *adj* pikant
savvy ['sævɪ] (*inf*) *n* Grips *m*; **he hasn't got much ~** er hat keine Ahnung
saw [sɔ:] (*pt* **~ed**, *pp* **sawed** *or* **~n**) *vt* sägen ▷ *n* Säge *f* ▷ *pt of* **see**; **to ~ sth up** etw zersägen
sawdust ['sɔ:dʌst] *n* Sägemehl *nt*
sawmill ['sɔ:mɪl] *n* Sägewerk *nt*
sawn [sɔ:n] *pp of* **saw**
sawn-off ['sɔ:nɔf], (*US*) **sawed-off** ['sɔ:dɔf] *adj*: **~ shotgun** Gewehr *nt* mit abgesägtem Lauf
saxophone ['sæksəfəun] *n* Saxofon *nt*
say [seɪ] (*pt, pp* **said**) *vt* sagen ▷ *n*: **to have one's ~** seine Meinung äußern; **could you ~ that again?** können Sie das wiederholen?; **my watch ~s 3 o'clock** auf meiner Uhr ist es 3 Uhr; **it ~s on the sign "No Smoking"** auf dem Schild steht „Rauchen verboten"; **shall we ~ Tuesday?** sagen wir Dienstag?; **come for dinner at, ~, 8 o'clock** kommt um, sagen wir mal 8 Uhr, zum Essen; **that doesn't ~ much for him** das spricht nicht gerade für ihn; **when all is said and done** letzten Endes; **there is something/a lot to be said for it** es spricht einiges/vieles dafür; **you can ~ that again!** das kann man wohl sagen!; **that is to ~** das heißt; **that goes without ~ing** das versteht sich von selbst; **to ~ nothing of ...** von ... ganz zu schweigen; **~ (that) ...** angenommen, (dass) ...; **to have a** *or* **some ~ in sth** ein Mitspracherecht bei etw haben
saying ['seɪɪŋ] *n* Redensart *f*
say-so ['seɪsəu] *n* Zustimmung *f*; **to do sth on sb's ~** etw auf jds Anweisung *acc* hin tun
SBA (*US*) *n abbr* (*= Small Business Administration*) *Regierungsstelle zur Unterstützung kleiner und mittelständischer Betriebe*
SC (*US*) *n abbr* = **Supreme Court** ▷ *abbr* (*Post*) = *South Carolina*
s/c *abbr* = **self-contained**
scab [skæb] *n* (*on wound*) Schorf *m*; (*pej*) Streikbrecher(in) *m(f)*
scabby ['skæbɪ] (*pej*) *adj* (*hands, skin*) schorfig
scaffold ['skæfəld] *n* (*for execution*) Schafott *nt*
scaffolding ['skæfəldɪŋ] *n* Gerüst *nt*
scald [skɔ:ld] *n* Verbrühung *f* ▷ *vt* (*burn*) verbrühen
scalding ['skɔ:ldɪŋ] *adj* (*also*: **scalding hot**) siedend heiß
scale [skeɪl] *n* Skala *f*; (*of fish*) Schuppe *f*; (*Mus*) Tonleiter *f*; (*size, extent*) Ausmaß *nt*, Umfang *m*; (*of map, model*) Maßstab *m* ▷ *vt* (*cliff, tree*) erklettern; **(pair of) scales** *npl* (*for weighing*) Waage *f*; **pay ~** Lohnskala *f*; **to draw sth to ~** etw maßstabgetreu zeichnen; **a small-~ model** ein Modell in verkleinertem Maßstab; **on a large ~** im großen Rahmen; **~ of charges** Gebührenordnung *f*
▸ **scale down** *vt* verkleinern; (*fig*) verringern
scaled-down [skeɪld'daun] *adj* verkleinert; (*project, forecast*) eingeschränkt
scale drawing *n* maßstabgetreue Zeichnung *f*
scallion ['skæljən] *n* Frühlingszwiebel *f*; (*US: shallot*) Schalotte *f*; (*: leek*) Lauch *m*
scallop ['skɔləp] *n* (*Zool*) Kammmuschel *f*;

(*Sewing*) Bogenkante *f*
scalp [skælp] *n* Kopfhaut *f* ▷ *vt* skalpieren
scalpel ['skælpl] *n* Skalpell *nt*
scalper ['skælpəʳ] (*US: inf*) *n* (*ticket tout*) (Karten) schwarzhändler(in) *m(f)*
scam [skæm] (*inf*) *n* Betrug *m*
scamp [skæmp] (*inf*) *n* Frechdachs *m*
scamper ['skæmpəʳ] *vi*: **to ~ away** *or* **off** verschwinden
scampi ['skæmpɪ] (*Brit*) *npl* Scampi *pl*
scan [skæn] *vt* (*horizon*) absuchen; (*newspaper etc*) überfliegen; (*TV, Radar*) abtasten ▷ *vi* (*poetry*) das richtige Versmaß haben ▷ *n* (*Med*) Scan *m*
scandal ['skændl] *n* Skandal *m*; (*gossip*) Skandalgeschichten *pl*
scandalize ['skændəlaɪz] *vt* schockieren
scandalous ['skændələs] *adj* skandalös
Scandinavia [skændɪ'neɪvɪə] *n* Skandinavien *nt*
Scandinavian [skændɪ'neɪvɪən] *adj* skandinavisch ▷ *n* Skandinavier(in) *m(f)*
scanner ['skænəʳ] *n* (*Med*) Scanner *m*; (*Radar*) Richtantenne *f*
scant [skænt] *adj* wenig
scantily ['skæntɪlɪ] *adv*: **~ clad** *or* **dressed** spärlich bekleidet
scanty ['skæntɪ] *adj* (*information*) dürftig; (*meal*) kärglich; (*bikini*) knapp
scapegoat ['skeɪpgəut] *n* Sündenbock *m*
scar [skɑ:] *n* Narbe *f*; (*fig*) Wunde *f* ▷ *vt* eine Narbe hinterlassen auf *+dat*; (*fig*) zeichnen
scarce [skɛəs] *adj* knapp; **to make o.s. ~** (*inf*) verschwinden
scarcely ['skɛəslɪ] *adv* kaum; (*certainly not*) wohl kaum; **~ anybody** kaum jemand; **I can ~ believe it** ich kann es kaum glauben
scarcity ['skɛəsɪtɪ] *n* Knappheit *f*; **~ value** Seltenheitswert *m*
scare [skɛəʳ] *n* (*fright*) Schreck(en) *m*; (*public fear*) Panik *f* ▷ *vt* (*frighten*) erschrecken; (*worry*) Angst machen *+dat*; **to give sb a ~** jdm einen Schrecken einjagen; **bomb ~** Bombendrohung *f*
▸ **scare away** *vt* (*animal*) verscheuchen; (*investor, buyer*) abschrecken
▸ **scare off** *vt* = **scare away**
scarecrow ['skɛəkrəu] *n* Vogelscheuche *f*
scared ['skɛəd] *adj*: **to be ~** Angst haben; **to be ~ stiff** fürchterliche Angst haben
scaremonger ['skɛəmʌŋgəʳ] *n* Panikmacher *m*
scarf [skɑ:f] (*pl* **~s** *or* **scarves**) *n* Schal *m*; (*headscarf*) Kopftuch *nt*
scarlet ['skɑ:lɪt] *adj* (scharlach)rot
scarlet fever *n* Scharlach *m*
scarper ['skɑ:pəʳ] (*Brit: inf*) *vi* abhauen
scarred [skɑ:d] *adj* narbig; (*fig*) gezeichnet
SCART socket ['skɑ:tsɔkɪt] *n* (*Comput*) SCART-Büchse *f*
scarves [skɑ:vz] *npl of* **scarf**
scary ['skɛərɪ] (*inf*) *adj* unheimlich; (*film*) gruselig
scathing ['skeɪðɪŋ] *adj* (*comments*) bissig; (*attack*) scharf; **to be ~ about sth** bissige Bemerkungen über etw *acc* machen
scatter ['skætəʳ] *vt* verstreuen; (*flock of birds*) aufscheuchen; (*crowd*) zerstreuen ▷ *vi* (*crowd*) sich zerstreuen
scatterbrained ['skætəbreɪnd] (*inf*) *adj* schusselig
scattered ['skætəd] *adj* verstreut; **~ showers** vereinzelte Regenschauer *pl*
scatty ['skætɪ] (*Brit: inf*) *adj* schusselig
scavenge ['skævəndʒ] *vi*: **to ~ for sth** nach etw suchen
scavenger ['skævəndʒəʳ] *n* (*person*) Aasgeier *m* (*inf*); (*animal, bird*) Aasfresser *m*
SCE *n abbr* (*= Scottish Certificate of Education*) *Schulabschlusszeugnis in Schottland*
scenario [sɪ'nɑ:rɪəu] *n* (*Theat, Cine*) Szenarium *nt*; (*fig*) Szenario *nt*
scene [si:n] *n* (*lit, fig*) Szene *f*; (*of crime*) Schauplatz *m*; (*of accident*) Ort *m*; (*sight*) Anblick *m*; **behind the ~s** (*fig*) hinter den Kulissen; **to make a ~** (*inf: fuss*) eine Szene machen; **to appear on the ~** (*fig*) auftauchen, auf der Bildfläche erscheinen; **the political ~** die politische Landschaft
scenery ['si:nərɪ] *n* (*Theat*) Bühnenbild *nt*; (*landscape*) Landschaft *f*
scenic ['si:nɪk] *adj* malerisch, landschaftlich schön
scent [sɛnt] *n* (*fragrance*) Duft *m*; (*track*) Fährte *f*; (*fig*) Spur *f*; (*liquid perfume*) Parfüm *nt*; **to put** *or* **throw sb off the ~** (*fig*) jdn von der Spur abbringen
sceptic, (US) **skeptic** ['skɛptɪk] *n* Skeptiker(in) *m(f)*
sceptical, (US) **skeptical** ['skɛptɪkl] *adj* skeptisch
scepticism, (US) **skepticism** ['skɛptɪsɪzəm] *n* Skepsis *f*
sceptre, (US) **scepter** ['sɛptəʳ] *n* Zepter *nt*
schedule ['ʃɛdju:l, (US) 'skɛdju:l] *n* (*of trains, buses*) Fahrplan *m*; (*of events*) Programm *nt*; (*of prices, details etc*) Liste *f* ▷ *vt* planen; (*visit, meeting etc*) ansetzen; **on ~** wie geplant, pünktlich; **we are working to a very tight ~** wir arbeiten nach einem sehr knappen Zeitplan; **everything went according to ~** alles ist planmäßig verlaufen; **to be ahead of/behind ~** dem Zeitplan voraus sein/im Rückstand sein; **he was ~d to leave yesterday** laut Zeitplan hätte er gestern abfahren sollen
scheduled ['ʃɛdju:ld, (US) 'skɛdju:ld] *adj* (*date, time*) vorgesehen; (*visit, event*) geplant; (*train, bus, stop*) planmäßig
scheduled flight *n* Linienflug *m*
schematic [skɪ'mætɪk] *adj* schematisch
scheme [ski:m] *n* (*personal plan*) Plan *m*; (*plot*) raffinierter Plan *m*, Komplott *nt*; (*formal plan*) Programm *nt* ▷ *vi* Pläne schmieden, intrigieren; **colour ~** Farbzusammenstellung *f*; **pension ~** Rentenversicherung *f*
scheming ['ski:mɪŋ] *adj* intrigierend ▷ *n*

Machenschaften *pl*
schism ['skızəm] *n* Spaltung *f*
schizophrenia [skıtsə'fri:nıə] *n* Schizophrenie *f*
schizophrenic [skıtsə'frɛnık] *adj* schizophren ▷ *n* Schizophrene(r) *f(m)*
scholar ['skɔləʳ] *n* Gelehrte(r) *f(m)*; (*pupil*) Student(in) *m(f)*, Schüler(in) *m(f)*; (*scholarship holder*) Stipendiat(in) *m(f)*
scholarly ['skɔləlı] *adj* gelehrt; (*text, approach*) wissenschaftlich
scholarship ['skɔləʃıp] *n* Gelehrsamkeit *f*; (*grant*) Stipendium *nt*
school [sku:l] *n* Schule *f*; (*US: inf: university*) Universität *f*; (*of whales, porpoises etc*) Schule *f*, Schwarm *m* ▷ *cpd* Schul-
school age *n* Schulalter *nt*
schoolbook ['sku:lbuk] *n* Schulbuch *nt*
schoolboy ['sku:lbɔı] *n* Schuljunge *m*, Schüler *m*
schoolchildren ['sku:ltʃıldrən] *npl* Schulkinder *pl*, Schüler *pl*
schooldays ['sku:ldeız] *npl* Schulzeit *f*
schooled [sku:ld] *adj* geschult; **to be ~ in sth** über etw *acc* gut Bescheid wissen
schoolgirl ['sku:lgə:l] *n* Schulmädchen *nt*, Schülerin *f*
schooling ['sku:lıŋ] *n* Schulbildung *f*
school-leaver [sku:l'li:vəʳ] (*Brit*) *n* Schulabgänger(in) *m(f)*
schoolmaster ['sku:lmɑ:stəʳ] *n* Lehrer *m*
schoolmistress ['sku:lmıstrıs] *n* Lehrerin *f*
school report (*Brit*) *n* Zeugnis *nt*
schoolroom ['sku:lru:m] *n* Klassenzimmer *nt*
schoolteacher ['sku:lti:tʃəʳ] *n* Lehrer(in) *m(f)*
schoolyard ['sku:ljɑ:d] *n* Schulhof *m*
schooner ['sku:nəʳ] *n* (*ship*) Schoner *m*; (*Brit: for sherry*) großes Sherryglas *nt*; (*US etc: for beer*) großes Bierglas *nt*
sciatica [saı'ætıkə] *n* Ischias *m or nt*
science ['saıəns] *n* Naturwissenschaft *f*; (*branch of knowledge*) Wissenschaft *f*; **the ~s** Naturwissenschaften *pl*
science fiction *n* Science-Fiction *f*
scientific [saıən'tıfık] *adj* wissenschaftlich
scientist ['saıəntıst] *n* Wissenschaftler(in) *m(f)*
sci-fi ['saıfaı] (*inf*) *n abbr* (= *science fiction*) SF
Scillies ['sılız] *npl* = **Scilly Isles**
Scilly Isles ['sılı'aılz] *npl*: **the ~** die Scillyinseln *pl*
scintillating ['sıntıleıtıŋ] *adj* (*fig: conversation*) faszinierend; (*wit*) sprühend
scissors ['sızəz] *npl* Schere *f*; **a pair of ~** eine Schere
sclerosis [sklı'rəusıs] *n* Sklerose *f*
scoff [skɔf] *vt* (*Brit: inf: eat*) futtern, verputzen ▷ *vi*: **to ~ (at)** (*mock*) spotten (über +*acc*), sich lustig machen (über +*acc*)
scold [skəuld] *vt* ausschimpfen
scolding ['skəuldıŋ] *n* Schelte *f*; **to get a ~** ausgeschimpft werden
scone [skɔn] *n* *brötchenartiges Teegebäck*
scoop [sku:p] *n* (*for flour etc*) Schaufel *f*; (*for ice cream etc*) Portionierer *m*; (*amount*) Kugel *f*; (*Press*) Knüller *m*
▸ **scoop out** *vt* aushöhlen
▸ **scoop up** *vt* aufschaufeln; (*liquid*) aufschöpfen
scooter ['sku:təʳ] *n* (*also*: **motor scooter**) Motorroller *m*; (*toy*) (Tret)roller *m*
scope [skəup] *n* (*opportunity*) Möglichkeiten *pl*; (*range*) Ausmaß *nt*, Umfang *m*; (*freedom*) Freiheit *f*; **within the ~ of** im Rahmen +*gen*; **there is plenty of ~ for improvement** (*Brit*) es könnte noch viel verbessert werden
scorch [skɔ:tʃ] *vt* versengen; (*earth, grass*) verbrennen
scorched earth policy *n* (*Mil*) Politik *f* der verbrannten Erde
scorcher ['skɔ:tʃəʳ] (*inf*) *n* heißer Tag *m*
scorching ['skɔ:tʃıŋ] *adj* (*day, weather*) brütend heiß
score [skɔ:ʳ] *n* (*number of points*) (Punkte)stand *m*; (*of game*) Spielstand *m*; (*Mus*) Partitur *f*; (*twenty*) zwanzig ▷ *vt* (*goal*) schießen; (*point, success*) erzielen; (*mark*) einkerben; (*cut*) einritzen ▷ *vi* (*in game*) einen Punkt/Punkte erzielen; (*Football etc*) ein Tor schießen; (*keep score*) (Punkte) zählen; **to settle an old ~ with sb** (*fig*) eine alte Rechnung mit jdm begleichen; **what's the ~?** (*Sport*) wie stehts?; **~s of** Hunderte von; **on that ~** in dieser Hinsicht; **to ~ well** gut abschneiden; **to ~ 6 out of 10** 6 von 10 Punkten erzielen; **to ~ (a point) over sb** (*fig*) jdn ausstechen
▸ **score out** *vt* ausstreichen
scoreboard ['skɔ:bɔ:d] *n* Anzeigetafel *f*
scorecard ['skɔ:kɑ:d] *n* (*Sport*) Spielprotokoll *nt*
score line *n* (*Sport*) Spielstand *m*; (*: final score*) Endergebnis *nt*
scorer ['skɔ:rəʳ] *n* (*Football etc*) Torschütze *m*, Torschützin *f*; (*person keeping score*) Anschreiber(in) *m(f)*
scorn [skɔ:n] *n* Verachtung *f* ▷ *vt* verachten; (*reject*) verschmähen
scornful ['skɔ:nful] *adj* verächtlich, höhnisch
Scorpio ['skɔ:pıəu] *n* Skorpion *m*; **to be ~** Skorpion sein
scorpion ['skɔ:pıən] *n* Skorpion *m*
Scot [skɔt] *n* Schotte *m*, Schottin *f*
Scotch [skɔtʃ] *n* Scotch *m*
scotch [skɔtʃ] *vt* (*rumour*) aus der Welt schaffen; (*plan, idea*) unterbinden
Scotch tape® *n* ≈ Tesafilm® *m*
scot-free ['skɔt'fri:] *adv*: **to get off ~** ungeschoren davonkommen
Scotland ['skɔtlənd] *n* Schottland *nt*
Scots [skɔts] *adj* schottisch
Scotsman ['skɔtsmən] (*irreg: like* **man**) *n* Schotte *m*
Scotswoman ['skɔtswumən] (*irreg: like* **woman**) *n* Schottin *f*
Scottish ['skɔtıʃ] *adj* schottisch
Scottish National Party *n* *Partei, die für die Unabhängigkeit Schottlands eintritt*
scoundrel ['skaundrl] *n* Schurke *m*

scour ['skauəʳ] *vt* (*search*) absuchen; (*clean*) scheuern
scourer ['skauərəʳ] *n* Topfkratzer *m*
scourge [skə:dʒ] *n* (*lit, fig*) Geißel *f*
scout [skaut] *n* (*Mil*) Kundschafter *m*, Späher *m*; (*also*: **boy scout**) Pfadfinder *m*; **girl ~** (*US*) Pfadfinderin *f*
▸ **scout around** *vi* sich umsehen
scowl [skaul] *vi* ein böses Gesicht machen ▹ *n* böses Gesicht *nt*; **to ~ at sb** jdn böse ansehen
scrabble ['skræbl] *vi* (*also*: **scrabble around**) herumtasten ▹ *n*: **S~®** Scrabble® *nt*; **to ~ at sth** nach etw krallen; **to ~ about** *or* **around for sth** nach etw herumsuchen
scraggy ['skrægɪ] *adj* (*animal*) mager; (*body, neck etc*) dürr
scram [skræm] (*inf*) *vi* abhauen, verschwinden
scramble ['skræmbl] *n* (*climb*) Kletterpartie *f*; (*rush*) Hetze *f*; (*struggle*) Gerangel *nt* ▹ *vi*: **to ~ up/over** klettern auf/über *+acc*; **to ~ for** sich drängeln um; **to go scrambling** (*Sport*) Querfeldeinrennen fahren
scrambled eggs ['skræmbld-] *n* Rührei *nt*
scrap [skræp] *n* (*bit*) Stückchen *nt*; (*fig*: *of truth, evidence*) Spur *f*; (*fight*) Balgerei *f*; (*also*: **scrap metal**) Altmetall *nt*, Schrott *m* ▹ *vt* (*machines etc*) verschrotten; (*fig*: *plans etc*) fallen lassen ▹ *vi* (*fight*) sich balgen; **scraps** *npl* (*leftovers*) Reste *pl*; **to sell sth for ~** etw als Schrott *or* zum Verschrotten verkaufen
scrapbook ['skræpbuk] *n* Sammelalbum *nt*
scrap dealer *n* Schrotthändler(in) *m(f)*
scrape [skreɪp] *vt* abkratzen; (*hand etc*) abschürfen; (*car*) verschrammen ▹ *n*: **to get into a ~** (*difficult situation*) in Schwulitäten *pl* kommen (*inf*)
▸ **scrape through** *vt* (*exam etc*) durchrutschen durch (*inf*)
▸ **scrape together** *vt* (*money*) zusammenkratzen
scraper ['skreɪpəʳ] *n* Kratzer *m*
scrap heap *n*: **to be on the ~** (*fig*) zum alten Eisen gehören
scrap merchant (*Brit*) *n* Schrotthändler(in) *m(f)*
scrap metal *n* Altmetall *nt*, Schrott *m*
scrap paper *n* Schmierpapier *nt*
scrappy ['skræpɪ] *adj* zusammengestoppelt (*inf*)
scrap yard *n* Schrottplatz *m*
scratch [skrætʃ] *n* Kratzer *m* ▹ *vt* kratzen; (*one's nose etc*) sich kratzen an *+dat*; (*paint, car, record*) verkratzen; (*Comput*) löschen ▹ *vi* sich kratzen ▹ *cpd* (*team, side*) zusammengewürfelt; **to start from ~** ganz von vorne anfangen; **to be up to ~** den Anforderungen entsprechen; **to ~ the surface** (*fig*) an der Oberfläche bleiben
scratch pad (*US*) *n* Notizblock *m*
scrawl [skrɔ:l] *n* Gekritzel *nt*; (*handwriting*) Klaue *f* (*inf*) ▹ *vt* hinkritzeln
scrawny ['skrɔ:nɪ] *adj* dürr
scream [skri:m] *n* Schrei *m* ▹ *vi* schreien; **to be a ~** (*inf*) zum Schreien sein; **to ~ at sb (to do sth)** jdn anschreien(, etw zu tun)
scree [skri:] *n* Geröll *nt*
screech [skri:tʃ] *vi* kreischen; (*tyres, brakes*) quietschen ▹ *n* Kreischen *nt*; (*of tyres, brakes*) Quietschen *nt*
screen [skri:n] *n* (*Cine*) Leinwand *f*; (*TV, Comput*) Bildschirm *m*; (*movable barrier*) Wandschirm *m*; (*fig*: *cover*) Tarnung *f*; (*also*: **windscreen**) Windschutzscheibe *f* ▹ *vt* (*protect*) abschirmen; (*from the wind etc*) schützen; (*conceal*) verdecken; (*film*) zeigen, vorführen; (*programme*) senden; (*candidates etc*) überprüfen; (*for illness*): **to ~ sb for sth** jdn auf etw *acc* (hin) untersuchen
screen editing *n* (*Comput*) Bildschirmaufbereitung *f*
screening ['skri:nɪŋ] *n* (*Med*) Untersuchung *f*; (*of film*) Vorführung *f*; (*TV*) Sendung *f*; (*for security*) Überprüfung *f*
screen memory *n* (*Comput*) Bildschirmspeicher *m*
screenplay ['skri:npleɪ] *n* Drehbuch *nt*
screen saver *n* (*Comput*) Bildschirmschoner *m*
screen test *n* Probeaufnahmen *pl*
screw [skru:] *n* Schraube *f* ▹ *vt* schrauben; (*inf!*) bumsen (*!*); **to ~ sth in** etw einschrauben; **to ~ sth to the wall** etw an der Wand festschrauben; **to have one's head ~ed on** (*fig*) ein vernünftiger Mensch sein
▸ **screw up** *vt* (*paper etc*) zusammenknüllen; (*inf*: *ruin*) vermasseln; **to ~ up one's eyes** die Augen zusammenkneifen
screwdriver ['skru:draɪvəʳ] *n* Schraubenzieher *m*
screwed-up ['skru:d'ʌp] (*inf*) *adj*: **to be/get ~ about sth** sich wegen etw ganz verrückt machen
screwy ['skru:ɪ] (*inf*) *adj* verrückt
scribble ['skrɪbl] *n* Gekritzel *nt* ▹ *vt, vi* kritzeln; **to ~ sth down** etw hinkritzeln
scribe [skraɪb] *n* Schreiber *m*
script [skrɪpt] *n* (*Cine*) Drehbuch *nt*; (*of speech, play etc*) Text *m*; (*alphabet*) Schrift *f*; (*in exam*) schriftliche Arbeit *f*
scripted ['skrɪptɪd] *adj* vorbereitet
scripture ['skrɪptʃəʳ] *n*, **scriptures** ['skrɪptʃəz] ▹ *npl* (heilige) Schrift *f*; **the S~(s)** (*the Bible*) die Heilige Schrift *f*
scriptwriter ['skrɪptraɪtəʳ] *n* (*Radio, TV*) Autor(in) *m(f)*; (*Cine*) Drehbuchautor(in) *m(f)*
scroll [skrəul] *n* Schriftrolle *f* ▹ *vi* (*Comput*) scrollen
scroll bar *n* (*Comput*) Bildaufleiste *f*
scrotum ['skrəutəm] *n* Hodensack *m*
scrounge [skraundʒ] (*inf*) *vt*: **to ~ sth off sb** etw bei jdm schnorren ▹ *vi* schnorren ▹ *n*: **on the ~** am Schnorren
scrounger ['skraundʒəʳ] (*inf*) *n* Schnorrer(in) *m(f)*
scrub [skrʌb] *n* Gestrüpp *nt* ▹ *vt* (*floor etc*) schrubben; (*inf*: *idea, plan*) fallen lassen
scrubbing brush ['skrʌbɪŋ-] *n* Scheuerbürste *f*
scruff [skrʌf] *n*: **by the ~ of the neck** am Genick

scruffy ['skrʌfɪ] *adj* gammelig, verwahrlost
scrum ['skrʌm], **scrummage** ['skrʌmɪdʒ] *n* (*Rugby*) Gedränge *nt*
scruple ['skru:pl] *n* (*gen pl*) Skrupel *m*, Bedenken *nt*; **to have no ~s about doing sth** keine Skrupel *or* Bedenken haben, etw zu tun
scrupulous ['skru:pjuləs] *adj* gewissenhaft; (*honesty*) unbedingt
scrupulously ['skru:pjuləslɪ] *adv* gewissenhaft; (*honest, fair*) äußerst; (*clean*) peinlich
scrutinize ['skru:tɪnaɪz] *vt* prüfend ansehen; (*data, records etc*) genau prüfen *or* untersuchen
scrutiny ['skru:tɪnɪ] *n* genaue Untersuchung *f*; **under the ~ of sb** unter jds prüfendem Blick
scuba ['sku:bə] *n* (Schwimm)tauchgerät *nt*
scuba diving *n* Sporttauchen *nt*
scuff [skʌf] *vt* (*shoes, floor*) abwetzen
scuffle ['skʌfl] *n* Handgemenge *nt*
scull [skʌl] *n* Skull *nt*
scullery ['skʌlərɪ] *n* (*old*) Spülküche *f*
sculptor ['skʌlptəʳ] *n* Bildhauer(in) *m(f)*
sculpture ['skʌlptʃəʳ] *n* (*art*) Bildhauerei *f*; (*object*) Skulptur *f*
scum [skʌm] *n* (*on liquid*) Schmutzschicht *f*; (*pej*) Abschaum *m*
scupper ['skʌpəʳ] (*Brit: inf*) *vt* (*plan, idea*) zerschlagen
scurrilous ['skʌrɪləs] *adj* verleumderisch
scurry ['skʌrɪ] *vi* huschen
▸ **scurry off** *vi* forthasten
scurvy ['skə:vɪ] *n* Skorbut *m*
scuttle ['skʌtl] *n* (*also:* **coal scuttle**) Kohleneimer *m* ▹ *vt* (*ship*) versenken ▹ *vi*: **to ~ away** *or* **off** verschwinden
scythe [saɪð] *n* Sense *f*
SD, **S.Dak.** (*US*) *abbr* (*Post*) = *South Dakota*
SDI (*US*) *n abbr* (*Mil:* = *Strategic Defense Initiative*) SDI *f*
SDLP (*Brit*) *n abbr* (*Pol:* = *Social Democratic and Labour Party*) *sozialdemokratische Partei in Nordirland*
SE *abbr* (= *south-east*) SO
sea [si:] *n* Meer *nt*, See *f*; (*fig*) Meer *nt* ▹ *cpd* See-; **by ~** (*travel*) mit dem Schiff; **beside** *or* **by the ~** (*holiday*) am Meer, an der See; (*village*) am Meer; **on the ~** (*boat*) auf See; **at ~** auf See; **to be all at ~** (*fig*) nicht durchblicken (*inf*); **out to ~** aufs Meer (hinaus); **to look out to ~** aufs Meer hinausblicken; **heavy/rough ~(s)** schwere/raue See *f*
sea anemone *n* Seeanemone *f*
sea bed *n* Meeresboden *m*
seaboard ['si:bɔ:d] *n* Küste *f*
seafarer ['si:fɛərəʳ] *n* Seefahrer *m*
seafaring ['si:fɛərɪŋ] *adj* (*life, nation*) Seefahrer-
seafood ['si:fu:d] *n* Meeresfrüchte *pl*
seafront ['si:frʌnt] *n* Strandpromenade *f*
seagoing ['si:gəuɪŋ] *adj* hochseetüchtig
seagull ['si:gʌl] *n* Möwe *f*
seal [si:l] *n* (*animal*) Seehund *m*; (*official stamp*) Siegel *nt*; (*in machine etc*) Dichtung *f*; (*on bottle etc*) Verschluss *m* ▹ *vt* (*envelope*) zukleben; (*crack, opening*) abdichten; (*with seal*) versiegeln; (*agreement, sb's fate*) besiegeln; **to give sth one's ~ of approval** einer Sache *dat* seine offizielle Zustimmung geben
▸ **seal off** *vt* (*place*) abriegeln
sea level *n* Meeresspiegel *m*; **2,000 ft above/below ~** 2000 Fuß über/unter dem Meeresspiegel
sealing wax ['si:lɪŋ-] *n* Siegelwachs *nt*
sea lion *n* Seelöwe *m*
sealskin ['si:lskɪn] *n* Seehundfell *nt*
seam [si:m] *n* Naht *f*; (*lit, fig: where edges join*) Übergang *m*; (*of coal etc*) Flöz *nt*; **the hall was bursting at the ~s** der Saal platzte aus allen Nähten
seaman ['si:mən] (*irreg: like* **man**) *n* Seemann *m*
seamanship ['si:mənʃɪp] *n* Seemannschaft *f*
seamless ['si:mlɪs] *adj* (*lit, fig*) nahtlos
seamy ['si:mɪ] *adj* zwielichtig; **the ~ side of life** die Schattenseite des Lebens
séance ['seɪɔns] *n* spiritistische Sitzung *f*
seaplane ['si:pleɪn] *n* Wasserflugzeug *nt*
seaport ['si:pɔ:t] *n* Seehafen *m*
search [sə:tʃ] *n* Suche *f*; (*inspection*) Durchsuchung *f*; (*Comput*) Suchlauf *m* ▹ *vt* durchsuchen; (*mind, memory*) durchforschen ▹ *vi*: **to ~ for** suchen nach; **"~ and replace"** (*Comput*) „suchen und ersetzen"; **in ~ of** auf der Suche nach
▸ **search through** *vt fus* durchsuchen
searcher ['sə:tʃəʳ] *n* Suchende(r) *f(m)*
searching ['sə:tʃɪŋ] *adj* (*question*) bohrend; (*look*) prüfend; (*examination*) eingehend
searchlight ['sə:tʃlaɪt] *n* Suchscheinwerfer *m*
search party *n* Suchtrupp *m*; **to send out a ~** einen Suchtrupp ausschicken
search warrant *n* Durchsuchungsbefehl *m*
searing ['sɪərɪŋ] *adj* (*heat*) glühend; (*pain*) scharf
seashore ['si:ʃɔ:ʳ] *n* Strand *m*; **on the ~** am Strand
seasick ['si:sɪk] *adj* seekrank
seasickness ['si:sɪknɪs] *n* Seekrankheit *f*
seaside ['si:saɪd] *n* Meer *nt*, See *f*; **to go to the ~** ans Meer *or* an die See fahren; **at the ~** am Meer, an der See
seaside resort *n* Badeort *m*
season ['si:zn] *n* Jahreszeit *f*; (*Agr*) Zeit *f*; (*Sport, of films etc*) Saison *f*; (*Theat*) Spielzeit *f* ▹ *vt* (*food*) würzen; **strawberries are in ~/out of ~** für Erdbeeren ist jetzt die richtige Zeit/nicht die richtige Zeit; **the busy ~** die Hochsaison *f*; **the open ~** (*Hunting*) die Jagdzeit *f*
seasonal ['si:znl] *adj* (*work*) Saison-
seasoned ['si:znd] *adj* (*fig: traveller*) erfahren; (*wood*) abgelagert; **she's a ~ campaigner** sie ist eine alte Kämpferin
seasoning ['si:znɪŋ] *n* Gewürz *nt*
season ticket *n* (*Rail*) Zeitkarte *f*; (*Sport*) Dauerkarte *f*; (*Theat*) Abonnement *nt*
seat [si:t] *n* (*chair, of government, Pol*) Sitz *m*; (*place*) Platz *m*; (*buttocks*) Gesäß *nt*; (*of trousers*) Hosenboden *m*; (*of learning*) Stätte *f* ▹ *vt* setzen; (*have room for*) Sitzplätze bieten für; **are there**

any ~s left? sind noch Plätze frei?; **to take one's ~** sich setzen; **please be ~ed** bitte nehmen Sie Platz; **to be ~ed** sitzen
seat belt *n* Sicherheitsgurt *m*
seating arrangements ['si:tɪŋ-] *npl* Sitzordnung *f*
seating capacity *n* Sitzplätze *pl*
SEATO ['si:təu] *n abbr* (= *Southeast Asia Treaty Organization*) SEATO *f*
sea urchin *n* Seeigel *m*
sea water *n* Meerwasser *nt*
seaweed ['si:wi:d] *n* Seetang *m*
seaworthy ['si:wə:ðɪ] *adj* seetüchtig
SEC (*US*) *n abbr* (= *Securities and Exchange Commission*) *amerikanische Börsenaufsichtsbehörde*
sec. *abbr* (= *second*) Sek.
secateurs [sɛkə'tə:z] *npl* Gartenschere *f*
secede [sɪ'si:d] *vi* (*Pol*): **to ~ (from)** sich abspalten (von)
secluded [sɪ'klu:dɪd] *adj* (*place*) abgelegen; (*life*) zurückgezogen
seclusion [sɪ'klu:ʒən] *n* Abgeschiedenheit *f*; **in ~** zurückgezogen
second[1] [sɪ'kɔnd] (*Brit*) *vt* (*employee*) abordnen
second[2] ['sɛkənd] *adj* zweite(r, s) ▷ *adv* (*come, be placed*) Zweite(r, s); (*when listing*) zweitens ▷ *n* (*time*) Sekunde *f*; (*Aut: also*: **second gear**) der zweite Gang; (*person*) Zweite(r) *f(m)*; (*Comm: imperfect*) zweite Wahl *f* ▷ *vt* (*motion*) unterstützen; **upper/lower ~** (*Brit: Univ*) ≈ Zwei plus/minus; **Charles the S~** Karl der Zweite; **just a ~!** einen Augenblick!; **~ floor** (*Brit*) zweiter Stock *m*; (*US*) erster Stock *m*; **to ask for a ~ opinion** ein zweites Gutachten einholen
secondary ['sɛkəndərɪ] *adj* weniger wichtig
secondary education *n* höhere Schulbildung *f*
secondary picketing *n Aufstellung von Streikposten bei nur indirekt beteiligten Firmen*
secondary school *n* höhere Schule *f*; *siehe Info-Artikel*

SECONDARY SCHOOL

Secondary school ist in Großbritannien eine weiterführende Schule für Kinder von 11 bis 18 Jahren. Manche Schüler gehen schon mit 16 Jahren, wenn die allgemeine Schulpflicht endet, von der Schule ab. Die meisten secondary schools sind heute Gesamtschulen, obwohl es auch noch selektive Schulen gibt. Siehe auch *comprehensive school, primary school*.

second-best [sɛkənd'bɛst] *adj* zweitbeste(r, s) ▷ *n*: **as a ~** als Ausweichlösung; **don't settle for ~** gib dich nur mit dem Besten zufrieden
second-class ['sɛkənd'klɑ:s] *adj* zweitklassig; (*citizen*) zweiter Klasse; (*Rail, Post*) Zweite-Klasse- ▷ *adv* (*Rail, Post*) zweiter Klasse; **to send sth ~** etw zweiter Klasse schicken; **to travel ~** zweiter Klasse reisen
second cousin *n* Cousin *m*/Cousine *f* zweiten Grades *f*
seconder ['sɛkəndə^r] *n* Befürworter(in) *m(f)*
second-guess ['sɛkənd'gɛs] *vt* vorhersagen; **to ~ sb** vorhersagen, was jd machen wird
second-hand ['sɛkənd'hænd] *adj* gebraucht; (*clothing*) getragen ▷ *adv* (*buy*) gebraucht; **to hear sth secondhand** etw aus zweiter Hand haben; **~ car** Gebrauchtwagen *m*; **~ smoking** (*US*) Passivrauchen *nt*
second hand *n* (*on clock*) Sekundenzeiger *m*
second-in-command ['sɛkəndɪnkə'mɑ:nd] *n* (*Mil*) stellvertretender Kommandeur *m*; (*Admin*) stellvertretender Leiter *m*
secondly ['sɛkəndlɪ] *adv* zweitens
secondment [sɪ'kɔndmənt] (*Brit*) *n* Abordnung *f*; **to be on ~** abgeordnet sein
second-rate ['sɛkənd'reɪt] *adj* zweitklassig
second thoughts *npl*: **on ~, on second thought** (*US*) wenn ich es mir (recht) überlege; **to have ~ (about doing sth)** es sich *dat* anders überlegen (und etw doch nicht tun)
Second World War *n*: **the ~** der Zweite Weltkrieg
secrecy ['si:krəsɪ] *n* Geheimhaltung *f*; (*of person*) Verschwiegenheit *f*; **in ~** heimlich
secret ['si:krɪt] *adj* geheim; (*admirer*) heimlich ▷ *n* Geheimnis *nt*; **in ~** heimlich; **~ passage** Geheimgang *m*; **to keep sth ~ from sb** etw vor jdm geheim halten; **can you keep a ~?** kannst du schweigen?; **to make no ~ of sth** kein Geheimnis *or* keinen Hehl aus etw machen
secret agent *n* Geheimagent(in) *m(f)*
secretarial [sɛkrɪ'tɛərɪəl] *adj* (*work*) Büro-; (*course*) Sekretärinnen-; (*staff*) Sekretariats-
secretariat [sɛkrɪ'tɛərɪət] *n* (*Pol, Admin*) Sekretariat *nt*
secretary ['sɛkrətərɪ] *n* (*Comm*) Sekretär(in) *m(f)*; (*of club*) Schriftführer(in) *m(f)*; **S~ of State (for)** (*Brit: Pol*) Minister(in) *m(f)* (für); **S~ of State** (*US: Pol*) Außenminister(in) *m(f)*
secretary-general ['sɛkrətərɪ'dʒɛnərl] (*pl* **secretaries-general**) *n* Generalsekretär(in) *m(f)*
secrete [sɪ'kri:t] *vt* (*Anat, Biol, Med*) absondern; (*hide*) verbergen
secretion [sɪ'kri:ʃən] *n* (*substance*) Sekret *nt*
secretive ['si:krətɪv] *adj* verschlossen; (*pej*) geheimnistuerisch
secretly ['si:krɪtlɪ] *adv* heimlich; (*hope*) insgeheim
secret police *n* Geheimpolizei *f*
secret service *n* Geheimdienst *m*
sect [sɛkt] *n* Sekte *f*
sectarian [sɛk'tɛərɪən] *adj* (*killing etc*) konfessionell motiviert; **~ violence** gewalttätige Konfessionsstreitigkeiten *pl*
section ['sɛkʃən] *n* (*part*) Teil *m*; (*department*) Abteilung *f*; (*of document*) Absatz *m*; (*cross-section*) Schnitt *m* ▷ *vt* (*divide*) teilen; **the business/sport ~** (*Press*) der Wirtschafts-/Sportteil

sectional ['sɛkʃənl] *adj*: ~ **drawing** Darstellung *f* im Schnitt
sector ['sɛktəʳ] *n* Sektor *m*
secular ['sɛkjuləʳ] *adj* weltlich
secure [sɪ'kjuəʳ] *adj* sicher; (*firmly fixed*) fest ▷ *vt* (*fix*) festmachen; (*votes etc*) erhalten; (*contract etc*) (sich *dat*) sichern; (*Comm: loan*) (ab)sichern; **to make sth** ~ etw sichern; **to ~ sth for sb** jdm etw sichern
secured creditor [sɪ'kjuəd-] *n* (*Comm*) abgesicherter Gläubiger *m*
securely [sɪ'kjuəlɪ] *adv* (*firmly*) fest; (*safely*) sicher
security [sɪ'kjuərɪtɪ] *n* Sicherheit *f*; (*freedom from anxiety*) Geborgenheit *f*; **securities** *npl* (*Stock Exchange*) Effekten *pl*, Wertpapiere *pl*; **securities market** Wertpapiermarkt *m*; **to increase/tighten** ~ die Sicherheitsvorkehrungen verschärfen; **~ of tenure** Kündigungsschutz *m*
Security Council *n* Sicherheitsrat *m*
security forces *npl* Sicherheitskräfte *pl*
security guard *n* Sicherheitsbeamte(r) *m*; (*transporting money*) Wachmann *m*
security risk *n* Sicherheitsrisiko *nt*
secy. *abbr* = **secretary**
sedan [sə'dæn] (*US*) *n* (*Aut*) Limousine *f*
sedate [sɪ'deɪt] *adj* (*person*) ruhig, gesetzt; (*life*) geruhsam; (*pace*) gemächlich ▷ *vt* (*Med*) Beruhigungsmittel geben *+dat*
sedation [sɪ'deɪʃən] *n* (*Med*) Beruhigungsmittel *pl*; **to be under** ~ unter dem Einfluss von Beruhigungsmitteln stehen
sedative ['sɛdɪtɪv] *n* (*Med*) Beruhigungsmittel *nt*
sedentary ['sɛdntrɪ] *adj* (*occupation, work*) sitzend
sediment ['sɛdɪmənt] *n* (*in bottle*) (Boden)satz *m*; (*in lake etc*) Ablagerung *f*
sedimentary [sɛdɪ'mɛntərɪ] *adj* (*Geog*) sedimentär; ~ **rock** Sedimentgestein *nt*
sedition [sɪ'dɪʃən] *n* Aufwiegelung *f*
seduce [sɪ'dju:s] *vt* verführen; **to ~ sb into doing sth** jdn dazu verleiten, etw zu tun
seduction [sɪ'dʌkʃən] *n* (*attraction*) Verlockung *f*; (*act of seducing*) Verführung *f*
seductive [sɪ'dʌktɪv] *adj* verführerisch; (*fig: offer*) verlockend
see [si:] (*pt* **saw**, *pp* **~n**) *vt* sehen; (*look at*) sich *dat* ansehen; (*understand*) verstehen, (ein)sehen; (*doctor etc*) aufsuchen ▷ *vi* sehen ▷ *n* (*Rel*) Bistum *nt*; **to ~ that** (*ensure*) dafür sorgen, dass; **to ~ sb to the door** jdn zur Tür bringen; **there was nobody to be ~n** es war niemand zu sehen; **to go and ~ sb** jdn besuchen (gehen); **to ~ a doctor** zum Arzt gehen; **~ you!** tschüss! (*inf*); **~ you soon!** bis bald!; **let me ~** (*show me*) lass mich mal sehen; (*let me think*) lass mich mal überlegen; **I** ~ ich verstehe, aha; (*annoyed*) ach so; **you** ~ weißt du, siehst du; **~ for yourself** überzeug dich doch selbst; **I don't know what she ~s in him** ich weiß nicht, was sie an ihm findet; **as far as I can ~** so wie ich das sehe
▸ **see about** *vt fus* sich kümmern um *+acc*
▸ **see off** *vt* verabschieden
▸ **see through** *vt fus* durchschauen ▷ *vt*: **to ~ sb through sth** jdm in etw *dat* beistehen; **to ~ sth through to the end** etw zu Ende bringen; **this should ~ you through** das müsste dir reichen
▸ **see to** *vt fus* sich kümmern um *+acc*
seed [si:d] *n* Samen *m*; (*of fruit*) Kern *m*; (*fig: usu pl*) Keim *m*; (*Tennis*) gesetzter Spieler *m*, gesetzte Spielerin *f*; **to go to ~** (*plant*) Samen bilden; (*lettuce etc*) schießen; (*fig: person*) herunterkommen
seedless ['si:dlɪs] *adj* kernlos
seedling ['si:dlɪŋ] *n* (*Bot*) Sämling *m*
seedy ['si:dɪ] *adj* (*person, place*) zwielichtig, zweifelhaft
seeing ['si:ɪŋ] *conj*: **~ as** *or* **that** da
seek [si:k] (*pt, pp* **sought**) *vt* suchen; **to ~ advice from sb** jdn um Rat fragen; **to ~ help from sb** jdn um Hilfe bitten
▸ **seek out** *vt* ausfindig machen
seem [si:m] *vi* scheinen; **there ~s to be a mistake** da scheint ein Fehler zu sein; **it ~s (that)** es scheint(, dass); **it ~s to me that ...** mir scheint, dass ...; **what ~s to be the trouble?** worum geht es denn?; (*doctor*) was fehlt Ihnen denn?
seemingly ['si:mɪŋlɪ] *adv* anscheinend
seemly ['si:mlɪ] *adj* schicklich
seen [si:n] *pp of* **see**
seep [si:p] *vi* sickern
seersucker ['sɪəsʌkəʳ] *n* Krepp *m*, Seersucker *m*
seesaw ['si:sɔ:] *n* Wippe *f*
seethe [si:ð] *vi*: **to ~ with** (*place*) wimmeln von; **to ~ with anger** vor Wut kochen
see-through ['si:θru:] *adj* durchsichtig
segment ['sɛgmənt] *n* Teil *m*; (*of orange*) Stück *nt*
segregate ['sɛgrɪgeɪt] *vt* trennen, absondern
segregation [sɛgrɪ'geɪʃən] *n* Trennung *f*
Seine [seɪn] *n*: **the** ~ die Seine *f*
seismic shock *n* Erdstoß *m*
seize [si:z] *vt* packen, ergreifen; (*fig: opportunity*) ergreifen; (*power, control*) an sich *acc* reißen; (*territory, airfield*) besetzen; (*hostage*) nehmen; (*Law*) beschlagnahmen
▸ **seize up** *vi* (*engine*) sich festfressen
▸ **seize (up)on** *vt fus* sich stürzen auf *+acc*
seizure ['si:ʒəʳ] *n* (*Med*) Anfall *m*; (*of power*) Ergreifung *f*; (*Law*) Beschlagnahmung *f*
seldom ['sɛldəm] *adv* selten
select [sɪ'lɛkt] *adj* exklusiv ▷ *vt* (aus)wählen; (*Sport*) aufstellen; **a ~ few** wenige Auserwählte *pl*
selection [sɪ'lɛkʃən] *n* (*being chosen*) Wahl *f*; (*range*) Auswahl *f*
selection committee *n* Auswahlkomitee *nt*
selective [sɪ'lɛktɪv] *adj* wählerisch; (*not general*) selektiv
selector [sɪ'lɛktəʳ] *n* (*Sport*) Mannschaftsaufsteller(in) *m(f)*; (*Tech*) Wählschalter *m*;

(: *button*) Taste *f*
self [sɛlf] (*pl* **selves**) *n* Selbst *nt*, Ich *nt*; **she was her normal ~ again** sie war wieder ganz die Alte
self ... [sɛlf] *pref* selbst-, Selbst-
self-addressed ['sɛlfə'drɛst] *adj*: **~ envelope** addressierter Rückumschlag *m*
self-adhesive [sɛlfəd'hi:zɪv] *adj* selbstklebend
self-appointed [sɛlfə'pɔɪntɪd] *adj* selbst ernannt
self-assertive [sɛlfə'sə:tɪv] *adj* selbstbewusst
self-assurance [sɛlfə'ʃuərəns] *n* Selbstsicherheit *f*
self-assured [sɛlfə'ʃuəd] *adj* selbstsicher
self-catering [sɛlf'keɪtərɪŋ] (*Brit*) *adj* (*holiday, flat*) für Selbstversorger
self-centred, (*US*) **self-centered** [sɛlf'sɛntəd] *adj* egozentrisch, ichbezogen
self-cleaning [sɛlf'kli:nɪŋ] *adj* selbstreinigend
self-confessed [sɛlfkən'fɛst] *adj* erklärt
self-confidence [sɛlf'kɔnfɪdns] *n* Selbstbewusstsein *nt*, Selbstvertrauen *nt*
self-confident [sɛlf'kɔnfɪdənt] *adj* selbstbewusst, selbstsicher
self-conscious [sɛlf'kɔnʃəs] *adj* befangen, gehemmt
self-contained [sɛlfkən'teɪnd] (*Brit*) *adj* (*flat*) abgeschlossen; (*person*) selb(st)ständig
self-control [sɛlfkən'trəul] *n* Selbstbeherrschung *f*
self-defeating [sɛlfdɪ'fi:tɪŋ] *adj* unsinnig
self-defence, (*US*) **self-defense** [sɛlfdɪ'fɛns] *n* Selbstverteidigung *f*; (*Law*) Notwehr *f*; **in ~** zu seiner/ihrer *etc* Verteidigung; (*Law*) in Notwehr
self-discipline [sɛlf'dɪsɪplɪn] *n* Selbstdisziplin *f*
self-employed [sɛlfɪm'plɔɪd] *adj* selbstständig
self-esteem [sɛlfɪs'ti:m] *n* Selbstachtung *f*
self-evident [sɛlf'ɛvɪdnt] *adj* offensichtlich
self-explanatory [sɛlfɪks'plænətrɪ] *adj* unmittelbar verständlich
self-financing [sɛlffaɪ'nænsɪŋ] *adj* selbstfinanzierend
self-governing [sɛlf'gʌvənɪŋ] *adj* selbst verwaltet
self-help ['sɛlf'hɛlp] *n* Selbsthilfe *f*
self-importance [sɛlfɪm'pɔ:tns] *n* Aufgeblasenheit *f*
self-indulgent [sɛlfɪn'dʌldʒənt] *adj* genießerisch; **to be ~** sich verwöhnen
self-inflicted [sɛlfɪn'flɪktɪd] *adj* selbst zugefügt
self-interest [sɛlf'ɪntrɪst] *n* Eigennutz *m*
selfish ['sɛlfɪʃ] *adj* egoistisch, selbstsüchtig
selfishly ['sɛlfɪʃlɪ] *adv* egoistisch, selbstsüchtig
selfishness ['sɛlfɪʃnɪs] *n* Egoismus *m*, Selbstsucht *f*
selfless ['sɛlflɪs] *adj* selbstlos
selflessly ['sɛlflɪslɪ] *adv* selbstlos
selflessness ['sɛlflɪsnɪs] *n* Selbstlosigkeit *f*
self-made ['sɛlfmeɪd] *adj*: **~ man** Selfmademan *m*
self-pity [sɛlf'pɪtɪ] *n* Selbstmitleid *nt*
self-portrait [sɛlf'pɔ:treɪt] *n* Selbstporträt *nt*, Selbstbildnis *nt*
self-possessed [sɛlfpə'zɛst] *adj* selbstbeherrscht
self-preservation ['sɛlfprɛzə'veɪʃən] *n* Selbsterhaltung *f*
self-raising ['sɛlf'reɪzɪŋ], (*US*) **self-rising** ['sɛlf'raɪzɪŋ] *adj*: **~ flour** *Mehl mit bereits beigemischtem Backpulver*
self-reliant [sɛlfrɪ'laɪənt] *adj* selb(st)ständig
self-respect [sɛlfrɪs'pɛkt] *n* Selbstachtung *f*
self-respecting [sɛlfrɪs'pɛktɪŋ] *adj* mit Selbstachtung; (*genuine*) der/die/das etwas auf sich hält
self-righteous [sɛlf'raɪtʃəs] *adj* selbstgerecht
self-rising [sɛlf'raɪzɪŋ] (*US*) *adj* = **self-raising**
self-sacrifice [sɛlf'sækrɪfaɪs] *n* Selbstaufopferung *f*
self-same ['sɛlfseɪm] *adj*: **the ~** genau derselbe/dieselbe/dasselbe
self-satisfied [sɛlf'sætɪsfaɪd] *adj* selbstzufrieden
self-sealing [sɛlf'si:lɪŋ] *adj* selbstklebend
self-service [sɛlf'sə:vɪs] *adj* (*shop, restaurant etc*) Selbstbedienungs-
self-styled ['sɛlfstaɪld] *adj* selbst ernannt
self-sufficient [sɛlfsə'fɪʃənt] *adj* (*country*) autark; (*person*) selb(st)ständig, unabhängig; **to be ~ in coal** seinen Kohlebedarf selbst decken können
self-supporting [sɛlfsə'pɔ:tɪŋ] *adj* (*business*) sich selbst tragend
self-taught [sɛlf'tɔ:t] *adj*: **to be ~** Autodidakt sein; **he is a ~ pianist** er hat sich das Klavierspielen selbst beigebracht
self-test ['sɛlftɛst] *n* (*Comput*) Selbsttest *m*
sell [sɛl] (*pt, pp* **sold**) *vt* verkaufen; (*shop: goods*) führen, haben (*inf*); (*fig: idea*) schmackhaft machen *+dat*, verkaufen (*inf*) ▷ *vi* sich verkaufen (lassen); **to ~ at** *or* **for 10 pounds** für 10 Pfund verkauft werden; **to ~ sb sth** jdm etw verkaufen; **to ~ o.s.** sich verkaufen
▸ **sell off** *vt* verkaufen
▸ **sell out** *vi*: **we/the tickets are sold out** wir/die Karten sind ausverkauft; **we have sold out of ...** wir haben kein ... mehr, ... ist ausverkauft
▸ **sell up** *vi* sein Haus/seine Firma *etc* verkaufen
sell-by date ['sɛlbaɪ-] *n* ≈ Haltbarkeitsdatum *nt*
seller ['sɛlə^r] *n* Verkäufer(in) *m(f)*; **~'s market** Verkäufermarkt *m*
selling point ['sɛlɪŋ-] *n* Verkaufsanreiz *m or* -argument *nt*
selling price ['sɛlɪŋ-] *n* Verkaufspreis *m*
sellotape® ['sɛləuteɪp] (*Brit*) *n* Klebeband *nt* ≈ Tesafilm® *m*
sellout ['sɛlaut] *n* (*inf: betrayal*) Verrat *m*; **the match was a ~** das Spiel war ausverkauft
selves [sɛlvz] *pl of* **self**
semantic [sɪ'mæntɪk] *adj* semantisch
semantics [sɪ'mæntɪks] *n* (*Ling*) Semantik *f*
semaphore ['sɛməfɔ:^r] *n* Flaggenalphabet *nt*
semblance ['sɛmblns] *n* Anschein *m*

semen ['si:mən] *n* Samenflüssigkeit *f*, Sperma *nt*
semester [sɪ'mɛstəʳ] (*esp US*) *n* Semester *nt*
semi ['sɛmɪ] *n* = **semidetached house**
semi ... ['sɛmɪ] *pref* halb-, Halb-
semibreve ['sɛmɪbri:v] (*Brit*) *n* (*Mus*) ganze Note *f*
semicircle ['sɛmɪsə:kl] *n* Halbkreis *m*
semicircular ['sɛmɪ'sə:kjuləʳ] *adj* halbkreisförmig
semicolon [sɛmɪ'kəulən] *n* Strichpunkt *m*, Semikolon *nt*
semiconductor [sɛmɪkən'dʌktəʳ] *n* Halbleiter *m*
semiconscious [sɛmɪ'kɔnʃəs] *adj* halb bewusstlos
semidetached
semidetached house (*Brit*) *n* Doppelhaushälfte *f*
semifinal [sɛmɪ'faɪnl] *n* Halbfinale *nt*
seminar ['sɛmɪnɑ:ʳ] *n* Seminar *nt*
seminary ['sɛmɪnərɪ] *n* (*Rel*) Priesterseminar *nt*
semi-precious stone *n* Halbedelstein *m*
semiquaver ['sɛmɪkweɪvəʳ] (*Brit*) *n* (*Mus*) Sechzehntelnote *f*
semiskilled [sɛmɪ'skɪld] *adj* (*work*) Anlern-; (*worker*) angelernt
semi-skimmed [sɛmɪ'skɪmd] *adj* (*milk*) teilentrahmt, Halbfett-
semitone ['sɛmɪtəun] *n* (*Mus*) Halbton *m*
semolina [sɛmə'li:nə] *n* Grieß *m*
Sen., sen. *abbr* (*US*) = **senator**; (*in names*: = *senior*) sen.
senate ['sɛnɪt] *n* Senat *m*; *siehe Info-Artikel*

SENATE

Senate ist das Oberhaus des amerikanischen Kongresses (das Unterhaus ist das *House of Representatives*. Der Senat besteht aus 100 Senatoren, zwei für jeden Bundesstaat, die für sechs Jahre gewählt werden, wobei ein Drittel alle zwei Jahre neu gewählt wird. Die Senatoren werden in direkter Wahl vom Volk gewählt. Siehe auch *congress*.

senator ['sɛnɪtəʳ] *n* Senator(in) *m(f)*
send [sɛnd] (*pt, pp* **sent**) *vt* schicken; (*transmit*) senden; **to ~ sth by post, to ~ sth by mail** (*US*) etw mit der Post schicken; **to ~ sb for sth** (*for check-up etc*) jdn zu etw schicken; **to ~ word that ...** Nachricht geben, dass ...; **she ~s (you) her love** sie lässt dich grüßen; **to ~ sb to Coventry** (*Brit*) jdn schneiden (*inf*); **to ~ sb to sleep** jdn einschläfern; **to ~ sth flying** etw umwerfen
▸ **send away** *vt* wegschicken
▸ **send away for** *vt fus* (per Post) anfordern
▸ **send back** *vt* zurückschicken
▸ **send for** *vt fus* (per Post) anfordern; (*doctor, police*) rufen
▸ **send in** *vt* einsenden, einschicken
▸ **send off** *vt* abschicken; (*Brit: player*) vom Platz weisen
▸ **send on** *vt* (*Brit: letter*) nachsenden; (*luggage etc*) vorausschicken
▸ **send out** *vt* verschicken; (*light, heat*) abgeben; (*signal*) aussenden
▸ **send round** *vt* schicken; (*circulate*) zirkulieren lassen
▸ **send up** *vt* (*astronaut*) hochschießen; (*price, blood pressure*) hochtreiben; (*Brit: parody*) verulken (*inf*)
sender ['sɛndəʳ] *n* Absender(in) *m(f)*
sending-off ['sɛndɪŋɔf] *n* (*Sport*) Platzverweis *m*
send-off ['sɛndɔf] *n*: **a good ~** eine große Verabschiedung
send-up ['sɛndʌp] *n* Verulkung *f* (*inf*)
Senegal [sɛnɪ'gɔ:l] *n* Senegal *nt*
Senegalese [sɛnɪgə'li:z] *adj* senegalesisch ▹ *n inv* Senegalese *m*, Senegalesin *f*
senile ['si:naɪl] *adj* senil
senility [sɪ'nɪlɪtɪ] *n* Senilität *f*
senior ['si:nɪəʳ] *adj* (*staff, manager*) leitend; (*officer*) höher; (*post, position*) leitend ▹ *n* (*Scol*): **the ~s** die Oberstufenschüler *pl*; **to be ~ to sb** jdm übergeordnet sein; **she is 15 years his ~** sie ist 15 Jahre älter als er; **P. Jones ~** P. Jones senior
senior citizen *n* Senior(in) *m(f)*
senior high school (*US*) *n* Oberstufe *f*
seniority [si:nɪ'ɔrɪtɪ] *n* (*in service*) (längere) Betriebszugehörigkeit *f*; (*in rank*) (höhere) Position *f*
sensation [sɛn'seɪʃən] *n* (*feeling*) Gefühl *nt*; (*great success*) Sensation *f*; **to cause a ~** großes Aufsehen erregen
sensational [sɛn'seɪʃənl] *adj* (*wonderful*) wunderbar; (*result*) sensationell; (*headlines etc*) reißerisch
sense [sɛns] *n* Sinn *m*; (*feeling*) Gefühl *nt*; (*good sense*) Verstand *m*, gesunder Menschenverstand *m*; (*meaning*) Bedeutung *f*, Sinn *m* ▹ *vt* spüren; **~ of smell** Geruchssinn *m*; **it makes ~** (*can be understood*) es ergibt einen Sinn; (*is sensible*) es ist vernünftig *or* sinnvoll; **there's no ~ in that** das hat keinen Sinn; **there is no ~ in doing that** es hat keinen Sinn, das zu tun; **to come to one's ~s** Vernunft annehmen; **to take leave of one's ~s** den Verstand verlieren
senseless ['sɛnslɪs] *adj* (*pointless*) sinnlos; (*unconscious*) besinnungslos, bewusstlos
sense of humour *n* Sinn *m* für Humor
sensibility [sɛnsɪ'bɪlɪtɪ] *n* Empfindsamkeit *f*; (*sensitivity*) Empfindlichkeit *f*; **to offend sb's sensibilities** jds Zartgefühl verletzen
sensible ['sɛnsɪbl] *adj* vernünftig; (*shoes, clothes*) praktisch
sensitive ['sɛnsɪtɪv] *adj* empfindlich; (*understanding*) einfühlsam; (*touchy: person*) sensibel; (*: issue*) heikel; **to be ~ to sth** in Bezug auf etw *acc* empfindlich sein; **he is very ~ about it/to criticism** er reagiert sehr empfindlich darauf/auf Kritik

sensitivity [sɛnsɪ'tɪvɪtɪ] *n* Empfindlichkeit *f*; (*understanding*) Einfühlungsvermögen *nt*; (*of issue etc*) heikle Natur *f*; **an issue of great ~** ein sehr heikles Thema
sensual ['sɛnsjuəl] *adj* sinnlich; (*person, life*) sinnenfroh
sensuous ['sɛnsjuəs] *adj* sinnlich
sent [sɛnt] *pt, pp of* **send**
sentence ['sɛntns] *n* (*Ling*) Satz *m*; (*Law: judgement*) Urteil *nt*; (*: punishment*) Strafe *f* ▷ *vt*: **to ~ sb to death/to 5 years in prison** jdn zum Tode/zu 5 Jahren Haft verurteilen; **to pass ~ on sb** das Urteil über jdn verkünden; (*fig*) jdn verurteilen; **to serve a life ~** eine lebenslängliche Freiheitsstrafe verbüßen
sentiment ['sɛntɪmənt] *n* Sentimentalität *f*; (*also pl: opinion*) Ansicht *f*
sentimental [sɛntɪ'mɛntl] *adj* sentimental
sentimentality [sɛntɪmɛn'tælɪtɪ] *n* Sentimentalität *f*
sentry ['sɛntrɪ] *n* Wachtposten *m*
sentry duty *n*: **to be on ~** auf Wache sein
Seoul [səul] *n* Seoul *nt*
separable ['sɛprəbl] *adj*: **to be ~ from** trennbar sein von
separate ['sɛprɪt] *adj* getrennt; (*occasions*) verschieden; (*rooms*) separat ▷ *vt* trennen ▷ *vi* sich trennen; **~ from** getrennt von; **to go ~ ways** getrennte Wege gehen; **under ~ cover** (*Comm*) mit getrennter Post; **to ~ into** aufteilen in *+acc*; *see also* **separates**
separately ['sɛprɪtlɪ] *adv* getrennt
separates ['sɛprɪts] *npl* (*clothes*) kombinierbare Einzelteile *pl*
separation [sɛpə'reɪʃən] *n* Trennung *f*
sepia ['si:pjə] *adj* sepiafarben
Sept. *abbr* (*= September*) Sept.
September [sɛp'tɛmbəʳ] *n* September *m*; *see also* **July**
septic ['sɛptɪk] *adj* vereitert, septisch; **to go ~** eitern
septicaemia, (US) **septicemia** [sɛptɪ'si:mɪə] *n* Blutvergiftung *f*
septic tank *n* Faulbehälter *m*
sequel ['si:kwl] *n* (*follow-up*) Nachspiel *nt*; (*of film, story*) Fortsetzung *f*
sequence ['si:kwəns] *n* Folge *f*; (*dance/film sequence*) Sequenz *f*; **in ~** der Reihe nach
sequential [sɪ'kwɛnʃəl] *adj* aufeinanderfolgend; **~ access** (*Comput*) sequenzieller Zugriff *m*
sequestrate [sɪ'kwɛstreɪt] *vt* (*Law, Comm*) sequestrieren, beschlagnahmen
sequin ['si:kwɪn] *n* Paillette *f*
Serbia ['sə:bɪə] *n* Serbien *nt*
Serbian ['sə:bɪən] *adj* serbisch ▷ *n* Serbier(in) *m(f)*; (*Ling*) Serbisch *nt*
Serbo-Croat ['sə:bəu'krəuæt] *n* (*Ling*) Serbokroatisch *nt*
serenade [sɛrə'neɪd] *n* Serenade *f* ▷ *vt* ein Ständchen *nt* bringen *+dat*
serene [sɪ'ri:n] *adj* (*landscape etc*) friedlich; (*expression*) heiter; (*person*) gelassen
serenity [sə'rɛnɪtɪ] *n* (*of landscape*) Friedlichkeit *f*; (*of expression*) Gelassenheit *f*
sergeant ['sɑ:dʒənt] *n* (*Mil etc*) Feldwebel *m*; (*Police*) Polizeimeister *m*
sergeant-major ['sɑ:dʒənt'meɪdʒəʳ] *n* Oberfeldwebel *m*
serial ['sɪərɪəl] *n* (*TV*) Serie *f*; (*Radio*) Sendereihe *f*; (*in magazine*) Fortsetzungsroman *m* ▷ *adj* (*Comput*) seriell
serialize ['sɪərɪəlaɪz] *vt* in Fortsetzungen veröffentlichen; (*TV, Radio*) in Fortsetzungen senden
serial killer *n* Serienmörder(in) *m(f)*
serial number *n* Seriennummer *f*
series ['sɪərɪz] *n inv* (*group*) Serie *f*, Reihe *f*; (*of books*) Reihe *f*; (*TV*) Serie *f*
serious ['sɪərɪəs] *adj* ernst; (*important*) wichtig; (*: illness*) schwer; (*: condition*) bedenklich; **are you ~ (about it)?** meinst du das ernst?
seriously ['sɪərɪəslɪ] *adv* ernst; (*talk, interested*) ernsthaft; (*ill, hurt, damaged*) schwer; (*not jokingly*) im Ernst; **to take sb/sth ~** jdn/etw ernst nehmen; **do you ~ believe that ...** glauben Sie ernsthaft *or* im Ernst, dass ...
seriousness ['sɪərɪəsnɪs] *n* Ernst *m*, Ernsthaftigkeit *f*; (*of problem*) Bedenklichkeit *f*
sermon ['sə:mən] *n* Predigt *f*; (*fig*) Moralpredigt *f*
serrated [sɪ'reɪtɪd] *adj* gezackt; **~ knife** Sägemesser *nt*
serum ['sɪərəm] *n* Serum *nt*
servant ['sə:vənt] *n* (*lit, fig*) Diener(in) *m(f)*; (*domestic*) Hausangestellte(r) *f(m)*
serve [sə:v] *vt* dienen *+dat*; (*in shop, with food/drink*) bedienen; (*food, meal*) servieren; (*purpose*) haben; (*apprenticeship*) durchmachen; (*prison term*) verbüßen ▷ *vi* (*at table*) auftragen, servieren; (*Tennis*) aufschlagen; (*soldier*) dienen; (*be useful*): **to ~ as/for** dienen als ▷ *n* (*Tennis*) Aufschlag *m*; **are you being ~d?** werden Sie schon bedient?; **to ~ its purpose** seinen Zweck erfüllen; **to ~ sb's purpose** jds Zwecken dienen; **it ~s him right** das geschieht ihm recht; **to ~ on a committee** einem Ausschuss angehören; **to ~ on a jury** Geschworene(r) *f(m)* sein; **it's my turn to ~** (*Tennis*) ich habe Aufschlag; **it ~s to show/explain ...** das zeigt/erklärt ...
▸ **serve out** *vt* (*food*) auftragen, servieren
▸ **serve up** *vt* = **serve out**
service ['sə:vɪs] *n* Dienst *m*; (*commercial*) Dienstleistung *f*; (*in hotel, restaurant*) Bedienung *f*, Service *m*; (*also:* **train service**) Bahnverbindung *f*; (*: generally*) Zugverkehr *m*; (*Rel*) Gottesdienst *m*; (*Aut*) Inspektion *f*; (*Tennis*) Aufschlag *m*; (*plates etc*) Service *nt* ▷ *vt* (*car, machine*) warten; **the Services** *npl* (*army, navy etc*) die Streitkräfte *pl*; **military/national ~** Militärdienst *m*; **to be of ~ to sb** jdm nützen; **to do sb a ~** jdm einen Dienst erweisen; **to put one's car in for a ~** sein Auto zur Inspektion geben; **dinner ~** Essservice *nt*
serviceable ['sə:vɪsəbl] *adj* zweckmäßig

service area *n* (*on motorway*) Raststätte *f*
service charge (*Brit*) *n* Bedienungsgeld *nt*
service contract *n* Wartungsvertrag *m*
service industry *n* Dienstleistungsbranche *f*
serviceman ['sə:vɪsmən] (*irreg*: *like* **man**) *n* Militärangehörige(r) *m*
service station *n* Tankstelle *f*
serviette [sə:vɪ'ɛt] (*Brit*) *n* Serviette *f*
servile ['sə:vaɪl] *adj* unterwürfig
session ['sɛʃən] *n* Sitzung *f*; (*US, Scot*: *Scol*) Studienjahr *nt*; (: *term*) Semester *nt*; **recording ~** Aufnahme *f*; **to be in ~** tagen
session musician *n* Session-Musiker(in) *m(f)*
set [sɛt] (*pt, pp* **~**) *n* (*of saucepans, books, keys etc*) Satz *m*; (*group*) Reihe *f*; (*of cutlery*) Garnitur *f*; (*also*: **radio set**) Radio(gerät) *nt*; (*also*: **TV set**) Fernsehgerät *nt*; (*Tennis*) Satz *m*; (*group of people*) Kreis *m*; (*Math*) Menge *f*; (*Theat*: *stage*) Bühne *f*; (: *scenery*) Bühnenbild *nt*; (*Cine*) Drehort *m*; (*Hairdressing*) (Ein)legen *nt* ▷ *adj* (*fixed*) fest; (*ready*) fertig, bereit ▷ *vt* (*table*) decken; (*place*) auflegen; (*time, price, rules etc*) festsetzen; (*record*) aufstellen; (*alarm, watch, task*) stellen; (*exam*) zusammenstellen; (*Typ*) setzen ▷ *vi* (*sun*) untergehen; (*jam, jelly, concrete*) fest werden; (*bone*) zusammenwachsen; **a ~ of false teeth** ein Gebiss *nt*; **a ~ of dining-room furniture** eine Esszimmergarnitur; **a chess ~** ein Schachspiel *nt*; **to be ~ on doing sth** etw unbedingt tun wollen; **to be all ~ to do sth** bereit sein, etw zu tun; **he's ~ in his ways** er ist in seinen Gewohnheiten festgefahren; **a ~ phrase** eine feste Redewendung; **a novel ~ in Rome** ein Roman, der in Rom spielt; **to ~ to music** vertonen; **to ~ on fire** anstecken; **to ~ free** freilassen; **to ~ sail** losfahren
▸ **set about** *vt fus* (*task*) anpacken; **to ~ about doing sth** sich daranmachen, etw zu tun
▸ **set aside** *vt* (*money etc*) beiseitelegen; (*time*) einplanen
▸ **set back** *vt*: **to ~ sb back 5 pounds** jdn 5 Pfund kosten; **to ~ sb back (by)** (*in time*) jdn zurückwerfen (um); **a house ~ back from the road** ein Haus, das etwas von der Straße abliegt
▸ **set in** *vi* (*bad weather*) einsetzen; (*infection*) sich einstellen; **the rain has ~ in for the day** es hat sich für heute eingeregnet
▸ **set off** *vi* (*depart*) aufbrechen ▷ *vt* (*bomb*) losgehen lassen; (*alarm, chain of events*) auslösen; (*show up well*) hervorheben
▸ **set out** *vi* (*depart*) aufbrechen ▷ *vt* (*goods etc*) ausbreiten; (*chairs etc*) aufstellen; (*arguments*) darlegen; **to ~ out to do sth** sich *dat* vornehmen, etw zu tun; **to ~ out from home** zu Hause aufbrechen
▸ **set up** *vt* (*organization*) gründen; (*monument*) errichten; **to ~ up shop** ein Geschäft eröffnen; (*fig*) sich selb(st)ständig machen
setback ['sɛtbæk] *n* Rückschlag *m*
set menu *n* Menü *nt*
set square *n* Zeichendreieck *nt*
settee [sɛ'ti:] *n* Sofa *nt*
setting ['sɛtɪŋ] *n* (*background*) Rahmen *m*; (*position*) Einstellung *f*; (*of jewel*) Fassung *f*
setting lotion *n* (Haar)festiger *m*
settle ['sɛtl] *vt* (*matter*) regeln; (*argument*) beilegen; (*accounts*) begleichen; (*affairs, business*) in Ordnung bringen; (*colonize*: *land*) besiedeln ▷ *vi* (*also*: **settle down**) sich niederlassen; (*sand, dust etc*) sich legen; (*sediment*) sich setzen; (*calm down*) sich beruhigen; **to ~ one's stomach** den Magen beruhigen; **that's ~d then!** das ist also abgemacht!; **to ~ down to work** sich an die Arbeit setzen; **to ~ down to watch TV** es sich *dat* vor dem Fernseher gemütlich machen
▸ **settle for** *vt fus* sich zufriedengeben mit
▸ **settle in** *vi* sich einleben; (*in job etc*) sich eingewöhnen
▸ **settle on** *vt fus* sich entscheiden für
▸ **settle up** *vi*: **to ~ up with sb** mit jdm abrechnen
settlement ['sɛtlmənt] *n* (*payment*) Begleichung *f*; (*Law*) Vergleich *m*; (*agreement*) Übereinkunft *f*; (*of conflict*) Beilegung *f*; (*village etc*) Siedlung *f*, Niederlassung *f*; (*colonization*) Besiedelung *f*; **in ~ of our account** (*Comm*) zum Ausgleich unseres Kontos
settler ['sɛtlə^r] *n* Siedler(in) *m(f)*
setup, set-up ['sɛtʌp] *n* (*organization*) Organisation *f*; (*system*) System *nt*; (*Comput*) Setup *nt*
seven ['sɛvn] *num* sieben
seventeen [sɛvn'ti:n] *num* siebzehn
seventh ['sɛvnθ] *num* siebte(r, s)
seventy ['sɛvntɪ] *num* siebzig
sever ['sɛvə^r] *vt* durchtrennen; (*fig*: *relations*) abbrechen; (: *ties*) lösen
several ['sɛvərl] *adj* einige, mehrere ▷ *pron* einige; **~ of us** einige von uns; **~ times** einige Male, mehrmals
severance ['sɛvərəns] *n* (*of relations*) Abbruch *m*
severance pay *n* Abfindung *f*
severe [sɪ'vɪə^r] *adj* (*damage, shortage*) schwer; (*pain*) stark; (*person, expression, dress, winter*) streng; (*punishment*) hart; (*climate*) rau
severely [sɪ'vɪəlɪ] *adv* (*damage*) stark; (*punish*) hart; (*wounded, ill*) schwer
severity [sɪ'vɛrɪtɪ] *n* (*gravity*: *of punishment*) Härte *f*; (: *of manner, voice, winter*) Strenge *f*; (: *of weather*) Rauheit *f*; (*austerity*) Strenge *f*
sew [səu] (*pt* **~ed**, *pp* **~n**) *vt, vi* nähen
▸ **sew up** *vt* (zusammen)nähen; **it is all ~n up** (*fig*) es ist unter Dach und Fach
sewage ['su:ɪdʒ] *n* Abwasser *nt*
sewage works *n* Kläranlage *f*
sewer ['su:ə^r] *n* Abwasserkanal *m*
sewing ['səuɪŋ] *n* Nähen *nt*; (*items*) Näharbeit *f*
sewing machine *n* Nähmaschine *f*
sewn [səun] *pp of* **sew**
sex [sɛks] *n* (*gender*) Geschlecht *nt*; (*lovemaking*) Sex *m*; **to have ~ with sb** (Geschlechts)verkehr mit jdm haben
sex act *n* Geschlechtsakt *m*
sex appeal *n* Sex-Appeal *m*
sex education *n* Sexualerziehung *f*

sexism ['sɛksɪzəm] *n* Sexismus *m*
sexist ['sɛksɪst] *adj* sexistisch
sex life *n* Sexualleben *nt*
sex object *n* Sexualobjekt *nt*
sextet [sɛks'tɛt] *n* Sextett *nt*
sexual ['sɛksjuəl] *adj* sexuell; (*reproduction*) geschlechtlich; (*equality*) der Geschlechter
sexual assault *n* Vergewaltigung *f*
sexual harassment *n* sexuelle Belästigung *f*
sexual intercourse *n* Geschlechtsverkehr *m*
sexually ['sɛksjuəlɪ] *adv* sexuell; (*segregate*) nach Geschlechtern; (*discriminate*) aufgrund des Geschlechts; (*reproduce*) geschlechtlich
sexual orientation *n* sexuelle Orientierung *f*
sexy ['sɛksɪ] *adj* sexy; (*pictures, underwear*) sexy, aufreizend
Seychelles [seɪ'ʃɛl(z)] *npl*: **the ~** die Seychellen *pl*
SF *n abbr* (*= science fiction*) SF
SG (*US*) *n abbr* (*Mil, Med*) = **Surgeon General**
Sgt *abbr* (*Police, Mil*) = **sergeant**
shabbiness ['ʃæbɪnɪs] *n* Schäbigkeit *f*
shabby ['ʃæbɪ] *adj* schäbig
shack [ʃæk] *n* Hütte *f*
▸ **shack up** (*inf*) *vi*: **to ~ up (with sb)** (mit jdm) zusammenziehen
shackles ['ʃæklz] *npl* Ketten *pl*; (*fig*) Fesseln *pl*
shade [ʃeɪd] *n* Schatten *m*; (*for lamp*) (Lampen)schirm *m*; (*of colour*) (Farb)ton *m*; (*US*: *also*: **window shade**) Jalousie *f*, Rollo *nt* ▹ *vt* beschatten; (*eyes*) abschirmen; **shades** *npl* (*inf*: *sunglasses*) Sonnenbrille *f*; **in the ~** im Schatten; **a ~ of blue** ein Blauton; **a ~ (more/too large)** (*small quantity*) etwas *or* eine Spur (mehr/zu groß)
shadow ['ʃædəu] *n* Schatten *m* ▹ *vt* (*follow*) beschatten; **without** *or* **beyond a ~ of a doubt** ohne den geringsten Zweifel
shadow cabinet (*Brit*) *n* Schattenkabinett *nt*
shadow economy *n* (*Econ*) Schattenwirtschaft *f*
shadowy ['ʃædəuɪ] *adj* schattig; (*figure, shape*) schattenhaft
shady ['ʃeɪdɪ] *adj* schattig; (*fig*: *dishonest*) zwielichtig; **~ deals** dunkle Geschäfte
shaft [ʃɑːft] *n* (*of arrow, spear*) Schaft *m*; (*Aut, Tech*) Welle *f*; (*of mine, lift*) Schacht *m*; (*of light*) Strahl *m*; **ventilation ~** Luftschacht *m*
shaggy ['ʃægɪ] *adj* zottelig; (*dog, sheep*) struppig
shake [ʃeɪk] (*pt* **shook**, *pp* **~n**) *vt* schütteln; (*weaken, upset, surprise*) erschüttern; (*weaken*: *resolve*) ins Wanken bringen ▹ *vi* zittern, beben; (*building, table*) wackeln; (*earth*) beben ▹ *n* Schütteln *nt*; **to ~ one's head** den Kopf schütteln; **to ~ hands with sb** jdm die Hand schütteln; **to ~ one's fist (at sb)** (jdm) mit der Faust drohen; **give it a good ~** schütteln Sie es gut durch; **a ~ of the head** ein Kopfschütteln
▸ **shake off** *vt* (*lit, fig*) abschütteln
▸ **shake up** *vt* schütteln; (*fig*: *upset*) erschüttern
shake-out ['ʃeɪkaut] *n* Freisetzung *f* von Arbeitskräften
shake-up ['ʃeɪkʌp] *n* (radikale) Veränderung *f*
shakily ['ʃeɪkɪlɪ] *adv* (*reply*) mit zittriger Stimme; (*walk, stand*) unsicher, wackelig
shaky ['ʃeɪkɪ] *adj* (*hand, voice*) zittrig; (*memory*) schwach; (*knowledge, prospects, future, start*) unsicher
shale [ʃeɪl] *n* Schiefer *m*
shall [ʃæl] *aux vb*: **I ~ go** ich werde gehen; **~ I open the door?** soll ich die Tür öffnen?; **I'll go, ~ I?** soll ich gehen?
shallot [ʃə'lɔt] (*Brit*) *n* Schalotte *f*
shallow ['ʃæləu] *adj* flach; (*fig*) oberflächlich; **the shallows** *npl* die Untiefen *pl*
sham [ʃæm] *n* Heuchelei *f*; (*person*) Heuchler(in) *m(f)*; (*object*) Attrappe *f* ▹ *adj* unecht; (*fight*) Schein- ▹ *vt* vortäuschen
shambles ['ʃæmblz] *n* heilloses Durcheinander *nt*; **the economy is (in) a complete ~** die Wirtschaft befindet sich in einem totalen Chaos
shambolic [ʃæm'bɔlɪk] (*inf*) *adj* chaotisch
shame [ʃeɪm] *n* Scham *f*; (*disgrace*) Schande *f* ▹ *vt* beschämen; **it is a ~ that …** es ist eine Schande, dass …; **what a ~!** wie schade!; **to bring ~ on** Schande bringen über *+acc*; **to put sb/sth to ~** jdn/etw in den Schatten stellen
shamefaced ['ʃeɪmfeɪst] *adj* betreten
shameful ['ʃeɪmful] *adj* schändlich
shameless ['ʃeɪmlɪs] *adj* schamlos
shampoo [ʃæm'puː] *n* Shampoo(n) *nt* ▹ *vt* waschen
shampoo and set *n* Waschen und Legen *nt*
shamrock ['ʃæmrɔk] *n* (*plant*) Klee *m*; (*leaf*) Kleeblatt *nt*
shandy ['ʃændɪ] *n* Bier *nt* mit Limonade, Radler *m*
shan't [ʃɑːnt] = **shall not**
shantytown ['ʃæntɪtaun] *n* Elendsviertel *nt*
SHAPE [ʃeɪp] *n abbr* (*Mil*: *= Supreme Headquarters Allied Powers, Europe*) *Hauptquartier der alliierten Streitkräfte in Europa während des 2. Weltkriegs*
shape [ʃeɪp] *n* Form *f* ▹ *vt* gestalten; (*form*) formen; (*sb's ideas*) prägen; (*sb's life*) bestimmen; **to take ~** Gestalt annehmen; **in the ~ of a heart** in Herzform; **I can't bear gardening in any ~ or form** ich kann Gartenarbeit absolut nicht ausstehen; **to get (o.s.) into ~** in Form kommen
▸ **shape up** *vi* sich entwickeln
-shaped [ʃeɪpt] *suff*: **heart-~** herzförmig
shapeless ['ʃeɪplɪs] *adj* formlos
shapely ['ʃeɪplɪ] *adj* (*woman*) wohlproportioniert; (*legs*) wohlgeformt
share [ʃɛəʳ] *n* (*part*) Anteil *m*; (*contribution*) Teil *m*; (*Comm*) Aktie *f* ▹ *vt* teilen; (*room, bed, taxi*) sich *dat* teilen; (*have in common*) gemeinsam haben; **to ~ in** (*joy, sorrow*) teilen; (*profits*) beteiligt sein an *+dat*; (*work*) sich beteiligen an *+dat*
▸ **share out** *vt* aufteilen
share capital *n* Aktienkapital *nt*
share certificate *n* Aktienurkunde *f*
shareholder ['ʃɛəhəuldəʳ] *n* Aktionär(in) *m(f)*
share index *n* Aktienindex *m*; **the 100 Share**

Index *Aktienindex der Financial Times*
share issue *n* Aktienemission *f*
shark [ʃɑ:k] *n* Hai(fisch) *m*
sharp [ʃɑ:p] *adj* scharf; (*point, nose, chin*) spitz; (*pain*) heftig; (*cold*) schneidend; (*Mus*) zu hoch; (*increase*) stark; (*person: quick-witted*) clever; (*: dishonest*) gerissen ▷ *n* (*Mus*) Kreuz *nt* ▷ *adv*: **at 2 o'clock ~** um Punkt 2 Uhr; **turn ~ left** biegen Sie scharf nach links ab; **to be ~ with sb** schroff mit jdm sein; **~ practices** (*Comm*) unsaubere Geschäfte *pl*; **C ~** (*Mus*) Cis *nt*; **look ~!** (ein bisschen) dalli! (*inf*)
sharpen ['ʃɑ:pn] *vt* schleifen, schärfen; (*pencil, stick etc*) (an)spitzen; (*fig: appetite*) anregen
sharpener ['ʃɑ:pnə^r] *n* (*also*: **pencil sharpener**) (Bleistift)spitzer *m*; (*also*: **knife sharpener**) Schleifgerät *nt*
sharp-eyed [ʃɑ:p'aɪd] *adj* scharfsichtig
sharpish ['ʃɑ:pɪʃ] (*inf*) *adj* (*instantly*) auf der Stelle
sharply ['ʃɑ:plɪ] *adv* scharf; (*stop*) plötzlich; (*retort*) schroff
sharp-tempered [ʃɑ:p'tɛmpəd] *adj* jähzornig
sharp-witted [ʃɑ:p'wɪtɪd] *adj* scharfsinnig
shatter ['ʃætə^r] *vt* zertrümmern; (*fig: hopes, dreams*) zunichtemachen; (*: confidence*) zerstören ▷ *vi* zerbrechen, zerspringen
shattered ['ʃætəd] *adj* erschüttert; (*inf: exhausted*) fertig, kaputt
shattering ['ʃætərɪŋ] *adj* erschütternd, niederschmetternd; (*exhausting*) äußerst anstrengend
shatterproof ['ʃætəpru:f] *adj* splitterfest, splitterfrei
shave [ʃeɪv] *vt* rasieren ▷ *vi* sich rasieren ▷ *n*: **to have a ~** sich rasieren
shaven ['ʃeɪvn] *adj* (*head*) kahl geschoren
shaver ['ʃeɪvə^r] *n* (*also*: **electric shaver**) Rasierapparat *m*
shaving ['ʃeɪvɪŋ] *n* Rasieren *nt*; **shavings** *npl* (*of wood etc*) Späne *pl*
shaving brush *n* Rasierpinsel *m*
shaving cream *n* Rasiercreme *f*
shaving foam *n* Rasierschaum *m*
shaving point *n* Steckdose *f* für Rasierapparate
shaving soap *n* Rasierseife *f*
shawl [ʃɔ:l] *n* (Woll)tuch *nt*
she [ʃi:] *pron* sie ▷ *pref* weiblich; **~-bear** Bärin *f*; **there ~ is** da ist sie
sheaf [ʃi:f] (*pl* **sheaves**) *n* (*of corn*) Garbe *f*; (*of papers*) Bündel *nt*
shear [ʃɪə^r] (*pt* **~ed**, *pp* **shorn**) *vt* scheren
▸ **shear off** *vi* abbrechen
shears ['ʃɪəz] *npl* (*for hedge*) Heckenschere *f*
sheath [ʃi:θ] *n* (*of knife*) Scheide *f*; (*contraceptive*) Kondom *nt*
sheathe [ʃi:ð] *vt* ummanteln; (*sword*) in die Scheide stecken
sheath knife *n* Fahrtenmesser *nt*
sheaves [ʃi:vz] *npl of* **sheaf**
shed [ʃɛd] (*pt, pp* **~**) *n* Schuppen *m*; (*Industry, Rail*) Halle *f* ▷ *vt* (*tears, blood*) vergießen; (*load*) verlieren; (*workers*) entlassen; **to ~ its skin** sich häuten; **to ~ light on** (*problem*) erhellen
she'd [ʃi:d] = **she had; she would**
sheen [ʃi:n] *n* Glanz *m*
sheep [ʃi:p] *n inv* Schaf *nt*
sheepdog ['ʃi:pdɔg] *n* Hütehund *m*
sheep farmer *n* Schaffarmer *m*
sheepish ['ʃi:pɪʃ] *adj* verlegen
sheepskin ['ʃi:pskɪn] *n* Schaffell *nt* ▷ *cpd* Schaffell-
sheer [ʃɪə^r] *adj* (*utter*) rein; (*steep*) steil; (*almost transparent*) (hauch)dünn ▷ *adv* (*straight up*) senkrecht; **by ~ chance** rein zufällig
sheet [ʃi:t] *n* (*on bed*) (Bett)laken *nt*; (*of paper*) Blatt *nt*; (*of glass, metal*) Platte *f*; (*of ice*) Fläche *f*
sheet feed *n* (*on printer*) Papiereinzug *m*
sheet lightning *n* Wetterleuchten *nt*
sheet metal *n* Walzblech *nt*
sheet music *n* Notenblätter *pl*
sheik, sheikh [ʃeɪk] *n* Scheich *m*
shelf [ʃɛlf] (*pl* **shelves**) *n* Brett *nt*, Bord *nt*; **set of shelves** Regal *nt*
shelf life *n* Lagerfähigkeit *f*
shell [ʃɛl] *n* (*on beach*) Muschel *f*; (*of egg, nut etc*) Schale *f*; (*explosive*) Granate *f*; (*of building*) Mauern *pl* ▷ *vt* (*peas*) enthülsen; (*Mil: fire on*) (mit Granaten) beschießen
▸ **shell out** (*inf*) *vt*: **to ~ out (for)** blechen (für)
she'll [ʃi:l] = **she will; she shall**
shellfish ['ʃɛlfɪʃ] *n inv* Schalentier *nt*; (*scallop etc*) Muschel *f*; (*as food*) Meeresfrüchte *pl*
shelter ['ʃɛltə^r] *n* (*building*) Unterstand *m*; (*refuge*) Schutz *m*; (*also*: **bus shelter**) Wartehäuschen *nt*; (*also*: **night shelter**) Obdachlosenasyl *nt* ▷ *vt* (*protect*) schützen; (*homeless, refugees*) aufnehmen; (*wanted man*) Unterschlupf gewähren *+dat* ▷ *vi* sich unterstellen; (*from storm*) Schutz suchen; **to take ~ (from)** (*from danger*) sich in Sicherheit bringen (vor *+dat*); (*from storm etc*) Schutz suchen (vor *+dat*)
sheltered ['ʃɛltəd] *adj* (*life*) behütet; (*spot*) geschützt; **~ housing** (*for old people*) Altenwohnungen *pl*; (*for handicapped people*) Behindertenwohnungen *pl*
shelve [ʃɛlv] *vt* (*fig: plan*) ad acta legen
shelves [ʃɛlvz] *npl of* **shelf**
shelving ['ʃɛlvɪŋ] *n* Regale *pl*
shepherd ['ʃɛpəd] *n* Schäfer *m* ▷ *vt* (*guide*) führen
shepherdess ['ʃɛpədɪs] *n* Schäferin *f*
shepherd's pie (*Brit*) *n* *Auflauf aus Hackfleisch und Kartoffelbrei*
sherbet ['ʃə:bət] *n* (*Brit: powder*) Brausepulver *nt*; (*US: water ice*) Fruchteis *nt*
sheriff ['ʃɛrɪf] (*US*) *n* Sheriff *m*
sherry ['ʃɛrɪ] *n* Sherry *m*
she's [ʃi:z] = **she is; she has**
Shetland ['ʃɛtlənd] *n* (*also*: **the Shetland Islands**) die Shetlandinseln *pl*
Shetland pony *n* Shetlandpony *nt*
shield [ʃi:ld] *n* (*Mil*) Schild *m*; (*trophy*) Trophäe *f*; (*fig: protection*) Schutz *m* ▷ *vt*: **to ~ (from)** schützen (vor *+dat*)
shift [ʃɪft] *n* (*change*) Änderung *f*; (*work-*

period, workers) Schicht *f* ▷ *vt* (*move*) bewegen; (*furniture*) (ver)rücken; (*stain*) herausbekommen ▷ *vi* (*move*) sich bewegen; (*wind*) drehen; **a ~ in demand** (*Comm*) eine Nachfrageverschiebung
shift key *n* Umschalttaste *f*
shiftless ['ʃɪftlɪs] *adj* träge
shift work *n* Schichtarbeit *f*; **to do ~** Schicht arbeiten
shifty ['ʃɪftɪ] *adj* verschlagen
Shiite ['ʃi:aɪt] *adj* schiitisch ▷ *n* Schiit(in) *m(f)*
shilling ['ʃɪlɪŋ] (*Brit: old*) *n* Shilling *m*
shilly-shally ['ʃɪlɪʃælɪ] *vi* unschlüssig sein
shimmer ['ʃɪmə^r] *vi* schimmern
shimmering ['ʃɪmərɪŋ] *adj* schimmernd
shin [ʃɪn] *n* Schienbein *nt* ▷ *vi*: **to ~ up a tree** einen Baum hinaufklettern
shindig ['ʃɪndɪg] (*inf*) *n* Remmidemmi *nt*
shine [ʃaɪn] (*pt, pp* **shone**) *n* Glanz *m* ▷ *vi* (*sun, light*) scheinen; (*eyes*) leuchten; (*hair: fig: person*) glänzen ▷ *vt* (*polish: pt, pp shined*) polieren; **to ~ a torch on sth** etw mit einer Taschenlampe anleuchten
shingle ['ʃɪŋgl] *n* (*on beach*) Kiesel(steine) *pl*; (*on roof*) Schindel *f*
shingles ['ʃɪŋglz] *npl* (*Med*) Gürtelrose *f*
shining ['ʃaɪnɪŋ] *adj* glänzend; (*example*) leuchtend
shiny ['ʃaɪnɪ] *adj* glänzend
ship [ʃɪp] *n* Schiff *nt* ▷ *vt* verschiffen; (*send*) versenden; (*water*) übernehmen; **on board ~** an Bord
shipbuilder ['ʃɪpbɪldə^r] *n* Schiffbauer *m*
shipbuilding ['ʃɪpbɪldɪŋ] *n* Schiffbau *m*
ship canal *n* Seekanal *m*
ship chandler [-'tʃɑ:ndlə^r] *n* Schiffsausrüster *m*
shipment ['ʃɪpmənt] *n* (*of goods*) Versand *m*; (*amount*) Sendung *f*
shipowner ['ʃɪpəunə^r] *n* Schiffseigner *m*; (*of many ships*) Reeder *m*
shipper ['ʃɪpə^r] *n* (*person*) Spediteur *m*; (*company*) Spedition *f*
shipping ['ʃɪpɪŋ] *n* (*transport*) Versand *m*; (*ships*) Schiffe *pl*
shipping agent *n* Reeder *m*
shipping company *n* Schifffahrtslinie *f*, Reederei *f*
shipping lane *n* Schifffahrtsstraße *f*
shipping line *n* = **shipping company**
shipshape ['ʃɪpʃeɪp] *adj* tipptopp (*inf*)
shipwreck ['ʃɪprɛk] *n* Schiffbruch *m*; (*ship*) Wrack *nt* ▷ *vt*: **to be ~ed** schiffbrüchig sein
shipyard ['ʃɪpjɑ:d] *n* Werft *f*
shire ['ʃaɪə^r] (*Brit*) *n* Grafschaft *f*
shirk [ʃə:k] *vt* sich drücken vor +*dat*
shirt [ʃə:t] *n* (Ober)hemd *nt*; (*woman's*) (Hemd)bluse *f*; **in (one's) ~ sleeves** in Hemdsärmeln
shirty ['ʃə:tɪ] (*Brit: inf*) *adj* sauer (*inf*)
shit [ʃɪt] (*inf!*) *excl* Scheiße (*!*)
shiver ['ʃɪvə^r] *n* Schauer *m* ▷ *vi* zittern; **to ~ with cold** vor Kälte zittern
shoal [ʃəul] *n* (*of fish*) Schwarm *m*; (*also*: **shoals**: *fig*) Scharen *pl*
shock [ʃɔk] *n* Schock *m*; (*impact*) Erschütterung *f*; (*also*: **electric shock**) Schlag *m* ▷ *vt* (*upset*) erschüttern; (*offend*) schockieren; **to be suffering from ~** (*Med*) einen Schock haben; **to be in ~** unter Schock stehen; **it gave us a ~** es hat uns erschreckt; **it came as a ~ to hear that ...** wir hörten mit Bestürzung, dass ...
shock absorber *n* (*Aut*) Stoßdämpfer *m*
shocker ['ʃɔkə^r] (*inf*) *n* (*film etc*) Schocker *m*, Reißer *m*; **that's a real ~** (*event etc*) das haut einen echt um
shocking ['ʃɔkɪŋ] *adj* schrecklich, fürchterlich; (*outrageous*) schockierend
shockproof ['ʃɔkpru:f] *adj* stoßfest
shock therapy *n* Schocktherapie *f*
shock treatment *n* = **shock therapy**
shock wave *n* (*lit*) Druckwelle *f*; (*fig*) Schockwelle *f*
shod [ʃɔd] *pt, pp of* **shoe**
shoddy ['ʃɔdɪ] *adj* minderwertig
shoe [ʃu:] (*pt, pp* **shod**) *n* Schuh *m*; (*for horse*) Hufeisen *nt*; (*also*: **brake shoe**) Bremsbacke *f* ▷ *vt* (*horse*) beschlagen
shoebrush ['ʃu:brʌʃ] *n* Schuhbürste *f*
shoehorn ['ʃu:hɔ:n] *n* Schuhanzieher *m*
shoelace ['ʃu:leɪs] *n* Schnürsenkel *m*
shoemaker ['ʃu:meɪkə^r] *n* Schuhmacher *m*, Schuster *m*
shoe polish *n* Schuhcreme *f*
shoe shop *n* Schuhgeschäft *nt*
shoestring ['ʃu:strɪŋ] *n* (*fig*): **on a ~** mit ganz wenig Geld
shoetree ['ʃu:tri:] *n* Schuhspanner *m*
shone [ʃɔn] *pt, pp of* **shine**
shoo [ʃu:] *excl* (*to dog etc*) pfui ▷ *vt* (*also*: **shoo away, shoo off,** *etc*) verscheuchen; (*somewhere*) scheuchen
shook [ʃuk] *pt of* **shake**
shoot [ʃu:t] (*pt, pp* **shot**) *n* (*on branch*) Trieb *m*; (*seedling*) Sämling *m*; (*Sport*) Jagd *f* ▷ *vt* (*gun*) abfeuern; (*arrow, goal*) schießen; (*kill, execute*) erschießen; (*wound*) anschießen; (*Brit: game birds*) schießen; (*film*) drehen ▷ *vi*: **to ~ (at)** schießen (auf +*acc*); **to ~ past (sb/sth)** (an jdm/etw) vorbeischießen
▸ **shoot down** *vt* abschießen
▸ **shoot in** *vi* hereingeschossen kommen
▸ **shoot out (of)** *vi* herausgeschossen kommen (aus +*dat*)
▸ **shoot up** *vi* (*fig: increase*) in die Höhe schnellen
shooting ['ʃu:tɪŋ] *n* Schießen *nt*, Schüsse *pl*; (*attack*) Schießerei *f*; (*murder*) Erschießung *f*; (*Cine*) Drehen *nt*; (*Hunting*) Jagen *nt*
shooting range *n* Schießplatz *m*
shooting star *n* Sternschnuppe *f*
shop [ʃɔp] *n* Geschäft *nt*, Laden *m*; (*workshop*) Werkstatt *f* ▷ *vi* (*also*: **go shopping**) einkaufen (gehen); **repair ~** Reparaturwerkstatt *f*; **to talk ~** (*fig*) über die Arbeit reden
▸ **shop around** *vi* Preise vergleichen; (*fig*) sich umsehen

shopaholic [ˈʃɔpəˈhɔlɪk] *(inf)* *n*: **to be a ~** einen Einkaufsfimmel haben
shop assistant *(Brit)* *n* Verkäufer(in) *m(f)*
shop floor *(Brit)* *n* *(workers)* Arbeiter *pl*; **on the ~** bei *or* unter den Arbeitern
shopkeeper [ˈʃɔpkiːpəʳ] *n* Geschäftsinhaber(in) *m(f)*, Ladenbesitzer(in) *m(f)*
shoplifter [ˈʃɔplɪftəʳ] *n* Ladendieb(in) *m(f)*
shoplifting [ˈʃɔplɪftɪŋ] *n* Ladendiebstahl *m*
shopper [ˈʃɔpəʳ] *n* Käufer(in) *m(f)*
shopping [ˈʃɔpɪŋ] *n* *(goods)* Einkäufe *pl*
shopping bag *n* Einkaufstasche *f*
shopping centre, *(US)* **shopping center** *n* Einkaufszentrum *nt*
shopping mall *n* Shoppingcenter *nt*
shop-soiled [ˈʃɔpsɔɪld] *adj* angeschmutzt
shop steward *(Brit)* *n* gewerkschaftlicher Vertrauensmann *m*
shop window *n* Schaufenster *nt*
shore [ʃɔːʳ] *n* Ufer *nt*; *(beach)* Strand *m* ▷ *vt*: **to ~ (up)** abstützen; **on ~** an Land
shore leave *n* *(Naut)* Landurlaub *m*
shorn [ʃɔːn] *pp of* **shear**; **to be ~ of** *(power etc)* entkleidet sein *+gen*
short [ʃɔːt] *adj* kurz; *(person)* klein; *(curt)* schroff, kurz angebunden *(inf)*; *(scarce)* knapp ▷ *n* *(also:* **short film***)* Kurzfilm *m*; **to be ~ of ...** zu wenig ... haben; **I'm 3 ~** ich habe 3 zu wenig, mir fehlen 3; **in ~** kurz gesagt; **to be in ~ supply** knapp sein; **it is ~ for ...** es ist die Kurzform von ...; **a ~ time ago** vor Kurzem; **in the ~ term** auf kurze Sicht; **~ of doing sth** außer etw zu tun; **to cut ~** abbrechen; **everything ~ of ...** alles außer ... *+dat*; **to fall ~ of sth** etw nicht erreichen; *(expectations)* etw nicht erfüllen; **to run ~ of ...** nicht mehr viel ... haben; **to stop ~** plötzlich innehalten; **to stop ~ of** haltmachen vor *+dat*; *see also* **shorts**
shortage [ˈʃɔːtɪdʒ] *n*: **a ~ of** ein Mangel *m* an *+dat*
shortbread [ˈʃɔːtbrɛd] *n* Mürbegebäck *nt*
short-change [ʃɔːtˈtʃeɪndʒ] *vt*: **to ~ sb** jdm zu wenig Wechselgeld geben
short circuit *n* Kurzschluss *m*
shortcoming [ˈʃɔːtkʌmɪŋ] *n* Fehler *m*, Mangel *m*
shortcrust pastry *(Brit)* *n* Mürbeteig *m*
short cut *n* Abkürzung *f*; *(fig)* Schnellverfahren *nt*
shorten [ˈʃɔːtn] *vt* verkürzen
shortening [ˈʃɔːtnɪŋ] *n* (Back)fett *nt*
shortfall [ˈʃɔːtfɔːl] *n* Defizit *nt*
shorthand [ˈʃɔːthænd] *n* Kurzschrift *f*, Stenografie *f*; *(fig)* Kurzform *f*; **to take sth down in ~** etw stenografieren
shorthand notebook *(Brit)* *n* Stenoblock *m*
shorthand typist *(Brit)* *n* Stenotypist(in) *m(f)*
short list *(Brit)* *n* Auswahlliste *f*; **to be on the ~** in der engeren Wahl sein
short-list [ˈʃɔːtlɪst] *(Brit)* *vt* in die engere Wahl ziehen; **to be ~ed** in die engere Wahl kommen
short-lived [ˈʃɔːtˈlɪvd] *adj* kurzlebig; **to be ~** nicht von Dauer sein
shortly [ˈʃɔːtlɪ] *adv* bald
shorts [ʃɔːts] *npl*: **(a pair of) ~** Shorts *pl*
short-sighted [ʃɔːtˈsaɪtɪd] *(Brit)* *adj* *(lit, fig)* kurzsichtig
short-sightedness [ʃɔːtˈsaɪtɪdnɪs] *n* Kurzsichtigkeit *f*
short-staffed [ʃɔːtˈstɑːft] *adj*: **to be ~** zu wenig Personal haben
short story *n* Kurzgeschichte *f*
short-tempered [ʃɔːtˈtɛmpəd] *adj* gereizt
short-term [ˈʃɔːttəːm] *adj* kurzfristig
short time *n*: **to work ~, to be on ~** kurzarbeiten, Kurzarbeit haben
short-wave [ˈʃɔːtweɪv] *(Radio)* *adj* auf Kurzwelle ▷ *n* Kurzwelle *f*
shot [ʃɔt] *pt, pp of* **shoot** ▷ *n* Schuss *m*; *(shotgun pellets)* Schrot *m*; *(injection)* Spritze *f*; *(Phot)* Aufnahme *f*; **to fire a ~ at sb/sth** einen Schuss auf jdn/etw abgeben; **to have a ~ at (doing) sth** etw mal versuchen; **to get ~ of sb/sth** *(inf)* jdn/etw loswerden; **a big ~** *(inf)* ein hohes Tier; **a good/poor ~** *(person)* ein guter/schlechter Schütze; **like a ~** sofort
shotgun [ˈʃɔtgʌn] *n* Schrotflinte *f*
should [ʃud] *aux vb*: **I ~ go now** ich sollte jetzt gehen; **he ~ be there now** er müsste eigentlich schon da sein; **I ~ go if I were you** an deiner Stelle würde ich gehen; **I ~ like to** ich möchte gerne, ich würde gerne; **~ he phone ...** falls er anruft ...
shoulder [ˈʃəuldəʳ] *n* Schulter *f* ▷ *vt* *(fig)* auf sich *acc* nehmen; **to rub ~s with sb** *(fig)* mit jdm in Berührung kommen; **to give sb the cold ~** *(fig)* jdm die kalte Schulter zeigen
shoulder bag *n* Umhängetasche *f*
shoulder blade *n* Schulterblatt *nt*
shoulder strap *n* *(on clothing)* Träger *m*; *(on bag)* Schulterriemen *m*
shouldn't [ˈʃudnt] = **should not**
shout [ʃaut] *n* Schrei *m*, Ruf *m* ▷ *vt* schreien, rufen ▷ *vi* *(also:* **shout out***)* aufschreien; **to give sb a ~** jdn rufen
▸ **shout down** *vt* niederbrüllen
shouting [ˈʃautɪŋ] *n* Geschrei *nt*
shouting match *(inf)* *n*: **to have a ~** sich gegenseitig anschreien
shove [ʃʌv] *vt* schieben; *(with one push)* stoßen, schubsen *(inf)* ▷ *n*: **to give sb a ~** jdn stoßen *or* schubsen *(inf)*; **to give sth a ~** etw verrücken; *(door)* gegen etw stoßen; **to ~ sth in sth** *(inf: put)* etw in etw *acc* stecken; **he ~d me out of the way** er stieß mich zur Seite
▸ **shove off** *(inf)* *vi* abschieben
shovel [ˈʃʌvl] *n* Schaufel *f*; *(mechanical)* Bagger *m* ▷ *vt* schaufeln
show [ʃəu] *(pt* **~ed**, *pp* **~n***)* *n* *(exhibition)* Ausstellung *f*, Schau *f*; *(Theat)* Aufführung *f*; *(TV)* Show *f*; *(Cine)* Vorstellung *f* ▷ *vt* zeigen; *(exhibit)* ausstellen ▷ *vi*: **it ~s** man sieht es; *(is evident)* man merkt es; **to ask for a ~ of hands** um Handzeichen bitten; **without any ~ of**

emotion ohne jede Gefühlsregung; **it's just for ~** es ist nur zur Schau; **on ~** ausgestellt, zu sehen; **who's running the ~ here?** (*inf*) wer ist hier verantwortlich?; **to ~ sb to his seat/to the door** jdn an seinen Platz/zur Tür bringen; **to ~ a profit/loss** Gewinn/Verlust aufweisen; **it just goes to ~ that ...** da sieht mans mal wieder, dass
▸ **show in** *vt* hereinführen
▸ **show off** (*pej*) *vi* angeben ▹ *vt* vorführen
▸ **show out** *vt* hinausbegleiten
▸ **show up** *vi* (*stand out*) sich abheben; (*inf: turn up*) auftauchen ▹ *vt* (*uncover*) deutlich erkennen lassen; (*shame*) blamieren

showbiz *n* = **show business**
show business *n* Showgeschäft *nt*
showcase ['ʃəukeɪs] *n* Schaukasten *m*; (*fig*) Werbung *f*
showdown ['ʃəudaun] *n* Kraftprobe *f*
shower ['ʃauə^r] *n* (*of rain*) Schauer *m*; (*of stones etc*) Hagel *m*; (*for bathing in*) Dusche *f*; (*US: party*) *Party, bei der jeder ein Geschenk für den Ehrengast mitbringt* ▹ *vi* duschen ▹ *vt*: **to ~ sb with** (*gifts etc*) jdn überschütten mit; (*missiles, abuse etc*) auf jdn niederhageln lassen; **to have** *or* **take a ~** duschen; **a ~ of sparks** ein Funkenregen *m*
showercap ['ʃauəkæp] *n* Duschhaube *f*
showerproof ['ʃauəpru:f] *adj* regenfest
showery ['ʃauərɪ] *adj* regnerisch
showground ['ʃəugraund] *n* Ausstellungsgelände *nt*
showing ['ʃəuɪŋ] *n* (*of film*) Vorführung *f*
show jumping *n* Springreiten *nt*
showman ['ʃəumən] (*irreg: like* **man**) *n* (*at fair*) Schausteller *m*; (*at circus*) Artist *m*; (*fig*) Schauspieler *m*
showmanship ['ʃəumənʃɪp] *n* Talent *nt* für effektvolle Darbietung
shown [ʃəun] *pp of* **show**
show-off ['ʃəuɔf] (*inf*) *n* Angeber(in) *m(f)*
showpiece ['ʃəupi:s] *n* (*of exhibition etc*) Schaustück *nt*; (*best example*) Paradestück *nt*; (*prime example*) Musterbeispiel *nt*
showroom ['ʃəurum] *n* Ausstellungsraum *m*
show trial *n* Schauprozess *m*
showy ['ʃəuɪ] *adj* auffallend
shrank [ʃræŋk] *pt of* **shrink**
shrapnel ['ʃræpnl] *n* Schrapnell *nt*
shred [ʃrɛd] *n* (*gen pl*) Fetzen *m*; (*fig*): **not a ~ of truth** kein Fünkchen Wahrheit; **not a ~ of evidence** keine Spur eines Beweises ▹ *vt* zerfetzen; (*Culin*) raspeln
shredder ['ʃrɛdə^r] *n* (*also*: **vegetable shredder**) Raspel *f*; (*also*: **document shredder**) Reißwolf *m*; (*also*: **garden shredder**) Häcksler *m*
shrew [ʃru:] *n* (*Zool*) Spitzmaus *f*; (*pej: woman*) Xanthippe *f*
shrewd [ʃru:d] *adj* klug
shrewdness ['ʃru:dnɪs] *n* Klugheit *f*
shriek [ʃri:k] *n* schriller Schrei *m* ▹ *vi* schreien; **to ~ with laughter** vor Lachen quietschen
shrift [ʃrɪft] *n*: **to give sb short ~** jdn kurz abfertigen
shrill [ʃrɪl] *adj* schrill
shrimp [ʃrɪmp] *n* Garnele *f*
shrine [ʃraɪn] *n* Schrein *m*; (*fig*) Gedenkstätte *f*
shrink [ʃrɪŋk] (*pt* **shrank**, *pp* **shrunk**) *vi* (*cloth*) einlaufen; (*profits, audiences*) schrumpfen; (*forests*) schwinden; (*also*: **shrink away**) zurückweichen ▹ *vt* (*cloth*) einlaufen lassen ▹ *n* (*inf: pej*) Klapsdoktor *m*; **to ~ from sth** vor etw *dat* zurückschrecken; **to ~ from doing sth** davor zurückschrecken, etw zu tun
shrinkage ['ʃrɪŋkɪdʒ] *n* (*of clothes*) Einlaufen *nt*
shrink-wrap ['ʃrɪŋkræp] *vt* einschweißen
shrivel ['ʃrɪvl] (*also*: **shrivel up**) *vt* austrocknen ▹ *vi* austrocknen, verschrumpeln
shroud [ʃraud] *n* Leichentuch *nt* ▹ *vt*: **~ed in mystery** von einem Geheimnis umgeben
Shrove Tuesday ['ʃrəuv-] *n* Fastnachtsdienstag *m*
shrub [ʃrʌb] *n* Strauch *m*, Busch *m*
shrubbery ['ʃrʌbərɪ] *n* Gebüsch *nt*
shrug [ʃrʌg] *n*: **~ (of the shoulders)** Achselzucken *nt* ▹ *vi, vt*: **to ~ (one's shoulders)** mit den Achseln zucken
▸ **shrug off** *vt* (*criticism*) auf die leichte Schulter nehmen; (*illness*) abschütteln

shrunk [ʃrʌŋk] *pp of* **shrink**
shrunken ['ʃrʌŋkn] *adj* (ein)geschrumpft
shudder ['ʃʌdə^r] *n* Schauder *m* ▹ *vi* schaudern; **I ~ to think of it** (*fig*) mir graut, wenn ich nur daran denke
shuffle ['ʃʌfl] *vt* (*cards*) mischen ▹ *vi* schlurfen; **to ~ (one's feet)** mit den Füßen scharren
shun [ʃʌn] *vt* meiden; (*publicity*) scheuen
shunt [ʃʌnt] *vt* rangieren
shunting yard ['ʃʌntɪŋ-] *n* Rangierbahnhof *m*
shush [ʃuʃ] *excl* pst!, sch!
shut [ʃʌt] (*pt, pp* **~**) *vt* schließen, zumachen (*inf*) ▹ *vi* sich schließen, zugehen; (*shop*) schließen, zumachen (*inf*)
▸ **shut down** *vt* (*factory etc*) schließen; (*machine*) abschalten ▹ *vi* schließen, zumachen (*inf*)
▸ **shut off** *vt* (*gas, electricity*) abstellen; (*oil supplies etc*) abschneiden
▸ **shut out** *vt* (*person*) aussperren; (*cold, noise*) nicht hereinlassen; (*view*) versperren; (*memory, thought*) verdrängen
▸ **shut up** *vi* (*inf: keep quiet*) den Mund halten ▹ *vt* (*silence*) zum Schweigen bringen

shutdown ['ʃʌtdaun] *n* Schließung *f*
shutter ['ʃʌtə^r] *n* Fensterladen *m*; (*Phot*) Verschluss *m*
shuttle ['ʃʌtl] *n* (*plane*) Pendelflugzeug *nt*; (*train*) Pendelzug *m*; (*also*: **space shuttle**) Raumtransporter *m*; (*also*: **shuttle service**) Pendelverkehr *m*; (*for weaving*) Schiffchen *nt* ▹ *vi*: **to ~ to and fro** pendeln; **to ~ between** pendeln zwischen ▹ *vt* (*passengers*) transportieren
shuttlecock ['ʃʌtlkɔk] *n* Federball *m*
shuttle diplomacy *n* Reisediplomatie *f*
shy [ʃaɪ] *adj* schüchtern; (*animal*) scheu ▹ *vi*: **to ~ away from doing sth** (*fig*) davor zurückschrecken, etw zu tun; **to fight ~ of**

aus dem Weg gehen *+dat*; **to be ~ of doing sth** Hemmungen haben, etw zu tun
shyly [ˈʃaɪlɪ] *adv* schüchtern, scheu
shyness [ˈʃaɪnɪs] *n* Schüchternheit *f*, Scheu *f*
Siam [saɪˈæm] *n* Siam *nt*
Siamese [saɪəˈmiːz] *adj*: **~ cat** Siamkatze *f*; **~ twins** siamesische Zwillinge *pl*
Siberia [saɪˈbɪərɪə] *n* Sibirien *nt*
sibling [ˈsɪblɪŋ] *n* Geschwister *nt*
Sicilian [sɪˈsɪlɪən] *adj* sizilianisch ▷ *n* Sizilianer(in) *m(f)*
Sicily [ˈsɪsɪlɪ] *n* Sizilien *nt*
sick [sɪk] *adj* krank; (*humour, joke*) makaber; **to be ~** (*vomit*) brechen, sich übergeben; **I feel ~** mir ist schlecht; **to fall ~** krank werden; **to be (off) ~** wegen Krankheit fehlen; **a ~ person** ein Kranker, eine Kranke; **to be ~ of** (*fig*) satthaben *+acc*
sickbag [ˈsɪkbæg] *n* Spucktüte *f*
sickbay [ˈsɪkbeɪ] *n* Krankenrevier *nt*
sickbed [ˈsɪkbɛd] *n* Krankenbett *nt*
sick building syndrome *n Kopfschmerzen, Allergien etc, die in modernen, vollklimatisierten Bürogebäuden entstehen*
sicken [ˈsɪkn] *vt* (*disgust*) anwidern ▷ *vi*: **to be ~ing for a cold/flu** eine Erkältung/Grippe bekommen
sickening [ˈsɪknɪŋ] *adj* (*fig*) widerlich, ekelhaft
sickle [ˈsɪkl] *n* Sichel *f*
sick leave *n*: **to be on ~** krankgeschrieben sein
sickle-cell anaemia *n* Sichelzellenanämie *f*
sick list *n*: **to be on the ~** auf der Krankenliste stehen
sickly [ˈsɪklɪ] *adj* kränklich; (*causing nausea*) widerlich, ekelhaft
sickness [ˈsɪknɪs] *n* Krankheit *f*; (*vomiting*) Erbrechen *nt*
sickness benefit *n* Krankengeld *nt*
sick note *n* Krankmeldung *f*
sick pay *n* Lohnfortzahlung *f* im Krankheitsfall; (*paid by insurance*) Krankengeld *nt*
sickroom [ˈsɪkruːm] *n* Krankenzimmer *nt*
side [saɪd] *n* Seite *f*; (*team*) Mannschaft *f*; (*in conflict etc*) Partei *f*, Seite *f*; (*of hill*) Hang *m* ▷ *adj* (*door, entrance*) Seiten-, Neben- ▷ *vi*: **to ~ with sb** jds Partei ergreifen; **by the ~ of** neben *+dat*; **~ by side** Seite an Seite; **the right/wrong ~** (*of cloth*) die rechte/linke Seite; **they are on our ~** sie stehen auf unserer Seite; **she never left my ~** sie wich mir nicht von der Seite; **to put sth to one ~** etw beiseitelegen; **from ~ to side** von einer Seite zur anderen; **to take ~s (with)** Partei ergreifen (für); **a ~ of beef** ein halbes Rind; **a ~ of bacon** eine Speckseite
sideboard [ˈsaɪdbɔːd] *n* Sideboard *nt*; **sideboards** (*Brit*) *npl* = **sideburns**
sideburns [ˈsaɪdbəːnz] *npl* Koteletten *pl*
sidecar [ˈsaɪdkɑːʳ] *n* Beiwagen *m*
side dish *n* Beilage *f*
side drum *n* kleine Trommel *f*
side effect *n* (*Med, fig*) Nebenwirkung *f*
sidekick [ˈsaɪdkɪk] (*inf*) *n* Handlanger *m*
sidelight [ˈsaɪdlaɪt] *n* (*Aut*) Begrenzungsleuchte *f*
sideline [ˈsaɪdlaɪn] *n* (*Sport*) Seitenlinie *f*; (*fig: job*) Nebenerwerb *m*; **to stand on the ~s** (*fig*) unbeteiligter Zuschauer sein; **to wait on the ~s** (*fig*) in den Kulissen warten
sidelong [ˈsaɪdlɔŋ] *adj* (*glance*) Seiten-; (*: surreptitious*) verstohlen; **to give sb a ~ glance** jdn kurz aus den Augenwinkeln ansehen
side plate *n* kleiner Teller *m*
side road *n* Nebenstraße *f*
side-saddle [ˈsaɪdsædl] *adv* (*ride*) im Damensitz
sideshow [ˈsaɪdʃəu] *n* Nebenattraktion *f*
sidestep [ˈsaɪdstɛp] *vt* (*problem*) umgehen; (*question*) ausweichen *+dat* ▷ *vi* (*Boxing etc*) seitwärts ausweichen
side street *n* Seitenstraße *f*
sidetrack [ˈsaɪdtræk] *vt* (*fig*) ablenken
sidewalk [ˈsaɪdwɔːk] (*US*) *n* Bürgersteig *m*
sideways [ˈsaɪdweɪz] *adv* seitwärts; (*lean, look*) zur Seite
siding [ˈsaɪdɪŋ] *n* Abstellgleis *nt*
sidle [ˈsaɪdl] *vi*: **to ~ up (to)** sich heranschleichen (an *+acc*)
SIDS *n abbr* (*Med: = sudden infant death syndrome*) plötzlicher Kindstod *m*
siege [siːdʒ] *n* Belagerung *f*; **to be under ~** belagert sein; **to lay ~ to** belagern
siege economy *n* Belagerungswirtschaft *f*
siege mentality *n* Belagerungsmentalität *f*
Sierra Leone [sɪˈɛrəlɪˈəun] *n* Sierra Leone *f*
siesta [sɪˈɛstə] *n* Siesta *f*
sieve [sɪv] *n* Sieb *nt* ▷ *vt* sieben
sift [sɪft] *vt* sieben; (*also*: **sift through**) durchgehen
sigh [saɪ] *n* Seufzer *m* ▷ *vi* seufzen; **to breathe a ~ of relief** erleichtert aufseufzen
sight [saɪt] *n* (*faculty*) Sehvermögen *nt*, Augenlicht *nt*; (*spectacle*) Anblick *m*; (*on gun*) Visier *nt* ▷ *vt* sichten; **in ~** in Sicht; **on ~** (*shoot*) sofort; **out of ~** außer Sicht; **at ~** (*Comm*) bei Sicht; **at first ~** auf den ersten Blick; **I know her by ~** ich kenne sie vom Sehen; **to catch ~ of sb/sth** jdn/etw sehen; **to lose ~ of sth** (*fig*) etw aus den Augen verlieren; **to set one's ~s on sth** ein Auge auf etw werfen
sighted [ˈsaɪtɪd] *adj* sehend; **partially ~** sehbehindert
sightseeing [ˈsaɪtsiːɪŋ] *n* Besichtigungen *pl*; **to go ~** auf Besichtigungstour gehen
sightseer [ˈsaɪtsiːəʳ] *n* Tourist(in) *m(f)*
sign [saɪn] *n* Zeichen *nt*; (*notice*) Schild *nt*; (*evidence*) Anzeichen *nt*; (*also*: **road sign**) Verkehrsschild *nt* ▷ *vt* unterschreiben; (*player*) verpflichten; **a ~ of the times** ein Zeichen unserer Zeit; **it's a good/bad ~** es ist ein gutes/schlechtes Zeichen; **plus/minus ~** Plus-/Minuszeichen *nt*; **there's no ~ of her changing her mind** nichts deutet darauf hin, dass sie es sich anders überlegen wird; **he was showing ~s of improvement** er ließ Anzeichen einer Verbesserung erkennen; **to ~**

one's name unterschreiben; **to ~ sth over to sb** jdm etw überschreiben
▸ **sign away** *vt* (*rights etc*) verzichten auf *+acc*
▸ **sign in** *vi* sich eintragen
▸ **sign off** *vi* (*Radio, TV*) sich verabschieden; (*in letter*) Schluss machen
▸ **sign on** *vi* (*Mil*) sich verpflichten; (*Brit: as unemployed*) sich arbeitslos melden; (*for course*) sich einschreiben ▹ *vt* (*Mil*) verpflichten; (*employee*) anstellen
▸ **sign out** *vi* (*from hotel etc*) sich (aus dem Hotelgästebuch *etc*) austragen
▸ **sign up** *vi* (*Mil*) sich verpflichten; (*for course*) sich einschreiben ▹ *vt* (*player, recruit*) verpflichten
signal ['sɪgnl] *n* Zeichen *nt*; (*Rail*) Signal *nt* ▹ *vi* (*Aut*) Zeichen/ein Zeichen geben ▹ *vt* ein Zeichen geben *+dat*; **to ~ a right/left turn** (*Aut*) rechts/links blinken
signal box *n* Stellwerk *nt*
signalman ['sɪgnlmən] (*irreg: like* **man**) *n* Stellwerkswärter *m*
signatory ['sɪgnətərɪ] *n* Unterzeichner *m*; (*state*) Signatarstaat *m*
signature ['sɪgnətʃə^r] *n* Unterschrift *f*; (*Zool, Biol*) Kennzeichen *nt*
signature tune *n* Erkennungsmelodie *f*
signet ring ['sɪgnət-] *n* Siegelring *m*
significance [sɪg'nɪfɪkəns] *n* Bedeutung *f*; **that is of no ~** das ist belanglos *or* bedeutungslos
significant [sɪg'nɪfɪkənt] *adj* bedeutend, wichtig; (*look, smile*) vielsagend, bedeutsam; **it is ~ that ...** es ist bezeichnend, dass ...
significantly [sɪg'nɪfɪkəntlɪ] *adv* bedeutend; (*smile*) vielsagend, bedeutsam
signify ['sɪgnɪfaɪ] *vt* bedeuten; (*person*) zu erkennen geben
sign language *n* Zeichensprache *f*
signpost ['saɪnpəust] *n* (*lit, fig*) Wegweiser *m*
Sikh [si:k] *n* Sikh *mf* ▹ *adj* (*province etc*) Sikh-
silage ['saɪlɪdʒ] *n* Silage *f*, Silofutter *nt*
silence ['saɪləns] *n* Stille *f*; (*of person*) Schweigen *nt* ▹ *vt* zum Schweigen bringen; **in ~** still; (*not talking*) schweigend
silencer ['saɪlənsə^r] *n* (*on gun*) Schalldämpfer *m*; (*Brit: Aut*) Auspufftopf *m*
silent ['saɪlənt] *adj* still; (*machine*) ruhig; **~ film** Stummfilm *m*; **to remain ~** still bleiben; (*about sth*) sich nicht äußern
silently ['saɪləntlɪ] *adv* lautlos; (*not talking*) schweigend
silent partner *n* stiller Teilhaber *m*
silhouette [sɪlu:'ɛt] *n* Sihouette *f*, Umriss *m* ▹ *vt*: **to be ~d against sth** sich als Silhouette gegen etw abheben
silicon ['sɪlɪkən] *n* Silizium *nt*
silicon chip *n* Silikonchip *m*
silicone ['sɪlɪkəun] *n* Silikon *nt*
silk [sɪlk] *n* Seide *f* ▹ *adj* (*dress etc*) Seiden-
silky ['sɪlkɪ] *adj* seidig
sill [sɪl] *n* (*also:* **window sill**) (Fenster)sims *m or nt*; (*of door*) Schwelle *f*; (*Aut*) Türleiste *f*
silly ['sɪlɪ] *adj* (*person*) dumm; **to do something ~** etwas Dummes tun
silo ['saɪləu] *n* Silo *nt*; (*for missile*) Raketensilo *nt*
silt [sɪlt] *n* Schlamm *m*, Schlick *m*
▸ **silt up** *vi* verschlammen ▹ *vt* verschlämmen
silver ['sɪlvə^r] *n* Silber *nt*; (*coins*) Silbergeld *nt* ▹ *adj* silbern
silver foil (*Brit*) *n* Alufolie *f*
silver paper (*Brit*) *n* Silberpapier *nt*
silver-plated [sɪlvə'pleɪtɪd] *adj* versilbert
silversmith ['sɪlvəsmɪθ] *n* Silberschmied(in) *m(f)*
silverware ['sɪlvəwɛə^r] *n* Silber *nt*
silver wedding, silver wedding anniversary *n* Silberhochzeit *f*
silvery ['sɪlvrɪ] *adj* silbern; (*sound*) silberhell
SIM card ['sɪmkɑ:d] *n* (*Tel: = Subscriber Identity Module card*) SIM-Karte *f*
similar ['sɪmɪlə^r] *adj*: **~ (to)** ähnlich (wie *or +dat*)
similarity [sɪmɪ'lærɪtɪ] *n* Ähnlichkeit *f*
similarly ['sɪmɪləlɪ] *adv* ähnlich; (*likewise*) genauso
simile ['sɪmɪlɪ] *n* (*Ling*) Vergleich *m*
simmer ['sɪmə^r] *vi* auf kleiner Flamme kochen
▸ **simmer down** (*inf*) *vi* (*fig*) sich abregen
simper ['sɪmpə^r] *vi* geziert lächeln
simpering ['sɪmprɪŋ] *adj* geziert
simple ['sɪmpl] *adj* einfach; (*dress*) einfach, schlicht; (*foolish*) einfältig; **the ~ truth is that ...** es ist einfach so, dass ...
simple interest *n* Kapitalzinsen *pl*
simple-minded [sɪmpl'maɪndɪd] (*pej*) *adj* einfältig
simpleton ['sɪmpltən] (*pej*) *n* Einfaltspinsel *m*
simplicity [sɪm'plɪsɪtɪ] *n* Einfachheit *f*; (*of dress*) Schlichtheit *f*
simplification [sɪmplɪfɪ'keɪʃən] *n* Vereinfachung *f*
simplify ['sɪmplɪfaɪ] *vt* vereinfachen
simply ['sɪmplɪ] *adv* (*just, merely*) nur, bloß; (*in a simple way*) einfach
simulate ['sɪmjuleɪt] *vt* vortäuschen, spielen; (*illness*) simulieren
simulated ['sɪmjuleɪtɪd] *adj* (*hair, fur*) imitiert; (*Tech*) simuliert
simulation [sɪmju'leɪʃən] *n* Vortäuschung *f*; (*simulated object*) Imitation *f*; (*Tech*) Simulation *f*
simultaneous [sɪməl'teɪnɪəs] *adj* gleichzeitig; (*translation, interpreting*) Simultan-
simultaneously [sɪməl'teɪnɪəslɪ] *adv* gleichzeitig
sin [sɪn] *n* Sünde *f* ▹ *vi* sündigen
since [sɪns] *adv* inzwischen, seitdem ▹ *prep* seit ▹ *conj* (*time*) seit(dem); (*because*) da; **~ then, ever since** seitdem
sincere [sɪn'sɪə^r] *adj* aufrichtig, offen; (*apology, belief*) aufrichtig
sincerely [sɪn'sɪəlɪ] *adv* aufrichtig, offen; **yours ~** (*in letter*) mit freundlichen Grüßen
sincerity [sɪn'sɛrɪtɪ] *n* Aufrichtigkeit *f*
sine [saɪn] *n* Sinus *m*
sine qua non [sɪnɪkwɑ:'nɔn] *n* unerlässliche Voraussetzung *f*
sinew ['sɪnju:] *n* Sehne *f*

sinful ['sɪnful] *adj* sündig, sündhaft
sing [sɪŋ] (*pt* **sang**, *pp* **sung**) *vt, vi* singen
Singapore [sɪŋgə'pɔːʳ] *n* Singapur *nt*
singe [sɪndʒ] *vt* versengen; (*lightly*) ansengen
singer ['sɪŋəʳ] *n* Sänger(in) *m(f)*
Singhalese [sɪŋə'liːz] *adj* = **Sinhalese**
singing ['sɪŋɪŋ] *n* Singen *nt*, Gesang *m*; **a ~ in the ears** ein Dröhnen in den Ohren
single ['sɪŋgl] *adj* (*solitary*) einzige(r, s); (*individual*) einzeln; (*unmarried*) ledig, unverheiratet; (*not double*) einfach ▷ *n* (*Brit*: *also*: **single ticket**) Einzelfahrschein *m*; (*record*) Single *f*; **not a ~ one was left** es war kein Einziges mehr übrig; **every ~ day** jeden Tag; **~ spacing** einfacher Zeilenabstand *m*
▸ **single out** *vt* auswählen; **to ~ out for praise** lobend erwähnen
single bed *n* Einzelbett *nt*
single-breasted ['sɪŋglbrɛstɪd] *adj* einreihig
Single European Market *n*: **the ~** der Europäische Binnenmarkt
single file *n*: **in ~** im Gänsemarsch
single-handed [sɪŋgl'hændɪd] *adv* ganz allein
single-minded [sɪŋgl'maɪndɪd] *adj* zielstrebig
single parent *n* Alleinerziehende(r) *f(m)*
single parent family *n* Einelternfamilie *f*
single room *n* Einzelzimmer *nt*
singles ['sɪŋglz] *npl* (*Tennis*) Einzel *nt*
singles bar *n* Singles-Bar *f*
single-sex school *n* reine Jungen-/Mädchenschule *f*; **education in ~s** nach Geschlechtern getrennte Schulerziehung
singly ['sɪŋglɪ] *adv* einzeln
singsong ['sɪŋsɔŋ] *adj* (*tone*) singend ▷ *n*: **to have a ~** zusammen singen
singular ['sɪŋgjuləʳ] *adj* (*odd*) eigenartig; (*outstanding*) einzigartig; (*Ling*: *form etc*) Singular- ▷ *n* (*Ling*) Singular *m*, Einzahl *f*; **in the ~** im Singular
singularly ['sɪŋgjuləlɪ] *adv* außerordentlich
Sinhalese [sɪnhə'liːz] *adj* singhalesisch
sinister ['sɪnɪstəʳ] *adj* unheimlich
sink [sɪŋk] (*pt* **sank**, *pp* **sunk**) *n* Spülbecken *nt* ▷ *vt* (*ship*) versenken; (*well*) bohren; (*foundations*) absenken ▷ *vi* (*ship*) sinken, untergehen; (*ground*) sich senken; (*person*) sinken; **to ~ one's teeth/claws into sth** die Zähne/seine Klauen in etw *acc* schlagen; **his heart/spirits sank at the thought** bei dem Gedanken verließ ihn der Mut; **he sank into the mud/a chair** er sank in den Schlamm ein/in einen Sessel
▸ **sink back** *vi* (zurück)sinken
▸ **sink down** *vi* (nieder)sinken
▸ **sink in** *vi* (*fig*) verstanden werden; **it's only just sunk in** ich begreife es erst jetzt
sinking ['sɪŋkɪŋ] *n* (*of ship*) Untergang *m*; (: *deliberate*) Versenkung *f* ▷ *adj*: **~ feeling** flaues Gefühl *nt* (im Magen)
sinking fund *n* Tilgungsfonds *m*
sink unit *n* Spüle *f*
sinner ['sɪnəʳ] *n* Sünder(in) *m(f)*
Sinn Féin [ʃɪn'feɪn] *n* *republikanisch-nationalistische irische Partei*
Sino- ['saɪnəu] *pref* chinesisch-
sinuous ['sɪnjuəs] *adj* (*snake*) gewunden; (*dance*) geschmeidig
sinus ['saɪnəs] *n* (Nasen)nebenhöhle *f*
sip [sɪp] *n* Schlückchen *nt* ▷ *vt* nippen an +*dat*
siphon ['saɪfən] *n* Heber *m*; (*also*: **soda siphon**) Siphon *m*
▸ **siphon off** *vt* absaugen; (*petrol*) abzapfen
SIPS *n abbr* (= *side impact protection system*) Seitenaufprallschutz *m*
sir [səʳ] *n* mein Herr, Herr X; **S~ John Smith** Sir John Smith; **yes, ~** ja(, Herr X); **Dear S~ (or Madam)** (*in letter*) Sehr geehrte (Damen und) Herren!
siren ['saɪərn] *n* Sirene *f*
sirloin ['səːlɔɪn] *n* (*also*: **sirloin steak**) Filetsteak *nt*
sirocco [sɪ'rɔkəu] *n* Schirokko *m*
sisal ['saɪsəl] *n* Sisal *m*
sissy ['sɪsɪ] (*inf*: *pej*) *n* Waschlappen *m* ▷ *adj* weichlich
sister ['sɪstəʳ] *n* Schwester *f*; (*nun*) (Ordens)schwester *f*; (*Brit*: *nurse*) Oberschwester *f* ▷ *cpd*: **~ organization** Schwesterorganisation *f*; **~ ship** Schwesterschiff *nt*
sister-in-law ['sɪstərɪnlɔː] *n* Schwägerin *f*
sit [sɪt] (*pt, pp* **sat**) *vi* (*sit down*) sich setzen; (*be sitting*) sitzen; (*assembly*) tagen; (*for painter*) Modell sitzen ▷ *vt* (*exam*) machen; **to ~ on a committee** in einem Ausschuss sitzen; **to ~ tight** abwarten
▸ **sit about** *vi* herumsitzen
▸ **sit around** *vi* = **sit about**
▸ **sit back** *vi* sich zurücklehnen
▸ **sit down** *vi* sich (hin)setzen; **to be ~ting down** sitzen
▸ **sit in on** *vt fus* dabei sein bei
▸ **sit up** *vi* sich aufsetzen; (*straight*) sich gerade hinsetzen; (*not go to bed*) aufbleiben
sitcom ['sɪtkɔm] *n abbr* (*TV*) = **situation comedy**
sit-down ['sɪtdaun] *adj*: **a ~ strike** ein Sitzstreik *m*; **a ~ meal** eine richtige Mahlzeit
site [saɪt] *n* (*place*) Platz *m*; (*of crime*) Ort *m*; (*also*: **building site**) Baustelle *f*; (*Comput*) Site *f* ▷ *vt* (*factory*) legen; (*missiles*) stationieren
sit-in ['sɪtɪn] *n* Sit-in *nt*
siting ['saɪtɪŋ] *n* (*location*) Lage *f*
sits vac *abbr* (= *situations vacant*) Stellenangebote *pl*
sitter ['sɪtəʳ] *n* (*for painter*) Modell *nt*; (*also*: **baby-sitter**) Babysitter *m*
sitting ['sɪtɪŋ] *n* Sitzung *f*; **we have two ~s for lunch** bei uns wird das Mittagessen in zwei Schüben serviert; **at a single ~** auf einmal
sitting member *n* (*Pol*) (derzeitiger) Abgeordnete(r) *m*, (derzeitige) Abgeordnete *f*
sitting room *n* Wohnzimmer *nt*
sitting tenant (*Brit*) *n* (derzeitiger) Mieter *m*
situate ['sɪtjueɪt] *vt* legen
situated ['sɪtjueɪtɪd] *adj* gelegen; **to be ~** liegen

situation [sɪtjuˈeɪʃən] *n* Situation *f*, Lage *f*; (*job*) Stelle *f*; (*location*) Lage *f*; **"~s vacant** *or* **wanted"** „Stellenangebote"
situation comedy *n* (*TV*) Situationskomödie *f*
six [sɪks] *num* sechs
six-pack [ˈsɪkspæk] *n* Sechserpack *m*
sixteen [sɪksˈtiːn] *num* sechzehn
sixth [sɪksθ] *num* sechste(r, s); **the upper/ lower ~** (*Brit: Scol*) ≈ die Ober-/Unterprima
sixty [ˈsɪkstɪ] *num* sechzig
size [saɪz] *n* Größe *f*; (*extent*) Ausmaß *nt*; **I take ~ 14** ich habe Größe 14; **the small/large ~** (*of soap powder etc*) die kleine/große Packung; **it's the ~ of ...** es ist so groß wie ...; **cut to ~** auf die richtige Größe zurechtgeschnitten
▸ **size up** *vt* einschätzen
sizeable [ˈsaɪzəbl] *adj* ziemlich groß; (*income etc*) ansehnlich
sizzle [ˈsɪzl] *vi* brutzeln
SK (*Canada*) *abbr* (= *Saskatchewan*)
skate [skeɪt] *n* (*also*: **ice skate**) Schlittschuh *m*; (*also*: **roller skate**) Rollschuh *m*; (*fish*: *pl inv*) Rochen *m* ▹ *vi* Schlittschuh laufen
▸ **skate around** *vt fus* (*problem, issue*) einfach übergehen
▸ **skate over** *vt fus* = **skate around**
skateboard [ˈskeɪtbɔːd] *n* Skateboard *nt*
skater [ˈskeɪtə^r] *n* Schlittschuhläufer(in) *m(f)*
skating [ˈskeɪtɪŋ] *n* Eislauf *m*
skating rink *n* Eisbahn *f*
skeleton [ˈskɛlɪtn] *n* Skelett *nt* ▹ *attrib* (*plan, outline*) skizzenhaft
skeleton key *n* Dietrich *m*; Nachschlüssel *m*
skeleton staff *n* Minimalbesetzung *f*
skeptic *etc* [ˈskɛptɪk] (*US*) = **sceptic** *etc*
sketch [skɛtʃ] *n* Skizze *f*; (*Theat, TV*) Sketch *m* ▹ *vt* skizzieren; (*also*: **sketch out**: *ideas*) umreißen
sketchbook [ˈskɛtʃbuk] *n* Skizzenbuch *nt*
sketchpad [ˈskɛtʃpæd] *n* Skizzenblock *m*
sketchy [ˈskɛtʃɪ] *adj* (*coverage*) oberflächlich; (*notes etc*) bruchstückhaft
skew [skjuː] *adj* schief
skewed [skjuːd] *adj* (*distorted*) verzerrt
skewer [ˈskjuːə^r] *n* Spieß *m*
ski [skiː] *n* Ski *m* ▹ *vi* Ski laufen *or* fahren
ski boot *n* Skistiefel *m*
skid [skɪd] *n* (*Aut*) Schleudern *nt* ▹ *vi* rutschen; (*Aut*) schleudern; **to go into a ~** ins Schleudern geraten *or* kommen
skid marks *npl* Reifenspuren *pl*; (*from braking*) Bremsspuren *pl*
skier [ˈskiːə^r] *n* Skiläufer(in) *m(f)*, Skifahrer(in) *m(f)*
skiing [ˈskiːɪŋ] *n* Skilaufen *nt*, Skifahren *nt*; **to go ~** Ski laufen *or* Ski fahren gehen
ski instructor *n* Skilehrer(in) *m(f)*
ski jump *n* (*event*) Skispringen *nt*; (*ramp*) Sprungschanze *f*
skilful, (*US*) **skillful** [ˈskɪlful] *adj* geschickt
skilfully *adv* geschickt
ski lift *n* Skilift *m*
skill [skɪl] *n* (*ability*) Können *nt*; (*dexterity*) Geschicklichkeit *f*; **skills** (*acquired abilities*) Fähigkeiten *pl*; **computer/language ~s** Computer-/Sprachkenntnisse *pl*; **to learn a new ~** etwas Neues lernen
skilled [skɪld] *adj* (*skilful*) geschickt; (*trained*) ausgebildet; (*work*) qualifiziert
skillet [ˈskɪlɪt] *n* Bratpfanne *f*
skillful *etc* [ˈskɪlful] (*US*) = **skilful** *etc*
skim [skɪm] *vt* (*also*: **skim off**: *cream, fat*) abschöpfen; (*glide over*) gleiten über +*acc* ▹ *vi*: **to ~ through** (*book etc*) überfliegen
skimmed milk [skɪmd-] *n* Magermilch *f*
skimp [skɪmp] (*also*: **skimp on**) *vt* (*work etc*) nachlässig machen; (*cloth etc*) sparen an +*dat*
skimpy [ˈskɪmpɪ] *adj* (*meagre*) dürftig; (*too small*) knapp
skin [skɪn] *n* Haut *f*; (*fur*) Fell *nt*; (*of fruit*) Schale *f* ▹ *vt* (*animal*) häuten; **wet** *or* **soaked to the ~** nass bis auf die Haut
skin cancer *n* Hautkrebs *m*
skin-deep [ˈskɪnˈdiːp] *adj* oberflächlich
skin diver *n* Sporttaucher(in) *m(f)*
skin diving *n* Sporttauchen *nt*
skinflint [ˈskɪnflɪnt] *n* Geizkragen *m*
skin graft *n* Hautverpflanzung *f*
skinhead [ˈskɪnhɛd] *n* Skinhead *m*
skinny [ˈskɪnɪ] *adj* dünn
skin test *n* Hauttest *m*
skintight [ˈskɪntaɪt] *adj* hauteng
skip [skɪp] *n* Sprung *m*, Hüpfer *m*; (*Brit*: *container*) (Müll)container *m* ▹ *vi* springen, hüpfen; (*with rope*) seilspringen ▹ *vt* überspringen; (*miss*: *lunch, lecture*) ausfallen lassen; **to ~ school** (*esp US*) die Schule schwänzen
ski pants *npl* Skihose *f*
ski pass *n* Skipass *nt*
ski pole *n* Skistock *m*
skipper [ˈskɪpə^r] *n* (*Naut*) Kapitän *m*; (*inf, Sport*) Mannschaftskapitän *m* ▹ *vt*: **to ~ a boat/team** Kapitän eines Schiffes/einer Mannschaft sein
skipping rope [ˈskɪpɪŋ-] (*Brit*) *n* Sprungseil *nt*
ski resort *n* Wintersportort *m*
skirmish [ˈskəːmɪʃ] *n* (*Mil*) Geplänkel *nt*; (*political etc*) Zusammenstoß *m*
skirt [skəːt] *n* Rock *m* ▹ *vt* (*fig*) umgehen
skirting board [ˈskəːtɪŋ-] (*Brit*) *n* Fußleiste *f*
ski run *n* Skipiste *f*
ski slope *n* Skipiste *f*
ski suit *n* Skianzug *m*
skit [skɪt] *n* Parodie *f*
ski tow *n* Schlepplift *m*
skittle [ˈskɪtl] *n* Kegel *m*
skittles [ˈskɪtlz] *n* (*game*) Kegeln *nt*
skive [skaɪv] (*Brit*: *inf*) *vi* blaumachen; (*from school*) schwänzen
skulk [skʌlk] *vi* sich herumdrücken
skull [skʌl] *n* Schädel *m*
skullcap [ˈskʌlkæp] *n* Scheitelkäppchen *nt*
skunk [skʌŋk] *n* Skunk *m*, Stinktier *nt*; (*fur*) Skunk *m*
sky [skaɪ] *n* Himmel *m*; **to praise sb to the skies** jdn in den Himmel heben

sky-blue [skaɪ'blu:] *adj* himmelblau
skydiving ['skaɪdaɪvɪŋ] *n* Fallschirmspringen *nt*
sky-high ['skaɪ'haɪ] *adj* (*prices, confidence*) himmelhoch ▷ *adv*: **to blow a bridge ~** eine Brücke in die Luft sprengen
skylark ['skaɪlɑ:k] *n* Feldlerche *f*
skylight ['skaɪlaɪt] *n* Dachfenster *nt*
skyline ['skaɪlaɪn] *n* (*horizon*) Horizont *m*; (*of city*) Skyline *f*, Silhouette *f*
skyscraper ['skaɪskreɪpə^r] *n* Wolkenkratzer *m*
slab [slæb] *n* (*stone*) Platte *f*; (*of wood*) Tafel *f*; (*of cake, cheese*) großes Stück *nt*
slack [slæk] *adj* (*loose*) locker; (*rope*) durchhängend; (*skin*) schlaff; (*careless*) nachlässig; (*Comm: market*) flau; (*: demand*) schwach; (*period*) ruhig ▷ *n* (*in rope etc*) durchhängendes Teil *nt*; **slacks** *npl* (*trousers*) Hose *f*; **business is ~** das Geschäft geht schlecht
slacken ['slækn] *vi* (*also*: **slacken off**: *speed, rain*) nachlassen; (*: pace*) langsamer werden; (*: demand*) zurückgehen ▷ *vt* (*grip*) lockern; (*speed*) verringern; (*pace*) verlangsamen
slag heap [slæg-] *n* Schlackenhalde *f*
slag off (*Brit: inf*) *vt* (*criticize*) (he)runtermachen
slain [sleɪn] *pp of* **slay**
slake [sleɪk] *vt* (*thirst*) stillen
slalom ['slɑ:ləm] *n* Slalom *m*
slam [slæm] *vt* (*door*) zuschlagen, zuknallen (*inf*); (*throw*) knallen (*inf*); (*criticize*) verreißen ▷ *vi* (*door*) zuschlagen, zuknallen (*inf*); **to ~ on the brakes** (*Aut*) auf die Bremse steigen (*inf*)
slammer ['slæmə^r] (*inf*) *n* (*prison*) Knast *m*
slander ['slɑ:ndə^r] *n* (*Law*) Verleumdung *f*; (*insult*) Beleidigung *f* ▷ *vt* verleumden
slanderous ['slɑ:ndrəs] *adj* verleumderisch
slang [slæŋ] *n* Slang *m*; (*jargon*) Jargon *m*
slanging match ['slæŋɪŋ-] *n* gegenseitige Beschimpfungen *pl*
slant [slɑ:nt] *n* Neigung *f*, Schräge *f*; (*fig: approach*) Perspektive *f* ▷ *vi* (*floor*) sich neigen; (*ceiling*) schräg sein
slanted ['slɑ:ntɪd] *adj* (*roof*) schräg; (*eyes*) schräg gestellt
slanting ['slɑ:ntɪŋ] *adj* = **slanted**
slap [slæp] *n* Schlag *m*, Klaps *m* ▷ *vt* schlagen ▷ *adv* (*inf: directly*) direkt; **to ~ sth on sth** etw auf etw *acc* klatschen; **it fell ~(-bang) in the middle** es fiel genau in die Mitte
slapdash ['slæpdæʃ] *adj* nachlässig, schludrig (*inf*)
slapstick ['slæpstɪk] *n* Klamauk *m*
slap-up ['slæpʌp] *adj*: **a ~ meal** (*Brit*) ein Essen mit allem Drum und Dran
slash [slæʃ] *vt* aufschlitzen; (*fig: prices*) radikal senken; **to ~ one's wrists** sich *dat* die Pulsadern aufschneiden
slat [slæt] *n* Leiste *f*, Latte *f*
slate [sleɪt] *n* Schiefer *m*; (*piece*) Schieferplatte *f* ▷ *vt* (*criticize*) verreißen
slaughter ['slɔ:tə^r] *n* (*of animals*) Schlachten *nt*; (*of people*) Gemetzel *nt* ▷ *vt* (*animals*) schlachten; (*people*) abschlachten
slaughterhouse ['slɔ:təhaus] *n* Schlachthof *m*
Slav [slɑ:v] *adj* slawisch ▷ *n* Slawe *m*, Slawin *f*
slave [sleɪv] *n* Sklave *m*, Sklavin *f* ▷ *vi* (*also*: **slave away**) sich abplagen, schuften (*inf*); **to ~ (away) at sth** sich mit etw herumschlagen
slave-driver ['sleɪvdraɪvə^r] *n* Sklaventreiber(in) *m(f)*
slave labour *n* Sklavenarbeit *f*; **it's just ~** (*fig*) es ist die reinste Sklavenarbeit
slaver ['slævə^r] *vi* (*dribble*) geifern
slavery ['sleɪvərɪ] *n* Sklaverei *f*
Slavic ['slævɪk] *adj* slawisch
slavish ['sleɪvɪʃ] *adj* sklavisch
slavishly ['sleɪvɪʃlɪ] *adv* sklavisch
Slavonic [slə'vɔnɪk] *adj* slawisch
slay [sleɪ] (*pt* **slew**, *pp* **slain**) *vt* (*liter*) erschlagen
sleazy ['sli:zɪ] *adj* schäbig
sledge [slɛdʒ] *n* Schlitten *m*
sledgehammer ['slɛdʒhæmə^r] *n* Vorschlaghammer *m*
sleek [sli:k] *adj* glatt, glänzend; (*car, boat etc*) schnittig
sleep [sli:p] (*pt, pp* **slept**) *n* Schlaf *m* ▷ *vi* schlafen ▷ *vt*: **we can ~ 4** bei uns können 4 Leute schlafen; **to go to ~** einschlafen; **to have a good night's ~** sich richtig ausschlafen; **to put to ~** (*euph: kill*) einschläfern; **to ~ lightly** einen leichten Schlaf haben; **to ~ with sb** (*euph: have sex*) mit jdm schlafen
▸ **sleep around** *vi* mit jedem/jeder schlafen
▸ **sleep in** *vi* (*oversleep*) verschlafen; (*rise late*) lange schlafen
sleeper ['sli:pə^r] *n* (*train*) Schlafwagenzug *m*; (*berth*) Platz *m* im Schlafwagen; (*Brit: on track*) Schwelle *f*; (*person*) Schläfer(in) *m(f)*
sleepily ['sli:pɪlɪ] *adv* müde, schläfrig
sleeping accommodation *n* (*beds etc*) Schlafgelegenheiten *pl*
sleeping arrangements *npl* Bettenverteilung *f*
sleeping bag *n* Schlafsack *m*
sleeping car *n* Schlafwagen *m*
sleeping partner (*Brit*) = **silent partner**
sleeping pill *n* Schlaftablette *f*
sleeping sickness *n* Schlafkrankheit *f*
sleepless ['sli:plɪs] *adj* (*night*) schlaflos
sleeplessness ['sli:plɪsnɪs] *n* Schlaflosigkeit *f*
sleepwalk ['sli:pwɔ:k] *vi* schlafwandeln
sleepwalker ['sli:pwɔ:kə^r] *n* Schlafwandler(in) *m(f)*
sleepy ['sli:pɪ] *adj* müde, schläfrig; (*fig: village etc*) verschlafen; **to be** *or* **feel ~** müde sein
sleet [sli:t] *n* Schneeregen *m*
sleeve [sli:v] *n* Ärmel *m*; (*of record*) Hülle *f*; **to have sth up one's ~** (*fig*) etw in petto haben
sleeveless ['sli:vlɪs] *adj* (*garment*) ärmellos
sleigh [sleɪ] *n* (Pferde)schlitten *m*
sleight [slaɪt] *n*: **~ of hand** Fingerfertigkeit *f*
slender ['slɛndə^r] *adj* schlank, schmal; (*small*) knapp

slept [slɛpt] *pt, pp of* **sleep**
sleuth [slu:θ] *n* Detektiv *m*
slew [slu:] *vi* (*Brit*: *also*: **slew round**) herumschwenken; **the bus ~ed across the road** der Bus rutschte über die Straße ▷ *pt of* **slay**
slice [slaɪs] *n* Scheibe *f*; (*utensil*) Wender *m* ▷ *vt* (in Scheiben) schneiden; **~d bread** aufgeschnittenes Brot *nt*; **the best thing since ~d bread** der/die/das Allerbeste
slick [slɪk] *adj* professionell; (*pej*) glatt ▷ *n* (*also*: **oil slick**) Ölteppich *m*
slid [slɪd] *pt, pp of* **slide**
slide [slaɪd] (*pt, pp* **slid**) *n* (*on ice etc*) Rutschen *nt*; (*fig*: *to ruin etc*) Abgleiten *nt*; (*in playground*) Rutschbahn *f*; (*Phot*) Dia *nt*; (*Brit*: *also*: **hair slide**) Spange *f*; (*microscope slide*) Objektträger *m*; (*in prices*) Preisrutsch *m* ▷ *vt* schieben ▷ *vi* (*slip*) rutschen; (*glide*) gleiten; **to let things ~** (*fig*) die Dinge schleifen lassen
slide projector *n* Diaprojektor *m*
slide rule *n* Rechenschieber *m*
sliding ['slaɪdɪŋ] *adj* (*door, window etc*) Schiebe-
sliding roof *n* (*Aut*) Schiebedach *nt*
sliding scale *n* gleitende Skala *f*
slight [slaɪt] *adj* zierlich; (*small*) gering; (*error, accent, pain etc*) leicht; (*trivial*) leicht ▷ *n*: **a ~ (on sb/sth)** ein Affront *m* (gegen jdn/etw); **the ~est noise** der geringste Lärm; **the ~est problem** das kleinste Problem; **I haven't the ~est idea** ich habe nicht die geringste Ahnung; **not in the ~est** nicht im Geringsten
slightly ['slaɪtlɪ] *adv* etwas, ein bisschen; **~ built** zierlich
slim [slɪm] *adj* schlank; (*chance*) gering ▷ *vi* eine Schlankheitskur machen, abnehmen
slime [slaɪm] *n* Schleim *m*
slimming ['slɪmɪŋ] *n* Abnehmen *nt*
slimy ['slaɪmɪ] *adj* (*lit, fig*) schleimig
sling [slɪŋ] (*pt, pp* **slung**) *n* Schlinge *f*; (*for baby*) Tragetuch *nt*; (*weapon*) Schleuder *f* ▷ *vt* schleudern; **to have one's arm in a ~** den Arm in der Schlinge tragen
slingshot ['slɪŋʃɔt] *n* Steinschleuder *f*
slink [slɪŋk] (*pt, pp* **slunk**) *vi*: **to ~ away** *or* **off** sich davonschleichen
slinky ['slɪŋkɪ] *adj* (*dress*) eng anliegend
slip [slɪp] *n* (*fall*) Ausrutschen *nt*; (*mistake*) Fehler *m*, Schnitzer *m*; (*underskirt*) Unterrock *m*; (*also*: **slip of paper**) Zettel *m* ▷ *vt* (*slide*) stecken ▷ *vi* ausrutschen; (*decline*) fallen; **he had a nasty ~** er ist ausgerutscht und böse gefallen; **to give sb the ~** jdm entwischen; **a ~ of the tongue** ein Versprecher *m*; **to ~ into/out of sth, to ~ sth on/off** in etw *acc*/ aus etw schlüpfen; **to let a chance ~ by** eine Gelegenheit ungenutzt lassen; **it ~ped from her hand** es rutschte ihr aus der Hand
▸ **slip away** *vi* sich davonschleichen
▸ **slip in** *vt* stecken in +*acc*
▸ **slip out** *vi* kurz weggehen
▸ **slip up** *vi* sich vertun (*inf*)
slip-on ['slɪpɔn] *adj* zum Überziehen; **~ shoes** Slipper *pl*
slipped disc [slɪpt-] *n* Bandscheibenschaden *m*
slipper ['slɪpə^r] *n* Pantoffel *m*, Hausschuh *m*
slippery ['slɪpərɪ] *adj* (*lit, fig*) glatt; (*fish etc*) schlüpfrig
slippy ['slɪpɪ] *adj* (*slippery*) glatt
slip road (*Brit*) *n* (*to motorway etc*) Auffahrt *f*; (*from motorway etc*) Ausfahrt *f*
slipshod ['slɪpʃɔd] *adj* schludrig (*inf*)
slipstream ['slɪpstri:m] *n* (*Tech*) Sog *m*; (*Aut*) Windschatten *m*
slip-up ['slɪpʌp] *n* Fehler *m*, Schnitzer *m*
slipway ['slɪpweɪ] *n* (*Naut*) Ablaufbahn *f*
slit [slɪt] (*pt, pp* **~**) *n* Schlitz *m*; (*tear*) Riss *m* ▷ *vt* aufschlitzen; **to ~ sb's throat** jdm die Kehle aufschlitzen
slither ['slɪðə^r] *vi* rutschen; (*snake etc*) gleiten
sliver ['slɪvə^r] *n* (*of glass, wood*) Splitter *m*; (*of cheese etc*) Scheibchen *nt*
slob [slɔb] (*inf*) *n* Drecksau *f* (!)
slog [slɔg] (*Brit*) *vi* (*work hard*) schuften ▷ *n*: **it was a hard ~** es war eine ganz schöne Schufterei; **to ~ away at sth** sich mit etw abrackern
slogan ['sləugən] *n* Slogan *m*
slop [slɔp] *vi* schwappen ▷ *vt* verschütten
▸ **slop out** *vi* (*in prison etc*) den Toiletteneimer ausleeren
slope [sləup] *n* Hügel *m*; (*side of mountain*) Hang *m*; (*ski slope*) Piste *f*; (*slant*) Neigung *f* ▷ *vi*: **to ~ down** abfallen; **to ~ up** ansteigen
sloping ['sləupɪŋ] *adj* (*upwards*) ansteigend; (*downwards*) abfallend; (*roof, handwriting*) schräg
sloppy ['slɔpɪ] *adj* (*work*) nachlässig; (*appearance*) schlampig; (*sentimental*) rührselig
slops [slɔps] *npl* Abfallbrühe *f*
slosh [slɔʃ] (*inf*) *vi*: **to ~ around** *or* **about** (*person*) herumplan(t)schen; (*liquid*) herumschwappen
sloshed [slɔʃt] (*inf*) *adj* (*drunk*) blau
slot [slɔt] *n* Schlitz *m*; (*fig*: *in timetable*) Termin *m*; (*: , Radio, TV*) Sendezeit *f* ▷ *vt*: **to ~ sth in** etw hineinstecken ▷ *vi*: **to ~ into** sich einfügen lassen in +*acc*
sloth [sləuθ] *n* (*laziness*) Trägheit *f*, Faulheit *f*; (*Zool*) Faultier *nt*
slot machine *n* (*Brit*) Münzautomat *m*; (*for gambling*) Spielautomat *m*
slot meter (*Brit*) *n* Münzzähler *m*
slouch [slautʃ] *vi* eine krumme Haltung haben; (*when walking*) krumm gehen ▷ *n*: **he's no ~** er hat etwas los (*inf*); **she was ~ed in a chair** sie hing auf einem Stuhl
Slovak ['sləuvæk] *adj* slowakisch ▷ *n* Slowake *m*, Slowakin *f*; (*Ling*) Slowakisch *nt*; **the ~ Republic** die Slowakische Republik
Slovakia [sləu'vækɪə] *n* die Slowakei
Slovakian [sləu'vækɪən] *adj, n* = **Slovak**
Slovene ['sləuvi:n] *n* Slowene *m*, Slowenin *f*; (*Ling*) Slowenisch *nt* ▷ *adj* slowenisch
Slovenia [sləu'vi:nɪə] *n* Slowenien *nt*
Slovenian [sləu'vi:nɪən] *adj, n* = **Slovene**
slovenly ['slʌvənlɪ] *adj* schlampig; (*careless*)

nachlässig, schludrig (*inf*)

slow [sləu] *adj* langsam; (*not clever*) langsam, begriffsstutzig ▷ *adv* langsam ▷ *vt* (*also*: **slow down, slow up**) verlangsamen; (*business*) verschlechtern ▷ *vi* (*also*: **slow down, slow up**) sich verlangsamen; (*business*) schlechter gehen; **to be ~** (*watch, clock*) nachgehen; **"~"** „langsam fahren"; **at a ~ speed** langsam; **to be ~ to act** sich *dat* Zeit lassen; **to be ~ to decide** lange brauchen, um sich zu entscheiden; **my watch is 20 minutes ~** meine Uhr geht 20 Minuten nach; **business is ~** das Geschäft geht schlecht; **to go ~** (*driver*) langsam fahren; (*Brit: in industrial dispute*) einen Bummelstreik machen

slow-acting [sləu'æktıŋ] *adj* mit Langzeitwirkung

slow food *n* Slow Food *nt*

slowly ['sləulı] *adv* langsam

slow motion *n*: **in ~** in Zeitlupe

slow-moving [sləu'mu:vıŋ] *adj* langsam; (*traffic*) kriechend

slowness ['sləunıs] *n* Langsamkeit *f*

sludge [slʌdʒ] *n* Schlamm *m*

slue [slu:] (*US*) *vi* = **slew**

slug [slʌg] *n* Nacktschnecke *f*; (*US: inf: bullet*) Kugel *f*

sluggish ['slʌgıʃ] *adj* träge; (*engine*) lahm; (*Comm*) flau

sluice [slu:s] *n* Schleuse *f*; (*channel*) (Wasch)rinne *f* ▷ *vt*: **to ~ down** *or* **out** abspritzen

slum [slʌm] *n* Slum *m*, Elendsviertel *nt*

slumber ['slʌmbə^r] *n* Schlaf *m*

slump [slʌmp] *n* Rezession *f* ▷ *vi* fallen; **~ in sales** Absatzflaute *f*; **~ in prices** Preissturz *m*; **he was ~ed over the wheel** er war über dem Steuer zusammengesackt

slung [slʌŋ] *pt, pp of* **sling**

slunk [slʌŋk] *pt, pp of* **slink**

slur [slə:^r] *n* (*fig*): **~ (on)** Beleidigung *f* (für) ▷ *vt* (*words*) undeutlich aussprechen; **to cast a ~ on** verunglimpfen

slurp [slə:p] (*inf*) *vt, vi* schlürfen

slurred [slə:d] *adj* (*speech, voice*) undeutlich

slush [slʌʃ] *n* (*melted snow*) Schneematsch *m*

slush fund *n* Schmiergelder *pl*, Schmiergeldfonds *m*

slushy ['slʌʃı] *adj* matschig; (*Brit: fig*) schmalzig

slut [slʌt] (*pej*) *n* Schlampe *f*

sly [slaı] *adj* (*smile, expression*) wissend; (*remark*) vielsagend; (*person*) schlau, gerissen; **on the ~** heimlich

S/M *n abbr* (= *sadomasochism*) S/M

smack [smæk] *n* Klaps *m*; (*on face*) Ohrfeige *f* ▷ *vt* (*hit*) schlagen; (: *child*) einen Klaps geben +*dat*; (: *on face*) ohrfeigen ▷ *vi*: **to ~ of** riechen nach ▷ *adv*: **it fell ~ in the middle** (*inf*) es fiel genau in die Mitte; **to ~ one's lips** schmatzen

smacker ['smækə^r] (*inf*) *n* (*kiss*) Schmatzer *m*

small [smɔ:l] *adj* klein ▷ *n*: **the ~ of the back** das Kreuz; **to get** *or* **grow ~er** (*thing*) kleiner werden; (*numbers*) zurückgehen; **to make ~er** (*amount, income*) kürzen; (*object, garment*) kleiner machen; **a ~ shopkeeper** der Inhaber eines kleinen Geschäfts; **a ~ business** ein Kleinunternehmen *nt*

small ads (*Brit*) *npl* Kleinanzeigen *pl*

small arms *n* Handfeuerwaffen *pl*

small business *n* Kleinunternehmen *nt*

small change *n* Kleingeld *nt*

small fry *npl* (*unimportant people*) kleine Fische *pl*

smallholder ['smɔ:lhəuldə^r] (*Brit*) *n* Kleinbauer *m*

smallholding ['smɔ:lhəuldıŋ] (*Brit*) *n* kleiner Landbesitz *m*

small hours *npl*: **in the ~** in den frühen Morgenstunden

smallish ['smɔ:lıʃ] *adj* ziemlich klein

small-minded [smɔ:l'maındıd] *adj* engstirnig

smallpox ['smɔ:lpɔks] *n* Pocken *pl*

small print *n*: **the ~** das Kleingedruckte

small-scale ['smɔ:lskeıl] *adj* (*map, model*) in verkleinertem Maßstab; (*business, farming*) klein angelegt

small talk *n* (oberflächliche) Konversation *f*

small-time ['smɔ:ltaım] *adj* (*farmer etc*) klein; **a ~ thief** ein kleiner Ganove

small-town ['smɔ:ltaun] *adj* kleinstädtisch

smarmy ['smɑ:mı] (*Brit: pej*) *adj* schmierig

smart [smɑ:t] *adj* (*neat*) ordentlich, gepflegt; (*fashionable*) chic *inv*, elegant; (*clever*) intelligent, clever (*inf*); (*quick*) schnell ▷ *vi* (*sting*) brennen; (*suffer*) leiden; **the ~ set** die Schickeria (*inf*); **and look ~ (about it)!** und zwar ein bisschen plötzlich! (*inf*)

smart card *n* Chipkarte *f*

smarten up ['smɑ:tn-] *vi* sich fein machen ▷ *vt* verschönern

smash [smæʃ] *n* (*also*: **smash-up**) Unfall *m*; (*sound*) Krachen *nt*; (*song, play, film*) Superhit *m*; (*Tennis*) Schmetterball *m* ▷ *vt* (*break*) zerbrechen; (*car etc*) kaputt fahren; (*hopes*) zerschlagen; (*Sport: record*) haushoch schlagen ▷ *vi* (*break*) zerbrechen; (*against wall, into sth etc*) krachen

▶ **smash up** *vt* (*car*) kaputt fahren; (*room*) kurz und klein schlagen (*inf*)

smash hit *n* Superhit *m*

smashing ['smæʃıŋ] (*inf*) *adj* super, toll

smattering ['smætərıŋ] *n*: **a ~ of Greek** *etc* ein paar Brocken Griechisch *etc*

smear [smıə^r] *n* (*trace*) verschmierter Fleck *m*; (*insult*) Verleumdung *f*; (*Med*) Abstrich *m* ▷ *vt* (*spread*) verschmieren; (*make dirty*) beschmieren; **his hands were ~ed with oil/ink** seine Hände waren mit Öl/Tinte beschmiert

smear campaign *n* Verleumdungskampagne *f*

smear test *n* Abstrich *m*

smell [smɛl] (*pt, pp* **smelt** *or* **~ed**) *n* Geruch *m*; (*sense*) Geruchssinn *m* ▷ *vt* riechen ▷ *vi* riechen; (*pej*) stinken; (*pleasantly*) duften; **to ~ of** riechen nach

smelly ['smɛlı] (*pej*) *adj* stinkend

smelt [smɛlt] *pt, pp of* **smell** ▷ *vt* schmelzen

smile [smaɪl] *n* Lächeln *nt* ▷ *vi* lächeln
smiling [ˈsmaɪlɪŋ] *adj* lächelnd
smirk [smə:k] *(pej) n* Grinsen *nt*
smithy [ˈsmɪðɪ] *n* Schmiede *f*
smitten [ˈsmɪtn] *adj*: **~ with** vernarrt in *+acc*
smock [smɔk] *n* Kittel *m*; *(US: overall)* Overall *m*
smog [smɔg] *n* Smog *m*
smoke [sməuk] *n* Rauch *m* ▷ *vi, vt* rauchen; **to have a ~** eine rauchen; **to go up in ~** in Rauch (und Flammen) aufgehen; *(fig)* sich in Rauch auflösen; **do you ~?** rauchen Sie?
smoked [sməukt] *adj* geräuchert, Räucher-; **~ glass** Rauchglas *nt*
smokeless fuel [ˈsməuklɪs-] *n* rauchlose Kohle *f*
smokeless zone *(Brit) n* rauchfreie Zone *f*
smoker [ˈsməukəʳ] *n* Raucher(in) *m(f)*; *(Rail)* Raucherabteil *nt*
smoke screen *n* Rauchvorhang *m*; *(fig)* Deckmantel *m*
smoke shop *(US) n* Tabakladen *m*
smoking [ˈsməukɪŋ] *n* Rauchen *nt*; **"no ~"** „Rauchen verboten"
smoking compartment, *(US)* **smoking car** *n* Raucherabteil *nt*
smoking room *n* Raucherzimmer *nt*
smoky [ˈsməukɪ] *adj* verraucht; *(taste)* rauchig
smolder [ˈsməuldəʳ] *(US) vi* = **smoulder**
smoochy [ˈsmu:tʃɪ] *adj (music, tape)* zum Schmusen
smooth [smu:ð] *adj (lit, fig: pej)* glatt; *(flavour, whisky)* weich; *(movement)* geschmeidig; *(flight)* ruhig
▸ **smooth out** *vt* glätten; *(fig: difficulties)* aus dem Weg räumen
▸ **smooth over** *vt*: **to ~ things over** *(fig)* die Sache bereinigen
smoothly [ˈsmu:ðlɪ] *adv* reibungslos, glatt; **everything went ~** alles ging glatt über die Bühne
smoothness [ˈsmu:ðnɪs] *n* Glätte *f*; *(of flight)* Ruhe *f*
smother [ˈsmʌðəʳ] *vt (fire, person)* ersticken; *(repress)* unterdrücken
smoulder, *(US)* **smolder** [ˈsməuldəʳ] *vi (lit, fig)* glimmen, schwelen
SMS *n abbr (= Short Message Service)* SMS *m*
smudge [smʌdʒ] *n* Schmutzfleck *m* ▷ *vt* verwischen
smug [smʌg] *(pej) adj* selbstgefällig
smuggle [ˈsmʌgl] *vt* schmuggeln; **to ~ in/out** einschmuggeln/herausschmuggeln
smuggler [ˈsmʌgləʳ] *n* Schmuggler(in) *m(f)*
smuggling [ˈsmʌglɪŋ] *n* Schmuggel *m*
smut [smʌt] *n (grain of soot)* Rußflocke *f*; *(in conversation etc)* Schmutz *m*
smutty [ˈsmʌtɪ] *adj (fig: joke, book)* schmutzig
snack [snæk] *n* Kleinigkeit *f* (zu essen); **to have a ~** eine Kleinigkeit essen
snack bar *n* Imbissstube *f*
snag [snæg] *n* Haken *m*, Schwierigkeit *f*
snail [sneɪl] *n* Schnecke *f*
snake [sneɪk] *n* Schlange *f*
snap [snæp] *n* Knacken *nt*; *(photograph)* Schnappschuss *m*; *(card game)* ≈ Schnippschnapp *nt* ▷ *adj (decision)* plötzlich, spontan ▷ *vt (break)* (zer)brechen ▷ *vi (break)* (zer)brechen; *(rope, thread etc)* reißen; **a cold ~** ein Kälteeinbruch *m*; **his patience ~ped** ihm riss der Geduldsfaden; **his temper ~ped** er verlor die Beherrschung; **to ~ one's fingers** mit den Fingern schnipsen *or* schnalzen; **to ~ open/shut** auf-/zuschnappen
▸ **snap at** *vt fus (dog)* schnappen nach; *(fig: person)* anschnauzen *(inf)*
▸ **snap off** *vt (break)* abbrechen
▸ **snap up** *vt (bargains)* wegschnappen
snap fastener *n* Druckknopf *m*
snappy [ˈsnæpɪ] *(inf) adj (answer)* kurz und treffend; *(slogan)* zündend; **make it ~** ein bisschen dalli!; **he is a ~ dresser** er zieht sich flott an
snapshot [ˈsnæpʃɔt] *n* Schnappschuss *m*
snare [snɛəʳ] *n* Falle *f* ▷ *vt (lit, fig)* fangen
snarl [snɑ:l] *vi* knurren ▷ *vt*: **to get ~ed up** *(plans)* durcheinanderkommen; *(traffic)* stocken
snarl-up [ˈsnɑ:lʌp] *n* Verkehrschaos *nt*
snatch [snætʃ] *n (of conversation)* Fetzen *m*; *(of song)* paar Takte *pl* ▷ *vt (grab)* greifen; *(steal)* stehlen, klauen *(inf)*; *(child)* entführen; *(fig: opportunity)* ergreifen; *(: look)* werfen ▷ *vi*: **don't ~!** nicht grapschen!; **to ~ a sandwich** schnell ein Butterbrot essen; **to ~ some sleep** etwas Schlaf ergattern
▸ **snatch up** *vt* schnappen
snazzy [ˈsnæzɪ] *(inf) adj* flott
sneak [sni:k] *(pt* **snuck***) (US) vi*: **to ~ in/out** sich einschleichen/sich hinausschleichen ▷ *vt*: **to ~ a look at sth** heimlich auf etw *acc* schielen ▷ *n (inf: pej)* Petze *f*
▸ **sneak up** *vi*: **to ~ up on sb** sich an jdn heranschleichen
sneakers [ˈsni:kəz] *npl* Freizeitschuhe *pl*
sneaking [ˈsni:kɪŋ] *adj*: **to have a ~ feeling/suspicion that ...** das ungute Gefühl/den leisen Verdacht haben, dass ...
sneaky [ˈsni:kɪ] *(pej) adj* raffiniert
sneer [snɪəʳ] *vi (smile nastily)* spöttisch lächeln; *(mock)*: **to ~ at** verspotten ▷ *n (smile)* spöttisches Lächeln *nt*; *(remark)* spöttische Bemerkung *f*
sneeze [sni:z] *n* Niesen *nt* ▷ *vi* niesen
▸ **sneeze at** *vt fus*: **it's not to be ~d at** es ist nicht zu verachten
snicker [ˈsnɪkəʳ] *vi see* **snigger**
snide [snaɪd] *(pej) adj* abfällig
sniff [snɪf] *n* Schniefen *nt*; *(smell)* Schnüffeln *nt* ▷ *vi* schniefen ▷ *vt* riechen, schnuppern an *+dat*; *(glue)* schnüffeln
sniffer dog [ˈsnɪfə-] *n* Spürhund *m*
snigger [ˈsnɪgəʳ] *vi* kichern
snip [snɪp] *n* Schnitt *m*; *(Brit: inf: bargain)* Schnäppchen *nt* ▷ *vt* schnippeln; **to ~ sth off/through sth** etw abschnippeln/durchschnippeln

sniper ['snaɪpəʳ] *n* Heckenschütze *m*
snippet ['snɪpɪt] *n* (*of information*) Bruchstück *nt*; (*of conversation*) Fetzen *m*
snivelling, (*US*) **sniveling** ['snɪvlɪŋ] *adj* heulend
snob [snɔb] *n* Snob *m*
snobbery ['snɔbərɪ] *n* Snobismus *m*
snobbish ['snɔbɪʃ] *adj* snobistisch, versnobt (*inf*)
snog [snɔg] (*Brit*: *inf*) *n* Knutscherei *f*; **to have a ~ with sb** mit jdm (rum)knutschen ▷ *vi* (rum)knutschen
snooker ['snu:kəʳ] *n* Snooker *nt* ▷ *vt* (*Brit*: *inf*): **to be ~ed** festsitzen
snoop [snu:p] *vi*: **to ~ about** herumschnüffeln; **to ~ on sb** jdm nachschnüffeln
snooper ['snu:pəʳ] *n* Schnüffler(in) *m(f)*
snooty ['snu:tɪ] *adj* hochnäsig
snooze [snu:z] *n* Schläfchen *nt* ▷ *vi* ein Schläfchen machen
snore [snɔ:ʳ] *n* Schnarchen *nt* ▷ *vi* schnarchen
snoring ['snɔ:rɪŋ] *n* Schnarchen *nt*
snorkel ['snɔ:kl] *n* Schnorchel *m*
snort [snɔ:t] *n* Schnauben *nt* ▷ *vi* (*animal*) schnauben; (*person*) prusten ▷ *vt* (*inf*: *cocaine*) schnüffeln
snotty ['snɔtɪ] (*inf*) *adj* (*handkerchief, nose*) Rotz-; (*pej*: *snobbish*) hochnäsig
snout [snaut] *n* Schnauze *f*
snow [snəu] *n* Schnee *m* ▷ *vi* schneien ▷ *vt*: **to be ~ed under with work** mit Arbeit reichlich eingedeckt sein; **it's ~ing** es schneit
snowball ['snəubɔ:l] *n* Schneeball *m* ▷ *vi* (*fig*: *problem*) eskalieren; (: *campaign*) ins Rollen kommen
snowbound ['snəubaund] *adj* eingeschneit
snow-capped ['snəukæpt] *adj* schneebedeckt
snowdrift ['snəudrɪft] *n* Schneewehe *f*
snowdrop ['snəudrɔp] *n* Schneeglöckchen *nt*
snowfall ['snəufɔ:l] *n* Schneefall *m*
snowflake ['snəufleɪk] *n* Schneeflocke *f*
snowline ['snəulaɪn] *n* Schneegrenze *f*
snowman ['snəumæn] (*irreg*: *like* **man**) *n* Schneemann *m*
snowplough, (*US*) **snowplow** ['snəuplau] *n* Schneepflug *m*
snowshoe ['snəuʃu:] *n* Schneeschuh *m*
snowstorm ['snəustɔ:m] *n* Schneesturm *m*
snowy ['snəuɪ] *adj* schneeweiß; (*covered with snow*) verschneit
SNP (*Brit*) *n abbr* (*Pol*) = **Scottish National Party**
snub [snʌb] *vt* (*person*) vor den Kopf stoßen ▷ *n* Abfuhr *f*
snub-nosed [snʌb'nəuzd] *adj* stupsnasig
snuff [snʌf] *n* Schnupftabak *m* ▷ *vt* (*also*: **snuff out**: *candle*) auslöschen
snuff movie *n Pornofilm, in dem jemand tatsächlich stirbt*
snug [snʌg] *adj* behaglich, gemütlich; (*well-fitting*) gut sitzend; **it's a ~ fit** es passt genau
snuggle ['snʌgl] *vi*: **to ~ up to sb** sich an jdn kuscheln; **to ~ down in bed** sich ins Bett kuscheln
snugly ['snʌglɪ] *adv* behaglich; **it fits ~** (*object in pocket etc*) es passt genau hinein; (*garment*) es passt wie angegossen
SO *n abbr* (*Banking*) = **standing order**

KEYWORD

so [səu] *adv* **1** (*thus, likewise*) so; **so saying he walked away** mit diesen Worten ging er weg; **if so** falls ja; **I didn't do it — you did so!** ich hab es nicht getan — hast du wohl!; **so do I, so am I** *etc* ich auch; **it's 5 o'clock — so it is!** es ist 5 Uhr — tatsächlich!; **I hope/think so** ich hoffe/glaube ja; **so far** bis jetzt
2 (*in comparisons etc*: *to such a degree*) so; **so big/quickly (that)** so groß/schnell(, dass); **I'm so glad to see you** ich bin ja so froh, dich zu sehen
3: **so much** so viel; **I've got so much work** ich habe so viel Arbeit; **I love you so much** ich liebe dich so sehr; **so many** so viele
4 (*phrases*): **10 or so** 10 oder so; **so long!** (*inf*: *goodbye*) tschüss!
▷ *conj* **1** (*expressing purpose*): **so as to do sth** um etw zu tun; **so (that)** damit
2 (*expressing result*) also; **so I was right after all** ich hatte also doch Recht; **so you see, I could have gone** wie Sie sehen, hätte ich gehen können; **so (what)?** na und?

soak [səuk] *vt* (*drench*) durchnässen; (*steep*) einweichen ▷ *vi* einweichen; **to be ~ed through** völlig durchnässt sein
▶ **soak in** *vi* einziehen
▶ **soak up** *vt* aufsaugen
soaking ['səukɪŋ] *adj* (*also*: **soaking wet**) patschnass
so-and-so ['səuənsəu] *n* (*somebody*) Soundso *no art*; **Mr/Mrs ~** Herr/Frau Soundso; **the little ~!** (*pej*) das Biest!
soap [səup] *n* Seife *f*; (*TV*: *also*: **soap opera**) Fernsehserie *f*, Seifenoper *f* (*inf*)
soapbox ['səupbɔks] *n* (*lit*) Seifenkiste *f*; (*fig*: *platform*) Apfelsinenkiste *f*
soapflakes ['səupfleɪks] *npl* Seifenflocken *pl*
soap opera *n* (*TV*) Fernsehserie *f*, Seifenoper *f* (*inf*)
soap powder *n* Seifenpulver *nt*
soapsuds ['səupsʌds] *npl* Seifenschaum *m*
soapy ['səupɪ] *adj* seifig; **~ water** Seifenwasser *nt*
soar [sɔ:ʳ] *vi* aufsteigen; (*price, temperature*) hochschnellen; (*building etc*) aufragen
soaring ['sɔ:rɪŋ] *adj* (*prices*) in die Höhe schnellend; (*inflation*) unaufhaltsam
sob [sɔb] *n* Schluchzer *m* ▷ *vi* schluchzen
s.o.b. (*US*: *inf!*) *n abbr* (= *son of a bitch*) Scheißkerl *m*
sober ['səubəʳ] *adj* nüchtern; (*serious*) ernst; (*colour*) gedeckt; (*style*) schlicht
▶ **sober up** *vt* nüchtern machen ▷ *vi* nüchtern werden
sobriety [sə'braɪətɪ] *n* Nüchternheit *f*;

(*seriousness*) Ernst *m*
sobriquet ['səubrɪkeɪ] *n* Spitzname *m*
sob story *n* rührselige Geschichte *f*
Soc. *abbr* (= *society*) Ges.
so-called ['səu'kɔːld] *adj* sogenannt
soccer ['sɔkəʳ] *n* Fußball *m*
soccer pitch *n* Fußballplatz *m*
soccer player *n* Fußballspieler(in) *m(f)*
sociable ['səuʃəbl] *adj* gesellig
social ['səuʃl] *adj* sozial; (*history*) Sozial-; (*structure*) Gesellschafts-; (*event, contact*) gesellschaftlich; (*person*) gesellig; (*animal*) gesellig lebend ▷ *n* (*party*) geselliger Abend *m*; ~ **life** gesellschaftliches Leben *nt*; **to have no ~ life** nicht mit anderen Leuten zusammenkommen
social class *n* Gesellschaftsklasse *f*
social climber (*pej*) *n* Emporkömmling *m*, sozialer Aufsteiger *m*
social club *n* Klub *m* für geselliges Beisammensein
Social Democrat *n* Sozialdemokrat(in) *m(f)*
social insurance (*US*) *n* Sozialversicherung *f*
socialism ['səuʃəlɪzəm] *n* Sozialismus *m*
socialist ['səuʃəlɪst] *adj* sozialistisch ▷ *n* Sozialist(in) *m(f)*
socialite ['səuʃəlaɪt] *n* Angehörige(r) *f(m)* der Schickeria
socialize ['səuʃəlaɪz] *vi* unter die Leute kommen; **to ~ with** (*meet socially*) gesellschaftlich verkehren mit; (*chat to*) sich unterhalten mit
socially ['səuʃəlɪ] *adv* (*visit*) privat; (*acceptable*) in Gesellschaft
social science *n* Sozialwissenschaft *f*
social security (*Brit*) *n* Sozialhilfe *f*; **Department of Social Security** Ministerium *nt* für Soziales
social services *npl* soziale Einrichtungen *pl*
social welfare *n* soziales Wohl *nt*
social work *n* Sozialarbeit *f*
social worker *n* Sozialarbeiter(in) *m(f)*
society [sə'saɪətɪ] *n* Gesellschaft *f*; (*people, their lifestyle*) die Gesellschaft; (*club*) Verein *m*; (*also*: **high society**) High Society *f* ▷ *cpd* (*party, lady*) Gesellschafts-
socioeconomic ['səusɪəuiːkə'nɔmɪk] *adj* sozioökonomisch
sociological [səusɪə'lɔdʒɪkl] *adj* soziologisch
sociologist [səusɪ'ɔlədʒɪst] *n* Soziologe *m*, Soziologin *f*
sociology [səusɪ'ɔlədʒɪ] *n* Soziologie *f*
sock [sɔk] *n* Socke *f* ▷ *vt* (*inf*: *hit*) hauen; **to pull one's ~s up** (*fig*) sich am Riemen reißen
socket ['sɔkɪt] *n* (*of eye*) Augenhöhle *f*; (*of joint*) Gelenkpfanne *f*; (*Brit*: *Elec*: *also*: **wall socket**) Steckdose *f*; (: *for light bulb*) Fassung *f*
sod [sɔd] *n* (*earth*) Sode *f*; (*Brit*: *inf!*) Sau *f* (*!*); **the poor ~** das arme Schwein
▸ **sod off** (*Brit*: *inf!*) *vi*: **~ off!** verpiss dich!
soda ['səudə] *n* Soda *nt*; (*also*: **soda water**) Soda(wasser) *nt*; (*US*: *also*: **soda pop**) Brause *f*
sodden ['sɔdn] *adj* durchnässt
sodium ['səudɪəm] *n* Natrium *nt*
sodium chloride *n* Natriumchlorid *nt*, Kochsalz *nt*
sofa ['səufə] *n* Sofa *nt*
Sofia ['səufɪə] *n* Sofia *nt*
soft [sɔft] *adj* weich; (*not rough*) zart; (*voice, music, light, colour*) gedämpft; (*lenient*) nachsichtig; **~ in the head** (*inf*) nicht ganz richtig im Kopf
soft benefits *npl* ▷ *econ* nicht monetäre (betriebliche) Leistungen *pl*
soft-boiled ['sɔftbɔɪld] *adj* (*egg*) weich (gekocht)
soft drink *n* alkoholfreies Getränk *nt*
soft drugs *npl* weiche Drogen *pl*
soften ['sɔfn] *vt* weich machen; (*effect, blow*) mildern ▷ *vi* weich werden; (*voice, expression*) sanfter werden
softener ['sɔfnəʳ] *n* (*also*: **water softener**) Enthärtungsmittel *nt*; (*also*: **fabric softener**) Weichspüler *m*
soft fruit (*Brit*) *n* Beerenobst *nt*
soft furnishings *npl* Raumtextilien *pl*
soft-hearted [sɔft'hɑːtɪd] *adj* weichherzig
softly ['sɔftlɪ] *adv* (*gently*) sanft; (*quietly*) leise
softness ['sɔftnɪs] *n* Weichheit *f*; (*gentleness*) Sanftheit *f*
soft option *n* Weg *m* des geringsten Widerstandes
soft sell *n* weiche Verkaufstaktik *f*
soft spot *n*: **to have a ~ for sb** eine Schwäche für jdn haben
soft target *n* leicht verwundbares Ziel *nt*
soft toy *n* Stofftier *nt*
software ['sɔftwɛəʳ] *n* (*Comput*) Software *f*
software package *n* (*Comput*) Softwarepaket *nt*
soft water *n* weiches Wasser *nt*
soggy ['sɔgɪ] *adj* (*ground*) durchweicht; (*sandwiches etc*) matschig
soil [sɔɪl] *n* Erde *f*, Boden *m* ▷ *vt* beschmutzen
soiled [sɔɪld] *adj* schmutzig
sojourn ['sɔdʒəːn] (*form*) *n* Aufenthalt *m*
solace ['sɔlɪs] *n* Trost *m*
solar ['səuləʳ] *adj* (*eclipse, power station etc*) Sonnen-
solarium [sə'lɛərɪəm] (*pl* **solaria**) *n* Solarium *nt*
solar panel *n* Sonnenkollektor *m*
solar plexus [-'plɛksəs] *n* (*Anat*) Solarplexus *m*, Magengrube *f*
solar power *n* Sonnenenergie *f*
solar system *n* Sonnensystem *nt*
solar wind *n* Sonnenwind *m*
sold [səuld] *pt, pp of* **sell**
solder ['səuldəʳ] *vt* löten ▷ *n* Lötmittel *nt*
soldier ['səuldʒəʳ] *n* Soldat *m* ▷ *vi*: **to ~ on** unermüdlich weitermachen; **toy ~** Spielzeugsoldat *m*
sold out *adj* ausverkauft
sole [səul] *n* Sohle *f*; (*fish*: *pl inv*) Seezunge *f* ▷ *adj* einzig, Allein-; (*exclusive*) alleinig; **the ~ reason** der einzige Grund
solely ['səullɪ] *adv* nur, ausschließlich; **I will hold you ~ responsible** ich mache Sie allein

dafür verantwortlich
solemn ['sɔləm] *adj* feierlich; (*person*) ernst
sole trader *n* (*Comm*) Einzelunternehmer *m*
solicit [sə'lɪsɪt] *vt* (*request*) erbitten, bitten um ▷ *vi* (*prostitute*) Kunden anwerben
solicitor [sə'lɪsɪtə^r] (*Brit*) *n* Rechtsanwalt *m*, Rechtsanwältin *f*
solid ['sɔlɪd] *adj* (*not hollow, pure*) massiv; (*not liquid*) fest; (*reliable*) zuverlässig; (*strong: structure*) stabil; (*: foundations*) solide; (*substantial: advice*) gut; (*: experience*) solide; (*unbroken*) ununterbrochen ▷ *n* (*solid object*) Festkörper *m*; **solids** *npl* (*food*) feste Nahrung *f*; **to be on ~ ground** (*fig*) sich auf festem Boden befinden; **I read for 2 hours ~** ich habe 2 Stunden ununterbrochen gelesen
solidarity [sɔlɪ'dærɪtɪ] *n* Solidarität *f*
solid fuel *n* fester Brennstoff *m*
solidify [sə'lɪdɪfaɪ] *vi* fest werden ▷ *vt* fest werden lassen
solidity [sə'lɪdɪtɪ] *n* (*of structure*) Stabilität *f*; (*of foundations*) Solidität *f*
solidly ['sɔlɪdlɪ] *adv* (*built*) solide; (*in favour*) geschlossen, einmütig; **a ~ respectable family** eine durch und durch respektable Familie
solid-state ['sɔlɪdsteɪt] *adj* (*Elec: equipment*) Halbleiter-
soliloquy [sə'lɪləkwɪ] *n* Monolog *m*
solitaire [sɔlɪ'tɛə^r] *n* (*gem*) Solitär *m*; (*game*) Patience *f*
solitary ['sɔlɪtərɪ] *adj* einsam; (*single*) einzeln
solitary confinement *n* Einzelhaft *f*
solitude ['sɔlɪtju:d] *n* Einsamkeit *f*; **to live in ~** einsam leben
solo ['səuləu] *n* Solo *nt* ▷ *adv* (*fly*) allein; (*play, perform*) solo; **~ flight** Alleinflug *m*
soloist ['səuləuɪst] *n* Solist(in) *m(f)*
Solomon Islands ['sɔləmən-] *npl*: **the ~** die Salomoninseln *pl*
solstice ['sɔlstɪs] *n* Sonnenwende *f*
soluble ['sɔljubl] *adj* löslich
solution [sə'lu:ʃən] *n* (*answer, liquid*) Lösung *f*; (*to crossword*) Auflösung *f*
solve [sɔlv] *vt* lösen; (*mystery*) enträtseln
solvency ['sɔlvənsɪ] *n* (*Comm*) Zahlungsfähigkeit *f*
solvent ['sɔlvənt] *adj* (*Comm*) zahlungsfähig ▷ *n* (*Chem*) Lösungsmittel *nt*
solvent abuse *n* Lösungsmittelmissbrauch *m*
Som. (*Brit*) *abbr* (*Post*) = *Somerset*
Somali [sə'mɑ:lɪ] *adj* somalisch ▷ *n* Somalier(in) *m(f)*
Somalia [sə'mɑ:lɪə] *n* Somalia *nt*
Somaliland *n* (*formerly*) Somaliland *nt*
sombre, (*US*) **somber** ['sɔmbə^r] *adj* (*dark*) dunkel, düster; (*serious*) finster

KEYWORD

some [sʌm] *adj* **1** (*a certain amount or number of*) einige; **some tea/water/money** etwas Tee/Wasser/Geld; **some biscuits** ein paar Plätzchen; **some children came** einige Kinder kamen; **he asked me some questions** er stellte mir ein paar Fragen
2 (*certain: in contrasts*) manche(r, s); **some people say that ...** manche Leute sagen, dass ...; **some films were excellent** einige *or* manche Filme waren ausgezeichnet
3 (*unspecified*) irgendein(e); **some woman was asking for you** eine Frau hat nach Ihnen gefragt; **some day** eines Tages; **some day next week** irgendwann nächste Woche; **that's some house!** das ist vielleicht ein Haus!
▷ *pron* **1** (*a certain number*) einige; **I've got some** (*books etc*) ich habe welche
2 (*a certain amount*) etwas; **I've got some** (*money, milk*) ich habe welche(s); **I've read some of the book** ich habe das Buch teilweise gelesen
▷ *adv*: **some 10 people** etwa 10 Leute

somebody ['sʌmbədɪ] *pron* = **someone**
someday ['sʌmdeɪ] *adv* irgendwann
somehow ['sʌmhau] *adv* irgendwie
someone ['sʌmwʌn] *pron* (irgend)jemand; **there's ~ coming** es kommt jemand; **I saw ~ in the garden** ich habe jemanden im Garten gesehen
someplace ['sʌmpleɪs] (*US*) *adv* = **somewhere**
somersault ['sʌməsɔ:lt] *n* Salto *m* ▷ *vi* einen Salto machen; (*vehicle*) sich überschlagen
something ['sʌmθɪŋ] *pron* etwas; **~ nice** etwas Schönes; **there's ~ wrong** da stimmt etwas nicht; **would you like ~ to eat/drink?** möchten Sie etwas zu essen/trinken?
sometime ['sʌmtaɪm] *adv* irgendwann; **~ last month** irgendwann letzten Monat; **I'll finish it ~** ich werde es irgendwann fertig machen
sometimes ['sʌmtaɪmz] *adv* manchmal
somewhat ['sʌmwɔt] *adv* etwas, ein wenig; **~ to my surprise** ziemlich zu meiner Überraschung
somewhere ['sʌmwɛə^r] *adv* (*be*) irgendwo; (*go*) irgendwohin; **~ (or other) in Scotland** irgendwo in Schottland; **~ else** (*be*) woanders; (*go*) woandershin
son [sʌn] *n* Sohn *m*
sonar ['səunɑ:^r] *n* Sonar(gerät) *nt*, Echolot *nt*
sonata [sə'nɑ:tə] *n* Sonate *f*
song [sɔŋ] *n* Lied *nt*; (*of bird*) Gesang *m*
songbook ['sɔŋbuk] *n* Liederbuch *nt*
songwriter ['sɔŋraɪtə^r] *n* Liedermacher *m*
sonic ['sɔnɪk] *adj* (*speed*) Schall-; **~ boom** Überschallknall *m*
son-in-law ['sʌnɪnlɔ:] *n* Schwiegersohn *m*
sonnet ['sɔnɪt] *n* Sonett *nt*
sonny ['sʌnɪ] (*inf*) *n* Junge *m*
soon [su:n] *adv* bald; (*a short time after*) bald, schnell; (*early*) früh; **~ afterwards** kurz *or* bald danach; **quite ~** ziemlich bald; **how ~ can you finish it?** bis wann haben Sie es fertig?; **how ~ can you come back?** wann können Sie frühestens wiederkommen?; **see you ~!** bis

bald!; *see also* **as**

sooner ['su:nəʳ] *adv* (*time*) früher, eher; (*preference*) lieber; **I would ~ do that** das würde ich lieber tun; **~ or later** früher oder später; **the ~ the better** je eher, desto besser; **no ~ said than done** gesagt, getan; **no ~ had we left than ...** wir waren gerade gegangen, da ...

soot [sut] *n* Ruß *m*

soothe [su:ð] *vt* beruhigen; (*pain*) lindern

soothing ['su:ðɪŋ] *adj* beruhigend; (*ointment etc*) schmerzlindernd; (*drink*) wohltuend; (*bath*) entspannend

SOP *n abbr* (*= standard operating procedure*) normale Vorgehensweise *f*

sop [sɔp] *n*: **that's only a ~** das soll nur zur Beschwichtigung dienen

sophisticated [sə'fɪstɪkeɪtɪd] *adj* (*woman, lifestyle*) kultiviert; (*audience*) anspruchsvoll; (*machinery*) hoch entwickelt; (*arguments*) differenziert

sophistication [səfɪstɪ'keɪʃən] *n* (*of person*) Kultiviertheit *f*; (*of machine*) hoher Entwicklungsstand *m*; (*of argument etc*) Differenziertheit *f*

sophomore ['sɔfəmɔ:ʳ] (*US*) *n Student(in) im 2. Studienjahr*

soporific [sɔpə'rɪfɪk] *adj* einschläfernd ▷ *n* Schlafmittel *nt*

sopping ['sɔpɪŋ] *adj*: **~ (wet)** völlig durchnässt

soppy ['sɔpɪ] (*pej*) *adj* (*person*) sentimental; (*film*) schmalzig

soprano [sə'prɑ:nəu] *n* Sopranist(in) *m(f)*

sorbet ['sɔ:beɪ] *n* Sorbet *nt or m*, Fruchteis *nt*

sorcerer ['sɔ:sərəʳ] *n* Hexenmeister *m*

sordid ['sɔ:dɪd] *adj* (*dirty*) verkommen; (*wretched*) elend

sore [sɔ:ʳ] *adj* wund; (*esp US: offended*) verärgert, sauer (*inf*) ▷ *n* wunde Stelle *f*; **to have a ~ throat** Halsschmerzen haben; **it's a ~ point** (*fig*) es ist ein wunder Punkt

sorely ['sɔ:lɪ] *adv*: **I am ~ tempted (to)** ich bin sehr in Versuchung(, zu)

soreness ['sɔ:nɪs] *n* (*pain*) Schmerz *m*

sorrel ['sɔrəl] *n* (*Bot*) (großer) Sauerampfer *m*

sorrow ['sɔrəu] *n* Trauer *f*; **sorrows** *npl* (*troubles*) Sorgen und Nöte *pl*

sorrowful ['sɔrəuful] *adj* traurig

sorry ['sɔrɪ] *adj* traurig; (*excuse*) faul; (*sight*) jämmerlich; **~!** Entschuldigung!, Verzeihung!; **~?** wie bitte?; **I feel ~ for him** er tut mir leid; **I'm ~ to hear that ...** es tut mir leid, dass ...; **I'm ~ about ...** es tut mir leid wegen ...

sort [sɔ:t] *n* Sorte *f*; (*make: of car etc*) Marke *f* ▷ *vt* (*also*: **sort out**) sortieren; (*: problems*) ins Reine bringen; (*Comput*) sortieren; **all ~s of reasons** alle möglichen Gründe; **what ~ do you want?** welche Sorte möchten Sie?; **what ~ of car?** was für ein Auto?; **I'll do nothing of the ~!** das kommt überhaupt nicht infrage!; **it's ~ of awkward** (*inf*) es ist irgendwie schwierig; **to ~ sth out** etw in Ordnung bringen

sort code *n* Bankleitzahl *f*

sortie ['sɔ:tɪ] *n* (*Mil*) Ausfall *m*; (*fig*) Ausflug *m*

sorting office ['sɔ:tɪŋ-] *n* Postverteilstelle *f*

SOS *n abbr* (*= save our souls*) SOS *nt*

so-so ['səusəu] *adv, adj* so lala

soufflé ['su:fleɪ] *n* Soufflé *nt*

sought [sɔ:t] *pt, pp of* **seek**

sought-after ['sɔ:tɑ:ftəʳ] *adj* begehrt, gesucht; **a much ~ item** ein viel begehrtes Stück

soul [səul] *n* Seele *f*; (*Mus*) Soul *m*; **the poor ~ had nowhere to sleep** der Ärmste hatte keine Unterkunft; **I didn't see a ~** ich habe keine Menschenseele gesehen

soul-destroying ['səuldɪstrɔɪɪŋ] *adj* geisttötend

soulful ['səulful] *adj* (*eyes*) seelenvoll; (*music*) gefühlvoll

soulless ['səullɪs] *adj* (*place*) seelenlos; (*job*) eintönig

soul mate *n* Seelenfreund(in) *m(f)*

soul-searching ['səulsə:tʃɪŋ] *n*: **after much ~** nach reiflicher Überlegung

sound [saund] *adj* (*healthy*) gesund; (*safe, secure*) sicher; (*not damaged*) einwandfrei; (*reliable*) solide; (*thorough*) gründlich; (*sensible, valid*) vernünftig ▷ *adv*: **to be ~ asleep** tief und fest schlafen ▷ *n* Geräusch *nt*; (*Mus*) Klang *m*; (*on TV etc*) Ton *m*; (*Geog*) Meerenge *f*, Sund *m* ▷ *vt*: **to ~ the alarm** Alarm schlagen ▷ *vi* (*alarm, horn*) ertönen; (*fig: seem*) sich anhören, klingen; **to be of ~ mind** bei klarem Verstand sein; **I don't like the ~ of it** das klingt gar nicht gut; **to ~ one's horn** (*Aut*) hupen; **to ~ like** sich anhören wie; **that ~s like them arriving** das hört sich so an, als ob sie ankommen; **it ~s as if ...** es klingt *or* es hört sich so an, als ob ...

▸ **sound off** (*inf*) *vi*: **to ~ off (about)** sich auslassen (über +*acc*)

▸ **sound out** *vt* (*person*) aushorchen; (*opinion*) herausbekommen

sound barrier *n* Schallmauer *f*

sound bite *n* prägnantes Zitat *nt*

sound effects *npl* Toneffekte *pl*

sound engineer *n* Toningenieur(in) *m(f)*

sounding ['saundɪŋ] *n* (*Naut*) Loten *nt*, Peilung *f*

sounding board *n* (*Mus*) Resonanzboden *m*; (*fig*): **to use sb as a ~ for one's ideas** seine Ideen an jdm testen

soundly ['saundlɪ] *adv* (*sleep*) tief und fest; (*beat*) tüchtig

soundproof ['saundpru:f] *adj* schalldicht ▷ *vt* schalldicht machen

sound system *n* Verstärkersystem *nt*

soundtrack ['saundtræk] *n* Filmmusik *f*

sound wave *n* Schallwelle *f*

soup [su:p] *n* Suppe *f*; **to be in the ~** (*fig*) in der Tinte sitzen

soup kitchen *n* Suppenküche *f*

soup plate *n* Suppenteller *m*

soupspoon ['su:pspu:n] *n* Suppenlöffel *m*

sour ['sauəʳ] *adj* sauer; (*fig: bad-tempered*) säuerlich; **to go** *or* **turn ~** (*milk, wine*) sauer

werden; (*fig: relationship*) sich trüben; **it's ~ grapes** (*fig*) die Trauben hängen zu hoch
source [sɔːs] *n* Quelle *f*; (*fig: of problem, anxiety*) Ursache *f*; **I have it from a reliable ~ that ...** ich habe es aus sicherer Quelle, dass ...
south [sauθ] *n* Süden *m* ▷ *adj* südlich, Süd- ▷ *adv* nach Süden; **(to the) ~ of** im Süden *or* südlich von; **to travel ~** nach Süden fahren; **the S~ of France** Südfrankreich *nt*
South Africa *n* Südafrika *nt*
South African *adj* südafrikanisch ▷ *n* Südafrikaner(in) *m(f)*
South America *n* Südamerika *nt*
South American *adj* südamerikanisch ▷ *n* Südamerikaner(in) *m(f)*
southbound ['sauθbaund] *adj* in Richtung Süden; (*carriageway*) Richtung Süden
south-east [sauθ'iːst] *n* Südosten *m*
South-East Asia *n* Südostasien *nt*
southerly ['sʌðəlɪ] *adj* südlich; (*wind*) aus südlicher Richtung
southern ['sʌðən] *adj* südlich, Süd-; **the ~ hemisphere** die südliche Halbkugel *or* Hemisphäre
South Korea *n* Südkorea *nt*
South Pole *n* Südpol *m*
South Sea Islands *npl* Südseeinseln *pl*
South Seas *npl* Südsee *f*
southward ['sauθwəd], **southwards** ['sauθwədz] *adv* nach Süden, in Richtung Süden
south-west [sauθ'wɛst] *n* Südwesten *m*
souvenir [suːvə'nɪəʳ] *n* Andenken *nt*, Souvenir *nt*
sovereign ['sɔvrɪn] *n* Herrscher(in) *m(f)*
sovereignty ['sɔvrɪntɪ] *n* Oberhoheit *f*, Souveränität *f*
soviet ['səuvɪət] (*formerly*) *adj* sowjetisch ▷ *n* Sowjetbürger(in) *m(f)*; **the S~ Union** die Sowjetunion *f*
sow¹ [sau] *n* Sau *f*
sow² [səu] (*pt* **~ed**, *pp* **~n**) *vt* (*lit, fig*) säen
soya ['sɔɪə], **soy** [sɔɪ] (*US*) *n*: **~ bean** Sojabohne *f*; **~ sauce** Sojasoße *f*
sozzled ['sɔzld] (*Brit: inf*) *adj* besoffen
spa [spɑː] *n* (*town*) Heilbad *nt*; (*US: also:* **health spa**) Fitnesszentrum *nt*
space [speɪs] *n* Platz *m*, Raum *m*; (*gap*) Lücke *f*; (*beyond Earth*) der Weltraum; (*interval, period*) Zeitraum *m* ▷ *cpd* Raum- ▷ *vt* (*also:* **space out**) verteilen; **to clear a ~ for sth** für etw Platz schaffen; **in a confined ~** auf engem Raum; **in a short ~ of time** in kurzer Zeit; **(with)in the ~ of an hour** innerhalb einer Stunde
space bar *n* (*on keyboard*) Leertaste *f*
spacecraft ['speɪskrɑːft] *n* Raumfahrzeug *nt*
spaceman ['speɪsmæn] (*irreg: like* **man**) *n* Raumfahrer *m*
spaceship ['speɪsʃɪp] *n* Raumschiff *nt*
space shuttle *n* Raumtransporter *m*
spacesuit ['speɪssuːt] *n* Raumanzug *m*
spacewoman ['speɪswumən] (*irreg: like* **woman**) *n* Raumfahrerin *f*
spacing ['speɪsɪŋ] *n* Abstand *m*; **single/double ~** einfacher/doppelter Zeilenabstand
spacious ['speɪʃəs] *adj* geräumig
spade [speɪd] *n* Spaten *m*; (*child's*) Schaufel *f*; **spades** *npl* (*Cards*) Pik *nt*
spadework ['speɪdwəːk] *n* (*fig*) Vorarbeit *f*
spaghetti [spə'gɛtɪ] *n* Spag(h)etti *pl*
Spain [speɪn] *n* Spanien *nt*
spam [spæm] (*Comput*) *n* Spam *m* ▷ *vt* wit Werbung bombardieren
span [spæn] *n* (*of bird, plane, arch*) Spannweite *f*; (*in time*) Zeitspanne *f* ▷ *vt* überspannen; (*fig: time*) sich erstrecken über *+acc*
Spaniard ['spænjəd] *n* Spanier(in) *m(f)*
spaniel ['spænjəl] *n* Spaniel *m*
Spanish ['spænɪʃ] *adj* spanisch ▷ *n* (*Ling*) Spanisch *nt*; **the Spanish** *npl* die Spanier *pl*; **~ omelette** *Omelett mit Paprikaschoten, Zwiebeln, Tomaten etc*
spank [spæŋk] *vt*: **to ~ sb's bottom** jdm den Hintern versohlen (*inf*)
spanner ['spænəʳ] (*Brit*) *n* Schraubenschlüssel *m*
spar [spɑːʳ] *n* (*Naut*) Sparren *m* ▷ *vi* (*Boxing*) ein Sparring *nt* machen
spare [spɛəʳ] *adj* (*free*) frei; (*extra: part, fuse etc*) Ersatz- ▷ *n* = **spare part** ▷ *vt* (*save: trouble etc*) (er)sparen; (*make available*) erübrigen; (*afford to give*) (übrig) haben; (*refrain from hurting*) verschonen; **these 2 are going ~** diese beiden sind noch übrig; **to ~** (*surplus*) übrig; **to ~ no expense** keine Kosten scheuen, an nichts sparen; **can you ~ the time?** haben Sie Zeit?; **I've a few minutes to ~** ich habe ein paar Minuten Zeit; **there is no time to ~** es ist keine Zeit; **~ me the details** verschone mich mit den Einzelheiten
spare part *n* Ersatzteil *nt*
spare room *n* Gästezimmer *nt*
spare time *n* Freizeit *f*
spare tyre *n* Reservereifen *m*
spare wheel *n* Reserverad *nt*
sparing ['spɛərɪŋ] *adj*: **to be ~ with** sparsam umgehen mit
sparingly ['spɛərɪŋlɪ] *adv* sparsam
spark [spɑːk] *n* (*lit, fig*) Funke *m*
sparking plug ['spɑːkɪŋ-] *n* = **spark plug**
sparkle ['spɑːkl] *n* Funkeln *nt*, Glitzern *nt* ▷ *vi* funkeln, glitzern
sparkler ['spɑːkləʳ] *n* (*firework*) Wunderkerze *f*
sparkling ['spɑːklɪŋ] *adj* (*water*) mit Kohlensäure; (*conversation*) vor Geist sprühend; (*performance*) glänzend; **~ wine** Schaumwein *m*
spark plug *n* Zündkerze *f*
sparring partner ['spɑːrɪŋ-] *n* (*also fig*) Sparringspartner *m*
sparrow ['spærəu] *n* Spatz *m*
sparse [spɑːs] *adj* spärlich; (*population*) dünn
spartan ['spɑːtən] *adj* (*fig*) spartanisch
spasm ['spæzəm] *n* (*Med*) Krampf *m*; (*fig: of anger etc*) Anfall *m*
spasmodic [spæz'mɔdɪk] *adj* (*fig*) sporadisch
spastic ['spæstɪk] (*old*) *n* Spastiker(in) *m(f)* ▷ *adj*

spastisch

spat [spæt] *pt, pp of* **spit** ▷ *n* (*US: quarrel*) Krach *m*

spate [speɪt] *n* (*fig*): **a ~ of** eine Flut von; **to be in full ~** (*river*) Hochwasser führen

spatial ['speɪʃl] *adj* räumlich

spatter ['spætəʳ] *vt* (*liquid*) verspritzen; (*surface*) bespritzen ▷ *vi* spritzen

spatula ['spætjulə] *n* (*Culin*) Spachtel *m*; (*Med*) Spatel *m*

spawn [spɔ:n] *vi* laichen ▷ *vt* hervorbringen, erzeugen ▷ *n* Laich *m*

SPCA (*US*) *n abbr* (= *Society for the Prevention of Cruelty to Animals*) Tierschutzverein *m*

SPCC (*US*) *n abbr* (= *Society for the Prevention of Cruelty to Children*) Kinderschutzbund *m*

speak [spi:k] (*pt* **spoke**, *pp* **spoken**) *vt* (*say*) sagen; (*language*) sprechen ▷ *vi* sprechen, reden; (*make a speech*) sprechen; **to ~ one's mind** seine Meinung sagen; **to ~ to sb/of** *or* **about sth** mit jdm/über etw *acc* sprechen *or* reden; **~ up!** sprich lauter!; **to ~ at a conference** bei einer Tagung einen Vortrag halten; **to ~ in a debate** in einer Debatte sprechen; **he has no money to ~ of** er hat so gut wie kein Geld; **so to ~** sozusagen ▸ **speak for** *vt fus*: **to ~ for sb** (*on behalf of*) in jds Namen *dat or* für jdn sprechen; **that picture is already spoken for** (*in shop*) das Bild ist schon verkauft *or* vergeben; **~ for yourself!** das meinst auch nur du!

speaker ['spi:kəʳ] *n* (*in public*) Redner(in) *m(f)*; (*also*: **loudspeaker**) Lautsprecher *m*; (*Pol*): **the S~** (*Brit, US*) der Sprecher, die Sprecherin; **are you a Welsh ~?** sprechen Sie Walisisch?

speaking ['spi:kɪŋ] *adj* sprechend; **Italian-~ people** Italienischsprechende *pl*; **to be on ~ terms** miteinander reden *or* sprechen; **~ clock** telefonische Zeitansage

spear [spɪəʳ] *n* Speer *m* ▷ *vt* aufspießen

spearhead ['spɪəhɛd] *vt* (*Mil, fig*) anführen

spearmint ['spɪəmɪnt] *n* Grüne Minze *f*

spec [spɛk] (*inf*) *n*: **on ~** auf Verdacht, auf gut Glück; **to buy/go on ~** auf gut Glück kaufen/hingehen

spec. *n abbr* (*Tech*) = **specification**

special ['spɛʃl] *adj* besondere(r, s); (*service, performance, adviser, permission, school*) Sonder- ▷ *n* (*train*) Sonderzug *m*; **take ~ care** pass besonders gut auf; **nothing ~** nichts Besonderes; **today's ~** (*at restaurant*) Tagesgericht *nt*

special agent *n* Agent(in) *m(f)*

special correspondent *n* Sonderberichterstatter(in) *m(f)*

special delivery *n* (*Post*): **by ~** durch Eilzustellung

special effects *npl* Spezialeffekte *pl*

specialist ['spɛʃəlɪst] *n* Spezialist(in) *m(f)*; (*Med*) Facharzt *m*, Fachärztin *f*; **heart ~** Facharzt *m*/Fachärztin *f* für Herzkrankheiten

speciality [spɛʃɪ'ælɪtɪ] *n* Spezialität *f*; (*study*) Spezialgebiet *nt*

specialize ['spɛʃəlaɪz] *vi*: **to ~ (in)** sich spezialisieren (auf +*acc*)

specially ['spɛʃlɪ] *adv* besonders, extra

special offer *n* Sonderangebot *nt*

specialty ['spɛʃəltɪ] (*esp US*) = **speciality**

species ['spi:ʃi:z] *n inv* Art *f*

specific [spə'sɪfɪk] *adj* (*fixed*) bestimmt; (*exact*) genau; **to be ~ to** eigentümlich sein für

specifically [spə'sɪfɪklɪ] *adv* (*specially*) speziell; (*exactly*) genau; **more ~** und zwar

specification [spɛsɪfɪ'keɪʃən] *n* genaue Angabe *f*; (*requirement*) Bedingung *f*; **specifications** *npl* (*Tech*) technische Daten *pl*

specify ['spɛsɪfaɪ] *vt* angeben; **unless otherwise specified** wenn nicht anders angegeben

specimen ['spɛsɪmən] *n* Exemplar *nt*; (*Med*) Probe *f*

specimen copy *n* Belegexemplar *nt*, Probeexemplar *nt*

specimen signature *n* Unterschriftsprobe *f*

speck [spɛk] *n* Fleckchen *nt*; (*of dust*) Körnchen *nt*

speckled ['spɛkld] *adj* gesprenkelt

specs [spɛks] (*inf*) *npl* Brille *f*

spectacle ['spɛktəkl] *n* (*scene*) Schauspiel *nt*; (*sight*) Anblick *m*; (*grand event*) Spektakel *nt*; **spectacles** *npl* (*glasses*) Brille *f*

spectacle case (*Brit*) *n* Brillenetui *nt*

spectacular [spɛk'tækjuləʳ] *adj* sensationell; (*success*) spektakulär ▷ *n* (*Theat etc*) Show *f*

spectator [spɛk'teɪtəʳ] *n* Zuschauer(in) *m(f)*; **~ sport** Publikumssport *m*

spectra ['spɛktrə] *npl of* **spectrum**

spectre, (*US*) **specter** ['spɛktəʳ] *n* Gespenst *nt*; (*fig*) (Schreck)gespenst *nt*

spectrum ['spɛktrəm] (*pl* **spectra**) *n* (*lit, fig*) Spektrum *nt*

speculate ['spɛkjuleɪt] *vi* (*Fin*) spekulieren; **to ~ about** spekulieren *or* Vermutungen anstellen über +*acc*

speculation [spɛkju'leɪʃən] *n* Spekulation *f*

speculative ['spɛkjulətɪv] *adj* spekulativ

speculator ['spɛkjuleɪtəʳ] *n* Spekulant(in) *m(f)*

sped [spɛd] *pt, pp of* **speed**

speech [spi:tʃ] *n* Sprache *f*; (*manner of speaking*) Sprechweise *f*; (*enunciation*) (Aus)sprache *f*; (*formal talk, Theat*) Rede *f*

speech day (*Brit*) *n* (*Scol*) ≈ Schulfeier *f*

speech impediment *n* Sprachfehler *m*

speechless ['spi:tʃlɪs] *adj* sprachlos

speech recognition software *n* (*Comput*) Spracherkennungssoftware *f*

speech therapist *n* Logopäde *m*, Logopädin *f*, Sprachtherapeut(in) *m(f)*

speech therapy *n* Logopädie *f*, Sprachtherapie *f*

speed [spi:d] (*pt, pp* **sped**) *n* Geschwindigkeit *f*, Schnelligkeit *f* ▷ *vi* (*exceed speed limit*) zu schnell fahren; **to ~ along** dahinsausen; **to ~ by** (*car etc*) vorbeischießen; (*years*) verfliegen; **at ~** (*Brit*) mit hoher Geschwindigkeit; **at full** *or* **top ~** mit Höchstgeschwindigkeit; **at a ~ of 70km/h** mit (einer Geschwindigkeit *or* einem

Tempo von) 70 km/h; **shorthand/typing ~s** Silben/Anschläge pro Minute; **a five-~ gearbox** ein Fünfganggetriebe *nt*
▸ **speed up** (*pt, pp* **~ed up**) *vi* beschleunigen; (*fig*) sich beschleunigen ▹ *vt* beschleunigen
speedboat ['spi:dbəut] *n* Rennboot *nt*
speed dial (*Tel*) *n* Kurzwahl *f* ▹ *adj* Kurzwahl-; ~ **button** Kurzwahltaste *f*
speedily ['spi:dɪlɪ] *adv* schnell
speeding ['spi:dɪŋ] *n* Geschwindigkeitsüberschreitung *f*
speed limit *n* Tempolimit *nt*, Geschwindigkeitsbegrenzung *f*
speedometer [spɪ'dɔmɪtə^r] *n* Tachometer *m*
speed trap *n* Radarfalle *f*
speedway ['spi:dweɪ] *n* (*also*: **speedway racing**) Speedway-Rennen *nt*
speedy ['spi:dɪ] *adj* schnell; (*reply, settlement*) prompt
speleologist [spɛlɪ'ɔlədʒɪst] *n* Höhlenkundler(in) *m(f)*
spell [spɛl] (*Brit*) (*pt, pp* **~ed**) *n* (*also*: **magic spell**) Zauber *m*; (*incantation*) Zauberspruch *m*; (*period of time*) Zeit *f*, Weile *f* ▹ *vt* schreiben; (*also*: **spell out**: *aloud*) buchstabieren; (*signify*) bedeuten; **to cast a ~ on sb** jdn verzaubern; **cold ~** Kältewelle *f*; **how do you ~ your name?** wie schreibt sich Ihr Name?; **can you ~ it for me?** können Sie das bitte buchstabieren?; **he can't ~** er kann keine Rechtschreibung
spellbound ['spɛlbaund] *adj* gebannt
spelling ['spɛlɪŋ] *n* Schreibweise *f*; (*ability*) Rechtschreibung *f*; **~ mistake** Rechtschreibfehler *m*
spelt [spɛlt] *pt, pp of* **spell**
spend [spɛnd] (*pt, pp* **spent**) *vt* (*money*) ausgeben; (*time, life*) verbringen; **to ~ time/money/effort on sth** Zeit/Geld/Mühe für etw aufbringen
spending ['spɛndɪŋ] *n* Ausgaben *pl*; **government ~** öffentliche Ausgaben *pl*
spending money *n* Taschengeld *nt*
spending power *n* Kaufkraft *f*
spendthrift ['spɛndθrɪft] *n* Verschwender(in) *m(f)*
spent [spɛnt] *pt, pp of* **spend** ▹ *adj* (*patience*) erschöpft; (*cartridge, bullets*) verbraucht; (*match*) abgebrannt
sperm [spə:m] *n* Samenzelle *f*, Spermium *nt*
sperm bank *n* Samenbank *f*
sperm whale *n* Pottwal *m*
spew [spju:] *vt* (*also*: **spew up**) erbrechen; (*fig*) ausspucken
sphere [sfɪə^r] *n* Kugel *f*; (*area*) Gebiet *nt*, Bereich *m*
spherical ['sfɛrɪkl] *adj* kugelförmig
sphinx [sfɪŋks] *n* Sphinx *f*
spice [spaɪs] *n* Gewürz *nt* ▹ *vt* würzen
spick-and-span ['spɪkən'spæn] *adj* blitzsauber
spicy ['spaɪsɪ] *adj* stark gewürzt
spider ['spaɪdə^r] *n* Spinne *f*; **~'s web** Spinnengewebe *nt*, Spinnennetz *nt*
spidery ['spaɪdərɪ] *adj* (*handwriting*) krakelig
spiel [spi:l] (*inf*) *n* Sermon *m*
spike [spaɪk] *n* (*point*) Spitze *f*; (*Bot*) Ähre *f*; (*Elec*) Spannungsspitze *f*; **spikes** *npl* (*Sport*) Spikes *pl*
spike heel (*US*) *n* Pfennigabsatz *m*
spiky ['spaɪkɪ] *adj* stachelig; (*branch*) dornig
spill [spɪl] (*pt, pp* **spilt** *or* **~ed**) *vt* verschütten ▹ *vi* verschüttet werden; **to ~ the beans** (*inf*: *fig*) alles ausplaudern
▸ **spill out** *vi* (*people*) herausströmen
▸ **spill over** *vi* überlaufen; (*fig*: *spread*) sich ausbreiten; **to ~ over into** sich auswirken auf *+acc*
spillage ['spɪlɪdʒ] *n* (*act*) Verschütten *nt*; (*quantity*) verschüttete Menge *f*
spin [spɪn] (*pt* **spun, span**, *pp* **spun**) *n* (*trip*) Spritztour *f*; (*revolution*) Drehung *f*; (*Aviat*) Trudeln *nt*; (*on ball*) Drall *m* ▹ *vt* (*wool etc*) spinnen; (*ball, coin*) (hoch)werfen; (*wheel*) drehen; (*Brit*: *also*: **spin-dry**) schleudern ▹ *vi* (*make thread*) spinnen; (*person*) sich drehen; (*car etc*) schleudern; **to ~ a yarn** Seemannsgarn spinnen; **to ~ a coin** (*Brit*) eine Münze werfen; **my head is ~ning** mir dreht sich alles
▸ **spin out** *vt* (*talk*) ausspinnen; (*job, holiday*) in die Länge ziehen; (*money*) strecken
spina bifida ['spaɪnə'bɪfɪdə] *n* offene Wirbelsäule *f*, Spina bifida *f*
spinach ['spɪnɪtʃ] *n* Spinat *m*
spinal ['spaɪnl] *adj* (*injury etc*) Rückgrat-
spinal column *n* Wirbelsäule *f*
spinal cord *n* Rückenmark *nt*
spindly ['spɪndlɪ] *adj* spindeldürr
spin doctor *n* PR-Fachmann *m*, PR-Fachfrau *f*
spin-dry ['spɪn'draɪ] *vt* schleudern
spin-dryer [spɪn'draɪə^r] (*Brit*) *n* (Wäsche)schleuder *f*
spine [spaɪn] *n* (*Anat*) Rückgrat *nt*; (*thorn*) Stachel *m*
spine-chilling ['spaɪntʃɪlɪŋ] *adj* schaurig, gruselig
spineless ['spaɪnlɪs] *adj* (*fig*) rückgratlos
spinner ['spɪnə^r] *n* (*of thread*) Spinner(in) *m(f)*
spinning ['spɪnɪŋ] *n* (*art*) Spinnen *nt*
spinning top *n* Kreisel *m*
spinning wheel *n* Spinnrad *nt*
spin-off ['spɪnɔf] *n* (*fig*) Nebenprodukt *nt*
spinster ['spɪnstə^r] *n* unverheiratete Frau; (*pej*) alte Jungfer
spiral ['spaɪərl] *n* Spirale *f* ▹ *vi* (*fig*: *prices etc*) in die Höhe klettern; **the inflationary ~** die Inflationsspirale
spiral staircase *n* Wendeltreppe *f*
spire ['spaɪə^r] *n* Turmspitze *f*
spirit ['spɪrɪt] *n* Geist *m*; (*soul*) Seele *f*; (*energy*) Elan *m*, Schwung *m*; (*courage*) Mut *m*; (*sense*) Geist *m*, Sinn *m*; (*frame of mind*) Stimmung *f*; **spirits** *npl* (*drink*) Spirituosen *pl*; **in good ~s** guter Laune; **community ~** Gemeinschaftssinn *m*
spirited ['spɪrɪtɪd] *adj* (*resistance, defence*) mutig; (*performance*) lebendig
spirit level *n* Wasserwaage *f*
spiritual ['spɪrɪtjuəl] *adj* geistig, seelisch;

(religious) geistlich ▷ *n* *(also:* **Negro spiritual***)* Spiritual *nt*
spiritualism ['spɪrɪtjuəlɪzəm] *n* Spiritismus *m*
spit [spɪt] *(pt, pp* **spat***)* *n* *(for roasting)* Spieß *m*; *(saliva)* Spucke *f* ▷ *vi* spucken; *(fire)* Funken sprühen; *(cooking)* spritzen; *(inf: rain)* tröpfeln
spite [spaɪt] *n* Boshaftigkeit *f* ▷ *vt* ärgern; **in ~ of** trotz *+gen*
spiteful ['spaɪtful] *adj* boshaft, gemein
spitroast ['spɪtrəust] *n* Spießbraten *m*
spitting ['spɪtɪŋ] *n*: **"~ prohibited"** „Spucken verboten" ▷ *adj*: **to be the ~ image of sb** jdm wie aus dem Gesicht geschnitten sein
spittle ['spɪtl] *n* Speichel *m*, Spucke *f*
spiv [spɪv] *(Brit: inf: pej)* *n* schmieriger Typ *m*
splash [splæʃ] *n* *(sound)* Platschen *nt*; *(of colour)* Tupfer *m* ▷ *excl* platsch! ▷ *vt* bespritzen ▷ *vi* *(also:* **splash about***)* herumplan(t)schen; *(water, rain)* spritzen; **to ~ paint on the floor** den Fußboden mit Farbe bespritzen
splashdown ['splæʃdaun] *n* *(Space)* Wasserung *f*
splayfooted ['spleɪfutɪd] *adj* mit nach außen gestellten Füßen
spleen [spli:n] *n* Milz *f*
splendid ['splɛndɪd] *adj* hervorragend, ausgezeichnet; *(impressive)* prächtig
splendour, (US) **splendor** ['splɛndəʳ] *n* Pracht *f*; **splendours** *npl* Pracht *f*
splice [splaɪs] *vt* spleißen, kleben
splint [splɪnt] *n* Schiene *f*
splinter ['splɪntəʳ] *n* Splitter *m* ▷ *vi* (zer)splittern
splinter group *n* Splittergruppe *f*
split [splɪt] *(pt, pp* **~***)* *n* *(tear)* Riss *m*; *(fig: division)* Aufteilung *f*; *(: difference)* Kluft *f*; *(Pol)* Spaltung *f* ▷ *vt* *(divide)* aufteilen; *(party)* spalten; *(share equally)* teilen ▷ *vi* *(divide)* sich aufteilen; *(tear)* reißen; **to do the ~s** (einen) Spagat machen; **let's ~ the difference** teilen wir uns die Differenz
▶ **split up** *vi* sich trennen; *(meeting)* sich auflösen
split-level ['splɪtlɛvl] *adj* mit versetzten Geschossen
split peas *npl* getrocknete (halbe) Erbsen *pl*
split personality *n* gespaltene Persönlichkeit *f*
split second *n* Bruchteil *m* einer Sekunde
splitting ['splɪtɪŋ] *adj*: **a ~ headache** rasende Kopfschmerzen *pl*
splutter ['splʌtəʳ] *vi* *(engine etc)* stottern; *(person)* prusten
spoil [spɔɪl] *(pt, pp* **spoilt** *or* **~ed***)* *vt* verderben; *(child)* verwöhnen; *(ballot paper, vote)* ungültig machen ▷ *vi*: **to be ~ing for a fight** Streit suchen
spoils [spɔɪlz] *npl* Beute *f*; *(fig)* Gewinn *m*
spoilsport ['spɔɪlspɔ:t] *(pej)* *n* Spielverderber *m*
spoilt [spɔɪlt] *pt, pp of* **spoil** ▷ *adj* *(child)* verwöhnt; *(ballot paper)* ungültig
spoke [spəuk] *pt of* **speak** ▷ *n* Speiche *f*
spoken ['spəukn] *pp of* **speak**
spokesman ['spəuksmən] *(irreg: like* **man***)* *n* Sprecher *m*
spokesperson ['spəukspə:sn] *n* Sprecher(in) *m(f)*
spokeswoman ['spəukswumən] *(irreg: like* **woman***)* *n* Sprecherin *f*
sponge [spʌndʒ] *n* Schwamm *m*; *(also:* **sponge cake***)* Biskuit(kuchen) *m* ▷ *vt* mit einem Schwamm waschen ▷ *vi*: **to ~ off** *or* **on sb** jdm auf der Tasche liegen
sponge bag *(Brit)* *n* Waschbeutel *m*, Kulturbeutel *m*
sponger ['spʌndʒəʳ] *(pej)* *n* Schmarotzer *m*
spongy ['spʌndʒɪ] *adj* schwammig
sponsor ['spɔnsəʳ] *n* Sponsor(in) *m(f)*, Geldgeber(in) *m(f)*; *(Brit: for charitable event)* Sponsor(in) *m(f)*; *(for application, bill etc)* Befürworter(in) *m(f)* ▷ *vt* sponsern, finanziell unterstützen; *(fund-raiser)* sponsern; *(applicant)* unterstützen; *(proposal, bill etc)* befürworten; **I ~ed him at 3p a mile** *(in fund-raising race)* ich habe mich verpflichtet, ihm 3 Pence pro Meile zu geben
sponsorship ['spɔnsəʃɪp] *n* finanzielle Unterstützung *f*
spontaneity [spɔntə'neɪɪtɪ] *n* Spontaneität *f*
spontaneous [spɔn'teɪnɪəs] *adj* spontan; **~ combustion** Selbstentzündung *f*
spoof [spu:f] *n* *(parody)* Parodie *f*; *(hoax)* Ulk *m*
spooky ['spu:kɪ] *(inf)* *adj* gruselig
spool [spu:l] *n* Spule *f*
spoon [spu:n] *n* Löffel *m*
spoon-feed ['spu:nfi:d] *vt* (mit dem Löffel) füttern; *(fig)* gängeln
spoonful ['spu:nful] *n* Löffel *m*
sporadic [spə'rædɪk] *adj* sporadisch, vereinzelt
sport [spɔ:t] *n* Sport *m*; *(type)* Sportart *f*; *(also:* **good sport***: person)* feiner Kerl *m* ▷ *vt* *(wear)* tragen; **indoor ~s** Hallensport *m*; **outdoor ~s** Sport *m* im Freien
sporting ['spɔ:tɪŋ] *adj* *(event etc)* Sport-; *(generous)* großzügig; **to give sb a ~ chance** jdm eine faire Chance geben
sport jacket *(US)* *n* = **sports jacket**
sports car *n* Sportwagen *m*
sports centre *n* Sportzentrum *nt*
sports ground *n* Sportplatz *m*
sports jacket *(Brit)* *n* Sakko *m*
sportsman ['spɔ:tsmən] *(irreg: like* **man***)* *n* Sportler *m*
sportsmanship ['spɔ:tsmənʃɪp] *n* Sportlichkeit *f*
sports page *n* Sportseite *f*
sportswear ['spɔ:tswɛəʳ] *n* Sportkleidung *f*
sportswoman ['spɔ:tswumən] *(irreg: like* **woman***)* *n* Sportlerin *f*
sporty ['spɔ:tɪ] *adj* sportlich
spot [spɔt] *n* *(mark)* Fleck *m*; *(dot)* Punkt *m*; *(on skin)* Pickel *m*; *(place)* Stelle *f*, Platz *m*; *(Radio, TV)* Nummer *f*, Auftritt *m*; *(also:* **spot advertisement***)* Werbespot *m*; *(small amount)*: **a ~ of** ein bisschen ▷ *vt* entdecken; **on the ~** *(in that place)* an Ort und Stelle; *(immediately)* auf der Stelle; **to be in a ~** in der Klemme

sitzen; **to put sb on the ~** jdn in Verlegenheit bringen; **to come out in ~s** Pickel bekommen
spot check *n* Stichprobe *f*
spotless ['spɔtlɪs] *adj* makellos sauber
spotlight ['spɔtlaɪt] *n* Scheinwerfer *m*; (*in room*) Strahler *m*
spot-on [spɔt'ɔn] (*Brit: inf*) *adj* genau richtig
spot price *n* Kassapreis *m*
spotted ['spɔtɪd] *adj* gepunktet
spotty ['spɔtɪ] *adj* pickelig
spouse [spaus] *n* (*male*) Gatte *m*; (*female*) Gattin *f*
spout [spaut] *n* (*of jug, teapot*) Tülle *f*; (*of pipe*) Ausfluss *m*; (*of liquid*) Strahl *m* ▹ *vi* spritzen; (*flames*) sprühen
sprain [spreɪn] *n* Verstauchung *f* ▹ *vt*: **to ~ one's ankle/wrist** sich *dat* den Knöchel/das Handgelenk verstauchen
sprang [spræŋ] *pt of* **spring**
sprawl [sprɔ:l] *vi* (*person*) sich ausstrecken; (*place*) wild wuchern ▹ *n*: **urban ~** wild wuchernde Ausbreitung des Stadtgebietes; **to send sb ~ing** jdn zu Boden werfen
spray [spreɪ] *n* (*small drops*) Sprühnebel *m*; (*sea spray*) Gischt *m or f*; (*container*) Sprühdose *f*; (*garden spray*) Sprühgerät *nt*; (*of flowers*) Strauß *m* ▹ *vt* sprühen, spritzen; (*crops*) spritzen ▹ *cpd* (*deodorant*) Sprüh-; **~ can** Sprühdose *f*
spread [sprɛd] (*pt, pp* **~**) *n* (*range*) Spektrum *nt*; (*selection*) Auswahl *f*; (*distribution*) Verteilung *f*; (*for bread*) (Brot)aufstrich *m*; (*inf: food*) Festessen *nt*; (*Press, Typ: two pages*) Doppelseite *f* ▹ *vt* ausbreiten; (*butter*) streichen; (*workload, wealth, repayments etc*) verteilen; (*scatter*) verstreuen; (*rumour, disease*) verbreiten ▹ *vi* (*disease, news*) sich verbreiten; (*also*: **spread out**: *stain*) sich ausbreiten; **to get a middle-age ~** in den mittleren Jahren Speck ansetzen
▸ **spread out** *vi* (*move apart*) sich verteilen
spread-eagled ['sprɛdi:gld] *adj* mit ausgestreckten Armen und Beinen; **to be** *or* **lie ~** mit ausgestreckten Armen und Beinen daliegen
spreadsheet ['sprɛdʃi:t] *n* (*Comput*) Tabellenkalkulation *f*
spree [spri:] *n*: **to go on a ~** (*drinking*) eine Zechtour machen; (*spending*) groß einkaufen gehen
sprig [sprɪg] *n* Zweig *m*
sprightly ['spraɪtlɪ] *adj* rüstig
spring [sprɪŋ] (*pt* **sprang**, *pp* **sprung**) *n* (*coiled metal*) Sprungfeder *f*; (*season*) Frühling *m*, Frühjahr *nt*; (*of water*) Quelle *f* ▹ *vi* (*leap*) springen ▹ *vt*: **to ~ a leak** (*pipe etc*) undicht werden; **in ~** im Frühling *or* Frühjahr; **to walk with a ~ in one's step** mit federnden Schritten gehen; **to ~ from** (*result*) herrühren von; **to ~ into action** aktiv werden; **he sprang the news on me** er hat mich mit der Nachricht überrascht
▸ **spring up** *vi* (*building, plant*) aus dem Boden schießen
springboard ['sprɪŋbɔ:d] *n* (*Sport, fig*) Sprungbrett *nt*
spring-clean [sprɪŋ'kli:n], **spring-cleaning** [sprɪŋ'kli:nɪŋ] *n* Frühjahrsputz *m*
spring onion (*Brit*) *n* Frühlingszwiebel *f*
spring roll *n* Frühlingsrolle *f*
springtime ['sprɪŋtaɪm] *n* Frühling *m*
springy ['sprɪŋɪ] *adj* federnd; (*mattress*) weich gefedert
sprinkle ['sprɪŋkl] *vt* (*liquid*) sprenkeln; (*salt, sugar*) streuen; **to ~ water on, ~ with water** mit Wasser besprengen; **to ~ sugar** *etc* **on, ~ with sugar** *etc* mit Zucker *etc* bestreuen
sprinkler ['sprɪŋklə^r] *n* (*for lawn*) Rasensprenger *m*; (*to put out fire*) Sprinkler *m*
sprinkling ['sprɪŋklɪŋ] *n*: **a ~ of** (*water*) ein paar Tropfen; (*salt, sugar*) eine Prise; (*fig*) ein paar ...
sprint [sprɪnt] *n* Sprint *m* ▹ *vi* rennen; (*Sport*) sprinten; **the 200 metres ~** der 200-Meter-Lauf
sprinter ['sprɪntə^r] *n* Sprinter(in) *m(f)*
sprite [spraɪt] *n* Kobold *m*
spritzer ['sprɪtsə^r] *n* Schorle *f*
sprocket ['sprɔkɪt] *n* Kettenzahnrad *nt*
sprout [spraut] *vi* sprießen; (*vegetable*) keimen
sprouts [sprauts] *npl* (*also*: **Brussels sprouts**) Rosenkohl *m*
spruce [spru:s] *n inv* Fichte *f* ▹ *adj* gepflegt, adrett
▸ **spruce up** *vt* auf Vordermann bringen (*inf*); **to ~ o.s. up** sein Äußeres pflegen
sprung [sprʌŋ] *pp of* **spring**
spry [spraɪ] *adj* rüstig
SPUC *n abbr* (*= Society for the Protection of the Unborn Child*) *Gesellschaft zum Schutz des ungeborenen Lebens*
spud [spʌd] (*inf*) *n* Kartoffel *f*
spun [spʌn] *pt, pp of* **spin**
spur [spə:^r] *n* Sporn *m*; (*fig*) Ansporn *m* ▹ *vt* (*also*: **spur on**: *fig*) anspornen; **on the ~ of the moment** ganz spontan
spurious ['spjuərɪəs] *adj* falsch
spurn [spə:n] *vt* verschmähen
spurt [spə:t] *n* (*of blood etc*) Strahl *m*; (*of energy*) Anwandlung *f* ▹ *vi* (*blood*) (heraus)spritzen; **to put on a ~** (*lit, fig*) einen Spurt einlegen
sputter ['spʌtə^r] *vi* = **splutter**
spy [spaɪ] *n* Spion(in) *m(f)* ▹ *vi*: **to ~ on** nachspionieren *+dat* ▹ *vt* sehen ▹ *cpd* (*film, story*) Spionage-
spying ['spaɪɪŋ] *n* Spionage *f*
Sq. *abbr* (*in address: = square*) ≈ Pl.
sq. *abbr* = **square**
squabble ['skwɔbl] *vi* (sich) zanken ▹ *n* Streit *m*
squad [skwɔd] *n* (*Mil*) Trupp *m*; (*Police*) Kommando *nt*; (*: drug/fraud squad*) Dezernat *nt*; (*Sport*) Mannschaft *f*; **flying ~** (*Police*) Überfallkommando *nt*
squad car (*Brit*) *n* (*Police*) Streifenwagen *m*
squaddie ['skwɔdɪ] (*Brit*) *n* (*private soldier*) Gefreite(r) *m*
squadron ['skwɔdrn] *n* (*Mil*) Schwadron *f*; (*Aviat*) Staffel *f*; (*Naut*) Geschwader *nt*
squalid ['skwɔlɪd] *adj* verkommen; (*conditions*) elend; (*sordid*) erbärmlich

squall [skwɔ:l] *n* Bö(e) *f*
squalor ['skwɔləʳ] *n* Elend *nt*
squander ['skwɔndəʳ] *vt* verschwenden; (*chances*) vertun
square [skwɛəʳ] *n* Quadrat *nt*; (*in town*) Platz *m*; (*US: block of houses*) Block *m*; (*also*: **set square**) Zeichendreieck *nt*; (*inf: person*) Spießer *m* ▹ *adj* quadratisch; (*inf: ideas, person*) spießig ▹ *vt* (*arrange*) ausrichten; (*Math*) quadrieren; (*reconcile*) in Einklang bringen ▹ *vi* (*accord*) übereinstimmen; **we're back to ~ one** jetzt sind wir wieder da, wo wir angefangen haben; **all ~** (*Sport*) unentschieden; (*fig*) quitt; **a ~ meal** eine ordentliche Mahlzeit; **2 metres ~** 2 Meter im Quadrat; **2 ~ metres** 2 Quadratmeter; **I'll ~ it with him** (*inf*) ich mache das mit ihm ab; **can you ~ it with your conscience?** können Sie das mit Ihrem Gewissen vereinbaren?
▸ **square up** (*Brit*) *vi* abrechnen
square bracket *n* eckige Klammer *f*
squarely ['skwɛəlɪ] *adv* (*directly*) direkt, genau; (*firmly*) fest; (*honestly*) ehrlich; (*fairly*) gerecht, fair
square root *n* Quadratwurzel *f*
squash [skwɔʃ] *n* (*Brit*): **lemon/orange ~** Zitronen-/Orangensaftgetränk *nt*; (*US: marrow etc*) Kürbis *m*; (*Sport*) Squash *nt* ▹ *vt* zerquetschen
squat [skwɔt] *adj* gedrungen ▹ *vi* (*also*: **squat down**) sich (hin)hocken; (*on property*): **to ~ (in a house)** ein Haus besetzen
squatter ['skwɔtəʳ] *n* Hausbesetzer(in) *m(f)*
squawk [skwɔ:k] *vi* kreischen
squeak [skwi:k] *vi* quietschen; (*mouse etc*) piepsen ▹ *n* Quietschen *nt*; (*of mouse etc*) Piepsen *nt*
squeaky-clean [skwi:kɪ'kli:n] (*inf*) *adj* blitzsauber
squeal [skwi:l] *vi* quietschen
squeamish ['skwi:mɪʃ] *adj* empfindlich
squeeze [skwi:z] *n* Drücken *nt*; (*Econ*) Beschränkung *f*; (*also*: **credit squeeze**) Kreditbeschränkung *f* ▹ *vt* drücken; (*lemon etc*) auspressen ▹ *vi*: **to ~ past sth** sich an etw *dat* vorbeidrücken; **to ~ under sth** sich unter etw *dat* durchzwängen; **to give sth a ~** etw drücken; **a ~ of lemon** ein Spritzer *m* Zitronensaft
▸ **squeeze out** *vt* (*juice etc*) (her)auspressen; (*fig: exclude*) hinausdrängen
squelch [skwɛltʃ] *vi* (*mud etc*) quatschen
squib [skwɪb] *n* Knallfrosch *m*
squid [skwɪd] *n* Tintenfisch *m*
squiggle ['skwɪgl] *n* Schnörkel *m*
squint [skwɪnt] *vi* (*in the sunlight*) blinzeln ▹ *n* (*Med*) Schielen *nt*; **he has a ~** er schielt
squire ['skwaɪəʳ] (*Brit*) *n* Gutsherr *m*; (*inf*) Chef *m*
squirm [skwə:m] *vi* (*lit, fig*) sich winden
squirrel ['skwɪrəl] *n* Eichhörnchen *nt*
squirt [skwə:t] *vi, vt* spritzen
Sr *abbr* (*in names*: = *senior*) sen.; (*Rel*) = **sister**
SRC (*Brit*) *n abbr* (= *Students' Representative Council*) *studentische Vertretung*
Sri Lanka [srɪ'læŋkə] *n* Sri Lanka *nt*
SRO (*US*) *abbr* (= *standing room only*) nur Stehplätze
SS *abbr* = **steamship**
SSA (*US*) *n abbr* (= *Social Security Administration*) *Sozialversicherungsbehörde*
SST (*US*) *n abbr* (= *supersonic transport*) Überschallverkehr *m*
ST (*US*) *abbr* = **standard time**
St *abbr* (= *saint*) St.; (= *street*) Str.
stab [stæb] *n* Stich *m*, Stoß *m*; (*inf: try*): **to have a ~ at sth** etw probieren ▹ *vt* (*person*) niederstechen; (*body*) einstechen auf +*acc*; **a ~ of pain** ein stechender Schmerz; **to ~ sb to death** jdn erstechen
stabbing ['stæbɪŋ] *n* Messerstecherei *f* ▹ *adj* (*pain*) stechend
stability [stə'bɪlɪtɪ] *n* Stabilität *f*
stabilization [steɪbəlaɪ'zeɪʃən] *n* Stabilisierung *f*
stabilize ['steɪbəlaɪz] *vt* stabilisieren ▹ *vi* sich stabilisieren
stabilizer ['steɪbəlaɪzəʳ] *n* (*Aviat*) Stabilisierungsfläche *f*; (*Naut, food additive*) Stabilisator *m*
stable ['steɪbl] *adj* stabil; (*marriage*) dauerhaft ▹ *n* Stall *m*; **riding ~s** Reitstall *m*
staccato [stə'kɑ:təu] *adv* (*Mus*) stakkato ▹ *adj* abgehackt
stack [stæk] *n* Stapel *m*; (*of books etc*) Stoß *m* ▹ *vt* (*also*: **stack up**) aufstapeln; **~s of time** (*Brit: inf*) jede Menge Zeit; **to ~ with** vollstapeln mit
stadia ['steɪdɪə] *npl of* **stadium**
stadium ['steɪdɪəm] (*pl* **stadia** *or* **~s**) *n* Stadion *nt*
staff [stɑ:f] *n* (*workforce, servants*) Personal *nt*; (*Brit: also*: **teaching staff**) (Lehrer)kollegium *nt*; (*stick, Mil*) Stab *m* ▹ *vt* (mit Personal) besetzen; **one of his ~** einer seiner Mitarbeiter; **a member of ~** ein(e) Mitarbeiter(in) *m(f)*; (*Scol*) ein(e) Lehrer(in) *m(f)*
staffroom ['stɑ:fru:m] *n* (*Scol*) Lehrerzimmer *nt*
Staffs (*Brit*) *abbr* (*Post*) = *Staffordshire*
stag [stæg] *n* Hirsch *m*; (*Brit: Stock Exchange*) Spekulant *m* (*der junge Aktien aufkauft*); **~ market** (*Brit: Stock Exchange*) Spekulantenmarkt *m*
stage [steɪdʒ] *n* Bühne *f*; (*platform*) Podium *nt*; (*point, period*) Stadium *nt* ▹ *vt* (*play*) aufführen; (*demonstration*) organisieren; (*perform: recovery etc*) schaffen; **the ~** das Theater, die Bühne; **in ~s** etappenweise; **to go through a difficult ~** eine schwierige Phase durchmachen; **in the early/final ~s** im Anfangs-/Endstadium
stagecoach ['steɪdʒkəutʃ] *n* Postkutsche *f*
stage door *n* Bühneneingang *m*
stage fright *n* Lampenfieber *nt*
stagehand ['steɪdʒhænd] *n* Bühnenarbeiter(in) *m(f)*
stage-manage ['steɪdʒmænɪdʒ] *vt* (*fig*) inszenieren

stage manager *n* Inspizient(in) *m(f)*
stagger ['stægəʳ] *vi* schwanken, taumeln ▷ *vt* (*amaze*) die Sprache verschlagen +*dat*; (*hours, holidays*) staffeln
staggering ['stægərɪŋ] *adj* (*amazing*) atemberaubend
staging post ['steɪdʒɪŋ-] *n* Zwischenstation *f*
stagnant ['stægnənt] *adj* (*water*) stehend; (*economy etc*) stagnierend
stagnate [stæg'neɪt] *vi* (*economy etc*) stagnieren; (*person*) verdummen
stagnation [stæg'neɪʃən] *n* Stagnation *f*
stag night, **stag party** *n* Herrenabend *m*; *siehe Info-Artikel*

STAG NIGHT

Als *stag night* bezeichnet man eine feuchtfröhliche Männerparty, die kurz vor einer Hochzeit vom Bräutigam und seinen Freunden meist in einem Gasthaus oder Nachtklub abgehalten wird. Diese Feiern sind oft sehr ausgelassen und können manchmal auch zu weit gehen (wenn dem betrunkenen Bräutigam ein Streich gespielt wird). Siehe auch *hen night*.

staid [steɪd] *adj* gesetzt
stain [steɪn] *n* Fleck *m*; (*colouring*) Beize *f* ▷ *vt* beflecken; (*wood*) beizen
stained glass window [steɪnd-] *n* buntes Glasfenster *nt*
stainless steel ['steɪnlɪs-] *n* (rostfreier) Edelstahl *m*
stain remover *n* Fleckentferner *m*
stair [stɛəʳ] *n* (*step*) Stufe *f*; **stairs** *npl* (*flight of steps*) Treppe *f*; **on the ~s** auf der Treppe
staircase ['stɛəkeɪs] *n* Treppe *f*
stairway ['stɛəweɪ] *n* = **staircase**
stairwell ['stɛəwɛl] *n* Treppenhaus *nt*
stake [steɪk] *n* (*post*) Pfahl *m*, Pfosten *m*; (*Comm*) Anteil *m*; (*Betting: gen pl*) Einsatz *m* ▷ *vt* (*money*) setzen; (*also*: **stake out**: *area*) abstecken; **to be at ~** auf dem Spiel stehen; **to have a ~ in sth** einen Anteil an etw *dat* haben; **to ~ a claim (to sth)** sich *dat* ein Anrecht (auf etw *acc*) sichern; **to ~ one's life on sth** seinen Kopf auf etw *acc* wetten; **to ~ one's reputation on sth** sich für etw verbürgen
stakeout ['steɪkaut] *n* (*surveillance*) Überwachung *f*
stalactite ['stæləktaɪt] *n* Stalaktit *m*
stalagmite ['stæləgmaɪt] *n* Stalagmit *m*
stale [steɪl] *adj* (*bread*) altbacken; (*food*) alt; (*smell*) muffig; (*air*) verbraucht; (*beer*) schal
stalemate ['steɪlmeɪt] *n* (*Chess*) Patt *nt*; (*fig*) Sackgasse *f*
stalk [stɔːk] *n* Stiel *m* ▷ *vt* sich heranpirschen an +*acc* ▷ *vi*: **to ~ out/off** hinaus-/davonstolzieren
stall [stɔːl] *n* (*Brit*: *in market etc*) Stand *m*; (*in stable*) Box *f* ▷ *vt* (*engine, car*) abwürgen; (*fig*: *person*) hinhalten; (: *decision etc*) hinauszögern ▷ *vi* (*engine*) absterben; (*car*) stehen bleiben; (*fig*: *person*) ausweichen; **stalls** *npl* (*Brit*: *in cinema, theatre*) Parkett *nt*; **a seat in the ~s** ein Platz im Parkett; **a clothes/flower ~** ein Kleidungs-/Blumenstand; **to ~ for time** versuchen, Zeit zu gewinnen
stallholder ['stɔːlhəuldəʳ] (*Brit*) *n* Standbesitzer(in) *m(f)*
stallion ['stæljən] *n* Hengst *m*
stalwart ['stɔːlwət] *adj* treu
stamen ['steɪmɛn] *n* Staubgefäß *nt*
stamina ['stæmɪnə] *n* Ausdauer *f*
stammer ['stæməʳ] *n* Stottern *nt* ▷ *vi* stottern; **to have a ~** stottern
stamp [stæmp] *n* (*lit, fig*) Stempel *m*; (*also*: **postage stamp**) Briefmarke *f* ▷ *vi* stampfen; (*also*: **stamp one's foot**) (mit dem Fuß) aufstampfen ▷ *vt* stempeln; (*with postage stamp*) frankieren; **~ed addressed envelope** frankierter Rückumschlag
▸ **stamp out** *vt* (*fire*) austreten; (*fig*: *crime*) ausrotten; (: *opposition*) unterdrücken
stamp album *n* Briefmarkenalbum *nt*
stamp collecting *n* Briefmarkensammeln *nt*
stamp duty (*Brit*) *n* (Stempel)gebühr *f*
stampede [stæm'piːd] *n* (*of animals*) wilde Flucht *f*; (*fig*) Massenandrang *m*
stamp machine *n* Briefmarkenautomat *m*
stance [stæns] *n* Haltung *f*; (*fig*) Einstellung *f*
stand [stænd] (*pt, pp* **stood**) *n* (*Comm*) Stand *m*; (*Sport*) Tribüne *f*; (*piece of furniture*) Ständer *m* ▷ *vi* stehen; (*rise*) aufstehen; (*remain*) bestehen bleiben; (*in election etc*) kandidieren ▷ *vt* stellen; (*tolerate, withstand*) ertragen; **to make a ~ against sth** Widerstand gegen etw leisten; **to take a ~ on sth** einen Standpunkt zu etw vertreten; **to take the ~** (*US*: *Law*) in den Zeugenstand treten; **to ~ at** (*value, score etc*) betragen; (*level*) liegen bei; **to ~ for parliament** (*Brit*) in den Parlamentswahlen kandidieren; **to ~ to gain/lose sth** etw gewinnen/verlieren können; **it ~s to reason** es ist einleuchtend; **as things ~** nach Lage der Dinge; **to ~ sb a drink/meal** jdm einen Drink/ein Essen spendieren; **I can't ~ him** ich kann ihn nicht leiden *or* ausstehen; **we don't ~ a chance** wir haben keine Chance; **to ~ trial** vor Gericht stehen
▸ **stand by** *vi* (*be ready*) sich bereithalten; (*fail to help*) (unbeteiligt) danebenstehen ▷ *vt fus* (*opinion, decision*) stehen zu; (*person*) halten zu
▸ **stand down** *vi* zurücktreten
▸ **stand for** *vt fus* (*signify*) bedeuten; (*represent*) stehen für; (*tolerate*) sich *dat* gefallen lassen
▸ **stand in for** *vt fus* vertreten
▸ **stand out** *vi* hervorstechen
▸ **stand up** *vi* aufstehen
▸ **stand up for** *vt fus* eintreten für
▸ **stand up to** *vt fus* standhalten +*dat*; (*person*) sich behaupten gegenüber +*dat*
stand-alone ['stændələun] *adj* (*Comput*) selb(st)ständig
standard ['stændəd] *n* (*level*) Niveau *nt*; (*norm*)

Norm *f*; (*criterion*) Maßstab *m*; (*flag*) Standarte *f* ▷ *adj* (*size, model, value etc*) Standard-; (*normal*) normal; **standards** *npl* (*morals*) (sittliche) Maßstäbe *pl*; **to be** *or* **to come up to ~** den Anforderungen genügen; **to apply a double ~** mit zweierlei Maß messen
Standard Grade (*Scot*) *n* (*Scol*) *Schulabschlusszeugnis*, ≈ mittlere Reife *f*
standardization [stændədaɪ'zeɪʃən] *n* Vereinheitlichung *f*
standardize ['stændədaɪz] *vt* vereinheitlichen
standard lamp (*Brit*) *n* Stehlampe *f*
standard of living *n* Lebensstandard *m*
standard time *n* Normalzeit *f*
stand-by, standby ['stændbaɪ] *n* Reserve *f*; (*also*: **standby ticket**) Stand-by-Ticket *nt* ▷ *adj* (*generator*) Reserve-, Ersatz-; **to be on ~** (*doctor*) Bereitschaftsdienst haben; (*crew, firemen etc*) in Bereitschaft sein, einsatzbereit sein
stand-by ticket *n* Stand-by-Ticket *nt*
stand-in ['stændɪn] *n* Ersatz *m*
standing ['stændɪŋ] *adj* (*permanent*) ständig; (*army*) stehend ▷ *n* (*status*) Rang *m*, Stellung *f*; **a ~ ovation** stürmischer Beifall; **of many years' ~** von langjähriger Dauer; **a relationship of 6 months' ~** eine seit 6 Monaten bestehende Beziehung; **a man of some ~** ein angesehener Mann
standing joke *n* Standardwitz *m*
standing order (*Brit*) *n* (*at bank*) Dauerauftrag *m*
standing room *n* Stehplätze *pl*
standoff *n* (*situation*) ausweglose *or* verfahrene Situation *f*
stand-offish [stænd'ɔfɪʃ] *adj* distanziert
standpat ['stændpæt] (*US*) *adj* konservativ
standpipe ['stændpaɪp] *n* Steigrohr *nt*
standpoint ['stændpɔɪnt] *n* Standpunkt *m*
standstill ['stændstɪl] *n*: **to be at a ~** stillstehen; (*fig: negotiations*) in eine Sackgasse geraten sein; **to come to a ~** (*traffic*) zum Stillstand kommen
stank [stæŋk] *pt of* **stink**
stanza ['stænzə] *n* Strophe *f*
staple ['steɪpl] *n* (*for papers*) Heftklammer *f*; (*chief product*) Hauptartikel *m* ▷ *adj* (*food, diet*) Grund-, Haupt- ▷ *vt* heften
stapler ['steɪplə^r] *n* Hefter *m*
star [stɑː^r] *n* Stern *m*; (*celebrity*) Star *m* ▷ *vt* (*Theat, Cine*) in der Hauptrolle zeigen ▷ *vi*: **to ~ in** die Hauptrolle haben in; **the stars** *npl* (*horoscope*) das Horoskop; **4-~ hotel** 4-Sterne-Hotel *nt*; **2-~ petrol** (*Brit*) Normal(benzin) *nt*; **4-~ petrol** (*Brit*) Super(benzin) *nt*
star attraction *n* Hauptattraktion *f*
starboard ['stɑːbɔːd] *adj* (*side*) Steuerbord-; **to ~** (nach) Steuerbord
starch [stɑːtʃ] *n* Stärke *f*
starched [stɑːtʃt] *adj* gestärkt
starchy ['stɑːtʃɪ] *adj* (*food*) stärkehaltig; (*pej: person*) steif
stardom ['stɑːdəm] *n* Berühmtheit *f*
stare [stɛə^r] *n* starrer Blick *m* ▷ *vi*: **to ~ at** anstarren
starfish ['stɑːfɪʃ] *n* Seestern *m*
stark [stɑːk] *adj* (*bleak*) kahl; (*simplicity*) schlicht; (*colour*) eintönig; (*reality, poverty*) nackt ▷ *adv*: **~ naked** splitternackt
starkers ['stɑːkəz] (*inf*) *adj* splitter(faser)nackt
starlet ['stɑːlɪt] *n* (Film)sternchen *nt*, Starlet *nt*
starlight ['stɑːlaɪt] *n* Sternenlicht *nt*
starling ['stɑːlɪŋ] *n* Star *m*
starlit ['stɑːlɪt] *adj* sternklar
starry ['stɑːrɪ] *adj* sternklar; **~ sky** Sternenhimmel *m*
starry-eyed [stɑːrɪ'aɪd] *adj* (*innocent*) arglos, blauäugig; (*from wonder*) verzückt
Stars and Stripes *n sing* Sternenbanner *nt*
star sign *n* Sternzeichen *nt*
star-studded ['stɑːstʌdɪd] *adj*: **a ~ cast** eine Starbesetzung *f*
START *n abbr* (*Mil: = Strategic Arms Reduction Talks*) START
start [stɑːt] *n* Beginn *m*, Anfang *m*; (*departure*) Aufbruch *m*; (*advantage*) Vorsprung *m* ▷ *vt* anfangen mit; (*panic*) auslösen; (*fire*) anzünden; (*found*) gründen; (*: restaurant etc*) eröffnen; (*engine*) anlassen; (*car*) starten ▷ *vi* anfangen; (*with fright*) zusammenfahren; (*engine etc*) anspringen; **at the ~** am Anfang, zu Beginn; **for a ~** erstens; **to make an early ~** frühzeitig aufbrechen; **to give a ~** zusammenfahren; **to wake up with a ~** aus dem Schlaf hochschrecken; **to ~ doing** *or* **to do sth** anfangen, etw zu tun; **to ~ (off) with ...** (*firstly*) erstens; (*at the beginning*) zunächst
▸ **start off** *vi* (*begin*) anfangen; (*begin moving*) losgehen/-fahren
▸ **start out** *vi* (*leave*) sich aufmachen
▸ **start over** (*US*) *vi* noch einmal von vorn anfangen
▸ **start up** *vt* (*business*) gründen; (*restaurant etc*) eröffnen; (*car*) starten; (*engine*) anlassen
starter ['stɑːtə^r] *n* (*Aut*) Anlasser *m*; (*Sport*): *official, runner, horse*) Starter *m*; (*Brit: Culin*) Vorspeise *f*; **for ~s** (*inf*) für den Anfang
starting point ['stɑːtɪŋ-] *n* (*lit, fig*) Ausgangspunkt *m*
starting price *n* (*at auction*) Ausgangsangebot *nt*
startle ['stɑːtl] *vt* erschrecken
startling ['stɑːtlɪŋ] *adj* (*news etc*) überraschend
star turn (*Brit*) *n* Sensation *f*, Hauptattraktion *f*
starvation [stɑː'veɪʃən] *n* Hunger *m*; **to die of/from ~** verhungern
starve [stɑːv] *vi* hungern; (*to death*) verhungern ▷ *vt* hungern lassen; (*fig: deprive*): **to ~ sb of sth** jdm etw vorenthalten; **I'm starving** ich sterbe vor Hunger
Star Wars *n* Krieg *m* der Sterne
stash [stæʃ] *vi* (*also*: **stash away**) beiseiteschaffen ▷ *n* (*secret store*) geheimes Lager *nt*
state [steɪt] *n* (*condition*) Zustand *m*; (*Pol*) Staat *m* ▷ *vt* (*say*) feststellen; (*declare*) erklären; **the**

States *npl* (*Geog*) die (Vereinigten) Staaten *pl*; **to be in a ~** aufgeregt sein; (*on edge*) nervös sein; (*in a mess*) in einem schrecklichen Zustand sein; **to get into a ~** durchdrehen (*inf*); **in ~** feierlich; **to lie in ~** (feierlich) aufgebahrt sein; **~ of emergency** Notstand *m*; **~ of mind** Verfassung *f*
state control *n* staatliche Kontrolle *f*
stated ['steɪtɪd] *adj* erklärt
State Department (*US*) *n* Außenministerium *nt*
state education (*Brit*) *n* staatliche Erziehung *f*; (*system*) staatliches Bildungswesen *nt*
stateless ['steɪtlɪs] *adj* staatenlos
stately ['steɪtlɪ] *adj* würdevoll; (*walk*) gemessen; **~ home** Schloss *nt*
statement ['steɪtmənt] *n* (*thing said*) Feststellung *f*; (*declaration*) Erklärung *f*; (*Fin*) (Konto)auszug *m*; **official ~** (amtliche) Erklärung *f*; **bank ~** Kontoauszug *m*
state of the art *n*: **the ~** der neueste Stand der Technik ▷ *adj*: **state-of-the-art** auf dem neuesten Stand der Technik; (*technology*) Spitzen-
state-owned ['steɪtəund] *adj* staatseigen
state school *n* öffentliche Schule *f*
state secret *n* Staatsgeheimnis *nt*
statesman ['steɪtsmən] (*irreg: like* **man**) *n* Staatsmann *m*
statesmanship ['steɪtsmənʃɪp] *n* Staatskunst *f*
static ['stætɪk] *n* (*Radio, TV*) atmosphärische Störungen *pl* ▷ *adj* (*not moving*) konstant
static electricity *n* Reibungselektrizität *f*
station ['steɪʃən] *n* (*Rail*) Bahnhof *m*; (*also*: **bus station**) Busbahnhof *m*; (*also*: **police station**) (Polizei)wache *f*; (*Radio*) Sender *m* ▷ *vt* (*guards etc*) postieren; (*soldiers etc*) stationieren; **action ~s** (*Mil*) Stellung *f*; **above one's ~** über seinem Stand
stationary ['steɪʃnərɪ] *adj* (*vehicle*) haltend; **to be ~** stehen
stationer ['steɪʃənəʳ] *n* Schreibwarenhändler(in) *m(f)*
stationer's, stationer's shop *n* Schreibwarenhandlung *f*
stationery ['steɪʃnərɪ] *n* Schreibwaren *pl*; (*writing paper*) Briefpapier *nt*
stationmaster ['steɪʃənmɑːstəʳ] *n* Bahnhofsvorsteher *m*
station wagon (*US*) *n* Kombi(wagen) *m*
statistic [stə'tɪstɪk] *n* Statistik *f*
statistical [stə'tɪstɪkl] *adj* statistisch
statistics [stə'tɪstɪks] *n* (*science*) Statistik *f*
statue ['stætjuː] *n* Statue *f*
statuesque [stætju'ɛsk] *adj* stattlich
statuette [stætju'ɛt] *n* Statuette *f*
stature ['stætʃəʳ] *n* Wuchs *m*, Statur *f*; (*fig: reputation*) Format *nt*
status ['steɪtəs] *n* Status *m*; (*position*) Stellung *f*; **the ~ quo** der Status quo
status line *n* (*Comput*) Statuszeile *f*
status symbol *n* Statussymbol *nt*
statute ['stætjuːt] *n* Gesetz *nt*; **statutes** *npl* (*of club etc*) Satzung *f*
statute book *n*: **to be on the ~** geltendes Recht sein
statutory ['stætjutrɪ] *adj* gesetzlich; **~ declaration** eidesstattliche Erklärung *f*
staunch [stɔːntʃ] *adj* treu ▷ *vt* (*flow*) stauen; (*blood*) stillen
stave [steɪv] *n* (*Mus*) Notensystem *nt*
▸ **stave off** *vt* (*attack*) abwehren; (*threat*) abwenden
stay [steɪ] *n* Aufenthalt *m* ▷ *vi* bleiben; (*with sb, as guest*) wohnen; (*in hotel*) übernachten; **~ of execution** (*Law*) Aussetzung *f*; **to ~ put** bleiben; **to ~ with friends** bei Freunden untergebracht sein; **to ~ the night** übernachten
▸ **stay behind** *vi* zurückbleiben
▸ **stay in** *vi* (*at home*) zu Hause bleiben
▸ **stay on** *vi* bleiben
▸ **stay out** *vi* (*of house*) wegbleiben; (*remain on strike*) weiterstreiken
▸ **stay up** *vi* (*at night*) aufbleiben
staying power ['steɪɪŋ-] *n* Stehvermögen *nt*, Durchhaltevermögen *nt*
STD *n abbr* (*Brit: Tel: = subscriber trunk dialling*) Selbstwählferndienst *m*; (*Med: = sexually transmitted disease*) durch Geschlechtsverkehr übertragene Krankheit *f*
stead [stɛd] *n*: **in sb's ~** an jds Stelle; **to stand sb in good ~** jdm zugute- *or* zustattenkommen
steadfast ['stɛdfɑːst] *adj* standhaft
steadily ['stɛdɪlɪ] *adv* (*regularly*) regelmäßig; (*constantly*) stetig; (*fixedly*) fest, unverwandt
steady ['stɛdɪ] *adj* (*job, boyfriend, girlfriend, look*) fest; (*income*) regelmäßig; (*speed*) gleichmäßig; (*rise*) stetig; (*person, character*) zuverlässig, solide; (*voice, hand etc*) ruhig ▷ *vt* (*stabilize*) ruhig halten; (*nerves*) beruhigen; **to ~ o.s. on sth** sich auf etw *acc* stützen; **to ~ o.s. against sth** sich an etw *dat* abstützen
steak [steɪk] *n* Steak *nt*; (*fish*) Filet *nt*
steakhouse ['steɪkhaus] *n* Steakrestaurant *nt*
steal [stiːl] (*pt* **stole**, *pp* **stolen**) *vt* stehlen ▷ *vi* stehlen; (*move secretly*) sich stehlen, schleichen
▸ **steal away** *vi* sich davonschleichen
stealth [stɛlθ] *n*: **by ~** heimlich
stealthy ['stɛlθɪ] *adj* heimlich, verstohlen
steam [stiːm] *n* Dampf *m* ▷ *vt* (*Culin*) dämpfen, dünsten ▷ *vi* dampfen; **covered with ~** (*window etc*) beschlagen; **under one's own ~** (*fig*) allein, ohne Hilfe; **to run out of ~** (*fig*) den Schwung verlieren; **to let off ~** (*inf: fig*) Dampf ablassen
▸ **steam up** *vi* (*window*) beschlagen; **to get ~ed up about sth** (*inf: fig*) sich über etw *acc* aufregen
steam engine *n* (*Rail*) Dampflok(omotive) *f*
steamer ['stiːməʳ] *n* Dampfer *m*; (*Culin*) Dämpfer *m*
steam iron *n* Dampfbügeleisen *nt*
steamroller ['stiːmrəuləʳ] *n* Dampfwalze *f*
steamship ['stiːmʃɪp] *n* = **steamer**

steamy ['sti:mɪ] *adj* (*room*) dampfig; (*window*) beschlagen; (*book, film*) heiß
steed [sti:d] (*liter*) *n* Ross *nt*
steel [sti:l] *n* Stahl *m* ▷ *adj* (*girder, wool etc*) Stahl-
steel band *n* (*Mus*) Steelband *f*
steel industry *n* Stahlindustrie *f*
steel mill *n* Stahlwalzwerk *nt*
steelworks ['sti:lwə:ks] *n* Stahlwerk *nt*
steely ['sti:lɪ] *adj* (*determination*) eisern; (*eyes, gaze*) hart, stählern
steep [sti:p] *adj* steil; (*increase, rise*) stark; (*price, fees*) gepfeffert ▷ *vt* einweichen; **to be ~ed in history** geschichtsträchtig sein
steeple ['sti:pl] *n* Kirchturm *m*
steeplechase ['sti:pltʃeɪs] *n* (*for horses*) Hindernisrennen *nt*; (*for runners*) Hindernislauf *m*
steeplejack ['sti:pldʒæk] *n* Turmarbeiter *m*
steeply ['sti:plɪ] *adv* steil
steer [stɪə^r] *vt* steuern; (*car etc*) lenken; (*person*) lotsen ▷ *vi* steuern; (*in car etc*) lenken; **to ~ for** zusteuern auf *+acc*; **to ~ clear of sb** (*fig*) jdm aus dem Weg gehen; **to ~ clear of sth** (*fig*) etw meiden
steering ['stɪərɪŋ] *n* (*Aut*) Lenkung *f*
steering column *n* (*Aut*) Lenksäule *f*
steering committee *n* Lenkungsausschuss *m*
steering wheel *n* (*Aut*) Lenkrad *nt*, Steuer *nt*
stellar ['stɛlə^r] *adj* stellar
stem [stɛm] *n* Stiel *m*; (*of pipe*) Hals *m* ▷ *vt* aufhalten; (*flow*) eindämmen; (*bleeding*) zum Stillstand bringen
▸ **stem from** *vt fus* zurückgehen auf *+acc*
stench [stɛntʃ] (*pej*) *n* Gestank *m*
stencil ['stɛnsl] *n* Schablone *f* ▷ *vt* mit Schablone zeichnen
stenographer [stɛ'nɔgrəfə^r] (*US*) *n* Stenograf(in) *m(f)*
stenography [stɛ'nɔgrəfɪ] (*US*) *n* Stenografie *f*
step [stɛp] *n* (*lit, fig*) Schritt *m*; (*of stairs*) Stufe *f* ▷ *vi*: **to ~ forward/back** vor-/zurücktreten; **steps** *npl* (*Brit*) = **stepladder**; **~ by step** (*fig*) Schritt für Schritt; **in/out of ~ (with)** im/nicht im Tritt (mit); (*fig*) im/nicht im Gleichklang (mit)
▸ **step down** *vi* (*fig: resign*) zurücktreten
▸ **step in** *vi* (*fig*) eingreifen
▸ **step off** *vt fus* aussteigen aus *+dat*
▸ **step on** *vt fus* treten auf *+acc*
▸ **step over** *vt fus* steigen über *+acc*
▸ **step up** *vt* (*efforts*) steigern; (*pace etc*) beschleunigen
stepbrother ['stɛpbrʌðə^r] *n* Stiefbruder *m*
stepchild ['stɛptʃaɪld] *n* Stiefkind *nt*
stepdaughter ['stɛpdɔ:tə^r] *n* Stieftochter *f*
stepfather ['stɛpfɑ:ðə^r] *n* Stiefvater *m*
stepladder ['stɛplædə^r] (*Brit*) *n* Trittleiter *f*
stepmother ['stɛpmʌðə^r] *n* Stiefmutter *f*
stepping stone ['stɛpɪŋ-] *n* Trittstein *m*; (*fig*) Sprungbrett *nt*
stepsister ['stɛpsɪstə^r] *n* Stiefschwester *f*
stepson ['stɛpsʌn] *n* Stiefsohn *m*
stereo ['stɛrɪəu] *n* (*system*) Stereoanlage *f* ▷ *adj* (*sound etc*) Stereo-; **in ~** in Stereo
stereotype ['stɪərɪətaɪp] *n* Klischee *nt*, Klischeevorstellung *f* ▷ *vt* in ein Klischee zwängen; **~d** stereotyp
sterile ['stɛraɪl] *adj* steril, keimfrei; (*barren*) unfruchtbar; (*fig: debate*) fruchtlos
sterility [stɛ'rɪlɪtɪ] *n* Unfruchtbarkeit *f*
sterilization [stɛrɪlaɪ'zeɪʃən] *n* Sterilisation *f*, Sterilisierung *f*
sterilize ['stɛrɪlaɪz] *vt* sterilisieren
sterling ['stə:lɪŋ] *adj* (*silver*) Sterling-; (*fig*) gediegen ▷ *n* (*Econ*) das Pfund Sterling, das englische Pfund; **one pound ~** ein Pfund Sterling
sterling area *n* (*Econ*) Sterlingländer *pl*
stern [stə:n] *adj* streng ▷ *n* Heck *nt*
sternum ['stə:nəm] *n* Brustbein *nt*
steroid ['stɪərɔɪd] *n* Steroid *nt*
stethoscope ['stɛθəskəup] *n* Stethoskop *nt*
stevedore ['sti:vədɔ:^r] *n* Stauer *m*, Schauermann *m*
stew [stju:] *n* Eintopf *m* ▷ *vt* schmoren; (*fruit, vegetables*) dünsten ▷ *vi* schmoren; **~ed tea** bitterer Tee *m*; **~ed fruit** (Obst)kompott *nt*
steward ['stju:əd] *n* Steward *m*; (*at public event*) Ordner(in) *m(f)*; (*also:* **shop steward**) gewerkschaftliche Vertrauensperson *f*
stewardess ['stjuədɛs] *n* Stewardess *f*
stewardship ['stjuədʃɪp] *n* Verwaltung *f*
stewing steak, (*US*) **stew meat** ['stju:ɪŋ-] *n* (Rinder)schmorfleisch *nt*
St. Ex. *abbr* = **stock exchange**
stg *abbr* = **sterling**
stick [stɪk] (*pt, pp* **stuck**) *n* Zweig *m*; (*of dynamite*) Stange *f*; (*of chalk etc*) Stück *nt*; (*as weapon*) Stock *m*; (*also:* **walking stick**) (Spazier)stock *m* ▷ *vt* (*with glue etc*) kleben; (*inf: put*) tun, stecken; (*: tolerate*) aushalten; (*thrust*) stoßen ▷ *vi*: **to ~ (to)** kleben (an *+dat*); (*remain*) (hängen) bleiben; (*door etc*) klemmen; (*lift*) stecken bleiben; **to get hold of the wrong end of the ~** (*Brit: fig*) es falsch verstehen; **to ~ in sb's mind** jdm im Gedächtnis (haften) bleiben
▸ **stick around** (*inf*) *vi* hier-/dableiben
▸ **stick out** *vi* (*ears etc*) abstehen ▷ *vt*: **to ~ it out** (*inf*) durchhalten
▸ **stick to** *vt fus* (*one's word, promise*) halten; (*agreement, rules*) sich halten an *+acc*; (*the truth, facts*) bleiben bei
▸ **stick up** *vi* hochstehen
▸ **stick up for** *vt fus* eintreten für
sticker ['stɪkə^r] *n* Aufkleber *m*
sticking plaster ['stɪkɪŋ-] *n* Heftpflaster *nt*
sticking point *n* Hindernis *nt*; (*in discussion etc*) strittiger Punkt *m*
stickleback ['stɪklbæk] *n* Stichling *m*
stickler ['stɪklə^r] *n*: **to be a ~ for sth** es mit etw peinlich genau nehmen
stick shift (*US*) *n* Schaltknüppel *m*; (*car*) Wagen *m* mit Handschaltung
stick-up ['stɪkʌp] (*inf*) *n* Überfall *m*
sticky ['stɪkɪ] *adj* klebrig; (*label, tape*) Klebe-; (*weather, day*) schwül

stiff [stɪf] *adj* steif; (*hard, firm*) hart; (*paste, egg-white*) fest; (*door, zip etc*) schwer gehend; (*competition*) hart; (*sentence*) schwer; (*drink*) stark ▷ *adv* (*bored, worried, scared*) zu Tode; **to be** *or* **feel ~** steif sein; **to have a ~ neck** einen steifen Hals haben; **to keep a ~ upper lip** (*Brit: fig*) die Haltung bewahren
stiffen ['stɪfn] *vi* steif werden; (*body*) erstarren
stiffness ['stɪfnɪs] *n* Steifheit *f*
stifle ['staɪfl] *vt* unterdrücken; (*heat*) erdrücken
stifling ['staɪflɪŋ] *adj* (*heat*) drückend
stigma ['stɪgmə] *n* Stigma *nt*; (*Bot*) Narbe *f*, Stigma *nt*; **stigmata** *npl* (*Med*) Wundmal *nt*
stile [staɪl] *n* Zaunübertritt *m*
stiletto [stɪ'lɛtəu] (*Brit*) *n* (*also*: **stiletto heel**) Bleistiftabsatz *m*
still [stɪl] *adj* (*motionless*) bewegungslos; (*tranquil*) ruhig; (*air, water*) still; (*Brit: drink*) ohne Kohlensäure ▷ *adv* (immer) noch; (*yet, even*) noch; (*nonetheless*) trotzdem ▷ *n* (*Cine*) Standfoto *nt*; **to stand ~** (*machine, motor*) stillstehen; (*motionless*) still stehen; **keep ~!** halte still!; **he ~ hasn't arrived** er ist immer noch nicht angekommen
stillborn ['stɪlbɔːn] *adj* tot geboren
still life *n* Stillleben *nt*
stilt [stɪlt] *n* (*pile*) Pfahl *m*; (*for walking on*) Stelze *f*
stilted ['stɪltɪd] *adj* gestelzt
stimulant ['stɪmjulənt] *n* Anregungsmittel *nt*
stimulate ['stɪmjuleɪt] *vt* anregen, stimulieren; (*demand*) ankurbeln
stimulating ['stɪmjuleɪtɪŋ] *adj* anregend, stimulierend
stimulation [stɪmju'leɪʃən] *n* Anregung *f*, Stimulation *f*
stimuli ['stɪmjulaɪ] *npl of* **stimulus**
stimulus ['stɪmjuləs] (*pl* **stimuli**) *n* (*incentive*) Anreiz *m*; (*Biol*) Reiz *m*; (*Psych*) Stimulus *m*
sting [stɪŋ] (*pt, pp* **stung**) *n* Stich *m*; (*pain*) Stechen *nt*; (*organ: of insect*) Stachel *m*; (*inf: confidence trick*) Ding *nt* ▷ *vt* stechen; (*fig*) treffen, verletzen ▷ *vi* stechen; (*eyes, ointment, plant etc*) brennen; **my eyes are ~ing** mir brennen die Augen
stingy ['stɪndʒɪ] (*pej*) *adj* geizig, knauserig
stink [stɪŋk] (*pt* **stank**, *pp* **stunk**) *n* Gestank *m* ▷ *vi* stinken
stinker ['stɪŋkə^r] (*inf*) *n* (*problem*) harter Brocken *m*; (*person*) Ekel *nt*
stinking ['stɪŋkɪŋ] (*inf*) *adj* (*fig*) beschissen (*!*); **a ~ cold** eine scheußliche Erkältung; **~ rich** stinkreich
stint [stɪnt] *n* (*period*) Zeit *f*; (*batch of work*) Pensum *nt*; (*share*) Teil *m* ▷ *vi*: **to ~ on** sparen mit
stipend ['staɪpɛnd] *n* Gehalt *nt*
stipendiary [staɪ'pɛndɪərɪ] *adj*: **~ magistrate** bezahlter Friedensrichter *m*
stipulate ['stɪpjuleɪt] *vt* festsetzen; (*condition*) stellen
stipulation [stɪpju'leɪʃən] *n* Bedingung *f*, Auflage *f*
stir [stəː^r] *n* (*fig*) Aufsehen *nt* ▷ *vt* umrühren; (*fig: emotions*) aufwühlen; (*: person*) bewegen ▷ *vi* sich bewegen; **to give sth a ~** etw umrühren; **to cause a ~** Aufsehen erregen
▸ **stir up** *vt*: **to ~ up trouble** Unruhe stiften; **to ~ things up** stänkern
stir-fry ['stəː'fraɪ] *vt* unter Rühren kurz anbraten ▷ *n* Pfannengericht *nt* (*das unter Rühren kurz angebraten wurde*)
stirring ['stəːrɪŋ] *adj* bewegend
stirrup ['stɪrəp] *n* Steigbügel *m*
stitch [stɪtʃ] *n* (*Sewing*) Stich *m*; (*Knitting*) Masche *f*; (*Med*) Faden *m*; (*pain*) Seitenstiche *pl* ▷ *vt* nähen; **he had to have ~es** er musste genäht werden
stoat [stəut] *n* Wiesel *nt*
stock [stɔk] *n* Vorrat *m*; (*Comm*) Bestand *m*; (*Agr*) Vieh *nt*; (*Culin*) Brühe *f*; (*descent, origin*) Abstammung *f*, Herkunft *f*; (*Fin*) Wertpapiere *pl*; (*Rail: also*: **rolling stock**) rollendes Material *nt* ▷ *adj* (*reply, excuse etc*) Standard- ▷ *vt* (*in shop*) führen; **in/out of ~** vorrätig/nicht vorrätig; **~s and shares** (Aktien und) Wertpapiere *pl*; **government ~** Staatsanleihe *f*; **to take ~ of** (*fig*) Bilanz ziehen über +*acc*; **well-~ed** (*shop*) mit gutem Sortiment
▸ **stock up** *vi*: **to ~ up (with)** sich eindecken (mit)
stockade [stɔ'keɪd] *n* Palisade *f*
stockbroker ['stɔkbrəukə^r] *n* Börsenmakler *m*
stock control *n* Bestandsüberwachung *f*
stock cube (*Brit*) *n* Brühwürfel *m*
stock exchange *n* Börse *f*
stockholder ['stɔkhəuldə^r] (*esp US*) *n* Aktionär(in) *m(f)*
Stockholm ['stɔkhəum] *n* Stockholm *nt*
stocking ['stɔkɪŋ] *n* Strumpf *m*
stock-in-trade ['stɔkɪn'treɪd] *n* (*fig*): **it's his ~** es gehört zu seinem festen Repertoire
stockist ['stɔkɪst] (*Brit*) *n* Händler *m*
stock market (*Brit*) *n* Börse *f*
stock phrase *n* Standardsatz *m*
stockpile ['stɔkpaɪl] *n* Vorrat *m*; (*of weapons*) Lager *nt* ▷ *vt* horten
stockroom ['stɔkruːm] *n* Lager *nt*, Lagerraum *m*
stocktaking ['stɔkteɪkɪŋ] (*Brit*) *n* Inventur *f*
stocky ['stɔkɪ] *adj* stämmig
stodgy ['stɔdʒɪ] *adj* (*food*) pampig (*inf*), schwer
stoic ['stəuɪk] *n* Stoiker(in) *m(f)* ▷ *adj* stoisch
stoical ['stəuɪkl] *adj* stoisch
stoke [stəuk] *vt* (*fire*) schüren; (*furnace, boiler*) heizen
stoker ['stəukə^r] *n* Heizer *m*
stole [stəul] *pt of* **steal** ▷ *n* Stola *f*
stolen ['stəuln] *pp of* **steal**
stolid ['stɔlɪd] *adj* phlegmatisch, stur (*inf*)
stomach ['stʌmək] *n* Magen *m*; (*belly*) Bauch *m* ▷ *vt* (*fig*) vertragen
stomach ache *n* Magenschmerzen *pl*
stomach pump *n* Magenpumpe *f*
stomach ulcer *n* Magengeschwür *nt*
stomp [stɔmp] *vi* stapfen
stone [stəun] *n* Stein *m*; (*Brit: weight*)

Gewichtseinheit (= 6,35 kg) ▷ *adj (wall, jar etc)* Stein-, steinern ▷ *vt (person)* mit Steinen bewerfen; *(fruit)* entkernen, entsteinen; **within a ~'s throw of the station** nur einen Katzensprung vom Bahnhof entfernt
Stone Age *n* Steinzeit *f*
stone-cold ['stəun'kəuld] *adj* eiskalt
stoned [stəund] *(inf) adj (on drugs)* stoned; *(drunk)* total zu
stone-deaf ['stəun'dɛf] *adj* stocktaub
stonemason ['stəunmeɪsn] *n* Steinmetz *m*
stonewall [stəun'wɔːl] *vi* mauern; *(in answering questions)* ausweichen
stonework ['stəunwəːk] *n* Mauerwerk *nt*
stony ['stəunɪ] *adj* steinig; *(fig: silence etc)* steinern
stood [stud] *pt, pp of* **stand**
stooge [stuːdʒ] *n (inf)* Handlanger(in) *m(f)*; *(Theat)* Stichwortgeber(in) *m(f)*
stool [stuːl] *n* Hocker *m*
stoop [stuːp] *vi (also:* **stoop down***)* sich bücken; *(walk)* gebeugt gehen; **to ~ to sth** *(fig)* sich zu etw herablassen; **to ~ to doing sth** sich dazu herablassen, etw zu tun
stop [stɔp] *n* Halt *m*; *(short stay)* Aufenthalt *m*; *(in punctuation: also:* **full stop***)* Punkt *m*; *(bus stop etc)* Haltestelle *f* ▷ *vt* stoppen; *(car etc)* anhalten; *(block)* sperren; *(prevent)* verhindern ▷ *vi (car etc)* anhalten; *(train)* halten; *(pedestrian, watch, clock)* stehen bleiben; *(end)* aufhören; **to come to a ~** anhalten; **to put a ~ to** einen Riegel vorschieben *+dat*; **to ~ doing sth** aufhören, etw zu tun; **to ~ sb (from) doing sth** jdn davon abhalten, etw zu tun; **~ it!** lass das!, hör auf!
▸ **stop by** *vi* kurz vorbeikommen
▸ **stop off** *vi* kurz haltmachen, Zwischenstation machen
▸ **stop up** *vt (hole)* zustopfen
stopcock ['stɔpkɔk] *n* Absperrhahn *m*
stopgap ['stɔpgæp] *n (person)* Lückenbüßer *m*; *(thing)* Notbehelf *m*; **~ measure** Überbrückungsmaßnahme *f*
stop-go [stɔp'gəu] *adj (economic cycle etc)* mit ständigem Auf und Ab
stoplights ['stɔplaɪts] *npl (Aut)* Bremslichter *pl*
stopover ['stɔpəuvəʳ] *n* Zwischenaufenthalt *m*; *(Aviat)* Zwischenlandung *f*
stoppage ['stɔpɪdʒ] *n (strike)* Streik *m*; *(blockage)* Unterbrechung *f*; *(of pay, cheque)* Sperrung *f*; *(deduction)* Abzug *m*
stopper ['stɔpəʳ] *n* Stöpsel *m*
stop press *n* letzte Meldungen *pl*
stopwatch ['stɔpwɔtʃ] *n* Stoppuhr *f*
storage ['stɔːrɪdʒ] *n* Lagerung *f*; *(also:* **storage space***)* Stauraum *m*; *(Comput)* Speicherung *f*
storage capacity *n (Comput)* Speicherkapazität *f*
storage heater *(Brit) n* (Nacht)speicherofen *m*
store [stɔːʳ] *n* Vorrat *m*; *(depot)* Lager *nt*; *(Brit: large shop)* Geschäft *nt*, Kaufhaus *nt*; *(US: shop)* Laden *m*; *(fig)*: **a ~ of** eine Fülle an *+dat* ▷ *vt* lagern; *(information etc, Comput)* speichern; *(food, medicines etc)* aufbewahren; *(in filing system)* ablegen; **stores** *npl (provisions)* Vorräte *pl*; **in ~** eingelagert; **who knows what's in ~ for us?** wer weiß, was uns bevorsteht?; **to set great/little ~ by sth** viel/wenig von etw halten
▸ **store up** *vt* einen Vorrat anlegen von; *(memories)* im Gedächtnis bewahren
storehouse ['stɔːhaus] *n (US: Comm)* Lager(haus) *nt*; *(fig)* Fundgrube *f*
storekeeper ['stɔːkiːpəʳ] *(US) n* Ladenbesitzer(in) *m(f)*
storeroom ['stɔːruːm] *n* Lagerraum *m*
storey, *(US)* **story** ['stɔːrɪ] *n* Stock *m*, Stockwerk *nt*
stork [stɔːk] *n* Storch *m*
storm [stɔːm] *n (lit, fig)* Sturm *m*; *(bad weather)* Unwetter *nt*; *(also:* **electrical storm***)* Gewitter *nt* ▷ *vi (fig)* toben ▷ *vt (attack)* stürmen
storm cloud *n* Gewitterwolke *f*
storm door *n* äußere Windfangtür *f*
stormy ['stɔːmɪ] *adj (lit, fig)* stürmisch
story ['stɔːrɪ] *n* Geschichte *f*; *(Press)* Artikel *m*; *(lie)* Märchen *nt*; *(US)* = **storey**
storybook ['stɔːrɪbuk] *n* Geschichtenbuch *nt*
storyteller ['stɔːrɪtɛləʳ] *n* Geschichtenerzähler(in) *m(f)*
stout [staut] *adj (strong)* stark; *(fat)* untersetzt; *(resolute)* energisch ▷ *n* Starkbier *nt*
stove [stəuv] *n* Herd *m*; *(small)* Kocher *m*; *(for heating)* (Heiz)ofen *m*; **gas ~** Gasherd *m*
stow [stəu] *vt (also:* **stow away***)* verstauen
stowaway ['stəuəweɪ] *n* blinder Passagier *m*
straddle ['strædl] *vt (sitting)* rittlings sitzen auf *+dat*; *(standing)* breitbeinig stehen über *+dat*; *(jumping)* grätschen über *+acc*; *(fig)* überspannen
strafe [strɑːf] *vt* beschießen
straggle ['strægl] *vi (houses etc)* verstreut liegen; *(people etc)* zurückbleiben
straggler ['stræglə ʳ] *n* Nachzügler *m*
straggly ['stræglɪ] *adj (hair)* unordentlich
straight [streɪt] *adj* gerade; *(hair)* glatt; *(honest)* offen, direkt; *(simple)* einfach; *(: fight)* direkt; *(Theat)* ernst; *(inf: heterosexual)* hetero; *(whisky etc)* pur ▷ *adv (in time)* sofort; *(in direction)* direkt; *(drink)* pur ▷ *n (Sport)* Gerade *f*; **to put** *or* **get sth ~** *(make clear)* etw klären; *(make tidy)* etw in Ordnung bringen; **let's get this ~** das wollen wir mal klarstellen; **10 ~ wins** 10 Siege hintereinander; **to win in ~ sets** *(Tennis)* ohne Satzverlust gewinnen; **to go ~ home** direkt nach Hause gehen; **~ out** rundheraus; **~ away, ~ off** sofort, gleich
straighten ['streɪtn] *vt (skirt, sheet etc)* gerade ziehen
▸ **straighten out** *vt (fig)* klären
straight-faced [streɪt'feɪst] *adj*: **to be/remain ~** ernst bleiben ▷ *adv* ohne zu lachen
straightforward [streɪt'fɔːwəd] *adj (simple)* einfach; *(honest)* offen
straight sets *npl (Tennis)*: **to win in ~** ohne Satzverlust gewinnen

strain [streɪn] *n* Belastung *f*; (*Med*: *also*: **back strain**) überanstrengter Rücken *m*; (: *tension*) Überlastung *f*; (*of virus*) Art *f*; (*breed*) Sorte *f* ▷ *vt* (*back etc*) überanstrengen; (*resources*) belasten; (*Culin*) abgießen ▷ *vi*: **to ~ to do sth** sich anstrengen, etw zu tun; **strains** *npl* (*Mus*) Klänge *pl*; **he's been under a lot of ~** er hat unter großem Stress gestanden
strained [streɪnd] *adj* (*back*) überanstrengt; (*muscle*) gezerrt; (*forced*) gezwungen; (*relations*) gespannt
strainer ['streɪnəʳ] *n* Sieb *nt*
strait [streɪt] *n* Meerenge *f*, Straße *f*; **straits** *npl* (*fig*): **to be in dire ~s** in großen Nöten sein
straitjacket ['streɪtdʒækɪt] *n* Zwangsjacke *f*
strait-laced [streɪt'leɪst] *adj* prüde, puritanisch
strand [strænd] *n* (*lit, fig*) Faden *m*; (*of wire*) Litze *f*; (*of hair*) Strähne *f*
stranded ['strændɪd] *adj*: **to be ~** (*traveller*) festsitzen; (*ship, sea creature*) gestrandet
strange [streɪndʒ] *adj* fremd; (*odd*) seltsam, merkwürdig
strangely ['streɪndʒlɪ] *adv* seltsam, merkwürdig; *see also* **enough**
stranger ['streɪndʒəʳ] *n* Fremde(r) *f*(*m*); **I'm a ~ here** ich bin hier fremd
strangle ['stræŋgl] *vt* erwürgen, erdrosseln; (*fig*: *economy etc*) ersticken
stranglehold ['stræŋglhəuld] *n* (*fig*) absolute Machtposition *f*
strangulation [stræŋgju'leɪʃən] *n* Erwürgen *nt*, Erdrosseln *nt*
strap [stræp] *n* Riemen *m*; (*of dress etc*) Träger *m* ▷ *vt* (*also*: **strap in**) anschnallen; (*also*: **strap on**) umschnallen
straphanging ['stræphæŋɪŋ] *n* Pendeln *nt* (als stehender Fahrgast)
strapless ['stræplɪs] *adj* trägerlos, schulterfrei
strapped [stræpt] (*inf*) *adj*: **~ (for cash)** pleite
strapping ['stræpɪŋ] *adj* stramm
Strasbourg ['stræzbəːg] *n* Straßburg *nt*
strata ['strɑːtə] *npl of* **stratum**
stratagem ['strætɪdʒəm] *n* List *f*
strategic [strə'tiːdʒɪk] *adj* strategisch; (*error*) taktisch
strategist ['strætɪdʒɪst] *n* Stratege *m*, Strategin *f*
strategy ['strætɪdʒɪ] *n* Strategie *f*
stratosphere ['strætəsfɪəʳ] *n* Stratosphäre *f*
stratum ['strɑːtəm] (*pl* **strata**) *n* Schicht *f*
straw [strɔː] *n* Stroh *nt*; (*also*: **drinking straw**) Strohhalm *m*; **that's the last ~!** das ist der Gipfel!
strawberry ['strɔːbərɪ] *n* Erdbeere *f*
stray [streɪ] *adj* (*animal*) streunend; (*bullet*) verirrt; (*scattered*) einzeln, vereinzelt ▷ *vi* (*children*) sich verirren; (*animals*) streunen; (*thoughts*) abschweifen
streak [striːk] *n* Streifen *m*; (*in hair*) Strähne *f*; (*fig*: *of madness etc*) Zug *m* ▷ *vt* streifen ▷ *vi*: **to ~ past** vorbeiflitzen; **a winning/losing ~** eine Glücks-/Pechsträhne
streaker ['striːkəʳ] (*inf*) *n* Blitzer(in) *m*(*f*)
streaky ['striːkɪ] *adj* (*bacon*) durchwachsen
stream [striːm] *n* (*small river*) Bach *m*; (*current*) Strömung *f*; (*of people, vehicles*) Strom *m*; (*of questions, insults etc*) Flut *f*, Schwall *m*; (*of smoke*) Schwaden *m*; (*Scol*) Leistungsgruppe *f* ▷ *vt* (*Scol*) in Leistungsgruppen einteilen ▷ *vi* strömen; **against the ~** gegen den Strom; **to come on ~** (*new power plant etc*) in Betrieb genommen werden
streamer ['striːməʳ] *n* Luftschlange *f*
stream feed *n* automatischer Papiereinzug *m*
streamline ['striːmlaɪn] *vt* Stromlinienform geben +*dat*; (*fig*) rationalisieren
streamlined ['striːmlaɪnd] *adj* stromlinienförmig; (*Aviat, Aut*) windschlüpfrig; (*fig*) rationalisiert
street [striːt] *n* Straße *f*; **the back ~s** die Seitensträßchen *pl*; **to be on the ~s** (*homeless*) obdachlos sein; (*as prostitute*) auf den Strich gehen
streetcar ['striːtkɑːʳ] (*US*) *n* Straßenbahn *f*
street cred [-krɛd] (*inf*) *n* Glaubwürdigkeit *f*
street lamp *n* Straßenlaterne *f*
street lighting *n* Straßenbeleuchtung *f*
street map *n* Stadtplan *m*
street market *n* Straßenmarkt *m*
street plan *n* Stadtplan *m*
streetwise ['striːtwaɪz] (*inf*) *adj*: **to be ~** wissen, wos langgeht
strength [strɛŋθ] *n* (*lit, fig*) Stärke *f*; (*physical*) Kraft *f*, Stärke *f*; (*of girder etc*) Stabilität *f*; (*of knot etc*) Festigkeit *f*; (*of chemical solution*) Konzentration *f*; (*of wine*) Schwere *f*; **on the ~ of** aufgrund +*gen*; **at full ~** vollzählig; **to be below ~** nicht die volle Stärke haben
strengthen ['strɛŋθn] *vt* (*lit, fig*) verstärken; (*muscle*) kräftigen; (*economy, currency, relationship*) festigen
strenuous ['strɛnjuəs] *adj* anstrengend; (*determined*) unermüdlich
strenuously ['strɛnjuəslɪ] *adv* energisch; **she ~ denied the rumour** sie leugnete das Gerücht hartnäckig
stress [strɛs] *n* Druck *m*; (*mental*) Belastung *f*, Stress *m*; (*Ling*) Betonung *f*; (*emphasis*) Akzent *m*, Gewicht *nt* ▷ *vt* betonen; **to lay great ~ on sth** großen Wert auf etw *acc* legen; **to be under ~** großen Belastungen ausgesetzt sein, unter Stress stehen
stressful ['strɛsful] *adj* anstrengend, stressig; (*situation*) angespannt
stretch [strɛtʃ] *n* (*of sand, water etc*) Stück *nt*; (*of time*) Zeit *f* ▷ *vi* (*person, animal*) sich strecken; (*land, area*) sich erstrecken ▷ *vt* (*pull*) spannen; (*fig*: *job, task*) fordern; **at a ~** an einem Stück, ohne Unterbrechung; **by no ~ of the imagination** beim besten Willen nicht; **to ~ to** *or* **as far as the frontier** (*extend*) sich bis zur Grenze erstrecken; **to ~ one's legs** sich *dat* die Beine vertreten
▶ **stretch out** *vi* sich ausstrecken ▷ *vt* ausstrecken

▸ **stretch to** *vt fus* (*be enough*) reichen für
stretcher ['strɛtʃəʳ] *n* (Trag)bahre *f*
stretcher-bearer ['strɛtʃəbɛərəʳ] *n* Krankenträger *m*
stretch marks *npl* Dehnungsstreifen *pl*; (*through pregnancy*) Schwangerschaftsstreifen *pl*
strewn [stru:n] *adj*: ~ **with** übersät mit
stricken ['strɪkən] *adj* (*person*) leidend; (*city, industry etc*) Not leidend; ~ **with** (*disease*) geschlagen mit; (*fear etc*) erfüllt von
strict [strɪkt] *adj* streng; (*precise*) genau; **in the ~est confidence** streng vertraulich; **in the ~ sense of the word** streng genommen
strictly ['strɪktlɪ] *adv* streng; (*exactly*) genau; (*solely*) ausschließlich; ~ **confidential** streng vertraulich; ~ **speaking** genau genommen; **not ~ true** nicht ganz richtig; ~ **between ourselves** ganz unter uns
strictness ['strɪktnɪs] *n* Strenge *f*
stridden ['strɪdn] *pp of* **stride**
stride [straɪd] (*pt* **strode**, *pp* **stridden**) *n* Schritt *m* ▹ *vi* schreiten; **to take sth in one's ~** (*fig*) mit etw spielend fertig werden
strident ['straɪdnt] *adj* schrill, durchdringend; (*demands*) lautstark
strife [straɪf] *n* Streit *m*, Zwietracht *f*
strike [straɪk] (*pt, pp* **struck**) *n* Streik *m*, Ausstand *m*; (*Mil*) Angriff *m* ▹ *vt* (*hit*) schlagen; (*fig*: *idea, thought*) in den Sinn kommen *+dat*; (*oil etc*) finden, stoßen auf *+acc*; (*bargain, deal*) aushandeln; (*coin, medal*) prägen ▹ *vi* streiken; (*illness, killer*) zuschlagen; (*disaster*) hereinbrechen; (*clock*) schlagen; **on ~** streikend; **to be on ~** streiken; **to ~ a balance** einen Mittelweg finden; **to be struck by lightning** vom Blitz getroffen werden; **to ~ a match** ein Streichholz anzünden
▸ **strike back** *vi* (*Mil*) zurückschlagen; (*fig*) sich wehren
▸ **strike down** *vt* niederschlagen
▸ **strike off** *vt* (*from list*) (aus)streichen; (*doctor etc*) die Zulassung entziehen *+dat*
▸ **strike out** *vi* losziehen, sich aufmachen ▹ *vt* (*word, sentence*) (aus)streichen
▸ **strike up** *vt* (*Mus*) anstimmen; (*conversation*) anknüpfen; (*friendship*) schließen
strikebreaker ['straɪkbreɪkəʳ] *n* Streikbrecher *m*
strike pay *n* Streikgeld *nt*
striker ['straɪkəʳ] *n* Streikende(r) *f(m)*; (*Sport*) Stürmer *m*
striking ['straɪkɪŋ] *adj* auffallend; (*attractive*) attraktiv
strimmer ['strɪməʳ] *n* Rasentrimmer *m*
string [strɪŋ] (*pt, pp* **strung**) *n* Schnur *f*; (*of islands*) Kette *f*; (*of people, cars*) Schlange *f*; (*series*) Serie *f*; (*Comput*) Zeichenfolge *f*; (*Mus*) Saite *f* ▹ *vt*: **to ~ together** aneinanderreihen; **the strings** *npl* (*Mus*) die Streichinstrumente *pl*; **to pull ~s** (*fig*) Beziehungen spielen lassen; **with no ~s attached** (*fig*) ohne Bedingungen; **to ~ sth out** etw verteilen
string bean *n* grüne Bohne *f*
stringed instrument *n* Saiteninstrument *nt*
stringent ['strɪndʒənt] *adj* streng; (*measures*) drastisch
string quartet *n* Streichquartett *nt*
strip [strɪp] *n* Streifen *m*; (*of metal*) Band *nt*; (*Sport*) Trikot *nt*, Dress *m* ▹ *vt* (*undress*) ausziehen; (*paint*) abbeizen; (*also*: **strip down**: *machine etc*) auseinandernehmen ▹ *vi* (*undress*) sich ausziehen
strip cartoon *n* Comic(strip) *m*
stripe [straɪp] *n* Streifen *m*; **stripes** *npl* (*Mil, Police*) (Ärmel)streifen *pl*
striped [straɪpt] *adj* gestreift
strip lighting (*Brit*) *n* Neonlicht *nt*
strip mall *n* Einkaufsmeile *nt*
stripper ['strɪpəʳ] *n* Stripper(in) *m(f)*, Stripteasetänzer(in) *m(f)*
strip-search ['strɪpsɛːtʃ] *n* Leibesvisitation *f* (*bei der man sich ausziehen muss*) ▹ *vt*: **to be ~ed** sich ausziehen müssen und durchsucht werden
striptease ['strɪpti:z] *n* Striptease *m or nt*
strive [straɪv] (*pt* **strove**, *pp* **~n**) *vi*: **to ~ for sth** nach etw streben; **to ~ to do sth** danach streben, etw zu tun
striven ['strɪvn] *pp of* **strive**
strobe [strəub] *n* (*also*: **strobe lights**) Stroboskoplicht *nt*
strode [strəud] *pt of* **stride**
stroke [strəuk] *n* Schlag *m*, Hieb *m*; (*Swimming*: *style*) Stil *m*; (*Med*) Schlaganfall *m*; (*of clock*) Schlag *m*; (*of paintbrush*) Strich *m* ▹ *vt* (*caress*) streicheln; **at a ~** mit einem Schlag; **on the ~ of 5** Punkt 5 (Uhr); **a ~ of luck** ein Glücksfall *m*; **a 2-~ engine** ein Zweitaktmotor *m*
stroll [strəul] *n* Spaziergang *m* ▹ *vi* spazieren; **to go for a ~, have** *or* **take a ~** einen Spaziergang machen
stroller ['strəuləʳ] (*US*) *n* (*pushchair*) Sportwagen *m*
strong [strɔŋ] *adj* stark; (*person, arms, grip*) stark, kräftig; (*healthy*) kräftig; (*object, material*) solide, stabil; (*letter*) geharnischt; (*measure*) drastisch; (*language*) derb; (*nerves*) gut; (*taste, smell*) streng ▹ *adv*: **to be going ~** (*company*) sehr erfolgreich sein; (*person*) gut in Schuss sein; **I have no ~ feelings about it** es ist mir ziemlich egal; **they are 50 ~** sie sind insgesamt 50
strong-arm ['strɔŋɑ:m] *adj* brutal
strongbox ['strɔŋbɔks] *n* (Geld)kassette *f*
stronghold ['strɔŋhəuld] *n* Festung *f*; (*fig*) Hochburg *f*
strongly ['strɔŋlɪ] *adv* (*solidly*) stabil; (*forcefully*) entschieden; (*deeply*) fest; **to feel ~ that ...** fest davon überzeugt sein, dass ...; **I feel ~ about it** mir liegt sehr viel daran; (*negatively*) ich bin sehr dagegen
strongman ['strɔŋmæn] (*irreg*: *like* **man**) *n* (*lit, fig*) starker Mann *m*
strongroom ['strɔŋru:m] *n* Tresorraum *m*
stroppy ['strɔpɪ] (*Brit*: *inf*) *adj* pampig; (*obstinate*) stur

strove [strəuv] *pt of* **strive**
struck [strʌk] *pt, pp of* **strike**
structural ['strʌktʃrəl] *adj* strukturell; (*damage*) baulich; (*defect*) Konstruktions-
structurally ['strʌktʃrəlı] *adv*: **~ sound** mit guter Bausubstanz
structure ['strʌktʃə^r] *n* Struktur *f*, Aufbau *m*; (*building*) Gebäude *nt*
struggle ['strʌgl] *n* Kampf *m*; (*difficulty*) Anstrengung *f* ▷ *vi* (*try hard*) sich abmühen; (*fight*) kämpfen; (*in self-defence*) sich wehren; **to have a ~ to do sth** Mühe haben, etw zu tun; **to be a ~ for sb** jdm große Schwierigkeiten bereiten
strum [strʌm] *vt* (*guitar*) klimpern auf *+dat*
strung [strʌŋ] *pt, pp of* **string**
strut [strʌt] *n* Strebe *f*, Stütze *f* ▷ *vi* stolzieren
strychnine ['strıkni:n] *n* Strychnin *nt*
stub [stʌb] *n* (*of cheque, ticket etc*) Abschnitt *m*; (*of cigarette*) Kippe *f* ▷ *vt*: **to ~ one's toe** sich *dat* den Zeh stoßen
▸ **stub out** *vt* (*cigarette*) ausdrücken
stubble ['stʌbl] *n* Stoppeln *pl*
stubborn ['stʌbən] *adj* hartnäckig; (*child*) störrisch
stubby ['stʌbı] *adj* kurz und dick
stucco ['stʌkəu] *n* Stuck *m*
stuck [stʌk] *pt, pp of* **stick** ▷ *adj*: **to be ~** (*jammed*) klemmen; (*unable to answer*) nicht klarkommen; **to get ~** stecken bleiben; (*fig*) nicht weiterkommen
stuck-up [stʌk'ʌp] (*inf*) *adj* hochnäsig
stud [stʌd] *n* (*on clothing etc*) Niete *f*; (*on collar*) Kragenknopf *m*; (*earring*) Ohrstecker *m*; (*on boot*) Stollen *m*; (*also*: **stud farm**) Gestüt *nt*; (*also*: **stud horse**) Zuchthengst *m* ▷ *vt* (*fig*): **~ded with** übersät mit; (*with jewels*) dicht besetzt mit
student ['stju:dənt] *n* Student(in) *m(f)*; (*at school*) Schüler(in) *m(f)* ▷ *cpd* Studenten-; **law/medical ~** Jura-/Medizinstudent(in) *m(f)*; **~ nurse** Krankenpflegeschüler(in) *m(f)*; **~ teacher** Referendar(in) *m(f)*
student driver (*US*) *n* Fahrschüler(in) *m(f)*
students' union ['stju:dənts-] (*Brit*) *n* Studentenvereinigung *f* ≈ AStA *m*; (*building*) Gebäude *nt* der Studentenvereinigung
studied ['stʌdıd] *adj* (*expression*) einstudiert; (*attitude*) berechnet
studio ['stju:dıəu] *n* Studio *nt*; (*sculptor's etc*) Atelier *nt*
studio flat, (*US*) **studio apartment** *n* Einzimmerwohnung *f*
studious ['stju:dıəs] *adj* lernbegierig
studiously ['stju:dıəslı] *adv* (*carefully*) sorgsam
study ['stʌdı] *n* Studium *nt*, Lernen *nt*; (*room*) Arbeitszimmer *nt* ▷ *vt* studieren; (*face*) prüfend ansehen; (*evidence*) prüfen ▷ *vi* studieren, lernen; **studies** *npl* (*studying*) Studien *pl*; **to make a ~ of sth** etw untersuchen; (*academic*) etw studieren; **to ~ for an exam** sich auf eine Prüfung vorbereiten
stuff [stʌf] *n* Zeug *nt* ▷ *vt* ausstopfen; (*Culin*) füllen; (*inf: push*) stopfen; **my nose is ~ed up** ich habe eine verstopfte Nase; **get ~ed!** (*inf!*) du kannst mich mal!
stuffed toy [stʌft-] *n* Stofftier *nt*
stuffing ['stʌfıŋ] *n* Füllung *f*; (*in sofa etc*) Polstermaterial *nt*
stuffy ['stʌfı] *adj* (*room*) stickig; (*person, ideas*) spießig
stumble ['stʌmbl] *vi* stolpern; **to ~ across** *or* **on** (*fig*) (zufällig) stoßen auf *+acc*
stumbling block ['stʌmblıŋ-] *n* Hürde *f*, Hindernis *nt*
stump [stʌmp] *n* Stumpf *m* ▷ *vt*: **to be ~ed** überfragt sein
stun [stʌn] *vt* betäuben; (*news*) fassungslos machen
stung [stʌŋ] *pt, pp of* **sting**
stunk [stʌŋk] *pp of* **stink**
stunning ['stʌnıŋ] *adj* (*news, event*) sensationell; (*girl, dress*) hinreißend
stunt [stʌnt] *n* (*in film*) Stunt *m*; (*publicity stunt*) (Werbe)gag *m*
stunted ['stʌntıd] *adj* verkümmert
stuntman ['stʌntmæn] (*irreg: like* **man**) *n* Stuntman *m*
stupefaction [stju:pı'fækʃən] *n* Verblüffung *f*
stupefy ['stju:pıfaı] *vt* benommen machen; (*fig*) verblüffen
stupendous [stju:'pɛndəs] *adj* enorm
stupid ['stju:pıd] *adj* dumm
stupidity [stju:'pıdıtı] *n* Dummheit *f*
stupidly ['stju:pıdlı] *adv* dumm
stupor ['stju:pə^r] *n* Benommenheit *f*; **in a ~** benommen
sturdily ['stə:dılı] *adv*: **~ built** (*person*) kräftig gebaut; (*thing*) stabil gebaut
sturdy ['stə:dı] *adj* (*person*) kräftig; (*thing*) stabil
sturgeon ['stə:dʒən] *n* Stör *m*
stutter ['stʌtə^r] *n* Stottern *nt* ▷ *vi* stottern; **to have a ~** stottern
Stuttgart ['stutgɑ:t] *n* Stuttgart *nt*
sty [staı] *n* Schweinestall *m*
stye [staı] *n* Gerstenkorn *nt*
style [staıl] *n* Stil *m*; (*design*) Modell *nt*; **in the latest ~** nach der neuesten Mode; **hair ~** Frisur *f*
styli ['staılaı] *npl of* **stylus**
stylish ['staılıʃ] *adj* elegant
stylist ['staılıst] *n* (*hair stylist*) Friseur *m*, Friseuse *f*; (*literary stylist*) Stilist(in) *m(f)*
stylized ['staılaızd] *adj* stilisiert
stylus ['staıləs] (*pl* **styli** *or* **~es**) *n* Nadel *f*
Styrofoam® ['staırəfəum] *n* ≈ Styropor® *nt*
suave [swɑ:v] *adj* zuvorkommend
sub [sʌb] *n abbr* (*Naut*) = **submarine**; (*Admin*) = **subscription**; (*Brit: Press*) = **subeditor**
sub ... [sʌb] *pref* Unter-, unter-
subcommittee ['sʌbkəmıtı] *n* Unterausschuss *m*
subconscious [sʌb'kɔnʃəs] *adj* unterbewusst
subcontinent [sʌb'kɔntınənt] *n*: **the (Indian) ~** der (indische) Subkontinent

subcontract [*vt* 'sʌbkən'trækt, *n* 'sʌb'kɔntrækt] *vt* (vertraglich) weitervergeben ▷ *n* Nebenvertrag *m*
subcontractor ['sʌbkən'træktə^r] *n* Subunternehmer *m*
subdivide [sʌbdɪ'vaɪd] *vt* unterteilen
subdivision ['sʌbdɪvɪʒən] *n* Unterteilung *f*
subdue [səb'dju:] *vt* unterwerfen; (*emotions*) dämpfen
subdued [səb'dju:d] *adj* (*light*) gedämpft; (*person*) bedrückt
subeditor [sʌb'ɛdɪtə^r] (*Brit*) *n* Redakteur(in) *m(f)*
subject [*n* 'sʌbdʒɪkt, *vt* səb'dʒɛkt] *n* (*matter*) Thema *nt*; (*Scol*) Fach *nt*; (*of country*) Staatsbürger(in) *m(f)*; (*Gram*) Subjekt *nt* ▷ *vt*: **to ~ sb to sth** jdn einer Sache *dat* unterziehen; (*expose*) jdn einer Sache *dat* aussetzen; **to change the ~** das Thema wechseln; **to be ~ to** (*law, tax*) unterworfen sein *+dat*; (*heart attacks etc*) anfällig sein für; **~ to confirmation in writing** vorausgesetzt, es wird schriftlich bestätigt
subjection [səb'dʒɛkʃən] *n* Unterwerfung *f*
subjective [səb'dʒɛktɪv] *adj* subjektiv
subject matter *n* Stoff *m*; (*content*) Inhalt *m*
sub judice [sʌb'dju:dɪsɪ] *adj* (*Law*): **to be ~** verhandelt werden
subjugate ['sʌbdʒugeɪt] *vt* unterwerfen
subjunctive [səb'dʒʌŋktɪv] *n* Konjunktiv *m*; **in the ~** im Konjunktiv
sublet [sʌb'lɛt] *vt* untervermieten
sublime [sə'blaɪm] *adj* erhaben, vollendet; **that's going from the ~ to the ridiculous** das ist ein Abstieg ins Profane
subliminal [sʌb'lɪmɪnl] *adj* unterschwellig
submachine gun ['sʌbmə'ʃi:n-] *n* Maschinenpistole *f*
submarine [sʌbmə'ri:n] *n* Unterseeboot *nt*, U-Boot *nt*
submerge [səb'mə:dʒ] *vt* untertauchen; (*flood*) überschwemmen ▷ *vi* tauchen; **~d** unter Wasser
submersion [səb'mə:ʃən] *n* Untertauchen *nt*; (*of submarine*) Tauchen *nt*; (*by flood*) Überschwemmung *f*
submission [səb'mɪʃən] *n* (*subjection*) Unterwerfung *f*; (*of plan, application etc*) Einreichung *f*; (*proposal*) Vorlage *f*
submissive [səb'mɪsɪv] *adj* gehorsam; (*gesture*) demütig
submit [səb'mɪt] *vt* (*proposal*) vorlegen; (*application etc*) einreichen ▷ *vi*: **to ~ to sth** sich einer Sache *dat* unterwerfen
subnormal [sʌb'nɔ:ml] *adj* (*below average*) unterdurchschnittlich; (*old: child etc*) minderbegabt; **educationally ~** lernbehindert
subordinate [sə'bɔ:dɪnət] *n* Untergebene(r) *f(m)*; (*Ling*): **~ clause** Nebensatz *m* ▷ *adj* untergeordnet; **to be ~ to sb** jdm untergeordnet sein
subpoena [səb'pi:nə] *n* (*Law*) Vorladung *f* ▷ *vt* vorladen
subroutine [sʌbru:'ti:n] *n* (*Comput*) Unterprogramm *nt*
subscribe [səb'skraɪb] *vi* spenden; **to ~ to** (*opinion, theory*) sich anschließen *+dat*; (*fund, charity*) regelmäßig spenden an *+acc*; (*magazine etc*) abonnieren
subscriber [səb'skraɪbə^r] *n* (*to magazine*) Abonnent(in) *m(f)*; (*Tel*) Teilnehmer(in) *m(f)*
subscript ['sʌbskrɪpt] *n* tiefgestelltes Zeichen *nt*
subscription [səb'skrɪpʃən] *n* (*to magazine etc*) Abonnement *nt*; (*membership dues*) (Mitglieds)beitrag *m*; **to take out a ~ to** (*magazine etc*) abonnieren
subsequent ['sʌbsɪkwənt] *adj* später, nachfolgend; (*further*) weiter; **~ to** im Anschluss an *+acc*
subsequently ['sʌbsɪkwəntlɪ] *adv* später
subservient [səb'sə:vɪənt] *adj* unterwürfig; (*less important*) untergeordnet; **to be ~ to** untergeordnet sein *+dat*
subside [səb'saɪd] *vi* (*feeling, pain*) nachlassen; (*flood*) sinken; (*earth*) sich senken
subsidence [səb'saɪdns] *n* Senkung *f*
subsidiarity [səbsɪdɪ'ærɪtɪ] *n* Subsidiarität *f*
subsidiary [səb'sɪdɪərɪ] *adj* (*question, role, Brit, Scol: subject*) Neben- ▷ *n* (*also*: **subsidiary company**) Tochtergesellschaft *f*
subsidize ['sʌbsɪdaɪz] *vt* subventionieren
subsidy ['sʌbsɪdɪ] *n* Subvention *f*
subsist [səb'sɪst] *vi*: **to ~ on sth** sich von etw ernähren
subsistence [səb'sɪstəns] *n* Existenz *f*; **enough for ~** genug zum (Über)leben
subsistence allowance *n* Unterhaltszuschuss *m*
subsistence level *n* Existenzminimum *nt*
substance ['sʌbstəns] *n* Substanz *f*, Stoff *m*; (*fig: essence*) Kern *m*; **a man of ~** ein vermögender Mann; **to lack ~** (*book*) keine Substanz haben; (*argument*) keine Durchschlagskraft haben
substance abuse *n* *Missbrauch von Alkohol, Drogen, Arzneimitteln etc*
substandard [sʌb'stændəd] *adj* minderwertig; (*housing*) unzulänglich
substantial [səb'stænʃl] *adj* (*solid*) solide; (*considerable*) beträchtlich, größere(r, s); (*meal*) kräftig
substantially [səb'stænʃəlɪ] *adv* erheblich; (*in essence*) im Wesentlichen
substantiate [səb'stænʃɪeɪt] *vt* erhärten, untermauern
substitute ['sʌbstɪtju:t] *n* Ersatz *m* ▷ *vt*: **to ~ A for B** B durch A ersetzen
substitute teacher (*US*) *n* Vertretung *f*
substitution [sʌbstɪ'tju:ʃən] *n* Ersetzen *nt*; (*Football*) Auswechseln *nt*
subterfuge ['sʌbtəfju:dʒ] *n* Tricks *pl*; (*trickery*) Täuschung *f*
subterranean [sʌbtə'reɪnɪən] *adj* unterirdisch
subtitle ['sʌbtaɪtl] *n* Untertitel *m*

subtle ['sʌtl] *adj* fein; (*indirect*) raffiniert
subtlety ['sʌtltɪ] *n* Feinheit *f*; (*art of being subtle*) Finesse *f*
subtly ['sʌtlɪ] *adv* (*change, vary*) leicht; (*different*) auf subtile Weise; (*persuade*) raffiniert
subtotal [sʌb'təutl] *n* Zwischensumme *f*
subtract [səb'trækt] *vt* abziehen, subtrahieren
subtraction [səb'trækʃən] *n* Abziehen *nt*, Subtraktion *f*
subtropical [sʌb'trɔpɪkl] *adj* subtropisch
suburb ['sʌbə:b] *n* Vorort *m*
suburban [sə'bə:bən] *adj* (*train etc*) Vorort-; (*lifestyle etc*) spießig, kleinbürgerlich
suburbia [sə'bə:bɪə] *n* die Vororte *pl*
subvention [səb'vɛnʃən] *n* Subvention *f*
subversion [səb'və:ʃən] *n* Subversion *f*
subversive [səb'və:sɪv] *adj* subversiv
subway ['sʌbweɪ] *n* (*US*) Untergrundbahn *f*, U-Bahn *f*; (*Brit: underpass*) Unterführung *f*
sub-zero [sʌb'zɪərəu] *adj*: **~ temperatures** Temperaturen unter null
succeed [sək'si:d] *vi* (*plan etc*) gelingen, erfolgreich sein; (*person*) erfolgreich sein, Erfolg haben ▷ *vt* (*in job*) Nachfolger werden *+gen*; (*in order*) folgen *+dat*; **sb ~s in doing sth** es gelingt jdm, etw zu tun
succeeding [sək'si:dɪŋ] *adj* folgend; **~ generations** spätere *or* nachfolgende Generationen *pl*
success [sək'sɛs] *n* Erfolg *m*; **without ~** ohne Erfolg, erfolglos
successful [sək'sɛsful] *adj* erfolgreich; **to be ~** erfolgreich sein, Erfolg haben; **sb is ~ in doing sth** es gelingt jdm, etw zu tun
successfully [sək'sɛsfəlɪ] *adv* erfolgreich, mit Erfolg
succession [sək'sɛʃən] *n* Folge *f*, Serie *f*; (*to throne etc*) Nachfolge *f*; **3 years in ~** 3 Jahre nacheinander *or* hintereinander
successive [sək'sɛsɪv] *adj* aufeinanderfolgend; **on 3 ~ days** 3 Tage nacheinander *or* hintereinander
successor [sək'sɛsə^r] *n* Nachfolger(in) *m(f)*
succinct [sək'sɪŋkt] *adj* knapp, prägnant
succulent ['sʌkjulənt] *adj* saftig ▷ *n* Fettpflanze *f*, Sukkulente *f*
succumb [sə'kʌm] *vi*: **to ~ to** (*temptation*) erliegen *+dat*; (*illness: become affected by*) bekommen; (*: die of*) erliegen *+dat*
such [sʌtʃ] *adj* (*of that kind*): **~ a book** so ein Buch; (*so much*): **~ courage** so viel Mut; (*emphasizing similarity*): **or some ~ place/name** *etc* oder so ähnlich ▷ *adv* so; **~ books** solche Bücher; **~ a lot of** so viel; **she made ~ a noise that ...** sie machte so einen Lärm, dass ...; **~ books as I have** was ich an Büchern habe; **I said no ~ thing** das habe ich nie gesagt; **~ a long trip** so eine lange Reise; **~ as** wie (zum Beispiel); **as ~** an sich
such-and-such ['sʌtʃənsʌtʃ] *adj* die und die, der und der, das und das
suchlike ['sʌtʃlaɪk] (*inf*) *pron*: **and ~** und dergleichen
suck [sʌk] *vt* (*sweet etc*) lutschen; (*ice-lolly*) lutschen an *+dat*; (*baby*) saugen an *+dat*; (*pump, machine*) saugen
sucker ['sʌkə^r] *n* (*Zool*) Saugnapf *m*; (*Tech*) Saugfuß *m*; (*Bot*) unterirdischer Ausläufer *m*; (*inf*) Dummkopf *m*
suckle ['sʌkl] *vt* (*baby*) stillen; (*animal*) säugen
sucrose ['su:krəuz] *n* (pflanzlicher) Zucker *m*
suction ['sʌkʃən] *n* Saugwirkung *f*
suction pump *n* Saugpumpe *f*
Sudan [su'dɑ:n] *n* der Sudan
Sudanese [su:də'ni:z] *adj* sudanesisch ▷ *n* Sudanese *m*, Sudanesin *f*
sudden ['sʌdn] *adj* plötzlich; **all of a ~** ganz plötzlich
sudden death *n* (*also*: **sudden-death play-off**) Stichkampf *m*
suddenly ['sʌdnlɪ] *adv* plötzlich
suds [sʌdz] *npl* Seifenschaum *m*
sue [su:] *vt* verklagen ▷ *vi* klagen, vor Gericht gehen; **to ~ sb for damages** jdn auf Schadenersatz verklagen; **to ~ for divorce** die Scheidung einreichen
suede [sweɪd] *n* Wildleder *nt* ▷ *cpd* Wildleder-
suet ['suɪt] *n* Nierenfett *nt*
Suez ['su:ɪz] *n*: **the ~ Canal** der Suezkanal
Suff. (*Brit*) *abbr* (*Post*) = *Suffolk*
suffer ['sʌfə^r] *vt* erleiden; (*rudeness etc*) ertragen ▷ *vi* leiden; **to ~ from** leiden an *+dat*; **to ~ the effects of sth** an den Folgen von etw leiden
sufferance ['sʌfərns] *n*: **he was only there on ~** er wurde dort nur geduldet
sufferer ['sʌfərə^r] *n* Leidende(r) *f(m)*
suffering ['sʌfərɪŋ] *n* Leid *nt*
suffice [sə'faɪs] *vi* genügen
sufficient [sə'fɪʃənt] *adj* ausreichend; **~ money** genug Geld
sufficiently [sə'fɪʃəntlɪ] *adv* genug, ausreichend; **~ powerful/enthusiastic** mächtig/begeistert genug
suffix ['sʌfɪks] *n* Suffix *nt*, Nachsilbe *f*
suffocate ['sʌfəkeɪt] *vi* (*lit, fig*) ersticken
suffocation [sʌfə'keɪʃən] *n* Ersticken *nt*
suffrage ['sʌfrɪdʒ] *n* Wahlrecht *nt*
suffragette [sʌfrə'dʒɛt] *n* Suffragette *f*
suffused [sə'fju:zd] *adj*: **~ with** erfüllt von; **~ with light** lichtdurchflutet
sugar ['ʃugə^r] *n* Zucker *m* ▷ *vt* zuckern
sugar beet *n* Zuckerrübe *f*
sugar bowl *n* Zuckerdose *f*
sugar cane *n* Zuckerrohr *nt*
sugar-coated ['ʃugə'kəutɪd] *adj* mit Zucker überzogen
sugar lump *n* Zuckerstück *nt*
sugar refinery *n* Zuckerraffinerie *f*
sugary ['ʃugərɪ] *adj* süß; (*fig: smile, phrase*) süßlich
suggest [sə'dʒɛst] *vt* vorschlagen; (*indicate*) andeuten, hindeuten auf *+acc*; **what do you ~ I do?** was schlagen Sie vor?
suggestion [sə'dʒɛstʃən] *n* Vorschlag *m*; (*indication*) Anflug *m*; (*trace*) Spur *f*
suggestive [sə'dʒɛstɪv] (*pej*) *adj* anzüglich

suicidal [suɪ'saɪdl] *adj* selbstmörderisch; (*person*) selbstmordgefährdet; **to be** *or* **feel ~** Selbstmordgedanken haben
suicide ['suɪsaɪd] *n* (*lit, fig*) Selbstmord *m*; (*person*) Selbstmörder(in) *m(f)*; *see also* **commit**
suicide attack *n* Selbstmordanschlag *m*
suicide attacker *n* Selbstmordattentäter(in) *m(f)*
suicide attempt, **suicide bid** *n* Selbstmordversuch *m*
suicide bomber *n* Selbstmordattentäter(in) *m(f)*
suit [su:t] *n* (*man's*) Anzug *m*; (*woman's*) Kostüm *nt*; (*Law*) Prozess *m*, Verfahren *nt*; (*Cards*) Farbe *f* ▷ *vt* passen *+dat*; (*colour, clothes*) stehen *+dat*; **to bring a ~ against sb** (*Law*) gegen jdn Klage erheben *or* einen Prozess anstrengen; **to follow ~** (*fig*) das Gleiche tun; **to ~ sth to** etw anpassen an *+acc*; **to be ~ed to do sth** sich dafür eignen, etw zu tun; **~ yourself!** wie du willst!; **well ~ed** (*couple*) gut zusammenpassend
suitability [su:tə'bɪlɪtɪ] *n* Eignung *f*
suitable ['su:təbl] *adj* (*convenient*) passend; (*appropriate*) geeignet; **would tomorrow be ~?** würde Ihnen morgen passen?; **Monday isn't ~** Montag passt nicht; **we found somebody ~** wir haben jemand Passenden gefunden
suitably ['su:təblɪ] *adv* passend; (*impressed*) gebührend
suitcase ['su:tkeɪs] *n* Koffer *m*
suite [swi:t] *n* (*of rooms*) Suite *f*, Zimmerflucht *f*; (*Mus*) Suite *f*; **bedroom/dining room ~** Schlafzimmer-/Esszimmereinrichtung *f*; **a three-piece ~** eine dreiteilige Polstergarnitur
suitor ['su:təʳ] *n* Kläger(in) *m(f)*
sulfate ['sʌlfeɪt] (*US*) *n* = **sulphate**
sulfur ['sʌlfəʳ] (*US*) *n* = **sulphur**
sulfuric [sʌl'fjuərɪk] (*US*) *adj* = **sulphuric**
sulk [sʌlk] *vi* schmollen
sulky ['sʌlkɪ] *adj* schmollend
sullen ['sʌlən] *adj* mürrisch, verdrossen
sulphate, (*US*) **sulfate** ['sʌlfeɪt] *n* Sulfat *nt*, schwefelsaures Salz *nt*
sulphur, (*US*) **sulfur** ['sʌlfəʳ] *n* Schwefel *m*
sulphur dioxide *n* Schwefeldioxid *nt*
sulphuric, (*US*) **sulfuric** [sʌl'fjuərɪk] *adj*: **~ acid** Schwefelsäure *f*
sultan ['sʌltən] *n* Sultan *m*
sultana [sʌl'tɑ:nə] *n* Sultanine *f*
sultry ['sʌltrɪ] *adj* schwül
sum [sʌm] *n* (*calculation*) Rechenaufgabe *f*; (*amount*) Summe *f*, Betrag *m*
▸ **sum up** *vt* zusammenfassen; (*evaluate rapidly*) einschätzen ▷ *vi* zusammenfassen
Sumatra [su'mɑ:trə] *n* Sumatra *nt*
summarize ['sʌməraɪz] *vt* zusammenfassen
summary ['sʌmərɪ] *n* Zusammenfassung *f* ▷ *adj* (*justice, executions*) im Schnellverfahren
summer ['sʌməʳ] *n* Sommer *m* ▷ *cpd* Sommer-; **in ~** im Sommer
summer camp (*US*) *n* Ferienlager *nt*
summer holidays *npl* Sommerferien *pl*
summerhouse ['sʌməhaus] *n* (*in garden*) Gartenhaus *nt*, Gartenlaube *f*
summertime ['sʌmətaɪm] *n* Sommer *m*, Sommerszeit *f*
summer time *n* Sommerzeit *f*
summery ['sʌmərɪ] *adj* sommerlich
summing-up [sʌmɪŋ'ʌp] *n* (*Law*) Resümee *nt*
summit ['sʌmɪt] *n* Gipfel *m*; (*also*: **summit conference/meeting**) Gipfelkonferenz *f*/-treffen *nt*
summon ['sʌmən] *vt* rufen, kommen lassen; (*help*) holen; (*meeting*) einberufen; (*Law: witness*) vorladen
▸ **summon up** *vt* aufbringen
summons ['sʌmənz] *n* (*Law*) Vorladung *f*; (*fig*) Aufruf *m* ▷ *vt* (*Law*) vorladen; **to serve a ~ on sb** jdn vor Gericht laden
sumo ['su:məu], **sumo wrestling** *n* Sumo(-Ringen) *nt*
sump [sʌmp] (*Brit*) *n* Ölwanne *f*
sumptuous ['sʌmptjuəs] *adj* (*meal*) üppig; (*costume*) aufwendig
Sun. *abbr* (= *Sunday*) So.
sun [sʌn] *n* Sonne *f*; **to catch the ~** einen Sonnenbrand bekommen; **everything under the ~** alles Mögliche
sunbathe ['sʌnbeɪð] *vi* sich sonnen
sunbeam ['sʌnbi:m] *n* Sonnenstrahl *m*
sunbed ['sʌnbɛd] *n* (*with sun lamp*) Sonnenbank *f*
sunblock *n* Sonnenschutzcreme *f*
sunburn ['sʌnbə:n] *n* Sonnenbrand *m*
sunburned ['sʌnbə:nd] *adj* = **sunburnt**
sunburnt ['sʌnbə:nt] *adj* sonnenverbrannt, sonnengebräunt; **to be ~** (*painfully*) einen Sonnenbrand haben
sun-cream ['sʌnkri:m] *n* Sonnencreme *f*
sundae ['sʌndeɪ] *n* Eisbecher *m*
Sunday ['sʌndɪ] *n* Sonntag *m*; *see also* **Tuesday**
Sunday paper *n* Sonntagszeitung *f*; *siehe Info-Artikel*

SUNDAY PAPERS

Die *Sunday papers* umfassen sowohl Massenblätter als auch seriöse Zeitungen. „The Observer" ist die älteste überregionale Sonntagszeitung der Welt. Die Sonntagszeitungen sind alle sehr umfangreich mit vielen Farb- und Sonderbeilagen. Zu den meisten Tageszeitungen gibt es parallele Sonntagsblätter, die aber separate Redaktionen haben.

Sunday school *n* Sonntagsschule *f*
sundial ['sʌndaɪəl] *n* Sonnenuhr *f*
sundown ['sʌndaun] (*esp US*) *n* Sonnenuntergang *m*
sundries ['sʌndrɪz] *npl* Verschiedenes *nt*
sundry ['sʌndrɪ] *adj* verschiedene; **all and ~** jedermann
sunflower ['sʌnflauəʳ] *n* Sonnenblume *f*
sunflower oil *n* Sonnenblumenöl *nt*

sung [sʌŋ] *pp of* **sing**
sunglasses ['sʌnglɑ:sɪz] *npl* Sonnenbrille *f*
sunk [sʌŋk] *pp of* **sink**
sunken ['sʌŋkn] *adj* versunken; (*eyes*) tief liegend; (*cheeks*) eingefallen; (*bath*) eingelassen
sunlamp ['sʌnlæmp] *n* Höhensonne *f*
sunlight ['sʌnlaɪt] *n* Sonnenlicht *nt*
sunlit ['sʌnlɪt] *adj* sonnig, sonnenbeschienen
sunny ['sʌnɪ] *adj* sonnig; (*fig*) heiter
sunrise ['sʌnraɪz] *n* Sonnenaufgang *m*
sun roof *n* (*Aut*) Schiebedach *nt*; (*on building*) Sonnenterrasse *f*
sun screen *n* Sonnenschutzmittel *nt*
sunset ['sʌnsɛt] *n* Sonnenuntergang *m*
sunshade ['sʌnʃeɪd] *n* Sonnenschirm *m*
sunshine ['sʌnʃaɪn] *n* Sonnenschein *m*
sunspot ['sʌnspɔt] *n* Sonnenfleck *m*
sunstroke ['sʌnstrəuk] *n* Sonnenstich *m*
suntan ['sʌntæn] *n* (Sonnen)bräune *f*; **to get a ~** braun werden
suntan lotion *n* Sonnenmilch *f*
suntanned ['sʌntænd] *adj* braun (gebrannt)
suntan oil *n* Sonnenöl *nt*
suntrap ['sʌntræp] *n* sonniges Eckchen *nt*
super ['su:pəʳ] (*inf*) *adj* fantastisch, toll
superannuation [su:pərænju'eɪʃən] *n* Beitrag *m* zur Rentenversicherung
superb [su:'pə:b] *adj* ausgezeichnet, großartig; (*meal*) vorzüglich
Super Bowl *n* Superbowl *m*, Super Bowl *m*, *American-Football-Turnier zwischen den Spitzenreitern der Nationalligen*
supercilious [su:pə'sɪlɪəs] *adj* herablassend
superconductor [su:pəkən'dʌktəʳ] *n* (*Phys*) Superleiter *m*
superficial [su:pə'fɪʃəl] *adj* oberflächlich
superficially [su:pə'fɪʃəlɪ] *adv* oberflächlich; (*from a superficial point of view*) oberflächlich gesehen
superfluous [su'pə:fluəs] *adj* überflüssig
superglue ['su:pəglu:] *n* Sekundenkleber *m*
superhighway (*US*) *n* ≈ Autobahn *f*; **information ~** Datenautobahn *f*
superhuman [su:pə'hju:mən] *adj* übermenschlich
superimpose ['su:pərɪm'pəuz] *vt* (*two things*) übereinanderlegen; **to ~ on** legen auf *+acc*; **to ~ with** überlagern mit
superintend [su:pərɪn'tɛnd] *vt* beaufsichtigen, überwachen
superintendent [su:pərɪn'tɛndənt] *n* Aufseher(in) *m(f)*; (*Police*) Kommissar(in) *m(f)*
superior [su'pɪərɪəʳ] *adj* besser, überlegen *+dat*; (*more senior*) höhergestellt; (*smug*) überheblich; (*: smile*) überlegen ▹ *n* Vorgesetzte(r) *f(m)*; **Mother S~** (*Rel*) Mutter Oberin
superiority [supɪərɪ'ɔrɪtɪ] *n* Überlegenheit *f*
superlative [su'pə:lətɪv] *n* Superlativ *m* ▹ *adj* überragend
superman ['su:pəmæn] (*irreg: like* **man**) *n* Übermensch *m*
supermarket ['su:pəmɑ:kɪt] *n* Supermarkt *m*
supermodel ['su:pəmɔdl] *n* Supermodell *nt*
supernatural [su:pə'nætʃərəl] *adj* übernatürlich ▹ *n*: **the ~** das Übernatürliche
supernova [su:pə'nəuvə] *n* Supernova *f*
superpower ['su:pəpauəʳ] *n* Supermacht *f*
superscript ['su:pəskrɪpt] *n* hochgestelltes Zeichen *nt*
supersede [su:pə'si:d] *vt* ablösen, ersetzen
supersonic [su:pə'sɔnɪk] *adj* (*aircraft etc*) Überschall-
superstar ['su:pəstɑ:ʳ] *n* Superstar *m*
superstition [su:pə'stɪʃən] *n* Aberglaube *m*
superstitious [su:pə'stɪʃəs] *adj* abergläubisch
superstore ['su:pəstɔ:ʳ] (*Brit*) *n* Großmarkt *m*
supertanker ['su:pətæŋkəʳ] *n* Supertanker *m*
supertax ['su:pətæks] *n* Höchststeuer *f*
supervise ['su:pəvaɪz] *vt* beaufsichtigen
supervision [su:pə'vɪʒən] *n* Beaufsichtigung *f*; **under medical ~** unter ärztlicher Aufsicht
supervisor ['su:pəvaɪzəʳ] *n* Aufseher(in) *m(f)*; (*of students*) Tutor(in) *m(f)*
supervisory ['su:pəvaɪzərɪ] *adj* beaufsichtigend, Aufsichts-
supine ['su:paɪn] *adj*: **to be ~** auf dem Rücken liegen ▹ *adv* auf dem Rücken
supper ['sʌpəʳ] *n* Abendessen *nt*; **to have ~** zu Abend essen
supplant [sə'plɑ:nt] *vt* ablösen, ersetzen
supple ['sʌpl] *adj* geschmeidig; (*person*) gelenkig
supplement ['sʌplɪmənt] *n* Zusatz *m*; (*of book*) Ergänzungsband *m*; (*of newspaper etc*) Beilage *f* ▹ *vt* ergänzen
supplementary [sʌplɪ'mɛntərɪ] *adj* zusätzlich, ergänzend
supplementary benefit (*Brit: old*) *n* ≈ Sozialhilfe *f*
supplementary budget *n* (*Pol*) ≈ Nachtragshaushalt *m or* -etat *m*
supplier [sə'plaɪəʳ] *n* Lieferant(in) *m(f)*
supply [sə'plaɪ] *vt* liefern; (*provide*) sorgen für; (*a need*) befriedigen ▹ *n* Vorrat *m*; (*supplying*) Lieferung *f*; **supplies** *npl* (*food*) Vorräte *pl*; (*Mil*) Nachschub *m*; **to ~ sth to sb** jdm etw liefern; **to ~ sth with sth** etw mit etw versorgen; **it comes supplied with an adaptor** es wird mit einem Adapter geliefert; **office supplies** Bürobedarf *m*; **to be in short ~** knapp sein; **the electricity/water/gas ~** die Strom-/Wasser-/Gasversorgung *f*; **~ and demand** Angebot *nt* und Nachfrage
supply teacher (*Brit*) *n* Vertretung *f*
support [sə'pɔ:t] *n* Unterstützung *f*; (*Tech*) Stütze *f* ▹ *vt* unterstützen, eintreten für; (*financially: family etc*) unterhalten; (*: party etc*) finanziell unterstützen; (*Tech*) (ab)stützen; (*theory etc*) untermauern; **they stopped work in ~ of ...** sie sind in den Streik getreten, um für ... einzutreten; **to ~ o.s.** (*financially*) finanziell unabhängig sein; **to ~ Arsenal** Arsenal-Fan sein
supporter [sə'pɔ:təʳ] *n* (*Pol etc*) Anhänger(in) *m(f)*; (*Sport*) Fan *m*

supporting [sə'pɔːtɪŋ] *adj*: **~ role** Nebenrolle *f*; **~ actor** Schauspieler *m* in einer Nebenrolle; **~ film** Vorfilm *m*
supportive [sə'pɔːtɪv] *adj* hilfreich; **to be ~ of sb/sth** jdn/etw unterstützen
suppose [sə'pəuz] *vt* annehmen, glauben; (*imagine*) sich *dat* vorstellen; **to be ~d to do sth** etw tun sollen; **it was worse than she'd ~d** es war schlimmer, als sie es sich vorgestellt hatte; **I don't ~ she'll come** ich glaube kaum, dass sie kommt; **he's about sixty, I ~** er muss wohl so um die Sechzig sein; **he's ~d to be an expert** er ist angeblich ein Experte; **I ~ so/not** ich glaube schon/nicht
supposedly [sə'pəuzɪdlɪ] *adv* angeblich
supposing [sə'pəuzɪŋ] *conj* angenommen
supposition [sʌpə'zɪʃən] *n* Annahme *f*
suppository [sə'pɔzɪtrɪ] *n* Zäpfchen *nt*
suppress [sə'prɛs] *vt* unterdrücken; (*publication*) verbieten
suppression [sə'prɛʃən] *n* Unterdrückung *f*
suppressor [sə'prɛsə[r]] *n* (*Elec etc*) Entstörungselement *nt*
supremacy [su'prɛməsɪ] *n* Vormachtstellung *f*
supreme [su'priːm] *adj* Ober-, oberste(r, s); (*effort*) äußerste(r, s); (*achievement*) höchste(r, s)
Supreme Court (*US*) *n* Oberster Gerichtshof *m*
supremo [su'priːməu] (*Brit: inf*) *n* Boss *m*
Supt *abbr* (*Police*) = **superintendent**
surcharge ['səːtʃɑːdʒ] *n* Zuschlag *m*
sure [ʃuə[r]] *adj* sicher; (*reliable*) zuverlässig, sicher ▷ *adv* (*inf: esp US*): **that ~ is pretty, that's ~ pretty** das ist aber schön; **to make ~ of sth** sich einer Sache *gen* vergewissern; **to make ~ that** sich vergewissern, dass; **I'm ~ of it** ich bin mir da sicher; **I'm not ~ how/why/when** ich bin mir nicht sicher *or* ich weiß nicht genau, wie/warum/wann; **to be ~ of o.s.** selbstsicher sein; **~!** klar!; **~ enough** tatsächlich
sure-fire ['ʃuəfaɪə[r]] (*inf*) *adj* todsicher
sure-footed [ʃuə'futɪd] *adj* trittsicher
surely ['ʃuəlɪ] *adv* sicherlich, bestimmt; **~ you don't mean that!** das meinen Sie doch bestimmt *or* sicher nicht (so)!
surety ['ʃuərətɪ] *n* Bürgschaft *f*, Sicherheit *f*; **to go** *or* **stand ~ for sb** für jdn bürgen
surf [səːf] *n* Brandung *f*
surface ['səːfɪs] *n* Oberfläche *f* ▷ *vt* (*road*) mit einem Belag versehen ▷ *vi* (*lit, fig*) auftauchen; (*feeling*) hochkommen; (*rise from bed*) hochkommen; **on the ~** (*fig*) oberflächlich betrachtet
surface area *n* Fläche *f*
surface mail *n* Post *f* auf dem Land-/Seeweg
surface-to-surface ['səːfɪstə'səːfɪs] *adj* (*missile*) Boden-Boden-
surfboard ['səːfbɔːd] *n* Surfbrett *nt*
surfeit ['səːfɪt] *n*: **a ~ of** ein Übermaß an *+dat*
surfer ['səːfə[r]] *n* Surfer(in) *m(f)*
surfing ['səːfɪŋ] *n* Surfen *nt*; **to go ~** surfen gehen
surge [səːdʒ] *n* Anstieg *m*; (*fig: of emotion*) Woge *f*; (*Elec*) Spannungsstoß *m* ▷ *vi* (*water*) branden; (*people*) sich drängen; (*vehicles*) sich wälzen; (*emotion*) aufwallen; (*Elec: power*) ansteigen; **to ~ forward** nach vorne drängen
surgeon ['səːdʒən] *n* Chirurg(in) *m(f)*
Surgeon General (*US*) *n* (*Med*) ≈ Gesundheitsminister(in) *m(f)*; (*Mil*) Sanitätsinspekteur(in) *m(f)*
surgery ['səːdʒərɪ] *n* Chirurgie *f*; (*Brit: room*) Sprechzimmer *nt*; (*: building*) Praxis *f*; (*also*: **surgery hours**): *of doctor, MP etc*) Sprechstunde *f*; **to have ~** operiert werden; **to need ~** operiert werden müssen
surgical ['səːdʒɪkl] *adj* chirurgisch; (*treatment*) operativ
surgical spirit (*Brit*) *n* Wundbenzin *nt*
surly ['səːlɪ] *adj* verdrießlich, mürrisch
surmise [səː'maɪz] *vt* vermuten, mutmaßen
surmount [səː'maunt] *vt* (*fig*) überwinden
surname ['səːneɪm] *n* Nachname *m*
surpass [səː'pɑːs] *vt* übertreffen
surplus ['səːpləs] *n* Überschuss *m* ▷ *adj* überschüssig; **it is ~ to our requirements** das benötigen wir nicht
surprise [sə'praɪz] *n* Überraschung *f* ▷ *vt* überraschen; (*astonish*) erstaunen; (*army*) überrumpeln; (*thief*) ertappen; **to take sb by ~** jdn überraschen
surprising [sə'praɪzɪŋ] *adj* überraschend; (*situation*) erstaunlich; **it is ~ how/that** es ist erstaunlich, wie/dass
surprisingly [sə'praɪzɪŋlɪ] *adv* überraschend, erstaunlich; **(somewhat) ~, he agreed** erstaunlicherweise war er damit einverstanden
surrealism [sə'rɪəlɪzəm] *n* Surrealismus *m*
surrealist [sə'rɪəlɪst] *adj* surrealistisch
surrender [sə'rɛndə[r]] *n* Kapitulation *f* ▷ *vi* sich ergeben ▷ *vt* aufgeben
surrender value *n* Rückkaufswert *m*
surreptitious [sʌrəp'tɪʃəs] *adj* heimlich, verstohlen
surrogate ['sʌrəgɪt] *n* Ersatz *m* ▷ *adj* (*parents*) Ersatz-
surrogate mother *n* Leihmutter *f*
surround [sə'raund] *vt* umgeben; (*Mil, Police etc*) umstellen
surrounding [sə'raundɪŋ] *adj* umliegend; **the ~ area** die Umgebung
surroundings [sə'raundɪŋz] *npl* Umgebung *f*
surtax ['səːtæks] *n* Steuerzuschlag *m*
surveillance [səː'veɪləns] *n* Überwachung *f*; **to be under ~** überwacht werden
survey ['səːveɪ] *n* (*of land*) Vermessung *f*; (*of house*) Begutachtung *f*; (*investigation*) Untersuchung *f*; (*report*) Gutachten *nt*; (*comprehensive view*) Überblick *m* ▷ *vt* (*land*) vermessen; (*house*) inspizieren; (*look at*) betrachten
surveying [sə'veɪɪŋ] *n* (*of land*) Vermessung *f*
surveyor [sə'veɪə[r]] *n* (*of land*) Landvermesser(in) *m(f)*; (*of house*) Baugutachter(in) *m(f)*

survival [sə'vaɪvl] *n* Überleben *nt*; (*relic*) Überbleibsel *nt*; **~ course/kit** Überlebenstraining *nt*/-ausrüstung *f*; **~ bag** Expeditionsschlafsack *m*
survive [sə'vaɪv] *vi* überleben; (*custom etc*) weiter bestehen ▷ *vt* überleben
survivor [sə'vaɪvəʳ] *n* Überlebende(r) *f(m)*
susceptible [sə'sɛptəbl] *adj*: **~ (to)** anfällig (für); (*influenced by*) empfänglich (für)
suspect ['sʌspɛkt] *adj* verdächtig ▷ *n* Verdächtige(r) *f(m)* ▷ *vt*: **to ~ sb of** jdn verdächtigen *+gen*; (*think*) vermuten; (*doubt*) bezweifeln
suspected [səs'pɛktɪd] *adj* (*terrorist etc*) mutmaßlich; **he is a ~ member of this organization** er steht im Verdacht, Mitglied dieser Organisation zu sein
suspend [səs'pɛnd] *vt* (*hang*) (auf)hängen; (*delay, stop*) einstellen; (*from employment*) suspendieren; **to be ~ed (from)** (*hang*) hängen (an *+dat*)
suspended animation [səs'pɛndɪd-] *n* *vorübergehender Stillstand aller Körperfunktionen*
suspended sentence *n* (*Law*) zur Bewährung ausgesetzte Strafe *f*
suspender belt [səs'pɛndəʳ-] *n* Strumpfhaltergürtel *m*
suspenders [səs'pɛndəz] *npl* (*Brit*) Strumpfhalter *pl*; (*US*) Hosenträger *pl*
suspense [səs'pɛns] *n* Spannung *f*; (*uncertainty*) Ungewissheit *f*; **to keep sb in ~** jdn auf die Folter spannen
suspension [səs'pɛnʃən] *n* (*from job*) Suspendierung *f*; (*from team*) Sperrung *f*; (*Aut*) Federung *f*; (*of driving licence*) zeitweiliger Entzug *m*; (*of payment*) zeitweilige Einstellung *f*
suspension bridge *n* Hängebrücke *f*
suspicion [səs'pɪʃən] *n* Verdacht *m*; (*distrust*) Misstrauen *nt*; (*trace*) Spur *f*; **to be under ~** unter Verdacht stehen; **arrested on ~ of murder** wegen Mordverdacht(s) festgenommen
suspicious [səs'pɪʃəs] *adj* (*suspecting*) misstrauisch; (*causing suspicion*) verdächtig; **to be ~ of** *or* **about sb/sth** jdn/etw mit Misstrauen betrachten
suss out [sʌs-] (*Brit: inf*) *vt* (*discover*) rauskriegen; (*understand*) durchschauen
sustain [səs'teɪn] *vt* (*continue*) aufrechterhalten; (*food, drink*) bei Kräften halten; (*suffer: injury*) erleiden
sustainable [səs'teɪnəbl] *adj*: **to be ~** aufrechtzuerhalten sein; **~ growth** stetiges Wachstum *nt*
sustained [səs'teɪnd] *adj* (*effort*) ausdauernd; (*attack*) anhaltend
sustenance ['sʌstɪnəns] *n* Nahrung *f*
suture ['su:tʃəʳ] *n* Naht *f*
SVQ *n abbr* (*= Scottish Vocational Qualification*) *Qualifikation für berufsbegleitende Ausbildungsinhalte in Schottland*
SW *abbr* (*= south-west*) SW; (*Radio: = short-wave*) KW
swab [swɔb] *n* (*Med*) Tupfer *m* ▷ *vt* (*Naut: also:* **swab down**) wischen
swagger ['swægəʳ] *vi* stolzieren
swallow ['swɔləu] *n* (*bird*) Schwalbe *f*; (*of food, drink etc*) Schluck *m* ▷ *vt* (herunter)schlucken; (*fig: story, insult, one's pride*) schlucken; **to ~ one's words** (*speak indistinctly*) seine Worte verschlucken; (*retract*) alles zurücknehmen
▶ **swallow up** *vt* verschlingen
swam [swæm] *pt of* **swim**
swamp [swɔmp] *n* Sumpf *m* ▷ *vt* (*lit, fig*) überschwemmen
swampy ['swɔmpɪ] *adj* sumpfig
swan [swɔn] *n* Schwan *m*
swank [swæŋk] (*inf*) *vi* angeben
swan song *n* (*fig*) Schwanengesang *m*
swap [swɔp] *n* Tausch *m* ▷ *vt*: **to ~ (for)** (ein)tauschen (gegen)
SWAPO ['swɑ:pəu] *n abbr* (*= South-West Africa People's Organization*) SWAPO *f*
swarm [swɔ:m] *n* Schwarm *m*; (*of people*) Schar *f* ▷ *vi* (*bees, people*) schwärmen; **to be ~ing with** wimmeln von
swarthy ['swɔ:ðɪ] *adj* (*person, face*) dunkelhäutig; (*complexion*) dunkel
swastika ['swɔstɪkə] *n* Hakenkreuz *nt*
SWAT (*US*) *n abbr* (*= Special Weapons and Tactics*): **~ team** ≈ schnelle Eingreiftruppe *f*
swat [swɔt] *vt* totschlagen ▷ *n* (*Brit: also:* **fly swat**) Fliegenklatsche *f*
swathe [sweɪð] *vt*: **to ~ in** wickeln in *+acc*
swatter ['swɔtəʳ] *n* (*also:* **fly swatter**) Fliegenklatsche *f*
sway [sweɪ] *vi* schwanken ▷ *vt* (*influence*) beeinflussen ▷ *n*: **to hold ~** herrschen; **to hold ~ over sb** jdn beherrschen *or* in seiner Macht haben
swear [swɛəʳ] (*pt* **swore**, *pp* **sworn**) *vi* (*curse*) fluchen ▷ *vt* (*promise*) schwören; **to ~ an oath** einen Eid ablegen
▶ **swear in** *vt* vereidigen
swearword ['swɛəwə:d] *n* Fluch *m*, Kraftausdruck *m*
sweat [swɛt] *n* Schweiß *m* ▷ *vi* schwitzen; **to be in a ~** schwitzen
sweatband ['swɛtbænd] *n* Schweißband *nt*
sweater ['swɛtəʳ] *n* Pullover *m*
sweatshirt ['swɛtʃə:t] *n* Sweatshirt *nt*
sweatshop ['swɛtʃɔp] (*pej*) *n* Ausbeuterbetrieb *m*
sweaty ['swɛtɪ] *adj* verschwitzt; (*hands*) schweißig
Swede [swi:d] *n* Schwede *m*, Schwedin *f*
swede [swi:d] (*Brit*) *n* Steckrübe *f*
Sweden ['swi:dn] *n* Schweden *nt*
Swedish ['swi:dɪʃ] *adj* schwedisch ▷ *n* Schwedisch *nt*
sweep [swi:p] (*pt, pp* **swept**) *n*: **to give sth a ~** etw fegen *or* kehren; (*curve*) Bogen *m*; (*range*) Bereich *m*; (*also:* **chimney sweep**) Kaminkehrer *m*, Schornsteinfeger *m* ▷ *vt* fegen, kehren; (*current*) reißen ▷ *vi* (*through air*) gleiten; (*wind*) fegen

▸ **sweep away** *vt* hinwegfegen
▸ **sweep past** *vi* vorbeirauschen
▸ **sweep up** *vi* zusammenfegen, zusammenkehren

sweeper ['swi:pəʳ] *n* (*Football*) Ausputzer *m*

sweeping ['swi:pɪŋ] *adj* (*gesture*) weit ausholend; (*changes, reforms*) weitreichend; (*statement*) verallgemeinernd

sweepstake ['swi:psteɪk] *n Pferdewette, bei der der Preis aus der Summe der Einsätze besteht*

sweet [swi:t] *n* (*candy*) Bonbon *nt or m*; (*Brit: Culin*) Nachtisch *m* ▹ *adj* süß; (*air, water*) frisch; (*kind*) lieb ▹ *adv*: **to smell/taste ~** süß duften/schmecken; **~ and sour** süß-sauer

sweetbread ['swi:tbrɛd] *n* Bries *nt*

sweetcorn ['swi:tkɔ:n] *n* Mais *m*

sweeten ['swi:tn] *vt* süßen; (*temper*) bessern; (*person*) gnädig stimmen

sweetener ['swi:tnəʳ] *n* Süßstoff *m*; (*fig*) Anreiz *m*

sweetheart ['swi:thɑ:t] *n* Freund(in) *m(f)*; (*in speech, writing*) Schatz *m*, Liebling *m*

sweetness ['swi:tnɪs] *n* Süße *f*; (*kindness*) Liebenswürdigkeit *f*

sweet pea *n* (Garten)wicke *f*

sweet potato *n* Süßkartoffel *f*, Batate *f*

sweet shop (*Brit*) *n* Süßwarengeschäft *nt*

sweet tooth *n*: **to have a ~** gern Süßes essen

swell [swɛl] (*pt* **~ed**, *pp* **swollen** *or* **~ed**) *n* Seegang *m* ▹ *adj* (*US: inf*) toll, prima ▹ *vi* (*increase*) anwachsen; (*sound*) anschwellen; (*feeling*) stärker werden; (*also*: **swell up**) anschwellen

swelling ['swɛlɪŋ] *n* Schwellung *f*

sweltering ['swɛltərɪŋ] *adj* (*heat*) glühend; (*weather, day*) glühend heiß

swept [swɛpt] *pt, pp of* **sweep**

swerve [swə:v] *vi* (*animal*) ausbrechen; (*driver, vehicle*) ausschwenken; **to ~ off the road** ausschwenken und von der Straße abkommen

swift [swɪft] *n* Mauersegler *m* ▹ *adj* schnell

swiftly ['swɪftlɪ] *adv* schnell

swiftness ['swɪftnɪs] *n* Schnelligkeit *f*

swig [swɪg] (*inf*) *n* Schluck *m* ▹ *vt* herunterkippen

swill [swɪl] *vt* (*also*: **swill out**) ausspülen; (*also*: **swill down**) abspülen ▹ *n* (*for pigs*) Schweinefutter *nt*

swim [swɪm] (*pt* **swam**, *pp* **swum**) *vi* schwimmen; (*before one's eyes*) verschwimmen ▹ *vt* (*the Channel etc*) durchschwimmen; (*a length*) schwimmen ▹ *n*: **to go for a ~** schwimmen gehen; **to go ~ming** schwimmen gehen; **my head is ~ming** mir dreht sich der Kopf

swimmer ['swɪməʳ] *n* Schwimmer(in) *m(f)*

swimming ['swɪmɪŋ] *n* Schwimmen *nt*

swimming baths (*Brit*) *npl* Schwimmbad *nt*

swimming cap *n* Badekappe *f*, Bademütze *f*

swimming costume (*Brit*) *n* Badeanzug *m*

swimmingly ['swɪmɪŋlɪ] (*inf*) *adv* glänzend

swimming pool *n* Schwimmbad *nt*

swimming trunks *npl* Badehose *f*

swimsuit ['swɪmsu:t] *n* Badeanzug *m*

swindle ['swɪndl] *n* Schwindel *m*, Betrug *m* ▹ *vt*: **to ~ sb (out of sth)** jdn (um etw) betrügen *or* beschwindeln

swindler ['swɪndləʳ] *n* Schwindler(in) *m(f)*

swine [swaɪn] (*inf!*) *n* Schwein *nt*

swing [swɪŋ] (*pt, pp* **swung**) *n* (*in playground*) Schaukel *f*; (*movement*) Schwung *m*; (*change*) Umschwung *m*; (*Mus*) Swing *m* ▹ *vt* (*arms, legs*) schwingen (mit); (*also*: **swing round**) herumschwenken ▹ *vi* schwingen; (*also*: **swing round**) sich umdrehen; (*vehicle*) herumschwenken; **a ~ to the left** (*Pol*) ein Linksruck *m*; **to get into the ~ of things** richtig reinkommen; **to be in full ~** (*party etc*) in vollem Gang sein

swing bridge *n* Drehbrücke *f*

swing door, (*US*) **swinging door** *n* Pendeltür *f*

swingeing ['swɪndʒɪŋ] (*Brit*) *adj* (*blow*) hart; (*attack*) scharf; (*cuts, increases*) extrem

swinging ['swɪŋɪŋ] *adj* (*music*) schwungvoll; (*movement*) schaukelnd

swipe [swaɪp] *vt* (*also*: **swipe at**) schlagen nach; (*inf: steal*) klauen ▹ *n* Schlag *m*

swirl [swə:l] *vi* wirbeln ▹ *n* Wirbeln *nt*

swish [swɪʃ] *vi* rauschen; (*tail*) schlagen ▹ *n* Rauschen *nt*; (*of tail*) Schlagen *nt* ▹ *adj* (*inf*) chic *inv*, schick

Swiss [swɪs] *adj* schweizerisch, Schweizer ▹ *n inv* Schweizer(in) *m(f)*

Swiss French *adj* französischschweizerisch

Swiss German *adj* deutsch-schweizerisch

Swiss roll *n* Biskuitrolle *f*

switch [swɪtʃ] *n* Schalter *m*; (*change*) Änderung *f* ▹ *vt* (*change*) ändern; (*exchange*) tauschen, wechseln; **to ~ (round** *or* **over)** vertauschen
▸ **switch off** *vt* abschalten; (*light*) ausschalten ▹ *vi* (*fig*) abschalten
▸ **switch on** *vt* einschalten; (*radio*) anstellen; (*engine*) anlassen

switchback ['swɪtʃbæk] (*Brit*) *n* (*road*) auf und ab führende Straße *f*; (*roller-coaster*) Achterbahn *f*

switchblade ['swɪtʃbleɪd] *n* Schnappmesser *nt*

switchboard ['swɪtʃbɔ:d] *n* Vermittlung *f*, Zentrale *f*

switchboard operator *n* Telefonist(in) *m(f)*

Switzerland ['swɪtsələnd] *n* die Schweiz *f*

swivel ['swɪvl] *vi* (*also*: **swivel round**) sich (herum)drehen

swollen ['swəulən] *pp of* **swell** ▹ *adj* geschwollen; (*lake etc*) angeschwollen

swoon [swu:n] *vi* beinahe ohnmächtig werden ▹ *n* Ohnmacht *f*

swoop [swu:p] *n* (*by police etc*) Razzia *f*; (*of bird etc*) Sturzflug *m* ▹ *vi* (*also*: **swoop down**: *bird*) herabstoßen; (*plane*) einen Sturzflug machen

swop [swɔp] = **swap**

sword [sɔ:d] *n* Schwert *nt*

swordfish ['sɔ:dfɪʃ] *n* Schwertfisch *m*

swore [swɔ:ʳ] *pt of* **swear**

sworn [swɔ:n] *pp of* **swear** ▹ *adj* (*statement*) eidlich; (*evidence*) unter Eid; (*enemy*)

geschworen
swot [swɔt] *vi* pauken ▷ *n* (*pej*) Streber(in) *m(f)*
▶ **swot up** *vt*: **to ~ up (on)** pauken (*+acc*)
swum [swʌm] *pp of* **swim**
swung [swʌŋ] *pt, pp of* **swing**
sycamore ['sɪkəmɔːʳ] *n* Bergahorn *m*
sycophant ['sɪkəfænt] *n* Kriecher *m*, Speichellecker *m*
sycophantic [sɪkə'fæntɪk] *adj* kriecherisch
Sydney ['sɪdnɪ] *n* Sydney *nt*
syllable ['sɪləbl] *n* Silbe *f*
syllabus ['sɪləbəs] *n* Lehrplan *m*; **on the ~** im Lehrplan
symbol ['sɪmbl] *n* Symbol *nt*
symbolic [sɪm'bɔlɪk], **symbolical** [sɪm'bɔlɪkl] *adj* symbolisch; **to be ~(al) of sth** etw symbolisieren, ein Symbol für etw sein
symbolism ['sɪmbəlɪzəm] *n* Symbolismus *m*
symbolize ['sɪmbəlaɪz] *vt* symbolisieren
symmetrical [sɪ'mɛtrɪkl] *adj* symmetrisch
symmetry ['sɪmɪtrɪ] *n* Symmetrie *f*
sympathetic [sɪmpə'θɛtɪk] *adj* (*understanding*) verständnisvoll; (*showing pity*) mitfühlend; (*likeable*) sympathisch; (*supportive*) wohlwollend; **to be ~ to a cause** (*well-disposed*) einer Sache wohlwollend gegenüberstehen
sympathetically [sɪmpə'θɛtɪklɪ] *adv* (*showing understanding*) verständnisvoll; (*showing support*) wohlwollend
sympathize ['sɪmpəθaɪz] *vi*: **to ~ with** (*person*) Mitleid haben mit; (*feelings*) Verständnis haben für; (*cause*) sympathisieren mit
sympathizer ['sɪmpəθaɪzəʳ] *n* (*Pol*) Sympathisant(in) *m(f)*
sympathy ['sɪmpəθɪ] *n* Mitgefühl *nt*; **sympathies** *npl* (*support, tendencies*) Sympathien *pl*; **with our deepest ~** mit aufrichtigem *or* herzlichem Beileid; **to come out in ~** (*workers*) in einen Sympathiestreik treten
symphonic [sɪm'fɔnɪk] *adj* sinfonisch
symphony ['sɪmfənɪ] *n* Sinfonie *f*
symphony orchestra *n* Sinfonieorchester *nt*
symposia [sɪm'pəuzɪə] *npl of* **symposium**
symposium [sɪm'pəuzɪəm] (*pl* **~s** *or* **symposia**) *n* Symposium *nt*
symptom ['sɪmptəm] *n* (*Med, fig*) Symptom *nt*, Anzeichen *nt*
symptomatic [sɪmptə'mætɪk] *adj*: **~ of** symptomatisch für
synagogue ['sɪnəgɔg] *n* Synagoge *f*
sync [sɪŋk] *n abbr* (*= synchronization*): **in ~** synchron; **out of ~** nicht synchron
synchromesh [sɪŋkrəu'mɛʃ] *n* Synchrongetriebe *nt*
synchronize ['sɪŋkrənaɪz] *vt* (*watches*) gleichstellen; (*movements*) aufeinander abstimmen; (*sound*) synchronisieren ▷ *vi*: **to ~ with** (*sound*) synchron sein mit
synchronized swimming ['sɪŋkrənaɪzd-] *n* Synchronschwimmen *nt*
syncopated ['sɪŋkəpeɪtɪd] *adj* synkopiert
syndicate ['sɪndɪkɪt] *n* Interessengemeinschaft *f*; (*of businesses*) Verband *m*; (*of newspapers*) Pressezentrale *f*
syndrome ['sɪndrəum] *n* Syndrom *nt*; (*fig*) Phänomen *nt*
synonym ['sɪnənɪm] *n* Synonym *nt*
synonymous [sɪ'nɔnɪməs] *adj* (*fig*): **~ (with)** gleichbedeutend (mit)
synopses [sɪ'nɔpsiːz] *npl of* **synopsis**
synopsis [sɪ'nɔpsɪs] (*pl* **synopses**) *n* Abriss *m*, Zusammenfassung *f*
syntactic [sɪn'tæktɪk] *adj* syntaktisch
syntax ['sɪntæks] *n* Syntax *f*
syntax error *n* (*Comput*) Syntaxfehler *m*
syntheses ['sɪnθəsiːz] *npl of* **synthesis**
synthesis ['sɪnθəsɪs] (*pl* **syntheses**) *n* Synthese *f*
synthesizer ['sɪnθəsaɪzəʳ] *n* Synthesizer *m*
synthetic [sɪn'θɛtɪk] *adj* synthetisch; (*speech*) künstlich; **synthetics** *npl* (*man-made fabrics*) Synthetik *f*
syphilis ['sɪfɪlɪs] *n* Syphilis *f*
syphon ['saɪfən] = **siphon**
Syria ['sɪrɪə] *n* Syrien *nt*
Syrian ['sɪrɪən] *adj* syrisch ▷ *n* Syrer(in) *m(f)*
syringe [sɪ'rɪndʒ] *n* Spritze *f*
syrup ['sɪrəp] *n* Sirup *m*; (*also*: **golden syrup**) (gelber) Sirup *m*
syrupy ['sɪrəpɪ] *adj* sirupartig; (*pej*: *fig*: *sentimental*) schmalzig
system ['sɪstəm] *n* System *nt*; (*body*) Körper *m*; (*Anat*) Apparat *m*, System *nt*; **it was a shock to his ~** er hatte schwer damit zu schaffen
systematic [sɪstə'mætɪk] *adj* systematisch
system disk *n* (*Comput*) Systemdiskette *f*
systems administrator ['sɪstəmz-] *n* (*Comput*) Systembetreuer(in) *m(f)*
systems analyst ['sɪstəmz-] *n* (*Comput*) Systemanalytiker(in) *m(f)*
systems engineer ['sɪstəmz-] *n* (*Comput*) Systemtechniker(in) *m(f)*

Tt

T, t [tiː] *n* (*letter*) T *nt*, t *nt*; **T for Tommy** ≈ T wie Theodor
TA (*Brit*) *n abbr* = **Territorial Army**
ta [tɑː] (*Brit: inf*) *interj* danke
tab [tæb] *n* (*on drinks can*) Ring *m*; (*on garment*) Etikett *nt*; **to keep ~s on sb/sth** (*fig*) jdn/etw im Auge behalten
tab [tæb] *n abbr* = **tabulator** ▷ *n* (*on drinks can*) Ring *m*; (*on garment*) Etikett *nt*; **to keep ~s on sb/sth** (*fig*) jdn/etw im Auge behalten
tabby ['tæbɪ] *n* (*also*: **tabby cat**) getigerte Katze *f*
tabernacle ['tæbənækl] *n* Tabernakel *nt*
table ['teɪbl] *n* Tisch *m*; (*Math, Chem etc*) Tabelle *f* ▷ *vt* (*Brit: Parl: motion etc*) einbringen; **to lay** *or* **set the ~** den Tisch decken; **to clear the ~** den Tisch abräumen; **league ~** (*Brit: Sport*) Tabelle *f*
tablecloth ['teɪblklɔθ] *n* Tischdecke *f*
table d'hôte [tɑːbl'dəut] *adj* (*menu, meal*) Tagesmenü *nt*
table lamp *n* Tischlampe *f*
tablemat ['teɪblmæt] *n* (*of cloth*) Set *nt or m*; (*for hot dish*) Untersatz *m*
table of contents *n* Inhaltsverzeichnis *nt*
table salt *n* Tafelsalz *nt*
tablespoon ['teɪblspuːn] *n* Esslöffel *m*; (*also*: **tablespoonful**) Esslöffel(voll) *m*
tablet ['tæblɪt] *n* (*Med*) Tablette *f*; (*Hist: for writing*) Tafel *f*; (*plaque*) Plakette *f*; **~ of soap** (*Brit*) Stück *nt* Seife
table tennis *n* Tischtennis *nt*
table wine *n* Tafelwein *m*
tabloid ['tæblɔɪd] *n* (*newspaper*) Boulevardzeitung *f*; **the ~s** die Boulevardpresse

TABLOID PRESS

Des Ausdruck *tabloid press* bezieht sich auf kleinformatige Zeitungen (ca 30 x 40 cm); diese sind in Großbritannien fast ausschließlich Massenblätter. Im Gegensatz zur *quality press* verwenden sie viele Fotos und einen knappern, oft reißerischen Stil. Sie kommen denjenigen Lesern entgegen, die mehr Wert auf Unterhaltung legen.

taboo [tə'buː] *n* Tabu *nt* ▷ *adj* tabu; **a ~ subject/word** ein Tabuthema/Tabuwort
tabulate ['tæbjuleɪt] *vt* tabellarisieren
tabulator ['tæbjuleɪtəʳ] *n* (*on typewriter*) Tabulator *m*
tachograph ['tækəgrɑːf] *n* Fahrtenschreiber *m*
tachometer [tæ'kɔmɪtəʳ] *n* Tachometer *m*
tacit ['tæsɪt] *adj* stillschweigend
taciturn ['tæsɪtəːn] *adj* schweigsam
tack [tæk] *n* (*nail*) Stift *m* ▷ *vt* (*nail*) anheften; (*stitch*) heften ▷ *vi* (*Naut*) kreuzen; **to change ~** (*fig*) den Kurs ändern; **to ~ sth on to (the end of) sth** etw (hinten) an etw *acc* anheften
tackle ['tækl] *n* (*for fishing*) Ausrüstung *f*; (*for lifting*) Flaschenzug *m*; (*Football, Rugby*) Angriff *m* ▷ *vt* (*deal with: difficulty*) in Angriff nehmen; (*challenge: person*) zur Rede stellen; (*physically, also Sport*) angreifen
tacky ['tækɪ] *adj* (*sticky*) klebrig; (*pej: cheap-looking*) schäbig
tact [tækt] *n* Takt *m*
tactful ['tæktful] *adj* taktvoll; **to be ~** taktvoll sein
tactfully ['tæktfəlɪ] *adv* taktvoll
tactical ['tæktɪkl] *adj* taktisch; **~ error** taktischer Fehler; **~ voting** taktische Stimmabgabe
tactician [tæk'tɪʃən] *n* Taktiker(in) *m(f)*
tactics ['tæktɪks] *npl* Taktik *f*
tactless ['tæktlɪs] *adj* taktlos
tactlessly ['tæktlɪslɪ] *adv* taktlos
tadpole ['tædpəul] *n* Kaulquappe *f*
taffy ['tæfɪ] (*US*) *n* (*toffee*) Toffee *nt*, Sahnebonbon *nt*
tag [tæg] *n* (*label*) Anhänger *m*; **price/name ~** Preis-/Namensschild *nt*; **(electronic) ~** (elektronische) Fußfessel *f*
▶ **tag along** *vi* sich anschließen
Tahiti [tɑː'hiːtɪ] *n* Tahiti *nt*
tail [teɪl] *n* (*of animal*) Schwanz *m*; (*of plane*) Heck *nt*; (*of shirt, coat*) Schoß *m* ▷ *vt* (*follow*) folgen *+dat*; **tails** *npl* (*formal suit*) Frack *m*; **to turn ~** die Flucht ergreifen; *see also* **head**
▶ **tail off** *vi* (*in size etc*) abnehmen; (*voice*) schwächer werden
tailback ['teɪlbæk] (*Brit*) *n* (*Aut*) Stau *m*
tail coat *n* = **tails**
tail end *n* Ende *nt*

tailgate ['teɪlgeɪt] *n* (*Aut*) Heckklappe *f*
taillight ['teɪllaɪt] *n* (*Aut*) Rücklicht *nt*
tailor ['teɪlə'] *n* Schneider(in) *m(f)* ▷ *vt*: **to ~ sth (to)** etw abstimmen (auf *+acc*); **~'s shop** Schneiderei *f*
tailoring ['teɪlərɪŋ] *n* (*craft*) Schneiderei *f*; (*cut*) Verarbeitung *f*
tailor-made ['teɪlə'meɪd] *adj* (*also fig*) maßgeschneidert
tailwind ['teɪlwɪnd] *n* Rückenwind *m*
taint [teɪnt] *vt* (*meat, food*) verderben; (*fig: reputation etc*) beschmutzen
tainted ['teɪntɪd] *adj* (*food, water, air*) verdorben; (*fig: profits, reputation etc*): **~ with** behaftet mit
Taiwan [taɪ'wɑːn] *n* Taiwan *nt*
Tajikistan [tɑːdʒɪkɪ'stɑːn] *n* Tadschikistan *nt*
take [teɪk] (*pt* **took**, *pp* **~n**) *vt* nehmen; (*photo, notes*) machen; (*decision*) fällen; (*require: courage, time*) erfordern; (*tolerate: pain etc*) ertragen; (*hold: passengers etc*) fassen; (*accompany: person*) begleiten; (*carry, bring*) mitnehmen; (*exam, test*) machen; (*conduct: meeting*) leiten; (*: class*) unterrichten ▷ *vi* (*have effect: drug*) wirken; (*: dye*) angenommen werden ▷ *n* (*Cine*) Aufnahme *f*; **to ~ sth from** (*drawer etc*) etw nehmen aus *+dat*; **I ~ it (that)** ich nehme an(, dass); **I took him for a doctor** (*mistake*) ich hielt ihn für einen Arzt; **to ~ sb's hand** jds Hand nehmen; **to ~ sb for a walk** mit jdm spazieren gehen; **to be ~n ill** krank werden; **to ~ it upon o.s. to do sth** es auf sich nehmen, etw zu tun; **~ the first (street) on the left** nehmen Sie die erste Straße links; **to ~ Russian at university** Russisch studieren; **it won't ~ long** es dauert nicht lange; **I was quite ~n with her/it** (*attracted to*) ich war von ihr/davon recht angetan
▸**take after** *vt fus* (*resemble*) ähneln *+dat*, ähnlich sein *+dat*
▸**take apart** *vt* auseinandernehmen
▸**take away** *vt* wegnehmen; (*carry off*) wegbringen; (*Math*) abziehen ▷ *vi*: **to ~ away from** (*detract from*) schmälern, beeinträchtigen
▸**take back** *vt* (*return*) zurückbringen; (*one's words*) zurücknehmen
▸**take down** *vt* (*write down*) aufschreiben; (*dismantle*) abreißen
▸**take in** *vt* (*deceive: person*) hereinlegen, täuschen; (*understand*) begreifen; (*include*) einschließen; (*lodger*) aufnehmen; (*orphan, stray dog*) zu sich nehmen; (*dress, waistband*) enger machen
▸**take off** *vi* (*Aviat*) starten; (*go away*) sich absetzen ▷ *vt* (*clothes*) ausziehen; (*glasses*) abnehmen; (*make-up*) entfernen; (*time*) freinehmen; (*imitate: person*) nachmachen
▸**take on** *vt* (*work, responsibility*) übernehmen; (*employee*) einstellen; (*compete against*) antreten gegen
▸**take out** *vt* (*invite*) ausgehen mit; (*remove: tooth*) herausnehmen; (*licence*) erwerben; **to ~ sth out of sth** (*drawer, pocket etc*) etw aus etw nehmen; **don't ~ it out on me!** lass es nicht an mir aus!
▸**take over** *vt* (*business*) übernehmen; (*country*) Besitz ergreifen von ▷ *vi* (*replace*): **to ~ over from sb** jdn ablösen
▸**take to** *vt fus* (*person, thing*) mögen; (*activity*) Gefallen finden an *+dat*; (*form habit of*): **to ~ to doing sth** sich *dat* angewöhnen, etw zu tun
▸**take up** *vt* (*hobby, sport*) anfangen mit; (*job*) antreten; (*idea etc*) annehmen; (*time, space*) beanspruchen; (*continue: task, story*) fortfahren mit; (*shorten: hem, garment*) kürzer machen ▷ *vi* (*befriend*): **to ~ up with sb** sich mit jdm anfreunden; **to ~ sb up on an offer/a suggestion** auf jds Angebot/Vorschlag eingehen
takeaway ['teɪkəweɪ] (*Brit*) *n* (*shop, restaurant*) ≈ Schnellimbiss *m*; (*food*) Imbiss *m* (*zum Mitnehmen*)
take-home pay ['teɪkhəum-] *n* Nettolohn *m*
taken ['teɪkən] *pp of* **take**
takeoff ['teɪkɔf] *n* (*Aviat*) Start *m*
takeout ['teɪkaut] (*US*) *n* = **takeaway**
takeover ['teɪkəuvə'] *n* (*Comm*) Übernahme *f*; (*of country*) Inbesitznahme *f*
takeover bid *n* Übernahmeangebot *nt*
takings ['teɪkɪŋz] *npl* Einnahmen *pl*
talc [tælk] *n* (*also*: **talcum powder**) Talkumpuder *nt*
tale [teɪl] *n* Geschichte *f*; **to tell ~s (to sb)** (*child*) (jdm) Geschichten erzählen
talent ['tælnt] *n* Talent *nt*
talented ['tæləntɪd] *adj* talentiert, begabt
talent scout *n* Talentsucher(in) *m(f)*
talisman ['tælɪzmən] *n* Talisman *m*
talk [tɔːk] *n* (*speech*) Vortrag *m*; (*conversation, discussion*) Gespräch *nt*; (*gossip*) Gerede *nt* ▷ *vi* (*speak*) sprechen; (*chat*) reden; (*gossip*) klatschen; **talks** *npl* (*Pol etc*) Gespräche *pl*; **to give a ~** einen Vortrag halten; **to ~ about** (*discuss*) sprechen *or* reden über; **~ing of films, have you seen ...?** da wir gerade von Filmen sprechen: hast du ... gesehen?; **to ~ sb into doing sth** jdn zu etw überreden; **to ~ sb out of doing sth** jdm etw ausreden
▸**talk over** *vt* (*problem etc*) besprechen, bereden
talkative ['tɔːkətɪv] *adj* gesprächig
talker ['tɔːkə'] *n*: **to be a good/entertaining/fast** *etc* **~** gut/amüsant/schnell *etc* reden können
talking point ['tɔːkɪŋ-] *n* Gesprächsthema *nt*
talking-to ['tɔːkɪŋtu] *n*: **to give sb a (good) ~** jdm eine (ordentliche) Standpauke halten (*inf*)
talk show *n* Talkshow *f*
tall [tɔːl] *adj* (*person*) groß; (*glass, bookcase, tree, building*) hoch; (*ladder*) lang; **to be 6 feet ~** (*person*) ≈ 1,80m groß sein; **how ~ are you?** wie groß bist du?
tallboy ['tɔːlbɔɪ] (*Brit*) *n* Kommode *f*
tallness ['tɔːlnɪs] *n* (*of person*) Größe *f*; (*of tree, building etc*) Höhe *f*
tall story *n* unglaubliche Geschichte *f*

tally ['tælɪ] *n* (*of marks, amounts etc*) aktueller Stand *m* ▷ *vi*: **to ~ (with)** (*figures, stories etc*) übereinstimmen mit; **to keep a ~ of sth** über etw *acc* Buch führen
talon ['tælən] *n* Kralle *f*
tambourine [tæmbə'ri:n] *n* Tamburin *nt*
tame [teɪm] *adj* (*animal, bird*) zahm; (*fig: story, party, performance*) lustlos, lahm (*inf*)
Tamil ['tæmɪl] *adj* tamilisch ▷ *n* Tamile *m*, Tamilin *f*; (*Ling*) Tamil *nt*
tamper ['tæmpəʳ] *vi*: **to ~ with sth** an etw *dat* herumpfuschen (*inf*)
tampon ['tæmpɔn] *n* Tampon *m*
tan [tæn] *n* (*also*: **suntan**) (Sonnen)bräune *f* ▷ *vi* (*person, skin*) braun werden ▷ *vt* (*hide*) gerben; (*skin*) bräunen ▷ *adj* (*colour*) hellbraun; **to get a ~** braun werden
tandem ['tændəm] *n* Tandem *nt*; (*together*): **in ~** (*fig*) zusammen
tandoori [tæn'duərɪ] *n*: **~ oven** Tandoori-Ofen *m*; **~ chicken** *im Tandoori-Ofen gebratenes* Huhn
tang [tæŋ] *n* (*smell*) Geruch *m*; (*taste*) Geschmack *m*
tangent ['tændʒənt] *n* (*Math*) Tangente *f*; **to go off at a ~** (*fig*) vom Thema abschweifen
tangerine [tændʒə'ri:n] *n* (*fruit*) Mandarine *f*; (*colour*) Orangerot *nt*
tangible ['tændʒəbl] *adj* greifbar; **~ assets** (*Comm*) Sachanlagevermögen *nt*
Tangier [tæn'dʒɪəʳ] *n* Tanger *nt*
tangle ['tæŋgl] *n* (*of branches, wire etc*) Gewirr *nt*; **to be in a ~** verheddert sein; (*fig*) durcheinander sein; **to get in a ~** sich verheddern; (*fig*) durcheinandergeraten
tango ['tæŋgəu] *n* Tango *m*
tank [tæŋk] *n* Tank *m*; (*for photographic processing*) Wanne *f*; (*also*: **fish tank**) Aquarium *nt*; (*Mil*) Panzer *m*
tankard ['tæŋkəd] *n* Bierkrug *m*
tanker ['tæŋkəʳ] *n* (*ship*) Tanker *m*; (*truck*) Tankwagen *m*
tanned [tænd] *adj* (*person*) braun gebrannt; (*hide*) gegerbt
tannin ['tænɪn] *n* Tannin *nt*
tanning ['tænɪŋ] *n* (*of leather*) Gerben *nt*
Tannoy® ['tænɔɪ] (*Brit*) *n* Lautsprechersystem *nt*; **over the Tannoy** über Lautsprecher
tantalizing ['tæntəlaɪzɪŋ] *adj* (*smell*) verführerisch; (*possibility*) verlockend
tantamount ['tæntəmaunt] *adj*: **~ to** gleichbedeutend mit
tantrum ['tæntrəm] *n* Wutanfall *m*; **to throw a ~** einen Wutanfall bekommen
Tanzania [tænzə'nɪə] *n* Tansania *nt*
Tanzanian [tænzə'nɪən] *adj* tansanisch ▷ *n* (*person*) Tansanier(in) *m(f)*
tap [tæp] *n* (*on sink, gas tap*) Hahn *m*; (*gentle blow*) leichter Schlag *m*, Klaps *m* ▷ *vt* (*hit gently*) klopfen; (*exploit: resources, energy*) nutzen; (*telephone*) abhören, anzapfen; **on ~** (*fig: resources, information*) zur Verfügung; (*beer*) vom Fass
tap-dancing ['tæpdɑ:nsɪŋ] *n* Stepptanz *m*
tape [teɪp] *n* (*also*: **magnetic tape**) Tonband *nt*; (*cassette*) Kassette *f*; (*also*: **sticky tape**) Klebeband *nt*; (*for tying*) Band *nt* ▷ *vt* (*record, conversation*) aufnehmen, aufzeichnen; (*stick with tape*) mit Klebeband befestigen; **on ~** (*song etc*) auf Band
tape deck *n* Tapedeck *nt*
tape measure *n* Bandmaß *nt*
taper ['teɪpəʳ] *n* (*candle*) lange, dünne Kerze ▷ *vi* sich verjüngen
tape recorder *n* Tonband(gerät) *nt*
tape recording *n* Tonbandaufnahme *f*
tapered ['teɪpəd] *adj* (*skirt, jacket*) nach unten enger werdend
tapering ['teɪpərɪŋ] *adj* spitz zulaufend
tapestry ['tæpɪstrɪ] *n* (*on wall*) Wandteppich *m*; (*fig*) Kaleidoskop *nt*
tapeworm ['teɪpwə:m] *n* Bandwurm *m*
tapioca [tæpɪ'əukə] *n* Tapioka *f*
tappet ['tæpɪt] *n* (*Aut*) Stößel *m*
tar [tɑ:] *n* Teer *m*; **low/middle ~ cigarettes** Zigaretten mit niedrigem/mittlerem Teergehalt
tarantula [tə'ræntjulə] *n* Tarantel *f*
tardy ['tɑ:dɪ] *adj* (*reply, letter*) verspätet; (*progress*) langsam
target ['tɑ:gɪt] *n* Ziel *nt*; (*fig: of joke, criticism etc*) Zielscheibe *f*; **to be on ~** (*project, work*) nach Plan verlaufen
target practice *n* Zielschießen *nt*
tariff ['tærɪf] *n* (*tax on goods*) Zoll *m*; (*Brit: in hotels etc*) Preisliste *f*
tariff barrier *n* Zollschranke *f*
tarmac® ['tɑ:mæk] *n* (*Brit: on road*) Asphalt *m*; (*Aviat*): **on the tarmac** auf dem Rollfeld ▷ *vt* (*Brit: road etc*) asphaltieren
tarn [tɑ:n] *n* Bergsee *m*
tarnish ['tɑ:nɪʃ] *vt* (*silver, brass etc*) stumpf werden lassen; (*fig: reputation etc*) beflecken, in Mitleidenschaft ziehen
tarot ['tærəu] *n* Tarot *nt or m*
tarpaulin [tɑ:'pɔ:lɪn] *n* Plane *f*
tarragon ['tærəgən] *n* Estragon *m*
tart [tɑ:t] *n* (*Culin*) Torte *f*; (*: small*) Törtchen *nt*; (*Brit: inf: prostitute*) Nutte *f* ▷ *adj* (*apple, grapefruit etc*) säuerlich
▸ **tart up** (*Brit: inf*) *vt* (*room, building*) aufmotzen; **to ~ o.s. up** sich fein machen; (*pej*) sich auftakeln
tartan ['tɑ:tn] *n* Tartan *m*, Schottenstoff *m* ▷ *adj* (*scarf etc*) mit Schottenmuster
tartar ['tɑ:təʳ] *n* (*on teeth*) Zahnstein *m*; (*pej: person*) Tyrann(in) *m(f)*
tartar sauce, **tartare sauce** ['tɑ:tə-] *n* Remouladensoße *f*
task [tɑ:sk] *n* Aufgabe *f*; **to take sb to ~** jdn ins Gebet nehmen
task force *n* (*Mil*) Sonderkommando *nt*; (*Police*) Spezialeinheit *f*
taskmaster ['tɑ:skmɑ:stəʳ] *n*: **a hard ~** ein strenger Lehrmeister
Tasmania [tæz'meɪnɪə] *n* Tasmanien *nt*
tassel ['tæsl] *n* Quaste *f*

taste [teɪst] *n* Geschmack *m*; (*sample*) Kostprobe *f*; (*fig: of suffering, freedom etc*) Vorgeschmack *m* ▷ *vt* (*get flavour of*) schmecken; (*test*) probieren, versuchen ▷ *vi*: **to ~ of/like sth** nach/wie etw schmecken; **sense of ~** Geschmackssinn *m*; **to have a ~ of sth** (*sample*) etw probieren; **to acquire a ~ for sth** (*liking*) Geschmack an etw *dat* finden; **to be in good/bad ~** (*joke etc*) geschmackvoll/geschmacklos sein; **you can ~ the garlic (in it)** (*detect*) man schmeckt den Knoblauch durch; **what does it ~ like?** wie schmeckt es?
taste buds *npl* Geschmacksknospen *pl*
tasteful ['teɪstful] *adj* geschmackvoll
tastefully ['teɪstfəlɪ] *adv* geschmackvoll
tasteless ['teɪstlɪs] *adj* geschmacklos
tasty ['teɪstɪ] *adj* schmackhaft
tattered ['tætəd] *adj* (*clothes, paper etc*) zerrissen; (*fig: hopes etc*) angeschlagen
tatters ['tætəz] *npl*: **to be in ~** (*clothes*) in Fetzen sein
tattoo [tə'tuː] *n* (*on skin*) Tätowierung *f*; (*spectacle*) Zapfenstreich *m* ▷ *vt*: **to ~ sth on sth** etw auf etw *acc* tätowieren
tatty ['tætɪ] (*Brit: inf*) *adj* schäbig
taught [tɔːt] *pt, pp of* **teach**
taunt [tɔːnt] *n* höhnische Bemerkung *f* ▷ *vt* (*person*) verhöhnen
Taurus ['tɔːrəs] *n* Stier *m*; **to be ~** (ein) Stier sein
taut [tɔːt] *adj* (*skin, thread etc*) straff
tavern ['tævən] *n* Taverne *f*
tawdry ['tɔːdrɪ] *adj* billig
tawny ['tɔːnɪ] *adj* gelbbraun
tawny owl *n* Waldkauz *m*
tax [tæks] *n* Steuer *f* ▷ *vt* (*earnings, goods etc*) besteuern; (*fig: memory, knowledge*) strapazieren; (*: patience etc*) auf die Probe stellen; **before/after ~** vor/nach Abzug der Steuern; **free of ~** steuerfrei
taxable ['tæksəbl] *adj* steuerpflichtig; (*income*) steuerbar
tax allowance *n* Steuerfreibetrag *m*
taxation [tæk'seɪʃən] *n* (*system*) Besteuerung *f*; (*money paid*) Steuern *pl*
tax avoidance *n* Steuerumgehung *f*
tax collector *n* Steuerbeamte(r) *m*, Steuerbeamtin *f*
tax disc (*Brit*) *n* (*Aut*) Steuerplakette *f*
tax evasion *n* Steuerhinterziehung *f*
tax exemption *n* Steuerbefreiung *f*
tax exile (*person*) *n* Steuerflüchtling *m*
tax-free ['tæksfriː] *adj* steuerfrei
tax haven *n* Steuerparadies *nt*
taxi ['tæksɪ] *n* Taxi *nt* ▷ *vi* (*Aviat: plane*) rollen
taxidermist ['tæksɪdəːmɪst] *n* Taxidermist(in) *m(f)*, Tierpräparator(in) *m(f)*
taxi driver *n* Taxifahrer(in) *m(f)*
tax inspector (*Brit*) *n* Steuerinspektor(in) *m(f)*
taxi rank (*Brit*) *n* Taxistand *m*
taxi stand *n* = **taxi rank**
taxpayer ['tækspeɪəʳ] *n* Steuerzahler(in) *m(f)*
tax rebate *n* Steuerrückvergütung *f*
tax relief *n* Steuernachlass *m*
tax return *n* Steuererklärung *f*
tax shelter *n* (*Comm*) *System zur Verhinderung von Steuerbelastung*
tax year *n* Steuerjahr *nt*
TB *n abbr* (*= tuberculosis*) Tb *f*, Tbc *f*
tbc *abbr* (*= to be confirmed*) noch zu bestätigen
TD (*US*) *n abbr* = **Treasury Department** (*Football*) = **touchdown**
tea [tiː] *n* (*drink*) Tee *m*; (*Brit: evening meal*) Abendessen *nt*; **afternoon ~** (*Brit*) Nachmittagstee *m*
tea bag *n* Teebeutel *m*
tea break (*Brit*) *n* Teepause *f*
teacake ['tiːkeɪk] (*Brit*) *n* Rosinenbrötchen *nt*
teach [tiːtʃ] (*pt, pp* **taught**) *vt*: **to ~ sb sth, ~ sth to sb** (*instruct*) jdm etw beibringen; (*in school*) jdn in etw *dat* unterrichten ▷ *vi* unterrichten; **it taught him a lesson** (*fig*) er hat seine Lektion gelernt
teacher ['tiːtʃəʳ] *n* Lehrer(in) *m(f)*; **German ~** Deutschlehrer(in) *m(f)*
teacher training college *n* (*for primary schools*) ≈ pädagogische Hochschule *f*; (*for secondary schools*) ≈ Studienseminar *nt*
teaching ['tiːtʃɪŋ] *n* (*work of teacher*) Unterricht *m*
teaching aids *npl* Lehrmittel *pl*
teaching hospital (*Brit*) *n* Ausbildungskrankenhaus *nt*
teaching staff (*Brit*) *n* Lehrerkollegium *nt*
tea cosy *n* Teewärmer *m*
teacup ['tiːkʌp] *n* Teetasse *f*
teak [tiːk] *n* Teak *nt*
tea leaves *npl* Teeblätter *pl*
team [tiːm] *n* (*of experts etc*) Team *nt*; (*Sport*) Mannschaft *f*, Team *nt*; (*of horses, oxen*) Gespann *nt*
▸ **team up** *vi*: **to ~ up (with)** sich zusammentun (mit)
team game *n* Mannschaftsspiel *nt*
team spirit *n* Teamgeist *m*
teamwork ['tiːmwəːk] *n* Teamwork *nt*, Teamarbeit *f*
tea party *n* Teegesellschaft *f*
teapot ['tiːpɔt] *n* Teekanne *f*
tear¹ [tɛəʳ] (*pt* **tore**, *pp* **torn**) *n* (*hole*) Riss *m* ▷ *vt* (*rip*) zerreißen ▷ *vi* (*become torn*) reißen; **to ~ sth to pieces** *or* **bits** *or* **shreds** (*lit, fig*) etw in Stücke reißen; **to ~ sb to pieces** jdn fertigmachen
▸ **tear along** *vi* (*rush: driver, car*) entlangrasen
▸ **tear apart** *vt* (*book, clothes, people*) auseinanderreißen; (*upset: person*) hin- und herreißen
▸ **tear away** *vt*: **to ~ o.s. away (from sth)** (*fig*) sich (von etw) losreißen
▸ **tear out** *vt* (*sheet of paper etc*) herausreißen
▸ **tear up** *vt* (*sheet of paper etc*) zerreißen
tear² [tɪəʳ] *n* (*in eye*) Träne *f*; **in ~s** in Tränen; **to burst into ~s** in Tränen ausbrechen
tearaway ['tɛərəweɪ] (*Brit: inf*) *n* Rabauke *m*
teardrop ['tɪədrɔp] *n* Träne *f*

tearful ['tɪəful] *adj* *(person)* weinend; *(face)* tränenüberströmt
tear gas *n* Tränengas *nt*
tearing ['tɛərɪŋ] *adj*: **to be in a ~ hurry** es unheimlich eilig haben
tearoom ['ti:ru:m] *n* = **teashop**
tease [ti:z] *vt* necken; *(unkindly)* aufziehen ▷ *n*: **she's a real ~** sie zieht einen ständig auf
tea set *n* Teeservice *nt*
teashop ['ti:ʃɔp] *(Brit)* *n* Teestube *f*
Teasmade® ['ti:zmeɪd] *n* Teemaschine *f* *(mit Zeiteinstellung)*
teaspoon ['ti:spu:n] *n* Teelöffel *m*; *(also*: **teaspoonful**: *measure)* Teelöffel(voll) *m*
tea strainer *n* Teesieb *nt*
teat [ti:t] *n* *(on bottle)* Sauger *m*
teatime ['ti:taɪm] *n* Teestunde *f*
tea towel *(Brit)* *n* Geschirrtuch *nt*
tea urn *n* Teespender *m*
tech [tɛk] *(inf)* *n abbr* = **technical college; technology**
technical ['tɛknɪkl] *adj* technisch; *(terms, language)* Fach-
technical college *(Brit)* *n* technische Fachschule *f*
technicality [tɛknɪ'kælɪtɪ] *n* *(point of law)* Formalität *f*; *(detail)* technische Einzelheit *f*; **on a (legal) ~** aufgrund einer (juristischen) Formalität
technically ['tɛknɪklɪ] *adv* *(strictly speaking)* genau genommen; *(regarding technique)* technisch (gesehen)
technician [tɛk'nɪʃən] *n* Techniker(in) *m(f)*
technique [tɛk'ni:k] *n* Technik *f*
techno ['tɛknəu] *n* *(Mus)* Techno *nt*
technocrat ['tɛknəkræt] *n* Technokrat(in) *m(f)*
technological [tɛknə'lɔdʒɪkl] *adj* technologisch
technologist [tɛk'nɔlədʒɪst] *n* Technologe *m*, Technologin *f*
technology [tɛk'nɔlədʒɪ] *n* Technologie *f*
technology college *n* *Oberstufenkolleg mit technischem Schwerpunkt*
teddy ['tɛdɪ], **teddy bear** *n* Teddy(bär) *m*
tedious ['ti:dɪəs] *adj* langweilig
tedium ['ti:dɪəm] *n* Langeweile *f*
tee [ti:] *n* *(Golf)* Tee *nt*
▶ **tee off** *vi* (vom Tee) abschlagen
teem [ti:m] *vi*: **to ~ with** *(tourists etc)* wimmeln von; **it is ~ing down** es gießt in Strömen
teenage ['ti:neɪdʒ] *adj* *(fashions etc)* Jugend-; *(children)* im Teenageralter
teenager ['ti:neɪdʒə^r] *n* Teenager *m*, Jugendliche(r) *f(m)*
teens [ti:nz] *npl*: **to be in one's ~** im Teenageralter sein
tee shirt *n* = **T-shirt**
teeter ['ti:tə^r] *vi* *(also fig)* schwanken, taumeln
teeth [ti:θ] *npl of* **tooth**
teethe [ti:ð] *vi* Zähne bekommen, zahnen
teething ring ['ti:ðɪŋ-] *n* Beißring *m*
teething troubles *npl* *(fig)* Kinderkrankheiten *pl*
teetotal ['ti:'təutl] *adj* *(person)* abstinent
teetotaller, *(US)* **teetotaler** ['ti:'təutlə^r] *n* Abstinenzler(in) *m(f)*, Antialkoholiker(in) *m(f)*
TEFL ['tɛfl] *n abbr* *(= Teaching of English as a Foreign Language)* *Unterricht in Englisch als Fremdsprache*
Teflon® ['tɛflɔn] *n* Teflon® *nt*
Teheran [tɛə'rɑ:n] *n* Teheran *nt*
tel. *abbr* *(= telephone)* Tel.
Tel Aviv ['tɛlə'vi:v] *n* Tel Aviv *nt*
telecast ['tɛlɪkɑ:st] *n* Fernsehsendung *f*
telecommunications ['tɛlɪkəmju:nɪ'keɪʃənz] *n* Nachrichtentechnik *f*
teleconferencing [tɛlɪ'kɔnfərənsɪŋ] *n* Telekonferenzen *pl*
telegram ['tɛlɪgræm] *n* Telegramm *nt*
telegraph ['tɛlɪgrɑ:f] *n* *(system)* Telegraf *m*
telegraphic [tɛlɪ'græfɪk] *adj* *(equipment)* telegrafisch
telegraph pole *n* Telegrafenmast *m*
telegraph wire *n* Telegrafenleitung *f*
telepathic [tɛlɪ'pæθɪk] *adj* telepathisch
telepathy [tə'lɛpəθɪ] *n* Telepathie *f*
telephone ['tɛlɪfəun] *n* Telefon *nt* ▷ *vt* *(person)* anrufen ▷ *vi* anrufen, telefonieren; **to be on the ~** *(talking)* telefonieren; *(possessing phone)* ein Telefon haben
telephone box, *(US)* **telephone booth** *n* Telefonzelle *f*
telephone call *n* Anruf *m*
telephone directory *n* Telefonbuch *nt*
telephone exchange *n* Telefonzentrale *f*
telephone number *n* Telefonnummer *f*
telephone operator *n* Telefonist(in) *m(f)*
telephone tapping *n* Abhören *nt* von Telefonleitungen
telephonist [tə'lɛfənɪst] *(Brit)* *n* Telefonist(in) *m(f)*
telephoto ['tɛlɪ'fəutəu] *adj*: **~ lens** Teleobjektiv *nt*
teleprinter ['tɛlɪprɪntə^r] *n* Fernschreiber *m*
Teleprompter® ['tɛlɪprɔmptə^r] *(US)* *n* Teleprompter *m*
telesales ['tɛlɪseɪlz] *n* Verkauf *m* per Telefon
telescope ['tɛlɪskəup] *n* Teleskop *nt* ▷ *vi* *(fig: bus, lorry)* sich ineinanderschieben ▷ *vt* *(make shorter)* zusammenschieben
telescopic [tɛlɪ'skɔpɪk] *adj* *(legs, aerial)* ausziehbar; **~ lens** Fernrohrlinse *f*
Teletext® ['tɛlɪtɛkst] *n* Videotext *m*
telethon ['tɛlɪθɔn] *n* *Spendenaktion für wohltätige Zwecke in Form einer vielstündigen Fernsehsendung*
televise ['tɛlɪvaɪz] *vt* (im Fernsehen) übertragen
television ['tɛlɪvɪʒən] *n* Fernsehen *nt*; *(set)* Fernseher *m*, Fernsehapparat *m*; **to be on ~** im Fernsehen sein
television licence *(Brit)* *n* Fernsehgenehmigung *f*
television programme *n* Fernsehprogramm *nt*
television set *n* Fernseher *m*, Fernsehapparat *m*
teleworking ['tɛlɪwə:kɪŋ] *n* Telearbeit *f*

telex ['tɛlɛks] *n* (*system, machine, message*) Telex *nt* ▷ *vt* (*message*) telexen; (*person*) ein Telex schicken +*dat* ▷ *vi* telexen

tell [tɛl] (*pt, pp* **told**) *vt* (*say*) sagen; (*relate: story*) erzählen; (*distinguish*): **to ~ sth from** etw unterscheiden von; (*be sure*) wissen ▷ *vi* (*have an effect*) sich auswirken; **to ~ sb to do sth** jdm sagen, etw zu tun; **to ~ sb of** *or* **about sth** jdm von etw erzählen; **to be able to ~ the time** (*know how to*) die Uhr kennen; **can you ~ me the time?** können Sie mir sagen, wie spät es ist?; **(I) ~ you what, let's go to the cinema** weißt du was? Lass uns ins Kino gehen!; **I can't ~ them apart** ich kann sie nicht unterscheiden
▸ **tell off** *vt*: **to ~ sb off** jdn ausschimpfen
▸ **tell on** *vt fus* (*inform against*) verpetzen

teller ['tɛləʳ] *n* (*in bank*) Kassierer(in) *m(f)*

telling ['tɛlɪŋ] *adj* (*remark etc*) verräterisch

telltale ['tɛlteɪl] *adj* verräterisch ▷ *n* (*pej*) Petzer *m*, Petze *f*

telly ['tɛlɪ] (*Brit: inf*) *n abbr* = **television**

temerity [tə'mɛrɪtɪ] *n* Unverschämtheit *f*

temp [tɛmp] (*Brit: inf*) *n abbr* (= *temporary office worker*) Zeitarbeitskraft *f* ▷ *vi* als Zeitarbeitskraft arbeiten

temper ['tɛmpəʳ] *n* (*nature*) Naturell *nt*; (*mood*) Laune *f* ▷ *vt* (*moderate*) mildern; **a (fit of) ~** ein Wutanfall *m*; **to be in a ~** gereizt sein; **to lose one's ~** die Beherrschung verlieren

temperament ['tɛmprəmənt] *n* Temperament *nt*

temperamental [tɛmprə'mɛntl] *adj* (*person, car*) launisch

temperate ['tɛmprət] *adj* gemäßigt

temperature ['tɛmprətʃəʳ] *n* Temperatur *f*; **to have** *or* **run a ~** Fieber haben; **to take sb's ~** bei jdm Fieber messen

temperature chart *n* (*Med*) Fiebertabelle *f*

tempered ['tɛmpəd] *adj* (*steel*) gehärtet

tempest ['tɛmpɪst] *n* Sturm *m*

tempestuous [tɛm'pɛstjuəs] *adj* (*also fig*) stürmisch; (*person*) leidenschaftlich

tempi ['tɛmpi:] *npl of* **tempo**

template ['tɛmplɪt] *n* Schablone *f*

temple ['tɛmpl] *n* (*building*) Tempel *m*; (*Anat*) Schläfe *f*

tempo ['tɛmpəu] (*pl* **~s** *or* **tempi**) *n* (*Mus, fig*) Tempo *nt*

temporal ['tɛmpərl] *adj* (*non-religious*) weltlich; (*relating to time*) zeitlich

temporarily ['tɛmpərərɪlɪ] *adv* vorübergehend; (*unavailable, alone etc*) zeitweilig

temporary ['tɛmpərərɪ] *adj* (*arrangement*) provisorisch; (*worker, job*) Aushilfs-; **~ refugee** Flüchtling *m* mit zeitlich begrenzter Aufenthaltserlaubnis; **~ secretary** Sekretärin zur Aushilfe; **~ teacher** Aushilfslehrer(in) *m(f)*

temporize ['tɛmpəraɪz] *vi* ausweichen

tempt [tɛmpt] *vt* in Versuchung führen; **to ~ sb into doing sth** jdn dazu verleiten, etw zu tun; **to be ~ed to do sth** versucht sein, etw zu tun

temptation [tɛmp'teɪʃən] *n* Versuchung *f*

tempting ['tɛmptɪŋ] *adj* (*offer*) verlockend; (*food*) verführerisch

ten [tɛn] *num* zehn ▷ *n*: **~s of thousands** Zehntausende *pl*

tenable ['tɛnəbl] *adj* (*argument, position*) haltbar

tenacious [tə'neɪʃəs] *adj* zäh, hartnäckig

tenacity [tə'næsɪtɪ] *n* Zähigkeit *f*, Hartnäckigkeit *f*

tenancy ['tɛnənsɪ] *n* (*of room*) Mietverhältnis *nt*; (*of land*) Pachtverhältnis *nt*

tenant ['tɛnənt] *n* (*of room*) Mieter(in) *m(f)*; (*of land*) Pächter(in) *m(f)*

tend [tɛnd] *vt* (*crops, sick person*) sich kümmern um ▷ *vi*: **to ~ to do sth** dazu neigen *or* tendieren, etw zu tun

tendency ['tɛndənsɪ] *n* (*of person*) Neigung *f*; (*of thing*) Tendenz *f*

tender ['tɛndəʳ] *adj* (*person, care*) zärtlich; (*heart*) gut; (*sore*) empfindlich; (*meat, age*) zart ▷ *n* (*Comm*) Angebot *nt*; (*money*): **legal ~** gesetzliches Zahlungsmittel *nt* ▷ *vt* (*offer*) vorlegen; (*resignation*) einreichen; (*apology*) anbieten; **to put in a ~ (for)** ein Angebot vorlegen (für); **to put work out to ~** (*Brit*) Arbeiten ausschreiben

tenderize ['tɛndəraɪz] *vt* (*meat*) zart machen

tenderly ['tɛndəlɪ] *adv* zärtlich, liebevoll

tenderness ['tɛndənɪs] *n* (*affection*) Zärtlichkeit *f*; (*of meat*) Zartheit *f*

tendon ['tɛndən] *n* Sehne *f*

tendril ['tɛndrɪl] *n* (*Bot*) Ranke *f*; (*of hair etc*) Strähne *f*

tenement ['tɛnəmənt] *n* Mietshaus *nt*

Tenerife [tɛnə'ri:f] *n* Teneriffa *nt*

tenet ['tɛnət] *n* Prinzip *nt*

Tenn. (*US*) *abbr* (*Post*) = *Tennessee*

tenner ['tɛnəʳ] (*Brit: inf*) *n* Zehner *m*

tennis ['tɛnɪs] *n* Tennis *nt*

tennis ball *n* Tennisball *m*

tennis club *n* Tennisklub *m*

tennis court *n* Tennisplatz *m*

tennis elbow *n* (*Med*) Tennisell(en)bogen *m*

tennis match *n* Tennismatch *nt*

tennis player *n* Tennisspieler(in) *m(f)*

tennis racket *n* Tennisschläger *m*

tennis shoes *npl* Tennisschuhe *pl*

tenor ['tɛnəʳ] *n* (*Mus*) Tenor *m*; (*of speech etc*) wesentlicher Gehalt *m*

tenpin bowling ['tɛnpɪn-] (*Brit*) *n* Bowling *nt*

tense [tɛns] *adj* (*person, muscle*) angespannt; (*smile*) verkrampft; (*period, situation*) gespannt ▷ *n* (*Ling*) Zeit *f*, Tempus *nt* ▷ *vt* (*muscles*) anspannen

tenseness ['tɛnsnɪs] *n* Gespanntheit *f*

tension ['tɛnʃən] *n* (*nervousness*) Angespanntheit *f*; (*between ropes etc*) Spannung *f*

tent [tɛnt] *n* Zelt *nt*

tentacle ['tɛntəkl] *n* (*Zool*) Fangarm *m*; (*fig*) Klaue *f*

tentative ['tɛntətɪv] *adj* (*person, smile*) zögernd;

(*step*) unsicher; (*conclusion, plans*) vorläufig
tentatively ['tɛntətɪvlɪ] *adv* (*suggest*) versuchsweise; (*wave etc*) zögernd
tenterhooks ['tɛntəhuks] *npl*: **to be on ~** wie auf glühenden Kohlen sitzen
tenth [tɛnθ] *num* zehnte(r, s) ▷ *n* Zehntel *nt*
tent peg *n* Hering *m*
tent pole *n* Zeltstange *f*
tenuous ['tɛnjuəs] *adj* (*hold, links etc*) schwach
tenure ['tɛnjuə^r] *n* (*of land etc*) Nutzungsrecht *nt*; (*of office*) Amtszeit *f*; (*Univ*): **to have ~** eine Dauerstellung haben
tepid ['tɛpɪd] *adj* (*also fig*) lauwarm
Ter. *abbr* (*in street names: = terrace*) ≈ Str.
term [tə:m] *n* (*word*) Ausdruck *m*; (*period in power etc*) Amtszeit *f*; (*Scol: three per year*) Trimester *nt* ▷ *vt* (*call*) nennen; **terms** *npl* (*also Comm*) Bedingungen *pl*; **in economic/political ~s** wirtschaftlich/politisch gesehen; **in ~s of business** was das Geschäft angeht *or* betrifft; **~ of imprisonment** Gefängnisstrafe *f*; **"easy ~s"** (*Comm*) „günstige Bedingungen"; **in the short/long ~** auf kurze/lange Sicht; **to be on good ~s with sb** sich mit jdm gut verstehen; **to come to ~s with** (*problem*) sich abfinden mit
terminal ['tə:mɪnl] *adj* (*disease, patient*) unheilbar ▷ *n* (*Aviat, Comm, Comput*) Terminal *nt*; (*Elec*) Anschluss *m*; (*Brit: also*: **bus terminal**) Endstation *f*
terminate ['tə:mɪneɪt] *vt* beenden ▷ *vi*: **to ~ in** enden in *+dat*
termination [tə:mɪ'neɪʃən] *n* Beendigung *f*; (*expiry: of contract*) Ablauf *m*; (*Med: of pregnancy*) Abbruch *m*
termini ['tə:mɪnaɪ] *npl of* **terminus**
terminology [tə:mɪ'nɔlədʒɪ] *n* Terminologie *f*
terminus ['tə:mɪnəs] (*pl* **termini**) *n* (*for buses, trains*) Endstation *f*
termite ['tə:maɪt] *n* Termite *f*
term paper (*US*) *n* (*Univ*) ≈ Semesterarbeit *f*
Terr. *abbr* (*in street names: = terrace*) ≈ Str.
terrace ['tɛrəs] *n* (*Brit: row of houses*) Häuserreihe *f*; (*Agr, patio*) Terrasse *f*; **the terraces** *npl* (*Brit: Sport*) die Ränge *pl*
terraced ['tɛrəst] *adj* (*house*) Reihen-; (*garden*) terrassenförmig angelegt
terracotta ['tɛrə'kɔtə] *n* (*clay*) Terrakotta *f*; (*colour*) Braunrot *nt* ▷ *adj* (*pot, roof etc*) Terrakotta-
terrain [tɛ'reɪn] *n* Gelände *nt*, Terrain *nt*
terrible ['tɛrɪbl] *adj* schrecklich, furchtbar
terribly ['tɛrɪblɪ] *adv* (*very*) furchtbar; (*very badly*) entsetzlich
terrier ['tɛrɪə^r] *n* Terrier *m*
terrific [tə'rɪfɪk] *adj* (*very great: thunderstorm, speed*) unheimlich; (*time, party*) sagenhaft
terrify ['tɛrɪfaɪ] *vt* erschrecken; **to be terrified** schreckliche Angst haben
terrifying ['tɛrɪfaɪɪŋ] *adj* entsetzlich, grauenvoll
territorial [tɛrɪ'tɔ:rɪəl] *adj* (*boundaries, dispute*) territorial, Gebiets-; (*waters*) Hoheits- ▷ *n* (*Mil*) Soldat *m* der Territorialarmee
Territorial Army (*Brit*) *n* (*Mil*): **the ~** die Territorialarmee
territorial waters *npl* Hoheitsgewässer *pl*
territory ['tɛrɪtərɪ] *n* (*also fig*) Gebiet *nt*
terror ['tɛrə^r] *n* (*great fear*) panische Angst *f*
terrorism ['tɛrərɪzəm] *n* Terrorismus *m*
terrorist ['tɛrərɪst] *n* Terrorist(in) *m(f)*
terrorize ['tɛrəraɪz] *vt* terrorisieren
terse [tə:s] *adj* knapp
tertiary ['tə:ʃərɪ] *adj* tertiär; **~ education** (*Brit*) Universitätsausbildung *f*
Terylene® ['tɛrɪli:n] *n* Terylen® *nt* ▷ *adj* Terylen-
TESL ['tɛsl] *n abbr* (*= Teaching of English as a Second Language*) *Unterricht in Englisch als Zweitsprache*
TESSA ['tɛsə] (*Brit*) *n abbr* (*= Tax Exempt Special Savings Account*) *steuerfreies Sparsystem mit begrenzter Einlagehöhe*
test [tɛst] *n* Test *m*; (*of courage etc*) Probe *f*; (*Scol*) Prüfung *f*; (*also*: **driving test**) Fahrprüfung *f* ▷ *vt* testen; (*check: ,, Scol*) prüfen; **to put sth to the ~** etw auf die Probe stellen; **to ~ sth for sth** etw auf etw *acc* prüfen
testament ['tɛstəmənt] *n* Zeugnis *nt*; **the Old/New T~** das Alte/Neue Testament; **last will and ~** Testament *nt*
test ban *n* (*also*: **nuclear test ban**) Teststopp *m*
test card *n* (*TV*) Testbild *nt*
test case *n* (*Law*) Musterfall *m*; (*fig*) Musterbeispiel *nt*
testes ['tɛsti:z] *npl* Testikel *pl*, Hoden *pl*
test flight *n* Testflug *m*
testicle ['tɛstɪkl] *n* Hoden *m*
testify ['tɛstɪfaɪ] *vi* (*Law*) aussagen; **to ~ to sth** (*Law, fig*) etw bezeugen
testimonial [tɛstɪ'məunɪəl] *n* (*Brit: reference*) Referenz *f*; (*Sport: also*: **testimonial match**) *Benefizspiel, dessen Erlös einem verdienten Spieler zugutekommt*
testimony ['tɛstɪmənɪ] *n* (*statement*) Aussage *f*; (*clear proof*): **to be (a) ~ to** ein Zeugnis *nt* sein für
testing ['tɛstɪŋ] *adj* schwierig
test match *n* (*Cricket, Rugby*) Testmatch *nt*, Test Match *nt*, Länderspiel *nt*
testosterone [tɛs'tɔstərəun] *n* Testosteron *nt*
test paper *n* (*Scol*) Klassenarbeit *f*
test pilot *n* Testpilot(in) *m(f)*
test tube *n* Reagenzglas *nt*
test-tube baby ['tɛsttju:b-] *n* Retortenbaby *nt*
testy ['tɛstɪ] *adj* gereizt
tetanus ['tɛtənəs] *n* Tetanus *m*
tetchy ['tɛtʃɪ] *adj* gereizt
tether ['tɛðə^r] *vt* (*animal*) festbinden ▷ *n*: **to be at the end of one's ~** völlig am Ende sein
text [tɛkst] *n* Text *m* ▷ *vt* (*on mobile phone*) eine SMS schreiben *+dat*
text [tɛkst] *vt* (*on mobile phone*) eine SMS schreiben *+dat*
textbook ['tɛkstbuk] *n* Lehrbuch *nt*
textiles ['tɛkstaɪlz] *npl* Textilien *pl*
text message *n* (*Tel*) SMS *f*

text messaging *n* (*Tel*) Textnachrichten *pl*
textual ['tɛkstjuəl] *adj* (*analysis etc*) Text-
texture ['tɛkstʃə^r] *n* Beschaffenheit *f*, Struktur *f*
TGWU (*Brit*) *n abbr* (= *Transport and General Workers' Union*) *Transportarbeitergewerkschaft*
Thai [taɪ] *adj* thailändisch ▷ *n* Thailänder(in) *m(f)*
Thailand ['taɪlænd] *n* Thailand *nt*
thalidomide® [θə'lɪdəmaɪd] *n* Contergan® *nt*
Thames [tɛmz] *n*: **the ~** die Themse
than [ðæn] *conj* (*in comparisons*) als; **more ~ 10** mehr als 10; **she is older ~ you think** sie ist älter, als Sie denken; **more ~ once** mehr als einmal
thank [θæŋk] *vt* danken *+dat*; **~ you** danke; **~ you very much** vielen Dank; **~ God!** Gott sei Dank!
thankful ['θæŋkful] *adj*: **~ (for/that)** dankbar (für/, dass)
thankfully ['θæŋkfəlɪ] *adv* dankbar; **~ there were few victims** zum Glück gab es nur wenige Opfer
thankless ['θæŋklɪs] *adj* undankbar
thanks [θæŋks] *npl* Dank *m* ▷ *excl* (*also*: **many thanks, thanks a lot**) danke, vielen Dank; **~ to** dank *+gen*
Thanksgiving ['θæŋksgɪvɪŋ], **Thanksgiving Day** (*US*) *n* Thanksgiving Day *m*

Thanksgiving (Day) ist ein Feiertag in den USA, der auf den vierten Donnerstag im November fällt. Er soll daran erinnern, wie die Pilgerväter die gute Ernte im Jahre 1621 feierten. In Kanada gibt es einen ähnlichen Erntedanktag (der aber nichts mit den Pilgervätern zu tun hat) am zweiten Montag im Oktober.

KEYWORD

that [ðæt, ðət] (*pl* **those**) *adj* (*demonstrative*) der/die/das; **that man** der Mann; **that woman** die Frau; **that book** das Buch; **that one** der/die/das da; **I want this one, not that one** ich will dieses (hier), nicht das (da)
▷ *pron* **1** (*demonstrative*) das; **who's/what's that?** wer/was ist das?; **is that you?** bist du das?; **will you eat all that?** isst du das alles?; **that's what he said** das hat er gesagt; **what happened after that?** was geschah danach?; **that is (to say)** das heißt; **and that's that!** und damit Schluss!
2 (*relative: subject*) der/die/das; (: (: *pl*) die; (: *direct object*) den/die/das; (: (: *pl*) die; (: *indirect object*) dem/der/dem; (: (: *pl*) denen; **the man that I saw** der Mann, den ich gesehen habe; **all that I have** alles was ich habe; **the people that I spoke to** die Leute, mit denen ich geredet habe
3 (*relative: of time*): **the day that he came** der Tag, an dem er kam; **the winter that he came to see us** der Winter, in dem er uns besuchte
▷ *conj* dass; **he thought that I was ill** er dachte, dass ich krank sei, er dachte, ich sei krank
▷ *adv* (*demonstrative*) so; **I can't work that much** ich kann nicht so viel arbeiten; **that high** so hoch

thatched [θætʃt] *adj* strohgedeckt
Thatcherism ['θætʃərɪzəm] *n* Thatcherismus *m*
Thatcherite ['θætʃəraɪt] *adj* thatcheristisch ▷ *n* Thatcher-Anhänger(in) *m(f)*
thaw [θɔː] *n* Tauwetter *nt* ▷ *vi* (*ice*) tauen; (*food*) auftauen ▷ *vt* (*also*: **thaw out**) auftauen; **it's ~ing** es taut

KEYWORD

the [ðiː, ðə] *def art* **1** (*before masculine noun*) der; (*before feminine noun*) die; (*before neuter noun*) das; (*before plural noun*) die; **to play the piano/violin** Klavier/Geige spielen; **I'm going to the butcher's/the cinema** ich gehe zum Metzger/ins Kino
2 (*+ adj to form noun*): **the rich and the poor** die Reichen und die Armen; **to attempt the impossible** das Unmögliche versuchen
3 (*in titles*): **Elizabeth the First** Elisabeth die Erste; **Peter the Great** Peter der Große
4 (*in comparisons*): **the more he works the more he earns** je mehr er arbeitet, desto mehr verdient er; **the sooner the better** je eher, desto besser

theatre, (*US*) **theater** ['θɪətə^r] *n* Theater *nt*; (*also*: **lecture theatre**) Hörsaal *m*; (*also*: **operating theatre**) Operationssaal *m*
theatre-goer ['θɪətəgəuə^r] *n* Theaterbesucher(in) *m(f)*
theatrical [θɪ'ætrɪkl] *adj* (*event, production*) Theater-; (*gestures etc*) theatralisch
theft [θɛft] *n* Diebstahl *m*
their [ðɛə^r] *adj* ihr
theirs [ðɛəz] *pron* ihre(r, s); **it is ~** es gehört ihnen; **a friend of ~** ein Freund/eine Freundin von ihnen; *see also* **my; mine¹**
them [ðɛm] *pron* (*direct*) sie; (*indirect*) ihnen; **I see ~** ich sehe sie; **give ~ the book** gib ihnen das Buch; **give me a few of ~** geben Sie mir ein paar davon; **with ~** mit ihnen; **without ~** ohne sie; *see also* **me**
theme [θiːm] *n* (*also Mus*) Thema *nt*
theme park *n* Themenpark *m*
theme song *n* Titelmusik *f*
theme tune *n* Titelmelodie *f*
themselves [ðəm'sɛlvz] *pl pron* (*reflexive, after prep*) sich; (*emphatic, alone*) selbst; **between ~** unter sich
then [ðɛn] *adv* (*at that time*) damals; (*next, later*) dann ▷ *conj* (*therefore*) also ▷ *adj*: **the ~ president** der damalige Präsident; **by ~** (*past*)

bis dahin; (*future*) bis dann; **from ~ on** von da an; **before ~** davor; **until ~** bis dann; **and ~ what?** und was dann?; **what do you want me to do ~?** was soll ich dann machen?; **... but ~ (again) he's the boss** ... aber er ist ja der Chef
theologian [θɪəˈləudʒən] *n* Theologe *m*, Theologin *f*
theological [θɪəˈlɔdʒɪkl] *adj* theologisch
theology [θɪˈɔlədʒɪ] *n* Theologie *f*
theorem [ˈθɪərəm] *n* Lehrsatz *m*
theoretical [θɪəˈrɛtɪkl] *adj* theoretisch
theorize [ˈθɪəraɪz] *vi* theoretisieren
theory [ˈθɪərɪ] *n* Theorie *f*; **in ~** theoretisch
therapeutic [θɛrəˈpjuːtɪk] *adj* therapeutisch
therapist [ˈθɛrəpɪst] *n* Therapeut(in) *m(f)*
therapy [ˈθɛrəpɪ] *n* Therapie *f*

KEYWORD

there [ðɛəʳ] *adv* **1: there is/are** da ist/sind; (*there exist(s)*) es gibt; **there are 3 of them** es gibt 3 davon; **there has been an accident** da war ein Unfall; **there will be a meeting tomorrow** morgen findet ein Treffen statt
2 (*referring to place*) da, dort; **down/over there** da unten/drüben; **put it in/on there** leg es dorthinein/-hinauf; **I want that book there** ich möchte das Buch da; **there he is!** da ist er ja!
3: there, there (*esp to child*) ist ja gut

thereabouts [ˈðɛərəˈbauts] *adv*: **or ~** (*place*) oder dortherum; (*amount, time*) oder so
thereafter [ðɛərˈɑːftəʳ] *adv* danach
thereby [ˈðɛəbaɪ] *adv* dadurch
therefore [ˈðɛəfɔːʳ] *adv* daher, deshalb
there's [ˈðɛəz] = **there is; there has**
thereupon [ðɛərəˈpɔn] *adv* (*at that point*) darauf(hin)
thermal [ˈθəːml] *adj* (*springs*) Thermal-; (*underwear, paper, printer*) Thermo-
thermodynamics [ˈθəːmədaɪˈnæmɪks] *n* Thermodynamik *f*
thermometer [θəˈmɔmɪtəʳ] *n* Thermometer *nt*
thermonuclear [ˈθəːməuˈnjuːklɪəʳ] *adj* thermonuklear
Thermos® [ˈθəːməs] *n* (*also*: **Thermos flask**) Thermosflasche® *f*
thermostat [ˈθəːməustæt] *n* Thermostat *m*
thesaurus [θɪˈsɔːrəs] *n* Synonymwörterbuch *nt*
these [ðiːz] *pl adj, pl pron* diese
theses [ˈθiːsiːz] *npl of* **thesis**
thesis [ˈθiːsɪs] (*pl* **theses**) *n* These *f*; (*for doctorate etc*) Dissertation *f*, Doktorarbeit *f*
they [ðeɪ] *pl pron* sie; **~ say that ...** (*it is said that*) man sagt, dass ...
they'd [ðeɪd] = **they had; = they would**
they'll [ðeɪl] = **they shall; they will**
they're [ðɛəʳ] = **they are**
they've [ðeɪv] = **they have**
thick [θɪk] *adj* dick; (*sauce etc*) dickflüssig; (*fog, forest, hair etc*) dicht; (*inf: stupid*) blöd ▷ *n*: **in the ~ of the battle** mitten im Gefecht; **it's 20 cm ~** es ist 20 cm dick
thicken [ˈθɪkn] *vi* (*fog etc*) sich verdichten ▷ *vt* (*sauce etc*) eindicken; **the plot ~s** die Sache wird immer verwickelter
thicket [ˈθɪkɪt] *n* Dickicht *nt*
thickly [ˈθɪklɪ] *adv* (*spread, cut*) dick; **~ populated** dicht bevölkert
thickness [ˈθɪknɪs] *n* (*of rope, wire*) Dicke *f*; (*layer*) Lage *f*
thickset [θɪkˈsɛt] *adj* (*person, body*) gedrungen
thick-skinned [θɪkˈskɪnd] *adj* (*also fig*) dickhäutig
thief [θiːf] (*pl* **thieves**) *n* Dieb(in) *m(f)*
thieves [θiːvz] *npl of* **thief**
thieving [ˈθiːvɪŋ] *n* Stehlen *nt*
thigh [θaɪ] *n* Oberschenkel *m*
thighbone [ˈθaɪbəun] *n* Oberschenkelknochen *m*
thimble [ˈθɪmbl] *n* Fingerhut *m*
thin [θɪn] *adj* dünn; (*fog*) leicht; (*hair, crowd*) spärlich ▷ *vt*: **to ~ (down)** (*sauce, paint*) verdünnen ▷ *vi* (*fog, crowd*) sich lichten; **his hair is ~ning** sein Haar lichtet sich
thing [θɪŋ] *n* Ding *nt*; (*matter*) Sache *f*; (*inf*): **to have a ~ about sth** (*be fascinated by*) wie besessen sein von etw; (*hate*) etw nicht ausstehen können; **things** *npl* (*belongings*) Sachen *pl*; **to do sth first ~ (every morning/ tomorrow morning)** etw (morgens/morgen früh) als Erstes tun; **I look awful first ~ in the morning** ich sehe frühmorgens immer furchtbar aus; **to do sth last ~ (at night)** etw als Letztes (am Abend) tun; **the ~ is ...** die Sache ist die: ...; **for one ~** zunächst mal; **don't worry about a ~** du brauchst dir überhaupt keine Sorgen zu machen; **you'll do no such ~!** das lässt du schön bleiben!; **poor ~** armes Ding; **the best ~ would be to ...** das Beste wäre, zu ...; **how are ~s?** wie gehts?
think [θɪŋk] (*pt, pp* **thought**) *vi* (*reflect*) nachdenken; (*reason*) denken ▷ *vt* (*be of the opinion*) denken; (*believe*) glauben; **to ~ of** denken an *+acc*; (*recall*) sich erinnern an *+acc*; **what did you ~ of them?** was hielten Sie von ihnen?; **to ~ about sth/sb** (*ponder*) über etw/ jdn nachdenken; **I'll ~ about it** ich werde es mir überlegen; **to ~ of doing sth** daran denken, etw zu tun; **to ~ highly of sb** viel von jdm halten; **to ~ aloud** laut nachdenken; **~ again!** denk noch mal nach!; **I ~ so/not** ich glaube ja/nein
▸ **think over** *vt* (*offer, suggestion*) überdenken; **I'd like to ~ things over** ich möchte mir die Sache noch einmal überlegen
▸ **think through** *vt* durchdenken
▸ **think up** *vt* sich *dat* ausdenken
thinking [ˈθɪŋkɪŋ] *n* Denken *nt*; **to my (way of) ~** meiner Meinung *or* Ansicht nach
think-tank [ˈθɪŋktæŋk] *n* Expertengremium *nt*
thinly [ˈθɪnlɪ] *adv* dünn; (*disguised, veiled*) kaum
thinness [ˈθɪnnɪs] *n* Dünne *f*
third [θəːd] *num* dritte(r, s) ▷ *n* (*fraction*) Drittel *nt*; (*Aut: also*: **third gear**) dritter Gang *m*;

(*Brit: Scol: degree*) ≈ Ausreichend *nt*; **a ~ of** ein Drittel *+gen*
third-degree burns ['θəːddɪgriː-] *npl* Verbrennungen *pl* dritten Grades
thirdly ['θəːdlɪ] *adv* drittens
third party insurance (*Brit*) *n* ≈ Haftpflichtversicherung *f*
third-rate ['θəːd'reɪt] (*pej*) *adj* drittklassig
Third World *n*: **the ~** die Dritte Welt ▹ *adj* der Dritten Welt
thirst [θəːst] *n* Durst *m*
thirsty ['θəːstɪ] *adj* durstig; **to be ~** Durst haben; **gardening is ~ work** Gartenarbeit macht durstig
thirteen [θəː'tiːn] *num* dreizehn
thirteenth ['θəː'tiːnθ] *num* dreizehnte(r, s)
thirtieth ['θəːtɪɪθ] *num* dreißigste(r, s)
thirty ['θəːtɪ] *num* dreißig

KEYWORD

this [ðɪs] (*pl* **these**) *adj* (*demonstrative*) diese(r, s); **this man** dieser Mann; **this woman** diese Frau; **this book** dieses Buch; **this one** diese(r, s) (hier)
▹ *pron* (*demonstrative*) dies, das; **who/what is this?** wer/was ist das?; **this is where I live** hier wohne ich; **this is what he said** das hat er gesagt; **this is Mr Brown** (*in introductions, photo*) das ist Herr Brown; (*on telephone*) hier ist Herr Brown
▹ *adv* (*demonstrative*): **this high/long** *etc* so hoch/lang *etc*

thistle ['θɪsl] *n* Distel *f*
thong [θɔŋ] *n* Riemen *m*
thorn [θɔːn] *n* Dorn *m*
thorny ['θɔːnɪ] *adj* dornig; (*fig: problem*) heikel
thorough ['θʌrə] *adj* gründlich
thoroughbred ['θʌrəbrɛd] *n* (*horse*) Vollblüter *m*
thoroughfare ['θʌrəfɛəʳ] *n* (*road*) Durchgangsstraße *f*; **"no ~"** (*Brit*) „Durchfahrt verboten"
thoroughgoing ['θʌrəgəuɪŋ] *adj* (*changes, reform*) grundlegend; (*investigation*) gründlich
thoroughly ['θʌrəlɪ] *adv* gründlich; (*very*) äußerst; **I ~ agree** ich stimme vollkommen zu
thoroughness ['θʌrənɪs] *n* Gründlichkeit *f*
those [ðəuz] *pl adj, pl pron* die (da); **~ (of you) who ...** diejenigen (von Ihnen), die ...
though [ðəu] *conj* obwohl ▹ *adv* aber; **even ~** obwohl; **it's not easy, ~** es ist aber nicht einfach
thought [θɔːt] *pt, pp of* **think** ▹ *n* Gedanke *m*; **thoughts** *npl* (*opinion*) Gedanken *pl*; **after much ~** nach langer Überlegung; **I've just had a ~** mir ist gerade etwas eingefallen; **to give sth some ~** sich *dat* Gedanken über etw *acc* machen
thoughtful ['θɔːtful] *adj* (*deep in thought*) nachdenklich; (*considerate*) aufmerksam
thoughtfully ['θɔːtfəlɪ] *adv* (*look etc*) nachdenklich; (*behave etc*) rücksichtsvoll; (*provide*) rücksichtsvollerweise
thoughtless ['θɔːtlɪs] *adj* gedankenlos
thoughtlessly ['θɔːtlɪslɪ] *adv* gedankenlos
thoughtlessness ['θɔːtlɪsnɪs] *n* Gedankenlosigkeit *f*
thought-out [θɔːt'aut] *adj* durchdacht
thought-provoking ['θɔːtprəvəukɪŋ] *adj*: **to be ~** Denkanstöße geben
thousand ['θauzənd] *num* (ein)tausend; **two ~** zweitausend; **~s of** Tausende von
thousandth ['θauzəntθ] *num* tausendste(r, s)
thrash [θræʃ] *vt* (*beat*) verprügeln; (*defeat*) (vernichtend) schlagen
▸ **thrash about** *vi* um sich schlagen
▸ **thrash around** *vi* = **thrash about**
▸ **thrash out** *vt* (*problem*) ausdiskutieren
thrashing ['θræʃɪŋ] *n*: **to give sb a ~** jdn verprügeln
thread [θrɛd] *n* (*yarn*) Faden *m*; (*of screw*) Gewinde *nt* ▹ *vt* (*needle*) einfädeln; **to ~ one's way between** sich hindurchschlängeln zwischen
threadbare ['θrɛdbɛəʳ] *adj* (*clothes*) abgetragen; (*carpet*) abgelaufen
threat [θrɛt] *n* Drohung *f*; (*fig*): **~ (to)** Gefahr *f* (für); **to be under ~ of** (*closure etc*) bedroht sein von
threaten ['θrɛtn] *vi* bedrohen ▹ *vt*: **to ~ sb with sth** jdm mit etw drohen; **to ~ to do sth** (damit) drohen, etw zu tun
threatening ['θrɛtnɪŋ] *adj* drohend, bedrohlich
three [θriː] *num* drei
three-dimensional [θriːdɪ'mɛnʃənl] *adj* dreidimensional
threefold ['θriːfəuld] *adv*: **to increase ~** dreifach *or* um das Dreifache ansteigen
three-piece suit ['θriːpiːs-] *n* dreiteiliger Anzug *m*
three-piece suite *n* dreiteilige Polstergarnitur *f*
three-ply [θriː'plaɪ] *adj* (*wool*) dreifädig; (*wood*) dreilagig
three-quarters [θriː'kwɔːtəz] *npl* drei Viertel *pl*; **~ full** drei viertel voll
three-wheeler ['θriː'wiːləʳ] *n* (*car*) Dreiradwagen *m*
thresh [θrɛʃ] *vt* dreschen
threshing machine ['θrɛʃɪŋ-] *n* Dreschmaschine *f*
threshold ['θrɛʃhəuld] *n* Schwelle *f*; **to be on the ~ of sth** (*fig*) an der Schwelle zu etw sein *or* stehen
threshold agreement *n* (*Econ*) *Tarifvereinbarung über der Inflationsrate angeglichene Lohnerhöhungen*
threw [θruː] *pt of* **throw**
thrift [θrɪft] *n* Sparsamkeit *f*
thrifty ['θrɪftɪ] *adj* sparsam
thrill [θrɪl] *n* (*excitement*) Aufregung *f*; (*shudder*) Erregung *f* ▹ *vi* zittern ▹ *vt* (*person, audience*) erregen; **to be ~ed** (*with gift etc*) sich riesig freuen

thriller [ˈθrɪləʳ] *n* Thriller *m*
thrilling [ˈθrɪlɪŋ] *adj* (*ride, performance etc*) erregend; (*news*) aufregend
thrive [θraɪv] (*pt* **~d** *or* **throve**, *pp* **~d**) *vi* gedeihen; **to ~ on sth** von etw leben
thriving [ˈθraɪvɪŋ] *adj* (*business, community*) blühend, florierend
throat [θrəut] *n* Kehle *f*; **to have a sore ~** Halsschmerzen haben
throb [θrɔb] *n* (*of heart*) Klopfen *nt*; (*pain*) Pochen *nt*; (*of engine*) Dröhnen *nt* ▷ *vi* (*heart*) klopfen; (*pain*) pochen; (*machine*) dröhnen; **my head is ~bing** ich habe rasende Kopfschmerzen
throes [θrəuz] *npl*: **in the ~ of** (*war, moving house etc*) mitten in *+dat*; **death ~** Todeskampf *m*
thrombosis [θrɔmˈbəusɪs] *n* Thrombose *f*
throne [θrəun] *n* Thron *m*; **on the ~** auf dem Thron
throng [ˈθrɔŋ] *n* Masse *f* ▷ *vt* (*streets etc*) sich drängen in *+dat* ▷ *vi*: **to ~ to** strömen zu; **a ~ of people** eine Menschenmenge; **to be ~ed with** wimmeln von
throttle [ˈθrɔtl] *n* (*in car*) Gaspedal *nt*; (*on motorcycle*) Gashebel *m* ▷ *vt* (*strangle*) erdrosseln
through [θruː] *prep* durch; (*time*) während; (*owing to*) infolge *+gen* ▷ *adj* (*ticket, train*) durchgehend ▷ *adv* durch; **(from) Monday ~ Friday** (US) von Montag bis Freitag; **to be ~** (*Tel*) verbunden sein; **to be ~ with sb/sth** mit jdm/etw fertig sein; **we're ~!** es ist aus zwischen uns!; **"no ~ road", "no ~ traffic"** (US) „keine Durchfahrt"; **to let sb ~** jdn durchlassen; **to put sb ~ to sb** (*Tel*) jdn mit jdm verbinden
throughout [θruːˈaut] *adv* (*everywhere*) überall; (*the whole time*) die ganze Zeit über ▷ *prep* (*place*) überall in *+dat*; (*time*): **~ the morning/afternoon** während des ganzen Morgens/Nachmittags; **~ her life** ihr ganzes Leben lang
throughput [ˈθruːput] *n* (*also Comput*) Durchsatz *m*
throve [θrəuv] *pt of* **thrive**
throw [θrəu] (*pt* **threw**, *pp* **~n**) *n* Wurf *m* ▷ *vt* werfen; (*rider*) abwerfen; (*fig: confuse*) aus der Fassung bringen; (*pottery*) töpfern; **to ~ a party** eine Party geben; **to ~ open** (*doors, windows*) aufreißen; (*debate*) öffnen
▸ **throw about** *vt* (*money*) herumwerfen mit
▸ **throw around** *vt* = **throw about**
▸ **throw away** *vt* wegwerfen; (*waste*) verschwenden
▸ **throw off** *vt* (*get rid of: burden*) abwerfen
▸ **throw out** *vt* (*rubbish*) wegwerfen; (*idea*) verwerfen; (*person*) hinauswerfen
▸ **throw together** *vt* (*meal*) hinhauen; (*clothes*) zusammenpacken
▸ **throw up** *vi* (*vomit*) sich übergeben
throwaway [ˈθrəuəweɪ] *adj* (*cutlery etc*) Einweg-; (*line, remark*) beiläufig
throwback [ˈθrəubæk] *n*: **it's a ~ to** (*reminder*) es erinnert an *+acc*
throw-in [ˈθrəuɪn] *n* (*Football*) Einwurf *m*
thrown [θrəun] *pp of* **throw**
thru [θruː] (US) *prep, adj, adv* = **through**
thrush [θrʌʃ] *n* (*bird*) Drossel *f*; (*Med: esp in children*) Soor *m*; (*: Brit: in women*) vaginale Pilzerkrankung *f*
thrust [θrʌst] (*pt, pp* **~**) *n* (*Tech*) Schubkraft *f*; (*push*) Stoß *m*; (*fig: impetus*) Stoßkraft *f* ▷ *vt* stoßen
thud [θʌd] *n* dumpfes Geräusch *nt*
thug [θʌg] *n* Schlägertyp *m*
thumb [θʌm] *n* Daumen *m* ▷ *vt*: **to ~ a lift** per Anhalter fahren; **to give sb/sth the ~s up** (*approve*) jdm/etw *dat* grünes Licht geben; **to give sb/sth the ~s down** (*disapprove*) jdn/etw ablehnen
▸ **thumb through** *vt fus* (*book*) durchblättern
thumb index *n* Daumenregister *nt*
thumbnail [ˈθʌmneɪl] *n* Daumennagel *m*
thumbnail sketch *n* kurze Darstellung *f*
thumbtack [ˈθʌmtæk] (US) *n* Heftzwecke *f*
thump [θʌmp] *n* (*blow*) Schlag *m*; (*sound*) dumpfer Schlag *m* ▷ *vt* schlagen auf *+acc* ▷ *vi* (*heart etc*) heftig pochen
thumping [ˈθʌmpɪŋ] *adj* (*majority, victory etc*) Riesen-; (*headache, cold*) fürchterlich
thunder [ˈθʌndəʳ] *n* Donner *m* ▷ *vi* donnern; (*shout angrily*) brüllen; **to ~ past** (*train etc*) vorbeidonnern
thunderbolt [ˈθʌndəbəult] *n* Blitzschlag *m*
thunderclap [ˈθʌndəklæp] *n* Donnerschlag *m*
thunderous [ˈθʌndrəs] *adj* donnernd
thunderstorm [ˈθʌndəstɔːm] *n* Gewitter *nt*
thunderstruck [ˈθʌndəstrʌk] *adj*: **to be ~** (*shocked*) wie von Donner gerührt sein
thundery [ˈθʌndərɪ] *adj* (*weather*) gewitterig
Thur., Thurs. *abbr* (= *Thursday*) Do.
Thursday [ˈθəːzdɪ] *n* Donnerstag *m*; *see also* **Tuesday**
thus [ðʌs] *adv* (*in this way*) so; (*consequently*) somit
thwart [θwɔːt] *vt* (*person*) einen Strich durch die Rechnung machen *+dat*; (*plans*) vereiteln
thyme [taɪm] *n* Thymian *m*
thyroid [ˈθaɪrɔɪd] *n* (*also*: **thyroid gland**) Schilddrüse *f*
tiara [tɪˈɑːrə] *n* Diadem *nt*
Tiber [ˈtaɪbəʳ] *n*: **the ~** der Tiber
Tibet [tɪˈbɛt] *n* Tibet *nt*
Tibetan [tɪˈbɛtən] *adj* tibetanisch ▷ *n* (*person*) Tibetaner(in) *m(f)*; (*Ling*) Tibetisch *nt*
tibia [ˈtɪbɪə] *n* Schienbein *nt*
tic [tɪk] *n* nervöse Zuckung *f*, Tic *m*, Tick *m*
tick [tɪk] *n* (*sound*) Ticken *nt*; (*mark*) Häkchen *nt*; (*Zool*) Zecke *f*; (*Brit: inf: moment*) Augenblick *m*; (*: credit*): **to buy sth on ~** etw auf Pump kaufen ▷ *vi* (*clock, watch*) ticken ▷ *vt* (*item on list*) abhaken; **to put a ~ against sth** etw abhaken; **what makes him ~?** was ist er für ein Mensch?
▸ **tick off** *vt* (*item on list*) abhaken; (*person*) rüffeln
▸ **tick over** *vi* (*engine*) im Leerlauf sein; (*fig: business etc*) sich über Wasser halten
ticker tape [ˈtɪkəteɪp] *n* Lochstreifen *m*; (*US: in*

celebrations) ≈ Luftschlangen *pl*

ticket ['tɪkɪt] *n (for public transport)* Fahrkarte *f*; *(for theatre etc)* Eintrittskarte *f*; *(in shop: on goods)* Preisschild *nt*; *(: from cash register)* Kassenbon *m*; *(for raffle)* Los *nt*; *(for library)* Ausweis *m*; *(also:* **parking ticket**: *fine)* Strafzettel *m*; *(US: Pol)* Wahlliste *f*; **to get a (parking) ~** *(Aut)* einen Strafzettel bekommen

ticket agency *n (Theat)* Vorverkaufsstelle *f*

ticket collector *n (Rail: at station)* Fahrkartenkontrolleur(in) *m(f)*; *(on train)* Schaffner(in) *m(f)*

ticket holder *n* Karteninhaber(in) *m(f)*

ticket inspector *n* Fahrkartenkontrolleur(in) *m(f)*

ticket office *n (Rail)* Fahrkartenschalter *m*; *(Theat)* Theaterkasse *f*

tickle ['tɪkl] *vt* kitzeln; *(fig: amuse)* amüsieren ▷ *vi* kitzeln; **it ~s!** das kitzelt!

ticklish ['tɪklɪʃ] *adj (person, situation)* kitzlig

tidal ['taɪdl] *adj (force)* Gezeiten-, der Gezeiten; *(river)* Tide-

tidal wave *n* Flutwelle *f*

tidbit ['tɪdbɪt] *(US) n* = **titbit**

tiddlywinks ['tɪdlɪwɪŋks] *n* Flohhüpfen *nt*

tide [taɪd] *n (in sea)* Gezeiten *pl*; *(fig: of events, opinion etc)* Trend *m*; **high ~** Flut *f*; **low ~** Ebbe *f*; **the ~ is in/out** es ist Flut/Ebbe; **the ~ is coming in** die Flut kommt

▸ **tide over** *vt* über die Runden helfen *+dat*

tidily ['taɪdɪlɪ] *adv* ordentlich

tidiness ['taɪdɪnɪs] *n* Ordentlichkeit *f*

tidy ['taɪdɪ] *adj (room, desk)* ordentlich, aufgeräumt; *(person)* ordnungsliebend; *(sum, income)* ordentlich ▷ *vt (also:* **tidy up***)* aufräumen

tie [taɪ] *n (Brit: also:* **necktie***)* Krawatte *f*; *(string etc)* Band *nt*; *(fig: link)* Verbindung *f*; *(Sport: match)* Spiel *nt*; *(in competition: draw)* Unentschieden *nt* ▷ *vt (parcel)* verschnüren; *(shoelaces)* zubinden; *(ribbon)* binden ▷ *vi (Sport etc)*: **to ~ with sb for first place** sich mit jdm den ersten Platz teilen; **"black ~"** „Abendanzug"; **"white ~"** „Frackzwang"; **family ~s** familiäre Bindungen; **to ~ sth in a bow** etw zu einer Schleife binden; **to ~ a knot in sth** einen Knoten in etw *acc* machen

▸ **tie down** *vt (fig: restrict)* binden; *(: to date, price etc)* festlegen

▸ **tie in** *vi*: **to ~ in with** zusammenpassen mit

▸ **tie on** *vt (Brit)* anbinden

▸ **tie up** *vt (parcel)* verschnüren; *(dog)* anbinden; *(boat)* festmachen; *(person)* fesseln; *(arrangements)* unter Dach und Fach bringen; **to be ~d up** *(busy)* zu tun haben, beschäftigt sein

tie-break ['taɪbreɪk], **tie-breaker** ['taɪbreɪkə^r] *n (Tennis)* Tiebreak *m*; *(in quiz)* Entscheidungsfrage *f*

tie-on ['taɪɔn] *(Brit) adj (label)* Anhänge-

tiepin ['taɪpɪn] *(Brit) n* Krawattennadel *f*

tier [tɪə^r] *n (of stadium etc)* Rang *m*; *(of cake)* Lage *f*

tie-tack ['taɪtæk] *(US) n* = **tiepin**

tiff [tɪf] *n* Krach *m*

tiger ['taɪgə^r] *n* Tiger *m*

tiger economy *n (Econ)* Tigerstaat *m*

tight [taɪt] *adj (screw, knot, grip)* fest; *(shoes, clothes, bend)* eng; *(security)* streng; *(budget, money)* knapp; *(schedule)* gedrängt; *(inf: drunk)* voll; *(: stingy)* knickerig ▷ *adv* fest; **to be packed ~** *(suitcase)* prallvoll sein; *(room)* gerammelt voll sein; **everybody hold ~!** alle festhalten!

tighten ['taɪtn] *vt (rope, strap)* straffen; *(screw, bolt)* anziehen; *(grip)* festigen; *(security)* verschärfen ▷ *vi (grip)* sich festigen; *(rope etc)* sich spannen

tightfisted [taɪt'fɪstɪd] *adj* knickerig *(inf)*

tight-lipped ['taɪt'lɪpt] *adj (fig: silence)* eisern; **to be ~ about sth** über etw *acc* schweigen

tightly ['taɪtlɪ] *adv* fest

tightrope ['taɪtrəup] *n* Seil *nt*; **to be on** *or* **walking a ~** *(fig)* einen Balanceakt vollführen

tightrope walker *n* Seiltänzer(in) *m(f)*

tights [taɪts] *(Brit) npl* Strumpfhose *f*

tigress ['taɪgrɪs] *n* Tigerin *f*

tilde ['tɪldə] *n* Tilde *f*

tile [taɪl] *n (on roof)* Ziegel *m*; *(on floor)* Fliese *f*; *(on wall)* Kachel *f* ▷ *vt (floor)* mit Fliesen auslegen; *(bathroom)* kacheln

tiled [taɪld] *adj (floor)* mit Fliesen ausgelegt; *(wall)* gekachelt

till [tɪl] *n (in shop etc)* Kasse *f* ▷ *vt (land)* bestellen ▷ *prep, conj* = **until**

tiller ['tɪlə^r] *n (Naut)* Ruderpinne *f*

tilt [tɪlt] *vt* neigen ▷ *vi* sich neigen ▷ *n (slope)* Neigung *f*; **to wear one's hat at a ~** den Hut schief aufhaben; **(at) full ~** mit Volldampf

timber ['tɪmbə^r] *n (material)* Holz *nt*; *(trees)* Nutzholz *nt*

time [taɪm] *n* Zeit *f*; *(occasion)* Gelegenheit *f*, Mal *nt*; *(Mus)* Takt *m* ▷ *vt (measure time of)* die Zeit messen bei; *(runner)* stoppen; *(fix moment for: visit etc)* den Zeitpunkt festlegen für; **a long ~** eine lange Zeit; **for the ~ being** vorläufig; **4 at a ~** 4 auf einmal; **from ~ to time** von Zeit zu Zeit; **~ after time, ~ and again** immer (und immer) wieder; **at ~s** manchmal, zuweilen; **in ~** *(soon enough)* rechtzeitig; *(eventually)* mit der Zeit; *(Mus)* im Takt; **in a week's ~** in einer Woche; **in no ~** im Handumdrehen; **any ~** jederzeit; **on ~** rechtzeitig; **to be 30 minutes behind/ahead of ~** 30 Minuten zurück/voraus sein; **by the ~ he arrived** als er ankam; **5 ~s 5** 5 mal 5; **what ~ is it?** wie spät ist es?; **to have a good ~** sich amüsieren; **we/they** *etc* **had a hard ~** wir/sie *etc* hatten es schwer; **~'s up!** die Zeit ist um!; **I've no ~ for it** *(fig)* dafür habe ich nichts übrig; **he'll do it in his own (good) ~** *(without being hurried)* er macht es, ohne sich hetzen zu lassen; **he'll do it in his own ~, he'll do it on his own ~** *(US: out of working hours)* er macht es in seiner Freizeit; **to be behind the ~s** rückständig sein; **to ~ sth well/badly** den richtigen/falschen Zeitpunkt für etw wählen; **the bomb was ~d to go off 5 minutes**

later die Bombe war so eingestellt, dass sie 5 Minuten später explodieren sollte
time-and-motion study ['taɪmənd'məuʃən-] *n* Arbeitsstudie *f*
time bomb *n (also fig)* Zeitbombe *f*
time card *n* Stechkarte *f*
time clock *n (in factory etc)* Stechuhr *f*
time-consuming ['taɪmkənsju:mɪŋ] *adj* zeitraubend
time difference *n* Zeitunterschied *m*
time frame *n* zeitlicher Rahmen *m*
time-honoured, (US) **time-honored** ['taɪmɔnəd] *adj* althergebracht
timekeeper ['taɪmki:pə^r] *n*: **she's a good ~** sie erfüllt ihr Zeitsoll
time-lag ['taɪmlæg] *n* Verzögerung *f*
timeless ['taɪmlɪs] *adj* zeitlos
time limit *n* zeitliche Grenze *f*
timely ['taɪmlɪ] *adj (arrival)* rechtzeitig; *(reminder)* zur rechten Zeit
time management *n* Zeitmanagement *nt*
time off *n*: **to take ~** sich *dat* freinehmen
timer ['taɪmə^r] *n (time switch)* Schaltuhr *f*; *(on cooker)* Zeitmesser *m*; *(on video)* Timer *m*
time-saving ['taɪmseɪvɪŋ] *adj* zeitsparend
timescale ['taɪmskeɪl] *(Brit) n* Zeitspanne *f*
time-share ['taɪmʃɛə^r] *n* Ferienwohnung *f* auf Timesharingbasis
time-sharing ['taɪmʃɛərɪŋ] *n (of property, Comput)* Timesharing *nt*
time sheet *n* = **time card**
time signal *n (Radio)* Zeitzeichen *nt*
time switch *n* Zeitschalter *m*
timetable ['taɪmteɪbl] *n (Rail etc)* Fahrplan *m*; *(Scol)* Stundenplan *m*; *(programme of events)* Programm *nt*
time zone *n* Zeitzone *f*
timid ['tɪmɪd] *adj (person)* schüchtern; *(animal)* scheu
timidity [tɪ'mɪdɪtɪ] *n (shyness)* Schüchternheit *f*
timing ['taɪmɪŋ] *n (Sport)* Timing *nt*; **the ~ of his resignation** der Zeitpunkt seines Rücktritts
timing device *n (on bomb)* Zeitzünder *m*
timpani ['tɪmpənɪ] *npl* Kesselpauken *pl*
tin [tɪn] *n (metal)* Blech *nt*; *(container)* Dose *f*; *(: for baking)* Form *f*; *(: Brit: can)* Büchse *f*, Dose *f*; **two ~s of paint** zwei Dosen Farbe
tinfoil ['tɪnfɔɪl] *n* Alufolie *f*
tinge [tɪndʒ] *n (of colour)* Färbung *f*; *(fig: of emotion etc)* Anflug *m*, Anstrich *m* ▷ *vt*: **~d with blue/red** leicht blau/rot gefärbt; **to be ~d with sth** *(fig: emotion etc)* einen Anstrich von etw haben
tingle ['tɪŋgl] *vi* prickeln; *(from cold)* kribbeln; **I was tingling with excitement** ich zitterte vor Aufregung
tinker ['tɪŋkə^r] *n (gipsy)* Kesselflicker *m*
▸ **tinker with** *vt fus* herumbasteln an *+dat*
tinkle ['tɪŋkl] *vi* klingeln ▷ *n (inf)*: **to give sb a ~** *(Tel)* bei jdm anklingeln
tin mine *n* Zinnbergwerk *nt*
tinned [tɪnd] *(Brit) adj (food, peas)* Dosen-, in Dosen
tinnitus ['tɪnɪtəs] *n* Tinnitus *m*, Ohrensummen *nt*
tinny ['tɪnɪ] *(pej) adj (sound)* blechern; *(car etc)* Schrott-
tin-opener ['tɪnəupnə^r] *(Brit) n* Dosenöffner *m*
tinsel ['tɪnsl] *n* Rauschgoldgirlanden *pl*
tint [tɪnt] *n (colour)* Ton *m*; *(for hair)* Tönung *f* ▷ *vt (hair)* tönen
tinted ['tɪntɪd] *adj* getönt
tiny ['taɪnɪ] *adj* winzig
tip [tɪp] *n (end)* Spitze *f*; *(gratuity)* Trinkgeld *nt*; *(Brit: for rubbish)* Müllkippe *f*; *(: for coal)* Halde *f*; *(advice)* Tipp *m*, Hinweis *m* ▷ *vt (waiter)* ein Trinkgeld geben *+dat*; *(tilt)* kippen; *(also:* **tip over**: *overturn)* umkippen; *(also:* **tip out**: *empty)* leeren; *(predict: winner etc)* tippen *or* setzen auf *+acc*; **he ~ped out the contents of the box** er kippte den Inhalt der Kiste aus
▸ **tip off** *vt* einen Tipp *or* Hinweis geben *+dat*
tip-off ['tɪpɔf] *n* Hinweis *m*
tipped ['tɪpt] *adj (Brit: cigarette)* Filter-; **steel-~** mit Stahlspitze
Tipp-Ex® ['tɪpɛks] *n* Tipp-Ex® *nt*
tipple ['tɪpl] *(Brit) vi* picheln ▷ *n*: **to have a ~** einen trinken
tipster ['tɪpstə^r] *n jd, der bei Pferderennen, Börsengeschäften etc Tipps gegen Bezahlung weitergibt*
tipsy ['tɪpsɪ] *(inf) adj* beschwipst
tiptoe ['tɪptəu] *n*: **on ~** auf Zehenspitzen
tip-top ['tɪp'tɔp] *adj*: **in ~ condition** tipptopp
tirade [taɪ'reɪd] *n* Tirade *f*
tire ['taɪə^r] *n (US)* = **tyre** ▷ *vt* müde machen, ermüden ▷ *vi (become tired)* müde werden; **to ~ of sth** genug von etw haben
▸ **tire out** *vt* erschöpfen
tired ['taɪəd] *adj* müde; **to be/look ~** müde sein/aussehen; **to feel ~** sich müde fühlen; **to be ~ of sth** etw satthaben; **to be ~ of doing sth** es satthaben, etw zu tun
tiredness ['taɪədnɪs] *n* Müdigkeit *f*
tireless ['taɪəlɪs] *adj* unermüdlich
tiresome ['taɪəsəm] *adj* lästig
tiring ['taɪərɪŋ] *adj* ermüdend, anstrengend
tissue ['tɪʃu:] *n (Anat, Biol)* Gewebe *nt*; *(paper handkerchief)* Papiertaschentuch *nt*
tissue paper *n* Seidenpapier *nt*
tit [tɪt] *n (bird)* Meise *f*; *(inf: breast)* Titte *f*; **~ for tat** wie du mir, so ich dir
titanium [tɪ'teɪnɪəm] *n* Titan *nt*
titbit, (US) **tidbit** ['tɪtbɪt] *n (food, news)* Leckerbissen *m*
titillate ['tɪtɪleɪt] *vt* erregen, reizen
titivate ['tɪtɪveɪt] *vt* fein machen
title ['taɪtl] *n* Titel *m*; *(Law)*: **~ to** Anspruch auf *+acc*
title deed *n* Eigentumsurkunde *f*
title page *n* Titelseite *f*
title role *n* Titelrolle *f*
title track *n* Titelstück *nt*
titter ['tɪtə^r] *vi* kichern
tittle-tattle ['tɪtltætl] *(inf) n* Klatsch *m*, Gerede *nt*

tizzy ['tɪzɪ] *n*: **to be in a ~** aufgeregt sein; **to get in a ~** sich aufregen
T-junction ['ti:'dʒʌŋkʃən] *n* T-Kreuzung *f*
TM *abbr (= trademark)* Wz = **transcendental meditation**
TN *(US) abbr (Post) = Tennessee*
TNT *n abbr (= trinitrotoluene)* TNT *nt*

KEYWORD

to [tu:] *prep* **1** *(direction)* nach *+dat*, zu *+dat*; **to go to France/London/school/the station** nach Frankreich/nach London/zur Schule/zum Bahnhof gehen; **to the left/right** nach links/rechts; **I have never been to Germany** ich war noch nie in Deutschland
2 *(as far as)* bis; **to count to 10** bis 10 zählen
3 *(with expressions of time)* vor *+dat*; **a quarter to 5** *(Brit)* Viertel vor 5
4 *(for, of)*: **the key to the front door** der Schlüssel für die Haustür; **a letter to his wife** ein Brief an seine Frau
5 *(expressing indirect object)*: **to give sth to sb** jdm etw geben; **to talk to sb** mit jdm sprechen; **I sold it to a friend** ich habe es an einen Freund verkauft; **you've done something to your hair** du hast etwas mit deinem Haar gemacht
6 *(in relation to)* zu; **A is to B as C is to D** A verhält sich zu B wie C zu D; **3 goals to 2** 3 zu 2 Tore; **40 miles to the gallon** 40 Meilen pro Gallone
7 *(purpose, result)* zu; **to sentence sb to death** jdn zum Tode verurteilen; **to my surprise** zu meiner Überraschung
▷ *with vb* **1** *(simple infinitive)*: **to go** gehen; **to eat** essen
2 *(following another vb)*: **to want to do sth** etw tun wollen; **to try/start to do sth** versuchen/anfangen, etw zu tun
3 *(with vb omitted)*: **I don't want to** ich will nicht; **you ought to** du solltest es tun
4 *(purpose, result)* (um ...) zu; **I did it to help you** ich habe es getan, um dir zu helfen
5 *(equivalent to relative clause)* zu; **he has a lot to lose** er hat viel zu verlieren; **the main thing is to try** die Hauptsache ist, es zu versuchen
6 *(after adjective etc)*: **ready to use** gebrauchsfertig; **too old/young to ...** zu alt/jung, um zu ...; **it's too heavy to lift** es ist zu schwer zu heben
▷ *adv*: **to push/pull the door to** die Tür zudrücken/zuziehen; **to and fro** hin und her

toad [təud] *n* Kröte *f*
toadstool ['təudstu:l] *n* Giftpilz *m*
toady ['təudɪ] *(pej) vi*: **to ~ to sb** vor jdm kriechen
toast [təust] *n (bread, drink)* Toast *m* ▷ *vt (bread etc)* toasten; *(drink to)* einen Toast *or* Trinkspruch ausbringen auf *+acc*; **a piece** *or* **slice of ~** eine Scheibe Toast
toaster ['təustəʳ] *n* Toaster *m*
toastmaster ['təustmɑ:stəʳ] *n* Zeremonienmeister *m*
toast rack *n* Toastständer *m*
tobacco [tə'bækəu] *n* Tabak *m*; **pipe ~** Pfeifentabak *m*
tobacconist [tə'bækənɪst] *n* Tabakhändler(in) *m(f)*
tobacconist's [tə'bækənɪsts], **tobacconist's shop** *n* Tabakwarenladen *m*
Tobago [tə'beɪgəu] *n see* **Trinidad**
toboggan [tə'bɔgən] *n* Schlitten *m*
today [tə'deɪ] *adv, n* heute; **what day is it ~?** welcher Tag ist heute?; **what date is it ~?** der Wievielte ist heute?; **~ is the 4th of March** heute ist der 4. März; **a week ago ~** heute vor einer Woche; **~'s paper** die Zeitung von heute
toddle ['tɔdl] *(inf) vi*: **to ~ in/off/along** herein-/davon-/entlangwatscheln
toddler ['tɔdləʳ] *n* Kleinkind *nt*
to-do [tə'du:] *n* Aufregung *f*, Theater *nt*
toe [təu] *n* Zehe *f*, Zeh *m*; *(of shoe, sock)* Spitze *f*; **to ~ the line** *(fig)* auf Linie bleiben; **big/little ~** großer/kleiner Zeh
toehold ['təuhəuld] *n (in climbing)* Halt *m* für die Fußspitzen; *(fig)*: **to get/gain a ~ (in)** einen Einstieg bekommen/sich *dat* einen Einstieg verschaffen (in *+dat*)
toenail ['təuneɪl] *n* Zehennagel *m*
toffee ['tɔfɪ] *n* Toffee *m*
toffee apple *(Brit) n* ≈ kandierter Apfel *m*
tofu ['təufu:] *n* Tofu *m*
toga ['təugə] *n* Toga *f*
together [tə'gɛðəʳ] *adv* zusammen; *(at the same time)* gleichzeitig; **~ with** gemeinsam mit
togetherness [tə'gɛðənɪs] *n* Beisammensein *nt*
toggle switch ['tɔgl-] *n (Comput)* Toggle-Schalter *m*
Togo ['təugəu] *n* Togo *nt*
togs [tɔgz] *(inf) npl* Klamotten *pl*
toil [tɔɪl] *n* Mühe *f* ▷ *vi* sich abmühen
toilet ['tɔɪlət] *n* Toilette *f* ▷ *cpd (kit, accessories etc)* Toiletten-; **to go to the ~** auf die Toilette gehen
toilet bag *(Brit) n* Kulturbeutel *m*
toilet bowl *n* Toilettenbecken *nt*
toilet paper *n* Toilettenpapier *nt*
toiletries ['tɔɪlətrɪz] *npl* Toilettenartikel *pl*
toilet roll *n* Rolle *f* Toilettenpapier
toilet soap *n* Toilettenseife *f*
toilet water *n* Toilettenwasser *nt*
to-ing and fro-ing ['tu:ɪŋən'frəuɪŋ] *(Brit) n* Hin und Her *nt*
token ['təukən] *n (sign, souvenir)* Zeichen *nt*; *(substitute coin)* Wertmarke *f* ▷ *adj (strike, payment etc)* symbolisch; **by the same ~** *(fig)* in gleicher Weise; **book/record/gift ~** *(Brit)* Bücher-/Platten-/Geschenkgutschein *m*
tokenism ['təukənɪzəm] *n*: **to be (pure) ~** (nur) eine Alibifunktion haben
Tokyo ['təukjəu] *n* Tokio *nt*
told [təuld] *pt, pp of* **tell**
tolerable ['tɔlərəbl] *adj (bearable)* erträglich;

(*fairly good*) passabel

tolerably ['tɔlərəblı] *adv*: **~ good** ganz annehmbar *or* passabel

tolerance ['tɔlərns] *n* Toleranz *f*

tolerant ['tɔlərnt] *adj* tolerant; **to be ~ of sth** tolerant gegenüber etw sein

tolerate ['tɔləreıt] *vt* (*pain, noise*) erdulden, ertragen; (*injustice*) tolerieren

toleration [tɔlə'reıʃən] *n* (*of person, pain etc*) Duldung *f*; (*Rel, Pol*) Toleranz *f*

toll [təul] *n* (*of casualties, deaths*) (Gesamt)zahl *f*; (*tax, charge*) Gebühr *f* ▷ *vi* (*bell*) läuten; **the work took its ~ on us** die Arbeit blieb nicht ohne Auswirkungen auf uns

tollbridge ['təulbrıdʒ] *n* gebührenpflichtige Brücke *f*, Mautbrücke *f*

toll call (*US*) *n* Ferngespräch *nt*

toll-free ['təulfri:] (*US*) *adj* gebührenfrei

toll road *n* gebührenpflichtige Straße *f*, Mautstraße *f*

tomato [tə'mɑ:təu] (*pl* **~es**) *n* Tomate *f*

tomato purée *n* Tomatenmark *nt*

tomb [tu:m] *n* Grab *nt*

tombola [tɔm'bəulə] *n* Tombola *f*

tomboy ['tɔmbɔı] *n* Wildfang *m*

tombstone ['tu:mstəun] *n* Grabstein *m*

tomcat ['tɔmkæt] *n* Kater *m*

tome [təum] (*form*) *n* Band *m*

tomorrow [tə'mɔrəu] *adv* morgen ▷ *n* morgen; (*future*) Zukunft *f*; **the day after ~** übermorgen; **a week ~** morgen in einer Woche; **~ morning** morgen früh

ton [tʌn] *n* (*Brit*) (britische) Tonne *f*; (*US*: *also*: **short ton**) (US-)Tonne *f* (*ca. 907 kg*); (*also*: **metric ton**) (metrische) Tonne *f*; **~s of** (*inf*) Unmengen von

tonal ['təunl] *adj* (*Mus*) klanglich, tonal

tone [təun] *n* Ton *m* ▷ *vi* (*also*: **tone in**: *colours*) (farblich) passen

▸ **tone down** *vt* (*also fig*) abschwächen

▸ **tone up** *vt* (*muscles*) kräftigen

tone-deaf [təun'dɛf] *adj* ohne Gefühl für Tonhöhen

toner ['təunə^r] *n* (*for photocopier*) Toner *m*

Tonga [tɔŋə] *n* Tonga *nt*

tongs [tɔŋz] *npl* Zange *f*; (*also*: **curling tongs**) Lockenstab *m*

tongue [tʌŋ] *n* Zunge *f*; (*form*: *language*) Sprache *f*; **~-in-cheek** (*speak, say*) ironisch

tongue-tied ['tʌŋtaıd] *adj* (*fig*) sprachlos

tongue-twister ['tʌŋtwıstə^r] *n* Zungenbrecher *m*

tonic ['tɔnık] *n* (*Med*) Tonikum *nt*; (*fig*) Wohltat *f*; (*also*: **tonic water**) Tonic *nt*; (*Mus*) Tonika *f*, Grundton *m*

tonight [tə'naıt] *adv* (*this evening*) heute Abend; (*this night*) heute Nacht ▷ *n* (*this evening*) der heutige Abend; (*this night*) die kommende Nacht; **(I'll) see you ~!** bis heute Abend!

tonnage ['tʌnıdʒ] *n* Tonnage *f*

tonne [tʌn] (*Brit*) *n* (*metric ton*) Tonne *f*

tonsil ['tɔnsl] *n* Mandel *f*; **to have one's ~s out** sich *dat* die Mandeln herausnehmen lassen

tonsillitis [tɔnsı'laıtıs] *n* Mandelentzündung *f*

too [tu:] *adv* (*excessively*) zu; (*also*) auch; **it's ~ sweet** es ist zu süß; **I went ~** ich bin auch mitgegangen; **~ much** (*adj*) zu viel; (*adv*) zu sehr; **~ many** zu viele; **~ bad!** das ist eben Pech!

took [tuk] *pt of* **take**

tool [tu:l] *n* (*also fig*) Werkzeug *nt*

tool box *n* Werkzeugkasten *m*

tool kit *n* Werkzeugsatz *m*

toot [tu:t] *n* (*of horn*) Hupton *m*; (*of whistle*) Pfeifton *m* ▷ *vi* (*with car-horn*) hupen

tooth [tu:θ] (*pl* **teeth**) *n* (*also Tech*) Zahn *m*; **to have a ~ out, to have a ~ pulled** (*US*) sich *dat* einen Zahn ziehen lassen; **to brush one's teeth** sich *dat* die Zähne putzen; **by the skin of one's teeth** (*fig*) mit knapper Not

toothache ['tu:θeık] *n* Zahnschmerzen *pl*; **to have ~** Zahnschmerzen haben

toothbrush ['tu:θbrʌʃ] *n* Zahnbürste *f*

toothpaste ['tu:θpeıst] *n* Zahnpasta *f*

toothpick ['tu:θpık] *n* Zahnstocher *m*

tooth powder *n* Zahnpulver *nt*

top [tɔp] *n* (*of mountain, tree, ladder*) Spitze *f*; (*of cupboard, table, box*) Oberseite *f*; (*of street*) Ende *nt*; (*lid*) Verschluss *m*; (*Aut*: *also*: **top gear**) höchster Gang *m*; (*also*: **spinning top**: *toy*) Kreisel *m*; (*blouse etc*) Oberteil *nt*; (*of pyjamas*) Jacke *f* ▷ *adj* höchste(r, s); (*highest in rank*) oberste(r, s); (*: golfer etc*) Top- ▷ *vt* (*poll, vote, list*) anführen; (*estimate etc*) übersteigen; **at the ~ of the stairs/page** oben auf der Treppe/Seite; **at the ~ of the street** am Ende der Straße; **on ~ of** (*above*) auf +*dat*; (*in addition to*) zusätzlich zu; **from ~ to bottom** von oben bis unten; **from ~ to toe** (*Brit*) von Kopf bis Fuß; **at the ~ of the list** oben auf der Liste; **at the ~ of his voice** so laut er konnte; **over the ~** (*inf*: *behaviour etc*) übertrieben; **to go over the ~** (*inf*) übertreiben; **at ~ speed** bei Höchstgeschwindigkeit

▸ **top up,** (*US*) **top off** *vt* (*drink*) nachfüllen; (*salary*) aufbessern

topaz ['təupæz] *n* Topas *m*

top-class ['tɔp'klɑ:s] *adj* erstklassig; (*hotel, player etc*) Spitzen-

topcoat ['tɔpkəut] *n* (*overcoat*) Mantel *m*; (*of paint*) Deckanstrich *m*

top floor *n* oberster Stock *m*

top hat *n* Zylinder *m*

top-heavy [tɔp'hɛvı] *adj* (*also fig*) kopflastig

topic ['tɔpık] *n* Thema *nt*

topical ['tɔpıkl] *adj* (*issue etc*) aktuell

topless ['tɔplıs] *adj* (*waitress*) Oben-ohne-; (*bather*) barbusig ▷ *adv* oben ohne

top-level ['tɔplɛvl] *adj* auf höchster Ebene

topmost ['tɔpməust] *adj* oberste(r, s)

top-notch ['tɔp'nɔtʃ] *adj* erstklassig

topography [tə'pɔgrəfı] *n* Topografie *f*

topping ['tɔpıŋ] *n* (*Culin*) Überzug *m*

topple ['tɔpl] *vt* (*government etc*) stürzen ▷ *vi* (*person*) stürzen; (*object*) fallen

top-ranking ['tɔpræŋkıŋ] *adj* (*official*)

hochgestellt
top-secret ['tɔp'si:krɪt] *adj* streng geheim
top-security ['tɔpsə'kjuərɪtɪ] *(Brit) adj (prison, wing)* Hochsicherheits-
topsy-turvy ['tɔpsɪ'tə:vɪ] *adj* auf den Kopf gestellt ▷ *adv* durcheinander; *(fall, land)* verkehrt herum
top-up ['tɔpʌp] *n*: **would you like a ~?** darf ich Ihnen nachschenken?
top-up loan *n* Ergänzungsdarlehen *nt*
torch [tɔ:tʃ] *n* Fackel *f*; *(Brit: electric)* Taschenlampe *f*
tore [tɔ:ʳ] *pt of* **tear**
torment [*n* 'tɔ:mɛnt, *vt* tɔ:'mɛnt] *n* Qual *f* ▷ *vt* quälen; *(annoy)* ärgern
torn [tɔ:n] *pp of* **tear'** ▷ *adj*: **~ between** *(fig)* hin- und hergerissen zwischen
tornado [tɔ:'neɪdəu] *(pl* **~es**) *n (storm)* Tornado *m*
torpedo [tɔ:'pi:dəu] *(pl* **~es**) *n* Torpedo *m*
torpedo boat *n* Torpedoboot *nt*
torpor ['tɔ:pəʳ] *n* Trägheit *f*
torrent ['tɔrnt] *n (flood)* Strom *m*; *(fig)* Flut *f*
torrential [tɔ'rɛnʃl] *adj (rain)* wolkenbruchartig
torrid ['tɔrɪd] *adj (weather, love affair)* heiß
torso ['tɔ:səu] *n* Torso *m*
tortoise ['tɔ:təs] *n* Schildkröte *f*
tortoiseshell ['tɔ:təʃɛl] *adj (jewellery, ornaments)* aus Schildpatt; *(cat)* braungelbschwarz, braun-gelb-schwarz
tortuous ['tɔ:tjuəs] *adj (path)* gewunden; *(argument, mind)* umständlich
torture ['tɔ:tʃəʳ] *n* Folter *f*; *(fig)* Qual *f* ▷ *vt* foltern; *(fig: torment)* quälen; **it was ~** *(fig)* es war eine Qual
torturer ['tɔ:tʃərəʳ] *n* Folterer *m*
Tory ['tɔ:rɪ] *(Brit: Pol) adj* konservativ ▷ *n* Tory *m*, Konservative(r) *f(m)*
toss [tɔs] *vt (throw)* werfen; *(one's head)* zurückwerfen; *(salad)* anmachen; *(pancake)* wenden ▷ *n*: **with a ~ of her head** mit einer Kopfbewegung; **to ~ a coin** eine Münze werfen; **to win/lose the ~** die Entscheidung per Münzwurf gewinnen/verlieren; **to ~ up for sth** etw per Münzwurf entscheiden; **to ~ and turn** *(in bed)* sich hin und her wälzen
tot [tɔt] *n (Brit: drink)* Schluck *m*; *(child)* Knirps *m*
▸ **tot up** *(Brit) vt (figures)* zusammenzählen
total ['təutl] *adj (number etc)* gesamt; *(failure, wreck etc)* völlig, total ▷ *n* Gesamtzahl *f* ▷ *vt (add up)* zusammenzählen; *(add up to)* sich belaufen auf; **in ~** insgesamt
totalitarian [təutælɪ'tɛərɪən] *adj* totalitär
totality [təu'tælɪtɪ] *n* Gesamtheit *f*
totally ['təutəlɪ] *adv* völlig
totem pole ['təutəm-] *n* Totempfahl *m*
totter ['tɔtəʳ] *vi (person)* wanken, taumeln; *(fig: government)* im Wanken sein
touch [tʌtʃ] *n (sense of touch)* Gefühl *nt*; *(contact)* Berührung *f*; *(skill: of pianist etc)* Hand *f* ▷ *vt* berühren; *(tamper with)* anrühren; *(emotionally)* rühren ▷ *vi (make contact)* sich berühren; **the personal ~** die persönliche Note; **to put the finishing ~es to sth** letzte Hand an etw *acc* legen; **a ~ of** *(fig: frost etc)* etwas, ein Hauch von; **in ~ with** *(person, group)* in Verbindung mit; **to get in ~ with sb** mit jdm in Verbindung treten; **I'll be in ~** ich melde mich; **to lose ~** *(friends)* den Kontakt verlieren; **to be out of ~ with sb** keine Verbindung mehr zu jdm haben; **to be out of ~ with events** nicht auf dem Laufenden sein; **~ wood!** hoffen wir das Beste!
▸ **touch on** *vt fus (topic)* berühren
▸ **touch up** *vt (car etc)* ausbessern
touch-and-go ['tʌtʃən'gəu] *adj (situation)* auf der Kippe; **it was ~ whether we'd succeed** es war völlig offen, ob wir Erfolg haben würden
touchdown ['tʌtʃdaun] *n (of rocket, plane)* Landung *f*; *(US: Football)* Touchdown *m*
touched [tʌtʃt] *adj (moved)* gerührt; *(inf: mad)* plemplem
touching ['tʌtʃɪŋ] *adj* rührend
touchline ['tʌtʃlaɪn] *n (Sport)* Seitenlinie *f*
touch-sensitive ['tʌtʃ'sɛnsɪtɪv] *adj* berührungsempfindlich; *(switch)* Kontakt-
touch-type ['tʌtʃtaɪp] *vi* blindschreiben
touchy ['tʌtʃɪ] *adj (person, subject)* empfindlich
tough [tʌf] *adj (strong, firm, difficult)* hart; *(resistant)* widerstandsfähig; *(meat, animal, person)* zäh; *(rough)* rau; **~ luck!** Pech!
toughen ['tʌfn] *vt (sb's character)* hart machen; *(glass etc)* härten
toughness ['tʌfnɪs] *n* Härte *f*
toupee ['tu:peɪ] *n* Toupet *nt*
tour ['tuəʳ] *n (journey)* Reise *f*, Tour *f*; *(of factory, museum etc)* Rundgang *m*; *(: also:* **guided tour**) Führung *f*; *(by pop group etc)* Tournee *f* ▷ *vt (country, factory etc: on foot)* ziehen durch; *(: in car)* fahren durch; **to go on a ~ of a museum/castle** an einer Museums-/Schlossführung teilnehmen; **to go on a ~ of the Highlands** die Highlands bereisen; **to go/be on ~** *(pop group, theatre company etc)* auf Tournee gehen/sein
tour guide *n* Reiseleiter(in) *m(f)*
touring ['tuərɪŋ] *n* Umherreisen *nt*
tourism ['tuərɪzm] *n* Tourismus *m*
tourist ['tuərɪst] *n* Tourist(in) *m(f)* ▷ *cpd (attractions, season)* Touristen-; **the ~ trade** die Tourismusbranche
tourist class *n* Touristenklasse *f*
tourist information centre *(Brit) n* Touristen-Informationszentrum *nt*
tourist office *n* Verkehrsamt *nt*
tournament ['tuənəmənt] *n* Turnier *nt*
tourniquet ['tuənɪkeɪ] *n* Aderpresse *f*
tour operator *(Brit) n* Reiseveranstalter *m*
tousled ['tauzld] *adj (hair)* zerzaust
tout [taut] *vi*: **to ~ for business** die Reklametrommel schlagen; **to ~ for custom** auf Kundenfang gehen ▷ *n (also:* **ticket tout**) *Schwarzhändler, der Eintrittskarten zu überhöhten Preisen verkauft*
tow [təu] *vt (vehicle)* abschleppen; *(caravan, trailer)* ziehen ▷ *n*: **to give sb a ~** *(Aut)* jdn

abschleppen; **"on ~", "in ~"** (*US*) „Fahrzeug wird abgeschleppt"
▸ **tow away** *vt* (*vehicle*) abschleppen
toward [tə'wɔːd], **towards** [tə'wɔːdz] *prep* (*direction*) zu; (*attitude*) gegenüber *+dat*; (*purpose*) für; (*in time*) gegen; **~(s) noon/the end of the year** gegen Mittag/Ende des Jahres; **to feel friendly ~(s) sb** jdm freundlich gesinnt sein
towel ['tauəl] *n* Handtuch *nt*; **to throw in the ~** (*fig*) das Handtuch werfen
towelling ['tauəlɪŋ] *n* Frottee *nt or m*
towel rail, (*US*) **towel rack** *n* Handtuchstange *f*
tower ['tauə^r] *n* Turm *m* ▹ *vi* aufragen; **to ~ above** *or* **over sb/sth** über jdm/etw aufragen
tower block (*Brit*) *n* Hochhaus *nt*
towering ['tauərɪŋ] *adj* hoch aufragend
towline ['təulaɪn] *n* Abschleppseil *nt*
town [taun] *n* Stadt *f*; **to go (in)to ~** in die Stadt gehen; **to go to ~ on sth** (*fig*) sich bei etw ins Zeug legen; **in ~** in der Stadt; **to be out of ~** (*person*) nicht in der Stadt sein
town centre *n* Stadtzentrum *nt*
town clerk *n* Stadtdirektor(in) *m(f)*
town council *n* Stadtrat *m*
town crier [-'kraɪə^r] *n* Ausrufer *m*
town hall *n* Rathaus *nt*
town house *n* (städtisches) Wohnhaus *nt*; (*US: in a complex*) Reihenhaus *nt*
townie ['taunɪ] (*inf*) *n* (*town-dweller*) Städter(in) *m(f)*
town plan *n* Stadtplan *m*
town planner *n* Stadtplaner(in) *m(f)*
town planning *n* Stadtplanung *f*
township ['taunʃɪp] *n* Stadt(gemeinde) *f*; (*formerly: in South Africa*) Township *f*
townspeople ['taunzpiːpl] *npl* Stadtbewohner *pl*
towpath ['təupɑːθ] *n* Leinpfad *m*
towrope ['təurəup] *n* Abschleppseil *nt*
tow truck (*US*) *n* Abschleppwagen *m*
toxic ['tɔksɪk] *adj* giftig, toxisch
toxin ['tɔksɪn] *n* Gift *nt*, Giftstoff *m*
toy [tɔɪ] *n* Spielzeug *nt*
▸ **toy with** *vt fus* (*object, idea*) spielen mit
toyshop ['tɔɪʃɔp] *n* Spielzeugladen *m*
trace [treɪs] *n* (*sign, small amount*) Spur *f* ▹ *vt* (*draw*) nachzeichnen; (*follow*) verfolgen; (*locate*) aufspüren; **without ~** (*disappear*) spurlos; **there was no ~ of it** es war spurlos verschwunden
trace element *n* Spurenelement *nt*
tracer ['treɪsə^r] *n* (*Mil: also:* **tracer bullet**) Leuchtspurgeschoss *nt*; (*Med*) Indikator *m*
trachea [trə'kɪə] *n* Luftröhre *f*
tracing paper ['treɪsɪŋ-] *n* Pauspapier *nt*
track [træk] *n* Weg *m*; (*of comet, Sport*) Bahn *f*; (*of suspect, animal*) Spur *f*; (*Rail*) Gleis *nt*; (*on tape, record*) Stück *nt*, Track *m* ▹ *vt* (*follow*) verfolgen; **to keep ~ of sb/sth** (*fig*) jdn/etw im Auge behalten; **to be on the right ~** (*fig*) auf der richtigen Spur sein
▸ **track down** *vt* aufspüren
tracker dog ['trækə-] (*Brit*) *n* Spürhund *m*
track events *npl* Laufwettbewerbe *f*
tracking station ['trækɪŋ-] *n* Bodenstation *f*
track meet (*US*) *n* (*Sport*) Leichtathletikwettkampf *m*
track record *n*: **to have a good ~** (*fig*) gute Leistungen vorzuweisen haben
tracksuit ['træksuːt] *n* Trainingsanzug *m*
tract [trækt] *n* (*Geog*) Gebiet *nt*; (*pamphlet*) Traktat *m or nt*; **respiratory ~** Atemwege *pl*
traction ['trækʃən] *n* (*power*) Zugkraft *f*; (*Aut: grip*) Bodenhaftung *f*; (*Med*): **in ~** im Streckverband
traction engine *n* Zugmaschine *f*
tractor ['træktə^r] *n* Traktor *m*
trade [treɪd] *n* (*activity*) Handel *m*; (*skill, job*) Handwerk *nt* ▹ *vi* (*do business*) handeln ▹ *vt*: **to ~ sth (for sth)** etw (gegen etw) eintauschen; **foreign ~** Außenhandel *m*; **Department of T~ and Industry** (*Brit*) ≈ Wirtschaftsministerium *nt*; **to ~ with** Handel treiben mit; **to ~ in** (*merchandise*) handeln in *+dat*
▸ **trade in** *vt* in Zahlung geben
trade barrier *n* Handelsschranke *f*
trade deficit *n* Handelsdefizit *nt*
Trade Descriptions Act (*Brit*) *n Gesetz über korrekte Warenbeschreibungen*
trade discount *n* Händlerrabatt *m*
trade fair *n* Handelsmesse *f*
trade figures *npl* Handelsziffern *pl*
trade-in ['treɪdɪn] *n*: **to take sth as a ~** etw in Zahlung nehmen
trade-in value *n* Gebrauchtwert *m*
trademark ['treɪdmɑːk] *n* Warenzeichen *nt*
trade mission *n* Handelsmission *f*
trade name *n* Handelsname *m*
trade-off ['treɪdɔf] *n* Handel *m*; **there's bound to be a ~ between speed and quality** es gibt entweder Einbußen bei der Schnelligkeit oder bei der Qualität
trader ['treɪdə^r] *n* Händler(in) *m(f)*
trade secret *n* (*also fig*) Betriebsgeheimnis *nt*
tradesman ['treɪdzmən] (*irreg: like* **man**) *n* (*shopkeeper*) Händler *m*
trade union *n* Gewerkschaft *f*
trade unionist [-'juːnjənɪst] *n* Gewerkschaftler(in) *m(f)*
trade wind *n* Passat *m*
trading ['treɪdɪŋ] *n* Handel *m*
trading estate (*Brit*) *n* Industriegelände *nt*
trading stamp *n* Rabattmarke *f*
tradition [trə'dɪʃən] *n* Tradition *f*
traditional [trə'dɪʃənl] *adj* traditionell
traditionally [trə'dɪʃnəlɪ] *adv* traditionell
traffic ['træfɪk] *n* Verkehr *m*; (*in drugs etc*) Handel *m* ▹ *vi*: **to ~ in** handeln mit
traffic calming *n* Verkehrsberuhigung *f*
traffic circle (*US*) *n* Kreisverkehr *m*
traffic island *n* Verkehrsinsel *f*
traffic jam *n* Verkehrsstauung *f*, Stau *m*
trafficker ['træfɪkə^r] *n* Händler(in) *m(f)*
traffic lights *npl* Ampel *f*

traffic offence (*Brit*) *n* Verkehrsdelikt *nt*
traffic sign *n* Verkehrszeichen *nt*
traffic violation (*US*) *n* = **traffic offence**
traffic warden *n* *Verkehrspolizist für Parkvergehen*; (*woman*) ≈ Politesse *f*
tragedy ['trædʒədɪ] *n* Tragödie *f*
tragic ['trædʒɪk] *adj* tragisch
tragically ['trædʒɪkəlɪ] *adv* tragisch
trail [treɪl] *n* (*path*) Weg *m*; (*track*) Spur *f*; (*of smoke, dust*) Wolke *f* ▷ *vt* (*drag*) schleifen; (*follow*) folgen +*dat* ▷ *vi* (*hang loosely*) schleifen; (*in game, contest*) zurückliegen; **to be on sb's ~** jdm auf der Spur sein
▸ **trail away** *vi* (*sound, voice*) sich verlieren
▸ **trail behind** *vi* hinterhertrotten
▸ **trail off** *vi* = **trail away**
trailer ['treɪləʳ] *n* (*Aut*) Anhänger *m*; (*US: caravan*) Caravan *m*, Wohnwagen *m*; (*Cine, TV*) Trailer *m*
trailer truck (*US*) *n* Sattelschlepper *m*
train [treɪn] *n* (*Rail*) Zug *m*; (*of dress*) Schleppe *f* ▷ *vt* (*apprentice etc*) ausbilden; (*dog*) abrichten; (*athlete*) trainieren; (*mind*) schulen; (*plant*) ziehen; (*point: camera, gun etc*): **to ~ on** richten auf +*acc* ▷ *vi* (*learn a skill*) ausgebildet werden; (*Sport*) trainieren; **~ of thought** Gedankengang *m*; **to go by ~** mit dem Zug fahren; **~ of events** Ereignisfolge *f*; **to ~ sb to do sth** jdn dazu ausbilden, etw zu tun
train attendant (*US*) *n* Schlafwagenschaffner *m*
trained [treɪnd] *adj* (*worker*) gelernt; (*teacher*) ausgebildet; (*animal*) dressiert; (*eye*) geschult
trainee [treɪ'ni:] *n* Auszubildende(r) *f(m)*
trainer ['treɪnəʳ] *n* (*Sport: coach*) Trainer(in) *m(f)*; (*: shoe*) Trainingsschuh *m*; (*of animals*) Dresseur(in) *m(f)*
training ['treɪnɪŋ] *n* (*for occupation*) Ausbildung *f*; (*Sport*) Training *nt*; **in ~** (*Sport*) im Training
training college *n* (*for teachers*) ≈ pädagogische Hochschule *f*
training course *n* Ausbildungskurs *m*
traipse [treɪps] *vi*: **to ~ in/out** hinein-/herauslatschen
trait [treɪt] *n* Zug *m*, Eigenschaft *f*
traitor ['treɪtəʳ] *n* Verräter(in) *m(f)*
trajectory [trə'dʒɛktərɪ] *n* Flugbahn *f*
tram [træm] (*Brit*) *n* (*also*: **tramcar**) Straßenbahn *f*
tramline ['træmlaɪn] *n* Straßenbahnschiene *f*
tramp [træmp] *n* Landstreicher *m*; (*pej: woman*) Flittchen *nt* ▷ *vi* stapfen ▷ *vt* (*walk through: town, streets*) latschen durch
trample ['træmpl] *vt*: **to ~ (underfoot)** niedertrampeln ▷ *vi* (*also fig*): **to ~ on** herumtrampeln auf +*dat*
trampoline ['træmpəli:n] *n* Trampolin *nt*
trance [trɑ:ns] *n* Trance *f*; **to go into a ~** in Trance verfallen
tranquil ['træŋkwɪl] *adj* ruhig, friedlich
tranquillity, (*US*) **tranquility** [træŋ'kwɪlɪtɪ] *n* Ruhe *f*
tranquillizer, (*US*) **tranquilizer** ['træŋkwɪlaɪzəʳ] *n* Beruhigungsmittel *nt*
transact [træn'zækt] *vt* (*business*) abwickeln
transaction [træn'zækʃən] *n* Geschäft *nt*; **cash ~** Bargeldtransaktion *f*
transatlantic ['trænzət'læntɪk] *adj* transatlantisch; (*phone-call*) über den Atlantik
transcend [træn'sɛnd] *vt* überschreiten
transcendental [trænsɛn'dɛntl] *adj*: **~ meditation** transzendentale Meditation *f*
transcribe [træn'skraɪb] *vt* transkribieren
transcript ['trænskrɪpt] *n* Niederschrift *f*, Transkription *f*
transcription [træn'skrɪpʃən] *n* Transkription *f*
transept ['trænsɛpt] *n* Querschiff *nt*
transfer ['trænsfəʳ] *n* (*of employees*) Versetzung *f*; (*of money*) Überweisung *f*; (*of power*) Übertragung *f*; (*Sport*) Transfer *m*; (*picture, design*) Abziehbild *nt* ▷ *vt* (*employees*) versetzen; (*money*) überweisen; (*power, ownership*) übertragen; **by bank ~** per Banküberweisung; **to ~ the charges** (*Brit: Tel*) ein R-Gespräch führen
transferable [træns'fə:rəbl] *adj* übertragbar; **"not ~"** „nicht übertragbar"
transfix [træns'fɪks] *vt* aufspießen; **~ed with fear** (*fig*) starr vor Angst
transform [træns'fɔ:m] *vt* umwandeln
transformation [trænsfə'meɪʃən] *n* Umwandlung *f*
transformer [træns'fɔ:məʳ] *n* (*Elec*) Transformator *m*
transfusion [træns'fju:ʒən] *n* (*also*: **blood transfusion**) Bluttransfusion *f*
transgress [træns'grɛs] *vt* (*go beyond*) überschreiten; (*violate: rules, law*) verletzen
transient ['trænzɪənt] *adj* vorübergehend
transistor [træn'zɪstəʳ] *n* (*Elec*) Transistor *m*; (*also*: **transistor radio**) Transistorradio *nt*
transit ['trænzɪt] *n*: **in ~** unterwegs
transit camp *n* Durchgangslager *nt*
transition [træn'zɪʃən] *n* Übergang *m*
transitional [træn'zɪʃənl] *adj* (*period, stage*) Übergangs-
transitive ['trænzɪtɪv] *adj* (*verb*) transitiv
transit lounge *n* Transithalle *f*
transitory ['trænzɪtərɪ] *adj* (*emotion, arrangement etc*) vorübergehend
transit visa *n* Transitvisum *nt*
translate [trænz'leɪt] *vt* übersetzen; **to ~ (from/into)** übersetzen (aus/in +*acc*)
translation [trænz'leɪʃən] *n* Übersetzung *f*; **in ~** als Übersetzung
translator [trænz'leɪtəʳ] *n* Übersetzer(in) *m(f)*
translucent [trænz'lu:snt] *adj* (*object*) lichtdurchlässig
transmission [trænz'mɪʃən] *n* (*also TV*) Übertragung *f*; (*of information*) Übermittlung *f*; (*Aut*) Getriebe *nt*
transmission rate *n* (*Tel, Comput*) Übertragungsrate *f*
transmit [trænz'mɪt] *vt* (*also TV*) übertragen; (*message, signal*) übermitteln

transmitter [trænz'mɪtəʳ] *n* (*TV, Radio*) Sender *m*
transparency [træns'pɛərnsɪ] *n* (*of glass etc*) Durchsichtigkeit *f*; (*Brit: Phot*) Dia *nt*
transparent [træns'pærnt] *adj* durchsichtig; (*fig: obvious*) offensichtlich
transpire [træns'paɪəʳ] *vi* (*turn out*) bekannt werden; (*happen*) passieren; **it finally ~d that ...** schließlich sickerte durch, dass ...
transplant [*vt* træns'plɑːnt, *n* 'trɑːnsplɑːnt] *vt* (*organ, seedlings*) verpflanzen ▷ *n* (*Med*) Transplantation *f*; **to have a heart ~** sich einer Herztransplantation unterziehen
transport ['trænspɔːt] *n* Transport *m*, Beförderung *f* ▷ *vt* transportieren; **do you have your own ~?** haben Sie ein Auto?; **public ~** öffentliche Verkehrsmittel *pl*; **Department of T~** (*Brit*) Verkehrsministerium *nt*
transportation ['trænspɔː'teɪʃən] *n* Transport *m*, Beförderung *f*; (*means of transport*) Beförderungsmittel *nt*; **Department of T~** (*US*) Verkehrsministerium *nt*
transport café (*Brit*) *n* Fernfahrerlokal *nt*
transpose [træns'pəuz] *vt* versetzen
transsexual [trænz'sɛksuəl] *adj* transsexuell ▷ *n* Transsexuelle(r) *f(m)*
transverse ['trænzvəːs] *adj* (*beam etc*) Quer-
transvestite [trænz'vɛstaɪt] *n* Transvestit *m*
trap [træp] *n* (*also fig*) Falle *f*; (*carriage*) zweirädriger Pferdewagen *m* ▷ *vt* (*animal*) (mit einer Falle) fangen; (*person: trick*) in die Falle locken; (*: confine*) gefangen halten; (*immobilize*) festsetzen; (*capture: energy*) stauen; **to set** *or* **lay a ~ (for sb)** (jdm) eine Falle stellen; **to shut one's ~** (*inf*) die Klappe halten; **to ~ one's finger in the door** sich *dat* den Finger in der Tür einklemmen
trap door *n* Falltür *f*
trapeze [trə'piːz] *n* Trapez *nt*
trapper ['træpəʳ] *n* Fallensteller *m*, Trapper *m*
trappings ['træpɪŋz] *npl* äußere Zeichen *pl*; (*of power*) Insignien *pl*
trash [træʃ] *n* (*rubbish*) Abfall *m*, Müll *m*; (*pej: nonsense*) Schund *m*, Mist *m*
trash can (*US*) *n* Mülleimer *m*
trashy ['træʃɪ] *adj* (*goods*) minderwertig, wertlos; (*novel etc*) Schund-
trauma ['trɔːmə] *n* Trauma *nt*
traumatic [trɔː'mætɪk] *adj* traumatisch
traumatize ['trɔːmətaɪz] *vt* traumatisieren
travel ['trævl] *n* (*travelling*) Reisen *nt* ▷ *vi* reisen; (*short distance*) fahren; (*move: car, aeroplane*) sich bewegen; (*sound etc*) sich fortpflanzen; (*news*) sich verbreiten ▷ *vt* (*distance*) zurücklegen; **travels** *npl* (*journeys*) Reisen *pl*; **this wine doesn't ~ well** dieser Wein verträgt den Transport nicht
travel agency *n* Reisebüro *nt*
travel agent *n* Reisebürokaufmann *m*, Reisebürokauffrau *f*
travel brochure *n* Reiseprospekt *m*
traveling *etc* (*US*) = **travelling** *etc*
traveller, (*US*) **traveler** ['trævləʳ] *n* Reisende(r) *f(m)*; (*Comm*) Vertreter(in) *m(f)*
traveller's cheque, (*US*) **traveler's check** *n* Reisescheck *m*
travelling, (*US*) **traveling** ['trævlɪŋ] *n* Reisen *nt* ▷ *cpd* (*circus, exhibition*) Wander-; (*bag, clock*) Reise-; **~ expenses** Reisespesen *pl*
travelling salesman *n* Vertreter *m*
travelogue ['trævəlɔg] *n* Reisebericht *m*
travel sickness *n* Reisekrankheit *f*
traverse ['trævəs] *vt* durchqueren
travesty ['trævəstɪ] *n* Travestie *f*
trawler ['trɔːləʳ] *n* Fischdampfer *m*
tray [treɪ] *n* (*for carrying*) Tablett *nt*; (*also:* **in-tray/out-tray**: *on desk*) Ablage *f* für Eingänge/Ausgänge
treacherous ['trɛtʃərəs] *adj* (*person, look*) verräterisch; (*ground, tide*) tückisch; **road conditions are ~** die Straßen sind in gefährlichem Zustand
treachery ['trɛtʃərɪ] *n* Verrat *m*
treacle ['triːkl] *n* Sirup *m*
tread [trɛd] (*pt* **trod**, *pp* **trodden**) *n* (*of tyre*) Profil *nt*; (*footstep*) Schritt *m*; (*of stair*) Stufe *f* ▷ *vi* gehen
▸ **tread on** *vt fus* treten auf *+acc*
treadle ['trɛdl] *n* Pedal *nt*
treas. *abbr* = **treasurer**
treason ['triːzn] *n* Verrat *m*
treasure ['trɛʒəʳ] *n* (*also fig*) Schatz *m* ▷ *vt* schätzen; **treasures** *npl* (*art treasures etc*) Schätze *pl*, Kostbarkeiten *pl*
treasure hunt *n* Schatzsuche *f*
treasurer ['trɛʒərəʳ] *n* Schatzmeister(in) *m(f)*
treasury ['trɛʒərɪ] *n*: **the T~, the T~ Department** (*US*) das Finanzministerium
treasury bill *n* kurzfristiger Schatzwechsel *m*
treat [triːt] *n* (*present*) (besonderes) Vergnügen *nt* ▷ *vt* (*also Med, Tech*) behandeln; **it came as a ~** es war eine besondere Freude; **to ~ sth as a joke** etw als Witz ansehen; **to ~ sb to sth** jdm etw spendieren
treatment ['triːtmənt] *n* Behandlung *f*; **to have ~ for sth** wegen etw in Behandlung sein
treaty ['triːtɪ] *n* Vertrag *m*
treble ['trɛbl] *adj* (*triple*) dreifach; (*Mus: voice, part*) (Knaben)sopran-; (*instrument*) Diskant- ▷ *n* (*singer*) (Knaben)sopran *m*; (*on hi-fi, radio etc*) Höhen *pl* ▷ *vt* verdreifachen ▷ *vi* sich verdreifachen; **to be ~ the amount/size of sth** dreimal so viel/so groß wie etw sein
treble clef *n* Violinschlüssel *m*
tree [triː] *n* Baum *m*
tree-lined ['triːlaɪnd] *adj* baumbestanden
treetop ['triːtɔp] *n* Baumkrone *f*
tree trunk *n* Baumstamm *m*
trek [trɛk] *n* Treck *m*; (*tiring walk*) Marsch *m* ▷ *vi* trecken
trellis ['trɛlɪs] *n* Gitter *nt*
tremble ['trɛmbl] *vi* (*voice, body, trees*) zittern; (*ground*) beben
trembling ['trɛmblɪŋ] *n* (*of ground*) Beben *nt*, Erschütterung *f*; (*of trees*) Zittern *nt* ▷ *adj* (*hand, voice etc*) zitternd

tremendous [trɪˈmɛndəs] *adj* (*amount, success etc*) gewaltig, enorm; (*holiday, view etc*) fantastisch
tremendously [trɪˈmɛndəslɪ] *adv* (*difficult, exciting*) ungeheuer; **he enjoyed it ~** es hat ihm ausgezeichnet gefallen
tremor [ˈtrɛməʳ] *n* Zittern *nt*; (*also*: **earth tremor**) Beben *nt*, Erschütterung *f*
trench [trɛntʃ] *n* Graben *m*
trench coat *n* Trenchcoat *m*
trench warfare *n* Stellungskrieg *m*
trend [trɛnd] *n* Tendenz *f*; (*fashion*) Trend *m*; **a ~ towards/away from sth** eine Tendenz zu/weg von etw; **to set a/the ~** richtungsweisend sein
trendy [ˈtrɛndɪ] *adj* modisch
trepidation [trɛpɪˈdeɪʃən] *n* (*apprehension*) Beklommenheit *f*; **in ~** beklommen
trespass [ˈtrɛspəs] *vi*: **to ~ on** (*private property*) unbefugt betreten; **"no ~ing"** „Betreten verboten"
trespasser [ˈtrɛspəsəʳ] *n* Unbefugte(r) *f(m)*; **"~s will be prosecuted"** „widerrechtliches Betreten wird strafrechtlich verfolgt"
tress [trɛs] *n* (*of hair*) Locke *f*
trestle [ˈtrɛsl] *n* Bock *m*
trestle table *n* Klapptisch *m*
trial [ˈtraɪəl] *n* (*Law*) Prozess *m*; (*test: of machine, drug etc*) Versuch *m*; (*worry*) Plage *f*; **trials** *npl* (*unpleasant experiences*) Schwierigkeiten *pl*; **~ by jury** Schwurgerichtsverfahren *nt*; **to be sent for ~** vor Gericht gestellt werden; **to be/go on ~** (*Law*) angeklagt sein/werden; **by ~ and error** durch Ausprobieren
trial balance *n* Probebilanz *f*
trial basis *n*: **on a ~** probeweise
trial period *n* Probezeit *f*
trial run *n* Versuch *m*
triangle [ˈtraɪæŋgl] *n* Dreieck *nt*; (*US: set square*) (Zeichen)dreieck *nt*; (*Mus*) Triangel *f*
triangular [traɪˈæŋgjuləʳ] *adj* dreieckig
triathlon [traɪˈæθlən] *n* Triathlon *nt*
tribal [ˈtraɪbl] *adj* (*warrior, warfare, dance*) Stammes-
tribe [traɪb] *n* Stamm *m*
tribesman [ˈtraɪbzmən] (*irreg: like* **man**) *n* Stammesangehörige(r) *m*
tribulations [trɪbjuˈleɪʃənz] *npl* Kümmernisse *pl*
tribunal [traɪˈbjuːnl] *n* Gericht *nt*
tributary [ˈtrɪbjutərɪ] *n* (*of river*) Nebenfluss *m*
tribute [ˈtrɪbjuːt] *n* Tribut *m*; **to pay ~ to** Tribut zollen *+dat*
trice [traɪs] *n*: **in a ~** im Handumdrehen
trick [trɪk] *n* Trick *m*; (*Cards*) Stich *m* ▷ *vt* hereinlegen; **to play a ~ on sb** jdm einen Streich spielen; **it's a ~ of the light** das Licht täuscht; **that should do the ~** das müsste hinhauen; **to ~ sb into doing sth** jdn (mit einem Trick) dazu bringen, etw zu tun; **to ~ sb out of sth** jdn um etw prellen
trickery [ˈtrɪkərɪ] *n* Tricks *pl*, Betrügerei *f*
trickle [ˈtrɪkl] *n* (*of water etc*) Rinnsal *nt* ▷ *vi* (*water, rain etc*) rinnen; (*people*) sich langsam bewegen
trick photography *n* Trickfotografie *f*
trick question *n* Fangfrage *f*
trickster [ˈtrɪkstəʳ] *n* Betrüger(in) *m(f)*
tricky [ˈtrɪkɪ] *adj* (*job, problem*) schwierig
tricycle [ˈtraɪsɪkl] *n* Dreirad *nt*
trifle [ˈtraɪfl] *n* (*detail*) Kleinigkeit *f*; (*Culin*) Trifle *nt* ▷ *adv*: **a ~ long** ein bisschen lang ▷ *vi*: **to ~ with sb/sth** jdn/etw nicht ernst nehmen; **he is not (someone) to be ~d with** mit ihm ist nicht zu spaßen
trifling [ˈtraɪflɪŋ] *adj* (*detail*) unbedeutend
trigger [ˈtrɪgəʳ] *n* Abzug *m*
▸ **trigger off** *vt fus* auslösen
trigonometry [trɪgəˈnɔmətrɪ] *n* Trigonometrie *f*
trilby [ˈtrɪlbɪ] (*Brit*) *n* (*also*: **trilby hat**) Filzhut *m*
trill [trɪl] *n* (*Mus*) Triller *m*; (*of birds*) Trillern *nt*
trilogy [ˈtrɪlədʒɪ] *n* Trilogie *f*
trim [trɪm] *adj* (*house, garden*) gepflegt; (*figure, person*) schlank ▷ *n* (*haircut etc*): **to have a ~** sich *dat* die Haare nachschneiden lassen; (*on clothes, car*) Besatz *m* ▷ *vt* (*hair, beard*) nachschneiden; (*decorate*): **to ~ (with)** besetzen (mit); (*Naut: a sail*) trimmen mit; **to keep o.s. in (good) ~** (gut) in Form bleiben
trimmings [ˈtrɪmɪŋz] *npl* (*Culin*): **with all the ~** mit allem Drum und Dran; (*cuttings: of pastry etc*) Reste *pl*
Trinidad and Tobago [ˈtrɪnɪdæd-] *n* Trinidad und Tobago *nt*
trinity [ˈtrɪnɪtɪ] *n* (*Rel*) Dreieinigkeit *f*
trinket [ˈtrɪŋkɪt] *n* (*ornament*) Schmuckgegenstand *m*; (*piece of jewellery*) Schmuckstück *nt*
trio [ˈtriːəu] *n* Trio *nt*
trip [trɪp] *n* (*journey*) Reise *f*; (*outing*) Ausflug *m* ▷ *vi* (*stumble*) stolpern; (*go lightly*) trippeln; **on a ~** auf Reisen
▸ **trip over** *vt fus* stolpern über *+acc*
▸ **trip up** *vi* stolpern ▷ *vt* (*person*) zu Fall bringen
tripartite [traɪˈpɑːtaɪt] *adj* (*agreement, talks*) dreiseitig
tripe [traɪp] *n* (*Culin*) Kaldaunen *pl*; (*pej: rubbish*) Stuss *m*
triple [ˈtrɪpl] *adj* dreifach ▷ *adv*: **~ the distance/the speed** dreimal so weit/schnell; **~ the amount** dreimal so viel
triple jump *n* Dreisprung *m*
triplets [ˈtrɪplɪts] *npl* Drillinge *pl*
triplicate [ˈtrɪplɪkət] *n*: **in ~** in dreifacher Ausfertigung
tripod [ˈtraɪpɔd] *n* (*Phot*) Stativ *nt*
Tripoli [ˈtrɪpəlɪ] *n* Tripolis *nt*
tripper [ˈtrɪpəʳ] (*Brit*) *n* Ausflügler(in) *m(f)*
tripwire [ˈtrɪpwaɪəʳ] *n* Stolperdraht *m*
trite [traɪt] (*pej*) *adj* (*comment, idea etc*) banal
triumph [ˈtraɪʌmf] *n* Triumph *m* ▷ *vi*: **to ~ (over)** triumphieren (über *+acc*)
triumphal [traɪˈʌmfl] *adj* (*return*) triumphal
triumphant [traɪˈʌmfənt] *adj* triumphal;

(*victorious*) siegreich
triumphantly [traɪ'ʌmfəntlɪ] *adv* triumphierend
trivia ['trɪvɪə] (*pej*) *npl* Trivialitäten *pl*
trivial ['trɪvɪəl] *adj* trivial
triviality [trɪvɪ'ælɪtɪ] *n* Trivialität *f*
trivialize ['trɪvɪəlaɪz] *vt* trivialisieren
trod [trɔd] *pt of* **tread**
trodden [trɔdn] *pp of* **tread**
trolley ['trɔlɪ] *n* (*for luggage*) Kofferkuli *m*; (*for shopping*) Einkaufswagen *m*; (*table on wheels*) Teewagen *m*; (*also*: **trolley bus**) Oberleitungsomnibus *m*, Obus *m*
trollop ['trɔləp] (*pej*) *n* (*woman*) Schlampe *f*
trombone [trɔm'bəun] *n* Posaune *f*
troop [tru:p] *n* (*of people, monkeys etc*) Gruppe *f* ▷ *vi*: **to ~ in/out** hinein-/hinausströmen; **troops** *npl* (*Mil*) Truppen *pl*
troop carrier *n* Truppentransporter *m*; (*Naut*: *also*: **troopship**) Truppentransportschiff *nt*
trooper ['tru:pəʳ] *n* (*Mil*) Kavallerist *m*; (*US*: *policeman*) Polizist *m*
trooping the colour ['tru:pɪŋ-] (*Brit*) *n* (*ceremony*) Fahnenparade *f*
troopship ['tru:pʃɪp] *n* Truppentransportschiff *nt*
trophy ['trəufɪ] *n* Trophäe *f*
tropic ['trɔpɪk] *n* Wendekreis *m*; **the tropics** *npl* die Tropen *pl*; **T~ of Cancer/Capricorn** Wendekreis des Krebses/Steinbocks
tropical ['trɔpɪkl] *adj* tropisch
trot [trɔt] *n* (*fast pace*) Trott *m*; (*of horse*) Trab *m* ▷ *vi* (*horse*) traben; (*person*) trotten; **on the ~** (*Brit*: *fig*) hintereinander
▸ **trot out** *vt* (*facts, excuse etc*) vorbringen
trouble ['trʌbl] *n* Schwierigkeiten *pl*; (*bother, effort*) Umstände *pl*; (*unrest*) Unruhen *pl* ▷ *vt* (*worry*) beunruhigen; (*disturb*: *person*) belästigen ▷ *vi*: **to ~ to do sth** sich *dat* die Mühe machen, etw zu tun; **troubles** *npl* (*personal*) Probleme *pl*; (*Pol etc*) Unruhen *pl*; **to be in ~** in Schwierigkeiten sein; **to have ~ doing sth** Schwierigkeiten *or* Probleme haben, etw zu tun; **to go to the ~ of doing sth** sich *dat* die Mühe machen, etw zu tun; **it's no ~!** das macht mir nichts aus!; **the ~ is ...** das Problem ist ...; **what's the ~?** wo fehlts?; **stomach** *etc* **~** Probleme mit dem Magen *etc*; **please don't ~ yourself** bitte bemühen Sie sich nicht
troubled [trʌbld] *adj* (*person*) besorgt; (*country, life, era*) von Problemen geschüttelt
trouble-free ['trʌblfri:] *adj* problemlos
troublemaker ['trʌblmeɪkəʳ] *n* Unruhestifter(in) *m(f)*
troubleshooter ['trʌblʃu:təʳ] *n* Vermittler(in) *m(f)*
troublesome ['trʌblsəm] *adj* (*child*) schwierig; (*cough etc*) lästig
trouble spot *n* (*Mil*) Unruheherd *m*
troubling ['trʌblɪŋ] *adj* (*question etc*) beunruhigend
trough [trɔf] *n* (*also*: **drinking trough**) Wassertrog *m*; (*also*: **feeding trough**) Futtertrog *m*; (*channel*) Rinne *f*; (*low point*) Tief *nt*; **a ~ of low pressure** ein Tiefdruckkeil *m*
trounce [trauns] *vt* (*defeat*) vernichtend schlagen
troupe [tru:p] *n* Truppe *f*
trouser press ['trauzə-] *n* Hosenpresse *f*
trousers ['trauzəz] *npl* Hose *f*; **short ~** kurze Hose; **a pair of ~** eine Hose
trouser suit (*Brit*) *n* Hosenanzug *m*
trousseau ['tru:səu] (*pl* **trousseaux** *or* **~s**) *n* Aussteuer *f*
trout [traut] *n inv* Forelle *f*
trowel ['trauəl] *n* (*garden tool*) Pflanzkelle *f*; (*builder's tool*) (Maurer)kelle *f*
truant ['truənt] (*Brit*) *n*: **to play ~** die Schule schwänzen
truce [tru:s] *n* Waffenstillstand *m*
truck [trʌk] *n* (*lorry*) Lastwagen *m*; (*Rail*) Güterwagen *m*; (*for luggage*) Gepäckwagen *m*; **to have no ~ with sb** nichts mit jdm zu tun haben
truck driver *n* Lkw-Fahrer(in) *m(f)*
trucker ['trʌkəʳ] (*US*) *n* Lkw-Fahrer(in) *m(f)*
truck farm (*US*) *n* Gemüsefarm *f*
trucking ['trʌkɪŋ] (*US*) *n* Transport *m*
trucking company (*US*) *n* Spedition *f*
truculent ['trʌkjulənt] *adj* aufsässig
trudge [trʌdʒ] *vi* (*also*: **trudge along**) sich dahinschleppen
true [tru:] *adj* wahr; (*accurate*) genau; (*genuine*) echt; (*faithful*: *friend*) treu; (*wall, beam*) gerade; (*circle*) rund; **to come ~** wahr werden; **~ to life** lebensecht
truffle ['trʌfl] *n* (*fungus, sweet*) Trüffel *f*
truly ['tru:lɪ] *adv* wahrhaft, wirklich; (*truthfully*) wirklich; **yours ~** (*in letter*) mit freundlichen Grüßen
trump [trʌmp] *n* (*also*: **trump card**: *also*: *fig*) Trumpf *m*; **to turn up ~s** (*fig*) sich als Retter in der Not erweisen
trumped-up *adj*: **a ~ charge** eine erfundene Anschuldigung
trumpet ['trʌmpɪt] *n* Trompete *f*
truncated [trʌŋ'keɪtɪd] *adj* (*message, object*) verstümmelt
truncheon ['trʌntʃən] (*Brit*) *n* Gummiknüppel *m*
trundle ['trʌndl] *vt* (*trolley etc*) rollen ▷ *vi*: **to ~ along** (*person*) dahinschlendern; (*vehicle*) dahinrollen
trunk [trʌŋk] *n* (*of tree*) Stamm *m*; (*of person*) Rumpf *m*; (*of elephant*) Rüssel *m*; (*case*) Schrankkoffer *m*; (*US*: *Aut*) Kofferraum *m*; **trunks** *npl* (*also*: **swimming trunks**) Badehose *f*
trunk call (*Brit*) *n* Ferngespräch *nt*
trunk road (*Brit*) *n* Fernstraße *f*
truss [trʌs] *n* (*Med*) Bruchband *nt*
▸ **truss (up)** *vt* (*Culin*) dressieren; (*person*) fesseln
trust [trʌst] *n* Vertrauen *nt*; (*Comm*: *for charity etc*) Stiftung *f* ▷ *vt* vertrauen +*dat*; **to take sth**

on ~ (*advice etc*) etw einfach glauben; **to be in ~** (*Law*) treuhänderisch verwaltet werden; **to ~ (that)** (*hope*) hoffen(, dass)
trust company *n* Trust *m*
trusted ['trʌstɪd] *adj* (*friend, servant*) treu
trustee [trʌs'ti:] *n* (*Law*) Treuhänder(in) *m(f)*; (*of school etc*) Aufsichtsratsmitglied *nt*
trustful ['trʌstful] *adj* vertrauensvoll
trust fund *n* Treuhandvermögen *nt*
trusting ['trʌstɪŋ] *adj* vertrauensvoll
trustworthy ['trʌstwə:ðɪ] *adj* (*person*) vertrauenswürdig
trusty ['trʌstɪ] *adj* getreu
truth [tru:θ] (*pl* **~s**) *n*: **the ~** die Wahrheit *f*
truthful ['tru:θful] *adj* (*person*) ehrlich; (*answer etc*) wahrheitsgemäß
truthfully ['tru:θfəlɪ] *adv* (*answer*) wahrheitsgemäß
truthfulness ['tru:θfəlnɪs] *n* Ehrlichkeit *f*
try [traɪ] *n* (*also Rugby*) Versuch *m* ▷ *vt* (*attempt*) versuchen; (*test*) probieren; (*Law*) vor Gericht stellen; (*strain: patience*) auf die Probe stellen ▷ *vi* es versuchen; **to have a ~** es versuchen, einen Versuch machen; **to ~ to do sth** versuchen, etw zu tun; **to ~ one's (very) best** *or* **hardest** sein Bestes versuchen *or* tun
▸ **try on** *vt* (*clothes*) anprobieren; **she's ~ing it on** (*fig*) sie probiert, wie weit sie gehen kann
▸ **try out** *vt* ausprobieren
trying ['traɪɪŋ] *adj* (*person*) schwierig; (*experience*) schwer
tsar [zɑ:ʳ] *n* Zar *m*
T-shirt ['ti:ʃə:t] *n* T-Shirt *nt*
T-square ['ti:skwɛəʳ] *n* (*Tech*) Reißschiene *f*
TT *adj abbr* (*Brit: inf*) = **teetotal** ▷ *abbr* (*US: Post: = Trust Territories*) *der US-Verwaltungshoheit unterstellte Gebiete*
tub [tʌb] *n* (*container*) Kübel *m*; (*bath*) Wanne *f*
tuba ['tju:bə] *n* Tuba *f*
tubby ['tʌbɪ] *adj* rundlich
tube [tju:b] *n* (*pipe*) Rohr *nt*; (*container*) Tube *f*; (*Brit: underground*) U-Bahn *f*; (*US: inf*): **the ~** (*television*) die Röhre
tubeless ['tju:blɪs] *adj* (*tyre*) schlauchlos
tuber ['tju:bəʳ] *n* (*Bot*) Knolle *f*
tuberculosis [tjubə:kju'ləusɪs] *n* Tuberkulose *f*
tube station (*Brit*) *n* U-Bahn-Station *f*
tubing ['tju:bɪŋ] *n* Schlauch *m*; **a piece of ~** ein Schlauch
tubular ['tju:bjuləʳ] *adj* röhrenförmig
TUC (*Brit*) *n abbr* (*= Trades Union Congress*) *britischer Gewerkschafts-Dachverband*
tuck [tʌk] *vt* (*put*) stecken ▷ *n* (*Sewing*) Biese *f*
▸ **tuck away** *vt* (*money*) wegstecken; **to be ~ed away** (*building*) versteckt liegen
▸ **tuck in** *vt* (*clothing*) feststecken; (*child*) zudecken ▷ *vi* (*eat*) zulangen
▸ **tuck up** *vt* (*invalid, child*) zudecken
tuck shop *n* Süßwarenladen *m*
Tue., Tues. *abbr* (*= Tuesday*) Di.
Tuesday ['tju:zdɪ] *n* Dienstag *m*; **it is ~ 23rd March** heute ist Dienstag, der 23. März; **on ~** am Dienstag; **on ~s** dienstags; **every ~** jeden Dienstag; **every other ~** jeden zweiten Dienstag; **last/next ~** letzten/nächsten Dienstag; **the following ~** am Dienstag darauf; **~'s newspaper** die Zeitung von Dienstag; **a week/fortnight on ~** Dienstag in einer Woche/in vierzehn Tagen; **the ~ before last** der vorletzte Dienstag; **the ~ after next** der übernächste Dienstag; **~ morning/lunchtime/afternoon/evening** Dienstag Morgen/Mittag/Nachmittag/Abend; **~ night** (*overnight*) Dienstag Nacht
tuft [tʌft] *n* Büschel *nt*
tug [tʌg] *n* (*ship*) Schlepper *m* ▷ *vt* zerren
tug of love *n* Tauziehen *nt* (*um das Sorgerecht für Kinder*)
tug-of-war [tʌgəv'wɔ:ʳ] *n* (*also fig*) Tauziehen *nt*
tuition [tju:'ɪʃən] *n* (*Brit*) Unterricht *m*; (*US: school fees*) Schulgeld *nt*
tulip ['tju:lɪp] *n* Tulpe *f*
tumble ['tʌmbl] *n* (*fall*) Sturz *m* ▷ *vi* (*fall*) stürzen
▸ **tumble to** (*inf*) *vt fus* kapieren
tumbledown ['tʌmbldaun] *adj* (*building*) baufällig
tumble dryer (*Brit*) *n* Wäschetrockner *m*
tumbler ['tʌmbləʳ] *n* (*glass*) Trinkglas *nt*
tummy ['tʌmɪ] (*inf*) *n* Bauch *m*
tumour, (*US*) **tumor** ['tju:məʳ] *n* (*Med*) Tumor *m*, Geschwulst *f*
tumult ['tju:mʌlt] *n* Tumult *m*
tumultuous [tju:'mʌltjuəs] *adj* (*welcome, applause etc*) stürmisch
tuna ['tju:nə] *n inv* (*also*: **tuna fish**) T(h)unfisch *m*
tune [tju:n] *n* (*melody*) Melodie *f* ▷ *vt* (*Mus*) stimmen; (*Radio, TV, Aut*) einstellen; **to be in/out of ~** (*instrument*) richtig gestimmt/verstimmt sein; (*singer*) richtig/falsch singen; **to be in/out of ~ with** (*fig*) in Einklang/nicht in Einklang stehen mit; **she was robbed to the ~ of 10,000 pounds** sie wurde um einen Betrag in Höhe von 10.000 Pfund beraubt
▸ **tune in** *vi* (*Radio, TV*) einschalten; **to ~ in to BBC1** BBC1 einschalten
▸ **tune up** *vi* (*Mus*) (das Instrument/die Instrumente) stimmen
tuneful ['tju:nful] *adj* melodisch
tuner ['tju:nəʳ] *n*: **piano ~** Klavierstimmer(in) *m(f)*; (*radio set*) Tuner *m*
tuner amplifier *n* Steuergerät *nt*
tungsten ['tʌŋstən] *n* Wolfram *nt*
tunic ['tju:nɪk] *n* Hemdbluse *f*
tuning fork ['tju:nɪŋ-] *n* Stimmgabel *f*
Tunis ['tju:nɪs] *n* Tunis *nt*
Tunisia [tju:'nɪzɪə] *n* Tunesien *nt*
Tunisian [tju:'nɪzɪən] *adj* tunesisch ▷ *n* (*person*) Tunesier(in) *m(f)*
tunnel ['tʌnl] *n* Tunnel *m*; (*in mine*) Stollen *m* ▷ *vi* einen Tunnel bauen
tunnel vision *n* (*Med*) Gesichtsfeldeinengung *f*; (*fig*) Engstirnigkeit *f*
tunny ['tʌnɪ] *n* T(h)unfisch *m*
turban ['tə:bən] *n* Turban *m*

turbid ['tə:bɪd] *adj* (*water*) trüb; (*air*) schmutzig
turbine ['tə:baɪn] *n* Turbine *f*
turbo ['tə:bəu] *n* Turbo *m*; **~ engine** Turbomotor *m*
turbojet [tə:bəu'dʒɛt] *n* Düsenflugzeug *nt*
turboprop [tə:bəu'prɔp] *n* (*engine*) Turbo-Prop-Turbine *f*
turbot ['tə:bət] *n inv* Steinbutt *m*
turbulence ['tə:bjuləns] *n* (*Aviat*) Turbulenz *f*
turbulent ['tə:bjulənt] *adj* (*water, seas*) stürmisch; (*fig: career, period*) turbulent
tureen [tə'ri:n] *n* Terrine *f*
turf [tə:f] *n* (*grass*) Rasen *m*; (*clod*) Sode *f* ▷ *vt* (*area*) mit Grassoden bedecken; **the T~** (*horse-racing*) der Pferderennsport
▸ **turf out** (*inf*) *vt* (*person*) rausschmeißen
turf accountant (*Brit*) *n* Buchmacher *m*
turgid ['tə:dʒɪd] *adj* geschwollen
Turin ['tjuə'rɪn] *n* Turin *nt*
Turk [tə:k] *n* Türke *m*, Türkin *f*
Turkey ['tə:kɪ] *n* die Türkei *f*
turkey ['tə:kɪ] *n* (*bird*) Truthahn *m*, Truthenne *f*; (*meat*) Puter *m*
Turkish ['tə:kɪʃ] *adj* türkisch ▷ *n* (*Ling*) Türkisch *nt*
Turkish bath *n* türkisches Bad *nt*
Turkish delight *n* *geleeartige Süßigkeit, mit Puderzucker oder Schokolade überzogen*
turmeric ['tə:mərɪk] *n* Kurkuma *f*
turmoil ['tə:mɔɪl] *n* Aufruhr *m*; **in ~** in Aufruhr
turn [tə:n] *n* (*change*) Wende *f*; (*in road*) Kurve *f*; (*rotation*) Drehung *f*; (*performance*) Nummer *f*; (*inf, Med*) Anfall *m* ▷ *vt* (*handle, key*) drehen; (*collar, steak*) wenden; (*page*) umblättern; (*shape: wood*) drechseln; (*: metal*) drehen ▷ *vi* (*object*) sich drehen; (*person*) sich umdrehen; (*change direction*) abbiegen; (*milk*) sauer werden; **to do sb a good ~** jdm einen guten Dienst erweisen; **a ~ of events** eine Wendung der Dinge; **it gave me quite a ~** (*inf*) das hat mir einen schönen Schrecken eingejagt; **"no left ~"** (*Aut*) „Linksabbiegen verboten"; **it's your ~** du bist dran; **in ~** der Reihe nach; **to take ~s (at)** sich abwechseln (bei); **at the ~ of the century/year** zur Jahrhundertwende/Jahreswende; **to take a ~ for the worse** (*events*) sich zum Schlechten wenden; **his health** *or* **he has taken a ~ for the worse** sein Befinden hat sich verschlechtert; **to ~ nasty/forty/grey** unangenehm/vierzig/grau werden
▸ **turn against** *vt fus* sich wenden gegen
▸ **turn around** *vi* sich umdrehen; (*in car*) wenden
▸ **turn away** *vi* sich abwenden ▷ *vt* (*applicants*) abweisen; (*business*) zurückweisen
▸ **turn back** *vi* umkehren ▷ *vt* (*person, vehicle*) zurückweisen
▸ **turn down** *vt* (*request*) ablehnen; (*heating*) kleiner stellen; (*radio etc*) leiser stellen; (*bedclothes*) aufschlagen
▸ **turn in** *vi* (*inf: go to bed*) sich hinhauen ▷ *vt* (*to police*) anzeigen; **to ~ o.s. in** sich stellen
▸ **turn into** *vt fus* (*change*) sich verwandeln in *+acc* ▷ *vt* machen zu
▸ **turn off** *vi* (*from road*) abbiegen ▷ *vt* (*light, radio etc*) ausmachen; (*tap*) zudrehen; (*engine*) abstellen
▸ **turn on** *vt* (*light, radio etc*) anmachen; (*tap*) aufdrehen; (*engine*) anstellen
▸ **turn out** *vt* (*light*) ausmachen; (*gas*) abstellen ▷ *vi* (*appear, attend*) erscheinen; **to ~ out to be** (*prove to be*) sich erweisen als; **to ~ out well/badly** (*situation*) gut/schlecht enden
▸ **turn over** *vi* (*person*) sich umdrehen ▷ *vt* (*object*) umdrehen, wenden; (*page*) umblättern; **to ~ sth over to** (*to sb*) etw übertragen *+dat*; (*to sth*) etw verlagern zu
▸ **turn round** *vi* sich umdrehen; (*vehicle*) wenden
▸ **turn up** *vi* (*person*) erscheinen; (*lost object*) wieder auftauchen ▷ *vt* (*collar*) hochklappen; (*heater*) höher stellen; (*radio etc*) lauter stellen
turnabout ['tə:nəbaut] *n* (*fig*) Kehrtwendung *f*
turnaround ['tə:nəraund] *n* = **turnabout**
turncoat ['tə:nkəut] *n* Überläufer(in) *m(f)*
turned-up ['tə:ndʌp] *adj*: **~ nose** Stupsnase *f*
turning ['tə:nɪŋ] *n* (*in road*) Abzweigung *f*; **the first ~ on the right** die erste Straße rechts
turning circle (*Brit*) *n* (*Aut*) Wendekreis *m*
turning point *n* (*fig*) Wendepunkt *m*
turning radius (*US*) *n* = **turning circle**
turnip ['tə:nɪp] *n* Rübe *f*
turnout ['tə:naut] *n* (*of voters etc*) Beteiligung *f*
turnover ['tə:nəuvə[r]] *n* (*Comm: amount of money*) Umsatz *m*; (*: of staff*) Fluktuation *f*; (*Culin*): **apple ~** Apfeltasche *f*; **there is a rapid ~ in staff** der Personalbestand wechselt ständig
turnpike ['tə:npaɪk] (*US*) *n* gebührenpflichtige Autobahn *f*
turnstile ['tə:nstaɪl] *n* Drehkreuz *nt*
turntable ['tə:nteɪbl] *n* (*on record player*) Plattenteller *m*
turn-up ['tə:nʌp] (*Brit*) *n* (*on trousers*) Aufschlag *m*; **that's a ~ for the books!** (*inf*) das ist eine echte Überraschung!
turpentine ['tə:pəntaɪn] *n* (*also:* **turps**) Terpentin *nt*
turquoise ['tə:kwɔɪz] *n* (*stone*) Türkis *m* ▷ *adj* (*colour*) türkis
turret ['tʌrɪt] *n* Turm *m*
turtle ['tə:tl] *n* Schildkröte *f*
turtleneck ['tə:tlnɛk], **turtleneck sweater** *n* Pullover *m* mit rundem Kragen
Tuscan ['tʌskən] *adj* toskanisch ▷ *n* (*person*) Toskaner(in) *m(f)*
Tuscany ['tʌskənɪ] *n* die Toskana
tusk [tʌsk] *n* (*of elephant*) Stoßzahn *m*
tussle ['tʌsl] *n* Gerangel *nt*
tutor ['tju:tə[r]] *n* Tutor(in) *m(f)*; (*private tutor*) Privatlehrer(in) *m(f)*
tutorial [tju:'tɔ:rɪəl] *n* Kolloquium *nt*
tuxedo [tʌk'si:dəu] (*US*) *n* Smoking *m*
TV [ti:'vi:] *n abbr* (*= television*) TV *nt*
TV dinner *n* Fertiggericht *nt*

twaddle ['twɔdl] (*inf*) *n* dummes Zeug *nt*
twang [twæŋ] *n* (*of instrument*) singender Ton *m*; (*of voice*) näselnder Ton *m* ▷ *vi* einen singenden Ton von sich geben ▷ *vt* (*guitar*) zupfen
tweak [twi:k] *vt* kneifen
tweed [twi:d] *n* Tweed *m* ▷ *adj* (*jacket, skirt*) Tweed-
tweezers ['twi:zəz] *npl* Pinzette *f*
twelfth [twɛlfθ] *num* zwölfte(r, s) ▷ *n* Zwölftel *nt*
Twelfth Night *n* ≈ Dreikönige *nt*
twelve [twɛlv] *num* zwölf; **at ~ (o'clock)** (*midday*) um zwölf Uhr (mittags); (*midnight*) um zwölf Uhr nachts
twentieth ['twɛntɪɪθ] *num* zwanzigste(r, s)
twenty ['twɛntɪ] *num* zwanzig
twenty-four seven ['twɛntɪfɔ:'sɛvn] *n* (*store*) Geschäft, das an sieben Tagen die Woche und 24 Stunden am Tag geöffnet hat ▷ *adj* rund um die Uhr; **~ service** Service, der rund um die Uhr zur Verfügung steht
twerp [twə:p] (*inf*) *n* Schwachkopf *m*
twice [twaɪs] *adv* zweimal; **~ as much** zweimal so viel; **~ a week** zweimal die Woche; **she is ~ your age** sie ist doppelt so alt wie du
twiddle ['twɪdl] *vt* drehen an *+dat* ▷ *vi*: **to ~ (with)** herumdrehen (an *+dat*); **to ~ one's thumbs** (*fig*) Däumchen drehen
twig [twɪg] *n* Zweig *m* ▷ *vi, vt* (*Brit: inf: realize*) kapieren
twilight ['twaɪlaɪt] *n* Dämmerung *f*; **in the ~** in der Dämmerung
twill [twɪl] *n* (*cloth*) Köper *m*
twin [twɪn] *adj* (*sister, brother*) Zwillings-; (*towers*) Doppel- ▷ *n* Zwilling *m*; (*room in hotel etc*) Zweibettzimmer *nt* ▷ *vt* (*towns etc*): **to be ~ned with ...** ... als Partnerstadt haben
twin-bedded room ['twɪn'bɛdɪd-] *n* Zweibettzimmer *nt*
twin beds *npl* zwei (gleiche) Einzelbetten *pl*
twin-carburettor ['twɪnkɑ:bju'rɛtəʳ] *adj* Doppelvergaser-
twine [twaɪn] *n* Bindfaden *m* ▷ *vi* sich winden
twin-engined [twɪn'ɛndʒɪnd] *adj* zweimotorig
twinge [twɪndʒ] *n* (*of pain*) Stechen *nt*; **a ~ of conscience** Gewissensbisse *pl*; **a ~ of fear/guilt** ein Angst-/Schuldgefühl *nt*
twinkle ['twɪŋkl] *vi* funkeln ▷ *n* Funkeln *nt*
twin town *n* Partnerstadt *f*
twirl [twə:l] *vt* herumwirbeln ▷ *vi* wirbeln ▷ *n* Wirbel *m*
twist [twɪst] *n* (*action*) Drehung *f*; (*in road*) Kurve; (*in coil, flex*) Biegung *f*; (*in story*) Wendung *f* ▷ *vt* (*turn*) drehen; (*injure: ankle etc*) verrenken; (*twine*) wickeln; (*fig: meaning etc*) verdrehen ▷ *vi* (*road, river*) sich winden; **~ my arm!** (*inf*) überreden Sie mich einfach!
twisted ['twɪstɪd] *adj* (*wire, rope*) gedreht; (*ankle*) verrenkt; (*fig: logic, mind*) verdreht
twit [twɪt] (*inf*) *n* Trottel *m*
twitch [twɪtʃ] *n* (*jerky movement*) Zucken *nt* ▷ *vi* zucken
two [tu:] *num* zwei; **~ by two, in twos** zu zweit; **to put ~ and ~ together** (*fig*) zwei und zwei zusammenzählen
two-bit [tu:'bɪt] (*inf*) *adj* (*worthless*) mies
two-door [tu:'dɔ:ʳ] *adj* zweitürig
two-faced [tu:'feɪst] (*pej*) *adj* scheinheilig
twofold ['tu:fəuld] *adv*: **to increase ~** um das Doppelte ansteigen ▷ *adj* (*increase*) um das Doppelte; (*aim, value etc*) zweifach
two-piece ['tu:pi:s] *n* (*also*: **two-piece suit**) Zweiteiler *m*; (*also*: **two-piece swimsuit**) zweiteiliger Badeanzug *m*
two-ply ['tu:plaɪ] *adj* (*wool*) zweifädig; (*tissues*) zweilagig
two-seater ['tu:'si:təʳ] *n* (*car*) Zweisitzer *m*
twosome ['tu:səm] *n* (*people*) Paar *nt*
two-stroke ['tu:strəuk] *n* (*also*: **two-stroke engine**) Zweitakter *m* ▷ *adj* (*engine*) Zweitakt-
two-tone ['tu:'təun] *adj* (*in colour*) zweifarbig
two-way ['tu:weɪ] *adj*: **~ traffic** Verkehr *m* in beiden Richtungen; **~ radio** Funksprechgerät *nt*
TX (*US*) *abbr* (*Post*) = *Texas*
tycoon [taɪ'ku:n] *n* Magnat *m*
type [taɪp] *n* (*category, model, example*) Typ *m*; (*Typ*) Schrift *f* ▷ *vt* (*letter etc*) tippen, (mit der) Maschine schreiben; **a ~ of** eine Art von; **what ~ do you want?** welche Sorte möchten Sie?; **in bold/italic ~** in Fett-/Kursivdruck
typecast ['taɪpkɑ:st] (*irreg: like* **cast**) *vt* (*actor*) (auf eine Rolle) festlegen
typeface ['taɪpfeɪs] *n* Schrift *f*, Schriftbild *nt*
typescript ['taɪpskrɪpt] *n* (maschinengeschriebenes) Manuskript *nt*
typeset ['taɪpsɛt] (*irreg: like* **set**) *vt* setzen
typesetter ['taɪpsɛtəʳ] *n* Setzer(in) *m(f)*
typewriter ['taɪpraɪtəʳ] *n* Schreibmaschine *f*
typewritten ['taɪprɪtn] *adj* maschine(n)geschrieben
typhoid ['taɪfɔɪd] *n* Typhus *m*
typhoon [taɪ'fu:n] *n* Taifun *m*
typhus ['taɪfəs] *n* Fleckfieber *nt*
typical ['tɪpɪkl] *adj* typisch; **~ (of)** typisch (für); **that's ~!** das ist typisch!
typify ['tɪpɪfaɪ] *vt* typisch sein für
typing ['taɪpɪŋ] *n* Maschine(n)schreiben *nt*
typing error *n* Tippfehler *m*
typing pool *n* Schreibzentrale *f*
typist ['taɪpɪst] *n* Schreibkraft *f*
typo ['taɪpəu] (*inf*) *n abbr* (= *typographical error*) Druckfehler *m*
typography [tɪ'pɔgrəfɪ] *n* Typografie *f*
tyranny ['tɪrənɪ] *n* Tyrannei *f*
tyrant ['taɪərnt] *n* Tyrann(in) *m(f)*
tyre, (*US*) **tire** ['taɪəʳ] *n* Reifen *m*
tyre pressure *n* Reifendruck *m*
Tyrol [tɪ'rəul] *n* Tirol *nt*
Tyrolean [tɪrə'li:ən] *adj* Tiroler ▷ *n* (*person*) Tiroler(in) *m(f)*
Tyrolese [tɪrə'li:z] = **Tyrolean**
Tyrrhenian Sea [tɪ'ri:nɪən-] *n*: **the ~** das Tyrrhenische Meer
tzar [zɑ:ʳ] *n* = **tsar**

Uu

U¹, u [ju:] *n* (*letter*) U *nt*, u *nt*; **U for Uncle** ≈ U wie Ulrich
U² [ju:] (*Brit*) *n abbr* (*Cine*: = *universal*) *Klassifikation für jugendfreie Filme*
UAW (*US*) *n abbr* (= *United Automobile Workers*) *Automobilarbeitergewerkschaft*
UB40 (*Brit*) *n abbr* (= *unemployment benefit form 40*) Arbeitslosenausweis *m*
U-bend ['ju:bɛnd] *n* (*in pipe*) U-Krümmung *f*
ubiquitous [ju:'bɪkwɪtəs] *adj* allgegenwärtig
UCCA ['ʌkə] (*Brit*) *n abbr* (= *Universities Central Council on Admissions*) *akademische Zulassungsstelle*, ≈ ZVS *f*
UDA (*Brit*) *n abbr* (= *Ulster Defence Association*) *paramilitärische protestantische Organisation in Nordirland*
UDC (*Brit*) *n abbr* (= *Urban District Council*) Stadtverwaltung *f*
udder ['ʌdə^r^] *n* Euter *nt*
UDI (*Brit*) *n abbr* (*Pol*: = *unilateral declaration of independence*) einseitige Unabhängigkeitserklärung *f*
UDR (*Brit*) *n abbr* (= *Ulster Defence Regiment*) *Regiment aus Teilzeitsoldaten zur Unterstützung der britischen Armee und Polizei in Nordirland*
UEFA [ju:'eɪfə] *n abbr* (= *Union of European Football Associations*) UEFA *f*
UFO ['ju:fəu] *n abbr* (= *unidentified flying object*) UFO *nt*
Uganda [ju:'gændə] *n* Uganda *nt*
Ugandan [ju:'gændən] *adj* ugandisch ▷ *n* Ugandaer(in) *m(f)*
UGC (*Brit*) *n abbr* (= *University Grants Committee*) *Ausschuss zur Verteilung von Geldern an Universitäten*
ugh [ə:h] *excl* igitt
ugliness ['ʌglɪnɪs] *n* Hässlichkeit *f*
ugly ['ʌglɪ] *adj* hässlich; (*nasty*) schlimm
UHF *abbr* (= *ultrahigh frequency*) UHF
UHT *abbr* (= *ultra heat treated*): **~ milk** H-Milch *f*
UK *n abbr* = **United Kingdom**
Ukraine [ju:'kreɪn] *n* Ukraine *f*
Ukrainian [ju:'kreɪnɪən] *adj* ukrainisch ▷ *n* Ukrainer(in) *m(f)*; (*Ling*) Ukrainisch *nt*
ulcer ['ʌlsə^r^] *n* (*stomach ulcer etc*) Geschwür *nt*; (*also*: **mouth ulcer**) Abszess *m* im Mund
Ulster ['ʌlstə^r^] *n* Ulster *nt*
ulterior [ʌl'tɪərɪə^r^] *adj*: **~ motive** Hintergedanke *m*
ultimata [ʌltɪ'meɪtə] *npl of* **ultimatum**
ultimate ['ʌltɪmət] *adj* (*final*) letztendlich; (*greatest*) größte(r, s); (: *deterrent*) äußerste(r, s); (: *authority*) höchste(r, s) ▷ *n*: **the ~ in luxury** das Äußerste *or* Höchste an Luxus
ultimately ['ʌltɪmətlɪ] *adv* (*in the end*) schließlich, letzten Endes; (*basically*) im Grunde (genommen)
ultimatum [ʌltɪ'meɪtəm] (*pl* **~s** *or* **ultimata**) *n* Ultimatum *nt*
ultrasonic [ʌltrə'sɔnɪk] *adj* (*sound*) Ultraschall-
ultrasound ['ʌltrəsaund] *n* Ultraschall *m*
ultraviolet ['ʌltrə'vaɪəlɪt] *adj* ultraviolett
umbilical cord [ʌm'bɪlɪkl-] *n* Nabelschnur *f*
umbrage ['ʌmbrɪdʒ] *n*: **to take ~ at** Anstoß nehmen an *+dat*
umbrella [ʌm'brɛlə] *n* (*for rain*) (Regen)schirm *m*; (*for sun*) Sonnenschirm *m*; (*fig*): **under the ~ of** unter der Leitung von
umlaut ['umlaut] *n* Umlaut *m*; (*mark*) Umlautzeichen *nt*
umpire ['ʌmpaɪə^r^] *n* Schiedsrichter(in) *m(f)* ▷ *vt* (*game*) als Schiedsrichter leiten
umpteen [ʌmp'ti:n] *adj* zig
umpteenth [ʌmp'ti:nθ] *adj*: **for the ~ time** zum x-ten Mal
UMWA *n abbr* (= *United Mineworkers of America*) *amerikanische Bergarbeitergewerkschaft*
UN *n abbr* (= *United Nations*) UNO *f*
unabashed [ʌnə'bæʃt] *adj*: **to be/seem ~** unbeeindruckt sein/scheinen
unabated [ʌnə'beɪtɪd] *adj* unvermindert ▷ *adv*: **to continue ~** nicht nachlassen
unable [ʌn'eɪbl] *adj*: **to be ~ to do sth** etw nicht tun können
unabridged [ʌnə'brɪdʒd] *adj* ungekürzt
unacceptable [ʌnək'sɛptəbl] *adj* unannehmbar, nicht akzeptabel
unaccompanied [ʌnə'kʌmpənɪd] *adj* (*child, song*) ohne Begleitung; (*luggage*) unbegleitet
unaccountably [ʌnə'kauntəblɪ] *adv* unerklärlich
unaccounted [ʌnə'kauntɪd] *adj*: **to be ~ for** (*passengers, money etc*) (noch) fehlen
unaccustomed [ʌnə'kʌstəmd] *adj*: **to be ~ to** nicht gewöhnt sein an *+acc*
unacquainted [ʌnə'kweɪntɪd] *adj*: **to be ~ with** nicht vertraut sein mit

unadulterated [ʌnəˈdʌltəreɪtɪd] *adj* rein
unaffected [ʌnəˈfɛktɪd] *adj (person, behaviour)* natürlich, ungekünstelt; **to be ~ by sth** von etw nicht berührt werden
unafraid [ʌnəˈfreɪd] *adj*: **to be ~** keine Angst haben
unaided [ʌnˈeɪdɪd] *adv* ohne fremde Hilfe
unanimity [juːnəˈnɪmɪtɪ] *n* Einstimmigkeit *f*
unanimous [juːˈnænɪməs] *adj* einstimmig
unanimously [juːˈnænɪməslɪ] *adv* einstimmig
unanswered [ʌnˈɑːnsəd] *adj* unbeantwortet
unappetizing [ʌnˈæpɪtaɪzɪŋ] *adj (food)* unappetitlich
unappreciative [ʌnəˈpriːʃɪətɪv] *adj (person)* undankbar; *(audience)* verständnislos
unarmed [ʌnˈɑːmd] *adj* unbewaffnet; **~ combat** Nahkampf *m* ohne Waffen
unashamed [ʌnəˈʃeɪmd] *adj (pleasure, greed etc)* unverhohlen
unassisted [ʌnəˈsɪstɪd] *adv* ohne fremde Hilfe
unassuming [ʌnəˈsjuːmɪŋ] *adj* bescheiden
unattached [ʌnəˈtætʃt] *adj (single: person)* ungebunden; *(unconnected)* ohne Verbindung
unattended [ʌnəˈtɛndɪd] *adj (car, luggage, child)* unbeaufsichtigt
unattractive [ʌnəˈtræktɪv] *adj* unattraktiv
unauthorized [ʌnˈɔːθəraɪzd] *adj (visit, use)* unbefugt; *(version)* nicht unautorisiert
unavailable [ʌnəˈveɪləbl] *adj (article, room)* nicht verfügbar; *(person)* nicht zu erreichen; **~ for comment** nicht zu sprechen
unavoidable [ʌnəˈvɔɪdəbl] *adj* unvermeidlich
unavoidably [ʌnəˈvɔɪdəblɪ] *adv (delayed etc)* auf unvermeidliche Weise
unaware [ʌnəˈwɛəʳ] *adj*: **he was ~ of it** er war sich *dat* dessen nicht bewusst
unawares [ʌnəˈwɛəz] *adv (catch, take)* unerwartet
unbalanced [ʌnˈbælənst] *adj (report)* unausgewogen; **(mentally) ~** geistig gestört
unbearable [ʌnˈbɛərəbl] *adj* unerträglich
unbeatable [ʌnˈbiːtəbl] *adj* unschlagbar
unbeaten [ʌnˈbiːtn] *adj* ungeschlagen
unbecoming [ʌnbɪˈkʌmɪŋ] *adj (language, behaviour)* unpassend; *(garment)* unvorteilhaft
unbeknown [ʌnbɪˈnəun], **unbeknownst** [ʌnbɪˈnəunst] *adv*: **~(st) to me/Peter** ohne mein/Peters Wissen
unbelief [ʌnbɪˈliːf] *n* Ungläubigkeit *f*
unbelievable [ʌnbɪˈliːvəbl] *adj* unglaublich
unbelievably [ʌnbɪˈliːvəblɪ] *adv* unglaublich
unbend [ʌnˈbɛnd] *(irreg: like* **bend**) *vi (relax)* aus sich herausgehen ▷ *vt (wire etc)* gerade biegen
unbending [ʌnˈbɛndɪŋ] *adj (person, attitude)* unnachgiebig
unbiased, unbiassed [ʌnˈbaɪəst] *adj* unvoreingenommen
unblemished [ʌnˈblɛmɪʃt] *adj (also fig)* makellos
unblock [ʌnˈblɔk] *vt (pipe)* frei machen
unborn [ʌnˈbɔːn] *adj* ungeboren
unbounded [ʌnˈbaundɪd] *adj* grenzenlos
unbreakable [ʌnˈbreɪkəbl] *adj (object)* unzerbrechlich
unbridled [ʌnˈbraɪdld] *adj* ungezügelt
unbroken [ʌnˈbrəukən] *adj (seal)* unversehrt; *(silence)* ununterbrochen; *(record, series)* ungebrochen
unbuckle [ʌnˈbʌkl] *vt* aufschnallen
unburden [ʌnˈbəːdn] *vt*: **to ~ o.s. (to sb)** (jdm) sein Herz ausschütten
unbusinesslike [ʌnˈbɪznɪslaɪk] *adj* ungeschäftsmäßig
unbutton [ʌnˈbʌtn] *vt* aufknöpfen
uncalled-for [ʌnˈkɔːldfɔːʳ] *adj (remark etc)* unnötig
uncanny [ʌnˈkænɪ] *adj* unheimlich
unceasing [ʌnˈsiːsɪŋ] *adj (search, flow etc)* unaufhörlich; *(loyalty)* unermüdlich
unceremonious [ʌnsɛrɪˈməunɪəs] *adj (abrupt, rude)* brüsk, barsch
uncertain [ʌnˈsəːtn] *adj (person)* unsicher; *(future, outcome)* ungewiss; **to be ~ about sth** unsicher über etw *acc* sein; **in no ~ terms** unzweideutig
uncertainty [ʌnˈsəːtntɪ] *n* Ungewissheit *f*; **uncertainties** *npl (doubts)* Unsicherheiten *pl*
unchallenged [ʌnˈtʃælɪndʒd] *adj* unbestritten ▷ *adv (walk, enter)* ungehindert; **to go ~** unangefochten bleiben
unchanged [ʌnˈtʃeɪndʒd] *adj* unverändert
uncharitable [ʌnˈtʃærɪtəbl] *adj (remark, behaviour etc)* unfreundlich
uncharted [ʌnˈtʃɑːtɪd] *adj (land, sea)* unverzeichnet
unchecked [ʌnˈtʃɛkt] *adv (grow, continue)* ungehindert
uncivil [ʌnˈsɪvɪl] *adj (person)* grob
uncivilized [ʌnˈsɪvɪlaɪzd] *adj* unzivilisiert
uncle [ˈʌŋkl] *n* Onkel *m*
unclear [ʌnˈklɪəʳ] *adj* unklar; **I'm still ~ about what I'm supposed to do** mir ist immer noch nicht klar, was ich tun soll
uncoil [ʌnˈkɔɪl] *vt (rope, wire)* abwickeln ▷ *vi (snake)* sich strecken
uncomfortable [ʌnˈkʌmfətəbl] *adj (person, chair)* unbequem; *(room)* ungemütlich; *(nervous)* unbehaglich; *(unpleasant: situation, fact)* unerfreulich
uncomfortably [ʌnˈkʌmfətəblɪ] *adv (sit)* unbequem; *(smile)* unbehaglich
uncommitted [ʌnkəˈmɪtɪd] *adj* nicht engagiert; **~ to** nicht festgelegt auf *+acc*
uncommon [ʌnˈkɔmən] *adj* ungewöhnlich
uncommunicative [ʌnkəˈmjuːnɪkətɪv] *adj (person)* schweigsam
uncomplicated [ʌnˈkɔmplɪkeɪtɪd] *adj* unkompliziert
uncompromising [ʌnˈkɔmprəmaɪzɪŋ] *adj (person, belief)* kompromisslos
unconcerned [ʌnkənˈsəːnd] *adj (person)* unbekümmert; **to be ~ about sth** sich nicht um etw kümmern
unconditional [ʌnkənˈdɪʃənl] *adj* bedingungslos; *(acceptance)* vorbehaltlos
uncongenial [ʌnkənˈdʒiːnɪəl] *adj (surroundings)* unangenehm

unconnected [ʌnkə'nɛktɪd] *adj* (*unrelated*) ohne Verbindung; **to be ~ with sth** nicht mit etw in Beziehung stehen
unconscious [ʌn'kɔnʃəs] *adj* (*in faint*) bewusstlos; (*unaware*): **~ of** nicht bewusst *+gen* ▷ *n*: **the ~** das Unbewusste; **to knock sb ~** jdn bewusstlos schlagen
unconsciously [ʌn'kɔnʃəslɪ] *adv* unbewusst
unconsciousness [ʌn'kɔnʃəsnɪs] *n* Bewusstlosigkeit *f*
unconstitutional ['ʌnkɔnstɪ'tju:ʃənl] *adj* verfassungswidrig
uncontested [ʌnkən'tɛstɪd] *adj* (*Pol: seat, election*) ohne Gegenkandidat; (*divorce*) ohne Einwände der Gegenseite
uncontrollable [ʌnkən'trəuləbl] *adj* unkontrollierbar; (*laughter*) unbändig
uncontrolled [ʌnkən'trəuld] *adj* (*behaviour*) ungezähmt; (*price rises etc*) ungehindert
unconventional [ʌnkən'vɛnʃənl] *adj* unkonventionell
unconvinced [ʌnkən'vɪnst] *adj*: **to be/remain ~** nicht überzeugt sein/bleiben
unconvincing [ʌnkən'vɪnsɪŋ] *adj* nicht überzeugend
uncork [ʌn'kɔ:k] *vt* (*bottle*) entkorken
uncorroborated [ʌnkə'rɔbəreɪtɪd] *adj* (*evidence*) unbestätigt
uncouth [ʌn'ku:θ] *adj* (*person, behaviour*) ungehobelt
uncover [ʌn'kʌvəʳ] *vt* aufdecken
unctuous ['ʌŋktjuəs] (*form*) *adj* (*person, behaviour*) salbungsvoll
undamaged [ʌn'dæmɪdʒd] *adj* unbeschädigt
undaunted [ʌn'dɔ:ntɪd] *adj* (*person*) unverzagt; **~, she struggled on** sie kämpfte unverzagt weiter
undecided [ʌndɪ'saɪdɪd] *adj* (*person*) unentschlossen; (*question*) unentschieden
undelivered [ʌndɪ'lɪvəd] *adj* (*goods*) nicht geliefert; (*letters*) nicht zugestellt; **if ~ return to sender** (*on envelope*) falls unzustellbar, zurück an Absender
undeniable [ʌndɪ'naɪəbl] *adj* unbestreitbar
undeniably [ʌndɪ'naɪəblɪ] *adv* (*true*) zweifellos; (*handsome*) unbestreitbar
under ['ʌndəʳ] *prep* (*position*) unter *+dat*; (*motion*) unter *+acc*; (*according to: law etc*) nach, gemäß *+dat* ▷ *adv* (*go, fly etc*) darunter; **to come from ~ sth** unter etw *dat* hervorkommen; **~ there** darunter; **in ~ 2 hours** in weniger als 2 Stunden; **~ anaesthetic** unter Narkose; **to be ~ discussion** diskutiert werden; **~ repair** in Reparatur; **~ the circumstances** unter den Umständen
under ... ['ʌndəʳ] *pref* Unter-, unter-
underage [ʌndər'eɪdʒ] *adj* (*person*) minderjährig; **~ drinking** Alkoholgenuss *m* von Minderjährigen
underarm ['ʌndərɑ:m] *adv* (*bowl, throw*) von unten ▷ *adj* (*throw, shot*) von unten; (*deodorant*) Achselhöhlen-
undercapitalized ['ʌndə'kæpɪtəlaɪzd] *adj* unterkapitalisiert
undercarriage ['ʌndəkærɪdʒ] *n* (*Aviat*) Fahrgestell *nt*
undercharge [ʌndə'tʃɑ:dʒ] *vt* zu wenig berechnen *+dat*
underclass ['ʌndəklɑ:s] *n* Unterklasse *f*
underclothes ['ʌndəkləuðz] *npl* Unterwäsche *f*
undercoat ['ʌndəkəut] *n* (*paint*) Grundierung *f*
undercover [ʌndə'kʌvəʳ] *adj* (*duty, agent*) Geheim- ▷ *adv* (*work*) insgeheim
undercurrent ['ʌndəkʌrnt] *n* (*also fig*) Unterströmung *f*
undercut [ʌndə'kʌt] (*irreg: like* **cut**) *vt* (*person, prices*) unterbieten
underdeveloped ['ʌndədɪ'vɛləpt] *adj* unterentwickelt
underdog ['ʌndədɔg] *n*: **the ~** der/die Benachteiligte
underdone [ʌndə'dʌn] *adj* (*food*) nicht gar; (*: meat*) nicht durchgebraten
underemployment ['ʌndərɪm'plɔɪmənt] *n* Unterbeschäftigung *f*
underestimate ['ʌndər'ɛstɪmeɪt] *vt* unterschätzen
underexposed ['ʌndərɪks'pəuzd] *adj* (*Phot*) unterbelichtet
underfed [ʌndə'fɛd] *adj* unterernährt
underfoot [ʌndə'fut] *adv*: **to crush sth ~** etw am Boden zerdrücken; **to trample sth ~** auf etw *dat* herumtrampeln
underfunded ['ʌndə'fʌndɪd] *adj* unterfinanziert
undergo [ʌndə'gəu] (*irreg: like* **go**) *vt* (*change*) durchmachen; (*test, operation*) sich unterziehen; **the car is ~ing repairs** das Auto wird gerade repariert
undergraduate [ʌndə'grædjuɪt] *n* Student(in) *m(f)* ▷ *cpd*: **~ courses** Kurse *pl* für nicht graduierte Studenten
underground ['ʌndəgraund] *adj* unterirdisch; (*Pol: newspaper, activities*) Untergrund- ▷ *adv* (*work*) unterirdisch; (*: miners*) unter Tage; (*Pol*): **to go ~** untertauchen ▷ *n*: **the ~** (*Brit*) die U-Bahn; (*Pol*) die Untergrundbewegung; **~ car park** Tiefgarage *f*
undergrowth ['ʌndəgrəuθ] *n* Unterholz *nt*
underhand [ʌndə'hænd], **underhanded** [ʌndə'hændɪd] *adj* (*fig: behaviour, person*) hinterhältig
underinsured [ʌndərɪn'ʃuəd] *adj* unterversichert
underlay [ʌndə'leɪ] *n* Unterlage *f*
underlie [ʌndə'laɪ] (*irreg: like* **lie**) *vt* (*fig: be basis of*) zugrunde liegen *+dat*; **the underlying cause** der eigentliche Grund
underline [ʌndə'laɪn] *vt* unterstreichen; (*fig: emphasize*) betonen
underling ['ʌndəlɪŋ] (*pej*) *n* Befehlsempfänger(in) *m(f)*
undermanning [ʌndə'mænɪŋ] *n* Personalmangel *m*
undermentioned [ʌndə'mɛnʃənd] *adj* unten genannt

undermine [ʌndə'maɪn] *vt* unterminieren, unterhöhlen
underneath [ʌndə'ni:θ] *adv* darunter ▷ *prep* (*position*) unter +*dat*; (*motion*) unter +*acc*
undernourished [ʌndə'nʌrɪʃt] *adj* unterernährt
underpaid [ʌndə'peɪd] *adj* unterbezahlt
underpants ['ʌndəpænts] *npl* Unterhose *f*
underpass ['ʌndəpɑ:s] (*Brit*) *n* Unterführung *f*
underpin [ʌndə'pɪn] *vt* (*argument*) untermauern
underplay [ʌndə'pleɪ] (*Brit*) *vt* herunterspielen
underpopulated [ʌndə'pɔpjuleɪtɪd] *adj* unterbevölkert
underprice [ʌndə'praɪs] *vt* (*goods*) zu billig anbieten
underprivileged [ʌndə'prɪvɪlɪdʒd] *adj* unterprivilegiert
underrate [ʌndə'reɪt] *vt* unterschätzen
underscore [ʌndə'skɔ:ʳ] *vt* unterstreichen
underseal [ʌndə'si:l] (*Brit*) *vt* (*car*) mit Unterbodenschutz versehen ▷ *n* (*of car*) Unterbodenschutz *m*
undersecretary ['ʌndə'sɛkrətərɪ] *n* (*Pol*) Staatssekretär(in) *m(f)*
undersell [ʌndə'sɛl] (*irreg: like* **sell**) *vt* (*competitors*) unterbieten
undershirt ['ʌndəʃə:t] (*US*) *n* Unterhemd *nt*
undershorts ['ʌndəʃɔ:ts] (*US*) *npl* Unterhose *f*
underside ['ʌndəsaɪd] *n* Unterseite *f*
undersigned ['ʌndə'saɪnd] *adj* unterzeichnet ▷ *n*: **the ~** der/die Unterzeichnete; **we the ~ agree that ...** wir, die Unterzeichneten, kommen überein, dass ...
underskirt ['ʌndəskə:t] (*Brit*) *n* Unterrock *m*
understaffed [ʌndə'stɑ:ft] *adj* unterbesetzt
understand [ʌndə'stænd] (*irreg: like* **stand**) *vt, vi* verstehen; **I ~ (that) you have ...** (*believe*) soweit ich weiß, haben Sie ...; **to make o.s. understood** sich verständlich machen
understandable [ʌndə'stændəbl] *adj* verständlich
understanding [ʌndə'stændɪŋ] *adj* verständnisvoll ▷ *n* Verständnis *nt*; **to come to an ~ with sb** mit jdm übereinkommen; **on the ~ that ...** unter der Voraussetzung, dass ...
understate [ʌndə'steɪt] *vt* herunterspielen
understatement ['ʌndəsteɪtmənt] *n* Understatement *nt*, Untertreibung *f*; **that's an ~!** das ist untertrieben!
understood [ʌndə'stud] *pt, pp of* **understand** ▷ *adj* (*agreed*) abgemacht; (*implied*) impliziert
understudy ['ʌndəstʌdɪ] *n* zweite Besetzung *f*
undertake [ʌndə'teɪk] (*irreg: like* **take**) *vt* (*task*) übernehmen ▷ *vi*: **to ~ to do sth** es übernehmen, etw zu tun
undertaker ['ʌndəteɪkəʳ] *n* (Leichen)bestatter *m*
undertaking ['ʌndəteɪkɪŋ] *n* (*job*) Unternehmen *nt*; (*promise*) Zusicherung *f*
undertone ['ʌndətəun] *n* (*of criticism etc*) Unterton *m*; **in an ~** mit gedämpfter Stimme
undervalue [ʌndə'vælju:] *vt* (*person, work etc*) unterbewerten
underwater ['ʌndə'wɔ:təʳ] *adv* (*swim etc*) unter Wasser ▷ *adj* (*exploration, camera etc*) Unterwasser-
underwear ['ʌndəwɛəʳ] *n* Unterwäsche *f*
underweight [ʌndə'weɪt] *adj*: **to be ~** Untergewicht haben
underworld ['ʌndəwə:ld] *n* Unterwelt *f*
underwrite [ʌndə'raɪt] *vt* (*Fin*) garantieren; (*Insurance*) versichern
underwriter ['ʌndəraɪtəʳ] *n* (*Insurance*) Versicherer(in) *m(f)*
undeserved [ʌndɪ'zə:vd] *adj* unverdient
undesirable [ʌndɪ'zaɪərəbl] *adj* unerwünscht
undeveloped [ʌndɪ'vɛləpt] *adj* (*land*) unentwickelt; (*resources*) ungenutzt
undies ['ʌndɪz] (*inf*) *npl* Unterwäsche *f*
undiluted ['ʌndaɪ'lu:tɪd] *adj* (*substance*) unverdünnt; (*emotion*) unverfälscht
undiplomatic ['ʌndɪplə'mætɪk] *adj* undiplomatisch
undischarged ['ʌndɪs'tʃɑ:dʒd] *adj*: **~ bankrupt** nicht entlasteter Konkursschuldner *m*, nicht entlastete Konkursschuldnerin *f*
undisciplined [ʌn'dɪsɪplɪnd] *adj* undiszipliniert
undiscovered ['ʌndɪs'kʌvəd] *adj* unentdeckt
undisguised ['ʌndɪs'gaɪzd] *adj* (*dislike, amusement etc*) unverhohlen
undisputed ['ʌndɪs'pju:tɪd] *adj* unbestritten
undistinguished ['ʌndɪs'tɪŋgwɪʃt] *adj* (*career, person*) mittelmäßig; (*appearance*) durchschnittlich
undisturbed [ʌndɪs'tə:bd] *adj* ungestört; **to leave sth ~** etw unberührt lassen
undivided [ʌndɪ'vaɪdɪd] *adj*: **you have my ~ attention** Sie haben meine ungeteilte Aufmerksamkeit
undo [ʌn'du:] (*irreg: like* **do**) *vt* (*unfasten*) aufmachen; (*spoil*) zunichtemachen
undoing [ʌn'du:ɪŋ] *n* Verderben *nt*
undone [ʌn'dʌn] *pp of* **undo** ▷ *adj*: **to come ~** (*shoelaces etc*) aufgehen
undoubted [ʌn'dautɪd] *adj* unzweifelhaft
undoubtedly [ʌn'dautɪdlɪ] *adv* zweifellos
undress [ʌn'drɛs] *vi* sich ausziehen ▷ *vt* ausziehen
undrinkable [ʌn'drɪŋkəbl] *adj* (*unpalatable*) ungenießbar; (*poisonous*) nicht trinkbar
undue [ʌn'dju:] *adj* (*excessive*) übertrieben
undulating ['ʌndjuleɪtɪŋ] *adj* (*movement*) Wellen-; (*hills*) sanft
unduly [ʌn'dju:lɪ] *adv* (*excessively*) übermäßig
undying [ʌn'daɪɪŋ] *adj* (*love, loyalty etc*) ewig
unearned [ʌn'ə:nd] *adj* (*praise*) unverdient; **~ income** Kapitaleinkommen *nt*
unearth [ʌn'ə:θ] *vt* (*skeleton etc*) ausgraben; (*fig: secrets etc*) ausfindig machen
unearthly [ʌn'ə:θlɪ] *adj* (*eerie*) unheimlich; **at some ~ hour** zu nachtschlafender Zeit
unease [ʌn'i:z] *n* Unbehagen *nt*
uneasy [ʌn'i:zɪ] *adj* (*person*) unruhig; (*feeling*) unbehaglich; (*peace, truce*) unsicher; **to feel**

~ about doing sth ein ungutes Gefühl dabei haben, etw zu tun
uneconomic ['ʌniːkəˈnɔmɪk] *adj* unwirtschaftlich
uneconomical ['ʌniːkəˈnɔmɪkl] *adj* unwirtschaftlich
uneducated [ʌnˈɛdjukeɪtɪd] *adj* ungebildet
unemployed [ʌnɪmˈplɔɪd] *adj* arbeitslos ▷ *npl*: **the ~** die Arbeitslosen *pl*
unemployment [ʌnɪmˈplɔɪmənt] *n* Arbeitslosigkeit *f*
unemployment benefit (*Brit*) *n* Arbeitslosenunterstützung *f*
unemployment compensation (*US*) *n* = **unemployment benefit**
unending [ʌnˈɛndɪŋ] *adj* endlos
unenviable [ʌnˈɛnvɪəbl] *adj* (*task, conditions etc*) wenig beneidenswert
unequal [ʌnˈiːkwəl] *adj* ungleich; **to feel ~ to** sich nicht gewachsen fühlen *+dat*
unequalled, (*US*) **unequaled** [ʌnˈiːkwəld] *adj* unübertroffen
unequivocal [ʌnɪˈkwɪvəkl] *adj* (*answer*) unzweideutig; **to be ~ about sth** eine klare Haltung zu etw haben
unerring [ʌnˈəːrɪŋ] *adj* unfehlbar
UNESCO [juːˈnɛskəu] *n abbr* (= *United Nations Educational, Scientific and Cultural Organization*) UNESCO *f*
unethical [ʌnˈɛθɪkl] *adj* (*methods*) unlauter; (*doctor's behaviour*) unethisch
uneven [ʌnˈiːvn] *adj* (*teeth, road etc*) uneben; (*performance*) ungleichmäßig
uneventful [ʌnɪˈvɛntful] *adj* ereignislos
unexceptional [ʌnɪkˈsɛpʃənl] *adj* durchschnittlich
unexciting [ʌnɪkˈsaɪtɪŋ] *adj* (*film, news*) wenig aufregend
unexpected [ʌnɪksˈpɛktɪd] *adj* unerwartet
unexpectedly [ʌnɪksˈpɛktɪdlɪ] *adv* unerwartet
unexplained [ʌnɪksˈpleɪnd] *adj* (*mystery, failure*) ungeklärt
unexploded [ʌnɪksˈpləudɪd] *adj* nicht explodiert
unfailing [ʌnˈfeɪlɪŋ] *adj* (*support, energy*) unerschöpflich
unfair [ʌnˈfɛə^r] *adj* unfair, ungerecht; (*advantage*) ungerechtfertigt; **~ to** unfair *or* ungerecht zu
unfair dismissal *n* ungerechtfertigte Entlassung *f*
unfairly [ʌnˈfɛəlɪ] *adv* (*treat*) unfair, ungerecht; (*dismiss*) ungerechtfertigt
unfaithful [ʌnˈfeɪθful] *adj* (*lover, spouse*) untreu
unfamiliar [ʌnfəˈmɪlɪə^r] *adj* ungewohnt; (*person*) fremd; **to be ~ with sth** mit etw nicht vertraut sein
unfashionable [ʌnˈfæʃnəbl] *adj* (*clothes, ideas*) unmodern; (*place*) unbeliebt
unfasten [ʌnˈfɑːsn] *vt* (*seat belt, strap*) lösen
unfathomable [ʌnˈfæðəməbl] *adj* unergründlich
unfavourable, (*US*) **unfavorable** [ʌnˈfeɪvrəbl] *adj* (*circumstances, weather*) ungünstig; (*opinion, report*) negativ
unfavourably, (*US*) **unfavorably** [ʌnˈfeɪvrəblɪ] *adv*: **to compare ~ (with sth)** im Vergleich (mit etw) ungünstig sein; **to compare ~ (with sb)** im Vergleich (mit jdm) schlechter abschneiden; **to look ~ on** (*suggestion etc*) ablehnend gegenüberstehen *+dat*
unfeeling [ʌnˈfiːlɪŋ] *adj* gefühllos
unfinished [ʌnˈfɪnɪʃt] *adj* unvollendet
unfit [ʌnˈfɪt] *adj* (*physically*) nicht fit; (*incompetent*) unfähig; **~ for work** arbeitsunfähig; **~ for human consumption** zum Verzehr ungeeignet
unflagging [ʌnˈflægɪŋ] *adj* (*attention, energy*) unermüdlich
unflappable [ʌnˈflæpəbl] *adj* unerschütterlich
unflattering [ʌnˈflætərɪŋ] *adj* (*dress, hairstyle*) unvorteilhaft; (*remark*) wenig schmeichelhaft
unflinching [ʌnˈflɪntʃɪŋ] *adj* unerschrocken
unfold [ʌnˈfəuld] *vt* (*sheets, map*) auseinanderfalten ▷ *vi* (*situation, story*) sich entfalten
unforeseeable [ʌnfɔːˈsiːəbl] *adj* unvorhersehbar
unforeseen ['ʌnfɔːˈsiːn] *adj* unvorhergesehen
unforgettable [ʌnfəˈgɛtəbl] *adj* unvergesslich
unforgivable [ʌnfəˈgɪvəbl] *adj* unverzeihlich
unformatted [ʌnˈfɔːmætɪd] *adj* (*disk, text*) unformatiert
unfortunate [ʌnˈfɔːtʃənət] *adj* (*unlucky*) unglücklich; (*regrettable*) bedauerlich; **it is ~ that ...** es ist bedauerlich, dass ...
unfortunately [ʌnˈfɔːtʃənətlɪ] *adv* leider
unfounded [ʌnˈfaundɪd] *adj* (*allegations, fears*) unbegründet
unfriendly [ʌnˈfrɛndlɪ] *adj* unfreundlich
unfulfilled [ʌnfulˈfɪld] *adj* (*ambition, prophecy*) unerfüllt; (*person*) unausgefüllt
unfurl [ʌnˈfəːl] *vt* (*flag etc*) entrollen
unfurnished [ʌnˈfəːnɪʃt] *adj* unmöbliert
ungainly [ʌnˈgeɪnlɪ] *adj* (*person*) unbeholfen
ungodly [ʌnˈgɔdlɪ] *adj* (*annoying*) heillos; **at some ~ hour** zu nachtschlafender Zeit
ungrateful [ʌnˈgreɪtful] *adj* undankbar
unguarded [ʌnˈgɑːdɪd] *adj*: **in an ~ moment** in einem unbedachten Augenblick
unhappily [ʌnˈhæpɪlɪ] *adv* (*miserably*) unglücklich; (*unfortunately*) leider
unhappiness [ʌnˈhæpɪnɪs] *n* Traurigkeit *f*
unhappy [ʌnˈhæpɪ] *adj* unglücklich; **~ about/with** (*dissatisfied*) unzufrieden über *+acc*/mit
unharmed [ʌnˈhɑːmd] *adj* (*person, animal*) unversehrt
UNHCR *n abbr* (= *United Nations High Commission for Refugees*) *Flüchtlingskommission der Vereinten Nationen*
unhealthy [ʌnˈhɛlθɪ] *adj* (*person*) nicht gesund; (*place*) ungesund; (*fig: interest*) krankhaft
unheard-of [ʌnˈhəːdɔv] *adj* (*unknown*) unbekannt; (*outrageous*) unerhört
unhelpful [ʌnˈhɛlpful] *adj* (*person*) nicht hilfreich; (*advice*) nutzlos

unhesitating [ʌn'hɛzɪteɪtɪŋ] *adj* (*loyalty*) bereitwillig; (*reply, offer*) prompt
unholy [ʌn'həulɪ] (*inf*) *adj* (*fig: alliance*) übel; (: *mess*) heillos; (: *row*) furchtbar
unhook [ʌn'huk] *vt* (*unfasten*) losmachen
unhurt [ʌn'hə:t] *adj* unverletzt
unhygienic ['ʌnhaɪ'dʒi:nɪk] *adj* unhygienisch
UNICEF ['ju:nɪsɛf] *n abbr* (= *United Nations International Children's Emergency Fund*) UNICEF *f*
unicorn ['ju:nɪkɔ:n] *n* Einhorn *nt*
unidentified [ʌnaɪ'dɛntɪfaɪd] *adj* (*unknown*) unbekannt; (*unnamed*) ungenannt; *see also* **UFO**
unification [ju:nɪfɪ'keɪʃən] *n* Vereinigung *f*
unification process *n* Einigungsprozess *m*
uniform ['ju:nɪfɔ:m] *n* Uniform *f* ▷ *adj* (*length, width etc*) einheitlich
uniformity [ju:nɪ'fɔ:mɪtɪ] *n* Einheitlichkeit *f*
unify ['ju:nɪfaɪ] *vt* vereinigen
unilateral [ju:nɪ'lætərəl] *adj* einseitig
unimaginable [ʌnɪ'mædʒɪnəbl] *adj* unvorstellbar
unimaginative [ʌnɪ'mædʒɪnətɪv] *adj* fantasielos
unimpaired [ʌnɪm'pɛəd] *adj* unbeeinträchtigt
unimportant [ʌnɪm'pɔ:tənt] *adj* unwichtig
unimpressed [ʌnɪm'prɛst] *adj* unbeeindruckt
uninhabited [ʌnɪn'hæbɪtɪd] *adj* unbewohnt
uninhibited [ʌnɪn'hɪbɪtɪd] *adj* (*person*) ohne Hemmungen; (*behaviour*) hemmungslos
uninjured [ʌn'ɪndʒəd] *adj* unverletzt
uninspiring [ʌnɪn'spaɪərɪŋ] *adj* wenig aufregend; (*person*) trocken, nüchtern
unintelligent [ʌnɪn'tɛlɪdʒənt] *adj* unintelligent
unintentional [ʌnɪn'tɛnʃənəl] *adj* unbeabsichtigt
unintentionally [ʌnɪn'tɛnʃnəlɪ] *adv* unabsichtlich
uninvited [ʌnɪn'vaɪtɪd] *adj* (*guest*) ungeladen
uninviting [ʌnɪn'vaɪtɪŋ] *adj* (*food*) unappetitlich; (*place*) wenig einladend
union ['ju:njən] *n* (*unification*) Vereinigung *f*; (*also*: **trade union**) Gewerkschaft *f* ▷ *cpd* (*activities, leader etc*) Gewerkschafts-; **the U~** (US) die Vereinigten Staaten
unionize ['ju:njənaɪz] *vt* (*employees*) gewerkschaftlich organisieren
Union Jack *n* Union Jack *m*
union shop *n* gewerkschaftspflichtiger Betrieb *m*
unique [ju:'ni:k] *adj* (*object etc*) einmalig; (*ability, skill*) einzigartig; **to be ~ to** charakteristisch sein für
unisex ['ju:nɪsɛks] *adj* (*clothes*) Unisex-; (*hairdresser*) für Damen und Herren
UNISON ['ju:nɪsn] *n Gewerkschaft der Angestellten im öffentlichen Dienst*
unison ['ju:nɪsn] *n*: **in ~** (*say, sing*) einstimmig; (*act*) in Übereinstimmung
unit ['ju:nɪt] *n* Einheit *f*; **production ~** Produktionsabteilung *f*; **kitchen ~** Küchen-Einbauelement *nt*
unitary ['ju:nɪtrɪ] *adj* (*state, system etc*) einheitlich
unit cost *n* (*Comm*) Stückkosten *pl*
unite [ju:'naɪt] *vt* vereinigen ▷ *vi* sich zusammenschließen
united [ju:'naɪtɪd] *adj* (*agreed*) einig; (*country, party*) vereinigt
United Arab Emirates *npl*: **the ~** die Vereinigten Arabischen Emirate *pl*
United Kingdom *n*: **the ~** das Vereinigte Königreich
United Nations *npl*: **the ~** die Vereinten Nationen *pl*
United States *n*: **the ~ (of America)** die Vereinigten Staaten *pl* (von Amerika)
unit price *n* (*Comm*) Einzelpreis *m*
unit trust (*Brit*) *n* (*Comm*) Investmenttrust *m*
unity ['ju:nɪtɪ] *n* Einheit *f*
Univ. *abbr* = **university**
universal [ju:nɪ'və:sl] *adj* allgemein
universe ['ju:nɪvə:s] *n* Universum *nt*
university [ju:nɪ'və:sɪtɪ] *n* Universität *f* ▷ *cpd* (*student, professor*) Universitäts-; (*education, year*) akademisch
university degree *n* Universitätsabschluss *m*
unjust [ʌn'dʒʌst] *adj* ungerecht; (*society*) unfair
unjustifiable ['ʌndʒʌstɪ'faɪəbl] *adj* nicht zu rechtfertigen
unjustified [ʌn'dʒʌstɪfaɪd] *adj* (*belief, action*) ungerechtfertigt; (*text*) nicht bündig
unkempt [ʌn'kɛmpt] *adj* ungepflegt
unkind [ʌn'kaɪnd] *adj* (*person, comment etc*) unfreundlich
unkindly [ʌn'kaɪndlɪ] *adv* unfreundlich
unknown [ʌn'nəun] *adj* unbekannt; **~ to me, …** ohne dass ich es wusste, …; **~ quantity** (*fig*) unbekannte Größe
unladen [ʌn'leɪdn] *adj* (*ship*) ohne Ladung; (*weight*) Leer-
unlawful [ʌn'lɔ:ful] *adj* gesetzwidrig
unleaded ['ʌn'lɛdɪd] *adj* (*petrol*) bleifrei, unverbleit; **I use ~** ich fahre bleifrei
unleash [ʌn'li:ʃ] *vt* (*fig: feeling, forces etc*) entfesseln
unleavened [ʌn'lɛvnd] *adj* (*bread*) ungesäuert
unless [ʌn'lɛs] *conj* es sei denn; **~ he comes** wenn er nicht kommt; **~ otherwise stated** wenn nicht anders angegeben; **~ I am mistaken** wenn ich mich nicht irre; **there will be a strike ~ …** es wird zum Streik kommen, es sei denn, …
unlicensed [ʌn'laɪsnst] (*Brit*) *adj* (*restaurant*) ohne Schankkonzession
unlike [ʌn'laɪk] *adj* (*not alike*) unähnlich ▷ *prep* (*different from*) verschieden von; **~ me, she is very tidy** im Gegensatz zu mir ist sie sehr ordentlich
unlikelihood [ʌn'laɪklɪhud] *n* Unwahrscheinlichkeit *f*
unlikely [ʌn'laɪklɪ] *adj* unwahrscheinlich; (*combination etc*) merkwürdig; **in the ~ event of/that …** im unwahrscheinlichen Fall *+gen*/dass …
unlimited [ʌn'lɪmɪtɪd] *adj* unbeschränkt

unlisted ['ʌn'lɪstɪd] *adj* (*Stock Exchange*) nicht notiert; (*US*: *Tel*): **to be ~** nicht im Telefonbuch stehen
unlit [ʌn'lɪt] *adj* (*room etc*) unbeleuchtet
unload [ʌn'ləud] *vt* (*box etc*) ausladen; (*car etc*) entladen
unlock [ʌn'lɔk] *vt* aufschließen
unlucky [ʌn'lʌkɪ] *adj* (*object*) Unglück bringend; (*number*) Unglücks-; **to be ~** (*person*) Pech haben
unmanageable [ʌn'mænɪdʒəbl] *adj* (*tool, vehicle*) kaum zu handhaben; (*person, hair*) widerspenstig; (*situation*) unkontrollierbar
unmanned [ʌn'mænd] *adj* (*station, spacecraft etc*) unbemannt
unmarked [ʌn'mɑ:kt] *adj* (*unstained*) fleckenlos; (*unscarred*) nicht gezeichnet; (*unblemished*) makellos; **~ police car** nicht gekennzeichneter Streifenwagen *m*
unmarried [ʌn'mærɪd] *adj* unverheiratet
unmarried mother *n* ledige Mutter *f*
unmask [ʌn'mɑ:sk] *vt* (*reveal*) enthüllen
unmatched [ʌn'mætʃt] *adj* unübertroffen
unmentionable [ʌn'mɛnʃnəbl] *adj* (*topic, word*) Tabu-; **to be ~** tabu sein
unmerciful [ʌn'mə:sɪful] *adj* erbarmungslos
unmistakable, **unmistakeable** [ʌnmɪs'teɪkəbl] *adj* unverkennbar
unmistakably, **unmistakeably** [ʌnmɪs'teɪkəblɪ] *adv* unverkennbar
unmitigated [ʌn'mɪtɪgeɪtɪd] *adj* (*disaster etc*) total
unnamed [ʌn'neɪmd] *adj* (*nameless*) namenlos; (*anonymous*) ungenannt
unnatural [ʌn'nætʃrəl] *adj* unnatürlich; (*against nature*: *habit*) widernatürlich
unnecessarily [ʌn'nɛsəsərɪlɪ] *adv* (*worry etc*) unnötigerweise; (*severe etc*) übertrieben
unnecessary [ʌn'nɛsəsərɪ] *adj* unnötig
unnerve [ʌn'nə:v] *vt* entnerven
unnoticed [ʌn'nəutɪst] *adj*: **to go** *or* **pass ~** unbemerkt bleiben
UNO ['ju:nəu] *n abbr* (= *United Nations Organization*) UNO *f*
unobservant [ʌnəb'zə:vənt] *adj* unaufmerksam
unobtainable [ʌnəb'teɪnəbl] *adj* (*item*) nicht erhältlich; **this number is ~** (*Tel*) kein Anschluss unter dieser Nummer
unobtrusive [ʌnəb'tru:sɪv] *adj* unauffällig
unoccupied [ʌn'ɔkjupaɪd] *adj* (*seat*) frei; (*house*) leer (stehend)
unofficial [ʌnə'fɪʃl] *adj* inoffiziell
unopened [ʌn'əupənd] *adj* ungeöffnet
unopposed [ʌnə'pəuzd] *adj*: **to be ~** (*suggestion*) nicht auf Widerstand treffen; (*motion, bill*) ohne Gegenstimmen angenommen werden
unorthodox [ʌn'ɔ:θədɔks] *adj* (*also Rel*) unorthodox
unpack [ʌn'pæk] *vt, vi* auspacken
unpaid [ʌn'peɪd] *adj* unbezahlt
unpalatable [ʌn'pælətəbl] *adj* (*meal*) ungenießbar; (*truth*) bitter
unparalleled [ʌn'pærəlɛld] *adj* beispiellos
unpatriotic ['ʌnpætrɪ'ɔtɪk] *adj* unpatriotisch
unplanned [ʌn'plænd] *adj* ungeplant
unpleasant [ʌn'plɛznt] *adj* unangenehm; (*person, manner*) unfreundlich
unplug [ʌn'plʌg] *vt* (*iron, record player etc*) den Stecker herausziehen *+gen*
unpolluted [ʌnpə'lu:tɪd] *adj* unverschmutzt
unpopular [ʌn'pɔpjulə^r] *adj* unpopulär; **to make o.s. ~ (with)** sich unbeliebt machen (bei)
unprecedented [ʌn'prɛsɪdɛntɪd] *adj* noch nie da gewesen; (*decision*) einmalig
unpredictable [ʌnprɪ'dɪktəbl] *adj* (*person, weather*) unberechenbar; (*reaction*) unvorhersehbar
unprejudiced [ʌn'prɛdʒudɪst] *adj* unvoreingenommen
unprepared [ʌnprɪ'pɛəd] *adj* unvorbereitet
unprepossessing ['ʌnpri:pə'zɛsɪŋ] *adj* (*person, place*) unattraktiv
unpretentious [ʌnprɪ'tɛnʃəs] *adj* (*building, person*) schlicht
unprincipled [ʌn'prɪnsɪpld] *adj* (*person*) charakterlos
unproductive [ʌnprə'dʌktɪv] *adj* (*land*) unfruchtbar, ertragsarm; (*discussion*) unproduktiv
unprofessional [ʌnprə'fɛʃənl] *adj* unprofessionell
unprofitable [ʌn'prɔfɪtəbl] *adj* nicht profitabel, unrentabel
UNPROFOR *n abbr* (= *United Nations Protection Force*) UNPROFOR *f*; **~ troops** UNPROFOR-Truppen, UNO-Schutztruppen
unprotected ['ʌnprə'tɛktɪd] *adj* ungeschützt
unprovoked [ʌnprə'vəukt] *adj* (*attack*) grundlos
unpunished [ʌn'pʌnɪʃt] *adj*: **to go ~** straflos bleiben
unqualified [ʌn'kwɔlɪfaɪd] *adj* unqualifiziert; (*disaster, success*) vollkommen
unquestionably [ʌn'kwɛstʃənəblɪ] *adv* fraglos
unquestioning [ʌn'kwɛstʃənɪŋ] *adj* bedingungslos
unravel [ʌn'rævl] *vt* (*also fig*) entwirren
unreal [ʌn'rɪəl] *adj* (*artificial*) unecht; (*peculiar*) unwirklich
unrealistic ['ʌnrɪə'lɪstɪk] *adj* unrealistisch
unreasonable [ʌn'ri:znəbl] *adj* (*person, attitude*) unvernünftig; (*demand, length of time*) unzumutbar
unrecognizable [ʌn'rɛkəgnaɪzəbl] *adj* nicht zu erkennen
unrecognized [ʌn'rɛkəgnaɪzd] *adj* (*talent etc*) unerkannt; (*Pol*: *regime*) nicht anerkannt
unreconstructed ['ʌnri:kən'strʌktɪd] (*esp US*) *adj* (*unwilling to accept change*) unverbesserlich
unrecorded [ʌnrə'kɔ:dɪd] *adj* (*piece of music etc*) nicht aufgenommen; (*incident, statement*) nicht schriftlich festgehalten
unrefined [ʌnrə'faɪnd] *adj* (*sugar, petroleum*) nicht raffiniert
unrehearsed [ʌnrɪ'hə:st] *adj* (*Theat etc*) nicht

geprobt; (*spontaneous*) spontan
unrelated [ʌnrɪ'leɪtɪd] *adj* (*incidents*) ohne Beziehung; (*people*) nicht verwandt
unrelenting [ʌnrɪ'lɛntɪŋ] *adj* (*person, behaviour etc*) unnachgiebig
unreliable [ʌnrɪ'laɪəbl] *adj* unzuverlässig
unrelieved [ʌnrɪ'li:vd] *adj* ungemindert
unremitting [ʌnrɪ'mɪtɪŋ] *adj* (*efforts, attempts*) unermüdlich
unrepeatable [ʌnrɪ'pi:təbl] *adj* (*offer*) einmalig; (*comment*) nicht wiederholbar
unrepentant [ʌnrɪ'pɛntənt] *adj*: **to be ~ about sth** etw nicht bereuen; **he's an ~ Marxist** er bereut es nicht, nach wie vor Marxist zu sein
unrepresentative ['ʌnrɛprɪ'zɛntətɪv] *adj*: **~ (of)** nicht repräsentativ (für)
unrepresented ['ʌnrɛprɪ'zɛntɪd] *adj* nicht vertreten
unreserved [ʌnrɪ'zə:vd] *adj* (*seat*) unreserviert; (*approval etc*) uneingeschränkt, vorbehaltlos
unreservedly [ʌnrɪ'zə:vɪdlɪ] *adv* ohne Vorbehalt
unresponsive [ʌnrɪs'pɔnsɪv] *adj* unempfänglich
unrest [ʌn'rɛst] *n* Unruhen *pl*
unrestricted [ʌnrɪ'strɪktɪd] *adj* unbeschränkt; **to have ~ access to** ungehinderten Zugang haben zu
unrewarded [ʌnrɪ'wɔ:dɪd] *adj* unbelohnt
unripe [ʌn'raɪp] *adj* unreif
unrivalled, (*US*) **unrivaled** [ʌn'raɪvəld] *adj* unübertroffen
unroll [ʌn'rəul] *vt* entrollen ▷ *vi* sich entrollen
unruffled [ʌn'rʌfld] *adj* unbewegt; (*hair*) unzerzaust
unruly [ʌn'ru:lɪ] *adj* (*child, behaviour*) ungebärdig; (*hair*) widerspenstig
unsafe [ʌn'seɪf] *adj* unsicher; (*machine, bridge, car etc*) gefährlich; **~ to eat/drink** ungenießbar
unsaid [ʌn'sɛd] *adj*: **to leave sth ~** etw ungesagt lassen
unsaleable, (*US*) **unsalable** [ʌn'seɪləbl] *adj* unverkäuflich
unsatisfactory ['ʌnsætɪs'fæktərɪ] *adj* unbefriedigend
unsatisfied [ʌn'sætɪsfaɪd] *adj* unzufrieden
unsavoury, (*US*) **unsavory** [ʌn'seɪvərɪ] *adj* (*fig: person, place*) widerwärtig
unscathed [ʌn'skeɪðd] *adj* unversehrt
unscientific ['ʌnsaɪən'tɪfɪk] *adj* unwissenschaftlich
unscrew [ʌn'skru:] *vt* losschrauben
unscrupulous [ʌn'skru:pjuləs] *adj* skrupellos
unseat [ʌn'si:t] *vt* (*rider*) abwerfen; (*from office*) aus dem Amt drängen
unsecured ['ʌnsɪ'kjuəd] *adj*: **~ creditor** nicht gesicherter Gläubiger *m*; **~ loan** Blankokredit *m*
unseeded [ʌn'si:dɪd] *adj* (*player*) nicht gesetzt
unseemly [ʌn'si:mlɪ] *adj* unschicklich
unseen [ʌn'si:n] *adj* (*person, danger*) unsichtbar
unselfish [ʌn'sɛlfɪʃ] *adj* selbstlos
unsettled [ʌn'sɛtld] *adj* (*person*) unruhig; (*future*) unsicher; (*question*) ungeklärt; (*weather*) unbeständig
unsettling [ʌn'sɛtlɪŋ] *adj* beunruhigend
unshakable, **unshakeable** [ʌn'ʃeɪkəbl] *adj* unerschütterlich
unshaven [ʌn'ʃeɪvn] *adj* unrasiert
unsightly [ʌn'saɪtlɪ] *adj* unansehnlich
unskilled [ʌn'skɪld] *adj* (*work, worker*) ungelernt
unsociable [ʌn'səuʃəbl] *adj* ungesellig
unsocial [ʌn'səuʃl] *adj*: **to work ~ hours** außerhalb der normalen Arbeitszeit arbeiten
unsold [ʌn'səuld] *adj* unverkauft
unsolicited [ʌnsə'lɪsɪtɪd] *adj* unerbeten
unsophisticated [ʌnsə'fɪstɪkeɪtɪd] *adj* (*person*) anspruchslos; (*method, device*) simpel
unsound [ʌn'saund] *adj* (*floor, foundations*) unsicher; (*policy, advice*) unklug; **of ~ mind** unzurechnungsfähig
unspeakable [ʌn'spi:kəbl] *adj* (*indescribable*) unsagbar; (*awful*) abscheulich
unspoken [ʌn'spəukn] *adj* (*word*) unausgesprochen; (*agreement etc*) stillschweigend
unstable [ʌn'steɪbl] *adj* (*piece of furniture*) nicht stabil; (*government*) instabil; (*person: mentally*) labil
unsteady [ʌn'stɛdɪ] *adj* (*step, voice, legs*) unsicher; (*ladder*) wack(e)lig
unstinting [ʌn'stɪntɪŋ] *adj* (*support*) vorbehaltlos; (*generosity*) unbegrenzt
unstuck [ʌn'stʌk] *adj*: **to come ~** (*label etc*) sich lösen; (*fig: plan, idea etc*) versagen
unsubstantiated ['ʌnsəb'stænʃɪeɪtɪd] *adj* (*rumour*) unbestätigt; (*accusation*) unbegründet
unsuccessful [ʌnsək'sɛsful] *adj* erfolglos; (*marriage*) gescheitert; **to be ~** keinen Erfolg haben
unsuccessfully [ʌnsək'sɛsfəlɪ] *adv* ohne Erfolg, vergeblich
unsuitable [ʌn'su:təbl] *adj* (*time*) unpassend; (*clothes, person*) ungeeignet
unsuited [ʌn'su:tɪd] *adj*: **to be ~ for** *or* **to sth** für etw ungeeignet sein
unsung ['ʌnsʌŋ] *adj*: **an ~ hero** ein unbesungener Held
unsure [ʌn'ʃuə[r]] *adj* unsicher; **to be ~ of o.s.** unsicher sein
unsuspecting [ʌnsəs'pɛktɪŋ] *adj* ahnungslos
unsweetened [ʌn'swi:tnd] *adj* ungesüßt
unswerving [ʌn'swə:vɪŋ] *adj* unerschütterlich
unsympathetic ['ʌnsɪmpə'θɛtɪk] *adj* (*showing little understanding*) abweisend; (*unlikeable*) unsympathisch; **to be ~ to(wards) sth** einer Sache *dat* ablehnend gegenüberstehen
untangle [ʌn'tæŋgl] *vt* entwirren
untapped [ʌn'tæpt] *adj* (*resources*) ungenutzt
untaxed [ʌn'tækst] *adj* (*goods, income*) steuerfrei
unthinkable [ʌn'θɪŋkəbl] *adj* undenkbar
unthinking [ʌn'θɪŋkɪŋ] *adj* (*uncritical*) bedenkenlos; (*thoughtless*) gedankenlos
untidy [ʌn'taɪdɪ] *adj* unordentlich
untie [ʌn'taɪ] *vt* (*knot, parcel*) aufschnüren;

(*prisoner, dog*) losbinden
until [ən'tɪl] *prep* bis *+acc*; (*after negative*) vor *+dat* ▷ *conj* bis; (*after negative*) bevor; **~ now** bis jetzt; **~ then** bis dann; **from morning ~ night** von morgens bis abends; **~ he comes** bis er kommt
untimely [ʌn'taɪmlɪ] *adj* (*moment*) unpassend; (*arrival*) ungelegen; (*death*) vorzeitig
untold [ʌn'təuld] *adj* (*joy, suffering, wealth*) unermesslich; **the ~ story** die Hintergründe
untouched [ʌn'tʌtʃt] *adj* unberührt; (*undamaged*) unversehrt; **~ by** (*unaffected*) unberührt von
untoward [ʌntə'wɔ:d] *adj* (*events, effects etc*) ungünstig
untrained ['ʌn'treɪnd] *adj* unausgebildet; (*eye, hands*) ungeschult
untrammelled [ʌn'træmld] *adj* (*person*) ungebunden; (*behaviour*) unbeschränkt
untranslatable [ʌntrænz'leɪtəbl] *adj* unübersetzbar
untried [ʌn'traɪd] *adj* (*policy, remedy*) unerprobt; (*prisoner*) noch nicht vor Gericht gestellt
untrue [ʌn'tru:] *adj* unwahr
untrustworthy [ʌn'trʌstwə:ðɪ] *adj* unzuverlässig
unusable [ʌn'ju:zəbl] *adj* (*object*) unbrauchbar; (*room*) nicht benutzbar
unused[1] [ʌn'ju:zd] *adj* (*new*) unbenutzt
unused[2] [ʌn'ju:st] *adj*: **to be ~ to sth** an etw *acc* nicht gewöhnt sein; **to be ~ to doing sth** nicht daran gewöhnt sein, etw zu tun
unusual [ʌn'ju:ʒuəl] *adj* ungewöhnlich; (*exceptional*) außergewöhnlich
unusually [ʌn'ju:ʒuəlɪ] *adv* (*large, high etc*) ungewöhnlich
unveil [ʌn'veɪl] *vt* (*also fig*) enthüllen
unwanted [ʌn'wɔntɪd] *adj* unerwünscht
unwarranted [ʌn'wɔrəntɪd] *adj* ungerechtfertigt
unwary [ʌn'wɛərɪ] *adj* unachtsam
unwavering [ʌn'weɪvərɪŋ] *adj* (*faith, support*) unerschütterlich; (*gaze*) fest
unwelcome [ʌn'wɛlkəm] *adj* (*guest*) unwillkommen; (*news*) unerfreulich; **to feel ~** sich nicht willkommen fühlen
unwell [ʌn'wɛl] *adj*: **to be ~, to feel ~** sich nicht wohlfühlen
unwieldy [ʌn'wi:ldɪ] *adj* (*object*) unhandlich; (*system*) schwerfällig
unwilling [ʌn'wɪlɪŋ] *adj*: **to be ~ to do sth** etw nicht tun wollen
unwillingly [ʌn'wɪlɪŋlɪ] *adv* widerwillig
unwind [ʌn'waɪnd] (*irreg: like* **wind**) *vt* abwickeln ▷ *vi* sich abwickeln; (*relax*) sich entspannen
unwise [ʌn'waɪz] *adj* unklug
unwitting [ʌn'wɪtɪŋ] *adj* (*accomplice*) unwissentlich; (*victim*) ahnungslos
unworkable [ʌn'wə:kəbl] *adj* (*plan*) undurchführbar
unworthy [ʌn'wə:ðɪ] *adj* unwürdig; **to be ~ of sth** einer Sache *gen* nicht wert *or* würdig sein; **to be ~ to do sth** es nicht wert sein, etw zu tun; **that remark is ~ of you** diese Bemerkung ist unter deiner Würde
unwrap [ʌn'ræp] *vt* auspacken
unwritten [ʌn'rɪtn] *adj* (*law*) ungeschrieben; (*agreement*) stillschweigend
unzip [ʌn'zɪp] *vt* aufmachen

KEYWORD

up [ʌp] *prep*: **to be up sth** (oben) auf etw *dat* sein; **to go up sth** (auf) etw *acc* hinaufgehen; **go up that road and turn left** gehen Sie die Straße hinauf und biegen Sie links ab
▷ *adv* **1** (*upwards, higher*) oben; **put it a bit higher up** stelle es etwas höher; **up there** dort oben; **up above** hoch oben
2: to be up (*out of bed*) auf sein; (*prices, level*) gestiegen sein; (*building, tent*) stehen; **time's up** die Zeit ist um *or* vorbei
3: up to (*as far as*) bis; **up to now** bis jetzt
4: to be up to (*depending on*) abhängen von; **it's up to you** das hängt von dir ab; **it's not up to me to decide** es liegt nicht bei mir, das zu entscheiden
5: to be up to (*equal to*) gewachsen sein *+dat*; **he's not up to it** (*job, task etc*) er ist dem nicht gewachsen; **his work is not up to the required standard** seine Arbeit entspricht nicht dem gewünschten Niveau
6: to be up to (*inf: be doing*) vorhaben; **what is he up to?** (*showing disapproval, suspicion*) was führt er im Schilde?
▷ *n*: **ups and downs** (*in life, career*) Höhen und Tiefen *pl*
▷ *vi* (*inf*): **she upped and left** sie sprang auf und rannte davon
▷ *vt* (*inf: price*) heraufsetzen

up-and-coming [ʌpənd'kʌmɪŋ] *adj* (*actor, company etc*) kommend
upbeat ['ʌpbi:t] *n* (*Mus*) Auftakt *m*; (*in economy etc*) Aufschwung *m* ▷ *adj* (*optimistic*) optimistisch
upbraid [ʌp'breɪd] *vt* tadeln
upbringing ['ʌpbrɪŋɪŋ] *n* Erziehung *f*
upcoming ['ʌpkʌmɪŋ] (*esp US*) *adj* kommend
update [ʌp'deɪt] *vt* aktualisieren
upend [ʌp'ɛnd] *vt* auf den Kopf stellen
upfront [ʌp'frʌnt] *adj* (*person*) offen ▷ *adv*: **20% ~** 20% (als) Vorschuss, 20% im Voraus
upgrade [ʌp'greɪd] *vt* (*house*) Verbesserungen durchführen in *+dat*; (*job*) verbessern; (*employee*) befördern; (*Comput*) nachrüsten
upheaval [ʌp'hi:vl] *n* Unruhe *f*
uphill ['ʌp'hɪl] *adj* bergaufwärts (führend); (*fig: task*) mühsam ▷ *adv* (*push, move*) bergaufwärts; (*go*) bergauf
uphold [ʌp'həuld] (*irreg: like* **hold**) *vt* (*law, principle*) wahren; (*decision*) unterstützen
upholstery [ʌp'həulstərɪ] *n* Polsterung *f*
upkeep ['ʌpki:p] *n* (*maintenance*) Instandhaltung *f*

up-market [ʌp'mɑːkɪt] *adj* anspruchsvoll
upon [ə'pɔn] *prep* (*position*) auf *+dat*; (*motion*) auf *+acc*
upper ['ʌpəʳ] *adj* obere(r, s) ▷ *n* (*of shoe*) Oberleder *nt*
upper class *n*: **the ~** die Oberschicht
upper-class ['ʌpə'klɑːs] *adj* vornehm
uppercut ['ʌpəkʌt] *n* Uppercut *m*
upper hand *n*: **to have the ~** die Oberhand haben
Upper House *n* (*Pol*) Oberhaus *nt*
uppermost ['ʌpəməust] *adj* oberste(r, s); **what was ~ in my mind** woran ich in erster Linie dachte
Upper Volta [-'vɔltə] *n* (*formerly*) Obervolta *nt*
upright ['ʌpraɪt] *adj* (*vertical*) vertikal; (*fig: honest*) rechtschaffen ▷ *adv* (*sit, stand*) aufrecht ▷ *n* (*Constr*) Pfosten *m*
uprising ['ʌpraɪzɪŋ] *n* Aufstand *m*
uproar ['ʌprɔːʳ] *n* Aufruhr *m*
uproarious [ʌp'rɔːrɪəs] *adj* (*laughter*) brüllend; (*joke*) brüllend komisch; (*mirth*) überwältigend
uproot [ʌp'ruːt] *vt* (*tree*) entwurzeln; (*fig: people*) aus der gewohnten Umgebung reißen; (*: in war etc*) entwurzeln
upset [*vt, adj* ʌp'sɛt, *n* 'ʌpsɛt] (*irreg: like* **set**) *vt* (*knock over*) umstoßen; (*person: offend, make unhappy*) verletzen; (*routine, plan*) durcheinanderbringen ▷ *adj* (*unhappy*) aufgebracht; (*stomach*) verstimmt ▷ *n*: **to have/get a stomach ~** (*Brit*) eine Magenverstimmung haben/bekommen; **to get ~** sich aufregen
upset price ['ʌpsɛt-] (*US, Scot*) *n* Mindestpreis *m*
upsetting [ʌp'sɛtɪŋ] *adj* (*distressing*) erschütternd
upshot ['ʌpʃɔt] *n* Ergebnis *nt*; **the ~ of it all was that ...** es lief schließlich darauf hinaus, dass ...
upside down ['ʌpsaɪd-] *adv* verkehrt herum; **to turn a room ~** (*fig*) ein Zimmer auf den Kopf stellen
upstage ['ʌp'steɪdʒ] *adv* (*Theat*) im Bühnenhintergrund ▷ *vt*: **to ~ sb** (*fig*) jdn ausstechen, jdm die Schau stehlen (*inf*)
upstairs [ʌp'stɛəz] *adv* (*be*) oben; (*go*) nach oben ▷ *adj* (*room*) obere(r, s); (*window*) im oberen Stock ▷ *n* oberes Stockwerk *nt*; **there's no ~** das Haus hat kein Obergeschoss
upstart ['ʌpstɑːt] (*pej*) *n* Emporkömmling *m*
upstream [ʌp'striːm] *adv, adj* flussaufwärts
upsurge ['ʌpsəːdʒ] *n* (*of enthusiasm etc*) Schwall *m*
uptake ['ʌpteɪk] *n*: **to be quick on the ~** schnell kapieren; **to be slow on the ~** schwer von Begriff sein
uptight [ʌp'taɪt] (*inf*) *adj* nervös
up-to-date ['ʌptə'deɪt] *adj* (*modern*) modern; (*person*) up to date
upturn ['ʌptəːn] *n* (*in economy*) Aufschwung *m*
upturned ['ʌptəːnd] *adj*: **~ nose** Stupsnase *f*
upward ['ʌpwəd] *adj* (*movement*) Aufwärts-; (*glance*) nach oben gerichtet
upwardly mobile ['ʌpwədlɪ-] *adj*: **to be ~** ein Aufsteigertyp *m* sein
upwards ['ʌpwədz] *adv* (*move*) aufwärts; (*glance*) nach oben; **upward(s) of** (*more than*) über *+acc*
URA (*US*) *n abbr* (= *Urban Renewal Administration*) *Stadtsanierungsbehörde*
Ural Mountains ['juərəl-] *npl*: **the ~** (*also*: **the Urals**) der Ural
uranium [juə'reɪnɪəm] *n* Uran *nt*
Uranus [juə'reɪnəs] *n* Uranus *m*
urban ['əːbən] *adj* städtisch; (*unemployment*) in den Städten
urbane [əː'beɪn] *adj* weltgewandt
urbanization ['əːbənaɪ'zeɪʃən] *n* Urbanisierung *f*, Verstädterung *f*
urchin ['əːtʃɪn] (*pej*) *n* Gassenkind *nt*
Urdu ['uəduː] *n* Urdu *nt*
urge [əːdʒ] *n* (*need, desire*) Verlangen *nt* ▷ *vt*: **to ~ sb to do sth** jdn eindringlich bitten, etw zu tun; **to ~ caution** zur Vorsicht mahnen
▸ **urge on** *vt* antreiben
urgency ['əːdʒənsɪ] *n* Dringlichkeit *f*
urgent ['əːdʒənt] *adj* dringend; (*voice*) eindringend
urgently ['əːdʒəntlɪ] *adv* dringend
urinal ['juərɪnl] *n* (*building*) Pissoir *nt*; (*vessel*) Urinal *nt*
urinate ['juərɪneɪt] *vi* urinieren
urine ['juərɪn] *n* Urin *m*
urn [əːn] *n* Urne *f*; (*also*: **tea urn**) Teekessel *m*
Uruguay ['juərəgwaɪ] *n* Uruguay *nt*
Uruguayan [juərə'gwaɪən] *adj* uruguayisch ▷ *n* (*person*) Uruguayer(in) *m(f)*
US *n abbr* (= *United States*) USA *pl*
us [ʌs] *pl pron* uns; (*emphatic*) wir; *see also* **me**
USA *n abbr* (= *United States of America*) USA *f*; (*Mil*: = *United States Army*) US-Armee *f*
usable ['juːzəbl] *adj* brauchbar
USAF *n abbr* (= *United States Air Force*) US-Luftwaffe *f*
usage ['juːzɪdʒ] *n* (*Ling*) (Sprach)gebrauch *m*
USB *abbr of* **universal serial bus**
USCG *n abbr* (= *United States Coast Guard*) *Küstenwache der USA*
USDA *n abbr* (= *United States Department of Agriculture*) *US-Landwirtschaftsministerium*
USDAW ['ʌzdɔː] (*Brit*) *n abbr* (= *Union of Shop, Distributive, and Allied Workers*) *Einzelhandelsgewerkschaft*
USDI *n abbr* (= *United States Department of the Interior*) *US-Innenministerium*
use [*n* juːs, *vt* juːz] *n* (*using*) Gebrauch *m*, Verwendung *f*; (*usefulness, purpose*) Nutzen *m* ▷ *vt* benutzen, gebrauchen; (*phrase*) verwenden; **in ~** in Gebrauch; **out of ~** außer Gebrauch; **to be of ~** nützlich *or* von Nutzen sein; **to make ~ of sth** Gebrauch von etw machen; **it's no ~** es hat keinen Zweck; **to have the ~ of sth** über etw *acc* verfügen können; **what's this ~d for?** wofür wird das gebraucht?; **to be ~d to sth** etw

gewohnt sein; **to get ~d to sth** sich an etw *acc* gewöhnen; **she ~d to do it** sie hat es früher gemacht
▸ **use up** *vt* (*food, leftovers*) aufbrauchen; (*money*) verbrauchen
used [ju:zd] *adj* gebraucht; (*car*) Gebraucht-
useful ['ju:sful] *adj* nützlich; **to come in ~** sich als nützlich erweisen
usefulness ['ju:sfəlnɪs] *n* Nützlichkeit *f*
useless ['ju:slɪs] *adj* nutzlos; (*person: hopeless*) hoffnungslos
user ['ju:zəʳ] *n* Benutzer(in) *m(f)*; (*of petrol, gas etc*) Verbraucher(in) *m(f)*
user-friendly ['ju:zə'frɛndlɪ] *adj* benutzerfreundlich
usher ['ʌʃəʳ] *n* (*at wedding*) Platzanweiser *m* ▹ *vt*: **to ~ sb in** jdn hineinführen
usherette [ʌʃə'rɛt] *n* Platzanweiserin *f*
USIA *n abbr* (= *United States Information Agency*) *US-Informations- und Kulturinstitut*
USM *n abbr* (= *United States Mint*) *US-Münzanstalt*; (= *United States Mail*) *US-Postbehörde*
USN *n abbr* (= *United States Navy*) US-Marine *f*
USPHS *n abbr* (= *United States Public Health Service*) *US-Gesundheitsbehörde*
USPO *n abbr* (= *United States Post Office*) *US-Postbehörde*
USS *abbr* (= *United States Ship*) *Namensteil von Schiffen der Kriegsmarine*
USSR *n abbr* (*formerly*: = *Union of Soviet Socialist Republics*) UdSSR *f*
usu. *abbr* = **usually**
usual ['ju:ʒuəl] *adj* üblich, gewöhnlich; **as ~** wie gewöhnlich
usually ['ju:ʒuəlɪ] *adv* gewöhnlich
usurer ['ju:ʒərəʳ] *n* Wucherer *m*
usurp [ju:'zə:p] *vt* (*title, position*) an sich *acc* reißen
usury ['ju:ʒurɪ] *n* Wucher *m*
UT (*US*) *abbr* (*Post*) = *Utah*
utensil [ju:'tɛnsl] *n* Gerät *nt*; **kitchen ~s** Küchengeräte *pl*
uterus ['ju:tərəs] *n* Gebärmutter *f*, Uterus *m*
utilitarian [ju:tɪlɪ'tɛərɪən] *adj* (*building, object*) praktisch; (*Philosophy*) utilitaristisch
utility [ju:'tɪlɪtɪ] *n* (*usefulness*) Nützlichkeit *f*; (*public utility*) Versorgungsbetrieb *m*
utility room *n* ≈ Hauswirtschaftsraum *m*
utilization [ju:tɪlaɪ'zeɪʃən] *n* Verwendung *f*
utilize ['ju:tɪlaɪz] *vt* verwenden
utmost ['ʌtməust] *adj* äußerste(r, s) ▹ *n*: **to do one's ~** sein Möglichstes tun; **of the ~ importance** von äußerster Wichtigkeit
utter ['ʌtəʳ] *adj* (*amazement*) äußerste(r, s); (*rubbish, fool*) total ▹ *vt* (*sounds, words*) äußern
utterance ['ʌtərəns] *n* Äußerung *f*
utterly ['ʌtəlɪ] *adv* (*totally*) vollkommen
U-turn ['ju:'tə:n] *n* (*also fig*) Kehrtwendung *f*
Uzbekistan [ʌzbɛkɪ'stɑ:n] *n* Usbekistan *nt*

Vv

V¹, v [vi:] *n* (*letter*) V *nt*, v *nt*; **V for Victor** ≈ V wie Viktor
V² *abbr* (= *volt*) V
v. *abbr* = **verse**; (= *versus*) vs.; (= *vide*) s.
VA (*US*) *abbr* (*Post*) = *Virginia*
vac [væk] (*Brit*: *inf*) *n* = **vacation**
vacancy ['veɪkənsɪ] *n* (*Brit*: *job*) freie Stelle *f*; (*room in hotel etc*) freies Zimmer *nt*; **"no vacancies"** „belegt"; **have you any vacancies?** (*hotel*) haben Sie Zimmer frei?; (*office*) haben Sie freie Stellen?
vacant ['veɪkənt] *adj* (*room, seat, job*) frei; (*look*) leer
vacant lot (*US*) *n* unbebautes Grundstück *nt*
vacate [və'keɪt] *vt* (*house*) räumen; (*one's seat*) frei machen; (*job*) aufgeben
vacation [və'keɪʃən] (*esp US*) *n* (*holiday*) Urlaub *m*; (*Scol*) Ferien *pl*; **to take a ~** Urlaub machen; **on ~** im Urlaub
vacation course *n* Ferienkurs *m*
vaccinate ['væksɪneɪt] *vt*: **to ~ sb (against sth)** jdn (gegen etw) impfen
vaccination [væksɪ'neɪʃən] *n* Impfung *f*
vaccine ['væksi:n] *n* Impfstoff *m*
vacuum ['vækjum] *n* (*empty space*) Vakuum *nt*
vacuum cleaner *n* Staubsauger *m*
vacuum flask (*Brit*) *n* Thermosflasche® *f*
vacuum-packed ['vækjum'pækt] *adj* vakuumverpackt
vagabond ['vægəbɔnd] *n* Vagabund *m*
vagary ['veɪgərɪ] *n*: **the vagaries of** die Launen *+gen*
vagina [və'dʒaɪnə] *n* Scheide *f*, Vagina *f*
vagrancy ['veɪgrənsɪ] *n* Landstreicherei *f*; (*in towns, cities*) Stadtstreicherei *f*
vagrant ['veɪgrənt] *n* Landstreicher(in) *m(f)*; (*in town, city*) Stadtstreicher(in) *m(f)*
vague [veɪg] *adj* (*memory*) vage; (*outline*) undeutlich; (*look, idea, instructions*) unbestimmt; (*person: not precise*) unsicher; (*: evasive*) unbestimmt; **to look ~** (*absent-minded*) zerstreut aussehen; **I haven't the ~st idea** ich habe nicht die leiseste Ahnung
vaguely ['veɪglɪ] *adv* (*unclearly*) vage, unbestimmt; (*slightly*) in etwa
vagueness ['veɪgnɪs] *n* Unbestimmtheit *f*
vain [veɪn] *adj* (*person*) eitel; (*attempt, action*) vergeblich; **in ~** vergebens; **to die in ~** umsonst sterben
vainly ['veɪnlɪ] *adv* vergebens
valance ['væləns] *n* (*of bed*) Volant *m*
valedictorian [vælɪdɪk'tɔ:rɪən] (*US*) *n* (*Scol*) *Abschiedsredner(in) bei der Schulentlassungsfeier*
valedictory [vælɪ'dɪktərɪ] *adj* (*speech*) Abschieds-; (*remarks*) zum Abschied
valentine ['væləntaɪn] *n* (*also*: **valentine card**) Valentinsgruß *m*; (*person*) *Freund/Freundin, dem/der man am Valentinstag einen Gruß schickt*
valet ['vælɪt] *n* Kammerdiener *m*
valet parking *n* Einparken *nt* (*durch Hotelangestellte etc*)
valet service *n* Reinigungsdienst *m*
valiant ['vælɪənt] *adj* (*effort*) tapfer
valid ['vælɪd] *adj* (*ticket, document*) gültig; (*argument, reason*) stichhaltig
validate ['vælɪdeɪt] *vt* (*contract, document*) für gültig erklären; (*argument, claim*) bestätigen
validity [və'lɪdɪtɪ] *n* (*soundness*) Gültigkeit *f*
valise [və'li:z] *n* kleiner Koffer *m*
valley ['vælɪ] *n* Tal *nt*
valour, (*US*) **valor** ['vælə^r] *n* Tapferkeit *f*
valuable ['væljuəbl] *adj* wertvoll; (*time*) kostbar
valuables ['væljuəblz] *npl* Wertsachen *pl*
valuation [vælju'eɪʃən] *n* (*of house etc*) Schätzung *f*; (*judgement of quality*) Einschätzung *f*
value ['vælju:] *n* Wert *m*; (*usefulness*) Nutzen *m* ▷ *vt* schätzen; **values** *npl* (*principles, beliefs*) Werte *pl*; **you get good ~ (for money) in that shop** in dem Laden bekommt man etwas für sein Geld; **to lose (in) ~** an Wert verlieren; **to gain (in) ~** im Wert steigen; **to be of great ~ (to sb)** (*fig*) von großem Wert (für jdn) sein
value-added tax [vælju:'ædɪd-] (*Brit*) *n* Mehrwertsteuer *f*
valued ['vælju:d] *adj* (*customer, advice*) geschätzt
valuer ['væljuə^r] *n* Schätzer(in) *m(f)*
valve [vælv] *n* Ventil *nt*; (*Med*) Klappe *f*
vampire ['væmpaɪə^r] *n* Vampir *m*
van [væn] *n* (*Aut*) Lieferwagen *m*; (*Brit: Rail*) Wa(g)gon *m*
V and A (*Brit*) *n abbr* (= *Victoria and Albert Museum*) *Londoner Museum*
vandal ['vændl] *n* Rowdy *m*
vandalism ['vændəlɪzəm] *n* Vandalismus *m*
vandalize ['vændəlaɪz] *vt* mutwillig zerstören

vanguard ['væŋgɑːd] *n (fig)*: **in the ~ of** an der Spitze *+gen*
vanilla [və'nɪlə] *n* Vanille *f*
vanilla ice cream *n* Vanilleeis *nt*
vanish ['vænɪʃ] *vi* verschwinden
vanity ['vænɪtɪ] *n (of person)* Eitelkeit *f*
vanity case *n* Kosmetikkoffer *m*
vantage point ['vɑːntɪdʒ-] *n* Aussichtspunkt *m*; *(fig)*: **from our ~** aus unserer Sicht
vaporize ['veɪpəraɪz] *vt* verdampfen ▷ *vi* verdunsten
vapour, *(US)* **vapor** ['veɪpə^r] *n (gas, steam)* Dampf *m*; *(mist)* Dunst *m*
vapour trail *n (Aviat)* Kondensstreifen *m*
variable ['vɛərɪəbl] *adj (likely to change: mood, quality, weather)* veränderlich, wechselhaft; *(able to be changed: temperature, height, speed)* variabel ▷ *n* veränderlicher Faktor *m*; *(Math)* Variable *f*
variance ['vɛərɪəns] *n*: **to be at ~ (with)** nicht übereinstimmen (mit)
variant ['vɛərɪənt] *n* Variante *f*
variation [vɛərɪ'eɪʃən] *n (change)* Veränderung *f*; *(different form: of plot, theme etc)* Variation *f*
varicose ['værɪkəus] *adj*: **~ veins** Krampfadern *pl*
varied ['vɛərɪd] *adj (diverse)* unterschiedlich; *(full of changes)* abwechslungsreich
variety [və'raɪətɪ] *n (diversity)* Vielfalt *f*; *(varied collection)* Auswahl *f*; *(type)* Sorte *f*; **a wide ~ of ...** eine Vielfalt an *+acc* ...; **for a ~ of reasons** aus verschiedenen Gründen
variety show *n* Varietévorführung *f*
various ['vɛərɪəs] *adj (reasons, people)* verschiedene; **at ~ times** *(different)* zu verschiedenen Zeiten; *(several)* mehrmals, mehrfach
varnish ['vɑːnɪʃ] *n* Lack *m* ▷ *vt (wood, one's nails)* lackieren
vary ['vɛərɪ] *vt* verändern ▷ *vi (be different)* variieren; **to ~ with** *(weather, season etc)* sich ändern mit
varying ['vɛərɪɪŋ] *adj* unterschiedlich
vase [vɑːz] *n* Vase *f*
vasectomy [væ'sɛktəmɪ] *n* Vasektomie *f*
Vaseline® ['væsɪliːn] *n* Vaseline *f*
vast [vɑːst] *adj (knowledge)* enorm; *(expense, area)* riesig
vastly ['vɑːstlɪ] *adv (superior, improved)* erheblich
vastness ['vɑːstnɪs] *n* ungeheure Größe *f*
VAT [væt] *(Brit) n abbr (= value-added tax)* MwSt *f*
vat [væt] *n* Fass *nt*
Vatican ['vætɪkən] *n*: **the ~** der Vatikan
vatman ['vætmæn] *(inf: irreg: like* **man***)* *n* ≈ Fiskus *m (bezüglich Einbehaltung der Mehrwertsteuer)*
vaudeville ['vəudəvɪl] *n* Varieté *nt*
vault [vɔːlt] *n (of roof)* Gewölbe *nt*; *(tomb)* Gruft *f*; *(in bank)* Tresorraum *m*; *(jump)* Sprung *m* ▷ *vt (also:* **vault over***)* überspringen
vaunted ['vɔːntɪd] *adj*: **much-~** viel gepriesen
VC *n abbr* = **vice-chairman**; *(Brit: = Victoria Cross)* Viktoriakreuz *nt*, *höchste britische Tapferkeitsauszeichnung*
VCR *n abbr* = **video cassette recorder**
VD *n abbr* = **venereal disease**
VDU *n abbr (Comput)* = **visual display unit**
veal [viːl] *n* Kalbfleisch *nt*
veer [vɪə^r] *vi (wind)* sich drehen; *(vehicle)* ausscheren
veg *(Brit: inf) n abbr* = **vegetable; vegetables**
vegan ['viːgən] *n* Veganer(in) *m(f)* ▷ *adj* radikal vegetarisch
vegeburger ['vɛdʒɪbəːgə^r] *n* vegetarischer Hamburger *m*
vegetable ['vɛdʒtəbl] *n (plant)* Gemüse *nt*; *(plant life)* Pflanzen *pl* ▷ *cpd (oil etc)* Pflanzen-; *(garden, plot)* Gemüse-
vegetarian [vɛdʒɪ'tɛərɪən] *n* Vegetarier(in) *m(f)* ▷ *adj* vegetarisch
vegetate ['vɛdʒɪteɪt] *vi (fig: person)* dahinvegetieren
vegetation [vɛdʒɪ'teɪʃən] *n (plants)* Vegetation *f*
vegetative ['vɛdʒɪtətɪv] *adj* vegetativ
veggieburger ['vɛdʒɪbəːgə^r] *n* = **vegeburger**
vehemence ['viːɪməns] *n* Vehemenz *f*, Heftigkeit *f*
vehement ['viːɪmənt] *adj* heftig
vehicle ['viːɪkl] *n (machine)* Fahrzeug *nt*; *(fig: means)* Mittel *nt*
vehicular [vɪ'hɪkjulə^r] *adj*: **"no ~ traffic"** „kein Fahrzeugverkehr"
veil [veɪl] *n* Schleier *m* ▷ *vt (also fig)* verschleiern; **under a ~ of secrecy** unter einem Schleier von Geheimnissen
veiled [veɪld] *adj (also fig: threat)* verschleiert
vein [veɪn] *n* Ader *f*; *(fig: mood, style)* Stimmung *f*
Velcro® ['vɛlkrəu] *n (also:* **Velcro fastener** *or* **fastening***)* Klettverschluss *m*
vellum ['vɛləm] *n (writing paper)* Pergament *nt*
velocity [vɪ'lɔsɪtɪ] *n* Geschwindigkeit *f*
velours [və'luə^r] *n* Velours *m*
velvet ['vɛlvɪt] *n* Samt *m* ▷ *adj (skirt, jacket)* Samt-
vendetta [vɛn'dɛtə] *n* Vendetta *f*; *(between families)* Blutrache *f*
vending machine ['vɛndɪŋ-] *n* Automat *m*
vendor ['vɛndə^r] *n* Verkäufer(in) *m(f)*; **street ~** Straßenhändler(in) *m(f)*
veneer [və'nɪə^r] *n (on furniture)* Furnier *nt*; *(fig)* Anstrich *m*
venerable ['vɛnərəbl] *adj* ehrwürdig; *(Rel)* hochwürdig
venereal [vɪ'nɪərɪəl] *adj*: **~ disease** Geschlechtskrankheit *f*
Venetian [vɪ'niːʃən] *adj (Geog)* venezianisch ▷ *n (person)* Venezianer(in) *m(f)*
Venetian blind *n* Jalousie *f*
Venezuela [vɛnɛ'zweɪlə] *n* Venezuela *nt*
Venezuelan [vɛnɛ'zweɪlən] *adj* venezolanisch ▷ *n (person)* Venezolaner(in) *m(f)*
vengeance ['vɛndʒəns] *n* Rache *f*; **with a ~** *(fig: fiercely)* gewaltig; **he broke the rules with a ~** er verstieß die Regeln – und nicht zu knapp
vengeful ['vɛndʒful] *adj* rachsüchtig

Venice ['vɛnɪs] *n* Venedig *nt*
venison ['vɛnɪsn] *n* Rehfleisch *nt*
venom ['vɛnəm] *n* (*poison*) Gift *nt*; (*bitterness, anger*) Gehässigkeit *f*
venomous ['vɛnəməs] *adj* (*snake, insect*) giftig; (*look*) gehässig
vent [vɛnt] *n* (*also*: **air vent**) Abzug *m*; (*in jacket*) Schlitz *m* ▷ *vt* (*fig: feelings*) abreagieren
ventilate ['vɛntɪleɪt] *vt* (*building*) belüften; (*room*) lüften
ventilation [vɛntɪ'leɪʃən] *n* Belüftung *f*
ventilation shaft *n* Luftschacht *m*
ventilator ['vɛntɪleɪtə^r] *n* (*Tech*) Ventilator *m*; (*Med*) Beatmungsgerät *nt*
ventriloquist [vɛn'trɪləkwɪst] *n* Bauchredner(in) *m(f)*
venture ['vɛntʃə^r] *n* Unternehmung *f* ▷ *vt* (*opinion*) zu äußern wagen ▷ *vi* (*dare to go*) sich wagen; **a business ~** ein geschäftliches Unternehmen; **to ~ to do sth** es wagen, etw zu tun
venture capital *n* Risikokapital *nt*
venue ['vɛnju:] *n* (*for meeting*) Treffpunkt *m*; (*for big events*) Austragungsort *m*
Venus ['vi:nəs] *n* Venus *f*
veracity [və'ræsɪtɪ] *n* (*of person*) Aufrichtigkeit *f*; (*of evidence etc*) Richtigkeit *f*
veranda, **verandah** [və'rændə] *n* Veranda *f*
verb [və:b] *n* Verb *nt*
verbal ['və:bl] *adj* verbal; (*skills*) sprachlich; (*translation*) wörtlich
verbally ['və:bəlɪ] *adv* (*communicate etc*) mündlich, verbal
verbatim [və:'beɪtɪm] *adj* wörtlich ▷ *adv* Wort für Wort
verbose [və:'bəus] *adj* (*person*) wortreich; (*writing*) weitschweifig
verdict ['və:dɪkt] *n* (*Law, fig*) Urteil *nt*; **~ of guilty/not guilty** Schuld-/Freispruch *m*
verge [və:dʒ] (*Brit*) *n* (*of road*) Rand *m*, Bankett *nt*; **"soft ~s"** (*Brit: Aut*) „Seitenstreifen nicht befahrbar"; **to be on the ~ of doing sth** im Begriff sein, etw zu tun
▸ **verge on** *vt fus* grenzen an *+acc*
verger ['və:dʒə^r] *n* (*Rel*) Küster *m*
verification [vɛrɪfɪ'keɪʃən] *n* (*see vt*) Bestätigung *f*; Überprüfung *f*
verify ['vɛrɪfaɪ] *vt* (*confirm*) bestätigen; (*check*) überprüfen
veritable ['vɛrɪtəbl] *adj* (*real*) wahr
vermin ['və:mɪn] *npl* Ungeziefer *nt*
vermouth ['və:məθ] *n* Wermut *m*
vernacular [və'nækjulə^r] *n* (*of country*) Landessprache *f*; (*of region*) Dialekt *m*
versatile ['və:sətaɪl] *adj* vielseitig
versatility [və:sə'tɪlɪtɪ] *n* Vielseitigkeit *f*
verse [və:s] *n* (*poetry*) Poesie *f*; (*stanza*) Strophe *f*; (*in bible*) Vers *m*; **in ~** in Versform
versed [və:st] *adj*: **(well-)~ in** (gut) bewandert in *+dat*
version ['və:ʃən] *n* Version *f*
versus ['və:səs] *prep* gegen
vertebra ['və:tɪbrə] (*pl* **~e**) *n* Rückenwirbel *m*
vertebrae ['və:tɪbri:] *npl of* **vertebra**
vertebrate ['və:tɪbrɪt] *n* Wirbeltier *nt*
vertical ['və:tɪkl] *adj* vertikal, senkrecht ▷ *n* Vertikale *f*
vertically ['və:tɪklɪ] *adv* vertikal
vertigo ['və:tɪgəu] *n* Schwindelgefühle *pl*; **to suffer from ~** leicht schwindlig werden
verve [və:v] *n* Schwung *m*
very ['vɛrɪ] *adv* sehr ▷ *adj*: **the ~ book which ...** genau das Buch, das ...; **the ~ last** der/die/das Allerletzte; **at the ~ least** allerwenigstens; **~ well/little** sehr gut/wenig; **~ much** sehr viel; (*like, hope*) sehr; **the ~ thought (of it) alarms me** der bloße Gedanke (daran) beunruhigt mich; **at the ~ end** ganz am Ende
vespers ['vɛspəz] *npl* (*Rel*) Vesper *f*
vessel ['vɛsl] *n* Gefäß *nt*; (*Naut*) Schiff *nt*; *see* **blood**
vest [vɛst] *n* (*Brit: underwear*) Unterhemd *nt*; (*US: waistcoat*) Weste *f* ▷ *vt*: **to ~ sb with sth, ~ sth in sb** jdm etw verleihen
vested interest ['vɛstɪd-] *n* (*Comm*) finanzielles Interesse *nt*; **to have a ~ in doing sth** ein besonderes Interesse daran haben, etw zu tun
vestibule ['vɛstɪbju:l] *n* Vorhalle *f*
vestige ['vɛstɪdʒ] *n* Spur *f*
vestment ['vɛstmənt] *n* (*Rel*) Ornat *nt*
vestry ['vɛstrɪ] *n* Sakristei *f*
Vesuvius [vɪ'su:vɪəs] *n* Vesuv *m*
vet [vɛt] (*Brit*) *n* = **veterinary surgeon**; (US) = **veteran** ▷ *vt* (*examine*) überprüfen
veteran ['vɛtərn] *n* Veteran(in) *m(f)* ▷ *adj*: **she's a ~ campaigner for ...** sie ist eine altgediente Kämpferin für ...
veteran car *n* Oldtimer *m* (*vor 1919 gebaut*)
veterinarian [vɛtrɪ'nɛərɪən] (*US*) *n* = **veterinary surgeon**
veterinary ['vɛtrɪnərɪ] *adj* (*practice, medicine*) Veterinär-; (*care, training*) tierärztlich
veterinary surgeon (*Brit*) *n* Tierarzt *m*, Tierärztin *f*
veto ['vi:təu] (*pl* **~es**) *n* Veto *nt* ▷ *vt* ein Veto einlegen gegen; **to put a ~ on sth** gegen etw ein Veto einlegen
vetting ['vɛtɪŋ] *n* Überprüfung *f*
vex [vɛks] *vt* (*irritate, upset*) ärgern
vexed [vɛkst] *adj* (*upset*) verärgert; (*question*) umstritten
VFD (*US*) *n abbr* (= *volunteer fire department*) ≈ freiwillige Feuerwehr *f*
VG (*Brit*) *n abbr* (*Scol etc*: = *very good*) ≈ "sehr gut"
VHF *abbr* (*Radio*: = *very high frequency*) VHF
VI (*US*) *abbr* (*Post*) = *Virgin Islands*
via ['vaɪə] *prep* über *+acc*
viability [vaɪə'bɪlɪtɪ] *n* (*see adj*) Durchführbarkeit *f*; Rentabilität *f*
viable ['vaɪəbl] *adj* (*project*) durchführbar; (*company*) rentabel
viaduct ['vaɪədʌkt] *n* Viadukt *m*
vial ['vaɪəl] *n* Fläschchen *nt*
vibes [vaɪbz] *npl* (*Mus*) *see* **vibraphone** (*inf: vibrations*): **I get good/bad ~ from it/him** das/er macht mich an/nicht an

vibrant ['vaɪbrnt] *adj* (*lively*) dynamisch; (*bright*) lebendig; (*full of emotion: voice*) volltönend
vibraphone ['vaɪbrəfəun] *n* Vibrafon *nt*
vibrate [vaɪ'breɪt] *vi* (*house*) zittern, beben; (*machine, sound etc*) vibrieren
vibration [vaɪ'breɪʃən] *n* (*act of vibrating*) Vibrieren *nt*; (*instance*) Vibration *f*
vibrator [vaɪ'breɪtəʳ] *n* Vibrator *m*
vicar ['vɪkəʳ] *n* Pfarrer *m*
vicarage ['vɪkərɪdʒ] *n* Pfarrhaus *nt*
vicarious [vɪ'kɛərɪəs] *adj* (*pleasure, experience*) indirekt
vice [vaɪs] *n* (*moral fault*) Laster *nt*; (*Tech*) Schraubstock *m*
vice- [vaɪs] *pref* Vize-
vice-chairman [vaɪs'tʃɛəmən] *n* stellvertretender Vorsitzender *m*
vice chancellor (*Brit*) *n* (*of university*) ≈ Rektor *m*
vice president *n* Vizepräsident(in) *m(f)*
viceroy ['vaɪsrɔɪ] *n* Vizekönig *m*
vice squad *n* (*Police*) Sittendezernat *nt*
vice versa ['vaɪsɪ'vəːsə] *adv* umgekehrt
vicinity [vɪ'sɪnɪtɪ] *n*: **in the ~ (of)** in der Nähe *or* Umgebung (*+gen*)
vicious ['vɪʃəs] *adj* (*attack, blow*) brutal; (*words, look*) gemein; (*horse, dog*) bösartig
vicious circle *n* Teufelskreis *m*
viciousness ['vɪʃəsnɪs] *n* Bösartigkeit *f*, Gemeinheit *f*
vicissitudes [vɪ'sɪsɪtjuːdz] *npl* Wechselfälle *pl*
victim ['vɪktɪm] *n* Opfer *nt*; **to be the ~ of an attack** einem Angriff zum Opfer fallen
victimization ['vɪktɪmaɪ'zeɪʃən] *n* Schikanierung *f*
victimize ['vɪktɪmaɪz] *vt* schikanieren
victor ['vɪktəʳ] *n* Sieger(in) *m(f)*
Victorian [vɪk'tɔːrɪən] *adj* viktorianisch
victorious [vɪk'tɔːrɪəs] *adj* (*team*) siegreich; (*shout*) triumphierend
victory ['vɪktərɪ] *n* Sieg *m*; **to win a ~ over sb** einen Sieg über jdn erringen
video ['vɪdɪəu] *n* (*film, cassette, recorder*) Video *nt* ▷ *vt* auf Video aufnehmen ▷ *cpd* Video-
video camera *n* Videokamera *f*
video cassette *n* Videokassette *f*
video cassette recorder *n* Videorekorder *m*
videodisc, videodisk ['vɪdɪəudɪsk] *n* Bildplatte *f*
video game *n* Videospiel *nt*, Telespiel *nt*
video nasty *n Video mit übertriebenen Gewaltszenen und/oder pornografischem Inhalt*
videophone ['vɪdɪəufəun] *n* Bildtelefon *nt*
video recorder *n* Videorekorder *m*
video recording *n* Videoaufnahme *f*
video tape *n* Videoband *nt*
vie [vaɪ] *vi*: **to ~ with sb/for sth** mit jdm/um etw wetteifern
Vienna [vɪ'ɛnə] *n* Wien *nt*
Viennese [vɪə'niːz] *adj* Wiener
Vietnam ['vjɛt'næm] *n* Vietnam *nt*
Viet Nam ['vjɛt'næm] *n* = **Vietnam**
Vietnamese [vjɛtnə'miːz] *adj* vietnamesisch ▷ *n inv* (*person*) Vietnamese *m*, Vietnamesin *f*; (*Ling*) Vietnamesisch *nt*
view [vjuː] *n* (*from window etc*) Aussicht *f*; (*sight*) Blick *m*; (*outlook*) Sicht *f*; (*opinion*) Ansicht *f* ▷ *vt* betrachten; (*house*) besichtigen; **to be on ~** (*in museum etc*) ausgestellt sein; **in full ~ of** vor den Augen *+gen*; **to take the ~ that ...** der Ansicht sein, dass ...; **in ~ of the weather/the fact that** in Anbetracht des Wetters/der Tatsache, dass ...; **in my ~** meiner Ansicht nach; **an overall ~ of the situation** ein allgemeiner Überblick über die Lage; **with a ~ to doing sth** mit der Absicht, etw zu tun
viewdata® ['vjuːdeɪtə] (*Brit*) *n* Bildschirmtext *m*
viewer ['vjuːəʳ] *n* (*person*) Zuschauer(in) *m(f)*; (*viewfinder*) Sucher *m*
viewfinder ['vjuːfaɪndəʳ] *n* Sucher *m*
viewpoint ['vjuːpɔɪnt] *n* (*attitude*) Standpunkt *m*; (*place*) Aussichtspunkt *m*
vigil ['vɪdʒɪl] *n* Wache *f*; **to keep ~** Wache halten
vigilance ['vɪdʒɪləns] *n* Wachsamkeit *f*
vigilance committee (*US*) *n* Bürgerwehr *f*
vigilant ['vɪdʒɪlənt] *adj* wachsam
vigilante [vɪdʒɪ'læntɪ] *n Mitglied einer Selbstschutzorganisation oder Bürgerwehr* ▷ *adj* (*group, patrol*) Bürgerwehr-, Selbstschutz-
vigorous ['vɪgərəs] *adj* (*action, campaign*) energisch, dynamisch; (*plant*) kräftig
vigour, (US) vigor ['vɪgəʳ] *n* (*of person, campaign*) Energie *f*, Dynamik *f*
vile [vaɪl] *adj* abscheulich
vilify ['vɪlɪfaɪ] *vt* diffamieren
villa ['vɪlə] *n* Villa *f*
village ['vɪlɪdʒ] *n* Dorf *nt*
villager ['vɪlɪdʒəʳ] *n* Dorfbewohner(in) *m(f)*
villain ['vɪlən] *n* (*scoundrel*) Schurke *m*; (*in novel etc*) Bösewicht *m*; (*Brit: criminal*) Verbrecher(in) *m(f)*
VIN (*US*) *n abbr* (= *vehicle identification number*) amtliches Kennzeichen *nt*
vinaigrette [vɪneɪ'grɛt] *n* Vinaigrette *f*
vindicate ['vɪndɪkeɪt] *vt* (*person*) rehabilitieren; (*action*) rechtfertigen
vindication [vɪndɪ'keɪʃən] *n* Rechtfertigung *f*
vindictive [vɪn'dɪktɪv] *adj* (*person*) nachtragend; (*action*) aus Rache
vine [vaɪn] *n* (*Bot: producing grapes*) Weinrebe *f*; (*: in jungle*) Rebengewächs *nt*
vinegar ['vɪnɪgəʳ] *n* Essig *m*
vine grower *n* Weinbauer *m*
vine-growing ['vaɪngrəuɪŋ] *adj* (*region*) Weinbau- ▷ *n* Weinbau *m*
vineyard ['vɪnjɑːd] *n* Weinberg *m*
vintage ['vɪntɪdʒ] *n* (*of wine*) Jahrgang *m* ▷ *cpd* (*classic*) klassisch; **the 1980 ~** (*of wine*) der Jahrgang 1980
vintage car *n* Oldtimer *m* (*zwischen 1919 und 1930 gebaut*)
vintage wine *n* erlesener Wein *m*
vinyl ['vaɪnl] *n* Vinyl *nt*; (*records*) Schallplatten *pl*
viola [vɪ'əulə] *n* Bratsche *f*

violate ['vaɪəleɪt] *vt* (*agreement*) verletzen; (*peace*) stören; (*graveyard*) schänden
violation [vaɪə'leɪʃən] *n* (*of agreement etc*) Verletzung *f*; **in ~ of** (*rule, law*) unter Verletzung *+gen*
violence ['vaɪələns] *n* Gewalt *f*; (*strength*) Heftigkeit *f*
violent ['vaɪələnt] *adj* (*behaviour*) gewalttätig; (*death*) gewaltsam; (*explosion, criticism, emotion*) heftig; **a ~ dislike of sb/sth** eine heftige Abneigung gegen jdn/etw
violently ['vaɪələntlɪ] *adv* heftig; (*ill*) schwer; (*angry*) äußerst
violet ['vaɪələt] *adj* violett ▷ *n* (*colour*) Violett *nt*; (*plant*) Veilchen *nt*
violin [vaɪə'lɪn] *n* Geige *f*, Violine *f*
violinist [vaɪə'lɪnɪst] *n* Violinist(in) *m(f)*, Geiger(in) *m(f)*
VIP *n abbr* (*= very important person*) VIP *m*
viper ['vaɪpəʳ] *n* Viper *f*
viral ['vaɪərəl] *adj* (*disease, infection*) Virus-
virgin ['vəːdʒɪn] *n* Jungfrau *f* ▷ *adj* (*snow, forest etc*) unberührt; **she is a ~** sie ist Jungfrau; **the Blessed V~** die Heilige Jungfrau
virgin birth *n* unbefleckte Empfängnis *f*; (*Biol*) Jungfernzeugung *f*
virginity [vəː'dʒɪnɪtɪ] *n* (*of person*) Jungfräulichkeit *f*
Virgo ['vəːgəu] *n* (*sign*) Jungfrau *f*; **to be ~** Jungfrau sein
virile ['vɪraɪl] *adj* (*person*) männlich
virility [vɪ'rɪlɪtɪ] *n* (*masculine qualities*) Männlichkeit *f*
virtual ['vəːtjuəl] *adj* (*Comput, Phys*) virtuell; **it's a ~ impossibility** es ist so gut wie unmöglich; **to be the ~ leader** eigentlich *or* praktisch der Führer sein
virtually ['vəːtjuəlɪ] *adv* praktisch, nahezu; **it is ~ impossible** es ist so gut wie unmöglich
virtual reality *n* virtuelle Realität *f*
virtue ['vəːtjuː] *n* Tugend *f*; (*advantage*) Vorzug *m*; **by ~ of** aufgrund *+gen*
virtuosi [vəːtju'əuzɪ] *npl of* **virtuoso**
virtuosity [vəːtju'ɔsɪtɪ] *n* Virtuosität *f*
virtuoso [vəːtju'əuzəu] (*pl* **~s** *or* **virtuosi**) *n* Virtuose *m*
virtuous ['vəːtjuəs] *adj* tugendhaft
virulence ['vɪruləns] *n* (*of disease*) Bösartigkeit *f*; (*hatred*) Feindseligkeit *f*
virulent ['vɪrulənt] *adj* (*disease*) bösartig; (*actions, feelings*) feindselig
virus ['vaɪərəs] *n* (*Med, Comput*) Virus *m or nt*
visa ['viːzə] *n* Visum *nt*
vis-à-vis [viːzə'viː] *prep* gegenüber
viscose ['vɪskəus] *n* (*also Chem*) Viskose *f*
viscount ['vaɪkaunt] *n* Viscount *m*
viscous ['vɪskəs] *adj* zähflüssig
vise [vaɪs] (*US*) *n* (*Tech*) = **vice**
visibility [vɪzɪ'bɪlɪtɪ] *n* (*range of vision*) Sicht(weite) *f*
visible ['vɪzəbl] *adj* sichtbar; **~ exports/imports** sichtbare Ausfuhren/Einfuhren
visibly ['vɪzəblɪ] *adv* sichtlich
vision ['vɪʒən] *n* (*sight*) Sicht *f*; (*foresight*) Weitblick *m*; (*in dream*) Vision *f*
visionary ['vɪʒənrɪ] *adj* (*with foresight*) vorausblickend
visit ['vɪzɪt] *n* Besuch *m* ▷ *vt* besuchen; **a private/official ~** ein privater/offizieller Besuch
visiting ['vɪzɪtɪŋ] *adj* (*speaker, team*) Gast-
visiting card *n* Visitenkarte *f*
visiting hours *npl* Besuchszeiten *pl*
visiting professor *n* Gastprofessor(in) *m(f)*
visitor ['vɪzɪtəʳ] *n* Besucher(in) *m(f)*
visitors' book ['vɪzɪtəz-] *n* Gästebuch *nt*
visor ['vaɪzəʳ] *n* (*of helmet etc*) Visier *nt*
VISTA ['vɪstə] (*US*) *n abbr* (*= Volunteers In Service To America*) *staatliches Förderprogramm für strukturschwache Gebiete*
vista ['vɪstə] *n* Aussicht *f*
visual ['vɪzjuəl] *adj* (*image etc*) visuell; **the ~ arts** die darstellenden Künste
visual aid *n* Anschauungsmaterial *nt*
visual display unit *n* (Daten)sichtgerät *nt*
visualize ['vɪzjuəlaɪz] *vt* sich *dat* vorstellen
visually ['vɪzjuəlɪ] *adv* visuell; **~ appealing** optisch ansprechend; **~ handicapped** sehbehindert
vital ['vaɪtl] *adj* (*essential*) unerlässlich; (*organ*) lebenswichtig; (*full of life*) vital; **of ~ importance (to sb/sth)** von größter Wichtigkeit (für jdn/etw)
vitality [vaɪ'tælɪtɪ] *n* (*liveliness*) Vitalität *f*
vitally ['vaɪtəlɪ] *adv*: **~ important** äußerst wichtig
vital statistics *npl* (*fig: of woman*) Körpermaße *pl*; (*of population*) Bevölkerungsstatistik *f*
vitamin ['vɪtəmɪn] *n* Vitamin *nt* ▷ *cpd* (*pill, deficiencies*) Vitamin-
vitiate ['vɪʃɪeɪt] *vt* (*spoil*) verunreinigen
vitreous ['vɪtrɪəs] *adj*: **~ china** Porzellanemail *nt*; **~ enamel** Glasemail *nt*
vitriolic [vɪtrɪ'ɔlɪk] *adj* (*fig: language, behaviour*) hasserfüllt
viva ['vaɪvə] *n* (*Scol: also:* **viva voce** [-'vəutʃɪ]) mündliche Prüfung *f*
vivacious [vɪ'veɪʃəs] *adj* lebhaft
vivacity [vɪ'væsɪtɪ] *n* Lebendigkeit *f*
vivid ['vɪvɪd] *adj* (*description*) lebendig; (*memory, imagination*) lebhaft; (*colour*) leuchtend; (*light*) hell
vividly ['vɪvɪdlɪ] *adv* (*describe*) lebendig; (*remember*) lebhaft
vivisection [vɪvɪ'sɛkʃən] *n* Vivisektion *f*
vixen ['vɪksn] *n* (*Zool*) Füchsin *f*; (*pej: woman*) Drachen *m*
viz [vɪz] *abbr* (*= videlicet*) nämlich
VLF *abbr* (*Radio: = very low frequency*) VLF
V-neck ['viːnɛk] *n* (*also:* **V-neck jumper** *or* **pullover**) Pullover *m* mit V-Ausschnitt
VOA *n abbr* (*= Voice of America*) Stimme *f* Amerikas
vocabulary [vəu'kæbjulərɪ] *n* (*words known*) Vokabular *nt*, Wortschatz *m*
vocal ['vəukl] *adj* (*of the voice*) stimmlich;

(*articulate*) lautstark
vocal cords *npl* Stimmbänder *pl*
vocalist ['vəukəlɪst] *n* Sänger(in) *m(f)*
vocals ['vəuklz] *npl* (*Mus*) Gesang *m*
vocation [vəu'keɪʃən] *n* (*calling*) Berufung *f*; (*profession*) Beruf *m*
vocational [vəu'keɪʃənl] *adj* (*training, guidance etc*) Berufs-
vociferous [və'sɪfərəs] *adj* (*protesters, demands*) lautstark
vodka ['vɔdkə] *n* Wodka *m*
vogue [vəug] *n* (*fashion*) Mode *f*; (*popularity*) Popularität *f*; **in ~** in Mode
voice [vɔɪs] *n* (*also fig*) Stimme *f* ▷ *vt* (*opinion*) zum Ausdruck bringen; **in a loud/soft ~** mit lauter/leiser Stimme; **to give ~ to** Ausdruck verleihen *+dat*
voice mail *n* (*Comput*) Voicemail *f*
voice-over ['vɔɪsəuvə^r] *n* (Film)kommentar *m*
void [vɔɪd] *n* (*hole*) Loch *nt*; (*fig: emptiness*) Leere *f* ▷ *adj* (*invalid*) ungültig; **~ of** (*empty*) ohne
voile [vɔɪl] *n* Voile *m*
vol. *abbr* (= *volume*) Bd.
volatile ['vɔlətaɪl] *adj* (*person*) impulsiv; (*situation*) unsicher; (*liquid etc*) flüchtig
volcanic [vɔl'kænɪk] *adj* (*rock, eruption*) vulkanisch, Vulkan-
volcano [vɔl'keɪnəu] (*pl* **~es**) *n* Vulkan *m*
volition [və'lɪʃən] *n*: **of one's own ~** aus freiem Willen
volley ['vɔlɪ] *n* (*of gunfire*) Salve *f*; (*of stones, questions*) Hagel *m*; (*Tennis etc*) Volley *m*
volleyball ['vɔlɪbɔːl] *n* Volleyball *m*
volt [vəult] *n* Volt *nt*
voltage ['vəultɪdʒ] *n* Spannung *f*; **high/low ~** Hoch-/Niederspannung *f*
volte-face ['vɔlt'fɑːs] *n* Kehrtwendung *f*
voluble ['vɔljubl] *adj* (*person*) redselig; (*speech*) wortreich
volume ['vɔljuːm] *n* (*space*) Volumen *nt*; (*amount*) Umfang *m*, Ausmaß *nt*; (*book*) Band *m*; (*sound level*) Lautstärke *f*; **~ one/two** (*of book*) Band eins/zwei; **his expression spoke ~s** sein Gesichtsausdruck sprach Bände
volume control *n* (*Radio, TV*) Lautstärkeregler *m*
volume discount *n* (*Comm*) Mengenrabatt *m*
voluminous [və'luːmɪnəs] *adj* (*clothes*) sehr weit; (*correspondence, notes*) umfangreich
voluntarily ['vɔləntrɪlɪ] *adv* freiwillig
voluntary ['vɔləntərɪ] *adj* freiwillig
voluntary liquidation *n* freiwillige Liquidation *f*
volunteer [vɔlən'tɪə^r] *n* Freiwillige(r) *f(m)* ▷ *vt* (*information*) vorbringen ▷ *vi* (*for army etc*) sich freiwillig melden; **to ~ to do sth** sich anbieten, etw zu tun
voluptuous [və'lʌptjuəs] *adj* sinnlich, wollüstig
vomit ['vɔmɪt] *n* Erbrochene(s) *nt* ▷ *vt* erbrechen ▷ *vi* sich übergeben
voracious [və'reɪʃəs] *adj* (*person*) gefräßig; **~ appetite** Riesenappetit *m*
vortal ['vɔːtl] *n* (*Comput*) Vortal *nt*
vote [vəut] *n* Stimme *f*; (*votes cast*) Stimmen *pl*; (*right to vote*) Wahlrecht *nt*; (*ballot*) Abstimmung *f* ▷ *vt* (*elect*): **to be ~d chairman** *etc* zum Vorsitzenden *etc* gewählt werden; (*propose*): **to ~ that** vorschlagen, dass ▷ *vi* (*in election etc*) wählen; **to put sth to the vote, (take a) ~ on sth** über etw *acc* abstimmen; **~ of censure** Tadelsantrag *m*; **to pass a ~ of confidence/no confidence** ein Vertrauens-/Misstrauensvotum annehmen; **to ~ to do sth** dafür stimmen, etw zu tun; **to ~ yes/no** mit Ja/Nein stimmen; **to ~ Labour/Green** *etc* Labour/die Grünen *etc* wählen; **to ~ for** *or* **in favour of sth/against sth** für/gegen etw stimmen
vote of thanks *n* Danksagung *f*
voter ['vəutə^r] *n* Wähler(in) *m(f)*
voting ['vəutɪŋ] *n* Wahl *f*
voting paper (*Brit*) *n* Stimmzettel *m*
voting right *n* Stimmrecht *nt*
vouch [vautʃ]: **~ for** *vt fus* bürgen für
voucher ['vautʃə^r] *n* Gutschein *m*; (*receipt*) Beleg *m*; **gift ~** Geschenkgutschein *m*; **luncheon ~** Essensmarke *f*; **travel ~** Reisegutschein *m*
vow [vau] *n* Versprechen *nt* ▷ *vt*: **to ~ to do sth/that** geloben, etw zu tun/dass; **to take** *or* **make a ~ to do sth** geloben, etw zu tun
vowel ['vauəl] *n* Vokal *m*
voyage ['vɔɪɪdʒ] *n* Reise *f*
voyeur [vwɑː'jəː^r] *n* Voyeur(in) *m(f)*
voyeurism [vwɑː'jəːrɪzəm] *n* Voyeurismus *m*
VP *n abbr* = **vice president**
vs *abbr* (= *versus*) vs.
V-sign ['viːsaɪn] (*Brit*) *n*: **to give sb the ~** ≈ jdm den Vogel zeigen
VSO (*Brit*) *n abbr* (= *Voluntary Service Overseas*) *britischer Entwicklungsdienst*
VT (*US*) *abbr* (*Post*) = *Vermont*
vulgar ['vʌlgə^r] *adj* (*remarks, gestures*) vulgär; (*decor, ostentation*) geschmacklos
vulgarity [vʌl'gærɪtɪ] *n* (*see adj*) Vulgarität *f*; Geschmacklosigkeit *f*
vulnerability [vʌlnərə'bɪlɪtɪ] *n* Verletzlichkeit *f*
vulnerable ['vʌlnərəbl] *adj* (*person, position*) verletzlich
vulture ['vʌltʃə^r] *n* (*also fig*) Geier *m*
vulva ['vʌlvə] *n* Vulva *f*

Ww

W¹, w ['dʌblju:] *n* (*letter*) W *nt*, w *nt*; **W for William** ≈ W wie Wilhelm
W² ['dʌblju:] *abbr* (*Elec*: = *watt*) W; (= *west*) W
WA *abbr* (*US: Post*) = *Washington*; (*Australia*) = *Western Australia*
wad [wɔd] *n* (*of cotton wool*) Bausch *m*; (*of paper, banknotes*) Bündel *nt*
wadding ['wɔdɪŋ] *n* Füllmaterial *nt*
waddle ['wɔdl] *vi* watscheln
wade [weɪd] *vi*: **to ~ across** (*a river, stream*) waten durch; **to ~ through** (*fig: a book*) sich durchkämpfen durch
wafer ['weɪfəʳ] *n* (*biscuit*) Waffel *f*
wafer-thin ['weɪfə'θɪn] *adj* hauchdünn
waffle ['wɔfl] *n* (*Culin*) Waffel *f*; (*inf: empty talk*) Geschwafel *nt* ▷ *vi* (*in speech etc*) schwafeln
waffle iron *n* Waffeleisen *nt*
waft [wɔft] *vt, vi* wehen
wag [wæg] *vt* (*tail*) wedeln mit; (*finger*) drohen mit ▷ *vi* (*tail*) wedeln; **the dog ~ged its tail** der Hund wedelte mit dem Schwanz
wage [weɪdʒ] *n* (*also*: **wages**) Lohn *m* ▷ *vt*: **to ~ war** Krieg führen; **a day's ~s** ein Tageslohn
wage claim *n* Lohnforderung *f*
wage differential *n* Lohnunterschied *m*
wage earner [-ə:nəʳ] *n* Lohnempfänger(in) *m(f)*
wage freeze *n* Lohnstopp *m*
wage packet *n* Lohntüte *f*
wager ['weɪdʒəʳ] *n* Wette *f* ▷ *vt* wetten
waggle ['wægl] *vt* (*ears etc*) wackeln mit ▷ *vi* wackeln
wagon, waggon ['wægən] *n* (*horse-drawn*) Fuhrwerk *nt*; (*Brit: Rail*) Wa(g)gon *m*
wail [weɪl] *n* (*of person*) Jammern *nt*; (*of siren*) Heulen *nt* ▷ *vi* (*person*) jammern; (*siren*) heulen
waist [weɪst] *n* (*Anat, of clothing*) Taille *f*
waistcoat ['weɪskəut] (*Brit*) *n* Weste *f*
waistline ['weɪstlaɪn] *n* Taille *f*
wait [weɪt] *n* Wartezeit *f* ▷ *vi* warten; **to lie in ~ for sb** jdm auflauern; **to keep sb ~ing** jdn warten lassen; **I can't ~ to ...** (*fig*) ich kann es kaum erwarten, zu ...; **to ~ for sb/sth** auf jdn/etw warten; **~ a minute!** Moment mal!; **"repairs while you ~"** „Reparaturen sofort"
▸ **wait behind** *vi* zurückbleiben
▸ **wait on** *vt fus* (*serve*) bedienen
▸ **wait up** *vi* aufbleiben; **don't ~ up for me** warte nicht auf mich
waiter ['weɪtəʳ] *n* Kellner *m*
waiting ['weɪtɪŋ] *n*: **"no ~"** (*Brit: Aut*) „Halten verboten"
waiting list *n* Warteliste *f*
waiting room *n* (*in surgery*) Wartezimmer *nt*; (*in railway station*) Wartesaal *m*
waitress ['weɪtrɪs] *n* Kellnerin *f*
waive [weɪv] *vt* (*rule*) verzichten auf *+acc*
waiver ['weɪvəʳ] *n* Verzicht *m*
wake [weɪk] (*pt* **woke, ~d**, *pp* **woken, ~d**) *vt* (*also*: **wake up**) wecken ▷ *vi* (*also*: **wake up**) aufwachen ▷ *n* (*for dead person*) Totenwache *f*; (*Naut*) Kielwasser *nt*; **to ~ up to** (*fig*) sich *dat* bewusst werden *+gen*; **in the ~ of** (*fig*) unmittelbar nach, im Gefolge *+gen*; **to follow in sb's ~** (*fig*) hinter jdm herziehen
waken ['weɪkn] *vt* = **wake**
Wales [weɪlz] *n* Wales *nt*; **the Prince of ~** der Prinz von Wales
walk [wɔ:k] *n* (*hike*) Wanderung *f*; (*shorter*) Spaziergang *m*; (*gait*) Gang *m*; (*path*) Weg *m*; (*in park, along coast etc*) (Spazier)weg *m* ▷ *vi* gehen; (*instead of driving*) zu Fuß gehen; (*for pleasure, exercise*) spazieren gehen ▷ *vt* (*distance*) gehen, laufen; (*dog*) ausführen; **it's 10 minutes' ~ from here** es ist 10 Minuten zu Fuß von hier; **to go for a ~** spazieren gehen; **to slow to a ~** im Schritttempo weitergehen; **people from all ~s of life** Leute aus allen Gesellschaftsschichten; **to ~ in one's sleep** schlafwandeln; **I'd rather ~ than take the bus** ich gehe lieber zu Fuß als mit dem Bus zu fahren; **I'll ~ you home** ich bringe dich nach Hause
▸ **walk out** *vi* (*audience*) den Saal verlassen; (*workers*) in Streik treten
▸ **walk out on** (*inf*) *vt fus* (*family etc*) verlassen
walkabout ['wɔ:kəbaut] *n*: **the Queen/president went on a ~** die Königin/der Präsident mischte sich unters Volk *or* nahm ein Bad in der Menge
walker ['wɔ:kəʳ] *n* (*person*) Spaziergänger(in) *m(f)*
walkie-talkie ['wɔ:kɪ'tɔ:kɪ] *n* Walkie-Talkie *nt*
walking ['wɔ:kɪŋ] *n* Wandern *nt*; **it's within ~ distance** es ist zu Fuß erreichbar
walking holiday *n* Wanderurlaub *m*

walking shoes *npl* Wanderschuhe *pl*
walking stick *n* Spazierstock *m*
Walkman® ['wɔːkmən] *n* Walkman® *m*
walk-on ['wɔːkɔn] *adj* (*Theat*): ~ **part** Statistenrolle *f*
walkout ['wɔːkaut] *n* (*of workers*) Streik *m*
walkover ['wɔːkəuvə^r] (*inf*) *n* (*competition, exam etc*) Kinderspiel *nt*
walkway ['wɔːkweɪ] *n* Fußweg *m*
wall [wɔːl] *n* Wand *f*; (*exterior, city wall etc*) Mauer *f*; **to go to the ~** (*fig: firm etc*) kaputtgehen
▸ **wall in** *vt* (*enclose*) ummauern
wall cupboard *n* Wandschrank *m*
walled [wɔːld] *adj* von Mauern umgeben
wallet ['wɔlɪt] *n* Brieftasche *f*
wallflower ['wɔːlflauə^r] *n* (*Bot*) Goldlack *m*; **to be a ~** (*fig*) ein Mauerblümchen sein
wall hanging *n* Wandbehang *m*
wallop ['wɔləp] (*Brit: inf*) *vt* verprügeln
wallow ['wɔləu] *vi* (*in mud, water*) sich wälzen; (*in guilt, grief*) schwelgen
wallpaper ['wɔːlpeɪpə^r] *n* Tapete *f* ▹ *vt* tapezieren
wall-to-wall ['wɔːltə'wɔːl] *adj*: ~ **carpeting** Teppichboden *m*
wally [wɔlɪ] (*inf*) *n* Trottel *m*
walnut ['wɔːlnʌt] *n* (*nut*) Walnuss *f*; (*tree*) Walnussbaum *m*; (*wood*) Nussbaumholz *nt*
walrus ['wɔːlrəs] (*pl* ~ *or* **walruses**) *n* Walross *nt*
waltz [wɔːlts] *n* Walzer *m* ▹ *vi* Walzer tanzen
wan [wɔn] *adj* bleich; (*smile*) matt
wand [wɔnd] *n* (*also*: **magic wand**) Zauberstab *m*
wander ['wɔndə^r] *vi* (*person*) herumlaufen; (*mind, thoughts*) wandern ▹ *vt* (*the streets, the hills etc*) durchstreifen
wanderer ['wɔndərə^r] *n* Wandervogel *m*
wandering ['wɔndrɪŋ] *adj* (*tribe*) umherziehend; (*minstrel, actor*) fahrend
wane [weɪn] *vi* (*moon*) abnehmen; (*influence etc*) schwinden
wangle ['wæŋgl] (*Brit: inf*) *vt* sich *dat* verschaffen
wanker ['wæŋkə^r] (*inf!*) *n* Wichser *m*
wannabe, wannabee ['wɔnəbiː] (*inf*) *n* Möchtegern *m*; **James Bond ~(e)** Möchtegern-James-Bond *m*
want [wɔnt] *vt* (*wish for*) wollen; (*need*) brauchen ▹ *n* (*lack*): **for ~ of** aus Mangel an +*dat*; **wants** *npl* (*needs*) Bedürfnisse *pl*; **to ~ to do sth** etw tun wollen; **to ~ sb to do sth** wollen, dass jd etw tut; **to ~ in/out** herein-/hinauswollen; **you're ~ed on the phone** Sie werden am Telefon verlangt; **he is ~ed by the police** er wird von der Polizei gesucht; **a ~ of foresight** ein Mangel *m* an Voraussicht
want ads (*US*) *npl* Kaufgesuche *pl*
wanted ['wɔntɪd] *adj* (*criminal etc*) gesucht; **"cook ~"** „Koch/Köchin gesucht"
wanting ['wɔntɪŋ] *adj*: **to be found ~** sich als unzulänglich erweisen
wanton ['wɔntn] *adj* (*violence*) mutwillig; (*promiscuous: woman*) schamlos

WAP [wæp] *n abbr* (*Comput*: = *wireless application protocol*) WAP *nt*
war [wɔː^r] *n* Krieg *m*; **to go to ~** (*start*) einen Krieg anfangen; **to be at ~ (with)** sich im Kriegszustand befinden (mit); **to make ~ (on)** Krieg führen (gegen); **a ~ on drugs/crime** ein Feldzug gegen Drogen/das Verbrechen
warble ['wɔːbl] *n* Trällern *nt* ▹ *vi* trällern
war cry *n* Kriegsruf *m*; (*fig: slogan*) Schlachtruf *m*
ward [wɔːd] *n* (*in hospital*) Station *f*; (*Pol*) Wahlbezirk *m*; (*Law*: *also*: **ward of court**) Mündel *nt* unter Amtsvormundschaft
▸ **ward off** *vt* (*attack, enemy, illness*) abwehren
warden ['wɔːdn] *n* (*of park etc*) Aufseher(in) *m(f)*; (*of jail*) Wärter(in) *m(f)*; (*Brit: of youth hostel*) Herbergsvater *m*, Herbergsmutter *f*; (*: in university*) Wohnheimleiter(in) *m(f)*; (*: also*: **traffic warden**) Verkehrspolizist(in) *m(f)*
warder ['wɔːdə^r] (*Brit*) *n* Gefängniswärter(in) *m(f)*
wardrobe ['wɔːdrəub] *n* (*for clothes*) Kleiderschrank *m*; (*collection of clothes*) Garderobe *f*; (*Cine, Theat*) Kostüme *pl*
warehouse ['wɛəhaus] *n* Lager *nt*
wares [wɛəz] *npl* Waren *pl*
warfare ['wɔːfɛə^r] *n* Krieg *m*
war game *n* Kriegsspiel *nt*
warhead ['wɔːhɛd] *n* Sprengkopf *m*
warily ['wɛərɪlɪ] *adv* vorsichtig
Warks (*Brit*) *abbr* (*Post*) = *Warwickshire*
warlike ['wɔːlaɪk] *adj* kriegerisch
warm [wɔːm] *adj* warm; (*thanks, applause, welcome, person*) herzlich; **it's ~** es ist warm; **I'm ~** mir ist warm; **to keep sth ~** etw warm halten; **with my ~est thanks/congratulations** mit meinem herzlichsten Dank/meinen herzlichsten Glückwünschen
▸ **warm up** *vi* warm werden; (*athlete*) sich aufwärmen ▹ *vt* aufwärmen
warm-blooded ['wɔːm'blʌdɪd] *adj* warmblütig
war memorial *n* Kriegerdenkmal *nt*
warm-hearted [wɔːm'hɑːtɪd] *adj* warmherzig
warmly ['wɔːmlɪ] *adv* (*applaud, welcome*) herzlich; (*dress*) warm
warmonger ['wɔːmʌŋgə^r] (*pej*) *n* Kriegshetzer *m*
warmongering ['wɔːmʌŋgrɪŋ] (*pej*) *n* Kriegshetze *f*
warmth [wɔːmθ] *n* Wärme *f*; (*friendliness*) Herzlichkeit *f*
warm-up ['wɔːmʌp] *n* Aufwärmen *nt*; **~ exercise** Aufwärmübung *f*
warn [wɔːn] *vt*: **to ~ sb that ...** jdn warnen, dass ...; **to ~ sb of sth** jdn vor etw *dat* warnen; **to ~ sb not to do sth** *or* **against doing sth** jdn davor warnen, etw zu tun
warning ['wɔːnɪŋ] *n* Warnung *f*; **without (any) ~** (*suddenly*) unerwartet; (*without notifying*) ohne Vorwarnung; **gale ~** Sturmwarnung *f*
warning light *n* Warnlicht *nt*
warning triangle *n* (*Aut*) Warndreieck *nt*
warp [wɔːp] *vi* (*wood etc*) sich verziehen ▹ *vt*

(*fig: character*) entstellen ▷ *n* (*Textiles*) Kette *f*
warpath ['wɔ:pɑ:θ] *n*: **to be on the ~** auf dem Kriegspfad sein
warped [wɔ:pt] *adj* (*wood*) verzogen; (*fig: character, sense of humour etc*) abartig
warrant ['wɔrnt] *n* (*Law: for arrest*) Haftbefehl *m*; (*: also*: **search warrant**) Durchsuchungsbefehl *m* ▷ *vt* (*justify, merit*) rechtfertigen
warrant officer *n* (*Mil*) *Dienstgrad zwischen Offizier und Unteroffizier*
warranty ['wɔrəntɪ] *n* Garantie *f*; **under ~** (*Comm*) unter Garantie
warren ['wɔrən] *n* (*of rabbits*) Bau *m*; (*fig: of passages, streets*) Labyrinth *nt*
warring ['wɔ:rɪŋ] *adj* (*nations*) Krieg führend; (*interests*) gegensätzlich; (*factions*) verfeindet
warrior ['wɔrɪə^r] *n* Krieger *m*
Warsaw ['wɔ:sɔ:] *n* Warschau *nt*
warship ['wɔ:ʃɪp] *n* Kriegsschiff *nt*
wart [wɔ:t] *n* Warze *f*
wartime ['wɔ:taɪm] *n*: **in ~** im Krieg
wary ['wɛərɪ] *adj* (*person*) vorsichtig; **to be ~ about** *or* **of doing sth** Bedenken haben, etw zu tun
was [wɔz] *pt of* **be**
wash [wɔʃ] *vt* waschen; (*dishes*) spülen, abwaschen; (*remove grease, paint etc*) ausspülen ▷ *vi* (*person*) sich waschen ▷ *n* (*clothes etc*) Wäsche *f*; (*washing programme*) Waschgang *m*; (*of ship*) Kielwasser *nt*; **he was ~ed overboard** er wurde über Bord gespült; **to ~ over/against sth** (*sea etc*) über/gegen etw *acc* spülen; **to have a ~** sich waschen; **to give sth a ~** etw waschen
▸ **wash away** *vt* wegspülen
▸ **wash down** *vt* (*wall, car*) abwaschen; (*food: with wine etc*) hinunterspülen
▸ **wash off** *vi* sich herauswaschen ▷ *vt* abwaschen
▸ **wash out** *vt* (*stain*) herauswaschen
▸ **wash up** *vi* (*Brit: wash dishes*) spülen, abwaschen; (*US: have a wash*) sich waschen
Wash. (*US*) *abbr* (*Post*) = *Washington*
washable ['wɔʃəbl] *adj* (*fabric*) waschbar; (*wallpaper*) abwaschbar
washbasin ['wɔʃbeɪsn], (*US*) **washbowl** ['wɔʃbəul] *n* Waschbecken *nt*
washcloth ['wɔʃklɔθ] (*US*) *n* Waschlappen *m*
washer ['wɔʃə^r] *n* (*on tap etc*) Dichtungsring *m*
washing ['wɔʃɪŋ] *n* Wäsche *f*
washing line (*Brit*) *n* Wäscheleine *f*
washing machine *n* Waschmaschine *f*
washing powder (*Brit*) *n* Waschpulver *nt*
Washington ['wɔʃɪŋtən] *n* Washington *nt*
washing-up [wɔʃɪŋ'ʌp] *n* Abwasch *m*; **to do the ~** spülen, abwaschen
washing-up liquid (*Brit*) *n* (Geschirr)spülmittel *nt*
wash-out ['wɔʃaut] (*inf*) *n* (*failed event*) Reinfall *m*
washroom ['wɔʃrum] (*US*) *n* Waschraum *m*
wasn't ['wɔznt] = **was not**
WASP, Wasp [wɔsp] (*US: inf*) *n abbr* (= *White Anglo-Saxon Protestant*) weißer angelsächsischer Protestant *m*
wasp [wɔsp] *n* Wespe *f*
waspish ['wɔspɪʃ] *adj* giftig
wastage ['weɪstɪdʒ] *n* Verlust *m*; **natural ~** natürliche Personalreduzierung
waste [weɪst] *n* Verschwendung *f*; (*rubbish*) Abfall *m* ▷ *adj* (*material*) Abfall-; (*left over: paper etc*) ungenutzt ▷ *vt* verschwenden; (*opportunity*) vertun; **wastes** *npl* (*area of land*) Wildnis *f*; **it's a ~ of money** das ist Geldverschwendung; **to go to ~** umkommen; **to lay ~** (*area, town*) verwüsten
▸ **waste away** *vi* verkümmern
wastebasket ['weɪstbɑ:skɪt] (*US*) *n* = **wastepaper basket**
waste disposal unit (*Brit*) *n* Müllschlucker *m*
wasteful ['weɪstful] *adj* (*person*) verschwenderisch; (*process*) aufwendig
waste ground (*Brit*) *n* unbebautes Grundstück *nt*
wasteland ['weɪstlənd] *n* Ödland *nt*; (*in town*) ödes Gebiet *nt*; (*fig*) Einöde *f*
wastepaper basket ['weɪstpeɪpə-] (*Brit*) *n* Papierkorb *m*
waste pipe *n* Abflussrohr *nt*
waste products *npl* Abfallprodukte *pl*
waster ['weɪstə^r] *n* Verschwender(in) *m(f)*; (*good-for-nothing*) Taugenichts *m*
watch [wɔtʃ] *n* (*also*: **wristwatch**) (Armband)uhr *f*; (*surveillance*) Bewachung *f*; (*Mil, Naut: group of guards*) Wachmannschaft *f*; (*Naut: spell of duty*) Wache *f* ▷ *vt* (*look at*) betrachten; (*: match, programme*) sich *dat* ansehen; (*spy on, guard*) beobachten; (*be careful of*) aufpassen auf +*acc* ▷ *vi* (*look*) zusehen; **to be on ~** Wache halten; **to keep a close ~ on sb/sth** jdn/etw genau im Auge behalten; **to ~ TV** fernsehen; **~ what you're doing!** pass auf!; **~ how you drive!** fahr vorsichtig!
▸ **watch out** *vi* aufpassen; **~ out!** Vorsicht!
watchband ['wɔtʃbænd] (*US*) *n* = **watchstrap**
watchdog ['wɔtʃdɔg] *n* (*dog*) Wachhund *m*; (*fig*) Aufpasser(in) *m(f)*
watchful ['wɔtʃful] *adj* wachsam
watchmaker ['wɔtʃmeɪkə^r] *n* Uhrmacher(in) *m(f)*
watchman ['wɔtʃmən] (*irreg: like* **man**) *n see* **night watchman**
watch stem (*US*) *n* (*winder*) Krone *f*, Aufziehrädchen *nt*
watchstrap ['wɔtʃstræp] *n* Uhrarmband *nt*
watchword ['wɔtʃwə:d] *n* Parole *f*
water ['wɔ:tə^r] *n* Wasser *nt* ▷ *vt* (*plant*) gießen; (*garden*) bewässern ▷ *vi* (*eyes*) tränen; **a drink of ~** ein Schluck Wasser; **in British ~s** in britischen (Hoheits)gewässern; **to pass ~** (*urinate*) Wasser lassen; **my mouth is ~ing** mir läuft das Wasser im Mund zusammen; **to make sb's mouth ~** jdm den Mund wässrig machen
▸ **water down** *vt* (*also fig*) verwässern
water biscuit *n* Cracker *m*

water cannon *n* Wasserwerfer *m*
water closet (*Brit: old*) *n* Wasserklosett *nt*
watercolour, (*US*) **watercolor** ['wɔːtəkʌləʳ] *n* (*picture*) Aquarell *nt*; **watercolours** *npl* (*paints*) Wasserfarben *pl*
water-cooled ['wɔːtəkuːld] *adj* wassergekühlt
water-cooler ['wɔːtəkuːləʳ] *n* Wasserkühler *m*; **~ talks** (*inf*) Flurfunk *m*
watercress ['wɔːtəkrɛs] *n* Brunnenkresse *f*
waterfall ['wɔːtəfɔːl] *n* Wasserfall *m*
waterfront ['wɔːtəfrʌnt] *n* (*at seaside*) Ufer *nt*; (*at docks*) Hafengegend *f*
water heater *n* Heißwassergerät *nt*
water hole *n* Wasserloch *nt*
water ice *n* Fruchteis *nt* (*auf Wasserbasis*)
watering can ['wɔːtərɪŋ-] *n* Gießkanne *f*
water level *n* Wasserstand *m*; (*of flood*) Pegelstand *m*
water lily *n* Seerose *f*
water line *n* Wasserlinie *f*
waterlogged ['wɔːtəlɔgd] *adj* (*ground*) unter Wasser
water main *n* Hauptwasserleitung *f*
watermark ['wɔːtəmɑːk] *n* (*on paper*) Wasserzeichen *nt*
watermelon ['wɔːtəmɛlən] *n* Wassermelone *f*
waterproof ['wɔːtəpruːf] *adj* (*trousers, jacket etc*) wasserdicht
water-repellent ['wɔːtərɪ'pɛlnt] *adj* Wasser abstoßend
watershed ['wɔːtəʃɛd] *n* (*Geog*) Wasserscheide *f*; (*fig*) Wendepunkt *m*
water-skiing ['wɔːtəskiːɪŋ] *n* Wasserski *nt*
water softener *n* Wasserenthärter *m*
water tank *n* Wassertank *m*
watertight ['wɔːtətaɪt] *adj* wasserdicht; (*fig: excuse, case, agreement etc*) hieb- und stichfest
water vapour *n* Wasserdampf *m*
waterway ['wɔːtəweɪ] *n* Wasserstraße *f*
waterworks ['wɔːtəwəːks] *n* Wasserwerk *nt*; (*inf: fig: bladder*) Blase *f*
watery ['wɔːtərɪ] *adj* (*coffee, soup etc*) wässrig; (*eyes*) tränend
watt [wɔt] *n* Watt *nt*
wattage ['wɔtɪdʒ] *n* Wattleistung *f*
wattle ['wɔtl] *n* Flechtwerk *nt*
wattle and daub *n* Lehmgeflecht *nt*
wave [weɪv] *n* (*also fig*) Welle *f*; (*of hand*) Winken *nt* ▷ *vi* (*signal*) winken; (*branches*) sich hin und her bewegen; (*grass*) wogen; (*flag*) wehen ▷ *vt* (*hand, flag etc*) winken mit; (*gun, stick*) schwenken; (*hair*) wellen; **short/medium/long ~** (*Radio*) Kurz-/Mittel-/Langwelle *f*; **the new ~** (*Cine, Mus*) die neue Welle *f*; **he ~d us over to his table** er winkte uns zu seinem Tisch hinüber; **to ~ goodbye to sb** jdm zum Abschied winken
▸ **wave aside** *vt* (*fig: suggestion etc*) zurückweisen
waveband ['weɪvbænd] *n* (*Radio*) Wellenbereich *m*
wavelength ['weɪvlɛŋθ] *n* (*Radio*) Wellenlänge *f*; **on the same ~** (*fig*) auf derselben Wellenlänge
waver ['weɪvəʳ] *vi* (*voice*) schwanken; (*eyes*) zucken; (*love, person*) wanken
wavy ['weɪvɪ] *adj* (*line*) wellenförmig; (*hair*) wellig
wax [wæks] *n* Wachs *nt*; (*for sealing*) Siegellack *m*; (*in ear*) Ohrenschmalz *nt* ▷ *vt* (*floor*) bohnern; (*car, skis*) wachsen ▷ *vi* (*moon*) zunehmen
waxed [wækst] *adj* (*jacket*) gewachst
waxen [wæksn] *adj* (*face*) wachsbleich
waxworks ['wækswəːks] *npl* (*models*) Wachsfiguren *pl* ▷ *n* (*place*) Wachsfigurenkabinett *nt*
way [weɪ] *n* Weg *m*; (*distance*) Strecke *f*; (*direction*) Richtung *f*; (*manner*) Art *f*; (*method*) Art und Weise *f*; (*habit*) Gewohnheit *f*; **which ~ to ...?** wo geht es zu ...?; **this ~, please** hier entlang, bitte; **on the ~** (*en route*) auf dem Weg, unterwegs; **to be on one's ~** auf dem Weg sein; **to fight one's ~ through a crowd** sich *acc* durch die Menge kämpfen; **to lie one's ~ out of sth** sich aus etw herauslügen; **to keep out of sb's ~** jdm aus dem Weg gehen; **it's a long ~ away** es ist weit entfernt; (*event*) das ist noch lange hin; **the village is rather out of the ~** das Dorf ist recht abgelegen; **to go out of one's ~ to do sth** sich sehr bemühen, etw zu tun; **to be in the ~** im Weg sein; **to lose one's ~** sich verirren; **under ~** (*project etc*) im Gang; **the ~ back** der Rückweg; **to make ~ (for sb/sth)** (für jdn/etw) Platz machen; **to get one's own ~** seinen Willen bekommen; **put it the right ~ up** (*Brit*) stell es richtig herum hin; **to be the wrong ~ round** verkehrt herum sein; **he's in a bad ~** ihm geht es schlecht; **in a ~** in gewisser Weise; **in some ~s** in mancher Hinsicht; **no ~!** (*inf*) kommt nicht infrage!; **by the ~ ...** übrigens ...; **"~ in"** (*Brit*) „Eingang"; **"~ out"** (*Brit*) „Ausgang"; **"give ~"** (*Brit: Aut*) „Vorfahrt beachten"; **~ of life** Lebensstil *m*
waybill ['weɪbɪl] *n* Frachtbrief *m*
waylay [weɪ'leɪ] (*irreg: like* **lay**) *vt* auflauern *+dat*; **to get waylaid** (*fig*) abgefangen werden
wayside ['weɪsaɪd] *adj* am Straßenrand ▷ *n* Straßenrand *m*; **to fall by the ~** (*fig*) auf der Strecke bleiben
way station (*US*) *n* (*Rail*) kleiner Bahnhof *m*; (*fig*) Zwischenstation *f*
wayward ['weɪwəd] *adj* (*behaviour*) eigenwillig; (*child*) eigensinnig
WC (*Brit*) *n abbr* (= *water closet*) WC *nt*
WCC *n abbr* (= *World Council of Churches*) Weltkirchenrat *m*
we [wiː] *pl pron* wir; **here we are** (*arriving*) da sind wir; (*finding sth*) na bitte
weak [wiːk] *adj* schwach; (*tea, coffee*) dünn; **to grow ~(er)** schwächer werden
weaken ['wiːkn] *vi* (*resolve, person*) schwächer werden; (*influence, power*) nachlassen ▷ *vt* schwächen

weak-kneed ['wi:k'ni:d] *adj* *(fig)* schwächlich
weakling ['wi:klɪŋ] *n* Schwächling *m*
weakly ['wi:klɪ] *adv* schwach
weakness ['wi:knɪs] *n* Schwäche *f*; **to have a ~ for** eine Schwäche haben für
wealth [wɛlθ] *n* Reichtum *m*; *(of details, knowledge etc)* Fülle *f*
wealth tax *n* Vermögenssteuer *f*
wealthy ['wɛlθɪ] *adj* wohlhabend, reich
wean [wi:n] *vt* *(also fig)* entwöhnen
weapon ['wɛpən] *n* Waffe *f*; **~s of mass destruction** Massenvernichtungswaffen *pl*
wear [wɛəʳ] *(pt* **wore**, *pp* **worn**) *vt* *(clothes, shoes, beard)* tragen; *(put on)* anziehen ▷ *vi* *(last)* halten; *(become old: carpet, jeans)* sich abnutzen ▷ *n* *(damage)* Verschleiß *m*; *(use)*: **I got a lot of/very little ~ out of the coat** der Mantel hat lange/nicht sehr lange gehalten; **baby~** Babykleidung *f*; **sports~** Sportkleidung *f*; **evening ~** Kleidung für den Abend; **to ~ a hole in sth** *(coat etc)* etw durchwetzen
▸ **wear away** *vt* verschleißen ▷ *vi* *(inscription etc)* verwittern
▸ **wear down** *vt* *(heels)* abnutzen; *(person, strength)* zermürben
▸ **wear off** *vi* *(pain etc)* nachlassen
▸ **wear on** *vi* sich hinziehen
▸ **wear out** *vt* *(shoes, clothing)* verschleißen; *(person, strength)* erschöpfen
wearable ['wɛərəbl] *adj* tragbar
wear and tear [-tɛəʳ] *n* Verschleiß *m*
wearer ['wɛərəʳ] *n* Träger(in) *m(f)*
wearily ['wɪərɪlɪ] *adv* *(say, sit)* lustlos, müde
weariness ['wɪərɪnɪs] *n* *(tiredness)* Müdigkeit *f*
wearisome ['wɪərɪsəm] *adj* *(boring)* langweilig; *(tiring)* ermüdend
weary ['wɪərɪ] *adj* *(tired)* müde; *(dispirited)* lustlos ▷ *vi*: **to ~ of sb/sth** jds/etw *gen* überdrüssig werden
weasel ['wi:zl] *n* Wiesel *nt*
weather ['wɛðəʳ] *n* Wetter *nt* ▷ *vt* *(storm, crisis)* überstehen; *(rock, wood)* verwittern; **what's the ~ like?** wie ist das Wetter?; **under the ~** *(fig: ill)* angeschlagen
weather-beaten ['wɛðəbi:tn] *adj* *(face)* vom Wetter gegerbt; *(building, stone)* verwittert
weathercock ['wɛðəkɔk] *n* Wetterhahn *m*
weather forecast *n* Wettervorhersage *f*
weatherman ['wɛðəmæn] *(irreg: like* **man**) *n* Mann *m* vom Wetteramt, Wetterfrosch *m* *(hum inf)*
weatherproof ['wɛðəpru:f] *adj* wetterfest
weather report *n* Wetterbericht *m*
weather vane [-veɪn] *n* = **weathercock**
weave [wi:v] *(pt* **wove**, *pp* **woven**) *vt* *(cloth)* weben; *(basket)* flechten ▷ *vi* *(fig: pt, pp* **weaved**: *move in and out)* sich schlängeln
weaver ['wi:vəʳ] *n* Weber(in) *m(f)*
weaving ['wi:vɪŋ] *n* Weberei *f*
web [wɛb] *n* *(also fig)* Netz *nt*; *(on duck's foot)* Schwimmhaut *f*
webbed ['wɛbd] *adj* *(foot)* Schwimm-
webbing ['wɛbɪŋ] *n* *(on chair)* Gewebe *nt*
website ['wɛbsaɪt] *n* *(Comput)* Website *f*, Webseite *f*
wed [wɛd] *(pt, pp* **~ded**) *vt, vi* heiraten ▷ *n*: **the newly-~s** die Jungvermählten *pl*
Wed. *abbr* *(= Wednesday)* Mi.
we'd [wi:d] = **we had; we would**
wedded ['wɛdɪd] *pt, pp of* **wed** ▷ *adj*: **to be ~ to sth** *(idea etc)* mit etw eng verbunden sein
wedding [wɛdɪŋ] *n* Hochzeit *f*; **silver/golden ~** silberne/goldene Hochzeit
wedding day *n* Hochzeitstag *m*
wedding dress *n* Hochzeitskleid *nt*
wedding present *n* Hochzeitsgeschenk *nt*
wedding ring *n* Trauring *m*
wedge [wɛdʒ] *n* Keil *m*; *(of cake)* Stück *nt* ▷ *vt* *(fasten)* festklemmen; *(pack tightly)* einkeilen
wedge-heeled shoes ['wɛdʒhi:ld-] *npl* Schuhe *pl* mit Keilabsätzen
wedlock ['wɛdlɔk] *n* Ehe *f*
Wednesday ['wɛdnzdɪ] *n* Mittwoch *m*; *see also* **Tuesday**
wee [wi:] *(Scot)* *adj* klein
weed [wi:d] *n* *(Bot)* Unkraut *nt*; *(pej: person)* Schwächling *m* ▷ *vt* *(garden)* jäten
▸ **weed out** *vt* *(fig)* aussondern
weedkiller ['wi:dkɪləʳ] *n* Unkrautvertilger *m*
weedy ['wi:dɪ] *adj* *(person)* schwächlich
week [wi:k] *n* Woche *f*; **once/twice a ~** einmal/zweimal die Woche; **in two ~s' time** in zwei Wochen; **a ~ today/on Friday** heute/Freitag in einer Woche
weekday ['wi:kdeɪ] *n* Wochentag *m*; *(Comm: Monday to Saturday)* Werktag *m*; **on ~s** an Wochentagen/Werktagen
weekend [wi:k'ɛnd] *n* Wochenende *nt*; **this/next/last ~** an diesem/am nächsten/am letzten Wochenende; **what are you doing at the ~?** was machen Sie am Wochenende?; **open at ~s** an Wochenenden geöffnet
weekly ['wi:klɪ] *adv* wöchentlich ▷ *adj* *(newspaper)* Wochen- ▷ *n* *(newspaper)* Wochenzeitung *f*; *(magazine)* Wochenzeitschrift *f*
weep [wi:p] *(pt, pp* **wept**) *vi* *(person)* weinen; *(wound)* nässen
weeping willow ['wi:pɪŋ-] *n* *(tree)* Trauerweide *f*
weepy ['wi:pɪ] *adj* *(person)* weinerlich; *(film)* rührselig ▷ *n* *(film etc)* Schmachtfetzen *m*
weft [wɛft] *n* Schussfaden *m*
weigh [weɪ] *vt* wiegen; *(fig: evidence, risks)* abwägen ▷ *vi* wiegen; **to ~ anchor** den Anker lichten
▸ **weigh down** *vt* niederdrücken
▸ **weigh out** *vt* *(goods)* auswiegen
▸ **weigh up** *vt* *(person, offer, risk)* abschätzen
weighbridge ['weɪbrɪdʒ] *n* Brückenwaage *f*
weighing machine ['weɪɪŋ-] *n* Waage *f*
weight [weɪt] *n* Gewicht *nt* ▷ *vt* *(fig)*: **to be ~ed in favour of sb/sth** jdn/etw begünstigen; **to be sold by ~** nach Gewicht verkauft werden; **to lose ~** abnehmen; **to put on ~** zunehmen; **~s and measures** Maße und Gewichte

weighting ['weɪtɪŋ] *n* (*allowance*) Zulage *f*
weightlessness ['weɪtlɪsnɪs] *n* Schwerelosigkeit *f*
weightlifter ['weɪtlɪftə^r] *n* Gewichtheber *m*
weight limit *n* Gewichtsbeschränkung *f*
weight training *n* Krafttraining *nt*
weighty ['weɪtɪ] *adj* schwer; (*fig: important*) gewichtig
weir [wɪə^r] *n* (*in river*) Wehr *nt*
weird [wɪəd] *adj* (*object, situation, effect*) komisch; (*person*) seltsam
weirdo ['wɪədəu] (*inf*) *n* verrückter Typ *m*
welcome ['wɛlkəm] *adj* willkommen ▷ *n* Willkommen *nt* ▷ *vt* begrüßen, willkommen heißen; **~ to London!** willkommen in London!; **to make sb ~** jdn freundlich aufnehmen; **you're ~ to try** du kannst es gern versuchen; **thank you — you're ~!** danke — nichts zu danken!
welcoming ['wɛlkəmɪŋ] *adj* (*smile, room*) einladend; (*person*) freundlich
weld [wɛld] *n* Schweißnaht *f* ▷ *vt* schweißen
welder ['wɛldə^r] *n* (*person*) Schweißer(in) *m(f)*
welding ['wɛldɪŋ] *n* Schweißen *nt*
welfare ['wɛlfɛə^r] *n* (*well-being*) Wohl *nt*; (*social aid*) Sozialhilfe *f*
welfare state *n* Wohlfahrtsstaat *m*
welfare work *n* Fürsorgearbeit *f*
well [wɛl] *n* (*for water*) Brunnen *m*; (*oil well*) Quelle *f* ▷ *adv* gut; (*for emphasis with adj*) durchaus ▷ *adj*: **to be ~** (*person*) gesund sein ▷ *excl* nun!, na!; **as ~** (*in addition*) ebenfalls; **you might as ~ tell me** sag es mir ruhig; **he did as ~ as he could** er machte es so gut er konnte; **pretty as ~ as rich** sowohl hübsch als auch reich; **~ done!** gut gemacht!; **to do ~** (*person*) gut vorankommen; (*business*) gut gehen; **~ before dawn** lange vor Tagesanbruch; **~ over 40** weit über 40; **I don't feel ~** ich fühle mich nicht gut *or* wohl; **get ~ soon!** gute Besserung!; **~, as I was saying ...** also, wie ich bereits sagte, ...
▸ **well up** *vi* (*tears, emotions*) aufsteigen
we'll [wi:l] = **we will; we shall**
well-behaved ['wɛlbɪ'heɪvd] *adj* wohlerzogen
well-being ['wɛl'bi:ɪŋ] *n* Wohl(ergehen) *nt*
well-bred ['wɛl'brɛd] *adj* (*person*) gut erzogen
well-built ['wɛl'bɪlt] *adj* gut gebaut
well-chosen ['wɛl'tʃəuzn] *adj* gut gewählt
well-deserved ['wɛldɪ'zə:vd] *adj* wohlverdient
well-developed ['wɛldɪ'vɛləpt] *adj* gut entwickelt
well-disposed ['wɛl'dɪspəuzd] *adj*: **~ to(wards)** freundlich gesonnen *+dat*
well-dressed ['wɛl'drɛst] *adj* gut gekleidet
well-earned ['wɛl'ə:nd] *adj* (*rest*) wohlverdient
well-groomed ['wɛl'gru:md] *adj* gepflegt
well-heeled ['wɛl'hi:ld] (*inf*) *adj* betucht
well-informed ['wɛlɪn'fɔ:md] *adj* gut informiert
Wellington ['wɛlɪŋtən] *n* (*Geog*) Wellington *nt*
wellingtons ['wɛlɪŋtənz] *npl* (*also*: **wellington boots**) Gummistiefel *pl*
well-kept ['wɛl'kɛpt] *adj* (*house, grounds*) gepflegt; (*secret*) gut gehütet
well-known ['wɛl'nəun] *adj* wohlbekannt
well-mannered ['wɛl'mænəd] *adj* wohlerzogen
well-meaning ['wɛl'mi:nɪŋ] *adj* (*person*) wohlmeinend; (*offer etc*) gut gemeint
well-nigh ['wɛl'naɪ] *adv*: **~ impossible** geradezu unmöglich
well-off ['wɛl'ɔf] *adj* (*rich*) begütert
well-read ['wɛl'rɛd] *adj* belesen
well-spoken ['wɛl'spəukn] *adj*: **to be ~** sich gut *or* gewandt ausdrücken
well-stocked ['wɛl'stɔkt] *adj* gut bestückt
well-timed ['wɛl'taɪmd] *adj* gut abgepasst
well-to-do ['wɛltə'du:] *adj* wohlhabend
well-wisher ['wɛlwɪʃə^r] *n* (*friend, admirer*) wohlmeinender Mensch *m*; **scores of ~s had gathered** eine große Gefolgschaft hatte sich versammelt; **letters from ~s** Briefe von Leuten, die es gut meinen
well-woman clinic ['wɛlwumən-] *n* ≈ Frauensprechstunde *f*
Welsh [wɛlʃ] *adj* walisisch ▷ *n* (*Ling*) Walisisch *nt*; **the Welsh** *npl* die Waliser *pl*
Welshman ['wɛlʃmən] (*irreg: like* **man**) *n* Waliser *m*
Welsh rarebit *n* überbackenes Käsebrot *nt*
Welshwoman ['wɛlʃwumən] (*irreg: like* **woman**) *n* Waliserin *f*
welter ['wɛltə^r] *n*: **a ~ of** eine Flut von
went [wɛnt] *pt of* **go**
wept [wɛpt] *pt, pp of* **weep**
were [wə:^r] *pt of* **be**
we're [wɪə^r] = **we are**
weren't [wə:nt] = **were not**
werewolf ['wɪəwulf] (*pl* **werewolves**) *n* Werwolf *m*
werewolves ['wɪəwulvz] *npl of* **werewolf**
west [wɛst] *n* Westen *m* ▷ *adj* (*wind, side, coast*) West-, westlich ▷ *adv* (*to or towards the west*) westwärts; **the W~** (*Pol*) der Westen
westbound ['wɛstbaund] *adj* (*traffic, carriageway*) in Richtung Westen
West Country (*Brit*) *n*: **the ~** Südwestengland *nt*
westerly ['wɛstəlɪ] *adj* westlich
western ['wɛstən] *adj* westlich ▷ *n* (*Cine*) Western *m*
westerner ['wɛstənə^r] *n* Abendländer(in) *m(f)*
westernized ['wɛstənaɪzd] *adj* (*society etc*) verwestlicht
West German *adj* westdeutsch ▷ *n* (*person*) Westdeutsche(r) *f(m)*
West Germany *n* (*formerly*) Bundesrepublik *f* Deutschland
West Indian *adj* westindisch ▷ *n* (*person*) Westinder(in) *m(f)*
West Indies [-'ɪndɪz] *npl*: **the ~** Westindien *nt*
Westminster ['wɛstmɪnstə^r] *n* Westminster *nt*; (*parliament*) das britische Parlament
westward ['wɛstwəd], **westwards** ['wɛstwədz] *adv* westwärts

wet [wɛt] *adj* nass ▷ *n* (*Brit: Pol*) Gemäßigte(r) *f(m)*, Waschlappen *m* (*pej*); **to get ~** nass werden; **"~ paint"** „frisch gestrichen"; **to be a ~ blanket** (*fig: pej: person*) ein(e) Spielverderber(in) *m(f)* sein; **to ~ one's pants/o.s.** sich *dat* in die Hosen machen
wetness ['wɛtnɪs] *n* Nässe *f*; (*of climate*) Feuchtigkeit *f*
wet suit *n* Taucheranzug *m*
we've [wi:v] = **we have**
whack [wæk] *vt* schlagen
whacked [wækt] (*Brit: inf*) *adj* (*exhausted*) erschlagen
whale [weɪl] *n* Wal *m*
whaler ['weɪlə[r]] *n* Walfänger *m*
whaling ['weɪlɪŋ] *n* Walfang *m*
wharf [wɔ:f] (*pl* **wharves**) *n* Kai *m*
wharves [wɔ:vz] *npl of* **wharf**

KEYWORD

what [wɔt] *adj* **1** (*in direct/indirect questions*) welche(r, s); **what colour/shape is it?** welche Farbe/Form hat es?; **for what reason?** aus welchem Grund?
2 (*in exclamations*) was für ein(e); **what a mess!** was für ein Durcheinander!; **what a fool I am!** was bin ich doch (für) ein Idiot!
▷ *pron* (*interrogative, relative*) was; **what are you doing?** was machst du?; **what are you talking about?** wovon redest du?; **what is it called?** wie heißt das?; **what about me?** und ich?; **what about a cup of tea?** wie wärs mit einer Tasse Tee?; **what about going to the cinema?** sollen wir ins Kino gehen?; **I saw what you did/what was on the table** ich habe gesehen, was du getan hast/was auf dem Tisch war; **tell me what you're thinking about** sag mir, woran du denkst
▷ *excl* (*disbelieving*) was, wie; **what, no coffee!** was *or* wie, kein Kaffee?

whatever [wɔt'ɛvə[r]] *adj*: **~ book** welches Buch auch immer ▷ *pron*: **do ~ is necessary/you want** tun Sie, was nötig ist/was immer Sie wollen; **~ happens** was auch passiert; **no reason ~** *or* **whatsoever** überhaupt kein Grund; **nothing ~** *or* **whatsoever** überhaupt nichts
whatsoever [wɔtsəu'ɛvə[r]] *adj* = **whatever**
wheat [wi:t] *n* Weizen *m*
wheatgerm ['wi:tdʒə:m] *n* Weizenkeim *m*
wheatmeal ['wi:tmi:l] *n* Weizenmehl *nt*
wheedle ['wi:dl] *vt*: **to ~ sb into doing sth** jdn beschwatzen, etw zu tun; **to ~ sth out of sb** jdm etw abluchsen
wheel [wi:l] *n* Rad *nt*; (*also*: **steering wheel**) Lenkrad *nt*; (*Naut*) Steuer *nt* ▷ *vt* (*pram etc*) schieben ▷ *vi* (*birds*) kreisen; (*also*: **wheel round**: *person*) sich herumdrehen
wheelbarrow ['wi:lbærəu] *n* Schubkarre *f*
wheelbase ['wi:lbeɪs] *n* Radstand *m*
wheelchair ['wi:ltʃɛə[r]] *n* Rollstuhl *m*
wheel clamp *n* Parkkralle *f*
wheeler-dealer ['wi:lə'di:lə[r]] (*pej*) *n* Geschäftemacher(in) *m(f)*
wheelie-bin ['wi:lɪbɪn] *n* Mülltonne *f* auf Rädern
wheeling ['wi:lɪŋ] *n*: **~ and dealing** (*pej*) Geschäftemacherei *f*
wheeze [wi:z] *vi* (*person*) keuchen ▷ *n* (*idea, joke etc*) Scherz *m*
wheezy ['wi:zɪ] *adj* (*person*) mit pfeifendem Atem; (*cough*) keuchend; (*breath*) pfeifend; (*laugh*) asthmatisch

KEYWORD

when [wɛn] *adv* wann
▷ *conj* **1** (*at, during, after the time that*) wenn; **she was reading when I came in** als ich hereinkam, las sie gerade; **be careful when you cross the road** sei vorsichtig, wenn du die Straße überquerst
2 (*on, at which*) als; **on the day when I met him** am Tag, als ich ihn traf
3 (*whereas*) wo ... doch, obwohl; **why did you buy that when you can't afford it?** warum hast du das gekauft, obwohl du es dir nicht leisten kannst?

whenever [wɛn'ɛvə[r]] *adv, conj* (*any time that*) wann immer; (*every time that*) (jedes Mal,) wenn; **I go ~ I can** ich gehe, wann immer ich kann
where [wɛə[r]] *adv, conj* wo; **this is ~ ...** hier ...; **~ possible** so weit möglich; **~ are you from?** woher kommen Sie?
whereabouts [wɛərə'bauts] *adv* wo ▷ *n*: **nobody knows his ~** keiner weiß, wo er ist
whereas [wɛər'æz] *conj* während
whereby [wɛə'baɪ] (*form*) *adv* wonach
whereupon [wɛərə'pɔn] *conj* worauf
wherever [wɛər'ɛvə[r]] *conj* (*position*) wo (auch) immer; (*motion*) wohin (auch) immer ▷ *adv* (*surprise*) wo (um alles in der Welt); **sit ~ you like** nehmen Sie Platz, wo immer Sie wollen
wherewithal ['wɛəwɪðɔ:l] *n*: **the ~ (to do sth)** (*money*) das nötige Kleingeld(, um etw zu tun)
whet [wɛt] *vt* (*appetite*) anregen; (*tool*) schleifen
whether ['wɛðə[r]] *conj* ob; **I don't know ~ to accept or not** ich weiß nicht, ob ich annehmen soll oder nicht; **~ you go or not** ob du gehst oder nicht; **it's doubtful ~ ...** es ist zweifelhaft, ob ...
whey ['weɪ] *n* Molke *f*

KEYWORD

which [wɪtʃ] *adj* **1** (*interrogative: direct, indirect*) welche(r, s); **which picture?** welches Bild?; **which books?** welche Bücher?; **which one?** welche(r, s) ?
2: in which case in diesem Fall; **by which time** zu dieser Zeit

▷ *pron* **1** (*interrogative*) welche(r, s); **which of you are coming?** wer von Ihnen kommt?; **I don't mind which** mir ist gleich, welche(r, s) **2** (*relative*) der/die/das; **the apple which you ate/which is on the table** der Apfel, den du gegessen hast/der auf dem Tisch liegt; **the chair on which you are sitting** der Stuhl, auf dem Sie sitzen; **the book of which you spoke** das Buch, wovon *or* von dem Sie sprachen; **he said he saw her, which is true** er sagte, er habe sie gesehen, was auch stimmt; **after which** wonach

whichever [wɪtʃˈɛvəʳ] *adj*: **take ~ book you want** nehmen Sie irgendein *or* ein beliebiges Buch; **~ book you take** welches Buch Sie auch nehmen
whiff [wɪf] *n* (*of perfume*) Hauch *m*; (*of petrol, smoke*) Geruch *m*; **to catch a ~ of sth** den Geruch von etw wahrnehmen
while [waɪl] *n* Weile *f* ▷ *conj* während; **for a ~** eine Weile (lang); **in a ~** gleich; **all the ~** die ganze Zeit (über); **I'll/we'll** *etc* **make it worth your ~** es wird sich für Sie lohnen
▸ **while away** *vt* (*time*) sich *dat* vertreiben
whilst [waɪlst] *conj* = **while**
whim [wɪm] *n* Laune *f*
whimper [ˈwɪmpəʳ] *n* (*cry, moan*) Wimmern *nt* ▷ *vi* wimmern
whimsical [ˈwɪmzɪkəl] *adj* wunderlich, seltsam; (*story*) kurios
whine [waɪn] *n* (*of pain*) Jammern *nt*; (*of engine, siren*) Heulen *nt* ▷ *vi* (*person*) jammern; (*dog*) jaulen; (*engine, siren*) heulen
whip [wɪp] *n* Peitsche *f*; (*Pol*) ≈ Fraktionsführer *m* ▷ *vt* (*person, animal*) peitschen; (*cream, eggs*) schlagen; (*move quickly*): **to ~ sth out/off** etw blitzschnell hervorholen/wegbringen
▸ **whip up** *vt* (*cream*) schlagen; (*inf*: *meal*) hinzaubern; (*arouse*: *support*) anheizen; (: *people*) mitreißen

WHIP

Der Ausdruck *whip* bezieht sich in der Politik auf einen Abgeordneten, der für die Einhaltung der Parteidisziplin zuständig ist, besonders für die Anwesenheit und das Wahlverhalten der Abgeordneten im Unterhaus. Die whips fordern die Abgeordneten ihrer Partei schriftlich zur Anwesenheit auf und deuten die Wichtigkeit der Abstimmungen durch ein-, zwei-, oder dreimaliges Unterstreichen an, wobei dreimaliges Unterstreichen (3-line whip) strengsten Fraktionszwang bedeutet.

whiplash [ˈwɪplæʃ] *n* Peitschenhieb *m*; (*Med*: *also*: **whiplash injury**) Schleudertrauma *nt*
whipped cream [wɪpt-] *n* Schlagsahne *f*
whipping boy [ˈwɪpɪŋ-] *n* (*fig*) Prügelknabe *m*
whip-round [ˈwɪpraund] (*Brit*: *inf*) *n* (Geld)sammlung *f*
whirl [wəːl] *vt* (*arms, sword etc*) herumwirbeln ▷ *vi* wirbeln ▷ *n* (*of activity, pleasure*) Wirbel *m*; **to be in a ~** (*mind, person*) völlig verwirrt sein
whirlpool [ˈwəːlpuːl] *n* (*lit*) Strudel *m*
whirlwind [ˈwəːlwɪnd] *n* (*lit*) Wirbelwind *m*
whirr [wəːʳ] *vi* (*motor etc*) surren
whisk [wɪsk] *n* (*Culin*) Schneebesen *m* ▷ *vt* (*cream, eggs*) schlagen; **to ~ sb away** *or* **off** jdn in Windeseile wegbringen
whiskers [ˈwɪskəz] *npl* (*of animal*) Barthaare *pl*; (*of man*) Backenbart *m*
whisky, (*US, Ireland*) **whiskey** [ˈwɪskɪ] *n* Whisky *m*
whisper [ˈwɪspəʳ] *n* Flüstern *nt*; (*fig*: *of wind*) Wispern *nt* ▷ *vt, vi* flüstern; **to ~ sth to sb** jdm etw zuflüstern
whispering [ˈwɪspərɪŋ] *n* Geflüster *nt*
whist [wɪst] (*Brit*) *n* Whist *nt*
whistle [ˈwɪsl] *n* (*sound*) Pfiff *m*; (*object*) Pfeife *f* ▷ *vi* pfeifen ▷ *vt*: **to ~ a tune** eine Melodie pfeifen
whistle-stop [ˈwɪslstɔp] *adj*: **to make a ~ tour of** (*fig*) eine Rundreise machen durch; (*Pol*) eine Wahlkampfreise machen durch
Whit [wɪt] *n* = **Whitsun**
white [waɪt] *adj* weiß ▷ *n* (*colour*) Weiß *nt*; (*person*) Weiße(r) *f(m)*; (*of egg, eye*) Weiße(s) *nt*; **to turn** *or* **go ~** (*person*: *with fear*) weiß *or* bleich werden; (: *with age*) weiße Haare bekommen; (*hair*) weiß werden; **the ~s** (*washing*) die Weißwäsche *f*; **tennis/cricket ~s** weiße Tennis-/Krickettrikots
whitebait [ˈwaɪtbeɪt] *n essbare Jungfische (Heringe, Sprotten etc)*
white coffee (*Brit*) *n* Kaffee *m* mit Milch
white-collar worker [ˈwaɪtkɔlə-] *n* Schreibtischarbeiter(in) *m(f)*
white elephant *n* (*fig*: *venture*) Fehlinvestition *f*
white food *n* weiße Lebensmittel *pl*, weißes Essen *nt*
white goods *npl* (*appliances*) große Haushaltsgeräte *pl*; (*linen etc*) Weißwaren *pl*
white-hot [waɪtˈhɔt] *adj* (*metal*) weiß glühend

WHITE HOUSE

White House, eine weiß gestrichene Villa in Washington, ist der offizielle Wohnsitz des amerikanischen Präsidenten. Im weiteren Sinne bezieht sich dieser Begriff auf die Exekutive der amerikanischen Regierung.

white lie *n* Notlüge *f*
whiteness [ˈwaɪtnɪs] *n* Weiß *nt*
white noise *n* weißes Rauschen *nt*
whiteout [ˈwaɪtaut] *n* starkes Schneegestöber *nt*
white paper *n* (*Pol*) Weißbuch *nt*
whitewash [ˈwaɪtwɔʃ] *n* (*paint*) Tünche *f*; (*inf, Sport*) totale Niederlage *f* ▷ *vt* (*building*)

tünchen; (*fig: incident, reputation*) reinwaschen

white water *n*: **white-water rafting** Wildwasserflößen *nt*

whiting ['waɪtɪŋ] *n inv* (*fish*) Weißling *m*

Whit Monday *n* Pfingstmontag *m*

Whitsun ['wɪtsn] *n* Pfingsten *nt*

whittle ['wɪtl] *vt*: **to ~ away** *or* **down** (*costs etc*) verringern

whizz [wɪz] *vi*: **to ~ past** *or* **by** vorbeisausen

whizz kid (*inf*) *n* Senkrechtstarter(in) *m(f)*

WHO *n abbr* (= *World Health Organization*) Weltgesundheitsorganisation *f*, WHO *f*

KEYWORD

who [hu:] *pron* **1** (*interrogative*) wer; (: *acc*) wen; (: *dat*) wem; **who is it?, who's there?** wer ist da?; **who did you give it to?** wem hast du es gegeben?

2 (*relative*) der/die/das; **the man/woman who spoke to me** der Mann, der/die Frau, die mit mir gesprochen hat

whodunit, whodunnit [hu:'dʌnɪt] (*inf*) *n* Krimi *m*

whoever [hu:'ɛvəʳ] *pron*: **~ finds it** wer (auch immer) es findet; **ask ~ you like** fragen Sie, wen Sie wollen; **~ he marries** ganz gleich *or* egal, wen er heiratet; **~ told you that?** wer um alles in der Welt hat dir das erzählt?

whole [həul] *adj* (*entire*) ganz; (*not broken*) heil ▷ *n* Ganze(s) *nt*; **the ~ lot (of it)** alles; **the ~ lot (of them)** alle; **the ~ (of the) time** die ganze Zeit; **~ villages were destroyed** ganze Dörfer wurden zerstört; **the ~ of** der/die/das ganze; **the ~ of Glasgow/Europe** ganz Glasgow/Europa; **the ~ of the town** die ganze Stadt; **on the ~** im Ganzen (gesehen)

wholefood ['həulfu:d] *n*, **wholefoods** ['həulfu:dz] ▷ *npl* Vollwertkost *f*

wholefood shop *n* ≈ Reformhaus *nt*

wholehearted [həul'hɑ:tɪd] *adj* (*agreement etc*) rückhaltlos

wholeheartedly [həul'hɑ:tɪdlɪ] *adv* (*agree etc*) rückhaltlos

wholemeal ['həulmi:l] (*Brit*) *adj* (*bread, flour*) Vollkorn-

whole note (*US*) *n* ganze Note *f*

wholesale ['həulseɪl] *n* (*business*) Großhandel *m* ▷ *adj* (*price*) Großhandels-; (*destruction etc*) umfassend ▷ *adv* (*buy, sell*) im Großhandel

wholesaler ['həulseɪləʳ] *n* Großhändler *m*

wholesome ['həulsəm] *adj* (*food*) gesund; (*effect*) zuträglich; (*attitude*) positiv

wholewheat ['həulwi:t] *adj* = **wholemeal**

wholly ['həulɪ] *adv* ganz und gar

KEYWORD

whom [hu:m] *pron* **1** (*interrogative*: *acc*) wen; (: *dat*) wem; **whom did you see?** wen hast du gesehen?; **to whom did you give it?** wem hast du es gegeben?

2 (*relative*: *acc*) den/die/das; (: *dat*) dem/der/dem; **the man whom I saw/to whom I spoke** der Mann, den ich gesehen habe/mit dem ich gesprochen habe

whooping cough ['hu:pɪŋ-] *n* Keuchhusten *m*

whoosh [wuʃ] *vi*: **to ~ along/past/down** entlang-/vorbei-/hinuntersausen ▷ *n* Sausen *nt*; **the skiers ~ed past, skiers came by with a ~** die Skifahrer sausten vorbei

whopper ['wɔpəʳ] (*inf*) *n* (*lie*) faustdicke Lüge *f*; (*large thing*) Mordsding *nt*

whopping ['wɔpɪŋ] (*inf*) *adj* Riesen-, riesig

whore [hɔ:ʳ] (*inf: pej*) *n* Hure *f*

KEYWORD

whose [hu:z] *adj* **1** (*possessive: interrogative*) wessen; **whose book is this?, whose is this book?** wessen Buch ist das?, wem gehört das Buch?; **I don't know whose it is** ich weiß nicht, wem es gehört

2 (*possessive: relative*) dessen/deren/dessen; **the man whose son you rescued** der Mann, dessen Sohn du gerettet hast; **the woman whose car was stolen** die Frau, deren Auto gestohlen worden war

▷ *pron*: **whose is this?** wem gehört das?; **I know whose it is** ich weiß, wem es gehört

Who's Who ['hu:z'hu:] *n* (*book*) Who's who *nt*

KEYWORD

why [waɪ] *adv* warum; **why not?** warum nicht?

▷ *conj* warum; **I wonder why he said that** ich frage mich, warum er das gesagt hat; **that's not why I'm here** ich bin nicht deswegen hier; **the reason why** der Grund, warum *or* weshalb

▷ *excl* (*expressing surprise, shock*) na so was; (*expressing annoyance*) ach; **why, yes (of course)** aber ja doch; **why, it's you!** na so was, du bists!

WI *n abbr* (*Brit*: = *Women's Institute*) *britischer Frauenverband* ▷ *abbr* = **West Indies**; (*US: Post*) = *Wisconsin*

wick [wɪk] *n* Docht *m*; **he gets on my ~** (*Brit: inf*) er geht mir auf den Geist

wicked ['wɪkɪd] *adj* (*crime, person*) böse; (*smile, wit*) frech; (*inf: prices*) unverschämt; (: *weather*) schrecklich

wicker ['wɪkəʳ] *adj* (*chair etc*) Korb-; (*basket*) Weiden-

wickerwork ['wɪkəʳwə:k] *adj* (*chair etc*) Korb-; (*basket*) Weiden- ▷ *n* (*objects*) Korbwaren *pl*

wicket ['wɪkɪt] *n* (*Cricket: stumps*) Tor *nt*, Wicket *nt*; (: *grass area*) Spielbahn *f*

wicket-keeper ['wɪkɪtki:pəʳ] *n* Torwächter *m*

wide [waɪd] *adj* breit; (*area*) weit; (*publicity*) umfassend ▷ *adv*: **to open sth ~** etw weit

öffnen; **it is 3 metres ~** es ist 3 Meter breit; **to go ~** vorbeigehen
wide-angle lens ['waɪdæŋgl-] *n* Weitwinkelobjektiv *nt*
wide-awake [waɪdə'weɪk] *adj* hellwach
wide-eyed [waɪd'aɪd] *adj* mit großen Augen; (*fig*) unschuldig, naiv
widely ['waɪdlɪ] *adv* (*differ, vary*) erheblich; (*travel*) ausgiebig, viel; (*spaced*) weit; (*believed, known*) allgemein; **to be ~ read** (*reader*) sehr belesen sein
widen ['waɪdn] *vt* (*road, river*) verbreitern; (*one's experience*) erweitern ▷ *vi* sich verbreitern
wideness ['waɪdnɪs] *n* (*of road, river, gap*) Breite *f*
wide open *adj* (*window, eyes, mouth*) weit geöffnet
wide-ranging [waɪd'reɪndʒɪŋ] *adj* (*effects*) weitreichend; (*interview, survey*) umfassend
widespread ['waɪdsprɛd] *adj* weitverbreitet
widow ['wɪdəu] *n* Witwe *f*
widowed ['wɪdəud] *adj* verwitwet
widower ['wɪdəuəʳ] *n* Witwer *m*
width [wɪdθ] *n* Breite *f*; (*in swimming pool*) (Quer)bahn *f*; **it's 7 metres in ~** es ist 7 Meter breit
widthways ['wɪdθweɪz] *adv* der Breite nach
wield [wi:ld] *vt* (*sword*) schwingen; (*power*) ausüben
wife [waɪf] (*pl* **wives**) *n* Frau *f*
wig [wɪg] *n* Perücke *f*
wigging ['wɪgɪŋ] (*Brit: inf*) *n* Standpauke *f*
wiggle ['wɪgl] *vt* wackeln mit
wiggly ['wɪglɪ] *adj*: **~ line** Schlangenlinie *f*
wigwam ['wɪgwæm] *n* Wigwam *m*
wild [waɪld] *adj* wild; (*weather*) rau, stürmisch; (*person, behaviour*) ungestüm; (*idea*) weit hergeholt; (*applause*) stürmisch ▷ *n*: **the ~** (*natural surroundings*) die freie Natur *f*; **the wilds** *npl* die Wildnis; **I'm not ~ about it** ich bin nicht versessen *or* scharf darauf
wild card *n* (*Comput*) Wildcard *f*, Ersatzzeichen *nt*
wildcat ['waɪldkæt] *n* Wildkatze *f*
wildcat strike *n* wilder Streik *m*
wilderness ['wɪldənɪs] *n* Wildnis *f*
wildfire ['waɪldfaɪəʳ] *n*: **to spread like ~** sich wie ein Lauffeuer ausbreiten
wild-goose chase [waɪld'gu:s-] *n* aussichtslose Suche *f*
wildlife ['waɪldlaɪf] *n* (*animals*) die Tierwelt *f*
wildly ['waɪldlɪ] *adv* wild; (*very: romantic*) wild-; (*: inefficient*) furchtbar
wiles [waɪlz] *npl* List *f*
wilful, (*US*) **willful** ['wɪlful] *adj* (*obstinate*) eigensinnig; (*deliberate*) vorsätzlich

KEYWORD

will [wɪl] *aux vb* **1** (*forming future tense*): **I will finish it tomorrow** ich werde es morgen fertig machen, ich mache es morgen fertig; **will you do it? — yes I will/no I won't** machst du es? — ja/nein
2 (*in conjectures, predictions*): **that will be the postman** das ist bestimmt der Briefträger
3 (*in commands, requests, offers*): **will you sit down** (*politely*) bitte nehmen Sie Platz; (*angrily*) nun setz dich doch; **will you be quiet!** seid jetzt still!; **will you help me?** hilfst du mir?; **will you have a cup of tea?** möchten Sie eine Tasse Tee?; **I won't put up with it!** das lasse ich mir nicht gefallen!
▷ *vt* (*pt, pp* **willed**) **to will sb to do sth** jdn durch Willenskraft dazu bewegen, etw zu tun; **he willed himself to go on** er zwang sich dazu, weiterzumachen
▷ *n* (*volition*) Wille *m*; (*testament*) Testament *nt*; **he did it against his will** er tat es gegen seinen Willen

willful ['wɪlful] (*US*) *adj* = **wilful**
willing ['wɪlɪŋ] *adj* (*having no objection*) gewillt; (*enthusiastic*) bereitwillig; **he's ~ to do it** er ist bereit, es zu tun; **to show ~** guten Willen zeigen
willingly ['wɪlɪŋlɪ] *adv* bereitwillig
willingness ['wɪlɪŋnɪs] *n* (*readiness*) Bereitschaft *f*; (*enthusiasm*) Bereitwilligkeit *f*
will-o'-the-wisp ['wɪləðə'wɪsp] *n* Irrlicht *nt*; (*fig*) Trugbild *nt*
willow ['wɪləu] *n* (*tree*) Weide *f*; (*wood*) Weidenholz *nt*
willpower ['wɪl'pauəʳ] *n* Willenskraft *f*
willy-nilly ['wɪlɪ'nɪlɪ] *adv* (*willingly or not*) wohl oder übel
wilt [wɪlt] *vi* (*plant*) welken
Wilts [wɪlts] (*Brit*) *abbr* (*Post*) = *Wiltshire*
wily ['waɪlɪ] *adj* listig, raffiniert
wimp [wɪmp] (*inf: pej*) *n* Waschlappen *m*
wimpish ['wɪmpɪʃ] (*inf*) *adj* weichlich
win [wɪn] (*pt, pp* **won**) *n* Sieg *m* ▷ *vt* gewinnen ▷ *vi* siegen, gewinnen
▶ **win over** *vt* (*persuade*) gewinnen
▶ **win round** (*Brit*) *vt* = **win over**
wince [wɪns] *vi* zusammenzucken
winch [wɪntʃ] *n* Winde *f*
Winchester disk ['wɪntʃɪstə-] *n* Winchesterplatte *f*
wind¹ [wɪnd] *n* (*air*) Wind *m*; (*Med*) Blähungen *pl*; (*breath*) Atem *m* ▷ *vt* (*take breath away from*) den Atem nehmen *+dat*; **the winds** *npl* (*Mus*) die Bläser *pl*; **into** *or* **against the ~** gegen den Wind; **to get ~ of sth** (*fig*) von etw Wind bekommen; **to break ~** Darmwind entweichen lassen
wind² [waɪnd] (*pt, pp* **wound**) *vt* (*thread, rope, bandage*) wickeln; (*clock, toy*) aufziehen ▷ *vi* (*road, river*) sich winden
▶ **wind down** *vt* (*car window*) herunterdrehen; (*fig: production*) zurückschrauben
▶ **wind up** *vt* (*clock, toy*) aufziehen; (*debate*) abschließen
windbreak ['wɪndbreɪk] *n* Windschutz *m*
windbreaker ['wɪndbreɪkəʳ] (*US*) *n* = **windcheater**
windcheater ['wɪndtʃi:təʳ] *n* Windjacke *f*

winder ['waɪndəʳ] *(Brit) n (on watch)* Krone *f*, Aufziehrädchen *nt*
windfall ['wɪndfɔːl] *n (money)* unverhoffter Glücksfall *m*; *(apple)* Fallobst *nt*
winding ['waɪndɪŋ] *adj* gewunden
wind instrument ['wɪnd-] *n* Blasinstrument *nt*
windmill ['wɪndmɪl] *n* Windmühle *f*
window ['wɪndəu] *n (also Comput)* Fenster *nt*; *(in shop)* Schaufenster *nt*
window box *n* Blumenkasten *m*
window cleaner *n* Fensterputzer(in) *m(f)*
window dresser *n* Schaufensterdekorateur(in) *m(f)*
window envelope *n* Fensterumschlag *m*
window frame *n* Fensterrahmen *m*
window ledge *n* Fenstersims *m*
window pane *n* Fensterscheibe *f*
window-shopping ['wɪndəuʃɔpɪŋ] *n* Schaufensterbummel *m*; **to go ~** einen Schaufensterbummel machen
windowsill ['wɪndəusɪl] *n* Fensterbank *f*
windpipe ['wɪndpaɪp] *n* Luftröhre *f*
wind power ['wɪnd-] *n* Windkraft *f*, Windenergie *f*
windscreen ['wɪndskriːn] *n* Windschutzscheibe *f*
windscreen washer *n* Scheibenwaschanlage *f*
windscreen wiper [-waɪpəʳ] *n* Scheibenwischer *m*
windshield ['wɪndʃiːld] *(US) n* = **windscreen**
windsurfing ['wɪndsəːfɪŋ] *n* Windsurfen *nt*
windswept ['wɪndswɛpt] *adj (place)* vom Wind gepeitscht; *(person)* vom Wind zerzaust
wind tunnel ['wɪnd-] *n* Windkanal *m*
windy ['wɪndɪ] *adj* windig; **it's ~** es ist windig
wine [waɪn] *n* Wein *m* ▷ *vt*: **to ~ and dine sb** jdm zu einem guten Essen ausführen
wine bar *n* Weinlokal *nt*
wine cellar *n* Weinkeller *m*
wine glass *n* Weinglas *nt*
wine list *n* Weinkarte *f*
wine merchant *n* Weinhändler(in) *m(f)*
wine tasting [-teɪstɪŋ] *n* Weinprobe *f*
wine waiter *n* Weinkellner *m*
wing [wɪŋ] *n (of bird, insect, plane)* Flügel *m*; *(of building)* Trakt *m*; *(of car)* Kotflügel *m*; **the wings** *npl (Theat)* die Kulissen *pl*
winger ['wɪŋəʳ] *n (Sport)* Flügelspieler(in) *m(f)*
wing mirror *(Brit) n* Seitenspiegel *m*
wing nut *n* Flügelmutter *f*
wingspan ['wɪŋspæn] *n* Flügelspannweite *f*
wingspread ['wɪŋsprɛd] *n* = **wingspan**
wink [wɪŋk] *n (of eye)* Zwinkern *m* ▷ *vi (with eye)* zwinkern; *(light etc)* blinken
winkle [wɪŋkl] *n* Strandschnecke *f*
winner ['wɪnəʳ] *n (of race, competition)* Sieger(in) *m(f)*; *(of prize)* Gewinner(in) *m(f)*
winning ['wɪnɪŋ] *adj (team, entry)* siegreich; *(shot, goal)* entscheidend; *(smile)* einnehmend; *see also* **winnings**
winning post *n (lit)* Zielpfosten *m*; *(fig)* Ziel *nt*
winnings ['wɪnɪŋz] *npl* Gewinn *m*
winsome ['wɪnsəm] *adj (expression)* gewinnend; *(person)* reizend
winter ['wɪntəʳ] *n* Winter *m* ▷ *vi (birds)* überwintern; **in ~** im Winter
winter sports *npl* Wintersport *m*
wintry ['wɪntrɪ] *adj (weather, day)* winterlich, Winter-
wipe [waɪp] *vt* wischen; *(dry)* abtrocknen; *(clean)* abwischen; *(erase: tape)* löschen; **to ~ one's nose** sich *dat* die Nase putzen ▷ *n*: **to give sth a ~** etw abwischen
▸ **wipe off** *vt* abwischen
▸ **wipe out** *vt (destroy: city etc)* auslöschen
▸ **wipe up** *vt (mess)* aufwischen
wire ['waɪəʳ] *n* Draht *m*; *(US: telegram)* Telegramm *nt* ▷ *vt (US)*: **to ~ sb** jdm telegrafieren; *(also:* **wire up**: *electrical fitting)* anschließen
wire brush *n* Drahtbürste *f*
wire cutters *npl* Drahtschere *f*
wireless ['waɪəlɪs] *(Brit: old) n* Funk *m*; *(set)* Rundfunkgerät *nt*
wireless phone *n* schnurloses Telefon *nt*
wire netting *n* Maschendraht *m*
wire service *(US) n* Nachrichtenagentur *f*
wire-tapping ['waɪə'tæpɪŋ] *n* Anzapfen *nt* von Leitungen
wiring ['waɪərɪŋ] *n* elektrische Leitungen *pl*
wiry ['waɪərɪ] *adj (person)* drahtig; *(hair)* borstig
Wis. *(US) abbr (Post)* = *Wisconsin*
wisdom ['wɪzdəm] *n (of person)* Weisheit *f*; *(of action, remark)* Klugheit *f*
wisdom tooth *n* Weisheitszahn *m*
wise *adj (person)* weise; *(action, remark)* klug; **I'm none the ~r** ich bin genauso klug wie vorher
▸ **wise up** *(inf) vi*: **to ~ up to sth** hinter etw *acc* kommen
...wise [waɪz] *suff*: **timewise/moneywise** *etc* zeitmäßig/geldmäßig *etc*
wisecrack ['waɪzkræk] *n* Witzelei *f*
wisely ['waɪzlɪ] *adv* klug, weise
wish [wɪʃ] *n* Wunsch *m* ▷ *vt* wünschen; **best ~es** *(for birthday etc)* herzliche Grüße, alle guten Wünsche; **with best ~es** *(in letter)* mit den besten Wünschen *or* Grüßen; **give her my best ~es** grüßen Sie sie herzlich von mir; **to make a ~** sich *dat* etw wünschen; **to ~ sb goodbye** jdm Auf Wiedersehen sagen; **he ~ed me well** er wünschte mir alles Gute; **to ~ to do sth** etw tun wollen; **to ~ sth on sb** jdm etw wünschen; **to ~ for sth** sich *dat* etw wünschen
wishbone ['wɪʃbəun] *n* Gabelbein *nt*
wishful ['wɪʃful] *adj*: **it's ~ thinking** das ist reines Wunschdenken
wishy-washy ['wɪʃɪ'wɔʃɪ] *(inf) adj (colour)* verwaschen; *(person)* farblos; *(ideas)* nichtssagend
wisp [wɪsp] *n (of grass)* Büschel *nt*; *(of hair)* Strähne *f*; *(of smoke)* Fahne *f*
wistful ['wɪstful] *adj* wehmütig
wit [wɪt] *n (wittiness)* geistreiche Art *f*; *(person)* geistreicher Mensch *m*; *(presence of mind)* Verstand *m*; **wits** *npl (intelligence)* Verstand *m*;

to be at one's ~s' end mit seinem Latein am Ende sein; **to have one's ~s about one** einen klaren Kopf haben; **to ~** (*namely*) und zwar
witch [wɪtʃ] *n* Hexe *f*
witchcraft ['wɪtʃkrɑːft] *n* Hexerei *f*
witch doctor *n* Medizinmann *m*
witch-hunt ['wɪtʃhʌnt] *n* (*fig*) Hexenjagd *f*

KEYWORD

with [wɪð] *prep* **1** (*accompanying, in the company of*) mit; **we stayed with friends** wir wohnten bei Freunden; **I'll be with you in a minute** einen Augenblick, ich bin sofort da; **I'm with you** (*I understand*) ich verstehe; **to be with it** (*inf: up-to-date*) auf dem Laufenden sein; (*: alert*) da sein
2 (*descriptive, indicating manner*) mit; **the man with the grey hat/blue eyes** der Mann mit dem grauen Hut/den blauen Augen; **with tears in her eyes** mit Tränen in den Augen; **red with anger** rot vor Wut

withdraw [wɪθ'drɔː] (*irreg: like* **draw**) *vt* (*object, offer*) zurückziehen; (*remark*) zurücknehmen ▷ *vi* (*troops*) abziehen; (*person*) sich zurückziehen; **to ~ money** (*from bank*) Geld abheben; **to ~ into o.s.** sich in sich *acc* selbst zurückziehen
withdrawal [wɪθ'drɔːəl] *n* (*of offer, remark*) Zurücknahme *f*; (*of troops*) Abzug *m*; (*of participation*) Ausstieg *m*; (*of services*) Streichung *f*; (*of money*) Abhebung *f*
withdrawal symptoms *npl* Entzugserscheinungen *pl*
withdrawn [wɪθ'drɔːn] *pp of* **withdraw** ▷ *adj* (*person*) verschlossen
wither ['wɪðəʳ] *vi* (*plant*) verwelken
withered ['wɪðəd] *adj* (*plant*) verwelkt; (*limb*) verkümmert
withhold [wɪθ'həuld] (*irreg: like* **hold**) *vt* vorenthalten
within [wɪð'ɪn] *prep* (*place*) innerhalb *+gen*; (*time, distance*) innerhalb von ▷ *adv* innen; **~ reach** in Reichweite; **~ sight (of)** in Sichtweite (*+gen*); **~ the week** vor Ende der Woche; **~ a mile of** weniger als eine Meile entfernt von; **~ an hour** innerhalb einer Stunde; **~ the law** im Rahmen des Gesetzes
without [wɪð'aut] *prep* ohne; **~ a coat** ohne Mantel; **~ speaking** ohne zu sprechen; **it goes ~ saying** das versteht sich von selbst; **~ anyone knowing** ohne dass jemand davon wusste
withstand [wɪθ'stænd] (*irreg: like* **stand**) *vt* widerstehen *+dat*
witness ['wɪtnɪs] *n* Zeuge *m*, Zeugin *f* ▷ *vt* (*event*) sehen, Zeuge/Zeugin sein *+gen*; (*fig*) miterleben; **to bear ~ to sth** Zeugnis für etw ablegen; **~ for the prosecution/defence** Zeuge/Zeugin der Anklage/Verteidigung; **to ~ to sth** etw bezeugen; **to ~ having seen sth** bezeugen, etw gesehen zu haben
witness box *n* Zeugenstand *m*
witness stand (*US*) *n* = **witness box**
witticism ['wɪtɪsɪzəm] *n* geistreiche Bemerkung *f*
witty ['wɪtɪ] *adj* geistreich
wives [waɪvz] *npl of* **wife**
wizard ['wɪzəd] *n* Zauberer *m*
wizened ['wɪznd] *adj* (*person*) verhutzelt; (*fruit, vegetable*) verschrumpelt
wk *abbr* = **week**
Wm. *abbr* = *William*
WO *n abbr* (*Mil*) = **warrant officer**
wobble ['wɔbl] *vi* wackeln; (*legs*) zittern
wobbly ['wɔblɪ] *adj* (*hand, voice*) zitt(e)rig; (*table, chair*) wack(e)lig; **to feel ~** sich wack(e)lig fühlen
woe [wəu] *n* (*sorrow*) Jammer *m*; (*misfortune*) Kummer *m*
woeful ['wəuful] *adj* traurig
wok [wɔk] *n* Wok *m*
woke [wəuk] *pt of* **wake**
woken ['wəukn] *pp of* **wake**
wolf [wulf] (*pl* **wolves**) *n* Wolf *m*
wolves [wulvz] *npl of* **wolf**
woman ['wumən] (*pl* **women**) *n* Frau *f*; **~ friend** Freundin *f*; **~ teacher** Lehrerin *f*; **young ~** junge Frau; **women's page** Frauenseite *f*
woman doctor *n* Ärztin *f*
womanize ['wumənaɪz] (*pej*) *vi* hinter Frauen her sein
womanly ['wumənlɪ] *adj* (*virtues etc*) weiblich
womb [wuːm] *n* Mutterleib *m*; (*Med*) Gebärmutter *f*
women ['wɪmɪn] *npl of* **woman**
women's lib ['wɪmɪnz-] (*inf*) *n* Frauenbefreiung *f*
Women's Liberation Movement, Women's Movement *n* Frauenbewegung *f*
won [wʌn] *pt, pp of* **win**
wonder ['wʌndəʳ] *n* (*miracle*) Wunder *nt*; (*awe*) Verwunderung *f* ▷ *vi*: **to ~ whether/why** *etc* sich fragen, ob/warum *etc*; **it's no ~ (that)** es ist kein Wunder(, dass); **to ~ at** (*marvel at*) staunen über *+acc*; **to ~ about** sich *dat* Gedanken machen über *+acc*; **I ~ if you could help me** könnten Sie mir vielleicht helfen
wonderful ['wʌndəful] *adj* wunderbar
wonderfully ['wʌndəfəlɪ] *adv* wunderbar
wonky ['wɔŋkɪ] (*Brit: inf*) *adj* wack(e)lig
wont [wəunt] *n*: **as is his ~** wie er zu tun pflegt
won't [wəunt] = **will not**
woo [wuː] *vt* (*woman, audience*) umwerben
wood [wud] *n* (*timber*) Holz *nt*; (*forest*) Wald *m* ▷ *cpd* Holz-
woodcarving ['wudkɑːvɪŋ] *n* (*act, object*) Holzschnitzerei *f*
wooded ['wudɪd] *adj* bewaldet
wooden ['wudn] *adj* (*also fig*) hölzern
woodland ['wudlənd] *n* Waldland *nt*
woodpecker ['wudpɛkəʳ] *n* Specht *m*
wood pigeon *n* Ringeltaube *f*
woodwind ['wudwɪnd] *adj* (*instrument*)

Holzblasinstrument *nt*; **the ~** die Holzbläser *pl*
woodwork ['wudwəːk] *n* (*skill*) Holzarbeiten *pl*
woodworm ['wudwəːm] *n* Holzwurm *m*
woof [wuf] *n* (*of dog*) Wau *nt* ▷ *vi* kläffen; **~, ~!** wau, wau!
wool [wul] *n* Wolle *f*; **to pull the ~ over sb's eyes** (*fig*) jdn hinters Licht führen
woollen, (*US*) **woolen** ['wulən] *adj* (*hat*) Woll-, wollen
woollens ['wulənz] *npl* Wollsachen *pl*
woolly, (*US*) **wooly** ['wulı] *adj* (*socks, hat etc*) Woll-; (*fig: ideas*) schwammig; (*person*) verworren ▷ *n* (*pullover*) Wollpullover *m*
woozy ['wuːzı] (*inf*) *adj* duselig
Worcs (*Brit*) *abbr* (*Post*) = *Worcestershire*
word [wəːd] *n* Wort *nt*; (*news*) Nachricht *f* ▷ *vt* (*letter, message*) formulieren; **~ for word** Wort für Wort, (wort)wörtlich; **what's the ~ for "pen" in German?** was heißt „pen" auf Deutsch?; **to put sth into ~s** etw in Worte fassen; **in other ~s** mit anderen Worten; **to break/keep one's ~** sein Wort brechen/halten; **to have ~s with sb** eine Auseinandersetzung mit jdm haben; **to have a ~ with sb** mit jdm sprechen; **I'll take your ~ for it** ich verlasse mich auf Sie; **to send ~ of sth** etw verlauten lassen; **to leave ~ (with sb/for sb) that ...** (bei jdm/für jdn) die Nachricht hinterlassen, dass ...; **by ~ of mouth** durch mündliche Überlieferung
wording ['wəːdıŋ] *n* (*of message, contract etc*) Wortlaut *m*, Formulierung *f*
word-perfect ['wəːd'pəːfıkt] *adj*: **to be ~** den Text perfekt beherrschen
word processing *n* Textverarbeitung *f*
word processor [-prəusɛsə^r] *n* Textverarbeitungssystem *nt*
wordwrap ['wəːdræp] *n* (*Comput*) (automatischer) Zeilenumbruch *m*
wordy ['wəːdı] *adj* (*book*) langatmig; (*person*) wortreich
wore [wɔː^r] *pt of* **wear**
work [wəːk] *n* Arbeit *f*; (*Art, Liter*) Werk *nt* ▷ *vi* arbeiten; (*mechanism*) funktionieren; (*be successful: medicine etc*) wirken ▷ *vt* (*clay, wood, land*) bearbeiten; (*mine*) arbeiten in; (*machine*) bedienen; (*create: effect, miracle*) bewirken; **to go to ~** zur Arbeit gehen; **to set to ~, to start ~** sich an die Arbeit machen; **to be at ~ (on sth)** (an etw *dat*) arbeiten; **to be out of ~** arbeitslos sein; **to be in ~** eine Stelle haben; **to ~ hard** hart arbeiten; **to ~ loose** (*part, knot*) sich lösen; **to ~ on the assumption that ...** von der Annahme ausgehen, dass ...
▶ **work on** *vt fus* (*task*) arbeiten an *+dat*; (*person: influence*) bearbeiten; **he's ~ing on his car** er arbeitet an seinem Auto
▶ **work out** *vi* (*plans etc*) klappen; (*Sport*) trainieren ▷ *vt* (*problem*) lösen; (*plan*) ausarbeiten; **it ~s out at 100 pounds** es ergibt 100 Pfund
▶ **work up** *vt*: **to get ~ed up** sich aufregen
workable ['wəːkəbl] *adj* (*system*) durchführbar; (*solution*) brauchbar
workaholic [wəːkə'hɔlık] *n* Arbeitstier *nt*
workbench ['wəːkbɛntʃ] *n* Werkbank *f*
worker ['wəːkə^r] *n* Arbeiter(in) *m(f)*; **office ~** Büroarbeiter(in) *m(f)*
workforce ['wəːkfɔːs] *n* Arbeiterschaft *f*
work-in ['wəːkın] (*Brit*) *n* Fabrikbesetzung *f*
working ['wəːkıŋ] *adj* (*day, conditions*) Arbeits-; (*population*) arbeitend; (*mother*) berufstätig; **a ~ knowledge of English** (*adequate*) Grundkenntnisse in Englisch
working capital *n* Betriebskapital *nt*
working class *n* Arbeiterklasse *f*
working-class ['wəːkıŋ'klɑːs] *adj* (*family, town*) Arbeiter-
working man *n* Arbeiter *m*
working order *n*: **in ~** in betriebsfähigem Zustand
working party (*Brit*) *n* Ausschuss *m*
working relationship *n* Arbeitsbeziehung *f*
working week *n* Arbeitswoche *f*
work-in-progress ['wəːkın'prəugrɛs] *n* laufende Arbeiten *pl*
workload ['wəːkləud] *n* Arbeitsbelastung *f*
workman ['wəːkmən] (*irreg: like* **man**) *n* Arbeiter *m*
workmanship ['wəːkmənʃıp] *n* Arbeitsqualität *f*
workmate ['wəːkmeıt] *n* Arbeitskollege *m*, Arbeitskollegin *f*
workout ['wəːkaut] *n* Fitnesstraining *nt*
work permit *n* Arbeitserlaubnis *f*
works [wəːks] (*Brit*) *n* (*factory*) Fabrik *f*, Werk *nt* ▷ *npl* (*of clock*) Uhrwerk *nt*; (*of machine*) Getriebe *nt*
work sheet *n* Arbeitsblatt *nt*
workshop ['wəːkʃɔp] *n* (*building*) Werkstatt *f*; (*practical session*) Workshop *nt*
work station *n* Arbeitsplatz *m*; (*Comput*) Workstation *f*
work-study ['wəːkstʌdı] *n* Arbeitsstudie *f*
worktop ['wəːktɔp] *n* Arbeitsfläche *f*
work-to-rule ['wəːktə'ruːl] (*Brit*) *n* Dienst *m* nach Vorschrift
world [wəːld] *n* Welt *f* ▷ *cpd* (*champion, power, war*) Welt-; **all over the ~** auf der ganzen Welt; **to think the ~ of sb** große Stücke auf jdn halten; **what in the ~ is he doing?** was um alles in der Welt macht er?; **to do sb a** *or* **the ~ of good** jdm unwahrscheinlich guttun; **W~ War One/Two** der Erste/Zweite Weltkrieg; **out of this ~** fantastisch
World Cup *n*: **the ~** (*Football*) die Fußballweltmeisterschaft *f*
world-famous [wəːld'feıməs] *adj* weltberühmt
worldly ['wəːldlı] *adj* weltlich; (*knowledgeable*) weltgewandt
world music *n* World Music *f*, *Richtung der Popmusik, die musikalische Stilelemente der Dritten Welt verwendet*
World Series (*US*) *n* *Endrunde der Baseball-Weltmeisterschaft zwischen den Tabellenführern der Spitzenligen*

worldwide ['wəːld'waɪd] *adj, adv* weltweit
worm [wəːm] *n* Wurm *m*
▸**worm out** *vt*: **to ~ sth out of sb** jdm etw entlocken
worn [wɔːn] *pp of* **wear** ▹ *adj* (*carpet*) abgenutzt; (*shoe*) abgetragen
worn-out ['wɔːnaut] *adj* (*object*) abgenutzt; (*person*) erschöpft
worried ['wʌrɪd] *adj* besorgt; **to be ~ about sth** sich wegen etw Sorgen machen
worrier ['wʌrɪə^r] *n*: **to be a ~** sich ständig Sorgen machen
worrisome ['wʌrɪsəm] *adj* besorgniserregend
worry ['wʌrɪ] *n* Sorge *f* ▹ *vt* beunruhigen ▹ *vi* sich *dat* Sorgen machen; **to ~ about** *or* **over sth/sb** sich um etw/jdn Sorgen machen
worrying ['wʌrɪɪŋ] *adj* beunruhigend
worse [wəːs] *adj* schlechter, schlimmer ▹ *adv* schlechter ▹ *n* Schlechtere(s) *nt*, Schlimmere(s) *nt*; **to get ~** (*situation etc*) sich verschlechtern *or* verschlimmern; **he is none the ~ for it** er hat keinen Schaden dabei erlitten; **so much the ~ for you!** um so schlimmer für dich!; **a change for the ~** eine Wendung zum Schlechten
worsen ['wəːsn] *vt* verschlimmern ▹ *vi* sich verschlechtern
worse off *adj* (*also fig*) schlechter dran; **he is now ~ than before** er ist jetzt schlechter dran als zuvor
worship ['wəːʃɪp] *n* (*act*) Verehrung *f* ▹ *vt* (*god*) anbeten; (*person, thing*) verehren; **Your W~** (*Brit: to mayor*) verehrter Herr Bürgermeister; (*: to judge*) Euer Ehren
worshipper ['wəːʃɪpə^r] *n* (*in church etc*) Kirchgänger(in) *m(f)*; (*fig*) Anbeter(in) *m(f)*, Verehrer(in) *m(f)*
worst [wəːst] *adj* schlechteste(r, s), schlimmste(r, s) ▹ *adv* am schlimmsten ▹ *n* Schlimmste(s) *nt*; **at ~** schlimmstenfalls; **if the ~ comes to the worst** wenn alle Stricke reißen
worst-case scenario ['wəːstkeɪs-] *n* Schlimmstfallszenario *nt*
worsted ['wustɪd] *n* Kammgarn *nt*
worth [wəːθ] *n* Wert *m* ▹ *adj*: **to be ~** wert sein; **£2 ~ of apples** Äpfel für £ 2; **how much is it ~?** was *or* wie viel ist es wert?; **it's ~ it** (*effort, time*) es lohnt sich; **it's ~ every penny** es ist sein Geld wert
worthless ['wəːθlɪs] *adj* wertlos
worthwhile ['wəːθ'waɪl] *adj* lohnend
worthy [wəːðɪ] *adj* (*person*) würdig; (*motive*) ehrenwert; **~ of** wert *+gen*

KEYWORD

would [wud] *aux vb* **1** (*conditional tense*): **if you asked him he would do it** wenn du ihn fragtest, würde er es tun; **if you had asked him he would have done it** wenn du ihn gefragt hättest, hätte er es getan
2 (*in offers, invitations, requests*): **would you like a biscuit?** möchten Sie ein Plätzchen?; **would you ask him to come in?** würden Sie ihn bitten hereinzukommen?
3 (*in indirect speech*): **I said I would do it** ich sagte, ich würde es tun
4 (*emphatic*): **it WOULD have to snow today!** ausgerechnet heute musste es schneien!
5 (*insistence*): **she wouldn't behave** sie wollte sich partout nicht benehmen
6 (*conjecture*): **it would have been midnight** es mochte etwa Mitternacht gewesen sein; **it would seem so** so scheint es wohl
7 (*indicating habit*): **he would go there on Mondays** er ging montags immer dorthin; **he would spend every day on the beach** er verbrachte jeden Tag am Strand

would-be ['wudbiː] *adj* (*singer, writer*) Möchtegern-
wouldn't ['wudnt] = **would not**
wound¹ [waund] *pt, pp of* **wind²**
wound² [wuːnd] *n* Wunde *f* ▹ *vt* verwunden; **~ed in the leg** am Bein verletzt
wove [wəuv] *pt of* **weave**
woven ['wəuvn] *pp of* **weave**
WP *n abbr* = **word processing; word processor** ▹ *abbr* (*Brit: inf: = weather permitting*) bei günstiger Witterung
WPC (*Brit*) *n abbr* (*= woman police constable*) Polizistin *f*
wpm *abbr* (*= words per minute*) Worte pro Minute (*beim Maschineschreiben*)
WRAC (*Brit*) *n abbr* (*= Women's Royal Army Corps*) *Frauenkorps der Armee*
WRAF (*Brit*) *n abbr* (*= Women's Royal Air Force*) *Frauenkorps der Luftwaffe*
wrangle ['ræŋgl] *n* Gerangel *nt* ▹ *vi*: **to ~ with sb over sth** sich mit jdm um etw zanken
wrap [ræp] *n* (*shawl*) Umhang *m*; (*cape*) Cape *nt* ▹ *vt* einwickeln; (*also*: **wrap up**: *pack*) einpacken; (*wind: tape etc*) wickeln; **under ~s** (*fig: plan*) geheim
wrapper ['ræpə^r] *n* (*on chocolate*) Papier *nt*; (*Brit: of book*) Umschlag *m*
wrapping paper ['ræpɪŋ-] *n* (*brown*) Packpapier *nt*; (*fancy*) Geschenkpapier *nt*
wrath [rɔθ] *n* Zorn *m*
wreak [riːk] *vt*: **to ~ havoc (on)** verheerenden Schaden anrichten (bei); **to ~ vengeance** *or* **revenge on sb** Rache an jdm üben
wreath [riːθ] (*pl* **~s**) *n* Kranz *m*
wreck [rɛk] *n* Wrack *nt*; (*vehicle*) Schrotthaufen *m* ▹ *vt* kaputt machen; (*car*) zu Schrott fahren; (*chances*) zerstören
wreckage ['rɛkɪdʒ] *n* (*of car, plane, building*) Trümmer *pl*; (*of ship*) Wrackteile *pl*
wrecker ['rɛkə^r] (*US*) *n* (*breakdown van*) Abschleppwagen *m*
Wren (*Brit*) *n abbr weibliches Mitglied der britischen Marine*
wren [rɛn] *n* (*Zool*) Zaunkönig *m*
wrench [rɛntʃ] *n* (*Tech*) Schraubenschlüssel *m*; (*tug*) Ruck *m*; (*fig*) schmerzhaftes Erlebnis *nt*

▹ *vt* (*pull*) reißen; (*injure*: *arm, back*) verrenken; **to ~ sth from sb** jdm etw entreißen

wrest [rɛst] *vt*: **to ~ sth from sb** jdm etw abringen

wrestle ['rɛsl] *vi*: **to ~ (with sb)** (mit jdm) ringen; **to ~ with a problem** mit einem Problem kämpfen

wrestler ['rɛsləʳ] *n* Ringer(in) *m(f)*

wrestling ['rɛslɪŋ] *n* Ringen *nt*; (*also*: **all-in wrestling**) Freistilringen *nt*

wrestling match *n* Ringkampf *m*

wretch [rɛtʃ] *n*: **poor ~** (*man*) armer Schlucker *m*; (*woman*) armes Ding *nt*; **little ~!** (*often humorous*) kleiner Schlingel!

wretched ['rɛtʃɪd] *adj* (*poor*) erbärmlich; (*unhappy*) unglücklich; (*inf*: *damned*) elend

wriggle ['rɪgl] *vi* (*also*: **wriggle about**: *person*) zappeln; (*fish*) sich winden; (*snake etc*) sich schlängeln ▹ *n* Zappeln *nt*

wring [rɪŋ] (*pt, pp* **wrung**) *vt* (*wet clothes*) auswringen; (*hands*) wringen; (*neck*) umdrehen; **to ~ sth out of sth/sb** (*fig*) etw/jdm etw abringen

wringer ['rɪŋəʳ] *n* Mangel *f*

wringing ['rɪŋɪŋ] *adj* (*also*: **wringing wet**) tropfnass

wrinkle ['rɪŋkl] *n* Falte *f* ▹ *vt* (*nose, forehead etc*) runzeln ▹ *vi* (*skin, paint etc*) sich runzeln

wrinkled ['rɪŋkld] *adj* (*fabric, paper*) zerknittert; (*surface*) gekräuselt; (*skin*) runzlig

wrinkly ['rɪŋklɪ] *adj* = **wrinkled**

wrist [rɪst] *n* Handgelenk *nt*

wristband ['rɪstbænd] (*Brit*) *n* (*of shirt*) Manschette *f*; (*of watch*) Armband *nt*

wristwatch ['rɪstwɔtʃ] *n* Armbanduhr *f*

writ [rɪt] *n* (*Law*) (gerichtliche) Verfügung *f*; **to issue a ~ against sb, serve a ~ on sb** eine Verfügung gegen jdn erlassen

write [raɪt] (*pt* **wrote**, *pp* **written**) *vt* schreiben; (*cheque*) ausstellen ▹ *vi* schreiben; **to ~ to sb** jdm schreiben

▸ **write away** *vi*: **to ~ away for sth** etw anfordern

▸ **write down** *vt* aufschreiben

▸ **write off** *vt* (*debt, project*) abschreiben; (*wreck*: *car etc*) zu Schrott fahren ▹ *vi* = **write away**

▸ **write out** *vt* (*put in writing*) schreiben; (*cheque, receipt etc*) ausstellen

▸ **write up** *vt* (*report etc*) schreiben

write-off ['raɪtɔf] *n* (*Aut*) Totalschaden *m*

write-protected ['raɪtprə'tɛktɪd] *adj* (*Comput*) schreibgeschützt

writer ['raɪtəʳ] *n* (*author*) Schriftsteller(in) *m(f)*; (*of report, document etc*) Verfasser(in) *m(f)*

write-up ['raɪtʌp] *n* (*review*) Kritik *f*

writhe [raɪð] *vi* sich krümmen

writing ['raɪtɪŋ] *n* Schrift *f*; (*of author*) Arbeiten *pl*; (*activity*) Schreiben *nt*; **in ~** schriftlich; **in my own ~** in meiner eigenen Handschrift

writing case *n* Schreibmappe *f*

writing desk *n* Schreibtisch *m*

writing paper *n* Schreibpapier *nt*

written ['rɪtn] *pp of* **write**

WRNS (*Brit*) *n abbr* (= *Women's Royal Naval Service*) *Frauenkorps der Marine*

wrong [rɔŋ] *adj* falsch; (*morally bad*) unrecht; (*unfair*) ungerecht ▹ *adv* falsch ▹ *n* (*injustice*) Unrecht *nt*; (*evil*): **right and ~** Gut und Böse ▹ *vt* (*treat unfairly*) unrecht *or* ein Unrecht tun *+dat*; **to be ~** (*answer*) falsch sein; (*in doing, saying sth*) unrecht haben; **you are ~ to do it** es ist ein Fehler von dir, das zu tun; **it's ~ to steal, stealing is wrong** Stehlen ist unrecht; **you are ~ about that, you've got it wrong** da hast du unrecht; **what's ~?** wo fehlts?; **there's nothing ~** es ist alles in Ordnung; **to go ~** (*person*) einen Fehler machen; (*plan*) schiefgehen; (*machine*) versagen; **to be in the ~** im Unrecht sein

wrongdoer ['rɔŋdu:əʳ] *n* Übeltäter(in) *m(f)*

wrong-foot [rɔŋ'fut] *vt*: **to ~ sb** (*Sport*) jdn auf dem falschen Fuß erwischen; (*fig*) jdn im falschen Moment erwischen

wrongful ['rɔŋful] *adj* unrechtmäßig

wrongly ['rɔŋlɪ] *adv* falsch; (*unjustly*) zu Unrecht

wrong number *n* (*Tel*): **you've got the ~** Sie sind falsch verbunden

wrong side *n*: **the ~** (*of material*) die linke Seite

wrote [rəut] *pt of* **write**

wrought [rɔ:t] *adj*: **~ iron** Schmiedeeisen *nt*

wrung [rʌŋ] *pt, pp of* **wring**

WRVS (*Brit*) *n abbr* (= *Women's Royal Voluntary Service*) *karitativer Frauenverband*

wry [raɪ] *adj* (*smile, humour*) trocken

wt. *abbr* = **weight**

WV (*US*) *abbr* (*Post*) = *West Virginia*

W.Va. (*US*) *abbr* (*Post*) = *West Virginia*

WWW *n abbr* (= *World Wide Web*) WWW *nt*

WY, Wyo. (*US*) *abbr* (*Post*) = *Wyoming*

WYSIWYG ['wɪzɪwɪg] *abbr* (*Comput*: = *what you see is what you get*) WYSIWYG *nt*

Xx

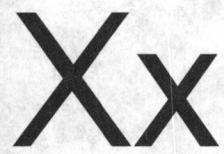

X, x [ɛks] *n* (*letter*) X *nt*, x *nt*; (*Brit*: *Cine*: *formerly*) *Klassifikation für nicht jugendfreie Filme*; **X for Xmas** ≈ X wie Xanthippe
Xerox® ['zɪərɔks] *n* (*also*: **Xerox machine**) Xerokopierer *m*; (*photocopy*) Xerokopie *f* ▷ *vt* xerokopieren
XL *abbr* (= *extra large*) XL
Xmas ['ɛksməs] *n abbr* = **Christmas**
XML *abbr* (*Comput*: = *extensible markup language*) XML
X-rated ['ɛks'reɪtɪd] (*US*) *adj* (*film*) nicht jugendfrei
X-ray ['ɛksreɪ] *n* Röntgenstrahl *m*; (*photo*) Röntgenbild *nt* ▷ *vt* röntgen; **to have an ~** sich röntgen lassen
xylophone ['zaɪləfəun] *n* Xylofon *nt*

Yy

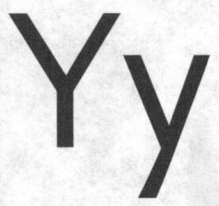

Y, y [waɪ] *n* (*letter*) Y *nt*, y *nt*; **Y for Yellow, Y for Yoke** (*US*) ≈ Y wie Ypsilon
yacht [jɔt] *n* Jacht *f*
yachting ['jɔtɪŋ] *n* Segeln *nt*
yachtsman ['jɔtsmən] (*irreg: like* **man**) *n* Segler *m*
yam [jæm] *n* Jamswurzel *f*, Yamswurzel *f*
Yank [jæŋk] (*pej*) *n* Ami *m*
yank [jæŋk] *vt* reißen ▷ *n* Ruck *m*; **to give sth a ~** mit einem Ruck an etw *dat* ziehen
Yankee ['jæŋkɪ] (*pej*) *n* = **Yank**
yap [jæp] *vi* (*dog*) kläffen
yard [jɑːd] *n* (*of house etc*) Hof *m*; (*US: garden*) Garten *m*; (*measure*) Yard *nt* (= 0,91 m); **builder's ~** Bauhof *m*
yardstick ['jɑːdstɪk] *n* (*fig*) Maßstab *m*
yarn [jɑːn] *n* (*thread*) Garn *nt*; (*tale*) Geschichte *f*
yawn [jɔːn] *n* Gähnen *nt* ▷ *vi* gähnen
yawning ['jɔːnɪŋ] *adj* (*gap*) gähnend
yd *abbr* = **yard**
yeah [jɛə] (*inf*) *adv* ja
year [jɪəʳ] *n* Jahr *nt*; (*referring to wine*) Jahrgang *m*; **every ~** jedes Jahr; **this ~** dieses Jahr; **a** *or* **per ~** pro Jahr; **~ in, ~ out** jahrein, jahraus; **to be 8 ~s old** 8 Jahre alt sein; **an eight-~-old child** ein achtjähriges Kind
yearbook ['jɪəbuk] *n* Jahrbuch *nt*
yearling ['jɪəlɪŋ] *n* (*horse*) Jährling *m*
yearly ['jɪəlɪ] *adj, adv* (*once a year*) jährlich; **twice ~** zweimal jährlich *or* im Jahr
yearn [jəːn] *vi*: **to ~ for sth** sich nach etwas sehnen; **to ~ to do sth** sich danach sehnen, etw zu tun
yearning ['jəːnɪŋ] *n*: **to have a ~ for sth** ein Verlangen nach etw haben; **to have a ~ to do sth** ein Verlangen danach haben, etw zu tun
yeast [jiːst] *n* Hefe *f*
yell [jɛl] *n* Schrei *m* ▷ *vi* schreien
yellow ['jɛləu] *adj* gelb ▷ *n* Gelb *nt*
yellow fever *n* Gelbfieber *nt*
yellowish ['jɛləuɪʃ] *adj* gelblich
Yellow Pages® *npl*: **the Yellow Pages** die gelben Seiten *pl*, das Branchenverzeichnis
Yellow Sea *n*: **the ~** das Gelbe Meer
yelp [jɛlp] *n* Jaulen *nt* ▷ *vi* jaulen
Yemen ['jɛmən] *n*: **(the) ~** (der) Jemen
Yemeni ['jɛmənɪ] *adj* jemenitisch ▷ *n* Jemenit(in) *m(f)*
yen [jɛn] *n* (*currency*) Yen *m*; (*craving*): **to have a ~ for** Lust auf etw haben; **to have a ~ to do sth** Lust darauf haben, etw zu tun
yeoman ['jəumən] (*irreg: like* **man**) *n*: **Y~ of the Guard** (königlicher) Leibgardist *m*
yes [jɛs] *adv* ja; (*in reply to negative*) doch ▷ *n* Ja *nt*; **to say ~** Ja sagen; **to answer ~** mit Ja antworten
yes-man ['jɛsmæn] (*irreg: like* **man**) (*pej*) *n* Jasager *m*
yesterday ['jɛstədɪ] *adv* gestern ▷ *n* Gestern *nt*; **~ morning/evening** gestern Morgen/Abend; **~'s paper** die Zeitung von gestern; **the day before ~** vorgestern; **all day ~** gestern den ganzen Tag (lang)
yet [jɛt] *adv* noch ▷ *conj* jedoch; **it is not finished ~** es ist noch nicht fertig; **must you go just ~?** musst du schon gehen?; **the best ~** der/die/das bisher Beste; **as ~** bisher; **it'll be a few days ~** es wird noch ein paar Tage dauern; **not for a few days ~** nicht in den nächsten paar Tagen; **~ again** wiederum
yew [juː] *n* (*tree*) Eibe *f*; (*wood*) Eibenholz *nt*
Y-fronts® ['waɪfrʌnts] *npl* (Herren-)Slip *m* (*mit y-förmiger Vorderseite*)
YHA (*Brit*) *n abbr* (= *Youth Hostels Association*) *britischer Jugendherbergsverband*
Yiddish ['jɪdɪʃ] *n* Jiddisch *nt*
yield [jiːld] *n* (*Agr*) Ertrag *m*; (*Comm*) Gewinn *m* ▷ *vt* (*surrender: control etc*) abtreten; (*produce: results, profit*) hervorbringen ▷ *vi* (*surrender, give way*) nachgeben; (*US: Aut*) die Vorfahrt achten; **a ~ of 5%** ein Ertrag *or* Gewinn von 5%
YMCA *n abbr* (*organization:* = *Young Men's Christian Association*) CVJM *m*
yob ['jɔb], **yobbo** ['jɔbəu] (*Brit: inf: pej*) *n* Rowdy *m*
yodel ['jəudl] *vi* jodeln
yoga ['jəugə] *n* Yoga *m or nt*
yoghourt, yogourt ['jəugət] *n* = **yoghurt**
yoghurt, yogurt ['jəugət] *n* Joghurt *m or nt*
yoke [jəuk] *n* (*also fig*) Joch *nt* ▷ *vt* (*also:* **yoke together**: *oxen*) einspannen
yolk [jəuk] *n* (*of egg*) Dotter *m*, Eigelb *nt*
yonder ['jɔndəʳ] *adv*: **(over) ~** dort drüben ▷ *adj*: **from ~ house** von dem Haus dort drüben

yonks [jɔŋks] (*inf*) *n*: **for ~** seit einer Ewigkeit
Yorks [jɔːks] (*Brit*) *abbr* (*Post*) = *Yorkshire*

KEYWORD

you [juː] *pron* **1** (*subject: familiar: singular*) du; (*: plural*) ihr; (*: polite*) Sie; **you Germans enjoy your food** ihr Deutschen esst gern gut
2 (*object: direct: familiar: singular*) dich; (*: plural*) euch; (*: polite*) Sie; (*: indirect: familiar: singular*) dir; (*: plural*) euch; (*: polite*) Ihnen; **I know you** ich kenne dich/euch/Sie; **I gave it to you** ich habe es dir/euch/Ihnen gegeben; **if I were you I would ...** an deiner/eurer/Ihrer Stelle würde ich ...
3 (*after prep, in comparisons*): **it's for you** es ist für dich/euch/Sie; **she's younger than you** sie ist jünger als du/ihr/Sie
4 (*impersonal: one*) man; **you never know** man weiß nie

you'd [juːd] = **you had; you would**
you'll [juːl] = **you will; you shall**
young [jʌŋ] *adj* jung; **the young** *npl* (*of animal*) die Jungen *pl*; (*people*) die jungen Leute *pl*; **a ~ man** ein junger Mann; **a ~ lady** eine junge Dame
younger [jʌŋgəʳ] *adj* jünger; **the ~ generation** die jüngere Generation
youngish [ˈjʌŋɪʃ] *adj* recht jung
youngster [ˈjʌŋstəʳ] *n* Kind *nt*
your [jɔːʳ] *adj* (*familiar: sing*) dein/deine/dein; (*: pl*) euer/eure/euer; (*polite*) Ihr/Ihre/Ihr; (*one's*) sein; **you mustn't eat with ~ fingers** man darf nicht mit den Fingern essen; *see also* **my**
you're [juəʳ] = **you are**
yours [jɔːz] *pron* (*familiar: sing*) deiner/deine/dein(e)s; (*: pl*) eurer/eure/eures; (*polite*) Ihrer/Ihre/Ihres; **a friend of ~** ein Freund von dir/Ihnen; **is it ~?** gehört es dir/Ihnen?; **~ sincerely/faithfully** mit freundlichen Grüßen; *see also* **mine**[1]
yourself [jɔːˈsɛlf] *pron* (*reflexive: familiar: sing: acc*) dich; (*: dat*) dir; (*: pl*) euch; (*: polite*) sich; (*emphatic*) selbst; **you ~ told me** das haben Sie mir selbst gesagt
yourselves [jɔːˈsɛlvz] *pl pron* (*reflexive: familiar*) euch; (*: polite*) sich; (*emphatic*) selbst; *see also* **oneself**
youth [juːθ] *n* Jugend *f*; (*young man: pl youths*) Jugendliche(r) *m*; **in my ~** in meiner Jugend
youth club *n* Jugendklub *m*
youthful [ˈjuːθful] *adj* jugendlich
youthfulness [ˈjuːθfəlnɪs] *n* Jugendlichkeit *f*
youth hostel *n* Jugendherberge *f*
youth movement *n* Jugendbewegung *f*
you've [juːv] = **you have**
yowl [jaul] *n* (*of animal*) Jaulen *nt*; (*of person*) Heulen *nt*
yr *abbr* (= *year*) J.
YT (*Canada*) *abbr* = *Yukon Territory*
yuck factor [ˈjʌkfæktəʳ] *n* (*inf*) Igitt-Faktor *m*
Yugoslav [ˈjuːgəuslɑːv] (*formerly*) *adj* jugoslawisch ▷ *n* Jugoslawe *m*, Jugoslawin *f*
Yugoslavia [ˈjuːgəuˈslɑːvɪə] (*formerly*) *n* Jugoslawien *nt*
Yugoslavian [ˈjuːgəuˈslɑːvɪən] (*formerly*) *adj* jugoslawisch
Yule log [juːl-] *n* *Biskuitrolle mit Überzug, die zu Weihnachten gegessen wird*
yuppie [ˈjʌpɪ] (*inf*) *n* Yuppie *m* ▷ *adj* yuppiehaft; (*job, car*) Yuppie-
YWCA *n abbr* (*organization*): = *Young Women's Christian Association*) CVJF *m*

Zz

Z, z [zɛd, (*US*) ziː] *n* (*letter*) Z *nt*, z *nt*; **Z for Zebra** ≈ Z wie Zacharias

Zaire [zɑːˈiːə^{r}] *n* Zaire *nt*

Zambia [ˈzæmbɪə] *n* Sambia *nt*

Zambian [ˈzæmbɪən] *adj* sambisch ▷ *n* Sambier(in) *m(f)*

zany [ˈzeɪnɪ] *adj* verrückt

zap [zæp] *vt* (*Comput: delete*) löschen

zeal [ziːl] *n* Eifer *m*

zealot [ˈzɛlət] *n* Fanatiker(in) *m(f)*

zealous [ˈzɛləs] *adj* eifrig

zebra [ˈziːbrə] *n* Zebra *nt*

zebra crossing (*Brit*) *n* Zebrastreifen *m*

zenith [ˈzɛnɪθ] *n* (*also fig*) Zenit *m*

zero [ˈzɪərəu] *n* (*number*) Null *f* ▷ *vi*: **to ~ in on sth** (*target*) etw einkreisen; **5 degrees below ~** 5 Grad unter null

zero hour *n* die Stunde X

zero option *n* (*esp Pol*) Nulllösung *f*

zero-rated [ˈziːrəureɪtɪd] (*Brit*) *adj* (*Tax*) mehrwertsteuerfrei

zest [zɛst] *n* (*for life*) Begeisterung *f*; (*of orange*) Orangenschale *f*

zigzag [ˈzɪgzæg] *n* Zickzack *m* ▷ *vi* sich im Zickzack bewegen

Zimbabwe [zɪmˈbɑːbwɪ] *n* Zimbabwe *nt*

Zimbabwean [zɪmˈbɑːbwɪən] *adj* zimbabwisch

zimmer® [ˈzɪmə^{r}] *n* (*also*: **zimmer frame**) Laufgestell *nt*

zinc [zɪŋk] *n* Zink *nt*

Zionism [ˈzaɪənɪzəm] *n* Zionismus *m*

Zionist [ˈzaɪənɪst] *adj* zionistisch ▷ *n* Zionist(in) *m(f)*

zip [zɪp] *n* (*also*: **zip fastener**) Reißverschluss *m* ▷ *vt* (*also*: **zip up**: *dress etc*) den Reißverschluss zumachen an +*dat*

zip code (*US*) *n* Postleitzahl *f*

zipper [ˈzɪpə^{r}] (*US*) *n* = **zip**

zither [ˈzɪðə^{r}] *n* Zither *f*

zodiac [ˈzəudɪæk] *n* Tierkreis *m*

zombie [ˈzɔmbɪ] *n* (*fig*) Schwachkopf *m*

zone [zəun] *n* (*also Mil*) Zone *f*, Gebiet *nt*; (*in town*) Bezirk *m*

zonked [zɔŋkt] (*inf*) *adj* (*tired*) total geschafft; (*high on drugs*) high; (*drunk*) voll

zoo [zuː] *n* Zoo *m*

zoological [zuəˈlɔdʒɪkl] *adj* zoologisch

zoologist [zuˈɔlədʒɪst] *n* Zoologe *m*, Zoologin *f*

zoology [zuːˈɔlədʒɪ] *n* Zoologie *f*

zoom [zuːm] *vi*: **to ~ past** vorbeisausen; **to ~ in (on sth/sb)** (*Phot, Cine*) (etw/jdn) näher heranholen

zoom lens *n* Zoomobjektiv *nt*

zucchini [zuːˈkiːnɪ] (*US*) *n(pl)* Zucchini *pl*

Zulu [ˈzuːluː] *adj* (*tribe, culture*) Zulu- ▷ *n* (*person*) Zulu *m/f*; (*Ling*) Zulu *nt*

Zürich [ˈzjuərɪk] *n* Zürich *nt*

Grammar
Grammatik

USING THE GRAMMAR

The Grammar section deals systematically and comprehensively with all the information you will need in order to communicate accurately in German. The user-friendly layout explains the grammar point on a left-hand page, leaving the facing page free for illustrative examples. The boxed numbers (→ [1]) direct you to the relevant example in every case.

The Grammar section also provides invaluable guidance on the dangers of translating English structures by identical structures in German. Important sections, explaining the use of Numbers and Punctuation are covered towards the end of this section. Finally, the index lists the main words and grammatical terms in both English and German.

ABBREVIATIONS

acc	accusative	***gen***	genitive
ctd	continued	***masc***	masculine
dat	dative	***neut***	neuter
fem	feminine	***nom***	nominative
ff	and following pages	***p(p)***	page(s)

Grammar

CONTENTS

CONTENTS

Grammar

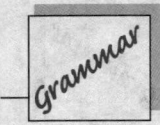

❒ Tense Formation

Tenses are either **simple** or **compound**. Once you know how to form the past participle, compound tenses are similar for all verbs (see pp 22 to 29). To form simple tenses you need to know whether a verb is **weak**, **strong** or **mixed**.

Simple tenses

In German these are:

Present indicative → [1]
Imperfect indicative → [2]
Present subjunctive → [3]
Imperfect subjunctive → [4]

Subjunctive forms are widely used in German, especially for indirect or reported speech (see pp 66 and 67).

The simple tenses are formed by adding endings to a verb **stem**. The endings show the number, person and tense of the subject of the verb → [5]

The types of verb you need to know to form simple tenses are:

- **Strong verbs** (pp 12 to 15), those whose vowel usually changes in forming the imperfect indicative → [6]

- **Weak verbs** (pp 8 to 11), which are usually completely regular and have no vowel changes. Their endings differ from those of strong verbs → [7]

- **Mixed verbs** (pp 16 and 17), which have a vowel change like strong verbs, but the endings of weak verbs → [8]

Examples

1	**ich hole**	I fetch I am fetching I do fetch
2	**ich holte**	I fetched I was fetching I used to fetch
3	**(dass) ich hole**	(that) I fetch/I fetched
4	**(dass) ich holte**	(that) I fetched
5	**ich hole** **wir holen** **du holtest**	I fetch we fetch you fetched
6	**singen** **er singt** **er sang**	to sing he sings he sang
7	**holen** **er holt** **er holte**	to fetch he fetches he fetched
8	**nennen** **er nennt** **er nannte**	to name he names he named

Weak Verbs

Weak verbs are usually **regular** in conjugation. Their simple tenses are formed as follows:

- **Present** and **imperfect** tenses are formed by adding the endings shown below to the verb **stem**. This stem is formed by removing the **–en** ending of the infinitive (the form found in the dictionary) → [1]
- Where the infinitive of a weak verb ends in **–eln** or **–ern**, only the **–n** is removed to form the verb stem → [2]
- The endings are as follows:

	PRESENT INDICATIVE	PRESENT SUBJUNCTIVE	
1st singular	**-e**	**-e**	
2nd	**-st**	**-est**	
3rd	**-t**	**-e**	→ [3]
1st plural	**-en**	**-en**	
2nd	**-t**	**-et**	
3rd	**-en**	**-en**	

	IMPERFECT INDICATIVE	IMPERFECT SUBJUNCTIVE	
1st singular	**-te**	**-te**	
2nd	**-test**	**-test**	
3rd	**-te**	**-te**	→ [3]
1st plural	**-ten**	**-ten**	
2nd	**-tet**	**-tet**	
3rd	**-ten**	**-ten**	

Examples

1

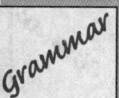

INFINITIVE		STEM
holen	*to fetch*	**hol-**
machen	*to make*	**mach-**
kauen	*to chew*	**kau-**

2

INFINITIVE		STEM
wandern	*to roam*	**wander-**
handeln	*to trade, to act*	**handel-**

3

holen *to fetch*

PRESENT INDICATIVE	PRESENT SUBJUNCTIVE	
ich hol**e**	ich hol**e**	I fetch
du hol**st**	du hol**est**	you fetch
er/sie/es hol**t**	er/sie/es hol**e**	he/she/it fetches
wir hol**en**	wir hol**en**	we fetch
ihr hol**t**	ihr hol**et**	you (*plural*) fetch
sie/Sie hol**en**	sie/Sie hol**en**	they/you (*polite*) fetch

IMPERFECT INDICATIVE AND SUBJUNCTIVE
(*These tenses are identical for weak verbs*)

ich hol**te**	I fetched
du hol**test**	you fetched
er/sie/es hol**te**	he/she/it fetched
wir hol**ten**	we fetched
ihr hol**tet**	you (*plural*) fetched
sie/Sie hol**ten**	they/you (*polite*) fetched

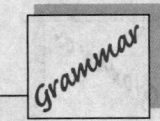

Weak Verbs (Continued)

- Where the stem of a weak verb ends in -**d** or -**t**, an extra -**e**- is inserted before those endings where this will ease pronunciation → 1

- Weak verbs whose stems end in -**m** or -**n** may take this extra -**e**-, or not, depending on whether its addition is necessary for pronunciation. If the -**m** or -**n** is preceded by a consonant *other than* **l**, **r** or **h**, the -**e**- is inserted → 2

- Weak (and strong) verbs whose stem ends in a sibilant sound (-**s**, -**z**, -**ss**, -**ß**) normally lose the -**s**- of the second person singular ending (the **du** form) in the present indicative → 3

⚠ NOTE: When this sibilant is -**sch**, the -**s**- of the ending remains → 4

Examples

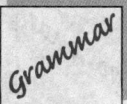

1 **reden** *to speak*

PRESENT	IMPERFECT
ich rede	ich redete
du redest	du redetest
er redet	er redete
wir reden	wir redeten
ihr redet	ihr redetet
sie reden	sie redeten

arbeiten *to work*

PRESENT	IMPERFECT
ich arbeite	ich arbeitete
du arbeitest	du arbeitetest
er arbeitet	er arbeitete
wir arbeiten	wir arbeiteten
ihr arbeitet	ihr arbeitetet
sie arbeiten	sie arbeiteten

2 **atmen** *to breathe*

PRESENT	IMPERFECT
ich atme	ich atmete
du atmest	du atmetest
er atmet	er atmete
wir atmen	wir atmeten
ihr atmet	ihr atmetet
sie atmen	sie atmeten

segnen *to bless*

PRESENT	IMPERFECT
ich segne	ich segnete
du segnest	du segnetest
er segnet	er segnete
wir segnen	wir segneten
ihr segnet	ihr segnetet
sie segnen	sie segneten

⚠ BUT:

umarmen *to embrace*

PRESENT	IMPERFECT
ich umarme	ich umarmte
du umarmst	du umarmtest
er umarmt	er umarmte
wir umarmen	wir umarmten
ihr umarmt	ihr umarmtet
sie umarmen	sie umarmten

lernen *to learn*

PRESENT	IMPERFECT
ich lerne	ich lernte
du lernst	du lerntest
er lernt	er lernte
wir lernen	wir lernten
ihr lernt	ihr lerntet
sie lernen	sie lernten

3 **grüßen** *to greet*

PRESENT
ich grüße
du **grüßt**
er grüßt
wir grüßen
ihr grüßt
sie grüßen

4 **löschen** *to extinguish*

PRESENT
ich lösche
du löschst
er löscht
wir löschen
ihr löscht
sie löschen

❒ Strong Verbs

A table of the most useful strong verbs is given on pp 86 to 97.

- What differentiates strong verbs from weak ones is that when forming their **imperfect indicative** tense, strong verbs undergo a vowel change and have a different set of endings → 1

  Their past participles are also formed differently (see p 24).

- To form the **imperfect subjunctive** of strong verbs, the endings from the appropriate table below are added to the stem of the imperfect indicative, but the vowel is modified by an umlaut where this is possible, i.e. **a** → **ä**, **o** → **ö**, **u** → **ü**. Exceptions to this are clearly shown in the table of strong verbs → 2

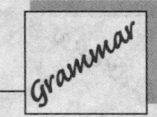

- The endings for the simple tenses of strong verbs are as follows:

	PRESENT INDICATIVE	PRESENT SUBJUNCTIVE	
1st singular	**-e**	**-e**	
2nd	**-st**	**-est**	
3rd	**-t**	**-e**	→ 3
1st plural	**-en**	**-en**	
2nd	**-t**	**-et**	
3rd	**-en**	**-en**	

	IMPERFECT INDICATIVE	IMPERFECT SUBJUNCTIVE	
1st singular	—	**-e**	
2nd	**-st**	**-(e)st**	
3rd	—	**-e**	→ 3
1st plural	**-en**	**-en**	
2nd	**-t**	**-(e)t**	
3rd	**-en**	**-en**	

Examples

Grammar

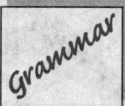

1	Compare:			
		INFINITIVE	PRESENT	IMPERFECT
	WEAK	**sagen** *to say*	**er sagt**	**er sagte**
	STRONG	**rufen** *to shout*	**er ruft**	**er rief**

2		IMPERFECT INDICATIVE	IMPERFECT SUBJUNCTIVE
		er gab *he gave*	**er gäbe** (*umlaut added*)
	⚠ BUT:	**er rief** *he shouted*	**er riefe** (*no umlaut possible*)

3	**singen** *to sing*	
	PRESENT INDICATIVE	PRESENT SUBJUNCTIVE
	ich sing**e**	ich sing**e**
	du sing**st**	du sing**est**
	er sing**t**	er sing**e**
	wir sing**en**	wir sing**en**
	ihr sing**t**	ihr sing**et**
	sie sing**en**	sie sing**en**
	Sie sing**en**	Sie sing**en**
	IMPERFECT INDICATIVE	IMPERFECT SUBJUNCTIVE
	ich sang	ich säng**e**
	du sang**st**	du säng**(e)st**
	er sang	er säng**e**
	wir sang**en**	wir säng**en**
	ihr sang**t**	ihr säng**(e)t**
	sie sang**en**	sie säng**en**
	Sie sang**en**	Sie säng**en**

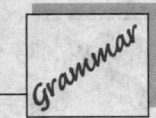

❒ Strong Verbs (Continued)

- In the present tense of strong verbs, the vowel also often changes for the second and third persons singular (the **du** and **er/sie/es** forms). The pattern of possible changes is as follows:

long **e**	→	**ie**
short **e**	→	**i**
a	→	**ä**
au	→	**äu**
o	→	**ö**

Verbs which undergo these changes are clearly shown in the table on p 86 → [1]

- Strong (and weak) verbs whose stem ends with a sibilant sound (**-s**, **-z**, **-ss**, **-ß**) normally lose the **-s-** of the second person singular ending (the **du** form) in the *present indicative*, unless the sibilant is **-sch**, when it remains → [2]

- In the second person singular of the *imperfect* tense of strong verbs whose stem ends in a sibilant sound (including **-sch**) the sibilant remains, and an **-e-** is inserted between it and the appropriate ending → [3]

1

sehen *to see*	helfen *to help*	fahren *to drive*
ich sehe	ich helfe	ich fahre
du s**ie**hst	du h**i**lfst	du f**ä**hrst
er/sie/es s**ie**ht	er/sie/es h**i**lft	er f**ä**hrt
wir sehen	wir helfen	wir fahren
ihr seht	ihr helft	ihr fahrt
sie sehen	sie helfen	sie fahren

saufen *to booze*	stoßen *to push*
ich saufe	ich stoße
du s**äu**fst	du st**ö**ßt
er s**äu**ft	er st**ö**ßt
wir saufen	wir stoßen
ihr sauft	ihr stoßt
sie saufen	sie stoßen

2

wachsen *to grow*	waschen *to wash*
ich wachse	ich wasche
du wächst	du wäsch**s**t
er wächst	er wäscht
wir wachsen	wir waschen
ihr wachst	ihr wascht
sie wachsen	sie waschen

3

lesen *to read*	schließen *to close*	waschen *to wash*
ich las	ich schloss	ich wusch
du las**e**st	du schloss**e**st	du wusch**e**st
er las	er schloss	er wusch
wir lasen	wir schlossen	wir wuschen
ihr last	ihr schlosst	ihr wuscht
sie lasen	sie schlossen	sie wuschen

❐ Mixed Verbs

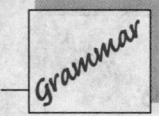

There are nine **mixed** verbs in German, and, as their name implies, they are formed according to a mixture of the rules already outlined for weak and strong verbs.

The mixed verbs are:

brennen *to burn*	**kennen** *to know*	**senden** *to send*
bringen *to bring*	**nennen** *to name*	**wenden** *to turn*
denken *to think*	**rennen** *to run*	**wissen** *to know*

Full details of their principal parts are given in the verb table beginning on p 86.

- Mixed verbs form their **imperfect** tense by adding the weak verb endings to a stem whose vowel has been changed as for a strong verb → [1]

  ⚠ NOTE: **Bringen** and **denken** have a consonant change too in their imperfect forms → [2]

- The **imperfect subjunctive** forms of mixed verbs are unusual and should be noted → [3]

- Other tenses of mixed verbs are formed as for strong verbs.

- The past participle of mixed verbs has characteristics of both weak and strong verbs, as shown on p 24.

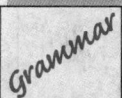

1 IMPERFECT INDICATIVE

kennen *to know*	**senden** *to send*	**wissen** *to know*
ich kann**te**	ich sand**te**	ich wuss**te**
du kann**test**	du sand**test**	du wuss**test**
er kann**te**	er sand**te**	er wuss**te**
wir kann**ten**	wir sand**ten**	wir wuss**ten**
ihr kann**tet**	ihr sand**tet**	ihr wuss**tet**
sie kann**ten**	sie sand**ten**	sie wuss**ten**

2 IMPERFECT INDICATIVE

bringen *to bring*	**denken** *to think*
ich **brachte**	ich **dachte**
du **brachtest**	du **dachtest**
er **brachte**	er **dachte**
wir **brachten**	wir **dachten**
ihr **brachtet**	ihr **dachtet**
sie **brachten**	sie **dachten**

3 IMPERFECT SUBJUNCTIVE

brennen	**kennen**	**senden**
ich brennte	ich kennte	ich sendete
du brenntest	du kenntest	du sendetest
er brennte *etc*	er kennte *etc*	er sendete *etc*
bringen	**nennen**	**wenden**
ich brächte	ich nennte	ich wendete
du brächtest	du nenntest	du wendetest
er brächte *etc*	er nennte *etc*	er wendete *etc*
denken	**rennen**	**wissen**
ich dächte	ich rennte	ich wüsste
du dächtest	du renntest	du wüsstest
er dächte *etc*	er rennte *etc*	er wüsste *etc*

❐ The Imperative

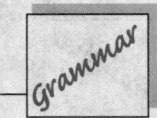

Ths is the form of a verb used to give an order or a command, or to make a request:

Come here/stand up/please bring me a beer → [1]

◆ German has three main imperative forms. These go with the three ways of addressing people - **Sie, du** and **ihr** (see p 160)

	FORMATION	EXAMPLES	
SINGULAR	stem (+ **e**)	**hol(e)!**	*fetch!*
PLURAL	stem + **t**	**holt**	*fetch!*
POLITE (*sing* and *pl*)	stem + **en Sie**	**holen Sie!**	*fetch!*

◆ The **-e** of the singular form is often dropped, ⚠ BUT not where the verb stem ends in **-chn**, **-ckn**, **-dn**, **-fn**, **-gn** or **-tm** → [2]

◆ **Weak verbs** ending in **-eln** or **-ern** take the **-e** ending in the singular form, but the additional **-e-** within the stem may be dropped → [3]

◆ Any vowel change in the present tense of a **strong verb** (see p 14) occurs also in its singular imperative form and no **-e** is added → [4]

⚠ BUT: If the vowel modification in the present tense of a **strong verb** is the addition of an umlaut, this is not added in the singular form of the imperative → [5]

◆ In the imperative form of a **reflexive verb** (see p 30) the pronoun is placed immediately after the verb → [6]

◆ **Separable prefixes** (see p 72) are placed at the end of an imperative statement → [7]

Examples

1

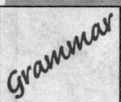

SINGULAR	**Komm mal her!**	Come here!
PLURAL	**Steht auf!**	Stand up!
POLITE	**Kommen Sie herein!**	Do come in

2

Hör zu! Listen!
Hol es! Fetch it!

⚠ BUT:
Öffne die Tür! Open the door!

3

wandern to walk
wand(e)re! walk!

handeln to act
hand(e)le! act!

4

nehmen to take
du nimmst you take
nimm! take!

helfen to help
du hilfst you help
hilf! help!

⚠ BUT:
sehen to see
sieh(e)! see!

5

laufen to run
du läufst you run
lauf(e)! run!

stoßen to push
du stößt you push
stoß(e)! push!

6

sich setzen to sit down
Setz dich! Sit down!
Setzt euch! Sit down!
Setzen Sie sich! Do sit down!

7

zumachen to close
Mach die Tür zu!
Close the door!

aufhören to stop
Hör aber endlich auf!
Do stop it!

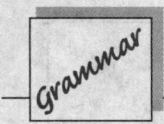

❒ The Imperative (Continued)

- Imperatives are followed in German by an exclamation mark, unless the imperative is not intended as a command → [1]

- **Du** and **ihr**, though not normally present in imperative forms, may be included for emphasis → [2]

- An imperative form also exists for the **wir** form of the verb. It consists of the normal present tense form, but with the pronoun **wir** *following* the verb. It is used for making suggestions → [3]

- The imperative forms of **sein** (*to be*) are irregular → [4]

- The particles **auch**, **nur**, **mal**, **doch** are frequently used with imperatives. They heighten or soften the imperative effect, or add a note of encouragement to a request or command. Often they have no direct equivalent in English and are therefore not always translated → [5]

Some alternatives to the imperative in German

- Infinitives are often used instead of the imperative in written instructions or public announcements → [6]

- The impersonal passive (see p 34) may be used → [7]

- Nouns, adjectives or adverbs can also be used with imperative effect → [8]
  Some of these have become set expressions → [9]

Examples

1 **Lass ihn in Ruhe!**
Leave him alone
Sagen Sie mir bitte, wie spät es ist
What's the time please?

2 **Geht ihr voran!** You go on ahead
Sag du ihm, was los ist You tell him what's wrong

3 **Nehmen wir an, dass ...**
Let's assume that ...
Sagen wir mal, es habe 2.000 Euro gekostet
Let's just say it cost 2,000 euros

4 sein to be
sei!
seid!
seien wir!
seien Sie!

5 **Geh doch!** Go on!/Get going!
Sag mal, ... Tell me ...
Versuchen Sie es mal! Do give it a try!
Komm schon! Do come/Please come
Mach es auch richtig! Be sure to do it properly

6 **Einsteigen!**
All aboard!
Zwiebeln abziehen und in Ringe schneiden
Peel the onions and slice them

7 **Jetzt wird aufgeräumt!**
You're going to clear up now!

8 **Ruhe!** Be quiet!/Silence!
Vorsicht! Careful!/Look out!

9 **Achtung!** Listen!/Attention!
Rauchen verboten! No smoking

❐ Compound Tenses

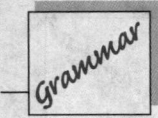

The present and imperfect tenses in German are **simple** tenses, as described on pp 6 to 17.

All other tenses, called **compound tenses**, are formed for all types of verb by using the appropriate tense of an **auxiliary verb** plus a part of the main verb.

There are three auxiliary verbs:

haben	for past tenses
sein	also for past tenses
werden	for future and conditional tenses

The **compound past tenses** in German are:

- Perfect indicative → [1]
- Perfect subjunctive → [2]
- Pluperfect indicative → [3]
- Pluperfect subjunctive → [4]

These are dealt with on p 26 ff.

The **future** and **conditional tenses** in German are all compound tenses. They are:

- Future indicative → [5]
- Future subjunctive → [6]
- Future perfect → [7]
- Conditional → [8]
- Conditional perfect → [9]

These are dealt with on p 28 ff.

Examples

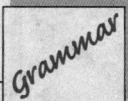

	WITH **haben**	WITH **sein**
1	**er hat geholt** he (has) fetched	**er ist gereist** he (has) travelled
2	**er habe geholt** he (has) fetched	**er sei gereist** he (has) travelled
3	**er hatte geholt** he had fetched	**er war gereist** he had travelled
4	**er hätte geholt** he had fetched	**er wäre gereist** he had travelled
5	**er wird holen** he will fetch	**er wird reisen** he will travel
6	**er werde holen** he will fetch	**er werde reisen** he will travel
7	**er wird geholt haben** he will have fetched	**er wird gereist sein** he will have travelled
8	**er würde holen** he would fetch	**er würde reisen** he would travel
9	**er würde geholt haben** he would have fetched	**er würde gereist sein** he would have travelled

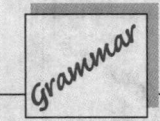

❒ Compound Past Tenses: Formation

- Compound past tenses are normally formed by using the auxiliary verb **haben**, plus the past participle of the main verb (see below) → [1]

- Certain types of verb take **sein** instead of **haben**, and this is clearly indicated in the verb table starting on p 86. They fall into three main types:

  1 intransitive verbs (those that take no direct object, often showing a change of state or place) → [2]
  2 certain verbs meaning "to happen" → [3]
  3 miscellaneous others, including:
  begegnen to meet, **bleiben** to remain,
  gelingen to succeed, **sein** to be, **werden** to become → [4]

- In some cases the verb can be conjugated with either **haben** or **sein**, depending on whether it is used transitively (with a direct object) or intransitively (where no direct object is possible) → [5]

The past participle: formation (see also p 50)

- **Weak** verbs add the prefix **ge**- and suffix -**t** to the verb stem → [6]
  Verbs ending in -**ieren** or -**eien** omit the **ge**- → [7]

- **Strong** verbs add the prefix **ge**- and the suffix -**en** to the verb stem → [8]
  The vowel of the stem may be modified (see verb table, p 86) → [9]

- **Mixed** verbs add the prefix **ge**- and the "weak" suffix -**t** to the stem. The stem vowel is modified as for many strong verbs → [10]

Examples

1 **Haben Sie gut geschlafen?**
Did you sleep well?
Die Kinder hatten fleißig gearbeitet
The children had worked hard

2 **Wir sind nach Bonn gefahren**
We went to Bonn
Er ist schnell eingeschlafen
He quickly fell asleep

3 **Was ist geschehen?**
What happened?

4 **Er ist zu Hause geblieben**
He stayed at home
Es ist uns nicht gelungen
We did not succeed
Er ist einem Freund begegnet
He met a friend

Er ist krank gewesen
He has been ill
Sie ist krank geworden
She became ill

5 **Er hat den Wagen nach Köln gefahren**
He drove the car to Cologne
Er ist nach Köln gefahren
He went to Cologne

6 **holen** to fetch
geholt fetched

7 **studieren** to study
studiert studied
prophezeien to prophesy
prophezeit prophesied

8 **laufen** to run
gelaufen run

9 **singen** to sing
gesungen sung

10 **senden** to send
gesandt sent
bringen to bring
gebracht brought

For a full list of strong and mixed verbs see p 86.

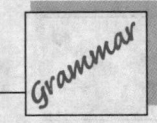

❒ Compound Past Tenses: Formation (Continued)

The formation of past participles for weak, strong and mixed verbs is described on p 24, and a comprehensive list of the principal parts of the most commonly used strong and mixed verbs is provided for reference on pp 86 to 97.

How to form the compound past tenses:

Perfect indicative	the present tense of **haben** or **sein** plus the past participle of the verb → [1]
Perfect subjunctive	(used in indirect or reported speech) the present subjunctive of **haben** or **sein** plus the past participle → [2]
Pluperfect indicative	imperfect indicative of **haben** or **sein** plus the past participle → [3]
Pluperfect subjunctive	(for indirect or reported speech) imperfect subjunctive of **haben** or **sein** plus the past participle → [4]

⚠ NOTE: The pluperfect subjunctive is a frequently used tense in German, since it can replace the much clumsier conditional perfect tense shown on p 28

Examples

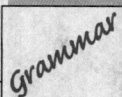

WITH **haben**	WITH **sein**
1 PERFECT INDICATIVE	
ich habe geholt	**ich bin gereist**
du hast geholt	**du bist gereist**
er/sie/es hat geholt	**er/sie/es ist gereist**
wir haben geholt	**wir sind gereist**
ihr habt geholt	**ihr seid gereist**
sie/Sie haben geholt	**sie/Sie sind gereist**
2 PERFECT SUBJUNCTIVE	
ich habe geholt	**ich sei gereist**
du habest geholt	**du sei(e)st gereist**
er/sie/es habe geholt	**er/sie/es sei gereist**
wir haben geholt	**wir seien gereist**
ihr habet geholt	**ihr seiet gereist**
sie/Sie haben geholt	**sie/Sie seien gereist**
3 PLUPERFECT INDICATIVE	
ich hatte geholt	**ich war gereist**
du hattest geholt	**du warst gereist**
er/sie/es hatte geholt	**er/sie/es war gereist**
wir hatten geholt	**wir waren gereist**
ihr hattet geholt	**ihr wart gereist**
sie/Sie hatten geholt	**sie/Sie waren gereist**
4 PLUPERFECT SUBJUNCTIVE	
ich hätte geholt	**ich wäre gereist**
du hättest geholt	**du wär(e)st gereist**
er/sie/es hätte geholt	**er/sie/es wäre gereist**
wir hätten geholt	**wir wären gereist**
ihr hättet geholt	**ihr wär(e)t gereist**
sie/Sie hätten geholt	**sie/Sie wären gereist**

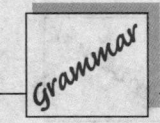

❐ Future and Conditional Tenses: Formation

- The **future** and **conditional** tenses are formed in the same way for all verbs, whether weak, strong or mixed.
- The auxiliary **werden** is used for all verbs together with the infinitive of the main verb.
- The infinitive is usually placed at the end of the clause (see p 224).

How to form the future and conditional tenses:

Future indicative	present tense of **werden** plus the infinitive of the verb → 1
Future subjunctive	present subjunctive of **werden** plus the infinitive → 2
Future perfect	present indicative of **werden** plus the **perfect infinitive** (see below) → 3
Conditional imperfect	subjunctive of **werden** plus the infinitive → 4
Conditional perfect	imperfect subjunctive of **werden** plus the **perfect infinitive** (see below) → 5

⚠ NOTE: The conditional perfect is often replaced by the pluperfect subjunctive.

- The **perfect infinitive** consists of the infinitive of **haben/sein** plus the past participle of the verb.

Examples

1 FUTURE INDICATIVE

ich werde holen	**wir werden holen**
du wirst holen	**ihr werdet holen**
er/sie/es wird holen	**sie/Sie werden holen**

2 FUTURE SUBJUNCTIVE

ich werde holen	**wir werden holen**
du werdest holen	**ihr werdet holen**
er/sie/es werde holen	**sie/Sie werden holen**

3 FUTURE PERFECT

ich werde geholt haben	**wir werden geholt haben**
du wirst geholt haben	**ihr werdet geholt haben**
er wird geholt haben	**sie/Sie werden geholt haben**

4 CONDITIONAL IMPERFECT

ich würde holen	**wir würden holen**
du würdest holen	**ihr würdet holen**
er/sie/es würde holen	**sie/Sie würden holen**

5 CONDITIONAL PERFECT [1]

ich würde geholt haben	**wir würden geholt haben**
du würdest geholt haben	**ihr würdet geholt haben**
er würde geholt haben	**sie/Sie würden geholt haben**

1 ⚠ NOTE: The conditional perfect is often replaced by the pluperfect subjunctive (see p 26).

❒ Reflexive Verbs

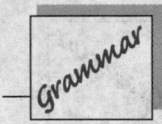

A verb whose action is reflected back to its subject may be termed reflexive:

she washes *herself*

Reflexive verbs in German are recognized in the infinitive by the preceding reflexive pronoun **sich** → [1]

German has many reflexive verbs, a great number of which are not reflexive in English → [1]

- Reflexive verbs are composed of the verb and a reflexive pronoun (see p 170). This pronoun may be either the direct object (and therefore in the accusative case) or the indirect object (and therefore in the dative case) → [2]

- Many verbs in German which are not essentially reflexive may become reflexive by the addition of a reflexive pronoun → [3]
  When a verb with an indirect object is made reflexive (see p 170) the pronoun is usually dative → [4]

- A direct object reflexive pronoun changes to the dative if another direct object is present → [5]

- In a main clause the reflexive pronoun follows the verb → [6]
  After inversion (see p 226), or in a subordinate clause, the reflexive pronoun must come after the subject if the subject is a personal pronoun → [7]
  It may precede or follow a noun subject → [8]

- Reflexive verbs are always conjugated with **haben** *except* where the pronoun is used to mean *each other*. Then the verb is normally conjugated with **sein**.

- The imperative forms are shown on p 19.

Examples

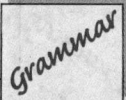

1 **sich beeilen**
to hurry

wir beeilen uns
we are hurrying

2 **sich** (*accusative*) **erinnern** to remember

ich erinnere mich	**wir erinnern uns**
du erinnerst dich	**ihr erinnert euch**
er/sie/es erinnert sich	**sie/Sie erinnern sich**

sich (*dative*) **erlauben** to allow oneself

ich erlaube mir	**wir erlauben uns**
du erlaubst dir	**ihr erlaubt euch**
er/sie/es erlaubt sich	**sie/Sie erlauben sich**

3 **etwas melden** to report something

sich melden
to report/to volunteer

Ich habe mich gemeldet
I volunteered

4 **wehtun** to hurt

sich wehtun
to get hurt

Hast du dir wehgetan?
Have you hurt yourself?

kaufen to buy

Er kaufte ihr einen Mantel
He bought her a coat

Er kaufte sich (*dative*) **einen neuen Mantel**
He bought himself a new coat

5 **Ich wasche mich**
I am having a wash

Ich wasche mir die Hände
I am washing my hands

6 **Er wird sich darüber freuen**
He'll be pleased about that

7 **Darüber wird er sich freuen**
He'll be pleased about that
Ich frage mich, ob er sich darüber freuen wird
I wonder if he'll be pleased about that

8 **Langsam drehten sich die Kinder um** OR:
Langsam drehten die Kinder sich um
The children slowly turned round

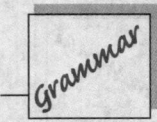

❐ Reflexive Verbs (Continued)

Some examples of verbs which can be used with a reflexive pronoun in the accusative case:

sich anziehen to get dressed → 1
sich aufregen to get excited → 2
sich beeilen to hurry → 3
sich beschäftigen mit[1] to be occupied with → 4
sich bewerben um[1] to apply for → 5
sich erinnern an[1] to remember → 6
sich freuen auf[1] to look forward to → 7
sich interessieren für[1] to be interested in → 8
sich irren to be wrong → 9
sich melden to report (for duty *etc*)/to volunteer
sich rasieren to shave
sich (hin)setzen to sit down → 10
sich trauen[2] to trust oneself
sich umsehen to look around → 11

Some examples of verbs which can be used with a reflexive pronoun in the dative case:

sich abgewöhnen to give up (something) → 12
sich aneignen to appropriate
sich ansehen to have a look at
sich einbilden to imagine (wrongly) → 13
sich erlauben to allow oneself → 14
sich leisten to treat oneself → 15
sich nähern to get close to
sich vornehmen to plan to do → 16
sich vorstellen to imagine → 17
sich wünschen to want → 18

[1] For verbs normally followed by a preposition, see p 76 ff.
[2] **trauen** when non-reflexive takes the dative case.

Examples

[1] **Du sollst dich sofort anziehen**
You are to get dressed immediately

[2] **Reg dich doch nicht so auf!**
Calm down!

[3] **Wir müssen uns beeilen**
We must hurry

[4] **Sie beschäftigen sich sehr mit den Kindern**
They spend a lot of time with the children

[5] **Hast du dich um diese Stelle beworben?**
Have you applied for this post?

[6] **Ich erinnere mich nicht daran**
I can't remember it

[7] **Ich freue mich auf die Fahrt**
I am looking forward to the journey

[8] **Interessierst du dich für Musik?**
Are you interested in music?

[9] **Er hat sich geirrt**
He was wrong

[10] **Bitte, setzt euch hin!**
Please sit down

[11] **Die Kinder sahen sich erstaunt um**
The children looked around in amazement

[12] **Eigentlich müsste man sich das Rauchen abgewöhnen**
One really ought to give up smoking

[13] **Bilde dir doch nichts ein!**
Don't kid yourself!

[14] **Eins könntest du dir doch erlauben**
You could surely allow yourself one

[15] **Wenn ich mir nur einen Mercedes leisten könnte!**
If only I could afford a Mercedes!

[16] **Du hast dir wieder zu viel vorgenommen!**
You've taken on too much again!

[17] **So hatte ich es mir oft vorgestellt**
I had often imagined it like this

[18] **Was wünscht ihr euch zu Weihnachten?**
What do you want for Christmas?

❐ The Passive

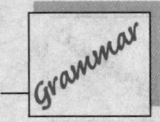

In active tenses, the subject of a verb carries out the action of the verb, but in passive tenses the subject of the verb has something done to it.

Compare the following:

Peter kicked the cat (subject: *Peter*)
The cat was kicked by Peter (subject: *the cat*)

- English uses the verb "to be" to form its passive tenses. German uses **werden** → 1

  A sample verb is conjugated in the passive on pp 39 to 41.

- In English, the word "by" usually introduces the agent through which the action of a passive tense is performed. In German this agent is introduced by:

  von for the performer of the action
  durch for an inanimate cause → 2

- The passive can be used to add impersonality or distance to an event → 3

  It may also be used where the identity of the cause of the deed is unknown or not important → 4

- In general, however, the passive is used less in German than in English. The following are common replacements for the passive:

  1 an active tense with the impersonal pronoun **man** as subject (meaning *they/one*). This resembles the use of *on* in French, and **man** is not always translated as *one* or *they* → 5

  2 **sich lassen** plus a verb in the infinitive → 6

Examples

[1] **Das Auto wurde gekauft**
The car was bought

[2] **Das ist von seinem Onkel geschickt worden**
It was sent by his uncle

Das Kind wurde von einem Hund gebissen
The child was bitten by a dog

Seine Bewerbung ist von der Firma abgelehnt worden
(*the firm is viewed as a human agent*)
His application was turned down by the firm

Die Tür wurde durch den Wind geöffnet
The door was opened by the wind

Das Getreide wurde durch den Sturm niedergeschlagen
The crop was flattened by the storm

[3] **Die Praxis ist von Dr. Disselkamp übernommen worden**
The practice has been taken over by Dr Disselkamp

Anfang 1993 wurde ein weiterer Anschlag auf sein Leben verübt
Another attempt was made on his life early in 1993

[4] **In letzter Zeit sind neue Gesetze eingeführt worden**
New laws have recently been introduced

[5] **Man hatte es schon verkauft**
It had already been sold

Man wird es verkauft haben
It will have been sold

[6] **Das lässt sich schnell herausfinden**
We'll/You'll/One will be able to find that out quickly

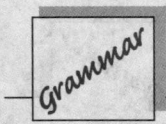

❐ The Passive (Continued)

- In English the indirect object of an active tense can become the subject of a passive statement e.g.

  Peter gave *him* a car (*him* = to him)
  He was given a car by Peter

  This is not possible in German, where the indirect object (*him*) must remain in the dative case (see p 110). There are two ways of handling this in German:

  1 with the direct object (*car*) as the subject of a passive verb → [1]
  2 by means of an impersonal passive construction, with or without the impersonal subject **es** → [1]

  These constructions would however normally be avoided in favour of an active tense, when the agent of the action is known → [2]

- Verbs which are normally followed by the dative case in German and so have only an indirect object (see p 80) should therefore be especially noted, as they can only adopt the impersonal or **man**-forms of the passive → [3]

- Some passive tenses are avoided in German, as they are inelegant (and difficult to use!). For instance, the future perfect passives should be replaced by an active tense or a construction using **man** → [4]

  The conditional perfect passives are also rarely used, past conditional being shown by the pluperfect subjunctives, either passive or active → [5]

- English passive constructions such as

  he was heard whistling/they were thought to be dying

  are not possible in German → [6]

Examples

1 **Ein Auto wurde ihm von Peter geschenkt**
OR:
Es wurde ihm von Peter ein Auto geschenkt
OR:
Ihm wurde von Peter ein Auto geschenkt
He was given a car by Peter

2 **Peter schenkte ihm ein Auto**
Peter gave him a car

3 **helfen** (+ *dative*) to help

Sie half mir	**Mir wurde von ihr geholfen**
She helped me	OR:
	Es wurde mir von ihr geholfen
	I was helped by her

4 **Er meint, es werde schon gesehen worden sein**
He thinks that it will already have been seen

✔ BETTER: **Er meint, man werde es schon gesehen haben**

5 **Es würde geholt worden sein / Man würde es geholt haben**
It would have been fetched

✔ BETTER: **Es wäre geholt worden / Man hätte es geholt**

6 **Man hörte ihn singen**
He was heard singing
Man sah sie ankommen
She was seen arriving
Man glaubte, er sei betrunken
He was thought to be drunk

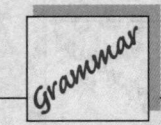

❐ Passive Tenses: Conjugation

Simple tenses

Present passive indicative e.g. *it is seen*	present indicative of **werden** + past participle of the verb → 1
Present passive subjunctive	present subjunctive of **werden** + past participle of the verb → 2
Imperfect passive indicative e.g. *it was seen*	imperfect indicative of **werden** + past participle of the verb → 3
Imperfect passive subjunctive	imperfect subjunctive of **werden** + past participle of the verb → 4

Compound tenses

Perfect passive indicative e.g. *it has been seen*	present indicative of **sein** + past participle of the verb + **worden** → 5
Perfect passive subjunctive	present subjunctive of **sein** + past participle of the verb + **worden** → 6
Pluperfect passive indicative e.g. *it had been seen*	imperfect indicative of **sein** + past participle of the verb + **worden** → 7

Examples

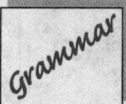

1 PRESENT PASSIVE INDICATIVE

ich werde gesehen	**wir werden gesehen**
du wirst gesehen	**ihr werdet gesehen**
er/sie/es wird gesehen	**sie/Sie werden gesehen**

OR: **man sieht mich/man sieht dich** *etc*

2 PRESENT PASSIVE SUBJUNCTIVE

ich werde gesehen	**wir werden gesehen**
du werdest gesehen	**ihr werdet gesehen**
er/sie/es werde gesehen	**sie/Sie werden gesehen**

OR: **man sehe mich/man sehe dich** *etc*

3 IMPERFECT PASSIVE INDICATIVE

ich wurde gesehen/wir wurden gesehen *etc*
OR: **man sah mich/man sah uns** *etc*

4 IMPERFECT PASSIVE SUBJUNCTIVE

ich würde gesehen/wir würden gesehen *etc*
OR: **man sähe mich/man sähe uns** *etc*

5 PERFECT PASSIVE INDICATIVE

ich bin gesehen worden/wir sind gesehen worden *etc*
OR: **man hat mich/uns gesehen** *etc*

6 PERFECT PASSIVE SUBJUNCTIVE

ich sei gesehen worden/wir seien gesehen worden *etc*
OR: **man habe mich/uns gesehen** *etc*

7 PLUPERFECT PASSIVE INDICATIVE

ich war gesehen worden/wir waren gesehen worden *etc*
OR: **man hatte mich/uns gesehen** *etc*

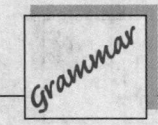

❒ Passive Tenses: Conjugation (Continued)

Pluperfect passive subjunctive	imperfect subjunctive of **sein** + past participle of the verb + **worden** → 1
Present passive infinitive e.g. *to be seen*	infinitive of **werden** + past participle of the verb → 2
Future passive indicative e.g. *it will be seen*	present indicative of **werden** + present passive infinitive of the verb → 3
Future passive subjunctive	present subjunctive of **werden** + present passive infinitive of the verb → 4
Perfect passive infinitive e.g. *to have been seen*	past participle of the verb + **worden sein** → 5
Future perfect passive e.g. *it will have been seen*	present indicative of **werden** + perfect passive infinitive of the verb → 6
Conditional passive e.g. *it would be seen*	imperfect subjunctive of **werden** + present passive infinitive of the verb → 7
Conditional perfect passive e.g. *it would have been seen*	imperfect subjunctive of **werden** + perfect passive infinitive of the verb → 8

1 PLUPERFECT PASSIVE SUBJUNCTIVE

ich wäre gesehen worden/wir wären gesehen worden *etc*
OR: **man hätte mich/uns gesehen** *etc*

2 PRESENT PASSIVE INFINITIVE

gesehen werden

3 FUTURE PASSIVE INDICATIVE

ich werde gesehen werden/wir werden gesehen werden *etc*
OR: **man wird mich/uns sehen** *etc*

4 FUTURE PASSIVE SUBJUNCTIVE

ich werde gesehen werden/wir werden gesehen werden *etc*
OR: **man werde mich/uns sehen** *etc*

5 PERFECT PASSIVE INFINITIVE

gesehen worden sein

6 FUTURE PERFECT PASSIVE

ich werde/wir werden gesehen worden sein *etc*
OR: **man wird mich/uns gesehen haben** *etc*

7 CONDITIONAL PASSIVE

ich würde gesehen werden/wir würden gesehen werden
OR: **man würde mich/uns sehen** *etc*

8 CONDITIONAL PERFECT PASSIVE

ich würde/wir würden gesehen worden sein *etc*
OR: **man würde mich/uns gesehen haben** *etc*
OR: pluperfect subjunctive: **man hätte mich/uns gesehen** *etc*

❐ Impersonal Verbs

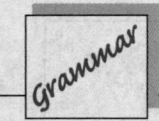

These verbs are used only in the third person singular, usually with the subject **es** meaning *it* → [1]

- Intransitive verbs (verbs with no direct object) are often made impersonal in the passive to describe activity of a general nature → [2]
  When the verb and subject are inverted (see p 226), the **es** is omitted → [3]
  Impersonal verbs in the passive can also be used as an imperative form (see p 20) → [4]

- In certain expressions in the active, the impersonal pronoun **es** can be omitted. In this case, a personal pronoun object begins the clause → [5]
  In the following lists * indicates that **es** may be omitted in this way:

Some common impersonal verbs and expressions

es donnert	it's thundering
es fällt mir ein, dass/zu*	it occurs to me that/to → [6]
es fragt sich, ob	one wonders whether → [7]
es freut mich, dass/zu	I am glad that/to → [8]
es friert	it is freezing → [9]
es gefällt mir	I like it → [10]
es geht mir gut/schlecht	I'm fine/not too good
es geht nicht	it's not possible
es geht um	it's about
es gelingt mir (zu)	I succeed (in) → [11]
es geschieht	it happens → [12]
es gießt	it's pouring
es handelt sich um	it's a question of

Examples

Grammar

1 **Es regnet** It's raining

2 **Es wurde viel gegessen und getrunken**
There was a lot of eating and drinking

3 **Auf der Hochzeit wurde viel gegessen und getrunken**
There was a lot of eating and drinking at the wedding

4 **Jetzt wird gearbeitet!** Now you're/we're going to work

5 **Mir ist warm** I'm warm

6 **Nachher fiel (es) mir ein, dass der Mann ziemlich komisch angezogen war**
Afterwards it occurred to me that the man was rather oddly dressed

7 **Es fragt sich, ob es sich lohnt, das zu machen**
One wonders if that's worth doing

8 **Es freut mich sehr, dass du gekommen bist**
I'm so pleased that you have come

9 **Heute Nacht hat es gefroren**
It was below freezing last night

10 **Ihm hat es gar nicht gefallen**
He didn't like it at all

11 **Es war ihnen gelungen, die letzten Karten zu kriegen**
They had succeeded in getting the last tickets

12 **Und so geschah es, dass ...**
And so it came about that ...

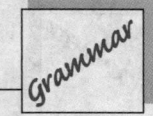

❒ Impersonal Verbs and Expressions (Continued)

es hängt davon ab	it depends
es hat keinen Zweck (zu)	there's no point (in) → [1]
es interessiert mich, dass/zu*	I am interested that/to
es ist mir egal (ob)*	it's all the same to me (if) → [2]
es ist möglich(, dass)	it's possible (that) → [3]
es ist nötig	it's necessary → [4]
es ist mir, als ob*	I feel as if
es ist mir gut/schlecht *etc* **zumute** *or* **zu Mute***	I feel good/bad *etc* → [5]
es ist schade(, dass)	it's a pity (that)
es ist (mir) wichtig*	it's important (to me)
es ist mir warm/kalt*	I'm warm/cold
es ist warm/kalt	it's *or* the weather is warm/cold
es ist zu hoffen/bedauern *etc**	it is to be hoped/regretted *etc*
es klingelt	someone's ringing the bell → [6]
es klopft	someone's knocking
es kommt darauf an(, ob)	it all depends (whether)
es kommt mir vor(, als ob)	it seems to me (as if)
es läutet	the bell is ringing → [7]
es liegt an	it is because of → [8]
es lohnt sich (nicht)	it's (not) worth it → [9]
es macht nichts	it doesn't matter
es macht nichts aus	it makes no difference → [10]
es macht mir (keinen) Spaß(, zu)	it's (no) fun (to) → [11]
es passiert	it happens → [12]
es regnet	it's raining → [13]
es scheint mir, dass/als ob*	it seems to me that/as if
es schneit	it's snowing
es stellt sich heraus, dass	it turns out that
es stimmt (nicht), dass	it's (not) true that
es tut mir Leid(, dass)	I'm sorry (that)
wie geht es (dir)?	how are you? → [14]
mir wird schlecht	I feel sick

Examples

1 **Es hat keinen Zweck, weiter darüber zu diskutieren**
There's no point in discussing this any further

2 **Es ist mir egal, ob du kommst oder nicht**
I don't care if you come or not

3 **Es ist doch möglich, dass der Zug Verspätung hat**
It's always possible the train has been delayed

4 **Es wird nicht nötig sein, uns darüber zu informieren**
It won't be necessary to inform us of it

5 **Mir ist heute seltsam zumute**
I feel strange today

6 **Es hat gerade geklingelt**
The bell just went/The phone just rang

7 **Es hat schon geläutet**
The bell has gone

8 **Woran liegt es?**
Why is that?

9 **Ich weiß nicht, ob es sich lohnt oder nicht**
I don't know if it's worth it or not

10 **Mir macht es nichts aus**
It makes no difference to me
Macht es Ihnen etwas aus, wenn ...
Would you mind if ...

11 **Hauptsache, es macht Spaß**
The main thing is to enjoy yourself

12 **Ihm ist bestimmt etwas passiert**
Something must have happened to him

13 **Es hat den ganzen Tag geregnet**
It rained the whole day

14 **Wie gehts denn? — Danke, es geht**
How are things? — All right, thank you

❒ The Infinitive

Forms

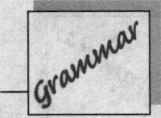

There are four forms of the infinitive → [1]. These forms are used in certain compound tenses (see p 28). The present active infinitive is the most widely used and is the form found in dictionaries.

Uses

- Preceded by **zu** (*to*)

  1 as in English, after other verbs ("I tried *to come*") → [2]
  2 as in English, after adjectives ("it was easy *to see*") → [3]
  3 where the English equivalent is not always an infinitive:
  - after nouns, where English may use an "-ing" form → [4]
  - after **sein**, where the English equivalent may be a passive tense → [5]

- Without **zu**, the infinitive is used after the following:

  modal verbs → [6]
  lassen → [7]
  heißen → [8]
  bleiben → [9]
  gehen → [10]
  verbs of perception → [11]

  ⚠ NOTE: Verbs of perception can also be followed by a subordinate clause beginning with **wie** or **dass**, especially if the sentence is long or involved → [12]

Examples

[1]	INFINITIVES:	
	PRESENT ACTIVE **holen** to fetch	PERFECT ACTIVE **geholt haben** to have fetched
	PRESENT PASSIVE **geholt werden** to be fetched	PERFECT PASSIVE **geholt worden sein** to have been fetched
[2]	**Ich versuchte zu kommen**	I tried to come
[3]	**Es war leicht zu sehen**	It was easy to see
[4]	**Ich habe nur wenig Gelegenheit, Musik zu hören** I have little opportunity to listen to music	
[5]	**Er ist zu bedauern**	He is to be pitied
[6]	**Er kann schwimmen**	He can swim
[7]	**Sie ließen uns warten**	They kept us waiting
[8]	**Er hieß ihn kommen**	He bade him come
[9]	**Er blieb sitzen**	He remained seated
[10]	**Sie ging einkaufen**	She went shopping
[11]	**Ich sah ihn kommen** **Er hörte sie singen**	I saw him coming He heard her singing
[12]	**Er sah, wie sie langsam auf und ab schlenderte** He watched her strolling slowly up and down	

❐ The Infinitive (Continued)

Used as an imperative

- The infinitive can be used as an imperative (see p 20) → [1]

Used as a noun

- The infinitive can be made into a noun by giving it a capital letter. Its gender is always neuter → [2]

Used with modal verbs (see p 52)

- An infinitive used with a modal verb is always placed at the end of a clause (see p 56) → [3]
- If the modal verb is in a compound tense, its auxiliary will follow the subject in a main clause in the normal way, and the modal participle comes after the infinitive.

  ⚠ BUT: In a subordinate clause, the auxiliary immediately precedes the infinitive and the modal participle, instead of coming at the end → [4]

- An infinitive expressing change of place may be omitted entirely after a modal verb (see p 56) → [5]

Used in infinitive phrases

Infinitive phrases can be formed with:

zu	**ohne ... zu**	→ [6]
um ... zu	**anstatt ... zu**	

- The infinitive comes at the end of its phrase → [7]
- In separable verbs, **zu** is inserted *between* the verb and its prefix in the present infinitive → [8]
- A reflexive pronoun comes first, immediately following an introductory word if there is one → [9]

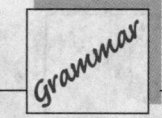

Examples

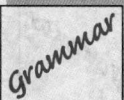

1 **Einsteigen und Türen schließen!**
All aboard! Close the doors!

2 <u>**rauchen** to smoke</u>
Er hat das Rauchen aufgegeben
He's given up smoking

3 **Wir müssen morgen einkaufen gehen**
We have to go shopping tomorrow

4 **Sie haben gestern aufräumen müssen**
They had to tidy up yesterday
⚠ BUT:
Da sie gestern haben aufräumen müssen, durften sie nicht kommen
They couldn't come as they had to tidy up yesterday

5 **Er will jetzt nach Hause**
He wants to go home now

6 <u>**es zu tun** to do it</u>

es getan zu haben	to have done it
um es zu tun	in order to do it
um es getan zu haben	in order to have done it
ohne es zu tun	without doing it
ohne es getan zu haben	without having done it
anstatt es zu tun	instead of doing it
anstatt es getan zu haben	instead of having done it

7 **Ohne ein Wort zu sagen, verließ er das Haus**
He left the house without saying a word
Er ging nach Hause, ohne mit ihr gesprochen zu haben
He went home without having spoken to her

8 <u>**aufgeben** to give up</u>

um es aufzugeben	in order to give it up

9 **Sie gingen weg, ohne sich zu verabschieden**
They left without saying goodbye

❐ The Present Participle

- The present participle for all verbs is formed by adding **-d** to the infinitive form → [1]
- The present participle may be used as an adjective. As with all adjectives, it is declined if used attributively (see p 140) → [2]
- The present participle may also be used as an adjectival noun (see p 148) → [3]

The past participle

- For weak verbs, the past participle is formed by prefixing **ge-** and adding **-t** to the verb stem → [4]
- For strong verbs, the past participle is formed by adding the prefix **ge-** and the ending **-en** to the verb stem → [5]
  The vowel is often modified too → [6]
  (See table of strong and mixed verbs beginning on p 86)
- Mixed verbs form their past participle by adding the **ge-** and **-t** of weak verbs, but they change their vowel as for strong verbs. (See table on p 86) → [7]
- The past participles of *separable* verbs are formed according to the above rules and are joined on to the separable prefix → [8]
- For *inseparable* verbs, past participles are formed without the **ge-** prefix → [9]
- Many past participles can also be used as adjectives and adjectival nouns → [10]

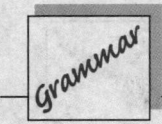

Examples

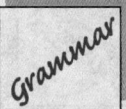

1	**lachen**	to laugh	**singen**	to sing
	lachend	laughing	**singend**	singing
2	**ein lachendes Kind**		a laughing child	
	mit klopfendem Herzen		with beating heart	
3	**der Vorsitzende/ein Vorsitzender**		the/a chairman	
4	**machen**	to do/make		
	gemacht	done/made		
5	**sehen**	to see		
	gesehen	seen		
6	**singen**	to sing		
	gesungen	sung		
7	**wissen**	to know		
	gewusst	known		
8	**aufstehen**	to get up	**nachmachen**	to copy/imitate
	aufgestanden	got up	**nachgemacht**	copied/imitated
9	**bestellen**	to order	**entscheiden**	to decide
	bestellt	ordered	**entschieden**	decided
10	**seine verlorene Brille**		his lost spectacles	
	Wir aßen Gebratenes		We ate fried food	

❒ Modal Auxiliary Verbs

Modal verbs, sometimes called modal auxiliaries, are used to *modify* other verbs (to show e.g. possibility, ability, willingness, permission, necessity) much as in English:

he *can* swim
may I come?
we *shouldn't* go

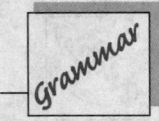

- In German the modal auxiliary verbs are: **dürfen**, **können**, **mögen**, **müssen**, **sollen** and **wollen**.
- Modal verbs have some important differences in their uses and in their conjugation from other verbs, and these are clearly shown in the verb tables on pp 86 to 97.
- Modal verbs have the following meanings:

dürfen	*to be allowed to/may* → [1] used negatively: *must not/may not* → [2] to show probability → [3] also used in some polite expressions → [4]
können	*to be able to/can* → [5] in its subjunctive forms: *would be able to/could* → [6] as an informal alternative to **dürfen** with the meaning: *to be allowed to/can* → [7] to show possibility → [8]
mögen	*to like/to like to* → [9] most common in its imperfect subjunctive form which expresses polite inquiry or request: *should like to/would like to* → [10] to show possibility or probability → [11]

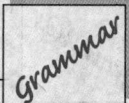

1 **Darfst du mit ins Kino kommen?**
Are you allowed to/can you come with us to the cinema?
Darf ich bitte mitkommen?
May I come with you please?
Ich dürfte schon, aber ich will nicht
I could/would be allowed to, but I don't want to

2 **Hier darf man nicht rauchen**
Smoking is prohibited here

3 **Das dürfte wohl das Beste sein**
That's probably the best thing

4 **Was darf es sein?**
Can I help you?/What would you like?

5 **Wir konnten es nicht schaffen**
We couldn't/weren't able to do it

6 **Er könnte noch früher kommen**
He could/would be able to come even earlier
Er meinte, er könne noch früher kommen
He though he could come earlier
Wir könnten vielleicht morgen hinfahren?
Perhaps we could go there tomorrow?

7 **Kann ich/darf ich ein Eis haben?**
Can I/may I have an ice cream?

8 **Wer könnte es gewesen sein?**
Who could it have been?
Das kann sein
That may be so
⚠ BUT: **Das kann nicht sein**
That cannot be so

9 **Magst du Butter?**
Do you like butter?

10 **Wir möchten bitte etwas trinken**
We should like something to drink
Möchtest du sie besuchen?
Would you like to visit her?

11 **Wie alt mag sie sein?**
How old might she be?

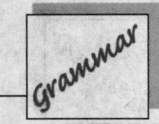

❐ Modal Auxiliary Verbs (Continued)

müssen *to have to/must/need to* → [1]

certain idiomatic uses → [2]

⚠ NOTE: For *must have …*, use the relevant tense of **müssen** + past participle of main verb + the auxiliary **haben** or **sein** → [3]

For *don't have to/need not*, a negative form of **brauchen** (*to need*) may be used instead of **müssen** → [4]

sollen *ought to/should* → [5]

to be (supposed) to where the demand is not self-imposed → [6]

to be said to be → [7]

as a command, either direct or indirect → [8]

wollen *to want/want to* → [9]

used as a less formal version of **mögen** to mean: *to want/wish* → [10]

to be willing to → [11]

to show previous intention → [12]

to claim or pretend → [13]

Examples

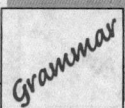

1 **Er hatte jeden Tag um sechs aufstehen müssen**
He had to get up at six o'clock every day
Man musste lachen
One had to laugh/One couldn't help laughing

2 **Muss das sein?** Is that really necessary?
Ein Millionär müsste man sein! Oh to be a millionaire!
Den Film muss man gesehen haben
That film is worth seeing

3 **Es muss geregnet haben** It must have been raining
Er meinte, es müsse am vorigen Abend passiert sein
He thought it must have happened the previous evening

4 **Das brauchtest du nicht zu sagen**
You didn't have to say that

5 **Man sollte immer die Wahrheit sagen**
One should always tell the truth
Er wusste nicht, was er tun sollte
He didn't know what to do (*what he should do*)

6 **Ich soll dir helfen**
I am to help you (*I have been told to help you*)
Du sollst sofort deine Frau anrufen
You are to phone your wife at once (*She has left a message asking you to ring*)

7 **Er soll sehr reich sein**
I've heard he's very rich/He is said to be very rich

8 **Es soll niemand sagen, dass die Schotten geizig sind!**
Let no-one say the Scots are mean!
Sie sagte mir, ich solle damit aufhören
She told me to stop it

9 **Das Kind will Lkw-Fahrer werden**
The child wants to become a lorry driver

10 **Willst du eins?** Do you want one?
Willst du/möchtest du etwas trinken?
Do you want/would you like something to drink?

11 **Er wollte nichts sagen** He refused to say anything

12 **Ich wollte gerade anrufen** I was just about to phone

13 **Keiner will es gewesen sein** No-one admits to doing it

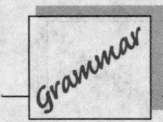

❐ Modal Auxiliary Verbs (Continued)

Conjugation and use

- Modal verbs have unusual present tenses → [1]

  Their principal parts are given in the verb tables on pp 86 to 97.

- Each modal verb has two past participles.

  The first, which is the more common, is the same as the infinitive form and is used where the modal is modifying a verb → [2]

  The second resembles a normal weak past participle and is used only where no verb is being modified (see the verb tables on p 86) → [3]

- The verb modified by the modal is placed in its infinitive form at the end of a clause → [4]

- Where the modal is used in a compound tense, its past participle in the form of the infinitive is also placed at the end of a clause, immediately after the modified verb → [5]

- If the modal verb is modifying a verb, and if the modal is used in a compound tense in a subordinate clause, then the normal word order for subordinate clauses (see p 228) does not apply. The auxiliary used to form the compound tense of the modal is not placed right at the end of the subordinate clause, but instead comes before both infinitives → [6]

  Such constructions are usually avoided in German, by using a simple tense in place of a compound. (For notes on the use of tenses in German, see p 58 ff) → [7]

- A modified verb which expresses motion may be omitted entirely if an adverb or adverbial phrase is present to indicate the movement or destination → [8]

Examples

1

dürfen	können
ich/er/sie/es darf	ich/er/sie/es kann
du darfst	du kannst
wir/sie/Sie dürfen	wir/sie/Sie können
ihr dürft	ihr könnt
mögen	**müssen**
ich/er/sie/es mag	ich/er/sie/es muss
du magst	du musst
wir/sie/Sie mögen	wir/sie/Sie müssen
ihr mögt	ihr müsst
sollen	**wollen**
ich/er/sie/es soll	ich/er/sie/es will
du sollst	du willst
wir/sie/Sie sollen	wir/sie/Sie wollen
ihr sollt	ihr wollt

2 **wollen**: Past participle **wollen**

Er hat kommen wollen

He wanted to come

3 **wollen**: Past participle **gewollt**

Hast du es gewollt?

Did you want it?

4 **Er kann gut schwimmen**

He can swim well

5 **Wir haben das Haus nicht kaufen wollen**

We didn't want to buy the house

Sie wird dich bald sehen wollen

She will want to see you soon

6 COMPARE:

Obwohl wir das Haus gekauft haben, ...

Although we bought the house ...

Obwohl wir das Haus haben kaufen wollen, ...

Although we wanted to buy the house ...

7 **Obwohl wir das Haus kaufen wollten ...**

Although we wanted to buy the house ...

8 **Ich muss nach Hause**

I must go home

Die Kinder sollen jetzt ins Bett

The children have to go to bed now

❒ Use of Tenses

Continuous forms

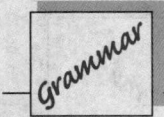

- Unlike English, the German verb does not distinguish between its simple and continuous forms → 1
- To emphasize continuity, the following may be used:
  - simple tense plus an adverb or adverbial phrase → 2
  - **am** or **beim** plus an infinitive used as a noun → 3
  - **eben/gerade dabei sein zu** plus an infinitive → 4

The present

- The present tense is used in German with **seit** or **seitdem** where English uses a past tense to show an action which began in the past and still continues → 5
  If the action is finished, or does not continue, a past tense is used → 6
- The present is commonly used with future meaning → 7

The future

- The present is often used as a future tense → 7
- The future tense is used however to:
  - emphasize the future → 8
  - express doubt or supposition about the future → 9
  - express future intention → 10

The future perfect

- The future perfect is used as in English to mean *shall/will have done* → 11
- It is used in German to express a supposition → 12
- In conversation it is replaced by the perfect → 13

The conditional

- The conditional may be used in place of the imperfect subjunctive to express improbable condition (see p 62) → 14
- It is used in indirect statements or questions to replace the future subjunctive in conversation or where the subjunctive form is not distinctive → 15

Examples

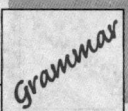

[1] **ich tue** I do (*simple form*) OR: I am doing (*continuous*)
er rauchte he smoked OR: he was smoking
sie hat gelesen she has read OR: she has been reading
es ist geschickt worden it is sent OR: it is being sent

[2] **Er kochte gerade das Abendessen**
He was cooking the supper
Nun spricht sie mit ihm Now she's talking to him

[3] **Ich bin am Bügeln** I am ironing

[4] **Wir waren eben dabei, einige Briefe zu schreiben**
We were just writing a few letters

[5] **Ich wohne seit drei Jahren hier**
I have been living here for three years

[6] **Seit er krank ist, hat er uns nicht besucht**
He hasn't visited us since he's been ill
Seit seiner Verlobung habe ich ihn nicht gesehen
I haven't seen him since his engagement

[7] **Wir fahren nächstes Jahr nach Griechenland**
We're going to Greece next year

[8] **Das werde ich erst nächstes Jahr machen können**
I won't be able to do that until next year

[9] **Wenn er zurückkommt, wird er mir bestimmt helfen**
He's sure to help me when he returns

[10] **Ich werde ihm helfen**
I'm going to help him

[11] **Bis Sonntag wird er es gelesen haben**
He will have read it by Sunday

[12] **Das wird Herr Keute gewesen sein**
That must have been Herr Keute

[13] **Bis du zurückkommst, haben wir alles aufgeräumt**
We'll have tidied up by the time you get back

[14] **Wenn ich eins hätte, würde ich es dir geben**
If I had one I would give it to you
Wenn er jetzt bloß kommen würde!
If only he would get here!

[15] **Er fragte, ob wir fahren würden**
He asked if we were going to go

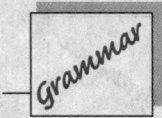

❒ Use of Tenses (Continued)

The conditional perfect

- May be used in place of the pluperfect subjunctive in a sentence containing a **wenn**-clause → 1
- But the pluperfect subjunctive is preferred → 2

The imperfect

- Is used in German with **seit** or **seitdem** where the pluperfect is used in English to show an action which began in the remote past and continued to a point in the more recent past → 3
  For discontinued actions the pluperfect is used → 4
- Is used to describe past actions which have no link with the present as far as the speaker is concerned → 5
  Is used for narrative purposes → 6
  Is used for repeated, habitual or prolonged past action → 7
  See also the ⚠ NOTE on **The Perfect** (below).

The perfect

- Is used to translate the English perfect tense, eg:
  I have spoken, he has been reading → 8
- Describes past actions or events which still have a link with the present or the speaker → 9
- Is used in conversation and similar communication → 10

⚠ NOTE: In practice however the perfect and imperfect are often interchangeable in German usage, and in spoken German a mixture of both is common.

The pluperfect

- Is used to translate *had done/had been doing*, except in conjunction with **seit/seitdem** (see **The Imperfect**) → 11

The subjunctive

- For uses of the subjunctive tenses, see pp 62 to 67.

Examples

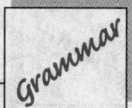

[1] **Wenn du es gesehen hättest, würdest dus geglaubt haben**
You would have believed it if you'd seen it

[2] **Hättest du es gesehen, so hättest du es geglaubt**
If you had seen it, you'd have believed it
Wenn ich das nur nicht gemacht hätte!
If only I hadn't done it!
Wäre ich nur da gewesen!
If I'd only been there

[3] **Sie war seit ihrer Heirat als Lehrerin beschäftigt**
She had been working as a teacher since her marriage

[4] **Ihren Sohn hatten sie seit zwölf Jahren nicht gesehen**
They hadn't seen their son for twelve years

[5] **Er kam zu spät, um teilnehmen zu können**
He arrived too late to take part

[6] **Das Mädchen stand auf, wusch sich das Gesicht und verließ das Haus**
The girl got up, washed her face and went out

[7] **Wir machten jeden Tag einen kleinen Spaziergang**
We went/We used to go for a little walk every day

[8] **Ich habe ihn heute nicht gesehen**
I haven't seen him today

[9] **Ich habe ihr nichts davon erzählt**
I didn't tell her anything about it
Gestern sind wir in die Stadt gefahren und haben uns ein paar Sachen gekauft
Yesterday we went into town and bought ourselves a few things

[10] **Hast du den Krimi gestern Abend im Fernsehen gesehen?**
Did you see the thriller on television last night?

[11] **Sie waren schon weggefahren**
They had already left
Diese Bücher hatten sie schon gelesen
They had already read these books

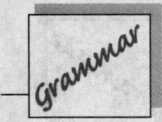

❐ The Subjunctive: when to use it

The subjunctive form in English has almost died out, leaving only a few examples such as:

> if I *were* rich
> if only he *were* to come
> so *be* it

German however makes much wider use of subjunctive forms, especially in formal, educated or literary contexts. Although there is a growing tendency to use indicatives in spoken German, subjunctives are still very common.

- The indicative tenses in German display fact or certainty. The subjunctives show unreality, uncertainty, speculation about a situation or any doubt in the speaker's mind → [1]

  Subjunctives are also used in indirect speech, as shown on pp 66 and 67.

- For how to form all tenses of the subjunctive, the reader is referred to the relevant sections on Simple Tenses (pp 6 to 17) and Compound Tenses (pp 22 to 29). See also the Subjunctive in Reported Speech (p 66).

- The **imperfect subjunctive** is very common. It is important to note that the imperfect subjunctive form does not always represent actions performed in the past → [2]

Uses of the subjunctive in German

- To show improbable condition (e.g. if he *came*, he would ...).
  The *if*-clause (**wenn** in German) has a verb in the imperfect subjunctive and the main clause can have either an imperfect subjunctive or a conditional → [3]

Examples

1 INDICATIVE

Das stimmt
That's true

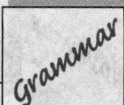

Es ist eine Unverschämtheit
It's a scandal

SUBJUNCTIVE

Es könnte doch war sein
It could well be true
Sie meint, es sei eine Unverschämtheit
She thinks it's a scandal
(*speaker not necessarily in agreement with her*)

2 *imperfect subjunctive expressing the future:*
Wenn ich morgen nur da sein könnte!
If only I could be there tomorrow!

expressing the present/immediate future:
Wenn er jetzt nur käme!
If only he would come now!

speaker's opinion, referring to present or future:
Sie wäre die Beste
She's the best

3 **Wenn du kämest, wäre ich froh**

OR:

Wenn du kämest, würde ich froh sein
I should be happy if you came

Wenn es mir nicht gefiele, würde ich es nicht bezahlen

OR:

Wenn es mir nicht gefiele, bezahlte ich es nicht
If I wasn't happy with it, I wouldn't pay for it
(*The second form is less likely, as the imperfect subjunctive and imperfect indicative forms of* **bezahlen** *are identical*)

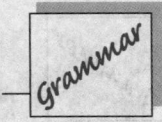

❒ The Subjunctive: when to use it (Continued)

- The imperfect of **sollen** or **wollen**, or a conditional tense might be used in the **wenn**-clause to replace an uncommon imperfect subjunctive, or a subjunctive which is not distinct from the same tense of the indicative → [1]

- To show unfulfilled condition (if he *had come*, he would have ...)

  The **wenn**-clause requires a pluperfect subjunctive, the main clause a pluperfect subjunctive or conditional perfect → [2]

  ⚠ NOTE: The indicative is used to express a *probable* condition, as in English → [3]

- **Wenn** can be omitted from conditional clauses. The verb must then follow the subject and **dann** or **so** usually begins the main clause → [4]

- With **selbst wenn** (*even if/even though*) → [5]

- With **wenn ... nur** (*if only ...*) → [6]

- To speculate or make assumptions → [7]

- After **als** (*as if/as though*) → [8]

- Where there is uncertainty or doubt → [9]

- To make a polite enquiry → [10]

- To indicate theoretical possibility or unreality → [11]

- As an alternative to the conditional perfect → [12]

Examples

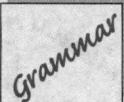

1 **Wenn er mich so sehen würde, würde er mich für verrückt halten!** OR:
Wenn er mich so sehen würde, hielte er mich für verrückt! OR:
Wenn er mich so sehen sollte, würde er mich für verrückt halten!
If he saw me like this, he would think I was mad!
(**Wenn er mich so sähe** *would sound rather stilted*)

2 **Wenn du pünktlich gekommen wärest, hättest du ihn gesehen**
OR:
Wenn du pünktlich gekommen wärest, würdest du ihn gesehen haben
If you had been on time, you would have seen him

3 **Wenn ich ihn sehe, gebe ich es ihm**
If I see him I'll give him it

4 **Hättest du mich nicht gesehen, so wäre ich schon weg**
If you hadn't seen me, I would have been gone by now

5 **Selbst wenn er etwas wüsste, würde er nichts sagen**
Even if he knew about it, he wouldn't say anything

6 **Wenn wir nur erfolgreich wären!**
If only we were successful!

7 **Und wenn er recht hätte?** What if he were right?
Eine Frau, die das sagen würde (OR: die das sagte), müsste Feministin sein!
Any woman who would say that must be a feminist!

8 **Er sah aus, als sei er krank**
He looked as if he were ill

9 **Er wusste nicht, wie es ihr jetzt ginge**
He didn't know how she was

10 **Wäre da sonst noch etwas?** Will there be anything else?

11 **Er stellte sich vor, wie gut er in dem Anzug aussähe**
He imagined how good he would look in the suit

12 **Ich hätte ihn gesehen** OR: **Ich würde ihn gesehen haben**
I would have seen him

❒ The Subjunctive in Indirect Speech

What a person asks or thinks can be reported in one of two ways, either **directly**:

Tom said, "I have been on holiday"

OR **indirectly**:

Tom said (that) he had been on holiday

- In English, indirect (or reported) speech can be indicated by a change in tense of what has been reported:

  He said, "*I know* your sister"
  He said (that) *he knew* my sister

  In German the change is not in tense, but from indicative to subjunctive → [1]

- There are two ways of introducing indirect speech in German, similar to the parallel English constructions:

  1 The clause which reports what is said may be introduced by **dass** (*that*). The finite verb or auxiliary comes at the end of the clause → [2]

  2 **dass** may be omitted. The verb in this case must stand in second position in the clause, instead of being placed at the end → [3]

Forms of the subjunctive in indirect speech

For conjugation of verbs in the subjunctive, see pp 8 to 15 and 26 to 31. In indirect (or reported) speech, wherever the present subjunctive is identical to the present indicative form, the imperfect subjunctive is used instead → [4]

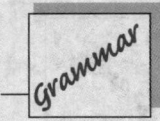

Examples

1 **Er sagte: „Sie kennt deine Schwester"**
He said, "She knows your sister"

Er sagte, sie kenne meine Schwester
He said she knew my sister

„Habe ich zu viel gesagt?", fragte er
"Have I said too much?", he asked

Er fragte, ob er zu viel gesagt habe
He asked if he had said too much

2 **Er hat uns gesagt, dass er Italienisch spreche**
He told us that he spoke Italian

3 **Er hat uns gesagt, er spreche Italienisch**
He told us he spoke Italian

4 PRESENT SUBJUNCTIVE IN INDIRECT SPEECH

WEAK VERBS

<u>**holen** to fetch</u>

ich holte	**wir holten**
du holest	ihr holet
er hole	**sie holten**

STRONG VERBS

<u>**singen** to sing</u>

ich sänge	**wir sängen**
du singest	ihr singet
er singe	**sie sängen**

❒ Verbs with Prefixes

Many verbs in German begin with a prefix. A prefix is a word or part of a word which precedes the verb stem → [1]

- Often the addition of a prefix changes the meaning of the basic verb → [2]
- Prefixes may be found in strong, weak or mixed verbs. Adding a prefix may occasionally change the verb conjugation → [3]

There are four kinds of prefix and each behaves in a slightly different way, as shown on the following pages. Prefixes may be inseparable, separable, double or variable (i.e. either separable or inseparable depending on the verb).

Inseparable prefixes

- The eight inseparable prefixes are:

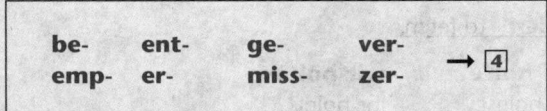

be-	**ent-**	**ge-**	**ver-**	→ [4]
emp-	**er-**	**miss-**	**zer-**	

- These exist only as prefixes, and cannot be words in their own right.
- They are never separated from the verb stem, whatever tense of the verb is used → [5]
- Inseparable prefixes are always unstressed → [6]

Examples

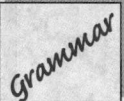

1 **zu + geben = zugeben**
an + ziehen = anziehen

2

nehmen	to take
zunehmen	to put on weight/to increase
sich benehmen	to behave

3

WEAK		STRONG	
suchen	to look for	**stehen**	to stand
versuchen	to try	**verstehen**	to understand
besuchen	to visit	**aufstehen**	to get up

WEAK		WEAK	
löschen	to extinguish	**fehlen**	to be missing

STRONG		STRONG	
erlöschen	to go out	**empfehlen**	to recommend

4

beschreiben	to describe
empfangen	to receive
enttäuschen	to disappoint
erhalten	to contain
gehören	to belong
misstrauen	to mistrust
verlieren	to lose
zerlegen	to dismantle

5 **besuchen** to visit

Er besucht uns regelmäßig	He visits us regularly
Er besuchte uns jeden Tag	He used to visit us every day
Er hat uns jeden Tag besucht	He visited us every day
Er wird uns morgen besuchen	He will visit us tomorrow
Besuche sofort deine Tante!	Visit your aunt at once

6 erlau**ben**, ver**stehen**, emp**fangen**, ver**gessen**

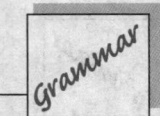

❐ Verbs with Prefixes (Continued)

Separable prefixes

Some common examples are:

ab	**fest**	**herunter**	**mit**
an	**frei**	**hervor**	**nach**
auf	**her**	**hin**	**nieder**
aus	**herab**	**hinab**	**vor**
bei	**heran**	**hinauf**	**vorbei**
da(r)	**herauf**	**hinaus**	**vorüber**
davon	**heraus**	**hindurch**	**weg**
dazu	**herbei**	**hinein**	**zu**
ein	**herein**	**hinüber**	**zurecht**
empor	**herüber**	**hinunter**	**zurück**
entgegen	**herum**	**los**	**zusammen**

- Unlike inseparable prefixes, separable prefixes may be words in their own right. Indeed, nouns, adjectives and adverbs are often used as separable prefixes → [1]

- The past participle of a verb with a separable prefix is formed with **ge**-. It comes between the verb and the prefix → [2]

- In main clauses, the prefix is placed at the end of the clause if the verb is in a simple tense (i.e. present, imperfect or imperative form) → [3]

- In subordinate clauses, whatever the tense of the verb, the prefix is attached to the verb and the resulting whole placed at the end of the clause → [4]

- Where an infinitive construction requiring **zu** is used (see p 48), the **zu** is placed between the infinitive and prefix to form one word → [5]

Examples

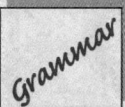

1 *noun + verb*: **teilnehmen** to take part
adjective + verb: **loswerden** to get free of
adverb + verb: **niederlegen** to lay down

2 **Er hat nicht teilgenommen**
He did not participate
Wir sind an der Grenze zurückgewiesen worden
We were turned back at the border

3 **wegbringen** to take for repair/to take away

PRESENT
Wir bringen das Auto weg
IMPERFECT
Wir brachten das Auto weg
IMPERATIVE
Bringt das Auto weg!
FUTURE
Wir werden das Auto wegbringen
CONDITIONAL
Wir würden das Auto wegbringen
PERFECT
Wir haben das Auto weggebracht
PERFECT PASSIVE
Das Auto ist weggebracht worden
PLUPERFECT SUBJUNCTIVE
Wir hätten das Auto weggebracht

4 PRESENT
Weil wir das Auto wegbringen, ...
IMPERFECT
Dass wir das Auto wegbrachten, ...
PERFECT
Nachdem wir das Auto weggebracht haben, ...
PLUPERFECT SUBJUNCTIVE
Wenn wir das Auto weggebracht hätten, ...
FUTURE
Obwohl wir das Auto wegbringen werden, ...

5 **Um das Auto rechtzeitig wegzubringen, müssen wir morgen früh aufstehen**
In order to take the car in on time we shall have to get up early tomorrow

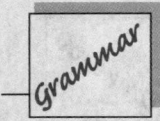

❐ Verbs with Prefixes (Continued)

Variable prefixes

These are:

durch	**über**	**unter**	**wider**
hinter	**um**	**voll**	**wieder**

- These can be separable or inseparable → [1]
- Often they are used separably and inseparably with the same verb. In such cases the verb and prefix will tend to retain their basic meanings if the prefix is used separably, but adopt figurative meanings when the prefix is used inseparably → [2]
- Variable prefixes behave as separable prefixes when used separably, and as inseparable prefixes when used inseparably → [3]

Double prefixes

These occur where a verb with an inseparable prefix is preceded by a separable prefix → [4]

- The separable prefix behaves as described on p 70, the verb plus inseparable prefix representing the basic verb to which the separable prefix is attached → [5]
- Unlike other separable verbs, however, verbs with double prefixes have no **ge**- in their past participles → [6]

Examples

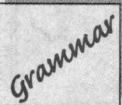

1 <u>**unternehmen** (*inseparable*) to undertake, take on</u>

Wir haben in den Ferien vieles unternommen

We did a great deal in the holidays

Du unternimmst zu viel

You take on too much

<u>**untergehen** (*separable*) to sink, go down</u>

Die Sonne geht unter

The sun is going down/is setting

Die Sonne ist untergangen

The sun has gone down/has set

2 **etwas wiederholen** (*separable*) to retrieve something

etwas wiederholen (*inseparable*) to repeat something

3 **Er holte ihr die Tasche wieder**

He brought her back her bag

Er wiederholte den Satz

He repeated the sentence

4 **ausverkaufen** to sell off

5 **Er verkauft alles aus**

He's selling everything off

Um alles auszuverkaufen …

In order to sell everything off …

Er wird alles ausverkaufen

He'll be selling everything off

6 **Aber er hat doch alles ausverkauft**

But he's sold everything off

❒ Verb Combinations

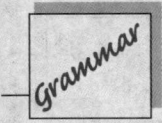

- *Noun* + *verb* combinations are written separately → 1

  ⚠ BUT: Compound verbs which are almost exclusively used in the infinitive or as participles are written as one word → 2

- *Infinitive* + *verb* combinations are written separately → 3

- *Participle* + *verb* combinations are written separately → 4

- *Adjective/adverb* + *verb* combinations are written as one word if the first component of the compound is not a word in its own right → 5

  Or if the first component of the compound cannot be qualified or compared → 6

- *Adjective* + *verb* combinations are written separately if the adjective can be qualified or compared (in this case, negation counts as a qualification) → 7

- *Adverb* + *verb* combinations are written separately if the adverb is a compound word → 8

- Verb combinations with -**ander** are written separately → 9

- Verb combinations with -**seits** and -**wärts** are written separately → 10

- Verb combinations with **sein** are written separately → 11

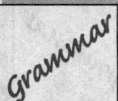

1 **Ski fahren, Eis laufen, Halt machen**

2 **bergsteigen, brustschwimmen, kopfrechnen, sonnenbaden**

3 **kennen lernen, sitzen bleiben, spazieren gehen**

4 **gefangen nehmen, verloren gehen**

5 **fehlschlagen, kundgeben, weismachen**

6 **bereithalten, fernsehen, totschlagen**

7 **bekannt machen, genau nehmen, kurz treten, nahe bringen**

8 **abhanden kommen, beiseite legen, überhand nehmen, zunichte machen**

9 **aneinander legen, auseinander laufen, durcheinander reden**

10 **abseits stehen, abwärts gehen**

11 **auf sein, zu sein**

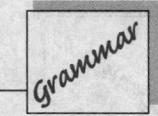

❒ Verbs followed by Prepositions

- Some verbs in English usage require a preposition (*for/with/by* etc) for their completion.
  This also happens in German, though the prepositions used with German verbs may not be those expected from their English counterparts → [1]

- The preposition used may significantly alter the meaning of a verb in German → [2]

- Occasionally German verbs use a preposition where their English equivalents do not → [3]

- Prepositions used with verbs behave as normal prepositions and affect the *case* of the following noun (see p198).

- A verb plus preposition may be followed by a clause containing another verb rather than by a noun or pronoun. This often corresponds to an *-ing* construction in English:

  Thank you for *coming*

  In German, this is dealt with in two ways:

  1 Where the "verb-plus-preposition" construction has the same subject as the following verb, the preposition is preceded by **da-** or **dar-** and the following verb becomes an infinitive used with **zu** → [4]

  2 Where the subject of the "verb-plus-preposition" is not the same as for the following verb, a **dass** clause is used → [5]

- Following clauses may also be introduced by interrogatives (**ob, wie** etc) if the meaning demands them → [6]

Examples

1 COMPARE:

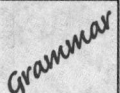

sich sehnen *nach*	to long *for*
warten *auf*	to wait *for*
bitten *um*	to ask *for*

2

bestehen	to pass (an examination/a test *etc*)
bestehen aus	to consist of
bestehen auf	to insist on
sich freuen auf	to look forward to
sich freuen über	to be pleased about

3 **diskutieren über** to discuss

4 **Ich freue mich sehr darauf, mal wieder mit ihm zu arbeiten**
I am looking forward to working with him again

5 **Ich freue mich sehr darauf, dass du morgen kommst**
I am looking forward to your coming tomorrow

Er sorgte dafür, dass die Kinder immer gut gepflegt waren
He saw to it that the children were always well cared for

6 **Er dachte lange darüber nach, ob er es wirklich kaufen wollte**
He thought for ages about whether he really wanted to buy it

Sie freut sich darüber, wie schnell ihre Schüler gelernt haben
She is pleased at how quickly her students have learned

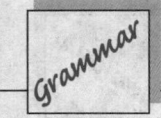

❒ Verbs followed by Prepositions (Continued)

COMMON VERBS FOLLOWED BY PREPOSITION PLUS ACCUSATIVE CASE:

achten auf	to pay attention to, keep an eye on → 1
sich amüsieren über	to laugh at, smile about
sich ärgern über	to get annoyed about/with
sich bewerben um	to apply for → 2
bitten um	to ask for → 3
denken an	to be thinking of → 4
denken über	to hold an opinion of, think about → 5
sich erinnern an	to remember
sich freuen auf	to look forward to
sich freuen über	to be pleased about → 6
sich gewöhnen an	to get used to → 7
sich interessieren für	to be interested in → 8
kämpfen um	to fight for
sich kümmern um	to take care of, see to
nachdenken über	to ponder, reflect on → 9
sich unterhalten über	to talk about
sich verlassen auf	to rely on, depend on → 10
warten auf	to wait for

COMMON VERBS FOLLOWED BY PREPOSITION PLUS DATIVE CASE:

abhängen von	to be dependent on → 11
sich beschäftigen mit	to occupy oneself with → 12
bestehen aus	to consist of → 13
leiden an/unter	to suffer from → 14
neigen zu	to be inclined to
riechen nach	to smell of → 15
schmecken nach	to taste of
sich sehnen nach	to long for
sterben an	to die of
teilnehmen an	to take part in → 16
träumen von	to dream of → 17
sich verabschieden von	to say goodbye to
sich verstehen mit	to get along with, get on with
zittern vor	to tremble with → 18

Examples

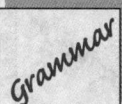

1 **Er musste auf die Kinder achten**
He had to keep an eye on the children

2 **Sie hat sich um die Stelle als Sekretärin beworben**
She applied for the post of secretary

3 **Die Kinder baten ihre Mutter um Plätzchen**
The children asked their mother for some biscuits

4 **Woran denkst du?** What are you thinking about?
Daran habe ich gar nicht mehr gedacht
I'd forgotten about that

5 **Wie denkt ihr darüber?** What do you think about it?

6 **Ich freute mich sehr darüber, Johannes besucht zu haben**
I was very glad I had visited Johannes

7 **Man gewöhnt sich an alles** One gets used to anything

8 **Sie interessiert sich sehr für Politik**
She is very interested in politics

9 **Er hatte schon lange darüber nachgedacht**
He had been thinking about it for a long time

10 **Er verlässt sich darauf, dass seine Frau alles tut**
He relies on his wife to do everything

11 **Das hängt davon ab** It all depends

12 **Sie sind im Moment sehr damit beschäftigt, ihr neues Haus in Ordnung zu bringen**
They are very busy sorting out their new house at the moment

13 **Dieser Kuchen besteht aus Eiern, Mehl und Zucker**
This cake consists of eggs, flour and sugar

14 **Sie hat lange an dieser Krankheit gelitten**
She suffered from this illness for a long time
Alte Leute können sehr unter der Einsamkeit leiden
Old people can suffer dreadful loneliness

15 **Der Kuchen roch nach Zimt**
The cake smelled of cinnamon

16 **Sie hat an der Bonner Tagung teilnehmen müssen**
She had to attend the Bonn conference

17 **Er hat von seinem Urlaub geträumt**
He dreamt of his holiday

18 **Er zitterte vor Freude** He was trembling with joy

❒ Verbs followed by the Dative

Some verbs have a direct object and an indirect object. In the English sentence "*He gave me a book*", *a book* is the direct object of *gave* and would be in the accusative and *me* (= *to me*) is the indirect object and would appear in the dative case in German → [1]

- In German, as in English, this type of verb is usually concerned with giving or telling something to someone, or with performing an action for someone → [2]
- The normal word order after such verbs is for the direct object to follow the indirect, *except* where the direct object is a personal pronoun (see p 224) → [2]
  This order may be reversed for emphasis → [3]
- Some examples of verbs followed by the dative in this way:

anbieten	gönnen	schicken	
bringen	kaufen	schreiben	
beweisen	leihen	schulden	→ [4]
erzählen	mitteilen	verkaufen	
geben	schenken	zeigen	

- Certain verbs in German however can be followed *only* by an indirect object in the dative case. These should be noted especially, since most of them are quite different from their English equivalents:

begegnen	gratulieren	schmeicheln	
danken	helfen	trauen	
fehlen	imponieren	trotzen	
gefallen	misstrauen	vorangehen	→ [5]
gehören	nachgehen	wehtun	
gelingen	schaden	widersprechen	
gleichen	schmecken	widerstehen	

- For how to form the passive of such verbs, see p 36.

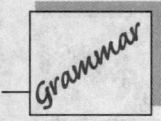

Examples

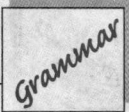

1 **Er gab mir ein Buch** He gave me a book

2 **Er wusch dem Kind** (*indirect*) **das Gesicht** (*direct*)
He washed the child's face
Er erzählte ihm (*indirect*) **eine Geschichte** (*direct*)
He told him a story
⚠ BUT:
Er hat sie (*direct*) **meiner Mutter** (*indirect*) **gezeigt**
He showed it to my mother
Kaufst du es (*direct*) **mir** (*indirect*)**?**
Will you buy it for me?

3 **Er wollte das Buch** (*direct*) **seiner Mutter** (*indirect*) **geben**
(*This emphasises* **seiner Mutter**)
He wanted to give the book to his mother

4 **Er bot ihr die Arbeitsstelle an** He offered her the job
Bringst du mir eins? Will you bring me one?
Ich gönne dir das neue Kleid
I want you to have the new dress
Er hat ihr mitgeteilt, dass ... He told her that ...
Ich schenke meiner Mutter Parfüm zum Geburtstag
I am giving my mother perfume for her birthday
Das schulde ich ihm I owe him that
Zeig es mir! Show me it!

5 **Er ist seinem Freund in der Stadt begegnet**
He bumped into his friend in town
Mir fehlt der Mut dazu I don't have the courage
Es ist ihnen gelungen They succeeded
Wem gehört dieses Buch? Whose book is this?
Er wollte ihr nicht helfen He refused to help her
Ich gratuliere dir! Congratulations!
Rauchen schadet der Gesundheit
Smoking is bad for your health
Das Essen hat ihnen gut geschmeckt
They enjoyed the meal

❒ There is/There are

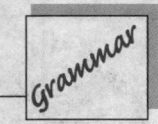

There are three ways of expressing this in German:

Es gibt

- This is always used in the singular form, and is followed by an accusative object which may be either singular or plural → [1]
- **Es gibt** is used to refer to things of a general nature or location → [2]
- It also has some idiomatic usages → [3]

Es ist/es sind

- The **es** here merely introduces the real subject. The verb therefore becomes plural where the real subject is plural. The real subject is in the nominative case → [4]
- The **es** is not required and is therefore omitted when the verb and real subject come together. This happens when inversion of subject and verb occurs (see p 226) and in subordinate clauses → [5]
- **Es ist** or **es sind** are used to refer to:
  1. subjects with a specific and confined location. This location must always be mentioned either by name or by **da, darauf, darin** *etc* → [6]
  2. temporary existence → [7]
  3. as a beginning to a story → [8]

The passive voice

Often *there is/there are* in English will be rendered by a verb in the passive voice in German → [9]

Examples

1 **Es gibt zu viele Probleme dabei**
There are too many problems involved
Es gibt kein besseres Bier
There's no better beer

2 **Es gibt bestimmt Regen**
It's definitely going to rain
Ruhe hat es bei uns nie gegeben
There has never been any peace here

3 **Was gibts (= gibt es) zum Essen?** What is there to eat?
Was gibts? What's wrong?, What's up?
So was gibts doch nicht! That's impossible!

4 **Es waren zwei ältere Leute unten im Hof**
There were two elderly people down in the yard
Es sind so viele Touristen da
There are so many tourists there

5 **Unten im Hof waren zwei ältere Leute**
Down in the yard were two elderly people
Wenn so viele Touristen da sind, ...
If there are so many tourists there, ...

6 **Es waren viele Flaschen Sekt im Keller**
There were a lot of bottles of champagne in the cellar
Ein Brief lag auf dem Tisch. Es waren auch zwei Bücher darauf
A letter lay on the table. There were also two books on it

7 **Es war niemand da**
There was no-one there

8 **Es war einmal ein König ...**
Once upon a time there was a king ...

9 **Es wurde auf der Party viel getrunken**
There was a lot of drinking at the party

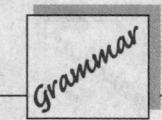

❒ Use of "es" as an Anticipatory Object

Many verbs can have as their object a **dass** clause or an infinitive with **zu** → [1]

- With some verbs **es** is used as an object to anticipate this clause or infinitive phrase → [2]
- When the clause or infinitive phrase begins the sentence, **es** is not used in the main clause but its place may be taken by an optional **das** → [3]

COMMON VERBS WHICH USUALLY HAVE THE "ES" OBJECT:

es ablehnen, zu	to refuse to
es aushalten, zu tun/dass	to stand doing → [4]
es ertragen, zu tun/dass	to endure doing
es leicht haben, zu	to find it easy to → [5]
es nötig haben, zu	to need to → [6]
es satt haben, zu	to have had enough of (doing)
es verstehen, zu	to know how to → [7]

COMMON VERBS WHICH OFTEN HAVE THE "ES" OBJECT:

es jemandem anhören/ansehen, dass	to tell by listening to/looking at someone that → [8]
es begreifen, dass/warum/wie	to understand that/why/how
es bereuen, zu tun/dass	to regret having done/that
es leugnen, dass	to deny that → [9]
es unternehmen, zu	to undertake to
es jemandem verbieten, zu	to forbid someone to
es jemandem vergeben, dass	to forgive someone for (doing)
es jemandem verschweigen, dass	not to tell someone that
es jemandem verzeihen, dass	to forgive someone for (doing)
es wagen zu	to dare to

Examples

1 **Er wusste, dass wir pünktlich kommen würden**
He knew that we would come on time
Sie fing an zu lachen
She began to laugh

2 **Er hatte es abgelehnt mitzufahren**
He had refused to come

3 **Dass es Wolfgang war, das haben wir ihr verschwiegen**
OR:
Dass es Wolfgang war, haben wir ihr verschwiegen
We didn't tell her that it was Wolfgang

4 **Ich halte es nicht mehr aus, bei ihnen zu arbeiten**
I can't stand working for them any longer

5 **Er hatte es nicht leicht, sie zu überreden**
He didn't have an easy job persuading them

6 **Ich habe es nicht nötig, mit dir darüber zu reden**
I don't have to talk to you about it

7 **Er versteht es, Autos zu reparieren**
He knows about repairing cars

8 **Man hörte es ihm sofort an, dass er kein Deutscher war**
OR:
Dass er kein Deutscher war, (das) hörte man ihm sofort an
One could tell immediately (from the way he spoke) that he wasn't German

Man sieht es ihm sofort an, dass er dein Bruder ist
OR:
Dass er dein Bruder ist, (das) sieht man ihm sofort an
One can tell at a glance that he's your brother

9 **Er hat es nie geleugnet, das Geld genommen zu haben**
He has never denied taking the money

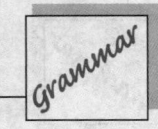

❒ Strong and Mixed Verbs - Principal Parts

INFINITIVE	TRANSLATION	3RD PERSON PRESENT ➠
backen	to bake	**er bäckt**
befehlen	to command	**er befiehlt**
beginnen	to begin	**er beginnt**
beißen	to bite	**er beißt**
bergen	to rescue	**er birgt**
bersten	to burst *intr*	**er birst**
betrügen	to deceive	**er betrügt**
biegen	to bend *tr*/to turn *intr*	**er biegt**
bieten	to offer	**er bietet**
binden	to tie	**er bindet**
bitten	to ask for	**er bittet**
blasen	to blow	**er bläst**
bleiben	to remain	**er bleibt**
braten	to fry	**er brät**
brechen	to break	**er bricht**
brennen	to burn	**er brennt**
bringen	to bring	**er bringt**
denken	to think	**er denkt**
dreschen	to thresh	**er drischt**
dringen	to penetrate	**er dringt**
dürfen	to be allowed to	**er darf**
empfehlen	to recommend	**er empfiehlt**
erlöschen	to go out (*fire, light*)	**er erlischt**
erschallen	to resound	**er erschallt**
erschrecken[1]	to be startled	**er erschrickt**
erwägen	to weigh up	**er erwägt**
essen	to eat	**er isst**
fahren	to travel	**er fährt**

[1] **erschrecken** meaning "to frighten" is weak:
erschrecken, erschreckt, erschreckte, hat erschreckt

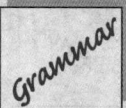

3RD PERSON IMPERFECT	PERFECT	IMPERFECT SUBJUNCTIVE
er backte	**er hat gebacken**	**er backte**
er befahl	**er hat befohlen**	**er befähle**
er begann	**er hat begonnen**	**er begänne**
er biss	**er hat gebissen**	**er bisse**
er barg	**er hat geborgen**	**er bärge**
er barst	**er ist geborsten**	**er bärste**
er betrog	**er hat betrogen**	**er betröge**
er bog	**er hat/ist gebogen**	**er böge**
er bot	**er hat geboten**	**er böte**
er band	**er hat gebunden**	**er bände**
er bat	**er hat gebeten**	**er bäte**
er blies	**er hat geblasen**	**er bliese**
er blieb	**er ist geblieben**	**er bliebe**
er briet	**er hat gebraten**	**er briete**
er brach	**er hat/ist gebrochen**	**er bräche**
er brannte	**er hat gebrannt**	**er brennte**
er brachte	**er hat gebracht**	**er brächte**
er dachte	**er hat gedacht**	**er dächte**
er drosch	**er hat gedroschen**	**er drösche**
er drang	**er ist gedrungen**	**er dränge**
er durfte	**er hat gedurft/dürfen**[1]	**er dürfte**
er empfahl	**er hat empfohlen**	**er empfähle**
er erlosch	**er ist erloschen**	**er erlösche**
er erschallte	**er ist erschollen**	**er erschölle**
er erschrak	**er ist erschrocken**	**er erschräke**
er erwog	**er hat erwogen**	**er erwöge**
er aß	**er hat gegessen**	**er äße**
er fuhr	**er ist gefahren**	**er führe**

[1] The second (infinitive) form is used when combined with an infinitive construction (see p 56).

❒ Strong and Mixed Verbs (Continued)

INFINITIVE	TRANSLATION	3RD PERSON PRESENT ➠
fallen	to fall	**er fällt**
fangen	to catch	**er fängt**
fechten	to fight	**er ficht**
finden	to find	**er findet**
fliegen	to fly	**er fliegt**
fliehen	to flee *tr/intr*	**er flieht**
fließen	to flow	**er fließt**
fressen	to eat (*of animals*)	**er frisst**
frieren	to be cold/to freeze over	**er friert**
gebären	to give birth to	**sie gebärt**
geben	to give	**er gibt**
gedeihen	to thrive	**er gedeiht**
gehen	to go	**er geht**
gelingen	to succeed	**es gelingt**
gelten	to be valid	**er gilt**
genesen	to get well	**er genest**
genießen	to enjoy	**er genießt**
geraten	to get into (*a state etc*)	**er gerät**
geschehen	to happen	**es geschieht**
gewinnen	to win	**er gewinnt**
gießen	to pour	**er gießt**
gleichen	to resemble/to equal	**er gleicht**
gleiten	to glide	**er gleitet**
glimmen	to glimmer	**er glimmt**
graben	to dig	**er gräbt**
greifen	to grip	**er greift**
haben	to have	**er hat**
halten	to hold/to stop	**er hält**
hängen[1]	to hang *intr*	**er hängt**
heben	to lift	**er hebt**
heißen	to be called	**er heißt**

[1] **hängen** is weak when used transitively.

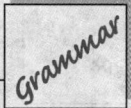

3RD PERSON IMPERFECT	PERFECT	IMPERFECT SUBJUNCTIVE
er fiel	**er ist gefallen**	**er fiele**
er fing	**er hat gefangen**	**er finge**
er focht	**er hat gefochten**	**er föchte**
er fand	**er hat gefunden**	**er fände**
er flog	**er hat/ist geflogen**	**er flöge**
er floh	**er hat/ist geflohen**	**er flöhe**
er floss	**er ist geflossen**	**er flösse**
er fraß	**er hat gefressen**	**er fräße**
er fror	**er hat/ist gefroren**	**er fröre**
sie gebar	**sie hat geboren**	**sie gebäre**
er gab	**er hat gegeben**	**er gäbe**
er gedieh	**er ist gediehen**	**er gediehe**
er ging	**er ist gegangen**	**er ginge**
es gelang	**es ist gelungen**	**es gelänge**
er galt	**er hat gegolten**	**er gälte**
er genas	**er ist genesen**	**er genäse**
er genoss	**er hat genossen**	**er genösse**
er geriet	**er ist geraten**	**er geriete**
es geschah	**es ist geschehen**	**es geschähe**
er gewann	**er hat gewonnen**	**er gewönne**
er goss	**er hat gegossen**	**er gösse**
er glich	**er hat geglichen**	**er gliche**
er glitt	**er ist geglitten**	**er glitte**
er glomm	**er hat geglommen**	**er glömme**
er grub	**er hat gegraben**	**er grübe**
er griff	**er hat gegriffen**	**er griffe**
er hatte	**er hat gehabt**	**er hätte**
er hielt	**er hat gehalten**	**er hielte**
er hing	**er hat gehangen**	**er hinge**
er hob	**er hat gehoben**	**er höbe**
er hieß	**er hat geheißen**	**er hieße**

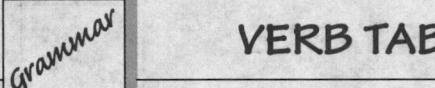

❐ Strong and Mixed Verbs (Continued)

INFINITIVE	TRANSLATION	3RD PERSON PRESENT ➠
helfen	to help	**er hilft**
kennen	to know (*someone etc*)	**er kennt**
klingen	to sound	**er klingt**
kommen	to come	**er kommt**
kneifen	to pinch	**er kneift**
können	to be able to	**er kann**
kriechen	to crawl	**er kriecht**
laden	to load	**er lädt**
lassen	to allow	**er lässt**
laufen	to walk/to run	**er läuft**
leiden	to suffer	**er leidet**
leihen	to lend	**er leiht**
lesen	to read	**er liest**
liegen	to lie	**er liegt**
lügen	to tell a lie	**er lügt**
mahlen	to grind	**er mahlt**
messen	to measure	**er misst**
misslingen	to fail	**es misslingt**
mögen	to like to	**er mag**
müssen	to have to	**er muss**
nehmen	to take	**er nimmt**
nennen	to call	**er nennt**
pfeifen	to whistle	**er pfeift**
preisen	to praise	**er preist**
quellen	to gush	**er quillt**
raten	to advise/to guess	**er rät**
reiben	to rub	**er reibt**
reißen	to tear *tr/intr*	**er reißt**
reiten	to ride *tr/intr*	**er reitet**

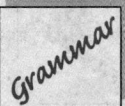

3RD PERSON IMPERFECT	PERFECT	IMPERFECT SUBJUNCTIVE
er half	**er hat geholfen**	**er hülfe**
er kannte	**er hat gekannt**	**er kennte**
er klang	**er hat geklungen**	**er klänge**
er kam	**er ist gekommen**	**er käme**
er kniff	**er hat gekniffen**	**er kniffe**
er konnte	**er hat gekonnt/können**[1]	**er könnte**
er kroch	**er ist gekrochen**	**er kröche**
er lud	**er hat geladen**	**er lüde**
er ließ	**er hat gelassen**	**er ließe**
er lief	**er ist gelaufen**	**er liefe**
er litt	**er hat gelitten**	**er litte**
er lieh	**er hat geliehen**	**er liehe**
er las	**er hat gelesen**	**er läse**
er lag	**er hat gelegen**	**er läge**
er log	**er hat gelogen**	**er löge**
er mahlte	**er hat gemahlen**	**er mahlte**
er maß	**er hat gemessen**	**er mäße**
es misslang	**es ist misslungen**	**es misslänge**
er mochte	**er hat gemocht/mögen**[1]	**er möchte**
er musste	**er hat gemusst/müssen**[1]	**er müsste**
er nahm	**er hat genommen**	**er nähme**
er nannte	**er hat genannt**	**er nennte**
er pfiff	**er hat gepfiffen**	**er pfiffe**
er pries	**er hat gepriesen**	**er priese**
er quoll	**er ist gequollen**	**er quölle**
er riet	**er hat geraten**	**er riete**
er rieb	**er hat gerieben**	**er riebe**
er riss	**er hat/ist gerissen**	**er risse**
er ritt	**er hat/ist geritten**	**er ritte**

[1] The second (infinitive) form is used when combined with an infinitive construction (see p 56).

❐ Strong and Mixed Verbs (Continued)

INFINITIVE	TRANSLATION	3RD PERSON PRESENT ➠
rennen	to run	**er rennt**
riechen	to smell	**er riecht**
ringen	to wrestle	**er ringt**
rinnen	to flow	**er rinnt**
rufen	to shout	**er ruft**
salzen	to salt	**er salzt**
saufen	to booze/to drink	**er säuft**
saugen	to suck	**er saugt**
schaffen[1]	to create	**er schafft**
scheiden	to separate *tr/intr*	**er scheidet**
scheinen	to seem/to shine	**er scheint**
schelten	to scold	**er schilt**
scheren	to shear	**er schert**
schieben	to shove	**er schiebt**
schießen	to shoot	**er schießt**
schlafen	to sleep	**er schläft**
schlagen	to hit	**er schlägt**
schleichen	to creep	**er schleicht**
schleifen	to grind	**er schleift**
schließen	to close	**er schließt**
schlingen	to wind	**er schlingt**
schmeißen	to fling	**er schmeißt**
schmelzen	to melt *tr/intr*	**er schmilzt**
schneiden	to cut	**er schneidet**
schreiben	to write	**er schreibt**
schreien	to shout	**er schreit**
schreiten	to stride	**er schreitet**
schweigen	to be silent	**er schweigt**

[1] **schaffen** meaning "to work hard/to manage" is weak:
schaffen, schafft, schaffte, hat geschafft

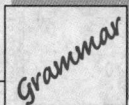

3RD PERSON IMPERFECT	PERFECT	IMPERFECT SUBJUNCTIVE
er rannte	**er ist gerannt**	**er rennte**
er roch	**er hat gerochen**	**er röche**
er rang	**er hat gerungen**	**er ränge**
er rann	**er ist geronnen**	**er ränne**
er rief	**er hat gerufen**	**er riefe**
er salzte	**er hat gesalzen**	**er salzte**
er soff	**er hat gesoffen**	**er söffe**
er sog	**er hat gesogen**	**er söge**
er schuf	**er hat geschaffen**	**er schüfe**
er schied	**er hat/ist geschieden**	**er schiede**
er schien	**er hat geschienen**	**er schiene**
er schalt	**er hat gescholten**	**er schölte**
er schor	**er hat geschoren**	**er schöre**
er schob	**er hat geschoben**	**er schöbe**
er schoss	**er hat geschossen**	**er schösse**
er schlief	**er hat geschlafen**	**er schliefe**
er schlug	**er hat geschlagen**	**er schlüge**
er schlich	**er ist geschlichen**	**er schliche**
er schliff	**er hat geschliffen**	**er schliffe**
er schloss	**er hat geschlossen**	**er schlösse**
er schlang	**er hat geschlungen**	**er schlänge**
er schmiss	**er hat geschmissen**	**er schmisse**
er schmolz	**er hat/ist geschmolzen**	**er schmölze**
er schnitt	**er hat geschnitten**	**er schnitte**
er schrieb	**er hat geschrieben**	**er schriebe**
er schrie	**er hat geschrie(e)n**	**er schriee**
er schritt	**er ist geschritten**	**er schritte**
er schwieg	**er hat geschwiegen**	**er schwiege**

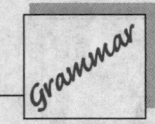

❒ Strong and Mixed Verbs (Continued)

INFINITIVE	TRANSLATION	3RD PERSON PRESENT ➠
schwellen[1]	to swell *intr*	**er schwillt**
schwimmen	to swim	**er schwimmt**
schwingen	to swing	**er schwingt**
schwören	to vow	**er schwört**
sehen	to see	**er sieht**
sein	to be	**er ist**
senden[2]	to send	**er sendet**
singen	to sing	**er singt**
sinken	to sink	**er sinkt**
sinnen	to ponder	**er sinnt**
sitzen	to sit	**er sitzt**
sollen	to be supposed to be	**er soll**
spalten	to split *tr/intr*	**er spaltet**
speien	to spew	**er speit**
spinnen	to spin	**er spinnt**
sprechen	to speak	**er spricht**
sprießen	to sprout	**er sprießt**
springen	to jump	**er springt**
stechen	to sting/to prick	**er sticht**
stehen	to stand	**er steht**
stehlen	to steal	**er stiehlt**
steigen	to climb	**er steigt**
sterben	to die	**er stirbt**
stinken	to stink	**er stinkt**
stoßen	to push	**er stößt**
streichen	to stroke/to wander	**er streicht**
streiten	to quarrel	**er streitet**

[1] **schwellen** is weak when used transitively:
schwellen, schwellt, schwellte, hat geschwellt

[2] **senden** meaning "to broadcast" is weak:
senden, sendet, sendete, hat gesendet

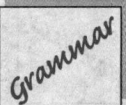

3RD PERSON IMPERFECT	PERFECT	IMPERFECT SUBJUNCTIVE
er schwoll	**er ist geschwollen**	**er schwölle**
er schwamm	**er ist geschwommen**	**er schwömme**
er schwang	**er hat geschwungen**	**er schwänge**
er schwor	**er hat geschworen**	**er schwüre**
er sah	**er hat gesehen**	**er sähe**
er war	**er ist gewesen**	**er wäre**
er sandte	**er hat gesandt**	**er sendete**
er sang	**er hat gesungen**	**er sänge**
er sank	**er ist gesunken**	**er sänke**
er sann	**er hat gesonnen**	**er sänne**
er saß	**er hat gesessen**	**er säße**
er sollte	**er hat gesollt/sollen**[1]	**er sollte**
er spaltete	**er hat/ist gespalten**	**er spaltete**
er spie	**er hat gespie(e)n**	**er spiee**
er spann	**er hat gesponnen**	**er spönne**
er sprach	**er hat gesprochen**	**er spräche**
er spross	**er ist gesprossen**	**er sprösse**
er sprang	**er ist gesprungen**	**er spränge**
er stach	**er hat gestochen**	**er stäche**
er stand	**er hat gestanden**	**er stünde**
er stahl	**er hat gestohlen**	**er stähle**
er stieg	**er ist gestiegen**	**er stiege**
er starb	**er ist gestorben**	**er stürbe**
er stank	**er hat gestunken**	**er stänke**
er stieß	**er hat/ist gestoßen**	**er stieße**
er strich	**er hat/ist gestrichen**	**er striche**
er stritt	**er hat gestritten**	**er stritte**

[1] The second (infinitive) form is used when combined with an infinitive construction (see p 56).

❒ Strong and Mixed Verbs (Continued)

INFINITIVE	TRANSLATION	3RD PERSON PRESENT ➠
tragen	to carry/to wear	**er trägt**
treffen	to meet	**er trifft**
treiben	to drive/to engage in	**er treibt**
treten	to kick/step	**er tritt**
trinken	to drink	**er trinkt**
tun	to do	**er tut**
verderben	to spoil/to go bad	**er verdirbt**
verdrießen	to irritate	**er verdrießt**
vergessen	to forget	**er vergisst**
verlieren	to lose	**er verliert**
vermeiden	to avoid	**er vermeidet**
verschwinden	to disappear	**er verschwindet**
verzeihen	to pardon	**er verzeiht**
wachsen	to grow	**er wächst**
waschen	to wash	**er wäscht**
weichen	to yield	**er weicht**
weisen	to point	**er weist**
wenden	to turn	**er wendet**
werben	to recruit	**er wirbt**
werden	to become	**er wird**
werfen	to throw	**er wirft**
wiegen[1]	to weigh	**er wiegt**
winden	to wind	**er windet**
wissen	to know	**er weiß**
wollen	to want to	**er will**
ziehen	to pull	**er zieht**
zwingen	to force	**er zwingt**

[1] **wiegen** meaning "to rock" is weak.

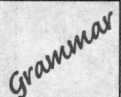

3RD PERSON IMPERFECT	PERFECT	IMPERFECT SUBJUNCTIVE
er trug	**er hat getragen**	**er trüge**
er traf	**er hat getroffen**	**er träfe**
er trieb	**er hat getrieben**	**er triebe**
er trat	**er hat/ist getreten**	**er träte**
er trank	**er hat getrunken**	**er tränke**
er tat	**er hat getan**	**er täte**
er verdarb	**er hat/ist verdorben**	**er verdürbe**
er verdross	**er hat verdrossen**	**er verdrösse**
er vergaß	**er hat vergessen**	**er vergäße**
er verlor	**er hat verloren**	**er verlöre**
er vermied	**er hat vermieden**	**er vermiede**
er verschwand	**er ist verschwunden**	**er verschwände**
er verzieh	**er hat verziehen**	**er verziehe**
er wuchs	**er ist gewachsen**	**er wüchse**
er wusch	**er hat gewaschen**	**er wüsche**
er wich	**er ist gewichen**	**er wiche**
er wies	**er hat gewiesen**	**er wiese**
er wandte	**er hat gewandt**	**er wendete**
er warb	**er hat geworben**	**er würbe**
er wurde	**er ist geworden**	**er würde**
er warf	**er hat geworfen**	**er würfe**
er wog	**er hat gewogen**	**er wöge**
er wand	**er hat gewunden**	**er wände**
er wusste	**er hat gewusst**	**er wüsste**
er wollte	**er hat gewollt/wollen**[1]	**er wollte**
er zog	**er hat gezogen**	**er zöge**
er zwang	**er hat gezwungen**	**er zwänge**

[1] The second (infinitive) form is used when combined with an infinitive construction (see p 56).

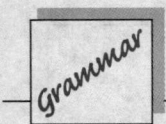

❒ The Declension of Nouns

In German, all nouns may be declined. This means that they may change their form according to their:

gender (i.e. masculine, feminine or neuter) → [1]

case (i.e. their function in the sentence) → [2]

number (i.e. singular or plural) → [3]

- Nearly all *feminine* nouns change in the *plural* form by adding -**n** or -**en**. Many *masculine* and *neuter* nouns also change → [4]

- *Masculine* and *neuter* nouns, with a few exceptions, add -**s** (-**s** or -**es** for nouns of one syllable) in the *genitive singular* (but see p 110) → [5]

- All nouns end in -**n** or -**en** in the *dative plural*. This is added to the nominative plural form, where this does not already end in -**n** → [6]

- A good dictionary will provide guidance on how to decline a noun:

  The nominative singular form is given in full, followed by the gender of the noun, then the genitive singular and nominative plural endings are shown where appropriate → [7]

- Adjectives used as nouns are declined as adjectives rather than nouns. Their declension endings are therefore dictated by the preceding article, as well as by number, case and gender (see p 140) → [8]

Examples

1

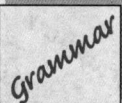

der Tisch (*masculine*)	the table
die Gabel (*feminine*)	the fork
das Mädchen (*neuter*)	the girl

2

des Tisches	of the table
auf den Tischen	on the tables

3

die Tische	the tables
die Gabeln	the forks
die Mädchen	the girls

4

	NOM SING	NOM PLURAL
MASC	**der Apfel**	**die Äpfel**
FEM	**die Schule**	**die Schulen**
NEUT	**das Kind**	**die Kinder**

5

	NOM SING	GEN SING
MASC	**der Apfel**	**des Apfels**
FEM	**die Schule**	**der Schule**
NEUT	**das Kind**	**des Kind(e)s**

6

	DAT PLURAL
MASC	**den Äpfeln**
FEM	**den Schulen**
NEUT	**den Kindern**

7 **Tiger** *m* **-s, -**

NOM SING	**der Tiger**	the tiger
GEN SING	**des Tigers**	of the tiger, the tiger's
NOM PLURAL	**die Tiger**	the tigers

8

der Angestellte	the employee
ein Angestellter	an employee
(die) Angestellten	(the) employees

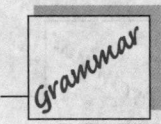

❐ The Gender of Nouns

In German a noun may be masculine, feminine or neuter. Gender is relatively unpredictable and has to be learned for each noun. This is best done by learning each noun with its definite article, i.e.

der Teppich
die Zeit
das Bild

The following are intended therefore only as guidelines in helping decide the gender of a word:

- Nouns denoting male people and animals are masculine → [1]
- Nouns denoting the female of the species, as shown on p 104, are feminine → [2]
- But nouns denoting an entire species can be of any gender → [3]
- Makes of cars identify with **der Wagen** and so are usually masculine → [4]
- Makes of aeroplane identify with **die Maschine** and so are usually feminine → [5]
- Seasons, months, days of the week, weather features and points of the compass are masculine → [6]
- Names of objects that perform an action are usually masculine → [7]
- Foreign nouns ending in **-ant**, **-ast**, **-ismus**, **-or** are masculine → [8]
- Nouns ending in **-ich**, **-ig**, **-ing**, **-ling** are masculine → [9]

Examples

1	**der Hörer**	(male) listener
	der Löwe	(male) lion
	der Onkel	uncle
	der Vetter	(male) cousin
2	**die Hörerin**	(female) listener
	die Löwin	lioness
	die Tante	aunt
	die Kusine	(female) cousin
3	**der Hund**	dog
	die Schlange	snake
	das Vieh	cattle
4	**der Mercedes**	Mercedes
	der VW	VW, Volkswagen
5	**die Boeing**	Boeing
	die Concorde	Concorde
6	**der Sommer**	summer
	der Winter	winter
	der August	August
	der Freitag	Friday
	der Wind	wind
	der Schnee	snow
	der Norden	north
	der Osten	east
7	**der Wecker**	alarm clock
	der Computer	computer
8	**der Ballast**	ballast
	der Chauvinismus	chauvinism
9	**der Essig**	vinegar
	der Schmetterling	butterfly

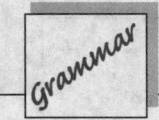

❒ The Gender of Nouns (Continued)

- Cardinal numbers are mostly feminine, but fractions are neuter → [1]

- Most nouns ending in -**e** are feminine → [2]

  ⚠ BUT: Male people or animals are masculine → [3]
  Nouns beginning with **Ge**- are normally neuter (*see below*)

- Nouns ending in -**heit**, -**keit**, -**schaft**, -**ung**, -**ei** are feminine → [4]

- Foreign nouns ending in -**anz**, -**enz**, -**ie**, -**ik**, -**ion**, -**tät**, -**ur** are generally feminine → [5]

- Nouns denoting the young of a species are neuter → [6]

- Infinitives used as nouns are neuter → [7]

- Most nouns beginning with **Ge**- are neuter → [8]

- -**chen** or -**lein** may be added to many words to give a diminutive form. These words are then neuter → [9]

  ⚠ NOTE: The vowel adds an umlaut where possible (i.e. on **a**, **o**, **u** or **au**) and a final -**e** is dropped before these endings → [10]

- Nouns ending in -**nis** or -**tum** are neuter → [11]

- Foreign nouns ending in -**at**, -**ett**, -**fon**, -**ma**, -**ment**, -**um**, -**ium** are mainly neuter → [12]

- Adjectives and participles may be used as masculine, feminine or neuter nouns (see p 148) → [13]

Examples

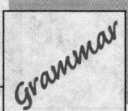

1	**Er hat eine Drei gekriegt**	He got a three (*mark*)
	ein Drittel davon	a third of it
2	**die Falte**	crease, wrinkle
	die Brücke	bridge
3	**der Löwe**	lion
	der Matrose	sailor
4	**die Eitelkeit**	vanity
	die Gewerkschaft	trade union
	die Scheidung	divorce
	die Druckerei	printing works
5	**die Distanz**	distance
	die Konkurrenz	rivalry
	die Theorie	theory
	die Panik	panic
	die Union	union
	die Elektrizität	electricity
	die Partitur	score (*musical*)
6	**das Baby**	baby
	das Kind	child
7	**das Schwimmen**	swimming
8	**das Geschirr**	crockery, dishes
	das Geschöpf	creature
	das Getreide	crop
9	**das Kindlein**	child
10	**das Bächlein** (*from* **der Bach**)	(small) stream
	das Kätzchen (*from* **die Katze**)	kitten
11	**das Ereignis**	event
	das Altertum	antiquity
12	**das Tablett**	tray
	das Telefon	telephone
	das Testament	will
	das Podium	platform, podium
13	**der Verwandte**	(male) relative
	die Verwandte	(female) relative
	das Gehackte	minced meat

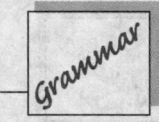

❐ The Gender of Nouns (Continued)

The following are some common exceptions to the gender guidelines shown on pp 100 to 103:

das Weib	woman, wife
die Person	person
die Waise	orphan
das Mitglied	member
das Genie	genius
die Wache	sentry, guard
das Restaurant	restaurant

The formation of feminine nouns

As in English, male and female forms are sometimes shown by two completely different words e.g.

mother/father
uncle/aunt etc → [1]

Where such separate forms do not exist, however, German often differentiates between male and female forms in one of two ways:

- The masculine form may sometimes be made feminine by the addition of -**in** in the singular and -**innen** in the plural → [2]

- An adjective may be used as a feminine noun (see p 148). It has feminine adjective endings which change according to the article which precedes it (see p 140) → [3]

Examples

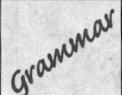

1	**der Vater** father	**die Mutter** mother
	der Bulle bull	**die Kuh** cow
	der Mann man	**die Frau** woman
2	**der Lehrer** (male) teacher	**die Lehrerin** (female) teacher
	der König king	**die Königin** queen
	der Hörer (male) listener	**die Hörerin** (female) listener

Liebe Hörer und Hörerinnen!
Dear listeners!

unsere Leser und Leserinnen
our readers

3

eine Deutsche
a German woman
Er ist mit einer Deutschen verheiratet
He is married to a German

die Abgeordnete
the female MP
Nur Abgeordnete durften dabei sein
Only MPs were allowed in

❒ The Gender of Nouns: Miscellaneous Points

Compound nouns

Compound nouns, i.e. nouns composed of two or more nouns put together, are a regular feature of German.

- They normally take their gender and declension from the last noun of the compound word → [1]
- Exceptions to this are compounds ending in **-mut**, **-scheu** and **-wort**, which do not always have the same gender as the last word when it stands alone → [2]

Nouns with more than one gender

- A few nouns have two genders, one of which may only be used in certain regions → [3]
- Other nouns have two genders, each of which gives the noun a different meaning → [4]

Abbreviations

- These take the gender of their principal noun → [5]

Examples

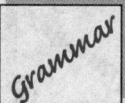

1	**die Armbanduhr** (*from* **die Uhr**)	wristwatch
	der Tomatensalat (*from* **der Salat**)	tomato salad
	der Fußballspieler (*from* **der Spieler**)	footballer
2	**der Mut**	courage
	die Armut	poverty
	die Demut	humility
	die Scheu	fear, shyness, timidity
	der Abscheu	repugnance, abhorrence
	das Wort	word
	die Antwort	reply
3	**das/der Marzipan**	marzipan
	das/der Keks	biscuit
4	**der Band**	volume, book
	das Band	ribbon, band, tape, bond
	der See	lake
	die See	sea
	der Leiter	leader, manager
	die Leiter	ladder
	der Tau	dew
	das Tau	rope, hawser
5	**der DGB** (*from* **der Deutsche Gewerkschaftsbund**)	the Federation of German Trade Unions
	die EU (*from* **die Europäische Union**)	the EU
	das AKW (*from* **das Atomkraftwerk**)	nuclear power station

❒ The Cases

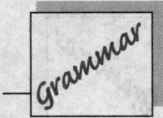

There are four grammatical *cases* - nominative, accusative, genitive and dative - which are generally shown by the form of the article used before the noun (see p 118).

The nominative case

- The nominative singular is the form shown in full in dictionary entries.

  The nominative plural is formed as described on p 98.

- The nominative case is used for:
  - the subject of a verb → [1]
  - the complement of **sein** or **werden** → [2]

The accusative case

- The noun in the accusative case usually has the same form as in the nominative → [3]

  Exceptions to this are "weak" masculine nouns (see p 115) and adjectives used as nouns (see p 148).

- It is used:
  - for the direct object of the verb → [4]
  - after those prepositions which always take the accusative case (see p 206 ff) → [5]
  - to show change of location after prepositions of place (see p 210) → [6]
  - in many expressions of time and place which do not contain a preposition → [7]
  - in certain fixed expressions → [8]

Examples

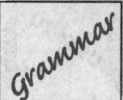

1 **Das Mädchen singt** The girl is singing

2 **Er ist ein guter Lehrer** He's a good teacher
Das wird ein Pullover It's going to be a jumper

3
das Lied	the song	(*nominative*)
das Lied	the song	(*accusative*)
der Wagen	the car	(*nominative*)
den Wagen	the car	(*accusative*)
die Dose	the tin	(*nominative*)
die Dose	the tin	(*accusative*)

4 **Er hat ein Lied gesungen** He sang a song

5 **für seine Freundin** for his girlfriend
ohne diesen Wagen without this car
durch das Rauchen through smoking

6 **in die Stadt** (*accusative*) into town
⚠ BUT:
in der Stadt (*dative*) in town

7 **Das macht sie jeden Donnerstag**
She does that every Thursday
Die Schule ist einen Kilometer entfernt
The school is a kilometre away

8 **Guten Abend!** Good evening!
Vielen Dank! Thank you very much!

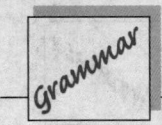

❒ The Cases (Continued)

The genitive case

- In the genitive singular, *masculine* and *neuter* nouns take endings as follows:
  1 **-s** is added to nouns ending in **-en**, **-el**, **-er** → [1]
  2 **-es** is added to nouns ending in **-tz**, **-sch**, **-st**, **-ss** or **-ß** → [2]
  3 For nouns of one syllable, either **-s** or **-es** may be added → [3]
- *Feminine singular* and all *plural* nouns have the same form as their nominative.
- The genitive is used:
  - to show possession → [3]
  - after prepositions taking the genitive (see p 212) → [4]
  - in expressions of time when the exact occasion is not specified → [5]

The dative case

- Singular nouns in the dative have the same form as in the nominative → [6]
- **-e** may be added to the dative singular of *masculine* and *neuter* nouns if the sentence rhythm needs it → [7]
  This **-e** is always used in certain set phrases → [8]
- Dative plural forms for all genders end in **-n** → [9]
  The only exceptions to this are some nouns of foreign origin that end in **-s** in all plural forms, including the dative plural (see p 114) → [10]
- The dative is used:
  - as the indirect object → [11]
  - after verbs taking the dative (see p 80) → [12]
  - after prepositions taking the dative (see p 202) → [13]
  - in certain idiomatic expressions → [14]
  - instead of the possessive adjective to refer to parts of the body and items of clothing (see p 122) → [15]

Examples

Grammar

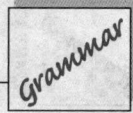

1	**der Wagen** car	→	**des Wagens** of the car
	das Rauchen smoking	→	**des Rauchens** of smoking
	der Computer computer	→	**des Computers** of the computer
	der Reiter rider	→	**des Reiters** of the rider
2	**der Sitz** seat; residence	→	**des Sitzes** of the seat/residence
	der Arzt doctor	→	**des Arztes** of the doctor
	das Schloss castle	→	**des Schlosses** of the castle

3 **das Kind** the child

Die Zähne des Kindes waren faul geworden

The child's teeth had decayed

Der Name des Kinds war ihm unbekannt

The child's name was not known to him

4	**wegen seiner Krankheit**	because of his illness
	trotz ihrer Bemühungen	despite her efforts
5	**eines Tages**	one day
6	**dem Wagen**	to the car
	der Frau	to the woman
	dem Mädchen	to the girl
7	**zu welchem Zwecke?**	to what purpose?
8	**nach Hause**	home

sich zu Tode trinken/arbeiten

to drink/work oneself to death

9	**mit den Anwälten**	with the lawyers
	nach den Kindern	after the children
10	SINGULAR	PLURAL
	das Auto	**die Autos**
	das Auto	**die Autos**
	des Autos	**der Autos**
	dem Auto	**den Autos**

11 **Er gab dem Mann das Buch**

He gave the man the book

12	**Sie half ihrer Mutter**	She helped her mother
13	**Nach dem Essen ...**	After eating ...
14	**Mir ist kalt**	I'm cold

15 **Ich habe mir die Hände gewaschen**

I've washed my hands

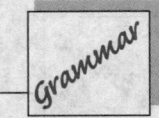

❐ The Formation of Plurals

The following pages show full noun declensions in all their singular and plural forms.
Those nouns shown represent the most common types of plural.

- Most feminine nouns add **-n**, **-en** or **-nen** to form their plurals:

	SINGULAR	PLURAL
NOM	**die Frau**	**die Frauen**
ACC	**die Frau**	**die Frauen**
GEN	**der Frau**	**der Frauen**
DAT	**der Frau**	**den Frauen**

- Many nouns have no plural ending.
  These are mainly masculine or neuter nouns ending in **-en**, **-er**, **-el**.
  An umlaut is sometimes added to the vowel in the plural forms:

	SINGULAR	PLURAL
NOM	**der Onkel**	**die Onkel**
ACC	**den Onkel**	**die Onkel**
GEN	**des Onkels**	**der Onkel**
DAT	**dem Onkel**	**den Onkeln**

	SINGULAR	PLURAL
NOM	**der Apfel**	**die Äpfel**
ACC	**den Apfel**	**die Äpfel**
GEN	**des Apfels**	**der Äpfel**
DAT	**dem Apfel**	**die Äpfeln**

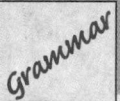

❒ The Formation of Plurals (Continued)

◆ Many nouns form their plurals by adding **¨e**:

	SINGULAR	PLURAL
NOM	**der Stuhl**	**die Stühle**
ACC	**den Stuhl**	**die Stühle**
GEN	**des Stuhl(e)s**	**der Stühle**
DAT	**dem Stuhl**	**den Stühlen**

	SINGULAR	PLURAL
NOM	**die Angst**	**die Ängste**
ACC	**die Angst**	**die Ängste**
GEN	**der Angst**	**der Ängste**
DAT	**der Angst**	**den Ängsten**

◆ Masculine and neuter nouns often add **-e** in the plural:

	SINGULAR	PLURAL
NOM	**das Schicksal**	**die Schicksale**
ACC	**das Schicksal**	**die Schicksale**
GEN	**des Schicksals**	**der Schicksale**
DAT	**dem Schicksal**	**den Schicksalen**

◆ Masculine and neuter nouns sometimes add **¨er** or **-er**:

	SINGULAR	PLURAL
NOM	**das Dach**	**die Dächer**
ACC	**das Dach**	**die Dächer**
GEN	**des Dach(e)s**	**der Dächer**
DAT	**dem Dach**	**den Dächern**

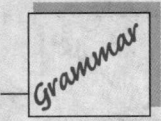

The Formation of Plurals (Continued)

Some unusual plurals

SINGULAR	TRANSLATION	PLURAL
das Ministerium	department	**die Ministerien**
das Prinzip	principle	**die Prinzipien**
das Thema	theme, topic, subject	**die Themen**
das Drama	drama	**die Dramen**
der Firma	firm	**die Firmen**
das Konto	bank account	**die Konten**
das Risiko	risk	**die Risiken**
das Komma	comma/decimal point	**die Kommas** *or* **Kommata**
das Baby	baby	**die Babys**
der Klub	club	**die Klubs**
der Streik	strike	**die Streiks**
der Park	park	**die Parks**
der Chef	boss, chief, head	**die Chefs**
der Israeli	Israeli	**die Israelis**
das Restaurant	restaurant	**die Restaurants**
das Bonbon	sweet	**die Bonbons**
das Hotel	hotel	**die Hotels**
das Niveau	standard, level	**die Niveaus**

German singular/English plural nouns

Some nouns are always plural in English, but singular in German.

- Some of the most common examples are:

  eine Brille glasses, spectacles
  eine Schere scissors
  eine Hose trousers

- They are only used in the plural in German to mean more than one pair, e.g. **zwei Hosen** *two pairs of trousers*

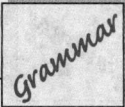

❒ The Declension of Nouns

"Weak" masculine nouns

Some masculine nouns have a weak declension, which means that in all cases apart from the nominative singular, they end in **-en** or, if the word ends in a vowel, in **-n**.

- The dictionary will often show such nouns as:
  Junge *m* **-n**, **-n** boy
  Held *m* **-en**, **-en** hero

- Weak masculine nouns are declined as follows:

	SINGULAR	PLURAL
NOM	**der Junge**	**die Jungen**
ACC	**den Jungen**	**die Jungen**
GEN	**des Jungen**	**der Jungen**
DAT	**dem Jungen**	**den Jungen**

- Masculine nouns falling into this category include:
  - those ending in **-og(e)** referring to males:
    der Psychologe, der Geologe, der Astrologe
  - those ending in **-aph** (*in many cases now spelt* **-af**) or **-oph**:
    der Graph, der Paragraf, der Philosoph
  - those ending in **-nom** referring to males:
    der Astronom, der Gastronom
  - those ending in **-ant**:
    der Elefant, der Diamant
  - those ending in **-t** referring to males:
    der Astronaut, der Komponist, der Architekt
  - miscellaneous others:
    der Bauer, der Chirurg, der Franzose, der Katholik, der Kollege, der Mensch, der Ochse, der Spatz

- **der Name** (*name*) has a different ending in the genitive singular, **-ns**: **des Namens**. Otherwise it is the same as **der Junge** shown above. Others in this category are: **der Buchstabe, der Funke, der Gedanke, der Glaube**.

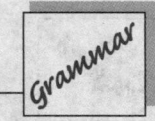

❒ The Declension of Proper Nouns

- Names of people and places add **-s** in the genitive singular unless they are preceded by the definite article or a demonstrative → [1]
- Where proper names end in a sibilant (**-s**, **-sch**, **-ss**, **-ß**, **-x**, **-z**, **-tz**) and this makes the genitive form with **-s** almost impossible to pronounce, they are best avoided altogether by using **von** followed by the dative case → [2]
- Personal names can be given diminutive forms if desired. These may be used as a sign of affection as well as with diminutive meaning → [3]
- **Herr** (*Mr*) is always declined where it occurs as part of a proper name → [4]
- When articles or adjectives form part of a proper name (e.g. in the names of books, plays, hotels, restaurants etc), these are declined in the normal way (see p 118 and 140) → [5]
- Surnames usually form their plurals by adding **-s**, unless they end in a sibilant, in which case they sometimes add **-ens**. They are often preceded by the definite article → [6]

Nouns of measurement and quantity

- These usually remain singular, even if preceded by a plural number → [7]
- The substance which they measure follows in the same case as the noun of quantity, and not in the genitive case as in English → [8]

Examples

1	**Annas Buch**	Anna's book
	Klaras Mantel	Klara's coat
	die Werke Goethes	Goethe's works

⚠ BUT: **die Versenkung der Bismarck**
the sinking of the Bismarck

2	**das Buch von Hans**	Hans' book
	die Werke von Marx	the works of Marx
	die Freundin von Klaus	Klaus's girlfriend
3	**von deinem Sabinchen**	from your Sabine

Das kleine Kläuschen hat uns dann ein Lied gesungen
Then little Klaus sang us a song

4	**an Herrn Schmidt**	to Mr Schmidt
	Sehr geehrte Herren	Dear Sirs
5	**im Weißen Schwan**	in the White Swan

Er hat den „Zauberberg" schon gelesen
He has already read "The Magic Mountain"

nach Karl dem Großen	after Charlemagne

6 **Die Schmidts haben uns eingeladen**
The Schmidts have invited us
Die Zeißens haben uns eingeladen
Mr and Mrs Zeiß have invited us

7 **Möchten Sie zwei Stück?**
Would you like two?

8 **Er wollte zwei Kilo Kartoffeln**
He wanted two kilos of potatoes
Sie hat drei Tassen Kaffee getrunken
She drank three cups of coffee
Drei Glas Weißwein, bitte!
Three glasses of white wine please

❒ The Definite Article

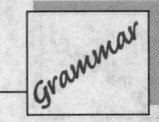

In English the definite article *the* always keeps the same form:

the book
the books
with *the* books

In German, however, the definite article has many forms:

- In its singular form it changes for masculine, feminine and neuter nouns → 1

- In its plural forms it is the same for all genders → 2

- The definite article is also used to show the function of the noun in the sentence by showing which case it is.

  There are four cases, as explained more fully on p 108:

  1 *nominative* for the subject or complement of the verb → 3
  2 *accusative* for the object of the verb and after some prepositions → 4
  3 *genitive* to show possession and after some prepositions → 5
  4 *dative* for an indirect object (*to* or *for*) and after some prepositions and certain verbs → 6

- The forms of the definite article are as follows:

	SINGULAR			PLURAL
	MASC	FEM	NEUT	ALL GENDERS
NOM	**der**	**die**	**das**	**die**
ACC	**den**	**die**	**das**	**die** → 7
GEN	**des**	**der**	**des**	**der**
DAT	**dem**	**der**	**dem**	**den**

Examples

Grammar

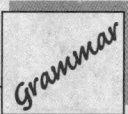

1 MASCULINE: **der Mann** the man
der Wagen the car
FEMININE: **die Frau** the wife/woman
die Blume the flower
NEUTER: **das Ding** the thing
das Mädchen the girl

2 **die Männer** the men
die Frauen the women
die Dinge the things

3 **Der Mann ist jung** The man is young
Die Frau/das Kind ist jung The woman/the child is young

4 **Ich kenne den Mann/die Frau/das Kind**
I know the man/the woman/the child

5 **der Kopf des Mannes/der Frau/des Kindes**
the man's/woman's/child's head
wegen des Mannes/der Frau/des Kindes
because of the man/the woman/the child

6 **Ich gab es dem Mann/der Frau/dem Kind**
I gave it to the man/to the woman/to the child

7 SINGULAR

	MASC	FEM	NEUT
NOM	**der Mann**	**die Frau**	**das Kind**
ACC	**den Mann**	**die Frau**	**das Kind**
GEN	**des Mann(e)s**	**der Frau**	**des Kind(e)s**
DAT	**dem Mann**	**der Frau**	**dem Kind**

PLURAL

	MASC	FEM	NEUT
NOM	**die Männer**	**die Frauen**	**die Kinder**
ACC	**die Männer**	**die Frauen**	**die Kinder**
GEN	**der Männer**	**der Frauen**	**der Kinder**
DAT	**den Männern**	**den Frauen**	**den Kindern**

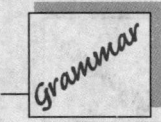

❒ Uses of the Definite Article

When to use and when not to use the definite article in German is one of the most difficult areas for the learner. The following guidelines show where German practice varies from English.

The definite article is used with:

- abstract and other nouns where something is being referred to as a whole or as a general idea → [1]

  Where these nouns are quantified or modified, the article is not used → [2]

- the genitive, unless the noun is a proper name or is acting as a proper name → [3]
- occasionally with proper names to make the sex or case clearer → [4]
- always with proper names preceded by an adjective → [5]
- sometimes with proper names in familiar contexts or for slight emphasis → [6]
- with masculine and feminine countries and districts → [7]
- with geographical names preceded by an adjective → [8]
- with names of seasons → [9]
- often with meals → [10]
- with the names of roads → [11]

Examples

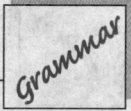

1	**Das Leben ist schön**	Life is wonderful
2	**Es braucht Mut**	It needs (some) courage
	Gibt es dort Leben?	Is there (any) life there?
3	**das Auto des Lehrers**	the teacher's car
	Günters Auto	Günter's car
	Muttis Auto	Mummy's car

4 **Er hat es Frau Lehmann gegeben**
Er hat es der Frau Lehmann gegeben
He gave it to Frau Lehmann

5 **Der alte Herr Brockhaus ist gestorben**
Old Mr Brockhaus has died

6 **Ich habe heute den Christoph gesehen**
I saw Christoph today
Du hast es aber nicht der Petra geschenkt!
You haven't given it to *Petra*!

7	**Deutschland is sehr schön**	Germany is very beautiful
	Die Schweiz ist auch schön	Switzerland is also lovely

8 **im (= in dem) heutigen Deutschland**
in today's Germany

9 **Im (= in dem) Sommer gehen wir schwimmen**
We go swimming in summer
Der Winter kommt bald
Soon it will be winter

10 **Das Abendessen wird ab acht Uhr serviert**
Dinner is served from eight o'clock
Was gibts zum (= zu dem) Mittagessen?
What's for lunch?
⚠ BUT:
Um acht Uhr ist Frühstück
Breakfast is at eight o'clock

11 **Sie wohnt jetzt in der Geisener Straße**
She lives in Geisener Road now

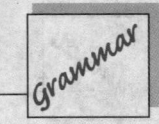

❐ Uses of the Definite Article (Continued)

- with months of the year except after **seit/nach/vor** → [1]

- instead of the possessive adjective to refer to parts of the body and items of clothing → [2]
  A reflexive pronoun or noun in the dative case is used if it is necessary to clarify to whom the parts of the body belong → [3]

- in expressions of price, to mean *each/per/a* → [4]

- with certain common expressions → [5]

Other uses

- The definite article can be used with demonstrative meaning → [6]

- After certain prepositions, forms of the definite article can be shortened (see p 198 ff).
  Some of these forms are best used in informal situations → [7]
  Others are commonly and correctly used in formal contexts → [1]
  → [5]
  → [8]

Omitting the definite article

The definite article may be omitted in German:

- in certain set expressions → [9]

- in *preposition* + *adjective* + *noun* combinations → [10]
  For the declension of adjectives without the article see p 142.

Examples

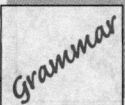

1 **Wir fahren im (= in dem) September weg**
We are going away in September
Wir sind seit September hier
We have been here since September

2 **Er legte den Hut auf den Tisch**
He laid his hat on the table
Ich drücke Ihnen die Daumen
I'm keeping my fingers crossed for you

3 **Er hat sich die Hände schon gewaschen**
He has already washed his hands
Er hat dem Kind schon die Hände gewaschen
He has already washed the child's hands

4	**Die kosten ...**	They cost ...
	... fünf Mark das Pfund	... five marks a pound
	... sechs Mark das Stück	... six marks each
5	**in die Stadt fahren**	to go into town
	zur (= zu der) Schule gehen	to go to school
	mit der Post	by post
	mit dem Zug/Bus/Auto	by train/bus/car
	im (= in dem) Gefängnis	in prison

6 **Du willst *das* Buch lesen!**
You want to read *that* book!

7 **für das ➤ fürs** **vor dem ➤ vorm** **um das ➤ ums** *etc*

8 **an dem ➤ am** **zu dem ➤ zum** **zu der ➤ zur** *etc*

9	**von Beruf**	by profession
	nach Wunsch	as desired
	Nachrichten hören	to listen to the news
10	**Mit gebeugtem Rücken ...**	Bending his back, ...

❒ The Indefinite Article

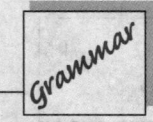

Like the definite article, the form of the indefinite article varies depending on the gender and case of the noun → [1]

It has no plural forms → [2]

The indefinite article is declined as follows:

	MASC	FEM	NEUT	
NOM	**ein**	**eine**	**ein**	
ACC	**einen**	**eine**	**ein**	→ [3]
GEN	**eines**	**einer**	**eines**	
DAT	**einem**	**einer**	**einem**	

◆ The indefinite article is omitted in the following:

- descriptions of people by profession, religion, nationality etc → [4]

- ⚠ BUT: Note that the article is included when an adjective precedes the noun → [5]

- in certain fixed expressions → [6]

- after **als** (*as a*) → [7]

Examples

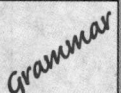

1 **Da ist ein Auto** There's a car
Er hat eine Wohnung He has a flat
Sie gab es einem Kind She gave it to a child

2 **Autos sind in letzter Zeit teurer geworden**
Cars have become more expensive recently

3

	SINGULAR		
	MASC	FEM	NEUT
NOM	**ein Mann**	**eine Frau**	**ein Kind**
ACC	**einen Mann**	**eine Frau**	**ein Kind**
GEN	**eines Mann(e)s**	**einer Frau**	**eines Kind(e)s**
DAT	**einem Mann**	**einer Frau**	**einem Kind**

4 **Sie ist Kinderärztin** She's a paediatrician
Sie ist Deutsche She's (a) German

5 **Sie ist eine sehr geschickte Kinderärztin**
She's a very clever paediatrician

6 **Es ist Geschmacksache** It's a question of taste
Tatsache ist … It's a fact …

7 **Als Ausländer ist er hier nicht wahlberechtigt**
As a foreigner he doesn't have the vote here

… und ich rede nun als Vater von vier Kindern
… and I'm talking now as a father of four

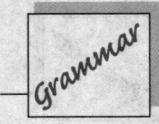

❒ The Indefinite Article (Continued)

In German, a separate negative form of the indefinite article exists. It is declined exactly like **ein** in the singular, and also has plural forms:

	SINGULAR			PLURAL
	MASC	FEM	NEUT	ALL GENDERS
NOM	**kein**	**keine**	**kein**	**keine**
ACC	**keinen**	**keine**	**kein**	**keine**
GEN	**keines**	**keiner**	**keines**	**keiner**
DAT	**keinem**	**keiner**	**keinem**	**keinen**

→ [1]

- It has the meaning *no/not a/not one/not any* → [2]

- It is used even where the equivalent *positive* phrase has no article → [3]

- It is also used in many idiomatic expressions → [4]

- **Nicht ein** may be used instead of **kein** where the **ein** is to be emphasized → [5]

1

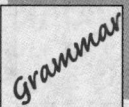

	SINGULAR		
	MASC	FEM	NEUT
NOM	**kein Mann**	**keine Frau**	**kein Kind**
ACC	**keinen Mann**	**keine Frau**	**kein Kind**
GEN	**keines Mann(e)s**	**keiner Frau**	**keines Kind(e)s**
DAT	**keinem Mann**	**keiner Frau**	**keinem Kind**

	PLURAL		
	MASC	FEM	NEUT
NOM	**keine Männer**	**keine Frauen**	**keine Kinder**
ACC	**keine Männer**	**keine Frauen**	**keine Kinder**
GEN	**keiner Männer**	**keiner Frauen**	**keiner Kinder**
DAT	**keinen Männern**	**keinen Frauen**	**keinen Kindern**

2

Er hatte keine Geschwister He had no brothers or sisters
Ich sehe keinen Unterschied I don't see any difference
Das ist keine richtige Antwort That's no answer
Kein Mensch hat es gesehen Not one person has seen it

3

Er hatte Angst davor He was frightened
Er hatte keine Angst davor He wasn't frightened

4

Er hatte kein Geld mehr All his money was gone
Es waren keine drei Monate vergangen, als ...
It was less than three months later that ...
Es hat mich keine zehn Euro gekostet
It cost me less than ten Euro

5

Nicht ein Kind hat es singen können
Not *one* child could sing it

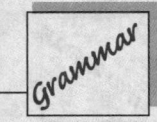

❒ Words declined like the Definite Article

The following have endings similar to those of the definite article shown on p 118:

aller, alle, alles	all, all of them
beide	both (*plural only*)
dieser, diese, dieses	this, this one, these
einiger, einige, einiges	some, a few, a little
irgendwelcher, -e, -es	some or other
jeder, jede, jedes	each, each one, every
jener, jene, jenes	that, that one, those
mancher, manche, manches	many a/some
sämtliche	all, entire (*usually plural*)
solcher, solche, solches	such/such a
welcher, welche, welches	which, which one

- These words can be used as:
  - articles → 1
  - pronouns → 2

- They have the following endings:

	SINGULAR			PLURAL
	MASC	FEM	NEUT	ALL GENDERS
NOM	**-er**	**-e**	**-es**	**-e**
ACC	**-en**	**-e**	**-es**	**-e**
GEN	**-es/-en**	**-er**	**-es/-en**	**-er**
DAT	**-em**	**-er**	**-em**	**-en**

Example declensions are shown on p 134 ff.

- **einiger** and **irgendwelcher** use the **-en** genitive ending before masculine or neuter nouns ending in **-s** → 3
  jeder, welcher, mancher and **solcher** may also do so → 4

Examples

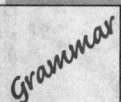

1 **Dieser Mann kommt aus Südamerika**
This man comes from South America

Er geht jeden Tag ins Büro
He goes to the office every day

Manche Leute können das nicht
A good many people can't do it

2 **Willst du diesen?**
Do you want this one?

In manchem hat er recht
He's right about some things

Man kann ja nicht alles wissen
You can't know everything

Es gibt manche, die keinen Alkohol mögen
There are some people who don't like alcohol

3 **wegen irgendwelchen Geredes**
on account of some gossip

4 **der Besitz solchen Reichtums**
the possession of such wealth

trotz jeden Versuchs
despite all attempts

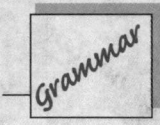

❐ Words declined like the Definite Article (Continued)

- Adjectives following these words have the weak declension (see p 140) → [1]

  Exceptions are the plural forms of **einige**, which are followed by the strong declension (see p 142) → [2]

Further points

- **Solcher**, **beide**, **sämtliche** may be used after another article or possessive adjective. They then take weak (see p 140) or mixed (see p 142) adjectival endings, as appropriate → [3]

- Although **beide** generally has plural forms only, one singular form does exist. This is in the neuter nominative and accusative: **beides** → [4]

- **Dies** often replaces the nominative and accusative **dieses** and **diese** when used as a pronoun → [5]

- A fixed form **all** exists which is used together with other articles or possessive pronouns → [6]

- **Ganz** can also be used to replace both the inflected form **aller/alle/alles** and the uninflected **all das/dieses/sein** *etc.*

  It is declined as a normal adjective (see p 140) → [7]

  It must be used with collective nouns, in time phrases and geographical references → [8]

Examples

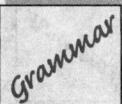

1 **dieses alte Auto**
this old car
aus irgendwelchem dummen Grund
for some stupid reason or other
welche neuen Waren?
which new goods?

2 **Dies sind einige gute Freunde von mir**
These are some good friends of mine

3 **Ein solches Kleid habe ich früher auch getragen**
I used to wear a dress like that too
Diese beiden Männer haben es gesehen
Both of these men have seen it

4 **Beides ist richtig**
Both are right
Sie hat beides genommen
She took both

5 **Hast du dies schon gelesen?**
Have you already read this?
Dies sind meine neuen Sachen
These are my new things

6 **All sein Mut war verschwunden**
All his courage had vanished
mit all diesem Geld
with all this money

7 **mit dem ganzen Geld**
with all the money

8 **die ganze Gesellschaft**
the entire company
Es hat den ganzen Tag geschneit
It snowed the whole day long
Im ganzen Land gab es keinen besseren Wein
There wasn't a better wine in the whole country

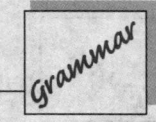

❒ Words declined like the Definite Article (Continued)

- **derjenige/diejenige/dasjenige** (*the one, those*) is declined exactly as the definite article plus an adjective in the weak declension (see p 140) → [1]

- **derselbe/dieselbe/dasselbe** (*the same, the same one*) is declined in the same way as **derjenige** → [2]

After prepositions, however, the normal contracted forms of the definite article are used for the appropriate parts of **derselbe** → [3]

1

SINGULAR

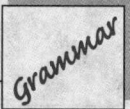

MASC	FEM	NEUT
derjenige Mann	**die**jenige Frau	**das**jenige Kind
denjenig**en** Mann	**die**jenige Frau	**das**jenige Kind
desjenig**en** Mann(e)s	**der**jenig**en** Frau	**des**jenig**en** Kind(e)s
demjenig**en** Mann	**der**jenig**en** Frau	**dem**jenig**en** Kind

PLURAL

MASC	FEM	NEUT
diejenig**en** Männer	**die**jenig**en** Frauen	**die**jenig**en** Kinder
diejenig**en** Männer	**die**jenig**en** Frauen	**die**jenig**en** Kinder
derjenig**en** Männer	**der**jenig**en** Frauen	**der**jenig**en** Kinder
denjenig**en** Männern	**den**jenig**en** Frauen	**den**jenig**en** Kindern

2

SINGULAR

MASC	FEM	NEUT
derselbe Mann	**die**selbe Frau	**das**selbe Kind
denselb**en** Mann	**die**selbe Frau	**das**selbe Kind
desselb**en** Mann(e)s	**der**selb**en** Frau	**des**selb**en** Kind(e)s
demselb**en** Mann	**der**selb**en** Frau	**dem**selb**en** Kind

PLURAL

MASC	FEM	NEUT
dieselb**en** Männer	**die**selb**en** Frauen	**die**selb**en** Kinder
dieselb**en** Männer	**die**selb**en** Frauen	**die**selb**en** Kinder
derselb**en** Männer	**der**selb**en** Frauen	**der**selb**en** Kinder
denselb**en** Männern	**den**selb**en** Frauen	**den**selb**en** Kindern

3

zur selben (= zu derselben) Zeit	at the same time
im selben (= in demselben) Zimmer	in the same room

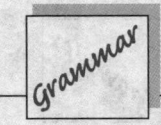

❐ Words declined like the Definite Article (Continued)

Sample declensions in full

◆ **dieser, diese, dieses** this, this one:

	SINGULAR		
	MASC	FEM	NEUT
NOM	dies**er** Mann	dies**e** Frau	dies**es** Kind
ACC	dies**en** Mann	dies**e** Frau	dies**es** Kind
GEN	dies**es** Mann(e)s	dies**er** Frau	dies**es** Kind(e)s
DAT	dies**em** Mann	dies**er** Frau	dies**em** Kind

	PLURAL		
	MASC	FEM	NEUT
NOM	dies**e** Männer	dies**e** Frauen	dies**e** Kinder
ACC	dies**e** Männer	dies**e** Frauen	dies**e** Kinder
GEN	dies**er** Männer	dies**er** Frauen	dies**er** Kinder
DAT	dies**en** Männern	dies**en** Frauen	dies**en** Kindern

◆ **jener, jene, jenes** that, that one:

	SINGULAR		
	MASC	FEM	NEUT
NOM	jen**er** Mann	jen**e** Frau	jen**es** Kind
ACC	jen**en** Mann	jen**e** Frau	jen**es** Kind
GEN	jen**es** Mann(e)s	jen**er** Frau	jen**es** Kind(e)s
DAT	jen**em** Mann	jen**er** Frau	jen**em** Kind

	PLURAL		
	MASC	FEM	NEUT
NOM	jen**e** Männer	jen**e** Frauen	jen**e** Kinder
ACC	jen**e** Männer	jen**e** Frauen	jen**e** Kinder
GEN	jen**er** Männer	jen**er** Frauen	jen**er** Kinder
DAT	jen**en** Männern	jen**en** Frauen	jen**en** Kindern

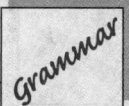

- **jeder, jede, jedes** each, every, everybody:

	SINGULAR		
	MASC	FEM	NEUT
NOM	jed**er** Wagen	jed**e** Minute	jed**es** Bild
ACC	jed**en** Wagen	jed**e** Minute	jed**es** Bild
GEN	jed**es** Wagens (jed**en** Wagens)	jed**er** Minute	jed**es** Bild(e)s (jed**en** Bild(e)s)
DAT	jed**em** Wagen	jed**er** Minute	jed**em** Bild

- **welcher, welche, welches** which?, which:

	SINGULAR		
	MASC	FEM	NEUT
NOM	welch**er** Preis	welch**e** Sorte	welch**es** Mädchen
ACC	welch**en** Preis	welch**e** Sorte	welch**es** Mädchen
GEN	welch**es** Preises (welch**en** Preises)	welch**er** Sorte	welch**es** Mädchens (welch**en** Mädchens)
DAT	welch**em** Preis	welch**er** Sorte	welch**em** Mädchen

	PLURAL		
	MASC	FEM	NEUT
NOM	welch**e** Preise	welch**e** Sorten	welch**e** Mädchen
ACC	welch**e** Preise	welch**e** Sorten	welch**e** Mädchen
GEN	welch**er** Preise	welch**er** Sorten	welch**er** Mädchen
DAT	welch**en** Preisen	welch**en** Sorten	welch**en** Mädchen

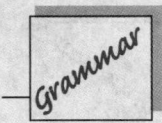

❒ Words declined like the Indefinite Article

The following have the same declension pattern as the indefinite articles **ein** and **kein** (see pp 124 and 126):

The possessive adjectives

mein	my → [1]
dein	your (*singular familiar*)
sein	his/its
ihr	her/its → [2]
unser	our
euer	your (*plural familiar*)
ihr	their → [2]
Ihr	your (*polite singular and plural*)

These words are declined as follows:

	SINGULAR			PLURAL
	MASC	FEM	NEUT	ALL GENDERS
NOM	—	**-e**	—	**-e**
ACC	**-en**	**-e**	—	**-e**
GEN	**-es**	**-er**	**-es**	**-er**
DAT	**-em**	**-er**	**-em**	**-en**

◆ Adjectives following these determiners have the mixed declension forms (see p 142), e.g.

sein altes Auto his old car

◆ **irgendein** (*some ... or other*) also follows this declension pattern in the singular.

Its plural form is **irgendwelche** (see p 128).

137 Examples

Grammar

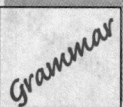

1 **mein, meine, mein** my:

	SINGULAR		
	MASC	FEM	NEUT
NOM	mein Bruder	mein**e** Schwester	mein Kind
ACC	mein**en** Bruder	mein**e** Schwester	mein Kind
GEN	mein**es** Bruders	mein**er** Schwester	mein**es** Kind(e)s
DAT	mein**em** Bruder	mein**er** Schwester	mein**em** Kind

	PLURAL		
	MASC	FEM	NEUT
NOM	mein**e** Brüder	mein**e** Schwestern	mein**e** Kinder
ACC	mein**e** Brüder	mein**e** Schwestern	mein**e** Kinder
GEN	mein**er** Brüder	mein**er** Schwestern	mein**er** Kinder
DAT	mein**en** Brüdern	mein**en** Schwestern	mein**en** Kindern

2 **ihr, ihre, ihr** her/its/their:

	SINGULAR		
	MASC	FEM	NEUT
NOM	ihr Bruder	ihr**e** Schwester	ihr Kind
ACC	ihr**en** Bruder	ihr**e** Schwester	ihr Kind
GEN	ihr**es** Bruders	ihr**er** Schwester	ihr**es** Kind(e)s
DAT	ihr**em** Bruder	ihr**er** Schwester	ihr**em** Kind

	PLURAL		
	MASC	FEM	NEUT
NOM	ihr**e** Brüder	ihr**e** Schwestern	ihr**e** Kinder
ACC	ihr**e** Brüder	ihr**e** Schwestern	ihr**e** Kinder
GEN	ihr**er** Brüder	ihr**er** Schwestern	ihr**er** Kinder
DAT	ihr**en** Brüdern	ihr**en** Schwestern	ihr**en** Kindern

❒ Indefinite Adjectives

These are adjectives used in place of, or together with, an article:

ander	other, different
mehrere (*plural only*)	several
viel	much, a lot, many
wenig	little, a little, few

- After the definite article and words declined like it (see p 128) these adjectives have weak declension endings → 1
  Adjectives following the indefinite adjectives are also weak → 2

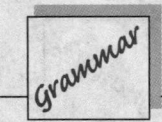

- After **ein**, **kein**, **irgendein** or the possessive adjectives they have mixed declension endings → 3
  Adjectives following the indefinite adjectives are also mixed in declension → 4

- When used without a preceding article, **ander** and **mehrere** have strong declension endings → 5

- When used without a preceding article, **viel** and **wenig** may be declined as follows, though in the singular they are usually undeclined → 6

	SINGULAR			PLURAL
	MASC	FEM	NEUT	ALL GENDERS
NOM	**viel**	**viel**	**viel**	**viele**
ACC	**viel**	**viel**	**viel**	**viele**
GEN	**vielen**	**vieler**	**vielen**	**vieler**
DAT	**viel(em)**	**vieler**	**viel(em)**	**vielen**

- Any adjective following **viel** or **wenig** has strong endings → 7

Examples

1 **Die wenigen Kuchen, die übrig geblieben waren …**
The few cakes which were left over …

2 **Die vielen interessanten Ideen, die ans Licht kamen**
The many interesting ideas which came to light

3 **Ihr anderes Auto ist in der Werkstatt**
Their other car is in for repair

4 **Mehrere gute Freunde waren gekommen**
Several good friends had come

5 **Mehrere prominente Gäste sind eingeladen**
Various prominent guests are invited

Er war anderer Meinung
He was of a different opinion

6 **Es wurde viel Bier getrunken**
They drank a lot of beer

Sie essen nur wenig Obst
They don't eat a lot of fruit

7 **Er kaufte viele billige Sachen**
He bought a lot of cheap things

Es wurde viel gutes Bier getrunken
They drank a lot of good beer

Sie essen wenig frisches Obst
They don't eat a lot of fresh fruit

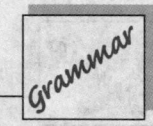

❒ The Declension of Adjectives

There are two ways of using adjectives:

1 They can be used **attributively**, where the adjective comes before the noun: *the new book*

2 They can be used **non-attributively**, where the adjective comes after the verb: *the book is new*

◆ In English the adjective does not change its form no matter how it is used.

In German, however, adjectives remain unchanged only when used non-attributively → [1]

Used attributively, adjectives change to show the number, gender and case of the noun they precede → [2]

The endings also depend on the nature of the article which precedes them → [3]

There are three sets of endings:

1) The weak declension

These are the endings used after **der** and those words declined like it as shown on p 128 → [4]

	SINGULAR			PLURAL
	MASC	FEM	NEUT	ALL GENDERS
NOM	**-e**	**-e**	**-e**	**-en**
ACC	**-en**	**-e**	**-e**	**-en**
GEN	**-en**	**-en**	**-en**	**-en**
DAT	**-en**	**-en**	**-en**	**-en**

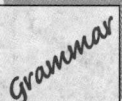

1 **Das Buch ist neu**
The book is new
Der Vortrag war sehr langweilig
The lecture was very boring

2 **Das neue Buch ist da**
The new book has arrived
Während des langweiligen Vortrags sind wir alle eingeschlafen
We all fell asleep during the boring lecture

3 **der junge Rechtsanwalt**
the young lawyer
ein junger Rechtsanwalt
a young lawyer
manch junger Rechtsanwalt
many a young lawyer

4

SINGULAR			
	MASC	FEM	NEUT
NOM	der alt**e** Mann	die alt**e** Frau	das alt**e** Haus
ACC	den alt**en** Mann	die alt**e** Frau	das alt**e** Haus
GEN	des alt**en** Mann(e)s	der alt**en** Frau	des alt**en** Hauses
DAT	dem alt**en** Mann	der alt**en** Frau	dem alt**en** Haus

PLURAL			
	MASC	FEM	NEUT
NOM	die alt**en** Männer	die alt**en** Frauen	die alt**en** Häuser
ACC	die alt**en** Männer	die alt**en** Frauen	die alt**en** Häuser
GEN	der alt**en** Männer	der alt**en** Frauen	der alt**en** Häuser
DAT	den alt**en** Männern	den alt**en** Frauen	den alt**en** Häusern

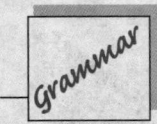

❐ The Declension of Adjectives (Continued)

2) The mixed declension

These are the endings used after **ein**, **kein**, **irgendein** and the possessive adjectives (see p 136) → [1]

	SINGULAR			PLURAL
	MASC	FEM	NEUT	ALL GENDERS
NOM	**-er**	**-e**	**-es**	**-en**
ACC	**-en**	**-e**	**-es**	**-en**
GEN	**-en**	**-en**	**-en**	**-en**
DAT	**-en**	**-en**	**-en**	**-en**

→ [2]

3) The strong declension

Strong declension endings:

	SINGULAR			PLURAL
	MASC	FEM	NEUT	ALL GENDERS
NOM	**-er**	**-e**	**-es**	**-e**
ACC	**-en**	**-e**	**-es**	**-e**
GEN	**-en**	**-er**	**-en**	**-er**
DAT	**-em**	**-er**	**-em**	**-en**

→ [3]

These endings are used where there is no preceding article. The article is omitted more frequently in German than in English, especially in *preposition* + *adjective* + *noun* combinations (see p 122).

These endings enable the adjective to do the work of the missing article by showing case, number and gender → [4]

143 Examples

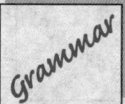

1 **Meine neue Stelle ist bei einer großen Druckerei**
My new job is with a large printing works
Ihre frühere Theorie ist jetzt bestätigt worden
Her earlier theory has now been proved true

2 SINGULAR

	MASC	FEM	NEUT
NOM	ein lang**er** Weg	eine lang**e** Reise	ein lang**es** Spiel
ACC	einen lang**en** Weg	eine lang**e** Reise	ein lang**es** Spiel
GEN	eines lang**en** Weg(e)s	einer lang**en** Reise	eines lang**en** Spiel(e)s
DAT	einem lang**en** Weg	einer lang**en** Reise	einem lang**en** Spiel

PLURAL
ALL GENDERS

NOM	ihre lang**en** Wege/Reisen/Spiele
ACC	ihre lang**en** Wege/Reisen/Spiele
GEN	ihrer lang**en** Wege/Reisen/Spiele
DAT	ihren lang**en** Wegen/Reisen/Spielen

3 SINGULAR

	MASC	FEM	NEUT
NOM	gut**er** Käse	gut**e** Marmelade	gut**es** Bier
ACC	gut**en** Käse	gut**e** Marmelade	gut**es** Bier
GEN	gut**en** Käses	gut**er** Marmelade	gut**en** Biers
DAT	gut**em** Käse	gut**er** Marmelade	gut**em** Bier

PLURAL
ALL GENDERS

NOM	gut**e** Käse/Marmeladen/Biere
ACC	gut**e** Käse/Marmeladen/Biere
GEN	gut**er** Käse/Marmeladen/Biere
DAT	gut**en** Käsen/Marmeladen/Bieren

4 **nach kurzer Fahrt** — after a short journey
mit gleichem Gehalt — with the same salary

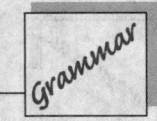

❐ The Declension of Adjectives (Continued)

◆ Strong declension endings are also used after any of the following where they are not preceded by an article or other determiner:

ein bisschen	a little, a bit of
ein wenig	a little
ein paar	a few, a couple → 1
weniger	fewer, less
einige (*plural forms only*)	some
allerlei/allerhand	all kinds of, all sorts of
keinerlei	no … whatsoever, no … at all
mancherlei	various, a number of
etwas	some, any (*singular*) → 2
mehr	more
lauter	nothing but, sheer, pure
solch	such
vielerlei	various, all sorts of, many different
mehrerlei	several kinds of
was für	what, what kind of
(⚠ NOTE: **Was für ein** takes the mixed declension)	
welcherlei	what kind of, what sort of
viel	much, many, a lot of
wievielerlei	how many kinds of
welch …!	what …! what a …! → 3
manch	many a
wenig	little, few, not much → 4
zweierlei/dreierlei *etc*	two/three *etc* kinds of
zwei, **drei** *etc*	two, three *etc* → 5
(⚠ NOTE: The mixed declension is used after **ein**)	

◆ The strong declension is also required after possessives where no other word indicates the case, gender and number → 6

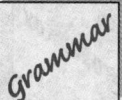

1 **ein paar gute Tipps** (*strong declension*)
a couple of good tips

2 **Etwas starken Pfeffer zugeben** (*strong*)
Add a little strong pepper

3 **Welch herrliches Wetter!** (*strong*)
What splendid weather!

4 **Es gab damals nur wenig frisches Obst** (*strong*)
At that time there was little fresh fruit

⚠ BUT:

Das wenige frische Obst, das es damals gab … (*weak*)
The little fresh fruit that was then available …

5 **Zwei große Jungen waren gekommen** (*strong*)
Two big boys had come along

⚠ BUT:

Die zwei großen Jungen, die gekommen waren (*weak*)
The two big boys who had come along

meine zwei großen Jungen (*mixed*)
my two big sons

6 **Herberts altes Buch** (*strong*)
Herbert's old book

Muttis neues Auto (*strong*)
Mum's new car

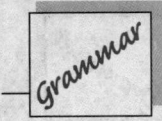

The Declension of Adjectives (Continued)

Some spelling changes when adjectives are declined

- When the adjective **hoch** (*high*) is declined, its stem changes to **hoh-** → [1]

- Adjectives ending in -**el** lose the -**e**- when inflected, i.e. when endings are added → [2]

- Adjectives with an -**er** ending often lose the -**e**- when inflected → [3]

The participles as adjectives

- The present participle can be used as an adjective with normal adjectival endings (pp 140 to 143) → [4]

  The present participles of **sein** and **haben** cannot be used in this way.

- The past participle can also be used as an adjective → [5]

Adjectives followed by the dative case

The *dative case* is required after many adjectives e.g.

ähnlich	similar to	
bekannt	familiar to	
dankbar	grateful to	
fremd	alien to	
gleich	all the same to/like	→ [6]
leicht	easy for	
nah	close to	
peinlich	painful for	
unbekannt	unknown to	

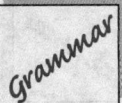

1 **Das Gebäude ist hoch**
The building is high

⚠ BUT: **ein hohes Gebäude**
a high building

2 **Das Zimmer ist dunkel**
The room is dark

⚠ BUT: **in dem dunklen Zimmer**
in the dark room

3 **Das Auto war teuer**
The car was expensive

⚠ BUT: **Er kaufte ein teures Auto**
He bought an expensive car

4 **die werdende Mutter**
the mother-to-be

ein lachendes Kind
a laughing child

5 **meine verlorene Sachen**
my lost things

die ausgebeuteten Arbeiter
the exploited workers

6 **Ist dir das bekannt?**
Do you know about it?

Ich wäre Ihnen dankbar, wenn ...
I should be grateful to you if ...

Diese Sache ist mir etwas peinlich
This matter is somewhat embarrassing for me

Solche Gedanken waren ihm fremd
Such thoughts were alien to him

❐ Adjectives used as Nouns

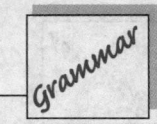

All adjectives in German, and those participles used as adjectives, can also be used as nouns. These are often called **adjectival nouns**.

- Adjectives and participles used as nouns have:

  - a capital letter like other nouns → [1]

  - declension endings like other adjectives, depending on the preceding article, if any (see below) → [2]

Declension endings for adjectives used as nouns

- After **der, dieser** and words like it shown on p 128, the normal *weak* adjective endings apply (see p 140) → [3]
  Der Junge (*the boy*) is an exception, and is declined like a weak masculine noun, as shown on p 115.

- After **ein, kein, irgendein** and the possessive adjectives shown on p 136, the *mixed* adjective endings apply (see p 142) → [4]

- Where no article is present, or after those words shown on p 144, the *strong* adjective endings are used (see p 142) → [5]

  When another adjective precedes the adjectival noun, the *strong* endings become *weak* in two instances:

  - in the *dative singular* → [6]

  - in the *nominative and accusative plural* after a possessive, where the strong endings might cause confusion with the singular feminine form → [7]

[1] **der Angestellte**
the employee

[2] **die Angestellte**
the (female) employee
das Neue daran ist ...
the new thing about it is ...
Es bleibt beim Alten
Things remain as they were
Er hat den ersten Besten genommen
He took the first that came to hand

[3] **für den Angeklagten**
for the accused
mit dieser Bekannten
with this (*female*) friend

[4] **Kein Angestellter darf hier rauchen**
No employee may smoke here
Sie machten einen Ausflug mit ihren Bekannten zusammen
They went on a trip with their friends

[5] **Etwas Besonderes ist geschehen**
Something special has happened

[6] **Ich hatte es Rudis jüngerem Verwandten versprochen**
I had promised it to Rudi's young relative

[7] **Rudis jüngere Verwandten wollten es haben**
Rudi's young relatives wanted to have it

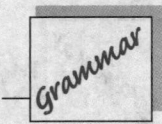

❐ Miscellaneous Points

Adjectives of nationality

- These are not spelt with a capital letter in German except in public or official names → [1]
- However, when used as a noun to refer to the language, a capital letter is used → [2]
- In German, for expressions like *he is English/he is German etc* a noun or adjectival noun is used instead of an adjective → [3]

Adjectives derived from place names

- These are formed by adding -**er** to names of towns → [4]
- They are never inflected → [5]
- Adjectives from **die Schweiz** and from certain regions can also be formed in this way → [6]
- Such adjectives may be used as nouns denoting the inhabitants of a town.
  They are then declined as normal nouns (see p 98 ff) → [7]
  The feminine form is made by adding -**in** in the singular and -**innen** in the plural → [8]
- Certain names ending in -**en** drop the -**e**- or the -**en** of their ending before adding -**er** → [9]
- A second type of adjective formed from place names exists, ending in -**isch** and spelt with a small letter. It is inflected as a normal adjective (see p 140).
  It is used mainly where the speaker is referring to the mood of, or something typical of, that place → [10]

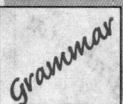

1 **die deutsche Sprache** the German language

das französische Volk the French people

⚠ BUT:

die Deutsche Bahn
the German railways

2 **Sie sprechen kein Englisch**
They don't speak English

3 **Er ist Deutscher** He is German

Sie ist Deutsche She is German

4 **Kölner, Frankfurter, Leipziger** *etc*

5 **der Kölner Dom** Cologne cathedral

ein Frankfurter Würstchen a frankfurter sausage

6 **Schweizer Käse**
Swiss cheese

7 **Die Sprache des Kölners heißt Kölsch**
von den Frankfurtern

8 **die Kölnerin, die Kölnerinnen**
die Londonerin, die Londonerinnen

9 **München → der Münchner**
Bremen → der Bremer
Göttingen → der Göttinger

10 **ein echt frankfurterischer Ausdruck**
a real Frankfurt expression
Er spricht etwas münchnerisch
He has something of a Munich accent

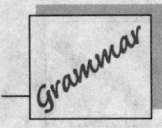

❒ The Comparison of Adjectives

Adjectives have three basic forms of comparison:

1) A simple form used to describe something or someone

e.g. a *little* house
the house is *little*

- This form is fully dealt with on pp 140 to 147.
- Simple forms are used in *as … as* / *not as … as* comparisons → [1]

2) A comparative form used to compare two things or persons

e.g. he is *bigger* than his brother

- In German, comparatives are formed by adding **-er** to the simple form → [2]
- *Than* in comparative statements is translated by **als** → [3]
- Unlike English, the vast majority of German adjectives, including those of several syllables, form their comparatives in this way → [4]
- Many adjectives modify the stem vowel when forming their comparatives → [5]

1 so ... wie as ... as
Er ist so gut wie sein Bruder
He is as good as his brother

ebenso ... wie just as ... as
Er war ebenso glücklich wie ich
He was just as happy as I was

zwei-/dreimal *etc* twice/three times etc
so ... wie as ... as

Er war zweimal so groß wie sein Bruder
He was twice as big as his brother

nicht so ... wie not as ... as
Er ist nicht so alt wie du
He is not as old as you

2

klein/kleiner	small/smaller
schön/schöner	lovely/lovelier

3 **Er ist kleiner als seine Schwester**
He is smaller than his sister

4

bequem/bequemer	comfortable/more comfortable
gebildet/gebildeter	educated/more educated
effektiv/effektiver	effective/more effective

5

alt/älter	old/older
stark/stärker	strong/stronger
schwach/schwächer	weak/weaker
scharf/schärfer	sharp/sharper
lang/länger	long/longer
kurz/kürzer	short/shorter
warm/wärmer	warm/warmer
kalt/kälter	cold/colder
hart/härter	hard/harder
groß/größer	big/bigger

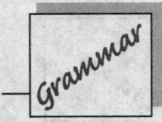

❒ The Comparison of Adjectives (Continued)

- Adjectives whose simple form ends in **-el** lose the **-e-** before adding the comparative ending **-er** → 1

- Adjectives with a diphthong followed by **-er** in their simple forms also drop the **-e-** before adding **-er** → 2

- Adjectives whose simple form ends in **-en** or **-er** may drop the **-e-** of the simple form when adjectival endings are added to their comparative forms → 3

- With a few adjectives, comparative forms may be used not only for comparison, but also to render the idea of "-ish" or "rather ..."
  Some common examples are:

älter	elderly	**jünger**	youngish
dünner	thinnish	**kleiner**	smallish
dicker	fattish	**kürzer**	shortish
größer	largish	**neuer**	newish

→ 4

- When used attributively (*before* the noun), comparative forms are declined in exactly the same way as simple adjectives (see pp 140 to 147) → 4 → 5

3) A superlative form used to compare three or more persons or things

e.g. he is *the biggest*/*the best*

- Superlatives are formed by adding **-st** to the simple adjective. The vowel is modified, as for comparative forms, where applicable. Superlative forms are generally used with an article and take endings accordingly (see p 140) → 6

Examples

1 **eitel/eitler** vain/vainer
dunkel/dunkler dark/darker

2 **sauer/saurer** sour/more sour
die saurere Zitrone
the sourer lemon
Der Wein ist saurer geworden
The wine has grown more sour

teuer/teurer expensive/more expensive
Das ist eine teurere Sorte
That is a more expensive kind
Die Neuen sind teurer
The new ones are more expensive

3 **finster/finsterer** dark/darker
ein finstreres Gesicht
OR:
ein finstereres Gesicht
a grimmer face

4 **ein älterer Herr**
an elderly gentleman
eine größere Summe
a rather large sum
von jüngerem Aussehen
of youngish appearance

5 **Die jüngere Schwester ist größer als die ältere**
The younger sister is bigger than the older one
Mein kleinerer Bruder geht jetzt zur Schule
My younger brother goes to school now

6 **Er ist der Jüngste**
He is the youngest
Ihr erfolgreichster Versuch war im Herbst 1998
Her most successful attempt was in the autumn of 1998

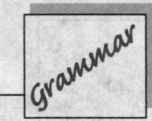

❒ The Comparison of Adjectives (Continued)

- Many adjectives form their superlative forms by adding **-est** instead of **-st** where pronunciation would otherwise be difficult or unaesthetic → [1]

- The English superlative "*most*" meaning "*very*" can be shown in German by any of the following → [2]

  äußerst

  sehr

  besonders

  außerordentlich

  höchst (*not with monosyllabic words*)

  furchtbar (*conversational only*)

  richtig (*conversational only*)

Some irregular comparative and superlative forms

SIMPLE FORM	COMPARATIVE	SUPERLATIVE
gut	**besser**	**der beste**
hoch	**höher**	**der höchste**
viel	**mehr**	**der meiste**
nah	**näher**	**der nächste**

1 **der/die/das schlechteste**
the worst

der/die/das schmerzhafteste
the most painful

der/die/das süßeste
the sweetest

der/die/das neueste
the newest

der/die/das stolzeste
the proudest

der/die/das frischeste
the freshest

2 **Er ist ein äußerst begabter Mensch**
He is a most gifted person

Das Essen war besonders schlecht
The food was really/most dreadful

Der Wein war furchtbar teuer!
The wine was dreadfully/most expensive!

Das sieht richtig komisch aus
That looks really/most funny

❐ Personal Pronouns

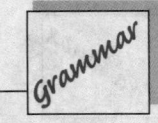

As in English, personal pronouns change their form depending on their function in the sentence:

I saw *him*
He saw *me* → 1
We saw *her*

The personal pronouns are declined as follows:

NOMINATIVE		ACCUSATIVE		DATIVE	
ich	I	**mich**	me	**mir**	to/for me
du	you (*familiar*)	**dich**	you	**dir**	to/for you
er	he/it	**ihn**	him/it	**ihm**	to/for him/it
sie	she/it	**sie**	her/it	**ihr**	to/for her/it
es	it/he/she	**es**	it/him/her	**ihm**	to/for it/him/her → 2
wir	we	**uns**	us	**uns**	to/for us
ihr	you (*plural*)	**euch**	you	**euch**	to/for you
sie	they	**sie**	them	**ihnen**	to/for them
Sie	you (*polite*)	**Sie**	you	**Ihnen**	to/for you
man	one	**einen**	one	**einem**	to/for one

- As can be seen from the above table, there are three ways of addressing people in German, by **du, ihr** or **Sie**.

  All three forms are illustrated on p 160.

- Personal pronouns in the dative require no preposition when acting as indirect object, i.e. *to* me, *to* him *etc* → 3

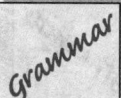

1 **Ich sah ihn**
I saw him

Er sah mich
He saw me

Wir sahen sie
We saw her

2 **Wir sind mit ihnen spazieren gegangen**
We went for a walk with them

Sie haben uns eine tolle Geschichte erzählt
They told us a great story

Soll ich Ihnen etwas mitbringen?
Shall I bring something back for you?

3 **Er hat es ihr gegeben**
He gave it to her

Ich habe ihm ein neues Buch gekauft
I bought a new book for him

OR:

I bought him a new book

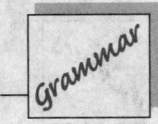

❐ Personal Pronouns (Continued)

◆ **Du** is a singular form, used only when speaking to one person. It is used to talk to children, close friends and relatives, animals and objects of affection such as a toy, one's car etc.

When in doubt it is always best to use the more formal **Sie** form.

◆ **Ihr** is simply the plural form of **du** and is used in exactly the same situations wherever more than one person is to be addressed → [1]

◆ The familiar forms and their possessives are written with a small letter → [2]

◆ **Sie** is the polite, or formal, way of addressing people. It is written in all its declined forms with a capital letter, including the possessive → [3]

Sie is used:

1. by children talking to adults outside their immediate family.
2. by adults talking to older children from mid-teens onwards. Teachers use it to their senior classes and bosses to their trainees etc.
3. among adult strangers meeting for the first time.
4. among colleagues, friends and acquaintances unless a suggestion has been formally made by one party and accepted by the other that the familiar forms should be used. Familiar forms must then continue to be used at all times, as a reversion to the formal might be considered insulting.

Examples

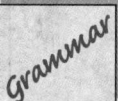

1 **Kinder, was wollt ihr essen?**

Children, what do you want to eat?

2 **Er hat mir gesagt, du sollst deine Frau mitbringen**

He told me you were to bring your wife

Gestern bin ich deinem Bruder begegnet

I met your brother yesterday

3 **Was haben Sie gesagt?**

What did you say?

Ich habe es Ihnen schon gegeben

I have already given it to you

Ja, Ihre Sachen sind jetzt fertig

Yes, your things are ready now

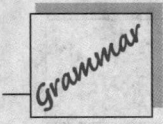

❒ Personal Pronouns (Continued)

Er/sie/es

- All German nouns are masculine, feminine or neuter → 1
- The personal pronoun must agree in number and in gender with the noun which it represents.

  Es is used only for neuter nouns, and not for all inanimate objects → 2

  Inanimate objects which are masculine use the pronoun **er** → 3

  Feminine inanimate objects use the pronoun **sie** → 4

  Neuter nouns referring to people have the neuter pronoun **es** → 5

  ⚠ NOTE: A common error for English speakers is to call all objects **es**.

Man

- This is used in much the same way as the pronoun **one** in English, but it is much more commonly used in German → 6
- It is also used to make an alternative passive form (see p 34) → 7

The genitive personal pronoun

- Genitive forms of the personal pronouns do exist → 8
- In practice, however, these are rarely used. Wherever possible, alternative expressions are found which do not require the genitive personal pronoun.
- Special genitive forms exist for use with the prepositions **wegen** and **willen** → 9

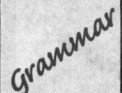

1 **der Tisch** the table (*masculine*)
die Gardine the curtain (*feminine*)
das Baby the baby (*neuter*)

2 **Das Bild ist schön** ➔ **Es ist schön**
The picture is beautiful ➔ It is beautiful

3 **Der Tisch ist groß** ➔ **Er ist groß**
The table is large ➔ It is large

4 **Die Gardine ist weiß** ➔ **Sie ist weiß**
The curtain is white ➔ It is white

5 **Das Kind stand auf** ➔ **Es stand auf**
The child stood up ➔ He/she stood up

6 **Es tut einem gut**
It does one good

7 **Man holt mich um sieben ab**
I am being picked up at seven

8

meiner	of me	**unser**	of us
deiner	of you	**euer**	of you (*plural*)
seiner	of him/it	**ihrer**	of them
ihrer	of her/it	**Ihrer**	of you (*polite*)

9 **meinetwegen** because of me, on my account
deinetwegen because of you, on your account *etc*
seinetwegen
ihretwegen
unsertwegen
euretwegen
Ihretwegen

meinetwillen for my sake, for me *etc*
deinetwillen
ihretwillen *etc*

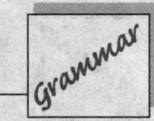

❐ Personal Pronouns (Continued)

The use of pronouns after prepositions

- Personal pronouns used after prepositions and referring to a person are in the *case* required by the preposition in question (see p 198 ff) → [1]

- When, however, a *thing* rather than a person is referred to, the construction

  preposition + pronoun

  becomes

  da- + *preposition* → [2]

  Before a preposition beginning with a vowel, the form **dar**- + *preposition* is used → [3]

This affects the following prepositions:

an	**bei**	**in**	**neben**	
auf	**durch**	**mit**	**über**	**zwischen**
aus	**für**	**nach**	**unter**	

- These contracted forms are used after verbs followed by a preposition (see p 76 ff) → [4]

- After prepositions used to express motion the form with **da(r)**- is not felt to be sufficiently strong. Forms with **hin** and **her** are used as follows:

  aus: heraus/hinaus
  auf: herauf/hinauf → [5]
  in: herein/hinein

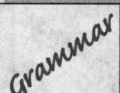

1 **Ich bin mit ihm spazieren gegangen**
I went for a walk with him

2 **Klaus hatte ein Messer geholt und wollte damit den Kuchen schneiden**
Klaus had brought a knife and was about to cut the cake with it

3 **Lege es bitte darauf**
Put it there please

4 **Der Unterschied liegt darin, dass …**
The difference is that …

Ich erinnere mich nicht daran
I don't remember (it)

5 **Er sah eine Treppe und ging leise hinauf**
He saw some stairs and went up them quietly

Endlich fand er unser Zelt und kam herein
He finally found our tent and came in

Er öffnete den Koffer und legte das Hemd hinein
He opened his suitcase and put in his shirt

Possessive Pronouns

meiner	mine
deiner	yours (*familiar*)
seiner	his/its
ihrer	hers/its
uns(e)rer	ours
eu(e)rer	yours (*plural*)
ihrer	theirs
Ihrer	yours (*polite*)

These have the same endings as **dieser**. Their declension is therefore the same as for possessive adjectives (see p 136) except in the masculine nominative singular and the neuter nominative and accusative singular:

		SINGULAR		PLURAL
	MASC	FEM	NEUT	ALL GENDERS
NOM	**-er**	**-e**	**-(e)s**	**-e**
ACC	**-en**	**-e**	**-(e)s**	**-e**
GEN	**-es**	**-er**	**-es**	**-er**
DAT	**-em**	**-er**	**-em**	**-en**

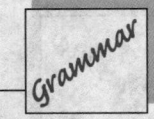

- The bracketed **(e)** is often omitted, especially in spoken German.
- Possessive pronouns must agree in number, gender and case with the noun they replace → [1]
- Note the translation of *of mine, of yours* etc → [2]
- **meiner** is declined in full opposite → [3]
  Deiner, seiner and **ihrer** are declined like **meiner**.
  Unserer and **euerer** are shown in full, since they have slightly different forms with an optional **-e-** → [4]

Examples

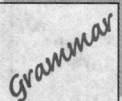

1 **Der Wagen da drüben ist meiner. Er ist kleiner als deiner**
The car over there is mine. It is smaller than yours

2 **Er ist ein Bekannter von mir**
He is an acquaintance of mine

3 **meiner** mine

	SINGULAR			PLURAL
	MASC	FEM	NEUT	ALL GENDERS
NOM	**meiner**	**meine**	**mein(e)s**	**meine**
ACC	**meinen**	**meine**	**mein(e)s**	**meine**
GEN	**meines**	**meiner**	**meines**	**meiner**
DAT	**meinem**	**meiner**	**meinem**	**meinen**

4 **uns(e)rer** ours

	SINGULAR			PLURAL
	MASC	FEM	NEUT	ALL GENDERS
NOM	**uns(e)rer**	**uns(e)re**	**uns(e)res**	**uns(e)re**
ACC	**uns(e)ren**	**uns(e)re**	**uns(e)res**	**uns(e)re**
GEN	**uns(e)res**	**uns(e)rer**	**uns(e)res**	**uns(e)rer**
DAT	**uns(e)rem**	**uns(e)rer**	**uns(e)rem**	**uns(e)ren**

eu(e)rer yours (*plural*)

	SINGULAR			PLURAL
	MASC	FEM	NEUT	ALL GENDERS
NOM	**eu(e)rer**	**eu(e)re**	**eu(e)res**	**eu(e)re**
ACC	**eu(e)ren**	**eu(e)re**	**eu(e)res**	**eu(e)re**
GEN	**eu(e)res**	**eu(e)rer**	**eu(e)res**	**eu(e)rer**
DAT	**eu(e)rem**	**eu(e)rer**	**eu(e)rem**	**eu(e)ren**

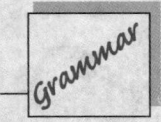

❒ Possessive Pronouns (Continued)

Alternative forms

There are two alternatives to the **meiner/deiner** *etc* forms shown on p 167:

der, die, das Meinige *or* **meinige**	mine
der, die, das Deinige *or* **deinige**	yours (*familiar*)
der, die, das Seinige *or* **seinige**	his/its
der, die, das Ihrige *or* **ihrige**	hers/its
der, die, das Uns(e)rige *or* **uns(e)rige**	ours
der, die, das Eu(e)rige *or* **eu(e)rige**	yours (*plural*)
der, die, das Ihrige *or* **ihrige**	theirs
der, die, das Ihrige	yours (*polite*)

- These are not as common as the **meiner/deiner** *etc* forms → [1]
- These forms are declined as the definite article followed by a weak adjective (see p 140) → [2]
- The bracketed **(e)** of the first and second person plural is often omitted in spoken German.

der, die, das Meine *or* **meine**	mine
der, die, das Deine *or* **deine**	yours (*familiar*)
der, die, das Seine *or* **seine**	his/its
der, die, das Ihre *or* **ihre**	hers/its
der, die, das Uns(e)re *or* **uns(e)re**	ours
der, die, das Eu(e)re *or* **eu(e)re**	yours (*plural*)
der, die, das Ihre *or* **ihre**	theirs
der, die, das Ihre	yours (*polite*)

- These forms are also less common than the **meiner/deiner** *etc* forms. They are declined as the definite article followed by a weak adjective (see p 140) → [3]

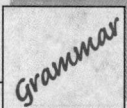

[1] **Ihr Auto ist aber neuer als das Meinige** *or* **meinige**
Your car is newer than mine
Paul hat seiner Freundin Blumen gekauft. Ich habe der Meinigen *or* **meinigen Parfüm geschenkt**
Paul bought his girlfriend some flowers. I bought mine perfume

[2]

SINGULAR

	MASC	FEM	NEUT
NOM	**der Meinige**	**die Meinige**	**das Meinige**
ACC	**den Meinigen**	**die Meinige**	**das Meinige**
GEN	**des Meinigen**	**der Meinigen**	**des Meinigen**
DAT	**dem Meinigen**	**der Meinigen**	**dem Meinigen**

PLURAL
ALL GENDERS

NOM	**die Meinigen**
ACC	**die Meinigen**
GEN	**der Meinigen**
DAT	**den Meinigen**

[3]

SINGULAR

	MASC	FEM	NEUT
NOM	**der Meine**	**die Meine**	**das Meine**
ACC	**den Meinen**	**die Meine**	**das Meine**
GEN	**des Meinen**	**der Meinen**	**des Meinen**
DAT	**dem Meinen**	**der Meinen**	**dem Meinen**

PLURAL
ALL GENDERS

NOM	**die Meinen**
ACC	**die Meinen**
GEN	**der Meinen**
DAT	**den Meinen**

⚠ NOTE: **Der/die/das Meinige** *etc* can also be spelt **der/die/das meinige** *etc* and **der/die/das Meine** *etc* can also be spelt **der/die/das meine** *etc*

❒ Reflexive Pronouns

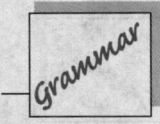

Reflexive pronouns, used to form reflexive verbs, have two forms, accusative and dative, as follows → 1

ACCUSATIVE	DATIVE	
mich	**mir**	myself
dich	**dir**	yourself (*familiar*)
sich	**sich**	himself/herself/itself/themselves
uns	**uns**	ourselves
euch	**euch**	yourselves (*plural*)
sich	**sich**	yourself/yourselves (*polite*)

- Unlike personal pronouns and possessives, the polite forms have no capital letter → 2
- For the position of reflexive pronouns within a sentence see p 30 (reflexive verbs) and pp 224 to 235 (sentence structure).
- Reflexive pronouns are also used after prepositions when the pronoun has the function of "reflecting back" to the subject of the sentence → 3
- A further use of reflexive pronouns in German is with transitive verbs where the action is performed for the benefit of the subject, as in the English phrase:

  I bought *myself* a new hat

  The pronoun is not always translated in English → 4

[1] **Er hat sich rasiert**

He had a shave

Du hast dich gebadet

You had a bath

Ich will es mir zuerst überlegen

I'll have to think about it first

[2] **Setzen Sie sich bitte**

Please take a seat

[3] **Er hatte nicht genug Geld bei sich** (⚠ NOT: **bei ihm**)

He didn't have enough money on him

[4] **Ich hole mir ein Bier**

I'm going to get a beer (for myself)

Er hat sich einen neuen Anzug gekauft

He bought (himself) a new suit

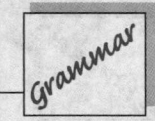

❒ Reflexive Pronouns (Continued)

- Reflexive pronouns may be used for *reciprocal* actions, usually rendered by "each other" in English → [1]

  Reciprocal actions may also be expressed by **einander**. This does not change in form → [2]

  Einander is always used in place of the reflexive pronoun after prepositions. Note that the preposition and **einander** come together to form one word → [3]

Emphatic reflexive pronouns

In English, these have the same forms as the normal reflexive pronouns:

The queen *herself* had given the order

I haven't read it *myself*, but ...

In German, this idea is expressed not by the reflexive pronouns, but by **selbst** or (in colloquial speech) **selber** placed at some point in the sentence after the noun or pronoun to which they refer → [4]

- **selbst/selber** do not change their form, regardless of number and gender of the noun to which they refer → [4]

- They are always stressed, regardless of their position in the sentence.

Examples

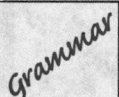

1 **Wir sind uns letzte Woche begegnet**

We met (each other) last week

Sie hatten sich auf einer Tagung kennengelernt

They had got to know each other at a conference

2 **Wir kennen uns schon**

OR:

Wir kennen einander schon

We already know each other

Sie kennen sich schon

OR:

Sie kennen einander schon

They already know each other

3 **Sie redeten miteinander**

They were talking to each other

4 **Die Königin selbst hat es befohlen**

The queen herself has given the order

Ich selbst habe es nicht gelesen, aber ...

I haven't read it myself, but ...

❐ Relative Pronouns

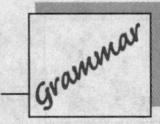

These have the same forms as the definite article, except in the dative plural and genitive cases.

They are declined as follows:

	SINGULAR			PLURAL
	MASC	FEM	NEUT	ALL GENDERS
NOM	**der**	**die**	**das**	**die**
ACC	**den**	**die**	**das**	**die**
GEN	**dessen**	**deren**	**dessen**	**deren**
DAT	**dem**	**der**	**dem**	**denen**

- Relative pronouns must agree in gender and number with the noun to which they refer. They take their case however from the function they have in their own relative clause → [1]

- The relative pronoun cannot be omitted in German as it sometimes is in English → [2]

- The genitive forms are used in relative clauses in much the same way as in English → [3]

  ⚠ NOTE, however, the translation of certain phrases → [4]

- When a preposition introduces the relative clause, the relative pronoun may be replaced by **wo**- or **wor**- if the noun or pronoun it stands for refers to an inanimate object or abstract concept → [5]
  The full form of relative pronoun plus preposition is however stylistically better.

- Relative clauses are always divided off by commas from the rest of the sentence → [1] - [5]

Examples

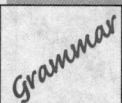

1 **Der Mann, den ich gestern gesehen habe, kommt aus Hamburg**

The man whom I saw yesterday comes from Hamburg

2 **Die Frau, mit der ich gestern gesprochen habe, kennt deine Mutter**

The woman I spoke to yesterday knows your mother

3 **Das Kind, dessen Fahrrad gestohlen worden war, ...**

The child whose bicycle had been stolen ...

4 **Die Kinder, von denen einige schon lesen konnten, ...**

The children, some of whom could read, ...

Meine Freunde, von denen einer ...

My friends, one of whom ...

5 **Das Buch, woraus ich vorgelesen habe, ...**

OR:

Das Buch, aus dem ich vorgelesen habe, ...

The book I read aloud from ...

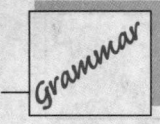

❒ Relative Pronouns (Continued)

Welcher

A second relative pronoun exists. This has the same forms as the interrogative adjective **welcher** without the genitive forms:

	SINGULAR			PLURAL
	MASC	FEM	NEUT	ALL GENDERS
NOM	**welcher**	**welche**	**welches**	**welche**
ACC	**welchen**	**welche**	**welches**	**welche**
GEN	—	—	—	—
DAT	**welchem**	**welcher**	**welchem**	**welchen**

- These forms are used only infrequently as relative pronouns, where sentence rhythm might benefit.

- They are also useful used as articles or adjectives to connect a noun in the relative clause with the contents of the main clause → 1

Wer, was

These are normally used as interrogative pronouns meaning *who*?, *what*? and are declined as such on p 178.

- They may, however, also be used without interrogative meaning to replace both subject and relative pronoun in English:

  he who
  a woman who → 2
  anyone who
  those who etc

- **Was** is the relative pronoun used in set expressions with certain neuter forms → 3

Examples

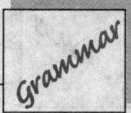

1 **Er glaubte, mit der Hausarbeit nicht helfen zu brauchen, mit welcher Idee seine Mutter nicht einverstanden war!**
He thought he didn't have to help in the house, an idea with which his mother was not in agreement!

2 **Wer das glaubt, ist verrückt**
Anyone who believes that is mad

Was mich angeht, ...
For my part, ...

Was du gestern gekauft hast, steht dir ganz gut
The things you bought yesterday suit you very well

3

alles, was ...	everything which
allerlei, was ...	all kinds of things that
das, was ...	that which
dasjenige, was ...	that which
dasselbe, was ...	the same one that
einiges, was ...	some that
Folgendes, was ...	the following which
manches, was ...	some which
nichts, was ...	nothing that
vieles, was ...	a lot that
wenig, was ...	little that

Nichts, was er sagte, hat gestimmt
Nothing that he said was right

Das, was du jetzt machst, ist reiner Unsinn!
What you are doing now is sheer nonsense!

Mit allem, was du gesagt hast, sind wir einverstanden
We agree with everything you said

❒ Interrogative Pronouns

These are the pronouns used to ask questions.

As in English, they have few forms, singular and plural being the same.

They are declined as follows:

	PERSONS	THINGS
NOM	**wer?**	**was?**
ACC	**wen?**	**was?**
GEN	**wessen?**	**wessen?**
DAT	**wem?**	—

- They are used in direct questions → 1

  or in indirect questions → 2

- When used as the subject of a sentence, they are always followed by a singular verb → 3

  ⚠ BUT: When followed by a verb and taking a noun complement, the verb may be plural if the sense demands it → 4

- The interrogative pronouns can be used in rhetorical questions or in exclamations → 5

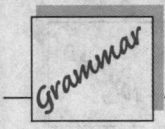

1 **Wer hat es gemacht?**

Who did it?

Mit wem bist du gekommen?

Who did you come with?

2 **Ich weiß nicht, wer es gemacht hat**

I don't know who did it

Er wollte wissen, mit wem er fahren sollte

He wanted to know who he was to travel with

3 **Wer kommt heute?**

Who's coming today?

4 **Wer sind diese Leute?**

Who are these people?

5 **Was haben wir gelacht!**

How we laughed!

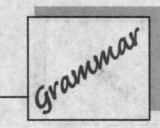

❐ Interrogative Pronouns (Continued)

- When used with prepositions, **was** usually becomes **wo**- and is placed in front of the preposition to form one word → 1

  Where the preposition begins with a vowel, **wor**- is used instead → 2

  This construction is similar to **da(r)**- + *preposition* shown on p 164.

  As with **da(r)**- + *preposition*, this construction is not used when the preposition is intended to convey movement.

  Wohin (*where to*) and **woher** (*where from*) are used instead → 3

Was für ein?, welcher?

- These are used to mean *what kind of one*? and *which one*?
- They are declined as shown on pp 124 and 128.
- They are used to form either direct or indirect questions → 4
- They may refer either to persons or to things with the appropriate declension endings → 5

1 **Wonach sehnst du dich?**

What do you long for?

Wodurch ist es zerstört worden?

How was it destroyed?

2 **Worauf kann man sich heutzutage noch verlassen?**

What is there left to rely on these days?

3 **Wohin fährst du?**

Where are you going?

Woher kommt das?

Where has this come from?/How has this come about?

4 **Was für eins hat er?**

What kind (of one) does he have?

Welches hast du gewollt?

Which one did you want?

5 **Für welchen hat sie sich entschieden?**

Which one (*man/hat etc*) did she choose?

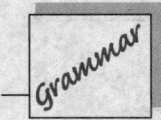

❒ Indefinite Pronouns

(Irgend)jemand someone, somebody

NOM	**(irgend)jemand**	→ [1]
ACC	**(irgend)jemanden, (irgend)jemand**	
GEN	**(irgend)jemand(e)s**	
DAT	**(irgend)jemandem, (irgend)jemand**	

Niemand no-one, nobody

NOM	**niemand**	→ [2]
ACC	**niemanden, niemand**	
GEN	**niemand(e)s**	
DAT	**niemandem, niemand**	

- The forms without endings are used in conversational German, but the inflected forms are preferred in literary and written styles.

- When **niemand** and **(irgend)jemand** are used with a following adjective, they are usually not declined, but the adjective takes a capital letter and is declined as follows:

NOM	**(irgend)jemand/niemand Neues**	→ [3]
ACC	**(irgend)jemand/niemand Neues**	
GEN	—	
DAT	**(irgend)jemand/niemand Neuem**	

- When **(irgend)jemand** and **niemand** are followed by **ander(e)s**, this is written with a small letter, e.g. **(irgend)jemand/niemand ander(e)s**.

Examples

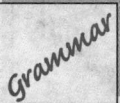

1 **Ich habe es (irgend)jemandem (*dat*) gegeben**

I gave it to someone

(Irgend)jemand (*nom*) hat es genommen

Someone has stolen it

2 **Er hat niemanden (*acc*) gesehen**

He didn't see anyone

Er ist unterwegs niemandem (*dat*) begegnet

He encountered no-one on the way

3 **Diese Aufgabe erfordert (irgend)jemand Intelligentes**

Someone intelligent is needed for this task

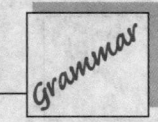

❐ Indefinite Pronouns (Continued)

Keiner none

	SINGULAR			PLURAL
	MASC	FEM	NEUT	ALL GENDERS
NOM	**keiner**	**keine**	**keins**	**keine**
ACC	**keinen**	**keine**	**keins**	**keine**
GEN	**keines**	**keiner**	**keines**	**keiner**
DAT	**keinem**	**keiner**	**keinem**	**keinen**

- It is declined like the article **kein**, **keine**, **kein** (see p 126) except in the nominative masculine and nominative and accusative neuter forms → [1]
- It may be used to refer to people or things → [1]

Einer one

	SINGULAR		
	MASC	FEM	NEUT
NOM	**einer**	**eine**	**ein(e)s**
ACC	**einen**	**eine**	**ein(e)s**
GEN	**eines**	**einer**	**eines**
DAT	**einem**	**einer**	**einem**

- This pronoun may be used to refer to either people or things → [2]
- It exists only in the singular forms.

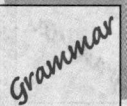

1 **Keiner von ihnen hat es tun können**

Not one of them was able to do it

Gibst du mir eine Zigarette? — Tut mir leid, ich habe keine

Will you give me a cigarette? — Sorry, I haven't got any

2 **Sie ist mit einem meiner Verwandten verlobt**

She is engaged to one of my relatives

Wo sind die anderen Kinder? Ich sehe hier nur eins

Where are the rest of the children? I can only see one here

Gibst du mir einen? (e.g. *einen Whisky, einen Zehner* etc) OR:
Gibst du mir eine? (e.g. *eine Zigarette, eine Blume* etc) OR:
Gibst du mir eins? (e.g. *ein Buch, ein Butterbrot* etc)

Will you give me one?

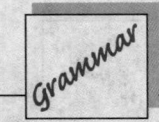

❒ Indefinite Pronouns (Continued)

- Certain adjectives and articles can be used as pronouns.

- The following are all declined to agree in gender and number with the noun or pronoun they represent → [1]

aller	all
ander	other
beide	both
derjenige	that one
derselbe	the same one
dieser	this one
einiger	some
irgendwelcher	someone or other/something or other
jeder	each (one), every one
jener	that one
mancher	some, quite a few
mehrere	several
sämtliche	all, the lot
solcher	such as that, such a one
welcher	which one

- The following do not change whatever the gender or number of the noun or pronoun they represent → [2]

ein bisschen	a bit, a little
ein paar	a few
ein wenig	a little, a few
(irgend)etwas	some, something
mehr	more
nichts	nothing, none

- When an adjective follows **etwas** or **nichts**, it takes a capital letter and declension endings, e.g. **etwas/nichts Gutes**

Examples

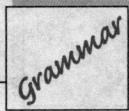

1 **Andere machen es besser** (e.g. *Leute, Waschmaschinen* etc)
Others do it better

Mit einem solchen kommst du nicht bis nach Hause (e.g. *Wagen* etc)
You won't make it home in one like that

Alles, was er ihr schenkte, schickte sie sofort zurück
Everything that he gave her she sent back at once

Er war mit beiden zufrieden (e.g. *Computern, Autos* etc)
He was satisfied with both

2 **Ich muss dir etwas sagen**
I must tell you something

(Irgend)etwas ist herausgefallen
Something fell out

Nichts ist geschehen
Nothing happened

Er ist mit nichts zufrieden
Nothing ever satisfies him

Gibst du mir bitte ein paar?
Will you give me a few?

Er hatte ein wenig bei sich
He had a little with him

Er braucht immer mehr um zu überleben
He needs more and more to survive

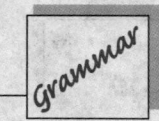

Use of Adverbs

- Adverbs, or phrases which are used as adverbs, may:

  1 modify a verb → [1]

  2 modify an adjective → [2]

  3 modify another adverb → [3]

  4 modify a conjunction → [4]

  5 ask a question → [5]

  6 form verb prefixes (see p 72) → [6]

- Adverbs are also used, in much the same way as in English, to make the meaning of certain tenses more precise e.g.

  1 with continuous tenses → [7]

  2 to show a future meaning where the tense used is not future → [8]

Examples

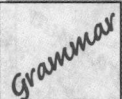

1 **Er ging langsam über die Brücke**
He walked slowly over the bridge

2 **Er ist ein ziemlich großer Kerl**
He's quite a big chap

3 **Sie arbeitet heute besonders tüchtig**
She's working exceptionally well today

4 **Wenn er es nur aufgeben wollte!**
If only he would give it up!

5 **Wann kommt er an?**
When does he arrive?

6 **falsch spielen**
to cheat (*at cards*)

hintragen
to carry (*to a place*)

7 **Er liest gerade die Zeitung**
He's just reading the paper

8 **Er wollte gerade aufstehen, als ...**
He was just about to get up when ...

Wir fahren morgen nach Köln
We're driving to Cologne tomorrow

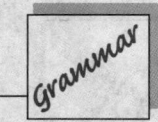

The Formation of Adverbs

- Many German adverbs are simply adjectives used as adverbs. Used in this way, unlike adjectives, they are not declined → 1

- Some adverbs are formed by adding **-weise** or **-sweise** to a noun → 2

- Some adverbs are also formed by adding **-erweise** to an uninflected adjective.

  Such adverbs are used mainly to show the speaker's opinion → 3

- There is also a class of adverbs which are not formed from other parts of speech e.g. **unten**, **oben**, **leider** → 4

  and those shown in the paragraphs below.

- For the position of adverbs within a clause or sentence, see the section on sentence structure, pp 224 to 235.

- The following are some common adverbs of time:

endlich	finally	
heute	today	
immer	always	→ 5
morgen	tomorrow	
morgens	in the mornings	
sofort	at once	

- The following are some common adverbs of degree:

äußerst	extremely	
besonders	especially	→ 6
beträchtlich	considerably	
ziemlich	fairly	

Examples

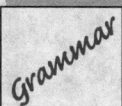

1 **Habe ich das richtig gehört?**
Is it true what I've heard?

Sie war modern angezogen
She was fashionably dressed

2

beispielsweise	for example
beziehungsweise	or/or rather/that is to say
schrittweise	step by step
zeitweise	at times
zwangsweise	compulsorily

3

erstaunlicherweise	astonishingly enough
glücklicherweise	fortunately
komischerweise	strangely enough

4 **Unten wohnte Frau Schmidt**
Mrs Schmidt lived downstairs

Leider können wir nicht kommen
Unfortunately we cannot come

5 **Ich kann erst morgen kommen**
I can't come till tomorrow

Das Kind hat immer Hunger
The child is always hungry

6 **Das Paket war besonders schwer**
The parcel was unusually heavy

Diese Übung ist ziemlich leicht
This exercise is quite easy

❐ Adverbs of place

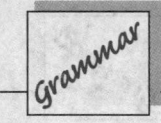

In certain respects German adverbs of place behave very differently from their English counterparts:

- Where no movement, or merely a movement within the same place, is involved, the adverb is used in its simple dictionary form → 1
- Movement *away from the speaker* is shown by the presence of **hin** → 2

  The following compound adverbs are therefore often used when movement away from the original position is concerned, even though a simple adverb would be used in English:

dahin	(to) there	
dorthin	there	
hierhin	here	
irgendwohin	(to) somewhere or other	→ 3
überallhin	everywhere	
wohin?	where (to)?	

- Movement *towards the speaker* or central person is shown by the presence of **her**.

  The following compound adverbs are therefore often used to show movement towards a person:

daher	from there	
hierher	here	
irgendwoher	from somewhere or other	→ 4
überallher	from all over	
woher?	where from?	

Examples

1 **Wo ist er?**

Where is he?

Er ist nicht da

He isn't there

Hier darf man nicht parken

You can't park here

2 **Klaus und Ulli geben heute eine Party. Gehen wir hin?**

Klaus and Ulli are having a party today. Shall we go?

3 **Wohin fährst du?**

Where are you going?

Sie liefen überallhin

They ran everywhere

4 **Woher kommst du?**

Where do you come from?

Woher hast du das?

Where did you get that from?

Das habe ich irgendwoher gekriegt

I got that from somewhere or other

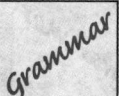

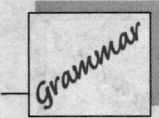

❐ Comparison of Adverbs

- The **comparative** form of the adverb is obtained in exactly the same way as that of adjectives, i.e. by adding **-er** → [1]

- The **superlative** form is produced as follows:

  am + *adverb* + **-sten/-esten**

  It is not declined → [2]

- Note the use of the comparative adverb with **immer** to show progression → [3]

- *the more ... the more ...* is expressed in German by:

  je ... desto ... or **je ... umso ...** → [4]

- Some adverbial superlatives are used to show the extent of a quality rather than a comparison with others. These are as follows:

bestens	very well/very warmly
höchstens	at the most/at best
meistens	mostly/most often
spätestens	at the latest
strengstens	strictly, absolutely
wenigstens	at least

→ [5]

- Two irregular comparatives and superlatives:

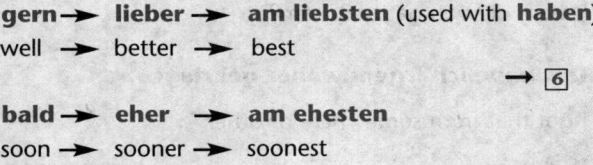

  gern → **lieber** → **am liebsten** (used with **haben**)
  well → better → best

  bald → **eher** → **am ehesten**
  soon → sooner → soonest

→ [6]

Examples

1 **Er läuft schneller als seine Schwester**
He runs faster than his sister

Ich sehe ihn seltener als früher
I see him less often than before

2 **Wer von ihnen arbeitet am schnellsten?**
Which of them works fastest?

Er isst am meisten
He eats most

3 **Die Mädchen sprachen immer lauter**
The girls were talking more and more loudly

Er fuhr immer langsamer
He drove more and more slowly

4 **Je eher, desto besser**
The sooner the better

5 **Er kommt meistens zu spät an**
He usually arrives late

Rauchen strengstens verboten!
Smoking strictly prohibited

6 **Welches hast du am liebsten?**
Which do you like best?

❒ Emphasizers

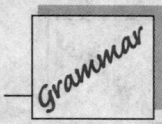

These are words commonly used in German, as indeed in English, especially in the spoken language, to emphasize or modify in some way the meaning of the sentence. The following are some of the most common:

Aber

Used to lend emphasis to a statement → [1]

Denn

As well as its uses as a conjunction (see p 214), **denn** is widely used to emphasize the meaning. It often cannot be directly translated → [2]

Doch

Used as a positive reply in order to correct negative assumptions or impressions → [3]

It can strengthen an imperative → [4]

It can make a question out of a statement → [5]

Mal

May be used with imperatives → [6]

It also has several idiomatic uses → [7]

Ja

Strengthens a statement → [8]

It also has several idiomatic uses → [9]

Schon

Is used familiarly with an imperative → [10]

It is also used in various idiomatic ways → [11]

Examples

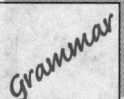

1	**Das ist aber schön!** Oh that's pretty!	**Aber ja!** Yes indeed!
2	**Was ist denn hier los?** What's going on here then?	**Wo denn?** Where?
3	**Hat es dir nicht gefallen? — Doch!** Didn't you like it? — Oh yes, I did!	
4	**Lass ihn doch!** Just leave him	
5	**Das schaffst du doch?** You'll manage it, won't you?	
6	**Komm mal her!** Come here!	**Moment mal!** Just a minute!
7	**Mal sehen** We'll see **Er soll es nur mal versuchen!** Just let him try it!	**Hören Sie mal ...** Look here now ...
8	**Er sieht ja wie seine Mutter aus** He looks like his mother **Das kann ja sein** That may well be	
9	**Ja und?** So what?/What then? **Das ist es ja** That's just it	**Das ist ja lächerlich** That's ridiculous
10	**Mach schon!** Get on with it!	
11	**schon wieder** again	**Schon gut** Okay/Very well

PREPOSITIONS

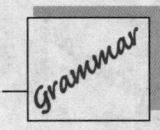

In English, a preposition does not affect the word or phrase which it introduces, e.g.

the women	a large meal	these events
with the women	*after* a large meal	*before* these events

In German, however, the noun following a preposition must be put in a certain *case*:

accusative → 1

dative → 2

genitive → 3

It is therefore important to learn each preposition with the case, or cases, it governs.

The following guidelines will help you:

- Prepositions which take the accusative or dative cases are much more common than those taking the genitive case.
- Certain prepositions may take a dative or accusative case, depending on whether *movement* is involved or not. This is explained further on p 202 ff → 4
- Prepositions are often used to complete the sense of certain verbs, as shown on p 76 ff → 5
- After many prepositions, a shortened or *contracted* form of the definite article may be merged with the preposition to form one word, e.g.

auf + das	→	**aufs**
bei + dem	→	**beim**
zu + der	→	**zur**

1 **Es ist für dich**

It's for you

Wir sind durch die ganze Welt gereist

We travelled all over the world

2 **Er ist mit seiner Frau gekommen**

He came with his wife

3 **Es ist ihm trotz seiner Bemühungen nicht gelungen**

Despite his efforts, he still didn't succeed

4 **Es liegt auf dem Tisch**

It's on the table

(*dative*: no movement implied)

Lege es bitte auf den Tisch

Please put it on the table

(*accusative*: movement *onto* the table)

5 **Ich warte auf meinen Mann**

I'm waiting for my husband

❒ Contracted forms

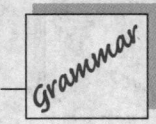

Contractions are possible with the following prepositions:

PREPOSITION	+ **das**	+ **den**	+ **dem**	+ **der**
an	ans		am	
auf	aufs*			
bei			beim	
durch	durchs*			
für	fürs*			
hinter	hinters*	hintern*	hinterm*	
in	ins		im	
über	übers*	übern*	überm*	
um	ums*			
unter	unters*	untern*	unterm*	
vor	vors*		vorm*	
von			vom	
zu			zum	zur

* ⚠ NOTE: Those forms marked with an asterisk are suitable only for use in colloquial, spoken German.
All other forms (not marked with an asterisk) may be safely used in any context, formal or informal → [1]

- Contracted forms are not used where the article is to be stressed → [2]

- Other contracted forms involving prepositions, as shown on pp 164 and 174, occur:

  1 in the introduction to relative clauses → [3]

  2 with personal pronouns representing inanimate objects → [4]

Examples

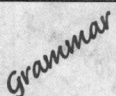

1 **Wir gehen heute Abend ins Theater**

We are going to the theatre this evening

Er geht zur Schule

He goes to school

Das kommt vom Trinken

That comes from drinking

2 **In dem Anzug kann ich mich nicht sehen lassen!**

I can't go out in that suit!

3 **Die Bank, worauf wir saßen, war etwas wackelig**

The bench we were sitting on was rather wobbly

4 **Er war damit zufrieden**

He was satisfied with that

Er hat es darauf gesetzt

He put it on it

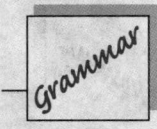

Prepositions followed by the Dative Case

Some of the most common prepositions taking the dative case are:

aus	**gegenüber**	**seit**
außer	**mit**	**von**
bei	**nach**	**zu**

Aus

- as a preposition meaning: *out of/from* → 1
- as a separable verbal prefix (see p 72) → 2

Außer

- as a preposition meaning: *out of* → 3
  except → 4

Bei

- as a preposition meaning: *at the home/shop/work* etc *of* → 5
  near → 6
  in the course of/during → 7
- as a separable verbal prefix (see p 72) → 8

Gegenüber

- as a preposition meaning: *opposite* → 9
  to(wards) → 10

⚠ NOTE: When used as a preposition, **gegenüber** is placed *after a pronoun*, but may be placed *before or after a noun.*

- as a separable verbal prefix → 11

[1] **Er trinkt aus der Flasche**
He is drinking out of the bottle
Er kommt aus Essen
He comes from Essen

[2] **aushalten** to endure
Ich halte es nicht mehr aus
I can't stand it any longer

[3] **außer Gefahr/Betrieb**
out of danger/order

[4] **alle außer mir**
all except me

[5] **bei uns in Schottland**
at home in Scotland
Er wohnt immer noch bei seinen Eltern
He still lives with his parents

[6] **Er saß bei mir**
He was sitting next to me

[7] **Ich singe immer beim Arbeiten**
I always sing when I'm working
Bei unserer Ankunft ...
On our arrival ...

[8] **Er stand seinem Freund bei**
He stood by his friend

[9] **Er wohnt uns gegenüber**
He lives opposite us

[10] **Er ist mir gegenüber immer sehr freundlich gewesen**
He has always been very friendly towards me

[11] **gegenüberstehen** to face/to have an attitude towards
Er steht ihnen kritisch gegenüber
He takes a critical view of them

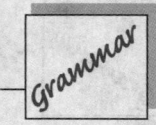

❒ Prepositions followed by the Dative Case (Continued)

Mit

- as a preposition meaning: *with* → 1
- as a separable verbal prefix (see p 72) → 2

Nach

- as a preposition meaning: *after* → 3
  to → 4
  according to (it can be placed after the noun with this meaning) → 5
- as a separable verbal prefix (see p 72) → 6

Seit

- as a preposition meaning: *since* → 7
  for (of time) → 8
  ⚠ NOTE: Beware of the tense!

Von

- as a preposition meaning: *from* → 9
  about → 10
- as an alternative, often preferred, to the genitive case → 11
- as a preposition meaning: *by* (to introduce the agent of a passive action, see p 34) → 12

Zu

- as a preposition meaning: *to* → 13
  for → 14
- as a separable verbal prefix (see p 72) → 15

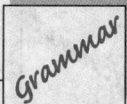

1 **Er ging mit seinen Freunden spazieren**
He went walking with his friends

2 **jemanden mitnehmen** to give someone a lift
Nimmst du mich bitte mit?
Will you give me a lift please?

3 **Nach zwei Stunden kam er wieder**
He returned two hours later

4 **Er ist nach London gereist**
He went to London

5 **Ihrer Sprache nach ist sie Süddeutsche**
From the way she spoke I would say she is from southern Germany

6 **nachmachen** to copy
Sie macht mir alles nach
She copies everything I do

7 **Seit der Zeit ...**
Since then ...

8 **Ich wohne seit zwei Jahren in Frankfurt**
I've been living in Frankfurt for two years

9 **Von Frankfurt sind wir weiter nach München gefahren**
From Frankfurt we went on to Munich

10 **Ich weiß nichts von ihm**
I know nothing about him

11 **Die Mutter von diesen Mädchen ...**
The mother of these girls ...
Sie ist eine Freundin von Horst
She is a friend of Horst's

12 **Er ist von unseren Argumenten überzeugt worden**
He was convinced by our arguments

13 **Er ging zum Arzt**
He went to the doctor's

14 **Wir sind zum Essen eingeladen**
We're invited for dinner

15 **zumachen** to shut
Mach die Tür zu!
Shut the door!

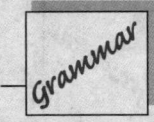

❐ Prepositions followed by the Accusative Case

The most common of these are:

durch	**für**	**ohne**	**wider**
entlang	**gegen**	**um**	

Durch

- as a preposition meaning: *through* → 1
- preceding the inanimate agent of a passive action (see p 34) → 2
- as a separable verbal prefix

Entlang

- as a preposition meaning: *along* (it follows the noun with this meaning) → 3
- as a separable verbal prefix → 4

Für

- as a preposition meaning: *for* → 5
to → 6
- in **was für/was für ein** *what kind of/what* (see p 144 and p 180) → 7

Gegen

- as a preposition meaning: *against* → 8
towards/getting on for → 9
- as a separable verbal prefix

Examples

1 **durch das Fenster blicken**
to look through the window

2 **Durch seine Bemühungen wurden alle gerettet**
Everyone was saved through his efforts

3 **die Straße entlang**
along the street

4 **Wir gingen die Straße entlang**
We went along the street

5 **Ich habe es für dich getan**
I did it for you

6 **Das ist für ihn sehr wichtig**
That is very important to him

7 **Was für Äpfel sind das?**
What kind of apples are they?

8 **Stelle es gegen die Mauer**
Put it against the wall

Haben Sie ein Mittel gegen Schnupfen?
Have you something for colds?

Ich habe nichts dagegen
I've got nothing against it

9 **Wir sind gegen vier angekommen**
We arrived at getting on for/around four o'clock

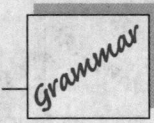

❒ Prepositions followed by the Accusative Case
(Continued)

Ohne

- as a preposition meaning: *without* → [1]

Um

- as a preposition meaning: *(a)round/round about* → [2]

  at (in time expressions) → [3]

  for (after certain verbs) → [4]

  about (after certain verbs) → [5]

  by (in expressions of quantity) → [6]

- as a variable verbal prefix (see p 74) → [7]

Wider

- as a preposition meaning: *contrary to/against* → [8]
- as a variable verbal prefix (see p 74) → [9]

Examples

Grammar

1 **Ohne ihn gehts nicht**
It won't work without him

2 **um die Ecke**
(a)round the corner

3 **Es fängt um neun Uhr an**
It begins at nine

4 **Sie baten ihre Mutter um Kekse**
They asked their mother for some biscuits

5 **Es handelt sich um dein Benehmen**
It's a question of your behaviour

6 **Es ist um zehn Euro billiger**
It is cheaper by ten euros

7 **umarmen** to embrace (*inseparable*)
Er hat sie umarmt
He gave her a hug

umfallen to fall over (*separable*)
Er ist umgefallen
He fell over

8 **Das geht mir wider die Natur**
That's against my nature

9 **widersprechen** to go against (*inseparable*)
Das hat meinen Wünschen widersprochen
That went against my wishes

(sich) widerspiegeln to reflect (*separable*)
Der Baum spiegelt sich im Wasser wider
The tree is reflected in the water

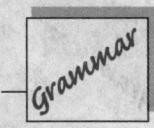

Prepositions followed by the Accusative or the Dative Case

These prepositions are followed by:

1 the **accusative** when *movement towards* a different place is involved.

2 the **dative** when *position* is described as opposed to movement, or when the movement is *within* the same place.

- The most common prepositions in this category are:

an	*on/at/to*
auf	*on/in/to/at*
hinter	*behind*
in	*in/into/to* → [1]
neben	*next to/beside*
über	*over/across/above*
unter	*under/among* → [2]
vor	*in front of/before*
zwischen	*between* → [3]

- These prepositions may also be used with figurative meanings as part of a *verb + preposition* construction (see p 76).

  The case following **auf** or **an** is then not the same after all verbs → [4]

  It is therefore best to learn such constructions together with the case which follows them.

- Many of these prepositions are also used as verbal prefixes in the same way as the prepositions described on pp 202 to 209 → [5]

Examples

[1] **Er ging ins Zimmer** (*acc*)
He entered the room

Im Zimmer (*dat*) **warteten viele Leute auf ihn**
A lot of people were waiting for him in the room

[2] **Er stellte sich unter den Baum** (*acc*)
He (came and) stood under the tree

Er lebte dort unter Freunden (*dat*)
There he lived among friends

[3] **Er legte es zwischen die beiden Teller** (*acc*)
He put it between the two plates

Das Dorf liegt zwischen den Bergen (*dat*)
The village lies between the mountains

[4]

sich verlassen auf (+*acc*)	to depend on
bestehen auf (+*dat*)	to insist on
glauben an (+*acc*)	to believe in
leiden an (+*dat*)	to suffer from

[5] **anrechnen** to charge for (*separable*)
Das wird Ihnen später angerechnet
You'll be charged for that later

aufsetzen to put on (*separable*)
Sie setzte sich den Hut auf
She put her hat on

überqueren to cross (*inseparable*)
Sie hat die Straße überquert
She crossed the street

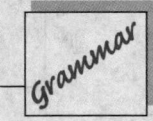

❐ Prepositions followed by the Genitive Case

The following are some of the more common prepositions which take the genitive case:

außerhalb	*outside*
beiderseits	*on both sides of*
diesseits	*on this side of*
... halber	*for ... sake/because of ...*
hinsichtlich	*with regard to*
infolge	*as a result of*
innerhalb	*within/inside* → [1]
jenseits	*on the other side of* → [2]
statt*	*instead of*
trotz*	*in spite of* → [3]
um ... willen	*for ... sake/because of ...*
während*	*during* → [4]
wegen*	*on account of* → [5]

* ⚠ NOTE: Those prepositions marked with an asterisk may also be followed by the dative case → [6]

⚠ NOTE: Special forms of the possessive and relative pronouns are used with **wegen, halber** and **willen** → [7]

Examples

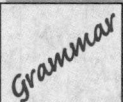

1 **innerhalb dieses Zeitraums**
within this period of time

2 **jenseits der Grenze**
on the other side of the frontier

3 **trotz seiner Befürchtungen**
despite his fears

4 **während der Vorstellung**
during the performance

5 **wegen der neuen Stelle**
because of the new job

6 **trotz allem**
in spite of everything

wegen mir
because of me

7

meinetwegen	on my account, because of me
deinetwegen	on your account, because of you (*familiar*)
seinetwegen	on his account, because of him
ihretwegen	on her/their account, because of her/them
unsertwegen	on our account, because of us
euertwegen	on your account, because of you (*plural*)
Ihretwegen	on your account, because of you (*polite*)
derentwegen	for whose sake, for her/their/its sake
dessentwegen	for whose sake, for his/its sake
meinethalben *etc*	on my *etc* account
derenthalben	on whose account, on her/their/its account
dessenthalben	on whose account, on his/its account
meinetwillen *etc*	for my *etc* sake
derentwillen	for whose sake, for her/its/their sake
dessentwillen	for whose sake, for his/its sake

Co-ordinating Conjunctions

These are used to link words, phrases or clauses.

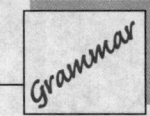

- These are the main co-ordinating conjunctions:

aber	*but* → 1
	however (with this meaning, **aber** is placed within the clause) → 2
denn	*for* → 3
oder	*or* → 4
sondern	*but* (after a negative construction) → 5
und	*and* → 6

- These do not cause the inversion of subject and verb, i.e. the verb follows the subject in the normal way (see p 224) → 1 - 6

- Inversion may however be caused by something other than the co-ordinating conjunction, e.g. **dann**, **trotzdem**, **montags** in the examples opposite → 7

Examples

1 **Wir wollten ins Kino, aber wir hatten kein Geld**
We wanted to go to the cinema but we had no money

2 **Ich wollte ins Theater; er aber wollte nicht mit**
I wanted to go to the theatre; however he wouldn't come

3 **Wir wollten heute fahren, denn montags ist weniger Verkehr**
We wanted to travel today because the traffic is lighter on Mondays

4 **Er hatte noch nie Whisky oder Schnaps getrunken**
He had never drunk whisky or schnapps

Willst du eins oder hast du vielleicht keinen Hunger?
Do you want one or aren't you hungry?

5 **Er ist nicht alt, sondern jung**
He isn't old, but young

6 **Horst und Veronika**
Horst and Veronika

Er ging in die Stadt und kaufte sich ein neues Hemd
He went into town and bought himself a new shirt

7 **Er hat sie besucht und dann ist er wieder nach Hause gegangen**
He paid her a visit and then went home again

Wir wollten doch ins Kino, aber trotzdem sind wir zu Hause geblieben
We wanted to go to the cinema, but even so we stayed at home

Wir wollten heute fahren, denn montags ist der Verkehr geringer
We wanted to travel today because there is less traffic on Mondays

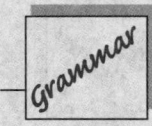

❒ Double Co-ordinating Conjunctions

These conjunctions consist of two separate elements, like their English counterparts, e.g.

not only ... but also ...

The following are widely used:

sowohl .. als auch *both ... and*

- This may link words or phrases → 1
- The verb is usually plural, whether the subjects are singular or plural → 1

weder ... noch *neither ... nor*

- This may link words or phrases → 2
- It may also link clauses, and inversion of subject and verb then takes place in both clauses → 3
- The verb is plural unless both subjects are singular → 4

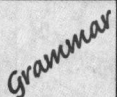

1 **Sowohl sein Vater als auch seine Mutter haben sich darüber gefreut**

Both his father and his mother were pleased about it

Sowohl unser Lehrkörper als auch unsere Schüler haben teilgenommen

Both our staff and our pupils took part

2 **Weder Georg noch sein Bruder kannte das Mädchen**

Neither Georg nor his brother knew the girl

3 **Weder mag ich ihn noch respektiere ich ihn**

I neither like nor respect him

4 **Weder die Befürworter noch die Gegner haben recht**

Neither the supporters nor the opponents are right

Weder du noch ich würde es schaffen

Neither you nor I would be able to do it

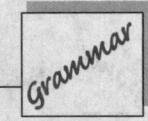

❒ Double Co-ordinating Conjunctions (Continued)

nicht nur ... sondern auch
not only ... but also

- This is used to link clauses as well as words and phrases → 1
- The word order is: inversion of subject and verb in the first clause, and normal order in the second → 2

  However, if **nicht nur** does not begin the clause, normal order prevails → 3
- The verb agrees in number with the subject nearest to it → 4

entweder ... oder
either ... or

- The verb agrees with the subject nearest it → 5
- The normal word order is: inversion in the first clause, and normal order in the second → 6

  However, it is possible to use normal order in the first clause, and this may lend a more threatening tone to the statement → 7

teils ... teils
partly ... partly

- The verb is normally plural unless both subjects are singular → 8
- Inversion of subject and verb takes place in both clauses → 9

Examples

1 **Er ist nicht nur geschickt, sondern auch intelligent** OR:
Nicht nur ist er geschickt, sondern er ist auch intelligent
He is not only skilful but also intelligent

2 **Nicht nur hat es die ganze Zeit geregnet, sondern ich habe mir auch noch das Bein gebrochen**
Not only did it rain the whole time, but I also broke my leg

3 **Es hat nicht nur die ganze Zeit geregnet, sondern ich habe mir auch noch das Bein gebrochen**
Not only did it rain the whole time, but I also broke my leg

4 **Nicht nur ich, sondern auch die Mädchen sind dafür verantwortlich**
Not just me, but the girls are also responsible

Nicht nur sie, sondern auch ich habe es gehört
They weren't the only ones to hear it — I heard it too

5 **Entweder du oder Georg muss es getan haben**
It must have been either you or Georg who did it

6 **Entweder komme ich morgen vorbei, oder ich rufe dich an**
I'll either drop in tomorrow or I'll give you a ring

7 **Entweder du gibst das sofort auf, oder du kriegst kein Taschengeld mehr**
Either you stop that immediately, or you get no more pocket money

8 **Die Studenten waren teils Deutsche, teils Ausländer**
The students were partly German and partly from abroad

9 **Teils bin ich überzeugt, teils bleibe ich skeptisch**
Part of me is convinced, and part remains sceptical

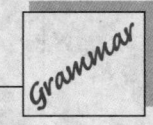

❒ Subordinating Conjunctions

These are used to link clauses in such a way as to make one clause dependent on another for its meaning. The dependent clause is called a **subordinate clause** and the other a **main clause**.

- The subordinate clause is always separated from the rest of the sentence by commas → [1]

- The subordinate clause may precede the main clause. When this happens, the verb and subject of the main clause are inverted, i.e. they swap places, as shown on p 226 → [2]

- The finite part of the verb (i.e. the conjugated part) is always at the end of a subordinate clause (see p 228) → [3]

- For compound tenses in subordinate clauses, it is the **auxiliary** (the main part of the verb) which comes last, after the participle or infinitive used to form the compound tense (see p 22 ff) → [4]

- Any **modal verb** (**mögen**, **können** etc, see p 52 ff) used in a subordinate clause is placed last in the clause → [5]

  ⚠ BUT: When the modal verb is in a compound tense, the order is as shown → [6]

Examples

1 MAIN CLAUSE — SUBORDINATE CLAUSE

Er ist zu Fuß gekommen, weil der Bus zu teuer ist
He came on foot because the bus is too dear

Ich trinke viel Bier, obwohl es nicht gesund ist
I drink a lot of beer although it isn't good for me

Wir haben weitergefeiert, nachdem sie gegangen waren
We carried on with the party after they went

2 SUBORDINATE CLAUSE — MAIN CLAUSE

Weil der Bus zu teuer ist, ist er zu Fuß gekommen

Obwohl es nicht gesund ist, trinke ich viel Bier

Nachdem sie gegangen waren, haben wir weitergefeiert

3 **Als er uns sah, ist er davongelaufen** OR:
Er ist davongelaufen, als er uns sah
He ran away when he saw us

4 **Nachdem er gegessen hatte, ging er hinaus**
He went out after he had eaten

5 **Da er nicht mit uns sprechen wollte, ist er davongelaufen**
Since he didn't want to speak to us he ran away

6 **Da er nicht mit uns hat sprechen wollen, ist er davongelaufen**
Since he didn't want to speak to us he ran away

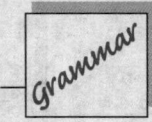

Subordinating conjunctions (Continued)

- Here are some common examples of subordinating conjunctions and their uses:

als	when → 1
als ob	as if, as though
bevor	before
bis	until → 2
da	as, since → 3
damit	so (that)
indem	while
inwiefern	to what extent
nachdem	after → 4
ob	whether, if
obwohl	although
wann	when (*interrogative*) → 5
während	while → 6
weil	because → 7
wenn	when, whenever/if → 8
wie	as, like
wo	where
wohin	to where
worauf	whereupon/on which
worin	in which
seitdem	since
sodass, so dass	such that, so that
sobald	as soon as
soweit	as far as

1 **Es regnete, als ich in Köln ankam** OR:
Als ich in Köln ankam, regnete es
It was raining when I arrived in Cologne

2 **Ich warte, bis du zurückkommst**
I'll wait till you get back

3 **Da er nicht kommen wollte, ...**
Since he didn't want to come ...

4 **Er wird uns Bescheid sagen können, nachdem er angerufen hat** OR:
Nachdem er angerufen hat, wird er uns Bescheid sagen können
He will be able to let us know for certain once he has phoned

5 **Er möchte wissen, wann der Zug ankommt**
He would like to know when the train is due to arrive

6 **Während seine Frau die Koffer auspackte, machte er das Abendessen** OR:
Er machte das Abendessen, während seine Frau die Koffer auspackte
He made the supper while his wife unpacked the cases

7 **Wir haben den Hund nicht mitgenommen, weil im Auto nicht genug Platz war** OR:
Weil im Auto nicht genug Platz war, haben wir den Hund nicht mitgenommen
We didn't take the dog because there wasn't enough room in the car

8 **Wenn ich ins Kino gehe ...**
When(ever) I go to the cinema ...

Ich komme, wenn du willst
I'll come if you like

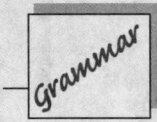

❒ Word Order: Main Clauses

- In a main clause the subject comes first and is followed by the verb, as in English:
  His mother (*subject*) drinks (*verb*) whisky → [1]

- If the verb is in a compound or passive tense, the auxiliary follows the subject and the past participle or infinitive goes to the end of the clause → [2]

- The verb is the second concept in a main clause. The first concept may be a word, phrase or clause (see p 226) → [3]

- Any reflexive pronoun follows the main verb in simple tenses and the auxiliary in compound tenses → [4]

- The order for articles, adjectives and nouns is as in English: *article + adjective(s) + noun* → [5]

- A direct object usually follows an indirect, except where the direct object is a personal pronoun.
  ⚠ BUT: The indirect object can be placed last for emphasis, providing it is not a pronoun → [6]

- The position of adverbial expressions (see p 188) is not fixed. As a general rule they are placed close to the words to which they refer.
  Adverbial items of *time* often come first in the clause, but this is flexible → [7]
  Adverbial items of *place* can be placed at the beginning of a clause when emphasis is required → [8]
  Adverbial items of *manner* are more likely to be within the clause, close to the word to which they refer → [9]

- Where there is more than one adverb, a useful rule of thumb is: "time, manner, place" → [10]

Examples

1 **Seine Mutter trinkt Whisky**
His mother drinks whisky

2 **Sie wird dir etwas sagen** **Sie hat mir nichts gesagt**
She will tell you something She told me nothing
Es ist für ihn gekauft worden
It was bought for him

3

1ST CONCEPT	2ND CONCEPT	
Die neuen Waren	**kommen**	**morgen**
(The new goods are coming tomorrow)		
Was du gesagt hast,	**stimmt**	**nicht**
(What you said isn't true)		

4 **Er rasierte sich** **Er hat sich rasiert**
He shaved He (has) shaved

5 **ein alter Mann** **diese alten Sachen**
an old man these old things

6 **Ich gab dem Mann das Geld**
I gave the man the money
Ich gab ihm das Geld **Ich gab es ihm**
I gave him the money I gave him it/Igave it to him
Er gab das Geld seiner Schwester
He gave the money to his sister (*not his brother*)

7 **Gestern gingen wir ins Theater** OR:
Wir gingen gestern ins Theater
We went to the theatre yesterday

8 **Dort haben sie Fußball gespielt** OR:
Sie haben dort Fußball gespielt
They played football there

9 **Sie spielen gut Fußball**
They play football well
Das war furchtbar teuer
It was terribly expensive

10 **Wir haben gestern gut hierhin gefunden**
We found our way here all right yesterday

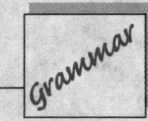

Word Order: Main Clauses (Continued)

- A pronoun object precedes all adverbs → [1]
- While the main verb must normally remain the second concept, the first concept need not always be the subject. Main clauses can begin with many things, including:

  an adverb → [2]
  a direct or indirect object → [3]
  an infinitive phrase → [4]
  a complement → [5]
  a past participle → [6]
  a prepositional phrase → [7]
  a clause acting as the object of the verb → [8]
  a subordinate clause → [9]

- If the subject does not begin a main clause, the verb and subject must be turned around or "inverted" → [2] - [9]
- Beginning a sentence with something other than the subject is frequent in German.
  It may however also be used for special effect to:

  highlight whatever is placed first in the clause → [10]
  emphasize the subject of the clause by forcing it from its initial position to the end of the clause → [11]

- After inversion, any reflexive pronoun precedes the subject, unless the subject is a pronoun → [12]
- The following do not cause inversion when placed at the beginning of a main clause, although inversion may be caused by something else placed after them:

  allein, **denn**, **oder**, **sondern**, **und** → [13]
  ja and **nein** → [14]
  certain exclamations: **ach**, **also**, **nun** *etc* → [15]
  words or phrases qualifying the subject: **auch**, **nur**, **sogar**, *etc* → [16]

1 **Sie haben es gestern sehr billig gekauft**
They bought it very cheaply yesterday

2 **Gestern sind wir ins Theater gegangen**
We went to the theatre yesterday

3 **So ein Kind habe ich noch nie gesehen!**
I've never seen such a child!
Seinen Freunden wollte er es nicht zeigen
He wouldn't show it to his friends

4 **Seinen Freunden zu helfen, hat er nicht versucht**
He didn't try to help his friends

5 **Deine Schwester war es** It was your sister

6 **Geraucht hatte er nie** He had never smoked

7 **In diesem Haus ist Mozart auf die Welt gekommen**
Mozart was born in this house

8 **Was mit ihm los war, haben wir nicht herausgefunden**
We never discovered what was wrong with him

9 **Nachdem ich ihn gesehen hatte, ging ich nach Hause**
I went home after seeing him

10 **Dem würde ich nichts sagen!**
I wouldn't tell *him* anything!

11 **An der Ecke stand eine riesengroße Fabrik**
A huge factory stood on the corner

12 **Daran erinnerten sich die Zeugen nicht**
The witnesses didn't remember that
Daran erinnerten sie sich nicht
They didn't remember that

13 **Peter ging nach Hause und Elsa blieb auf der Party**
Peter went home and Elsa stayed at the party
⚠ BUT: **Peter ging nach Hause und unterwegs sah er Kurt**
Peter went home and on the way he saw Kurt

14 **Nein, ich will nicht** No, I don't want to
⚠ BUT: **Nein, das tue ich nicht** No, I won't do that

15 **Also, wir fahren nach Hamburg**
So we'll go to Hamburg
⚠ BUT: **Also, nach Hamburg wollt ihr fahren**
So you want to go to Hamburg

16 **Sogar seine Mutter wollte es ihm nicht glauben**
Even his mother wouldn't believe him
⚠ BUT: **Sogar mit dem Zug ginge es nicht schneller**
It would be no faster even by train

❐ Word Order: Subordinate Clauses

- A subordinate clause may be introduced by:

  1 a relative pronoun (see p 174) → [1]

  2 a subordinating conjunction (see p 222) → [2] - [3]

- The subject follows the opening conjunction or relative pronoun - see **wir** and **er** → [1] - [3]

- The main verb almost always goes to the end of a subordinate clause → [1] - [3]

  The exceptions to this are:

  1 in a **wenn** clause where **wenn** is omitted (see p 64) → [4]

  2 in an indirect statement without **dass** (see p 64) → [5]

- The order for articles, nouns, adjectives, adverbs, direct and indirect objects is the same as for main clauses (see p 224), but they are all placed between the subject of the clause and the verb → [6]

- If the subject of a reflexive verb in a subordinate clause is a pronoun, the order is *subject pronoun* + *reflexive pronoun* → [7]

  If the subject is a noun, the reflexive pronoun may follow or precede it → [8]

- Where one subordinate clause lies inside another, both still obey the order rule for subordinate clauses → [9]

Examples

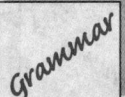

1 **Die Kinder, die wir gesehen haben …**
The children whom we saw …

2 **Da er nicht schwimmen wollte, ist er nicht mitgekommen**
As he didn't want to swim he didn't come

3 **Ich weiß, dass er zur Zeit in London wohnt**
I know he's living in London at the moment
Ich weiß nicht, ob er kommt
I don't know if he's coming

4 **Findest du meine Uhr, so ruf mich bitte an**
(= Wenn du meine Uhr findest, ruf mich bitte an)
If you find my watch, please give me a ring

5 **Er meint, er werde es innerhalb einer Stunde schaffen**
(= Er meint, dass er es innerhalb einer Stunde schaffen werde)
He thinks (that) he will manage it inside an hour

6 MAIN CLAUSE
Er ist gestern mit seiner Mutter in die Stadt gefahren
He went to town with his mother yesterday
SUBORDINATE CLAUSES
Da er gestern mit seiner Mutter in die Stadt gefahren ist, …
Since he went to town with his mother yesterday …
Der Junge, der gestern mit seiner Mutter in die Stadt gefahren ist, …
The boy who went to town with his mother yesterday …
Ich weiß, dass er gestern mit seiner Mutter in die Stadt gefahren ist
I know that he went to town with his mother yesterday

7 **Weil er sich nicht setzen wollte, …**
Because he wouldn't sit down …

8 **Weil das Kind sich nicht setzen wollte, …** OR:
Weil sich das Kind nicht setzen wollte, …
Because the child wouldn't sit down …

9 **Er wusste, dass der Mann, mit dem er gesprochen hatte, bei einer Baufirma arbeitete**
He knew that the man he had been speaking to worked for a construction company

❐ Word Order

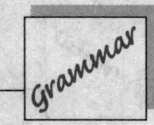

In the imperative

1 normal order → [1]

2 with reflexive verbs → [2]

3 with separable verbs → [3]

4 with separable reflexive verbs → [4]

In direct and indirect speech

- the verb of saying ("he replied/he said") must be inverted if it is placed within a quotation → [5]
- the position of the verb in indirect speech depends on whether or not **dass** (see p 66) is used → [6]

Verbs with separable prefixes (see pp 72 to 75)

- in main clauses the verb and prefix are separated in simple tenses and imperative forms → [7]
- for compound tenses of main clauses and all tenses of subordinate clauses, the verb and its prefix are united at the end of the clause → [8]
- in a present infinitive phrase (see p 46), the verb and prefix are joined together by **zu** and placed at the end of the phrase → [9]

Examples

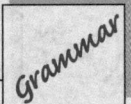

1 **Hol mir das Buch!** (*singular*)
Holt mir das Buch! (*plural*) — Fetch me that book!
Holen Sie mir das Buch! (*polite*)

2 **Wasch dich sofort!** (*singular*)
Wascht euch sofort! (*plural*) — Wash yourself/yourselves
Waschen Sie sich sofort! (*polite*) — at once!

3 **Hör jetzt auf!** (*singular*)
Hört jetzt auf! (*plural*) — Stop it!
Hören Sie jetzt auf! (*polite*)

4 **Dreh dich um!** (*singular*)
Dreht euch um! (*plural*) — Turn round!
Drehen Sie sich um! (*polite*)

5 **„Meine Mutter" sagte er, „kommt erst morgen an"**
"My mother", he said, "won't arrive till tomorrow"

6 **Er sagte, dass sie erst am nächsten Tag ankomme**
He said that she would not arrive until the next day
Er sagte, sie komme erst am nächsten Tag an
He said she would not arrive until the next day

7 **Er machte die Tür zu**
He closed the door
Ich räume zuerst auf
I'll clean up first
Hol mich um 7 ab!
Pick me up at 7!

8 **Er hat die Tür zugemacht**
He closed the door
Ich werde zuerst aufräumen
I'll clean up first
Er wurde um 7 abgeholt
He was picked up at 7
Wenn du mich um 7 abholst, ...
If you pick me up at 7 ...
Nachdem du mich abgeholt hast, ...
After you've picked me up ...

9 **Um frühzeitig anzukommen, fuhren wir sofort ab**
In order to arrive early we left immediately

❐ Question Forms

Direct questions

- In German, a direct question is formed by simply inverting the verb and subject → [1]
- In compound tenses (see p 22 ff) the past participle or infinitive goes to the end of the clause → [2]
- A statement can be made into a question by the addition of **nicht**, **nicht wahr** or **doch**, as with "isn't it" in English → [3]

  Questions formed in this way normally expect the answer to be "yes".
- When a question is put in the negative, **doch** can be used to answer it more positively than **ja** → [4]

Questions formed using interrogative words

- When questions are formed with **interrogative adverbs**, the subject and verb are inverted → [5]
- When questions are formed with **interrogative pronouns** and **adjectives** (see pp 144 and 176 to 178), the word order is that of direct statements:

  1 as the subject of the verb at the beginning of the clause they do not cause inversion → [6]

  2 if *not* the subject of the verb *and* at the beginning of the clause they do cause inversion → [7]

Indirect questions

These are questions following verbs of asking and wondering etc. The verb comes at the end of an indirect question → [8]

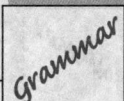

1 **Magst du ihn?**
Do you like him?

Gehst du ins Kino?
Do you go to the cinema? OR: Are you going to the cinema?

2 **Hast du ihn gesehen?**
Did you see him? OR: Have you seen him?

Wird sie mit ihm kommen?
Will she come with him?

3 **Das stimmt, nicht (wahr)?**
That's true, isn't it?

Das schaffst du doch?
You'll manage, won't you?

4 **Glaubst du mir nicht? — Doch!**
Don't you believe me? — Yes I do!

5 **Wann ist er gekommen?**
When did he come?

Wo willst du hin?
Where are you off to?

6 **Wer hat das gemacht?**
Who did this?

7 **Wem hast du es geschenkt?**
Who did you give it to?

8 **Er fragte, ob du mitkommen wolltest**
He asked if you wanted to come

Er möchte wissen, warum du nicht gekommen bist
He would like to know why you didn't come

Negatives

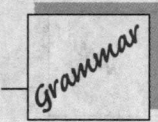

A statement or question is made negative by adding:

nicht (*not*) or **nie** (*never*)

- The negative may be placed next to the phrase or word to which it refers. The negative meaning can be shifted from one element of the sentence to another in this way → [1]
- **nie** can be placed at the beginning of a sentence for added emphasis, in which case the subject and verb are inverted → [2]
- **nicht** comes at the end of a negative imperative, except when the verb is separable, in which case **nicht** *precedes* the separable prefix → [3]
- The combination **nicht ein** is usually replaced by forms of **kein** (see p 126) → [4]
- **doch** (see p 196) is used in place of **ja** to contradict a negative statement → [5]
- Negative comparison is made with **nicht ... sondern** (*not ... but*).

  This construction is used to correct a previous false impression or idea → [6]

Examples

1 **Mit ihr wollte er nicht sprechen**
He didn't want to speak to *her*
Er wollte nicht mit ihr sprechen
He didn't *want* to speak to her

Er will nicht morgen nach Hause
OR: **Morgen will er nicht nach Hause**
He doesn't want to go home *tomorrow*
Er will morgen nicht nach Hause
He doesn't want to go *home* tomorrow

Wohnen Sie nicht in Dortmund?
Don't you live in Dortmund?
Warum ist er nicht mitgekommen?
Why didn't he come with you?
Waren Sie nie in Dortmund?
Have you never been to Dortmund?

2 **Nie war sie glücklicher gewesen**
She had never been happier

3 **Iss das nicht!**
Don't eat that!
Beeilen Sie sich nicht!
Don't hurry!
⚠ BUT: **Geh nicht weg!**
Don't go away!

4 **Gibt es keine Plätzchen?**
Aren't there any biscuits?
Kein einziges Kind hatte die Arbeit geschrieben
Not a single child had done the work

5 **Du kommst nicht mit — Doch, ich komme mit**
You're not coming — Yes I am

6 **Nicht Joachim, sondern sein Bruder war es**
It wasn't Joachim, but his brother

Cardinal (*one, two etc*)		**Ordinal** (*first, second etc*)	
null	0		
eins	1	**der erste** [2]	1.
zwei [1]	2	**der zweite** [1]	2.
drei	3	**der dritte**	3.
vier	4	**der vierte**	4.
fünf	5	**der fünfte**	5.
sechs	6	**der sechste**	6.
sieben	7	**der siebte**	7.
acht	8	**der achte**	8.
neun	9	**der neunte**	9.
zehn	10	**der zehnte**	10.
elf	11	**der elfte**	11.
zwölf	12	**der zwölfte**	12.
dreizehn	13	**der dreizehnte**	13.
vierzehn	14	**der vierzehnte**	14.
fünfzehn	15	**der fünfzehnte**	15.
sechzehn	16	**der sechzehnte**	16.
siebzehn	17	**der siebzehnte**	17.
achtzehn	18	**der achtzehnte**	18.
neunzehn	19	**der neunzehnte**	19.
zwanzig	20	**der zwanzigste**	20.
einundzwanzig	21	**der einundzwanzigste**	21.
zweiundzwanzig [1]	22	**der zweiundzwanzigste** [1]	22.
dreißig	30	**der dreißigste**	30.
vierzig	40	**der vierzigste**	40.
fünfzig	50	**der fünfzigste**	50.
sechzig	60	**der sechzigste**	60.

[1] **zwo** often replaces **zwei** in speech, to distinguish it clearly from **drei**: **zwo, zwoundzwanzig** *etc.*

[2] The ordinal number and the preceding definite article (and adjective if there is one) are declined, e.g.:

bei seinem dritten Versuch *at his third attempt*

siebzig	70	**der siebzigste**	70.
achtzig	80	**der achtzigste**	80.
neunzig	90	**der neunzigste**	90.
hundert	*a hundred*	**der hundertste**	100.
einhundert	*one hundred*		
hunderteins	101	**der hunderterste**	101.
hundertzwei	102	**der hundertzweite**	102.
hunderteinundzwanzig	121	**der hunderteinundzwanzigste**	121.
zweihundert	200	**der zweihundertste**	200.
tausend	*a thousand*	**der tausendste**	1000.
eintausend	*one thousand*		
tausendeins	1001	**der tausenderste**	1001.
zweitausend	2000	**der zweitausendste**	2000.
hunderttausend	100 000	**der hunderttausendste**	100 000.
eine Million	1 000 000	**der millionste**	1 000 000.

- With large numbers, spaces or full stops are used where English uses a comma, e.g.:
  1.000.000 or 1 000 000 for 1,000,000 (*a million*)

- Decimals are written with a comma instead of a full stop, e.g.:
  7,5 (**sieben Komma fünf**) for 7.5 (*seven point five*)

- When ordinal numbers are used as nouns, they are written with a capital letter, e.g.:
  sie ist die Zehnte *she's the tenth*

Fractions

halb	**die Hälfte**	**eine halbe Stunde**
half (a)	half (the)	half an hour
das Drittel	**zwei Drittel**	**das Viertel**
third	two thirds	quarter
drei viertel	**anderthalb, eineinhalb**	**zweieinhalb**
three quarters	one and a half	two and a half

Wie spät ist es? / Wie viel Uhr ist es?
What time is it?

Es ist ...
It's ...

00.00	**Mitternacht / null Uhr / vierundzwanzig Uhr / zwölf Uhr**
00.10	**zehn (Minuten) nach zwölf / null Uhr zehn**
00.15	**Viertel nach zwölf / null Uhr fünfzehn**
00.30	**halb eins / null Uhr dreißig**
00.40	**zwanzig (Minuten) vor eins / null Uhr vierzig**
00.45	**Viertel vor eins / drei viertel eins / null Uhr fünfundvierzig**
01.00	**ein Uhr**
01.10	**zehn (Minuten) nach eins / ein Uhr zehn**
01.15	**Viertel nach eins / ein Uhr fünfzehn**
01.30	**halb zwei /ein Uhr dreißig**
01.40	**zwanzig (Minuten) vor zwei / ein Uhr vierzig**
01.45	**Viertel vor zwei / drei viertel zwei / ein Uhr fünfundvierzig**
01.50	**zehn (Minuten) vor zwei / ein Uhr fünfzig**
12.00	**zwölf Uhr**
12.30	**halb eins / zwölf Uhr dreißig**
13.00	**ein Uhr / dreizehn Uhr**
16.30	**halb fünf / sechzehn Uhr dreißig**
22.00	**zehn Uhr / zweiundzwanzig Uhr / zwoundzwanzig Uhr**

morgen um halb drei
at half past two tomorrow

um drei Uhr (nachmittags)
at three (pm)

kurz vor zehn Uhr
just before ten o'clock

gegen vier Uhr (nachmittags)
towards four o'clock (in the afternoon)

erst um halb neun
not until half past eight

ab neun Uhr
from nine o'clock onwards

morgen früh/Abend
tomorrow morning/evening

Dates

Der Wievielte ist heute? / Welches Datum haben wir heute?
What's the date today?

Heute ist ...	It's ...
der zwanzigste März	the twentieth of March
der Zwanzigste	the twentieth
Heute haben wir ...	It's ...
den zwanzigsten März	the twentieth of March
den Zwanzigsten	the twentieth
Am Wievielten findet es statt?	When does it take place?
Es findet am ersten April statt ...	... on the first of April
Es findet am Ersten statt	... on the first

Es findet (am) Montag, den ersten April statt OR:
Es findet Montag, den 1. April statt
It takes place on Monday, the first of April / April 1st

Years

Er wurde 1970 geboren	**(im Jahre) 1994**
He was born in 1970	in 1994

Other expressions

im Dezember/Januar *etc*	**im Winter/Sommer/Herbst/Frühling**
in December/January *etc*	in winter/summer/autumn/spring
nächstes Jahr	**Anfang September**
next year	at the beginning of September

Punctuation

German punctuation differs from English in the following cases:

Commas

- Decimal places are always shown by a comma → [1]
- Large numbers are separated off by means of a space or a full stop → [2]
- Subordinate clauses are always marked off from the rest of the sentence by a comma → [3]

  This applies to all types of subordinate clause, e.g.:

  1 clauses with an adverbial function → [3]

  2 relative clauses → [4]

  3 clauses containing indirect speech → [5]
- A comma is not required between two main clauses linked by **und** or **oder** → [6]

Exclamation marks

- Exclamation marks are used after imperative forms unless these are not intended as commands → [7]
- An exclamation mark is occasionally used after the name at the beginning of a letter, but this tends to be rather old-fashioned → [8]

Examples

1 **3,4 (drei Komma vier)**
3.4 (three point four)

2 **20 000**
OR: **20.000 (zwanzigtausend)**
20,000 (twenty thousand)

3 **Als er nach Hause kam, war sie schon weg**
She had already gone when he came home

Er bleibt gesund, obwohl er zu viel trinkt
He stays healthy, even though he drinks too much

4 **Der Mann, mit dem sie verheiratet ist, soll sehr reich sein**
The man she is married to is said to be very rich

5 **Er sagt, es gefällt ihm nicht**
He says he doesn't like it

6 **Wir gehen ins Kino oder wir bleiben zu Hause**
We'll go to the cinema or stay at home

7 **Steh auf!**
Get up!

Bitte nehmen Sie doch Platz
Do please sit down

8 **Liebe Elke! ...**
Dear Elke, ...

Sehr geehrter Herr Braun!...
Dear Mr Braun, ...

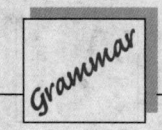

The following index lists comprehensively both grammatical terms and *key words* in **German** and English contained in this book.

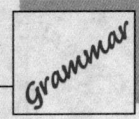

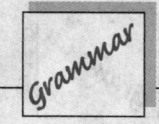

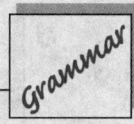

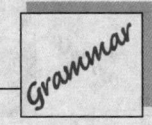

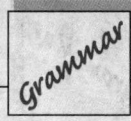

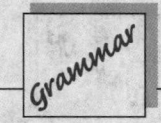

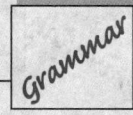